S0-BIJ-584

The Everyday Life Bible

Containing the

Amplified Old Testament

and the

Amplified New Testament

FEATURING NOTES *and* COMMENTARY
BY

JOYCE MEYER

Faith
Words

New York • Nashville

The Everyday Life Bible

Additional text copyright © 2006, 2018 by Joyce Meyer

Cover copyright © 2020 by Hachette Book Group, Inc.

Hachette Book Group supports the right to free expression and
the value of copyright. The purpose of copyright is to encourage writers
and artists to produce the creative works that enrich our culture.

The scanning, uploading, and distribution of this book without permission
is a theft of the author's intellectual property. If you would like permission
to use material from the book (other than for review purposes), please
contact permissions@hbgusa.com.
Thank you for your support of the author's rights.

FaithWords

Hachette Book Group

1290 Avenue of the Americas, New York, NY 10104

faithwords.com

twitter.com/faithwords

Originally published in hardcover by FaithWords in October 2006
under the title *The Everyday Life Bible*
First Edition: March 2020

FaithWords is a division of Hachette Book Group, Inc. The FaithWords
name and logo are trademarks of Hachette Book Group, Inc.

The publisher is not responsible for websites (or their content)
that are not owned by the publisher.

The Hachette Speakers Bureau provides a wide range of authors
for speaking events. To find out more, go to
www.hachettespeakersbureau.com or call (866) 376-6591.

The Holy Bible, Amplified Bible, copyright © 1954, 1958, 1962, 1964, 1965,
1987, 2015 by The Lockman Foundation, all rights reserved

Print book interior design and composition by Koechel Peterson & Associates

ISBNs: 978-1-4789-2295-7 (hardcover),
978-1-4789-2296-4 (pink imitation leather),
978-1-4789-2298-8 (gray imitation leather),
978-1-4789-2291-9 (paperback),
978-1-4789-2297-1 (ebook)
978-1-4789-2293-3 (teal LeatherLuxe®)
978-1-4789-2294-0 (blush LeatherLuxe®)

Printed in China
RRD

10   9   8   7   6   5   4

FOREWORD

Scriptural Promise

"The grass withers, the flower fades,
But the word of our God stands forever."

ISAIAH 40:8

The *Amplified* Bible has been produced with the conviction that the words of Scripture as originally penned in the Hebrew, Aramaic, and Greek were inspired by God. Since they are the eternal Word of God, the Holy Scriptures speak with fresh power to each generation, to give wisdom that leads to salvation, that people may serve Christ to the glory of God.

The Fourfold Aim of The Lockman Foundation

1. The publications shall be true to the original Hebrew, Aramaic, and Greek.
2. They shall be grammatically correct.
3. They shall be understandable to the people.
4. They shall give the Lord Jesus Christ His proper place, the place which the Word gives Him; therefore, no translation work will ever be personalized.

PREFACE

In 1958 The Lockman Foundation and Zondervan Publishing House issued the first edition of the *Amplified* New Testament. In 1962 and 1964 the two-volume *Amplified* Old Testament was released. In 1965 the complete *Amplified* Bible was published, and in 1987 the *Amplified* Bible, *Expanded Edition* was completed. Over fifty years have passed since the *Amplified* New Testament was translated and during that time there have been changes in both the style and usage of the English language; therefore, it seemed appropriate for The Lockman Foundation to revisit this well-loved translation of God's Word. Accordingly, Dr. Robert G. Lambeth, President of The Lockman Foundation, established a translation team and under his leadership the project was developed and completed.

The Lockman Foundation is now pleased to present the *Amplified* Bible of 2015. The English has been updated based on contemporary usage, a substantial number of new amplifications have been added to the Old Testament, and original amplifications have been updated, expanded, refined, or clarified where needed. The translation team has also added a significant number of new footnotes and references.

The result is a translation that is contemporary and firmly based on the foundation established by the *Amplified* Bible of 1965. That original translation project was envisioned and led by Frances Siewert (1881-1967), an amazing and gifted woman who devoted her life to serving the Lord and to making His Word available in an entirely new format. Her contribution to the spread of the Gospel through the *Amplified* Bible is impossible to quantify and her vision continues to speak to the hearts of people today.

The *Amplified* Bible of 2015 has been editorially recast so that a verse may be read either with or without amplification. The basic verse is the literal equivalent translation of the Hebrew, Aramaic, or Greek text. The basic verse is then amplified in a way that permits the reader to have a greater understanding of the relationship between the crispness of contemporary English and the depth of meaning in the biblical languages.

EXPLANATION OF GENERAL FORMAT

Amplification is indicated within the English text by parentheses, brackets, and italicized conjunctions.

Parentheses in Roman type ( ) supply the definition in context of the preceding name, place, or word. When the *Amplified* Bible is read aloud the definition in context may be skipped over.

Parentheses in **bold** type () indicate a parenthetical phrase that is part of the original language and should be included when Scripture is read aloud.

Brackets in Roman type [ ] contain justified words, phrases, or brief commentary not fully expressed in the preceding English text, but which are validated by the meaning of the original Hebrew, Aramaic, or Greek, or are validated elsewhere by Scripture. The amplifications within brackets serve many purposes. They may expand the depth of meaning in the underlying Hebrew, Aramaic, or Greek word; they may clarify a theological word or concept; they may expand a teaching or principle; they may supply information that helps the reader grasp the context of the passage.

Brackets in **bold** type [ ] are footnoted and indicate text not found in early mss or found only in some early mss.

Italicized conjunctions: *and, or, nor* are not in the original text, but are used to connect additional English words indicated by the original Hebrew, Aramaic, or Greek.

Italicized words are not found in the original language, but implied by it.

Proper names of persons, places, or things are often used to replace pronouns. When pronouns are retained in the text they may be followed by a name placed in parentheses.

Pronouns referring to God, the Father; Jesus, the Son; and the Holy Spirit are always capitalized, so that the reader immediately recognizes Deity in the text.

Paragraphs are identified by **bold** verse numbers or **bold** letters. This allows paragraphs to be clearly identified without displaying the verses in paragraph format. The text can still be read or studied by paragraphs, but individual verses are much easier to find when each verse begins on a new line.

Small capital letters are used in the New Testament to indicate Old Testament quotations or obvious references to Old Testament texts. Variations of Old Testament wording are found in New Testament citations depending on whether the New Testament writer translated from a Hebrew text, used existing Greek or Aramaic translations, or restated the material. It should be noted that modern rules for the indication of direct quotations were not used in biblical times; therefore, the ancient writer would use exact quotations or references to quotations without specific indication of such.

The proper name of God in the Old Testament is most significant and understandably so. The most common name for the Deity is God, a translation of the Hebrew word, *Elohim*. One of the titles for God is Lord, a translation of *Adonai*. There is yet another name which is particularly assigned to God as His special or proper name, that is, the four letters YHWH (Exodus 3:14 and Isaiah 42:8). This name has not been pronounced by the Jews because of reverence for the great sacredness of the divine name. Therefore, it has been consistently translated LORD. The only exception to this translation of YHWH is when it occurs in immediate proximity to the word *Lord,* that is, *Adonai*. In that case it is regularly translated GOD in order to avoid confusion. When the name of God appears within parentheses or brackets, the context of the verse determines which name and type style is used.

Verse references are placed in brackets at the end of some verses. If a verse contains more than one Scripture reference, the references are listed in biblical order.

Section headings are included in the text, but are not part of the original language.

ABBREVIATIONS
AND SPECIAL MARKINGS

Aram   = Aramaic

c   = about

DSS   = Dead Sea Scrolls

etc.   = and so on

e.g.   = for example

Gr   = Greek translation of O.T. (Septuagint or LXX) or Greek text of N.T.

Heb   = Hebrew text, usually Masoretic

i.e.,   = that is

Lat   = Latin

MT   = Masoretic text

Syr   = Syriac

Lit   = A literal translation

Or   = An alternate translation justified by the Hebrew, Aramaic, or Greek

ch, chs   = chapter, chapters

cf   = compare

f, ff   = following verse or verses

mg   = Refers to a marginal reading on another verse

ms, mss   = manuscript, manuscripts

v, vv   = verse, verses

THE LOCKMAN FOUNDATION

The Lockman Foundation wishes to express deepest gratitude to all those who have contributed to the development of the 2015 edition of the Amplified Bible. Throughout these years of translation many people have shared their time, talent, prayers and very best effort to bring this Bible translation to completion.

It is our prayer that each participant—whether scholar or staff, professor or proofreader, consultant or critical reader—will look at these pages of Scripture and know that each one's contribution is treasured . . . nothing is insignificant when dealing with God's Word.

To quote F. Dewey "Granddad" Lockman (1898–1974), "This work is a symphony, not a solo!" May each of you be specially blessed and always hold a special joy in your heart whenever you read the new Amplified Bible 2015. Thank you beloved.

Phoebe McAuley Lambeth
Coordinating Editor

A Personal Word from Joyce Meyer

For more than forty years, I have enjoyed and greatly benefitted from the *Amplified* Bible. It gives insights I have not found in other translations I have used. Because God has used the *Amplified* Bible in my life to open up many truths from His Word to me, I wanted to share the insight He has given me to help others. I prayed for many years to get permission from the publisher to produce a specialty Bible using this version and was thrilled when permission was finally granted.

God's Word is very precious to me. I can truly say that I love God's Word. It has changed me, and it has changed my life. I have also witnessed transformation in the lives of multitudes of people over the years through studying and believing God's Word. God's words are not ordinary words, as the words of people are. His words are filled with power. The power of God is actually inherent in His Word and it heals, delivers, comforts, saves, corrects, and encourages us.

When people are very discouraged, they can actually take God's Word as medicine for their souls. It encourages the discouraged, lifts up the lowly and downtrodden, heals the sick, saves the lost, fills the empty, and counsels those who need to make a decision.

Jesus is the Word of God Who took on human flesh and dwelt for a while among people (see John 1:14). When we read, study, meditate on, or confess the Word of God, we are fellowshipping with Jesus. We are actually taking Him as our nourishment and we find that only He can satisfy our souls. God's Word is our spiritual food and we need it regularly, just as we need natural food. The prophet Jeremiah said, "Your words were found and I ate them, and Your words became a joy to me and the delight of my heart" (Jeremiah 15:16).

God's Word is very important to Him. The Bible says in Psalm 138:2 that He has magnified together His name and His word. We should always respect and honor God's Word and give it a place of priority in our everyday lives. I truly believe that God's Word contains an answer to every problem and situation we encounter in life. It is certainly spiritual, but it is also very practical and has been given for our everyday lives. This is why, when we first produced this Bible, using the *Amplified Classic* Bible, we called it *The Everyday Life Bible*. This new edition uses the most current *Amplified* Bible translation (2015). I believe that many people have connected the Bible only with church or some other spiritual activity when it really is a life-giving Book we can apply to our lives daily.

I also believe the Bible is largely a book about relationships. It offers in-depth information about our relationships with God, ourselves, and our fellow human beings. Much of the difficulty we face in life is the result of poor relationships. I have learned through God's Word how to receive His love, love myself in a balanced way, and let His love flow through me to others. I pray that this would be your goal because Jesus said that the thing we should concentrate on is loving God and loving others as we love ourselves (see Matthew 27:37–39).

Let me encourage you to be a "lifetime learner." Apply God's Word to situations in your life as you would apply medicine to an injury. If you are having a particular struggle such as anger, depression, or fear, go to God's Word and select passages that deal with these subjects (I have provided in the back of this Bible a topical index called "The Word for Your Everyday Life," which makes finding these passages easy for you). As you read these verses, slowly take them in, and roll them over and over in your mind. You will find a change taking place in your heart and life. I encourage you to love God's Word, for in it you will find resurrection power and contentment far greater than anything the world has to offer.

Now, I want to make sure you are aware of the special features *The Everyday Life Bible* has to offer because I believe they will help tremendously as you live your life by the Word of God.

Book Introductions: At the beginning of every book of the Bible, you will find basic historical background information on that particular book, along with my thoughts on why each book is important and how it relates to practical living. You will also find "Everyday Life Principles," which summarize the key points and general themes of each book.

Everyday Life Articles: These articles are the longest, most thorough entries in the Bible. They correspond to specific verses or passages, and provide great insight and advice on a variety of topics. I wrote many of them especially for *The Everyday Life Bible*, and I believe they will help you tremendously in your everyday life.

Life Points: If you have followed my teaching ministry for long, you may realize that I often use short, catchy, to-the-point phrases or "one-liners" to emphasize certain principles or truths. Life Points include many of these well-known phrases, as well and other nuggets of encouragement and exhortation.

Speak the Word: I believe that confessing God's Word is vital to a successful Christian life. Anywhere you see an entry entitled, "Speak the Word," you will find a Scripture verse or passage adapted as a first-person confession or prayer. I encourage you to speak and pray these words as you come across them in this Bible and use them to teach you how to pray and confess other verses throughout God's Word.

Putting the Word to Work: We all need to apply the truths of God's Word to our lives. The "Putting the Word to Work" feature takes biblical principles and gives you opportunities to meditate on them, answer questions about them, and think about how you can specifically apply them to the situations in your life.

The Word for Your Everyday Life: Located in the back of this Bible, "The Word for Your Everyday Life" is a list of topics you are likely to face over the course of your life—perhaps many times. Under each topic heading, you will find Scripture references pertaining to that topic. Read those verses and passages, and you will discover biblical answers and guidance to help you overcome every challenge and live your life victoriously.

How To Receive Jesus as Your Personal Lord and Savior: The most important relationship of your life is a personal relationship with Jesus Christ. If you would like to receive Him as your Lord and Savior, and enter into the greatest relationship you have ever known, please pray the prayer at the back of the Bible on the page entitled, "How To Receive Jesus as Your Personal Lord and Savior."

Contents

Contents

Old Testament

Genesis

Author:
Moses

Date:
About 1440 BC

Everyday Life Principles:
Beginnings are important and, thankfully, God continually gives us opportunities for a fresh start.

Be watching for the opportunities God brings your way. They will present themselves in the situations of your everyday life, such as your relationships, your workplace, the way you choose to spend your time, and issues of personal integrity.

Only as you take advantage of these opportunities can you move forward in God's plans for your life.

We often hear the book of Genesis described as a "book of beginnings," but I also like to think of it as a book of opportunities. From its start to its finish, we read stories of people who were presented with opportunities.

First, we see Eve with the opportunity to choose between good and evil—between God's instruction and the serpent's deception. We read about Noah and his opportunity to demonstrate his faith when everyone around him thought he was crazy. We see Abraham with an opportunity to believe God's promise when it was naturally impossible and then to obey God when obedience required a willingness to sacrifice the promised son for whom he waited so long. We learn about Jacob's opportunity to deceive, which resulted in all kinds of trouble—and later with an opportunity to surrender completely to God, which resulted in great blessing. We see Joseph with opportunities to forgive and to trust God.

Throughout Genesis, people were blessed when they took advantage of opportunities to choose well—to choose truth over deception, faith over fear, peace over strife, forgiveness over bitterness, patience and waiting on God over trying to force something to happen. I hope the stories and principles in this book will help you recognize the opportunities God gives you and help you make wise choices that will lead to greater blessings than you have ever known.

1 IN THE beginning God (*Elohim*) created [by forming from nothing] the heavens and the earth. [Heb 11:3]

²The earth was formless and void *or* a waste and emptiness, and darkness was upon the face of the deep [primeval ocean that covered the unformed earth]. The Spirit of God was moving (hovering, brooding) over the face of the waters.

³And God said, "Let there be light"; and there was light.

⁴God saw that the light was good (pleasing, useful) *and* He affirmed and sustained it; and God separated the light [distinguishing it] from the darkness. [2 Cor 4:6]

⁵And God called the light day, and the darkness He called night. And there was evening and there was morning, one day.

⁶And God said, "Let there be an expanse [of the sky] in the midst of the waters, and let it separate the waters [below the expanse] from the waters [above the expanse]."

⁷And God made the expanse [of sky] and separated the waters which were under the expanse from the waters which were above the expanse; and it was so [just as He commanded].

⁸God called the expanse [of sky] heaven. And there was evening and there was morning, a second day.

⁹Then God said, "Let the waters below the heavens be gathered into one place [of standing, pooling together], and let the dry land appear"; and it was so.

¹⁰God called the dry land earth, and the gathering of the waters He called seas; and God saw that this was good (pleasing, useful) *and* He affirmed and sustained it.

¹¹So God said, "Let the earth sprout [tender] vegetation, plants yielding seed, and fruit trees bearing fruit according to (limited to, consistent with) their kind, whose seed is in them upon the earth"; and it was so.

¹²The earth sprouted *and* abundantly produced vegetation, plants yielding seed according to their kind, and trees bearing fruit with seed in them, according to their kind; and God saw that it was good *and* He affirmed and sustained it.

¹³And there was evening and there was morning, a third day.

¹⁴Then God said, "Let there be light-bearers (sun, moon, stars) in the expanse of the heavens to separate the day from the night, and let them be *useful* for signs (tokens) [of God's provident care], and for *marking* seasons, days, and years; [Gen 8:22]

¹⁵and let them be *useful* as lights in the expanse of the heavens to provide light on the earth"; and it was so, [just as He commanded].

¹⁶God made the two great lights—the greater light (the sun) to rule the day, and the lesser light (the moon) to rule the night; *He made* the [galaxies of] stars also [that is, all the amazing wonders in the heavens].

¹⁷God placed them in the expanse of the heavens to provide light upon the earth,

¹⁸to rule over the day and the night, and to separate the light from the darkness; and God saw that it was good *and* He affirmed and sustained it.

speak the Word

Lord, I thank You that You have blessed me and called me to be fruitful in my life. I pray that I will use the resources You have created to serve You and to serve others.

—ADAPTED FROM GENESIS 1:28

¹⁹And there was evening and there was morning, a fourth day.

²⁰Then God said, "Let the waters swarm *and* abundantly produce living creatures, and let birds soar above the earth in the open expanse of the heavens."

²¹God created the great sea monsters and every living creature that moves, with which the waters swarmed according to their kind, and every winged bird according to its kind; and God saw that it was good *and* He affirmed and sustained it.

²²And God blessed them, saying, "Be fruitful, multiply, and fill the waters in the seas, and let birds multiply on the earth."

²³And there was evening and there was morning, a fifth day.

²⁴Then God said, "Let the earth bring forth living creatures according to (limited to, consistent with) their kind: livestock, crawling things, and wild animals of the earth according to their kinds"; and it was so [because He had spoken them into creation].

²⁵So God made the wild animals of the earth according to their kind, and the cattle according to their kind, and

enjoy your life

When God had completed His six days of creation, He took time to look over everything and He saw that "it was very good and He validated it completely" (Genesis 1:31). God took time to enjoy the work of His hands, and we should do the same. In our passion to possess more and more, we often fall into the trap of working, working, working—and we never enjoy the fruit of our labor. Sometimes we should simply take time to relax and enjoy what we have accomplished.

The writer of Ecclesiastes said there is nothing better for a person than to see "good in his labor" (Ecclesiastes 2:24). I have always been a hard worker. A few years ago, I realized I was working hard but not taking time to enjoy what I was doing. I made a decision to include enjoyment in my life. I no longer just "do" conferences; I enjoy them. When my house is clean and pretty, I take time to look at it and enjoy it. At the end of a year I go over my calendar and remember the various things I have done, and I enjoy the sense of accomplishment it brings. I look at what God has enabled me to do, and I say, "It is good."

Many people feel worthless, insecure, and unacceptable, but God looked at *everything* He had created, including man, and said, "It is very good." He validated it completely. God knows everything about each of us, and He loves us unconditionally. God approves of us; He may not approve of everything we do, but He does approve of us as His beloved children. I encourage you to make a decision to not only enjoy the labor of your hands, but to approve of and enjoy yourself as well.

Choosing to enjoy and accept myself is one of the best decisions I have ever made. God does not create anything worthless. He is good, and everything He does is good. We cannot believe that God created us and also believe we are worthless. Begin to accept and enjoy yourself where you are, and God will help you get to where you need to be.

everything that creeps *and* crawls on the earth according to its kind; and God saw that it was good (pleasing, useful) *and* He affirmed and sustained it.

²⁶Then God said, "Let Us (Father, Son, Holy Spirit) make man in Our image, according to Our likeness [not physical, but a spiritual personality and moral likeness]; and let them have complete authority over the fish of the sea, the birds of the air, the cattle, and over the entire earth, and over everything that creeps *and* crawls on the earth." [Ps 104:30; Heb 1:2; 11:3]

²⁷So God created man in His own image, in the image *and* likeness of God He created him; male and female He created them. [Col 3:9, 10; James 3:8, 9]

²⁸And God blessed them [granting them certain authority] and said to them, "Be fruitful, multiply, and fill the earth, and subjugate it [putting it under your power]; and rule over (dominate) the fish of the sea, the birds of the air, and every living thing that moves upon the earth."

²⁹So God said, "Behold, I have given you every plant yielding seed that is on the surface of the entire earth, and every tree which has fruit yielding seed; it shall be food for you;

³⁰and to all the animals on the earth and to every bird of the air and to everything that moves on the ground—to everything in which there is the breath of life—*I have given* every green plant for food"; and it was so [because He commanded it].

³¹God saw everything that He had made, and behold, it was very good *and* He validated it completely. And there was evening and there was morning, a sixth day.

life point

Here in the very first chapter of the Bible, God clearly communicates His desire for our lives to be fruitful. Two of the things necessary to live fruitful lives are balance and pruning. To stay balanced we need to make sure we get the right amounts of healthy nourishment, rest, work, play, time alone with God, and time to enjoy godly relationships.

Pruning is not always pleasant, but it does ensure that the situations, activities, or relationships that are depleting us will not continue to do so. It means something must be cut off or removed from our lives, but God promises great reward as a result—more fruitfulness than ever!

Stay balanced by letting God, the wise Master Gardener, prune your life as He sees fit, and you will enjoy years of fruitfulness and fulfillment.

2 SO THE heavens and the earth were completed, and all their hosts (inhabitants). ²And by the seventh day God completed His work which He had done, and He rested (ceased) on the seventh day from all His work which He had done. [Heb 4:9, 10] ³So God blessed the seventh day and sanctified it [as His own, that is, set it apart as holy from other days], because in it He rested from all His work which He had created and done. [Ex 20:11] ⁴This is the history of [the origin of] the heavens and of the earth when they were created, in the day [that is, days of creation] that the LORD God made the earth and the heavens— ⁵no shrub *or* plant of the field was yet in the earth, and no herb of the field had yet sprouted, for the LORD God had not caused it to rain on the earth, and there was no man to cultivate the ground, ⁶but a mist (fog, dew, vapor) used to rise from the land and water the entire surface of the ground—

⁷then the Lord God formed [that is, created the body of] man from the dust of the ground, and breathed into his nostrils the breath of life; and the man became a living being [an individual complete in body and spirit]. [1 Cor 15:45–49]

⁸And the Lord God planted a garden (oasis) in the east, in Eden (delight, land of happiness); and He put the man whom He had formed (created) there.

⁹And [in that garden] the Lord God

a very creative God

I cannot imagine what a job it must have been for Adam to name all the birds and animals. He certainly had to be creative to do that!

I could go on and on about how diverse and imaginative God was in creation, but I am sure, if you think about it, you will agree that our God is awesome not only in His power and His love, but also in His creativity.

Simply take a walk and look around. Watch something about nature on a video or on television. Find out what is in the ocean, or learn about how bees and flowers work together. Then realize that the same Holy Spirit present at Creation is living inside you if you have truly accepted Jesus Christ as your Lord and Savior.

So much creativity lies within each one of us, and we need to learn to tap into it and express it without fear. Often, instead of exercising creativity, we keep repeating the same things, even when we are bored with them, simply because we are afraid to step out and do something different. Even if we like the familiar, we all need variety in our lives.

Some people keep the same job or live in the same geographic area all of their lives because they feel those activities or environments are safe. Even if they feel unfulfilled and unhappy at work, at least they know how to do their jobs (they're familiar) and are comfortable with them—and the thought of getting other jobs is frightening to them! In other cases, people do want to make changes in their lives, but they do not want to fail at something new, so they refuse to try and they stick with the familiar.

I do not encourage people to pursue every whim that crosses their minds or to latch onto every fad that comes their way. But there is a definite time to step out of the ordinary—out of the comfort zone—and into new things.

God has created us to need diversity and variety. We are designed to require freshness and newness in our lives, and there is nothing wrong with feeling that you "just need a change." On the other hand, never being satisfied and always trying the next new thing is another type of problem. Stay within reason, but do not be afraid of something new. Embrace the fresh and different opportunities, experiences, and environments God brings your way. He is a creative God; His creativity did not stop in the Garden of Eden, but is still active today as He continues to shape and refine the wonderful creation He is making in you!

caused to grow from the ground every tree that is desirable *and* pleasing to the sight and good (suitable, pleasant) for food; the tree of life was also in the midst of the garden, and the tree of the [experiential] knowledge (recognition) of [the difference between] good and evil. [Rev 2:7; 22:14, 19]

¹⁰Now a river flowed out of Eden to water the garden; and from there it divided and became four [branching] rivers.

¹¹The first [river] is named Pishon; it flows around the entire land of Havilah, where there is gold.

¹²The gold of that land is good; bdellium (a fragrant, valuable resin) and the onyx stone are found there.

¹³The name of the second river is Gihon; it flows around the entire land of Cush [in Mesopotamia].

¹⁴The third river is named Hiddekel (Tigris); it flows east of Assyria. And the fourth river is the Euphrates.

¹⁵So the LORD God took the man [He had made] and settled him in the Garden of Eden to cultivate and keep it.

¹⁶And the LORD God commanded the man, saying, "You may freely (unconditionally) eat [the fruit] from every tree of the garden;

¹⁷but [only] from the tree of the knowledge (recognition) of good and evil you shall not eat, otherwise on

life point

Adam did what God told him not to do (see Genesis 3:1–6). As a result, Adam became a captive of Satan, who had lured him into going against what God had said. By listening to Satan instead of to God, Adam surrendered to Satan the authority to rule the earth that God had originally given to man. Always listen to God and obey His Word.

life point

God created Adam as a living being, in His image (see Genesis 1:26–27), and gave him authority over everything else He had created (see Genesis 1:28). Man was created to rule under God and to be the physical carrier of God's Spirit in the earth. Part of human nature is that we, as living beings like Adam, have a free will. Why? Because God is too loving to force submission from anyone. He wants us to freely choose to love and serve Him. I hope that today you will make a fresh and willful commitment to love and serve Him with all your heart.

the day that you eat from it, you shall most certainly die [because of your disobedience]."

¹⁸Now the LORD God said, "It is not good (beneficial) for the man to be alone; I will make him a helper [one who balances him—a counterpart who is] suitable *and* complementary for him."

¹⁹So the LORD God formed out of the ground every animal of the field and every bird of the air, and brought them to Adam to see what he would call them; and whatever the man called a living creature, that was its name.

²⁰And the man gave names to all the livestock, and to the birds of the air, and to every animal of the field; but for Adam there was not found a helper [that was] suitable (a companion) for him.

²¹So the LORD God caused a deep sleep to fall upon Adam; and while he slept, He took one of his ribs and closed up the flesh at that place.

²²And the rib which the LORD God had taken from the man He made (fashioned, formed) into a woman, and He brought her *and* presented her to the man.

²³Then Adam said,

"This is now bone of my bones,
And flesh of my flesh;
She shall be called Woman,
Because she was taken out of Man."

²⁴For this reason a man shall leave his father and his mother, and shall be joined to his wife; and they shall become one flesh. [Matt 19:5; 1 Cor 6:16; Eph 5:31–33] ²⁵And the man and his wife were both naked and were not ashamed *or* embarrassed.

3 NOW THE serpent was more crafty (subtle, skilled in deceit) than any living creature of the field which the Lᴏʀᴅ God had made. And the serpent (Satan) said to the woman, "Can it really be that God has said, 'You shall not eat from any tree of the garden'?" [Rev 12:9–11] ²And the woman said to the serpent, "We may eat fruit from the trees of the garden, ³except the fruit from the tree which is in the middle of the garden. God

becoming one

The minute two people marry, they are legally joined together. Experientially, though, they do not immediately "become one" when they say, "I do"; they simply begin the *process* of becoming one (see Genesis 2:24). As the process works itself out, each partner should hold marriage in honor and esteem the relationship as worthy and precious. They should treat each other as being very valuable.

Note in this passage a three-step progression that demonstrates how to become one: (1) *Leave.* Sometimes a wife clings excessively to her mother and her mother's opinions about what she ought to do, or a husband runs to his father for advice, when the couple should be trusting and leaning on each other. If two people are married but have not left home (both physically and mentally), they need to do so. (2) *Be joined.* In practical terms, this means to stick to each other like glue. (3) *Become one.* Becoming one means the complete union of body, soul, and spirit—and again, this takes time.

If both people in a marriage relationship are born again, then the spiritual union is in place. The most difficult part of the "becoming one" process is usually the uniting of two souls—the joining of two minds, wills, and sets of emotions. Most marital problems in the arena of the soul result from strife over lack of communication, sexual misunderstanding, money, goals, and the disciplining of children. All of these things need to be worked out in the soulish realm of the marriage union, and in order to become one in that area, a husband and a wife need to give their issues to God and say, "Father, change my mind, my will, or my feelings if I'm wrong." God is the One Who will bring them into agreement with His will and purpose. If each marriage partner is willing to be brought into agreement with the other, they no longer try to force each other to be someone they are not, but realize they need each other to be exactly who God created them to be. They no longer pick on each other's weaknesses. Instead, they partake of their strengths, they enjoy one another, and they enjoy the process of becoming one.

said, 'You shall not eat from it nor touch it, otherwise you will die.'"

[4]But the serpent said to the woman, "You certainly will not die! [2 Cor 11:3]

[5]"For God knows that on the day you eat from it your eyes will be opened [that is, you will have greater awareness], and you will be like God, knowing [the difference between] good and evil."

[6]And when the woman saw that the tree was good for food, and that it was delightful to look at, and a tree to be desired in order to make one wise *and* insightful, she took some of its fruit and ate it; and she also gave some to her husband with her, and he ate.

[7]Then the eyes of the two of them were opened [that is, their awareness increased], and they knew that they were naked; and they fastened fig leaves together and made themselves coverings.

[8]And they heard the sound of the LORD God walking in the garden in the cool [afternoon breeze] of the day, so the man and his wife hid *and* kept themselves hidden from the presence of the LORD God among the trees of the garden.

[9]But the LORD God called to Adam, and said to him, "Where are you?"

[10]He said, "I heard the sound of You [walking] in the garden, and I was afraid because I was naked; so I hid myself."

[11]God said, "Who told you that you were naked? Have you eaten [fruit] from the tree of which I commanded you not to eat?"

[12]And the man said, "The woman

the devil's doom

I believe that Adam was clothed with God's glory before he sinned. As soon as Adam and Eve sinned, they realized they were naked. We might say that they lost their "covering." As long as they obeyed God, they were protected from everything the devil wanted to do to them—and, ultimately, through them. Upon seeing what the devil had done, God immediately announced his doom and told him how it would take place.

Satan did not really understand what God was saying; nevertheless, God said it, and it had to come to pass: "And I will put enmity (open hostility) between you and the woman, and between your seed (offspring) and her Seed; He shall [fatally] bruise your head, and you shall [only] bruise His heel" (Genesis 3:15).

To "bruise the head" symbolizes a weakening of authority. God has said that the woman's offspring (Jesus) will take away Satan's authority. Satan will bruise Jesus' heel (afflict His body—both on the cross and by afflicting mankind).

Through Jesus' death on the cross, God took Satan's authority (which Adam had given him) and gave it first to Jesus and then to every person who will believe—not only that Jesus died for them, but also that Satan has lost authority over them. We need to understand not only that Jesus died for us, but also that He has *redeemed* us!

No matter what the devil tries to do to you, he is doomed to defeat, and you are redeemed and victorious over him through Jesus Christ.

whom You gave to be with me—she gave me [fruit] from the tree, and I ate it."

¹³Then the Lord God said to the woman, "What is this that you have done?" And the woman said, "The serpent beguiled *and* deceived me, and I ate [from the forbidden tree]." [2 Cor 11:3; 1 Tim 2:14]

¹⁴The Lord God said to the serpent,

"Because you have done this,
You are cursed more than all
    the cattle,
And more than any animal of
    the field;
On your belly you shall go,
And dust you shall eat
All the days of your life.
¹⁵"And I will put enmity (open
    hostility)
Between you and the woman,
And between your seed (offspring)
    and her Seed;
He shall [fatally] bruise your head,
And you shall [only] bruise His
    heel." [Gal 4:4]

¹⁶To the woman He said,

"I will greatly multiply
Your pain in childbirth;
In pain you will give birth to
    children;
Yet your desire *and* longing will
    be for your husband,
And he will rule [with authority]
    over you *and* be responsible
    for you."

¹⁷Then to Adam the Lord God said, "Because you have listened [attentively] to the voice of your wife, and have eaten [fruit] from the tree about which I commanded you, saying, 'You shall not eat of it';

The ground is [now] under a curse
    because of you;
In sorrow *and* toil you shall eat
    [the fruit] of it
All the days of your life.

¹⁸"Both thorns and thistles it shall
    grow for you;
And you shall eat the plants of
    the field.
¹⁹"By the sweat of your face
You will eat bread
Until you return to the ground,
For from it you were taken;
For you are dust,
And to dust you shall return."

²⁰The man named his wife Eve (life spring, life giver), because she was the mother of all the living. ²¹The Lord God made tunics of [animal] skins for Adam and his wife and clothed them. ²²And the Lord God said, "Behold, the man has become like one of Us (Father, Son, Holy Spirit), knowing [how to distinguish between] good and evil; and now, he might stretch out his hand, and take from the tree of life as well, and eat [its fruit], and live [in this fallen, sinful condition] forever"— ²³therefore the Lord God sent Adam away from the Garden of Eden, to till *and* cultivate the ground from which he was taken. ²⁴So God drove the man out; and at the east of the Garden of Eden He [permanently] stationed the cherubim and the sword with the flashing blade which turned round and round [in every direction] to protect *and* guard the way (entrance, access) to the tree of life. [Rev 2:7; 22:2, 14, 19]

4 NOW THE man Adam knew Eve as his wife, and she conceived and gave birth to Cain, and she said, "I have obtained a man (baby boy, son) with *the help of* the Lord." ²And [later] she gave birth to his brother Abel. Now Abel kept the flocks [of sheep and goats], but Cain cultivated the ground. ³And in the course of time Cain

brought to the LORD an offering of the fruit of the ground.

[4]But Abel brought [an offering of] the [finest] firstborn of his flock and the fat portions. And the LORD had respect (regard) for Abel and for his offering; [Heb 11:4]

[5]but for Cain and his offering He had no respect. So Cain became extremely angry (indignant), and he looked annoyed *and* hostile.

[6]And the LORD said to Cain, "Why are you so angry? And why do you look annoyed?

[7]"If you do well [believing Me and doing what is acceptable and pleasing to Me], will you not be accepted? And if you do not do well [but ignore My instruction], sin crouches at your door; its desire is for you [to overpower you], but you must master it."

[8]Cain talked with Abel his brother [about what God had said]. And when they were [alone, working] in the field, Cain attacked Abel his brother and killed him. [1 John 3:12]

[9]Then the LORD said to Cain, "Where is Abel your brother?" And he [lied and] said, "I do not know. Am I my brother's keeper?"

[10]The LORD said, "What have you done? The voice of your brother's [innocent] blood is crying out to Me from the ground [for justice]. [Num 35:33; Deut 21:1–9]

[11]"And now you are cursed from the ground, which has opened its mouth to receive your brother's [shed] blood from your hand. [Deut 28:15–20]

[12]"When you cultivate the ground, it shall no longer yield its strength [it will resist producing good crops] for you; you shall be a fugitive and a vagabond [roaming aimlessly] on the earth [in perpetual exile without a home, a degraded outcast]."

[13]Cain said to the LORD, "My punishment is greater than I can bear.

[14]"Behold, You have driven me out this day from the face of the land; and from Your face (presence) I will be hidden, and I will be a fugitive and an [aimless] vagabond on the earth, and whoever finds me will kill me."

[15]And the LORD said to him, "Therefore, whoever kills Cain, a sevenfold vengeance [that is, punishment seven times worse] shall be taken on him [by Me]." And the LORD set a [protective] mark (sign) on Cain, so that no one who found (met) him would kill him. [Gen 4:24]

[16]So Cain went away from the [manifested] presence of the LORD, and lived in the land of Nod [wandering in exile], east of Eden.

[17]Cain knew his wife [one of Adam's descendants] and she conceived and gave birth to Enoch; and Cain built a city and named it Enoch, after the name of his son.

[18]Now to Enoch was born Irad, and Irad became the father of Mehujael, and Mehujael became the father of Methushael, and Methushael became the father of Lamech.

[19]And Lamech took for himself two wives; the name of the one was Adah, and the name of the other, Zillah.

[20]Adah gave birth to Jabal; he became the father of those [nomadic

putting the Word to work

Cain did not relate well to his brother, Abel. We know that their interests and pursuits were different, because Abel was a shepherd and Cain tilled the ground. We do not know what their other differences were, but Cain's resentment of Abel eventually led to murder (see Genesis 4:8).

How do you respond to those who are close to you, yet have different personalities, gifts, or pursuits? Ask God to help you when you are tempted to resent them.

herdsmen] who live in tents and have cattle *and* raise livestock.

²¹His brother's name was Jubal; he became the father of all those [musicians] who play the lyre and flute.

²²Zillah gave birth to Tubal-cain, the smith (craftsman) *and* teacher of every artisan in instruments of bronze and iron. The sister of Tubal-cain was Naamah.

²³Lamech said to his wives,

"Adah and Zillah,
Hear my voice;
You wives of Lamech,
Listen to what I say;
For I have killed a man [merely]
   for wounding me,
And a boy [only] for striking
   (bruising) me.
²⁴"If Cain is avenged sevenfold [as
   the LORD said he would be],
Then Lamech [will be avenged]
   seventy-sevenfold."

²⁵Adam knew [Eve as] his wife again; and she gave birth to a son, and named him Seth, for [she said], "God has granted another child for me in place of Abel, because Cain killed him."

²⁶To Seth, also, a son was born, whom he named Enosh (mortal man, mankind). At that [same] time men began to call on the name of the LORD [in worship through prayer, praise, and thanksgiving]. [Joel 2:32; Luke 3:38; Acts 2:21]

5 THIS IS the book (the written record, the history) of the generations of [the descendants of] Adam. When God created man, He made him in the likeness of God [not physical, but a spiritual personality and moral likeness].

²He created them male and female, and blessed them and named them *Mankind at the time they were created.

³When Adam had lived a hundred and thirty years, he *became the father

of *a son* in his own likeness, according to his image, and named him Seth.

⁴After he became the father of Seth, Adam lived eight hundred years and had *other* sons and daughters.

⁵So Adam lived nine hundred and thirty years in all, and he died.

⁶When Seth was a hundred and five years old, he became the father of Enosh.

⁷Seth lived eight hundred and seven years after the birth of Enosh, and he had *other* sons and daughters.

⁸So Seth lived nine hundred and twelve years, and he died.

⁹When Enosh was ninety years old, he became the father of Kenan.

¹⁰Enosh lived eight hundred and fifteen years after the birth of Kenan and had *other* sons and daughters.

¹¹So Enosh lived nine hundred and five years, and he died.

¹²When Kenan was seventy years old, he became the father of Mahalalel.

¹³Kenan lived eight hundred and forty years after the birth of Mahalalel and had *other* sons and daughters.

¹⁴So Kenan lived nine hundred and ten years, and he died.

¹⁵When Mahalalel was sixty-five years old, he became the father of Jared.

¹⁶Mahalalel lived eight hundred and thirty years after the birth of Jared and had *other* sons and daughters.

¹⁷So Mahalalel lived eight hundred and ninety-five years, and he died.

¹⁸When Jared was a hundred and sixty-two years old, he became the father of Enoch.

¹⁹Jared lived eight hundred years after the birth of Enoch and had *other* sons and daughters.

²⁰So Jared lived nine hundred and sixty-two years, and he died.

²¹When Enoch was sixty-five years old, he became the father of Methuselah.

²²Enoch walked [in habitual fellowship] with God three hundred years

5:2 Lit *Adam*.   5:3 Lit *begot*, and so throughout chapter.

after the birth of Methuselah and had *other* sons and daughters.

²³So all the days of Enoch were three hundred and sixty-five years.

²⁴And [in reverent fear and obedience] Enoch walked with God; and he was not [found among men], because God took him [away to be home with Him]. [Heb 11:5]

²⁵When Methuselah was a hundred and eighty-seven years old, he became the father of Lamech.

²⁶Methuselah lived seven hundred and eighty-two years after the birth of Lamech and had *other* sons and daughters.

²⁷So Methuselah lived nine hundred and sixty-nine years, and he died.

²⁸When Lamech was a hundred and eighty-two years old, he became the father of a son.

²⁹He named him Noah, saying, "This one shall bring us rest *and* comfort from our work and from the [dreadful] toil of our hands because of the ground which the LORD cursed."

³⁰Lamech lived five hundred and ninety-five years after the birth of Noah and had *other* sons and daughters.

³¹So all the days of Lamech were seven hundred and seventy-seven years, and he died.

³²After Noah was five hundred years old, he became the father of Shem, Ham, and Japheth.

6 NOW IT happened, when men began to multiply on the face of the land, and daughters were born to them,

²that the sons of God saw that the daughters of men were beautiful *and* desirable; and they took wives for

putting the Word to work

According to Genesis 6:12, the world around Noah was "debased and degenerate." People had "corrupted their way on the earth and lost their true direction." In the midst of corruption and evil around you today, how can you be like Noah and be righteous before God in your generation?

themselves, whomever they chose *and* desired.

³Then the LORD said, "My Spirit shall not strive *and* remain with man forever, because he is indeed flesh [sinful, corrupt—given over to sensual appetites]; nevertheless his days shall yet be a hundred and twenty years."

⁴There were Nephilim (men of stature, notorious men) on the earth in those days—and also afterward—when the sons of God lived with the daughters of men, and they gave birth to their *children*. These were the mighty men who were of old, men of renown (great reputation, fame). [Num 13:33]

⁵The LORD saw that the wickedness (depravity) of man was great on the earth, and that every imagination *or* intent of the thoughts of his heart were only evil continually.

⁶The LORD regretted that He had made mankind on the earth, and He was [deeply] grieved in His heart.

⁷So the LORD said, "I will destroy (annihilate) mankind whom I have created from the surface of the earth—not only man, but the animals and the crawling things and the birds of the air—because it [deeply] grieves Me [to see mankind's sin] *and* I regret that I have made them."

speak the Word

Father, I thank You that I have found grace and favor in Your sight.
–ADAPTED FROM GENESIS 6:8

[8]But Noah found favor *and* grace in the eyes of the LORD.

[9]These are *the records of* the generations (family history) of Noah. Noah was a righteous man [one who was just and had right standing with God], blameless in his [evil] generation; Noah walked (lived) [in habitual fellowship] with God.

[10]Now Noah became the father of three sons: Shem, Ham, and Japheth. [11]The [population of the] earth was corrupt [absolutely depraved—spiritually and morally putrid] in

the importance of a right heart

Genesis 6:5–8 reveals two things that displease God: wickedness, and evil imaginations and intentions of the heart. Because those things described the condition of people's hearts during Noah's day, God decided to destroy all mankind—everyone, that is, except Noah and his family. God spared Noah's life because Noah had found grace and favor in His eyes.

I can only surmise that Noah must have had a right heart; otherwise, he would have been destroyed with all the other people who practiced wickedness, evil imaginations, and evil intentions in their hearts.

One of the lessons we can learn from Noah's story is that many people today are being destroyed for the simple reason that their hearts are not right before God. In their hearts they regard wickedness, they allow impure imaginations, and they think bad thoughts.

We cannot imagine how many areas of our lives would be straightened out if we would just get our hearts right with God! Our hearts may not be filled with the blatant evil we read about in Noah's time, but bad attitudes and wrong thinking certainly qualify as evil imaginations and evil intentions. We need to have right attitudes toward everything we do, because our attitudes basically determine everything else about our situations. If our hearts are full of bad attitudes and our minds are full of "stinking thinking," we will not make much progress in life.

We need to have pure, tender hearts. We need to hear and heed the voice of conscience so that the moment we realize we have a bad attitude about something or someone, we can make the necessary adjustments. That is why Proverbs 4:23 instructs us: "Watch over your heart with all diligence, for from it flow the springs of life."

So often, we fail to guard our hearts as diligently as we should, and we allow too many negative feelings into our hearts and too many negative thoughts into our minds. We need to remember the familiar phrase "garbage in, garbage out," and realize that we cannot take in garbage and produce good things. We must be attentive not only to our actions, but also to our thoughts, imaginations, motives, intentions, and attitudes. God looks at these things because He is a God of hearts. Whatever you do, make sure you have a right heart before the Lord, and you will reap abundant life instead of destruction.

God's sight, and the land was filled with violence [desecration, infringement, outrage, assault, and lust for power].

¹²God looked on the earth and saw how debased *and* degenerate it was, for all humanity had corrupted their way on the earth *and* lost their true direction.

¹³God said to Noah, "I intend to make an end of all that lives, for through men the land is filled with violence; and behold, I am about to destroy them together with the land.

¹⁴"Make yourself an ark of gopher wood; make in it rooms (stalls, pens, coops, nests, cages, compartments) and coat it inside and out with pitch (bitumen).

¹⁵"This is the way you are to make it: the length of the ark shall be three hundred cubits, its width fifty cubits, and its height thirty cubits (450' x 75' x 45').

¹⁶"You shall make a window [for light and ventilation] for the ark, and finish it to at least a cubit (eighteen inches) from the top—and set the [entry] door of the ark in its side; and you shall make it with lower, second and third decks.

¹⁷"For behold, I, even I, will bring a flood of waters on the earth, to destroy all life under the heavens in which there is the breath *and* spirit of life; everything that is on the land shall die.

¹⁸"But I will establish My covenant (solemn promise, formal agreement) with you; and you shall come into the ark—you and your [three] sons and your wife, and your sons' wives with you.

¹⁹"And of every living thing [found on land], you shall bring two of every kind into the ark, to keep them alive with you; they shall be male and female.

²⁰"Of fowls *and* birds according to their kind, of animals according to their kind, of every crawling thing of the ground according to its kind—two of every kind shall come to you to keep them alive.

²¹"Also take with you every kind of food that is edible, and you shall collect *and* store it; and it shall be food for you and for them."

²²So Noah did this; according to all that God commanded him, that is what he did.

7 THEN THE LORD said to Noah, "Come into the ark, you with all your household, for you [alone] I have seen as righteous (doing what is right) before Me in this generation. [Ps 27:5; 33:18, 19; 2 Pet 2:9]

²"Of every clean animal you shall take with you seven pair, the male and his female, and of animals that are not clean, two each the male and his female; [Lev 11:1–13]

³also of the birds of the air, seven pair, the male and the female, to keep the offspring alive on the surface of the earth.

⁴"For in seven days I am going to cause it to rain on the earth for forty days and forty nights; and I will destroy (blot out, wipe away) every living thing that I have made from the surface of the earth."

⁵So Noah did all that the LORD commanded him. [Heb 11:7]

⁶Noah was six hundred years old when the flood (deluge) of water came on the earth [covering all of the land].

⁷Then Noah and his sons and his

speak the Word

God, I pray that I will be like Noah and do all that You have commanded me to do.
–ADAPTED FROM GENESIS 7:5

wife and his sons' wives with him entered the ark to escape the flood waters. [Matt 24:38; Luke 17:27]

⁸Of clean animals and animals that are not clean and birds *and* fowls and everything that crawls on the ground,

⁹they came [motivated by God] into the ark with Noah two by two, the male and the female, just as God had commanded Noah.

¹⁰And after the seven days [God released the rain and] the floodwaters came on the earth.

¹¹In the six hundredth year of Noah's life, on the seventeenth day of the second month, on that same day all the fountains of the great deep [subterranean waters] burst open, and the windows *and* floodgates of the heavens were opened.

¹²It rained on the earth for forty days and forty nights.

¹³On the very same day Noah and Shem and Ham and Japheth, the sons of Noah, and Noah's wife and the three wives of his sons with them, entered the ark,

¹⁴they and every animal according to its kind, all the livestock according to their kinds, every moving thing that crawls on the earth according to its kind, and every bird according to its kind, every winged thing of every sort.

¹⁵So they went into the ark with Noah, two by two of all living beings in which there was the breath *and* spirit of life.

¹⁶Those which entered, male and female of all flesh (creatures), entered as God had commanded Noah; and the LORD closed *the door* behind him.

¹⁷The flood [the great downpour of rain] was forty days *and* nights on the earth; and the waters increased and lifted up the ark, and it floated [high] above the land.

¹⁸The waters became mighty and increased greatly on the earth, and the ark floated on the surface of the waters.

¹⁹The waters prevailed so greatly *and* were so mighty *and* overwhelming on the earth, so that all the high mountains everywhere under the heavens were covered.

²⁰[In fact] the waters became fifteen cubits higher [than the highest ground], and the mountains were covered.

²¹All living beings that moved on the earth perished—birds and cattle (domestic animals), [wild] animals, all things that swarm *and* crawl on the earth, and all mankind.

²²Everything on the dry land, all in whose nostrils was the breath *and* spirit of life, died.

²³God destroyed (blotted out, wiped away) every living thing that was on the surface of the earth; man and animals and the crawling things and the birds of the heavens were destroyed from the land. Only Noah and those who were with him in the ark remained alive. [Matt 24:37–44]

²⁴The waters covered [all of] the earth for a hundred and fifty days (five months).

8 AND GOD remembered *and* thought kindly of Noah and every living thing and all the animals that were with him in the ark; and God made a wind blow over the land, and the waters receded.

²Also the fountains of the deep [subterranean waters] and the windows of the heavens were closed, the [pouring] rain from the sky was restrained,

³and the waters receded steadily from the earth. At the end of a hundred and fifty days the waters had diminished.

⁴On the seventeenth day of the seventh month [five months after the rain began], the ark came to rest on the mountains of Ararat [in Turkey].

⁵The waters continued to decrease until the tenth month; on the first day of the tenth month the tops of the mountains were seen.

⁶At the end of [another] forty days Noah opened the window of the ark which he had made;

⁷and he sent out a raven, which flew here and there until the waters were dried up from the earth.

⁸Then Noah sent out a dove to see if the water level had fallen below the surface of the land.

⁹But the dove found no place on which to rest the sole of her foot, and she returned to him to the ark, for the waters were [still] on the face of the entire earth. So he reached out his hand and took the dove, and brought her into the ark.

¹⁰He waited another seven days and again sent the dove out from the ark.

¹¹The dove came back to him in the evening, and there, in her beak, was a fresh olive leaf. So Noah knew that the water level had subsided from the earth.

¹²Then he waited another seven days and sent out the dove, but she did not return to him again.

¹³Now in the six hundred and first year [of Noah's life], on the first day of the first month, the waters were drying up from the earth. Then Noah removed the covering of the ark and looked, and the surface of the ground was drying.

¹⁴On the twenty-seventh day of the second month the land was [entirely] dry.

¹⁵And God spoke to Noah, saying,

¹⁶"Go out of the ark, you and your wife and your sons and their wives with you.

¹⁷"Bring out with you every living thing from all flesh—birds and animals and every crawling thing that crawls on the earth—that they may breed abundantly on the earth, and be fruitful and multiply on the earth."

¹⁸So Noah went out, and his wife and his sons and their wives with him [after being in the ark one year and ten days].

¹⁹Every animal, every crawling thing, every bird—and whatever moves on the land—went out by families (types, groupings) from the ark.

²⁰And Noah built an altar to the Lord, and took of every [ceremonially] clean animal and of every clean bird and offered burnt offerings on the altar.

²¹The Lord smelled the pleasing aroma [a soothing, satisfying scent] and the Lord said to Himself, "I will never again curse the ground because of man, for the intent (strong inclination, desire) of man's heart is wicked from his youth; and I will never again destroy every living thing, as I have done.

²²"While the earth remains,
Seedtime and harvest,
Cold and heat,
Winter and summer,
And day and night
Shall not cease."

9 AND GOD blessed Noah and his sons and said to them, "Be fruitful and multiply, and fill the earth.

²"The fear and the terror of you shall be [instinctive] in every animal of the land and in every bird of the air; and together with everything that moves on the ground, and with all the fish of the sea; they are given into your hand.

³"Every moving thing that lives shall be food for you; I give you everything, as I gave you the green plants and vegetables.

⁴"But you shall not eat meat along with its life, that is, its blood. [Lev 7:26; Acts 15:20; 21:25]

⁵"For your lifeblood I will most certainly require an accounting; from every animal [that kills a person] I will require it. And from man, from every man's brother [that is, anyone who murders] I will require the life of man. [Ex 21:28, 29]

⁶"Whoever sheds man's blood [unlawfully],

By man (judicial government)
   shall his blood be shed,
For in the image of God
He made man. [Rom 13:4]
⁷"As for you, be fruitful and multiply;
   Populate the earth abundantly and
   multiply in it."

⁸Then God spoke to Noah and to his sons with him, saying,

⁹"Now behold, I am establishing My covenant (binding agreement, solemn promise) with you and with your descendants after you

¹⁰and with every living creature that is with you—the birds, the livestock, and the wild animals of the earth along with you, of everything that comes out of the ark—every living creature of the earth.

¹¹"I will establish My covenant with you: Never again shall all flesh be cut off by the water of a flood, nor shall there ever again be a flood to destroy *and* ruin the earth."

¹²And God said, "This is the token (visible symbol, memorial) of the [solemn] covenant which I am making between Me and you and every living creature that is with you, for all future generations;

¹³I set My rainbow in the clouds, and it shall be a sign of a covenant between Me and the earth.

¹⁴"It shall come about, when I bring clouds over the earth, that the rainbow shall be seen in the clouds,

¹⁵and I will [compassionately] remember My covenant, which is between Me and you and every living creature of all flesh; and never again will the water become a flood to destroy all flesh.

¹⁶"When the rainbow is in the clouds and I look at it, I will [solemnly] remember the everlasting covenant between God and every living creature of all flesh that is on the earth."

¹⁷And God said to Noah, "This [rainbow] is the sign of the covenant (solemn pledge, binding agreement) which I have established between Me and all living things on the earth."

¹⁸The sons of Noah who came out of the ark were Shem and Ham and Japheth. Ham would become the father of Canaan.

¹⁹These are the three sons of Noah, and from these [men] the whole earth was populated *and* scattered with inhabitants.

²⁰And Noah began to farm *and* cultivate the ground and he planted a vineyard.

²¹He drank some of the wine and became drunk, and he was uncovered *and* lay exposed inside his tent.

²²Ham, the father of Canaan, saw [by accident] the nakedness of his father, and [to his father's shame] told his two brothers outside.

²³So Shem and Japheth took a robe and put it on both their shoulders, and walked backwards and covered the nakedness of their father; their faces were turned away so that they did not see their father's nakedness.

²⁴When Noah awoke from his wine [induced stupor], he knew what his younger son [Ham] had done to him.

²⁵So he said,

"Cursed be Canaan [the son of Ham];
A servant of servants
He shall be to his brothers."
   [Deut 27:16]

²⁶He also said,

"Blessed be the Lᴏʀᴅ,
The God of Shem;
And let Canaan be his servant.
²⁷"May God enlarge [the land of] Japheth,
And let him dwell in the tents of Shem;
And let Canaan be his servant."

²⁸Noah lived three hundred and fifty years after the flood.

²⁹So all the days of Noah were nine hundred and fifty years, and he died.

10 THESE ARE *the records of* the generations (descendants) of Shem, Ham, and Japheth, the sons of Noah; and the sons born to them after the flood:

²the sons of Japheth: Gomer, Magog, Madai, Javan, Tubal, Meshech, and Tiras;

³the sons of Gomer: Ashkenaz, Riphath, and Togarmah;

⁴the sons of Javan: Elishah, Tarshish, Kittim, and Dodanim.

⁵From these, [the people of] the coastlands of the nations were separated *and* spread into their lands, every one according to his own language, according to their constituent groups (families), *and* into their nations:

⁶the sons of Ham: Cush, Mizraim [from whom descended the Egyptians], Put, and Canaan;

⁷the sons of Cush: Seba, Havilah, Sabtah, Raamah, and Sabteca; and the sons of Raamah; Sheba and Dedan.

⁸Cush became the father of Nimrod; he became a mighty one on the earth.

⁹He was a mighty hunter before the Lᴏʀᴅ; therefore it is said, "Like Nimrod a mighty hunter before the Lᴏʀᴅ."

¹⁰The beginning of his kingdom was *Babel and Erech and Accad and Calneh, in the land of Shinar [in Babylonia].

¹¹From that land Nimrod went to Assyria, and built Nineveh, and Rehoboth-Ir, and Calah,

¹²and [Nimrod built] Resen, which is between Nineveh and Calah; all these [combined to form] the great city [Nineveh]. [Jon 1:2; 3:2]

¹³Mizraim [the ancestor of the Egyptians] became the father of Ludim, Anamim, Lehabim, Naphtuhim

¹⁴and Pathrusim and Casluhim— from whom came the Philistines—and Caphtorim.

¹⁵Canaan became the father of Sidon, his firstborn, and Heth

¹⁶and the Jebusite and the Amorite and the Girgashite

¹⁷and the Hivite and the Arkite and the Sinite

¹⁸and the Arvadite and the Zemarite and the Hamathite. Afterward the families of the Canaanite were spread abroad.

¹⁹The territory of the Canaanite extended from Sidon as one goes to Gerar, as far as Gaza; and as one goes to Sodom and Gomorrah and Admah and Zeboiim, as far as Lasha.

²⁰These are the descendants of Ham according to their constituent groups, according to their languages, by their lands, and by their nations.

²¹Also to Shem, the father of all the children of Eber [including the Hebrews], the older brother of Japheth, children were born.

²²The sons of Shem: Elam, Asshur, Arpachshad, Lud and Aram;

²³the sons of Aram [ancestor of the Syrians]: Uz, Hul, Gether and Mash.

²⁴Arpachshad became the father of Shelah; and Shelah became the father of Eber.

²⁵Two sons were born to Eber; the name of one was Peleg (division), for [the inhabitants of] the earth were divided in his days; and his brother's name was Joktan.

²⁶Joktan became the father of Almodad, Sheleph, Hazarmaveth, Jerah,

²⁷and Hadoram, Uzal, Diklah,

²⁸and Obal, Abimael, Sheba,

²⁹and Ophir, Havilah, and Jobab; all these were the sons of Joktan.

³⁰Now their territory extended from Mesha as one goes toward Sephar, to the hill country of the east.

³¹These are Shem's descendants according to their constituent groups (families), according to their languages, by their lands, according to their nations.

³²These are the families of the sons

10:10 Or *Babylon.*

of Noah, according to their descendants, by their nations; and from these [people] the nations were separated *and* spread abroad on the earth after the flood. [Acts 17:26]

11 NOW THE whole earth spoke one language and used the same words (vocabulary). ²And as people journeyed eastward, they found a plain in the land of Shinar and they settled there. [Gen 10:10] ³They said one to another, "Come, let us make bricks and fire them thoroughly [in a kiln, to harden and strengthen them]." So they used brick for stone [as building material], and they used tar (bitumen, asphalt) for mortar. ⁴They said, "Come, let us build a city for ourselves, and a tower whose top *will reach* into the heavens, and let us make a [famous] name for ourselves, so that we will not be scattered [into separate groups] *and* be dispersed over the surface of the entire earth [as the LORD instructed]." [Gen 9:1] ⁵Now the LORD came down to see the city and the tower which the sons of men had built. ⁶And the LORD said, "Behold, they are one [unified] people, and they all have the same language. This is only the beginning of what they will do [in rebellion against Me], and now no evil thing they imagine they can do will be impossible for them. ⁷"Come, let Us (Father, Son, Holy Spirit) go down and there confuse *and* mix up their language, so that they will not understand one another's speech." ⁸So the LORD scattered them abroad from there over the surface of the entire earth; and they stopped building the city. ⁹Therefore the name of the city was Babel—because there the LORD confused the language of the entire earth; and from that place the LORD scattered *and* dispersed them over the surface of all the earth.

¹⁰These are *the records of* the generations of Shem [from whom Abraham descended]. Shem was a hundred years old when he became the father of Arpachshad, two years after the flood. ¹¹And Shem lived five hundred years after Arpachshad was born, and he had *other* sons and daughters. ¹²When Arpachshad had lived thirty-five years, he became the father of Shelah. ¹³Arpachshad lived four hundred and three years after Shelah was born, and he had *other* sons and daughters. ¹⁴When Shelah had lived thirty years, he became the father of Eber. ¹⁵Shelah lived four hundred and three years after Eber was born, and he had *other* sons and daughters. ¹⁶When Eber had lived thirty-four years, he became the father of Peleg. ¹⁷And Eber lived four hundred and thirty years after Peleg was born, and he had *other* sons and daughters. ¹⁸When Peleg had lived thirty years, he became the father of Reu. ¹⁹And Peleg lived two hundred and nine years after Reu was born, and he had *other* sons and daughters. ²⁰When Reu had lived thirty-two years, he became the father of Serug. ²¹And Reu lived two hundred and seven years after Serug was born, and he had *other* sons and daughters. ²²When Serug had lived thirty years, he became the father of Nahor. ²³And Serug lived two hundred years after Nahor was born, and he had *other* sons and daughters. ²⁴When Nahor had lived twenty-nine years, he became the father of Terah. ²⁵And Nahor lived a hundred and nineteen years after Terah was born, and he had *other* sons and daughters. ²⁶After Terah had lived seventy years, he became the father of Abram and Nahor and Haran [his firstborn].

²⁷Now these are *the records of* the descendants of Terah. Terah was the father of Abram (Abraham), Nahor, and Haran; and Haran was the father of Lot. ²⁸Haran died before his father Terah in the land of his birth, in Ur of the Chaldeans. ²⁹Abram and Nahor took wives for themselves. The name of Abram's wife was Sarai (later called Sarah), and the name of Nahor's wife was Milcah, the daughter of Haran, the father of Milcah and Iscah. ³⁰But Sarai was barren; she did not have a child. ³¹Terah took Abram his son, and Lot the son of Haran, his grandson, and Sarai his daughter-in-law, his son Abram's wife; and they went out together to go from Ur of the Chaldeans into the land of Canaan; but when they came to Haran [about five hundred and fifty miles northwest of Ur], they settled there. ³²Terah lived two hundred and five years; and Terah died in Haran.

12

NOW [in Haran] the LORD had said to Abram,

"Go away from your country,
And from your relatives
And from your father's house,
To the land which I will show you;
   [Heb 11:8–10]
²And I will make you a great nation,
And I will bless you [abundantly],
And make your name great
   (exalted, distinguished);
And you shall be a blessing [a
   source of great good to others];
³And I will bless (do good for,
   benefit) those who bless you,
And I will curse [that is, subject to
   My wrath and judgment] the one
   who curses (despises, dishonors,
   has contempt for) you.

And in you all the families
   (nations) of the earth will be
   blessed." [Gal 3:8]

⁴So Abram departed [in faithful obedience] as the LORD had directed him; and Lot [his nephew] left with him. Abram was seventy-five years old when he left Haran. ⁵Abram took Sarai his wife and Lot his nephew, and all their possessions which they had acquired, and the people (servants) which they had acquired in Haran, and they set out to go to the land of Canaan. When they came to the land of Canaan, ⁶Abram passed through the land as far as the site of Shechem, to the [great] terebinth (oak) tree of Moreh. Now the Canaanites were in the land at that time. ⁷Then the LORD appeared to Abram and said, "I will give this land to your descendants." So Abram built an altar there to [honor] the LORD who had appeared to him. ⁸Then he moved on from there to the mountain on the east of Bethel, and pitched his tent, with Bethel on the west and Ai on the east; and there he built an altar to the LORD and called

life point

We can read God's promise to Abraham in Genesis 12:2 and think, *Oh, hallelujah! That applies to me, too*! But we cannot forget that God required a sacrifice of obedience before Abraham could receive the promise. Abraham had to be willing to leave the place where he was comfortable; he had to leave his father and all of his relatives. And he did; he simply moved in faith to the place God said He would show him. If you are willing to have Abraham's kind of obedience, you can have Abraham's kind of blessing.

on the name of the LORD [in worship through prayer, praise, and thanksgiving].

⁹Then Abram journeyed on, continuing toward the Negev (the South country of Judah).

¹⁰Now there was a famine in the land; and Abram went down into Egypt to live temporarily, for the famine in the land was oppressive *and* severe.

¹¹And when he was about to enter Egypt, he said to Sarai his wife, "Listen: I know that you are a beautiful woman;

¹²so when the Egyptians see you, they will say, 'This is his wife'; and they will kill me [to acquire you], but they will let you live.

¹³"Please tell them that you are my sister so that things will go well for me for your sake, and my life will be spared because of you."

¹⁴And when Abram entered Egypt, the Egyptians saw that Sarai was very beautiful.

¹⁵Pharaoh's princes (officials) also saw her and praised her to Pharaoh; and the woman was taken [for the purpose of marriage] into Pharaoh's house (harem).

¹⁶Therefore Pharaoh treated Abram well for her sake; he acquired sheep, oxen, male and female donkeys, male and female servants, and camels.

¹⁷But the LORD punished Pharaoh

one step at a time

Abraham learned to trust God to lead him one step at a time. God essentially told him, "Trust Me with this first step, because it is best for you to go where I lead you." At that time, Abraham might have wondered whether or not packing up his tent and leaving his family and his country would be to his advantage, but God told him to go to the place that He would show him, and Abraham simply obeyed.

When God gave Abraham this instruction, He gave him only step one, not step two. Abraham would not get to step two until he had accomplished step one. This is so simple, but so profound: God gives us direction *one step at a time.*

You may be like many people who refuse to take step one until they think they understand steps two, three, four, and five. If so, I hope you will be inspired to go forward in God's plan for your life by trusting Him with the first step. Understanding that His will for you is revealed a step at a time should build your confidence to do at least what you already know to do. After the first few steps, your faith will grow because you will realize there is always sure footing beneath each step God instructs you to take.

Know that God has a good plan for your life and that you will be blessed when you obey Him. You can miss out on blessings by not obeying what God clearly tells you to do. He shows you the way to go, and you are to walk in that direction. Sometimes God may be gracious enough to carry you part of the way, but there comes a time when the carrying is over, and He says, "Now walk."

God wants you to obey Him quickly. He does not want you to argue with Him for three or four weeks before you will do a simple little thing. He wants you to trust Him and, like Abraham, take in faith the first step He calls you to take.

and his household with severe plagues because of Sarai, Abram's wife.

¹⁸Then Pharaoh called Abram and said, "What is this that you have done to me? Why did you not tell me that she was your wife?

¹⁹"Why did you say, 'She is my sister,' so that I took her as my wife? Now then, here is your wife; take her and go!"

²⁰So Pharaoh commanded his men concerning him; and they escorted him on his way, with his wife and all that he had.

13 SO ABRAM went up out of Egypt, he and his wife and all that he had, and Lot [his nephew] with him, into the Negev (the South country of Judah).

²Now Abram was extremely rich in livestock and in silver and in gold.

³He journeyed on from the Negev as far as Bethel, to the place where his tent had been at the beginning, between Bethel and Ai,

⁴where he had first built an altar; and there Abram called on the name of the LORD [in prayer]. [Gal 3:6–9]

lift up your eyes

In Genesis 13, we read that the herdsmen of Abraham and his nephew, Lot, argued because there was not enough space for both their flocks and herds to graze. Abraham suggested that Lot go one way and said that he would go the other way so there would be room enough for both of their animals and households. Lot chose the best land for himself and left Abraham with an inferior portion (see Genesis 13:10, 11).

At that point, the Lord said to Abraham, "Now lift up your eyes and look from the place where you are standing, northward and southward and eastward and westward; for all the land which you see I will give to you and to your descendants forever" (Genesis 13:14, 15).

We would do well to remember this story today. Instead of becoming discouraged, depressed, or angry when people disappoint us, God wants us to lift up our eyes, look around us, and trust Him to lead us into an even better situation. He wants us to look around and count our blessings instead of focusing on what we *do not* have. He wants us to fix our eyes on Him, not on the work of the enemy, because He has plans to bless us and bring us increase.

No matter how your life has turned out to this point, you have two options. One is to give up and quit; the other is to keep going. If you decide to keep going, you again have two choices. One is to live in misery and depression; the other is to live in faith, hope, and joy.

Choosing to live in faith, hope, and joy does not mean you will no longer have disappointments, but it does mean you have decided that your disappointments will not defeat you. Instead, you can lift up your eyes, your head, your hands, and your heart, not focusing on your problems, but looking at the Lord, Who has promised to see you through to abundance and victory.

⁵But Lot, who went with Abram, also had flocks and herds and tents.

⁶Now the land was not able to support them [that is, sustain all their grazing and water needs] while they lived near one another, for their possessions were too great for them to stay together.

⁷And there was strife *and* quarreling between the herdsmen of Abram's cattle and the herdsmen of Lot's cattle. Now the Canaanite and the Perizzite were living in the land at that same time [making grazing of the livestock difficult].

⁸So Abram said to Lot, "Please let there be no strife *and* disagreement between you and me, nor between your herdsmen and my herdsmen, because we are relatives.

⁹"Is not the entire land before you? Please separate [yourself] from me. If you take the left, then I will go to the right; or if you choose the right, then I will go to the left."

¹⁰So Lot looked and saw that the valley of the Jordan was well watered everywhere—this was before the Lord destroyed Sodom and Gomorrah; [it was all] like the garden of the Lord, like the land of Egypt, as you go to Zoar [at the south end of the Dead Sea].

¹¹Then Lot chose for himself all the valley of the Jordan, and he traveled east. So they separated from each other.

¹²Abram settled in the land of Canaan, and Lot settled in the cities of the valley and camped as far as Sodom *and* lived there.

¹³But the men of Sodom were extremely wicked and sinful against the Lord [unashamed in their open sin before Him].

¹⁴The Lord said to Abram, after Lot had left him, "Now lift up your eyes and look from the place where you are *standing*, northward and southward and eastward and westward;

¹⁵for all the land which you see I will give to you and to your descendants forever. [Acts 7:5]

¹⁶"I will make your descendants [as numerous] as the dust of the earth, so that if a man could count the [grains of] dust of the earth, then your descendants could also be counted. [Gen 28:14]

¹⁷"Arise, walk (make a thorough reconnaissance) around in the land, through its length and its width, for I will give it to you."

¹⁸Then Abram broke camp *and* moved his tent, and came and settled by the [grove of the great] terebinths (oak trees) of Mamre [the Amorite], which are in Hebron, and there he built an altar to [honor] the Lord.

14 IN THE days of the [Eastern] kings Amraphel of Shinar, Arioch of Ellasar, Chedorlaomer of Elam, and Tidal of Goiim,

²they [invaded the Jordan Valley near the Dead Sea, and] made war with Bera king of Sodom, Birsha king of Gomorrah, Shinab king of Admah, Shemeber king of Zeboiim, and the king of Bela (that is, Zoar).

³All of these [kings] joined together [as allies] in the Valley of Siddim (that is, the Sea of Salt).

⁴Twelve years they had served Chedorlaomer [the most powerful king in the invading confederacy], but in the thirteenth year they rebelled.

⁵In the fourteenth year Chedorlaomer and the [three] kings who were with him attacked and subdued the Rephaim in Ashteroth-karnaim, the Zuzim in Ham, and the Emim in Shaveh-kiriathaim,

⁶and the Horites in their mountainous country of Seir, as far as El-paran, which is on the border of the wilderness.

⁷Then they turned back and came to En-mishpat (that is, Kadesh), and subdued all the country of the Amalekites,

and also the Amorites who lived in Hazazon-tamar.

⁸Then the kings of Sodom, Gomorrah, Admah, Zeboiim, and Bela (that is, Zoar) came out; and they joined together for battle with the invading kings in the Valley of Siddim,

⁹against Chedorlaomer king of Elam and Tidal king of Goiim and Amraphel king of Shinar and Arioch king of Ellasar—four kings against five.

¹⁰Now the Valley of Siddim was full of tar (bitumen) pits; and as the kings of Sodom and Gomorrah fled, they fell into them. But the remainder [of the kings] who survived fled to the hill country.

¹¹Then the victors took all the possessions of Sodom and Gomorrah and all their food supply *and* provisions and left.

¹²And they also took [captive] Lot, Abram's nephew, and his possessions and left, for he was living in Sodom.

¹³Then a survivor who had escaped [from the invading forces on the other side of the Jordan] came and told Abram the Hebrew. Now he was living by the terebinths (oaks) of Mamre the Amorite, brother of Eshcol and brother of Aner—they were allies of Abram.

¹⁴When Abram heard that his nephew [Lot] had been captured, he armed *and* led out his trained men, born in his own house, [numbering] three hundred and eighteen, and went in pursuit as far [north] as Dan.

¹⁵He divided his forces against them by night, he and his servants, and attacked *and* defeated them, and pursued them as far as Hobah, which is north of Damascus.

¹⁶And he brought back all the goods, and also brought back his nephew Lot and his possessions, and also the women, and the people.

¹⁷Then after Abram's return from the defeat (slaughter) of Chedorlaomer and the kings who were with him, the king of Sodom went out to meet him at the Valley of Shaveh (that is, the King's Valley).

¹⁸Melchizedek king of Salem (ancient Jerusalem) brought out bread and wine [for them]; he was the priest of God Most High.

¹⁹And Melchizedek blessed Abram and said,

"Blessed (joyful, favored) be
   Abram by God Most High,
Creator *and* Possessor of heaven
   and earth;
²⁰ And blessed, praised, *and* glorified
   be God Most High,
Who has given your enemies into
   your hand."

And Abram gave him a tenth of all [the treasure he had taken in battle]. [Heb 7:1–10]

²¹The king of Sodom said to Abram, "Give me the people and keep the goods (spoils of battle) for yourself."

²²But Abram said to the king of Sodom, "I have raised my hand *and* sworn an oath to the Lᴏʀᴅ God Most High, the Creator *and* Possessor of heaven and earth,

²³that I would not take anything that is yours, from a thread to a sandal strap, so you could not say, 'I [the King of Sodom] have made Abram rich.'

²⁴"I will take nothing except what my young men have eaten, and the share of the spoils belonging to the men [my allies] who went with me—Aner, Eshcol, and Mamre; let them take their share of the spoils."

life point

If Abraham had bowed his knee to fear, the rest of the story would never have come to pass. He would never have experienced God as his shield, and he would never have received his very great reward (see Genesis 15:1).

15

AFTER THESE things the word of the Lord came to Abram in a vision, saying,

"Do not be afraid, Abram,
I am your shield;
Your reward [for obedience] shall
   be very great."

[2]Abram said, "Lord God, what *reward* will You give me, since I am [leaving this world] childless, and he who will be the owner *and* heir of my house is this [servant] Eliezer from Damascus?"

[3]And Abram continued, "Since You have given no child to me, one (a servant) born in my house is my heir."

[4]Then behold, the word of the Lord came to him, saying, "This man [Eliezer] will not be your heir but he who shall come from your own body shall be your heir."

[5]And the Lord brought Abram outside [his tent into the night] and said, "Look now toward the heavens and count the stars—if you are able to count them." Then He said to him, "So [numerous] shall your descendants be." [Heb 11:12]

[6]Then Abram believed in (affirmed, trusted in, relied on, remained steadfast to) the Lord; and He counted (credited) it to him as righteousness (doing right in regard to God and man). [Rom 4:3, 18–22; Gal 3:6; James 2:23]

[7]And He said to him, "I am the [same] Lord who brought you out of Ur of the Chaldeans, to give you this land as an inheritance."

[8]But Abram said, "Lord God, by what [proof] will I know that I will inherit it?"

[9]So God said to him, "Bring Me a three-year-old heifer, a three-year-old female goat, a three-year-old ram, a turtledove, and a young pigeon."

[10]So Abram brought all these to Him and cut them down the middle, and laid each half opposite the other; but he did not cut the birds.

[11]The birds of prey swooped down on the carcasses, but Abram drove them away.

[12]When the sun was setting, a deep sleep overcame Abram; and a horror (terror, shuddering fear, nightmare) of great darkness overcame him.

[13]*God* said to Abram, "Know for sure that your descendants will be strangers [living temporarily] in a land (Egypt) that is not theirs, where they will be enslaved and oppressed for four hundred years. [Ex 12:40]

[14]"But on that nation whom your descendants will serve I will bring judgment, and afterward they will come out [of that land] with great possessions. [Ex 12:35, 36; Acts 7:6, 7]

[15]"As for you, you shall [die and] go to your fathers in peace; you shall be buried at a good old age.

[16]"Then in the fourth generation your descendants shall return here [to Canaan, the land of promise], for the wickedness *and* guilt of the Amorites is not yet complete (finished)." [Josh 24:15]

[17]When the sun had gone down and a [deep] darkness had come, *there appeared* a smoking brazier and a flaming torch which passed between the [divided] pieces [of the animals]. [Jer 34:18, 19]

[18]On the same day the Lord made a covenant (promise, pledge) with Abram, saying,

"To your descendants I have given
   this land,
From the river of Egypt to the
   great river Euphrates—

speak the Word

God, I will not fear, because You are my shield. In You my reward shall be very great.
—ADAPTED FROM GENESIS 15:1

¹⁹[the land of] the Kenites and the Kenizzites and the Kadmonites ²⁰and the Hittites and the Perizzites and the Rephaim, ²¹the Amorites and the Canaanites and the Girgashites and the Jebusites."

16 NOW SARAI, Abram's wife, had not borne him any *children,* and she had an Egyptian maid whose name was Hagar.

²So Sarai said to Abram, "See here, the LORD has prevented me from bearing *children.* I am asking you to go in to [the bed of] my maid [so that she may bear you a child]; perhaps I will obtain children by her." And Abram listened to Sarai *and* did as she said.

³After Abram had lived in the land of Canaan ten years, Abram's wife Sarai took Hagar the Egyptian [maid], and gave her to her husband Abram to be his [secondary] wife.

⁴He went in to [the bed of] Hagar, and she conceived; and when she realized that she had conceived, she looked with contempt on her mistress [regarding Sarai as insignificant because of her infertility].

⁵Then Sarai said to Abram, "May [the responsibility for] the wrong done to me [by the arrogant behavior of Hagar] be upon you. I gave my maid into your arms, and when she realized that she had conceived, I was despised *and* looked on with disrespect. May the LORD judge [who has done right] between you and me."

⁶But Abram said to Sarai, "Look, your maid is *entirely* in your hands

give God time

Abraham had a definite word from God about his future. He knew what God had promised, but he had no indication about when the promise would be fulfilled. The same is often true for us. While we are waiting for our manifestation to come forth—waiting for a breakthrough—we may grow frustrated or impatient. Sitting in the waiting room of life is not always easy!

Once God speaks to us or shows us something, we tend to be excited and focus on that revelation. It is as though we are "pregnant" with what God has said. He has planted a seed in us—and then we have to enter a time of preparation before that seed can bear fruit. These seasons of preparation equip us to handle whatever God has promised to give to us or do for us.

This process parallels the development and birth of a child. First, a seed is planted in the mother's womb, then a time of preparation (nine months of waiting) is required, and then, finally, the baby is born. During the nine months, so much happens in the mother and in the child. The seed grows to maturity, while the mother's body prepares to give birth, and the family prepares everything necessary for a new baby in the house.

Just as so much development takes place in the hidden place of the mother's womb, there is also much activity taking place in the spiritual realm concerning God's promises in our lives—and we cannot see this, any more than we can watch cells multiply in an unborn baby. The fact that we cannot see or feel any progress does not mean nothing is happening. God does some of His best work in secret; He delights in surprising His children; and whether you know it or not, He is busy bringing good things to pass for you, right this minute! Just give Him time—and you will see.

and subject to your authority; do as you please with her." So Sarai treated her harshly *and* humiliated her, and Hagar fled from her.

7But the Angel of the LORD found her by a spring of water in the wilderness, on the road to [Egypt by way of] Shur.

8And He said, "Hagar, Sarai's maid, where did you come from and where are you going?" And she said, "I am running away from my mistress Sarai."

9The Angel of the LORD said to her, "Go back to your mistress, and submit humbly to her authority."

10Then the Angel of the LORD said to her, "I will greatly multiply your descendants so that they will be too many to count."

11The Angel of the LORD continued,

"Behold, you are with child,

And you will bear a son;
And you shall name him Ishmael (God hears),
Because the LORD has heard *and* paid attention to your persecution (suffering).

12"He (Ishmael) will be a wild donkey of a man;
His hand *will be* against every man [continually fighting]
And every man's hand against him;
And he will dwell in defiance of all his brothers."

13Then she called the name of the LORD who spoke to her, "You are God Who Sees"; for she said, "Have I not even here [in the wilderness] remained alive after seeing Him [who sees me with understanding and compassion]?"

14Therefore the well was called

don't have an Ishmael

Abram and Sarai got tired of waiting. They were weary as they watched for God's promise to come to pass, and they wondered if they might do something to help move things along. Sarai decided to see if her handmaid, Hagar, would conceive a child by Abram (see Genesis 16:2). She thought that could be God's way of giving her and Abram the child He had promised. God had promised Abram a son *by Sarai* (see Genesis 17:16), but since it appeared God was not doing anything, she must have reasoned that she knew how to help!

Does that sound familiar? Have you ever tried or wanted to "help" God in your life?

In Sarai's case, Abram heeded her advice and Hagar conceived. The child, named Ishmael, was indeed a son, as God had spoken, but he was not the child of the promise. Abram and Sarai waited another fourteen years before Isaac, the true promised son, arrived. I wonder if it took so long because once we give birth to the "Ishmaels" in our lives, we must deal with the consequences. In other words, once an Ishmael is born, we have to change his diapers and take care of him!

We would like to carry out our own plans and then have God bless them, but He taught me years ago that He is not obligated to bless or care for the things I give birth to out of the strength of my flesh. The psalmist affirms this point: "Unless the LORD builds the house, they labor in vain who build it" (Psalm 127:1).

God has great things in store for you, and He will bring them to pass in His perfect timing. Let me encourage you to wait on Him. An Ishmael will be a burden in your life, but God's "Isaacs" will bring blessing and delight.

Beer-lahai-roi (Well of the Living One Who Sees Me); it is between Kadesh and Bered.

¹⁵So Hagar gave birth to Abram's son; and Abram named his son, to whom Hagar gave birth, Ishmael (God hears). ¹⁶Abram was eighty-six years old when Hagar gave birth to Ishmael.

17 WHEN ABRAM was ninety-nine years old, the LORD appeared to him and said,

"I am God Almighty;
Walk [habitually] before Me [with integrity, knowing that you are always in My presence], and be blameless *and* complete [in obedience to Me].
²"I will establish My covenant (everlasting promise) between Me and you,
And I will multiply you exceedingly [through your descendants]."

³Then Abram fell on his face [in worship], and God spoke with him, saying,

⁴"As for Me, behold, My covenant is with you,
And [as a result] you shall be the father of many nations.
⁵"No longer shall your name be Abram (exalted father),
But your name shall be Abraham (father of a multitude);
For I will make you the father of many nations.

⁶"I will make you exceedingly fruitful, and I will make nations of you, and kings will come from you. ⁷"I will establish My covenant between Me and you and your descendants after you throughout their generations for an everlasting covenant, to be God to you and to your descendants after you. [Gal 3:16]

⁸"I will give to you and to your descendants after you the land in which you are a stranger [moving from place to place], all the land of Canaan, as an everlasting possession [of property]; and I will be their God." [Acts 7:5]

⁹Further, God said to Abraham, "As for you [your part of the agreement], you shall keep *and* faithfully obey [the terms of] My covenant, you and your descendants after you throughout their generations. ¹⁰"This is [the sign of] My covenant, which you shall keep *and* faithfully obey, between Me and you and your descendants after you: Every male among you shall be circumcised. ¹¹"And you shall be circumcised in the flesh of your foreskins, and it shall

life point

When God entered into covenant with Abraham, He told him to circumcise himself and all the males eight days old and older (see Genesis 17:10–12). Blood was shed at what we might refer to as "the fountain of life"—the place from which the seed for future generations would come—and circumcision was a sign of the covenant between God and Abraham.

Blood is a powerful entity, and that is because life is in the blood (see Leviticus 17:11). When anything is covered by blood, in God's way of looking at it, it is covered with life and thus cleansed. Therefore, when we receive Jesus as our Savior, we are covered by His blood, and God sees us as clean and pure before Him.

speak the Word

Thank You, God Almighty, for helping me to walk habitually before You with integrity, knowing that I am always in Your presence, and for helping me to be blameless and complete in obedience to You.
—ADAPTED FROM GENESIS 17:1

be the sign (symbol, memorial) of the covenant between Me and you.

¹²"Every male among you who is eight days old shall be circumcised throughout your generations, [including] a *servant* whether born in the house or one who is purchased with [your] money from any foreigner, who is not of your descendants.

¹³"A *servant* who is born in your house or one who is purchased with your money must be circumcised; and [the sign of] My covenant shall be in your flesh for an everlasting covenant.

¹⁴"And the male who is not circumcised in the flesh of his foreskin, that person shall be cut off from his people; he has broken My covenant."

¹⁵Then God said to Abraham, "As for Sarai your wife, you shall not call her name Sarai (my princess), but her name will be Sarah (Princess).

what's in a name?

Names meant so much more to people during Bible times than they do to many of us today. Even here in the early chapters of the Bible, we see that names were tremendously important, because they described a person's character.

In Genesis 17, we read that God gave new names to Abram and Sarai (see Genesis 17:4, 5, 15, 16). He was changing things in their lives, and He wanted to give them new names to declare what He was doing in and through them. Abram and Sarai knew well the importance of names, so they understood the profound significance of God's changing their names. When He gave them new names, He was beginning to speak of "nonexistent things" as though they already existed (see Romans 4:17). The name changes indicated to Abram and Sarai that God was beginning to fulfill His promise when He said to Abram: "'Look now toward the heavens and count the stars—if you are able to count them.' Then He said to him, 'So [numerous] shall your descendants be'" (Genesis 15:5).

So what's in a name? A lot more than many of us realize. Think about Sarai, for instance. She was a barren woman, who probably had a poor self-image because, in biblical societies, so much of a woman's worth depended on her ability to bear children. She was an old woman, and, biologically, she had no hope of ever being able to conceive and deliver a baby. But God changed her name.

Sarah means "princess." So when Abraham or anyone else called Sarai by her new name, Sarah, they were helping her change her image of herself. They were calling her beautiful and valuable, a king's daughter—and they were speaking forth the image of the mother God had destined her to be. As a result, she must have begun to see herself differently. She must have felt faith rising in her heart. She must have begun to be sure God would keep His word to her.

Similarly, Abram must have undergone his own transformation and had his own faith bolstered when God changed his name to Abraham, meaning "father of a multitude."

Following this idea through to the New Testament and to our lives today, I encourage you to remember the significance of a name when you speak the name of Jesus. Remember, His is not just a name; it is a word loaded with meaning and filled with life. It declares His character; it proclaims all that He is, all He has done, and all He will do in your life.

¹⁶"I will bless her, and indeed I will also give you a son by her. Yes, I will bless her, and she shall be a *mother of* nations; kings of peoples will come from her."

¹⁷Then Abraham fell on his face and laughed, and said in his heart, "Shall a child be born to a man who is a hundred years old? And shall Sarah, who is ninety years old, bear *a child?*"

¹⁸And Abraham said to God, "Oh, that Ishmael [my firstborn] might live before You!"

¹⁹But God said, "No, Sarah your wife shall bear you a son indeed, and you shall name him Isaac (laughter); and I will establish My covenant with him for an everlasting covenant and with his descendants after him.

²⁰"As for Ishmael, I have heard *and* listened to you; behold, I will bless him, and will make him fruitful and will greatly multiply him [through his descendants]. He will be the father of twelve princes (chieftains, sheiks), and I will make him a great nation. [Gen 25:12–18]

²¹"But My covenant [My promise, My solemn pledge], I will establish with Isaac, whom Sarah will bear to you at this time next year."

²²And God finished speaking with him and went up from Abraham.

²³Then Abraham took Ishmael his son, and all *the servants* who were born in his house and all who were purchased with his money, every male among the men of Abraham's household, and circumcised the flesh of their foreskin the very same day, as God had said to him.

²⁴So Abraham was ninety-nine years old when he was circumcised.

²⁵And Ishmael his son was thirteen years old when he was circumcised.

²⁶On the very same day Abraham was circumcised, as well as Ishmael his son.

²⁷All the men [servants] of his household, both those born in the house and those purchased with money from a foreigner, were circumcised along with him [as the sign of God's covenant with Abraham].

18 NOW THE Lᴏʀᴅ appeared to Abraham by the terebinth *trees* of Mamre [in Hebron], while he was sitting at the tent door in the heat of the day.

²When he raised his eyes and looked up, behold, three men were standing [a little distance] from him. When he saw them, he ran from the tent door to meet them and bowed down [with his face] to the ground,

³and Abraham said, "My lord, if now I have found favor in your sight, please do not pass by your servant [without stopping to visit].

⁴"Please let a little water be brought [by one of my servants] and [you may] wash your feet, and recline *and* rest comfortably under the tree.

⁵And I will bring a piece of bread to refresh *and* sustain you; after that you may go on, since you have come to your servant." And they replied, "Do as you have said."

⁶So Abraham hurried into the tent to Sarah, and said, "Quickly, get ready three measures of fine meal, knead it and bake cakes."

⁷Abraham also ran to the herd and brought a calf, tender and choice, and he gave it to the servant [to butcher], and he hurried to prepare it.

⁸Then he took curds and milk and the calf which he had prepared, and set it before the men; and he stood beside them under the tree while they ate.

⁹Then they said to him, "Where is Sarah your wife?" And he said, "There, in the tent."

¹⁰He said, "I will surely return to you at this *time next year; and behold,

18:10 Lit *when the time revives.*

Sarah your wife will have a son." And Sarah was listening at the tent door, which was behind him. [Rom 9:9–12]

¹¹Now Abraham and Sarah were old, well advanced in years; she was past [the age of] childbearing.

¹²So Sarah laughed to herself [when she heard the Lord's words], saying, "After I have become old, shall I have pleasure *and* delight, my lord (husband) being also old?" [1 Pet 3:6]

¹³And the Lord asked Abraham, "Why did Sarah laugh [to herself], saying, 'Shall I really give birth [to a child] when I am so old?'

¹⁴"Is anything too difficult *or* too wonderful for the Lord? At the appointed time, when the season [for her delivery] comes, I will return to you and Sarah will have a son." [Matt 19:26]

¹⁵Then Sarah denied it, saying, "I did not laugh"; because she was afraid. And He (the Lord) said, "No, but you did laugh."

¹⁶Then the men got up from there, and looked toward Sodom; and Abraham walked with them to send them on the way.

¹⁷The Lord said, "Shall I keep secret from Abraham [My friend and servant] what I am going to do, [Gal 3:8]

¹⁸since Abraham is destined to become a great and mighty nation, and all the nations of the earth will be blessed through him? [Gen 12:2, 3]

¹⁹"For I have known (chosen, acknowledged) him [as My own], so that he may teach *and* command his children and [the sons of] his household after him to keep the way of the Lord by doing what is righteous and just, so that the Lord may bring upon Abraham what He has promised him."

²⁰And the Lord said, "The outcry [of the sin] of Sodom and Gomorrah is indeed great, and their sin is exceedingly grave.

²¹"I will go down now, and see whether they have acted [as vilely and wickedly] as the outcry which has come to Me [indicates]; and if not, I will know."

²²Now the [two] men (angelic beings) turned away from there and went toward Sodom, but Abraham remained standing before the Lord.

²³Abraham approached [the Lord] and said, "Will You really sweep away the righteous (those who do right) with the wicked (those who do evil)?

²⁴"Suppose there are fifty righteous [people] within the city; will You really sweep it away and not spare it for the sake of the fifty righteous who are in it?

²⁵"Far be it from You to do such a thing—to strike the righteous with the wicked, so that the righteous and the wicked are *treated* alike. Far be it from You! Shall not the Judge of all the earth do right [by executing just and righteous judgment]?"

²⁶So the Lord said, "If I find within the city of Sodom fifty righteous [people], then I will spare the entire place for their sake."

²⁷Abraham answered, "Now behold, I who am but dust [in origin] and ashes have decided to speak to the Lord. [Gen 3:19; Job 30:19]

²⁸"If five of the fifty righteous are lacking, will You destroy the entire city for lack of five?" And He said, "If I find [at least] forty-five [righteous people] there, I will not destroy it."

²⁹Abraham spoke to Him yet again and said, "Suppose [only] forty are

speak the Word

Father, I thank You that there is nothing too difficult for You!
—adapted from Genesis 18:14

found there." And He said, "I will not do it for the sake of the forty [who are righteous]."

[30]Then Abraham said [to Him], "Oh, may the Lord not be angry, and I will speak; suppose thirty [righteous people] are found there?" And He said, "I will not do it if I find thirty there."

[31]And he said, "Now behold, I have decided to speak to the Lord [again]. Suppose [only] twenty [righteous people] are found there?" And the Lord said, "I will not destroy it for the sake of the twenty."

[32]Then Abraham said, "Oh may the Lord not be angry [with me], and I will speak only this once; suppose ten [righteous people] are found there?" And He said, "I will not destroy it for the sake of the ten."

[33]As soon as He had finished speaking with Abraham the LORD departed, and Abraham returned to his own place.

19 IT WAS evening when the two angels came to Sodom. Lot was sitting at Sodom's [city] gate. Seeing them, Lot got up to meet them and bowed down *with his* face to the ground.

[2]And he said, "See here, my lords, please turn aside *and* come into your servant's house, and spend the night, and wash your feet; then you may get up early and go on your way." But they said, "No, we shall spend the night in the open plaza [of the city]."

[3]However, Lot strongly urged them, so they turned aside and entered his house; and he prepared a feast for them [with wine], and baked unleavened bread, and they ate.

[4]But before they lay down [to sleep], the men of the city, the men of Sodom, both young and old, surrounded the house, all the men from every quarter;

[5]and they called out to Lot and said to him, "Where are the men who came to you tonight? Bring them out to us so that we may know them [intimately]."

[6]But Lot went out of the doorway to the men, and shut the door after him, [7]and said, "Please, my brothers, do not do something so wicked.

[8]"See here, I have two daughters who have not known a man [intimately]; please let me bring them out to you [instead], and you can do as you please with them; only do nothing to these men, because they have in fact come under the shelter of my roof [for protection]."

[9]But they said, "Get out of the way!" And they said, "This man (Lot) came [as an outsider] to live here temporarily, and now he is acting like a judge. Now we will treat you worse than your visitors!" So they rushed forward *and* pressed violently against Lot and came close to breaking down the door [of his house].

[10]But the men (angels) reached out with their hands and pulled Lot into the house with them, and shut the door [after him].

[11]They struck (punished) the men who were at the doorway of the house with blindness, from the young men to the old men, so that they exhausted *themselves trying* to find the doorway.

[12]And the [two] men (angels) asked Lot, "Have you any others here [in

putting the Word to work

Lot and his wife had to leave the city where they lived in order to escape the destruction God would bring upon that city because of the sin of the people who lived there. They were instructed not to look back as they left the city. In what situations in your life do you need to heed God's instruction not to look back? How can you look ahead instead of behind you in those areas?

Sodom]—a son-in-law, and your sons, and your daughters? Whomever you have in the city, take them out of here;

¹³for we are destroying this place, because the outcry [for judgment] against them has grown so great before the Lord that the Lord has sent us to destroy *and* ruin it."

¹⁴So Lot went out and spoke to his sons-in-law, who were [betrothed, and legally promised] to marry his daughters, and said, "Get up, get out of this place, for the Lord is about to destroy this city!" But to his sons-in-law he appeared to be joking.

¹⁵When morning dawned, the angels urged Lot [to hurry], saying, "Get up! Take your wife and two daughters who are here [and go], or you will be swept away in the punishment of the city."

¹⁶But Lot hesitated *and* lingered. The men took hold of his hand and the hand of his wife and the hands of his two daughters, because the Lord was merciful to him [for Abraham's sake]; and they brought him out, and left him outside the city [with his family].

¹⁷When they had brought them outside, one [of the angels] said, "Escape for your life! Do not look behind you, or stop anywhere in the entire valley; escape to the mountains [of Moab], or you will be consumed *and* swept away."

¹⁸But Lot said to them, "Oh no, [not that place] my lords!

¹⁹"Please listen, your servant has found favor in your sight, and you have magnified your lovingkindness (mercy) to me by saving my life; but I cannot escape to the mountains, because the disaster will overtake me and I will be killed.

²⁰"Now look, this town [in the distance] is near *enough for us* to flee to, and it is small [with only a few people]. Please, let me escape there (is it not small?) so that my life will be saved."

²¹And the angel said to him, "Behold, I grant you this request also; I will not destroy this town of which you have spoken.

²²"Hurry and take refuge there, for I cannot do anything [to punish Sodom] until you arrive there." For this reason the town was named Zoar (few, small).

²³The sun had risen over the earth when Lot came to Zoar.

²⁴Then the Lord rained down brimstone (flaming sulfur) and fire on Sodom and on Gomorrah from the Lord out of heaven,

²⁵and He overthrew (demolished, ended) those cities, and the entire valley, and all the inhabitants of the cities, and whatever grew on the ground.

²⁶But Lot's wife, from behind him, [foolishly, longingly] looked [back toward Sodom in an act of disobedience], and she became a pillar of salt. [Luke 17:32]

²⁷Abraham started out early the next morning to the place where he [only the day before] had stood before the Lord;

²⁸and he looked down toward Sodom and Gomorrah, and toward all the land of the valley [of the Dead Sea]; and he saw, and behold, the smoke of the land went up like the smoke of a kiln (pottery furnace).

²⁹Now when God ravaged *and* destroyed the cities of the plain [of Siddim], He remembered Abraham [and for that reason], and He sent [Abraham's nephew] Lot out of the midst of the destruction, when He destroyed the cities in which Lot had lived.

³⁰Now Lot went up from Zoar, and lived in the mountain together with his two daughters, for he was afraid to stay [any longer] in Zoar; and he lived in a cave with his two daughters.

³¹The firstborn said to the younger, "Our father is aging, and there is not a man on earth [available] to be intimate with us in the customary way [so that we may have children].

³²"Come, let us make our father drunk with wine, and we will lie with

him so that we may preserve our family through our father."

³³So they gave their father wine that night, and the firstborn went in and lay with her father; and he did not know when she lay down or when she got up [because he was completely intoxicated].

³⁴Then the next day, the firstborn said to the younger, "Behold, I lay with my father last night; let us make him drunk with wine tonight also, and then you go in and lie with him, so that we may preserve our family through our father."

³⁵So they gave their father wine that night also, and the younger got up and lay with him; and *again* he did not know when she lay down or when she got up.

³⁶Thus both the daughters of Lot conceived by their father.

³⁷The firstborn gave birth to a son, and named him Moab (from father); he is the father of the Moabites to this day.

³⁸The younger also gave birth to a son and named him Ben-ammi (son of my people); he is the father of the Ammonites to this day.

20 NOW ABRAHAM journeyed from there toward the Negev (the South country), and settled between Kadesh and Shur; then he lived temporarily in Gerar.

²Abraham said [again] of Sarah his wife, "She is my sister." So Abimelech king of Gerar sent and took Sarah [into his harem].

³But God came to Abimelech in a dream during the night, and said, "Behold, you are a dead man because of the woman whom you have taken [as your wife], for she is another man's wife."

⁴Now Abimelech had not yet come near her; so he said, "Lord, will you kill a people who are righteous *and* innocent *and* blameless [regarding Sarah]?

⁵"Did Abraham not tell me, 'She is my sister?' And she herself said, 'He is my brother.' In the integrity of my heart and innocence of my hands I have done this."

⁶Then God said to him in the dream, "Yes, I know you did this in the integrity of your heart, for it was I who kept you back *and* spared you from sinning against Me; therefore I did not give you an opportunity to touch her.

⁷"So now return the man's wife, for he is a prophet, and he will pray for you and you will live. But if you do not return *her* [to him], know that you shall die, you and all who are yours (your household)."

⁸So Abimelech got up early in the morning and called all his servants and told them all these things; and the men were terrified.

⁹Then Abimelech called Abraham and said to him, "What have you done to us? And how have I offended you that you have brought on me and my kingdom a great sin? You have done to me what ought not to be done [to anyone]."

¹⁰And Abimelech said to Abraham, "What have you encountered *or* seen [in us or our customs], that you have done this [unjust] thing?"

¹¹Abraham said, "Because I thought, 'Surely there is no fear *or* reverence of God in this place, and they will kill me because of my wife.'

¹²"Besides, she actually is my [half] sister; she is the daughter of my father [Terah], but not of my mother; and she became my wife.

¹³"When God caused me to wander from my father's house, I said to her, 'This kindness *and* loyalty you can show me: at every place we stop, say of me, "He is my brother."'"

¹⁴Then Abimelech took sheep and oxen and male and female slaves, and gave them to Abraham, and returned Sarah his wife to him [as God commanded].

¹⁵So Abimelech said, "Behold, my

16Then to Sarah he said, "Look, I have given this brother of yours a thousand pieces of silver; it is to compensate you [for all that has happened] *and* to vindicate your honor before all who are with you; before all men you are cleared *and* compensated."

17So Abraham prayed to God, and God healed Abimelech and his wife and his maids, and they *again* gave birth to *children,*

18for the LORD had securely closed the wombs of all [the women] in Abimelech's household because of Sarah, Abraham's wife. [1 Pet 3:1–6]

21 THE LORD graciously remembered *and* visited Sarah as He had said, and the LORD did for her as He had promised.

2So Sarah conceived and gave birth to a son for Abraham in his old age, at the appointed time of which God had spoken to him.

3Abraham named his son Isaac (laughter), *the son* to whom Sarah gave birth.

4So Abraham circumcised his son Isaac when he was eight days old, just as God had commanded him.

5Abraham was a hundred years old when his son Isaac was born.

6Sarah said, "God has made me laugh; all who hear [about our good news] will laugh with me."

7And she said, "Who would have said

putting the Word to work

Abraham and Sarah had to wait a long time before God's promise came to pass, but it finally did, as we read in Genesis 21:1–3. What promises of God are you waiting to have fulfilled in your life? How can you be like Abraham and wait with a heart full of faith?

to Abraham that Sarah would nurse children? For I have given birth to a son by him in his old age." [Heb 11:12]

8The child [Isaac] grew and was weaned, and Abraham held a great feast on the day that Isaac was weaned.

9Now [as time went on] Sarah saw [Ishmael] the son of Hagar the Egyptian, whom she had borne to Abraham, mocking [Isaac]. [Gal 4:29]

10Therefore she said to Abraham, "Drive out this maid and her son, for the son of this maid shall not be an heir with my son Isaac." [Gal 4:28–31]

11The situation distressed Abraham greatly because of his son [Ishmael].

12God said to Abraham, "Do not let it distress you because of Ishmael and your maid; whatever Sarah tells you, listen to her *and* do what she asks, for your descendants will be named through Isaac. [Rom 9:7]

13"And I will also make a nation of [Ishmael] the son of the maid, because he is your descendant."

14So Abraham got up early in the morning and took bread and a skin of water and gave them to Hagar, putting them on her shoulder, and *gave her* the boy, and sent her away. And she left [but lost her way] and wandered [aimlessly] in the Wilderness of Beersheba.

15When the water in the skin was all gone, Hagar abandoned the boy under one of the bushes.

16Then she went and sat down opposite him, about a bowshot away, for she said, "Do not let me see the boy die." And as she sat down opposite him, she raised her voice and wept.

17God heard the voice of the boy, and the angel of God called to Hagar from heaven and said to her, "What troubles you, Hagar? Do not be afraid, for God has heard the voice of the boy from where he is [resting].

18"Get up, help the boy up, and hold him by the hand, for I will make him a great nation."

¹⁹Then God opened her eyes and she saw a well of water; and she went and filled the [empty] skin with water and gave the boy a drink.

²⁰God was with Ishmael, and he grew *and* developed; and he lived in the wilderness and became an [expert] archer.

²¹He lived in the wilderness of Paran; and his mother took a wife for him from the land of Egypt.

²²Now at that time Abimelech and Phicol, the commander of his army, said to Abraham, "God is with you in everything you do;

²³so now, swear to me here by God that you will not deal unfairly with me [by breaking any agreements we have] or with my son or with my descendants, but as I have treated you with kindness, you shall do the same to me and to the land in which you have sojourned (temporarily lived)."

²⁴And Abraham said, "I will swear."

²⁵Then Abraham complained to Abimelech about a well of water which the servants of Abimelech had [violently] seized [from him],

²⁶Abimelech said, "I do not know who did this thing. Indeed, you did not tell me, and I did not hear of it until today."

²⁷So Abraham took sheep and oxen and gave them to Abimelech, and the two men made a covenant (binding agreement).

²⁸Then Abraham set apart seven ewe lambs of the flock,

²⁹and Abimelech said to Abraham, "What is the meaning of these seven ewe lambs which you have set apart?"

³⁰Abraham said, "You are to accept these seven ewe lambs from me as a witness for me, that I dug this well."

³¹Therefore that place was called Beersheba (Well of the Oath or Well of the Seven), because there the two of them swore an oath.

³²So they made a covenant at Beersheba; then Abimelech and Phicol, the commander of his army, got up and returned to the land of the Philistines.

³³Abraham planted a tamarisk tree at Beersheba, and there he called on the name of the LORD [in prayer], the Eternal God.

³⁴And Abraham lived [as a resident alien] in the land of the Philistines for many days.

22 NOW AFTER these things, God tested [the faith and commitment of] Abraham and said to him, "Abraham!" And he answered, "Here I am."

²God said, "Take now your son, your only son [of promise], whom you love, Isaac, and go to the region of Moriah, and offer him there as a burnt offering on one of the mountains of which I shall tell you."

³So Abraham got up early in the morning, saddled his donkey, and took two of his young men with him and his son Isaac; and he split the wood for the burnt offering, and then he got up and went to the place of which God had told him.

⁴On the third day [of travel] Abraham looked up and saw the place in the distance.

⁵Abraham said to his servants, "Settle down *and* stay here with the donkey; the young man and I will go over there and worship [God], and we will come back to you." [Heb 11:17–19]

⁶Then Abraham took the wood for the burnt offering and laid it on [the shoulders of] Isaac his son, and he took the fire (firepot) in his own hand and the [sacrificial] knife; and the two of them walked on together.

⁷And Isaac said to Abraham, "My father!" And he said, "Here I am, my son." Isaac said, "Look, the fire and the wood, but where is the lamb for the burnt offering?"

⁸Abraham said, "My son, God will provide for Himself a lamb for the

burnt offering." So the two walked on together.

⁹When they came to the place of which God had told him, Abraham built an altar there and arranged the wood, and bound Isaac his son and placed him on the altar, on top of the wood. [Matt 10:37]

¹⁰Abraham reached out his hand and took the knife to kill his son. [Heb 11:17–19]

¹¹But the Angel of the Lᴏʀᴅ called to him from heaven and said, "Abraham, Abraham!" He answered, "Here I am."

¹²The Lᴏʀᴅ said, "Do not reach out [with the knife in] your hand against the boy, and do nothing to [harm] him; for now I know that you fear God [with reverence and profound respect], since you have not withheld from Me your son, your only son [of promise]."

¹³Then Abraham looked up and glanced around, and behold, behind him was a ram caught in a thicket by his horns. And Abraham went and took the ram and offered it up for a burnt offering (ascending sacrifice) instead of his son.

¹⁴So Abraham named that place The Lᴏʀᴅ Will Provide. And it is said to this day, "On the mountain of the Lᴏʀᴅ it will be seen *and* provided."

¹⁵The Angel of the Lᴏʀᴅ called to Abraham from heaven a second time

¹⁶and said, "By Myself (on the basis of Who I Am) I have sworn [an oath], declares the Lᴏʀᴅ, that since you have done this thing and have not withheld [from Me] your son, your only son [of promise],

¹⁷indeed I will greatly bless you, and I will greatly multiply your descendants like the stars of the heavens and like the sand on the seashore; and your seed shall possess the gate of their enemies [as conquerors]. [Heb 6:13, 14; 11:12]

¹⁸"Through your seed all the nations of the earth shall be blessed, because you have heard *and* obeyed My voice."

[Gen 12:2, 3; 13:16; 22:18; 26:4; 28:14; Acts 3:25, 26; Gal 3:16]

¹⁹So Abraham returned to his servants, and they got up and went with him to Beersheba; and Abraham settled in Beersheba.

²⁰Now after these things Abraham was told, "Milcah has borne children to your brother Nahor:

²¹Uz the firstborn and Buz his brother and Kemuel the father of Aram,

²²Chesed and Hazo and Pildash and Jidlaph and Bethuel."

²³Bethuel became the father of Rebekah. These eight [children] Milcah bore to Nahor, Abraham's brother.

²⁴Nahor's concubine, whose name was Reumah, gave birth to Tebah and Gaham and Tahash and Maacah.

23 SARAH LIVED a hundred and twenty-seven years; this was the length of the life of Sarah.

²Sarah died in Kiriath-arba (that is, Hebron) in the land of Canaan, and Abraham went to mourn for Sarah and to weep for her.

³Then Abraham stood up before his dead [wife's body], and spoke to the sons of Heth (Hittites), saying,

⁴"I am a stranger and a sojourner (resident alien) among you; give (sell) me property for a burial place among you so that I may bury my dead [in the proper manner]."

⁵The Hittites replied to Abraham,

⁶"Listen to us, my lord; you are a prince of God [a mighty prince] among us; bury your dead in the choicest of our graves; none of us will refuse you his grave *or* hinder you from burying your dead [wife]."

⁷So Abraham stood up and bowed to the people of the land, the Hittites.

⁸And Abraham said to them, "If you are willing to grant my dead a [proper] burial, listen to me, and plead with Ephron the son of Zohar for me,

⁹so that he may give (sell) me the cave of Machpelah which he owns—it is at the end of his field; let him give it to me here in your presence for the full price as a burial site [which I may keep forever among you]."

¹⁰Now Ephron was present there among the sons of Heth; so within the hearing of all the sons of Heth and all who were entering the gate of his city, Ephron the Hittite answered Abraham, saying,

¹¹"No, my lord, hear me; I give you the [entire] field, and I also give you the cave that is in it. In the presence of the men of my people I give (sell) it to you; bury your dead [there]."

¹²Then Abraham bowed down before the people of the land.

¹³He said to Ephron in the presence of the people of the land, "If you will only please listen to me and accept my offer. I will give you the price of the field; accept it from me and I will bury my dead there."

¹⁴Ephron replied to Abraham,

¹⁵"My lord, listen to me. The land [you seek] is worth four hundred shekels of silver; what is that between you and me? So bury your dead."

¹⁶So Abraham listened to Ephron [and agreed to his terms]; and he weighed out for Ephron the [amount of] silver which he had named in the hearing of the Hittites: four hundred shekels of silver, according to the weights current among the merchants.

¹⁷So the field of Ephron in Machpelah, which was to the east of Mamre (Hebron)—the field and the cave which was in it, and all the trees that were in the field and in all its borders around it—were deeded over [legally]

¹⁸to Abraham as his possession in the presence of the Hittites, before all who were entering at the gate of his city.

¹⁹After this, Abraham buried Sarah his wife in the cave of the field of Machpelah to the east of Mamre (that is, Hebron) in the land of Canaan.

²⁰The field and the cave in it were deeded over to Abraham by the Hittites as a [permanent] possession and burial place.

24 NOW ABRAHAM was old, [well] advanced in age; and the LORD had blessed Abraham in all things.

²Abraham said to his servant [Eliezer of Damascus], the oldest of his household, who had charge over all that Abraham owned, "Please, put your hand under my thigh [as is customary for affirming a solemn oath], [Gen 15:2]

³and I will make you swear by the LORD, the God of heaven and the God of earth, that you will not take a wife for my son from the daughters of the Canaanites, among whom I live,

⁴but you will [instead] go to my [former] country (Mesopotamia) and to my relatives, and take a wife for my son Isaac [the heir of the covenant promise]."

⁵The servant said to him, "Suppose the woman will not be willing to follow me back to this country; should I take your son back to the country from which you came?"

⁶Abraham said to him, "See to it that you do not take my son back there!

⁷"The LORD, the God of heaven, who took me from my father's house, from the land of my family and my birth, who spoke to me and swore to me, saying, 'To your descendants I will give this land'—He will send His angel before you [to guide you], and you will take a wife from there for my son [and bring her here].

⁸"If the woman is not willing to follow you [to this land], then you will be free from this my oath and blameless; only you must never take my son back there."

⁹So the servant put his hand under the thigh of Abraham his master, and swore to him concerning this matter.

¹⁰Then the servant took ten of his master's camels, and set out, taking some of his master's good things with him; so he got up and journeyed to Mesopotamia [between the Tigris and the Euphrates Rivers], to the city of Nahor [the home of Abraham's brother].

¹¹He made the camels kneel down outside the city by the well of water at the time of the evening when women go out to draw water.

¹²And he said, "O Lord, God of my master Abraham, please grant me success today, and show lovingkindness (faithfulness) to my master Abraham.

¹³"Behold, I stand here at the spring of water, and the daughters of the men of the city are coming out to draw water;

¹⁴now let it be that the girl to whom I say, 'Please, let down your jar so that I may [have a] drink,' and she replies, 'Drink, and I will also give your camels water to drink'—may she *be the one* whom You have selected [as a wife] for Your servant Isaac; and by this I will know that You have shown lovingkindness (faithfulness) to my master."

¹⁵Before Eliezer had finished speaking (praying), Rebekah came out with her [water] jar on her shoulder. Rebekah was the daughter of Bethuel the son of Milcah, who was the wife of Abraham's brother Nahor.

¹⁶The girl was very beautiful, a virgin and unmarried; and she went down to the spring and filled her jar and came up.

¹⁷Then the servant ran to meet her, and said, "Please let me drink a little water from your jar."

¹⁸And she said, "Drink, my lord"; and she quickly lowered her jar to her hand, and gave him a drink.

¹⁹When she had given Eliezer a drink, she said, "I will also draw water for your camels until they have finished drinking."

²⁰So she quickly emptied her jar into the trough, and ran again to the well and drew water for all his camels.

²¹Meanwhile, the man stood gazing at Rebekah in [reverent] silence, [waiting] to know if the Lord had made his trip successful or not.

²²When the camels had finished drinking, Eliezer took a gold ring weighing a half-shekel and two bracelets for her hands weighing ten shekels in gold,

²³and said, "Whose daughter are you? Please tell me, is there room in your father's house for us to lodge?"

²⁴And she said to him, "I am the daughter of Bethuel, Milcah's son, whom she bore to [her husband] Nahor."

²⁵Again she said to him, "We have plenty of both straw and feed, and also room to lodge."

²⁶The man bowed his head and worshiped the Lord.

²⁷He said, "Blessed be the Lord, the God of my master Abraham, who has not denied His lovingkindness and His truth to my master. As for me, the Lord led me to the house of my master's brothers."

²⁸Then the girl ran and told her mother's household what had happened.

²⁹Now Rebekah had a brother whose name was Laban; and Laban ran out to the man at the well.

³⁰When he saw the ring and the bracelets on his sister's arms, and when he heard Rebekah his sister, saying, "The man said this to me," he went to Eliezer and found him standing by the camels at the spring.

speak the Word

God, I pray that I will walk before You habitually and obediently, that You will send Your angel with me to make my journey successful.
—ADAPTED FROM GENESIS 24:40

³¹And Laban said, "Come in, blessed of the Lᴏʀᴅ! Why do you stand outside since I have made the house ready and have prepared a place for the camels?"

³²So the man came into the house, and Laban unloaded his camels and gave them straw and feed, and [he gave] water to [Eliezer to] wash his feet and the feet of the men who were with him.

³³But when food was set before him, he said, "I will not eat until I have stated my business." And Laban said, "Speak on."

³⁴So he said, "I am Abraham's servant. ³⁵The Lᴏʀᴅ has greatly blessed my master, and he has become great (wealthy, powerful); He has given him flocks and herds, and silver and gold, and servants and maids, and camels and donkeys.

³⁶"Now Sarah my master's wife bore a son to my master when she was in her old age, and he has given everything that he has to him.

³⁷"My master made me swear [an oath], saying, 'You must not take a wife for my son from the daughters of the Canaanites, in whose land I live;

³⁸but you shall [instead] go to my father's house and to my family and take a wife for my son [Isaac].'

³⁹"Then I said to my master, 'But suppose the woman will not follow me [back to this land].'

⁴⁰"He said to me, 'The Lᴏʀᴅ, before whom I walk [habitually and obediently], will send His angel with you to make your journey successful, and you will take a wife for my son from my relatives and from my father's house;

⁴¹then you will be free of my oath, when you come to my relatives; and if they do not give her to you, you will [also] be free of my oath.'

⁴²"I came today to the spring, and said, 'O Lᴏʀᴅ, God of my master Abraham, if now You will make my journey on which I go successful;

⁴³please look, I am standing by the spring of water; now let it be that when the maiden [whom You have chosen for Isaac] comes out to draw [water], and to whom I say, "Please, give me a little water to drink from your jar";

⁴⁴and if she says to me, "You drink, and I will also draw [water] for your camels"; let that woman be the one whom the Lᴏʀᴅ has selected *and* chosen [as a wife] for my master's son.'

⁴⁵"Before I had finished praying in my heart, behold, Rebekah came out with her [water] jar on her shoulder, and she went down to the spring and drew water. And I said to her, 'Please, let me have a drink.'

⁴⁶"And she quickly let down her jar from her *shoulder,* and said, 'Drink, and I will also water your camels'; so I drank, and she also watered the camels.

⁴⁷"Then I asked her, 'Whose daughter are you?' She said, 'The daughter of Bethuel, Nahor's son, whom Milcah bore to him'; and I put the ring in her nose, and the bracelets on her arms.

⁴⁸"And I bowed down my head and worshiped the Lᴏʀᴅ, and blessed the Lᴏʀᴅ, the God of my master Abraham, who had led me in the right way to take the daughter of my master's brother to his son [as a wife].

⁴⁹"So now if you are going to show kindness and truth to my master [being faithful to him], tell me; and if not, tell me, that I may turn to the right or to the left [and go on my way]."

⁵⁰Then Laban and Bethuel answered, "The matter has come from the Lᴏʀᴅ; so we dare not speak bad or good [to you about it—we cannot interfere].

⁵¹"Rebekah is before you; take her and go, and let her be the wife of your master's son, as the Lᴏʀᴅ has spoken."

⁵²When Abraham's servant heard their words, he bowed himself to the ground [in worship] before the Lᴏʀᴅ.

⁵³Then the servant brought out jewelry of silver, jewelry of gold, and articles of clothing, and gave them to Rebekah; he also gave precious things to her brother and her mother.

⁵⁴Then he and the men who were with him ate and drank and spent the night [there]. In the morning when they got up, he said, "Now send me back to my master."

⁵⁵But Rebekah's brother and mother said, "Let the girl stay with us a few days—at least ten; then she may go."

⁵⁶But Eliezer said to them, "Do not delay me, since the LORD has prospered my way. Send me away, so that I may go back to my master."

⁵⁷And they said, "We will call the girl and ask her what she prefers."

⁵⁸So they called Rebekah and said, "Will you go with this man?" And she answered, "I will go."

⁵⁹So they sent off their sister Rebekah and her nurse [Deborah, as her attendant] and Abraham's servant [Eliezer] and his men.

⁶⁰They blessed Rebekah and said to her,

"May you, our sister,
Become [the mother of] thousands
    of ten thousands,
And may your descendants
    possess (conquer)
The [city] gate of those who hate
    them."

⁶¹Then Rebekah and her attendants stood, and they mounted camels and followed the man. So the servant took Rebekah and went on his way.

⁶²Now Isaac had returned from going to Beer-lahai-roi (Well of the Living One Who Sees Me), for he was living in the Negev. [Gen 16:14]

⁶³Isaac went out to bow down [in prayer] in the field in the [early] evening; he raised his eyes and looked, and camels were coming.

⁶⁴Rebekah also raised her eyes *and* looked, and when she saw Isaac, she dismounted from her camel.

⁶⁵She said to the servant, "Who is that man there walking across the field to meet us?" And the servant said, "He is my master [Isaac]." So she took a veil and covered herself [as was customary].

⁶⁶The servant told Isaac everything that he had done.

⁶⁷Then Isaac brought her into his mother Sarah's tent, and he took Rebekah [in marriage], and she became his wife, and he loved her; therefore Isaac was comforted after his mother's death.

25 ABRAHAM TOOK another wife, whose name was Keturah.

²She gave birth to Zimran, Jokshan, Medan, Midian, Ishbak, and Shuah.

³Jokshan was the father of Sheba and Dedan. The sons of Dedan were Asshurim, Letushim, and Leummim.

⁴The sons of Midian were Ephah, Epher, Hanoch, Abida, and Eldaah. All these were the sons of Keturah.

⁵Now Abraham gave everything that he had to Isaac;

⁶but to the sons of his concubines [Hagar and Keturah], Abraham gave gifts while he was still living and he sent them to the east country, away from Isaac his son [of promise].

⁷The days of Abraham's life were a hundred and seventy-five years.

⁸Then Abraham breathed his last and he died at a good old age, an old man who was satisfied [with life]; and he was gathered to his people [who had preceded him in death]. [Gen 15:15; Heb 11:13–16]

⁹So his sons Isaac and Ishmael buried him in the cave of Machpelah, in the field of Ephron the son of Zohar the Hittite, which is east of Mamre,

¹⁰the field which Abraham purchased from the sons of Heth; there Abraham was buried with Sarah his wife.

[11]Now after the death of Abraham, God blessed his son Isaac; and Isaac lived at Beer-lahai-roi.

[12]Now these are *the records of* the descendants of Ishmael, Abraham's son, whom Hagar the Egyptian, Sarah's maid, bore to Abraham;

[13]and these are the names of the [twelve] sons of Ishmael, named in the order of their births: Nebaioth, the firstborn of Ishmael, and Kedar, Adbeel, Mibsam,

[14]Mishma, Dumah, Massa,

[15]Hadad, Tema, Jetur, Naphish, and Kedemah.

[16]These are the sons of Ishmael and these are their names, by their settlements, and by their encampments (sheepfolds); twelve princes (sheiks) according to their tribes. [Foretold in Gen 17:20]

[17]Ishmael lived a hundred and thirty-seven years; then he breathed his last and died, and was gathered to his people [who had preceded him in death].

[18]Ishmael's sons (descendants) settled from Havilah to Shur which is east of Egypt as one goes toward Assyria; he settled opposite (east) of all his relatives.

[19]Now these are *the records of* the descendants of Isaac, Abraham's son: Abraham was the father of Isaac.

[20]Isaac was forty years old when he married Rebekah, the daughter of Bethuel the Aramean (Syrian) of Paddan-aram, the sister of Laban the Aramean.

[21]Isaac prayed to the LORD for his wife, because she was unable to conceive children; and the LORD granted his prayer and Rebekah his wife conceived [twins].

[22]But the children struggled together within her [kicking and shoving one another]; and she said, "If it is so [that the LORD has heard our prayer], why then am I *this way?*" So she went to inquire of the LORD [praying for an answer].

[23]The LORD said to her,

"[The founders of] two nations are
   in your womb;
And the separation of two nations
   has begun in your body;
The one people shall be stronger
   than the other;
And the older shall serve the
   younger."

[24]When her days to be delivered were fulfilled, behold, there were twins in her womb.

[25]The first came out reddish all over like a hairy garment; and they named him Esau (hairy).

[26]Afterward his brother came out, and his hand grasped Esau's heel, so he was named Jacob (one who grabs by the heel, supplanter). Isaac was sixty years old when Rebekah gave birth to them.

[27]When the boys grew up, Esau was an able *and* skilled hunter, a man of the outdoors, but Jacob was a quiet *and* peaceful man, living in tents.

[28]Now Isaac loved [and favored] Esau, because he enjoyed eating his game, but Rebekah loved [and favored] Jacob.

[29]Jacob had cooked [reddish-brown lentil] stew [one day], when Esau came from the field and was famished;

[30]and Esau said to Jacob, "Please, let me have a quick swallow of that red stuff there, because I am exhausted *and* famished." For that reason Esau was [also] called Edom (Red).

[31]Jacob answered, "First sell me your birthright (the rights of a firstborn)."

[32]Esau said, "Look, I am about to die [if I do not eat soon]; so of what use is this birthright to me?"

[33]Jacob said, "Swear [an oath] to me today [that you are selling it to me for this food]"; so he swore [an oath] to him, and sold him his birthright.

³⁴Then Jacob gave Esau bread and lentil stew; and he ate and drank, and got up and went on his way. In this way Esau scorned his birthright. [Heb 12:15–17]

26 NOW THERE was a famine in the land [of Canaan], besides the previous famine that had occurred in the days of Abraham. So Isaac went to Gerar, to Abimelech king of the Philistines.

²The Lord appeared to him and said, "Do not go down to Egypt; stay in the land of which I will tell you.

³"Live temporarily [as a resident] in this land and I will be with you and will bless *and* favor you, for I will give all these lands to you and to your descendants, and I will establish *and* carry out the oath which I swore to Abraham your father. [Gen 22:16–18; Ps 105:9]

⁴"I will make your descendants multiply as the stars of the heavens, and will give to your descendants all these lands; and by your descendants shall all the nations of the earth be blessed, [Gen 22:18; Acts 3:25, 26; Gal 3:16]

⁵because Abraham listened to *and* obeyed My voice and [consistently] kept My charge, My commandments, My statutes, and My laws."

⁶So Isaac stayed in Gerar.

⁷The men of the place asked him about his wife, and he said, "She is my sister," for he was afraid to say, "my wife"—thinking, "the men of the place might kill me on account of Rebekah, since she is very beautiful."

⁸It happened when he had been there a long time, that Abimelech king of the Philistines looked out of a window and saw Isaac caressing Rebekah his wife.

⁹Then Abimelech called Isaac and said, "See here, Rebekah is in fact your wife! How did you [dare to] say to me, 'She is my sister'?" And Isaac said to him, "Because I thought I might be killed because of her [desirability]."

¹⁰Abimelech said, "What is this that you have done to us? One of the men [among our people] might easily have been intimate with your wife, and you would have brought guilt on us [before God]."

¹¹Then Abimelech commanded all his people, "Whoever touches this man [Isaac] or his wife [Rebekah] shall without exception be put to death."

¹²Then Isaac planted [seed] in that land [as a farmer] and reaped in the same year a hundred times [as much as he had planted], and the Lord blessed *and* favored him.

¹³And the man [Isaac] became great and gained more and more until he became very wealthy *and* extremely distinguished;

¹⁴he owned flocks and herds and a great household [with a number of servants], and the Philistines envied him.

¹⁵Now all the wells which his father's servants had dug in the days of Abraham his father, the Philistines stopped up by filling them with dirt.

¹⁶Then Abimelech said to Isaac, "Go away from here, because you are far too powerful for us."

¹⁷So Isaac left that region and camped in the Valley of Gerar, and settled there.

¹⁸Now Isaac again dug [and reopened] the wells of water which had been dug in the days of Abraham his father, because the Philistines had filled them up [with dirt] after the death of Abraham; and he gave the wells the same names that his father had given them.

¹⁹But when Isaac's servants dug in the valley and found there a well of flowing [spring] water,

²⁰the herdsmen of Gerar quarreled with Isaac's herdsmen, saying, "The water is ours!" So Isaac named the well Esek (quarreling), because they quarreled with him.

²¹Then his servants dug another

well, and they quarreled over that also, so Isaac named it Sitnah (enmity).

²²He moved away from there and dug another well, and they did not quarrel over that one; so he named it Rehoboth (broad places), saying, "For now the LORD has made room for us, and we shall be prosperous in the land."

²³Then he went up from there to Beersheba.

²⁴The LORD appeared to him the same night and said,

"I am the God of Abraham your
    father;
Do not be afraid, for I am with you.
I will bless *and* favor you, and
    multiply your descendants,
For the sake of My servant
    Abraham."

²⁵So Isaac built an altar there and called on the name of the LORD [in prayer]. He pitched his tent there; and there Isaac's servants dug a well.

²⁶Then Abimelech came to him from Gerar with Ahuzzath, his [close friend and confidential] adviser, and Phicol, the commander of his army.

²⁷Isaac said to them, "Why have you [people] come to me, since you hate me and have sent me away from you?"

²⁸They said, "We see clearly that the LORD has been with you; so we said, 'There should now be an oath between us [with a curse for the one who breaks it], that is, between you and us, and let us make a covenant (binding agreement, solemn promise) with you,

²⁹that you will not harm us, just as we have not touched you and have done nothing but good to you and have sent you away in peace. You are now the blessed *and* favored of the LORD!'"

³⁰Then Isaac held a [formal] banquet (covenant feast) for them, and they ate and drank.

³¹They got up early in the morning and swore oaths [pledging to do nothing but good to each other]; and Isaac

sent them on their way and they left him in peace.

³²Now on the same day, Isaac's servants came and told him about the well they had dug, saying, "We have found water."

³³So he named the well Shibah; therefore the name of the city is Beersheba to this day. [Gen 21:31]

³⁴When Esau was forty years old he married Judith the daughter of Beeri the Hittite, and Basemath the daughter of Elon the Hittite as his wives;

³⁵and they were a source of grief to [Esau's parents] Isaac and Rebekah.

27 NOW WHEN Isaac was old and his eyes were too dim to see, he called his elder [and favorite] son Esau and said to him, "My son." And Esau answered him, "Here I am."

²Isaac said, "See here, I am old; I do not know when I may die.

³"So now, please take your [hunting] gear, your quiver [of arrows] and your bow, and go out into the open country and hunt game for me;

⁴and make me a savory *and* delicious

life point

One of the things Isaac did when he grew to adulthood was to open the wells of his father, Abraham, wells that had been stopped up by their enemies (see Genesis 26:18). The very name Isaac, the one who caused the wells to flow again, means "laughter." I think we may draw from this story the idea that laughter and joy in the Holy Spirit will open the deep wells of life inside us—wells that may have been stopped up by the enemy through depression, discouragement, or disappointment. Go ahead and laugh; and let God's joy bubble up in you right now!

dish [of meat], the kind I love, and bring it to me to eat, so that my soul may bless you [as my firstborn son] before I die."

⁵But Rebekah overheard what Isaac said to Esau his son; and when Esau had gone to the open country to hunt for game that he might bring back,

⁶Rebekah said to Jacob her [younger and favorite] son, "Listen carefully: I heard your father saying to Esau your brother,

⁷'Bring me some game and make me a savory *and* delicious dish [of meat], so that I may eat it, and declare my blessing on you in the presence of the Lord before my death.'

⁸"So now, my son, listen [carefully] to me [and do exactly] as I command you.

⁹"Go now to the flock and bring me two good *and* suitable young goats, and I will make them into a savory dish [of meat] for your father, the kind he loves [to eat].

¹⁰"Then you shall bring it to your father to eat, so that he may bless you before his death."

¹¹Jacob said to Rebekah his mother, "Listen, Esau my brother is a hairy man and I am a smooth [skinned] man.

¹²"Suppose my father touches me *and* feels my skin; then I will be seen by him as a cheat (imposter), and I will bring his curse on me and not a blessing."

¹³But his mother said to him, "May your curse be on me, my son; only listen *and* obey me, and go, bring the young goats to me."

¹⁴So Jacob went and got the two young goats, and brought them to his mother; and his mother prepared a delicious *dish of* food [with a delightful aroma], the kind his father loved [to eat].

¹⁵Then Rebekah took her elder son Esau's best clothes, which were with her in her house, and put them on Jacob her younger son.

¹⁶And she put the skins of the young goats on his hands and on the smooth part of his neck.

¹⁷Then she gave her son Jacob the delicious meat and the bread which she had prepared.

¹⁸So he went to his father and said, "My father." And Isaac said, "Here I am. Who are you, my son?"

¹⁹Jacob said to his father, "I am Esau your firstborn; I have done what you told me to do. Now please, sit up and eat some of my game, so that you may bless me."

²⁰Isaac said to his son, "How is it that you have found the game so quickly, my son?" And he said, "Because the Lord your God caused it to come to me."

²¹But Isaac [wondered and] said to Jacob, "Please come close [to me] so that I may touch you, my son, *and* determine if you are really my son Esau or not."

²²So Jacob approached Isaac, and his father touched him and said, "The voice is Jacob's voice, but the hands are the hands of Esau."

²³He could not recognize him [as Jacob], because his hands were hairy like his brother Esau's hands; so he blessed him.

²⁴But he said, "Are you really my son Esau?" Jacob answered, "I am."

²⁵Then Isaac said, "Bring the food to me, and I will eat some of my son's game, so that I may bless you." He brought it to him, and he ate; and he brought him wine and he drank.

²⁶Then his father Isaac said to him, "Please come, my son, and kiss me."

²⁷So he came and kissed him; and Isaac smelled his clothing and blessed him and said,

"The scent of my son [Esau]
Is like the aroma of a field which
    the Lord has blessed;
²⁸Now may God give you of the dew
    of heaven [to water your land],

And of the fatness (fertility) of the
   earth,
And an abundance of grain and
   new wine; [Gen 27:39; Deut
   33:13, 28]
²⁹ May peoples serve you,
And nations bow down to you;
Be lord *and* master over your
   brothers,
And may your mother's sons bow
   down to you.
May those who curse you be
   cursed,
And may those who bless you be
   blessed."

³⁰Now as soon as Isaac had finished blessing Jacob, and Jacob had scarcely left the presence of Isaac his father, Esau his brother came in from his hunting. ³¹Esau also made a delicious dish [of meat] and brought it to his father and said to him, "Let my father get up and eat some of his son's game, so that you may bless me." ³²Isaac his father said to him, "Who are you?" And he replied, "I am your son, your firstborn, Esau." ³³Then Isaac trembled violently, and he said, "Then who was the one [who was just here] who hunted game and brought it to me? I ate all of it before you came, and I blessed him. Yes, and he [in fact] shall be (shall remain) blessed." ³⁴When Esau heard the words of his father, he cried out with a great and extremely bitter cry and said to his father, "Bless me, even me also, O my father!" [Heb 12:16, 17] ³⁵Isaac said, "Your brother came deceitfully and has [fraudulently] taken away your blessing [for himself]." ³⁶Esau replied, "Is he not rightly named Jacob (the supplanter)? For he has supplanted me these two times: he took away my birthright, and now he has taken away my blessing. Have you not reserved a blessing for me?"

³⁷But Isaac replied to Esau, "Listen carefully: I have made Jacob your lord *and* master; I have given him all his brothers *and* relatives as servants; and I have sustained him with grain and new wine. What then, can I do for you, my son?" ³⁸Esau said to his father, "Have you only one blessing, my father? Bless me, even me also, O my father." Then Esau [no longer able to restrain himself] raised his voice and wept [loudly]. ³⁹Then Isaac his father answered and [prophesied and] said to him,

"Your dwelling shall be away from
   the fertility of the earth
And away from the dew of heaven
   above;
⁴⁰ But you shall live by your sword,
And serve your brother;
However it shall come to pass
   when you break loose [from your
   anger and hatred],
That you will tear his yoke off your
   neck [and you will be free of
   him]."

⁴¹So Esau hated Jacob because of the blessing with which his father blessed him; and Esau said in his heart, "The days of mourning for my father are very near; then I will kill my brother Jacob." ⁴²When these words of her elder son Esau were repeated to Rebekah, she sent for Jacob her younger son, and said to him, "Listen carefully, your

putting the Word to work

When Isaac was old and sick, his son Jacob deceived him into thinking that he (Jacob) was his brother Esau (see Genesis 27:30–32). That way, Jacob tricked Isaac into giving him the birthright that should haven gone to Esau. Have you, like Isaac, ever been deceived by someone? Have you forgiven that person?

brother Esau is comforting himself concerning you *by planning* to kill you.

⁴³"So now, my son, listen *and* do what I say; go, escape to my brother Laban in Haran!

⁴⁴"Stay with him for a while, until your brother's anger subsides.

⁴⁵"When your brother's anger toward you subsides and he forgets what you did to him, then I will send and bring you back from there. Why should I be deprived of you both in a single day?"

⁴⁶Then Rebekah said to Isaac, "I am tired of living because of the daughters of Heth [these insolent wives of Esau]. If Jacob takes a wife from the daughters of Heth, like these daughters of the land, what good will my life be to me?" [Gen 26:34]

28 SO ISAAC called Jacob and blessed him and charged him, and said to him, "You shall not marry one of the women of Canaan.

²"Arise, go to Paddan-aram, to the house of Bethuel your mother's father; and take from there as a wife for yourself one of the daughters of Laban your mother's brother.

³"May God Almighty bless you and make you fruitful and multiply you, so that you may become a [great] company of peoples.

⁴"May He also give the blessing of Abraham to you and your descendants with you, that you may inherit the [promised] land of your sojournings, which He gave to Abraham."

⁵Then Isaac sent Jacob away, and he went to Paddan-aram, to Laban, son of Bethuel the Aramean, the brother of Rebekah, the mother of Jacob and Esau.

⁶Now Esau noticed that Isaac had blessed Jacob and sent him to Paddan-aram to take a wife for himself from there, and that as he blessed him he gave him a prohibition, saying, "You shall not take a wife from the daughters of Canaan,"

⁷and that Jacob obeyed his father and his mother and had gone to Paddan-aram.

⁸So Esau realized that [his two wives] the daughters of Canaan displeased Isaac his father;

⁹and [to appease his parents] Esau went to [the family of] Ishmael and took as his wife, in addition to the wives he [already] had, Mahalath the daughter of Ishmael, Abraham's son, the sister of Nebaioth [Ishmael's firstborn son].

¹⁰Now Jacob left Beersheba [never to see his mother again] and traveled toward Haran.

¹¹And he came to a certain place and stayed overnight there because the sun had set. Taking one of the stones of the place, he put it under his head and lay down there [to sleep].

¹²He dreamed that there was a ladder (stairway) placed on the earth, and the top of it reached [out of sight] toward heaven; and [he saw] the angels of God ascending and descending on it [going to and from heaven]. [John 1:51]

¹³And behold, the Lᴏʀᴅ stood above *and* around him and said, "I am the Lᴏʀᴅ, the God of Abraham your [father's] father and the God of Isaac; I will give to you and to your descendants the land [of promise] on which you are lying.

¹⁴"Your descendants shall be as [countless as] the dust of the earth, and you shall spread abroad to the west and the east and the north and the south; and all the families (nations) of the earth shall be blessed through you and your descendants. [Gen 12:2, 3; 13:16; 22:18; 26:4; Acts 3:25, 26; Gal 3:8, 16]

¹⁵"Behold, I am with you and will keep [careful watch over you and guard] you wherever you may go, and I will bring you back to this [promised] land; for I will not leave you until I have done what I have promised you."

¹⁶Then Jacob awoke from his sleep and he said, "Without any doubt the LORD is in this place, and I did not realize it."

¹⁷So he was afraid and said, "How fearful *and* awesome is this place! This is none other than the house of God, and this is the gateway to heaven."

¹⁸So Jacob got up early in the morning, and took the stone he had put under his head and he set it up as a pillar [that is, a monument to the vision in his dream], and he poured [olive] oil on the top of it [to consecrate it].

¹⁹He named that place Bethel (the house of God); the previous name of that city was Luz (Almond Tree).

²⁰Then Jacob made a vow (promise), saying, "If God will be with me and will keep me on this journey that I take, and will give me food to eat and clothing to wear,

²¹and if [He grants that] I return to my father's house in safety, then the LORD will be my God.

²²"This stone which I have set up as a pillar (monument, memorial) will be God's house [a sacred place to me], and of everything that You give me I will give the tenth to You [as an offering to signify my gratitude and dependence on You]." [Deut 12:8–11; 14:22–26; 26:1–11]

29 THEN JACOB went on his way and came to the land of the people of the East [near Haran].

²As he looked, he saw a well in the field, and three flocks of sheep lying there [resting] beside it because the flocks were watered from that well. Now the stone on the mouth of the well [that covered and protected it] was large,

³and when all the flocks were gathered there, the shepherds would roll the stone from the mouth of the well, water the sheep, and [afterward] replace the stone on the mouth of the well.

⁴Jacob said to them, "My brothers, where are you from?" And they said, "We are from Haran."

⁵So he said to them, "Do you know Laban the grandson of Nahor [Abraham's brother]?" And they replied, "We know him."

⁶And he asked them, "Is it well with him?" And they said, "He is doing well; look, here comes his daughter Rachel with the sheep!"

⁷Jacob said, "Look, the sun is still high [overhead]; it is a long time before the flocks need to be gathered [in their folds for the night]. Water the sheep, and go, and return them to their pasture."

⁸But they said, "We cannot [leave] until all the flocks are gathered together, and the shepherds roll the stone from the mouth of the well; then we will water the sheep."

⁹While he was still speaking with them, Rachel came with her father's sheep, for she was a shepherdess.

¹⁰When Jacob saw [his cousin] Rachel, the daughter of Laban, his mother's brother, and Laban's sheep, he came up and rolled the stone away from the mouth of the well and watered the flock of Laban, his uncle.

¹¹Then Jacob kissed Rachel [in greeting], and he raised his voice and wept.

speak the Word

Father, I thank You that You are with me and that You are keeping careful watch over me and guarding me wherever I go.
—ADAPTED FROM GENESIS 28:15

¹²Jacob told Rachel he was her father's relative, Rebekah's son; and she ran and told her father.

¹³When Laban heard of the arrival of Jacob, his sister's son, he ran to meet him, and embraced and kissed him and brought him to his house. Then he told Laban all these things.

¹⁴Then Laban said to him, "You are my bone and my flesh." And Jacob stayed with him a month.

¹⁵Then Laban said to Jacob, "Just because you are my relative, should you work for me for nothing? Tell me, what should your wages be?"

¹⁶Now Laban had two daughters; the name of the older was Leah, and the name of the younger was Rachel.

¹⁷Leah's eyes were weak, but Rachel was beautiful in form and appearance.

¹⁸Jacob loved Rachel, so he said, "I will serve you [as a hired workman] for seven years [in return] for [the privilege of marrying] Rachel your younger daughter."

¹⁹Laban said, "It is better that I give her [in marriage] to you than give her to another man. Stay *and* work with me."

²⁰So Jacob served [Laban] for seven years for [the right to marry] Rachel, but they seemed like only a few days to him because of his love for her.

²¹Finally, Jacob said to Laban, "Give me my wife, for my time [of service] is completed, so that I may take her to me [as my wife]."

²²So Laban gathered together all the men of the place and prepared a [wedding] feast [with wine].

²³But in the evening he took Leah his daughter and brought her to Jacob, and Jacob went in to [consummate the marriage with] her.

²⁴Laban also gave Zilpah his maid to his daughter Leah as a maid.

²⁵But in the morning [when Jacob awoke], it was Leah [who was with him]! And he said to Laban, "What is

putting the Word to work

The Bible indicates that Leah was not nearly as beautiful or desirable as Rachel (see Genesis 29:17). Have you ever felt rejected, as she must have? Remember that God loves you; He wants you, and He has an awesome plan for your life!

this that you have done to me? Did I not work for you [for seven years] for Rachel? Why have you deceived *and* betrayed me [like this]?"

²⁶But Laban only said, "It is not the tradition here to give the younger [daughter in marriage] before the older.

²⁷"Finish the week [of the wedding feast] for Leah; then we will give you Rachel also, and in return you shall work for me for seven more years."

²⁸So Jacob complied and fulfilled Leah's week [of celebration]; then Laban gave him his daughter Rachel as his [second] wife.

²⁹Laban also gave Bilhah his maid to his daughter Rachel as a maid.

³⁰So Jacob consummated his marriage *and* lived with Rachel [as his wife], and he loved Rachel more than Leah, and he served with Laban for another seven years.

³¹Now when the LORD saw that Leah was unloved, He made her able to bear children, but Rachel was barren.

³²Leah conceived and gave birth to a son and named him Reuben (See, a son!), for she said, "Because the LORD has seen my humiliation *and* suffering; now my husband will love me [since I have given him a son]."

³³Then she conceived again and gave birth to a son and said, "Because the LORD heard that I am unloved, He has given me this son also." So she named him Simeon (God hears).

³⁴She conceived again and gave birth to a son and said, "Now this time my husband will become attached to me [as a

companion], for I have given him three sons." Therefore he was named Levi.

35Again she conceived and gave birth to a [fourth] son, and she said, "Now I will praise the LORD." So she named him Judah; then [for a time] she stopped bearing [children].

30 WHEN RACHEL saw that she conceived no children for Jacob, she envied her sister, and said to Jacob, "Give me children, or else I will die."

2Then Jacob became furious with Rachel, and he said, "Am I in the place of God, who has denied you children?"

3She said, "Here, take my maid Bilhah and go in to her; and [when the baby comes] she shall deliver it [while sitting] on my knees, so that by her I may also have children [to count as my own]."

4So she gave him Bilhah her maid as a [secondary] wife, and Jacob went in to her.

5Bilhah conceived and gave birth to a son for Jacob.

6Then Rachel said, "God has judged and vindicated me, and has heard my plea and has given me a son [through my maid]." So she named him Dan (He judged).

7Bilhah, Rachel's maid, conceived again and gave birth to a second son for Jacob.

8So Rachel said, "With mighty wrestlings [in prayer to God] I have struggled with my sister and have prevailed." So she named him Naphtali (my wrestlings).

9When Leah saw that she had stopped bearing [children], she took Zilpah her maid and gave her to Jacob as a [secondary] wife.

10Zilpah, Leah's maid, gave birth to a son for Jacob.

11Then Leah said, "How fortunate!" So she named him Gad (good fortune).

12Zilpah, Leah's maid, gave birth to a second son for Jacob.

13Then Leah said, "I am happy! For women will call me happy." So she named him Asher (happy).

14Now at the time of wheat harvest Reuben [the eldest child] went and found some mandrakes in the field, and brought them to his mother Leah. Then Rachel said to Leah, "Please give me some of your son's mandrakes."

15But Leah answered, "Is it a small thing that you have taken my husband? Would you take away my son's mandrakes also?" So Rachel said, "Jacob shall sleep with you tonight in exchange for your son's mandrakes."

16When Jacob came in from the field in the evening, Leah went out to meet him and said, "You must sleep with me [tonight], for I have in fact hired you with my son's mandrakes." So he slept with her that night.

17God listened and answered [the prayer of] Leah, and she conceived and gave birth to a fifth son for Jacob.

18Then Leah said, "God has given me my reward because I have given my maid to my husband." So she named him Issachar.

19Leah conceived again and gave birth to a sixth son for Jacob.

20Then Leah said, "God has endowed me with a good [marriage] gift [for my husband]; now he will live with me [regarding me with honor as his wife], because I have given birth to six sons." So she named him Zebulun.

21Afterward she gave birth to a daughter and named her Dinah.

22Then God remembered [the prayers of] Rachel, and God thought of her and opened her womb [so that she would conceive].

23So she conceived and gave birth to a son; and she said, "God has taken away my disgrace and humiliation."

24She named him Joseph (may He add) and said, "May the LORD add to me another son."

25Now when Rachel had given birth

to Joseph, Jacob said to Laban, "Send me away, that I may go back to my own place and to my own country.

²⁶"Give me my wives and my children for whom I have served you, and let me go; for you know the work which I have done for you."

²⁷But Laban said to him, "If I have found favor in your sight, *stay with me;* for I have learned [from the omens in divination and by experience] that the Lᴏʀᴅ has blessed me because of you."

²⁸He said, "Name your wages, and I will give it [to you]."

²⁹Jacob answered him, "You know how I have served you and how your possessions, your cattle *and* sheep *and* goats, have fared with me.

³⁰"For you had little before I came and it has increased *and* multiplied abundantly, and the Lᴏʀᴅ has favored you with blessings wherever I turned. But now, when shall I provide for my own household?"

³¹Laban asked, "What shall I give you?" Jacob replied, "You shall not give me anything. But if you will do this one thing for me [which I now propose], I will again pasture and keep your flock:

³²Let me pass through your entire flock today, removing from it every speckled and spotted sheep and every dark *or* black one among the lambs and the spotted and speckled among the goats; and those shall be my wages.

³³"So my honesty will be evident for me later, when you come [for an accounting] concerning my wages. Every one that is not speckled and spotted among the goats and dark among the young lambs, *if found* with me, shall be considered stolen."

³⁴And Laban said, "Good! Let it be done as you say."

³⁵So on that same day Laban [secretly] removed the male goats that were streaked and spotted and all the female goats that were speckled and spotted, every one with white on it, and all the dark ones among the sheep, and put them in the care of his sons.

³⁶And he put [a distance of] three days' journey between himself and Jacob, and Jacob was then left in care of the rest of Laban's flock.

³⁷Then Jacob took branches of fresh poplar and almond and plane trees, and peeled white stripes in them, exposing the white in the branches.

³⁸Then he set the branches which he had peeled in front of the flocks in the watering troughs, where the flocks came to drink; and they mated *and* conceived when they came to drink.

³⁹So the flocks mated *and* conceived by the branches, and the flocks gave birth to streaked, speckled, and spotted offspring.

⁴⁰Jacob separated the lambs, and [as he had done with the peeled branches] he made the flocks face toward the streaked and all the dark *or* black in the [new] flock of Laban; and he put his own herds apart by themselves and did not put them [where they could breed] with Laban's flock.

⁴¹Furthermore, whenever the stronger [animals] of the flocks were breeding, Jacob would place the branches in the sight of the flock in the watering troughs, so that they would mate *and* conceive among the branches;

⁴²but when the flock was sickly, he did not put *the branches* there; so the sicker [animals] were Laban's and the stronger Jacob's.

⁴³So Jacob became exceedingly prosperous, and had large flocks [of sheep and goats], and female and male servants, and camels and donkeys.

31 JACOB HEARD that Laban's sons were saying: "Jacob has taken away everything that was our father's, and from what belonged to our father he has acquired all this wealth *and* honor."

²Jacob noticed [a change in] the attitude of Laban, and saw that it was not *friendly* toward him as before.

³Then the LORD said to Jacob, "Return to the land of your fathers and to your people, and I will be with you."

⁴So Jacob sent and called Rachel and Leah to his flock in the field,

⁵and he said to them, "I see [a change in] your father's attitude, that he is not *friendly* toward me as [he was] before; but the God of my father [Isaac] has been with me.

⁶"You know that I have served your father with all my strength.

⁷"Yet your father has cheated me [as often as possible] and changed my wages ten times; but God did not allow him to hurt me.

⁸"If he said, 'The speckled shall be your wages,' then the entire flock gave birth to speckled [young]; and if he said, 'The streaked shall be your wages,' then the entire flock gave birth to streaked [young].

⁹"Thus God has taken away the flocks of your father and given them to me.

¹⁰"And it happened at the time when the flock conceived that I looked up and saw in a dream that the rams which mated [with the female goats] were streaked, speckled, and spotted.

¹¹"And the Angel of God said to me in the dream, 'Jacob.' And I said, 'Here I am.'

¹²"He said, 'Look up and see, all the rams which are mating [with the flock] are streaked, speckled, and spotted; for I have seen all that Laban has been doing to you.

¹³'I am the God of Bethel, where you anointed the pillar, and where you made a vow to Me; now stand up, leave this land, and return to the land of your birth.'"

¹⁴Rachel and Leah answered him, "Is there still any portion or inheritance for us in our father's house?

¹⁵"Are we not counted by him as foreigners? For he sold us [to you in marriage], and has also entirely used up our purchase price.

¹⁶"Surely all the riches which God has taken from our father are ours and our children's. Now then, whatever God has told you to do, do it."

¹⁷Then Jacob stood [and took action] and put his children and his wives on camels;

¹⁸and he drove away all his livestock and [took along] all his property which he had acquired, the livestock he had obtained and accumulated in Paddan-aram, to go to his father Isaac in the land of Canaan.

¹⁹When Laban had gone to shear his sheep, Rachel [went inside the house and] stole her father's household gods.

²⁰And Jacob deceived Laban the Aramean (Syrian) by not telling him that he intended to leave *and* he slipped away secretly.

²¹So he fled with everything that he had, and got up and crossed the river [Euphrates], and set his face toward the hill country of Gilead [east of the Jordan River].

²²On the third day [after his departure] Laban was told that Jacob had fled.

²³So he took his relatives with him and pursued him for seven days, and they overtook him in the hill country of Gilead.

²⁴God came to Laban the Aramean in a dream at night and said to him, "Be careful that you do not speak to Jacob, either good or bad."

²⁵Then Laban overtook Jacob. Now Jacob had pitched his tent on the hill, and Laban with his relatives camped on the same hill of Gilead.

²⁶Then Laban said to Jacob, "What do you mean by deceiving me *and* leaving without my knowledge, and carrying off my daughters as if [they were] captives of the sword?

²⁷"Why did you run away secretly

and deceive me and not tell me, so that [otherwise] I might have sent you away with joy and with songs, with [music on the] tambourine and lyre?

28"And why did you not allow me to kiss my grandchildren and my daughters [goodbye]? Now you have done a foolish thing [in behaving like this].

29"It is in my power to harm you, but the God of your father spoke to me last night, saying, 'Be careful not to speak to Jacob, either good or bad.'

30"Now [I suppose] you felt you must go because you were homesick for your father's house and family; but why did you steal my [household] gods?"

31Jacob answered Laban, "[I left secretly] because I was afraid, for I thought you would take your daughters away from me by force.

32"The one with whom you find your gods shall not live; in the presence of our relatives [search my possessions and] point out whatever you find that belongs to you and take it." For Jacob did not know that Rachel had stolen the idols.

33So Laban went into Jacob's tent and into Leah's tent and the tent of the two maids, but he did not find them. Then he came out of Leah's tent and entered Rachel's tent.

34Now Rachel had taken the household idols and put them in the camel's saddlebag and sat on them. Laban searched through all her tent, but did not find them.

35So Rachel said to her father, "Do not be displeased, my lord, that I cannot rise before you, for the manner of women is on me and I am unwell." He searched [further] but did not find the household idols.

36Then Jacob became angry and argued with Laban. And he said to Laban, "What is my fault? What is my sin that you pursued me like this?

37"Although you have searched through all my possessions, what have you found of your household goods? Put it here before my relatives and your relatives, so that they may decide [who has done right] between the two of us.

38"These twenty years I have been with you; your ewes and your female goats have not lost their young, nor have I eaten the rams of your flocks.

39"I did not bring you the torn carcasses [of the animals attacked by predators]; I [personally] took the loss. You required of me [to make good] everything that was stolen, whether it occurred by day or night.

40"This was my situation: by day the heat consumed me and by night the cold, and I could not sleep.

41"These twenty years I have been in your house; I served you fourteen years for your two daughters and six years for [my share of] your flocks, and you have changed my wages ten times.

42"If the God of my father, the God of Abraham, and [the Feared One] of Isaac, had not been with me, most certainly you would have sent me away now empty-handed. God has seen my affliction and humiliation and the [exhausting] labor of my hands, so He rendered judgment and rebuked you last night."

43Laban answered Jacob, "These women [that you married] are my daughters, these children are my grandchildren, these flocks are [from] my flocks, and all that you see [here] is mine. But what can I do today to these my daughters or to their children to whom they have given birth?

44"So come now, let us make a covenant, you and I, and let it serve as a witness between you and me."

45So Jacob took a stone and set it up as a [memorial] pillar.

46Jacob said to his relatives, "Gather stones." And they took stones and made a mound [of stones], and they ate [a ceremonial meal together] there on the mound [of stones]. [Prov 16:7]

⁴⁷Laban called it Jegar-sahadutha (stone monument of testimony in Aramaic), but Jacob called it Galeed.

⁴⁸Laban said, "This mound [of stones] is a witness [a reminder of the oath taken] today between you and me." Therefore he [also] called the name Galeed,

⁴⁹and Mizpah (watchtower), for Laban said, "May the Lord watch between you and me when we are absent from one another.

⁵⁰"If you should mistreat (humiliate, oppress) my daughters, or if you should take other wives besides my daughters, although no one is with us [as a witness], see *and* remember, God is witness between you and me."

⁵¹Laban said to Jacob, "Look at this mound [of stones] and look at this pillar which I have set up between you and me.

⁵²"This mound is a witness, and this pillar is a witness, that I will not pass by this mound to harm you, and that you will not pass by this mound and this pillar to harm me.

⁵³"The God of Abraham [your father] and the God of Nahor [my father], and the god [the image of worship] of their father [Terah, an idolater], judge between us." But Jacob swore [only] by [the one true God] the Fear of his father Isaac. [Josh 24:2]

⁵⁴Then Jacob offered a sacrifice [to the Lord] on the mountain, and called his relatives to the meal; and they ate food and spent the night on the mountain.

⁵⁵Early in the morning Laban got up and kissed his grandchildren and his daughters [goodbye] and pronounced a blessing [asking God's favor] on them. Then Laban left and returned home.

32

THEN AS Jacob went on his way, the angels of God met him [to reassure and protect him].

²When Jacob saw them, he said, "This is God's camp." So he named that place Mahanaim (double camps). [Gen 32:7, 10]

³Then Jacob sent messengers ahead of him to his brother Esau in the land of Seir, the country of Edom.

⁴He commanded them, saying, "This is what to say to my lord Esau: 'Your servant Jacob says this, "I have been living temporarily with Laban, and have stayed there until now;

⁵I have oxen, donkeys, flocks, male servants, and female servants; and I have sent [this message] to tell my lord, so that I may find grace *and* kindness in your sight."'"

⁶The messengers returned to Jacob, saying, "We went to your brother Esau, and now he is coming to meet you, and there are four hundred men with him."

⁷Jacob was greatly afraid and distressed; and he divided the people who were with him, and the flocks and herds and camels, into two camps;

⁸and he said, "If Esau comes to the one camp and attacks it, then the other camp which is left will escape."

⁹Jacob said, "O God of my father Abraham and God of my father Isaac, the Lord, who said to me, 'Return to your country and to your people, and I will make you prosper,'

¹⁰I am unworthy of all the loving-kindness *and* compassion and of all the faithfulness which You have shown to Your servant. With only my staff [long ago] I crossed over

speak the Word

Father, thank You for all the loving-kindness, compassion, and faithfulness
You show to me, even though I am unworthy.
−ADAPTED FROM GENESIS 32:10

this Jordan, and now I have become [blessed and increased into these] two groups [of people].

11"Save me, please, from the hand of my brother, from the hand of Esau; for I fear him, that he will come and attack me and the mothers with the children.

12"And You [LORD] said, 'I will certainly make you prosper and make your descendants as [numerous as] the sand of the sea, which is too great to be counted.'"

13So Jacob spent the night there. Then he selected a present for his brother Esau from the livestock he had acquired:

14two hundred female goats, twenty male goats, two hundred ewes, twenty rams,

15thirty milking camels with their colts, forty cows, ten bulls, twenty female donkeys, and ten [donkey] colts.

16He put them into the care of his servants, every herd by itself, and said to his servants, "Go on ahead of me, and put an interval [of space] between the *individual* herds."

17Then he commanded the one in front, saying, "When Esau my brother meets you and asks to whom you belong, and where you are going, and whose are the *animals* in front of you?

18then you shall say, 'They are your servant Jacob's; they are a gift sent to my lord Esau. And he also is behind us.'"

19And so Jacob commanded the second and the third as well, and all that followed the herds, saying, "This is

everybody limps

Jacob was a man with many weaknesses, yet he pressed on with God and was determined to receive God's blessing. God likes that kind of determination. He actually told Jacob in Genesis 32:28 that he (Jacob) had struggled with God and men and had prevailed. Because of that struggle, God would be glorified in him. God can always be glorified through people who do not allow their personal weaknesses to stop Him from flowing through them.

In order for God to flow through us, we must first come face-to-face with the fact that we have weaknesses—and then we must determine not to let them bother us. Our imperfections will not stop God from working through us unless we let them. We need to accept ourselves completely—weaknesses and all—because God does.

I am going to ask you to do something very important. Right now, stop and wrap your arms around yourself. Give yourself a great big hug and say aloud: "I accept myself. I love myself. I know I have weaknesses and imperfections, but I will not let them stop me, and I will not allow them to stop God from working through me." Try doing that several times per day, and you will soon develop a new attitude toward yourself, a new outlook on life, and a greater level of confidence in God.

Jacob wrestled with the angel of the Lord, who touched the hollow of his thigh. As a result of that encounter, he developed a limp (see Genesis 32:24–32). I like to say that Jacob limped away from the fight, but he took his blessing with him! God will bless all of us even though we limp, even though we are not perfect. Remember, God looks at our hearts. If we have faith in Him and hearts that long to obey Him and bring Him glory, then He will work wonders through us in spite of our weaknesses.

what you shall say to Esau when you meet him;

²⁰and you shall say, 'Look, your servant Jacob is behind us.'" For he said [to himself], "I will try to appease him with the gift that is going ahead of me. Then afterward I will see him; perhaps he will accept *and* forgive me."

²¹So the gift [of the herds of livestock] went on ahead of him, and he himself spent that night back in the camp.

²²But he got up that same night and took his two wives, his two female servants, and his eleven children, and waded over the ford of the Jabbok.

²³Then he took them and sent them across the brook. And he also sent across whatever he had.

²⁴So Jacob was left alone, and a Man [came and] wrestled with him until daybreak.

²⁵When the Man saw that He had not prevailed against Jacob, He touched his hip joint; and Jacob's hip was dislocated as he wrestled with Him.

²⁶Then He said, "Let Me go, for day is breaking." But Jacob said, "I will not let You go unless You declare a blessing on me."

²⁷So He asked him, "What is your name?" And he said, "Jacob."

²⁸And He said, "Your name shall no longer be Jacob, but Israel; for you have struggled with God and with men and have prevailed." [Hos 12:3, 4]

²⁹Then Jacob asked Him, "Please tell me Your name." But He said, "Why is it that you ask My name?" And He declared a blessing [of the covenant promises] on Jacob there.

³⁰So Jacob named the place Peniel (the face of God), *saying,* "For I have seen God face to face, yet my life has not been snatched away."

³¹Now the sun rose on him as he passed Penuel (Peniel), and he was limping because of his hip.

³²Therefore, to this day the Israelites do not eat the tendon of the hip which is on the socket of the thigh, because He touched the socket of Jacob's thigh by the tendon of the hip.

33 THEN JACOB looked up, and saw Esau coming with four hundred men. So he divided the children among Leah and Rachel and the two maids.

²He put the maids and their children in front, Leah and her children after them, and Rachel and Joseph last of all.

³Then Jacob crossed over [the stream] ahead of them and bowed himself to the ground seven times [bowing and moving forward each time], until he approached his brother.

⁴But Esau ran to meet him and embraced him, and hugged his neck and kissed him, and they wept [for joy]. [Luke 15:20]

⁵Esau looked up and saw the women and the children, and said, "Who are these with you?" So Jacob replied, "They are the children whom God has graciously given your servant."

⁶Then the maids approached with their children, and they bowed down.

⁷Leah also approached with her children, and they bowed down. Afterward Joseph and Rachel approached, and they bowed down.

⁸Esau asked, "What do you mean by all this company which I have met?" And he answered, "[These are] to find favor in the sight of my lord."

⁹But Esau said, "I have plenty, my brother; keep what you have for yourself."

¹⁰Jacob replied, "No, please, if now I have found favor in your sight, then accept my gift [as a blessing] from my hand, for I see your face as if I had seen the face of God, and you have received me favorably.

¹¹"Please accept my blessing (gift) which has been brought to you, for God has dealt graciously with me and I have everything [that I could possibly

want]." So Jacob kept urging him and Esau accepted it.

¹²Then Esau said, "Let us get started on our journey and I will go in front of you [to lead the way]."

¹³But Jacob replied, "You know, my lord, that the children are frail *and* need gentle care, and the nursing flocks and herds [with young] are of concern to me; for if the men should drive them hard for a single day, all the flocks will die.

¹⁴"Please let my lord go on ahead of his servant, and I will move on slowly, governed by the pace of the livestock that are in front of me and according to the endurance of the children, until I come to my lord in Seir [in Edom]."

¹⁵Then Esau said, "Please let me leave with you some of the people who are with me." But Jacob said, "What need is there [for it]? Let me find favor in the sight of my lord."

¹⁶So Esau turned back [toward the south] that day on his way to Seir.

¹⁷But Jacob journeyed [north] to Succoth, and built himself a house and made shelters for his livestock; so the name of the place is Succoth (huts, shelters).

¹⁸When Jacob came from Paddan-aram, he arrived safely *and* in peace at the city of Shechem, in the land of Canaan, and camped in front of the [walled] city.

¹⁹Then he bought the piece of land on which he had pitched his tents from the sons of Hamor, Shechem's father, for a hundred pieces of money.

²⁰There he erected an altar and called it El-Elohe-Israel.

34 NOW DINAH the daughter of Leah, whom she had borne to Jacob, went out [unescorted] to visit the girls of the land.

²When Shechem the son of Hamor the Hivite, prince (sheik) of the land, saw her, he kidnapped her and lay [intimately] with her by force [humbling and offending her].

³But his soul longed for and clung to Dinah daughter of Jacob, and he loved the girl and spoke comfortingly to her young heart's wishes.

⁴So Shechem said to his father Hamor, "Get me this young woman as a wife."

⁵Now Jacob heard that Shechem had defiled (violated) Dinah his daughter; but his sons were in the field with his livestock, so Jacob said nothing until they came in.

⁶But Shechem's father Hamor went to Jacob to talk with him.

⁷Now when Jacob's sons heard of it they came in from the field; they were deeply grieved, and they were very angry, for Shechem had done a disgraceful thing to Israel by lying with Jacob's daughter, for such a thing is not to be done.

⁸But Hamor conferred with them, saying, "The soul of my son Shechem [deeply] longs for your daughter [and sister]. Please give her to him as his wife.

⁹"And [beyond that] intermarry with us; give your daughters to us [as wives] and take our daughters for yourselves. [Ex 34:15, 16; Deut 7:3; Josh 23:12, 13]

¹⁰"In this way you shall live with us; the country will be open to you; live and do business in it and acquire property *and* possessions in it."

¹¹Shechem also said to Dinah's father and to her brothers, "Let me find favor in your sight, and I will give you whatever you ask of me.

putting the Word to work

Have you, like Dinah, ever been an innocent victim? I can assure you that even in the worst circumstances, God gives us grace to forgive so that we can go on with our lives.

¹²"Demand of me a very large bridal payment and gift [as compensation for giving up your daughter and sister], and I will give you whatever you tell me; only give me the girl to be my wife."

¹³Jacob's sons answered Shechem and Hamor his father deceitfully, because Shechem had defiled *and* disgraced their sister Dinah.

¹⁴They said to them, "We cannot do this thing and give our sister [in marriage] to one who is not circumcised, because that would be a disgrace to us.

¹⁵"But we will consent to you only on this *condition:* if you will become like us, in that every male among you *consents to* be circumcised,

¹⁶then we will give our daughters to you [in marriage], and we will take your daughters for ourselves, and we will live with you and become one people.

¹⁷"But if you do not listen to us *and* refuse to be circumcised, then we will take our daughter [Dinah] and go."

¹⁸Their words seemed reasonable to Hamor and his son Shechem,

¹⁹and the young man did not hesitate to do the [required] thing, for he was delighted with Jacob's daughter. Now he was more respected *and* honored than all [others] in the household of his father.

²⁰Then Hamor and Shechem his son came to the gate of their [walled] city [where the leading men would meet] and spoke with the men of the city, saying,

²¹"These men are peaceful *and* friendly with us; so let them live in the land and do business in it, for the land is large enough [for us and] for them; let us take their daughters for wives and let us give them our daughters [in marriage].

²²"But only on this *condition* will the men consent to our request that they live among us and become one people:

that every male among us become circumcised just as they are circumcised.

²³"Will not their cattle and their possessions and all their animals be ours [if we do this]? Let us consent [to do as they ask], and they will live here with us."

²⁴And every [Canaanite] man who went out of the city gate listened *and* considered what Hamor and Shechem said; and every male who was a resident of that city was circumcised.

²⁵Now on the third day [after the circumcision], when all the men were [terribly] sore *and* in pain, two of Jacob's sons, Simeon and Levi, Dinah's [full] brothers, took their swords, boldly entered the city [without anyone suspecting them of evil intent], and they killed every male.

²⁶They killed Hamor and his son Shechem with the edge of the sword, and took Dinah out of Shechem's house [where she was staying], and left.

²⁷Then Jacob's [other] sons came upon those who were killed and looted the town, because their sister had been defiled *and* disgraced.

²⁸They took the Canaanites' flocks and their herds and their donkeys, and whatever was in the city and in the field;

²⁹they looted all their wealth, and [took captive] all their children and their wives, even everything that was in the houses.

³⁰Then Jacob said to Simeon and Levi, "You have ruined me, making me a stench to the inhabitants of the land, the Canaanites and the Perizzites! My men are few in number, and the men of the land will band together against me and attack me; I shall be destroyed, I and my household."

³¹But they said, "Should he [be permitted to] treat our sister as a prostitute?"

35

THEN GOD said to Jacob, "Go up to Bethel and live there, and make an altar there to God, who appeared to you [in a distinct manifestation] when you fled [years ago] from Esau your brother." [Gen 28:11–22]

²Then Jacob said to his household and to all who were with him, "Get rid of the [idols and images of] foreign gods that are among you, and ceremonially purify yourselves and change [into fresh] clothes;

³then let us get up and go up to Bethel, and I will make an altar there to God, who answered me in the day of my distress and has been with me wherever I have gone."

⁴So they gave Jacob all the [idols and images of the] foreign gods they had and the rings which were in their ears [worn as charms against evil], and Jacob buried them under the oak tree near Shechem.

⁵As they journeyed, there was a great [supernatural] terror [sent from God] on the cities around them, and [for that reason] the Canaanites did not pursue the sons of Jacob.

⁶So Jacob came to Luz (that is, Bethel), which is in the land of Canaan, he and all the people who were with him.

⁷There he built an altar [to worship the LORD], and called the place El-bethel (God of the House of God), because there God had revealed Himself to him when he escaped from his brother.

⁸Now Deborah, [who once was] Rebekah's nurse, died and was buried below Bethel under the oak; and the name of it was called Allon-bacuth (Oak of Weeping).

⁹Then God [in a visible manifestation] appeared to Jacob again when he came out of Paddan-aram, and declared a blessing on him. [Gen 32:28]

¹⁰Again God said to him,

"Your name is Jacob;
You shall no longer be called Jacob,
But Israel shall be your name."

So he was called Israel.
¹¹And God said to him,

"I am God Almighty.
Be fruitful and multiply;
A nation and a company of nations
    shall come from you,
And kings shall be born of your
    loins.
¹²"The land which I gave Abraham
    and Isaac
I will give to you,
and to your descendants after you
    I will give the land."

¹³Then God ascended from Jacob in the place where He had spoken with him.

¹⁴Jacob set up a pillar (memorial, monument) in the place where he had talked with God, a pillar of stone, and he poured a drink offering [of wine] on it; he also poured oil on it [to declare it sacred for God's purpose].

¹⁵So Jacob named the place where God had spoken with him, Bethel (the House of God).

¹⁶Then they journeyed from Bethel; and when there was still some distance to go to Ephrath (Bethlehem), Rachel began to give birth and had difficulty *and* suffered severely.

¹⁷When she was in hard labor the midwife said to her, "Do not be afraid; you now have another son."

¹⁸And as her soul was departing, (for she died), she named him Ben-oni (son of my sorrow); but his father called him Benjamin (son of the right hand).

¹⁹So Rachel died and was buried on the way to Ephrath (that is, Bethlehem).

²⁰Jacob set a pillar (memorial, monument) on her grave; that is the pillar of Rachel's grave to this day.

²¹Then Israel (Jacob) journeyed on and pitched his tent on the other side of the tower of Eder [the lookout point used by shepherds].

22While Israel was living in that land, Reuben [his eldest son] went and lay with Bilhah his father's concubine, and Israel heard about it.

Now Jacob had twelve sons—

23The sons of Leah: Reuben, Jacob's firstborn, then Simeon, Levi, Judah, Issachar, and Zebulun;

24and the sons of Rachel: Joseph and Benjamin;

25and the sons of Bilhah, Rachel's maid: Dan and Naphtali;

26and the sons of Zilpah, Leah's maid: Gad and Asher. These are the sons of Jacob born to him in Paddan-aram.

27Jacob came to Isaac his father at Mamre of Kiriath-arba (that is, Hebron), where Abraham and Isaac had lived temporarily.

28Now the days of Isaac were a hundred and eighty years.

29Isaac's spirit departed and he died and was gathered to his people [who had preceded him in death], an old man full of days (satisfied, fulfilled); his sons Esau and Jacob buried him [in the cave of Machpelah with his parents Abraham and Sarah].

36 NOW THESE are *the records of* the descendants of Esau, (that is, Edom).

2Esau took his [three] wives from the daughters of Canaan: Adah the daughter of Elon the Hittite, and Oholibamah the daughter of Anah, the son of Zibeon the Hivite,

3and Basemath, Ishmael's daughter, sister of Nebaioth.

4Adah bore Eliphaz to Esau, and Basemath bore Reuel,

5and Oholibamah bore Jeush, Jalam, and Korah. These are the sons of Esau born to him in Canaan.

6Now Esau took his wives and his sons and his daughters and all the members of his household, and his livestock and all his cattle and all his possessions which he had acquired in the land of Canaan, and he went to a land away from his brother Jacob.

7For their [great flocks and herds and] possessions made it impossible for them to live together [in the same region]; the land in which they lived temporarily could not support them because of their livestock.

8So Esau lived in the hill country of Seir; Esau is Edom.

9These are *the records of* the generations of Esau the father of the Edomites in the hill country of Seir.

10These are the names of Esau's sons: Eliphaz, the son of Adah, Esau's wife, and Reuel, the son of Basemath, Esau's wife.

11And the sons of Eliphaz were Teman, Omar, Zepho, Gatam, and Kenaz.

12And Timna was a concubine of Eliphaz, Esau's son; and she bore Amalek to Eliphaz. These are the sons of Adah, Esau's wife.

13These are the sons of Reuel: Nahath, Zerah, Shammah, and Mizzah. These are the sons of Basemath, Esau's wife.

14And these are the sons of Oholibamah, Esau's wife, the daughter of Anah, the son of Zibeon. She bore to Esau: Jeush, Jalam, and Korah.

15These are the *tribal* chiefs of the sons of Esau: The sons of Eliphaz, the firstborn of Esau: Chiefs Teman, Omar, Zepho, Kenaz,

16Korah, Gatam, and Amalek. These are the chiefs of Eliphaz in the land of Edom; they are the sons of Adah.

17These are the sons of Reuel, Esau's son: Chiefs Nahath, Zerah, Shammah, Mizzah. These are the chiefs of Reuel in the land of Edom; they are the sons of Basemath, Esau's wife.

18These are the sons of Oholibamah, Esau's wife: Chiefs Jeush, Jalam, and Korah. These are the chiefs born of Oholibamah, daughter of Anah, Esau's wife.

19These are the sons of Esau, (that is, Edom), and these are their chiefs.

²⁰These are the sons of Seir the Horite, the inhabitants of the land: Lotan, Shobal, Zibeon, Anah,

²¹Dishon, Ezer, and Dishan. These are the chiefs of the Horites, the sons of Seir in the land of Edom.

²²The sons of Lotan are Hori and Hemam; and Lotan's sister is Timna.

²³The sons of Shobal are these: Alvan, Manahath, Ebal, Shepho, and Onam.

²⁴These are the sons of Zibeon: Aiah and Anah. This is the Anah who found the hot springs in the wilderness as he pastured the donkeys of Zibeon his father.

²⁵The children of Anah are these: Dishon and Oholibamah [Esau's wife], the daughter of Anah.

²⁶These are the sons of Dishon: Hemdan, Eshban, Ithran, and Cheran.

²⁷Ezer's sons are these: Bilhan, Zaavan, and Akan.

²⁸The sons of Dishan are these: Uz and Aran.

²⁹The Horite chiefs are these: Chiefs Lotan, Shobal, Zibeon, Anah,

³⁰Dishon, Ezer, Dishan. These are the Horite chiefs, according to their various clans in the land of Seir.

³¹And these are the kings who reigned in the land of Edom before any king reigned over the Israelites:

³²Bela the son of Beor reigned in Edom, and the name of his city was Dinhabah.

³³Now Bela died, and Jobab the son of Zerah of Bozrah reigned as his successor.

³⁴Then Jobab died, and Husham of the land of the Temanites reigned as his successor.

³⁵And Husham died, and Hadad the son of Bedad, who defeated Midian in the country of Moab, reigned as his successor. The name of his [walled] city was Avith.

³⁶Hadad died, and Samlah of Masrekah succeeded him.

³⁷Then Samlah died, and Shaul of Rehoboth on the river [Euphrates] reigned as his successor.

³⁸And Shaul died, and Baal-hanan son of Achbor reigned as his successor.

³⁹Baal-hanan the son of Achbor died, and then Hadar reigned [as his successor]. His [walled] city was Pau; his wife's name was Mehetabel the daughter of Matred, the daughter of Mezahab.

⁴⁰And these are the names of the *tribal* chiefs of Esau, according to their families and places of residence, by their names: Chiefs Timna, Alvah, Jetheth,

⁴¹Oholibamah, Elah, Pinon,

⁴²Kenaz, Teman, Mibzar,

⁴³Magdiel, and Iram. These are the *tribal* chiefs of Edom (that is, of Esau the father of the Edomites), according to their dwelling places in the land of their possession.

37 SO JACOB (Israel) lived in the land where his father [Isaac] had been a stranger (sojourner, resident alien), in the land of Canaan.

²These are the generations of Jacob. Joseph, when he was seventeen years old, was shepherding the flock with his brothers [Dan, Naphtali, Gad, and Asher]; the boy was with the sons of Bilhah and Zilpah, his father's [secondary] wives; and Joseph brought back a bad report about them to their father.

³Now Israel (Jacob) loved Joseph more than all his children, because he was the son of his old age; and he made him a [distinctive] multicolored tunic.

⁴His brothers saw that their father loved Joseph more than all of his brothers; so they hated him and could not [find it within themselves to] speak to him on friendly terms.

⁵Now Joseph dreamed a dream, and he told it to his brothers, and they hated him even more.

⁶He said to them, "Please listen to [the details of] this dream which I have dreamed;

⁷we [brothers] were binding sheaves [of grain stalks] in the field, and lo, my sheaf [suddenly] got up and stood upright *and* remained standing; and behold, your sheaves stood all around my sheaf and bowed down [in respect]."

⁸His brothers said to him, "Are you actually going to reign over us? Are you really going to rule *and* govern us as your subjects?" So they hated him even more for [telling them about] his dreams and for his [arrogant] words.

⁹But Joseph dreamed still another dream, and told it to his brothers [as well]. He said, "See here, I have again dreamed a dream, and lo, [this time I saw] eleven stars and the sun and the moon bowed down [in respect] to me!"

¹⁰He told it to his father as well as to his brothers; but his father rebuked him and said to him [in disbelief], "What is [the meaning of] this dream that you have dreamed? Shall I and your mother and your brothers actually come to bow down to the ground [in respect] before you?"

¹¹Joseph's brothers were envious *and* jealous of him, but his father kept the words [of Joseph] *in mind* [wondering about their meaning].

life point

God gave Joseph dreams of greatness, but in his zeal and excitement, Joseph unwisely told his dreams to his brothers, who did not share his enthusiasm (see Genesis 37:5). As a result, they sold him as a slave, and he had to endure some hard years and difficult experiences. During those years, though, God developed wisdom in Joseph and thereby prepared him for his life's call. Just as He did for Joseph, God is able to develop in you whatever you may lack today so that you can fulfill His purpose for your life.

¹²Then his brothers went to pasture their father's flock near Shechem.

¹³Israel (Jacob) said to Joseph, "Are not your brothers pasturing [the flock] at Shechem? Come, and I will send you to them." And he said, "Here I am [ready to obey you]."

¹⁴Then Jacob said to him, "Please go and see whether everything is all right with your brothers and all right with the flock; then bring word [back] to me." So he sent him from the Hebron Valley, and he went to Shechem.

¹⁵Now a certain man found Joseph, and saw that he was wandering around *and* had lost his way in the field; so the man asked him, "What are you looking for?"

¹⁶He said, "I am looking for my brothers. Please tell me where they are pasturing *our flocks.*"

¹⁷Then the man said, "[They were here, but] they have moved on from this place. I heard them say, 'Let us go to Dothan.'" So Joseph went after his brothers and found them at Dothan.

¹⁸And when they saw him from a distance, even before he came close to them, they plotted to kill him.

¹⁹They said to one another, "Look, here comes this dreamer.

²⁰"Now then, come and let us kill him and throw him into one of the pits (cisterns, underground water storage); then we will say [to our father], 'A wild animal killed *and* devoured him'; and we shall see what will become of his dreams!"

²¹Now Reuben [the eldest] heard this and rescued him from their hands and said, "Let us not take his life."

²²Reuben said to them, "Do not shed his blood, but [instead] throw him [alive] into the pit that is here in the wilderness, and do not lay a hand on him [to kill him]"—[he said this so] that he could rescue him from them and return him [safely] to his father.

²³Now when Joseph reached his

brothers, they stripped him of his tunic, the [distinctive] multicolored tunic which he was wearing;

²⁴then they took him and threw him into the pit. Now the pit was empty; there was no water in it.

²⁵Then they sat down to eat their meal. When they looked up, they saw a caravan of Ishmaelites coming from Gilead [east of the Jordan], with their camels bearing ladanum resin [for perfume] and balm and myrrh, going on their way to carry the cargo down to Egypt.

²⁶Judah said to his brothers, "What do we gain if we kill our brother and cover up his blood (murder)?

²⁷"Come, let us [instead] sell him to these Ishmaelites [and Midianites] and not lay our hands on him, because he is our brother and our flesh." So his brothers listened to him and agreed. [Gen 22:24; 25:2]

²⁸Then as the Midianite [and Ishmaelite] traders were passing by, the brothers pulled Joseph up and lifted him out of the pit, and they sold him to the Ishmaelites for twenty shekels of silver. And so they took Joseph [as a captive] into Egypt.

²⁹Now Reuben [unaware of what had happened] returned to the pit, and [to his great alarm found that] Joseph was not in the pit; so he tore his clothes [in deep sorrow].

³⁰He rejoined his brothers and said, "The boy is not there; as for me, where shall I go [to hide from my father]?"

³¹Then they took Joseph's tunic, slaughtered a male goat and dipped the tunic in the blood;

³²and they brought the multicolored tunic to their father, saying, "We have found this; please examine it and decide whether or not it is your son's tunic."

³³He recognized it and said, "It is my son's tunic. A wild animal has devoured him; Joseph is without doubt torn in pieces!"

³⁴So Jacob tore his clothes [in grief],

put on sackcloth and mourned many days for his son.

³⁵Then all his sons and daughters attempted to console him, but he refused to be comforted and said, "I will go down to Sheol (the place of the dead) in mourning for my son." And his father wept for him.

³⁶Meanwhile, in Egypt the Midianites sold Joseph [as a slave] to Potiphar, an officer of Pharaoh and the captain of the [royal] guard.

38

NOW AT that time, Judah left his brothers and went down to [stay with] a certain Adullamite named Hirah.

²There Judah saw a daughter of Shua, a Canaanite, and he took her [as his wife] and lived with her.

³So she conceived and gave birth to a son and Judah named him Er.

⁴Then she conceived again and gave birth to a son and named him Onan.

⁵Again she conceived and gave birth to still another son and named him Shelah. It was at Chezib that she gave birth to him.

⁶Now Judah took a wife for Er his firstborn; her name was Tamar.

⁷But Er, Judah's firstborn, was evil in the sight of the Lord, and the Lord killed him [in judgment].

⁸Then Judah told Onan, "Go in to your brother's widow, and perform your duty as a brother-in-law [under the levirate marriage custom]; [be her husband and] raise children for [the name of] your brother." [Deut 25:5–10]

⁹Onan knew that the child (heir) would not be his [but his dead brother's]; so whenever he lay with his brother's widow, he spilled his seed on the ground [to prevent conception], so that he would not give a child to his brother.

¹⁰But what he did was displeasing in the sight of the Lord; therefore He killed him also [in judgment].

¹¹Then Judah said to Tamar, his

daughter-in-law, "Remain a widow at your father's house until Shelah my [youngest] son is grown"; [but he was deceiving her] for he thought that [if Shelah should marry her] he too might die like his brothers did. So Tamar went and lived in her father's house.

¹²But quite a while later, Judah's wife, the daughter of Shua, died; and when the time of mourning was ended, he went up to his sheepshearers at Timnah with his friend Hirah the Adullamite.

¹³Tamar was told, "Listen, your father-in-law is going up to Timnah to shear his sheep."

¹⁴So she removed her widow's clothes and covered herself with a veil, and wrapped herself up [in disguise], and sat in the gateway of Enaim, which is on the road to Timnah; for she saw that Shelah had grown up, and she had not been given to him as a wife [as Judah had promised].

¹⁵When Judah saw her, he thought she was a [temple] prostitute, for she had covered her face [as such women did].

¹⁶He turned to her by the road, and said, "Please come, let me lie with you"; for he did not know that she was his daughter-in-law. And she said, "What will you give me, that you may lie with me?"

¹⁷He answered, "I will send you a young goat from the flock." And she said, "Will you give me a pledge [as a deposit] until you send it?"

¹⁸He said, "What pledge shall I give you?" She said, "Your seal and your cord, and the staff that is in your hand." So he gave them to her and was intimate with her, and she conceived by him.

¹⁹Then she got up and left, and removed her veil and put on her widow's clothing.

²⁰When Judah sent the young goat by his friend the Adullamite, to get his pledge [back] from the woman, he was unable to find her.

²¹He asked the men of that place, "Where is the temple prostitute who was by the roadside at Enaim?" They said, "There was no prostitute here."

²²So he returned to Judah, and said, "I cannot find her; also the local men said, 'There was no prostitute around here.'"

²³Then Judah said, "Let her keep the things (pledge articles) for herself, otherwise we will be a laughingstock [searching everywhere for her]. After all, I sent this young goat, but you did not find her."

²⁴About three months later Judah was told, "Tamar your daughter-in-law has played the [role of a] prostitute, and she is with child because of her immorality." So Judah said, "Bring her out and let her be burned [to death as punishment]!"

²⁵While she was being brought out, she [took the things Judah had given her and] sent [them along with a message] to her father-in-law, saying, "I am with child by the man to whom these articles belong." And she added, "Please examine [them carefully] and see [clearly] to whom these things belong, the seal and the cord and staff."

²⁶Judah recognized the articles, and said, "She has been more righteous [in this matter] than I, because I did not give her to my son Shelah [as I had promised]." And Judah did not have [intimate] relations with her again.

²⁷Now when the time came for her to give birth, there were twins in her womb.

²⁸And when she was in labor, one [baby] put out his hand, and the midwife took his hand and tied a scarlet thread on it, saying, "This one was born first."

²⁹But he pulled back his hand, and his brother was born first. And she said, "What a breach you have made for yourself [to be the firstborn]!" So he was named Perez (breach, break forth). [Matt 1:3]

³⁰Afterward his brother who had the scarlet [thread] on his hand was born and was named Zerah (brightness).

39

NOW JOSEPH had been taken down to Egypt; and Potiphar, an Egyptian officer of Pharaoh, the captain of the [royal] guard, bought him from the Ishmaelites, who had taken him down there.

²The LORD was with Joseph, and he [even though a slave] became a successful *and* prosperous man; and he was in the house of his master, the Egyptian.

³Now his master saw that the LORD was with him and that the LORD caused all that he did to prosper (succeed) in his hand. [Gen 21:22; 26:27, 28; 41:38, 39]

⁴So Joseph pleased Potiphar *and* found favor in his sight and he served him as his personal servant. He made Joseph overseer over his house, and he put all that he owned in Joseph's charge.

⁵It happened that from the time that he made Joseph overseer in his house and [put him in charge] over all that he owned, that the LORD blessed the Egyptian's house because of Joseph; so the LORD's blessing was on everything that Potiphar owned, in the house and in the field.

⁶So Potiphar left all that he owned in Joseph's charge; and with Joseph there he did not [need to] pay attention to anything except the food he ate.

life point

While we are waiting on God, it is important for us to take our positions and stay faithful. Then, like Joseph, God will raise us up in His timing (see Genesis 39:2–5). Be faithful as you wait on God, do your work well, and people will see that God's hand is upon you for good.

Now Joseph was handsome *and* attractive in form and appearance. [Gen 43:32]

⁷Then after a time his master's wife looked at Joseph with desire, and she said, "Lie with me."

⁸But he refused and said to his master's wife, "Look, with me in the house, my master does not concern himself with anything; he has put everything that he owns in my charge.

⁹"He is not greater in this house than I am, nor has he kept anything from me except you, because you are his wife. How then could I do this great evil and sin against God [and your husband]?"

¹⁰And so it was that she spoke to Joseph [persistently] day after day, but he did not listen to her [plea] to lie beside her or be with her.

¹¹Then it happened one day that Joseph went into the house to attend to his duties, and none of the men of the household was there in the house.

¹²She caught Joseph by his [outer] robe, saying, "Lie with me!" But he left his robe in her hand and ran, and got outside [the house].

¹³When she saw that he had left his robe in her hand and had run outside,

¹⁴she called to the men of her household and said to them, "Look at this, your master has brought a Hebrew [into the household] to mock *and* insult us; he came to me to lie with me, and I screamed.

¹⁵"When he heard me screaming, he left his robe with me and ran outside [the house]."

¹⁶So she left Joseph's [outer] robe beside her until his master came home.

¹⁷Then she told her husband the same story, saying, "The Hebrew servant, whom you brought among us, came to me to mock *and* insult me;

¹⁸then as soon as I raised my voice and screamed, he left his robe with me and ran outside [the house]."

¹⁹And when Joseph's master heard

the words of his wife, saying, "This is the way your servant treated me," his anger burned.

²⁰So Joseph's master took him and put him in the prison, a place where the king's prisoners were confined; so he was there in the prison.

²¹But the LORD was with Joseph and extended lovingkindness to him, and gave him favor in the sight of the warden.

²²The warden committed to Joseph's care (management) all the prisoners who were in the prison; so that whatever was done there, he was in charge of it.

²³The warden paid no attention to anything that was in Joseph's care because the LORD was with him; whatever Joseph did, the LORD made to prosper.

40 NOW SOME time later, the cupbearer (butler) and the baker for the king of Egypt offended their lord, Egypt's king.

²Pharaoh (Sesostris II) was extremely angry with his two officials, the chief of the cupbearers and the chief of the bakers.

³He put them in confinement in the house of the captain of the guard, in the same prison where Joseph was confined.

⁴The captain of the guard put Joseph in charge of them, and he served them; and they continued to be in custody for some time.

⁵Then the cupbearer and the baker of the king of Egypt, who were confined in the prison, both dreamed a dream in the same night, each man

receive God's favor

Joseph had been unjustly accused and imprisoned, but the Lord was with him and showed him mercy and grace. In Genesis 39:20–23, we see that God gave him favor in the eyes of the prison warden, who basically put Joseph in charge of running the prison. Even in the dismal circumstances of incarceration, the Lord caused Joseph to prosper.

God's favor is also available to us, His children. But like many other good things in life, the fact that something is available to us does not mean that we will ever partake of it. The Lord offers us many things that we never enjoy because we do not activate our faith to receive what He has provided.

Favor is actually a part of grace. In the English New Testament, the word *grace* and the word *favor* are both translated from the same Greek word *charis*. So the grace of God is the favor of God. And the favor of God is the grace of God—that which causes things to happen in our lives through the channel of our faith. It is the power of God doing something for us that we do not earn or deserve. For example, if you ask someone, "Can you do me a favor?" you are asking that person to do something for you that you have not earned or paid for. You are depending on that individual's goodness to manifest in the form of a blessing, even though there is no natural reason for that person to extend it to you.

God wants to give you favor, just as He did Joseph. But in order to receive that favor, it's necessary to follow Joseph's example and believe God for it. Joseph maintained a good attitude in a bad situation, and his "faith attitude" led to God's favor. Expect God's favor and keep your attitude of faith in every situation you face.

with his [own significant] dream and each dream with its [personal] interpretation.

⁶When Joseph came to them in the morning and looked at them, [he saw that] they were sad *and* depressed.

⁷So he asked Pharaoh's officials who were in confinement with him in his master's house, "Why do you look so down-hearted today?"

⁸And they said to him, "We have [each] dreamed [distinct] dreams and there is no one to interpret them." So Joseph said to them, "Do not interpretations belong to God? Please tell me [your dreams]."

⁹So the chief cupbearer told his dream to Joseph, and said to him, "In my dream there was a grapevine in front of me;

¹⁰and on the vine were three branches. Then as soon as it budded, its blossoms burst open, and its clusters produced ripe grapes [in rapid succession].

¹¹"Now Pharaoh's cup was in my hand, and I took the grapes and squeezed them into Pharaoh's cup; then I placed the cup into Pharaoh's hand."

¹²Then Joseph said to him, "This is the interpretation of it: the three branches represent three days;

¹³within three more days Pharaoh will lift up your head (present you in public) and restore you to your position; and you will [again] put Pharaoh's cup into his hand just as [you did] when you were his cupbearer.

¹⁴"Only think of me when it goes well with you, and please show me kindness by mentioning me to Pharaoh and get me out of this house.

¹⁵"For in fact I was taken (stolen) from the land of the Hebrews by [unlawful] force, and even here I have done nothing for which they should put me in the dungeon."

¹⁶When the chief baker saw that the interpretation [of the dream] was good, he said to Joseph, "I also dreamed, and [in my dream] there were three cake baskets on my head;

¹⁷and in the top basket there were some of all sorts of baked food for Pharaoh, but the birds [of prey] were eating [these foods] out of the basket on my head."

¹⁸Joseph answered, "This is the interpretation of it: the three baskets represent three days;

¹⁹within three more days Pharaoh will lift up your head and will hang you on a tree (gallows, pole), and [you will not so much as be given a burial, but] the birds will eat your flesh."

²⁰Now on the third day, [which was] the Pharaoh's birthday, he [released the two men from prison and] made a feast for all his servants; and he lifted up the head of the chief cupbearer and the head of the chief baker [that is, presented them in public] among his servants.

²¹He restored the chief cupbearer to his office, and the cupbearer [once again] put the cup into Pharaoh's hand;

²²but Pharaoh hanged the chief baker, just as Joseph had interpreted [the meaning of the dreams] to them.

²³Yet [even after all that] the chief cupbearer did not remember Joseph, but forgot [all about] him.

41 NOW IT happened at the end of two full years that Pharaoh dreamed that he was standing by the Nile.

²And lo, there came up out of the Nile seven [healthy] cows, sleek *and* handsome and fat; and they grazed in the reed grass [in a marshy pasture].

³Then behold, seven other cows came up after them out of the Nile, ugly and gaunt *and* raw-boned, and stood by the *fat* cows on the bank of the Nile.

⁴Then the ugly and gaunt *and* raw-boned cows ate up the seven sleek and fat cows. Then Pharaoh awoke.

⁵Then he fell asleep and dreamed a second time; and behold, seven ears of

grain came up on a single stalk, plump and good.

⁶Then behold, seven ears [of grain], thin and dried up by the east wind, sprouted after them.

⁷Then the thin ears swallowed the seven plump and full ears. And Pharaoh awoke, and it was a dream.

⁸So when morning came his spirit was troubled *and* disturbed and he sent and called for all the magicians and all the wise men of Egypt. And Pharaoh told them his dreams, but no one could interpret them to him.

⁹Then the chief cupbearer spoke to Pharaoh, saying, "I would mention my faults today.

¹⁰"[Two years ago] Pharaoh was angry with his servants, and he put me in confinement in the house of the captain of the guard, both me and the chief baker.

¹¹"We dreamed a dream on the same night, he and I; each of us dreamed according to [the significance of] the interpretation of his own dream.

¹²"Now there was with us [in the prison] a young man, a Hebrew, servant to the captain of the guard; and we told him, and he interpreted our dreams for us, to each man according to the significance of his own dream.

¹³"And just as he interpreted [the dreams] for us, so it happened; I was restored to my office [as chief cupbearer], and the baker was hanged."

¹⁴Then Pharaoh sent and called for Joseph, and they hurriedly brought him out of the dungeon; and when Joseph shaved himself and changed his clothes [making himself presentable], he came to Pharaoh.

life point

God can speak to us today through dreams, just as He did in Joseph's time (see Genesis 41). But we need to be balanced in our approach because many of our dreams are not spiritual. If God is trying to show you something or speak to you through a dream, I believe He will confirm it in your heart if you ask Him for wisdom, use discernment, and stay in balance with His Word.

¹⁵Pharaoh said to Joseph, "I have dreamed a dream, and there is no one who can interpret it; and I have heard it said about you that you can understand a dream and interpret it."

¹⁶Joseph answered Pharaoh, "It is not in me [to interpret the dream]; God [not I] will give Pharaoh a favorable answer [through me]."

¹⁷So Pharaoh said to Joseph, "In my dream, I was standing on the bank of the Nile;

¹⁸and seven fat, sleek *and* handsome cows came up out of the river, and they grazed in the reed grass [of a marshy pasture].

¹⁹"Lo, seven other cows came up after them, very ugly and gaunt [just skin and bones]; such emaciated animals as I have never seen in all the land of Egypt.

²⁰"And the lean and ugly cows ate up the first seven fat cows.

²¹"Yet when they had devoured them, it could not be detected that they had eaten them, because they

speak the Word

God, I thank You for causing me to be fruitful and very successful even when I am suffering.
–ADAPTED FROM GENESIS 41:52

were still as thin *and* emaciated as before. Then I awoke [but again I fell asleep and dreamed].

²²"I saw in my [second] dream, seven ears [of grain], plump and good, growing on a single stalk;

²³and lo, seven [other] ears, withered, thin, and scorched by the east wind, sprouted after them;

²⁴and the thin ears devoured the seven good ears. Now I told this to the magicians *and* soothsayers, but there was no one who could explain it [to me]."

²⁵Then Joseph said to Pharaoh, "The [two] dreams are one [and the same and have one interpretation]; God has shown Pharaoh what He is about to do.

²⁶"The seven good cows are seven years, and the seven good ears are seven years; the [two] dreams are one [and the same].

²⁷"The seven thin and ugly cows that came up after them are seven years; and also the seven thin ears, dried up *and* scorched by the east wind, they are seven years of famine *and* hunger.

from the pit to the palace

Because his brothers hated him, Joseph was thrown into a pit and left there to die (see Genesis 37:23–24). But God had other plans! As it turned out, Joseph was sold as a slave in Egypt, became a servant to a wealthy ruler, and then was thrown into a pit again for a crime he did not commit (see Genesis 39). Ultimately, Joseph was freed from prison and ended up in the palace, second in command to Pharaoh, the ruler over all Egypt.

How did Joseph get from the pit to the palace? I believe he made that journey by staying positive, refusing to be bitter, being confident in God, and trusting Him. Even though Joseph was labeled a "slave," he refused to have a slave mentality. Even though he appeared to be defeated on many occasions, he kept standing up on the inside. In other words, Joseph had a right attitude. Without a right attitude, we can start in the palace and end up in the pit. This happens to a lot of people. Some people have great opportunities given to them, and they do nothing with their lives. Others may get a very bad start in life, but then overcome all obstacles and succeed.

I also believe Joseph believed in the dreams God had given him. Joseph was a dreamer; he made big plans and refused to give them up (see Genesis 37:5–10). The devil does not want us to have dreams and visions of better things. He wants us to stay in the pit and be "do-nothings."

I challenge you to make up your mind right now to do something great for God. *No matter where you started, you can have a great finish.* If people have mistreated and abused you, do not waste your time trying to get revenge—leave them in God's hands and trust Him to bring justice into your life. Know what you want out of life and what you want to do. Don't be vague; be confident! To be confident means to be bold, open, plain, and straightforward—that does not sound like a vague, sheepish, fearful individual who is uncertain about everything. Decide to leave your mark in this world. When you depart from this earth, people should know that you have been here. Even if you are in a "pit" today, God can still raise you up and do great things in you and through you!

²⁸"This is the message just as I have told Pharaoh: God has shown Pharaoh what He is about to do.

²⁹"Listen very carefully: seven years of great abundance will come throughout all the land of Egypt;

³⁰but afterward seven years of famine *and* hunger will come, and [there will be such desperate need that] all the great abundance [of the previous years] will be forgotten in the land of Egypt [as if it never happened], and famine *and* destitution will ravage *and* destroy the land.

³¹"So the great abundance will become forgotten in the land because of that subsequent famine, for it will be very severe.

³²"That the dream was repeated twice to Pharaoh [and in two different ways] indicates that this matter is fully determined *and* established by God, and God will bring it to pass very quickly.

³³"So now let Pharaoh [prepare ahead and] look for a man discerning *and* clear-headed and wise, and set him [in charge] over the land of Egypt [as governor under Pharaoh].

³⁴"Let Pharaoh take action to appoint overseers *and* officials over the land, and set aside one-fifth [of the produce] of the [entire] land of Egypt in the seven years of abundance.

³⁵"Let them gather [as a tax] all [of the fifth of] the food of these good years that are coming, and store up grain under the direction *and* authority of Pharaoh, and let them guard the food [in fortified granaries] in the cities.

³⁶"That food shall be put [in storage] as a reserve for the land against the seven years of famine *and* hunger which will occur in the land of Egypt, so that the land (people) will not be ravaged during the famine."

³⁷Now the plan seemed good to Pharaoh and to all of his servants.

³⁸So Pharaoh said to his servants,

"Can we find a man like this [a man equal to Joseph], in whom is the divine spirit [of God]?"

³⁹Then Pharaoh said to Joseph, "Since [your] God has shown you all this, there is no one as discerning *and* clear-headed and wise as you are.

⁴⁰"You shall have charge over my house, and all my people shall be governed according to your word and pay respect [to you with reverence, submission, and obedience]; only in [matters of] the throne will I be greater than you [in Egypt]."

⁴¹Then Pharaoh said to Joseph, "See, I have set you [in charge] over all the land of Egypt."

⁴²Then Pharaoh took off his signet ring from his hand and put it on Joseph's hand, and dressed him in [official] vestments of fine linen and put a gold chain around his neck.

⁴³He had him ride in his second chariot; and runners proclaimed before him, "[Attention,] bow the knee!" And he set him over all the land of Egypt.

⁴⁴Moreover, Pharaoh said to Joseph, "*Though* I am Pharaoh, yet without your permission shall no man raise his hand [to do anything] or set his foot [to go anywhere] in all the land of Egypt [all classes of people shall submit to your authority]."

⁴⁵Then Pharaoh named Joseph Zaphenath-paneah; and he gave him Asenath, the daughter of Potiphera, priest of On (Heliopolis in Egypt), as his wife. And Joseph went out over all the land of Egypt [to inspect and govern it].

⁴⁶Now Joseph [had been in Egypt thirteen years and] was thirty years old when he stood before Pharaoh, king of Egypt. Joseph departed from the presence of Pharaoh and went through all the land of Egypt [performing his duties].

⁴⁷In the seven abundant years the earth produced handfuls [for each seed planted].

48And Joseph gathered all the [surplus] food of the seven [good] years in the land of Egypt and stored [enormous quantities of] the food in the cities. He stored away in every city the food [collected] from its own surrounding fields.

49Thus Joseph gathered *and* stored up grain in great abundance like the sand of the sea, until he stopped counting it, for it could not be measured.

50Now two sons were born to Joseph before the years of famine came, whom Asenath, the daughter of Potiphera, priest of On, bore to him.

51Joseph named the firstborn Manasseh (causing to forget), for *he said,* "God has made me forget all my trouble *and* hardship and all [the sorrow of the loss of] my father's household."

52He named the second [son] Ephraim (fruitfulness), for "God has caused me to be fruitful *and* very successful in the land of my suffering."

53When the seven years of plenty came to an end in the land of Egypt,

54the seven years of famine began to come, just as Joseph had said [they would]; the famine was in all the [surrounding] lands, but in the land of Egypt there was bread (food).

55So when all the land of Egypt was famished, the people cried out to Pharaoh for food; and Pharaoh said to all the Egyptians, "Go to Joseph; do whatever he says to you."

56When the famine was *spread* over all the land, Joseph opened all the storehouses, and sold [surplus grain] to the Egyptians; and the famine grew [extremely] severe in the land of Egypt.

57And [the people of] all countries came to Egypt to Joseph to buy grain, because the famine was severe over all the [known] earth.

42

NOW WHEN Jacob (Israel) learned that there was grain in Egypt, he said to his sons, "Why are you staring at one another [in bewilderment and not taking action]?"

2He said, "I have heard that there is grain in Egypt; go down there and buy [some] grain for us, so that we may live and not die [of starvation]."

3So ten of Joseph's brothers went down to buy grain in Egypt.

4But Jacob did not send Benjamin, Joseph's [younger] brother, with his brothers, for he said, "I am afraid that some harm *or* injury may come to him."

5So the sons of Israel came [to Egypt] to buy grain along with the others who were coming, for famine was in the land of Canaan *also.*

6Now Joseph was the ruler over the land, and he was the one who sold [grain] to all the people of the land; and Joseph's [half] brothers came and bowed down before him with *their* faces to the ground.

7When Joseph saw his brothers he recognized them, but [hiding his identity] he treated them as strangers and spoke harshly to them. He said to them, "Where have you come from?" And they said, "From the land of Canaan, to buy food."

8Joseph recognized his brothers, but they did not recognize him.

9Joseph remembered the dreams he had dreamed about them, and said to them, "You are spies; you have come [with a malicious purpose] to observe the undefended parts of our land."

10But they said to him, "No, my lord, for your servants have [only] come to buy food.

11"We are all the sons of one man; we are honest men, your servants are not spies."

12Yet he said to them, "No, you have come to see the undefended parts of our land."

¹³But they said, "Your servants are twelve brothers [in all], the sons of one man in the land of Canaan; please listen: the youngest is with our father today, and one is no longer alive."

¹⁴Joseph said to them, "It is as I said to you, you are spies.

¹⁵"In this way you shall be tested: by the life of Pharaoh, you shall not leave this place unless your youngest brother comes here!

¹⁶"Send one of you [back home], and let him bring your brother [here], while [the rest of] you remain confined, so that your words may be tested, [to see] whether there is any truth in you [and your story]; or else, by the life of Pharaoh, certainly you are spies."

¹⁷Then Joseph put them all in prison for three days.

¹⁸Now Joseph said to them on the third day, "Do this and [you may] live, for I fear God:

¹⁹if you are honest men, let one of your brothers be confined in your [place here in] prison; but as for *the rest of* you, go, carry grain for the famine in your households,

²⁰but bring your youngest brother to me, so your words will be verified and you will not die." And they did so.

²¹And they said to one another, "Truly we are guilty regarding our brother [Joseph], because we saw the distress *and* anguish of his soul when he pleaded with us [to let him go], yet we would not listen [to his cry]; so this distress *and* anguish has come on us."

²²Reuben answered them, "Did I not tell you, 'Do not sin against the boy'; and you would not listen? Now the accounting for his blood is required [of us for we are guilty of his death]."

²³They did not know that Joseph understood [their conversation], because he spoke to them through an interpreter.

²⁴He turned away from his brothers and [left the room and] wept; then he returned and talked with them, and took Simeon from them and bound him in front of them [to be kept as a hostage in Egypt].

²⁵Then Joseph gave orders [privately] that their bags be filled with grain, and that every man's money [used to pay for the grain] be put back in his sack, and that provisions be given to them for the journey. And so this was done for them.

²⁶They loaded their donkeys with grain and left from there.

²⁷And at the lodging place, as one *of them* opened his sack to feed his donkey, he saw his money in the opening of his sack.

²⁸And he said to his brothers, "My money has been returned! Here it is in my sack!" And their hearts sank, and they were afraid *and* turned trembling to one another, saying, "What is this that God has done to us?"

²⁹When they came to Jacob their father in the land of Canaan, they told him everything that had happened to them, saying,

³⁰"The man who is the lord of the land spoke harshly to us, and took us for spies of the land.

³¹"But we told him, 'We are honest men; we are not spies.

³²'We are twelve brothers, sons of our father; one is no longer alive, and the youngest is with our father today in the land of Canaan.'

³³"And the man, the lord of the country, said to us, 'By this [test] I will know that you are honest men: leave one of your brothers here with me and take *grain for* your starving households and go.

³⁴'Bring your youngest brother to me; then I will know that you are not spies, but that you are honest men. Then I will return your [imprisoned] brother [back] to you, and you may trade *and* do business in the land.'"

³⁵Now when they emptied their

sacks, every man's bundle of money [paid to buy grain] was in his sack. When they and their father saw the bundles of money, they were afraid.

36Jacob their father said to them, "You have bereaved me [by causing the loss] of my children. Joseph is no more, and Simeon is no more, and you would take Benjamin [from me]. All these things are [working] against me."

37Then Reuben spoke to his father, "You may put my two sons to death if I do not bring Benjamin back to you; put him in my care, and I will return him to you."

38But Jacob said, "My son shall not go down [to Egypt] with you; for his brother is dead, and he alone is left [of Rachel's children]. If any harm *or* accident should happen to him on the journey you are taking, then you will bring my gray hair down to Sheol (the place of the dead) in sorrow."

43 NOW THE famine was very severe in the land [of Canaan]. 2And it happened that when the families of Jacob's sons had finished eating [all of] the grain which they had brought from Egypt, their father said to them, "Go again, buy us a little food."

3But Judah said to him, "The man [representing Pharaoh] solemnly *and* sternly warned us, saying, 'You will not see my face [again] unless your brother is with you.'

4"If you will send our brother with us, we will go down [to Egypt] and buy you food.

5"But if you will not send him, we will not go down there; for the man said to us, 'You will not see my face unless your brother is with you.'"

6And Israel (Jacob) said, "Why did you treat me so badly by telling the man that you had *another* brother?"

7And they said, "The man asked us straightforward questions about ourselves and our relatives. He said, 'Is your father still alive? Have you *another* brother?' And we answered him accordingly. How could we possibly know that he would say, 'Bring your brother down [here to Egypt]'? "

8Judah said to Israel his father, "Send the young man with me and we will get up and go [buy food], so that we may live and not die [of starvation], we as well as you and our little ones.

9"I will be security (a guarantee) for him; you may hold me [personally] responsible for him. If I do not bring him [back] to you and place him [safely] before you, then let me bear the blame before you forever.

10"For if we had not delayed like this, surely by now we would have returned the second time."

11Then their father Israel said to them, "If *it must be* so, then do this; take some of the choicest products of the land in your sacks, and carry it as a present [of tribute] to the man [representing Pharaoh], a little balm and a little honey, aromatic spices *or* gum, resin, pistachio nuts, and almonds.

12"Take double the [amount of] money with you, and take back the money that was returned in the opening of your sacks; perhaps it was an oversight.

13"Take your brother [Benjamin] also, and get up, and go to the man;

14and may God Almighty grant you compassion *and* favor before the man, so that he will release to you your other brother [Simeon] and Benjamin. And as for me, if I am bereaved of my children [Joseph, Simeon, and Benjamin], I am bereaved."

15Then the men took the present, and they took double the [amount of] money with them, and Benjamin; then they left and went down to Egypt and stood before Joseph.

16When Joseph saw Benjamin with them, he said to the steward of his house, "Bring the men into the house, and kill an animal and make [a meal] ready; for the men will dine with me at noon."

¹⁷So the man did as Joseph said, and brought the men to Joseph's house. ¹⁸The men were afraid, because they were brought to Joseph's house; and [expecting the worst] they said, "It is because of the money that was returned in our sacks the first time [we came] that we are being brought in, so that he may find a reason to accuse us and assail us, and take us as slaves, and *seize* our donkeys." ¹⁹So they approached the steward of Joseph's house, and talked with him at the entrance of the house, ²⁰and said, "Oh, my lord, we indeed came down here the first time to buy food; ²¹and when we arrived at the inn [after leaving here], we opened our sacks and there was each man's money [with which he had paid for grain], in full, returned in the mouth of his sack. So we have brought it back [this time]. ²²"We have also brought down with us additional money to buy food; we do not know who put our money [back] in our sacks [last time]." ²³But the steward [encouraged them and] said, "Peace be to you, do not be afraid; your God and the God of your father has [miraculously] given you treasure in your sacks. I [already] had your money [which you paid to us]." Then he brought Simeon out to them. ²⁴Then the steward brought the men into Joseph's house and gave them water, and they washed [the dust off] their feet; and he gave their donkeys feed. ²⁵So they prepared the present [of tribute] for Joseph before his arrival at noon; for they had heard that they were to eat a meal there. ²⁶When Joseph came home, they brought into the house to him the present [of tribute] which they had with them and bowed to the ground before him.

²⁷He asked them about their well-being, and said, "Is your old father well, of whom you spoke? Is he still alive?" ²⁸And they answered, "Your servant our father is in good health; he is still alive." And they bowed down [their heads before Joseph] in respect. ²⁹And he looked up and saw his brother Benjamin, his mother's [only other] son, and said, "Is this your youngest brother, of whom you spoke to me?" And Joseph said, "God be gracious to you *and* show you favor, my son." ³⁰Then Joseph hurried out [of the room] because his heart was deeply touched over his brother, and he sought *privacy* to weep; so he entered his chamber and wept there. ³¹Then he washed his face and came out, and, restraining himself, said, "Let the meal be served." ³²So the servants served Joseph by himself [in honor of his rank], and his brothers by themselves, and the Egyptians who ate with him by themselves, because [according to custom] the Egyptians could not eat food with the Hebrews, for that is loathsome to the Egyptians. ³³Now Joseph's brothers were seated [by the steward] before him [in the order of their birth]—the firstborn according to his birthright and the youngest according to his youth; and the men looked at one another in astonishment [because so much was known about them]. ³⁴Joseph selected *and* sent portions to them from his own table, but Benjamin's portion was five times as much as any of theirs. So they feasted and drank freely *and* celebrated with him.

44 AND HE commanded the steward of his house, saying, "Fill the men's sacks with food, as much as they can carry, and put every man's [grain] money in the mouth of the sack.

²"Put my [personal] cup, the silver cup, in the mouth of the sack of the youngest, with his grain money." And the steward did as Joseph had told him.

³As soon as the morning was light, the men were sent away, they and their donkeys.

⁴When they had left the city, and were not yet far away, Joseph said to his steward, "Get up, follow after the men; and when you overtake them, say to them, 'Why have you repaid evil [to us] for good [paid to you]?

⁵'Is this not my lord's drinking cup and the one which he uses for divination? You have done [a great and unforgivable] wrong in doing this.'"

⁶So the steward overtook them and he said these words to them.

⁷They said to him, "Why does my lord speak these things? Far be it from your servants to do such a thing!

⁸"Please remember, the money which we found in the mouths of our sacks we have brought back to you from the land of Canaan. Is it likely then that we would steal silver or gold from your master's house?

⁹"With whomever of your servants your master's cup is found, let him die, and the rest of us will be my lord's slaves."

¹⁰And the steward said, "Now let it be as you say; he with whom the cup is found will be my slave, but *the rest of* you shall be blameless."

¹¹Then every man quickly lowered his sack to the ground and each man opened his sack [confident the cup would not be found among them].

¹²The steward searched, beginning with the eldest and ending with the youngest, and the cup was found in Benjamin's sack.

¹³Then they tore their clothes [in grief]; and after each man had loaded his donkey again, they returned to the city.

¹⁴When Judah and his brothers came to Joseph's house, he was still there; and they fell to the ground before him.

¹⁵Joseph spoke harshly to them, "What is this thing that you have done? Do you not realize that such a man as I can indeed practice divination *and* foretell [everything you do without outside knowledge of it]?"

¹⁶So Judah said, "What can we say to my lord? What can we reply? Or how can we clear ourselves, since God has exposed the sin *and* guilt of your servants? Behold, we are my lord's slaves, the rest of us as well as he with whom the cup is found."

¹⁷But Joseph said, "Far be it from me that I should do that; but the man in whose hand the cup has been found, he will be my servant; and as for [the rest of] you, get up and go in peace to your father."

¹⁸Then Judah approached him, and said, "O my lord, please let your servant say a word to you in private, and do not let your anger blaze against your servant, for you are equal to Pharaoh [so I speak as if directly to him].

¹⁹"My lord asked his servants, saying, 'Have you a father or a brother?'

²⁰"We said to my lord, 'We have an old father and a young [brother, Benjamin, the] child of his old age. Now his brother [Joseph] is dead, and he alone is left of [the two sons born of] his mother, and his father loves him.'

²¹"Then you said to your servants, 'Bring him down to me that I may actually see him.'

²²"But we said to my lord, 'The young man cannot leave his father, for if he should leave his father, his father would die.'

23"You said to your servants, 'Unless your youngest brother comes with you, you shall not see my face again.'

24"So when we went back to your servant my father, we told him what my lord had said.

25"Our father said, 'Go back [to Egypt], and buy us a little food.'

26"But we said, 'We cannot go down [to Egypt]. If our youngest brother is with us, then we will go down [there]; for we [were sternly told that we] cannot see the man's face unless our youngest brother is with us.'

27"Your servant my father said to us, 'You know that my wife [Rachel] bore me [only] two sons.

28'And one [son] went out from me, and I said, "Surely he is torn to pieces," and I have not seen him since.

29'If you take this one also from me, and harm or an accident happens to him, you will bring my gray hair down to Sheol in sorrow.'

30"Now, therefore, when I come to your servant my father, and the young man is not with us, since his life is bound up in the young man's life,

31when he sees that the young man is not with us, he will die; and your servants will bring the gray hair of your servant our father down to Sheol in [great] sorrow.

32"For your servant became security for the young man to my father, saying, 'If I do not bring him back to you, then let me bear the blame before my father forever.'

33"Now, therefore, please let your servant (Judah) remain here instead of the youth [to be] a slave to my lord, and let the young man go home with his brothers.

34"How can I go up to my father if the young man is not with me—for fear that I would see the tragedy that would overtake my [elderly] father [if Benjamin does not return]?"

45 THEN JOSEPH could not control himself [any longer] in front of all those who attended him, and he called out, "Have everyone leave me." So no man stood there when Joseph revealed himself to his brothers.

2Joseph wept aloud, and the Egyptians [who had just left him] heard it, and the household of Pharaoh heard of it.

3Then Joseph said to his brothers, "I am Joseph! Is my father still alive?" But his brothers were speechless, for they were stunned and dismayed by [the fact that they were in] Joseph's presence.

4And Joseph said to his brothers, "Please come closer to me." And they approached him. And he said, "I am Joseph your brother, whom you sold into Egypt.

5"Now do not be distressed or angry with yourselves because you sold me here, for God sent me ahead of you to save life and preserve our family.

6"For the famine has been in the land these two years, and there are still five more years in which there will be no plowing and harvesting.

7"God sent me [to Egypt] ahead of you to preserve for you a remnant on the earth, and to keep you alive by a great escape.

8"So now it was not you who sent me here, but God; and He has made me a father to Pharaoh and lord of all his household and ruler over all the land of Egypt.

9"Hurry and go up to my father, and tell him, 'Your son Joseph says this to you: "God has made me lord of all Egypt; come down to me, do not delay.

10"You shall live in the land of Goshen [the best pasture land of Egypt], and you shall be close to me—you and your children and your grandchildren, your flocks and your herds and all you have.

11"There I will provide for you *and* sustain you, so that you and your household and all that are yours may not become impoverished, for there are still five years of famine *to come*."'

12"Look! Your eyes see, and the eyes of my brother Benjamin see, that I am speaking to you [personally in your language and not through an interpreter].

13"Now you must tell my father of all my splendor *and* power in Egypt, and of everything that you have seen; and you must hurry and bring my father down here."

14Then he embraced his brother Benjamin's neck and wept, and Benjamin wept on his neck.

15He kissed all his brothers and wept on them, and afterward his brothers talked with him.

16When the news was heard in Pharaoh's house that Joseph's brothers had come, it pleased Pharaoh and his servants.

17Then Pharaoh said to Joseph, "Tell your brothers, 'Do this: load your animals and return to the land of Canaan [without delay],

18and get your father and your households and come to me. I will give you the best of the land of Egypt and you will eat the fat (the finest produce) of the land.'

19"Now you [brothers of Joseph] are ordered [by Pharaoh], 'Do this: take wagons from the land of Egypt for your little ones and for your wives, and bring your father and come.

20'Do not be concerned with your goods, for the best of all the land of Egypt is yours.'"

21Then the sons of Israel did so; and Joseph gave them wagons according to the command of Pharaoh, and gave them provisions for the journey.

22To each of them Joseph gave changes of clothing, but to Benjamin he gave three hundred *pieces of* silver and five changes of clothing.

23To his father he sent the following: ten *male* donkeys loaded with the good things of Egypt, and ten female donkeys loaded with grain and bread and provision for his father [to supply all who were with him] on the journey.

24So he sent his brothers away, and as they departed, he said to them, "See that you do not quarrel on the journey [about how to explain this to our father]."

25So they went up from Egypt, and came to the land of Canaan to Jacob their father,

26and they said to him, "Joseph is still alive, and indeed he is ruler over all the land of Egypt." But Jacob was stunned *and* his heart almost stopped beating, because he did not believe them.

27When they told him everything that Joseph had said to them, and when he saw the wagons which Joseph had sent to carry him, the spirit of their father Jacob revived.

28And Israel (Jacob) said, "It is enough! Joseph my son is still alive. I will go and see him before I die."

46 SO ISRAEL set out with all that he had, and came to Beersheba [where both his father and grandfather had worshiped God], and offered sacrifices to the God of his father Isaac. [Gen 21:33; 26:23–25]

2And God spoke to Israel in visions of the night and said, "Jacob, Jacob!" And he said, "Here I am."

3And He said, "I am God, the God of your father; do not be afraid to go down to Egypt, for I will make you (your descendants) a great nation there.

4"I will go down with you to Egypt, and I will also surely bring you (your people) up again; and Joseph will put his hand on your eyes [to close them at the time of your death]."

5So Jacob set out from Beersheba; and the sons of Israel carried their father Jacob and their children and their wives in the wagons that Pharaoh had sent to carry him.

6And they took their livestock and the possessions which they had acquired in the land of Canaan and came to Egypt, Jacob and all his descendants with him.

7His sons and his grandsons, his daughters and his granddaughters, and all his descendants he brought with him to Egypt.

8Now these are the names of the sons of Israel, Jacob and his sons, who went to Egypt: Reuben, Jacob's firstborn.

9The sons of Reuben: Hanoch, Pallu, Hezron, and Carmi.

10The sons of Simeon: Jemuel, Jamin, Ohad, Jachin, Zohar, and Shaul the son of a Canaanite woman.

11The sons of Levi: Gershon, Kohath, and Merari.

12The sons of Judah: Er, Onan, Shelah, Perez, and Zerah—but Er and Onan died in the land of Canaan. And the sons of Perez were Hezron and Hamul.

13The sons of Issachar: Tola, Puvah, Job, and Shimron.

14The sons of Zebulun: Sered, Elon, and Jahleel.

15These are the sons of Leah, whom she bore to Jacob in Paddan-aram, with his daughter Dinah; all of his sons and daughters *numbered* thirty-three.

16The sons of Gad: Ziphion, Haggi, Shuni, Ezbon, Eri, Arodi, and Areli.

17The sons of Asher: Imnah, Ishvah, Ishvi, Beriah, and Serah their sister. And the sons of Beriah: Heber and Malchiel.

18These are the sons of Zilpah, [the maid] whom Laban gave to Leah his daughter [when she married Jacob]; and she bore to Jacob these sixteen persons [two sons and fourteen grandchildren].

19The sons of Rachel, Jacob's wife: Joseph and Benjamin.

20Now to Joseph in the land of Egypt were born Manasseh and Ephraim, whom Asenath, the daughter of Potiphera, priest of On (Heliopolis in Egypt), bore to him.

21And the sons of Benjamin: Bela, Becher, Ashbel, Gera, Naaman, Ehi, Rosh, Muppim, Huppim, and Ard.

22These are the sons of Rachel, who were born to Jacob; [there were] fourteen persons in all [two sons and twelve grandchildren].

23The son of Dan: Hushim.

24The sons of Naphtali: Jahzeel, Guni, Jezer, and Shillem.

25These are the sons of Bilhah, [the maid] whom Laban gave to Rachel his daughter [when she married Jacob]. And she bore these to Jacob; [there were] seven persons in all [two sons and five grandchildren].

26All the persons who came with Jacob into Egypt—who were his direct descendants, not counting the wives of [Jacob or] Jacob's sons, were sixty-six persons in all,

27and the sons of Joseph, who were born to him in Egypt, were two. All the persons of the house of Jacob [including Jacob, and Joseph and his sons], who came into Egypt, were seventy.

28Now Jacob (Israel) sent Judah ahead of him to Joseph, to direct him to Goshen; and they came into the land of Goshen.

29Then Joseph prepared his chariot and went up to meet Israel his father in Goshen; as soon as he presented himself before him (authenticating his identity), he fell on his [father's] neck and wept on his neck a [very] long time.

30And Israel said to Joseph, "Now let me die [in peace], since I have seen your face [and know] that you are still alive."

31Joseph said to his brothers and to his father's household, "I will go up and tell Pharaoh, and say to him, 'My brothers and my father's household, who were in the land of Canaan, have come to me;

³²and the men are shepherds, for they have been keepers of livestock; and they have brought their flocks and their herds and all that they have.'

³³"And it shall be that when Pharaoh calls you and says, 'What is your occupation?'

³⁴you shall say, 'Your servants have been keepers of livestock from our youth until now, both we and our fathers [before us],' in order that you may live [separately and securely] in the land of Goshen; for every shepherd is repulsive to the Egyptians."

47

THEN JOSEPH came and told Pharaoh, "My father and my brothers, with their flocks and their herds and all that they own, have come from the land of Canaan, and they are in the land of Goshen."

²He took five men from among his brothers and presented them to Pharaoh.

³And Pharaoh said to his brothers [as Joseph expected], "What is your occupation?" And they said to Pharaoh, "Your servants are shepherds, both we and our fathers [before us]."

⁴Moreover, they said to Pharaoh, "We have come to live temporarily (sojourn) in the land [of Egypt], for there is no pasture for the flocks of your servants [in our land], for the famine is very severe in Canaan. So now, please let your servants live in the land of Goshen."

⁵Then Pharaoh spoke to Joseph, saying, "Your father and your brothers have come to you.

⁶"The land of Egypt is before you; settle your father and your brothers in the best of the land. Let them live in the land of Goshen; and if you know of any men of ability among them, put them in charge of my livestock."

⁷Then Joseph brought Jacob (Israel) his father and presented him before Pharaoh; and Jacob blessed Pharaoh.

⁸And Pharaoh asked Jacob, "How old are you?"

⁹Jacob said to Pharaoh, "The years of my pilgrimage are a hundred and thirty. Few and unpleasant have been the years of my life, and they have not reached the years that my fathers lived during the days of their pilgrimage."

¹⁰And Jacob blessed Pharaoh, and departed from his presence.

¹¹So Joseph settled his father and brothers and gave them a possession in Egypt, in the best of the land, in the land of Rameses (Goshen), as Pharaoh commanded.

¹²Joseph provided *and* supplied his father and his brothers and all his father's household with food, according to [the needs of] their children.

¹³Now [in the course of time] there was no food in all the land, for the famine was distressingly severe, so that the land of Egypt and all the land of Canaan languished [in destitution and starvation] because of the famine.

¹⁴Joseph gathered all the money that was found in the land of Egypt and in the land of Canaan [in payment] for the grain which they bought, and Joseph brought the money into Pharaoh's house.

¹⁵And when the money was exhausted in the land of Egypt and in the land of Canaan, all the Egyptians came to Joseph and said, "Give us food! Why should we die before your very eyes? For our money is gone."

¹⁶Joseph said, "Give up your livestock, and I will give you food in exchange for your livestock, since the money is gone."

¹⁷So they brought their livestock to Joseph, and he gave them food in exchange for the horses and the flocks and the herds and the donkeys; and he supplied them with food in exchange for all their livestock that year.

¹⁸When that year was ended, they came to him the next year and said to

him, "We will not hide from my lord [the fact] that our money is spent; my lord also has our herds of livestock; there is nothing left in the sight of my lord but our bodies and our lands.

¹⁹"Why should we die before your eyes, both we and our land? Buy us and our land in exchange for food, and we and our land will be servants to Pharaoh. And give us seed [to plant], that we may live and not die, and that the land may not be desolate."

²⁰So Joseph bought all the land of Egypt for Pharaoh; for every Egyptian sold his field because the famine was severe upon them. So the land became Pharaoh's.

²¹And as for the people, he relocated them [temporarily] to cities from one end of Egypt's border to the other.

²²Only the land of the priests he did not buy, for the priests had an allotment from Pharaoh, and they lived on the amount which Pharaoh gave them, so they did not sell their land.

²³Then Joseph said to the people, "Look, today I have bought you and your land for Pharaoh; now, here is seed for you, and you shall plant the land.

²⁴"At harvest time [when you reap the increase] you shall give one-fifth of it to Pharaoh, and four-fifths will be your own to use for seed for the field and as food for you and those of your households and for your little ones."

²⁵And they said, "You have saved our lives! Let us find favor in the sight of my lord, and we will be Pharaoh's servants."

²⁶And Joseph made it a law over the land of Egypt—valid to this day—that Pharaoh should have the fifth part [of the crops]; only the land of the priests did not become Pharaoh's.

²⁷Now [the people of] Israel lived in the country of Egypt, in [the land of] Goshen, and they gained possessions and acquired property there and were fruitful and multiplied greatly.

²⁸And Jacob lived in the land of Egypt seventeen years; so the length of Jacob's life was a hundred and forty-seven years.

²⁹And when the time drew near for Israel to die, he called his son Joseph and said to him, "If now I have found favor in your sight, please put your hand under my thigh and [promise to] deal loyally and faithfully with me. Please do not bury me in Egypt,

³⁰but when I lie down with my fathers [in death], you will carry me out of Egypt and bury me in their burial place [at Hebron in the cave of Machpelah]." And Joseph said, "I will do as you have directed."

³¹Then he said, "Swear to me [that you will do it]." So he swore to him. Then Israel (Jacob) bowed *in worship* at the head of the bed.

48 NOW SOME time after these things happened, Joseph was told, "Your father is sick." So he took his two sons Manasseh and Ephraim with him [to go to Goshen].

²And when Jacob (Israel) was told, "Look now, your son Joseph has come to you," Israel strengthened himself and sat up on the bed.

³Then Jacob said to Joseph, "God Almighty appeared to me at Luz (Bethel) in the land of Canaan and blessed me,

⁴and said to me, 'Behold, I will make you fruitful and numerous, and I will make you a great company of people, and will give this land to your descendants after you as an everlasting possession.' [Gen 28:13–22; 35:6–15]

⁵"Now your two sons [Ephraim and Manasseh], who were born to you in the land of Egypt before I came to you in Egypt, are mine; Ephraim and Manasseh shall be mine [that is, adopted as my heirs and sons as surely], as Reuben and Simeon are *my sons.*

⁶"But other sons who were born to

you after them shall be your own; they shall be called by the names of their [two] brothers in their inheritance.

[7]"Now as for me, when I came from Paddan [in Mesopotamia], Rachel died beside me in the land of Canaan on the journey, when there was still some distance to go to Ephrath; and I buried her there on the way to Ephrath (that is, Bethlehem)."

[8]When Israel [who was almost blind] saw Joseph's sons, he said, "Who are these?"

[9]Joseph said to his father, "They are my sons, whom God has given me here [in Egypt]." So he said, "Please bring them to me, so that I may bless them."

[10]Now Israel's eyes were so dim from age that he could not see [clearly]. Then Joseph brought them close to him, and he kissed and embraced them.

[11]Israel said to Joseph, "I never expected to see your face, but see, God has shown me your children as well."

[12]Then Joseph took the boys [from his father's embrace], and he bowed [before him] with his face to the ground.

[13]Then Joseph took them both, Ephraim with his right hand toward Israel's left, and Manasseh with his left hand toward Israel's right, and brought them close to him.

[14]But Israel reached out his right hand and laid it on the head of Ephraim, who was the younger, and his left hand on Manasseh's head, crossing his hands [intentionally], even though Manasseh was the firstborn.

[15]Then Jacob (Israel) blessed Joseph, and said,

"The God before whom my fathers
   Abraham and Isaac walked [in
   faithful obedience],
The God who has been my
   Shepherd [leading and caring for
   me] all my life to this day,

[16]The Angel [that is, the LORD
   Himself] who has redeemed me
   [continually] from all evil,
Bless the boys;
And may my name live on in them
   [may they be worthy of having
   their names linked with mine],
And the names of my fathers
   Abraham and Isaac;
And may they grow into a [great]
   multitude in the midst of the
   earth."

[17]When Joseph saw that his father laid his right hand on Ephraim's head, it displeased him [because he was not the firstborn]; and he grasped his father's hand to move it from Ephraim's head to Manasseh's head.

[18]Joseph said to his father, "Not so, my father, for this is the firstborn; place your right hand on Manasseh's head."

[19]But his father refused and said, "I know, my son, I know; Manasseh also will become a people and he will be great; but his younger brother shall be greater than he, and his descendants shall become a multitude of nations."

[20]Then Jacob blessed them that day, saying,

"By you Israel will pronounce a
   blessing, saying,
'May God make you like Ephraim
   and Manasseh.'"

And he put Ephraim before Manasseh. [21]Then Israel said to Joseph, "Behold, I am about to die, but God will be with you, and bring you back to [Canaan] the land of your fathers. [22]"Moreover, I have given you [the birthright,] one portion [Shechem, one mountain ridge] more than any of your brothers, which I took [reclaiming it] from the hand of the Amorites with my sword and with my bow." [Gen 33:18, 19; Josh 24:32, 33; John 4:5]

49

THEN JACOB called for his sons and said, "Assemble yourselves [around me] that I may tell you what will happen to you *and* your descendants in the days to come.

2 "Gather together and hear, O sons of Jacob;
And listen to Israel (Jacob) your father.
3 "Reuben, you are my firstborn;
My might, the beginning of my strength *and* vigor,
Preeminent in dignity and preeminent in power [that should have been your birthright].
4 "But unstable *and* reckless *and* boiling over like water [in sinful lust], you shall not excel *or* have the preeminence [of the firstborn],
Because you went up to your father's bed [with Bilhah];
You defiled it—he went up to my couch. [Gen 35:22]

5 "Simeon and Levi are brothers [equally headstrong, deceitful, vindictive, and cruel];
Their swords are weapons of violence *and* revenge. [Gen 34:25–30]
6 "O my soul, do not come into their secret council;
Let not my glory (honor) be united with their assembly [for I knew nothing of their plot];
Because in their anger they killed men [an honored man, Shechem, and the Shechemites],
And in their self-will they lamed oxen.
7 "Cursed be their anger, for it was fierce;
And their wrath, for it was cruel.
I will divide *and* disperse them in Jacob,

And scatter them in [the midst of the land of] Israel.

8 "Judah, you are the one whom your brothers shall praise;
Your hand will be on the neck of your enemies;
Your father's sons shall bow down to you.
9 "Judah, a lion's cub;
With the prey, my son, you have gone high up [the mountain].
He stooped down, he crouched like a lion,
And like a lion—who dares rouse him? [Rev 5:5]
10 "The scepter [of royalty] shall not depart from Judah,
Nor the ruler's staff from between his feet,
Until Shiloh [the Messiah, the Peaceful One] comes,
And to Him *shall be* the obedience of the peoples. [Num 24:17; Ps 60:7; Ezek 21:27]
11 "Tying his foal to the [strong] vine
And his donkey's colt to the choice vine,
He washes his clothing in wine [because the grapevine produces abundantly],
And his robes in the blood of grapes.
[Is 63:1–3; Zech 9:9; Rev 19:11–16]
12 "His eyes are darker *and* sparkle more than wine,
And his teeth whiter than milk.

13 "Zebulun shall dwell at the seashore;
And he shall be a haven (landing place) for ships,
And his flank shall be toward Sidon.

14 "Issachar is [like] a strong-boned donkey,
Crouching down between the sheepfolds.
15 "When he saw that the resting place was good

And that the land was pleasant,
He bowed his shoulder to bear
[burdens],
And became a servant at forced
labor.

16 "Dan shall judge his people,
As one of the tribes of Israel.
17 "Dan shall be a [venomous]
serpent in the way,
A fanged snake in the path,
That bites the horse's heels,
So that his rider falls backward.
18 "I wait for Your salvation, O Lord.

19 "As for Gad—a raiding troop shall
raid him,
But he shall raid at their heels *and*
assault them [victoriously].

20 "Asher's food [supply] shall be rich
and bountiful,
And he shall yield *and* deliver
royal delights.

21 "Naphtali is a doe let loose, [a swift
warrior,]
Which yields branched antlers
(eloquent words).

22 "Joseph is a fruitful bough (a main
branch of the vine),
A fruitful bough by a spring (a
well, a fountain);
Its branches run over the wall
[influencing others].

23 "The [skilled] archers have bitterly
attacked *and* provoked him;
They have shot [at him] and
harassed him.

24 "But his bow remained firm *and*
steady [in the Strength that does
not fail],
For his arms were made strong
and agile
By the hands of the Mighty One of
Jacob,
(By the name of the Shepherd, the
Stone of Israel), [Gen 48:15; Deut
32:4; Is 9:6; 49:26]

25 By the God of your father who will
help you,

And by the Almighty who
blesses you
With blessings of the heavens
above,
Blessings lying in the deep that
couches beneath,
Blessings of the [nursing] breasts
and of the [fertile] womb.

26 "The blessings of your father
Are greater than the blessings
of my ancestors [Abraham and
Isaac]
Up to the utmost bound of the
everlasting hills;
They shall be on the head of Joseph,
Even on the crown of the head of
him who was the distinguished
one *and* the one who is prince
among (separate from) his
brothers.

27 "Benjamin is a ravenous wolf;
In the morning he devours the prey,
And at night he divides the spoil."

28 All these are the [beginnings of the]
twelve tribes of Israel, and this is what
their father said to them as he blessed
them, blessing each one according to
the blessing appropriate to him.

29 He charged them and said to them,
"I am to be gathered to my people; bury
me with my fathers in the cave that is
in the field of Ephron the Hittite,
30 in the cave in the field at Machpelah,
east of Mamre, in the land of Canaan,
that Abraham bought, along with the
field from Ephron the Hittite, to possess
as a burial site. [Gen 23:17–20]
31 "There they buried Abraham and
Sarah his wife, there they buried Isaac
and Rebekah his wife, and there I
buried Leah—
32 the field and the cave that is in it
was purchased from the sons of Heth."
33 When Jacob (Israel) had finished
commanding his sons, he drew his feet
into the bed and breathed his last, and
was gathered to his people [who had
preceded him in death].

50 THEN JOSEPH fell upon his father's face, and wept over him and kissed him [tenderly].

²Then Joseph ordered his servants the physicians to embalm (mummify) his father. So the physicians embalmed Israel (Jacob).

³Now forty days were required for this, for that is the customary number of days [of preparation] required for embalming. And the Egyptians wept *and* grieved for him [in public mourning as they would for royalty] for seventy days.

⁴When the days of weeping *and* public mourning for him were past, Joseph spoke to [the nobles of] the house of Pharaoh, saying, "If now I have found favor in your sight, please speak to Pharaoh, saying,

⁵'My father made me swear [an oath], saying, "Hear me, I am about to die; bury me in my tomb which I prepared for myself in the land of Canaan." So now let me go up [to Canaan], please, and bury my father; then I will return.'"

⁶And Pharaoh said, "Go up and bury your father, as he made you swear."

turn your mess into your message

Joseph's brothers were afraid he would never forgive them for wanting him dead and for selling him into slavery. In Genesis 50:20, we see that Joseph had a good and loving attitude as he gave his brothers the assurance that he had forgiven their wrongdoing. They may have meant to do evil against him, but God meant it for good.

It is amazing how many times Satan will set a trap for us, meaning it for our harm and destruction. But when God gets involved, He takes what Satan meant to destroy us and turns it so that it works for our good instead. Nobody else can make things work out that way, but God can. He can take any negative situation, and through His miracle-working power use it to make us stronger and more dangerous to the enemy than we would have been without it.

My own situation bears this out. I was sexually, mentally, and emotionally abused for many years during my childhood. This was certainly a terrible thing to happen to a child, and it was definitely a work of Satan, but God has worked it out for good. My mess has become my message; my misery has become my ministry, and I am using the experience I gained from my pain to help multitudes of others who are hurting.

I encourage you not to waste your pain. God will use it if you give it to Him. He has given me beauty for ashes, just as He promised in Isaiah 61:3 (see the Amplified Classic or KJV, NKJV, or NIV translations of this verse), but I had to let go of the ashes. I had to learn to have a good attitude, as Joseph did. I had to learn to let go of the bitterness, resentment, and unforgiveness I felt toward the people who hurt me.

When we have been hurt, it is important not to let the pain go on and on by having a bitter attitude. We hurt only ourselves when we hate people. We would not waste our time hating people if we realized that they are probably enjoying their lives and are not the least concerned with how we feel about them. Remember, God is our Vindicator, and He will bring good out of what the enemy intended for evil.

⁷So Joseph went up [to Canaan] to bury his father, and with him went all the officials of Pharaoh, [the nobles of his court and] the elders of his household and all [the nobles and] the elders of the land of Egypt—

⁸and all the household of Joseph and his brothers and his father's household. They left only their little ones and their flocks and herds in the land of Goshen.

⁹Both chariots and horsemen also went up [to Canaan] with Joseph; and it was a very great company.

¹⁰When they came to the threshing floor of Atad, which is beyond the Jordan, they mourned there with a great lamentation (expressions of mourning for the deceased) and [extreme demonstrations of] sorrow [according to Egyptian custom]; and Joseph observed a seven-day mourning for his father.

¹¹When the inhabitants of the land, the Canaanites, saw the mourning at the threshing floor of Atad, they said, "This is a grievous mourning for the Egyptians." Therefore the place was named Abel-mizraim (mourning of Egypt); it is west of the Jordan.

¹²So Jacob's sons did for him as he had commanded them;

¹³for his sons carried him to the land of Canaan and buried him in the cave of the field of Machpelah, east of Mamre, which Abraham bought along with the field as a burial site from Ephron the Hittite.

¹⁴After he had buried his father, Joseph returned to Egypt, he and his brothers, and all who had gone up with him.

¹⁵When Joseph's brothers saw that their father was dead, they said, "What if Joseph carries a grudge against us and pays us back in full for all the wrong which we did to him?"

¹⁶So they sent *word* to Joseph, saying, "Your father commanded us before he died, saying,

¹⁷'You are to say to Joseph, "I beg you, please forgive the transgression of your brothers and their sin, for they did you wrong."' Now, please forgive the transgression of the servants of the God of your father." And Joseph wept when they spoke to him.

life point

So often in our lives, Satan thinks he is doing some terrible thing to bring about our destruction, and yet God has another plan entirely (see Genesis 50:20). He intends to take what Satan means for our harm and work it out not only for our good, but for the good of the many to whom we will minister.

¹⁸Then his brothers went and fell down before him [in confession]; then they said, "Behold, we are your servants (slaves)."

¹⁹But Joseph said to them, "Do not be afraid, for am I in the place of God? [Vengeance is His, not mine.]

²⁰"As for you, you meant evil against me, but God meant it for good in order to bring about this present outcome, that many people would be kept alive [as they are this day].

²¹"So now, do not be afraid; I will provide for you *and* support you and your little ones." So he comforted them [giving them encouragement

speak the Word

Father, I thank You that when others mean evil against me, You mean it for good.
–ADAPTED FROM GENESIS 50:20

and hope] and spoke [with kindness] to their hearts. ²²Now Joseph lived in Egypt, he and his father's household, and Joseph lived a hundred and ten years. ²³Joseph saw the third generation of Ephraim's children; also the children of Machir, the son of Manasseh, were born *and* raised on Joseph's knees. ²⁴Joseph said to his brothers, "I am about to die, but God will surely take care of you and bring you up out of this land to the land which He promised to Abraham, to Isaac, and to Jacob [to give you]." ²⁵Then Joseph made the sons of Israel (Jacob) swear [an oath], saying, "God will surely visit you *and* take care of you [returning you to Canaan], and [when that happens] you shall carry my bones up from here." ²⁶So Joseph died, being a hundred and ten years old; and they embalmed him and he was put in a coffin in Egypt.

Exodus

Author:
Moses

Date:
About 1440 BC

Everyday Life Principles:
When God leads us out of a situation, He always takes us into something better.

Deliverance from any kind of bondage is a process, and God takes us through it one step at a time.

Allow God to teach you how to trust Him and how to follow Him as He leads you into a place of fulfilled promises and great blessing.

The entire book of Exodus is a story of deliverance, a story of people who broke free from oppression and began a journey toward the good land that God had promised them. From beginning to end, Exodus teaches us how God brings us out of situations that keep us in bondage in order to take us into something better.

Just as God prepared Moses to deliver Israel, He has sent Jesus to be our deliverer. Just as He led the Israelites with a cloud by day and a pillar of fire by night, the Holy Spirit in our hearts leads us today. Just as the Israelites' deliverance was a process, a journey that could be completed only *one step* at a time, God almost always leads us step-by-step instead of moving us instantly from one situation to the next. Just as the Israelites' murmuring and complaining slowed them down, bad attitudes will also impede our progress in God. Just as He gave the Israelites the Ten Commandments as laws to show them how to live a blessed life, He has given us the Bible as a guidebook for our journey through life. Just as He used the Israelites' journey to develop the faith, trust, strength, and character they would need in the Promised Land, He does the same for us in our journey.

As you read Exodus and consider the ways God is leading you out of any area of bondage or oppression in your life right now, determine that you will follow Him faithfully. Keep a good attitude so that you can get where He wants to take you and enjoy the fulfillment of His promises in your life.

1 NOW THESE are the names of the sons of Israel who came to Egypt with Jacob; each came with his household:

²Reuben, Simeon, Levi, and Judah; ³Issachar, Zebulun, and Benjamin; ⁴Dan and Naphtali, Gad, and Asher. ⁵All the descendants of Jacob were seventy people; Joseph was [already] in Egypt.

⁶Then Joseph died, and all his brothers and all that generation,

⁷but the Israelites were prolific and increased greatly; they multiplied and became extremely strong, so that the land was filled with them.

⁸Now a new king arose over Egypt, who did not know Joseph [nor the history of his accomplishments].

⁹He said to his people, "Behold, the people of the sons of Israel are too many and too mighty for us [they greatly outnumber us].

¹⁰"Come, let us deal shrewdly with them, so that they will not multiply and in the event of war, join our enemies, and fight against us and escape from the land."

¹¹So they set taskmasters over them to oppress them with hard labor. And the sons of Israel built Pithom and Raamses as storage cities for Pharaoh.

¹²But the more the Egyptians oppressed them, the more they multiplied and expanded, so that the Egyptians dreaded *and* were exasperated by the Israelites.

¹³And the Egyptians made the Israelites serve rigorously [forcing them into severe slavery].

¹⁴They made their lives bitter with hard labor in mortar, brick, and all kinds of field work. All their labor was harsh *and* severe.

¹⁵Then the king of Egypt said to the Hebrew midwives, one of whom was named Shiphrah (beauty) and the other named Puah (splendor),

¹⁶"When you act as midwives to the Hebrew women and see them on the birthstool, if it is a son, you shall kill him; but if it is a daughter, she shall live."

¹⁷But the midwives feared God [with profound reverence] and did not do as the king of Egypt commanded, but they let the boy babies live.

¹⁸So the king of Egypt called for the midwives and said to them, "Why have you done this thing, and allowed the boy babies to live?"

¹⁹The midwives answered Pharaoh, "Because the Hebrew women are not like the Egyptian women; they are vigorous and give birth quickly and their babies are born before the midwife can get to them."

²⁰So God was good to the midwives, and the people [of Israel] multiplied and became very strong.

²¹And because the midwives feared God [with profound reverence], He established families *and* households for them.

²²Then Pharaoh commanded all his people, saying, "Every son who is born [to the Hebrews] must be thrown into the Nile, but every daughter you shall keep alive."

2 NOW A man of the house of Levi [the priestly tribe] went and took as his wife a daughter of Levi. [Ex 6:18, 20; Num 26:59]

²The woman conceived and gave birth to a son; and when she saw that he was [especially] beautiful *and*

putting the Word to work

When the Hebrew midwives had to choose between fearing God and obeying the orders of the king of Egypt, they chose to fear God (see Exodus 1:15–17). How will you respond when you are faced with a choice between pleasing man and obeying God.

healthy, she hid him for three months [to protect him from the Egyptians]. [Acts 7:20; Heb 11:23]

³When she could no longer hide him, she got him a basket (chest) made of papyrus reeds and covered it with tar and pitch [making it waterproof]. Then she put the child in it and set it among the reeds by the bank of the Nile.

⁴And his sister [Miriam] stood some distance away to find out what would happen to him.

⁵Now the daughter of Pharaoh came down to bathe at the Nile, and [she, together with] her maidens walked along the river's bank; she saw the basket among the reeds and sent her maid [to get it], and she brought it *to her*.

⁶When she opened it, she saw the child, and behold, the baby was crying. And she took pity on him and said, "This is one of the Hebrews' children."

⁷Then his sister said to Pharaoh's daughter, "Shall I go and call a wet-nurse from the Hebrew women to nurse the child for you?"

⁸And Pharaoh's daughter said to her, "Go *ahead*." So the girl went and called the child's mother.

⁹Then Pharaoh's daughter said to her, "Take this child away and nurse him for me, and I will give you your wages." So the woman took the child and nursed him.

¹⁰And the child grew, and she brought him to Pharaoh's daughter and he became her son. And she named him Moses, and said, "Because I drew him out of the water."

¹¹One day, after Moses had grown [into adulthood], it happened that he went to his countrymen and looked [with compassion] at their hard labors; and he saw an Egyptian beating a Hebrew, one of his countrymen.

¹²He turned to look around, and seeing no one, he killed the Egyptian and hid him in the sand.

¹³He went out the next day and saw two Hebrew men fighting with each other; and he said to the aggressor, "Why are you striking your friend?"

¹⁴But the man said, "Who made you a prince and a judge over us? Do you intend to kill me as you killed the Egyptian?" Then Moses was afraid and said, "Certainly this incident is known."

¹⁵When Pharaoh heard about this matter, he tried to kill Moses. Then Moses fled from Pharaoh's presence and took refuge in the land of Midian, where he sat down by a well.

¹⁶Now the priest of Midian had seven daughters; and they came and drew water [from the well where Moses was resting] and filled the troughs to water their father's flock.

¹⁷Then shepherds came and drove them away, but Moses stood up and helped them and watered their flock.

¹⁸When they came to Reuel (Jethro) their father, he said, "How is it that you have come back so soon today?"

¹⁹They said, "An Egyptian saved us from the shepherds. He even drew water [from the well] for us and watered the flock."

²⁰Then he said to his daughters, "Where is he? Why have you left the man behind? Invite him to have something to eat."

²¹Moses was willing to remain with the man, and he gave Moses his daughter Zipporah [to be his wife].

²²She gave birth to a son, and he named him Gershom (stranger); for he said, "I have been a stranger in a foreign land."

²³Now it happened after a long time [about forty years] that the king of Egypt died. And the children of Israel (Jacob) groaned *and* sighed because of the bondage, and they cried out. And their cry for help because of their bondage ascended to God.

²⁴So God heard their groaning and God remembered His covenant with Abraham, Isaac, and Jacob (Israel).

[Gen 12:1–3; 15:18–21; 17:3–8, 21; 35:10–12]

²⁵God saw the sons of Israel, and God took notice [of them] *and* was concerned about them [knowing all, understanding all, remembering all]. [Ps 56:8, 9; 139:2]

3 NOW MOSES was keeping the flock of Jethro (Reuel) his father-in-law, the priest of Midian; and he led his flock to the west side of the wilderness and came to Horeb (Sinai), the mountain of God.

²The Angel of the LORD appeared to him in a blazing flame of fire from the midst of a bush; and he looked, and behold, the bush was on fire, yet it was not consumed.

³So Moses said, "I must turn away [from the flock] and see this great sight—why the bush is not burned up."

⁴When the LORD saw that he turned away [from the flock] to look, God called to him from the midst of the bush and said, "Moses, Moses!" And he said, "Here I am."

⁵Then God said, "Do not come near; take your sandals off your feet [out of respect], because the place on which you are standing is holy ground."

⁶Then He said, "I am the God of your father, the God of Abraham, the God of Isaac, and the God of Jacob." Then Moses hid his face, because he was afraid to look at God.

⁷The LORD said, "I have in fact seen the affliction (suffering, desolation) of My people who are in Egypt, and

life point

To hear clearly from God, it's important to be willing to live on holy ground (a life of purity), and that means keeping your thoughts in line with God's Word. Remember that Jesus said the pure in heart would see God (see Matthew 5:8).

have heard their cry because of their taskmasters (oppressors); for I know their pain *and* suffering.

⁸"So I have come down to rescue them from the hand (power) of the Egyptians, and to bring them up from that land to a land [that is] good and spacious, to a land flowing with milk and honey [a land of plenty]—to the place of the Canaanite, the Hittite, the Amorite, the Perizzite, the Hivite, and the Jebusite.

⁹"Now, behold, the cry of the children of Israel has come to Me; and I have also seen how the Egyptians oppress them.

¹⁰"Therefore, come now, and I will send you to Pharaoh, and then bring My people, the children of Israel, out of Egypt."

¹¹But Moses said to God, "Who am I, that I should go to Pharaoh, and that I should bring the children of Israel out of Egypt?"

¹²And God said, "Certainly I will be with you, and this shall be the sign to you that it is I who have sent you: when you have brought the people out of Egypt, you shall serve *and* worship God at this mountain."

¹³Then Moses said to God, "Behold, when I come to the Israelites and say to them, 'The God of your fathers (ancestors) has sent me to you,' and they say to me, 'What is His name?' What shall I say to them?"

¹⁴God said to Moses, "I AM WHO I AM"; and He said, "You shall say this to the Israelites, 'I AM has sent me to you.'"

¹⁵Then God also said to Moses, "This is what you shall say to the Israelites, 'The LORD, the God of your fathers, the God of Abraham, the God of Isaac, and the God of Jacob (Israel), has sent me to you.' This is My Name forever, and this is My memorial [name] to all generations.

¹⁶"Go, gather the elders (tribal leaders) of Israel together, and say to them,

'The LORD, the God of your fathers, the God of Abraham, of Isaac, and of Jacob, appeared to me, saying, "I am indeed concerned about you and what has been done to you in Egypt.

[17]"So I said I will bring you up out of the suffering *and* oppression of Egypt to the land of the Canaanite, the Hittite, the Amorite, the Perizzite, the Hivite, and the Jebusite, to a land flowing with milk and honey."'

[18]"The elders [of the tribes] will listen *and* pay attention to what you say; and you, with the elders of Israel, shall go to the king of Egypt and you shall say to him, 'The LORD, the God of the Hebrews, has met with us; so now, please, [we ask and plead with you,] let us go on a three days' journey into the wilderness, so that we may sacrifice to the LORD our God.'

[19]"But I know that the king of Egypt will not let you go unless [he is forced] by a strong hand.

[20]"So I will reach out My hand and strike Egypt with all My wonders which I shall do in the midst of it; and after that he will let you go.

[21]"And I will grant this people favor *and* respect in the sight of the Egyptians; therefore, it shall be that when you go, you will not go empty-handed.

[22]"But every woman shall [insistently] ask her neighbor and any woman who lives in her house, for articles of silver and articles of gold, and clothing; and you shall put them on your sons and daughters. In this way

"I AM."

If you have ever wondered, "Who am I?" You are not alone. When Moses had this thought, God responded with Who He is: "I AM" (Exodus 3:14). I have pondered these awesome words for a long time, and I believe they are much more significant than we realize.

What was God really saying when He referred to Himself as "I AM"? For one thing, He is *so much* that there is no way to explain Him properly. How can we describe Someone Who is *everything* and wrap it up in one name? When Moses asked the question about God's identity in Exodus 3:13, evidently the Lord did not want to get into a long dissertation about Who He was because He simply told Moses, "You shall say . . . . I AM has sent me to you" (verse 14). By way of explanation, He preceded His statement with "I AM WHO I AM and WHAT I AM, and I WILL BE WHAT I WILL BE" (verse 14 Amplified Classic). God was saying to Moses, "You don't have to worry about Pharaoh or anybody else. I AM able to take care of anything you encounter. Whatever you need, I AM it. Either I have it or I can get it. If it does not exist, I will create it. I have everything covered, not just now but for all time. Relax!"

We need not worry about who we are, what we can do, what we cannot do, or anything else. The great "I AM" strengthens us in our weaknesses. As long as He is with us, we can do whatever we need to do. A great piece of advice for us is to be more concerned about Who God is than about who we are.

Even as I write these words about Who God is, I can sense His presence and anointing. There is power in His name! He can handle what we think is difficult or impossible. God's answer to our "Who am I?" is "I AM WHO I AM." Almighty God is more than sufficient in the face of our lack. He is truly everything.

you are to plunder the Egyptians [leaving bondage with great possessions that are rightfully yours]." [Gen 15:14]

4 THEN MOSES answered [the LORD] and said, "What if they will not believe me or take seriously what I say? For they may say, 'The LORD has not appeared to you.'"

²And the LORD said to him, "What is that in your hand?" And he said, "A staff."

³Then He said, "Throw it on the ground." So Moses threw it on the ground, and it became a [living] serpent [like the royal symbol on the crown of Pharaoh]; and Moses ran from it.

⁴But the LORD said to Moses, "Reach out your hand and grasp it by the tail." So he reached out his hand and caught it, and it became a staff in his hand—

⁵["You shall do this," said the LORD,] "so that the elders may believe that the LORD, the God of their fathers, the God of Abraham, the God of Isaac, and the God of Jacob, has [most certainly] appeared to you."

⁶The LORD also said to him, "Put your hand into your robe [where it covers your chest]." So he put his hand into his robe, and when he took it out, his hand was leprous, as white as snow.

⁷Then God said, "Put your hand into your robe again." So he put his hand back into his robe, and when he took it out, it was restored [and was] like the rest of his body.

⁸"If they will not believe you or pay attention to the evidence of the first sign, they may believe the evidence of the second sign.

⁹"But if they will not believe these two signs or pay attention to what you say, you are to take some water from the Nile and pour it on the dry ground; and the water which you take out of the river will turn into blood on the dry ground."

¹⁰Then Moses said to the LORD, "Please, Lord, I am not a man of words (eloquent, fluent), neither before nor since You have spoken to Your servant; for I am slow of speech and tongue."

¹¹The LORD said to him, "Who has made man's mouth? Or who makes the mute or the deaf, or the seeing or the blind? Is it not I, the LORD?

¹²"Now then go, and I, even I, will be with your mouth, and will teach you what you shall say."

¹³But he said, "Please my Lord, send *the message* [of rescue to Israel] by [someone else,] whomever else You will [choose]."

¹⁴Then the anger of the LORD was kindled *and* burned against Moses; He said, "Is there not your brother, Aaron the Levite? I know that he speaks fluently. Also, he is coming out to meet you, and when he sees you, he will be overjoyed.

¹⁵"You must speak to him and put the words in his mouth; I, even I, will be with your mouth and with his mouth, and I will teach you what you are to do.

¹⁶"Moreover, he shall speak for you to the people; he will act as a mouthpiece for you, and you will be as God to him [telling him what I say to you].

¹⁷"You shall take in your hand this staff, with which you shall perform the signs [the miracles which prove I sent you]."

¹⁸Then Moses went away and returned to Jethro his father-in-law, and said to him, "Please, let me go back so that I may return to my relatives in

speak the Word

God, I pray that You will teach me what to say in every situation.
–ADAPTED FROM EXODUS 4:12

Egypt, and see if they are still alive." And Jethro said to Moses, "Go in peace."

¹⁹Then the LORD said to Moses in Midian, "Go back to Egypt, for all the men who were seeking your life [for killing the Egyptian] are dead." [Ex 2:11, 12]

²⁰So Moses took his wife [Zipporah] and his sons [Gershom and Eliezer] and seated them on donkeys, and returned to the land of Egypt. Moses also took the staff of God in his hand.

²¹The LORD said to Moses, "When you return to Egypt, see that you perform before Pharaoh all the wonders (miracles) which I have put in your hand, but I will harden his heart *and* make him stubborn so that he will not let the people go.

²²"Then you shall say to Pharaoh, 'Thus says the LORD, "Israel is My son, My firstborn.

²³"So I say to you, 'Let My son go so that he may serve Me'; and if you refuse to let him go, behold, I will kill your son, your firstborn."'"

²⁴Now it happened at the lodging place, that the LORD met Moses and sought to kill him [making him deathly ill because he had not circumcised one of his sons]. [Gen 17:9–14]

²⁵Then Zipporah took a flint knife and cut off the foreskin of her son and threw it at Moses' feet, and said, "Indeed you are a husband of blood to me!"

²⁶So He let Moses alone [to recover]. At that time Zipporah said, *"You are* a husband of blood"—because of the circumcision.

²⁷The LORD said to Aaron, "Go into the wilderness to meet Moses." So he went and met him at the mountain of God (Sinai) and kissed him.

²⁸Moses told Aaron all the words of the LORD with which He had sent him, and all the signs that He had commanded him to do.

²⁹Then Moses and Aaron went [into Egypt] and assembled all the elders of the Israelites;

³⁰and Aaron said all the words which the LORD had spoken to Moses. Then Moses performed the signs [given to him by God] before the people.

³¹So the people believed; and when they heard that the LORD was concerned about the Israelites and that He had looked [with compassion] on their suffering, then they bowed their heads and worshiped [the LORD].

5 AFTERWARD MOSES and Aaron came and said to Pharaoh, "Thus says the LORD, the God of Israel, 'Let My people go, so that they may celebrate a feast to Me in the wilderness.'"

²But Pharaoh said, "Who is the LORD that I should obey His voice to let Israel go? I do not know the LORD, nor will I let Israel go."

³Then they said, "The God of the Hebrews has met with us. Please, let us go on a three days' journey into the wilderness and sacrifice to the LORD our God, so that He does not discipline us with pestilence or with the sword."

⁴But the king of Egypt said to Moses and Aaron, "Why do you take the people away from their work? Get back to your burdens!"

⁵Pharaoh said, "Look, the people of the land are now many, and you would have them stop their work!"

⁶The very same day Pharaoh gave orders to the [Egyptian] taskmasters in charge of the people and their [Hebrew] foremen, saying,

⁷"You will no longer give the people straw to make brick as before; let them go and gather straw for themselves.

⁸"But the number of bricks which they were making before, you shall [still] require of them; you are not to reduce it in the least. For they are idle *and* lazy; that is why they cry, 'Let us go and sacrifice to our God.'

⁹"Let labor be heavier on the men, and let them work [hard] at it so that

they will pay no attention to [their God's] lying words."

¹⁰Then the [Egyptian] taskmasters [in charge] of the people and their [Hebrew] foremen went out and said to the people, "Thus says Pharaoh, 'I will not give you any straw.

¹¹'Go, get straw for yourselves wherever you can find it, but your work [quota] will not be reduced in the least.'"

¹²So the people were scattered throughout the land of Egypt to gather stubble to use for straw.

¹³And the taskmasters pressured them, saying, "Finish your work, [fulfill] your daily quotas, just as when there was straw [given to you]."

¹⁴And the Hebrew foremen, whom Pharaoh's taskmasters had set over them, were beaten and were asked, "Why have you not fulfilled your required quota of making bricks yesterday and today, as before?"

¹⁵Then the Hebrew foremen came to Pharaoh and cried, "Why do you deal like this with your servants?

¹⁶"No straw is given to your servants, yet they say to us, 'Make bricks!' And look, your servants are being beaten, but it is the fault of your own people."

¹⁷But Pharaoh said, "You are lazy, very lazy *and* idle! That is why you say, 'Let us go *and* sacrifice to the LORD.'

¹⁸"Get out now and get to work; for no straw will be given to you, yet you are to deliver the same quota of bricks."

¹⁹The Hebrew foremen saw that they were in a bad situation because they were told, "You must not reduce [in the least] your daily quota of bricks."

²⁰When they left Pharaoh's presence, the foremen met Moses and Aaron, who were waiting for them.

²¹And the foremen said to them, "May the LORD look upon you and judge you, because you have made us odious (something hated) in the sight of Pharaoh and his servants, and you have put a sword in their hand to kill us."

²²Then Moses turned again to the LORD and said, "O Lord, why have You brought harm *and* oppression to this people? Why did You ever send me? [I cannot understand Your purpose!]

²³"Ever since I came to Pharaoh to speak in Your name, he has harmed *and* oppressed this people, and You have done nothing at all to rescue Your people."

6 THEN THE LORD said to Moses, "Now you shall see what I will do to Pharaoh; for under compulsion he will [not only] let them go, but under compulsion he will drive them out of his land."

²Then God spoke further to Moses and said to him, "I am the LORD. [Ex 3:14]

³"I appeared to Abraham, to Isaac, and to Jacob (Israel) as God Almighty [El Shaddai], but by My name, LORD, I did not make Myself known to them [in acts and great miracles]. [Gen 17:1]

⁴"I also established My covenant with them, to give them the land of Canaan, the land in which they lived as strangers (temporary residents, foreigners). [Gen 12:1–3; 13:14–17; 15:18–21; 17:19; 26:3, 4; 28:13]

⁵"And I have also heard the groaning of the sons of Israel, whom the Egyptians have enslaved, and I have [faithfully] remembered My covenant [with Abraham, Isaac, and Jacob].

⁶"Therefore, say to the children of

speak the Word

Thank You, Lord, for bringing me out from under burdens and freeing me from bondage. Thank You for redeeming and rescuing me with Your outstretched arm.
—ADAPTED FROM EXODUS 6:6

Israel, 'I am the LORD, and I will bring you out from under the burdens of the Egyptians, and I will free you from their bondage. I will redeem *and* rescue you with an outstretched (vigorous, powerful) arm and with great acts of judgment [against Egypt].

⁷'Then I will take you for My people, and I will be your God; and you shall know that I am the LORD your God, who redeemed you *and* brought you out from under the burdens of the Egyptians.

⁸'I will bring you to the land which I swore to give to Abraham, Isaac, and Jacob (Israel); and I will give it to you as a possession. I am the LORD [you have the promise of My changeless omnipotence and faithfulness].'"

⁹Moses told this to the Israelites, but they did not listen to him because of their impatience *and* despondency, and because of their forced labor.

¹⁰The LORD spoke to Moses, saying, ¹¹"Go, tell Pharaoh king of Egypt to let the children of Israel go out of his land."

¹²But Moses said to the LORD, "Look, [my own people] the Israelites have not listened to me; so how then will Pharaoh listen to me, for I am unskilled *and* inept in speech?"

¹³Then the LORD spoke to Moses and Aaron, and gave them a command concerning the Israelites and Pharaoh king of Egypt, to bring the Israelites out of the land of Egypt.

¹⁴These are the heads of their fathers' households. The sons of Reuben, Israel's (Jacob's) firstborn: Hanoch and Pallu, Hezron and Carmi; these are the families of Reuben.

¹⁵The sons of Simeon: Jemuel, Jamin, Ohad, Jachin, Zohar, and Shaul the son of a Canaanite woman; these are the families of Simeon.

¹⁶These are the names of the sons of Levi according to their births: Gershon, Kohath, and Merari; and Levi lived a hundred and thirty-seven years.

¹⁷The sons of Gershon: Libni and Shimei, by their families.

¹⁸The sons of Kohath: Amram (Moses' father), Izhar, Hebron, and Uzziel; and Kohath lived a hundred and thirty-three years.

¹⁹The sons of Merari: Mahli and Mushi. These are the families of Levi according to their generations.

²⁰Amram married his father's sister Jochebed, and she gave birth to Aaron and Moses; and Amram lived a hundred and thirty-seven years.

²¹The sons of Izhar: Korah, Nepheg, and Zichri.

²²The sons of Uzziel: Mishael, Elzaphan, and Sithri.

²³Aaron married Elisheba, the daughter of Amminadab and the sister of Nahshon, and she gave birth to Nadab, Abihu, Eleazar, and Ithamar.

²⁴The sons of Korah: Assir, Elkanah, and Abiasaph. These are the [extended] families of the Korahites.

²⁵Eleazar, Aaron's son, married one of the daughters of Putiel, and she gave birth to Phinehas. These are the heads of the fathers' households of the Levites by their families.

²⁶These are [the same] Aaron and Moses to whom the LORD said, "Bring the children of Israel out of the land of Egypt by their armies."

²⁷They were the ones who spoke to Pharaoh king of Egypt about bringing the Israelites out of Egypt; these are [the same] Moses and Aaron.

²⁸Now it happened on the day when the LORD spoke to Moses in the land of Egypt,

²⁹that He said, "I am the LORD; tell Pharaoh king of Egypt everything that I say to you."

³⁰But Moses said before the LORD, "Look, I am unskilled *and* inept in speech; how then will Pharaoh listen to me *and* pay attention to what I say?"

7 THEN THE Lord said to Moses, "Now hear this: I make you as God to Pharaoh [to declare My will and purpose to him]; and your brother Aaron shall be your prophet.

²"You shall speak all that I command you, and your brother Aaron shall tell Pharaoh to let the children of Israel go out of his land.

³"And I will make Pharaoh's heart hard, and multiply My signs and My wonders (miracles) in the land of Egypt.

⁴"But Pharaoh will not listen to you, and I shall lay My hand on Egypt and bring out My hosts [like a defensive army, tribe by tribe], My people the children of Israel, out of the land of Egypt by great acts of judgment (the plagues).

⁵"The Egyptians shall know that I am the Lord, when I stretch out My hand on Egypt and bring out the children of Israel from among them."

⁶And Moses and Aaron did so; just as the Lord commanded them, so they did.

⁷Now Moses was eighty years old and Aaron eighty-three years old when they spoke to Pharaoh.

⁸Now the Lord said to Moses and Aaron,

⁹"When Pharaoh says to you, 'Work a miracle [to prove your authority],' then you say to Aaron, 'Take your staff and throw it down before Pharaoh, so that it may become a serpent.'"

¹⁰So Moses and Aaron came to Pharaoh, and did just as the Lord had commanded; Aaron threw down his staff before Pharaoh and his servants, and it became a serpent.

¹¹Then Pharaoh called for the wise men [skilled in magic and omens] and the sorcerers [skilled in witchcraft], and they also, these magicians (soothsayer-priests) of Egypt, did the same with their secret arts *and* enchantments.

¹²For every man threw down his staff and they turned into serpents; but Aaron's staff swallowed up their staffs.

¹³Yet Pharaoh's heart was hardened and he would not listen to them, just as the Lord had said.

¹⁴Then the Lord said to Moses, "Pharaoh's heart is hard; he refuses to let the people go.

¹⁵"Go to Pharaoh in the morning as he is going out to the water, and wait for him on the bank of the Nile; and you shall take in your hand the staff that was turned into a serpent.

¹⁶"You shall say to him, 'The Lord, the God of the Hebrews, has sent me to you, saying, "Let My people go, so that they may serve Me in the wilderness. But behold, you have not listened until now."

¹⁷'Thus says the Lord, "By this you shall know *and* recognize *and* acknowledge that I am the Lord: look, with the staff in my hand I will strike the water in the Nile, and it shall be turned to blood.

¹⁸"The fish in the Nile will die, and the Nile will become foul, and the Egyptians will not be able to drink water from the Nile."'"

¹⁹Then the Lord said to Moses, "Say to Aaron, 'Take your staff and stretch out your hand over the waters of Egypt, over their rivers, over their streams, over their pools, and over all their reservoirs of water, so that they may become blood; and there shall be blood throughout all the land of Egypt, in *containers* both of wood and of stone.'"

²⁰So Moses and Aaron did as the Lord commanded; Aaron lifted up the staff and struck the waters in the Nile, in the sight of Pharaoh and in the sight of his servants, and all the water that was in the Nile was turned into blood.

²¹The fish in the Nile died, and the river became foul smelling, and the Egyptians could not drink its water, and there was blood throughout all the land of Egypt.

²²But the magicians of Egypt did the same by their secret arts *and* enchantments; so Pharaoh's heart was hardened, and he did not listen to Moses and Aaron, just as the LORD had said.

²³Then Pharaoh turned and went into his house, and he did not take even this [divine sign] to heart.

²⁴So all the Egyptians dug near the river for water to drink, because they could not drink the water of the Nile.

²⁵Seven days passed after the LORD had struck the Nile.

8 THEN THE LORD said to Moses, "Go to Pharaoh and say to him, 'Thus says the LORD, "Let My people go, so that they may serve Me.

²"However, if you refuse to let them go, hear this: I am going to strike your entire land with frogs.

³"The Nile will swarm with frogs, which will come up and go into your home, into your bedroom and on to your bed, and into the houses of your servants and on your people, and into your ovens and your kneading bowls.

⁴"So the frogs will come up on you and on your people and all your servants." ' "

⁵Then the LORD said to Moses, "Say to Aaron, 'Stretch out your hand with your staff over the rivers, over the streams *and* canals, over the pools [among the reeds], and make frogs come up on the land of Egypt.' "

⁶So Aaron stretched out his hand [with his staff] over the waters of Egypt, and the frogs came up and covered the land of Egypt.

⁷But the magicians (soothsayer-priests) did the same thing with their secret arts *and* enchantments, and brought up [more] frogs on the land of Egypt.

⁸Then Pharaoh called for Moses and Aaron and said, "Plead with the LORD that He may take away the frogs from me and my people; and I will let the people go, so that they may sacrifice to the LORD."

⁹And Moses said to Pharaoh, "I am entirely at your service: when shall I plead [with the Lord] for you and your servants and your people, so that the frogs may leave you and your houses and remain only in the Nile?"

¹⁰Then Pharaoh said, "Tomorrow." Moses replied, "*May it be* as you say, so that you may know [without any doubt] *and* acknowledge that there is no one like the LORD our God.

¹¹"The frogs will leave you and your houses and leave your servants and your people; they will remain only in the Nile."

¹²So Moses and Aaron left Pharaoh, and Moses cried out to the LORD [as he had agreed to do] concerning the frogs which God had inflicted on Pharaoh.

¹³The LORD did as Moses asked, and the frogs died out of the houses, out of the courtyards *and* villages, and out of the fields.

¹⁴So they piled them up in heaps, and the land was detestable *and* stank.

¹⁵But when Pharaoh saw that there was [temporary] relief, he hardened his heart and would not listen *or* pay attention to them, just as the LORD had said.

¹⁶Then the LORD said to Moses, "Say to Aaron, 'Stretch out your staff and strike the dust of the ground, and it will become [biting] gnats (lice) throughout the land of Egypt.' "

¹⁷They did so; Aaron stretched out his hand with his staff and struck the dust of the earth, and there were [biting] gnats on man and animal. All the

speak the Word

God, I declare that there is no one like You!
−ADAPTED FROM Exodus 8:10

dust of the land became gnats through all the land of Egypt.

18The magicians (soothsayer-priests) tried by their secret arts *and* enchantments to create gnats, but they could not; and there were gnats on man and animal.

19Then the magicians said to Pharaoh, "This is the [supernatural] finger of God." But Pharaoh's heart was hardened and he would not listen to them, just as the LORD had said.

20Now the LORD said to Moses, "Get up early in the morning and stand before Pharaoh as he is coming out to the water [of the Nile], and say to him, 'Thus says the LORD, "Let My people go, so that they may serve Me.

21"For if you do not let My people go, hear this: I will send swarms of [bloodsucking] insects on you and on your servants and on your people and into your houses; and the houses of the Egyptians will be full of swarms of insects, as well as the ground on which they stand.

22"But on that day I will separate *and* set apart the land of Goshen, where My people are living, so that no swarms of insects will be there, so that you may know [without any doubt] *and* acknowledge that I, the LORD, am in the midst of the earth.

23"I will put a division (distinction) between My people and your people. By tomorrow this sign shall be in evidence." ' "

24Then the LORD did so. And there came heavy *and* oppressive swarms of [bloodsucking] insects into the house of Pharaoh and his servants' houses; in all the land of Egypt the land was corrupted *and* ruined because of the [great invasion of] insects.

25Then Pharaoh called for Moses and Aaron and said, "Go, sacrifice to your God [here] in the land [of Egypt]."

26But Moses said, "It is not right [or even possible] to do that, for we will sacrifice to the LORD our God what is repulsive *and* unacceptable to the Egyptians [that is, animals that the Egyptians consider sacred]. If we sacrifice what is repulsive *and* unacceptable to the Egyptians, will they not riot *and* stone us?

27"We must go a three days' journey into the wilderness and sacrifice to the LORD our God as He commands us."

28So Pharaoh said, "I will let you go, so that you may sacrifice to the LORD your God in the wilderness; only you shall not go very far away. Plead [with your God] for me."

29Moses said, "I am going to leave you, and I will urgently petition (pray, entreat) the LORD that the swarms of insects may leave Pharaoh, his servants, and his people tomorrow; only do not let Pharaoh act deceitfully again by not letting the people go to sacrifice to the LORD."

30So Moses left Pharaoh and prayed to the LORD [on behalf of Pharaoh].

31The LORD did as Moses asked, and removed the swarms of [bloodsucking] insects from Pharaoh, from his servants and from his people; not one remained.

32But Pharaoh hardened his heart this time also, and he did not let the people go.

9 THEN THE LORD said to Moses, "Go to Pharaoh and tell him, 'Thus says the LORD, the God of the Hebrews: "Let My people go, so that they may serve Me.

2"But if you refuse to let them go and continue to hold them,

3now hear this: the hand of the LORD will fall on your livestock which are out in the field, on the horses, the donkeys, the camels, the herds, and the flocks—a horrible plague shall come.

4"But the LORD will make a distinction between the livestock of Israel and the livestock of Egypt, so that nothing that belongs to the Israelites will die.'"

⁵The Lord set a [definite] time, saying, "Tomorrow the Lord will do this thing in the land."

⁶And the Lord did this thing the next day, and all [kinds of] the livestock of Egypt died; but of the livestock of the Israelites, not one died.

⁷Then Pharaoh sent [men to investigate], and not even one of the livestock of the Israelites had died. But the heart of Pharaoh was hardened [and his mind was firmly set], and he did not let the people go.

⁸Then the Lord said to Moses and Aaron, "Take handfuls of soot from the brick kiln, and let Moses throw it toward the sky in the sight of Pharaoh.

⁹"It will become fine dust over the entire land of Egypt, and it will become boils breaking out in sores on man and animal in all the land [occupied by the Egyptians]."

¹⁰So they took soot from the kiln, and stood before Pharaoh; and Moses threw it toward the sky, and it became boils erupting in sores on man and animal.

¹¹The magicians (soothsayer-priests) could not stand before Moses because of the boils, for the boils were on the magicians as well as on all the Egyptians.

¹²But the Lord hardened the heart of Pharaoh, and he did not listen or pay attention to them, just as the Lord had told Moses.

¹³Then the Lord said to Moses, "Get up early in the morning and stand before Pharaoh and say to him, 'Thus says the Lord, the God of the Hebrews, "Let My people go, so that they may serve Me.

¹⁴"For this time I will send all My plagues on you [in full force,] and on your servants and on your people, so that you may know [without any doubt] and acknowledge that there is no one like Me in all the earth.

¹⁵"For by now I could have put out My hand and struck you and your people with a pestilence, and you would then have been cut off (obliterated) from the earth.

¹⁶"But indeed for this very reason I have allowed you to live, in order to show you My power and in order that My name may be proclaimed throughout all the earth. [Rom 9:17–24]

¹⁷"Since you are still [arrogantly] exalting yourself [in defiance] against My people by not letting them go,

¹⁸hear this: tomorrow about this time I will send a very heavy and dreadful hail, such as has not been seen in Egypt from the day it was founded until now.

¹⁹"Now therefore send [a message], bring your livestock and whatever you have in the field to safety. Every man and animal that is in the field and is not brought home shall be struck by the hail and shall die."'"

²⁰Then everyone among the servants of Pharaoh who feared the word of the Lord made his servants and his livestock flee into the houses and shelters;

²¹but everyone who ignored and did not take seriously the word of the Lord left his servants and his livestock in the field.

²²Now the Lord said to Moses, "Stretch out your hand [with your staff] toward the sky, so that there may be hail in all the land of Egypt, on man and on animal and on all the vegetation of the field, throughout the land of Egypt."

²³Moses stretched out his staff toward the sky, and the Lord sent thunder and hail, and lightning (fireballs) ran down to the earth and along the ground. And the Lord rained hail on the land of Egypt.

²⁴So there was hail, and lightning (fireballs) flashing intermittently in the midst of the extremely heavy hail, such as had not been in all the land of Egypt since it became a nation.

²⁵The hail struck down everything that was in the field throughout all the land of Egypt, both man and animal; the hail struck *and* beat down all the plants in the field and shattered every tree in the field.

²⁶Only in the land of Goshen, where the children of Israel lived, was there no hail.

²⁷Then Pharaoh sent for Moses and Aaron, and said to them, "I have sinned this time; the Lᴏʀᴅ is righteous, and I and my people are wicked.

²⁸"Pray *and* entreat the Lᴏʀᴅ, for there has been enough of God's thunder and hail; I will let you go, and you shall stay here no longer."

²⁹Moses said to him, "As soon as I leave the city, I will stretch out my hands to the Lᴏʀᴅ; the thunder will cease and there will be no more hail, so that you may know [without any doubt] *and* acknowledge that the earth is the Lᴏʀᴅ's.

³⁰"But as for you and your servants, I know that you do not yet fear the Lᴏʀᴅ God."

³¹(Now the flax and the barley were battered *and* ruined [by the hail], because the barley was in the ear (ripe, but soft) and the flax was in bud,

³²but the wheat and spelt (coarse wheat) were not battered *and* ruined, because they *ripen* late in the season.)

³³So Moses left the city and Pharaoh, and stretched out his hands to the Lᴏʀᴅ; then the thunder and hail ceased, and rain no longer poured on the earth.

³⁴But when Pharaoh saw that the rain and the hail and the thunder had ceased, he sinned again and hardened his heart, both he and his servants.

³⁵Pharaoh's heart was hardened, and he did not let the Israelites go, just as the Lᴏʀᴅ had said through Moses. [Ex 4:21]

10 THEN THE Lᴏʀᴅ said to Moses, "Go to Pharaoh, for I have hardened his heart and the heart of his servants [making them determined and unresponsive], so that I may exhibit My signs [of divine power] among them,

²and that you may recount *and* explain in the hearing of your son, and your grandson, what I have done [repeatedly] to make a mockery of the Egyptians—My signs [of divine power] which I have done among them—so that you may know [without any doubt] *and* recognize [clearly] that I am the Lᴏʀᴅ."

³So Moses and Aaron went to Pharaoh and said to him, "Thus says the Lᴏʀᴅ, the God of the Hebrews: 'How long will you refuse to humble yourself before Me? Let My people go, so that they may serve Me.

⁴'For if you refuse to let My people go, then hear this: tomorrow I will bring [migratory] locusts into your country.

⁵'They shall cover the [visible] surface of the land, so that no one will be able to see the ground, and they will eat the rest of what has remained—that is, the *vegetation* left after the hail—and they will eat every one of your trees that grows in the field;

⁶your houses and those of all your servants and of all the Egyptians shall be filled *with locusts*, as neither your fathers nor your grandfathers have seen, from their birth until this day.' " Then Moses turned and left Pharaoh.

⁷Pharaoh's servants said to him, "How long shall this man be a trap to us? Let the men go, so that they may serve the Lᴏʀᴅ their God. Do you not realize that Egypt is destroyed?"

⁸So Moses and Aaron were brought back to Pharaoh, and he said to them, "Go, serve the Lᴏʀᴅ your God! Who specifically are the ones that are going?"

⁹Moses said, "We will go with our young and our old, with our sons and our daughters, with our flocks and our

herds [all of us and all that we have], for we must hold a feast to the Lord."

¹⁰Pharaoh said to them, "The Lord be with you [to help you], if I ever let you go with your children [because you will never return]! Look [be forewarned], you have an evil plan in mind.

¹¹"No! Go now, you who are men, [without your families] and serve the Lord, if that is what you want." So Moses and Aaron were driven from Pharaoh's presence.

¹²Then the Lord said to Moses, "Stretch out your hand over the land of Egypt for the locusts, so that they may come up on the land of Egypt and eat all the plants of the land, all that the hail has left."

¹³So Moses stretched out his staff over the land of Egypt, and the Lord brought an east wind on the land all that day and all that night; when it was morning, the east wind had brought the [swarms of] locusts.

¹⁴The locusts came up over all the land of Egypt and settled down in the whole territory, a very dreadful mass of them; never before were there such locusts as these, nor will there ever be again.

¹⁵For they covered the [visible] surface of the land, so that the ground was darkened; and they ate every plant of the land and all the fruit of the trees which the hail had left. There remained not a green thing on the trees or the plants of the field throughout all the land of Egypt.

¹⁶Then Pharaoh hurried to call for Moses and Aaron, and he said, "I have sinned against the Lord your God and against you.

¹⁷"Now therefore, please forgive my sin only this once [more], and pray and entreat the Lord your God, so that He will remove this [plague of] death from me."

¹⁸Moses left Pharaoh and entreated the Lord.

¹⁹So the Lord shifted *the wind* to a violent west wind which lifted up the locusts and drove them into the Red Sea; not one locust remained within the border of Egypt.

²⁰But the Lord hardened Pharaoh's heart [so that it was even more resolved and obstinate], and he did not let the Israelites go.

²¹Then the Lord said to Moses, "Stretch out your hand toward the sky, so that darkness may come over the land of Egypt, a darkness which [is so awful that it] may be felt."

²²So Moses stretched out his hand toward the sky, and for three days a thick darkness was all over the land of Egypt [no sun, no moon, no stars].

²³The Egyptians could not see one another, nor did anyone leave his place for three days, but all the Israelites had [supernatural] light in their dwellings.

²⁴Then Pharaoh called to Moses, and said, "Go, serve the Lord; only your flocks and your herds must be left behind. Even your children may go with you."

²⁵But Moses said, "You must also let us have sacrifices and burnt offerings, so that we may sacrifice them to the Lord our God.

²⁶"Therefore, our livestock must also go with us; not one hoof shall be left behind, for we must take some of them to serve the Lord our God. Even we do not know with what we will serve the Lord until we arrive there."

²⁷But the Lord hardened Pharaoh's heart, and he was not willing to let them go.

²⁸Then Pharaoh said to Moses, "Get away from me! See that you never enter my presence again, for on the day that you see my face again you will die!"

²⁹Then Moses said, "You are correct; I will never see your face again!"

11

THEN THE LORD said to Moses, "I will bring yet one more plague on Pharaoh and on Egypt; after that he will let you go. When he lets you go, he will most certainly drive you out of here completely.

²"Speak so that all of the people [of Israel] may hear, and tell every man to ask from his neighbor, and every woman to ask from her neighbor, articles of silver, and articles of gold."

³The LORD gave the people favor in the sight of the Egyptians. Moreover, the man Moses was greatly esteemed in the land of Egypt, [both] in the sight of Pharaoh's servants and in the sight of the people.

⁴Then Moses said, "Thus says the LORD: 'At midnight I am going out into the midst of Egypt,

⁵and all the firstborn in the land [the pride, hope, and joy] of Egypt shall die, from the firstborn of Pharaoh who sits on his throne, to the firstborn of the slave girl who is behind the hand-mill, and all the firstborn of cattle as well.

⁶'There shall be a great cry [of heartache and sorrow] throughout the land of Egypt, such as has never been before and such as shall never be again.

⁷'But not even a dog will threaten any of the Israelites, whether man or animal, so that you may know [without any doubt] and acknowledge how the LORD makes a distinction between Egypt and Israel.'

⁸"All these servants of yours will come down to me and bow down before me, saying, 'Get out, you and all the people who follow you.' After that I will leave." And he left Pharaoh in the heat of anger.

⁹Then the LORD said to Moses, "Pharaoh will not listen to you, so that My wonders (miracles) may be multiplied in the land of Egypt."

¹⁰Moses and Aaron did all these wonders (miracles) before Pharaoh; yet the LORD hardened Pharaoh's heart, and he did not let the Israelites go out of his land.

12

THE LORD said to Moses and Aaron in the land of Egypt,

²"This month shall be the beginning of months to you; it is to be the first month of the year to you.

³"Tell all the congregation of Israel, 'On the tenth [day] of this month they are to take a lamb *or* young goat for themselves, according to [the size of] the household of which he is the father, a lamb *or* young goat for each household.

⁴'Now if the household is too small for a lamb [to be consumed], let him and his next door neighbor take one according to the number of people [in the households]; according to what each man can eat, you are to divide the lamb.

⁵'Your lamb *or* young goat shall be [perfect] without blemish *or* bodily defect, a male a year old; you may take it from the sheep or from the goats. [1 Pet 1:19, 20]

⁶'You shall keep it until the fourteenth day of the same month, then the whole assembly of the congregation of Israel is to slaughter it at twilight.

⁷'Moreover, they shall take some of the blood and put it on the two doorposts and on the lintel [above the door] of the houses in which they eat it. [Matt 26:28; John 1:29; Heb 9:14]

putting the Word to work

Do you need favor with the people you work for, as the Israelites did in the sight of the Egyptians? Ask God to give you the favor you need, just as He gave the Israelites favor in the eyes of their taskmasters so long ago (see Exodus 11:3).

⁸'They shall eat the meat that same night, roasted in fire, and they shall eat it with unleavened bread and bitter herbs.

⁹'Do not eat any of it raw or boiled in water, but roasted in fire—both its head and its legs, along with its inner parts.

¹⁰'You shall let none of the meat remain until the morning, and anything that remains left over until morning, you shall burn completely in the fire.

¹¹'Now you are to eat it in this manner: [be prepared for a journey] with your loins girded [that is, with the outer garment tucked into the band], your sandals on your feet, and your staff in your hand; you shall eat it quickly—it is the Lord's Passover.

¹²'For I [the Lord] will pass through the land of Egypt on this night, and will strike down all the firstborn in the land of Egypt, both man and animal; against all the gods of Egypt I will execute judgments [exhibiting their worthlessness]. I am the Lord.

¹³'The blood shall be a sign for you on [the doorposts of] the houses where you live; when I see the blood I shall pass over you, and no affliction shall happen to you to destroy you when I strike the land of Egypt. [1 Cor 5:7; Heb 11:28]

¹⁴'Now this day will be a memorial to you, and you shall keep it as a feast to the Lord; throughout your generations you are to celebrate it as an ordinance forever.

apply the blood to your life

God instructed the Israelites to use the blood of a lamb as a token or a sign that they were not to be harmed under the Old Covenant. Notice that the Lord said to them, "When I see the blood I shall pass over you" (Exodus 12:13). In order for the people to be protected from the angel of death, God had to *see* the blood, and He could not *see* it if they did not *put* it on the side posts and tops of their doorframes.

You and I live under the New Covenant, which is far better than the Old Covenant because the applied blood of Jesus is permanent (see Hebrews 9:12–26). How do we "put" the blood on our lives and homes? We do it by believing in Jesus Christ as we simply say in faith, "I believe the blood of Jesus is on my life and my home, cleansing and protecting me." We can apply the blood in any practical situation we face.

Start applying the blood by faith over yourself and that which belongs to you—your children, your car, your home, your body. Are you battling with wounded emotions? Then cover your emotions with the blood of Jesus so you will not continue to be devastated by people who do not seem to know how to give you what you feel you need from them. Are you in financial difficulty? Lay your hands on your wallet; pray your funds will be protected by the blood of Jesus. Ask God to cause your money to multiply in the work of the Lord and to see to it that Satan does not steal any of it from you. Are you sick? Release your faith for the blood of Jesus to cover and protect your body. The life is in the blood; it cleanses us from all sin and protects us from things that will harm us.

Pray with me: "Father, I come to You in Jesus' name, and I apply the blood of Jesus to my life, to all that belongs to me, and to everything You have given me to steward. I put the blood of Jesus on my mind, my body, my emotions, and my will. I put the blood on my family, my coworkers, and my friends. Thank You for protecting me with Your blood. Amen."

15'[In the celebration of the Passover in future years,] seven days you shall eat unleavened bread, but on the first day you shall remove the leaven from your houses [because it represents the spread of sin]; for whoever eats leavened bread on the first day through the seventh day, that person shall be cut off *and* excluded from [the atonement made for] Israel.

16'On the first day [of the feast] you shall have a holy *and* solemn assembly, and on the seventh day there shall be another holy *and* solemn assembly; no work of any kind shall be done on those days, except for the preparation of food which every person must eat— only that may be done by you.

17'You shall also observe the Feast of Unleavened Bread, because on this very day I brought your hosts [grouped according to tribal armies] out of the land of Egypt; therefore you shall observe this day throughout your generations as an ordinance forever.

18'In the first *month,* on the fourteenth day of the month at evening, you shall eat unleavened bread, [and continue] until the twenty-first day of the month at evening.

19'Seven days no leaven shall be found in your houses; whoever eats what is leavened shall be cut off *and* excluded from [the atonement made for] the congregation of Israel, whether a stranger or native-born. [1 Cor 5:6–8]

20'You shall eat nothing leavened; in all your dwellings you shall eat unleavened bread.'"

21'Then Moses called for all the elders of Israel and said to them, "Go and take a lamb for yourselves according to [the size of] your families and slaughter the Passover *lamb.*

22'"You shall take a bunch of hyssop, dip it in the blood which is in the basin, and touch some of the blood to the lintel [above the doorway] and to the two doorposts; and none of you shall go outside the door of his house until morning.

23'"For the LORD will pass through to strike the Egyptians; and when He sees the blood on the lintel [above the entry way] and on the two doorposts, the LORD will pass over the door and will not allow the destroyer to come into your houses to slay you.

24'"You shall observe this event [concerning Passover] as an ordinance for you and for your children forever.

25'"When you enter the land which the LORD will give you, as He has promised, you shall keep *and* observe this service.

26'"When your children say to you, 'What does this service mean to you?'

27'you shall say, 'It is the sacrifice of the LORD's Passover, for He passed over the houses of the Israelites in Egypt when He struck the Egyptians, but spared our houses.'" And the people bowed [their heads] low and worshiped [God].

28'Then the Israelites went and did [as they had been told]: just as the LORD had commanded Moses and Aaron, so they did.

29'Now it happened at midnight that the LORD struck every firstborn in the land of Egypt, from the firstborn of Pharaoh who sat on his throne to the firstborn of the prisoner who was in the dungeon, and all the firstborn of the cattle.

30'Pharaoh got up in the night, he and all his servants and all the Egyptians, and there was a great cry [of heartache and sorrow] in Egypt, for there was no house where there was not someone dead.

31'Then he called for Moses and Aaron at night and said, "Get up, get out from among my people, both you and the Israelites; and go, serve the LORD, as you said.

32'"Take both your flocks and your

herds, as you have said, and go, and [ask your God to] bless me also."

³³The Egyptians [anxiously] urged the people [to leave], to send them out of the land quickly, for they said, "We will all be dead."

³⁴So the people took their dough before it was leavened, their kneading bowls being bound up in their clothes on their shoulders.

³⁵Now the Israelites had acted in accordance with the word of Moses; and they had asked the Egyptians for articles of silver and articles of gold, and clothing.

³⁶The LORD gave the people favor in the sight of the Egyptians, so that they gave them what they asked. And so they plundered the Egyptians [of those things].

³⁷Now the Israelites journeyed from Rameses to Succoth, about six hundred thousand men on foot, besides [the women and] the children.

³⁸A mixed multitude [of non-Israelites from foreign nations] also went with them, along with both flocks and herds, a very large number of livestock. [Num 11:4; Deut 29:11]

³⁹And they baked unleavened cakes of the dough which they brought from Egypt; it was not leavened, since they were driven [quickly] from Egypt and could not delay, nor had they prepared any food for themselves.

⁴⁰Now the period of time the children of Israel lived in Egypt was four hundred and thirty years. [Gen 15:13, 14]

⁴¹At the end of the four hundred and thirty years, to that very day, all the hosts of the LORD [gathered into tribal armies] left the land of Egypt.

⁴²It is a night of watching to be observed for the LORD for having brought them out of the land of Egypt; this [same] night is for the LORD, to be observed and celebrated by all the Israelites throughout their generations.

⁴³The LORD said to Moses and Aaron,

"This is the ordinance of the Passover; no foreigner is to eat it;

⁴⁴but every man's slave who is bought with money, after you have circumcised him, then he may eat it.

⁴⁵"No stranger (temporary resident, foreigner) or hired servant shall eat it.

⁴⁶"It is to be eaten inside one house; you shall not take any of the meat outside the house, nor shall you break any of its bones. [John 19:33, 36]

⁴⁷"The entire congregation of Israel shall keep and celebrate it.

⁴⁸"If a stranger living temporarily among you wishes to celebrate the Passover to the LORD, all his males must be circumcised, and then he may participate and celebrate it like one that is born in the land. But no uncircumcised person may eat it.

⁴⁹"The same law shall apply to the native-born and to the stranger who lives temporarily among you."

⁵⁰Then all the Israelites did so; they did just as the LORD had commanded Moses and Aaron.

⁵¹And on that very same day the LORD brought the Israelites out of the land of Egypt by their hosts (tribal armies).

13

THE LORD spoke to Moses, saying,

²"Sanctify to Me [that is, set apart for My purpose] every firstborn, the first offspring of every womb among the children of Israel, both of man and of animal; it is Mine."

³Moses said to the people, "Remember [solemnly observe and commemorate] this day on which you came out of Egypt, out of the house of bondage and slavery; for by a strong and powerful hand the LORD brought you out of this place. And nothing leavened shall be eaten.

⁴"On this day in the month Abib, you are about to go onward.

⁵"And it shall be when the LORD brings you into the land of the Canaanite, the

13:5

rite, the Hivite, and
h He swore to your
ou, a land [of abun-
ing with milk and honey,
ou shall keep *and* observe this
rite (service) in this month.

[6]"For seven days you shall eat unleavened bread, and on the seventh
day there shall be a feast to the LORD.
[7]"Unleavened bread shall be eaten
throughout the seven days; no leavened bread shall be seen with you, nor
shall there be leaven within the borders of your territory.

[8]"You shall explain this to your son
on that day, saying, 'It is because of
what the LORD did for me when I came
out of Egypt.'

[9]"It shall serve as a sign to you on
your hand (arm), and as a reminder on
your forehead, so that the instruction
(law) of the LORD may be in your mouth;
for with a strong *and* powerful hand the
LORD brought you out of Egypt.

[10]"Therefore, you shall keep this ordinance at this time from year to year.

[11]"Now it shall be when the LORD
brings you into the land of the Canaanite, as He swore to you and your
fathers, and gives it to you,

[12]you shall set apart *and* dedicate to
the LORD all that first opens the womb.
All the firstborn males of your livestock shall be the LORD's.

[13]"Every firstborn of a donkey you
shall redeem by [substituting] a lamb
[as a sacrifice for it], but if you do not
[wish to] redeem it, then you shall
break its neck; and every firstborn
among your sons you shall redeem

when life gets difficult

Sometimes God leads us the hard way instead of the easy way because He is doing a special work in us. How will we ever learn to lean on Him if everything in our lives is easy enough for us to handle by ourselves? God led the children of Israel the long, difficult way through the wilderness to prepare them for the battles they would face in possessing the Promised Land. He was concerned that when they saw the enemy they might run back to Egypt and become enslaved again in their former bondage. God wanted to teach them Who He was and that they could depend on Him to fight their battles.

Many of us think that when we enter into our Promised Land we will have no more spiritual battles. Not so! After the Israelites crossed the Jordan River and went in to possess the land of promise, they fought one battle after another. But as they learned to fight in God's strength and under His direction, they won their battles.

If you know God has asked you to do something, do not back down just because it gets hard. When things get tough, spend more time with Him, lean more on Him, and receive more grace from Him. Realize that grace comes at no cost to you; grace is the power of God working in you and through you to do those things you cannot do. As you face challenges in your life, beware of thoughts that say, *I can't do this; it's just too hard*. Do not let your mind give up! Satan knows that if he can defeat you in your mind, he can defeat you in your experience. That is why it is so impor-tant not to lose heart and not to grow weary or faint. You can be sure that wherever God leads you, He is able to keep you. He never will allow more temptation to come to you than you can bear (see 1 Corinthians 10:13). You do not have to live in a con-stant struggle if you learn to continually lean on Him for the strength you need.

[that is, "buy back" from God with a suitable sacrifice].

[14]"And it shall be when your son asks you in time to come, saying, 'What does this mean?' you shall say to him, 'With a strong *and* powerful hand the LORD brought us out of Egypt, from the house of bondage *and* slavery.

[15]'For it happened, when Pharaoh stubbornly refused to let us go, that the LORD struck every firstborn in the land of Egypt, both the firstborn of man and the firstborn of animal. Therefore, I sacrifice to the LORD all the males, the first [to be born] of every womb, but every firstborn of my sons I redeem.'

[16]"So it shall serve as a sign *and* a reminder on your [left] hand (arm) and as frontlets between your eyes, for by a strong *and* powerful hand the LORD brought us out of Egypt."

[17]So it happened, when Pharaoh let the people go, God did not lead them by way of the land of the Philistines, even though it was nearer; for God said, "The people might change their minds when they see war [that is, that there will be war], and return to Egypt."

[18]But God led the people around by the way of the wilderness toward the Red Sea; the sons of Israel went up in battle array (orderly ranks, marching formation) out of the land of Egypt.

[19]Moses took the bones of Joseph with him, for Joseph had solemnly ordered (placed under an oath) the Israelites, saying, "God will assuredly take care of you, and you must carry my bones away from here with you." [Gen 50:25]

[20]They journeyed from Succoth [in Goshen] and camped at Etham on the edge of the wilderness.

[21]The [presence of the] LORD was going before them by day in a pillar (column) of cloud to lead them along the way, and in a pillar of fire by night to give them light, so that they could travel by day and by night.

[22]He did not withdraw the pillar of cloud by day, nor the pillar of fire by night, from going before the people.

14 NOW THE LORD spoke to Moses, saying, [2]"Tell the sons of Israel to turn back and camp in front of Pihahiroth, between Migdol and the sea. You shall camp in front of Baal-zephon, opposite it, by the sea.

[3]"For Pharaoh will say of the Israelites, 'They are wandering aimlessly in the land; the wilderness has shut them in.'

[4]"I will harden (make stubborn, defiant) Pharaoh's heart, so that he will pursue them; and I will be glorified *and* honored through Pharaoh and all his army, and the Egyptians shall know [without any doubt] *and* acknowledge that I am the LORD." And they did so.

[5]When the king of Egypt was told that the people had fled, Pharaoh and his servants had a change of heart toward the people, and they said, "What is this that we have done? We have let Israel go from serving us!"

[6]So Pharaoh harnessed *horses to* his war-chariots [for battle] and took his army with him;

[7]and he took six hundred chosen war-chariots, and all the other war-chariots of Egypt with fighting charioteers over all of them.

[8]The LORD hardened the heart of Pharaoh, king of Egypt, and he pursued the Israelites, as they were leaving confidently *and* defiantly. [Acts 13:17]

[9]The Egyptians chased them with all the horses and war-chariots of Pharaoh, his horsemen and his army, and they overtook them as they camped by the sea, beside Pi-hahiroth, in front of Baal-zephon.

[10]As Pharaoh approached, the Israelites looked up and saw the Egyptians marching after them, and they were very frightened; so the Israelites cried out to the LORD.

¹¹Then they said to Moses, "Is it because there are no graves in Egypt that you have taken us away to die in the wilderness? What is this that you have done to us by bringing us out of Egypt?

¹²"Did we not say to you in Egypt, 'Leave us alone; let us serve the Egyptians?' For it would have been better for us to serve the Egyptians [as slaves] than to die in the wilderness."

¹³Then Moses said to the people, "Do not be afraid! Take your stand [be firm and confident and undismayed] and see the salvation of the LORD which He will accomplish for you today; for those Egyptians whom you have seen today, you will never see again.

¹⁴"The LORD will fight for you while you [only need to] keep silent *and* remain calm."

¹⁵The LORD said to Moses, "Why do you cry to Me? Tell the sons of Israel to move forward [toward the sea].

¹⁶"As for you, lift up your staff and stretch out your hand over the sea and divide it, so that the sons of Israel may go through the middle of the sea on dry land.

¹⁷"As for Me, hear this: I will harden the hearts of the Egyptians, and they will go in [the sea] after them; and I will be glorified *and* honored through Pharaoh and all his army, and his war-chariots and his horsemen.

¹⁸"And the Egyptians shall know [without any doubt] *and* acknowledge that I am the LORD, when I am glorified *and* honored through Pharaoh, through his war-chariots and his charioteers."

¹⁹The angel of God, who had been going in front of the camp of Israel, moved and went behind them. The pillar of the cloud moved from in front and stood behind them.

²⁰So it came between the camp of Egypt and the camp of Israel. It was a cloud along with darkness [even by day to the Egyptians], but it gave light by night [to the Israelites]; so one [army] did not come near the other all night.

²¹Then Moses stretched out his hand over the sea; and the LORD swept the sea back by a strong east wind all that night and turned the seabed into dry land, and the waters were divided.

²²The Israelites went into the middle of the sea on dry land, and the waters formed a wall to them on their right hand and on their left.

²³Then the Egyptians pursued them into the middle of the sea, even all Pharaoh's horses, his war-chariots and his charioteers.

²⁴So it happened at the early morning watch [before dawn], that the LORD looked down on the army of the Egyptians through the pillar of fire and cloud and put them in a state of confusion.

²⁵He made their chariot wheels hard to turn, and the chariots difficult to drive; so the Egyptians said, "Let us flee from Israel, for the LORD is fighting for them against the Egyptians."

²⁶Then the LORD said to Moses, "Stretch out your hand over the sea so that the waters may come back over the Egyptians, on their war-chariots and their charioteers."

speak the Word

God, I pray that You will help me not to be afraid, but to take my stand—firm, confident, and undismayed—and see the salvation of the Lord, which You will accomplish for me today.
—ADAPTED FROM EXODUS 14:13

²⁷So Moses stretched out his hand over the sea, and the sea returned to its normal flow at sunrise; and the Egyptians retreated right into it [being met by the returning water]; so the Lord overthrew the Egyptians *and* tossed them into the midst of the sea.

²⁸The waters returned and covered the chariots and the charioteers, and all the army of Pharaoh that had gone into the sea after them; not even one of them survived.

²⁹But the Israelites walked on dry land in the middle of the sea, and the waters formed a wall to them on their right hand and on their left.

³⁰The Lord saved Israel that day from the hand of the Egyptians, and Israel saw the Egyptians [lying] dead on the seashore.

³¹When Israel saw the great power which the Lord had used against the Egyptians, they feared the Lord [with reverence and awe-filled respect], and they believed in the Lord, and in His servant Moses.

15 THEN MOSES and the children of Israel sang this song to the Lord, singing,

"I will sing to the Lord, for He has triumphed gloriously;
The horse and its rider He has thrown into the sea.
²"The Lord is my strength and my song,
And He has become my salvation;
This is my God, and I will praise Him;
My father's God, and I will exalt Him.
³"The Lord is a warrior;
The Lord is His name.
⁴"Pharaoh's chariots and his army He has thrown into the sea;
His chosen captains are drowned in the *Red Sea.
⁵"The deep [water] covers them;

[Clad in armor] they sank into the depths like a stone.
⁶"Your right hand, O Lord, is glorious in power;
Your right hand, O Lord, shatters the enemy.
⁷"In the greatness of Your majesty You overthrow *and* annihilate those [adversaries] who rise [in rebellion] against You;
You send out Your fury, and it consumes them like chaff.
⁸"With the blast of Your nostrils the waters piled up,
The flowing waters stood up like a mound;
The deeps were congealed in the heart of the sea.
⁹"The enemy said, 'I will pursue, I will overtake, I will divide the spoil;
My desire shall be satisfied against them;
I will draw my sword, my hand shall dispossess them *and* drive them out.'
¹⁰"You blew with Your wind, the sea covered them;
[Clad in armor] they sank like lead in the mighty waters.
¹¹"Who is like You among the gods, O Lord?
Who is like You, majestic in holiness,
Awesome in splendor, working wonders?
¹²"You stretched out Your right hand,
The sea swallowed them.
¹³"You in Your lovingkindness *and* goodness have led the people whom You have redeemed;
In Your strength You have guided them with care to Your holy habitation.
¹⁴"The peoples have heard [about You], they tremble;
Anguish *and* fear has gripped the inhabitants of Philistia.

15:4 Lit. *Sea of Reeds.*

15"Then the [tribal] chiefs of Edom
  were dismayed *and* horrified;
The [mighty] leaders of Moab,
  trembling grips them;
All the inhabitants of Canaan have
  melted away [in despair]—
16Terror and dread fall on them;
Because of the greatness of Your
  arm they are as still as a stone;
Until Your people pass by *and* [into
  Canaan], O Lord,
Until the people pass by whom You
  have purchased.
17"You will bring them [into the land
  of promise] and plant them on
  the mountain (Mt. Moriah in
  Jerusalem) of Your inheritance,
The place, O Lord, You have made
  for Your dwelling [among them],
The sanctuary, O Lord, which Your
  hands have established.
18"The Lord shall reign to eternity
  and beyond."

19For the horses of Pharaoh went
with his war-chariots and his charioteers into the sea, and the Lord
brought back the waters of the sea on
them, but the sons of Israel walked on
dry land in the middle of the sea.
20Then Miriam the prophetess, the
sister of Aaron [and Moses], took
a timbrel in her hand, and all the
women followed her with timbrels and
dancing. [Mic 6:4]
21Miriam answered them,

"Sing to the Lord, for He has
  triumphed gloriously *and* is
  highly exalted;
The horse and its rider He has
  hurled into the sea."

22Then Moses led Israel from the Red
Sea, and they went into the Wilderness
of Shur; they went [a distance of] three
days (about thirty-three miles) in the
wilderness and found no water.
23Then they came to Marah, but
they could not drink its waters because they were bitter; therefore it
was named Marah (bitter).
24The people [grew discontented
and] grumbled at Moses, saying,
"What are we going to drink?"
25Then he cried to the Lord [for
help], and the Lord showed him a tree,
[a branch of] which he threw into the
waters, and the waters became sweet.
There the Lord made a statute and
an ordinance for them, and there He
tested them,
26saying, "If you will diligently listen
and pay attention to the voice of the
Lord your God, and do what is right in
His sight, and listen to His commandments, and keep [foremost in your
thoughts and actively obey] all His
precepts *and* statutes, then I will not
put on you any of the diseases which
I have put on the Egyptians; for I am
the Lord who heals you."
27Then the children of Israel came to
Elim where there were twelve springs
of water and seventy date palms, and
they camped there beside the waters.

16 THEY SET out from Elim,
and all the congregation of
Israel came to the Wilderness of Sin, which is between Elim
and Sinai, on the fifteenth day of the
second month after they left the land
of Egypt.

speak the Word

*I declare, God, that You are majestic in holiness, that You are awesome in
splendor, that You work wonders, and that in Your loving-kindness
and goodness You will lead me.*
—ADAPTED FROM Exodus 15:11, 13

²The whole congregation of the Israelites [grew discontented and] murmured *and* rebelled against Moses and Aaron in the wilderness,

³and the Israelites said to them, "Would that we had died by the hand of the Lord in the land of Egypt, when we sat by the pots of meat and ate bread until we were full; for you have brought us out into this wilderness to kill this entire assembly with hunger."

⁴Then the Lord said to Moses, "Behold, I will cause bread to rain from heaven for you; the people shall go out and gather a day's portion every day,

so that I may test them [to determine] whether or not they will walk [obediently] in My instruction (law).

⁵"And it shall be that on the sixth day, they shall prepare to bring in twice as much as they gather daily [so that they will not need to gather on the seventh day]."

⁶So Moses and Aaron said to all Israel, "At evening you shall know that the Lord has brought you out of the land of Egypt,

⁷and in the morning you will see the glory of the Lord, for He hears your murmurings against the Lord. What

grace for today and every day

God miraculously fed the Israelites as they traveled through the wilderness, but He gave them only enough for one day at a time (see Exodus 16:4). Through this, we see one of God's principles at work—that we are to trust Him each day for what we need that day and not worry about tomorrow. Jesus knew this principle when He taught His disciples to pray in Matthew 6:11, saying, "Give us this day our daily bread."

We all like to have what we need for today and plenty set aside for the future. It makes us feel secure to already have all of our provision in hand and not have to trust God for it. We rather enjoy being in control and having everything all neatly planned out, but God does not always allow us to do that. Just about the time we think we have everything all figured out and that we have taken good care of ourselves, something happens we did not expect and we have to trust God anyway.

God said the Israelites could gather a day's portion every day so that He might test them to determine whether or not they would obey His instructions. Giving them what they needed as they needed it was His way of teaching them to trust Him and testing them to see if they would walk in obedience to His commandments. If they did try to gather more than enough for one day, what they gathered became rotten and started to stink (see Exodus 16:20).

When we worry about tomorrow, we waste today. I believe that we become discouraged and think our lives are worthless because we have never learned to trust God one day at a time.

Trust requires that we have unanswered questions. God's ways are not our ways, but His ways are always best. Trust God and learn to live one day at a time. As you do, you will enjoy life more than ever before.

are we, that you murmur *and* rebel against us?"

⁸Moses said, "*This will happen* when the LORD gives you meat to eat in the evening, and in the morning [enough] bread to be fully satisfied, because the LORD has heard your murmurings against Him; for what are we? Your murmurings are not against us, but against the LORD."

⁹Then Moses said to Aaron, "Say to all the congregation of Israel, 'Approach the LORD, because He has heard your murmurings.'"

¹⁰So it happened that as Aaron spoke to the whole congregation of Israel, they looked toward the wilderness, and behold, the glory *and* brilliance of the LORD appeared in the cloud!

¹¹Then the LORD spoke to Moses, saying,

¹²"I have heard the murmurings of the Israelites; speak to them, saying, 'At twilight you shall eat meat, and in the morning you shall be filled with bread; and you shall know that I am the LORD your God.'"

life point

Many of us have real and pressing concerns about the future. We may be dealing with uncertainties in our jobs, our health, our families, or our environments. If you are anxious about what the future holds for you and your loved ones, the first thing to do is make a decision not to worry. In the same way God provided manna for the Israelites in the wilderness, He will supply what you need today. Believe that He will show you what to do when the time comes. God wants you to know that what you need will be there when you need it. He encourages you to believe and enter His rest—just as the children of Israel rested from the toil of gathering manna on the Sabbath day (see Exodus 16:29, 30).

¹³So in the evening the quails came up and covered the camp, and in the morning there was a blanket of dew around the camp.

¹⁴When the layer of dew evaporated, on the surface of the wilderness there was a fine, flake-like thing, as fine as frost on the ground.

¹⁵When the Israelites saw it, they said to one another, "What is it?" For they did not know what it was. And Moses said to them, "This is the bread which the LORD has given you to eat. [John 6:31, 33]

¹⁶"This is what the LORD has commanded: 'Let every man gather as much of it as he needs. Take an omer for each person, according to the number of people each of you has in his tent.'"

¹⁷The Israelites did so, and some gathered much [of it] and some [only a] little.

¹⁸When they measured it with an omer, he who had gathered a large amount had no excess, and he who had gathered little had no lack; every man gathered according to his need (family size).

¹⁹Moses said, "Let none of it be left [overnight] until [the next] morning."

²⁰But they did not listen to Moses, and some left a supply of it until morning, and it bred worms and became foul *and* rotten; and Moses was angry with them.

²¹So they gathered it every morning, each as much as he needed, because when the sun was hot it melted.

²²Now on the sixth day they gathered twice as much bread, two omers for each person; and all the leaders of the congregation came and told Moses.

²³He said to them, "This is what the LORD has said: 'Tomorrow is a solemn rest, a holy Sabbath to the LORD'; bake and boil what you will bake and boil [today], and all that remains left over put aside for yourselves to keep until morning."

²⁴They put it aside until morning, as Moses told them, and it did not become foul nor was it wormy.

²⁵Then Moses said, "Eat that today, for today is a Sabbath to the LORD; today you will not find it in the field.

²⁶"Six days you shall gather it, but on the seventh day, the Sabbath, there will be none [in the field]."

²⁷Now on the seventh day some of the people went out to gather, but they found none.

²⁸Then the LORD said to Moses, "How long do you [people] refuse to keep My commandments and My instructions (laws)?

²⁹"See, the LORD has given you the Sabbath; therefore He gives you the bread for two days on the sixth day. Let every man stay in his place; no man is to leave his place on the seventh day."

³⁰So the people rested on the seventh day.

³¹The house of Israel called the bread manna; it was like coriander seed, white, and it tasted like flat pastry (wafers) made with honey.

³²Then Moses said, "This is the word which the LORD commands, 'Let an omer of it be kept throughout your generations, that they may see the bread with which I fed you in the wilderness, when I brought you out of the land of Egypt.'"

³³So Moses said to Aaron, "Take a pot and put an omer of manna in it, and place it before the LORD to be kept throughout your generations."

³⁴As the LORD commanded Moses, so Aaron [eventually] placed it in the presence of the Testimony, to be kept. [Heb 9:4]

³⁵The Israelites ate manna forty years, until they reached an inhabited land; they ate the manna until they came to the border of the land of Canaan.

³⁶(Now an omer is the tenth of an ephah.)

17 THEN ALL the congregation of the children of Israel moved on from the Wilderness of Sin by stages, according to the commandment of the LORD, and camped at Rephidim, but there was no water for the people to drink.

²Therefore the people quarreled with Moses and said, "Give us water so we may [have something to] drink." And Moses said to them, "Why do you quarrel with me? Why do you tempt the LORD *and* try His patience?"

³But the people were thirsty for water; and the people murmured against Moses and said, "Why did you bring us up from Egypt to kill us and our children and our livestock with thirst?"

⁴So Moses cried out to the LORD for help, saying, "What shall I do with this people? They are almost ready to stone me."

⁵Then the LORD said to Moses, "Pass before the people and take with you some of the elders of Israel; and take in your hand the staff with which you struck the Nile, and go.

⁶"Behold, I will stand before you there on the rock at Horeb; there you shall strike the rock, and water will come out of it, so that the people may [have something to] drink." And Moses did so in the sight of the elders of Israel. [1 Cor 10:4]

⁷He named the place [where this miracle occurred] Massah (test) and Meribah (contention) because of the quarreling of the sons of Israel, and because they tested the [patience of the] LORD, saying, "Is the LORD among us, or not?"

⁸Then Amalek [and his people] came and fought with Israel at Rephidim.

⁹So Moses said to Joshua, "Choose men for us and go out, fight against Amalek [and his people]. Tomorrow I will stand on the top of the hill with the staff of God in my hand."

¹⁰So Joshua did as Moses said, and fought with Amalek; and Moses, Aaron, and Hur went up to the hilltop.

¹¹Now when Moses held up his hand, Israel prevailed, and when he lowered his hand [due to fatigue], Amalek prevailed.

¹²But Moses' hands were heavy *and* he grew tired. So they took a stone and put it under him, and he sat on it. Then Aaron and Hur held up his hands, one on one side and one on the other side; so it was that his hands were steady until the sun set.

¹³So Joshua overwhelmed *and* defeated Amalek and his people with the edge of the sword.

¹⁴Then the LORD said to Moses, "Write this in the book as a memorial and recite it to Joshua, that I will utterly wipe out the memory of Amalek [and his people] from under heaven." [1 Sam 15:2–8]

¹⁵And Moses built an altar and named it The LORD Is My Banner;

¹⁶saying, "The LORD has sworn [an oath]; the LORD will have war against [the people of] Amalek from generation to generation."

18 NOW JETHRO (Reuel), the priest of Midian, Moses' father-in-law, heard of all that God had done for Moses and for Israel His people, and that the LORD had brought Israel out of Egypt.

²Then Jethro, Moses' father-in-law,

putting the Word to work

If you are in a position of leadership, do you have people who will be as Aaron and Hur to you, strengthening you when you are weary? If not, ask God to give you people like that in your life.

no one can do everything

Moses was a man with many responsibilities. All day, every day, the Israelites came to him for everything. Wanting to please the people, Moses tried to meet all of their needs. When God told Moses through his father-in-law that his task was too heavy for him, the message came through loud and clear: "The thing that you are doing is not good . . . you cannot do it alone" (Exodus 18:17, 18).

One of the fastest ways for a person to grow weary in ministry is to be a "people-pleaser" rather than a "God-pleaser." For many years, I did everything in my ministry except lead the worship. I taught in all the sessions, and I prayed for sometimes hundreds of people after the meetings. Between sessions I would greet people at the cassette tape table, sign books, and do just about anything that was asked of me, because I was trying to give people everything I thought they wanted. I finally realized if I kept up that frantic pace, it would physically kill me. I quickly learned that God did not anoint my efforts to be a people-pleaser.

People-pleasers have a hard time setting proper boundaries in ministry. But we need to understand that setting limits is wise and is a sign of strength, not weakness. Like Moses, we need to learn that we cannot do it all. We are on the road to burnout if we try to keep everyone happy and do everything we think they want us to do all of the time. Seek to please God alone, and you will experience peace, freedom, and enjoyment you have never known.

took Moses' wife Zipporah, after he had sent her away [from Egypt],

³along with her two sons, of whom one was named Gershom (stranger), for Moses said, "I have been a stranger in a foreign land."

⁴The other [son] was named Eliezer (my God is help), for *Moses said*, "The God of my father was my help, and He rescued me from the sword of Pharaoh."

⁵Then Jethro, his father-in-law, came with Moses' sons and his wife to [join] Moses in the wilderness where he was camped, at the mountain of God [that is, Mt. Sinai in Horeb].

⁶He sent a message to Moses, "I, your father-in-law Jethro, am coming to you with your wife and her two sons [who are] with her."

⁷So Moses went out to meet his father-in-law, and he bowed down [in respect] and kissed him. They asked each other about their well-being and went into the tent.

⁸Moses told his father-in-law about all that the LORD had done to Pharaoh and the Egyptians for Israel's sake, and about all the hardship that had happened during the journey, and how the LORD had rescued them.

⁹Jethro rejoiced over all the good things the LORD had done to Israel, in that He had rescued them from the hand of the Egyptians.

¹⁰Jethro said, "Blessed be the LORD, who has rescued you from the hand of the Egyptians and from the hand of Pharaoh, and who has rescued the people from under the hand of the Egyptians.

¹¹"Now I know that the LORD is greater than all gods; indeed, it was proven when they acted insolently toward Israel [and the LORD showed Himself infinitely superior to all their gods]."

¹²Then Jethro, Moses' father-in-law, took a burnt offering and [other] sacrifices [to offer] to God, and Aaron came with all the elders of Israel to eat a meal with Moses' father-in-law before God.

¹³Now the next day Moses sat to judge [the disputes] the people [had with one another], and the people stood around Moses from dawn to dusk.

¹⁴When Moses' father-in-law saw everything that he was doing for the people, he said, "What is this that you are doing for the people? Why are you sitting alone [as a judge] with all the people standing around you from dawn to dusk?"

life point

When God calls a leader, He not only anoints that person to do a certain work, but He also places and anoints people around the leader to do part of that work. That is the great truth Moses discovered when he learned to delegate some of his work to others. Because Moses heeded the wise counsel of his father-in-law (see Exodus 18:18–22), he was better able to endure the stress of his task, and at the same time others were given the opportunity to grow in leadership.

God places certain people in each of our lives to help us. If we do not receive their help, we can become frustrated and overworked. Likewise, they feel unfulfilled because they are not using their gifts and are unable to develop their own sense of accomplishment.

Do you feel overburdened with the enormity of your task? Are you in danger of falling apart emotionally or physically? Learn to delegate. Let as many people help you as possible. If you do, you will last a lot longer and will enjoy yourself a lot more—and others will be blessed as they find purpose in doing their part. God has created us to be interdependent on one another. We need each other!

¹⁵Moses said to his father-in-law, "Because the people come to me to ask [about the will] of God.

¹⁶"When they have a dispute they come to me, and I judge between a man and his neighbor and I make known the statutes of God and His laws."

¹⁷Moses' father-in-law said to him, "The thing that you are doing is not good.

¹⁸"You will certainly wear out both yourself and these people who are with you, because the task is too heavy for you [to bear]; you cannot do it alone.

¹⁹"Now listen to me; I will advise you, and may God be with you [to confirm my advice]. You shall represent the people before God. You shall bring their disputes *and* causes to Him.

²⁰"You shall teach them the decrees and laws. You shall show them the way they are to live and the work they are to do.

²¹"Furthermore, you shall select from all the people competent men who [reverently] fear God, men of

dealing with overload

Have you ever told God, "I don't know how much longer I can endure this strain"? I have learned an important truth that has helped me keep in balance and avoid anxiety in ministry: God does not have to anoint anything He does not tell me to do. It is true that Jesus is the Author and the Perfecter of my faith (see Hebrews 12:2), but He does not have to finish anything He did not start!

In Exodus 18:23, Moses was told that he would be able to endure the responsibility if he would do what God commanded him. We need to realize that God does not give us more than we can stand or endure. He will give us the ability to perform the assignments He has given us, and we will not have to drag ourselves around, exhausted with stress. Remember, Jesus said He came that we might "have and enjoy life, and have it in abundance [to the full, till it overflows]" (John 10:10). We are out of balance if we think we can do anything, no matter what it is, without God's direction and anointing. Sooner or later we must hear God say, "No, you cannot do just anything. You can do only the part that I have anointed you to do."

Note also in Exodus 18:23 that Moses was told if he followed wise advice, the people would go home in peace. I believe that when God puts people around us who are anointed to help us, they will be frustrated if we do not let them use their gifts. They will have no peace because they are not able to make progress in their own lives. But if we will allow God to use them as He intended, we will be able to stand the strain and they will be happy and fulfilled.

Everyone in a family needs to contribute to making the home a great place to live. If a mother wears herself out trying to do everything herself, she is in danger of feeling that the other family members are taking advantage of her.

Ask for help and realize that when you allow others to help you, they may not do everything exactly the way you would do it, but you need the help more than you need perfection. Look around you. Do you need to make any adjustments in order to keep yourself in balance? If you will make those adjustments as Moses did, then you will have more joy and peace in your life, you will be releasing others to help and minister, and you will be more effective than ever in ministry and in life.

truth, those who hate dishonest gain; you shall place these over the people as leaders of thousands, of hundreds, of fifties and of tens.

²²"They shall judge the people at all times; have them bring every major dispute to you, but let them judge every minor dispute themselves. So it will be easier for you, and they will bear *the burden* with you.

²³"If you will do this thing and God so commands you, then you will be able to endure [the responsibility], and all these people will also go [back] to their tents in peace."

²⁴So Moses listened to his father-in-law and did everything that he had said.

²⁵Moses chose able men from all Israel and made them heads over the people, leaders of thousands, of hundreds, of fifties and of tens [from the highest to the lowest judicial levels].

²⁶And they judged the people at all times; they would bring the difficult cases to Moses, but every minor dispute they judged *and* decided themselves.

²⁷Then Moses said goodbye to his father-in-law, and Jethro went back to his own land (Midian).

19 IN THE third month after the children of Israel had left the land of Egypt, the very same day, they came into the Wilderness of Sinai.

²When they moved out from Rephidim, they came to the Wilderness of Sinai and they camped there; Israel camped at the base of the mountain [of Sinai].

³Moses went up to God [on the mountain], and the Lord called to him from the mountain, saying, "Say this to the house of Jacob and tell the Israelites:

⁴'You have seen what I did to the Egyptians, and how I carried you on eagles' wings, and brought you to Myself.

⁵'Now therefore, if you will in fact obey My voice and keep My covenant (agreement), then you shall be My own special possession *and* treasure from among all peoples [of the world], for all the earth is Mine;

⁶and you shall be to Me a kingdom of priests and a holy nation [set apart for My purpose].' These are the words that you shall speak to the Israelites."

⁷So Moses called for the elders of the people, and told them all these words which the Lord commanded him.

⁸All the people answered together and said, "We will do everything that the Lord has spoken." And Moses reported the words of the people to the Lord.

⁹The Lord said to Moses, "Behold, I will come to you in a thick cloud, so that the people may hear when I speak with you and may believe *and* trust in you forever." Then Moses repeated the words of the people to the Lord.

¹⁰The Lord also said to Moses, "Go to the people and consecrate them today and tomorrow [that is, prepare them for My sacred purpose], and have them wash their clothes

¹¹and be ready by the third day, because on the third day the Lord will come down on Mount Sinai [in the cloud] in the sight of all the people.

¹²"You shall set barriers for the people all around [the mountain], saying, 'Beware that you do not go up on the mountain or touch its border; whoever touches the mountain must be put to death.

¹³'No hand shall touch him [that is, no one shall try to save the guilty party], but the offender must be stoned or shot through [with arrows]; whether man or animal [that touches the mountain], he shall not live.' When the ram's horn sounds a long blast, they shall come up to the mountain." [Num 24:8]

¹⁴So Moses went down from the mountain to the people and sanctified them [for God's sacred purpose], and they washed their clothes.

¹⁵He said to the people, "Be prepared for the third day; do not be intimate with a woman."

¹⁶So it happened on the third day, when it was morning, that there were thunder and flashes of lightning, and a thick cloud was on the mountain, and a very loud blast was sounded on a ram's horn, so that all the people who were in the camp trembled. ¹⁷Then Moses brought the people out of the camp to meet God, and they stood *and* presented themselves at the foot of the mountain. ¹⁸Mount Sinai was wrapped in smoke because the LORD descended upon it in fire; its smoke ascended like the smoke of a furnace, and the whole mountain quaked violently. ¹⁹And it happened, as the blast of the ram's horn grew louder and louder, Moses spoke and God answered him with [a voice of] thunder. [Deut 4:12] ²⁰The LORD came down on Mount Sinai, to the top of the mountain; and the LORD called Moses to the top of the mountain, and he went up. ²¹Then the LORD spoke to Moses, "Go down, warn the people, so that they do not break through [the barriers around the mountain] to the LORD to see [Me], and many of them perish [as a result]. ²²"Also have the priests who approach the LORD consecrate (sanctify, set apart) themselves [for My sacred purpose], or else the LORD will break forth [in judgment] against them [and destroy them]."

²³Moses said to the LORD, "The people cannot come up to Mount Sinai, because You warned us, saying, 'Set barriers around the mountain and consecrate it.'"

²⁴Then the LORD said to him, "Go down and come up again, you and Aaron with you; but do not let the priests and the people break through [the barriers] to come up to the LORD, or He will break forth [in judgment] against them [and destroy them]."

²⁵So Moses went down to the people and told them [again about God's warning].

20 THEN GOD spoke all these words:

²"I am the LORD your God, who has brought you out of the land of Egypt, out of the house of slavery.

³"You shall have no other gods before Me.

⁴"You shall not make for yourself any idol, or any likeness (form, manifestation) of what is in heaven above or on the earth beneath or in the water under the earth [as an object to worship].

⁵"You shall not worship them nor serve them; for I, the LORD your God, am a jealous (impassioned) God [demanding what is rightfully and uniquely mine], visiting (avenging) the iniquity (sin, guilt) of the fathers on the children [that is, calling the children to account

speak the Word

Lord, I know that You are a jealous God, and I declare that I will not worship nor serve anyone or anything but You.
−ADAPTED FROM EXODUS 20:5

Thank You, God, that You show graciousness and steadfast loving-kindness to me and to thousands of generations of those who love You and keep Your commandments.
−ADAPTED FROM EXODUS 20:6

for the sins of their fathers], to the third and fourth generations of those who hate Me, [Is 42:8; 48:11]

⁶but showing graciousness *and* steadfast lovingkindness to thousands [of generations] of those who love Me and keep My commandments.

⁷"You shall not take the name of the LORD your God in vain [that is, irreverently, in false affirmations or in ways that impugn the character of God]; for the LORD will not hold guiltless *nor* leave unpunished the one who takes His name in vain [disregarding its reverence and its power].

⁸"Remember the Sabbath (seventh) day to keep it holy (set apart, dedicated to God).

⁹"Six days you shall labor and do all your work,

¹⁰but the seventh day is a Sabbath [a day of rest dedicated] to the LORD your God; on that day you shall not do any

work, you or your son, or your daughter, or your male servant, or your female servant, or your livestock or the temporary resident (foreigner) who stays within your [city] gates.

¹¹"For in six days the LORD made the heavens and the earth, the sea and everything that is in them, and He rested (ceased) on the seventh day. That is why the LORD blessed the Sabbath day and made it holy [that is, set it apart for His purposes].

¹²"Honor (respect, obey, care for) your father and your mother, so that your days may be prolonged in the land the LORD your God gives you.

¹³"You shall not commit murder (unjustified, deliberate homicide). [Gen 9:6; Ex 21:12, 14, 18]

¹⁴"You shall not commit adultery. [Prov 6:25, 26; Matt 5:27, 28; Rom 1:24; Eph 5:3]

¹⁵"You shall not steal [secretly,

speak God's name with purpose

Do you want to see the power of God released when you speak His name? Then it is important not to take His name lightly or frivolously. I had always thought that to "take the Lord's name in vain" meant to attach a curse word to His name. But it is so much more than that alone. To take the Lord's name in vain means to speak His name in such a way that our words are useless, fruitless, foolish, or irreverent. This sometimes happens when we casually use His name as a verbal exclamation. Let me explain.

The Holy Spirit convicted me early in my walk with the Lord that I had a habit that actually was causing me to break the third commandment (see Exodus 20:7), but I had been deceived and did not even realize I was doing it. I used to say things like "Oh, my God" when I saw something shocking or heard surprising news—even when I dropped something or when one of the children broke something. The Lord revealed to me that His name is more than just a phrase, and when I realized that, I was grieved in my heart and repented thoroughly.

The name of the Lord represents awesome power, and we need to reverently fear it (see Malachi 1:14). I believe the church has lost many things because it has lost reverence for God. It is vital that we return to a reverential fear and awe of God, His name, and His work. We need to have such respect for the Lord and all of His expressive names that we are very careful not to speak any of those holy names without purpose. Ask God to reveal to you the power and weight of His name, and when you do use it, honor it and remember how awesome it is.

openly, fraudulently, or through carelessness]. [Prov 11:1; 16:8; 21:6; 22:16; Jer 17:11; Mal 3:8]

¹⁶"You shall not testify falsely [that is, lie, withhold, or manipulate the truth] against your neighbor (any person). [Ex 23:1; Prov 19:9; 24:28]

¹⁷"You shall not covet [that is, selfishly desire and attempt to acquire] your neighbor's house; you shall not covet your neighbor's wife, or his male servant, or his female servant, or his ox, or his donkey, or anything that belongs to your neighbor." [Luke 12:15; Col 3:5]

¹⁸Now all the people witnessed the thunder and the flashes of lightning and the sound of the trumpet and the smoking mountain; and as they looked, the people were afraid, and they trembled [and moved backward] and stood at a [safe] distance.

¹⁹Then they said to Moses, "You speak to us and we will listen, but do not let God speak to us or we will die."

²⁰Moses said to the people, "Do not be afraid; for God has come in order to test you, and in order that the fear of Him [that is, a profound reverence for Him] will remain with you, so that you do not sin."

²¹So the people stood at a [safe] distance, but Moses approached the thick cloud where God was.

²²Then the Lord said to Moses, "Thus you shall say to the Israelites, 'You have seen for yourselves that I have spoken to you from heaven.

²³'You shall not make *other gods* [to worship] besides Me; gods of silver or gods of gold, you shall not make [these lifeless idols] for yourselves.

²⁴'You shall make an altar of earth for Me, and sacrifice on it your burnt offerings and your peace offerings, your sheep and your oxen. In every place where I cause My Name to be recorded *and* remembered [through revelation of My divine nature] I will come to you and bless you.

²⁵'If you make an altar of stone for Me, you shall not build it of cut stones, for if you use a chisel on it, you will profane it.

²⁶'Nor shall you go up to My altar on steps, so that your nakedness will not be exposed on it.'

21 "NOW THESE are the ordinances (laws) which you shall set before the Israelites:

²"If you purchase a Hebrew servant [because of his debt or poverty], he shall serve six years, and in the seventh [year] he shall leave as a free man, paying nothing. [Lev 25:39]

³"If he came [to you] alone, he shall leave alone; if he came married, then his wife shall leave with him.

⁴"If his master gives him a wife, and she gives birth to sons or daughters, the wife and her children shall belong to her master, and he shall leave [your service] alone.

⁵"But if the servant plainly says, 'I love my master, my wife and my children; I will not leave as a free man,'

⁶then his master shall bring him to God [that is, to the judges who act in God's name], then he shall bring him to the door or doorpost. And his master shall pierce his ear with an awl (strong needle); and he shall serve him for life.

⁷"If a man sells his daughter to be a female servant, she shall not go free [after six years] as male servants do.

⁸"If she does not please her master who has chosen her for himself [as a wife], he shall let her be redeemed [by her family]. He does not have the authority to sell her to a foreign people, because he has been unfair to her.

⁹"If her master chooses her [as a wife] for his son, he shall act toward her as if she were legally his daughter.

¹⁰"If her master marries another wife, he may not reduce her food, her clothing, or her privilege as a wife.

¹¹"If he does not do these three things for her, then shall she leave free, without *payment of* money.

¹²"Whoever strikes a man so that he dies must be put to death.

¹³"However, if he did not lie in wait [for him], but God allowed him to fall into his hand, then I will establish for you a place to which he may escape [for protection until duly tried]. [Num 35:22–28]

¹⁴"But if a man acts intentionally against another and kills him by [design through] treachery, you are to take him from My altar [to which he may have fled for protection], so that he may be put to death.

¹⁵"Whoever strikes his father or his mother must be put to death.

¹⁶"Whoever kidnaps a man, whether he sells him or is found with him in his possession, must be put to death.

¹⁷"Whoever curses his father or his mother *or* treats them contemptuously must be put to death.

¹⁸"If men quarrel and one strikes another with a stone or with his fist, and he does not die but is confined to bed,

¹⁹if he gets up and walks around leaning on his cane, then the one who struck him shall be left [physically] unpunished; he must only pay for his loss of time [at work], and the costs [of treatment and recuperation] until he is thoroughly healed.

²⁰"If a man strikes his male or his female servant with a staff and the servant dies at his hand, he must be punished.

²¹"If, however, the servant survives for a day or two, the offender shall not be punished, for the [injured] servant is his own property.

²²"If men fight with each other and injure a pregnant woman so that she gives birth prematurely [and the baby lives], yet there is no *further* injury, the one who hurt her must be punished

with a fine [paid] to the woman's husband, as much as the judges decide.

²³"But if there is *any further* injury, then you shall require [as a penalty] life for life,

²⁴eye for eye, tooth for tooth, hand for hand, foot for foot,

²⁵burn for burn, wound for wound, bruise for bruise.

²⁶"If a man hits the eye of his male servant or female servant and it is destroyed, he must let the servant go free because of [the loss of] the eye.

²⁷"And if he knocks out the tooth of his male servant or female servant, he must let the servant go free because of [the loss of] the tooth.

²⁸"If an ox gores a man or a woman to death, the ox must be stoned and its meat shall not be eaten; but the owner of the ox shall be cleared [of responsibility].

²⁹"But if the ox has tried to gore on a previous occasion, and its owner has been warned, but has not kept it confined and it kills a man or a woman, the ox shall be stoned and its owner shall be put to death as well.

³⁰"If a ransom is demanded of him [in return for his life], then he shall give whatever is demanded for the redemption of his life.

³¹"If the ox has gored another's son or daughter, he shall be dealt with according to this same rule.

³²"If the ox gores a male or a female servant, the owner shall give to the servant's master thirty shekels of silver [the purchase price for a slave], and the ox shall be stoned.

³³"If a man leaves a pit open, or digs a pit and does not cover it, and an ox or a donkey falls into it,

³⁴the owner of the pit shall make restitution; he shall give money to the animal's owner, but the dead [animal] shall be his.

³⁵"If one man's ox injures another's so that it dies, then they shall sell

the live ox and divide the proceeds equally; they shall also divide the dead ox [between them].

36"Or if it is known that the ox was previously in the habit of goring, and its owner has not kept it confined, he must make restitution of ox for ox, and the dead [animal] shall be his.

22 "IF A man steals an ox or sheep and kills or sells it, he shall make restitution of five oxen for an ox or four sheep for a sheep.

2"If a thief is caught breaking in [after dark] and is struck [by the owner] so that he dies, there shall be no bloodguilt for him.

3"But if the sun has risen, there will be bloodguilt for him. The thief [if he lives] must make [full] restitution; if he has nothing, then he shall be sold [as a slave to make restitution] for his theft.

4"If the animal that he stole is found alive in his possession, whether it is ox or donkey or sheep, he shall pay double [for it].

5"If a man causes a field or vineyard to be grazed bare or lets his livestock loose so that it grazes in another man's field, he shall make restitution from the best of his own field and the best of his own vineyard.

6"If fire breaks out and spreads to thorn bushes so that the stacked grain or standing grain or the field is consumed, he who started the fire shall make full restitution.

7"If a man gives his neighbor money or [other] goods to keep [for him while he is away] and it is stolen from the neighbor's house, then, if the thief is caught, he shall pay double [for it].

8"If the thief is not caught, the owner of the house shall appear before the judges [who act in God's name], to determine whether or not he had stolen his neighbor's goods.

9"For every offense involving property, whether it concerns ox, donkey, sheep, clothing, or any piece of lost property, which another identifies as his, the case of both parties shall come before the judges [who act in God's name]. Whomever the judges pronounce guilty shall pay double to his neighbor.

10"If a man gives his neighbor a donkey or an ox or a sheep or any [other] animal to keep [for him], and it dies or is injured or taken away while no one is looking,

11then an oath before the LORD shall be made by the two of them that he has not taken his neighbor's property; and the owner of it shall accept his word and not require him to make restitution.

12"But if it is actually stolen from him [when in his care], he shall make restitution to its owner.

13"If it is torn to pieces [by some predator or by accident], let him bring the mangled carcass as evidence; he shall not make restitution for what was torn to pieces.

14"And if a man borrows an animal from his neighbor, and it gets injured or dies while its owner is not with it, the borrower shall make full restitution.

15"But if the owner is with it [when the damage is done], the borrower shall not make restitution. If it was hired, the damage is included in [the price of] its fee.

16"If a man seduces a virgin who is not betrothed, and lies with her, he must pay a dowry (marriage price) for her to be his wife.

17"If her father absolutely refuses to give her to him, he must [still] pay money equivalent to the dowry of virgins.

18"You shall not allow a woman who practices sorcery to live.

19"Whoever lies with an animal must be put to death. [Lev 18:23]

²⁰"He who sacrifices to any god, other than to the LORD alone, shall be put under a ban (designated) for destruction (execution).

²¹"You shall not wrong a stranger or oppress him, for you were strangers in the land of Egypt.

²²"You shall not harm or oppress any widow or fatherless child.

²³"If you harm or oppress them in any way, and they cry at all to Me [for help], I will most certainly hear their cry;

²⁴and My wrath shall be kindled and burn; I will kill you with the sword, and your wives shall become widows and your children fatherless.

²⁵"If you lend money to any one of My people with you who is poor, you shall not act as a creditor (professional moneylender) to him; you shall not charge him interest.

²⁶"If you ever take your [poor] neighbor's robe in pledge, you must return it to him before sunset,

²⁷for that is his only covering; it is his clothing for his body. In what shall he sleep? And when he cries to Me [for help], I will hear him, for I am compassionate and gracious.

²⁸"You shall not curse God, nor curse the ruler of your people [since he administers God's law]. [Acts 23:5]

²⁹"You shall not delay the offering from your harvest and your vintage. You shall give (consecrate, dedicate) to Me the firstborn of your sons. [Ex 34:19, 20]

³⁰"You shall do the same with your oxen and with your sheep. It shall be with its mother for seven days; on the eighth day you shall give it [as an offering] to Me.

³¹"You shall be holy men to Me; therefore you shall not eat meat [from any animal] that has been torn to pieces [by predators] in the field; you shall throw it to the dogs.

23 "YOU SHALL not give a false report; you shall not join hands with the wicked to be a malicious witness [promoting wrong and violence].

²"You shall not follow a crowd to do [something] evil, nor shall you testify at a trial or in a dispute so as to side with a crowd in order to pervert justice;

³nor shall you favor or be partial to a poor man in his dispute [simply because he is poor].

⁴"If you meet your enemy's ox or his donkey wandering off, you must bring it back to him.

⁵"If you see the donkey of one who hates you lying helpless under its load, you shall not leave the man to deal with it [alone]; you must help him release the animal [from its burden].

⁶"You shall not pervert (bend) the justice due to your poor in his dispute.

⁷"Keep far away from a false charge or action, and do not condemn to death the innocent or the righteous, for I will not justify and acquit the guilty.

⁸"You shall not accept a bribe, for a bribe blinds the clear-sighted and subverts the testimony and the cause of the righteous.

⁹"You shall not oppress a stranger, for you know the soul [the feelings, thoughts, and concerns] of a stranger, for you were strangers in Egypt.

¹⁰"You shall sow your land six years and harvest its yield,

¹¹but the seventh year you shall let it rest and lie uncultivated, so that the poor among your people may eat [what the land grows naturally]; whatever they leave the animals of the field may eat. You shall do the same with your vineyard and olive grove.

¹²"Six days [each week] you shall do your work, but on the seventh day you shall stop [working] so that your ox and your donkey may settle down and rest, and the son of your female servant, as well as your stranger, may be refreshed.

¹³"Now concerning everything which I have said to you, be on your guard; do not mention the name of other gods [either in a blessing or in a curse]; do not let such speech be heard [coming] from your mouth.

¹⁴"Three times a year you shall celebrate a feast [dedicated] to Me.

¹⁵"You shall observe the Feast of Unleavened Bread; for seven days you shall eat unleavened bread, as I commanded you, at the appointed time in the month of Abib, for in it you came out of Egypt. No one shall appear before Me empty-handed [but you shall bring sacrificial offerings].

¹⁶"Also [you shall observe] the Feast of Harvest (Weeks, Pentecost, or First Fruits), acknowledging the first fruits of your labor, of what you sow in the field. And [third] the Feast of Ingathering (Booths or Tabernacles) at the end of the year when you gather in [the fruit of] your labors from the field.

¹⁷"Three times a year all your males shall appear before the Lord GOD.

¹⁸"You shall not offer the blood of My sacrifice with leavened bread; and the fat of My feast is not to be left overnight until morning.

¹⁹"You shall bring the choice first fruits of your ground into the house of the LORD your God.

"You shall not boil a young goat in its mother's milk.

²⁰"Behold, I am going to send an Angel before you to keep *and* guard you on the way and to bring you to the place I have prepared.

²¹"Be on your guard before Him, listen to *and* obey His voice; do not be rebellious toward Him *or* provoke Him, for He will not pardon your transgression, since My Name (authority) is in Him. [Ex 32:34; 33:14; Is 63:9]

²²"But if you will indeed listen to *and* truly obey His voice and do everything that I say, then I will be an enemy to your enemies and an adversary to your adversaries.

²³"When My Angel goes before you and brings you to [the land of] the Amorite, the Hittite, the Perizzite, the Canaanite, the Hivite, and the Jebusite, I will reject them *and* completely destroy them.

²⁴"You shall not bow down to worship their gods, nor serve them, nor do [anything] in accordance with their practices. You shall completely overthrow them and break down their [sacred] pillars *and* images [of pagan worship].

²⁵"You shall serve [only] the LORD your God, and He shall bless your bread and water. I will also remove sickness from among you.

²⁶"No one shall suffer miscarriage or be barren in your land; I will fulfill the number of your days.

²⁷"I will send My terror ahead of you, and I will throw into confusion all the people among whom you come, and I will make all your enemies turn their backs to you [in flight].

speak the Word

Thank You, God, for sending angels ahead of me to keep me and guard me on my way.
—ADAPTED FROM EXODUS 23:20

God, I thank You for driving out my enemies from before me little by little, until I am strong enough to take possession of everything You have for me.
—ADAPTED FROM EXODUS 23:30

²⁸"I will send hornets ahead of you which shall drive out the Hivite, the Canaanite, and the Hittite before you.

²⁹"I will not drive them out before you in a single year, so that the land does not become desolate [due to lack of attention] and the [wild] animals of the field do not become too numerous for you.

³⁰"I will drive them out before you little by little, until you have increased and are strong enough to take possession of the land.

³¹"I will establish your borders from the Red Sea to the Sea of the Philistines (the Mediterranean), and from the wilderness to the River *Euphrates;* for I will hand over the residents of the land to you, and you shall drive them out before you.

³²"You shall not make a covenant with them or with their gods.

³³"They shall not live in your land, because they will make you sin against Me; for if you serve their gods, it is certain to be a trap for you [resulting in judgment]."

24 THEN GOD said to Moses, "Come up to the LORD, you and Aaron, Nadab and Abihu (Aaron's older sons), and seventy of Israel's elders, and you shall worship at a [safe] distance.

²"Moses alone shall approach the LORD, but the others shall not come near, nor shall the people come up with him."

³Then Moses came and told the people everything that the LORD had said and all the ordinances. And all the people answered with one voice, "Everything the LORD has said we will do."

⁴Moses wrote down all the words of the LORD. Then he got up early in the morning, and built an altar [for worship] at the foot of the mountain with twelve pillars (memorial stones) representing the twelve tribes of Israel.

⁵Then he sent young Israelite men, and they offered burnt offerings and sacrificed young bulls as peace offerings to the LORD.

⁶Moses took half of the blood and put it in large basins, and [the other] half of the blood he sprinkled on the altar.

⁷Then he took the Book of the Covenant and read it aloud to the people; and they said, "Everything that the LORD has said we will do, and we will be obedient."

⁸So Moses took the blood [which had been placed in the large basins] and sprinkled it on the people, and said, "Behold the blood of the covenant, which the LORD has made with you in accordance with all these words." [1 Cor 11:25; Heb 8:6; 10:28, 29]

⁹Then Moses, Aaron, Nadab, and Abihu, and seventy of the elders of Israel went up [the mountainside],

¹⁰and they saw [a manifestation of] the God of Israel; and under His feet there appeared to be a pavement of sapphire, just as clear as the sky itself. [Ex 33:20–23; Deut 4:12; Ezek 28:14]

¹¹Yet He did not stretch out His hand against the nobles of the Israelites; and they saw [the manifestation of the presence of] God, and ate and drank. [Ex 19:21]

¹²Now the LORD said to Moses, "Come up to Me on the mountain and stay there, and I will give you the stone tablets with the law and the commandments which I have written for their instruction." [2 Cor 3:2, 3]

¹³So Moses arose with Joshua his

speak the Word

God, I declare as the Israelites did: Everything that You have said, I will do.
–ADAPTED FROM EXODUS 24:3

attendant, and he went up to the mountain of God.

¹⁴And he said to the elders, "Wait here for us until we come back to you. Remember that Aaron and Hur are with you; whoever has a legal matter, let him go to them."

¹⁵Then Moses went up to the mountain, and the cloud covered the mountain.

¹⁶The glory *and* brilliance of the LORD rested on Mount Sinai, and the cloud covered it for six days. On the seventh day God called to Moses from the midst of the cloud.

¹⁷In the sight of the Israelites the appearance of the glory *and* brilliance of the LORD was like consuming fire on the top of the mountain.

¹⁸Moses entered the midst of the cloud and went up the mountain; and he was on the mountain forty days and forty nights.

25 THEN THE LORD spoke to Moses, saying, ²"Tell the children of Israel to take an offering for Me. From every man whose heart moves him [to give willingly] you shall take My offering.

check your "want to"

In Exodus 25:1, 2, we read about giving from a willing heart. Giving to God willingly and ungrudgingly basically boils down to whether or not we desire to give. I call this attitude our "want to," and I believe without it, we will never do anything significant.

Throughout many years of ministry I have had to press through a lot of negative things. Yes, I have a call from God on my life, but I need something in addition to His call. I need to have a lot of "want to." Another word for that is passion. It is the thing that motivates us to work hard and make sacrifices with a good attitude.

"Want to" is a powerful thing. With it we can do a job well, lose weight, keep our houses clean, save money, get out of debt, or reach any other goal in life. We do not like to face the fact that our victory or defeat is connected to our "want to." We are often really good at laying the blame for our failures on someone or something else. We like to blame the devil, other people, the past, and on and on, when usually the bottom line is that we do not have enough of the right kind of "want to."

We really need to recognize that we end up doing what we want to do in life. If we have a strong desire to do something, we will somehow find a way to do it. Many of us need to sit down and take a good old-fashioned inventory of our "want to." We should be honest enough to admit, "Lord, I didn't win the victory because I really didn't want to. I didn't pray or read the Bible because I didn't want to. I didn't spend time meditating on the Word and talking with You because I didn't want to. Instead, I sat around all night on the couch watching television because I wanted to." There is nothing wrong with rest and entertainment, but we need to keep our priorities right.

Taking full responsibility for our lives is difficult emotionally, but we should remember that only "the truth" sets us free (see John 8:32).

If you and I are going to serve God and be examples to others, we need to have sanctified "want to." God is not interested in our good works if we are not doing them with a willing heart. Ask God to give you His desires and cause you to want what He wants.

³"This is the offering you are to receive from them: gold, silver, and bronze,

⁴blue, purple, and scarlet fabric, fine twisted linen, goats' *hair,*

⁵rams' skins dyed red, porpoise skins, acacia wood,

⁶[olive] oil for lighting, balsam for the anointing oil and for the fragrant incense,

⁷onyx stones and setting stones for the [priest's] ephod and for the breastpiece.

⁸"Have them build a sanctuary for Me, so that I may dwell among them. [Heb 8:1, 2; 10:1]

⁹"You shall construct it in accordance with everything that I am going to show you, as the pattern of the tabernacle and the pattern of all its furniture.

¹⁰"They shall make an ark of acacia wood two and a half cubits long, one and a half cubits wide, and one and a half cubits high.

¹¹"You shall overlay the ark with pure gold, overlay it inside and out, and you shall make a gold border (frame) around its top.

¹²"You shall cast four gold rings for it and attach them to the four feet, two rings on either side.

¹³"You shall make [carrying] poles of acacia wood and overlay them with gold,

¹⁴and put the poles through the rings on the sides of the ark, by which to carry it.

¹⁵"The poles shall remain in the rings of the ark; they shall not be removed from it [so that the ark itself need not be touched].

¹⁶"You shall put into the ark the Testimony (Ten Commandments) which I will give you.

¹⁷"You shall make a mercy seat (cover) of pure gold, two and a half cubits long and one and a half cubits wide.

¹⁸"You shall make two cherubim (winged angelic figures) of [solid] hammered gold at the two ends of the mercy seat.

¹⁹"Make one cherub at each end, making the cherubim *of one piece* with the mercy seat at its two ends.

²⁰"The cherubim shall have their wings spread upward, covering the mercy seat with their wings and facing each other. The faces of the cherubim are to be *looking downward* toward the mercy seat.

²¹"You shall put the mercy seat on the top of the ark, and in the ark you shall put the Testimony which I will give you.

²²"There I will meet with you; from above the mercy seat, from between the two cherubim which are on the ark of the Testimony, I will speak [intimately] with you regarding every commandment that I will give you for the Israelites.

²³"You shall make a table of acacia wood, two cubits long, one cubit wide, and one and a half cubits high.

²⁴"You shall overlay it with pure gold and make a border of gold around the top of it.

²⁵"You shall make a rim of a hand width around it; you shall make a gold border for the rim around it.

²⁶"You shall make four gold rings for it and fasten them at the four corners that are on the table's four legs.

²⁷"The rings shall be close against the rim as holders for the poles to carry the table.

²⁸"You shall make the poles of acacia wood and overlay them with gold, so that the table may be carried with them.

²⁹"You shall make its plates [for the showbread] and its cups [for incense] and its pitchers and bowls for sacrificial drink offerings; you shall make them of pure gold.

³⁰"You shall set the bread of the Presence (showbread) on the table before Me at all times. [John 6:58]

31"You shall make a lampstand of pure gold. The lampstand and its base and its shaft shall be made of hammered work; its cups, its calyxes and its flowers shall be *all of one piece* with it.

32"Six branches shall come out of its sides; three branches of the lampstand out of the one side and three branches of the lampstand out of its other side [the shaft being the seventh branch].

33"Three cups shall be made like almond *blossoms,* each with a calyx and a flower on one branch, and three cups made like almond *blossoms* on the other branch with a calyx and a flower—so for the six branches coming out of the lampstand;

34and in the [center shaft of the] lampstand [you shall make] four cups shaped like almond *blossoms,* with their calyxes and their flowers.

35"A calyx shall be under the *first* pair of branches coming out of it, and a calyx under the *second* pair of branches coming out of it, and a calyx under the *third* pair of branches coming out of it, for the six branches coming out of the lampstand.

36"Their calyxes and their branches *shall be of one piece* with it; all of it shall be one piece of hammered work of pure gold.

37"Then you shall make the lamps [of the lampstand] seven *in number* [with one lamp at the top of the shaft]. The priests shall set up its *seven* lamps so that they will light the space in front of it.

38"Its snuffers and their trays shall be of pure gold.

39"It shall be made from a talent (50–80 lbs.) of pure gold, including all these utensils.

40"See that you make them [exactly] after their pattern which was shown to you on the mountain. [Heb 8:5, 6]

26 "MOREOVER, YOU shall make the tabernacle (sacred tent of worship) with ten [interior] curtains of fine twisted linen, and blue, purple, and scarlet fabric; you shall make them with [embroidered] cherubim, the handwork of a skillful craftsman.

2"The length of each curtain shall be twenty-eight cubits, and the width of each curtain four cubits; all of the curtains shall measure the same.

3"The five curtains shall be joined to one another, and *the other* five curtains shall be joined to one another.

4"You shall make loops of blue on the *outer* edge of the last curtain in the *first* set, and likewise in the second set.

5"You shall make fifty loops on the one curtain, and fifty loops on the edge of the *last* curtain that is in the second set. The loops on one curtain correspond to the loops on the other.

6"You shall make fifty gold hooks, and fasten the curtains together with the hooks; and the tabernacle shall be one unit.

7"Then you shall make [exterior] curtains of goats' *hair* as a tent over the tabernacle. You shall make eleven curtains in all.

8"Each curtain shall be thirty cubits long and four cubits wide. The eleven curtains shall all measure the same.

9"You shall join five curtains by themselves and the *other* six curtains by themselves, and you shall double over the sixth curtain at the front of the tent [to make a closed door].

10"Make fifty loops on the edge of the outermost curtain in the *first* set, and fifty loops on the edge of the *outermost* curtain in the second set.

11"You shall make fifty bronze hooks and put the hooks into the loops and join the tent together so that it may be one unit.

12"The overlapping part that is left over from the tent curtains, the half curtain that is left over, shall lap over the back of the tabernacle.

¹³"The cubit on one side and the cubit on the other, of what is left over in the length of the curtains of the tent shall lap over the sides of the tabernacle on one side and the other side, to cover it.

¹⁴"You shall make a *third* covering for the tent of rams' skins dyed red, and a *fourth* covering above that of porpoise skins.

¹⁵"Then you shall make the boards for the tabernacle of acacia wood, standing upright [as a trellis-like frame].

¹⁶"The length of each board shall be ten cubits and the width of each board shall be one and a half cubits.

¹⁷"Make two dovetails in each board for fitting [them] together; you shall do the same for all the tabernacle boards.

¹⁸"You shall make the boards for the tabernacle [in the following quantities]: twenty boards for the south side.

¹⁹"You shall make forty silver sockets under the twenty boards, two sockets under each board for its two dovetails, and two sockets under another board for its two dovetails;

²⁰for the north side of the tabernacle there shall be twenty boards,

²¹and their forty silver sockets, two sockets under each board.

²²"For the back or west side of the tabernacle you shall make six boards.

²³"Make two boards for the corners of the tabernacle at the rear [on both sides].

²⁴"They shall be joined together underneath, and joined together on top with one ring. So shall it be for both of them; they shall form the two [rear] corners.

²⁵"There shall be eight boards and sixteen silver sockets; two sockets under each board.

²⁶"Then you shall make [fifteen] bars of acacia wood: five for the boards of one side of the tabernacle,

²⁷and five bars for the boards of the other side of the tabernacle, and five bars for the boards of the rear end of the tabernacle, for the back wall toward the west.

²⁸"And the middle bar in the center of the boards shall pass through [horizontally] from end to end.

²⁹"You shall overlay the boards with gold and make their rings of gold to hold the bars. You shall overlay the bars with gold.

³⁰"You shall erect the tabernacle according to its plan [the direction corresponding to its meaning and purpose] which has been shown to you on the mountain.

³¹"You shall make a veil [to divide the two rooms] of blue, purple, and scarlet fabric and fine twisted linen, skillfully worked with cherubim on it.

³²"You shall hang it on four pillars (support poles) of acacia wood overlaid with gold, with gold hooks, on four silver sockets.

³³"You shall hang the veil from the hooks [that connect the curtains together], and you shall bring the ark of the Testimony there within the veil. The veil shall separate for you the Holy Place and the Holy of Holies.

³⁴"You shall put the mercy seat on the ark of the Testimony in the Holy of Holies.

³⁵"You shall set the table [for the bread] outside the veil [in the Holy Place] on the north side, and the lampstand opposite the table on the south side of the tabernacle.

³⁶"You shall make a screen [to provide a covering] for the doorway of the tent of blue, purple, and scarlet fabric and finely woven [embroidered] linen, the work of an embroiderer. [John 10:9]

³⁷"You shall make five pillars (support poles) of acacia wood to support the hanging curtain and overlay them with gold. Their hooks shall be of gold, and you shall cast five [base] sockets of bronze for them.

27

"AND YOU shall make the altar [for burnt offerings] of acacia wood, five cubits long and five cubits wide; the altar shall be square, and its height shall be three cubits.

²"Make horns (horn-shaped projections) for it on its four corners; the horns shall be of one piece with it, and you shall overlay it with bronze.

³"You shall make pots to remove its ashes, and shovels, basins [to catch the blood of the sacrificed animal], meat-forks, and firepans [to store live coals]. You shall make all its utensils of bronze.

⁴"Also make a grate for it, a network of bronze; and on the grid you are to make four bronze rings at its four corners.

⁵"And you shall put it under the ledge of the altar, so that the grid will extend halfway up the altar.

⁶"You shall make [carrying] poles for the altar, poles of acacia wood, overlaid with bronze.

⁷"The poles shall be inserted through the rings on the two sides of the altar so that it may be carried. [Num 4:14, 15]

⁸"You are to make the altar hollow with planks; as you were shown on the mountain [of Sinai], so shall it be made.

⁹"You shall make the court of the tabernacle. The south side of the court is to have curtains of fine twisted linen, a hundred cubits long for one side;

¹⁰it shall have twenty pillars and twenty bronze sockets; but the hooks of the pillars and their fasteners shall be silver;

¹¹likewise for the north side there shall be curtains, a hundred *cubits* long, and its twenty pillars and twenty bronze sockets; but the hooks of the pillars and their fasteners shall be silver.

¹²"For the width of the court on the west side there shall be curtains of fifty cubits, with ten pillars (support poles) and ten sockets.

¹³"The width of the court [to the front], on the east side shall be fifty cubits.

¹⁴"The curtains for one side [of the gate] shall be fifteen cubits with three pillars and three sockets.

¹⁵"On the other side [of the gate] the curtains shall be fifteen cubits with three pillars and three sockets.

¹⁶"For the gate of the court there shall be a screen [to provide a covering] of twenty cubits, of blue, purple, and scarlet fabric and finely woven [embroidered] linen, the work of an embroiderer, with four pillars and four [base] sockets.

¹⁷"All the pillars (support poles) around the court shall be joined together with silver rods; their hooks shall be of silver and their sockets of bronze.

¹⁸"The length of the court shall be a hundred cubits, and the width fifty [cubits] throughout, and the height five cubits of fine twisted linen, and their sockets of bronze.

¹⁹"All the tabernacle's utensils *and* instruments used in all its service, and all its stakes, and all the stakes for the court, shall be of bronze.

²⁰"You shall command the Israelites to provide you with clear oil of beaten olives for the light, to make a lamp burn continually [every night].

²¹"In the Tent of Meeting [of God with His people], outside the veil which is in front of the [ark of the] Testimony [and sets it apart], Aaron [the high priest] and his sons shall keep the lamp burning from evening to morning before the LORD. It shall be a perpetual statute [to be observed] throughout their generations on behalf of the Israelites.

28

"NOW BRING your brother Aaron near, and his sons with him from among the sons of Israel, so that he may serve as priest to Me—Aaron, Nadab and Abihu, Eleazar and Ithamar, Aaron's sons.

2"You are to make sacred garments [official clothing reserved for holy services] for Aaron your brother, for honor and for beauty (ornamentation).

3"Tell all the skilled *and* talented people whom I have endowed with a spirit of wisdom, that they are to make Aaron's garments to sanctify him *and* set him apart to serve as a priest for Me.

4"These are the garments which they shall make: a breastpiece and an ephod [for the breastpiece] and a robe and a tunic of checkered work, a turban, and a sash. They shall make sacred garments for Aaron your brother and his sons, so that he may serve as a priest to Me.

5"They are to use the gold and the blue and the purple and the scarlet fabric and fine twisted linen [from the people],

6and they shall make the ephod of gold and blue, purple, and scarlet fabric and fine twisted linen, skillfully woven *and* [beautifully] worked.

7"It is to have two shoulder pieces joined to its two [back and front] ends, so that it may be joined together.

8"And the skillfully woven sash, which is on the ephod shall be made of the same material: of gold, of blue, purple, and scarlet fabric and fine twisted linen.

9"You shall take two onyx stones and engrave on them the names of the [twelve] sons of Israel,

10six of their names on one stone and the remaining six names on the other stone, arranged in the order of their births.

11"With the work of a jeweler, like the engravings of a signet, you shall engrave the two stones according to the names of the sons of Israel. You shall have them set in filigree [settings] of gold.

12"You shall put the two stones on the [two] shoulder pieces of the ephod [of the high priest], as memorial stones for Israel; and Aaron shall bear their names on his two shoulders as a memorial before the LORD.

13"You shall make filigree [settings] of gold,

14and you are to make two chains of pure gold like twisted cords, and fasten the corded chains to the *settings*.

15"You are to make a breastpiece of judgment, the work of a skilled *and* talented craftsman; like the work of the ephod you shall make it: of gold, of blue, purple, and scarlet fabric and of fine twisted linen.

16"The breastpiece shall be square and folded double; a span [about nine inches] in length and a span in width.

17"You shall mount on it four rows of stones: the first row shall be a row of ruby, topaz, and emerald;

18the second row a turquoise, a sapphire, and a diamond;

19the third row a jacinth, an agate, and an amethyst;

20and the fourth row a beryl and an onyx and a jasper; they shall be set in gold filigree.

21"The [engraved] stones shall be twelve, according to the names of

life point

Skill without wisdom will not take us very far. In its simplest form, wisdom is just plain old common sense. If you want to succeed in life and in ministry, you need to have spiritual gifts, natural talent, and wisdom. Seek God for wisdom to accompany your spiritual gifts and talents, and He will give it to you (see James 1:5).

There are people who have a gift, an ability, or a skill that can help them climb the ladder of success, but once they arrive they do not have enough wisdom to keep them there. Use plenty of wisdom and common sense, and you will succeed in life.

[the twelve tribes of] the sons of Israel; they shall be like the engravings of a signet, each with its name for the twelve tribes.

²²"You shall make for the breastpiece chains of pure gold twisted like cords.

²³"You shall make on the breastpiece two rings of gold, and shall put the two rings on the two ends of the breastpiece.

²⁴"You shall put the two twisted cords of gold in the two rings which are on the ends of the breastpiece.

²⁵"The *other* two ends of the two cords you shall fasten in the two filigree *settings* in front, putting them on the shoulder pieces of the ephod.

²⁶"You shall make two gold rings and put them at the two ends of the breastpiece, on its inside edge next to the ephod.

²⁷"You are to make two gold rings and attach them to the lower part of the two shoulder pieces of the ephod in front, close to the place where it is joined, above the skillfully woven sash of the ephod.

²⁸"They shall bind the breastpiece by its rings to the rings of the ephod with a blue cord, so that it will be above the skillfully woven sash of the ephod, so that the breastpiece will not come loose from the ephod.

²⁹"So Aaron shall carry the names of the sons of Israel (Jacob) in the breastpiece of judgment over his heart when he enters the Holy Place, to bring them in continual remembrance before the LORD.

³⁰"In the breastpiece of judgment you shall put the Urim (Lights) and the Thummim (Perfections) [to be used for determining God's will in a matter]. They shall be over Aaron's heart whenever he goes before the LORD, and Aaron shall always carry the judgment (verdict, judicial decisions) of the sons of Israel over his heart before the LORD.

³¹"And you shall make the robe of the ephod all of blue.

³²"There shall be an opening at its top in the center [for the head], with a binding of woven work around the opening, like the opening in a coat of armor, so that it will not tear *or* fray.

³³"You shall make pomegranates of blue, purple, and scarlet fabric all around its hem, with gold bells between them;

³⁴a golden bell and a pomegranate, a golden bell and a pomegranate, all around the [bottom] hem of the robe.

³⁵"Aaron shall wear the robe when he ministers, and its sound shall be heard when he goes [alone] into the Holy Place before the LORD, and when he comes out, so that he will not die there.

³⁶"You shall also make a plate of pure gold and engrave on it, like the engravings of a signet, 'Holy to the LORD.' [Ex 39:30]

³⁷"You shall fasten it on the front of the turban with a blue cord.

³⁸"It shall be on Aaron's forehead, and Aaron shall take away the guilt from the holy things which the sons of Israel dedicate, with regard to all their holy gifts. It shall always be on his forehead, so that they may be accepted before the LORD. [Luke 24:44; Heb 8:1, 2]

³⁹"You shall weave the tunic of checkered work of fine linen, and make a turban of fine linen. You shall make a sash, the work of an embroiderer.

⁴⁰"For Aaron's sons you shall make tunics and sashes and [ornamental] caps, for glory *and* honor and beauty.

⁴¹"You shall put the various articles of clothing on Aaron your brother and on his sons with him, and shall anoint them and ordain and sanctify them, so that they may serve Me as priests.

⁴²"You shall make for them [white] linen undergarments to cover their bare flesh, reaching from the waist to the thighs.

⁴³"The various articles of clothing shall be on Aaron and on his sons when they enter the Tent of Meeting,

or when they approach the altar [of incense] to minister in the Holy Place, so that they do not incur guilt and die. It shall be a statute forever to Aaron and to his descendants after him.

29 "THIS IS what you shall do to consecrate Aaron and his sons so that they may serve Me as priests: take one young bull and two rams, without blemish,

²and unleavened bread and unleavened cakes mixed with oil, and unleavened wafers spread with oil; you shall make them of fine wheat flour.

³"You shall put them in one basket, and present them in the basket along with the bull and the two rams.

⁴"Then bring Aaron and his sons to the doorway of the Tent of Meeting [out where the basin is] and wash them with water.

⁵"Then you shall take the garments, and put on Aaron the tunic and the robe of the ephod and the ephod and the breastpiece, and wrap him with the skillfully woven sash of the ephod;

⁶and you shall put the turban on his head and put the holy crown on the turban.

⁷"Then you shall take the anointing oil and pour it on his head and anoint him.

⁸"You shall bring his sons and put tunics on them.

⁹"And you shall wrap them with sashes, Aaron and his sons, and put the [ornamental] caps on them; and the priest's office shall be theirs by a perpetual statute. So you shall ordain Aaron and his sons.

¹⁰"Then you shall bring the bull before the Tent of Meeting, and Aaron and his sons shall lay their hands on the bull's head.

¹¹"Then you shall kill the bull before the LORD by the doorway of the Tent of Meeting.

¹²"And you shall take some of the blood of the bull and with your finger put it on the horns of the altar [of burnt offering], and you shall pour out the remainder of the blood at the base of the altar.

¹³"You shall take all the fat that covers the intestines and the lobe of the liver, and the two kidneys and the fat that is on them, and offer them up in smoke on the altar.

¹⁴"But the meat of the bull, its hide, and the contents of its intestines you shall burn in the fire outside the camp; it is a sin offering. [Heb 13:11–13]

¹⁵"And you shall take one of the rams, and Aaron and his sons shall lay their hands on the head of the ram;

¹⁶then you shall kill the ram and you shall take its blood and sprinkle it around the altar [of burnt offering].

¹⁷"Then you shall cut the ram into pieces, and wash its intestines and legs, and place them with its pieces and its head,

¹⁸and you shall burn the whole ram on the altar. It is a burnt offering to the LORD: it is a sweet *and* soothing aroma, an offering by fire to the LORD.

¹⁹"Then you shall take the other ram, and Aaron and his sons shall lay their hands on the head of the ram.

²⁰"Then you shall kill the ram, and take some of its blood and put it on the tip of the right ears of Aaron and his sons and on the thumbs of their right hands and on the big toes of their right feet, and sprinkle the [rest of the] blood around on the altar [of burnt offering].

²¹"Then you shall take some of the blood that is on the altar and some of the anointing oil, and sprinkle it on Aaron and his garments and on his sons and their garments. Now Aaron and his garments and his sons and their garments shall be consecrated (dedicated, made holy, declared sacred for God's purpose).

²²"You shall also take the fat of the ram, the fat tail, the fat that covers the

intestines, the lobe of the liver, the two kidneys with the fat that is on them, and the right thigh; (for it is a ram of ordination),

23and one loaf of bread and one cake of oiled bread and one wafer out of the basket of the unleavened bread that is before the LORD;

24and you shall put all these in the hands of Aaron and his sons, and wave them as a wave offering before the LORD.

25"Then you shall take them from their hands, add them to the burnt offering, and burn them on the altar for a sweet *and* soothing aroma before the LORD; it is an offering by fire to the LORD.

26"Then you shall take the breast of the ram of Aaron's ordination, and wave it as a wave offering before the LORD; and it shall be your (Moses) portion.

27"You shall consecrate the waved breast offering [of the ram] used in the ordination and the waved thigh offering of the priests' portion, since it is [a contribution] for Aaron and for his sons.

28"It shall be for Aaron and his sons as their due portion from the Israelites forever, for it is a heave offering. It shall be a heave offering to the LORD from the Israelites from the sacrifices of their peace offerings.

29"The holy garments of Aaron shall be for his sons after him, to be anointed and ordained in them.

30"That son who is [high] priest in his place shall put them on [each day for] seven days when he comes into the Tent of Meeting to minister in the Holy Place.

31"You shall take the ram of the ordination and boil its meat in a holy place.

32"Aaron and his sons shall eat the meat of the ram and the bread in the basket, at the doorway of the Tent of Meeting.

33"They shall eat those things by which atonement was made at their ordination and consecration; but a layman shall not eat them, because they are holy [that is, set apart to the worship of God].

34"And if any of the meat of ordination or the bread remains until morning, you shall burn it in the fire; it shall not be eaten, because it is holy.

35"So you shall do to Aaron and to his sons in accordance with all I have commanded you; during seven days you are to ordain them.

36"You shall offer a bull every day as a sin offering for atonement. You shall cleanse the altar *from sin* when you make atonement for it, and you shall anoint it to consecrate it [for God's sacred purpose].

37"For seven days you shall make atonement for the altar [of burnt offering] and consecrate it; then the altar shall be most holy. Whatever touches the altar must be holy (set apart for God's service).

38"Now this is what you shall offer on the altar: two one year old lambs shall be offered each day, continuously.

39"One lamb you shall offer in the morning and the other lamb at twilight;

40and with the one lamb there shall be one-tenth of *a measure* of fine flour mixed with one-fourth of a hin of beaten [olive] oil, and one-fourth of a hin of wine for a drink offering [to be poured out].

41"And the other lamb you shall offer at twilight, and do with it as with the grain offering of the morning and with the drink offering, for a sweet *and* soothing aroma [to appease God], an offering by fire to the LORD.

42"This will be a continual burnt offering throughout your generations at the doorway of the Tent of Meeting before the LORD, where I will meet with you, to speak to you there.

43"There I will meet with the Israelites, and the Tent of Meeting shall be sanctified by My glory [the Shekinah, God's dwelling presence].

⁴⁴"I will sanctify the Tent of Meeting and the altar [of burnt offering]; also I will sanctify Aaron and his sons to serve as priests to Me.

⁴⁵"I will dwell among the sons of Israel and be their God.

⁴⁶"They shall know [from personal experience] *and* acknowledge that I am the Lord their God who brought them out of the land of Egypt so that I might dwell among them; I am the Lord their God.

30
"YOU SHALL make an altar upon which to burn incense; you shall make it of acacia wood.

²"It shall be a cubit long and a cubit wide. It shall be square and it shall be two cubits high. Its horns of one piece with it.

³"You shall overlay it with pure gold, its top and its sides all around, and its horns; and you shall make a gold molding all around it.

⁴"You shall make two gold rings under its molding, make them on the two side walls—on opposite sides—they shall be holders for the poles with which to carry it.

⁵"You shall make the poles of acacia wood overlaid with gold.

⁶"You shall put the altar of incense [in the Holy Place] in front *and* outside

the blood makes atonement

Exodus 30:10 foreshadows Jesus' crucifixion and the sufficiency of His sacrifice to atone for our sins once and for all. When the high priest went into the Holy of Holies on the Day of Atonement to offer sacrifices for his own sins and the sins of the people, he had to do so with the blood of animals as a substitute. The Bible tells us that the life is in the blood and that the blood has been given on the altar to make atonement for our souls (see Leviticus 17:11). Note that the priest had to go year after year and make the same sacrifices. The priest's sins and the sins of the people were not washed away; they were merely covered over. The blood of animals was placed on their sins to atone for them, but it was not a finished work. It had to be done again and again.

The action by the high priest who repeatedly offered the blood of animals was a type, a mere shadow, of what was to come. The book of Hebrews teaches that when Jesus finished the work of His sacrifice on the cross, He put an end to continual sacrifices (see Hebrews 8:1–10:14). How beautifully Hebrews 9:12 communicates the permanence of Christ's atonement. It says Jesus "went once for all into the Holy Place [the Holy of Holies of heaven, into the presence of God], and not through the blood of goats and calves, but through His own blood, having obtained and secured eternal redemption [that is, the salvation of all who personally believe in Him as Savior]."

Jesus offered Himself once as a sacrifice for our sins. He does not have to keep doing it. My husband likes to quip, "If you do the job right, you won't have to keep doing it over and over." That's what Jesus did for us, once and for all. He did it right. His atonement lasts. Forever.

We no longer have to make sacrifices every time we sin. We can now live by faith, trusting God that the sacrifice Jesus made is more than enough to cleanse us and make us whole.

of the veil that screens the ark of the Testimony, before the mercy seat that is over the Testimony, where I will meet with you.

7"Aaron shall burn sweet *and* fragrant incense on it; he shall burn it every morning when he trims *and* tends the lamps. [Ps 141:2; Rev 5:8; 8:3, 4]

8"When Aaron sets up the lamps at twilight, he shall burn incense, a perpetual incense before the LORD throughout your generations.

9"You shall not offer any strange incense on this altar, or burnt offering or meal offering; you shall not pour out a drink offering on it.

10"Once a year Aaron shall make atonement [for sin] on its horns. He shall make atonement on it with the blood of the sin offering of atonement once a year throughout your generations. It is most holy to the LORD."

11Then the LORD said to Moses,

12"When you take the census of the Israelites, each one shall give a ransom for himself to the LORD when you count them, so that no plague will come on them when you number them. [Rom 8:1–4]

13"This is what everyone who is counted shall give [as he joins those already counted]: a half shekel, according to the sanctuary shekel (the shekel is twenty gerahs); a half shekel as a contribution to the LORD.

14"Everyone who is counted, from twenty years old and over, [as he joins those already counted], shall give this contribution to the LORD. [Matt 10:24; 1 Pet 1:18, 19]

15"The rich shall not give more and the poor shall not give less than half a shekel, when you give this contribution to the LORD to make atonement for yourselves.

16"You shall take the atonement money from the Israelites and use it [exclusively] for the service of the Tent of Meeting, so that it may be a memorial for the Israelites before the LORD, to make atonement for yourselves."

17Then the LORD said to Moses,

18"You shall also make a basin of bronze, with a base of bronze, for washing. You shall put it [outside in the court] between the Tent of Meeting and the altar [of burnt offering], and you shall put water in it.

19"Aaron and his sons shall wash their hands and their feet.

20"When they enter the Tent of Meeting, they shall wash with water, so that they will not die. Also, when they approach the altar to minister, to burn an offering in the fire to the LORD [they shall do the same]. [John 13:6–8]

21"They shall wash their hands and their feet, so that they will not die; it shall be a perpetual statute for them, for Aaron and his descendants throughout their generations."

22Moreover, the LORD said to Moses,

23"Take for yourself the best spices: five hundred *shekels* of liquid myrrh, half as much—two hundred and fifty—of sweet-scented cinnamon, and two hundred and fifty of fragrant cane,

24and five hundred *shekels* of cinnamon blossom according to the sanctuary shekel, and a hin of olive oil.

25"You shall make of these a holy anointing oil, a perfume mixture, the work of a perfumer; it shall be a sacred anointing oil.

26"You shall anoint the Tent of Meeting with it, and the ark of the Testimony,

27and the table [for the bread] and all its utensils, and the lampstand and its utensils, and the altar of incense,

28and the altar of burnt offering with all its utensils, and the basin [for cleansing] and its base.

29"You shall consecrate them, that they may be most holy; whatever touches them must be holy (set apart for God).

30"You shall anoint Aaron and his

sons, and consecrate them, that they may serve as priests to Me.

³¹"You shall say to the Israelites, 'This shall be a holy *and* sacred anointing oil, to Me [alone] throughout your generations. [Rom 8:9; 1 Cor 12:3]

³²'It shall not be poured on anyone's body, nor shall you make any like it in the same composition. It is holy, and it shall be sacred to you.

³³'Whoever prepares any like it or puts any of it on a layman shall be cut off from his people [excluding him from the atonement made for them].'"

³⁴Then the LORD said to Moses, "Take sweet *and* fragrant spices—stacte, onycha, and galbanum, sweet *and* fragrant spices with pure frankincense; there shall be an equal amount of each—

³⁵and make incense with it, a perfume, the work of a perfumer, salted, pure and sacred.

³⁶"You shall crush some of it [into a] very fine [powder], and put some of it before the Testimony in the Tent of Meeting, where I will meet with you; it shall be most holy to you.

³⁷"The incense which you shall make, you shall not make in the same proportions for yourselves; it shall be holy to you for the LORD.

³⁸"Whoever makes any like it, to use as perfume shall be cut off from his people [excluding him from the atonement made for them]."

31 NOW THE LORD said to Moses, ²"See, I have called by name Bezalel, son of Uri, the son of Hur, of the tribe of Judah.

³"I have filled him with the Spirit of God in wisdom *and* skill, in understanding *and* intelligence, in knowledge, and in all kinds of craftsmanship,

⁴to make artistic designs for work in gold, in silver, and in bronze,

⁵and in the cutting of stones for settings, and in the carving of wood, to work in all kinds of craftsmanship.

⁶"And behold, I Myself have appointed with him Oholiab, son of Ahisamach, of the tribe of Dan; to all who are wise-hearted I have given the skill *and* ability to make everything that I have commanded you:

⁷the Tent of Meeting, the ark of the Testimony, the mercy seat that is upon it, all the furnishings of the tent—

⁸the table [for the bread] and its utensils, the pure *gold* lampstand with all its utensils, the [golden] altar of incense,

⁹the [bronze] altar of burnt offering with all its utensils, the basin and its base—

¹⁰the finely worked garments, the holy garments for Aaron the [high] priest and the garments for his sons to minister as priests,

¹¹and the anointing oil and the sweet *and* fragrant incense for the Holy Place. They are to make *them* according to all that I have commanded you."

¹²And the LORD said to Moses,

¹³"But as for you, say to the Israelites, 'You shall most certainly observe My Sabbaths, for it is a sign between Me and you throughout your generations, so that you may know [without any doubt] *and* acknowledge that I am the LORD who sanctifies you *and* sets you apart [for Myself].

¹⁴"Therefore, you shall keep the

speak the Word

I pray, God, that You will fill me with Your Spirit, with wisdom and skill, with understanding and intelligence, and with knowledge. And I pray that You will help me do what You have called me to do.

—ADAPTED FROM EXODUS 31:3

Sabbath, for it is holy to you. Everyone who profanes it must be put to death; for whoever does work on the Sabbath, that person (soul) shall be cut off from among his people [excluding him from the atonement made for them].

¹⁵'For six days work may be done, but the seventh is the Sabbath of complete rest, sacred to the LORD; whoever does work on the Sabbath day must be put to death.

¹⁶'So the Israelites shall observe the Sabbath, to celebrate the Sabbath throughout their generations as a perpetual covenant.'

¹⁷"It is a sign between Me and the Israelites forever; for in six days the LORD made the heavens and the earth, and on the seventh day He ceased and was refreshed."

¹⁸When He had finished speaking with him on Mount Sinai, He gave Moses the two tablets of the Testimony, tablets of stone, written with the finger of God.

32 NOW WHEN the people saw that Moses delayed coming down from the mountain, they gathered together before Aaron and said to him, "Come, make us a god who will go before us; as for this Moses, the man who brought us up from the land of Egypt, we do not know what has become of him."

²So Aaron replied to them, "Take off

putting the Word to work

We all need regular Sabbaths in our lives (see Exodus 31:14)—times of rest, relaxation, refreshing, and renewal. Do you incorporate such times of refreshing in your life? If so, keep it up! If not, what changes can you make in your schedule so that you can have regular times of rest and renewal?

the gold rings that are in the ears of your wives, your sons and daughters, and bring them to me."

³So all the people took off the gold rings that were in their ears and brought them to Aaron.

⁴And he took *the gold* from their hands, and fashioned it with an engraving tool and made it into a molten calf; and they said, "This is your god, O Israel, who brought you up from the land of Egypt."

⁵Now when Aaron saw the molten calf, he built an altar before it; and Aaron made a proclamation, and said, "Tomorrow shall be a feast to the LORD!"

⁶So they got up early the next day and offered burnt offerings, and brought peace offerings; then the people sat down to eat and drink, and got up to play [shamefully—without moral restraint].

⁷Then the LORD said to Moses, "Go down at once, for your people, whom you brought up from the land of Egypt, have corrupted themselves.

⁸"They have quickly turned aside from the way which I commanded them. They have made themselves a molten calf, and have worshiped it and sacrificed to it, and said, 'This is your god, O Israel, who brought you up from the land of Egypt!'"

⁹The LORD said to Moses, "I have seen this people, and behold, they are a stiff-necked (stubborn, rebellious) people.

¹⁰"Now therefore, let Me alone *and* do not interfere, so that My anger may burn against them and that I may destroy them; and I will make of you (your descendants) a great nation."

¹¹But Moses appeased *and* entreated the LORD his God, and said, "LORD, why does Your anger burn against Your people whom You have brought out of the land of Egypt with great power and a mighty hand?

¹²"Why should the Egyptians say, 'With evil [intent] their God brought

them out to kill them in the mountains and destroy them from the face of the earth'? Turn away from Your burning anger and change Your mind about harming Your people.

13"Remember Abraham, Isaac, and Israel (Jacob), Your servants to whom You swore [an oath] by Yourself, and said to them, 'I will multiply your descendants as the stars of the heavens, and all this land of which I have spoken I will give to your descendants, and they shall inherit it forever.'"

14So the LORD changed His mind about the harm which He had said He would do to His people.

15Then Moses turned and went down from the mountain with the two tablets of the Testimony in his hand; tablets that were written on both sides—they were written on one side and on the other.

16The tablets were the work of God; the writing was the writing of God engraved on the tablets.

17Now when Joshua heard the noise of the people as they shouted, he said to Moses, "There is a sound of battle in the camp."

18But Moses said,

"It is not the sound of the cry of
    victory,
Nor is it the sound of the cry of
    defeat;
But I hear the sound of singing."

19And as soon as he approached the camp and he saw the calf and the dancing, Moses' anger burned; and he threw the tablets from his hands and smashed them at the foot of the mountain.

20Then Moses took the calf they had made and burned it in the fire, and ground it to powder, and scattered it on the surface of the water and made the Israelites drink it.

21Then Moses said to Aaron, "What did this people do to you, that you have brought so great a sin on them?"

22Aaron said, "Do not let the anger of my lord burn; you know the people yourself, that they are prone to evil.

23"For they said to me, 'Make us a god who will go before us; as for this Moses, the man who brought us out of the land of Egypt, we do not know what has become of him.'

24"I said to them, 'Let whoever has gold [jewelry], take it off.' So they gave it to me; then I threw it into the fire, and out came this calf."

25Now when Moses saw that the people were out of control—for Aaron had let them get out of control to the point of being an object of mockery among their enemies—

26then Moses stood in the gate of the camp, and said, "Whoever is on the LORD's side, come to me!" And all the sons of Levi [the priestly tribe] gathered together to him.

27He said to them, "Thus says the LORD God of Israel, 'Every man strap his sword on his thigh and go back and forth from gate to gate throughout the camp, and every man kill his brother, and every man his friend, and every man his neighbor [all who continue pagan worship].' "

28So the sons of Levi did as Moses instructed, and about three thousand men of the people [of Israel] were killed that day.

29Then Moses said [to the Levites],

speak the Word

God, I dedicate myself to You and pray that You will restore me and bestow Your blessing upon me.
—ADAPTED FROM EXODUS 32:29

"Dedicate yourselves today to the LORD—for each man has been against his own son and his own brother [in his attempt to escape execution]—so that He may restore *and* bestow His blessing on you this day."

³⁰Then the next day Moses said to the people, "You have committed a great sin. Now I will go up to the LORD; perhaps I can make atonement for your sin."

³¹So Moses returned to the LORD, and said, "Oh, these people have committed a great sin [against You], and have made themselves a god of gold.

³²"Yet now, if You will, forgive their sin—and if not, please blot me out of Your book which You have written (kill me)!"

³³But the LORD said to Moses, "Whoever has sinned against Me, I will blot him out of My book [not you]. [Ps 69:28; Dan 12:1; Phil 4:3; Rev 3:5]

³⁴"But now go, lead the people [to the place] where I have told you. Behold, My Angel shall go before you; nevertheless, in the day when I punish, I will punish them for their sin!" [Ex 23:20; 33:2, 3]

³⁵So the LORD struck the people with a plague, because of what they had done with the calf which Aaron had made [for them].

33 THE LORD spoke to Moses, saying, "Depart, go up from here, you and the people whom you have brought from the land of Egypt, to the land which I swore to Abraham, Isaac, and Jacob (Israel), saying, 'To your descendants I will give it.'

²"I will send an Angel before you and I will drive out the Canaanite, the Amorite, the Hittite, the Perizzite, the Hivite, and the Jebusite. [Ex 23:23; 34:11]

³"Go up to a land [of abundance] flowing with milk and honey; for I

time to grow up

The Israelites did not want to take responsibility for their actions. Moses sought God for them, he did their praying for them, and he even tried to do their repenting when they got themselves into trouble (see Exodus 32:30–32). However, this eventually came to an end, and the Israelites had to become responsible.

A baby has no responsibility when he is born. But as the child grows up, he is expected to take on more and more responsibility. One of the most important things parents can do is to teach their children to accept responsibility. God desires that His children learn to be responsible also.

The Lord has given me the opportunity to be in full-time ministry—to teach His Word on television and radio and to preach the gospel all over the world. I can assure you that there is a responsibility to that call, a responsibility many people know nothing of. A lot of people say they want to be in ministry. They expect constant excitement and think they will be involved in a continual spiritual event.

The truth is that people in ministry do not float around on a cloud all day singing "The Hallelujah Chorus." We work, and we work hard. We have to get up on time, follow a daily routine, and submit to authority. We walk in integrity and try to do so with excellence. It is a privilege to work in ministry, but it also requires a willingness to take responsibility for our attitudes and actions. Let's not be people who passively let others do for us what we need to do. Let's rise up in faith and be ready to take responsibility for our own lives and ministries.

will not go up in your midst, because you are a stiff-necked (stubborn, rebellious) people, and I might destroy you on the way."

⁴When the people heard this sad word, they mourned, and none of them put on his ornaments.

⁵For the LORD had said to Moses, "Say to the sons of Israel, 'You are a stiff-necked (stubborn, rebellious) people! If I should come among you for one moment, I would destroy you. Now therefore, [penitently] take off your ornaments, so that I may know what to do with you.'"

⁶So the Israelites left off all their ornaments [in repentance], from Mount Horeb (Sinai) *onward*.

⁷Now Moses used to take his own tent and pitch it outside the camp, far away from the camp, and he called it the tent of meeting [of God with His own people]. And everyone who sought the LORD would go out to the [temporary] tent of meeting which was outside the camp.

⁸Whenever Moses went out to the tent, all the people would rise and stand, each at his tent door, and look at Moses until he entered the tent.

⁹Whenever Moses entered the tent, the pillar of cloud would descend and stand at the doorway of the tent; and the LORD would speak with Moses.

¹⁰When all the people saw the pillar of cloud standing at the tent door, all the people would rise and worship, each at his tent door.

¹¹And so the LORD used to speak to Moses face to face, just as a man speaks to his friend. When Moses returned to the camp, his attendant Joshua, the son of Nun, a young man, would not depart from the tent.

¹²Moses said to the LORD, "See, You say to me, 'Bring up this people,' but You have not let me know whom You will send with me. Yet You have said, 'I know you by name, and you have also found favor in My sight.'

¹³"Now therefore, I pray you, if I have found favor in Your sight, let me know Your ways so that I may know You [becoming more deeply and intimately acquainted with You, recognizing and understanding Your ways more clearly] and that I may find grace *and* favor in Your sight. And consider also, that this nation is Your people."

¹⁴And the LORD said, "My presence shall go *with you,* and I will give you rest [by bringing you and the people into the promised land]." [Deut 3:20]

¹⁵And Moses said to Him, "If Your presence does not go [with me], do not lead us up from here.

¹⁶"For how then can it be known that Your people and I have found favor in Your sight? Is it not by Your going with us, so that we are distinguished, Your people and I, from all the [other] people on the face of the earth?"

¹⁷The LORD said to Moses, "I will also do this thing that you have asked; for you have found favor (lovingkindness, mercy) in My sight and I have known you [personally] by name." [Rev 2:17]

¹⁸Then Moses said, "Please, show me Your glory!"

¹⁹And God said, "I will make all My goodness pass before you, and I will proclaim the Name of the LORD before you; for I will be gracious to whom I will be gracious, and will show compassion

speak the Word

God, I do not ever want to be without You. Do not let me go anywhere that Your presence does not go with me.
–ADAPTED FROM EXODUS 33:15

rest in His presence

Moses had a big job on his hands. He knew he needed God's presence and sought the assurance that God would go with him and help him (see Exodus 33:12–14). That is all we need too—God's presence and His rest. No matter how difficult our circumstance, the knowledge of His presence will strengthen and enable us to do the job at hand. It's important that we remember to seek God's presence, not His "presents."

In ministry, sometimes we can get upset and frustrated as we try to bring hope and healing to others, but over the years the Lord has taught me and my ministry team to remain calm, cool, and steady in the face of the challenges. He has shown us the importance of being adaptable, keeping our eyes on Him, and not focusing on our own plans. If things do not work out the way we want them to, we need to stay relaxed and trust Him to show us what to do. I have learned that when I am upset I cannot hear clearly from the Lord; therefore, I pursue peace at all times.

How do you react when your plans fall through and it seems you have no options? Some of us just give up, saying, "Well, that does it! Now my plan is ruined!" We need to think about who did the "ruining." If God ruined our plan, we had the wrong plan to begin with. If the devil ruined our plan, the Lord will give us another plan, one that will be ten times better than the one that failed. Too often we start blaming the devil as a conditioned response when things do not work out just as we want them to. Not everything is the devil's fault. There are times when we are trying to do something that was never God's will. Even though there are things that we want, we must learn to want what God wants even more than we want what we want!

Any time our plans are not working, we must submit it to God and simply rest in His presence. Psalm 91:1 encourages us, "He who dwells in the shelter of the Most High will remain secure and rest in the shadow of the Almighty [whose power no enemy can withstand]." We need to realize that God is our Refuge and our Fortress. We can rely and confidently trust in Him. If the devil is resisting you and causing trouble, God will show you that. Then you can take authority over him, reminding him that the greater One lives inside you. As you resist the devil and steadfastly trust God, His plan will always prevail.

Moses asked God to show him His way so he could get to know Him better. The Lord answered by assuring Moses that His presence would be with him and that He would give him rest. What Moses really needed at that difficult time of his life was the presence of God and the rest of God. The same is true for us. As much as we would like to know God's plans for us, what we need most of all is His presence, which will give us rest wherever He sends us and in whatever task He assigns us.

I encourage you to want God's will more than your own. When things do not work out as you planned, remain peaceful and trust God. Seek His presence at all times. If your trouble and delay are the result of satanic opposition, remember that Satan may come against you one way, but he will have to flee before you seven ways if you keep your eyes on God (see Deuteronomy 28:7).

(lovingkindness) on whom I will show compassion." [Rom 9:15, 16]

²⁰But He said, "You cannot see My face, for no man shall see Me and live!"

²¹Then the Lord said, "Behold, there is a place beside Me, and you shall stand there on the rock;

²²and while My glory is passing by, I will put you in a cleft of the rock and *protectively* cover you with My hand until I have passed by.

²³"Then I will take away My hand and you shall see My back; but My face shall not be seen."

34 THEN THE Lord said to Moses, "Cut two tablets of stone like the first, and I will write on these tablets the words that were on the first tablets which you smashed [when you learned of Israel's idolatry].

²"So be ready by morning, and come up in the morning to Mount Sinai, and present yourself there to Me on the top of the mountain.

³"No man is to come up with you, nor let any man be seen anywhere on the mountain; nor let flocks or herds feed in front of that mountain."

⁴So Moses cut two tablets of stone like the first ones, and he got up early in the morning and went up on Mount Sinai, as the Lord had commanded him, and took the two tablets of stone in his hand.

⁵Then the Lord descended in the cloud and stood there with Moses as he proclaimed the Name of the Lord.

⁶Then the Lord passed by in front of him, and proclaimed, "The Lord, the Lord God, compassionate and gracious, slow to anger, and abounding in lovingkindness and truth (faithfulness);

⁷keeping mercy *and* lovingkindness for thousands, forgiving iniquity and transgression and sin; but He will by no means leave *the guilty* unpunished, visiting (avenging) the iniquity (sin, guilt) of the fathers upon the children and the grandchildren to the third and fourth generations [that is, calling the children to account for the sins of their fathers]."

⁸Moses bowed to the earth immediately and worshiped [the Lord].

⁹And he said, "If now I have found favor *and* lovingkindness in Your sight, O Lord, let the Lord, please, go in our midst, though it is a stiff-necked (stubborn, rebellious) people, and pardon our iniquity and our sin, and take us as Your possession."

¹⁰Then God said, "Behold, I am going to make a covenant. Before all your people I will do wondrous works (miracles) such as have not been created *or* produced in all the earth nor among any of the nations; and all the people among whom you live shall see the working of the Lord, for it is a fearful *and* awesome thing that I am going to do with you.

¹¹"Be sure to observe what I am commanding you this day: behold, I am going to drive out the Amorite before you, and the Canaanite, the Hittite, the Perizzite, the Hivite, and the Jebusite.

¹²"Watch yourself so that you do not make a covenant (solemn agreement, treaty) with the inhabitants of the land into which you are going, or it will become a [dangerous] trap among you.

¹³"But you shall tear down *and* destroy their [pagan] altars, smash in pieces their [sacred] pillars (obelisks, images) and cut down their Asherim

¹⁴—for you shall not worship any other god; for the Lord, whose name is Jealous, is a jealous (impassioned) God [demanding what is rightfully and uniquely His]—

¹⁵otherwise you might make a covenant with the inhabitants of the land and they would play the prostitute with their gods and sacrifice to their gods, and someone might invite you to eat his sacrifice (meal),

¹⁶and you might take some of his daughters for your sons, and his daughters would play the prostitute with their gods and cause your sons also to play the prostitute (commit apostasy) with their gods [that is, abandon the true God for man-made idols].

¹⁷"You shall make for yourselves no molten gods.

¹⁸"You shall observe the Feast of Unleavened Bread (Passover). For seven days you shall eat unleavened bread, as I have commanded you, at the appointed time in the month of Abib; for in the month of Abib you came out of Egypt.

¹⁹"All the firstborn males among your livestock belong to Me, whether cattle or sheep.

²⁰"You shall redeem the firstborn of a donkey with a lamb; but if you do not redeem it, then you shall break its neck. You shall redeem all the firstborn of your sons. None of you are to appear before Me empty-handed.

²¹"You shall work for six days, but on the seventh day you shall rest; [even] in plowing time and in harvest you shall rest [on the Sabbath].

²²"You shall observe *and* celebrate the Feast of Weeks (Harvest, First Fruits, or Pentecost), the first fruits of the wheat harvest, and the Feast of Ingathering (Booths or Tabernacles) at the year's end.

²³"Three times a year all your males shall appear before the Lord GOD, the God of Israel.

²⁴"For I will drive out *and* dispossess nations before you and enlarge your borders; nor shall any man covet (actively seek for himself) your land when you go up to appear before the LORD your God three times a year.

²⁵"You shall not offer the blood of My sacrifice with leavened bread, nor shall the sacrifice of the Feast of the Passover (Unleavened Bread) be left over until morning.

²⁶"You shall bring the very first of the first fruits of your ground to the house of the LORD your God.

"You shall not boil a young goat in his mother's milk [as some pagans do]."

²⁷Then the LORD said to Moses, "Write these words, for in accordance with these words I have made a covenant with you and with Israel."

²⁸Moses was there with the LORD forty days and forty nights; he ate no bread and drank no water. And he wrote on the tablets the words of the covenant, the Ten Commandments.

²⁹When Moses came down from Mount Sinai with the two tablets of the Testimony in his hand, he did not know that the skin of his face was shining [with a unique radiance] because he had been speaking with God.

³⁰When Aaron and all the Israelites saw Moses, behold, the skin of his face shone, and they were afraid to approach him.

³¹But Moses called to them, and Aaron and all the leaders of the congregation returned to him; and he spoke to them.

³²Afterward all the Israelites approached him, and he commanded them to do everything that the LORD had said to him on Mount Sinai.

³³When Moses had finished speaking with them, he put a veil over his face.

³⁴But whenever Moses went in before the LORD to speak with Him, he would take off the veil until he came out. When he came out and he told the Israelites what he had been commanded [by God],

³⁵the Israelites would see the face of Moses, how his skin shone [with a unique radiance]. So Moses put the veil on his face again until he went in to speak with God.

35 MOSES GATHERED all the congregation of the sons of Israel together, and said to them, "These are the things which the LORD has commanded you to do:

²"For six days work may be done, but the seventh day shall be a holy day for you, a Sabbath of complete rest to the LORD; whoever does any kind of work on that day shall be put to death.

³"You shall not kindle a fire in any of your dwellings on the Sabbath day."

⁴And Moses said to all the congregation of the sons of Israel, "This is the thing which the LORD has commanded:

⁵'Take from among you an offering to the LORD. Whoever has a willing heart, let him bring it as the LORD's offering: gold, silver, and bronze,

⁶blue, purple, and scarlet fabric, fine linen, goats' *hair,*

⁷and rams' skins dyed red, and skins of porpoises, and acacia wood,

⁸and [olive] oil for the lighting, and balsam for the anointing oil, and for the fragrant incense,

how to get stirred up for God

The people who built the tabernacle of the Lord were stirred up about the things of God, and they gave with willing hearts. You may be thinking, *I wish I could be excited about the Lord's work, but I just don't feel that way. I don't really know how to get myself stirred up.* What can you do to be stirred up for God?

1. Stay around people who are excited about the things of God. Before long, you will be excited and stirred up too. If you associate with a person who is a visionary, you will soon get a vision. But if you stay around lifeless people who want to do nothing but complain, sit on the couch, eat doughnuts, and watch soap operas, then soon you will be doing the same things.

2. Decide to take action about the negative way you feel instead of just wishing things were different. Realize that if you want to have victory over your feelings strongly enough, you will do whatever it takes to get it. If you do not want the victory, no one can motivate you to want it. We need to stop feeling sorry for ourselves. We need to stop whining, "I wish I had this," or "I wish I didn't have that. I wish my parents loved me more. I wish I had more money. I wish my back didn't hurt. I wish . . . I wish . . . I wish . . ." I used to do that. For years I went around "wishing," until the Lord spoke to me and said, "You can be pitiful or you can be powerful, but you cannot be both. So take your pick."

3. Avoid passivity, procrastination, and laziness. A passive person waits to be moved by an outside force before he or she will take action. We are to be motivated and led by the Holy Spirit within us, not by things on the outside. The best way we can guard against the spirit of passivity is to do what we need to do now, and do it with all our might (see Ecclesiastes 9:10).

4. Stay on fire for God. Romans 12:11 encourages us to be "never lagging behind in diligence; aglow in the Spirit, enthusiastically serving the Lord." In order to always be aglow and burning, we have to stay on fire. I have discovered that the best way to fan the fire is to speak the Word of God in the form of prayer, praise, preaching, or confession. Those disciplines stir up the gift within, keep the fire burning, and prevent my spirit from sinking within me.

Remember, everything we do is to be done unto the Lord and for His glory. We should do it through Him, to Him, for Him, by Him, and with Him. And we should do it willingly, with our whole hearts stirred up within us.

⁹and onyx stones and other stones to be set for the ephod and the breastpiece.

¹⁰'Let every skilled *and* talented man among you come, and make everything that the LORD has commanded:

¹¹the tabernacle (sacred dwelling of God), its tent and its covering, its hooks, its boards, its bars, its pillars, and its sockets;

¹²the ark [of the covenant] and its carrying poles, with the mercy seat and the veil (partition curtain) of the screen [to hang between the Holy Place and the Holy of Holies];

¹³the table and its carrying poles, and all its utensils, and the bread of the [divine] Presence (showbread);

¹⁴the lampstand also for the light and its utensils and its lamps, and the oil for the light;

¹⁵and the altar of incense and its carrying poles, the anointing oil and the fragrant incense, the screen (curtain) for the doorway at the entrance of the tabernacle;

¹⁶the altar of burnt offering with its bronze grating, its carrying poles, and all its utensils, the wash basin and its base (stand);

¹⁷the court's curtains, its support poles and their sockets, and the curtain for the gate of the courtyard;

¹⁸the pegs of the tabernacle and the pegs of the court and their cords;

¹⁹the finely-woven garments for ministering in the Holy Place, the holy garments for Aaron the priest and the garments for his sons, to minister as priests.'"

²⁰Then all the congregation of the Israelites left Moses' presence.

²¹Everyone whose heart stirred him and everyone whose spirit moved him came and brought the LORD's offering to be used for the Tent of Meeting, for all its service, and for the holy garments.

²²Then all whose hearts moved them, both men and women, came and brought brooches, earrings *or* nose rings, signet rings, and necklaces, all jewels of gold; everyone bringing an offering of gold to the LORD.

²³Every man who had in his possession blue or purple or scarlet fabric, and fine linen, and goats' *hair*, and rams' skins dyed red and porpoise skins, brought them.

²⁴Everyone who could make an offering of silver or bronze brought it as the LORD's offering; every man who had in his possession acacia wood for any work of the service brought it.

²⁵All the skilled *and* talented women spun thread with their hands, and brought what they had spun, blue and purple and scarlet fabric and fine linen.

²⁶All the women whose heart stirred with a skill spun the goats' *hair*.

²⁷The leaders brought onyx stones and other stones to be put in settings for the ephod and for the breastpiece,

life point

Sometimes when we see a person as gifted as Bezalel, we try to emulate him instead of exercising our own gifts. We become so busy attempting to do somebody else's ministry that we never get around to doing our own! It is important for us to see that God has given each person different gifts to be used for the benefit of the whole body of Christ (see 1 Corinthians 12:4–30). Often we are not satisfied with what the Lord has given us to do because we are insecure and do not realize who we are in Christ. If God has not given you a ministry of standing in front of people and ministering to them, then do not try to minister that way. You will not be happy or successful if you try to minister with gifts you have not been given. Celebrate and embrace who you are. You will find the most wonderful fulfillment as you do your very best with the gifts God has given you.

28and spice and [olive] oil for the light and for the anointing oil and for the fragrant incense.

29The Israelites, all the men and women whose heart moved them to bring *material* for all the work which the Lord had commanded through Moses to be done, brought a freewill (voluntary) offering to the Lord.

30Then Moses said to the Israelites, "See, the Lord called by name Bezalel son of Uri, the son of Hur, of the tribe of Judah;

31and He has filled him with the Spirit of God, with wisdom *and* skill, with intelligence *and* understanding, and with knowledge in all [areas of] craftsmanship,

32to devise artistic designs to work in gold, silver, and bronze,

33and in the cutting of stones for setting and in the carving of wood, for work in every skilled craft.

34"He has also put in Bezalel's heart [the willingness] to teach [others the same skills], both he and Oholiab, son of Ahisamach, of the tribe of Dan.

35"He has filled them with skill to do the work of an engraver, of a designer, and of an embroiderer, in blue, purple, and scarlet fabric, and in fine linen, and of a weaver; makers of every work and embroiderers of [excellent] designs.

36 "BEZALEL AND Oholiab, and every skilled person in whom the Lord has put ability and understanding to know how to do all the work in the construction of the sanctuary, shall work according to all that the Lord has commanded."

2So Moses called Bezalel and Oholiab and every skilled person in whom the Lord had put ability, everyone whose heart stirred him, to come to do the work.

3They received from Moses all the offerings which the Israelites had brought for the construction of the sanctuary, to prepare it for service. And they continued to bring him freewill (voluntary) offerings every morning.

4And all the skilled men who were doing all the work on the sanctuary came, each one from the work which he was doing,

5and they said to Moses, "The people are bringing much more than enough for the construction work which the Lord commanded us to do."

6So Moses issued a command, and it was proclaimed throughout the camp, "Let neither man nor woman do any more work for the sanctuary offering." So the people were restrained from bringing *anything more;*

7for the material they had was sufficient and more than enough to do all the work.

8All the skilled men among them who were doing the work on the tabernacle made ten curtains of fine twisted linen and blue, purple, and scarlet fabric, with cherubim [worked into them], the work of an embroiderer, Bezalel made them.

9Each curtain was twenty-eight cubits long and four cubits wide; all the curtains were one size.

10Bezalel joined five curtains one to another, and [the other] five curtains he joined one to another.

11He made loops of blue on the edge of the outermost curtain in the first set; he also did this on the edge of the curtain that was outermost in the second set.

12He made fifty loops in the one curtain [of the first set] and fifty loops on the edge of the curtain which was in the second set; the loops were opposite one another.

13He made fifty gold hooks and joined the curtains together with the hooks, so that the tabernacle became a unit.

14Then he made curtains of goats'

hair for a tent over the tabernacle; he made eleven curtains in all.

¹⁵Each curtain was thirty cubits long and four cubits wide; the eleven curtains were of equal size.

¹⁶Bezalel joined five curtains by themselves and [the other] six curtains by themselves.

¹⁷He made fifty loops on the edge of the outermost curtain in the *first* set, and he made fifty loops on the edge of the *outermost* curtain of the second set.

¹⁸He made fifty bronze hooks to join the tent together into a unit.

¹⁹He made a [third] covering for the tent of rams' skins dyed red, and above it a [fourth] covering of porpoise skins.

²⁰Bezalel made boards of acacia wood for the upright framework of the tabernacle.

²¹Each board was ten cubits long and one and a half cubits wide.

²²Each board had two tenons (dovetails), fitted to one another; he did this for all the boards of the tabernacle.

²³And [this is how] he made the boards [for frames] for the tabernacle: twenty boards for the south side;

²⁴and he made under the twenty boards forty silver sockets; two sockets under one board for its two tenons (dovetails), and two sockets under another board for its two tenons.

²⁵For the other side of the tabernacle, the north side, he made twenty boards,

²⁶and their forty silver sockets; two sockets under [the end of] each board.

²⁷And for the rear of the tabernacle, to the west, he made six [frame] boards.

²⁸And he made two boards for each corner of the tabernacle in the rear.

²⁹They were separate below, but linked together at the top with one ring; thus he made both of them in both corners.

³⁰There were eight boards with sixteen silver sockets, and under [the end of] each board two sockets.

³¹Bezalel made bars of acacia wood, five for the [frame] boards of the one side of the tabernacle,

³²and five bars for the boards of the tabernacle's other side, and five bars for the boards at the rear side to the west.

³³And he made the middle bar pass through [horizontally] halfway up the boards from one end to the other.

³⁴He overlaid the boards and the bars with gold and made their rings of gold as holders for the bars.

³⁵Further, Bezalel made the veil of blue and purple and scarlet fabric, and fine twisted linen; he made it with cherubim, the work of an embroiderer. [Matt 27:50, 51; Heb 10:19–22]

³⁶For the veil (partition curtain) he made four support poles of acacia wood and overlaid them with gold; their hooks were gold, and he cast for them four silver sockets.

³⁷He made a screen (curtain) for the doorway of the tent, of blue, purple, and scarlet fabric, and fine twisted linen, the work of an embroiderer;

³⁸and [he made] the five support poles with their hooks, and overlaid their [ornamental] tops and connecting rings with gold; but their five sockets were bronze.

37 BEZALEL MADE the ark [of the covenant] of acacia wood—it was two and a half cubits long, and one and a half cubits wide, and one and a half cubits high.

²And he overlaid it with pure gold inside and out, and made a molding (border) of gold to go all around [the top of it].

³He cast four rings of gold for it on its four feet, two rings on one side and two rings on the other side.

⁴He made carrying poles of acacia wood and overlaid them with gold.

⁵He put the carrying poles through the rings at the sides of the ark, to carry it.

⁶Bezalel made the mercy seat of pure gold; it was two and a half cubits long, and one and a half cubits wide. ⁷He made two cherubim of hammered gold; he made them at the two ends of the mercy seat, ⁸one cherub at one end and one cherub at the other end; he made the cherubim [of one piece] with the mercy seat at the two ends. ⁹The cherubim spread out their wings upward, covering *and* protecting the mercy seat with their wings, with their faces toward each other; the faces of the cherubim were [looking downward] toward the mercy seat. [Heb 9:23–26]

¹⁰Bezalel made the table [for the bread] of acacia wood; it was two cubits long, a cubit wide, and one and a half cubits high. ¹¹He overlaid it with pure gold, and made a border of gold for it all around [its top]. ¹²He made a rim for it [just under the top] a hand width wide all around, and a border of gold around its rim. ¹³He cast four rings of gold for it and fastened the rings to the four corners that were at its four legs. ¹⁴Close by the rim were the rings, the holders for the poles [to pass through] to carry the table. ¹⁵Bezalel made the carrying poles of acacia wood to carry the table and overlaid them with gold. ¹⁶He made the utensils which were to be on the table, its dishes and its pans [for bread], its bowls and its jars for pouring drink offerings, of pure gold.

¹⁷Then he made the lampstand (menorah) of pure gold. He made the lampstand of hammered work, its base and its [center] shaft; its cups, its calyxes, and its flowers were *all of one piece* with it. ¹⁸There were six branches coming out of the sides of the lampstand, three branches from one side of *the center shaft* and three branches from the other side of it;

¹⁹three cups shaped like almond *blossoms*, a calyx and a flower in one branch, and three cups shaped like almond *blossoms*, a calyx and a flower in the opposite branch—so for the six branches coming out of *the center shaft of* the lampstand. ²⁰On *the center shaft of* the lampstand there were four cups shaped like almond *blossoms*, with calyxes and flowers [one at the top]; ²¹and a calyx was under the *first* pair of branches *coming* out of it, and a calyx under the *second* pair of branches, *coming* out of it, and a calyx under the *third* pair of branches *coming* out of it, for the six branches coming out of the lampstand. ²²Their calyxes and their branches were *of one piece* with it; all of it was a single hammered work of pure gold. ²³He made its seven lamps with its snuffers and its trays of pure gold. ²⁴He made the lampstand and all its utensils from a talent of pure gold. [John 1:4, 5, 9; 2 Cor 4:6]

²⁵Then Bezalel made the incense altar of acacia wood; its top was a cubit square and it was two cubits high; the horns were *of one piece* with it. ²⁶He overlaid it with pure gold, its top, its sides all around and its horns; he also made a rim of gold around it. ²⁷He made two rings of gold for it under its rim, on its two opposite sides, as holders for the poles [to pass through] to carry it. ²⁸He made the poles of acacia wood and overlaid them with gold. ²⁹He also made the holy anointing oil and the pure, fragrant incense of spices, the work of a perfumer.

38 THEN BEZALEL made the altar of burnt offering of acacia wood; its top was square, five cubits long and five cubits wide, and three cubits high. ²And he made its horns (horn-shaped projections) on the four corners of it; the horns were *of one piece* with it, and he overlaid it with bronze.

³He made all the utensils *and* vessels of the altar [of burnt offering], the pots, shovels, basins [to catch the blood of the sacrificed animal], meat hooks and the firepans [to store live coals]. He made all its utensils of bronze.

⁴He made for the altar a grating of bronze mesh under its rim, extending halfway up it.

⁵He cast four rings for the four corners of the bronze grating as holders for the carrying poles.

⁶And he made the carrying poles of acacia wood and overlaid them with bronze.

⁷He put the poles through the rings on the sides of the altar, with which to carry it; he made it hollow with planks.

⁸Bezalel made the basin and its base of bronze from the mirrors of the attending women who served *and* ministered at the doorway of the Tent of Meeting.

⁹Then he made the court: for the south side the curtains of the court were of fine twisted linen, a hundred cubits;

¹⁰their twenty support poles, and their twenty bronze sockets; the hooks of the support poles and their connecting rings were silver.

¹¹And for the north side [of the court the curtains were also] a hundred cubits; their twenty support poles and their twenty bronze sockets; the hooks of the support poles and their connecting rings were silver.

¹²For the west side [of the court] there were curtains of fifty cubits with their ten support poles and their ten sockets; the hooks of the support poles and their connecting rings were silver.

¹³For the east side [the front of the courtyard, there were curtains of] fifty cubits.

¹⁴The curtains for one side *of the court gate were* fifteen cubits, with their three support poles and their three sockets;

¹⁵and *the same* for the other side [of the court gate]. Left and right of the court gate there were curtains of fifteen cubits; with their three support poles and their three sockets.

¹⁶All the curtains around the court were of fine twisted linen.

¹⁷The sockets for the support poles were *made of* bronze, the hooks of the support poles and their connecting rings were *made of* silver; and silver overlaid their tops. All the support poles of the court had silver connecting rings.

¹⁸The screen (curtain) for the gate of the courtyard [on the east side] was the work of an embroiderer, in blue, purple, and scarlet fabric, and fine twisted linen; it was twenty cubits long and five cubits high, corresponding to the curtains of the court.

¹⁹Their four support poles and their four sockets were bronze; their hooks were silver, and silver overlaid their tops and their connecting rings.

²⁰All the pegs for the tabernacle and the court were bronze.

²¹This is the sum of the things for the tabernacle, the tabernacle of the Testimony, as counted according to the command of Moses, for the work of the Levites, under the direction of Ithamar the son of Aaron the priest.

²²Now Bezalel the son of Uri, the son of Hur, of the tribe of Judah, made everything that the Lord commanded Moses.

²³With him was Oholiab the son of Ahisamach, of the tribe of Dan, an engraver and a skillful craftsman and an embroiderer in blue and in purple and in scarlet fabric, and in fine linen.

²⁴All the gold that was used for the work, in all the building *and* furnishing of the sanctuary, the gold from the wave offering, was twenty-nine

talents and seven hundred and thirty shekels, according to the shekel of the sanctuary.

²⁵The silver from those of the congregation who were assembled *and* counted was 100 talents and 1,775 shekels, according to the shekel of the sanctuary;

²⁶a beka for each man (that is, half a shekel according to the shekel of the sanctuary) for everyone who was counted, from twenty years old and upward, for 603,550 men.

²⁷The hundred talents of silver were for casting the sockets of the sanctuary and the sockets of the veil (partition curtain); a hundred sockets for the hundred talents, a talent for a socket.

²⁸Of the 1,775 *shekels*, he made hooks for the support poles and overlaid their tops and made connecting rings for them.

²⁹The bronze of the wave offering was seventy talents and 2,400 shekels.

³⁰With it Bezalel made the sockets for the doorway of the Tent of Meeting, and the bronze altar and its bronze grating, and all the utensils of the altar,

³¹and the sockets of the court all around and the sockets of the court gate, and all the pegs of the tabernacle and all the pegs around the court.

39

MOREOVER, FROM the blue and purple and scarlet fabric, they made finely woven garments for serving *and* ministering in the Holy Place; they made the holy garments for Aaron, just as the LORD had commanded Moses.

²Bezalel made the ephod of gold, and of blue, purple, and scarlet fabric, and fine twisted linen.

³Then Bezalel and Oholiab hammered the gold [into thin sheets] and cut it into threads to work into the blue, purple, and scarlet fabric, and into the fine linen, the work of a skilled craftsman.

⁴They made attaching shoulder pieces for the ephod; it was attached at its two [upper] edges.

⁵The skillfully woven sash with which to bind it, which was on the ephod [to hold it in place], was like its workmanship, of the same material: of gold and of blue, purple, and scarlet fabric, and fine twisted linen, just as the LORD had commanded Moses.

⁶They made the onyx stones, set in settings of gold filigree; they were engraved as signets are engraved, with the names of [the twelve tribes of] the sons of Israel.

⁷And he put them on the shoulder pieces of the ephod to be memorial stones (a remembrance) for the sons of Israel (Jacob), just as the LORD had commanded Moses.

⁸Bezalel made the breastpiece, the work of a skillful craftsman, like the workmanship of the ephod: of gold and of blue, purple, and scarlet fabric, and fine twisted linen.

⁹It was square; they made the breastpiece folded double, a [hand's] span long and a [hand's] span wide when folded double.

¹⁰And they mounted four rows of stones on it. The first row was a row of ruby, topaz, and emerald;

¹¹and the second row, a turquoise, a sapphire, and a diamond;

¹²and the third row, a jacinth, an agate, and an amethyst;

¹³and the fourth row, a beryl, an onyx, and a jasper; they were mounted in settings of gold filigree.

¹⁴The stones corresponded to the names of the sons of Israel; they were twelve [in all], corresponding to their names, engraved like a signet, each with its name, for the twelve tribes.

¹⁵And they made on the breastpiece twisted chains like cords of pure gold.

¹⁶They made two settings of gold filigree and two gold rings, and put the two rings on the two ends of the breastpiece.

¹⁷Then they put the two twisted cords of gold in the two rings on the ends of the breastpiece.

¹⁸They put the [other] two ends of the two cords on the two filigree settings, and put them on the shoulder pieces of the ephod at the front of it.

¹⁹They made two rings of gold and put them on the two ends of the breastpiece, on its inner edge which was next to the ephod.

²⁰Furthermore, they made two [other] gold rings and attached them to the bottom of the two shoulder pieces of the ephod, at the front of it, close to the place where it is joined, above the woven sash of the ephod.

²¹They bound the breastpiece by its rings to the rings of the ephod with a blue cord, so that it would lie on the woven sash of the ephod, and so that the breastpiece would not come loose from the ephod, just as the LORD commanded Moses.

²²Then Bezalel made the robe of the ephod of woven work, all of blue;

²³there was an opening [for the head] in the middle of the robe, like the opening in a coat of armor, with a hem around it, so that it would not be frayed or torn.

²⁴On the hem of the robe they made pomegranates of blue, purple, and scarlet fabric, and fine twisted linen.

²⁵They also made bells of pure gold, and put the bells between the pomegranates around the hem of the robe;

²⁶a bell and a pomegranate, a bell and a pomegranate, all [the way] around the hem of the robe, for service and ministering, just as the LORD commanded Moses.

²⁷And they made tunics of finely woven linen for Aaron and his sons,

²⁸and the turban of fine linen, and the ornamental caps of fine linen, and the linen undergarments of fine twisted linen,

²⁹and the sash of fine twisted linen, and blue, purple, and scarlet fabric, the work of an embroiderer, just as the LORD commanded Moses.

³⁰They made the plate of the holy crown of pure gold, and wrote on it an inscription, like the engravings of a signet, "Holy to the LORD." [Ex 28:36]

³¹They tied a blue cord to it, to fasten it on the turban above, just as the LORD commanded Moses.

³²Thus all the work of the tabernacle of the Tent of Meeting was finished; and the Israelites did according to all that the LORD had commanded Moses; that is what they did.

³³They brought the tabernacle to Moses [for him to inspect]: the tent and all its furnishings, its hooks, its [frame] boards, its bars, its support poles, its sockets or bases;

³⁴and the covering of rams' skins dyed red, and the covering of porpoise skins, and the veil (partition) of the screen (curtain);

³⁵the ark of the Testimony, its carrying poles and the mercy seat;

³⁶the table and all its utensils and the bread of the Presence (showbread);

³⁷the pure gold lampstand and its lamps, with the lamps placed in order, all its utensils, and the oil for the light;

³⁸the golden altar [of incense], the anointing oil and the fragrant incense, and the [hanging] veil for the doorway of the tent;

³⁹the bronze altar [of burnt offering] and its grating of bronze, its poles and all its utensils, the basin and its base;

⁴⁰the curtains of the courtyard, its support poles and sockets, and the screen (curtain) for the courtyard gate, its cords and pegs, and all the utensils for the service of the tabernacle, for the Tent of Meeting [of God with His people]; [Ex 29:42, 43]

⁴¹the [finely] woven garments for serving and ministering in the Holy Place, the holy garments for Aaron the priest, and the garments of his sons to minister as priests.

⁴²So the Israelites did all the work according to all that the Lᴏʀᴅ had commanded Moses.

⁴³And Moses [carefully] inspected all the work, and behold, they had done it; just as the Lᴏʀᴅ had commanded, so had they done it. So Moses blessed them.

40

THEN THE Lᴏʀᴅ spoke to Moses, saying, ²"On the first day of the first month (Abib) you shall set up the tabernacle of the Tent of Meeting [of God with you].

³"You shall place the ark of the Testimony there, and you shall screen off the ark [from the Holy Place of God's Presence] with the veil (partition curtain). [Heb 10:19–23]

⁴"You shall bring in the table [for the bread] and arrange its setting; you shall bring in the lampstand and mount *and* light its lamps. [Rev 21:23–25]

⁵"You shall set the golden altar of incense in front of the ark of the Testimony [outside the veil], and put the [hanging] veil at the doorway of the tabernacle.

⁶"You shall set the [bronze] altar of burnt offering in front of the doorway of the tabernacle of the Tent of Meeting.

⁷"You shall set the basin between the Tent of Meeting and the altar [of burnt offering], and put water in it.

⁸"You shall set up the courtyard [curtains] all around and hang up the screen (curtain) for the gateway of the courtyard.

⁹"Then you shall take the anointing oil and anoint the tabernacle and all that is in it, and consecrate it and all its furniture; and it shall be holy (declared sacred, separated from secular use).

¹⁰"You shall anoint the altar of burnt offering and all its utensils, and consecrate the altar, and the altar shall be most holy.

¹¹"You shall anoint the basin and its base, and consecrate it.

¹²"Then you shall bring Aaron and his sons to the doorway of the Tent of Meeting and wash them with water. [John 17:17–19]

¹³"You shall put the holy garments on Aaron and anoint him and consecrate him, that he may serve as a priest to Me.

¹⁴"You shall bring his sons and put tunics on them;

¹⁵you shall anoint them just as you anointed their father, so that they may serve as priests to Me; and their anointing shall qualify them for an everlasting priesthood throughout their generations."

¹⁶Thus Moses did; in accordance with all that the Lᴏʀᴅ commanded him, so he did.

¹⁷Now it happened on the first day of the first month (Abib) in the second year [after the exodus from Egypt], that the tabernacle was erected.

¹⁸Moses erected the tabernacle, laid its sockets, set up its boards, put in its bars and erected its support poles.

¹⁹He spread the tent over the tabernacle and put the covering of the tent over it, just as the Lᴏʀᴅ had commanded him.

²⁰He took the Testimony [the stones inscribed with the Ten Commandments] and put it into the ark [of the covenant], and placed the poles [through the rings] on the ark, and put the mercy seat on top of the ark.

²¹Moses brought the ark into the tabernacle, and set up a veil (partition) for the screen (curtain), and screened off the ark of the Testimony, just as the Lᴏʀᴅ had commanded him.

²²Then he put the table in the Tent of Meeting on the north side of the tabernacle, outside the veil.

²³He set the bread [of the Presence] in order on it before the Lᴏʀᴅ, just as the Lᴏʀᴅ had commanded him. [John 6:32–35]

²⁴Then he put the lampstand in the

Tent of Meeting, opposite the table, on the south side of the tabernacle.

²⁵Moses mounted *and* lighted the lamps [on the lampstand] before the LORD, just as the LORD commanded him.

²⁶He put the golden altar [of incense] in the Tent of Meeting in front of the veil;

²⁷he burned fragrant incense [as a symbol of prayer] on it, just as the LORD commanded him. [Ps 141:2; Rev 8:3]

²⁸Then he set up the screen (curtain) at the doorway of the tabernacle.

²⁹He set the altar of burnt offering before the doorway of the tabernacle of the Tent of Meeting, and offered on it the burnt offering and the grain offering, just as the LORD commanded him.

³⁰He placed the basin between the Tent of Meeting and the altar [of burnt offering], and put water in it for washing.

putting the Word to work

The cloud that led the Israelites on their journey (see Exodus 40:36–38) symbolizes the leading of the Holy Spirit in our lives today. Are you following the "cloud" in your life, patiently waiting on God to lead you on the next phase of your journey and being quick to obey when He does?

³¹Then from it Moses and Aaron and his sons washed their hands and their feet.

³²When they entered the Tent of Meeting, and when they approached the altar, they washed, just as the LORD commanded Moses.

³³And he erected the courtyard all around the tabernacle and the altar, and hung the screen (curtain) at the gateway of the courtyard. So Moses finished the work.

³⁴Then the cloud [the Shekinah, God's visible, dwelling presence] covered the Tent of Meeting, and the glory *and* brilliance of the LORD filled the tabernacle. [Rev 15:8]

³⁵Moses was not able to enter the Tent of Meeting because the cloud remained on it, and the glory *and* brilliance of the LORD filled the tabernacle.

³⁶In all their journeys, whenever the cloud was taken up from over the tabernacle, the Israelites would set out;

³⁷but if the cloud was not taken up, then they did not journey on until the day when it was taken up.

³⁸For throughout all their journeys, the cloud of the LORD was on the tabernacle by day, and there was fire in it by night, in the sight of all the house of Israel.

Leviticus

Author:
Moses

Date:
About 1440 BC

Everyday Life Principles:
God's laws are in place for our good. He has established them so that we can enjoy His blessings.

Serious consequences result when we do not obey God.

God calls us to live holy lives and to have purity and integrity in every aspect of our everyday lives.

The basic message of Leviticus is: "If you obey God, you will be blessed. If you don't, you won't." The laws and instructions we find in Leviticus, and the commands to obey, all have one purpose: blessing. God knows that sin and disobedience will separate us from Him, so He gives us guidelines for living so we can stay close to Him and live under His blessing. God requires our obedience so that we can stay in fellowship with Him and live in His favor.

In addition to showing us the need to obey the laws of God so we can be blessed, Leviticus also calls us to holiness in our everyday lives. The Israelites' idea of holiness was based on laws and rituals; our concept of holiness is much different because of what Jesus did on the cross. While there are certain actions we can take to express holiness, actions alone do not make us holy. Holiness begins in our hearts with faith in Jesus, and He leads us to desire to obey God in everything we do.

I hope you will look beyond the animal sacrifices and elaborate rituals in Leviticus and see the rich symbolism in this book. I hope it will stir you to live a more holy life in the midst of your everyday circumstances and bring about greater obedience in your heart so that you can live in greater and greater blessing.

1

THE LORD called to Moses and spoke to him from the Tent of Meeting, saying,

[2]"Speak to the children of Israel and say to them, 'When any one of you brings an offering to the LORD, you shall bring your offering of [domestic] animals from the herd (cattle, oxen) or from the flock (sheep, goats).

[3]'If his offering is a burnt offering from the herd, he shall offer a male without blemish; he shall offer it at the doorway of the Tent of Meeting so that he may be accepted before the LORD. [Rom 12:1; Phil 1:20]

[4]'He shall lay his hand on the head of the burnt offering [transferring symbolically his guilt to the sacrifice], that it may be accepted for him to make atonement on his behalf. [Heb 13:15, 16; 1 Pet 1:2]

[5]'He shall kill the young bull before the LORD; and Aaron's sons the priests shall present the blood and sprinkle the blood around on the altar that is at the doorway of the Tent of Meeting.

[6]'Then he shall skin the burnt offering and cut it into pieces.

[7]'The sons of Aaron the [high] priest shall put fire on the altar [of burnt offering] and arrange wood on the fire.

[8]'Then Aaron's sons the priests shall arrange the pieces, the head and the fat, on the wood which is on the fire that is on the altar.

[9]'But he shall wash its entrails and its legs with water. The priest shall offer all of it up in smoke on the altar as a burnt offering. It is an offering by fire, a sweet *and* soothing aroma to the LORD. [Eph 5:2; Phil 4:18; 1 Pet 2:5]

[10]'But if his offering is from the flock, of the sheep or of the goats, as a burnt offering, he shall offer a male without blemish.

[11]'He shall kill it on the north side of the altar before the LORD, and Aaron's sons the priests shall sprinkle its blood around on the altar.

[12]'He shall cut it into pieces, with its head and its fat, and the priest shall arrange them on the wood which is on the fire that is on the altar.

[13]'But he shall wash the entrails and legs with water. The priest shall offer all of it, and offer it up in smoke on the altar. It is a burnt offering, an offering by fire, a sweet *and* soothing aroma to the LORD.

[14]'But if his offering to the LORD is a burnt offering of birds, then he shall bring turtledoves or young pigeons as his offering.

[15]'The priest shall bring it to the altar, and wring off its head, and offer it up in smoke on the altar; and its blood is to be drained out on the side of the altar.

[16]'He shall remove its crop with its feathers and throw it next to the east side of the altar, in the place for ashes.

[17]'Then he shall tear it open by its wings, but shall not sever it. And the priest shall offer it up in smoke on the altar, on the wood that is on the fire. It is a burnt offering, an offering by fire, a sweet *and* soothing aroma to the LORD.

2

'WHEN ANYONE presents a grain offering to the Lord, his offering shall be of fine flour, and he shall pour [olive] oil over it and put frankincense on it.

[2]'He shall bring it to Aaron's sons the priests. Out of it he shall take a handful of the fine flour and oil, with all of its frankincense, and the priest shall offer this up in smoke on the altar [of burnt offering] as the memorial portion of it. It is an offering by fire, a sweet *and* soothing aroma to the LORD.

speak the Word

God, I pray that everything I offer You will be pure and without blemish.
–ADAPTED FROM LEVITICUS 1:3

³'What is left of the grain offering belongs to Aaron and his sons; it is a most holy part of the offerings to the LORD by fire.

⁴'When you bring an offering of grain baked in the oven, it shall be unleavened cakes of fine flour mixed with oil, or unleavened wafers spread with oil.

⁵'If your offering is grain baked on a griddle, it shall be of fine unleavened flour, mixed with oil.

⁶'You are to break it into pieces, and you shall pour oil on it; it is a grain offering.

⁷'Now if your offering is grain cooked in a lidded pan, it shall be made of fine flour with oil.

⁸'When you bring the grain offering that is made of these things to the LORD, it shall be presented to the priest, and he shall bring it to the altar [of burnt offering].

⁹'The priest shall take from the grain offering its memorial portion and offer it up in smoke on the altar. It is an offering by fire, a sweet *and* soothing aroma to the LORD.

¹⁰'What is left of the grain offering belongs to Aaron and his sons; it is a most holy part of the offerings to the LORD by fire.

¹¹'No grain offering that you bring to the LORD shall be made with leaven, for you shall not offer up in smoke any leaven [which symbolizes the spread of sin] or any honey [which, like leaven, is subject to fermentation] in any offering by fire to the LORD. [1 Cor 5:8]

¹²'As an offering of first fruits you may offer them [leaven and honey] to the LORD, but they shall not go up [in smoke] on the altar as a sweet *and* soothing aroma.

¹³'You shall season every grain offering with salt so that the salt (preservation) of the covenant of your God will not be missing from your grain offering. You shall offer salt with all your offerings. [Mark 9:49, 50]

¹⁴'If you bring a grain offering of early ripened things to the LORD, you shall bring fresh heads of grain roasted in the fire, crushed grain of new growth, for the grain offering of your early ripened things.

¹⁵'You shall put oil on it and lay incense on it; it is a grain offering.

¹⁶'The priest shall offer up in smoke its memorial portion, part of the crushed grain and part of its oil with all its incense; it is an offering by fire to the LORD.

3 'IF A man's offering is a sacrifice of peace offerings, if he offers an animal from the herd, whether male or female, he shall offer it without blemish before the LORD.

²'He shall lay his hand on the head of his offering [transferring symbolically his guilt to the sacrifice] and kill it at the doorway of the Tent of Meeting; and Aaron's sons the priests shall sprinkle the blood around on the altar.

³'From the sacrifice of the peace offerings, an offering by fire to the LORD, he shall present the fat that covers the entrails, and all the fat which is on the entrails,

⁴and the two kidneys with the fat that is on them at the loins, and the lobe of the liver which he shall remove with the kidneys.

⁵'Aaron's sons shall offer it up in smoke on the altar [placing it] on the burnt offering which is on the wood that is on the fire. It is an offering by fire, a sweet *and* soothing aroma to the LORD.

⁶'If his peace offering to the LORD is an animal from the flock, male or female, he shall offer the animal without blemish.

⁷'If he offers a lamb as his offering, then he shall present it before the LORD,

⁸and he shall lay his hand on the head of his offering and kill it before the Tent of Meeting, and Aaron's sons shall sprinkle its blood around on the altar.

⁹'From the sacrifice of peace offerings he shall bring as an offering by fire to the LORD, its fat, the entire fat tail which he shall remove close to the backbone, and the fat that covers the entrails, and all the fat which is on the entrails,

¹⁰and the two kidneys with the fat that is on them at the loins, and the lobe of the liver, which he shall remove with the kidneys.

¹¹'The priest shall offer it up in smoke on the altar as food, an offering by fire to the LORD.

¹²'If his offering is a goat, he shall present it before the LORD,

¹³and he shall lay his hand on its head [transferring symbolically his guilt to the sacrifice], and kill it before the Tent of Meeting; and the sons of Aaron shall sprinkle its blood around on the altar.

¹⁴'Then he shall present from it as his offering, an offering by fire to the LORD: the fat that covers the entrails, and all the fat that is on the entrails,

¹⁵and the two kidneys with the fat that is on them at the loins, and the lobe of the liver which he shall remove with the kidneys.

¹⁶'The priest shall offer them up in smoke on the altar as food. It is an offering by fire, a sweet *and* soothing aroma; all the fat is the LORD's.

¹⁷'It is a permanent statute for your generations wherever you may be, that you shall not eat any fat or any blood.'"

4 THEN THE LORD spoke to Moses, saying,

²"Speak to the children of Israel, 'If a person sins unintentionally in any of the things which the LORD has commanded not to be done, and commits any of them—

³if the anointed priest sins, bringing guilt on the people, then he shall offer to the LORD a young bull without blemish as a sin offering for the sin he has committed. [Heb 7:27, 28]

⁴'He shall bring the bull to the doorway of the Tent of Meeting before the LORD, and shall lay his hand on the bull's head [transferring symbolically his guilt to the sacrifice] and kill the bull before the LORD.

⁵'Then the anointed priest is to take some of the bull's blood and bring it into the Tent of Meeting;

⁶and the priest shall dip his finger in the blood and sprinkle some of it seven times before the LORD in front of the veil (curtain) of the sanctuary.

⁷'The priest shall also put some of the blood on the horns of the altar of fragrant incense which is before the LORD in the Tent of Meeting. All the *rest of the* blood of the bull he shall pour out at the base of the altar of the burnt offering which is at the doorway of the Tent of Meeting.

⁸'He shall remove all the fat from the bull of the sin offering—the fat that covers the entrails, and all the fat which is on the entrails,

⁹and the two kidneys with the fat that is on them at the loins, and the lobe of the liver, which he shall remove with the kidneys

¹⁰(just as these are removed from the ox of the sacrifice of peace offerings), and the priest is to offer them up in smoke on the altar of burnt offering.

¹¹'But the hide of the bull and all its meat, with its head, its legs, its entrails, and its refuse,

¹²that is, *all the rest of* the bull, he is to bring outside the camp to a clean place where the ashes are poured out, and burn it on a fire of wood. Where the ashes are poured out it shall be burned. [Heb 13:11–13]

¹³'Now if the whole congregation of Israel sins unintentionally, and the matter escapes the notice of the assembly, and they have done any one of the things which the LORD has commanded not to be done, and they become guilty;

[14]when the sin which they have committed becomes known, then the congregation shall offer a young bull of the herd as a sin offering and bring it before the Tent of Meeting.

[15]'Then the elders of the congregation shall lay their hands on the head of the bull before the LORD [to transfer symbolically the congregation's guilt to the sacrifice], and they shall kill the bull before the LORD.

[16]'The anointed priest is to bring some of the bull's blood to the Tent of Meeting,

[17]and the priest shall dip his finger in the blood, and sprinkle it seven times before the LORD, in front of the veil [which screens off the Holy of Holies and the ark of the covenant].

[18]'He shall put some of the blood on the horns of the altar [of incense] which is before the LORD in the Tent of Meeting; and he shall pour out all the rest of the blood at the base of the altar of burnt offering which is at the doorway of the Tent of Meeting.

[19]'He shall remove all its fat from the bull and offer it up in smoke on the altar.

[20]'He shall also do with the bull just as he did with the bull of the sin offering; that is what he shall do with this. So the priest shall make atonement for [the sin of] the people, and they will be forgiven.

[21]'Then the priest is to bring the bull outside the camp and burn it as he burned the first bull; it is the sin offering for the congregation.

[22]'When a ruler or leader sins and unintentionally does any one of the things the LORD his God has commanded not to be done, and he becomes guilty,

[23]if his sin which he has committed is made known to him, he shall bring a goat, a male without blemish as his offering.

[24]'He shall lay his hand on the head of the male goat [transferring symbolically his guilt to the sacrifice], and kill it in the place where they kill the burnt offering before the LORD; it is a sin offering.

[25]'Then the priest is to take some of the blood of the sin offering with his finger and put it on the horns of the altar of burnt offering; and the rest of its blood he shall pour out at the base of the altar of burnt offering.

[26]'And he shall offer all its fat up in smoke on the altar like the fat from the sacrifice of peace offerings; so the priest shall make atonement for him in regard to his sin, and he will be forgiven.

[27]'If anyone of the common people sins unintentionally by doing any of the things the LORD has commanded not to be done, and becomes guilty,

[28]if his sin which he has committed is made known to him, then he shall bring a goat, a female without blemish as his offering for the sin which he has committed.

[29]'He shall lay his hand on the head of the sin offering [transferring symbolically his guilt to the sacrifice], and kill it at the place of the burnt offering.

[30]'The priest shall take some of its blood with his finger and put it on the horns of the altar of burnt offering and shall pour out all the rest of its blood at the base of the altar.

[31]'Then he shall remove all its fat, just as the fat was removed from the sacrifice of peace offerings; and the priest shall offer it up in smoke on the altar as a sweet and soothing aroma to the LORD. In this way the priest shall make atonement for him, and he will be forgiven.

[32]'If he brings a lamb as his offering for a sin offering, he shall bring a female without blemish.

[33]'He shall lay his hand on the head of the sin offering [transferring symbolically his guilt to the sacrifice], and

kill it as a sin offering in the place where they kill the burnt offering.

³⁴'The priest is to take some of the blood of the sin offering with his finger and put it on the horns of the altar of burnt offering and all *the rest of* the blood of the lamb he shall pour out at the base of the altar.

³⁵'Then he shall remove all its fat, just as the fat of the lamb is removed from the sacrifice of the peace offerings, and the priest shall offer it up in smoke on the altar, on the offerings by fire to the LORD. In this way the priest shall make atonement for him in regard to the sin which he has committed, and he will be forgiven. [Heb 9:13, 14]

5 'IF ANYONE sins after he hears a public adjuration (solemn command to testify) when he is a witness, whether he has seen or [otherwise] known [something]—if he fails to report it, then he will bear his guilt *and* be held responsible.

²'Or if someone touches any [ceremonially] unclean thing—whether the carcass of an unclean wild animal or the carcass of an unclean domestic animal or the carcass of unclean creeping things—even if he is unaware of it, he has become unclean, and he will be guilty.

³'Or if he touches human uncleanness—whatever kind it may be—and he becomes unclean, but he is unaware of it, when he recognizes it, he will be guilty.

⁴'Or if anyone swears [an oath] thoughtlessly *or* impulsively aloud that he will do either evil or good, in whatever manner a person may speak thoughtlessly *or* impulsively with an oath, but he is unaware of it, when he recognizes it, he will be guilty in one of these. [Mark 6:23]

⁵'So it shall be when a person is guilty in one of these, that he shall confess the sin he has committed.

⁶'He shall bring his guilt offering to the LORD for the sin which he has committed, a female from the flock, a lamb or a goat as a sin offering. So the priest shall make atonement on his behalf for his sin.

⁷'But if he cannot afford a lamb, then he shall bring two turtledoves or two young pigeons as his guilt offering for his sin to the LORD, one as a sin offering and the other as a burnt offering.

⁸'He shall bring them to the priest, who shall offer first the one for the sin offering, and shall nip its head at the front of its neck, but shall not sever it [completely].

⁹'He shall also sprinkle some of the blood of the sin offering on the side of the altar, and the rest of the blood shall be drained out at the base of the altar; it is a sin offering.

¹⁰'The second [bird] he shall prepare as a burnt offering, according to the ordinance. So the priest shall make atonement on his behalf for the sin which he has committed, and it will be forgiven him.

¹¹'But if he cannot afford to bring two turtledoves or two young pigeons, then he shall bring as his offering for his sin the tenth part of an ephah of fine flour as a sin offering; he shall not put [olive] oil or incense on it, for it is a sin offering.

¹²'He shall bring it to the priest, who shall take a handful of it as a memorial portion and offer it up in smoke on the altar, with the offerings by fire to the LORD; it is a sin offering.

¹³'In this way the priest shall make atonement for him for the sin which he has committed in one of these things, and it will be forgiven him; then *the rest* shall be for the priest, like the grain offering.'"

¹⁴Then the LORD spoke to Moses, saying,

¹⁵"If a person commits a breach of faith and sins unintentionally against

the holy things of the Lord, then he shall bring his guilt offering to the Lord, a ram without blemish from the flock, valued by you in shekels of silver, that is, the shekel of the sanctuary, as a guilt offering.

16"He shall make restitution for the sin which he has committed against the holy thing, and shall add a fifth [of the ram's value] to it, and give it to the priest. The priest shall then make atonement for him with the ram of the guilt offering, and he shall be forgiven.

17"Now if anyone sins and does any of the things which the Lord has forbidden, though he was not aware of it, still he is guilty and shall bear his punishment. [Luke 12:48]

18"He is then to bring to the priest a ram without blemish from the flock, according to your valuation, for a guilt offering. In this way the priest shall make atonement for him regarding the error which he committed unintentionally and did not know it, and he shall be forgiven.

19"It is a guilt offering; he was certainly guilty before the Lord."

6 THEN THE Lord spoke to Moses, saying, 2"When anyone sins and acts unfaithfully against the Lord by deceiving his neighbor (companion, associate) in regard to a deposit or a security entrusted to him, or through robbery, or if he has extorted from his neighbor,

3or has found what was lost and lied about it and sworn falsely, so that he sins in regard to any one of the things a man may do—

4then if he has sinned and is guilty, he shall restore what he took by robbery, or what he got by extortion, or the deposit which was entrusted to him, or the lost thing which he found,

5or anything about which he has sworn falsely; he shall not only restore it in full, but shall add to it one-fifth

more. He shall give it to the one to whom it belongs on the day of his guilt offering.

6"Then he shall bring to the priest his guilt offering to the Lord, a ram without blemish from the flock, as valued by you, as a guilt offering.

7"The priest shall make atonement for him before the Lord, and he will be forgiven for any one of the things which he may have done to incur guilt."

8Then the Lord spoke to Moses, saying,

9"Command Aaron and his sons, saying, 'This is the law of the burnt offering: the burnt offering *shall remain* on the hearth *that is* on the altar all night until morning and the fire is to be kept burning on the altar.

10'The priest is to put on his linen robe, with his linen undergarments next to his body. Then he shall take up the ashes of the burnt offering which the fire has consumed on the altar and put them beside the altar.

11'Then he shall take off his garments and put on something else, and take the ashes outside the camp to a (ceremonially) clean place.

12'The fire on the altar shall be kept burning; it shall not [be allowed to] go out. The priest shall burn wood on it every morning, and he shall arrange the burnt offering on it and offer the fat portions of the peace offerings up in smoke on it.

13'The fire shall be burning continually on the altar; it shall not [be allowed to] go out.

14'Now this is the law of the grain offering: the sons of Aaron shall present it before the Lord in front of the altar.

15'One of them shall take up from it a handful of the fine flour of the grain offering with its oil and all the incense that is on the grain offering, and he shall offer it up in smoke on the altar, a sweet *and* soothing aroma, as the memorial offering to the Lord.

16'What is left of it Aaron and his

sons are to eat. It shall be eaten as un-leavened bread in a holy place; they are to eat it in the courtyard of the Tent of Meeting. [1 Cor 9:13, 14]

[17]"It shall not be baked with leaven [which represents corruption or sin]. I have given it as their share of My offer-ings by fire; it is most holy, like the sin offering and the guilt offering.

[18]"Every male among the sons of Aaron may eat it [as his share]; it is a permanent ordinance throughout your generations, from offerings by fire to the LORD. Whatever touches them will become consecrated (cer-emonially clean).' "

[19]Then the LORD spoke to Moses, saying,

[20]"This is the offering which Aaron and his sons are to present to the LORD on the day when he is anointed: the tenth of an ephah of fine flour as a regular grain offering, half of it in the morning and half of it in the evening.

[21]"It shall be prepared with oil on a griddle. When it is well stirred, you shall bring it. You shall present the grain offering in baked pieces as a sweet *and* soothing aroma to the LORD.

[22]"The priest from among the sons of Aaron who is anointed in his place shall offer it. By a permanent statute it shall be entirely offered up in smoke to the LORD.

[23]"So every grain offering of the priest shall be burned entirely. It shall not be eaten."

[24]Then the LORD spoke to Moses, saying,

[25]"Speak to Aaron and his sons, say-ing, 'This is the law of the sin offering: the sin offering shall be killed before the LORD in the [same] place where the burnt offering is killed; it is most holy.

[26]"The priest who offers it for sin shall eat it. It shall be eaten in a holy place, in the courtyard of the Tent of Meeting.

[27]"Whatever touches its meat will become consecrated (ceremonially clean). When any of its blood splashes on a garment, you shall wash what was splashed on in a holy place.

[28]"Also the earthenware vessel in which it was boiled shall be broken; and if it was boiled in a bronze vessel, then that vessel shall be scoured and rinsed in water.

[29]"Every male among the priests may eat this offering; it is most holy.

[30]"But no sin offering from which any of the blood is brought into the Tent of Meeting to make atonement in the Holy Place shall be eaten; it shall be [completely] burned in the fire. [Heb 13:11–13]

7 'THIS IS the law of the guilt of-fering; it is most holy.
[2]'In the place where they kill the burnt offering they are to kill the guilt offering, and he shall sprinkle its blood around on the altar.

[3]'Then he shall offer all its fat, the fat tail and the fat that covers the entrails,

[4]and the two kidneys with the fat that is on them at the loins, and the lobe of the liver, which he shall re-move with the kidneys.

[5]'The priest shall offer them up in smoke on the altar as an offering by fire to the LORD; it is a guilt offering.

[6]'Every male among the priests may eat it; it shall be eaten in a holy place; it is most holy.

[7]'The guilt offering is like the sin of-fering, there is one law for [both of] them: the priest who makes atone-ment with it shall have it for himself.

[8]'The priest who presents any man's burnt offering shall have for himself the hide of the burnt offering which he has presented.

[9]'Likewise, every grain offering that is baked in the oven and every-thing that is prepared in a pan or on a griddle shall belong to the priest who presents it.

[10]'Every grain offering, mixed with

[olive] oil or dry, all the sons of Aaron may have, one as well as another.

¹¹'Now this is the law of the sacrifice of peace offerings which shall be presented to the Lord:

¹²'If one offers it as a *sacrificial meal of* thanksgiving, then along with the sacrifice of thanksgiving he shall offer unleavened cakes mixed with oil, and unleavened wafers spread with oil, and cakes of fine flour mixed with oil.

¹³'With the sacrifice of his peace offerings for thanksgiving, he shall present his offering with cakes of leavened bread.

¹⁴'Of this he shall present one [cake] from each offering as a contribution to the Lord; it shall belong to the priest who sprinkles the blood of the peace offerings.

¹⁵'The meat of the sacrifice of thanksgiving presented as a peace offering shall be eaten on the day that it is offered; none of it shall be left until morning.

¹⁶'But if the sacrifice of his offering is a vow or a freewill offering, it shall be eaten on the day that he offers his sacrifice, and on the next day that which remains of it may be eaten;

¹⁷but what is left over from the meat of the sacrifice on the third day shall be [completely] burned in the fire.

¹⁸'If any of the meat of the sacrifice of his peace offerings is ever eaten on the third day, then it will not be accepted, and the one who brought it will not be credited with it. It shall be an abhorred (offensive) thing; the one who eats it shall bear his own guilt.

¹⁹'The meat that comes in contact with anything that is unclean shall not be eaten; it shall be burned in the fire. As for other meat, everyone who is [ceremonially] clean may eat it.

²⁰'But the one who eats meat from the sacrifice of peace offerings which belong to the Lord, in his uncleanness, that person shall be cut off from his people [excluding him from the atonement made for them].

²¹'When anyone touches any unclean thing—human uncleanness, or an unclean animal, or any unclean detestable thing—and then eats the meat of the sacrifice of the Lord's peace offerings, that person shall be cut off from his people [excluding him from the atonement made for them].'"

²²Then the Lord spoke to Moses, saying,

²³"Speak to the children of Israel, saying, 'You shall not eat any fat from an ox, a sheep, or a goat.

²⁴'The fat of an animal which dies [of natural causes] and the fat of one which is torn [to pieces by a predator] may be put to any other use, but under no circumstances are you to eat it.

²⁵'For whoever eats the fat of the animal from which an offering by fire is presented to the Lord, that person who eats shall be cut off from his people [excluding him from the atonement made for them].

²⁶'Moreover, you are not to eat any blood [of any kind], whether of bird or animal, in any of your dwelling places.

²⁷'Whoever eats any blood, that person shall be cut off from his people.'"

²⁸Then the Lord spoke to Moses, saying,

²⁹"Speak to the children of Israel, saying, 'He who offers the sacrifice of his peace offerings to the Lord shall bring his offering to the Lord from the sacrifice of his peace offerings.

putting the Word to work

Throughout the book of Leviticus, we read about the sacrifices required to atone for sin. Aren't you thankful that God sent His Son, Jesus, to fulfill all of the laws enumerated in the Old Testament and to be the once-and-for-all, perfect sacrifice for our sins? Tell Him today how grateful you are.

³⁰'With his own hands he is to bring offerings by fire to the Lᴏʀᴅ; he shall bring the fat with the breast, so that the breast may be presented as a wave offering before the Lᴏʀᴅ.

³¹'The priest shall offer up the fat in smoke on the altar, but the breast shall be for Aaron and his sons.

³²'You shall give the right thigh to the priest as a contribution from the sacrifices of your peace offerings.

³³'The son of Aaron who offers the blood of the peace offerings and the fat shall have the right thigh as his portion.

³⁴'For I have taken the breast of the wave offering and the thigh of the heave offering from the Israelites, from the sacrifices of their peace offerings, and I have given them to Aaron the priest and to his sons as their perpetual portion from the Israelites.

³⁵'This is the *consecrated* portion from the offerings by fire to the Lᴏʀᴅ that was designated for Aaron and his sons on the day he presented them to serve as priests to the Lᴏʀᴅ.

³⁶'The Lᴏʀᴅ commanded this to be given to the priests by the Israelites on the day that He anointed them. It is *their* portion perpetually throughout their generations.'"

³⁷This is the law of the burnt offering, the grain offering, the sin offering, the guilt offering, the consecration (ordination) offering, and the sacrifice of peace offerings,

³⁸which the Lᴏʀᴅ commanded Moses at Mount Sinai on the day He commanded the Israelites to present their offerings to the Lᴏʀᴅ, in the Wilderness of Sinai.

8 THEN THE Lᴏʀᴅ spoke to Moses, saying, ²"Take Aaron and his sons with him, and the garments [which are symbols of their office], and the anointing oil, and the bull for the sin offering, and the two rams, and the basket of unleavened bread;

³and assemble the entire congregation at the doorway of the Tent of Meeting."

⁴Moses did as the Lᴏʀᴅ commanded him, and the congregation was assembled at the doorway of the Tent of Meeting.

⁵Moses said to the congregation, "This is what the Lᴏʀᴅ has commanded us to do."

⁶Then Moses brought Aaron and his sons and washed them with water.

⁷He put the undertunic on Aaron, tied the sash around him, clothed him in the robe, and put the ephod (an upper vestment) on him. He tied the [skillfully woven] band of the ephod around him, with which he secured it to Aaron.

⁸Moses then put the breastpiece on Aaron, and he put in the breastpiece the Urim and the Thummim [the sacred articles the high priest used when seeking God's will concerning the nation].

⁹He also put the turban on Aaron's head, and on it, in the front, Moses placed the golden plate, the holy crown, just as the Lᴏʀᴅ had commanded him.

¹⁰Then Moses took the anointing oil and anointed the tabernacle and all that was in it, and consecrated them.

¹¹He sprinkled some of the oil on the altar seven times and anointed the altar and all its utensils, and the basin and its stand, to consecrate them.

¹²Then he poured some of the anointing oil on Aaron's head and anointed him, to consecrate him.

¹³Next Moses brought Aaron's sons forward, put undertunics on them, belted them with sashes, and bound caps on them, just as the Lᴏʀᴅ had commanded Moses.

¹⁴Then he brought the bull for the sin offering, and Aaron and his sons laid their hands on the head of the bull.

¹⁵Next Moses killed it and took the blood and with his finger put *some of it* around on the horns of the altar and purified it [from sin]. Then he poured out the *rest of the* blood at the base of the altar and consecrated it, to make atonement for it.

¹⁶He took all the fat that was on the entrails, and the lobe of the liver, and the two kidneys with their fat, and Moses offered them up in smoke on the altar.

¹⁷But the bull (the sin offering) and its hide, its meat, and its refuse he burned in the fire outside the camp, just as the Lord had commanded Moses.

¹⁸He brought the ram for the burnt offering, and Aaron and his sons laid their hands on the head of the ram.

¹⁹Moses killed it and sprinkled the blood around on the altar.

²⁰When he had cut the ram into pieces, Moses offered up the head, the pieces, and the fat in smoke.

²¹After he had washed the entrails and the legs in water, Moses offered up the whole ram in smoke on the altar. It was a burnt offering for a sweet *and* soothing aroma, an offering by fire to the Lord, just as the Lord had commanded Moses.

²²Then he brought the second ram, the ram of consecration (ordination), and Aaron and his sons laid their hands on the head of the ram.

why the ceremony?

In Leviticus 8:1–30, God detailed to Moses the ritual required to consecrate Aaron and his sons to serve the Lord as priests in His sanctuary, the Tent of Meeting. The meaningful ceremony these priests went through so many centuries ago is filled with significance for us today.

Note in Leviticus 8:23, 24 that Moses put ram's blood on the priests' right ears, the thumbs of their right hands, and the big toes of their right feet. Verse 30 tells us Moses also sprinkled anointing oil and blood from the altar upon Aaron and his garments and upon his sons and their garments in order to sanctify them and make them holy (see also Exodus 29:20, 21).

The significance of God's instruction to Moses to put the blood on the right side of the body is that in the Bible, the right side represents power. The ear was anointed so the priest would hear clearly and not be deceived, the thumb so that what he laid his hand to do would be right and blessed, and the right toe so that everywhere he went would be holy and sanctified.

I believe this ceremony is a physical picture of our spiritual sanctification as priests unto the Lord today (see Revelation 1:5, 6). The shedding of Jesus' blood for our sin sanctifies those it covers; the anointing of the Holy Spirit, represented by the oil, is poured out to empower for service and good works those who are made righteous by the blood of Jesus. We can hear, take action, and go in directions that are safe and divinely led. Just as Aaron and his sons were set apart for God's use, we believers are also set apart for holy use.

Ask God to give you ears that hear what He wants to say, not just what you want to hear. Ask for consecrated ears that are anointed to hear His voice with clear discernment and without the interference of fleshly desires. Ask Him to sanctify your hands to do right and lead your feet to walk in the right path.

²³Moses killed it and took some of its blood and put it on the lobe of Aaron's right ear, and on the thumb of his right hand, and on the big toe of his right foot.

²⁴He also brought Aaron's sons forward and put some of the blood on the lobes of their right ears, and the thumbs of their right hands, and the big toes of their right feet; and Moses sprinkled the *rest of the* blood around on the altar.

²⁵He took the fat, the fat tail, all the fat that was on the entrails, the lobe of the liver, and the two kidneys and their fat, and the right thigh;

²⁶and from the basket of unleavened bread that was before the LORD, he took one unleavened cake, a cake of oiled bread, and one wafer and put them on the fat and on the right thigh;

²⁷and he put all *these things* in Aaron's hands and his sons' hands and presented them as a wave offering before the LORD.

²⁸Then Moses took these things from their hands and offered them up in smoke on the altar with the burnt offering. They were a consecration (ordination) offering for a sweet *and* soothing aroma, an offering by fire to the LORD.

²⁹Moses also took the breast and presented it as a wave offering before the LORD; it was Moses' portion of the ram of consecration (ordination), just as the LORD had commanded Moses.

³⁰So Moses took some of the anointing oil and some of the blood which was on the altar and sprinkled it on Aaron and his garments, and also on his sons and their garments with him; so Moses consecrated Aaron and his garments, and his sons and his sons' garments with him.

³¹Then Moses said to Aaron and to his sons, "Boil the meat at the doorway of the Tent of Meeting and eat it there together with the bread that is in the basket of the consecration (ordination) offering, just as I commanded, saying, 'Aaron and his sons shall eat it.'

³²"And what remains of the meat and of the bread you shall burn in the fire.

³³"You shall not go outside the doorway of the Tent of Meeting for seven days, until the days of your consecration (ordination) are ended; for it will take seven days to consecrate you.

³⁴"As has been done this day, so the LORD has commanded to do for your atonement.

³⁵"You shall remain day and night for seven days at the doorway of the Tent of Meeting, doing what the Lord has required you to do, so that you will not die; for so I (Moses) have been commanded."

³⁶So Aaron and his sons did all the things which the LORD had commanded through Moses.

9 AND IT happened on the eighth day that Moses called Aaron and his sons and the elders of Israel;

²and he said to Aaron, "Take a bull calf as a sin offering and a ram as a burnt offering, [each] without blemish, and offer *both* before the LORD. [Heb 10:10–12]

³"Then say to the Israelites, 'Take a male goat as a sin offering, and a calf and a lamb, both one year old, without blemish, as a burnt offering,

⁴and a bull and a ram as peace offerings to sacrifice before the LORD, and a grain offering mixed with [olive] oil, for today the LORD will appear to you.'"

⁵So they took what Moses had commanded to the front of the Tent of Meeting, and all the congregation approached and stood before the LORD.

⁶Moses said, "This is the thing which the LORD has commanded you to do, so that the glory of the LORD may appear to you."

⁷Moses said to Aaron, "Approach the altar and present your sin offering and your burnt offering and make atonement for yourself and for the people;

and present the offering of the people and make atonement for them, just as the LORD has commanded." [Heb 5:1–5; 7:27]

⁸So Aaron approached the altar and killed the calf as the sin offering, which was *designated* for himself.

⁹The sons of Aaron presented the blood to him; he dipped his finger in the blood and put *some of it* on the horns of the altar, and poured out the *rest of the* blood at the altar's base;

¹⁰but the fat, the kidneys, and the lobe of the liver from the sin offering he offered up in smoke on the altar, just as the LORD had commanded Moses.

¹¹And Aaron burned the meat and the hide in the fire outside the camp.

¹²Then he killed the burnt offering; and Aaron's sons handed the blood to him and he sprinkled it around on the altar.

¹³They brought the burnt offering to him piece by piece, with the head, and Aaron offered them up in smoke on the altar.

¹⁴He also washed the entrails and the legs, and offered them up in smoke with the burnt offering on the altar.

¹⁵Then Aaron presented the people's offering. He took the goat for the sin offering of the people, and killed it and offered it for sin, as *he did* the first. [Heb 2:16, 17]

¹⁶He also presented the burnt offering and offered it according to the ordinance.

¹⁷Next Aaron presented the grain offering and took a handful of it and offered it up in smoke on the altar in addition to the burnt offering of the morning.

¹⁸He also killed the bull and the ram, the sacrifice of peace offerings which was for the people; and Aaron's sons handed the blood to him and he sprinkled it around on the altar,

¹⁹As for the portions of fat from the bull and from the ram—the fat tail, and the fat covering the internal organs, and the kidneys, and the lobe of the liver—

²⁰they now put the portions of fat on the breasts; and Aaron offered the fat up in smoke on the altar.

²¹But the breasts and the right thigh Aaron presented as a wave offering before the LORD, just as Moses had commanded.

²²Then Aaron lifted his hands toward the people and blessed them, and came down [from the altar of burnt offering] after presenting the sin offering, the burnt offering, and the peace offerings.

²³Moses and Aaron went into the Tent of Meeting, and when they came out they blessed the people, and the glory *and* brilliance of the LORD [the Shekinah cloud] appeared to all the people [as promised]. [Lev 9:6]

²⁴Then fire came out from before the LORD and consumed the burnt offering and the portions of fat on the altar; and when all the people saw it, they shouted and fell face downward [in awe and worship].

10 NOW NADAB and Abihu, the sons of Aaron, took their respective [ceremonial] censers, put fire in them, placed incense on it and offered strange (unauthorized, unacceptable) fire before the LORD, [an act] which He had not commanded them to do.

²And fire came out from the presence of the LORD and devoured them, and they died before the LORD.

³Then Moses said to Aaron, "This is what the LORD said:

'I will be treated as holy by those
   who approach Me,
And before all the people I will be
   honored.'"

So Aaron, therefore, said nothing.

⁴Moses called Mishael and Elzaphan,

the sons of Uzziel who was Aaron's uncle, and said to them, "Come here, carry your relatives away from the front of the sanctuary and *take them* outside the camp."

⁵So they came forward and carried them, still in their undertunics, outside the camp, as Moses had said.

⁶Then Moses said to Aaron and to his [younger] sons Eleazar and Ithamar, "Do not uncover your heads *nor* let your hair hang loose nor tear your clothes [as expressions of mourning], so that you will not die [also] and so that He will not express His wrath *and* anger toward all the congregation. But your relatives, the whole house of Israel, may mourn the burning which the Lᴏʀᴅ has brought about.

⁷"You shall not even go out of the doorway of the Tent of Meeting, or you will die; for the Lᴏʀᴅ's anointing oil is upon you." So they did [everything] according to the word of Moses.

⁸Then the Lᴏʀᴅ spoke to Aaron, saying,

⁹"Do not drink wine or intoxicating drink, neither you nor your sons with you, when you come into the Tent of Meeting, so that you will not die—it is a permanent statute throughout your generations—

¹⁰and to make a distinction *and* recognize a difference between the holy (sacred) and the common (profane), and between the [ceremonially] unclean and the clean; [Ezek 44:23]

¹¹and *you are* to teach the Israelites

all the statutes which the Lᴏʀᴅ has spoken to them through Moses."

¹²Then Moses said to Aaron, and to his surviving sons, Eleazar and Ithamar, "Take the grain offering that is left over from the offerings by fire to the Lᴏʀᴅ, and eat it unleavened beside the altar, for it is most holy.

¹³"You shall eat it in a holy place, because it is your portion and your sons' portion, from the offerings by fire to the Lᴏʀᴅ; for so I have been commanded.

¹⁴"But the breast of the wave offering and the thigh of the heave offering you may eat in a clean place, you and your sons and daughters with you; for the breast and the thigh are your portion and your sons' portion, given out of the sacrifices of the peace offerings of the Israelites.

¹⁵"They shall bring the thigh presented by lifting up and the breast presented by waving, along with the offerings by fire of the fat, to present as a wave offering before the Lᴏʀᴅ. This shall be yours and your sons' with you, as your perpetual portion, just as the Lᴏʀᴅ has commanded."

¹⁶But Moses diligently tried to find the goat [that had been offered] as the sin offering, and discovered that it had been burned up [as waste, not eaten]! So he was angry with Aaron's surviving sons Eleazar and Ithamar, saying,

¹⁷"Why did you not eat the sin offering in the holy place? For it is most holy; and God gave it to you to remove

speak the Word

God, I declare that You are holy and that You are honored in my life.
—ADAPTED FROM Lᴇᴠɪᴛɪᴄᴜs 10:3

God, I pray that You will help me distinguish between what is holy and what is unholy, between what is sacred and what is profane, because I want to live a pure, holy life before You.
—ADAPTED FROM Lᴇᴠɪᴛɪᴄᴜs 10:10

the guilt of the congregation, to make atonement for them before the Lord.

¹⁸"Behold, its blood was not brought into the Holy Place; you certainly should have eaten the goat in the sanctuary, just as I commanded."

¹⁹Then Aaron said to Moses, "This very day they have [obediently] presented their sin offering and their burnt offering before the Lord, but [such terrible things] as these have happened to me [and to them]; if I [and my sons] had eaten a sin offering today would it have been acceptable *and* pleasing in the sight of the Lord?" [Hos 9:4]

²⁰When Moses heard that, he was satisfied.

11 THE LORD spoke again to Moses and Aaron, saying to them,

²"Speak to the children of Israel, saying, 'Among all the animals which are on the earth, these are the animals which you may eat. [Mark 7:15–19]

³'You may eat any animal that has a divided hoof [that is, a hoof split into two parts especially at its distal extremity] and chews the cud.

⁴'Nevertheless, you are not to eat these, among those which chew the cud or divide the hoof: the camel, because it chews the cud but does not divide the hoof; it is [ceremonially] unclean to you.

⁵'And the shaphan, because it chews the cud but does not divide the hoof; it is unclean to you.

⁶'And the hare, because it chews the cud but does not divide the hoof; it is unclean to you.

⁷'And the swine, because it divides the hoof and makes a split hoof, but does not chew the cud; it is unclean to you.

⁸'You shall not eat their meat nor touch their carcasses; they are unclean to you.

putting the Word to work

Leviticus contains much instruction on eating. Do you have any eating habits that you know are unwise or displeasing to the Lord? Ask Him to help you eat healthfully!

⁹'These you may eat, whatever is in the water: whatever has fins and scales in the waters, in the seas, and in the rivers, these you may eat;

¹⁰but whatever does not have fins and scales in the seas and in the rivers, of all the teeming life in the waters, and of all the living creatures that are in the waters, they are [to be considered] detestable to you. [1 Cor 8:8–13]

¹¹'They shall be hated things to you. You may not eat their meat; you shall detest their carcasses.

¹²'Everything in the water that does not have fins and scales is detestable to you.

¹³'These you shall detest among the birds; they are not to be eaten, for they are hated things: the eagle and the vulture and the buzzard,

¹⁴the kite, every kind of falcon,

¹⁵every kind of raven,

¹⁶the ostrich, the nighthawk, the sea gull, every species of hawk,

¹⁷the little owl and the cormorant and the great owl,

¹⁸the white owl, the pelican, the carrion vulture,

¹⁹the stork, all kinds of heron, the hoopoe, and the bat.

²⁰'All winged insects that walk on all fours are detestable to you;

²¹yet of all winged insects that walk on all fours you may eat those which have legs above their feet with which to leap on the ground.

²²'Of these you may eat: the whole species of migratory locust, of bald locust, of cricket, and of grasshopper. [Matt 3:4]

²³'But all other winged insects which are four footed are detestable to you.

²⁴'By [contact with] these you will become unclean; whoever touches their carcasses becomes unclean until the evening (dusk),

²⁵and whoever picks up any of their carcasses shall wash his clothes and be unclean until the evening.

²⁶'Concerning all the animals which divide the hoof, but do not have a split hoof, or which do not chew the cud,

please God with your eating

Leviticus 11 sets forth all kinds of guidelines about what the Israelites could and could not eat. Over the years, I have needed God's help in the area of eating, just as the Israelites did. I would like to share ten tips I have learned that have enabled me to eat wisely, healthfully, and in a way that pleases God:

1. Eat when you are truly hungry and not just because someone offers you food or because it is sitting in front of you.

2. If you listen carefully to your body, it will let you know what it needs and wants. Sometimes I actually crave vegetables; at other times I want fish or red meat. That is my body letting me know what it needs. There are times I want something sweet, and it is not wrong to eat sweets if we do so in moderation. Eating a variety of foods is one of the keys to good nutrition.

3. Enjoy what you eat.

4. Eat sitting down. People tend to eat more than they realize when they are standing while they eat.

5. Eat slowly. After about twenty minutes of eating, your brain receives a signal that you are full.

6. Stop eating when you are no longer hungry. Take small portions, planning to have another portion if you want it. Many times, the first small portion will satisfy you.

7. Eat small portions more frequently rather than one or two huge meals a day. Anything your body cannot metabolize and use is stored as fat. Keeping your metabolism working by eating several small meals a day or healthy snacks between meals will actually help you stay fit and trim.

8. Do not make provision for "eating binges" by keeping your refrigerator and pantry full of high-calorie, high-fat, low-quality foods that you know you should not eat.

9. Stay focused on things you need to do and keep your mind off food.

10. Eat necessary food. We all consume many calories that are truly unnecessary every day—a bite of this or that, the piece of bread and butter before the meal, the second helping when in reality we are already getting full. Ask yourself if you really need something before you mindlessly put it in your mouth.

I think it is amazing that the Bible tells us what to eat. God cares about every area of our lives, not just the spiritual parts. He wants us to be healthy, filled with energy, and looking our best!

they are unclean to you; whoever touches them becomes unclean.

²⁷'Also all *animals* that walk on their paws, among all *kinds of* animals that walk on four *legs*, are unclean to you; whoever touches their carcasses becomes unclean until the evening,

²⁸and the one who picks up their carcasses shall wash his clothes and be unclean until the evening; they are unclean to you.

²⁹'These also are unclean to you among the swarming things that crawl around on the ground [and multiply profusely]: the mole, the mouse, and any kind of great lizard,

³⁰the gecko, the crocodile, the lizard, the sand reptile, and the chameleon.

³¹'These [creatures] are unclean to you among all that swarm; whoever touches them when they are dead becomes unclean until evening.

³²'Also anything on which one of them falls after dying becomes unclean, whether it is an article of wood or clothing, or a skin, or a sack—any article that is used—it must be put in water, and will be unclean until the evening; then it becomes clean.

³³'As for any earthenware container into which any of these [crawling things] falls, whatever is in it becomes unclean, and you shall break the container.

³⁴'Any of the food which may be eaten, but on which [unclean] water falls, shall become unclean, and any liquid that may be drunk in every container shall become unclean.

³⁵'Everything that part of their carcass falls on becomes unclean; an oven, or a small stove shall be smashed; they are unclean, and shall be unclean to you.

³⁶'Nevertheless a spring or a cistern (reservoir) collecting water shall be clean; but whoever touches one of these carcasses shall be unclean.

³⁷'If a part of their carcass falls on any seed for sowing which is to be sown, it is clean;

³⁸but if water is put on the seed and a part of their carcass falls on it, it is unclean to you.

³⁹'If one of the animals that you may eat dies [of natural causes], whoever touches its carcass becomes unclean until the evening.

⁴⁰'And whoever eats some of its meat shall wash his clothes, and be unclean until evening; also whoever picks up its carcass shall wash his clothes, and be unclean until the evening.

⁴¹'Now everything that swarms on the ground is detestable; it is not to be eaten.

⁴²'Whatever crawls on its belly, and whatever walks on all fours, and whatever has many feet among all things that swarm on the ground, you shall not eat; for they are detestable.

⁴³'Do not make yourselves loathsome (impure, repulsive) by [eating] any swarming thing; you shall not make yourselves unclean by them so as to defile yourselves.

⁴⁴'For I am the LORD your God; so consecrate yourselves and be holy, for I am holy. You shall not make yourselves unclean with any of the swarming things that swarm *or* crawls on the ground. [1 Thess 4:7, 8]

⁴⁵'For I am the LORD who brought you up from the land of Egypt to be your

speak the Word

Thank You, God, for bringing me out of every form of bondage that has attempted to ensnare me, just as You brought the Israelites out of Egypt. Help me now to be holy, just as You are holy.
–ADAPTED FROM LEVITICUS 11:45

God; therefore you shall be holy, for I am holy.'" [1 Pet 1:14–16]

⁴⁶This is the law regarding the animal and the bird and every living thing that moves in the waters and everything that swarms on the earth,

⁴⁷to make a distinction between the [ceremonially] unclean and the [ceremonially] clean, and between the animal that may be eaten and the animal that may not be eaten.

12 THEN THE LORD spoke to Moses, saying,
²"Speak to the children of Israel, saying,

'If a woman conceives and gives birth to a male child, she shall be [ceremonially] unclean for seven days, unclean as during her monthly period.

³'On the eighth day the flesh of the male child's foreskin shall be circumcised.

⁴'Then she shall remain [intimately separated] thirty-three days to be purified from the blood; she shall not touch any consecrated thing nor enter the [courtyard of the] sanctuary until the days of her purification are over.

⁵'But if she gives birth to a female child, then she shall be unclean for two weeks, as during her monthly period, and she shall remain [intimately separated] sixty-six days to be purified from the blood.

⁶'When the days of her purification are completed, whether for a son or for a daughter, she shall bring to the priest at the doorway of the Tent of Meeting a one year old lamb as a burnt offering and a young pigeon or a turtledove as a sin offering;

⁷and he shall offer it before the LORD and make atonement for her, and she shall be cleansed from the flow of her blood. This is the law for her who gives birth to a child, whether a male or a female child.

⁸'If she cannot afford a lamb then she shall take two turtledoves or young pigeons, one as a burnt offering, the other as a sin offering; the priest shall make atonement for her, and she will be clean.'" [Luke 2:22, 24]

13 THEN THE LORD spoke to Moses and to Aaron, saying,
²"When a man has a swelling on the skin of his body, a scab, or a bright spot, and it becomes the infection of leprosy on the skin of his body, then he shall be brought to Aaron the priest, or to one of his sons the priests.

³"The priest shall look at the diseased spot on the skin of his body, and if the hair in the infection has turned white and the infection appears deeper than the skin of his body, it is an infection of leprosy; when the priest has looked at him, he shall pronounce him [ceremonially] unclean.

⁴"If the bright spot is white on the skin of his body and does not appear to be deeper than the skin, and the hair on it has not turned white, the priest shall isolate *the person who has* the infection for seven days.

⁵"The priest shall examine it on the seventh day, and if in his estimation the infection has not changed and has not spread on the skin, then the priest shall isolate him for seven more days.

⁶"The priest shall examine him again on the seventh day, and if the infection has a more normal color and the spot has not spread on the skin, the priest shall pronounce him clean; it is *only* a scab; and he shall wash his clothes and be clean.

⁷"But if the scab spreads farther on the skin after he has shown himself to the priest for his [ceremonial] cleansing, he shall show himself to the priest again.

⁸"The priest shall look, and if the scab has spread on the skin, then he shall pronounce him unclean; it is leprosy.

⁹"When a leprous infection is on a person, he shall be brought to the priest.

¹⁰"The priest shall examine him, and if there is a white swelling on the skin and it has turned the hair white and there is new raw flesh in the swelling,

¹¹it is a chronic leprosy on the skin of his body, and the priest shall pronounce him unclean; he shall not isolate him because he is [clearly] unclean.

¹²"But if the [suspected] leprosy breaks out farther on the skin, and it covers all of the skin of the *one who has the* outbreak—from his head to his foot—wherever the priest looks,

¹³the priest shall examine him. If the [suspected] leprosy has covered his entire body, he shall pronounce him clean of the disease; it has all turned white, and he is clean.

¹⁴"But whenever raw flesh appears on him, he shall be unclean.

¹⁵"The priest shall examine the raw flesh, and he shall pronounce him unclean; the raw flesh is unclean, it is leprosy.

¹⁶"But if the raw flesh turns again and is changed to white, then he shall come to the priest,

¹⁷and the priest shall examine him, and if the diseased part is changed to white, then the priest shall pronounce *him who had* the disease to be clean; he is clean.

¹⁸"And when there is on the skin of the body [the scar of] a boil that is healed,

¹⁹and in the place of the boil there is a white swelling or a bright spot, reddish white, then it shall be shown to the priest;

²⁰and the priest shall look, and if it looks deeper than the skin and the hair on it has turned white, the priest shall pronounce him unclean; it is the disease of leprosy; it has broken out in the boil.

²¹"But if the priest examines it and finds no white hair in it and it is not deeper than the skin and is dull in color, then the priest shall isolate him for seven days.

²²"If it spreads farther on the skin, then the priest shall pronounce him unclean; it is a disease.

²³"But if the bright spot remains where it is and does not spread, it is the scar of the boil, and the priest shall pronounce him clean.

²⁴"Or if the body has on its skin a burn from fire and the new flesh of the burn becomes a bright spot, reddish white or white,

²⁵then the priest shall examine it, and if the hair in the bright spot has turned white, and it appears deeper than the skin, then leprosy has broken out in the burn. So the priest shall pronounce him unclean; it is the disease of leprosy.

²⁶"But if the priest examines it and there is no white hair in the bright spot and it is not deeper than [the rest of] the skin but is dull in color, then the priest shall isolate him for seven days.

²⁷"And the priest shall examine him on the seventh day; if it is spreading farther on the skin, then the priest shall pronounce him unclean; it is leprosy.

²⁸"But if the bright spot remains in its place and has not spread in the skin, but is dull in color, it is a swelling from the burn, and the priest shall pronounce him clean; for it is the scar of the burn.

²⁹"When a man or woman has a disease on the head or in the beard (face),

³⁰the priest shall examine the diseased place; if it appears to be deeper than the skin, with yellow, thin hair in it, the priest shall pronounce him unclean; it is a scale, it is leprosy of the head or beard.

³¹"But if the priest examines the spot infected by the scale, and it does not appear deeper than the skin and there is no black hair in it, the priest shall isolate the *person with the* scaly infection for seven days.

³²"On the seventh day the priest shall examine the diseased spot; if the scale has not spread and has no yellow

hair in it, and the scale does not look deeper than the skin,

³³then he shall shave himself, but he shall not shave the scale; and the priest shall isolate the *person with the* scale for seven more days.

³⁴"Then on the seventh day the priest shall look at the scale; if the scale has not spread on the skin and appears to be no deeper than the skin, the priest shall pronounce him clean; he shall wash his clothes and be clean.

³⁵"But if the scale spreads farther on the skin after his cleansing,

³⁶then the priest shall examine him, and if the scale has spread on the skin, the priest need not look for the yellowish hair; he is unclean.

³⁷"If, in the priest's estimation, the scale has remained [without spreading], and black hair has grown in it, the scale is healed; he is clean, and the priest shall pronounce him clean.

³⁸"When a man or a woman has bright spots on the skin of the body, *even* white bright spots,

³⁹then the priest shall look, and if the bright spots on the skin of their bodies is a dull white, it is [only] a rash that has broken out on the skin; he is clean.

⁴⁰"If a man loses the hair on his head, he is bald, but he is clean.

⁴¹"And if he loses the hair on front of his head, he is bald on the forehead, but he is clean.

⁴²"But if there is a reddish-white infection on the bald head or forehead, it is leprosy breaking out on his bald head or forehead.

⁴³"Then the priest shall examine him, and if the diseased swelling is reddish-white on his bald head or forehead like the appearance of leprosy on the skin of the body,

⁴⁴he is a leprous man; he is unclean; the priest shall most certainly pronounce him unclean; his disease is on his head.

⁴⁵"As for the leper who has the infection, his clothes shall be torn, and the hair of his head shall be uncovered (disheveled), and he shall cover his mustache and call out, 'Unclean! Unclean!'

⁴⁶"He shall remain [ceremonially] unclean as long as the disease is on him; he is unclean. He shall live alone; he shall live outside the camp.

⁴⁷"When a garment has a mark of leprosy in it, whether it is a wool garment or a linen garment, [Jude 23; Rev 3:4]

⁴⁸whether in woven or knitted material or in the warp (lengthwise strands) or woof (crosswise strands) of linen or of wool, or in a skin or on anything made of leather,

⁴⁹if the mark is greenish or reddish in the garment or in the leather or in the warp or woof or in any article made of leather, it is an infestation of leprosy and shall be shown to the priest.

⁵⁰"The priest shall examine the mark and shall quarantine the article with the mark for seven days.

⁵¹"He shall examine the mark on the seventh day; if it has spread in the garment, whether in the warp or the woof, or in the leather, whatever the leather's purpose, the mark is a malignant leprosy; it is unclean.

⁵²"So he shall burn the garment, whether the warp or woof, in wool or linen, or on anything made of leather in which the mark occurs; for it is a malignant leprosy; it shall be burned in the fire.

⁵³"But if the priest sees that the mark has not spread in the garment, either in the warp or the woof, or on anything made of leather,

⁵⁴then the priest shall order that they wash the thing in which the mark occurs, and he shall quarantine it for seven more days.

⁵⁵"The priest shall examine the article with the mark after it has been washed, and if the mark has not changed color, even though the mark has not spread,

it is unclean; you shall burn it in the fire; it is a corroding mildew, whether on the top or on the front of it.

⁵⁶"If the priest looks and the mark has faded after it is washed, he shall tear it out of the garment, or the leather, or out of the warp or woof.

⁵⁷"If it still appears in the garment, either in the warp or in the woof, or on anything made of leather, it is an outbreak; you shall burn the marked part in the fire.

⁵⁸"The garment, whether the warp or the woof, or anything made of leather from which the mildew has departed after washing, shall then be washed a second time and it will be [ceremonially] clean."

⁵⁹This is the law for a leprous disease in a garment of wool or linen, either in the warp or woof, or on anything made of leather, to pronounce it clean or unclean.

14 THEN THE LORD spoke to Moses, saying, ²"This shall be the law of the leper on the day of his [ceremonial] cleansing. He shall be brought to the priest [at a meeting place outside the camp];

³the priest shall go out of the camp [to meet him]; and the priest shall examine him, and if the leper has been healed of the infection of leprosy,

⁴then the priest shall give orders to take two live clean birds and cedar wood and scarlet string and hyssop for the one to be cleansed. [Heb 9:19–22]

⁵"Next the priest shall order that one of the birds be killed [as a sacrifice] in an earthenware container over [fresh] running water.

⁶"As for the live bird, he shall take it together with the cedar wood and the scarlet string and the hyssop, and shall dip them and the live bird in the blood of the bird sacrificed over the running water.

⁷"He shall sprinkle [the blood] seven times on the one to be cleansed from the leprosy and shall pronounce him [ceremonially] clean. Then he shall let the live bird go free over the open field. [Heb 9:13–15]

⁸"The one to be cleansed shall wash his clothes, shave off all his hair, and bathe in water; and he shall be clean. After that he may come into the camp, but he shall stay outside of his tent for seven days.

⁹"On the seventh day he shall shave off all his hair: he shall shave his head and his beard and his eyebrows, even all his hair [on his body]. Then he shall wash his clothes and bathe his body in water, and be clean.

¹⁰"Now on the eighth day he shall take two male lambs without blemish, and a yearling ewe lamb without blemish, and three-tenths *of an ephah* of fine flour mixed with [olive] oil as a grain offering, and one log (about a pint) of oil;

¹¹and the priest who cleanses him shall present the man to be cleansed and his offerings before the LORD at the doorway of the Tent of Meeting.

¹²"Then the priest shall take one of the male lambs and offer it as a guilt offering, with the log of oil, and present them as a wave offering before the LORD.

¹³"He shall kill the male lamb in the place where they kill the sin offering and the burnt offering, in the sacred place [the courtyard of the tabernacle]; for the guilt offering, like the sin offering, belongs to the priest; it is most holy.

¹⁴"The priest shall take some of the blood of the guilt offering and put it on the lobe of the right ear of the one to be cleansed, and on the thumb of his right hand, and on the big toe of his right foot.

¹⁵"The priest shall also take some of the log of oil, and pour it into the palm of his own left hand;

¹⁶and the priest shall dip his right finger in the oil that is in his left palm,

and with his finger sprinkle some of the oil seven times before the LORD.

17"Of the rest of the oil which is in his palm, the priest shall put some on the lobe of the right ear of the one to be cleansed, and on the thumb of his right hand, and on the big toe of his right foot, on top of the blood of the guilt offering.

18"The remaining oil that is in the priest's palm shall be put on the head of the one to be cleansed. The priest shall make atonement for him before the LORD.

19"Next the priest shall offer the sin offering and make atonement for the one to be cleansed from his uncleanness, and afterward kill the burnt offering.

20"The priest shall offer the burnt offering and the grain offering on the altar; and the priest shall make atonement for him, and he shall be clean.

21"But if the cleansed leper is poor and his means are insufficient, then he is to take one lamb as a guilt offering to be waved to make atonement for him, and one tenth *of an ephah* of fine flour mixed with oil as a grain offering, and a log of oil,

22and two turtledoves or two young pigeons, such as he can afford, one shall be a sin offering, the other a burnt offering.

23"He shall bring them on the eighth day for his [ceremonial] cleansing to the priest at the doorway of the Tent of Meeting, before the LORD.

24"The priest shall take the lamb of the guilt offering, and the log of oil, and shall present them as a wave offering before the LORD.

25"Next he shall kill the lamb of the guilt offering; and the priest is to take some of the blood of the guilt offering and put it on the lobe of the right ear of the one to be cleansed, and on the thumb of his right hand, and on the big toe of his right foot.

26"The priest shall pour some of the oil into his left palm,

27and with his right finger the priest shall sprinkle some of the oil that is in his left palm seven times before the LORD.

28"The priest shall put some of the oil in his palm on the lobe of the right ear of the one to be cleansed, and on the thumb of his right hand, and on the big toe of his right foot, on the places where he has put the blood of the guilt offering.

29"The rest of the oil that is in the priest's palm shall be put on the head of the one to be cleansed, to make atonement for him before the LORD.

30"Then he shall offer one of the turtledoves or young pigeons, which are within his means.

31"*He shall offer* what he can afford, one as a sin offering and the other as a burnt offering, together with the grain offering. The priest shall make atonement before the LORD on behalf of the one to be cleansed.

32"This is the law for the one in whom there is an infection of leprosy, whose means are limited for his [ceremonial] cleansing."

33The LORD further spoke to Moses and Aaron, saying,

34"When you come into the land of Canaan, which I am giving you as a possession, and I put a mark of leprosy on a house in your land,

35then the one who owns the house shall come and tell the priest, 'I have seen *something that looks like* a mark *of leprosy* in my house.'

36"The priest shall order that they empty the house before he goes in to examine the mark, so that everything in the house will not have to be declared unclean; afterward he shall go in to see the house.

37"He shall examine the mark, and if the mark on the walls of the house has greenish or reddish depressions and appears deeper than the surface,

³⁸the priest shall go out of the house, to the doorway, and quarantine the house for seven days.

³⁹"The priest shall return on the seventh day and look; and if the mark has spread on the walls of the house,

⁴⁰he shall order them to tear out the contaminated stones and throw them into an unclean place outside the city.

⁴¹"He shall have the entire inside area of the house scraped, and the plaster that is scraped off shall be dumped in an unclean place outside the city.

⁴²"Then they shall take new stones and replace the [contaminated] stones, and he shall take plaster and replaster the house.

⁴³"If, however, the mark breaks out again in the house after he has removed the stones and has scraped and replastered the house,

⁴⁴then the priest shall come and look *again*, and if the mark has spread in the house, it is a malignant leprosy in the house; it is [ceremonially] unclean.

⁴⁵"He shall tear down the house— its stones and its timber and all the plaster of the house—and shall take *everything* outside the city to an unclean place.

⁴⁶"Moreover, whoever goes into the house during the time that it is quarantined becomes unclean until evening.

⁴⁷"And whoever lies down in the house [to rest] shall wash his clothes, and whoever eats in the house shall wash his clothes.

⁴⁸"But if the priest comes in and inspects it and the mark has not spread in the house after the house has been replastered, he shall pronounce the house clean because the mark has not reappeared.

⁴⁹"To cleanse the house then, he shall take two birds and cedar wood and scarlet string and hyssop;

⁵⁰and he shall kill one of the birds in an earthenware container over running water,

⁵¹and he shall take the cedar wood and the hyssop and the scarlet string, and the living bird, and dip them in the blood of the slain bird as well as in the running water, and sprinkle the house seven times.

⁵²"So he shall cleanse the house with the blood of the bird and with the running water, along with the live bird and the cedar wood and the hyssop and the scarlet string.

⁵³"But he shall let the live bird go free outside the city into the open field. So he shall make atonement for the house, and it will be clean."

⁵⁴This is the law for any mark of leprosy—even for a scale,

⁵⁵and for the leprous garment or house,

⁵⁶and for a swelling, and for a scab, and for a bright spot on the skin—

⁵⁷to teach when they are unclean and when they are clean. This is the law of leprosy [in regard to both persons and property].

15 THE LORD spoke to Moses and Aaron, saying,
²"Speak to the children of Israel, and say to them, 'When any man has a bodily discharge, his discharge is unclean.

³'This shall be [the law concerning] his uncleanness in his discharge: whether his body allows its discharge to flow or obstructs its flow; it is uncleanness in him.

⁴'Every bed on which the one who has the discharge lies becomes unclean, and everything on which he sits becomes unclean.

⁵'Whoever touches his bed shall wash his clothes, and bathe in water, and be unclean until evening;

⁶and whoever sits on anything on which the man with the discharge has been sitting shall wash his clothes and bathe in water, and be unclean until evening.

⁷'Also whoever touches the man with the discharge shall wash his clothes and bathe in water, and be unclean until evening.

⁸'And if he who has the discharge spits on one who is clean, then he shall wash his clothes and bathe in water, and be unclean until evening.

⁹'Any saddle on which the man with the discharge rides becomes unclean.

¹⁰'Whoever touches anything that has been under him shall be unclean until evening; and whoever carries those things shall wash his clothes and bathe in water, and be unclean until evening.

¹¹'Whomever the one with the discharge touches without rinsing his hands in water shall wash his clothes and bathe in water, and be unclean until evening.

¹²'An earthenware container that the one with the discharge touches shall be broken, and every wooden container shall be rinsed in water.

¹³'When the man with the discharge becomes cleansed from his discharge, he shall count off seven days for his purification; he shall then wash his clothes and bathe his body in running water and will become clean.

¹⁴'On the eighth day he shall take two turtledoves or two young pigeons and come before the LORD to the doorway of the Tent of Meeting, and give them to the priest;

¹⁵and the priest shall offer them, one as a sin offering and the other as a burnt offering. So the priest shall make atonement for the man before the LORD because of his discharge.

¹⁶'Now if any man has a seminal emission, he shall wash all his body in water, and be unclean until evening.

¹⁷'Every garment and every leather on which there is semen shall be washed with water, and shall be unclean until evening.

¹⁸'If a man lies with a woman so that there is a seminal emission, they shall both bathe in water and be unclean until evening.

¹⁹'When a woman has a discharge, if her bodily discharge is blood, she shall continue in her menstrual impurity for seven days; and whoever touches her shall be unclean until evening.

²⁰'Everything on which she lies during her menstrual impurity shall be unclean; and everything on which she sits shall be unclean.

²¹'Anyone who touches her bed shall wash his clothes and bathe in water, and be unclean until evening.

²²'Whoever touches anything on which she sits shall wash his clothes and bathe in water, and be unclean until evening.

²³'And if it is on her bed or on the thing on which she is sitting, when he touches it, he shall be unclean until evening.

²⁴'If a man actually lies with her so that her menstrual impurity is on him, he shall be unclean for seven days; and every bed on which he lies shall be unclean.

²⁵'Now if a woman has a flow of blood for many days, not during the time of her menstruation, or if she has a discharge beyond that period, as long as the impure discharge continues she shall be as she is in the days of her [normal] menstrual impurity; she is unclean. [Matt 9:20]

²⁶'Every bed on which she lies during the time of her discharge shall be to her like the bed of her menstrual impurity, and whatever she sits on shall be unclean, like the uncleanness of her monthly period.

²⁷'And whoever touches those things shall be unclean, and shall wash his clothes and bathe in water, and be unclean until evening.

²⁸'When she is cleansed from her discharge, then she shall count off for herself seven days, and after that she will be clean.

²⁹"Then on the eighth day she shall take for herself two turtledoves or two young pigeons and bring them to the priest at the doorway of the Tent of Meeting;

³⁰and the priest shall offer one as a sin offering and the other as a burnt offering; and he shall make atonement for her before the LORD for her unclean discharge.'

³¹"Thus you shall separate the Israelites from their uncleanness, so that they do not die in their uncleanness by their defiling My tabernacle that is among them."

³²This is the law for the one who has a discharge and for the one who has a seminal emission, so that he is unclean by it;

³³and for the woman who is ill because of her monthly period, and for the one who has a discharge, whether man or woman, or for a man who lies with a woman who is [ceremonially] unclean.

16 THEN THE LORD spoke to Moses after the death of the two sons of Aaron who had died when they [irreverently] approached the presence of the LORD. [Lev 10:1, 2]

²The LORD said to Moses,

"Tell Aaron your brother that he must not enter at any time into the Holy Place inside the veil (the Holy of Holies), before the mercy seat which is on the ark, or he will die, for I will appear in the cloud over the mercy seat. [Heb 9:7–15, 25–28]

³"Aaron [as high priest] shall enter the Holy Place in this way: with [the blood of] a young bull as a sin offering and [the blood of] a ram as a burnt offering.

⁴"He shall put on the holy linen tunic, and the linen undergarments shall be next to his body, and he shall be belted with the linen sash, and dressed with the linen turban (these are the holy garments). He shall bathe his body in water and put them on.

⁵"He shall take from the congregation of the Israelites [at their expense] two male goats as a sin offering and one ram as a burnt offering.

⁶"Then Aaron shall present the bull as the sin offering for himself, and make atonement for himself and for his house.

⁷"He shall take the two goats and present them before the LORD at the doorway of the Tent of Meeting.

⁸"Aaron shall cast lots for the two goats—one lot for the LORD, the other lot for the scapegoat.

⁹"Then Aaron shall bring the goat on which the LORD's lot fell and offer it as a sin offering.

¹⁰"But the goat on which the lot fell for the scapegoat shall be presented alive before the LORD to make atonement on it; it shall be sent into the wilderness as the scapegoat.

¹¹"Aaron shall present the bull as the sin offering for himself and make atonement for himself and for his household (the other priests), and he shall kill the bull as the sin offering for himself.

¹²"He shall take a censer full of burning coals from the [bronze] altar before the LORD, and two handfuls of finely ground sweet incense, and bring it inside the veil [into the Most Holy Place],

¹³and put the incense on the fire [in the censer] before the LORD, so that the cloud of the incense may cover the mercy seat that is on [the ark of] the Testimony, otherwise he will die.

¹⁴"He shall take some of the bull's blood and sprinkle it with his finger on the east side of the mercy seat; also in front of the mercy seat he shall sprinkle some of the blood with his finger seven times.

¹⁵"Then he shall kill the goat of the sin offering that is for [the sins of] the

people and bring its blood within the veil [into the Most Holy Place] and do with its blood as he did with the blood of the bull, and sprinkle it on the mercy seat and in front of the mercy seat. [Heb 2:17]

16"So he shall make atonement for the Holy Place (Holy of Holies) because of the uncleanness and transgressions of the Israelites, for all their sins. He shall also do this for the Tent of Meeting which is among them in the midst of their uncleanness (impurities). [Heb 9:22–24]

17"There shall be no person in the Tent of Meeting when the high priest goes in to make atonement in the Holy Place [within the veil] until he comes out, so that he may make atonement for himself (his own sins) and for his household and for all the congregation of Israel.

18"Then he shall go out to the altar [of burnt offering in the court] which is before the Lord and make atonement for it, and shall take some of the blood of the bull and of the goat and put it on the horns of the altar on all sides.

19"With his finger he shall sprinkle some of the blood on the altar of burnt offering seven times and cleanse it and consecrate it from the uncleanness of the Israelites.

20"When he has finished atoning for the Holy Place and the Tent of Meeting and the altar, he shall present the live goat.

21"Then Aaron shall lay both of his hands on the head of the live goat, and confess over it all the wickedness of the sons of Israel and all their transgressions in regard to all their sins; and he shall lay them on the head of the goat [the scapegoat, the sin-bearer], and send it away into the wilderness by the hand of a man who is prepared [for the task].

22"The goat shall carry on itself all their (the Israelites) wickedness,

carrying them to a solitary (infertile) land; and he shall release the goat in the wilderness. [Ps 103:12; Is 53:11, 12; John 1:29]

23"Then Aaron shall come into the Tent of Meeting and take off the linen garments which he put on when he went into the Holy Place (Holy of Holies), and shall leave them there.

24"He shall bathe his body with water in a holy place and put on his clothes, and come out and offer his burnt offering and that of the people, and make atonement for himself and for the people.

25"And he shall offer up in smoke the fat of the sin offering on the altar.

26"The man who released the goat as the [sin-bearing] scapegoat shall wash his clothes and bathe his body in water, and afterward he may come into the camp.

27"The bull for the sin offering and the goat for the sin offering, whose blood was brought in to make atonement in the Holy Place (Holy of Holies), shall be taken outside the camp; their skins, their meat, and their waste shall be burned in the fire. [Heb 13:11–13]

28"Then he who burns them shall wash his clothes and bathe his body with water, and afterward he may come into the camp.

29"This shall be a permanent statute for you: in the seventh month (nearly October) on the tenth day of the month you shall humble yourselves [by fasting] and not do any work, whether the native-born or the stranger who lives temporarily among you;

30for it is on this day that atonement shall be made for you, to cleanse you; you will be clean from all your sins before the Lord. [Heb 10:1, 2; 1 John 1:7, 9]

31"It is a Sabbath of solemn rest for you, and you shall humble yourselves; it is a permanent statute.

32"So the priest who is anointed and ordained to serve *and* minister as priest in his father's place shall make atonement: he shall wear the holy linen garments,

[33]and make atonement for the Holy Sanctuary, and he shall make atonement for the Tent of Meeting, and for the altar [of burnt offering in the court]. He shall also make atonement for the priests and for all the people of the assembly.

[34]"This shall be a permanent statute for you, so that atonement may be made for the children of Israel for all their sins once a year." So he did just as the LORD had commanded Moses.

17 THEN THE LORD spoke to Moses, saying, [2]"Speak to Aaron and his sons and all the children of Israel, and say to them, 'This is what the LORD has commanded, saying,

[3]"Any man from the house of Israel who kills an ox or lamb or goat in the camp, or kills it outside the camp

[4]and has not brought it to the doorway of the Tent of Meeting to offer it as an offering to the LORD before the tabernacle of the LORD, that man shall be guilty of bloodshed. He has shed blood and shall be cut off from his people [excluding him from the atonement made for them].

[5]"This is so that the sons of Israel may bring their sacrifices which they were sacrificing [to idols] in the open field [where they killed them], that they may bring them in to the LORD, at the doorway of the Tent of Meeting to the priest, and sacrifice them as sacrifices of peace offerings to the LORD.

[6]"The priest shall sprinkle the blood on the altar of the LORD at the doorway of the Tent of Meeting and offer the fat up in smoke as a sweet *and* soothing aroma to the LORD.

[7]"So they shall no longer offer their sacrifices to goat-idols *or* demons *or* field spirits with which they have

played the prostitute. This shall be a permanent statute for them throughout their generations."'

[8]"Then you shall say to them, 'Any man from the house of Israel or any of the strangers living temporarily among you, who offers a burnt offering or sacrifice

[9]and does not bring it to the doorway of the Tent of Meeting to offer it to the LORD shall be cut off from his people [excluding him from the atonement made for them].

[10]"Any man from the house of Israel, or any stranger living temporarily among you, who eats any blood, against that person I shall set My face and I will cut him off from his people [excluding him from the atonement made for them]. [Ezek 33:25]

[11]'For the life of the flesh is in the blood, and I have given it to you on the altar to make atonement for your souls; for it is the blood that makes atonement, by reason of the life [which it represents].' [Rom 3:24–26]

[12]"Therefore I have said to the sons of Israel, 'No person among you may eat blood, nor may any stranger living temporarily among you eat blood.'

life point

The Bible speaks of blood from Genesis to Revelation. In Leviticus 17:11, we read that there is life in the blood. In Genesis 4:10 we see Abel's blood crying out to God from the ground after Cain murdered him, and in Revelation 19:13 we see Jesus dressed in a robe that was dipped in blood. Why does the Word of God speak so much about the blood? Because the life is in the blood, and it is through blood that atonement is made for our souls. In Hebrews 10:18, 19 we learn that Christ's blood was shed for us to permanently atone for our sins. That's good news!

¹³"So when any Israelite or any stranger living temporarily among them, catches any ceremonially clean animal or bird when hunting, he shall pour out its blood and cover it with earth.

¹⁴"For in regard to the life of all flesh, its blood is [the same] as its life; therefore I said to the Israelites, 'You are not to eat the blood of any flesh, for the life of all flesh is its blood. Whoever eats it shall be cut off [excluding him from the atonement made for them].'

¹⁵"Every person who eats an animal which dies [of natural causes] or was torn by a predator, whether he is native-born or a stranger, he shall wash his clothes and bathe in water, and be [ceremonially] unclean until evening; then he will become clean. [Acts 15:20]

¹⁶"But if he does not wash *his clothes* or bathe his body, he shall bear his guilt [for it will not be borne by the sacrifice of atonement]."

life point

Just as light is the only force that can conquer or overcome darkness, so life is the only force that can conquer death. When God created Adam, He formed him from dust and "breathed into his nostrils the breath of life; and the man became a living being [an individual complete in body and spirit]" (Genesis 2:7). Adam's blood was already flowing through his body, but there was no life in it until God breathed His own life into him.

The chemical substance that we call blood carries life. If a person loses his blood, he loses his life. No blood means no life, because the blood carries the life. Life is a spiritual substance, but it must have a physical carrier. As believers in Jesus Christ, our bodies are the temple of the Holy Spirit. The Spirit and the life of God are in us.

18 THEN THE LORD spoke to Moses, saying, ²"Speak to the children of Israel and say to them, 'I am the LORD your God.

³'You shall not do what is done in the land of Egypt where you lived, and you shall not do what is done in the land of Canaan where I am bringing you. You shall not follow their statutes (practices, customs).

⁴'You are to follow My judgments (precepts, ordinances) and keep My statutes and live by them. I am the LORD your God.

⁵'So you shall keep My statutes and My judgments, by which, if a person keeps them, he shall live; I am the LORD. [Luke 10:25–28; Rom 10:4, 5; Gal 3:12]

⁶'No one shall approach any blood relative of his to uncover nakedness (have intimate relations). I am the LORD.

⁷'You shall not uncover the nakedness of your father, that is, the nakedness of your mother. She is your mother. You shall not uncover her nakedness.

⁸'You shall not uncover the nakedness of your father's wife; it is your father's nakedness.

⁹'You shall not uncover the nakedness of your sister, *either* the daughter of your father or of your mother, whether born at home or born elsewhere.

¹⁰'You shall not uncover the nakedness of your son's daughter or your daughter's daughter; their nakedness you shall not uncover, for they are your own nakedness [that is, your own descendants].

¹¹'You shall not uncover the nakedness of your father's wife's daughter; born to your father, she is your sister.

¹²'You shall not uncover the nakedness of your father's sister; she is your father's blood relative.

¹³'You shall not uncover the nakedness of your mother's sister, for she is your mother's blood relative.

¹⁴'You shall not uncover the nakedness of your father's brother's wife; you shall not approach his wife; she is your aunt.

¹⁵'You shall not uncover the nakedness of your daughter-in-law; she is your son's wife. You shall not uncover her nakedness.

¹⁶'You shall not uncover the nakedness of your brother's wife; it is your brother's nakedness.

¹⁷'You shall not uncover the nakedness of a woman and her daughter, nor shall you take her son's daughter or her daughter's daughter to uncover their nakedness (have intimate relations with them); they are [her] blood relatives; it is an outrageous offense.

¹⁸'You shall not marry a woman in addition to her sister as a rival while she is alive, to uncover her nakedness.

¹⁹'Also you shall not approach a woman to uncover her nakedness during her menstrual impurity *and* ceremonial uncleanness.

²⁰'You shall not have intimate relations with your neighbor's wife, to be defiled with her.

²¹'You shall not give any of your children to offer them [by fire as a sacrifice] to Molech [the god of the Ammonites], nor shall you profane the name of your God [by honoring idols as gods]. I am the LORD.

²²'You shall not lie [intimately] with a male as one lies with a female; it is repulsive. [1 Cor 6:9, 10]

²³'You shall not have intimate relations with any animal to be defiled with it; nor shall a woman stand before an animal to mate with it; it is a perversion.

²⁴'Do not defile yourselves by any of

these things; for by all these the nations which I am casting out before you have become defiled.

²⁵'For the land has become defiled; therefore I have brought its punishment upon it, and the land vomits out its inhabitants.

²⁶'But as for you, you are to keep My statutes and My judgments (precepts) and shall not commit any of these repulsive acts, neither the native-born, nor the stranger who lives temporarily among you

²⁷(for all these repulsive acts have been done by the men who lived in the land before you, and the land has become defiled);

²⁸[do none of these things] so that the land will not vomit you out, should you defile it, as it has vomited out the nation which has been before you.

²⁹'For whoever commits any of these repulsive acts, those persons who do so shall be cut off from among their people [excluding them from the atonement made for them].

³⁰'So keep My command: do not practice any of the repulsive customs which have been practiced before you, so as not to defile yourselves by them; I am the LORD your God.'"

19 THEN THE LORD spoke to Moses, saying, ²"Say to all the congregation of the children of Israel, 'You shall be holy, for I the LORD your God am holy. [1 Pet 1:15]

³'Each of you shall respect his mother and his father, and you shall keep My Sabbaths; I am the LORD your God.

⁴'Do not turn to idols or make for

speak the Word

Lord, help me to follow Your judgments and to keep your statutes and live by them. You are the Lord my God.
—ADAPTED FROM LEVITICUS 18:4, 5

yourselves molten gods (images cast in metal); I am the LORD your God.

⁵'Now when you offer a sacrifice of peace offerings to the LORD, you shall offer it so that you may be accepted.

⁶'It shall be eaten the same day you offer it and on the day following; and if anything remains until the third day, it shall be burned in the fire.

⁷'But if it is eaten at all on the third day, it is repulsive; it will not be accepted [by God as an offering].

⁸'Everyone who eats it will bear [the responsibility for] his wickedness, for he has profaned a holy thing of the LORD; and that person shall be cut off from his people [excluding him from the atonement made for them].

⁹'Now when you reap the harvest of your land, you shall not reap to the very corners of your field, nor shall you gather the gleanings (grain left after reaping) of your harvest.

¹⁰'And you shall not glean your vineyard, nor shall you gather its fallen grapes; you shall leave them for the poor and for the stranger. I am the LORD your God.

¹¹'You shall not steal, nor deal deceptively, nor lie to one another. [Col 3:9, 10]

¹²'You shall not swear [an oath] falsely by My name, so as to profane the name of your God; I am the LORD.

¹³'You shall not oppress *or* exploit your neighbor, nor rob him. You shall not withhold the wages of a hired man overnight until morning.

putting the Word to work

The Bible specifically instructs us not to gossip. Let me ask you, how do you handle the things you hear? Remember to always keep confidences, honor other people's "business," and keep their secrets. Do not be what Leviticus 19:16 calls a "gossip among your people."

putting the Word to work

Do you hold grudges? Remember that the Bible teaches us not to hold grudges (see Leviticus 19:18), but instead to love our neighbors as we love ourselves. Let go of anything that you may be holding against anyone.

¹⁴'You shall not curse a deaf man nor put a stumbling block before the blind, but you shall fear your God [with profound reverence]; I am the LORD.

¹⁵'You shall not do injustice in judgment; you shall not be partial to the poor nor show a preference for the great, but judge your neighbor fairly.

¹⁶'You shall not go around as a gossip among your people, and you are not to act against the life of your neighbor [with slander or false testimony]; I am the LORD.

¹⁷'You shall not hate your brother in your heart; you may most certainly rebuke your neighbor, but shall not incur sin because of him. [Gal 6:1; 1 John 2:9, 11; 3:15]

¹⁸'You shall not take revenge nor bear any grudge against the sons of your people, but you shall love your neighbor (acquaintance, associate, companion) as yourself; I am the LORD. [Matt 5:43–46; Rom 12:17, 19]

¹⁹'You are to keep My statutes. You shall not breed together two kinds of your cattle; you shall not sow your field with two kinds of seed, nor wear clothing of two kinds of material mixed together.

²⁰'Now if a man has intimate relations with a woman who is a slave acquired for [marriage to] *another* man, but who has not been redeemed nor given her freedom, there shall be punishment [after an investigation]; they shall not be put to death, because she was not free;

²¹but he shall bring his guilt offering

to the LORD to the doorway of the Tent of Meeting, a ram as a guilt offering.

²²'The priest shall make atonement for him with the ram of the guilt offering before the LORD for his sin which he has committed; and he shall be forgiven for his sin.

²³'When you enter the land and plant all kinds of trees for food, then you shall consider their fruit forbidden. For three years the fruit shall be forbidden to you; it shall not be eaten.

²⁴'In the fourth year all the fruit shall be holy, an offering of praise to the LORD.

²⁵'In the fifth year you may eat the fruit [of the trees], this is so that their yield may increase for you; I am the LORD your God.

²⁶'You shall not eat *anything* with the blood, nor practice divination [using omens or witchcraft] or soothsaying.

²⁷'You shall not trim *and* round off the side-growth of [the hair on] your heads, nor mar the edges of your beard.

²⁸'You shall not make any cuts on your body [in mourning] for the dead, nor make any tattoo marks on yourselves; I am the LORD.

²⁹'Do not profane your daughter by making her a prostitute, so that the land will not fall to prostitution and become full of wickedness.

³⁰'You shall keep My Sabbaths and revere My sanctuary. I am the LORD.

³¹'Do not turn to mediums [who pretend to consult the dead] or to spiritists [who have spirits of divination]; do not seek them out to be defiled by them. I am the LORD your God.

³²'You shall rise before the gray-headed and honor the aged, and you shall fear your God [with profound reverence]; I am the LORD.

³³'When a stranger resides with you in your land, you shall not oppress *or* mistreat him.

³⁴'But the stranger who resides with you shall be to you like someone native-born among you; and you shall love him as yourself, for you were strangers in the land of Egypt; I am the LORD your God.

life point

Many people, including some who consider themselves Christians, participate in practices that God considers vile and evil. They innocently think there is nothing wrong with such things as reading horoscopes and consulting psychics; then they wonder why they do not have peace.

The Bible says that in the latter days many false prophets will rise up and tell people what their itching ears want to hear. People will search for one teacher after another who will tell them something pleasing and gratifying. To suit their own desires, they will turn away from hearing the truth and wander off into listening to myths and man-made fictions (see 2 Timothy 4:3, 4).

Never before have we seen such an influx of psychics vying for a ready ear. Television programs feature mediums who claim to be connecting with departed loved ones, but the tragic truth is that psychics such as these are taking advantage of grieving people. These mediums are really communicating with familiar spirits who tell half-truths about the past and lies about the future. God's Word clearly says to turn away from mediums and spiritists because they will deceive and defile us. This is a serious command! Fortune-telling, physics, horoscopes, mediums, palm readers, tarot card readers, divination, witchcraft, and the like are all forbidden in God's Word. We are to be led and guided by the Holy Spirit. We do not need a phony substitute when the real thing is available.

³⁵'You shall do no wrong in judgment, in measurement of weight or quantity. ³⁶'You shall have just *and* accurate balances, just weights, a just ephah, and a just hin. I am the LORD your God, who brought you out of the land of Egypt.

³⁷'You shall observe *and* keep all My statutes and all My ordinances and do them. I am the LORD.'"

20 THEN THE LORD spoke to Moses, saying, ²"Moreover, you shall say to the children of Israel,

'Any Israelite or any stranger residing in Israel who gives any of his children to Molech (the god of the Ammonites) [as a human sacrifice] shall most certainly be put to death;

in God alone

God says that He will set His face against anyone who turns to mediums and spiritists to prostitute themselves by following them instead of following their Maker (see Leviticus 20:6). Multitudes of people consult the stars before making decisions, even for things as simple as when to cut their hair. However, a study of God's Word shows clearly that these things are an abomination to God. Even wearing and depending on "good-luck charms" is an affront to God. Our faith must be in God alone, not God plus a lot of other things. Those of us who believe in Jesus Christ do not need to depend on luck; we can trust God that He will bless us.

It is wrong to seek guidance for our lives through any means but God Himself, His Word, or a godly friend or counselor that God approves of. He is offended when we look to these other sources, and when we do, we will not have the peaceful, joy-filled, and prosperous lives He intended for us.

If you have been involved in seeking guidance through mediums, spirit guides, horoscopes, or any other occult activity, I strongly encourage you to thoroughly repent, ask God to forgive you, and completely turn away from it. Then I encourage you to keep your heart pure and be careful what you read, watch, and listen to.

Just as you cannot effectively listen to two radio stations at once, neither can you serve two masters (see Luke 16:13). You may have to choose new friends if they are filling you with things contrary to the Word of God. You may have to change television stations at home and choose new radio stations to listen to while you are riding in your car to prevent filling yourself with things not pleasing to God. Do not poison your inner man by being a garbage dump for the devil. Pay attention: if negative, ungodly talk is filling the air around you, change your listening habits. Also, make sure that negative, ungodly talk does not come out of your own mouth for yourself and others to hear.

Jesus said, "Blessed . . . are the pure in heart [those with integrity, moral courage, and godly character], for they will see God" (Matthew 5:8). If you have a pure heart, you will enjoy having clarity of mind. You will perceive clearly God's plan for your life, and you will not feel aimless or confused. To keep your heart pure before the Lord, turn away from the things that defile you. Live a pure, clean life that flows like pure, clean water because God alone is your source.

the people of the land shall stone him with stones.

³'I will also set My face against that man [opposing him, withdrawing My protection from him] and will cut him off from his people [excluding him from the atonement made for them], because he has given some of his children to Molech, so as to defile My sanctuary and profane My holy name.

⁴'If the people of the land should ever tolerate that man when he gives any of his children [as a burnt offering] to Molech, and fail to put him to death [as My law requires],

⁵then I shall set My face against that man and against his [extended] family, and I will cut off from their people both him and all who follow him in playing the prostitute (commit apostasy) with Molech.

⁶'As for the person who turns to mediums [who consult the dead] or to spiritists, to play the prostitute after them, I shall set My face against that person and will cut him off from his people [excluding him from the atonement made for them]. [Is 54:5]

⁷'You shall consecrate yourselves therefore, and be holy; for I am the LORD your God.

⁸'You shall keep My statutes and do them. I am the LORD who sanctifies you.

⁹'If anyone curses his father or mother, he shall most certainly be put to death; he has cursed his father or mother; his blood is on him [that is, he bears full responsibility for the consequences].

¹⁰'The man who commits adultery with another's wife, even his neighbor's wife, the adulterer and the adulteress shall most certainly be put to death. [John 8:4–11]

¹¹'The man who lies [intimately] with his father's wife has uncovered his father's nakedness; both of them shall most certainly be put to death; their blood is on them.

¹²'If a man lies [intimately] with his daughter-in-law, both of them shall most certainly be put to death; they have committed incest; their blood is on them.

¹³'If a man lies [intimately] with a male as if he were a woman, both men have committed a detestable (perverse, unnatural) act; they shall most certainly be put to death; their blood is on them.

¹⁴'It is immoral *and* shameful if a man marries a woman and her mother; all three shall be burned in fire, so that there will be no immorality among you. [Josh 7:15, 25]

¹⁵'If a man has intimate relations with an animal, he shall most certainly be put to death; you shall kill the animal also.

¹⁶'If a woman approaches any animal to mate with it, you shall kill the woman and the animal; they shall most certainly be put to death; their blood is on them.

¹⁷'If a man takes his sister, his father's daughter or his mother's daughter, so that he sees her nakedness and she sees his nakedness, it is a disgrace; and they shall be cut off in the sight of the sons of their people. He has uncovered his sister's nakedness; he bears [responsibility for] his guilt.

¹⁸'If a man lies [intimately] with a woman during her menstrual cycle and uncovers her nakedness, he has exposed her flow, and she has uncovered the flow of her blood; both of them shall be cut off from their people [excluding them from the atonement made for them].

speak the Word

Thank You, God, that You are the One Who sanctifies me and makes me holy.
−ADAPTED FROM LEVITICUS 20:8

¹⁹'You shall not uncover the nakedness of (have intimate relations with) your mother's sister or your father's sister, for such a one has uncovered his blood relative; they will bear their guilt.

²⁰'If *there is* a man who lies [intimately] with his uncle's wife, he has uncovered his uncle's nakedness; they will bear their sin. They will die childless.

²¹'If a man takes his brother's wife, it is a hated *and* unclean thing; he has uncovered his brother's nakedness. They will be childless.

²²'Therefore keep all My statutes and all My ordinances and do them, so that the land where I am bringing you to live may not vomit you out [as it did those before you]. [Lev 18:28]

²³'You shall not follow the statutes (laws, practices, customs) of the nation which I am driving out before you; for they did all these things, and therefore I have loathed them.

²⁴'But I have said to you, "You are to inherit *and* take possession of their land, and I will give it to you to possess, a land [of plenty] flowing with milk and honey." I am the LORD your God, who has separated you from the peoples (pagan nations).

²⁵'You are therefore to make a distinction between the [ceremonially] clean animal and the unclean, and between the unclean bird and the clean; and you shall not make yourselves detestable by animal or by bird or by anything that crawls on the ground, which I have set apart from you as unclean.

²⁶'You are to be holy to Me; for I the LORD am holy, and have set you apart from the peoples (nations) to be Mine.

²⁷'A man or woman who is a medium [who pretends to consults the dead] or who is a spiritist shall most certainly be put to death, and be stoned with stones; their blood is on them.'"

21

THEN THE LORD said to Moses, "Speak to the priests, the sons of Aaron, and say to them:

'No one shall defile himself [that is, become ceremonially unclean] for the dead among his people [by touching a corpse or assisting in preparing it for burial],

²except for his relatives who are nearest to him, his mother, his father, his son, his daughter, and his brother,

³also his virgin sister, who is near to him because she has had no husband; for her he may become unclean.

⁴'He shall not become unclean as a relative by marriage among his people, and so profane himself.

⁵'The priests shall not shave their heads, nor shave off the edges of their beards, nor make any cuts in their body.

⁶'They shall be holy to their God and not profane the name of their God; for they present the offerings by fire to

life point

God never speaks words to make us feel bad about ourselves. True godly conviction is a positive thing that moves us into a new level of holiness. The devil's condemnation presses us down under a heavy burden so that we cannot even hear from God. If you sense God speaking to you about something in your behavior, how do you know it is God? You will know because He will not shame you or put you down, but He will motivate you and empower you to change. I could not make progress until I learned to discern the difference between conviction and condemnation, and I do not believe you can either. Remember: conviction makes you aware of a problem and then lifts you up and out of it. Condemnation makes you feel guilty and presses you down.

the LORD, the food of their God; so they shall be holy.

⁷'They shall not take [as a wife] a woman who is a prostitute, nor a woman who is divorced from her husband; for the priest is holy to his God.

⁸'You shall consecrate him, therefore, for he offers the food of your God; he shall be holy to you; for I the LORD, who sanctifies you, am holy.

⁹'The daughter of any priest who profanes herself by prostitution profanes her father; she shall be burned in fire. [Josh 7:15, 25]

¹⁰'But he who is the high priest among his brothers, on whose head the anointing oil has been poured and who has been consecrated to wear the [sacred] garments, shall not uncover his head nor tear his clothes [in mourning],

¹¹nor shall he approach any dead person, nor defile himself [by doing so, even] for his father or for his mother;

¹²nor shall he go out of the sanctuary nor profane (make ceremonially unclean) the sanctuary of his God, for the consecration of the anointing oil of his God is on him; I am the LORD.

¹³'He shall take a wife in her virginity.

¹⁴'He may not marry a widow or a divorced woman or one who is profaned by prostitution, but he is to marry a virgin from his own people, [1 Tim 3:2–7; Titus 1:7–9]

¹⁵so that he will not profane or dishonor his children among his people; for I am the LORD who sanctifies the high priest.'"

¹⁶Then the LORD spoke to Moses, saying,

¹⁷"Say to Aaron, 'Throughout their generations none of your descendants who has any [physical] defect shall approach [the altar] to present the food of his God.

¹⁸'For no man who has a defect shall approach [God's altar as a priest]: no man who is blind or lame, or who has a disfigured face, or any deformed limb,

¹⁹or a man who has a broken foot or a broken hand,

²⁰or a hunchback or a dwarf, or one who has a defect in his eye or eczema or scabs or crushed testicles.

²¹'No man among the descendants of Aaron the priest who has a [physical] defect and is disfigured or deformed is to approach [the altar] to present the offerings of the LORD by fire. He has a defect; he shall not approach [the altar] to present the food of his God.

²²'He may eat the food of his God, both of the most holy and of the holy things,

²³but he shall not go within the veil or approach the altar [of incense], because he has a defect, so that he will not profane My sanctuaries; for I am the LORD who sanctifies them.'" [Heb 7:28]

²⁴So Moses spoke to Aaron and to his sons, and to all the Israelites.

22 THEN THE LORD spoke to Moses, saying,

²"Tell Aaron and his sons to be careful with the holy things (offerings, gifts) which the children of Israel dedicate to Me, so that they do not profane My holy name; I am the LORD.

³"Say to them, 'Any one of your descendants throughout your generations who approaches the holy things which the Israelites dedicate to the LORD, while he is [ceremonially] unclean, that person shall be cut off from My presence and excluded from the sanctuary; I am the LORD.

⁴'No man of the descendants of Aaron who is a leper or has a discharge may eat the holy things [the offerings and the showbread] until he is clean. And whoever touches any person or thing made unclean by contact with a corpse or a man who has had a seminal emission,

⁵or whoever touches any crawling thing by which he is made unclean, or any person by whom he is made unclean, whatever it may be, [Lev 11:24–28]

⁶the person who touches any such thing shall be unclean until evening and shall not eat the holy things unless he has bathed his body in water. [Heb 10:22]

⁷'When the sun sets, he will be clean, and afterward he may eat the holy things, for it is his food.

⁸'He shall not eat that which dies [of natural causes] or is torn by a predator, becoming unclean by it; I am the LORD.

⁹'Therefore the priests shall observe My ordinance, so that they will not bear sin because of it and die if they profane it; I am the LORD who sanctifies them.

¹⁰'No layman [that is, someone outside of Aaron's family] is to eat the holy *gift* [which has been offered to God]; a foreigner residing with the priest or a hired man shall not eat the holy thing.

¹¹'But if a priest buys a slave as his property with his money, the slave may eat the holy thing, and those who are born in the priest's house; they may eat his food.

¹²'If a priest's daughter is married to a layman [one not part of the priestly tribe], she shall not eat the offering of the holy things.

¹³'But if a priest's daughter is a widow or divorced, and has no child, and returns to her father's house as in her youth, she shall eat her father's food; but no layman shall eat it.

¹⁴'But if a person unknowingly eats a holy *gift* [which has been offered to God], then he shall add one-fifth of its value to it and give the holy *gift* to the priest.

¹⁵'The priests shall not profane the holy things the Israelites offer to the LORD,

¹⁶and so cause them [by neglect of any essential observance] to bear the punishment of guilt when they eat their holy things; for I am the LORD who sanctifies them.'"

¹⁷Then the LORD spoke to Moses, saying,

¹⁸"Speak to Aaron and his sons and to all the Israelites and say to them, 'Any man of the house of Israel or any stranger in Israel who presents his offering, whether to *fulfill* any of their vows or as any of their freewill (voluntary) offerings which they presented to the LORD as a burnt offering—

¹⁹so that you may be accepted—it must be a male without blemish from the cattle, the sheep, or the goats.

²⁰'You shall not offer anything which has a blemish, because it will not be accepted for you. [1 Pet 1:19]

²¹'Whoever offers a sacrifice of peace offerings to the LORD to fulfill a special vow to the LORD or as a freewill offering from the herd or from the flock, it must be perfect to be accepted; there shall be no blemish in it.

²²'Animals *that are* blind or fractured or mutilated, or have a sore or a running wound or an itch or scabs, you shall not offer to the LORD nor make an offering of them by fire on the altar to the LORD.

²³'For a freewill offering you may offer either a bull or a lamb which has an overgrown or stunted member (deformity), but for [the payment of] a vow it will not be accepted.

²⁴'You shall not offer to the LORD any animal which has its testicles bruised or crushed or torn or cut off, or sacrifice it in your land.

²⁵'Nor shall you offer as the food of your God any such [animals obtained] from a foreigner, because their corruption *and* blemish makes them unfit; there is a defect in them, they shall not be accepted for you.'"

²⁶Then the LORD spoke to Moses, saying,

²⁷"When a bull or a sheep or a goat is born, it shall remain for seven days with its mother; and after the eighth day it shall be accepted as an offering by fire to the LORD.

²⁸"And whether [the mother] is a cow

life point

I urge you to be a thankful person. The Bible says we are to thank God in every situation (see 1 Thessalonians 5:18). That means we are not to complain, murmur, grumble, or find fault, no matter what is going on in our lives. Whining shows that we have no faith in God's ability to make things better, but thankfulness opens the door to His blessing.

or a sheep, you shall not kill both it and its young in one day.

29"When you sacrifice an offering of thanksgiving to the LORD, you shall sacrifice it so that you may be accepted.

30"It shall be eaten on the same day; you shall leave none of it until *the next* morning; I am the LORD.

31"So you shall keep My commandments and do them; I am the LORD.

32"You shall not profane My holy name [using it to honor an idol, or treating it with irreverence or contempt or as a byword]; but I will be sanctified (set apart as holy) among the Israelites. I am the LORD, who sanctifies *and* declares you holy,

33who brought you out of the land of Egypt to be your God; I am the LORD."

23 THE LORD spoke again to Moses, saying, 2"Speak to the children of Israel and say to them, 'The appointed times (established feasts) of the LORD which you shall proclaim as holy convocations—My appointed times are these:

3'For six days work may be done, but the seventh day is the Sabbath of complete rest, a holy convocation (calling together). You shall not do any work [on that day]; it is the Sabbath of the LORD wherever you may be.

4'These are the appointed times of the LORD, holy convocations which you shall proclaim at their appointed times:

5'The LORD's Passover is on the fourteenth day of the first month at twilight.

6'The Feast of Unleavened Bread to the LORD is on the fifteenth day of the same month; for seven days you shall eat unleavened bread. [1 Cor 5:7, 8]

7'On the first day you shall have a holy convocation (calling together); you shall not do any laborious work [on that day].

8'But you shall present an offering by fire to the LORD for seven days; on the seventh day there shall be a holy convocation; you shall not do any laborious work [on that day].'"

9Then the LORD spoke to Moses, saying,

10"Speak to the children of Israel and say to them, 'When you enter the land which I am giving you and reap its harvest, you shall bring the sheaf of the first fruits of your harvest to the priest.

11'He shall wave the sheaf before the LORD so that you may be accepted; the priest shall wave it on the day after the Sabbath.

12'Now on the day when you wave the sheaf you shall offer a male lamb one year old without blemish as a burnt offering to the LORD.

13'Its grain offering shall be two-tenths of an ephah of fine flour mixed with [olive] oil, an offering by fire to the LORD for a sweet *and* soothing aroma, with its drink offering [to be poured out], a fourth of a hin of wine.

14'You shall not eat any bread or roasted grain or new growth, until this same day when you bring in the offering to your God; it is a permanent statute throughout your generations wherever you may be.

15'You shall count from the day after the Sabbath, from the day when you brought in the sheaf (tied bundle of grain) of the wave offering; there shall be seven complete Sabbaths (seven full weeks).

¹⁶'You shall count fifty days to the day after the seventh Sabbath; then you shall present a new grain offering to the Lord.

¹⁷'You shall bring in from your places two loaves of bread as a wave offering, made from two-tenths *of an ephah* of fine flour; they shall be baked with leaven as first fruits to the Lord.

¹⁸'And you shall offer with the bread seven unblemished lambs, one year old, and one young bull and two rams. They are to be a burnt offering to the Lord, with their grain offering and their drink offerings. It is an offering by fire, a sweet *and* soothing aroma to the Lord.

¹⁹'And you shall sacrifice one male goat as a sin offering and two male lambs, one year old as a sacrifice of peace offerings.

²⁰'The priest shall wave them before the Lord as a wave offering, together with the bread of the first fruits and the two lambs. They are to be holy to the Lord for the priest.

²¹'On this same day you shall make a proclamation, you are to have a holy convocation (calling together); you shall not do any laborious work [on that day]. It is to be a permanent statute throughout your generations wherever you may be.

²²'When you reap the harvest of your land, you shall not reap to the edges of your field, nor gather the gleaning of your harvest; you are to leave them for the poor and for the stranger. I am the Lord your God.' "

²³Again the Lord spoke to Moses, saying,

²⁴"Say to the children of Israel, 'On the first day of the seventh month (almost October), you shall observe a day of solemn sabbatical rest, a memorial day announced by the blowing *of trumpets*, a holy convocation.

²⁵'You shall not do any laborious work [on that day], but you shall present an offering by fire to the Lord.' "

²⁶The Lord spoke to Moses, saying,

²⁷"Also the tenth day of this seventh month is the Day of Atonement; it shall be a holy convocation for you, and you shall humble yourselves [by fasting] and present an offering by fire to the Lord.

²⁸"You shall not do any work on this same day, for it is the Day of Atonement, to make atonement on your behalf before the Lord your God.

²⁹"If there is any person who will not humble himself on this same day, he shall be cut off from his people [excluding him from the atonement made for them].

³⁰"If there is any person who does any work on this same day, I will destroy that person from among his people.

³¹"You shall do no work at all [on that day]. It is a permanent statute throughout your generations wherever you may be.

³²"It is to be to you a Sabbath of complete rest, and you shall humble yourselves. On the ninth day of the month at evening, from evening to evening you shall keep your Sabbath."

³³Again the Lord spoke to Moses, saying,

³⁴"Say to the children of Israel, 'On the fifteenth day of this seventh month, and for seven days, is the Feast of Booths (Tabernacles) to the Lord.

³⁵'The first day is a holy convocation (calling together); you shall not do any laborious work [on that day].

³⁶'For seven days you shall present an offering by fire to the Lord. On the eighth day you shall have a holy convocation and present an offering by fire to the Lord. It is a festive assembly; you shall not do any laborious work [on that day].

³⁷'These are the appointed times (established feasts) of the Lord, which

you shall proclaim to be holy convocations, to present an offering by fire to the Lord, a burnt offering and a grain offering, sacrifices and drink offerings, each on its own day.

³⁸'This is in addition to the [weekly] Sabbaths of the Lord, and in addition to your gifts and all your vowed offerings and all your freewill offerings, which you give to the Lord.

³⁹'On exactly the fifteenth day of the seventh month (nearly October), when you have gathered in the crops of the land, you shall celebrate the feast of the Lord for seven days, with a Sabbath rest on the first day and a Sabbath rest on the eighth day.

⁴⁰'Now on the first day you shall take for yourselves the foliage of beautiful trees, branches of palm trees, and boughs of thick (leafy) trees, and willows of the brook [and make booths of them]; and you shall rejoice before the Lord your God for seven days.

⁴¹'You shall celebrate it as a feast to the Lord for seven days in the year. It shall be a permanent statute throughout your generations; you shall celebrate it in the seventh month.

⁴²'You shall live in booths (temporary shelters) for seven days; all native-born in Israel shall live in booths,

⁴³so that your generations may know that I had the sons of Israel live in booths when I brought them out of the land of Egypt. I am the Lord your God.'"

⁴⁴So Moses declared to the Israelites the appointed feasts of the Lord.

24 THEN THE Lord spoke to Moses, saying, ²"Command the children of Israel to bring to you clear oil from beaten olives for the light [of the golden lampstand], to make a lamp burn continually.

³"Outside the veil of the Testimony [between the Holy Place and the Most Holy Place] in the Tent of Meeting,

Aaron shall always keep the lamps burning before the Lord from evening until morning; it shall be a permanent statute throughout your generations.

⁴"He shall keep the lamps burning on the pure *gold* lampstand before the Lord continually. [Rev 1:12–18]

⁵"Then you shall take fine flour and bake twelve cakes (bread of the Presence, showbread) with it; two-tenths of *an ephah* shall be in each cake (loaf).

⁶"You shall set the bread of the Presence (showbread) in two rows, six in a row, on the pure *gold* table before the Lord.

⁷"You shall put pure frankincense [in two censers, one] beside each row, so that it may be with the bread as a memorial portion, an offering by fire to the Lord.

⁸"Every Sabbath day Aaron shall arrange the showbread before the Lord continually; it is an everlasting covenant for the Israelites.

⁹"The bread of the Presence shall be for Aaron and his sons, and they shall eat it in a sacred place, for it is for Aaron a most holy portion of the offerings by fire to the Lord, his portion forever."

¹⁰Now the son of an Israelite woman, whose father was an Egyptian, went out among the Israelites, and he and a man of Israel quarreled *and* struggled with each other in the camp.

¹¹The Israelite woman's son blasphemed the Name [of the Lord] and cursed. So they brought him to Moses. (Now his mother's name was Shelomith, the daughter of Dibri, of the tribe of Dan.)

¹²They put him in custody until the will *and* command of the Lord might be made clear to them.

¹³Then the Lord spoke to Moses, saying,

¹⁴"Bring the one who has cursed [the Lord] outside the camp, and let all who heard him lay their hands on his head

[as witnesses to his guilt]; then let all the congregation stone him.

15"You shall speak to the Israelites, saying, 'Whoever curses his God will bear his sin [through his own death].

16'Further, the one who blasphemes the name of the Lord shall most certainly be put to death; all the congregation shall stone him. The stranger as well as the native-born shall be put to death when he blasphemes the Name [of the Lord].

17'If a man takes the life of any human being [unlawfully], he shall most certainly be put to death.

18'The one who kills an animal shall replace it, animal for animal.

19'If a man injures his neighbor (fellow citizen), whatever he has done shall be done to him:

20fracture for fracture, eye for eye, tooth for tooth; just as he has injured a man, so shall the same be done to him. [Matt 5:38–42; 7:2]

21'The one who kills an animal shall replace it; but he who kills a human being [unlawfully] shall be put to death.

22'You shall have one standard of law for the stranger *among you* as well as for the native, for I am the Lord your God.'"

23Then Moses spoke to the Israelites, and they brought the one who had cursed [the Lord] outside the camp and stoned him with stones. Thus the Israelites did just as the Lord had commanded Moses.

putting the Word to work

Much of our modern society seems to have lost respect for the name of the Lord. Do you honor His name in your speech? Do not use the name God, Lord, or Jesus in a frivolous or disrespectful way. Always remember that His name represents all that He is, and His name is to be honored not only in our hearts but also in our speech.

25

THE LORD spoke to Moses at Mount Sinai, saying, 2"Speak to the children of Israel and say to them, 'When you come into the land which I am giving you, then the land shall keep a Sabbath to the Lord.

3'For six years you shall sow your field, and for six years you shall prune your vineyard and gather in its crop.

4'But in the seventh year there shall be a Sabbath of rest for the land, a Sabbath to the Lord; you shall not sow [seed in] your field nor prune your vineyard.

5'Whatever reseeds itself (uncultivated) in your harvest you shall not reap, nor shall you gather the grapes from your uncultivated vine, it shall be a year of sabbatical rest for the land.

6'And all of you shall have for food whatever the [untilled] land produces during its Sabbath year; yourself, and your male and female slaves, your hired servant, and the foreigners who reside among you,

7even your domestic animals and the [wild] animals that are in your land shall have all its crops to eat.

8'You are also to count off seven Sabbaths of years for yourself, seven times seven years, so that you have the time of the seven Sabbaths of years, namely, forty-nine years.

9'Then you shall sound the ram's horn everywhere on the tenth day of the seventh month (almost October); on the Day of Atonement you shall sound the trumpet throughout your land.

10'And you shall consecrate the fiftieth year and proclaim freedom [for the slaves] throughout the land to all its inhabitants. It shall be a Jubilee (year of remission) for you, and each of you shall return to his own [ancestral] property [that was sold to another because of poverty], and each of you shall return to his family [from whom he was separated by bondage].

¹¹'That fiftieth year shall be a Jubilee for you; you shall not sow [seed], nor reap what reseeds itself, nor gather the grapes of the uncultivated vines.

¹²'For it is the Jubilee; it shall be holy to you; you shall eat its crops out of the field.

¹³'In this Year of Jubilee each of you shall return to his own [ancestral] property.

¹⁴'If you sell anything to your friend or buy from your friend, you shall not wrong one another.

¹⁵'According to the number of years after the Jubilee, you shall buy from your friend. And he is to sell to you according to the number of years of crops [which may be harvested before you must restore the property to him].

¹⁶'If the years [until the next Jubilee] are many, you shall increase the price, but if the years remaining are few, you shall reduce the price, because it is the number of crops that he is selling to you.

¹⁷'You shall not wrong one another, but you shall fear your God [with profound reverence]; for I am the Lord your God.

¹⁸'Therefore you shall carry out My statutes and keep My ordinances and do them, so that you may live securely on the land.

¹⁹'Then the land will yield its produce, so that you can eat your fill and live securely on it.

²⁰'And if you say, "What are we going to eat in the seventh year if we do not sow [seed] or gather in our crops?"

²¹then [this is My answer:] I will order My [special] blessing for you in the sixth year, so that it will produce [sufficient] crops for three years.

²²'When you are sowing the eighth

life point

We must have reverential fear and awe of God in order to hear from Him and to receive His wisdom and knowledge. Reverential fear is to know that God is God and that He means what He says. God has called us His friends, even His sons and daughters, but we are to respect Him and honor Him with profound reverence.

year, you can still eat old things from the crops, eating the old until the ninth year when its crop comes in.

²³'The land shall not be sold permanently, for the land is Mine; you are [only] foreigners and temporary residents with Me. [Heb 11:13; 1 Pet 2:11–17]

²⁴'So in all the country that you possess, you are to provide for the redemption of the land [in the Year of Jubilee].

²⁵'If a fellow countryman of yours becomes so poor he has to sell some of his property, then his nearest relative is to come and buy back (redeem) what his relative has sold.

²⁶'Or in case a man has no relative [to redeem his property], but he has become more prosperous *and* has enough to buy it back,

²⁷then he shall calculate the years since its sale and refund the balance to the man to whom he sold it, and so return to his [ancestral] property. [1 Kin 21:2, 3]

²⁸'But if he is unable to redeem it, then what he has sold shall remain in the hands of the purchaser until the Year of Jubilee; but at the Jubilee it shall revert, and he may return to his property.

²⁹'If a man sells a house in a walled

speak the Word

I thank You, God, that as I carry out Your statutes, I will live securely in the land where You have placed me.
—ADAPTED FROM LEVITICUS 25:18, 19

city, then his right of redemption remains valid for a full year after its sale; his right of redemption lasts a full year.

³⁰'But if it is not redeemed for him within a full year, then the house that is in the walled city passes permanently *and* irrevocably to the purchaser throughout his generations. It does not revert back in the Year of Jubilee.

³¹'The houses of the villages that have no surrounding walls, however, shall be considered as open fields. They may be redeemed, and revert in the Year of Jubilee.

³²'As for the cities of the Levites, the Levites have a permanent right of redemption for the houses in the cities which they possess.

³³'Therefore, what is [purchased] from the Levites may be redeemed [by a Levite], and the house that was sold in the city they possess reverts in the Year of Jubilee, for the houses in the Levite cities are their [ancestral] property among the Israelites.

³⁴'But the pasture lands of their cities may not be sold, for that is their permanent possession.

³⁵'Now if your fellow countryman becomes poor and his hand falters with you [that is, he has trouble repaying you for something], then you are to help *and* sustain him, [with courtesy and consideration] like [you would] a stranger or a temporary resident [without property], so that he may live among you. [1 John 3:17]

³⁶'Do not charge him usurious interest, but fear your God [with profound reverence], so your countryman may [continue to] live among you.

³⁷'You shall not give him your money at interest, nor your food at a profit.

³⁸'I am the LORD your God, who brought you out of the land of Egypt to give you the land of Canaan and to be your God.

release your grudges

In Leviticus 25 we read about the Year of Jubilee, in which all debts were forgiven and all debtors were pardoned and set free.

When we are in Christ, every day can be the Year of Jubilee. We can say to those who are in debt to us by their mistreatment of us, "I forgive you and release you from your debt. You are free to go. I leave you in God's hands to let Him deal with you, because as long as I am trying to deal with you, He won't."

According to the Bible, we are not to hold a person in perpetual debt, just as we ourselves are not to be indebted to anyone else. Romans 13:8 instructs us, "Owe nothing to anyone except to love and seek the best for one another." We need to learn to forgive people by canceling their debts to us. We also need to realize we can have our own sins forgiven continually through repentance and faith in Jesus Christ. We can enjoy a continual Year of Jubilee.

Can you imagine the joy of a person who learns that he has been pardoned from a ten- or twenty-year prison sentence? That's the good news of the Cross. Because Jesus paid our debt for us, God can say to us, "You don't owe Me anything anymore!" Our trouble is either that we are still trying to pay our debt to the Lord, or that we are still trying to collect our debts from others. Just as God canceled our debt and forgave us of it, so are we to cancel the debts of others and forgive them what they owe us.

[39]'And if your fellow countryman becomes so poor [in his dealings] with you that he sells himself to you [as payment for a debt], you shall not let him do the work of a slave [who is ineligible for redemption],

[40]but he is to be with you as a hired man, as if he were a temporary resident; he shall serve with you until the Year of Jubilee,

[41]and then he shall leave you, he and his children with him, and shall go back to his own family and return to the property of his fathers.

[42]'For the Israelites are My servants whom I brought out of the land of Egypt; they shall not be sold in a slave sale. [1 Cor 7:23]

[43]'You shall not rule over him with harshness (severity, oppression), but you are to fear your God [with profound reverence]. [Eph 6:9; Col 4:1]

[44]As for your male and female slaves whom you may have—you may acquire male and female slaves from the pagan nations that are around you.

[45]'Moreover, from the children of the strangers who live as aliens among you, from them you may buy *slaves* and from their families who are with you, whom they have produced in your land; they may become your possession.

[46]'You may even bequeath them as an inheritance to your children after you, to receive as a possession; you can use them as permanent slaves. But in respect to your fellow countrymen, the children of Israel, you shall not rule over one another with harshness (severity, oppression).

[47]'Now if the financial means of a stranger or temporary resident among you become sufficient, and your fellow countryman becomes poor *in comparison* to him and sells himself to the stranger who is living among you or to the descendants of the stranger's family,

[48]then after he is sold he shall have the right of redemption. One of his relatives may redeem him:

[49]either his uncle or his uncle's son may redeem him, or one of his blood relatives from his family may redeem him; or if he prospers, he may redeem himself.

[50]'Then he [or his redeemer] shall calculate with his purchaser from the year when he sold himself to the purchaser to the Year of Jubilee, and the [original] price of his sale shall be adjusted according to the number of years. The time he was with his owner shall be considered as that of a hired man.

[51]'If there are still many years [before the Year of Jubilee], in proportion to them he must refund [to the purchaser] part of the price of his sale for his redemption *and* release.

[52]'And if *only* a few years remain until the Year of Jubilee, he shall so calculate it with him. He is to refund the proportionate amount for his release.

[53]'Like a man hired year by year he shall deal with him; he shall not rule over him with harshness in your sight.

[54]'Even if he is not redeemed during these years *and* under these provisions, then he shall go free in the Year of Jubilee, he and his children with him.

[55]'For the children of Israel are My servants; My servants, whom I brought out of the land of Egypt. I am the Lord your God.

26 'YOU SHALL not make idols for yourselves, nor shall you erect an image, a sacred pillar *or* an obelisk, nor shall you place any figured stone in your land so that you may bow down to it; for I am the Lord your God.

[2]'You shall keep My Sabbaths and have reverence for My sanctuary. I am the Lord.

[3]'If you walk in My statutes and keep My commandments and [obediently] do them,

⁴then I will give you rain in its season, and the land will yield her produce and the trees of the field bear their fruit.

⁵And your threshing season will last until grape gathering and the grape gathering [time] will last until planting, and you will eat your bread and be filled and live securely in your land.

⁶I will also grant peace in the land, so that you may lie down and there will be no one to make you afraid. I will also eliminate harmful animals from the land, and no sword will pass through your land.

⁷And you will chase your enemies, and they will fall before you by the sword.

⁸Five of you will chase a hundred, and a hundred of you will put ten

wait for God's timing

Leviticus 26:4 says, "I will give you rain in its season." When is *its season*? I believe it is when God knows we are ready, when everyone else involved is ready, and when it fits into God's corporate plan. God has an individual plan for our individual lives, but He also has a corporate plan for the entire world.

I remember a time when I was frustrated because nothing was happening in my ministry. I knew I was anointed to teach God's Word, but absolutely no doors opened to me. It seemed I had waited so long. I felt ready. I had been cooperating with God. He had done major work in me, and I just could not understand why something was not happening. I remember asking, "God, what are You waiting for now? Am I not ready?" He responded in my heart, "You are ready, but some of the others who will be involved with you are not yet ready. I am still working some things out in them, and you will need to wait on them now."

God does not push, shove, demand, manipulate, or force people. He leads, guides, prompts, and suggests. Then, each individual is responsible to give his or her will over to Him for His purpose. Sometimes this takes longer for one person than for another. An excellent example of this is the single person who is praying for the right mate. God is, in fact, preparing that mate, but the one praying gets tired of waiting since he or she does not know what is happening behind the scenes. God's good plan does take time, and often more time than we anticipated. Seeing the fulfillment of it requires a willingness to wait for the blessing "in its season."

Our wait is easier to endure when we believe God's timing is perfect, and He is never late, not one single day. Whatever the reason for the delay, Galatians 6:9 encourages us not to "grow weary or become discouraged in doing good, for at the proper time we will reap, if we do not give in." Also, 1 Peter 5:6 exhorts us to humble ourselves under God's mighty hand so that He may exalt you "at the appropriate time."

There is a right time for all things in our lives, and there is safety in being in God's perfect timing. I pray to be in God's perfect will with His perfect timing—not one step ahead of Him, nor one step behind. I hope you will pray that way too.

I also want to remind you to enjoy where you are while you are on the way to where you are going. God's timing is perfect, and being frustrated will not make Him hurry! Enjoy today, because right now it's all you have!

life point

A continual theme throughout the Bible is that you will be blessed if you will keep God's commandments. The Amplified Bible explains that "blessed" means you will be "spiritually prosperous and happy" (Matthew 5:3) "with life-joy in God's favor" (Matthew 5:9), regardless of your outward condition. That sounds like a good thing to me! However, you must not miss what you need to do to receive God's blessing. Do you see that little word *if* in Leviticus 26:3? It may be a small word, but it has a big meaning. It means that God has a condition for receiving blessing. He does not require you to be perfect, because no one is perfect, but you do need to be aggressively attempting to do what God instructs you to do—to walk in His statutes and keep and do His commandments.

thousand to flight; your enemies will fall before you by the sword.

⁹'For I will turn toward you [with favor and regard] and make you fruitful and multiply you, and I will establish *and* confirm My covenant with you. [2 Kin 13:23]

¹⁰'You will eat the old supply of [abundant] produce, and clear out the old [to make room] for the new.

¹¹'I will make My dwelling among you, and My soul will not reject *nor* separate itself from you.

¹²'I will walk among you and be your God, and you shall be My people.

¹³'I am the LORD your God, who brought you out of the land of Egypt so that you would not be their slaves; and I broke the bars of your yoke and made you walk upright [with heads held high as free men].

¹⁴'But if you do not obey Me and do not [obediently] do all these commandments,

¹⁵if, instead, you reject My statutes, and if your soul rejects My ordinances, so that you will not [obediently] do all My commandments, and in this way break My covenant,

¹⁶I, in turn, will do this to you: I will appoint over you sudden terror, consumption, and fever that will waste away the eyes and cause the soul to languish also. And you will sow your seed uselessly, for your enemies will eat what you plant.

¹⁷'I will set My face against you so that you will be struck down before your enemies; those who hate you will rule over you, and you will flee when no one is pursuing you. [1 Sam 4:10; 31:1]

¹⁸'If in spite of all this you still will not listen to Me *and* be obedient, then I will punish you seven times more for your sins.

¹⁹'I will break your pride in your power, and I will make your sky like iron [giving no rain and blocking all prayers] and your ground like bronze [hard to plow and yielding no produce]. [1 Kin 17:1]

speak the Word

Thank You, God, for turning toward me with favor and regard, making me fruitful and establishing Your covenant with me.
—ADAPTED FROM LEVITICUS 26:9

God, I thank You that You walk with me, that You are my God and that I belong to You.
—ADAPTED FROM LEVITICUS 26:12

²⁰'Your strength will be spent uselessly, for your land will not yield its produce and the trees of the land will not yield their fruit.

²¹'If then, you act with hostility toward Me and are unwilling to obey Me, I will increase the plague on you seven times in accordance with your sins.

²²'I will let loose the [wild] animals of the field among you, which will bereave you of your children and destroy your livestock and make you so few in number that your roads will lie deserted *and* desolate. [2 Kin 17:25, 26]

²³'And if by these things you are not turned to Me, but act with hostility against Me,

²⁴then I also will act with hostility against you, and I will strike you seven times for your sins.

²⁵'I will bring a sword on you that will execute vengeance for [breaking] the covenant; and when you gather together in your cities, I will send pestilence (virulent disease) among you, and you shall be handed over to the enemy. [Num 16:49; 2 Sam 24:15]

²⁶'When I break your staff of bread [that is, cut off your supply of food], ten women will bake your bread in one oven, and they will ration your bread; and you will eat and not be satisfied. [Hag 1:6]

²⁷'Yet if in spite of this you will not [attentively] listen to Me but act with hostility against me,

²⁸then I will act with hostility against you in wrath, and I also will punish you seven times for your sins.

²⁹'You will eat the flesh of your sons and the flesh of your daughters. [2 Kin 6:28, 29]

³⁰'I will destroy your high places [devoted to idolatrous worship], and cut down your incense altars, and heap your dead bodies upon the [crushed] bodies of your idols, and My soul will detest you [with deep and unutterable loathing]. [2 Kin 23:8, 20]

³¹'I will lay waste your cities as well and will make your sanctuaries desolate, and I will not smell your sweet *and* soothing aromas [of offerings by fire]. [2 Kin 25:4–10; 2 Chr 36:19]

³²'I will make the land desolate, and your enemies who settle in it will be appalled at it.

³³'I will scatter you among the nations and draw out the sword [of your enemies] after you; your land will become desolate and your cities will become ruins. [Ps 44:11–14]

³⁴'Then the land [of Israel] will enjoy its Sabbaths as long as it lies desolate, while you are in your enemies' land; then the land will rest and enjoy its Sabbaths.

³⁵'As long as it lies desolate, it will have rest, the rest it did not have on your Sabbaths, while you were living on it. [2 Chr 36:21]

³⁶'As for those who are left of you, I will bring despair (lack of courage, weakness) into their hearts in the lands of their enemies; the sound of a scattered leaf will put them to flight, and they will flee as if [running] from the sword, and will fall even when no one is chasing them.

³⁷'They shall stumble over one another as if *to escape* from a sword when no one is chasing them; and you will have no power to stand before your enemies.

³⁸'You will perish among the nations; the land of your enemies will consume you.

³⁹'Those of you who are left will rot away because of their wickedness in the lands of your enemies; also because of the wickedness of their forefathers they will rot away like them.

⁴⁰'If they confess their wickedness and the wickedness of their forefathers, in their unfaithfulness which they have committed against Me—and also in their acting with hostility toward Me—

⁴¹I also was acting with hostility toward them and brought them into the land of their enemies—then if their uncircumcised (sin-filled) hearts are humbled and they accept the punishment for their wickedness, [2 Kin 24:10–14; Dan 9:11–14]

⁴²then I will remember My covenant with Jacob, and also My covenant with Isaac, and also My covenant with Abraham, and remember the land. [Ps 106:44–46]

⁴³'But the land will be abandoned by them and will enjoy its Sabbaths while it lies desolate without them; and they will accept the punishment for their wickedness *and* make amends because they rejected My ordinances and their soul rejected My statutes.

⁴⁴'Yet in spite of this, when they are in the land of their enemies, I will not reject them, nor will I so despise them as to destroy them, breaking My covenant with them; for I am the LORD their God. [Deut 4:31–35; Jer 33:4, 5, 23–26; Rom 11:2–5]

⁴⁵'But I will, for their sake, [earnestly] remember the covenant with their forefathers, whom I have brought out of the land of Egypt in the sight of the nations, that I might be their God. I am the LORD.'"

⁴⁶These are the statutes, ordinances, and laws which the LORD established between Himself and the Israelites through Moses at Mount Sinai.

27 AGAIN, THE LORD spoke to Moses, saying, ²"Speak to the children of Israel and say to them, 'When a man makes a special vow [consecrating himself or a member of his family], he *shall be valued* according to your [established system of] valuation of people belonging to the LORD [that is, the priest accepts from the man making the vow a specified amount of money for the temple treasury in place of the actual person].

³'If your valuation is of a male between twenty and sixty years of age, then your valuation shall be fifty shekels of silver, according to the shekel of the sanctuary.

⁴'Or if the person is a female, then your valuation shall be thirty shekels.

⁵'If the person is between five years and twenty years of age, then your valuation for the male shall be twenty shekels and for the female ten shekels.

⁶'But if the child is between one month and five years of age, then your valuation shall be five shekels of silver for the male and three shekels for the female.

⁷'If the person is sixty years old and above, your valuation shall be fifteen shekels for the male, and ten shekels for the female.

⁸'But if the person is too poor to pay your valuation, then he shall be placed before the priest, and the priest shall value him; according to the ability of the one who vowed, the priest shall value him.

⁹'Now if it is an animal of the kind which men can present as an offering to the LORD, any such that one gives to the LORD shall be holy.

¹⁰'He shall not replace it or exchange it, a good for a bad, or a bad for a good; but if he does exchange an animal for an animal, then both the original offering and its substitute shall be holy.

¹¹'If it is any unclean animal of the kind which men do not present as an offering to the LORD, then he shall bring the animal before the priest,

¹²and the priest shall value it as either good or bad; it shall be as you, the priest, value it.

¹³'But if he ever *wishes to* redeem it, then he shall add one-fifth of it to your valuation.

¹⁴'If a man consecrates his house as sacred to the LORD, the priest shall appraise it as either good or bad; as the priest appraises it, so shall it stand.

¹⁵'If the one who consecrates his

house should *wish to* redeem it, then he shall add one-fifth of your valuation price to it, so that it may be his.

¹⁶'And if a man consecrates to the LORD part of a field of his own property, then your valuation shall be proportionate to the seed needed for it; a homer of barley seed shall be valued at fifty shekels of silver.

¹⁷'If he consecrates his field during the Year of Jubilee, it shall stand according to your valuation.

¹⁸'But if he consecrates his field after the Jubilee, then the priest shall calculate the price for him in proportion to the years that remain until the Year of Jubilee; and it shall be deducted from your valuation.

¹⁹'If the one who consecrates the field should ever wish to redeem it, then he shall add one-fifth of the appraisal price to it, so that it may return to him.

²⁰'If he does not redeem the field, but has sold it to another man, it may no longer be redeemed.

²¹'When the field reverts in the Jubilee, the field shall be holy to the LORD, like a field set apart (devoted); the priest shall possess it as his property.

²²'Or if a man consecrates to the LORD a field which he has bought, which is not part of the field of his [ancestral] property,

²³then the priest shall calculate for him the amount of your valuation up to the Year of Jubilee; and the man shall give that [amount] on that day as a holy thing to the LORD.

²⁴'In the Year of Jubilee the field shall return to the one from whom it was purchased, to whom the land belonged [as his ancestral inheritance].

²⁵'Every valuation of yours shall be in accordance with the sanctuary shekel; twenty gerahs shall make a shekel.

²⁶'However, the firstborn among animals, which as a firstborn belongs to the LORD, no man may consecrate, whether an ox or a sheep. It is [already] the LORD's.

²⁷'If it is among the unclean animals, the owner may redeem it in accordance with your valuation, and add one-fifth to it; or if it is not redeemed, then it shall be sold in accordance with your valuation.

²⁸'But nothing that a man sets apart [that is, devotes as an offering] to the LORD out of all that he has, of man or of animal or of the fields of his own property, shall be sold or redeemed. Anything devoted to destruction (banned, cursed) is most holy to the LORD.

²⁹'No one who may have been set apart among men shall be ransomed [from death], he shall most certainly be put to death.

³⁰'And all the tithe (tenth part) of the land, whether the seed of the land or the fruit of the tree, is the LORD's; it is holy to the LORD. [1 Cor 9:11; Gal 6:6]

³¹'If a man wishes to redeem any part of his tithe, he shall add one-fifth to it.

³²'For every tithe of the herd or flock, whatever passes under the [shepherd's] staff, the tenth one shall be holy to the LORD. [2 Cor 9:7–9]

³³'The man is not to be concerned whether *the animal is* good or bad, nor shall he exchange it. But if he does exchange it, then both it and its substitute shall become holy; it shall not be redeemed.'"

³⁴These are the commandments which the LORD commanded Moses on Mount Sinai for the children of Israel. [Rom 10:4; Heb 4:2; 12:18–29]

Numbers

Author:
Moses

Date:
About 1440 BC

Everyday Life Principles:
Let God lead you. Move when He says to move, and be still when He says not to move.

When God has brought you out of a place of bondage, do not be tempted to go back. Persevere until you reach the place where He is leading you.

Approach life with a positive attitude and with faith so that obstacles or challenges in life will not intimidate you.

One of the primary themes in Numbers is God's guidance. The Israelites never knew when God was going to ask them to move as they made their journey toward the Promised Land. When He did call them to stop or to resume their travel, He made His leading clear in the appearance of a cloud by day and fire by night.

Even though God's guidance was so evident and the Israelites knew He was leading them into the Promised Land, they grew weary and discouraged along the way. In fact, they became so disheartened that they wanted to go back to Egypt where they had been miserable!

In order to live victorious lives, we need to be sensitive to God's Spirit and keep making progress without looking back. We need to move when He says to move, and we need to stay where we are when He instructs us to be still. I encourage you to do everything you can to develop an intimate relationship with the Holy Spirit so you can sense His leading in your life. Do not grow weary or become discouraged if you walk through "wilderness" times, but keep pressing on with a good attitude. It's important to refuse any inclination to go back to an old place, a place of bondage, or oppression, and instead follow God into all the great things He has for you.

1 THE LORD spoke [by special revelation] to Moses in the Wilderness of Sinai in the Tent of Meeting (tabernacle) on the first day of the second month in the second year after the Israelites came out of the land of Egypt, saying,

²"Take a census of all the congregation of the sons of Israel, by their families (clans), by their fathers' households, according to the number of names, every male, head by head ³from twenty years old and upward, all in Israel who *are able to* go out to war. You and Aaron shall number them, army by army.

⁴"And with you there shall be a man [to assist you] from each tribe, each being the head of his father's household.

⁵"These then are the names of the men who shall stand with you: from [the tribe of] Reuben, Elizur the son of Shedeur;

⁶from [the tribe of] Simeon, Shelumiel the son of Zurishaddai;

⁷from [the tribe of] Judah, Nahshon the son of Amminadab;

⁸from [the tribe of] Issachar, Nethanel the son of Zuar;

⁹from [the tribe of] Zebulun, Eliab the son of Helon;

¹⁰from the sons (descendants) of Joseph: from [the tribe of] Ephraim, Elishama the son of Ammihud; from [the tribe of] Manasseh, Gamaliel the son of Pedahzur;

¹¹from [the tribe of] Benjamin, Abidan the son of Gideoni;

¹²from [the tribe of] Dan, Ahiezer the son of Ammishaddai;

¹³from [the tribe of] Asher, Pagiel the son of Ochran;

¹⁴from [the tribe of] Gad, Eliasaph the son of Deuel;

¹⁵from [the tribe of] Naphtali, Ahira the son of Enan.

¹⁶"These men were the ones called from the congregation, the leaders of their fathers' (ancestors') tribes; they were the heads of thousands [the highest ranking officers] in Israel."

¹⁷So Moses and Aaron took these men who were designated by name,

¹⁸and assembled all the congregation on the first day of the second month, and they registered by ancestry in their families (clans), by their fathers' households, according to the number of names from twenty years old and upward, head by head,

¹⁹just as the LORD had commanded Moses. So he numbered them in the Wilderness of Sinai.

²⁰The sons of Reuben, Israel's (Jacob's) firstborn, their generations, by their families (clans), by their fathers' households, according to the number of names, head by head, every male from twenty years old and upward, all who *were able to* go to war:

²¹those of the tribe of Reuben numbered 46,500.

²²Of the sons of Simeon, their descendants, by their families (clans), by their fathers' households, their numbered men according to the number of names, head by head, every male from twenty years old and upward, all who *were able to* go to war:

²³those of the tribe of Simeon numbered 59,300.

²⁴Of the sons of Gad, their descendants, by their families (clans), by their fathers' households, according to the number of names, from twenty years old and upward, all who *were able to* go to war:

²⁵those of the tribe of Gad numbered 45,650.

²⁶Of the sons of Judah, their descendants, by their families (clans), by their fathers' households, according to the number of names, from twenty years old and upward, all who *were able to* go to war:

²⁷those of the tribe of Judah numbered 74,600.

²⁸Of the sons of Issachar, their descendants, by their families (clans), by

their fathers' households, according
to the number of names, from twenty
years old and upward, all who *were*
able to go to war:

²⁹those of the tribe of Issachar numbered 54,400.

³⁰Of the sons of Zebulun, their descendants, by their families (clans), by
their fathers' households, according
to the number of names, from twenty
years old and upward, all who *were*
able to go to war:

³¹those of the tribe of Zebulun numbered 57,400.

³²Of the sons of Joseph: the sons
(descendants) of Ephraim, their descendants, by their families (clans), by
their fathers' households, according
to the number of names, from twenty
years old and upward, all who *were*
able to go to war:

³³those of the tribe of Ephraim numbered 40,500.

³⁴Of the sons of Manasseh, their descendants, by their families (clans), by
their fathers' households, according
to the number of names, from twenty
years old and upward, all who *were*
able to go to war:

³⁵those of the tribe of Manasseh
numbered 32,200.

³⁶Of the sons of Benjamin, their descendants, by their families (clans),
by their fathers' households, according to the number of names, from
twenty years old and upward, all who
were able to go to war:

³⁷those of the tribe of Benjamin
numbered 35,400.

³⁸Of the sons of Dan, their descendants, by their families (clans), by
their fathers' households, according
to the number of names, from twenty
years old and upward, all who *were*
able to go to war:

³⁹those of the tribe of Dan numbered
62,700.

⁴⁰Of the sons of Asher, their descendants, by their families (clans), by

their fathers' households, according
to the number of names, from twenty
years old and upward, all who *were*
able to go to war:

⁴¹those of the tribe of Asher numbered 41,500.

⁴²Of the sons of Naphtali, their descendants, by their families (clans), by
their fathers' households, according
to the number of names, from twenty
years old and upward, all who *were*
able to go to war:

⁴³those of the tribe of Naphtali numbered 53,400.

⁴⁴These were the ones who were
numbered, whom Moses and Aaron
numbered, with the leaders of Israel,
twelve men, each representing his fathers' household.

⁴⁵So all those numbered of the sons
of Israel, by their fathers' households,
from twenty years old and upward, all
who *were able to* go to war in Israel,

⁴⁶all who were numbered were
603,550.

⁴⁷The Levites, however, were not
numbered among them by their fathers' tribe.

⁴⁸For the Lᴏʀᴅ had said to Moses,

⁴⁹"Only the tribe of Levi you shall
not number, nor shall you take their
census among the sons of Israel [since
they are unavailable to go to war].

⁵⁰"But appoint the Levites over the
tabernacle (sanctuary) of the Testimony, and over all its furnishings and
all things that belong to it. They shall
carry the tabernacle [when traveling]
and all its furnishings, and they shall
take care of it and camp around it.

⁵¹"When the tabernacle is to go forward, the Levites shall take it down;
and when the tabernacle is to [be set
up for] camp, the Levites shall set it
up. But the layman (non-Levite) who
approaches the tabernacle shall be put
to death.

⁵²"The Israelites shall camp according to their armies, every man by his

own camp and every man by his own [tribal] standard (banner).

⁵³"But the Levites shall camp around the tabernacle of the Testimony, so that there will be no wrath against the congregation of the Israelites. The Levites shall be in charge of the tabernacle of the Testimony."

⁵⁴Thus the sons of Israel did *these things;* according to all that the Lᴏʀᴅ had commanded Moses, so they did.

2 THE LORD spoke to Moses and Aaron, saying, ²"The sons of Israel shall camp, each by his own standard, with the banners of their fathers' households; they shall camp around the Tent of Meeting (tabernacle), but at a distance. ³"Those who camp on the east side toward the sunrise *shall be* of the standard of the camp of Judah, by their armies; and Nahshon the son of Amminadab shall lead the sons of Judah, ⁴and his army as numbered totaled 74,600.

⁵"Next to Judah [on the east side] the tribe of Issachar shall encamp; and Nethanel the son of Zuar shall lead the sons of Issachar, ⁶and his army as numbered totaled 54,400.

⁷"Then [also on the east side] the tribe of Zebulun; and Eliab the son of Helon shall lead the sons of Zebulun, ⁸and his army as numbered totaled 57,400.

⁹"The total of the numbered men [in the three tribes on the east side] in the camp of Judah was 186,400, by their armies. They shall move out first [on the march].

¹⁰"On the south side shall be the standard of the camp of Reuben, by their armies; and Elizur the son of Shedeur shall lead the sons of Reuben, ¹¹and his army as numbered totaled 46,500.

¹²"Those who camp next to Reuben

[on the south side] shall be the tribe of Simeon; and Shelumiel the son of Zurishaddai shall lead the sons of Simeon, ¹³and his army as numbered totaled 59,300.

¹⁴"Then [completing the south side] the tribe of Gad; and Eliasaph the son of Reuel (Deuel) shall lead the sons of Gad, ¹⁵and his army as numbered totaled 45,650.

¹⁶"The total of the numbered men [in the three tribes on the south side] in the camp of Reuben was 151,450, by their armies. They shall move out second [on the march].

¹⁷"Then the Tent of Meeting (tabernacle) shall move out with the camp of the Levites in the middle of the [other] camps; just as they camp so shall they move out, every man in his place by their standards.

¹⁸"On the west side shall be the standard of the camp of Ephraim, by their armies; and Elishama the son of Ammihud shall lead the sons of Ephraim, ¹⁹and his army as numbered totaled 40,500.

²⁰"Beside Ephraim [on the west side] shall be the tribe of Manasseh; and Gamaliel the son of Pedahzur shall lead the sons of Manasseh, ²¹and his army as numbered totaled 32,200.

²²"Then [completing the west side shall be] the tribe of Benjamin; and Abidan the son of Gideoni shall lead the sons of Benjamin, ²³and his army as numbered totaled 35,400.

²⁴"The total of the numbered men [of the three tribes on the west side] in the camp of Ephraim was 108,100, by their armies. They shall move out in third place.

²⁵"On the north side shall be the standard of the camp of Dan, by their armies; and Ahiezer the son of Ammishaddai shall lead the sons of Dan,

²⁶and his army as numbered totaled 62,700.

²⁷"Encamped next to Dan [on the north side] shall be the tribe of Asher; and Pagiel the son of Ochran shall lead the sons of Asher,

²⁸and his army as numbered totaled 41,500.

²⁹"Then [completing the north side] *comes* the tribe of Naphtali; and Ahira the son of Enan shall lead the sons of Naphtali,

³⁰and his army as numbered totaled 53,400.

³¹"The total of the numbered men [of the three tribes on the north side] in the camp of Dan was 157,600. They shall move out last, standard after standard."

³²These are the men of the Israelites [twenty years old and upward] as numbered by their fathers' households. The total of the numbered men of the camps by their armies, 603,550.

³³But the Levites were not numbered with the [other] Israelites, just as the LORD had commanded Moses.

³⁴Thus the Israelites did [as ordered]; according to everything the LORD had commanded Moses, so they camped by their standards, and so they moved out, everyone with his family (clan), according to his fathers' household.

3 NOW THESE are the *records of the* generations of Aaron and Moses in the day when the LORD spoke [by special revelation] with Moses on Mount Sinai.

²These are the names of the sons of Aaron: Nadab the firstborn, Abihu, Eleazar, and Ithamar.

³These are the names of the sons of Aaron, the priests who were anointed, whom Aaron consecrated *and* ordained to minister in the priest's office.

⁴But Nadab and Abihu died in the presence of the LORD when they offered strange (unholy, unacceptable, inappropriate) fire before the LORD

in the Wilderness of Sinai; and they had no sons. So Eleazar and Ithamar served as priests in the presence *and* under the supervision of Aaron their father. [Lev 10:1–4]

⁵Then the LORD spoke to Moses, saying,

⁶"Bring the tribe of Levi near and present them before Aaron the priest, so that they may serve him.

⁷"They shall carry out the duties for him and for the whole congregation before the Tent of Meeting, doing the service of the tabernacle.

⁸"They shall also take care of all the furnishings *and* utensils of the Tent of Meeting, and [attend to] the duties of the Israelites, doing the service of the tabernacle.

⁹"You shall give the Levites to Aaron and to his sons [as servants and helpers]; they are to be given wholly to him from among the Israelites.

¹⁰"So you shall appoint Aaron and his sons, and they shall observe *and* attend to their priesthood; but the layman (non-Levite) who approaches [the holy things] shall be put to death."

¹¹Again the LORD spoke to Moses, saying,

¹²"Behold, I have taken the Levites from among the sons of Israel instead of *and* as a substitute for every firstborn, that is, the first that opens the womb among the Israelites. So the Levites shall be Mine,

¹³for all the firstborn are Mine. On the day that I killed all the firstborn in the land of Egypt, I consecrated for Myself all the firstborn in Israel, both man and animal. They shall be mine; I am the LORD."

¹⁴Then the LORD spoke to Moses in the Wilderness of Sinai, saying,

¹⁵"Number the sons of Levi by their fathers' households, by their families (clans). You shall number every male from a month old and upward."

¹⁶So Moses numbered them just

as he was commanded by the word (mouth) of the LORD.

¹⁷These are the [three] sons of Levi by their names: Gershon, Kohath, and Merari.

¹⁸These are the names of the [two] sons of Gershon by their families: Libni and Shimei;

¹⁹and the [four] sons of Kohath by their families: Amram, Izhar, Hebron, and Uzziel;

²⁰and the [two] sons of Merari by their families: Mahli and Mushi. These are the families of the Levites by their fathers' households.

²¹Of Gershon were the families of the Libnites and of the Shimeites. These are the families of the Gershonites.

²²The males who were numbered, every male from a month old and upward totaled 7,500.

²³The families of the Gershonites were to camp behind the tabernacle on the west,

²⁴and the leader of the fathers' households of the Gershonites was Eliasaph the son of Lael.

²⁵Now the responsibilities of the sons of Gershon in the Tent of Meeting *involved* the tabernacle and the tent, its covering, and the curtain for the doorway of the Tent of Meeting,

²⁶and the hangings of the courtyard, the curtain for the doorway of the courtyard which is around the tabernacle and the altar, its tent ropes, and all the service concerning them.

²⁷Of Kohath were the families of the Amramites, the Izharites, the Hebronites, and the Uzzielites; these are the families of the Kohathites.

²⁸The males who were numbered, every male from a month old and upward *totaled* 8,600, attending to the duties of the sanctuary.

²⁹The families of the sons of Kohath were to camp on the south side of the tabernacle,

³⁰and the leader of the fathers'

households of the families of the Kohathites was Elizaphan the son of Uzziel.

³¹Now their responsibilities *involved* the ark, the table [on which the bread of the Presence was placed], the lampstand, the altars, the utensils of the sanctuary with which the priests minister, and the curtain, and all the service concerning them.

³²Eleazar, the son of Aaron the priest, was chief of the leaders of the Levites; he supervised those who performed the duties of the sanctuary.

³³Of Merari were the families of the Mahlites and the Mushites; these are the families of Merari.

³⁴The males who were numbered, every male from a month old and upward *totaled* 6,200.

³⁵The leader of the fathers' households of the families of Merari was Zuriel the son of Abihail. The Merarites were to camp on the north side of the tabernacle.

³⁶Now the appointed responsibilities of the sons of Merari *involved* the frames of the tabernacle, its bars, its pillars, its sockets *or* bases, and all the equipment, and all the service concerning them,

³⁷and the pillars around the courtyard with their bases and their pegs and their cords (tent ropes).

³⁸Now those to camp before the tabernacle toward the east, before the Tent of Meeting, toward the sunrise, were to be Moses, and Aaron and his sons, performing the duties of the sanctuary for whatever was required of the Israelites; and the layman (non-Levite) who approached [the sanctuary] was to be put to death.

³⁹All the men of the Levites whom Moses and Aaron numbered at the command of the LORD, by their families, every male from a month old and upward, were 22,000.

⁴⁰Then the LORD said to Moses,

"Number every firstborn male of the Israelites from a month old and upward, and make a list of their names. ⁴¹"You shall take the Levites for Me instead of *and* as a substitute for all the firstborn among the Israelites. I am the LORD; and *you shall take* the cattle of the Levites instead of *and* as a substitute for all the firstborn among the cattle of the Israelites."

⁴²So Moses numbered all the firstborn among the Israelites, just as the LORD had commanded him;

⁴³and all the firstborn males from a month old and upward as numbered were 22,273 [273 more than the Levites].

⁴⁴Then the LORD spoke to Moses, saying,

⁴⁵"Take the Levites [for Me] instead of all the firstborn among the sons of Israel, and the cattle of the Levites instead of their cattle. And the Levites shall be Mine. I am the LORD.

⁴⁶"For the ransom (redemption price) of the 273 of the firstborn of the Israelites who outnumber the Levites,

⁴⁷you shall take five shekels apiece, per head, you shall take them in terms of the sanctuary shekel (the shekel is twenty gerahs),

⁴⁸and give the money, the ransom (redemption price) of those who outnumber the Levites to Aaron and to his sons."

⁴⁹So Moses took the ransom (redemption) money from those who were in excess, beyond those ransomed by the Levites;

⁵⁰from the firstborn of the Israelites he took the money in terms of the sanctuary shekel, 1,365 shekels.

⁵¹Then Moses gave the ransom money to Aaron and to his sons at the command of the LORD, just as the LORD had commanded Moses.

4 THEN THE LORD spoke to Moses and Aaron, saying, ²"Take a census of the sons of Kohath from among the sons of Levi, by their families (clans), by their fathers' households,

³from thirty years old and upward, even to fifty years old, all who enter the service to do the work in the Tent of Meeting (tabernacle).

⁴"This is the work *and* responsibility of the sons of Kohath in the Tent of Meeting (tabernacle): the most holy things.

⁵"When the camp prepares to move out, Aaron and his sons shall come into *the sanctuary* and take down the veil (curtain) screening off *the Holy of Holies,* and cover the ark of the testimony with it;

⁶and they shall put on it a covering of porpoise skin (fine leather), and shall spread over that a cloth of pure blue, and shall insert the carrying poles of the ark.

⁷"Over the table of the bread of the Presence they shall spread a cloth of blue and put on it the plates, the dishes [for incense], the sacrificial bowls, the jars for the drink offering, and the continual bread [of the Presence] shall be on it.

⁸"They shall spread over them a cloth of scarlet, and cover that with a covering of porpoise skin, and they shall insert its carrying poles.

⁹"Then they shall take a blue cloth and cover the lampstand for the light,

putting the Word to work

In Numbers 4, God gave specific responsibilities to the sons of Kohath and to the sons of Aaron. What specific responsibilities has God given you in the various areas of your life? Ask Him to help you fulfill your responsibilities in ways that are pleasing to Him.

along with its lamps, its wick cutters, its trays, and all the oil vessels, by which it is supplied;

¹⁰and they shall put the lampstand and all its utensils in a covering of porpoise skin, and shall put it on the carrying bars.

¹¹"Over the golden [incense] altar they shall spread a blue cloth, and cover it with a covering of porpoise skin, and shall insert its carrying poles;

¹²and they shall take all the utensils of the service with which they minister in the sanctuary, and put them in a blue cloth, and cover them with a covering of porpoise skin, and put them on the carrying bars.

¹³"Then they shall clean away the ashes from the altar [of burnt offering], and spread a purple cloth over it.

¹⁴"They shall also put on it all its utensils with which they minister in connection with it: the pans, the meat-forks, the shovels, the basins, and all the utensils of the altar; and they shall spread a covering of porpoise skin over it, and insert its carrying poles.

¹⁵"When Aaron and his sons have finished covering the sanctuary and all its furniture, as the camp sets out, after all that [is done, but not before], the sons of Kohath shall come to carry them [using the poles], so that they do not touch the holy things, and die. These are the things in the Tent of Meeting (tabernacle) which the sons of Kohath are to carry.

¹⁶"The responsibility of Eleazar, the son of Aaron the priest, is the oil for the light, the fragrant incense, the continual grain offering, and the anointing oil—the responsibility of all the tabernacle and everything that is in it, with the sanctuary and its furnishings."

¹⁷Then the LORD spoke to Moses and Aaron, saying,

¹⁸"Do not cut off (eliminate, destroy) the tribe of the families of the Kohathites [who are only Levites and not priests], from among the Levites [by exposing them to the sin of touching the most holy things].

¹⁹"But deal with them in this way, so that they may live and not die when they approach the most holy things: Aaron and his sons shall go in and assign each of them to his [specific] work and to his load [to be carried on the march].

²⁰"But the Kohathites shall not go in to see the holy things, even for an instant, or they will die."

²¹Then the LORD spoke to Moses, saying,

²²"Take a census of the sons of Gershon also, by their fathers' households, by their families.

²³"From thirty years and upward to fifty years old, you shall number them; all who enter for service to do the work in the Tent of Meeting.

²⁴"This is the service of the families of the Gershonites, in serving and in carrying [when on the march]:

²⁵they shall carry the tent curtains of the tabernacle, and the Tent of Meeting, its covering and the covering of porpoise skin (fine leather) that is on top of it, and the curtain for the doorway of the Tent of Meeting (tabernacle),

²⁶and the hangings of the courtyard, and the curtain for the entrance of the gate of the courtyard which is around the tabernacle and the altar, and their tent ropes, and all the equipment for their service; and all that is to be done, they shall perform.

²⁷"Aaron and his sons shall direct all the service of the sons of the Gershonites, all they have to carry and all they have to do. You shall assign to them as a duty all that they are to carry [on the march].

²⁸"This is the service of the families of the sons of Gershon in the Tent of Meeting (tabernacle); and their duties shall be under the direction of Ithamar the son of Aaron, the [high] priest.

²⁹"As for the sons of Merari, you shall number them by their families (clans), by their fathers' households; ³⁰from thirty years and upward to fifty years old, you shall number them, everyone who enters the service to do the work of the Tent of Meeting (tabernacle). ³¹"This is what they are assigned to carry [on the march], according to all their service in the Tent of Meeting: the boards [for the framework] of the tabernacle and its bars and its pillars and its sockets *or* bases, ³²and the pillars around the courtyard with their sockets *or* bases and their pegs and their cords (tent ropes), with all their equipment and with all their [accessories for] service; and you shall assign *each man* by name the items he is to carry [on the march]. ³³"This is the work of the families of the sons of Merari, according to all their tasks in the Tent of Meeting (tabernacle), under the direction of Ithamar the son of Aaron, the priest."

³⁴So Moses and Aaron and the leaders of the congregation numbered the sons of the Kohathites by their families (clans) and by their fathers' households, ³⁵from thirty years and upward even to fifty years old, everyone who enters the service to do the work in the Tent of Meeting (tabernacle); ³⁶the men who were numbered by their families were 2,750. ³⁷These were numbered of the families of the Kohathites, all who did service in the Tent of Meeting (tabernacle), whom Moses and Aaron numbered according to the commandment of the LORD through Moses. ³⁸The men who were numbered of the sons of Gershon, by their families (clans), and by their fathers' households, ³⁹from thirty years and upward even to fifty years old, everyone who entered the service to do the work in the Tent of Meeting (tabernacle); ⁴⁰the men who were numbered by their families, by their fathers' households, were 2,630. ⁴¹These were numbered men of the families of the sons of Gershon, everyone who served in the Tent of Meeting (tabernacle), whom Moses and Aaron numbered just as the LORD had commanded. ⁴²The men who were numbered of the sons of Merari, by their families (clans), by their fathers' households, ⁴³from thirty years and upward even to fifty years old, everyone who entered the service for work in the Tent of Meeting (tabernacle); ⁴⁴the men who were numbered by their families were 3,200. ⁴⁵These are the men who were numbered of the families of the sons of Merari, whom Moses and Aaron numbered in accordance with the commandment of the LORD through Moses. ⁴⁶All the men who were numbered of the Levites, whom Moses and Aaron and the leaders of Israel counted by their families (clans) and by their fathers' households, ⁴⁷from thirty years and upward even to fifty years old, everyone who could enter to do the work of service and the work of carrying in the Tent of Meeting (tabernacle); ⁴⁸the men that were numbered were 8,580. ⁴⁹According to the commandment of the LORD through Moses, they were numbered, each *assigned* to his work of serving and carrying. Thus they were numbered by him, just as the LORD had commanded Moses.

5 THE LORD spoke to Moses, saying, ²"Command the Israelites to send away from the camp every leper and everyone who has a discharge, and whoever is defiled [that is, ceremonially

unclean] by [coming in contact with] the dead.

³"You shall send away both male and female; you shall send them outside the camp so that they will not defile their camp where I dwell in their midst."

⁴The Israelites did so, and sent them outside the camp; just as the Lord had said to Moses, so the Israelites did.

⁵And the Lord spoke to Moses, saying,

⁶"Say to the Israelites, 'When a man or woman commits any of the sins of mankind [against other people], thus breaking faith with the Lord, and that person is guilty,

⁷then he shall confess the sin which he has committed, and he shall make restitution for his wrong in full, and add a fifth to it, and give it to [the person] whom he has wronged.

⁸'But if the man [who was wronged] has no redeemer (relative) to whom the restitution may be made, it is to be given to the Lord for the priest, besides the ram of atonement with which atonement is made for the offender.

⁹'Also every contribution pertaining to all the holy gifts of the Israelites which they offer to the priest, shall be his.

¹⁰'And every man's holy gifts shall be the priest's; whatever any man gives the priest, it becomes his.'"

¹¹Then the Lord spoke to Moses, saying,

¹²"Speak to the Israelites and say to them, 'If any man's wife goes astray (deviates) and is unfaithful to him,

¹³and a man is intimate with her, and it is hidden from the eyes of her husband and it is kept secret, although she has defiled herself, and there is no witness against her and she has not been caught in the act,

¹⁴and if a spirit (sense, attitude) of jealousy comes over him and he is jealous *and* angry at his wife who has defiled herself—or if a spirit of jealousy comes over him and he is jealous of his wife when she has not defiled herself—

¹⁵then the man shall bring his wife to the priest, and he shall bring as an offering for her, a tenth of an ephah of barley meal; he shall not pour oil on it nor put frankincense on it [the symbols of favor and joy], because it is a grain offering of jealousy, a memorial grain offering, a reminder of [the consequences of] wickedness.

¹⁶'Then the priest shall have her approach and have her stand before the Lord,

¹⁷and the priest shall take holy water [from the sacred basin] in an earthenware vessel; and he shall take some of the dust that is on the floor of the tabernacle and put it in the water.

¹⁸'The priest shall then have the woman stand before the Lord, and let the hair of the woman's head hang loose, and put the memorial grain offering in her hands, which is the jealousy offering, and in the hand of the priest is to be the water of bitterness that brings a curse.

¹⁹'Then the priest shall have her take an oath and say to the woman, "If no man has lain with you and if you have not gone astray into uncleanness [while married], then be immune to this water of bitterness that brings a curse;

²⁰but if you have gone astray [while married] and you have defiled yourself and a man other than your husband has been intimate with you"

²¹(then the priest shall have the woman swear the oath of the curse, and say to the woman), "The Lord make you a curse and an oath among your people when the Lord makes your thigh waste away and your abdomen swell;

²²and this water that brings a curse shall go into your stomach, and make your abdomen swell and your thigh waste away." And the woman shall say, "Amen. Amen (so let it be)."

²³'The priest shall then write these curses on a scroll and shall wash them off into the water of bitterness;

²⁴and he shall make the woman drink the water of bitterness that brings a curse, and the water that brings the curse will go into her and *cause* bitterness.

²⁵'Then the priest shall take the grain offering of jealousy out of the woman's hand, and he shall wave the grain offering before the LORD and offer it on the altar.

²⁶'Then the priest shall take a handful of the grain offering as the memorial portion of it and offer it up in smoke on the altar, and afterward he shall make the woman drink the water.

²⁷'When he has made her drink the water, then it shall come about, that if she has defiled herself and has been unfaithful to her husband, the curse water will go into her and *cause* bitterness and cause her abdomen to swell and her thigh to waste away, and the woman will become a curse among her people.

²⁸'But if the woman has not defiled herself and is clean, then she will be free and conceive children.

²⁹'This is the law of jealousy: when a wife goes astray [while married] and defiles herself,

³⁰or when a spirit (sense, attitude) of jealousy *and* suspicion comes on a man and he is jealous of his wife; then he shall have the woman stand before the LORD, and the priest shall apply this law to her.

³¹'Further, the husband will be free from guilt, but that woman [if guilty] shall bear her guilt.'"

6 AGAIN THE LORD spoke to Moses, saying,

²"Say to the sons of Israel, 'When a man or a woman makes a special vow, the vow of a Nazirite, that is, one separated *and* dedicated to the LORD,

³he shall abstain from wine and strong drink; he shall drink no vinegar, whether made from wine or strong drink, nor shall he drink any grape juice nor eat fresh or dried grapes. [Luke 1:15]

⁴'All the time of his separation he shall not eat anything produced from the grapevine, from the seeds even to the skins.

⁵'All the time of the vow of his separation no razor shall be used on his head. Until the time of his separation to the LORD is completed, he shall be holy, and shall let the hair of his head grow long.

⁶'All the time that he separates himself to the LORD he shall not go near a dead body.

⁷'He shall not make himself [ceremonially] unclean for his father, mother, brother, or sister, when they die, because [the responsibility for] his separation to God is on his head.

⁸'All the time of his separation he is holy to the LORD.

⁹'If a man dies very suddenly beside him, and he defiles his dedicated head, then he shall shave his head on the day that he becomes [ceremonially] clean; he shall shave it on the seventh day [the end of the purification period].

¹⁰'On the eighth day he shall bring two turtledoves or two young pigeons to the priest, to the doorway of the Tent of Meeting (tabernacle).

¹¹'The priest shall offer the one as a sin offering and the other as a burnt offering and make atonement for him concerning his sin because of the [dead] body. He shall consecrate his head the same day,

¹²and he shall dedicate himself to the LORD for the time of his separation and shall bring a male lamb a year old as a guilt offering; but the previous days will be void *and* lost, because his separation was defiled.

¹³'Now this is the law of the Nazirite when the days of his separation *and* dedication are fulfilled: he shall bring the offering to the doorway of the Tent of Meeting (tabernacle).

¹⁴and he shall offer his gift to the LORD: one male lamb a year old without blemish as a burnt offering, and one female lamb a year old without blemish as a sin offering, and one ram without blemish as a peace offering,

¹⁵and a basket of unleavened bread, cakes of fine flour mixed with oil, and wafers of unleavened bread spread with oil, along with their grain offering and their drink offering.

¹⁶'Then the priest shall present them before the LORD and shall offer the person's sin offering and his burnt offering.

¹⁷'He shall also offer the ram as a sacrifice of peace offerings to the LORD, together with the basket of unleavened bread; the priest shall offer also its grain offering and its drink offering.

¹⁸'The Nazirite shall shave his dedicated head at the doorway of the Tent of Meeting (tabernacle), and take the dedicated hair of his head and put it on the fire which is under the sacrifice of the peace offerings.

aglow with God's glory

God pronounced a blessing upon His people, saying that His face would shine upon them and that He would lift up His countenance upon them (see Numbers 6:25, 26).

Our countenance is simply the way we look. When people look at us, we want them to see something about us that is different from what they see about everyone else. They cannot read our minds or see into our hearts, but they can see from the glow on our faces that we have something awesome and wonderful.

Our countenance is important. The look we have on our faces at work and our tone of voice at home are important. It is important that we smile at one another, that we are pleasant and just downright nice to each other. We are supposed to be loving people who reflect God's joy on our faces. But how do we do that?

The Bible talks about Jesus' countenance and how it "changed dramatically" when He communed with God the Father on the mountain: "His face shone [with heavenly glory, clear and bright] like the sun" (Matthew 17:2). We need that same experience, and it comes to us as it did to Jesus—through worshiping God. We look better when we worship God. Worship puts a smile on our faces. It is almost impossible to scowl while we are praising, worshiping, and thanking God. If we regularly spend time fellowshipping with God and worshiping Him, our countenance will carry His presence. We will look strong, joyful, and peaceful instead of frustrated or stressed.

I remember one time when I was at a conference, a woman looked at my face and said, "I can tell you have been with Jesus." She was right. I had spent a long time that morning in prayer and fellowship with the Lord, preparing for the teaching I would do that day. How could she tell I had been with Jesus? Something about my countenance let her know. Perhaps I looked happy and satisfied, or peaceful. I do not know exactly what she saw, but something about the look on my face let her know Who I was spending my time with.

It is important that we spend more time talking to God, thanking Him and worshiping Him; then our faces will carry His glory. We need to ask, "Does my countenance reflect the greatness of my God?"

[19]'The priest shall take the boiled shoulder of the ram, and one unleavened [ring-shaped] loaf out of the basket, and one unleavened flat cake and shall put them on the hands of the Nazirite after he has shaved his dedicated *hair*.

[20]'Then the priest shall wave them as a wave offering before the LORD; they are a holy portion for the priest, together with the breast that is waved and the thigh that is offered by lifting up; and afterward the Nazirite may drink wine.'

[21]"This is the law for the Nazirite who vows his offering to the LORD for his separation, besides what else he is able to afford, according to the vow which he has vowed; so shall he do according to the law for his separation *and* abstinence [as a Nazirite]." [Acts 21:24, 26]

[22]Then the LORD spoke to Moses, saying,

[23]"Speak to Aaron and his sons, saying, 'This is the way you shall bless the Israelites. Say to them:

[24]The LORD bless you, and keep you [protect you, sustain you, and guard you];

[25]The LORD make His face shine upon you [with favor],
And be gracious to you [surrounding you with lovingkindness];

[26]The LORD lift up His countenance (face) upon you [with divine approval],
And give you peace [a tranquil heart and life].'

[27]"So Aaron and his sons shall put My name upon the children of Israel, and I will bless them."

7 ON THE day that Moses had finished setting up the tabernacle and had anointed and consecrated it and all its furniture, and the altar and all its utensils; he also anointed them and consecrated them [for holy use].

[2]Then the leaders of Israel, the heads of their fathers' households, made offerings. (These were the leaders of the tribes; they were the ones who were over the men who were numbered.)

[3]They brought their offering before the LORD, six covered carts and twelve oxen; a cart for each two of the leaders and an ox for each one; and they presented them before the tabernacle.

[4]Then the LORD spoke to Moses, saying,

[5]"Accept *these things* from them, so that they may be used in the service of the Tent of Meeting (tabernacle), and give them to the Levites, to each man according to his service."

[6]So Moses took the carts and the oxen and gave them to the Levites.

[7]He gave two carts and four oxen to the sons of Gershon, according to their service [in transporting the tabernacle];

[8]and he gave four carts and eight oxen to the sons of Merari, according to their service [in transporting the tabernacle], under the supervision of Ithamar the son of Aaron, the [high] priest.

[9]But to the sons of Kohath he gave nothing, because they were assigned the care of the holy things which they

speak the Word

God, I thank You that You are blessing me and keeping me.
Let Your face continue to shine upon me with favor. Thank You for being
gracious to me and surrounding me with loving-kindness. Thank You that
Your divine approval is upon me and that You give me peace.
–ADAPTED FROM NUMBERS 6:24-26

carried on their shoulders [when the tabernacle was moved].

¹⁰The leaders offered the dedication *sacrifices* for the altar on the day that it was anointed; and they offered their sacrifice before the altar.

¹¹Then the LORD said to Moses, "Let them present their offerings, one leader each day, for the dedication of the altar."

¹²Now the one who presented his offering on the first day was Nahshon the son of Amminadab, of the tribe of Judah;

¹³and his offering was one silver dish, the weight of which was a hundred and thirty *shekels*, one silver basin of seventy shekels, according to the shekel of the sanctuary, both of them full of fine flour mixed with oil as a grain offering;

¹⁴one golden bowl of ten *shekels*, full of incense;

¹⁵one young bull, one ram, one male lamb one year old, as a burnt offering;

¹⁶one male goat as a sin offering;

¹⁷and for the sacrifice of peace offerings, two oxen, five rams, five male goats, five male lambs one year old. This was the offering of Nahshon the son of Amminadab [from the tribe of Judah].

¹⁸On the second day Nethanel the son of Zuar, leader [of the tribe] of Issachar, presented [his offering];

¹⁹he presented as his offering one silver dish, the weight of which was a hundred and thirty *shekels*, one silver basin of seventy shekels, according to the shekel of the sanctuary, both of them full of fine flour mixed with oil as a grain offering;

²⁰one golden bowl of ten *shekels*, full of incense;

²¹one young bull, one ram, and one male lamb one year old, as a burnt offering;

²²one male goat as a sin offering;

²³and for the sacrifice of peace offerings, two oxen, five rams, five male goats, five male lambs one year old.

This was the offering of Nethanel the son of Zuar [from the tribe of Issachar].

²⁴On the third day [it was] Eliab the son of Helon, leader [of the tribe] of the sons of Zebulun [who presented his offering];

²⁵his offering was one silver dish, the weight of which was a hundred and thirty *shekels*, and one silver basin of seventy shekels, according to the shekel of the sanctuary, both of them full of fine flour mixed with oil as a grain offering;

²⁶one golden bowl of ten *shekels*, full of incense;

²⁷one young bull, one ram, one male lamb one year old, as a burnt offering;

²⁸one male goat as a sin offering;

²⁹and for the sacrifice of peace offerings, two oxen, five rams, five male goats, five male lambs one year old. This was the offering of Eliab the son of Helon [from the tribe of Zebulun].

³⁰On the fourth day [it was] Elizur the son of Shedeur, leader [of the tribe] of the sons of Reuben [who presented his offering];

³¹his offering was one silver dish, the weight of which was a hundred and thirty *shekels*, and one silver basin of seventy shekels, according to the shekel of the sanctuary, both of them full of fine flour mixed with oil for a grain offering;

³²one golden bowl of ten *shekels*, full of incense;

³³one young bull, one ram, one male lamb one year old, as a burnt offering;

³⁴one male goat as a sin offering;

³⁵and for the sacrifice of peace offerings, two oxen, five rams, five male goats, five male lambs one year old. This was the offering of Elizur the son of Shedeur [from the tribe of Reuben].

³⁶On the fifth day [it was] Shelumiel the son of Zurishaddai, leader [of the tribe] of the sons of Simeon [who presented his offering];

³⁷his offering was one silver dish, the

weight of which was a hundred and thirty *shekels*, and one silver basin of seventy shekels, according to the shekel of the sanctuary, both of them full of fine flour mixed with oil as a grain offering; ³⁸one golden bowl of ten *shekels*, full of incense; ³⁹one young bull, one ram, one male lamb one year old, for a burnt offering; ⁴⁰one male goat as a sin offering; ⁴¹and for the sacrifice of peace offerings, two oxen, five rams, five male goats, five male lambs one year old. This was the offering of Shelumiel the son of Zurishaddai [from the tribe of Simeon].

⁴²On the sixth day [it was] Eliasaph the son of Deuel, leader [of the tribe] of the sons of Gad [who presented his offering];

⁴³his offering was one silver dish the weight of which was a hundred and thirty *shekels*, and a silver basin of seventy shekels, according to the shekel of the sanctuary, both of them full of fine flour mixed with oil as a grain offering; ⁴⁴one golden bowl of ten *shekels*, full of incense; ⁴⁵one young bull, one ram, one male lamb one year old, as a burnt offering; ⁴⁶one male goat as a sin offering; ⁴⁷and for the sacrifice of peace offerings, two oxen, five rams, five male goats, five male lambs one year old. This was the offering of Eliasaph the son of Deuel [from the tribe of Gad].

⁴⁸On the seventh day [it was] Elishama the son of Ammihud, leader [of the tribe] of the sons of Ephraim [who presented his offering];

⁴⁹his offering was one silver dish, the weight of which was a hundred and thirty *shekels*, and one silver basin of seventy shekels, according to the shekel of the sanctuary, both of them full of fine flour mixed with oil as a grain offering; ⁵⁰one golden bowl of ten *shekels*, full of incense;

⁵¹one young bull, one ram, one male lamb one year old, as a burnt offering; ⁵²one male goat as a sin offering; ⁵³and for the sacrifice of peace offerings, two oxen, five rams, five male goats, five male lambs one year old. This was the offering of Elishama the son of Ammihud [from the tribe of Ephraim].

⁵⁴On the eighth day [it was] Gamaliel the son of Pedahzur, leader [of the tribe] of the sons of Manasseh [who presented his offering];

⁵⁵his offering was one silver dish the weight of which was a hundred and thirty *shekels*, and one silver basin of seventy shekels, according to the shekel of the sanctuary, both of them full of fine flour mixed with oil as a grain offering; ⁵⁶one golden bowl of ten *shekels*, full of incense; ⁵⁷one young bull, one ram, one male lamb one year old, as a burnt offering; ⁵⁸one male goat as a sin offering; ⁵⁹and for the sacrifice of peace offerings, two oxen, five rams, five male goats, five male lambs one year old. This was the offering of Gamaliel the son of Pedahzur [from the tribe of Manasseh].

⁶⁰On the ninth day [it was] Abidan the son of Gideoni, leader [of the tribe] of the sons of Benjamin [who presented his offering];

⁶¹his offering was one silver dish, the weight of which was a hundred and thirty *shekels*, and one silver basin of seventy shekels, according to the shekel of the sanctuary, both of them full of fine flour mixed with oil as a grain offering; ⁶²one golden bowl of ten *shekels*, full of incense; ⁶³one young bull, one ram, one male lamb one year old, as a burnt offering; ⁶⁴one male goat as a sin offering; ⁶⁵and as the sacrifice of peace offerings, two oxen, five rams, five male goats, five male lambs one year old.

This was the offering of Abidan the son of Gideoni [from the tribe of Benjamin].

⁶⁶On the tenth day [it was] Ahiezer the son of Ammishaddai, leader [of the tribe] of the sons of Dan [who presented his offering];

⁶⁷his offering was one silver dish, the weight of which was a hundred and thirty *shekels*, and one silver basin of seventy shekels, according to the shekel of the sanctuary, both of them full of fine flour mixed with oil as a grain offering;

⁶⁸one golden bowl of ten *shekels*, full of incense;

⁶⁹one young bull, one ram, one male lamb one year old, as a burnt offering;

⁷⁰one male goat as a sin offering;

⁷¹and for the sacrifice of peace offerings, two oxen, five rams, five male goats, five male lambs one year old. This was the offering of Ahiezer the son of Ammishaddai [from the tribe of Dan].

⁷²On the eleventh day [it was] Pagiel the son of Ochran, leader [of the tribe] of the sons of Asher [who presented his offering];

⁷³his offering was one silver dish, the weight of which was a hundred and thirty *shekels*, and one silver basin of seventy shekels, according to the shekel of the sanctuary, both of them full of fine flour mixed with oil as a grain offering;

⁷⁴one golden bowl of ten *shekels*, full of incense;

⁷⁵one young bull, one ram, and one male lamb one year old, as a burnt offering;

⁷⁶one male goat as a sin offering;

⁷⁷and for the sacrifice of peace offerings, two oxen, five rams, five male goats, five male lambs one year old. This was the offering of Pagiel the son of Ochran [from the tribe of Asher].

⁷⁸On the twelfth day [it was] Ahira the son of Enan, leader [of the tribe] of the sons of Naphtali [who presented his offering];

⁷⁹his offering was one silver dish, the weight of which was a hundred and thirty *shekels*, and one silver basin of seventy shekels, according to the shekel of the sanctuary, both of them full of fine flour mixed with oil as a grain offering;

⁸⁰one golden bowl of ten *shekels*, full of incense;

⁸¹one young bull, one ram, one male lamb one year old, as a burnt offering;

⁸²one male goat as a sin offering;

⁸³and for the sacrifice of peace offerings, two oxen, five rams, five male goats, five male lambs one year old. This was the offering of Ahira the son of Enan [from the tribe of Naphtali].

⁸⁴This was the dedication offering for the altar from the leaders of Israel on the day when it was anointed: twelve dishes of silver, twelve silver basins, twelve golden bowls;

⁸⁵each dish of silver weighing a hundred and thirty *shekels*, each basin seventy [shekels]; all the silver vessels *weighed* 2,400 shekels, according to the shekel of the sanctuary;

⁸⁶the twelve golden bowls, full of incense, *weighing* ten shekels apiece, according to the shekel of the sanctuary, all the gold of the bowls being a hundred and twenty *shekels*;

⁸⁷all the oxen for the burnt offering were twelve bulls, the rams twelve, the male lambs one year old twelve, together with their grain offering; and the male goats as a sin offering twelve;

⁸⁸and all the oxen for the sacrifice of the peace offerings were twenty-four bulls, the rams sixty, the male goats sixty, the male lambs one year old sixty. This was the dedication for the altar [of burnt offering] after it was anointed.

⁸⁹Now when Moses went into the Tent of Meeting (tabernacle) to speak with the Lᴏʀᴅ, he heard the voice speaking to him from above the mercy seat (the gold cover) that was on the ark of the Testimony from between

the two cherubim; and He spoke [by special revelation] to him.

8 THEN THE Lord spoke to Moses, saying, 2"Speak to Aaron and say to him, 'When you set up *and* light the lamps, the seven lamps will shine in front of the lampstand.'"

3And Aaron did so; he set up the lamps at the front of the lampstand, just as the Lord had commanded Moses.

4Now this was the workmanship of the lampstand: hammered work of gold; from its base to its flowers it was hammered work; according to the pattern which the Lord had shown Moses, so he made the lampstand.

5Again the Lord spoke to Moses, saying,

6"Take the Levites from among the sons of Israel and cleanse them.

7"This is what you shall do to them to [ceremonially] cleanse them: sprinkle the water of purification on them, and let them use a razor over their whole body and wash their clothes, and they will be clean. [Num 19:17, 18]

8"Then let them take a young bull and its grain offering of fine flour mixed with oil, and you shall take another young bull as a sin offering.

9"You shall present the Levites before the Tent of Meeting (tabernacle), and you shall also assemble the whole congregation of the children of Israel,

10and present the Levites before the Lord, and the Israelites shall lay their hands on the Levites.

11"Aaron shall present the Levites before the Lord as a wave offering from the Israelites, so that they may perform the service of the Lord.

12"Then the Levites shall lay their hands on the heads of the bulls, then you are to offer the one as a sin offering and the other as a burnt offering to the Lord, to make atonement for the Levites.

13"You shall have the Levites stand before Aaron and his sons and present them as a wave offering to the Lord.

14"Thus you shall separate the Levites from among the Israelites, and the Levites shall be Mine [in a very special sense].

15"Then after that the Levites may go in to serve the Tent of Meeting (tabernacle), but you shall cleanse them [first] and present them as a wave offering;

16for they are wholly given to Me from among the Israelites. I have taken them for Myself instead of all who are born first, the firstborn of all the Israelites.

17"For all the firstborn among the Israelites are Mine, among the men and among the animals; on the day that I struck down every firstborn in the land of Egypt, I sanctified *and* set the Israelites apart for Myself.

18"And I have taken the Levites instead of every firstborn among the Israelites.

19"I have given the Levites as a gift to Aaron and to his sons from among the Israelites, to perform the service of the Israelites at the Tent of Meeting (tabernacle) and to make atonement for them, so that there will be no plague among the Israelites if they should approach the sanctuary."

20Thus Moses and Aaron and all the congregation of the children of Israel did [these things] to the Levites; in accordance with all that the Lord had commanded Moses concerning the Levites, so the Israelites did to them.

21The Levites, too, purified themselves from sin and they washed their clothes; and Aaron presented them as a wave offering before the Lord, and Aaron made atonement for them to cleanse them.

22Then after that the Levites went in to perform their service in the Tent of Meeting before Aaron and his sons; just as the Lord had commanded Moses concerning the Levites, so they did to them.

²³Now the LORD spoke to Moses, saying,

²⁴"This is what *applies* to the Levites: from twenty-five years old and upward they shall enter to perform service in the work of the Tent of Meeting,

²⁵but at the age of fifty years, they shall retire from the service of the [tabernacle] work and serve no longer.

²⁶They may assist their brothers in the Tent of Meeting to keep an obligation, but they shall do no [heavy or difficult] work. Thus you shall deal with the Levites concerning their obligations."

9 THE LORD spoke to Moses in the Wilderness of Sinai in the first month of the second year after they had come out of the land of Egypt, saying,

²"The sons of Israel are to keep the Passover at its appointed time.

³"On the fourteenth day of this month at twilight, you shall keep it at its appointed time; according to all its statutes and ordinances you shall keep it."

⁴So Moses told the Israelites to observe the Passover.

⁵They observed the Passover on the fourteenth day of the first month at twilight in the Wilderness of Sinai; in accordance with all that the LORD had commanded Moses, so the Israelites did.

⁶But there were certain men who were [ceremonially] unclean because of [touching] the dead body of a man, so they could not observe the Passover on that day; so they came before Moses and Aaron that same day.

⁷Those men said to Moses, "We are [ceremonially] unclean because of [touching] a dead body. Why are we being restrained from presenting the LORD's offering at its appointed time among the Israelites?"

⁸Therefore, Moses said to them, "Wait, and I will listen to what the LORD will command concerning you."

⁹Then the LORD spoke to Moses, saying,

¹⁰"Say to the Israelites, 'If any one of you or of your descendants becomes [ceremonially] unclean because of [touching] a dead body or is on a distant journey, he may, however, observe the Passover to the LORD.

¹¹'On the fourteenth day of the second month [thirty days later] at twilight, they shall observe it; they shall eat it with unleavened bread and bitter herbs.

¹²'They shall leave none of it until morning nor break any of its bones; in accordance with all the statutes of the Passover they shall observe it. [John 19:36]

¹³'But the man who is [ceremonially] clean and is not on a journey, and yet does not observe the Passover, that person shall be cut off from among his people [excluding him from the atonement made for them] because he did not bring the LORD's offering at its appointed time; that man will bear [the penalty of] his sin.

¹⁴'If a stranger lives among you as a resident alien and observes the Passover to the LORD, in accordance with its statutes and its ordinances, so shall he do; you shall have one statute, both for the resident alien and for the native of the land.'"

¹⁵Now on the day that the tabernacle was erected, the cloud [of God's presence] covered the tabernacle, that is, the tent of the Testimony; and in the evening it was over the tabernacle, appearing like [a pillar of] fire until the morning. [Ex 13:21]

putting the Word to work

In the midst of your busy life, are you able to be like Moses and "wait" (see Numbers 9:8) to hear what the Lord wants to say to you? Ask Him to help you hear His voice more clearly.

¹⁶So it was continuously; the cloud covered it *by day*, and the appearance of fire by night. ¹⁷Whenever the cloud was lifted from over the tent (tabernacle), afterward the Israelites would set out; and in the place where the cloud stopped, there the Israelites would camp. ¹⁸At the Lᴏʀᴅ's command the Israelites would journey on, and at His command they would camp. As long as the cloud remained over the tabernacle they remained camped. ¹⁹Even when the cloud lingered over the tabernacle for many days, the Israelites would keep their obligation to the Lᴏʀᴅ and not set out. ²⁰Sometimes the cloud remained only a few days over the tabernacle, and in accordance with the command of the Lᴏʀᴅ they remained camped. Then at His command they set out. ²¹If sometimes the cloud remained [over the tabernacle] from evening only until morning, when the cloud was lifted in the morning, they would journey on; whether in the daytime or at night, whenever the cloud was lifted, they would set out. ²²Whether it was two days or a month or a year that the cloud [of the Lᴏʀᴅ's presence] lingered over the tabernacle, staying above it, the Israelites remained camped and did not set out; but when it was lifted, they set out. ²³At the command of the Lᴏʀᴅ they camped, and at the command of the Lᴏʀᴅ they journeyed on; they kept their obligation to the Lᴏʀᴅ, in accordance with the command of the Lᴏʀᴅ through Moses.

10 THE LORD spoke further to Moses, saying, ²"Make two trumpets of silver; you shall make them of hammered work. You shall use them to summon the congregation and to have the camps move out.

³"When both are blown, all the congregation [that is, all adult males] shall gather before you at the doorway of the Tent of Meeting (tabernacle). ⁴"However, if a single trumpet is blown, then the leaders, heads of the tribes of Israel, shall gather themselves to you. ⁵"When you blow an alarm, the camps on the east side [of the tabernacle] shall set out. ⁶"When you blow an alarm the second time, then the camps on the south side [of the tabernacle] shall set out. They shall blow an alarm whenever they are to move out [on their journeys]. ⁷"When the assembly is to be gathered, you shall blow [the trumpets in short, sharp tones], but without sounding an alarm. ⁸"The sons of Aaron, the priests, shall blow the trumpets; and the trumpets shall be for you a perpetual statute throughout your generations. ⁹"When you go to war in your land against the enemy that attacks you, then sound an alarm with the trumpets, so that you may be remembered before the Lᴏʀᴅ your God, and you shall be saved from your enemies. ¹⁰"Also in the day of rejoicing, and in your appointed feasts, and at the beginnings of your months, you shall sound the trumpets over your burnt offerings, and over the sacrifice of your peace offerings; and they shall be as a reminder of you before your God. I am the Lᴏʀᴅ your God."

¹¹On the twentieth day of the second month in the second year [since leaving Egypt], the cloud [of the Lord's presence] was lifted from over the tabernacle of the Testimony, ¹²and the Israelites set out on their journey from the Wilderness of Sinai, and the cloud [of the Lᴏʀᴅ's guiding presence] settled down in the Wilderness of Paran. ¹³So they moved out for the first time

in accordance with the command of the LORD through Moses.

¹⁴The standard of the camp of the sons of Judah, according to their armies, moved out first, Nahshon the son of Amminadab was [commander] over its army,

¹⁵and Nethanel the son of Zuar was [commander] over the tribal army of the sons of Issachar;

¹⁶and Eliab the son of Helon was [commander] over the tribal army of the sons of Zebulun.

¹⁷Then the tabernacle was taken down; and the sons of Gershon and the sons of Merari, who were carrying the tabernacle, moved out.

¹⁸Next the standard of the camp of the sons of Reuben, according to their armies, moved out, with Elizur the son of Shedeur [commander] over its army,

¹⁹and Shelumiel the son of Zurishaddai was [commander] over the tribal army of the sons of Simeon,

²⁰and Eliasaph the son of Deuel was [commander] over the tribal army of the sons of Gad.

²¹Then the Kohathites moved out, carrying the holy things, and the tabernacle was set up before they arrived.

²²Next the standard of the camp of the sons of Ephraim moved out, according to their armies, with Elishama the son of Ammihud [commander] over its army,

²³and Gamaliel the son of Pedahzur was [commander] over the tribal army of the sons of Manasseh,

²⁴and Abidan the son of Gideoni was [commander] over the tribal army of the sons of Benjamin.

²⁵Then the standard of the camp of

life point

When the Israelites journeyed from Egypt (the land of bondage) to Canaan (the land of promise), the cloud of the Lord went before them, leading the way. Each time the ark of the covenant was lifted up and carried out before them, Moses cried out to God, "Rise up, O LORD! Let Your enemies be scattered" (Numbers 10:35). I love that! May we be reminded each day to praise the Lord and expect His power to bring us victory.

the sons of Dan, according to their armies, which formed the rear guard for all the camps, moved out, with Ahiezer the son of Ammishaddai [commander] over its army,

²⁶and Pagiel the son of Ochran was [commander] over the tribal army of the sons of Asher,

²⁷and Ahira the son of Enan was [commander] over the tribal army of the sons of Naphtali.

²⁸This was the order of march of the sons of Israel by their armies as they moved out.

²⁹Then Moses said to Hobab the son of Reuel the Midianite, Moses' father-in-law, "We are going to the place of which the LORD said, 'I will give it to you.' Come with us, and we will be good to you, for the LORD has promised good [things] concerning Israel."

³⁰But Hobab [Moses' brother-in-law] said to him, "I will not go; I will return to my own land and to my family."

³¹Then Moses said, "Please do not leave us, for you know how we are to

speak the Word

Thank You, God, that You have promised good things concerning me, just as You did for the Israelites so long ago.
—ADAPTED FROM NUMBERS 10:29

camp in the wilderness, and you will serve as eyes for us [as we make our trek through the desert].

³²"So if you will go with us, it shall be that whatever good the LORD does for us, we will do *the same* for you."

³³So they set out from the mountain of the LORD (Sinai) three days' journey; and the ark of the covenant of the LORD went in front of them during the three days' journey to seek out a resting place for them.

³⁴The cloud of the LORD was over them by day when they set out from the camp.

³⁵Whenever the ark set out, Moses said,

"Rise up, O LORD!
Let Your enemies be scattered;

And let those who hate You flee before You." [Ps 68:1, 2]

³⁶And when the ark rested, Moses said,

"Return, O LORD,
To the myriad (many) thousands of Israel."

11 NOW THE people became like those who complain *and* whine about their hardships, and the LORD heard it; and when the LORD heard it, His anger was kindled, and the fire of the LORD burned among them and devoured those in the outlying parts of the camp.

²So the people cried out to Moses, and when Moses prayed to the LORD, the fire died out.

³He named that place Taberah (the

don't turn back

The Israelites spent a great deal of time grumbling and hating their hardships as they traveled through the wilderness on their way to the Promised Land. The way we behave and the attitudes we display during our "wilderness experiences" may well be the determining factors in how long we stay there. Some people never stop complaining, and as a result, they never make progress in their lives.

Not only did the children of Israel complain, they also frequently wanted to turn around and go back to the place they had come from. They had made the mistake of bringing unbelieving Egyptians out of Egypt with them. Called in Numbers 11:4 "the rabble," these people did not love God and tempted the Israelites by reminding them of the dubious benefits of Egypt. Similarly, the devil reminds people today of the benefits they had while they were in the world and doing things their own way.

When we decide to live for God, the enemy tries in all kinds of ways to get us to grumble and complain. In 1976, God called me to quit my job and prepare for ministry. In order to do so, my husband and I had to trust God for money to pay the bills because his salary alone was not enough. Many times in those days, the devil tried to influence me to go back to work and take care of myself. He reminded me of the days when we had plenty of money, new cars, new clothes, and cash left over. But he failed to remind me of how miserable I was because I was not following God's will for my life.

There are plenty of places on the road of life where we can park or even turn around and go back the way we came. But if we press on and follow God's plan for our lives, we will be greatly blessed in the end. Being in God's perfect will is the most comfortable place in the world to be. Don't ever turn back. Keep pressing on!

place of burning), because the fire of the LORD burned among them.

⁴The rabble among them [who followed Israel from Egypt] had greedy desires [for familiar and delicious food], and the Israelites wept again and said, "Who will give us meat to eat?

⁵"We remember the fish we ate freely *and* without cost in Egypt, the cucumbers, melons, leeks, onions, and garlic.

⁶"But now our appetite is gone; there is nothing at all [in the way of food] to be seen but this manna."

⁷The manna was like coriander seed, and it looked like bdellium.

⁸The people went about and gathered it, and ground it in mills or beat it in mortars, and boiled it in pots, and made cakes with it; and it tasted like cakes baked with fresh [olive] oil.

⁹When the dew fell on the camp at night, the manna fell with it.

¹⁰Now Moses heard the people weeping [in self-pity] throughout their families, every man at the doorway of his tent; and the anger of the LORD blazed hotly, and Moses regarded their behavior as evil.

¹¹So Moses said to the LORD, "Why have You been so hard on Your servant? And why have I not found favor in Your sight, that You have placed the burden of all these people on me?

¹²"Was it I who conceived all these people? Was it I who brought them forth, that You should say to me, 'Carry them in your arms as a nurse carries the nursing infant, to the land which You swore to their fathers'?

¹³"Where am I to get meat to give to all these people? For they weep before me and say, 'Give us meat, so that we may eat.'

¹⁴"I am not able to carry all these people alone, because the burden is too heavy for me.

¹⁵"So if this is the way You are going to deal with me, please kill me at once, if I have found favor in your sight, and do not let me see my wretchedness."

¹⁶Accordingly, the LORD said to Moses, "Gather for Me seventy men from among the elders of Israel whom you know to be the elders of the people and their officers; bring them to the Tent of Meeting (tabernacle) and let them stand there with you.

¹⁷"Then I will come down and speak with you there, and I will take away some of the Spirit who is upon you, and will put *Him* upon them; and they shall bear the burden of the people with you, so that you will not have to bear it all alone.

¹⁸"Say to the people, 'Consecrate (separate as holy) yourselves for tomorrow, and you shall eat meat; for you have wept [in self-pity] in the ears of the LORD, saying, "Who will give us meat to eat? For we were well-off in Egypt." Therefore the LORD will give you meat, and you shall eat.

¹⁹'You shall eat, not one day, nor two days, nor five days, nor ten days, nor twenty days,

²⁰but a whole month—until it comes out of your nostrils and is disgusting to you—because you have rejected *and* despised the LORD who is among you, and have wept [in self-pity] before Him, saying, "Why did we come out of Egypt?"'" [Ps 106:13–15]

²¹But Moses said, "The people, among whom I am, are 600,000 [fighting men] on foot [besides all the women and children]; yet You have said, 'I will give them meat, so that they may eat it for a whole month!'

putting the Word to work

Do you ever feel, as Moses did, that you are carrying burdens that are too heavy for you? At those times, remember to cast your cares upon God because He cares for you (see 1 Peter 5:7).

²²"Should flocks and herds be slaughtered for them, to be sufficient for them? Or should all the fish of the sea be collected for them to be sufficient for them?"

²³The Lord said to Moses, "Is the Lord's hand (ability, power) limited (short, inadequate)? You shall see now whether My word will come to pass for you or not." [Is 50:2]

²⁴So Moses went out and spoke to the people the words of the Lord, and he gathered seventy men from among the elders of the people and stationed them around the Tent (tabernacle).

²⁵Then the Lord came down in the cloud and spoke to him; and He took some of the Spirit who was upon Moses and put *Him* upon the seventy elders. When the Spirit rested upon them, they prophesied [praising God and declaring His will], but they did not do it again. [Num 11:29]

²⁶But two men had remained in the camp; one named Eldad and the other named Medad. The Spirit rested upon them (now they were among those who had been registered, but had not gone out to the Tent), and they prophesied in the camp.

²⁷So a young man ran and told Moses and said, "Eldad and Medad are prophesying [extolling the praises of God and declaring His will] in the camp."

²⁸Then Joshua the son of Nun, the attendant of Moses from his youth, said, "My lord Moses, stop them!"

²⁹But Moses said to him, "Are you jealous for my sake? Would that all the Lord's people were prophets and that the Lord would put His Spirit upon them!" [Luke 9:49, 50]

³⁰Then Moses went back into the camp, he and the elders of Israel.

³¹Now there went forth a wind from the Lord and it brought quails from the sea, and let *them* fall [so they flew low] beside the camp, about a day's journey on this side and on the other side, all around the camp, about two cubits (three feet) *deep* on the surface of the ground.

³²The people spent all that day and all night and all the next day and caught *and* gathered the quail (the one who gathered least gathered ten homers) and they spread them out for themselves around the camp [to cure them by drying].

³³While the meat was still between their teeth, before it was chewed, the anger of the Lord was kindled against the people, and the Lord struck them with a very severe plague.

³⁴So that place was named Kibroth-hattaavah (the graves of greediness), because there they buried the people who had been greedy [for more than the manna that God provided them]. [1 Cor 10:1–13]

³⁵From Kibroth-hattaavah the people set out for Hazeroth, and they remained at Hazeroth.

12

NOW MIRIAM and Aaron spoke against Moses because of the Cushite woman whom he had married (for he had married a Cushite woman);

²and they said, "Has the Lord really spoken only through Moses? Has He not spoken also through us?" And the Lord heard it.

³(Now the man Moses was very humble (gentle, kind, devoid of self-righteousness), more than any man who was on the face of the earth.)

⁴Suddenly the Lord said to Moses, Aaron, and Miriam, "Come out, you three, to the Tent of Meeting (tabernacle)." And the three of them came out.

⁵The Lord came down in a pillar of cloud and stood at the doorway of the tabernacle, and He called Aaron and Miriam, and they came forward.

⁶And He said,

"Hear now My words:
If there is a prophet among you,

I the LORD will make Myself known
to him in a vision
And I will speak to him in a
dream.
7 "But it is not so with My servant
Moses;
He is entrusted *and* faithful in all
My house. [Heb 3:2, 5, 6]
8 "With him I speak mouth to mouth
[directly],
Clearly *and* openly and not in
riddles;
And he beholds the form of the
LORD.

Why then were you not afraid
to speak against My servant
Moses?"

9 And the anger of the LORD was kindled against Miriam and Aaron, and He departed. 10 But when the cloud had withdrawn from over the tent, behold, Miriam was leprous, as *white as* snow. And Aaron turned *and* looked at Miriam, and, behold, she was leprous. 11 Then Aaron said to Moses, "Oh, my lord, I plead with you, do not account

the meaning of meekness

For years, I read Numbers 12:3 in the Amplified Classic translation, which says that Moses was "very meek" (see also KJV).

When you think of a meek person, what image comes to mind? I would like to explain the character trait of meekness to you because we rarely hear much about it. *Meek* does not mean "weak." I believe an illustration of true meekness is *getting angry at the right time in the right measure for the right reason.*

Moses was the meekest man on the face of the earth. Said another way, he was able to maintain a careful balance between emotional extremes. What was Moses like? He was patient and long-suffering with the Israelites. When he could have blasted them for their sins and rebellion, he prayed for them instead. As their God-ordained leader and guide, he put up with decades of griping and complaining and insolence from these people who never seemed to tire of testing his patience and endurance. Yet when he came down from meeting with the Lord on the mountaintop and saw the Israelites bowing down and worshiping the golden calf they had made, he became so angry he threw down the tablets with the Ten Commandments written on them!

There is a time to repress anger, and there is a time to express anger—and wisdom knows the difference. A meek person is not someone who never shows anger, but someone who never allows his anger to get out of control. Although Moses was a meek man, he was not a perfect man. There was a time when Moses allowed his anger to get out of control, and God punished him for it. Meekness does not mean being without emotion; it means being in charge of emotion and channeling it in the right direction for the right purpose. Moses was a man to whom God entrusted great power and responsibility. God had given him a great deal, and He expected a great deal from him.

I encourage you to develop true meekness in your life. As you do, remember God's promise in Matthew 5:5: "Blessed . . . are the meek . . . , for they shall inherit the earth!" (Amplified Classic).

this sin to us, in which we have acted foolishly and in which we have sinned.

¹²"Oh, do not let her be like one dead, already half decomposed when he comes from his mother's womb."

¹³So Moses cried out to the LORD, saying, "Heal her please, O God, I plead with You!"

¹⁴But the LORD said to Moses, "If her father had but spit in her face, would she not bear her shame for seven days? Let her be shut up outside the camp for seven days, and afterward she may return."

¹⁵So Miriam was shut up outside the camp for seven days, and the people did not move on until Miriam was brought in again [and declared ceremonially clean from her leprosy].

¹⁶Afterward the people moved on from Hazeroth and camped in the Wilderness of Paran.

13

THEN THE LORD spoke to Moses, saying, ²"Send men to spy out the land of Canaan, which I am going to give to the sons of Israel. From each of their fathers' tribes you shall send a man, every one a leader among them."

³So Moses sent spies from the Wilderness of Paran at the command of the LORD, all of them men who were heads of the Israelites.

⁴These were their names: from the tribe of Reuben, Shammua the son of Zaccur;

⁵from the tribe of Simeon, Shaphat the son of Hori;

⁶from the tribe of Judah, Caleb the son of Jephunneh;

⁷from the tribe of Issachar, Igal the son of Joseph;

⁸from the tribe of Ephraim, Hoshea [that is, Joshua] the son of Nun;

⁹from the tribe of Benjamin, Palti the son of Raphu;

¹⁰from the tribe of Zebulun, Gaddiel the son of Sodi;

¹¹from the tribe of Joseph, that is, of the tribe of Manasseh, Gaddi the son of Susi;

¹²from the tribe of Dan, Ammiel the son of Gemalli;

¹³from the tribe of Asher, Sethur the son of Michael;

¹⁴from the tribe of Naphtali, Nahbi the son of Vophsi;

¹⁵from the tribe of Gad, Geuel the son of Machi.

¹⁶These are the names of the men whom Moses sent to spy out the land; but Moses called Hoshea the son of Nun, Joshua (the LORD is salvation).

¹⁷Moses sent them to spy out the land of Canaan, and said to them, "Go up this way into the Negev (the South country); then go up into the hill country.

¹⁸"See what the land is like and whether the people who live there are strong or weak, few or many,

¹⁹and whether the land in which they live is good or bad, and whether the cities in which they live are [open] camps or fortifications,

²⁰and what the land is, whether it is fat (productive) or lean, whether there is timber on it or not. Make an effort to get some of the fruit of the land." Now the time was the time of the first ripe grapes.

²¹So they went up and spied out the land from the Wilderness of Zin to

speak the Word

God, I pray that I will be like Moses and be faithful in Your house and that You will speak clearly and openly to me.
—ADAPTED FROM NUMBERS 12:7, 8

giant-sized problems

The children of Israel faced giants they feared would stop them from entering their Promised Land. Moses had sent Joshua, Caleb, and ten other men to spy out the land of Canaan and bring back a report (see Numbers 13:17–20). The ten came back and said that the land was full of good fruit, but it was also full of giants who would be difficult to defeat (see Numbers 13:27, 28).

Joshua and Caleb had a different attitude. They too had seen the giants but preferred to keep their eyes on God, Whom they believed was greater than the giants. Caleb urged, "Let us go up at once and take possession of it; for we will certainly conquer it" (Numbers 13:30). How did the negative people respond? They answered, "We are not able . . . they are too strong for us" (Numbers 13:31).

Isn't this the way it is with life? There are positive people who try to go forward, and there are negative people who try to contaminate everything good and positive with their bad attitudes. Ten of the spies were negative and two were positive. Based on those figures, the great majority of the people said they were not able to defeat the giants, and only a small fraction believed God was greater than the problem. The same thing is true today. If a higher percentage of people believed in the great power of God, we would see more people succeeding in life. Evil would not be rampant, because the righteous in the land would be aggressively going forth in faith, conquering everything that is not in harmony with God.

Sadly, we often stare at our giant-sized problems instead of at our God. We lose our focus; we become entangled with the problem and lose sight of what God has called us to do. I believe that more time spent worshiping and praising God would help us keep a clear focus and enable us to go forward with a strong, positive attitude, believing we can do anything God tells us to do.

How much time do you spend fellowshipping with your problems compared to the time you spend fellowshipping with God? Sometimes when we supposedly spend time with God, all we do is talk to Him about our problems. We still are not *really* spending time with Him; we have just found another way to talk about things we are unhappy about. We can tell God about what concerns us and ask Him to help, but we need to spend more time praising than we do petitioning.

Joshua and Caleb reminded the others that God had promised to give them the land. They encouraged them not to rebel against the Lord and not to fear the giants. They encouraged the people: "The Lord is with us. Do not fear them" (Numbers 14:9).

God is not with the enemy; He is with us. And if God is for us, who can be against us? I encourage you to practice maintaining a good attitude. Be content, thankful. Pay attention to what God is doing, and do not simply take note of what you think He is not doing for you. Beware of complaining. Instead, worship God and keep worshiping Him until your breakthrough comes. Having a good attitude will bring your breakthrough faster than being grouchy. However long you have to wait, you might as well be happy while you wait. Enjoy *where* you are—on *the way* to where you are going! Do not fear the giants; slay them with your faith. God is greater than any giant or any giant-sized problem you face.

Rehob [a town in Lebanon], at Lebo-
hamath [in the far north].

²²When they had gone up into the
Negev (the South country), they came
to Hebron; and Ahiman, Sheshai, and
Talmai the descendants of Anak were
there. (Now Hebron was built seven
years before Zoan in Egypt.)

²³Then they came to the Valley of
Eshcol (cluster of grapes), and from
there cut down a branch with a single
cluster of grapes; and they carried it
on a pole between two of them, with
some of pomegranates and the figs.

²⁴That place was called the Valley of
Eshcol (cluster of grapes) because of
the cluster of grapes which the sons of
Israel cut down there.

²⁵When they returned from spying
out the land, at the end of forty days,
²⁶they came to Moses and Aaron and
to all the congregation of the sons of
Israel in the Wilderness of Paran at
Kadesh, and brought back word to
them and to all the congregation, and
showed them the land's fruit.

²⁷They reported to Moses and said,
"We went in to the land where you
sent us; and it certainly does flow with
milk and honey, and this is its fruit.
²⁸"But the people who live in the land
are strong, and the cities are fortified
(walled) and very large; moreover, we
saw there the descendants of Anak
[people of great stature and courage].
²⁹"[The people descended from] Amalek live in the land of the Negev (South
country); the Hittite, the Jebusite, and
the Amorite live in the hill country; and
the Canaanites live by the [Dead] Sea
and along the side of the Jordan."

³⁰Then Caleb quieted the people before Moses, and said, "Let us go up at
once and take possession of it; for we
will certainly conquer it."

³¹But the men who had gone up with
him said, "We are not able to go up
against the people [of Canaan], for
they are too strong for us."

life point

Possessing the land (see Numbers 13:30)
involves dispossessing the current
occupants. To the Israelites, the occupants were people; to us, they may be
people, situations, or even the devil and
his demons. Our spiritual enemy, Satan,
seeks to divert the good things that are
ours. In order to possess the land and
enjoy the many blessings available to
God's children, we need to learn how to
deal with the devil. We cannot fight him
through ordinary means; we must combat
him with spiritual warfare (see Ephesians
6:11–18). As we do, we cannot be lazy or
irresponsible. We need to be aggressively
walking in the righteousness of God. We
must wear our shoes of peace and wear
our helmets of salvation. We should wield
the two-edged sword of the Spirit, which
to me means to speak God's Word in every
situation. It's also important to walk in
truth, stay in faith, and pray at all times.
We cannot make excuses, because an
excuse is just a reason stuffed with a lie.

I think each one of us carries an invisible
"excuse bag." When God puts something
on our hearts to do what we do not want
to do, we just reach into that bag and
draw out an excuse, such as "It's too
hard" or "I'm afraid"—just as the ten
spies did. We think an excuse relieves us
of our responsibility to do what God has
said. But God's answer to us is, "Then do
it afraid! As you go, I will help you conquer your fear."

Who said that you cannot do what God
has told you, even if you have to start off
afraid? As you shed your excuses, you
will find that God is more than sufficient.
Learn from the two men who were confident God would help them possess the
land He had given them. Know that God
wants you to enter your land of promise,
confidently waging spiritual warfare and
going forward without excuse.

³²So they gave the Israelites a bad report about the land which they had spied out, saying, "The land through which we went, in spying it out, is a land that devours its inhabitants. And all the people that we saw in it are men of great stature.

³³"There we saw the Nephilim (the sons of Anak are part of the Nephilim); and we were like grasshoppers in our own sight, and so we were in their sight."

14 THEN ALL the congregation [of Israel] raised their voices and cried out, and the people wept that night.

²All the Israelites murmured [in discontent] against Moses and Aaron; and the whole congregation said to them, "Oh that we had died in the land

life point

Do you see how negative the Israelites were in Numbers 14:1–3? They were complaining, ready to give up too easily, preferring to go back into bondage instead of pressing through the wilderness into the Promised Land. Actually, they did not have a problem; they were the problem! These people felt exceedingly sorry for themselves. Every inconvenience became a new excuse to engage in self-pity. I remember when the Lord showed me during one of my "pity parties" that I could make a choice: I could be pitiful or powerful, but I could not be both. It is vitally important to understand that we cannot entertain self-pity and also walk in the power of God!

slaying the giants in your land

How do you see yourself? How do you look at the obstacles in your way? If we feel we are nothing, it will be hard to accomplish much in life. We will probably shrink back in fear from every challenge, just like the ten men Moses sent into Canaan to spy out the land. They saw it was a good land with abundant fruit, but there was one problem—there were giants in the land. As these men looked at the giants and then at themselves, their courage diminished and they said, "We were like grasshoppers in our own sight, and so we were in their sight" (Numbers 13:33). The big mistake these men made was that they looked at the giants and they looked at themselves, but *they did not look at God.*

In and of ourselves we are nothing and can do very little, but in Christ we can do all things He asks us to do (see Philippians 4:13). We must keep our eyes on Jesus and not on ourselves or our weaknesses. (We all have weaknesses, but God will show His strength through them if we believe He is greater than they are!) The giants in this world do not have to frighten us if we keep our eyes on God and put our trust in Him. God says we do not have to live in fear, because He is with us at all times. He has promised never to leave us or forsake us. If God is on our side, why should we be afraid of anybody or anything?

Twelve men were sent into the land to see if they could conquer it, but only Joshua and Caleb believed that God is greater than any obstacle. Make a decision today that you will not stand with those who see only their limitations when facing their giants. Decide to stand with those who see God and believe the giants can be slain. Believe that He will take care of the giants and bring you to a place of abundant blessing.

of Egypt! Or that we had died in this wilderness!

³"Why is the LORD bringing us to this land [of Canaan], to fall by the sword? Our wives and children will become plunder. Would it not be better for us to return to Egypt?" [Acts 7:37–39]

⁴So they said one to another, "Let us appoint a [new] leader and return to Egypt."

⁵Then Moses and Aaron fell on their faces before all the assembly of the congregation of the Israelites.

⁶Joshua the son of Nun and Caleb the son of Jephunneh, who were among those who had spied out the land, tore their clothes [as a sign of grief],

⁷and they spoke to all the congregation of the sons of Israel, saying, "The land through which we passed as spies is an exceedingly good land.

⁸"If the LORD delights in us, then He will bring us into this land and give it to us, a land which flows with milk and honey.

⁹"Only do not rebel against the LORD; and do not fear the people of the land, for they will be our prey. Their protection has been removed from them, and the LORD is with us. Do not fear them."

¹⁰But all the congregation said to stone Joshua and Caleb with stones. But the glory and brilliance of the LORD appeared at the Tent of Meeting (tabernacle) before all the sons of Israel.

¹¹The LORD said to Moses, "How long will these people treat me disrespectfully and reject Me? And how long will they not believe in Me, despite all the [miraculous] signs which I have performed among them?

¹²"I will strike them with the pestilence (plague) and dispossess them, and will make you into a nation greater and mightier than they."

¹³But Moses said to the LORD, "Then the Egyptians will hear of it, for by Your strength You brought up these people from among them,

¹⁴and they will tell it to the inhabitants

on your face

Notice in Numbers 14:5 how Moses and Aaron reacted to the Israelites' murmuring and complaining: they fell on their faces. This action of falling on one's face is found throughout the Bible. It was an act of humility and seeking God in prayer. If all the Israelites had been on their faces before God, I believe they would have seen miracle after miracle. But they were too busy getting tripped up by feeling sorry for themselves, talking negatively, finding fault with God and Moses, and wanting to go back to Egypt. I thank God for Moses and Aaron. As they fell on their faces and worshiped God, they demonstrated their reverence for Him. I believe they took this action before the whole assembly to show them they needed to do the same.

Joshua and Caleb would not allow negative, unbelieving people to adversely affect them either. These two men remained full of faith and confidence that they could conquer their enemies. Likewise, we need to keep our faith positive by not letting pessimistic people steal our joy. We should not let doubters destroy our confidence; we can believe that God is a good God and has a good plan for our lives. Satan uses negative people to drain us, but we can choose not to let their misery and negativism affect or infect our joy.

When you are tempted to complain, shun the negative talk; instead, worship and honor the Lord. Rather than getting sidetracked by all the things in your way, fall on your face before God in humility and prayer. You will see Him work on your behalf.

of this land. They have heard that You, Lord, are among these people [of Israel], that You, Lord, are seen face to face, while Your cloud stands over them; and that You go before them in a pillar of cloud by day and in a pillar of fire by night.

¹⁵"Now if You kill these people as one man, then the nations (Gentiles) that have heard of Your fame will say,

¹⁶'Because the Lord was not able to bring these people into the land which He promised to give them, therefore He slaughtered them in the wilderness.'

¹⁷"But now, please, let the power of the Lord be great, just as You have declared, saying,

¹⁸'The Lord is slow to anger, and abundant in lovingkindness, forgiving wickedness and transgression; but He will by no means clear *the guilty*, visiting (avenging) the wickedness *and* guilt of the fathers on the children, to the third and fourth *generations* [that is, calling the children to account for the sins of their fathers].' [Ex 34:6, 7]

¹⁹"Please pardon the wickedness *and* guilt of these people according to the greatness of Your lovingkindness, just as You have forgiven these people, from Egypt even until now."

²⁰So the Lord said, "I have pardoned *them* according to your word;

²¹but indeed as I live, all the earth will be filled with the glory of the Lord. [Is 6:3; 11:9]

²²"Surely all the men who have seen My glory and My [miraculous] signs which I performed in Egypt and in the wilderness, yet have put Me to the test these ten times and have not listened to My voice,

²³will by no means see the land which I swore to [give to] their fathers; nor will any who treated me disrespectfully *and* rejected Me see it. [Heb 6:4–11]

²⁴"But My servant Caleb, because he has a different spirit and has followed Me fully, I will bring into the land into which he entered, and his descendants shall take possession of it.

²⁵"Now the Amalekites and the Canaanites live in the valley; tomorrow turn and set out for the wilderness by way of the Red Sea."

²⁶The Lord spoke to Moses and Aaron, saying,

²⁷"How long *shall I put up with* this evil congregation who murmur [in discontent] against Me? I have heard the complaints of the Israelites, which they are making against Me.

²⁸"Say to them, 'As I live,' says the Lord, 'just what you have spoken in My hearing I will most certainly do to you;

²⁹your dead bodies will fall in this wilderness, even all who were numbered of you, your entire number from twenty years old and upward, who have murmured against Me. [Heb 3:17–19]

³⁰'Except for Caleb the son of Jephunneh and Joshua the son of Nun, not one of you shall enter the land in which I swore [an oath] to settle you.

³¹'But your children whom you said would become plunder, I will bring in, and they will know the land which you have despised *and* rejected.

³²'But as for you, your dead bodies will fall in this wilderness.

³³'Your sons shall be wanderers *and* shepherds in the wilderness for forty years, and they will suffer for your unfaithfulness (spiritual infidelity),

speak the Word

God, let people hear about me what they heard about the Israelites—that You are in the midst of everything I do, that I know You intimately, that Your presence stands over me, and that You go before me in every situation.
—ADAPTED FROM NUMBERS 14:14

until your corpses are consumed in the wilderness.

³⁴'According to the number of days in which you spied out the land [of Canaan], forty days, for each day, you shall bear *and* suffer a year for your sins *and* guilt, for forty years, and you shall know My displeasure [the revoking of My promise and My estrangement because of your sin].

³⁵'I, the LORD, have spoken. I will most certainly do this to all this evil congregation who are gathered together against Me. In this wilderness they shall be consumed [by war, disease, and plagues], and here they shall die.'" [1 Cor 10:10, 11]

³⁶As for the men whom Moses sent to spy out the land, and who returned and made all the congregation murmur *and* complain against him by bringing back a bad report concerning the land,

³⁷even those [ten] men who brought back the very bad report of the land died by a plague before the LORD. [Heb 3:17–19; Jude 5–7]

³⁸But Joshua the son of Nun and Caleb the son of Jephunneh remained alive out of those men who went to spy out the land.

³⁹Moses spoke the Lord's words to all the Israelites, and the people mourned greatly.

⁴⁰They got up early in the morning and went up to the ridge of the hill country, saying, "Look, here we are; we have indeed sinned, but we will go up to the place which the LORD has promised."

⁴¹But Moses said, "Why then are you transgressing the commandment of the LORD, when it will not succeed?

⁴²"Do not go up, or you will be struck down before your enemies, for the LORD is not among you.

⁴³"For the Amalekites and the Canaanites will be there in front of you, and you will fall by the sword, because you have turned away from following the LORD; therefore the LORD will not be with you."

⁴⁴But [in their arrogance] they dared to go up to the ridge of the hill country; however, neither the ark of the covenant of the LORD nor Moses left the camp.

⁴⁵Then the Amalekites and the Canaanites who lived in that hill country came down and struck the Israelites and scattered them as far as Hormah.

15

NOW THE LORD spoke to Moses, saying, ²"Speak to the Israelites and say to them, 'When you come into the land where you are to live, which I am giving you,

³then make an offering by fire to the LORD, a burnt offering or a sacrifice to fulfill a special vow, or as a freewill offering or in your appointed feasts, to make a sweet *and* soothing aroma to the LORD, from the herd or from the flock.

⁴'The one who presents his offering shall present to the LORD a grain offering of a tenth *of an ephah* of fine flour mixed with a fourth of a hin of oil,

⁵and you shall prepare wine for the drink offering, a fourth of a hin, with the burnt offering or for the sacrifice, for each lamb.

⁶'Or for a ram you shall prepare as a grain offering two-tenths *of an ephah* of fine flour mixed with a third of a hin of oil,

⁷'And for the drink offering you shall offer a third of a hin of wine, as a sweet *and* soothing aroma to the LORD.

⁸'When you prepare a bull as a burnt offering or as a sacrifice, in fulfilling a special vow or peace offering to the LORD,

⁹then you shall offer with the bull a grain offering of three-tenths *of an ephah* of fine flour mixed with half a hin of oil;

¹⁰and you shall bring as the drink

offering one-half a hin of wine as an offering by fire, as a sweet *and* soothing aroma to the LORD.

¹¹'Thus shall it be done for each bull, or for each ram, or for each of the male lambs, or of the goats.

¹²'According to the number that you prepare, so shall you do to everyone according to their number.

¹³'All who are native-born shall do these things in this way, in presenting an offering by fire, as a sweet *and* soothing aroma to the LORD.

¹⁴'If a stranger lives as a resident alien with you, or whoever may be among you throughout your generations, and he *wishes to* make an offering by fire, as a sweet *and* soothing aroma to the LORD, just as you do, so shall he do.

¹⁵'As for the assembly, there shall be one [and the same] statute for you [of the congregation] and for the stranger who is a resident alien with you, a permanent statute throughout your generations; as you are, so shall the stranger be before the LORD.

¹⁶'There is to be one law and one ordinance for you and for the stranger who lives with you as a resident alien.'"

¹⁷Then the LORD spoke to Moses, saying,

¹⁸"Speak to the Israelites and say to them, 'When you enter the land to which I am bringing you,

¹⁹then, when you eat the food of the land, you shall lift up an offering (heave offering) to the LORD.

²⁰'You shall lift up a cake *made* of the first of your [ground grain which has been made into] dough as an offering [to the Lord]; as an offering from the threshing floor, so shall you lift it up.

²¹'From the first of your dough (ground grain) you shall give to the LORD an offering throughout your generations.

²²'But when you unintentionally fail and do not observe all these commandments, which the LORD has spoken to Moses,

²³*even* all that the LORD has commanded you through Moses, from the day that the LORD gave commandments and onward throughout your generations,

²⁴then it shall be, if it was done unintentionally without the knowledge of the congregation, that all the congregation shall offer one young bull as a burnt offering, as a sweet *and* soothing aroma to the LORD, with its grain offering and its drink offering, according to the ordinance, and one male goat as a sin offering.

²⁵'Then the priest shall make atonement for all the congregation of the sons of Israel, and they will be forgiven, for it was an error and they have brought their offering, an offering by fire to the LORD, and their sin offering before the LORD, for their error.

²⁶'So all the congregation of the Israelites will be forgiven as well as the stranger who lives among them as a resident alien, because all the people were involved in the error.

²⁷'Also if one person sins unintentionally, then he shall offer a female goat one year old as a sin offering.

²⁸'The priest shall make atonement before the LORD for the person who commits an error when he sins unintentionally, making atonement for him so that he may be forgiven.

²⁹'You shall have one law for him who sins unintentionally, whether he is native-born among the Israelites or a stranger who is living among them as a resident alien.

³⁰'But the person who does [anything wrong] willfully *and* defiantly, whether he is native-born or a stranger, that one is blaspheming the LORD, and that person shall be cut off from among his people [excluding him from the atonement made for them].

³¹'Because he has despised *and* rejected the word of the LORD, and has broken His commandment, that person

shall be utterly cut off; [the responsibility for] his wickedness *and* guilt will be upon him.'"

³²Now while the Israelites were in the wilderness, they found a man who was gathering wood on the Sabbath day.

³³Those who found him gathering wood brought him to Moses and Aaron and to all the congregation;

³⁴and they put him in custody, because it had not been explained [by God] what should be done to him.

³⁵Then the LORD said to Moses, "The man shall certainly be put to death. All the congregation shall stone him with stones outside the camp."

³⁶So all the congregation brought him outside the camp and stoned him to death with stones, just as the LORD had commanded Moses.

³⁷The LORD said to Moses,

³⁸"Speak to the sons of Israel and tell them to make for themselves tassels on the hems of their garments throughout their generations, and put a cord of blue on the tassel of each hem.

³⁹"It shall be a tassel for you to look at and remember all the commandments of the LORD, to do them, so that you do not follow after [the desires of] your own heart and eyes, [desires] after which you used to follow *and* play the prostitute,

⁴⁰so that you may remember to do all My commandments and be holy (set apart) to your God.

⁴¹"I am the LORD your God, who brought you out of the land of Egypt to be your God. I am the LORD your God."

16

NOW KORAH the son of Izhar, the son of Kohath, the son of Levi, with Dathan and Abiram the sons of Eliab, and On the son of Peleth, descendants of Reuben, took *action,*

²and they rose up [in rebellion] before Moses, together with some of the Israelites, two hundred and fifty leaders of the congregation chosen in the assembly, men of distinction.

³They assembled together against Moses and Aaron, and said to them, "You have gone far enough, for all the congregation are holy, every one of them, and the LORD is among them. Why then do you exalt yourselves above the assembly of the LORD?"

⁴And when Moses heard this, he fell face downward;

⁵and he spoke to Korah and all his company, saying, "In the morning the LORD will show who belongs to Him, and who is holy, and will bring him near to Himself; the one whom He will choose He will bring near to Himself. [2 Tim 2:19]

⁶"Do this: Take censers for yourselves, Korah and all your company,

⁷then put fire in them and place incense on them in the presence of the LORD tomorrow; and the man whom the LORD chooses shall be the one who is holy. You have gone far enough, you sons of Levi."

⁸Then Moses said to Korah, "Hear now, you sons of Levi,

⁹does it seem but a small thing to you that the God of Israel has separated you from the congregation of Israel, to bring you near to Himself, to do the service of the tabernacle of

speak the Word

God, I thank You that I belong to You, that You have chosen me, and that through Jesus, I can draw near to You.
–ADAPTED FROM NUMBERS 16:5

the LORD, and to stand before the congregation to minister to them;

¹⁰and that He has brought you near [to Him], *Korah* and all your brothers, sons of Levi with you? Would you seek the priesthood also?

¹¹"Therefore you and all your company are gathered together against the LORD; but as for Aaron, who is he that you murmur against him?"

¹²Then Moses sent to call Dathan and Abiram, the sons of Eliab; but they said [defiantly], "We will not come up.

¹³"Is it a small thing that you have brought us up out of a land [of plenty] flowing with milk and honey to kill us in the wilderness, but you would also lord it over us?

¹⁴"Indeed, you have not brought us into a land flowing with milk and honey, nor given us an inheritance of fields and vineyards. Will you gouge out the eyes of these men? We will not come up!"

¹⁵Then Moses became very angry and said to the LORD, "Pay no attention to their offering! I have not taken one donkey from them, nor have I harmed any one of them."

¹⁶Moses said to Korah, "You and all your company are to appear before the LORD tomorrow, both you and they along with Aaron.

¹⁷"Each of you take his censer and put incense on it, and each of you bring his censer before the LORD, two hundred and fifty censers; also you and Aaron *shall* each *bring* his censer."

¹⁸So they each took his own censer and put fire on it and laid incense on it; and they stood at the doorway of the Tent of Meeting (tabernacle), with Moses and Aaron.

¹⁹Then Korah assembled all the congregation against Moses and Aaron at the doorway of the Tent of Meeting (tabernacle). And the glory *and* brilliance of the LORD appeared to all the congregation.

²⁰Then the LORD spoke to Moses and Aaron, saying,

²¹"Separate yourselves from among this congregation, so that I may consume them immediately."

²²But they fell on their faces [before the LORD], and said, "O God, God of the spirits of all flesh! When one man sins, will You be angry with the entire congregation?"

²³Then the LORD spoke to Moses, saying,

²⁴"Say to the congregation, 'Get away from around the tents of Korah, Dathan, and Abiram.'"

²⁵Then Moses arose and went to Dathan and Abiram, and the elders of Israel followed him.

²⁶And he said to the congregation, "Get away from the tents of these wicked men, and touch nothing of theirs, or you will be swept away in all their sin."

²⁷So they got back from around the tents of Korah, Dathan, and Abiram; and Dathan and Abiram came out and stood at the doorway of their tents with their wives and their sons and their little children.

²⁸Then Moses said, "By this you shall know that the LORD has sent me to do all these works; for I do not act of my own accord.

²⁹"If these men die the common death of all mankind or if what happens to everyone happens to them, then [you will know for sure that] the LORD has not sent me.

³⁰"But if the LORD creates an entirely new thing, and the ground opens its mouth and swallows them up, along with all that belongs to them, and they descend alive into Sheol (the nether world, the place of the dead), then you will understand that these men have spurned *and* rejected the LORD!"

³¹As soon as Moses finished speaking all these words, the ground under them split open;

³²and the earth opened its mouth

and swallowed them and their house-
holds, and all the men who supported
Korah, with all their possessions.
[Num 26:10, 11]

³³So they and all that belonged to
them went down alive to Sheol; and
the earth closed over them, and they
perished from among the assembly.

³⁴All Israel who were around them
fled at their outcry, for they said, "The
earth may swallow us *also*."

³⁵Fire also came forth from the Lord
and consumed the two hundred and
fifty men who were offering the incense.

³⁶Then the Lord spoke to Moses,
saying,

³⁷"Tell Eleazar the son of Aaron, the
priest, that he is to pick up the censers
from the midst of the blaze for they
are holy; and you scatter the burning
coals abroad.

³⁸"As for the censers of these people
who have sinned at the cost of their
lives, have the censers made into
hammered sheets as a plating for the
altar [of burnt offering], for they were
presented before the Lord and they
are sacred. They shall be a [warning]
sign to the sons of Israel."

³⁹So Eleazar the priest took the
bronze censers which the Levites
who were burned had offered, and
they were hammered out [into broad
sheets] as a plating for the [bronze]
altar [of burnt offering],

⁴⁰as a reminder to the sons of Israel
so that no layman—that is, one who is
not of the descendants of Aaron should
approach to offer incense before the
Lord; so that he will not become like
Korah and as his company—just as the
Lord had said to him through Moses.

⁴¹But on the next day the entire con-
gregation of the Israelites murmured
against Moses and Aaron, saying,
"You have caused the death of the
people of the Lord."

⁴²When the congregation was as-
sembled against Moses and Aaron,

they turned *and* looked at the Tent of
Meeting (tabernacle), and behold, the
cloud covered it and the glory *and* brilliance of the Lord appeared.

⁴³Then Moses and Aaron came to
the front of the Tent of Meeting (tabernacle),

⁴⁴and the Lord spoke to Moses saying,

⁴⁵"Get away from among this con-
gregation, so that I may consume them
immediately." Then Moses and Aaron
fell on their faces [in silence before
the Lord].

⁴⁶Moses said to Aaron, "Take a censer
and put fire in it from the altar and lay
incense on it; then bring it quickly to
the congregation and make atonement
for them, for wrath has gone forth from
the Lord; the plague has begun!"

⁴⁷So Aaron took the burning censer
as Moses commanded, and ran into the
midst of the assembly; and behold, the
plague had [already] begun among the
people; and he put on the incense and
made atonement for the people.

⁴⁸He stood between the dead and the
living, so that the plague was brought
to an end.

⁴⁹But those who died in the plague
were 14,700, besides those who died
because of Korah.

⁵⁰Then Aaron returned to Moses at
the doorway of the Tent of Meeting
(tabernacle), for the plague had been
brought to an end.

17 THEN THE Lord spoke to
Moses, saying,
²"Speak to the sons of Israel
and get rods from them, a rod for each
father's household, from all their leaders according to their fathers' households, twelve rods. Write every man's
name on his rod,

³and write Aaron's name on the rod
of Levi [his ancestor]; for there is one
rod for the head of each of their fathers' households.

⁴"You shall then deposit them in the

Tent of Meeting (tabernacle) in front of [the ark of] the Testimony, where I meet with you.

⁵"It shall be that the rod of the man whom I choose will bud, and I will no longer hear the constant grumblings of the Israelites, who are grumbling against you."

⁶So Moses spoke to the Israelites, and each of their leaders gave him a rod, one for each leader according to their fathers' households, twelve rods, and the rod of Aaron was among their rods.

⁷So Moses deposited the rods before the LORD in the Tent of the Testimony (tabernacle).

⁸Now on the next day Moses went into the Tent of the Testimony, and the rod of Aaron of the tribe of Levi had sprouted and put out buds and produced blossoms and yielded [ripe] almonds.

⁹Moses brought out all the rods from the presence of LORD to all the Israelites; and they looked, and each man took his rod.

¹⁰But the LORD said to Moses, "Put Aaron's rod back before the Testimony [in the ark], to be kept as a [warning] sign for the rebellious *and* contentious, so that you may put an end to their murmurings [of discontent] against Me, so that they do not die."

¹¹And Moses did so; just as the LORD had commanded him, so he did.

¹²The sons of Israel said to Moses, "Look, we perish, we are doomed, all doomed!

¹³"Everyone who approaches, who approaches the tabernacle of the LORD, must die. Are we to perish completely?"

18 SO THE LORD said to Aaron, "You and your sons and your father's household (family) with you shall bear the guilt in connection with the sanctuary [that is, through your service as priests you will atone for the offenses which the people unknowingly commit when brought into contact with the manifestations of God's presence]; and you and your sons with you shall bear the guilt in connection with your priesthood [that is, your own unintentional offenses].

²"But bring with you also your brothers, the tribe of Levi, the tribe of your father (ancestor), so that they may join with you and serve you [as assistants], while you and your sons with you are before the Tent of the Testimony [the Holy Place where only priests may go, and the Most Holy Place which only the high priest may enter].

³"And the Levites shall attend to your duty [as assistants] and to the duties of all the tent (tabernacle); only they shall not approach the articles of the sanctuary and the altar, or both they and you will die.

⁴"They shall join you and attend to the duties of the Tent of Meeting—all the service of the tent—and no stranger [no layman, anyone who is not a Levite] may approach you [and your sons].

⁵"So you shall attend to the duties of the sanctuary and the duties of the altar [of burnt offering and the altar of incense], so that there will no longer be wrath on the Israelites [as with Korah, Dathan, and Abiram]. [Num 16:42–50]

⁶"Behold, I Myself have taken your fellow Levites from among the sons of Israel; they are a gift to you, given (dedicated) to the LORD, to do the service for the Tent of Meeting (tabernacle).

⁷"Therefore you and your sons with you shall attend to your priesthood for everything concerning the altar [of burnt offering and the altar of incense] and [of the Holy of Holies] within the veil, and you are to serve. I am giving you the priesthood as a bestowed service, but the stranger (outsider, layman) who approaches shall be put to death." [Ex 40:18, 20, 26]

⁸Then the LORD spoke to Aaron, "Now behold, I [the LORD] have entrusted you with My heave offerings, even all the holy gifts of the Israelites, I have given them to you as a portion, and to your sons as a continual allotment. [Lev 7:35]

⁹"This shall be yours of the most holy things, [reserved] from the fire: every offering of the people, every grain offering and sin offering and guilt offering, which they shall render (give) to Me, shall be most holy for you and for your sons.

¹⁰"You shall eat it as the most holy thing; every male [of your family] shall eat it. It shall be holy to you. [Lev 22:10–16]

¹¹"This also is yours: the heave offering of their gift, including all the wave offerings of the Israelites. I have given them to you and to your sons and to your daughters with you as a continual allotment; everyone in your household who is [ceremonially] clean may eat it.

¹²"All the best of the fresh [olive] oil, and all the best of the new wine and of the grain, the first fruits of those which they give to the LORD, I give them to you.

¹³"The first ripe fruits of all that is in the land, which they bring to the LORD, shall be yours; everyone in your household who is [ceremonially] clean may eat it.

¹⁴"Every devoted thing in Israel [everything that has been promised to the Lord with an oath] shall be yours.

¹⁵"Every firstborn of the womb of all flesh, whether it is man or animal, which they bring to the LORD, shall be yours; nevertheless, the firstborn of man you shall most certainly redeem, and the firstborn of unclean animals you shall redeem.

¹⁶"And their redemption price, from a month old you shall redeem, according to your valuation, for the [fixed] price of five shekels in silver, in accordance with the shekel of the sanctuary, which is twenty gerahs.

¹⁷"But the firstborn of a cow or of a sheep or of a goat you shall not redeem; they are holy [and belong to the LORD]. You shall sprinkle their blood on the altar and shall offer up their fat in smoke as an offering by fire, for a sweet *and* soothing aroma to the LORD.

¹⁸"Their meat shall be yours, like the breast of a wave offering and like the right thigh.

¹⁹"All the offerings of the holy things, which the Israelites offer to the LORD I have given to you and to your sons and your daughters with you as a continual allotment. It is an everlasting covenant of salt [that cannot be dissolved or violated] before the LORD to you and to your descendants with you."

²⁰Then the LORD said to Aaron, "You shall have no inheritance in the land [of the Israelites], nor have any portion [of land] among them. I am your portion and your inheritance among the children of Israel.

²¹"Behold, I have given the Levites all the tithe in Israel as an inheritance, in return for their service which they perform, the service of the Tent of Meeting (tabernacle).

²²"The Israelites shall never again approach the Tent of Meeting [the covered sanctuary, the Holy Place, and the Holy of Holies], or they [who do] will incur sin and die.

²³"Only the Levites shall perform the service of the Tent of Meeting (tabernacle), and they shall bear their iniquity; it shall be a statute forever throughout your generations, that the Levites shall have no inheritance [of land] among the children of Israel.

²⁴"But the tithe of the Israelites, which they present as an offering to the LORD, I have given to the Levites as an inheritance; therefore I have said to them, 'They shall have no inheritance among the children of Israel.'"

²⁵Then the Lord spoke to Moses, saying,

²⁶"Moreover, you shall speak to the Levites and say to them, 'When you take from the Israelites the tithe which I have given to you from them as your inheritance, then you shall present an offering from it to the Lord, a tithe of the tithe [paid by the people].

²⁷'Your offering shall be credited to you as the grain from the threshing floor or as the full produce from the wine vat.

²⁸'Likewise you shall also present an offering to the Lord from all your tithes, which you receive from the Israelites; and from it you shall give the Lord's offering to Aaron the priest.

²⁹'Out of all your gifts, you shall present every offering due to the Lord, from all the best of it, *even* the sacred part from them.'

³⁰"Therefore you shall say to them, 'When you have offered the best from it, then *the rest* shall be credited to the Levites as the product of the threshing floor, and as the product of the wine vat.

³¹'You may eat it anywhere, you and [the members of] your households, for it is your compensation in return for your service in the Tent of Meeting (tabernacle).

³²'You will bear no sin because of it when you have offered the best of it; but you shall not profane the sacred gifts of the children of Israel, or you will die [because of it].'"

19 THEN THE Lord spoke to Moses and Aaron, saying, ²"This is the statute of the law which the Lord has commanded: 'Tell the Israelites to bring you an unblemished red heifer in which there is no defect and on which a yoke has never been placed.

³'You shall give it to Eleazar the priest, and it shall be brought outside the camp and be slaughtered in his presence.

⁴'Next Eleazar the priest shall take some of its blood with his finger and sprinkle some of it toward the front of the Tent of Meeting (tabernacle) seven times.

⁵'Then the heifer shall be burned in his sight; its skin, its flesh, its blood, and its waste, shall be burned (reduced to ash).

⁶'The priest shall take cedar wood and hyssop and scarlet [material] and cast them into the midst of the burning heifer.

⁷'Then the priest shall wash his clothes and bathe his body in water; and afterward come into the camp, but he shall be [ceremonially] unclean until evening.

⁸'The one who burns the heifer shall wash his clothes and bathe his body in water, and shall be unclean until evening.

⁹'Now a man who is [ceremonially] clean shall collect the ashes of the heifer and deposit them outside the camp in a clean place, and the congregation of the Israelites shall keep it for water to remove impurity; it is [to be used for] purification from sin.

¹⁰'The one who gathers the ashes of the heifer shall wash his clothes, and be unclean until evening. This shall be a perpetual statute to the Israelites and to the stranger who lives as a resident alien among them.

¹¹'The one who touches the dead body of any person shall be unclean for seven days.

¹²'That one shall purify himself from uncleanness with the water [made with the ashes of the burned heifer] on the third day and on the seventh day, and then he will be clean; but if he does not purify himself on the third day and on the seventh day, he will not be clean.

¹³'Whoever touches a corpse, the body of anyone who has died, and does not purify himself, defiles the tabernacle of the Lord; and that person shall

be cut off from Israel [that is, excluded from the atonement made for them]. Because the water for impurity was not sprinkled on him, he shall be unclean; his uncleanness is still on him.

¹⁴"This is the law when a man dies in a tent: everyone who comes into the tent and everyone who is in the tent shall be [ceremonially] unclean for seven days.

¹⁵'Every open container [in the tent], which has no covering tied down on it, is unclean.

¹⁶'Also, anyone in the open field who touches one who has been killed with a sword or who has died [of natural causes], or a human bone or a grave, shall be unclean for seven days.

¹⁷'Then for the unclean person they shall take some of the ashes of the heifer burnt for the purification from sin, and running water shall be added to them in a container.

¹⁸'A clean person shall take hyssop and dip it in the water and sprinkle it on the tent and on all the furnishings and on the people who were there, and on the one who touched the bone or the one who was killed or the one who died [naturally] or the grave.

¹⁹'Then the clean person shall sprinkle [the water for purification] on the unclean person on the third day and on the seventh day, and on the seventh day the unclean man shall purify himself, and wash his clothes and bathe himself in water, and shall be [ceremonially] clean at evening.

²⁰'But the man who is unclean and does not purify himself, that person shall be cut off from among the assembly, because he has defiled the sanctuary of the LORD. The water for purification has not been sprinkled on him; he is unclean.

²¹'So it shall be a perpetual statute to them. He who sprinkles the water for impurity [on another] shall wash his clothes, and he who touches the water for impurity shall be unclean until evening.

²²'Furthermore, anything the unclean person touches shall be unclean, and anyone who touches it shall be [ceremonially] unclean until evening.'"

20 THEN THE Israelites, the whole congregation, came into the Wilderness of Zin in the first month [in the fortieth year after leaving Egypt]. And the people lived in Kadesh. Miriam died there and was buried there.

²Now there was no water for the congregation, and they gathered together against Moses and Aaron.

³The people contended with Moses, and said, "If only we had perished when our brothers perished [in the plague] before the LORD! [Num 16:49]

⁴"Why have you brought up the assembly of the LORD into this wilderness to die here, we and our livestock?

⁵"Why have you made us come up from Egypt, to bring us to this wretched place? It is not a place of grain or of figs or of vines or of pomegranates, and there is no water to drink."

⁶Then Moses and Aaron went from the presence of the assembly to the doorway of the Tent of Meeting (tabernacle) and fell on their faces [before

life point

The words the Israelites spoke in Numbers 20:3–5 revealed their total lack of trust in God. They had a negative attitude and had decided they were going to fail before they ever really got started, simply because every circumstance was not perfect. They displayed an attitude that came from a wrong mind-set. Bad attitudes are the fruit of bad thoughts. Ask God to give you thoughts in line with His Word, and watch your attitude change!

the LORD in prayer]. Then the glory *and* brilliance of the LORD appeared to them;

⁷and the LORD spoke to Moses, saying,

⁸"Take the rod; and you and your brother Aaron assemble the congregation and speak to the rock in front of them, so that it will pour out its water. In this way you shall bring water for them out of the rock and let the congregation and their livestock drink [fresh water]."

⁹So Moses took the rod from before the LORD, just as He had commanded him;

¹⁰and Moses and Aaron gathered the assembly before the rock. Moses said to them, "Listen now, you rebels; must we bring you water out of this rock?"

¹¹Then Moses raised his hand [in anger] and with his rod he struck the rock twice [instead of speaking to the rock as the LORD had commanded]. And the water poured out abundantly, and the congregation and their livestock drank [fresh water].

¹²But the LORD said to Moses and Aaron, "Because you have not believed (trusted) Me, to treat Me as holy in the sight of the sons of Israel, you therefore shall not bring this assembly into the land which I have given them." [Ps 106:32, 33]

¹³These are the waters of Meribah (contention, strife), where the sons of Israel contended with the LORD, and He showed Himself holy among them.

¹⁴Moses sent messengers from Kadesh to the king of Edom: "Thus says your brother Israel, 'You know all the hardship that has come upon us [as a nation];

¹⁵that our fathers (ancestors) went down to Egypt, and we lived there for a long time, and the Egyptians treated [both] us and our fathers badly.

¹⁶'But when we cried out to the LORD [for help], He heard us and sent an angel and brought us out of Egypt. Now look, we are in Kadesh, a city on the edge of your territory.

¹⁷'Please let us pass through your land. We will not pass through a field or through a vineyard; we will not even drink water from a well. We will go along the king's highway, not turning [off-course] to the right or to the left until we have passed through your territory.'"

¹⁸But [the king of] Edom said to him, "You shall not pass through my territory, or I will come out against you with the sword."

¹⁹Again, the Israelites said to him, "We will go by the highway [trade route], and if I and my livestock drink any of your water, then I will pay for it. Only let me pass through on foot, nothing else."

²⁰But the king of Edom said, "You shall not pass through [my territory]." And Edom came out against Israel with many people and a strong hand.

²¹Thus [the king of] Edom refused to give Israel passage through his territory, so Israel turned away from him.

²²Now when they set out from Kadesh, the Israelites, the whole congregation, came to Mount Hor.

²³Then the LORD spoke to Moses and Aaron at Mount Hor, by the border of the land of Edom, saying,

²⁴"Aaron will be gathered to his people [in death]; for he shall not enter the land which I have given to the children of Israel, because you [both] rebelled against My command at the waters of Meribah. [Num 20:7-12]

²⁵"Take Aaron and Eleazar his son and bring them up to Mount Hor;

²⁶and strip Aaron of his garments and put them on Eleazar his son. So Aaron will be gathered *to his fathers*, and will die there."

²⁷So Moses did just as the LORD had commanded; and they went up Mount Hor in the sight of all the congregation.

²⁸After Moses stripped Aaron of his

[priestly] garments and put them on Eleazar his son, Aaron died there on the mountain top. Then Moses and Eleazar came down from the mountain.

[29]When all the congregation saw that Aaron had died, all the house of Israel wept (mourned) for him thirty days.

21 WHEN THE Canaanite, the king of Arad, who lived in the Negev (the South country) heard that Israel was coming by the way of Atharim [the route traveled by the spies sent out by Moses], he fought against Israel and took some of them captive.

[2]So Israel made a vow to the LORD, and said, "If You will indeed hand over these people to me, then I will utterly destroy their cities."

[3]The LORD heard the voice of Israel and handed over the Canaanites; then they utterly destroyed them and their cities. So the name of the place was called Hormah (dedicate to destruction).

[4]Then they set out from Mount Hor by the way of the [branch of the] Red Sea [called the Gulf of Aqabah], to go around the land of Edom; and the people became impatient, because [of the challenges] of the journey.

[5]So the people spoke against God and against Moses, "Why have you brought us out of Egypt to die in the wilderness? For there is no bread, nor is there any water, and we loathe this miserable food."

[6]Then the LORD sent fiery (burning) serpents among the people; and they bit the people, and many Israelites died.

[7]So the people came to Moses, and said, "We have sinned, for we have spoken against the LORD and against

look and live

The Israelites were dying in large numbers because a plague of snakes came upon them and were biting them as a result of their sin (see Numbers 21:6). What did Moses do? He prayed. To solve the problem, Moses turned his attention immediately to God, not to himself or anyone else.

I have found that victorious people in the Bible faced their problems with prayer. They did not worry—they prayed. I ask you today: Do you worry or do you take your needs to God in prayer?

Moses sought God about how to handle the snakes. He did not make his own plan and ask God to bless it; he did not try to reason out an answer, nor did he worry. He prayed, and his action brought a response from God. God told Moses to make a bronze serpent, set it on a pole, and put it in front of the people. Every snake-bitten person who looked at it would live. The New Testament tells us this action represented the Cross and Jesus' taking our sin upon Himself: "Just as Moses lifted up the [bronze] serpent in the desert [on a pole], so must the Son of Man be lifted up [on the cross], so that whoever believes in Him will have eternal life [after physical death, and will actually live forever]" (John 3:14, 15).

The message is still the same today: "Look and live." Look at Jesus and at what He has done, not at yourself and what you have done or can do. The answer to your problem, whatever it may be, is not worry, but trusting God and praying. Pray and worship God because He is good, and His goodness will be released in your life.

you; pray to the LORD, so that He will remove the serpents from us." So Moses prayed for the people.

⁸Then the LORD said to Moses, "Make a fiery *serpent* [of bronze] and set it on a pole; and everyone who is bitten will live when he looks at it."

⁹So Moses made a serpent of bronze and put it on the pole, and it happened that if a serpent had bitten any man, when he looked to the bronze serpent, he lived.

¹⁰Now the sons of Israel moved out and camped at Oboth.

¹¹They journeyed on from Oboth and camped at Iye-abarim, in the wilderness facing Moab, toward the sunrise.

¹²From there they set out and camped in the Wadi Zered.

¹³From there they journeyed on and camped on the other side of [the river] Arnon, which is in the wilderness that extends from the boundary of the Amorites; for [the river] Arnon is the boundary of Moab, between Moab and the Amorites.

¹⁴That is why it is said in the Book of the Wars of the LORD:

life point

Along with other bad attitudes (see Numbers 21:4, 5), the children of Israel lacked gratitude. They simply could not quit thinking about where they had come from—and where they were—long enough to get where they were going! What could have helped them? They could have considered their forefather, Abraham. He went through some disappointing experiences in his life, but he did not allow those challenges to negatively affect his future. When things get tough, rehearse the good things the Lord has done. That kind of gratitude to God will help you get through any trial with faith and emerge victorious.

"Waheb in Suphah,
And the wadis of the Arnon [River],
¹⁵And the slope of the wadis
That stretches toward the site of Ar
And leans to the border of Moab."

¹⁶From there *the Israelites went on* to Beer, that is the well where the LORD said to Moses, "Gather the people together and I will give them water." [John 7:37–39]

¹⁷Then Israel sang this song,

"Spring up, O well! Sing to it, [Rom 14:17]
¹⁸The well which the leaders dug,
Which the nobles of the people hollowed out
With the scepter and with their staffs."

And from the wilderness *Israel journeyed* to Mattanah,
¹⁹and from Mattanah to Nahaliel, and from Nahaliel to Bamoth,
²⁰and from Bamoth to the valley that is in the field of Moab, to the top of Pisgah which looks down on the wasteland.

²¹Then Israel sent messengers to Sihon, king of the Amorites, saying,

²²"Let me pass through your land; we will not turn away [from the road] into field or vineyard; we will not drink the water of the wells. We will go by the king's highway until we have crossed your border."

²³But Sihon would not allow Israel to pass through his border. Instead Sihon gathered all his people together and went out against Israel into the wilderness, and came to Jahaz, and he fought against Israel.

²⁴Then Israel struck the king of the Amorites with the edge of the sword and took possession of his land from the Arnon to the Jabbok, as far as the Ammonites, for the boundary of the Ammonites was strong.

²⁵Israel took all these cities, and settled in all the cities of the Amorites, in Heshbon and in all its towns.

²⁶For Heshbon was the city of Sihon, king of the Amorites, who had fought against the former king of Moab and had taken all his land out of his hand, as far as the Arnon.
²⁷That is why those who use proverbs say,

"Come to Heshbon,
Let the city of Sihon be built and
    established.
²⁸"For fire has gone out of Heshbon,
A flame from the city of Sihon;
It devoured Ar of Moab
And the lords of the heights of the
    Arnon.
²⁹"Woe (judgment is coming) to you,
    Moab!
You are destroyed, O people of [the
    god] Chemosh!
Moab has given his sons as
    fugitives [that is, survivors of
    battle],
And his daughters into captivity
To Sihon king of the Amorites.
³⁰"We have shot them down [with
    arrows];
Heshbon is destroyed as far as
    Dibon,
And we have laid them waste as
    far as Nophah,
Which reaches to Medeba."

³¹Thus Israel settled in the land of the Amorites.
³²Now Moses sent *men* to spy out Jazer, and they overthrew its villages and dispossessed the Amorites who were there.
³³Then they turned and went up by the way of Bashan; and Og the king of Bashan went out against them, he and all his people, to battle at Edrei.
³⁴But the LORD said to Moses, "Do not fear him, for I have handed over him and all his people and his land to you; and you shall do to him just as you did to Sihon king of the Amorites, who lived at Heshbon."
³⁵So the sons of Israel killed Og and his sons and all his people, until there was no survivor left to him; and they took possession of his land.

22 THE ISRAELITES journeyed, and camped in the plains of Moab, on the east side of the Jordan [River] across from Jericho.
²And Balak [the king of Moab] the son of Zippor saw all that Israel had done to the Amorites.
³So Moab was terrified because of the people, for they were numerous. Moab was overcome with fear because of the sons of Israel.
⁴Moab said to the elders of Midian, "Now this horde will lick up all that is around us, just as the ox licks up the grass of the field." And Balak the son of Zippor was the king of Moab at that time.
⁵So he sent messengers to Balaam [a famous prophet-diviner] the son of Beor at Pethor, which is by the [Euphrates] River, in the land of the descendants of his people, to call for him, saying, "There is a people who have come out of Egypt; behold, they cover the surface of the land, and they are living opposite me.
⁶"Now please come, curse these people for me, for they are too powerful for me; perhaps I will be able to defeat them and drive them out of the land. For I know [your reputation] that he whom you bless is blessed, and he whom you curse is cursed."
⁷So the elders of Moab and of Midian departed with *fees for* divination (foretelling) in hand; and they came to Balaam and told him the words of Balak.
⁸Balaam said to them, "Spend the night here and I will bring word back to you as the LORD may speak to me." So the leaders of Moab stayed with Balaam [that night].
⁹God came to Balaam, and said, "Who are these men with you?"

¹⁰Balaam said to God, "Balak the son of Zippor, king of Moab, has sent *word* to me:

¹¹'Hear this, the people who came out of Egypt cover the surface of the land; come now, curse them for me. Perhaps I may be able to fight against them and drive them out.'"

¹²God said to Balaam, "Do not go with them; you shall not curse the people [of Israel], for they are blessed."

¹³Balaam got up in the morning, and said to the leaders of Balak, "Go back to your own land [of Moab], for the LORD has refused to let me go with you."

¹⁴The leaders of Moab arose and went to Balak, and said, "Balaam refused to come with us."

¹⁵Then Balak again sent leaders, more numerous and [men who were] more distinguished than the first ones.

¹⁶They came to Balaam, and said to him, "Thus says Balak the son of Zippor, 'I beg you, let nothing hinder you from coming to me.

¹⁷'For I will give you a very great honor and I will do whatever you tell me; so please come, curse these people [of Israel] for me.'"

¹⁸Balaam answered the servants of Balak, "Even if Balak were to give me his house full of silver and gold, I could not do anything, either small or great, contrary to the command of the LORD my God.

¹⁹"Now please, you also stay here tonight, and I will find out what else the LORD will say to me."

²⁰God came to Balaam at night and said to him, "If the men have come to call you, get up and go with them, but you shall *still* do only what I tell you."

²¹So Balaam got up in the morning and saddled his donkey and went with the leaders of Moab.

²²But God's anger was kindled because he was going, and the Angel of the LORD took His stand in the way as an adversary against him. Now he was riding on his donkey, and his two servants were with him.

²³When the donkey saw the Angel of the LORD standing in the way and His drawn sword in His hand, the donkey turned off the path and went into the field; but Balaam struck the donkey to turn her back toward the path.

²⁴But the Angel of the LORD stood in a narrow path of the vineyards, with a [stone] wall on this side and a [stone] wall on that side.

²⁵When the donkey saw the Angel of the LORD, she pressed herself against the wall and crushed Balaam's foot against it, and he struck her again.

²⁶The Angel of the LORD went further, and stood in a narrow place where there was no room to turn, either to the right or to the left.

²⁷When the donkey saw the Angel of the LORD, she lay down under Balaam, so Balaam was angry and he struck the donkey [a third time] with his staff.

²⁸And the LORD opened the mouth of the donkey, and she said to Balaam, "What have I done to you that you have struck me these three times?"

²⁹Then Balaam said to the donkey, "Because you have made a mockery of me! If there had been a sword in my hand, I would have killed you by now!"

³⁰The donkey said to Balaam, "Am I not your donkey on which you have ridden all your life until this day? Have I ever been accustomed to do so to you?" And he said, "No."

speak the Word

God, I pray that my behavior will never be willfully obstinate or contrary before You, but that You will help me keep my heart and actions pleasing to You.
–ADAPTED FROM NUMBERS 22:32

³¹Then the Lᴏʀᴅ opened Balaam's eyes, and he saw the Angel of the Lᴏʀᴅ standing in the way with His drawn sword in His hand; and he bowed his head and lay himself face down.

³²The Angel of the Lᴏʀᴅ said to him, "Why have you struck your donkey these three times? Behold, I have come out to stand against you, because your behavior was obstinate *and* contrary to Me.

³³"The donkey saw Me and turned away from Me these three times. If she had not turned away from Me, I would have certainly killed you now, and let her live."

³⁴Balaam said to the Angel of the Lᴏʀᴅ, "I have sinned, for I did not know that You were standing in the way against me. But now, if my going displeases You, I will turn back."

³⁵The Angel of the Lᴏʀᴅ said to Balaam, "Go with the men, but you shall speak only what I tell you." So Balaam went along with the leaders of Balak.

³⁶When Balak heard that Balaam was coming, he went out to meet him at the city of Moab, which is on the border at the Arnon [River], at the farthest end of the border.

³⁷Balak said to Balaam, "Did I not urgently send *word* to you to call you? Why did you not come to me [immediately]? Am I really unable to honor (pay) you?"

³⁸So Balaam said to Balak, "Indeed I have come to you now, but am I able to say anything at all? The word that God puts in my mouth, that I shall speak."

³⁹And Balaam went with Balak, and they came to Kiriath-huzoth.

⁴⁰Balak sacrificed oxen and sheep, and sent *some* to Balaam and to the leaders who were with him.

⁴¹Then it came about in the morning that Balak took Balaam and brought him up to the high places of Baal; from there he saw a portion of the Israelites.

23 THEN BALAAM said to Balak, "Build seven altars for me here, and prepare for me seven bulls and seven rams here."

²Balak did just as Balaam had said, and Balak and Balaam offered a bull and a ram on each altar.

³Then Balaam said to Balak, "Stand beside your burnt offering and I will go. Perhaps the Lᴏʀᴅ will come to meet me; and whatever He shows me I will tell you." So he went to a desolate hill.

⁴Now God met Balaam, who said to Him, "I have prepared seven altars, and I have offered a bull and a ram on each altar."

⁵Then the Lᴏʀᴅ put a speech in Balaam's mouth, and said, "Return to Balak, and you shall speak thus."

⁶Balaam returned to Balak, and behold, he was standing by his burnt sacrifice, he and all the leaders of Moab.

⁷Balaam took up his [first] discourse (oracle) and said:

"Balak, the king of Moab, has
  brought me from Aram (Syria),
from the mountains of the east,
  [saying,]
'Come, curse [the descendants of]
  Jacob for me;
And come, [violently] denounce
  Israel.'
⁸"How shall I curse those whom
  God has not cursed?
Or how can I [violently] denounce
  those the Lᴏʀᴅ has not
  denounced?
⁹"For from the top of the rocks I
  see Israel,
And from the hills I look at him.
Behold, the people [of Israel] shall
  dwell alone
And will not be reckoned among
  the nations.
¹⁰"Who can count the dust (the
  descendants) of Jacob
And the number of *even* the fourth
  part of Israel?

Let me die the death of the
  righteous [those who are upright
  and in right standing with God],
And let my end be like his!" [Ps
  37:37; Rev 14:13]

¹¹Then Balak said to Balaam, "What have you done to me? I brought you to curse my enemies, but here you have [thoroughly] blessed them instead!"

¹²Balaam answered, "Must I not be obedient *and* careful to speak what the LORD has put in my mouth?"

¹³Balak said to him, "Come with me, I implore you, to another place from where you can see them, although you will see only the nearest and not all of them; and curse them for me from there."

¹⁴So he took Balaam to the field of Zophim to the top of [Mount] Pisgah, and built seven altars, and offered a bull and a ram on each altar.

¹⁵Balaam said to Balak, "Stand here beside your burnt offering while I go to meet the LORD over there."

¹⁶Then the LORD met Balaam and put a speech in his mouth, and said, "Go back to Balak and you shall speak thus."

¹⁷When Balaam returned to Balak, he was standing beside his burnt offering, and the leaders of Moab were with him. And Balak said to him, "What has the LORD spoken?"

¹⁸Balaam took up his [second] discourse (oracle) and said:

"Rise up, O Balak, and hear;
Listen [closely] to me, son of Zippor.
¹⁹"God is not a man, that He should
  lie,
Nor a son of man, that He should
  repent.
Has He said, and will He not do it?

Or has He spoken and will He not
  make it good *and* fulfill it?
²⁰"Behold, I have received *His
  command* to bless [Israel].
He has blessed, and I cannot
  reverse it.
²¹"God has not observed wickedness
  in Jacob [for he is forgiven],
Nor has He seen trouble in Israel.
The LORD their God is with Israel,
And the shout of their King is
  among the people. [Rom 4:7, 8;
  1 John 3:1, 2]
²²"God brought them out of Egypt;
They have the strength of a
  wild ox.
²³"For there is no enchantment *or*
  omen against Jacob,
Nor is there any divination against
  Israel.
At the proper time it shall be said
  to Jacob
And to Israel, what has God done!
²⁴"Behold, a people rises up like a
  lioness
And lifts itself up like a lion;
He will not lie down until he
  devours the prey
And drinks the blood of the slain."

²⁵Then Balak said to Balaam, "Neither curse them at all nor bless them at all!"

²⁶But Balaam answered Balak, "Did I not say to you, 'All that the LORD speaks, that I must do?'"

²⁷Then Balak said to Balaam, "Please come; I will take you to another place. Perhaps it will please God to let you curse them for me from there."

²⁸So Balak brought Balaam to the top of [Mount] Peor, that overlooks the wasteland.

speak the Word

Thank You, God, that You are not a man that You should lie, but that You will make good on everything You have spoken and fulfill it.
–ADAPTED FROM NUMBERS 23:19

²⁹And Balaam said to Balak, "Build seven altars for me here, and prepare for me seven bulls and seven rams here."

³⁰Balak did just as Balaam had said, and offered a bull and a ram on each altar.

24 WHEN BALAAM saw that it pleased the LORD to bless Israel, he did not go as he had done each time before [superstitiously] to seek omens and signs [in the natural world], but he set his face toward the wilderness (desert).

²And Balaam raised his eyes and he saw Israel living in their tents tribe by tribe; and the Spirit of God came on him.

³He took up his [third] discourse (oracle) and said:

"The oracle of Balaam the son of
    Beor,
And the oracle of the man whose
    eye is opened [at last, to see
    clearly the purpose and will of
    God],
⁴The oracle of one who hears the
    words of God,
Who sees the vision of the
    Almighty,
Falling down, but having his eyes
    open and uncovered,
⁵How fair are your tents, O Jacob,
And your tabernacles, O Israel!
⁶"Like valleys that stretch out,
Like gardens beside the river,
Like aloes planted by the LORD,
Like cedars beside the waters. [Ps
    1:3]
⁷"Water [that is, great blessings]
    will flow from his buckets,
And his offspring will live by many
    waters,
And his king will be higher than
    Agag,
And his kingdom shall be exalted.
⁸"God brought Israel out of Egypt;
Israel has strength like the wild ox;

He will devour [Gentile] nations,
    his adversaries (enemies),
And will crush their bones in
    pieces,
And shatter them with his arrows.
⁹"He bowed down [to rest], he lies
    down as a lion;
And as a lioness, who dares to
    rouse him?
Blessed [of God] is he who blesses
    you,
And cursed [of God] is he who
    curses you." [Matt 25:40]

¹⁰Then Balak's anger was kindled against Balaam, and he struck his hands together; and Balak said to Balaam, "I called you to curse my enemies, but behold, you have done nothing but bless them these three times.

¹¹"Therefore now flee to your place! I had intended to honor you greatly, but behold, the LORD has held you back from honor."

¹²Balaam said to Balak, "Did I not tell your messengers whom you had sent to me,

¹³'Even if Balak would give me his house full of silver and gold, I could not go beyond the command of the LORD, to do either good or bad of my own accord. What the LORD speaks, that I will speak?'

¹⁴"And now, look, I am going to my people; come, I will advise you as to what this people [Israel] will do to your people [Moab] in the days to come."

¹⁵He took up his [fourth] discourse (oracle) and said:

"The oracle of Balaam the son of
    Beor,
The oracle of the man whose eye is
    opened,
¹⁶The oracle of him who hears the
    words of God
And knows the knowledge of the
    Most High,
Who sees the vision of the
    Almighty,

Falling down, but having his eyes
open *and* uncovered:
¹⁷"I see Him, but not now;
I behold Him, but not near.
A star shall come forth from [the
descendants of] Jacob,
A scepter shall rise out of [the
descendants of] Israel
And shall crush the forehead of
Moab
And destroy all the sons of Sheth.
[Matt 2:2; Rom 15:12]
¹⁸"Edom shall be [taken as] a
possession,
[Mount] Seir, Israel's enemies, also
will be a possession,
While Israel performs valiantly.
¹⁹"One from [the descendants of]
Jacob shall have dominion
And will destroy the remnant from
the city."

²⁰Balaam looked at Amalek and took
up his [fifth] discourse (oracle) and
said:

"Amalek was the first of the
[neighboring] nations [to oppose
the Israelites after they left
Egypt],
But his end shall be destruction."

²¹And Balaam looked at the Kenites
and took up his [sixth] discourse (oracle) and said:

"Strong is your dwelling place,
And you set your nest in the cliff.
²²"Nevertheless the Kenites will be
consumed.
How long will Asshur (Assyria)
keep you (Israel) captive?"

²³Then he took up his [seventh] discourse (oracle) and said:

"Alas, who can live unless God has
ordained it?
²⁴"But ships *shall come* from the
coast of Kittim,
And shall afflict Asshur (Assyria)
and Eber;

So they (the victors) also *will come*
to destruction."

²⁵Then Balaam arose and departed
and returned to his place, and Balak
also went on his way.

25 ISRAEL SETTLED *and* remained in Shittim, and the
people began to play the
prostitute with the women of Moab
[by being unfaithful to God].
²For they invited the Israelites to
the sacrifices of their gods, and the
Israelites ate [food offered to idols]
and bowed down to Moab's gods.
³So Israel joined themselves to Baal
of Peor [in worship]. And the anger of
the LORD was kindled against Israel.
⁴The LORD said to Moses, "Take all
the leaders of the people [who have
committed sin with the Moabites], and
execute them in broad daylight before
the LORD, so that the fierce anger of
the LORD may turn away from Israel."
⁵So Moses said to the judges of Israel,
"Each one of you must kill his men
who have joined themselves to Baal
of Peor [in worship]."
⁶Then one of the Israelites came and
presented to his relatives a Midianite
woman, in the sight of Moses and the
whole congregation of the Israelites,
while they were weeping [over God's
judgment] at the doorway of the Tent
of Meeting (tabernacle).
⁷When Phinehas the son of Eleazar,
the son of Aaron the priest, saw this,
he left the congregation and took a
spear in his hand,
⁸and he went after the man of Israel
into the tent, and pierced both of them
through the body, the man of Israel
and the woman. Then the plague on
the Israelites stopped.
⁹Nevertheless, those [Israelites] who
died in the plague numbered 24,000.
¹⁰Then the LORD spoke to Moses,
saying,
¹¹"Phinehas the son of Eleazar, the

son of Aaron the priest, has turned my wrath away from the Israelites because he was jealous with My jealousy among them, so that I did not destroy the Israelites in My jealousy.

¹²"Therefore say, 'Behold, I give to Phinehas My covenant of peace.

¹³'And it shall be for him and his descendants after him, a covenant of an everlasting priesthood, because he was jealous (impassioned) for [the unique honor and respect owed to] his God and made atonement for the sons of Israel.'" [Ps 106:28–31]

¹⁴Now the name of the man of Israel who was killed with the Midianite woman was Zimri the son of Salu, a leader of a father's household among the Simeonites.

¹⁵The name of the Midianite woman who was killed was Cozbi the daughter of Zur, who was the tribal head of a father's household in Midian.

¹⁶Then the Lord spoke to Moses, saying,

¹⁷"Provoke hostilities with the Midianites and attack them,

¹⁸for they harass you with their tricks, the tricks with which they have deceived you in the matter [of the Baal] of Peor, and in the matter of Cozbi, the daughter of the leader of Midian, their sister, who was killed on the day of the plague because [of the Baal] of Peor."

26 THEN IT happened after the plague that the Lord said to Moses and Eleazar the son of Aaron the priest,

²"Take a census of all the [males in the] congregation of the sons of Israel from twenty years old and upward, by their fathers' households, all in Israel who are able to go to war."

³So Moses and Eleazar the priest spoke with the people in the plains of Moab by the Jordan at Jericho, saying,

⁴"A census of the people shall be taken from twenty years old and upward, just as the Lord has commanded Moses."

Now the Israelites who came out of the land of Egypt were:

⁵Reuben, the firstborn of Israel (Jacob), the sons of Reuben: of Hanoch, the family of the Hanochites; of Pallu, the family of the Palluites;

⁶of Hezron, the family of the Hezronites; of Carmi, the family of the Carmites.

⁷These are the families (clans) of the Reubenites; and those who were numbered of them were 43,730.

⁸The son of Pallu: Eliab.

⁹The sons of Eliab: Nemuel and Dathan and Abiram. These are the Dathan and Abiram who were called by the congregation, who contended against Moses and Aaron in the company of Korah, when they contended against the Lord,

¹⁰and the earth opened its mouth and swallowed them up along with Korah, when that company died, when the fire devoured two hundred and fifty men, so that they became a [warning] sign.

¹¹But Korah's sons did not die [because they did not participate in the rebellion].

¹²The sons of Simeon according to their families: of Nemuel, the family of the Nemuelites; of Jamin, the family of the Jaminites; of Jachin, the family of the Jachinites;

¹³of Zerah, the family of the Zerahites; of Shaul, the family of the Shaulites.

¹⁴These are the families (clans) of the Simeonites, 22,200.

¹⁵The sons of Gad according to their families: of Zephon, the family of the Zephonites; of Haggi, the family of the Haggites; of Shuni, the family of the Shunites;

¹⁶of Ozni, the family of the Oznites; of Eri, the family of the Erites;

¹⁷of Arod, the family of the Arodites; of Areli, the family of the Arelites.

¹⁸These are the families (clans) of the sons of Gad according to those who were numbered, 40,500.

¹⁹The sons of Judah were Er and Onan, but Er and Onan [were judged by God and] died in the land of Canaan. [Gen 38:7–10]

²⁰The sons of Judah according to their families: of Shelah, the family of the Shelanites; of Perez, the family of the Perezites; of Zerah, the family of the Zerahites.

²¹The sons of Perez: of Hezron, the family of the Hezronites; of Hamul, the family of the Hamulites.

²²These are the families (clans) of Judah according to those who were numbered, 76,500.

²³The sons of Issachar according to their families: of Tola, the family of the Tolaites; of Puvah, the family of the Punites;

²⁴of Jashub, the family of the Jashubites; of Shimron, the family of the Shimronites.

²⁵These are the families (clans) of Issachar according to those who were numbered, 64,300.

²⁶The sons of Zebulun according to their families: of Sered, the family of the Seredites; of Elon, the family of the Elonites; of Jahleel, the family of the Jahleelites.

²⁷These are the families (clans) of the Zebulunites according to those who were numbered, 60,500.

²⁸The sons of Joseph according to their families were Manasseh and Ephraim.

²⁹The sons of Manasseh: of Machir, the family of the Machirites; and Machir was the father of Gilead; of Gilead, the family of the Gileadites.

³⁰These are the sons of Gilead: of Iezer, the family of the Iezerites; of Helek, the family of the Helekites;

³¹of Asriel, the family of the Asrielites; of Shechem, the family of the Shechemites;

³²of Shemida, the family of the Shemidaites; and of Hepher, the family of the Hepherites.

³³Zelophehad the son of Hepher had no sons, but only daughters, and the names of Zelophehad's daughters were Mahlah, Noah, Hoglah, Milcah, and Tirzah.

³⁴These are the families (clans) of Manasseh; and those who were numbered of them were 52,700.

³⁵These are the sons of Ephraim according to their families: of Shuthelah, the family of the Shuthelahites; of Becher, the family of the Becherites; of Tahan, the family of the Tahanites.

³⁶And these are the sons of Shuthelah: of Eran, the family of the Eranites.

³⁷These are the families (clans) of the sons of Ephraim according to those who were numbered, 32,500. These are the descendants of Joseph according to their families (clans).

³⁸The sons of Benjamin according to their families: of Bela, the family of the Belaites; of Ashbel, the family of the Ashbelites; of Ahiram, the family of the Ahiramites;

³⁹of Shephupham, the family of the Shuphamites; of Hupham, the family of the Huphamites.

⁴⁰The sons of Bela were Ard and Naaman: *of Ard*, the family of the Ardites; of Naaman, the family of the Naamites.

⁴¹These are the sons of Benjamin according to their families (clans); and those who were numbered, 45,600.

⁴²These are the sons of Dan according to their families: of Shuham, the family of the Shuhamites. These are the families of Dan according to their families.

⁴³All the families (clans) of the Shuhamites according to those who were numbered, 64,400.

⁴⁴Of the sons of Asher according to their families: of Imnah, the family of the Imnites; of Ishvi, the family of the Ishvites; of Beriah, the family of the Beriites.

⁴⁵Of the sons of Beriah: of Heber, the

family of the Heberites; of Malchiel, the family of the Malchielites.

⁴⁶And the name of the daughter of Asher was Serah.

⁴⁷These are the families (clans) of the sons of Asher according to those who were numbered, 53,400.

⁴⁸Of the sons of Naphtali according to their families: of Jahzeel, the family of the Jahzeelites; of Guni, the family of the Gunites;

⁴⁹of Jezer, the family of the Jezerites; of Shillem, the family of the Shillemites.

⁵⁰These are the families (clans) of Naphtali according to their families; and those who were numbered of them were 45,400.

⁵¹This was the [total] number of the [male] Israelites, 601,730 [twenty years old and upward who were able to go to war].

⁵²And the LORD spoke to Moses, saying,

⁵³"Among these the land shall be divided as an inheritance according to the number of names.

⁵⁴"To the larger *tribe* you shall give the larger inheritance, and to the smaller *tribe* the smaller inheritance; each *tribe* shall be given its inheritance according to its numbers.

⁵⁵"But the land shall be divided by lot. They shall receive their inheritance according to the names of the tribes of their fathers (tribal ancestors).

⁵⁶"According to the [location selected by] lot, their inheritance shall be divided between the larger and the smaller [groups]."

⁵⁷These are those who were numbered of the Levites according to their families: of Gershon, the family of the Gershonites; of Kohath, the family of the Kohathites; of Merari, the family of the Merarites.

⁵⁸These are the families of Levi: the family of the Libnites, the family of the Hebronites, the family of the Mahlites, the family of the Mushites,

the family of the Korahites. And Kohath was the father of Amram.

⁵⁹The name of Amram's wife was Jochebed, the daughter of Levi, who was born to Levi in Egypt; and to Amram she bore Aaron, Moses, and Miriam their sister.

⁶⁰To Aaron were born Nadab, Abihu, Eleazar, and Ithamar.

⁶¹But Nadab and Abihu died [in the presence of God] when they offered [in their ceremonial censers] strange [unholy, unacceptable, unauthorized] fire before the LORD. [Lev 10:1–3]

⁶²Those numbered of the Levites were 23,000, every male from a month old and upward; for they were not numbered among the sons of Israel, since no inheritance [of land] was given to them among the Israelites.

⁶³These are those numbered by Moses and Eleazar the priest, who numbered the sons of Israel [for the second time] in the plains of Moab by the Jordan [River] at Jericho.

⁶⁴But among these there was not a man [left] of those numbered by Moses and Aaron the priest, who numbered the sons of Israel [for the first time] in the Wilderness of Sinai.

⁶⁵For the LORD had said of them, "They shall certainly die in the wilderness." And not a man was left of them except Caleb the son of Jephunneh and Joshua the son of Nun.

27 THEN THE [five] daughters of Zelophehad the son of Hepher, the son of Gilead, the son of Machir, the son of Manasseh, from the tribes of Manasseh [who was] the son of Joseph, approached [with a request]. These are the names of his daughters: Mahlah, Noah, Hoglah, Milcah, and Tirzah.

²They stood before Moses, Eleazar the priest, the leaders, and all the congregation at the doorway of the Tent of Meeting (tabernacle), saying,

³"Our father died in the wilderness. He was not among those who assembled together against the LORD in the company of Korah, but he died for his own sin [as did all those who rebelled at Kadesh], and he had no sons. [Num 14:26–35]

⁴"Why should the name of our father be removed from his family because he had no son? Give to us a possession (land) among our father's brothers."

⁵So Moses brought their case before the LORD.

⁶Then the LORD said to Moses,

⁷"The request of the daughters of Zelophehad is justified. You shall certainly give them a possession as an inheritance among their father's brothers, and you shall transfer their father's inheritance to them.

⁸"Further, you shall say to the Israelites, 'If a man dies and has no son, you shall transfer his inheritance to his daughter.

⁹'If a man has no daughter, then you shall give his inheritance to his brothers.

¹⁰'If a man has no brothers, then you shall give his inheritance to his father's brothers.

¹¹'If his father has no brothers, then you shall give his inheritance to his nearest relative in his own family, and he shall take possession of it. It shall be a statute and ordinance to the Israelites, just as the LORD has commanded Moses.'"

¹²Then the LORD said to Moses, "Go up to this mountain (Nebo) [in the] Abarim [range] and look at the land I have given to the sons of Israel.

¹³"When you have seen it, you too will be gathered to your people [in death], just as Aaron your brother was gathered;

¹⁴because in the Wilderness of Zin, during the strife of the congregation, you rebelled against My command to treat me as holy [by following My instruction] before their eyes at the water." (These are the waters of Meribah in Kadesh in the Wilderness of Zin.) [Num 20:10–12]

¹⁵Then Moses spoke to the LORD, saying,

¹⁶"Let the LORD, the God of the spirits of all flesh, appoint a man over the congregation

¹⁷who will go out and come in before them, and will lead them out and bring them in, so that the congregation of the LORD will not be as sheep without a shepherd."

¹⁸The LORD said to Moses, "Take Joshua the son of Nun, a man in whom is the Spirit, and lay your hand on him;

¹⁹and have him stand before Eleazar the priest and before the whole congregation, and give him a commission in their sight.

²⁰"You shall put some of your authority *and* honor on him, so that all the congregation of the Israelites will obey him.

²¹"He shall stand before Eleazar the priest, who shall inquire before the LORD for him by the judgment (decision) of the Urim. At Joshua's command the people shall go out and at

speak the Word

God, I pray that I will never be as a sheep without a shepherd, but that You will always guide me to wise, godly leaders.
–ADAPTED FROM NUMBERS 27:16, 17

God, I pray that I will be like Joshua and that Your Spirit will be in me.
–ADAPTED FROM NUMBERS 27:18

his command they shall come in, he and all the congregation of Israel with him."

²²Moses did as the Lord commanded him. He took Joshua and had him stand before Eleazar the priest and the whole congregation,

²³and Moses laid his hands on Joshua and commissioned him, just as the Lord had commanded through Moses.

28 THEN THE Lord spoke to Moses, saying, ²"Command the Israelites and say to them, 'You shall be careful to present at its appointed time [during the year] My offering, My food for My offerings by fire as a sweet *and* soothing aroma to Me.'

³"You shall say to the people, 'This is the offering by fire which you shall present to the Lord every day: two male lambs one year old without blemish as a continual burnt offering.

⁴'You shall offer one lamb in the morning and you shall offer the other lamb at twilight,

⁵also a tenth of an ephah of finely-milled flour as a grain offering, mixed with a fourth of a hin of pressed oil.

⁶'It is a continual burnt offering which was ordained on Mount Sinai as a sweet *and* soothing aroma, an offering by fire to the Lord.

⁷'Its drink offering shall be a fourth of a hin for each lamb, in the holy place you shall pour out a strong drink offering to the Lord.

⁸'The other lamb you shall offer at twilight; as the grain offering of the morning and as its drink offering, you shall offer it, an offering by fire, a sweet *and* soothing aroma to the Lord.

⁹'Then on the Sabbath day two male lambs one year old without blemish, and two-tenths [of an ephah] of fine flour mixed with oil as a grain offering, and its drink offering.

¹⁰'This is the burnt offering of every Sabbath, in addition to the continual burnt offering and its drink offering.

¹¹'Then at the beginning of [each of] your months you shall present a burnt offering to the Lord: two bulls, one ram, seven male lambs one year old without blemish;

¹²and three-tenths [of an ephah] of fine flour mixed with oil as a grain offering, for each bull; and two-tenths [of an ephah] of fine flour mixed with oil as a grain offering, for the one ram;

¹³and a tenth [of an ephah] of fine flour mixed with oil as a grain offering for each lamb, as a burnt offering of a sweet *and* soothing aroma, an offering by fire to the Lord.

¹⁴'Their drink offerings shall be half a hin of wine for a bull, and a third of a hin for a ram, and a fourth of a hin for a lamb. This is the burnt offering of each month throughout the months of the year.

¹⁵'And one male goat as a sin offering to the Lord; it shall be offered with its drink offering in addition to the continual burnt offering.

¹⁶'The Lord's Passover shall be on the fourteenth day of the first month [of each year].

¹⁷'There shall be a feast on the fifteenth day of this month; unleavened bread shall be eaten for seven days.

¹⁸'On the first day there shall be a holy [summoned] assembly; you shall do no laborious work *that day*.

¹⁹'But you shall present an offering by fire, a burnt offering to the Lord: two bulls, one ram, and seven male lambs one year old, without blemish.

²⁰'For their grain offering you shall offer fine flour mixed with oil; three-tenths [of an ephah] for the bull, and two-tenths for the ram;

²¹you shall offer a tenth [of an ephah] for each of the seven male lambs;

²²and one male goat as a sin offering to make atonement for you.

²³'You shall present these in addition

to the burnt offering of the morning, which is for a continual burnt offering. ²⁴"In this way you shall present daily, for seven days, the food of the offering by fire, a sweet *and* soothing aroma to the Lord; it shall be presented with its drink offering in addition to the continual burnt offering.

²⁵"On the seventh day you shall have a holy [summoned] assembly; you shall do no laborious work.

²⁶"Also on the day of the first fruits, when you offer a new grain offering to the Lord at your *Feast of* Weeks, you shall have a holy [summoned] assembly; you shall do no laborious work.

²⁷"You shall present the burnt offering as a sweet *and* soothing aroma to the Lord: two young bulls, one ram, seven male lambs one year old;

²⁸and their grain offering of fine flour mixed with oil; three-tenths [of an ephah] for each bull, two-tenths for the one ram,

²⁹a tenth for each of the seven male lambs,

³⁰and one male goat to make atonement for you.

³¹"In addition to the continual burnt offering and its grain offering, you shall present them with their drink offerings. They shall be without blemish.

29 'ON THE first day of the seventh month, you shall have a holy [summoned] assembly; you shall do no laborious work. It will be for you a day of blowing the trumpets (the shophar, ram's horn).

²"You shall offer a burnt offering as a sweet *and* soothing aroma to the Lord: one bull, one ram, and seven male lambs one year old without blemish;

³also their grain offering, fine flour mixed with oil, three-tenths [of an ephah] for the bull, two-tenths for the ram,

⁴and one-tenth [of an ephah] for each of the seven lambs,

⁵and one male goat as a sin offering to make atonement for you.

⁶"*These are* in addition to the burnt offering of the New Moon and its grain offering, and the continual burnt offering and its grain offering, and their drink offerings, according to the ordinance for them, as a sweet *and* soothing aroma, an offering by fire to the Lord.

⁷"Then on the tenth day of this seventh month you shall have a holy [summoned] assembly [for the Day of Atonement]; and you shall humble yourselves; you shall not do any work.

⁸"You shall present a burnt offering to the Lord as a sweet *and* soothing aroma: one bull, one ram, and seven male lambs one year old, which are without blemish;

⁹and their grain offering, fine flour mixed with oil, three-tenths [of an ephah] for the bull, two-tenths for the one ram,

¹⁰a tenth [of an ephah] for each of the seven lambs,

¹¹one male goat as a sin offering, in addition to the sin offering of atonement, and the continual burnt offering and its grain offering, and their drink offerings.

¹²"Then on the fifteenth day of the seventh month you shall have a holy [summoned] assembly; you shall do no laborious work, and you shall observe a Feast [of Booths] to the Lord for seven days.

¹³"You shall present a burnt offering, an offering by fire as a sweet *and* soothing aroma to the Lord: thirteen bulls, two rams, and fourteen male lambs one year old, which are without blemish;

¹⁴and their grain offering, fine flour mixed with oil, three-tenths [of an ephah] for each of the thirteen bulls, two-tenths for each of the two rams,

¹⁵and a tenth [of an ephah] for each of the fourteen lambs;

¹⁶also one male goat as a sin offering,

in addition to the continual burnt offering, its grain offering and its drink offering.

¹⁷'Then on the second day [of the Feast of Booths]: twelve bulls, two rams, fourteen male lambs one year old without blemish,

¹⁸with their grain offering and their drink offerings for the bulls, the rams, and the lambs, by their number according to the ordinance,

¹⁹also one male goat as a sin offering, in addition to the continual burnt offering, its grain offering, and their drink offerings.

²⁰'Then on the third day [of the Feast of Booths]: eleven bulls, two rams, fourteen male lambs one year old without blemish,

²¹with their grain offering and drink offerings for the bulls, the rams, and the lambs, by their number according to the ordinance,

²²and one male goat as a sin offering, in addition to the continual burnt offering, its grain offering, and its drink offering.

²³'Then on the fourth day [of the Feast of Booths]: ten bulls, two rams, and fourteen male lambs one year old without blemish;

²⁴their grain offering and their drink offerings for the bulls, the rams, and the lambs, by their number according to the ordinance,

²⁵and one male goat as a sin offering, besides the continual burnt offering, its grain offering, and its drink offering.

²⁶'Then on the fifth day [of the Feast of Booths]: nine bulls, two rams, and fourteen male lambs one year old without blemish,

²⁷and their grain offering and drink offerings for the bulls, the rams, and the lambs, by their number according to the ordinance;

²⁸and one male goat as a sin offering, in addition to the continual burnt

offering, and its grain offering, and its drink offering.

²⁹'Then on the sixth day [of the Feast of Booths]: eight bulls, two rams, and fourteen male lambs one year old without blemish;

³⁰and their grain offering and their drink offerings for the bulls, the rams, and the lambs, by their number according to the ordinance,

³¹and one male goat as a sin offering, in addition to the continual burnt offering, its grain offering, and its drink offerings.

³²'Then on the seventh day [of the Feast of Booths]: seven bulls, two rams, and fourteen male lambs one year old without blemish,

³³and their grain offering and drink offerings for the bulls, the rams, and the lambs, by their number according to the ordinance;

³⁴and one male goat as a sin offering, in addition to the continual burnt offering, and its grain offering, and its drink offering.

³⁵'On the eighth day you shall have a solemn assembly [to mark the end of the feast]; you shall do no laborious work.

³⁶'You shall present a burnt offering, an offering by fire, as a sweet *and* soothing aroma to the LORD: one bull, one ram, seven male lambs one year old without blemish;

³⁷their grain offering and drink offerings for the bull, the ram, and the lambs, by their number according to the ordinance,

³⁸and one male goat as a sin offering, in addition to the continual burnt offering, and its grain offering, and its drink offering.

³⁹'You shall present these to the LORD at your appointed times, in addition the offerings you have vowed and your freewill offerings, as your burnt offerings, grain offerings, drink offerings, and as your peace offerings.'"

⁴⁰So Moses spoke to the Israelites in accordance with everything that the Lᴏʀᴅ had commanded him.

30 THEN MOSES spoke to the leaders of the tribes of the Israelites, saying, "This is the thing which the Lᴏʀᴅ has commanded:

²"If a man makes a vow to the Lᴏʀᴅ or swears an oath to bind himself with a pledge [of abstinence], he shall not break (violate, profane) his word; he shall do according to all that proceeds out of his mouth.

³"Also if a woman makes a vow to the Lᴏʀᴅ and binds herself by a pledge [of abstinence], while *living* in her father's house in her youth,

⁴and her father hears her vow and her pledge by which she has bound herself, and he offers no objection, then all her vows shall stand and every pledge by which she has bound herself shall stand.

⁵"But if her father disapproves of her [making her vow] on the day that he hears about it, none of her vows or her pledges by which she has bound herself shall stand; and the Lᴏʀᴅ will forgive her because her father has disapproved of her [making the vow].

⁶"But if she marries while under her vows or if she has bound herself by a rash statement,

⁷and her husband hears of it and says nothing about it on the day he hears it, then her vows shall stand and her pledge by which she bound herself shall stand.

⁸"But if her husband disapproves of her [making her vow or pledge] on the day that he hears of it, then he shall annul her vow which she is under and the rash statement of her lips by which she bound herself; and the Lᴏʀᴅ will forgive her.

⁹"But the vow of a widow or of a divorced woman, everything by which she has bound herself, shall stand against her.

¹⁰"However, if she vowed in her husband's house or bound herself by a pledge with an oath,

¹¹and her husband heard it, but said nothing to her and did not disapprove of her [making the vow], then all her vows and every pledge by which she bound herself shall stand.

¹²"But if her husband absolutely annuls them on the day he heard them, then whatever proceeds from her lips concerning her vows or concerning her pledge shall not stand. Her husband has annulled them, and the Lᴏʀᴅ will forgive her.

¹³"Every vow and every binding oath to humble herself, her husband may confirm it or her husband may annul it.

¹⁴"But if her husband says nothing to her [concerning the matter] from day to day, then he confirms all her vows or all her pledges which are on her. He has confirmed them because he said nothing to her on the day he heard them.

¹⁵"But if he indeed nullifies them after he hears of them, then he shall be responsible for *and* bear her guilt [for breaking her promise]."

¹⁶These are the statutes which the Lᴏʀᴅ commanded Moses, between a man and his wife, and between a father and his daughter while she is a youth in her father's house.

31 THE LORD spoke to Moses, saying, ²"Take vengeance for the Israelites on the Midianites; afterward you will be gathered to your people [in death]."

³Moses spoke to the people, saying, "Arm men from among you for war, so that they may go against Midian to execute the Lᴏʀᴅ's vengeance on Midian [for seducing Israel to participate in idolatry]. [Num 25:16–18]

⁴"A thousand [fighting men] from each tribe of all the tribes of Israel you shall send to the war."

⁵So out of the thousands of Israel, a thousand from each tribe were selected, twelve thousand armed for war.

⁶Moses sent them, a thousand from each tribe, to the war, and Phinehas the son of Eleazar the priest, to war with them, and the sacred vessels [of the sanctuary] and the trumpets to blow the alarm in his hand.

⁷They made war against Midian, just as the LORD had commanded Moses, and they killed every male.

⁸They killed the kings of Midian along with *the rest of* their slain: Evi and Rekem and Zur [the father of Cozbi] and Hur and Reba, the five kings of Midian; also Balaam the son of Beor they killed with the sword. [Num 22:31–35; Neh 13:1, 2]

⁹The sons of Israel captured the women of Midian and their children; and all their cattle, all their livestock, and all their property they took as spoil [of war].

¹⁰They burned all the cities where they lived, and all their encampments with fire.

¹¹They took all the plunder and all the spoils of war, both people and livestock.

¹²Then they brought the captives, the spoils, and the plunder to Moses and to Eleazar the priest and to the congregation of the Israelites at the camp on the plains of Moab by the Jordan [River] across from Jericho.

¹³Moses and Eleazar the priest and all the leaders of the congregation went out to meet them outside the camp.

¹⁴But Moses was angry with the officers of the army, the commanders of thousands and of hundreds, who served in the war.

¹⁵And Moses said to them, "Have you let all the women live?

¹⁶"Look, these [are the women who] caused the Israelites, by the counsel of Balaam, to trespass against the LORD in the matter of Peor, and so a plague came among the congregation of the LORD. [Num 25:1–9; 31:8]

¹⁷"Now therefore, kill every male among the children, and kill every woman who is not a virgin.

¹⁸"But all the young girls who have not known a man intimately, keep alive for yourselves [to marry].

¹⁹"Camp outside the camp for seven days; whoever has killed any person and whoever has touched any dead body, purify yourselves and your captives, on the third day and on the seventh day.

²⁰"You shall purify every garment and every article made of leather and all the things made of goats' hair, and every article made of wood."

²¹Then Eleazar the priest said to the men of war who had gone to battle, "This is the statute of the law which the LORD has commanded Moses:

²²only the gold, the silver, the bronze, the iron, the tin, and the lead,

²³everything that can stand fire, you shall pass through fire, and it shall be clean. Nevertheless, it shall also be purified with the water of purification [to remove its impurity]; and all that cannot stand fire [such as fabrics] you shall pass through water.

²⁴"And you shall wash your clothes on the seventh day and be clean, and afterward you may come into the camp."

²⁵Then the LORD spoke to Moses, saying,

²⁶"You and Eleazar the priest and the leaders of the fathers' households of the congregation are to take a count of the spoil of war that was captured, both people and livestock.

²⁷"Divide the spoil into two [equal] parts between those who were involved in the war, that is, those who went out to battle and all [the rest of] the congregation.

²⁸"Levy a tax for the LORD from the

warriors who went to battle, one in five hundred of the persons, the oxen, the donkeys, and the flocks.

²⁹"Take this tribute from the warriors' half and give it to Eleazar the priest as an offering to the LORD.

³⁰"From the Israelites' half [of the spoil] you shall take one out of every fifty of the persons, the oxen, the donkeys, the flocks, and of all the livestock, and give them to the Levites who are in charge of the tabernacle of the LORD."

³¹Moses and Eleazar the priest did just as the LORD had commanded Moses.

³²The plunder that remained from the spoil of war which the warriors had taken, was 675,000 sheep,

³³and 72,000 cattle,

³⁴and 61,000 donkeys,

³⁵and 32,000 persons in all, of the [Midianite] women who were virgins.

³⁶The half share, the portion of those who went to war, was 337,500 sheep in number,

³⁷and the LORD's levy (tax) of the sheep was 675;

³⁸the cattle were 36,000, from which the LORD's levy was 72;

³⁹the donkeys were 30,500, from which the LORD's levy was 61;

⁴⁰the persons were 16,000, from whom the LORD's levy was 32 persons.

⁴¹Moses gave the levy which was the LORD's offering to Eleazar the priest, just as the LORD had commanded Moses.

⁴²As for the Israelites' half, which Moses separated from that of the warriors—

⁴³now the congregation's half was 337,500 sheep,

⁴⁴and 36,000 cattle,

⁴⁵and 30,500 donkeys,

⁴⁶and 16,000 people—

⁴⁷and from the Israelites' half, Moses took one out of every fifty, both of persons and animals, and gave them to the Levites, who were in charge of the tabernacle of the LORD, just as the LORD had commanded Moses.

⁴⁸Then the officers who were over the thousands of the army, the commanders of thousands and hundreds, approached Moses,

⁴⁹and they said to him, "Your servants have counted the warriors under our command, and not one man of us is missing.

⁵⁰"So we have brought as an offering to the LORD what each man obtained—articles of gold, armlets, bracelets, signet rings, earrings, necklaces—to make atonement for ourselves before the LORD."

⁵¹Moses and Eleazar the priest took the gold from them, all the handmade articles.

⁵²All the gold of the offering which they presented to the LORD from the commanders of thousands and of hundreds was 16,750 shekels.

⁵³For the men of war had taken plunder, every man for himself.

⁵⁴So Moses and Eleazar the priest received the gold from the commanders of thousands and of hundreds, and brought it into the Tent of Meeting (tabernacle) as a memorial for the sons of Israel before the LORD.

32 NOW THE sons of Reuben and the sons of Gad had very large herds of cattle, and they saw the land of Jazer and the land of Gilead [on the east side of the Jordan River], and indeed, the place was suitable for raising livestock.

²So the sons of Gad and of Reuben came and spoke to Moses, to Eleazar the priest, and to the leaders of the congregation, saying,

³"[The country around] Ataroth, Dibon, Jazer, Nimrah, Heshbon, Elealeh, Sebam, Nebo, and Beon,

⁴the land which the LORD conquered before the congregation of Israel, is a land [suitable] for livestock, and your servants have [very large herds of] livestock."

⁵They said, "If we have found favor in your sight, let this land be given to your servants as a possession. Do not take us across the Jordan [River]."

⁶But Moses said to the sons of Gad and the sons of Reuben, "Shall your brothers go to war while you sit here?

⁷"Now why are you discouraging the hearts of the Israelites from crossing over into the land which the LORD has given them?

⁸"This is what your fathers did when I sent them from Kadesh-barnea to see the land!

⁹"For when they went up to the Valley of Eshcol and saw the land, they discouraged the hearts of the Israelites so that they did not go into the land which the LORD had given them.

¹⁰"And the LORD's anger was kindled on that day and He swore an oath, saying,

¹¹'None of the men who came up from Egypt, from twenty years old and upward, shall see the land which I promised to Abraham, to Isaac, and to Jacob, because they have not followed Me completely,

¹²except Caleb the son of Jephunneh the Kenizzite and Joshua the son of Nun, for they have followed the LORD completely.'

¹³"So the LORD's anger was kindled against the sons of Israel (Jacob) and He made them wander in the wilderness forty years, until the entire generation of those who had done evil in the sight of the LORD was destroyed.

¹⁴"Now look, you [the tribes of Reuben and Gad] have risen up in your fathers' place, a brood of sinful men, to add still more to the fierce anger of the LORD against Israel.

¹⁵"For if you turn back from following Him [completely], He will once again leave them in the wilderness, and you will destroy all these people."

¹⁶But the people of Reuben and Gad approached Moses and said, "We will build sheepfolds here for our flocks and [walled] cities for our children,

¹⁷but we will be armed and ready to go to war before the [other tribes of the] Israelites, until we have brought them to their place, while our children live in the fortified cities because of the inhabitants of the land.

¹⁸"We will not return to our homes until every one of the [other] sons of Israel has taken possession of his inheritance.

¹⁹"For we will not inherit with them on the west side of the Jordan and beyond, because our inheritance has come to us on this side of the Jordan [River] toward the east."

²⁰Moses replied, "If you will do as you say, if you will arm yourselves before the LORD for war,

²¹and every armed man of yours will cross the Jordan before the LORD until He has driven out His enemies before Him,

²²and the land [west of the Jordan] is subdued before the LORD, then afterward you shall return and be blameless [in this matter] before the LORD and before Israel, and this land [east of the Jordan] shall be yours as a possession before the LORD.

²³"But if you do not do this, behold, you will have sinned against the LORD; and be sure that your sin will find you out.

²⁴"Build yourselves cities for your children, and folds for your sheep, and do that of which you have spoken."

²⁵Then the descendants of Gad and of Reuben said to Moses, "Your servants will do just as my lord commands.

²⁶"Our children, our wives, our livestock, and all our cattle shall be there in the cities of Gilead.

²⁷"But your servants will cross over, every man armed for war, before the LORD to the battle, just as my lord says."

²⁸So Moses gave the command concerning them to Eleazar the priest, and to Joshua the son of Nun, and to

the leaders of the fathers' *households* of the tribes of the Israelites.

²⁹Moses said to them, "If the sons of Gad and the sons of Reuben will cross over the Jordan with you, every man armed for battle before the Lᴏʀᴅ, and the land is subdued before you, then you shall give them the land of Gilead [east of the Jordan River] as a possession;

³⁰but if they will not cross over with you armed, they shall have possessions among you in the land of Canaan [and surrender their right to their land east of the Jordan River]."

³¹The sons of Gad and the sons of Reuben answered, "As the Lᴏʀᴅ has said to your servants, so will we do.

³²"We will cross over armed before the Lᴏʀᴅ into the land of Canaan, so that the possession of our inheritance on [the east] side of the Jordan may be ours."

³³So Moses gave to them, to the sons of Gad and to the sons of Reuben and to the half-tribe of Manasseh the son of Joseph, the kingdom of Sihon, the king of the Amorites and the kingdom of Og, the king of Bashan, the land with its cities and territories, the cities of the surrounding land.

³⁴The sons of Gad built Dibon, At-aroth, Aroer,

³⁵Atroth-shophan, Jazer, Jogbehah,

³⁶Beth-nimrah, and Beth-haran, fortified (walled) cities, and sheep-folds for sheep.

³⁷The sons of Reuben built Heshbon, Elealeh, Kiriathaim,

³⁸Nebo, and Baal-meon (their names being changed) and Sibmah; and they gave other names to the cities which they built.

³⁹The sons of Machir the son of Manasseh went to Gilead and took it, and drove out the Amorites who were in it.

⁴⁰So Moses gave Gilead to [the tribe of] Machir the son of Manasseh, and they settled in it.

⁴¹[The sons of] Jair the son of Manasseh went and took its towns (tent villages) and called them Havvoth-jair.

⁴²Nobah went and took Kenath and its villages, and called it Nobah after his own name.

33

THESE ARE the stages of the journeys of the Israelites, by which they came out of the land of Egypt by their [tribal] armies, under the leadership of Moses and Aaron.

²Moses recorded their points of departure, as the Lᴏʀᴅ commanded, stage by stage; and these are their journeys according to their points of departure:

³They set out from Rameses on the fifteenth day of the first month; on the day after the Passover the Israelites moved out triumphantly in the sight of all the Egyptians,

⁴while the Egyptians were burying all their firstborn whom the Lᴏʀᴅ had struck down among them. Upon their gods the Lᴏʀᴅ also executed judgments.

⁵Then the Israelites moved out from Rameses [where they had all joined together], and camped in Succoth.

⁶They moved out from Succoth and camped in Etham, which is on the edge of the wilderness.

⁷They moved out from Etham and turned back to Pi-hahiroth, east of Baal-zephon, and they camped before Migdol.

⁸They moved out from before Pi-hahiroth and passed through the midst of the [Red] Sea into the wilderness; and they went a three days' journey in the Wilderness of Etham and camped at Marah.

⁹They moved out from Marah and came to Elim; in Elim there were twelve springs of water and seventy palm trees, and they camped there.

¹⁰They moved out from Elim and camped by the Red Sea (Sea of Reeds).

¹¹They moved out from the Red Sea and camped in the Wilderness of Sin.

¹²They moved out from the Wilderness of Sin and camped at Dophkah.

¹³They moved out from Dophkah and camped at Alush.

¹⁴They moved out from Alush and camped at Rephidim; now it was there that the people had no water to drink.

¹⁵They moved out from Rephidim and camped in the Wilderness of Sinai [where they remained for about a year].

¹⁶They moved out from the Wilderness of Sinai and camped at Kibroth-hattaavah.

¹⁷They moved out from Kibroth-hattaavah and camped at Hazeroth.

¹⁸They moved out from Hazeroth and camped at Rithmah [near Kadesh, the place from which the twelve spies were sent to spy out the land of Canaan].

¹⁹They moved out from Rithmah and camped at Rimmon-perez.

²⁰They moved out from Rimmon-perez and camped at Libnah.

²¹They moved out from Libnah and camped at Rissah.

²²They moved out from Rissah and camped at Kehelathah.

²³They moved out from Kehelathah and camped at Mount Shepher.

²⁴They moved out from Mount Shepher and camped at Haradah.

²⁵They moved out from Haradah and camped at Makheloth.

²⁶They moved out from Makheloth and camped at Tahath.

²⁷They moved out from Tahath and camped at Terah.

²⁸They moved out from Terah and camped at Mithkah.

²⁹They moved out from Mithkah and camped at Hashmonah.

³⁰They moved out from Hashmonah and camped at Moseroth.

³¹They moved out from Moseroth and camped at Bene-jaakan.

³²They moved out from Bene-jaakan and camped at Hor-haggidgad.

³³They moved out from Hor-haggidgad and camped at Jotbathah.

³⁴They moved out from Jotbathah and camped at Abronah.

³⁵They moved out from Abronah and camped at Ezion-geber [or Elath on the gulf of Aqabah].

³⁶They moved out from Ezion-geber and camped in the Wilderness of Zin, which is Kadesh.

³⁷They moved out from Kadesh and camped at Mount Hor, on the edge of the land of Edom.

³⁸Aaron the priest went up on Mount Hor at the command of the Lord, and died there in the fortieth year after the Israelites came out of the land of Egypt, on the first day of the fifth month. [Num 20:23–29]

³⁹Aaron was a hundred and twenty-three years old when he died on Mount Hor.

⁴⁰The Canaanite king of Arad, who lived in the Negev (the South country) in the land of Canaan, heard that the sons of Israel were coming.

⁴¹They moved out from Mount Hor and camped at Zalmonah.

⁴²Then they moved out from Zalmonah and camped at Punon.

⁴³They moved out from Punon and camped at Oboth.

⁴⁴They moved out from Oboth and camped at Iye-abarim, on the border of Moab.

⁴⁵They moved out from Iyim (Iye-abarim) and camped at Dibon-gad.

⁴⁶They moved out from Dibon-gad and camped at Almon-diblathaim.

⁴⁷They moved out from Almon-diblathaim and camped in the mountains of Abarim, before [Mount] Nebo.

⁴⁸They moved out from the mountains of Abarim and camped in the plains of Moab by the Jordan across from Jericho [their last stop on the journey to Canaan].

⁴⁹They camped by the Jordan from Beth-jeshimoth as far as Abel-shittim in the plains of Moab.

⁵⁰Then the Lord spoke to Moses

in the plains of Moab by the Jordan *across from* Jericho, saying,

⁵¹"Say to the children of Israel, 'When you cross the Jordan into the land of Canaan,

⁵²then you shall drive out all the inhabitants of the land before you and destroy all their sculpted images, and destroy all their cast idols and completely eliminate all their [idolatrous] high places,

⁵³and you shall take possession of the land and live in it, for I have given the land to you to possess.

⁵⁴'You shall inherit the land by lot according to your families; to the large *tribe* you shall give a larger inheritance, and to the small *tribe* you shall give a smaller inheritance. Wherever the lot falls to any man, that shall be [the location of] his [inheritance]. According to the tribes of your fathers (ancestors) you shall inherit.

⁵⁵'But if you do not drive out the inhabitants of the land from before you, then those you let remain of them will be like pricks in your eyes and like thorns in your sides, and they will attack you in the land in which you live.

⁵⁶'And as I [the LORD] planned to do to them, so I will do to you.'"

34 THEN THE LORD spoke to Moses, saying, ²"Command the Israelites, 'When you enter the land of Canaan, this is the land that shall be yours as an inheritance, the land of Canaan according to its boundaries,

³your southern region shall be from the Wilderness of Zin along the side of Edom, and your southern boundary from the end of the Salt (Dead) Sea eastward.

⁴'Your boundary shall turn from the south to the ascent of Akrabbim, and continue on to Zin, and its limit shall be south of Kadesh-barnea. Then it

shall go on to Hazar-addar and pass on to Azmon.

⁵'Then the boundary shall turn from Azmon to the Brook of Egypt (Wadi el-arish), and its limit shall be at the [Mediterranean] Sea.

⁶'As the western boundary you shall have the Great [Mediterranean] Sea and its coastline. This shall be your western boundary.

⁷'And this shall be your north border: from the Great [Mediterranean] Sea mark out your boundary line to Mount Hor;

⁸from Mount Hor you shall mark out your boundary to the entrance of Hamath, and the limit of the border shall be at Zedad;

⁹then the [northern] boundary shall go on to Ziphron, and its limit shall be at Hazar-enan. This shall be your northern boundary.

¹⁰'You shall mark out your eastern boundary from Hazar-enan to Shepham;

¹¹the [eastern] boundary shall go down from Shepham to Riblah on the east side of Ain and shall descend and reach to the slope on the east of the Sea of Chinnereth [the Sea of Galilee];

¹²and the [eastern] boundary shall go down to the Jordan [River], and its limit shall be at the Salt (Dead) Sea. This shall be your land according to its boundaries all around.'"

¹³So Moses commanded the Israelites, saying, "This is the land you are to inherit by lot, which the LORD has commanded to be given to the nine tribes and the half-tribe [of Manasseh],

¹⁴for the tribe of the sons of Reuben and the tribe of the sons of Gad have received *their inheritance* by their fathers' households, and the half-tribe of Manasseh have received their possession.

¹⁵"The two and a half tribes have received their inheritance across the

Jordan [River] opposite Jericho, eastward toward the sunrise."

[16]Then the LORD spoke to Moses, saying,

[17]"These are the names of the men who shall divide the land among you as an inheritance: Eleazar the priest and Joshua the son of Nun.

[18]"You shall take one leader from every tribe to divide the land for the inheritance.

[19]"These are the names of the men: From the tribe of Judah, Caleb the son of Jephunneh;

[20]from the tribe of the sons of Simeon, Samuel the son of Ammihud;

[21]from the tribe of Benjamin, Elidad the son of Chislon;

[22]from the tribe of the sons of Dan a leader, Bukki the son of Jogli;

[23]of the sons of Joseph: from the tribe of the sons of Manasseh a leader, Hanniel the son of Ephod;

[24]from the tribe of the sons of Ephraim a leader, Kemuel the son of Shiphtan;

[25]from the tribe of the sons of Zebulun a leader, Elizaphan the son of Parnach;

[26]from the tribe of the sons of Issachar a leader, Paltiel the son of Azzan;

[27]from the tribe of the sons of Asher a leader, Ahihud the son of Shelomi;

[28]from the tribe of the sons of Naphtali a leader, Pedahel the son of Ammihud."

[29]These are the [twelve] men whom the LORD commanded [to work with Joshua and Eleazar] to divide the inheritance to the sons of Israel in the land of Canaan.

35 THEN THE LORD spoke to Moses in the plains of Moab by the Jordan [across from] Jericho, saying,

[2]"Command the Israelites to give to the Levites cities to live in from the inheritance of their possession; and you shall give to the Levites pasture lands around the cities.

[3]"The cities shall be theirs to live in; and their pasture lands shall be for their cattle and for their herds and for all their livestock.

[4]"The pasture lands around the cities which you shall give to the Levites *shall reach* from the wall of the city and outward a thousand cubits (1,500 ft.) around.

[5]"You shall also measure outside the city on the east, south, west, and north sides two thousand cubits (3,000 ft.), with the city in the center. This shall belong to the Levites as pasture lands for the cities.

[6]"[Among] the cities which you give to the Levites shall be the six cities of refuge, which you shall provide for the one who commits manslaughter to flee to; and in addition to them you shall give forty-two cities [to the Levites].

[7]"So you shall give to the Levites forty-eight cities in all, together with their pasture lands.

[8]"As for the cities which you shall give from the possession of the Israelites, from the larger *tribes* you shall take many and from the smaller *tribes* few; each *tribe* shall give [at least some] of its cities to the Levites in proportion to [the size of] its inheritance which it possesses."

[9]Then the LORD spoke to Moses, saying,

[10]"Tell the Israelites, 'When you cross the Jordan [River] into the land of Canaan,

[11]then you shall select for yourselves cities to be cities of refuge, so that the one who kills any person unintentionally may escape there.

[12]'The cities shall be to you as a refuge from the avenger, so that the one who has caused the death of another will not be killed until he has had a [fair] trial before the congregation.

[13]'The cities which you are to provide shall be your six cities of refuge.

[14]"You shall provide three cities on this

[east] side of the Jordan [River], and three [more] cities in the land of Canaan; they are to be the cities of refuge.

¹⁵'These six cities shall be a refuge for the Israelites and for the stranger and the resident alien among them; so that anyone who kills a person unintentionally may escape there.

¹⁶'But if he struck his victim down [intentionally] with an iron object so that he died, he is a murderer; the murderer shall certainly be put to death.

¹⁷'If he struck his victim down [intentionally] with a stone in hand, which may cause a person to die, and he died, he is a murderer; the murderer shall certainly be put to death.

¹⁸'Or if he struck his victim down [intentionally] with a wooden object in hand, which may cause a person to die, and he died, he is a murderer; the murderer shall certainly be put to death.

¹⁹'The blood avenger shall himself put the murderer to death; he shall put him to death when he meets him.

²⁰'But if he pushed his victim out of hatred or threw something at him with malicious intent, and he died,

²¹or if, in enmity, he struck the victim down with his hand, and he died, the one that struck the victim shall certainly be put to death; he is a murderer. The blood avenger shall put the murderer to death when he meets him.

²²'But if he pushed the victim suddenly, not in enmity, or threw anything at him without malicious intent,

²³or without seeing him hit him [accidentally] with a stone object that could kill him, and he died, and [the offender] was not his enemy nor intending to harm him,

²⁴then the congregation shall judge between the offender and the blood avenger according to these ordinances.

²⁵'The congregation shall rescue the offender from the hand of the blood avenger and return him to his city of refuge, [the place] to which he had

escaped; and he shall live there until the death of the high priest who was anointed with the sacred oil.

²⁶'But if at any time the one guilty of manslaughter comes outside the border of his city of refuge to which he fled,

²⁷and the blood avenger finds him outside the border of his city of refuge and kills the offender, the blood avenger will not be guilty of murder,

²⁸because the offender should have remained in his city of refuge until the death of the high priest. But after the high priest's death the offender shall return to the land of his possession.

²⁹'These things shall be a statute for you throughout your generations wherever you may be.

³⁰'If anyone kills a person [intentionally], the murderer shall be put to death on the testimony of [two or more] witnesses; but no one shall be put to death on the testimony of [only] one witness.

³¹'Moreover, you shall not accept a ransom [in exchange] for the life of a murderer guilty *and sentenced* to death; but he shall certainly be put to death.

³²'You shall not accept a ransom for him who has escaped to his city of refuge, so that he may return to live in his [own] land before the death of the high priest.

³³'So you shall not pollute *and* defile the land in which you live; for [the shedding of innocent] blood pollutes *and* defiles the land. No atonement (expiation) can be made for the land for the [innocent] blood shed in it, except by the blood (execution) of him who shed it.

³⁴'You shall not defile the land in which you live, in the midst of which I live, for I, the LORD, live among the people of Israel.'"

36 THE LEADERS of the fathers' *households* of the family of the sons of Gilead, the son of Machir, the son of Manasseh, of the families of the sons of Joseph,

approached and spoke before Moses and before the leaders, the heads of the fathers' *households* of the Israelites,

²and they said, "The LORD commanded my lord [Moses] to give the land by lot to the sons of Israel as an inheritance, and my lord was commanded by the LORD to give the inheritance of Zelophehad our brother to his daughters.

³"But if the daughters marry any of the men from any of the *other* tribes of Israel, then their inheritance will be taken away from that of our fathers (tribal ancestors) and will be added to the inheritance of the tribe to which they belong; so it will be taken away from our allotted inheritance.

⁴"When the [year of] Jubilee of the Israelites comes, then their inheritance will be added [permanently] to that of the tribe to which they belong; so their inheritance will be taken away from that of the tribe of our fathers (tribal ancestors)."

⁵Then Moses commanded the Israelites in accordance with the word of the LORD, saying, "The statement of the tribe of the sons of Joseph is correct.

⁶"This is what the LORD commands regarding the daughters of Zelophehad: 'Let them marry whom they wish; only they must marry within the family of the tribe of their father.'

⁷"So no inheritance of the Israelites shall be transferred from tribe to tribe, for every one of the Israelites shall hold to the inheritance of the tribe of his fathers (tribal ancestors).

⁸"Every daughter who possesses an inheritance [of land] in any one of the tribes of the Israelites shall marry [only] a man whose family is of her father's tribe, so that the Israelites may each possess the inheritance of his fathers (tribal ancestors).

⁹"So no inheritance shall be transferred from one tribe to another, but each of the tribes of the Israelites shall hold to its own inheritance."

¹⁰The daughters of Zelophehad did as the LORD commanded Moses.

¹¹For Mahlah, Tirzah, Hoglah, Milcah, and Noah, the daughters of Zelophehad, were married to sons of their father's brothers.

¹²They married into the families of the descendants of Manasseh the son of Joseph, and their inheritance remained in the tribe of the family of their father.

¹³These are the commandments and the ordinances (judgments) which the LORD commanded through Moses to the sons of Israel in the plains of Moab by the Jordan [across from] Jericho.

Deuteronomy

Author:
Moses

Date:
About 1440 BC

Everyday Life Principles:
Blessings and curses are set before us. We need to choose life and continually make good, godly decisions.

We do not live "by bread alone." In other words, real life is not in our possessions, positions, or worldly prestige, but in knowing God, fellowshipping with Him, and trusting Him.

We do not need to strive to be blessed. When we obey God, blessings come as long are we are seeking Him for Who He is and not what He can do for us.

Deuteronomy is a book about our never-ending need for God and His presence in our everyday lives. It is about trusting Him for daily miracles, learning to live in the blessings He gives us, and relying on His guidance in every situation we face.

In Deuteronomy, we see that the Israelites had to learn to worship God in the wilderness, to honor and obey Him while they were *on the way* to the Promised Land, when the journey was difficult. God asks us today, just as He did the Israelites, to worship Him and trust Him when life's journey gets tough. He knows that we will not consistently worship during the good times if we will not worship Him in the hard times. He also knows that our trust in Him is developed and strengthened in difficulty and not when everything is going well for us.

Let Deuteronomy provoke you to trust God and to seek His presence more fervently than ever. Remember that we do not live "by bread alone," but by the Word of God and in the presence of God. Let this book encourage you to live in the blessings of obedience to God and teach you to handle those blessings wisely. Let it inspire you to worship your way through the wilderness times in your own life and to keep choosing life in every situation (see Deuteronomy 30:19).

1 THESE ARE the words which Moses spoke to all Israel [while they were still] beyond [that is, on the east side of] the Jordan [River] in the wilderness [across from Jerusalem], in the Arabah [the long, deep valley running north and south from the eastern arm of the Red Sea to beyond the Dead Sea] opposite Suph, between Paran and Tophel and Laban and Hazeroth and Dizahab (place of gold).

²It is [only] eleven days' *journey* from Horeb (Mount Sinai) by way of Mount Seir to Kadesh-barnea [on Canaan's border; yet Israel wandered in the wilderness for forty years before crossing the border and entering Canaan, the promised land].

³In the fortieth year, on the first day of the eleventh month, Moses spoke to the children of Israel in accordance with all that the LORD had commanded him *to say* to them,

⁴after he had defeated Sihon the king of the Amorites, who lived in Heshbon, and Og the king of Bashan, who lived at Ashtaroth in Edrei.

⁵Beyond (east of) the Jordan in the land of Moab, Moses began to explain this law, saying,

⁶"The LORD our God spoke to us at Horeb, saying, 'You have stayed long enough on this mountain.

⁷'Turn and resume your journey, and go to the hill country of the Amorites, and to all their neighbors in the Arabah, in the hill country and in the lowland (the Shephelah), in the Negev (South country) and on the coast of the [Mediterranean] Sea, the land of the Canaanites, and Lebanon, as far as the great river, the river Euphrates.

⁸'Look, I have set the land before you; go in and take possession of the land which the LORD swore (solemnly promised) to your fathers, to Abraham, to Isaac, and to Jacob, to give to them and to their descendants after them.'

walk out of your wilderness

Moses pointed out to the Israelites that it was only an *eleven-day* journey to the border of Canaan (the Promised Land); yet it had taken them *forty years* to get there. Then Moses said these great words: "The LORD our God spoke . . . You have stayed long enough on this mountain" (Deuteronomy 1:6).

Have you dwelt long enough on the same mountain? Have you spent forty years in the wilderness trying to make an eleven-day trip?

In my own life, there was a time when I finally had to wake up and realize that I was going nowhere. I was a Christian without victory. I had many wrong mind-sets and many mental strongholds that had built up through the years. The devil had lied to me, and I had believed him. I did not even realize I was deceived. I decided I had been on the same mountain long enough. I had spent forty years making what could have been a much shorter journey had I only known the truth of God's Word.

God showed me that the Israelites stayed in the wilderness because they had a "wilderness mentality"—certain types of wrong thinking that kept them in bondage. Let me urge you to make a quality decision to renew your mind and learn to choose your thoughts carefully. Make up your mind that you will not give up until victory is complete and you have taken possession of your rightful inheritance. Do not stay too long in any one place, but keep moving toward everything God has for you.

⁹"I spoke to you at that time, saying, 'I am not able to bear *the burden* of you alone.

¹⁰"The LORD your God has multiplied you, and look, today you are as numerous as the stars of heaven.

¹¹"May the LORD, the God of your fathers, add to you a thousand times as many as you are and bless you, just as He has promised you!

¹²"How can I alone bear the weight *and* pressure and burden of you and your strife (contention) *and* complaining?

¹³"Choose for yourselves wise, understanding, experienced, *and* respected men from your tribes, and I will appoint them as heads (leaders) over you.'

¹⁴"And you answered me, 'The thing which you have said to do is good.'

¹⁵"So I took the leaders of your tribes, wise and experienced men, and made them leaders over you, commanders of thousands, and hundreds, and fifties, and tens, and officers (administrators) for your tribes.

¹⁶"Then I commanded your judges at that time, saying, 'Hear *the matters* between your brothers [your fellow countrymen], and judge righteously *and* fairly between a man and his brother, or the stranger (resident alien, foreigner) who is with him.

¹⁷"You shall not show partiality in judgment; you shall hear *and* pay attention to the [cases of the] least [important] as well as the great. You shall not fear man, for the judgment is God's. The case that is too hard for you [to judge], you shall bring to me, and I will hear it.'

¹⁸"I commanded you at that time [regarding] all the things that you should do.

¹⁹"Then we set out from Horeb (Sinai), and went through all that great and terrible wilderness which you saw on the way to the hill country of the Amorites, just as the LORD our God commanded us; and we came to Kadesh-barnea.

²⁰"And I said to you, 'You have come to the hill country of the Amorites which the LORD our God is about to give us.

²¹"Behold, the LORD your God has set the land before you; go up and take possession *of it*, just as the LORD, the God of your fathers, has spoken to you. Do not fear or be dismayed.'

²²"Then all of you approached me and said, 'Let us send men [into the land] before us, so that they may explore *and* search the area for us, and bring back to us word regarding the way we should go, and the cities we should enter.'

²³"The plan pleased me and I took twelve of your men, one man from each tribe.

²⁴"They turned and went up into the hill country, and came to the Valley of Eshcol and spied it out.

²⁵"Then they took some of the fruit of the land in their hands and brought it down to us; and they reported back to us, and said, 'It is a good land which the LORD our God is about to give us.'

²⁶"Yet you were not willing to go up [to take possession of it], but rebelled against the command of the LORD your God.

²⁷"You murmured *and* were ill-tempered (discontented) in your tents, and said, 'Because the LORD hates us He has brought us from the land of Egypt to hand us over to the Amorites to destroy us.

²⁸"Where can we go up? Our brothers (spies) have made our hearts melt [in fear] *and* demoralized us by saying, "The people are bigger and taller than we; the cities are large, and fortified [all the way up] to heaven. And besides, we saw the [giant-like] sons of the Anakim there."'

²⁹"Then I said to you, 'Do not be shocked, nor fear them.

³⁰'The LORD your God who goes before you will fight for you Himself, just as He did for you in Egypt before your [very] eyes,

³¹and in the wilderness where you saw how the LORD your God carried *and* protected you, just as a man carries his son, all along the way which you traveled until you arrived at this place.'

³²"Yet in spite of this word, you did not trust [that is, confidently rely on and believe] the LORD your God,

³³who went before you along the way, in fire by night and in a cloud by day, to seek a place for you to make camp and to show you the way in which you should go.

³⁴"And the LORD heard the sound of your words, and He was angry and took an oath, saying,

³⁵'Not one of these men, this evil generation, shall see the good land which I swore (solemnly promised) to give to your fathers,

³⁶except Caleb the son of Jephunneh; he shall see it, and to him and to his children I will give the land on which he has walked, because he has followed the LORD completely [and remained true to Him].'

³⁷"The LORD was angry with me also because of you, saying, 'Not even you shall enter Canaan.

³⁸'Joshua the son of Nun, who stands before you, he shall enter there. Encourage *and* strengthen him, for he shall cause Israel to inherit it.

³⁹'Moreover, your little ones whom you said would become prey, and your sons, who today have no knowledge of good or evil, shall enter Canaan, and I will give it to them and they shall possess it.

⁴⁰'But as for you, turn around and set out for the wilderness by way of the Red Sea (Sea of Reeds).'

⁴¹"Then you answered and said to me, 'We have sinned against the LORD. We will go up and fight, just as the LORD our God has commanded us.' So you equipped every man with weapons of war, and regarded it as easy to go up into the hill country.

⁴²"But the LORD said to me, 'Say to them, "Do not go up and do not fight, for I am not among you [because of your rebellion]; otherwise you will be [badly] defeated by your enemies."'

⁴³"So I spoke to you, but you would not listen. Instead you rebelled against the command of the LORD, and acted presumptuously and went up into the hill country.

⁴⁴"Then the Amorites who lived in that hill country came out against you and chased you as bees do, and struck you down in Seir as far as Hormah.

⁴⁵"And you returned and wept before the LORD; but the LORD would not listen to your voice nor pay attention to you.

⁴⁶"So you stayed in Kadesh; many days you stayed there.

2 "THEN WE turned and set out for the wilderness by the way of the Red Sea, just as the LORD had told me; and we circled Mount Seir for many days.

²"And the LORD spoke to me, saying,

³'You have circled this mountain long enough; turn northward,

⁴and command the people, saying, "You are passing through the territory of your brothers the sons of Esau (the Edomites), who live in Seir; and they will be afraid of you. So be very careful;

speak the Word

Thank You, Lord, that You are the God who goes before me and You will fight for me, just as You did for the Israelites in Egypt.
−ADAPTED FROM DEUTERONOMY 1:30, 31

⁵do not provoke them, for I will not give you any of their land, not even *as little as* a footstep, because I have given Mount Seir to Esau as a possession.

⁶"You shall buy food from them with money so that you may [have something to] eat, and you shall also buy water from them with money so that you may [have something to] drink.

⁷"For the LORD your God has blessed you in all that you have done; He has known about your wanderings through this great wilderness. These forty years the LORD your God has been with you; you have lacked nothing."'

⁸"So we passed beyond our brothers the sons of Esau, who lived in Seir, away from the Arabah (wilderness) road, away from Elath and from Ezion-geber. Then we turned and passed through by the way of the Wilderness of Moab.

life point

If we choose to serve God and live His way, we can avoid long wrestling matches with Him. Wisdom tells us to let God do with us what He wants, when He wants, so that we do not waste time going around in circles like the Israelites did (see Deuteronomy 2:3). I have met people who have been going around the same obstacles and issues for twenty or thirty years. Had they simply obeyed God in the beginning, they would have moved on with their lives long ago. They would now be enjoying the blessings of God, but instead they are still miserable and frustrated.

No matter how much we may enjoy where we are, God will not let us stay there and become stagnant. He has new places to take us and new lessons to teach us. He wants to keep us fresh and full of life, full of growth, and full of His great purposes for our lives.

⁹"And the LORD said to me, 'Do not harass [the descendants of] Moab, nor provoke them to war, for I will not give you any of their land as a possession, because I have given Ar to the sons (Moab and Ammon) of Lot as a possession.' [Gen 19:30–38]

¹⁰(The Emim lived there in times past, a people great and numerous, and as tall as the Anakim.

¹¹These also are regarded as Rephaim [an ancient people], as are the Anakim, but the Moabites call them Emim.

¹²The Horites also used to live in Seir, but the sons of Esau dispossessed them. They destroyed them from before them and settled in their place, just as Israel did in the land which the LORD gave them as their possession.)

¹³'Now arise and cross the valley of the Zered.' So we crossed the Zered Valley.

¹⁴"Now thirty-eight years passed from the time we left Kadesh-barnea until we crossed the Zered Valley, until that entire generation of the men of war had died from within the camp, just as the LORD had sworn to them.

¹⁵"Moreover the hand of the LORD was against them, to destroy them from within the camp, until they were all dead.

¹⁶"So it came about when all the men of war had finally died from among the people,

¹⁷that the LORD spoke to me, saying,

¹⁸'Today you are to pass through Ar, the border of Moab.

¹⁹'When you come opposite the territory of the sons of Ammon, do not harass them nor provoke them, for I will not give you any of the land of the sons of Ammon as a possession, because I have given it to the sons of Lot as a possession.'

²⁰(It is also regarded as the land of the Rephaim [of giant stature], for Rephaim used to live there, but the Ammonites call them Zamzummin,

[21]a great, numerous people, and tall as the Anakim, but the LORD destroyed them before the sons of Ammon. And they dispossessed them and settled in their place,

[22]just as He did for the sons of Esau, who live in Seir, when He destroyed the Horites from before them; and the sons of Esau (the Edomites) dispossessed them and settled in their place [and remain there] even to this day.

[23]As for the Avvim, who lived in villages as far as Gaza, the Caphtorim (Cretans, later Philistines) who came from Caphtor (Crete) destroyed them and settled in their place.)

[24]'Now arise, continue on, and go through the valley of the Arnon. Look, I have handed over to you Sihon the Amorite, king of Heshbon, and his land. Begin! Take possession [of it] and fight with him in battle.

[25]'This day I will begin to put the dread and the fear of you on the peoples (pagans) under the whole heaven, who, when they hear the reports about you, will tremble and be in anguish because of you.'

[26]"So I sent messengers from the Wilderness of Kedemoth to Sihon king of Heshbon with words of peace, saying,

[27]'Let me pass through your land [with my people]. I will travel [with them] only on the highway; I will not turn away to the right or to the left.

[28]'You will sell me food for money so that I [along with my people] will eat, and you will give me water for money so that I [along with my people] will drink; only let me [and my people] travel through [the land] on foot,

[29]just as the sons of Esau, who live in Seir, and the Moabites, who live in Ar, did for me, until I cross the Jordan into the land which the LORD our God is giving us.'

[30]"But Sihon king of Heshbon was not willing for us to travel through his land; for the LORD your God hardened his spirit and made his heart obstinate, in order to hand him over to you, as he is today.

[31]"The LORD said to me, 'Look, I have begun to hand over to you Sihon and his land. Begin! Take possession [of it], so that you may possess his land.'

[32]"Then at Jahaz, Sihon and all his people came out to meet us in battle.

[33]"So the LORD our God handed him over to us [and gave us the victory], and we defeated him and his sons and all his people.

[34]"At the same time we took all his cities and utterly destroyed every city—men, women and children. We left no survivor.

[35]"We took only the cattle as plunder for ourselves and the spoil of the cities which we had captured.

[36]"From Aroer, which is on the edge of the Arnon Valley, and *from* the city which is in the valley, as far as Gilead, there was no city [whose wall was] too high *and* too strong for us; the LORD our God handed over everything to us.

[37]"Only you did not go near the land of the sons of Ammon, all along the river Jabbok and the cities of the hill country, and wherever the LORD our God had forbidden us.

3 "THEN WE turned and went up the road toward Bashan, and at Edrei, Og king of Bashan, with all his people came out to meet us in battle.

[2]"And the LORD said to me, 'Do not fear him, for I have handed him over to you, him and all his people and his land; and you shall do to him just as you did to Sihon king of the Amorites, who lived at Heshbon.'

[3]"So the LORD our God also handed over Og king of Bashan, and all his people, into our hand and we struck him until no survivor was left.

[4]"We captured all his cities at that time; there was not a city which we did

not take from them: sixty cities, the whole region of Argob, the kingdom of Og in Bashan.

⁵"All these cities were fortified *and* unassailable with their high walls, gates, and bars; in addition, [there were] a very great number of unwalled villages.

⁶"We utterly destroyed them, just as we did to Sihon king of Heshbon, utterly destroying every city—the men, women, and children.

⁷"But we took all the cattle and the spoil of the cities as plunder for ourselves.

⁸"So we took the land at that time from the hand of the two kings [Sihon and Og] of the Amorites who were beyond the Jordan, from the valley of the Arnon to Mount Hermon

⁹(the Sidonians call Hermon Sirion, and the Amorites call it Senir):

¹⁰all the cities of the plain and all Gilead and all Bashan, as far as Salecah and Edrei, cities of the kingdom of Og in Bashan."

¹¹(For only Og king of Bashan was left of the remnant of the [the giants known as the] Rephaim. Behold, his bed frame was a bed frame of iron; is it not in Rabbah of the Ammonites? It was nine cubits (12 ft.) long and four cubits (6 ft.) wide, using the cubit of a man [the forearm to the end of the middle finger].)

¹²"So we took possession of this land at that time. I gave *the territory* from Aroer, which is by the valley of the Arnon, along with half of the hill country of Gilead and its cities to the Reubenites and to the Gadites.

¹³"The rest of Gilead and all of Bashan, the kingdom of Og, I gave to the half-tribe of Manasseh, that is, all the region

of Argob (concerning all Bashan, it is called the land of Rephaim.

¹⁴Jair the son (descendant) of Manasseh took all the region of Argob as far as the border of the Geshurites and the Maacathites, *that is* Bashan, and called it after his own name, Havvoth (the villages of) Jair, *as it is called* to this day.)

¹⁵"I gave Gilead to Machir [of Manasseh].

¹⁶"To the Reubenites and Gadites I gave *the territory* from Gilead as far as the Valley of Arnon, with the middle of the Valley as a boundary, and as far as the Jabbok River, the boundary of the sons of Ammon;

¹⁷the Arabah also, with the Jordan as its boundary, from Chinnereth (the Sea of Galilee) as far as the sea of the Arabah, the Salt Sea (Dead Sea), at the foot of the slopes of Pisgah on the east.

¹⁸"Then I commanded you [Reuben, Gad, and the half-tribe of Manasseh] at that time, saying, 'The LORD your God has given you this land to possess; all you who are brave men shall cross over [the Jordan] armed before your brothers, the sons of Israel.

¹⁹'But your wives and your children and your cattle—I know that you have much livestock—shall remain in your cities which I have given you,

²⁰until the LORD gives rest to your fellow countrymen as [He has] to you, and they also possess the land which the LORD your God has given them beyond the Jordan. Then each of you may return to the land (possession) which I have given to you.'

²¹"I commanded Joshua at that time, saying, 'Your eyes have seen everything that the LORD your God has done to these two kings [Sihon and Og]; so

speak the Word

Thank You, God, that You are fighting for me. Because You are, I will not fear.
–ADAPTED FROM DEUTERONOMY 3:22

the Lord shall do the same to all the kingdoms into which you are about to cross.

²²'Do not fear them, for it is the Lord your God who is fighting for you.'

²³"Then I pleaded with the Lord at that time [for His favor], saying,

²⁴'O Lord God, You have only begun to show Your servant Your greatness and Your mighty hand; for what god is there in heaven or on earth that can do such works and mighty acts (miracles) as Yours?

²⁵'I pray, let me go over and see the good land that is beyond the Jordan, that good hill country [with Hermon] and Lebanon.'

²⁶"But the Lord was angry with me because of you [and your rebellion at Meribah], and would not listen to me; and the Lord said to me, 'Enough! Speak to Me no longer about this matter. [Num 20:8]

²⁷'Go up to the top of [Mount] Pisgah and raise your eyes toward the west and north and south and east, and see it with your eyes, for you shall not cross this Jordan.

²⁸'But command Joshua and encourage and strengthen him, for he shall go across and lead this people, and he will give them the land which you see as an inheritance.'

²⁹"So we stayed in the Valley opposite Beth-peor.

4 "NOW, O Israel, listen *and* pay attention to the statutes and the judgments (God's legal decisions) which I am teaching you to do, so that you may live and go in and take possession of the land which the Lord, the God of your fathers, is giving you.

²"You shall not add to the word which I am commanding you, nor take away from it, so that you may keep the commandments of the Lord your God which I am commanding you.

³"Your eyes have seen what the Lord did at Baal-peor; for all the men who followed [and participated in the worship of] Baal of Peor, the Lord your God destroyed them from among you, [Num 25:1–9]

⁴but you who held tightly to the Lord your God are alive today, every one of you.

⁵"Look, I have taught you statutes and judgments just as the Lord my God has commanded me, so that you may do them in the land which you are entering to possess.

⁶"So keep and do them, for that is your wisdom and your understanding in the sight of the peoples who will hear all these statutes and say, 'Surely this great nation is a wise and understanding people.'

⁷"For what great nation is there that has a god so near to it as the Lord our God [is to us] whenever we call on Him?

⁸"Or what great nation has statutes and judgments so righteous (upright, just) as this whole law which I am placing before you today?

⁹"Only pay attention and watch yourselves closely so that you do not forget the things which your eyes have seen and they do not depart from your heart all the days of your life. Make them known to your children and your grandchildren [impressing these things on their mind and penetrating their heart with these truths]—

¹⁰*especially* the day you stood before the Lord your God at Horeb (Mount Sinai), when the Lord said to me, 'Assemble the people to Me and I will let them hear My words, so that they may learn to fear Me [with awe-filled reverence and profound respect] all the days they live on the land, and so that they may teach their children.'

¹¹"You approached and stood at the foot of the mountain, and the mountain burned with fire to the [very] heart of the heavens: darkness, cloud and thick gloom.

¹²"Then the Lord spoke to you from the midst of the fire; you heard the sound of the words, but you saw no form—there was only a voice.

¹³"So He declared to you His covenant which He commanded you to follow, the Ten Commandments; and He wrote them on two tablets of stone.

¹⁴"The Lord commanded me at that time to teach you the statutes and judgments, so that you might do them in the land which you are going over to possess.

¹⁵"So pay attention *and* watch yourselves carefully—for you did not see any form [of God] on the day the Lord spoke to you at Horeb from the midst of the fire—

¹⁶so that you do not act corruptly and make for yourselves a carved *or* sculpted image [to worship] in the form of any figure, the likeness of male or female,

¹⁷the likeness of any animal that is on the earth, or of any winged bird that flies in the sky,

¹⁸the likeness of anything that crawls on the ground, or of any fish that is in the waters beneath the earth.

¹⁹"And *beware* that you do not raise your eyes toward heaven and see the sun and the moon and the stars, all the host of heaven, and let yourselves be led astray and worship them and serve them, [mere created bodies] which the Lord your God has allotted to [serve and benefit] all the peoples under the whole heaven.

²⁰"But the Lord has taken you and brought you out of the iron [smelting] furnace, out of Egypt, to be a people for His own possession, as [you are] this day.

²¹"Now the Lord was angry with me [at the waters of Meribah] because of you, and He swore [an oath] that I would not cross the Jordan, and that I would not enter the good land which the Lord your God is giving you as an inheritance.

²²"For I am going to die in this land, I am not going to cross the Jordan, but you shall cross over and take possession of this good land.

²³"So be on your guard *and* watch yourselves, so that you do not forget the covenant of the Lord your God which He has made with you, and make for yourselves a carved *or* sculpted image in the form of anything which the Lord your God has forbidden you.

²⁴"For the Lord your God is a consuming fire; He is a jealous (impassioned) God [demanding what is rightfully and uniquely His].

²⁵"When you become the father of children and grandchildren and have grown old in the land, then if you corrupt yourselves by making a carved *or* sculpted image in the form of anything [for the purpose of worship], and do evil [things] in the sight of the Lord your God, provoking Him to anger,

²⁶I call heaven and earth as witnesses against you today, that you will soon utterly perish from the land which you are crossing the Jordan to possess. You shall not live long on it, but will be utterly destroyed.

²⁷"The Lord will scatter *and* disperse you among the peoples (pagan nations), and you will be left few in number among the nations where the Lord drives you.

²⁸"And there you will serve [false and foreign] gods, the work of human hands, [lifeless images of] wood and stone, which neither see nor hear nor eat nor smell [the offerings of food given to them].

²⁹"But from there you will seek the Lord your God, and you will find *Him* if you search for Him with all your heart and all your soul.

³⁰"When you are in distress *and* tribulation and all these things come on you, in the latter days you will return to the Lord your God and listen to His voice.

³¹"For the LORD your God is a merciful *and* compassionate God; He will not fail you, nor destroy you, nor forget the covenant with your fathers which He swore to them.

³²"Indeed, ask now about the days that are past, [those days] which were before you, since the day that God created man on the earth, and ask from one end of the heavens to the other. Has *anything* been done like this great thing, or has *anything* been heard like it?

³³"Did [any] people ever hear the voice of God speaking out of the midst of the fire, as you heard, and [still] live?

³⁴"Or has any [man-made] god ever tried to go and take for himself a nation from within *another* nation by trials, by signs and wonders and by war and by a mighty hand and by an outstretched arm and by great terrors, as the LORD your God did for you in Egypt before your [very] eyes?

³⁵"It was shown to you so that you might have [personal] knowledge *and* comprehend that the LORD is God; there is no other besides Him.

³⁶"Out of the heavens He let you hear His voice to discipline *and* admonish you; and on earth He let you see His great fire, and you heard His words from the midst of the fire.

³⁷"And because He loved your fathers, He chose their descendants who followed them, and brought you from Egypt with His Presence, with His great *and* awesome power,

³⁸dispossessing *and* driving out from before you nations, [nations that were] greater and mightier than you, to bring you in, to give you their land as an inheritance, as it is this day.

³⁹Therefore know *and* understand today, and take it to your heart, that the LORD is God in the heavens above and on the earth below; there is no other.

⁴⁰"So you shall keep His statutes and His commandments which I am commanding you today, so that it may go well with you and with your children after you, and so that you may live long on the land which the LORD your God is giving you for all time."

⁴¹Then Moses set apart three cities [of refuge] beyond the Jordan toward the rising of the sun (eastward),

⁴²so that someone who committed manslaughter could flee there, [that is, a person] who killed his neighbor unintentionally and without previously having hostility toward him, and that by escaping to one of these cities he might [claim the right of asylum and] save his life:

⁴³Bezer in the wilderness on the plateau for the Reubenites, and Ramoth in Gilead for the Gadites, and Golan in Bashan for the Manassites.

⁴⁴This is the law which Moses placed before the sons of Israel;

⁴⁵these are the testimonies (legal provisions) and the statutes and the judgments which Moses spoke to the sons of Israel when they came out of Egypt,

speak the Word

God, help me to seek You always. If I search for You with all of my heart and all of soul, I will find You.
—ADAPTED FROM DEUTERONOMY 4:29

Thank You, God, that You are a merciful and compassionate God. I declare that You will never fail me or forget the covenant You have with me.
—ADAPTED FROM DEUTERONOMY 4:31

⁴⁶beyond the Jordan in the Valley opposite Beth-peor, in the land of Sihon king of the Amorites who lived at Heshbon, whom Moses and the sons of Israel defeated when they came out from Egypt.

⁴⁷They took possession of his land and the land of Og king of Bashan, the two kings of the Amorites, who *reigned* across the Jordan to the east,

⁴⁸from Aroer, which is on the edge of the valley of the [river] Arnon, as far as Mount Sion (that is, Hermon),

⁴⁹with all the Arabah (desert lowlands) across the Jordan to the east, even as far as the sea of the Arabah (the Dead Sea), at the foot of the slopes of Pisgah.

5 THEN MOSES summoned all Israel and said to them:
"Hear, O Israel, the statutes and judgments (legal decisions) which I am speaking today in your hearing, so that you may learn them and observe them carefully.

²"The LORD our God made a covenant with us at Horeb.

³"The LORD did not make this covenant with our fathers, but with us, all of us who are alive here today.

⁴"The LORD spoke with you face to face at the mountain from the midst of the fire.

⁵"I was standing between the LORD and you at that time, to declare to you the word of the LORD; for you were afraid because of the fire and did not go up the mountain. He said,

⁶'I am the LORD your God who brought you out of the land of Egypt, out of the house of slavery.

⁷'You shall have no other gods before Me.

⁸'You shall not make for yourself an idol [as an object to worship], or any likeness (form, manifestation) of what is in heaven above or on the earth beneath or in the water under the earth.

putting the Word to work

Deuteronomy 5:16 tells us that things will go well with us if we honor our parents. How can you better honor your mother and your father?

⁹'You shall not worship them or serve them; for I, the LORD your God, am a jealous (impassioned) God [demanding what is rightfully and uniquely mine], visiting (avenging) the iniquity (sin, guilt) of the fathers on the children [that is, calling the children to account for the sins of their fathers], to the third and the fourth *generations* of those who hate Me, [Is 42:8; 48:11]

¹⁰but showing graciousness *and* lovingkindness to thousands [of generations] of those who love Me and keep My commandments.

¹¹'You shall not take the name of the LORD your God in vain [that is, irreverently, in false affirmations or in ways that impugn the character of God]; for the LORD will not hold guiltless *nor* leave unpunished the one who takes His name in vain [disregarding its reverence and its power].

¹²'Observe the Sabbath day to keep it holy (set apart, dedicated to God), as the LORD your God commanded you.

¹³'Six days you shall labor and do all your work,

¹⁴but the seventh day is a Sabbath [a day of rest dedicated] to the LORD your God; on that day you shall not do any work, you or your son or your daughter or your male servant or your female servant or your ox or your donkey or any of your livestock or the stranger who stays inside your [city] gates, so that your male servant and your female servant may rest as well as you.

¹⁵'You shall remember [with thoughtful concern] that you were a slave in the land of Egypt, and that the LORD your God brought you out of

there with a mighty hand and by an outstretched arm; therefore the LORD your God has commanded you to observe the Sabbath day.

¹⁶'Honor (respect, obey, care for) your father and your mother, as the LORD your God has commanded you, so that your days [on the earth] may be prolonged and so that it may go well with you in the land which the LORD your God gives you.

¹⁷'You shall not murder.

¹⁸'You shall not commit adultery. [Prov 6:25, 26; Matt 5:27, 28; Rom 1:24; Eph 5:3]

¹⁹'You shall not steal. [Prov 11:1; 16:8; 21:6; 22:16; Jer 17:11; Mal 3:8]

²⁰'You shall not give false testimony [that is, lie, withhold, or manipulate the truth] against your neighbor (any person). [Ex 23:1; Prov 19:9; 24:28]

²¹'You shall not covet [that is, desire and seek to acquire] your neighbor's wife, nor desire your neighbor's house, his field, his male servant or his female servant, his ox or his donkey or anything that belongs to your neighbor.' [Luke 12:15; Col 3:5]

²²"The LORD spoke these words with a great voice to all your assembly at the mountain out of the midst of the fire, the cloud, and the thick darkness, and He added no more. He wrote these commandments on two tablets of stone and gave them to me.

²³"And when you heard the voice from the midst of the darkness, while the mountain was burning with fire, you approached me, all the leaders (heads) of your tribes and your elders;

²⁴and you said, 'Behold, the LORD our God has shown us His glory and His greatness, and we have heard His voice from the midst of the fire; we have seen today that God speaks with man, yet he [still] lives.

²⁵'Now then why should we die? For this great fire will consume us; if we hear the voice of the LORD our God any longer, then we will die.

²⁶'For who is there of all flesh (mankind) who has heard the voice of the living God speaking from the midst of the fire, as we have, and lived?

²⁷'You, Moses, go near and listen to everything that the LORD our God says; then speak to us everything that the LORD our God speaks to you, and we will listen and do it.'

²⁸"The LORD heard your words when you spoke to me, and the LORD said to me, 'I have heard the words of this people which they have spoken to you. They have done well in all that they have spoken.

²⁹'Oh that they had such a heart in them, that they would fear [and worship Me with awe-filled reverence and profound respect] and keep all My commandments always, so that it may go well with them and with their children forever!

³⁰'Go and say to them, "Return to your tents."

³¹'But as for you, stand here by Me, and I will tell you all the commandments and the statutes and the judgments which you shall teach them, so that they may obey them in the land which I give them to possess.'

³²"Therefore you shall pay attention *and* be careful to do just as the LORD your God has commanded you; you shall not turn aside to the right or to the left [deviating from My commandments].

speak the Word

Help me, God, to live each and every day in all the ways which You have commanded me, so that I may live and so that it may go well with me.
–ADAPTED FROM DEUTERONOMY 5:32, 33

33"You shall walk [that is, live each and every day] in all the ways which the Lord your God has commanded you, so that you may live and so that it may be well with you, and that you may live long in the land which you will possess.

6 "NOW THIS is the command; the statutes and the judgments (precepts) which the Lord your God has commanded me to teach you, so that you might do (follow, obey) them in the land which you are crossing over [the Jordan] to possess,

2so that you and your son and your grandson may fear *and* worship the Lord your God [with awe-filled reverence and profound respect], to keep [and actively do] all His statutes and His commandments which I am commanding you, all the days of your life, so that your days may be prolonged.

3"Therefore listen, O Israel, and be careful to do *them*, that it may go well with you and that you may increase greatly [in numbers], as the Lord, the God of your fathers, has promised you, in a land flowing with milk and honey.

4"Hear, O Israel! The Lord is our God, the Lord is one [the only God]!

5"You shall love the Lord your God with all your heart *and* mind and with all your soul and with all your strength [your entire being].

6"These words, which I am commanding you today, shall be [written] on your heart *and* mind.

7"You shall teach them diligently to your children [impressing God's precepts on their minds and penetrating their hearts with His truths] and shall speak of them when you sit in your house and when you walk on the road and when you lie down and when you get up.

8"And you shall bind them as a sign on your hand (forearm), and they shall be used as bands (frontals, frontlets) on your forehead.

9"You shall write them on the doorposts of your house and on your gates.

10"Then it shall come about when the Lord your God brings you into the land which He swore (solemnly promised) to [give] your fathers—to Abraham, Isaac, and Jacob—to give you, [a land with] great and splendid cities which you did not build,

11and houses full of all good things which you did not fill, and hewn (excavated) cisterns (wells) which you did not dig out, and vineyards and olive trees which you did not plant, and you eat and are full *and* satisfied,

12then beware that you do not forget the Lord who brought you out of the land of Egypt, out of the house of slavery.

13"You shall fear [only] the Lord your God; and you shall serve Him [with awe-filled reverence and profound respect] and swear [oaths] by His name [alone].

14"You shall not follow other gods, any of the gods of the peoples who surround you,

15for the Lord your God who is among you is a jealous (impassioned) God [demanding what is rightfully and uniquely His]—otherwise the anger of the Lord your God will be kindled *and* burn against you, and He will destroy you from the face of the earth.

16"You shall not put the Lord your

speak the Word

Thank You, God, that as I am watchful to do Your commandments, things will go well for me and I will increase exceedingly.
—ADAPTED FROM DEUTERONOMY 6:3

God to the test, as you tested Him at Massah. [Ex 17:7]

17"You shall diligently keep [foremost in your thoughts and actively do] the commandments of the LORD your God, and His testimonies and His statutes which He has commanded you.

18"You shall do what is right and good in the sight of the LORD, so that it may be well with you and that you may go in and possess the good land which the LORD swore to [give] your fathers,

19by driving out all your enemies from before you, as the LORD has spoken.

20"When your son asks you in time to come, saying, 'What *is the meaning* of the testimonies and statutes and judgments (precepts) which the LORD our God has commanded you?'

21then you shall say to your son, 'We were Pharaoh's slaves in Egypt, and the LORD brought us out of Egypt with a mighty hand.

22'Moreover, the LORD showed great and terrible signs and wonders before our eyes against Egypt, Pharaoh and all his household;

23He brought us out from there in order to bring us in, to give us the land which He had sworn to [give] our fathers.'

24"So the LORD commanded us to do all these statutes, to fear [and worship] the LORD our God [with awe-filled reverence and profound respect] for our

putting the Word to work

We know from Deuteronomy 6:23 that God "brings us out to take us in." What has God brought you out of in order to take you into something better? Thank Him today!

good always and so that He might preserve us alive, as it is today.

25"It will be [considered] righteousness for us [that is, right standing with God] if we are careful to observe all this commandment before the LORD our God—just as He has commanded us.

7 "WHEN THE LORD your God brings you into the land which you are entering to possess, and has cleared away many nations before you, the Hittite and the Girgashite and the Amorite and the Canaanite and the Perizzite and the Hivite and the Jebusite, seven nations greater and mightier than you,

2and when the LORD your God gives them over to you and you defeat them, then you shall utterly destroy them. You shall not make a covenant (treaty) with them nor show mercy *and* compassion to them.

3"You shall not intermarry with them; you shall not give your daughter to his son, nor shall you take his daughter for your son;

4for they will turn your sons away from following Me to serve other gods; then the anger of the LORD will be kindled *and* burn against you and He will quickly destroy you.

5"But this is how you shall deal with them: you shall tear down their altars and smash to pieces their *sacred* pillars, and cut down their Asherim (symbols of the goddess Asherah), and burn their carved *or* sculpted images in the fire.

6"For you are a holy people [set apart] to the LORD your God; the LORD

speak the Word

Thank You, God, that You have chosen me to be holy, set apart to You, Your very special treasure.
—ADAPTED FROM DEUTERONOMY 7:6

your God has chosen you out of all the peoples on the face of the earth to be a people for His own possession [that is, His very special treasure].

7"The LORD did not love you and choose you because you were greater in number than any of the *other* peoples, for you were the fewest of all peoples.

8"But because the LORD loves you and is keeping the oath which He swore to your fathers, the LORD has brought you out with a mighty hand and redeemed (bought) you from the house of slavery, from the hand of Pharaoh king of Egypt.

9"Therefore know [without any doubt] *and* understand that the LORD your God, He is God, the faithful God, who is keeping His covenant and His [steadfast] lovingkindness to a thousand generations with those who love Him and keep His commandments;

10but repays those who hate Him to their faces, by destroying them; He will not hesitate with him who hates Him, He will repay him to his face.

11"Therefore, you shall keep (follow, obey) the commandment and the statutes and judgments (precepts) which I am commanding you today.

12"Then it shall come about, because you listen to these judgments and keep and do them, that the LORD your God will keep with you the covenant and the [steadfast] lovingkindness which He swore to your fathers.

13"He will love you and bless you and multiply you; He will also bless the fruit of your womb and the fruit of your land, your grain and your new wine and your [olive] oil, the offspring

life point

Just before they entered the Promised Land, the Lord told the Israelites that He would drive out their enemies before them "little by little" (Deuteronomy 7:22), lest the beasts of the field increase among them. I believe pride is one of the "beasts" that will consume us if we receive too much freedom too quickly, and the best way to gain lasting freedom and wholeness is to be liberated one area at a time. That way, we appreciate our freedom more; we realize it is truly a gift from God and not something we can make happen in our own strength. If it seems that freedom is slow in coming to any area of your life, remember that true progress often happens little by little.

of your cattle and the young of your flock, in the land which He swore to your fathers to give you.

14"You shall be blessed above all peoples; there will be no male or female barren (childless, infertile) among you or among your cattle.

15"The LORD will take away from you all sickness; and He will not subject you to any of the harmful diseases of Egypt which you have known, but He will impose them on all [those] who hate you.

16"And you shall consume all the peoples whom the LORD your God will give over to you; your eye shall not pity them, nor shall you serve their gods, for that would be a [deadly] trap to you.

17"If you say in your heart, 'These

speak the Word

God, I know without any doubt and understand that You are the faithful God Who is keeping covenant and steadfast loving-kindness for a thousand generations with those who love You and keep Your commandments.
—ADAPTED FROM DEUTERONOMY 7:9

nations are greater than I am; how can I dispossess them?'

¹⁸you shall not be afraid of them; you shall remember [with confidence] what the LORD your God did to Pharaoh and to all Egypt—

¹⁹the great trials which you saw with your own eyes, and the signs, the wonders, the mighty hand and the outstretched arm by which the LORD

life point

I once went through a difficult and upsetting set of circumstances in my ministry. One week I would have a meeting with a large crowd; the next week only half as many would attend. Satan would say to me, "Well, the people didn't like what you said last week, so they didn't come back." When circumstances conveyed to me I was doing well, my emotions were up. When circumstances indicated I was not doing very well, my emotions were down. The devil had me on the run. Every good experience elated me; every bad circumstance deflated me. (I call this "yo-yo" Christianity.)

One day I said to God, "Why is this happening?" He impressed upon my heart, "I am teaching you that man does not live by bread alone, but by every word that proceeds out of the mouth of the Lord" (see Deuteronomy 8:3). Bread was the daily sustenance for the children of Israel. Bread kept them going. When the Lord spoke to me about bread, He was saying, "I am trying to teach you that you cannot live by all these other things that seem to keep you going. You must look to Me for your daily strength." The same is true for you. I encourage you to seek God first and most of all, instead of seeking what He can do for you.

your God brought you out. So shall the LORD your God do to all the peoples of whom you are afraid.

²⁰"Moreover, the LORD your God will send the hornet (His terror) against them, until those who are left and hide themselves from you perish.

²¹"You shall not dread them, for the LORD your God is in your midst, a great and awesome God.

²²"The LORD your God will clear away these nations before you little by little; you will not be able to put an end to them quickly, for [if you did] the wild animals would become too numerous for you.

²³"But the LORD your God will hand them over to you, and will confuse them with a great panic until they are destroyed.

²⁴"And He will hand over their kings to you, and you will make their name perish from under heaven; no man will be able to stand before you until you have destroyed them.

²⁵"You shall burn the carved *and* sculpted images of their gods in the fire. You shall not covet the silver or gold that is on them, nor take it for yourselves, so that you will not be ensnared by it [in a deadly trap], for it is an abomination (repulsive) to the LORD your God.

²⁶"You shall not bring an abomination (idol) into your house, and like it come under the ban (doomed to destruction); you shall utterly detest and you shall utterly hate it, for it is something banned.

8 "EVERY COMMANDMENT that I am commanding you today you shall be careful to do, so that you may live and multiply, and go in and possess the land which the LORD swore [to give] to your fathers.

²"And you shall remember [always] all the ways which the LORD your God

has led you these forty years in the wilderness, so that He might humble you and test you, to know what was in your heart (mind), whether you would keep His commandments or not.

³"He humbled you and allowed you to be hungry and fed you with manna, [a substance] which you did not know, nor did your fathers know, so that He might make you understand [by personal experience] that man does not live by bread alone, but man lives by every *word* that proceeds out of the mouth of the LORD.

⁴"Your clothing did not wear out on you, nor did your feet swell these forty years.

⁵"Therefore, know in your heart (be fully cognizant) that the LORD your God disciplines *and* instructs you just as a man disciplines *and* instructs his son.

⁶"Therefore, you shall keep the commandments of the LORD your God, to

seek God's presence, not His presents

The Israelites wandered around and around the wilderness, going through the same struggles time and time again. God said He allowed this to teach them the truth of Deuteronomy 8:3: that man does not live by bread alone (worldly things) but by every word that proceeds out of the mouth of God (His promises). God met their basic necessities in the wilderness, but they were a long way from having their desires fulfilled. God wanted them to have abundant life, but first they needed to learn to obey Him and trust Him at all times.

Sooner or later God has to teach us that our true life is in Him, not in anything the world has to offer. It would be great if He could simply tell us that truth and we could believe it, turn our backs on the world, and totally trust Him. It does not happen that way, though. God deals with us and allows us to go through tests and trials so we can learn by experience that doing things His way is the best way. God knows that if we will not serve and worship Him in the hard times of life (the valleys), we will not consistently serve and worship Him in the good times (the mountaintops). He wants to bless us with the desires of our hearts, but He wants to see that He is in first place in our lives at all times.

There is a fine line between serving God because of what He can do for us and serving Him because of Who He is. We can easily be deceived into seeking His hand (His presents) and not seeking His face (His presence) in our lives. We need to seek first the kingdom of God and His righteousness, and then all the other things will be given to us also (see Matthew 6:33).

Are you in a valley? Worship God! Are you on top of the mountain? Worship God! Are all of your needs met? Worship God! Are you in want? Worship God! When all things become the same to you in the light of His glory, He is free to give you all things. Seek His presence, not His presents. Keep God first in your life, and you will be amazed at what He will do for you.

life point

Often, our first impulse when someone disciplines us is to find fault with him or her. Satan tempts us to do this so we will divert the conversation away from the real issue. God disciplines us too, according to Deuteronomy 8:5. Being corrected by God through people in authority, such as employers, parents, or teachers, is something we all encounter throughout our lives. We may not always like the person or source God chooses to bring correction to us, but we are wise to accept good discipline and instruction in order to make progress in our lives.

walk [that is, to live each and every day] in His ways and fear [and worship] Him [with awe-filled reverence and profound respect]. [Prov 8:13]

⁷"For the Lᴏʀᴅ your God is bringing you into a good land, a land of brooks of water, of fountains and springs, flowing forth in valleys and hills;

⁸a land of wheat and barley, and vines and fig trees and pomegranates, a land of olive oil and honey;

⁹a land where you will eat bread without shortage, in which you will lack nothing; a land whose stones are iron, and out of whose hills you can dig copper.

¹⁰"When you have eaten and are satisfied, then you shall bless the Lᴏʀᴅ your God for the good land which He has given you.

¹¹"Beware that you do not forget the Lᴏʀᴅ your God by failing to keep His commandments and His judgments (precepts) and His statutes which I am commanding you today;

¹²otherwise, when you have eaten and are satisfied, and have built good houses and lived *in them,*

¹³and when your herds and flocks multiply, and your silver and gold multiply, and all that you have increases,

¹⁴then your heart will become lifted up [by self-conceit and arrogance] and you will forget the Lᴏʀᴅ your God who brought you from the land of Egypt, out of the house of slavery.

¹⁵"He led you through the great and terrible wilderness, *with its* fiery serpents and scorpions and thirsty ground where there was no water; it was He who brought water for you out of the flinty rock.

¹⁶"He fed you manna in the wilderness, [a substance] which your fathers did not know, so that He might humble you [by dependence on Him] and that He might test you, to do good [things] for you at the end.

¹⁷"Otherwise, you may say in your heart, 'My power and the strength of my hand made me this wealth.'

¹⁸"But you shall remember [with profound respect] the Lᴏʀᴅ your God, for it is He who is giving you power to make wealth, that He may confirm His covenant which He swore (solemnly promised) to your fathers, as it is this day.

¹⁹"And it shall come about if you ever forget the Lᴏʀᴅ your God and follow other gods and serve them and worship them, I testify against you today that you will most certainly perish.

life point

Apart from God, we really are powerless. Our joy must be in Him, our peace must be in Him, our achievements come through Him, and our abilities are the results of His grace. Take the advice of Deuteronomy 8:17, and do not let your mind and heart try to convince you that your own power and the strength of your hands profit anything. It's all God!

[20]"Like the nations which the LORD causes to perish before you, so shall you perish; because you would not listen to *and* obey the voice of the LORD your God.

life point

Many people believe and act on the biblical principles of tithing and giving offerings, yet they never seem to be able to leave what I call the "land of even." Though their basic needs are met, they are living from paycheck to paycheck. They never get ahead; they simply break even. They live "little lives" and miss the joy-filled, fruitful, peaceful, and abundant lives that God has for them.

God's Word clearly teaches that He desires for us to live in the "land of plenty" (see Deuteronomy 8:7–9). God brought the Israelites out of the land of *lack*, through the land of *even*, and into the land of *plenty*. He wanted every one of the Israelites to live in abundance, but, sadly, only two of the original Israelites who came out of Egypt actually crossed over the Jordan and lived in the land of promise, the land of plenty.

The same situation appears in every generation. Only a few people enter into the best God has provided for them through Jesus Christ, while the majority barely get by and have little joy or peace. They struggle and struggle, hearing about a better land but not understanding why they cannot take up residence there.

Be one who makes it all the way to the Promised Land. Remember that God has abundance for you, and determine to live the good life that God prearranged for you to live (see Ephesians 2:10).

9 "HEAR, O Israel! You are crossing the Jordan today to go in to dispossess nations greater and more powerful than you, great cities fortified to heaven,

[2]a people great and tall, sons of Anakim, whom you know and of whom you have heard *it said,* 'Who can stand before the sons of Anak?'

[3]"So know today [with confident assurance] that the LORD your God is crossing [the Jordan] before you like a devouring fire. He will destroy them and He will subdue them before you, and you shall drive them out and destroy them quickly, just as the LORD has promised you.

[4]"Do not say in your heart when the LORD your God has driven them out before you, 'Because of my righteousness the LORD has brought me in to possess this land,' but because of the wickedness of these nations the LORD is dispossessing them before you.

[5]"It is not for your righteousness or for the uprightness of your heart that you are going to possess their land, but because of the wickedness of these nations the LORD your God is driving them out before you, and to confirm the oath which the LORD swore to your fathers, to Abraham, Isaac, and Jacob.

[6]"Know [without any doubt], that the LORD your God is not giving you this good land to possess because of your righteousness, for you are a stiff-necked (stubborn, obstinate) people.

[7]"Remember [with remorse] and do not forget how you provoked the LORD your God to wrath in the wilderness; from the day you left the land of Egypt until you arrived in this place, you have been rebellious against the LORD.

[8]"And at Horeb (Sinai) you provoked the LORD to wrath, and the LORD was so angry with you that He would have destroyed you.

[9]"When I went up the mountain to receive the tablets of stone, the tablets

of the covenant which the Lord made with you, I remained on the mountain forty days and forty nights; I did not eat food or drink water.

¹⁰"The Lord gave me the two tablets of stone written with the finger of God; and on them *were written* all the words which the Lord had spoken to you at the mountain from the midst of the fire on the day of the assembly.

¹¹"It came about at the end of forty days and forty nights that the Lord gave me the two tablets of stone, the tablets of the covenant.

¹²"Then the Lord said to me, 'Arise, go down from here quickly, for your people whom you brought from Egypt have acted corruptly. They have quickly turned aside from the way which I commanded them; they have made (cast) a molten image for themselves.'

¹³"Furthermore, the Lord said to me, 'I have seen this people, and indeed, they are stiff-necked (stubborn, obstinate) people.

¹⁴'Let Me alone, so that I may destroy them and wipe out their name from under heaven; and I will make of you a nation mightier and greater than they.'

¹⁵"So I turned and came down from the mountain while the mountain was burning with fire, and the two tablets of the covenant were in my two hands.

¹⁶"And I saw that you had indeed sinned against the Lord your God. You had made for yourselves a molten calf (idol). You had turned aside quickly from the way which the Lord had commanded you. [Ex 32:1–10]

¹⁷"So I took hold of the two tablets and threw them from my two hands and smashed them before your very eyes!

¹⁸"Then, as before, I fell down before the Lord for [another] forty days and forty nights; I did not eat food or drink water, because of all the sin you had committed by doing what was evil in the sight of the Lord to provoke Him to anger.

¹⁹"For I was afraid of the anger and absolute fury which the Lord held against you, [enough divine fury] to destroy you, but the Lord listened to me that time also.

²⁰"The Lord was very angry with Aaron, angry [enough] to destroy him, so I also prayed for Aaron at the same time.

²¹"I took your sinful *thing,* the calf which you had made, and burned it in the fire and thoroughly crushed it, grinding the metal thoroughly until it was as fine as dust; and I threw its dust into the brook that came down from the mountain.

²²"At Taberah also and at Massah and at Kibroth-hattaavah you provoked the Lord to wrath.

²³"And when the Lord sent you from Kadesh-barnea, saying, 'Go up and take possession of the land which I have given you,' then you rebelled against the command of the Lord your God, and you did not believe *and* rely on Him, nor did you obey His voice.

²⁴"You have been rebellious against the Lord from the [first] day that I knew you.

²⁵"So I fell down *and* lay face down before the Lord forty days and nights because the Lord had said He would destroy you.

²⁶"Then I prayed to the Lord and said, 'O Lord God, do not destroy Your people, even Your inheritance, whom You have redeemed through Your greatness, whom You have brought from Egypt with a mighty hand.

²⁷'Remember [with compassion] Your servants, Abraham, Isaac, and Jacob; do not look at the stubbornness of this people or at their wickedness or at their sin,

²⁸so that the [people of the] land from which You brought us will not say, "Because the Lord was not capable of bringing them into the land which He had promised them and because He hated them He has brought them

out to the wilderness [in order] to kill them."

²⁹'Yet they are Your people and Your inheritance, whom You have brought out by Your great power and by Your outstretched arm.'

10 "AT THAT time the LORD said to me, 'Cut out for yourself two tablets of stone like the first, and come up to Me on the mountain, and make an ark (chest) of wood for yourself.

²'I will write on the tablets the words that were on the first tablets which you shattered, and you shall put them in the ark.'

³"So I made an ark of acacia wood and cut out two tablets of stone like the first, and went up the mountain with the two tablets in my hand.

⁴"The LORD wrote on the tablets, like the first writing, the Ten Commandments which the LORD had spoken to you on the mountain from the midst of the fire on the day of the assembly; then the LORD gave them to me.

⁵"Then I turned and came down from the mountain and put the tablets in the ark which I had made; and they are there, just as the LORD commanded me."

⁶(Now the sons of Israel traveled from the wells of the sons of Jaakan to Moserah. There Aaron died and there he was buried and Eleazar his son ministered as priest in his place.

⁷From there they traveled to Gudgodah, and from Gudgodah to Jotbathah, a land of brooks of water.

⁸At that time the LORD set apart the tribe of Levi to carry the ark of the

putting the Word to work

Deuteronomy 10:16 instructs us not to be stubborn or obstinate. Is there any stubbornness or hardness in your heart or in your mind? Confess your sin in these areas and ask for God's help.

covenant of the LORD, to stand before the LORD to serve Him and to bless in His name until this day.

⁹Therefore, Levi does not have a portion or inheritance [of tribal land] with his brothers; the LORD is his inheritance, as the LORD your God has promised him.)

¹⁰"And I stayed on the mountain, like the first time, forty days and nights, and the LORD listened to me at that time also; the LORD was not willing to destroy you.

¹¹"Then the LORD said to me, 'Arise, go on your journey ahead of the people, so that they may go in and take possession of the land which I swore to their fathers to give to them.'

¹²"And now, Israel, what does the LORD your God require from you, but to fear [and worship] the LORD your God [with awe-filled reverence and profound respect], to walk [that is, to live each and every day] in all His ways and to love Him, and to serve the LORD your God with all your heart and with all your soul [your choices, your thoughts, your whole being],

¹³and to keep the commandments of the LORD and His statutes which I am commanding you today for your good?

¹⁴"Behold, the heavens and the highest of heavens belong to the LORD your God, the earth and all that is in it.

speak the Word

Help me, God, to fear and worship You, to walk in all Your ways, to love You, and to serve You with all my mind and with all my soul—my choices, my thoughts, my entire being.
—ADAPTED FROM DEUTERONOMY 10:12, 13

¹⁵"Yet the LORD had a delight in loving your fathers *and* set His affection on them, and He chose their descendants after them, you above all peoples, as it is this day.

¹⁶"So circumcise [that is, remove sin from] your heart, and be stiff-necked (stubborn, obstinate) no longer.

¹⁷"For the LORD your God is the God of gods and the Lord of lords, the great, the mighty, the awesome God who does not show partiality nor take a bribe.

life point

There are many things that can become "gods" to us and we are not to turn our hearts toward them (see Deuteronomy 11:16, 17). Even a ministry can become a god if we let it become more important than God Himself. We must never forget that it is the Lord Who places the vision for ministry in our hearts. It is He Who calls us and gives us the desire to minister. He must always have the first and most preeminent place in our lives. Putting the things with which He blesses us before Him is offensive to Him.

We are not going to experience the blessings God desires for us if our hearts are not right before Him. Sometimes we erroneously blame the devil for our lack of blessing; we think everything would be just fine if the devil would just leave us alone. That is not so. We have it backward. If we would live right, then the door into our lives would be closed to the devil. He might pester us, but he would have no real power over us, just as he had no real power over Jesus. Let nothing stand between you and God. Put Him first, and you will be blessed.

11:4 Lit *Sea of Reeds.*

¹⁸"He executes justice for the orphan and the widow, and shows His love for the stranger (resident alien, foreigner) by giving him food and clothing.

¹⁹"Therefore, show your love for the stranger, for you were strangers in the land of Egypt.

²⁰"You shall fear [and worship] the LORD your God [with awe-filled reverence and profound respect]; you shall serve Him and cling to Him [hold tightly to Him, be united with Him], and you shall swear [oaths] by His name.

²¹"He is your praise *and* glory; He is your God, who has done for you these great and awesome things which you have seen with your own eyes.

²²"Your fathers went down to Egypt, seventy persons [in all], and now the LORD your God has made you as numerous as the stars of heaven.

11 "THEREFORE YOU shall love the LORD your God, and always keep His charge, His statutes, His precepts, and His commandments [it is your obligation to Him].

²"Know this day that I am not *speaking* to your children who have not known [by personal experience] and who have not seen [firsthand] the instruction *and* discipline of the LORD your God—His greatness, His mighty hand and His outstretched arm;

³and His signs and His works which He did in the midst of Egypt to Pharaoh the king of Egypt and to all his land;

⁴and what He did to the army of Egypt, to its horses and its chariots, when He made the water of the *Red Sea engulf them as they pursued you, and how the LORD completely destroyed them;

⁵and what He did to you in the wilderness until you came to this place;

⁶and what He did to Dathan and

Abiram, the sons of Eliab, the son of Reuben, when the earth opened its mouth and swallowed them, their households, their tents, and every living thing that followed them, in the midst of all Israel. [Num 26:9, 10]

⁷"For your eyes have seen all the great work of the LORD which He did.

⁸"Therefore, you shall keep all the commandments which I am commanding you today, so that you may be strong and go in and take possession of the land which you are crossing over [the Jordan] to possess;

⁹so that you may live long on the land which the LORD swore (solemnly

defeating deception

In Deuteronomy 11:18–21 God told the people to write His words on the doors of their houses, on their gates, on their foreheads, and on their hands. They were to let the Word permeate their entire being, whether they were sitting, lying down, or walking around. Why did God say to do all this? Because He is aware that knowing the Word keeps a person from having a deceived heart. This is what Jesus taught in John 8:31, 32 when He said: "If you abide in My word [continually obeying My teachings and living in accordance with them, then] you are truly My disciples. And you will know the truth [regarding salvation], and the truth will set you free [from the penalty of sin]."

If we do not really care enough about the Word of God to abide in it, we are going to be in for trouble in these last days in which we live. Religious fluff is not going to be enough to get us through; we have to be deeply serious about learning the Word. When we know the Word, God will protect us and keep us. If we do not, we will be sucked up into deception. Simply stated, deception happens when we believe a lie, and Satan lies to us continually. Without a thorough knowledge of God's Word, we do not even recognize the lies.

Some people deceive themselves by reasoning contrary to God's truth. Earlier in my life, before I learned how to really surrender to the will of God, He sometimes impressed me to give something away I wanted to keep, or to do something I did not want to do. I learned from making mistakes that it was very easy to deceive myself when God asked for something I did not want to release.

We make all kinds of excuses to keep ourselves from doing what God asks of us. Sometimes we pretend, "Well, it must not have been God dealing with me about that. It probably was just my imagination or the devil trying to make me miserable by asking for what's precious to me." We can quickly become "spiritually deaf" to the voice of God when He says something we really do not want to hear.

A deceived heart will not do for Christian leaders or for anyone who intends to be victorious in life. We should be diligent to root out any areas of our lives where we are susceptible to deception. We need to live openly and honestly, abiding in the light of God's truth as He reveals it in His Word.

promised) to your fathers to give to them and to their descendants, a land [of great abundance,] flowing with milk and honey.

¹⁰"For the land which you are entering to possess is not like the land of Egypt from which you have come, where you sowed your seed and watered it with your foot like a garden of vegetables.

¹¹"But the land into which you are about to cross to possess, a land of hills and valleys, drinks water from the rain of heaven,

life point

God has given us the power of choice. We must choose one way or the other, and whatever pathway we choose will lead to a specific destination (see Deuteronomy 11:26–28). If we choose disobedience, we end up with curses and every kind of misery; but if we choose life, we are blessed. I often wonder why anyone would choose to be miserable when we could be blessed; yet multitudes do just that.

We have an enemy, Satan, who tells us we can do what is wrong and still have good lives, but we have to remember that God's Word tells us he is a liar. Satan told Eve the same lie in the Garden of Eden, and that is where our troubles began. I strongly encourage you to make right choices. Do not procrastinate or delay, because that is one of Satan's favorite ways to deceive us. We intend to do what is right, but say we are not ready just yet. We live as if tomorrow will never come, but it always does. I believe wisdom is choosing to do now what we will be satisfied with later. Remember, we always reap what we have sown. Make a decision to keep God's commands and open the door to the blessed life He wants to give you.

¹²a land for which the LORD your God cares; the eyes of the LORD your God are always on it, from the beginning of the year to the end of the year.

¹³"It shall come about, if you listen obediently *and* pay attention to My commandments which I command you today—to love the LORD your God and to serve Him with all your heart and with all your soul [your choices, your thoughts, your whole being]—

¹⁴that He will give the rain for your land in its season, the early [fall] rain and the late [spring] rain, so that you may gather in your grain and your new wine and your [olive] oil.

¹⁵"And He will give grass in your fields for your cattle, and you will eat and be satisfied.

¹⁶"Beware that your hearts are not deceived, and that you do not turn away [from the LORD] and serve other gods and worship them,

¹⁷or [else] the LORD's anger will be kindled *and* burn against you, and He will shut up the heavens so that there will be no rain and the land will not yield its fruit; and you will perish quickly from the good land which the LORD is giving you.

¹⁸"Therefore, you shall impress these words of mine on your heart and on your soul, and tie them as a sign on your hand, and they shall be as bands (frontals, frontlets) on your forehead.

¹⁹"You shall teach them [diligently] to your children [impressing God's precepts on their minds and penetrating their hearts with His truths], speaking of them when you sit in your house and when you walk along the road and when you lie down and when you rise up.

²⁰"You shall write them on the doorposts of your house and on your gates,

²¹so that your days and the days of your children may be multiplied in the land which the LORD swore to your

fathers to give them, as long as the heavens are above the earth.

²²"For if you are careful to keep all this commandment which I am commanding you to do, to love the Lord your God, to walk [that is, to live each and every day] in all His ways and to hold tightly to Him—

²³then the Lord will drive out all these nations from before you, and you shall dispossess nations greater and mightier than you.

²⁴"Every place on which the sole of your foot treads shall become yours; your territory shall be from the wilderness to Lebanon, and from the river, the river Euphrates, as far as the western sea (the Mediterranean).

²⁵"No man will be able to stand before you; the Lord your God will lay the fear and the dread of you on all the land on which you set foot, just as He has spoken to you.

²⁶"Behold, today I am setting before you a blessing and a curse—

²⁷the blessing, if you listen to *and* obey the commandments of the Lord your God, which I am commanding you today;

²⁸and the curse, if you do not listen to *and* obey the commandments of the Lord your God, but turn aside from the way which I am commanding you today, by following (acknowledging, worshiping) other gods which you have not known.

²⁹"It shall come about, when the Lord your God brings you into the land which you are entering to possess, that you shall place the blessing on Mount Gerizim and the curse on Mount Ebal. [Josh 8:30–35]

³⁰"Are they not across the Jordan, west of the road, toward the sunset, in the land of the Canaanites who live in the Arabah, opposite Gilgal, beside the oaks of Moreh?

³¹"For you are about to cross the Jordan to go in to possess the land which the Lord your God is giving you, and you shall possess it and live in it,

³²and you shall be careful to do all the statutes and the judgments which I am setting before you today.

12

"THESE ARE the statutes and judgments (precepts) which you shall be careful to do in the land which the Lord, the God of your fathers, has given you to possess as long as you live on the earth.

²"You shall utterly destroy all the places where the nations whom you shall dispossess serve their gods, on the high mountains and the hills and under every green [leafy] tree.

³"You shall tear down their altars and smash their [idolatrous] pillars and burn their Asherim in the fire; you shall cut down the carved *and* sculpted images of their gods and obliterate their name from that place.

⁴"You shall not act like this toward the Lord your God.

⁵"But you shall seek *the Lord* at the place which the Lord your God will choose out of all your tribes to establish His Name there for His dwelling [place], and there you shall come [to worship Him].

⁶"There you shall bring your burnt offerings, your sacrifices, your tithes, the contribution of your hand, your votive (pledged, vowed) offerings, your freewill (voluntary) offerings, and the firstborn of your herd and of your flock.

⁷"And there you and your households shall eat before the Lord your God, and rejoice in all to which you put your hand, in which the Lord your God has blessed you.

⁸"You shall not do at all what we are doing here [in the camp] today, every man doing whatever is right in his [own] eyes.

⁹"For you have not yet come to the

resting place and to the inheritance which the LORD your God is giving you.

¹⁰"When you cross the Jordan and live in the land which the LORD your God is giving you to inherit, and He gives you rest from all your enemies around you so that you live in security,

¹¹then it shall come about that the place which the LORD your God will choose for His Name [and Presence] to dwell; there you shall bring everything that I am commanding you: your burnt offerings, your sacrifices, your tithes and the [voluntary] contribution of your hand [as a first gift from the fruits of the ground], and all your choice votive offerings which you vow to the LORD.

¹²"And you shall rejoice before the LORD your God, you and your sons and your daughters, and your male and female servants, and the Levite who is within your [city] gates, since he has no portion or inheritance with you.

¹³"Be careful that you do not offer your burnt offerings in every [cultic] place you see,

¹⁴but [only] in the place which the LORD will choose in one of your tribes, there you shall offer your burnt offerings, and there you shall do everything that I am commanding you.

¹⁵"However, you may slaughter and eat meat within any of your [city] gates, whatever you wish, according to the blessing of the LORD your God which He has given you [as His generous provision for daily life]. The [ceremonially] unclean and the clean may eat it, such as the gazelle and the deer.

¹⁶"Only you shall not eat the blood; you are to pour it out on the ground like water.

¹⁷"You are forbidden to eat within your [city] gates the tithe of your grain or new wine or oil, or the firstborn of your herd or flock, or any of your votive offerings, or your freewill offerings, or the contribution of your hand.

life point

Deuteronomy 13:4 commands us to obey God. Obedience keeps us from defiling our consciences and empowers us to live for God's glory.

¹⁸"But you shall eat them before the LORD your God in the place which the LORD your God will choose, you and your son and your daughter, and your male and female servants, and the Levite who is within your [city] gates; and you shall rejoice before the LORD your God in all that you undertake.

¹⁹"Be careful that you do not neglect the Levite [who serves God] as long as you live in your land.

²⁰"When the LORD your God extends your territory, as He promised you, and you say, 'I will eat meat,' because you want to eat meat, then you may eat meat, whatever you wish.

²¹"If the place which the LORD your God chooses to put His Name (Presence) is too far away from you, then you may slaughter [animals] from your herd or flock which the LORD has given you, just as I have commanded you; and you may eat within your [city] gates whatever you wish.

²²"Just as the gazelle or the deer is eaten, so you may eat it [but not make it an offering]; the [ceremonially] unclean and the clean alike may eat it.

²³"Only be sure that you do not eat the blood, for the blood is the life (soul), and you shall not eat the life with the meat.

²⁴"You shall not eat it; you shall pour it out on the ground like water.

²⁵"You shall not eat it, so that all may be well with you and with your children after you, because you will be doing what is right in the sight of the LORD.

²⁶"However, you shall take your holy things which you have [to offer] and

your votive (pledged, vowed) offerings, you shall take *them* and go to the place which the Lord will choose.

27"And you shall offer your burnt offerings, the meat and the blood, on the altar of the Lord your God; and the blood of your sacrifices shall be poured out on the altar of the Lord your God, and you shall eat the meat.

28"Be careful to listen to all these words which I am commanding you, so that it may be well with you and with your children after you forever, because you will be doing what is good and right in the sight of the Lord your God.

29"When the Lord your God cuts off *and* destroys before you the nations which you are going in to dispossess, and you dispossess them and settle in their land,

30beware that you are not lured (ensnared) into following them, after they have been destroyed before you, and that you do not inquire about their gods, saying, 'How did these nations serve their gods, so that I too may do likewise?'

31"You shall not behave this way toward the Lord your God, for they have done for their gods every repulsive thing which the Lord hates; for they even burn their sons and their daughters in the fire [as sacrifices] to their gods.

32"Everything I command you, you shall be careful to do it; you shall not add to it nor take away from it.

13 "IF A prophet arises among you, or a dreamer of dreams, and gives you a sign or a wonder,

2and the sign or the wonder which he spoke (foretold) to you comes to pass, and if he says, 'Let us follow after other gods (whom you have not known) and let us serve *and* worship them,'

3you shall not listen to the words of that prophet or that dreamer of dreams;

for the Lord your God is testing you to know whether you love the Lord your God with all your heart *and* mind and all your soul [your entire being].

4"You shall walk after the Lord your God and you shall fear [and worship] Him [with awe-filled reverence and profound respect], and you shall keep His commandments and you shall listen to His voice, and you shall serve Him, and cling to Him.

5"But that prophet or that dreamer of dreams shall be put to death, because he has counseled rebellion against the Lord your God who brought you from the land of Egypt and redeemed you from the house of slavery, to draw you away from the way in which the Lord your God has commanded you to walk. So you shall remove the evil from among you.

6"If your brother, the son of your mother, or your son or daughter, or the wife you cherish, or your friend who is as [precious to you as] your own life (soul), entices you secretly, saying, 'Let us go and serve other gods' (*gods* whom neither you nor your fathers have known,

7of the gods of the peoples who are around you, near you or far from you, from one end of the earth to the other),

8you shall not consent to him or listen to him; and your eye shall not pity him, nor shall you spare him or conceal him.

9"Instead, you shall most certainly execute him; your hand shall be first [to be raised] against him to put him to death, and afterwards the hand of all the people.

10"So you shall stone him to death with stones, because he has tried to draw you away from the Lord your God who brought you from the land of Egypt, from the house of slavery.

11"Then all Israel will hear and be afraid, and will never again do such a wicked thing among you.

¹²"If you hear [it said] in one of your cities, which the Lord your God gives you to live in,

¹³that some worthless *and* evil men have gone out from among you and have tempted the inhabitants of their city [to sin], saying, 'Let us go and serve other gods' (whom you have not known),

¹⁴then you shall investigate and search out [witnesses] and ask thorough *questions*. If it is true and the matter is established that this loathsome thing has been done among you,

¹⁵you shall most certainly strike the inhabitants of that city with the edge of the sword, utterly destroying it and all that is in it, even its livestock with the edge of the sword.

¹⁶"Then you shall collect all its spoil (plunder) into the middle of its open square and burn the city and set fire to the spoil as a whole burnt offering to the Lord your God. It shall be a ruin forever. It shall not be built again.

¹⁷"Nothing from that which is put under the ban (designated for destruction) shall cling to your hand, so that the Lord may turn away from His burning anger and show mercy to you, and have compassion on you and make you increase, just as He swore to your fathers,

¹⁸because you have listened to *and* obeyed the voice of the Lord your God, keeping all His commandments which I am commanding you today, and doing what is right in the eyes of the Lord your God.

14 "YOU ARE the sons of the Lord your God; you shall not cut yourselves nor shave your forehead for the sake of the dead,

²for you are a holy people [set apart] to the Lord your God; and the Lord has chosen you out of all the peoples who are on the earth to be a people for His own possession.

³"You shall not eat anything that is detestable [to the Lord and forbidden by Him].

⁴"These are the animals that you may eat: the ox, the sheep, the goat,

⁵the deer, the gazelle, the roebuck, the wild goat, the ibex, the antelope and the mountain sheep.

⁶"Among the animals, you may eat any animal that has the divided hoof [that is, a hoof] split into two parts [especially at its distal extremity] and that chews the cud.

⁷"However, you are not to eat any of these [animals] among those which chew the cud, or among those that divide the hoof in two: the camel, the hare and the shaphan, for though they chew the cud, they do not split the hoof; they are unclean for you.

⁸"The swine, because it has a divided hoof but *does* not *chew* the cud; it is unclean for you. You shall not eat their meat nor touch their carcasses.

⁹"Of all [creatures] that are in the waters, you may eat these: anything that has fins and scales you may eat,

¹⁰but you may not eat anything that does not have fins and scales; it is unclean for you.

¹¹"You may eat any clean bird.

¹²"But these are the ones which you shall not eat: the eagle, the vulture, and the black buzzard,

¹³and the red kite, the falcon, and the birds of prey of any variety,

¹⁴and every raven of any variety,

¹⁵and the ostrich, the owl, the seagull, the hawk of any variety,

¹⁶the little owl, the great owl, the long-eared owl,

¹⁷the pelican, the carrion vulture, the cormorant,

¹⁸the stork, and the heron of any variety, and the hoopoe, and the bat.

¹⁹"And all flying insects are unclean for you; they shall not be eaten.

²⁰"You may eat any clean bird.

²¹"You shall not eat anything that dies *on its own*. You may give it to the stranger (resident alien, foreigner)

who is in your [city] gates, so that he may eat it, or you may sell it to a foreigner [since they are not under God's law], but you are a people holy (set apart) to the LORD your God. You shall not boil a young goat *or* a lamb in its mother's milk.

²²"Every year you shall certainly tithe [a tenth] of all the yield of your seed which is produced by your field.

²³"You shall eat the tithe (tenth) of your grain, your new wine, your oil, and the firstborn of your herd and your flock before the LORD your God in the place where He chooses to establish His Name (Presence), so that you may learn to fear [and worship] the LORD your God [with awe-filled reverence and profound respect] always.

²⁴"If the place where the LORD your God chooses to set His Name (Presence) is a great distance from you and you are not able to carry *your tithe,* because the LORD your God has blessed you [with such an abundance],

²⁵then you shall exchange *your tithe* for money, and take the money in your hand and go to the place [of worship] which the LORD your God chooses.

²⁶"You may spend the money for anything your heart desires: for oxen, or sheep, or wine, or [other] strong drink, or anything else you want. You shall eat there in the presence of the LORD your God and rejoice, you and your household.

²⁷"Also you shall not neglect the Levite who is within your [city] gates, for he does not have a share [of land] or an inheritance among you.

²⁸"At the end of every third year you shall bring out all the tithe of your

putting the Word to work

God commands us in Deuteronomy 15:11 to "freely open" our hands to those who are less fortunate than we are. In what ways can you be more generous or more attentive to the poor and needy people around you?

produce for that year, and shall store it up within your [city] gates.

²⁹"The Levite, because he has no share [of land] or an inheritance among you, and the stranger, and the orphan and the widow who are within your [city] gates, shall come and eat and be satisfied, so that the LORD your God may bless you in all the work of your hands.

15 "AT THE end of every seven years you shall grant a release (remission, pardon) *from debt.*

²"This is the regulation for the release: every creditor shall forgive what he has loaned to his neighbor; he shall not require repayment from his neighbor and his brother, because the LORD's release has been proclaimed.

³"You may require repayment from a foreigner, but whatever of yours is with your brother [Israelite] your hand shall release.

⁴"However, there will be no poor among you, since the LORD will most certainly bless you in the land which the LORD your God is giving you as an inheritance to possess,

⁵if only you will listen to *and* obey the voice of the LORD your God, to observe

speak the Word

God, help me to always open my hands wide to the poor and give to those in need.
–ADAPTED FROM DEUTERONOMY 15:8

carefully all these commandments which I am commanding you today.

⁶"When the LORD your God blesses you as He has promised you, then you will lend to many nations, but you will not borrow; and you will rule over many nations, but they will not rule over you.

⁷"If there is a poor man among you, one of your fellow Israelites, in any of your cities in the land that the LORD your God is giving you, you shall not be heartless, nor close-fisted with your poor brother;

⁸but you shall freely open your hand to him, and shall generously lend to him whatever he needs.

⁹"Beware that there is no wicked thought in your heart, saying, 'The seventh year, the year of release (remission, pardon), is approaching,' and your eye is hostile (unsympathetic) toward your poor brother, and you give him nothing [since he would not have to repay you]; for he may cry out to the LORD against you, and it will become a sin for you.

¹⁰"You shall freely *and* generously give to him, and your heart shall not be resentful when you give to him, because for this [generous] thing the LORD your God will bless you in all your work and in all your undertakings.

¹¹"For the poor will never cease to be in the land; therefore I command you, saying, 'You shall freely open your hand to your brother, to your needy, and to your poor in your land.'

¹²"If your fellow Israelite, a Hebrew man or woman, is sold to you, and serves you for six years, then in the seventh year you shall set him free [from your service].

¹³"When you set him free, you shall not let him go away empty-handed.

¹⁴"You shall give him generous provisions from your flock, from your threshing floor and from your wine press; you shall give to him as the LORD your God has blessed you.

¹⁵"And you shall remember *and* thoughtfully consider that you were [once] a slave in the land of Egypt, and the LORD your God redeemed you; therefore, I am commanding you these things today.

¹⁶"Now if the servant says to you, 'I will not leave you,' because he loves you and your household, since he is doing well with you;

¹⁷then take an awl and pierce it through his ear into the door, and he shall [willingly] be your servant always. Also you shall do the same for your maidservant. [Ex 21:6]

¹⁸"It shall not seem hard to you when you set him free, for he has served you six years *with* double the service of a hired man; so the LORD your God will bless you in everything you do.

¹⁹"You shall consecrate (set apart) to the LORD your God all the firstborn males that are born of your herd and flock. You shall not work with the firstborn of your herd, nor shear the firstborn of your flock.

²⁰"You and your household shall eat it every year before the LORD your God in the place [for worship] which the LORD chooses.

²¹"But if it has any defect *or* injury, *such as* lameness or blindness, or any serious defect, you shall not sacrifice it to the LORD your God.

²²"You shall eat it within your [city] gates; the [ceremonially] unclean and the clean alike *may eat it*, as [if it were] a gazelle or a deer.

²³"Only you shall not eat its blood; you are to pour it out on the ground like water.

16 "OBSERVE THE month of Abib and celebrate the Passover to the LORD your God, for in the month of Abib the LORD your God brought you out of Egypt by night.

²"You shall sacrifice the Passover [lamb] to the Lord your God from the flock or the herd, in the place where the Lord chooses to establish His Name (Presence).

³"You shall not eat leavened bread with it; *instead,* for seven days you shall eat the Passover with unleavened bread, the bread of affliction (for you left the land of Egypt in haste); [do this] so that all the days of your life you may remember [thoughtfully] the day when you came out of the land of Egypt.

⁴"For seven days no leaven shall be seen with you in all your territory, and none of the meat which you sacrificed the evening of the first day shall remain overnight until morning.

⁵"You are not allowed to sacrifice the Passover [lamb] in any of your cities which the Lord your God is giving you;

⁶but at the place where the Lord your God chooses to establish His Name (Presence), you shall sacrifice the Passover [lamb] in the evening at sunset, at the time that you came out of Egypt.

⁷"You shall cook and eat it in the place which the Lord your God chooses. In the morning you are to return to your tents.

⁸"For six days you shall eat unleavened bread, and on the seventh day there shall be a celebration to the Lord your God; so you shall do no work [on that day].

⁹"You shall count seven weeks for yourself; you shall begin to count seven weeks from the time you first put the sickle to the standing grain.

¹⁰"Then you shall celebrate the Feast of Weeks to the Lord your God with a tribute of a freewill offering from your hand, which you shall give [to Him] just as the Lord your God blesses you;

¹¹and you shall rejoice before the Lord your God, you and your son and your daughter and your male and female servants and the Levite who is within your [city] gates, and the stranger and the orphan and the widow who are among you, at the place where the Lord your God chooses to establish His Name (Presence).

¹²"You shall remember that you were a slave in Egypt, and you shall be careful to obey these statutes.

¹³"You shall celebrate the Feast of Booths (Tabernacles) seven days, when you have gathered in [the grain] from your threshing floor and [the wine] from your wine vat.

¹⁴"You shall rejoice in your feast, you and your son and your daughter and your male and female servants and the Levite and the stranger and the orphan and the widow who are within your city.

¹⁵"Seven days you shall celebrate a feast to the Lord your God in the place which the Lord chooses, because the Lord your God will bless you in all your produce and in all the work of your hands, so that you will be altogether joyful.

¹⁶"Three times a year all your males shall appear before the Lord your God in the place which He chooses, at the Feast of Unleavened Bread (Passover) and at the Feast of Weeks (Pentecost) and at the Feast of Booths (Tabernacles), and they shall not appear before the Lord empty-handed.

¹⁷"Every man shall give as he is able, in accordance with the blessing which the Lord your God has given you.

¹⁸"You shall appoint judges and officers in all your cities (gates) which the Lord your God is giving you, according to your tribes, and they shall judge the people with righteous judgment.

¹⁹"You shall not distort justice; you shall not be partial, and you shall not take a bribe, for a bribe blinds the eyes of the wise and perverts the words of the righteous.

²⁰"You shall pursue justice, *and only* justice [that which is uncompromisingly

righteous], so that you may live and take possession of the land which the Lᴏʀᴅ your God is giving you.

²¹"You shall not plant for yourself an Asherah of any kind of tree *or* wood beside the altar of the Lᴏʀᴅ your God, which you shall make.

²²"You shall not set up for yourself a *sacred* pillar which the Lᴏʀᴅ your God hates.

presumption kills

In Old Testament days, God dealt differently with His people than He does now. I am so glad to be living under the dispensation of grace. But if we look at how God dealt with sin under the Old Covenant, we can see how serious it is and be warned not to wink at it or to be passive about eliminating it from our lives. We are being presumptuous if we think that we can purposely sin and get by with it.

In Deuteronomy 17:12, 13, God was telling His people that if one of their leaders acted presumptuously, he was to be killed. This was because leaders communicate through their actions that whatever they do is acceptable for everyone. But God is saying to us, "I will not let a presumptuous leader get by with wrong behavior, because if I do, everyone is going to think it is all right to act the same way." That is exactly why we must keep right heart attitudes if we want God to continue to use us. Leadership carries with it great responsibility. Ministry is more than standing up in front of people and exercising spiritual gifts. We must live our lives with integrity behind the scenes, and that involves living without presumption. It means we do what is right when nobody but God can see us.

Why is it so important to be on guard against presumption? Presumption causes disrespect and a rebellious attitude toward authority. Presumptuous people think they do not have to listen to those who have been placed in authority over them. Often they are overconfident in their arrogance and unreasonably bold. Presumptuous people talk when they should be quiet. They try to dictate direction to those from whom they should be receiving counsel. They give orders when they should be taking orders. They do things without asking permission. They assume things instead of asking. They think they can make wrong choices and get right results, which does not work because it goes against God's principles.

Presumption is a big problem that comes from a wrong heart, as we learn from 2 Peter 2:10–11, which tells of "those who indulge in the corrupt passions of the sin nature and despise authority. Presumptuous and reckless, self-willed and arrogant [creatures, despising the majesty of the Lord], they do not tremble when they revile angelic majesties, whereas even angels who are superior in might and power do not bring a reviling (defaming) accusation against them before the Lord."

God does not want us to be presumptuous. He wants us to be humble so others can come to know and honor Him through the way we live our lives.

17 "YOU SHALL not sacrifice to the LORD your God an ox or sheep with a blemish or any defect, for that is a detestable thing to the LORD your God.

²"If there is discovered among you, within any of your cities, which the LORD your God is giving you, a man or a woman who does evil in the sight of the LORD your God, by transgressing (violating) His covenant,

³and has gone and served other gods and worshiped them, or the sun or the moon or any of the heavenly host, [doing these things] which I have commanded not to do,

⁴and if it is told to you and you hear about it, then you shall investigate thoroughly [all the charges]. If it is confirmed beyond doubt that this detestable thing has been done in Israel,

⁵then you shall bring that man or that woman who has done this evil thing to the gates [of your city] and you shall stone the man or the woman to death.

⁶"On the evidence of two or three witnesses, he who is to die shall be put to death; he shall not be put to death on the evidence of [only] one witness.

⁷"The hand of the witnesses shall be the first against him to put him to death, and afterward the hand of all the people. So you shall remove the evil from among you.

⁸"If any case is too difficult for you to judge—between one kind of homicide and another, between one kind of lawsuit and another, between one kind of assault and another, being controversial issues in your courts—then you shall arise and go to the place which the LORD your God chooses.

⁹"So you shall come to the Levitical priests or to the judge who is *in office* at that time, and you shall consult them and they will declare to you the verdict in the case.

¹⁰"You shall act in accordance with the terms of the verdict which they declare to you from that place which the LORD chooses. You shall be careful to act in accordance with all of their instructions.

¹¹"You shall act in accordance with the law which they teach you and the judgment which they tell you. You shall not turn aside from their verdict, to the right or to the left.

¹²"The man who acts presumptuously *and* insolently by not listening to the priest who stands there to serve the LORD your God, nor to the judge, that man shall die; so you shall remove the evil from Israel.

¹³"Then all the people will hear and be afraid, and will not act presumptuously again.

¹⁴"When you enter the land which the LORD your God is giving you, and you take possession of it and live there, and you say, 'I will set a king over me like all the nations who are around me,'

¹⁵you shall most certainly set a king over you whom the LORD your God chooses. You shall set a king over you from among your countrymen (brothers); you may not choose a foreigner [to rule] over you who is not your countryman.

¹⁶"Further, he shall not acquire many [war] horses for himself, nor make the people return to Egypt in order to acquire horses [to expand his military power], since the LORD said to you, 'You shall never return that way again.'

¹⁷"He shall not acquire multiple wives for himself, or else his heart will turn away [from God]; nor [for the same reason] shall he acquire great amounts of silver and gold.

¹⁸"Now it shall come about when he sits on the throne of his kingdom, he shall write for himself a copy of this law on a scroll in the presence of the Levitical priests.

¹⁹"And it shall be with him and he shall read it all the days of his life, so that he may learn to fear [and worship] the LORD his God [with awe-filled reverence and profound respect], by carefully obeying (keeping foremost in his thoughts and actively doing) all the words of this law and these statutes, ²⁰so that his heart will not be lifted up above his countrymen [by a false sense of self-importance and self-reliance] and that he will not turn away (deviate) from the commandment, to the right or to the left, so that he and his sons may continue [to

reign] for a long time in his kingdom in Israel.

18 "THE LEVITICAL priests, the entire tribe of Levi, shall own [privately] no portion [of land] or inheritance with Israel; they shall eat the LORD's offerings by fire and His portion. ²"They shall have no inheritance [of land] among their countrymen (brothers, brethren); the LORD is their inheritance, as He promised them. ³"Now this shall be the priests' portion from the people, from those

the danger of occult practices

Today many people are going to fortune-tellers and tarot card readers or calling psychics who charge them so much per minute to tell them their futures. There are millions of people who follow horoscopes, making decisions based on the stars. You may be one of them, and if so, I want you to know that there is no need to worship the stars when you can worship the God Who made them.

The Bible has much to say about consulting with mediums and soothsayers and other kinds of activities that God considers repulsive (see also Leviticus 20:6, 7). You may not be familiar with some of the words used in Deuteronomy 18:10–12, but it's talking about such things as horoscopes, tarot cards, psychic readings, mediums, and what we call "New Age" practices.

While the Bible says these occult practices are repulsive to God, I think many people today do not realize that God is opposed to such things. In fact, some churches do not even teach people that those activities are wrong. One of the women in a church I attended for a period of time was getting involved in transcendental meditation. Since she did not know whether there was anything wrong with it or not, she asked the pastor. He told her, "I'm not really sure. Let me know whether it works or not; I might even try it myself." I didn't know any better than that either. Had God not intervened in my life, I might have fallen into the dangerous trap of New Age activity. There is no telling how many people are sucked into occult practices and the New Age movement simply because they really do not know God's Word well enough to stay away from such dangerous pursuits.

God's Living Word is the only source of truth, and His Spirit is the only One Who can lead us into peace, joy, and victory in our everyday lives. Don't waste your money calling up people who supposedly can tell you about your future. Let God lead your future.

offering a sacrifice, either an ox or a sheep: they shall give to the priest the shoulder and the two cheeks and the stomach.

⁴"You shall also give him the first fruits of your grain, your new wine [the first of the season], and your [olive] oil, and the first sheared fleece of your sheep.

⁵"For the Lord your God has chosen him, him and his sons from all your tribes, to stand and serve in the name of the Lord forever.

⁶"Now if a Levite comes from any of your cities throughout Israel where he resides, and comes whenever he wishes to [the sanctuary] the place which the Lord chooses;

⁷then he shall serve in the name of the Lord his God, like all his fellow Levites who stand there before the Lord.

⁸"They shall have equal portions to eat, except *what they receive* from the sale of their fathers' *estates*. [Jer 32:6–15]

⁹"When you enter the land which the Lord your God is giving you, you shall not learn to imitate the detestable (repulsive) practices of those nations.

¹⁰"There shall not be found among you anyone who makes his son or daughter pass through the fire [as a sacrifice], one who uses divination *and* fortune-telling, one who practices witchcraft, or one who interprets omens, or a sorcerer,

¹¹or one who casts a charm *or* spell, or a medium, or a spiritist, or a necromancer [who seeks the dead].

¹²"For everyone who does these things is utterly repulsive to the Lord; and because of these detestable practices the Lord your God is driving them out before you.

¹³"You shall be blameless (complete, perfect) before the Lord your God.

¹⁴"For these nations which you shall dispossess listen to those who practice witchcraft and to diviners *and*

fortune-tellers, but as for you, the Lord your God has not allowed you to do so.

¹⁵"The Lord your God will raise up for you a prophet like me [Moses] from among you, from your countrymen (brothers, brethren). You shall listen to him. [Matt 21:11; John 1:21]

¹⁶"This is according to all that you asked of the Lord your God at Horeb (Mount Sinai) on the day of the assembly, saying, 'Let me not hear the voice of the Lord my God again, nor see this great fire anymore, so that I will not die.'

¹⁷"The Lord said to me, 'They have spoken well.

¹⁸'I will raise up a prophet from among their countrymen like you, and I will put My words in his mouth, and he shall speak to them all that I command him.

¹⁹'It shall come about that whoever will not listen to My words which he shall speak in My name, I Myself will require it of him [and there will be consequences].

²⁰'But the prophet who presumes to speak a word in My name which I have not commanded him to speak, or which he speaks in the name of other gods—that prophet shall die.'

²¹"If you say in your heart, 'How will we know *and* recognize the word which the Lord has not spoken?'

²²"When a prophet speaks in the name of the Lord and the thing does not happen or come true, that is the thing which the Lord has not spoken. The prophet has spoken it presumptuously; you shall not be afraid of him.

19

"WHEN THE Lord your God cuts off (destroys) the nations whose land He is giving you, and you dispossess them and live in their cities and in their houses, ²you shall designate three cities for yourself in the central area of the land, which the LORD your God is giving you to possess.

³"You shall prepare *and* maintain for yourself the roads [to these cities], and divide the territory of your land into three parts, so that anyone who kills another unintentionally may escape there [for asylum].

⁴"Now this is the case of the offender (manslayer) who may escape there and live [protected from vengeance]: when he kills his neighbor unintentionally, not having hated him previously—

⁵as [for example] when *a man* goes into the forest with his neighbor to cut wood, and his hand swings the axe to cut down the tree, but the iron *head* slips off the wooden handle and hits his companion and he dies—the offender may escape to one of these cities and live;

⁶otherwise the avenger of blood might pursue the offender in the heat of anger, and overtake him, because it is a long way, and take his life, even though he did not deserve to die, since he did not hate his neighbor beforehand.

⁷"Therefore, I command you, saying, 'You shall set aside three cities [of refuge] for yourself.'

⁸"If the LORD your God enlarges your border, as He has sworn to your fathers to do, and gives you all the land which He promised to give to your fathers—

⁹if you keep *and* carefully observe all these commandments which I am commanding you today, to love the LORD your God, and to walk [that is, to live each and every day] always in His ways—then you shall add three more cities [of refuge] for yourself, besides these three,

¹⁰so that innocent blood will not be shed [by blood avengers] in your land which the LORD your God is giving you as an inheritance, and blood guilt will not be on you [for the death of an innocent man].

¹¹"But if there is a man who hates his neighbor and lies in wait *and* ambush for him and attacks him and strikes him down so that he dies, and the assailant escapes to one of these cities,

¹²then the elders of his own city shall send for him and have him taken back from there and turn him over to the avenger of blood, so that he may be put to death.

¹³"You shall not pity him [the guilty one], but you shall purge the blood of the innocent from Israel, so that it may go well with you.

¹⁴"You shall not move your neighbor's boundary mark, which the forefathers [who first divided the territory] have set, in the land which you will inherit in the land which the LORD your God is giving you to possess.

¹⁵"A single witness shall not appear *in a trial* against a man for any wrong or any sin which he has committed; [only] on the testimony *or* evidence of two or three witnesses shall a charge be confirmed.

¹⁶"If a malicious witness rises up against a man to [falsely] accuse him of wrongdoing,

¹⁷then both parties to the controversy shall stand before the LORD, before the priests and the judges who will be *in office* at that time.

¹⁸"The judges shall investigate thoroughly, and if the witness is a false witness, and he has accused his brother falsely,

¹⁹then you shall do to him just as he had intended to do to his brother. So you shall remove the evil from among you.

²⁰"Those who remain will hear and be afraid, and will never again do such an evil thing among you.

²¹"You shall not show pity [to the guilty one]: *it shall be* life for life, eye for eye, tooth for tooth, hand for hand, foot for foot.

gentle as a lamb, bold as a lion

What happens when we lack courage? In our hearts we say, "I can't do this. It's just too hard." If we are going to be faithful believers in the kingdom of God, we cannot quit when things get tough. We need to be as bold as a lion.

Being bold-hearted does not mean we should be tough and harsh. It is possible to be tender and tough at the same time, and the key is to know when to be tender and when to be tough. We need to be meek, sweet, and gentle toward people, but bold, tough, and aggressive with the devil—because that is the way he is with us.

I used to have a problem understanding how a person could be both tough and tender. When I read the Bible one verse seemed to say I was to be as gentle as a lamb, while another passage (such as Deuteronomy 20:1–4) seemed to instruct me to be lionhearted. I did not have any trouble with the lion part, but I did have problems with the lamb part. I had a lot of natural lion in me, but I needed to develop the lamb part of me. Gentleness did not come easily to me, partly because I was not raised in a gentle atmosphere, and partly because my personality was not gentle by nature.

Jesus is humble, gentle, meek, and lowly—not harsh, hard, sharp, or pressing. I was not like Jesus, but I wanted to be, so I went to the extreme of collecting little stuffed lambs and placing them all over my house. I had pictures of lambs and paintings of lambs. I had images of Jesus holding lambs, Jesus sitting among groups of lambs, and Jesus carrying lambs on His shoulders. I had so many lambs in my house that it started to look silly, so I cleaned out many and kept only the ones I liked best. But all of the lambs served a purpose: they reminded me to be more gentle. They helped me form new habits in how I dealt with people.

We should resist Satan and all of his evil works as aggressively and boldly as a lion, but in our dealings with people, we usually should be very gentle unless a situation calls for us to apply some tough love.

The Holy Spirit is very gentle and sensitive. If we are harsh and hard with people, we can easily offend the Holy Spirit, and we certainly do not want to do that.

Are you more like a lion, or are you more like a lamb? You may be shy and timid, as gentle and meek as a lamb, preferring to avoid hard or controversial issues. So God has to put a bit of lion in you. Or you may have a strong lion in you, as I did, and need to have some lamb qualities developed in you.

No matter what your temperament is, we all face times that call for a lion as well as times that call for a lamb. When we lack courage, we need to dig in our heels and exclaim in lion-like faith, "I am not going to shrink back! God will help me! I am not going to give up or quit, no matter how hard it gets or how long it takes! I will be courageous!"

20

"WHEN YOU go out to battle against your enemies and see horses and chariots and people more numerous than you, do not be afraid of them; for the LORD your God, who brought you up from the land of Egypt, is with you.

²"When you approach the battle, the priest shall come forward and speak to the people,

³and shall say to them, 'Hear, O Israel: you are advancing today to battle against your enemies. Do not lack courage. Do not be afraid, or panic, or tremble [in terror] before them,

⁴for the LORD your God is He who goes with you, to fight for you against your enemies, to save you.' [1 Sam 17:45]

⁵"The officers shall also speak to the soldiers, saying, 'What man is there who has built a new house and has not yet dedicated it? Let him go and return to his house, otherwise he might die in the battle and another man would dedicate it.

⁶'What man has planted a vineyard and has not put it to use [harvesting its fruit]? Let him go and return to his house, otherwise he might die in the battle and another man would begin to use its fruit.

⁷'And who is the man who is engaged (legally promised) to a woman and has not married her? Let him go and return to his house, otherwise he might die in the battle and another man would marry her.'

⁸"Then the officers shall speak further to the soldiers and say, 'Who is the man who is afraid and lacks courage? Let him go and return to his house, so that he does not cause his brothers' courage to fail like his own.'

⁹"And it shall be when the officers have finished speaking to the soldiers, they shall appoint commanders of armies over them.

¹⁰"When you advance to a city to fight against it, you shall [first] offer it terms of peace.

¹¹"If that city accepts your terms of peace and opens *its gates* to you, then all the people who are found in it shall become your forced labor and shall serve you.

¹²"However, if it does not make peace with you, but makes war against you, then you shall lay siege to it.

¹³"When the LORD your God gives it into your hand, you shall strike down all the men in it with the edge of the sword.

¹⁴"Only the women and the children and the animals and everything that is in the city, all its spoil, you shall take as plunder for yourself; and you shall use the spoil of your enemies which the LORD your God has given you.

¹⁵"That is what you shall do to all the cities that are very far away from you, which are not among the cities of these nations nearby [which you are to dispossess].

¹⁶"Only in the cities of these peoples that the LORD your God is giving you as an inheritance, you shall not leave alive anything that breathes.

¹⁷"But you shall utterly destroy them, the Hittite, the Amorite, the Canaanite, the Perizzite, the Hivite and the Jebusite, just as the LORD your God has commanded you,

¹⁸so that they will not teach you to act in accordance with all the detestable practices which they have done [in worship and service] for their gods, and in this way cause you to sin against the LORD your God.

¹⁹"When you besiege a city for a *long time, making war against it in order to capture it, you shall not destroy its [fruit-bearing] trees by swinging an axe against them; for you may eat from them, and you shall not cut them down. For is the tree of the field a man, that it should be besieged (destroyed) by you?

20:19 Lit *many days*.

²⁰"Only the trees which you know are not fruit trees shall you destroy and cut down, so that you may build siegeworks against the city that is making war with you until it falls.

21 "IF SOMEONE is found slain, lying in the field, in the land which the Lᴏʀᴅ your God gives you to possess, and it is not known who has killed him,

²then your elders and judges shall go out and measure *the distance* to the cities which are around the dead person.

³"It shall be that the elders of the city which is nearest to the dead man shall take a heifer of the herd, one which has not been worked and which has not pulled in a yoke;

⁴and the elders of that city shall bring the heifer down to a [river] valley with running water, which has not been plowed or planted, and shall break the heifer's neck there in the valley.

⁵"Then the priests, the sons of Levi, shall approach, for the Lᴏʀᴅ your God has chosen them to serve Him and to bless in the Name (Presence) of the Lᴏʀᴅ; and every dispute and every assault (violent crime) shall be settled by them.

⁶"All the elders of that city nearest to the dead man shall wash their hands over the heifer whose neck was broken in the valley;

⁷and they shall respond, and say, 'Our hands did not shed this blood, nor did our eyes see it.

⁸'Forgive Your people Israel whom You have redeemed, O Lᴏʀᴅ, and do not put the guilt of innocent blood among Your people Israel.' And the guilt of blood shall be forgiven them.

⁹"So shall you remove the guilt of innocent blood from among you, when you do what is right in the sight of the Lᴏʀᴅ.

¹⁰"When you go out to battle against your enemies, and the Lᴏʀᴅ your God hands them over to you and you lead them away captive,

¹¹and you see a beautiful woman among the captives, and desire her and would take her as your wife,

¹²then you shall bring her [home] to your house, and she shall shave her head and trim her nails [in preparation for mourning].

¹³"She shall take off the clothes of her captivity and remain in your house, and weep (mourn) for her father and her mother a full month. After that you may go in to her and be her husband and she shall be your wife.

¹⁴"But it shall be that if you have no delight *and* take no pleasure in her, then you shall let her go wherever she wishes. You certainly shall not sell her for money; you shall not deal with her as a slave *or* mistreat her, because you have humbled her [by forced marriage].

¹⁵"If a man has two wives, one loved and the other unloved, and both the loved and the unloved have born him sons, and the firstborn son belongs to the unloved *wife,*

¹⁶then on the day when he wills his possessions to his sons, he cannot treat the son of his loved wife as firstborn in place of the son of the unloved wife—the [actual] firstborn.

¹⁷"Instead he shall acknowledge the son of the unloved as the firstborn, by giving him a double portion of all that he has, for he was the beginning of his strength (generative power); to him belongs the right of the firstborn.

¹⁸"If any man has a stubborn and rebellious son who will not obey the voice of his father or of his mother, and when they reprimand *and* discipline him, he will not listen to them,

¹⁹then his father and mother shall take hold of him, and bring him out to the elders of his city at the gateway of his hometown.

²⁰"They shall say to the elders of his city, 'This son of ours is stubborn and

rebellious; he will not obey us, he is a glutton and a drunkard.' [Prov 23:20–22]

²¹"Then all the men of his city shall stone him to death; so you shall remove the evil from among you, and all Israel will hear of it and be afraid.

²²"And if a man has committed a sin worthy of death, and he is put to death and [afterward] you hang him on a tree [as a public example], [Josh 10:26, 27]

²³his body shall not hang all night on the tree, but you shall most certainly bury him on the same day (for he who is hanged is cursed by God), so that you do not defile your land which the LORD your God gives you as an inheritance. [Gal 3:13]

22 "YOU SHALL not see your countryman's ox or his sheep straying away *or* being stolen, and ignore [your duty to help] them; you shall certainly take them back to him. [Prov 24:12]

²"If your countryman is not nearby or you do not know him, you shall bring the animal to your house, and it shall stay with you until he searches for it; then you shall return it to him.

³"You shall do this with his donkey or with his garment or with anything that your countryman has lost and you have found. You are not allowed to ignore [your duty to help] them.

⁴"You shall not see your countryman's donkey or his ox fall down along the road, and ignore [your duty to help] them; you shall certainly help him lift it up.

⁵"A woman shall not wear a man's clothing, nor shall a man put on a woman's clothing; for whoever does these things is utterly repulsive to the LORD your God.

⁶"If you happen to come upon a bird's nest along the road, in any tree or on the ground, with young ones or eggs, and the mother [bird] is sitting on the young or on the eggs, you shall not take the mother with the young.

⁷"You shall certainly let the mother go, but you may take the young for yourself, so that it may be well with you and that you may prolong your days.

⁸"When you build a new house, you shall make a railing (parapet) around your [flat] roof, so that you do not bring the guilt of [innocent] blood on your house if someone falls from it.

⁹"You shall not sow your vineyard with two kinds of seed, or everything produced by the seed which you have sown and the yield of the vineyard will become defiled [and banned for use].

¹⁰"You shall not plow with an ox [a clean animal] and a donkey [an unclean animal] together. [2 Cor 6:14–16]

¹¹"You shall not wear a fabric made of wool and linen blended together [a fabric pagans believed to be magical]. [Ezek 44:18; Rev 19:8]

¹²"You shall make tassels for yourself on the four corners of your outer garment with which you cover yourself. [Num 15:37–40]

¹³"If any man takes a wife and goes in to her and then scorns *and* hates her,

¹⁴and charges her [without cause] with shameful behavior and publicly defames her, and says, 'I took this woman, but when I approached her, I did not find in her evidence of virginity,'

¹⁵then the young woman's father and her mother shall get and bring out the evidence of her virginity to the elders of the city at the gate [where court is held].

¹⁶"The father of the young woman shall say to the elders, 'I gave my daughter to this man as a wife, but he hates her *and* has turned against her;

¹⁷and behold, he has made baseless charges against her, saying, "I did not find in your daughter the evidence of her virginity." But this is the evidence of my daughter's virginity.' And they shall spread out the garment before the elders of the city.

¹⁸"Then the elders of that city shall take the man and reprimand him,

¹⁹and they shall fine him a hundred *shekels* of silver and give it to the father of the young woman, because he publicly defamed a virgin of Israel. And she shall remain his wife; he is not allowed to divorce her as long as he lives.

²⁰"But if this charge is true that the evidence of virginity was not found in the young woman,

²¹then they shall bring her out to the doorway of her father's house, and the men of her city shall stone her to death because she has committed a deliberate sin in Israel by playing the prostitute in her father's house. So you shall remove the evil from among you.

²²"If a man is intimate with a woman who is another man's wife, they shall both be put to death, the man who lay with the woman, and the woman. So you shall remove the evil from Israel.

²³"If a young woman who is a virgin is engaged (legally betrothed) to a man, and *another* man finds her in the city and is intimate with her,

²⁴then you shall bring them both out to the gate of that city and stone them to death—the young woman because she did not cry out for help [though she was] in the city, and the man because he has violated his neighbor's [promised] wife. So you shall remove the evil from among you.

²⁵"However, if the man finds the girl who is engaged (legally betrothed) in the [open] field, and seizes her and is intimate with her [by force], then only the man who lies with her shall be put to death.

²⁶"But you shall do nothing to the young woman; she has committed no sin worthy of death, for this is the same as when a man attacks his neighbor and murders him.

²⁷When he found her in the [open] field, the engaged girl [may have] cried out for help, but there was no one to [hear and] save her.

²⁸"If a man finds a girl who is a virgin, who is not engaged, and seizes her and is intimate with her and they are discovered,

²⁹then the man who was intimate with her shall give fifty *shekels* of silver to the girl's father, and she shall become his wife because he has violated her; he can never divorce her.

³⁰"A man shall not take his father's [former] wife, so that he will not expose his father's wife.

23 "HE WHO has been castrated by *having his testicles* crushed or his male organ cut off shall not enter the congregation of the LORD.

²"A person of illegitimate birth shall not enter the assembly of the LORD; none of his *descendants*, even to the tenth generation.

³"An Ammonite or Moabite shall not enter the assembly of the LORD; none of their *descendants*, even to the tenth generation, shall ever enter the assembly of the LORD,

⁴because they did not meet you with bread (food) and water on the road as you came out of Egypt, and because they hired [to act] against you Balaam the son of Beor from Pethor of Mesopotamia, to curse you.

⁵"Nevertheless, the LORD your God was not willing to listen to Balaam, but the LORD your God turned the curse into a blessing for you because the LORD your God has loved you.

speak the Word

God, thank You for turning curses into blessings in my life because You love me.
–ADAPTED FROM DEUTERONOMY 23:5

⁶"You shall never seek their peace nor their prosperity all your days.

⁷"You shall not detest an Edomite, for he is your brother [Esau's descendant]. You shall not detest an Egyptian, because you were a stranger (resident alien, foreigner) in his land.

⁸"Their children of the third generation who are born to them may enter the assembly of the LORD.

⁹"When you go out as an army [to fight] against your enemies, you shall keep yourselves from every evil [thing].

¹⁰"If there is any man among you who is [ceremonially] unclean because of nocturnal emission, then he must go outside the camp; he shall not come back to the camp.

¹¹"But when evening comes, he shall bathe in water, and at sundown he may return to the camp.

¹²"You shall also have a place outside the camp to which you may go,

¹³and you shall have a spade among your tools, and when you [prepare to] sit down outside [to relieve yourself], you shall dig a hole with it and shall turn and cover up your waste.

¹⁴"Since the LORD your God walks in the midst of your camp to rescue you and to defeat your enemies before you, therefore your camp must be holy (undefiled); and He must not see anything indecent among you or He will turn away from you.

¹⁵"You shall not hand over to his master a slave who has escaped from his master to you.

¹⁶"He shall live among you, in the place he chooses in one of your cities where it pleases him; you shall not mistreat or oppress him.

¹⁷"There shall be no cult prostitute among the daughters of Israel, nor shall there be a cult prostitute (a sodomite) among the sons of Israel.

¹⁸"You shall not bring the wages of a prostitute or the price of a dog [that is, a male prostitute] into the house of the LORD your God as payment for any vow, for both of these [the gift and the giver] are utterly repulsive to the LORD your God.

¹⁹"You shall not charge interest to your fellow Israelite—interest on money, food or anything that may be loaned for interest.

²⁰"You may charge interest to a foreigner, but to your fellow Israelite you shall not charge interest, so that the LORD your God may bless you in all that you undertake in the land which you are about to enter to possess.

²¹"When you make a vow to the LORD your God, you shall not delay to pay it, for He will most certainly require it of you, and a delay would cause you to sin.

²²"But if you refrain from making a vow, that would not be [counted as] sin in you.

²³"You shall be careful to perform that [vow] which passes your lips, just as you have made a voluntary vow to the LORD your God, just as you have promised with your own words (mouth).

²⁴"When you enter your neighbor's vineyard, you may eat your fill of grapes, as many as you please, but you shall not put any in your basket [to take with you].

²⁵"When you come into the standing grain of your neighbor, you may pluck the ears of grain with your hand, but you shall not wield a sickle in your neighbor's standing grain [to harvest it].

24 "WHEN A man takes a wife and marries her, and it happens that she loses his favor because he has found something indecent or unacceptable about her, and he writes her a certificate of divorce, puts it in her hand and sends her out of his house,

²and after she leaves his house, she goes and becomes another man's wife,

³and if the latter husband *turns against her and writes her a certificate of divorce, puts it in her hand, and sends her out of his house, or if the latter husband dies who took her as his wife, ⁴then her former husband who [first] sent her away may not take her again as his wife, since she has been defiled; for that is an outrage before the LORD, and you shall not bring sin on the land which the LORD your God gives you as an inheritance.

⁵"When a man takes a new wife, he shall not go out [to fight] with the army nor be charged with any duty; he shall be free at home for one year and shall bring happiness to his wife whom he has taken.

⁶"No one shall take a handmill or an upper millstone [used to grind grain into bread] as security [for a debt], for he would be taking a [person's] life in pledge.

⁷"If a man is caught kidnapping any of his countrymen from the sons of Israel, and he treats him violently or sells him [as a slave], then that thief shall die. So you shall remove the evil from among you.

⁸"Be careful during an outbreak of leprosy, that you diligently observe and do according to all that the Levitical priests teach you; just as I have commanded them, so you shall be careful to do. [Lev 13:14, 15]

⁹"Remember [with thoughtful concern] what the LORD your God did to Miriam on the road as you came out of Egypt. [Num 12:10]

¹⁰"When you lend your neighbor anything, you shall not go into his house to get his pledge (security deposit).

¹¹"You shall stand outside, and the man to whom you lend shall bring the pledge out to you.

¹²"If the man is poor, you shall not keep his pledge overnight.

¹³"You shall certainly restore the pledge (security deposit) to him at sunset, so that he may sleep in his garment and bless you; and it will be credited to you as righteousness (right standing) before the LORD your God.

¹⁴"You shall not take advantage of a hired servant who is poor and needy, whether [he is] one of your countrymen or one of the strangers (resident aliens, foreigners) who is in your land inside your cities.

¹⁵"You shall give him his wages on the day that he earns them before the sun sets—for he is poor and is *counting on it—so that he does not cry out to the LORD against you, and it becomes a sin for you.

¹⁶"The fathers shall not be put to death for [the sins of] their children, nor shall the children be put to death for their fathers; [only] for his own sin shall anyone be put to death.

¹⁷"You shall not pervert the justice due a stranger or an orphan, nor seize (impound) a widow's garment as security [for a loan].

¹⁸"But you shall remember that you were a slave in Egypt, and the LORD your God redeemed you from there; therefore I am commanding you to do this thing.

¹⁹"When you reap your harvest in your field and have forgotten a sheaf [of grain] in the field, you shall not go back to get it; it shall be for the stranger, for the orphan, and for the widow, so that the LORD your God may bless you in all the work of your hands.

²⁰"When you beat [the olives off of] your olive tree, do not search through the branches again; [whatever is left] shall be for the stranger, for the orphan, and for the widow.

²¹"When you gather the grapes of your vineyard, you shall not glean it afterward; it shall be for the stranger, for the orphan, and for the widow.

24:3 Lit *hates*.   24:15 Lit *sets his heart*.

²²"You shall [thoughtfully] remember [the fact] that you were a slave in the land of Egypt; therefore I am commanding you to do this thing.

25 "IF THERE is a controversy between men, and they go to court, and the judges decide [the issue] between them, and they judge in favor of the innocent and condemn the guilty,

²then it shall be that if the guilty man deserves to be beaten, the judge shall make him lie down and be beaten in his presence with a [certain] number of stripes in proportion to his offense.

³"He may have him beaten forty times, but no more. He is not to be beaten with more stripes than these and he is not to be degraded [that is, treated like an animal] in your sight.

⁴"You shall not muzzle the ox while he is threshing [to prevent him from eating any of the grain]. [1 Cor 9:9, 10; 1 Tim 5:17, 18]

⁵"If brothers are living together and one of them dies without a son, the widow of the deceased shall not

when weariness attacks

Amalek's attack on the Israelites, mentioned in Deuteronomy 25:17, 18, is a type and shadow of Satan and the method he uses to assault, hinder, and stop believers today (see John 10:10). Amalek chose to attack the Israelites when they were tired and weary. Satan tries to wear us down to the point of exhaustion so that once we are in that position, he can intensify his attack to bring us down.

If you, a Christian, are struggling with weariness—if you want to just give up and quit—you are not alone. Satan brings attacks of weariness on the body of Christ to keep us from receiving the harvest God has for us. And God is preparing a great spiritual harvest!

When we plant seed in the natural world, a lot happens underground that we cannot see. The root system needs to grow and be established before we notice any harvest. Because God's kingdom is based on the principle of seed planting and harvest (see Mark 4:26–32), God is doing much work "under the ground," out of our sight, to bring our planted seeds to fruition.

This "growing stage" is the point when many of us become weary and want to faint. When we are doing everything we know to do in God—and we are doing it again and again without seeing the results we desire in the natural world—we can become weary in well-doing. We may have planted our seeds of obedience in faithfulness and diligence, but we have lost sight of the manner in which the kingdom of God operates to grow fruit. We need to remember the wonderful promise of Galatians 6:9: "Let us not grow weary or become discouraged in doing good, for at the proper time we will reap, if we do not give in."

When the enemy attacks you in times of weakness or fatigue, stir up your courage, muster your strength, and rise up against him with the truth of God's Word! This is a good time to behave as a bold, aggressive lion.

be *married* outside *the family* to a stranger. Her husband's brother shall be intimate with her after taking her as his wife and perform the duty of a husband's brother to her.

⁶"It shall be that her firstborn [son] will be given the name of the dead brother, so that his name will not be blotted out of Israel.

⁷"But if the man does not want to marry his brother's [widowed] wife, then she shall go up to the gate [of the city, where court is held] to the elders, and say, 'My brother-in-law refuses to continue his brother's name in Israel; he is not willing to perform the duty of a husband's brother.'

⁸"Then the elders of his city will summon him and speak to him. And if he stands firm and says, 'I do not want to marry her,'

⁹then his brother's widow shall approach him in the presence of the elders, and pull his sandal off his foot and spit in his face; and she shall answer and say, 'So it is done to that man who does not build up his brother's household.'

¹⁰"In Israel his [family] name shall be, 'The house of him whose sandal was removed.'

¹¹"If [two] men, a man and his countryman, are fighting and the wife of one approaches to rescue her husband from the man who is striking him, and she reaches out with her hand and grabs the aggressor's genitals,

¹²then you shall cut off her hand; you shall not show pity [for her].

¹³"You shall not have in your bag inaccurate weights, a heavy and a light [so you can cheat others].

¹⁴"You shall not have in your house inaccurate measures, a large and a small.

¹⁵"You shall have a perfect (full) and just weight, and a perfect and just measure, so that your days may be long in the land which the Lᴏʀᴅ your God gives you.

¹⁶"For everyone who does such things, everyone who acts unjustly [without personal integrity] is utterly repulsive to the Lᴏʀᴅ your God.

¹⁷"Remember what Amalek did to you along the road when you came from Egypt,

¹⁸how he met you along the road and attacked all the stragglers at your rear when you were tired and weary; and he did not *fear God. [Ex 17:14]

¹⁹"Therefore when the Lᴏʀᴅ your God has given you rest from all your surrounding enemies, in the land which the Lᴏʀᴅ your God gives you as an inheritance to possess, you shall wipe out the memory of Amalek from under heaven; you must not forget.

26 "THEN IT shall be, when you enter the land which the Lᴏʀᴅ your God gives you as an inheritance, and you take possession of it and live in it,

²that you shall take some of the first of all the produce of the ground which you harvest from the land that the Lᴏʀᴅ your God gives you, and you shall put it in a basket and go to the place where the Lᴏʀᴅ your God chooses to establish His Name (Presence).

³"You shall go to the priest who is in office at that time and say to him, 'I declare this day to the Lᴏʀᴅ my God that I have entered the land which the Lᴏʀᴅ swore to our fathers to give us.'

⁴"Then the priest will take the basket from you and place it before the altar of the Lᴏʀᴅ your God.

⁵"And you shall say before the Lᴏʀᴅ your God, 'My father [Jacob] was a wandering Aramean, and he [along with his family] went down to Egypt and lived there [as strangers], few in number; but while there he became a great, mighty and populous nation.

25:18 Or *reverence.*

6'And the Egyptians treated us badly and oppressed us, and imposed hard labor on us.

7"Then we cried out to the Lord, the God of our fathers for help, and He heard our voice and saw our suffering and our labor and our [cruel] oppression;

8and the Lord brought us out of Egypt with a mighty hand and with an outstretched arm and with great terror [suffered by the Egyptians] and with signs and with wonders;

9and He has brought us to this place and has given us this land, a land flowing with milk and honey.

10'And now, look, I have brought the first of the produce of the ground which You, O Lord, have given me.' And you shall place it before the Lord your God, and shall worship before the Lord your God;

11and you and the Levite and the stranger (resident alien, foreigner) among you shall rejoice in all the good which the Lord your God has given you and your household.

12"When you have finished paying all the tithe of your produce the third year, [which is] the year of tithing, then you shall give it to the Levite, to the stranger, to the orphan, and to the widow, so that they may eat within the gates of your cities and be satisfied.

13"You shall say before the Lord your God, 'I have removed the sacred *portion* (the tithe) from my house and also have given it to the Levite, to the stranger, to the orphan, and to the widow, in accordance with all that You have commanded me. I have not transgressed or forgotten any of Your commandments.

14'I have not eaten from the tithe while mourning, nor have I removed any of it when I was [ceremonially] unclean [making the tithe ceremonially unclean], nor offered any of it to the dead. I have listened to the voice of the Lord my God; I have done *everything* in accordance with all that You have commanded me.

15'Look down from Your holy dwelling above, from heaven, and bless Your people Israel, and the land which You have given us, as You have sworn to our fathers, a land [of plenty] flowing with milk and honey.'

16"This day the Lord your God commands you to do these statutes and judgments (precepts). Therefore, you shall be careful to do them with all your heart and with all your soul (your entire being).

17"Today you have [openly] declared the Lord to be your God, and that you will walk [that is, live each and every day] in His ways and keep His statutes, His commandments, and His judgments (precepts), and listen to His voice.

18"Today the Lord has declared that you are His people, His treasured possession, just as He promised you, and that you are to keep all His commandments;

19and that He will set you high above all the nations which He has made, for praise, fame, and honor: and that you shall be a holy people [set apart and consecrated] to the Lord your God, just as He has spoken."

27 THEN MOSES and the elders of Israel commanded the people, saying, "Keep (remember, obey) all the commandments which I am commanding you today.

2"So it shall be on the day when you cross the Jordan to [enter] the land which the Lord your God gives you, that you shall set up for yourself large stones and coat them with plaster (lime, whitewash).

3"You shall write on the stones all the words of this law when you cross over, so that you may go into the land which the Lord your God gives you, a land [of plenty] flowing with milk and honey, just as the LORD, the God of your fathers has promised you.

⁴"Now when you cross the Jordan you shall set up these stones on Mount Ebal, just as I am commanding you today and coat them with plaster.

⁵"There you shall build an altar to the LORD your God, an altar of stones; you shall not use an iron tool on them.

⁶"You shall build the altar of the LORD your God with whole [uncut] stones, and offer burnt offerings on it to the LORD your God;

⁷and you shall sacrifice peace offerings and shall eat there, and shall rejoice before the LORD your God.

⁸"And you shall write very clearly on the stones all the words of this law."

⁹Then Moses and the Levitical priests said to all Israel, "Be silent and listen, O Israel! This day you have become a people for the LORD your God.

¹⁰"So you shall obey the voice of the LORD your God, and do His commandments and statutes which I am commanding you today."

¹¹Moses also commanded the people that day, saying,

¹²"These [tribes] shall stand on

life point

Obedience is not to be an occasional event; it is to be a way of life. There is a big difference between people who are willing to obey God daily and those who are willing to obey only in order to get out of trouble. God certainly shows people how to get out of trouble, but He showers blessings on those who decide to live wholeheartedly for Him and make obedience to Him their lifestyle.

speak the Word

Mount Gerizim to bless the people when you have crossed the Jordan: Simeon, Levi, Judah, Issachar, Joseph, and Benjamin.

¹³"These [tribes] shall stand on Mount Ebal to *pronounce* the curse [for disobedience]: Reuben, Gad, Asher, Zebulun, Dan, and Naphtali.

¹⁴"The Levites shall answer with a loud voice to all the men of Israel:

¹⁵'Cursed is the man who makes a carved or cast image (idol), a repulsive thing to the LORD, the work of the hands of the artisan, and sets it up in secret.' All the people shall answer and say, 'Amen.'

¹⁶'Cursed is he who dishonors (treats with contempt) his father or his mother.' And all the people shall say, 'Amen.'

¹⁷'Cursed is he who moves his neighbor's boundary mark.' And all the people shall say, 'Amen.'

¹⁸'Cursed is he who misleads a blind person on the road.' And all the people shall say, 'Amen.'

¹⁹'Cursed is he who distorts (perverts) the justice due to a stranger, an orphan, and a widow.' And all the people shall say, 'Amen.'

²⁰'Cursed is he who is intimate with his father's [former] wife, because he has violated what belongs to his father.' And all the people shall say, 'Amen.'

²¹'Cursed is he who is intimate with any animal.' And all the people shall say, 'Amen.'

²²'Cursed is he who is intimate with his [half] sister, whether his father's or his mother's daughter.' And all the people shall say, 'Amen.'

²³'Cursed is he who is intimate with his mother-in-law.' And all the people shall say, 'Amen.'

God, I will listen diligently to Your voice and obey it, being careful to do all of Your commandments. And I am expecting Your favor and blessings in my life.
—ADAPTED FROM DEUTERONOMY 28:1, 2

²⁴'Cursed is he who strikes his neighbor in secret.' And all the people shall say, 'Amen.'

²⁵'Cursed is he who accepts a bribe to strike down an innocent person.' And all the people shall say, 'Amen.'

²⁶'Cursed is he who does not confirm the words of this law by doing them [keeping them, taking them to heart as the rule of his life].' And all the people shall say, 'Amen.'

28 "NOW IT shall be, if you diligently listen to *and* obey the voice of the LORD your God, being careful to do all of His commandments which I am commanding you today, the LORD your God will set you high above all the nations of the earth.

²"All these blessings will come upon you and overtake you if you pay attention to the voice of the LORD your God.

³"You *will be* blessed in the city, and you *will be* blessed in the field.

⁴"The offspring of your body and the produce of your ground and the offspring of your animals, the offspring of your herd and the young of your flock *will be* blessed.

⁵"Your basket and your kneading bowl *will be* blessed.

⁶"You *will be* blessed when you come in and you *will be* blessed when you go out.

⁷"The LORD will cause the enemies who rise up against you to be defeated before you; they will come out against you one way, but flee before you seven ways.

⁸"The LORD will command the blessing upon you in your storehouses and in all that you undertake, and He will bless you in the land which the LORD your God gives you.

⁹"The LORD will establish you as a people holy [and set apart] to Himself, just as He has sworn to you, if you keep the commandments of the LORD your God and walk [that is, live your life each and every day] in His ways.

¹⁰"So all the peoples of the earth will see that you are called by the name of the LORD, and they will be afraid of you.

¹¹"The LORD will give you great prosperity, in the offspring of your body and in the offspring of your livestock and the produce of your ground, in the land which the LORD swore to your fathers to give you.

¹²"The LORD will open for you His good treasure house, the heavens, to give rain to your land in its season and to bless all the work of your hand; and you will lend to many nations, but you will not borrow.

¹³"The LORD will make you the head (leader) and not the tail (follower); and you will be above only, and you will not be beneath, if you listen *and* pay attention to the commandments of the LORD your God, which I am commanding you today, to observe them carefully.

¹⁴"Do not turn aside from any of the words which I am commanding you today, to the right or to the left, to follow and serve other gods.

¹⁵"But it shall come about, if you do not listen to *and* obey the voice of the LORD your God, being careful to do all His commandments and His statutes which I am commanding you today, then all these curses will come upon you and overtake you:

speak the Word

Thank You, God, that You have made me the head and not the tail, that I am above only and not beneath anything or anyone if I listen and pay attention to Your commandments.
—ADAPTED FROM DEUTERONOMY 28:13

¹⁶"You *will be* cursed in the city and cursed in the field.

¹⁷"Your basket and your kneading bowl *will be* cursed.

¹⁸"The offspring of your body and the produce of your land, the offspring of your herd and the young of your flock *will be* cursed.

¹⁹"You *will be* cursed when you come in and you *will be* cursed when you go out.

²⁰"The LORD will send upon you curses, confusion, and rebuke in everything that you undertake to do, until you are destroyed, perishing quickly because of the evil of your deeds, because you have turned away from Me.

²¹"The LORD will make the pestilence *and* plague cling to you until He has consumed *and* eliminated you from the land which you are entering to possess.

²²"The LORD will strike you with consumption [causing you to waste away] and with fever and with inflammation and with fiery heat and with the sword and with blight and with mildew [on your crops]; and they will pursue you until you perish.

²³"The heaven which is over your head shall be bronze [giving no rain and blocking all prayers], and the earth which is under you, iron [hard to plow and yielding no produce].

²⁴"The LORD will make the rain of your land powder and dust; from heaven it will come down on you until you are destroyed.

²⁵"The LORD will cause you to be defeated before your enemies; you will go out against them one way, but flee

receiving outrageous blessings

God's promises usually come with conditions. He is merciful, and He does certain things for us that we do not deserve. Even when we have not behaved correctly, we can still pray for mercy and ask God to help us. But anybody who wants to live in the radical, outrageous, chase-you-down-the-street-and-overtake-you blessings of God has to do something to receive them.

The blessing package described in Deuteronomy 28:1–14 is conditional. Listen to the condition: "If you diligently listen to and obey the voice of the LORD your God . . . if you keep the commandments of the LORD your God and walk [that is, live your life each and every day] in His ways," then "all these blessings will come upon you and overtake you" (Deuteronomy 28:1, 2, 9). The promised blessings are many: blessings wherever you are or whatever you do; blessings in your family, with your work, and in your possessions; victory over your enemies; blessings of being established as God's holy people.

While we want all these blessings, many times we are not willing to do what it takes to receive them. Radical and outrageous blessings come from radical and outrageous obedience. They come from a willingness to obey God when He tells us to do something in His Word or by speaking in our hearts. We really do not need to complain about doing what God tells us because He gives us the ability to do the things He calls us to do. Our part is simply to listen to His voice and do what He says without reservation. That's when the blessings come.

before them seven ways, and you will be *an example of* terror to all the kingdoms of the earth [when they see your destruction]. [2 Chr 29:8]

26"Your carcasses will be food for all the birds of the sky and the beasts of the earth, and there will be no one to frighten them away.

27"The LORD will strike you with the boils of Egypt and with tumors and with the scab and the itch that you cannot heal.

28"The LORD will strike you with madness and with blindness and with bewilderment of heart *and* mind;

29and you will be groping at noon [in broad daylight], just as the blind grope in the darkness, and nothing you do will prosper; but you will only be oppressed *and* exploited and robbed continually, with no one to save you.

30"You will be pledged to marry a wife, but another man will be intimate with her [before you]; you will build a house, but you will not live in it; you will plant a vineyard, but you will not use its fruit.

31"Your ox will be slaughtered before your eyes, but you will not eat any of it; your donkey will be torn away from you, and it will not be returned to you; your sheep will be given to your enemies, and you will have no one to save you.

32"Your sons and daughters will be given to another people, while your eyes look on and long for them continually; but there will be nothing you can do. [2 Chr 29:9]

33"A people whom you do not know will eat the produce of your land and all the products of your labors, and you will never be anything but oppressed *and* exploited and crushed continually. [Judg 6:1–6; 13:1]

34You shall be driven mad by the sight of the things you see.

35"The LORD will strike you on the knees and on the legs with sore boils that you cannot heal, from the sole of your foot to the crown of your head.

36"The LORD will bring you and your king, whom you appoint over you, to a nation which you and your fathers have never known; there you will [be forced to] serve other gods, [lifeless gods of] wood and stone. [2 Kin 17:4, 6; 24:12, 14; 25:7, 11; Dan 6:11, 12]

37"And you will become a horror, a proverb [a mere object lesson], and a taunt [a derisive joke] among all the people to which the LORD drives you.

38"You will bring out a great quantity of seed to the field, but you will gather in little, because the locusts will consume it. [Hag 1:6]

39"You will plant vineyards and cultivate them, but you will not drink the wine or gather *the grapes,* because the worm will eat them.

40"You will have olive trees throughout your territory but you will not anoint yourselves with the oil, because your olives will drop off.

41"You will have sons and daughters, but they will not be yours [for long], because they will go into captivity. [Lam 1:5]

42"The cricket will take possession of all your trees and the produce of your ground. [Joel 1:4]

43"The stranger who lives among you will rise above you higher and higher, and you will go down lower and lower.

44"He will lend to you [out of his affluence], but you will not lend to him [because of your poverty]; he will be the head, and you the tail.

45"So all these curses will come on you and pursue you and overtake you until you are destroyed, because you would not obey the voice of the LORD your God by keeping His commandments and His statutes which He has commanded you.

46"They will be a sign and a wonder to you and your descendants forever.

47"Because you did not serve the

Lord your God with a heart full of joy and gladness for the abundance of all things [with which He blessed you],

⁴⁸you will therefore serve your enemies whom the Lord sends against you, in hunger and in thirst, in nakedness and in lack of all things; and He will put an iron yoke [of slavery] on your neck until He has destroyed you.

⁴⁹"The Lord will bring a nation against you from far away, from the end of the earth, [as swift] as the eagle swoops down [to attack], a nation whose language you will not understand,

⁵⁰a defiant nation who will have no respect for the old, nor show favor to the young,

⁵¹and it will eat the offspring of your herd and the produce of your ground until you are destroyed, who will leave you no grain, new wine, or oil, nor the offspring of your herd or the young of your flock until they have caused you to perish.

⁵²"They will besiege you in all your cities until your high and fortified walls in which you trusted come down throughout your land; and they will besiege you in all your cities throughout your land which the Lord your God has given you.

⁵³"Then you will eat the offspring of your own body [to avoid starvation], the flesh of your sons and daughters whom the Lord your God has given you, during the siege and the misery by which your enemy will oppress you. [2 Kin 6:24–29]

⁵⁴"The man who is most refined and well-bred among you will be cruel and hostile toward his brother and toward the wife he cherishes and toward the rest of his children who remain,

⁵⁵so that he will not give even one of them any of the flesh of his children which he will eat, because he has nothing else left, during the siege and the misery by which your enemy will oppress you in all your cities.

⁵⁶"The most refined and well-bred woman among you, who would not venture to set the sole of her foot on the ground because she is so delicate and pampered, will be cruel and hostile toward the husband she cherishes and toward her son and daughter,

⁵⁷and toward her afterbirth that comes from between her legs and toward the children whom she bears; for she will eat them secretly for lack of anything else, during the siege and the misery by which your enemy will oppress you in your cities.

⁵⁸"If you are not careful to do all the words of this law that are written in this book, to fear and honor with reverence this glorious and awesome name, the Lord your God,

⁵⁹then the Lord will bring extraordinary plagues on you and your descendants, even severe and lasting plagues, and miserable and chronic sicknesses.

⁶⁰"Moreover, He will bring on you all the diseases of Egypt of which you were afraid, and they will cling to you.

⁶¹"Also the Lord will bring on you every sickness and every plague which is not written in this book of this law, until you are destroyed.

⁶²"Because you did not obey the voice of the Lord your God, you who were as numerous as the stars of heaven shall be left few in number.

⁶³"It shall come about that just as the Lord delighted over you to make you prosper and multiply, so the Lord will delight over you to bring you to ruin and destruction; and you will be uprooted [violently] from the land which you are entering to possess.

⁶⁴"And the Lord will scatter you among all the nations, from one end of the earth to the other; and there you will [be forced to] serve other gods,

[lifeless gods of] wood and stone, which neither you nor your fathers have known. [Dan 3:6]

⁶⁵"Among those nations you will find no peace (rest), and there will be no resting place for the sole of your foot; but there the Lord will give you a trembling heart, failing eyes, and a despairing soul.

⁶⁶"Your life will hang in doubt before you; night and day you will be filled with anxiety and have no assurance of living.

⁶⁷"In the morning you will say, 'I wish it were evening!' and in the evening you will say, 'I wish it were morning!'—because of the dread in your heart with which you tremble, and because of the sight of your eyes which you will see.

⁶⁸"The Lord will bring you back to Egypt in ships, by the way about which I said to you, 'You will never see it again!' And there you will offer yourselves for sale to your enemies as male and female slaves, but there will be no one to buy you. [Hos 8:13]

29

THESE ARE the words of the covenant which the Lord commanded Moses to make with the sons of Israel in the land of Moab, in addition to the covenant which He made with them at Horeb (Sinai).

²Moses summoned all Israel and said to them, "You have seen all that the Lord did before your eyes in the land of Egypt to Pharaoh, to all his servants, and to all his land;

³the great trials [of Pharaoh] which your eyes have seen, the signs and those great wonders.

⁴"Yet to this day the Lord has not given you a heart *and* mind to understand, nor eyes to see, nor ears to hear.

⁵"I have led you in the wilderness forty years; your clothes have not worn out on you, and your sandals have not worn out on your feet.

⁶"You have not eaten bread, nor have you drunk wine or strong drink, so that you might know that I am the Lord your God [on whom you must depend].

⁷"When you reached this place, Sihon the king of Heshbon and Og the king of Bashan came out to meet us in battle, but we defeated them;

⁸and we took their land and gave it as an inheritance to the tribe of Reuben, the tribe of Gad, and the half-tribe of Manasseh.

⁹"So keep the words of this covenant and obey them, so that you may prosper *and* be successful in everything that you do.

¹⁰"All of you stand today before the Lord your God—your chiefs, your tribes, your elders and your officers, *even* all the men of Israel,

¹¹your little ones, your wives, and the stranger (resident alien, foreigner) who is in your camps, from the one who chops *and* gathers your firewood to the one who draws your water—

¹²so that you may enter into the covenant of the Lord your God, and into His oath *and* agreement which the Lord your God is making with you today,

¹³so that He may establish you today as His people and that He may be your God, just as He spoke to you and as He swore to your fathers, to Abraham, Isaac, and Jacob.

¹⁴"It is not with you alone that I am making this covenant and this oath,

¹⁵but with those [future Israelites] who are not here with us today, as well as with those who stand here with us today in the presence of the Lord our God

¹⁶(for you know how we lived in the land of Egypt, and how we passed through the nations along the way;

¹⁷and you have seen their detestable acts and their [repulsive] idols of wood and stone, [lifeless images] of silver and gold, which *they had* with them),

¹⁸so that there will not be among you

a man or woman, or family or tribe, whose heart turns away today from the Lord our God, to go and serve the [false] gods of these nations; so that there will not be among you a root [of idolatry] bearing poisonous fruit and wormwood (bitterness).

¹⁹"It will happen that when he (a renegade) hears the words of this oath, and he imagines himself as blessed, saying, 'I will have peace *and* safety even though I walk within the stubbornness of my heart [rejecting God and His law], in order that the watered *land* dwindles away along with the dry [destroying everything],'

²⁰the Lord will not be willing to forgive him, but then the anger of the Lord and His jealousy will burn against that man, and every curse which is written in this book will rest on him; the Lord will blot out his name from under heaven.

²¹"Then the Lord will single him out for disaster from all the tribes of Israel [making an example of him], according to all the curses of the covenant that are written in this Book of the Law.

²²"Now the next generation, your children who come after you and the foreigner who comes from a distant land, when they see the plagues of this land and the diseases with which the Lord has afflicted it, will say,

²³'The whole land is brimstone and salt, a burning waste, unsown and unproductive, and no grass grows in it; it is like the overthrow of Sodom and Gomorrah, Admah and Zeboiim, which the Lord overthrew in His anger and wrath.'

²⁴"All the nations will say, 'Why has the Lord done this thing to this land? Why this great outburst of anger?'

²⁵"Then *people* will say, 'It is because they abandoned (broke) the covenant of the Lord, the God of their fathers,

choose life

Thousands of thoughts are presented to our minds every day, and we must allow our minds to be renewed after the Spirit and not after the flesh. Our carnal (worldly, fleshly) minds have had so much practice operating freely that we can think wrong thoughts without much effort at all. On the other hand, we have to purposefully choose to think right thoughts. After we have finally decided to be like-minded with God, then we will need to *choose* and *continue to choose* right thoughts.

When we begin to feel that the battle of the mind is just too difficult and that we are not going to make it, we must cast down that negative kind of thinking. We need to choose to think that we are going to make it and decide not to quit. When bombarded with doubts and fears, we need to take a stand and say: "I will never give up! God is on my side. He loves me, and He is helping me!"

You and I will have many choices to make throughout our lives. In Deuteronomy 30:19, the Lord told His people that He had set before them life and death and urged them to choose life. Proverbs 18:21 also tells us we can choose life or death. It says, "Death and life are in the power of the tongue, and those who love it and indulge it will eat its fruit and bear the consequences of their words."

Our thoughts become our words. Therefore, it is vitally important that we *choose* life-giving thoughts.

life point

Deuteronomy 30:2 encourages us to obey God wholeheartedly. To whatever degree we love God, we obey Him. To whatever degree we obey God, that's the measure of our love for Him. Our love for Jesus grows as we obey Him.

which He made with them when He brought them out of the land of Egypt.

²⁶'For they went and served other gods and worshiped them, [false] gods whom they have not known and whom He had not allotted (given) to them.

²⁷'So the anger of the LORD burned against this land, bringing on it every curse that is written in this book;

²⁸and the LORD uprooted them from their land in anger and in wrath and in great indignation, and cast them into another land, as it is this day.'

²⁹"The secret things belong to the LORD our God, but the things which are revealed *and* disclosed belong to us and to our children forever, so that we may do all of the words of this law.

30

"SO IT shall be when all these things have come on you, the blessing and the curse which I have set before you, and you call them to mind in all the nations where the LORD your God has driven you,

²and you have returned to the LORD your God and have listened to *and* obeyed His voice with all your heart and with all your soul, in accordance with everything that I am commanding you today, you and your children,

³then the LORD your God will restore your fortunes [in your return from exile], and have compassion on you, and will gather you together again from all the peoples (nations) where He has scattered you.

⁴"Even if any of your dispersed are at the ends of the earth, the LORD your God will gather you together from there, and from there He will bring you back.

⁵"The LORD your God will bring you into the land which your fathers possessed, and you will take possession of it; and He shall make you prosper and multiply—even more than your fathers.

⁶"And the LORD your God will circumcise your heart and the hearts of your descendants [that is, He will remove the desire to sin from your heart], so that you will love the LORD your God with all your heart and all your soul, so that you may live [as a recipient of His blessing].

⁷"The LORD your God will inflict all these curses on your enemies and on those who hate you, who have persecuted you.

⁸"And you shall again listen to *and* obey the voice of the LORD, and do all His commandments which I command you today.

⁹"Then the LORD your God shall make you abundantly prosperous in everything that you do, in the offspring of your body and in the offspring of your cattle and in the produce of your land; for the LORD will again delight over you for good, just as He delighted over your fathers,

¹⁰if you listen to *and* obey the voice of the LORD your God to keep His commandments and His statutes which are written in this Book of the Law,

speak the Word

Thank You, God, that as I live in obedience to You, You will make me abundantly prosperous in everything I do, in my family, and in everything that concerns me.
—ADAPTED FROM DEUTERONOMY 30:9

and if you turn to the LORD your God with all your heart and with all your soul (your entire being).

¹¹"For this commandment which I am commanding you today is not too difficult for you, nor is it out of reach.

¹²"It is not [a secret hidden] in heaven, that you should say, 'Who will go up to heaven for us and bring it to us, so that we may hear it and obey it?'

¹³"Nor is it beyond the sea, that you should say, 'Who will cross the sea for us and bring it to us, so that we may hear it and obey it?'

¹⁴"But the word is very near you, in your mouth and in your heart, so that you may obey it.

¹⁵"Listen closely, I have set before you today life and prosperity (good), and death and adversity (evil);

¹⁶in that I command you today to love the LORD your God, to walk [that is, to live each and every day] in His ways and to keep His commandments and His statutes and His judgments (precepts), so that you will live and multiply, and that the LORD your God will bless you in the land which you are entering to possess.

¹⁷"But if your heart turns away and you will not hear *and* obey, but are drawn away and worship other gods and serve them,

¹⁸I declare to you today that you will certainly perish. You will not live long

life point

Sometimes we think we have to wait until we are no longer afraid before we try to do something. But we probably will not accomplish much for God, for others, or even for ourselves if we wait until all our fear is gone. We need to face our fear with courage and do some things despite feelings of trepidation. We can learn to "do it afraid." God promises us that He will be with us (see Deuteronomy 31:6).

in the land which you cross the Jordan to enter and possess.

¹⁹"I call heaven and earth as witnesses against you today, that I have set before you life and death, the blessing and the curse; therefore, you shall choose life in order that you may live, you and your descendants,

²⁰by loving the LORD your God, by obeying His voice, and by holding closely to Him; for He is your life [your good life, your abundant life, your fulfillment] and the length of your days, that you may live in the land which the LORD promised (swore) to give to your fathers, to Abraham, Isaac, and Jacob."

31 SO MOSES went and spoke these words to all Israel. ²And he said to them, "I am a hundred and twenty years old today; I am no longer able to come in and go out [as your spiritual and military leader], and the LORD has said to me, 'You shall not cross this Jordan.'

³"It is the LORD your God who will cross ahead of you; He will destroy these nations before you, and you shall dispossess them. Joshua is the one who will go across before you [to lead you], just as the LORD has said.

⁴"The LORD will do to them just as He did to Sihon and Og, the kings of the Amorites, and to their land, when He destroyed them.

⁵"The LORD will hand them over to you, and you shall do to them in accordance with all the commandments which I have commanded you.

⁶"Be strong and courageous, do not be afraid or tremble in dread before them, for it is the LORD your God who goes with you. He will not fail you or abandon you."

⁷Then Moses called to Joshua and said to him in the sight of all [the people of] Israel, "Be strong and courageous, for you will go with this people into the land which the LORD has sworn

to their fathers to give them, and you will give it to them as an inheritance.

⁸"It is the LORD who goes before you; He will be with you. He will not fail you or abandon you. Do not fear or be dismayed."

⁹So Moses wrote this law and gave it to the priests, the sons of Levi who carried the ark of the covenant of the LORD, and to all the elders of Israel.

¹⁰Then Moses commanded them, saying, "At the end of *every* seven years, at the time of year when debts are forgiven, at the Feast of Booths (Tabernacles),

¹¹when all Israel comes to appear before the LORD your God in the place which He chooses, you shall read this law before all [the people of] Israel so that they may hear.

God will go with you

I first read Deuteronomy 31:6 in the Amplified Classic version, and in it, Moses told the Israelites to be "strong, courageous, and firm." Do you know what it means to be firm? It means to stick to what you know is right without letting anything or anyone talk you out of it.

Moses also told Joshua that he was to be strong, courageous, and firm because he was to lead the people into the land that the Lord had given them. He assured him that the Lord would never fail him or forsake him and that *God would go with him* to lead him to victory. God makes that same promise to you and me today.

It is comforting to know that everywhere we go, God has been before us to prepare the way. Our ministry does many conferences, and prior to our conferences in other states or countries, someone always goes ahead of us to get things ready. They make sure all the arrangements are properly made before Dave and I arrive. For example, we once had a conference planned in another part of the world. When our employee arrived ahead of us, he realized that the arena we had planned to use was in an inaccessible part of the city. The traffic would be heavy before and after meetings, there was only one road in and one road out, and it could take as long as four hours for people to get through. We were glad we had sent him months in advance because he was able to change the meeting place and save us a lot of time.

Also, at least two days before we arrive in a city, a team scouts out the arrangements and takes care of details so that when we arrive we can wholly focus on ministering to the people. This makes our ministry much more fruitful. Knowing that someone has gone before me comforts me; it gives me confidence. Likewise, knowing that God has gone before me in every situation of my life gives me great confidence, and I am free to live without fear.

Whatever your situation, know that God promises to go with you. If you have a court case coming up, you need to understand that God has already gone ahead of you into the court before you arrive. Or, if you need to confront your employer about some issue at work, believe what the Word says. Trust God that He will give you favor and give you the right words to speak in loving ways when the time comes.

Whenever you go, whatever your circumstances, ask God to go before you and prepare the way. He will do it—then all you have to do is follow.

¹²"Assemble the people, the men and the women and children and the stranger (resident alien, foreigner) within your cities, so that they may hear and learn and fear the Lord your God [with awe-filled reverence and profound respect], and be careful to obey all the words of this law.

¹³"Their children, who have not known [the law], will hear and learn to fear [and worship] the Lord your God, as long as you live in the land which you are crossing the Jordan to possess."

¹⁴Then the Lord said to Moses, "Behold, the time for you to die is near; call Joshua, and present yourselves at the Tent of Meeting, so that I may commission him." So Moses and Joshua went and presented themselves at the Tent of Meeting.

¹⁵Then the Lord appeared in the tent in a pillar of cloud, and the pillar of cloud stood beside the doorway of the tent.

¹⁶The Lord said to Moses, "Behold, you are about to lie down [in death] with your fathers; and this people will arise and play the prostitute (commit apostasy) with the foreign gods [of the people] of the land, where they go to be among them. They will abandon (turn away from) Me and break My covenant which I have made with them.

¹⁷"Then My anger will be kindled and burn against them in that day, and I will abandon (turn away from) them and hide My face from them. They will be devoured, and many evils and troubles will come on them, so that they will say in that day, 'Is it not because our God is not among us that these evils have come on us?'

¹⁸"But I will certainly hide My face [from them] in that day because of all the evil which they will do, for they will turn to other gods [to worship lifeless idols, to honor handmade relics].

¹⁹"Now then, write this song for yourselves, and teach it to the sons of Israel; put it in their mouth, so that this song may be a witness for Me against the sons of Israel.

²⁰"For when I bring them into the land which I have sworn to their fathers, a land [of plenty] flowing with milk and honey, and they have eaten and are satisfied and become prosperous, then they will turn to other gods and serve them, and despise and reject Me and break My covenant.

²¹"Then it shall come about, when many evils and troubles have come on them, that this [sacred] song will confront them as a witness; for it will not be forgotten from the mouth of their descendants. For I know their inclination which is developing even now, before I bring them into the land which I have sworn to give them."

²²So Moses wrote this song the same day, and taught it to the children of Israel. [Deut 32:1–43]

²³Then He commanded and commissioned Joshua, the son of Nun, and said, "Be strong and courageous, for you will bring the sons of Israel into the land which I have sworn to give them, and I will be with you."

²⁴And when Moses completely finished writing the words of this law in a book,

²⁵he commanded the Levites who carried the ark of the covenant of the Lord, saying,

²⁶"Take this Book of the Law and put it beside the ark of the covenant of the Lord your God, so that it may remain there as a witness against you.

²⁷"For I know your rebellion and contention and your stubbornness; behold, while I am still alive with you today, you have been rebellious against the Lord; how much more, then, after my death?

²⁸"Assemble before me all the elders of your tribes and your officers, so

that I may speak these words in their hearing and call heaven and earth as witnesses against them.

29"For I know that after my death you will behave corruptly and turn from the way which I have commanded you; and evil will come upon you in the latter days, because you will do evil in the sight of the LORD, provoking Him to anger with the work of your hands."

30Then Moses spoke in the hearing of all the congregation of Israel the words of this song, until they were ended:

32 "LISTEN, O heavens, and I will speak;
And let the earth hear the words of my mouth.
2"Let my teaching drop as the rain,
My speech distill as the dew,
As the light rain upon the tender grass,
And as the spring showers upon the herb.
3"For I proclaim the name [and presence] of the LORD;
Ascribe greatness and honor to our God!
4"The Rock! His work is perfect,
For all His ways are just;
A God of faithfulness without iniquity (injustice),
Just and upright is He.
5"They (Israel) have acted corruptly toward Him.
They are not His children, because of their [moral] defect;
But are a perverse and crooked generation.
6"Do you thus repay the LORD,
O foolish and unwise people?
Is not He your Father who has acquired you [as His own]?
He has made you and established you [as a nation].
7"Remember the days of old,

Consider the years of many generations.
Ask your father, and he will inform you,
Your elders, and they will tell you.
8"When the Most High gave the nations their inheritance,
When He separated the sons of man,
He set the boundaries of the peoples
According to the number of the sons of Israel.
9"For the LORD's portion and chosen share is His people;
Jacob (Israel) is the allotment of His inheritance.
10"He found him in a desert land,
In the howling wasteland of a wilderness;
He kept circling him, He took care of him,
He protected him as the apple of His eye.
11"As an eagle that protects its nest,

life point

God is our Rock (see Deuteronomy 32:4) and place of refuge. He is solid, stable, steadfast, dependable, always there, always the same, always good and loving, always kind and merciful. He is great and unfailing, faithful and just, perfect and right in all His doings! We may have emotional ups and downs as we encounter the influences of negative circumstances and feelings. But the Lord changes not, and He cannot be moved by circumstances that would flatten us. We can trust our Rock because He does not waver in His faithfulness to us. We can learn to respond to life as He does as we allow ourselves to be molded and transformed into His image. He is our Rock, but He is also our Example. I encourage you to be like He is—faithful and steadfast.

That flutters over its young,
He spread out His wings and took
   them,
He carried them on His pinions.
   [Luke 13:34]
¹²"So the LORD alone led him;
There was no foreign god with
   him.
¹³"He made him (Israel) ride on the
   high places of the earth,
And he ate the produce of the field;
And He made him suck honey
   from the rock,
And [olive] oil from the flinty rock,
¹⁴Butter *and* curds of cows, and milk
   of the flock,
With fat of lambs,
And rams, the breed of Bashan,
   and goats,
With the finest of the wheat;
And you drank wine, the blood of
   grapes.
¹⁵"But Jeshurun (Israel) became fat
   and kicked [at God].
You became fat, thick, sleek, *and*
   obstinate!
Then he abandoned God who had
   made him,
And scorned the Rock of his
   salvation.
¹⁶"They provoked Him to jealousy
   with strange *gods* [by denying
   Him the honor and loyalty that is
   rightfully and uniquely His];
And with repulsive acts they
   provoked Him to anger.
¹⁷"They sacrificed to demons, not to
   God,
To gods whom they have not
   known,
New *gods* who came lately,
Whom your fathers never feared.
¹⁸"You were unmindful of the Rock
   who bore you,
And you forgot the God who gave
   you birth.
¹⁹"The LORD saw it, and rejected
   them,

Out of indignation with His sons
   and His daughters.
²⁰"Then He said, 'I will hide My face
   from them,
I will see what their end *shall be;*
For they are a perverse generation,
Sons in whom there is no
   faithfulness.
²¹'They have made Me jealous with
   what is not God;
They have provoked Me to anger
   with their idols.
So I will make them jealous with
   those who are not a people;
I will provoke them to anger with a
   foolish nation.
²²'For a fire is kindled by My anger,
And it burns to the depths of Sheol
   (the place of the dead, the nether
   world),
It devours the earth with its yield,
And sets on fire the foundations of
   the mountains.
²³'I will heap misfortunes on them;
I will use My arrows on them.
²⁴'They will be wasted by hunger,
   and consumed by plague
And a bitter destruction;
And I will send the teeth of beasts
   against them,
With the venom of crawling things
   of the dust.
²⁵'Outside the sword will bereave,
And inside [the chambers] terror—
For both young man and virgin,
For the nursing child and the man
   of gray hair.
²⁶'I would have said, "I will cut them
   to pieces [scattering them far
   away],
I will remove the memory of them
   from men,"
²⁷Had I not feared the provocation of
   the enemy,
That their adversaries would
   misjudge,
That they would say, "Our [own]
   hand has prevailed,

And the Lord has not done all this.'"

28 "For they are a nation devoid of counsel,
And there is no understanding in them.
29 "O that they were wise, that they understood this,
That they could discern their future *and* ultimate fate!
30 "How could one chase a thousand,
And two put ten thousand to flight,
Unless their Rock had sold them,
And the Lord had given them up?
31 "For their rock is not like our Rock,
Even our enemies themselves judge this.
32 "For their vine is from the vine of Sodom,
And from the fields of Gomorrah;
Their grapes are grapes of poison,
Their clusters, bitter.
33 "Their wine is the venom of serpents,
And the deadly poison of vipers.
34 'Is it not laid up in store with Me,
Sealed up in My treasuries?
35 'Vengeance is Mine, and retribution,
In due time their foot will slip;
For the day of their disaster is at hand,
And their doom hurries to meet them.'
36 "For the Lord will vindicate His people,
And will have compassion on His servants,
When He sees that their strength (hand) is gone,
And none remains, whether bond or free.
37 "And He will say, 'Where are their gods,
The rock in which they took refuge?
38 'Who ate the fat of their sacrifices,
And drank the wine of their drink offering?
Let them rise up and help you,
Let them be your hiding place!
39 'See now that I, I am He,
And there is no god besides Me;
It is I who put to death and I who give life.
I have wounded and it is I who heal,
And there is no one who can deliver from [the power of] My hand.
40 'Indeed, I lift up My hand to heaven,
And say (swear an oath), as I live forever,
41 If I sharpen the lightning of My sword,
And My hand takes hold of judgment,
I will render vengeance on My adversaries,
And I will repay those who hate Me.
42 'I will make My arrows drunk with blood,
And My sword will devour flesh,
With the blood of the slain and the captives,
From the heads of the leaders of the enemy.'
43 "Rejoice, O nations, with His people;
For He will avenge the blood of His servants,
And will render vengeance on His adversaries,
And will atone for His land *and* His people."

44 Then Moses came and spoke all the words of this song in the hearing of the people, he and Joshua the son of Nun.
45 When Moses had finished speaking all these words to all [the people of] Israel,
46 he said to them, "Take to heart all the words of warning which I am

speaking to you today; and you shall command your children to observe them carefully—to do all the words of this law.

⁴⁷"For it is not an empty *or* trivial matter for you; indeed it is your [very] life. By [honoring and obeying] this word you will live long in the land, which you are crossing the Jordan to possess."

⁴⁸And the LORD said to Moses that very same day,

⁴⁹"Go up to this mountain of the Abarim, Mount Nebo, which is in the land of Moab opposite Jericho, and look at the land of Canaan, which I am giving to the sons of Israel as a possession.

⁵⁰"Then die on the mountain which you climb, and be gathered to your people [in death], just as Aaron your brother died on Mount Hor and was gathered to his people,

⁵¹because you broke faith with Me among of the sons of Israel at the waters of Meribah-kadesh, in the Wilderness of Zin, and because you did not treat Me as holy among of the sons of Israel. [Num 20:8–12; 27:14]

⁵²"For you shall see the land opposite you from a distance, but you shall not go there, into the land which I am giving to the children of Israel."

33 THIS IS the blessing with which Moses the man of God blessed the sons of Israel before his death.

²He said,

"The LORD came from Sinai,
And dawned on them from Seir;
He shone forth from Mount Paran,
And He came from among ten
  thousand holy ones;
At His right hand was a flaming
  fire, a law, for them.
³"Indeed, He loves His people;
All Your holy ones are in Your
  hand.

They followed in Your steps;
They accept *and* receive direction
  from You.
⁴"Moses commanded us with a law,
As a possession for the assembly of
  Jacob.
⁵"The LORD was King in Jeshurun
  (Israel),
When the heads of the people
  were gathered,
The tribes of Israel together.

⁶"May [the tribe of] Reuben live
  and not die out,
But let his men be few."

⁷And [Moses said] this of Judah:

"Hear, O LORD, the voice of Judah,
And bring him to his people.
With his hands he contended for
  them,
And may You be a help against his
  enemies."

⁸Of Levi he said,

"Your Thummim and Your Urim
  belong to Your godly man
  [Aaron],
Whom You tested *and* proved at
  Massah,
With whom You contended at the
  waters of Meribah; [Num 20:1–13]
⁹Who said of his father and mother,
'I did not consider them';
Nor did he acknowledge his
  brothers,
Nor did he regard his own sons,
For the priests observed Your word,
And kept Your covenant.
¹⁰"The priests shall teach Your
  ordinances (judgments) to Jacob,
And Your law to Israel.
They shall put incense before You,
And whole burnt offerings on Your
  altar.
¹¹"O LORD, bless Levi's substance
  (ability),
And accept *and* take pleasure in
  the work of his hands;

Crush *and* shatter the loins of
those who rise up against him,
And of those who hate him, so that
they do not rise *again*."

¹²Of Benjamin he said,

"May the beloved of the Lord dwell
in safety by Him;
He shields *and* covers him all the
day long,
And he dwells between His
shoulders."

¹³And of Joseph he said,

"Blessed by the Lord be his land,
With the precious things of
heaven, with the dew,
And from the deep *water* that lies
beneath,
¹⁴With the precious fruits of the sun,
And with the precious produce of
the months.
¹⁵"With the best things of the
ancient mountains,
And with the precious things of
the everlasting hills,
¹⁶With the precious things of the
earth and its fullness,
And the favor *and* goodwill of Him
who dwelt in the bush.
Let *these blessings* come upon the
head of Joseph,
And upon the crown of the head
of him who was distinguished
[as a prince] among his brothers.
[Ex 3:4]
¹⁷"His majesty is like a firstborn
young bull,

And his horns like the horns of the
wild ox;
With them he will gore the
peoples,
All of them together, to the ends of
the earth.
And those are the ten thousands of
Ephraim,
And those are the thousands of
Manasseh."

¹⁸Of Zebulun he said,

"Rejoice, Zebulun, in your interests
abroad,
And, Issachar, in your tents [at
home].
¹⁹"They will call the peoples to the
mountain (Mount Carmel);
There they will offer sacrifices of
righteousness;
For they will draw out the
abundance of the seas,
And the hidden treasures of the
sand."

²⁰Of Gad he said,

"Blessed is the one who enlarges
Gad;
He lurks like a lioness,
And tears the arm and the crown
of the head.
²¹"He selected the best [land] for
himself,
For there the leader's portion was
reserved;
Yet he came with the leaders of the
people;
He carried out the justice
(righteous will) of the Lord,

speak the Word

*Thank You, God, that You love me, that I am in Your hand, that I can follow
in Your steps and receive direction for my life from You.*
—ADAPTED FROM Deuteronomy 33:3

*I pray, God, that You will bless everything I have, as You did for Levi, and that
You will accept and take pleasure in the work of my hands.*
—ADAPTED FROM Deuteronomy 33:11

And His ordinances (judgments) with Israel." [Num 32:29–33]

²²Of Dan he said,

"Dan is a lion's cub,
That leaps forth from Bashan."

²³Of Naphtali he said,

"O Naphtali, satisfied with favor,
And full of the blessing of the LORD,
Take possession of the sea [of Galilee] and the south."

²⁴Of Asher he said,

"More blessed than sons is Asher;
May he be favored by his brothers,
And may he dip his foot in oil.
²⁵"Your strongholds will be iron and bronze,
And as your days are, so will your strength, your rest *and* security be.
²⁶"There is none like the God of Jeshurun (Israel),
Who rides the heavens to your help,
And through the skies in His majestic glory.
²⁷"The eternal God is your refuge *and* dwelling place,
And underneath are the everlasting arms;
He drove out the enemy from before you,
And said, 'Destroy!'
²⁸"So Israel dwells in safety *and* security,

life point

It is comforting to know that underneath us are God's everlasting arms (see Deuteronomy 33:27). No matter what our circumstances, His loving arms come down to where we are and lift us up. As we make the conscious decision to lean on the arm of the Lord and no longer lean on the arm of the flesh, we will experience the manifest presence of God.

The fountain of Jacob alone *and* secluded,
In a land of grain and new wine;
His heavens also drop down dew.
²⁹"Happy *and* blessed are you, O Israel;
Who is like you, a people saved by the LORD,
The Shield of your help,
And the Sword of your majesty!
Your enemies will cringe before you,
And you will tread on their high places [tramping down their idolatrous altars]."

34 NOW MOSES went up from the plains of Moab to Mount Nebo, to the top of Pisgah, that is opposite Jericho. And the LORD showed him all the land, from Gilead to Dan,
²and all Naphtali and the land of Ephraim and Manasseh, and all the land of Judah to the western sea (Mediterranean Sea),
³and the Negev (South country) and the plain in the Valley of Jericho, the city of palm trees, as far as Zoar.
⁴Then the LORD said to him, "This is the land which I swore to Abraham, Isaac, and Jacob, saying, 'I will give it to your descendants.' I have let you see it with your eyes, but you shall not go over there."
⁵So Moses the servant of the LORD died there in the land of Moab, according to the word of the LORD.
⁶And He buried him in the valley in the land of Moab, opposite Beth-peor; but no man knows where his burial place is to this day.
⁷Although Moses was a hundred and twenty years old when he died, his eyesight was not dim, nor his natural strength abated. [Deut 31:2]
⁸So the sons of Israel wept for Moses in the plains of Moab for thirty days; then the days of weeping and mourning for Moses were ended.

⁹Now Joshua the son of Nun was filled with the spirit of wisdom, for Moses had laid his hands on him; so the sons of Israel listened to him and did as the Lord commanded Moses.

¹⁰Since that time no prophet has risen in Israel like Moses, whom the Lord knew face to face,

¹¹[none equal to him] in all the signs and wonders which the Lord sent him to perform in the land of Egypt against Pharaoh, all his servants, and all his land,

¹²and in all the mighty power and all the great *and* terrible deeds which Moses performed in the sight of all Israel.

speak the Word

Lord, cause me to be like Joshua, filled with the spirit of wisdom.
−ADAPTED FROM DEUTERONOMY 34:9

Joshua

Author:
Uncertain; attributed to Joshua

Date:
1400 BC–1375 BC

Everyday Life Principles:
We may have to fight for the things God promises us.

Following God requires boldness and brings blessing.

God doesn't tell us *not to feel* fear; He tells us *not to give in* to it.

The book of Joshua teaches us much about the kind of courage we need if we are going to possess God's promises and enjoy the blessings He has for us. God had already given the Israelites the Promised Land, but they did have to fight for possession of it. They had to believe that God would help them conquer the enemies who stood between them and the Promised Land, and they had to trust that He would miraculously get them across the strong, swift current of the Jordan River when it was so high that it overflowed its banks. Not only did they have enemies to fight on their way to the Promised Land, they also had enemies to fight once they got there.

As their leader, Joshua not only needed to be courageous himself; he also needed to inspire courage in the people. When God spoke to him to "fear not," He wasn't telling him not to feel fear; He was telling him not to let fear hold him back. In other words, He was saying to Joshua, "Do it afraid." And Joshua did.

I pray that you, like Joshua, will be strong and courageous in your everyday life and that you will inspire others to be bold as well. Do not give in to fear, but take action in spite of it. Press forward with boldness into everything God has for you, and do not allow fear to rob you of any of the blessings God wants to give you.

1 NOW IT happened after the death of Moses the servant of the LORD, that the LORD spoke to Joshua the son of Nun, Moses' servant (attendant), saying, [Deut 34:4–8]

²"Moses My servant is dead; now therefore arise [to take his place], cross over this Jordan, you and all this people, into the land which I am giving to them, to the sons of Israel.

³"I have given you every place on which the sole of your foot treads, just as I promised to Moses.

⁴"From the wilderness [of Arabia in the south] and this Lebanon [in the north], even as far as the great river, the river Euphrates [in the east], all the land of the Hittites (Canaan), and as far as the Great [Mediterranean] Sea toward the west shall be your territory.

⁵"No man will [be able to] stand before you [to oppose you] as long as you live. Just as I was [present] with Moses, so will I be with you; I will not fail you or abandon you.

⁶"Be strong *and* confident and courageous, for you will give this people as an inheritance the land which I swore to their fathers (ancestors) to give them.

⁷"Only be strong and very courageous; be careful to do [everything] in accordance with the entire law which Moses My servant commanded you;

leave the past behind

After Moses' death, the law allowed the Israelites thirty days to mourn. After those days were completed, God told Joshua it was time for him to take his new position (see Joshua 1:2). It was time to start moving toward new things. Joshua would miss Moses, but he knew he had to obey God and move on. There is a proper time for mourning the things that we have lost or that have come to an end. But, ultimately, we must choose to start living and making progress again. We all have a past, but thank God we all have a future—and a good one, according to His Word (see Jeremiah 29:11).

Because Moses had done so much for Joshua and the Israelites before he died, they needed to learn how to handle new responsibilities after his death. They may not have felt prepared to step out into new things, but God knew they were ready. It is actually good when we do not "feel" ready, because then we are more likely to totally lean on God. If we feel self-sufficient, God can't really use us.

New things always seem frightening, but soon they will become old and familiar, and God will have another "new thing" on the horizon of our lives. We need to grow accustomed to stepping out into new things. The more we do, the more we realize that we don't have to be comfortable to be obedient. In order to take hold of something new, we must let go of the old and allow ourselves time to get acquainted with the new. I believe that when God reminded Joshua that Moses was dead, He was encouraging him to let go of the past and press on. I encourage you to do the same.

Remember the blessings of your past, but do not get stuck there. God is always doing something new! When God called Abraham to a new place, he did not even think about where he was to go. He simply trusted God because he knew God was faithful. Do not be afraid to release and walk away from what God is finished with; He has wonderful new things waiting for you!

do not turn from it to the right or to the left, so that you may prosper *and* be successful wherever you go.

⁸"This Book of the Law shall not depart from your mouth, but you shall read [and meditate on] it day and night, so that you may be careful to do [everything] in accordance with all that is written in it; for then you will make your way prosperous, and then you will be successful.

⁹"Have I not commanded you? Be strong and courageous! Do not be terrified or dismayed (intimidated), for the LORD your God is with you wherever you go."

¹⁰Then Joshua commanded the officers of the people, saying,

¹¹"Go throughout the camp and command the people, saying, 'Prepare your provisions, for within three days you are to cross this [river] Jordan, to go in to take possession of the land which the LORD your God is giving you to possess [as an inheritance].'"

¹²To the Reubenites and to the Gadites and to the half-tribe of Manasseh, Joshua said,

¹³"Remember the word which Moses the servant of the LORD commanded you, saying, 'The LORD your God is giving you rest (peace) and will give you this land [east of the Jordan].'

life point

"Moses My servant is dead" (Joshua 1:2). With those words plainly said, God opened a new chapter in Joshua's life. God told Joshua that he was to accept a new responsibility—to lead the people across the Jordan into the Promised Land. Like Joshua, we also need to be willing to take responsibility as we go forward to claim our spiritual inheritance. Every blessing God gives us comes with a measure of responsibility, and we need to take that responsibility seriously.

life point

How much time do you spend thinking about the Word of God? The Bible says that if you want to make your journey through life prosperous and be successful, the key is to meditate on the Word of God day and night (see Joshua 1:8).

For most of my life, I did not think about what I was thinking about. I simply thought whatever crossed my mind because I did not know that Satan could inject thoughts into my brain. Most of my thoughts were either lies from Satan or just plain nonsense—things that wasted my time because they were not truly important. The devil was controlling my life because he was controlling my thoughts. I did not know that if I would simply meditate on God's Word, I could push back the enemy. When we fill our minds with God's truth, we will find that our thoughts are thoughts of truth, freedom, victory, and peace.

¹⁴"Your wives, your children, and your cattle shall [be allowed to] stay in the land which Moses gave you on this [eastern] side of the Jordan, but you shall go across [the river] before your brothers (the other tribes) armed for battle, all your brave warriors, and you shall help them [conquer and take possession of their land],

¹⁵until the LORD gives your brothers rest, as *He has given* you, and they also take possession of the land which the LORD your God is giving them. Then you shall [be allowed to] return to your own land, and take possession of that which Moses the servant of the LORD gave you beyond the Jordan toward the sunrise."

¹⁶They answered Joshua, saying, "All that you have commanded us we

will do, and wherever you send us we will go.

¹⁷"Just as we obeyed Moses in all things, so will we obey you; only may the Lᴏʀᴅ your God be with you as He was with Moses.

¹⁸"Any man who rebels against your command and does not obey everything that you command him, shall be put to death; only be strong and courageous."

2 JOSHUA THE son of Nun sent two men as scouts secretly from Shittim, saying, "Go, view the land, especially Jericho [the walled city]." So they went and came to the house of a prostitute named Rahab, and lodged there.

²Now the king of Jericho was told, "Behold, men from the sons of Israel have come here tonight to spy *and* search out the land."

³So the king of Jericho sent *word* to Rahab, saying, "Bring out the men who have come to you, who entered your house, because they have come [as spies] to search out all the land."

⁴But the woman had taken the two men and hidden them; so she said, "Yes, two men came to me, but I did not know where they were from.

⁵"When *it was time* to close the [city] gate at dark, the men left; I do not know where they went. Pursue them quickly, for [if you do] you will overtake them."

⁶But [in fact] she had brought the

passing the faithfulness test

Moses was faithful to God's people during the forty years they wandered in the wilderness. Time and time again, he successfully passed the "faithfulness test." But God had spent many years preparing Moses to lead the people out of bondage. On the back side of the desert, God had taught him how to be faithful (see Exodus 2:23–3:1). Likewise, Joshua had learned to be faithful throughout the years and had served loyally under Moses. When God chose Joshua to lead Israel after Moses' death, He knew Joshua would be a faithful leader because he had been trustworthy in the past. Joshua is an excellent example of a faithful person, and his life reminds us that God rewards faithfulness.

God works through and blesses faithful people—people who are faithful in the wilderness (in times of testing) as well as in the Promised Land (in times of blessing). Being faithful means being devoted, supportive, and loyal. Faithful people are worthy of trust or belief; they are reliable, consistent, constant, and steadfast. They will stay wherever God places them and be true to those God has given them to work with.

If we want to exercise authority, we must first learn to come under authority and stay wherever God has placed us until He moves us. Like Joshua, we must respect and be obedient to those in authority over us. It's important to do the right thing simply because it is right, even though we may never understand the "*why*" of every situation—which is a real test of our faithfulness and obedience. We need to be faithful to stay where God has placed us and perhaps under the leadership of an authority figure we do not particularly like.

Do you want to have authority and be respected? Then learn to be reliable and loyal. God loves to reward the faithful.

life point

I love the fact that Rahab was able to get past her past. Before she met the two Israelite spies, she had worked as a prostitute (see Joshua 2:1). But by the end of her life, she too had come to love the God of Israel and is mentioned as an ancestor of Jesus Christ (see Matthew 1:5). No matter how bad your past is, always know that God has a new beginning for you. Like Rahab, you may have a past, but you also have a future. You can get past your past!

scouts up to the roof and had hidden them under the stalks of flax which she had laid in order on the roof [to dry].

⁷So the [king's] men pursued them on the road to the Jordan as far as the fords [east of Jericho]; as soon as the pursuers had gone out after them, the gate [of the city] was shut.

⁸Now before the two men lay down [to sleep], Rahab came up to them on the roof,

⁹and she said to the men, "I know that the LORD has given you the land, and that the terror *and* dread of you has fallen on us, and that all the inhabitants of the land have melted [in despair] because of you.

¹⁰"For we have heard how the LORD dried up the water of the Red Sea for you when you came out of Egypt, and what you did to the two kings of the Amorites who were beyond the Jordan [on the east], to Sihon and Og, whom you utterly destroyed.

¹¹"When we heard it, our hearts melted [in despair], and a [fighting] spirit no longer remained in any man because of you; for the LORD your God, He is God in heaven above and on earth beneath. [Heb 11:31]

¹²"And now, please swear [an oath] to me by the LORD, since I have shown you kindness, that you also will show kindness to my father's household (family), and give me a pledge of truth *and* faithfulness,

¹³and spare my father and my mother and my brothers and my sisters, along with everyone who belongs to them, and let us all live."

¹⁴So the men said to her, "Our lives for yours if you do not tell [anyone about] this business of ours; then when the LORD gives us the land we will show you kindness and faithfulness [and keep our agreement with you]."

¹⁵Then she let them down by a rope through the window, for her house was built into the city wall, so that she was living on the wall.

¹⁶And she said to them, "Go [west] to the hill country, so that the pursuers [who have headed east] will not encounter you; hide yourselves there for three days until the pursuers return. Then afterward you can go your way."

¹⁷The men said to her, "We *shall be* blameless *and* free from this oath which you have made us swear,

¹⁸unless, when we come into the land, you tie this cord of scarlet thread in the window through which you let us down, and bring into the house your father and your mother and your brothers and all your father's household [so that they will be safe].

¹⁹"But if anyone goes out the doors of your house into the street, his blood *shall be* on his own head [that is, his own responsibility], and we *shall be* blameless *and* free [from our oath]; however, if a hand is *laid* on anyone who is with you in the house, his blood *shall be* on our head.

²⁰"But if you tell [anyone] this business of ours, we shall be blameless *and* free from the oath which you made us swear."

²¹She said, "According to your words, so be it." Then Rahab sent them off, and they departed; and she tied the scarlet cord in the window.

²²They left and went [on their way] to the hill country [west of Jericho], and stayed there [hidden in the caves] three days until the pursuers returned. The pursuers had searched all along the road but had not found *them*. ²³Then the two men turned back and came down from the hill country and crossed over [the Jordan] and came to Joshua the son of Nun [at Shittim], and told him everything that had happened to them. ²⁴They said to Joshua, "Certainly the Lord has given all the land into our hands; for all the inhabitants of the land have melted [in despair] because of us."

3 JOSHUA GOT up early in the morning; then he and all the children of Israel set out from Shittim and came to the Jordan, and they spent the night there before they crossed [the river]. ²And it happened at the end of three days that the officers went throughout the camp, ³and they commanded the people, "When you see the ark of the covenant of the Lord your God being carried by the Levitical priests, then you shall set out from where you are and follow it. ⁴"However, there shall be a distance between you and it of about 2,000 cubits (3,000 ft.) by measurement. Do not come near it, so that you may [be able to see the ark and] know the way you are to go, for you have not passed this way before." ⁵Then Joshua said to the people, "Sanctify yourselves [for His purpose], for tomorrow the Lord will do wonders (miracles) among you." ⁶Joshua said to the priests, "Take up the ark of the covenant and cross over [the river] ahead of the people." So they took up the ark of the covenant and went on ahead of the people. ⁷The Lord said to Joshua, "This day I will begin to magnify *and* exalt you in

common people, uncommon things

Do you want God to use you as a leader? It can happen. God is always looking for people to promote—and you can be one of them. Like Joshua, you have tremendous capabilities and potential; all you need to do is develop them. That involves allowing God to change you. The process may hurt at times, but it will benefit you in the long term.

Is a good leader born or made? Some people are born with natural leadership qualities, but they still have to go through a process of development that makes them into all they can be. Do not look at leadership as something attainable only by rare individuals who have great talents. God delights in using common people to accomplish uncommon things. Common people with *uncommon* goals who make an *uncommon* commitment can help an *uncommon* number of other people.

As you develop the leadership qualities God has placed in you, remember that you are investing in the future. You can fulfill the plan God has for you if you are determined and refuse to be anything less than all you can be. A major key to moving from where you are to where you want to be is to "keep on keeping on."

Let me encourage you to develop your potential to the full, and as you do, you can encourage others to do the same. Be all you can be, and then help others fulfill the purpose for which they were created.

the sight of all Israel, so that they may know that just as I was with Moses, I will [also] be with you.

8"You shall command the priests who carry the ark of the covenant, saying, 'When you come to the edge of the waters of the Jordan, you shall stand *still* in the Jordan.'"

9Joshua said to the Israelites, "Come here, and listen to the words of the LORD your God."

10Joshua said, "By this you shall know that the living God is among you, and that He will, without fail, drive out from before you the Canaanite, the Hittite, the Hivite, the Perizzite, the Girgashite, the Amorite, and the Jebusite.

11"Behold, the ark of the covenant of the Lord of all the earth is crossing over ahead of you [leading the way] into the Jordan.

12"So now take for yourselves twelve men from the tribes of Israel, one man from each tribe.

13"When the soles of the feet of the priests who carry the ark of the LORD, the Lord of all the earth, [come to] rest in the waters of the Jordan, the waters of the Jordan flowing down from above will be cut off, and they will stand in one mass [of water]."

14So when the people set out from their tents to cross over the Jordan with the priests who were carrying the ark of the covenant before the people,

putting the Word to work

Have you ever had to believe God for something miraculous in your life, as the Israelites did when they stood ready to cross the Jordan River (see Joshua 3:15, 16)? Are you in that position right now? As you read about how God led the Israelites across the Jordan on dry ground and about other miracles in the Bible, be encouraged and remember that God is still a God of miracles!

life point

Joshua 3:17 lets us know that the nation of Israel finally did cross the Jordan to enter the Promised Land. The sad thing is that they could have crossed over much sooner than they did. Why the delay? Wilderness mentalities, patterns of thinking that kept them wandering in the wilderness—and out of the Promised Land—for forty years. One of the Israelites' wilderness mentalities was an impatient attitude. They did not know how to stay calm and to be long-suffering through the hardships of their journey. How could these people possibly be ready to go into the Promised Land and drive off the current occupants so they could possess the land if they could not even remain patient and steadfast during a little inconvenience?

I encourage you to work with the Holy Spirit as He develops the fruit of patience in you. The more you resist Him, the longer the process will take. Learn to respond patiently in all kinds of trials, and you will find yourself living not in the wilderness, but in the joy of God's promises for your life, your own Promised Land.

15and when those who were carrying the ark came up to the Jordan, and the feet of the priests carrying the ark were submerged at the edge of the water (for the Jordan overflows all of its banks throughout the time of harvest),

16the waters which were flowing down from above stopped and rose up in one mass a great distance away at Adam, the city that is beside Zarethan. Those [waters] flowing downward toward the sea of the Arabah, the Salt Sea, were completely cut off. So the people crossed [the river] opposite Jericho. [Ps 114]

17And while all [the people of] Israel

crossed over on dry ground, the priests who carried the ark of the covenant of the LORD stood firm on dry ground in the midst of the Jordan [riverbed], until all the nation had finished crossing over the Jordan.

4 SO IT was when all the nation had finished crossing the Jordan, the LORD said to Joshua, ²"Take for yourselves the twelve men [chosen] from among the people, one man from each tribe, ³and command them, 'Pick up for yourselves twelve stones [one each] from here out of the midst of the Jordan, from the place where the priests' feet are standing firm; carry them over with you and lay them down at the place where you will spend the night tonight.'"

⁴Then Joshua called the twelve men whom he had appointed from the sons of Israel, one man from each tribe; ⁵and Joshua said to them, "Cross over again to the ark of the LORD your God into the midst of the Jordan, and each of you take up a stone on his shoulder, according to the number of the tribes of the sons of Israel, ⁶so that this may be a sign among you; when your children ask later, 'What do these stones mean to you?' ⁷then you shall say to them that the waters of the Jordan were cut off before the ark of the covenant of the LORD; when it crossed the Jordan, the waters of the Jordan were cut off. So these stones shall become a memorial for Israel forever."

⁸So the [twelve men chosen from the] sons of Israel did as Joshua commanded, and took up twelve stones out of the midst of the Jordan, according to the number of the tribes of the sons of Israel, just as the LORD had spoken to Joshua; and they carried them over with them to the place where they were spending the night and put them down there.

⁹Then Joshua set up [a second monument of] twelve stones in the midst of the Jordan at the place where the feet of the priests who carried the ark of the covenant were standing, and they are there to this day.

¹⁰For the priests who carried the ark were standing in the midst of the Jordan until everything was finished that the LORD had commanded Joshua to tell the people, in accordance with everything that Moses had commanded Joshua. The people hurried and crossed [the dry riverbed]; ¹¹and when all the people had finished crossing, the ark of the LORD and the priests crossed over in the presence of the people.

¹²The sons of Reuben and the sons of Gad and half the tribe of Manasseh crossed over armed for battle before the [other] sons of Israel, just as Moses had spoken to them; ¹³about 40,000 [men] armed *and* equipped for war crossed for battle before the LORD to the desert plains of Jericho.

¹⁴On that day the LORD magnified *and* exalted Joshua in the sight of all Israel; so they feared him [with profound awe and reverence], just as they had feared Moses all the days of his life.

¹⁵Now the LORD said to Joshua, ¹⁶"Order the priests carrying the ark of the Testimony to come up out of the Jordan." ¹⁷So Joshua commanded the priests, saying, "Come up out of the Jordan." ¹⁸When the priests who carried the ark of the covenant of the LORD had come up from the midst of the Jordan, and the soles of their feet were raised up to the dry land, the waters of the Jordan returned to their place, and flowed over all its banks as before.

¹⁹Now the people came up from the Jordan on the tenth [day] of the first month and encamped at Gilgal on the eastern border of Jericho.

²⁰And those twelve stones which they had taken from the Jordan, Joshua set up in Gilgal.

²¹He said to the sons of Israel, "When your children ask their fathers in time to come, 'What do these stones mean?'

²²then you shall let your children know, 'Israel crossed this Jordan on dry ground.'

²³"For the LORD your God dried up the waters of the Jordan for you until you crossed over, just as the LORD your God did to the Red Sea, which He dried up before us until we had crossed;

²⁴so that all the peoples of the earth may know [without any doubt] *and* acknowledge that the hand of the LORD is mighty *and* extraordinarily powerful, so that you will fear the LORD your God [and obey and worship Him with profound awe and reverence] forever."

5 NOW IT happened when all the kings of the Amorites who were beyond the Jordan to the west, and all the kings of the Canaanites who were by the sea, heard that the LORD had dried up the waters of the Jordan before the Israelites until they had crossed over, their hearts melted [in despair], and there was no [fighting] spirit in them any longer because of the Israelites [and what God had done for them].

²At that time the LORD said to Joshua, "Make for yourself flint knives and circumcise the [new generation of the] sons of Israel as [was done] before."

³So Joshua made flint knives and circumcised the sons of Israel at Gibeath-haaraloth.

⁴This is the reason why Joshua circumcised them: all the people who came out of Egypt who were males, all the men of war, had died in the wilderness along the way after they left Egypt.

⁵All the males who came out were circumcised, but all the males who were born in the wilderness on the way as they left Egypt had not been circumcised.

⁶For the Israelites walked forty years in the wilderness, until all the nation, *that is,* the men of war who came out of Egypt, died because they did not listen to the voice of the LORD; to them the LORD had sworn [an oath] that He would not let them see the land which He had promised to their fathers to give us, a land [of abundance] flowing with milk and honey.

⁷So it was their uncircumcised sons whom He raised up in their place, whom Joshua circumcised, because circumcision had not been performed on the way.

⁸Then, when they had finished circumcising all [the males of] the nation, they stayed in their places in the camp until they were healed.

⁹Then the LORD said to Joshua, "This day I have rolled away the reproach (derision, ridicule) of Egypt from you." So the name of that place is called Gilgal (rolling) to this day.

¹⁰While the Israelites camped at Gilgal they observed the Passover on the evening of the fourteenth day of the month on the desert plains of Jericho.

¹¹On the day after Passover, on that very day, they ate some of the produce of the land, unleavened bread, and roasted *grain*. [Lev 23:14]

¹²And the manna ceased on the day

speak the Word

Thank You, God, that Your hand is mighty and extraordinarily powerful. Help me to fear You, obey You, and worship You with profound awe and reverence forever!
—ADAPTED FROM JOSHUA 4:24

after they had eaten some of the produce of the land, so that the Israelites no longer had manna, but they ate some of the produce of the land of Canaan during that year.

¹³Now when Joshua was by Jericho, he looked up, and behold, a man was standing opposite him with his drawn sword in his hand, and Joshua went to him and said to him, "Are you for us or for our adversaries?"

¹⁴He said, "No; rather I have come

roll away the reproach

After Joshua led the Israelites into the Promised Land, they needed to be circumcised before they would be ready to conquer and occupy their first city, Jericho (see Joshua 5:2–7). After the men had been circumcised, the Lord told Joshua that He had "rolled away" the reproach of Egypt from His people. Now they were ready to overcome and capture Jericho (see Joshua 6). Why did reproach have to be lifted off them first? What exactly is a reproach?

The word *reproach* means "blame, disgrace, or shame" or, as the amplification of verse 9 indicates, "derision or ridicule." When God said that He had "rolled away" the reproach of Egypt from the Israelites, He was making a strong point. Egypt represents the world. After a few years of being in the world and becoming worldly, we all need the world's reproach to be rolled away.

After many years in ministry, I am convinced that most of our problems stem from the way we feel about ourselves. Personally, I had a shame-based nature because of things I had done and things that had been done to me. I blamed myself for what had happened to me. This is despite the fact that most of these things happened in my childhood, and there was nothing I could have done to stop them. Disgrace told me that I was no good—not worthy of God's love or help. Shame poisoned my inner being. I was not only ashamed of what had been done to me, but I was ashamed of myself. Deep down inside, I did not like myself. I needed God to roll away my reproach. He was willing and ready, but I had to believe it was possible. I did believe, and I am a totally different person today. No more shame, blame, or disgrace! I am a new creature in Jesus Christ (see 2 Corinthians 5:17).

I have said that grace is the power of God coming to us (as a free gift from Him) to help us do with ease what we cannot do ourselves. God wants to give us grace, and Satan wants to give us *dis*grace, which is another word for "reproach." God's action of rolling away our reproach means that we receive the forgiveness He is offering for all our past sins.

Self-hatred, self-rejection, refusal to accept God's forgiveness (by not forgiving yourself), not understanding righteousness through the blood of Jesus, and any related problems will definitely keep us wandering in the wilderness. Our minds must be renewed concerning the right standing we have with God through Jesus—not through our own works. We can never deserve God's blessings or be worthy of them. We can only humbly accept and appreciate them, and be in awe of how good He is and how much He loves us. The Bible says we are joint-heirs with Christ (see Romans 8:17). He earned our blessings by carrying our reproach to the Cross.

Let God roll the reproach off you, and experience the freedom from shame that Jesus wants to give you.

now as captain of the army of the LORD." Then Joshua fell with his face toward the earth and bowed down, and said to him, "What does my lord have to say to his servant?"

¹⁵The captain of the LORD's army said to Joshua, "Remove your sandals from your feet, because the place where you are standing is holy (set apart to the LORD)." And Joshua did so. [Ex 3:5]

6 NOW JERICHO [a fortified city with high walls] was tightly closed because [of the people's fear] of the sons of Israel; no one went out or came in.

²The LORD said to Joshua, "See, I have given Jericho into your hand, with its king and the mighty warriors.

³"Now you shall march around the city, all the men of war circling the city once. You shall do this [once each day] for six days.

⁴"Also, seven priests shall carry seven trumpets [made] of rams' horns ahead of the ark; then on the seventh day you shall march around the city seven times, and the priests shall blow the trumpets.

⁵"When they make a long blast with the ram's horn, and when you hear the sound of the trumpet, all the people shall cry out with a great shout (battle cry); and the wall of the city will fall down in its place, and the people shall go up, each man [going] straight ahead [climbing over the rubble]."

⁶So Joshua the son of Nun called for the priests and said to them, "Take up the ark of the covenant, and have seven priests carry seven trumpets made of rams' horns ahead of the ark of the LORD."

⁷He said to the people, "Go forward! March around the city, and let the armed men go ahead of the ark of the LORD."

⁸And it was so, that when Joshua had spoken to the people, the seven priests carrying the seven trumpets made of rams' horns went on before the LORD and blew the trumpets; then the ark of the covenant of the LORD went behind them.

⁹The armed men went in front of the priests who blew the trumpets, and the rear guard came after the ark, while the priests continued to blow the trumpets.

¹⁰But Joshua commanded the people, "You shall not shout [the battle cry] nor let your voice be heard nor let a word come out of your mouth, until the day I tell you to shout. Then you shall shout!"

¹¹So Joshua had the ark of the LORD taken around the city [on the first day], circling it once; then they came back into the camp and spent the night in the camp.

¹²Then Joshua got up early in the morning [on the second day], and the priests took up the ark of the LORD.

¹³The seven priests carrying the seven trumpets made of rams' horns ahead of the ark of the LORD went on continually, blowing the trumpets; and the armed men went ahead of them and the rear guard came after the ark of the LORD, while the priests continued to blow the trumpets.

¹⁴On the second day they marched around the city once, and returned to the camp; they did this for six days.

¹⁵Then on the seventh day they got up early at daybreak and marched around the city in the same way seven

putting the Word to work

Israel had to fight their way into possession of the Promised Land. Have you ever had to fight for God's promises in your life? Remember that He goes before you, He fights for you, and He always gives you the victory. Stand your ground, and refuse to give up!

times; only on that day they marched around the city seven times.

¹⁶And the seventh time, when the priests had blown the trumpets, Joshua said to the people, "Shout! For the Lord has given you the city.

¹⁷"The city and everything that is in it shall be under the ban [that is, designated to be destroyed as a form of tribute] to the Lord; only Rahab the prostitute and all [the people] who are with her in her house shall [be allowed to] live, because she hid *and* protected the messengers (scouts) whom we sent.

¹⁸"But as for you, keep yourselves [away] from the things under the ban [which are to be destroyed], so that you do not covet *them* and take some of the things under the ban [for personal gain], and put the camp of Israel under the ban (doomed to destruction), and bring disaster upon it.

¹⁹"All the silver and gold and articles of bronze and iron are holy (consecrated) to the Lord; they shall go into the treasury of the Lord."

²⁰So the people shouted [the battle cry], and the priests blew the trumpets. When the people heard the sound of the trumpet, they raised a great shout and the wall [of Jericho] fell down, so that the sons of Israel went up into the city, every man straight ahead [climbing over the rubble], and they overthrew the city.

²¹Then they utterly destroyed everything that was in the city, both man and woman, young and old, and ox and sheep and donkey, with the edge of the sword.

²²But Joshua said to the two men who had spied out the land, "Go into the prostitute's house and bring the woman and all that she has out of there, as you have sworn to her."

²³So the young men, the spies, went in and brought out Rahab and her father and her mother and her brothers and everything that she had; they also brought out all her relatives and allowed them to stay outside the camp of Israel [at Gilgal during the time required for ceremonial cleansing]. [Num 31:19]

²⁴Then they completely burned the city and everything that was in it. They put only the silver and the gold, and the articles of bronze and of iron, into the treasury of the house (tabernacle) of the Lord.

²⁵So Joshua spared Rahab the prostitute, with her father's household and everything that she had; and she has lived among Israel to this day, because she hid the messengers (scouts) whom Joshua sent to spy out Jericho.

²⁶Then Joshua made them take an oath at that time, saying, "Cursed before the Lord is the man who rises up and rebuilds this city, Jericho; with *the loss of* his firstborn he shall lay its foundation, and with *the loss of* his youngest son he shall set up its gates." [1 Kin 16:34]

²⁷So the Lord was with Joshua, and his fame was in all the land.

7 BUT THE sons of Israel acted unfaithfully *and* violated their obligation in regard to the things [off limits] under the ban [those things belonging to the Lord], for Achan, the son of Carmi, the son of Zabdi, the son of Zerah, from the tribe of Judah, took some of the things under the ban [for personal gain]. Therefore the anger of the Lord burned against the Israelites.

²Now Joshua sent men from Jericho to Ai, which is near Beth-aven, east of Bethel, and said to them, "Go up and spy out the land." So the men went up and spied out Ai.

³Then they returned to Joshua and said to him, "Do not make all the people go up [to fight]; have *only* about two thousand or three thousand men go up and attack Ai; do not make the entire army go up there, for they [of Ai] are few."

⁴So about three thousand men from the sons of Israel went up there, but they fled [in retreat] from the men of Ai.

⁵The men of Ai killed about thirty-six of Israel's men, and chased them from the gate as far as [the bluffs of] Shebarim and struck them down as they descended [the steep pass], so the hearts of the people melted [in despair and began to doubt God's promise] and became like water (disheartened).

⁶Then Joshua tore his clothes and fell face downward on the ground before the ark of the LORD until evening, he and the elders of Israel; and [with great sorrow] they put dust on their heads.

⁷Joshua said, "Alas, O Lord GOD, why have You brought this people across the Jordan at all, only to hand us over to the Amorites, to destroy us? If only we had been willing to live beyond the Jordan!

⁸"O Lord, what can I say now that [the army of] Israel has turned back [in retreat and fled] before their enemies?

⁹"For the Canaanites and all the inhabitants of the land will hear about it, and will surround us and cut off our name from the earth. And what will You do for Your great name [to keep it from dishonor]?"

¹⁰So the LORD said to Joshua, "Get up! Why is it that you have fallen on your face?

¹¹"Israel has sinned; they have also transgressed My covenant which I commanded them [to keep]. They have even taken some of the things under the ban, and they have both stolen and denied [the theft]. Moreover, they have also put *the stolen objects* among their own things.

¹²"That is why the soldiers of Israel could not stand [and defend themselves] before their enemies; they turned their backs [and ran] before them, because they have become accursed. I will not be with you anymore unless you destroy the things under the ban from among you.

¹³"Rise up! Consecrate the people and say, 'Consecrate yourselves for tomorrow, for thus says the LORD, the God of Israel: "There are things under the ban among you, O Israel. You cannot stand [victorious] before your enemies until you remove the things under the ban from among you."

¹⁴'In the morning you shall come forward by your tribes. And it shall be that the tribe which the LORD chooses *by lot* shall come forward by families, and the family which the LORD chooses shall come forward by [separate] households, and the household which the LORD chooses shall come forward man by man.

¹⁵'It shall be that the one who is chosen with the things under the ban shall be [killed and his body] burned with fire, he and all that belongs to him, because he has transgressed the covenant of the LORD, and because he has done a disgraceful *and* disobedient thing in Israel.'" [Josh 7:25]

¹⁶So Joshua got up early in the morning and had Israel come forward by tribes, and the tribe of Judah was chosen [by lot].

¹⁷He had the families of Judah come forward, and the family of the Zerahites was chosen; and he had the family of the Zerahites come forward man by man, and Zabdi was chosen.

¹⁸He brought his household forward man by man; and Achan the son of Carmi, son of Zabdi, son of Zerah, of the tribe of Judah, was chosen.

¹⁹Then Joshua said to Achan, "My son, I implore you, give glory to the LORD, the God of Israel, and give praise to Him [in recognition of His righteous judgments]; and tell me now what you have done. Do not hide it from me."

²⁰So Achan answered Joshua and said, "In truth, I have sinned against

the LORD, the God of Israel, and this is what I have done:

²¹when I saw among the spoils [in Jericho] a beautiful robe from Shinar (southern Babylon) and two hundred shekels of silver and a bar of gold weighing fifty shekels, I wanted them and took them. Behold, they are hidden in the ground inside my tent, with the silver underneath."

²²So Joshua sent messengers, and they ran to the tent; and they saw the stolen objects hidden in his tent, with the silver underneath.

²³And they took them from the tent and brought them to Joshua and to all the sons of Israel, and spread them out before the LORD.

²⁴Then Joshua and all Israel with him, took Achan the son of Zerah, the silver, the [royal] robe, the bar of gold, his sons, his daughters, his oxen, his donkeys, his sheep, his tent, and everything that he had; and they brought them up to the Valley of Achor (Disaster).

²⁵Joshua said, "Why have you brought disaster on us? The LORD will bring you disaster this day." Then all Israel stoned them [to death] with stones; afterward they burned their bodies in the fire.

²⁶Then they piled up over him a great heap of stones that remains to this day. Then the LORD turned from the fierceness of His anger. Therefore the name of that place has been called the Valley of Achor (Disaster) to this day.

8 NOW THE LORD said to Joshua, "Do not fear or be dismayed (intimidated). Take all the men of war with you and set out, go up to Ai; see, I have given the king of Ai, his people, his city, and his land into your hand.

²"You shall do [the same] to Ai and its king as you did to Jericho and its king; [except that] you shall take only its spoil and its cattle as plunder for

life point

No matter what we face in life, Jesus is the Mighty Warrior, the Captain of the Host. He is our Leader, and He is leading His people into victory. I do not believe that we have to live in fear. God has promised to provide for His own. He has assured us, just as He did Joshua, that we will triumph if we listen to Him and obey. Whatever obstacles are before you today, do not be afraid or dismayed, because God is with you.

yourselves. Set up an ambush for the city behind it [on the west side]."

³So Joshua set out with all the people of war to go up against Ai; then Joshua chose thirty thousand valiant men, and sent them out at night.

⁴He commanded them, saying, "Listen closely, you are going to lie in wait *and* ambush the city from behind it. Do not go very far away from the city, but all of you be ready.

⁵"Then I and all the people who are with me will approach the city. And when they come out to meet us [for battle] as [they did] the first time, we will run away from them.

⁶"They will come out after us until we have lured them away from the city, because they will say, 'They are running from us as [they did] before.' So we will run from them.

⁷"Then you will emerge from the ambush and take possession of the city, for the LORD your God will hand it over to you.

⁸"When you have taken the city, you shall set it on fire; you shall do [exactly] as the LORD commanded. See, I have commanded you."

⁹So Joshua sent them off, and they went to the place for the ambush and stayed [hidden] between Bethel and Ai, on the west side of Ai; but Joshua spent that night among the people [in Gilgal].

¹⁰Now Joshua got up early in the morning and assembled the people, and went up with the elders of Israel before the people to Ai.

¹¹Then all the fighting men who were with him went up and advanced and arrived in front of the city, and camped on the north side of Ai. Now there was a ravine between them and Ai.

¹²And Joshua took about five thousand men and set them in ambush between Bethel and Ai, on the west side of the city.

¹³So they stationed the people, all the army—the main encampment that was north of the city, and their rear guard on the west side of the city—and Joshua spent that night in the valley.

¹⁴Now when the king [and the people] of Ai saw it, the men of the city hurried and got up early and went out to meet Israel in battle, the king and all his people at the appointed [time and] place before the desert plain (the Arabah). But he did not know that there was an ambush against him [waiting] behind the city [on the west side].

¹⁵So Joshua and all Israel pretended to be defeated by them, and ran toward the wilderness.

¹⁶Then all the people who were in the city were called together to pursue them, and they pursued Joshua and were lured away from the city.

¹⁷Not a man was left in Ai or Bethel who had not gone out after Israel; so they left the city open *and* unguarded and they pursued Israel.

¹⁸Then the LORD said to Joshua, "Reach out with the spear that is in your hand [and point it] toward Ai, for I will give it into your hand." So Joshua reached out with the spear in his hand [and pointed it] toward the city.

¹⁹The [men in] ambush emerged quickly from their [hiding] place, and when Joshua stretched out his hand

they ran and entered the city and captured it, and quickly set the city on fire.

²⁰When the men of Ai turned back and looked, behold, the smoke of the city was ascending toward the sky, and they had no opportunity to run this way or that way. Then the people who had been running to the wilderness turned back toward the pursuers.

²¹When Joshua and all Israel saw that the [men in] ambush had taken the city and that the smoke of the city was ascending, they turned back and struck down the men of Ai.

²²Then the others came out of the city to confront the men of Ai [as they returned], so that they were *trapped* in the midst of Israel, some on this side and some on that side; then Israel struck them until none of them survived or escaped.

²³But they took the king of Ai alive and brought him to Joshua.

²⁴When Israel had finished killing all the inhabitants of Ai in the field in the wilderness where they pursued them, and they had all fallen by the edge of the sword until they were destroyed, then all Israel returned to Ai and struck it with the edge of the sword.

²⁵And all who fell that day, both men and women, were twelve thousand, all the people of Ai.

²⁶For Joshua did not withdraw his hand with which he stretched out the spear until he had utterly destroyed all the inhabitants of Ai.

²⁷Israel took only the livestock and the spoil of that city as plunder for themselves, according to the word of the LORD which He had commanded Joshua.

²⁸So Joshua burned Ai and made it a rubbish heap forever, a desolation until this day.

²⁹He hanged [the body of] the king of Ai on a tree [leaving it there] until

evening; at sunset Joshua gave a command and they took the body down from the tree and dumped it at the entrance of the city gate, and piled a great heap of stones over it *that stands* to this day.

³⁰Then Joshua built an altar to the LORD, the God of Israel, on Mount Ebal, ³¹just as Moses the servant of the LORD had commanded the sons of Israel, as it is written in the Book of the Law of Moses, an altar of uncut stones on which no one has wielded an iron *tool;* and they offered on it burnt offerings to the LORD, and sacrificed peace offerings. ³²And there, in the presence of the sons of Israel, Joshua wrote on the stones a copy of the Law of Moses which *Moses* had written. ³³All Israel, the stranger as well as the native born [among them], with their elders and officers and their judges, stood on either side of the ark before the Levitical priests who carried the ark of the covenant of the LORD. Half of them *stood* in front of Mount Gerizim and half of them in front of Mount Ebal, just as Moses the servant of the LORD had commanded at first to bless the people of Israel. ³⁴Then afterward Joshua read all the words of the law, the blessing and curse, according to all that is written in the Book of the Law. ³⁵There was not a word of all that Moses had commanded which Joshua did not read before the entire assembly of Israel, including the women and the children and the foreigners who were living among them.

9 NOW WHEN all the kings who were beyond the Jordan, in the hill country and in the lowland [at the western edge of the hills of Judea], and all along the coast of the Great [Mediterranean] Sea toward Lebanon, the Hittite and the Amorite, the Canaanite, the Perizzite, the Hivite and the Jebusite, heard of this [army and its victories over Jericho and Ai], ²they gathered together with one purpose to fight with Joshua and with Israel.

³But when the people of Gibeon [the Hivites] heard what Joshua had done to Jericho and Ai, ⁴they too acted craftily *and* cunningly, and set out and took along provisions, but took worn-out sacks on their donkeys, and wineskins (leather bottles) that were worn out and split open and patched together, ⁵and worn-out and patched sandals on their feet, and worn-out clothes; and all their supply of food was dry and had turned to crumbs. ⁶They went to Joshua in the camp at Gilgal and said to him and the men of Israel, "We have come from a far country; so now, make a covenant (treaty) with us." ⁷But the men of Israel said to the Hivites, "Perhaps you are living within our land; how then can we make a covenant (treaty) with you?" ⁸They said to Joshua, "We are your servants." Then Joshua said to them, "Who are you, and where do you come from?" ⁹They said to him, "Your servants have come from a country that is very far away because of the fame of the LORD your God; for we have heard the news about Him and all [the remarkable things] that He did in Egypt, ¹⁰and everything that He did to the two kings of the Amorites who were beyond the Jordan, to Sihon the king of Heshbon and to Og the king of Bashan who *lived* in Ashtaroth. ¹¹"So our elders and all the residents of our country said to us, 'Take provisions for the journey and go to meet the sons of Israel and say to them, "We are your servants; now make a covenant (treaty) with us." '

¹²"This bread of ours was hot (fresh) when we took it along as our provision from our houses on the day we left to come to you; now look, it is dry and has turned to crumbs.

¹³"These wineskins which we filled were new, and look, they are split; our clothes and our sandals are worn out because of the very long journey [that we had to make]."

¹⁴So the men [of Israel] took some of their own provisions [and offered them in friendship], and [foolishly] did not ask for the counsel of the LORD.

¹⁵Joshua made peace with them and made a covenant (treaty) with them, to let them live; and the leaders of the congregation [of Israel] swore *an oath* to them.

¹⁶It happened that three days after they had made a covenant (treaty) with them, the Israelites heard that they were [actually] their neighbors and that they were living among them.

¹⁷Then the sons of Israel set out and came to their cities on the third day. Now the cities [of the Hivites] were Gibeon and Chephirah and Beeroth and Kiriath-jearim.

¹⁸But the sons of Israel did not strike

life point

Joshua 9:12 mentions bread that has become dry and crumbled. If a loaf of bread is left on a table for very long, a person can touch it and tell it is getting stale. It is on its way to becoming hard and tasteless. The same thing can happen in our lives. If we are not careful, the enemy will deceive us into allowing our lives to become dry and stale. We must resist this by staying fresh—being creative and having different experiences, breaking our routines once in a while, and allowing God to do new things in us, for us, and through us.

them because the leaders of the congregation had sworn to them by the LORD the God of Israel [to spare them]. And all the congregation murmured [expressing great dissatisfaction] against the leaders.

¹⁹But all the leaders said to the whole congregation, "We have sworn to them by the LORD, the God of Israel, so now we cannot touch them.

²⁰"This [is what] we will do to them: we will let them live, so that the wrath [of God] does not come upon us for [violating] the oath which we have sworn to them."

²¹The leaders said to them, "Let them live [as our slaves]." So they became the cutters *and* gatherers of firewood and water carriers for the entire congregation, just as the leaders had said of them.

²²Joshua called the [Hivite] men and said, "Why did you deceive us, saying, 'We *live* very far away from you,' when [in fact] you live among us?

²³"Now therefore, you are cursed, and you shall always be slaves, both cutters *and* gatherers of firewood and water carriers for the house of my God."

²⁴They replied to Joshua and said, "Because your servants were told in no uncertain terms that the LORD your God commanded His servant Moses to give you all the land, and to destroy all the land's inhabitants before you, we feared greatly for our lives because of you, and so we did this [deceptive] thing.

²⁵"Now look, we are in your hands; do to us as it seems good and right in your sight."

²⁶So that is what he did to them; he rescued them from the hands of the Israelites and they did not kill them.

²⁷Now on that day Joshua made them cutters *and* gatherers of firewood and water carriers for the congregation and for the altar of the LORD, to this day, in the place which He would choose.

10 WHEN ADONI-ZEDEK king of Jerusalem heard that Joshua had captured Ai, and had utterly destroyed it—as he had done to Jericho and its king, so he had done to Ai and its king—and that the residents of Gibeon had made peace with Israel and were [living] among them,

²he [and his people] feared greatly, because Gibeon was a great city, like one of the royal cities, and because it was greater than Ai, and all its men were mighty.

³So Adoni-zedek king of Jerusalem sent *word* to Hoham king of Hebron, and to Piram king of Jarmuth, to Japhia king of Lachish, and to Debir king of Eglon, saying,

⁴"Come up to me and help me, and let us attack Gibeon [with a combined army], because it has made peace with Joshua and with the sons (people) of Israel."

⁵Then the five kings of the Amorites, the king of Jerusalem, the king of Hebron, the king of Jarmuth, the king of Lachish, and the king of Eglon, gathered together and went up, they with all their armies, and they camped by Gibeon and fought against it.

⁶So the men of Gibeon sent *word* to Joshua at the camp in Gilgal, saying, "Do not abandon your servants; come up to us quickly and save us and help us, for all [five of] the kings of the Amorites who live in the hill country have assembled against us."

⁷So Joshua went up from Gilgal, he and all the people of war with him, and all the men of valor.

⁸The LORD said to Joshua, "Do not fear them, because I have given them into your hand; not one of them shall stand before you."

⁹So Joshua came upon them suddenly, [surprising them] by marching [uphill] all night from Gilgal.

¹⁰And the LORD caused them to panic *and* be confused before Israel, and He struck them dead in a great slaughter at Gibeon, and chased them along the way that goes up to Beth-horon and struck them as far as Azekah and Makkedah.

¹¹As they fled before Israel, while they were at the descent of Beth-horon, the LORD threw down large stones [of hail] from heaven on them as far as Azekah, and they died. More [Amorites] died because of the hailstones than those whom the sons of Israel killed with the sword.

¹²Then Joshua spoke to the LORD on the day when the LORD handed over the Amorites to the sons of Israel, and Joshua said in the sight of Israel,

"Sun, stand still at Gibeon,
And moon, in the Valley of
    Aijalon."
¹³So the sun stood still, and the
    moon stopped,
Until the nation [of Israel] took
    vengeance upon their enemies.

Is it not written in the Book of Jashar? So the sun stood still in the middle of the sky and was in no hurry to go down for about a whole day.

¹⁴There has not been a day like that before it or after it, when the LORD listened to (heeded) the voice of a man; for the LORD was fighting for Israel.

¹⁵Then Joshua and all Israel with him returned to the camp at Gilgal.

¹⁶Now these five [Amorite] kings fled and hid themselves in the cave at Makkedah.

¹⁷And Joshua was told, "The five kings have been found and are hidden in the cave at Makkedah."

¹⁸Joshua said, "Roll large stones against the mouth of the cave, and assign men by it to guard them,

¹⁹but do not stay there yourselves; pursue your enemies and attack them from the rear. Do not allow them to enter their cities, for the LORD your God has given them into your hand."

²⁰Now when Joshua and the sons of

Israel had finished striking the Amorites dead in a very great defeat, until they were wiped out, and the surviving remnant among them had entered the fortified cities,

²¹all the people returned to the camp to Joshua at Makkedah in peace. No one uttered a [threatening] word against any of the sons of Israel.

²²Then Joshua said, "Open the mouth of the cave and bring out to me those five [Amorite] kings from the cave."

²³They did so, and brought these five [Amorite] kings out of the cave to him—the king of Jerusalem, the king of Hebron, the king of Jarmuth, the king of Lachish, and the king of Eglon.

²⁴When they brought these kings out to Joshua, Joshua called for all the men of Israel, and told the commanders of the men of war who had gone with him, "Come up close, put your feet on the necks of these kings." So they came forward and put their feet on the necks [of the five kings].

²⁵Joshua said to them, "Do not fear or be dismayed (intimidated)! Be strong and courageous, for this is what the LORD will do to all your enemies against whom you [are about to] fight."

²⁶Then afterward Joshua struck them [with his sword] and put them to death, and he hung them on five trees; and they hung on the trees until evening.

²⁷At sunset Joshua gave a command, and they took the bodies down from the trees and threw them into the cave where the kings had hidden themselves, and placed large stones over the mouth of the cave, [where they remain] to this very day.

²⁸Now Joshua captured Makkedah on that day, and struck it and its king with the edge of the sword; he utterly destroyed it and everyone who was in it. He left no survivor. So he did to the king of Makkedah just as he had done to the king of Jericho. [Josh 6:21]

²⁹Then Joshua and all Israel with him went on from Makkedah to Libnah, and fought against Libnah.

³⁰The LORD gave it also along with its king into the hands of Israel, and Joshua struck it and every person who was in it with the edge of the sword. He left no survivor in it. So he did to the king of Libnah just as he had done to the king of Jericho.

³¹And Joshua and all Israel with him moved on from Libnah to Lachish, and they camped by it and fought against it.

³²The LORD gave Lachish into the hands of Israel; and Joshua captured it on the second day, and struck it and every person who was in it with the edge of the sword, just as he had done to Libnah.

life point

Fear is not from God. Fear is from the enemy. It is the spirit Satan uses to try to keep God's people from coming under the leadership of our true Master, Jesus Christ. The only acceptable attitude (and confession) that a Christian can have toward fear is this: "It is not from God, and I will not put up with it or let it control my life! *I will confront fear*, because it is a spirit sent from hell to torment me."

I believe God works powerfully in us to bring us out of bondage, to take us from fear into liberty. The Bible is full of instructions to "fear not." Events in my own life have led me to understand that "Fear not" means "Do not run; face it." I encourage you to press on, and if need be, "do it afraid"—whatever "it" is in your life. Do not run from fear; instead, "Be strong and courageous," as Joshua 10:25 exhorts. Confront fear in prayer and take whatever actions God leads you to take.

³³Then Horam king of Gezer went up to help Lachish, and Joshua struck him and his people down until he had left him no survivor.

³⁴And Joshua and all Israel with him went on from Lachish to Eglon, and they camped by it and fought against it.

³⁵They captured it on that day and struck it with the edge of the sword; and on that day he utterly destroyed every person who was in it, just as he had done to Lachish.

³⁶Then Joshua and all Israel with him went up from Eglon to Hebron, and they fought against it

³⁷and captured it and struck it and its king and all its cities and all the persons who were in it with the edge of the sword. He left no survivor, just as he had done to Eglon. He utterly destroyed it and every person who was in it.

³⁸Then Joshua and all Israel with him returned to Debir, and fought against it.

³⁹He captured it with its king and all its cities, and they struck them with the edge of the sword, and utterly destroyed every person who was in it. He left no survivor. Just as he had done to Hebron, so Joshua did to Debir and its king, as he had done also to Libnah and its king.

⁴⁰So Joshua struck all the land, the hill country, the Negev (South country) and the lowland and the slopes [that descend to the Dead Sea] and all their kings. He left no survivor, but he utterly destroyed all who breathed, just as the LORD, the God of Israel, had commanded. [Deut 20:16]

⁴¹Joshua struck them from Kadesh-barnea even as far as Gaza, and all the country of Goshen even as far as Gibeon.

⁴²Joshua captured all these kings and their land at one time, because the LORD, the God of Israel, fought for Israel.

⁴³So Joshua and all Israel with him returned to the camp at Gilgal.

life point

Joshua fought many battles in order to finally enter the Promised Land. As the Lord gave him direction all along the way, He repeatedly told him to be of good courage. Courage means having a good attitude in the face of dangerous or frightening circumstances.

Have you ever wondered what would have happened had Joshua not listened to God's advice to take courage? When the enemy repeatedly came against him, Joshua could have given up, the children of Israel would never have defeated all their enemies, and they would not have enjoyed living in the Promised Land.

The same is true in our daily walk. Joy and cheer in the Lord give us the strength to pursue the goal that He has given us and to fight the battles we face along the way. When you are tempted to lose courage, remember that the joy of the Lord is your strength (see Nehemiah 8:10). Like Joshua, all of your enemies will be utterly defeated as you stay strong in God.

11 THEN WHEN Jabin king of Hazor heard [of Israel's other victories] he sent *word* to Jobab king of Madon, and to the king of Shimron, and to the king of Achshaph,

²and to the kings who were in the north, in the hill country, and in the Arabah [the plain] south of Chinnereth (the Sea of Galilee) and in the lowland and on the hills of Dor on the west;

³to the Canaanite in the east and in the west, and to the Amorite, the Hittite, the Perizzite, and the Jebusite in the hill country, and the Hivite at the foot of [Mount] Hermon in the land of Mizpeh.

⁴They went out, they and all their armies with them, as many people as

the sand on the seashore, with very many horses and chariots.

⁵So all these kings met and they came and encamped together at the waters of Merom, to fight against Israel.

⁶Then the LORD said to Joshua, "Do not be afraid because of them, for tomorrow by this time I am going to hand over all of them slain [by the sword] to Israel; you shall hamstring (disable) their horses and set fire to their chariots."

⁷So Joshua and all the people of war with him came against them suddenly by the waters of Merom, and attacked them.

⁸The LORD handed them over to Israel, who struck them and pursued them as far as Great Sidon and Misrephoth-maim and eastward as far as the Valley of Mizpeh; they struck them down until no survivor was left.

⁹Joshua did to them as the LORD had told him; he hamstrung (disabled) their horses and set fire to their chariots.

¹⁰At that time Joshua turned back and captured Hazor and struck its king dead with the sword; for Hazor previously was the head of all these kingdoms.

¹¹They struck all the people who were in it with the edge of the sword, utterly destroying them; there was no one left who breathed. And he set fire to Hazor.

¹²Joshua captured all the cities of these kings, and all their kings, and he struck them with the edge of the sword, utterly destroying them, just as Moses the servant of the LORD had commanded. [Deut 20:16]

¹³But Israel did not burn any of the cities that stood [walled and fortified] on their mounds, except Hazor alone, which Joshua burned.

¹⁴The sons of Israel took as their plunder all the spoil of these cities and the cattle; but they struck every man with the edge of the sword, until they had destroyed them. They left no one alive.

¹⁵Just as the LORD had commanded Moses His servant, so Moses had commanded Joshua, and so Joshua did; he left nothing undone of all that the LORD had commanded Moses.

¹⁶So Joshua took all this land: the hill country, all the Negev (South country), all the land of Goshen, the lowland, the Arabah [plain], the hill country of Israel and its lowland

¹⁷from Mount Halak, that rises toward Seir [in the south], even as far as Baal-gad in the Valley of Lebanon at the foot of Mount Hermon [in the north]. He captured all their kings and struck them and put them to death.

¹⁸Joshua waged war with all these kings a long time [at least five years].

¹⁹There was no city that made peace with the Israelites except the Hivites living in Gibeon; they took all *the others* in battle.

²⁰For it was [the purpose] of the LORD to harden their hearts, to meet Israel in battle so that Israel would utterly destroy them, that they would receive no mercy, but that Israel would destroy them, just as the LORD had commanded Moses.

²¹Then Joshua came at that time and cut off the Anakim from the hill country, from Hebron, from Debir, from Anab and from all the hill country of Judah and all the hill country of Israel. Joshua utterly destroyed them with their cities.

²²There were no Anakim left in the land of the children of Israel; only in Gaza, in Gath, and in Ashdod [of Philistia] some remained.

²³So Joshua took the whole land [of Canaan], according to all that the LORD had spoken to Moses, and Joshua gave it as an inheritance to Israel according to their divisions by their tribes. So the land had rest from war.

12 NOW THESE are the kings of the land whom the sons of Israel defeated, and whose land they possessed beyond the Jordan toward the east, from the valley of the [river] Arnon to Mount Hermon, and all the Arabah [plain] to the east:

²Sihon king of the Amorites, who lived in Heshbon, and ruled from Aroer, which is on the edge of the valley of the [river] Arnon, both the middle of the valley and half of Gilead, and as far as the brook Jabbok, [which is] the border of the sons of Ammon;

³and the Arabah [plain] as far as the Sea of Chinnereth (Galilee) eastward, and as far as the sea of the Arabah, the Salt (Dead) Sea, eastward toward Beth-jeshimoth, and southward to the foot of the slopes of [Mount] Pisgah;

⁴and the territory of Og king of Bashan, one of the remnant of the Rephaim, who lived at Ashtaroth and at Edrei,

⁵and ruled over Mount Hermon and Salecah and all of Bashan to the border of the Geshurites and the Maacathites, and over half of Gilead, *as far as* the border of Sihon king of Heshbon.

⁶Moses the servant of the Lord and the sons of Israel defeated them; and Moses the servant of the Lord gave their land as a possession to the Reubenites and the Gadites and the half-tribe of Manasseh. [Num 21; 32:33; Deut 2; 3]

⁷These are the kings of the land whom Joshua and the sons of Israel defeated on the west side of the Jordan, from Baal-gad in the Valley of Lebanon to Mount Halak, which rises toward Seir. Joshua gave their land to the tribes of Israel as a possession according to their divisions,

⁸in the hill country, in the lowland (foothills), in the Arabah [plain], on the slopes [descending to the Dead Sea], and in the wilderness, and in the Negev (South country)—the [lands of the] Hittite, the Amorite and the Canaanite, the Perizzite, the Hivite and the Jebusite:

⁹the king of Jericho, one; the king of Ai, which is beside Bethel, one;

¹⁰the king of Jerusalem, one; the king of Hebron, one;

¹¹the king of Jarmuth, one; the king of Lachish, one;

¹²the king of Eglon, one; the king of Gezer, one;

¹³the king of Debir, one; the king of Geder, one;

¹⁴the king of Hormah, one; the king of Arad, one;

¹⁵the king of Libnah, one; the king of Adullam, one;

¹⁶the king of Makkedah, one; the king of Bethel, one;

¹⁷the king of Tappuah, one; the king of Hepher, one;

¹⁸the king of Aphek, one; the king of Lasharon, one;

¹⁹the king of Madon, one; the king of Hazor, one;

²⁰the king of Shimron-meron, one; the king of Achshaph, one;

²¹the king of Taanach, one; the king of Megiddo, one;

²²the king of Kedesh, one; the king of Jokneam in Carmel, one;

²³the king of Dor in the heights of Dor, one; the king of Goiim in Gilgal, one;

²⁴the king of Tirzah, one: in all, thirty-one kings.

13 NOW JOSHUA was old and advanced in years, and the Lord said to him, "You have grown old and advanced in years, and very substantial portions of the land remain to be possessed.

²"This is the land that remains: all the regions of the Philistines and all those of the Geshurites;

³from the Shihor [waterway] which is east of Egypt [at the southern end of Canaan], northward to the border

of Ekron (all of it regarded as Canaanite); the five rulers of the Philistines: the Gazite, Ashdodite, the Ashkelonite, the Gittite, the Ekronite; and the Avvite

⁴in the south, all the land of the Canaanite, and Mearah that belongs to the Sidonians, as far as Aphek, to the border of the Amorite;

⁵and the land of the Gebalite, and all Lebanon, toward the east, from Baal-gad below Mount Hermon to the entrance of Hamath.

⁶"As for all the inhabitants of the hill country from Lebanon to Misrephoth-maim, even all the Sidonians, I will drive them out before Israel; only allot the land to Israel as an inheritance just as I have commanded you.

⁷"So now, divide this land [west of the Jordan] as an inheritance for the nine tribes and the half-tribe of Manasseh."

⁸With the other half-tribe [of Manasseh], the Reubenites and the Gadites received their inheritance which Moses gave them beyond the Jordan eastward, just as Moses the servant of the LORD gave to them;

⁹from Aroer on the edge of the valley of the [river] Arnon, and the city in the middle of the valley, and all the plain of Medeba, as far as Dibon;

¹⁰and all the cities of Sihon king of the Amorites, who reigned in Heshbon, as far as the border of the Ammonites;

¹¹and Gilead, and the territory of the Geshurites and Maacathites, and all Mount Hermon, and all Bashan as far as Salecah;

¹²the entire kingdom of Og in Bashan, who reigned in Ashtaroth and Edrei—he alone was left of the remnant of the Rephaim [giants]—for Moses had struck them and dispossessed them.

¹³But the sons of Israel did not dispossess the Geshurites or the Maacathites; for Geshur and Maacath live among Israel to this day.

¹⁴It was only to the tribe of Levi that Moses gave no [territory as an] inheritance; the offerings by fire to the LORD, the God of Israel, are their inheritance, as He told him.

¹⁵So Moses gave *an inheritance* to the tribe of the sons of Reuben according to their families.

¹⁶Their territory was from Aroer, which is on the edge of the valley of the [river] Arnon, and the city which is in the middle of the valley and all the plain by Medeba;

¹⁷with Heshbon, and all its cities which are on the plain: Dibon and Bamoth-baal and Beth-baal-meon,

¹⁸and Jahaz and Kedemoth and Mephaath,

¹⁹and Kiriathaim and Sibmah and Zereth-shahar on the hill of the valley,

²⁰and Beth-peor and the slopes of Pisgah and Beth-jeshimoth,

²¹even all the cities of the plain and all the kingdom of Sihon king of the Amorites who reigned in Heshbon, whom Moses struck down along with the leaders of Midian, Evi and Rekem and Zur and Hur and Reba, the princes of Sihon, who lived in the land.

²²The sons of Israel also killed Balaam the son of Beor, the diviner (soothsayer), with the sword among [the rest of] their slain. [Num 31:16]

²³The border of the sons of Reuben was the Jordan. This was the inheritance of the sons of Reuben according to their families, with their cities and villages.

²⁴Moses also gave *an inheritance* to the tribe of Gad, to the sons of Gad, according to their families.

²⁵Their territory was Jazer, and all the cities of Gilead, and half the land of the sons of Ammon, as far as Aroer east of Rabbah;

²⁶and from Heshbon as far as Ramath-mizpeh and Betonim, and from Mahanaim as far as the border of Debir;

²⁷and in the valley, Beth-haram and Beth-nimrah and Succoth and Zaphon,

the rest of the kingdom of Sihon king of Heshbon, with the Jordan as a border, as far as the *lower* end of the Sea of Chinnereth (Galilee) east of the Jordan. [28]This is the inheritance of the sons of Gad according to their families, with their cities and their villages. [29]Moses also gave *an inheritance* to the half-tribe of Manasseh; and it was for the half-tribe of the sons of Manasseh according to their families. [30]Their region extended from Mahanaim, all Bashan, the entire kingdom of Og king of Bashan, and all the towns of Jair, which are in Bashan, sixty cities; [31]also half of Gilead, with Ashtaroth and Edrei, the cities of the kingdom of Og in Bashan; these were for the sons of Machir the son of Manasseh, for half of the sons of Machir according to their families (clans). [32]These are *the territories* which Moses distributed as an inheritance in the plains of Moab, beyond the Jordan at Jericho to the east. [33]But to the tribe of Levi, Moses did not give an inheritance; the LORD, the God of Israel, is their inheritance, as He told them.

14 NOW THESE are *the territories* which the tribes of Israel inherited in the land of Canaan, which Eleazar the priest, and Joshua the son of Nun, and the heads of the households of the tribes of Israel apportioned to them as an inheritance, [2]by the lot of their inheritance, as the LORD had commanded through Moses, for the nine tribes and the half-tribe. [3]For Moses had given an inheritance to the two tribes and the half-tribe beyond the Jordan; but he did not give [any territory as] an inheritance to the Levites among them. [4]For the sons of Joseph were two tribes, Manasseh and Ephraim, and no portion was given in the land to the Levites except cities in which to live, with their pasture lands for their livestock and for their property. [5]The Israelites did just as the LORD had commanded Moses, and they divided the land.

[6]Then the [tribe of the] sons of Judah approached Joshua in Gilgal, and Caleb the son of Jephunneh the Kenizzite said to him, "You know the word which the LORD said to Moses the man of God concerning me and you in Kadesh-barnea. [7]"I was forty years old when Moses the servant of the LORD sent me from Kadesh-barnea to scout the land [of Canaan], and I brought a report back to him as it was in my heart. [8]"My brothers (fellow spies) who went up with me made the heart of the people melt with fear; but I followed the LORD my God completely. [9]"So Moses swore [an oath to me] on that day, saying, 'Be assured that the land on which your foot has walked will be an inheritance to you and to your children always, because you have followed the LORD my God completely.' [Deut 1:35, 36] [10]"And now, look, the LORD has let me live, just as He said, these forty-five years since the LORD spoke this word to Moses, when Israel wandered in the wilderness; and now, look at me, I am eighty-five years old today. [11]"I am still as strong today as I was the day Moses sent me; as my strength was then, so is my strength now, for war and for going out and coming in. [12]"So now, give me this hill country about which the LORD spoke that day, for you heard on that day that the [giant-like] Anakim were there, with great fortified cities; perhaps the LORD will be with me, and I shall drive them out just as the LORD said." [13]So Joshua blessed him and gave Hebron to Caleb the son of Jephunneh as an inheritance.

¹⁴Therefore, Hebron became the inheritance of Caleb the son of Jephunneh the Kenizzite to this day, because he followed the LORD, the God of Israel, completely.

¹⁵The name of Hebron was formerly Kiriath-arba [city of Arba]; *for Arba* was the greatest man among the [giant-like] Anakim. Then the land had rest from war.

15 NOW THE lot (allotment) for the tribe of the sons of Judah according to their families reached [southward to] the border of Edom, southward to the wilderness of Zin at its most southern part.

²Their southern border was from the lower end of the Salt (Dead) Sea, from the bay that turns southward.

³Then it proceeded southward to the ascent of Akrabbim and continued along to Zin, and then went by the south of Kadesh-barnea and continued along to Hezron, and went up to Addar and turned about to Karka.

⁴It continued along to Azmon and proceeded to the Brook of Egypt (Wadi el-Arish), and the border ended at the

boundaries are a good thing

After the children of Israel came in and possessed the land, they wisely established clear boundaries (Joshua 15–19 describes this in great detail). Likewise, it is smart for us to draw healthy boundary lines in our lives and relationships.

Just as a person puts up a fence around his property to keep intruders out, so you would be wise to establish limits and margins—invisible lines you draw in your life to protect yourself from being used and abused. If you had a privacy fence around your yard, and on a sunny afternoon you looked out into your yard and saw your neighbors sunbathing there while their children played on your swing set without your permission, what would you do? You certainly would not simply say, "Oh, my, I do wish those neighbors would leave me alone." You would probably inform them, maybe quite forcefully, that your yard is off-limits to them for their leisure without your permission. It's important to be just as lovingly forceful in letting people know you expect them to respect the limits and margins you have erected around your personal life.

People-pleasers do not live within limits or margins. In their efforts to please people, they push themselves beyond reasonable boundaries. Let's face it—people often expect us to do things we either should not do or cannot do. People-pleasers will push beyond the bounds of reason, if they think it means everyone will be happy with them.

Some people will take advantage of us if we let them; that is just human nature. And if they *do* take advantage of us, often we become bitter or resentful toward them; we do not realize that we are just as guilty as they are, if not more so. It is impossible for others to keep taking advantage of us unless we allow them to do so. We need to be the ones to take responsibility for ourselves and make sure we do not let people treat us inappropriately.

My responsibility is to manage my life under the direction of the Holy Spirit, and so is yours. Clear-cut boundaries will help keep it that way. If you have a problem setting proper boundaries in your life, ask the Lord to help you set up boundaries with grace and balance. He will do it because He knows that boundaries are a good thing!

[Mediterranean] sea. This was their southern border.

⁵The eastern border was the Salt (Dead) Sea, as far as the mouth of the Jordan. The northern border was from the bay of the sea at the mouth of the Jordan.

⁶Then the border went up to Beth-hoglah, and continued along north of Beth-arabah, and the border went up to the [landmark of the] stone of Bohan the son of Reuben.

⁷The border went up to Debir from the Valley of Achor, and turned northward toward Gilgal which is opposite the ascent of Adummim, which is on the south side of the valley; and the border continued on to the waters of En-shemesh and ended at En-rogel.

⁸Then the border went up by the Valley of Ben-hinnom (son of Hinnom) at the southern slope of the Jebusite [city] (that is, Jerusalem); and the border went up to the top of the mountain that lies before the Valley of Hinnom to the west, which is at the northern end of the Valley of Rephaim.

⁹Then the border extended from the top of the mountain to the spring of the waters of Nephtoah and proceeded to the cities of Mount Ephron; then the border curved to Baalah (that is, Kiriath-jearim).

¹⁰The border went around west from Baalah to Mount Seir, and passed along to the northern slope of Mount Jearim (that is, Chesalon), and went down to Beth-shemesh and then continued on through Timnah.

¹¹The border proceeded to the slope [of the hill] of Ekron northward, then curved to Shikkeron and continued to Mount Baalah and proceeded to Jabneel. Then the border ended at the [Mediterranean] sea.

¹²The western border was at the Great Sea, with its coastline. This is the border around the tribe of the sons of Judah according to their families.

¹³Now to Caleb the son of Jephunneh Joshua gave a portion among the sons of Judah, as the LORD commanded him, *namely,* Kiriath-arba, *Arba being* the father of Anak (that is, Hebron).

¹⁴So Caleb drove out from there the three sons of Anak: Sheshai and Ahiman and Talmai, the children of Anak.

¹⁵Then he went up from there against the people of Debir; Debir was formerly named Kiriath-sepher.

¹⁶Caleb said, "I will give Achsah my daughter as wife to the man who attacks Kiriath-sepher and captures it."

¹⁷And Othniel the son of Kenaz, Caleb's brother, captured it; so he gave him Achsah his daughter as a wife.

¹⁸Now it came about that when Achsah came *to Othniel,* she persuaded him [to allow her] to ask her father for a field. Then she [rode up to Caleb and] dismounted from her donkey, and Caleb said to her, "What do you want?"

¹⁹Achsah answered, "Give me a blessing; since you have given me the [dry] land of the Negev (South country), give me springs of water, too." So he gave her the upper springs and the lower springs.

²⁰This is the inheritance of the tribe of the sons of Judah according to their families (clans).

²¹The cities of the tribe of the sons of Judah in the extreme south toward the border of Edom were Kabzeel and Eder and Jagur,

²²and Kinah and Dimonah and Adadah,

²³and Kedesh and Hazor and Ithnan,

²⁴Ziph and Telem and Bealoth,

²⁵and Hazor-hadattah and Kerioth-hezron (that is, Hazor),

²⁶Amam and Shema and Moladah,

²⁷and Hazar-gaddah and Heshmon and Beth-pelet,

²⁸and Hazar-shual and Beersheba and Biziothiah,

²⁹Baalah and Iim and Ezem,

30and Eltolad and Chesil and Hormah,

31and Ziklag and Madmannah and Sansannah,

32and Lebaoth and Shilhim and Ain and Rimmon; in all twenty-nine cities with their villages.

33In the lowland: Eshtaol and Zorah and Ashnah,

34and Zanoah and En-gannim, Tappuah and Enam,

35Jarmuth and Adullam, Socoh and Azekah,

36and Shaaraim and Adithaim and Gederah and Gederothaim; fourteen cities with their villages.

37Zenan and Hadashah and Migdal-gad,

38and Dilean and Mizpeh and Joktheel,

39Lachish and Bozkath and Eglon,

40and Cabbon and Lahmas and Chitlish,

41and Gederoth, Beth-dagon and Naamah and Makkedah; sixteen cities with their villages.

42Libnah and Ether and Ashan,

43and Iphtah and Ashnah and Nezib,

44and Keilah and Achzib and Mareshah; nine cities with their villages.

45Ekron, with its towns and villages;

46from Ekron even to the sea, all that were beside Ashdod, with their villages;

47Ashdod, with its towns and its villages; Gaza, with its towns and its villages; as far as the Brook of Egypt (Wadi el-Arish) and the Great [Mediterranean] Sea with its coastline.

48In the hill country: Shamir and Jattir and Socoh,

49and Dannah and Kiriath-sannah (that is, Debir),

50and Anab and Eshtemoh and Anim,

51and Goshen and Holon and Giloh; eleven cities with their villages.

52Arab and Dumah and Eshan,

53and Janum and Beth-tappuah and Aphekah,

54and Humtah and Kiriath-arba (that is, Hebron), and Zior; nine cities with their villages.

55Maon, Carmel and Ziph and Juttah,

56and Jezreel and Jokdeam and Zanoah,

57Kain, Gibeah and Timnah; ten cities with their villages.

58Halhul, Beth-zur and Gedor,

59and Maarath and Beth-anoth and Eltekon; six cities with their villages.

60Kiriath-baal (that is, Kiriath-jearim), and Rabbah; two cities with their villages.

61In the wilderness [that slopes downward toward the Dead Sea]: Beth-arabah, Middin and Secacah,

62and Nibshan and the City of Salt and Engedi; six cities with their villages.

63But as for the Jebusites, the inhabitants of Jerusalem, the [tribe of the] sons of Judah were not able to drive them out; so the Jebusites live with the sons of Judah in Jerusalem to this day.

16

THEN THE lot (allotment) for the sons of Joseph went from the Jordan Valley at Jericho to the waters of Jericho on the east into the wilderness, going up from Jericho through the hill country to Bethel.

2Then it went from Bethel to Luz, and continued to Ataroth, the border of the Archites.

3It went down westward to the territory of the Japhletites, as far as the outskirts of lower Beth-horon, then to Gezer, and it ended at the sea.

4The sons of Joseph, Manasseh and Ephraim, received their inheritance.

5Now this was the territory of the sons of Ephraim according to their families: on the east side the border of their inheritance was Ataroth-addar, as far as upper Beth-horon.

6Then the border went westward at Michmethath on the north, and turned eastward to Taanath-shiloh and continued beyond it to the east of Janoah.

⁷It went down from Janoah to Ataroth and to Naarah, touched Jericho and ended at the Jordan.

⁸The border continued from Tappuah westward to the Brook Kanah, and it ended at the [Mediterranean] sea. This is the inheritance of the tribe of the sons of Ephraim according to their families (clans),

⁹with the cities which were set apart for the sons of Ephraim within the inheritance of the sons of Manasseh, all the cities with their villages.

¹⁰But they did not drive out the Canaanites who lived in Gezer, so the Canaanites live among Ephraim to this day, and they became forced laborers.

17 NOW THIS was the lot (allotment) for the tribe of Manasseh, for he was the firstborn of Joseph. To Machir the firstborn of Manasseh, the father of Gilead, were allotted Gilead and Bashan, because he was a man of war.

²So *the lot* was also made for the rest of the sons of Manasseh according to their families—for the sons of Abiezer and for the sons of Helek and for the sons of Asriel and for the sons of Shechem and for the sons of Hepher and for the sons of Shemida; these were the male descendants of Manasseh the son of Joseph according to their families (clans).

³But Zelophehad the son of Hepher, the son of Gilead, the son of Machir, the son of Manasseh, had no sons, only daughters; and these are the names of his daughters: Mahlah and Noah, Hoglah, Milcah and Tirzah.

⁴They came before Eleazar the priest and before Joshua the son of Nun and before the leaders and said, "The LORD commanded Moses to give us an inheritance among our brothers." So according to the command of the LORD Joshua gave them an inheritance among their father's brothers.

⁵So ten portions fell to Manasseh, besides the land of Gilead and Bashan, which is beyond the Jordan [on the east side of the river],

⁶because the daughters of [Zelophehad, a descendant of] Manasseh had received an inheritance among his [other] sons [whose inheritance went to their male descendants]. The land of Gilead belonged to the rest of the sons of Manasseh. [Num 36:5–12]

⁷The territory of Manasseh reached from Asher to Michmethath which was east of Shechem; then the border went southward to the inhabitants of En-tappuah.

⁸The land of Tappuah belonged to Manasseh, but [the city of] Tappuah on the border of Manasseh belonged to the sons of Ephraim.

⁹Then the border went down to the brook of Kanah, south of the brook (these cities *belonged* to Ephraim,

life point

Once the Israelites possessed the land, they got very involved in setting up their boundary lines. This reminds me that normal Christian life should be lived within the boundaries of balanced living. Once a person has a serious case of burnout, it is not easy to fix. None of us, not even those of us "called by God," can break His natural laws without consequences. Even though we may work for God, we cannot live without limits. I encourage you to take care of yourself. You have only one body, and you need it to live here on the earth. Be sure you rest physically, mentally, and emotionally. Doing some things for yourself while you are also busy doing for others is not wrong. In fact, it's healthy. Stay in balance, and you will be able to run your race well and cross the finish line.

among the cities of Manasseh), and Manasseh's border was on the north side of the brook and it ended at the sea.

¹⁰The land on the south side *belonged* to Ephraim and that on the north side was Manasseh's, and the sea was their border; they reached to [the territory of] Asher on the north and to [the territory of] Issachar on the east.

¹¹Also, in Issachar and in Asher, Manasseh had Beth-shean and its towns and Ibleam and its towns, and the inhabitants of Dor and its towns, and the inhabitants of En-dor and its towns, and the inhabitants of Taanach and its towns, and the inhabitants of Megiddo and its towns; the third is Napheth.

¹²But the sons of Manasseh were not able to [drive out the inhabitants and] take possession of these cities, because the Canaanites persisted in living in that land.

¹³When the Israelites became strong, they put the Canaanites to forced labor, but they did not drive them out completely.

¹⁴The sons of Joseph spoke to Joshua, saying, "Why have you given us only one lot and one portion as an inheritance, when we are a numerous people whom the LORD has so far blessed?"

¹⁵Then Joshua replied, "If you are a numerous people, go up to the forest and clear ground for yourselves there in the land of the Perizzites and the Rephaim, since the hill country of Ephraim is too narrow for you."

¹⁶The sons of Joseph said, "The hill country is not enough for us, and all the Canaanites who live in the valley have iron chariots, both those who are in Beth-shean and its towns and those in the Valley of Jezreel."

¹⁷Joshua said to the house of Joseph, to Ephraim and to Manasseh, "You are a numerous people and have great power; you shall not have *only* one lot,

¹⁸but the hill country shall be yours. For though it is a forest, you shall clear

it and possess it to its farthest borders; for you shall drive out the Canaanites, even though they have iron chariots and though they are strong."

18 THEN THE whole congregation of the Israelites assembled at Shiloh [in the tribal territory of Ephraim], and set up the Tent of Meeting there; and the land was subdued before them.

²There remained among the Israelites seven tribes who had not yet divided their inheritance.

³So Joshua asked them, "How long will you put off entering to take possession of the land which the LORD, the God of your fathers, has given you?

⁴"Provide for yourselves three men from each tribe so that I may send them, and that they may go through the land and write a description of it with regard to their [tribal] inheritance; then they shall return to me.

⁵"They shall divide it into seven parts; [the tribe of] Judah shall remain in its territory on the south, and the house of Joseph shall remain in its territory on the north.

⁶"You shall describe the land in seven divisions, and bring *the description* here to me. I will cast lots for you here before the LORD our God.

⁷"But the Levites have no portion among you, because the priesthood of the LORD is their inheritance. Gad and Reuben and half the tribe of Manasseh also have received their inheritance eastward beyond the Jordan, which Moses the servant of the LORD gave them."

⁸So the men arose and went [on their way], and Joshua commanded those who went to describe the land, saying, "Go and walk throughout the land and describe it, and return to me; and I will cast lots for you here before the LORD in Shiloh."

⁹So the men set out and passed

through the land, and described it by cities in seven divisions in a book; and they came back to Joshua to the camp at Shiloh.

¹⁰Joshua cast lots for them in Shiloh before the LORD, and there Joshua divided the land to the sons of Israel, [to each tribe] according to their portions.

¹¹Now the lot (allotment) of the tribe of the sons of Benjamin came up according to their families, and the territory of their lot fell between [the tribes of] the sons of Judah and the sons of Joseph.

¹²On the north side their border began at the Jordan, then it went up the slope of Jericho on the north, and up through the hill country westward, and it ended at the Beth-aven wilderness.

¹³Then the border continued southward toward Luz, to the slope of Luz (that is, Bethel); then the border went down to Ataroth-addar, by the hill that lies south of lower Beth-horon.

¹⁴The border changed course [from there] and turned around on the western side southward, from the hill that lies to the south opposite Beth-horon; it ended at Kiriath-baal (that is, Kiriath-jearim), a city of [the tribe of] the sons of Judah. This *formed* the western side [of Benjamin's territory].

¹⁵The southern side was from the edge of Kiriath-jearim, and the border went on westward and went to the source of the waters of Nephtoah.

¹⁶Then the border went down to the edge of the hill overlooking the Valley of Ben-hinnom (son of Hinnom), which is at the north end of the Valley of Rephaim; and it descended to the Valley of Hinnom, south to the slope of the Jebusite, and went on down to En-rogel.

¹⁷Then it turned toward the north and went on to En-shemesh and on to Geliloth, which is opposite the ascent of Adummim, and it went down to the stone of Bohan the son of Reuben.

¹⁸It continued to the north to the side opposite [Beth-] Arabah and went down to the Arabah.

¹⁹The border continued along to the north of the slope of Beth-hoglah; and the border ended at the northern bay of the Salt (Dead) Sea, at the south end of the Jordan. This was the southern border.

²⁰And the Jordan River was its border on the east side. This was the inheritance of the sons of Benjamin, according to their families and according to its borders all around.

²¹Now the cities of the tribe of the sons of Benjamin according to their families were Jericho and Beth-hoglah and Emek-keziz,

²²and Beth-arabah and Zemaraim and Bethel,

²³and Avvim and Parah and Ophrah,

²⁴and Chephar-ammoni and Ophni and Geba; twelve cities with their villages;

²⁵Gibeon and Ramah and Beeroth,

²⁶and Mizpeh and Chephirah and Mozah,

²⁷and Rekem and Irpeel and Taralah,

²⁸and Zelah, Haeleph and the Jebusite (that is, Jerusalem), Gibeah, Kiriath; fourteen cities with their villages. This is the inheritance of [the tribe of] the sons of Benjamin according to their families (clans).

putting the Word to work

Do you have good boundaries in your life? Ask God to show you where you may need to improve. Are you stressed out all the time? Make some changes so you can enjoy a peaceful life.

19 THEN THE second lot fell to Simeon, to the tribe of the sons of Simeon according to their families (clans), and their inheritance was within the inheritance of the sons of Judah.

²So they had as their inheritance Beersheba or Sheba and Moladah,

³and Hazar-shual and Balah and Ezem,

⁴and Eltolad and Bethul and Hormah,

⁵and Ziklag and Beth-marcaboth and Hazar-susah,

⁶and Beth-lebaoth and Sharuhen; thirteen cities with their villages;

⁷Ain, Rimmon and Ether and Ashan; four cities with their villages;

⁸and all the villages which were around these cities as far as Baalath-beer, Ramah of the Negev (South country). This was the inheritance of the tribe of the sons of Simeon according to their families.

⁹The inheritance of the sons of Simeon *was taken* from the portion of the sons of Judah, for the share of the sons of Judah was too large for them; so the sons of Simeon received an inheritance within Judah's inheritance.

¹⁰The third lot came up for [the tribe of] the sons of Zebulun according to their families. The territory of their inheritance extended to Sarid.

¹¹Then its border went up westward and on to Maralah, and reached to Dabbesheth and reached to the brook east of Jokneam.

¹²Then it turned from Sarid east toward the sunrise as far as the border of Chisloth-tabor, and it proceeded to Daberath and on up to Japhia.

¹³From there it continued east toward the sunrise to Gath-hepher and to Eth-kazin, and proceeded to Rimmon which turns toward Neah.

¹⁴The border circled it on the north to Hannathon, ending at the Valley of Iphtahel.

¹⁵Included were Kattah and Nahalal and Shimron and Idalah and Bethlehem; twelve cities with their villages.

¹⁶This was the inheritance of the sons of Zebulun according to their families, these cities with their villages.

¹⁷The fourth lot fell to [the tribe of] Issachar, to the sons of Issachar according to their families.

¹⁸Their territory included: Jezreel and Chesulloth and Shunem,

¹⁹and Hapharaim and Shion and Anaharath,

²⁰and Rabbith and Kishion and Ebez,

²¹and Remeth and En-gannim and En-haddah and Beth-pazzez.

²²The border reached to Tabor and Shahazumah and Beth-shemesh, and their border ended at the Jordan; sixteen cities with their villages.

²³This was the inheritance of the tribe of the sons of Issachar according to their families, the cities and their villages.

²⁴The fifth lot fell to the tribe of the sons of Asher according to their families.

²⁵Their territory was Helkath and Hali and Beten and Achshaph,

²⁶and Allammelech and Amad and Mishal; and on the west it reached to Carmel and to Shihor-libnath.

²⁷Then it turned eastward to Beth-dagon and reached Zebulun and the Valley of Iphtahel northward to Beth-emek and Neiel, and continued in the north to Cabul,

²⁸and Ebron and Rehob and Hammon and Kanah, as far as Great Sidon.

²⁹Then the border turned to Ramah, [reaching] to the fortified city of Tyre; and it turned to Hosah, and it ended at the [Mediterranean] sea at the region of Achzib.

³⁰Included were Ummah, and Aphek and Rehob; twenty-two cities with their villages.

³¹This was the inheritance of the tribe of the sons of Asher according to their families, these cities with their villages.

³²The sixth lot fell to [the tribe of] the sons of Naphtali according to their families.

³³Their border ran from Heleph, from the oak in Zaanannim and

Adami-nekeb and Jabneel, as far as Lakkum, and it ended at the Jordan.

³⁴Then the border turned westward to Aznoth-tabor and went from there to Hukkok; and it reached Zebulun on the south and reached Asher on the west, and to Judah toward the east at the Jordan.

³⁵The fortified cities were Ziddim, Zer, and Hammath, Rakkath and Chinnereth,

³⁶and Adamah and Ramah and Hazor,

³⁷and Kedesh and Edrei and En-hazor,

³⁸and Yiron and Migdal-el, Horem and Beth-anath and Beth-shemesh; nineteen cities with their villages.

³⁹This was the inheritance of the tribe of the sons of Naphtali according to their families, the cities and their villages.

⁴⁰The seventh lot fell to the tribe of the sons of Dan according to their families.

⁴¹The territory of their inheritance included Zorah and Eshtaol and Ir-shemesh,

⁴²and Shaalabbin and Aijalon and Ithlah,

⁴³and Elon and Timnah and Ekron,

⁴⁴and Eltekeh and Gibbethon and Baalath,

⁴⁵and Jehud and Bene-berak and Gath-rimmon,

⁴⁶and Me-jarkon and Rakkon, with the territory opposite Joppa.

⁴⁷The territory of the sons of Dan went beyond these; so the sons of Dan went up to fight against Leshem (Laish) and captured it. Then they struck it with the edge of the sword and took possession of it and settled there [between the tribes of Naphtali and Manasseh]; they renamed Leshem, Dan, after the name of their father (ancestor) Dan. [Judg 1:34; 18:7–10, 27]

⁴⁸This was the inheritance of the tribe of the sons of Dan according to their families (clans), these cities with their villages.

⁴⁹When they had finished dividing the land for inheritance by its borders, the Israelites gave an inheritance among them to Joshua the son of Nun.

⁵⁰According to the command of the LORD they gave him the city for which he asked—Timnath-serah in the hill country of Ephraim. So he built the city and settled in it.

⁵¹These are the inheritances which Eleazar the priest, Joshua the son of Nun, and the heads of the households of the tribes of the sons of Israel distributed by lot in Shiloh before the LORD at the doorway of the Tent of Meeting. So they finished dividing the land.

20 THE LORD spoke to Joshua, saying, ²"Speak to the Israelites, saying, 'Designate the cities of refuge (asylum), of which I spoke to you through Moses,

³so that the person (manslayer) who kills any person unintentionally, without premeditation, may flee there, and they shall be your refuge from the blood avenger. [Num 35:10ff]

⁴'He shall flee to one of these cities, and shall stand at the entrance of the gate of the city and explain his case to the elders of that city; and they shall take him into [the protection of] the city and give him a place [to stay], so that he may live among them.

⁵'If the blood avenger pursues him, they shall not hand the offender (manslayer) over to him, because he killed his neighbor unintentionally and without premeditation and did not hate him beforehand.

⁶'He shall live in that city until he has stood before the congregation for judgment [and if acquitted of murder he must stay there], until the death of the one who is the high priest in those days. Then the offender (manslayer)

shall return to his own city and his own house from which he fled.'"

⁷So they set apart *and* consecrated Kedesh in Galilee in the hill country of Naphtali, and Shechem in the hill country of Ephraim, and Kiriath-arba (that is, Hebron) in the hill country of Judah.

⁸Beyond the Jordan east of Jericho, they designated Bezer in the wilderness on the plain from the tribe of Reuben, and Ramoth in Gilead from the tribe of Gad, and Golan in Bashan from the tribe of Manasseh.

⁹These were the appointed cities for all the Israelites and for the stranger sojourning (living temporarily) among them, so that whoever killed any person unintentionally may flee there, and not die by the hand of the blood avenger until he had stood before the congregation [for judgment].

21 THEN THE heads of the households of the Levites came to Eleazar the priest, and Joshua the son of Nun, and the heads of the households of the tribes of the sons of Israel.

²They spoke to them at Shiloh in the land of Canaan, saying, "The LORD commanded Moses to give us cities to live in, with their pasture lands for our cattle."

³So the sons of Israel gave the Levites from their inheritance these [forty-eight] cities and their pasture lands, in accordance with the command of the LORD.

⁴The [first] lot (allotment) came out for the families of the Kohathites. So those Levites who were sons (descendants) of Aaron the priest received thirteen cities by lot from the tribe of Judah and from the tribe of Simeon and from the tribe of Benjamin.

⁵The rest of the sons of Kohath received ten cities by lot from the families of the tribe of Ephraim and from

the tribe of Dan and from the half-tribe of Manasseh.

⁶The sons of Gershon received thirteen cities by lot from the families of the tribe of Issachar and from the tribe of Asher and from the tribe of Naphtali and from the half-tribe of Manasseh in Bashan.

⁷The sons of Merari according to their families received twelve cities from the tribe of Reuben and from the tribe of Gad and from the tribe of Zebulun.

⁸The sons of Israel gave by lot to the Levites these cities with their pasture lands, as the LORD had commanded through Moses.

⁹They gave these cities which are mentioned here by name from the tribe of the sons of Judah and from the tribe of the sons of Simeon;

¹⁰and they were for the sons of Aaron, one of the families of the Kohathites, of the sons of Levi, because the lot fell to them first.

¹¹They gave them [the city of] Kiriath-arba, *Arba being* the father of Anak (that is, Hebron) in the hill country of Judah, with its surrounding pasture lands.

¹²But the fields of the city and its villages they had given to Caleb the son of Jephunneh as his property.

¹³So to the sons of Aaron the priest they gave Hebron, the city of refuge for anyone who committed manslaughter, with its pasture lands, and Libnah with its pasture lands,

¹⁴and Jattir with its pasture lands and Eshtemoa with its pasture lands,

¹⁵and Holon with its pasture lands and Debir with its pasture lands,

¹⁶and Ain with its pasture lands and Juttah with its pasture lands *and* Beth-shemesh with its pasture lands; nine cities from these two tribes (Judah and Simeon).

¹⁷From the tribe of Benjamin, Gibeon with its pasture lands, and Geba with its pasture lands,

¹⁸Anathoth with its pasture lands and Almon with its pasture lands; four cities.

¹⁹All the cities of the sons of Aaron, the priests, were thirteen cities with their pasture lands.

²⁰Then the cities from the tribe of Ephraim were allotted to the families of the sons of Kohath, the Levites, *even to* the rest of the sons of Kohath.

²¹They gave them Shechem, the city of refuge for anyone who committed manslaughter, with its pasture lands, in the hill country of Ephraim, and Gezer with its pasture lands,

²²and Kibzaim with its pasture lands and Beth-horon with its pasture lands; four cities.

²³From the tribe of Dan, Eltekeh with its pasture lands, Gibbethon with its pasture lands,

²⁴Aijalon with its pasture lands, Gath-rimmon with its pasture lands; four cities.

²⁵From the half-tribe of Manasseh, *they allotted* Taanach with its pasture lands and Gath-rimmon with its pasture lands; two cities.

²⁶All the cities with their pasture lands for the families of the rest of the sons of Kohath *totaled* ten.

²⁷To the sons of Gershon, one of the families of the Levites, *they gave* from the other half-tribe of Manasseh, [the city of] Golan in Bashan, the city of refuge for anyone who committed manslaughter, with its pasture lands, and Be-eshterah with its pasture lands; two cities.

²⁸From the tribe of Issachar, *they gave* Kishion with its pasture lands, Daberath with its pasture lands,

²⁹Jarmuth with its pasture lands, and En-gannim with its pasture lands; four cities.

³⁰From the tribe of Asher, *they gave* Mishal with its pasture lands, Abdon with its pasture lands,

³¹Helkath with its pasture lands and Rehob with its pasture lands; four cities.

³²From the tribe of Naphtali, *they gave* Kedesh in Galilee, the city of refuge for anyone who committed manslaughter, with its pasture lands and Hammoth-dor with its pasture lands and Kartan with its pasture lands; three cities.

³³All the cities of the Gershonites according to their families were thirteen cities with their pasture lands.

³⁴To the families of the sons of Merari, the rest of the Levites, *they gave* from the tribe of Zebulun, Jokneam with its pasture lands and Kartah with its pasture lands,

³⁵Dimnah with its pasture lands and Nahalal with its pasture lands; four cities.

³⁶From the tribe of Reuben, *they gave* Bezer with its pasture lands and Jahaz with its pasture lands,

³⁷Kedemoth with its pasture lands and Mephaath with its pasture lands; four cities.

³⁸From the tribe of Gad, *they gave* Ramoth in Gilead, the city of refuge for anyone who committed manslaughter, with its pasture lands and Mahanaim with its pasture lands,

³⁹Heshbon with its pasture lands and Jazer with its pasture lands; four cities in all.

⁴⁰All [these were] the cities of the sons of Merari according to their families, the rest of the families of the Levites; and their lot was twelve cities.

⁴¹All the cities of the Levites in the midst of the property of the sons of Israel were forty-eight cities with their pasture lands.

⁴²These cities each had its surrounding pasture lands; so it was with all these cities.

⁴³So the LORD gave Israel all the land which He had sworn to give to their fathers (ancestors), and they took possession of it and lived in it.

⁴⁴The Lᴏʀᴅ gave them rest [from conflict] on every side, in accordance with everything that He had sworn to their fathers, and not one of all their enemies stood before them [in battle]; the Lᴏʀᴅ handed over all their enemies to them. ⁴⁵Not one of the good promises which the Lᴏʀᴅ had spoken to the house of Israel failed; all had come to pass.

22 THEN JOSHUA called the Reubenites and the Gadites and the half-tribe of Manasseh, ²and said to them, "You have kept all that Moses the servant of the Lᴏʀᴅ commanded you, and have listened to and obeyed my voice in everything that I commanded you. ³"You have not deserted your brothers these many days to this day, but have [carefully] kept the obligation of the commandment of the Lᴏʀᴅ your God. ⁴"And now the Lᴏʀᴅ your God has given rest to your brothers, as He has promised them; so turn now and go to your tents, to the land of your possession, which Moses the servant of the Lᴏʀᴅ gave you beyond the [east side of the] Jordan. ⁵"Only be very careful and diligently observe the commandment and the law which Moses the servant of the Lᴏʀᴅ has commanded you to love the Lᴏʀᴅ your God and walk in all His ways and keep His commandments and hold fast to Him and serve Him with all your heart and with all your soul [your very life]."

⁶So Joshua blessed them and sent them away, and they went to their tents. ⁷Now to the one-half of the tribe of Manasseh Moses had given a possession in Bashan, but to the other half Joshua gave a possession on the west side of the Jordan among their brothers. So when Joshua sent them away to their tents, he blessed them, ⁸and he said to them, "Return to your tents with great riches and with very much livestock, with silver, gold, bronze, iron, and with very many clothes; divide the spoil of your enemies with your brothers (fellow tribesmen)." ⁹So the sons (descendants) of Reuben and the sons of Gad and the half-tribe of Manasseh returned home and departed from the [other] sons (western tribes) of Israel at Shiloh which is in the land of Canaan, to go to the land of Gilead, to the land of their own which they had possessed, in accordance with the command of the Lᴏʀᴅ through Moses. ¹⁰When they came to the region of the Jordan which is in the land of Canaan, the sons of Reuben and the sons of Gad and the half-tribe of Manasseh built an altar there by the Jordan, an altar that was great to behold. ¹¹And the [other] sons of Israel heard it said, "Look, the sons of Reuben and the sons of Gad and the half-tribe of Manasseh have built an altar at the edge of the land of Canaan, in

speak the Word

Thank You, God, that not one of my enemies can stand before me, but that You hand over all of them to me.
–ᴀᴅᴀᴘᴛᴇᴅ ꜰʀᴏᴍ Jᴏsʜᴜᴀ 21:44

God, help me to love You, to walk in all Your ways and keep Your commandments. Help me to hold fast to You and to serve You with all my heart and soul, with my very life.
–ᴀᴅᴀᴘᴛᴇᴅ ꜰʀᴏᴍ Jᴏsʜᴜᴀ 22:5

the region [west] of the Jordan, on the side *belonging to* the sons of Israel."

¹²When the sons of Israel heard of it, the whole congregation of the Israelites gathered at Shiloh to make war against them.

¹³Then the sons of Israel sent Phinehas the son of Eleazar the priest to the sons of Reuben and the sons of Gad and the half-tribe of Manasseh, in the land of Gilead,

¹⁴and with him ten leaders, one leader from each father's household from each of the tribes of Israel; and each one was the head of his father's household among the thousands of Israel.

¹⁵They came to the sons of Reuben and the sons of Gad and the half-tribe of Manasseh, in the land of Gilead, and they said to them,

¹⁶"This is what the entire congregation of the LORD says, 'What is this disloyal *and* unfaithful act which you have committed against the God of Israel, so as to turn away from following the LORD this day, by building yourselves an altar, to rebel against the LORD this day?

¹⁷'Is the wrongdoing (idolatry) of Peor not enough for us, from which we have not cleansed ourselves to this day, even though the affliction [in which twenty-four thousand died] came on the congregation of the LORD, [Num 25:1–9]

¹⁸that you would turn away this day from following the LORD? If you rebel against the LORD today, He will be angry with the entire congregation of Israel tomorrow.

¹⁹'If, however, the land of your possession is unclean, then cross into the land of the possession of the LORD, where the LORD's tabernacle is situated, and settle down among us. But do not rebel against the LORD, or rebel against us by building an altar for yourselves, besides the altar of the LORD our God [at Shiloh].

²⁰'Did not Achan the son of Zerah act unfaithfully in the things under the ban, and [as a result God's] wrath came on the entire congregation of Israel? And that man did not perish alone in his wrongdoing.'" [Josh 7:1–26]

²¹Then the sons of Reuben and the sons of Gad and the half-tribe of Manasseh answered and said to the heads of the families of Israel,

²²"The Mighty One, God, the LORD, the Mighty One, God, the LORD! He knows, and may Israel itself know. If it was in rebellion, or if in an unfaithful act against the LORD, do not save us this day!

²³"If we have built an altar for ourselves to turn away from following the LORD, or if [we did so] to offer a burnt offering or grain offering on it, or if to offer sacrifices of peace offerings on it, may the LORD Himself require it [of us and hold us responsible].

²⁴"But in truth we have done this out of concern, for a reason, saying, 'In time to come your sons (descendants) may say to our sons, "What claim do you have to the LORD, the God of Israel?

²⁵"For the LORD has made the Jordan a border between us and you, you sons of Reuben and sons of Gad; you have no part in the LORD." So your sons (descendants) may cause our sons to stop fearing the LORD.'

²⁶"So we said, 'Let us prepare *and* build an altar, not for burnt offering or for sacrifice,

²⁷but to be a witness between us and you and between the generations after us, that we are to perform the service of the LORD before Him with our burnt offerings, and with our sacrifices and with our peace offerings, so that your sons (descendants) will not say to our sons in time to come, "You have no part in the LORD."'

²⁸"So we said, 'If your descendants should say this to us or to our descendants in time to come, then we

can reply, "See the copy of the altar of the LORD which our fathers made, not for burnt offering or for sacrifice, but rather it is a witness between us and you."'

²⁹"Far be it from us that we should rebel against the LORD and turn away from following the LORD this day, by building an altar for burnt offering, for grain offering or for sacrifice, besides the altar of the LORD our God which is before His tabernacle [in Shiloh]."

³⁰So when Phinehas the priest and the leaders of the congregation and heads of the families of Israel who were with him, heard the words which the sons of Reuben and the sons of Gad and the sons of Manasseh spoke, it pleased them.

³¹Phinehas the son of Eleazar the priest said to the sons of Reuben and the sons of Gad and the sons of Manasseh, "Today we know that the LORD is among us, because you have not committed this unfaithful act against the LORD; indeed you have saved Israel from the hand of the LORD."

³²Then Phinehas the son of Eleazar the priest and the leaders returned from the sons of Reuben and the sons of Gad, from the land of Gilead to the land of Canaan, to the sons of Israel, and brought back word to them.

³³The report pleased the sons of Israel, and the sons of Israel blessed God; and they said no more about going to battle against them to destroy the land in which the sons of Reuben and the sons of Gad were living.

³⁴The sons of Reuben and the sons of Gad called the altar *Witness*; "For it is a witness between us that the LORD is God."

23 A LONG time after that, when the LORD had given Israel rest from all their enemies on every side, and Joshua had grown old and advanced in years, ²that Joshua called all Israel, their

elders and their heads and their judges and their officers, and said to them, "I am old and advanced in years.

³"And you have seen all that the LORD your God has done to all these nations for your sake; for the LORD your God is He who has been fighting for you. [Ex 14:14]

⁴"See, I have allotted to you these nations that remain as an inheritance for your tribes, with all the nations which I have cut off, from the Jordan [on the east] to the Great [Mediterranean] Sea toward the setting sun.

⁵"The LORD your God will push them away from before you and drive them out of your sight and you will take possession of their land, just as the LORD your God promised you.

⁶"Be steadfast *and* very determined to keep and to do everything that is written in the Book of the Law of Moses, so that you do not turn aside from it to the right or the left,

⁷so that you do not associate with these nations which remain among you, or mention the name of their gods, or make anyone swear [an oath by them], or serve them, or bow down to them.

⁸"But you are to cling to the LORD your God, just as you have done to this day.

⁹"For the LORD has driven out great and mighty nations from before you; and as for you, no man has been able to stand [in opposition] before you to this day.

¹⁰"One of your men puts to flight a thousand, for the LORD your God is He who is fighting for you, just as He promised you.

¹¹"So be very careful *and* watchful of yourselves to love the LORD your God.

¹²"For if you ever turn back and cling to the rest of these nations, these that are left among you, and intermarry with them, so that you associate with them and they with you,

¹³know *and* understand with certainty that the LORD your God will not

continue to drive these nations out from before you; but they will be a snare and trap to you, and a whip on your sides and thorns in your eyes, until you perish from this good land which the Lord your God has given you.

14"Now behold, today I am going the way of all the earth, and you know in all your hearts and in all your souls that not one word of all the good words which the Lord your God has promised concerning you has failed; all have been fulfilled for you, not one of them has failed.

15"It shall come about that just as every good word which the Lord your God spoke *and* promised to you has been fulfilled for you, so the Lord will bring upon you every bad thing [about which He warned you], until He has destroyed *and* eliminated you from this good land which the Lord your God has given you.

16"When you transgress (violate) the covenant of the Lord your God, which He commanded you [to follow], and you go and serve other gods and bow down to them, then the anger of the Lord will be kindled against you, and you shall perish quickly from the good land which He has given you."

24 THEN JOSHUA gathered all the tribes of Israel to Shechem, and called for the elders of Israel and for their heads and for their judges and for their officers; they presented themselves before God.

2Joshua said to all the people, "This is what the Lord, the God of Israel, says, 'Your fathers, including Terah, the father of Abraham and the father of Nahor, lived beyond the [Euphrates] River in ancient times; and they served other gods.

3'Then I took your father Abraham from beyond the [Euphrates] River and led him through all the land of Canaan, and multiplied his descendants, and I gave him Isaac.

4'To Isaac I gave Jacob and Esau, and to Esau I gave [the hill country of] Mount Seir to possess; but Jacob and his sons went down to Egypt.

5'Then I sent Moses and Aaron, and I plagued Egypt by what I did in its midst; and afterward I brought you out.

6'Then I brought your fathers out of Egypt, and you came to the sea; and the Egyptians pursued your fathers with chariots and horsemen to the Red Sea.

7'When they cried out to the Lord [for help], He put darkness between you and the Egyptians, and brought the sea upon them and covered them; and your own eyes saw what I did in Egypt. And you lived in the wilderness a long time (forty years). [Josh 5:6]

8'Then I brought you into the land of the Amorites who lived on the other side of the Jordan, and they fought with you; and I gave them into your hand, and you took possession of their land and I destroyed them before you.

9'Then Balak the son of Zippor, king of Moab, arose and fought against Israel, and he sent and called Balaam the son of Beor to curse you.

10'But I would not listen to Balaam. Therefore he had to bless you, so I saved you from Balak's hand. [Deut 23:5]

11'You crossed the Jordan and came to Jericho; and the citizens of Jericho fought against you, as did the Amorite and the Perizzite and the Canaanite and the Hittite and the Girgashite, the Hivite and the Jebusite; and so I gave them into your hand.

speak the Word

I know in my heart, God, that not one of all the good words You have promised concerning me will fail, but that all will be fulfilled for me.
—ADAPTED FROM JOSHUA 23:14

¹²'I sent the hornet [that is, the ter-ror of you] before you, which drove the two kings of the Amorites out before you; but it was not by your sword or by your bow. [Ex 23:27, 28; Deut 2:25; 7:20]

¹³'I gave you a land for which you did not labor, and cities which you did not build, and you live in them; you eat from vineyards and olive groves which you did not plant.'

¹⁴"Now, therefore, fear the LORD and serve Him in sincerity and in truth; remove the gods which your fathers served on the other side of the [Eu-phrates] River and in Egypt, and serve the LORD.

¹⁵"If it is unacceptable in your sight to serve the LORD, choose for your-selves this day whom you will serve: whether the gods which your fathers served that were on the other side of the River, or the gods of the Amorites in whose land you live; but as for me and my house, we will serve the LORD."

¹⁶The people answered, "Far be it from us to abandon (reject) the LORD to serve other gods;

¹⁷for the LORD our God is He who brought us and our fathers up out of the land of Egypt, from the house of bondage, and who did these great signs (miracles) in our sight and kept us safe

"i will serve the Lord."

Regardless of what other people may think, serving and following God really is the only way to live a fulfilling, victorious life.

In Jesus' day, many leaders believed in Jesus but would not confess their faith to others. They feared they would be expelled from the synagogue if they went public with their belief in Him (see John 12:42–43). They were hindered from a relation-ship with Jesus because they were addicted to approval. Although they wanted a relationship with the Lord, they loved other people's approval more. That is sad, but it happens all the time.

Joshua, on the other hand, in Old Testament times, was bold about his belief in God, declaring that, "as for me and my house, we will serve the LORD" (Joshua 24:15). Be like Joshua, and determine that you and your household will serve the Lord. Follow God, not people!

The leaders of Jesus' day knew that He was real. They believed in Him, but their love of approval would not permit them to have a true relationship with Him. I wonder how their lives turned out. What did they miss because they said *yes* to people and *no* to God? I wonder how many of them were never mentioned in the Bible again. I wonder if they faded into oblivion and never fulfilled their destinies because they loved the approval of men more than the approval of God. How many of them spent their lives disrespecting themselves because they were people-pleasers?

We need to realize that not everyone is going to like us. If we live our lives wor-rying about what other people think, we will never take risks or stretch ourselves into new realms. We will give up our dreams. Satan is a dream thief, and he works through people who are selfish enough to steal our dreams in order to have theirs.

Do not let anyone steal from you what Jesus died to give you—the freedom to follow the leading of the Holy Spirit for you as an individual. As you follow Him, I guarantee that He will lead you into a rewarding life. Like Joshua, make a deliberate, personal decision to serve the Lord and boldly declare: "As for me and my house, we will serve the LORD."

all along the way that we went and among all the peoples among whom we passed.

¹⁸"The LORD drove all the peoples out from before us, even the Amorites who lived in the land. We also will serve the LORD, for He is our God."

¹⁹Then Joshua said to the people, "You will not be able to serve the LORD [if you serve any other gods], for He is a holy God; He is a jealous God [demanding what is rightfully and uniquely His]. He will not forgive your transgression [of His law] or your sins.

²⁰"If you do abandon (reject) the LORD and serve foreign gods, then He will turn and do you harm and consume *and* destroy you after He has done you good."

²¹The people said to Joshua, "No, but we will serve [only] the LORD."

²²Joshua then said to the people, "You are witnesses against yourselves that you have chosen for yourselves the LORD, to serve Him." And they said, "We are witnesses."

²³"Now then, remove the foreign gods which are among you, and incline your hearts toward the LORD, the God of Israel."

²⁴The people said to Joshua, "We will serve the LORD our God and we will listen to *and* obey His voice."

²⁵So Joshua made a covenant with the people that day, and made for them a statute and an ordinance at Shechem.

²⁶And Joshua wrote these words in the Book of the Law of God. Then he took a large stone and set it up there under the oak that was in [the courtyard of] the sanctuary of the LORD.

²⁷Joshua then said to all the people, "Look, this stone shall serve as a witness against us, for it has heard all the words of the LORD which He spoke to us; so it shall be a witness against you, so that [afterward] you do not deny your God."

²⁸Then Joshua sent the people away, each to [the territory of] his inheritance.

²⁹It happened after these things that Joshua the son of Nun, the servant of the LORD, died, at the age of a hundred and ten years.

³⁰They buried him in the territory of his inheritance in Timnath-serah, which is in the hill country of Ephraim, on the north side of Mount Gaash.

³¹Israel served the LORD all the days of Joshua and all the days of the elders who outlived Joshua, and had known all the works of the LORD which He had done for Israel.

³²Now they buried the bones of Joseph, which the children of Israel brought up from Egypt, at Shechem, in the plot of land which Jacob had bought from the sons of Hamor the father of Shechem for a hundred pieces of money; and it became the inheritance of the sons of Joseph.

³³And Eleazar [the priest], the son of Aaron died; and they buried him at Gibeah [on the hill] of Phinehas his son, which had been given to him in the hill country of Ephraim.

speak the Word

God, I declare as Joshua did: As for me and my house, we will serve the Lord.
—ADAPTED FROM JOSHUA 24:15

Lord, I declare with the Israelites of long ago: I will serve the Lord my God and I will listen to and obey His voice.
—ADAPTED FROM JOSHUA 24:24

Judges

Author:
Unknown

Date:
About 1050 BC–1000 BC

Everyday Life Principles:
Disobeying and dishonoring God always brings trouble to our lives.

God is merciful, and He sends deliverance when we cry out to Him.

The Spirit of God works through people to do miraculous things.

The book of Judges teaches us about a time when the people of Israel departed from God as they settled in the Promised Land. After Joshua died and they were left with no leader, they stopped honoring and obeying God. They disregarded His laws, forgot their covenant with Him, and began to do whatever they wanted (see Judges 21:25). Because of His mercy, God raised up good leaders such as Deborah, Gideon, and Samson; He also sent His Spirit among the Israelites and upon certain people to lead them, help them, and give them victory over their enemies.

Judges clearly shows us that the Israelites had so much trouble simply because they would not obey God. They found themselves in a continual cycle of turning from God, then becoming oppressed by their enemies, then crying out to God in their misery. When they cried out, God was faithful to answer in His mercy by sending a person empowered by the Holy Spirit to deliver them in miraculous ways. After a period of time they would forget God and, slowly but surely, sink back into being oppressed by their enemies again.

Let me encourage you not to follow the pattern of the Israelites in the book of Judges by departing from God and getting yourself in trouble. Instead, remember how important obedience is, and do everything you can to honor God in every way, keeping your heart loyal and faithful to Him.

1 NOW IT came about after the death of Joshua, that the sons (descendants) of Israel (Jacob) asked the LORD, "Who shall go up first for us against the Canaanites, to fight against them?"

²And the LORD said, "Judah shall go up [first]; behold, I have given the land into his hand."

³And [the tribe of the sons of] Judah said to [the tribe of the sons of] Simeon his brother, "Come up with me into my allotted territory, so that we may fight against the Canaanites; and I likewise will go with you into your allotted territory." So Simeon went with him.

⁴Then Judah went up, and the LORD gave the Canaanites and the Perizzites into their hand, and they struck down in defeat ten thousand men at Bezek.

⁵Then they found Adoni-bezek in Bezek and fought against him, and they struck down in defeat the Canaanites and the Perizzites.

⁶But Adoni-bezek fled; and they pursued him and caught him and cut off his thumbs and his big toes.

⁷Adoni-bezek said, "Seventy kings with their thumbs and big toes cut off used to gather up *scraps of food* under my table; as I have done [to others], so God has repaid me." So they brought him to Jerusalem, and he died there.

⁸Then the sons of Judah fought against [Jebusite] Jerusalem and captured it and struck it with the edge of the sword and set the city on fire.

⁹Afterward the sons of Judah went down to fight against the Canaanites who lived in the hill country, in the Negev (South country) and in the lowland.

¹⁰So Judah went against the Canaanites who lived in Hebron (the name of Hebron formerly was Kiriath-arba); and they defeated Sheshai and Ahiman and Talmai.

¹¹From there [the tribe of] Judah went against the inhabitants of Debir (the name of Debir formerly was Kiriath-sepher [city of books and scribes]).

¹²And Caleb said, "Whoever attacks Kiriath-sepher and captures it, I will even give him my daughter Achsah as a wife."

¹³Othniel the son of Kenaz, Caleb's younger brother, captured it; so he gave him his daughter Achsah as a wife.

¹⁴When she came *to Othniel,* she persuaded him to [allow her to] ask her father [Caleb] for a field. Then she [rode up to Caleb and] dismounted from her donkey, and Caleb said to her, "What do you want?"

¹⁵She said to him, "Give me a blessing; since you have given me the land of the Negev (South country), give me springs of water, too." So Caleb gave her the upper springs and the lower springs.

¹⁶The sons of [Jethro] the Kenite, Moses' father-in-law, went up from the City of Palms (Jericho) with the sons of Judah, to the wilderness of Judah which is in the Negev (South country) *near* Arad; and they went and lived with the people. [Ex 3:1]

¹⁷Then [the warriors of the tribe of] Judah went with [the warriors of the tribe of] Simeon his brother, and they struck the Canaanites living in Zephath and utterly destroyed it. So the city was called Hormah (destruction).

¹⁸Also [the warriors of] Judah captured Gaza with its territory and Ashkelon with its territory and Ekron with its territory.

¹⁹The LORD was with Judah, and [the tribe of] Judah took possession of the hill country, but they could not dispossess *and* drive out those inhabiting the valley because they had iron chariots.

²⁰Then they gave Hebron to Caleb, as Moses had said, and he drove out from there the three sons of Anak. [Josh 14:6, 9]

²¹But the sons of Benjamin did not drive out the Jebusites who inhabited Jerusalem; so the Jebusites have lived

with the sons of Benjamin in Jerusalem to this day.

²²The house of Joseph also went up against Bethel, and the LORD was with them.

²³The house of Joseph spied out Bethel (now the name of the city was formerly Luz).

²⁴The spies saw a man coming out of the city and they said to him, "Please show us the entrance to the city and we will treat you kindly."

²⁵So he showed them the entrance to the city, and they struck the city with the edge of the sword, but they let the man and all his family go free.

²⁶The man went into the land of the Hittites and built a city and named it Luz, which is its name to this day.

²⁷But [the tribe of] Manasseh did not take possession of Beth-shean and its villages, or Taanach and its villages, or the inhabitants of Dor and its villages, or the inhabitants of Ibleam and its villages, or the inhabitants of Megiddo and its villages; so the Canaanites remained in that land.

²⁸It happened when Israel became strong, that they put the Canaanites to forced labor, but they did not drive them out completely.

²⁹Neither did [the warriors of] Ephraim drive out the Canaanites who were living in Gezer; so the Canaanites lived in Gezer among them.

³⁰[The warriors of the tribe of] Zebulun did not drive out the inhabitants of Kitron or of Nahalol; so the Canaanites lived among them and were put to forced labor.

³¹[The warriors of the tribe of] Asher did not drive out the inhabitants of Acco, or the inhabitants of Sidon, or of Ahlab, or of Achzib, or of Helbah, or of Aphik, or of Rehob.

³²So the Asherites lived among the Canaanites, the inhabitants of the land, because they did not drive them out.

³³Neither did [the warriors of] Naphtali drive out the inhabitants of Beth-shemesh, or the inhabitants of Beth-anath, but they lived among the Canaanites, the inhabitants of the land; and the inhabitants of Beth-shemesh and of Beth-anath became forced labor for them.

³⁴Then the Amorites forced the sons of Dan [back] into the hill country, for they would not allow them to come down into the valley;

³⁵yet the Amorites persisted in living on Mount Heres (the mountain of the sun), in Aijalon, and in Shaalbim; but when the power of the house (descendants) of Joseph became strong *and* prevailed, they became forced labor.

³⁶The border of the Amorites ran from the ascent of Akrabbim, from Sela (rock) and upward.

2 NOW THE Angel of the LORD came up from Gilgal to Bochim. And he said, "I brought you up from Egypt and led you to the land which I swore [to give] to your fathers; and I said, 'I will never break My covenant with you, [Ex 20:2; 23:32]

²and as for you, you shall not make a covenant with the inhabitants of this land; you shall tear down their altars.' But you have not obeyed Me; what is this that you have done?

³"So I also said, 'I will not drive your enemies out before you; but they will be *like thorns* in your sides and their gods will be a snare to you.'"

⁴When the Angel of the LORD had spoken these words to all the Israelites, the people raised their voices and wept.

⁵So they named that place Bochim

speak the Word

Thank You, God, that You will never break Your covenant with me.
–ADAPTED FROM JUDGES 2:1

(weepers); and there they offered sacrifices to the Lord.

⁶And when Joshua had sent the people away, the [tribes of the] Israelites went each to his inheritance, to take possession of the land.

⁷The people served the Lord all the days of Joshua and all the days of the elders who outlived Joshua, who had seen all the great work of the Lord which He had done for Israel.

⁸Then Joshua the son of Nun, the servant of the Lord, died at the age of a hundred and ten.

⁹And they buried him in the territory of his inheritance in Timnath-heres, in the hill country of Ephraim, north of Mount Gaash.

¹⁰Also, all [the people of] that generation were gathered to their fathers [in death]; and another generation arose after them who did not know (recognize, understand) the Lord, nor even the work which He had done for Israel.

¹¹Then the Israelites did evil in the sight of the Lord and worshiped *and* served the Baals,

¹²and they abandoned the Lord, the God of their fathers, who brought them out of the land of Egypt. They followed other gods from the gods of the peoples who were around them, and they bowed down to them, and offended *and* provoked the Lord to anger.

¹³So they abandoned the Lord and served Baal [the pagan god of the Canaanites] and the Ashtaroth.

¹⁴So the anger of the Lord burned against Israel, and He gave them into the hands (power) of plunderers who robbed them; and He sold them into the hands of their surrounding enemies, so that they could no longer stand [in opposition] before their enemies.

¹⁵Wherever they went, the hand of the Lord was against them for evil (misfortune), as the Lord had spoken, and as the Lord had sworn to them, so that they were severely distressed. [Lev 26:14–46]

¹⁶Then the Lord raised up judges who rescued them from the hands of those who robbed them.

¹⁷Yet they did not listen to their judges, for they played the prostitute after other gods and they bowed down to them. They quickly turned aside from the way in which their fathers had walked in obeying the commandments of the Lord; they did not do as *their fathers*.

¹⁸When the Lord raised up judges for them, He was with the judge and He rescued them from the hand of their enemies all the days of the judge; for the Lord was moved to pity by their groaning because of those who oppressed and afflicted them.

¹⁹But when the judge died, they turned back and behaved more corruptly than their fathers, in following and serving other gods, and bowing down to them. They did not abandon their practices or their stubborn ways.

²⁰So the anger of the Lord burned against Israel, and He said, "Because this nation has transgressed (violated) My covenant (binding agreement) which I commanded their fathers, and has not listened to My voice,

²¹I also will no longer drive out before them any of the nations which Joshua left [to be conquered] when he died,

²²in order to test [the loyalty of] Israel by them, whether Israel will keep the way of the Lord to walk in it, as their fathers did, or not."

²³So the Lord allowed those nations to remain, not driving them out at once; and He did not give them into the hand of Joshua.

3 NOW THESE are the nations which the Lord left [in order] to test Israel by them (*that is*, all [the people of Israel] who had not [previously] experienced any of the wars in Canaan;

²only in order that the generations of the sons of Israel might be taught war,

at least those who had not experienced it previously).

³*The remaining nations are:* the five lords (governors) of the Philistines, all the Canaanites, the Sidonians, and the Hivites who lived on Mount Lebanon from Mount Baal-hermon to the entrance of Hamath.

⁴They were [allowed to remain] for the testing of Israel, to determine whether Israel would listen to *and* obey the commandments of the LORD, which He had commanded their fathers (ancestors) through Moses.

⁵And the Israelites lived among the Canaanites, Hittites, Amorites, Perizzites, Hivites, and Jebusites;

⁶and they took their daughters for themselves as wives and gave their own daughters to their sons, and served their [pagan] gods. [Ex 34:12–16]

⁷And the Israelites did evil in the sight of the LORD, and they forgot the LORD their God and served the Baals and the Asheroth. [Judg 2:13]

⁸So the anger of the LORD was kindled against Israel, and He sold them into the hand of Cushan-rishathaim king of Mesopotamia; and the Israelites served Cushan-rishathaim eight years.

⁹But when the Israelites cried out to the LORD [for help], the LORD raised up a man to rescue the people of Israel, Othniel the son of Kenaz, Caleb's younger brother.

¹⁰The Spirit of the LORD came upon him, and he judged Israel. He went out to war, and the LORD gave Cushan-rishathaim king of Mesopotamia into his hand, and he prevailed over Cushan-rishathaim.

¹¹And the land was at rest [from oppression for] forty years. Then Othniel the son of Kenaz died.

¹²Now the Israelites again did evil in the sight of the LORD, and the LORD strengthened Eglon king of Moab against Israel, since they had done what was evil in the sight of the LORD.

¹³And Eglon gathered to him the sons of Ammon and Amalek, and went and struck down Israel [in defeat], and they took possession of the City of Palm Trees (Jericho).

¹⁴And the Israelites served Eglon king of Moab eighteen years.

¹⁵But when the Israelites cried out to the LORD [for help], the LORD raised up a man to rescue them, Ehud the son of Gera, a Benjamite, a left-handed man. And the Israelites sent *a gift* of tribute by him to Eglon king of Moab.

¹⁶Now Ehud made for himself a sword a cubit long, which had two edges, and he bound it on his right thigh under his robe.

¹⁷And he brought the tribute to Eglon king of Moab. Now Eglon was a very fat man.

¹⁸And when Ehud had finished presenting the tribute, he sent away the people who had carried it.

¹⁹But Ehud himself turned back from the sculptured stones at Gilgal, [and he returned to Eglon] and said [to him], "I have a secret message for you, O king." Eglon said "Keep silence." And all who attended him left him.

²⁰Ehud came to him as he was sitting alone in his [private] cool upper chamber, and Ehud said, "I have a

life point

Throughout the Old Testament, as in Judges 3:10, we see that the Spirit of the Lord "came upon" people and gave them power, wisdom, or ability beyond what they naturally possessed.

Outward power comes from inner purity, and that inner purification (or sanctification) is a work of the Holy Spirit living within us. He wants to fill us with His Spirit and give us the power to live the abundant life that is available through believing in Jesus Christ.

message from God for you." And the king got up from his seat.

²¹Then Ehud reached out with his left hand and took the sword from his right thigh, and plunged it into Eglon's belly.

²²And the hilt also went in after the blade, and the fat closed over the blade, because Ehud did not draw the sword out of his belly; and the refuse came out.

²³Then Ehud went out into the vestibule and shut the doors of the upper chamber behind him, and locked *them*.

²⁴When Ehud departed, Eglon's servants came. And when they saw that the doors of the upper room were locked, they said, "He is only relieving himself in the cool room."

²⁵They waited [a very long time] until they became embarrassed *and* uneasy, but he still did not open the doors of the upper room. So [finally] they took the key and opened them, and behold, their master had fallen to the floor, dead.

²⁶Now Ehud escaped while they lingered, and he passed beyond the sculptured stones and escaped to Seirah.

²⁷When he had arrived, he blew a trumpet in the hill country of Ephraim; and the sons of Israel went down with him from the hill country, and he was in front of them.

²⁸And he said to them, "Pursue *them,* for the Lord has handed over your enemies the Moabites to you." So they went down after him and seized the fords of the Jordan opposite Moab and did not allow anyone to cross.

²⁹They struck down at that time about ten thousand Moabite men, all strong, courageous men; not a man escaped.

³⁰So Moab was subdued *and* humbled that day under the hand of Israel, and the land was at rest for eighty years.

³¹After Ehud came Shamgar the son of Anath, who struck down six hundred Philistine men with an oxgoad. He too saved Israel.

4 BUT THE Israelites again did evil in the sight of the Lord, after Ehud died. ²So the Lord sold them into the hand of Jabin king of Canaan, who reigned in Hazor. The commander of his army was Sisera, who lived in Harosheth-hagoyim.

³Then the Israelites cried out to the Lord [for help], for Jabin had nine hundred iron chariots and had oppressed *and* tormented the sons of Israel severely for twenty years.

⁴Now Deborah, a prophetess, the wife of Lappidoth, was judging Israel at that time.

⁵She used to sit [to hear and decide disputes] under the palm tree of Deborah between Ramah and Bethel in the hill country of Ephraim; and the Israelites came up to her for judgment.

⁶Now she sent *word* and summoned Barak the son of Abinoam from Kedesh-naphtali, and said to him, "Behold, the Lord, the God of Israel, has commanded, 'Go and march to Mount Tabor, and take with you ten thousand men [of war] from the tribes of Naphtali and Zebulun.

⁷'I will draw out Sisera, the commander of Jabin's army, with his chariots and his infantry to meet you at the river Kishon, and I will hand him over to you.'"

⁸Then Barak said to her, "If you will go with me, then I will go; but if you will not go with me, I will not go."

⁹She said, "I will certainly go with you; nevertheless, the journey that you are about to take will not be for your honor *and* glory, because the Lord will sell Sisera into the hand of a woman." Then Deborah got up and went with Barak to Kedesh.

¹⁰And Barak summoned [the fighting men of the tribes of] Zebulun and Naphtali to Kedesh, and ten thousand men went up under his command; Deborah also went up with him.

¹¹Now Heber the Kenite had separated himself from the Kenites, from the sons of Hobab the father-in-law of Moses, and had pitched his tent as far away as the terebinth tree in Zaanannim, which is near Kedesh.

¹²When someone told Sisera that Barak the son of Abinoam had gone up to Mount Tabor,

¹³Sisera called together all his chariots, nine hundred iron chariots, and all the people who were with him, from Harosheth-hagoyim to the river Kishon.

¹⁴Deborah said to Barak, "Arise! For this is the day when the LORD has given Sisera into your hand. Has the LORD not gone out before you?" So Barak went down from Mount Tabor with ten thousand men following him.

¹⁵And the LORD routed Sisera and all his chariots and [confused] all his army with the edge of the sword before Barak; and Sisera dismounted from his chariot and fled away on foot.

¹⁶But Barak pursued the chariots and the army to Harosheth-hagoyim, and the entire army of Sisera fell by the sword; not even one man was left.

¹⁷But Sisera fled on foot to the tent of Jael, the wife of Heber the Kenite, because there was peace between Jabin the king of Hazor and the house of Heber the Kenite.

¹⁸Jael went out to meet Sisera, and said to him, "Turn aside, my lord, turn aside to me! Have no fear." So he turned aside to her [and went] into the tent, and she covered him with a rug.

¹⁹And he said to her, "Please give me a little water to drink because I am thirsty." And she opened a skin of milk and gave him a drink; then she covered him.

²⁰And he said to her, "Stand at the door of the tent, and if any man comes and asks you, 'Is there anyone here?' tell him, 'No.'"

²¹But Jael, Heber's wife, took a tent peg and a hammer in her hand, and came up quietly to him and drove the peg through his temple, and it went through into the ground; for he was sound asleep and exhausted. So he died.

²²And behold, as Barak pursued Sisera, Jael came out to meet him and said to him, "Come, and I will show you the man whom you are seeking." And he entered [her tent] with her, and behold Sisera lay dead with the tent peg in his temple.

²³So on that day God subdued and humbled Jabin king of Canaan before the sons of Israel.

²⁴And the hand of the sons of Israel pressed down heavier and heavier on Jabin king of Canaan, until they had destroyed him.

5 THEN DEBORAH and Barak the son of Abinoam sang on that day, saying,

²"For the leaders who took the lead in Israel,
For the people who volunteered [for battle],
Bless the LORD!
³"Hear, O kings; listen, O rulers!
I will sing to the LORD,
I will sing praise to the LORD, the God of Israel.
⁴"LORD, when You went out from Seir,
When You marched from the field of Edom,
The earth quaked, the heavens also dripped,
Yes, the clouds dripped water.
⁵"The mountains quaked at the presence of the LORD,
Yes, this Sinai, at the presence of the LORD, the God of Israel.

⁶"In the days of Shamgar the son of Anath,
In the days of Jael, the highways were deserted,

And travelers went by roundabout
ways.
7 "The villagers ceased *to be;* they
ceased in Israel
Until I, Deborah, arose,
Until I arose, a mother in Israel.
8 "They chose new gods;
Then war was in the gates.
Was there a shield or spear seen
Among forty thousand in Israel?
9 "My heart *goes out* to the
commanders of Israel,
The volunteers among the people;
Bless the LORD!
10 "Sing of it, you who ride on white
donkeys,
You who sit on *rich* carpets,
And you who walk by the way.
11 "At the sound of those who divide
flocks among the watering
places,
There they shall recount the
righteous acts of the LORD,
The righteous acts toward His
villagers in Israel.
Then the people of the LORD went
down to the gates.
12 "Awake, awake, Deborah;
Awake, awake, sing a song!

life point

Deborah and Barak gave God glory for
their victory over the king of Canaan (see
Judges 5:1–5). Let me assure you: God
uses people who will give Him the credit
and the praise for their accomplishments.
According to 1 Corinthians 1:29, God will
not allow a human being to boast in His
presence. He will not allow us to steal
His glory, which is why He chooses to
use and promote those who know they
are nothing without Him and who give
Him the glory and the credit for all their
accomplishments. Every time you have a
"success" in your life, remember to give
God the glory.

Arise, Barak, and lead away your
captives, you son of Abinoam.
13 "Then down marched the
survivors to the nobles;
The people of the LORD marched
down for Me against the mighty.
14 "From Ephraim those whose root
is in Amalek *came down,*
After you, Benjamin, with your
relatives;
From Machir came down
commanders *and* rulers,
And from Zebulun those who
handle the scepter of the [office
of] scribe.
15 "And the heads of Issachar *came*
with Deborah;
As Issachar, so was Barak;
Into the valley they rushed at his
heels;
Among the divisions of Reuben
There were great searchings of
heart.
16 "Why [Reuben] did you linger
among the sheepfolds,
To hear the piping for the flocks?
Among the divisions of Reuben
There were great searchings of
heart.
17 "Gilead remained beyond the
Jordan;
And why did Dan live as an alien
on ships?
Asher sat [still] on the seacoast,
And remained by its landings.
[These did not come to battle for
God's people.]
18 "But Zebulun was a people who
risked their lives to the [point of]
death;
Naphtali also, on the heights of the
field.
19 "The kings came and fought;
Then the kings of Canaan fought
At Taanach by the waters of
Megiddo.
Spoils of silver they did not obtain.
20 "From the heavens the stars
fought,

From their courses they fought
against Sisera.
21 "The torrent Kishon swept the
enemy away,
The ancient torrent, the torrent
Kishon.
O my soul, march on with
strength.
22 "Then the horses' hoofs beat
[loudly]
Because of the galloping—the
galloping of his valiant and
powerful steeds.
23 'Curse Meroz,' said the messenger
of the LORD,
'Utterly curse its inhabitants;
Because they did not come to the
help of the LORD,
To the help of the LORD against the
mighty.'
24 "Most blessed of women is Jael,
The wife of Heber the Kenite;
Most blessed is she of women in
the tent.
25 "Sisera asked for water and she
gave him milk;
She brought him curds in a
magnificent bowl.
26 "She reached out her [left] hand
for the tent peg,
And her right hand for the
workmen's hammer.
Then she struck Sisera, she
smashed his head;
And she shattered and pierced his
temple.
27 "He bowed, he fell, he lay [still] at
her feet;
At her feet he bowed, he fell;
Where he bowed, there he fell
dead.
28 "Out of the window she looked
down and lamented (cried out in
a shrill voice),
The mother of Sisera through the
lattice,
'Why is his chariot delayed in
coming?

Why have the hoofbeats of his
chariots delayed?'
29 "Her wise ladies answered her,
Indeed, she repeated her words to
herself,
30 'Are they not finding and dividing
the spoil?
A maiden (concubine) or two for
every man;
A spoil of dyed garments for
Sisera,
A spoil of dyed garments
embroidered,
Two pieces of dyed garments
embroidered for the neck of the
plunderer?'
31 "So let all Your enemies perish,
O LORD;
But let those who love Him be like
the rising of the sun in its might."

And the land was at rest for forty
years.

6 THEN THE Israelites did evil
in the sight of the LORD; and the
LORD gave them into the hand of
Midian for seven years. 2 The [powerful] hand of Midian
prevailed against Israel. Because of
Midian the sons of Israel made for
themselves the dens (hideouts) which
were in the mountains, and the caves
and the [mountain] strongholds. 3 For it was whenever Israel had
sown [their seed] that the Midianites
would come up with the Amalekites
and the people of the east and go up
against them. 4 So they would camp against them
and destroy the crops of the land as far
as Gaza, and leave no sustenance in Israel as well as no sheep, ox, or donkey. 5 For they would come up with their
livestock and their tents, and they
would come in as numerous as locusts;
both they and their camels were innumerable. So they came into the land to
devastate it. 6 So Israel was greatly impoverished

because of the Midianites, and the Israelites cried out to the LORD [for help].

⁷Now it came about when they cried out to the LORD because of Midian,

⁸that the LORD sent a prophet to the Israelites, and he said to them, "Thus says the LORD, the God of Israel, 'I brought you up from Egypt and brought you out of the house of slavery.

⁹'And I rescued you from the hand of the Egyptians and from the hand of all who oppressed you, and drove them out before you and gave you their land,

¹⁰and I said to you, "I am the LORD your God; you shall not fear the gods of the Amorites in whose land you live." But you have not listened to *and* obeyed My voice.' "

¹¹Now the Angel of the LORD came and sat under the terebinth tree at Ophrah, which belonged to Joash the Abiezrite, and his son Gideon was beating wheat in the wine press [instead of the threshing floor] to [hide it and] save it from the Midianites.

¹²And the Angel of the LORD appeared to him and said to him, "The LORD is with you, O brave man."

¹³But Gideon said to him, "Please my lord, if the LORD is with us, then why has all this happened to us? And where are all His wondrous works which our fathers told us about when they said, 'Did not the LORD bring us up from Egypt?' But now the LORD has abandoned us and put us into the hand of Midian."

¹⁴The LORD turned to him and said, "Go in this strength of yours and save Israel from the hand of Midian. Have I not sent you?"

¹⁵But Gideon said to Him, "Please Lord, how am I to rescue Israel? Behold, my family is the least [significant] in Manasseh, and I am the youngest (smallest) in my father's house."

¹⁶The LORD answered him, "I will certainly be with you, and you will strike down the Midianites as [if they were only] one man."

¹⁷Gideon replied to Him, "If I have found any favor in Your sight, then show me a sign that it is You who speaks with me.

what about prophecy?

Throughout the Bible, we read about God sending prophets to speak on His behalf to an individual or a group, as He did in Judges 6:8. I believe that the prophetic ministry is still operative today and that a true God-inspired prophecy can strengthen, encourage, and comfort the person who receives it (see 1 Corinthians 14:3).

There is a difference between a person who has a gift of prophecy and someone who is appointed to the office of prophet in the body of Christ. A prophet has a stronger word for the church at large than someone who is operating in the gift of prophecy to simply strengthen and encourage individual believers.

The Word of God encourages us to welcome divinely inspired prophecy (see 1 Corinthians 14:1, 3, 4). Prophecy must be consistent with the Word of God, and a personal word of prophecy should confirm something that is already in your heart. If a word is truly from God, *He will make it happen* in His own time. Hold the prophecy in your heart and wait to see if God brings it to pass. He does still speak today through prophecy, and He will confirm prophetic words to you when the prophecies truly represent His heart.

¹⁸"Please do not depart from here until I come back to You, and bring my offering and place it before You." And He said, "I will wait until you return."

¹⁹Then Gideon went and prepared a young goat and unleavened bread from an ephah of flour. The meat he put in a basket and the broth in a pot, and he brought *the food* to Him under the oak (terebinth) and presented it.

²⁰The Angel of God said to him, "Take the meat and unleavened bread

how to have a healthy self-image

Gideon did not have a very good self-image (see Judges 6:15)! Sometimes, Christians believe that speaking negatively about themselves is an indicator of humility or holiness. It isn't! So, what is a normal, healthy Christian attitude toward "self"? Here are a few thoughts that reflect a wholesome, God-centered self-image:

1. I know God created me, and He loves me.

2. I have faults and weaknesses, and I want to change. I believe God is working in my life. He is changing me bit by bit, day by day. While He is doing so, I can still enjoy myself and enjoy my life.

3. Everyone has faults, so I am not a complete failure just because I am not perfect.

4. I am going to work with God to overcome my weaknesses, but I realize that I will always have something to deal with; therefore, I will not become discouraged when God convicts me of areas in my life that need improvement.

5. I want to make people happy and I want them to like me, but my sense of worth is not dependent on what others think of me. Jesus has already affirmed my value by His willingness to die for me.

6. I will not be controlled by what people think, say, or do. Even if they totally reject me, I will survive. I can rest in the fact that God loves me!

7. No matter how often I fail, I am not a failure unless I quit trying. Therefore, I will not give up, because God is with me to strengthen and sustain me. He has promised never to desert me, forsake me, let me down, or relax His hold on me (see Hebrews 13:5).

8. I like myself. I don't like everything I do, and I want to change—but I refuse to reject myself.

9. I am in right standing with God through Jesus Christ.

10. God has a good plan for my life. I am going to fulfill my destiny and be all I can be for His glory. I have God-given gifts and talents, and I intend to use them to help others.

11. I am nothing, and yet I am everything! In myself I am nothing, and yet in Jesus I am everything I need to be.

12. I can do all the things I need to do, and everything that God calls me to do, through His Son, Jesus Christ (see Philippians 4:13).

and lay them on this rock, and pour out the broth [over them]." And he did so.

²¹Then the Angel of the LORD put out the end of the staff that was in His hand and touched the meat and the unleavened bread; and fire flared up from the rock and consumed the meat and the unleavened bread. Then the Angel of the LORD vanished from his sight.

²²When Gideon realized [without any doubt] that He was the Angel of the LORD, he declared, "Oh no, Lord GOD! For now I have seen the Angel of the LORD face to face [and I am doomed]!"

²³The LORD said to him, "Peace to you, do not be afraid; you shall not die."

²⁴Then Gideon built an altar there to the LORD and named it The LORD is Peace. To this day it is still in Ophrah, of the Abiezrites.

²⁵Now on that same night the LORD said to Gideon, "Take your father's bull, the second bull seven years old, and tear down the altar of Baal that belongs to your father, and cut down the Asherah that is beside it;

²⁶and build an altar to the LORD your God on top of this mountain stronghold [with stones laid down] in an orderly way. Then take the second bull and offer a burnt sacrifice using the wood of the Asherah which you shall cut down."

²⁷Then Gideon took ten men of his servants and did just as the LORD had told him; but because he was too afraid of his father's household (relatives) and the men of the city to do it during daylight, he did it at night.

²⁸Early the next morning when the men of the city got up, they discovered that the altar of Baal was torn down, and the Asherah which was beside it was cut down, and the second bull was offered on the altar which had been built.

²⁹So they said to one another, "Who has done this thing?" When they searched about and inquired, they were told, "Gideon the son of Joash did it."

³⁰Then the men of the city said to Joash, "Bring out your son, so that he may be executed, because he has torn down the altar of Baal and cut down the Asherah which was beside it."

³¹But Joash said to all who stood against him, "Will you plead for Baal? Will you save him? Whoever pleads for Baal shall be put to death while it is still morning. If Baal is a god, let him defend himself, because someone has torn down his altar."

³²Therefore on that day he named Gideon Jerubbaal, meaning, "Let Baal plead," because he had torn down his altar.

³³Then all the Midianites and the Amalekites and the people of the east assembled together; and they crossed over [the Jordan] and camped in the Valley of Jezreel.

³⁴So the Spirit of the LORD clothed Gideon [and empowered him]; and he blew a trumpet, and the Abiezrites were called together [as a militia] to follow him.

³⁵He sent messengers throughout [the tribe of] Manasseh, and the fighting men were also called together to follow him; and he sent messengers to [the tribes of] Asher, Zebulun, and Naphtali, and they came up to meet them.

life point

As believers we are not to be self-confident but God-confident—and that kind of confidence comes only by the Holy Spirit. The Bible says repeatedly that we are not supposed to have confidence in *ourselves*. Instead, we are to have confidence in God—that He will work mightily *through* us, just as He did through Gideon (see Judges 6:34).

³⁶Then Gideon said to God, "If You are going to rescue Israel through me, as You have spoken,

³⁷behold, I will put a fleece of [freshly sheared] wool on the threshing floor. If there is dew only on the fleece, and it is dry on all the ground [around it], then I will know that You will rescue Israel through me, as You have said."

³⁸And it was so. When he got up early the next morning and squeezed the dew out of the fleece, he wrung from it a bowl full of water.

³⁹Then Gideon said to God, "Do not let your anger burn against me, so that I may speak once more. Please let me make a test once more with the fleece; now let only the fleece be dry, and let there be dew on all the ground."

⁴⁰God did so that night; for it was dry only on the fleece, and there was dew on all the ground [around it].

7 THEN JERUBBAAL (that is, Gideon) and all the people who were with him got up early and camped beside the spring of Harod; and the camp of Midian was north of them by the hill of Moreh in the valley. ²Then the LORD said to Gideon, "There are too many people with you for Me to hand over Midian to them, otherwise Israel will boast [about

life point

Sometimes people want God to speak to them through a sign, as Gideon did when he laid out a fleece on the threshing floor (see Judges 6:36–40). Even though God did honor Gideon's request, Gideon missed out on God's best. God will sometimes give us a sign, as He did for Gideon, when we are young Christians. However, as we mature in our knowledge of God's leading, He is pleased when we learn to operate in faith, which requires no signs in order to believe and obey.

life point

The Lord instructed Gideon to tell the men who were fearful to turn around and go home (see Judges 7:3); twenty-two thousand of them left, leaving ten thousand behind to face the enemy. That tells us there were more men who were afraid than were courageous.

How many times does God put something on our hearts to do, but then we cower when fear comes along, causing us to hesitate and become double-minded? In this circumstance, we may feel fear, but we *can* do things afraid. Remember, God's Word to us is, "Fear not, for I am with you." When fear knocks on your door, let faith answer!

themselves] against Me, saying, 'My own power has rescued me.'

³"So now, proclaim in the hearing of the people, 'Whoever is afraid and trembling, let him turn back and leave Mount Gilead.'" So twenty-two thousand men returned [home], but ten thousand remained.

⁴Then the LORD said to Gideon, "There are still too many people; bring them down to the water and I will test them for you there. Therefore it shall be that he of whom I say to you, 'This one shall go with you,' he shall go with you; but everyone of whom I say to you, 'This one shall not go with you,' he shall not go."

⁵So he brought the people down to the water, and the LORD said to Gideon, "You shall separate everyone who laps the water with his tongue as a dog laps, as well as everyone who kneels down to drink."

⁶Now the number of those who lapped [the water], putting their hand to their mouth, was three hundred men, but all the rest of the people kneeled down to drink water.

⁷And the Lᴏʀᴅ told Gideon, "With the three hundred men who lapped I will rescue you, and will hand over the Midianites to you. Let all the *other* people go, each man to his home."

⁸So the three hundred men took people's provisions [for the journey] and their trumpets [made of rams' horns] in their hands. And Gideon sent [away] all the *other* men of Israel, each to his tent, but kept the three hundred men. And the camp of Midian was below him in the valley.

⁹Now on that same night the Lᴏʀᴅ said to Gideon, "Arise, go down against their camp, for I have given it into your hand.

¹⁰"But if you are afraid to go down [by yourself], go with Purah your servant down to the camp,

¹¹and you will hear what they say; and afterward you will have the courage to go down against the camp." Then he went down with Purah his servant to the outposts of the army that was in the camp.

¹²Now the Midianites and the Amalekites and all the sons of the east were lying [camped] in the valley, as countless as locusts; and their camels were without number, as numerous as the sand on the seashore.

¹³When Gideon arrived, there was a man telling a dream to his friend. And he said, "Listen carefully, I had a dream: there was a loaf of barley bread tumbling into the camp of Midian, and it came to the tent and struck it so that it fell, and turned it upside down so that the tent lay flat."

¹⁴And his friend replied, "This [dream] is nothing less than the sword of Gideon the son of Joash, a man of Israel. God has given Midian and the entire camp into his hand."

¹⁵When Gideon heard the account of the dream and its interpretation, he bowed down in worship. Then he

the reward of relying on God

Instead of telling Gideon that He would give him more men, God told him that he had too many men to gain victory over the enemy. Interestingly, sometimes God works through our weaknesses instead of through our strengths. There are times when we have too much on our side, from a natural perspective, for God to give the victory. If we depend too much on ourselves and on our own strength, God does not work. Our problem is not big enough for God to give us a miracle if anyone but God can help us.

In Judges 7, God was telling Gideon that his men were too strong in themselves and that He wanted them in a position where they would have to depend entirely on Him. He cut their army down to a size that made victory impossible without His divine intervention.

Pride and boasting ruin the best of people, so God has to help us stay humble and totally dependent on Him. Israel had repeated the same cycle over and over since their exodus from Egypt. They would lean entirely on God, and He would help them. Then they would become self-sufficient, disobedient, and rebellious, thinking that they did not need God, and their circumstances would once again become bad. When they trusted God, they defeated their enemies; when they did not, their enemies defeated them. Trust God and experience victory in your life.

returned to the camp of Israel and said, "Arise, for the LORD has given the camp of Midian into your hand."

¹⁶He divided the three hundred men into three companies, and he put trumpets and empty pitchers into the hands of all of them, with torches inside the pitchers.

¹⁷And he said to them, "Look at me, then do likewise. When I come to the edge of the camp, do just as I do.

¹⁸"When I and all who are with me blow the trumpet (ram's horn), then all around the camp you also blow the trumpets and shout, 'For the LORD and for Gideon!'"

¹⁹So Gideon and the hundred men who were with him came to the edge of the camp at the beginning of the middle watch, when the guards had just been changed, and they blew the trumpets and smashed the pitchers that were in their hands.

²⁰When three companies blew the trumpets and broke the pitchers, they held the torches in their left hands, and the trumpets in their right hands to blow, and they shouted, "A sword for the LORD and for Gideon!"

²¹Then each stood in his place around the camp; and the entire [Midianite] army ran, crying out as they fled.

²²When Gideon's men blew the three hundred trumpets, the LORD set the sword of one [Midianite] against another even throughout the whole army; and the army fled as far as Beth-shittah toward Zererah, as far as the border of Abel-meholah, by Tabbath.

²³The men of Israel were summoned together from [the tribes of] Naphtali and Asher and all Manasseh, and they pursued Midian.

²⁴Then Gideon sent messengers throughout the hill country of [the tribe of] Ephraim, saying, "Come down against the Midianites and take [control of] the waters before them [thereby cutting off the Midianites], as far as Beth-barah and the Jordan [River]." So all the men of Ephraim were assembled together and they

praise God preemptively

As soon as Gideon received a personal word from God, he began to talk about the battle before him as though it were already won (see Judges 7:14, 15). He did not wait to see the results of the battle before he proclaimed the triumph of the Lord, but he began to praise and worship God as though he had already won the victory.

In the book of Exodus, the Israelites sang the right song after they had passed through the Red Sea and their enemies had been drowned: "For He has triumphed gloriously; the horse and its rider He has thrown into the sea" (Exodus 15:1). However, they sang this song of victory on the wrong side of the river. They were all excited. They had their tambourines out and were singing and dancing. They went into a long dissertation about the greatness of God—*after* they had seen the manifestation of His power. They sang the right song at the wrong time. It would have been so much better had they sung their victory song before they crossed the river.

We would certainly be remiss if we did not praise and worship God after the victories in our lives, but Gideon did the right thing in worshiping *before* he won his battle. All he needed was to hear from God that he would win—and then he started worshiping. Learning to worship God before the battle gets His attention, demonstrates our faith, and inspires us to boldly embrace any challenge we face.

took *control of* the waters, as far as Beth-barah and the Jordan.

25Then the men of Ephraim took the two leaders of Midian, Oreb and Zeeb, and they killed Oreb at the rock of Oreb, and they killed Zeeb at the wine press of Zeeb, and pursued Midian; and they brought the heads of Oreb and Zeeb to Gideon from across the Jordan.

8 AND THE men of [the tribe of] Ephraim said to Gideon, "What is this thing that you have done to us, not calling us when you went to fight with Midian?" And they quarreled with him vehemently.

2But he said to them, "What have I done now [that is so significant] in comparison with you? Is not the gleaning (leftovers) *of the grapes* of [your tribe of]

life point

Notice that each man in Gideon's tiny army held a torch in one hand and a trumpet in the other, leaving them no chance to use swords (Judges 7:20). When God sent them to battle against a vastly superior host of Midianites, He intentionally put these items in their hands so they could not draw their swords to fight on their own. Think about it: God sent out three hundred fearless men who were focused on what they were called to do, and He made sure they had something in each hand so they could not possibly fight their own battle; they had to depend on Him to fight it for them. All they had to do was break a pitcher, hold up a torch, and cry, "For the Lᴏʀᴅ and for Gideon!" (Judges 7:20). We can learn from them to put all of our confidence and trust in God instead of in our ability to help ourselves. What God has asked you to do may be impossible for you, but it is not impossible for Him.

Ephraim better than the vintage (entire harvest) of [my clan of] Abiezer?

3"God has given the leaders of Midian, Oreb and Zeeb into your hands; and what was I able to do in comparison with you?" Then their anger toward him subsided when he made this statement.

4So Gideon came to the Jordan and crossed over [the river], he and the three hundred men who were with him—exhausted, yet [still] pursuing [the enemy].

5He said to the men of Succoth, "Please give loaves of bread to the people who are following me since they are exhausted, and I am pursuing Zebah and Zalmunna, kings of Midian."

6But the leaders of Succoth said, "Are Zebah and Zalmunna already in your hands, that we should give bread to your army?"

7Gideon said, "For that [response], when the Lᴏʀᴅ has handed over Zebah and Zalmunna to me, I will thrash your bodies with the thorns and briars of the wilderness."

8He went from there up to Penuel and spoke similarly to them; and the men of Penuel answered him just as the men of Succoth had answered.

9So Gideon said also to the men of Penuel, "When I come again in peace, I will tear down this tower."

10Now Zebah and Zalmunna were in Karkor with their armies, about fifteen thousand [fighting] men, all who were left of the entire army of the sons of the east; for a hundred and twenty thousand swordsmen had fallen.

11Gideon went up by the route of those who lived in tents to the east of Nobah and Jogbehah, and he attacked their camp when the camp was unsuspecting.

12When Zebah and Zalmunna fled, he pursued them and captured the two kings of Midian, Zebah and Zalmunna, and terrified the entire army.

¹³Then Gideon the son of Joash returned from the battle by the ascent of Heres.

¹⁴He captured a young man of Succoth and questioned him. And *the youth* wrote down for him [the names of] the leaders of Succoth and its elders, seventy-seven men.

¹⁵He came to the men of Succoth and said, "Look here, Zebah and Zalmunna, about whom you taunted me, saying, 'Are Zebah and Zalmunna now in your hand, that we should give bread to your men who are exhausted?'"

¹⁶He took the elders of the city, and thorns of the wilderness and briars, and with them he punished the men of Succoth.

¹⁷He tore down the tower of Penuel and killed the men of the city.

¹⁸Then Gideon said to Zebah and Zalmunna, "What kind of men were they whom you killed at Tabor?" And they replied, "They were like you, each one of them resembled the son of a king."

¹⁹He said, "They were my brothers, the sons of my mother. As the LORD lives, if only you had let them live, I would not kill you."

²⁰So [to humiliate them] Gideon said to Jether his firstborn, "Stand up, and kill them!" But the youth did not draw his sword, because he was afraid, for he was still [just] a boy.

²¹Then Zebah and Zalmunna said, "Rise up yourself and strike us; for as the man is, so is his strength." So Gideon arose and killed Zebah and Zalmunna, and took the crescent amulets that were on their camels' necks.

²²Then the men of Israel said to Gideon, "Rule [as king] over us, both you and your son, also your son's son, for you have rescued us from the hand of Midian."

²³But Gideon said to them, "I will not rule over you, and my son will not rule over you; the LORD shall rule over you."

²⁴And Gideon said to them, "I would make a request of you, that each one of you give me an earring from his spoil." For the Midianites had gold earrings, because they were Ishmaelites [who customarily wore them].

²⁵They answered, "We will certainly give them *to you.*" And they spread out a garment, and every one of them threw an earring there from his spoil.

²⁶And the weight of the golden earrings that he requested was seventeen hundred *shekels* of gold, apart from the crescent amulets and pendants and the purple garments which were worn by the kings of Midian, and apart from the chains that were on their camels' necks.

²⁷Gideon made [all the golden earrings into] an ephod [a sacred, high priest's garment], and put it in his city of Ophrah, and all Israel worshiped it as an idol there, and it became a trap for Gideon and his household.

²⁸So Midian was subdued *and* humbled before the sons of Israel, and they no longer lifted up their heads [in pride]. And the land was at rest for forty years in the days of Gideon.

²⁹Jerubbaal (Gideon) the son of Joash went and lived in his own house.

³⁰Now Gideon had seventy sons born to him, because he had many wives.

³¹And his concubine who was in Shechem also bore him a son, whom he named Abimelech.

³²Gideon the son of Joash died at a good advanced age and was buried in the tomb of Joash his father in Ophrah of the Abiezrites.

³³Then it came about, as soon as Gideon was dead, that the Israelites again played the prostitute with the Baals, and made Baal-berith their god.

³⁴And the Israelites did not remember the LORD their God, who had rescued them from the hand of all their enemies on every side;

³⁵nor did they show kindness to the family of Jerubbaal (*that is,* Gideon)

in return for all the good that he had done for Israel.

9 NOW ABIMELECH the son of Jerubbaal (Gideon) went to Shechem to his mother's relatives, and said to them and to the whole clan of the household of his mother's father,

²"Speak now in the hearing of all the leaders of Shechem, 'Which is better for you, that seventy men, all of the sons of Jerubbaal rule over you, or that one man rule over you?' Also, remember that I am your *own* bone and flesh."

³So his mother's relatives spoke all these words concerning him so that all the leaders of Shechem could hear; and their hearts were inclined to follow Abimelech, for they said, "He is our relative."

⁴And they gave him seventy *pieces* of silver from the house of Baal-berith, with which Abimelech hired worthless and undisciplined men, and they followed (supported) him.

⁵Then he went to his father's house at Ophrah and murdered his brothers the sons of Jerubbaal, seventy men, [in a public execution] on one stone. But Jotham the youngest son of Jerubbaal was left *alive*, because he had hidden himself.

⁶All the men of Shechem and all of Beth-millo assembled together, and they went and made Abimelech king, by the oak (terebinth) of the pillar (memorial stone) at Shechem.

⁷When they told Jotham, he went and stood at the top of Mount Gerizim and shouted to them, "Hear me, O men of Shechem, so that God may hear you.

⁸"Once the trees went forth to anoint a king over them, and they said to the olive tree, 'Reign over us!'

⁹"But the olive tree said to them, 'Should I give up my fatness by which God and men are honored, and go to wave over the trees?'

¹⁰"Then the trees said to the fig tree, 'You come and reign over us!'

¹¹"But the fig tree said to them, 'Should I give up my sweetness and my good fruit, and go to wave over the trees?'

¹²"Then the trees said to the vine, 'You come and reign over us.'

¹³"And the vine replied, 'Should I give up my new wine, which makes God and men happy, and go to wave over the trees?'

¹⁴"Then all the trees said to the bramble, 'You come and reign over us.'

¹⁵"So the bramble said to the trees, 'If in truth you are anointing me king over you, then come and take refuge in my shade; but if not, let fire come out of the bramble and devour the cedars of Lebanon.'

¹⁶"Now then, if you acted in truth and integrity when you made Abimelech king, and if you have dealt well with Jerubbaal and his house, and have dealt with him as he deserved—

¹⁷for my father fought for you and risked his life and rescued you from the hand of Midian;

¹⁸but you have risen against my father's house today and have murdered his sons, seventy men, on one stone, and have made Abimelech, son of his maidservant, king over the people of Shechem, because he is your relative—

¹⁹if then you have acted in truth and integrity with Jerubbaal and his house this day, then rejoice in Abimelech, and let him also rejoice in you.

²⁰"But if not, may fire come out from Abimelech and devour the people of Shechem and Beth-millo; and may fire come out from the people of Shechem and Beth-millo, and devour Abimelech."

²¹Then Jotham escaped and fled, and went to Beer and lived there because of Abimelech his brother.

²²Abimelech ruled over Israel for three years.

²³Then God sent an evil spirit between Abimelech and the leaders of Shechem; and the leaders of Shechem acted treacherously against Abimelech,

²⁴so that the violence done to the seventy sons of Jerubbaal (Gideon) might come [on the guilty], and that their [innocent] blood might be laid on Abimelech their brother, who had killed them, and on the leaders of Shechem, who strengthened his hands (encouraged him) to kill his brothers.

²⁵The leaders of Shechem set men in ambush against Abimelech on the mountaintops, and they robbed all who passed by them along the road; and it was reported to Abimelech.

²⁶Now Gaal the son of Ebed came with his relatives, and moved into Shechem; and the leaders of Shechem trusted him.

²⁷They went out into the field, gathered the grapes of their vineyard and trod them, and held a festival; and they entered the house of their god, and they ate and drank, and cursed Abimelech.

²⁸Gaal the son of Ebed said, "Who is Abimelech, and who is Shechem, that we should serve him? Is he not [merely] the son of Jerubbaal and is Zebul not his lieutenant? Serve the men of Hamor the father (founder) of Shechem. Why then should we serve Abimelech?

²⁹"If only this people were under my authority! Then I would remove Abimelech and say to him, 'Increase [the size of] your army and come out [to fight].'"

³⁰When Zebul the ruler of the city heard the words of Gaal the son of Ebed, his anger burned.

³¹He sent messengers to Abimelech secretly, saying, "Behold, Gaal the son of Ebed and his relatives have come to Shechem; and they are stirring up the city against you.

³²"Now then, get up during the night, you and the people who are with you, and set up an ambush in the field.

³³"Then in the morning, at sunrise, you will get up early and rush upon *and* attack the city; and when Gaal and the people who are with him come out against you, you shall do to them whatever you can."

³⁴So Abimelech and all the people who were with him got up during the night, and set up an ambush against Shechem, in four companies.

³⁵Now Gaal the son of Ebed came out and stood in the entrance of the city gate; then Abimelech and the people who were with him got up from the ambush.

³⁶When Gaal saw the people, he said to Zebul, "Look, people are coming down from the mountaintops." But Zebul said to him, "You are *only* seeing the shadow of the mountains as *if they were* men."

³⁷Gaal spoke again and said, "Look! People are coming down from the highest part of the land, and one company is coming by way of the sorcerers' oak tree."

³⁸Then Zebul said to Gaal, "Where is your [boasting] mouth now, you who said, 'Who is Abimelech that we should serve him?' Is this not the people whom you despised? Go out now and fight with them!"

³⁹So Gaal went out ahead of the leaders of Shechem and fought with Abimelech.

⁴⁰Abimelech chased him, and he fled before him; and many fell wounded as far as the entrance of the gate.

⁴¹Then Abimelech stayed at Arumah, and Zebul drove out Gaal and his relatives so that they could not remain in Shechem.

⁴²The next day the people went out to the field, and it was reported to Abimelech.

⁴³So he took his people and divided them into three companies, and set

an ambush in the field; and he looked and saw the people coming out of the city. And he rose up against them and struck them down.

⁴⁴Then Abimelech and the company with him advanced forward and stood in the entrance of the city gate; the two other companies attacked all who were in the field and killed them.

⁴⁵Abimelech fought against the city that entire day. He took the city and killed the people who were in it; he demolished the city and sowed it with salt.

⁴⁶When all the leaders of the Tower of Shechem heard about it, they entered the inner chamber (stronghold) of the temple of El-berith (the god of a covenant).

⁴⁷Abimelech was told that all the leaders of the Tower of Shechem were assembled together.

⁴⁸So Abimelech went up to Mount Zalmon, he and all the people with him; and Abimelech took an axe in his hand and cut down a branch from the trees, picked it up, and laid it on his shoulder. And he said to the people with him, "What you have seen me do, hurry and do just as I have done."

⁴⁹So everyone of the people also cut down his branch and followed Abimelech, and they put *the branches* on top of the inner chamber and set it on fire over those *inside*, so that all the people in the Tower of Shechem also died, about a thousand men and women.

⁵⁰Then Abimelech went to Thebez, and camped against Thebez and took it.

⁵¹But there was a strong (fortified) tower in the center of the city, and all the men and women with all the leaders of the city fled to it and shut themselves in; and they went up on the roof of the tower.

⁵²So Abimelech came to the tower and fought against it, and approached the entrance of the tower to burn it down with fire.

⁵³But a certain woman threw an upper millstone [down] on Abimelech's head and crushed his skull.

⁵⁴Then he called quickly to the young man who was his armor bearer, and said to him, "Draw your sword and kill me, so that it will not be said of me, 'A woman killed him.'" So the young man pierced him through, and he died.

⁵⁵When the men of Israel saw that Abimelech was dead, each departed to his home.

⁵⁶In this way God repaid the wickedness of Abimelech, which he had done to his father [Jerubbaal] by killing his seventy brothers.

⁵⁷Also God repaid all the wickedness of the men of Shechem on their heads, and the curse of Jotham the son of Jerubbaal (Gideon) came upon them. [Judg 9:19, 20]

10 AFTER ABIMELECH died, Tola the son of Puah, the son of Dodo, a man of Issachar, arose to save Israel; and he lived in Shamir, in the hill country of Ephraim.

²Tola judged Israel for twenty-three years; then he died and was buried in Shamir.

³After him, Jair the Gileadite arose, and he judged Israel for twenty-two years.

⁴He had thirty sons who rode on thirty donkeys, and they had thirty towns in the land of Gilead that are called Havvoth-jair (towns of Jair) to this day.

⁵And Jair died and was buried in Kamon.

⁶Then the Israelites again did what was evil in the sight of the LORD; they served the Baals, the Ashtaroth (female deities), the gods of Aram (Syria), the gods of Sidon, the gods of Moab, the gods of the Ammonites, and the gods of the Philistines. They abandoned the LORD and did not serve Him.

⁷So the anger of the LORD was kindled

against Israel, and He sold them into the hands of the Philistines and the Ammonites,

⁸and they oppressed and crushed Israel that year. For eighteen years they *oppressed* all the Israelites who were beyond the Jordan in the land of the Amorites, which is in Gilead.

⁹The Ammonites crossed the Jordan to fight against Judah, Benjamin, and the house of Ephraim, so that Israel was greatly distressed.

¹⁰Then the Israelites cried out to the Lord [for help], saying, "We have sinned against You, because we have abandoned (rejected) our God and have served the Baals."

¹¹The Lord said to the Israelites, "Did I not rescue you from the Egyptians, the Amorites, the Ammonites, and the Philistines?

¹²"Also when the Sidonians, the Amalekites, and the Maonites oppressed *and* crushed you, you cried out to Me, and I rescued you from their hands.

¹³"Yet you have abandoned (rejected) Me and served other gods; therefore I will no longer rescue you.

¹⁴"Go, cry out to the gods you have chosen; let them rescue you in your time of distress."

¹⁵The Israelites said to the Lord, "We have sinned, do to us whatever seems good to You; only please rescue us this day."

¹⁶So they removed the foreign gods from among them and served the Lord; and He could bear the misery of Israel no longer.

¹⁷Then the Ammonites were assembled together and they camped in Gilead. And the sons of Israel assembled and camped at Mizpah.

¹⁸The people, the leaders of Gilead (Israel) said to one another, "Who is the man who will begin to fight against the Ammonites? He shall become head over all the inhabitants of Gilead."

11 NOW JEPHTHAH the Gileadite was a brave warrior, but he was the son of a prostitute. Gilead was the father of Jephthah.

²Gilead's wife bore him sons, and when his wife's sons grew up, they drove Jephthah out and said to him, "You shall not have an inheritance in our father's house, because you are the son of another woman."

³Then Jephthah fled from his brothers and lived in the land of Tob; and worthless *and* unprincipled men gathered around Jephthah, and went out [on raids] with him.

⁴Now it happened after a while that the Ammonites fought against Israel.

⁵When the Ammonites fought against Israel, the elders of Gilead went to get Jephthah from the land of Tob;

⁶and they said to Jephthah, "Come and be our leader, so that we may fight against the Ammonites."

⁷But Jephthah said to the elders of Gilead, "Did you not hate me and drive me from the house of my father? Why have you come to me now when you are in trouble?"

⁸The elders of Gilead said to Jephthah, "This is why we have turned to you now: that you may go with us and fight the Ammonites and become head over all the inhabitants of Gilead."

⁹So Jephthah said to the elders of Gilead, "If you take me back [home] to fight against the Ammonites and the Lord gives them over to me, will I [really] become your head?"

speak the Word

God, I pray that I will never abandon You, but that I will always serve You.
−ADAPTED FROM JUDGES 10:6

[10]The elders of Gilead said to Jephthah, "The LORD is the witness between us; be assured that we will do as you have said."

[11]So Jephthah went with the elders of Gilead, and the people made him head and leader over them. And Jephthah repeated everything that he had promised before the LORD at Mizpah.

[12]Now Jephthah sent messengers to the king of the Ammonites, saying, "What is [the problem] between you and me, that you have come against me to fight in my land?"

[13]The Ammonites' king replied to the messengers of Jephthah, "It is because Israel took away my land when they came up from Egypt, from the [river] Arnon as far as the Jabbok and [east of] the Jordan; so now, return those lands peaceably."

[14]But Jephthah sent messengers again to the king of the Ammonites,

[15]and they said to him, "This is what Jephthah says: 'Israel did not take the land of Moab or the land of the Ammonites.

[16]'For when they came up from Egypt, Israel walked through the wilderness to the Red Sea and came to Kadesh;

[17]then Israel sent messengers to the king of Edom, saying, "Please let us pass through your land," but the king of Edom would not listen. Also they sent word to the king of Moab, but he would not consent. So Israel stayed at Kadesh.

[18]'Then they went through the wilderness and went around the land of Edom and the land of Moab, and came to the east side of the land of Moab, and they camped on the other side of the [river] Arnon; but they did not enter the territory of Moab, for the Arnon was the [northern] boundary of Moab.

[19]'Then Israel sent messengers to Sihon king of the Amorites, king of Heshbon, and Israel said to him, "Please let us pass through your land to our place."

[20]'But Sihon did not trust Israel to pass through his territory; so Sihon gathered together all his people and camped at Jahaz and fought against Israel.

[21]'The LORD, the God of Israel, gave Sihon and all his people into the hand of Israel, and they defeated them; so Israel took possession of all the land of the Amorites, the inhabitants of that country.

[22]'They took possession of all the territory of the Amorites, from the Arnon as far as the Jabbok, and from the wilderness [westward] as far as the Jordan.

[23]'And now the LORD God of Israel has dispossessed *and* driven out the Amorites from before His people Israel, so [why] should you possess it?

[24]'Do you not possess what Chemosh your god gives you to possess? And everything that the LORD our God dispossessed before us, we will possess.

[25]'Now are you any better than Balak the son of Zippor, king of Moab? Did he ever strive against Israel, or did he ever go to war against them?

[26]'While Israel lived in Heshbon and its villages, and in Aroer and its villages, and in all the cities along the banks of the Arnon for three hundred years, why did you not recover your lost lands during that time?

[27]'So I have not sinned against you, but you are doing me wrong by making war against me; may the LORD, the [righteous] Judge, judge this day between the Israelites and the Ammonites.'"

[28]But the king of the Ammonites disregarded the message of Jephthah, which he sent to him.

[29]Then the Spirit of the LORD came upon Jephthah, and he passed through Gilead and Manasseh, and Mizpah of Gilead, and from Mizpah of Gilead he passed on to the Ammonites.

[30]Jephthah made a vow to the LORD

and said, "If You will indeed give the Ammonites into my hand,

³¹then whatever comes out of the doors of my house to meet me when I return in peace from the Ammonites, it shall be the Lord's, and I will offer it up as a burnt offering."

³²Then Jephthah crossed over to the Ammonites to fight with them; and the Lord gave them into his hand.

³³And from Aroer to the entrance of Minnith he struck them, twenty cities, and as far as Abel-keramim (brook by the vineyard), with a very great defeat. So the Ammonites were subdued *and* humbled before the Israelites.

³⁴Then Jephthah came to his house at Mizpah, and this is what he saw: his daughter coming out to meet him with tambourines and with dancing. And she was his only child; except for her he had no son or daughter.

³⁵And when he saw her, he tore his clothes [in grief] and said, "Alas, my daughter! You have brought me great disaster, and you are the cause of ruin to me; for I have made a vow to the Lord, and I cannot take it back."

³⁶And she said to him, "My father, you have made a vow to the Lord; do to me as you have vowed, since the Lord has taken vengeance for you on your enemies, the Ammonites."

³⁷And she said to her father, "Let this *one* thing be done for me; let me alone for two months, so that I may go to the mountains and weep over my virginity, I and my companions."

³⁸And he said, "Go." So he sent her away for two months; and she left with her companions, and wept over her virginity on the mountains.

³⁹At the end of two months she returned to her father, who did to her as he had vowed; and she had no relations with a man. It became a custom in Israel,

⁴⁰that the daughters of Israel went yearly to tell the story of the daughter of Jephthah the Gileadite four days in the year.

12 THE MEN of [the tribe of] Ephraim were summoned [to action], and they crossed over to Zaphon and said to Jephthah, "Why did you cross over to fight with the Ammonites without calling us to go with you? [For that] we will burn your house down upon you."

²And Jephthah said to them, "My people and I were in a major conflict with the Ammonites, and when I called you [for help], you did not rescue me from their hand.

³"So when I saw that you were not coming to help me, I took my life in my hands and crossed over against the Ammonites, and the Lord handed them over to me. So why have you come up to me this day to fight against me?"

⁴Then Jephthah assembled all the men of Gilead and fought with [the tribe of] Ephraim; and the men of Gilead defeated Ephraim, because they had said, "You Gileadites are fugitives of Ephraim, in the midst of [the tribes of] Ephraim and Manasseh."

⁵And the Gileadites took the fords of the Jordan opposite the Ephraimites; and when *any of* the fugitives of Ephraim said, "Let me cross over," the men of Gilead would say to him, "Are you an Ephraimite?" If he said, "No,"

⁶they said to him, "Then say 'Shibboleth.'" And he said, "Sibboleth," for he could not pronounce it correctly. Then they seized him and killed him at the fords of the Jordan. At that time forty-two thousand of the Ephraimites fell.

⁷Jephthah judged Israel for six years. Then Jephthah the Gileadite died and was buried in *one of* the cities of Gilead.

⁸And after him Ibzan of Bethlehem judged Israel.

⁹He had thirty sons, and thirty daughters whom he gave in marriage outside *the family,* and he brought in

thirty daughters [-in-law] from outside for his sons. He judged Israel for seven years.

[10]Then Ibzan died and was buried at Bethlehem.

[11]After him Elon the Zebulunite judged Israel; and he judged Israel for ten years.

[12]Then Elon the Zebulunite died and was buried at Aijalon in the land of Zebulun.

[13]Now after him Abdon the son of Hillel the Pirathonite judged Israel.

[14]He had forty sons and thirty grandsons who rode on seventy donkeys; and he judged Israel for eight years.

[15]Then Abdon the son of Hillel the Pirathonite died and was buried at Pirathon in the land of Ephraim, in the hill country of the Amalekites.

13 NOW ISRAEL again did what was evil in the sight of the LORD, and the LORD gave them into the hands of the Philistines for forty years.

[2]And there was a certain man of Zorah, of the family of the Danites, whose name was Manoah; and his wife was infertile and had no *children*.

[3]And the Angel of the LORD appeared to the woman and said to her, "Behold, you are infertile and have no *children*, but you shall conceive and give birth to a son.

[4]"Therefore, be careful not to drink wine or [any other] intoxicating drink, and do not eat anything [ceremonially] unclean.

[5]"For behold, you shall conceive and give birth to a son. No razor shall come upon his head, for the boy shall be a Nazirite [dedicated] to God from birth; and he shall begin to rescue Israel from the hands of the Philistines."

[6]Then the woman went and told her husband, saying, "A Man of God came to me and his appearance was like the appearance of the Angel of God, very

awesome. I did not ask Him where he came from, and he did not tell me his name.

[7]"But He said to me, 'Behold, you shall conceive and give birth to a son, and now you shall not drink wine or [any other] intoxicating drink, nor eat anything [ceremonially] unclean, for the boy shall be a Nazirite to God from birth to the day of his death.'"

[8]Then Manoah pleaded with the LORD and said, "O Lord, please let the Man of God whom You sent come again to us and teach us what we are to do for the boy who is to be born."

[9]And God listened to the voice of Manoah; and the Angel of God came again to the woman as she sat in the field, but Manoah her husband was not with her.

[10]So the woman ran quickly and told her husband, "Behold, the Man who came to me the other day has appeared to me."

[11]Then Manoah got up and followed his wife, and came to the Man and said to him, "Are you the Man who spoke to this woman?" He said, "I am."

[12]And Manoah said, "Now when your words come *true,* what shall be the boy's manner of life, and his vocation?"

[13]The Angel of the LORD said to Manoah, "The woman must pay attention to everything that I said to her.

[14]"She may not eat anything that comes from the vine nor drink wine or [any other] intoxicating drink, nor eat anything [ceremonially] unclean. She shall observe everything that I commanded her."

[15]Then Manoah said to the Angel of the LORD, "Please let us detain you and let us prepare a young goat for you [to eat]."

[16]The Angel of the LORD said to Manoah, "Though you detain me, I will not eat your food, but if you prepare a burnt offering, offer it to the LORD." For Manoah did not know that he was the Angel of the LORD.

¹⁷Manoah said to the Angel of the Lord, "What is your name, so that when your words come *true,* we may honor you?"

¹⁸But the Angel of the Lord said to him, "Why do you ask my name, seeing it is wonderful (miraculous)?" [Is 9:6]

¹⁹So Manoah took the young goat with the grain offering and offered it on the rock to the Lord, and He performed miracles while Manoah and his wife looked on.

²⁰For when the flame went up toward heaven from the altar, the Angel of the Lord ascended in the altar flame. When Manoah and his wife saw this they fell on their faces to the ground.

²¹The Angel of the Lord did not appear again to Manoah or his wife. Then Manoah knew that he was the Angel of the Lord.

²²So Manoah said to his wife, "We will certainly die, because we have seen God."

²³But his [sensible] wife said to him, "If the Lord had desired to kill us, He would not have received a burnt offering and a grain offering from our hands, nor would He have shown us all these things, nor would He have announced *such things* as these at this time."

²⁴So the woman [in due time] gave birth to a son and named him Samson; and the boy grew and the Lord blessed him.

²⁵And the Spirit of the Lord began to stir him at times in Mahaneh-dan, between Zorah and Eshtaol.

14 SAMSON WENT down to Timnah and at Timnah he saw a woman, one of the daughters of the Philistines.

²So he went back and told his father and his mother, "I saw a woman in Timnah, one of the daughters of the Philistines; now get her for me as a wife."

³But his father and mother said to him, "Is there no woman among the daughters of your relatives, or among all our people, that you must go to take a wife from the uncircumcised (pagan) Philistines?" And Samson said to his father, "Get her for me, because she looks pleasing to me."

⁴His father and mother did not know that it was of the Lord, and that He was seeking an occasion [to take action] against the Philistines. Now at that time the Philistines were ruling over Israel.

⁵Then Samson went down to Timnah with his father and mother [to arrange the marriage], and they came as far as the vineyards of Timnah; and suddenly, a young lion *came* roaring toward him.

⁶The Spirit of the Lord came upon him mightily, and he tore the lion apart as one tears apart a young goat, and he had nothing at all in his hand; but he did not tell his father or mother what he had done.

⁷So he went down and talked with the woman; and she looked pleasing to Samson.

⁸When he returned later to take her, he turned aside to see the carcass of the lion; and behold, a swarm of bees and honey were in the body of the lion.

⁹So he scraped the honey out into his hands and went on, eating as he went. When he came to his father and mother, he gave them *some,* and they ate it; but he did not tell them he had taken the honey from the body of the lion.

¹⁰His father went down to the woman, and Samson prepared a feast there, for that was the customary thing for young men to do.

¹¹When the people saw him, they brought thirty companions (wedding attendants) to be with him.

¹²Then Samson said to them, "Let me now ask you a riddle; if you can tell me what it is within the seven days of the feast, and solve it, then I will give you thirty linen tunics (undergarments) and thirty changes of [outer] clothing.

¹³"But if you are unable to tell me

[the answer], then you shall give me thirty linen tunics (undergarments) and thirty changes of [outer] clothing." And they said to him, "Ask your riddle, so that we may hear it."

¹⁴So he said to them,

"Out of the eater came something
    to eat,
And out of the strong came
    something sweet."

And they could not solve the riddle in three days.

¹⁵Then on the fourth day they said to Samson's wife, "Persuade your husband to tell us [through you] the [answer to the] riddle, or we will burn you and your father's household with fire. Have you invited us to make us poor? Is this not *true?*"

¹⁶So Samson's wife wept before him and said, "You only hate me, you do not love me; you have asked my countrymen a riddle, and have not told [the answer] to me." And he said to her, "Listen, I have not told my father or my mother [either], so [why] should I tell you?"

¹⁷However Samson's wife wept before him seven days while their [wedding] feast lasted, and on the seventh day he told her because she pressed him so hard. Then she told the [answer to the] riddle to her countrymen.

¹⁸So the men of the city said to Samson on the seventh day before sundown,

"What is sweeter than honey?
What is stronger than a lion?"

And he said to them,

"If you had not plowed with my
    heifer,
You would not have solved my
    riddle."

¹⁹Then the Spirit of the Lᴏʀᴅ came upon him mightily, and he went down to Ashkelon and killed thirty of them and took their gear, and gave changes *of clothes* to those who had explained the riddle. And his anger burned, and he went up to his father's house.

²⁰But Samson's wife was *given* to his companion who had been his friend.

15 BUT AFTER a while, in the time of wheat harvest, Samson went to visit his wife with a young goat [as a gift of reconciliation]; and he said, "I will go in to my wife in *her* room." But her father would not allow him to go in.

²Her father said, "I really thought you utterly hated her; so I gave her to your companion. Is her younger sister not more beautiful than she? Please take her [as your wife] instead."

³Samson said to them, "This time I shall be blameless in regard to the Philistines when I do them harm."

⁴So Samson went and caught three hundred foxes, and took torches and turning *the foxes* tail to tail, he put a torch between each pair of tails.

⁵When he had set the torches ablaze, he let the foxes go into the standing grain of the Philistines, and he burned up the heap of sheaves and the standing grain, along with the vineyards and olive groves.

⁶Then the Philistines said, "Who did this?" And they were told, "Samson, the son-in-law of the Timnite, because he took Samson's wife and gave her to his [chief] companion [at the wedding feast]." So the Philistines came up and burned her and her father with fire.

⁷Samson said to them, "If this is the way you act, be certain that I will take revenge on you, and [only] after that I will stop."

⁸Then he struck them without mercy, a great slaughter; and he went down and lived in the cleft of the rock of Etam.

⁹Then the [army of the] Philistines came up and camped in [the tribal territory of] Judah, and overran Lehi (Jawbone).

¹⁰The men of Judah said, "Why have you come up against us?" And they answered, "We have come up to bind Samson, in order to do to him as he has done to us."

¹¹Then three thousand men of Judah went down to the cleft of the rock of Etam and said to Samson, "Have you not known that the Philistines are rulers over us? What is this that you have done to us?" He said to them, "As they did to me, so I have done to them."

¹²They said to him, "We have come down to bind you, so that we may hand you over to the Philistines." And Samson said to them, "Swear to me that you will not kill me."

¹³So they said to him, "No, we will [only] bind you securely and place you into their hands; but we certainly will not kill you." So they bound him with two new ropes and brought him up from the rock [of Etam].

¹⁴When he came to Lehi, the Philistines came shouting to meet him. And the Spirit of the LORD came upon him mightily, and the ropes on his arms were like flax (linen) that had been burned, and his bonds dropped off his hands.

¹⁵He found a fresh jawbone of a donkey, so he reached out his hand and took it and killed a thousand men with it.

¹⁶Then Samson said,

"With the jawbone of a donkey,
Heaps upon heaps,
With the jawbone of a donkey
I have struck down a thousand
    men."

¹⁷When he finished speaking, he threw the jawbone from his hand; and he named that place Ramath-lehi (hill of the jawbone).

¹⁸Then Samson was very thirsty, and he called out to the LORD and said, "You have given this great victory through the hand of Your servant, and now am I to die of thirst and fall into the hands of the uncircumcised (pagans)?"

¹⁹So God split open the hollow place that was at Lehi, and water came out of it. When Samson drank, his spirit (strength) returned and he was revived. Therefore he named it En-hakkore (spring which is calling), which is at Lehi to this day.

²⁰And Samson judged Israel in the days of [occupation by] the Philistines for twenty years. [Judg 17:6]

16

THEN SAMSON went to Gaza and saw a prostitute there, and went in to her. ²The Gazites *were told*, "Samson has come here." So they surrounded *the place* and waited all night at the gate of the city to ambush him. They kept quiet all night, saying, "In the morning, when it is light, we will kill him."

³But Samson lay [resting] until midnight, then at midnight he got up and took hold of the doors of the city gate and the two door-posts, and pulled them up, [security] bar and all, and he put them on his shoulders and carried them up to the top of the hill which is opposite Hebron.

⁴After this he fell in love with a [Philistine] woman [living] in the Valley of Sorek, whose name was Delilah.

⁵So the [five] lords (governors) of the Philistines came to her and said to her, "Persuade him, and see where his great strength *lies* and [find out] how we may overpower him so that we may bind him to subdue him. And each of us will give you eleven hundred *pieces* of silver."

⁶So Delilah said to Samson, "Please tell me where your great strength lies and with what you may be bound and subdued."

⁷Samson said to her, "If they bind me with seven fresh cords (tendons) that have not been dried, then I will be weak and be like any [other] man."

⁸Then the Philistine lords brought her seven fresh cords that had not been dried, and she bound him with them.

⁹Now she had men lying in ambush in an inner room. And she said to him, "The Philistines are upon you, Samson!" And he broke the cords as a string of tow breaks when it touches fire. So [the secret of] his strength was not discovered.

¹⁰Then Delilah said to Samson, "See now, you have mocked me and told me lies; now please tell me [truthfully] how you may be bound."

¹¹He said to her, "If they bind me tightly with new ropes that have not been used, then I will become weak and be like any [other] man."

¹²So Delilah took new ropes and bound him with them and said to him, "The Philistines are upon you, Samson!" And the men lying in ambush were in the inner room. But he snapped the ropes off his arms like [sewing] thread.

¹³Then Delilah said to Samson, "Until now you have mocked me and told me lies; tell me [truthfully] with what you may be bound." And he said to her, "If you weave the seven braids of my hair with the web [and fasten it with a pin, then I will become weak and be like any other man."

resisting temptation

We can learn a lot from Samson's story (see Judges 13:24—16:31). Samson had extraordinary strength from God, and his might and ability were directly tied to obedience. God had told Samson not to cut his hair and promised that as long as he obeyed, he would have special strength and be able to do awesome feats. Satan wanted to weaken and destroy Samson, so he sent temptation in the form of a woman named Delilah. Day after day, she pressed him to reveal his secret. Eventually Samson was "annoyed to death," the Bible tells us, so he finally gave in and told Delilah his secret (see Judges 16:15–17). While he was sleeping, she cut his hair and robbed him of his strength.

When Satan comes to tempt us, he is persistent. He keeps up his attack, hoping to eventually wear us out. This is exactly what happened with Samson. He had a weakness for women, and, just as Satan knew Samson's weakness and used it against him, he also knows our weaknesses and tries to take advantage of them.

Let me encourage you to be aware of your weaknesses and to pray regularly for God to strengthen you in the weak spots in your life. Do not wait until you are deep in trouble and then begin to pray. Instead, pray ahead of time. For example, if an overactive appetite is a weakness for you, then every time you sit down to eat, pray that God will help you control yourself. Do not wait until you have eaten too much and then spend the rest of the day feeling guilty. Let your new motto be: "I won't delay; I'll pray right away."

Jesus told His disciples to pray that they come not into temptation, and He said, "the spirit is willing, but the body is weak" (Matthew 26:41). He never told them that temptation would not come. He said to pray that they would not give in when temptation comes. We will all be tempted, but God will give us the ability to resist if we will be faithful to pray for His strength to recognize and resist whatever attack Satan sends our way, especially when he tries to hit us in our weak spots.

¹⁴So while he slept, Delilah took the seven locks (braids) of his hair and wove them into the web]. And she fastened it with the pin [of the loom] and said to him, "The Philistines are upon you, Samson!" And he awoke from his sleep and pulled out the pin of the [weaver's] loom and the web.

¹⁵Then she said to him, "How can you say, 'I love you,' when your heart is not with me? You have mocked me these three times and have not told me where your great strength lies."

¹⁶When she pressured him day after day with her words and pleaded with him, he was annoyed to death.

¹⁷Then [finally] he told her everything that was in his heart and said to her, "A razor has never been used on my head, for I have been a Nazirite to God from my mother's womb. If I am shaved, then my strength will leave me, and I will become weak and be like any [other] man."

¹⁸Then Delilah realized that he had told her everything in his heart, so she sent and called for the Philistine lords, saying, "Come up this once, because he has told me everything in his heart." Then the Philistine lords came up to her and brought the money [they had promised] in their hands.

¹⁹She made Samson sleep on her knees, and she called a man and had him shave off the seven braids of his head. Then she began to abuse Samson, and his strength left him.

²⁰She said, "The Philistines are upon you, Samson!" And he awoke from his sleep and said, "I will go out as I have time after time and shake myself free." For Samson did not know that the LORD had departed from him.

²¹Then the Philistines seized him and gouged out his eyes; and they brought him down to Gaza and bound him with [two] bronze chains; and he was *forced to be* a grinder [of grain into flour at the mill] in the prison.

²²But the hair of his head began to grow again after it had been shaved off.

²³Now the Philistine lords gathered together to offer a great sacrifice to Dagon their god, and to celebrate, for they said,

"Our god has given Samson our
    enemy into our hands!"

²⁴When the people saw Samson, they praised their god, for they said,

"Our god has handed over our
    enemy to us,
The ravager of our country,
Who has killed many of us."

²⁵Now when they were in high spirits, they said, "Call for Samson, so that he may amuse us." So they called Samson out of the prison, and he entertained them. They made him stand between the pillars.

²⁶Then Samson said to the boy who held him by the hand, "Let me feel the pillars on which the [roof of the] house rests, so that I may lean against them."

²⁷Now the house was full of men and women; all the Philistine lords were there, and on the flat roof were about three thousand men and women who looked on while Samson was entertaining them.

²⁸Then Samson called to the LORD and said, "O Lord GOD, please remember me and please strengthen me just this one time, O God, and let me take vengeance on the Philistines for my two eyes."

²⁹Samson took hold of the two middle [support] pillars on which the house rested, and braced himself against them, one with his right hand and the other with his left.

³⁰And Samson said, "Let me die with the Philistines!" And he stretched out with all his might [collapsing the support pillars], and the house fell on the lords and on all the people who were in it. So the dead whom he killed at his

death were more than those whom he had killed during his life.

³¹Then his brothers and his father's entire [tribal] household came down, took him, and brought him up; and they buried him in the tomb of Manoah his father, [which was] between Zorah and Eshtaol. So Samson had judged Israel for twenty years. [Judg 17:6; Heb 11:32]

17 THERE WAS a man of the hill country of Ephraim whose name was Micah. ²And he said to his mother, "The eleven hundred *pieces* of silver which were taken from you, about which you cursed [the thief] and also spoke about in my hearing, behold, the silver is with me; I took it." And his mother said, "Blessed be my son before the LORD."

³He returned the eleven hundred *pieces* of silver to his mother, and she said, "I had truly dedicated the silver from my hand to the LORD for my son (in his name) to make an image [carved from wood and plated with silver] and a cast image [of solid silver]; so now, I will return it to you."

⁴So when he returned the silver to his mother, she took two hundred *pieces* of silver and gave them to the silversmith who made of it an image [of silver-plated wood] and a cast image [of solid silver]; and they were in the house of Micah.

⁵Now the man Micah had a house of gods (shrine), and he made an ephod and teraphim and dedicated *and* installed one of his sons, who became his [personal] priest.

⁶In those days there was no king in Israel; every man did what was right in his own eyes.

⁷Now there was a young man from Bethlehem in Judah, from the family [of the tribe] of Judah, who was a Levite; and he was staying there [temporarily].

⁸Then the man left the town of Bethlehem in Judah, to stay wherever he could find *a place;* and as he journeyed, he came to the hill country of Ephraim, to the house of Micah.

⁹Micah said to him, "Where do you come from?" And he said to him, "I am a Levite from Bethlehem in Judah, and I am going to stay wherever I can find *a place.*"

¹⁰And Micah said to him, "Live here with me and be a father and a [personal] priest to me, and I will give you ten *pieces* of silver each year, a supply of clothing, and your sustenance (room and board)." So the Levite went in.

¹¹The Levite agreed to live with the man, and the young man became to Micah like one of his sons.

¹²So Micah dedicated (installed) the Levite, and the young man became his priest and lived in the house of Micah.

¹³Then Micah said, "Now I know that the LORD will favor me *and* make me prosper because I have a Levite as my priest."

18 IN THOSE days there was no king in Israel; and in those days the tribe of the Danites was seeking an inheritance [of land] for themselves to live in, for until then an inheritance had not been allotted to them as a possession among the tribes of Israel.

²So the sons of Dan sent from the total number of their [extended] family five brave men from Zorah and Eshtaol, to scout the land and to explore it; and they said to them, "Go, explore the land." They came to the hill country of Ephraim, to the house of Micah, and lodged there.

³When they passed near Micah's house, they recognized the voice of the young man, the Levite, and they turned aside there and said to him, "Who brought you here? And what are you doing in this place? And what do you have here?"

⁴And he said to them, "Micah has

done this and that for me, and he has hired me and I have become his priest."

⁵And they said to him, "Please ask of God, so that we may know whether our journey on which we are going will be successful."

⁶The priest said to them, "Go in peace; the journey on which you are going is acceptable to the LORD."

⁷Then the five men went on and came to Laish and saw the people who were there, [how they were] living securely in the style of the Sidonians, quiet and peaceful; and there was no oppressive magistrate in the land humiliating *them* in anything, and they were far from the Sidonians and had no dealings with anyone.

⁸The five men came back [home] to their brothers at Zorah and Eshtaol, and their brothers said to them, "What *do* you *have to report?*"

⁹They said, "Arise, let us go up against them; for we have seen the land, and behold, it is very good (fertile). Will you sit still *and* do nothing? Do not hesitate to go, to enter, to take possession of the land.

¹⁰"When you enter, you will come to people [feeling] safe and secure with a spacious land [widely extended on all sides]; for God has given it into your hands—a place where there is no lack of anything that is on the earth."

¹¹Then from the [tribal] family of the Danites, from Zorah and from Eshtaol, six hundred men armed with weapons of war set out.

¹²They went up and camped at Kiriath-jearim in Judah. Therefore they have called that place Mahaneh-dan to this day; it is west of Kiriath-jearim.

¹³They went on from there to the hill country of Ephraim and came to Micah's house.

¹⁴Then the five men who had gone to scout the country of Laish said to their relatives, "Do you know that there are in these houses an ephod, teraphim,

an image [of silver-plated wood], and a cast image [of solid silver]? Now therefore, consider what you should do."

¹⁵So they turned in that direction and came to the house of the young Levite, at the home of Micah, and asked him how he was doing.

¹⁶Now the six hundred men armed with their weapons of war, who were of the sons of Dan, stood at the entrance of the gate.

¹⁷Now the five men who had gone to scout the land went up and entered the house and took the image [of silver-plated wood], the ephod, the teraphim, and the cast image [of solid silver], while the priest stood by the entrance of the gate with the six hundred men armed with weapons of war.

¹⁸When these [five men] went into Micah's house and took the [plated] image, the ephod, the teraphim, and the cast image, the priest asked them, "What are you doing?"

¹⁹They said to him, "Keep quiet, put your hand over your mouth and come with us, and be a father and a priest to us. Is it better for you to be a priest to the house of one man, or to be a priest to a tribe and family in Israel?"

²⁰The priest's heart was glad [to hear that], and he took the ephod, the teraphim, and the image, and went among the people.

²¹So they turned and left, and they put the children, the livestock, and the valuables *and* supplies in front of them.

²²When they had gone some distance from the house of Micah, the men who were [living] in the houses near Micah's house assembled [as a militia] and overtook the sons of Dan.

²³They shouted to the Danites, who turned and said to Micah, "What is your *reason* for assembling [against us]?"

²⁴He said, "You have taken away my gods which I have made, and the priest, and have gone away; what else

do I have left? How can you say to me, 'What is your *reason*?'"

²⁵The sons of Dan said to him, "Do not let your voice [of complaint] be heard among us, or else angry men will assault you and you will lose your life, along with the lives of [everyone in] your household."

²⁶Then the Danites went on their way; and Micah saw that they were too strong for him, so he turned and went back to his house.

²⁷They took the [idolatrous] things that Micah had made, and his priest, and they came to Laish, to a people who were quiet and secure; and they struck them with the edge of the sword and burned the city with fire.

²⁸And there was no one to rescue them because it was far from Sidon and they had no dealings with anyone. It was in the valley which belongs to Beth-rehob. And they rebuilt the city and lived in it.

²⁹They named the city Dan, after Dan their forefather who was born to Israel (Jacob); however, the original name of the city was Laish.

³⁰The [tribe of] the sons of Dan set up the image [of silver-plated wood] for themselves; and Jonathan the son of Gershom, the son of Moses, and his sons were priests to the tribe of the Danites until the day of the captivity *and* exile from the land.

³¹So they set up for themselves Micah's [silver-plated wooden] image which he had made, *and kept it* throughout the time that the house (tabernacle) of God was at Shiloh.

19 NOW IT happened in those days, when there was no king in Israel, that a certain Levite living [as an alien] in the most remote part of the hill country of Ephraim, who took a concubine for himself from Bethlehem in Judah. ²But his concubine was unfaithful

putting the Word to work

Notice in Judges 19:5 that the Levite's father-in-law encouraged him to "strengthen yourself with a piece of bread." In today's language, we might call that "emotional eating." Are you an "emotional eater"? If so, ask God to help you learn to find emotional strength in His Word and in no other source.

to him, and left him and went to her father's house in Bethlehem of Judah, and stayed there for a period of four months.

³Then her husband arose and went after her to speak kindly *and* tenderly to her in order to bring her back, taking with him his servant and a pair of donkeys. So she brought him into her father's house, and when the father of the girl saw him, he was happy to meet him.

⁴So his father-in-law, the girl's father, detained him; and he stayed there with him for three days. So they ate and drank, and he lodged there.

⁵On the fourth day they got up early in the morning, and the Levite prepared to leave; but the girl's father said to his son-in-law, "Strengthen yourself with a piece of bread, and afterward go your way."

⁶So both men sat down and ate and drank together; and the girl's father said to the man, "Please be willing to spend the night and enjoy yourself."

⁷Then the man got up to leave, but his father-in-law urged him [strongly to remain]; so he spent the night there again.

⁸On the fifth day he got up early in the morning to leave, but the girl's father said, "Please strengthen yourself, and wait until the end of the day." So both of them ate.

⁹When the man and his concubine and his servant got up to leave, his

father-in-law, the girl's father, said to him, "Behold, now the day has drawn to a close; please spend the night. Look, now the day comes to an end; spend the night here and celebrate, enjoy yourself. Then tomorrow you may get up early for your journey and go home."

¹⁰But the man was not willing to stay the night; so he got up and left and came to *a place* opposite Jebus (that is Jerusalem). With him were two saddled donkeys [and his servant] and his concubine.

¹¹When they were near Jebus, the day was almost gone, and the servant said to his master, "Please come and let us turn aside into this Jebusite city and spend the night in it."

¹²But his master said to him, "We will not turn aside into a city of foreigners who are not of the sons (descendants) of Israel. We will go on as far as Gibeah."

¹³And he said to his servant, "Come and let us approach one of *these* places: and we will spend the night in Gibeah or in Ramah."

¹⁴So they passed by and went on their way, and the sun set on them near Gibeah, which belongs to [the tribe of] Benjamin,

¹⁵and they turned aside there to go in and spend the night in Gibeah. And the Levite went in and sat down in the open square of the city, because no man invited them into his house to spend the night.

¹⁶Then behold, *there was* an old man *who* was coming out of the field from his work at evening. He was from the hill country of Ephraim but was staying in Gibeah, and the men of the place were sons (descendants) of Benjamin.

¹⁷When he looked up, he saw the traveler [and his companions] in the city square; and the old man said, "Where are you going, and where do you come from?"

¹⁸The Levite replied, "We are passing through from Bethlehem [in the territory] of Judah to the most remote part of the hill country of Ephraim; I am from there. I went to Bethlehem of Judah, but I am *now* going [home] to my house, and there is no man [in the city] who will take me into his house [for the night].

¹⁹"Yet we have both straw and feed for our donkeys, and also bread and wine for me, and for your handmaid, and for the young man who is with your servant; there is no lack of anything."

²⁰Then the old man said, "Peace be to you. Only *leave* all your needs to me; and do not spend the night in the open square."

²¹So he brought him into his house and fed the donkeys; and they washed their feet and ate and drank.

²²While they were celebrating, behold, men of the city, certain worthless *and* evil men, surrounded the house, pounding on the door; and they spoke to the master of the house, the old man, saying, "Bring out the man who came to your house so that we may have relations with him."

²³Then the man, the master of the house, went out and said to them, "No, my fellow citizens, please do not act so wickedly. Since this man has come to my house [as my guest], do not commit this sacrilege.

²⁴"Here is my virgin daughter and this man's concubine. I will bring them out now; abuse *and* humiliate them and do to them whatever you want, but do not commit this act of sacrilege against this man."

²⁵But the men would not listen to him. So the man took the Levite's concubine and brought her outside to them; and they had relations with her and abused her all night until morning; and when daybreak came, they let her go.

²⁶At daybreak the woman came and collapsed at the door of the man's house where her master was, until it was [fully] light.

²⁷When her master got up in the morning and opened the doors of the house and went out to go on his way, he saw his concubine lying at the door of the house, and her hands were on the threshold.

²⁸He said to her, "Get up, and let us go." But there was no answer [for she had died]. Then he put her [body] on the donkey; and the man left and went home.

²⁹When he arrived at his house, he took a knife, and taking hold of his [dead] concubine, he cut her [corpse] limb by limb into twelve pieces, and sent her [body parts] throughout all the territory of Israel.

³⁰All who saw *the dismembered parts* said, "Nothing like this has *ever* happened or been seen from the day that the sons of Israel came up from the land of Egypt to this day. Consider it, take counsel, and speak [your minds]!"

20 THEN ALL the sons of Israel from Dan [in the north] to Beersheba [in the south], including the land of Gilead came out, and the congregation assembled as one man to the LORD at Mizpah.

²The chiefs of all the people of all the tribes of Israel, presented themselves in the assembly of the people of God, four hundred thousand men on foot who drew the sword.

³(Now the Benjamites [in whose territory the crime was committed] heard that the [other tribes of the] sons of Israel had gone up to Mizpah.) And the sons of Israel said, "How did this evil thing happen?"

⁴So the Levite, the husband of the woman who was murdered, replied, "I had come with my concubine to spend the night in Gibeah, [a town] which belongs to [the tribe of] Benjamin.

⁵"But the men of Gibeah rose up against me and surrounded the house at night because of me. They intended to kill me, but instead they raped my concubine [so brutally] that she died.

⁶"So I took my concubine and cut her [corpse] in pieces and sent her [body parts] throughout the land of the inheritance of Israel; for the men of Gibeah have committed a lewd and disgraceful act in Israel.

⁷"Now then, all you sons of Israel, all of you, give your advice and counsel here [regarding what should be done]."

⁸Then all the people stood [unified] as one man, saying, "None of us will go to his tent, and none of us will return to his home [until this is settled].

⁹"But now this is the thing which we will do to Gibeah; *we will go up* by lot against it,

¹⁰and we will take ten men out of a hundred throughout the tribes of Israel, and a hundred out of a thousand, and a thousand out of ten thousand to bring provisions for the men, so that when they come to Gibeah of Benjamin, they may punish them for all the despicable acts which they have committed in Israel."

¹¹So all the men of Israel assembled against the city, united as one man.

¹²Then the tribes of Israel sent men through the entire tribe of Benjamin, saying, "What is this evil thing that has been done among you?

¹³"Now therefore, turn over the men [involved], the worthless *and* wicked men in Gibeah, so that we may put them to death and remove *this* wickedness from Israel." But the Benjamites would not listen to the voice of their brothers, the sons of Israel.

¹⁴Then the [tribe of the] sons of Benjamin gathered from the cities to Gibeah, to go out to battle against the [other] sons of Israel.

¹⁵And the Benjamites assembled out of their cities at that time twenty-six thousand men who drew the sword, besides the inhabitants of Gibeah, who assembled seven hundred chosen men.

¹⁶Out of all these people were seven hundred choice left-handed men; each one could sling stones at [a target no wider than] a hair and not miss.

¹⁷Then the men of Israel, other than Benjamin, assembled four hundred thousand men who drew the sword; all of these were men of war.

¹⁸The men of Israel arose and went up to Bethel and asked of God and said, "Which of us shall take the lead to battle against the sons [tribe] of Benjamin?" And the Lord said, "Judah [shall go up] first."

¹⁹Then the [fighting men of the] sons of Israel arose in the morning and camped against Gibeah.

²⁰The men of Israel went out to battle against Benjamin, and assembled in battle formation against them at Gibeah.

²¹The sons of Benjamin came out of Gibeah and struck to the ground on that day twenty-two thousand [fighting] men of Israel.

²²But the people, the [fighting] men of Israel, took courage *and* strengthened themselves and again set their battle line in the same place where they formed it the first day.

²³The sons of Israel went up and wept before the Lord until evening, and asked of the Lord, "Shall we advance again to battle against the sons of our brother Benjamin?" And the Lord said, "Go up against them."

²⁴So the sons of Israel came against the sons of Benjamin the second day.

²⁵And [the fighting men from the tribe of] Benjamin went out of Gibeah against them the second day and again struck to the ground the sons of Israel, eighteen thousand men, all of whom were swordsmen.

²⁶Then all the sons of Israel and all the people went up and came to Bethel and wept; and they sat there before the Lord and fasted that day until evening and offered burnt offerings and peace offerings before the Lord.

²⁷And the sons of Israel inquired of the Lord (for the ark of the covenant of God was there [at Bethel] in those days,

²⁸and Phinehas the son of Eleazar, the son of Aaron, *ministered* before it in those days), saying, "Shall I yet again go out to battle against the sons of my brother Benjamin, or shall I quit?" And the Lord said, "Go up, for tomorrow I will hand them over to you."

²⁹So Israel set men in ambush around Gibeah.

³⁰The [fighting men of the] sons of Israel went up against the sons of Benjamin on the third day and placed themselves in battle formation against Gibeah as at other times.

³¹The Benjamites went out against their army and were lured away from the city, and they began to strike and kill some of the people as at other times, on the highways, one of which goes up to Bethel and the other to Gibeah, and in the open country, about thirty men of Israel.

³²And the Benjamites said, "They are defeated before us, as at the first." But the sons of Israel said, "Let us flee and lure them away from the city to the highways."

³³Then all the men of Israel got up from their places and placed themselves in battle formation at Baal-tamar; and the men of Israel [who were] in ambush rushed from their place in the plain of Maareh-geba.

³⁴When the ten thousand choice [fighting] men from all Israel came against Gibeah, the battle was hard *and* fierce; but the Benjamites did not realize that disaster was about to strike them.

³⁵And the Lord struck down [the tribe of] Benjamin before Israel, so that the sons of Israel destroyed twenty-five thousand one hundred men of Benjamin that day, all of whom were swordsmen.

³⁶So the Benjamites realized that they were defeated. Then men of Israel gave

ground to the Benjamites, because they relied on the men in ambush whom they had placed against Gibeah.

37Then the men in ambush quickly rushed and attacked Gibeah; and the men in ambush also deployed and struck the entire city with the edge of the sword.

38Now the appointed signal between the men of Israel and the men in ambush was that they would make a great cloud of smoke rise from the city.

39So the men of Israel turned in the battle, and Benjamin began to strike and kill about thirty men of Israel, for they said, "Certainly they are defeated before us as in the first battle!"

40But when the [signal] cloud began to rise out of the city in a column of smoke, the Benjamites looked behind them; and behold, the entire city went up *in smoke* to heaven.

41When the men of Israel turned back *again*, the men of Benjamin were terrified, for they saw that disaster had fallen upon them.

42Therefore, they turned their backs before the men of Israel [and fled] toward the direction of the wilderness, but the battle followed *and* overtook them. As the [fighting men of the] sons of Benjamin ran among them, the Israelites of the cities came out and destroyed them.

43They surrounded [the men of] Benjamin, pursued them relentlessly, and overtook them opposite Gibeah toward the east.

44Thus eighteen thousand men of Benjamin fell, all of these brave *and* able warriors.

45The survivors [of Benjamin] turned and fled toward the wilderness to the rock of Rimmon, and Israel caught five thousand of them on the roads and overtook them at Gidom and killed two thousand of them.

46So all of Benjamin who fell that day were twenty-five thousand men who drew the sword, all of them brave *and* able warriors.

47But six hundred men turned and fled toward the wilderness to the rock of Rimmon and stayed at the rock of Rimmon for four months.

48The men of Israel turned back against [the tribe of] the sons of Benjamin and struck them with the edge of the sword, both the entire city [of Gibeah] and the livestock and all that they found. They also set on fire all the [surrounding] towns which they found.

21 NOW THE men of Israel had sworn [an oath] at Mizpah, "None of us shall give his daughter in marriage to [a man of] Benjamin."

2So the people came to Bethel and sat there before God until evening, and lifted up their voices and wept bitterly. [Judg 20:27]

3They said, "O LORD, God of Israel, why has this come about in Israel, that there should be today one tribe missing from Israel?"

4And the next day the people got up early and built an altar there and offered burnt offerings and peace offerings.

5Then the sons of Israel said, "Which one from all the tribes of Israel did not come up in the assembly to the LORD?" For they had taken a great oath concerning him who did not come up to the LORD at Mizpah, saying, "He shall certainly be put to death."

6And the sons of Israel felt sorry [and had compassion] for their brother Benjamin and said, "One tribe has been cut off from Israel today.

7"What shall we do for wives for those who are left, since we have sworn [an oath] by the LORD that we will not give them any of our daughters as wives?"

8And they said, "Which one is there of the tribes from Israel that did not come up to Mizpah to the LORD?" And behold, [it was discovered that] no one had come to the camp from Jabesh-gilead, to the assembly.

⁹For when the people were assembled, behold, there was not one of the inhabitants of Jabesh-gilead there.

¹⁰And the congregation sent twelve thousand of the most courageous men there, and commanded them saying, "Go and strike the inhabitants of Jabesh-gilead with the sword, including the women and the children.

¹¹"And this is the thing that you shall do; you shall utterly destroy every male and every woman who is not a virgin."

¹²And they found among the inhabitants of Jabesh-gilead four hundred young virgins who had not known a man intimately; and they brought them to the camp at Shiloh, which is in the land of Canaan.

¹³Then the whole congregation sent *word* to the [surviving] sons of Benjamin who were at the rock of Rimmon, and proclaimed peace to them.

¹⁴So [the survivors of] Benjamin returned at that time, and they gave them the women whom they had kept alive from the women of Jabesh-gilead; but there were not enough [to provide wives] for them.

¹⁵And the people were sorry [and had compassion] for [the survivors of the tribe of] Benjamin because the Lᴏʀᴅ had made a gap in the tribes of Israel.

¹⁶Then the elders of the congregation said, "What shall we do for wives for those [men] who are left, since the women of Benjamin have been destroyed?"

¹⁷They said, "*There must be* an inheritance for the survivors of Benjamin, so that a tribe will not be wiped out from Israel.

¹⁸"But we cannot give them wives from our daughters." For the sons of Israel had sworn [an oath], "Cursed is he who gives a wife to [a man from the tribe of] Benjamin."

¹⁹So they said, "Listen, there is the yearly feast of the Lᴏʀᴅ at Shiloh, which is on the north side of Bethel, on the east side of the highway that goes up from Bethel to Shechem, and on the south side of Lebonah."

²⁰So they instructed the sons of Benjamin, saying, "Go, set an ambush in the vineyards,

²¹and watch; if the daughters of Shiloh come out to dance in the dances, then you shall come out of the vineyards and each of you shall catch his wife from the daughters of Shiloh, and go to the land of [the tribe of] Benjamin.

²²"When their fathers or their brothers come to complain to us, we shall say to them, 'Give them to us voluntarily, because we did not take a wife for each man *of Benjamin* in battle, nor did you give *wives* to them, for that would have made you guilty [of breaking your oath].'"

²³So the sons of [the tribe of] Benjamin did as instructed and took wives according to their number, from the dancers whom they carried away. Then they went and returned to their inheritance, and rebuilt the towns and lived in them.

²⁴The sons of Israel departed from there at that time, each man to his tribe and family, and each man went from there to his inheritance.

²⁵In those days [when the judges governed] there was no king in Israel; every man did what was right in his own eyes.

speak the Word

God, I pray that I will always seek Your ways and Your will instead of doing what is right in my own eyes.
–ᴀᴅᴀᴘᴛᴇᴅ ꜰʀᴏᴍ Jᴜᴅɢᴇs 21:25

Ruth

Author:
Unknown; traditionally Samuel

Date:
Between 1050 BC and 500 BC

Everyday Life Principles:
The power of commitment and faithfulness cannot be overemphasized.

Wise, godly choices put us in position for God to bless us.

God rewards faithfulness and sacrifice for others.

The book of Ruth is an awesome story of the power of faithfulness, sacrifice, and wise choices. Ruth made a difficult choice when she decided not to return to her homeland, choosing instead to endure the hardships of going to Bethlehem with her bitter, widowed mother-in-law. Even though Ruth's husband had died and she did not *have* to stay with Naomi, she made the courageous choice to be faithful and merciful to Naomi, to care for her, and to follow Naomi's God. Orpah, on the other hand, made the choice that was easy for her at the moment—and we never hear of her again.

Ruth's hard choice in the present brought great blessing to her future. It meant that she would have to endure some suffering for a season, but it put her in position for God to reward her faithfulness. God gave Ruth a good, wealthy husband in Boaz, who gave her a child. God caused her to be happy again; and He placed Ruth in the lineage of Jesus Christ.

As you read the book of Ruth, I hope you will commit to be like Ruth— to make wise choices, to be more faithful than ever to the people God has placed in your life, to be merciful, and to have a good attitude when you have to struggle and work hard. When you act on such commitments, God will delight to bless you as powerfully as He did Ruth.

1 IN THE days when the judges governed [Israel], there was a famine in the land [of Canaan]. And a certain man of Bethlehem in Judah went to live temporarily in the country of Moab with his wife and his two sons.

²The man's name was Elimelech and his wife's name was Naomi and his two sons were named Mahlon and Chilion. They were Ephrathites from Bethlehem in Judah. They went to the country of Moab and stayed there.

³Then Elimelech, Naomi's husband, died, and she was left [a widow] with her two sons.

⁴They took wives from the Moabite women; the name of the one was Orpah, and the name of the other was Ruth. They lived there about ten years;

⁵and then both Mahlon and Chilion also died, so the woman [Naomi] was left without her two sons and her husband.

⁶Then she set out with her daughters-in-law to return from the country of Moab, for she had heard in Moab how the LORD had taken care of His people [of Judah] in giving them food.

⁷So she left the place where she was living, her two daughters-in-law with her, and they started on the way back to the land of Judah.

⁸But Naomi said to her two daughters-in-law, "Go back, each of you return to your mother's house. May the LORD show kindness to you as you have shown kindness to the dead and to me.

⁹"May the LORD grant that you find rest, each one in the home of her husband." Then she kissed them [good-bye], and they wept aloud.

¹⁰And they said to her, "No, we will go with you to your people [in Judah]."

¹¹But Naomi said, "Go back, my daughters, why should you go with me? Do I still have sons in my womb that may become your husbands?

¹²"Go back, my daughters, go, for I am too old to have a husband. If I said I have hope, and if I actually had a husband tonight and even gave birth to sons,

¹³would you wait until they were

life point

If you have lost your spouse to death, as Ruth and Naomi did (see Ruth 1:3-5), or to divorce, you will face many adjustments as you learn to function alone. You may have to learn to do things you have forgotten how to do or have never done before. You may have to get a job or learn to cook and care for children or make decisions you are not accustomed to making concerning matters you know nothing about.

While you are doing these new things, you may still hurt, but you can take satisfaction in knowing you are moving forward. Each day you are making progress. God promises to be with you in trouble. While you are waiting for Him to deliver you, you can be comforted by knowing He is with you and working on your behalf even though you cannot always see with your natural eyes how He is working for your good. Take comfort in these words that Jesus spoke in Matthew 28:20: "I am with you always [remaining with you perpetually—regardless of circumstance, and on every occasion], even to the end of the age."

In the book of Ruth, we see three women who have lost their husbands. One of them, Naomi, not only lost her husband, but her two sons as well. We see Ruth and Naomi recover from their losses and go on to live joy-filled, fruitful lives. When we suffer loss in our lives, we also can recover with God's comfort and help.

grown? Would you go without marrying? No, my daughters; for it is much more difficult for me than for you, because the LORD's hand has gone against me."

¹⁴Then they wept aloud again; and Orpah kissed her mother-in-law [goodbye], but Ruth clung to her.

¹⁵Then Naomi said, "Look, your sister-in-law has gone back to her people and to her gods; turn back *and* follow your sister-in-law."

¹⁶But Ruth said, "Do not urge me to leave you or to turn back from following you; for where you go, I will go, and where you lodge, I will lodge.

Your people will be my people, and your God, my God.

¹⁷"Where you die, I will die, and there I will be buried. May the LORD do the same to me [as He has done to

life point

God is a God of purpose. We may not always understand His purpose, but we can be sure He definitely has one. Something may initially look terrible to us, as Ruth's situation must have looked to her and Naomi after the loss of their husbands, and yet all the while God intends to show His glory by working something good from it.

commitment over comfort

Ruth was a woman who experienced loss and tragedy. Her husband, brother-in-law, and father-in-law were all dead. Ruth and her sister-in-law Orpah had a decision to make. Would they stay with Naomi, their mother-in-law, or would they return to their own country?

Naomi had nothing to offer them. She had no more sons, she was elderly, and she had no money. She encouraged her daughters-in-law to leave her and go back home where they would be guaranteed a good life. Orpah did leave, but Ruth insisted on staying with Naomi. Ruth knew that without divine intervention her future looked dim, but she insisted on being faithful to Naomi anyway. Ruth swore she would not leave her, saying that she wanted to live in Naomi's homeland and to know and serve Naomi's God (see Ruth 1:16, 17). Many people choose comfort over commitment, but in the end they miss out on the best that God had for them. Ruth did not know what her future held, but she determined to be a woman of godly character, which includes faithfulness. Together Ruth and Naomi went through some lean and difficult times; however, they kept a good attitude, they were thankful for what little they did have, and God kept making special arrangements to bless them. As it turned out, Naomi had a relative named Boaz who was very wealthy and also happened to be single. God gave Ruth favor with him, and they eventually married (see Ruth 4:10).

Faithfulness led Ruth from poverty to abundance. Proverbs 28:20 states that a faithful person will "abound with blessings." Being faithful means we will have to endure some difficulty along the way. We will encounter things that we would rather run away from, but if we wait patiently for the Lord, we will see His salvation in every situation.

you], and more also, if anything but death separates me from you."

¹⁸When Naomi saw that Ruth was determined to go with her, she said nothing more.

¹⁹So the two of them went on until they came to Bethlehem. And when they arrived in Bethlehem, the whole city was stirred because of them, and the women asked, "Is this Naomi?"

²⁰She said to them, "Do not call me Naomi (sweetness); call me Mara (bitter), for the Almighty has caused me great grief *and* bitterness.

²¹"I left full [with a husband and two sons], but the LORD has brought me back empty. Why call me Naomi, since the LORD has testified against me and the Almighty has afflicted me?"

²²So Naomi returned from the country of Moab, and with her Ruth the Moabitess, her daughter-in-law. And

better, not bitter

After losing her husband, enduring a famine, and moving back to Judah from Moab, Naomi became bitter (see Ruth 1:20). The word *bitter* refers to something that is pungent or sharp to the taste. Bondage leads to bitterness! Naomi was bitter because she was in bondage to the pain, the disappointments, and the difficulties of her circumstances.

We remember that God instructed the children of Israel to prepare a Passover meal that included bitter herbs when they were about to be led out of Egypt, on the very eve of their departure. Why? God wanted them to eat those bitter herbs as a reminder of the bitterness they had experienced under Egyptian oppression.

It is said that the bitter herbs the Israelites ate were probably akin to horseradish. If you have ever taken a big bite of horseradish, you know it can cause quite a physical reaction. Bitterness causes precisely the same type of reaction in us spiritually.

How does bitterness begin? According to the Bible, it grows from a root. Hebrews 12:15 speaks of bitterness as a "root of resentment" that "springs up and causes trouble, and by it many be defiled." Because Naomi was bitter inside, she accused the Lord of causing her "great grief and bitterness" (Ruth 1:20).

Bitterness can result from the many minor offenses we simply will not let go of, the little things we rehearse over and over inside us until they become monumental. It can also result from significant hurts, offenses, traumas, or losses when we do not deal with them properly.

The longer we allow pain, anger, or disappointment to grow and fester, the more powerful these negative emotions become, and the more they infect our entire being: our personalities, our attitudes and behaviors, our perspectives, and our relationships.

Just as God turned Naomi's situation around and made it good, we can expect Him to do the same for us if we will release our bitterness, ask Him to help us and heal us, and continue believing that He is good, no matter what we face.

they arrived in Bethlehem at the beginning of the barley harvest.

2 NOW NAOMI had a relative of her husband, a man of great wealth *and* influence, from the family of Elimelech, whose name was Boaz.

²And Ruth the Moabitess said to Naomi, "Please let me go to the field and glean among the ears of grain after one [of the reapers] in whose sight I may find favor." Naomi said to her, "Go, my daughter."

³So Ruth went and picked up the leftover grain in a field after the reapers; and she happened to stop at the plot of land belonging to Boaz, who was of the family of Elimelech.

⁴It was then that Boaz came back from Bethlehem and said to the reapers, "The LORD be with you!" And they answered him, "The LORD bless you!"

⁵Then Boaz said to his servant who was in charge of the reapers, "Whose young woman is this?"

⁶The servant in charge of the reapers answered, "She is the young Moabite woman who came back with Naomi from the country of Moab.

⁷"And she said, 'Please let me glean and gather after the reapers among the sheaves.' So she came and has continued [gathering grain] from early morning until now, except when she sat [resting] for a little while in the [field] house."

⁸Then Boaz said to Ruth, "Listen carefully, my daughter. Do not go to glean in another field or leave this one, but stay here close by my maids.

⁹"Watch which field they reap, and follow behind them. I have commanded the servants not to touch you. And when you are thirsty, go to the [water] jars and drink from what the servants draw."

¹⁰Then she kneeled face downward, bowing to the ground, and said to him, "Why have I found favor in your eyes that you should notice me, when I am a foreigner?"

¹¹Boaz answered her, "I have been made fully aware of everything that you have done for your mother-in-law since the death of your husband, and how you have left your father and mother and the land of your birth, and have come to a people that you did not know before.

¹²"May the LORD repay you for your kindness, and may your reward be full from the LORD, the God of Israel, under whose wings you have come to take refuge."

¹³Then she said, "Let me find favor in your sight, my lord, for you have comforted me and have spoken kindly to your maidservant, though I am not as one of your maidservants."

¹⁴At mealtime Boaz said to her,

life point

You and I must resist the temptation to speak negatively even when we feel negative, as Naomi did in Ruth 1:21. Blurting out negative statements based on our emotions is extremely unfruitful. Speaking out of our emotions is not the right thing to do. Our emotions usually do not serve us well in times of testing. But we do have hope, because as we mature in Christ, we learn to control our emotions and our mouths.

speak the Word

God, I declare that like Ruth, I have come to take refuge under Your wings.
–ADAPTED FROM RUTH 2:12

"Come over here and eat some bread and dip your bread in the vinegar." So she sat beside the reapers; and he served her roasted grain, and she ate until she was satisfied and she had some left [for Naomi].

15When she got up to glean, Boaz ordered his servants, "Let her glean even among the sheaves, and do not insult her.

16"Also you shall purposely pull out for her some stalks [of grain] from the sheaves and leave them so that she may collect them, and do not rebuke her."

17So she gleaned in the field until evening. Then she beat out what she had gleaned, and it was about an ephah of barley.

18She picked it up and went into the city, and her mother-in-law saw what she had gleaned. Ruth also took out and gave to Naomi what she had saved after she [had eaten and] was satisfied.

19Her mother-in-law said to her, "Where did you glean today? Where did you work? Blessed be the man who took notice of you." So she told her mother-in-law with whom she had worked and said, "The name of

life point

In response to Ruth's kindness to Naomi, God spoke to Boaz, the owner of the field where Ruth was gleaning and the richest man in the county. God led him to leave "stalks" or handfuls of grain for her "purposely" (Ruth 2:16).

If you are kind to people everywhere you go, you will find "handfuls" of kindness God has left on purpose, lying around for you. God will return a harvest of kindness to you because you have sown seeds of kindness. His heart is to bless you, so be on the lookout, because His "handfuls" are everywhere.

the man with whom I worked today is Boaz."

20Naomi said to her daughter-in-law, "May he be blessed of the LORD who has not ceased His kindness to the living and to the dead." Again Naomi said to her, "The man is one of our closest relatives, one who has the right to redeem us." [Lev 25:25]

21Then Ruth the Moabitess said, "He also said to me, 'Stay close to my servants until they have harvested my entire crop.'"

22Naomi said to Ruth, "It is good, my daughter, for you to go out [to work] with his maids, so that others do not assault you in another field."

23So she stayed close to the maids of Boaz, gleaning until the end of the barley and wheat harvests. And she lived with her mother-in-law.

3 THEN NAOMI her mother-in-law said to Ruth, "My daughter, shall I not look for security and a home for you, so that it may be well with you?

2"Now Boaz, with whose maids you were [working], is he not our relative? See now, he is winnowing barley at the threshing floor tonight.

3"So wash and anoint yourself [with olive oil], then put on your [best] clothes, and go down to the threshing floor; but stay out of the man's sight until he has finished eating and drinking.

4"When he lies down, notice the place where he is lying, and go and uncover his feet and lie down. Then he will tell you what to do."

5Ruth answered her, "I will do everything that you say."

6So she went down to the threshing floor and did just as her mother-in-law had told her.

7When Boaz had eaten and drunk and his heart was happy, he went to lie down at the end of the stack of grain.

Then Ruth came secretly, and uncovered his feet and lay down.

[8]In the middle of the night the man was startled and he turned over, and found a woman lying at his feet.

[9]So he said, "Who are you?" And she answered, "I am Ruth your maid. Spread the hem of your garment over me, for you are a close relative *and* redeemer."

life point

One of the lessons we learn from Ruth is that loss does not mean everything in your life is over; just that one part of it has ended. One season has passed and another can now begin—if you are willing to believe that you can go forward.

Do not just passively sit around and wait for something to happen or someone to come along. Pray, and then step out in faith. That is what Ruth did, and that was when she stepped into God's plan of restoration in her life (see Ruth 3:1–5).

If you are lonely, do not simply sit and wish you would meet other people. *Go make new friends!* Find someone else who is lonely too—someone even lonelier than you are—and be a friend to that individual. You will reap what you sow. God will return that friendship to you, multiplied many times over. If you are hurting, go find someone else who is hurting and help him or her. As you sow into the lives of other hurting people, God will heal your wounds.

The Bible teaches us that faith moves us to take God-inspired action (see James 2:17). I am not suggesting works of the flesh, or just fleshly zeal, but I am saying to be bold and step out as God leads. Be like Ruth and put "hands and feet" to your prayers.

[10]Then he said, "May you be blessed by the LORD, my daughter. You have made your last kindness better than the first; for you have not gone after young men, whether poor or rich.

[11]"Now, my daughter, do not be afraid. I will do for you whatever you ask, since all my people in the city know that you are a woman of excellence.

[12]"It is true that I am your close relative *and* redeemer; however, there is a relative closer [to you] than I.

[13]"Spend the night [here], and in the morning if he will redeem you, fine; let him do it. But if he does not wish to redeem you, then, as the LORD lives, I will redeem you. Lie down until the morning."

[14]So she lay at his feet until the morning, but got up before anyone could recognize another; Boaz said, "Do not let it be known that the woman came to the threshing floor [last night]."

[15]He also said, "Give me the shawl you are wearing and hold it out." So Ruth held it and he measured out six measures of barley [into it] and placed it on her. And she went into the city.

[16]When she came home, her mother-in-law said, "How did it go, my daughter?" And Ruth told her everything that the man had done for her.

[17]She said, "He gave me these six measures of barley, and he said to me, 'Do not go back to your mother-in-law empty-handed.'"

[18]Then Naomi said, "Sit *and* wait, my daughter, until you learn how this matter turns out; for the man will not rest until he has settled it today."

4 THEN BOAZ went up to the city gate [where business and legal matters were settled] and sat down, and then the close relative (redeemer) of whom Boaz had spoken came by. He said to him, "Come over here, friend, and sit down." So he came and sat down.

putting the Word to work

The book of Ruth is a wonderful story of restoration and redemption in Ruth's life and in Naomi's. Is there anything you are believing God to restore in your life right now? Begin to thank Him for doing that in His way and in His timing.

²Then Boaz took ten men from the elders of the city and said, "Sit down here." And they sat down.

³He said to the closest relative (redeemer), "Naomi, who has returned from the country of Moab, must sell the plot of land which belonged to our brother Elimelech.

⁴"So I thought to let you hear of it, saying, 'Buy it in the presence of those sitting here, and before the elders of my people. If you will redeem it, redeem it; but if not, then tell me, so that I may know; for there is no one besides you to redeem it, and I am [next of kin] after you.'" And he said, "I will redeem it."

⁵Then Boaz said, "The day that you buy the field from Naomi, you must also acquire Ruth the Moabitess, the widow of the deceased, to restore the name of the deceased to his inheritance."

⁶The closest relative (redeemer) said, "I cannot redeem it for myself, because [by marrying a Moabitess] I would jeopardize my own inheritance. Take my right of redemption (purchase) yourself, because I cannot redeem it." [Deut 23:3, 4]

⁷Now formerly in Israel this was the custom concerning redeeming and exchanging *property*. To confirm a transaction, a man pulled off his sandal and gave it to the other. This was the *way of* confirming *and* attesting in Israel.

⁸So, when the closest relative (redeemer) said to Boaz, "Buy it for yourself," he pulled off his sandal [and gave it to Boaz to confirm the agreement].

⁹Then Boaz said to the elders and to all the people, "You are witnesses this day that I have bought everything that was Elimelech's and everything that was Chilion's and Mahlon's from the hand of Naomi.

¹⁰"I have also acquired Ruth the Moabitess, the widow of Mahlon, to be my wife to restore the name of the deceased to his inheritance, so that the name of the deceased will not be cut off from his brothers or from the gate of his birthplace. You are witnesses today."

¹¹All the people at the gate and the

life point

Even though Ruth did not believe in the God of Israel when she chose to extend kindness to her widowed mother-in-law, Naomi, she was obeying what we now recognize as the biblical principle to be kind and good to others, especially widows (see James 1:27). In fact, Naomi's friends even remarked that Ruth had been better to her than seven sons (see Ruth 4:15).

Being good to someone else helps us overcome the pain, loss, or disappointments we experience; it also releases joy in our lives. Many times people who have been hurt experience depression. I believe this is partially due to the fact that their attention is on their own pain instead of on what they can do to relieve someone else's pain. God has not called us to "in-reach," He has called us to "outreach." When we reach out to others, God reaches into our souls and heals us. He is the only One Who can heal the brokenhearted and make the wounded better than new. This was certainly true in Ruth's case, as God gave her a kind, godly husband, a baby boy, and a place in the bloodline of Jesus Christ.

elders said, "We are witnesses. May the LORD make the woman who is coming into your house like Rachel and Leah, the two who built the household of Israel. May you achieve wealth *and* power in Ephrathah and become famous in Bethlehem.

¹²"Further, may your house be like the house of Perez whom Tamar bore to Judah, because of the offspring which the LORD will give you by this young woman."

¹³So Boaz took Ruth, and she became his wife. And he went in to her, and the LORD enabled her to conceive, and she gave birth to a son.

¹⁴Then the women said to Naomi, "Blessed is the LORD who has not left you without a redeemer (grandson, as heir) today, and may his name become famous in Israel.

¹⁵"May he also be to you one who restores life and sustains your old age; for your daughter-in-law, who loves you and is better to you than seven sons, has given birth to him."

¹⁶Then Naomi took the child and placed him in her lap, and she became his nurse.

¹⁷The neighbor women gave him a name, saying, "A son (grandson) has been born to Naomi." They named him Obed (worshiper). He is the father of Jesse, the father of David [the ancestor of Jesus Christ].

¹⁸Now these are the descendants of Perez: Perez was the father of Hezron,

¹⁹Hezron was the father of Ram, Ram the father of Amminadab,

²⁰Amminadab the father of Nahshon, Nahshon the father of Salmon,

²¹Salmon the father of Boaz, Boaz the father of Obed,

²²Obed the father of Jesse, and Jesse the father of David [the king of Israel and the ancestor of Jesus Christ].

First Samuel

Author:
Uncertain

Date:
Between 931 BC and 722 BC

Everyday Life Principles:
God will answer the cries of a pure, desperate heart like Hannah's.

God will expose an evil, rebellious heart like Saul's.

Our actions are important, but God looks beyond them to see the motives and intentions of our hearts.

First Samuel tells the story of Samuel, a priest in Israel, and Saul, Israel's first king. It introduces us to David and gives us extensive background on this man who would later succeed Saul as the ruler of God's people. Among other things and in the midst of some dramatic stories and adventure, this book reveals the importance of the heart. In the beginning of 1 Samuel, we see a barren woman with a desperate heart, who prays fervently to God out of a pure heart. God answers with a miracle and gives her Samuel as her son. Samuel, in turn, served God with a faithful heart as a prophet and a priest. He anointed Saul as king, and though God had clearly chosen Saul to rule, we see that his heart was evil, jealous, fearful, and angry. Against the backdrop of Saul's wickedness, we see God raising up the future king, David, who is called a man "after His own heart" (see 1 Samuel 13:14). So we know that David's heart was pure and honorable before the Lord.

First Samuel 16:7 tells us that "man looks at the outward appearance, but the LORD looks at the heart." Determine today that whatever the Lord sees when He looks into your heart will be pleasing to Him.

1 THERE WAS a certain man of Ramathaim-zophim, of the hill country of Ephraim, named Elkanah the son of Jeroham, the son of Elihu, the son of Tohu, the son of Zuph, an Ephraimite.

²He had two wives, one named Hannah and the other named Peninnah. Peninnah had children, but Hannah had none.

³This man went up from his city each year to worship and sacrifice to the LORD of hosts at Shiloh. Hophni and Phinehas, the two sons of Eli, were priests to the LORD there.

⁴When the day came that Elkanah sacrificed, he would give portions [of the sacrificial meat] to Peninnah his wife and all her sons and daughters.

⁵But to Hannah he would give a double portion, because he loved Hannah, but the LORD had given her no children.

⁶Hannah's rival provoked her bitterly, to irritate *and* embarrass her, because the LORD had left her childless.

⁷So it happened year after year, whenever she went up to the house of the LORD, Peninnah provoked her; so she wept and would not eat.

⁸Then Elkanah her husband said to her, "Hannah, why do you cry and why do you not eat? Why are you so sad *and* discontent? Am I not better to you than ten sons?"

⁹So Hannah got up after eating and drinking in Shiloh. Now Eli the priest was sitting on his seat beside the doorpost of the temple (tabernacle) of the LORD.

¹⁰Hannah was greatly distressed, and she prayed to the LORD and wept in anguish.

¹¹She made a vow, saying, "O LORD of hosts, if You will indeed look on the affliction (suffering) of Your maidservant and remember, and not forget Your maidservant, but will give Your maidservant a son, then I will give

him to the LORD all the days of his life; a razor shall never touch his head."

¹²Now it happened as she continued praying before the LORD, that Eli was watching her mouth.

¹³Hannah was speaking in her heart (mind); only her lips were moving, and her voice was not heard, so Eli thought she was drunk.

¹⁴Eli said to her, "How long will you make yourself drunk? Get rid of your wine."

¹⁵But Hannah answered, "No, my lord, I am a woman with a despairing spirit. I have not been drinking wine or *any* intoxicating drink, but I have poured out my soul before the LORD. [Gen 19:34]

¹⁶"Do not regard your maidservant as a wicked *and* worthless woman, for I have spoken until now out of my great concern and [bitter] provocation."

¹⁷Then Eli answered and said, "Go in peace; and may the God of Israel grant your petition that you have asked of Him."

¹⁸Hannah said, "Let your maidservant find grace *and* favor in your sight." So the woman went on her way and ate, and her face was no longer *sad*.

¹⁹The family got up early the next morning, worshiped before the LORD, and returned to their home in Ramah. Elkanah knew Hannah his wife, and the LORD remembered her [prayer].

²⁰It came about in due time, after Hannah had conceived, that she gave birth to a son; she named him Samuel, *saying*, "Because I have asked for him from the LORD."

putting the Word to work

Are you praying fervently for something to happen in your life, as Hannah was praying for a son (see 1 Samuel 1:1–20)? Remember Hannah and know that God hears your desperate cry, and He will answer.

²¹Then the man Elkanah and all his household went up to offer to the LORD the yearly sacrifice and *pay* his vow. ²²But Hannah did not go up, for she said to her husband, *"I will not go up* until the child is weaned; and then I will bring him, so that he may appear before the LORD and remain there as long as he lives." ²³Elkanah her husband said to her, "Do what seems best to you. Wait until you have weaned him; only may the LORD establish *and* confirm His word." So the woman remained [behind] and nursed her son until she weaned him. ²⁴Now when she had weaned him, she took him up with her, along with a three-year-old bull, an ephah of flour, and a leather bottle of wine [to pour over the burnt offering for a sweet fragrance], and she brought Samuel to the LORD's house in Shiloh, although the child was young. ²⁵Then they slaughtered the bull, and brought the child to Eli. ²⁶Hannah said, "Oh, my lord! As [surely as] your soul lives, my lord, I am the woman who stood beside you here, praying to the LORD. ²⁷"For this child I prayed, and the LORD has granted me my request which I asked of Him. ²⁸"Therefore I have also dedicated him to the LORD; as long as he lives he is dedicated to the LORD." And they worshiped the LORD there.

2

HANNAH PRAYED and said,

"My heart rejoices *and* triumphs in the LORD;
My horn (strength) is lifted up in the LORD,
My mouth has opened wide [to speak boldly] against my enemies,
Because I rejoice in Your salvation.
²"There is no one holy like the LORD,
There is no one besides You,
There is no Rock like our God.
³"Do not go on boasting so very proudly,
Do not let arrogance come out of your mouth;
For the LORD is a God of knowledge,
And by Him actions are weighed (examined).
⁴"The bows of the mighty are broken,
But those who have stumbled equip themselves with strength.
⁵"Those who were full hire themselves out for bread,
But those who were hungry cease [to hunger].
Even the barren [woman] gives birth to seven,
But she who has many children withers away.
⁶"The LORD puts to death and makes alive;
He brings down to Sheol (the grave) and raises up [from the grave].

speak the Word

God, my heart rejoices and triumphs in You. My strength is in You. My mouth is opened wide to speak boldly against my enemies because I rejoice in Your salvation.
—ADAPTED FROM 1 SAMUEL 2:1

God, I declare that there is none holy as You are holy; there is no god besides You; there is no Rock in my life like You.
—ADAPTED FROM 1 SAMUEL 2:2

7"The LORD makes poor and makes
　　rich;
He brings low and He lifts up.
8"He raises up the poor from the dust,
He lifts up the needy from the ash
　　heap
To make them sit with nobles,
And inherit a seat of honor *and*
　　glory;
For the pillars of the earth are the
　　LORD's,
And He set the land on them.
9"He guards the feet of His godly
　　(faithful) ones,
But the wicked ones are silenced
　　and perish in darkness;
For a man shall not prevail by
　　might.
10"The adversaries of the LORD will
　　be broken to pieces;
He will thunder against them in
　　the heavens,
The LORD will judge the ends of the
　　earth;
And He will give strength to His
　　king,
And will exalt the horn (strength)
　　of His anointed." [Luke 1:46]

11Elkanah [and his wife Hannah]
returned to Ramah to his house. But
the child [Samuel] served the LORD
under the guidance of Eli the priest.
12The sons of Eli [Hophni and
Phinehas] were worthless (dishonorable, unprincipled) men; they did not
know [nor respect] the LORD

life point

We must remember that what goes up can
come down. God lifts up, and God brings
down (see 1 Samuel 2:7). If we are to be
leaders in His kingdom, we must develop
and maintain strong, godly character and
the most intimate communion with God
we possibly can so we will be able to stay
in the positions to which He elevates us.

13and the custom of the priests with
[the sacrifices of] the people. When
any man was offering a sacrifice, the
priest's servant would come while
the meat was boiling, with a three-
pronged [meat] fork in his hand;
14then he would thrust it into the pan,
or kettle, or caldron, or pot; everything
that the fork brought up the priest
would take for himself. This is what
they did in Shiloh to all [the sacrifices
of] the Israelites who came there.
15Also, before they burned (offered)
the fat, the priest's servant would
come and say to the man who was sacrificing, "Give the priest meat to roast,
since he will not accept boiled meat
from you, only raw."
16If the man said to him, "Certainly
they are to burn (offer) the fat first,
and then you may take as much as you
want," then the priest's servant would
say, "No! You shall give *it to me* now or
I will take it by force."
17So the sin of the [two] young men
[Hophni and Phinehas] was very
great before the LORD, for the men
treated the offering of the LORD disrespectfully.
18Now Samuel was ministering before the LORD, as a child dressed in a
linen ephod [a sacred item of priestly
clothing].
19Moreover, his mother would make
him a little robe and would bring it up
to him each year when she came up
with her husband to offer the yearly
sacrifice.
20Then Eli would bless Elkanah and
his wife and say, "May the LORD give
you children by this woman in place of
the one she asked for which was dedicated to the LORD." Then they would
return to their own home.
21And [the time came when] the LORD
visited Hannah, so that she conceived
and gave birth to three sons and two
daughters. And the boy Samuel grew
before the LORD.

²²Now Eli was very old; and he heard about everything that his sons were doing to all [the people of] Israel, and how they were lying with the women who served at the entrance to the Tent of Meeting (tabernacle).

²³Eli said to them, "Why do you do such things, the evil things that I hear from all these people?

²⁴"No, my sons; for the report that I keep hearing from the passers-by among the Lord's people is not good.

²⁵"If one man does wrong *and* sins against another, God will intercede (arbitrate) for him; but if a man does wrong to the Lord, who can intercede for him?" But they would not listen to their father, for it was the Lord's will to put them to death.

²⁶But the boy Samuel continued to grow in stature and in favor both with the Lord and with men.

²⁷Then a man of God (prophet) came to Eli and said to him, "Thus says the Lord: 'Did I *not* plainly reveal Myself to the house of your father (ancestor) when they were in Egypt *in bondage* to Pharaoh's house?

²⁸'Moreover, I selected him out of all the tribes of Israel to be My priest, to go up to My altar, to burn incense, to wear an ephod before Me. And [from then on] I gave to the house of your father all the fire *offerings* of the sons of Israel.

²⁹'Why then do you kick at (despise) My sacrifice and My offering which I commanded in My dwelling place, and honor your sons more than Me, by fattening yourselves with the choicest part of every offering of My people Israel?'

³⁰"Therefore the Lord God of Israel declares, 'I did indeed say that your house and that of [Aaron] your father would walk [in priestly service] before Me forever.' But now the Lord declares, 'Far be it from Me—for those who honor Me I will honor, and those who despise Me will be insignificant *and* contemptible.

³¹'Behold, the time is coming when I will cut off your strength and the strength of your father's house, so that there will not be an old man in your house.

³²'You will look at the distress of *My* house (the tabernacle), in *spite of* all the good which God will do for Israel, and there will never again be an old man in your house.

³³'Yet I will not cut off every man of yours from My altar; your eyes will fail *from weeping* and your soul will grieve, and all those born in your house will die as men [in the prime of life]. [1 Sam 22:17–20]

³⁴"This will be the sign to you which shall come concerning your two sons, Hophni and Phinehas: on the same day both of them shall die. [1 Sam 4:17, 18]

³⁵'But I will raise up for Myself a faithful priest who will do according to what is in My heart and in My soul; and I will build him a permanent *and* enduring house, and he will walk before My anointed forever. [1 Sam 2:10]

³⁶'And it will happen that everyone who is left in your house will come and bow down to him for a piece of silver and a loaf of bread and say, "Please assign me to one of the priest's offices so I may eat a piece of bread."'"

3 NOW THE boy Samuel was attending to the service of the Lord under the supervision of Eli. The word of the Lord was rare *and* precious in those days; visions [that is, new revelations of divine truth] were not widespread.

²Yet it happened at that time, as Eli was lying down in his own place (now his eyesight had begun to grow dim and he could not see *well*).

³and the [oil] lamp of God had not yet gone out, and Samuel was lying down in the temple of the Lord, where the ark of God was,

how to hear God's voice

When God started calling to Samuel, Samuel thought his master, Eli, was speaking to him (see 1 Samuel 3:4–6). Both times Eli said to Samuel, "I did not call you." After this happened a third time, Eli finally realized God was calling Samuel. God spoke to Samuel in a voice that was familiar to him so that he would not be frightened.

Samuel was accustomed to hearing Eli's voice; therefore, when God called to him, it sounded like Eli. Likewise, God wants us to listen to Him, so He speaks to us through a voice that we will recognize. Sometimes it may sound like our own voice; sometimes it may sound like the voice of someone we know. But the point is that the voice will bring peace when God speaks to us.

People who listen to my teachings tell me that frequently when they are about to make a decision, they will hear me say something that gives them direction or correction. What they are really hearing is God speaking through His Word, but they have heard my voice speaking it to them for so long, it sounds like me when it comes to them.

A woman told me at a meeting, "I was in an intense situation with my husband. God led me to know what to do by reminding me of something you said on one of your tapes. All of a sudden I heard your voice saying just what I needed to remember. God reminded me of it as a *word in due season*." Even though she heard my voice playing back from her memory bank, it was the Holy Spirit Who called forth that memory just when she needed it.

When God speaks to us, He does not usually boom from heaven. Often He speaks to us through what the New King James Bible calls "a still small voice" (1 Kings 19:12) that comes from our inner man. In such situations, we may think we are talking to ourselves, but God's words in our spirit are always filled with wisdom we could never have on our own.

People have said to me, "You're always saying, 'God said.' You sound like you have conversations with God all the time." I do have fellowship with God regularly, and He speaks to me in many different ways—and God is trying to talk to everyone else all the time, too. We all can hear Him if we will simply ask Him to speak clearly to us, then listen to our "inner man" (our conscience), and wait for Him to speak (see Psalm 5:3).

God speaks to us in many different ways. Many people think they do not hear from God because they are looking for some kind of supernatural manifestation that is not likely to happen. Most of the time, God speaks in our hearts through peace or a lack of it. If we have peace, we may proceed with our intended action, but if we do not have peace, that is a word from God to stop. God also speaks through wisdom and common sense. He does not lead us to do foolish things. He speaks to us through His Word and never tells us to do anything that does not agree with His Word. He speaks to us through other people and even our circumstances. Let me encourage you to begin to ask God to speak to you and then listen for His voice. He has so many good things to say to you!

⁴that the LORD called Samuel, and he answered, "Here I am."

⁵He ran to Eli and said, "Here I am, for you called me." But Eli said, "I did not call you; lie down again." So he went and lay down.

⁶Then the LORD called yet again, "Samuel!" So Samuel got up and went to Eli and said, "Here I am, for you called me." But Eli answered, "I did not call, my son; lie down again."

⁷Now Samuel did not yet know [or personally experience] the LORD, and the word of the LORD was not yet revealed [directly] to him.

⁸So the LORD called Samuel a third time. And he stood and went to Eli and said, "Here I am, for you did call me." Then Eli understood that it was the LORD [who was] calling the boy.

⁹So Eli said to Samuel, "Go, lie down, and it shall be that if He calls you, you shall say, 'Speak, LORD, for Your servant is listening.'" So Samuel went and lay down in his place.

¹⁰Then the LORD came and stood and called as at the previous times, "Samuel! Samuel!" Then Samuel answered, "Speak, for Your servant is listening."

¹¹The LORD said to Samuel, "Behold, I am about to do a thing in Israel at which both ears of everyone who hears it will ring.

¹²"On that day I will carry out against Eli everything that I have spoken concerning his house (family), from beginning to end.

¹³"Now I have told him that I am about to judge his house forever for the sinful behavior which he knew [was happening], because his sons were bringing a curse on themselves [dishonoring and blaspheming God] and he did not rebuke them.

¹⁴"Therefore I have sworn to the house of Eli that the sinful behavior of Eli's house (family) shall not be atoned for by sacrifice or offering forever."

¹⁵So Samuel lay down until morning. Then he opened the doors of the LORD's house. But Samuel was afraid to tell the vision to Eli.

¹⁶But Eli called Samuel and said, "Samuel, my son." And he answered, "Here I am."

¹⁷Then Eli said, "What is it that He said to you? Please do not hide it from me. May God do the same to you, and more also, if you hide from me anything of all that He said to you."

¹⁸So Samuel told him everything, hiding nothing from him. And Eli said, "It is the LORD; may He do what seems good to Him."

¹⁹Now Samuel grew; and the LORD was with him and He let none of his words fail [to be fulfilled]. [Josh 23:14]

²⁰And all Israel from Dan [in the north] to Beersheba [in the south] knew that Samuel was appointed as a prophet of the LORD.

²¹And the LORD continued to appear in Shiloh, for the LORD revealed Himself to Samuel in Shiloh by the word of the LORD.

speak the Word

Speak to me, Lord. I am listening for Your voice.
—ADAPTED FROM 1 SAMUEL 3:10

God, I pray that as I continue to grow spiritually, You will be with me and let none of my words fail to be fulfilled.
—ADAPTED FROM 1 SAMUEL 3:19

4 AND THE word of [the LORD through] Samuel came to all Israel. Now Israel went out to meet the Philistines in battle and they camped beside Ebenezer while the Philistines camped at Aphek. ²The Philistines assembled in battle formation to meet Israel, and when the battle was over, Israel was defeated by the Philistines, who killed about four thousand men on the battlefield. ³When the people (soldiers) came into the camp, the elders of Israel said, "Why has the LORD defeated us today before the Philistines? Let us bring the ark of the covenant of the LORD here from Shiloh, so that He may come among us and save us from the hand of our enemies." ⁴So the people sent *word* to Shiloh, and from there they carried the ark of the covenant of the LORD of hosts who sits *above* the cherubim; and the two sons of Eli, Hophni and Phinehas, were with the ark of the covenant of God.

⁵So it happened that as the ark of the covenant of the LORD came into the camp, all [the people of] Israel shouted with a great shout, and the earth resounded. ⁶When the Philistines heard the noise of the shout, they said, "What *does* the noise of this great shout in the camp of the Hebrews *mean?*" Then they understood that the ark of the LORD had come into the camp. ⁷The Philistines were afraid, for they said, "God has come into the camp." And they said, "Woe [disaster is coming] to us! For nothing like this has happened before. ⁸"Woe to us! Who will rescue us from the hand of these mighty gods? These are the gods who struck the Egyptians with all kinds of plagues in the wilderness. ⁹"Take courage, and be men, O Philistines, so that you do not become servants to the Hebrews, as they have been servants to you; act like men and fight!"

¹⁰So the Philistines fought; Israel was defeated and every man fled to his tent. It was a very great defeat, for thirty thousand foot soldiers of Israel fell. ¹¹Also the ark of God was taken; and the two sons of Eli, Hophni and Phinehas, were killed. [1 Sam 2:34] ¹²Now a man [from the tribe] of Benjamin ran from the battle line and came to Shiloh that same day with his clothes torn and dust on his head [as signs of mourning over the disaster]. ¹³When he arrived, Eli was sitting on his seat by the road, keeping watch, because his heart was anxious about the ark of God. When the man arrived to report [the news] in the city, everyone in the city cried out [to God, for help]. ¹⁴When Eli heard the noise of the outcry, he asked, "What is the noise of this uproar?" And the man came hurriedly and told Eli. ¹⁵Now Eli was ninety-eight years old; his eyes were dim so that he could not see. ¹⁶The man said to Eli, "I have come from the battle line. Indeed, I escaped from the battle line today." Eli said, "How did things go, my son?" ¹⁷The messenger replied, "Israel has fled before the Philistines and there has also been a great slaughter among the people. Also your two sons, Hophni and Phinehas, are dead, and the ark of God has been taken." ¹⁸When he mentioned the ark of God, Eli fell off the seat backwards by the side of the [city] gate. His neck was broken and he died, for he was old and heavy. He had judged Israel for forty years.

¹⁹Now his daughter-in-law, Phinehas' wife, was pregnant, and was about to give birth; so when she heard the news that the ark of God had been taken and that her father-in-law and

her husband had died, she kneeled down and gave birth, because her [labor] pains began.

²⁰And about the time of her death [following the sudden birth] the women attending her said to her, "Do not be afraid, for you have given birth to a son." But she did not answer or pay any attention.

²¹And she named the boy Ichabod, saying, "The glory has left Israel," because the ark of God had been taken and because of [the deaths of] her father-in-law and her husband.

²²She said, "The glory has left Israel, for the ark of God has been taken."

5 THEN THE Philistines took the ark of God, and they brought it from Ebenezer to Ashdod. ²They took the ark of God and brought it into the house of Dagon and set it beside [the image of] Dagon [their chief idol].

³When the people of Ashdod got up early the next day, behold, Dagon had fallen on his face on the ground before the ark of the Lord. So they took Dagon and returned him to his place.

⁴But when they got up early the next morning, behold, Dagon had [again] fallen on his face on the ground before the ark of the Lord, and his head and both palms of his hands were [lying] cut off on the threshold; only the trunk [portion] of [the idol of] Dagon was left on him.

⁵This is the reason neither the priests of Dagon nor any who enter Dagon's house step on the threshold of Dagon in Ashdod to this day.

⁶Then the hand of the Lord was heavy on the people of Ashdod, and He caused them to be dumbfounded and struck them with tumors, both Ashdod and its territory.

⁷When the men of Ashdod saw what had happened, they said, "The ark of the God of Israel must not remain with

us, for His hand is heavy on us and on Dagon our god."

⁸So they sent word and gathered all the lords (governors) of the Philistines to them and said, "What shall we do with the ark of the God of Israel?" They answered, "Let the ark of the God of Israel be brought around to Gath." So they took the ark of the God of Israel there.

⁹But it happened that after they had taken it to Gath, the hand of the Lord was against the city, causing an extremely great panic [because of the deaths from the plague], for He struck the people of the city, both young and old, and tumors broke out on them.

¹⁰So they sent the ark of God to Ekron. And as the ark of God came to Ekron, the Ekronites cried out, "They have brought the ark of the God of Israel [from Gath] to us, to kill us and our people."

¹¹So they sent word and gathered all the lords of the Philistines and said, "Send away the ark of the God of Israel; let it be returned to its own place, so that it will not kill us and our people." For there was a deadly panic throughout the city; the hand of God was very heavy (severe) there.

¹²The men who had not died were stricken with tumors and the cry of the city [for help] went up to heaven.

6 NOW THE ark of the Lord had been in the country of the Philistines for seven months. ²And the Philistines called for the priests and the diviners (seers), saying, "What shall we do with the ark of the Lord? Let us know how we can send it back to its place."

³They said, "If you send away the ark of the God of Israel, do not send it empty [without a gift]; but be sure to return [it] to Him [together with] a guilt offering. Then you will be healed, and it will be known to you why His hand is not removed from you."

[4]Then they said, "What shall the guilt offering be which we shall return to Him?" They answered, "Five golden tumors and five golden mice, according to the number of the lords (governors) of the Philistines, for one plague was on all of you and on your lords.

[5]"So you shall make replicas of your tumors and of your mice that ravage the land, and give glory to the God of Israel; perhaps He will lighten His hand [of judgment] on you and your gods and your land.

[6]"Why then do you harden your hearts [allowing pride to cause your downfall] just as the Egyptians and Pharaoh hardened their hearts? When He had severely dealt with them *and* mocked them, did they not allow the people [of Israel] to go, and they departed?

[7]"Now then, make a new cart and prepare two milk cows on which a yoke has never been placed; and hitch the cows to the cart and take their calves back home, away from them.

[8]"Then take the ark of the LORD and put it on the cart; and put the articles of gold which you are returning to Him as a guilt offering in a box beside it. Then send it away [without a driver].

[9]"But watch, if it goes up by the way of its own territory to Beth-shemesh, then [you will know that] He has done us this great evil. But if not, then we will know that it was not His hand that struck us; this disaster happened to us by chance."

[10]And the men did so, and took two milk cows and hitched them to the cart, and corralled their calves at home.

[11]They put the ark of the LORD on the cart, and the box containing the golden mice and the replicas of their tumors.

[12]And the cows went straight toward Beth-shemesh along the highway, lowing as they went, and did not turn away to the right or the left. And the Philistine lords (governors) followed them to the border of Beth-shemesh.

[13]Now *the men of* Beth-shemesh were gathering their wheat harvest in the valley, and they looked up and saw the ark and rejoiced to see it.

[14]The cart came into the field of Joshua of Beth-shemesh and stopped there. A large stone was there; and the men split up the wood of the cart [for firewood] and offered the cows as a burnt offering to the LORD.

[15]The Levites had taken down the ark of the LORD and the box beside it, in which were the articles of gold, and put them on the large stone. And the men of Beth-shemesh offered burnt offerings and made sacrifices that day to the LORD.

[16]When the five lords of the Philistines saw what happened, they returned to Ekron that day.

[17]These are the golden tumors which the Philistines returned as a guilt offering to the LORD: one for Ashdod, one for Gaza, one for Ashkelon, one for Gath and one for Ekron [the five chief cities of the Philistines];

[18]also the golden mice, *according* to the number of all the cities of the Philistines belonging to the five lords, both fortified cities and [unwalled] country villages. The large stone on which the Levites set the ark of the LORD *remains a witness* to this day in the field of Joshua of Beth-shemesh.

[19]The LORD struck down some of the men of Beth-shemesh because they had looked into the ark of the LORD. He struck down 50,070 men among the people, and the people mourned because the LORD had struck the people with a great slaughter.

[20]The men of Beth-shemesh said, "Who is able to stand before the LORD, this holy God? And to whom shall He go up from us?"

[21]So they sent messengers to the residents of Kiriath-jearim, saying, "The Philistines have returned the ark of the LORD. Come down and take it up to you."

7 SO THE men of Kiriath-jearim came and took up the ark of the Lord and brought it into the house of Abinadab on the hill, and they consecrated Eleazar his son to care for the ark of the Lord.

²And from that day the ark remained in Kiriath-jearim for a very long time, for it was twenty years [until the reign of King David]; and all the house of Israel lamented (wailed) *and* grieved after the LORD. [2 Sam 6:3, 4; 1 Chr 13:5–7]

³Then Samuel said to all the house of Israel, "If you are returning to the LORD with all your heart, remove the foreign gods and the Ashtaroth (pagan goddesses) from among you and direct your hearts to the LORD and serve Him only; and He will rescue you from the hand of the Philistines."

⁴So the Israelites removed the Baals and the Ashtaroth and served the LORD alone.

⁵Samuel said, "Gather all Israel together at Mizpah and I will pray to the LORD for you."

⁶So they gathered at Mizpah, and drew water and poured it out before the LORD, and fasted on that day and said there, "We have sinned against the LORD." And Samuel judged the Israelites at Mizpah.

⁷Now when the Philistines heard that the Israelites had gathered at Mizpah, the lords (governors) of the Philistines went up against Israel. And when the Israelites heard it, they were afraid of the Philistines.

⁸And the sons of Israel said to Samuel, "Do not cease to cry out to the LORD our God for us, so that He may save us from the hand of the Philistines."

⁹So Samuel took a nursing lamb and offered it as a whole burnt offering to the LORD; and Samuel cried out to the LORD for Israel and the LORD answered him.

¹⁰As Samuel was offering up the burnt offering, the Philistines approached for the battle against Israel. Then the LORD thundered with a great voice that day against the Philistines and threw them into confusion, and they were defeated *and* fled before Israel.

¹¹And the men of Israel came out of Mizpah and pursued the Philistines, and struck them down as far as [the territory] below Beth-car.

¹²Then Samuel took a stone and set it between Mizpah and Shen, and he named it Ebenezer (stone of help), saying, "Thus far the LORD has helped us."

¹³So the Philistines were subdued and they did not come anymore into Israelite territory. And the hand of the LORD was against the Philistines all the days of Samuel.

¹⁴The cities which the Philistines had taken from Israel were restored to Israel, from Ekron to Gath; and Israel recovered the cities' territory from the Philistines. Also there was peace between Israel and the Amorites.

¹⁵Now Samuel judged Israel all the days of his life.

¹⁶He used to go annually on a circuit to Bethel, Gilgal, and Mizpah, and he judged Israel in all these places.

¹⁷Then he would return to Ramah, because his home was there; and there he judged Israel, and there he built an altar to the LORD.

8 AND IT came about when Samuel was old that he appointed his sons as judges over Israel.

²Now the name of his firstborn was Joel, and the name of his second, Abijah; they were judging in Beersheba.

³His sons, however, did not walk in his ways, but turned aside after dishonest gain, took bribes, and perverted justice.

⁴Then all the elders of Israel gathered together and came to Samuel at Ramah

⁵and said to him, "Look, you have grown old, and your sons do not walk

in your ways. Now appoint us a king to judge us [and rule over us] like all the other nations."

⁶But their demand displeased Samuel when they said, "Give us a king to judge *and* rule over us." So Samuel prayed to the LORD.

⁷The LORD said to Samuel, "Listen to the voice of the people in regard to all that they say to you, for they have not rejected you, but they have rejected Me from being King over them.

⁸"Like all the deeds which they have done since the day that I brought them up from Egypt even to this day—in that they have abandoned (rejected) Me and served other gods—so they are doing to you also.

⁹"So now listen to their voice; only solemnly warn them and tell them the ways of the king who will reign over them."

¹⁰So Samuel told all the words of the LORD to the people who were asking him for a king.

¹¹He said, "These will be the ways of the king who will reign over you: he will take your sons and appoint them for himself to his chariots and among his horsemen and they will run before his chariots.

¹²"He will appoint them for himself to be commanders over thousands and over fifties, and *some* to do his plowing and to reap his harvest and to make his implements of war and equipment for his chariots.

¹³"He will take your daughters to be perfumers, cooks, and bakers.

¹⁴"He will take the best of your fields, your vineyards, and your olive groves, and give them to his servants.

¹⁵"He will take a tenth of your grain and of your vineyards and give it to his officers and to his servants.

¹⁶"He will take your male servants and your female servants and your best young men and your donkeys and use them for his work.

¹⁷"He will take a tenth of your flocks, and you yourselves shall be his servants.

¹⁸"Then you will cry out on that day because of your king whom you have chosen for yourselves, but the LORD will not answer you on that day [because you have rejected Him as King]."

¹⁹Nevertheless, the people refused to listen to the voice of Samuel, and they said, "No, but there shall be a king over us,

²⁰so that we too may be like all the nations [around us], that our king may judge [and govern] us and go out before us and fight our battles."

²¹Samuel had heard all the words of the people and repeated them to the LORD.

²²And the LORD said to Samuel, "Listen to their request and appoint a king for them." So Samuel said to the men of Israel, "Go, each man to his own city."

9 THERE WAS a man of [the tribe of] Benjamin whose name was Kish the son of Abiel, the son of Zeror, the son of Becorath, the son of Aphiah, a Benjamite, a mighty man of influence *and* wealth.

²Kish had a son named Saul, a choice and handsome man; among the sons of Israel there was not a man more handsome than he. From his shoulders and up he was [a head] taller than any of the people.

³Now the donkeys of Kish, Saul's father, had wandered off *and* were lost. Kish said to his son Saul, "Please take one of the servants with you and arise, go look for the donkeys."

⁴And they passed through the hill country of Ephraim and the land of Shalishah, but did not find *them*. Then they passed through the land of Shaalim, but they were not *there* and the land of the Benjamites, but they [still] did not find *them*.

⁵When they came to the land of

Zuph, Saul said to his servant who was with him, "Come, let us return, otherwise my father will stop *worrying* about the donkeys and become anxious about us."

6The servant said to him, "Look here, in this city there is a man of God, and the man is held in honor; everything that he says comes true. Now let us go there; perhaps he can advise us about our journey [and tell us where we should go]."

7Then Saul said to his servant, "But look, if we go [to see him], what shall we bring to the man? For the bread from our sacks is gone and there is no gift to bring to the man of God. What do we have [to offer]?"

8The servant replied again to Saul, "Here in my hand I have a quarter of a shekel of silver; I will give that to the man of God, and he will advise us as to [where we should go on] our journey [to find the donkeys]."

9(Formerly in Israel, when a man went to inquire of God, he would say, "Come, let us go to the seer"; for *he who is called* a prophet today was formerly called a seer.)

10Saul said to his servant, "Well said; come, let us go." So they went to the city where the man of God was living.

11As they went up the hill to the city, they met some young women going out to draw water, and said to them, "Is the seer (prophet) here?"

12They answered them, "He is; look, he is ahead of you. Hurry now, for he has come into the city today because the people have a sacrifice on the high place today.

13"As you enter the city you will find him before he goes up to the high place to eat, for the people will not eat until he comes, because he must ask the blessing on the sacrifice; afterward, those who are invited will eat. So go up now, for about now you will find him."

14So they went up to the city. And as they came into the city, there was Samuel coming out toward them to go up to the high place.

15Now a day before Saul came, the LORD had informed Samuel [of this], saying,

16"About this time tomorrow I will send you a man from the land of Benjamin, and you shall anoint him as leader over My people Israel; and he will save My people from the hand of the Philistines. For I have looked upon [the distress of] My people, because their cry [for help] has come to Me."

17When Samuel saw Saul, the LORD said to him, "There is the man of whom I spoke to you. This one shall rule over My people [as their king]."

18Then Saul approached Samuel in the [city] gate and said, "Please tell me where the seer's house is."

19Samuel answered Saul, "I am the seer. Go on ahead of me to the high place, for you shall eat with me today; and in the morning I will let you go, and will tell you all that is on your mind.

20"As for your donkeys which were lost three days ago, do not be concerned about them, for they have been found. And for whom are all things that are desirable in Israel? Are they not for you and for all your father's household (family)?"

21Saul replied, "Am I not a Benjamite, of the smallest of the tribes of Israel? And is not my family the smallest of all the families of the tribe of Benjamin? Why then have you spoken this way to me [as if I were very important]?"

22Then Samuel took Saul and his servant and brought them into the hall [at the high place] and gave them a place [to sit] at the head of the persons—about thirty men—who were invited [while the rest ate outside].

23Samuel said to the cook, "Bring the [priests'] portion that I gave you, regarding which I told you, 'Set it aside.'"

24Then the cook lifted up the leg

(thigh) with *the meat* that was on it [indicating that it was the priest's honored portion] and placed it before Saul. Samuel said, "Here is what has been reserved [for you]. Set it before you and eat, because it has been kept for you until the appointed time, ever since I invited the people." So Saul ate with Samuel that day.

²⁵When they came down from the high place into the city, Samuel spoke with Saul on the roof [of his house].

²⁶They got up early [the next day]; and at dawn Samuel called Saul [who was sleeping] on the roof, saying, "Get up, so that I may send you on your way." Saul got up, and both he and Samuel went outside.

²⁷As they were going down to the outskirts of the city, Samuel said to Saul, "Tell the servant to go on ahead of us so that he may pass by but you stand still now so that I may proclaim the word of God to you."

10 THEN SAMUEL took the flask of oil and poured it on Saul's head, kissed him, and said, "Has the LORD not anointed you as ruler over His inheritance (Israel)?

²"When you leave me today, you will meet two men beside Rachel's tomb in the territory of Benjamin at Zelzah; they will say to you, 'The donkeys you went to look for have been found. And your father has stopped caring about them and is worried about you, saying, "What shall I do about my son?"'

³"Then you will go on further from there, and you will come to the terebinth tree of Tabor, and three men going up to [sacrifice to] God at Bethel will meet you there, one carrying three young goats, another carrying three loaves of bread, and another carrying a jug of wine.

⁴They will greet you and give you two *loaves* of bread, which you will accept from their hand.

⁵"After that you will come to the hill of God where the garrison of the Philistines is; and when you come there to the city, you will meet a group of prophets coming down from the high place [of worship] with harp, tambourine, flute, and lyre before them, and they will be prophesying.

⁶"Then the Spirit of the LORD will come upon you mightily, and you will prophesy with them, and you will be changed into another man.

⁷"When these signs come to you, do for yourself whatever the situation requires, for God is with you.

⁸"You shall go down ahead of me to Gilgal; and behold, I will be coming down to you to offer burnt offerings and to sacrifice peace offerings. You shall wait seven days until I come to you and show you what you must do."

⁹Then it happened when Saul turned his back to leave Samuel, God changed his heart; and all those signs came to pass that day.

¹⁰When they came to the hill [Gibeah], behold, a group of prophets met him; and the Spirit of God came on him mightily, and he prophesied [under divine guidance] among them.

¹¹Now when all who knew Saul previously saw that he actually prophesied now [by inspiration] with the prophets, the people said one to another, "What has happened to [Saul, who is nobody but] the son of Kish? Is Saul also among the prophets?"

speak the Word

God, I pray that Your Spirit will come upon me so mightily and make me so new that people will hardly recognize me!
–ADAPTED FROM 1 SAMUEL 10:6

¹²And a man from there answered, "But who is the father of the others?" So it became a proverb, "Is Saul also among the prophets?"

¹³When Saul had finished prophesying, he went to the high place [of worship].

¹⁴Saul's uncle said to him and to his servant, "Where did you go?" And Saul said, "To look for the donkeys. And when we saw that they were nowhere to be found, we went to Samuel [for help]."

¹⁵Saul's uncle said, "Please tell me, what did Samuel say to you?"

¹⁶And Saul said to his uncle, "He told us plainly that the donkeys had been found." But he did not tell him about the matter of the kingdom which Samuel had mentioned.

changed by the Holy Spirit

When the Spirit of God truly comes upon a person, that person will be changed. First Samuel 10:6 tells us that Saul would be "changed into another man," which really means that he would be so thoroughly changed that people would think he was someone else.

The most important evidences of the Spirit-filled life are a change of character and the development of the fruit of the Holy Spirit described in Galatians 5:22, 23. God fills people with the Holy Spirit to enable them to live for Him. If they are not doing that, they are not showing forth the proper evidence of being a believer in Jesus Christ. Speaking in tongues was one of the evidences of the outpouring of the Holy Spirit at Pentecost, and it still is one today. But the most important evidence was then—and always will be—changed men and women (see Acts 2:1–4).

At Jesus' trial, Peter denied Christ three times because he was afraid of the Jews (see Luke 22:56–62); but after being filled with the Holy Spirit on the Day of Pentecost, he stood and preached an extremely bold message. Three thousand souls were added to the kingdom of God as the result of Peter's preaching that day (see Acts 2:14–41). The baptism of the Holy Spirit changed Peter; it turned him into another man. His fear suddenly disappeared, and he became as bold as a lion.

Peter was not the only person who took a courageous stand that day; all eleven of the remaining apostles did the same. They had all been hiding behind closed doors for fear of the Jews when Jesus came to them after His resurrection (see John 20:19–22), but suddenly, after being filled with the Holy Spirit, they all became fearless and brave.

There was a common thread that ran through the lives of Jesus' disciples—their fear was turned to boldness through the power of the Holy Spirit. Like them, you do not need to live with the torment of being afraid. Your fear can also be turned to boldness.

There is help available to you through the infilling of the Holy Spirit. The baptism of the Holy Spirit changed Saul; it changed Peter and the disciples; it changed me; and it continues to change earnest seekers all over the world. Ask God to fill you completely with His precious Holy Spirit. Surrender all of yourself to Him, holding nothing back. Paul prayed for the church that they would become bodies wholly filled with God Himself (see Ephesians 3:16). This is my desire, and I pray that it is also yours.

¹⁷Then Samuel called the people together to the LORD at Mizpah,

¹⁸and he said to Israel, "Thus says the LORD, the God of Israel, 'It was I who brought Israel up from Egypt, and I rescued you from the hand of the Egyptians and from all the kingdoms that were oppressing you.'

¹⁹"But today you have rejected your God, who Himself saves you from all your disasters and distresses; yet you have said, 'No! Set a king over us.' Now then, present yourselves before the LORD by your tribes and by your families (clans)."

²⁰And when Samuel brought all the tribes of Israel near, the tribe of Benjamin was chosen by lot.

²¹Then he brought the tribe of Benjamin near by their families, and the family of Matri was chosen by lot. And Saul the son of Kish was chosen by lot; but when they looked for him, he could not be found.

²²So they inquired further of the LORD, "Has the man come here yet?" And the LORD answered, "He is there, hiding himself by the provisions *and* supplies." [Ex 28:30]

²³So they ran and took him from there, and when he stood among the people, he was taller than any of the people from his shoulders upward.

²⁴Samuel said to all the people, "Do you see him whom the LORD has chosen? For there is no one like him among all the people." So all the people shouted and said, "*Long* live the king!"

²⁵Then Samuel told the people the requirements of the kingdom, and wrote them in a book and placed it before the LORD. And Samuel sent all the people away, each one to his home.

²⁶Saul also went home to Gibeah; and the brave men whose hearts God had touched went with him.

²⁷But some worthless men said, "How can this man save *and* rescue us?" And they regarded Saul with contempt and did not bring him a gift. But he ignored the insult *and* kept silent.

11 NOW NAHASH the Ammonite [king] went up and besieged Jabesh-gilead; and all the men of Jabesh said to Nahash, "Make a treaty [of peace] with us and we will serve you."

²But Nahash the Ammonite told them, "I will make *a treaty* with you on this condition, that I will gouge out the right eye of every one of you, and make it a disgrace upon all Israel."

³The elders of Jabesh said to Nahash, "Give us seven days so that we may send messengers throughout the territory of Israel. Then, if there is no one to save us, we will come out [and surrender] to you."

⁴Then the messengers came to Gibeah of Saul and told the news to the people; and all the people raised their voices and wept aloud.

⁵Now Saul was coming out of the field behind the oxen, and he said, "What is *the matter* with the people that they are weeping?" So they told him about the report of the men of Jabesh.

⁶The Spirit of God came upon Saul mightily when he heard these words, and he became extremely angry.

⁷He took a team of oxen and cut them in pieces, and sent them throughout the territory of Israel by the hand of messengers, saying, "Whoever does not come out to follow Saul and Samuel, the same shall be done to his oxen." Then fear of the LORD fell on the people, and they came out [united] as one man [with one purpose].

⁸He assembled *and* counted them at Bezek; and the sons of Israel numbered 300,000, and the men of Judah 30,000.

⁹They said to the messengers who had come, "You shall say to the men of Jabesh-gilead: 'Tomorrow, by the time the sun is hot, you will have help [against the Ammonites].'" So the

messengers came and reported this to the men of Jabesh; and they were overjoyed.

¹⁰So the men of Jabesh said [to Nahash the Ammonite], "Tomorrow we will come out to you [to surrender], and you may do to us whatever seems good to you."

¹¹The next morning Saul put the men into three companies; and they entered the [Ammonites'] camp during the [darkness of the early] morning watch and killed the Ammonites until the heat of the day; and the survivors were scattered, and no two of them were left together.

¹²The people said to Samuel, "Who is the one who said, 'Shall Saul reign over us?' Bring the men, and we will put them to death."

¹³But Saul said, "No man shall be put to death this day, for today the Lord has brought victory to Israel."

¹⁴Samuel said to the people, "Come, let us go to Gilgal and there restore the kingdom."

¹⁵So all the people went to Gilgal, and there they made Saul king before the Lord in Gilgal. There they also sacrificed peace offerings before the Lord; and there Saul and all the men of Israel rejoiced greatly.

12 THEN SAMUEL said to all Israel, "Behold, I have listened to your voice in everything that you have said to me and have appointed a king over you.

²"And now, here is the king walking before you. As for me, I am old and gray, and here are my sons with you. I have walked before you from my childhood to this day.

³"Here I am; testify against me before the Lord and [Saul] His anointed [if I have done someone wrong]. Whose ox have I taken, or whose donkey have I taken, or whom have I exploited? Whom have I oppressed or from whose hand have I taken a bribe to blind my eyes [to the truth]? [Tell me and] I will restore it to you."

⁴They said, "You have not exploited us or oppressed us or taken anything at all from a man's hand."

⁵Samuel said to them, "The Lord is a witness against you, and [Saul] His anointed is a witness this day that you have not found anything in my hand." And they answered, "*He is* a witness."

⁶Then Samuel said to the people, "It is the Lord who appointed Moses and Aaron and brought your fathers (ancestors) up from the land of Egypt.

⁷"Now then, take your stand, so that I may plead *and* contend with you before the Lord concerning all the righteous acts of the Lord which He did for you and for your fathers.

⁸"When Jacob [and his sons] had come into Egypt [and later when the Egyptians oppressed them] and your fathers cried out to the Lord, then the Lord sent Moses and Aaron who brought your fathers out of Egypt and settled them in this place.

⁹"But when they forgot the Lord their God, He sold them into the hand of Sisera, commander of Hazor's army, and into the hand of the Philistines and of the king of Moab, and they fought against them.

¹⁰"They cried out to the Lord, saying, 'We have sinned because we have abandoned (rejected) the Lord and have served the Baals and the Ashtaroth; but now rescue us from the hands of our enemies, and we will serve You.'

speak the Word

God, I declare that You are my King!
–ADAPTED FROM 1 SAMUEL 12:12

[11]"Then the LORD sent Jerubbaal (Gideon) and Bedan and Jephthah and Samuel, and He rescued you from the hand of your enemies on every side, and you lived in security. [12]"But when you saw that Nahash king of the Ammonites had come against you, you said to me, 'No, but a king shall reign over us'—although the LORD your God was your King. [13]"Now therefore, here is [Saul] the king whom you have chosen, and for whom you asked; behold, the LORD has set a king over you. [14]"If you will fear the LORD [with awe and profound reverence] and serve Him and listen to His voice and not rebel against His commandment, then both you and your king will follow the LORD your God [and it will be well]. [15]"But if you do not listen to the LORD's voice, but rebel against His command, then the hand of the LORD will be against you [to punish you], as it was against your fathers. [16]"So now, take your stand and see this great thing which the LORD will do before your eyes. [17]"Is it not [the beginning of the] wheat harvest today? I will call to the LORD and He will send thunder and rain; then you will know [without any doubt], and see that your evil which you have done is great in the sight of the LORD by asking for yourselves a king." [18]So Samuel called to the LORD [in prayer], and He sent thunder and rain that day; and all the people greatly feared the LORD and Samuel. [19]Then all the people said to Samuel, "Pray to the LORD your God for your servants, so that we will not die, for we

have added to all our sins *this* evil—to ask for a king for ourselves." [20]Samuel said to the people, "Do not be afraid. You have [indeed] done all this evil; yet do not turn away from following the LORD, but serve the LORD with all your heart. [21]"You must not turn away, for *then you would go* after futile things which cannot profit or rescue, because they are futile. [22]"The LORD will not abandon His people for His great name's sake, because the LORD has been pleased to make you a people for Himself. [23]"Moreover, as for me, far be it from me that I should sin against the LORD by ceasing to pray for you; but I will instruct you in the good and right way. [24]"Only fear the LORD [with awe and profound reverence] and serve Him faithfully with all your heart; for consider what great things He has done for you. [25]"But if you still do evil, both you and your king will be swept away [to destruction]."

13

SAUL WAS *thirty* years old when he began to reign, and he reigned *forty*-two years over Israel. [2]Saul chose for himself 3,000 men of Israel; of whom 2,000 were with him in Michmash and in the hill country of Bethel, while 1,000 were with Jonathan at Gibeah of Benjamin. But he sent the rest of the people away, each one to his own tent. [3]Jonathan attacked *and* defeated the Philistine garrison which was at Geba, and the Philistines heard about it. Then Saul blew the trumpet

speak the Word

Lord, I give You reverence and I want to serve You faithfully, with all my heart. Help me to always remember the great things You have done for me.
—ADAPTED FROM 1 SAMUEL 12:24

throughout the land, saying, "Let the Hebrews hear."

4All Israel heard that Saul had defeated the Philistine garrison, and also that Israel had become despicable to the Philistines. And the people were summoned to join Saul at Gilgal.

5Now the Philistines gathered to fight against Israel, 30,000 chariots and 6,000 horsemen, and troops in multitude, like sand on the seashore. They came up and camped at Michmash, east of Beth-aven.

6When the men of Israel saw that they were in a tight situation (for their troops were hard-pressed), they hid in caves, in thickets, in cellars, and in [dry] cisterns (pits).

7Also *some of* the Hebrews had crossed the [river] Jordan to the land of Gad and Gilead. As for Saul, he was still in Gilgal, and all the people followed him, trembling [in fear and anticipation].

8Now Saul waited seven days, according to the appointed time which Samuel had set, but Samuel had not come to Gilgal; and the people were scattering away from Saul.

9So Saul said, "Bring me the burnt offering and the peace offerings." And he offered the burnt offering [which he was forbidden to do].

10As soon as he finished offering the burnt offering, Samuel finally came; Saul went out to meet and to welcome him.

11But Samuel said, "What have you done?" Saul said, "Since I saw that the people were scattering away from me, and that you did not come within the appointed time, and that the Philistines were assembling at Michmash,

12therefore, I said, 'Now the Philistines will come down against me at Gilgal, and I have not asked for the LORD's favor [by making supplication to Him].' So I forced myself to offer the burnt offering."

13Samuel said to Saul, "You have acted foolishly; you have not kept the commandment of the LORD your God, which He commanded you, for [if you had obeyed] the LORD would have established your kingdom over Israel forever.

14"But now your kingdom shall not endure. The LORD has sought out for

life point

First Samuel 13:1–14 gives us great insight into Saul's character. Saul was anointed king of Israel. He had an opportunity to enjoy a great and glorious future, but he had some character weaknesses that proved to be his downfall. Saul was a people-pleaser. He loved the approval of other people so much that he disobeyed God's instructions in order to get it. God instructed Saul to wait until the prophet Samuel arrived to offer up a burnt offering. When Samuel did not arrive at the expected time, the people became restless and impatient. Although Saul knew in his heart that he was being disobedient, he went ahead and offered the sacrifice he had been forbidden to offer. Saul's reply to the question of why he had done this was, "Since I saw that the people were scattering away from me . . ." (1 Samuel 13:11). Samuel told Saul he had done a foolish thing, and because of his disobedience he would lose his kingdom. Saul was so addicted to approval that he did lose his kingdom because of it.

It is important that we do not follow Saul's example. We need to resist the urge to please others when they lead us contrary to God's ways. We need to be obedient to God, following Him wholeheartedly. When we aim to please God, and not man, we open the door for God's blessing.

Himself a man (David) after His own heart, and the Lord has appointed him as leader *and* ruler over His people, because you have not kept (obeyed) what the Lord commanded you."

¹⁵Then Samuel arose and went up from Gilgal to Gibeah of Benjamin. And Saul assembled *and* counted the people who were still with him, [only] about six hundred [fighting] men.

¹⁶Saul and his son Jonathan and the people with them were staying in Geba of Benjamin, while the Philistines camped at Michmash.

¹⁷And the raiding party came from the Philistine camp in three companies: one company turned toward Ophrah, to the land of Shual,

¹⁸another company turned toward Beth-horon, and another toward the border overlooking the Valley of Zeboim toward the wilderness.

¹⁹Now no blacksmith (metal-worker) could be found in all the land of Israel, for the Philistines said, "Otherwise the Hebrews will make swords or spears."

²⁰So all [the men of] Israel went down to the Philistines, each to get his plowshare, pick, axe, or sickle sharpened.

²¹The fee [for sharpening] was a pim (two-thirds of a shekel) for the plowshares, the picks, the pitchforks, and the axes, and to straighten the goads (cattle prods).

²²So it came about on the day of battle that neither sword nor spear was found in the hands of any of the people who were with Saul and Jonathan; but Saul and Jonathan his son had them.

²³And the garrison of the Philistines went out to the pass at Michmash.

14 ONE DAY Jonathan the son of Saul said to his young armor bearer, "Come, let us go over to the Philistine garrison on the other side." But he did not tell his father.

²Saul was staying in the outskirts of Gibeah under a pomegranate tree in Migron; and with him were about six hundred men,

³and Ahijah the son of Ichabod's brother Ahitub the son of Phinehas, the son of Eli, the Lord's priest at Shiloh, was wearing the ephod. And the people did not know that Jonathan had gone.

⁴Between the passes by which Jonathan sought to cross over to get to the Philistine garrison, there was a rocky crag on the one side and a rocky crag on the other side; one [crag] was named Bozez, and the other, Seneh.

⁵The one crag was on the north in front of Michmash, and the other on the south in front of Geba.

⁶Jonathan said to his young armor bearer, "Come, let us cross over to the garrison of these uncircumcised men; it may be that the Lord will work for us. For there is nothing to prevent the Lord from saving, whether by many or by few."

⁷And his armor bearer said to him, "Do everything that is in your heart (mind); here I am with you in whatever you think [best]."

⁸Jonathan said, "See now, we are going to cross over to the [Philistine] men and reveal ourselves to them.

⁹"If they say to us, 'Wait until we come to you,' then we will stand in our place and not go up to them.

¹⁰"But if they say, 'Come up to us,' we will go up, for the Lord has handed them over to us; and this shall be the sign to us."

speak the Word

God, I pray that I will be like David and be a person after Your own heart.
—ADAPTED FROM 1 SAMUEL 13:14

[11]When both of them revealed themselves to the garrison of the Philistines, the Philistines said, "Look, the Hebrews are coming out of the holes where they have hidden themselves."

[12]So the men of the garrison responded to Jonathan and his armor bearer, "Come up to us and we will tell you something." Jonathan said to his armor bearer, "Climb up after me, for the LORD has given them into the hands of Israel."

[13]Then Jonathan climbed up on his hands and feet, his armor bearer following after him. The enemy fell before Jonathan [in combat], and his armor bearer killed *some of them* after him.

[14]That first slaughter which Jonathan and his armor bearer made was about twenty men within about half a [plow] furrow in a plot of land [the area of which a yoke of oxen could plow in a day].

[15]And there was trembling in the [Philistine] camp, in the field, and among all the people; even the garrison and the raiding party trembled [in fear], and the earth quaked and it became a trembling *and* terror from God.

[16]Saul's watchmen in Gibeah of Benjamin looked, and behold, the multitude melted away and they went here and there.

[17]Then Saul said to the people with him, "Take a count and see who has left us." When they had taken a count, behold, Jonathan and his armor bearer were missing.

[18]Saul said to Ahijah [the priest], "Bring the ark of God here." For at that time the ark of God was with the sons of Israel.

[19]While Saul talked to the priest, the commotion in the Philistine camp continued and increased, so Saul said to the priest, "Withdraw your hand."

[20]Then Saul and all the people who were with him rallied and went into the battle; and behold, every [Philistine] man's sword was against his companion, in wild confusion.

[21]Now the Hebrews who were with the Philistines previously, who went up with them all around in the camp, they also *turned* to be with the Israelites who were with Saul and Jonathan.

[22]When all the men of Israel who had hidden themselves in the hill country of Ephraim heard that the Philistines had fled, they too pursued them closely in the battle.

[23]So the LORD saved Israel that day, and the battle spread beyond Beth-aven.

[24]But the men of Israel were hard-pressed that day, because Saul had put the people under a curse, saying, "Cursed be the man who eats food before evening, and before I have taken vengeance on my enemies." So none of the people ate any food.

[25]All *the people of* the land came to a forest, and there was honey on the ground.

[26]When the people entered the forest, the honey was dripping, but no man put his hand to his mouth [to taste it], because the people feared the oath [of Saul].

[27]But Jonathan had not heard when his father put the people under the oath. So he put out the end of the staff that was in his hand and dipped it into a honeycomb, and then he put his hand to his mouth, and his energy was restored.

[28]But one of the people told him, "Your father strictly put the people under an oath, saying, 'Cursed be the man who eats food today.'" And the people were exhausted [and hungry].

[29]Then Jonathan said, "My father has troubled the land [with his foolish curse]. See how my energy is restored because I tasted a little of this honey.

[30]How much better [it would have been] if only the people had eaten freely today from the spoil of their enemies which they found! For now

the slaughter among the Philistines has not been great."

³¹They struck the Philistines that day from Michmash to Aijalon. And the people were very tired.

³²[When night came and the oath ended] the people rushed greedily upon the spoil. They took sheep, oxen, and calves, and slaughtered them on the ground; and they ate them [raw] with the blood [still in them].

³³Then Saul was told, "Look, the people are sinning against the Lord by eating [the meat] with the blood." And he said, "You have violated [the Law] *and* acted treacherously; roll a large stone to me today." [Lev 7:26, 27]

³⁴Saul said, "Spread out among the people and tell them, 'Each one of you bring me his ox or his sheep, and butcher it [properly] here and eat; and do not sin against the Lord by eating [the meat with] the blood.'" So that night each one brought his ox with him and butchered it there.

³⁵And Saul built an altar to the Lord; it was the first altar that he built to the Lord.

³⁶Then Saul said, "Let us go down after the Philistines by night and plunder them until the morning light, and let us not leave a man of them [alive]." They said, "Do whatever seems good to you." Then the priest said, "Let us approach God here."

³⁷Saul asked [counsel] of God, "Shall I go down after the Philistines? Will You hand them over to Israel?" But He did not answer him that day.

³⁸Then Saul said, "Come here, all you who are leaders of the people, and let us find out how this sin [causing God's silence] happened today.

³⁹"For as the Lord lives, who saves Israel, for *even* if *the guilt* is in my son Jonathan, he shall most certainly die." But not one of all the people answered him.

⁴⁰Then he said to all the Israelites, "You shall be on one side; I and my son Jonathan will be on the other side." The people said to Saul, "Do what seems good to you."

⁴¹Therefore, Saul said to the Lord, the God of Israel, "Give a perfect lot [identifying the transgressor]." Then Saul and Jonathan were selected [by lot], but the other men went free.

⁴²Saul said, "Cast [lots] between me and my son Jonathan." And Jonathan was selected.

⁴³Saul said to Jonathan, "Tell me what you have done." So Jonathan told him, "I tasted a little honey with the end of the staff that was in my hand. Here I am, I must die!"

⁴⁴Saul answered, "May God do so [to me], and more also [if I do not keep my word], for you shall most certainly die, Jonathan."

⁴⁵But the people said to Saul, "Must Jonathan, who has brought about this great victory in Israel, be put to death? Far from it! As the Lord lives, not one hair of his head shall fall to the ground, for he has worked with God this day." So the people rescued Jonathan and he was not put to death.

⁴⁶Then Saul stopped pursuing the Philistines, and the Philistines went to their own place.

⁴⁷When Saul assumed control of the kingdom of Israel, he fought against all his enemies on every side: Moab, the sons (descendants) of Ammon, Edom, the kings of Zobah, and the Philistines. Wherever he turned, he inflicted punishment.

⁴⁸He acted valiantly and defeated the Amalekites, and rescued Israel from the hands of those who had plundered them.

⁴⁹Now Saul's sons were Jonathan, Ishvi, and Malchi-shua. The names of his two daughters *were these:* the name of the firstborn was Merab, and the name of the younger, Michal.

⁵⁰The name of Saul's wife was Ahinoam the daughter of Ahimaaz. The

commander of his army was named Abner, the son of Ner, Saul's uncle.

⁵¹Kish was the father of Saul, and Ner the father of Abner was the son of Abiel.

⁵²Now the war against the Philistines was severe (brutal, relentless) all the days of Saul; and whenever Saul saw any mighty or courageous man, he recruited him for his staff.

15 SAMUEL SAID to Saul, "The Lord sent me to anoint you king over His people Israel. Now listen *and* pay close attention to the words of the Lord.

²"Thus says the Lord of hosts (armies), 'I will punish Amalek for what he did to Israel, how he set himself against him on the way when Israel came up from Egypt.

³'Now go and strike Amalek and completely destroy everything that they have; do not spare them, but kill both man and woman, child and infant, ox and sheep, camel and donkey.'"

⁴So Saul summoned the people and numbered them at Telaim—200,000 foot soldiers and 10,000 men of Judah.

⁵Saul came to the city of Amalek and set an ambush in the valley.

⁶Saul said to the Kenites, "Go, leave, go down from the Amalekites, so that I do not destroy you along with them; for you showed kindness to all the Israelites when they went up from Egypt." So the Kenites departed from among the Amalekites.

⁷Saul defeated the Amalekites, from Havilah as far as Shur, which is east of Egypt.

⁸He captured Agag the king of the Amalekites alive, though he totally destroyed all [the rest of] the people with the sword.

⁹Saul and the people spared Agag and the best of the sheep, the oxen, the fatlings, the lambs, and everything that was good, and they were not willing to destroy them entirely; but everything that was undesirable or worthless they destroyed completely.

¹⁰Then the word of the Lord came to Samuel, saying,

¹¹"I regret that I made Saul king, for he has turned away from following Me and has not carried out My commands." Samuel was angry [over Saul's failure] and he cried out to the Lord all night.

¹²When Samuel got up early in the morning to meet Saul, he was told, "Saul came to Carmel, and behold, he set up for himself a monument [commemorating his victory], then he turned and went on and went down to Gilgal."

¹³So Samuel came to Saul, and Saul said to him, "Blessed are you of the Lord. I have carried out the command of the Lord."

¹⁴But Samuel said, "What then is this bleating of the sheep in my ears, and the lowing of the oxen which I hear?"

¹⁵Saul said, "They have brought them from the Amalekites, for the people spared the best of the sheep and oxen to sacrifice to the Lord your God; but the rest we have destroyed completely."

¹⁶Then Samuel said to Saul, "Stop, and let me tell you what the Lord said to me last night." Saul said to him, "Speak."

¹⁷Samuel said, "Is it not true that even though you were small (insignificant) in your own eyes, you were *made* the head of the tribes of Israel? And the Lord anointed you king over Israel,

¹⁸and the Lord sent you on a mission, and said, 'Go, totally destroy the sinners, the Amalekites, and fight against them until they are eliminated.'

¹⁹"Why did you not obey the voice of the Lord, but [instead] swooped down on the plunder [with shouts of victory] and did evil in the sight of the Lord?"

²⁰Saul said to Samuel, "I have obeyed the voice of the Lord, and have gone

on the mission on which the Lord sent me, and have brought back Agag the king of Amalek, and have completely destroyed the Amalekites.

²¹"But the people took some of the spoil, sheep and oxen, the best of the things [that were] to be totally destroyed, to sacrifice to the Lord your God at Gilgal."

²²Samuel said,

"Has the Lord as great a delight in burnt offerings and sacrifices
As in obedience to the voice of the Lord?
Behold, to obey is better than sacrifice,
And to heed [is better] than the fat of rams.
²³"For rebellion is as [serious as] the sin of divination (fortune-telling),
And disobedience is as [serious as] false religion and idolatry.
Because you have rejected the word of the Lord,
He also has rejected you as king."

²⁴Then Saul said to Samuel, "I have sinned; for I have transgressed

obedience is better than sacrifice

When the Lord called me into ministry, He asked me to quit my job, trust Him to provide what we needed above my husband's salary, and spend my time preparing for my future teaching ministry. I struggled tremendously with the thought of not working, and, frankly, I was frightened by it. I had been working since I was thirteen years old and was accustomed to taking care of myself. Out of fear, I decided to quit my full-time job and get a part-time job, instead of stopping work altogether as God had asked me to do. I only had that job for a short while before I was fired. I was normally a good employee and not the type who would be fired. Actually, the reason for my being fired was not related to my work; the office manager did not like me personally. I had disobeyed God, and He had withheld His favor in that job situation. I had tried to partially obey God and still needed to learn that obedience is not true obedience unless it is complete.

Like Saul, I had given a sacrifice instead of obedience (see 1 Samuel 15:22). God led me to quit my job, and I did, but I got a part-time job to replace it. My part-time job represented part-time obedience. So often we think we can bargain with God, but it never works. There is only one way, and that is His way. It is all or nothing!

The Lord is very clear about disobedience. He says it is rebellion and some Bible translations say that rebellion is like witchcraft (see 1 Samuel 15:23). We may think our ideas are better than God's, but He calls this attitude stubbornness and says it is equivalent to idolatry. Why idolatry? Because we are idolizing our own ideas, exalting them above God's command.

Saul rebelled and lost the opportunity to be king. I wonder how many people think they are obeying God when actually they are offering Him an unacceptable sacrifice. Those same people live miserable, unfulfilled lives and often blame God for what really is their own doing.

God requires prompt, complete obedience; nothing less is acceptable. We may feel that some of the things He asks us to do are too hard, but we must remember that He promises to give us grace to do whatever He asks of us; we only need to be willing.

the command of the LORD and your words, because I feared the people and obeyed their voice.

²⁵"Now, please, pardon my sin and return with me, so that I may worship the LORD."

²⁶But Samuel said to Saul, "I will not return with you; for you have rejected the word of the LORD, and the LORD has rejected you from being king over Israel."

²⁷As Samuel turned to go [away], *Saul* grabbed the hem of his robe [to stop him], and it tore.

²⁸So Samuel said to him, "The LORD has torn the kingdom of Israel from you today and has given it to your neighbor, who is better than you.

²⁹"Also the Splendor *and* Glory *and* Eminence of Israel will not lie or change His mind; for He is not a man that He should change His mind."

breaking the cycle of abuse and rebellion

First Samuel 15:23 teaches us that "rebellion is as [serious as] the sin of divination (fortune-telling)." I believe a great deal of rebellion is the result of abuse. When a person has been repeatedly hurt by others, there usually comes a time when he makes up his mind, "Nobody is ever going to push me around again. As long as I live, nobody is going to tell me what to do. Why should I submit to somebody I can't trust to do what's best for me? From now on, I'm going to look out for myself and make my own decisions."

So often, the end result of abuse is willfulness, stubbornness, and rebellion. I know from my own bitter experience that being subjected to continual abuse has a lasting effect on a strong-willed person. It was a nightmare for someone of my personality type to be controlled and manipulated for years on end. In my case, I submitted to the Lord, and He used that experience to make me strong for ministry so I could help others caught in similar situations.

The sad thing is that once people do manage to escape from an abusive environment, the effects of that abuse do not suddenly end. Many times, hurting, wounded people are drawn to other hurting, wounded people. Victims of long-term abuse often marry other such victims. The result is that they end up hurting and wounding each other. Their children pick up the tendency to abuse and pass it on from one generation to the next. The abusive tendency will go on until someone stops it with God's help.

Do you desire to break free from the pattern of abuse and rebellion? You do not have to end up like Saul. You can choose to follow God and His way rather than mindlessly following after your feelings and emotions. Boldly declare: "That's enough! This curse of abuse is not going any further! It is stopping right here!" Choose God's way, apply the victory that Jesus won at the cross to your life, and watch Him work for you.

You might feel that you have inherited some bad habits and character flaws through your bloodline, but the blood of Jesus, when applied to your life by faith, is able to erase the adverse effects of natural inheritance. Do not look back to your past and get stuck there; instead, look forward to the great future God has planned for you!

life point

Saul had his own ideas about things. One time when Samuel the prophet was correcting Saul for not doing what he had been instructed to do, Saul's reply was, "I said . . ." (1 Samuel 13:12). He then proceeded to express his idea of how he said things should have been done, because he thought that was the way they should be done (compare 1 Samuel 10:6–8 with 13:8–14). Samuel's answer to King Saul's attitude is in this verse: ". . . to obey is better than sacrifice" (1 Samuel 15:22).

How many of God's children fail to "reign as kings in life" (Romans 5:17, Amplified Classic) because they substitute what God really requires with what they think He wants? When faced with a point of obedience, it is dangerous for us to say, "I think this" or "I want that." Rather we need to ask God, "What do You want me to do?" and be obedient to what He says. If Jesus is not Lord of all, then He is not our Lord at all. He may be our Savior, but not our Lord and Master. Let God take His rightful place in your life, which is "first place" in everything.

³⁰Saul said, "I have sinned; but please honor me now before the elders of my people and before Israel, and go back with me, so that I may worship the LORD your God."

³¹So Samuel went back following Saul, and Saul worshiped the LORD.

³²Then Samuel said, "Bring me Agag, the king of the Amalekites." And Agag came to him cheerfully. And Agag said, "Surely the bitterness of death has come to an end."

³³Samuel said, "As your sword has made women childless, so shall your mother be childless among women." And Samuel cut Agag in pieces before the LORD in Gilgal.

³⁴Then Samuel went to Ramah, but Saul went up to his house in Gibeah of Saul.

³⁵Samuel did not see Saul again until the day of his death, for Samuel grieved over Saul. And the LORD regretted that He had made Saul king over Israel.

16 THE LORD said to Samuel, "How long will you grieve for Saul, when I have rejected him as king over Israel? Fill your horn with oil and go; I will send you to Jesse the Bethlehemite, for I have chosen a king for Myself among his sons."

²But Samuel said, "How can I go? When Saul hears *about it,* he will kill me." And the LORD said, "Take a heifer from the herd with you and say, 'I have come to sacrifice to the Lord.'

³"You shall invite Jesse to the sacrifice, and I will show you what you shall do [after that]; and you shall anoint for Me the one whom I designate."

⁴So Samuel did what the LORD said, and came to Bethlehem. And the elders of the city came trembling to meet him and said, "Do you come in peace?"

⁵And he said, "In peace; I have come to sacrifice to the LORD. Consecrate yourselves and come with me to the sacrifice." He also consecrated Jesse and his sons and invited them to the sacrifice.

⁶So it happened, when they had come, he looked at Eliab [the eldest son] and thought, "Surely the LORD's anointed is before Him."

⁷But the LORD said to Samuel, "Do not look at his appearance or at the height of his stature, because I have rejected him. For the LORD sees not as man sees; for man looks at the outward appearance, but the LORD looks at the heart."

⁸Then Jesse called Abinadab and had him pass before Samuel. But Samuel said, "The LORD has not chosen this one either."

⁹Next Jesse had Shammah pass by. And Samuel said, "The LORD has not chosen him either."

¹⁰Jesse had seven of his sons pass before Samuel. But Samuel said to Jesse, "The LORD has not chosen [any of] these."

¹¹Then Samuel said to Jesse, "Are all your sons here?" Jesse replied, "There is still one left, the youngest; he is tending the sheep." Samuel said to Jesse, "Send *word* and bring him; because we will not sit down [to eat the sacrificial meal] until he comes here."

¹²So Jesse sent *word* and brought him in. Now he had a ruddy complexion, with beautiful eyes and a handsome appearance. The LORD said [to Samuel], "Arise, anoint him; for this is he."

¹³Then Samuel took the horn of oil and anointed David in the presence of his brothers; and the Spirit of the LORD came mightily upon David from that day forward. And Samuel arose and went to Ramah.

¹⁴Now the Spirit of the LORD departed from Saul, and an evil spirit from the Lord tormented *and* terrified him.

¹⁵Saul's servants said to him, "Behold, an evil spirit from God is tormenting you.

¹⁶"Let our lord now command your servants who are here before you to find a man who plays skillfully on the harp; and when the evil spirit from God is on you, he shall play *the harp* with his hand, and you will be well."

¹⁷So Saul told his servants, "Find me a man who plays well and bring him to me."

¹⁸One of the young men said, "Behold, I have seen a son of Jesse the Bethlehemite who is a skillful musician, a brave *and* competent man, a warrior, discerning (prudent, eloquent) in speech, and a handsome man; and the LORD is with him."

¹⁹So Saul sent messengers to Jesse and said, "Send me David your son, who is with the flock."

²⁰Jesse took a donkey [loaded with] bread and a jug of wine and a young goat, and sent them to Saul with David his son.

²¹Then David came to Saul and attended him. Saul loved him greatly and [later] David became his armor bearer.

²²Saul sent *word* to Jesse, saying, "Please let David be my attendant, for he has found favor in my sight."

life point

God is the God of hearts. He does not look at the exterior of a person—or even the things a person does—and judge an individual by that criterion. Man judges after the flesh, but 1 Samuel 16:7 teaches us that God judges according to the heart.

It is possible to put up a good front and still have a lousy heart. It is also possible to be dealing with personality problems or bad habits on the outside and still have a right heart on the inside. God is much more inclined to use a person with a good heart and a few problems than He is to use a person who appears to be perfect outwardly, but who has a wicked heart.

If we want to have success as a Christian or be used by God as a leader in His kingdom, it is important that we get in touch with our inner lives and our heart attitudes. Our motives, thoughts, and feelings need to be consistent with God's heart. Having a pure heart is vital. Start taking a regular inventory of your inner thoughts and attitudes, and work with the Holy Spirit to let the thoughts and attitudes of Jesus reside in you (see Philippians 2:5).

²³So it came about that whenever the [evil] spirit from God was on Saul, David took a harp and played it with his hand; so Saul would be refreshed and be well, and the evil spirit would leave him.

17 NOW THE Philistines gathered their armies for battle and were assembled at Socoh, which belongs to Judah; and they camped between Socoh and Azekah, in Ephes-dammim.

²Saul and the men of Israel were gathered together and they camped in the Valley of Elah, and assembled in battle formation to meet the Philistines.

³The Philistines were standing on the mountain on one side and Israel was standing on the mountain on the other side, with the valley between them.

⁴Then a champion came out from the camp of the Philistines named Goliath of Gath, whose height was six cubits and a span.

⁵*He had* a bronze helmet on his head, and wore a coat of scale-armor (overlapping metal plates) which weighed 5,000 shekels of bronze.

⁶*He had* bronze shin protectors on his legs and a bronze javelin hung between his shoulders.

⁷The [wooden] shaft of his spear was like a weaver's beam; the blade-head of his spear *weighed* six hundred shekels of iron. And a shield-bearer walked in front of him.

⁸Goliath stood and shouted to the battle lines of Israel, saying to them, "Why have you come out to draw up for battle? Am I not the Philistine and are you not servants of Saul? Choose a man for yourselves and have him come down to me.

⁹"If he is able to fight with me and kill me, then we will become your servants; but if I prevail against him and kill him, then you shall become our servants and serve us."

¹⁰Again the Philistine said, "I defy the battle lines of Israel this day; give me a man so that we may fight together."

¹¹When Saul and all Israel heard these words of the Philistine, they were dismayed and greatly afraid.

¹²Now David was the son of the Ephrathite of Bethlehem in Judah, named Jesse, who had eight sons. Jesse was old in the days of Saul, advanced *in years* among men.

¹³His three older sons had followed Saul into battle. The names of his three sons who went to battle were Eliab, the firstborn; next, Abinadab; and third, Shammah.

¹⁴David was the youngest. Now the three oldest followed Saul,

¹⁵but David went back and forth from Saul to tend his father's flock at Bethlehem.

¹⁶The Philistine [Goliath] came out morning and evening, and took his stand for forty days.

¹⁷Then Jesse said to David his son, "Take for your brothers an ephah of this roasted grain and these ten loaves of bread and run quickly to the camp to your brothers.

¹⁸"Also take these ten cuts of cheese to the commander of the unit. See how your brothers are doing and bring back news of them.

¹⁹"Now they are with Saul and all the men of Israel in the Valley of Elah, fighting with the Philistines."

²⁰So David got up early in the morning, left the flock with a keeper, picked up *the provisions* and went just as Jesse had directed him. And he came to the encampment as the army was going out in battle formation shouting the battle cry.

²¹Israel and the Philistines drew up in battle formation, army against army.

²²Then David left his provisions in the care of the supply keeper, and ran to the ranks and came and greeted his brothers.

²³As he was talking with them, behold, the champion, the Philistine of Gath named Goliath, was coming up from the army of the Philistines, and he spoke these same words *again;* and David heard *him*.

²⁴When the men of Israel all saw the man, they fled from him, and were very frightened.

²⁵The men of Israel said, "Have you seen this man who is coming up? Surely he is coming up to defy Israel. The king will reward the man who kills him with great riches, and will give him his daughter [in marriage] and make his father's house (family) free [from taxes and service] in Israel."

²⁶Then David spoke to the men who

reject rejection

David believed that with God's help, he could slay the giant Goliath, but his brother Eliab accused him of presumption and having an evil heart (see 1 Samuel 17:28). Eliab's accusation came from a jealous attitude toward David. He tried to make David feel small and worthless. David was a wise young man, and his response to Eliab was an important key to his future: "David turned away from Eliab" (1 Samuel 17:30).

When we take a step of faith to do something for God or to help hurting people, Satan attacks. He often works through someone we love to make us feel worthless, rejected, unacceptable, inept, or out of place. We must stand against these attacks and keep our eyes on God and His direction to us. God fills our hearts with faith, enabling us to believe He can use us, but Satan comes against us with fears—often with fears about ourselves and our abilities.

David's older brothers did not include David in the things they did because they thought he was too young, and they probably were jealous of him. As a result, I am sure he felt rejected. Many times God will choose to use people who have felt rejected and been excluded. He selects those whom society would reject in order to show Himself strong. He also purposely chooses what the world would call "weak and foolish" so no one takes the credit that is due to Him alone (see 1 Corinthians 1:26–29).

If you have been rejected or treated badly, I encourage you to do as David did. Turn away from it! Forgive your enemies, and do not let offense fill your heart. Do not pay attention to what the devil is trying to do; keep your eyes on God and follow His instructions. Yes, God can use you to do great things. God is looking for someone with *availability* more than He is looking for someone with *ability*. He is not looking for someone with perfect attributes, but someone with a perfect heart toward Him. Keep your heart pure by refusing to allow hatred, strife, offense, bitterness, resentment, or unforgiveness to dwell in it.

Always believe what God says about you instead of believing your own feelings about yourself or believing what others have to say. God says you belong to Him. He loves you and will work through you if you will simply let Him. You are special to God. You have infinite worth and value. Perhaps the world would not consider you usable material for God, but He sees differently than the world does. Say, "Here I am God, use me," and watch Him go to work!

were standing by him, "What will be done for the man who kills this Philistine and removes the disgrace [of his taunting] from Israel? For who is this uncircumcised Philistine that he has taunted *and* defied the armies of the living God?"

²⁷The men told him, "That is what will be done for the man who kills him."

²⁸Now Eliab his oldest brother heard what he said to the men; and Eliab's anger burned against David and he said, "Why have you come down here? With whom did you leave those few sheep in the wilderness? I know your presumption (overconfidence) and the

life point

When David volunteered to go out and fight the giant Goliath, nobody encouraged him. Everyone told him, "You're too young. You don't have the right armor or weapons. He's much bigger and more experienced than you are," and on and on. Even King Saul questioned David's ability to overcome the boastful Philistine (see 1 Samuel 17:33). But David encouraged himself by recounting the victories God had given him in the past.

If you want to do something for God, it's important to understand that there will be hundreds, maybe thousands of times when Satan will come against you to discourage you. Why? Because he knows you must have courage to go forward and fulfill God's good plan for your life. When you become discouraged, you become weak and lose the courage you need to go forward. What must you do in times of discouragement? Shake it off in faith and recount the victories God has already given you. Have confidence that He will be strong in your weakness and use you for His glory.

evil of your heart; for you have come down in order to see the battle."

²⁹But David said, "What have I done now? Was it not just a [harmless] question?"

³⁰Then David turned away from Eliab to someone else and asked the same question; and the people gave him the same answer as the first time.

³¹When the words that David spoke were heard, the men reported them to Saul, and he sent for him.

³²David said to Saul, "Let no man's courage fail because of him (Goliath). Your servant will go out and fight with this Philistine."

³³Then Saul said to David, "You are not able to go against this Philistine to fight him. For you are [only] a young man and he has been a warrior since his youth."

³⁴But David said to Saul, "Your servant was tending his father's sheep. When a lion or a bear came and took a lamb out of the flock,

³⁵I went out after it and attacked it and rescued the lamb from its mouth; and when it rose up against me, I seized it by its whiskers and struck and killed it.

³⁶"Your servant has killed both the lion and the bear; and this uncircumcised Philistine will be like one of them, since he has taunted *and* defied the armies of the living God."

³⁷David said, "The Lᴏʀᴅ who rescued me from the paw of the lion and from the paw of the bear, He will rescue me from the hand of this Philistine." And Saul said to David, "Go, and may the Lᴏʀᴅ be with you."

³⁸Then Saul dressed David in his garments and put a bronze helmet on his head, and put a coat of mail (armor) on him.

³⁹Then David fastened his sword over his armor and tried to walk, [but he could not,] because he was not used to them. And David said to Saul, "I

cannot go with these, because I am not used to them." So David took them off.

⁴⁰Then he took his [shepherd's] staff in his hand and chose for himself five smooth stones out of the stream bed, and put them in his shepherd's bag which he had, that is, in his shepherd's pouch. With his sling in his hand, he approached the Philistine.

⁴¹The Philistine came and approached David, with his shield-bearer in front of him.

⁴²When the Philistine looked around and saw David, he derided *and* disparaged him because he was [just] a young man, with a ruddy *complexion,* and a handsome appearance.

⁴³The Philistine said to David, "Am I a dog, that you come to me with [shepherd's] staffs?" And the Philistine cursed David by his gods.

⁴⁴The Philistine also said to David, "Come to me, and I will give your flesh to the birds of the sky and the beasts of the field."

⁴⁵Then David said to the Philistine, "You come to me with a sword, a spear, and a javelin, but I come to you in the name of the Lord of hosts, the God of the armies of Israel, whom you have taunted.

⁴⁶"This day the Lord will hand you over to me, and I will strike you down and cut off your head. And I will give the corpses of the army of the Philistines this day to the birds of the sky and the wild beasts of the earth, so that all the earth may know that there is a God in Israel,

⁴⁷and that this entire assembly may know that the Lord does not save with the sword or with the spear; for the battle is the Lord's and He will hand you over to us."

life point

When young David looked at the giant, he "ran quickly toward the battle line" (1 Samuel 17:48). I think David knew that if he thought too long about Goliath, he might run away. He took action and obeyed God immediately, and we need to always do the same. When God prompts you to take action, run to do it. His grace will be present to help you. Do not procrastinate! Frequently, those who do put things off never get around to obeying God. They have good intentions to do what God has asked of them at the right time, but, sadly, the "right time" never seems to come, and they lose out merely because they did not take faith-filled action at the right time.

⁴⁸When the Philistine rose and came forward to meet David, David ran quickly toward the battle line to meet the Philistine.

⁴⁹David put his hand into his bag and took out a stone and slung it, and it struck the Philistine on his forehead. The stone penetrated his forehead, and he fell face down on the ground.

⁵⁰So David triumphed over the Philistine with a sling and a stone, and he struck down the Philistine and killed him; but there was no sword in David's hand.

⁵¹So he ran and stood over the Philistine, grasped his sword and drew it out of its sheath and killed him, and cut off his head with it. When the Philistines saw that their [mighty] champion was dead, they fled.

⁵²The men of Israel and Judah stood with a shout and pursued the Philistines as far as the entrance to the

speak the Word

Thank You, God, that in my battles You will hand my enemies over to me.
—ADAPTED FROM 1 SAMUEL 17:47

valley and the gates of Ekron. And the [fatally] wounded Philistines fell along the way to Shaaraim, even as far as Gath and Ekron. ⁵³The sons of Israel returned from their pursuit of the Philistines and plundered their camp.

⁵⁴Then David took the head of the Philistine and brought it to Jerusalem, but he put his weapons in his tent.

⁵⁵When Saul saw David going out against the Philistine, he said to Abner the captain of the army, "Abner, whose son is this young man?" And Abner answered, "By your life, O king, I do not know."

⁵⁶The king said, "Ask whose son the young man is."

⁵⁷When David returned from killing [Goliath] the Philistine, Abner took him and brought him before Saul with the head of the Philistine in his hand.

⁵⁸Saul asked him, "Whose son are you, young man?" And David answered, "I am the son of your servant Jesse of Bethlehem."

18 WHEN DAVID had finished speaking to Saul, the soul of Jonathan was bonded to the soul of David, and Jonathan loved him as himself.

²Saul took David that day and did not let him return to his father's house.

³Then Jonathan made a covenant with David because he loved him as himself.

⁴Jonathan stripped himself of the outer robe that he was wearing and

putting the Word to work

David and Jonathan were truly great friends to one another (see 1 Samuel 18:3). Do you have a great friend, someone you love as much as you love your own life? Thank God for that person today.

gave it to David, with his armor, including his sword, his bow, and his belt.

⁵So David went out wherever Saul sent him, and he acted wisely *and* prospered; and Saul appointed him over the men of war. And it pleased all the people and also Saul's servants.

⁶As they were coming [home], when David returned from killing the Philistine, the women came out of all the

life point

One day I just happened to notice 1 Samuel 18:5, and I underlined it in my Bible. David was a man who was anointed to be king, yet he was put in the household of Saul for some training and some crucifixion of the flesh.

Anyone who is anointed for leadership has to be around a person like Saul sometime in his life. God uses the "Sauls" in our lives to get the "Saul" out of us. God tends to put us around someone who is like sandpaper to smooth off our rough edges.

It's important we grasp this truth: *Just because we are anointed for leadership does not mean that we get to move immediately into a position of leadership.* There is a work that has to be done in us, a testing that has to take place before we get promoted.

After I had noticed and underlined this verse about David's serving under King Saul, my attention was drawn to verse 14, which says, "David acted wisely and prospered in all his ways, and the LORD was with him." Why did David succeed? Not just because he was anointed, but also because he acted wisely and allowed the Lord to be with him. If we want to lead, we must first serve in circumstances that may not be ideal and learn to behave wisely. This prepares us to be greatly used by God.

cities of Israel, singing and dancing, to meet King Saul with tambourines, [songs of] joy, and musical instruments.

⁷The women sang as they played *and* danced, saying,

"Saul has slain his thousands,
And David his ten thousands."

⁸Then Saul became very angry, for this saying displeased him; and he said, "They have ascribed to David ten thousands, but to me they have ascribed [only] thousands. Now what more can he have but the kingdom?"

⁹Saul looked at David with suspicion [and jealously] from that day forward.

¹⁰Now it came about on the next day that an evil spirit from God came forcefully on Saul, and he raved [madly] inside his house, while David was playing *the harp* with his hand, as usual; and there was a spear in Saul's hand.

¹¹Saul hurled the spear, for he thought, "I will pin David to the wall." But David evaded him twice.

¹²Now Saul was afraid of David, because the Lord was with him, but had departed from Saul.

¹³So Saul had David removed from his presence and appointed him as his commander of a thousand; and he publicly associated with the people.

¹⁴David acted wisely *and* prospered in all his ways, and the Lord was with him.

¹⁵When Saul saw that he was prospering greatly, he was afraid of him.

¹⁶But all Israel and Judah loved David, because he publicly associated with them.

¹⁷Then Saul said to David, "Behold I will give you my older daughter Merab as a wife; only be brave for me and fight the Lord's battles." For Saul thought, "My hand shall not be against him, but let the hand of the Philistines be against him."

¹⁸David said to Saul, "Who am I, and what is my life or my father's family in Israel, that I should be the king's son-in-law?"

¹⁹But at the time when Merab, Saul's daughter, should have been given to David, she was [instead] given to Adriel the Meholathite as a wife.

²⁰Now Michal, Saul's daughter, loved David; and when they told Saul, it pleased him.

²¹Saul said, "I will give her to him so that she may become a snare (bad influence, source of trouble) to him, and that the hand of the Philistines may be against him." So Saul said to David for a second time, "You shall be my son-in-law today."

²²Then Saul commanded his servants, "Speak to David secretly, saying, 'Listen, the king delights in you, and all his servants love you; now then, become the king's son-in-law.'"

²³So Saul's servants spoke these words to David. But David said, "Is it a trivial thing in your sight to become a king's son-in-law, seeing that I am a poor man and insignificant?"

²⁴The servants of Saul told him what David said.

²⁵Then Saul said, "This is what you shall say to David: 'The king wants no dowry except a hundred foreskins of the Philistines, to take vengeance on the king's enemies.'" Now Saul's intention was to cause David's death at the hand of the Philistines.

²⁶When his servants told David these words, it pleased him to become

speak the Word

God, I pray that I will act wisely and prosper in all my ways, and that You will be with me.
—adapted from 1 Samuel 18:14

the king's son-in-law. Before the time [for the marriage] arrived, ²⁷David arose and went, he and his men, and killed two hundred Philistine men, and David brought their foreskins [as proof of death] and presented every one of them to the king, so that he might become the king's son-in-law. So Saul gave him Michal, his [younger] daughter, as a wife. ²⁸When Saul saw and knew that the LORD was with David, and that Michal, his daughter, loved him, ²⁹Saul was even more afraid of David; and Saul became David's constant enemy. ³⁰Then the Philistine commanders (princes) came out *to battle,* and it happened as often as they did, that David acted more wisely *and* had more success than all Saul's servants. So his name was highly esteemed.

putting the Word to work

Is there anyone who treats you as a "constant enemy" (1 Samuel 18:29), as Saul treated David? Remember the Bible's instructions about enemies: forgive them, love them, and pray for them (see Matthew 5:44).

19 NOW SAUL told his son Jonathan and all his servants to kill David, but Jonathan, Saul's son, greatly delighted in David. ²So he told David, "Saul my father is seeking to kill you. Now then, please be on guard in the morning, and stay in a secret place and hide yourself. ³"As for me, I will go out and stand beside my father in the field where you are, and I will speak with my father about you, and if I learn anything, then I will tell you." ⁴Then Jonathan spoke well of David to Saul his father and said to him,

"May the king not sin against his servant David, since he has not sinned against you, and since his deeds have been very beneficial to you. ⁵"For he took his life in his hand and killed the Philistine, and the LORD brought about a great victory for all Israel; you saw it and rejoiced. Why then would you sin against innocent blood by killing David without a cause?" ⁶Saul listened to Jonathan and swore [an oath], "As the LORD lives, he shall not be put to death." ⁷So Jonathan called David and told him all these things. And Jonathan brought David to Saul, and he was in his presence [serving him] as previously. ⁸Then there was war again, and David went out and fought with the Philistines and defeated them with a great slaughter, and they fled before him. ⁹Then an evil spirit from the LORD came on Saul as he was sitting in his house with his spear in his hand, and David was playing the harp with his hand. ¹⁰Saul tried to pin David to the wall with the spear, but he escaped from Saul's presence, so that Saul only stuck the spear into the wall. Then David fled and escaped that night. ¹¹Then Saul sent messengers to David's house to watch for him, so that he might kill him in the morning. But Michal, David's wife, told him, "If you do not save your life tonight, tomorrow you will be killed." ¹²So Michal let David down through the window, and he fled and escaped. ¹³And Michal took the household idol and laid it on the bed, put a pillow of goats' *hair* at its head, and covered it with clothes. ¹⁴And when Saul sent messengers to take David, she said, "He is sick." ¹⁵Then Saul sent the messengers [again] to see David, saying, "Bring him up to me on his bed [if necessary], so that I may kill him."

¹⁶When the messengers came in, there was the household idol on the bed with a quilt of goats' *hair* at its head.

¹⁷Saul said to Michal, "Why have you deceived me like this and let my enemy go, so that he has escaped?" Michal answered Saul, "He said to me, 'Let me go! Why should I kill you?'"

¹⁸So David fled and escaped and came to Samuel at Ramah, and told him everything that Saul had done to him. And he and Samuel went and stayed in Naioth.

¹⁹Saul was told, "David is at Naioth in Ramah."

²⁰Then Saul sent messengers to take David; but when they saw the group of prophets prophesying, and Samuel standing and presiding over them, the Spirit of God came on the messengers of Saul; and they also prophesied.

²¹When Saul was informed, he sent other messengers, and they also prophesied. So Saul sent messengers again, the third time, and they prophesied as well.

²²Then Saul went to Ramah himself and came to the great well that is in Secu; and he asked, "Where are Samuel and David?" And he was told, "They are at Naioth [with the prophets] in Ramah."

²³So he went on to Naioth in Ramah; and the Spirit of God came upon him too, and he went along continually prophesying until he came to Naioth in Ramah.

²⁴He also took off his [royal] robes [and armor] and prophesied before Samuel and lay down naked all that day and night. So they say, "Is Saul also among the prophets?" [1 Sam 10:10]

20 DAVID FLED from Naioth in Ramah and he came and said to Jonathan, "What have I done? What is my guilt? What is my sin before (against) your father, that he is seeking my life?"

²Jonathan said to him, "Far from it! You shall not die. My father does nothing important or insignificant without telling me. So why would he hide this thing from me? It is not so!"

³But David vowed again, saying "Your father certainly knows that I have found favor in your sight, and he has said, 'Do not let Jonathan know this, or he will be worried.' But truly as the LORD lives and as your soul lives, there is hardly a step between me and death."

⁴Then Jonathan said to David, "Whatever you say, I will do for you."

⁵David said to Jonathan, "Behold, tomorrow is the New Moon [observance], and I should sit at the table to eat [the sacrificial meal] with the king; but let me go, so that I may hide myself in the field until the third evening.

⁶"If your father misses me at all, then say, 'David earnestly asked *permission* from me to go to Bethlehem, his city, because it is the yearly sacrifice there for the entire family.'

⁷"If he says, 'All right,' your servant will be safe; but if he is very angry, then be certain that he has decided on evil.

⁸"Therefore show kindness to your servant, because you have brought your servant into a covenant of the LORD with you. But if there is iniquity (guilt) in me, kill me yourself; for why should you bring me to your father [to be killed]?"

⁹Jonathan said, "Far be it from [happening to] you! In fact, if I indeed learn that my father has decided to harm you, would I not tell you about it?"

¹⁰Then David said to Jonathan, "Who will tell me if your father answers you harshly?"

¹¹Jonathan said to David, "Come, let us go out into the field [to talk]." So they went out to the field.

¹²Then Jonathan said to David, "The LORD, the God of Israel, *is my witness!* When I have sounded out my father about this time tomorrow, or the third

day, behold, if he has a good *feeling* toward you, shall I not then send *word* to you and make it known to you?

¹³"But if it pleases my father *to do* you harm, may the LORD do so to Jonathan, and more if I do not let you know about it and send you away, so that you may go in safety. And may the LORD be with you as He has been with my father.

¹⁴"If I am still alive, will you not show me the lovingkindness *and* faithfulness of the LORD, so that I will not die?

¹⁵"You shall never cut off your lovingkindness *and* faithfulness from my house, not even when the LORD cuts off every one of the enemies of David from the face of the earth."

¹⁶So Jonathan made a *covenant* with the house of David. [He added,] "May the LORD require it at the hands of

life point

In ancient Israel, when two people entered into a covenant relationship, everything they possessed as individuals was made freely available to the other. The covenant relationship also meant that they would help one another, fight for one another, and do anything necessary to meet each other's needs.

David and Jonathan had a covenant relationship that included all of their descendants (see 1 Samuel 20:14–16; 18:3). We know from later chapters that Jonathan was killed and David became king. David kept the covenant he made with Jonathan by actively searching for Jonathan's heirs so that he could bless them. King David found Jonathan's son, brought him to the royal palace, and restored him (see 2 Samuel 9:1–13). Just as David honored his covenant with Jonathan, God will honor the covenant He makes with us. God is looking for someone He can bless for Jesus' sake. It can be you, if you are willing.

David's enemies. [that is, hold them accountable for any harm they inflict on David]."

¹⁷Jonathan made David vow again because of his love for him, for Jonathan loved him as himself.

¹⁸Then Jonathan said to David, "Tomorrow is the New Moon [festival], and you will be missed because your seat will be empty.

¹⁹"When you have stayed for three days, you shall go down quickly and come to the place where you hid yourself on that eventful day [when my father tried to kill you], and shall stay by the stone Ezel.

²⁰"I will shoot three arrows to the side of it, as though I shot at a target.

²¹"And I will send a boy, *saying,* 'Go, find the arrows.' If I specifically say to the boy, 'Look, the arrows are on this side of you, get them,' then come [back to my father's table]; for it is safe for you and there is no danger, as the LORD lives.

²²"But if I say to the boy, 'Look, the arrows are beyond you,' then go, for the LORD has sent you away.

²³"As for the agreement of which you and I have spoken, behold, the LORD is between you and me forever [making sure that we each keep our word]."

²⁴So David hid in the field; and when the New Moon [festival] came, the king sat down to eat food.

²⁵The king sat on his seat as on previous occasions, on his seat by the wall; then Jonathan stood up, and Abner [his commander] sat down by Saul's side, but David's place was empty.

²⁶Yet Saul did not say anything that day, for he thought, "It is an incident [of some kind] and he is not [ceremonially] clean—surely he is unclean."

²⁷But on the next day, the second *day* of the new moon, David's place was empty [again]; and Saul said to Jonathan his son, "Why has the son of Jesse not come to the meal, either yesterday or today?"

²⁸Jonathan answered Saul, "David

earnestly asked me for permission *to go* to Bethlehem.

²⁹He said, 'Please let me go because our family is holding a sacrifice in the city, and my brother has commanded me to attend. Now, if I have found favor in your eyes, please let me slip away so that I may see my brothers.' That is why he has not come to the king's table."

³⁰Then Saul's anger burned against Jonathan and he said to him, "You son of a wayward, rebellious woman! Do I not know that you have chosen the son of Jesse [over me] to your own shame, and to the shame of your mother's nakedness?

³¹"For as long as the son of Jesse lives on the earth, neither you [as heir to the throne] nor your kingdom will be established. So now, send [someone] and bring him to me, for he must die."

³²Jonathan answered Saul his father, "Why must he be put to death? What has he done?"

³³Then Saul hurled his spear at him to strike him down, so Jonathan knew [without any doubt] that his father had decided to put David to death.

³⁴Then Jonathan stood up from the table in the heat of anger, and ate no food on that second day of the new moon (month), for he grieved *and* worried about David because his father had dishonored him.

³⁵In the morning Jonathan went out to the field for the meeting with David, and a young boy was with him.

³⁶And he said to his boy, "Run, please find the arrows which I am about to shoot." As the boy ran, he shot an arrow past him.

³⁷When the boy came to the place where Jonathan had shot the arrow, Jonathan called to him, "Is the arrow not beyond you?"

³⁸And Jonathan called out after the boy, "Hurry, be quick, do not stay!" So Jonathan's boy picked up the arrow and came back to his master.

³⁹But the boy was not aware of anything; only Jonathan and David knew about the matter.

⁴⁰Jonathan gave his weapons to his boy and said to him, "Go, take them to the city."

⁴¹As soon as the boy was gone, David got up from the south side [beside the mound of stones] and fell on his face to the ground [in submission and respect], and bowed three times. Then they kissed one another and wept together, but David *wept* more.

⁴²Jonathan told David, "Go in safety, inasmuch as we have sworn to each other in the name of the LORD, saying, 'The LORD shall be between me and you, and between my descendants and yours forever.'" Then he stood and left, while Jonathan went into the city.

21 THEN DAVID went to Nob to Ahimelech the priest; and Ahimelech came trembling [in fear] to meet David and said to him, "Why are you alone, and no one with you?"

²David said to Ahimelech the priest, "The king has commissioned me with a matter and has told me, 'Let no one know anything about the matter for which I am sending you and with which I have commissioned you. I have directed the young men to a certain place.'

³"Now what [food] do you have on hand? Give me five loaves of bread, or whatever can be found."

⁴The priest answered David, "There is no ordinary (unconsecrated) bread on hand, but there is consecrated bread; [you may have it] if only the young men have kept themselves from women."

⁵David answered the priest, "Be assured that women have been kept from us in these three days since I set out, and the bodies of the young men were consecrated (ceremonially

clean), although it was an ordinary (unconsecrated) journey; so how much more will their vessels be holy today?"

⁶So the priest gave him the consecrated *bread;* for there was no bread there except the bread of the Presence which was removed from before the LORD in order to put hot bread *in its place* when it was taken away.

⁷Now one of Saul's servants was there that day, detained before the LORD; his name was Doeg the Edomite, the chief of Saul's shepherds.

⁸David said to Ahimelech, "Do you not have a sword or spear here on hand? For I brought neither my sword nor my [other] weapons with me, because the king's business was urgent."

⁹Then the priest said, "The sword of Goliath the Philistine, whom you killed in the Valley of Elah, is here wrapped in a cloth behind the ephod; if you would take it for yourself, do so. For there is no other here except for it." And David said, "There is none like that; give it to me."

¹⁰Then David arose and fled from Saul that day, and went to Achish king of Gath.

¹¹The servants of Achish said to him, "Is this not David the king of the land? Did they not sing in praise of this one as they danced, saying,

'Saul has slain his thousands,
And David his ten thousands'?"

¹²David took these words to heart and was greatly afraid of Achish king of Gath.

¹³So [fearing for his life] he changed his behavior in their sight, and acted insanely in their hands, and he scribbled on the doors of the gate, and drooled on his beard.

¹⁴Then Achish said to his servants, "Look, you see that the man is insane. Why have you brought him to me?

¹⁵"Do I lack madmen, that you bring this one to behave like a madman in my presence? Shall this one come into my house?"

22 SO DAVID departed from there and escaped to the cave of Adullam; and when his brothers and all his father's house heard about it, they went down there to him.

²Everyone who was suffering hardship, and everyone who was in debt, and everyone who was discontented gathered to him; and he became captain over them. There were about four hundred men with him.

³And David went from there to Mizpah of Moab; and he said to the king of Moab, "Please let my father and my mother come [out of Judah] and stay with you until I know what God will do for me."

⁴Then he left them with the king of Moab; and they stayed with him all the time that David was in the stronghold.

⁵Then the prophet Gad said to David, "Do not stay in the stronghold; leave, and go into the land of Judah." So David left and went into the forest of Hereth.

⁶But Saul heard that David and the men who were with him had been discovered. Now Saul was in Gibeah, sitting under the tamarisk tree on the high place with his spear in his hand, and all his servants were standing around him.

⁷Saul said to his servants who were standing around him, "Listen now, you Benjamites! Will the son of Jesse also give every one of you fields and vineyards? Will he make you all commanders of thousands and hundreds?

⁸"For all of you have conspired against me so that no one informs me when my son [Jonathan] makes *a covenant* with the son of Jesse. None of you cares about me or informs me that my son has stirred up my servant

against me to lie in ambush, as *he does* this day?"

⁹Then Doeg the Edomite, who was standing with Saul's servants, replied, "I saw the son of Jesse coming to Nob, to Ahimelech [the priest] the son of Ahitub.

¹⁰"Ahimelech inquired of the LORD for him, and gave him provisions and the sword of Goliath the Philistine."

¹¹Then the king sent someone to call Ahimelech the priest, the son of Ahitub, and all his father's household, the priests who were at Nob; and all of them came to the king.

¹²Then Saul said, "Listen now, son of Ahitub." He replied, "Here I am [at your service], my lord."

¹³Saul said to him, "Why have you and the son of Jesse conspired against me, in that you have given him bread and a sword and have inquired of God for him, so he would rebel against me by lying in ambush, as *he does* this day?"

¹⁴Then Ahimelech answered the king, "And who among all your servants is as faithful *and* trustworthy as David, who is the king's son-in-law, and who is captain over your guard [and your confidant], and is honored in your house?

¹⁵"Did I *just* begin to inquire of God for him today? Far be it from me! Do not let the king impute any *guilt* to his servant or to any of the household of my father, for your servant knows nothing at all about this entire matter."

¹⁶But Saul said, "Be assured that you shall die, Ahimelech, you and all your father's household (extended family)."

¹⁷And the king said to the guards who stood around him, "Turn around and kill the priests of the LORD, because their loyalty also is with David, and because they knew that he was fleeing and did not inform me." But the servants of the king were not willing to put out their hands to attack the LORD's priests.

¹⁸So the king said to Doeg, "You turn around and attack the priests." And Doeg the Edomite turned and attacked the priests, and that day he killed eighty-five men who wore the [priest's] linen ephod.

¹⁹And he struck Nob the city of the priests with the edge of the sword, both men and women, children and infants; also *he struck* oxen and donkeys and sheep with the edge of the sword.

²⁰But one of the sons of Ahimelech the son of Ahitub, named Abiathar, escaped and fled to David.

²¹Abiathar told David that Saul had murdered the LORD's priests.

²²Then David said to Abiathar, "I knew that day, when Doeg the Edomite was there, that he would certainly tell Saul. I have brought about *the death* of everyone in your father's household (extended family).

²³"Stay with me; do not be afraid, for he who seeks my life seeks your life, but you are safe with me."

23

THEN THEY told David, saying, "Behold, the Philistines are fighting against Keilah and are plundering (robbing) the threshing floors [of the grain]."

²So David inquired of the LORD, saying, "Shall I go and attack these Philistines?" And the Lord said to David, "Go and attack the Philistines and save Keilah."

putting the Word to work

In 1 Samuel 23:2, and throughout the biblical accounts of David's life, we see that David "inquired of the LORD." Do you inquire of God when faced with a need or a decision, or do you run to your friends for advice? "Don't run to the phone; run to the throne," as I like to say. Remember that God cares for you, and He will answer when you inquire of Him.

457 1 Samuel 23:25

³But David's men said to him, "Listen, we are afraid here in Judah. How much more then if we go to Keilah against the battle lines of the Philistines?"

⁴Then David inquired of the LORD again. And the LORD answered him, "Arise, go down to Keilah, for I will hand over the Philistines to you."

⁵So David and his men went to Keilah and fought the Philistines; he drove away their cattle and struck them with a great slaughter. So David rescued the inhabitants of Keilah.

⁶When Abiathar the son of Ahimelech fled to David at Keilah, he came down with an ephod in his hand.

⁷Now when Saul was informed that David had come to Keilah, Saul said, "God has handed him over to me, for he shut himself in by entering a city that has double gates and bars."

⁸So Saul summoned all the people (soldiers) for war, to go down to Keilah to besiege David and his men.

⁹But David knew that Saul was plotting evil against him; and he said to Abiathar the priest, "Bring the ephod here."

¹⁰Then David said, "O LORD, the God of Israel, Your servant has heard for certain that Saul intends to come to Keilah, to destroy the city on my account.

¹¹"Will the men of Keilah hand me over to him? Will Saul come down just as Your servant has heard? O LORD, God of Israel, I pray, tell Your servant." And the LORD said, "He will come down."

¹²Then David asked, "Will the men of Keilah surrender me and my men to Saul?" The LORD said, "They will surrender you."

¹³Then David and his men, about six hundred, arose and left Keilah, and they went wherever they could go. When Saul was told that David had escaped from Keilah, he gave up the pursuit.

¹⁴David stayed in the wilderness in strongholds, in the hill country of the Wilderness of Ziph. Saul searched for him every day, but God did not hand David over to him.

¹⁵Now David became aware that Saul had come out to seek his life. David was in the Wilderness of Ziph [in the woods] at Horesh.

¹⁶And Jonathan, Saul's son, arose and went [into the woods] to David at Horesh, and encouraged him in God.

¹⁷He said to him, "Do not be afraid; the hand of my father Saul will not find you. You will be king over Israel and I will be second in command to you; my father Saul knows this too."

¹⁸So the two of them made a covenant before the LORD; and David stayed [in the woods] at Horesh and Jonathan went to his house.

¹⁹Then the Ziphites came to Saul at Gibeah, saying, "Is David not hiding with us in strongholds of Horesh, on the hill of Hachilah, which is south of Jeshimon?

²⁰"Now then, O king, come down [to Ziph] in accordance with all your heart's desire to do so [and capture him]; and our part shall be to hand him over to the king."

²¹Saul said, "May you be blessed by the LORD, because you have had compassion on me.

²²"Go now, be very persistent and investigate, and see where his haunt is and who has seen him there; for I am told he is very cunning.

²³"So look, and take note of all the places where he hides and come back to me with the established facts, then I will go with you. If he is [anywhere] in the land, I will search him out among all the thousands of Judah."

²⁴So they arose and went to Ziph ahead of Saul. Now David and his men were in the Wilderness of Maon, in the Arabah south of Jeshimon.

²⁵Then Saul and his men went to

search for him. When David was told *about it*, he went down to the rock and stayed [there] in the Wilderness of Maon. When Saul heard it, he pursued David in the Wilderness of Maon.

²⁶Saul went on one side of the mountain, and David and his men on the other side of the mountain. And David was hurrying to get away from Saul, for Saul and his men were surrounding David and his men to capture them.

²⁷But a messenger came to Saul, saying, "Hurry and come, because the Philistines have attacked the land."

²⁸So Saul returned from pursuing David and went to meet the Philistines; therefore they called that place the Rock of Escape.

²⁹David went up from there and stayed in the strongholds of Engedi.

24 WHEN SAUL returned from following the Philistines, he was told, "Behold, David is in the Wilderness of Engedi."

²Then Saul took three thousand chosen men out of all Israel and went to search for David and his men in front of the Rocks of the Wild Goats.

³On the way he came to the sheepfolds where there was a cave; and Saul went in to relieve himself. Now David and his men were sitting in the cave's innermost recesses.

⁴David's men said to him, "Behold, *this is* the day of which the LORD said to you, 'Behold, I will hand over your enemy to you, and you shall do to him as seems good to you.'" Then David arose [in the darkness] and stealthily cut off the hem (edge) of Saul's robe.

⁵Afterward, David's conscience bothered him because he had cut off the hem of Saul's *robe*.

⁶He said to his men, "The LORD forbid that I should do this thing to my master, the LORD's anointed, to put out my hand against him, since he is the anointed of the LORD."

⁷So David strongly rebuked his men with these words and did not let them rise up against Saul. Saul got up, left the cave and went on his way.

⁸Then David also got up afterward and went out of the cave and called after Saul, saying, "My lord the king!" And when Saul looked behind him, David bowed with his face to the ground and lay himself face down.

⁹David said to Saul, "Why do you listen to the words of men who say, 'David seeks to harm you?'

¹⁰"Behold, your eyes have seen today how the LORD had given you into my hand in the cave. Some told me to kill you, but I spared you; I said, 'I will not reach out my hand against my lord, for he is the LORD's anointed.'

¹¹"Look, my father! Indeed, see the hem of your robe in my hand! Since I cut off the hem of your robe and did not kill you, know and understand [without question] that there is no evil or treason in my hands. I have not sinned against you, though you are lying in wait to take my life.

¹²"May the LORD judge between me and you; and may the LORD avenge me on you; but my hand shall not be against you.

¹³"As the proverb of the ancients says, 'Out of the wicked comes wickedness'; but my hand shall not be against you.

¹⁴"After whom has the king of Israel come out? Whom do you pursue [with three thousand men]? A dead dog, a single flea?

¹⁵"May the LORD be the judge and render judgment between me and you; and may He see and plead my cause and vindicate me *by saving me* from your hand." [Ps 142]

¹⁶When David had finished saying these words to Saul, Saul said, "Is this your voice, my son David?" Then Saul raised his voice and wept.

¹⁷He said to David, "You are more

righteous *and* upright [in God's eyes] than I; for you have done good to me, but I have done evil to you.

[18]"You have declared today the good that you have done to me, for when the LORD put me into your hand, you did not kill me.

[19]"For if a man finds his enemy, will he let him go away unharmed? So may the LORD reward you with good in return for what you have done for me this day.

[20]"Now, behold, I know that you will certainly be king and that the kingdom of Israel will be established in your hand.

[21]"So now swear to me by the LORD that you will not cut off my descendants after me and that you will not destroy my name from my father's household (extended family)."

[22]David gave Saul his oath; and Saul went home, but David and his men went up to the mountain stronghold.

25 NOW SAMUEL died; and all Israel assembled and mourned for him, and they buried him at his house in Ramah. Then David left and went down to the Wilderness of Paran.

[2]Now *there was* a man in Maon whose business *and* possessions were in Carmel; and the man was very rich. He had three thousand sheep and a thousand goats, and he was shearing his sheep in Carmel

[3](now the man's name was Nabal and his wife's name was Abigail. She was intelligent and beautiful in appearance, but the man was harsh and evil in his dealings; he was a Calebite).

[4]David heard in the wilderness that Nabal was shearing his sheep.

[5]So David sent ten young men; and David said to the young men, "Go up to Carmel and go to Nabal, and greet him in my name;

[6]and this is what you shall say, 'Have a long life! Peace be to you, and peace to your house, and peace to all that you have.

[7]'Now I have heard that you have shearers. Now your shepherds have been with us and we have not harmed them, nor were they missing anything all the time they were in Carmel.

[8]'Ask your young men and they will tell you. Therefore let my young men find favor in your sight [and be well-treated], for we have come on a good (festive) day. Please, give whatever you find at hand to your servants and to your son David.' "

[9]When David's young men came, they spoke to Nabal according to all these words in the name of David; then they waited.

[10]But Nabal answered David's servants and said, "Who is David? And who is the son of Jesse? There are many servants today, each of whom is breaking away from his master.

[11]"So should I take my bread and my water and my meat that I have slaughtered for my shearers, and give it to men when I do not know where they are from?"

[12]So David's young men made their way back and returned; and they came and told him everything that was said [to them by Nabal].

[13]David said to his men, "Each man put on your sword." So each man put on his sword. David also put on his sword, and about four hundred men went up behind David while two hundred stayed *back* with the provisions and supplies.

[14]But one of *Nabal's* young men told Abigail, Nabal's wife, "Listen, David sent messengers out of the wilderness to bless (greet) our master, and he shouted at them [in contempt].

[15]"But *David's* men were very good to us, and we were not harmed *or* treated badly, nor did we miss anything as long as we were with them, when we were in the fields.

¹⁶"They were a wall [of protection] to us both night and day, all the time that we were with them tending the sheep.

¹⁷"Now then, know this and consider what you should do, for evil is [already] planned against our master and against all his household; but he is such a worthless *and* wicked man that one cannot speak [reasonably] to him."

¹⁸Then Abigail hurried and took two hundred *loaves* of bread, two jugs of wine, five sheep already prepared [for roasting], five measures of roasted grain, a hundred clusters of raisins, and two hundred cakes of figs, and loaded them on donkeys.

¹⁹She said to her young men (servants), "Go on ahead of me; behold, I am coming after you." But she did not tell her husband Nabal.

²⁰It happened that as she was riding on her donkey and coming down by [way of] the hidden part of the mountain, that suddenly David and his men were coming down toward her, and she met them.

²¹Now David had said, "Surely in vain I have protected *and* guarded all that this man has in the wilderness, so that nothing was missing of all that belonged to him; and he has repaid me evil for good.

²²"May God do so to the enemies of David, and more also, if by morning I leave [alive] even one male of any who belong to him."

²³When Abigail saw David, she hurried and dismounted from the donkey, and kneeled face downward before David and bowed down to the ground [in respect].

²⁴Kneeling at his feet she said, "My lord, let the blame *and* guilt be on me alone. And please let your maidservant speak to you, and listen to the words of your maidservant.

²⁵"Please do not let my lord pay attention to this worthless man, Nabal, for as his name is, so is he. Nabal (fool)

is his name and foolishness (stupidity) is with him; but I your maidservant did not see my lord's young men whom you sent.

²⁶"So now, my lord, as the LORD lives, and as your soul lives, since the LORD has prevented you from shedding blood, and from avenging yourself by your own hand, now then let your enemies and those who seek to do evil to my lord, be as [self-destructive as] Nabal.

²⁷"Now this gift, which your maidservant has brought my lord, let it be given to the young men who accompany *and* follow my lord.

²⁸"Please forgive the transgression of your maidservant; for the LORD will certainly make my lord a secure *and* enduring house, because my lord is fighting the battles of the LORD, and evil will not be found in you all your days.

²⁹"Should anyone rise up to pursue you and to seek your life, then the life of my lord will be bound in the [precious] bundle of the living with the LORD your God; but the lives of your enemies—those He will hurl out as from the center of a sling.

³⁰"And it will happen when the LORD does for my lord according to all the good that He has spoken (promised) concerning you, and appoints you ruler over Israel,

³¹that this [incident] will not cause grief or [bring] a troubled conscience to my lord, both by having shed blood without cause and by my lord having avenged himself. When the LORD deals well with my lord, then remember [with favor] your maidservant."

³²David said to Abigail, "Blessed be the LORD, the God of Israel, who sent you to meet me this day.

³³"And blessed be your discretion *and* discernment, and blessed be you, who has kept me from bloodshed this day and from avenging myself by my own hand.

³⁴"Nevertheless, as the Lᴏʀᴅ the God of Israel lives, who has prevented me from harming you, if you had not come quickly to meet me, most certainly by the morning light there would not have been left to Nabal so much as one male."

³⁵So David accepted what she had brought to him and said to her, "Go up to your house in peace. See, I have listened to you and have granted your request."

³⁶Then Abigail came to Nabal, and he was holding a feast in his house [for the shearers], like the feast of a king. And Nabal's mood was joyous because he was very drunk; so she told him nothing at all until the morning light.

³⁷But in the morning, when Nabal was sober, and his wife told him these things, his heart died within him and he became [paralyzed and helpless] like a stone.

³⁸About ten days later, the Lᴏʀᴅ struck Nabal and he died.

³⁹When David heard that Nabal was dead, he said, "Blessed be the Lᴏʀᴅ, who has pleaded the cause of my reproach [suffered] at the hand of Nabal and has kept His servant from [retaliating with] evil. For the Lord has returned the wickedness of Nabal on his own head." Then David sent word to Abigail, proposing to take her as his wife.

⁴⁰When the servants of David came to Abigail at Carmel, they said to her, "David sent us to you to take you [to him] to be his wife."

⁴¹And she stood and bowed with her face to the ground and said, "Behold, your maidservant is [ready to be] a maid to wash the feet of the servants of my lord."

⁴²Then Abigail quickly got up, and rode on a donkey, with five of her maidens who attended her; and she followed the messengers of David and became his wife.

⁴³David had also taken Ahinoam of Jezreel, and they both became his wives.

⁴⁴But Saul had given Michal his [younger] daughter, David's wife, to Palti the son of Laish, who was from Gallim.

26 THE ZIPHITES came to Saul at Gibeah, saying, "Is David not hiding on the hill of Hachilah, *east of* Jeshimon?"

²So Saul arose and went down to the Wilderness of Ziph, taking with him three thousand chosen men of Israel, to search for David [there] in the wilderness of Ziph.

³Saul camped on the hill of Hachilah, which is beside the road east of Jeshimon, but David stayed in the wilderness. When he saw that Saul came into the wilderness after him,

⁴David sent out spies, and he learned that Saul was definitely coming.

⁵So David arose and went to the place where Saul had camped, and saw the spot where Saul lay, as well as Abner the son of Ner, the commander of his army; and Saul was lying inside the circle of the camp, with the army camped around him.

⁶Then David said to Ahimelech the Hittite and to Abishai the son of Zeruiah, brother of Joab, "Who will go down with me to Saul in the camp?" And Abishai said, "I will go down with you."

⁷So David and Abishai went to the army during the night, and there was Saul lying asleep inside the circle of the camp with his spear stuck in the ground by his head; and Abner and the people were lying around him.

⁸Then Abishai said to David, "God has given your enemy into your hand this day; now then, please let me strike him with the spear *driving it* to the ground with one stroke, and I will not strike him the second time."

⁹But David said to Abishai, "Do not kill him, for who can put out his hand against the Lᴏʀᴅ's anointed [king] and be guiltless (innocent)?"

life point

David remained loyal and faithful to King Saul, recognizing and respecting God's anointing on him, even though Saul was trying to kill him. In his training for leadership, David learned to stay under God's protective hand by refusing to rise up against Saul—even when he had an opportunity (see 1 Samuel 26:7–11). Instead, he patiently waited for God to deliver him. If you are a leader, follow David's example and refuse to rebel against those in authority over you. Wait patiently for the Lord to deliver you, vindicate you, and raise you up as well.

¹⁰David also said, "As the Lord lives, most certainly the Lord will strike him [in His own time and way], or his day will come and he will die, or he will go down into battle and be carried off [dead]. ¹¹The Lord forbid that I would put out my hand against the Lord's anointed; but now take the spear that is by his head and the jug of water, and let us go." ¹²So David took the spear and the jug of water from *beside* Saul's head, and they left, and no one saw or knew nor did anyone awaken, because they were all *sound* asleep, for a deep sleep from the Lord had fallen on them. ¹³Then David crossed over to the other side and stood on the top of the mountain at a distance, with a large area between them. ¹⁴David called to the army and to Abner the son of Ner, "Will you not answer, Abner?" Abner replied, "Who are you who calls [and disturbs] the king?" ¹⁵David said to Abner, "Are you not a [brave] man? Who is like you in Israel? Why then have you not guarded your lord the king? For one of the people came [into your camp] to kill the king your lord.

¹⁶"This thing that you have done is not good. As the Lord lives, you surely deserve to die, because you have not guarded your lord, the Lord's anointed. And now, see where the king's spear is, and the jug of water that was by his head." ¹⁷Then Saul recognized David's voice and said, "Is this your voice, my son David?" And David said, "It is my voice, my lord the king!" ¹⁸And David said, "Why is my lord pursuing his servant? For what have I done? Or what evil is in my hand? ¹⁹"Now therefore, please let my lord the king hear the words of his servant. If the Lord has incited you against me, let Him accept an offering [from me]; but if it is men, may they be cursed before the Lord, because they have driven me out this day to keep me from sharing in the inheritance of the Lord, saying, 'Go, serve other gods.' ²⁰"Now then, do not let my blood fall to the ground away from the presence of the Lord; for the king of Israel has come out to search for a single flea, just as when one hunts a [defenseless] partridge in the mountains." ²¹Then Saul said, "I have sinned. Return, my son David, for I will not harm you again because my life was precious in your sight this day. Hear me, I have played the fool and have done a very great wrong [to you]." ²²David answered, "Look, here is the king's spear! Now let one of the young men come over and get it. ²³"The Lord will repay each man for his righteousness and his faithfulness; for the Lord handed you over to me today, but I refused to put out my hand against the Lord's anointed. ²⁴"Now behold, just as your life was precious in my sight this day, so let my life be precious in the sight of the Lord, and may He rescue me from all distress." ²⁵Then Saul said to David, "May you

be blessed, my son David; you will both accomplish much and certainly prevail." So David went on his way, and Saul returned to his place.

27 BUT DAVID said in his heart, "Now I will die one day by the hand of Saul. There is nothing better for me than to escape to the land of the Philistines. Then Saul will give up searching for me inside the borders of Israel, and I will escape from his hand [once and for all]."

²So David and the six hundred men who were with him arose and crossed over to Achish the son of Maoch, king of Gath.

³And David lived with Achish at Gath, he and his men, each man with his household, and David with his two wives, Ahinoam the Jezreelitess, and Abigail the Carmelitess, [who was] Nabal's widow.

⁴When Saul was told that David had fled to Gath, he no longer searched for him.

⁵Then David said to Achish, "If I have found favor in your sight, let me be given a place [of my own] in one of the cities in the country, so that I may live there; for why should your servant live in the royal city with you?"

⁶Then Achish gave David [the town of] Ziklag that day. Therefore Ziklag has belonged to the kings of Judah to this day.

⁷The number of days that David lived in the country of the Philistines was a year and four months.

⁸Now David and his men went up and raided the Geshurites, the Girzites, and the Amalekites [the enemies of Israel that Joshua had failed to annihilate]; for they had inhabited the land from ancient times, as one comes to Shur even as far as the land of Egypt. [Deut 25:19; Josh 13:1, 2, 13]

⁹David attacked the land and did not leave a man or a woman alive, but he took the sheep, the cattle, the donkeys, the camels, and the clothing, and returned to Achish.

¹⁰When Achish asked, "Where did you raid today?" David replied, "Against the Negev (the South country) of Judah, and against the Negev of the Jerahmeelites, and against the Negev of the Kenites."

¹¹David did not leave a man or a woman alive to bring news to Gath, saying [to himself], "Otherwise they will tell about us, saying, 'This is what David has done, and this has been his practice all the time that he has lived in the country of the Philistines.'"

¹²Achish believed David, saying, "He has certainly become hated by his people in Israel; so he will always be my servant."

28 IN THOSE days the Philistines gathered their forces for war to fight against Israel. Achish said to David, "Understand for certain that you and your men will go out with me to battle."

²David said to Achish, "All right, you shall know what your servant can do." So Achish said to David, "Therefore I will make you my bodyguard for life."

³Now Samuel had died, and all Israel had mourned for him and buried him in Ramah, his own city. And Saul had removed the mediums and the spiritists (soothsayers) from the land.

⁴The Philistines assembled and came and camped at Shunem; and Saul gathered all the Israelites and they camped at Gilboa.

⁵When Saul saw the Philistine army, he was afraid and badly shaken.

⁶So Saul inquired of the LORD, but the LORD did not answer him, either by dreams or by Urim [used like lots by the priest to determine the will of God] or by prophets. [Prov 1:24–30]

⁷Then Saul said to his servants, "Find for me a woman who is a medium

[between the living and the dead], so that I may go to her and ask her advice." His servants said to him, "There is a woman who is a medium at En-dor."

8So Saul disguised himself by wearing different clothes, and he left with two men, and they came to the woman at night. He said *to her,* "Conjure up for me, please, and bring up [from the dead] for me [the spirit] whom I shall name to you."

9But the woman said to him, "See here, you know what Saul has done, how he has cut off (eliminated) those who are mediums and spiritists from the land. So why are you laying a trap for my life, to cause my death?"

10Then Saul swore [an oath] to her by the Lord, saying, "As the Lord lives, no punishment shall come upon you for this."

11So the woman said, "Whom shall I bring up for you?" He said, "Bring up Samuel for me."

12When the woman saw Samuel, she screamed with a loud voice; and she said to Saul, "Why have you deceived me? You are Saul!"

13The king said to her, "Do not be afraid; but [tell me] what do you see?" The woman said to Saul, "I see a divine [superhuman] being coming up from the earth."

14He said to her, "What is his appearance?" And she said, "An old man is coming up, wrapped in a robe." Then Saul knew that it was Samuel, and he bowed with his face to the ground and paid respect [to him].

15Then Samuel said to Saul, "Why have you disturbed me by bringing me up?" Saul answered, "I am greatly distressed; for the Philistines are making war against me, and God has left me and no longer answers me, either through prophets or by dreams; therefore I have called you to make known to me what I should do."

16Samuel said, "Why then do you ask me, since the Lord has left you and has become your enemy?

17"The Lord has done [to you] just as He said through me [when I was with you]; for the Lord has torn the kingdom out of your hand and given it to your neighbor, to David. [1 Sam 15:22–28]

18"Because you did not obey the voice of the Lord and did not execute His fierce wrath on Amalek, therefore the Lord has done this thing to you this day.

19"Moreover, the Lord will also put Israel along with you into the hands of the Philistines, and tomorrow you and your sons will be with me [among the dead]. Indeed, the Lord will put the army of Israel into the hands of the Philistines."

20Then Saul immediately fell full length on the earth [floor of the medium's house], and was very afraid because of Samuel's words; and he was thoroughly exhausted because he had not eaten all day and all night.

21The woman came to Saul and saw that he was greatly troubled, and she said to him, "Look, your maidservant has obeyed you, and I have taken my life in my hand and have listened to everything you said to me.

22"So now, please listen to the voice of your maidservant, and let me set a piece of bread before you, and eat, so that you may have strength when you go on your way."

23But he refused and said, "I will not eat." But his servants together with the woman urged him, and he [finally] listened to them. So he got up from the ground and sat on the bed.

24The woman had a fattened calf in the house; she quickly killed it, and took flour, kneaded it and baked unleavened bread.

25She brought it before Saul and his servants, and they ate. Then they got up and went away that night.

29 NOW THE Philistines gathered all their forces at Aphek, while Israel camped by the spring in Jezreel. ²As the Philistine lords (governors) were proceeding on [marching] by hundreds and by thousands, and David and his men were proceeding on in the rear with Achish [the king of Gath], ³the Philistine commanders [having noticed David] said, "What are these Hebrews *doing here?*" Achish said to the Philistine commanders, "Is this not David, the servant of Saul king of Israel, who has been with me these days and years, and I have found no fault in him from the day he deserted *to me* to this day?"

⁴But the Philistine commanders were angry with Achish and they said to him, "Make this man return, so that he may go back to his place where you have assigned him, and do not let him go down to battle with us, or in the battle he may [turn and] become our adversary. For how could David reconcile himself to his lord [Saul]? *Would it* not be with the heads of these [Philistine] men?

⁵"Is this not David, of whom they used to sing in dances,

'Saul killed his thousands,
And David his ten thousands'?"

⁶Then Achish called David and said to him, "As the Lord lives, you *have been* upright (righteous), and your behavior in the army is pleasing in my sight. For from the day you came to me to this day I have found no evil in you. Nevertheless, the [Philistine] lords do not approve of you.

⁷"So return now and go in peace [to your place], so that you do not displease the Philistine lords."

⁸David said to Achish, "But what have I done? What have you found in your servant from the day when I [first] came before you to this day, that I may not go and fight against the enemies of my lord the king?"

⁹Achish answered David, "I know that you are blameless in my sight, like an angel of God; nevertheless the commanders of the Philistines have said, 'He must not go up with us to the battle.'

¹⁰"So now, get up early in the morning with your master's servants who have come with you, and as soon as you are up in the morning and have light, leave."

¹¹So David and his men got up early to leave in the morning, to return to the land of the Philistines. But the Philistines went up to Jezreel [to fight against Israel].

30 NOW IT happened when David and his men came [home] to Ziklag on the third day, [they found] that the Amalekites had made a raid on the Negev (the South country) and on Ziklag, and had overthrown Ziklag and burned it with fire; ²and they had taken captive the women [and all] who were there, both small and great. They killed no one, but carried them off [to be used as slaves] and went on their way. ³When David and his men came to the town, it was burned, and their wives and their sons and their daughters had been taken captive. ⁴Then David and the people who were with him raised their voices and wept until they were too exhausted to weep [any longer]. ⁵Now David's two wives had been captured, Ahinoam the Jezreelitess and Abigail the widow of Nabal the Carmelite. ⁶Further, David was greatly distressed because the people spoke of stoning him, for all of them were embittered, each man for his sons and daughters. But David felt strengthened *and* encouraged in the Lord his God.

[7]David said to Abiathar the priest, Ahimelech's son, "Please bring me the ephod." So Abiathar brought him the ephod.

[8]David inquired of the LORD, saying, "Shall I pursue this band [of raiders]? Will I overtake them?" And He answered him, "Pursue, for you will certainly overtake them, and you will certainly rescue [the captives]."

[9]So David went, he and the six hundred men who were with him, and came to the brook Besor; there those [who could not continue] remained behind.

[10]But David pursued [the Amalekites], he and four hundred men, for two hundred who were too exhausted to cross the brook Besor stayed *behind*.

[11]They found an Egyptian [who had collapsed] in the field and brought him to David, and gave him bread and he ate, and they gave him water to drink,

[12]and they gave him a piece of a fig cake and two clusters of raisins; and when he had eaten, his energy returned, for he had not eaten bread or had any water to drink for three days and three nights.

[13]David said to him, "To whom do you belong, and where are you from?" He said, "I am a young man from Egypt, a servant of an Amalekite; and my master abandoned me [as useless] when I fell sick three days ago.

[14]"We made a raid on the Negev of the Cherethites, and on that which belongs to Judah, and on the Negev of Caleb, and we burned Ziklag with fire."

[15]Then David said to him, "Will you take me down to this band [of raiders]?" And he said, "Swear to me by God that you will not kill me or turn me over to the hand of my master, and I will bring you down to this band."

[16]When he brought David down, the Amalekites had disbanded *and* spread over all the land, eating and drinking and dancing because of all the great spoil they had taken from the land of the Philistines and from the land of Judah.

[17]Then David [and his men] struck them down [in battle] from twilight until the evening of the next day; and not a man of them escaped, except four hundred young men who rode camels and fled.

[18]So David recovered all that the Amalekites had taken, and rescued his two wives.

[19]Nothing of theirs was missing whether small or great, sons or daughters, spoil or anything that had been taken; David recovered it all.

[20]So David captured all the flocks and herds [which the enemy had], and [the people] drove those animals before him and said, "This is David's spoil."

[21]David came to the two hundred men who were so exhausted that they could not follow him and had been left at the brook Besor [with the provisions]. They went out to meet David and the people with him, and when he approached the people, he greeted them.

[22]Then all the wicked and worthless men among those who went with David said, "Because they did not go with us, we will give them none of the spoil that we have recovered, except that each man may take his wife and children away and leave."

[23]David said, "You must not do so, my brothers, with what the LORD has given us. He has kept us safe and has handed over to us the band [of Amalekites] that came against us.

[24]"And who will listen to you in regard to this matter? For as is the share of him who goes down into the battle, so shall his share be who stays by the provisions and supplies; they shall share alike."

[25]So from that day forward he made it a statute and an ordinance for Israel to this day.

[26]When David came to Ziklag, he

encourage yourself!

If you need encouragement and no one is around to give it, encourage yourself as David did (see 1 Samuel 30:6). He had a positive attitude about himself, and you should also. We all should be careful of having a prideful attitude, but it is not wrong to have a good and confident attitude toward ourselves.

David was in a seemingly hopeless situation—his city was destroyed, its women and children captured, and his men blamed him for their misfortune. What did David do? He encouraged and strengthened himself in the Lord. Later on, that situation was totally turned around (see 1 Samuel 30:7–20).

Earlier in his life, when David was just a boy, everyone around him discouraged him concerning his ability to fight Goliath. David, however, was confident in God. He believed that God would be strong in his weakness and give him the victory. He went out in the name of the Lord, with a heart full of confidence, and became a giant-killer who was eventually crowned king (see 1 Samuel 17). David had no one to believe in him but God, so he believed about himself what God believed about him; he believed in God's ability in him.

The Lord once told me that if I did not have confidence in myself, I really did not have confidence in Him. He said, "I am in you; I am your confidence, but I can only do through you what you believe." Self-doubt is absolutely tormenting. I lived in it for many years, and I personally prefer confidence.

You may be thinking, *Well, Joyce, I wish I had confidence too*.

Confidence is something we decide to have. It is more than a feeling; it is a decision to step out boldly into whatever we feel God is leading us to do. We learn about God—about His love, His ways, and His Word—then ultimately we must *decide* whether we believe or not. If we do believe, then we have confidence. If we do not believe, we live in doubt about everything. Self-doubt makes us double-minded, and James 1:8 teaches us that a double-minded person is unstable and restless about everything. We really cannot go forward until we decide to have confidence in God and in ourselves.

I encourage you to take a big step of faith and *stop doubting yourself*. As the old saying goes, "Don't sell yourself short." You have more capabilities than you think you do. You are able to do a lot more than you have ever done in the past. God will help you, if you will put your trust in Him and stop doubting yourself.

Like everyone else, you will make mistakes—but God will allow you to learn from them and will actually work them out for your good if you will decide not to be defeated by them. When doubt begins to torment your mind, speak the Word of God and you will win the battle. Believe wholeheartedly in God, believe that He is in you, and you are able to do whatever you need to do through Him.

sent part of the spoil to the elders of Judah, his friends, saying, "Here is a blessing (gift) for you from the spoil of the enemies of the LORD:

²⁷For those in Bethel, Ramoth of the Negev, Jattir,

²⁸Aroer, Siphmoth, Eshtemoa,

²⁹Racal, the cities of the Jerahmeelites, the cities of the Kenites,

³⁰Hormah, Bor-ashan, Athach,

³¹Hebron, and for [those elders in] all the places where David himself and his men were accustomed to go."

31 NOW THE Philistines fought against Israel, and the men of Israel fled before them and fell slain on Mount Gilboa. ²The Philistines overtook Saul and his sons; and they killed Jonathan and Abinadab and Malchi-shua, Saul's sons. ³The battle went heavily against Saul, and the archers hit him; and he was severely wounded by the archers. ⁴Saul said to his armor bearer, "Draw your sword and pierce me through with it, otherwise these uncircumcised [Philistines] will come and pierce me through and abuse *and* mock me." But his armor bearer would not, because he was terrified [of doing such a thing]. So Saul took his sword and fell on it. ⁵When his armor bearer saw that Saul was dead, he also fell on his sword and died with him. ⁶So Saul, his three sons, his armor bearer, and all his men died together on that day.

⁷When the men of Israel who were on the other side of the valley [of Jezreel], and those who were beyond the Jordan, saw that the *other* men of Israel had fled and that Saul and his sons were dead, they abandoned the cities and fled; then the Philistines came and lived in them. ⁸The next day, when the Philistines came to plunder the dead, they found Saul and his three sons fallen on Mount Gilboa. ⁹So they cut off Saul's head and stripped off his weapons *and* armor and sent them throughout the land of the Philistines, to bring the good news to the house of their idols and to the people. ¹⁰And they put Saul's weapons *and* armor in the temple of the Ashtaroth (female goddesses), and they fastened his body to the wall of Beth-shan. ¹¹When the inhabitants of Jabesh-gilead heard what the Philistines had done to Saul, ¹²all the brave men stood and walked all night, and they took the bodies of Saul and his sons from the wall of Beth-shan, and they came to Jabesh and cremated them there. ¹³They took their bones and buried them under the tamarisk tree at Jabesh, and fasted [as a sign of mourning and respect] for seven days.

Second Samuel

Author:
Uncertain

Date:
Between 931 BC and 722 BC

Everyday Life Principles:
We position ourselves to receive God's blessings by getting into the places God has called us and staying there. Do not go to a place unless God leads you to go, and do not leave a place until God instructs you to leave.

Being in the wrong place at the wrong time can have serious consequences, both short-term and long-term.

God will help us get into proper position and stay there as we follow and obey Him.

One of the major life lessons we learn from 2 Samuel is that being in the right place at the right time brings God's blessings, and being out of position can keep God's blessings from flowing in our lives. In 2 Samuel, we learn this lesson primarily through people who were not in their proper places at the proper time.

Examples of people who were out of place include Uzzah, Mephibosheth, and even King David. Uzzah got out of position when, against God's instruction, he touched the ark when it became unstable. As a result, he died (see 2 Samuel 6:6, 7). Jonathan's son, Mephibosheth, was also in the wrong place, living in the wilderness of Lo-debar and thinking of himself as a "dead dog" (2 Samuel 9:8), when his family's covenant with David entitled him to live in the palace and eat at the king's table (see 2 Samuel 9:1–13). We also see King David tragically out of place when he committed sin with Bathsheba. Second Samuel 11:1 tells us that he sinned with her "in the spring, at the time when the kings go out to battle." If David had been at war where he was supposed to be instead of at home, he could have avoided falling into adultery and the tragedies that resulted from it.

Learn from those who were out of place in 2 Samuel. Ask God to help you hear His voice so that you will know where you are supposed to be and be there at the proper time.

1 NOW IT happened after the death of Saul, when David had returned from the slaughter of the Amalekites, that he stayed two days in Ziklag.

²On the third day a man came [unexpectedly] from Saul's camp with his clothes torn and dust on his head [as in mourning]. When he came to David, he bowed to the ground and lay himself face down [in an act of great respect and submission].

³Then David asked him, "Where do you come from?" He said, "I have escaped from the camp of Israel."

⁴David said to him, "How did it go? Please tell me." He answered, "The people have fled from the battle. Also, many of the people have fallen and are dead; Saul and Jonathan his son are also dead."

⁵So David said to the young man who informed him, "How do you know Saul and his son Jonathan are dead?"

⁶And the young man who told him explained, "By chance I happened to be on Mount Gilboa, and there was Saul leaning on his spear, and the chariots and horsemen [of the Philistines] were close behind him.

⁷"When he turned to look behind him, he saw me, and called to me. And I answered, 'Here I am.'

⁸"He asked me, 'Who are you?' I answered him, 'I am an Amalekite.'

⁹"He said to me, 'Stand up facing me and kill me, for [terrible] agony has come over me, yet I still live [and I will be taken alive].'

¹⁰"So I stood facing him and killed him, because I knew that he could not live after he had fallen. Then I took the crown which was on his head and the band which was on his arm, and I have brought them here to my lord." [1 Sam 31:4]

¹¹Then David grasped his own clothes and tore them [in mourning]; so did all the men who were with him.

¹²They mourned and wept and fasted until evening for Saul and Jonathan his son, and for the LORD's people and the house of Israel, because they had fallen by the sword [in battle].

¹³David said to the young man who informed him, "Where are you from?"

life point

David and Jonathan had a special bond (see 1 Samuel 18:1), and when Jonathan died, David lamented his death greatly (see 2 Samuel 1:11, 12).

Any time a person loses a loved one as David did or suffers a significant loss, he or she will need to grieve. The grieving *process* is necessary and healthy—mentally, emotionally, and even physically. Note that David rent his clothing and mourned his loss with weeping. Often a person who refuses to go through the grieving process is not facing reality, which ultimately has a devastating effect on his entire being.

A *spirit* of grief is another matter entirely. Usually a spirit of grief clings to an individual and brings with it severe regret and crushing guilt. A spirit of grief will not allow people to go on with their lives after their loss. If a person does not resist a spirit of grief, it will take over and destroy the life of the one who has suffered a loss. If not confronted and controlled, it will rob a person's health, strength, and vitality—and even life itself.

God's will is to comfort those who mourn. Are you having difficulty grieving a loss? I encourage you to face your grief with God's comfort. If need be, resist a spirit of grief with God's power. Stay in balance and receive the assurance Jesus gives: "Blessed . . . are those who mourn . . . , for they will be comforted" (Matthew 5:4).

He answered, "I am the son of a foreigner (resident alien, sojourner), an Amalekite."

¹⁴David said to him, "How is it that you were not afraid to put out your hand to destroy the LORD's anointed?"

¹⁵David called one of the young men and said, "Go, execute him." So he struck the Amalekite and he died.

¹⁶David said to the [fallen] man, "Your blood is on your own head, for your own mouth has testified against you, saying, 'I have killed the LORD's anointed.'"

¹⁷Then David sang this dirge (funeral song) over Saul and his son Jonathan,

¹⁸and he told *them* to teach the sons of Judah, *the song of* the bow. Behold, it is written in the Book of Jashar:

¹⁹"Your glory *and* splendor, O Israel,
 is slain upon your high places!
How the mighty have fallen!
²⁰"Tell it not in Gath,
 Proclaim it not in the streets of
  Ashkelon,
 Or the daughters of the Philistines
  will rejoice,
 The daughters of the uncircumcised
  (pagans) will exult.
²¹"O mountains of Gilboa,
 Let not dew or rain be upon you,
  nor fields with offerings;
 For there the shield of the mighty
  was defiled,
 The shield of Saul, [dry, cracked]
  not anointed with oil.
²²"From the blood of the slain, from
  the fat of the mighty,
 The bow of Jonathan did not turn
  back,
 And the sword of Saul did not
  return empty.
²³"Saul and Jonathan, beloved and
  lovely *and* friends in their lives,
 And in their death they were not
  separated;
 They were swifter than eagles,
 They were stronger than lions.

²⁴"O daughters of Israel, weep over
 Saul,
 Who clothed you luxuriously in
  scarlet,
 Who put ornaments of gold on
  your apparel.
²⁵"How the mighty have fallen in the
  midst of the battle!
 Jonathan lies slain upon your high
  places.
²⁶"I am distressed for you, my
  brother Jonathan;
 You have been a good friend to me.
 Your love toward me was more
  wonderful
 Than the love of women.
²⁷"How the mighty have fallen,
 And the weapons of war have
  perished!"

2 SO IT happened after this that David inquired of the LORD, saying, "Shall I go up into one of the cities of Judah?" And the LORD said to him, "Go up." David asked, "Where shall I go?" And He said, "To Hebron."

²So David went up there [to Hebron] with his two wives also, Ahinoam of Jezreel and Abigail the widow of Nabal of Carmel [in Judah].

³And David brought up his men who were with him, each one with his household; and they lived in the cities of Hebron.

⁴Then the men of Judah came and there they anointed David king over the house of Judah.

Then they told David, "It was the men of Jabesh-gilead who buried Saul." [1 Sam 31:11–13]

⁵So David sent messengers to the men of Jabesh-gilead, and said to them, "May you be blessed by the LORD because you showed this graciousness *and* loyalty to Saul your lord (king), and buried him.

⁶"Now may the LORD show lovingkindness and truth *and* faithfulness to you. I too will show this goodness to you, because you have done this thing.

7"So now, let your hands be strong and be valiant; for your lord Saul is dead, and also the house of Judah has anointed me king over them."

8Now [Saul's cousin] Abner the son of Ner, commander of Saul's army, had taken Ish-bosheth the son of Saul and brought him over to Mahanaim.

9He made him king over Gilead, over the Ashurites, over Jezreel, over Ephraim, over Benjamin, even over all Israel [except Judah].

10Ish-bosheth, Saul's son, was forty years old when he became king over Israel, and he reigned for two years. But the house of Judah followed David.

11And the time that David was king in Hebron over the house of Judah was seven years and six months.

12Now Abner the son of Ner and the servants of Ish-bosheth the son of Saul went out from Mahanaim to Gibeon.

13Joab [David's nephew] the son of Zeruiah and the servants of David also went out and met them by the pool of Gibeon. They sat down, with one group on one side of the pool and the other group on the other side of the pool.

14Then Abner said to Joab, "Let the young men now stand and have a contest before us." And Joab said, "Let them stand."

15So they stood up and went over by number, twelve for Benjamin and Ish-bosheth the son of Saul, and twelve of the servants of David.

16Each one of them seized his opponent by the head and *thrust* his sword into his opponents side; so they fell down together. Therefore that place was called Helkath-hazzurim [that is, the Field of Sides], which is in Gibeon.

17There was a very fierce battle that day, and Abner and the men of Israel were beaten before the servants of David.

18Three sons of Zeruiah [the half sister of David] were there: Joab, Abishai, and Asahel. Now Asahel was as light *and* swift-footed as one of the [wild] gazelles in the field.

19Asahel pursued Abner and did not turn to the right or to the left as he followed him.

20Then Abner looked behind him and said, "Is that you, Asahel?" He answered, "It is I."

21So Abner said to him, "Turn to your right or to your left, and grab one of the young men and take his armor for yourself." But Asahel was not willing to turn away from pursuing Abner.

22Abner repeated again, "Turn away from following me. Why should I have to strike you to the ground? How would I be able to face Joab your brother [and look him in the eye]?"

23But Asahel refused to turn away; so Abner struck him in the abdomen with the butt end of his spear, and the spear came out his back; and he fell there and died on that spot. And it came about that everyone who came to the place where Asahel fell and died, stood still [and reflected].

24But Joab and Abishai [Asahel's brothers] pursued Abner. When the sun was going down, they came to the hill of Ammah, which is in front of Giah on the way to the wilderness of Gibeon.

25And the sons of [the tribe of] Benjamin gathered together behind Abner and became one troop, and took their stand on the top of a hill.

26Then Abner called to Joab, "Must

speak the Word

God, I pray that You would show loving-kindness, truth, and faithfulness to me, and that You would strengthen my hands and cause me to be valiant.
−ADAPTED FROM 2 SAMUEL 2:6, 7

the sword devour forever? Do you not know that it will be bitter in the end? How long [will it be] before you tell the people to stop pursuing their brothers?"

²⁷Joab said, "As God lives, if you had not spoken, then the people certainly would have stopped pursuing their brothers in the morning."

²⁸So Joab blew the trumpet; and all the people halted and no longer pursued Israel, nor did they fight anymore.

²⁹Then Abner and his men went through the Arabah (desert region) all that night, crossed the Jordan, went through Bithron and walked the whole morning and came to Mahanaim [where Ish-bosheth ruled Israel].

³⁰Joab returned from pursuing Abner; and when he had gathered all the people together, nineteen of David's servants were missing, besides Asahel.

³¹But the servants of David had struck down many of Benjamin and Abner's men; so that three hundred and sixty men died.

³²And they picked up [the body of] Asahel and buried him in the tomb of his father in Bethlehem. Then Joab and his men walked all night and they arrived in Hebron at daybreak.

3 THERE WAS a long war between the house of Saul and the house of David; but David grew steadily stronger, while the house of Saul grew weaker and weaker [to the point of being powerless].

²Sons were born to David in Hebron: his firstborn was Amnon, by Ahinoam of Jezreel;

³his second, Chileab, by Abigail the widow of Nabal of Carmel; the third, Absalom the son of [his wife] Maacah, daughter of Talmai the king of Geshur;

⁴the fourth, Adonijah the son of [his wife] Haggith; the fifth, Shephatiah the son of [his wife] Abital;

⁵and the sixth, Ithream, by David's wife Eglah. These [sons] were born to David in Hebron.

⁶Now while war continued between the houses of Saul and David, Abner was proving himself strong in the house of Saul.

⁷Now Saul had a concubine whose name was Rizpah the daughter of Aiah; and Ish-bosheth said to Abner, "Why have you gone in to my father's concubine?"

⁸Then Abner was very angry at the words of Ish-bosheth, and he said, "Am I a dog's head [a despicable traitor] that belongs to Judah? Today I show loyalty and kindness to the house of Saul your father, to his brothers and his friends, by not having you handed over to David; and yet you charge me today with guilt concerning this woman.

⁹"May God do so to Abner, and more also, if I do not do for David just as the Lord has sworn to him,

¹⁰to transfer the kingdom from the house of Saul, and establish the throne of David over Israel and Judah from Dan [in the north] to Beersheba [in the south]."

¹¹And Ish-bosheth could not say another word to Abner, because he was afraid of him.

¹²Then Abner sent messengers to David [who was] in his place [at Hebron], saying, "Whose is the land? Make your covenant (treaty) with me, and behold, my hand shall be with you to bring all Israel over to you."

¹³David said, "Good! I will make a covenant (treaty) with you, but I require one thing of you: you shall not see my face unless you first bring Michal, Saul's daughter, when you come to see me."

¹⁴So David sent messengers to Ish-bosheth, Saul's son, saying, "Give me my wife Michal, to whom I was betrothed for [the price of] a hundred foreskins of the Philistines."

¹⁵So Ish-bosheth sent and took her from her husband, from Paltiel the son of Laish [to whom Saul had given her].

¹⁶But her husband went with her, weeping continually behind her as far as Bahurim. Then Abner told him, "Go, return." And he did so.

¹⁷Abner talked with the elders (tribal leaders) of Israel, saying, "In times past you were seeking for David to be king over you.

¹⁸"Now then, do it [and make him king]! For the Lord has spoken of David, saying, 'By the hand of My servant David I will save My people Israel from the hand of the Philistines and the hand of all their enemies.'" [1 Sam 9:16]

¹⁹Abner also spoke to [the men of] Benjamin. Then he also went to tell David at Hebron everything that seemed good to Israel and to the entire house of Benjamin.

²⁰So Abner came to David at Hebron, and [brought] twenty men along with him. And David prepared a feast for Abner and the men with him.

²¹Abner said to David, "Let me stand up and go, and gather all Israel to my lord the king, so that they may make a covenant (treaty) with you, and that you may reign over all that your soul desires." So David sent Abner away, and he went in peace.

²²Then the servants of David came with Joab from a raid and brought a great quantity of spoil with them; but Abner was not with David at Hebron, because David had sent him away, and he had gone in peace.

²³When Joab and all the army that was with him arrived, they told Joab, "Abner the son of Ner came to the king, and he has sent him away, and he has gone in peace."

²⁴Then Joab came to the king and said, "What have you done? Behold, Abner came to you; why did you send him away, so that he is already gone?

²⁵"You know Abner the son of Ner, that he [only] came to deceive you [with flattering words] and to learn of your going out and coming in, and to find out what you are doing."

²⁶When Joab left David, he sent messengers after Abner, and they brought him back from the well of Sirah; but David knew nothing [about Joab's action].

²⁷So when Abner returned to Hebron, Joab took him aside to the middle of the gate to speak to him privately, and there he struck Abner in the abdomen so that he died, to avenge the blood of Asahel, Joab's brother.

²⁸Afterward, when David heard of it, he said, "I and my kingdom are forever innocent before the Lord of the blood of Abner the son of Ner.

²⁹"Let the guilt fall on the head of Joab and on all his father's house (family); and may there never disappear from the house of Joab one who suffers with a discharge or one who is a leper or one who walks with a crutch [being unfit for war], or one who falls by the sword, or one who lacks food."

³⁰So Joab and Abishai his brother murdered Abner because he had killed their brother Asahel in the battle at Gibeon.

³¹Then David said to Joab and to all the people with him, "Tear your clothes, put on sackcloth, and mourn before Abner." And King David walked behind the bier.

³²They buried Abner in Hebron; and the king raised his voice and wept at the grave of Abner, and all the people wept.

³³And the king sang a dirge (funeral song) over Abner and said,

"Should Abner [the great warrior]
   die as a fool dies?
³⁴"Your hands were not bound, nor
   your feet put in fetters;
As a man falls before the wicked,
   so you have fallen."

And all the people wept again over him.

35All the people came to urge David to eat food while it was still day; but David took an oath, saying, "May God do so to me, and more also, if I taste bread or anything else before the sun sets."

36And all the people took notice of it and it pleased them, just as everything that the king did pleased all the people.

37So all the people and all Israel understood that day that it had not been the will of the king to put Abner the son of Ner to death.

38Then the king said to his servants, "Do you not know that a prince and a great man has fallen this day in Israel?

39"Today I am weak, though anointed king; these men, the sons of Zeruiah, are too difficult for me. May the LORD repay the evildoer [Joab] in accordance with his wickedness!"

4 WHEN SAUL'S son Ish-bosheth [king of Israel], heard that Abner had died in Hebron, he lost courage, and all Israel was horrified.

2Saul's son had two men who were commanders of [raiding] bands [of soldiers]. One was named Baanah and the other Rechab, the sons of Rimmon the Beerothite of the sons (tribe) of Benjamin (for Beeroth is also considered part of [the tribe of] Benjamin,

3and the Beerothites fled to Gittaim, and have been resident aliens there to this day).

4Jonathan, Saul's son, had a son whose feet were crippled. He was five years old when the news [of the deaths] of Saul and Jonathan came from Jezreel. And the boy's nurse picked him up and fled; but it happened that while she was hurrying to flee, he fell and became lame. His name was Mephibosheth.

5So the sons of Rimmon the Beerothite, Rechab and Baanah, left and came to the house of Ish-bosheth in the heat of the day while he was taking his midday rest.

6They came into the interior of the house as if to get wheat [for the soldiers], and they struck him in the stomach. Then Rechab and Baanah his brother escaped [unnoticed].

7Now when they entered the house he was lying on his bed in his bedroom. They [not only] struck and killed him, [but] they also beheaded him. Then they took his head and traveled all night by way of the Arabah.

8They brought the head of Ish-bosheth

life point

Second Samuel 4:4 tells the story of Jonathan's young son named Mephibosheth. When Mephibosheth's nurse heard the dreadful news that Saul and Jonathan had been killed in battle, she feared that David might try to take vengeance on the boy because of the terrible way Saul had treated David. She ran from the palace with the young child in her arms, dropping him in her escape attempt. This left him lame in both feet. He would have to live the rest of his life handicapped because of something that was not even his fault.

Many of us have crippled self-images that prevent us from receiving all God has for us. If you have a poor self-image, as I did, I recommend that you read the end of Mephibosheth's story, which is found in 2 Samuel, chapter 9. The story of his restoration greatly affected my life, and I believe it will do the same for you. It will help you see not only why you are living far below the level that God intends for you now, but also why you are in danger of missing out on what He has in mind for you in the future—and I do not want you to miss the great things He has in store for you!

to David at Hebron, and said to the king, "Look, the head of Ish-bosheth the son of Saul, your enemy, who sought your life; thus the Lord has granted my lord the king vengeance this day on Saul and on his descendants."

⁹David replied to Rechab and Baanah his brother, the sons of Rimmon the Beerothite, and said to them, "As the Lord lives, who has redeemed my life from every adversity,

¹⁰when a man told me, 'Behold, Saul is dead,' thinking that he was bringing good news, I seized and killed him in Ziklag, to reward him for his news.

¹¹"How much more, when wicked men have killed a righteous *and* just man in his own house on his bed, shall I not require his blood from your hand and remove you from the earth?"

¹²So David commanded his young men, and they killed them and cut off their hands and feet and hung them beside the pool in Hebron. But they took Ish-bosheth's head and buried it in Hebron in the tomb of Abner [his relative].

5 THEN ALL the tribes of Israel came to David at Hebron and said, "Behold, we are your bone and your flesh.

²"In times past, when Saul was king over us, it was you who led Israel out [to war] and brought Israel in [from battle]. And the Lord told you, 'You shall shepherd My people Israel and be ruler over them.'" [1 Sam 15:27–29; 16:1]

³So all the elders (tribal leaders) of Israel came to the king at Hebron, and King David made a covenant with them at Hebron before the Lord; and they anointed him king over Israel.

⁴David was thirty years old when he became king, and he reigned forty years.

⁵In Hebron he reigned over Judah seven years and six months, and in Jerusalem he reigned thirty-three years over all Israel and Judah.

⁶Now the king and his men went to Jerusalem against the Jebusites, the inhabitants of the land, who said to David, "You shall not enter here, for the blind and the lame [even the weakest among us] will turn you away"; they thought, "David cannot come in here [because the walls are impenetrable]."

⁷Nevertheless, David captured the stronghold (fortress) of Zion, that is, the City of David.

⁸Then David said on that day, "Whoever strikes the Jebusites, let him go up through the [underground] water shaft to strike the lame and the blind, who are detested by David's soul [because of their arrogance]." So [for that reason] they say, "The blind or the lame (Jebusites) shall not come into the [royal] house [of Israel]." [1 Chr 11:6]

⁹So David lived in the stronghold and called it the City of David. And he built all around [the surrounding area] from the Millo [fortification] and inward.

¹⁰David became greater and greater, for the Lord, the God of hosts (armies), was with him.

¹¹Now Hiram the king of Tyre sent messengers to David with cedar trees, carpenters, and stonemasons; and they built a house (palace) for David.

¹²And David knew that the Lord had established him as king over Israel, and that He had exalted his kingdom for His people Israel's sake.

¹³David took more concubines and

speak the Word

God, I pray that You would make me greater and greater in You and for You because You are with me.
–ADAPTED FROM 2 SAMUEL 5:10

wives from Jerusalem, after he came from Hebron; and more sons and daughters were born to him.

¹⁴And these are the names of those who were born to him in Jerusalem: Shammua, Shobab, Nathan, Solomon, ¹⁵Ibhar, Elishua, Nepheg, Japhia, ¹⁶Elishama, Eliada, and Eliphelet.

¹⁷When the Philistines heard that David had been anointed king over Israel, all the Philistines went up to look for him, but he heard about it and went down to the stronghold. ¹⁸Now the Philistines had come and spread out [for battle] in the Valley of Rephaim.

¹⁹David inquired of the LORD, saying, "Shall I go up against the Philistines? Will You hand them over to me?" And the LORD said to David, "Go up, for I will certainly hand them over to you." ²⁰So David came to Baal-perazim, and he defeated them there, and said, "The LORD has broken through my enemies before me, like a breakthrough of water." So he named that place Baal-perazim (master of breakthroughs).

putting the Word to work

In 2 Samuel 5:12, we see that David "knew that the LORD had established him as king over Israel, and that He had exalted his kingdom for His people Israel's sake." Do you know what God wants to do in you and through you and why? Ask Him to help you understand what He is establishing in you right now and what purposes of His can be served through you, just as His purposes were served through David.

²¹The Philistines abandoned their [pagan] idols there, so David and his men took them away [to be burned]. ²²The Philistines came up once again and spread out in the Valley of Rephaim. ²³When David inquired of the LORD, He said, "You shall not go up, but circle around behind them and come at them in front of the balsam trees. ²⁴"And when you hear the sound of marching in the tops of the balsam trees, then you shall pay attention *and* act promptly, for at that time the LORD will have gone out before you to strike the army of the Philistines." ²⁵David did just as the LORD had commanded him, and struck down the Philistines from Geba as far as Gezer.

6 AGAIN DAVID gathered together all the chosen men of Israel, thirty thousand. ²And David arose and went with all those who were with him to Baale-judah [Kiriath-jearim], to bring up from there [to Jerusalem] the ark of God which is called by the Name—the very Name of the LORD of hosts, who dwells enthroned *above* the cherubim. ³They placed the ark of God on a new cart and brought it out of the house of Abinadab, which was on the hill; and Uzzah and Ahio, sons of Abinadab, were leading the new cart. ⁴So they brought it with the ark of God from the house of Abinadab, which was on the hill; and Ahio was walking in front of the ark. [1 Sam 7:2] ⁵Meanwhile, David and all the house of Israel were celebrating *and* dancing before the LORD with all kinds of *instruments made of* fir *or* cypress wood,

speak the Word

Thank You, God, that You break through my enemies before me, like a breakthrough of water.
–ADAPTED FROM 2 SAMUEL 5:20

with lyres, harps, tambourines, casta-
nets, and cymbals.

⁶When they came to Nacon's threshing floor, Uzzah reached out [with his
hand] to the ark of God and took hold
of it, because the oxen [stumbled and]
nearly overturned it.

⁷And the anger of the LORD burned
against Uzzah, and God struck him
there for his irreverence; and he died
there by the ark of God.

life point

Uzzah disobeyed God by touching the
ark, and, as a result, he was killed (see
2 Samuel 6:6, 7). I believe that Uzzah
reached out to steady the ark because it
had been kept in his father's house for
a long time and had become familiar to
him. We must not ever regard the holy as
commonplace, but keep a reverent attitude toward sacred things (God's Word,
prayer, worship, God's presence, etc.)
and not allow them to become so familiar
that we dishonor them.

We should always keep a sense of awe
and wonder about the things of God.

⁸David became angry and grieved
and offended because of the LORD's
outburst against Uzzah, and that place
has been called Perez-uzzah (outburst
against Uzzah) to this day.

⁹So David was afraid of the LORD that
day; and he said, "How can the ark of
the LORD come to me?"

¹⁰David was unwilling to move the
ark of the LORD into the City of David
with him; instead he took it aside to
the house of Obed-edom the Gittite.

¹¹So the ark of the LORD remained in
the house of Obed-edom the Gittite for
three months, and the LORD blessed
Obed-edom and all his household
(family).

¹²Now King David was told, "The
LORD has blessed the house of Obed-
edom and all that belongs to him,
because of the ark of God." So David
went and brought up the ark of God
from the house of Obed-edom into
the City of David with rejoicing and
gladness.

¹³And when those who were carrying the ark of the LORD [by its poles]
had gone six paces, he sacrificed an
ox and a fatling.

¹⁴And David was dancing before
the LORD with great enthusiasm, and
David was wearing a linen ephod [a
priest's upper garment].

¹⁵So David and all the house of Israel
were bringing the ark of the LORD up
[to the City of David] with shouts [of
joy] and with the sound of the trumpet.

¹⁶Then, as the ark of the LORD came
into the City of David, Michal, Saul's
daughter [David's wife], looked down
from the window above and saw King
David leaping and dancing before the
LORD; and she felt contempt for him in
her heart [because she thought him
undignified].

¹⁷They brought in the ark of the LORD
and set it in its place inside the tent
which David had pitched for it; and
David offered burnt offerings and
peace offerings before the LORD.

¹⁸When David had finished offering
the burnt offerings and peace offerings,

putting the Word to work

When the ark of the Lord, which represents God's presence, was in Obed-
edom's house, Obed-edom and all of his
household were blessed (see 2 Samuel
6:11). Is God welcome in your home,
and are you enjoying the blessings of
His presence upon your house and your
family? Tell Him today that you want
His presence to fill your home and to be
with everyone who lives there.

putting the Word to work

In 2 Samuel 6:14–16, King David danced and worshiped God in a very demonstrative way, and his wife was embarrassed and despised him for his display of praise to God. In 2 Samuel 6:21–23, David tells her that he will continue to worship even more fervently and boldly than before. Are you expressing your worship to God as passionately as you possibly can, regardless of what people think? Go ahead; follow David's example in 2 Samuel 6:21, and express your "pure enjoyment" in God.

he blessed the people in the name of the LORD of hosts (armies),

¹⁹and distributed to all the people, the entire multitude of Israel, both to men and women, to each a [ring-shaped] loaf of bread, a cake of dates, and a cake of raisins. Then all the people departed, each to his house.

²⁰Then David returned to bless his household. But [his wife] Michal the daughter of Saul came out to meet David and said, "How glorious *and* distinguished was the king of Israel today, who uncovered himself *and* stripped [off his kingly robes] in the eyes of his servants' maids like one of the riffraff who shamelessly uncovers himself!"

²¹So David said to Michal, "It was before the LORD [that I did this], who chose me above your father and all his house, to appoint me as ruler over Israel, the people of the LORD. Therefore I will celebrate [in pure enjoyment] before the LORD.

²²"Yet I will demean myself *even* more than this, and will be humbled (abased) in my own sight [and yours, as I please], but by the maids whom you mentioned, by them I shall be held in honor."

²³Michal the daughter of Saul had no child to the day of her death.

7 WHEN KING David lived in his house (palace) and the LORD had given him rest from all his surrounding enemies,

²the king said to Nathan the prophet, "See now, I dwell in a house of cedar, but the ark of God dwells within tent curtains."

³And Nathan said to the king, "Go, do everything that is in your heart, for the LORD is with you."

⁴But it happened that night that the word of the LORD came to Nathan, saying,

⁵"Go and tell My servant David, 'Thus says the LORD, "Should you be the one to build Me a house in which to dwell?

⁶"For I have not dwelt in a house since the day I brought the sons (descendants) of Israel up from Egypt, even to this day; but I have been moving about in a tent, even in a tabernacle.

⁷"Wherever I have gone with all the Israelites, did I speak a word to any from the tribes of Israel, whom I commanded to shepherd My people Israel, asking, 'Why have you not built Me a house of cedar?'"'

⁸"So now, say this to My servant David, 'Thus says the LORD of hosts, "I took you from the pasture, from following the sheep, to be ruler over My people Israel.

⁹"I have been with you wherever you have gone, and have cut off all your enemies from before you; and I will make you a great name, like that of the great men of the earth.

¹⁰"I will appoint a place for My people Israel and will plant them, so that they may live in a place of their own and not be disturbed again. The wicked will not afflict them again, as formerly,

¹¹even from the day that I appointed judges over My people Israel; and I will give you rest from all your enemies. The LORD also declares to you that He will make a house (royal dynasty) for you.

¹²"When your days are fulfilled and you lie down [in death] with your fathers (ancestors), I will raise up your descendant after you, who shall be born to you, and I will establish his kingdom.

¹³"He [is the one who] shall build a house for My Name *and* My Presence, and I will establish the throne of his kingdom forever.

¹⁴"I will be his Father, and he shall be My son. When he commits iniquity (wrongdoing), I will discipline him with the rod of men and with the strokes of the sons of man.

¹⁵"But My lovingkindness *and* mercy will not depart from him, as I took it from Saul, whom I removed from before you.

¹⁶"Your house (royal dynasty) and your kingdom will endure forever before Me; your throne will be established forever."'"

¹⁷Nathan spoke to David in accordance with all these words and all of this vision.

¹⁸Then King David went in and sat [in prayer] before the LORD, and said, "Who am I, O Lord GOD, and what is my house (family), that You have brought me this far?

¹⁹"Yet this was very insignificant in Your eyes, O Lord GOD, for You have spoken also of Your servant's house (royal dynasty) in the distant future. And this is the law *and* custom of man, O Lord GOD.

²⁰"What more can David say to You? For You know (acknowledge, choose) Your servant, O Lord GOD.

²¹"Because of Your word (promise), and in accordance with Your own heart, You have done all these great

and astounding things to let Your servant know (understand).

²²"Therefore You are great, O Lord GOD; for there is none like You, and there is no God besides You, according to all that we have heard with our ears.

²³"What one nation on earth is like Your people Israel, whom God went to redeem for Himself as a people and to make a name for Himself, and to do great and awesome things for Yourself and for Your land, before Your people whom You have redeemed for Yourself from Egypt, *from* nations and their gods?

²⁴"You established for Yourself Your people Israel as Your people forever, and You, O LORD, have become their God.

²⁵"Now, O LORD God, confirm forever the word [of the covenant] that You have spoken in regard to Your servant and his house (royal dynasty); and do just as You have spoken,

²⁶so that Your Name may be magnified forever, saying, 'The LORD of hosts (armies) is God over Israel;' and may the house (royal dynasty) of Your servant David be established before You.

²⁷"For You, O LORD of hosts, God of Israel, have revealed this to Your servant, saying, 'I will build you a house (royal dynasty).' For that reason Your servant has found courage to pray this prayer to You.

²⁸"And now, O Lord GOD, You are God, and Your words are truth, and You have promised this good thing to Your servant.

²⁹"Therefore now, may it please You to bless the house (royal dynasty) of Your servant, so that it may continue forever before You; for You, O Lord

speak the Word

Thank You, God, that Your loving-kindness
and mercy will not ever depart from me.
–ADAPTED FROM 2 SAMUEL 7:15

GOD, have spoken it, and with Your blessing may the house of Your servant be blessed forever."

8 NOW IT came about after this that David defeated the Philistines and subdued (humbled) them, and he took control of Methegammah [the main city] from the hand of the Philistines.

²He defeated Moab, and measured them with a length of rope, making them lie down on the ground; he measured two lengths to [choose those to] put to death, and one full length to [choose those to] be kept alive. And the [surviving] Moabites became servants to David, bringing tribute.

³Then David defeated Hadadezer the son of Rehob, king of Zobah, as he went to restore his power at the River [Euphrates].

⁴David captured from him 1,700 horsemen and 20,000 foot soldiers. David also hamstrung all the chariot horses (making them lame), but reserved *enough* of them for a hundred chariots.

⁵When the Arameans (Syrians) of Damascus came to help Hadadezer, king of Zobah, David struck down 22,000 Arameans.

⁶Then David put garrisons among the Arameans in Damascus, and the Arameans became his servants and brought tribute. The LORD helped David wherever he went.

⁷David took the shields of gold that were carried by the servants of Hadadezer, and brought them to Jerusalem.

⁸And from Betah and Berothai, cities of Hadadezer, King David took an immense quantity of bronze.

⁹When Toi king of Hamath heard about David's defeat of all the forces of Hadadezer,

¹⁰Toi sent Joram his son to King David to greet and congratulate him for his battle and defeat of Hadadezer; for

Hadadezer had been at war with Toi. *Joram* brought with him articles of silver, gold, and bronze [as gifts].

¹¹King David also dedicated these [gifts] to the LORD, along with the silver and gold that he had dedicated from all the nations which he subdued:

¹²from Aram (Syria), Moab, the Ammonites, the Philistines, and Amalek, and from the spoil of Hadadezer the son of Rehob, king of Zobah.

¹³So David made a name *for himself* when he returned from killing 18,000 Arameans (Syrians) in the Valley of Salt.

¹⁴He put garrisons in Edom; in all Edom he put garrisons, and all the Edomites became servants to David. And the LORD helped him wherever he went.

¹⁵So David reigned over all Israel, and continued to administer justice and righteousness for all his people.

¹⁶Joab the son of Zeruiah was [commander] over the army; Jehoshaphat the son of Ahilud was recorder (secretary);

¹⁷Zadok the son of Ahitub and Ahimelech the son of Abiathar were the [chief] priests, and Seraiah was the scribe;

¹⁸Benaiah the son of Jehoiada was [head] over both the Cherethites and Pelethites [the king's bodyguards]; and David's sons were chief [confidential] advisers (officials) [to the king]. [1 Chr 18:17]

9 AND DAVID said, "Is there still anyone left of the house (family) of Saul to whom I may show kindness for Jonathan's sake?"

²There was a servant of the house of Saul whose name was Ziba, so they called him to David. And the king said to him, "Are you Ziba?" He said, "*I am* your servant."

³And the king said, "Is there no longer anyone *left* of the house (family)

of Saul to whom I may show the goodness *and* graciousness of God?" Ziba replied to the king, "There is still a son of Jonathan, [one] whose feet are crippled." [1 Sam 20:14–17]

⁴So the king said to him, "Where is he?" And Ziba replied to the king, "He is in the house of Machir the son of Ammiel, in Lo-debar."

⁵Then King David sent *word* and had him brought from the house of Machir the son of Ammiel, from Lo-debar.

⁶Mephibosheth the son of Jonathan, the son of Saul, came to David and fell face down and lay himself down [in respect]. David said, "Mephibosheth." And he answered, "Here is your servant!"

⁷David said to him, "Do not be afraid, for I will certainly show you kindness for the sake of your father Jonathan, and will restore to you all the land of your grandfather Saul; and you shall always eat at my table."

⁸Again Mephibosheth lay himself face down and said, "What is your servant, that you would be concerned for a dead dog like me?"

⁹Then the king summoned Ziba, Saul's servant, and said to him, "I have

looking for people to bless

David desired to bless someone in Saul's family because of a covenant he had made with his friend Jonathan (see 1 Samuel 18:3; 20:14–16). As he looked for Jonathan's descendants, he discovered that Jonathan's crippled son, Mephibosheth, was alive, but living in less-than-desirable circumstances (see 2 Samuel 9:3, 4).

Just as David searched for someone he could be kind to for Jonathan's sake, God looks for people He can be kind to for Jesus' sake. God is merciful and kind; He is constantly extending His kindness toward us, but we must be willing to accept it.

David's covenant relationship with Jonathan included all of Jonathan's children. I believe Mephibosheth never exercised his covenant rights because of the negative way he felt about himself. Many of God's children do the same thing. They shrink back from God in fear rather than approaching Him boldly. They feel badly about themselves; they look at everything that is wrong with them instead of looking at Jesus and the righteousness He offers through faith in Him. Mephibosheth actually referred to himself as a "dead dog" (2 Samuel 9:8). He had a poor self-image and, although David would have helped him at any time had he only asked, he never asked because he felt unworthy.

We can all learn a good lesson from Mephibosheth. God's goodness and mercy, and His willingness to help us, are not based on our perfection, but on our covenant with His Son, Jesus. When we are in Christ, we are included in that covenant and can go boldly to the throne and receive mercy and help in plenty of time to meet all of our needs. Even though Mephibosheth was lame in both feet, he ultimately received the mercy David offered and ate at the king's table (see 2 Samuel 9:13).

We do not have to talk God into being good to us. He is good; and He is looking for someone to bless for Jesus' sake. Make a decision to start receiving what you do not deserve and have not earned. As you do, you will be living in God's awesome grace, which is freely available to all who will receive it.

given your master's grandson everything that belonged to Saul and to all his house (family).

¹⁰"You and your sons and your servants shall cultivate the land for him, and you shall bring in *the produce,* so that your master's grandson may have

life point

Mephibosheth had been living for years in a small town called Lo-debar (see 2 Samuel 9:3, 4). The name *Lo-debar* means "pasture-less." In an agricultural society, a place without pastures was probably a place of poverty; it certainly was not a nice or popular town.

When our self-image is poor, we often choose surroundings that seem to fit the way we feel about ourselves. I have noticed that some people who are filled with self-loathing will not bother to fix themselves up or even try to dress or look nice. The way they feel about themselves inside shows on the outside. Other people go to the opposite extreme. They feel so bad about themselves inwardly that they try to hide it by becoming perfectionists outwardly. Everything around them has to appear to be perfect—their homes, personal appearance, children, spouse, and everything else. They live under tremendous pressure, and they put pressure on the people around them. We all need to realize that God wants to bless us in spite of our imperfections. Our worth and value are not found in outward things but knowing in our hearts who we are in Christ. Relax and learn to receive from God.

God wants you to have peace knowing that your imperfections will not and cannot stop Him from working in your life. Like Mephibosheth, God does not want you to live in a barren place, but to experience His unlimited kindness. He delights in being merciful!

food to eat; but Mephibosheth, your master's grandson, shall always eat at my table." Now Ziba had fifteen sons and twenty servants.

¹¹Then Ziba said to the king, "Your servant will do according to everything that my lord the king commands." So Mephibosheth ate at David's table as one of the king's sons.

¹²Mephibosheth had a young son whose name was Mica. And all who lived in Ziba's house were servants to Mephibosheth.

¹³So Mephibosheth lived in Jerusalem, for he always ate at the king's table. And he was lame in both feet.

10 NOW IT happened later that [Nahash] the king of the Ammonites died, and his son Hanun became king in his place.

²Then David said, "I will show kindness to Hanun the son of Nahash, just as his father did to me." So David sent [a letter along with] some of his servants to console him in regard to his father's death; and David's servants came into the land of the Ammonites.

³But the princes of the Ammonites [were suspicious and] said to Hanun their lord, "Do you think that David is honoring your father because he has sent comforters to you? Has David not sent his servants to you in order to search the city, to spy it out and overthrow it?"

⁴So Hanun took David's servants and shaved off half their beards, and cut off their robes in the middle as far as their hips, and sent them away.

⁵When David was informed, he sent [messengers] to meet them [before they reached Jerusalem], for the men were greatly ashamed *and* humiliated. And the king said, "Stay at Jericho until your beards grow, and *then* return."

⁶When the Ammonites saw that they had become an object of hatred to David, they sent *word* and hired the

Arameans (Syrians) of Beth-rehob and the Arameans of Zobah, 20,000 foot soldiers, and the king of Maacah with 1,000 men, and the men of Tob with 12,000 men [to fight for them].

⁷When David heard about it, he sent Joab and the entire army, the strong *and* brave men.

⁸The Ammonites came out and lined up for battle at the entrance of the [city] gate, but the Arameans of Zobah and Rehob and the men of Tob and Maacah were [stationed] by themselves in the field.

⁹Now when Joab saw that the battlefront was against him in front and

no more dead dogs

Mephibosheth had a poor self-image, a dead-dog image (see 2 Samuel 9:8). He did not think very well of himself. Instead of seeing himself as the rightful heir of Jonathan (King David's covenant friend), he saw himself as someone who would be rejected. If this were not true, he would have already gone to the palace long before to claim his inheritance.

A poor self-image causes us to operate in fear instead of faith. We look at what is wrong with us instead of what is right with Jesus. He has taken our wrongness and given us His righteousness (see 2 Corinthians 5:21). We need to walk in the reality of that truth.

When I saw that Mephibosheth thought of himself as a "dead dog," I realized that I also had a dead-dog image that was hindering me from being all I could be and having all I could have in life. I started changing my attitude toward myself. It took time and a lot of help from the Holy Spirit, but I determined that I would not live below the blessed life Jesus had provided for me.

God's Word says that because of His covenant with you, you can be the "head (leader) and not the tail (follower) . . . above only, and you will not be beneath" (Deuteronomy 28:13). I am sure that, like me, you have been the tail long enough. It is time to take a stand and start receiving your rightful inheritance.

David blessed Mephibosheth. He gave him servants and provided for all of his needs. The story ends by saying that Mephibosheth dwelled in Jerusalem and ate at the king's table, even though "he was lame in both feet" (2 Samuel 9:13).

I absolutely love the end of the story! I relate Mephibosheth's lameness to our own weaknesses. We may also fellowship and eat with our King, Jesus—even though we have faults and weaknesses. We still have a covenant with God, sealed and ratified in the blood of Jesus Christ. A blood covenant was, and still is, one of the strongest agreements that can be made between two parties.

We offer God what we have, and He gives us what He has. He takes all of our sins, faults, weaknesses, and failures, and gives us His ability, His righteousness, and His strength. He takes our poverty and gives us His riches. He takes our diseases and sicknesses and gives us His healing and health. He takes our messed up, failure-filled pasts and gives us the hope of bright futures. In ourselves we are nothing; our own righteousness is like "filthy rags" (Isaiah 64:6). But in Christ we have a future. We are in covenant with Almighty God. What an awesome truth!

in the rear, he selected some of all the choice men in Israel and set them in battle formation to meet the Arameans (Syrians).

¹⁰But he placed the rest of the men in the hand of his brother Abishai, and he placed them in battle formation to meet the Ammonites.

¹¹Joab said [to Abishai], "If the Arameans are too strong for me, then you shall help me; but if the Ammonites are too strong for you, I will come to help you.

¹²"Be courageous, and let us show ourselves courageous for the benefit of our people and the cities of our God. And may the LORD do what is good in His sight."

¹³So Joab and the people who were with him approached the battle against the Arameans, and they fled before him.

¹⁴When the Ammonites saw that the Arameans had fled, they also fled before Abishai and entered the city. So Joab returned from *battling* against the Ammonites and came to Jerusalem.

¹⁵When the Arameans saw that they were defeated by Israel, they gathered together.

¹⁶Hadadezer sent *word* and brought out the Arameans who were beyond the River [Euphrates]; and they came to Helam; and Shobach the commander of the army of Hadadezer led them.

¹⁷When David was informed, he gathered all Israel together and crossed the Jordan, and came to Helam. Then the Arameans assembled in battle formation to meet David and fought against him.

¹⁸But the Arameans fled before Israel, and David killed 700 Aramean charioteers and 40,000 horsemen, and struck Shobach the commander of their army, and he died there.

¹⁹When all the kings serving Hadadezer saw that they had been defeated by Israel, they made peace with Israel and served them. So the Arameans (Syrians) were afraid to help the Ammonites anymore.

11 THEN IT happened in the spring, at the time when the kings go out *to battle,* that David sent Joab and his servants with him, and all [the fighting men of] Israel, and they destroyed the Ammonites and besieged Rabbah. But David remained in Jerusalem.

²One evening David got up from his couch and was walking on the [flat] roof of the king's palace, and from there he saw a woman bathing; and she was very beautiful in appearance.

³David sent *word* and inquired about the woman. *Someone* said, "Is this not Bathsheba, the daughter of Eliam, the wife of Uriah the Hittite?"

⁴David sent messengers and took her. When she came to him, he lay with her. And when she was purified from her uncleanness, she returned to her house.

⁵The woman conceived; and she sent *word* and told David, "I am pregnant."

⁶Then David sent *word* to Joab, *saying,* "Send me Uriah the Hittite." So Joab sent Uriah to David.

putting the Word to work

One reason David fell into sin with Bathsheba was that he was not where he was supposed to be when he was supposed to be there. According to 2 Samuel 11:1, during the springtime, he should have been on the battlefield instead of in Jerusalem. Do you try to follow God's leading in every situation so that you will be at the right place at the right time? Ask Him to help you. He wants you to be perfectly positioned, far away from sin and in a place where you can receive His blessings.

⁷When Uriah came to him, David asked him how Joab was, how the people were doing, and how the war was progressing.

⁸Then David said to Uriah, "Go down to your house, and wash your feet (spend time at home)." Uriah left the king's palace, and a gift from the king was sent out after him.

⁹But Uriah slept at the entrance of the king's palace with all the servants of his lord, and did not go down to his house.

¹⁰When they told David, "Uriah did not go down to his house," David said to Uriah, "Have you not [just] come from a [long] journey? Why did you not go to your house?"

¹¹Uriah said to David, "The ark and Israel and Judah are staying in huts (temporary shelters), and my lord Joab and the servants of my lord are camping in the open field. Should I go to my house to eat and drink and lie with my wife? By your life and the life of your soul, I will not do this thing."

¹²Then David said to Uriah, "Stay here today as well, and tomorrow I will let you leave." So Uriah remained in Jerusalem that day and the next.

life point

Sin always leads to more sin, as it did when David ordered that Uriah be killed after he had committed adultery with his wife (see 2 Samuel 11:15). When we do sin, we must repent and receive God's forgiveness quickly. That way, we do not become ensnared in a web of sin, but we stay clean and pure before God. David did not repent for a long time, and, in God's eyes, the fact that he covered up his sin was worse than the original sin he had committed. We can receive forgiveness if we admit we have sinned and repent, but if we hide sin and make excuses, we remain in it and live deceived lives.

¹³Now David called him [to dinner], and he ate and drank with him, so that he made Uriah drunk; in the evening he went out to lie on his bed with the servants of his lord, and [still] did not go down to his house.

¹⁴In the morning David wrote a letter to Joab and sent it with Uriah.

¹⁵He wrote in the letter, "Put Uriah in the front line of the heaviest fighting and leave him, so that he may be struck down and die."

¹⁶So it happened that as Joab was besieging the city, he assigned Uriah to the place where he knew the [enemy's] valiant men were *positioned*.

¹⁷And the men of the city came out and fought against Joab, and some of the people among the servants of David fell; Uriah the Hittite also died.

¹⁸Then Joab sent *word* and informed David of all the events of the war.

¹⁹And he commanded the messenger, "When you have finished reporting all the events of the war to the king,

²⁰then if the king becomes angry and he says to you, 'Why did you go so near to the city to fight? Did you not know that they would shoot [arrows] from the wall?

²¹'Who killed Abimelech the son of Jerubbesheth (Gideon)? Was it not a woman who threw an upper millstone on him from the wall so that he died at Thebez? Why did you go so near the wall?' Then you shall say, 'Your servant Uriah the Hittite is also dead.'" [Judg 9:35, 53]

²²So the messenger left, and he came and told David everything that Joab had sent him *to report*.

²³The messenger said to David, "The men indeed prevailed against us and came out to us in the field, but we were on them *and* pushed them as far as the entrance of the [city] gate.

²⁴"Then the archers shot at your servants from the wall. Some of the king's

servants are dead, and your servant Uriah the Hittite is also dead."

²⁵Then David said to the messenger, "Tell Joab this, 'Do not let this thing disturb you, for the sword devours one [side] as well as another. Strengthen your battle against the city and overthrow it'; and so encourage Joab."

²⁶When Uriah's wife [Bathsheba] heard that her husband Uriah was dead, she mourned for her husband.

²⁷And when the time of mourning was past, David sent *word* and had her brought to his house, and she became his wife and bore him a son. But the thing that David had done [with Bathsheba] was evil in the sight of the LORD.

12

AND THE LORD sent Nathan [the prophet] to David. He came and said to him,

"There were two men in a city, one rich and the other poor. ²"The rich man had a very large number of flocks and herds,

³But the poor man had nothing but one little ewe lamb
Which he had purchased and nourished;
And it grew up together with him and his children.
It ate his food, drank from his cup, it lay in his arms,
And was like a daughter to him.
⁴"Now a traveler (visitor) came to the rich man,
And to avoid taking one from his own flock or herd
To prepare [a meal] for the traveler who had come to him,
He took the poor man's ewe lamb and prepared it for his guest."

⁵Then David's anger burned intensely against the man, and he said to Nathan, "As the LORD lives, the man who has done this deserves to die. ⁶"He shall make restitution for the ewe lamb four times as much [as the lamb was worth], because he did this thing and had no compassion."

the gift of repentance

David had committed adultery with Bathsheba and made arrangements to have her husband killed so he could cover his sin (see 2 Samuel 11:1–15). Time had passed, and he was still ignoring the issue. He was probably doing what we are all tempted to do when we sin—he was making excuses and being deceived by his own reasoning. All of us may not deal with sins as serious as what David was facing, but sin is sin, and it has a similar effect on us, no matter what type of sin it is. The point is, until we admit it, confess, and repent of our sin (which is to turn entirely away from it and go in another direction), we will not be able to worship God out of a pure heart or with a clean conscience. King David was quite miserable until he finally repented of his sin. His joy returned only after he repented (see Psalm 32:1–7).

I am very thankful for the gift of repentance. Why do I refer to repentance as a gift? I have seen people who could not feel sorry for their sins, and that is a terrible thing. When the conscience is seared (hardened), people are unable to feel the weight and seriousness of their wrong behavior. Because of this, we should all pray for a tender conscience toward God.

First John 1:9 states that we can admit our sins, confess them, and that God is faithful to completely cleanse us of all unrighteousness. What good news! We can live before God with a perfectly clear conscience.

⁷Then Nathan said to David, "You are the man! Thus says the Lord, the God of Israel, 'I anointed you as king over Israel, and I spared you from the hand of Saul.

⁸'I also gave you your master's house, and put your master's wives into your care *and* under your protection, and I gave you the house (royal dynasty) of Israel and of Judah; and if *that had been* too little, I would have given you much more!

⁹'Why have you despised the word of the Lord by doing evil in His sight? You have struck down Uriah the Hittite with the sword and have taken his wife to be your wife. You have killed him with the sword of the Ammonites. [Lev 20:10; 24:17]

¹⁰'Now, therefore, the sword shall never depart from your house, because you have despised Me and have taken the wife of Uriah the Hittite to be your wife.'

¹¹"Thus says the Lord, 'Behold, I will stir up evil against you from your own household; and I will take your wives before your eyes and give them to your companion, and he will lie with your wives in broad daylight.

¹²'Indeed you did it secretly, but I will do this thing before all Israel, and in broad daylight.'" [2 Sam 16:21, 22]

¹³David said to Nathan, "I have sinned against the Lord." And Nathan said to David, "The Lord also has allowed your sin to pass [without further punishment]; you shall not die. [Ps 51]

¹⁴"Nevertheless, because by this deed you have given [a great] opportunity to the enemies of the Lord to blaspheme [Him], the son that is born to you shall certainly die."

¹⁵Then Nathan went [back] to his home.

And the Lord struck the child that Uriah's widow bore to David, and he was very sick.

¹⁶David therefore appealed to God for the child [to be healed]; and David fasted and went in and lay all night on the ground.

beyond grief

What was David saying in 2 Samuel 12:20–23? He was saying: "When my child was sick, I did everything I could to save him. Now that he is dead, there is nothing more I can do. Why should I sit around mourning over something I cannot change? It is much better for me if I get up and get on with my life."

That is what the Lord is encouraging us to do today. He is telling us to stop mourning over what has happened in the past and to make the decision to live today and every day for the rest of our lives. He is telling us not to ruin the time we have left by grieving what has been lost.

I am not saying that we should not go through a period of mourning when we experience loss. Going through a grief process is normal and right. What I *am* saying is that when we allow our grief to go on and on without a resolution, it becomes destructive and turns into self-pity.

Make a vow right now that from this moment on you will not waste any more of your valuable time feeling sorry for yourself and grieving over things you cannot change. Instead, pledge that you are going to live each day to the fullest, looking forward to what God has in store for you as you follow Him.

¹⁷The elders of his household stood by him [in the night] to lift him up from the ground, but he was unwilling [to get up] and would not eat food with them.

¹⁸Then it happened on the seventh day that the child died. David's servants were afraid to tell him that the child was dead, for they said, "While the child was still alive, we spoke to him and he would not listen to our voices. How then can we tell him the child is dead, since he might harm himself [or us]?"

¹⁹But when David saw that his servants were whispering to one another, he realized that the child was dead. So David said to them, "Is the child dead?" And they said, "He is dead."

²⁰Then David got up from the ground, washed, anointed *himself* [with olive oil], changed his clothes, and went into the house of the LORD and worshiped. Then he came [back] to his own house, and when he asked, they set food before him and he ate.

²¹Then his servants said to him, "What is this thing that you have done? While the child was alive you fasted and wept, but when the child died, you got up and ate food."

²²David said, "While the child was still alive, I fasted and wept; for I thought, 'Who knows, the LORD may be gracious to me and the child may live.'

²³"But now he is dead; why should I [continue to] fast? Can I bring him back again? I will go to him [when I die], but he will not return to me."

²⁴David comforted his wife Bathsheba, and went to her and lay with her; and she gave birth to a son, and David named him Solomon. And the LORD loved the child;

²⁵and He sent *word* through Nathan the prophet, and he named him Jedidiah (beloved of the LORD) for the sake of the LORD [who loved the child].

²⁶Now Joab fought against Rabbah of the Ammonites and captured the royal city.

²⁷Joab sent messengers to David and said, "I have fought against Rabbah; I have even taken the city of waters.

²⁸"So now, assemble the rest of the men, and camp against the city and capture it, or I will take the city myself, and it will be named after me."

²⁹So David gathered all the men together and went to Rabbah, then fought against it and captured it.

³⁰And he took the crown of their king from his head; it weighed a talent of gold, and [set in it was] a precious stone; and it was *placed* on David's head. And he brought the spoil out of the city in great amounts.

³¹He also brought out the people who were there, and put them to [work with] the saws and sharp iron instruments and iron axes, and made them work at the brickkiln. And he did this to all the Ammonite cities. Then David and all the men returned to Jerusalem.

13 IT HAPPENED afterwards that Absalom the son of David had a beautiful sister whose name was Tamar, and Amnon [her half brother] the son of David was in love with her.

²Amnon was so frustrated because of his [half-] sister Tamar that he made himself sick, for she was a virgin, and Amnon thought it impossible for him to do anything to her.

³But Amnon had a friend whose name was Jonadab the son of Shimeah, David's brother; and Jonadab was a very shrewd (cunning) man.

⁴He said to Amnon, "Why are you, the king's son, so depressed morning after morning? Will you not tell me?" And Amnon said to him, "I am in love with Tamar, my [half-] brother Absalom's sister."

⁵Jonadab said to him, "Go to bed and pretend you are sick; and when your

father [David] comes to see you, say to him, 'Just let my sister Tamar come and serve me food, and let her prepare it in my sight, so that I may see it and eat it from her hand.'"

⁶So Amnon lay down and pretended to be sick; and when the king came to see him, Amnon said to the king, "Please let my sister Tamar come and make me a couple of cakes in my sight, so that I may eat from her hand."

⁷Then David sent *word* to the house for Tamar, saying, "Go now to your brother Amnon's house, and prepare some food for him."

⁸So Tamar went to her brother Amnon's house, and he was in bed. And she took dough and kneaded it, and made cakes in his sight, and baked them.

⁹She took the pan and dished them out before him, but he refused to eat. And Amnon said, "Have everyone leave me." So everyone left him [except Tamar].

¹⁰Then Amnon said to Tamar, "Bring the food into the bedroom, so that I may eat from your hand." So Tamar took the cakes she had made and brought them into the bedroom to her [half-] brother Amnon.

¹¹When she brought them to him to eat, he took hold of her and said, "Come, lie with me, my sister."

¹²She replied, "No, my brother! Do not violate me, for such a thing is not done in Israel; do not do this disgraceful thing! [Gen 34:7]

¹³"As for me, how could I get rid of my shame *and* disgrace? And you, you

the deepest kind of shame

The Bible does not ignore the issue of sexual abuse; we find it in 2 Samuel 13:1–14, in the story of Tamar. I believe that sexual abuse is the worst, most offensive, and most damaging of all types of abuse. When an individual is forced to engage in sex against his or her will, something that is meant to be given only willingly as a gift is violently taken from that person. If that individual is abused in a perverted manner, he or she may suffer lasting damage to the soul as well as to the physical body.

When people, especially children, are abused sexually, their minds, wills, and emotions may be tremendously damaged. They may become negative, suspicious, critical, judgmental, worried, and unsettled. They may also become what I would call "mentally deep," always reasoning, always trying to figure everything out, always asking, "How can I take care of myself? How can I keep life under control so I don't get hurt anymore?" The problem with such a deep thinker is that he or she never gets to enjoy life.

In almost every case, an abuse victim like Tamar will be rooted in shame and will develop a shame-based nature. Because my father sexually abused me, I felt shame, which I internalized. Along the way, I made an unhealthy transition in my thinking: I moved from being ashamed of what my father had done to me to being ashamed of myself because of what he did. This is a very common thought process for abuse victims.

The nature of shame is to be embarrassed or feel defective because of bad things that happen to us, and the only way to be healed of shame is to apply the medicine of God's Word to our lives. God's Word has healed me, not instantly, but over time. It will do the same for you if you diligently apply it to your life.

will be considered one of the fools in Israel. So now, just speak to the king [about taking me as your wife], for he will not withhold me from you."

¹⁴But he would not listen to her; and since he was stronger than she, he violated her and lay with her.

¹⁵Then Amnon became extremely hateful toward her, for his hatred toward her was greater than the love which he had for her. And Amnon said to her, "Get up and get out!"

¹⁶But she said, "No, because this wrong of sending me away is worse than the other that you have done to me!" But he would not listen to her.

¹⁷Instead, he called his young man who was his personal servant and said, "Now throw this woman out of my *presence* and bolt the door behind her."

¹⁸Now Tamar was wearing a [long-sleeved] robe of various colors; for that is how the virgin daughters of the king dressed themselves in robes. Then Amnon's personal servant took her out and bolted the door behind her.

¹⁹So Tamar put dust on her head [in grief] and tore the long-sleeved robe which she had on, and she put her hand on her head and went away crying out [for help].

²⁰So her brother Absalom said to her, "Has your brother Amnon been with you? But now keep silent, my sister; he is your brother; do not take this matter to heart." So Tamar remained secluded in her brother Absalom's house.

²¹Now when King David heard about all these things, he was very angry [but failed to take any action].

²²But Absalom did not speak to Amnon either good or bad; for Absalom hated Amnon because he had violated his sister Tamar.

²³Now it came about after two full years that Absalom had sheepshearers at Baal-hazor near Ephraim, and Absalom invited all the king's sons [to a party].

²⁴Absalom came to [his father] the king and said, "Behold, your servant has sheepshearers; please let the king and his servants go with your servant."

²⁵But the king said to Absalom, "No, my son, we should not all go, for we will be a burden to you." Although Absalom [strongly] urged David, still he would not go, but he gave him his blessing.

²⁶Then Absalom said, "If not, then at least let my brother Amnon go with us." And the king said to him, "Why should he go with you?"

²⁷But Absalom urged him [again], and he let Amnon and all the king's sons go with him.

²⁸Now Absalom commanded his servants, "Notice carefully, when Amnon's heart is joyous with wine, and when I say to you, 'Strike Amnon,' then kill him. Do not be afraid; have I not commanded you myself [and in doing so have I not taken full responsibility for his death]? Be courageous and brave."

²⁹So the servants of Absalom did to Amnon just as Absalom had commanded. Then all the king's sons got up, and every man mounted his mule and fled.

³⁰Now it happened while they were on the way [back home], that the [exaggerated] report came to David, "Absalom has killed all the king's sons, and not one of them is left."

³¹Then the king stood and tore his clothes and lay on the ground [in mourning]; and all his servants were standing by with their clothes torn.

³²But Jonadab the son of Shimeah, David's brother, responded, "Do not let my lord assume that all the king's sons have been put to death; for only Amnon is dead. This *act of revenge* has been on Absalom's mind since the day Amnon violated his sister Tamar.

³³"So now, do not let my lord the king take the report to heart that all the king's sons are dead; for Amnon alone is dead."

³⁴Now Absalom fled. And the young man who kept watch looked up, and behold, many people were coming from the road behind him by the side of the mountain.

³⁵And Jonadab said to the king, "Look, the king's sons are coming. It has turned out just as your servant said."

³⁶And when he finished speaking, the king's sons came, and they raised their voices and wept; and the king and all his servants also wept very bitterly.

³⁷But Absalom fled and went to [his mother's father] Talmai the son of Ammihud, king of Geshur. And David mourned for his son every day.

³⁸So Absalom fled and went to Geshur, and was there for three years.

³⁹And *the heart of* King David longed to go to Absalom; for he was comforted regarding Amnon, since he was dead.

14 NOW JOAB the son of Zeruiah knew that the king's heart *longed* for Absalom. ²So Joab sent *word* to Tekoa and had a wise woman brought from there and told her, "Please pretend to be a mourner, and put on mourning clothes, and do not anoint yourself with oil, but act like a woman who has for many days been in mourning for the dead. ³"Then go to the king and speak to him in this way." So Joab told her what to say.

⁴When the woman of Tekoa spoke to the king, she bowed with her face to the ground and lay herself down, and said, "Help, O king."

⁵The king asked her, "What is the matter?" She said, "Truly I am a widow; my husband is dead.

⁶"Your maidservant had two sons, but the two of them struggled *and* fought in the field. There was no one to separate them, so one struck the other and killed him.

⁷"Now behold, the entire family has risen against your maidservant, and they say, 'Hand over the one who killed his brother, so that we may put him to death [to pay] for the life of his brother whom he killed and destroy the heir also.' By doing this they will extinguish my coal that is left, leaving my husband without a name or a remnant (heir) on the face of the earth."

⁸Then David said to the woman, "Go to your home, and I will give orders concerning you."

⁹The woman of Tekoa said to the king, "My lord, O king, the guilt is on me and on my father's house, but the king and his throne are guiltless."

¹⁰The king said, "If anyone speaks to you [about this matter], bring him to me [for judgment], and he will not touch you again."

¹¹Then she said, "Please let the king remember the Lord your God, so that the avenger of blood will not continue to destroy, otherwise they will destroy my son." And David said, "As the Lord lives, not a single hair [from the head] of your son shall fall to the ground."

¹²Then the woman said, "Please let your maidservant speak *one more* word to my lord the king." He said, "Speak."

¹³The woman said, "Now why have you planned such a thing against God's people? For in speaking this word the king is like a guilty man, in that the king does not bring back his banished one.

¹⁴"For we will certainly die and are like water that is spilled on the ground and cannot be gathered up again. Yet God does not [simply] take away life, but devises plans so that the one who is banished is not driven away from Him.

¹⁵"Now I came to speak of this matter to my lord the king because the people have made me afraid. So your maidservant thought, 'I will just speak to the king; perhaps the king will do what his maidservant requests.

¹⁶'For the king will hear and save his maidservant from the hand of the man

who would destroy me and my son to-gether from the inheritance of God.'

¹⁷"Then your maidservant said, 'Please let the word of my lord the king be comforting, for my lord the king is as the angel of God to discern good and evil. May the Lord your God be with you.'"

¹⁸Then the king answered and said to the woman, "Do not hide from me anything that I ask you." And the woman said, "Let my lord the king please speak."

¹⁹The king said, "Is the hand of Joab with you in all of this?" And the woman answered, "As your soul lives, my lord the king, no one can turn to the right or to the left from anything that my lord the king has said. Indeed, it was your servant Joab who com-manded me; he put all these words in the mouth of your maidservant.

²⁰"In order to change the appearance of things [between Absalom and you, his father] your servant Joab did this thing. But my lord has wisdom like the wisdom of the angel of God, to know everything that is in the earth."

²¹Then the king said to Joab, "Listen, I will most certainly do this thing; now go, bring back the young man Absalom."

²²Joab bowed his face toward the ground and lay himself down and blessed the king. Then Joab said, "To-day your servant knows that I have found favor in your sight, my lord, O king, in that the king has done the re-quest of his servant."

²³So Joab got up, went to Geshur, and brought Absalom to Jerusalem.

²⁴However, the king said, "Let him go to his own house, and do not let him see my face." So Absalom went to his own house and did not see the king's face.

²⁵Now in all Israel there was no man as handsome as Absalom, so highly praised [for that]; from the sole of his foot to the crown of his head there was no blemish in him.

²⁶When he cut the hair of his head (for at the end of each year he cut it, because its weight was heavy on him) he weighed the hair of his head at 200 shekels by the king's weight.

²⁷To Absalom were born three sons and one daughter whose name was Tamar; she was a beautiful woman.

²⁸Absalom lived two full years in Je-rusalem, without seeing the king's face.

²⁹So Absalom sent for Joab, to send him to the king, but he would not come to him; even when he sent again a sec-ond time, he [still] would not come.

³⁰Therefore Absalom said to his ser-vants, "See, Joab's property is near mine, and he has barley there; go and set it on fire." So Absalom's servants set the field on fire.

³¹Then Joab took action and went to Absalom at his house and said to him, "Why did your servants set my field on fire?"

³²Absalom answered Joab, "I sent for you, saying, 'Come here, so that I may send you to the king to ask, "Why have I come [back] from Geshur? It would be better for me to still be there."' Now then, let me see the king's face, and if there is guilt in me, let him put me to death."

³³So Joab came to the king and told him. Then David called for Absalom, and he came to the king and bowed his face to the ground before the king; and the king kissed Absalom.

15 AFTER THIS, Absalom pro-vided for himself a chariot and horses, and fifty men as runners before him.

²He would get up early and stand be-side the road to the gate [of the city, where court was held]; and when any man who had a dispute came to the king for judgment, Absalom would call to him, "From what city are you?" And he would say, "Your servant is from one of the tribes of Israel."

³Then Absalom would say to him, "See, your claims are good and right, but there is no man appointed as the king's agent to listen to you."

⁴Moreover Absalom would say, "Oh, that I were appointed judge in the land! Then every man who had a dispute could come to me and I would get justice for him."

⁵And whenever a man approached to bow down before him, he would put out his hand, take hold of him, and kiss him.

⁶This is how Absalom dealt with everyone in Israel who came to the king for judgment. So Absalom stole the hearts of the men of Israel.

⁷And after four years, Absalom said to the king, "Please let me go and pay my vow which I have made to the Lᴏʀᴅ at Hebron [my birthplace].

⁸"For your servant made a vow while I lived at Geshur in Aram (Syria), 'If the Lᴏʀᴅ will in fact bring me back to Jerusalem, then I will serve the Lord [by offering a sacrifice of thanksgiving].'"

⁹And [David] the king said to him, "Go in peace." So he arose and went to Hebron.

¹⁰But Absalom sent spies throughout all the tribes of Israel, saying, "As soon as you hear the sound of the trumpet, you shall say, 'Absalom is king in Hebron.'"

¹¹Then two hundred men from Jerusalem who were invited [as guests to his sacrificial feast] went with Absalom. They went innocently and knew nothing [about his plan against David].

¹²And Absalom sent for Ahithophel the Gilonite, David's counselor, from his city Giloh, while he was offering sacrifices. And the conspiracy grew strong, for the people with Absalom increased continually.

¹³Then a messenger came to David, saying, "The hearts of the men of Israel are with Absalom."

¹⁴David said to all his servants who were with him at Jerusalem, "Arise, let us flee, or none of us will escape from Absalom! Go in haste, or he will overtake us quickly and bring disaster on us and strike the city with the edge of the sword."

¹⁵The king's servants said to him, "Listen, your servants *are ready to do* whatever my lord the king decides."

¹⁶So the king left, and all his household with him. But the king left behind ten women *who were* concubines to take care of the house (palace). [2 Sam 12:11; 20:3]

¹⁷The king left, and all the people with him, and they stopped at the last house.

¹⁸All of David's servants passed on beside him, and all the Cherethites, Pelethites and the Gittites, six hundred men who had come with him from Gath, passed on before the king.

¹⁹Then the king said to Ittai the Gittite, "Why should you go with us, too? Go back and stay with the king [of your own country], for you are a foreigner and an exile as well; *return* to your own place.

²⁰"You came *only* yesterday, so should I make you wander with us today while I go where I will? Return and take your brothers back with you also. May lovingkindness and faithfulness be with you."

²¹But Ittai answered the king, "As the Lᴏʀᴅ lives, and as my lord the king lives, most certainly wherever my lord the king may be, whether for death or life, there will your servant be also."

²²So David said to Ittai, "Go on and cross over [the Brook Kidron]." So Ittai the Gittite crossed over with all his men and all the little ones who were with him.

²³While all the country was weeping with a loud voice, all the people crossed over. The king also crossed the Brook Kidron, and all the people went on toward the way of the wilderness

[that lies between Jerusalem and the Jordan River].

²⁴Now Zadok also *came*, and all the Levites with him carrying the ark of the covenant of God. And they set down the ark of God, and Abiathar [the priest] came up [and officiated] until all the people had finished passing from the city.

²⁵Then the king told Zadok, "Take the ark of God back to [its rightful place in] the city [of Jerusalem, the capital]. If I find favor in the LORD's sight, He will bring me back again and let me see both it and His dwelling place (habitation).

²⁶"But if He should say, 'I have no delight in you,' then here I am; let Him do to me what seems good to Him."

²⁷The king also said to Zadok the priest, "Are you not a seer? Return to the city in peace [you and Abiathar], and your two sons with you, your son Ahimaaz and Jonathan the son of Abiathar.

²⁸"See, I am going to wait at the fords [of the Jordan] in the wilderness until word comes from you to inform me."

²⁹So Zadok and Abiathar brought the ark of God back to Jerusalem, and they stayed there.

³⁰And David went up the ascent of the *Mount of* Olives, weeping as he went, with his head covered and walking barefoot [in despair]. And all the people who were with him covered their heads and went up, weeping as they went.

³¹David was told, "Ahithophel [your counselor] is among the conspirators with Absalom." David said, "O LORD, I pray You, turn Ahithophel's counsel into foolishness."

³²It happened when David came to the summit [of the Mount of Olives], where he worshiped God, behold, Hushai the Archite came to meet him with his tunic torn and dust on his head [as if in mourning].

³³David said to him, "If you go on with me, you will be a burden to me.

³⁴"But if you return to the city, and say to Absalom, 'I will be your servant, O king; as I have been your father's servant in the past, so I will be your servant now;' then you can thwart (make useless) the advice of Ahithophel for me.

³⁵"Are not Zadok and Abiathar the priests with you there? So it shall be that every word you hear from the king's palace, you shall report it to them.

³⁶"Their two sons are there with them, Ahimaaz, Zadok's son and Jonathan, Abiathar's son; and by them you shall send to me everything that you hear."

³⁷So Hushai, David's friend, returned to the city, and [at about the same time] Absalom came into Jerusalem.

16

WHEN DAVID was a little past the summit [of the Mount of Olives], behold, Ziba, the servant of Mephibosheth, met him with a team of saddled donkeys, and on them were two hundred loaves of bread, a hundred clusters of raisins, a hundred summer fruits, and a jug of wine.

²The king said to Ziba, "Why do you have these?" Ziba said, "The donkeys are for the king's household (family) to ride on, the bread and summer fruit for the young men to eat, and the wine is for anyone to drink who becomes weary in the wilderness."

³Then the king said, "And where is your master's son [Mephibosheth]?" Ziba said to the king, "Behold, he remains in Jerusalem, for he said, 'Today the house of Israel will give me back the kingdom of my father.'"

⁴Then the king said to Ziba, "Behold, everything that belonged to Mephibosheth is [now] yours." Ziba said, "I bow down [in honor and gratitude];

let me find favor in your sight, O my lord the king."

⁵When King David came to Bahurim, a man named Shimei, the son of Gera, came out from there. He was of the family of Saul's household and he was cursing continually as he came out.

⁶He threw stones at David and at all the servants of King David; yet all the people and all the warriors *remained* on his right and on his left.

⁷This is what Shimei said as he cursed: "Get out, get out, you man of bloodshed, you worthless *and* useless man!

⁸"The LORD has returned upon you all the bloodshed of the house of Saul, in whose place you have reigned; and the LORD has given the kingdom into the hands of Absalom your son. And behold, you are *caught* in your own evil, for you are a man of bloodshed!"

⁹Then Abishai [David's nephew], the son of Zeruiah, said to the king, "Why should this dead dog (despicable person) curse my lord the king? Let me go over and take off his head."

¹⁰But the king said, "What business is this of yours, O sons of Zeruiah? If Shimei is cursing because the LORD said to him, 'Curse David,' then who should say, 'Why have you done so?'"

¹¹Then David said to Abishai and to all his servants, "Look, my son [Absalom] who came from my own body, is seeking my life; how much more [reason] now [does] this Benjamite [have to curse me]? Let him alone and let him curse, for [it could be that] the LORD has told him [to do it].

¹²"Perhaps the LORD will look on the wrong done to me [by Shimei, if he is acting on his own]; and [in that case perhaps] the Lord will this day return good to me in place of his cursing."

¹³So David and his men went on the road; and Shimei went along on the hillside close beside David and cursed as he went and threw stones and dust at him.

¹⁴The king and all the people who were with him arrived [at the Jordan River] weary, and he refreshed himself there.

¹⁵Then Absalom and all the people, the men of Israel, entered Jerusalem, and Ahithophel with him.

¹⁶Now it happened when Hushai the Archite, David's friend, came to Absalom, Hushai said to him, "*Long* live the king! *Long* live the king!"

¹⁷Absalom said to Hushai, "Is this your loyalty to your friend? Why did you not go with your friend?"

¹⁸Hushai said to Absalom, "No! For whomever the LORD and this people and all the men of Israel have chosen [as king], I will be his, and I will remain with him.

¹⁹"Besides, whom should I serve? *Should I* not *serve* in the presence of David's son? As I have served in your father's presence, so I shall serve in your presence."

²⁰Then Absalom said to Ahithophel, "Give *me* your advice. What should we do?"

²¹Ahithophel said to Absalom, "Go in to your father's concubines, whom he has left behind to take care of the house; then all Israel will hear that you have made yourself odious to your father. Then the hands of all who are with you will be strengthened [by your boldness and audacity]."

²²So they pitched a tent for Absalom on the roof [of the king's palace], and Absalom went in to his father's concubines in the sight of all Israel. [2 Sam 12:11, 12]

²³The advice of Ahithophel, which he gave in those days, was as if a man had consulted the word of God; that is how all Ahithophel's counsel was *regarded* by both David and Absalom.

17 THEN, AHITHOPHEL said to Absalom, "Please let me choose 12,000 men, and I will set out and pursue David tonight.

²"I will strike while he is weary and

exhausted, and terrify him; and all the people with him will flee [in terror]. Then I will attack the king alone,

³and I will bring all the people [who follow David] back to you. The return of everyone depends on the [death of the] man you are seeking; then all the people will be at peace [and accept you as king]."

⁴So the plan pleased Absalom and all the elders of Israel.

⁵Nevertheless, Absalom said, "Now call Hushai the Archite also, and let us hear what he has to say."

⁶When Hushai came to Absalom, Absalom said to him, "Ahithophel has advised this [plan of action]. Should we do what he says? If not, you speak [and explain why not]."

⁷So Hushai said to Absalom, "Ahithophel has not given good advice this time."

⁸And Hushai said, "You know your father and his men, that they are brave men, and they are enraged *and* fierce, like a bear deprived of her cubs in the field. Your father is a [shrewd] man of war, and will not spend the night with the people [knowing that you seek his life].

⁹"Behold, he has hidden himself [even] now in one of the ravines or in another place; and when some of your troops fall at the first attack, whoever hears *about it* will say, 'There has been a defeat among the people who follow Absalom.'

¹⁰"And even the one who is brave, whose heart is like the heart of a lion, will completely lose heart *and* melt away; for all Israel knows that your father is a mighty man, and that those who are with him are brave men.

¹¹"But I advise that all [the men of] Israel be summoned to you, from Dan [in the north] to Beersheba [in the south], like the sand that is by the sea in abundance, and that you personally go into battle.

¹²"So shall we come upon David in one of the places where he can be found, and we *will fall* on him as the dew falls [unseen and unheard] on the ground; and of him and of all the men who are with him, not even one will be left.

¹³"If he retreats into a city, then all Israel shall bring ropes to that city, and we will drag it into the ravine until not even a pebble [of it] is found there."

¹⁴Then Absalom and all the men of Israel said, "The advice of Hushai the Archite is better than that of Ahithophel." For the Lord had ordained to thwart the good advice of Ahithophel, so that the Lord could bring disaster upon Absalom.

¹⁵Then Hushai said to Zadok and Abiathar the priests, "This is the advice that Ahithophel gave to Absalom and the elders of Israel, and this is the advice that I have given.

¹⁶"Now then, send *word* quickly and tell David, 'Do not spend the night at the fords [on the west side of the Jordan] in the wilderness, but by all means cross over [to the east side of the river], or else the king and all the people with him will be destroyed [if Ahithophel is allowed by Absalom to lead an attack].'"

¹⁷Now Jonathan and Ahimaaz [the priests' sons] were staying at En-rogel, and a maidservant [appearing to go for water] would go and tell them [what was happening], and they would go [secretly] and inform King David; for they could not [allow themselves to] be seen coming into the city [of Jerusalem].

¹⁸But a boy saw them and told Absalom; so the two of them left quickly and came to the house of a man in Bahurim, who had a well in his courtyard, and [with his permission] they went down into it.

¹⁹And the woman [of the house] took a covering and spread it over the mouth of the well and scattered grain on it; so nothing was discovered.

²⁰Then Absalom's servants came to the woman at the house and asked, "Where are Ahimaaz and Jonathan?" And the woman said to them, "They have crossed over the brook." When they searched and could not find them, they returned to Jerusalem.

²¹After they left, Jonathan and Ahimaaz came up out of the well and went and informed King David, and said to David, "Arise and cross over the Jordan River quickly, for Ahithophel has advised [an attack] against you."

²²Then David and all the people who were with him departed and crossed over the Jordan. By daybreak, not even one was left who had not crossed the Jordan.

²³Now when Ahithophel saw that his advice had not been followed, he saddled his donkey and set out and went to his home, to his city. Then he put his household in order, and hanged himself. So he died and was buried in the tomb of his father.

²⁴Then David came to Mahanaim. And Absalom crossed over the Jordan, he and all the men of Israel with him.

²⁵Absalom put Amasa in command of the army instead of Joab. Now Amasa was the son of a man named Ithra the Israelite, who had married Abigail the daughter of Nahash, [the half sister of David and] the sister of Zeruiah, Joab's mother.

²⁶So Israel and Absalom camped in the land of Gilead.

²⁷When David came to Mahanaim, Shobi the son of Nahash from Rabbah of the Ammonites, and Machir the son of Ammiel from Lo-debar, and Barzillai the Gileadite from Rogelim

²⁸brought beds, basins, pottery, wheat, barley, flour, roasted grain, broad beans, lentils, and [other] roasted *grain,*

²⁹honey, cream, sheep, and cheese of the herd, for David and the people who were with him, to eat; for they said, "The people are hungry and weary and thirsty in the wilderness."

18 DAVID NUMBERED the men who were with him and set over them commanders of thousands and commanders of hundreds.

²Then David sent the army out, a third under the command of Joab, a third under Abishai the son of Zeruiah, Joab's brother, and a third under the command of Ittai the Gittite. And the king said to the men, "I myself will certainly go out [to fight] with you."

³But the men said, "You should not go out [to battle with us]. For if in fact we retreat, they will not care about us; even if half of us die, they will not care about us. But you are worth ten thousand of us. So now it is better that you be *ready* to help us from the city [of Mahanaim]."

⁴Then the king said to them, "I will do whatever seems best to you." So the king stood beside the gate [of Mahanaim], and all the army went out in groups of hundreds and of thousands.

⁵The king commanded Joab and Abishai and Ittai, saying, "*Deal* gently with the young man Absalom for my sake." And all the men heard when the king gave orders to all the commanders about Absalom.

⁶So the men went out into the field against Israel, and the battle was *fought* in the forest of Ephraim.

⁷The men of Israel [who supported Absalom] were defeated there by the men of David, and a great slaughter took place there that day, 20,000 men.

⁸For the battle there was spread out over the surface of the entire countryside, and the [hazards of the] forest devoured more men that day than did the sword.

⁹Now Absalom met the servants of David. Absalom was riding on his mule, and the mule went under the thick branches of a massive tree, and

his head was caught in [the thick branches of] the tree; and he was left hanging [in midair] between heaven and earth, while the mule that had been under him kept going.

¹⁰A certain man saw it and informed Joab, saying, "I saw Absalom hanging in a tree."

¹¹Joab said to the man who informed him, "You saw *him!* Why then did you not strike him there to the ground? I would have given you ten *pieces* of silver and a belt."

¹²The man told Joab, "Even if I were to feel the weight of a thousand *pieces* of silver in my hands, I would not put out my hand against the king's son; for we all heard the king command you, Abishai, and Ittai, saying, 'Protect the young man Absalom, for my sake.'

¹³"Otherwise, if I had acted treacherously against his life (for nothing is hidden from the king) you yourself would have taken sides against me."

¹⁴Joab said, "I will not waste time with you." So he took three spears in his hand and thrust them through the heart of Absalom while he was still alive [and caught] in the midst of the tree.

¹⁵And ten young men, Joab's armor bearers, surrounded and struck Absalom and killed him.

¹⁶Then Joab blew the trumpet [to signal the end of the combat], and the men returned from pursuing Israel, for Joab held them back.

¹⁷They took [down the body of] Absalom and threw him into a deep pit in the forest and set up a huge mound of stones over him. Then all Israel fled, everyone to his own tent.

¹⁸Now Absalom in his lifetime had taken and set up for himself a memorial pillar which is in the King's Valley, for he said, "I have no son to keep my name in remembrance." He named the memorial pillar after himself, and to this day it is called Absalom's Monument.

¹⁹Then Ahimaaz the son of Zadok, said, "Let me run and bring the king news that the LORD has vindicated him *by rescuing him* from [the power of] his enemies."

²⁰But Joab told him, "You are not the man to carry news [to King David] today, but you shall carry news another day. On this day you shall carry no news, because the king's son is dead."

²¹Then Joab said to the Cushite (Ethiopian), "Go, tell the king what you have seen." And the Cushite bowed to Joab and ran.

²²Then Ahimaaz the son of Zadok said again to Joab, "But whatever happens, please let me also run after the Cushite." Joab said, "Why should you run, my son, seeing you will have no messenger's reward for going [because you have only bad news]?"

²³"But whatever happens, Let me run." So Joab said to him, "Run." Then Ahimaaz ran by the way of the plain [of the Jordan River] and outran the Cushite.

²⁴Now David was sitting between the two gates; and the lookout went up to the roof of the gate by the wall, and when he raised his eyes and looked, he saw a man running alone.

²⁵The lookout called *down* and told the king. The king said, "If he is alone, he has good news to tell." And he came nearer and nearer.

²⁶Then the lookout saw another man running, and he called to the gatekeeper and said, "Look, *another* man running alone." The king said, "He also is bringing good news."

²⁷The lookout said, "I think the man in front runs like Ahimaaz the son of Zadok." The king said, "He is a good man and is coming with good news."

²⁸And Ahimaaz called out and said to the king, "All is well." And he bowed before the king with his face to the ground and said, "Blessed be the LORD your God, who has handed over the men who lifted up their hands [to fight] against my lord the king."

²⁹The king asked, "Is the young man Absalom safe?" Ahimaaz answered, "When Joab sent the king's servant, and your servant, I saw a great turmoil, but I do not know what *it was about*."

³⁰The king told him, "Step aside; stand here." And he stepped aside and stood still.

³¹Behold, the Cushite (Ethiopian) arrived, and said, "Let my lord the king receive good news, for the LORD has vindicated you today *by rescuing you* from the hand (power) of all those who stood against you."

³²The king asked the Cushite, "Is the young man Absalom [my son] safe?" The Cushite replied, "May the enemies of my lord the king, and all those who rise against you to do evil, be [dead] like that young man is."

³³The king was deeply moved and went to the upper room over the gate and wept [in sorrow]. And this is what he said as he walked: "O my son Absalom, my son, my son Absalom! How I wish that I had died instead of you, O Absalom, my son, my son!"

19 IT WAS told to Joab, "Behold, the king is weeping and mourning for Absalom."
²So the victory on that day was turned into mourning for all the people, for the people heard it said on that day, "The king grieves for his son."

³The people stole into the city [of Mahanaim] that day, as people who are humiliated *and* ashamed steal away when they retreat in battle.

⁴But the king covered his face and cried out with a loud voice, "O my son Absalom, O Absalom, my son, my son!"

⁵Then Joab came into the house to the king and said, "Today you have put all your servants to shame who this day have saved your life and the lives of your sons and your daughters, and the lives of your wives and concubines.

⁶"For you love those who hate you and hate those who love you. For you have shown today that commanders and servants are nothing to you; for today I know that if Absalom had lived and all the rest of us had died today, then you would be pleased.

⁷"So now stand up, go out and speak kindly *and* encouragingly to your servants; for I swear by the LORD that if you do not go out, not a man will stay with you tonight. And this will be worse for you than all the evil that has come upon you from your youth until now."

⁸Then the king stood and sat at the gate [of Mahanaim]. And they told all the people, "The king is sitting at the gate," and all the people came before the king.

But Israel [Absalom's troops] had fled, every man to his tent.

⁹All the people were quarreling throughout the tribes of Israel, saying, "The king rescued us from the hands of our enemies, and he saved us from the hands of the Philistines, but now he has fled out of the land from Absalom.

¹⁰"And Absalom, whom we anointed over us, has died in battle. So now, why are you [leaders] doing nothing about bringing back the king?"

¹¹Then King David sent *word* to Zadok and to Abiathar the priests, saying, "Say to the elders of Judah, 'Why are you the last to bring the king back to his house [in Jerusalem], since the

speak the Word

Thank You, God, that You are a God Who vindicates and rescues me from the power of all who stand against me!
–ADAPTED FROM 2 SAMUEL 18:31

word of all Israel has come to the king, and to his house?

¹²'You are my brothers (relatives, relations); you are my bone and my flesh. Why then are you the last to bring back the king?'

¹³"Say to Amasa [the commander of Absalom's troops], 'Are you not my bone and my flesh? May God do so to me, and more also, if you will not be commander of my army from now on in place of Joab.'"

¹⁴In this way he changed the hearts of all the men of Judah as one man, so they sent *word* to the king, "Return, you and all your servants."

¹⁵So David returned and came to the Jordan. And [supporters from] Judah came to Gilgal to meet the king, to escort him across the Jordan.

¹⁶Then Shimei the son of Gera, a Benjamite of Bahurim, hurried and came down with the men [from the tribe of] of Judah to meet King David,

¹⁷and a thousand men [from the tribe] of Benjamin with him. And Ziba, the servant of the house of Saul, and his fifteen sons and twenty servants with him, rushed down to the Jordan before the king.

¹⁸Then they [repeatedly] crossed the ford to bring over the king's household (family), and to do what pleased him. And Shimei the son of Gera fell down before the king as he was about to cross the Jordan,

¹⁹and said to the king, "Let not my lord consider me guilty, nor remember what your servant did wrong on the day my lord the king left Jerusalem, so that the king would take it to heart.

²⁰"For your servant knows that I have sinned; therefore, behold, I have come today, the first of all the house of Joseph to come down to meet my lord the king."

²¹But Abishai the son of Zeruiah said, "Should not Shimei be put to death for this, because he cursed the LORD's anointed?"

²²David said, "What business is this of yours, you sons of Zeruiah, that you should be an adversary to me today? Should anyone be put to death in Israel today? For do I not know that today I am king over Israel?"

²³Therefore the king said to Shimei, "You shall not be put to death." And so the king gave him his promise. [1 Kin 2:44–46]

²⁴Then Mephibosheth the [grand] son of Saul came down to meet the king, but he had not cared for his feet, nor trimmed his mustache, nor washed his clothes from the day the king left until the day he returned in peace *and* safety.

²⁵And when he came to Jerusalem to meet the king, the king said to him, "Why did you not go with me, Mephibosheth?"

²⁶He said, "My lord the king, my servant [Ziba] betrayed me; for I said, 'Saddle a donkey for me so that I may ride on it and go with the king,' for your servant is lame [but he took the donkeys and left without me]. [2 Sam 16:1–4]

²⁷"Further, he has slandered your servant to my lord the king; but my lord the king is like the angel of God; so do what is good in your eyes.

²⁸"For were not all of my father's household (family) nothing but dead men before my lord the king; yet you set your servant among those who ate at your own table. So what right do I still have to cry out anymore to the king [for help]?"

²⁹The king said to him, "Why speak anymore of your affairs? I have said, 'You and Ziba shall divide the land.'"

³⁰Mephibosheth said to the king, "Let him even take it all, since my lord the king has returned to his own house in safety *and* peace."

³¹Now Barzillai the Gileadite came down from Rogelim and went on to the Jordan with the king to escort him over the Jordan.

³²Barzillai was a very old man, eighty years old; and he had provided the king with food while he stayed at Mahanaim, for he was a very great *and* wealthy man.

³³The king said to Barzillai, "Cross over with me and I will provide for you in Jerusalem with me."

³⁴But Barzillai said to the king, "How much longer have I to live, that I should go up with the king to Jerusalem?

³⁵"I am this day eighty years old. Can I [be useful to advise you to] discern between good and bad? Can your servant taste what I eat or drink? Can I still hear the voices of singing men and women? Why then should your servant be an added burden to my lord the king?

³⁶"Your servant would merely cross over the Jordan with the king. Why should the king compensate me with this reward?

³⁷"Please let your servant return, so that I may die in my own city [and be buried] by the grave of my father and mother. But here is your servant Chimham [my son]; let him cross over with my lord the king, and do for him what seems good to you." [1 Kin 2:7]

³⁸The king answered, "Chimham shall cross over with me, and I will do for him what seems good to you; and whatever you ask of me, I will do for you."

³⁹So all the people crossed over the Jordan. When the king had crossed over, he kissed Barzillai and blessed him, and he returned to his place.

⁴⁰Then the king went on to Gilgal, and Chimham went on with him; and all the people of Judah and also half the people of Israel accompanied the king.

⁴¹And all the men of Israel came to the king and said to him, "Why have our brothers (relatives), the men [from the tribe] of Judah, stolen you away and brought the king and his household and all David's men with him over the Jordan [instead of waiting for us to arrive]?"

⁴²Then all the men of Judah answered the men of Israel, "Because the king is a close relative to us. So why then are you angry about this matter? Have we eaten at all at the king's *expense?* Or has anything been taken for us?"

⁴³Then the men of Israel answered the men of Judah, "We have ten [tribes'] shares in the king, and we have more *claim* on David than you. Why then did you treat us with contempt *and* ignore us [by rushing ahead]? Were we not the first to speak of bringing back our king?" But the words of the men of Judah were harsher than those of the men of Israel.

20 THERE HAPPENED to be there a worthless *and* wicked man named Sheba the son of Bichri, a Benjamite. He blew a trumpet [to call Israel to revolt] and said,

"We have no portion in David
And no inheritance in the son of Jesse,
Every man to his tents, O Israel!"

²So all the men of Israel deserted David and followed Sheba the son of Bichri; but the men of Judah stayed faithfully with their king, from the Jordan to Jerusalem.

³Then David came to his house (palace) at Jerusalem, and the king took the ten women, his concubines whom he had left to take care of the house, and placed them under guard and provided for them, but did not go in to them. So they were confined, and lived as widows until the day of their death.

⁴Now the king said to Amasa [the commander of his army], "Summon the [fighting] men of Judah to me within three days, and be present here yourself."

⁵So Amasa went to summon [the fighting men of] Judah, but he delayed longer than the time which David had set for him.

⁶And David said to Abishai [his nephew], "Now Sheba the son of Bichri will do us more harm than Absalom did. Take your lord's servants and pursue him, so that he does not find fortified cities for himself and escape from our sight."

⁷So Joab's men went after him, along with [David's bodyguards] the Cherethites and Pelethites and all the warriors; they went out from Jerusalem to pursue Sheba the son of Bichri.

⁸When they were at the great stone in Gibeon, Amasa came to meet them. Now Joab was wearing his military uniform, and over it he had a belt with a sheathed sword strapped around his hips; and as he went forward, it fell out.

⁹Joab said to Amasa, "Is it going well with you, my brother?" And with his right hand Joab took hold of Amasa by the beard [as if] to kiss him [in greeting].

¹⁰But Amasa [who had replaced Joab as David's commander] was off guard *and* not attentive to the sword in Joab's hand. So Joab struck Amasa in the abdomen with the sword, spilling his intestines to the ground. Without another blow Amasa died. Then Joab and Abishai his brother pursued Sheba the son of Bichri.

¹¹Now one of Joab's young men stood by him and said, "Whoever favors Joab and is for David, let him follow Joab!"

¹²But Amasa was wallowing in his blood in the middle of the highway. And when the man saw that all the people who came by stopped [to look], he moved Amasa from the highway into the field and threw a garment over him when he saw that everyone who came by Amasa stopped.

¹³When [the body of] Amasa was removed from the highway, everyone followed after Joab to pursue Sheba the son of Bichri.

¹⁴Now Joab went through all the tribes of Israel to Abel, even Beth-maacah,

and all the Berites; and they assembled and also went after Sheba.

¹⁵And the army of Joab came and besieged Sheba in Abel Beth-maacah, and they built up an assault ramp against the city, and it stood against the outer rampart; and all the people who were with Joab were wreaking destruction to make the wall fall.

¹⁶Then a wise woman cried out from the city, "Hear, hear! Tell Joab, 'Come here so that I may speak to you.'"

¹⁷So when he approached her, the woman asked, "Are you Joab?" He answered, "I am." Then she said to him, "Listen to the words of your maidservant." He answered, "I am listening."

¹⁸Then she said, "In the past people used to say, 'They will certainly ask *advice* at Abel,' and so they settled *the dispute*.

¹⁹"I am one of the peaceable and faithful in Israel. You are seeking to destroy a city, and a mother in Israel. Why would you swallow up (devour) the inheritance of the LORD?"

²⁰Joab answered, "Far be it, far be it from me that I would swallow up or destroy!

²¹"That is not true. But a man of the hill country of Ephraim, Sheba the son of Bichri by name, has lifted up his hand [in rebellion] against King David. Only hand him over, and I will leave the city." And the woman said to Joab, "Behold, his head shall be thrown to you over the wall."

²²Then the woman in her wisdom went to all the people [to inform them of the agreement]. And they beheaded Sheba the son of Bichri and threw his head [down] to Joab. So he blew the trumpet [signaling the end of the attack], and they dispersed from the city, every man to his own tent. And Joab returned to Jerusalem to [David] the king. [Eccl 9:13–16]

²³Now Joab was [commander] over the entire army of Israel; Benaiah the

son of Jehoiada was [commander] over the Cherethites and Pelethites [the king's bodyguards];

²⁴Adoram was over the forced labor; Jehoshaphat the son of Ahilud was recorder;

²⁵Sheva was the scribe; and Zadok and Abiathar were priests;

²⁶also Ira the Jairite was a priest to David.

21 THERE WAS famine in the days of David for three consecutive years; and David sought the presence (face) of the LORD [asking the reason]. The LORD replied, "It is because of Saul and his bloody house, because he put the Gibeonites to death."

²So the king called the Gibeonites and spoke to them (now the Gibeonites were not of the sons (descendants) of Israel but of the remnant (survivors) of the Amorites. The Israelites had sworn [an oath] to [spare] them, but Saul in his zeal for the sons of Israel and Judah had sought to strike down the Gibeonites).

³So David said to the Gibeonites, "What should I do for you? How can I make it good so that you will bless the LORD's inheritance (Israel)?"

⁴The Gibeonites said to him, "We will not accept silver or gold belonging to Saul or his household (descendants); nor is it for us to put any man to death in Israel." David said, "I will do for you whatever you say."

⁵So they said to the king, "The man who consumed us and planned to exterminate us from remaining in any territory of Israel,

⁶let seven men [chosen] from his sons (descendants) be given to us and we will hang them before the LORD [that is, put them on display, impaled with broken legs and arms] in Gibeah of Saul, the chosen one of the LORD." And the king said, "I will give them."

⁷But the king spared Mephibosheth the son of Jonathan, the son of Saul, because of the LORD's oath that was between David and Saul's son Jonathan.

⁸So the king took the two sons of Rizpah the daughter of Aiah, whom she bore to Saul, Armoni and Mephibosheth, and the five sons of Merab the daughter of Saul, whom she had borne to Adriel the son of Barzillai the Meholathite.

⁹He handed them over to the Gibeonites, and they hanged them on the hill before the LORD, and the seven died together. They were put to death in the first days of the grain harvest, the beginning of the barley harvest [in the spring].

¹⁰Rizpah the daughter of Aiah took sackcloth and spread it out for herself on the rock, from the beginning of harvest [in the spring] until [the autumn] rain fell on them; and she allowed neither the birds of the sky to rest on their bodies by day, nor the beasts of the field [to feed on them] by night.

¹¹David was told what Rizpah the daughter of Aiah, the concubine of Saul, had done.

¹²Then David went and took the bones of Saul and Jonathan his son from the men of Jabesh-gilead, who had stolen them from the open square of Beth-shan, where the Philistines had hanged them on the day when the Philistines had killed Saul in Gilboa.

¹³He brought up the bones of Saul and of Jonathan his son from there, and they gathered the bones of those who had been hanged [with their arms and legs broken].

¹⁴They buried the bones of Saul and Jonathan his son in the country of Benjamin in Zela, in the tomb of Kish his father; and they did all that the king commanded. After that, God was moved by prayer for the land.

¹⁵Now the Philistines were at war again with Israel. David went down with

his servants, and as they fought against the Philistines, David became weary.

¹⁶Then Ishbi-benob, who was among the descendants of the giant, the weight of whose spear was three hundred *shekels* (six pounds) of bronze, was armed with a new *sword,* and he intended to kill David.

¹⁷But Abishai the son of Zeruiah came to David's aid, and struck and killed the Philistine. Then David's men swore to him, "You shall not go out again with us to battle, so that you do not extinguish the lamp of Israel."

¹⁸After this, there was war again with the Philistines at Gob (Gezer). At that time Sibbecai the Hushathite killed Saph (Sippai), who was among the descendants of the giant.

¹⁹There was war with the Philistines again at Gob, and Elhanan the son of Jaare-oregim, a Bethlehemite, killed Goliath the Gittite, whose spear shaft was like a weaver's beam.

²⁰There was war at Gath again,

life point

Why does praising the Lord and calling Him "worthy to be praised" (2 Samuel 22:4) defeat our enemies? If you and I will go through the gates of praise into God's presence and begin to worship Him there, our enemies will become confused and destroy one another. When the devil tries to upset us and we react by singing praise to God, it confuses him and his demons so badly that they begin to attack each other. In the process we are delivered from the destruction they want to render to us, and we enter into new levels of joy.

where there was a man of *great* stature who had six fingers on each hand and six toes on each foot, twenty-four in number; he also was a descendant of the giants.

²¹And when he taunted *and* defied Israel, Jonathan the son of Shimei, David's brother, killed him.

²²These four [warriors] were descended from the giant in Gath, and they fell by the hands of David and his servants.

22 DAVID SPOKE the words of this song to the LORD when the LORD rescued him from the hands of all his enemies and from the hand of Saul.

²He said:

"The LORD is my rock and my fortress [on the mountain] and my rescuer; [1 Sam 23:14, 25, 28]
³My God, my rock, in whom I take refuge;
My shield and the horn of my salvation, my stronghold and my refuge,
My Savior—You save me from violence. [Gen 15:1]
⁴"I call on the LORD, who is worthy to be praised,
And I am saved from my enemies.
⁵"For the waves of death encompassed me;
The torrents of destruction overwhelmed *and* terrified me.
⁶"The cords of Sheol surrounded me;
The snares of death confronted me.
⁷"In my distress I called upon the LORD;
I cried out to my God,

speak the Word

Thank You, God, for hearing me when I call upon You in times of distress. Thank You that my cry reaches Your ears and that You are listening to my voice.
–ADAPTED FROM 2 SAMUEL 22:7

And from His temple [in the
heavens] He heard my voice;
My cry for help *came* into His ears.
8 "Then the earth shook and quaked,
The foundations of the heavens
trembled
And were shaken, because He was
angry.
9 "Smoke went up out of His nostrils,
And devouring fire from His
mouth;
Coals were kindled by it.
10 "He bowed the heavens also, and
came down
With thick darkness under His feet.
11 "He rode on a cherub and flew;
He appeared upon the wings of the
wind.
12 "He made darkness canopies
around Him,
A mass of waters, thick clouds of
the skies.
13 "Out of the brightness before Him
Coals of fire were set aflame.
14 "The LORD thundered from heaven,
And the Most High uttered His
voice.
15 "He sent out arrows and scattered
them;
Lightning, and confused them.
16 "The channels of the sea appeared,
The foundations of the world were
uncovered
At the rebuke of the LORD,
At the blast of the breath of His
nostrils.
17 "He sent from above, He took me;
He drew me out of great waters.
18 "He rescued me from my strong
enemy,
From those who hated me, for they
were too mighty for me.
19 "They came upon me in the day of
my calamity,
But the LORD was my support.
20 "He also brought me out to an open
place;
He rescued me because He
delighted in me.

21 "The LORD has dealt with me
according to my righteousness;
According to the cleanness of my
hands He has rewarded me.
22 "For I have kept the ways of the
LORD,
And have not acted wickedly
against my God.
23 "For all His judgments (legal
decisions) were before me,
And from His statutes I did not
turn aside.
24 "I was also blameless before Him,
And kept myself from wrongdoing.
25 "Therefore the LORD has
rewarded me according to my
righteousness,
According to my cleanness in His
sight.
26 "With the loving *and* loyal You
show Yourself loving *and* loyal,
With the blameless You show
Yourself blameless.
27 "With the pure You show Yourself
pure,
With the perverted You show
Yourself astute.

life point

God is our strength, our rock, and our
fortress (see 2 Samuel 22:33, 34). He asks
us to put our faith in Him and to believe
that we can do whatever He asks us to
do. He is mighty to uphold us and make
us stand. He will support us and keep
us from failing. God's strength is readily
available to us, and we receive it through
believing the promise He has made to
give it to us. If we believe we are weak,
then we will only manifest weakness, but
the Bible says, "Let the weak say, 'I am
strong!'" (Joel 3:10). When we can say we
are strong with a heart of conviction—
even though we are weak in ourselves—
the Lord will be strong in us, and we will
experience victory in our lives!

²⁸"And You save the afflicted people;
But Your eyes are on the haughty
   whom You abase (humiliate).
²⁹"For You, O Lᴏʀᴅ, are my lamp;
The Lᴏʀᴅ illumines *and* dispels my
   darkness.
³⁰"For by You I can run upon a troop;
By my God I can leap over a wall.
³¹"As for God, His way is blameless
   and perfect;
The word of the Lᴏʀᴅ is tested.

He is a shield to all those who take
   refuge *and* trust in Him.
³²"For who is God, besides the Lᴏʀᴅ?
And who is a rock, besides our
   God? [1 Sam 2:2]
³³"God is my strong fortress;
He sets the blameless in His way.
³⁴"He makes my feet like the doe's
   feet [firm and swift];
He sets me [secure and confident]
   on my high places.
³⁵"He trains my hands for war,

let God be your strength

David said, "God is my strong fortress" (2 Samuel 22:33). God does not want to just *give* us strength; He wants to *be* our strength.

Many of the men and women in the Bible knew that God was their strength; they became examples to encourage us today to trust in God's strength. David wrote in Psalm 18:29 that by his God he could crush a troop and leap over a wall. In 1 Kings 19:4–8 an angel came and ministered to Elijah, who was tired and depressed, and he went forty days and nights in the strength that he received from that one visit. The Apostle Paul found the strength of God so wonderful that in 2 Corinthians 12:9, 10 he wrote that he would boast in his weaknesses, knowing that when he was weak, he was actually powerful because he could draw from God's strength. To put it in our language today, Paul was saying that he was glad when he was weak because then he got to experience the strength of God.

How does a person receive strength from God? By faith. Start receiving the strength of God by *believing* His promise to strengthen you. That faith will quicken your body, as well as your spirit and soul. For example, if you have a weak back, it can be made strong. At our conferences, the Holy Spirit has strengthened weak knees, ankles, and backs as we have prayed for those who asked God for strength. His healing power came as we waited in His presence and received it from Him.

By faith you can receive strength to stay in a difficult marriage, raise a difficult child, or stick with a difficult job in which you have a difficult boss. You can receive strength to do great things even though you may have a physical impairment yourself.

Have you been trying to push through difficulties on your own? If so, make a change right now. Start gaining strength from deep within you, where the Holy Spirit dwells. If that divine strength does not yet dwell in you, all you need to do to receive it is admit your sins, repent of them, and ask Jesus to be your Savior and Lord. Surrender your life, all that you are and all that you are not, to Him. Ask Him to baptize you in the Holy Spirit and to fill you through and through with the power of the Holy Spirit. Let God be your strength. Say with David, "My God, my rock, in whom I take refuge; my shield and the horn of my salvation, my stronghold and my refuge, my Savior" (2 Samuel 22:3).

So that my arms can bend (pull
back) a bow of bronze.
36 "You have also given me the shield
of Your salvation,
And Your help *and* gentleness
make me great.
37 "You enlarge my steps under me,
And my feet have not slipped.
38 "I pursued my enemies and
destroyed them,
And I did not turn back until they
were consumed (eliminated).
39 "I consumed them and shattered
them, so that they did not rise;
They fell under my feet.
40 "For You have surrounded me with
strength for the battle;
You have subdued under me those
who stood against me.
41 "You have also made my enemies
turn their backs to me [in retreat],
And I destroyed those who
hated me.
42 "They looked, but there was no
savior *for them*—
Even to the LORD [they looked], but
He did not answer them.
43 "Then I beat them as [small as] the
dust of the earth;
I crushed and stamped them as the
mire (dirt, mud) of the streets.
44 "You also have rescued me from
strife with my [own] people;
You have kept me as the head of
the nations.
People whom I have not known
served me.
45 "Foreigners pretend obedience to
me;
As soon as they hear [me], they
obey me.
46 "Foreigners lose heart;
They come trembling out of their
strongholds.
47 "The LORD lives, and blessed be
my rock,

putting the Word to work

Second Samuel 23:3, 4 offers valuable
insight to leaders. When we lead others
in righteousness and in the fear of God,
good things result. If you are a leader,
ask God to help you increase more and
more in righteousness and in the fear of
the Lord as you lead those God has put
under your care.

And exalted be my God, the rock
of my salvation.
48 "It is God who executes vengeance
for me,
And brings down [and disciplines]
the peoples under me,
49 Who also brings me out from my
enemies.
You even lift me above those who
rise up against me;
You rescue me from the violent
man.
50 "For this I will give thanks *and*
praise You, O LORD, among the
nations;
I will sing praises to Your name.
51 "He is a tower of salvation *and*
great deliverance to His king,
And shows lovingkindness to His
anointed,
To David and his offspring forever."

23

NOW THESE are the last
words of David.

David the son of Jesse declares,
The man who was raised on high
declares,
The anointed of the God of Jacob,
And the sweet psalmist of Israel,
2 "The Spirit of the LORD spoke by me,
And His word was on my tongue.
3 "The God of Israel,

speak the Word

*Thank You, God, that You have surrounded me
with strength for every battle that I face.*
—ADAPTED FROM 2 SAMUEL 22:40

The Rock of Israel spoke to me,
'He who rules over men
   righteously,
Who rules in the fear of God,
⁴Is like the morning light *when* the
   sun rises,

A morning without clouds,
When the fresh grass *springs* out of
   the earth
Through sunshine after rain.'
⁵"Truly is not my house so [blessed]
   with God?

fear God, not people

David understood one of the essential qualities of a leader, as we see in 2 Samuel 23:3. Anyone who wants to lead well must fear the Lord. When we talk about fearing God, we are not talking about a wrong kind of fear. We are talking about the reverential fear that causes us to bow in His presence and even to prostrate ourselves before Him and worship Him in awe of Who He is.

The Apostle Paul wrote something in Galatians 1:10 that has always gripped my heart. He said, "Am I now trying to win the favor and approval of men, or of God? Or am I seeking to please someone? If I were still trying to be popular with men, I would not be a bond-servant of Christ."

I know firsthand how Satan uses rejection to prevent us from going forward with the call of God on our lives. Have you ever been attacked by rejection? Of course you have; we all have. The devil uses it to keep us from making progress. He knows that we will be blessed if we are in the will of God, so he uses the fear of rejection to hold us back.

When I was filled with the Holy Spirit in 1976, I experienced rejection from most of my friends, my church, and my family. They did not understand my new zeal and enthusiasm and thought I was being deceived. The rejection grew even worse when God called me to teach and preach His Word. Everywhere I turned, I was being rejected by someone I loved and cared about. It was very difficult to go on. Many times I wanted to give in to the pressure and make decisions that would please people. I look back now and shudder to think what I might have sacrificed had I bowed down to the pressure. There have also been other important times in my life and ministry when the devil launched attacks of rejection against me, and each of them came at a time when God was trying to promote me into the next level of what He had for my life.

Anyone who is going to do the will of God must have more fear of God than of other human beings. I wanted acceptance, but I did not want to be out God's will, and I knew that I would be if I did what my friends wanted me to do. I thank God for His grace that sustained and strengthened me through those difficult testing times.

Those who want to do God's will need to remember what Jesus told His disciples: "'A servant is not greater than his master.' If they persecuted Me, they will also persecute you" (John 15:20). He was saying, "If they reject you, in effect they are rejecting Me." I believe the Lord takes it personally when people reject you because you are trying to do the right thing. He knows how you feel about being rejected, because He felt the same thing. He is your Vindicator, your reward comes from Him, and you must reverentially fear and honor Him more than anything or anyone else.

For He has made an everlasting
  covenant with me,
Ordered in all things, and secured.
For will He not cause to grow *and*
  prosper
All my salvation and my every
  wish?
Will He not make it grow *and*
  prosper?
⁶"But the wicked *and* worthless
  are all to be thrown away like
  thorns,
Because they cannot be taken with
  the hand;
⁷"But the man who touches them
Must be armed with iron and the
  shaft of a spear,
And they are utterly burned *and*
  consumed by fire in their place."

⁸These are the names of the mighty men (warriors) whom David had: Josheb-basshebeth, a Tahchemonite, chief of the captains, *also called* Adino the Eznite (spear) because of the eight hundred men killed [by him] at one time. [1 Chr 11:11]

⁹Next to him was Eleazar the son of Dodo the son of Ahohi. He was one of the three mighty men with David when they taunted *and* defied the Philistines assembled there for battle, and the men of Israel had gone.

¹⁰Eleazar stood up and struck down the Philistines until his hand was weary and clung to the sword. The Lord brought about a great victory that day; the people returned after him only to take the spoil [of the slain].

¹¹Next to Eleazar was Shammah the son of Agee the Hararite. The Philistines were gathered into an army where there was a plot of ground full of lentils, and the people [of Israel] fled from the Philistines.

¹²But he took his stand in the center of the plot and defended it and struck down the Philistines; and the Lord brought about a great victory.

¹³Then three of the thirty chief men went down and came to David at harvest time in the cave of Adullam, while an army of Philistines was encamped in the Valley of Rephaim.

¹⁴David was then in the stronghold, and the garrison of the Philistines was then in Bethlehem.

¹⁵And David had a craving and said, "Oh that someone would give me water to drink from the well of Bethlehem, which is by the gate!"

¹⁶So the three mighty men broke through the camp of the Philistines, and drew water from the well of Bethlehem by the gate, and carried and brought it to David. But he would not drink it, but poured it out [in worship] to the Lord.

¹⁷And he said, "Far be it from me, O Lord, that I should drink this. [Is it not the same as] the blood of the men who went at the risk of their lives?" So he would not drink it. These things the three mighty men did.

¹⁸Now Abishai the brother of Joab the son of Zeruiah was chief of the thirty. He wielded his spear against three hundred men and killed them, and gained a reputation beside the three.

¹⁹He was the most honored of the thirty, so he became their commander; however, he did not attain to the [greatness of the] three.

²⁰Then Benaiah the son of Jehoiada, the son of a valiant man of Kabzeel, who had done many notable acts, killed two [famous] warriors of Moab. He also went down and killed a lion in the middle of a pit on a snowy day.

²¹And he killed an Egyptian, an impressive *and* handsome man. The Egyptian had a spear in his hand, but Benaiah went down to him with a club, snatched the spear out of the Egyptian's hand and killed the man with his own spear.

²²These things Benaiah the son of Jehoiada did, and gained a reputation beside the three mighty men.

²³He was honored among the thirty, but he did not attain to the [greatness of the] three. David appointed him over his guard.

²⁴Asahel the brother of Joab was one of the thirty; *then* Elhanan the son of Dodo of Bethlehem,

²⁵Shammah of Harod, Elika of Harod,

²⁶Helez the Paltite, Ira the son of Ikkesh of Tekoa,

²⁷Abiezer of Anathoth, Mebunnai the Hushathite,

²⁸Zalmon the Ahohite, Maharai of Netophah,

²⁹Heleb the son of Baanah of Netophah, Ittai the son of Ribai of Gibeah of the Benjamites,

³⁰Benaiah of Pirathon, Hiddai of the brooks of Gaash,

³¹Abi-albon the Arbathite, Azmaveth the Barhumite,

³²Eliahba of Shaalbon, the sons of Jashen, Jonathan,

³³Shammah the Hararite, Ahiam the son of Sharar the Ararite,

³⁴Eliphelet the son of Ahasbai the son of Maacah, Eliam the son of Ahithophel of Giloh,

³⁵Hezro (Hezrai) of Carmel, Paarai the Arbite,

³⁶Igal the son of Nathan of Zobah, Bani the Gadite,

³⁷Zelek the Ammonite, Naharai of Beeroth, armor bearer of Joab the son of Zeruiah,

³⁸Ira the Ithrite, Gareb the Ithrite,

³⁹Uriah the Hittite—thirty-seven in all.

24 NOW AGAIN the anger of the LORD burned against Israel, and He incited David against them to say, "Go, count [the people of] Israel and Judah."

²So the king said to Joab the commander of the army who was with him, "Go now through all the tribes of Israel, from Dan [in the north] to Beersheba [in the south], and conduct a census of the people, so that I may know the number of the people."

³But Joab said to the king, "May the LORD your God add to the people a hundred times as many as there are, and let the eyes of my lord the king see

life point

David's heart "troubled" him after he had sinned against the Lord (2 Samuel 24:10). This means that his heart condemned him. A condemned heart steals confidence.

Anyone who wants to be a leader must learn how to handle condemnation. When he sins, he must know how to admit it, repent, and receive forgiveness. We must shake off mistakes from the past and go on, because no one is perfect. We may have a perfect heart, a heart after God's own, but still we will not be perfect in our every thought, word, and deed.

As a leader and teacher of God's Word, I know how condemning it is to teach others about what is right and then make mistakes in that very area myself. When we leaders do that, we feel a double dose of condemnation because the devil will say to us, "You, of all people, ought to know better." If we listen to him, he will make us feel that we are not worthy to be a leader of God's people.

God *convicts* us of our wrongdoing; He does not *condemn* us. Conviction helps us to repent and be lifted out of the problem; condemnation only pushes us down and makes us feel bad about ourselves. We must shake off the feeling of condemnation because if we don't, we won't have confidence before God. Without confidence, we will have no faith. And without faith, we cannot please God or receive His empowerment to fulfill His calling.

it; but why does my lord the king want to do this thing?"

⁴Nevertheless, the king's word prevailed against Joab and the commanders of the army. So they went from the king's presence to take a census of the people of Israel.

⁵They crossed over the Jordan and camped in Aroer, on the south side of the city which is in the middle of the river valley [of the Arnon] toward Gad, and on toward Jazer.

⁶Then they came to Gilead and to the land of Tahtim-hodshi, and they came to Dan-jaan and around to Sidon,

⁷and they came to the stronghold of Tyre and to all the cities of the Hivites and Canaanites, and they went out to the south of Judah, to Beersheba.

⁸So when they had gone about through all the land [taking the census], they came to Jerusalem at the end of nine months and twenty days.

⁹And Joab gave the sum of the census of the people to the king. In Israel there were 800,000 valiant men who drew the sword, and the men of Judah were 500,000.

¹⁰But David's heart (conscience) troubled him after he had counted the people. David said to the LORD, "I have sinned greatly in what I have done. But now, O LORD, please take away the sin of Your servant, for I have acted very foolishly."

¹¹When David got up in the morning, the word of the LORD came to the prophet Gad, David's seer, saying,

¹²"Go and say to David, 'Thus says the LORD, "I am giving you three *choices;* select one of them for yourself, and I will do it to you."'"

¹³So Gad came to David and told him, and said to him, "Shall seven years of famine come to you in your land? Or will you flee three months before your enemies as they pursue you? Or shall there be three days of pestilence (plague) in your land? Now consider this and decide what answer I shall return to Him who sent me."

¹⁴Then David said to Gad, "I am in great distress. Let us fall into the hands of the LORD, for His mercies are great, but do not let me fall into the hands of man."

¹⁵So the LORD sent a pestilence (plague) [lasting three days] upon Israel from the morning until the appointed time, and seventy thousand men of the people from Dan to Beersheba died.

¹⁶When the [avenging] angel stretched out his hand toward Jerusalem to destroy it, the LORD relented from the disaster and said to the angel who destroyed the people, "It is enough! Now relax your hand." And the angel of the LORD was by the threshing floor of Araunah the Jebusite.

¹⁷When David saw the angel who was striking down the people, he spoke to the LORD and said, "Behold, I [alone] am the one who has sinned and done wrong; but these sheep (people of Israel), what have they done [to deserve this]? Please let Your hand be [only] against me and my father's house (family)."

¹⁸Then Gad [the prophet] came to David that day and said to him, "Go up, set up an altar to the LORD on the threshing floor of Araunah the Jebusite [where you saw the angel]."

¹⁹So David went up according to Gad's word, as the LORD commanded.

²⁰Araunah looked down and saw the king and his servants crossing over

speak the Word

God, I pray that when I am in distress, I will fall into
Your merciful hands and not into the hands of man.
—ADAPTED FROM 2 SAMUEL 24:14

toward him; and he went out and bowed before the king with his face toward the ground.

²¹Araunah said, "Why has my lord the king come to his servant?" And David said, "To buy the threshing floor from you, to build an altar to the LORD, so that the plague may be held back from the people."

²²Araunah said to David, "Let my lord the king take and offer up whatever seems good to him. Look, here are oxen for the burnt offering, and threshing sledges and the yokes of the oxen for the wood.

²³"All of this, O king, Araunah gives to the king." And Araunah said to the king, "May the LORD your God be favorable to you."

²⁴But the king said to Araunah, "No, but I will certainly buy it from you for a price. I will not offer burnt offerings to the LORD my God which cost me nothing." So David purchased the threshing floor and the oxen for fifty shekels of silver.

²⁵David built an altar to the LORD there, and offered burnt offerings and peace offerings. So the LORD was moved [to compassion] by [David's] prayer for the land, and the plague was held back from Israel.

First Kings

Author:
Unknown

Date:
600 BC–550 BC

Everyday Life Principles:
God values and works through relationships.

Honor your covenant with God. Your relationship with Him will be a powerful legacy for your descendants.

Remember that the character traits and standards of other people affect you, so be sure to associate with godly people who will be good influences on you.

In many ways, the everyday life lessons we learn from 1 Kings are woven through the stories of four men—the natural father-son team of David and Solomon, and the spiritual father-son team of Elijah and Elisha. Indeed, 1 Kings tells the stories of the division of the kingdom and of various rulers in the north and in the south, but much of its practical instruction for our lives is found in the context of relationships.

In David and Solomon, we see a son fulfilling his father's dream—the building of the temple. We also see God fulfilling to Solomon the covenant He made with David. Even when Solomon went astray and married foreign women, God left him on the throne for David's sake. In this, we see that a person who has a powerful relationship with God, as David did, will leave an awesome legacy for his or her descendants.

In the relationship between two prophets, Elijah and Elisha, we see Elisha learning from Elijah, observing him, and doing everything he can to develop in his life the qualities he saw in his mentor. Elisha reminds us that other people affect us, and we can incorporate their character qualities into our lives. Elisha's faithfulness, as we learn in 2 Kings, resulted in his having a double portion of Elijah's spirit after Elijah was taken to heaven.

Remember that relationships are important, and be sure to connect with godly people who can be a blessing in your life and whom you can bless in return.

1 NOW KING David was old, advanced in years; they covered him with clothes, but he could not get warm.

²So his servants said to him, "Let a young virgin be found for my lord the king and let her attend him and become his nurse; let her lie against your chest, so that my lord the king may feel warm."

³So they searched for a beautiful girl throughout the territory of Israel, and found Abishag the Shunammite, and brought her to the king.

⁴The girl was very beautiful; and she became the king's nurse and served him, but the king was not intimate with her.

⁵Then Adonijah the son of [David's wife] Haggith exalted himself, saying, "I [the eldest living son] will be king." So [following Absalom's example] he prepared for himself chariots and horsemen, and fifty men to run before him. [2 Sam 15:1]

⁶His father [David] had never rebuked him at any time by asking, "Why have you done this?" Adonijah was also a very handsome man, and he was born after Absalom.

⁷He had conferred with Joab the son of Zeruiah [David's half sister] and with Abiathar the priest; and they followed Adonijah and helped him.

⁸But Zadok the priest, Benaiah the son of Jehoiada, Nathan the prophet, Shimei, Rei, and David's most formidable warriors did not side with Adonijah [in his desire to become king].

⁹Adonijah sacrificed sheep and oxen and fattened steers by the Stone of Zoheleth, which is beside [the well] En-rogel; and he invited all his brothers, the king's sons, and all the men of Judah, the king's servants [to this feast]. [2 Sam 15:7–12]

¹⁰But he did not invite Nathan the prophet, Benaiah, the most formidable warriors, or his brother Solomon.

¹¹Then Nathan spoke to Bathsheba the mother of Solomon, "Have you not heard that Adonijah the son of Haggith has become king, and David our lord does not know about it?

¹²"Come now, please let me advise you and save your life and the life of your son Solomon. [2 Sam 12:24, 25]

¹³"Go at once to King David and say to him, 'Did you not, my lord, O king, swear to your maidservant, saying, "Solomon your son shall certainly be king after me, and he shall sit on my throne"? Why then has Adonijah become king?'

¹⁴"Behold, while you are still there speaking with the king, I will come in after you and confirm your words."

¹⁵So Bathsheba went to the king in his bedroom. Now the king was very old *and* weak, and Abishag the Shunammite was attending the king.

¹⁶So Bathsheba bowed down and paid respect to the king. And the king said, "What do you wish?"

¹⁷She said to him, "My lord, you swore by the LORD your God to your maidservant, *saying*, 'Solomon your son shall certainly be king after me and he shall sit on my throne.'

¹⁸"But now, behold, Adonijah is [acting as] king; and now [as things stand], my lord the king, you do not know it.

¹⁹"He has sacrificed oxen and fattened steers and sheep in abundance, and has invited all the king's sons and Abiathar the priest and Joab the commander of the army [to a feast], but he did not invite your servant Solomon.

²⁰"Now as for you, my lord the king, the eyes of all Israel are on you [waiting for you] to tell them who shall sit on the throne of my lord the king after him.

²¹"Otherwise it will come about when my lord the king lies down [in death] with his fathers, that I and my son Solomon will be considered political enemies."

²²While she was still speaking with the king, Nathan the prophet came in.

²³The king was told, "Here is Nathan the prophet." And when he came before the king, he bowed before the king with his face to the ground.

²⁴Then Nathan said, "My lord the king, have you said, 'Adonijah shall be king after me, and he shall sit on my throne'?

²⁵"Because he has gone down today [to En-Rogel] and has sacrificed oxen and fattened steers and sheep in abundance, and has invited all the king's sons, the commanders of the army and Abiathar the priest [to this feast]; and [right now] they are eating and drinking in his presence; and they say, 'Long live King Adonijah!'

²⁶"But he has not invited me, your servant, nor Zadok the priest, nor Benaiah the son of Jehoiada, nor your servant Solomon.

²⁷"If this thing has been done by my lord the king, why have you not shown your servants who shall sit on the throne of my lord the king after him?"

²⁸King David answered, "Call Bathsheba to me." And she came into the king's presence and stood before him.

²⁹Then the king swore an oath and said, "As the LORD lives, who has redeemed my soul from all distress,

³⁰even as I swore to you by the LORD, the God of Israel, saying, 'Solomon your son shall certainly be king after me, and he shall sit on my throne in my place'; I will indeed do so this very day."

³¹Bathsheba bowed down with her face to the ground, and laid herself face down before the king and said, "May my lord King David live forever!"

³²Then King David said, "Call Zadok the priest, Nathan the prophet, and Benaiah the son of Jehoiada to me." And they came before the king.

³³The king told them, "Take the servants of your lord with you and have Solomon my son ride on my own mule, and bring him down to [the spring at] Gihon [in the Kidron Valley].

³⁴"Let Zadok the priest and Nathan the prophet anoint him there as king over Israel. Then blow the trumpet and say, 'Long live King Solomon!'

³⁵"Then you shall come up [to Jerusalem] after him, and he shall come and sit on my throne and he shall reign as king in my place; for I have appointed him to be ruler over Israel and Judah."

³⁶Benaiah [the overseer of the king's bodyguards], the son of Jehoiada answered the king and said, "Amen! (So be it!) May the LORD, the God of my lord the king, say so too.

³⁷"Just as the LORD has been with my lord the king, so may He be with Solomon, and make his throne greater than the throne of my lord King David!"

³⁸So Zadok the priest, Nathan the prophet, Benaiah the son of Jehoiada, the Cherethites, and the Pelethites [the king's bodyguards] went down [from Jerusalem] and had Solomon ride on King David's mule, and brought him to [the spring at] Gihon.

³⁹Zadok the priest took a horn of [olive] oil from the [sacred] tent and anointed Solomon. They blew the trumpet, and all the people said, "Long live King Solomon!"

⁴⁰All the people went up after him, and they were playing on flutes and rejoicing with great joy, so that the earth shook and seemed to burst open with their [joyful] sound.

⁴¹Now Adonijah and all the guests who were with him heard it as they finished eating. When Joab heard the trumpet sound, he said, "Why is the city in such an uproar?"

⁴²While he was still speaking, behold, Jonathan the son of Abiathar the priest arrived. And Adonijah said, "Come in, for you are a valiant and trustworthy man and you bring good news." [2 Sam 17:17–21]

⁴³But Jonathan replied to Adonijah,

"No, *on the contrary,* our lord King David has made Solomon king!

⁴⁴"The king has sent him with Zadok the priest, Nathan the prophet, Benaiah the son of Jehoiada, the Cherethites, and the Pelethites; and they have had him ride on the king's [own royal] mule.

⁴⁵"Also, Zadok the priest and Nathan the prophet have anointed him king in Gihon, and they have come up from there celebrating, so the city is in an uproar. This is the noise which you have heard.

⁴⁶"Besides, Solomon has taken his seat on the throne of the kingdom.

⁴⁷"Moreover, the king's servants came to bless (congratulate) our lord King David, saying, 'May your God make the name of Solomon better (more famous) than your name and make his throne greater than your throne.' And the king bowed himself [before God] upon the bed.

⁴⁸"The king has also said this: 'Blessed be the Lᴏʀᴅ, the God of Israel, who has granted one [of my descendants] to sit on my throne today and *allowed* my eyes to see it.'"

⁴⁹Then all Adonijah's guests were terrified [of being branded as traitors] and stood up *and* left the feast, and each one went on his way.

⁵⁰And Adonijah feared Solomon, and he got up and went [to the tabernacle on Mt. Zion] and took hold of the horns of the altar [seeking asylum].

⁵¹Now Solomon was told, "Behold, Adonijah is afraid of King Solomon, and behold, he has grasped the horns of the altar [seeking God's protection], saying, 'King Solomon must swear to me today that he will not kill his servant with the sword.'"

⁵²Solomon said, "If he [proves he] is a worthy man, not *even* one of his hairs shall fall to the ground; but if wickedness is found in him, he shall die."

⁵³So King Solomon sent [soldiers], and they brought Adonijah down from the altar [that was in front of the tabernacle]. And he came and bowed down to King Solomon, and Solomon said to him, "Go to your house."

2 WHEN DAVID'S time to die approached, he gave instructions to Solomon his son, saying,

²"I am going the way of all the earth [as dust to dust]. Be strong and prove yourself a man.

³"Keep the charge of the Lᴏʀᴅ your God, [that is, fulfill your obligation to] walk in His ways, keep His statutes, His commandments, His precepts, and His testimonies, as it is written in the Law of Moses, so that you may succeed in everything that you do and wherever you turn,

⁴so that the Lᴏʀᴅ may fulfill His promise concerning me, saying, 'If your sons are careful regarding their way [of life], to walk before Me in truth with all their heart *and* mind and with all their soul, you shall not fail to have a man (descendant) on the throne of Israel.'

⁵"Now you also know what Joab the son of Zeruiah [my sister] did to me, and what he did to the two commanders of the armies of Israel, to Abner the son of Ner and to Amasa the son of Jether, [both of] whom he murdered; avenging the blood of war in [a time

speak the Word

God, I pray that I will keep Your charge, walk in Your ways, and keep Your statutes and commandments, that I may succeed in everything that I do, wherever I turn.
—ᴀᴅᴀᴘᴛᴇᴅ ꜰʀᴏᴍ 1 Kɪɴɢꜱ 2:3

of] peace. And he put the [innocent] blood of war [of Abner and Amasa] on his belt that was around his waist, and on his sandals on his feet.

⁶"So act in accordance with your wisdom, but do not let his gray head go down to Sheol (the place of the dead) in peace.

⁷"But be gracious *and* kind to the sons of Barzillai the Gileadite, and let them be among those who [have the honor to] eat at your table; for they met me [with kindness] when I fled from your brother Absalom. [2 Sam 17:27–29]

⁸"And look, you have with you Shimei the son of Gera, the Benjamite of Bahurim; he is the one who cursed me with a sinister curse the day I went to Mahanaim. But he came down to meet me at the Jordan [on my return], and I swore to him by the Lord, saying, 'I will not put you to death with the sword.'

⁹"But now do not let him go unpunished, for you are a wise man; and you will know what to do to him, and you will bring his gray head down to Sheol [covered] with blood."

¹⁰So David lay down with his fathers [in death] and was buried in the City of David.

¹¹The time that David reigned over Israel was forty years: he reigned seven years in Hebron and thirty-three years in Jerusalem.

¹²Then Solomon sat on the throne of David his father, and his kingdom was firmly established.

¹³Now Adonijah the son of [David and] Haggith came to Bathsheba the mother of Solomon. She said, "Do you come in peace?" And he said, "In peace."

¹⁴Then he said, "I have something *to say* to you." And she said, "Speak."

¹⁵So he said, "You know that the kingdom belonged to me [as the eldest living son] and all Israel looked to me *and* expected me to be king. However, the kingdom has passed [from

me] and became my brother's, for it was his from the Lord.

¹⁶"So now I am making one request of you; do not refuse me." And she said to him, "Speak."

¹⁷He said, "Please speak to King Solomon, for he will not refuse you; *ask* that he may give me Abishag the Shunammite as a wife." [1 Kin 1:1–4]

¹⁸Bathsheba replied, "Very well; I will speak to the king for you."

¹⁹So Bathsheba went to King Solomon to speak to him for Adonijah. And the king rose to meet her, bowed before her, and sat down on his throne; then he had a throne set for her, the king's mother, and she sat on his right.

²⁰Then she said, "I am making one small request of you; do not refuse me." And the king said to her, "Ask, my mother, for I will not refuse you."

²¹So she said, "Let Abishag the Shunammite be given to your brother Adonijah as a wife."

²²King Solomon answered and said to his mother, "And why are you asking for Abishag the Shunammite for

putting the Word to work

Today's world is full of examples of people who have maneuvered or manipulated their way into positions of authority that were not rightfully theirs. Have you ever felt that you have been cheated out of a promotion or a position of leadership? Like Solomon, you can rest confidently in the knowledge that if such a position is God's purpose for you, nothing or no one can keep you from being established in that place. Place your faith in God and His power to promote you, and do not ever let resentment or bitterness take root in your heart. Always remember that God's timing and ways are perfect!

Adonijah? Ask the kingdom for him also—since he is my older brother—[ask it] for him and for Abiathar the priest and Joab the son of Zeruiah [his supporters]!"

²³Then King Solomon swore by the Lord, saying, "May God do the same to me, and more also, if Adonijah has not requested this [deplorable] thing against his own life.

²⁴"So now, as the Lord lives, who has established me and set me on the throne of David my father, and who has made me a house as He promised, Adonijah shall indeed be put to death today."

²⁵So King Solomon sent Benaiah the son of Jehoiada, and he struck Adonijah and he died.

²⁶Then the king said to Abiathar the priest, "Go to Anathoth to your own fields, for you certainly deserve to die; but I will not put you to death this day, because you carried the ark of the Lord God before my father David, and you suffered everything that my father endured."

²⁷So Solomon dismissed Abiathar [a descendant of Eli] from being priest to the Lord, fulfilling the word of the Lord, which He had spoken concerning the house (descendants) of Eli in Shiloh. [1 Sam 2:27–36]

²⁸Now the news reached Joab, for Joab had supported *and* followed Adonijah, although he had not followed Absalom. So Joab fled to the [sacred] tent of the Lord and took hold of the horns of the altar [to seek asylum].

²⁹King Solomon was told that Joab had fled to the tent of the Lord and was at that moment beside the altar. Then Solomon sent Benaiah the son of Jehoiada, saying, "Go, strike him down."

³⁰So Benaiah came to the tent of the Lord and told Joab, "This is what the king commands, 'Come out *of there.*'"

But Joab said, "No, for I will die here." Then Benaiah brought word to the king again, saying, "This is what Joab said, and this is how he answered me."

³¹The king said to him, "Do as he has said. Strike him down and bury him, so that you may remove from me and from my father's house the innocent blood which Joab shed.

³²"The Lord will return his bloody deeds upon his own head, because he struck down two men more righteous and honorable than he and killed them with the sword, without my father David knowing: Abner the son of Ner, commander of the army of Israel, and Amasa the son of Jether, commander of the army of Judah.

³³"So shall their blood return on the head of Joab and the heads of his descendants forever. But for David, his descendants, his house, and his throne, may there be peace from the Lord forever."

³⁴So Benaiah the son of Jehoiada went up [to the tabernacle] and struck and killed Joab, and he was buried at his own house in the wilderness [of Judah].

³⁵The king appointed Benaiah the son of Jehoiada over the army in Joab's place, and appointed Zadok the priest in place of Abiathar.

³⁶Now the king sent *word* and called for Shimei and said to him, "Build yourself a house in Jerusalem and live there. Do not go from there to any other place.

³⁷"For on the day you leave and cross over the Brook Kidron, know for certain that you shall surely die; your blood shall be on your own head."

³⁸Shimei said to the king, "The word (ruling) is good. As my lord the king has said, so will your servant do." So Shimei lived in Jerusalem for many days.

³⁹But it happened after three years, that two of Shimei's servants ran away to Achish the son of Maacah, the king

of Gath. And Shimei was told, "Behold, your [runaway] servants are in Gath."

⁴⁰So Shimei arose, saddled his donkey, and went to Gath to [King] Achish to look for his servants. And Shimei went and brought them *back* from Gath.

⁴¹Now Solomon was told that Shimei had gone from Jerusalem to Gath, and had returned.

⁴²So the king sent *word* and called for Shimei and said to him, "Did I not make you swear by the LORD and solemnly warn you, saying, 'Know for certain that on the day you leave [Jerusalem] and go anywhere, you shall surely die'? And you said to me, 'The word (ruling) I have heard is good.'

⁴³"Why then have you not kept the oath of the LORD, and the command which I gave you?"

⁴⁴The king also said to Shimei, "You are aware in your own heart of all the evil you did to my father David; so the LORD shall return your evil on your own head.

⁴⁵"But King Solomon shall be blessed, and the throne of David shall be established before the LORD forever."

⁴⁶So the king commanded Benaiah the son of Jehoiada, and he went out and struck down Shimei, and he died.

So the kingdom was established in the hands of Solomon.

3 NOW SOLOMON became a son-in-law to Pharaoh king of Egypt [and formed an alliance] by taking Pharaoh's daughter [in marriage]. He brought her to the City of David [where she remained temporarily] until he had finished building his own house (palace) and the house of the LORD and the wall around Jerusalem.

putting the Word to work

If God came to you and said, "Ask [Me] what I shall give you" as He did to Solomon (see 1 Kings 3:5), how do you think you would respond? Solomon could have asked for riches beyond imagining, great fame, or unsurpassable power. Yet Solomon's response is an amazing demonstration of humility and recognition of his need for God and for wisdom. When you take your requests before God, ask Him to show you those things you truly need, and always remember that your greatest need is for *Him*, not the things He can do for you.

²But [in the meantime] the people were still sacrificing [to God] on the high places (hilltops) [as the pagans did to their idols], for there was no [permanent] house yet built for the Name of the LORD.

³Now Solomon loved the LORD, walking [at first] in the statutes of David his father, except [for the fact that] he sacrificed and burned incense in the high places [ignoring the law that required all sacrifices to be offered at the tabernacle]. [Lev 17:3, 4]

⁴The king went to Gibeon [near Jerusalem, where the tabernacle and the bronze altar stood] to sacrifice there, for that was the great high place. Solomon offered a thousand burnt offerings on that altar.

⁵In Gibeon the LORD appeared to Solomon in a dream at night; and God said, "Ask [Me] what I shall give you."

⁶Then Solomon said, "You have shown Your servant David my father

speak the Word

God, I pray that You would give me an understanding mind and heart that hears Your voice so that I can discern between good and evil.
—ADAPTED FROM 1 KINGS 3:9

great lovingkindness, because he walked before You in faithfulness and righteousness and with uprightness of heart toward You; and You have kept for him this great lovingkindness, in that You have given him a son to sit on his throne, as it is today.

⁷"So now, O Lord my God, You have made Your servant king in place of David my father; and as for me, I am but a little boy [in wisdom and experience]; I do not know how to go out or come in [that is, how to conduct business as a king].

⁸"Your servant is among Your people whom You have chosen, a great people who are too many to be numbered or counted.

⁹"So give Your servant an understanding mind *and* a hearing heart [with which] to judge Your people, so that I may discern between good and evil. For who is able to judge *and* rule this great people of Yours?" [James 1:5]

¹⁰Now it pleased the Lord that Solomon had asked this thing.

¹¹God said to him, "Because you have asked this and have not asked

seek the best

If God were to tell you that you could ask for anything and He would give it to you, what would you ask for? Solomon had this opportunity, and God was extremely pleased with his request (see 1 Kings 3:5–10). He asked for wisdom, an understanding mind, and a hearing heart so that he might discern between good and evil.

It would be a great blessing if all God's children understood the value of wisdom, understanding, discretion, discernment, and prudence. Proverbs teaches us that these things are more valuable than anything else we could desire. They are more valuable than silver and gold, rubies, pearls, or other precious gems (see Proverbs 3:13–15).

What we seek after in life reveals so much about our character. Too many of us seek the wrong things, and, as a result, we are never satisfied and fulfilled. If we will seek God as our number one necessity in life and ask for understanding of His ways, we will be content and God will add other things, as He did for Solomon. God was so pleased with Solomon's request for wisdom that He also gave him popularity, fame, an abundance of wealth and possessions, friends, family, success, and anything else he could ever want in life.

What are you seeking? God confronted me with this question several years ago, and I discovered that my answer was not pleasing to Him. I was ashamed when I realized how much more concerned I was with my circumstances than with my spiritual life. At that point, God began to teach me what is truly valuable, and His grace enabled me to change my focus. I am eternally glad that God asked me that question, and I now ask it of myself on a regular basis. I always want to seek those things that are pleasing to my Lord, and I am sure you feel the same way.

Do not feel condemned if you find that the focus of your desires needs to be adjusted. Just ask God to help you make the necessary changes. Seek wisdom; seek to have a heart that understands other people's hurts and needs. Ask for the ability to discern between good and evil and the grace to always make the right choices. As you seek these things, you will enjoy a life that is beyond anything you could ever imagine.

for yourself a long life nor for wealth, nor for the lives of your enemies, but have asked for yourself understanding to recognize justice,

¹²behold, I have done as you asked. I have given you a wise and discerning heart (mind), so that no one before you was your equal, nor shall anyone equal to you arise after you.

¹³"I have also given you what you have not asked, both wealth and honor, so that there will not be anyone equal to you among the kings, for all your days.

¹⁴"If you walk in My ways, keeping My statutes and My commandments, as your father David did, then I will lengthen your days."

¹⁵Then Solomon awoke, and he realized that it was a dream. He came [back] to Jerusalem and stood before the ark of the covenant of the LORD; he offered burnt offerings and peace offerings, and he prepared a feast for all his servants. [2 Sam 6:17]

¹⁶Then two women who were prostitutes came to the king and stood before him.

¹⁷And the one woman said, "O my lord, this woman and I live in the same house; and I gave birth to a child while she was in the house.

¹⁸"And on the third day after I gave birth, this woman also gave birth. And we were [alone] together; no one else was with us in the house, just we two.

¹⁹"Now this woman's son died during the night, because she lay on him [and smothered him].

²⁰"So she got up in the middle of the night and took my son from [his place] beside me while your maidservant was asleep, and laid him on her bosom, and laid her dead son on my bosom.

²¹"When I got up in the morning to nurse my son, behold, he was dead. But when I examined him carefully in the morning, behold, it was not my son, *the one* whom I had borne."

²²Then the other woman said, "No! For my son is the one who is living, and your son is the dead one." But the first woman said, "No! For your son is the dead one, and my son is the living one." [This is how] they were speaking before the king.

²³Then the king said, "This woman says, 'This is my son, the one who is alive, and your son is the dead one'; and the other woman says, 'No! For your son is the dead one, and my son is the one who is alive.'"

²⁴Then the king said, "Bring me a sword." So they brought a sword before the king.

²⁵Then the king said, "Cut the living child in two, and give half to the one [woman] and half to the other."

²⁶Then the woman whose child was the living one spoke to the king, for she was deeply moved over her son, "O my lord, give her the living child, and by no means kill him." But the other said, "He shall be neither mine nor yours; cut *him!*"

²⁷Then the king said, "Give the first woman [who is pleading for his life] the living child, and by no means kill him. She is his mother."

putting the Word to work

Have you ever thought that a law or perhaps a court verdict was unfair or unjust? Under Solomon's rule, the Israelites were greatly blessed by his God-given wisdom in administering justice among them (see 1 Kings 3:28). Some governing officials today are like Solomon, but not all of them are. Remember to pray for those in the legislative and legal systems, that they might have great wisdom and discernment in matters of justice. Pray that they will all totally submit their lives to God and make laws based on His Word and principles.

²⁸When all [the people of] Israel heard about the judgment which the king had made, they [were in awe and reverently] feared the king, for they saw that the wisdom of God was within him to administer justice.

4 KING SOLOMON was king over all [the people of] Israel. ²These were his [chief] officials: Azariah the son of Zadok was the *high* priest;

³Elihoreph and Ahijah the sons of Shisha, were scribes; Jehoshaphat the son of Ahilud was the recorder [of important events];

⁴Benaiah the son of Jehoiada was in command of the army; Zadok and Abiathar were priests;

⁵Azariah the son of Nathan was in charge of the deputies; Zabud the son of Nathan was priest and was the king's friend [and trusted advisor];

⁶Ahishar was in charge of the household (palace); and Adoniram the son of Abda was in charge of the forced labor.

⁷Solomon had twelve deputies over all Israel, who secured provisions for the king and his household; each man had to provide for a month in the year.

⁸These were their names: Ben-hur, in the hill country of [the tribe of] Ephraim;

⁹Ben-deker in Makaz and Shaalbim and Beth-shemesh and Elon-beth-hanan;

¹⁰Ben-hesed, in Arubboth (to him belonged Socoh and all the land of Hepher);

¹¹Ben-abinadab, in all the hills of Dor (Taphath, Solomon's daughter, was his wife);

¹²Baana the son of Ahilud, in Taanach, Megiddo, and all Beth-shean which is beside Zarethan below Jezreel, from Beth-shean to Abel-meholah as far as beyond Jokmeam;

¹³Ben-geber, in Ramoth-gilead (the villages of Jair the son of Manasseh, which are in Gilead belonged to him, also the region of Argob, which is in Bashan, sixty great cities with walls and bronze bars);

¹⁴Ahinadab the son of Iddo, in Mahanaim;

¹⁵Ahimaaz, in [the tribe of] Naphtali (he also married Basemath, Solomon's daughter);

¹⁶Baana the son of Hushai, in [the tribe of] Asher and Bealoth;

¹⁷Jehoshaphat the son of Paruah, in [the tribe of] Issachar;

¹⁸Shimei the son of Ela, in [the tribe of] Benjamin;

¹⁹Geber the son of Uri, in the land of Gilead, the country of Sihon king of the Amorites and of Og king of Bashan; and *he was* the only officer who was in the land.

²⁰[The people of] Judah and Israel were as numerous as the sand that is in abundance by the sea; they were eating and drinking and rejoicing.

²¹Now Solomon reigned over all the kingdoms from the [Euphrates] River to the land of the Philistines and to the border of Egypt; they brought tribute (money) and served Solomon all the days of his life.

²²Solomon's food [for the royal household] for one day was thirty kors of finely milled flour, sixty kors of wheat flour,

²³ten fat oxen, twenty pasture-fed oxen, a hundred sheep not counting fallow deer, gazelles, roebucks, and fattened fowl.

²⁴For he was ruling over everything west of the [Euphrates] River, from Tiphsah to Gaza, over all the kings west of the [Euphrates] River; and he had peace on all sides around him.

²⁵Judah and Israel lived in security, every man under his vine and fig tree [in peace and prosperity], from Dan [in the north] to Beersheba [in the south], during all the days of Solomon. [Mic 4:3, 4]

²⁶Solomon also had 40,000 stalls of horses for his chariots, and 12,000 horsemen.

²⁷Those deputies provided food for King Solomon and for all [the staff] who came to King Solomon's table, each in his month; they let nothing be lacking.

²⁸They also brought the barley and straw for the horses and swift steeds (warhorses, chargers) to the place where it was needed, each man according to his assignment.

²⁹Now God gave Solomon [exceptional] wisdom and very great discernment and breadth of mind, like the sand of the seashore.

³⁰Solomon's wisdom surpassed the wisdom of all the sons of the east and all the wisdom of Egypt.

³¹For he was wiser than all [other] men, [wiser] than Ethan the Ezrahite, and Heman, Calcol, and Darda, the sons of Mahol. His fame was *known* in all the surrounding nations.

³²He also spoke 3,000 proverbs, and his songs were 1,005.

³³He spoke of trees, from the cedar which is in Lebanon to the hyssop [vine] that grows on the wall; he spoke also of animals, of birds, of creeping things, and fish.

³⁴People came from all the peoples (nations) to hear the wisdom of Solomon, and from all the kings of the earth who had heard of his wisdom.

5 HIRAM KING of Tyre sent his servants to Solomon when he heard that they had anointed him king in place of his father, for Hiram had always been a friend of David.

²Then Solomon sent *word* to Hiram, saying,

³"You know that David my father could not build a house (temple) for the Name (Presence) of the Lord his God because of the wars which surrounded him, until the Lord put his enemies under his feet. [2 Sam 7:4ff; 1 Chr 22:8]

⁴"But now that the Lord my God has given me rest [from war] on every side, there is neither adversary nor misfortune [confronting me].

⁵"Behold, I intend to build a house (temple) to the Name of the Lord my God, just as the Lord said to my father David: 'Your son whom I will put on your throne in your place shall build the house for My Name *and* Presence.'

⁶"So now, command that they cut cedar trees from Lebanon for me, and my servants will join your servants, and I will give you whatever wages you set for your servants. For you know that there is no one among us who knows how to cut timber like the men of Sidon."

⁷When Hiram heard the words of Solomon, he rejoiced greatly and said, "Blessed be the Lord this day, who has given David a wise son [to be king] over this great people."

⁸So Hiram sent *word* to Solomon, saying, "I have heard *the message* which you sent to me; I will do everything you wish concerning the cedar and cypress timber.

⁹"My servants will bring the logs down from Lebanon to the [Mediterranean] sea, and I will have them made into rafts *to go* by sea to the place (port) that you direct me; then I will have them broken up there, and

speak the Word

Lord, I pray that You would do for me what You did for Solomon and give me exceptional wisdom, very great discernment, and breadth of mind like the sand of the seashore.

–ADAPTED FROM 1 KINGS 4:29

you shall carry *them* away. Then you shall return the favor by providing food for my household."

[10]So Hiram gave Solomon all the cedar and cypress timber he desired,

[11]and Solomon gave Hiram 20,000 kors of wheat as food for his household, and 20 kors of pure [olive] oil. Solomon gave all these to Hiram each year.

[12]The LORD gave Solomon wisdom, just as He promised him; and there was peace between Hiram and Solomon, and the two of them made a treaty.

[13]King Solomon levied forced laborers from all Israel; and the forced laborers numbered 30,000 men.

[14]He sent them to Lebanon, 10,000 a month in shifts; one month they were in Lebanon and two months at home. Adoniram was in charge of the forced laborers.

[15]Solomon had 70,000 burden bearers (transporters) and 80,000 stonemasons in the hill country [of Judah],

[16]besides Solomon's 3,300 chief deputies who were in charge of the project and who were in charge of the people doing the work.

[17]The king gave orders, and they quarried great stones, valuable stones, to lay the foundation of the house (temple) with cut stones.

[18]So Solomon's builders and Hiram's builders and the men of Gebal cut *and* chiseled *the stones,* and prepared the timber and the stones to build the house (temple).

handling your relationships wisely

Solomon asked God for wisdom, and God gave it to him (see 1 Kings 5:12). Solomon wrote the book of Proverbs, a collection of wise truths that have helped many people successfully live their day-to-day lives.

The Bible teaches us that it is hard to succeed at anything if we do not possess wisdom. Many people have gifts, but they do not operate in wisdom or develop good character because they simply will not grow up and allow God to do the things He needs to do in their lives. As believers in Jesus Christ, His wisdom is in us, but it does us no good if we do not use it. Nothing works right in life or relationships if we do not seek and walk in wisdom.

Let me give you an example of what can happen when people do not use wisdom in relationships. So many people get hurt because they tell a friend what is on their heart, and that friend betrays them. Then they become angry with their friend. If they had used wisdom and kept their mouth shut in the first place, they would have avoided that whole situation. I know this is true because it has happened to me many times. God once impressed upon me, "Joyce, if you don't want your friends hurting your feelings and betraying you, then just learn to keep quiet about things you don't want anyone to know." If we expect God to share His secrets with us, we must be able to keep His secrets. Not telling people things I do not want repeated has taken a great deal of pressure out of my relationships. I no longer have to worry about their telling things I do not want known.

I cannot overemphasize the importance of using wisdom as we deal with other people—family, friends, coworkers, neighbors, and even casual acquaintances. Ask God to give you wisdom in your relationships. He'll do it!

6 NOW IT came about in the four hundred and eightieth year after the Israelites came out of the land of Egypt, in the fourth year of Solomon's reign over Israel, in the month of Ziv (April-May) which is the second month, that he began to build the Lord's house (temple).

²The length of the house which King Solomon built for the LORD was sixty cubits (90 ft.), its width twenty (30 ft.), and its height thirty cubits (45 ft.).

³The porch in front of the main room of the house (temple) was twenty cubits long, corresponding to the width of the house, and its depth in front of the house was ten cubits.

⁴He also made framed (artistic) window openings for the house.

⁵Against the wall of the house he built extensions around the walls of the house, around both the main room (Holy Place) and the Holy of Holies; and he made side chambers all around.

⁶The lowest story was five cubits wide, the middle was six cubits wide, and the third was seven cubits wide; for he made offsets (niches) *in the walls* all around on the outside of the house so that *the supporting beams* would not be inserted into the walls of the house.

⁷While it was being built, the house was built of stone prepared *and* finished (precut) at the quarry, and no hammer, axe, or iron tool of any kind was heard in the house while it was under construction.

⁸The entrance to the lowest side chamber was on the right [or south] side of the house; and they would go up winding stairs to the middle [level], and from the middle to the third.

⁹So Solomon built the house (temple) and finished it, and roofed the house with beams and boards of cedar.

¹⁰Then he built the extensions [of rooms] against the entire house, each [story] five cubits high; and they were attached to the house with timbers of cedar.

¹¹Now the word of the LORD came to Solomon, saying,

¹²*"Concerning* this house which you are building, if you will walk in My statutes and execute My precepts and keep all My commandments by walking in them, then I will carry out My word (promises) with you which I made to David your father.

¹³"I will dwell among the sons (descendants) of Israel, and will not abandon My people Israel."

¹⁴So Solomon built the house (temple) and finished it.

¹⁵He built the walls of the interior of the house [that is, the Holy Place and the Holy of Holies] with boards of cedar, from the floor of the house to the rafters of the ceiling. He overlaid the interior with wood, and he overlaid the floor of the house with boards of cypress.

¹⁶He built twenty cubits on the rear of the house with boards of cedar from the floor to the ceiling; he built its interior as the [inner] sanctuary, the Holy of Holies.

¹⁷The [rest of the] house, that is, the temple in front of *the Holy of Holies,* was forty cubits long.

¹⁸The cedar on the house within had wood carvings *in the shape* of gourds and open flowers. Everything was cedar; no stone was visible.

putting the Word to work

Do you sometimes wonder whether God is concerned with the details of your life? Take heart in knowing that the God Who gave such precise instructions for the construction of the temple (see 1 Kings 6:14—7:51) is even more concerned about the particulars of your life. If something matters to you, it matters to Him!

¹⁹Then he prepared the Holy of Holies within the house in order to put the ark of the covenant of the LORD there. ²⁰The Holy of Holies was twenty cubits in length, twenty cubits in width, and twenty cubits in height (a cube), and he overlaid it with pure gold. He also overlaid the cedar altar [with gold]. ²¹Solomon overlaid the interior of the house with pure gold, and he drew chains of gold across the front of the Holy of Holies (inner sanctuary), and he overlaid it with gold. ²²Then he overlaid the entire house with gold, until the whole house was finished. He also overlaid the entire [incense] altar which was by the Holy of Holies with gold. ²³Within the Holy of Holies he made two cherubim (sculptured figures) of olive wood, each ten cubits high. ²⁴One wing of the cherub was five cubits long, and the other wing was *also* five cubits long; it was ten cubits from the tip of one wing to the tip of the other. ²⁵The [wingspan of the] other cherub was also ten cubits. The measurements and cut (shape) of the two cherubim were the same; ²⁶the height of the one cherub was ten cubits, as was the other. ²⁷He put the cherubim [above the ark] inside the innermost room of the

life point

As you read about the construction of the temple, notice that God's house was built with extreme excellence (see 1 Kings 6:18–21). Today, we, His people, are His "house," the place where He lives and reveals Himself. We modern-day believers need to be diligent to follow the example of the Old Testament temple and provide excellence to the world around us by being excellent people.

house, and their wings were spread out so that the wing of the one touched one wall, and the wing of the other cherub was touching the other wall; and their inner wings were touching each other in the middle of the house. ²⁸Solomon also overlaid the cherubim with gold. ²⁹He carved all the walls of the house all around with carved engravings of cherubim, palm-shaped decorations, and open flowers, [both] the inner and the outer *sanctuaries*. ³⁰He overlaid the floor of the house with gold, [both] the inner and outer *sanctuaries*. ³¹For the entrance of the Holy of Holies he made two [folding] doors of olive wood, the lintel (header above the door) and five-sided doorposts (frames). ³²So *he made* two doors of olive wood, and he carved on them carvings of cherubim, palm-shaped decorations, and open flowers; and overlaid them with gold; and he hammered out overlays of gold on the cherubim and palm decorations. ³³Also he made for the entrance of the [outer] sanctuary (the Holy Place) four-sided doorposts (frames) of olive wood ³⁴and two doors of cypress wood; the two leaves of the one door turned on pivots *and* were folding, and the two leaves of the other door also turned on pivots. ³⁵He carved cherubim, palm-shaped decorations, and open flowers *on the doors*, and overlaid them with gold evenly applied on the carved work. ³⁶He built the inner courtyard with three rows of cut stone and a row of cedar beams. ³⁷In the fourth year [of King Solomon's reign] the foundation of the LORD's house was laid, in the [second] month, Ziv (April-May). ³⁸In the eleventh year [of King Solomon's reign] in the month of Bul (October-November), that is, the eighth month, the house was finished throughout all its parts and in accordance with all its specifications. So he built it in seven years.

7 NOW SOLOMON built his own house (palace) in thirteen years, and he finished all of his house [in that time].

²He also built the House of the Forest of Lebanon; its length was a hundred cubits (150 ft.), its width fifty cubits (75 ft.), and its height thirty cubits (45 ft.), upon four rows of cedar pillars, with cedar beams upon the pillars.

³And it was covered with cedar [as a roof] on the supporting beams that were upon the forty-five pillars, fifteen in each row.

⁴*There were artistic window* frames in three rows, and window was opposite window in three tiers.

⁵All the doorways and doorposts [and windows] had squared [artistic] frames, and window was opposite window in three tiers.

⁶He also made the Hall of Pillars; its length was fifty cubits (75 ft.) and its width thirty cubits (45 ft.). There was a porch in front, and pillars and a threshold in front of them.

⁷He made the hall for the throne where he was to judge, the Hall of Judgment; it was paneled with cedar from [one] floor to [another] floor.

⁸His house where he was to live, the other courtyard behind the hall, was of similar workmanship. Solomon also made a house like this hall for Pharaoh's daughter, whom he had married.

⁹All these were of expensive stones, of stone cut according to measure, sawed with saws, inside and outside; even from the foundation to the coping, and from the outside to the great courtyard.

¹⁰The foundation was of expensive stones, large stones, stones of ten cubits and stones of eight cubits.

¹¹And above [the foundation] were expensive stones, stones cut according to measure, and cedar.

¹²So the great courtyard all around had three rows of cut stone and a row of cedar beams like the inner courtyard of the house of the LORD, and the porch of the house.

¹³Now King Solomon sent *word* and brought Hiram [a skilled craftsman] from Tyre.

¹⁴He was the son of a widow from the tribe of Naphtali, and his father was a man of Tyre, a craftsman in bronze. Hiram was filled with wisdom, understanding, and skill for doing any [kind of] work in bronze. So he came to King Solomon and did all his [bronze] work.

¹⁵He cast the two pillars of bronze; the one pillar was eighteen cubits high, and a [measuring] line of twelve cubits measured the circumference of both.

¹⁶He also made two capitals (crowns) of cast bronze to put on the tops of the pillars; the height of one capital was five cubits, and the height of the other capital was five cubits.

¹⁷*There were* nets of network (latticework) and twisted threads (wreaths) of chainwork for the capitals which were on the tops of the pillars, seven for one capital and seven for the other.

¹⁸So Hiram made the pillars [in this manner], and two rows around on the one network to cover the capitals which were on the top of the pomegranates; and he did the same for the other capital.

¹⁹The capitals which were upon the top of the pillars in the porch were of lily work (design), four cubits.

²⁰The capitals were on the two pillars and also above and close to the rounded projection which was beside the network. There were two hundred pomegranates in rows around both capitals.

²¹Hiram set up the pillars at the porch of the temple; he set up the right pillar and named it Jachin (may he establish),

and he set up the left pillar and named it Boaz (in it is strength).

²²On the tops of the pillars was lily work (design). So the work of the pillars was finished.

²³Now he made the Sea (basin) of cast *metal,* ten cubits from brim to brim, circular in form, five cubits high and thirty cubits in circumference. [Ex 30:17–21; 2 Chr 4:6]

²⁴Under its brim were gourds encircling it ten to a cubit, completely surrounding the Sea; the gourds were in two rows, cast in one piece with it.

²⁵It stood on twelve oxen, three facing north, three west, three south, and three east; the Sea *was set* on top of them, and all their rear parts *pointed* inward.

²⁶It was a hand width thick, and its brim was made like the brim of a cup, like a lily blossom. It held two thousand baths.

²⁷Then Hiram made ten bronze stands [for smaller basins]; the length of each stand was four cubits, its width was four cubits and its height was three cubits.

²⁸This was the design of the stands: they had borders between the frames.

²⁹On the borders between the frames were lions, oxen, and cherubim; and on the frames there was a pedestal above. Beneath the lions and oxen were borders of hanging work.

³⁰Now each stand had four bronze wheels with bronze axles, and its four feet had supports [for a basin]. Beneath the basin were cast supports with borders at each side.

³¹Its opening inside the crown at the top *measured* a cubit, and its opening was round like the design of a pedestal, a cubit and a half. Also on its opening were carvings, and their borders were square, not round.

³²Underneath the borders were four wheels, and the axles of the wheels were on the stand. And the height of a wheel was a cubit and a half.

³³The wheels were made like a chariot wheel: their axles, their rims, their spokes, and their hubs were all cast.

³⁴Now there were four supports at the four corners of each stand; the supports were part of the stand itself.

³⁵On the top of the stand there was a circular piece half a cubit high, and on the top of the stand its supports and borders were part of it.

³⁶And on the surface of its supports and its borders Hiram engraved cherubim, lions, and palm-shaped decorations, according to the [available] space for each, with borders all around.

³⁷He made the ten stands like this: they all had one casting, one measure, and one form.

³⁸Then he made ten basins of bronze; each basin held forty baths and was four cubits, and there was one basin on each of the ten stands.

³⁹Then he placed the bases, five on the right [or south] side of the house and five on the left [or north] side; and he set the Sea [of cast metal] on the right side of the house toward the southeast.

⁴⁰Now Hiram made the basins and the shovels and the bowls. So Hiram finished all the work which he did for King Solomon on the house of the Lᴏʀᴅ:

⁴¹the two pillars and the [two] bowls of the capitals which were on the top of the two pillars, and the two networks to cover the two bowls of the capitals which were on top of the pillars;

⁴²and the four hundred pomegranates for the two networks, two rows of pomegranates for each network to cover the two bowls of the capitals that were on the tops of the pillars;

⁴³the ten stands and the ten basins on the stands;

⁴⁴one Sea (basin), and the twelve oxen under the Sea;

⁴⁵the pails, the shovels, and the bowls; all these utensils which Hiram made for King Solomon in the house of the Lᴏʀᴅ were of polished bronze.

⁴⁶In the plain of the Jordan [River] the king cast them, in the clay ground between Succoth and Zarethan.

⁴⁷Solomon left all the utensils *unweighed*, because there were so many; the weight of the bronze could not be determined.

⁴⁸Solomon made all the [other] furniture which was in the house of the LORD: the [incense] altar of gold; the table of gold on which was the bread of the Presence;

⁴⁹the lampstands of pure gold, five on the right side and five on the left, in front of the Holy of Holies (inner sanctuary); with the flowers, the lamps, and the tongs of gold;

⁵⁰the cups, snuffers, bowls, spoons, firepans—of pure gold; and the hinges of gold [both] for the doors of the inner house, the Holy of Holies, and for the doors of the house, the main room [the Holy Place].

⁵¹So all the work that King Solomon did on the house of the LORD was completed. Solomon brought in the things which David his father had dedicated—the silver, the gold, and the utensils—and he put them in the treasuries of the LORD's house.

8 THEN SOLOMON assembled the elders of Israel and all the heads of the tribes, the leaders of the fathers' *households* of the sons of Israel, to King Solomon in Jerusalem, to bring up the ark of the covenant of the Lord from the City of David, which is Zion.

²All the men of Israel assembled before King Solomon at the feast in the month of Ethanim (September-October), that is, the seventh month.

³All the elders of Israel came, and the priests carried the ark.

⁴They brought up the ark of the LORD and the Tent of Meeting and all the holy utensils that were in the tent; the priests and the Levites brought them up.

⁵King Solomon and all the congregation of Israel, who had assembled before him, were with him before the ark, sacrificing sheep and oxen, so many that they could not be counted or numbered.

⁶Then the priests brought the ark of the covenant of the LORD to its place, into the inner sanctuary of the house, into the Holy of Holies, under the wings of the cherubim.

⁷For the cherubim spread their two wings over the place of the ark, and the cherubim covered the ark and its [carrying] poles from above.

⁸The poles were so long that the ends of the poles were visible from the Holy Place that was in front of the Holy of Holies, but they were not visible from the outside; they are there to this day (the date of this writing).

⁹There was nothing in the ark except the two tablets of stone which Moses put there at Horeb (Sinai), where the LORD made a covenant with the Israelites when they came out of the land of Egypt. [Deut 10:2–5]

¹⁰Now it happened that when the priests had come out of the Holy Place, the cloud filled the LORD's house,

¹¹so the priests could not stand [in their positions] to minister because of the cloud, for the glory *and* brilliance of the LORD had filled the LORD's house (temple).

¹²Then Solomon said,

"The LORD has said that He would
    dwell in the thick darkness [of
    the cloud].
¹³"I have certainly built You a lofty
    house,
A place for You to dwell in forever."

¹⁴Then the king turned around and blessed all the assembly of Israel, while all the assembly of Israel was standing.

¹⁵He said, "Blessed be the LORD, the God of Israel, who spoke with His

mouth to my father David and has fulfilled it with His hand, saying,

¹⁶'Since the day that I brought My people Israel out of Egypt, I did not choose a [particular] city out of all the tribes of Israel *in which* to build a house so that My Name (Presence) would be in it, but I chose David to be over My people Israel.'

¹⁷"Now it was [determined] in the heart of my father David to build a house (temple) for the Name of the LORD, the God of Israel.

¹⁸"But the LORD said to my father David, 'Because it was in your heart to build a house for My Name, you did well, in that it was in your heart.

¹⁹'Nevertheless, you shall not build the house, but your son, who shall be born to you, it is he who shall build it for My Name [and My Presence].'

²⁰"Now the LORD has fulfilled His word which He spoke; I have risen in the place of my father David and have taken my seat on the throne of Israel, just as the LORD promised, and have

His awesome presence

In the Old Testament, the ark of the covenant represented the presence of the Lord. I cannot stress enough how much we need God's presence in our lives—in fact, we need His presence more than we need anything else.

When God called Moses to tell Pharaoh to let God's people go, Moses was scared and insecure about his lack of abilities. But God said to him, "Certainly I will be with you" (see Exodus 3:10–14). Later God told Moses, "My presence shall go with you, and I will give you rest" (Exodus 33:14). I love Moses' reply: "If Your presence does not go [with me], do not lead us up from here" (Exodus 33:15). In other words, "God, if You're not going to be there, don't send me!" That's exactly the way I feel when I start to minister to others.

We need to really understand the awesomeness of the presence of God and the magnitude of what is available to us as believers if only we will take the time to be in His presence. Why in the world would we not want to spend time with God? We spend time on the telephone, we hang out in the shopping center, we spend hours in front of the television—and we seem to have no problem investing our time in those pursuits. The truth is this: *The devil fights us more in the area of our spending time with God than he does in any other area of our Christian lives.* In fact, Satan would much prefer that we get involved in all kinds of religious activity rather than spend time with the Lord.

There is only one way I know to maintain the anointing on my life, and that is by spending time in the presence of God. You may be wondering, "But what do I do when I spend time with God?" You simply set aside a portion of your time for that purpose. Try not to be legalistic about it, but do try to be as regular with it as you can. During that time period, read the Bible and Christian books that minister to you. Talk to God. Sometimes you may want to listen to Christian music and worship; other times you may want to sit there and enjoy the silence. These are wonderful ways to begin to feel and sense the presence of the Lord.

built the house (temple) for the Name of the LORD, the God of Israel.

²¹"There I have made a place [in the Holy of Holies] for the ark, in which is the covenant (solemn agreement) of the LORD, which He made with our fathers when He brought them out of the land of Egypt." [Ex 34:28]

²²Then Solomon stood [in the court-yard] before the altar of the LORD in the presence of all the assembly of Is-rael and spread out his hands toward heaven.

²³He said, "O LORD, the God of Israel, there is no God like You in heaven above or on earth below, who keeps the covenant and shows lovingkind-ness to Your servants who walk before You with all their heart;

²⁴You who have kept what You promised to Your servant my father David. You have spoken with Your mouth and have fulfilled Your word with Your hand, as it is this day.

²⁵"Now therefore, O LORD, the God of Israel, keep for Your servant my father David that which You promised him when You said, 'You shall not be without a man (descendant) to sit on the throne of Israel, if only your sons take heed to their way [of life] to walk before Me [ac-cording to my laws] as you have done.'

²⁶"Now, O God of Israel, please let Your word which You have spoken to Your servant David my father be con-firmed.

²⁷"But will God indeed dwell on the earth? Behold, heaven and the highest heaven cannot contain You; how much less this house which I have built!

²⁸"Yet graciously consider the prayer of Your servant and his supplication, O LORD my God, to listen to the [loud]

life point

There are many facets of God's charac-ter, and each one of them seems to be more wonderful than the next. In 1 Kings 8:23, Solomon referred to God's faith-fulness to keep His covenant and to His loving-kindness. He is also long-suffering, just, and honest—among many other wonderful attributes. We need to get acquainted with God's qualities because they reveal God's character to us. The better we know His character, the better we know His heart for us, and the easier it becomes to trust and obey Him.

cry and to the prayer which Your ser-vant prays before You today;

²⁹that Your eyes may be open toward this house night and day, toward the place of which You have said, 'My Name (Presence) shall be there,' that You may listen to the prayer which Your servant shall pray toward this place.

³⁰"Listen to the prayer of Your servant and of Your people Israel which they pray toward this place. Hear in heaven, Your dwelling place; hear and forgive.

³¹"If a man sins against his neighbor and is made to take an oath [of inno-cence] and he comes to take the oath before Your altar in this house (temple),

³²then hear from heaven and act and judge Your servants, condemn-ing the wicked by bringing his guilt on his own head, and justifying the righteous by rewarding him in accor-dance with his righteousness.

³³"When Your people Israel are de-feated before an enemy because they have sinned against You, and *then*

speak the Word

Thank You, God, for graciously considering my prayers and supplications and for hearing the requests that I make of You today.
−ADAPTED FROM 1 KINGS 8:28

they turn to You again and praise Your Name and pray and ask for Your favor *and* compassion in this house (temple),

³⁴then hear in heaven, and forgive the sin of Your people Israel, and bring them back to the land which You gave their fathers.

³⁵"When the heavens are shut up and there is no rain because they have sinned against You, and they pray toward this place and praise Your name and turn from their sin when You afflict them,

³⁶then hear in heaven and forgive the sin of Your servants and of Your people Israel; indeed, teach them the good way in which they should walk (live). And send rain on Your land which You have given to Your people as an inheritance.

³⁷"If there is famine in the land, or if there is pestilence (plague), blight, mildew, migratory locusts, or grasshoppers, if their enemy besieges them in the land of their cities, whatever affliction *or* plague, whatever sickness [there is],

³⁸whatever prayer or pleading is made by any individual, or by Your people Israel, each knowing the affliction of his own heart, and spreading his hands out toward this house;

³⁹then hear in heaven Your dwelling place, and forgive and act and give to each according to his ways, whose heart (mind) You know, for You and You alone know the hearts of all the children of men,

⁴⁰so that they may fear You [with reverence and awe] all the days that they live in the land which You have given to our fathers.

⁴¹"Moreover, concerning a foreigner who is not of Your people Israel, but comes from a far (distant) country for the sake of Your name [to plead with You]

⁴²(for they will hear of Your great name, Your strong hand [of power], and outstretched arm); when he comes and prays toward this house (temple),

⁴³hear in heaven, Your dwelling place, and do according to all for which the foreigner calls upon (prays to) You, so that all peoples of the earth may know Your name and fear You [with reverence and awe], as *do* Your people Israel, and that they may know [without any doubt] that this house which I have built is called by Your name.

⁴⁴"When Your people go out to battle against their enemy, by whatever way You send them, and they pray to the LORD toward the city which You have chosen and the house that I have built for Your Name *and* Presence,

⁴⁵then hear in heaven their prayer and their pleading, and maintain their right *and* defend their cause.

⁴⁶"When they sin against You (for there is no man who does not sin) and You are angry with them and hand them over to the enemy, so that they are carried away captive to the enemy's land, [whether] far away or near;

⁴⁷if they take it to heart in the land where they have been taken captive, and they repent and pray to You in the land of their captors, saying, 'We have sinned and done wrong and we have acted wickedly;'

⁴⁸if they return to You with all their heart and with all their soul in the land of their enemies who have taken them captive, and they pray to You toward their land [of Israel] which You gave

speak the Word

God, I pray that all peoples of the earth may know Your Name and fear You with reverence and awe.
–ADAPTED FROM 1 KINGS 8:43

to their fathers, the city [of Jerusalem] which You have chosen, and the house which I have built for Your Name *and* Presence;

⁴⁹then hear their prayer and their supplication in heaven Your dwelling place, and maintain their right *and* defend their cause,

⁵⁰and forgive Your people who have sinned against You and all the transgressions which they have committed against You, and make them *objects of* compassion before their captors, that they will be merciful to them

⁵¹(for they are Your people and Your heritage, whom You brought out of Egypt, from the midst of the iron furnace [of slavery and oppression]),

⁵²that Your eyes may be open to the supplication of Your servant and to the supplication of Your people Israel, to listen to them *and* be attentive to them whenever they call to You.

⁵³"For You singled them out from all the peoples of the earth as Your heritage, just as You declared through Moses Your servant, when You brought our fathers out of Egypt, O Lord GOD."

⁵⁴When Solomon finished offering this entire prayer and supplication to the LORD, he arose from before the LORD's altar, where he had knelt down with his hands stretched toward heaven.

⁵⁵And he stood and blessed all the assembly of Israel with a loud voice, saying,

⁵⁶"Blessed be the LORD, who has given rest to His people Israel, in accordance with everything that He promised. Not one word has failed of all His good promise, which He spoke through Moses His servant.

⁵⁷"May the LORD our God be with us as He was with our fathers; may He not leave us nor abandon us [to our enemies],

⁵⁸that He may guide our hearts to Himself, to walk in all His ways [following Him] and to keep His commandments, His statutes, and His precepts which He commanded our fathers.

⁵⁹"Let these words of mine, with which I have made supplication before the LORD, be near to the LORD our God day and night, so that He will maintain the cause *and* right of His servant and of His people Israel as each day requires,

⁶⁰so that all the peoples of the earth may know that the LORD is God; there is no one else.

⁶¹"Therefore, your hearts are to be wholly devoted to the LORD our God, to walk in His statutes and to keep His commandments, as [you are doing] today."

⁶²Then the king and all [the people of] Israel with him [repeatedly] offered sacrifice before the LORD.

⁶³Solomon offered as peace offerings to the LORD: 22,000 oxen and 120,000 sheep. So the king and all the Israelites dedicated the house (temple) of the LORD.

⁶⁴On that same day the king consecrated the middle of the courtyard that was in front of the house (temple) of the LORD; for he offered there the burnt offerings, the grain offerings, and the fat of the peace offerings, because the bronze altar that was before the LORD was too small to hold [all] the burnt offerings, the grain offerings and the fat of the peace offerings.

⁶⁵So at that time Solomon held the

speak the Word

Lord, I pray that my heart would be wholly devoted to You, to walk in Your statutes and to keep Your commandments.
–ADAPTED FROM 1 KINGS 8:61

feast, and all Israel with him, a great assembly, from the entrance of Hamath [on the northern border of Israel] to the Brook of Egypt [at Israel's southern border], before the LORD our God, for seven days and seven *more* days [beyond the prescribed period for the Feast of Booths], fourteen days in all. [66]On the eighth (fifteenth) day he sent the people away and they blessed the king. Then they went to their tents joyful and in good spirits because of all the goodness which the LORD had shown to David His servant and Israel His people.

9 NOW IT happened when Solomon had finished building the house (temple) of the LORD and the king's house (palace), and all else which he was pleased to do,

[2]that the LORD appeared to Solomon a second time, just as He had appeared to him at Gibeon.

[3]The LORD told him, "I have heard your prayer and supplication which you have made before Me; I have consecrated this house which you have built by putting My Name *and* My Presence there forever. My eyes and My heart shall be there perpetually.

[4]"As for you, if you walk (live your life) before Me, as David your father walked, in integrity of heart and in uprightness, acting in accordance with everything that I have commanded you, and will keep My statutes and My precepts,

[5]then I will establish the throne of your kingdom over Israel forever, just as I promised your father David, saying, 'You shall not be without a man (descendant) on the throne of Israel.'

[6]"But if you or your sons turn away from following Me, and do not keep My commandments and My statutes which I have set before you, but go and serve other gods and worship them,

[7]then I will cut off Israel from the land which I have given them, and I will cast out of My sight the house which I have consecrated for My Name *and* Presence. Then Israel will become a proverb (a saying) and a byword (object of ridicule) among all the peoples.

[8]"This house (temple) will become a heap of ruins; everyone who passes by will be appalled and sneer and say, 'Why has the LORD done such a thing to this land and to this house?'

[9]"And they [who know] will say, 'Because they abandoned the LORD their God, who brought their fathers out of the land of Egypt, and they have chosen other gods and have worshiped and served them; that is the reason the LORD has brought on them all this adversity.'"

[10]Now at the end of twenty years, in which Solomon had built the two houses, the temple of the LORD and the palace of the king

[11](Hiram king of Tyre had supplied Solomon with as much cedar and cypress timber [from Lebanon] and gold as he desired), at that time King Solomon gave Hiram twenty cities in the land of Galilee (northern Israel).

[12]So Hiram came from Tyre to see the cities which Solomon had given him, and they did not please him.

[13]He said, "What are these cities [good for] which you have given me, my brother?" So they have been called the land of Cabul (like nothing, unproductive) to this day.

[14]And Hiram sent to the king 120 talents of gold.

[15]Now this is the account of the forced labor which King Solomon conscripted to build the house of the LORD, his own house, the Millo (fortification), the wall of Jerusalem, [and the fortress cities of] Hazor, Megiddo, and Gezer.

[16]*For* Pharaoh king of Egypt had gone up and taken Gezer, burned it with fire and killed the Canaanites who lived in the city, and he had

given it as a dowry to his daughter, Solomon's wife.

¹⁷So Solomon rebuilt [and fortified] Gezer and Lower Beth-horon,

¹⁸Baalath and Tamar in the wilderness, in the land *of Judah,*

¹⁹and all the storage cities [for surplus provisions] which Solomon had, and the cities for his chariots and cities for his horsemen, and whatever it pleased Solomon to build in Jerusalem, in Lebanon, and in all the land under his rule.

²⁰*As for* all the people who were left of the Amorites, Hittites, Perizzites, Hivites, and Jebusites, who were not of the sons (descendants) of Israel,

²¹their children who were left after them in the land, whom the Israelites were unable to completely destroy, from them Solomon levied (conscripted) forced laborers, even to this day (the date of this writing).

²²But Solomon did not make slaves of the sons of Israel; for they were men of war (soldiers), his servants, his officers, his captains, his chariot commanders, and his horsemen.

²³These were the chief officers who were over Solomon's work, five hundred and fifty, who ruled over the people doing the work.

²⁴As soon as Pharaoh's daughter came up from the City of David to her house which Solomon had built for her, then he built the Millo (fortification).

²⁵Three times a year [during the major annual festivals] Solomon offered burnt offerings and peace offerings on the altar he had built to the LORD, and he burned incense with them before the LORD. So he finished the house [of the LORD].

²⁶King Solomon built a fleet of ships in Ezion-geber, which is near Eloth on the shore of the Red Sea (Sea of Reeds), in the land of Edom.

²⁷And Hiram [king of Tyre] sent his servants with the fleet, sailors who knew the sea, along with the servants of Solomon.

²⁸They came to Ophir and took four hundred and twenty talents of gold from there, and brought it to King Solomon.

10 NOW WHEN the queen of Sheba heard of the fame of Solomon concerning the name of the LORD, she came to test him with riddles.

²So she came to Jerusalem with a very large caravan (entourage), with camels carrying spices, a great quantity of gold, and precious stones. When she came to Solomon, she spoke with him about everything that was on her mind [to discover the extent of his wisdom].

³Solomon answered all her questions; there was nothing hidden from the king which he did not explain to her.

⁴When the queen of Sheba had seen all the wisdom of Solomon, and the house (palace) which he had built,

⁵the food on his table, the seating of his servants (court officials), the attendance of his waiters and their attire, his cupbearers, his stairway by which

putting the Word to work

People who do not really know God often have questions about Him, and will sometimes even try to "stump" us with hard questions. The queen of Sheba did this to Solomon (see 1 Kings 10:1–3). Is there someone in your life who is asking you questions about God? Scripture talks about the importance of being prepared to respond to people's questions. Reading the Bible, praying, and listening to Christian teaching are all ways to prepare ourselves. As you prepare, ask God to give you wisdom, as Solomon did, that you will know how to answer.

he went up to the house (temple) of the LORD, she was breathless *and* awed [by the wonder of it all].

⁶Then she told the king, "The report which I heard in my own land about your words and wisdom is true!

⁷"I did not believe the report until I came and saw it with my own eyes. Behold, the half of it was not told to me. You exceed in wisdom and prosperity the report which I heard.

⁸"How blessed (fortunate, happy) are your men! How blessed are these your servants who stand continually before you, hearing your wisdom!

⁹"Blessed be the LORD your God who delighted in you to set you on the throne of Israel! Because the LORD loved Israel forever, He made you king to execute justice and righteousness."

¹⁰She gave the king a hundred and twenty talents of gold and a very great *quantity* of spices and precious stones. Never again did such an abundance of spices come in [to Israel] as that which the queen of Sheba gave King Solomon.

¹¹Also the ships of Hiram, which brought gold from Ophir, brought in from Ophir a great *quantity* of almug wood (sandalwood) and precious stones.

¹²From the almug wood (sandalwood) the king made pillars for the house of the LORD and for the king's palace, and also lyres and harps for the singers. Such almug wood did not come in [to Israel] *again,* nor has it been seen to this day.

¹³King Solomon [in turn] gave to the queen of Sheba everything that she wanted, whatever she asked, besides what he gave to her from his royal bounty. So she returned to her own country, she and her servants.

¹⁴Now the weight of the gold that came to Solomon in one [particular] year was six hundred and sixty-six talents of gold,

¹⁵besides *the taxes* from the traders and from the wares of the merchants, and [the tribute money] from all the kings of the Arabs (Bedouins) and the governors of the country.

¹⁶King Solomon made two hundred large shields of beaten (hammered) gold; six hundred *shekels of* gold went into each shield.

¹⁷*He made* three hundred *smaller* shields of beaten gold; three minas of gold went into each shield. The king put them in the House of the Forest of Lebanon [the king's armory].

¹⁸Also the king made a great throne of ivory and overlaid it with the finest gold.

¹⁹The throne had six steps, and a round top *was attached* to the throne from the back. On either side of the seat were armrests, and two lions stood beside the armrests.

²⁰Twelve lions stood there, one on either end of each of the six steps; there was nothing like it made for any other kingdom.

²¹All King Solomon's drinking vessels were of gold, and all vessels of the House of the Forest of Lebanon were of pure gold. None were of silver; it was not considered valuable in the days of Solomon.

²²For the king had at sea the [large cargo] ships of Tarshish with the ships of Hiram. Once every three years the ships of Tarshish came bringing gold, silver, ivory, monkeys, and peacocks.

²³So King Solomon exceeded all the kings of the earth in wealth and in wisdom.

²⁴All the earth was seeking the presence of Solomon, to hear his wisdom which God had put in his mind.

²⁵Every man brought a gift [of tribute]: articles of silver and gold, garments, weapons, spices, horses, and mules, so much year by year.

²⁶Now Solomon collected chariots and horsemen; he had 1,400 chariots and 12,000 horsemen, which he stationed

in the chariot cities and with the king in Jerusalem.

²⁷The king made silver *as common* in Jerusalem as stones, and cedars as plentiful as the sycamore trees that are in the lowland.

²⁸Solomon's horses were imported from Egypt and from Kue, and the king's merchants acquired them from Kue, for a price. [Deut 17:15, 16]

²⁹A chariot could be imported from Egypt for six hundred *shekels* of silver, and a horse for a hundred and fifty; and in the same way they exported them, by the king's merchants, to all the kings of the Hittites and to the kings of Aram (Syria).

11 NOW KING Solomon [defiantly] loved many foreign women along with the daughter of Pharaoh: Moabite, Ammonite, Edomite, Sidonian, and Hittite women,

²from the very nations of whom the LORD said to the Israelites, "You shall not associate with them, nor shall they associate with you, for the result will be that they will turn away your hearts to follow their gods." Yet Solomon clung to these in love. [Deut 17:17]

³He had seven hundred wives, princesses, and three hundred concubines,

life point

Even though God had given Solomon a great gift of wisdom, he did not use wisdom in every area of his life (see 1 Kings 11:1). You see, godly wisdom does not automatically lead to obedience. Solomon defied God and loved foreign women. Having wisdom does not mean that a person uses wisdom. Let's thank God that His wisdom is in us as believers in Him, but let's also ask for the ability to act on the wisdom He gives us and to have hearts that are obedient to Him.

putting the Word to work

Even though Solomon did so much right, Scripture tells us that his heart was not *completely devoted* to God, and this was evil in God's sight (see 1 Kings 11:1–6). Ask God to identify anything in your life that is keeping you from following Him fully, repent and receive His forgiveness, and ask Him to help you to trust and follow Him completely.

and his wives turned his heart away [from God].

⁴For when Solomon was old, his wives turned his heart away after other gods; and his heart was not completely devoted to the LORD his God, as was the heart of his father David.

⁵For Solomon went after Ashtoreth, the [fertility] goddess of the Sidonians, and after Milcom the horror (detestable idol) of the Ammonites. [1 Kin 9:6–9]

⁶Solomon did evil [things] in the sight of the LORD, and did not follow the LORD fully, as his father David *had done*.

⁷Then Solomon built a high place for [worshiping] Chemosh the horror (detestable idol) of Moab, on the hill which is east of Jerusalem, and for Molech the horror (detestable idol) of the sons of Ammon.

⁸And he did the same for all of his foreign wives, who burned incense and sacrificed to their gods.

⁹So the LORD became angry with Solomon because his heart was turned away from the LORD, the God of Israel, who had appeared to him twice,

¹⁰and had commanded him concerning this thing, that he should not follow other gods; but he did not observe (remember, obey) what the LORD had commanded.

¹¹Therefore the LORD said to Solomon, "Because you have done this and have not kept My covenant and My statutes,

which I have commanded you, I will certainly tear the kingdom away from you and give it to your servant.

¹²"However, I will not do it in your lifetime, for the sake of your father David, but I will tear it out of the hand of your son (Rehoboam).

¹³"However, I will not tear away all the kingdom; I will give one tribe (Judah) to your son for the sake of My servant David and for the sake of Jerusalem which I have chosen."

¹⁴Then the LORD stirred up an adversary against Solomon, Hadad the Edomite; he was of royal descent in Edom.

¹⁵For it came about, when David was in Edom, and Joab the commander of the army had gone up to bury those killed [in battle] and had struck down every male in Edom

¹⁶(for Joab and all [the army of] Israel stayed there six months, until he had killed every male in Edom),

¹⁷that Hadad escaped to Egypt, he and some Edomites from his father's servants with him, while Hadad was [still] a little boy.

¹⁸They set out from Midian [south of Edom] and came to Paran, and took men with them from Paran and came to Egypt, to Pharaoh king of Egypt, who gave [young] Hadad a house and ordered food *and* provisions for him and gave him land.

¹⁹Hadad found great favor with Pharaoh, so that he gave Hadad in marriage the sister of his own wife, the sister of Tahpenes the queen.

²⁰The sister of Tahpenes gave birth to Genubath, Hadad's son, whom Tahpenes weaned in Pharaoh's house; and Genubath was in Pharaoh's household among the sons of Pharaoh.

²¹But when Hadad heard in Egypt that David had died and that Joab the commander of the army was dead, Hadad said to Pharaoh, "Let me leave, so that I may go to my own country."

²²Then Pharaoh said to him, "But what have you lacked with me that now you ask to go to your own country?" He replied, "Nothing; nevertheless you must let me go."

²³God also stirred up *another* adversary for Solomon, Rezon the son of Eliada, who had fled from his master, Hadadezer king of Zobah.

²⁴Rezon gathered men to himself and became leader of a marauding band, after David killed those *in Zobah.* They went to Damascus and stayed there and they reigned in Damascus. [2 Sam 10:8, 18]

²⁵So Rezon was an adversary to Israel all the days of Solomon, along with the evil that Hadad *inflicted.* Rezon hated Israel and reigned over Aram (Syria).

²⁶Jeroboam, Solomon's servant, the son of Nebat, an Ephrathite of Zeredah whose mother's name was Zeruah, a widow, also rebelled against the king.

²⁷Now this is the reason why he rebelled against the king: Solomon built the Millo (fortification) and he repaired *and* closed the breach of the city of his father David.

²⁸The man Jeroboam was a brave warrior and when Solomon saw that the young man was industrious, he put him in charge of all the forced labor of the house of Joseph.

²⁹It came about at that time, when Jeroboam left Jerusalem, that the prophet Ahijah the Shilonite met him on the road. Now Ahijah had covered himself with a new cloak; and the two of them were alone in the field.

³⁰Then Ahijah took hold of the new cloak which he was wearing and tore it into twelve pieces.

³¹He said to Jeroboam, "Take ten pieces for yourself; for thus says the LORD, the God of Israel, 'Behold, I am going to tear the kingdom from the hand of Solomon and give you ten tribes—

³²but he [and his descendants] shall have one tribe (Benjamin was annexed

to Judah), for the sake of My servant David and for the sake of Jerusalem, the city which I have chosen out of all the tribes of Israel—

³³because they have abandoned Me and have worshiped Ashtoreth the goddess of the Sidonians, Chemosh the god of the Moabites, and Milcom the god of the sons of Ammon; and they have not walked in My ways *and* followed My commandments, doing what is right in My sight and *keeping* My statutes and My ordinances as did his father David.

³⁴'However, I will not take the entire kingdom out of his hand; but I will make him ruler all the days of his life for the sake of My servant David, whom I chose because he kept My commandments and My statutes.

³⁵'But I will take the kingdom out of his son's hand and give it to you: ten tribes.

³⁶'Yet to his son I will give one tribe, so that My servant David may have a lamp always before Me in Jerusalem, the city where I have chosen to put My Name *and* Presence.

³⁷'I will take you [Jeroboam], and you shall reign over whatever your soul desires; and you shall be king over Israel (the ten northern tribes).

³⁸'Then it shall be, that if you listen to all that I command you and walk in My ways, and do what is right in My sight, keeping *and* observing My statutes and My commandments, as My servant David did, then I will be with you and build you an enduring house, as I built for David, and I will give Israel to you.

³⁹'And in this way I will afflict the descendants of David for this (their sin), but not forever.'"

⁴⁰So Solomon attempted to kill Jeroboam; but Jeroboam set out and escaped to Egypt, to Shishak king of Egypt, and stayed in Egypt until Solomon died.

⁴¹The rest of the acts of Solomon—and all that he did, and his wisdom—are they not written in the book of the acts of Solomon?

⁴²The time Solomon reigned in Jerusalem over all Israel was forty years.

⁴³And Solomon slept [in death] with his fathers and was buried in the city of his father David. Rehoboam his son reigned in his place.

12 REHOBOAM WENT to Shechem, for all Israel had come to Shechem to make him king.

²Now when Jeroboam the son of Nebat heard about it, he was living in Egypt (for he was still in Egypt, where he had fled from King Solomon).

³So they sent *word* and called for him, and Jeroboam and all the assembly of Israel came and spoke to Rehoboam, saying,

⁴"Your father made our yoke (burden) heavy; so now lighten the hard labor and the heavy yoke your father imposed on us, and we will serve you."

⁵Rehoboam replied to them, "Leave for three days, then come back to me [for my decision]." So the people left.

⁶King Rehoboam consulted with the elders who had served *and* advised his father Solomon while he was still alive and said, "How do you advise me to answer this people?"

⁷They spoke to him, saying, "If you will be a servant to this people today, and will serve them and grant their request, and speak good words to them, then they will be your servants forever."

⁸But he ignored the advice which the elders gave him and consulted the young men who grew up with him and served him.

⁹He said to them, "What do you advise that we answer this people who have said to me, 'Lighten the yoke (burden) which your father put on us'?"

¹⁰The young men who had grown up

with him answered, "This is what you should say to this people who told you, 'Your father made our yoke heavy, but as for you, make our yoke lighter'—say this to them: 'My little finger is thicker than my father's loins [and my reign will be even more severe].

¹¹'And now, whereas my father loaded you with a heavy yoke, I will add to your yoke. My father disciplined you with whips, but I will discipline you with scorpions.'"

¹²Jeroboam and all the people came back to Rehoboam on the third day, just as the king had instructed, saying, "Return to me on the third day."

¹³The king answered the people harshly and ignored the advice which the elders had given him,

¹⁴and spoke to them in accordance with the advice of the young men, saying, "My father made your yoke heavy, but as for me, I will add to your yoke; my father disciplined you with whips, but I will discipline you with scorpions."

¹⁵So the king did not listen to the people; for the situation was from the LORD, so that He might fulfill His word which He spoke through Ahijah the Shilonite to Jeroboam the son of Nebat. [1 Kin 11:29–33]

¹⁶So when all [the ten northern tribes of] Israel saw that the king did not listen to them, the people replied to the king, saying,

"What portion do we have in David?
We have no inheritance in the son of Jesse;
To your tents, O Israel!
Look now after your own house, David!"

Then Israel went back to their tents.

¹⁷But as for the sons (descendants) of Israel who lived in the cities of Judah [including Benjamin], Rehoboam reigned over them.

¹⁸Then King Rehoboam sent Adoram, who was in charge of the forced labor [to represent him], and all Israel stoned him to death. And King Rehoboam quickly mounted his chariot to escape to Jerusalem.

¹⁹So Israel (the ten northern tribes) has rebelled against the house (royal line) of David to this day (the date of this writing).

²⁰It came about when all Israel heard that Jeroboam had returned, that they sent word and called him to the assembly and made him king over all Israel. None followed the house of David except the tribe of Judah [including Benjamin].

²¹Now when Rehoboam arrived in Jerusalem, he assembled all the [fighting men from the] house of Judah, with the tribe of Benjamin, 180,000 chosen warriors, to fight against the house of Israel to bring the kingdom back to Rehoboam the son of Solomon.

²²But the word of God came to Shemaiah the man of God, saying,

²³"Tell Rehoboam the son of Solomon, king of Judah, and all the house (fighting men) of Judah and Benjamin and the rest of the people,

²⁴'Thus says the LORD, "You shall not go up and fight against your brothers, the sons of Israel. Let every man return to his house, for this thing has come about from Me."'" So they listened to the word of the LORD and returned to go home, in accordance with the word of the LORD.

²⁵Then Jeroboam built Shechem [as his royal city] in the hill country of Ephraim and lived there. He went out from there and rebuilt Penuel [as a stronghold].

²⁶Jeroboam [doubted God's promise to him and] said in his heart, "Now the kingdom will return to the house of David. [1 Kin 11:38]

²⁷"If these people go up to the house of the LORD in Jerusalem to offer sacrifices, then their heart will turn to

their lord, to Rehoboam king of Judah; and they will kill me and return to Rehoboam king of Judah."

²⁸So the king took counsel [and followed bad advice] and made two calves of gold. And he said to the people, "It is too much for you to go [all the way] up to Jerusalem; behold your gods, O Israel, who brought you up out of the land of Egypt."

²⁹He set the one [golden calf] in Bethel, and the other he put in Dan.

³⁰Now this thing became a sin [for Israel]; because the people went *to worship* before the one [or the other of them] as far as Dan.

³¹And Jeroboam also made houses on high places, and he made priests from all people who were not of the sons (descendants) of Levi.

³²Jeroboam held a feast on the fifteenth day of the eighth month, like the feast which is *kept* in Judah, and he went up to the altar; he did this in Bethel, sacrificing to the calves which he had made. And he stationed in Bethel the priests of the high places which he had made. [Lev 23:34]

³³So he went up to the altar which he had made in Bethel on the fifteenth day of the eighth month, in the month which he had devised in his own heart [in defiance of God's commandments]; and he held a feast for the Israelites and he went up to the altar to burn incense [in defiance of God's law.]

13 NOW BEHOLD, there came a man of God from Judah to Bethel by the word (command) of the Lord, while Jeroboam was standing by the altar [which he had built] to burn incense.

²The man cried out against the [idolatrous] altar by the word of the Lord, "O altar, altar, thus says the Lord: 'Behold, a son shall be born to the house of David, Josiah by name; and on you shall he sacrifice [the bodies of] the priests of the high places who burn incense on you, and human bones shall be burned on you.'"

³And he gave a sign the same day, saying, "This is the sign which the Lord has spoken: 'Behold, the altar shall be split apart and the ashes that are on it shall be poured out.'" [2 Kin 23:15, 16]

⁴When the king heard the words which the man of God cried out against the altar in Bethel, Jeroboam put out his hand from the altar, saying, "Seize him!" And his hand which he had put out against him withered, so that he was unable to pull it back to himself.

⁵The altar also was split apart and the ashes were poured out from the altar in accordance with the sign which the man of God had given by the word of the Lord.

⁶The king answered and said to the man of God, "Please entreat [the favor of] the Lord your God and pray for me, that my hand may be restored to me." So the man of God entreated the Lord, and the king's hand was restored to him and became as it was before.

⁷And the king said to the man of God, "Come home with me and refresh yourself, and I will give you a reward."

⁸But the man of God said to the king, "*Even* if you were to give me half your house (wealth), I would not go with you, nor would I eat bread or drink water in this place.

⁹"For I was commanded by the word of the Lord, 'You shall not eat bread or drink water, nor shall you return by the way you came.'"

¹⁰So he went another way and did not return by the way that he came to Bethel.

¹¹Now there was an old prophet living in Bethel; and his sons came and told him everything that the man of God had done that day in Bethel; they also told their father the words which he had spoken to the king.

¹²Their father asked them, "Which

way did he go?" For his sons had seen which way the man of God who came from Judah had gone.

¹³He said to his sons, "Saddle the donkey for me." So they saddled the donkey for him and he rode away on it,

¹⁴and he went after the man of God. And he found him sitting under an oak (terebinth) tree, and he said to him, "Are you the man of God who came from Judah?" And he said, "I am."

¹⁵Then he said to him, "Come home with me and eat bread."

¹⁶He said, "I cannot return with you nor go in with you, nor will I eat bread or drink water with you in this place.

¹⁷"For I was told by the word of the LORD, 'You shall not eat bread nor drink water there, nor shall you return by going the way that you came.'"

¹⁸He answered him, "I too am a prophet, as you are; and an angel spoke to me by the word of the LORD, saying, 'Bring him back with you to your house, so that he may eat bread and drink water.'" *But* he lied to him.

¹⁹So the man of God went back with him, and ate bread in his house and drank water.

²⁰Now it happened as they were sitting at the table, that the word of the LORD came to the prophet who had brought him back.

²¹And he cried out to the man of God who had come from Judah, "Thus says the LORD, 'Because you have disobeyed the word of the LORD and have not kept the commandment which the LORD your God commanded you,

²²but have come back and have eaten bread and drunk water in the place of which the LORD said to you, "You shall not eat bread nor drink water"; your body shall not come to the tomb of your fathers (ancestors).'"

²³After the prophet of the house had eaten bread and after he had drunk, he saddled the donkey for the prophet whom he had brought back.

²⁴Now when he had gone, a lion met him by the road and killed him, and his body was thrown in the road, with the donkey standing beside it; the lion was also standing beside the body.

²⁵And there were men passing by, and they saw the body thrown in the road, and the lion standing beside the body. So they came and told about it in the city [of Bethel] where the old prophet lived.

²⁶When the prophet who had brought him back from the road heard about it, he said, "It is the man of God who was disobedient to the word of the LORD; therefore the LORD has given him to the lion, which has torn him and killed him, in accordance with the word of the LORD which He spoke to him."

²⁷And he said to his sons, "Saddle the donkey for me." And they saddled it.

²⁸And he went and found the body thrown on the road, and the donkey and the lion standing beside the body; the lion [miraculously] had not eaten the body or attacked the donkey.

²⁹Then the prophet picked up the body of the man of God and laid it on the donkey and brought it back, and he came into the city (Bethel) of the old prophet to mourn and to bury him.

³⁰And he laid the body in his own grave, and they mourned over him, saying, "Alas, my brother!"

³¹Then after he had buried him, he said to his sons, "When I am dead, bury me in the grave in which the man of God is buried; lay my bones beside his bones.

³²"For the words which he cried out by the word of the LORD against the altar in Bethel and against all the houses of the high places which are in the cities of Samaria shall certainly come to pass."

³³After this event, Jeroboam [still] did not turn from his evil way, but again made priests for the high places from among all the people. He ordained anyone who was willing, so

that there would be priests for the high places.

³⁴And this thing (idol worship) became the sin of the house of Jeroboam to blot it out and eliminate it from the face of the earth.

14 AT THAT time Abijah the son [and crown prince, heir] of Jeroboam became sick. ²Jeroboam said to his wife, "Please get up and disguise yourself, so that people will not know that you are Jeroboam's wife, and go to Shiloh. Ahijah the prophet is there, the one who told me that *I would be* king over this people.

³"Take with you ten loaves of bread, *some* cakes, and a bottle of honey, and go to him. He will tell you what will happen to the boy."

⁴Jeroboam's wife did so. She got up and went [twenty miles] to Shiloh, and came to the house of Ahijah. Now Ahijah could not see, because his eyes were dim from old age.

⁵And the Lord said to Ahijah, "Behold, the wife of Jeroboam is coming to inquire of you about her son, because he is sick. You shall say such and such to her, for when she arrives, she will pretend to be another woman."

⁶So when Ahijah heard the sound of her feet as she came in the doorway, he said, "Come in, wife of Jeroboam. Why do you pretend to be another woman? For I have been sent to you [by God] with a harsh *message*.

⁷"Go, tell Jeroboam, 'This is what the Lord, the God of Israel, says: "Because I exalted you from among the people and made you leader over My people Israel,

⁸and tore the kingdom away from the house of David and gave it to you— but you have not been like My servant David, who kept My commandments and followed Me with all his heart, to do only what was right in My eyes,

⁹but have done more evil than all [the kings] who were before you; for you have gone and made for yourself other gods and molten images to provoke Me to anger, and have cast Me behind your back—

¹⁰therefore behold, I am bringing evil on the house (royal line) of Jeroboam, and I will cut off (destroy) from Jeroboam every male, both bond and free, in Israel, and will *utterly* sweep away the house of Jeroboam as one sweeps away dung until it is all gone.

¹¹"The dogs will eat [the carcass of] anyone belonging to Jeroboam who dies in the city, and the birds of the sky will eat [the carcass of] anyone who dies in the field, for the Lord has spoken it."' [Deut 28:26]

¹²"Now as for you (Jeroboam's wife), arise, go to your own house. When your feet enter the city, the child [Abijah] will die.

¹³"All Israel shall mourn for him and bury him, for he alone of Jeroboam's *family* will come to [be placed in] the grave, because in him there was found something good *and* pleasing toward the Lord, the God of Israel, in the house of Jeroboam.

¹⁴"Moreover, the Lord will raise up for Himself a king over Israel who will cut off the house (royal line) of Jeroboam this day and from now on.

¹⁵"The Lord will strike Israel, as a reed is shaken in the water; and He will uproot Israel from this good land which He gave to their fathers, and He will scatter them beyond the [Euphrates] River, because they have made their Asherim, provoking the Lord to anger.

¹⁶"He will give up Israel because of the sins of Jeroboam which he has committed, and with which he has made Israel sin [by leading them into idolatry]."

¹⁷So Jeroboam's wife arose and left and came to Tirzah [the king's residence]. As she was entering the threshold of the house, the child [Abijah] died.

¹⁸And all Israel buried him and mourned for him, in accordance with

the word of the LORD which He spoke through His servant Ahijah the prophet.

¹⁹Now as for the rest of the acts of Jeroboam, how he made war and how he reigned, behold, they are written in the Book of the Chronicles of the Kings of Israel.

²⁰The time that Jeroboam reigned was twenty-two years, and he slept with his fathers [in death]; and Nadab his son reigned in his place.

²¹Now Rehoboam the son of Solomon reigned in Judah. Rehoboam was forty-one years old when he became king, and he reigned seventeen years in Jerusalem, the city the LORD had chosen from all the tribes of Israel in which to put His Name (Presence). His mother's name was Naamah the Ammonitess.

²²And [the people of] Judah did evil in the sight of the LORD. They provoked Him to jealousy more than all that their fathers had done, with their sins which they had committed.

²³For they also built for themselves high places [to worship idols] and *sacred* pillars and Asherim [for the goddess Asherah]. *These were* on every high hill and under every luxuriant tree.

²⁴There were also male cult prostitutes in the land. They committed all the repulsive acts of the nations which the LORD dispossessed before the Israelites.

²⁵Now in the fifth year of King Rehoboam, Shishak king of Egypt [Jeroboam's brother-in-law] came up against Jerusalem.

²⁶He took away the treasures of the house (temple) of the LORD and the treasures of the king's house; he took away everything, he even took all the shields of gold which Solomon had made.

²⁷So King Rehoboam made bronze shields to replace them and handed them over to the captains of the palace guard who guarded the doorway of the king's house.

²⁸And as often as the king went into the house of the LORD, the guards would carry them and bring them back into the guardroom.

²⁹Now as for the rest of the acts of Rehoboam, and everything that he did, are they not written in the Book of the Chronicles of the Kings of Judah?

³⁰There was also war between Rehoboam and Jeroboam continually.

³¹And Rehoboam slept with his fathers [in death] and was buried with his fathers in the City of David. His mother's name was Naamah the Ammonitess. Abijam (Abijah) his son became king in his place.

15

IN THE eighteenth year of King Jeroboam the son of Nebat, Abijam became king over Judah.

²He reigned three years in Jerusalem. His mother was Maacah [grand]daughter of Abishalom (Absalom).

³He walked in all the sins [of idol worship] that his father [Rehoboam] committed before him; and his heart was not entirely devoted to the LORD his God, like the heart of his father (forefather) David.

⁴Nevertheless, for David's sake the LORD his God gave him a lamp (descendant on the throne) in Jerusalem, setting up his son after him and establishing Jerusalem,

⁵because David did what was right in the eyes of the LORD, and had not turned aside from anything that He

speak the Word

God, may I do what is right in Your eyes, turning not aside from anything You have commanded me all the days of my life.
—ADAPTED FROM 1 KINGS 15:5

commanded him all the days of his life, except in the matter of [the betrayal of] Uriah the Hittite.

⁶There was war between Rehoboam [Abijam's father] and Jeroboam all the days of Rehoboam's life.

⁷Now as for the rest of the acts of Abijam and everything that he did, are they not written in the Book of the Chronicles of the Kings of Judah? And there was war between Abijam and Jeroboam.

⁸Abijam slept with his fathers [in death] and they buried him in the City of David. Asa his son became king in his place.

⁹So in the twentieth year of Jeroboam king of Israel, Asa began to reign as king over Judah.

¹⁰He reigned forty-one years in Jerusalem. His [great-grand]mother was Maacah the daughter of Abishalom (Absalom). [1 Kin 15:2]

¹¹Asa did what was right in the eyes of the LORD, as did his father (forefather) David.

¹²He expelled the male cult prostitutes (sodomites) from the land and removed all the idols that his fathers [Solomon, Rehoboam, and Abijam] had made. [1 Kin 11:5–11; 14:22]

¹³He also deposed his [great-grand] mother Maacah from *being* queen mother, because she had made a horrid (obscene, vulgar) image for [the goddess] Asherah. Asa cut down her horrid image, and burned it by the Brook Kidron.

¹⁴But the high places [of idol worship] were not removed. Nevertheless, Asa's heart was entirely devoted to the LORD all his days.

¹⁵He brought the things which his father had dedicated and the things which he had dedicated into the house of the LORD—silver, gold, and utensils *and* accessories.

¹⁶Now there was war between Asa and Baasha king of Israel all their days.

¹⁷Baasha king of Israel went up against Judah and fortified Ramah [north of Jerusalem], in order to prevent *anyone* from going out or coming in to Asa king of Judah.

¹⁸Then Asa took all the silver and gold left in the treasuries of the house of the LORD and the treasuries of the palace of the king and handed them over to his servants. And King Asa sent them to Ben-hadad the son of Tabrimmon, the son of Hezion, king of Aram (Syria), who lived in Damascus, saying,

¹⁹"*Let there be* a treaty between me and you, *as there was* between my father and your father. Behold, I have sent you a gift of silver and gold; go, break your treaty with Baasha king of Israel, so that he will withdraw from me."

²⁰So Ben-hadad listened to king Asa and sent the commanders of his armies against the cities of Israel, and conquered Ijon, Dan, Abel-bethmaacah, and all Chinneroth [the region of the Sea of Galilee], along with all the land of Naphtali.

²¹When Baasha heard about it, he stopped fortifying Ramah and stayed in Tirzah.

²²Then King Asa made a proclamation to all Judah—none was exempt—and they carried away the stones of Ramah and its timber with which Baasha had built [the fortifications]. And King Asa built with them [border fortresses at] Geba of Benjamin and Mizpah.

²³Now as for the rest of all the acts of Asa, all his might, everything that he did, and the cities which he built, are they not written in the Book of the Chronicles of the Kings of Judah? But during the time of his old age he had a foot disease.

²⁴Asa slept with his fathers [in death] and was buried with his fathers in the city of his father David. Jehoshaphat his son reigned in his place.

²⁵Now Nadab the son of Jeroboam

began to reign over Israel in the second year of Asa king of Judah, and he reigned over Israel for two years.

²⁶He did evil in the sight of the Lord and walked in the way of his father [Jeroboam] and in his sin [of idolatry], with which he made Israel sin.

²⁷Baasha the son of Ahijah of the house (tribe) of Issachar conspired against Nadab, and Baasha struck him down at Gibbethon, which belonged to the Philistines, while Nadab and all Israel were laying siege to Gibbethon.

²⁸So Baasha killed Nadab in the third year of Asa king of Judah, and reigned in his place.

²⁹As soon as he was king, Baasha struck down all the household of Jeroboam. He did not leave for Jeroboam anyone alive, but he destroyed them in accordance with the word of the Lord which He had spoken through His servant Ahijah the Shilonite— [1 Kin 14:9–16]

³⁰because of the sins committed by Jeroboam and which he made Israel commit, and because he provoked the Lord God of Israel to anger.

³¹Now as for the rest of Nadab's acts and everything that he did, are they not written in the Book of the Chronicles of the Kings of Israel?

³²There was war between Asa and Baasha king of Israel all their days.

³³In the third year of Asa king of Judah, Baasha the son of Ahijah became king over all Israel in Tirzah [the capital city], and reigned twenty-four years.

³⁴He did evil in the sight of the Lord and walked in the way of Jeroboam and in his sin [of idolatry] with which he made Israel sin.

16 NOW THE word of the Lord came to Jehu the son of Hanani against Baasha, saying,

²"Because I exalted you [Baasha] from the dust and made you leader over My people Israel, and you walked in the way of Jeroboam and made My people Israel sin, provoking Me to anger with their sins [of idol worship],

³behold, I am going to sweep away Baasha and his household (family), and I will make your house (royal line) like that of Jeroboam the son of Nebat.

⁴"The dogs will eat anyone belonging to Baasha who dies in the city, and the birds of the sky will eat anyone belonging to him who dies in the field."

⁵Now as for the rest of the acts of Baasha, what he did and his might, are they not written in the Book of the Chronicles of the Kings of Israel?

⁶Baasha slept with his fathers [in death] and was buried in Tirzah. Elah his son became king in his place.

⁷Moreover, the word of the Lord came against Baasha and his household through the prophet Jehu the son of Hanani, both for all the evil that Baasha did in the sight of the Lord in provoking Him to anger with the work of his hands (idolatry), in being like the house of Jeroboam, and because he [willingly] destroyed it (the family of Jeroboam).

⁸In the twenty-sixth year of Asa king of Judah, Elah the son of Baasha became king over Israel in Tirzah, and reigned two years.

⁹His servant Zimri, commander of half his chariots, conspired against Elah. Now Elah was in Tirzah, getting drunk in the house of Arza, who was in charge of the [king's] household in Tirzah.

¹⁰Then Zimri came in and struck and killed Elah in the twenty-seventh year of Asa king of Judah, and became king in his place.

¹¹When he became king, as soon as he sat on his throne, he killed the entire household of Baasha; he did not leave a single male [alive], either of his relatives or his friends.

¹²Thus Zimri destroyed the entire household of Baasha, in accordance

with the word of the LORD which He spoke against Baasha through Jehu the prophet, [1 Kin 16:3]

¹³for all the sins of Baasha and the sins of Elah his son, which they committed, and made Israel commit, provoking the LORD God of Israel to anger with their idols.

¹⁴Now as for the rest of the acts of Elah and everything that he did, are they not written in the Book of the Chronicles of the Kings of Israel?

¹⁵In the twenty-seventh year of Asa king of Judah, Zimri reigned [over Israel] for seven days at Tirzah. Now the troops were camped against Gibbethon, [a city] which belonged to the Philistines,

¹⁶and the people who were camped heard it said, "Zimri has conspired and has also struck down the king." So all Israel made Omri, the commander of the army, king over Israel that day in the camp.

¹⁷Then Omri went up from Gibbethon, and all Israel with him, and they besieged Tirzah.

¹⁸When Zimri saw that the city was taken, he went into the fortress of the king's palace; and *while inside,* he set fire to the king's palace and died,

¹⁹because of the sins he had committed, doing evil in the sight of the LORD, by walking in the way of Jeroboam, and because of his sin he caused Israel to sin.

²⁰Now as for the rest of the acts of Zimri, and his [treasonous] conspiracy which he committed, are they not written in the Book of the Chronicles of the Kings of Israel?

²¹Then the people of Israel were divided in half. Half of the people followed Tibni the son of Ginath, to make him king, and the *other* half followed Omri.

²²But the people who followed Omri prevailed over the people who followed Tibni the son of Ginath. So Tibni died and Omri became king.

²³In the thirty-first year of Asa king of Judah, Omri became king over Israel *and reigned* for twelve years. He reigned six years at Tirzah.

²⁴Omri bought the hill Samaria from Shemer for two talents of silver, and he built *a city* on the hill [and fortified it], and named the city which he built Samaria, after the owner of the hill, Shemer.

²⁵But Omri did evil in the sight of the LORD, and acted more wickedly than all who *came* before him.

²⁶He walked in all the ways of Jeroboam the son of Nebat and in his sin, which he made Israel commit, provoking the LORD God of Israel, [to anger] with their idols.

²⁷Now as for the rest of the acts of Omri which he did, and his might which he showed, are they not written in the Book of the Chronicles of the Kings of Israel?

²⁸So Omri slept with his fathers [in death] and was buried in Samaria. Ahab his son became king in his place.

²⁹Ahab the son of Omri became king over Israel in the thirty-eighth year of Asa king of Judah, and Ahab the son of Omri reigned over Israel in Samaria for twenty-two years.

³⁰Ahab the son of Omri did evil in the sight of the LORD more than all [the kings] who were before him.

³¹It came about, as if it had been a trivial thing for Ahab to walk in the sins of Jeroboam the son of Nebat, that he married Jezebel the daughter of Ethbaal king of the Sidonians, and went and served Baal and worshiped him.

³²So he erected an altar for Baal in the house of Baal which he built in Samaria.

³³Ahab also made the Asherah. Ahab did more to provoke the LORD God of Israel than all the kings of Israel who were before him.

³⁴In his days, Hiel the Bethelite rebuilt Jericho. He laid its foundations with the

loss of Abiram his firstborn, and set up its gates with the *loss of* his youngest son Segub, in accordance with the word of the LORD, which He spoke through Joshua the son of Nun. [Josh 6:26]

17 NOW ELIJAH the Tishbite, who was of the settlers of Gilead, said to Ahab, "As the LORD, the God of Israel lives, before whom I stand, there shall be neither dew nor rain these years, except by my word." [Deut 11:16, 17]

²And the word of the LORD came to him, saying,

³"Go from here and turn eastward and hide yourself by the brook Cherith, which is east of the Jordan [River].

⁴"You shall drink from the brook, and I have commanded the ravens to sustain you there [with food]."

⁵So he went and did in accordance with the word of the LORD; he went and lived by the brook Cherith, which is east of the Jordan.

⁶And the ravens brought him bread and meat in the morning, and bread and meat in the evening; and he would drink from the brook.

⁷It happened after a while that the brook dried up, because there was no rain in the land.

⁸Then the word of the LORD came to him, saying,

putting the Word to work

Have you ever wondered how all the bills were going to get paid, or perhaps even where your next meal was coming from? God can be very creative when it comes to providing for His people, as Elijah found out in 1 Kings 17:1–9. As you follow God, you can always trust Him to provide for you, even if it is in ways you don't expect! Be sure to thank Him for His faithful provision every day.

life point

In the story that begins at 1 Kings 17:9, God sends Elijah to Zarephath. I believe God sent Elijah to the widow at Zarephath not because God wanted to do something in Elijah, but because God wanted to do something in the widow. If God relocates you or sends you into a situation you do not understand, He will bless you, but it may be for someone else's sake. If your "brook" dries up, as it did for Elijah in 1 Kings 17 before he went to Zarephath, that does not mean you have done anything wrong; it more likely means God needs you somewhere else. If God closes one door, you can always expect Him to open another one.

⁹"Arise, go to Zarephath, which belongs to Sidon, and stay there. Behold, I have commanded a widow there to provide for you."

¹⁰So he set out and went to Zarephath, and when he came to the gate of the city, behold, a widow was there gathering sticks [for firewood]. He called out to her and said, "Please bring me a little water in a jar, so that I may drink."

¹¹As she was going to get it, he called to her and said, "Please bring me a piece of bread in your hand."

¹²But she said, "As the LORD your God lives, I have no bread, only a handful of flour in the bowl and a little oil in the jar. See, I am gathering a few sticks so that I may go in and bake it for me and my son, that we may eat it [as our last meal] and die."

¹³Elijah said to her, "Do not fear; go and do as you have said. Just make me a little bread from it first and bring it out to me, and afterward you may make one for yourself and for your son.

¹⁴"For this is what the LORD God of Israel says: 'The bowl of flour shall not be exhausted nor shall the jar of oil be

empty until the day that the Lᴏʀᴅ sends rain [again] on the face of the earth.'"

¹⁵She went and did as Elijah said. And she and he and her household ate for *many* days.

¹⁶The bowl of flour was not exhausted nor did the jar of oil become empty, in accordance with the word of the Lᴏʀᴅ which He spoke through Elijah.

¹⁷It happened after these things, that the son of the woman, the mistress of the house, became sick; and his illness was so severe that there was no breath left in him.

¹⁸So she said to Elijah, "What [problem] is there between you and me, O man of God? Have you come to me to bring my sin to mind and to put my son to death?"

¹⁹He said to her, "Give me your son." Then he took him from her arms and carried him up to the upper room where he was living, and laid him on his own bed.

²⁰He called to the Lᴏʀᴅ and said, "O Lᴏʀᴅ my God, have You brought further tragedy to the widow with whom I am staying, by causing her son to die?"

²¹Then he stretched himself out upon the child three times, and called to the Lᴏʀᴅ and said, "O Lᴏʀᴅ my God, please let this child's life return to him."

²²The Lᴏʀᴅ heard the voice of Elijah, and the life of the child returned to him and he revived.

putting the Word to work

Is there something that God is asking you to do that seems like a hardship or involves great personal cost, as it did for the widow at Zarephath (see 1 Kings 17:8–16)? Know that God's instructions may not seem to make sense, but when you obey you will discover, like the widow, that God will do amazing things in you, through you, and for you.

²³Elijah took the child and brought him down from the upper room into the [lower part of the] house and gave him to his mother; and Elijah said, "See, your son is alive."

²⁴Then the woman said to Elijah, "Now I know that you are a man of God and that the word of the Lᴏʀᴅ in your mouth is truth."

18 NOW IT happened after many days that the word of the Lord came to Elijah in the third year, saying, "Go, show yourself to Ahab, and I will send rain on the face of the earth."

²So Elijah went to show himself to Ahab. Now the famine was severe in Samaria.

³Ahab called Obadiah who was the governor of his house. (Now Obadiah feared the Lᴏʀᴅ greatly;

⁴for when Jezebel destroyed the prophets of the Lᴏʀᴅ, Obadiah took a hundred prophets and hid them by fifties in a cave, and provided them with bread and water.)

⁵Then Ahab said to Obadiah, "Go into the land to all the sources of water and to all the streams; perhaps we may find grass and keep the horses and mules alive, and not have to kill some of the cattle."

⁶So they divided the land between them to survey it. Ahab went one way by himself and Obadiah went another way by himself.

⁷As Obadiah was on the way, behold, Elijah met him. He recognized him and fell face downward [out of respect] and said, "Is it you, my lord Elijah?"

⁸He answered him, "It is I. Go tell your master, 'Elijah is here.'"

⁹But he said, "What sin have I committed, that you would hand over your servant to Ahab to put me to death?

¹⁰"As the Lᴏʀᴅ your God lives, there is no nation or kingdom where my master has not sent *messengers* to seek you;

and when they said, 'He is not here,' Ahab made the kingdom or nation swear that they had not found you.

¹¹"And now you are saying, 'Go, tell your master, "Behold, Elijah [is here]."'

¹²"And as soon as I leave you, the Spirit of the LORD will carry you to a place I do not know; so when I come to tell Ahab and he does not find you, he will kill me. Yet your servant has [reverently] feared the LORD from my youth.

¹³"Has it not been told to my lord [Elijah] what I did when Jezebel killed the prophets of the LORD, how I hid a hundred of the LORD's prophets by

fifties in a cave, and provided them with bread and water?

¹⁴"And now you are saying, 'Go, tell your master, "Elijah is here"'; and he will kill me."

¹⁵Elijah said, "As the LORD of hosts (armies) lives, before whom I stand, I will certainly show myself to Ahab today."

¹⁶So Obadiah went to meet Ahab and told him; and Ahab went to meet Elijah.

¹⁷When Ahab saw Elijah, Ahab said to him, "Are you the one who is bringing disaster on Israel?"

the truth about doubt

When we read in 1 Kings 18:21 about halting and limping "between two opinions," we can interpret that phrase quite simply as "doubting." I once heard a story that offers valuable insight into the doubt that so often affects Christians.

There was a man who had a financial need and was confessing God's Word over his life, quoting Scriptures, and believing that God had already provided a way for him. He was just waiting for his breakthrough to become a reality. While doing so, he was intermittently attacked with thoughts of doubt. After he had suffered a particularly difficult time and was beginning to get discouraged, God opened his eyes to the spiritual world. This is what he saw: a demon (an evil spirit) speaking lies to him, telling him that he was not going to get the help he needed and that confessing God's Word was not going to work. But he also saw that each time he confessed the Word, light would come out of his mouth like a sword, and the demon would cower and fall backward.

As God showed him this vision, the man then understood why it is so important to keep speaking the Word. He saw that he did have faith, which was why the evil spirit was attacking him with doubt.

Doubt is not something God puts in us. Romans 12:3 says that God gives every man the "measure of faith" (KJV). God has placed faith in our hearts, but the devil tries to negate our faith by attacking us with doubt.

Doubt comes in the form of thoughts that are in opposition to the Word of God. This is why it is so important for us to know the Bible. If we know the Word, then we can recognize when the devil is lying to us. Be assured that he lies to us in order to steal what Jesus purchased for us through His death and resurrection.

I encourage you to be like that man who sought help from the Lord: speak God's Word because His Word is true, and because confessing the truth sends the demons of doubt away!

18Elijah said, "I have not brought disaster on Israel, but you and your father's household *have,* by abandoning (rejecting) the commandments of the LORD and by following the Baals.

19"Now then, send *word* and gather to me all Israel at Mount Carmel, together with the 450 prophets of Baal and the 400 prophets of [the goddess] Asherah, who eat at [Queen] Jezebel's table."

20So Ahab sent *word* to all the Israelites and assembled the [pagan] prophets together at Mount Carmel.

21Elijah approached all the people and said, "How long will you hesitate between two opinions? If the LORD is God, follow Him; but if Baal, follow him." But the people [of Israel] did not answer him [so much as] a word.

22Then Elijah said to the people, "I alone remain a prophet of the LORD, while Baal's prophets are 450 men.

23"Now let them give us two oxen, and let them choose one ox for themselves and cut it in pieces, and lay it on the wood, but put no fire *under it.* I will prepare the other ox and lay it on the wood, and I will not put a fire *under it.*

24"Then you call on the name of your god, and I will call on the name of the LORD; and the god who answers by fire, He is God." And all the people answered, "It is well spoken."

25Elijah said to the prophets of Baal, "Choose one bull for yourselves and prepare it first, since there are many of you; and call on the name of your god, but put no fire *under it.*"

26So they took the bull that was given

putting the Word to work

Do you sometimes feel that God does not really hear you when you pray? The prophets of Baal went through quite a routine to try to get their god to hear them—without success (see 1 Kings 18:25–39). But you can have the confidence of Elijah when you pray, knowing that you pray to the living God, Who hears every prayer and is ready to act on your behalf.

right as rain

God had brought drought and famine on Israel to show His power to Ahab. God was letting Ahab and his wicked wife, Jezebel, know that they needed to change their wicked ways, and if they did not, the circumstances would not be good. After three years of famine, God sent His prophet Elijah to tell Ahab it was going to rain. Elijah said to Ahab that he was hearing "the sound of the roar of an abundance of rain" (1 Kings 18:41). He told him to get ready because there was going to be a downpour.

Ahab and Jezebel could not stand the sight of Elijah because he was a prophet and servant of God. Have you ever noticed how wicked people hate righteous people for no reason at all? They will hate the righteous simply because we represent the One they are rebelling against. All Elijah did in 1 Kings 18 was to show up; that alone was enough to send Ahab into a rage. Although Ahab wanted rain, he did not want Elijah to be right or to be the one in control.

I do not believe Elijah really heard the sound of rain with his natural ears. He heard it in the spiritual realm by faith. He was listening to the Spirit of God; he believed what God said and began to act on it before he saw the manifestation of it. We need that kind of faith!

to them and prepared it, and called on the name of Baal from morning until noon, saying, "O Baal, hear *and* answer us." But there was no voice and no one answered. And they leaped about the altar which they had made.

²⁷At noon Elijah mocked them, saying, "Cry out with a loud voice, for he is a god; either he is occupied, or he is out [at the moment], or he is on a journey. Perhaps he is asleep and must be awakened!"

²⁸So they cried out with a loud voice [to get Baal's attention] and cut themselves with swords and lances in accordance with their custom, until the blood flowed out on them.

²⁹As midday passed, they played the part of prophets *and* raved dramatically until the time for offering the *evening* sacrifice; but there was no voice, no one answered, and no one paid attention.

³⁰Then Elijah said to all the people, "Come near to me." So all the people approached him. And he repaired *and* rebuilt the [old] altar of the LORD that had been torn down [by Jezebel]. [1 Kin 18:13; 19:10]

³¹Then Elijah took twelve stones in accordance with the number of the tribes of the sons of Jacob, to whom the word of the LORD had come, saying, "Israel shall be your name." [Gen 32:28]

³²So with the stones Elijah built an altar in the name of the LORD. He made

worship before the rain

After announcing to Ahab what was going to happen—rain was coming—Elijah went to the top of Mount Carmel. There he got down on his knees with his forehead on the ground (see 1 Kings 18:42). Can't you just see him? In that position of worship, Elijah sent his servant to run back and forth several times to see if the rain had started.

Six times his servant came back with a bad report, but Elijah did not get out of his worship position. Imagine how Elijah must have felt every time the report came back that nothing was happening! But each time Elijah just said, "Go back" (see 1 Kings 18:43). Despite the repeated negative reports, Elijah never gave up. He stayed right where he was, worshiping God.

Worship strengthens our faith. Doubt could have caused Elijah to give up, but his worship kept him strong. Romans 4 tells us of another person in the Bible who had absolutely no human reason to hope. Doubt and unbelief came against Abraham but did not defeat him; he became strong as he gave praise and glory to God. If praise and worship worked for Abraham and Elijah, it will work for us also.

Elijah's servant could have been saying to him, "Elijah, you must have missed God this time because nothing is happening; there's not even a cloud out there." But each time Elijah refused to give up! Finally, Elijah's servant came back and reported that he saw a cloud as small as a man's hand. At that word, Elijah came up shouting, "Hallelujah! Go tell Ahab to hurry home and seek shelter because it's beginning to rain" (see 1 Kings 18:44).

When you worship God, He will send the rain of His Spirit upon you, and it will drown all the "Ahabs" and all the other resistances in your life. Take your position and praise the Lord, worshiping before it begins to "rain" in your life.

a trench around the altar large enough to hold two measures of seed.

³³Then he laid out the wood and cut the ox in pieces and laid it on the wood.

³⁴And he said, "Fill four pitchers with water and pour it on the burnt offering and the wood." And he said, "Do it the second time." And they did it the second time. And he said, "Do it the third time." And they did it a third time.

³⁵The water flowed around the altar, and he also filled the trench with water.

³⁶At the time of the offering of the *evening* sacrifice, Elijah the prophet approached [the altar] and said, "O Lord, the God of Abraham, Isaac, and Israel (Jacob), let it be known today that You are God in Israel and that I am Your servant and that I have done all these things at Your word.

³⁷"Answer me, O Lord, answer me, so that this people may know that You, O Lord, are God, and that You have turned their hearts back [to You]."

³⁸Then the fire of the Lord fell and consumed the burnt offering and the wood, and *even* the stones and the dust; it also licked up the water in the trench.

³⁹When all the people saw it, they fell face downward; and they said, "The Lord, He is God! The Lord, He is God!"

⁴⁰Then Elijah said to them, "Seize the prophets of Baal; do not let one of them escape." They seized them; and Elijah brought them down to the brook Kishon, and [as God's law required] killed them there. [Deut 13:5, 12–15; 18:20]

⁴¹Now Elijah said to Ahab, "Go up, eat and drink, for there is the sound of the roar *of an abundance* of rain."

⁴²So Ahab went up to eat and to drink. And Elijah went up to the top of Carmel; and he crouched down to the earth and put his face between his knees,

⁴³and he said to his servant, "Go up, look toward the sea." So he went up and looked and said, "There is nothing." Elijah said, "Go back" seven times.

⁴⁴And at the seventh *time* the servant said, "A cloud as small as a man's hand is coming up from the sea." And Elijah said, "Go up, say to Ahab, 'Prepare *your chariot* and go down, so that the rain shower does not stop you.'"

⁴⁵In a little while the sky grew dark with clouds and wind, and there were heavy showers. And Ahab mounted *and* rode [his chariot] and went [inland] to Jezreel.

⁴⁶Then the hand of the Lord came upon Elijah [giving him supernatural strength]. He girded up his loins and outran Ahab to the entrance of Jezreel [nearly twenty miles].

19

NOW AHAB told Jezebel all that Elijah had done, and how he had killed all the prophets [of Baal] with the sword.

²Then Jezebel sent a messenger to Elijah, saying, "So may the gods do to me, and even more, if by this time tomorrow I do not make your life like the life of one of them."

³And Elijah was afraid and arose and ran for his life, and he came to Beersheba which belongs to Judah, and he left his servant there.

life point

Nothing in life looks good to us when we are exhausted. It seems that nobody loves us, nobody helps us, and nobody is concerned about us. We think we have to do all the work. We think we are being abused, misused, misunderstood, and mistreated. Many times when we feel we have a deep problem, all that really is wrong is that we (like Elijah) are just plain tired (see 1 Kings 19:4). When people are already exhausted and they continue to do more and more, they usually become very confused and cranky. We must learn to listen to our bodies and rest when we need it. Rest is not a luxury, it is essential to living a balanced, fruitful life.

keep your balance

Why in the world would a man like Elijah, who the previous day had made fools of 450 prophets of Baal and then personally slayed every one of them, suddenly allow himself to become so intimidated by the threats of a solitary woman named Jezebel that he ran away in fear (see 1 Kings 19:1–3)? I doubt very much that Jezebel was so fearsome that Elijah had to do that. I believe he responded in such an unbalanced way because he was exhausted.

Many of the problems we face in relationships come from being out of balance, and often that imbalance is the result of simply being worn out. When we are totally exhausted, we respond to people differently than we do when we are fully rested. We tend to respond emotionally and get our feelings hurt easily. We are touchier and more likely to get upset over the slightest thing that goes wrong. Even our creative ability dries up when we are overly tired. Like Elijah, we become vulnerable to depression and discouragement. I know from personal experience that my faith is affected when I am too tired; it is even difficult to want to pray at those times.

In many of today's families, both husband and wife need to work full-time just to provide for themselves and their children. After working all day, they then have to go home and take care of the children, prepare meals, do laundry and housework, go grocery shopping, see to the yard work, pay bills, and on and on. Sooner or later, they may become exhausted. If they are Christians, they will want to attend church and may also take on other church commitments.

While many of these activities are good, they may not all be commitments that are Spirit-led. If the people are not careful, they may end up trying to be everything to everybody, which wears them out. They may begin to feel that they are being pulled apart because everywhere they look, someone wants them to do something. Although serving in church and community is a very important part of our overall duty and desire, we must be Spirit-led and simply realize that we can do some things, but we cannot do everything.

I know all about this because I have gone through it in my own life. Not only am I a minister with an international ministry to operate, I am also a wife, a mother of four grown children, a grandmother, and a friend with many other duties, responsibilities, and relationships.

I am extremely busy; we all are, which is why we need balance in our lives. That may mean having to cut off some things we do not really want to get rid of, but that will cause problems if we do not allow God to prune them. In some cases, that may mean giving up a second job. We may have told ourselves that we took the job for our family, but the truth may be that our family needs *us* more than they need the money we could earn for them.

Let Elijah's story in 1 Kings 19:1–3 remind you to maintain balance in every aspect of your life: physical, mental, emotional, social, and spiritual. God wants you blessed, and in order to receive, enjoy, and wisely steward His blessings, it's vital for you to be strong and refreshed, not stressed and exhausted.

⁴But he himself traveled a day's journey into the wilderness, and he came and sat down under a juniper tree and asked [God] that he might die. He said, "It is enough; now, O LORD, take my life, for I am no better than my fathers."

⁵He lay down and slept under the juniper tree, and behold, an angel touched him and said to him, "Get up and eat."

⁶He looked, and by his head there was a bread cake baked on hot coal, and a pitcher of water. So he ate and drank and lay down again.

⁷Then the angel of the LORD came again a second time and touched him and said, "Get up, and eat, for the journey is too long for you [without adequate sustenance]."

⁸So he got up and ate and drank, and with the strength of that food he traveled forty days and nights to Horeb (Sinai), the mountain of God.

⁹There he came to a cave and spent the night in it; and behold, the word of the LORD *came* to him, and He said to him, "What are you doing here, Elijah?"

¹⁰He said, "I have been very zealous (impassioned) for the LORD God of hosts (armies) [proclaiming what is rightfully and uniquely His]; for the sons of Israel have abandoned (broken) Your covenant, torn down Your altars, and killed Your prophets with the sword. And I, only I, am left; and they seek to take away my life."

¹¹So He said, "Go out and stand on the mountain before the LORD." And

avoiding burnout

I have observed that after a person goes through a real emotional high, he or she will usually bottom out with an emotional low.

We see this in the life of Elijah the prophet. One day he is on Mount Carmel, in triumph and at the height of his victory. The next day he is sitting under a tree in the wilderness, asking God to let him die because he feels so depressed (see 1 Kings 19:4).

In my own life, I have noticed when I minister in a long series of meetings, I spend everything I have spiritually, emotionally, and mentally, praying for people and meeting their needs. And when I return from something exciting like that to normal, everyday life, it is quite a transition. This might be compared to climbing an emotional mountain, then falling off it. Who would want to go from doing miracles one day to hiding from Jezebel the next?

Often we get the idea, *Oh, if I could just stay on this emotional high forever!* But God knows we could not stand to maintain that level of intense emotion. Too many emotional highs and lows wear us out in every way. When I have finished an extensive ministry trip and I feel completely drained, I have learned to rest. It usually takes about two days for me to totally recuperate physically, mentally, emotionally, and even spiritually. I need to sleep, have some quality food for nourishment, spend extra time with God, do something fun for my emotions, and not make decisions that would require any mental effort.

When you feel "low" after an emotional high, do not do as Elijah did and get down on yourself. Resist allowing the devil to take advantage of you during those times. Use wisdom and get the rest you need—it will make a huge difference.

behold, the LORD was passing by, and a great and powerful wind was tearing out the mountains and breaking the rocks in pieces before the LORD; but the LORD was not in the wind. And after the wind, [there was] an earthquake, but the LORD was not in the earthquake.

¹²After the earthquake, [there was] a fire, but the LORD was not in the fire; and after the fire, [there was] the sound of a gentle blowing.

¹³When Elijah heard *the sound*, he

life point

How did the Lord through His angel get Elijah to the place where he was strong enough to go on with the next phase of his ministry? He gave him two good meals and a nice long nap (see 1 Kings 19:5, 6). That was all He gave him, and in the strength of that food and rest, Elijah went forty days and nights on a journey to Horeb! There was nothing great, spiritual, or supernatural about this. Elijah was worn out from everything he had done the day before and everything he had been through since. His body was broken down, and his emotions had fallen apart. He was not handling himself the way he normally would. He was afraid, depressed, discouraged, and even suicidal.

The Lord said to him, "You're worn out. You need a couple of hot meals and a good night's rest." And after Elijah was refreshed and made the journey to Horeb, the word of the Lord came to him there. With a fresh word from God, he was sent off again to do the work of the Lord.

Remember, staying spiritually strong does include natural wisdom. Take care of your body, exercise, and eat healthfully so you will have the physical stamina and alertness necessary to complete God's next assignment for you.

wrapped his face in his mantle (cloak) and went out and stood in the entrance of the cave. And behold, a voice came to him and said, "What are you doing here, Elijah?"

¹⁴He said, "I have been very zealous for the LORD God of hosts (armies), because the sons of Israel have abandoned (broken) Your covenant, torn down Your altars and killed Your prophets with the sword. And I, only I, am left; and they seek to take away my life."

¹⁵The LORD said to him, "Go, return on your way to the Wilderness of Damascus; and when you arrive, you shall anoint Hazael as king over Aram (Syria);

¹⁶and you shall anoint Jehu the son of Nimshi as king over Israel; and anoint Elisha the son of Shaphat of Abel-meholah as prophet in your place.

¹⁷"It shall come about that Jehu shall put to death whoever escapes from the sword of Hazael, and Elisha shall put to death whoever escapes the sword of Jehu.

¹⁸"Yet I will leave 7,000 [survivors] in Israel, all the knees that have not bowed down to Baal and every mouth that has not kissed him."

¹⁹So Elijah departed from there and found Elisha the son of Shaphat, while he was plowing with twelve pairs *of oxen* before him, and he with the twelfth. Elijah went over to him and threw his mantle (coat) on him.

²⁰He left the oxen and ran after Elijah and said, "Please let me kiss my father and mother [goodbye], then I will follow you." And he said to him,

life point

The ways of the Holy Spirit are gentle; most of the time He speaks to us as He did to Elijah, in "a still small voice" (1 Kings 19:12, KJV).

"Go on back; for what have I done to [stop] you?"

²¹So Elisha left him and went back. Then he took a pair of oxen and sacrificed them and boiled their meat with the implements of the oxen [as fuel], and gave *the meat* to the people, and they ate. Then he stood and followed Elijah, and served him. [2 Kin 3:11]

20 BEN-HADAD KING of Aram (Syria) gathered all his army together; thirty-two kings were [allied] with him, with horses and chariots. And he went up

and besieged Samaria [Israel's capital], and fought against it.

²Then he sent messengers to the city to Ahab king of Israel; and he said to him, "Thus says Ben-hadad:

³'Your silver and your gold are mine; your wives and your children, even the fairest, also are mine [as conditions of peace].'"

⁴The king of Israel [conceded his defeat and] answered, "By your word, my lord, O king, I am yours, and all that I have."

⁵The messengers returned and said, "Thus says Ben-hadad: 'I indeed sent

hearing God's still small voice

I was fascinated to learn that some horses have what their trainers call a "reining ear." While most horses are guided and led by a strap fastened to the bit in their mouth, some horses keep one ear turned to their master's voice. One ear is open for warnings in the natural world; the other is sensitive to the trusted trainer.

Elijah needed to hear from God, and thankfully he had a reining ear toward God even though his circumstances had frightened him. He had experienced tremendous victory but afterward he ran for his life, hid in a cave, and prayed to God to die. Knowing Elijah's need, God taught Elijah a wonderful lesson about what His voice sounds like. As Elijah waited on God, He demonstrated His power through wind, earthquake, and fire. But God was not in those things; instead, He spoke to Elijah through what the King James Version calls a "still small voice" (1 Kings 19:12) and gave instructions for Elijah's next mission. Later in this chapter we will see that Elijah obeyed the still small voice of the Lord.

Elijah's story helps us understand how to hear God when we need direction. God did not reassure Elijah with a showy, flashy manifestation of power, although He had already proven that He was capable of doing so. Instead, God spoke to His prophet through a still small voice—and He still chooses to communicate directly to His children through a whisper deep within our spirits.

The Bible tells us that God is a spiritual Being, and those who worship Him must worship Him in spirit and truth (see John 4:24). Jesus explained that some people do not hear the voice of God because they do not believe Him and thus do not have His Word living in their hearts (see John 5:37–40). He taught us that we must be born again in order to hear God's voice: "You must be born again. . . . The wind blows where it wishes and you hear its sound, but you do not know where it is coming from and where it is going; so it is with everyone who is born of the Spirit" (John 3:7, 8). When we are born again, we are made alive in our spirits to be sensitive to the voice of God. We hear His whisper even though we cannot tell where it comes from. We become tuned in our ears to hear our Master's voice. He whispers to convict, correct, and direct us by a still small voice deep within our hearts.

word to you, saying, "You shall give me your silver, your gold, your wives, and your children,"

⁶but about this time tomorrow I will send my servants to you, and they will search your house and the houses of your servants; and they will take with their hands (confiscate) whatever is desirable in your eyes and carry it away.'"

⁷Then the king of Israel summoned all the elders of the land and said, "Please observe and see how this man is seeking our destruction. For he sent *messengers* to me for my wives, my children, my silver, and my gold, and I did not refuse him."

⁸All the elders and all the people said to him, "Do not listen or consent [to this additional demand]."

⁹So he said to Ben-hadad's messengers, "Tell my lord the king, 'Every *demand* you first sent to your servant I will do, but I cannot do this [additional] thing [as a condition of peace].'" And the messengers left; then they brought him word again.

¹⁰Ben-hadad sent *word* to him and said, "May the gods do so to me, and more also, if there is enough dust left of Samaria for handfuls for all the [armed] people who follow me."

¹¹The king of Israel answered, "Tell him, 'A man who puts on [his armor to go to battle] should not boast like the man who takes it off [after the battle has been won].'"

¹²When Ben-hadad heard this message, as he and the kings were drinking in the temporary shelters, he said to his servants, "Station *yourselves.*" So they stationed *themselves* against the city [of Samaria].

¹³Then a prophet approached Ahab king of Israel and said, "Thus says the LORD: 'Have you seen all this great army? Behold, I will hand them over to you, and you shall know [without any doubt] that I am the LORD.'"

¹⁴Ahab said, "By whom?" And he said,

"Thus says the LORD: 'By the young men [the attendants or bodyguards] of the governors of the districts.'" Then Ahab said, "Who shall begin the battle?" And he answered, "You."

¹⁵Then Ahab assembled *and* counted the young men of the governors of the districts, and there were 232. After them he assembled *and* counted all the people, all the sons of Israel, 7,000. [1 Kin 19:18]

¹⁶They went out at noon, while Ben-hadad was getting drunk in the temporary shelters, he and the thirty-two kings who were helping him.

¹⁷The young men of the governors of the districts went out first; and Ben-hadad sent *men* out and they told him, saying, "Men have come out of Samaria."

¹⁸And he said, "Whether they have come out for peace or for war, take them alive."

¹⁹So these young men of the governors of the districts went out of the city, and the army followed them.

²⁰And each one killed his man; and the Arameans (Syrians) fled and Israel pursued them. Ben-hadad king of Aram escaped on a horse with horsemen.

²¹The king of Israel went out and struck [the riders of] the horses and chariots, and killed the Arameans in a great slaughter.

²²Then the prophet approached the king of Israel and said to him, "Go, strengthen yourself and observe and see what you have to do; for at the first of next year the king of Aram (Syria) will come up against you."

²³Now the servants of the king of Aram said to him, "Israel's god is a god of the hills; that is why they were stronger than we. But let us fight against them in the plain, and surely we will be stronger than they.

²⁴"Do this: remove the [thirty-two allied] kings, each from his place, and put captains in their place,

²⁵and assemble an army like the army that you have lost *in battle,* horse for horse and chariot for chariot. Then we will fight against them in the plain, and surely we shall be stronger than they." And he listened to their words and did so.

²⁶At the first of the year [in spring], Ben-hadad assembled *and* counted the Arameans (Syrians) and went up to Aphek [east of the Sea of Galilee] to fight against Israel.

²⁷The sons of Israel were counted and given provisions, and they went to meet them. The Israelites camped before the enemy like two little flocks of goats [with everything against them, except God], and the Arameans filled the country.

²⁸A man of God approached and said to the king of Israel, "Thus says the LORD, 'Because the Arameans have said, "The LORD is a god of the hills, but He is not a god of the valleys," I will give this great army into your hand, and you shall know [by experience] that I am the LORD.'" [Phil 4:13]

²⁹So they camped opposite each other for seven days. Then on the seventh day the battle began, and the sons of Israel killed 100,000 of the Aramean foot soldiers in a single day.

³⁰But the rest ran to the city of Aphek, and the [city] wall fell on 27,000 of the men who were left. Ben-hadad escaped and came into the city, going into an inner chamber [to hide].

³¹But his servants said to him, "We have heard that the kings of the house (royal line) of Israel are merciful kings. Please let us put sackcloth around our loins and ropes on our necks [as symbols of submission], and go out to the king of Israel; perhaps he will spare your life."

³²So they put sackcloth around their loins and ropes on their necks, and came to the king of Israel and said, "Your servant Ben-hadad says, 'Please

let me live.'" And Ahab asked, "Is he still alive? He is my brother."

³³Now the men took it as a *good* omen, and quickly understanding his meaning said, "Yes, your brother Ben-hadad *lives.*" Then the king said, "Go, bring him." Then Ben-hadad came out to him, and Ahab had him come up into the chariot.

³⁴Ben-hadad [tempting him] said to him, "I will restore the cities which my father took from your father; and you may set up bazaars (shops) of your own in Damascus, as my father did in Samaria." Then, *Ahab replied,* "I will let you go with this covenant (treaty)." So he made a covenant with him and let him go.

³⁵Now a certain man of the sons of the prophets said to another by the word of the LORD, "Please strike me." But the man refused to strike him.

³⁶Then the prophet said to him, "Because you have not obeyed the voice of the LORD, behold, as soon as you leave me, a lion will kill you." And as soon as he left him, a lion found him and killed him.

³⁷Then the prophet found another man and said, "Please strike me." So the man struck him hard, wounding him.

³⁸So the prophet left and waited for King Ahab by the road, and disguised himself [as a wounded soldier] with a bandage over his eyes.

³⁹As the king passed by, the prophet called out to the king and said, "Your servant went out into the middle of the battle, and behold, a man turned aside and brought a man to me and said, 'Guard this man; if for any reason he is missing, then your life shall be *required* for his life, or else you shall pay a talent of silver.'

⁴⁰"But while your servant was busy here and there, he [escaped and] was gone." And the king of Israel said to him, "Such is your own judgment (verdict); you have determined it."

⁴¹Then the prophet quickly removed the bandage from his eyes, and [Ahab] the king of Israel recognized him as one of the prophets.

⁴²He said to the king, "Thus says the Lᴏʀᴅ: 'Because you have released from your hand the man [Ben-hadad] whom I had devoted to destruction, your life shall be *required* for his life, and your people for his people.'"

⁴³So the king of Israel went to his house resentful and sullen, and came to Samaria. [1 Kin 22:34–36]

21 NOW IT came about after these things that Naboth the Jezreelite had a vineyard in Jezreel, close beside the [winter] palace of Ahab king of Samaria;

²Ahab spoke to Naboth, saying, "Give me your vineyard, so that I may have it for a garden of vegetables *and* herbs, because it is near my house. I will give you a better vineyard for it, or, if you prefer, I will give you what it is worth in money."

³But Naboth said to Ahab, "The Lᴏʀᴅ forbid me that I should give the inheritance of my fathers to you."

⁴So Ahab [already upset by the Lord's message] came into his house [feeling more] resentful and sullen because of what Naboth the Jezreelite had said to him; for he had said, "I will not give you the inheritance of my fathers." And he lay down on his bed and turned away his face, and would not eat any food.

⁵Then Jezebel his wife came to him and asked him, "Why is your spirit so troubled that you have not eaten?"

⁶And he said to her, "Because I spoke to Naboth the Jezreelite and said to him, 'Give me your vineyard for money; or if you prefer, I will give you *another* vineyard for it.' But he answered, 'I will not give you my vineyard.'"

⁷Jezebel his wife said to him, "Do you now reign over Israel? Get up, eat food, and let your heart rejoice; I will give you the vineyard of Naboth the Jezreelite."

⁸So she wrote letters in Ahab's name and sealed them with his seal, and sent them to the elders and nobles who lived with Naboth in his city.

⁹Now in the letters she wrote, "Proclaim a fast and seat Naboth at the head of the people;

¹⁰and seat two worthless *and* unprincipled men opposite him, and have them testify against him, saying, 'You cursed God and the king.' Then take him out and stone him to death."

¹¹So the men of his city, the elders and the nobles who lived there, did as Jezebel had sent *word* to them, just as it was written in the letters which she had sent to them.

¹²They proclaimed a fast and seated Naboth at the head of the people.

¹³Two worthless *and* unprincipled men came in and sat down opposite him; and they testified against Naboth before the people, saying, "Naboth cursed *and* renounced God and the king." Then they brought him outside the city and stoned him to death.

¹⁴Then they sent *word* to Jezebel, saying, "Naboth has been stoned to death."

¹⁵When Jezebel heard that Naboth had been stoned and was dead, she said to Ahab, "Arise, take possession of the vineyard of Naboth the Jezreelite which he refused to sell you, because Naboth is no longer alive, but dead."

¹⁶When Ahab heard that Naboth was dead, he arose to go down to the vineyard of Naboth the Jezreelite, to take possession of it.

¹⁷Then the word of the Lᴏʀᴅ came to Elijah the Tishbite, saying,

¹⁸"Arise, go down to meet Ahab king of Israel, who is in Samaria. Behold, he is in the vineyard of Naboth, where he has gone to take possession of it.

¹⁹"You shall speak to him, saying, 'Thus says the Lᴏʀᴅ: "Have you murdered and also taken possession [of

the victim's property]?"' And you shall speak to him, saying, 'Thus says the Lord: "In the place where dogs licked up the blood of Naboth, dogs will lick up your blood as well."'"

²⁰Ahab said to Elijah, "Have you found me, O my enemy?" And he answered, "I have found you, because you have sold yourself to do evil in the sight of the LORD.

²¹"Behold [says the LORD], I am bringing evil (catastrophe) on you, and will utterly sweep you away, and will cut off from Ahab every male, both bond and free in Israel;

²²and I will make your house (descendants) like that of Jeroboam the son of Nebat, and like the house of Baasha the son of Ahijah, for provoking Me to anger and making Israel sin.

²³"The LORD also spoke in regard to Jezebel, saying, 'The dogs will eat [the body of] Jezebel in the district of Jezreel.'

²⁴"The dogs will eat anyone belonging to Ahab who dies in the city, and the birds of the air will eat anyone who dies in the field." [1 Kin 14:11; 16:4]

²⁵There certainly was no one like Ahab who sold himself to do evil in the sight of the LORD, because Jezebel his wife incited him.

²⁶He acted very repulsively in following idols, in accordance with everything the Amorites had done, whom the LORD expelled [from the land] before the sons of Israel.

²⁷Now when Ahab heard these words [of Elijah], he tore his clothes, put on sackcloth and fasted, and he lay in sackcloth and went about dejectedly (mourning).

²⁸Then the word of the LORD came to Elijah the Tishbite, saying,

²⁹"Do you see how Ahab has humbled himself before Me? Because he has humbled himself before Me, I will not bring the evil (catastrophe) in his lifetime, but in his son's days I will bring evil upon his house."

22

ARAM (SYRIA) and Israel continued without war for three years.

²In the third year Jehoshaphat king of Judah came down to the king of Israel.

³Now the king of Israel said to his servants, "Do you know that Ramoth in Gilead is ours, yet we are still doing nothing to take it from the hand of the king of Aram?"

⁴And Ahab said to Jehoshaphat, "Will you go with me to battle at Ramoth-gilead?" Jehoshaphat said to the king of Israel, "I am as you are, my people as your people, my horses as your horses."

⁵But Jehoshaphat said to the king of Israel, "Please inquire first for the word of the LORD."

⁶Then the king of Israel gathered the prophets together, about four hundred men, and said to them, "Shall I go to battle against Ramoth-gilead, or should I not?" And they said, "Go up, for the LORD has handed it over to the king."

⁷But Jehoshaphat [doubted and] said, "Is there not another prophet of the LORD here whom we may ask?"

⁸The king of Israel said to Jehoshaphat, "There is one more man, Micaiah the son of Imlah, by whom we may inquire of the LORD, but I hate him, because he never prophesies good *news* for me, but *only* evil." But Jehoshaphat said, "May the king not say that [Micaiah only tells bad news]."

⁹Then the king of Israel summoned an officer and said, "Bring quickly Micaiah the son of Imlah."

¹⁰Now the king of Israel and Jehoshaphat king of Judah were each sitting on his throne, dressed in *their* [royal] robes, [in an open place] at the threshing floor at the entrance of the gate of Samaria; and all the prophets were prophesying before them.

¹¹Then Zedekiah the son of Chenaanah made for himself horns of iron and said, "Thus says the LORD: 'With these you will gore the Arameans (Syrians) until they are destroyed.'"

¹²All the prophets were prophesying in the same way [to please Ahab], saying, "Go up to Ramoth-gilead and be successful, for the LORD will hand it over to the king."

¹³Then the messenger who went to summon Micaiah said to him, "Listen carefully, the words of the prophets are unanimously favorable to the king. Please let your words be like the word of one of them, and speak favorably."

¹⁴But Micaiah said, "As the LORD lives, I will speak what the LORD says to me."

¹⁵So when he came to the king, the king said to him, "Micaiah, shall we go against Ramoth-gilead in battle, or shall we not?" And he answered him, "Go up and be successful, for the LORD will hand it over to the king."

¹⁶But the king [doubted him and] said to him, "How many times must I make you swear to tell me nothing but the truth in the name of the LORD?"

¹⁷And he said,

"I saw all Israel
Scattered upon the mountains,
Like sheep that have no shepherd.
And the LORD said,
'These have no master.
Let each of them return to his
    house in peace.'"

¹⁸Then the king of Israel said to Jehoshaphat, "Did I not tell you that he would not prophesy good concerning me, but evil?"

¹⁹Micaiah said, "Therefore, hear the word of the LORD. I saw the LORD sitting on His throne, and all the host (army) of heaven standing by Him on His right hand and on His left.

²⁰"The LORD said, 'Who will entice Ahab to go up and fall at Ramoth-gilead?' And one said this, while another said that.

²¹"Then a spirit came forward and stood before the LORD and said, 'I will entice him.'

²²"The LORD said to him, 'How?' And he said, 'I will go out and be a deceiving spirit in the mouth of all his prophets.' Then the LORD said, 'You are to entice him and also succeed. Go and do so.'

²³"Now then, behold, the LORD has put a deceiving spirit in the mouth of all these prophets; and the LORD has proclaimed disaster against you."

²⁴But Zedekiah the son of Chenaanah approached and struck Micaiah on the cheek and said, "How did the Spirit of the LORD pass from me to speak to you?"

²⁵Micaiah said, "Behold, you shall see on that day [of the king's defeat] when you enter an inner room [looking for a place] to hide yourself."

²⁶Then the king of Israel said, "Take Micaiah and return him to Amon, the governor of the city, and to Joash, the king's son,

²⁷and say, 'Thus says the king, "Put this man in prison, and feed him sparingly with the bread and water until I return safely."'"

²⁸Micaiah said, "If you indeed return safely, the LORD has not spoken by me." Then he said, "Listen, all you people."

²⁹So [Ahab] the king of Israel and Jehoshaphat the king of Judah went up to Ramoth-gilead.

³⁰The king of Israel said to Jehoshaphat, "I will disguise myself and enter the battle, but you put on your [royal] clothing." So the king of Israel disguised himself and went into the battle.

³¹Now the king of Aram (Syria) had commanded the thirty-two captains of his chariots, saying, "Do not fight with

speak the Word

Lord, may I be obedient and always speak what You say to me.
–ADAPTED FROM 1 KINGS 22:14

[anyone, either] small or great, but with [Ahab] the king of Israel alone."

³²When the captains of the chariots saw Jehoshaphat, they said, "Surely it is the king of Israel." They turned to fight against him, and Jehoshaphat shouted out [in fear].

³³When the captains of the chariots saw that it was not the king of Israel, they turned back from pursuing him.

³⁴But one man drew a bow at random and struck the king of Israel in a joint of the armor. So he said to the driver of his chariot, "Turn around and take me out of the fight, because I have been seriously wounded."

³⁵The battle raged that day, and [Ahab] the king was propped up in his chariot facing the Arameans (Syrians). And in the evening he died, and the blood from his wound ran down into the bottom of the chariot.

³⁶Then about sundown a resounding cry passed throughout the army, saying, "Every man to his city and every man to his own country!"

³⁷So the king died and was brought to Samaria, and they buried the king in Samaria.

³⁸They washed the chariot by the pool [on the outskirts] of Samaria, where the prostitutes bathed, and the dogs licked up his blood, in accordance with the word of the Lord which He had spoken. [1 Kin 21:19]

³⁹Now the rest of Ahab's acts, and everything that he did, the ivory palace which he built and all the cities which he built, are they not written in the Book of the Chronicles of the Kings of Israel?

⁴⁰So Ahab slept with his fathers [in death], and Ahaziah his son became king in his place.

⁴¹Now Jehoshaphat the son of Asa became king over Judah in the fourth year of Ahab king of Israel.

⁴²Jehoshaphat was thirty-five years old when he became king, and he reigned twenty-five years in Jerusalem. His mother's name was Azubah the daughter of Shilhi.

⁴³He walked in all the ways of Asa his father, without turning from them, doing right in the sight of the Lord. However, the high places were not removed; the people still sacrificed and burned incense on the high places.

⁴⁴Jehoshaphat also made peace with the king of Israel.

⁴⁵Now the rest of the acts of Jehoshaphat, his might which he displayed and how he made war, are they not written in the Book of the Chronicles of the Kings of Judah?

⁴⁶And the remnant of the sodomites (male cult prostitutes) who remained in the days of his father Asa, Jehoshaphat expelled from the land.

⁴⁷Now there was no king in Edom; a deputy (governor) was [serving as] king.

⁴⁸Jehoshaphat had [large cargo] ships of Tarshish constructed to go to Ophir for gold, but they did not go, because the ships were wrecked at Ezion-geber.

⁴⁹Then Ahaziah the son of Ahab said to Jehoshaphat, "Let my servants go with your servants in the ships," But Jehoshaphat was unwilling *and* refused.

⁵⁰Jehoshaphat slept with his fathers [in death] and was buried with his fathers in the city of his father David, and Jehoram his son became king in his place.

⁵¹Ahaziah the son of Ahab became king over Israel in Samaria in the seventeenth year of Jehoshaphat king of Judah, and he reigned over Israel for two years.

⁵²He did evil in the sight of the Lord and walked in the [idolatrous] way of his father [Ahab] and of his mother [Jezebel], and in the way of Jeroboam the son of Nebat, who made Israel sin.

⁵³He served Baal and worshiped him, and he provoked the Lord God of Israel to anger, in accordance with everything that his father [Ahab] had done.

Second Kings

Author:
Unknown

Date:
600 BC–550 BC

Everyday Life Principles:
Obeying God leads to blessings;
disobeying or dishonoring Him brings
curses.

The ministries of both Elijah and Elisha
can remind us that God is a God of miracles and He still does miracles today.

A double portion awaits those who are
faithful until the very end.

Second Kings, like 1 Kings, continues the biblical record of the names, reigns, and some of the actions of the rulers of the divided kingdom. On the time line of history, 2 Kings picks up where 1 Kings leaves off. Throughout 2 Kings, we see good kings and bad kings, those who sought to serve God and those who did not. We continue to see Israel as a nation go back and forth between honoring God and dishonoring Him. One of the same truths we see throughout the Old Testament is reiterated yet again in 2 Kings: When we obey God, we are blessed; when we are living in disobedience to God, we cannot expect Him to bless us.

One noteworthy event in 2 Kings is the death of Elijah, which was not a typical death—he was simply caught up in a whirlwind and taken to heaven in a chariot of fire. Elisha remained faithful to Elijah until the very end, and after Elijah died, Elisha received a double portion of his spirit and went on to witness and be used by God in great signs, wonders, and miracles.

As you read 2 Kings, remember that obedience brings blessings and disobedience brings curses. Remember too that God will reward your faithfulness, just as He did Elisha's. Many people give up just prior to a breakthrough, but the double portion awaits those who will stay faithful until the end.

1 NOW MOAB rebelled against Israel after the death of Ahab.
²Ahaziah [the king of Israel] fell through the lattice (grid) in his upper chamber which was in Samaria, and became sick [from the injury]. So he sent messengers, saying to them, "Go, inquire of Baal-zebub, the god of Ekron, if I will recover from this sickness."

³But the angel of the LORD said to Elijah the Tishbite, "Arise, go up to meet the messengers of the king of Samaria, and say to them, 'Is it because there is no God in Israel that you are going to inquire of Baal-zebub, the god of Ekron?'

⁴"Therefore this is what the LORD says: 'You [Ahaziah] will not leave the bed on which you lie, but you will certainly die.'" So Elijah departed.

⁵When the messengers returned to Ahaziah, he said to them, "Why have you returned [so soon]?"

⁶They replied, "A man came up to meet us and said to us, 'Go, return to the king who sent you and tell him, "Thus says the LORD: 'Is it because there is no God in Israel that you send to inquire of Baal-zebub, the god of Ekron? Therefore you will not leave the bed on which you lie, but you will certainly die.'"'"

⁷The king asked them, "What was the appearance of the man who came up to meet you and said these things to you?"

⁸They answered him, "*He was* a hairy man with a [wide] leather band bound around his loins." And Ahaziah said, "It is Elijah the Tishbite."

⁹Then the king sent to Elijah a captain of fifty with his fifty [fighting men to seize the prophet]. And he went up to him, and behold, he was sitting on the top of a hill. And the captain said to him, "Man of God, the king says, 'Come down.'"

¹⁰Elijah replied to the captain of fifty, "So if I am a man of God, then let fire come down from heaven and consume you and your fifty [fighting men]." Then fire fell from heaven and consumed him and his fifty.

¹¹So King Ahaziah again sent to him another captain of fifty with his fifty [fighting men]. And he said to him, "Man of God, thus says the king, 'Come down quickly.'"

¹²Elijah answered them, "If I am a man of God, let fire come down from heaven and consume you and your fifty [fighting men]." And the fire of God came down from heaven and consumed him and his fifty.

¹³So Ahaziah again sent a captain of a third fifty with his fifty [fighting men]. And the third captain of fifty went up and came bowed down on his knees before Elijah, and begged him [for compassion] and said to him, "O man of God, please let my life and the lives of your servants, these fifty, be precious in your sight.

¹⁴"Behold, fire came down from heaven and consumed the first two captains of fifty with their fifties; but now let my life be precious in your sight."

¹⁵The angel of the LORD said to Elijah, "Go down with him; do not be afraid of him." So he stood and went down with him to the king.

¹⁶Then Elijah said to Ahaziah, "Thus says the LORD: 'Since you have sent messengers to inquire of Baal-zebub, god of Ekron—is it because there is no God in Israel to inquire of His word?—therefore you will not leave the bed on which you lie, but will certainly die.'"

¹⁷So Ahaziah [the son of King Ahab] died in accordance with the word of the LORD which Elijah had spoken. And because he had no son, Jehoram [his younger brother] became king [of Israel, the northern kingdom] in his place in the second year of Jehoram the son of Jehoshaphat, king of Judah [the southern kingdom].

¹⁸Now the rest of the acts of Ahaziah

which he did, are they not written in the Book of the Chronicles of the Kings of Israel?

2 WHEN THE LORD was about to take Elijah up to heaven by a whirlwind, Elijah and Elisha were traveling from Gilgal.

²And Elijah said to Elisha, "Please stay here, for the LORD has sent me to Bethel." But Elisha replied, "As the LORD lives and as your soul lives, I will not leave you." So they went down to Bethel.

³Now the sons of the prophets who were at Bethel came out to Elisha and said to him, "Do you know that the LORD will take your master away from you today?" He said, "Yes, I know it; be quiet [about it]."

⁴Elijah said to him, "Elisha, please stay here, for the LORD has sent me to Jericho." But he said, "As the LORD lives and as your soul lives, I will not leave you." So they came to Jericho.

⁵The sons of the prophets who were at Jericho approached Elisha and said to him, "Do you know that the LORD will take your master away from you today?" And he answered, "Yes, I know it; be quiet [about it]."

⁶Elijah said to him, "Please stay here, for the LORD has sent me to the Jordan." But he said, "As the LORD lives and as your soul lives, I will not leave you." So the two of them went on.

⁷Fifty men of the sons of the prophets also went and stood opposite them [to watch] at a distance; and the two of them stood by the Jordan.

⁸And Elijah took his mantle (coat) and rolled it up and struck the waters, and they were divided this way and that, so that the two of them crossed over on dry ground.

⁹And when they had crossed over, Elijah said to Elisha, "Ask what I shall do for you before I am taken from you."

putting the Word to work

Having a spiritual mentor is a great gift. Is there a more mature Christian in your life who is helping you to grow in your relationship with God? If not, ask God to identify someone who can be a mentor to you, as Elijah was to Elisha (see 1 Kings 2:2–8). If you do have a spiritual mentor, one way to show your appreciation is through faithful support of and loyalty to that individual.

And Elisha said, "Please let a double portion of your spirit be upon me."

¹⁰He said, "You have asked for a difficult thing. *However,* if you see me when I am taken from you, it shall be so for you; but if not, it shall not be so."

¹¹As they continued along and talked, behold, a chariot of fire with horses of fire [appeared suddenly and] separated the two of them, and Elijah went up to heaven in a whirlwind.

¹²Elisha saw it and cried out, "My father, my father, the chariot of Israel and its horsemen!" And he no longer saw Elijah. Then he took hold of his own clothes and tore them into two pieces [in grief].

¹³He picked up the mantle of Elijah that fell off him, and went back and stood by the bank of the Jordan.

¹⁴He took the mantle of Elijah that fell from him and struck the waters and said, "Where is the LORD, the God of Elijah?" And when he too had struck the waters, they divided this way and that, and Elisha crossed over.

¹⁵When the sons of the prophets who were [watching] opposite at Jericho saw him, they said, "The spirit of Elijah rests on Elisha." And they came to meet him and bowed down to the ground before him [in respect].

¹⁶Then they said to Elisha, "Behold

now, there are among your servants fifty strong men; please let them go and search for your master. It may be that the Spirit of the LORD has taken him up and cast him on some mountain or into some valley." And he said, "You shall not send *anyone*."

¹⁷But when they urged him until he was embarrassed [to refuse them], he said, "Send *them*." So they sent fifty men, and they searched for three days but did not find Elijah.

¹⁸They returned to Elisha while he was staying at Jericho; and he said to them, "Did I not tell you, 'Do not go'?"

¹⁹Then the men of the city said to Elisha, "Look, this city is in a pleasant place, as my lord [Elisha] sees; but the water is bad and the land is barren."

²⁰He said, "Bring me a new jar, and put salt in it." So they brought it to him.

²¹Then Elisha went to the spring of water and threw the salt in it and said, "Thus says the LORD: 'I [not the salt]

double-portion blessings

Seeing an assignment or a project from God through to the finish is extremely important. Many people start things enthusiastically but never finish them, and this is not pleasing to God. The Bible says in Luke 14:28–30 that we should count the cost before we begin to build and make sure we have what will be needed to finish the project.

Elisha was Elijah's servant and had been chosen and anointed to take Elijah's place when he was gone. As Elijah neared the end of his time on earth, he asked Elisha what he could do for him. We read in 2 Kings 2:9 that Elisha requested a double portion of his mentor's spirit, or anointing. Elisha had asked for a hard thing, but was told he could have it if he saw Elijah when God took him away.

I have always felt that Elijah was saying, "If you stick with me until the very end, if you finish what you started many years ago—then you may have what you asked for." Many people ask for things and then are not willing to do what is required of them to have their requests granted. Asking is easy, but seeing things through to the finish is not. Beginnings are exciting, and they come with zeal and enthusiasm. Many times, in the beginning of an endeavor, lots of people are willing to help. However, the way becomes tougher when the newness wears off and some of the people who originally committed to help lose interest or grow weary.

We must be able to endure hard work, wait longer for results than we expected to, endure loneliness, betrayal, misunderstanding, and many other unpleasant things if needed. Jesus endured all these things in order to complete God's will for His life, and we are to follow in His footsteps. Jesus said, "Take up your cross and follow Me" (see Luke 9:23). I believe the cross we are called on to carry is the challenge of living an unselfish life. That means we cannot quit or give up just because we do not enjoy the difficult work of pressing on. We must live beyond how we feel, what we think or want, and, in the face of hardship, do all that God asks us to do.

Make a decision today that from now on, by God's grace, you will always finish what you start. It may be cleaning out your closet, or keeping a commitment at church or to a friend. It could be paying for the things you have purchased or going to a Bible college. Whatever it is, just do it! God has a double-portion blessing waiting for you, but you will find it at the finish line.

have purified *and* healed these waters; there shall no longer be death or barrenness because of it.'"

²²So the waters have been purified to this day, in accordance with the word spoken by Elisha.

²³Then Elisha went up from Jericho to Bethel. On the way, young boys came out of the city and mocked him and said to him, "Go up, you baldhead! Go up, you baldhead!"

²⁴When he turned around and looked at them, he cursed them in the name of the Lord. Then two female bears came out of the woods and tore to pieces forty-two of the boys.

²⁵Elisha went from there to Mount Carmel, and from there he returned to Samaria.

3 JEHORAM THE son of Ahab became king over Israel in Samaria in the eighteenth year of Jehoshaphat king of Judah, and reigned twelve years.

²He did evil in the sight of the Lord, but not like his father and mother; for he put away the *sacred* pillar of Baal that his father had made.

³Nevertheless, he continued in the [idolatrous] sins of Jeroboam the son of Nebat, who made Israel sin; he did not depart from them.

⁴Mesha the king of Moab was a sheep breeder, and he used to pay [an annual tribute] to the king of Israel 100,000 lambs and the wool of 100,000 rams.

⁵But when Ahab died, the king of Moab rebelled against the king of Israel.

⁶So King Jehoram left Samaria at that time and assembled all [the fighting men of] Israel.

⁷Then he went and sent *word* to Jehoshaphat king of Judah, saying, "The king of Moab has rebelled against me. Will you go with me to fight against Moab?" And he replied, "I will go; I am as you are, my people as your people, my horses as your horses."

⁸Jehoram said, "Which way shall we go up?" Jehoshaphat answered, "The way through the Wilderness of Edom."

⁹So the king of Israel went with the king of Judah and the king of Edom. They made a circuit of seven days' journey, but there was no water for the army or for the cattle that followed them.

¹⁰Then the king of Israel said, "We are doomed, for the Lord has called these three kings to be handed over to Moab."

¹¹But Jehoshaphat said, "Is there no prophet of the Lord here from whom we may inquire of the Lord?" One of the servants of the king of Israel answered, "Elisha the son of Shaphat is here, who used to pour water over Elijah's hands."

¹²Jehoshaphat said, "The word of the Lord is with him." So the king of Israel and Jehoshaphat and the king of Edom went down to Elisha.

¹³Now Elisha said to the king of Israel, "What *business* do you have with me? Go to the prophets of your [wicked] father [Ahab] and to the prophets of your [pagan] mother [Jezebel]." But the king of Israel said to him, "No, for the Lord has called these three kings *together* to be handed over to Moab."

¹⁴Elisha said, "As the Lord of hosts (armies) lives, before whom I stand, were it not that I have regard for Jehoshaphat king of Judah, I would not look at you nor see you [king of Israel].

¹⁵"But now bring me a musician." And it came about while the musician played, that the hand (power) of the Lord came upon Elisha.

¹⁶He said, "Thus says the Lord, 'Make this valley (the Arabah) full of trenches.'

¹⁷"For thus says the Lord, 'You will not see wind or rain, yet that valley will be filled with water, so you and your cattle and your *other* animals may drink.

¹⁸'This is but a simple thing in the sight of the Lord; He will also hand over the Moabites to you.

¹⁹'You shall strike every fortified city and every choice (principal) city, and cut down every good tree and stop up all sources of water, and ruin every good piece of land with stones.'"

²⁰It happened in the morning, when the sacrifice was offered, that suddenly water came [miraculously] from the area of Edom, and the country was filled with water.

²¹Now all the Moabites heard that the [three] kings had come up to fight against them, and all who were able to put on armor, as well as those who were older, were summoned and stood [together in battle formation] at the border.

²²When they got up early the *next* morning, the sun shone on the water, and the Moabites saw the water across from *them* as red as blood.

²³And they said, "This is blood! Clearly the kings have fought together, and have killed one another. Now then, Moab, to the spoil [and the plunder of the dead soldiers]!"

²⁴But when they came to the camp of Israel, the Israelites rose up and struck the Moabites, so that they fled before them; and they went forward into the land, killing the Moabites [as they went].

²⁵They destroyed the [walls of the] cities, and each man threw a stone on every piece of good land, covering it [with stones]. And they stopped up all the springs of water and cut down all the good trees, until they left *nothing* in Kir-hareseth [Moab's capital city] but its stones. Then the [stone] slingers surrounded the city and destroyed it.

²⁶When the king of Moab saw that the battle was too fierce for him, he took with him seven hundred swordsmen

flow freely again

In Old Testament times, stopping up wells with stones was one of the weapons used to defeat one's enemies (see 1 Kings 3:19). Our enemy, the devil, still uses that weapon against us today.

I believe that you and I are born open and free with an ability to flow. But over time our enemy, Satan, comes along and starts throwing stones into the well of our inner being—stones of abuse, hurt, rejection, abandonment, misunderstanding, bitterness, rejection, resentment, self-pity, revenge, depression, hopelessness, and on and on. By the time we become adults, our wells are so filled with stones that they have become stopped up and no longer flow freely within us. Every now and then we may feel a little gurgle down inside, but we never seem to experience the full release needed for the waters of our souls to flow freely once again.

It is interesting that when Jesus went to raise His friend Lazarus from the dead, He ordered, "Take away the stone" (John 11:39). In a similar sense, I believe the Holy Spirit wants to take away the stones that have been clogging our wells of living water.

When speaking of living water in John 7:37–39, Jesus did not say that from those who believe in Him there will flow rivers of living water *once in a while*. He said these rivers of living water would flow *continually*. That living water is the Holy Spirit. What Jesus was talking about here is the outpouring of the Holy Spirit, which we (who have accepted Jesus as Lord and Savior) have received. Let the power of the Holy Spirit remove the stones that block the wellspring of your life, and let the water of life within you be released to flow again.

to break through to the king of Edom; but they could not.

[27]Then the king of Moab took his eldest son, who was to reign in his place, and offered him [publicly] as a burnt offering [to Chemosh] on the [city] wall [horrifying everyone]. And there was great wrath against Israel, and Israel's allies [Judah and Edom] withdrew from King Jehoram and returned to their own land.

4 NOW ONE of the wives *of a man* of the sons of the prophets cried out to Elisha [for help], saying "Your servant my husband is dead, and you know that your servant [reverently] feared the LORD; but the creditor is coming to take my two sons to be his slaves [in payment for a loan]."

[2]Elisha said to her, "What shall I do for you? Tell me, what do you have [of value] in the house?" She said, "Your

the first step to fullness

The key to value and worth is knowing who we are in Jesus. When we know that, there is nothing for us to do but stand in awe of the Lord and give Him thanks and praise for what He has done for us in Christ. Like the poor widow in 2 Kings 4:1–7, the first step to fullness is to recognize we are empty.

All of us are empty vessels. None of us has anything in us of any value except the power of God that is resident there to flow out of us. What do we have to offer to God? Nothing. God is not needy. He does not need you or me; He can do His own work without us. We are not indispensable. I do not make this observation to make us feel bad about ourselves, but to remind us all that being used by God is a great privilege and an honor, not a right.

We do have value—more than we can imagine—because of the value the Lord assigns to us because of the blood of His Son, Jesus Christ. We have nothing in and of ourselves. In Christ, we are and have everything. But in our flesh, there is nothing of any value or worth. What is born of the flesh is flesh, and it profits us nothing.

When I first started ministering, I wanted to help people. The Lord showed me during that time that when we are empty of ourselves so that all we have left within us is the ability to depend on the Holy Spirit, when we have learned that everything we are and have comes from Him, *then* He will send us to those we know to fill their empty vessels with the life He has poured into our empty vessels.

Arriving at the place of being empty of ourselves is not an easy task, and it does not happen quickly. I spent many years wondering if I would ever reach a place of manifesting humility instead of pride—of being dependent on God instead of independent—of trusting in the strength of His arm instead of my arm. If you feel the same way, let me encourage you that *as long as you don't give up, you are making progress*.

It may seem as though reaching the place you desire to go is taking forever, but "He who began a good work in you will continue until the day of Jesus Christ [right up to the time of His return], developing [that good work] and perfecting and bringing it to full completion in you" (Philippians 1:6 Amplified Classic).

If we press on and are sincere about spiritual maturity, we will eventually be like the woman in 2 Kings 4:1–7—empty of ourselves and ready to be used by God to fulfill His great purposes for our lives.

maidservant has nothing in the house except a [small] jar of [olive] oil."

³Then he said, "Go, borrow containers from all your neighbors, empty containers—and not *just* a few.

⁴"Then you shall go in and shut the door behind you and your sons, and pour out [the oil you have] into all these containers, and you shall set aside each one when it is full."

⁵So she left him and shut the door behind her and her sons; they were bringing her *the containers* as she poured [the oil].

⁶When the containers were all full, she said to her son, "Bring me another

owe no man anything but love

The Bible teaches us that we are to owe no man anything except to love him (see Romans 13:8). In 2 Kings 4:7, we see that we are to pay our debts. When we allow debt to overwhelm us, we can quickly and easily become discouraged and depressed.

Have you realized that one of the main reasons people get into debt is that their emotions are out of control? When a desire for personal pleasure, a sense of prestige, or the ability to impress others causes us to live beyond our means, we end up in debt.

When Dave and I were young marrieds, we got into trouble with debt. We did it by running up our credit cards to their maximum limit, buying things we wanted for ourselves and our children. We made the minimum payments on our balances each month, but the interest was so high we never seemed to make any progress toward paying off what we owed. In fact, we just kept getting deeper and deeper into debt.

What caused that? Emotions and a lack of wisdom.

If you and I are ever going to get anywhere in the kingdom of God, we must learn to live by wisdom and not by our carnal desire, which is human emotion (Proverbs 3:13–15).

Wisdom makes the decision today that it will be comfortable with tomorrow. Emotion does what feels good today and takes no thought of tomorrow. When tomorrow arrives, the wise enjoy it in peace and security, but the foolish end up discouraged and depressed. Why? Because the wise have prepared for tomorrow and are able to enjoy the fruits of their labor, while the foolish, who have put pleasure first, now must pay for yesterday.

It is much better to work now and play later, than to play now and worry later!

It is so discouraging to go to the mailbox every day and find nothing there but bills, bills, and more bills. Eventually that discouragement leads to depression because of the pressure of not being able to see a way out. When we charge things we cannot pay for, we are spending tomorrow's prosperity today. Then when tomorrow comes, all we have is debt.

To live a disciplined life, which is what it takes to produce good fruit in our lives, we have to be willing to invest today so that we can reap tomorrow. To relieve the discouragement and depression that come from being in debt, we must get out of debt by becoming self-disciplined enough to think not of today's sacrifices, but of tomorrow's rewards.

container." And he said to her, "There is not a one left." Then the oil stopped [multiplying].

⁷Then she came and told the man of God. He said, "Go, sell the oil and pay your debt, and you and your sons can live on the rest."

⁸Now there came a day when Elisha went over to Shunem, where there was a prominent *and* influential woman, and she persuaded him to eat a meal. Afterward, whenever he passed by, he stopped there for a meal.

⁹She said to her husband, "Behold, I sense that this is a holy man of God who frequently passes our way.

¹⁰"Please, let us make a small, fully-walled upper room [on the housetop] and put a bed there for him, with a table, a chair, and a lampstand. Then whenever he comes to *visit* us, he can turn in there."

¹¹One day he came there and turned in to the upper room and lay down to rest.

¹²And he said to Gehazi his servant, "Call this Shunammite." So he called her and she stood before him.

¹³Now he said to Gehazi, "Say to her now, 'You have gone to all this trouble for us; what can I do for you? Would you *like* to be mentioned to the king or to the captain of the army?'" She answered, "I live among my own people [in peace and security and need no special favors]."

putting the Word to work

Would you like to bless your pastor or some other Christian leader in your life? Offering hospitality in various forms is a wonderful way to demonstrate both your appreciation and God's love. As the Shunammite woman discovered (see 2 Kings 4:8–17), you can be sure that God honors those who provide hospitality!

¹⁴Later Elisha said, "What then is to be done for her?" Gehazi answered, "Well, she has no son and her husband is old."

¹⁵He said, "Call her." So Gehazi called her, and she [came and] stood in the doorway.

¹⁶Elisha said, "At this season next year, you will embrace a son." She said, "No, my lord. O man of God, do not lie to your maidservant."

¹⁷But the woman conceived and gave birth to a son at that season the next year, just as Elisha had said to her.

¹⁸When the child was grown, the day came that he went out to his father, to the reapers.

¹⁹But he said to his father, "My head, my head." The man said to his servant, "Carry him to his mother."

²⁰When he had carried and brought him to his mother, he sat on her lap until noon, and *then* he died.

²¹She went up and laid him on the bed of the man of God, and shut *the door* [of the small upper room] behind him and left.

²²Then she called to her husband and said, "Please send me one of the servants and one of the donkeys, so that I may run to the man of God and return."

²³He said, "Why are you going to him today? It is neither the New Moon nor the Sabbath." And she said, "*It will be* all right."

²⁴Then she saddled the donkey and said to her servant, "Drive [the animal] fast; do not slow down the pace for me unless I tell you."

²⁵So she set out and came to the man of God at Mount Carmel.

When the man of God saw her at a distance, he said to Gehazi his servant, "Look, there is the Shunammite *woman*.

²⁶"Please run now to meet her and ask her, 'Is it well with you? Is it well with your husband? Is it well with the child?'" And she answered, "It is well."

²⁷When she came to the mountain to

the man of God, she took hold of his feet. Gehazi approached to push her away; but the man of God said, "Let her alone, for her soul is desperate *and* troubled within her; and the LORD has hidden *the reason* from me and has not told me."

²⁸Then she said, "Did I ask for a son from my lord? Did I not say, 'Do not give me false hope'?"

²⁹Then he said to Gehazi, "Gird up your loins (prepare now!) and take my staff in your hand, and go [to the woman's house]; if you meet any man [along the way], do not greet him and if a man greets you, do not [stop to] answer him; and lay my staff on the face of the boy [as soon as you reach the house]."

³⁰The mother of the child said, "As the LORD lives and as your soul lives, I will not leave you." So Elisha arose and followed her.

³¹Gehazi went on ahead of them and laid the staff on the boy's face, but there was no sound or response [from the boy]. So he turned back to meet Elisha and told him, "The boy has not awakened (revived)."

³²When Elisha came into the house, the child was dead and lying on his bed. ³³So he went in, shut the door behind the two of them, and prayed to the LORD. ³⁴Then he went up and lay on the child and put his mouth on his mouth, his eyes on his eyes, and his hands on his hands. And as he stretched himself out on him *and* held him, the boy's skin became warm. [1 Kin 17:21] ³⁵Then he returned and walked in the house once back and forth, and went up [again] and stretched himself out on him; and the boy sneezed seven times and he opened his eyes.

³⁶Then Elisha called Gehazi and said, "Call this Shunammite." So he called her. And when she came to him, he said, "Pick up your son." ³⁷She came and fell at his feet, bowing

herself to the ground [in respect and gratitude]. Then she picked up her son and left.

³⁸Elisha came back to Gilgal during a famine in the land. The sons of the prophets were sitting before him, and he said to his servant, "Put on the large pot and cook stew for the sons of the prophets."

³⁹Then one [of them] went into the field to gather herbs, and found a wild vine and gathered from it a lapful of wild gourds, and came and cut them up into the pot of stew, although they did not know *what they were.* ⁴⁰So they served it for the men to eat. But as they ate the stew, they cried out, "O man of God, there is death in the pot." And they could not eat it. ⁴¹But he said, "Bring flour." And he threw it into the pot and said, "Serve it for the people so that they may eat." Then there was nothing harmful in the pot.

⁴²Now [at another time] a man from Baal-shalisha came and brought the man of God bread of the first fruits, twenty loaves of barley bread, and fresh ears of grain [in the husk] in his sack. And Elisha said, "Give it to the people [affected by the famine] so that they may eat." ⁴³His servant said, "How am I to set [only] this before a hundred [hungry]

putting the Word to work

Do you ever feel that you do not have much to offer in ministry? The man from Baal-shalisha had only a little bit of food to offer one hundred men, but he gave it willingly (see 2 Kings 4:42–44). Not only did the men eat, but there was food left over! As you freely offer what you have to give in service to God, ask Him to multiply what you have given and make it a blessing beyond what you can imagine.

men?" He said, "Give it to the people so that they may eat, for thus says the LORD, 'They shall eat and have *some* left.' "

⁴⁴So he set it before them, and they ate and left *some*, in accordance with the word of the LORD.

5 NOW NAAMAN, commander of the army of the king of Aram (Syria), was *considered* a great man by his king, and was highly respected because through Naaman the LORD had given victory to Aram (Syria). He was also a man of courage, *but he was* a leper.

²The Arameans (Syrians) had gone out in bands [as raiders] and had taken captive a little girl from the land of Israel; and she waited on Naaman's wife [as a servant].

³She said to her mistress, "I wish that my master [Naaman] were with the prophet who is in Samaria! Then he would heal him of his leprosy."

⁴Naaman went in and told his master [the king], "The girl who is from the land of Israel said such and such."

⁵Then the king of Aram (Syria) said, "Go now, and I will send a letter to the king of Israel (Jehoram the son of Ahab)." So he left and took with him ten talents of silver and 6,000 *shekels* of gold, and ten changes of clothing.

⁶And he brought the letter to the king of Israel. It said, "And now when this letter comes to you, I will have sent my servant Naaman to you, so that you may heal him of his leprosy."

⁷When the king of Israel read the letter, he tore his clothes [in shock and outrage at the request] and said, "Am I God, to kill and to make alive, that this man sends to me [a request] to heal a man of his leprosy? Just consider [what he is asking] and see how he is seeking an opportunity [for a battle] with me."

⁸Now when Elisha the man of God heard that the king of Israel had torn his clothes, he sent *word* to the king,

putting the Word to work

Second Kings 5:9–14 tells the story of Naaman's healing. This man's pride almost kept him from receiving the healing God wanted to give him. Do you struggle with pride, perhaps thinking you should be treated a certain way because of your station in life? Ask God to identify areas of pride and to teach you humility. Do not let pride keep you from experiencing all God wants to do in your life.

asking, "Why have you torn your clothes? Just let Naaman come to me, and he shall know that there is a [true] prophet in Israel."

⁹So Naaman came with his horses and chariots and stopped at the entrance of Elisha's house.

¹⁰Elisha sent a messenger to him, saying, "Go and wash in the Jordan seven times, and your flesh will be restored to you and *you will* be clean."

¹¹But Naaman was furious and went away and said, "Indeed! I thought 'He would at least come out to [see] me and stand and call on the name of the LORD his God, and wave his hand over the place [of leprosy] and heal the leper.'

¹²"Are not Abana and Pharpar, the rivers of Damascus [in Aram], better than all the waters of Israel? Could I not wash in them and be clean?" So he turned and went away in a rage.

¹³Then his servants approached and said to him, "My father, if the prophet had told you *to do some* great thing, would you not have done it? How much more then, when he has said to you, 'Wash, and be clean?' "

¹⁴So he went down and plunged himself into the Jordan seven times, just as the man of God had said; and his flesh was restored like that of a little child and he was clean.

¹⁵Then Naaman returned to the man

of God, he and all the people in his group, and stood before him. He said, "Behold, I know that there is no God in all the earth, except in Israel; so now accept a blessing *and* gift from your servant."

¹⁶But Elisha said, "As the LORD lives, before whom I stand, I will accept nothing." He urged him to take it, but Elisha refused.

¹⁷Naaman said, "If not, then please, let your servant be given a load of earth for a team of mules; for [from this day on] your servant will no longer offer a burnt offering nor a sacrifice to other gods, but only to the LORD, [the God of Israel].

¹⁸"In this matter may the LORD pardon your servant: when my master [the king] goes into the house of [his god] Rimmon to worship there, and he leans on my hand and I bow in the house of Rimmon, when I bow down in the house of Rimmon, may the LORD pardon your servant in this matter [of attending the king when he worships]."

¹⁹Elisha said to him, "Go in peace." So Naaman departed and was a good distance away from him,

²⁰when Gehazi, the servant of Elisha the man of God, said, "My master has spared this Naaman the Aramean (Syrian), by not accepting from him what he brought. As the LORD lives, I will run after him and get something from him."

²¹So Gehazi pursued Naaman. When Naaman saw someone running after him, he got down from the chariot to meet him and said, "Is all well?"

²²And he said, "All is well. My master has sent me to say, 'Just now two young men of the sons of the prophets have come to me from the hill country of Ephraim. Please give them a talent of silver and two changes of clothes.'"

²³Naaman said, "Please take two talents." And he urged him [to accept], and tied up two talents of silver in two bags with two changes of clothes and

putting the Word to work

Are you ever tempted to seek material gain even at the cost of your integrity? Elisha's servant Gehazi learned the hard way that greed is evil in the eyes of God (see 2 Kings 5:20–27). Ask God to teach you to be content and trust His provision for you.

gave them to two of his servants; and they carried them in front of Gehazi.

²⁴When he came to the hill, he took them from their hand and put them in the house [for safekeeping]; and he sent the men away, and they left.

²⁵Then he went in and stood before his master. Elisha asked him, "Where have you been, Gehazi?" He said, "Your servant went nowhere."

²⁶Elisha said to him, "Did my heart not go *with you,* when the man turned from his chariot to meet you? Is it a [proper] time to accept money and clothing and olive orchards and vineyards and sheep and oxen and male and female servants?

²⁷"Therefore, the leprosy of Naaman shall cling to you and to your descendants forever." So Gehazi departed from his presence, a leper *as white* as snow. [Ex 4:6; Num 12:10]

6 NOW THE sons of the prophets said to Elisha, "Look now, the place where we live near you is too small for us.

²"Please let us go to the Jordan [River] and let each man take from there a beam [for the building]; and let us make a place there for ourselves where we may live." And he answered, "Go."

³Then one said, "Please be willing to go with your servants." So he answered, "I shall go."

⁴So he went with them; and when they came to the Jordan, they cut down [some of] the trees.

⁵But it happened that as one was cutting down a beam, the axe head fell into the water; and he cried out and said, "Oh no, my master! It was borrowed!"

⁶The man of God said, "Where did it fall?" When he showed him the place, Elisha cut off a stick and threw it in there, and made the iron [axe head] float.

⁷He said, "Pick it up for yourself." So he reached out with his hand and took it.

⁸Now the king of Aram (Syria) was making war against Israel, and he consulted with his servants, saying, "My camp shall be in such and such a place."

⁹The man of God sent *word* to the king of Israel saying, "Be careful not to pass by this place, because the Arameans are pulling back to there."

¹⁰Then the king of Israel sent *word* to the place about which Elisha had warned him; so he guarded himself there repeatedly.

¹¹Now the heart of the king of Aram (Syria) was enraged over this thing. He called his servants and said to them, "Will you not tell me which of us is helping the king of Israel?"

¹²One of his servants said, "None [of us is helping him], my lord, O king; but Elisha, the prophet who is in Israel, tells the king of Israel the words that you speak in your bedroom."

¹³So he said, "Go and see where he is, so that I may send [men] and seize him." And he was told, "He is in Dothan."

¹⁴So he sent horses and chariots and a powerful army there. They came by night and surrounded the city.

¹⁵The servant of the man of God got up early and went out, and behold, there was an army with horses and chariots encircling the city. Elisha's servant said to him, "Oh no, my master! What are we to do?"

¹⁶Elisha answered, "Do not be afraid, for those who are with us are more than those who are with them."

¹⁷Then Elisha prayed and said, "Lord, please, open his eyes that he may see." And the Lord opened the servants eyes and he saw; and behold, the mountain was full of horses and chariots of fire surrounding Elisha.

¹⁸When the Arameans came down to him, Elisha prayed to the Lord and said, "Please strike this people (nation) with blindness." And God struck them with blindness, in accordance with Elisha's request.

¹⁹Then Elisha said to the Arameans, "This is not the way, nor is this the city. Follow me and I will lead you to the man whom you are seeking." And he led them to Samaria.

²⁰When they had come into Samaria, Elisha said, "Lord, open the eyes of these *men,* so that they may see." And the Lord opened their eyes and they saw. Behold, they were in the midst of Samaria.

²¹When the king of Israel (Jehoram) saw them, he said to Elisha, "My father, shall I kill them? Shall I kill them?"

²²Elisha answered, "You shall not kill them. Would you kill those you have taken captive with your sword and bow? Serve them bread and water, so that they may eat and drink, and go back to their master [King Ben-hadad]."

²³So the king prepared a great feast for them; and when they had eaten and drunk he sent them away, and they went to their master. And the marauding

speak the Word

Thank You, God, that I do not need to fear because there are more with me than with my enemies.
–ADAPTED FROM 2 KINGS 6:16

bands of Aram did not come into the land of Israel again.

²⁴But it came about after this, that Ben-hadad king of Aram (Syria) gathered his whole army together and went up and besieged Samaria.

²⁵Now there was a great famine in Samaria; and they besieged it until a donkey's head was sold for eighty *shekels* of silver, and a fourth of a kab of dove's dung for five *shekels* of silver.

²⁶As the king of Israel (Jehoram) was passing by on the [city] wall a woman cried out to him, "Help, my lord, O king!"

²⁷He said, "If the LORD does not help you, from where shall I get you help? From the threshing floor, or from the wine press?"

²⁸And the king said to her, "What is the matter with you?" She answered, "This woman said to me, 'Give your son so we may eat him today, and we will eat my son tomorrow.'

²⁹"So we cooked my son and ate him. The next day I said to her, 'Give your son so that we may eat him'; but she had hidden her son."

³⁰When the king heard the woman's words, he tore his clothes—now he was still walking along on the wall—and the people looked [at him], and he had on sackcloth underneath [his royal robe] next to his skin.

³¹Then he said, "May God do so to me and more also, if the head of Elisha the son of Shaphat remains on him today!"

³²Now Elisha was sitting in his house, and the elders were sitting with him. And *the king* sent a man ahead of him [to behead Elisha]; but before the messenger arrived, Elisha told the elders, "Do you see how this son of [Jezebel] a murderer has sent [a man] to remove my head? Look, when the messenger comes, shut the door and hold it securely against him. Is not the sound of his master's feet [just] behind him?"

³³While Elisha was still talking with them, the messenger came down to him [followed by the king] and the king said, "This evil [situation] is from the LORD! Why should I wait for [help from] the LORD any longer?"

7 THEN ELISHA said, "Hear the word of the LORD. Thus says the LORD, 'Tomorrow about this time a measure of finely-milled flour will sell for a shekel, and two measures of barley for a shekel, at the gate of Samaria.'"

²Then the royal officer on whose arm the king leaned answered the man of God and said, "If the LORD should make windows in heaven [for the rain], could this thing take place?" Elisha said, "Behold, you will see it with your own eyes, but [because you doubt] you will not eat of it."

³Now four men who were lepers were at the entrance of the [city's] gate; and they said to one another, "Why should we sit here until we die?

⁴"If we say, 'We will enter the city'— then the famine is in the city and we will die there; and if we sit still here, we will also die. So now come, let us go over to the camp of the Arameans (Syrians). If they let us live, we will live; and if they kill us, we will only die."

⁵So they got up at twilight to go to the Aramean camp. But when they came to the edge of the camp, there was no one there.

⁶For the LORD had caused the Aramean army to hear the sound of chariots, and the sound of horses, the sound of a great army. They had said to one another, "The king of Israel has hired against us the kings of the Hittites, and the kings of the Egyptians, to come [and fight] against us."

⁷So the Arameans set out and fled during the twilight, and left their tents, horses, and donkeys, *even left* the camp just as it was, and fled for their lives.

⁸When these lepers came to the edge of the camp, they went into one tent and ate and drank, and carried away from

there silver, gold, and clothing, and went and hid them. Then they went back and entered another tent and carried [some valuable things] from there *also*, and went and hid them.

⁹Then they said one to another, "We are not doing the right thing. This is a day of good news, yet we are keeping silent. If we wait until the morning light, some punishment [for not reporting this now] will come on us. So now come, let us go and tell the king's household."

¹⁰So they came and called to the gatekeepers of the city. They told them, "We went to the camp of the Arameans (Syrians), and behold, there was no one there, nor the sound of man there—only the horses and donkeys tied up, and the tents [had been left] just as they were."

¹¹Then the gatekeepers called out and it was reported to the king's household inside [the city].

¹²Then the king got up in the night and said to his servants, "I will tell you what the Arameans have done to us. They know that we are hungry; so they have left the camp to hide themselves in the open country, thinking, 'When they come out of the city, we shall take them alive and get into the city.'"

¹³One of his servants replied, "Please let some *men* take five of the horses which remain inside the city. Consider this: [if they are caught then at worst] they will be like all the people of Israel who are left in the city; [even if they are killed then] they will be like all the people of Israel who have already died. So let us send [them] and see [what happens]."

¹⁴So they took two chariots with horses, and the king sent them after the Aramean army, saying, "Go and see."

¹⁵They went after them to the Jordan, and all the road was entirely littered with clothing and equipment which the Arameans (Syrians) had

thrown away when they hurriedly fled. And the messengers returned and told the king.

¹⁶Then the people [of Israel] went out and plundered the camp of the Arameans. So [goods were so plentiful that] a measure of finely-milled flour [was sold] for a shekel, and two measures of barley for a shekel, in accordance with the word of the LORD [as spoken through Elisha]. [2 Kin 7:1]

¹⁷Now the king had appointed the royal officer on whose arm he leaned to be in charge of the [city] gate; and the [starving] people trampled him at the gate [as they struggled to get through for food], and he died, just as the man of God had foretold when the king came down to him.

¹⁸It happened just as [Elisha] the man of God had spoken to the king, saying, "Two measures of barley will be sold for a shekel and a measure of finely-milled flour for a shekel tomorrow about this time at the gate of Samaria."

¹⁹The royal officer had answered the man of God and said, "Now behold, [even] if the LORD should make windows in heaven, could such a thing happen?" And Elisha had answered, "You will see it with your own eyes, but [because of your doubt] you will not eat it." [2 Kin 7:2]

²⁰And so it happened to him; for the people trampled him at the gate, and he died.

8 NOW ELISHA had said to the [Shunammite] woman whose son he had restored to life, "Prepare and go, you and your household, and stay temporarily wherever you can; for the LORD has called for a famine, and moreover, it will come on the land [and continue] for seven years."

²So the woman set out and did everything in accordance with the word

of the man of God. She and her household went and stayed temporarily as foreigners in the land of the Philistines for seven years.

³At the end of the seven years the woman returned from the land of the Philistines; and she went to appeal to the king [of Israel] for her house and for her land.

⁴Now the king was talking with Gehazi, the servant of the man of God, saying, "Tell me all the great things that Elisha has done."

⁵And [just] as Gehazi was telling the king how Elisha had restored the dead to life, behold, the woman whose son he had restored to life appealed to the king for her house and for her land. And Gehazi said, "My lord, O king, this is the woman and this is her son, whom Elisha restored to life."

⁶When the king asked the woman, she told him [everything]. So the king appointed for her a certain high official, saying, "Restore everything that was hers, including all the produce of the field since the day that she left the land until now."

⁷Now Elisha came to Damascus, and Ben-hadad king of Aram (Syria) was sick; and he was told, "The man of God has come here."

⁸And the king said to Hazael, "Take a gift with you and go to meet the man of God, and inquire of the LORD by him, saying, 'Will I recover from this illness?'"

⁹So Hazael went to meet Elisha and took a gift with him of every good thing of Damascus, forty camels' loads; and he came and stood before him and said, "Your son Ben-hadad king of Aram has sent me to you, asking, 'Will I recover from this illness?'"

¹⁰And Elisha said to him, "Go, say to him, 'You will certainly recover,' but the LORD has shown me that he will certainly die."

¹¹Elisha stared steadily at Hazael until he was embarrassed, and then the man of God wept.

¹²Hazael said, "Why are you weeping, my lord?" He answered, "Because I know the evil that you will do to the sons (descendants) of Israel. You will set their strongholds on fire, kill their young men with the sword, smash their children to pieces, and rip up their pregnant women."

¹³Then Hazael said, *"Surely not!* For what is your servant, *who is nothing more than* a dog, that he would do this monstrous thing?" And Elisha answered, "The LORD has shown me that you will be king over Aram."

¹⁴Then Hazael departed from Elisha and came to his master, who said to him, "What did Elisha say to you?" And he answered, "He told me you would certainly recover."

¹⁵But the next day Hazael took the bedspread and dipped it in water and covered the king's face, so that he died. And Hazael became king in his place.

¹⁶Now in the fifth year of Joram (Jehoram) the son of Ahab king of Israel, when Jehoshaphat was king of Judah, Jehoram the son of Jehoshaphat king of Judah became king.

¹⁷He was thirty-two years old when he became king, and he reigned for eight years in Jerusalem.

¹⁸He walked in the ways of the kings of Israel, just as the house of Ahab had done, for [Athaliah] the daughter of Ahab became his wife. He did evil in the sight of the LORD.

¹⁹Yet for the sake of His servant David the LORD was not willing to destroy Judah, since He had promised to give him a lamp (enthroned descendant) through his sons always.

²⁰In his days Edom revolted from the rule of Judah, and set up a king over themselves.

²¹So Jehoram [king of Judah] went over to Zair [in Edom] with all his chariots. He set out by night and struck

down the Edomites who had surrounded him and the captains of his chariots; but the people [of his army] fled to their tents.

²²So Edom revolted against Judah to this day. Then Libnah revolted at the same time.

²³The rest of the acts of Jehoram and everything that he did, are they not written in the Book of the Chronicles of the Kings of Judah?

²⁴Jehoram slept with his fathers [in death] and was buried with them in the City of David. Ahaziah his son became king in his place.

²⁵In the twelfth year of Joram (Jehoram) the son of Ahab king of Israel, Ahaziah the son of Jehoram king of Judah began to reign.

²⁶Ahaziah was twenty-two years old when he became king, and he reigned one year in Jerusalem. His mother's name was Athaliah, the granddaughter of Omri king of Israel.

²⁷He walked in the ways of the house of Ahab and did evil in the sight of the Lord, as *did* the house of Ahab, for he was a son-in-law of the house of Ahab.

²⁸Ahaziah went with Joram the son of Ahab to battle against Hazael king of Aram (Syria) in Ramoth-gilead; and the Arameans wounded Joram.

²⁹King Joram returned to Jezreel to be healed of the wounds which the Arameans had inflicted on him at Ramah when he fought against Hazael king of Aram. And Ahaziah the son of Jehoram king of Judah went down to see Joram the son of Ahab in Jezreel, because he was sick.

9 NOW ELISHA the prophet called one of the sons of the prophets and said to him, "Gird up your loins (prepare for action), take this flask of oil in your hand and go to Ramoth-gilead.

²"When you arrive there, look for Jehu the son of Jehoshaphat the son of Nimshi, and go in and have him arise from among his brothers, and take him into an inner room.

³"Then take the flask of oil and pour it on his head and say, 'Thus says the Lord: "I have anointed you king over Israel."' Then open the door and flee and do not delay."

⁴So the young man, the servant of the prophet, went to Ramoth-gilead.

⁵When he arrived, the captains of the army were sitting [outside]; and he said, "I have a message for you, O captain." Jehu said, "To which one of us?" And he said, "For you, O captain."

⁶So Jehu got up, and they went into the house. And he poured the oil on Jehu's head and said to him, "Thus says the Lord, the God of Israel: 'I have anointed you king over the people of the Lord, over Israel.

⁷'You shall strike the house of Ahab your master, so that I may avenge the blood of My servants the prophets, and the blood of all the servants of the Lord, [who have died] at the hands of Jezebel.

⁸'For the entire house of Ahab shall perish, and I will cut off from Ahab every male, both bond and free, in Israel.

⁹'I will make the house of Ahab like the house of Jeroboam the son of Nebat, and like the house of Baasha the son of Ahijah. [1 Kin 21:22]

¹⁰'And the dogs will eat Jezebel in the territory of Jezreel, and there will be no one to bury her.'" Then he opened the door and fled. [2 Kin 9:33–37]

¹¹When Jehu came out to the servants of his master, one said to him, "Is all well? Why did this madman come to you?" And he said to them, "You know [very well] the man and his talk."

¹²And they said, "It is a lie; tell us now." And he said, "Thus and thus he spoke to me, saying, 'Thus says the Lord: "I have anointed you king over Israel."'"

¹³Then they hurried and each man took his garment and placed it [as a cushion] under Jehu on the top of the

[outside] stairs, and blew the trumpet, saying, "Jehu is king!"

¹⁴So Jehu the son of Jehoshaphat, the son of Nimshi, conspired against Joram [to dethrone and kill him]. Now Joram with all Israel was protecting Ramoth-gilead against Hazael king of Aram (Syria),

¹⁵but King Joram had returned to Jezreel to heal from the wounds which the Arameans had inflicted on him when he fought with Hazael king of Aram. So Jehu said, "If this is your intent, let no one survive and leave the city (Ramoth-gilead) to go and tell *of the plan* in Jezreel [the capital]."

¹⁶So Jehu rode in a chariot and went to Jezreel, for Joram was lying there. And Ahaziah king of Judah had come down to see Joram.

¹⁷Now the watchman was standing on the tower in Jezreel and he saw the crowd with Jehu as he approached, and said, "I see a company." And Joram said, "Send a horseman to meet them and have him ask, 'Do you come in peace?'"

¹⁸So the horseman went to meet him and said, "Thus says the king: 'Do you come in peace?'" And Jehu said, "What have you to do with peace? Rein in behind me." And the watchman reported, "The messenger approached them, but he has not returned."

¹⁹Then Joram sent out a second horseman, who approached them and said, "Thus says the king: 'Do you come in peace?'" Jehu replied, "What have you to do with peace? Rein in behind me."

²⁰And the watchman reported, "He approached them, but he has not returned; and the driving [of the chariot] is like that of Jehu the son of Nimshi, for he drives furiously."

²¹Then Joram said, "Harness [the chariot]." When they harnessed his chariot *horses*, Joram king of Israel and Ahaziah king of Judah went out, each in his chariot, and they went out

to meet Jehu and met him on the property of Naboth the Jezreelite.

²²When Joram saw Jehu, he said, "Do you come in peace, Jehu?" And he answered, "What peace [can exist] as long as the fornications of your mother Jezebel and her sorceries are so many?"

²³So Joram reined [his chariot] around and fled, and he said to Ahaziah, "Treachery *and* betrayal, Ahaziah!"

²⁴But Jehu drew his bow with his full strength and shot Joram between his shoulders; and the arrow went out through his heart and he sank down in his chariot.

²⁵Then Jehu said to Bidkar his officer, "Pick him up and throw him on the property of the field of Naboth the Jezreelite; for I remember when you and I were riding together after his father Ahab, that the LORD uttered this prophecy against him:

²⁶'I certainly saw the blood of Naboth and the blood of his sons yesterday,' says the LORD, 'and I will repay you on this property,' says the LORD. Now then, pick him up and throw him into the property [of Naboth], in accordance with the word of the LORD." [1 Kin 21:15–29]

²⁷When Ahaziah the king of Judah saw this, he fled by the way of the garden house. Jehu pursued him and said, "Shoot him too, [while he is] in the chariot." *So they shot him* at the ascent to Gur, which is by Ibleam. And Ahaziah fled to Megiddo and died there.

²⁸Then his servants carried him in a chariot to Jerusalem and buried him in his grave with his fathers in the City of David.

²⁹In the eleventh year of Joram, the son of Ahab, Ahaziah became king over Judah.

³⁰So when Jehu came to Jezreel, Jezebel heard about it, and she painted her eyes and adorned her head and looked down from the [upper] window.

[31]As Jehu entered in at the gate, she said, "Is it well, Zimri, your master's murderer?" [1 Kin 16:9, 10]

[32]Then Jehu raised his face toward the window and said, "Who is on my side? Who?" And two or three officials looked down at him.

[33]And he said, "Throw her down." So they threw her down, and some of her blood spattered on the wall and on the horses, and he trampled her underfoot.

[34]When he came in, he ate and drank, and said, "See now to this cursed woman and bury her, for she is a king's daughter."

[35]They went to bury her, but they found nothing left of her except the skull and the feet and the palms of her hands.

[36]So they returned and told Jehu. Then he said, "This is the word of the LORD, which He spoke through His servant Elijah the Tishbite, saying, 'In the property of Jezreel the dogs shall eat the flesh of Jezebel. [1 Kin 21:23]

[37]'The corpse of Jezebel will be like dung on the surface of the field in the property of Jezreel, so they cannot say, "This is Jezebel."' "

10 AHAB HAD seventy sons [and grandsons] in Samaria. So Jehu wrote letters and sent them to Samaria, to the rulers of Jezreel, to the elders, and to the guardians of *the children of* Ahab, saying,

[2]"Now as soon as this letter comes to you, since your master's sons (male descendants) are with you, as well as chariots and horses and a fortified city and weapons,

[3]select the best and most capable of your master's sons, and set him on his father's throne, and fight for your master's [royal] house."

[4]But they were extremely afraid and said, "Look, the two kings did not stand before Jehu; so how can we stand?"

[5]And the one who was in charge of the household, and the one who was overseer of the city, the elders, and the guardians [of the children] sent *word* to Jehu, saying, "We are your servants and we will do whatever you tell us, *but* we will not make any man king; do what is good in your eyes."

[6]Then Jehu wrote a second letter to them, saying, "If you are with me and will obey me, take the heads of your master's sons, and come to me at Jezreel tomorrow about this time." Now the [dead] king's sons, seventy persons, were with the great men of the city, who were rearing them.

[7]When the letter came to them, they took the king's sons and slaughtered them, seventy persons, and put their heads in baskets, and sent them to Jehu at Jezreel.

[8]When a messenger came and told him, "They have brought the heads of the king's sons," he said, "Put them in two heaps at the entrance of the city gate until morning."

[9]The next morning he went out and stood and said to all the people, "You are just *and* innocent; behold, I conspired against [Joram] my master and killed him, but who killed all these?

[10]"Know then [without any doubt] that there shall fall to the earth nothing of the word of the LORD, which the LORD spoke concerning the house of Ahab, for the LORD has done what He said through His servant Elijah." [1 Kin 19:17]

[11]So Jehu killed all who remained of the house of Ahab in Jezreel, and all his great men and his familiar friends and his priests, until he left him without a survivor.

[12]And he set out and went to Samaria. On the way as he was at the place of the sand heaps [meeting place] for the shepherds,

[13]Jehu met the relatives of Ahaziah king of Judah and said, "Who are

you?" They answered, "We are the relatives of Ahaziah; and we came down to greet the royal princes and the sons of the queen mother [Jezebel]."

¹⁴Then Jehu said, "Take them alive." So they took them alive and [later] slaughtered them at the well by the place of the sand heaps, forty-two men; he left none of them [alive].

¹⁵When Jehu went on from there, he met Jehonadab the son of Rechab *coming* to meet him. He greeted him and said to him, "Is your heart right, as my heart is with yours?" Jehonadab answered, "It is." *Jehu said* "If it is, give me your hand." He gave him his hand, and Jehu pulled him up into the chariot.

¹⁶And he said, "Come with me and see my zeal for the Lᴏʀᴅ." So he had Jehonadab in his chariot.

¹⁷When Jehu came to Samaria, he killed everyone who remained of Ahab's family in Samaria, until he had destroyed all of them, in accordance with the word of the Lᴏʀᴅ which He spoke to Elijah.

¹⁸Jehu assembled all the people and said [in pretense] to them, "Ahab served Baal a little; Jehu will serve him much [more].

¹⁹"Now, summon unto me all the prophets of Baal, all his worshipers and all his priests. Let no one be missing, for I have a great sacrifice for Baal; whoever is missing shall not live." But Jehu did it with trickery, in order to destroy the worshipers of Baal.

²⁰Jehu said, "Consecrate a festive assembly (celebration) for Baal." And they proclaimed it.

²¹Then Jehu sent throughout Israel, and all the worshipers of Baal came; there was no one left who did not come. They went to the house (temple) of Baal, and the house of Baal was filled from one end to the other.

²²He said to the man in charge of the wardrobe, "Bring out garments for all the worshipers of Baal." And he brought the garments out to them.

²³Then Jehu with Jehonadab the son of Rechab went into the house of Baal; and he said to the worshipers of Baal, "Search carefully and see that there are no servants of the Lᴏʀᴅ here with you, but only the worshipers of Baal."

²⁴Then they went in to offer sacrifices and burnt offerings.

Now Jehu had stationed eighty men outside for himself and said, "If any of the men whom I have brought into your hands escape, the one who lets him go shall forfeit his own life for that man's life."

²⁵Then it came about, as soon as he had finished offering the burnt offering, that Jehu said to the guards and to the royal officers, "Go in and kill them; let no one come out." And they killed them with the edge of the sword; and the guard and the royal officers threw *their bodies* out, and went to the inner room of the house of Baal.

²⁶They brought out the *sacred* pillars (obelisks) of the house of Baal and burned them.

²⁷They also tore down the *sacred* pillar of Baal and tore down the house of Baal, and made it into a latrine [forever unclean] to this day.

²⁸Thus Jehu eradicated Baal from Israel.

²⁹However, Jehu did not turn from the [idolatrous] sins of Jeroboam the son of Nebat, who made Israel sin, that is, [led them to worship] the golden

speak the Word

God, I pray that I will be such a passionate believer that others will be able to clearly see my zeal for You.
−ᴀᴅᴀᴘᴛᴇᴅ ꜰʀᴏᴍ 2 Kɪɴɢs 10:16

calves which were at Bethel and Dan.
[1 Kin 12:28ff]

³⁰The LORD said to Jehu, "Because
you have done well in executing what
is right in My eyes, and have done to
the house of Ahab in accordance with
everything that was in My heart, your
sons (descendants) shall sit on Israel's throne to the fourth generation."
[2 Kin 15:12]

³¹But Jehu did not take care to walk
in the law of the LORD, the God of Israel, with all his heart; he did not turn
from the sins of Jeroboam, who made
Israel sin.

³²*So* in those days the LORD began
to cut off *portions* of Israel; Hazael [of
Aram] defeated them throughout the
territory of Israel:

³³from the Jordan eastward, all the
land of Gilead, the Gadites and the
Reubenites and the Manassites, from
Aroer, which is by the Arnon River,
even Gilead and Bashan.

³⁴Now the rest of the acts of Jehu
and everything that he did and all his
might, are they not written in the Book
of the Chronicles of the Kings of Israel?

³⁵Jehu slept with his fathers [in
death], and they buried him in Samaria. Jehoahaz his son became king
in his place.

³⁶The time that Jehu reigned over
Israel in Samaria was twenty-eight
years.

11 WHEN ATHALIAH the
mother of Ahaziah [king of
Judah] saw that her son was
dead, she arose and destroyed all the
royal offspring.

²But Jehosheba, the daughter of
King Joram [of Judah and half] sister
of Ahaziah, took Joash the son of Ahaziah and abducted him from among
the king's sons who were to be killed,
and hid him and his nurse in the bedroom. So they hid him from Athaliah,
and he was not put to death.

³Joash was hidden with his nurse in
the house (temple) of the LORD for six
years, while Athaliah reigned over the
land.

⁴Now in the seventh year Jehoiada
[the priest, Jehosheba's husband] sent
for the captains of hundreds of the
Carites and of the guard and brought
them to him to the house of the LORD.
Then he made a covenant with them
and put them under oath in the house
of the LORD, and showed them the
king's [hidden] son.

⁵He commanded them, saying, "This
is the thing that you shall do: a third of
you who come in [reporting for duty]
on the Sabbath shall keep watch over
the king's house

⁶(a third shall also be at the [city]
gate Sur, and a third at the gate behind
the guards); so you shall keep watch
over the palace [from three posts] for
defense.

⁷"Two units of you, all those who go
out [off duty] on the Sabbath, shall also
keep watch over the house (temple) of
the LORD for [the protection of] the king.

⁸"You shall surround the [young]
king, each man with weapons in his
hand; and whoever comes through the
ranks shall be put to death. You are to
be with the king when he goes out and
when he comes in."

⁹The captains of hundreds acted in
accordance with everything that Jehoiada the priest commanded; and
each of them took his men who were
to come in (on duty) on the Sabbath,
with those who were to go out (off
duty) on the Sabbath, and they came
to Jehoiada the priest.

¹⁰The priest gave to the captains of
hundreds the spears and shields that
had been King David's, which were in
the house of the LORD.

¹¹And the guards stood, each man
with weapons in his hand, from the
right side to the left side of the temple
area, by the altar [in the courtyard]

and by the temple [proper], all around the king.

¹²Then Jehoiada brought out the king's son and put the crown on him and gave him the Testimony [a copy of the Mosaic Law]; and they made him king and anointed him, and they clapped their hands and said, "*Long live the king!*"

¹³When Athaliah heard the sound of the guards and of the people, she went into the house of the LORD to the people.

¹⁴When she looked, behold, there stood the [young] king [on the platform] by the pillar, as was customary [on such occasions], and the captains and the trumpeters were beside the king; and all the people of the land rejoicing and blowing the trumpets. Then Athaliah tore her clothes and cried, "Treason! Treason!"

¹⁵Then Jehoiada the priest commanded the captains of hundreds appointed over the army and said to them, "Take her out between the ranks, and whoever follows her put to death with the sword." For the priest had said, "Let her not be put to death in the house (temple) of the LORD."

¹⁶So they seized her, and she went through the horses' entrance to the king's house (palace), and she was put to death there.

¹⁷Then Jehoiada made a covenant between the LORD, the king, and the people, that they would be the LORD's people—also between the king and the people [to be his subjects].

¹⁸Then all the people of the land went to the house of Baal and tore it down. They utterly smashed his altar and his images to pieces, and they put Mattan the priest of Baal to death in front of the altars. And [Jehoiada] the priest appointed officers over the house of the LORD.

¹⁹Then he took the captains of hundreds, the Carites (royal bodyguards),

the guard, and all the people of the land; and they brought the [young] king down from the house of the LORD, and came by way of the guards' gate to the king's house. And [little] Joash sat on the throne of the kings.

²⁰So all the people of the land rejoiced and the city [of Jerusalem] was quiet. For they had put Athaliah to death with the sword at the king's house.

²¹Jehoash (Joash) was seven years old when he became king.

12 IN THE seventh year of Jehu [king of Israel], Jehoash became king [over Judah], and he reigned forty years in Jerusalem. His mother's name was Zibiah of Beersheba.

²Jehoash did right in the sight of the LORD all his days in which Jehoiada the priest instructed him.

³Only the high places were not removed; the people were still sacrificing and burning incense [to the LORD] on the high places [rather than at the temple].

⁴Jehoash said to the priests, "All the money for the dedicated things which is brought into the house of the LORD, in current money, *both* the money of each man's assessment [for all those bound by vows], *and* all the money which any man's heart prompts him to bring into the house (temple) of the LORD,

⁵let the priests receive such contributions for themselves, each from his acquaintance; and they shall repair any breach in the house *of the LORD*, wherever a breach is found."

⁶But it came about in the twenty-third year of [the reign of] King Jehoash, that the priests *still* had not repaired the damages of the LORD's house.

⁷Then King Jehoash called for Jehoiada the priest and the [other] priests and said to them, "Why are you not repairing the damage of the house (temple)? Now then, do not take any

more money from your acquaintances, but turn it all over for [the repair of] the damages of the house." [You are no longer responsible for this work. I will take it into my own hands.]

⁸So the priests agreed that they would receive no [more] money from the people, nor [be responsible to] repair the damages of the house.

⁹Then Jehoiada the priest took a chest and bored a hole in its lid and set it beside the altar, on the right side as one enters the house of the LORD; and the priests who guarded the door put in the chest all the money that was brought [by the people] into the house of the LORD.

¹⁰And whenever they saw that there was a large amount of money in the chest, the king's scribe and the high priest came up and tied it in bags and counted the money that was found in the house of the LORD.

¹¹Then they gave the money, which was weighed out into the hands of those who were doing the work, who had the oversight of the house of the LORD; and they paid it out to the carpenters and builders who worked on the house (temple) of the LORD,

¹²and to the masons and stonecutters, and to buy timber and hewn (cut) stone to repair any breach in the house of the LORD, and for all that was laid out for repairing the house.

¹³However, there were not made for the house of the LORD basins of silver, snuffers, bowls, trumpets, any gold containers or [other] silver containers, from the money that was brought into the house of the LORD;

¹⁴but they gave that to those who did the work, and with it they repaired the house of the LORD.

¹⁵Moreover, they did not require an accounting from the men into whose hands they placed the money to be paid to those who did the work, for they acted in good faith.

¹⁶Money from the guilt offerings and money from the sin offerings was not brought into the house of the LORD [for repairs]; it was for the priests.

¹⁷Then Hazael king of Aram (Syria) went up, fought against Gath [in Philistia], and captured it. And Hazael resolved to go up to Jerusalem.

¹⁸So Jehoash the king of Judah took all the sacred things that Jehoshaphat and Jehoram and Ahaziah, his fathers, kings of Judah, had dedicated, and his own sacred things and all the gold that was found in the treasuries of the house (temple) of the LORD and of the king's house, and sent them to Hazael king of Aram; and Hazael departed from Jerusalem. [1 Kin 15:18]

¹⁹Now the rest of the acts of Joash and everything that he did, are they not written in the Book of the Chronicles of the Kings of Judah?

²⁰His servants arose and formed a conspiracy [against him] and struck down Joash [in revenge] at the house of Millo, [on the way] that goes down to Silla. [2 Chr 24:22–25]

²¹For Jozacar (Jozachar) the son of Shimeath and Jehozabad the son of Shomer, his servants, struck him and he died; and they buried Joash with his fathers in the City of David. Amaziah his son became king in his place.

13 IN THE twenty-third year of Joash the son of Ahaziah, king of Judah, Jehoahaz the son of Jehu became king over Israel in Samaria, *and he reigned* seventeen years.

²He did evil in the sight of the LORD, and followed the [idolatrous] sins of Jeroboam the son of Nebat, who made Israel sin; he did not turn from them.

³So the anger of the LORD was kindled *and* burned against Israel, and He handed them over time and again to Hazael the king of Aram (Syria), and of Ben-hadad the son of Hazael.

⁴But Jehoahaz sought the favor of the LORD, and the LORD listened to him; for He saw the oppression of Israel, how the king of Aram oppressed them.

⁵Then the LORD gave Israel a savior [to rescue them and give them peace], so that they escaped from under the hand of the Arameans; and the sons (descendants) of Israel lived in their tents as before.

⁶Yet they did not turn from the [idolatrous] sins of the [royal] house of Jeroboam, who made Israel sin; but walked in them. And the Asherah [set up by Ahab] also remained standing in Samaria [Israel's capital].

⁷For he left to Jehoahaz [king of Israel] an army of no more than fifty horsemen, ten chariots, and 10,000 footmen, for the king of Aram (Benhadad) had destroyed them and made them like dust to be trampled.

⁸Now the rest of the acts of Jehoahaz, everything that he did and his might, are they not written in the Book of the Chronicles of the Kings of Israel?

⁹Jehoahaz slept with his fathers [in death], and they buried him in Samaria; Joash his son became king in his place.

¹⁰In the thirty-seventh year of Joash king of Judah, Jehoash (Joash) the son of Jehoahaz became king over Israel in Samaria, *and reigned* sixteen years. ¹¹He did evil in the sight of the LORD; he did not turn away from all the [idolatrous] sins of Jeroboam the son of Nebat, who made Israel sin; but he walked in them.

¹²Now the rest of the acts of Joash, everything that he did, and his might with which he fought against Amaziah king of Judah, are they not written in the Book of the Chronicles of the Kings of Israel?

¹³Joash slept with his fathers [in death], and Jeroboam [II] sat on his throne. Joash was buried in Samaria with the kings of Israel.

¹⁴Now Elisha had become sick with the illness by which he would die. And Joash the king of Israel came down to him and wept over him and said, "O my father, my father, the chariot of Israel and its horsemen!" [2 Kin 2:12]

¹⁵And Elisha said to him, "Take a bow and arrows." So he took a bow and arrows.

¹⁶Then he said to the king of Israel, "Put your hand on the bow." And he put his hand on it, and Elisha put his hands on the king's hands.

¹⁷And he said, "Open the window to the east," and he opened it. Then Elisha said, "Shoot!" And he shot. And Elisha said, "The LORD's arrow of victory, the arrow of victory over Aram (Syria); for you will strike the Arameans in Aphek until you have destroyed them."

¹⁸Then he said, "Take the arrows," and he took them. And Elisha said to the king of Israel, "Strike the ground," and he struck *it* three times and stopped.

¹⁹So the man of God was angry with him and said, "You should have struck five or six times; then you would have struck down Aram until you had destroyed it. But now you shall strike Aram *only* three times."

²⁰Elisha died, and they buried him. Now marauding bands of Moabites would invade the land in the spring of the year. ²¹And it happened that as a man was being buried [on an open bier], they saw a marauding band [coming]; and they threw the man into Elisha's grave. But when the [body of the] man [was being let down and] touched the bones of Elisha he revived and stood up on his feet.

²²Hazael the king of Aram oppressed Israel all the days of Jehoahaz. ²³But the LORD was gracious to them and had compassion on them and turned toward them for the sake of His covenant with Abraham, Isaac,

and Jacob, and He was unwilling to destroy them, and did not cast them from His presence until now. [Mal 3:6] ²⁴Hazael king of Aram (Syria) died; Ben-hadad his son became king in his place. ²⁵Then Jehoash (Joash) the son of Jehoahaz recovered from Ben-hadad the son of Hazael the cities which he had taken from Jehoahaz his father by war. Three times Joash defeated Ben-hadad and recovered the cities of Israel. [2 Kin 13:19]

14 IN THE second year of Joash the son of Jehoahaz, king of Israel, Amaziah the son of Joash king of Judah became king. ²He was twenty-five years old when he became king, and he reigned twenty-nine years in Jerusalem. His mother's name was Jehoaddin of Jerusalem. ³He did right in the sight of the Lord, though not like David his father (ancestor). He acted in accordance with everything that his father Joash had done. ⁴However, the high places were not removed; the people were still sacrificing and burning incense on the high places. ⁵As soon as the kingdom was firmly in Amaziah's hand, he executed his servants who had killed his father the king. [2 Kin 12:20] ⁶But he did not put the sons of the murderers to death, in compliance with what is written in the Book of the Law of Moses, in which the Lord commanded, saying, "The fathers shall not be put to death for the sons, nor shall the sons be put to death for the fathers; but each shall be put to death [only] for his own sin." [Deut 24:16] ⁷Amaziah killed 10,000 [men] of Edom in the Valley of Salt, and took Sela (rock) by war, and renamed it Joktheel, to this day. ⁸Then Amaziah sent messengers to Jehoash (Joash) the son of Jehoahaz,

the son of Jehu, king of Israel, saying, "Come, let us face each other [in combat]." ⁹Jehoash the king of Israel sent *word* to Amaziah king of Judah, saying, "The [little] thorn-bush in Lebanon sent *word* to the [tall] cedar in Lebanon, saying, 'Give your daughter to my son as wife.' But a wild beast that was in Lebanon passed by and trampled the thorn-bush. ¹⁰"You have indeed defeated Edom, and your heart has lifted you up [in pride]. Enjoy your glory but stay at home; for why should you plunge into misery so that you, even you, would fall [at my hand], and Judah with you?" ¹¹But Amaziah would not listen. So Jehoash king of Israel went up; and he and Amaziah king of Judah faced each other [in combat] at Beth-shemesh, which belongs to Judah. ¹²Judah was defeated by Israel, and every man fled to his tent. ¹³Then Jehoash king of Israel captured Amaziah the king of Judah, the son of Jehoash (Joash), the son of Ahaziah, at Beth-shemesh, and came to Jerusalem and broke through the wall of Jerusalem from the Gate of Ephraim to the Corner Gate, 400 cubits (600 feet). ¹⁴He seized all the gold and silver and all the utensils found in the house (temple) of the Lord and in the treasuries of the king's house, as well as hostages, and returned to Samaria. ¹⁵Now the rest of the acts of Jehoash which he did, and his might and how he fought with Amaziah the king of Judah, are they not written in the Book of the Chronicles of the Kings of Israel? ¹⁶Jehoash slept with his fathers [in death] and was buried in Samaria with the kings of Israel. His son Jeroboam [II] became king in his place. ¹⁷Amaziah the son of Joash king of Judah lived for fifteen years after the death of Jehoash the son of Jehoahaz king of Israel.

¹⁸The rest of the acts of Amaziah, are they not written in the Book of the Chronicles of the Kings of Judah?

¹⁹Now a conspiracy was formed against him in Jerusalem, and Amaziah fled [south] to Lachish; but they sent [men] after him to Lachish and killed him there.

²⁰Then they carried him on horses and he was buried at Jerusalem with his fathers in the City of David.

²¹And all the people of Judah took Azariah, who was [only] sixteen years old, and made him king in place of his father Amaziah.

²²He built Elath and restored it to Judah after the king [his father Amaziah] slept with his fathers [in death].

²³In the fifteenth year of Amaziah the son of Joash king of Judah, Jeroboam [II] the son of Joash (Jehoash) king of Israel became king in Samaria, *and reigned* forty-one years.

²⁴He did evil in the sight of the Lord; he did not turn from all the [idolatrous] sins of Jeroboam [I] the son of Nebat, who made Israel sin.

²⁵Jeroboam restored Israel's border from the entrance of Hamath to the Sea of the Arabah (Dead Sea), in accordance with the word of the Lord, the God of Israel, which He spoke through His servant Jonah the son of Amittai, the prophet who was from Gath-hepher.

²⁶For the Lord saw the affliction (suffering) of Israel as very bitter; there was no one left, bond or free, nor any helper for Israel.

²⁷But the Lord had not said that He would blot out the name of Israel from under the heavens, so He saved them by the hand of Jeroboam [III] the son of Joash [king of Israel].

²⁸The rest of the acts of Jeroboam [II], all that he did, his might, how he fought, and how he recovered Damascus and Hamath for Israel, *which had belonged* to Judah, are they not written in the Book of the Chronicles of the Kings of Israel?

²⁹Jeroboam [II] slept with his fathers [in death], even with the kings of Israel. Zechariah his son became king in his place.

15 IN THE twenty-seventh year of Jeroboam [II] king of Israel, Azariah (Uzziah) the son of Amaziah king of Judah became king.

²He was sixteen years old when he became king, and he reigned fifty-two years in Jerusalem. His mother's name was Jecoliah of Jerusalem.

³He did right in the sight of the Lord, in accordance with all that his father Amaziah had done.

⁴Only [the altars on] the high places were not removed; the people still sacrificed and burned incense on the high places [instead of worshiping God at the temple].

⁵And the Lord struck (afflicted) the king, and he was a leper until the day of his death, and lived in a separate house. Jotham the king's son was in charge of the household, judging the people of the land. [2 Chr 26:16–21]

⁶Now the rest of Azariah's acts, and everything that he did, are they not written in the Book of the Chronicles of the Kings of Judah?

⁷Azariah slept with his fathers [in death], and they buried him with his fathers in the City of David. His son Jotham became king in his place.

⁸In the thirty-eighth year of Azariah king of Judah, Zechariah the son of Jeroboam [II] became king over Israel in Samaria for six months.

⁹He did evil in the sight of the Lord, just as his fathers had done; he did not turn from the sins of Jeroboam [I] the son of Nebat, who made Israel sin.

¹⁰But Shallum the son of Jabesh conspired against Zechariah and struck and killed him in the presence of the people and reigned in his place.

¹¹Now the rest of the acts of Zechariah,

behold, they are written in the Book of the Chronicles of the Kings of Israel.

¹²This is [the fulfillment of] the word of the LORD which He spoke to Jehu, saying, "Your sons (descendants) shall sit on the throne of Israel to the fourth generation." And so it came to pass. [2 Kin 10:30]

¹³Shallum the son of Jabesh became king in the thirty-ninth year of Uzziah (Azariah) king of Judah, and he reigned one month in Samaria.

¹⁴For Menahem the son of Gadi went up from Tirzah and came to Samaria, and struck and killed Shallum the son of Jabesh in Samaria and became king in his place.

¹⁵The rest of Shallum's acts, and his conspiracy which he made, they are written in the Book of the Chronicles of the Kings of Israel.

¹⁶Then Menahem struck [the town of] Tiphsah and all who were in it and its borders from Tirzah; [he attacked it] because they did not surrender *to him;* so he struck it and ripped up all the women there who were pregnant.

¹⁷In the thirty-ninth year of Azariah king of Judah, Menahem the son of Gadi became king over Israel, *and reigned* ten years in Samaria.

¹⁸He did evil in the sight of the LORD; for all his days he did not turn from the sins of Jeroboam the son of Nebat, who caused Israel to sin.

¹⁹Pul, [Tiglath-pileser III] king of Assyria, came against the land [of Israel], and Menahem gave Pul a thousand talents of silver [as a bribe], so that he might help him to strengthen his control of the kingdom.

²⁰Menahem exacted the money from Israel, from all the wealthy, influential men, fifty shekels of silver from each man to give to the king of Assyria. So the king of Assyria turned back and did not stay there in the land.

²¹Now the rest of Menahem's acts, and everything that he did, are they not written in the Book of the Chronicles of the Kings of Israel?

²²And Menahem slept with his fathers [in death]; his son Pekahiah became king in his place.

²³In the fiftieth year of Azariah king of Judah, Pekahiah the son of Menahem became king over Israel, *and reigned* two years in Samaria.

²⁴He did evil in the sight of the LORD; he did not turn from the [idolatrous] sins of Jeroboam [I] the son of Nebat, who made Israel sin.

²⁵But Pekah the son of Remaliah, his officer, conspired against Pekahiah and struck him in Samaria, in the citadel of the king's house, with Argob and Arieh; and with Pekah were fifty Gileadites. So he killed Pekahiah and became king in his place.

²⁶Now the rest of the acts of Pekahiah, all that he did, they are written in the Book of the Chronicles of the Kings of Israel.

²⁷In the fifty-second year of Azariah king of Judah, Pekah the son of Remaliah became king over Israel, *and reigned* twenty years in Samaria.

²⁸He did evil in the sight of the LORD; he did not turn from the [idolatrous] sins of Jeroboam [I] the son of Nebat, who made Israel sin.

²⁹In the days of Pekah king of Israel, Tiglath-pileser king of Assyria came and took Ijon, Abel-beth-maacah, Janoah, Kedesh, Hazor, Gilead, and Galilee, all the land of [the tribe of] Naphtali, and he carried the people captive to Assyria.

³⁰Hoshea the son of Elah conspired against Pekah the son of Remaliah [of Israel]; he struck and killed him, and became king in his place in the twentieth year of Jotham the son of Uzziah [king of Judah].

³¹Now the rest of Pekah's acts, and everything that he did, they are written in the Book of the Chronicles of Israel's Kings.

³²In the second year of Pekah the son of Remaliah king of Israel, Jotham the son of Uzziah king of Judah became king.

³³When he was twenty-five years old, he became king [over Judah], and he reigned sixteen years in Jerusalem. His mother's name was Jerusha daughter of Zadok.

³⁴He did what was right in the sight of the LORD, in accordance with everything that his father Uzziah had done.

³⁵Only [the altars on] the high places were not removed; the people still sacrificed and burned incense on the high places [rather than in the temple]. He built the upper gate of the house of the LORD.

³⁶Now the rest of the acts of Jotham, and all that he did, are they not written in the Book of the Chronicles of Judah's Kings?

³⁷In those days the LORD began sending Rezin the king of Aram (Syria) and [Israel's king] Pekah the son of Remaliah against Judah.

³⁸Jotham slept with his fathers [in death], and was buried with them in the City of David his father (ancestor). Ahaz his son became king in his place.

16 IN THE seventeenth year of Pekah the son of Remaliah, Ahaz the son of Jotham, king of Judah, became king.

²Ahaz was twenty years old when he became king, and he reigned sixteen years in Jerusalem. He did not do what was right in the sight of the LORD his God, as his father (ancestor) David had done.

³Instead he walked in the way of the [idolatrous] kings of Israel, and even made his son pass through the fire [as a human sacrifice], in accordance with the repulsive [and idolatrous] practices of the [pagan] nations whom the LORD drove out before the Israelites.

⁴He also sacrificed and burned incense on the high places and on the hills and under every green tree.

⁵Then Rezin the king of Aram (Syria) and Pekah the son of Remaliah, king of Israel, came up to Jerusalem to wage war. They besieged Ahaz, but could not overcome *and* conquer him.

⁶At that time Rezin king of Aram recovered Elath [in Edom] for Aram, and drove the Jews away from it. The Arameans came to Elath, and live there to this day.

⁷So Ahaz sent messengers to Tiglath-pileser king of Assyria, saying, "I am your servant and son. Come up and rescue me from the hand of the kings of Aram and of Israel, who are rising up against me."

⁸And Ahaz took the silver and gold that was found in the house of the LORD and in the treasuries of the king's house, and sent a gift to the king of Assyria.

⁹So the king of Assyria listened to him; and he went up against Damascus and captured it, and carried *its people* away into exile to Kir, and put Rezin [king of Aram] to death.

¹⁰Now King Ahaz went to Damascus to meet Tiglath-pileser the king of Assyria, and saw the *pagan* altar which was at Damascus. Then King Ahaz sent a model of the altar to Urijah the priest along with a [detailed] pattern for all its construction.

¹¹So Urijah the priest built an altar; in accordance with everything that King Ahaz had sent from Damascus, that is how Urijah the priest made it before King Ahaz returned from Damascus.

¹²When the king came from Damascus, he saw the altar; then the king approached the altar and offered [sacrifices] on it,

¹³and burned his burnt offering and his grain offering, and poured out his drink offering, and sprinkled the blood of his peace offerings on the altar.

¹⁴He brought the bronze altar, which was before the LORD, from the front of the house (temple), from between the [new] altar and the house of the LORD, and put it on the north side of the [new] altar.

¹⁵Then King Ahaz commanded Urijah the priest, saying, "Upon the great [new] altar, burn the morning burnt offering and the evening grain offering, and the king's burnt offering and his grain offering, with the burnt offering of all the people of the land and their grain offering and their drink offerings; and sprinkle on the new altar all the blood of the burnt offering and all the blood of the sacrifice. But the [old] bronze altar shall be kept for me to use to examine the sacrifices."

¹⁶Urijah the priest acted in accordance with everything that King Ahaz commanded.

¹⁷Then King Ahaz cut away the frames of the basin stands [in the temple], and removed the basin from [each of] them; and he took down the [large] Sea from the bronze oxen which were under it, and put it on a plastered stone floor.

¹⁸He removed from the house of the LORD the covered way for the Sabbath which they had built in the house, and the outer entrance of the king, because of the king of Assyria [who might confiscate them].

¹⁹Now the rest of the acts of Ahaz, are they not written in the Book of the Chronicles of the Kings of Judah?

²⁰So Ahaz slept with his fathers [in death] and was buried with his fathers in the City of David; and his son Hezekiah became king in his place.

17

IN THE twelfth year of Ahaz king of Judah, Hoshea the son of Elah became king over Israel in Samaria, *and reigned* for nine years.

²He did evil in the sight of the LORD, but not as the kings of Israel who came before him.

putting the Word to work

We learn from 2 Kings 17:6–23 that the Lord allowed Israel to be taken captive and led away into exile because of their disobedience. Do you ever get careless about doing what God has asked you to do, letting sin creep into your life? Do not let our enemy, the devil, lead you into the captivity of sin and disobedience; it leads only to destruction.

³Shalmaneser [V] king of Assyria came up against him, and Hoshea became his servant and paid him tribute (money).

⁴But the king of Assyria discovered a conspiracy in Hoshea, who sent messengers to So, king of Egypt, and offered no tribute to the king of Assyria, as *he had done* year by year; therefore the king of Assyria arrested him and bound him in prison.

⁵Then the king of Assyria invaded all the land [of Israel] and went up to Samaria and besieged it for three years.

⁶In the ninth year of Hoshea, the king of Assyria took Samaria and carried [the people of] Israel into exile to Assyria, and settled them in Halah and in Habor, by the river of Gozan, and in the cities of the Medes.

⁷Now this came about because the Israelites had sinned against the LORD their God, who had brought them up from the land of Egypt, from under the hand of Pharaoh king of Egypt; and they had feared [and worshiped] other gods

⁸and walked in the customs of the [pagan] nations whom the LORD had driven out before the sons (descendants) of Israel, and *in the pagan customs of* the kings of Israel which they had introduced.

speak the Word

God, I pray that I will not give in to the influence and customs of the world around me, but that I will always honor You.
—ADAPTED FROM 2 KINGS 17:8

⁹The Israelites ascribed things to the LORD their God which were not true. They built for themselves high places [of worship] in all their towns, from [the lonely] lookout tower to the [populous] fortified city.

¹⁰They set up for themselves *sacred* pillars (memorial stones) and Asherim on every high hill and under every green tree.

¹¹There they burned incense on all the high places, just as the [pagan] nations whom the LORD had deported before them; and they did evil *and* contemptible things, provoking the LORD [to anger].

¹²And they served idols, of which the LORD had said to them, "You shall not do this thing."

¹³Yet the LORD warned Israel and Judah through all His prophets and every seer, saying, "Turn from your evil ways and keep My commandments and My statutes, in accordance with all the Law which I commanded your fathers, and which I sent to you by My servants the prophets."

¹⁴However they did not listen, but stiffened their necks as did their fathers who did not believe (trust in, rely on, remain steadfast to) the LORD their God.

¹⁵They rejected His statutes and His covenant which He made with their fathers, as well as His warnings that he gave them. And they followed vanity [that is, false gods, idols] and became vain (empty-headed). They followed the [pagan practices of the] nations which surrounded them, although the LORD had commanded that they were not to do as they did.

¹⁶They abandoned all the commandments of the LORD their God and made for themselves cast images of two calves; and they made an Asherah [idol] and worshiped all the [starry] host of heaven and served Baal.

¹⁷They made their sons and their daughters pass through the fire [as human sacrifices], and used divination [to foretell the future] and enchantments; and they sold themselves to do evil in the sight of the LORD, provoking Him to anger.

¹⁸Therefore the LORD was very angry with Israel and removed them from His sight; none [of the tribes] was left except the tribe of Judah.

¹⁹Judah did not keep the commandments of the LORD their God either, but walked in the customs which Israel introduced.

²⁰So the LORD rejected all the descendants of Israel (Jacob) and [repeatedly] afflicted them and handed them over to plunderers, until He had cast them out of His sight.

²¹When He had torn Israel from the [royal] house of David, they made Jeroboam the son of Nebat king. And Jeroboam drove Israel away from following the LORD and made them commit a great sin.

²²For the Israelites walked in all the [idolatrous] sins which Jeroboam committed; they did not turn from them

²³until the LORD removed Israel from His sight, just as He had foretold through all His servants the prophets. So Israel went into exile from their own land to Assyria to this day [the date of this writing].

²⁴The king of Assyria brought *men* from Babylon and from Cuthah and from Avva and from Hamath and Sepharvaim, and settled them in the cities of Samaria in place of the sons (people) of Israel. They took possession of Samaria and lived in its cities.

²⁵Now when they began to live there, they did not fear the LORD; therefore the LORD sent lions among them which killed some of them.

²⁶So the king of Assyria was told, "The nations whom you have sent into exile and settled in the cities of Samaria do not know the custom of the

god of the land; so He has sent lions among them, and they are killing them because they do not know the manner of [worship demanded by] the god of the land."

²⁷Then the king of Assyria commanded, "Take back [to Samaria] one of the priests whom you brought from there, and have him go and live there; and have him teach the people the custom of the god of the land."

²⁸So one of the priests whom they had exiled from Samaria came [back] and lived in Bethel and taught them how they should fear [and worship] the LORD.

²⁹But every nation still made gods of its own and put them in the houses (shrines) of the high places which the Samaritans had made, every nation in the cities where they lived.

³⁰The men of Babylon made Succoth-benoth, the men of Cuth made Nergal, the men of Hamath made Ashima,

³¹the Avvites made Nibhaz and Tartak; and the Sepharvites burned their children in the fire to Adrammelech and Anammelech, the gods of Sepharvaim.

³²They also feared the LORD and appointed from among themselves priests of the high places, who sacrificed for them in the houses of the high places.

³³They feared the LORD, yet served their own gods, following the custom of the nations from among whom they had been sent into exile.

³⁴To this day they act in accordance with their former [pagan] customs: they do not [really] fear the LORD, nor do they obey their statutes and ordinances, nor the law, nor the commandments which the LORD commanded the

sons (descendants) of Jacob, whom He named Israel;

³⁵with whom the LORD had made a covenant and commanded them, saying, "You shall not fear other gods or bow yourselves to them nor serve them, nor sacrifice to them.

³⁶"But the LORD, who brought you up from the land of Egypt with great power and an outstretched arm, Him you shall fear, and to Him you shall bow yourselves down, and to Him you shall sacrifice.

³⁷"The statutes and the ordinances and the law and the commandment which He wrote for you [by the hand of Moses], you shall observe and do forever. You shall not fear (worship, serve) other gods.

³⁸"The covenant that I have made with you, you shall not forget; you shall not fear other gods.

³⁹"But the LORD your God you shall fear [and worship]; then He will rescue you from the hands of all your enemies."

⁴⁰However, they did not listen, but they acted in accordance with their former custom.

⁴¹So these nations [superficially] feared the LORD; they also served their idols, as did their children and their children's children, just as their fathers did, so do they to this day [the date of this writing].

18 NOW IT came about in the third year of Hoshea the son of Elah king of Israel, Hezekiah the son of Ahaz king of Judah became king.

²He was twenty-five years old when he became king, and he reigned

speak the Word

Thank You, God, that You will deliver me out of the hands of my enemies as I fear and worship You.
—ADAPTED FROM 2 KINGS 17:39

twenty-nine years in Jerusalem. His mother's name was Abi the daughter of Zechariah.

³Hezekiah did right in the sight of the LORD, in accordance with everything that David his father (ancestor) had done.

⁴He removed the high places [of pagan worship], broke down the images (memorial stones) and cut down the Asherim. He also crushed to pieces the bronze serpent that Moses had made, for until those days the Israelites had burned incense to it; and it was called Nehushtan [a bronze sculpture]. [Num 21:8]

⁵Hezekiah trusted in *and* relied confidently on the LORD, the God of Israel; so that after him there was no one like him among all the kings of Judah, nor *among those* who were before him.

⁶For he clung to the LORD; he did not turn away from [faithfully] following Him, but he kept His commandments, which the LORD had commanded Moses.

⁷And the LORD was with Hezekiah; he was successful wherever he went. And he rebelled against the king of Assyria and refused to serve him.

⁸He defeated the Philistines as far as Gaza [the most distant city] and its borders, from the [isolated] lookout tower to the [populous] fortified city.

⁹Now in the fourth year of King Hezekiah, which was the seventh of Hoshea the son of Elah king of Israel, Shalmaneser the king of Assyria went up against Samaria and besieged it.

¹⁰At the end of three years they captured it; in the sixth year of Hezekiah, which was the ninth year of Hoshea the king of Israel, Samaria was taken.

¹¹Then the king of Assyria sent Israel into exile to Assyria, and put them in Halah, and on the Habor, the river of [the city of] Gozan, and in the cities of the Medes,

¹²because they did not obey the voice of the LORD their God, but broke His covenant, everything that Moses the servant of the LORD had commanded; and they would not listen nor do it.

¹³In the fourteenth year of King Hezekiah, Sennacherib king of Assyria went up against all the fortified cities of Judah [except Jerusalem] and captured them.

¹⁴Then Hezekiah king of Judah sent *word* to the king of Assyria at Lachish, saying, "I have done wrong. Withdraw from me; whatever you impose on me I will bear." So the king of Assyria imposed on Hezekiah king of Judah [a tribute tax of] three hundred talents of silver and thirty talents of gold.

¹⁵Hezekiah gave him all the silver that was found in the house (temple) of the LORD, and in the treasuries of the king's house (palace).

putting the Word to work

One of the first things Hezekiah did when he became king was to get rid of the things that kept his people from walking in obedience to God (see 2 Kings 18:1–7). What keeps you from obeying God? It may be something that seems very important to you, but there is nothing more important than obeying God. Ask God to help you do what is right in His eyes, and know that He will honor your obedience, as He did Hezekiah's (see 2 Kings 18:8).

speak the Word

God, may I be like Hezekiah, trusting in and relying confidently in You. May I cling to You, never turning away from faithfully following You.
—ADAPTED FROM 2 KINGS 18:5, 6

¹⁶At that time Hezekiah cut away *the gold framework from* the doors of the temple of the Lᴏʀᴅ and from the door-posts which he had overlaid, and gave it to the king of Assyria.

¹⁷Then the king of Assyria sent the Tartan and the Rab-saris and the Rabshakeh [his highest officials] with a large army, from Lachish to King Hezekiah at Jerusalem. They went up and came to Jerusalem, and when they went up and arrived, they stood by the aqueduct of the upper pool, which is on the road of the Fuller's Field. [2 Chr 32:9–19; Is 36:1–22]

¹⁸When they called for the king, Eliakim the son of Hilkiah, who was in charge of the [king's] household, and Shebna the scribe, and Joah the son of Asaph the secretary went out to [meet] them.

¹⁹Then the Rabshakeh said to them, "Say to Hezekiah, 'Thus says the great king, the king of Assyria, "What is [the reason for] this confidence that you have?

²⁰"You say (but they are only empty words) '*I have* counsel and strength for the war.' Now on whom do you rely, that you have rebelled against me?

²¹"Now pay attention: you are rely-ing on Egypt, on that staff of crushed reed; if a man leans on it, it will *only* go into his hand and pierce it. So is Pharaoh king of Egypt to all who trust *and* rely on him.

²²"But if you tell me, 'We trust in *and* rely on the Lᴏʀᴅ our God,' is it not He whose high places and altars Heze-kiah has removed, and has said to Ju-dah and Jerusalem, 'You shall worship [only] before this altar in Jerusalem'?

²³"Now then, make a bargain with my lord the king of Assyria, and I will give you two thousand horses, if on your part you can put riders on them.

²⁴"How then can you drive back *even* one official of the least of my master's servants, when you rely on Egypt for chariots and horsemen?

²⁵"Now have I come up against this place to destroy it without the Lᴏʀᴅ's approval? The Lᴏʀᴅ said to me, 'Go up against this land and destroy it.'"'"

²⁶Then Eliakim the son of Hilkiah, and Shebna and Joah, said to the Rab-shakeh, "Please speak to your servants in the Aramaic (Syrian) language, because we understand it; and do not speak with us in the Judean (Hebrew) language in the hearing of the people who are on the wall."

²⁷But the Rabshakeh said to them, "Has my master sent me *only* to your master and to you to say these things? Has he not sent me to the men who sit on the wall, [who are doomed by the siege] to eat their own excrement and drink their own urine along with you?"

²⁸Then the Rabshakeh stood and shouted out with a loud voice in Ju-dean (Hebrew), "Hear the word of the great king, the king of Assyria.

²⁹"Thus says the king, 'Do not let Hezekiah deceive you, for he will not be able to rescue you from my hand;

³⁰nor let Hezekiah make you trust in *and* rely on the Lᴏʀᴅ, saying, "The Lᴏʀᴅ will certainly rescue us, and this city [of Jerusalem] will not be given into the hand of the king of Assyria."

³¹'Do not listen to Hezekiah, for thus says the king of Assyria: "Surrender to me and come out to [meet] me, and every man may eat from his own vine and fig tree, and every man may drink the waters of his own well,

³²until I come and take you away to a land like your own land, a land of grain and new wine, a land of bread and vineyards, a land of olive trees and honey, so that you may live and not die." Do not listen to Hezekiah when he misleads *and* incites you, saying, "The Lᴏʀᴅ will rescue us!"

³³'Has any one of the gods of the na-tions ever rescued his land from the hand of the king of Assyria?

³⁴'Where are the gods of Hamath

and Arpad [in Aram]? Where are the gods of Sepharvaim, Hena, and Ivvah [in the valley of the Euphrates]? Have they rescued Samaria (Israel's capital) from my hand?

³⁵'Who among all the gods of the lands have rescued their lands from my hand, that the Lᴏʀᴅ would rescue Jerusalem from my hand?'"

³⁶But the people kept silent and did not answer him, for the king had commanded, "Do not answer him."

³⁷Then Eliakim the son of Hilkiah, who was in charge of the [royal] household, and Shebna the scribe and Joah the son of Asaph the secretary, came to Hezekiah with their clothes torn [in grief and despair] and told him what the Rabshakeh had said.

19 WHEN KING Hezekiah heard it, he tore his clothes and he covered himself with sackcloth and went into the house (temple) of the Lᴏʀᴅ. [Is 37:1–13]

²Then he sent Eliakim who was in charge of his household, Shebna the scribe, and the elders of the priests, covered with sackcloth, to Isaiah the prophet the son of Amoz.

³They said to him, "Thus says Hezekiah, 'This is a day of distress *and* anxiety, of punishment and humiliation; for children have come to [the time of their] birth and there is no strength to rescue them.

⁴'It may be that the Lᴏʀᴅ your God will hear all the words of the Rabshakeh, whom his master the king of Assyria has sent to taunt *and* defy the living God, and will rebuke the words which the Lᴏʀᴅ your God has heard.

So offer a prayer for the remnant [of His people] that is left [in Judah].'"

⁵So the servants of King Hezekiah came to Isaiah.

⁶Isaiah said to them, "Say this to your master: 'Thus says the Lᴏʀᴅ, "Do not be afraid because of the words that you have heard, with which the servants of the king of Assyria have reviled (blasphemed) Me.

⁷"Behold, I will put a spirit in him so that he will hear a rumor and return to his own land. And I will make him fall by the sword in his own land."'"

⁸So the Rabshakeh returned and found the king of Assyria fighting against Libnah [a fortified city of Judah]; for he had heard that the king had left Lachish.

⁹When the king heard them say concerning Tirhakah king of Ethiopia, "Behold, he has come out to make war against you," he sent messengers again to Hezekiah, saying,

¹⁰"Say this to Hezekiah king of Judah, 'Do not let your God on whom you rely deceive you by saying, "Jerusalem shall not be handed over to the king of Assyria."

¹¹"Listen, you have heard what the Assyrian kings have done to all the lands, destroying them completely. So will you be spared?

¹²'Did the gods of the nations whom my forefathers destroyed rescue them—Gozan and Haran [of Mesopotamia] and Rezeph and the people of Eden who were in Telassar?

¹³'Where is the king of Hamath, the king of Arpad [of northern Syria], the king of the city of Sepharvaim, and of Hena and Ivvah?'"

¹⁴Hezekiah received the letter from

speak the Word

God, I declare that You alone are God of all the kingdoms of the earth! You have made the heavens and the earth.
–ᴀᴅᴀᴘᴛᴇᴅ ꜰʀᴏᴍ 2 Kɪɴɢs 19:15

the hand of the messengers and read it. Then he went up to the house (temple) of the LORD and spread it out before the LORD. [Is 37:14–20]

¹⁵Hezekiah prayed before the LORD and said, "O LORD, the God of Israel, who is enthroned *above* the cherubim [of the ark in the temple], You are the God, You alone, of all the kingdoms of the earth. You have made the heavens and the earth.

¹⁶"O LORD, bend down Your ear and hear; LORD, open Your eyes and see; hear the [taunting] words of Sennacherib, which he has sent to taunt *and* defy the living God.

¹⁷"It is true, LORD, that the Assyrian kings have devastated the nations and their lands

¹⁸and have thrown their gods into the fire, for they were not [real] gods but [only] the work of men's hands, wood and stone. So they [could destroy them and] have destroyed them.

¹⁹"Now, O LORD our God, please, save us from his hand so that all the kingdoms of the earth may know [without any doubt] that You alone, O LORD, are God."

²⁰Then Isaiah the son of Amoz sent *word* to Hezekiah, saying, "Thus says the LORD, the God of Israel: 'I have heard your prayer to Me regarding Sennacherib king of Assyria.' [Is 37:21–38]

²¹"This is the word that the LORD has spoken against him:

'The virgin daughter of Zion
Has despised you and mocked you;
The daughter of Jerusalem
Has shaken her head behind you!
²²'Whom have you taunted and
   blasphemed?
Against whom have you raised your
   voice,
And haughtily lifted up your eyes?
Against the Holy One of Israel!
²³'Through your messengers you
   have taunted *and* defied the Lord,

And have said [boastfully], "With
   my many chariots
I came up to the heights of the
   mountains,
To the remotest parts of Lebanon;
I cut down its tall cedar trees and
   its choicest cypress trees.
I entered its most distant lodging,
   its densest forest.
²⁴"I dug *wells* and drank foreign
   waters,
And with the sole of my feet I
   dried up
All the rivers of [the Lower Nile of]
   Egypt."
²⁵'Have you not heard [asks the God
   of Israel]?
Long ago I did it;
From ancient times I planned it.
Now I have brought it to pass,
That you [king of Assyria] should
   [be My instrument to] turn
   fortified cities into ruinous
   heaps.
²⁶'Therefore their inhabitants were
   powerless,
They were shattered [in spirit] and
   put to shame;
They were like plants of the field,
   the green herb,
As grass on the housetops is
   scorched before it is grown up.
²⁷'But I [the LORD] know your sitting
   down [O Sennacherib],
Your going out, your coming in,
And your raging against Me.
²⁸'Because of your raging against Me,
And because your arrogance *and*
   complacency have come up to My
   ears,
I will put My hook in your nose,
And My bridle in your lips,
And I will turn you back [to Assyria]
   by the way that you came.

²⁹'Then this shall be the sign [of these things] to you [Hezekiah]: this year you will eat what grows of itself, in the second year what springs up

voluntarily, and in the third year sow and reap, plant vineyards, and eat their fruit.

³⁰'The survivors who remain of the house of Judah will again take root downward and bear fruit upward.

³¹'For a remnant will go forth from Jerusalem, and [a band of] survivors from Mount Zion. The zeal of the Lᴏʀᴅ of hosts shall perform this.

³²'Therefore thus says the Lᴏʀᴅ concerning the king of Assyria: "He will not come to this city [Jerusalem] nor shoot an arrow there; nor will he come before it with a shield nor throw up a siege ramp against it.

³³"By the way that he came, by the same way he will return, and he will not come into this city," ' declares the Lᴏʀᴅ.

³⁴'For I will protect this city to save it, for My own sake and for My servant David's sake.' "

³⁵Then it came to pass that night, that the angel of the Lᴏʀᴅ went forth and struck down 185,000 [men] in the camp of the Assyrians; when *the survivors* got up early in the morning, behold, all [185,000] of them were dead.

³⁶So Sennacherib king of Assyria left and returned *home,* and lived at Nineveh.

³⁷It came about as he was worshiping in the house of Nisroch his god, that his sons Adrammelech and Sharezer killed him with a sword; and they escaped to the land of Ararat. And Esarhaddon his son became king in his place.

20

IN THOSE days [when Sennacherib first invaded Judah] Hezekiah became deathly ill. The prophet Isaiah the son of Amoz came and said to him, "Thus says the Lᴏʀᴅ, 'Set your house in order, for you shall die and not recover.' " [2 Chr 32:24–26; Is 38:1–8]

²Then Hezekiah turned his face to the wall and prayed to the Lᴏʀᴅ, saying,

³"Please, O Lᴏʀᴅ, remember now [with

life point

God answered Hezekiah's prayer by healing him and adding fifteen years to his life. (Of course, God does not always respond this way, but in Hezekiah's case, He did.) During that time, many horrible things happened (see 2 Kings 20:17), and Hezekiah suffered greatly. It seems that although God answered Hezekiah's request, it was not God's best for him. We need to remember that the only safe prayer policy is for God's will. The best prayer always acknowledges that we do not really know in most instances what is best for us; therefore, we must be willing to say, "whatever You want, Lord." As Proverbs 16:9 reminds us: "A man's mind plans his way [as he journeys through life], but the Lᴏʀᴅ directs his steps and establishes them."

compassion] how I have walked before You in faithfulness *and* truth and with a whole heart [entirely devoted to You], and have done what is good in Your sight." And Hezekiah wept bitterly.

⁴Before Isaiah had gone out of the middle courtyard, the word of the Lᴏʀᴅ came to him, saying,

⁵"Go back and tell Hezekiah the leader of My people, 'Thus says the Lᴏʀᴅ, the God of David your father (ancestor): "I have heard your prayer, I have seen your tears. Behold, I am healing you; on the third day you shall go up to the house of the Lᴏʀᴅ.

⁶"I will add fifteen years to your life and save you and this city [Jerusalem] from the hand of the king of Assyria; and I will protect this city for My own sake and for My servant David's sake." ' "

⁷Then Isaiah said, "Bring a cake of figs. And they brought it and placed it on the [painful] inflammation, and he recovered."

⁸Hezekiah said to Isaiah, "What will

be the sign that the LORD will [com-pletely] heal me, and that I shall go up to the house of the LORD on the third day?"

⁹Isaiah said, "This will be the sign to you from the LORD, that He will do the thing that He has spoken: shall the shadow [indicating the time of day] go forward ten steps, or go backward ten steps?"

¹⁰Hezekiah answered, "It is easy for the shadow to go forward ten steps; no, but let the shadow turn backward ten steps."

¹¹So Isaiah the prophet called out to the LORD, and He brought the shadow on the steps ten steps backward by which it had gone down on the sun-dial of Ahaz.

¹²At that time Berodach-baladan a son of Baladan, king of Babylon, sent letters and a gift to Hezekiah, for he had heard that Hezekiah had been sick. [Is 39:1–8]

¹³Hezekiah listened to *and* welcomed them and [foolishly] showed them all his treasure house—the silver and gold and spices and precious oil and his ar-mory and everything that was found in his treasuries. There was nothing in his house (palace) nor in all his realm that Hezekiah did not show them.

¹⁴Then Isaiah the prophet came to King Hezekiah and said to him, "What did these men say [that would cause you to do this for them]? From where have they come to you?" Hezekiah said, "They have come from a far country, from Babylon."

¹⁵Isaiah said, "What have they seen in your house?" Hezekiah answered, "They have seen everything that is in my house (palace). There is nothing in my treasuries that I have not shown them."

¹⁶Then Isaiah said to Hezekiah, "Hear the word of the LORD.

¹⁷'Behold, the time is coming when everything that is in your house, and that your fathers have stored up until this day, will be carried to Babylon; nothing will be left,' says the LORD.

¹⁸'And some of your sons (descen-dants) who will be born to you will be taken away [as captives]; and they will become eunuchs in the palace of the king of Babylon.'"

¹⁹Then Hezekiah said to Isaiah, "The word of the LORD which you have spo-ken is good." For he thought, "Is it not good, if [at least] there will be peace and security in my lifetime?"

²⁰The rest of the acts of Hezekiah and all his might, and how he made the [Siloam] pool and the aqueduct and brought water into the city, are they not written in the Book of the Chronicles of the Kings of Judah?

²¹Hezekiah slept with his fathers [in death], and Manasseh his son became king in his place.

21

MANASSEH WAS twelve years old when he became king, and he reigned for fifty-five years in Jerusalem. His mother's name was Hephzibah.

²He did [great] evil in the sight of the LORD, in accordance with the [idol-atrous] repulsive acts of the [pagan] nations whom the LORD dispossessed before the sons (descendants) of Israel.

³For he rebuilt the high places [for the worship of pagan gods] which his father Hezekiah had destroyed; and he set up altars for Baal and made an [image of] Asherah, just as Ahab king of Israel had done, and he worshiped all the [starry] host of heaven and served them.

⁴And he built [pagan] altars in the house (temple) of the LORD, of which the LORD had said, "In Jerusalem I will put My Name (Presence)."

⁵And he built altars for all the host of heaven in the two courtyards of the house of the LORD.

⁶He made his son pass through the fire *and* burned him [as an offering to Molech]; he practiced witchcraft and

divination, and dealt with mediums and soothsayers. He did great evil in the sight of the Lord, provoking *Him to anger.*

⁷He made a carved image of the [goddess] Asherah and set it up in the house (temple), of which the Lord said to David and to his son Solomon, "In this house and in Jerusalem [in the tribe of Judah], which I have chosen from all the tribes of Israel, I will put My Name forever.

⁸"And I will not make the feet of Israel wander anymore from the land which I gave their fathers, if only they will be careful to act in accordance with everything that I have commanded them, and with all the law that My servant Moses commanded them."

⁹But they did not listen; and Manasseh seduced them to do more evil than the nations whom the Lord destroyed before the sons (descendants) of Israel.

¹⁰Now the Lord spoke through His servants the prophets, saying,

¹¹"Because Manasseh king of Judah has committed these repulsive acts, having done more evil than all the Amorites did who were before him, and has also made Judah sin with his idols;

¹²therefore thus says the Lord, the God of Israel: 'Behold, I am bringing *such* catastrophe on Jerusalem and Judah, that everyone who hears of it, both of his ears will ring [from the shock].

¹³'I will stretch over Jerusalem the measuring line of Samaria and the plummet of the house of Ahab; and I will wipe Jerusalem clean just as one wipes a [dirty] bowl clean, wiping it and turning it upside down.

¹⁴'I will abandon the remnant (remainder) of My inheritance and hand them over to their enemies; and they will become plunder and spoil to all their enemies,

¹⁵because they have done evil in My sight, and have been provoking Me to anger, since the day their fathers came from Egypt to this day.'"

¹⁶Moreover, Manasseh shed a very great quantity of innocent blood, until he had filled Jerusalem from one end to another; besides his sin with which he made Judah sin, by doing evil in the sight of the Lord. [2 Chr 33:1–10]

¹⁷Now the rest of the acts of Manasseh, everything that he did, and the sin that he committed, are they not written in the Book of the Chronicles of the Kings of Judah?

¹⁸Manasseh slept with his fathers [in death] and was buried in the garden of his own house, in the garden of Uzza. And his son Amon became king in his place.

¹⁹Amon was twenty-two years old when he became king, and he reigned two years in Jerusalem. His mother's name was Meshullemeth the daughter of Haruz of Jotbah.

²⁰He also did evil in the sight of the Lord, just as his father Manasseh had done. [2 Kin 23:26, 27; 24:3, 4]

²¹He walked in all the [evil] ways that his father had walked; and he served the idols that his father had served, and worshiped them;

²²he abandoned the Lord, the God of his fathers, and did not walk in the way of the Lord.

²³But the servants of Amon conspired against him and killed the king in his own house (palace).

²⁴Then the people of the land [of Judah] killed all those who had conspired against King Amon, and the

speak the Word

God, may I never forsake You or fail to walk in Your way.
—ADAPTED FROM 2 KINGS 21:22

people of the land made his son Josiah king in his place.

²⁵Now the rest of the acts of Amon which he did, are they not written in the Book of the Chronicles of the Kings of Judah?

²⁶He was buried in his tomb in the garden of Uzza, and his son Josiah became king in his place.

22 JOSIAH WAS eight years old when he became king, and reigned for thirty-one years in Jerusalem. His mother's name was Jedidah daughter of Adaiah of Bozkath.

²He did what was right in the sight of the LORD and walked in all the ways of his father (ancestor) David, and did not turn aside to the right or to the left.

like a child

In 2 Kings 22:1, we see that Josiah became king when he was only eight years old. In 2 Kings 11:21, Jehoash became king at age seven; and in 2 Kings 21:1, Manasseh became king at age twelve. These boys were forced to grow up quickly!

Many people feel that they, like these young kings, were forced to grow up too fast. When that happened, they lost something, and that loss was detrimental to their enjoyment of adulthood.

As adults we should be able to accomplish things in our lives without feeling burdened. We should be responsible and yet lighthearted enough to enjoy our daily lives, even our work, as we read in Ecclesiastes 5:18: "Behold, here is what I have seen to be good and fitting: to eat and drink, and to find enjoyment in all the labor in which he labors under the sun during the few days of his life which God gives him—for this is his [allotted] reward."

I believe we should be able to enjoy every single thing we do. Some years ago this fact was brought to my attention because I realized I was past forty years of age, married with four children, and yet I could not say I had ever really enjoyed much of my life.

John 10:10 tells us Jesus came to this earth so that you and I might have life and have it in abundance. I really think we have forgotten how to enjoy life the way God intends for us to. We need to learn how to be childlike, because if there is one thing a child knows how to do, it is to enjoy anything and everything! But when a child is forced to grow up too quickly without being permitted to be a child, he or she often ends up with tremendous emotional problems.

Not being permitted to play will steal a person's childhood and his or her enjoyment of adulthood. My problem was thinking I had to deserve every bit of fun, enjoyment, or blessing that came my way. Now I have learned to work until quitting time and then leave whatever I am doing for the next day. If you and I don't do that, we open ourselves up to burnout—and once we get burned out, it is very hard to recover.

The good things that come to us in this life are given to us by the Lord (see James 1:17). He wants to give them to us. He wants us to enjoy life to the fullest. If you lost part of your childhood because you had to grow up too quickly, pray and ask God to restore your joy, your childlike faith, and your ability to celebrate life.

³In the eighteenth year of King Josiah, the king sent Shaphan the son of Azaliah, the son of Meshullam the scribe to the house of the LORD, saying,

⁴"Go up to Hilkiah the high priest, so that he may count the entire amount of money brought into the house of the LORD, which the doorkeepers have collected from the people. [2 Kin 12:4]

⁵"And have them deliver it to the hands of the workmen who have been appointed over the house of the LORD, and have them give it to the workmen who are in the house of the LORD to repair the damages of the house—

⁶that is, [have them give the money] to the carpenters and the builders and the masons—and to buy timber and cut stones to repair the house (temple).

⁷"However, no accounting shall be required of them for the money placed in their hands, because they act faithfully."

⁸Hilkiah the high priest said to Shaphan the scribe, "I have found the Book of the Law in the house (temple) of the LORD." Hilkiah gave the book to Shaphan, and he read it.

⁹Shaphan the scribe came to the king and brought back word to him: "Your servants have emptied out the money that was found in the house, and have placed it in the hands of the workmen who have been appointed over the house of the LORD."

putting the Word to work

Have you ever doubted someone's spiritual leadership because he or she was young? Josiah was a young king (see 2 Kings 22:1), yet he led his people in great spiritual renewal, restoring worship and leading the people back into a right relationship with God. Encourage and pray for your children and other Christian young people, that they would walk in the destiny God has for them.

putting the Word to work

Do you ever wonder if it is just too late, or perhaps that your sin is too great, to receive forgiveness from God? Even though the sin of the people was enormous, God responded to Josiah's repentant heart (see 2 Kings 22:18, 19). Do not hesitate to seek God's forgiveness; He will not turn away a humble, tender heart.

¹⁰Then Shaphan the scribe told the king, "Hilkiah the priest has given me a book." And Shaphan read it [aloud] before the king.

¹¹Now when the king heard the words of the Book of the Law, he tore his clothes.

¹²Then the king commanded Hilkiah the priest, Ahikam the son of Shaphan, Achbor the son of Micaiah, Shaphan the scribe, and Asaiah the servant of the king, saying,

¹³"Go, inquire of the LORD for my sake and for the sake of the people and for all Judah concerning the words of this book which has been found, for great is the wrath of the LORD which has been kindled against us, because our fathers have not listened to *and* obeyed the words of this book, so as to act in accordance with everything that is written concerning us."

¹⁴So Hilkiah the priest, Ahikam, Achbor, Shaphan, and Asaiah went to Huldah the prophetess, the wife of Shallum the son of Tikvah, the son of Harhas, keeper of the wardrobe (she was living in Jerusalem, in the Second Quarter [the new part of the city]); and they spoke to her.

¹⁵She said to them, "Thus says the LORD, the God of Israel: 'Tell the man who sent you to me,

¹⁶thus says the LORD: "Behold, I am bringing a catastrophe on this place (Judah) and on its inhabitants, [according

to] all the words of the book which the king of Judah has read.

17"Because they have abandoned (rejected) Me and have burned incense to other gods, that they might provoke Me to anger with all the work of their hands, therefore My wrath burns against this place, and it will not be quenched."'

18"But to the king of Judah who sent you to inquire of the LORD, you shall say this to him: 'Thus says the LORD God of Israel, "*Regarding* the words which you have heard,

19because your heart was tender (receptive, penitent) and you humbled yourself before the LORD when you heard what I said against this

the gift of a tender heart

In 2 Kings 22:19, Huldah the prophetess, speaking for the Lord, declared that King Josiah had a tender heart. Having a tender heart is equivalent to having a tender conscience, and tenderness of conscience is vital to being used by God.

It is dangerous to become hard-hearted and develop a seared conscience so that we cannot really tell if we are doing anything wrong or not. One way we develop a tender conscience is by repenting quickly if God convicts us of something and by not making excuses for our behavior.

When God shows us we have done something wrong, we need to say, "You're right, Lord, I'm wrong. There is no excuse, so please forgive me and help me not do it again." It is amazing how much that will help us have a tender conscience toward God. But as soon as we start trying to reason things out and make excuses for our wrongs, we start getting a little callus on our consciences. It becomes just a little bit harder for us to feel than it was the time before.

For example, if I mistreat someone without repenting, my conscience starts to become calloused. The next time I do it, my conscience becomes a little more calloused. Soon, although I go around presenting myself as a person who loves God, He cannot use me anymore because I am mistreating people and talking wrongly to them. The worst thing is that I do not even realize I am doing it, because I no longer have a tender heart and a tender conscience toward God.

We must remember that God does not care how gifted or talented we are; His primary concern is our heart attitude. If we have willing hearts, stirred-up hearts, wise hearts, perfect hearts, and tender consciences, then the devil is no real threat to us or to our future, because nothing can stop God from using us.

Acts 23:1 describes the good conscience Paul had. He said, "Kinsmen, I have lived my life before God with a perfectly good conscience until this very day." How many of us can go to bed at night saying, "Well, Lord, I can go to sleep with a perfectly good conscience"? Paul goes on to describe what he did to keep his conscience tender: "In view of this, I also do my best and strive always to have a clear conscience before God and before men" (Acts 24:16).

Why did Paul strive to keep a clear conscience? Because he knew he could not minister to others out of a hard heart. He knew that if he wanted to help people, he had to keep a tender conscience toward God. I believe all of us should pray regularly, "Lord, help me to have a tender heart and a tender conscience toward You."

place and against its inhabitants, that they should become a desolation and a curse, and because you have torn your clothes and wept before Me, I have heard you," declares the LORD.

[20]"Therefore, behold, [King Josiah,] I will gather you to your fathers, and you will be taken to your grave in peace, and your eyes will not see all the evil (catastrophe) which I will bring on this place."'" So they brought back word to the king.

23 KING JOSIAH sent *word* and they brought to him all the elders of Judah and of Jerusalem.

[2]The king went up to the house of the LORD, and with him all the men of Judah and all the inhabitants of Jerusalem, the priests, the prophets, and all the people, both small and great; and he read in their hearing all the words of the book of the covenant which was found in the house (temple) of the LORD.

[3]The king stood by the pillar and made a covenant before the LORD, to walk after the LORD and to keep His commandments, His testimonies, and His statutes with all his heart and soul, to confirm the words of this covenant that were written in this book. And all the people entered into the covenant.

[4]Then the king commanded Hilkiah the high priest and the priests of the second rank and the doorkeepers to bring out of the temple of the LORD all the articles made for Baal, for [the goddess] Asherah, and for all the [starry] host of heaven; and he burned them outside Jerusalem in the fields of the Kidron, and carried their

putting the Word to work

Do you have difficulty in figuring out what it means to follow God or to know how He would want you to respond in certain situations? Josiah realized that if he and those he ruled were to know how they were to follow God, they had to know His law (see 2 Kings 23:1–3). Likewise, if you want to walk in God's ways, it is important that you learn all you can about God and His ways by reading Scripture and doing what it says.

ashes to Bethel [where Israel's idolatry began]. [1 Kin 12:28, 29]

[5]He got rid of the idolatrous priests whom the kings of Judah had ordained to burn incense [to pagan gods] in the high places in Judah's cities and all around Jerusalem—also those who burned incense to Baal, to the sun, to the moon, to the constellations [of the zodiac], and to all the [starry] host of heaven.

[6]Josiah brought out the Asherah from the house of the LORD to the Brook Kidron outside Jerusalem, and burned it there, and ground it to dust, and threw its dust on the graves of the common people [who had sacrificed to it].

[7]And he tore down the houses of the [male] cult prostitutes, which were at the house (temple) of the LORD, where the women were weaving [tent] hangings for the Asherah [shrines].

[8]Then Josiah brought all the [idolatrous] priests from the cities of Judah, and desecrated the high places where the priests had burned incense [to

speak the Word

God, help me to keep my heart tender, receptive, penitent, and humble before You.
−ADAPTED FROM 2 KINGS 22:19

idols], from Geba to Beersheba, [that is, north to south]; and he tore down the high places of the gates which were at the entrance of the gate of Joshua the governor of the city, which were on one's left at the city gate.

⁹However, the priests of the high places were not allowed to go up to the altar of the LORD in Jerusalem [to serve], but they ate unleavened bread among their brothers.

¹⁰Josiah also defiled Topheth, which is in the Valley of Ben-hinnom (son of Hinnom), so that no man could make his son or his daughter pass through the fire [as a burnt offering] for Molech. [Ezek 16:21]

¹¹And he got rid of the horses that the kings of Judah had given [in worship] to the sun at the entrance of the house of the LORD, by the chamber of Nathan-melech the official, which was in the annex; and he burned the chariots of the sun.

¹²The altars [dedicated to the starry host of heaven] which were on the roof, the upper chamber of Ahaz, which the kings of Judah had made, and the altars which Manasseh had made in the two courtyards of the house of the LORD, the king tore down; and he smashed them there and threw their dust into the Brook Kidron.

¹³The king desecrated the high places which were opposite [east of] Jerusalem, which were on the right (south) of the mount of corruption which Solomon the king of Israel had built for Ashtoreth the repulsiveness of the Sidonians, for Chemosh the repulsiveness of Moab, and for Milcom the repulsiveness of the sons (descendants) of Ammon.

¹⁴He broke in pieces the *sacred* pillars (cultic memorial stones, images) and cut down the Asherim and replaced them with human bones [to desecrate the places forever].

¹⁵Further, the altar that was at Bethel, the high place which Jeroboam the son of Nebat, who made Israel sin, had made, even that altar and the high place he tore down. Then he demolished its stones, ground them to dust, and burned the Asherah.

¹⁶And as Josiah turned, he saw the graves that were there on the mountain, and he sent *men* and had the bones taken from the graves, and burned them on the altar and [thereby] desecrated it, in accordance with the word of the LORD which the man of God prophesied, who proclaimed these things [about this altar, naming Josiah before he was born]. [1 Kin 13:2–5]

¹⁷Then Josiah said, "What is this monument (gravestone) that I see?" The men of the city told him, "It is the grave of the man of God who came from Judah and proclaimed these things which you have done to the altar of Bethel."

¹⁸He said, "Let him alone; let no one disturb his bones." So they left his bones undisturbed, with the bones of the prophet who came from Samaria. [1 Kin 13:31, 32]

¹⁹Josiah also removed all the houses of the high places which were in the cities of Samaria, which the kings of Israel had made provoking the LORD [to anger]; and he did to them just as he had done [to those] in Bethel.

²⁰All the priests of the high places who were there he slaughtered on the altars, and burned human bones on them [to desecrate the places forever]. Then he returned to Jerusalem.

²¹Then the king commanded all the people, saying, "Celebrate the Passover to the LORD your God as it is written in this book of the covenant."

²²Indeed, such a Passover as this had not been held since the days of the judges who judged Israel, nor in all the days of the kings of Israel and the kings of Judah.

²³But in the eighteenth year of King

Josiah, this Passover to the LORD was kept in Jerusalem.

²⁴Moreover, Josiah removed the mediums and the soothsayers and the teraphim (household gods) and the idols and all the repulsive things that were seen in Judah and in Jerusalem, so that he might fulfill the words of the law written in the book which Hilkiah the priest found in the house (temple) of the LORD.

²⁵Before him there was no king like Josiah who turned to the LORD with all his heart and all his soul and all his might, in accordance with all the Law of Moses; nor did anyone like him arise after him.

²⁶However, the LORD did not turn from the fierceness of His great wrath which was kindled against Judah because of all the despicable acts with which Manasseh had provoked Him.

²⁷The LORD said, "I will also remove Judah from My sight, just as I have removed Israel; and will reject this city which I have chosen, this Jerusalem, and the house, of which I said, 'My Name [and the pledge of My Presence] shall be there.'"

²⁸Now the rest of the acts of Josiah, everything that he did, are they not written in the Book of the Chronicles of the Kings of Judah?

²⁹In his days Pharaoh Neco (Necho) king of Egypt went up to the king of Assyria to the river Euphrates [to help him fight Nabopolassar the king of Babylon]. King Josiah went out to meet him, but Pharaoh killed Josiah at Megiddo when he saw him.

³⁰Josiah's servants carried his dead body in a chariot from Megiddo, brought him to Jerusalem, and buried him in his own tomb. Then the people of the land took Jehoahaz the son of Josiah and anointed him and made him king in his father's place.

³¹Jehoahaz was twenty-three years old when he became king, and he reigned for [only] three months in Jerusalem. His mother's name was Hamutal daughter of Jeremiah of Libnah.

³²He did evil in the sight of the LORD, in accordance with everything that his forefathers had done.

³³Pharaoh Neco imprisoned him at Riblah in the land of Hamath, so that he would not reign in Jerusalem, and imposed a fine on the land of a hundred talents of silver and a talent of gold.

³⁴Pharaoh Neco made Eliakim the son of Josiah king in place of his father Josiah, and changed his name to Jehoiakim. But he took Jehoahaz and brought him to Egypt, where he died.

³⁵Jehoiakim gave the silver and the gold to Pharaoh, but he taxed the land to give the money as Pharaoh commanded. He collected the silver and gold from the people of the land, from everyone according to his assessment, to give it to Pharaoh Neco.

³⁶Jehoiakim was twenty-five years old when he became king, and he reigned for eleven years in Jerusalem. His mother's name was Zebidah daughter of Pedaiah of Rumah.

³⁷He did evil in the sight of the LORD, in accordance with everything that his forefathers had done.

24 IN HIS days, Nebuchadnezzar king of Babylon came up, and Jehoiakim became his servant for three years; then he turned and rebelled against him.

²The LORD sent marauding bands of Chaldeans, Arameans (Syrians), Moabites, and Ammonites against Jehoiakim. And He sent them against Judah to destroy it, in accordance with the word of the LORD which He spoke through His servants the prophets.

³Surely this came on Judah at the command of the LORD, to remove them from His sight because of the sins of [King] Manasseh, in accordance with everything that he had done,

⁴and also for the innocent blood that he shed, for he filled Jerusalem with innocent blood; and the LORD would not pardon it.

⁵Now the rest of the acts of Jehoiakim, and everything that he did, are they not written in the Book of the Chronicles of the Kings of Judah?

⁶So Jehoiakim slept with his fathers [in death], and his son Jehoiachin became king in his place.

⁷The king of Egypt did not come out of his land again, because the king of Babylon had taken everything that belonged to the king of Egypt, from the river of Egypt to the river Euphrates.

⁸Jehoiachin was eighteen years old when he became king, and he reigned [only] three months in Jerusalem. His mother's name was Nehushta daughter of Elnathan of Jerusalem.

⁹He did evil in the sight of the LORD, in accordance with everything that his father had done.

¹⁰At that time the servants of Nebuchadnezzar king of Babylon went up to Jerusalem, and the city came under siege.

¹¹Nebuchadnezzar king of Babylon came to the city while his servants were besieging it.

¹²Jehoiachin king of Judah surrendered to the king of Babylon, he and his mother and his servants and his captains and his [palace] officials. So the king of Babylon took him prisoner in the eighth year of his [own] reign.

¹³He carried out of there (Jerusalem) all the treasures of the house (temple) of the LORD, and the treasures of the house (palace) of the king, and cut in pieces all the articles of gold in the temple of the LORD, which Solomon king of Israel had made, just as the LORD had said.

¹⁴He led away into exile all Jerusalem and all the captains and all the brave men, ten thousand captives, and all the craftsmen and the smiths.

None remained except the poorest people of the land.

¹⁵Nebuchadnezzar led Jehoiachin away into exile to Babylon; also he took the king's mother and the king's wives and his officials and the leading men of the land [including Ezekiel] as exiles from Jerusalem to Babylon. [Ezek 1:1]

¹⁶And the king of Babylon brought as exiles to Babylon all the brave men, seven thousand [of them], and the craftsmen and the smiths, a thousand [of them], all strong and fit for war.

¹⁷Then the king of Babylon made Mattaniah, Jehoiachin's uncle, king in his place, and changed his name to Zedekiah.

¹⁸Zedekiah was twenty-one years old when he became king, and he reigned for eleven years in Jerusalem. His mother's name was Hamutal daughter of Jeremiah of Libnah. [2 Kin 23:31]

¹⁹He did evil in the sight of the LORD, in accordance with everything that Jehoiakim had done.

²⁰Because of the anger of the LORD *these things* happened in Jerusalem and Judah, and it [finally] came to the point that He cast them from His presence. And Zedekiah rebelled against the king of Babylon.

25 NOW IN the ninth year of Zedekiah's reign, on the tenth day of the tenth month, Nebuchadnezzar king of Babylon came, he with all his army, against Jerusalem, and camped against it and built siege works surrounding it.

²The city came under siege [for nearly two years] until the eleventh year of King Zedekiah.

³On the ninth day of the *fourth* month the famine [caused by the siege] was severe in the city; there was no food for the people of the land.

⁴Then the city [wall] was broken into [and conquered]; all the men of war *fled* by night by way of the gate

between the two walls by the king's garden, though the Chaldeans (Babylonians) were all around the city. And they went by way of the Arabah (the plain of the Jordan).

⁵The army of the Chaldeans pursued the king and overtook him in the plains of Jericho. Then his entire army was dispersed from him.

⁶So they seized the king (Zedekiah) and brought him to the king of Babylon at Riblah [on the Orontes River], and sentence was passed on him.

⁷They slaughtered the sons of Zedekiah before his eyes, then put out the eyes of Zedekiah and bound him [hand and foot] with bronze fetters and brought him to Babylon. [Jer 34:3; Ezek 12:13]

⁸On the seventh day of the fifth month in the nineteenth year of King Nebuchadnezzar of Babylon, Nebuzaradan, captain of the bodyguard, a servant of the king of Babylon, came to Jerusalem.

⁹He burned the house (temple) of the LORD, the king's house, and all the houses of Jerusalem; every great house he burned down.

¹⁰All the army of the Chaldeans (Babylonians) who *were with* the captain of the bodyguard tore down the walls around Jerusalem.

¹¹Then Nebuzaradan the captain of the bodyguard deported [into exile] the rest of the people who were left in the city and the deserters who had joined the king of Babylon, and the rest of the multitude.

¹²But the captain of the bodyguard left some of the unimportant *and* poorest people of the land to be vineyard workers and farmers.

¹³Now the Chaldeans (Babylonians) smashed the bronze pillars which were in the house of the LORD and their bases and the bronze sea (large basin) which were in the house of the LORD, and carried the bronze to Babylon.

¹⁴They took away the pots, the shovels, the snuffers, the spoons, and all the bronze articles which were used in the *temple* service,

¹⁵the captain of the bodyguard also took away the firepans and basins, anything made of fine gold and anything made of fine silver.

¹⁶The two pillars, the one sea (large basin), and the bases which Solomon had made for the house of the LORD, the bronze of all these articles was incalculable.

¹⁷The height of the one pillar was eighteen cubits (27 ft.), and a capital of bronze was on top of it. The height of the capital was three cubits (4.5 ft.); a network (lattice work) and pomegranates around the capital were all of bronze. And the second pillar had the same as these, with a network.

¹⁸The captain of the bodyguard took [captive] Seraiah the chief priest, Zephaniah the second priest, and the three doorkeepers [of the temple].

¹⁹And from the city [of Jerusalem] he took an officer who was in command of the men of war, and five men from the king's personal advisors who were found in the city, and the scribe of the captain of the army who mustered the people of the land [for military service] and sixty men from the people of the land who were found in the city.

²⁰Nebuzaradan the captain of the bodyguard took them and brought them to the king of Babylon at Riblah.

²¹Then the king of Babylon struck them down and killed them at Riblah in the land of Hamath [north of Damascus]. So Judah was taken into exile from its land.

²²Now over the people whom Nebuchadnezzar king of Babylon had left in the land of Judah, he appointed [as governor] Gedaliah the son of Ahikam, the son of Shaphan.

²³When all the captains of the forces, they and their men, heard that

the king of Babylon had appointed Gedaliah *governor,* they came with their men to Gedaliah at Mizpah, namely, Ishmael the son of Nethaniah, and Johanan the son of Kareah, and Seraiah the son of Tanhumeth the Netophathite, and Jaazaniah the son of the Maacathite.

²⁴Gedaliah swore [an oath] to them and their men, and said to them, "Do not be afraid of the servants (officials) of the Chaldeans. Live in the land and serve the king of Babylon, and it will be well with you."

²⁵But in the seventh month Ishmael the son of Nethaniah, the son of Elishama, of the royal family [who had a claim to be governor], came with ten men and struck and killed Gedaliah and the Jews and the Chaldeans who were with him at Mizpah.

²⁶Then all the people, both small and great, and the captains of the forces set out and went to Egypt; for they were afraid of the Chaldeans (Babylonians).

²⁷Now it came about in the thirty-seventh year of the exile of Jehoiachin king of Judah, on the twenty-seventh day of the twelfth month, that Evil-merodach king of Babylon, in the year that he became king, showed favor to Jehoiachin king of Judah *and* released him from prison;

²⁸and he spoke kindly to him and set his throne above the throne of the [other] kings [of captive peoples] who were with him in Babylon.

²⁹Jehoiachin changed his prison clothes [for palace garments] and he dined regularly in the king's presence for the remainder of his life;

³⁰and his allowance, a continual one, was given to him by the king (Evil-meridach), a portion every day, for the rest of his life.

First Chronicles

Author:
Attributed to Ezra

Date:
Probably between 425 BC and 400 BC

Everyday Life Principles:
God is faithful.

Faithfulness to God results in rewards from God.

God's presence makes all the difference in our everyday lives.

First Chronicles is full of encouragement to stay faithful to God. Its first nine chapters chronicle the family line of the godly King David, and its remaining twenty chapters tell the story of his righteous reign over God's people.

A key theme we find throughout 1 Chronicles is the theme of God's faithfulness to His people. His faithfulness brings blessings, which is why He continually calls for faithfulness and warns against unfaithfulness.

One of the highlights of this book is David's bringing the ark (the symbol of God's presence) back to Jerusalem. This ancient story reminds us of how desperately we need God's presence in every part of our lives today.

As you read 1 Chronicles, remember that faithfulness has its rewards, and unfaithfulness leads to trouble. When we are unfaithful, God always takes us back because of His mercy, but we often suffer the consequences of breaking fellowship with Him. Let me encourage you today to stay faithful to God in every situation in your life. Remember that He is faithful to you. He is always near you, always watching over you, and always wanting the best for you.

When you come across the story of the ark's return to Jerusalem, consider the various aspects of your life—your family, your work, your friendships, your home, your spiritual life, your entertainment, your hobbies, your finances, and the other things that concern you—and ask God to increase His presence more and more in your life.

1 ADAM [HIS genealogical line], Seth, Enosh, [2]Kenan, Mahalalel, Jared, [3]Enoch, Methuselah, Lamech, [4]Noah, [and his sons] Shem, Ham, and Japheth.

[5]The sons (descendants) of Japheth: Gomer, Magog, Madai, Javan, Tubal, Meshech, and Tiras.

[6]The sons of Gomer: Ashkenaz, Diphath, and Togarmah.

[7]The sons of Javan: Elishah, Tarshish, Kittim, and Rodanim.

[8]The sons of Ham: Cush, Mizraim, Put, and Canaan.

[9]The sons of Cush: Seba, Havilah, Sabta, Raama, and Sabteca. The sons of Raamah: Sheba and Dedan.

[10]Cush became the father of Nimrod; he began to be a mighty one upon the earth.

[11]Mizraim became the father of the people of Lud, Anam, Lehab, Naphtuh,

[12]Pathrus, and Casluh, from whom came the Philistines, and Caphtor.

do things God's way

As believers, we need to be reminded of our heritage in God. The author of 1 Chronicles (presumed to be Ezra) provides us with a list of families among God's people, and as he does, we can remember and honor the legacy of faith in our own lives.

First Chronicles 1:27 mentions Abram. We recall that Genesis 12 teaches us that God called Abram to leave his family, his home, and all he was familiar with and go to a place God would show him. Just imagine—Abram left everything, not having any idea where he was supposed to go. As a result of his radical obedience, God made some very radical promises to him—promises of blessing, wealth, fame, leadership, descendants, and so on. God entered into covenant with Abram, changing his name to Abraham (see Genesis 17:5). God told Abraham that if he would believe, it would be counted to him as right standing with God, and he would be taken care of in every way (see Genesis 15:5, 6).

Abraham believed God! That is all God asks of us: "Believe." Not just *for* things, but *in* and *through* things. Abraham believed God for a child that would be his heir, but he had to believe God through some difficult and lengthy things before he saw the promised child. You might say that those years of waiting were his "silent years," years during which he believed God, even though neither he nor anyone else saw any outward evidence that God had truly spoken to him.

During those silent years of waiting, Abraham took action that was not God-inspired when he followed his wife's advice and took her maid to be his secondary wife. Abraham's name has the prophetic meaning "father of a multitude" because God was planning to make him the father of many nations. But because Abraham and his wife, Sarah, got tired of waiting for God's promise, they took matters into their own hands, and Sarah's maid by Abraham gave birth to Ishmael. Although Abraham loved Ishmael, he was not the promised child and eventually brought great pain and difficulty into Abraham's life.

There are times in our lives, as in Abraham's, when God simply lets us go our own way so we can learn by experience that "our way" does not work. We suffer during these years. We experience confusion and frustration, but we eventually emerge from our struggles as changed people, finally ready to do things God's way!

¹³Canaan became the father of Sidon his firstborn, and Heth,

¹⁴the Jebusites, Amorites, Girgashites,

¹⁵Hivites, Arkites, Sinites,

¹⁶Arvadites, Zemarites, and Hamathites.

¹⁷The sons of Shem: Elam, Asshur, Arpachshad, Lud, Aram, Uz, Hul, Gether, and Meshech.

¹⁸Arpachshad became the father of Shelah, and Shelah became the father of Eber.

¹⁹To Eber were born two sons: the name of the one was Peleg, because in his days [the population of] the earth was divided [according to its languages], and his brother's name was Joktan.

²⁰Joktan became the father of Almodad, Sheleph, Hazarmaveth, Jerah,

²¹Hadoram, Uzal, Diklah,

²²Ebal, Abimael, Sheba,

²³Ophir, Havilah, and Jobab. All these were the sons of Joktan.

²⁴Shem [his genealogical line], Arpachshad, Shelah,

²⁵Eber, Peleg, Reu,

²⁶Serug, Nahor, Terah,

²⁷Abram, the same as Abraham.

²⁸The sons of Abraham: Isaac [by his wife Sarah] and Ishmael [by Hagar her maid].

²⁹These are their descendants: The firstborn of Ishmael, Nebaioth; then Kedar, Adbeel, Mibsam,

³⁰Mishma, Dumah, Massa, Hadad, Tema,

³¹Jetur, Naphish, and Kedemah. These are the sons of Ishmael.

³²Now the sons of Keturah, Abraham's concubine: she gave birth to Zimran, Jokshan, Medan, Midian, Ishbak, and Shuah. The sons of Jokshan: Sheba and Dedan.

³³The sons of Midian: Ephah, Epher, Hanoch, Abida, and Eldaah. All these are the sons [and grandsons] of Keturah.

³⁴Abraham became the father of Isaac. The sons of Isaac: Esau and Israel (Jacob).

³⁵The sons of Esau: Eliphaz, Reuel, Jeush, Jalam, and Korah.

³⁶The sons of Eliphaz: Teman, Omar, Zephi, Gatam, Kenaz, Timna, and Amalek.

³⁷The sons of Reuel: Nahath, Zerah, Shammah, and Mizzah.

³⁸The sons of Seir: Lotan, Shobal, Zibeon, Anah, Dishon, Ezer, and Dishan.

³⁹The sons of Lotan: Hori and Homam; and Timna was Lotan's sister.

⁴⁰The sons of Shobal: Alian, Manahath, Ebal, Shephi, and Onam. The sons of Zibeon: Aiah and Anah.

⁴¹The son of Anah: Dishon. The sons of Dishon: Hamran, Eshban, Ithran, and Cheran.

⁴²The sons of Ezer: Bilhan, Zaavan, and Jaakan. The sons of Dishan: Uz and Aran.

⁴³These are the kings who reigned in the land of Edom before any king reigned over the sons (descendants) of Israel (Jacob): Bela the son of Beor; the name of his city was Dinhabah.

⁴⁴When Bela died, Jobab the son of Zerah of Bozrah became king in his place.

⁴⁵When Jobab died, Husham of the land of the Temanites became king in his place.

⁴⁶When Husham died, Hadad [I of Edom] the son of Bedad, who defeated Midian in the field of Moab, became king in his place; the name of his city was Avith.

⁴⁷When Hadad [I] died, Samlah of Masrekah became king in his place.

⁴⁸When Samlah died, Shaul of Rehoboth on the River [Euphrates] became king in his place.

⁴⁹When Shaul died, Baal-hanan the son of Achbor became king in his place.

⁵⁰When Baal-hanan died, Hadad [II] became king in his place; the name of his city was Pai; his wife's name was

Mehetabel daughter of Matred, the daughter of Mezahab.

⁵¹Hadad died also.

The chiefs of Edom were: chiefs Timna, Aliah, Jetheth,

⁵²Oholibamah, Elah, Pinon,

⁵³Kenaz, Teman, Mibzar,

⁵⁴Magdiel, and Iram. These are the chiefs of Edom.

2 THESE ARE the sons of Israel: Reuben, Simeon, Levi, Judah, Issachar, Zebulun,

²Dan, Joseph, Benjamin, Naphtali, Gad, and Asher.

³The sons of Judah: Er, Onan, and Shelah; the three were born to him by Shua's daughter the Canaanitess. Er, Judah's eldest, was evil in the LORD's sight, and He put him to death.

⁴Tamar, Judah's daughter-in-law, bore him Perez and Zerah. Judah's sons were five in all. [Gen 38]

⁵The sons of Perez: Hezron and Hamul.

⁶The sons of Zerah: Zimri, Ethan, Heman, Calcol, and Dara—five in all. [1 Kin 4:31]

⁷The son of Carmi: Achar, the troubler of Israel, who violated the ban [by taking things from Jericho that had been banned]. [Josh 7:1]

⁸The son of Ethan: Azariah.

⁹The sons of Hezron who were born to him: Jerahmeel, Ram, and Chelubai [that is, Caleb].

¹⁰Ram became the father of Amminadab, and Amminadab became the father of Nahshon, leader of the sons of Judah.

¹¹Nahshon became the father of Salma, Salma became the father of Boaz,

¹²Boaz became the father of Obed, and Obed became the father of Jesse.

¹³Jesse became the father of Eliab

be faithful and be blessed

One thing we remember when we see Joseph's name in 1 Chronicles 2:2 is that he was faithful to God. Even though he was a slave in Potiphar's house, God blessed him and prospered him because He was with him everywhere he went (see Genesis 39:1–6).

Even when we are going through difficult times, God will bless us in the midst of them, not just when they are over. The important thing for us to do is keep a good attitude, which includes being thankful for what we do have and giving praise to God, worshiping Him for Who He is.

For example, even if your boss treats you improperly, does not recognize your true value, and will not let you do anything but sweep the floor, if God is with you, He can prosper you and make you successful in so many other ways. God can certainly promote you in His timing because all true promotion comes from Him (see Psalm 75:6, 7). Do not look to anything on this earth as your source; look only to God as your Source.

The world will soon recognize that God is with His people. Some of the individuals who have rejected us in the past will come to realize that God is with us; they will see the evidence of His presence in our lives. If we, like Joseph, will take our positions and be faithful in them while we wait on Him, God will raise us up in His timing, and it will become obvious that God's hand is upon us for good.

his firstborn, Abinadab the second, Shimea the third,

¹⁴Nethanel the fourth, Raddai the fifth,

¹⁵Ozem the sixth, David the seventh.

¹⁶Their sisters were Zeruiah and Abigail. The sons of Zeruiah: Abishai, Joab, and Asahel, three.

¹⁷Abigail gave birth to Amasa, and the father of Amasa was Jether the Ishmaelite.

¹⁸And Caleb the son of Hezron had sons by his wife Azubah and by Jerioth. Azubah's sons were: Jesher, Shobab, and Ardon.

¹⁹Azubah died, and Caleb married Ephrath, who bore him Hur.

²⁰Hur became the father of Uri, and Uri became the father of Bezalel [the skillful craftsman who made the furnishings of the tabernacle]. [Ex 31:2–5]

²¹Later, when Hezron was sixty years old, he married the daughter of Machir the father of Gilead, and she bore him Segub.

²²Segub became the father of Jair, who [later] had twenty-three cities in the land of Gilead.

²³But Geshur and Aram took from them Havvoth-jair, with Kenath and its villages, sixty towns *in all*. All these were the sons (descendants) of Machir, the father of Gilead.

²⁴After Hezron died in Caleb-ephrathah, Abijah, Hezron's wife, bore him Ashhur the father of Tekoa.

²⁵The sons of Jerahmeel the first-born of Hezron: Ram the firstborn, Bunah, Oren, Ozem, and Ahijah.

²⁶Jerahmeel had another wife, named Atarah; she was the mother of Onam.

²⁷The sons of Ram the firstborn of Jerahmeel were: Maaz, Jamin, and Eker.

²⁸The sons of Onam: Shammai and Jada. The sons of Shammai: Nadab and Abishur.

²⁹The name of Abishur's wife was Abihail; she bore him Ahban and Molid.

³⁰The sons of Nadab: Seled and Appaim. Seled died childless.

³¹The son of Appaim: Ishi. The son of Ishi: Sheshan. The son of Sheshan: Ahlai.

³²The sons of Jada the brother of Shammai: Jether and Jonathan. Jether died childless.

³³The sons of Jonathan: Peleth and Zaza. These were the sons (descendants) of Jerahmeel.

³⁴Sheshan had no sons—only daughters. But Sheshan had a servant, an Egyptian, whose name was Jarha.

³⁵So Sheshan gave his daughter to Jarha his servant as a wife; she bore him Attai.

³⁶Attai became the father of Nathan, and Nathan became the father of Zabad.

³⁷Zabad became the father of Ephlal, and Ephlal became the father of Obed.

³⁸Obed became the father of Jehu, and Jehu became the father of Azariah.

³⁹Azariah became the father of Helez, and Helez became the father of Eleasah.

⁴⁰Eleasah became the father of Sismai, and Sismai became the father of Shallum.

⁴¹Shallum became the father of Jekamiah, and Jekamiah became the father of Elishama.

⁴²The sons of Caleb, the brother of Jerahmeel: Mesha his firstborn was the father of Ziph; and his son Mareshah was the father of Hebron.

⁴³The sons of Hebron: Korah, Tappuah, Rekem, and Shema.

⁴⁴Shema became the father of Raham, the father of Jorkeam. And Rekem became the father of Shammai.

⁴⁵The son of Shammai was Maon; Maon became the father of Bethzur.

⁴⁶Ephah, Caleb's concubine, gave birth to Haran, Moza, and Gazez; Haran became the father of Gazez.

⁴⁷The sons of Jahdai: Regem, Jotham, Geshan, Pelet, Ephah, and Shaaph.

⁴⁸Maacah, Caleb's concubine, gave birth to Sheber and Tirhanah.

⁴⁹She also bore Shaaph the father of Madmannah and Sheva the father of Machbena and of Gibea; and the daughter of Caleb was Achsah.

⁵⁰These were the sons (descendants) of Caleb.

The sons of Hur, the firstborn of Ephrathah: Shobal the father of Kiriath-jearim,

⁵¹Salma the father of Bethlehem and Hareph the father of Beth-gader.

⁵²Shobal the father of Kiriath-jearim had [other] sons (descendants): Haroeh, half of the Manahathites [in Judah],

⁵³and the families of Kiriath-jearim: the Ithrites, Puthites, Shumathites, and Mishraites. From these came the Zorathites and the Eshtaolites.

⁵⁴The sons (descendants) of Salma: Bethlehem, the Netophathites, Atroth-beth-joab, and half of the Manahathites, the Zorites.

⁵⁵The families of scribes who lived at Jabez: the Tirathites, Shimeathites, and Sucathites. These are the Kenites who came from Hammath, the father of the house of Rechab.

3 THESE WERE the sons of David who were born to him in Hebron: the firstborn was Amnon, by Ahinoam the Jezreelitess; second, Daniel (Chileab), by Abigail the Carmelitess;

²third, Absalom the son of Maacah, daughter of Talmai king of Geshur; fourth, Adonijah, the son of Haggith;

³fifth, Shephatiah, by Abital; sixth, Ithream, by his wife Eglah.

⁴These six were born to David in Hebron; he reigned there seven years and six months, and in Jerusalem he reigned thirty-three years.

⁵These were born to David in Jerusalem: Shimea (Shammua), Shobab, Nathan, Solomon—four by Bath-shua (Bathsheba) daughter of Ammiel (Eliam);

⁶then Ibhar, Elishama (Elishua), Eliphelet (Elpelet),

⁷Nogah, Nepheg, Japhia,

⁸Elishama, Eliada (Beeliada), and Eliphelet—nine in all.

⁹All these were the sons of David, besides the sons of the concubines; and Tamar was their sister.

¹⁰Solomon's son was Rehoboam. Abijah was his son, Asa his son, Jehoshaphat his son,

¹¹Joram (Jehoram) his son, Ahaziah his son, Joash his son,

¹²Amaziah his son, Azariah his son, Jotham his son,

¹³Ahaz his son, Hezekiah his son, Manasseh his son,

¹⁴Amon his son, Josiah his son.

¹⁵The sons of Josiah: firstborn, Johanan; second, Jehoiakim (Eliakim); third, Zedekiah; fourth, Shallum (Jehoahaz).

¹⁶The sons (descendants) of Jehoiakim: Jehoiachin (Jeconiah) his son, Zedekiah his son.

¹⁷The sons (descendants) of Jehoiachin (Jeconiah) the prisoner: Shealtiel his son,

¹⁸Malchiram, Pedaiah, Shenazzar, Jekamiah, Hoshama and Nedabiah.

¹⁹The sons of Pedaiah: Zerubbabel and Shimei. The sons of Zerubbabel: Meshullam and Hananiah, and Shelomith was their sister;

putting the Word to work

Have you ever wondered why the Bible contains so many genealogies? First Chronicles is full of them! Clearly, family is important to God. When you asked Jesus to forgive your sins and to come into your life, God adopted you into His family. Thank Him for your brothers and sisters in Christ, and ask Him to help you fully enjoy and experience the blessings of belonging to His family.

²⁰and Hashubah, Ohel, Berechiah, Hasadiah, and Jushab-hesed—five *in all*.

²¹The sons of Hananiah: Pelatiah and Jeshaiah, the sons of Rephaiah, the sons of Arnan, the sons of Obadiah, the sons of Shecaniah.

²²The sons (descendants) of Shecaniah: Shemaiah. The sons of Shemaiah: Hattush, Igal, Bariah, Neariah, and Shaphat—six *in all*.

²³The sons of Neariah: Elioenai, Hizkiah, and Azrikam—three *in all*.

²⁴The sons of Elioenai: Hodaviah, Eliashib, Pelaiah, Akkub, Johanan, Delaiah, and Anani—seven *in all*.

4 THE SONS of Judah: Perez, Hezron, Carmi, Hur, and Shobal.

²Reaiah the son of Shobal became the father of Jahath, and Jahath became the father of Ahumai and Lahad. These were the families of the Zorathites.

³These were the sons of Etam: Jezreel, Ishma, and Idbash; and the name of their sister was Hazzelelponi.

⁴Penuel was the father of Gedor, and Ezer the father of Hushah. These were the sons of Hur, the eldest of Ephrathah (Ephrath), the father of Bethlehem.

⁵Ashhur, the father of Tekoa, had two wives, Helah and Naarah.

⁶Naarah bore him Ahuzzam, Hepher, Temeni and Haahashtari. These were Naarah's sons.

⁷The sons of Helah: Zereth, Izhar, and Ethnan.

⁸Koz fathered Anub, Zobebah, and the families of Aharhel the son of Harum.

⁹Jabez was more honorable than his brothers; but his mother named him Jabez, saying, "Because I gave birth to him in pain."

¹⁰Jabez cried out to the God of Israel, saying, "Oh that You would indeed bless me and enlarge my border [property], and that Your hand would be with me, and You would keep me from evil so that it does not hurt me!" And God granted his request.

¹¹Chelub the brother of Shuhah became the father of Mehir, the father of Eshton.

¹²Eshton became the father of Beth-rapha, Paseah, and Tehinnah the father of Ir-nahash. These are the men of Recah.

¹³The sons of Kenaz: Othniel and Seraiah. The sons of Othniel: Hathath and Meonothai.

¹⁴Meonothai became the father of Ophrah, and Seraiah became the father of Joab the father of Ge-harashim [the Valley of Craftsmen, so named] because they were craftsmen.

¹⁵The sons of Caleb [Joshua's companion] the son of Jephunneh: Iru, Elah, and Naam. The son of Elah: Kenaz.

¹⁶The sons of Jehallelel: Ziph, Ziphah, Tiria, and Asarel.

¹⁷The sons of Ezrah: Jether, Mered, Epher, and Jalon. These are the sons of Bithia daughter of Pharaoh, whom Mered took: she conceived *and gave birth to* Miriam, Shammai, and Ishbah the father of Eshtemoa.

¹⁸Mered's Jewish wife gave birth to Jered the father of Gedor, Heber the father of Soco, and Jekuthiel the father of Zanoah.

¹⁹The sons of the wife of Hodiah, the sister of Naham, were: the fathers of Keilah the Garmite and Eshtemoa the Maacathite.

speak the Word

God, I pray like Jabez that You will bless me and enlarge my border, and that Your hand would be with me, and that You would keep me from evil.
—ADAPTED FROM 1 CHRONICLES 4:10

[20]The sons of Shimon: Amnon, Rinnah, Benhanan, and Tilon. The sons of Ishi: Zoheth and Ben-zoheth.

[21]The sons of Shelah son of Judah: Er the father of Lecah and Laadah the father of Mareshah, and the families of the house of the linen workers at Beth-ashbea;

[22]and Jokim, the men of Cozeba, Joash, and Saraph, who ruled in Moab, and Jashubi-lehem. These are ancient words (genealogical records).

[23]These were the potters and those who lived [among plantations and hedges] at Netaim and Gederah; they lived there with the king for his work.

[24]The sons of Simeon: Nemuel, Jamin, Jarib, Zerah, and Shaul;

[25]Shallum was Shaul's son, Mibsam his son, Mishma his son.

[26]The sons of Mishma: Hammuel his son, Zaccur his son, Shimei his son.

[27]Shimei had sixteen sons and six daughters; but his brothers did not have many sons, neither did all their family multiply like the sons of Judah.

[28]They lived at Beersheba, Moladah, Hazar-shual,

[29]Bilhah, Ezem, Tolad,

[30]Bethuel, Hormah, Ziklag,

[31]Beth-marcaboth, Hazar-susim, Beth-biri, and at Shaaraim. These were their cities until the reign of David.

[32]*These were* their villages: Etam, Ain, Rimmon, Tochen, and Ashan—five cities—

[33]and all their villages that were around these towns as far as Baal. These were their settlements, and they have their genealogical record.

[34]Meshobab, Jamlech, Joshah the son of Amaziah,

[35]Joel, Jehu the son of Joshibiah, the son of Seraiah, the son of Asiel,

[36]also Elioenai, Jaakobah, Jeshohaiah, Asaiah, Adiel, Jesimiel, Benaiah,

[37]Ziza the son of Shiphi, the son of Allon, the son of Jedaiah, the son of Shimri, the son of Shemaiah;

[38]these mentioned by name were leaders in their families; and their fathers' houses increased greatly [so they needed more land].

[39]So they journeyed to the entrance of Gedor, to the east side of the valley, to seek pasture for their flocks.

[40]They found rich, good pasture, and the [cleared] land was wide, quiet, and peaceful; for those who had lived there previously came from Ham [and had left it a better place for those who came after them].

[41]These, registered by name, came in the days of Hezekiah king of Judah, and they attacked their tents and the Meunites (foreigners) who were found there, and utterly destroyed them to this day; and they settled in their place, because there was pasture there for their flocks.

[42]From them, from the sons of Simeon, five hundred men went to Mount Seir, with Pelatiah, Neariah, Rephaiah, and Uzziel, the sons of Ishi, as their leaders.

[43]They destroyed the remnant of the Amalekites who escaped, and they have lived there to this day (the date of this writing).

5 NOW [WE come to] the sons of Reuben the firstborn of Israel—for Reuben was the eldest, but because he defiled his father's bed [with Bilhah his father's concubine], his birthright was given to [Manasseh and Ephraim] the sons of Joseph [the favorite] son of Israel, so that he is not enrolled in the genealogy according to the birthright. [Gen 35:22; 48:15–22; 49:3, 4]

[2]Though Judah prevailed over his brothers, and from him came [David] the leader [and eventually the Messiah], yet the birthright was Joseph's—[Gen 49:10; Mic 5:2]

[3]the sons of Reuben the firstborn of Israel: Hanoch, Pallu, Hezron, and Carmi.

⁴The sons of Joel: Shemaiah his son, Gog his son, Shimei his son,

⁵Micah his son, Reaiah his son, Baal his son,

⁶Beerah his son, whom Tilgath-pilneser king of Assyria carried away into exile; he was a leader of the tribe of Reuben.

⁷And his brothers (relatives) by their families, in the genealogy of their generations, were the chief Jeiel, and Zechariah,

⁸Bela the son of Azaz, the son of Shema, the son of Joel, who lived in Aroer as far as Nebo and Baal-meon.

⁹To the east Bela settled as far as the entrance into the desert from the river Euphrates, because their cattle had multiplied in the land of Gilead.

¹⁰In the days of King Saul they made war with the Hagrites, who fell by their hands; and they lived in their tents throughout all the land east of Gilead.

¹¹The sons of Gad lived opposite them in the land of Bashan, as far as Salecah:

life point

Notice in 1 Chronicles 5:1 that Reuben's birthright was given to the sons of Joseph. Why? Because Reuben "defiled his father's bed" (1 Chronicles 5:1) with his father's concubine. A birthright was an enormous and extremely valuable blessing to a man during Bible times. Whoever had the birthright inherited "the best of the best" from his father. But Reuben forfeited all the blessings of the birthright for a few moments with a concubine. He lost a great inheritance because he could not control his emotions.

Ask God to help you perceive what is truly valuable and to never allow the lust of the flesh or your emotions to cause you to miss out on a blessing.

¹²Joel was the chief, Shapham the second, then Janai and Shaphat in Bashan.

¹³Their relatives from the households of their fathers: Michael, Meshullam, Sheba, Jorai, Jacan, Zia, and Eber—seven *in all*.

¹⁴These were the sons of Abihail the son of Huri, the son of Jaroah, the son of Gilead, the son of Michael, the son of Jeshishai, the son of Jahdo, the son of Buz;

¹⁵Ahi the son of Abdiel, the son of Guni, was chief in their fathers' households.

¹⁶They lived in Gilead, in Bashan and in its towns, and in all the [surrounding] pasture lands of Sharon, as far as their borders.

¹⁷All these were enrolled in the genealogies in the days of Jotham king of Judah and in the days of Jeroboam [II] king of Israel.

¹⁸The sons of Reuben, the Gadites, and the half-tribe of Manasseh—valiant men able to bear shield and sword, and to shoot with the bow, and skillful in war—were 44,760 who went to war.

¹⁹And these Israelites, [on the east side of the Jordan River] made war with the Hagrites [a tribe of northern Arabia], Jetur, Naphish, and Nodab.

²⁰They were given help against them, and the Hagrites were handed over to them, and all who were *allied* with them; for they cried out to God [for help] in the battle; and He granted their entreaty because they relied on *and* trusted in Him.

²¹These Israelites took away their livestock: their 50,000 camels, and 250,000 sheep, and 2,000 donkeys; and 100,000 people.

²²For a great number fell mortally wounded, because the battle was of God. And these Israelites settled in their territory until the exile [by Assyria more than five centuries later]. [2 Kin 15:29]

²³Now the sons (people) of the half-tribe of Manasseh lived in the land; their settlements spread from Bashan to Baal-hermon and Senir and Mount Hermon.

²⁴These were the heads of their fathers' households: Epher, Ishi, Eliel, Azriel, Jeremiah, Hodaviah, and Jahdiel, warriors of valor [willing and able to encounter danger], famous men, and heads of the households of their fathers.

²⁵But they acted treacherously against the God of their fathers and played the prostitute with the gods of the peoples of the land, whom God had destroyed before them.

²⁶So the God of Israel stirred up the spirit of Pul, king of Assyria, [that is,] the spirit of Tilgath-pilneser king of Assyria, and he carried them away into exile—the Reubenites, the Gadites, and the half-tribe of Manasseh—and brought them to Halah, Habor, Hara, and the river Gozan, [where they remain] to this day.

6 THE SONS of Levi: Gershom, Kohath and Merari. ²The sons of Kohath: Amram, Izhar, Hebron, and Uzziel. ³The sons of Amram: Aaron, Moses and Miriam. And the sons of Aaron: Nadab, Abihu, Eleazar, and Ithamar.

⁴Eleazar became the father of Phinehas, Phinehas became the father of Abishua,

⁵and Abishua became the father of Bukki, and Bukki became the father of Uzzi,

⁶and Uzzi became the father of Zerahiah, and Zerahiah became the father of Meraioth,

⁷Meraioth became the father of Amariah, and Amariah became the father of Ahitub,

⁸and Ahitub became the father of Zadok, and Zadok became the father of Ahimaaz,

⁹and Ahimaaz became the father of Azariah, and Azariah became the father of Johanan,

¹⁰and Johanan became the father of Azariah (it was he who was priest in the house (temple) which Solomon built in Jerusalem)

¹¹and Azariah became the father of Amariah, and Amariah became the father of Ahitub,

¹²and Ahitub became the father of Zadok, and Zadok became the father of Shallum,

¹³and Shallum became the father of Hilkiah, and Hilkiah became the father of Azariah,

¹⁴and Azariah became the father of Seraiah, and Seraiah became the father of Jehozadak;

¹⁵and Jehozadak went into captivity when the Lord sent [the people of] Judah and Jerusalem into exile by the hand of Nebuchadnezzar.

¹⁶The sons of Levi: Gershom, Kohath, and Merari.

¹⁷These are the names of the sons of Gershom: Libni and Shimei.

¹⁸The sons of Kohath: Amram, Izhar, Hebron, and Uzziel.

¹⁹The sons of Merari: Mahli and Mushi. These are the families of the Levites according to their fathers.

²⁰Of Gershom: Libni his son, Jahath his son, Zimmah his son,

²¹Joah his son, Iddo his son, Zerah his son, Jeatherai his son.

²²The sons of Kohath: Amminadab his son, Korah his son, Assir his son,

²³Elkanah his son, Ebiasaph his son, Assir his son,

²⁴Tahath his son, Uriel his son, Uzziah his son, and Shaul his son.

²⁵The sons of Elkanah: Amasai and Ahimoth.

²⁶*As for* Elkanah, the sons of Elkanah: Zophai his son and Nahath his son,

²⁷Eliab his son, Jeroham his son, Elkanah [Samuel's father] his son.

²⁸The sons of Samuel: Joel the first-born and Abijah the second.

²⁹The sons of Merari: Mahli, Libni his son, Shimei his son, Uzza his son, ³⁰Shimea his son, Haggiah his son, Asaiah his son.

³¹Now these are those whom David appointed over the service of song in the house of the Lᴏʀᴅ after the ark [of the covenant] rested *there*. ³²They ministered with singing before the tabernacle of the Tent of Meeting, until Solomon had built the Lᴏʀᴅ's house (temple) in Jerusalem, performing their service in due order.

³³These men and their sons served from the Kohathites: Heman the singer, the son of Joel, the son of Samuel [the great prophet and judge], ³⁴the son of Elkanah [III], the son of Jeroham, the son of Eliel, the son of Toah, ³⁵the son of Zuph, the son of Elkanah [II], the son of Mahath, the son of Amasai, ³⁶the son of Elkanah [I], the son of Joel, the son of Azariah, the son of Zephaniah, ³⁷the son of Tahath, the son of Assir, the son of Ebiasaph, the son of Korah, ³⁸the son of Izhar, the son of Kohath, the son of Levi, the son of Israel (Jacob).

³⁹Heman's [tribal] brother Asaph stood at his right hand: Asaph the son of Berechiah, the son of Shimea, ⁴⁰the son of Michael, the son of Baaseiah, the son of Malchijah, ⁴¹the son of Ethni, the son of Zerah, the son of Adaiah, ⁴²the son of Ethan, the son of Zimmah, the son of Shimei, ⁴³the son of Jahath, the son of Gershom, the son of Levi.

⁴⁴Their relatives the sons of Merari *stood* at the left hand: Ethan the son of Kishi, the son of Abdi, the son of Malluch, ⁴⁵the son of Hashabiah, the son of Amaziah, the son of Hilkiah, ⁴⁶the son of Amzi, the son of Bani, the son of Shemer, ⁴⁷the son of Mahli, the son of Mushi, the son of Merari, the son of Levi.

⁴⁸Their relatives the Levites [who were not descended from Aaron] were appointed for all *the other kinds of* service of the tabernacle of the house of God.

⁴⁹But [the line of] Aaron and his sons made offerings on the altar of burnt offering and on the altar of incense, *ministering* for all the work of the Holy of Holies (Most Holy Place), and [they did so] to make atonement for Israel, according to all that Moses, God's servant, had commanded. ⁵⁰These are the sons of Aaron: Eleazar his son, Phinehas his son, Abishua his son, ⁵¹Bukki his son, Uzzi his son, Zerahiah his son, ⁵²Meraioth his son, Amariah his son, Ahitub his son, ⁵³Zadok his son, Ahimaaz his son.

⁵⁴Now these are their settlements according to their camps within their borders: to the sons of Aaron of the families of the Kohathites (for theirs was the *first* allocation by lot) [Josh 21:10] ⁵⁵to them they gave Hebron in the land of Judah and its surrounding pasture land; ⁵⁶but the fields of the city and its villages they gave to Caleb the son of Jephunneh. ⁵⁷To the sons of Aaron they gave the *following* cities of refuge: Hebron, Libnah with its pasture lands, Jattir, Eshtemoa with its pasture lands, [Josh 21:13] ⁵⁸Hilen with its pasture lands, Debir with its pasture lands, ⁵⁹Ashan with its pasture lands, and Beth-shemesh with its pasture lands; ⁶⁰and from the tribe of Benjamin: Geba, Alemeth, and Anathoth, with their pasture lands. All their cities throughout their families were thirteen cities.

⁶¹Then to the rest of the sons of Kohath *were given* ten cities by lot from the family of the tribe [of Ephraim and of Dan and], from the half-tribe, the half of Manasseh. [Josh 21:5]

⁶²To the sons of Gershom, according to their families, *were given* thirteen cities from the tribes of Issachar, Asher, Naphtali, and [the other half of] Manasseh in Bashan.

⁶³To the sons of Merari *were given* twelve cities by lot, according to their families, from the tribes of Reuben, Gad, and Zebulun.

⁶⁴So the sons of Israel gave to the Levites these cities with their pasture lands.

⁶⁵They gave by lot from the tribes of the sons of Judah, Simeon, and Benjamin these cities which are mentioned by name.

⁶⁶Some of the families of the sons of Kohath had cities of their [allotted] territory from the tribe of Ephraim.

⁶⁷They gave to the Levites the *following* cities of refuge: Shechem in the hill country of Ephraim with its pasture lands, Gezer with its pasture lands;

⁶⁸Jokmeam and Beth-horon with their pasture lands,

⁶⁹Aijalon and Gath-rimmon, with their pasture lands;

⁷⁰and from the half-tribe of Manasseh [these cities], with their pasture lands: Aner and Bileam, for the rest of the families of the sons of Kohath.

⁷¹To the sons of Gershom *were given* from the family of the half-tribe of Manasseh: Golan in Bashan and Ashtaroth, with their pasture lands;

⁷²from the tribe of Issachar: Kedesh and Daberath with their pasture lands,

⁷³Ramoth and Anem with their pasture lands;

⁷⁴from the tribe of Asher: Mashal and Abdon with their pasture lands,

⁷⁵Hukok and Rehob with their pasture lands;

⁷⁶and from the tribe of Naphtali: Kedesh in Galilee, Hammon, and Kiriathaim with their pasture lands.

⁷⁷To the rest of *the Levites,* the sons of Merari *were given,* from the tribe of Zebulun: Rimmono and Tabor, with their pasture lands;

⁷⁸and on the other side of the Jordan at Jericho, on the east side of the Jordan *the Levites were given,* from the tribe of Reuben: Bezer in the wilderness and Jahzah with their pasture lands,

⁷⁹Kedemoth and Mephaath with their pasture lands;

⁸⁰from the tribe of Gad: Ramoth in Gilead and Mahanaim with their pasture lands,

⁸¹Heshbon and Jazer with their pasture lands.

7 THE SONS of Issachar were: Tola, Puah, Jashub, and Shimron—four *in all.*

²The sons of Tola: Uzzi, Rephaiah, Jeriel, Jahmai, Ibsam, and Samuel, heads of their fathers' households. *The sons* of Tola were courageous men in their generations; their number in the days of David was 22,600.

³The son of Uzzi: Izrahiah. The sons of Izrahiah: Michael, Obadiah, Joel, Isshiah; all five of them were chief men.

⁴With them by their generations according to their fathers' households were 36,000 troops of the army for war, for they had many wives and children.

⁵Their relatives among all the families of Issachar, courageous men, registered by genealogies, were 87,000 in all.

⁶*The sons of* Benjamin were three: Bela, Becher, and Jediael.

⁷The sons of Bela were five: Ezbon, Uzzi, Uzziel, Jerimoth, and Iri. They were heads of the households of their fathers, courageous men. By their genealogies they were 22,034.

⁸The sons of Becher: Zemirah, Joash, Eliezer, Elioenai, Omri, Jeremoth, Abijah, Anathoth, and Alemeth, all these were sons of Becher.

⁹They were registered by their genealogies according to their generations, as heads of their fathers' households, courageous men, 20,200 *in number*.

¹⁰The son of Jediael: Bilhan. The sons of Bilhan: Jeush, Benjamin, Ehud, Chenaanah, Zethan, Tarshish, and Ahishahar.

¹¹All these were the sons of Jediael, according to the heads of their fathers' households, 17,200 courageous men of valor, fit for military service.

¹²Shuppim and Huppim were the sons of Ir, and Hushim the son of Aher.

¹³The sons of Naphtali: Jahziel, Guni, Jezer, and Shallum, the sons of Bilhah.

¹⁴The sons of Manasseh: Asriel, whom his Aramean concubine bore; she gave birth to Machir the father of Gilead.

¹⁵Machir took as a wife the sister of Huppim and Shuppim; her name was Maacah. The name of a second [descendant, the first being Gilead], was Zelophehad; and Zelophehad had [only] daughters. [Num 27:1–7]

¹⁶Maacah the wife of Machir gave birth to a son; she named him Peresh. The name of his brother was Sheresh; his sons were Ulam and Rakem.

¹⁷The son of Ulam: Bedan. These were the sons of Gilead the son of Machir, the son of Manasseh.

¹⁸His sister Hammolecheth gave birth to Ishhod and Abiezer and Mahlah.

¹⁹The sons of Shemida were: Ahian, Shechem, Likhi, and Aniam.

²⁰The sons of Ephraim: Shuthelah and Bered his son, Tahath [I] his son, Eleadah his son, Tahath [II] his son,

²¹Zabad his son, Shuthelah his son, and Ezer and Elead were killed by men who were natives of Gath, because they came down to take their livestock.

²²Their father Ephraim mourned for many days, and his relatives came to comfort him.

²³Then he went in to his wife, and she conceived and gave birth to a son, and he named him Beriah (on misfortune), because tragedy had come on his house.

²⁴Beriah's daughter was Sheerah, who built both Lower and Upper Beth-horon, and also Uzzen-sheerah.

²⁵Rephah was his son *along* with Resheph; Resheph's son was Telah, Tahan his son,

²⁶Ladan his son, Ammihud his son, Elishama his son,

²⁷Non (Nun) his son, and Joshua [Moses' successor] his son.

²⁸Their possessions and settlements were Bethel and its towns, and eastward Naaran, and westward Gezer, and Shechem, and as far as Ayyah with all their towns,

²⁹and along the borders of the sons of Manasseh, Beth-shean, Taanach, Megiddo, Dor, with all their towns. In these [places] lived the sons of Joseph the son of Israel (Jacob).

³⁰The sons of Asher: Imnah, Ishvah, Ishvi, and Beriah; and Serah their sister.

³¹The sons of Beriah: Heber and Malchiel, who was the father of Birzaith.

³²Heber became the father of Japhlet, Shomer, Hotham, and Shua their sister.

³³The sons of Japhlet: Pasach, Bimhal, and Ashvath. These were the sons of Japhlet.

³⁴The sons of Shemer (Shomer) [his brother]: Ahi and Rohgah, Jehubbah, and Aram.

³⁵The sons of his brother Helem (Hotham): Zophah, Imna, Shelesh, and Amal.

³⁶The sons of Zophah: Suah, Harnepher, Shual, Beri, Imrah,

³⁷Bezer, Hod, Shamma, Shilshah, Ithran, and Beera.

³⁸The sons of Jether: Jephunneh, Pispa, and Ara.

³⁹The sons of Ulla: Arah, Hanniel, and Rizia.

⁴⁰All these were sons (descendants) of Asher, heads of their fathers' houses,

choice men, courageous men, chiefs of the leaders. Their number, enrolled by genealogies for service in war, was 26,000 men.

8 BENJAMIN BECAME the father of Bela his firstborn, Ashbel the second, Aharah the third, ²Nohah the fourth and Rapha the fifth.

³Bela had sons: Addar, Gera, Abihud, ⁴Abishua, Naaman, Ahoah, ⁵Gera, Shephuphan, and Huram.

⁶These are the sons of Ehud: These are the heads of the fathers' *households* of the inhabitants of Geba; they were exiled to Manahath: ⁷Naaman, Ahijah, and Gera—he forced them into exile; he became the father of Uzza and Ahihud.

⁸Shaharaim became the father of children in the country of Moab after he had sent away (divorced) Hushim and Baara his wives. ⁹By Hodesh his wife he became the father of Jobab, Zibia, Mesha, Malcam, ¹⁰Jeuz, Sachia, and Mirmah. These were his sons, heads of fathers' *households*. ¹¹By Hushim he became the father of Abitub and Elpaal.

¹²The sons of Elpaal: Eber, Misham, and Shemed, who built Ono and Lod, with its towns; ¹³and Beriah and Shema, who were heads of fathers' *households* of the inhabitants of Aijalon, who drove out the inhabitants of Gath; ¹⁴and Ahio, Shashak, and Jeremoth, ¹⁵Zebadiah, Arad, Eder, ¹⁶Michael, Ishpah, and Joha *were* the sons of Beriah.

¹⁷Zebadiah, Meshullam, Hizki, Heber, ¹⁸Ishmerai, Izliah, and Jobab were the sons of Elpaal. ¹⁹Jakim, Zichri, Zabdi, ²⁰Elienai, Zillethai, Eliel, ²¹Adaiah, Beraiah, and Shimrath were the sons of Shimei.

²²Ishpan, Eber, Eliel, ²³Abdon, Zichri, Hanan, ²⁴Hananiah, Elam, Anthothijah, ²⁵Iphdeiah and Penuel were the sons of Shashak.

²⁶Shamsherai, Shehariah, Athaliah, ²⁷Jaareshiah, Elijah, and Zichri were the sons of Jeroham.

²⁸These [men] were heads of the fathers' *households*, according to their generations, chief men who lived in Jerusalem.

²⁹Now in Gibeon, *Jeiel,* the father of Gibeon lived, and his wife's name was Maacah; ³⁰and his firstborn son was Abdon, then Zur, Kish, Baal, Nadab, ³¹Gedor, Ahio, and Zecher. ³²Mikloth became the father of Shimeah. They also lived with their relatives in Jerusalem opposite their other relatives.

³³Ner became the father of Kish, and Kish became the father of [King] Saul, and Saul became the father of Jonathan, Malchi-shua, Abinadab and Eshbaal (Ish-bosheth).

³⁴The son of Jonathan was Merib-baal (Mephibosheth), and Merib-baal became the father of Micah. ³⁵The sons of Micah: Pithon, Melech, Tarea, and Ahaz. ³⁶Ahaz became the father of Je-hoaddah, and Jehoaddah became the father of Alemeth, Azmaveth, and Zimri; and Zimri became the father of Moza. ³⁷Moza became the father of Binea; Raphah was his son, Eleasah his son, Azel his son. ³⁸Azel had six sons, and these were their names: Azrikam, Bocheru, Ish-mael, Sheariah, Obadiah, and Hanan. All these were the sons of Azel. ³⁹The sons of Eshek his brother: Ulam his firstborn, Jeush the second, and Eliphelet the third.

⁴⁰The sons of Ulam were courageous men, archers, and had many sons and

grandsons—150 *in all*. All these were of the sons (descendants) of Benjamin.

9 SO ALL Israel was enrolled by genealogies; and they are written in the Book of the Kings of Israel. And Judah was carried away into exile to Babylon because of their unfaithfulness [to God].

²Now the first [of the returned exiles] who lived [again] in their possessions in their cities were Israel, the priests, the Levites, and the Nethinim (temple servants).

³Some of the sons (people) of Judah, Benjamin, Ephraim, and Manasseh lived in Jerusalem:

⁴Uthai the son of Ammihud, the son of Omri, the son of Imri, the son of Bani, of the sons of Perez the son of Judah.

⁵From the Shilonites: Asaiah the firstborn and his sons.

⁶From the sons of Zerah: Jeuel and their relatives, 690 [of them].

⁷From the sons of Benjamin: Sallu the son of Meshullam, the son of Hodaviah, the son of Hassenuah;

⁸Ibneiah the son of Jeroham, Elah the son of Uzzi, the son of Michri, and Meshullam son of Shephatiah, the son of Reuel, the son of Ibnijah;

⁹and their relatives according to their generations, 956. All these men were heads of fathers' *households* according to their fathers' houses.

¹⁰Of the priests: Jedaiah, Jehoiarib, Jachin,

¹¹Azariah the son of Hilkiah, the son of Meshullam, the son of Zadok, the son of Meraioth, the son of Ahitub, the chief officer of the house of God;

¹²and Adaiah the son of Jeroham, the son of Pashhur, the son of Malchijah; Maasai the son of Adiel, the son of Jahzerah, the son of Meshullam, the son of Meshillemith, the son of Immer;

¹³and their relatives, heads of their fathers' households, 1,760—very able men for the work of the service of the house of God.

¹⁴Of the Levites: Shemaiah the son of Hasshub, the son of Azrikam, the son of Hashabiah, of the sons of Merari;

¹⁵and Bakbakkar, Heresh, Galal, and Mattaniah son of Mica, the son of Zichri, the son of Asaph;

¹⁶and Obadiah the son of Shemaiah, the son of Galal, the son of Jeduthun, and Berechiah the son of Asa, the son of Elkanah, who lived in the villages of the Netophathites [near Jerusalem].

¹⁷The gatekeepers were: Shallum, Akkub, Talmon, Ahiman, and their relatives (Shallum the chief

¹⁸who until now *was assigned* to the king's gate on the east side) they were the gatekeepers for the camp of the Levites.

¹⁹Shallum the son of Kore, the son of Ebiasaph, the son of Korah, and his relatives of his father's house, the Korahites, were in charge of the work of the service, doorkeepers of the Tent; and their fathers had been in charge of the camp of the LORD, keepers of the entrance.

²⁰Phinehas the son of Eleazar was ruler over them in times past, and the LORD was with him.

²¹Zechariah son of Meshelemiah was gatekeeper at the entrance of the Tent of Meeting.

²²All those chosen to be gatekeepers at the thresholds were 212. They were enrolled by their genealogies in their villages [around Jerusalem], these men [whose grandfathers] David and Samuel the seer had appointed to their official duty.

²³So they and their sons were in charge of the gates of the house of the LORD, that is, the house of the tabernacle, as guards.

²⁴The gatekeepers were *stationed* on the four sides —on the east, west, north, and south.

²⁵Their relatives in their villages were to come in every seven days from time to time to be with them;

²⁶for these Levites, the four chief

gatekeepers, had an official duty, and were in charge of the chambers and treasuries of the house of God.

²⁷They spent the night around the house of God, for the [night] watch was theirs, and they were in charge of opening *the house* morning after morning.

²⁸Now some of them were in charge of the serving utensils, being required to count them when they brought them in or took them out.

²⁹Some of them also were appointed over the furniture and over all the [sacred] utensils of the sanctuary, as well as over the fine flour and the wine and the [olive] oil and the frankincense and the spices.

³⁰Other sons of the priests prepared the mixture of spices.

³¹Mattithiah, one of the Levites, the firstborn of Shallum the Korahite, was responsible for the things baked in pans.

³²Some of their Kohathite relatives were in charge of the showbread to prepare it every Sabbath.

³³Now these are the singers, heads of the fathers' *households* of the Levites, *living* in the *temple* chambers, free *from other service* because they were on duty day and night.

³⁴These were heads of fathers' *households* of the Levites according to their generations, chief men, who lived in Jerusalem.

³⁵Jeiel the father of Gibeon lived in Gibeon, and his wife's name was Maacah,

³⁶and his firstborn son was Abdon, then Zur, Kish, Baal, Ner, Nadab,

³⁷Gedor, Ahio, Zechariah, and Mikloth.

³⁸Mikloth became the father of Shimeam. They also lived with their relatives in Jerusalem, opposite their *other* relatives.

³⁹Ner became the father of Kish, and Kish became the father of [King] Saul,

and Saul became the father of Jonathan, Malchi-shua, Abinadab, and Esh-baal.

⁴⁰The son of Jonathan was Meribbaal (Mephibosheth); Merib-baal became the father of Micah.

⁴¹The sons of Micah: Pithon, Melech, Tahrea [and Ahaz].

⁴²Ahaz became the father of Jarah, and Jarah became the father of Alemeth, Azmaveth, and Zimri; and Zimri became the father of Moza,

⁴³Moza became the father of Binea and Rephaiah his son, Eleasah his son, Azel his son.

⁴⁴Azel had six sons, and these are their names: Azrikam, Bocheru, Ishmael, Sheariah, Obadiah, and Hanan. These were the sons of Azel.

10 NOW THE Philistines fought against Israel; and the men of Israel fled from them and fell slain on Mount Gilboa.

²The Philistines followed closely after Saul and his sons *and* overtook them, and the Philistines killed Jonathan, Abinadab, and Malchi-shua, the sons of Saul.

³The battle became heavy against Saul, and the archers found him; and he was [mortally] wounded by the archers.

⁴Then Saul said to his armor bearer, "Draw your sword and run me through with it, otherwise these uncircumcised [Philistines] will come and abuse *and* humiliate me." But his armor bearer would not, for he was terrified. So Saul took his own sword and fell on it.

⁵When his armor bearer saw that Saul was dead, he also fell on his sword and died.

⁶So Saul died with his three sons and all *those* of his house died together.

⁷When all the men of Israel who were in the valley saw that the army had fled, and that Saul and his sons were dead, they abandoned their cities

and fled; and the Philistines came and lived in them.

⁸It came about the next day, when the Philistines came to strip (plunder) the slain, that they found Saul and his sons fallen on Mount Gilboa.

⁹So they stripped Saul and took his head and his armor and sent *messengers* around the land of the Philistines to bring the good news to their idols and to the people.

¹⁰They put Saul's armor in the house of their gods and nailed up his head in the house (temple) of Dagon.

¹¹When all Jabesh-gilead heard about everything that the Philistines had done to Saul,

¹²all the brave men arose, took away the body of Saul and the bodies of his sons and brought them to Jabesh, and they buried their bones under the oak in Jabesh; then they fasted seven days. [1 Sam 31:12]

¹³So Saul died for his trespass which he committed against the LORD, for his failure to keep the word of the LORD; and also because he consulted a medium [regarding a spirit of the dead], to inquire *of her,*

¹⁴and did not inquire of the LORD [instead]. Therefore the LORD killed him

life point

Saul lost his kingdom because he did not keep God's Word and he consulted a medium (see 1 Chronicles 10:13, 14). No doubt he thought this person would speak truth to him, but such people are not only deceived themselves, they also speak deception to others and present it as truth. The world we live in would have us believe that there are many sources of truth. Remember to love, honor, know, study, and obey God's Word so that you can live by "the truth, the whole truth, and nothing but the truth," because it is "the Truth" that sets you free (see John 8:32).

and turned the kingdom over to David the son of Jesse. [1 Sam 28:6]

11 THEN ALL Israel gathered to David at Hebron, saying, "Behold, we are your bone and your flesh. [2 Sam 2:8–10]

²"In times past, even when Saul was king, it was you who led out and brought in Israel; and the LORD your God said to you, 'You shall shepherd My people Israel, and you shall be prince *and* leader over My people Israel.'"

³So all the elders of Israel came to the king at Hebron, and David made a covenant (solemn agreement) with them there before the LORD; and they anointed him king over Israel, in accordance with the word of the LORD through Samuel. [1 Sam 16:1, 12, 13]

⁴Then David and all Israel went to Jerusalem (that is Jebus); and the Jebusites, the inhabitants of the land, were there.

⁵Then the Jebusites said to David, "You shall not come in here." But David captured the stronghold of Zion (that is, the City of David).

⁶Now David said, "Whoever strikes down a Jebusite first shall be chief and commander." Joab the son of Zeruiah [David's half sister] went up first, and so he was made chief.

⁷Then David lived in the stronghold; so it was called the City of David.

⁸He built the city around it, from the Millo (fortification) to the surrounding area; and Joab repaired the rest of the [old Jebusite] city.

⁹David became greater and greater, for the LORD of hosts was with him.

¹⁰Now these are the chiefs of David's mighty men, who strongly supported him in his kingdom, together with all Israel, to make him king, in accordance with the word of the LORD concerning Israel.

¹¹This is the list of David's mighty men: Jashobeam, the son of a Hachmonite,

the chief of the thirty [heroes]. He lifted up his spear against three hundred whom he killed at one time.

¹²Next to him [in rank] was Eleazar the son of Dodo the Ahohite, who was one of the three mighty men.

¹³He was with David at Pasdammim [where David had killed Goliath] and there the Philistines were gathered together for battle, and there was a plot of ground full of barley; and the people [of Israel] fled before the Philistines.

¹⁴But they took their stand in the midst of that plot and defended it, and killed the Philistines; and the LORD rescued them by a great victory. [2 Sam 23:9, 10]

¹⁵Three of the thirty chief men went down to the rock to David, into the cave of Adullam, while the army of the Philistines was camped in the Valley of Rephaim.

¹⁶David was then in the stronghold, while the garrison of the Philistines was in Bethlehem.

¹⁷David had a craving and said, "Oh that someone would give me a drink of water from the well of Bethlehem, which is next to the gate!"

¹⁸Then the three [mighty men] broke through the camp of the Philistines and drew water out of the well of Bethlehem which was next to the gate, and brought it to David. But David would not drink it; he poured it out to the LORD [as an offering];

¹⁹and he said, "Far be it from me before my God that I would do this thing! Shall I drink the blood of these men who have put their lives in jeopardy? For they brought it at the risk of their lives." So he would not drink it. These things the three mighty men did.

²⁰Abishai the brother of Joab was chief of the [other] three, and he lifted up his spear against three hundred and killed them, and he had a name as well as the three.

²¹Of the three in the second [rank] he was the most honored and became their captain; however, he did not attain to the *first* three [Jashobeam, Eleazar, and Shammah].

²²Benaiah the son of Jehoiada, the son of a courageous man of Kabzeel who had done great things, killed the two *sons of* Ariel of Moab. Also he went down and killed a lion in a pit on a snowy day.

²³He killed an Egyptian also, a man of *great* stature, five cubits tall. In the Egyptian's hand was a spear like a weaver's beam, and Benaiah went down to him with [only] a staff (rod) and grabbed the spear from the Egyptian's hand and killed him with his own spear.

²⁴Benaiah the son of Jehoiada did these *things,* and had a name as well as the three mighty men.

²⁵He was honored among the thirty, but he did not attain to [the rank of] the [first] three. David appointed him over his bodyguard.

²⁶Now the mighty men of the armies were: Asahel the brother of Joab, Elhanan the son of Dodo of Bethlehem,

²⁷Shammoth the Harorite, Helez the Pelonite,

²⁸Ira the son of Ikkesh of Tekoa, Abiezer of Anathoth,

²⁹Sibbecai the Hushathite, Ilai the Ahohite,

³⁰Maharai the Netophathite, Heled the son of Baanah the Netophathite,

³¹Ithai the son of Ribai of Gibeah of the Benjamites, Benaiah the Pirathonite,

³²Hurai of the brooks of Gaash, Abiel the Arbathite,

³³Azmaveth the Baharumite, Eliahba the Shaalbonite,

³⁴the sons of Hashem the Gizonite, Jonathan the son of Shagee the Hararite,

³⁵Ahiam the son of Sacar the Hararite, Eliphal the son of Ur,

³⁶Hepher the Mecherathite, Ahijah the Pelonite,

³⁷Hezro the Carmelite, Naarai the son of Ezbai,

³⁸Joel the brother of Nathan, Mibhar the son of Hagri,

³⁹Zelek the Ammonite, Naharai the Berothite, the armor bearer of Joab the son of Zeruiah [David's half sister],

⁴⁰Ira the Ithrite, Gareb the Ithrite,

⁴¹Uriah the Hittite [Bathsheba's husband], Zabad the son of Ahlai,

⁴²Adina the son of Shiza the Reubenite, a chief of the Reubenites, and thirty [heroes] with him,

⁴³Hanan the son of Maacah, and Joshaphat the Mithnite,

⁴⁴Uzzia the Ashterathite, Shama and Jeiel the sons of Hotham the Aroerite,

⁴⁵Jediael the son of Shimri, and his brother Joha, the Tizite,

⁴⁶Eliel the Mahavite, Jeribai and Joshaviah the sons of Elnaam, Ithmah the Moabite,

⁴⁷Eliel and Obed and Jaasiel the Mezobaite.

12 THESE ARE the ones who came to David at Ziklag, while he still concealed himself from Saul the son of Kish; they were among the courageous men who helped him in battle.

²They were armed with bows, and could use the right hand or the left to *sling* stones and *shoot* arrows from the bow; *they were* Saul's relatives from [the tribe of] Benjamin.

³The chief was Ahiezer and then Joash, the sons of Shemaah of Gibeah; Jeziel and Pelet the sons of Azmaveth; Beracah, and Jehu of Anathoth,

⁴Ishmaiah of Gibeon, a mighty man among the thirty, and [a leader] over them; Jeremiah, Jahaziel, Johanan, Jozabad of Gederah,

⁵Eluzai, Jerimoth, Bealiah, Shemariah, Shephatiah the Haruphite,

⁶Elkanah, Isshiah, Azarel, Joezer, and Jashobeam, the Korahites,

⁷and Joelah and Zebadiah the sons of Jeroham of Gedor.

⁸Courageous men from the Gadites came over to David in the stronghold in the wilderness, men trained for war, who could handle shield and spear, whose faces were like the faces of lions, and who were swift as gazelles on the mountains.

⁹Ezer was the first, Obadiah the second, Eliab the third,

¹⁰Mishmannah the fourth, Jeremiah the fifth,

¹¹Attai the sixth, Eliel the seventh,

¹²Johanan the eighth, Elzabad the ninth,

¹³Jeremiah the tenth, Machbannai the eleventh.

¹⁴These from the sons (descendants) of Gad were captains of the army; he who was least was equal to a hundred, and the greatest was equal to a thousand.

¹⁵These are the men who crossed over the Jordan in the first month when it had overflowed all its banks and they put to flight all those in the valleys, east and west.

¹⁶Then some of the men of Benjamin and Judah came to the stronghold to David.

¹⁷David went out to meet them and said to them, "If you have come peacefully to me to help me, my heart shall be united with you; but if *you have come* to betray me to my adversaries, since there is no violence *or* wrong in my hands, may the God of our fathers look on [what you are doing] and punish [you]."

¹⁸Then the [Holy] Spirit came on

speak the Word

Thank You, God, that I have peace because You are helping me.
–ADAPTED FROM 1 CHRONICLES 12:18

Amasai, who was chief of the thirty, *and he said,*

"We are yours, O David,
And with you, O son of Jesse!
Peace, peace be to you,
And peace be to him who helps you;
For your God helps you."

Then David accepted *and* received them and made them officers of his troops.

[19]Some [of the men] of Manasseh also defected to David when he came with the Philistines to go to battle against Saul. But David's men did not [actually] assist the Philistines, for the

the power of focus

In 1 Chronicles 12:33 the writer describes the brave men who helped David wage war. As we see, they had undivided hearts; they were focused, stable, and trustworthy. They stuck to their sole purpose in life.

God taught others in the Bible to be single-minded in purpose. When God called Abraham, He told him to leave the past behind and to focus on the place that God would show him (see Genesis 12:1). Being single-hearted was what Paul spoke of when he said to let go of what lies behind and press on to what lies ahead (see Philippians 3:14, 15). Being single in purpose was what the Lord was encouraging Israel to do through the prophet Isaiah: "Do not remember the former things, or ponder the things of the past. Listen carefully, I am about to do a new thing" (Isaiah 43:18, 19).

Our problem is that we always want to hold on to the past and still go into the future. There are times when God tells us to move on, but our souls are still tied to the place we need to leave behind. That causes a divided heart, and when we have divided hearts it is difficult to find peace of mind.

Jesus said, "No one can serve two masters; for either he will hate the one and love the other, or he will be devoted to the one and despise the other . . . " (Matthew 6:24). In James 1:8 we read that a person who is double-minded is unstable and restless about everything he thinks, feels, or decides.

We need to avoid having a double heart and a dual purpose in life. Instead, we should be decisive people. Leaders especially should be able to make decisions and then stick to them. If we make decisions and then continue to go back and forth in our minds about whether we did the right thing or not, we are unstable in our ways. We need to hear from God, and then make a decision based on what He has said to us. Once we have decided something, we need to do it with all our hearts, putting our whole selves into it.

Also, we need to be focused and single-hearted with respect to God's gifts and calling. In Romans 12:6–8 the apostle Paul talks about the different gifts of grace that have been given to the individual members of the body of Christ. He says that if you are a teacher, you should give yourself to your teaching. If you are a giver, you should give generously. If you are an encourager, you should excel in encouraging people. In other words, Paul says not to get overly involved in things God has not gifted you for and called you to do, but to focus on what you are called to do. Resist the temptation to get entangled in things that do not help you accomplish your goals. Do not be double-minded. If you believe you are supposed to do something specific with your life, then be consistent in it. Stay on track and remain focused and stable, always pressing toward your goal through the power of the Holy Spirit.

lords (governors) of the Philistines after consultation sent him away, saying, "At *the cost of* our heads he may defect to his master Saul." [1 Sam 29:2–9]

²⁰As David went to Ziklag, *these men* defected to him from Manasseh: Adnah, Jozabad, Jediael, Michael, Jozabad, Elihu, and Zillethai, captains of thousands who belonged to Manasseh.

²¹They helped David against the band of raiders, for they were all courageous men, and [all seven] became commanders in his army.

²²For day by day men kept coming to David to help him, until there was a great army, like the army of God.

²³These are the numbers of the [armed] units equipped for war who came to David at Hebron to turn [over] the kingdom of Saul to him, in accordance with the word of the LORD.

²⁴Those of the tribe of Judah who carried shield and spear were 6,800, armed for war;

²⁵of the tribe of Simeon, brave warriors, 7,100;

²⁶of the tribe of Levi, 4,600.

²⁷Jehoiada was the leader of [the house of] Aaron, and with him were 3,700,

²⁸and Zadok, a courageous young man, and twenty-two captains from his father's house.

²⁹Of the tribe of Benjamin, the relatives of [King] Saul, 3,000; for until now the majority of them had kept their allegiance to the house of Saul.

³⁰Of the tribe of Ephraim, 20,800, courageous men, famous in their fathers' houses.

³¹Of the half-tribe of Manasseh, 18,000, who were designated by name to come and make David king.

³²Of the tribe of Issachar, men who understood the times, with knowledge of what Israel should do, two hundred chiefs; and all their relatives were at their command;

³³of the tribe of Zebulun, there were 50,000 in military service who could draw up in battle formation with all kinds of weapons of war and helped *David, men* with an undivided heart.

³⁴Of the tribe of Naphtali, *there were* 1,000 captains, and with them 37,000 [of the rank and file armed] with shield and spear.

³⁵Of the tribe of Dan, 28,600 men who could draw up in battle formation.

³⁶Of the tribe of Asher, 40,000 men in military service, able to draw up in battle formation.

³⁷From the other side [east] of the Jordan *River*, of [the tribes of] Reuben and Gad and the half-tribe of Manasseh, 120,000 men, *armed* with all kinds of weapons of war for the battle.

³⁸All these, being men of war arrayed in battle formation, came to Hebron with a perfect (committed) heart to make David king over all Israel; and all the rest of Israel were also of one mind to make David king.

³⁹They were there with David for three days, eating and drinking, for their relatives had prepared for them.

⁴⁰Also those who were [living] near them [from] as far as [the tribes of] Issachar, Zebulun, and Naphtali, brought food on donkeys, camels, mules, and oxen, abundant supplies of flour, cakes of figs and raisins, wine, [olive] oil, oxen, and sheep, for there was joy in Israel.

speak the Word

God, I pray that You would make me like the men of Issachar and give me understanding of the times, so that I will know what I should do.
—ADAPTED FROM 1 CHRONICLES 12:32

13 DAVID CONSULTED with the captains of the thousands and the hundreds, even with every leader.

²David said to all the assembly of Israel, "If it seems good to you, and if it is from the LORD our God, let us send *word* everywhere to our fellow countrymen who remain in all the land of Israel, and to the priests and Levites who are with them in their cities with pasture lands, so that they may meet with us;

³and let us bring back the ark of our God to us, for we did not seek it during the days of Saul."

⁴Then all the assembly agreed to do so, for the thing was right in the eyes of all the people.

⁵So David gathered all Israel together, from the Shihor [watercourse] of Egypt, to the entrance of Hamath [in the north], to bring the ark of God from Kiriath-jearim.

⁶David and all Israel went up to Baalah, *that is,* to Kiriath-jearim, which belongs to Judah, to bring up from there the ark of God the LORD who sits enthroned *above* the cherubim, *the ark* which is called by *His* name.

⁷They carried the ark of God on a new cart and brought it out of the house of Abinadab, and Uzza and Ahio [his brother] drove the cart.

⁸David and all Israel celebrated [joyfully] before God with all their might,

with songs, lyres, harps, tambourines, cymbals, and trumpets.

⁹When they came to the threshing floor of Chidon, Uzza put out his hand to hold *and* steady the ark, for the oxen [that were drawing the cart] nearly overturned it.

¹⁰The anger of the LORD burned against Uzza, and He struck him down because he touched the ark; and there he died before God. [Num 4:15]

¹¹David became angry because of the LORD's outburst against Uzza; so that place is called Perez-uzza to this day.

¹²David was afraid of God that day, and he said, "How can I bring the ark of God *home* with me?"

¹³So David did not bring the ark with him to the City of David, but took it aside to the house of Obed-edom the Gittite. [Josh 21:20, 24; 1 Chr 15:24]

¹⁴So the ark of God remained with the family of Obed-edom in his house three months; and the LORD blessed the house of Obed-edom and all that he had.

14 NOW HIRAM king of Tyre sent messengers to David with cedar timbers, masons and carpenters, to build a house (palace) for him.

²And David understood that the LORD had established *and* confirmed him as king over Israel, for his kingdom was highly exalted for the sake of His people Israel.

³Then David took more wives at Jerusalem, and he became the father of more sons and daughters.

⁴Now these are the names of the children born [to him] in Jerusalem: Shammua, Shobab, Nathan, Solomon,

⁵Ibhar, Elishua, Elpelet,

⁶Nogah, Nepheg, Japhia,

⁷Elishama, Beeliada, and Eliphelet.

⁸When the Philistines heard that David had been anointed king over all Israel, they all went up in search

putting the Word to work

When you are facing a challenge, do you depend on your own wits to see you through or do you seek the counsel of others? David, even with all of his might and power, knew the value of trusted counsel (see 1 Chronicles 13:1). Seek people who can provide upright and reliable counsel to you, and avail yourself of their wisdom.

of David; and he heard about it and went out against them.

9Now the Philistines had come and made a raid in the Valley of Rephaim.

10So David inquired of God, "Shall I go up against the Philistines? And will You hand them over to me?" Then the LORD said to him, "Go up, and I will hand them over to you."

11So Israel came up to Baal-perazim, and David defeated the Philistines there. Then David said, "God has broken through my enemies by my hand, like the breakthrough of waters." Therefore they named that place Baal-perazim.

12The Philistines abandoned their gods (idols) there; so David gave a command and they were burned in a fire [as the Law of Moses required]. [Deut 7:5]

13The Philistines again made a raid in the valley.

14So David inquired again of God, and God said to him, "Do not go up after them; circle around behind them and come at them in front of the balsam trees.

15"It shall be when you hear the sound of marching in the tops of the balsam trees, then you shall go out to battle, for God has gone out before you to strike the Philistine army."

16So David did just as God had commanded him, and they struck down the army of the Philistines from Gibeon as far as Gezer.

17Then David's fame spread into all the lands; and the LORD caused all nations to fear him.

15 DAVID BUILT houses for himself in the City of David; and he prepared a place for the ark of God and pitched a tent for it.

2Then David said, "No one is to carry the ark of God except the Levites; for the LORD chose them to carry the ark of God and to minister to Him forever."

3And David assembled all Israel at Jerusalem to bring up the ark of the LORD to the place which he had prepared for it.

4David gathered together the sons of Aaron and the Levites:

5of the sons of Kohath, Uriel the chief, with 120 of his relatives;

6of the sons of Merari, Asaiah the chief, with 220 of his relatives;

7of the sons of Gershom, Joel the chief, with 130 of his relatives;

8of the sons of Elizaphan, Shemaiah the chief, with 200 of his relatives;

9of the sons of Hebron, Eliel the chief, with 80 of his relatives;

10of the sons of Uzziel, Amminadab the chief, with 112 of his relatives.

11Then David called for Zadok and Abiathar the priests, and for the Levites—Uriel, Asaiah, Joel, Shemaiah, Eliel, and Amminadab,

12and he said to them, "You are the heads of the fathers' *households* of the Levites; consecrate yourselves, both you and your relatives, so that you may bring up the ark of the LORD God of Israel, to *the place* that I have prepared for it.

13"Because you did not [carry it as God directed] the first time, the LORD our God made an [angry] outburst against us, for we did not seek Him in accordance with the ordinance." [Num 1:50; 1 Chr 13:7–10]

14So the priests and the Levites consecrated (dedicated) themselves to bring up the ark of the LORD God of Israel.

15The Levites carried the ark of God on their shoulders with the poles, as Moses commanded in accordance with the word of the LORD.

16Then David told the chiefs of the Levites to appoint their relatives as the singers, with instruments of music—harps, lyres, and cymbals—to play loudly *and* to raise sounds of joy [with their voices].

[17]So the Levites appointed Heman the son of Joel, and from his relatives, Asaph the son of Berechiah; and from the sons of Merari their relatives, Ethan the son of Kushaiah,

[18]and with them their relatives of the second rank: Zechariah, Ben, Jaaziel, Shemiramoth, Jehiel, Unni, Eliab, Benaiah, Maaseiah, Mattithiah, Eliphelehu, and Mikneiah, Obed-edom, and Jeiel, the gatekeepers.

[19]So the singers, Heman, Asaph, and Ethan *were appointed* to sound aloud the bronze cymbals;

[20]and Zechariah, Aziel, Shemiramoth, Jehiel, Unni, Eliab, Maaseiah, and Benaiah [were to play] with harps *tuned* to Alamoth [that is, a high pitch];

[21]and Mattithiah, Eliphelehu, Mikneiah, Obed-edom, Jeiel, and Azaziah were to lead with lyres set to Sheminith [that is, the eighth string, a low pitch].

[22]Chenaniah, leader of the Levites, was *in charge of* the singing; he gave instruction in singing because he was skilled.

[23]Berechiah and Elkanah were gatekeepers for the ark.

[24]Shebaniah, Joshaphat, Nethanel, Amasai, Zechariah, Benaiah, and Eliezer the priests blew the trumpets before the ark of God. Obed-edom and Jehiah (Jeiel) were also gatekeepers for the ark.

[25]So David, with the elders of Israel and the captains over thousands, went to bring up the ark of the covenant of the LORD from the house of Obed-edom with joy.

[26]Because God was helping the Levites who carried the ark of the covenant of the LORD [to do it carefully and safely], they sacrificed seven bulls and seven rams.

[27]David was clothed with a robe of fine linen, as were all the Levites who carried the ark, and the singers and Chenaniah, director of the music of the singers. David also wore an ephod (a priestly upper garment) of linen.

[28]Thus all Israel brought up the ark of the covenant of the LORD with shouting, and with the sound of the horn, with trumpets, with loud-sounding cymbals, with harps and lyres.

[29]It happened that as the ark of the covenant of the LORD came to the City of David, Michal [David's wife] the daughter of Saul, looking down through a window, saw King David leaping and dancing [in celebration]; and she despised him in her heart.

16

SO THEY brought the ark of God and set it inside the tent which David had pitched for it, and they offered burnt offerings and peace offerings before God.

[2]When David had finished offering the burnt offerings and the peace offerings, he blessed the people in the name of the LORD.

[3]He distributed to everyone in Israel, both man and woman, to everyone a loaf of bread, a portion *of meat,* and a raisin cake.

[4]He appointed some of the Levites to minister before the ark of the LORD and to profess [God's name] and to thank and praise the LORD, the God of Israel:

[5]Asaph the chief, and second to him Zechariah, *then* Jeiel (Jaaziel), Shemiramoth, Jehiel, Mattithiah, Eliab, Benaiah, Obed-edom, and Jeiel with musical instruments, harps and lyres; also Asaph *played* loud-sounding cymbals;

[6]and Benaiah and Jahaziel the priests *blew* trumpets continually before the ark of the covenant of God.

[7]Then on that day David first entrusted to Asaph and his relatives to give thanks to the LORD [as their chief task].

take a praise pause

When the ark of God was placed in the tabernacle, David stopped everything and began to worship God (see 1 Chronicles 16:1–7). I do not think anything blesses God more than when we stop right in the middle of what we are doing and lift our hands to worship Him, or take a moment to bow down before Him and say, "I love You, Lord." In Psalm 119:164, the psalmist says he took time to praise God seven times a day and all day long too!

Think about a businessman, for example, maybe the president of a large company. Wouldn't it be wonderful if several times a day, he closed the door to his office, turned the lock, knelt, and said, "God, I just want to take some time to worship You. Father, all these things You are giving me—the business, the money, the success—are great, but I just want to worship You. I magnify You. You are so wonderful. I love You. You are all I need. Father, I worship You. Jesus, I worship You. Holy Spirit, I worship You." I do not think a businessman with such a habit would ever need to be concerned about his business, his finances, or his success. All of those things would be taken care of (see Matthew 6:33).

The same is true for students, stay-at-home moms, retired people, secretaries, flight attendants, brain surgeons, clerks, and salespeople—anyone you can think of. All of them would have many more fruitful, productive, and peaceful days if they took time to praise the Lord throughout the day.

We all would benefit greatly from taking a "praise pause." I encourage you to take one today.

8 O give thanks to the LORD, call on His name;
Make His deeds known among the people.
9 Sing to Him, sing praises to Him;
Speak of all His wonders.
10 Glory in His holy name;
Let the hearts of those who seek the LORD rejoice.
11 Seek the LORD and His strength;
Seek His face continually [longing to be in His presence].
12 Remember [with gratitude] His marvelous deeds which He has done,

His miracles and the judgments from His mouth,
13 O seed of Israel His servant,
Children of Jacob, His chosen ones!
14 He is the LORD our God;
His judgments are in all the earth.
15 Be mindful of His covenant forever,
The promise which He commanded and established to a thousand generations,
16 The covenant which He made with Abraham,

speak the Word

*I give thanks to You, God, and I call upon Your name.
I will make known Your deeds among the people around me.
I will sing praise to You and speak of all Your wonders!*
—ADAPTED FROM 1 CHRONICLES 16:8, 9

And His oath (sworn promise) to
Isaac.
¹⁷He confirmed it as a statute to
Jacob,
And to Israel as an everlasting
covenant, [Gen 35:11, 12]
¹⁸Saying, "To you I will give the land
of Canaan,
As the portion of your possession
and inheritance."
¹⁹When you were few in number,
Even a very few, and strangers
in it,
²⁰When they wandered from nation
to nation,
And from *one* kingdom to another
people,
²¹He allowed no man to oppress *or*
exploit them,
And, He reproved *and* punished
kings for their sakes, *saying,*
[Gen 12:17; 20:3; Ex 7:15–18]
²²"Do not touch My anointed ones,
And do My prophets no harm."
[Gen 20:7]
²³Sing to the LORD, all the earth;
Proclaim the good news of His
salvation from day to day.
²⁴Declare His glory among the
nations,

life point

Reverential fear, as is mentioned in
1 Chronicles 16:25, is to know that God is
God and that He means business. He has
called us His friends (see John 15:14, 15)
and His children, but He is still an awesome, holy God. We need to honor Him,
respect Him, obey Him, and revere Him in
all things.

speak the Word

putting the Word to work

1 Chronicles 16:7–36 helps us understand the value and necessity of
thanksgiving. What are you most
thankful for? Be sure to give thanks
to God every day. Like David, remember to thank Him for His wondrous
works, for His everlasting mercy, for
the good news of His salvation, for
His beauty and holiness, and for His
goodness. Keep your thank-tank full
and you, like David, will marvel at the
greatness of God.

His marvelous works among all
peoples.
²⁵For great is the LORD, and greatly to
be praised;
He is also to be feared [with awe-
filled reverence] above all gods.
²⁶For all the gods of the peoples are
[lifeless] idols,
But the LORD made the heavens.
²⁷Splendor and majesty are [found]
in His presence;
Strength and joy are [found] in His
place (sanctuary).
²⁸Ascribe to the LORD, O families of
the peoples,
Ascribe to the LORD glory *and*
honor and strength.
²⁹Ascribe to the LORD the glory *and*
honor due His name;
Bring an offering [of
thanksgiving], and come before
Him;
Worship the LORD in the splendor
of holiness.
³⁰Tremble [reverently] before Him,
all the earth;

*Thank You, God, that splendor, majesty, strength,
and joy are found in Your presence.*
–ADAPTED FROM 1 CHRONICLES 16:27

The world is firmly established, it will not be moved.

31 Let the heavens be glad, and let the earth rejoice;
And let them say among the nations, "The LORD reigns."

32 Let the sea roar, and all the things that fill it;
Let the field rejoice, and all that is in it.

33 Then the trees of the forest will sing for joy before the LORD;
For He comes to judge *and* govern the earth.

34 O give thanks to the LORD, for *He is* good;
For His lovingkindness endures forever.

35 Then say, "Save us, O God of our salvation;
Gather us together and rescue us from the nations,
That we may give thanks to Your holy name,
And glory in Your praise."

36 Blessed be the LORD, the God of Israel,
Forever and ever.

And all the people said, "Amen," and praised the LORD.

37 So David left Asaph and his relatives there before the ark of the covenant of the LORD to minister before the ark continually, as each day's work required;

life point

David loved God very much, yet he made serious mistakes. His passions gained mastery over him and caused him to commit adultery and have a man murdered. I believe David talked so much about the mercy of God (one example is in 1 Chronicles 16:34) because he had experienced it firsthand in his life and ministry. That same mercy is available today to all who will seek God for it.

life point

When I was learning to hear from God and desiring with all my heart to be led by the Spirit, 1 Chronicles 17:1–4 really helped me to realize that we can move about with some degree of freedom following our sanctified desires, as long as we are ready to immediately go in another direction if God shows us we need to do so. It is not wrong to have a plan and follow it if we are willing to give up that plan when God does not approve of it.

In John 15:7 Jesus said, "If you remain in Me and My words remain in you [that is, if we are vitally united and My message lives in your heart], ask whatever you wish and it will be done for you." How can this be possible unless there really is a merging of our desires with God's as we mature in Him?

The goal of every true believer is to be one with God. This happens spiritually when we are born again; and it occurs in our minds, wills, and emotions as we grow and mature spiritually. In Ephesians 4:15 the apostle Paul urges us, "Let us grow up in all things into Him [following His example] who is the Head—Christ." As we do so, our desires become His desires, and we are safe in acting on them.

38 and Obed-edom with his sixty-eight relatives; also Obed-edom the son of Jeduthun, and Hosah, were to be gatekeepers.

39 *David left* Zadok the priest and his relatives the priests before the dwelling place (tabernacle) of the LORD in the high place which was at Gibeon, [1 Chr 21:29]

40 to offer burnt offerings to the LORD on the altar of burnt offering continually, morning and evening, in accordance with all that is written in

the Law of the LORD, which He commanded Israel.

⁴¹With them were Heman and Jeduthun, and the rest who were chosen and designated by name, to give thanks to the LORD, for His lovingkindness endures forever.

⁴²With them were Heman and Jeduthun *with* trumpets and cymbals for those who *were to* sound aloud, and instruments for [accompanying] the songs of God. And the sons of Jeduthun were to be at the gate.

⁴³Then all the people departed, each to his house, and David returned [home] to bless his household.

17

AS DAVID sat in his house (palace), he said to Nathan the prophet, "Behold, I live in a house of cedars, while the ark of the covenant of the LORD is under tent curtains."

²Then Nathan said to David, "Do all that is in your heart, for God is with you."

³But it came about that same night that the word of God came to Nathan, saying,

⁴"Go and tell David My servant, 'Thus says the LORD, "You shall not build a house for Me to dwell in;

⁵for I have not dwelt in a house since the day that I brought Israel up [from

words and actions

Must we always have a specific word from God before we take any action? I do not think so. David wanted to build a house for God, and the prophet Nathan told him to do all that was in his heart, for God was with him (see 1 Chronicles 17:1–4). That night, however, God spoke to David through Nathan and gave instructions that David was not to build His house, but that one of his sons would do it (see 1 Chronicles 17:11).

It seems to me that the general guideline on taking action is simply to follow our hearts unless God gives a specific word. We are told in Proverbs 3:6 to acknowledge God in all of our ways and He will remove the obstacles that block our way. To acknowledge God means to care about what He thinks. We are never told in Scripture that we must have specific direction from God before taking any action at all. God gives us wisdom, and He expects us to use it. As we study His Word we learn His ways, and He expects us to follow them. God gives us freedom; He believes in us and believes we can make good choices, and He lets us do so. In all our prayers we should tell our Lord that we want His will in all things and then trust Him to lead and guide us.

Note that David was planning to build God a house until the moment God said no. When He did, David immediately praised God for choosing one of his family members and never showed any disappointment or rebellion against God's choice. David had a heart after God. He wanted what God wanted.

This story was particularly helpful to me as a young believer who wanted God's will, but did not know what to do when God was not speaking. I learned that because we have His Spirit and heart, we should trust the inner witness that we sense about what we should or should not do. Do what you believe to be best based on the knowledge you have, and be willing to change if and when God shows you something definite.

Egypt] until this day, but I have gone from tent to tent and from *one* dwelling place *to another*.

6"Wherever I have walked with all Israel, did I say a word to any of the judges of Israel, whom I commanded to shepherd My people, saying, 'Why have you not built for Me a house of cedar?' " '

7"Now, therefore, this is what you shall say to My servant David: 'Thus says the LORD of hosts, "I took you from the pasture, from following the sheep, to be leader over My people Israel.

8"I have been with you wherever you have gone, and I have cut off all your enemies from before you; and I will make your name like the name of the great ones of the earth.

9"I will appoint a place for My people Israel, and will plant them, so that they may live in their own place and not be moved again [nor tremble with fear]; and the wicked will not waste (persecute) them anymore, as formerly,

10since the time that I commanded judges to be over My people Israel. And I will humble *and* subdue all your enemies.

"**F**urthermore, I tell you that the LORD will build you a house (a blessed posterity).

11"And it shall come to pass that when your days are completed and you must go to be with your fathers [in death], I will raise up *one of* your descendants after you, one of your own sons; and I will establish his kingdom.

12"He shall build Me a house, and I will establish his throne forever. [1 Chr 28:7]

13"I will be his father and he shall be My son; and I will not take My steadfast love *and* mercy away from him,

as I took it from him (King Saul) who was before you. [Heb 1:5, 6]

14"But I will settle him in My house and in My kingdom forever, and his throne shall be established forevermore." ' " [Is 9:7]

15According to all these words and according to all this vision, so Nathan spoke to David.

16Then David the king went in and sat before the LORD and said, "Who am I, O LORD God, and what is my house *and* family that You have brought me this far?

17"This was a small thing in Your eyes, O God; but You have spoken of Your servant's house for a great while to come, and have regarded me according to the standard *and* estate of a man of high degree (prominence), O LORD God.

18"What more can David say to You for the honor *granted to* Your servant? For You know Your servant.

19"O LORD, for Your servant's sake, and in accordance with Your own heart, You have accomplished all this greatness, to make known all these great things.

20"O LORD, there is no one like You, nor is there any God except You, according to all that we have heard with our ears.

21"And what one nation on the earth is like Your people Israel, whom God went to redeem for Himself as a people, to make a name for Yourself by great and awesome *and* terrible things, by driving out nations from before Your people, whom You redeemed out of Egypt?

22"You made Your people Israel Your own people forever, and You, LORD, became their God.

23"Therefore now, O LORD, let the word which You have spoken concerning Your servant and his house endure forever, and do as You have said.

speak the Word

God, I thank You that the word You have spoken concerning me and my household will endure and do as You have said.
—ADAPTED FROM 1 CHRONICLES 17:23

²⁴"Let Your name [and the character that it denotes] endure and be magnified forever, saying, 'The Lᴏʀᴅ of hosts is the God of Israel, yes, a God to Israel; and the house of Your servant David is established before You.'

²⁵"For You, O my God, have revealed to Your servant that You will build for him a house (descendants); therefore Your servant has found *courage* to pray before You.

²⁶"And now, O Lᴏʀᴅ, You are God, and you have spoken *and* promised this good thing to Your servant.

²⁷"Therefore may it please You to bless the house (descendants) of Your servant, that it may continue before You forever; for what You bless, O Lᴏʀᴅ, is blessed forever."

18 AFTER THIS it came about that David defeated and subdued the Philistines, and he took Gath and its villages out of the hand of the Philistines.

²He defeated Moab, and the Moabites became David's servants and brought tribute (gifts).

³David also defeated Hadadezer king of Zobah *as far as* Hamath, as he went to establish his dominion to the Euphrates River.

⁴David took from him 1,000 chariots, 7,000 horsemen, and 20,000 foot soldiers (infantrymen). David also hamstrung [nearly] all the chariot horses [to make them lame and useless], but left enough of them for 100 chariots.

⁵When the Arameans (Syrians) of Damascus came to help Hadadezer king of Zobah, David killed 22,000 of the Arameans.

⁶Then David put *military outposts* among the Arameans in Damascus; and the Arameans became David's servants and brought tribute. Thus the Lᴏʀᴅ helped David wherever he went.

⁷David took the shields of gold which were carried by the servants of Hadadezer and brought them to Jerusalem.

⁸Likewise from Tibhath and from Cun, cities of Hadadezer, David brought a very large amount of bronze, with which Solomon later made the bronze Sea (large basin), the pillars, and the utensils of bronze. [1 Kin 7:13–47; 2 Chr 4:2–18]

⁹When Tou king of Hamath heard how David had defeated all the army of Hadadezer king of Zobah,

¹⁰he sent Hadoram his son to King David to greet him and to bless (congratulate) him, because he had fought against Hadadezer and had defeated him; for Hadadezer had been at war with Tou. And *Hadoram brought* all kinds of articles of gold and silver and bronze.

¹¹King David also dedicated these to the Lᴏʀᴅ [setting them apart for sacred use], with the silver and the gold which he brought from all the nations: from Edom, Moab, the Ammonites, the Philistines, and from Amalek.

¹²Also Abishai the son of Zeruiah [David's half sister] defeated 18,000 Edomites in the Valley of Salt.

¹³He put military outposts in Edom, and all the Edomites became David's servants. Thus the Lᴏʀᴅ helped David wherever he went.

¹⁴So David reigned over all Israel and administered justice and righteousness for all his people.

¹⁵Joab the son of Zeruiah was in command of the army, and Jehoshaphat the son of Ahilud was the recorder;

¹⁶Zadok the son of Ahitub and Abimelech the son of Abiathar were the priests, and Shavsha was secretary (state scribe);

speak the Word

Thank You, Lord, that You are God and You have promised good things to me!
– ᴀᴅᴀᴘᴛᴇᴅ ꜰʀᴏᴍ 1 Cʜʀᴏɴɪᴄʟᴇs 17:26

¹⁷and Benaiah the son of Jehoiada was in charge of the Cherethites and the Pelethites [David's bodyguards], and the sons of David were chiefs at the king's side.

19 NOW IT came about after this, that Nahash king of the Ammonites died, and his son became king in his place.

²David said, "I will be kind (gracious) to Hanun son of Nahash, because his father was kind to me." So David sent messengers to comfort him concerning [the death of] his father. And the servants of David came to the land of the Ammonites to comfort Hanun.

³But the leaders of the Ammonites said to Hanun, "Do you think that David has sent people to console *and* comfort you because he honors your father? Have his servants not come to you to search and to overthrow and to spy out the land?"

⁴Therefore Hanun took David's servants, shaved them [cutting off half their beards], and cut off their garments in the middle as far as their buttocks, and sent them away [in humiliation].

⁵When David was told how the men were treated, he sent *messengers* to meet them, for they were very humiliated *and* ashamed [to return]. So the king said, "Stay in Jericho until your beards grow [back], and *then* return."

⁶When the Ammonites saw that they had made themselves hateful to David, Hanun and his people sent 1,000 talents of silver to hire for themselves chariots and horsemen from Mesopotamia, Aram-maacah, and Zobah.

⁷So they hired for themselves 32,000 chariots and the king of Maacah and his troops, who came and camped before Medeba. And the Ammonites gathered together from their cities and came to battle.

⁸When David heard *about it*, he sent Joab and all the army of courageous men.

⁹The Ammonites came out and lined up in battle formation at the entrance of the city [Medeba], while the kings who had come were by themselves in the open country.

¹⁰Now when Joab saw that the battle was set against him in the front and in the rear, he chose *warriors* from all the choice men of Israel and put them in formation against the Arameans (Syrians).

¹¹The rest of the soldiers he placed in the hand of Abishai his brother, and they lined up against the Ammonites.

¹²He said, "If the Arameans are too strong for me, then you shall help me; but if the Ammonites are too strong for you, I will help you.

¹³"Be strong and let us show ourselves courageous for the sake of our people and for the cities of our God; and may the LORD do what is good in His sight."

¹⁴So Joab and the people who were with him approached the Arameans for battle, and they fled before him.

¹⁵When the Ammonites saw that the Arameans fled, they also fled before Abishai, Joab's brother, and entered the city [Medeba]. Then Joab came to Jerusalem.

¹⁶When the Arameans (Syrians) saw that they had been defeated by Israel, they sent messengers and brought out the Arameans who were beyond the [Euphrates] River, with Shophach the commander of the army of Hadadezer leading them.

¹⁷When this was told to David, he gathered all Israel and crossed the Jordan, and came upon them and drew up in formation against them. So when David drew up in battle array against the Arameans, they fought against him.

¹⁸But the Arameans fled before Israel, and David killed of the Arameans 7,000 charioteers and 40,000 foot soldiers, and put to death Shophach the commander of the army.

¹⁹When the servants of Hadadezer saw that they had been defeated by Israel, they made peace with David and became subject to *and* served him. And the Arameans (Syrians) were not willing to help the Ammonites anymore.

20 THEN IT happened at the end of the year, at the time when kings go out *to battle,* Joab led out the army and ravaged *and* devastated the land of the Ammonites, and came and besieged Rabbah. But David stayed at Jerusalem [with Bathsheba]. Joab struck Rabbah and overthrew it. [2 Sam 12:24–29]

²David took the crown of their king from his head and found that it weighed a talent of gold and that there was a precious stone in it; so it was set on David's head. He also brought a very great amount of spoil (plunder) out of the city [of Rabbah].

³He brought out the people who were in it, and put them [to work] with saws, iron picks, and axes. David dealt *in this way* with all the Ammonite cities. Then David and all the people returned to Jerusalem.

⁴Now it came about after this that war broke out at Gezer with the Philistines; then Sibbecai the Hushathite killed Sippai, one of the descendants of the giants, and they were subdued.

⁵There was war again with the Philistines, and Elhanan the son of Jair killed Lahmi the brother of Goliath the Gittite, the shaft of whose spear was like a weaver's beam.

⁶Again there was war at Gath, where there was a man of *great* stature who had twenty-four fingers and toes, six *fingers on each hand* and six *toes on each foot;* and he also was descended from the giants.

⁷When he taunted Israel, Jonathan the son of Shimea, David's brother, killed him.

⁸These were descended from the giants in Gath, and they fell by the hand of David and by the hand of his servants.

21 SATAN [THE adversary] stood up against Israel and incited David to count [the population of] Israel.

²So David said to Joab and the leaders of the people, "Go, count Israel from Beersheba to Dan, and bring me their total, so that I may know it."

³Joab said, "May the Lord add to His people a hundred times as many as they are! But, my lord the king, are they not all my lord's servants? Why then does my lord require this? Why will he bring guilt on Israel?"

⁴But the king's word prevailed over Joab. So Joab left and went throughout all Israel and came to Jerusalem.

⁵Then Joab gave the total of the census of the people to David. And all Israel were 1,100,000 men who drew the sword; and in Judah 470,000 men who drew the sword.

⁶But he did not count Levi and Benjamin among them, because the king's order was detestable to Joab.

⁷Now God was displeased with this act [of arrogance and pride], and He struck Israel.

⁸Then David said to God, "I have sinned greatly because I have done this thing. But now, I beseech You, take away the wickedness *and* guilt of Your servant, for I have acted very foolishly."

⁹And the Lord said to Gad, David's seer,

¹⁰"Go and tell David, saying, 'Thus says the Lord, "I offer you three *choices;* choose for yourself one of them, which I will do to you [as punishment for your sin]." ' "

¹¹So Gad came to David and said to him, "Thus says the Lord: 'Choose for yourself

¹²either three years of famine, or

three months to be swept away before your enemies, while the sword of your enemies overtakes you, or else three days of the sword of the Lord and plague in the land, and the angel of the Lord bringing destruction throughout all the territory of Israel.' Now therefore, consider what answer I shall return to Him who sent me."

¹³David said to Gad, "I am in great distress; please let me fall into the hands of the Lord, for His mercies are very great; but do not let me fall into the hand of man."

¹⁴So the Lord sent a plague on Israel, and 70,000 men of Israel fell.

¹⁵God sent an angel to Jerusalem to destroy it; and as he was destroying it, the Lord looked, and relented concerning the catastrophe and said to the destroying angel, "It is enough; now remove your hand [of judgment]." And the angel of the Lord was standing by the threshing floor of Ornan the Jebusite.

¹⁶Then David raised his eyes and saw the angel of the Lord standing between earth and heaven, having a drawn sword in his hand stretched out over Jerusalem. Then David and the elders, covered in sackcloth, fell on their faces.

¹⁷David said to God, "Is it not I who commanded the people to be counted? I am the one who has sinned and done evil; but as for these sheep [the people of Israel], what have they done? O Lord my God, please let Your hand be against me and my father's house, but not against Your people that they should be plagued."

¹⁸Then the angel of the Lord commanded Gad to say to David, that David should go up and build an altar to the Lord on the threshing floor of Ornan the Jebusite.

¹⁹So David went up at Gad's word, which he spoke in the name of the Lord.

²⁰Now Ornan was threshing wheat, and he turned back and saw the angel; and his four sons who were with him hid themselves.

²¹As David came to Ornan, Ornan looked and saw him, and went out from the threshing floor and bowed down before David with his face to the ground.

²²Then David said to Ornan, "Give me the site of this threshing floor, so that I may build an altar on it to the Lord. You shall charge me the full price for it, so that the plague may be averted from the people."

²³Ornan said to David, "Take it for yourself; and let my lord the king do what is good in his eyes. See, I will give you the oxen also for burnt offerings and the threshing sledges (heavy wooden platforms) for wood and the wheat for the grain offering; I give it all."

²⁴But King David said to Ornan, "No, I will certainly pay the full price; for I will not take what is yours for the Lord, nor offer a burnt offering which costs me nothing."

²⁵So David gave Ornan 600 shekels of gold by weight for the site. [2 Chr 3:1]

²⁶Then David built an altar to the Lord there and presented burnt offerings and peace offerings. And he called on the Lord, and He answered him with fire from heaven on the altar of burnt offering.

²⁷Then the Lord commanded the [avenging] angel, and he put his sword back into its sheath.

²⁸At that time, when David saw that the Lord had answered him on the threshing floor of Ornan the Jebusite, he sacrificed there.

²⁹For the tabernacle of the Lord, which Moses made in the wilderness, and the altar of burnt offering were at that time in the high place at Gibeon.

³⁰But David could not go before it to inquire of God, for he was terrified by the sword of the angel of the Lord.

22

THEN DAVID said, "This is the house of the LORD God, and this is the altar of burnt offering for Israel."

²So David gave orders to gather the foreigners who were in the land of Israel, and he assigned stonecutters to hew out stones to build the house of God.

³David prepared large quantities of iron to make nails for the doors of the gates and for the clamps (trusses), and more bronze than could be weighed;

⁴and cedar trees beyond number, for the Sidonians and Tyrians brought large quantities of cedar timber to David.

⁵David said, "Solomon my son is young and inexperienced, and the house that is to be built for the LORD shall be exceedingly magnificent, famous, and an object of glory *and* splendor throughout all lands [of the earth]. So now I will make preparations for it." Therefore, David made ample preparations before his death.

⁶Then he called for Solomon his son and ordered him to build a house for the LORD, the God of Israel.

⁷David said to Solomon, "My son, I had intended to build a house for the Name (Presence) of the LORD my God.

⁸"But the word of the LORD came to me, saying, 'You have shed much blood and have waged great wars; you shall not build a house for My Name, because you have shed so much blood on the earth before me.

⁹'Behold, a son will be born to you,

putting the Word to work

Have you ever been disappointed when someone else was given the privilege of doing something in ministry that you wanted to do? Rather than be frustrated or discouraged, you can follow David's example in 1 Chronicles 22:6–11. Bless the efforts of others; pray for them that they might have wisdom; and encourage them to keep following the Lord in all they do, that they might prosper. God will be faithful to honor you.

who will be a man of peace. I will give him rest from all his enemies on every side; for his name shall be Solomon, and I will give peace and quiet to Israel in his days. [2 Sam 12:24, 25]

¹⁰'He shall build a house for My Name (Presence). He shall be My son and I will be his father; and I will establish his royal throne over Israel forever.'

¹¹"Now, my son, may the LORD be with you so that you may be successful and build the house of the LORD your God, just as He has spoken concerning you.

¹²"Only may the LORD give you wisdom and understanding, and give you charge over Israel, so that you may keep the law of the LORD your God.

¹³"Then you will prosper, if you are careful to observe *and* fulfill the statutes and ordinances which the LORD commanded Moses concerning Israel.

putting the Word to work

Many of us spend hours preparing for a special event, a big project at work, or a test at school. David did all he could do to prepare for the building of the temple (see 1 Chronicles 22:1–5). Will you put the same diligent preparation into the work God calls you to do?

life point

First Chronicles 22:13 warns us not to fear or be dismayed. Fear and dismay will not only keep us from fulfilling God's Word, but will also hinder our prosperity. Fear never brings a blessing. Instead of being dismayed over the things that frighten you, take courage in the Lord.

Be strong and courageous, do not fear nor be dismayed.

¹⁴"Now listen, with great trouble I have prepared *and* provided for the house of the LORD 100,000 talents of gold, 1,000,000 talents of silver, and bronze and iron beyond weighing, for they are great in quantity. I have also prepared *and* provided timber and stone, and you may add to them.

¹⁵"Further, you have workmen in abundance: stonecutters and stonemasons and carpenters, and all men who are skillful in every kind of work.

¹⁶"As for the gold, the silver, the

life point

King David was an exceptional leader for many reasons, but what stands out to me about him in 1 Chronicles 22:14 is that he took a lead role in providing for the house of God even while he was troubled and afflicted. He did not expect others to do what he would not do, and he wanted to make sure that a good example for giving had been set so that all the people would follow. That's what an effective leader does—leads by example even when it requires pain or sacrifice.

give when it hurts

God said that David was a man after His own heart—one who would do all of His will and carry out His program fully (see Acts 13:22). David was a giving man, and he gave generously toward the building of God's house. Even in his own times of trouble and affliction, he continued to give generously (see 1 Chronicles 22:14).

It is tempting to stop giving to others when we are hurting. During those times, we do not feel like being a blessing to someone else; we want someone to comfort us and make us feel better. But when we are hurting, we can choose to behave as we would if we were not hurting. We should keep all our commitments, including our financial commitments to the work of God.

We all go through times of testing, and our behavior during those times clearly reveals our level of spiritual maturity. Spiritual babies do what is right only if they are quickly being noticed and rewarded. But mature Christians do what is right because it is right—and they never quit. They do not change when their circumstances change.

To me there is a big difference between giving and being a "giver." People who are givers look for opportunities to give to others; they do not look for reasons to get out of giving. It is easy to use personal problems as an excuse to be selfish, but I believe that seeds sown during hard times are more powerful than any other kind. God appreciates our faithfulness no matter what we are going through. Do not be an emotional giver, but choose to be one who does what is right on purpose, no matter how you feel.

If I am hurting from a trial I am going through and the devil tempts me not to give because of my personal pain, I purposefully give a little extra, just to let the enemy know where I stand. When Jesus died for us He was hurting, yet He still gave His best. Let's always go the extra mile and never compromise on our commitments.

bronze, and the iron, there is no limit. So arise and begin working, and may the LORD be with you."

¹⁷David also commanded all the leaders of Israel to help Solomon his son, *saying,*

¹⁸"Is not the LORD your God with you? And has He not given you rest *and* peace on every side? For He has given the inhabitants of the land into my hand, and the land is subdued before the LORD and before His people.

¹⁹"Now set your heart and your soul to seek (inquire of, require as your vital necessity) the LORD your God. Arise and build the sanctuary of the LORD God, so that you may bring the ark of the covenant of the LORD and the holy articles *and* utensils of God into the house built for the Name (Presence) of the LORD."

putting the Word to work

Are you looking for purpose and meaning in your life? Take heed of David's counsel in 1 Chronicles 22:19, and set your heart and soul to seek the Lord your God. As you do, you will find that God has plans and purposes for your life beyond anything you can dream of.

23 WHEN DAVID reached old age, he made his son Solomon king over Israel.

²And he assembled together all the leaders of Israel with the priests and Levites.

³The Levites thirty years old and upward were counted, and their number man by man was 38,000.

⁴Of these 24,000 were to oversee *and* inspect the work of the house of the LORD and 6,000 were to be administrators and judges,

⁵and 4,000 were gatekeepers, and 4,000 [musicians] were to praise the LORD with the instruments which David made for giving praise.

⁶And David organized them into divisions according to the sons of Levi: Gershon, Kohath, and Merari.

⁷Of the Gershonites: Ladan (Libni) and Shimei.

⁸The sons of Ladan: Jehiel the first and Zetham and Joel—three *in all.*

⁹The sons of Shimei: Shelomoth, Haziel, and Haran—three *in all.* These were the heads of the fathers' *households* of Ladan.

¹⁰The sons of Shimei: Jahath, Zina (Zizah), Jeush, and Beriah. These were the four sons of Shimei.

¹¹Jahath was the first and Zizah the second; but Jeush and Beriah did not have many sons [not enough for a father's house or clan], so they were [counted together] as one father's household, one working group.

¹²The sons of Kohath: Amram, Izhar, Hebron, and Uzziel—four *in all.*

¹³The sons of Amram: Aaron and Moses. Aaron was set apart to consecrate him as most holy, he and his sons forever, to burn incense before the LORD, attend to His service, and to bless [worshipers] in His name forever.

¹⁴But as for Moses the man of God, his sons were counted among the tribe of Levi.

¹⁵The sons of Moses: Gershom and Eliezer.

¹⁶The son of Gershom: Shebuel the chief.

¹⁷The son of Eliezer was Rehabiah the chief. Eliezer had no other sons, but Rehabiah's sons were very many [in number].

¹⁸The son of Izhar: Shelomith the chief.

¹⁹The sons of Hebron: Jeriah the first, Amariah the second, Jahaziel the third, and Jekameam the fourth.

²⁰The sons of Uzziel: Micah the first and Isshiah the second.

²¹The sons of Merari: Mahli and

Mushi. The sons of Mahli: Eleazar and Kish.

²²Eleazar died and had no sons, but daughters only, and their relatives, the sons of Kish, took them as wives.

²³The sons of Mushi: Mahli, Eder, and Jeremoth—three *in all.*

²⁴These were the Levites by their fathers' households, the heads of the fathers' *households* of those registered, according to the number of names of the individuals who were the servants of the house of the LORD, from twenty years old and upward.

²⁵For David said, "The LORD God of Israel, has given peace *and* rest to His people, and He dwells in Jerusalem forever.

²⁶"Also, the Levites will no longer need to carry the tabernacle and all its utensils for its service."

²⁷For by the last words of David, the Levites from twenty years old and above were counted.

²⁸For their duty is to assist [the priests] the sons of Aaron in the service of the house of the LORD, in [caring for] the courtyards, the chambers, the purifying of all holy things, and any work of the service of the house of God,

²⁹and with the showbread, and the fine flour for a grain offering, and unleavened wafers, or *what is baked in* the pan or what is well-mixed, and all measures of volume and size [as the Law of Moses required].

³⁰They are to stand every morning to thank and praise the LORD, and likewise at evening,

³¹and to offer all burnt sacrifices to the LORD on the Sabbaths, the new moons, and the festivals by number according to the ordinance concerning them, continually before the LORD.

³²So they shall be responsible for the Tent of Meeting, the Holy Place, and the sons of Aaron their relatives, for the service of the house of the LORD.

life point

First Chronicles 23:30 teaches us about those who were to worship the Lord morning and evening. I hope you will also begin to worship early in the morning. I suggest starting before you even get out of bed. Worship while you get ready for work; worship on the way to work; worship when you get home in the evening and as you go to sleep. You will be amazed to see how things begin to change. Worship creates an atmosphere where God can do mighty things in your life.

Worship is not difficult. It simply means to adore the Lord and be thankful for Him and all He does for you. Tell Him regularly how much you love Him and how wonderful He is!

24 THE DIVISIONS of the descendants of Aaron *were these:* the sons of Aaron were Nadab, Abihu, Eleazar, and Ithamar.

²But Nadab and Abihu died before their father and had no sons; therefore Eleazar and Ithamar served as priests.

³David, with Zadok of the sons of Eleazar and Ahimelech of the sons of Ithamar, divided them according to their offices for their *assigned* duties.

⁴Since there were more chief men found among the descendants of Eleazar than among the descendants of Ithamar [because of Eli's misfortunes, and Saul's massacre of the priests at Nob], they were divided in this way: sixteen heads of fathers' households of the descendants of Eleazar and eight of the descendants of Ithamar, corresponding to their fathers' households.

⁵So they were divided by lot, one group with the other; for they were officers of the sanctuary and officers (high priests) of God, both from the descendants of Eleazar and from the descendants of Ithamar.

⁶Shemaiah, the son of Nethanel the scribe, from the Levites, recorded them in the presence of the king, the officers, Zadok the priest, Ahimelech the son of Abiathar [the priest who escaped Saul's massacre at Nob], and the heads of the fathers' *households* of the priests and of the Levites; one father's household taken for Eleazar and one taken for Ithamar.

⁷The lots fell, the first one to Jehoiarib, the second to Jedaiah,

⁸the third to Harim, the fourth to Seorim,

⁹the fifth to Malchijah, the sixth to Mijamin,

¹⁰the seventh to Hakkoz, the eighth to Abijah,

¹¹the ninth to Jeshua, the tenth to Shecaniah,

¹²the eleventh to Eliashib, the twelfth to Jakim,

¹³the thirteenth to Huppah, the fourteenth to Jeshebeab,

¹⁴the fifteenth to Bilgah, the sixteenth to Immer,

¹⁵the seventeenth to Hezir, the eighteenth to Happizzez,

¹⁶the nineteenth to Pethahiah, the twentieth to Jehezkel,

¹⁷the twenty-first to Jachin, the twenty-second to Gamul,

¹⁸the twenty-third to Delaiah, the twenty-fourth to Maaziah.

¹⁹These were their offices *and* positions for their service in the house of the Lᴏʀᴅ according to the ordinance given to them by their father (ancestor) Aaron, just as the Lᴏʀᴅ God of Israel had commanded him.

²⁰Now as for the rest of the sons of Levi: of the sons of Amram: Shubael; of the sons of Shubael: Jehdeiah.

²¹Of Rehabiah: of the sons of Rehabiah: Isshiah the first.

²²Of the Izharites: Shelomoth; of the sons of Shelomoth, Jahath.

²³The sons *of Hebron:* Jeriah *the first,* Amariah the second, Jahaziel the third, Jekameam the fourth.

²⁴Of the sons of Uzziel, Micah; of the sons of Micah, Shamir.

²⁵The brother of Micah, Isshiah; of the sons of Isshiah, Zechariah.

²⁶The sons of Merari: Mahli and Mushi; the sons of Jaaziah, Beno.

²⁷The sons of Merari: by Jaaziah were Beno, Shoham, Zaccur, and Ibri.

²⁸By Mahli: Eleazar, who had no sons.

²⁹By Kish: the sons of Kish, Jerahmeel.

³⁰The sons of Mushi: Mahli, Eder, and Jerimoth. These were the sons of the Levites according to their fathers' households.

³¹These also cast lots as did their relatives the sons of Aaron in the presence of David the king, Zadok, Ahimelech, and the heads of the fathers' *households* of the priests and of the Levites—the head of father's *households* as well as those of his younger brother.

25 MOREOVER, DAVID and the commanders of the army selected for the [temple] service some of the sons of Asaph, Heman, and Jeduthun, who were to prophesy with lyres, harps, and cymbals. The list of the musicians who performed their service was *as follows:*

²Of the sons of Asaph: Zaccur, Joseph, Nethaniah, and Asharelah; the sons of Asaph were under the direction of Asaph, who prophesied under the direction of the king.

³Of Jeduthun, the sons of Jeduthun: Gedaliah, Zeri, Jeshaiah, Shimei, Hashabiah, and Mattithiah, six, under the direction of their father Jeduthun, who prophesied with the lyre in thanksgiving and praise to the Lᴏʀᴅ.

⁴Of Heman, the sons of Heman: Bukkiah, Mattaniah, Uzziel, Shebuel, Jerimoth, Hananiah, Hanani, Eliathah, Giddalti, Romamti-ezer, Joshbekashah, Mallothi, Hothir, and Mahazioth.

⁵All these [men] were the sons of Heman the king's seer to exalt him in accordance with the words of God; for God gave Heman fourteen sons and three daughters. [Ps 68:25]

⁶All these were under the direction of their father to sing in the house of the LORD, with cymbals, harps, and lyres, for the service of the house of God. Asaph, Jeduthun, and Heman were under the order *and* direction of the king.

⁷So their number [who led the remainder of the 4,000], with their relatives who were trained in singing to the LORD, all who were skillful, was 288. [1 Chr 23:5]

⁸The musicians cast lots for their duties, everyone alike, the small (younger) as well as the great (older), the teacher *as well* as the student.

⁹The first lot for Asaph fell to Joseph; the second to Gedaliah, to him, his relatives and his sons, twelve;

¹⁰the third to Zaccur, his sons and his relatives, twelve;

¹¹the fourth to Izri, his sons and his relatives, twelve;

¹²the fifth to Nethaniah, his sons and his relatives, twelve;

¹³the sixth to Bukkiah, his sons and his relatives, twelve;

¹⁴the seventh to Jesharelah, his sons and his relatives, twelve;

¹⁵the eighth to Jeshaiah, his sons and his relatives, twelve;

¹⁶the ninth to Mattaniah, his sons and his relatives, twelve;

¹⁷the tenth to Shimei, his sons and his relatives, twelve;

¹⁸the eleventh to Azarel, his sons and his relatives, twelve;

¹⁹the twelfth to Hashabiah, his sons and his relatives, twelve;

²⁰the thirteenth to Shubael, his sons and his relatives, twelve;

²¹the fourteenth to Mattithiah, his sons and his relatives, twelve;

²²the fifteenth to Jeremoth, his sons and his relatives, twelve;

²³the sixteenth to Hananiah, his sons and his relatives, twelve;

²⁴the seventeenth of Joshbekashah, his sons and his relatives, twelve;

²⁵the eighteenth to Hanani, his sons and his relatives, twelve;

²⁶the nineteenth to Mallothi, his sons and his relatives, twelve;

²⁷the twentieth to Eliathah, his sons and his relatives, twelve;

²⁸the twenty-first to Hothir, his sons and his relatives, twelve;

²⁹the twenty-second to Giddalti, his sons and his relatives, twelve;

³⁰the twenty-third to Mahazioth, his sons and his relatives, twelve;

³¹the twenty-fourth to Romamti-ezer, his sons and his relatives, twelve.

26

FOR THE divisions of the gatekeepers: Of the Korahites: Meshelemiah the son of Kore, of the sons of Asaph.

²Meshelemiah had sons: Zechariah the firstborn, Jediael the second, Zebadiah the third, Jathniel the fourth,

³Elam the fifth, Jehohanan the sixth, Eliehoenai the seventh.

⁴Obed-edom had sons: Shemaiah the firstborn, Jehozabad the second, Joah the third, Sacar the fourth, Nethanel the fifth,

⁵Ammiel the sixth, Issachar the seventh, Peullethai the eighth; for God had blessed him.

⁶Also to his son Shemaiah sons were born who ruled over the house of their father, for they were courageous men of ability.

⁷The sons of Shemaiah: Othni, Rephael, Obed, and Elzabad, whose brothers were courageous *and* able men, Elihu and Semachiah.

⁸All these were sons of Obed-edom [in whose house the ark was kept], they and their sons and relatives, strong *and* able men for the service—sixty-two from Obed-edom. [1 Chr 13:13, 14]

[9]Meshelemiah had sons and relatives, eighteen courageous men.

[10]Also Hosah, one of the sons of Merari, had sons: Shimri the first *and* chief (although he was not the first-born, his father made him first),

[11]Hilkiah the second, Tebaliah the third, Zechariah the fourth; the sons and relatives of Hosah were thirteen in all.

[12]To these divisions of the gatekeepers, the chief men, *were given* duties, like their relatives, to minister in the house of the LORD.

[13]They cast lots, the small (younger) and great (older) alike, in accordance with their fathers' households, for every gate.

[14]The lot for the east [gates] fell to Shelemiah. They cast lots also for his son Zechariah, a wise counselor, and his lot came out for the north [gates].

[15]To Obed-edom [it came out] for the south [gates], and the storehouse *was allotted* to his sons.

[16]To Shuppim and Hosah [the lot fell] for the west [gates], by the gate of Shallecheth, on the ascending highway, division by division.

[17]On the east were six Levites, on the north four a day, on the south four a day, and two by two at the storehouse.

[18]At the colonnade on the west side [of the outer court of the temple] *there were* four at the road and two at the colonnade.

[19]These were the divisions of the gatekeepers among the Korahites and the sons of Merari.

[20]Of the Levites, Ahijah was in charge of the treasuries of the house of God and the treasuries of the dedicated gifts.

[21]The sons of Ladan, the sons of the Gershonites belonging to Ladan, *namely,* the Jehielites, *were* the heads of the fathers' *households,* belonging to Ladan the Gershonite.

[22]The sons of Jehieli, Zetham and his brother Joel, were in charge of the treasuries of the house of the LORD.

[23]Of the Amramites, Izharites, Hebronites, and Uzzielites:

[24]Shebuel the son of Gershom, the son of Moses, was supervisor over the treasuries.

[25]His relatives by Eliezer were his son Rehabiah, his son Jeshaiah, his son Joram, his son Zichri, and his son Shelomoth.

[26]This Shelomoth and his relatives were in charge of all the treasuries of the dedicated gifts which King David, the heads of the fathers' *households,* the commanders of thousands and hundreds, and the commanders of the army, had dedicated.

[27]From spoil won in battles they dedicated *gifts* to maintain *and* repair the house of the LORD.

[28]Also all that Samuel the seer had dedicated, and Saul the son of Kish, Abner the son of Ner and Joab the son of Zeruiah, everyone who had dedicated *anything,* this was in the care of Shelomoth and his relatives.

[29]Of the Izharites: Chenaniah and his sons were *appointed* to outside duties for Israel, as administrators and judges.

[30]Of the Hebronites: Hashabiah and his relatives, 1,700 capable men, were in charge of the affairs of Israel west of the Jordan, for all the work of the LORD and the service of the king.

[31]Of the Hebronites: Jerijah was the chief (these Hebronites were examined according to their descendants and fathers' *households* in the fortieth [and final] year of David's reign, and men of courage *and* ability were found among them at Jazer in Gilead)

[32]and Jerijah's relatives, 2,700 capable men, were heads of fathers' *households;* and King David made them overseers of the Reubenites, the Gadites, and the half-tribe of Manasseh, for everything pertaining to God and to the king.

27 THIS IS the list of the sons (descendants) of Israel, the heads of fathers' *house-holds*, the commanders of thousands and of hundreds, and their officers who served the king in all matters of the divisions which came in and went out month by month throughout the year, each division *numbering* 24,000:

²Jashobeam the son of Zabdiel was in charge of the first division for the first month; and in his division were 24,000.

³*He was* descended from Perez, *and was* chief of all the commanders of the army for the first month.

⁴Dodai the Ahohite and his division was in charge of the division for the second month, Mikloth was the chief officer; and in his division were 24,000.

⁵The third commander of the army for the third month was Benaiah, the son of Jehoiada the priest, as chief; and in his division were 24,000.

⁶This is the Benaiah who was the mighty man of the thirty and was in charge of the thirty; and Ammizabad his son was *over* his division.

⁷The fourth, for the fourth month was Asahel the brother of Joab, and Zebadiah his son after him; and in his division were 24,000.

⁸The fifth, for the fifth month was the commander Shamhuth the Izrahite; and in his division were 24,000.

⁹The sixth, for the sixth month was Ira the son of Ikkesh the Tekoite; and in his division were 24,000.

¹⁰The seventh, for the seventh month was Helez the Pelonite of the sons of Ephraim; and in his division were 24,000.

¹¹The eighth, for the eighth month was Sibbecai the Hushathite of the Zerahites; and in his division were 24,000.

¹²The ninth, for the ninth month was Abiezer of Anathoth, a Benjamite; and in his division were 24,000.

¹³The tenth, for the tenth month was Maharai from Netophah of the Zera-hites; and in his division were 24,000.

¹⁴The eleventh, for the eleventh month was Benaiah the Pirathonite of the sons of Ephraim; and in his division were 24,000.

¹⁵The twelfth, for the twelfth month was Heldai the Netophathite of Othniel; and in his division were 24,000.

¹⁶Now in charge of the tribes of Israel [were the following]: chief officer of the Reubenites was Eliezer the son of Zichri; of the Simeonites, Shephatiah the son of Maacah;

¹⁷of Levi, Hashabiah the son of Kemuel; of Aaron, Zadok;

¹⁸of Judah, Elihu, one of David's brothers; of Issachar, Omri the son of Michael;

¹⁹of Zebulun, Ishmaiah the son of Obadiah; of Naphtali, Jeremoth the son of Azriel;

²⁰of the Ephraimites, Hoshea the son of Azaziah; of the half-tribe of Manasseh, Joel the son of Pedaiah;

²¹of the half-tribe of Manasseh in Gilead, Iddo the son of Zechariah; of Benjamin, Jaasiel the son of Abner;

²²of Dan, Azarel the son of Jeroham. These were the leaders of the tribes of Israel.

²³But David did not count those twenty years of age and under, for the LORD had said he would multiply Israel as the stars of heaven.

²⁴Joab the son of Zeruiah began a census but did not finish; and because of this, [God's] wrath came on Israel, and the number was not recorded in the chronicles of King David.

²⁵Azmaveth the son of Adiel was in charge of the king's storerooms; and Jonathan the son of Uzziah was in charge of the storehouses in the country, in the cities, in the villages, and in the towers.

²⁶Ezri the son of Chelub was in charge of those who did the work of the field, tilling the soil.

²⁷Shimei the Ramathite was in charge

of the vineyards; Zabdi the Shiphmite was in charge of the produce of the vineyards for the wine cellars.

²⁸Baal-hanan the Gederite was in charge of the olive and sycamore trees in Shephelah (the lowlands); and Joash was in charge of the stores of [olive] oil.

²⁹Shitrai the Sharonite was in charge of the cattle grazing in Sharon; Shaphat the son of Adlai was in charge of the cattle in the valleys.

³⁰Obil the Ishmaelite was in charge of the camels; and Jehdeiah the Meronothite was in charge of the donkeys.

³¹Jaziz the Hagrite was in charge of the flocks. All these were overseers *and* stewards of the property which belonged to King David.

³²Also Jonathan, David's uncle, was a counselor *and* advisor, a man of understanding *and* wisdom, and a scribe; and Jehiel the son of Hachmoni attended (tutored) the king's sons. [2 Kin 10:6]

³³Ahithophel was counselor to the king; and Hushai the Archite was the king's companion *and* friend.

³⁴Ahithophel was succeeded by Jehoiada the son of Benaiah and by Abiathar; and Joab was the commander of the king's army.

28 DAVID ASSEMBLED at Jerusalem all the leaders (officials) of Israel, the leaders of the tribes, and the commanders of the divisions that served the king, and the commanders of thousands, and the commanders of hundreds, and the overseers of all the property and livestock of the king and his sons, with the palace officers and the mighty men, and all the brave warriors.

²Then David the king rose to his feet and said, "Hear me, my brothers [in arms] and my people. I had intended to build a permanent home for the ark of the covenant of the LORD and as a footstool for our God, and I prepared materials for the building.

³"But God said to me, 'You shall not build a house for My Name (Presence), because you are a man of war and have shed blood.'

⁴"However, the LORD, the God of Israel, chose me from all in my father's house to be king over Israel forever. For He has chosen Judah to be the leader; and in the house (tribe) of Judah he chose the house of my father; and among the sons of my father He was pleased to make me king over all Israel.

⁵"Of all my sons (for the LORD has given me many sons) He has chosen my son Solomon to sit on the throne of the kingdom of the LORD over Israel.

⁶"He said to me, 'Solomon your son shall build My house and My courts; for I have chosen him to be a son to Me, and I will be a father to him.

⁷'I will establish his kingdom forever if he loyally *and* continually obeys My commandments and My ordinances, as is done today.'

⁸"Now therefore, in the sight of all Israel, the assembly of the LORD, and in the hearing of our God, observe and seek after all the commandments of the LORD your God so that you may possess the good land and leave it as an inheritance to your sons after you forever.

⁹"As for you, Solomon my son, know the God of your father [have personal

speak the Word

God, may I heed David's instructions and know You, understand You, appreciate You, heed You, cherish You, and serve You with a blameless heart and a willing mind. I know that if I seek You and require You as my first and vital necessity, I will find You.
—ADAPTED FROM 1 CHRONICLES 28:9

knowledge of Him, be acquainted with, and understand Him; appreciate, heed, and cherish Him] and serve Him with a blameless heart and a willing mind; for the LORD searches all hearts *and* minds, and understands every intent *and* inclination of the thoughts. If you seek Him [inquiring for and of Him and requiring Him as your first and vital necessity] He will let you find Him; but if you abandon (turn away from) Him, He will reject you forever.

¹⁰"Consider this carefully, for the LORD has chosen you to build a house for the sanctuary. Be courageous *and* strong and do it."

¹¹Then David gave to his son Solomon the plan for the porch *of the temple,* its buildings, its treasuries, its upper chambers, its inner rooms, and for the place for the [ark and its] mercy seat;

¹²and the plan of all that he had in mind, for the courts of the house of the LORD, and for all the surrounding rooms, for the storerooms of the house of God and for the storerooms for the dedicated gifts *and* offerings;

¹³*the plan* for the divisions of the priests and the Levites and for all the work of the service in the house of the LORD and for all the utensils for service in the house of the LORD;

¹⁴for the golden *utensils,* the weight of gold and silver for all the gold and silver articles for every kind of service;

¹⁵and the weight *of gold* for the golden lampstands and their golden lamps, with the weight of each lampstand and its lamps; and the *weight of silver* for the silver lampstands, with the weight of each lampstand and its lamps according to the use of each lampstand;

¹⁶the gold by weight for each table of showbread, and the silver for the tables of silver;

¹⁷and the forks, the basins, and the pitchers of pure gold; and for the golden bowls with the weight for each bowl; and for the silver bowls with the weight for each bowl;

¹⁸and for the altar of incense refined gold by weight; and gold for the model of the chariot of the cherubim that spread *their wings* and covered the ark of the LORD's covenant.

¹⁹"All *this,*" said David, "the LORD made me understand in writing by His hand upon me, all the work *and* details [to be done] according to this plan."

²⁰Then David said to his son Solomon, "Be strong and courageous, and take action; do not fear nor be dismayed, for the LORD God, my God, is with you. He will not fail you nor abandon you [but will guide you in the construction] until you have finished all the work for the service of the house of the LORD.

²¹"And see, [you have] the divisions of the priests and Levites for all the service of God's house, and every willing, skillful man will be with you in all the kinds of work for any kind of service. Also the officers and all the people will be entirely at your command."

29 AND KING David said to all the assembly, "My son Solomon, whom alone God has chosen, is still young and inexperienced and the work is great; for the temple is not for man but for the LORD God.

speak the Word

God, I will be strong and courageous and will do what You have asked me to do. I will not fear or be dismayed, because You are with me and You will not fail me nor abandon me.
—ADAPTED FROM 1 CHRONICLES 28:20

²"So with all my ability I have provided for the house of my God the gold for the *things of* gold, silver for the *things of* silver, bronze for the *things of* bronze, iron for the *things of* iron, and wood for the *things of* wood, *as well as* onyx stones and stones to be inlaid, stones of antimony (a brittle, silvery-white metal) and stones of various colors, and all kinds of precious stones and alabaster in abundance.

³"Moreover, because I delight in the house of my God, the [personal] treasure that I have of gold and silver, I give to the house of my God, in addition to all that I have already provided for the holy house:

⁴*namely*, 3,000 talents of gold from the gold of Ophir, and 7,000 talents of refined silver, to overlay the walls of the buildings;

⁵gold for the *things of* gold, silver for the *things of* silver, that is, for all the work to be done by craftsmen. Now who is willing to consecrate himself today to the LORD?"

⁶Then the rulers of the fathers' *households*, and leaders of the tribes of Israel, and the commanders of thousands and of hundreds, with the overseers of the king's work, offered willingly

⁷and gave for the service of the house of God: 5,000 talents and 10,000 darics of gold, and 10,000 talents of silver, and 18,000 talents of bronze, and 100,000 talents of iron.

⁸Whoever had *precious* stones gave

putting the Word to work

Do you regularly give of your finances to the work of God? As David's people willingly gave, they were filled with joy (see 1 Chronicles 29:2–16)! Remember, anything you have to give came from God in the first place, and one way to honor Him is by joyfully giving of your resources.

putting the Word to work

Have you ever had your heart set on something, only to be disappointed? David knew that only by fixing their hearts on God would the people he led prosper and have joy (see 1 Chronicles 29:3). Ask God to help you fix your heart on Him; He will never disappoint or fail you.

them to the treasury of the house of the LORD, in the care of Jehiel the Gershonite.

⁹Then the people rejoiced because they had given willingly, for with a whole *and* blameless heart they had offered freely to the LORD. King David also rejoiced greatly.

¹⁰Therefore David blessed the LORD in the sight of all the assembly and said, "Blessed (praised, adored, and thanked) are You, O LORD God of Israel (Jacob) our father, forever and ever.

¹¹"Yours, O LORD, is the greatness and the power and the glory and the victory and the majesty, indeed everything that is in the heavens and on the earth; Yours is the dominion *and* kingdom, O LORD, and You exalt Yourself as head over all.

life point

It is important to look at our attitudes and motives for working. If we are lazy and do not want to work, we will not work. We will make all kinds of excuses and end up in ruin. But if we have strong desires, they will motivate us to work and work hard; we will do whatever it takes to get the job done, as the people mentioned in 1 Chronicles 29:6 did. Smart people realize that nothing worthwhile is ever accomplished without dedication and a lot of hard work.

¹²"Both riches and honor *come* from You, and You rule over all. In Your hand is power and might; and it is in Your hands to make great and to give strength to everyone.

¹³"Now therefore, our God, we thank You, and praise Your glorious name.

¹⁴"But who am I, and who are my people, that we should be able to offer as generously as this? For all things come from You, and from Your own hand we have given to You.

¹⁵"For we are sojourners before You, and tenants, as all our fathers were; our days on the earth are like a shadow, and there is no hope [of remaining].

¹⁶"O LORD our God, all this abundance that we have prepared to build You a house for Your holy Name, it is from Your hand, and is all Your own.

¹⁷"I know also, my God, that You test the heart and delight in uprightness *and* integrity. In the uprightness of my heart I have willingly offered all these *things*. So now with joy I have seen Your people who are present here, make their offerings willingly *and* freely to You.

¹⁸"O LORD, God of Abraham, Isaac, and Israel, our fathers, keep forever such purposes *and* thoughts in the minds of Your people, and direct their hearts toward You;

¹⁹and give to my son Solomon a perfect heart to keep Your commandments, Your testimonies, and Your statutes, and to do all [that is necessary]

be willing to be willing

Do you like it when people do something for you, but you know they do not really want to do it? I don't like that at all. I believe this comes from my upbringing. It seemed to me that even when my father allowed me to do things, he really did not want me to do them. So to this day if people do not really want to do something for me, I would rather they not do anything at all.

If we feel that way, how much more must God feel that way? We human beings do a halfway decent job of hiding our true feelings from people, but we cannot hide our hearts from God. We may as well start being honest about the way we feel and start doing things out of a willing heart—or at least start praying for God to give us a willing heart—so we can do them for the right reasons.

Sometimes we may have to pray, "Lord, make me willing to be willing." And sometimes we may have to pray, "Lord, make me willing to be willing to be willing—because I don't even really feel that I want to be willing at all!"

God examines our heart attitudes, and whatever we do for Him needs to be done willingly. I particularly like 1 Chronicles 29:9 because it emphasizes that people can truly rejoice when they give to God willingly and with a whole heart. According to 2 Corinthians 9:7, "God loves a cheerful giver [and delights in the one whose heart is in his gift]." He does not take pleasure in those who give legalistically or under compulsion.

There are times when we obey God even though it is difficult for us, but we still do it because we love Him and want to please Him. In those cases I still see us as willing. We are willing to go beyond our own fleshly feelings about a particular thing and honor God anyway. Even if you have to ask God to make you willing, be willing—and be one in whom God delights!

to build the temple [for You], for which I have made provision."

²⁰Then David said to all the assembly, "Now bless (praise, thank) the LORD your God." And all the assembly blessed the LORD, the God of their fathers, and bowed down and honored the LORD and to the king [as His earthly representative].

²¹The next day they offered sacrifices and burnt offerings to the LORD: 1,000 bulls, 1,000 rams, and 1,000 lambs, with their drink offerings (libations) and sacrifices in abundance for all Israel.

²²They ate and drank that day before the LORD with great rejoicing.

They made Solomon the son of David king a second time, and anointed him as ruler for the LORD and Zadok as [high] priest.

²³Then Solomon sat on the throne of the LORD as king in place of David his father; and he prospered, and all Israel obeyed him.

²⁴All of the leaders and warriors, and also all the sons of King David, pledged allegiance to King Solomon.

²⁵The LORD highly exalted Solomon in the sight of all Israel, and bestowed on him royal majesty which had not been on any king before him in Israel.

²⁶Thus David the son of Jesse reigned over all Israel.

²⁷The time that he reigned over Israel was forty years; he reigned seven years in Hebron and thirty-three years in Jerusalem.

²⁸He died in a good old age [his seventy-first year], full of days (satisfied), riches and honor. Solomon his son reigned in his place.

²⁹Now the acts of King David, from first to last, are written in the chronicles (records) of Samuel the seer, in the chronicles of Nathan the prophet, and in the chronicles of Gad the seer,

³⁰with [accounts of] all his reign, and his power, and the times *and* circumstances which came on him, on Israel, and on all the kingdoms of the [surrounding] lands.

Second Chronicles

Author:
Attributed to Ezra

Date:
Probably between 425 BC and 400 BC

Everyday Life Principles:
We need to see ourselves as a temple, a place where God is pleased to abide.

God blesses us when we seek Him.

Remember, the battle belongs to the Lord.

Just as 1 Chronicles recounts the reign of King David, 2 Chronicles records the rule of David's son, King Solomon, who is often called the wisest man who ever lived. No doubt, Solomon's greatest achievement was the completion of the temple—a permanent place where God would be pleased to dwell and be worshiped in the midst of His people.

One of the ongoing themes of 2 Chronicles is the instruction to seek God. Because of their history, God's people knew how miserable their lives could be when they did not seek Him and how blessed they could be when they did inquire of Him. Nevertheless, God continually reminded them in various ways throughout 2 Chronicles to consult Him in every situation.

I believe that one of the greatest truths in Scripture—one we need to keep in the forefront of our minds as we go about our everyday lives—is found in 2 Chronicles 20: *The battle belongs to the Lord*. When we belong to God, our battles belong to Him too. We do not have to fight life's wars in our own strength, but we fight in the power of our God, Who always gains the victory.

I hope that 2 Chronicles will serve as a reminder to you to seek God continually and make a place for Him in every area of your life.

1 SOLOMON THE son of David established himself securely over his kingdom, and the LORD his God was with him and made him exceedingly great.

²Solomon spoke to all Israel, to the commanders of thousands and of hundreds and to the judges and to every leader in all Israel, the heads of the fathers' (ancestors') *households*.

³Then Solomon and all the assembly went to the high place at Gibeon [to offer sacrifices, where the Canaanites had habitually worshiped], for God's Tent of Meeting was there, which Moses the servant of the LORD had made in the wilderness.

⁴But David had brought up the ark of God from Kiriath-jearim to the place he had prepared for it, because he had pitched a tent for it in Jerusalem.

⁵Now the bronze altar, which Bezalel the son of Uri, the son of Hur, had made was there before the tabernacle of the LORD, and Solomon and the assembly sought it out.

⁶And Solomon went up to the bronze altar before the LORD at the Tent of Meeting, and offered a thousand burnt offerings on it.

⁷That night God appeared to Solomon and said to him, "Ask what I shall give to you."

⁸Then Solomon said to God, "You have shown great lovingkindness *and* mercy to my father David, and have made me king in his place.

⁹"Now, O LORD God, Your promise to my father David is fulfilled, for You have made me king over a people as numerous as the dust of the earth.

¹⁰"Give me wisdom and knowledge, so that I may go out and come in [performing my duties] before this people, for [otherwise] who can rule *and* administer justice to this great people of Yours?"

¹¹God replied to Solomon, "Because this was in your heart and you did not

putting the Word to work

Do you sometimes feel overwhelmed by everything you are supposed to be doing? Solomon certainly seemed to struggle with such feelings. Ask God, as Solomon did, for wisdom as to how you are to carry out your tasks (see 2 Chronicles 1:9, 10). He has promised to give wisdom to those who ask.

ask for riches, possessions or honor *and* personal glory, or the life of those who hate you, nor have you even asked for long life, but you have asked for wisdom and knowledge for yourself so that you may rule *and* administer justice to My people over whom I have made you king,

¹²wisdom and knowledge have been granted you. I will also give you riches, possessions, and honor, such as none of the kings who were before you has possessed nor will those who will come after you."

¹³So Solomon went from the high place at Gibeon, from the Tent of Meeting, to Jerusalem. And he reigned over Israel.

¹⁴Solomon acquired chariots and horsemen; he had 1,400 chariots and 12,000 horsemen, and he stationed them in the cities [suited for the use] of chariots and with the king at Jerusalem.

¹⁵The king made silver and gold as plentiful *and* common in Jerusalem as stones, and he made cedar as plentiful as the sycamore-fig trees in the lowland.

¹⁶Solomon's horses were imported from Egypt and from Kue. The king's merchants purchased them [in large numbers] from Kue at a price.

¹⁷And they imported chariots from Egypt for 600 *shekels* of silver apiece, and horses for 150 apiece; and in the same way they exported horses to all the kings of the Hittites and the kings of the Arameans (Syrians).

2 NOW SOLOMON decided to build a house (temple) for the Name of the LORD, and a royal palace for himself.

²So Solomon assigned 70,000 men to carry loads, 80,000 men to quarry stone in the mountains, and 3,600 to supervise them.

³Then Solomon sent *word* to Hiram king of Tyre, saying, "As you dealt with my father David and sent him cedars to build himself a house in which to live, [please] do the same for me.

⁴"Observe, I am about to build a house for the Name of the LORD my God, dedicated to Him, to burn fragrant incense [of sweet spices] before Him, to set out the showbread continually, and to offer burnt offerings morning and evening, on Sabbaths, New Moons, and on the festivals of the LORD our God, as *ordained* forever in Israel.

⁵"The house I am going to build will be great, for our God is greater than all the gods.

⁶"But who is able to build a house for Him, since the heavens and [even] the highest heavens cannot contain Him? Who am I to build a house for Him, except [as a place] to burn *incense* before Him?

⁷"Now send me a man who is skilled to work in gold, silver, bronze, and iron, and in purple, crimson, and blue *fabrics,* and who knows how to make engravings, *to work* with the skilled men who are with me in Judah and Jerusalem, whom my father David provided.

⁸"Send me also cedar, cypress, and algum timber, for I know that your servants know how to cut timber in Lebanon. And indeed my servants *will work* with your servants

⁹to prepare for me an abundance of

life point

When Solomon was building the temple, a dwelling place for God, he chose laborers who were skilled in their crafts (see 2 Chronicles 2:7). These men knew what they were gifted to do, and they were skilled at doing it. When I think about them, I am reminded of how many people today are asking, *What am I supposed to do with my life? What is my purpose on earth? Does God have a calling for my life?* God answers these questions through our natural gifts and abilities, and He helps us discover our purposes through the natural skills and unique talents He bestows upon us.

God-given gifts are the skills a person easily performs without formal training. Although training and education may help to perfect our skills, the skills are readily recognized prior to the training. Many great artists know exactly how to put shapes and colors together, and so they enjoy designing buildings or sculpting beautiful and useful items. Many songwriters simply write down the music they hear in their heads. Some people are great at organizing, while others are natural counselors, helping people sort out their lives and their relationships. I have always been a good communicator. No matter what our gifts are, we all derive great pleasure from doing what we are naturally good at doing. We do not have to try to do it; it comes naturally.

If you are unsure of your purpose in life, just do what you are good at doing, and watch God confirm you by blessing your endeavors. Then be diligent to develop your gifts, so you can be skilled at what you are gifted to do.

speak the Word

I declare, God, that You are greater than all other so-called gods!
–ADAPTED FROM 2 CHRONICLES 2:5

timber, because the house I am about to build will be great and wonderful.

10"And I will give to your servants who cut timber, 20,000 measures of crushed wheat and 20,000 measures of barley, and 20,000 baths of wine and 20,000 baths of [olive] oil."

11Then Hiram, king of Tyre replied in a letter sent to Solomon: "Because the Lord loves His people, He has made you king over them."

12Hiram said also, "Blessed be the Lord, the God of Israel, who made heaven and earth, who has given King David a wise son, endowed with discretion and understanding, who will build a house for the Lord and a royal palace for himself.

13"Now I am sending a skilled man, endowed with understanding, Huram-abi,

14the son of a Danite woman and a Tyrian father. He is trained to work in gold, silver, bronze, iron, stone, and wood; in purple, blue, and crimson fabrics, and in fine linen. He is able to make any kind of engraving and to carry out any design given him. *He will work* with your skilled men and those of my lord, David your father.

15"Now then, let my lord send to his servants the wheat, the barley, the oil, and the wine of which he has spoken.

16"We will cut whatever timber you need from Lebanon and bring it to you on rafts by sea to Joppa, so that you may take it up to Jerusalem."

17Then Solomon took a count of all the aliens in the land of Israel, like the census that his father David had taken; and they were found to be 153,600.

18He assigned 70,000 of them to carry loads and 80,000 to quarry stone in the mountain, and 3,600 as overseers to make the people work.

3 THEN SOLOMON began to build the house of the Lord in Jerusalem on Mount Moriah, where the Lord appeared to his father David, in the place that David had prepared, on the threshing floor of Ornan the Jebusite. [1 Chr 21:20–22]

2Solomon began to build on the second day of the second month in the fourth year of his reign.

3Now this is the [measurement of the] foundation which Solomon laid for the house of God: the length in cubits—by the old standard of measure—was sixty cubits (90 ft.), and the width was twenty cubits (30 ft.).

4The porch in front of the house was as long as the width of the house, twenty cubits, and the height was 120 cubits. He overlaid it inside with pure gold.

5He overlaid the main room [the Holy Place] with cypress wood and overlaid it with fine gold, and decorated it with palm trees and chains.

6And he adorned the house with precious stones; and the gold was gold from Parvaim.

7He also overlaid the house [the Holy Place] with gold—the beams, the thresholds, and its walls and its doors; and he carved cherubim on the walls.

8Now he made the room of the Holy of Holies: its length equaling the width of the house was twenty cubits, and its width was twenty cubits; and he overlaid it with 600 talents of fine gold.

9The weight of the nails was fifty shekels of gold. He also overlaid the upper rooms with gold.

10And in the Holy of Holies he made two sculptured cherubim, and overlaid them with gold.

11The wingspan of the cherubim was twenty cubits: one wing of one cherub was five cubits, reaching to the wall of the house, and its other wing, of five cubits, touched the other cherub's wing.

12The wing of the other cherub, of five cubits, touched the wall of the house; and its other wing of five cubits touched the wing of the first cherub.

13The wings of these cherubim extended twenty cubits. The cherubim stood on their feet, their faces toward the Holy Place (the main room).

[14]He made the veil [between the Holy Place and the Holy of Holies] of blue, purple, and crimson colors, and fine linen, and embroidered cherubim on it. [15]He also made two pillars for the front of the house, thirty-five cubits high, and the capital on the top of each one was five cubits. [16]He made chains [like a necklace] in the inner sanctuary and put them on the tops of the pillars; and he made a hundred pomegranates and put them on the chains. [17]He erected the pillars in front of the temple, one on the right, the other on the left, and named the one on the right Jachin (may He establish) and the one on the left Boaz (in Him is strength).

4 THEN SOLOMON made an altar of bronze, twenty cubits in length, twenty cubits in width, and ten cubits in height. [2]He also made the Sea [that is, the large basin used for ceremonial washing] of cast metal, ten cubits from brim to brim, circular in form, and five cubits in height, and its circumference was thirty cubits. [3]Under it and entirely encircling it were figures of oxen, ten to a cubit. The oxen were in two rows, cast in one piece. [4]It stood on twelve oxen, three facing north, three facing west, three facing south, three facing east; and the Sea was set on top of them and all their hindquarters turned inward. [5]It was a handbreadth (the width of the four fingers) thick; its brim was made like the brim of a cup, like a lily blossom. It could hold 3,000 baths (measures). [6]He also made ten [portable] basins in which to wash, and he put five on the right (south) side and five on the

left (north). They would rinse things for the burnt offering in them, but the Sea was for the priests to wash in. [7]And he made ten golden lampstands just as directed and set them in the temple, five on the right side and five on the left. [8]He made also ten tables and placed them in the temple, five on the right side and five on the left side, and he made a hundred [ceremonial] basins of gold. [9]Moreover, he made the courtyard of the priests, and the great courtyard [for the people] and doors for the courtyard, and he overlaid their doors with bronze. [10]He set the Sea on the right side at the southeast corner [of the house]. [11]And Huram also made the pails [for ashes], the shovels, and the basins. So Huram finished the work that he did for King Solomon in the house of God: [12]the two pillars, the bowls, the capitals on top of the two pillars, and the two lattice works to cover the two bowls of the capitals which were on top of the pillars, [13]and the four hundred pomegranates for the two lattice works, two rows of pomegranates for each lattice to cover the two bowls of the capitals on the pillars. [14]He also made the stands and he made the basins on the stands; [15]and the one Sea with the twelve oxen under it. [16]The pails, the shovels, and the meat-forks, and all the utensils Huramabi made of polished bronze for King Solomon for the house of the LORD. [17]The king cast them on the plain of the Jordan, in the clay ground between Succoth and Zeredah. [18]Solomon made all these utensils in such great quantity that the weight of the bronze could not be determined. [19]Solomon also made all the articles that were in the house of God:

the golden altar, and the tables for the bread of the Presence (showbread),

²⁰and the lampstands with their lamps of pure gold, to burn in front of the inner sanctuary (the Holy of Holies) as directed;

²¹the flowers, the lamps, and the tongs of gold, of purest gold;

²²and the snuffers, the basins, the dishes [for incense], and the firepans, of pure gold; and for the entrance of the house (temple), the inner doors for the Holy of Holies and the doors of the Holy Place (main room), were of gold.

5 THUS ALL the work that Solomon did for the house of the LORD was finished. He brought in the things that his father David had dedicated, and he put the silver and the gold and all the utensils in the treasuries of the house of God.

²Then Solomon assembled the elders of Israel and all the heads of the tribes, the leaders of the fathers' *households* of the Israelites, in Jerusalem to bring the ark of the covenant of the LORD up from the City of David, which is Zion.

³All the men of Israel gathered before the king at the feast in the seventh month.

⁴And all the elders of Israel came, and the Levites took up the ark.

⁵The Levitical priests brought up the ark, the Tent of Meeting, and all the holy utensils that were in the Tent.

⁶And King Solomon and all the assembly of Israel who gathered together

putting the Word to work

Worship is a powerful way for us to draw near to God, just as it was in Solomon's day (see 2 Chronicles 5:11–14). Do you long to experience His presence in your life? Then worship, worship, worship!

with him before the ark were sacrificing so many sheep and oxen that they could not be counted or numbered.

⁷Then the priests brought the ark of the covenant of the LORD to its place, to the inner sanctuary of the house, into the Holy of Holies, under the wings of the cherubim;

⁸for the cherubim spread out their wings over the place of the ark, making a covering above the ark and its carrying poles.

⁹The poles were so long that the ends of the poles of the ark were visible from the front of the Holy of Holies (inner sanctuary), but were not visible from the outside. They are there to this day.

¹⁰There was nothing in the ark except the two tablets [of the Ten Commandments] which Moses put there at Mount Horeb, when the LORD made a covenant with the Israelites, when they came out of Egypt. [Ex 31:18]

¹¹When the priests came out of the Holy Place (for all the priests who were present had sanctified themselves [separating themselves from everything unclean], without regard to their assigned divisions),

¹²and all of the Levitical singers, Asaph, Heman, and Jeduthun, with their sons and relatives, clothed in fine linen, with cymbals, harps, and lyres were standing at the east end of the altar, and with them a hundred and twenty priests blowing trumpets

¹³in unison when the trumpeters and singers were to make themselves heard with one voice praising and thanking the LORD, and when they raised their voices accompanied by the trumpets and cymbals and [other] instruments of music, and when they praised the LORD, *saying,* "For *He* is good, for His mercy *and* lovingkindness endure forever," then the house of the LORD was filled with a cloud,

¹⁴so that the priests could not remain

life point

In the Old Testament, God's glory visibly filled the temple and overwhelmed the priests to the point that they could not remain standing (see 2 Chronicles 5:13, 14). Today, under the New Covenant, you and I *are* God's temple (see 1 Corinthians 6:19). God wants to display His glory in and through us as dramatically as He did in the physical temple of Solomon's day. When God's glory is manifested in your life, others will look at you and say, "Wow, what a great God you serve," because the power of His goodness toward you is visually evident to them. God wants to "wow" you as He fills your temple with His power and glory.

standing to minister because of the cloud; for the glory *and* brilliance of the LORD filled the house of God.

6 THEN SOLOMON said,

"The LORD has said that He would dwell in the thick cloud. ²"I have built You a lofty house, A place for You to dwell forever."

³Then the king turned around and blessed the entire assembly of Israel, while they were all standing. ⁴And he said, "Blessed be the LORD, the God of Israel, who spoke with His mouth to my father David and has fulfilled with His hands *what He promised,* saying, ⁵'Since the day that I brought My people out of the land of Egypt, I did not choose a city among all the tribes of Israel *in which* to build a house so that My Name (Presence) might be there, nor did I choose any man to be a leader over My people Israel; ⁶but I have chosen Jerusalem that My Name might be there, and I have chosen David to be over My people Israel.' ⁷"Now it was in the heart of my father David to build a house for the Name of the LORD, the God of Israel. ⁸"But the LORD said to my father David, 'Because it was in your heart to build a house for My Name, you did well that it was in your heart. ⁹'Nevertheless you shall not build the house, but your son who will be born to you, he shall build the house for My Name.' ¹⁰"Now the LORD has fulfilled His word which He spoke; for I have risen in place of my father David and I sit on the throne of Israel, just as the LORD promised, and have built the house for the Name of the LORD, the God of Israel. ¹¹"There I have placed the ark [the symbol of His Presence] in which is the covenant of the LORD [the Ten Commandments], which He made with the people (descendants) of Israel." ¹²Then Solomon stood before the altar of the LORD in the presence of the entire assembly of Israel and spread out his hands. ¹³For Solomon had made a bronze platform, five cubits square and three cubits high, and had set it in the midst of the courtyard; and he stood on it, and he knelt down on his knees in the presence of all the assembly of Israel and spread out his hands toward heaven, ¹⁴and he said, "O LORD, God of Israel, there is no god like You in heaven or on the earth, keeping covenant and *showing* mercy *and* lovingkindness to Your servants who walk before You [in obedience] with all their heart, ¹⁵[You] who have kept Your promise

speak the Word

I bless You, Lord, because You fulfill with Your hands what You speak with Your mouth.
—ADAPTED FROM 2 CHRONICLES 6:4

to Your servant David, my father, that which You told him; You have spoken with Your mouth and have fulfilled it with Your hand, as it is today.

[16]"Now therefore, O LORD, the God of Israel, keep with Your servant David, my father, that which You promised him, saying, 'You shall not fail to have a man to sit on the throne of Israel, provided your sons are careful to walk in My law as you, [David,] have walked before Me.'

[17]"Now then, O LORD, the God of Israel, let Your word which You have spoken to Your servant David be confirmed (verified).

[18]"But will God actually dwell with mankind on the earth? Behold, heaven and the highest heaven cannot contain You; how much less this house which I have built!

[19]"Yet have regard for the prayer of Your servant and for his supplication, O LORD my God, to listen to the cry and to the prayer which Your servant prays before You,

[20]that Your eyes may be open toward this house day and night, toward the place in which You have said that *You would* put Your Name (Presence), to listen to the prayer which Your servant shall pray toward this place.

[21]"So listen to the requests of Your servant and Your people Israel when

putting the Word to work

God is faithful to fulfill every one of His promises to us. How do you respond to Him when He brings one of His promises to pass in your life? Be like Solomon; tell others about God's greatness and worship Him with thanksgiving (see 2 Chronicles 6:12–15).

life point

Throughout 2 Chronicles 6, we see Solomon crying out for God to hear his prayers. In order to accomplish what God has called us to do in this life, we need to be assured He does hear our prayers and does respond to them (see Psalm 65:2). Never neglect to pray, because God is always listening and ready to answer. Where there is prayer, there is power!

they pray toward this place. Hear from Your dwelling place, from heaven; and *when You* hear, forgive.

[22]"If a man sins against his neighbor, and he is required to take an oath, and he comes and takes the oath before Your altar in this house,

[23]then hear from heaven and act and judge Your servants, punishing the wicked by bringing his conduct on his own head, and providing justice to the righteous by giving to him in accordance with his righteousness (innocence).

[24]"If Your people Israel have been defeated by an enemy because they have sinned against You, and they return *to You* and confess Your name, and pray and make supplication before You in this house,

[25]then hear from heaven and forgive the sin of Your people Israel, and bring them again to the land which You gave to them and to their fathers.

[26]"When the heavens are shut up and there is no rain because Your people have sinned against You, and they pray toward this place and confess Your name, and turn from their sin when You afflict *and* humble them;

[27]then hear in heaven and forgive the sin of Your servants and Your people Israel, indeed, teach them the

speak the Word

I thank You, God, for giving me Your Word to teach me the good way in which I should walk.
–ADAPTED FROM 2 CHRONICLES 6:27

good way in which they should walk. And send rain on Your land which You have given to Your people as an inheritance.

²⁸"If there is famine in the land, if there is pestilence, if there is blight or mildew, if there are [migratory] locusts or grasshoppers, if their enemies besiege them in the land of their cities, whatever plague or whatever sickness *there is,*

²⁹then whatever prayer or request is made by any man or all of Your people Israel, each knowing his own suffering and his own pain, and stretching out his hands toward this house,

³⁰then hear from heaven, Your dwelling place, and forgive, and render to each in accordance with all his ways, whose heart You know; for You alone know the hearts of the sons of men,

³¹so that they may fear You, to walk in Your ways [in obedience to You] as long as they live in the land which You have given to our fathers.

³²"Also in regard to the foreigner who is not from Your people Israel, but has come from a far country for the sake of Your great name and Your mighty power and Your outstretched arm—when they come and pray toward this house,

³³then hear from heaven, from Your dwelling place, and do according to all for which the foreigner calls to You, so that all the peoples of the earth may know Your name, and fear You [reverently and worshipfully], as *do* Your people Israel, and that they may know that this house which I have built is called by Your Name.

³⁴"When Your people go out to war against their enemies, by the way that You send them, and they pray to You

facing this city [Jerusalem] which You have chosen and the house which I have built for Your Name,

³⁵then hear from heaven their prayer and their request, and maintain their cause *and* do justice.

³⁶"When they sin against You (for there is no man who does not sin) and You are angry with them and hand them over to an enemy, so that they take them away captive to a land far away or near,

³⁷if they take it to heart in the land where they have been taken captive, and repent and pray to You in the land of their captivity, saying, 'We have sinned, we have done wrong and have acted wickedly';

³⁸if they return to You with all their heart and with all their soul in the land of their captivity, and pray facing their land which You have given to their fathers and toward the city which You have chosen, and toward the house which I have built for Your Name;

³⁹then hear from heaven, from Your dwelling place, their prayer and requests, and maintain their cause *and* do justice and forgive Your people who have sinned against You.

⁴⁰"Now, O my God, I pray, let Your eyes be open and Your ears attentive to the prayer *offered* in this place.

⁴¹"Now then arise, O Lord God, [and come] to Your resting place, You and the ark of Your strength *and* power. Let Your priests, O Lord God, be clothed with salvation and let Your godly ones rejoice in [Your] goodness.

⁴²"O Lord God, do not turn away *and* reject the face of Your anointed; remember *Your* lovingkindness *and* faithfulness to Your servant David."

speak the Word

Lord, I rejoice in You and in Your goodness!
–ADAPTED FROM 2 CHRONICLES 6:41

7 WHEN SOLOMON had finished praying, fire came down from heaven and consumed the burnt offering and the sacrifices, and the [Shekinah] glory *and* brilliance of the LORD filled the house. [Lev 9:24]

²The priests could not enter the house of the LORD because the glory *and* brilliance of the LORD had filled the LORD's house.

³When all the people of Israel saw how the fire came down and *saw* the glory *and* brilliance of the LORD upon the house, they bowed down on the stone pavement with their faces to the ground, and they worshiped and praised the LORD, *saying,* "For He is good, for His mercy *and* lovingkindness endure forever."

⁴Then the king and all the people offered a sacrifice before the LORD.

⁵King Solomon offered a sacrifice of 22,000 oxen and 120,000 sheep. In this way the king and all the people dedicated God's house.

⁶The priests stood at their posts [ready for service], and the Levites also, with the musical instruments of the LORD which King David had made to praise the LORD, *saying,* "For His lovingkindness *and* mercy endure forever," whenever David offered praise through their ministry. The priests were opposite the Levites blowing the trumpets and all Israel was standing.

⁷Moreover, Solomon consecrated the middle of the courtyard that was in front of the house of the LORD, for it was there that he offered burnt offerings and the fat of the peace offerings because the bronze altar which he had made was not sufficient to hold the burnt offerings, the grain offerings, and the fat [all together].

⁸At that time Solomon observed the feast for seven days, and all Israel with him, a very large assembly, from the entrance of Hamath to the Brook of Egypt.

⁹On the eighth day they held a celebration, for they had observed the dedication of the altar for seven days, and the feast for seven days.

¹⁰And on the twenty-third day of the seventh month Solomon sent the people to their tents, rejoicing and happy in heart because of the goodness that the LORD had shown to David, to Solomon, and to His people Israel.

¹¹And so Solomon finished the house (temple) of the LORD and the palace of the king. He successfully accomplished all that he had planned to do in the house of the LORD and in his palace.

¹²Then the LORD appeared to Solomon by night and said to him: "I have heard your prayer and have chosen this place for Myself as a house of sacrifice.

¹³"If I shut up the heavens so that no rain falls, or if I command locusts to devour the land, or if I send pestilence *and* plague among My people,

¹⁴and My people, who are called by My Name, humble themselves, and pray and seek (crave, require as a necessity) My face and turn from their wicked ways, then I will hear [them] from heaven, and forgive their sin and heal their land.

putting the Word to work

God is very clear about what is necessary for a nation to receive His blessing (see 2 Chronicles 7:14). Did you know that you can help to bring about God's blessing upon your country? In humility, pray on behalf of your nation, identifying its sins and confessing them. Seek God's face, and pray that anyone who may be doing evil in your nation will turn from their wicked ways. God has promised forgiveness and healing to those nations that come to Him in humility and repentance.

¹⁵"Now My eyes will be open and My ears attentive to prayer *offered* in this place.

¹⁶"For now I have chosen and sanctified *and* set apart for My purpose this house that My Name may be here forever, and My eyes and My heart will be here perpetually.

¹⁷"As for you [Solomon], if you will walk before me as your father David walked, and do everything that I have commanded you, and observe My statutes and My ordinances, [1 Kin 11:1–11]

¹⁸then I will establish your royal throne just as I covenanted with your father David, saying, 'You will not fail to have a man as ruler in Israel.'

¹⁹"But if you [people] turn away and abandon My statutes and My commandments which I have set before you, and you go and serve other gods and worship them,

²⁰then I will uproot Israel from My land which I have given them; and I will cast this house, which I have consecrated for My Name, out of My sight, and will make it a proverb and an object of scorn among all nations. [Jer 24:9, 10]

²¹"And as for this house, which was so exalted, everyone who passes by it will be astonished *and* appalled and say, 'Why has the LORD done thus to this land and to this house?'

²²"Then people will say, 'It is because they abandoned the LORD, the God of their fathers, who brought them out of the land of Egypt, and they adopted other gods, and worshiped them and served them; therefore He has brought all this adversity *and* evil on them.'"

8 NOW IT came about at the end of the twenty years, in which Solomon had built the house of the LORD and his own house (palace),

²that he built *and* fortified the cities which Huram (Hiram) had given to him, and settled the Israelites there.

³Then Solomon went to Hamath-zobah and captured it.

⁴He built Tadmor in the wilderness, and all his storage cities in Hamath.

⁵He also built upper Beth-horon and lower Beth-horon, fortified cities with walls, gates, and bars [to lock the gates];

⁶and Baalath and all the storage cities that Solomon had, and all the cities for his chariots and the cities for his horsemen, and all that Solomon desired to build in Jerusalem, in Lebanon, and in all the land under his rule.

⁷All the people who were left of the Hittites, the Amorites, the Perizzites, the Hivites, and the Jebusites, who were not of Israel,

⁸*but were* descendants of those who were left in the land, whom the Israelites had not destroyed—Solomon brought them up as forced laborers to this day.

⁹But Solomon did not make slaves of the Israelites for his work; they were men of war, his chief captains, and commanders of his chariots and his horsemen.

¹⁰These were the chief officers of King Solomon, two hundred and fifty [in authority] who ruled over the people.

¹¹Then Solomon brought the daughter of Pharaoh up from the City of David into the house (palace) he had built for her, for he said, "My wife shall not live in the house of David king of Israel, because the places where the ark of the LORD has entered are holy."

¹²Then Solomon offered burnt offerings to the LORD on the altar of the LORD which he had built in front of the porch [of the temple],

¹³a certain number every day, offering them up as Moses commanded for the Sabbaths, the New Moons, and the three annual feasts—the Feast of Unleavened Bread, the Feast of Weeks, and the Feast of Booths (Tabernacles).

[14]Now in accordance with the ordinance of his father David, he appointed the divisions of the priests for their service, and the Levites for their duties of praise and ministering *and* serving before the priests as every day required, and the gatekeepers by their divisions at every gate; for David the man of God had so commanded.

[15]And they did not deviate from the commandment of the king to the priests and Levites in any respect or in regard to the storehouses *or* treasuries.

[16]Thus all the work of Solomon was carried out from the day the foundation of the house of the LORD was laid until it was finished. So the house of the LORD was completed.

[17]Then Solomon went to Ezion-geber and to Eloth on the shore of the [Red] Sea in the land of Edom.

[18]And Huram (Hiram) sent him, by his servants, ships and servants familiar with the sea; and they went with Solomon's servants to Ophir, and took from there four hundred and fifty talents of gold, and brought them to King Solomon.

9 WHEN THE queen of Sheba heard of the fame of Solomon, she came to Jerusalem to test Solomon with riddles. She was accompanied by a very large number of attendants, with camels bearing spices (balsam oil) and a large amount of gold and precious stones. And when she came to Solomon, she talked with him about all that was on her mind.

[2]Solomon answered all her questions; nothing was hidden from him which he did not make clear to her.

[3]So when the queen of Sheba saw the [depth of] Solomon's wisdom, and the house which he had built,

[4]and the food of his table, the [vast] seating order of his officials, the attendance *and* service of his ministers and their attire, his cupbearers and their attire, and his stairway by which he went up to the house of the LORD, she was breathless.

[5]She said to the king, "The report which I heard in my own land regarding your [accomplishments and your] words and your wisdom was true,

[6]but I did not believe the reports until I came and saw it with my own eyes. Behold, the half of the greatness of your wisdom was not told to me; you have surpassed the report that I heard.

[7]"Blessed *and* fortunate are your people, how blessed *and* fortunate are these servants of yours who stand before you continually and hear your wisdom!

[8]"Blessed be the LORD your God, who delighted in you, setting you on His throne as king for the LORD your God; because your God loved Israel, establishing them forever, therefore He made you king over them, to do justice and righteousness."

[9]Then she gave the king a hundred and twenty talents of gold, a very large *amount of* spices (balsam oil) and precious stones; there was no such spice [anywhere] like that which the queen of Sheba gave to King Solomon.

[10]The servants of Huram and those of Solomon, who brought gold from Ophir, also brought almug trees and precious stones.

[11]From the almug timber the king made stairways for the house of the LORD and for the king's palace, and lyres and harps for the singers; none like that was seen before in the land of Judah.

[12]King Solomon gave to the queen of Sheba all [the things] she desired, whatever she asked, besides *a return for* what she had brought to the king. So she returned to her own land with her servants.

[13]Now the weight of gold which came to Solomon in one year was 666 talents,

[14]besides what the traders and merchants brought; and all the kings of

Arabia and the governors of the country brought gold and silver to Solomon.

¹⁵King Solomon made two hundred large shields of beaten gold, using six hundred *shekels of* beaten gold on each large shield.

¹⁶And *he made* three hundred [smaller] shields of beaten gold, using three hundred shekels of gold on each shield; and the king put them in the house of the Forest of Lebanon.

¹⁷Moreover, the king made a great throne of ivory and overlaid it with pure gold.

¹⁸*There were* six steps to the throne and a golden footstool attached to the throne, and arms on each side of the seat, with two lions standing beside the arms.

¹⁹Also, twelve lions were standing there, one on each side of the six steps. Nothing like it had ever been made for any [other] kingdom.

²⁰All King Solomon's drinking vessels were of gold, and all the vessels of the house of the Forest of Lebanon were of pure gold; silver was not considered valuable in the days of Solomon.

²¹For the king's ships went to Tarshish with the servants of Huram; once every three years the ships of Tarshish came bringing gold and silver, ivory and apes and peacocks.

²²So King Solomon surpassed all the kings of the earth in wealth and wisdom.

²³And all the kings of the earth were seeking the presence of Solomon, to hear his wisdom which God had put into his heart.

²⁴Each man brought his gift, articles of silver and gold, garments, weapons, spices, horses and mules, so much year by year.

²⁵Now Solomon had 4,000 stalls for horses and chariots, and 12,000 horsemen, and he stationed them in the chariot cities or with the king at Jerusalem. [Deut 17:16, 17]

²⁶He ruled over all the kings from the Euphrates River to the land of the Philistines, and as far as the border of Egypt.

²⁷The king made silver in Jerusalem *as common* as stones, and cedar wood as plentiful as the sycamore-fig trees that are in the lowland.

²⁸And they were importing horses for Solomon from Egypt and from all [the other] countries.

²⁹Now the rest of the acts of Solomon, from the first to the last, are they not written in the records of Nathan the prophet, and in the prophecy of Ahijah the Shilonite, and in the visions of Iddo the seer concerning Jeroboam the son of Nebat?

³⁰Solomon reigned forty years in Jerusalem over all Israel.

³¹And Solomon slept with his fathers [in death]; he was buried in the city of his father David. Rehoboam his son reigned in his place.

putting the Word to work

If someone wanted to give you either wealth or wise counsel, which would you choose? Although the riches of Solomon surpassed those of all the kings of the earth, it was his wisdom that other rulers sought (see 2 Chronicles 9:23). Recognize, like the kings in Solomon's day, that God-given wisdom is far more valuable than wealth.

10 THEN REHOBOAM went to Shechem, because all Israel had come to Shechem to make him king.

²When Jeroboam the son of Nebat heard *about the new king* (for he was in Egypt, where he had fled from the presence of King Solomon), Jeroboam returned from Egypt. [1 Kin 11:26–40]

³And the people sent *messengers* and summoned him. So when Jeroboam

and all Israel came, they spoke to Rehoboam, saying,

⁴"Your father [King Solomon] made our yoke hard (heavy, difficult); so now lighten the hard service of your father and his heavy yoke which he put on us, and we will serve you."

⁵Rehoboam replied, "Come back to me again in three days." So the people departed.

⁶Then King Rehoboam consulted with the elders who had served his father Solomon [as advisers] while he was alive, asking, "What advice do you give me in answer to these people?"

⁷They answered him, saying, "If you are kind to these people and please them and speak good words to them, then they will be your servants forever."

⁸But the king rejected the advice which the elders gave him, and consulted with the young men who grew up with him and served him [as advisers].

⁹He asked them, "What advice do you give to us regarding the answer to these people, who have spoken to me, saying, 'Lighten the yoke which your father put on us'?"

¹⁰The young men who grew up with him told him, "Tell the people who said to you, 'Your father made our yoke heavy, but you make it lighter for us': 'My little finger is thicker than my father's loins!

¹¹'Now my father loaded you with a heavy yoke, but I will add [more weight] to your yoke. My father disciplined you with whips, but I *will discipline you* with scorpions (extremely painful scourges).'"

¹²So on the third day Jeroboam and all the people returned to Rehoboam just as the king had directed, saying, "Return to me on the third day."

¹³The king answered them harshly, for King Rehoboam rejected the counsel of the elders.

¹⁴He spoke to them in accordance with the advice of the young men, saying, "My father made your yoke heavy, but I will add to it; my father disciplined you with whips, but I *will discipline you* with scorpions."

¹⁵So the king did not listen to the people, for the turn of events was from God that the LORD might fulfill His word, which He had spoken through Ahijah the Shilonite to Jeroboam the son of Nebat. [1 Kin 11:29–39]

¹⁶When all Israel saw that the king did not listen *and* pay attention to them, the people answered him,

"What portion do we have in David?
We have no inheritance in the son
   of Jesse.
Every man to your tents, O Israel;
Now, [Rehoboam, descendant of]
   David, see to your own house."

So all Israel went to their tents. ¹⁷But as for the Israelites who lived in Judah's cities, Rehoboam ruled over them.

¹⁸Then King Rehoboam sent Hadoram, who was over the forced labor, and the Israelites stoned him and he died. And King Rehoboam hurried to mount his [royal] chariot to escape to Jerusalem.

¹⁹And Israel has rebelled against the house of David to this day.

11 NOW WHEN Rehoboam came to Jerusalem, he assembled the house of Judah and Benjamin, 180,000 chosen warriors to fight against [the ten tribes of] Israel to restore the kingdom to Rehoboam.

²But the word of the LORD came to Shemaiah the man of God, saying,

³"Say to Rehoboam the son of Solomon, king of Judah, and to all Israel in Judah and Benjamin,

⁴'Thus says the LORD: "You shall not go up nor fight against your brothers (countrymen); return, every man to his house, for this thing is from Me."'"

And they listened to *and* obeyed the words of the Lord and turned back from going against Jeroboam.

⁵Rehoboam lived in Jerusalem and built [fortified] cities for defense in Judah.

⁶He built Bethlehem, Etam, Tekoa, ⁷Beth-zur, Soco, Adullam, ⁸Gath, Mareshah, Ziph, ⁹Adoraim, Lachish, Azekah, ¹⁰Zorah, Aijalon, and Hebron, which are fortified cities in Judah and Benjamin.

¹¹He strengthened the fortresses and put officers in them, with supplies of food, [olive] oil, and wine.

¹²And in each city he put [large] shields and spears, and made them very strong. So he held Judah and Benjamin.

¹³Further, the priests and the Levites who were in all Israel took their stand with Rehoboam from all their districts.

¹⁴For the Levites left their pasture lands and their property and came to Judah and Jerusalem, because Jeroboam and his sons had excluded them from serving as priests to the Lord.

¹⁵Jeroboam appointed his own priests for the high places, for the satyrs (goat demons) and calves (idols) which he had made. [1 Kin 12:28]

¹⁶Those from all the tribes of Israel who set their hearts on seeking the Lord God of Israel followed them to Jerusalem, to sacrifice to the Lord God of their fathers.

¹⁷So they strengthened the kingdom of Judah and supported Rehoboam the son of Solomon for three years; for they walked in the way of David and Solomon for three years.

¹⁸Rehoboam took as his wife Mahalath, the daughter of Jerimoth the son of David, and of Abihail the daughter of Eliab the son of Jesse.

¹⁹She bore him sons: Jeush, Shemariah, and Zaham.

²⁰After her he took Maacah the daughter (granddaughter) of Absalom, and she bore him Abijah, Attai, Ziza, and Shelomith.

²¹Rehoboam loved Maacah the daughter (granddaughter) of Absalom more than all his wives and concubines—for he had taken eighteen wives and sixty concubines, and he fathered twenty-eight sons and sixty daughters.

²²Rehoboam appointed Abijah the son of Maacah the chief leader among his brothers, because he *intended* to make him king.

²³He acted wisely and distributed some of his sons throughout the territories of Judah and Benjamin to all the fortified cities. He gave them abundant provisions, and he sought many wives *for them*.

12 WHEN THE kingdom of Rehoboam was established and strong, he and all Israel with him abandoned the law of the Lord.

²And it came about in King Rehoboam's fifth year, because they had been unfaithful to the Lord, that Shishak king of Egypt came up against Jerusalem ³with 1,200 chariots and 60,000 horsemen. The people who came with him from Egypt were beyond counting—the Lubim, the Sukkiim, and the Ethiopians.

⁴Shishak took the fortified cities of Judah and came as far as Jerusalem.

⁵Then Shemaiah the prophet came to Rehoboam and the leaders of Judah who had gathered at Jerusalem because of Shishak, and said to them, "Thus says the Lord: 'You have abandoned (turned away from) Me, so I have abandoned you into the hands of Shishak.'"

⁶Then the leaders of Israel and the king humbled themselves and said, "The Lord is righteous."

[7]When the LORD saw that they humbled themselves, the word of the LORD came to Shemaiah, saying, "They have humbled themselves so I will not destroy them, but I will grant them some *measure* of a remnant [that escapes]; and My wrath shall not be poured out on Jerusalem by means of Shishak.

[8]"Nevertheless they will become his slaves, so that they may know [the difference between] My service and the service of the kingdoms of the countries."

[9]So Shishak king of Egypt went up against Jerusalem; he took the treasures of the house of the LORD and the treasures of the king's house (palace). He took everything. He even took the shields of gold which Solomon had made.

[10]In their place King Rehoboam made shields of bronze and entrusted them to the care of the officers of the guard who guarded the door of the king's house.

[11]And whenever the king entered the house of the LORD, the guards came and carried the shields and *then* brought them back into the guards' room.

[12]When Rehoboam humbled himself, the wrath of the LORD turned away from him, so as not to destroy him completely; and also conditions were good in Judah.

[13]So King Rehoboam established himself in Jerusalem and reigned. Rehoboam was forty-one years old when he began to reign, and he reigned seventeen years in Jerusalem, the city in which the LORD had chosen from all the tribes of Israel to put His Name. And his mother was Naamah the Ammonitess.

[14]He did evil because he did not set his heart to seek *and* worship *and* honor the LORD.

[15]Now the acts of Rehoboam, from the first to the last, are they not written in the records of Shemaiah the prophet and of Iddo the seer, according to genealogical enrollment? *There were* wars between Rehoboam [of Judah] and Jeroboam [of Israel] continually.

[16]And Rehoboam slept with his fathers [in death] and was buried in the City of David; and Abijah his son became king in his place.

13 IN THE eighteenth year of King Jeroboam, Abijah became king over Judah.

[2]He reigned three years in Jerusalem. His mother's name was Micaiah the daughter of Uriel of Gibeah.

And there was war between Abijah and Jeroboam [of Israel].

[3]Abijah began the battle with an army of brave soldiers, 400,000 chosen men. Jeroboam drew up in battle formation against him with 800,000 chosen men, valiant men.

[4]Then Abijah stood on Mount Zemaraim, which is in the hill country of Ephraim, and said, "Listen to me, Jeroboam and all Israel:

[5]"Do you not know that the LORD God of Israel, gave rule over Israel forever to David and to his sons by a covenant of salt [a permanent pact, extending to each generation of Israel]? [Num 18:19]

[6]"Yet Jeroboam the son of Nebat, a servant of Solomon the son of David, rose up and rebelled against his lord [the king],

[7]and worthless (unprincipled, unethical) men gathered around him, useless *and* wicked men, who proved too strong for Rehoboam the son of Solomon when Rehoboam was young and timid, and could not assert himself against them.

[8]"And now you intend to assert yourselves against the kingdom of the LORD which is in the hands of the sons of David, since you are a great multitude and have with you the golden calves (idols) which Jeroboam made for you as gods.

[9]"Have you not driven out the priests

of the LORD, the sons of Aaron and the Levites, and made priests for yourselves like the peoples of *other* lands? So whoever comes to consecrate himself with a young bull and seven rams, even he may become a priest of nonexistent gods (idols).

¹⁰"But as for us, the LORD is our God, and we have not abandoned (turned away from) Him. The sons of Aaron are ministering to the LORD as priests, and the Levites attend to their service.

¹¹"Every morning and every evening they offer the burnt offerings and the fragrant incense to the LORD; and the showbread is set on the clean table [of pure gold], and the golden lampstand with its lamps is ready to light every evening; for we keep the charge of the LORD our God [that is, the obligation we have to Him], but you have abandoned (turned away from) Him.

¹²"Behold, God is with us at our head, and His priests [are here] with their signal trumpets to sound an alarm against you. O sons of Israel, do not fight against the LORD God of your fathers, for you cannot succeed."

¹³But Jeroboam had set an ambush to come from the rear, so that Israel was in front of Judah and the ambush was behind them.

¹⁴When [the men of] Judah turned around, they were attacked from both front and rear; so they cried out to the LORD [for help], and the priests blew the trumpets.

¹⁵Then the men of Judah raised a war cry; and as they shouted, God struck Jeroboam and all Israel [with defeat] before Abijah and Judah.

¹⁶And the sons of Israel fled before Judah, and God handed over the sons of Israel to them.

¹⁷Abijah and his people inflicted on them a great defeat, so that 500,000 chosen men of Israel fell slain.

¹⁸Thus the sons of Israel were subdued (humbled) at that time, and the sons of Judah prevailed because they relied on the LORD, the God of their fathers.

¹⁹Abijah pursued Jeroboam and captured [several] cities from him: Bethel, Jeshanah, and Ephraim (Ephron), with their villages.

²⁰Jeroboam did not recover strength again during the time of [the reign of] Abijah. And the LORD struck him and he died.

²¹But Abijah became powerful. He took fourteen wives for himself and fathered twenty-two sons and sixteen daughters.

²²Now the rest of the acts of Abijah, and his ways and his sayings, are written in the writing of the prophet Iddo.

14 SO ABIJAH slept with his fathers [in death], and they buried him in the City of David; and Asa his son became king in his place. The land was at peace for ten years during his days. ²Asa did what was good and right in the sight of the LORD his God. ³He removed the foreign altars and high places and tore down the [pagan] pillars (obelisks, memorial stones), and cut to pieces the Asherim [the symbols of the goddess Asherah].

⁴And he commanded Judah to seek the LORD God of their fathers [to inquire of and for Him and seek Him as a vital necessity], and to observe the law [given to Moses] and the commandment.

⁵Asa also removed the [idolatrous] high places and the incense altars from all the cities of Judah. The kingdom was at rest *and* undisturbed under his reign.

⁶He built fortified cities in Judah, since the land was at rest, and there was no one at war with him in those years, because the LORD had given him rest.

⁷So he said to Judah, "Let us build these cities and surround them with walls, towers, gates and bars [to secure the doors]. The land is still ours because we have sought the Lord our God; we have sought Him [longing for Him with all our heart] and He has given us peace on every side." So they built and prospered.

⁸Now Asa had an army of 300,000 men from Judah, who carried large shields and spears, and 280,000 from Benjamin, who carried shields and drew bows, all courageous men.

⁹Now Zerah the Ethiopian (Cushite) came out against Judah with an army of a million men and three hundred chariots, and he came as far as Mareshah.

¹⁰Then Asa went out against him, and they drew up in battle formation in the Valley of Zephathah at Mareshah.

¹¹Asa called out to the Lord his God, saying, "O Lord, there is no one besides You to help *in the battle* between the powerful and the weak; so help us, O Lord our God, for we trust in *and* rely on You, and in Your name we have come against this multitude. O Lord, You are our God; let not man prevail against You."

¹²So the Lord struck the Ethiopians [with defeat] before Asa and Judah, and the Ethiopians fled.

¹³Asa and the people who were with him pursued them as far as Gerar; and so many Ethiopians fell that none of them *were found* alive; for they were destroyed before the Lord and His army. And they carried away a very large amount of spoil.

¹⁴They attacked *and* destroyed all the cities around Gerar, for the dread of the Lord had fallen on them. They plundered all the cities, for there was a large amount of spoil in them.

¹⁵They also struck down the people [living] in tents who had livestock, and took captive large numbers of sheep and camels. Then they returned to Jerusalem.

15 NOW THE Spirit of God came on Azariah the son of Oded,

²and he went out to meet Asa and said to him, "Hear me, Asa, and all Judah and Benjamin: the Lord is with you while you are with Him. If you seek Him [inquiring for and of Him, as your soul's first necessity], He will let you find Him; but if you abandon (turn away from) Him, He will abandon (turn away from) you.

³"Now for a long time Israel was without the true God and without a teaching priest, and without [God's] law.

⁴"But when they were in their trouble *and* distress they turned to the Lord God of Israel, and [in desperation earnestly] sought Him, and He let them find Him.

⁵"In those times there was no peace for him who went out or for him who

putting the Word to work

Have you ever felt that God is hiding from you? Second Chronicles 15:1–4 provides us with encouragement as we seek God. He promises that when you seek Him, you *will* find Him. Always remember that He draws near to all those who draw near to Him.

speak the Word

God, there is none besides You to help me, and it makes no difference whether I am feeling mighty or powerless, I still need Your help. Help me, God; I am trusting in and relying on You alone.
—ADAPTED FROM 2 CHRONICLES 14:11

came in, for great suffering came on all the inhabitants of the lands.

⁶"Nation was crushed by nation, and city by city, for God troubled them with every kind of distress.

⁷"But as for you, be strong and do not lose courage, for there is reward for your work."

⁸And when Asa heard these words, the prophecy of Azariah the son of Oded the prophet, he took courage and removed the repulsive idols from all the land of Judah and Benjamin and from the cities which he had captured in the hill country of Ephraim. Then he restored the altar [of burnt offering] of the Lord which was in front of the porch [of the temple] of the Lord.

⁹He gathered all Judah and Benjamin and the strangers who were with them out of Ephraim, Manasseh, and Simeon, for they came over to Asa from Israel in large numbers when they saw that the Lord his God was with him.

¹⁰So they assembled at Jerusalem in the third month of the fifteenth year of Asa's reign.

¹¹They sacrificed to the Lord on that day from the spoil they had brought—700 oxen and 7,000 sheep.

¹²They entered into a covenant (solemn agreement) to seek the Lord God of their fathers with all their heart and soul;

¹³and that whoever would not seek the Lord God of Israel, was to be put to death, whether young or old, man or woman.

¹⁴They swore an oath to the Lord with a loud voice, with [jubilant] shouting, with trumpets, and with horns.

¹⁵All Judah rejoiced over the oath, for they had sworn with all their heart and had sought Him with their whole heart, and He let them find Him. So the Lord gave them rest on every side.

¹⁶He also removed Maacah, King Asa's mother, from *the position of* queen mother, because she had made a repulsive image for [the goddess] Asherah. Asa cut down her idol, crushed it, and burned it at the Brook Kidron.

¹⁷But the high places [of pagan worship] were not removed from Israel. Nevertheless Asa's heart was blameless all his days.

¹⁸He brought the things that his father [Abijah] had dedicated and those things that he had dedicated into the house of God—silver and gold and utensils.

¹⁹And there was no war until the thirty-fifth year of Asa's reign.

16 IN THE thirty-sixth year of Asa's reign Baasha king of Israel came up against Judah and fortified Ramah in order to prevent *anyone* from going out or coming in to [meet with] Asa king of Judah.

²Then Asa brought out silver and gold from the treasuries of the house of the Lord and from the king's house, and sent them to Ben-hadad king of Aram (Syria), who lived in Damascus, saying,

³"*Let there be* a treaty between you and me, as there was between my father and your father. Look, I am sending you silver and gold; go, break your treaty with Baasha king of Israel, so that he will withdraw from me."

⁴Ben-hadad listened to King Asa and sent the commanders of his armies against the cities of Israel; and they

speak the Word

God, help me to be strong and not to lose courage, knowing that there is reward for my work.
—adapted from 2 Chronicles 15:7

does your heart belong completely to God?

When I first read 2 Chronicles 16:9 in the Amplified Classic version of the Bible, I saw that it said God looks for those whose hearts are "blameless" toward Him. In the King James Version, it says He is looking for those whose hearts are "perfect" toward Him.

Based on those readings, I misunderstood this truth and thought, *Boy, I had better straighten up.* Then I realized that the verse meant that God is looking for someone whose heart is perfect toward Him, or as it is rendered in the 2015 Amplified Bible, whose heart is "completely His." What does it mean for our hearts to be completely His? It does not mean to do everything "right"; it means to have a heartfelt desire to do right and to please God.

People whose hearts belong completely to God truly love Him, though they may not be perfect. They may still have things in the flesh to deal with. They may say things they should not say. They may make mistakes or lose their tempers. But when they do, they are quick to repent and make things right with God again. If they have offended someone, they will humble themselves and apologize.

If our hearts belong completely to the Lord, He counts us as perfect or blameless and works with us while that perfection becomes more and more real in our lives.

I am not a perfect person, but I do believe my heart is completely God's. I am sure there are things I am unaware of in my heart that need to be exposed and rooted out, but I believe God holds us responsible for only those things we are aware of. I do not have a perfect performance. Every day, I still do things I wish I did not do. But I love God with all my heart. There are many people with right hearts, and those are the ones God uses. Keep working on the things you need to work on in your life, and while you're at it, make sure your heart belongs completely to the Lord.

attacked *and* conquered Ijon, Dan, Abel-maim, and all the storage cities of Naphtali.

⁵When Baasha heard about it, he ceased fortifying Ramah and stopped his work.

⁶Then King Asa brought all Judah, and they carried away the stones of Ramah and its timber with which Baasha had been building, and with them he fortified Geba and Mizpah.

⁷At that time Hanani the seer came to Asa king of Judah and said to him,

"Because you relied on the king of Aram (Syria) and did not rely on the LORD your God, the army of the king of Aram (Syria) has escaped out of your hand.

⁸"Were not the Ethiopians and Lubim a huge army with a great number of chariots and horsemen? Yet because you relied on the LORD, He placed them in your hand.

⁹"For the eyes of the LORD move to and fro throughout the earth so that He may support those whose heart is

speak the Word

Thank You, God, that You support those whose hearts are completely Yours. Let my heart belong completely to You!
—ADAPTED FROM 2 CHRONICLES 16:9

completely His. You have acted foolishly in this; therefore, from now on you will have wars."

[10]Then Asa was angry with the seer and put him in prison [in the stocks], for he was enraged with him because of this. And at the same time Asa oppressed some of the people.

[11]Now the acts of Asa, from the first to the last, are written in the Book of the Kings of Judah and Israel.

[12]In the thirty-ninth year of his reign Asa developed a disease in his feet. His disease was severe, yet even in his illness he did not seek the LORD, but [relied only on] the physicians.

[13]So Asa slept with his fathers [in death], dying in the forty-first year of his reign.

[14]They buried him in his own tomb which he had cut out for himself in the City of David, and they laid him on a bier which he had filled with various kinds of spices blended by the perfumers' art; and they made a very great fire in his honor.

17 JEHOSHAPHAT HIS son then became king [of Judah] in Asa's place, and strengthened his position over Israel.

[2]He placed troops in all the fortified cities of Judah, and set garrisons in the land of Judah and in the cities of Ephraim which his father Asa had captured.

[3]The LORD was with Jehoshaphat because he followed the example of his father (ancestor) David. He did not seek [to follow] the Baals [the false gods],

[4]but sought the God of his father, and walked in (obeyed) His commandments, and did not act as Israel did.

[5]Therefore the LORD established the kingdom in his hand; and all Judah brought tribute to Jehoshaphat, and he had great wealth and honor.

[6]His heart was encouraged and he took great pride in the ways of the LORD; moreover, he again removed the high places [of pagan worship] and the Asherim from Judah.

[7]Then in the third year of his reign he sent his officials, Ben-hail, Obadiah, Zechariah, Nethanel, and Micaiah, to teach in the cities of Judah;

[8]and with them were the Levites— Shemaiah, Nethaniah, Zebadiah, Asahel, Shemiramoth, Jehonathan, Adonijah, Tobijah, and Tobadonijah; and with them the priests Elishama and Jehoram.

[9]They taught in Judah having the Book of the Law of the LORD with them; they went throughout all the cities of Judah and taught among the people.

[10]Now the dread of the LORD was on all the kingdoms of the lands surrounding Judah, so that they did not make war against Jehoshaphat.

[11]Some of the Philistines brought gifts and silver as tribute to Jehoshaphat; the Arabians also brought him flocks: 7,700 rams and 7,700 male goats.

[12]So Jehoshaphat became greater and greater. He built fortresses and storage cities in Judah.

[13]He had large supplies in the cities of Judah, and soldiers, courageous men, in Jerusalem.

[14]This was the number of them by their fathers' (ancestors') households: of Judah, the commanders of thousands, Adnah the commander, and with him 300,000 courageous men;

[15]and next to him was Jehohanan the commander, and with him 280,000;

[16]and next to him Amasiah the son of Zichri, who volunteered for the LORD, and with him 200,000 courageous men;

[17]and of Benjamin: Eliada, a brave man, and with him 200,000 men armed with bow and shield;

[18]and next to him was Jehozabad, and with him 180,000 armed and ready for military service.

¹⁹These are the ones who were in the service of the king, besides those he had placed in fortified cities throughout Judah.

18

NOW JEHOSHAPHAT had great wealth and honor, and was allied by marriage with Ahab.

²Some years later he went down to [visit] Ahab in Samaria. And Ahab slaughtered many sheep and oxen for him and the people who were with him, and induced him to go up against Ramoth-gilead.

³Ahab king of Israel said to Jehoshaphat king of Judah, "Will you go with me to [fight against] Ramoth-gilead?" He answered, "I am as you are, and my people as your people [your hopes and concerns are ours]; we will be with you in the battle."

⁴Further, Jehoshaphat said to the king of Israel, "Please inquire first for the word of the LORD."

⁵Then the king of Israel assembled the prophets, four hundred men, and said to them, "Shall we go against Ramoth-gilead to battle, or shall I refrain?" And they said, "Go up, for God will hand it over to the king."

⁶But Jehoshaphat said, "Is there no prophet of the LORD still here by whom we may inquire?"

⁷The king of Israel said to Jehoshaphat, "There is still one man by whom we may inquire of the LORD, but I hate him, for he never prophesies [anything] good for me, but always evil. He is Micaiah the son of Imla" And Jehoshaphat said, "Let not the king say so [perhaps this time it will be different]."

⁸Then the king of Israel called for an officer and said, "Bring Micaiah the son of Imla quickly."

⁹Now the king of Israel and Jehoshaphat the king of Judah were sitting, each on his throne, arrayed in their robes; they were sitting at the threshing floor at the entrance of the gate of Samaria; and all the prophets were prophesying before them.

¹⁰Zedekiah the son of Chenaanah had made horns of iron for himself; and said, "Thus says the LORD: 'With these you shall gore the Arameans (Syrians) until they are destroyed.'"

¹¹All the prophets prophesied this, saying, "Go up to Ramoth-gilead and succeed; the LORD will hand it over to the king."

¹²The messenger who went to call Micaiah said to him, "Listen, the words of the prophets are of one accord, foretelling a favorable outcome for the king. So just let your word be like one of them and speak favorably."

¹³But Micaiah said, "As the LORD lives, I will [only] speak what my God says."

¹⁴When he came to the king, the king said to him, "Micaiah, shall we go to Ramoth-gilead to battle, or shall I refrain?" And he said, "Go up and succeed, for they will be handed over to you."

¹⁵Then the king said to him, "How many times must I warn you (make you swear an oath) to tell me nothing but the truth in the name of the LORD?"

¹⁶Then Micaiah said,

"I saw all [the people of] Israel
Scattered on the mountains,
As sheep that have no shepherd;
And the LORD said,
'These have no master.
Let each one return to his house in
    peace.'"

¹⁷Then the king of Israel said to Jehoshaphat, "Did I not tell you that he would not prophesy good in regard to me, but [only] evil?"

¹⁸So Micaiah said, "Therefore, hear the word of the LORD: I saw the LORD sitting on His throne, and all the host (army) of heaven standing on His right and on His left.

¹⁹"Then the Lᴏʀᴅ said, 'Who will entice Ahab king of Israel to go up and fall [defeated] at Ramoth-gilead?' And one said this and another said that.

²⁰"Then a spirit came forward and stood before the Lᴏʀᴅ and said, 'I will entice him.' The Lᴏʀᴅ said to him, 'By what means?'

²¹"He said, 'I will go out and be a deceptive spirit in the mouth of all his prophets.' Then the Lᴏʀᴅ said, 'You are to entice him and also succeed. Go and do so.'

²²"Now, you see, the Lᴏʀᴅ put a deceptive spirit in the mouth of these prophets of yours; and the Lᴏʀᴅ has [actually] proclaimed disaster against you."

²³Then Zedekiah the son of Chenaanah came up and struck Micaiah on the cheek and said, "Which way did the Spirit of the Lᴏʀᴅ go [when he departed] from me to speak to you?"

²⁴Micaiah said, "Behold, you will see on that day when you go into an inner room [desperately trying] to hide yourself."

²⁵Then the king of Israel said, "Take Micaiah and return him to Amon the governor of the city and to Joash the king's son,

²⁶and say, 'Thus says the king: "Put this man in prison and feed him just enough bread and water to survive until I return in peace (safely)."'"

²⁷But Micaiah said, "If you actually return in peace, the Lᴏʀᴅ has not spoken by me." And he added, "Listen [to what I have said], you people, all of you."

²⁸So [Ahab] the king of Israel and Jehoshaphat king of Judah went up against Ramoth-gilead.

²⁹The king of Israel said to Jehoshaphat, "I will disguise myself and will go into battle, but you put on your [royal] robes." So the king of Israel disguised himself, and they went into the battle.

³⁰Now the king of Aram (Syria) had commanded the captains of his chariots, saying, "Do not fight with the small or the great, but only with the king of Israel."

³¹So when the captains of the chariots saw Jehoshaphat [of Judah], they said, "It is the king of Israel!" So they turned to fight against him, but Jehoshaphat called out [for God's help], and the Lᴏʀᴅ helped him; and God diverted them away from him.

³²When the captains of the chariots saw that it was not the king of Israel, they turned back from pursuing him.

³³Then a certain man drew his bow at random and struck [Ahab] the king of Israel between the scales of *his* armor. So Ahab said to his chariot driver, "Turn around and take me out of the battle, because I am seriously wounded."

³⁴The battle raged that day, and the king of Israel propped himself up in his chariot in front of the Arameans (Syrians) until the evening, and at sunset he died.

19 JEHOSHAPHAT THE king of Judah returned safely to his house (palace) in Jerusalem.

²Jehu the son of Hanani the seer went out to meet him and said to King Jehoshaphat, "Should you help the ungodly and love those who hate the Lᴏʀᴅ and in doing so *bring* wrath from the Lᴏʀᴅ on yourself?

³"But there are *some* good things found in you, for you have removed the Asherim (idols) from the land and you have set your heart to seek God [with all your soul's desire]."

⁴So Jehoshaphat lived in Jerusalem, and he went out again among the people from Beersheba to the hill country of Ephraim and brought them back to the Lᴏʀᴅ, the God of their fathers.

⁵He appointed judges in the land in all the fortified cities of Judah, city by city,

⁶and he said to the judges, "Be careful what you do, for you do not judge

for man, but for the LORD who is with you in the matter of judgment.

7"So now let the fear (reverent awe) of the LORD be on you [to keep you from making unjust decisions]; be careful in what you do, for there is no injustice with the LORD our God, or partiality, or acceptance of a bribe."

8In Jerusalem also Jehoshaphat appointed some of the Levites, priests, and heads of the fathers' *households* of Israel to *render* the judgment of the LORD and to judge disputes among the inhabitants of Jerusalem.

9Then the king commanded them, "Do this in the fear of the LORD, faithfully and wholeheartedly.

10"Whenever any dispute comes to you from your brothers (relatives) who live in their cities, between blood and blood, between law and commandment, or between statutes and judgments, you are to warn [and instruct] them so that they may not

be guilty before the LORD; otherwise [God's] wrath will come on you and your brothers. Do this and you will not be guilty.

11"Behold, Amariah the chief priest will be over you in all matters of the LORD, and Zebadiah the son of Ishmael, the governor of the house of Judah, in all the king's matters; and the Levites will serve you as officers. Deal courageously, and may the LORD be with the upright."

20 NOW IT happened after this that the Moabites and the Ammonites, together with some of the Meunites, came to make war against Jehoshaphat.

2Then it was reported to Jehoshaphat, "A great multitude has come against you from beyond the [Dead] Sea, out of Aram (Syria); and behold, they are in Hazazon-tamar (that is, Engedi)."

run to the throne

Are the "-ites" after you? In 2 Chronicles 20:1–3 it was the Moabites, the Ammonites, and the Menuites who were after King Jehoshaphat and the people of Judah. In other places in the Old Testament it was the Jebusites, the Hittites, and the Canaanites who were the troublemakers for God's people.

But with us it is the "fear-ites," "disease-ites," "poverty-ites," "bad marriage-ites," "stress-ites," "grouchy neighbor-ites," "insecurity-ites," "rejection-ites," and on and on.

How many "-ites" are chasing you around? However many there are, let's look at what King Jehoshaphat did to turn his attention on God instead of focusing on all those "-ites" that were trying to rise and rule.

When Jehoshaphat was told that the "-ites" were coming against him, the first thing he did was to fear. But then he did something else: He set himself to seek the Lord. Determined to hear from Him, he proclaimed a fast throughout the land for that very purpose. He knew he needed to hear from God. He needed a battle plan, and only God could give him one that was sure to succeed.

When we have trouble, we should develop the habit of running to God instead of to people. We should seek God rather than our own minds or other people's thoughts. Ask yourself, "When trouble comes, do I run to the phone or to the throne?" God might direct us to a person for advice, but we should always go to Him first to show that we honor and trust Him above all else.

³Then Jehoshaphat was afraid and set himself [determinedly, as his vital need] to seek the LORD; and he proclaimed a fast throughout all Judah.

⁴So [the people of] Judah gathered together to seek help from the LORD; indeed they came from all the cities of Judah to seek the LORD [longing for Him with all their heart].

⁵Then Jehoshaphat stood in the assembly of Judah and Jerusalem, in the house of the LORD in front of the new courtyard,

⁶and said, "O LORD, God of our fathers, are You not God in heaven? And do You not rule over all the kingdoms of the nations? Power and might are in Your hand, there is no one able to take a stand against You.

⁷"O our God, did You not drive out the inhabitants of this land before Your people Israel and give it forever

putting the Word to work

Have you ever found yourself in circumstances that made you fearful? Jehoshaphat found himself surrounded by enemies, but instead of giving in to fear, he sought God's advice (see 2 Chronicles 20:1–4). When you are afraid or uncertain how to handle a difficult challenge, ask the Lord to help you know how to best deal with the situation. He will give you the guidance you need.

to the descendants of Your friend Abraham?

⁸"They have lived in it, and have built You a sanctuary in it for Your Name, saying,

⁹'If evil comes on us, or the sword of judgment, or plague, or famine,

these are fighting words

The words in 2 Chronicles 20:6–11 are fighting words! If we listen to what the Lord is saying to us through them, we will learn something that will change our battle plan forever and give us victory after victory.

After starting his prayer by acknowledging how great, awesome, powerful, and wonderful the Lord is, Jehoshaphat then began relating specific mighty acts God had performed in the past to protect His people and uphold the promises He had made to them. And in finally presenting his request, he expressed his confidence that God would handle the problem. Jehoshaphat said in so many words, "Oh, by the way, our enemies are coming against us to try to take away the possession that You gave us for our inheritance. I just thought I would mention this little problem. But You are so great; I know You already have it all under control."

When we do ask God for help, we should remember that He hears us the first time we ask Him for something. We do not need to spend our prayer time asking Him for the same things over and over. We may keep talking to Him about our needs until we have assurance in our hearts that we have a breakthrough, but we do not have to do that to move God.

God has a plan for our deliverance from every situation, even before those situations present themselves. He knows what we need before we ask Him. God is not surprised when the enemy attacks, and He is not in heaven wringing His hands, trying to figure out what to do. Our job is to focus on Him and His mighty power, worshiping Him and praising Him for the manifestation of His solution, and listening for a word or direction from Him. He always has a winning battle plan!

we will stand before this house and before You (for Your Name *and* Your Presence is in this house) and we will cry out to You in our distress, and You will hear and save us.'

¹⁰"Now behold, the sons of Ammon and Moab and Mount Seir, whom You would not allow Israel to invade when they came from the land of Egypt (for they turned away from them and did not destroy them), [Deut 2:9]

¹¹here they are, rewarding us by coming to drive us out of Your possession which You have given us as an inheritance.

¹²"O our God, will You not judge them? For we are powerless against this great multitude which is coming against us. We do not know what to do, but our eyes are on You."

¹³So all Judah stood before the LORD, with their infants, their wives, and their children.

¹⁴Then in the midst of the assembly the Spirit of the LORD came upon Jahaziel the son of Zechariah, the son of Benaiah, the son of Jeiel, the son of Mattaniah, a Levite of the sons of Asaph.

¹⁵He said, "Listen carefully, all [you people of] Judah, and you inhabitants of Jerusalem, and King Jehoshaphat.

rest in the storm

I love 2 Chronicles 20:12 because it tells us what to pray when we are facing a big battle: "We do not know what to do, but our eyes are on You." The people in this war realized three things: (1) They had no might against their enemies, (2) they did not know what to do, and (3) they needed to have their eyes focused on God.

The Lord responded with these powerful, assuring words: "You need not fight in this battle; take your positions, stand and witness the salvation of the LORD who is with you. . . . Do not fear or be dismayed" (2 Chronicles 20:17).

What is our position? It is one of abiding in Jesus and entering the rest of God. It is one of waiting on the Lord continually with our eyes focused upon Him, doing what He directs us to do and otherwise having a "reverential fear" of moving in the flesh.

Concerning entering God's rest, I would like to say this: There is no such thing as "the rest of God" without opposition. To illustrate, let me share a story I once heard involving two artists who were asked to paint pictures of "peace" as they perceived it. One painted a quiet, still lake, far back in the mountains. The other painted a raging, rushing waterfall that had a birch tree leaning out over it with a bird resting in a nest on one of the branches.

Which painting truly depicts peace? The second one does, because there is no such thing as peace without opposition. The first painting represents stagnation. The scene it sets forth may be serene; a person might be motivated to want to go there to recuperate. It may offer a pretty picture, but it does not depict the rest of God.

Jesus said, "Peace I leave with you; My [perfect] peace I give to you; not as the world gives do I give to you" (John 14:27). His peace is a spiritual peace, and His rest is one that operates in the midst of the storm—not in its absence. Jesus did not come to remove all opposition from our lives, but rather to give us a different approach to the storms of life. As we learn His ways and approach life in the same way He did, we will experience His rest in the midst of our storms.

The LORD says this to you: 'Be not afraid or dismayed at this great multitude, for the battle is not yours, but God's.

[16]'Go down against them tomorrow. Behold, they will come up by the ascent of Ziz, and you will find them at the end of the river valley, in front of the Wilderness of Jeruel.

[17]'You *need* not fight in this *battle;* take your positions, stand and witness the salvation of the LORD who is with you, O Judah and Jerusalem. Do not fear or be dismayed; tomorrow go out against them, for the LORD is with you.'"

[18]Jehoshaphat bowed with his face

life point

When "all Judah" was assembled before the Lord in 2 Chronicles 20:13–17, a person began to prophesy and speak God's direction to them. I believe the Spirit of God came upon this person because everyone was waiting on God.

When we learn to seek God and wait on Him, He will answer us. That answer may be very plain and simple, as Judah's was. The Lord told Judah to not be afraid because the battle was not to be their battle, but His. That does not sound too mystical or deeply spiritual, but it was all they needed to hear.

The battle is not yours, but God's. What good news! God did not say there was nothing for them to do in the battle; He was saying that He was going to show them their part. They could do it in the strength and wisdom of the Lord, but the battle was still His to win.

After God gave them that word of encouragement, He gave them a word of specific instruction (see 2 Chronicles 20:17). We are to wait on the Lord until He has told us what to do, and then we are to do it in the strength He gave us while we were waiting on Him.

life point

Second Chronicles 20:22 says that while the people of Judah were singing praise to God, He set ambushes against their enemies. What happened next was astounding: the enemy soldiers slaughtered one another! Praise confused the enemy!

Just think about it. The people of Judah set themselves to seek God rather than live in fear. They told God how awesome He is; they stood and waited on God. He sent a prophet with a word for them, telling them the battle was not theirs but His. He told them to take their position and stand still. They worshiped and praised. Jehoshaphat appointed singers to sing and praise, and the Lord defeated their enemies by confusing them so much that they killed each other! What an awesome God we serve!

to the ground, and all Judah and the inhabitants of Jerusalem fell down before the LORD, worshiping Him.

[19]The Levites, from the sons of the Kohathites and the sons of the Korahites, stood up to praise the LORD God of Israel, with a very loud voice.

[20]So they got up early in the morning and went out into the Wilderness of Tekoa; and as they went out, Jehoshaphat stood and said, "Hear me, O Judah, and you inhabitants of Jerusalem! Believe *and* trust in the LORD your God and you will be established (secure). Believe *and* trust in His prophets and succeed."

[21]When he had consulted with the people, he appointed those who sang to the LORD and those who praised Him in their holy (priestly) attire, as they went out before the army and said, "Praise *and* give thanks to the LORD, for His mercy *and* lovingkindness endure forever."

[22]When they began singing and praising, the LORD set ambushes against the

sons of Ammon, Moab, and Mount Seir, who had come against Judah; so they were struck down [in defeat].

²³For the sons of Ammon and Moab [suspecting betrayal] rose up against the inhabitants of Mount Seir, completely destroying them; and when they had finished with the inhabitants of Seir, they helped to destroy one another.

²⁴When [the men of] Judah came to the lookout tower of the wilderness, they looked toward the multitude, and behold, they were dead bodies lying on the ground, and no one had escaped.

²⁵When Jehoshaphat and his people came to take their spoil, they found much among them, *including* equipment, garments, and valuable things which they took for themselves, more than they could carry away; so much that they spent three days gathering the spoil.

²⁶Then on the fourth day they assembled in the Valley of Beracah, for it was there that they blessed the LORD. For that reason they named that place "The Valley of Beracah (blessing)" until today.

²⁷Then they returned to Jerusalem with joy, every man of Judah and Jerusalem, led by Jehoshaphat, for the LORD had made them rejoice over their enemies.

²⁸They came to Jerusalem with harps, lyres, and trumpets to the house (temple) of the LORD.

²⁹And the fear of God came on all the kingdoms of those countries when they heard that the LORD had fought against the enemies of Israel.

³⁰So the kingdom of Jehoshaphat was quiet, for his God gave him rest on all sides.

³¹Now Jehoshaphat reigned over Judah. He was thirty-five years old when he became king, and he reigned in Jerusalem for twenty-five years.

His mother's name was Azubah the daughter of Shilhi.

³²He walked in the way of his father Asa and did not depart from it, doing what was right in the sight of the LORD.

³³Only the high places [for pagan sacrifices] were not removed, for the people had not yet set their hearts firmly on the God of their fathers.

³⁴Now the rest of the acts of Jehoshaphat, from the first to the last, behold, they are written in the records of Jehu the son of Hanani, which are recorded in the Book of the Kings of Israel.

³⁵After [all] this Jehoshaphat king of Judah made an alliance with Ahaziah king of Israel, and he acted wickedly in doing so.

³⁶He joined him in building ships to go to Tarshish [for trade], and they built them in Ezion-geber.

³⁷Then Eliezer the son of Dodavahu of Mareshah prophesied against Jehoshaphat, saying, "Because you have allied yourself with Ahaziah, the LORD has broken down what you have built." So the ships were wrecked and were unable to go to Tarshish.

21

JEHOSHAPHAT SLEPT with his fathers [in death] and was buried with them in the City of David; and his son Jehoram became king in his place.

²He had brothers, the sons of Jehoshaphat: Azariah, Jehiel, Zechariah, Azaryahu, Michael, and Shephatiah. All of these were the sons of Jehoshaphat king of Israel.

³Their father gave them many gifts of silver, gold, and valuable things, in addition to fortified cities in Judah; but he gave the kingdom to Jehoram because he was the firstborn.

⁴When Jehoram had ascended over the kingdom of his father and made himself secure, he killed all his brothers with the sword [to eliminate any

rivals], and some of the leaders of Israel as well.

⁵Jehoram was thirty-two years of age when he became king, and he reigned eight years in Jerusalem. ⁶He walked in the way of the kings of Israel, just as the house of Ahab had done (for he married the daughter of Ahab), and he did what was evil in the sight of the LORD.

⁷Yet the LORD would not destroy the house of David because of the covenant which He had made with David, and because He had promised to give a lamp to him and to his sons forever. [2 Sam 7:12–17; 1 Kin 11:36; Ps 132:17]

⁸In the days of Jehoram Edom revolted against the rule of Judah and set up a king over themselves. ⁹Then Jehoram crossed over [the Jordan River] with his commanders and all his chariots, and rose up by night and struck down the Edomites who were surrounding him and the commanders of the chariots. ¹⁰So Edom revolted against the rule of Judah to this day. Then Libnah revolted at the same time against Jehoram's rule, because he had abandoned (turned away from) the LORD God of his fathers. ¹¹Moreover, he made [idolatrous] high places in the hill country of Judah, and caused the inhabitants of Jerusalem to be unfaithful [to God], and he led Judah astray [compelling the people's cooperation].

¹²Then a letter came to Jehoram from Elijah the prophet, saying, "Thus says the LORD God of David your father (ancestor): 'Because you have not walked in the ways of your father Jehoshaphat nor in the ways of Asa king of Judah, ¹³but have walked in the way of the kings of Israel, and caused Judah and the inhabitants of Jerusalem to be unfaithful [to God] as the house of Ahab was unfaithful, and you have also murdered your brothers, your father's house (your own family), who were better than you,

¹⁴behold, the LORD is going to strike your people, your sons, your wives, and all your possessions with a great disaster; ¹⁵and you will suffer a severe illness, an intestinal disease, until your intestines come out because of the sickness, day after day.'"

¹⁶Then the LORD stirred up against Jehoram the spirit (anger) of the Philistines and of the Arabs who bordered the Ethiopians. ¹⁷They came against Judah and invaded it, and carried away all the possessions found in the king's house (palace), together with his sons and his wives; so there was not a son left to him except Jehoahaz, the youngest of his sons.

¹⁸After all this, the LORD struck Jehoram with an incurable intestinal disease. ¹⁹Now it came about in the course of time, at the end of two years, that his intestines came out because of his disease and he died in excruciating pain. And his people did not make a funeral fire *to honor* him, like the fire for his fathers.

²⁰Jehoram was thirty-two years old when he became king, and he reigned in Jerusalem eight years; and he departed with no one's regret (sorrow). They buried him in the City of David, but not in the tombs of the kings.

22 THEN THE inhabitants of Jerusalem made Ahaziah, his youngest son, king in his place, because the band of men (raiders) who came with the Arabs to the camp had killed all the older *sons*. So Ahaziah the son of Jehoram king of Judah began to reign. ²Ahaziah was twenty-two years old when he became king and he reigned one year in Jerusalem. His mother's

name was Athaliah, a granddaughter of Omri. [2 Kin 8:26]

³He also walked in the ways of the house of Ahab, for his mother was his adviser [and she encouraged him] to act wickedly.

⁴So he did evil in the sight of the LORD like the house of Ahab, for they were his advisers after the death of his father, resulting in his destruction. ⁵He also walked in accordance with their advice, and he went with Jehoram the son of Ahab king of Israel to wage war against Hazael king of Aram (Syria) at Ramoth-gilead. And the Arameans wounded Joram (Jehoram). [2 Kin 8:28ff]

⁶Then he returned to Jezreel to recover from the wounds they had inflicted on him at Ramah when he fought against Hazael king of Aram. And Ahaziah, the son of Jehoram king of Judah, went down to see Jehoram the son of Ahab in Jezreel, because he was sick.

⁷But the downfall of Ahaziah was ordained by God, in that he went to Joram (Jehoram). For when he arrived there he went out [as an ally] with Jehoram against Jehu the son of Nimshi, whom the LORD had anointed to destroy the house of Ahab.

⁸It came about that when Jehu was executing judgment on the house of Ahab, he found the leaders of Judah and the sons of Ahaziah's [murdered] brothers ministering to Ahaziah, and he killed them.

⁹Jehu also searched for Ahaziah, who was hiding in Samaria; he was captured, brought to Jehu, and put to death. They buried him, for they said, "After all, he is the grandson of Jehoshaphat, who sought the LORD with all his heart." So the house of Ahaziah had no one left to retain the power to rule over the kingdom.

¹⁰Now when Athaliah the mother of Ahaziah saw that her son was dead, she rose and destroyed all the royal family of the house of Judah.

¹¹But Jehoshabeath, the king's daughter, took Joash the [infant] son of Ahaziah and stole him away from among the king's sons who were being put to death, and she placed him and his nurse in the bedroom. So Jehoshabeath, the daughter of King Jehoram [of Judah] and wife of Jehoiada the priest, hid Joash from [his grandmother] Athaliah so that she did not murder him (for Jehoshabeath was the sister of Ahaziah).

¹²Joash was hidden with them in the house (temple) of God for six years, and Athaliah reigned over the land.

23 IN THE seventh year Jehoiada [the priest] summoned his courage and took the captains of hundreds: Azariah the son of Jeroham, Ishmael the son of Johanan, Azariah the son of Obed, Maaseiah the son of Adaiah, and Elishaphat the son of Zichri, *and they entered* into a covenant with him.

²They went throughout Judah and gathered the Levites out of all the cities of Judah, and the heads of the *households of the* fathers (ancestors) in Israel, and they came to Jerusalem.

³Then all the assembly made a covenant in the house of God with the king [that is, with the child Joash, to overthrow Athaliah by proclaiming his sovereignty]. And Jehoiada [the priest] said to them, "Behold, the king's son [Joash] shall reign, as the LORD has said in regard to the sons of David.

⁴"This is what you shall do: a third of you, of the priests and Levites who are resuming service on the Sabbath, shall be gatekeepers,

⁵a [second] third *shall be* at the king's house (palace), and a [final] third at the Gate of the Foundation; and all the people shall be in the courtyards of the house of the LORD.

6"But let no one enter the house (temple) of the LORD except the priests and the Levites who minister; they may enter, for they are holy. And let all the people carefully observe the law of the LORD.

7"The Levites shall surround the [young] king, every man with his weapons in his hand; and whoever comes into the temple [breaking through the ranks of the guard to get near Joash] is to be killed. You are to be with the king when he comes in [from the temple chamber where he is hiding] and when he goes out."

8So the Levites and all Judah acted in accordance with everything that Jehoiada the priest had commanded; and every man took his men who were to resume duty on the Sabbath, with those who were to go off duty on the Sabbath, for Jehoiada the priest did not dismiss [any of] the divisions [from their duties].

9Then Jehoiada the priest gave to the captains of hundreds the spears and the large and small shields which had been King David's, which were in the house of God.

10He stationed all the people around the king [as guards for him], every man with his weapon in his hand, from the right side to the left side of the house (temple), by the altar and by the house.

11Then they brought out the king's son and put the crown on him, and gave him the testimony [a copy of the Mosaic Law] and made him king. And Jehoiada and his sons anointed him and said, "Long live the king!" [Ex 25:16, 21]

12When Athaliah heard the sound of the people running and praising the king, she went into the house of the LORD to [see what] the people [were doing].

13She looked, and there was the [young] king, standing by his pillar at the entrance, and the captains and the

trumpeters were beside him. And all the people of the land were rejoicing and blowing trumpets, and the singers with their musical instruments were directing the [singing of] praise. Then Athaliah tore her clothes and cried, "Treason! Treason!"

14So Jehoiada the priest brought out the captains of hundreds who were appointed over the army and said to them, "Bring her out between the ranks [of soldiers]; and whoever follows her shall be put to death with the sword." For the priest had said, "Do not let her be put to death in the temple of the LORD."

15So they seized Athaliah, and when she arrived at the entrance of the Horse Gate of the king's house (palace), they put her to death there.

16Then Jehoiada made a covenant between himself, all the people, and the king, that they would be the LORD's people.

17Then all the people went to the house of Baal and tore it down, and they smashed its altars and its images to pieces, and killed Mattan, the priest of Baal, in front of the altars.

18Also Jehoiada placed the offices and officers of the house of the LORD under the authority of the Levitical priests, whom David had [previously] assigned over the house of the LORD, to offer the burnt offerings of the LORD, as it is written in the Law of Moses, with rejoicing and singing in accordance with the order of David.

19Jehoiada stationed the gatekeepers [at the gates] of the house of the LORD, so that no one would enter who was in any way unclean.

20He took the captains of hundreds, the nobles, the rulers of the people, and all the people of the land, and brought the king down from the house of the LORD; and they came through the upper gate to the king's house (palace) and set the king on the throne of the kingdom.

21So all the people of the land rejoiced, and the city was quiet after Athaliah had been put to death with the sword.

24 JOASH WAS seven years old when he became king, and he reigned for forty years in Jerusalem. His mother's name was Zibiah from Beersheba.

²Joash did what was right in the sight of the LORD all the days of Jehoiada the priest [his uncle].

³Jehoiada took two wives for him, and he fathered sons and daughters.

⁴Now it came about after this that Joash decided to restore the house (temple) of the LORD.

⁵He gathered the priests and the Levites and said to them, "Go out to the cities of Judah and collect money from all Israel to repair the house of your God from year to year; and see that you do it quickly." But the Levites did not act quickly.

⁶So the king called for Jehoiada the high *priest* and said to him, "Why have you not required the Levites to bring in from Judah and Jerusalem the tax for the tent of the testimony which was *authorized by* Moses, the servant of the LORD and *the servant* of the assembly of Israel?"

⁷For the sons of Athaliah, that wicked woman, had broken into the house of God and also had used all the holy *and* dedicated things of the house of the LORD for the Baals.

⁸So at the king's command they made a chest and set it outside by the gate of the house of the LORD.

⁹Then they made a proclamation in Judah and Jerusalem to bring in for the LORD the tax that Moses the servant of God imposed on Israel in the wilderness.

¹⁰All the officers and all the people rejoiced and brought their tax and dropped it into the chest until they had finished [and the chest was full].

¹¹It came about that whenever the Levites brought the chest to the king's official, and whenever they saw that there was a large amount of money, the king's secretary and the chief priest's representative would come and empty the chest, and take it, and return it to its place. They did this day after day and collected a large amount of money.

¹²The king and Jehoiada gave it to those who did the work of the service of the house of the LORD; and they would hire masons and carpenters (craftsmen) and also those who worked in iron and bronze to repair *and* restore the house of the LORD.

¹³So the workmen labored, and the repair work progressed in their hands; and they restored *and* organized the house of God in accordance with its specifications and strengthened it.

¹⁴When they had finished, they brought the rest of the money before the king and Jehoiada; and it was [melted down and] made into utensils for the house of the LORD, utensils for ministering and for burnt offerings, and bowls and utensils of gold and silver. And they offered burnt offerings in the house of the LORD continually all the days of Jehoiada.

¹⁵Now when Jehoiada grew old and was full of days, he died. He was a hundred and thirty years old at his death.

¹⁶They buried him in the City of David among the kings, because he had done good [things] in Israel and toward God and His house.

¹⁷Now after the death of Jehoiada [the priest, who had hidden Joash], the officials of Judah came and bowed down to King Joash; then the king listened to them.

¹⁸They abandoned the house of the LORD, the God of their fathers, and served the Asherim and the idols; so [God's] wrath came on Judah and Jerusalem for their sin *and* guilt.

¹⁹Yet God sent prophets among them to bring them back to the LORD; these prophets testified against them, but they would not listen.

²⁰Then the Spirit of God came over Zechariah the son of Jehoiada the priest, and he stood above the people and said to them, "This is what God has said: 'Why do you transgress the commandments of the LORD so that you cannot prosper? Because you have abandoned (turned away from) the LORD, He has also abandoned (turned away from) you.'"

²¹So they conspired against Zechariah and stoned him [to death] at the command of the king, in the courtyard of the house of the LORD.

²²Thus Joash the king did not remember the kindness which Jehoiada, Zechariah's father, had shown him, but he murdered his son. And when Zechariah was dying, he said, "May the LORD see this and require an accounting!"

²³Now it happened at the end of the year, that the army of Aram (Syria) went up against Joash. They came to Judah and Jerusalem and killed all the leaders among the people and sent all their spoil to the king of Damascus.

²⁴Though the army of the Arameans came with a small company of men, the LORD handed over a very large army into their hands, because Joash and Judah had abandoned (turned away from) the LORD, the God of their fathers. So the Arameans executed judgment against Joash.

²⁵When they left Joash (for they left him very ill), his own servants conspired against him because of the blood of the son of Jehoiada the priest, and they murdered him on his bed. So he died, and they buried him in the City of David, but they did not bury him in the tombs of the kings.

²⁶The conspirators against Joash were Zabad the son of Shimeath the Ammonitess, and Jehozabad the son of Shimrith the Moabitess.

²⁷Now as to his sons and the many prophecies uttered against him and the rebuilding of the house of God, they are written in the commentary on the Book of Kings. Then his son Amaziah became king in his place.

25 AMAZIAH WAS twenty-five years old when he became king, and he reigned for twenty-nine years in Jerusalem. His mother's name was Jehoaddan of Jerusalem.

²He did right in the sight of the LORD, yet not wholeheartedly.

³When his kingdom was firmly established, he killed his servants who had struck down his father the king.

⁴But he did not kill their children; for *he did* as it is written in the Law, in the Book of Moses, where the LORD commanded, "The fathers shall not die for the children, nor the children die for the fathers, but each shall be put to death for his own sin."

⁵Amaziah assembled [the men of] Judah and appointed them in accordance with *their* fathers' (ancestors') households under commanders of thousands and of hundreds throughout Judah and Benjamin. He numbered them from twenty years old and above and found there to be 300,000 choice men fit for war and *able to* handle spear and shield.

⁶He also hired 100,000 brave warriors from Israel for a hundred talents of silver.

⁷But a man of God came to him, saying, "O king, do not let this army of Israel go with you, for the LORD is not with Israel *nor with* any of the sons of Ephraim.

⁸"But if you do go [in spite of this warning], be strong *and* courageous for battle; yet God will cause you to stumble *and* fall before the enemy, for

God has power to help and to cause *people* to stumble."

⁹Amaziah said to the man of God, "But what *shall we* do about the hundred talents which I gave to the troops of Israel?" The man of God answered, "The Lord is able to give you much more than this."

¹⁰So Amaziah dismissed the troops that came to him from Ephraim, to go home. So their anger was kindled *and* burned greatly against Judah, and they returned home in the heat of anger.

¹¹Now Amaziah took courage and led his people out to the Valley of Salt, and he struck down 10,000 of the men of Seir (Edom).

¹²The sons of Judah also captured 10,000 alive and brought them to the top of the cliff. They threw them down from the top of the cliff and they were all crushed to pieces.

¹³But the troops whom Amaziah sent back, *those* not allowed to go with him to battle, attacked *and* raided the cities of Judah, from Samaria to Beth-horon, and struck down 3,000 men and took a large amount of spoil.

¹⁴After Amaziah came back from the slaughter of the Edomites, he brought the gods of the sons of Seir, and set them up to be his gods, bowed before them, and burned incense to them.

¹⁵So the anger of the Lord burned against Amaziah, and He sent him a prophet who said to him, "Why have you desired the gods of the people who did not save their own people from your hand?"

¹⁶As he was talking, the king said to him, "Have we made you the king's counselor? Stop! Why should you be put to death?" Then the prophet stopped and said, "I know that God has decided to destroy you because you have done this and have ignored my advice."

doing the right thing with the right heart

There are many conditions of the heart. Some are positive, and some are negative. Of course, many people do have a right heart. They love God with all their hearts, and they really want to do the right thing in every situation. But there are others who have a wrong heart, and they do the right thing, but with the wrong motive.

In 2 Chronicles 25:1, 2 we read about a king who had a negative condition of the heart. This passage says that King Amaziah did all the right things, but his heart was not right. Therefore, God was not pleased with him. That's a scary situation. We can do the right thing, and yet it still will not be acceptable to God because we do it with a wrong heart.

Let's take giving, for example. In 2 Corinthians 9:7 we are told that God loves a cheerful giver, one who gives not out of compulsion or with a bad attitude, but out of a willing heart. God wants us to give joyfully. In fact, this verse says that God loves a cheerful giver so much, He is absolutely unwilling to abandon or do without a person whose heart is in his giving.

There is a physical heart and a spiritual heart, and the two are parallel. Physically speaking, the heart is the most important organ in our bodies. Spiritually speaking, I believe the heart of an individual is the most important aspect of his or her spiritual life. And it is the most important thing we can give to God. That is why the condition of our hearts is so important. Make sure that you are not only doing the right things, but also that the attitude of your heart is pleasing to the Lord.

¹⁷Then Amaziah king of Judah took counsel and sent *word* to Joash the son of Jehoahaz the son of Jehu, king of Israel, saying, "Come [to battle], let us face each other." [2 Kin 14:8–20]

¹⁸Then Joash king of Israel sent *word* to Amaziah king of Judah, saying, "The [little] thorn bush in Lebanon sent *word* to the [great] cedar in Lebanon, saying, 'Give your daughter to my son in marriage.' But a wild beast in Lebanon passed by and trampled down the thorn bush.

¹⁹"You say, 'See, I have struck down *and* defeated Edom.' Your heart lifts you up to boast [about your victory]. Now stay at home; why should you meddle *and* court disaster so that you, even you, will fall and Judah with you?"

²⁰But Amaziah would not listen, for it was from God, so that He might hand Judah over *to Joash* because they had desired the gods of Edom.

²¹So Joash king of Israel went up; and he and Amaziah king of Judah faced one another at Beth-shemesh, which belonged to Judah.

²²And Judah was defeated by Israel, and they fled, every man to his tent.

²³Then Joash king of Israel captured Amaziah king of Judah, the son of Joash the son of Jehoahaz (Ahaziah), at Beth-shemesh, and brought him to Jerusalem and broke down the wall of Jerusalem from the Ephraim Gate to the Corner Gate, 400 cubits.

²⁴*He took* all the gold and silver and all the utensils which were found in the house of God with [the door-keeper] Obed-edom, and the treasures of the king's house (palace), and the hostages, and returned to Samaria.

²⁵And Amaziah the son of Joash king of Judah lived fifteen years after the death of Joash the son of Jehoahaz king of Israel.

²⁶Now the rest of the acts of Amaziah, from the first to the last, are they not written in the Book of the Kings of Judah and Israel?

²⁷Now from the time that Amaziah turned away from following the Lord, they conspired against him in Jerusalem, and he fled to Lachish; but they sent *men* after him to Lachish and killed him there.

²⁸Then they brought him on horses and buried him with his fathers in the City of [David in] Judah.

26 THEN ALL the people of Judah took Uzziah, who was sixteen years old, and made him king in place of his father Amaziah.

²He built Eloth and restored it to Judah after the king [Amaziah] slept with his fathers [in death].

³Uzziah was sixteen years old when he became king, and he reigned fifty-two years in Jerusalem. His mother's name was Jechiliah of Jerusalem.

⁴He did right in the sight of the Lord, in accordance with everything that his father Amaziah had done.

⁵He continued to seek God in the days of Zechariah, who had understanding through the vision of God; and as long as he sought (inquired of, longing for) the Lord, God caused him to prosper.

⁶He went out and made war against the Philistines, and broke through the wall of Gath, the wall of Jabneh, and the wall of Ashdod; and he built cities near Ashdod and [elsewhere] among the Philistines.

⁷God helped him against the Philistines, and against the Arabs who lived in Gur-baal, and the Meunites.

⁸The Ammonites paid tribute (money) to Uzziah, and his fame spread abroad, even as far as the border of Egypt, for he became very strong.

⁹Uzziah also built towers in Jerusalem at the Corner Gate, the Valley Gate, and at the corner buttress [of the wall], and fortified them.

¹⁰He also built towers in the wilderness and dug many cisterns, for he had a great deal of livestock, both in the lowlands and in the plain. *He also had* farmers and vinedressers in the hill country and in the fertile fields, for he loved the soil.

¹¹Moreover, Uzziah had an army ready for battle, which went into combat by divisions according to the number of their muster as recorded by Jeiel the scribe and Maaseiah the official, under the direction of Hananiah, one of the king's commanders.

¹²The total number of the heads of the fathers' households, of valiant men, was 2,600.

¹³Under their command was an army of 307,500, who could wage war with great power, to help the king against the enemy.

¹⁴Moreover, Uzziah prepared shields, spears, helmets, body armor, bows, and sling stones for the entire army.

¹⁵In Jerusalem he made machines of war invented by skillful men to be put on the towers and on the [corner] battlements for the purpose of shooting arrows and large stones. And his fame spread far, for he was marvelously helped until he was strong.

¹⁶But when Uzziah became strong, he became so proud [of himself and his accomplishments] that he acted corruptly, and he was unfaithful *and* sinned against the LORD his God, for he went into the temple of the LORD to burn incense on the altar of incense. [Num 3:38]

¹⁷Then Azariah the priest went in after him, and with him eighty priests of the LORD, men of courage.

¹⁸They opposed King Uzziah and said to him, "It is not for you, Uzziah, to burn incense to the LORD, but for the priests, the sons of Aaron who have been consecrated to burn incense. Get out of the sanctuary, for you have been unfaithful and will have no honor from the LORD God."

¹⁹Then Uzziah, with a censer in his hand to burn incense, was enraged; and while he was enraged with the priests, leprosy broke out on his forehead before the priests in the house of the LORD, beside the incense altar.

²⁰As Azariah the chief priest and all the priests looked toward him, behold, he was leprous on his forehead; and they hurried him out of there, and he also hurried to get out because the LORD had stricken him.

²¹King Uzziah was a leper to the day of his death; and, being a leper, he lived in a separate house, for he was excluded from the house of the LORD. And his son Jotham took charge of the king's household, judging *and* governing the people of the land.

²²Now the rest of the acts of Uzziah, from the first to the last, Isaiah the prophet, the son of Amoz, has written. [Is 1:1]

²³So Uzziah slept with his fathers [in death], and they buried him with his fathers in the burial field of the kings [outside the royal tombs], for they said, "He is a leper." And his son Jotham became king in his place.

27 JOTHAM WAS twenty-five years old when he became king, and he reigned for sixteen years in Jerusalem. His mother's name was Jerushah the daughter of Zadok.

²He did right in the sight of the LORD, in accordance with everything that his father Uzziah had done; however, he did not enter the temple of the LORD. But the people continued behaving corruptly.

³He built the upper gate of the house of the LORD, and did extensive building on the wall of Ophel.

⁴Moreover, he built cities in the hill country of Judah, and in the forests he built fortresses and towers.

⁵He also fought with the king of the

Ammonites and prevailed over them. As a result the Ammonites gave him during that year a hundred talents of silver and ten thousand measures each of wheat and of barley. The Ammonites also paid him that much in the second year and third year. ⁶So Jotham grew powerful, because he directed his ways before the LORD his God. ⁷Now the rest of the acts of Jotham, and all his wars and his ways, behold, they are written in the Book of the Kings of Israel and Judah. ⁸He was twenty-five years old when he became king, and he reigned for sixteen years in Jerusalem. ⁹And Jotham slept with his fathers [in death], and they buried him in the City of David. Ahaz his son became king in his place.

28 AHAZ WAS twenty years old when he became king, and he reigned for sixteen years in Jerusalem. He did not do right in the sight of the LORD, as his father (forefather) David *had done*. ²Instead he walked in the ways of the kings of Israel, and even made cast images for the Baals. ³And he burned incense in the Valley of Ben-hinnom and burned his sons [as an offering], in accordance with the repulsive acts of the [pagan] nations whom the LORD had driven out before the sons (descendants) of Israel. ⁴He also sacrificed and burned incense on the high places [of pagan worship], on the hills and under every green tree. ⁵Therefore the LORD his God handed over Ahaz to the king of Aram (Syria), who defeated him and led away a great number [of the people] as captives, and brought them to Damascus. And he was also handed over to the king of Israel, who struck Judah with a great slaughter. ⁶For Pekah son of Remaliah killed

120,000 in Judah in one day, all courageous men, because they had abandoned (turned away from) the LORD God of their fathers. ⁷And Zichri, a warrior of Ephraim, killed Maaseiah the king's son, and Azrikam the governor of the house, and Elkanah, who was second [in power] to the king. ⁸And the sons of Israel led away captive 200,000 of their kinsmen [of Judah]—women, sons, and daughters—and they also took a great quantity of spoil from them and brought it to Samaria. ⁹But a prophet of the LORD was there, whose name was Oded; and he went out to meet the army that was returning to Samaria and said to them, "Behold, because the LORD, the God of your fathers, was angry with Judah, He handed them over to you; but you have killed them in a rage that has reached as far as heaven. ¹⁰"And now you intend to subjugate the people of Judah and Jerusalem as male and female slaves for yourselves. But are you yourselves not guilty *of transgressions* against the LORD your God? ¹¹"Now therefore, hear me and return the captives whom you have captured from your brothers (fellow descendants of Israel, i.e. Jacob), for the burning anger of the LORD is against you." ¹²Then some of the heads of the Ephraimites (Israel)—Azariah the son of Johanan, Berechiah the son of Meshillemoth, Jehizkiah the son of Shallum, and Amasa the son of Hadlai—took a stand against those who were returning from the battle, ¹³and said to them, "You must not bring the captives in here; for we are guilty before the LORD *already*, and *what* you intend to *do will* add more to our sins and our guilt. For our guilt is so great that His burning anger is against Israel."

[14]So the armed men [of Israel] left the captives and the spoil [of Judah] before the officers and all the assembly.

[15]Then the men who were designated by name rose up and took the captives, and from the spoil they clothed all those who were naked; they clothed them and gave them sandals, and fed them and gave them [something to] drink, anointed them [with oil, as was a host's duty], and led all the feeble ones on donkeys, and they brought them to Jericho, the City of Palm Trees, to their brothers (fellow descendants of Israel, i.e. Jacob). Then they returned to Samaria. [Luke 10:25–37]

[16]At that time King Ahaz sent *word* to the king of Assyria [to ask him] for help.

[17]For the Edomites had come again and attacked Judah and led away captives.

[18]The Philistines had also invaded the cities of the low country and of the Negev (the South country) of Judah, and had taken Beth-shemesh, Aijalon, Gederoth, and Soco with their villages, and also Timnah with its villages, and Gimzo with its villages, and they settled there.

[19]For the Lord humbled Judah because of Ahaz king of Israel, for Ahaz had allowed unrestrained *and* undisciplined behavior in Judah and had been very unfaithful to the Lord.

[20]So Tilgath-pilneser king of Assyria came against him and harassed him instead of strengthening *and* supporting him.

[21]Although Ahaz took a portion [of treasure] from the house of the Lord and from the house (palace) of the king and from the leaders, and gave it [as tribute] to the king of Assyria, it did not help Ahaz.

[22]In the time of his distress, this same King Ahaz became yet more unfaithful to the Lord.

[23]For he sacrificed to the gods of Damascus, which had defeated him, and he said, "Since the gods of the kings of Aram (Syria) helped them, I will sacrifice to them so that they may help me." But they became the ruin *and* downfall of him and all of Israel.

[24]Then Ahaz collected the utensils of the house of God and he cut them in pieces; and he shut the doors of the house of the Lord and made altars for himself in every corner of Jerusalem.

[25]In every city of Judah he made high places to burn incense to other gods, provoking to anger the Lord, the God of his fathers.

[26]Now the rest of his acts and of all his ways, from the first to the last, behold, they are written in the Book of the Kings of Judah and Israel.

[27]And Ahaz slept with his fathers [in death], and they buried him in the city, in Jerusalem, but they did not bring him into the tombs of the kings of Israel. And his son Hezekiah reigned in his place.

29 HEZEKIAH BECAME king when he was twenty-five years old, and he reigned twenty-nine years in Jerusalem. His mother's name was Abijah the daughter of Zechariah.

[2]He did right in the sight of the Lord, in accordance with everything that David his father (forefather) had done.

[3]In the first year of his reign, in the first month, he opened the doors of the house of the Lord [which his father had closed] and repaired them [and replaced the gold overlay]. [2 Kin 18:16]

[4]He brought in the priests and Levites and gathered them into the square on the east.

[5]Then he said to them, "Levites, listen to me! Now consecrate (dedicate) yourselves and consecrate the house of the Lord, the God of your fathers, and get the filth [of idol worship] out of the Holy Place.

6"For our fathers have been unfaithful and have done evil in the sight of the LORD our God, and they have abandoned Him and have turned their faces away from the dwelling place of the LORD, and have turned their backs [toward Him].

7"They have also closed the doors of the [temple] porch and put out the lamps, and they have not burned incense nor offered burnt offerings in the Holy Place to the God of Israel. [2 Kin 16:10–16]

8"Therefore the wrath of the LORD has been against Judah and Jerusalem, and He has made them an object of terror, of horror, and of hissing, just as you see with your own eyes.

9"For behold, our fathers have fallen by the sword, and our sons and our daughters and our wives are in captivity because of this.

10"Now it is in my heart to make a covenant (solemn agreement) with the LORD God of Israel, so that His burning anger will turn away from us.

11"My sons, do not be negligent *and* careless now, for the LORD has chosen you to stand in His presence, to attend to His service, and to be His ministers and burn incense."

12Then the Levites arose: Mahath the son of Amasai and Joel the son of Azariah, from the sons of the Kohathites; from the sons of Merari: Kish the son of Abdi, Azariah the son of Jehallelel; from the Gershonites: Joah the son of Zimmah and Eden the son of Joah;

13from the sons of Elizaphan: Shimri and Jeiel; from the sons of Asaph: Zechariah, and Mattaniah;

14from the sons of Heman: Jehiel and Shimei; and from the sons of Jeduthun: Shemaiah and Uzziel.

15They gathered their brothers (fellow Levites) together, consecrated themselves, and went in to cleanse the house of the LORD, as the king had commanded by the words of the LORD.

16The priests went into the inner part of the house of the LORD to cleanse it, and every unclean thing they found in the temple of the LORD they brought out to the courtyard of the LORD's house. Then the Levites received it to take out to the Kidron Valley [for disposal].

17Now they began the consecration on the first [day] of the first month, and on the eighth day of the month they came to the porch of the LORD. Then for eight days they consecrated the house of the LORD, and on the sixteenth day of the first month they finished.

18Then they went inside to King Hezekiah and said, "We have cleansed the entire house (temple) of the LORD, the altar of burnt offering with all of its utensils, and the table of showbread with all its utensils.

19"Moreover, we have prepared and consecrated all the utensils which King Ahaz had discarded during his reign in his unfaithfulness; and behold, they are in front of the altar of the LORD."

20Then King Hezekiah arose early and assembled the officials of the city, and went up to the house of the LORD.

21They brought seven bulls, seven rams, seven lambs, and seven male goats for a sin offering for the kingdom, the sanctuary, and Judah. He commanded the priests, the sons of Aaron, to offer them on the altar of the LORD.

22So they slaughtered the bulls, and the priests took the blood and sprinkled it on the altar. They also slaughtered the rams and sprinkled the blood on the altar; then they slaughtered the lambs and sprinkled the blood on the altar.

23Then they brought the male goats for the sin offering before the king and the assembly, and they laid their hands on them [to symbolize the transference of their sin].

24The priests slaughtered them and cleansed the altar from sin with their blood to atone for all Israel, because the king commanded that the burnt offering and the sin offering *be made* for all Israel.

²⁵Hezekiah stationed the Levites in the house of the LORD with cymbals, with harps, and with lyres, in accordance with the command of David [his ancestor] and of Gad the king's seer, and of Nathan the prophet; for the command was from the LORD through His prophets.

²⁶The Levites stood with the *musical* instruments of David, and the priests with the trumpets.

²⁷Then Hezekiah gave the order to offer the burnt offering on the altar. And when the burnt offering began, the song to the LORD also began with the trumpets *accompanied* by the instruments of David, king of Israel.

²⁸The entire congregation worshiped, the singers also sang, and the trumpets sounded; all this *continued* until the burnt offering was finished.

²⁹When the burnt offerings were completed, the king and all who were present with him bowed down and worshiped [God].

³⁰Also King Hezekiah and the officials ordered the Levites to exclaim praises to the LORD with the words of David and of Asaph the seer. And they exclaimed praises with joy, and bowed down and worshiped.

³¹Then Hezekiah said, "Now you have consecrated yourselves to the LORD; approach and bring sacrifices and thank offerings into the house of the LORD." And the assembly brought in sacrifices and thank offerings, and all those who were willing *brought* burnt offerings. [Ex 35:5, 22]

³²The number of the burnt offerings which the assembly brought was 70 bulls, 100 rams, and 200 lambs. All these were for a burnt offering to the LORD.

³³The consecrated things were 600 bulls and 3,000 sheep.

³⁴But there were too few priests and they were unable to skin all the burnt offerings; so until the *other* priests had consecrated themselves, their brothers, the Levites, helped them until the work was done. For the Levites were more upright in heart *and* more conscientious than the priests in consecrating themselves.

³⁵There were also many burnt offerings with the fat of the peace offerings and with the drink offerings for the burnt offerings. So the service of the house of the LORD was established again.

³⁶Then Hezekiah and all the people rejoiced because of what God had prepared for the people, for the thing came about suddenly.

30 HEZEKIAH SENT *word* to all Israel and to Judah and also wrote letters to Ephraim and Manasseh to come to the house of the LORD at Jerusalem to celebrate the Passover *Feast* to the LORD God of Israel.

²For the king and his officials and all the assembly in Jerusalem had decided to celebrate the Passover in the second month, [Num 9:10, 11]

³since they could not celebrate it at that time because a sufficient number of priests had not consecrated themselves, nor had the people assembled at Jerusalem.

⁴Thus the [decision to set a] new time pleased the king and the entire assembly.

⁵So they decided to circulate a proclamation throughout Israel, from Beersheba to Dan, that the people were to come to celebrate the Passover to the LORD God of Israel, at Jerusalem. For they had not celebrated it in great numbers as it was prescribed [for a long time].

⁶So the runners went throughout Israel and Judah with the letters from

the hand of the king and his officials, in accordance with the command of the king, saying, "O sons (descendants) of Israel, return to the Lord God of Abraham, Isaac, and Israel (Jacob), so that He will return to those of you who escaped and are left from the hand (power) of the kings of Assyria.

⁷"Do not be like your fathers and your brothers, who were unfaithful to the Lord God of their fathers, so that He made them a horror (lifeless, desolate), just as you see.

⁸"Now do not stiffen your neck [becoming obstinate] like your fathers, but yield to the Lord and come to His sanctuary which He has sanctified *and* set apart forever, and serve the Lord your God, so that His burning anger will turn away from you.

⁹"For if you return to the Lord, your brothers (relatives) and your children will find compassion in the presence of those who led them away captive and will return to this land. For the Lord your God is gracious and merciful, and He will not turn His face away from you if you return to Him."

¹⁰So the runners (couriers) passed from city to city through the country of Ephraim and Manasseh, as far as Zebulun; but the people laughed at them with scorn and mocked them.

¹¹Yet *some of* the men of Asher, Manasseh, and Zebulun humbled themselves and came to Jerusalem.

¹²Also the hand of God was on Judah to give them one heart to do that which the king and the officials had commanded by the word of the Lord.

¹³Now many people were gathered at Jerusalem to celebrate the Feast of Unleavened Bread in the second month; it was a very large assembly.

¹⁴They took action and removed the [pagan] altars which were in Jerusalem; they also removed all the incense altars and threw them into the Brook Kidron [the dumping place for the ashes of such repulsive things].

¹⁵Then they slaughtered the Passover *lambs* on the fourteenth day of the second month. And the priests and the Levites were ashamed of themselves, and consecrated themselves and brought burnt offerings to the house of the Lord.

¹⁶They stood at their accustomed stations, in accordance with the Law of Moses, the man of God. The priests sprinkled the blood [which they received] from the hand of the Levites [on the altar].

¹⁷For there were many in the assembly who had not consecrated themselves [that is, become ceremonially clean and free from all sin]; so the Levites had to slaughter the Passover *lambs* for everyone who was not clean, in order to make them holy for the Lord.

¹⁸For the majority of the people, many from Ephraim and Manasseh, Issachar and Zebulun, had not purified themselves, and yet they ate the Passover contrary to what had been prescribed. For Hezekiah had prayed for them, saying, "May the good Lord pardon

¹⁹everyone who sets his heart to seek God—the Lord God of his fathers— even though it is not in accordance with the [ceremonial] purification [rules] of the sanctuary."

²⁰So the Lord listened to Hezekiah and healed the people [of their uncleanness].

²¹The Israelites who were present in Jerusalem celebrated the Feast of Unleavened Bread for seven days

speak the Word

Help me, God, to not be stiff-necked or obstinate, but to always yield to You.
—ADAPTED FROM 2 CHRONICLES 30:8

with great joy. The Levites and priests praised the Lord day after day, *singing* to the Lord with loud instruments.

²²Hezekiah spoke encouragingly to all the Levites who showed good understanding *in the things* of the Lord. So the people ate for the appointed seven days, sacrificing peace offerings and giving thanks to the Lord God of their fathers.

²³Then the whole assembly decided to celebrate [the feast] for another seven days; and they celebrated it *another* seven days with joy.

²⁴For Hezekiah king of Judah gave to the assembly 1,000 bulls and 7,000 sheep, and the officials gave the assembly 1,000 bulls and 10,000 sheep. And a large number of priests consecrated themselves [for service].

²⁵All the assembly of Judah rejoiced, with the priests and the Levites and all the assembly that came from Israel, both the sojourners (resident aliens, foreigners) who came from the land of Israel and those living in Judah.

²⁶So there was great joy in Jerusalem, because there had been nothing like this in Jerusalem since the time of Solomon the son of David, king of Israel.

²⁷Then the priests and Levites stood and blessed the people; and their voice was heard and their prayer came up to His holy dwelling place, to heaven.

31 NOW WHEN all of this was finished, all Israel who were present went out to the cities of Judah, and smashed the [pagan] pillars (obelisks, memorial stones) in pieces, cut down the Asherim (wooden symbols of a female deity), and tore down the high places and the altars [of idolatry] throughout all Judah and Benjamin, as well as in Ephraim and Manasseh, until they had destroyed them all. Then all the sons (descendants) of Israel returned to their own cities, each to his own property.

²And Hezekiah appointed the divisions of the priests, and the Levites by their divisions, each in accordance with his service, both the priests and Levites, for burnt offerings and for peace offerings, to minister and to give thanks and to praise in the gates of the camp of the Lord.

³Hezekiah also *appointed* the king's [personal] portion of his goods: for the morning and evening burnt offerings, and the burnt offerings for the Sabbaths and for the New Moons and for the appointed feasts, as it is written in the Law of the Lord.

⁴He also told (ordered) the people living in Jerusalem to give the portion that was due to the priests and Levites, so that they might [be free to] devote themselves to the Law of the Lord.

⁵As soon as the *king's* order spread, the Israelites gave in abundance the first fruits of grain, new wine, [olive] oil, honey, and of all the produce of the field; and they brought in the tithe of everything abundantly.

⁶The sons of Israel and Judah who lived in the cities of Judah also brought in the tithe of oxen and sheep, and the tithe of sacred gifts which were consecrated to the Lord their God, and placed them in heaps.

⁷In the third month [at the end of wheat harvest] they began to make the heaps, and they finished them in the seventh month.

⁸When Hezekiah and the rulers came and saw the heaps, they blessed the Lord and His people Israel.

⁹Then Hezekiah questioned the priests and Levites about the heaps.

¹⁰Azariah the high priest of the house of Zadok answered him, "Since the people began to bring the offerings into the house of the Lord, we have had enough to eat with plenty left over, for the Lord has blessed His people, and this great quantity is left over."

¹¹Then Hezekiah told them to prepare

rooms [for storage] in the house of the LORD, and they prepared them.

¹²They faithfully brought in the contributions, the tithes, and the sacred (dedicated) things. Conaniah the Levite was in charge of them, and Shimei his brother was second [in authority].

¹³Jehiel, Azaziah, Nahath, Asahel, Jerimoth, Jozabad, Eliel, Ismachiah, Mahath, and Benaiah were overseers directed by Conaniah and Shimei his brother by the appointment of King Hezekiah, and Azariah was the *chief* officer of the house of God.

¹⁴Kore the son of Imnah the Levite, keeper of the East Gate, was in charge of the voluntary offerings to God, to apportion the contributions for the LORD and the most holy things.

¹⁵Under his authority were Eden, Miniamin, Jeshua, Shemaiah, Amariah, and Shecaniah in the cities of the priests, to distribute faithfully *their portions* to their brothers (relatives) by divisions, whether great or small,

¹⁶without regard to their genealogical registration, to the males from thirty years old and upward—everyone who entered the house of the LORD for his daily obligations—for their service in accordance with their duties by their divisions;

¹⁷as well as the priests who were registered genealogically according to their fathers' households, and the Levites from twenty years old and upward, by their duties and by their divisions.

¹⁸The genealogical registration *included* all their little children, their wives, and their sons and daughters, for the whole assembly, because they consecrated themselves faithfully in holiness.

¹⁹Also for the sons of Aaron, the priests, who were in the pasture lands of their cities or in each and every city, there were men who were designated by name to give portions to every male among the priests and to everyone

genealogically registered among the Levites.

²⁰This is what Hezekiah did throughout Judah; and he did what was good, right, and true before the LORD his God.

²¹Every work which he began in the service of the house of God in keeping with the law and the commandment, seeking *and* inquiring of his God [and longing for Him], he did with all his heart and prospered.

32 AFTER THESE things and this faithfulness, Sennacherib king of Assyria came and invaded Judah and besieged the fortified cities, intending to take them for himself.

²When Hezekiah saw that Sennacherib had come and that he intended to go to war against Jerusalem,

³he decided, together with his officers and his soldiers, to stop up the water [supply] from the springs which were outside the city [by enclosing them with masonry and concealing them], and they helped him.

⁴So many people came together, and they stopped up all the springs and the brook which flowed [underground] through the region, saying, "Why should the kings of Assyria come and find an abundance of water?"

⁵Also Hezekiah resolutely set to work and rebuilt all the wall that had been broken down, and erected towers on it, and *he built* another wall outside and strengthened the Millo (fortification) in the City of David, and made a great number of weapons and shields.

⁶He also appointed military officers over the people and gathered them to him in the square at the city gate, and spoke encouragingly to them, saying,

⁷"Be strong and courageous. Do not fear or be dismayed because of the king of Assyria, nor because of all the army that is with him; for the One with us is greater than the one with him.

⁸"With him there is only an arm of flesh, but with us is the LORD our God to help us and to fight our battles." And the people relied on the words of Hezekiah king of Judah.

⁹After this, Sennacherib king of Assyria, while he was at Lachish [besieging it] with all his forces, sent his servants to Jerusalem, to Hezekiah king of Judah, and to all Judah who were at Jerusalem, saying,

¹⁰"Thus says Sennacherib king of Assyria, 'In what do you trust that you are remaining in Jerusalem under siege?

¹¹'Is not Hezekiah misleading you in order to let you die by famine and thirst, *while* saying, "The LORD our God will rescue us from the hand of the king of Assyria?'

¹²'Has the same Hezekiah not taken away his [Baal's] high places and his altars, and commanded Judah and Jerusalem, "You shall worship before [only] one altar and burn incense on it"?

¹³'Do you not know what I and my fathers (ancestors) have done to all the peoples of the [other] lands? Were the gods of the nations of those lands able to rescue their lands from my hand at all?

¹⁴'Who [was there] among all the gods of those nations that my fathers utterly destroyed who was able to rescue his people from my hand, that your God should be able to rescue you from my hand?

¹⁵'So now, do not let Hezekiah deceive or mislead you like this, and do not believe him, for no god of any nation or kingdom has been able to rescue his people from my hand or the hand of my fathers. How much less will your God rescue you from my hand!'"

¹⁶And his servants said *even* more

God's strong arm

When the Assyrians came in great strength to invade Judah and lay siege to Jerusalem, King Hezekiah inspired courage in the people with strong words of encouragement: "Do not trust in the arm of flesh, but trust in the Lord" (see 2 Chronicles 32:7, 8).

That is the attitude you and I need to have in the face of seemingly overwhelming problems. Rather than looking at our past failures, our present fallacies, or our future fears, we need to be looking to the Lord and trusting in His wisdom, strength, and power. We should be reminding ourselves that no matter how many problems may be facing us, the One Who is with us is greater than all those who oppose us. With them is the arm of the flesh, but with us is the arm of the Lord.

In Jeremiah 17:5–8 we read that those who put their trust in the arm of the flesh are "cursed" (Jeremiah 17:5). They are like a shrub in the desert, dry and destitute. They will not see any good happen. But those who put their trust in the arm of the Lord are blessed. They are like a tree planted by a river that produces fruit even in the midst of a drought. No matter what comes, they will flourish and not be anxious. Jeremiah says, "Blessed [with spiritual security] is the man who believes and trusts in and relies on the LORD and whose hope and confident expectation is the LORD" (Jeremiah 17:7).

If we lean on the arm of flesh, meaning other people or ourselves, we will end up disappointed and perhaps devastated. We need to love and enjoy people, but we also need to realize that they have the ability to ultimately let us down. We must rely on the strong arm of the Lord to help us, because He will never fail us nor abandon us.

against the LORD God and against His servant Hezekiah.

¹⁷The Assyrian king also wrote letters insulting *and* taunting the LORD God of Israel, and speaking against Him, saying, "As the gods of the nations of other lands have not rescued their people from my hand, so the God of Hezekiah will not rescue His people from my hand."

¹⁸They shouted it loudly in the language of Judah to the people of Jerusalem who were on the wall, to frighten and terrify them, so that they might take the city [without a long siege].

¹⁹They spoke of the God of Jerusalem as [they spoke of] the gods of the peoples of the earth, [which are only] the work of the hands of men.

²⁰But Hezekiah the king and the

looking up

In answer to the prayers of King Hezekiah and the prophet Isaiah, the Lord intervened and saved Hezekiah and Judah from their enemies. As a result, Hezekiah began to be exalted in the sight of the people (see 2 Chronicles 32:22, 23).

God is not against that. If you become a leader, people will look up to you and honor you. They may want to do nice things for you. That is not all bad, but it can be dangerous. As happened with Hezekiah, people's admiration for a leader, or the leader's view of that admiration, can lead to pride if not kept under control. In his pride, Hezekiah fell ill and almost died. But he humbled himself and repented of his proud heart and things were straightened out (see 2 Chronicles 32:24–26).

It is interesting that when Hezekiah turned to God, the Lord began to honor, promote, and bless him again (see 2 Chronicles 32:27). That is exactly what happens to people who commit wholeheartedly to the Lord. Sooner or later their ministry starts increasing, and they start moving up. People begin looking up to them. But if they become proud, God will deal with them about their pride. Like Hezekiah, they can quickly repent and come back to a place of humility; and God can continue to bless them in amazing ways. Or, if they refuse to repent, they will begin to lose God's blessing and eventually their place of honor.

This is a key issue in Christian leadership. Everyone who is doing anything of importance for the Lord must resist the attacks and temptations of the spirit of pride. That is why no one automatically always has a right heart; it takes effort to keep our hearts right. We have to work at it all the time. And one of the most powerful things we have to guard against is a spirit of self-righteousness, which is rooted in pride.

Our enemy, Satan, is going to use every opportunity he can to get us into places where our hearts are not right. When that happens, we need to repent to God immediately.

If you and I want to stand before God one day and say, as Jesus did in John 17:4, "I have glorified You [down here] on the earth by completing the work that You gave Me to do," then we must be careful to keep a right heart. Psalm 101:5 says that God will not tolerate anyone who has a haughty look and a proud and arrogant heart. We need to be diligent to guard against pride and make sure that we walk before God and others with a humbled heart. God's Word teaches us to watch over our hearts "with all diligence," for from them "flow the springs of life" (Proverbs 4:23).

prophet Isaiah the son of Amoz prayed about this and cried out to heaven [for help].

²¹And the LORD sent an angel who destroyed every brave warrior, commander, and officer in the camp of the king of Assyria. So the king returned to his own land in shame. And when he entered the house (temple) of his god, some of his own children killed him there with the sword. [2 Kin 19:35–37]

²²Thus the LORD saved Hezekiah and the inhabitants of Jerusalem from the hand of Sennacherib the king of Assyria and from the hand of all *others,* and He gave them rest on every side.

²³And many brought gifts to the LORD at Jerusalem and valuable presents to Hezekiah king of Judah; so from then on he was exalted in the sight of all nations.

²⁴In those days Hezekiah became terminally ill; and he prayed to the LORD, and He answered him and gave him a [miraculous] sign.

²⁵But Hezekiah did nothing [for the LORD] in return for the benefit *bestowed* on him, because his heart had become proud; therefore *God's* wrath came on him and on Judah and Jerusalem.

²⁶However, Hezekiah humbled his proud heart, both he and the inhabitants of Jerusalem, so that the wrath of the LORD did not come on them during the days of Hezekiah.

²⁷Now Hezekiah had immense wealth and honor; and he made for himself treasuries for silver, gold, precious stones, spices, shields, and all kinds of delightful articles,

²⁸and storehouses for the produce of grain, new wine, and [olive] oil, and stalls for all kinds of cattle, and sheepfolds for the flocks.

²⁹Moreover, he made cities for himself and *acquired* an abundance of flocks and herds, for God gave him very many possessions.

³⁰This same Hezekiah also stopped

life point

Notice in 2 Chronicles 32:31 that God left Hezekiah "alone only to test him, in order to know everything that was in his heart." Do not be discouraged if you feel there are times when God has left you "alone" when you do not sense His presence or hear His voice. Sometimes He is quiet and seemingly imperceptible, just to see if we will continue to be faithful to Him. Determine right now that you will always be faithful in hard times as well as in good times!

up the upper outlet of the waters of Gihon and channeled them down to the west side of the City of David. Hezekiah succeeded in everything that he did.

³¹And so *in the matter of* the envoys of the rulers of Babylon, who were sent to him to inquire about the wonder that had happened in the land, God left him *alone only* to test him, in order to know everything that was in his heart. [Is 39:1–7]

³²Now the rest of the acts of Hezekiah and his godly achievements, behold, they are written in the vision of Isaiah the prophet, the son of Amoz, in the Book of the Kings of Judah and Israel.

³³So Hezekiah slept with his fathers [in death] and they buried him in the upper section of the tombs of the descendants of David; and all Judah and the inhabitants of Jerusalem honored him at his death. And his son Manasseh became king in his place.

33 MANASSEH WAS twelve years old when he became king, and he reigned for fifty-five years in Jerusalem.

²But he did evil in the sight of the LORD, like the repulsive acts of the [pagan] nations whom the LORD dispossessed before the sons (descendants) of Israel.

³For he rebuilt the [idolatrous] high places which his father Hezekiah had torn down; and he set up altars for the Baals and made the Asherim, and worshiped all the host of heaven [the sun, the moon, stars and planets] and served them. [Deut 4:19]

⁴He built [pagan] altars in the house of the Lord, of which the Lord had said, "My Name shall be in Jerusalem forever."

⁵He built altars for all the host of heaven in the two courts of the house of the Lord.

⁶He made his sons pass through the fire [as an offering to his gods] in the Valley of Ben-hinnom; and he practiced witchcraft, used divination, and practiced sorcery, and dealt with mediums and spiritists. He did much evil in the sight of the Lord, provoking Him to anger.

⁷Then he set the carved image of the idol which he had made in the house of God, of which God had said to David and to Solomon his son, "In this house and in Jerusalem, which I have chosen from all the tribes of Israel, I will put My Name [and the symbol of my Presence] forever;

⁸and I will not again remove Israel from the land which I appointed for your fathers, if they will only be careful to do everything that I have commanded them in regard to all the law, the statutes, and the ordinances *given* through Moses."

⁹So Manasseh caused Judah and the inhabitants of Jerusalem to sin, by doing more evil than the [pagan] nations whom the Lord had destroyed before the sons of Israel.

¹⁰Now the Lord spoke to Manasseh and to his people, but they paid no attention.

¹¹So the Lord brought the commanders of the army of the king of Assyria against them, and they captured Manasseh with hooks [through his nose or cheeks] and bound him with bronze [chains] and took him to Babylon.

¹²But when he was in distress, he sought the Lord his God and humbled himself greatly before the God of his fathers.

¹³When he prayed to Him, He was moved by his entreaty and heard his pleading, and brought him back to Jerusalem to his kingdom. Then Manasseh knew that the Lord is God.

¹⁴After this he built an outer wall for the City of David on the west side of Gihon, in the river valley, to the entrance of the Fish Gate; and he encircled the Ophel *with it* and made it very high. Then he put military commanders in all the fortified cities of Judah.

¹⁵He also removed the foreign gods and the idol from the house of the Lord, as well as all the altars which he had built on the mountain of the house of the Lord and in Jerusalem; and he threw them outside the city.

¹⁶Then he set up the altar of the Lord and sacrificed peace offerings and thank offerings on it; and he ordered Judah to serve the Lord God of Israel. [Ex 35:5, 22]

¹⁷Yet the people still sacrificed on the high places, *but* only to the Lord their God.

¹⁸Now the rest of the acts of Manasseh, and his prayer to his God, and the words of the seers who spoke to him in the name of the Lord God of Israel, behold, they are among the records of the kings of Israel.

¹⁹His prayer also and how God heard him, and all his sin, his unfaithfulness, and the sites on which he built high places and set up the Asherim and the carved images, before he humbled himself, behold, they are written in the records of the Hozai.

²⁰So Manasseh slept with his fathers [in death], and they buried him in [the garden of] his own house. And his son Amon became king in his place.

²¹Amon was twenty-two years old when he became king, and he reigned for two years in Jerusalem.

²²But he did evil in the sight of the LORD, just as his father Manasseh had done. Amon sacrificed to all the carved images which his father Manasseh had made, and he served them.

²³Further, he did not humble himself before the LORD as his father Manasseh [finally] had done, but Amon multiplied his guilt *and* his sin.

²⁴And his servants conspired against him and killed him in his own house (palace).

²⁵But the people of the land struck down all those who had conspired against King Amon, and they made his son Josiah king in his place.

34 JOSIAH WAS eight years old when he became king, and he reigned for thirty-one years in Jerusalem.

²He did what was right in the sight of the LORD, and walked in the ways of David his father (forefather) and did not turn aside either to the right or to the left.

³For in the eighth year of his reign, while he was still young (sixteen), he began to seek after *and* inquire of the God of his father David; and in the twelfth year he began to purge Judah and Jerusalem of the high places, the Asherim, and the carved and cast images.

⁴They tore down the altars of the Baals in his presence; he cut to pieces the incense altars that were high above them; he also smashed the Asherim and the carved images and the cast images to pieces, and ground them to dust and scattered it on the graves of those who had sacrificed to them.

⁵Then Josiah burned the bones of the [pagan] priests on their altars and purged *and* cleansed Judah and Jerusalem.

⁶In the cities of Manasseh, Ephraim, Simeon, and as far as Naphtali, in their surrounding ruins,

⁷he tore down the altars and beat *and* crushed the Asherim and the carved images into powder, and cut to pieces all the incense altars throughout the land of Israel. Then he returned to Jerusalem.

⁸In the eighteenth year of Josiah's reign, when he had purged the land and the [LORD's] house, he sent Shaphan the son of Azaliah, and Maaseiah the governor of the city, and Joah the son of Joahaz the recorder (secretary), to repair the house of the LORD his God.

⁹When they came to Hilkiah the high priest, they delivered the money that had been brought into the house of God, which the Levites, who guarded the doors, had collected from Manasseh and Ephraim, and from all the remnant of Israel, and from all Judah and Benjamin, and the inhabitants of Jerusalem.

¹⁰Then they gave it to the workmen who were appointed over the house of the LORD, and the workmen who were working in the house of the LORD gave it [to others] to repair and restore the house (temple).

¹¹They in turn gave it to the carpenters and builders to buy quarried stone and timber for couplings (trusses, braces) and to make beams for the houses which the kings of Judah had let go to ruin.

¹²The men did the work faithfully with foremen over them to supervise *and* inspect [their work]: Jahath and Obadiah, the Levites of the sons of Merari, and Zechariah and Meshullam of the sons of the Kohathites, and the Levites, all who were skillful with musical instruments.

¹³*They were* also in charge of the burden bearers [who carried heavy loads], and supervised all the workmen in any kind of service; and some

of the Levites were scribes and officials and gatekeepers.

¹⁴When they were bringing out the money which had been brought into the house of the LORD, Hilkiah the priest found the Book of the Law of the LORD *given* by Moses.

¹⁵Hilkiah told Shaphan the scribe, "I have found the Book of the Law in the house of the LORD." And he gave the book to Shaphan.

¹⁶Shaphan brought the book to the king, but [first] reported further to him, "Your servants are doing everything that was entrusted to them.

¹⁷"They have emptied out the money that was found in the house of the LORD, and have delivered it into the hands of the overseers and the workmen."

¹⁸Then Shaphan the scribe told the king, "Hilkiah the priest has given me a book." And Shaphan read from it in the presence of the king.

¹⁹When the king heard the words of the Law, he tore his clothes.

²⁰Then the king commanded Hilkiah, Ahikam the son of Shaphan, Abdon the son of Micah, Shaphan the scribe, and Asaiah a servant of the king, saying,

²¹"Go, inquire of the LORD for me and for those who are left in Israel and in Judah in regard to the words of the book which has been found; for great is the wrath of the LORD which has been poured out on us because our fathers have not kept *and* obeyed the word of the LORD, to act in accordance with everything that is written in this book."

²²So Hilkiah and those whom the king had told went to Huldah the prophetess, the wife of Shallum the son of Tokhath, the son of Hasrah, keeper of the wardrobe (now she lived in Jerusalem, in the Second Quarter); and they spoke to her about this.

²³And she answered them, "Thus says the LORD, the God of Israel: 'Tell the man who sent you to me,

²⁴thus says the LORD: "Behold, I am bringing evil on this place and on its inhabitants, all the curses that are written in the book which they have read in the presence of the king of Judah.

²⁵"Because they have abandoned (rejected) Me and have burned incense to other gods, in order to provoke Me to anger with all the works of their hands, My wrath will be poured out on this place and it will not be extinguished."'

²⁶"But you shall say the following to King Josiah of Judah, who sent you to inquire of the LORD: 'Thus says the LORD God of Israel, *concerning* the words which you have heard,

²⁷"Because your heart was gentle *and* penitent and you humbled yourself before God when you heard His words against this place and its inhabitants, and humbled yourself before Me, and tore your clothes and wept before Me, I also have heard you," declares the LORD.

²⁸"Behold, I will gather you to your fathers [in death], and you shall be gathered to your grave in peace, and your eyes shall not see all the evil which I am going to bring on this place and on its inhabitants."'" So they brought back word to the king.

²⁹Then the king sent *word* and gathered all the elders of Judah and Jerusalem.

³⁰And the king went up to the house of the LORD with all the men of Judah, the inhabitants of Jerusalem, the priests, the Levites, and all the people, from the greatest to the least; and he read aloud so they could hear all the words of the Book of the Covenant which was found in the house of the LORD.

³¹Then the king stood in his place and made a covenant before the LORD—to walk after (obey) the LORD, and to keep His commandments, His testimonies, and His statutes with all his heart and

with all his soul, to perform the words of the covenant written in this book.

³²Further, he made all who were present in Jerusalem and Benjamin stand [with him, in confirmation of it]. So the inhabitants of Jerusalem acted in accordance with the covenant of God, the God of their fathers.

³³Josiah removed all the [pagan] repulsive things from all the lands belonging to the sons (descendants) of Israel, and made all who were present in Israel serve the LORD their God. Throughout his lifetime they did not turn from following the LORD God of their fathers.

35 JOSIAH CELEBRATED the Passover to the LORD in Jerusalem; they slaughtered the Passover *lambs* on the fourteenth *day* of the first month.

²He appointed the priests to their positions and encouraged them in the service of the house of the LORD.

³To the Levites who taught all Israel and were holy to the LORD he said, "Put the holy ark in the house (temple) which Solomon the son of David king of Israel built; it shall not be a burden [carried] on your shoulders any longer. Now serve the LORD your God and His people Israel.

⁴"Prepare *yourselves* according to your fathers' (ancestors') households by your divisions, in accordance with the instructions of David king of Israel, and the instructions of his son Solomon.

⁵"And stand in the holy place [of the priests] according to the sections of the fathers' households of your fellow kinsmen the lay people, and according to the Levites, by division of [the families of] a father's household.

⁶"Slaughter the Passover *lambs* and consecrate yourselves, and prepare for your fellow countrymen to carry out (obey) the word of the LORD *given* by Moses."

⁷Then Josiah contributed to the lay people, to all who were present, flocks of lambs and young goats numbering 30,000, all as Passover offerings, and 3,000 bulls—these were from the king's property.

⁸His officers also contributed a voluntary offering to the people, the priests and the Levites. Hilkiah, Zechariah, and Jehiel, the officials of the house of God, gave to the priests for the Passover offerings 2,600 *from the flocks* [of lambs and young goats], and 300 bulls.

⁹Conaniah also, and Shemaiah and Nethanel, his brothers, and Hashabiah and Jeiel and Jozabad, officers of the Levites, contributed to the Levites for the Passover offerings 5,000 *from the flocks* [of lambs and young goats], and 500 bulls.

¹⁰When the service was ready, the priests stood in their [assigned] places and the Levites by their divisions, in accordance with the king's command.

¹¹They slaughtered the Passover *lambs,* and while the priests sprinkled the blood *received* from their hand, the Levites skinned *the animals.*

¹²Then they removed the burnt offerings, to distribute them to the sections of the fathers' households of the lay people to offer to the LORD, as it is written in the Book of Moses. *They did* the same with the bulls.

¹³So they roasted the Passover *lambs* on the fire according to the ordinance; and they cooked the holy offerings in pots, in kettles, and in pans, and quickly brought them to all the lay people.

¹⁴Afterward the Levites prepared for themselves and for the priests, because the priests, the sons of Aaron, *were busy* offering the burnt offerings and the fat until night; so the Levites prepared for themselves and for the priests, the sons of Aaron.

¹⁵The singers, the sons of Asaph, were also in their places in accordance with the command of David, Asaph, Heman,

and Jeduthun the king's seer; and the gatekeepers at each gate did not need to leave their service, because their kinsmen the Levites prepared for them. ¹⁶So all the service of the LORD was prepared on that day to celebrate the Passover, and to offer burnt offerings on the altar of the LORD, in accordance with the command of King Josiah. ¹⁷Thus the sons of Israel who were present celebrated the Passover at that time, and the Feast of Unleavened Bread for seven days. ¹⁸No Passover like it had been celebrated in Israel since the days of Samuel the prophet; nor had any of the kings of Israel celebrated such a Passover as Josiah did with the priests, the Levites, all Judah and Israel who were present, and the inhabitants of Jerusalem. ¹⁹In the eighteenth year of Josiah's reign this Passover was celebrated.

²⁰After all this, when Josiah had prepared the temple, Neco king of Egypt came up to make war at Carchemish on the Euphrates, and Josiah went out to meet him. ²¹But Neco sent messengers to Josiah, saying, "What business do we have with each other, O King of Judah? *I am* not *coming* against you today, but against the house with which I am at war, and God has ordered me to hurry. Stop for your own sake from *interfering with* God who is with me, so that He will not destroy you." ²²Yet Josiah would not turn away from him, but disguised himself in order to fight against him. He did not listen to the words of Neco from the mouth of God, but came to fight against him on the plain of Megiddo. ²³The archers shot King Josiah, and the king said to his servants, "Take me away, for I am badly wounded." ²⁴So his servants took him out of the chariot and carried him in the second chariot which he had, and brought him to Jerusalem where he died and

was buried in the tombs of his fathers. All Judah and Jerusalem mourned for Josiah. ²⁵Then Jeremiah sung a lament (funeral song) for Josiah, and all the male and female singers have spoken about Josiah in their laments to this day. They made the songs an ordinance in Israel; behold, they are written in the Lamentations. [Lam 4:20] ²⁶Now the rest of the acts of Josiah and his deeds of devotion *and* godly achievements as written in the Law of the LORD, ²⁷and his acts, from the first to the last, behold, they are written in the Book of the Kings of Israel and Judah.

36 THEN THE people of the land took Joahaz the son of Josiah, and made him king in Jerusalem in place of his father. ²Joahaz was twenty-three years old when he became king, and he reigned [only] three months in Jerusalem. ³Then the king of Egypt deposed him at Jerusalem, and imposed a fine on the land of a hundred talents of silver and one talent of gold. ⁴The king of Egypt made Eliakim, the brother *of Joahaz,* king over Judah and Jerusalem, and changed his name to Jehoiakim. But Neco took Joahaz his brother, and brought him to Egypt.

⁵Jehoiakim was twenty-five years old when he became king, and he reigned for eleven years in Jerusalem; and he did evil in the sight of the LORD his God. ⁶Nebuchadnezzar king of Babylon came up against him and bound him with bronze [chains] to take him to Babylon. ⁷Nebuchadnezzar also brought some of the articles of the house (temple) of the LORD to Babylon and put them in his temple there. ⁸Now the rest of the acts of Jehoiakim and the repulsive acts which he committed, and what was found against

him, behold, they are written in the Book of the Kings of Israel and Judah. And his son Jehoiachin became king in his place.

⁹Jehoiachin was eight[teen] years old when he became king, and he reigned for three months and ten days in Jerusalem, and he did evil in the sight of the LORD. [2 Kin 24:8]

¹⁰Now at the turn of the year [in the spring], King Nebuchadnezzar sent *word* and had him brought to Babylon with the valuable articles of the house of the LORD, and made his brother Zedekiah king over Judah and Jerusalem.

¹¹Zedekiah was twenty-one years old when he became king, and he reigned for eleven years in Jerusalem.

¹²He did evil in the sight of the LORD his God; he did not humble himself before Jeremiah the prophet, *who spoke* for the LORD.

¹³He also rebelled against King Nebuchadnezzar who had made him swear *allegiance* by God. He stiffened his neck and hardened his heart against turning to the LORD God of Israel.

¹⁴Also, all the officials of the priests and the people were very unfaithful, *following* all the repulsive acts of the [pagan] nations; and they defiled the house of the LORD which He had sanctified in Jerusalem.

¹⁵The LORD, the God of their fathers, sent *word* to them again and again by His messengers, because He had compassion on His people and on His dwelling place.

¹⁶But they kept mocking the messengers of God and despising His words and scoffing at His prophets until the wrath of the LORD arose against His people, until there was no remedy *or* healing.

¹⁷Therefore He brought the king of the Chaldeans against them, who killed their young men with the sword in the house of their sanctuary, and had no compassion on young man or virgin, old man or infirm; He gave them all into his hand.

¹⁸And as for all the articles of the house of God, great and small, and the treasures of the house of the LORD, and the treasures of the king and of his officials, he brought them all to Babylon.

¹⁹Then they burned the house of God and tore down the wall of Jerusalem, and burned all its fortified buildings with fire, and destroyed all its valuable articles.

²⁰He deported to Babylon those who had escaped from the sword; and they were servants to him and to his sons until the kingdom of Persia was established there,

²¹to fulfill the word of the LORD by the mouth of Jeremiah, until the land had restored its Sabbaths; for as long as the land lay desolate it kept Sabbath until seventy years were complete. [Lev 25:4; 26:43; Jer 25:11; 29:10]

²²Now in the first year of Cyrus king of Persia—in order to fulfill the word of the LORD by the mouth of Jeremiah—the LORD stirred up the spirit of Cyrus king of Persia, so that he sent a proclamation throughout his kingdom, and also *put it* in writing, saying,

²³"Thus says Cyrus king of Persia: 'The LORD, the God of heaven, has given me all the kingdoms of the earth, and He has appointed me to build Him a house in Jerusalem, which is in Judah. Whoever there is among you of all His people, may the LORD his God be with him, and let him go up [to Jerusalem]!'"

Ezra

Author:
Probably Ezra

Date:
538 BC–457 BC

Everyday Life Principles:
The enemy always wants to oppose people who are doing something for God so he can stop their work.

You do not have to be afraid when you experience opposition, because God is with you.

Even though the enemy does not give up easily, he is a defeated foe, and you will eventually overcome him if you stay courageous.

The events recounted in the book of Ezra cover a period of about eighty years and tell the story of diligent, faithful people who overcame opposition and resistance in order to rebuild God's temple and restore it to its former glory.

When the people grew weary and discouraged because of the taunts of their enemies, God sent the two prophets Haggai and Zechariah to remind them of God's faithfulness and to encourage them to finish the work. In fact, we can read some of the words that inspired the people and their leaders to continue in Haggai 2:4, 5: "'be courageous, all you people of the land,' declares the LORD, 'and work; for I am with you,' declares the LORD of hosts . . . 'My Spirit stands [firm and immovable] and continues with you; do not fear.'"

I believe that God has a great plan for your life and that you are called to do something special for Him. The enemy will resist you, but let the book of Ezra remind you that God is on your side and the enemy is a defeated foe. Whatever battles the enemy wages against you, do not become discouraged, but stay courageous in God. Do not fear, but remember that God is faithful and He is with you; He always wins and in Him, you do too.

1 NOW IN the first year of Cyrus king of Persia [that is, the first year he ruled Babylon], in order to fulfill the word of the LORD by the mouth of Jeremiah [the prophet], the LORD stirred up (put in motion) the spirit of Cyrus king of Persia, so that he sent a proclamation throughout all his kingdom, and also *put it* in writing, saying: [Jer 29:10–14]

2"Thus says Cyrus king of Persia, 'The LORD, the God of heaven, has given me all the kingdoms of the earth and He has appointed me to build Him a house at Jerusalem, which is in Judah.

3'Whoever there is among you of all His people, may his God be with him! Let him go up to Jerusalem, which is in Judah and rebuild the house of the LORD, the God of Israel; He is God who is in Jerusalem.

4'In any place where a survivor (Jewish exile) may live, let the men (Gentiles) of that place support him with silver and gold, with goods and cattle, together with freewill offerings for the house of God in Jerusalem.'"

5Then the heads of the fathers' *households* of Judah and Benjamin, and the priests and Levites, all those whose spirits God had stirred up, arose to go up and rebuild the house of the LORD which is in Jerusalem.

6All those who were around them encouraged them with articles of silver, with gold, with goods, with cattle, and with valuable things, in addition to all that was given as a freewill offering.

7Also King Cyrus brought out the articles of the house of the LORD, which Nebuchadnezzar had carried away from Jerusalem [when he captured that city] and had put in the house of his gods.

8And Cyrus, king of Persia, had Mithredath the treasurer bring them out, and he counted them out to Sheshbazzar, the governor (leader) of Judah.

9And they counted: 30 dishes (basins) of gold, 1,000 dishes of silver, 29 duplicates;

1030 [small] gold bowls, 410 [small] silver bowls of a second *kind,* and 1,000 other articles.

11All the articles of gold and of silver *totaled* 5,400. All these Sheshbazzar [the governor] brought up with the exiles who went from Babylon up to Jerusalem.

2 NOW THESE are the people of the province [of Judah] who came up from the captivity of the exiles, whom Nebuchadnezzar the king of Babylon had deported to Babylon, and who returned to Jerusalem and Judah, each to his own city.

2These came with Zerubbabel: Jeshua, Nehemiah, Seraiah, Reelaiah, Mordecai, Bilshan, Mispar, Bigvai, Rehum, Baanah.

The number of the men of the people of Israel:

3the sons (descendants) of Parosh, 2,172;

4the sons of Shephatiah, 372;

5the sons of Arah, 775;

6the sons of Pahath-moab of the sons of Jeshua and Joab, 2,812;

7the sons of Elam, 1,254;

8the sons of Zattu, 945;

9the sons of Zaccai, 760;

10the sons of Bani, 642;

11the sons of Bebai, 623;

12the sons of Azgad, 1,222;

13the sons of Adonikam, 666;

14the sons of Bigvai, 2,056;

15the sons of Adin, 454;

16the sons of Ater of Hezekiah, 98;

17the sons of Bezai, 323;

18the sons of Jorah, 112;

19the sons of Hashum, 223;

20the sons of Gibbar, 95;

21the men of Bethlehem, 123;

22the men of Netophah, 56;

23the men of Anathoth, 128;

24the sons of Azmaveth, 42;

²⁵the sons of Kiriath-arim, Chephirah and Beeroth, 743;

²⁶the sons of Ramah and Geba, 621;

²⁷the men of Michmas, 122;

²⁸the men of Bethel and Ai, 223;

²⁹the sons of Nebo, 52;

³⁰the sons of Magbish, 156;

³¹the sons of the other Elam, 1,254;

³²the sons of Harim, 320;

³³the sons of Lod, Hadid and Ono, 725;

³⁴the men of Jericho, 345;

³⁵the sons of Senaah, 3,630.

³⁶The priests: the sons of Jedaiah of the house of Jeshua, 973;

³⁷the sons of Immer, 1,052;

³⁸the sons of Pashhur, 1,247;

³⁹the sons of Harim, 1,017.

⁴⁰The Levites: the sons of Jeshua and Kadmiel, of the sons of Hodaviah, 74.

⁴¹The singers: the sons of Asaph, 128.

⁴²The sons of the gatekeepers: of Shallum, Ater, Talmon, Akkub, Hatita, and Shobai, in all 139.

⁴³The temple servants: the sons of Ziha, Hasupha, Tabbaoth,

⁴⁴the sons of Keros, Siaha, Padon,

⁴⁵the sons of Lebanah, Hagabah, Akkub,

⁴⁶the sons of Hagab, Shalmai, Hanan,

⁴⁷the sons of Giddel, Gahar, Reaiah,

⁴⁸the sons of Rezin, Nekoda, Gazzam,

⁴⁹the sons of Uzza, Paseah, Besai,

⁵⁰the sons of Asnah, Meunim, Nephisim,

⁵¹the sons of Bakbuk, Hakupha, Harhur,

⁵²the sons of Bazluth, Mehida, Harsha,

⁵³the sons of Barkos, Sisera, Temah,

⁵⁴the sons of Neziah, Hatipha.

⁵⁵The sons of [King] Solomon's servants: the sons of Sotai, Hassophereth (Sophereth), Peruda,

⁵⁶the sons of Jaalah, Darkon, Giddel,

⁵⁷the sons of Shephatiah, Hattil, Pochereth-hazzebaim, Ami.

⁵⁸All the temple servants and the sons of Solomon's servants totaled 392.

⁵⁹Now these are the ones who came up from Tel-melah, Tel-harsha, Cherub, Addan, and Immer, but they could not provide evidence of their fathers' households and their descendants, whether they were of Israel:

⁶⁰the sons of Delaiah, Tobiah, and Nekoda, 652.

⁶¹Of the sons of the priests: the sons of Hobaiah, of Hakkoz, and of Barzillai, who took a wife from the daughters of Barzillai the Gileadite, and he was known by their name. [2 Sam 17:27, 28; 19:31–39]

⁶²These searched [for their names] among those registered in the genealogies, but they were not found; so they *were excluded* from the priesthood as [ceremonially] unclean.

⁶³The governor told them that they should not eat of the most holy things [the priests' food] until a priest stood up with Urim and Thummim [who by consulting these articles in his breastplate could determine God's will in the matter].

⁶⁴The whole assembly totaled 42,360,

⁶⁵besides their male and female servants who numbered 7,337; and [among them] they had 200 male and female singers.

⁶⁶Their horses totaled 736; their mules, 245;

⁶⁷their camels totaled 435; their donkeys, 6,720.

⁶⁸Some of the heads of the fathers' *households* (extended families), when they arrived at the house of the LORD in Jerusalem, made voluntary contributions for the house of God to rebuild it on its [old] foundation.

⁶⁹They gave according to their ability to the treasury for the work, 61,000 drachmas of gold, 5,000 minas of silver, and 100 priestly [linen] garments.

⁷⁰So the priests, the Levites, some of the people, the singers, the gatekeepers, and the temple servants settled in their [own] cities, and all Israel [gradually settled] into their cities.

3 WHEN THE seventh month came and the sons of Israel were in the cities, the people gathered together as one man to Jerusalem.

²Then Jeshua the son of Jozadak and his brothers the priests, and Zerubbabel the son of Shealtiel and his brothers arose, and they built the altar of the God of Israel, to offer burnt offerings on it, as it is written in the Law of Moses, the man of God.

³So they set up the altar on its [old] foundation, for they were terrified because of the peoples of the lands; and they offered burnt offerings on it to the LORD, morning and evening.

⁴They celebrated the Feast of Booths, as it is written, and offered the fixed number of daily burnt offerings, in accordance with the ordinances, as each day required;

⁵and afterward, there was the continual burnt offering, the offering at the New Moons, and at all the appointed festivals of the LORD that were consecrated, and the offerings of everyone who made a voluntary offering to the LORD.

life point

God moves on our behalf when we focus on Him instead of on our fears. Thoughts and feelings of fear are simply the result of our enemy, Satan, trying to distract us from God and His will for our lives. We would do well to follow the Israelites' example in Ezra 3:3 and focus on God, worshiping Him with all our hearts. The Israelites worshiped by offering burnt offerings, which was a requirement of the Old Covenant. Under the New Covenant, we worship Him by offering everything we have and everything we are for His use and glory. He no longer wants animal sacrifices; now He wants us to come to Him as a "living sacrifice, holy and well-pleasing" to Him (Romans 12:1).

putting the Word to work

Have you seen evidence of God fulfilling His plans in your life or ministry? Be sure to thank Him for His faithfulness from the very beginning, as the Israelites did when the foundation of the second temple was laid (see Ezra 3:10, 11).

⁶From the first day of the seventh month they began to offer burnt offerings to the LORD, but the foundation of the temple of the LORD had not been laid.

⁷They gave money to the masons and to the carpenters, and gave food, drink, and [olive] oil to the people from Sidon and Tyre, to bring cedar wood from Lebanon to the seaport of Joppa, in accordance with the authorization they had from Cyrus king of Persia.

⁸In the second year of their coming to God's house at Jerusalem, in the second month, Zerubbabel the son of Shealtiel and Jeshua the son of Jozadak began [the work], with the rest of their brothers—the priests and Levites and all who came to Jerusalem from the captivity. They appointed the Levites, from twenty years old and upward, to oversee the work of the house of the LORD.

⁹Then Jeshua with his sons and brothers stood united with Kadmiel and his sons, the sons of Judah and the sons of Henadad with their sons and brothers the Levites, to oversee the workmen in the house of God.

¹⁰Now when the builders had laid the foundation of the temple of the LORD, the priests stood in their apparel with trumpets, and the Levites, the sons of Asaph, with their cymbals, to praise the LORD in accordance with the directions of David king of Israel.

¹¹They sang [responsively], praising and giving thanks to the LORD, *saying,*

life point

The children of Israel faced much opposition as they worked to restore the temple, but they never lost sight of God's goodness (see Ezra 3:11). Like the Israelites, we need to remember that God is good all the time. He wants us to understand and experience His goodness in every situation.

When resistance attempts to stand in your way as you seek to obey God, remember not to question His goodness. Instead, let opposition provoke you to praise and declare the goodness of God. Be like the children of Israel and refuse to be discouraged. Instead, believe and proclaim God's goodness more aggressively. He *is* good, and His goodness is available to you, no matter what obstacles are in your way.

"For He is good, for His lovingkindness (mercy) toward Israel *endures* forever." And all the people shouted with a great shout when they praised the LORD because the foundation of the house of the LORD was laid.

¹²But many of the priests and Levites and heads of fathers' *households,* the old men who had seen the first house (temple), wept with a loud voice when the foundation of this house was laid before their eyes, while many shouted aloud for joy,

¹³so that the people could not distinguish the sound of the shout of joy from the sound of the weeping of the people, for the people shouted with a loud shout, and the sound was heard far away.

4 NOW WHEN [the Samaritans] the adversaries of Judah and Benjamin heard that the exiles from the captivity were building a temple to the LORD God of Israel,

²they came to Zerubbabel [who was now governor] and to the heads of the

putting the Word to work

Is change happening in the midst of your personal life or in the life of your church or ministry? Experiencing mixed emotions during times of change is not uncommon (see Ezra 3:12, 13). Do not try to make serious decisions during emotional times. As I like to say, "Let emotions subside and then decide!"

fathers' *households* and said to them, "Let us build with you, for we seek your God [and worship] just as you do; and we have sacrificed to Him since the days of Esarhaddon king of Assyria, who brought us up here." [2 Kin 17:24–29]

³But Zerubbabel and Jeshua and the rest of the heads of fathers' *households* of Israel said to them, "You have nothing in common with us in building a house to our God; but we ourselves will together build to the LORD God of Israel, just as King Cyrus, the king of Persia, has commanded us."

⁴Then [the Samaritans and others of] the people of the land discouraged the people of Judah, and frightened them [to deter them] from building,

⁵and hired advisers [to work] against them to frustrate their plans during the entire time that Cyrus king of Persia reigned, [and this lasted] even until the reign of Darius king of Persia.

⁶Now in the reign of Ahasuerus (Xerxes), in the beginning of his reign, the Samaritans wrote [to him] an accusation against the inhabitants of Judah and Jerusalem [who had returned from exile].

⁷Later, in the days of [King] Artaxerxes, Bishlam, Mithredath, Tabeel and the rest of their associates wrote to Artaxerxes king of Persia; and the text of the letter was written in Aramaic and translated *from* Aramaic.

grace to overcome opposition

In Ezra 4:1–5, we read about the two tribes of Judah and Benjamin, who received permission from Cyrus, the king of Persia, to build a temple to the Lord. When the Samaritans heard what was going on, they went to the governor, Zerubbabel, and to the other leaders of the people and asked to join in rebuilding the temple, because they claimed to worship the same God.

If we investigate this, we will discover that although it is true that these Samaritans were worshiping the God of Israel, they were worshiping Him for the wrong reason. They were doing it because, basically, they had been taught to do so in order to keep evil out of their camp. These people were not Israelites; they were Assyrians who had simply added the Lord God of Israel to the list of other gods they worshiped. While they did worship the one true God, Jehovah, they also kept their false gods and idols.

Since the Israelites were well aware of this fact, they told the Samaritans, their long-time enemies, that they would have no part in building a temple to the Lord. This made the Samaritans so angry that they began to do everything in their power to harass and cause trouble for the Israelites, to frustrate their purpose and plans.

How should godly people respond to that kind of opposition and persecution? Jesus said we should "calm down" and "cheer up" (see John 14:27; 16:33). I believe the willingness to do so is a key to enjoying the life of grace that God provides and wants for His people.

If we think we can do anything for God without opposition, we are mistaken. Jesus warned us that in this life we will have tribulation (see John 16:33). He said that if people persecuted Him, they will also persecute us, because we belong to Him (see John 15:18, 20). We know that we cannot go through life on this earth without encountering some kind of trouble. Yet often it is trouble that frustrates us and makes us miserable and unhappy. If we know that trials are a fact of life, we should make the decision not to let them steal our peace and joy. If they do, they will also steal our power.

Often, when people first come to the Lord, they suddenly begin to be attacked in ways that are totally different from anything they have experienced before. Many times they do not understand what is happening to them or why. If they do not have proper instruction in this area, their misunderstanding and frustration can cause them to give up and fall away from God.

We need to remember that the devil is not going to sit back and allow us to take new ground without putting up a fight. Any time we begin to make progress in building the kingdom of God, our enemy will come against us. Many times the mistake we make is one I made in my early Christian life—trying to use faith to get to the place where there is total freedom from trouble. I am sure you know by now that it simply does not work that way.

The purpose of faith is not always to keep us *from* trouble; it is often to carry us *through* trouble. If we never had any trouble, we would not need any faith. What we need in the midst of trouble is grace—God's powerful, overcoming grace.

⁸Rehum the [Persian] commander [of the Samaritans] and Shimshai the scribe wrote a letter against Jerusalem to Artaxerxes the king as follows—

⁹then *wrote* Rehum the [Persian] commander, Shimshai the scribe, and the rest of their associates, the judges, the lesser governors, the officials, the secretaries, the men of Erech, the Babylonians, the men of Susa, that is, the Elamites,

¹⁰and the rest of the nations whom the great and noble Osnappar deported and settled in the city of Samaria, and in the rest of the region west of the [Euphrates] River. Now

¹¹this is a copy of the letter which they sent to him:

"To King Artaxerxes from your servants, the men in the region west of the [Euphrates] River; and now:

¹²Let it be known to the king that the Jews who came up from you have come to us at Jerusalem. They are rebuilding this rebellious and evil city and are finishing its walls and repairing the foundations.

¹³"Now let it be known to the king, that if that city is rebuilt and the walls are finished, then they will not pay tax, custom, or toll, and the revenue of the kings will be diminished.

¹⁴"Now because we are in the service of the palace, and it is not proper for us to witness the king's dishonor, for that reason we have sent *word* and informed the king,

¹⁵in order that a search may be made in the record books of your fathers. And you will discover in the record books and learn that this is a rebellious city, damaging to kings and provinces, and that in the past they have incited rebellion within it. That is why that city was laid waste (destroyed).

¹⁶"We are informing the king that if that city is rebuilt and its walls finished, it will mean that you will have no possession in *the province* west of the [Euphrates] River."

¹⁷*Then* the king sent an answer to Rehum the [Persian] commander, to Shimshai the scribe, and to the rest of their colleagues who live in Samaria and in the rest of *the provinces* west of the River: "Peace (Greetings). And now,

¹⁸The document which you sent to us has been translated and read before me.

¹⁹"I have issued a command and a search has been made, and it has been discovered that this city [Jerusalem] in earlier times has revolted against the kings, and that rebellion and sedition have been perpetrated in it.

²⁰"There have also been mighty kings over Jerusalem who have ruled over all *the provinces* west of the [Euphrates] River, and tax, custom, and toll were paid to them.

²¹"So, now issue a decree to make these men stop [work], so that this city is not rebuilt until a [new] command is issued by me.

²²"Beware of being negligent in carrying out this *matter*. Why should damage increase to the detriment of the kings?"

²³Then as soon as the copy of King Artaxerxes' document was read before Rehum and Shimshai the scribe, and their colleagues, they went up hurriedly to Jerusalem to the Jews, and made them stop [work] by force of arms.

²⁴Then the work on the house of God in Jerusalem stopped. It was suspended until the second year of the reign of Darius king of Persia.

5 NOW WHEN the prophets, Haggai the prophet and Zechariah, the son (grandson) of Iddo, prophesied to the Jews who were in Judah and Jerusalem in the name of the God of Israel, *whose Spirit was* over them,

²then Zerubbabel the son of Shealtiel [heir to the throne of Judah] and Jeshua the son of Jozadak arose and

717   Ezra 5:17

began to rebuild the house of God in Jerusalem; and the prophets of God [Haggai and Zechariah] were with them, supporting *and* encouraging them. [Hag 1:12–14; Matt 1:12, 13]

³At that time Tattenai, the governor of *the province* on the west side of the [Euphrates] River, and Shethar-bozenai and their colleagues came to them and said, "Who issued you a decree *and* authorized you to rebuild this temple and to restore this wall (shrine)?"

⁴Then, accordingly, we told them the names of the men who were reconstructing this building.

⁵But the eye of their God was on the elders of the Jews, so they [Tattenai and the others] did not stop them until a report could come before Darius, and then an answer was returned by letter concerning it.

⁶*This is* a copy of the letter that Tattenai, governor of *the province* west of the [Euphrates] River, and Shethar-bozenai and his associates, the officials who were west of the River, sent to Darius the king.

⁷They sent a report to him in which it was written: "To Darius the king, all peace.

⁸"Let it be known to the king that we have gone to the province of Judah, to the house of the great God. It is being built with huge stones, with beams laid in the walls; and this work goes on with diligence *and* care and is succeeding in their hands.

⁹"Then we asked those elders, 'Who issued you a decree to rebuild this temple and to finish this structure?'

¹⁰"We also asked them their names so that we might notify you, and so

that we might record the names of the men in charge.

¹¹"They replied, 'We are servants of the God of heaven and earth, and are rebuilding the temple which was erected many years ago, which a great king of Israel built and finished.

¹²'But because our fathers provoked the God of heaven to wrath, He handed them over to Nebuchadnezzar king of Babylon, the Chaldean, who destroyed this temple and exiled the people to Babylon.

¹³'But in the first year of Cyrus king of Babylon, [the same] King Cyrus issued a decree to rebuild this house of God.

¹⁴'Also the gold and silver utensils of the house of God which Nebuchadnezzar had taken from the temple in Jerusalem and had brought into the temple of Babylon, King Cyrus took from the temple of Babylon and had them given to a man whose name was Sheshbazzar, whom he had appointed governor.

¹⁵'And Cyrus said to him, "Take these utensils, go and deposit them in the temple in Jerusalem, and let the house of God be rebuilt on its site."

¹⁶'Then that Sheshbazzar came and laid the foundations of the house of God in Jerusalem; and from then until now it has been under construction and is not yet completed.'

¹⁷"So now, if it pleases the king, let a search be conducted in the king's treasure house [in the royal archives] there in Babylon to see if it is true that a decree was issued by King Cyrus to rebuild this house of God at Jerusalem; and let the king send us his decision concerning this matter."

speak the Word

Thank You, God, for giving me the diligence and care I need in order to press on in the work You have given me to do and for causing it to succeed in my hands.
–ADAPTED FROM EZRA 5:8

6 THEN KING Darius issued a decree, and a search was conducted in Babylon in the archives where the treasures [and records] were stored.

2In Ecbatana in the fortress (palace) in the province of Media, a scroll was found on which this was recorded: "Memorandum—

3"In the first year of King Cyrus, Cyrus the king issued a decree: 'Concerning the house of God in Jerusalem, let the temple (house), the place where sacrifices are offered, be rebuilt and let its foundations be strongly laid, its height and its width each 60 cubits,

4with three layers of huge stones and one layer of timbers. Let the cost be paid from the royal treasury.

5'Also let the gold and silver utensils of the house of God, which Nebuchadnezzar took from the temple in Jerusalem and brought to Babylon, be returned and brought back to their [proper] places in the temple in Jerusalem; and you shall put them in the house of God.'

6"Now therefore, Tattenai, governor of the province west of the [Euphrates] River, Shethar-bozenai and your associates, the officials who are west of the River, keep far away from there.

7"Leave the work on this house of God alone; let the governor of the Jews and the Jewish elders rebuild this house of God on its site.

8"Also, I issue a decree as to what you are to do for these Jewish elders for the rebuilding of this house of God: the full cost is to be paid to these people from the royal treasury out of the taxes of the provinces west of the River, and that without delay.

9"Whatever is needed, including young bulls, rams, and lambs for the burnt offerings to the God of heaven, and wheat, salt, wine, and anointing oil, according to the request of the priests at Jerusalem, let it all be given to them daily without fail,

10so that they may offer pleasing (sweet-smelling) sacrifices to the God of heaven and pray for the life of the king and his sons.

11"I have also issued a decree that if there is any man who violates this edict, a beam of timber shall be pulled from his house [and set up]; then he shall be impaled on it, and his house shall be turned into a refuse heap for this [violation].

12"May the God who has caused His Name to dwell there overthrow any king or people who attempts to alter this command, so as to destroy this house of God in Jerusalem. I, Darius, have issued this decree; let it be carried out quickly and with due diligence."

13Then Tattenai, governor of the province west of the [Euphrates] River, with Shethar-bozenai and their associates carried out the decree with due diligence, just as King Darius had sent and commanded.

14And the Jewish elders built and prospered through the prophesying of Haggai the prophet and Zechariah the son of Iddo. They finished their building as commanded by the God of Israel and in accordance with the decree of Cyrus and Darius and Artaxerxes king of Persia.

15This temple was finished on the third day of the month of Adar, in the sixth year of the reign of King Darius.

16And all Israel—the priests, the Levites, and the rest of the [former] exiles—celebrated the dedication of this house of God with joy.

17They offered at the dedication of this house of God 100 bulls, 200 rams, 400 lambs, and, as a sin offering for all Israel, 12 male goats, according to the number of Israel's tribes.

18Then they appointed the priests to their divisions and the Levites in their orders for the service of God at Jerusalem, as it is written in the book of Moses.

¹⁹The [former] exiles kept the Passover on the fourteenth [day] of the first month.

²⁰For the priests and the Levites had purified themselves together; all of them were [ceremonially] clean. So they slaughtered the Passover *lamb* for all the exiles, for their brothers the priests, and for themselves.

²¹The *Passover* was eaten by the sons (descendants) of Israel (Jacob) who returned from exile and by all those who had separated themselves from the [ceremonial] uncleanness of the nations of the land to *join* them, *in order* to seek the LORD God of Israel.

²²They observed the Feast of Unleavened Bread for seven days with joy, for the LORD had caused them to rejoice and had turned the heart of the king of Assyria toward them, so that he encouraged them *and* strengthened their hands in the work of the house of God, the God of Israel.

7 NOW AFTER this, in the reign of Artaxerxes I [son of Ahasuerus (Xerxes)] king of Persia, Ezra the son (descendant) of Seraiah, the son of Azariah, the son of Hilkiah,

²the son of Shallum, the son of Zadok, the son of Ahitub,

³the son of Amariah, the son of Azariah, the son of Meraioth,

⁴the son of Zerahiah, the son of Uzzi, the son of Bukki,

the truth about hard work

It is easy to drift backward when we face obstacles and persecution, but like those who rebuilt the temple, we need to press on and go forward. *Effortless living* is never effective. Everyone thinks that the more we can do with *less effort*, the better life is—but that is not true!

Think about the number of buttons we push each day to make our lives easier. We push a button to get on an elevator and push another one to get to the next floor; we put dirty dishes in a washer and push a button and the dishes come out clean; we put dirty clothes in a machine, push a button, and they are washed; throw them into another machine, push a button, and they are dried—and if we remove them from the dryer quickly enough, they do not even wrinkle enough to need ironing. Still, we complain and grumble because we have to load and unload the machines!

Speaking of effortless living and its effects, consider this story about a science experiment: Some bees were taken along on a space flight to see how they would do in a gravity-free environment. Because the bees floated in space, they did not have to make any effort to fly. When the astronauts were asked how the bees seemed to respond to the experiment, they replied, "They enjoyed the ride, but they died."

We may think we would enjoy an effortless life, but it would not be good for us. We are created to make effort. Whether we know it or not, we are created for work, involvement, participation, and struggle. We are not supposed to struggle with everything, but we are also not supposed to be the kind of people who always take the easy way out.

Look at what the people mentioned in Ezra accomplished with their hard work— they rebuilt God's beautiful temple, restoring worship to the Lord their God in Jerusalem (see Ezra 6:14, 15). Let their story restore diligence in your heart to faithfully serve the Lord.

⁵the son of Abishua, the son of Phinehas, the son of Eleazar, the son of Aaron the chief priest—

⁶this Ezra went up from Babylon. He was a scribe skilled in the Law (the five books) of Moses, which the LORD God of Israel had given; and the king granted him everything that he asked, for the hand of the LORD his God was on him.

⁷Some of the sons of Israel, with some of the priests and Levites, the singers and gatekeepers, and the temple servants also went up [from Babylon] to Jerusalem in the seventh year of King Artaxerxes.

⁸Ezra came to Jerusalem in the fifth month of the seventh year of the king.

⁹For on the first of the first month he started out from Babylon, and on the first of the fifth month he arrived in Jerusalem, because the good hand of his God was on him.

¹⁰For Ezra had set his heart (resolved) to study *and* interpret the Law of the LORD, and to practice it and teach *His* statutes and ordinances in Israel.

¹¹Now this is a copy of the decree that King Artaxerxes gave to Ezra the priest, the scribe [who was] learned in the words of the commandments of the LORD and of His statutes to Israel:

¹²"Artaxerxes, king of kings, to Ezra the priest, the scribe of the Law of the God of heaven, perfect *peace* (greetings). And now

¹³I have issued a decree that all of the people of Israel and their priests and the Levites in my kingdom who are willing to go to Jerusalem, may go with you.

¹⁴"For you are sent by the king and his seven advisers to inquire about Judah and Jerusalem in accordance with the Law of your God, which is in your hand,

¹⁵and to bring [with you] the silver and gold which the king and his advisers have freely offered to the God of Israel, whose dwelling is in Jerusalem,

¹⁶and all the silver and gold which you find in the whole province of Babylon, along with the freewill offering of the people and of the priests for the house of their God in Jerusalem.

¹⁷"Therefore with this money, you shall diligently buy bulls, rams, and lambs, with their grain offerings and drink offerings, and offer them on the altar of the house of your God which is in Jerusalem.

¹⁸"And whatever seems good to you and to your brothers to do with the rest of the silver and the gold, you may do in accordance with the will of your God.

¹⁹"As for the utensils which are given to you for the service of the house of your God, deliver [those] in full before the God of Jerusalem.

²⁰"The rest of the things required for the house of your God, which you may have occasion to provide, provide it from the royal treasury.

²¹"And I, Artaxerxes the king, issue a decree to all the treasurers *in the provinces* west of the [Euphrates] River, that whatever Ezra the priest, the scribe of the Law of the God of heaven, may require of you, it shall be done diligently *and* at once—

²²*even* up to 100 talents of silver, 100 kors (measures) of wheat, 100 baths of wine, 100 baths of [olive] oil, and salt as needed.

speak the Word

Lord, I pray that You would help me set my heart to study Your Word and seek Your will.
—ADAPTED FROM EZRA 7:10

23"Whatever is commanded by the God of heaven, let it be done diligently *and* with enthusiasm for the house of the God of heaven, so that there will not be wrath against the kingdom of the king and his sons.

24"We also inform you that it is not authorized to impose tax, tribute, or toll on any of the priests, Levites, singers, doorkeepers, temple servants or *other* servants of this house of God.

25"You, Ezra, are to appoint magistrates and judges in accordance with the wisdom *and* instruction of your God which is in your hand, so that they may judge all the people who are in *the province* west of the [Euphrates] River; *appoint* those who know the laws of your God; and you may teach anyone who does not know *them*.

26"Whoever does not observe *and* practice the law of your God and the law of the king, let judgment be executed upon him strictly *and* promptly, whether it be for death or banishment or confiscation of property or imprisonment."

27Blessed be the LORD, the God of our fathers [said Ezra], who put *such a thing* as this in the king's heart, to adorn *and* glorify the house of the LORD in Jerusalem,

28and has extended His mercy *and* lovingkindness to me before the king, his advisers, and all the king's mighty officials. I was strengthened *and* encouraged, for the hand of the LORD my God was upon me, and I gathered together outstanding men of Israel to go up with me [to Jerusalem].

8 THESE ARE the heads of their fathers' *households* and *this is* the genealogy of those who went up with me from Babylon in the reign of King Artaxerxes:

2of the sons of Phinehas, Gershom; of the sons of Ithamar, Daniel; of the sons of David, Hattush;

3of the sons of Shecaniah *who was* of the sons of Parosh, Zechariah, and with him were registered 150 men by genealogy;

4of the sons of Pahath-moab, Eliehoenai son of Zerahiah, with 200 men;

5of the sons of Zattu, Shecaniah son of Jahaziel, with 300 men;

6of the sons of Adin, Ebed son of Jonathan, with 50 men;

7of the sons of Elam, Jeshaiah son of Athaliah, with 70 men;

8of the sons of Shephatiah, Zebadiah son of Michael, with 80 men;

9of the sons of Joab, Obadiah son of Jehiel, with 218 men;

10of the sons of Bani, Shelomith son of Josiphiah, with 160 men;

11of the sons of Bebai, Zechariah son of Bebai, with 28 men;

12of the sons of Azgad, Johanan son of Hakkatan, with 110 men;

13of the sons of Adonikam, the last to come, their names are Eliphelet, Jeiel, and Shemaiah, with 60 men;

14and of the sons of Bigvai, Uthai and Zabbud, with 70 men.

15Now I gathered them together at the river that runs to Ahava, where we camped for three days. I observed the people and the priests, and I did not find any Levites there.

speak the Word

God, whatever You command me to do, I will do it diligently and with enthusiasm.
–ADAPTED FROM EZRA 7:23

God, I bless You because Your mercy and loving-kindness are extended to me. I am strengthened and encouraged because Your hand is upon me.
–ADAPTED FROM EZRA 7:27, 28

¹⁶So I sent for Eliezer, Ariel, She-maiah, Elnathan, Jarib, Elnathan, Nathan, Zechariah, and Meshullam, [who were] leading men, and also for Joiarib and Elnathan, [who were] teachers.

¹⁷And I sent them to Iddo, the leading man at the place Casiphia, telling them what to say to Iddo and his brothers, the temple servants at the place Casiphia, *that is,* to bring us servants (ministers) for the house of our God.

¹⁸And as the good hand of our God was upon us, they brought us a man of understanding (insight) from the sons of Mahli, the son of Levi, the son of Israel, *named* Sherebiah, with his sons and his brothers (relatives), 18 men;

¹⁹and Hashabiah, and with him Jeshaiah of the sons of Merari, with his brothers (relatives) and their sons, 20 men;

²⁰also 220 of the temple servants, whom David and the leaders had set apart [with their descendants] for the service of the Levites. They were all designated by name.

²¹Then I proclaimed a fast there at the river Ahava, so that we might humble ourselves before our God to seek from Him a safe journey for us, our children, and all our possessions.

²²For I was ashamed to request troops and horsemen from the king to protect us from the enemy along the way, because we had told the king, "The hand of our God is favorable toward all those who seek Him, but His power and His anger are against all those who abandon (turn away from) Him."

²³So we fasted and sought [help from] our God concerning this [matter], and He heard our plea.

²⁴Then I set apart twelve leading

putting the Word to work

Ezra knew that the exiled Jews needed guidance and protection as they prepared to return to Jerusalem (see Ezra 8:21–23). Are you facing a challenging situation or opposition from the enemy? Humble yourself before God, seek Him desperately, and trust Him to honor your dependence on Him.

priests, Sherebiah, Hashabiah, and ten of their brothers (relatives),

²⁵and I weighed out to them the silver, the gold, and the utensils, the offering for the house of our God which the king, his advisers, his officials, and all Israel who were present there had offered.

²⁶I weighed into their hands 650 talents of silver, and silver utensils *worth* 100 talents, and 100 talents of gold;

²⁷also 20 bowls of gold *worth* 1,000 darics, and two utensils of fine shiny bronze, precious as gold.

²⁸Then I said to them, "You are holy to the LORD, the utensils are holy, and the silver and the gold are a freewill offering to the LORD God of your fathers.

²⁹"Guard and keep them until you weigh them before the leading priests and the Levites and the leaders of the fathers' *households* of Israel in Jerusalem, in the chambers of the house of the LORD."

³⁰So the priests and the Levites received the weighed out silver and gold, and the utensils, to bring them to Jerusalem to the house of our God.

³¹We set out from the river Ahava on the twelfth [day] of the first month to go to Jerusalem; and the hand of our God was upon us, and He rescued us from

speak the Word

God, I thank You that Your hand is favorable toward me because I seek You.
–ADAPTED FROM EZRA 8:22

the hand of the enemy and those who lay in ambushes along the way. ³²So we came to Jerusalem and remained there for three days. ³³On the fourth day the silver and the gold and the utensils were weighed out in the house of our God into the hand of Meremoth the son of Uriah the priest, and with him was Eleazar the son of Phinehas; and with them were the Levites—Jozabad the son of Jeshua and Noadiah the son of Binnui. ³⁴Every piece was counted and weighed, and all the weight was recorded at that time. ³⁵Also the [former] exiles who had come from the captivity offered burnt offerings to the God of Israel: 12 bulls for all Israel, 96 rams, 77 lambs, and 12 male goats for a sin offering. All this was a burnt offering to the LORD. ³⁶And they delivered the king's edicts to the king's satraps (lieutenants) and to the governors west of the [Euphrates] River, and they supported the people and God's house.

9 WHEN THESE things were completed, the officials came to me and said, "The people of Israel and the priests and Levites have not separated themselves from the peoples of the lands, but have committed the repulsive acts of the Canaanites, Hittites, Perizzites, Jebusites, Ammonites, Moabites, Egyptians, and Amorites. ²"For they have taken some of their daughters *as wives* for themselves and for their sons, so that the holy race has intermingled with the peoples of the lands. Indeed, the officials and chief men have been foremost in this unfaithful act *and* direct violation [of God's will]." [Deut 7:3, 4] ³When I heard this, I tore my clothing and my robe [in grief], I pulled out some of the hair from my head and my beard, and sat down appalled [at the shame of it]. ⁴Then everyone who trembled at the words of the God of Israel because of the unfaithfulness of the exiles gathered

seek God desperately

In Ezra 8:23, we read that Ezra proclaimed a fast to show God his desperation when the Israelites required protection and needed to know what to do. Missing a few meals and taking that time to seek God is not a bad idea. Turning the television off and spending the time you would normally spend watching it with God instead is not a bad idea either. Let me encourage you to stay home a few evenings and spend extra time with the Lord instead of going out with your friends and repeating your problems over and over to them.

Ezra and the Israelites sought God and inquired of Him (see Ezra 8:23). When we seek God we pursue, crave, and go after Him with all our might. In other words, we act like a starving person in search of food to keep us alive. We need to seek God all the time, not just when we are in trouble.

I'm convinced one reason so many people have so many problems is that the only time they seek God is when they are in trouble. He once showed me that if He removed their problems, those people would not spend any time with Him. He spoke to my heart, "Seek Me as if you are desperate all the time, and then you will not find yourself desperate as often in reality." I think this is good advice, and I highly recommend that we all follow it. Hearing from God is vital, and we need to do whatever it takes to hear His voice clearly.

to me as I sat appalled until the evening offering.

⁵At the evening offering I arose from my [time of] humiliation *and* penitence and having torn my clothing and my robe, I fell on my knees and stretched out my hands to the Lord my God,

⁶and I said, "O my God, I am ashamed and embarrassed to lift up my face to You, my God, for our wrongdoings have risen higher than our heads and our guilt has grown to the heavens.

⁷"Since the days of our fathers to this day we have been exceedingly guilty; and on account of our wrongdoings we, our kings, and our priests have been handed over to the kings of the lands, to the sword, to captivity, to plundering, and to complete shame, as it is today.

⁸"But now for a brief moment grace has been [shown to us] from the Lord our God, who has left us a surviving remnant and has given us a peg (secure hold) in His holy place, that our God may enlighten our eyes and give us a little reviving in our bondage.

⁹"For we are slaves; yet our God has not abandoned us in our bondage, but has extended lovingkindness to us before the kings of Persia, to revive us to rebuild the house of our God, to repair the site of its ruins and to give us a wall [of protection] in Judah and Jerusalem.

¹⁰"Now, O our God, what shall we say after this? For we have abandoned (turned away from) Your commandments,

¹¹which You have commanded by Your servants the prophets, saying, 'The land which you are entering to possess is a defiled land with the uncleanness of the peoples of the lands, through their repulsive acts which have filled it from one end to the other *along* with their impurity.

¹²'So now do not give your daughters to their sons or take their daughters for your sons; and never seek their peace or their prosperity, so that you may be strong and eat the good *things*

putting the Word to work

Have you ever been tempted to take sin lightly? Remember, in the eyes of the Lord, there is no distinction between "small" sins or "large" sins: sin is sin. We need to be like Ezra and approach God with true sorrow and humility when we ask for forgiveness (see Ezra 9:1–6).

of the land and leave it as an inheritance to your children forever.'

¹³"And after everything that has come upon us for our evil deeds and for our great guilt, since You our God have punished us less than our wrongdoings *deserve,* and have given us survivors like these,

¹⁴shall we again break Your commandments and intermarry with the peoples who practice these repulsive acts? Would You not be angry with us to the point of total destruction, so that there would be no remnant nor survivor? [Deut 7:2–4]

¹⁵"O Lord God of Israel, You are [uncompromisingly] just (righteous), for we have been left as survivors, as it is this day. Behold, we are before You in our guilt, for no one can stand before You because of this."

10 NOW WHILE Ezra was praying and confessing, weeping and laying himself face down before the house of God, a very large group from Israel, of men, women, and children, gathered to him, for the people wept bitterly.

²Shecaniah the son of Jehiel, of the sons of Elam, said to Ezra, "We have been unfaithful to our God and have married foreign women from the peoples of the land; yet now there is hope for Israel in spite of this.

³"Therefore let us now make a covenant with our God to send away all the [foreign] wives and their children,

in accordance with the advice of my lord and of those who tremble [in reverent obedience] at the commandment of our God; and let it be done in accordance with the Law.

⁴"Stand up, for it is your duty, and we will be with you. Be brave and act."

⁵Then Ezra stood and made the leaders of the priests, the Levites, and all Israel, take an oath that they would act in accordance with this proposal; so they took the oath.

⁶Then Ezra got up from before the house of God and went into the chamber of Jehohanan the son of Eliashib [and spent the night there]. He did not eat bread nor drink water, for he was mourning over the [former] exiles' faithlessness.

⁷They made a proclamation throughout Judah and Jerusalem to all the [former] exiles, that they were to assemble at Jerusalem,

⁸and that whoever would not come within three days, by order of the counsel of the leaders and the elders, all his possessions *and* property would be forfeited and he himself would be excluded from the assembly of the exiles.

⁹So all the men of Judah and Benjamin gathered at Jerusalem within three days. It was the twentieth [day] of the ninth month, and all the people sat in the open square *in front of* the house of God, trembling because of [the seriousness of] this matter and because of the heavy rain.

¹⁰Then Ezra the priest stood up and said to them, "You have been unfaithful [to God] and have married foreign (pagan) women, adding to the guilt of Israel.

¹¹"So now, make confession to the Lᴏʀᴅ God of your fathers and do His will. Separate yourselves from the peoples of the land and from [your] foreign wives."

¹²Then all the assembly replied with a loud voice, "It is our responsibility to do just as you have said.

¹³"But there are many people and it is the season of heavy rain; so we are unable to stand outside. Nor *can* the task *be done* in a day or two, for we have transgressed greatly in this matter.

¹⁴"Let our leaders stand for *and* represent the entire assembly; let all those in our cities who have married foreign wives come at appointed times, together with the elders and judges of each city, until the burning anger of our God over this matter is turned away from us."

¹⁵Only Jonathan the son of Asahel and Jahzeiah the son of Tikvah opposed this, and Meshullam and Shabbethai the Levite supported them.

¹⁶Then the [former] exiles did so. Ezra the priest and men *who were* heads of fathers' *households* were selected, according to their fathers' households, each of them by name; and they sat down on the first day of the tenth month to investigate the matter.

¹⁷And by the first day of the first month they finished *investigating* all the men married to foreign wives.

¹⁸Now among the sons of the priests who had married foreign women were found: of the sons of Jeshua [the high priest] the son of Jozadak, and his brothers—Maaseiah, Eliezer, Jarib, and Gedaliah.

¹⁹They vowed to send away their [pagan] wives, and being guilty, *they each offered* a ram of the flock for their offense.

²⁰Of the sons of Immer: Hanani and Zebadiah;

²¹and of the sons of Harim: Maaseiah, Elijah, Shemaiah, Jehiel, and Uzziah;

²²and of the sons of Pashhur: Elioenai, Maaseiah, Ishmael, Nethanel, Jozabad, and Elasah.

²³Of the Levites: Jozabad, Shimei, Kelaiah, that is, Kelita, Pethahiah, Judah, and Eliezer.

²⁴Of the singers: Eliashib; and of the gatekeepers: Shallum, Telem, and Uri.

²⁵Of Israel, of the sons of Parosh:

Ramiah, Izziah, Malchijah, Mijamin, Eleazar, Malchijah (Hashabiah), and Benaiah;

²⁶and of the sons of Elam: Mattaniah, Zechariah, Jehiel, Abdi, Jeremoth, and Elijah;

²⁷and of the sons of Zattu: Elioenai, Eliashib, Mattaniah, Jeremoth, Zabad, and Aziza;

²⁸and of the sons also of Bebai: Jehohanan, Hananiah, Zabbai, and Athlai;

²⁹and of the sons of Bani: Meshullam, Malluch, Adaiah, Jashub, Sheal, and Jeremoth;

³⁰and of the sons of Pahath-moab: Adna, Chelal, Benaiah, Maaseiah, Mattaniah, Bezalel, Binnui, and Manasseh;

³¹and of the sons of Harim: Eliezer, Isshijah, Malchijah, Shemaiah, Shimeon,

³²Benjamin, Malluch, and Shemariah;

³³of the sons of Hashum: Mattenai, Mattattah, Zabad, Eliphelet, Jeremai, Manasseh, and Shimei;

³⁴of the sons of Bani: Maadai, Amram, Uel,

³⁵Benaiah, Bedeiah, Cheluhi,

³⁶Vaniah, Meremoth, Eliashib,

³⁷Mattaniah, Mattenai, Jaasu,

³⁸Bani, Binnui, Shimei,

³⁹Shelemiah, Nathan, Adaiah,

⁴⁰Machnadebai, Shashai, Sharai,

⁴¹Azarel, Shelemiah, Shemariah,

⁴²Shallum, Amariah, and Joseph.

⁴³Of the sons of Nebo: Jeiel, Mattithiah, Zabad, Zebina, Jaddai, Joel, and Benaiah.

⁴⁴All these had married foreign women, and some of them had wives *by whom* they had children.

Nehemiah

Author:
Nehemiah

Date:
Approximately 423 BC

Everyday Life Principles:
God wants to repair every broken thing in your life and restore everything that has been lost.

The enemy's resistance should be an encouragement that God is doing something significant in your life, because he does not oppose anything that does not threaten him.

The enemy will oppose restoration in your life, but be like Nehemiah and stay focused and prayerful. You *will* overcome!

The book of Nehemiah is the story of a man who had a burden from God to rebuild the walls of the ruined city of Jerusalem. It is also the story of people who came together for a common purpose, worked and prayed in unity, resisted their enemies, responded to Nehemiah's good leadership, achieved their goal, celebrated their victory, enjoyed the rewards of their labors, and experienced spiritual renewal.

But in order to accomplish the task set before them, Nehemiah and the people had to be totally dedicated to the restoration to which God had called them. As their leader, Nehemiah stayed focused on his assignment, steadfastly refusing to be distracted or discouraged. Even in the midst of intense mocking and persecution and all kinds of resistance, he remained diligent and prayerful until his God-given assignment was complete.

Just as Nehemiah's enemies were relentless in their various efforts to stop the rebuilding of Jerusalem's walls, the devil will use multiple strategies as he repeatedly tries to thwart the restoration and rebuilding God wants to do in your life. The enemy does not oppose anything that does not threaten him, so let his resistance be a sign that God is indeed doing a great work in you. Be like Nehemiah; fight back with frequent, fervent prayer and with increased diligence as you partner with God to bring His purposes to pass in you.

1 THE WORDS of Nehemiah son of Hacaliah:
Now it happened in the month of Chislev, in the twentieth year [of the Persian king], as I was in the capitol of Susa,

2Hanani, one of my brothers, and some men from Judah came; and I asked them about the surviving Jews who had escaped and survived the captivity, and about Jerusalem.

3They said to me, "The remnant there in the province who survived the captivity are in great distress and reproach; the wall of Jerusalem is broken down and its [fortified] gates have been burned (destroyed) by fire."

4Now it came about when I heard these words, I sat down and wept and mourned for days; and I was fasting and praying [constantly] before the God of heaven.

5And I said, "Please, O LORD God of heaven, the great and awesome God, who keeps the covenant and lovingkindness for those who love Him and keep His commandments,

6please let Your ear be attentive and Your eyes open to hear the prayer of Your servant which I am praying before

life point

Nehemiah was not afraid of emotion; notice that he wept and mourned in Nehemiah 1:4. Some people refuse to weep or show any kind of outward emotion, which is not healthy. Pent-up emotions are powerful and need to be released. If we do not release our emotions at appropriate times, as Nehemiah did when he heard that the walls of Jerusalem had been destroyed, then our emotions will eat away at us on the inside. Since God has given us tear glands and the ability to cry, that must mean there will be times in life when we, like Nehemiah, need to weep.

life point

Like Nehemiah, we are to confess our sins and failures to the Lord (see Nehemiah 1:6, 7), confident that He will forgive us of those sins and failures and cleanse us from all unrighteousness, as He has promised in His Word (see 1 John 1:9).

You, day and night, on behalf of Your servants, the sons (descendants) of Israel (Jacob), confessing the sins of the sons of Israel which we have committed against You; I and my father's house have sinned.

7"We have acted very corruptly against You and have not kept the commandments, nor the statutes, nor the ordinances which You commanded Your servant Moses. [Deut 6:1–9]

8"Please remember the word which You commanded Your servant Moses, saying, 'If you are unfaithful and violate your obligations to Me I will scatter you [abroad] among the peoples; [Lev 26:33]

9but if you return to Me and keep My commandments and do them, though those of you who have been scattered are in the most remote part of the heavens, I will gather them from there and will bring them to the place where I have chosen for My Name to dwell.' [Deut 30:1–5]

10"Now they are Your servants and Your people whom You have redeemed by Your great power and by Your strong hand.

putting the Word to work

Nehemiah waited for God to respond to his prayers (see Nehemiah 1:5–11). When you pray, do you give God time to answer or do you try to push ahead? Remember Nehemiah, and always wait on God to respond to your prayers in His timing.

11"Please, O Lord, let Your ear be attentive to the prayer of Your servant and the prayer of Your servants who delight to [reverently] fear Your Name [Your essence, Your nature, Your attributes, with awe]; and make Your servant successful this day and grant him compassion in the sight of this man [the king]."

For I was cupbearer to the king [of Persia].

2 IN THE month of Nisan, in the twentieth year of King Artaxerxes, when wine was *placed* before him, I took the wine and gave it to the king. Now I had not [previously] been sad in his presence.

2So the king said to me, "Why do you look sad when you are not sick? This is nothing but sadness of heart." Then I was very frightened,

3and I said to the king, "Let the king live forever. Why should my face not be sad when the city, the place of my fathers' tombs, lies desolate and its gates have been consumed by fire?"

4The king said to me, "What do you request?" So I prayed to the God of heaven.

5I said to the king, "If it pleases the king, and if your servant has found favor in your presence, [I ask] that you send me to Judah, to the city of my fathers' tombs, so that I may rebuild it."

6The king, beside whom the queen was sitting, asked me, "How long will your journey take, and when will you return?" So it pleased the king to send me, and I gave him a definite time [for my return].

7Then I said to the king, "If it pleases the king, let letters be given to me for the governors *of the provinces* beyond the [Euphrates] River, so that they will allow me to pass through until I reach Judah,

8and a letter to Asaph, the keeper of the king's forest, so that he will give me timber to construct beams for the gates of the fortress which is by the temple, and for the city wall and for the house which I will occupy." And the king granted me *what I asked,* for the good hand of my God was upon me.

9Then I came to the governors *of the provinces* beyond the [Euphrates] River and gave them the king's letters. Now the king had sent officers of the army and horsemen with me.

10When Sanballat the Horonite and Tobiah the Ammonite official heard this, it caused them great displeasure that someone had come to see about the welfare *and* prosperity of the Israelites.

11So I came to Jerusalem and was there for three days.

12Then I got up in the night, I and a few men with me. I did not tell anyone what my God was putting in my heart to do for Jerusalem, and there was no animal with me except the one on which I was riding [so as not to attract attention].

13So I went out at night by the Valley Gate toward the Dragon's Well and to the Refuse Gate and inspected the walls of Jerusalem which were broken down and its gates which were consumed by fire.

14Then I passed over to the Fountain Gate and to the King's Pool, but there was no place for the animal that I was riding to pass.

15So I went up at night by the ravine [of Kidron] and inspected the wall; then I turned back and entered [the city] by the Valley Gate, and returned.

speak the Word

I thank You, Lord, that Your good hand is upon me!
—ADAPTED FROM NEHEMIAH 2:8

¹⁶The officials did not know where I had gone or what I had done; nor had I yet told the Jews, the priests, the nobles, the officials, or the rest who did the work.

¹⁷Then I said to them, "You see the bad situation that we are in—how Jerusalem is desolate *and* lies in ruins and its gates have been burned with fire. Come, and let us rebuild the wall of Jerusalem, so that we will no longer be a disgrace."

¹⁸Then I told them how the hand of my God had been favorable to me and also about the words that the king had spoken to me. And they said, "Let us rise up and build." So they thoroughly supported the good *work*.

¹⁹But when Sanballat the Horonite and Tobiah the Ammonite official and Geshem the Arab heard about it, they mocked us and regarded us with contempt and said, "What is this thing you are doing? Are you rebelling against the king?"

²⁰I answered them, "The God of heaven [has appointed us for His purpose and] will give us success; therefore we His servants will arise and build, but you have no portion, right, or memorial in Jerusalem."

3 THEN ELIASHIB the high priest rose up with his brothers the priests and built the Sheep Gate. They consecrated it and set up its doors; and they consecrated the wall [westward] to the Tower of the Hundred, as far as the Tower of Hananel.

²Next to Eliashib the men of Jericho built, and next to them Zaccur the son of Imri built.

³Now the sons of Hassenaah built the Fish Gate; they laid its beams and set up its doors with its bolts and its bars.

⁴Next to them Meremoth the son of Uriah, the son of Hakkoz, made repairs. Next to him Meshullam the son of Berechiah, the son of Meshezabel, made repairs. And next to him Zadok the son of Baana *also* made repairs.

⁵Next to him the men of Tekoa made repairs, but their nobles did not support the work of their overseers.

⁶Joiada the son of Paseah and Meshullam the son of Besodeiah repaired the Old Gate. They laid its beams and set up its doors with its bolts and its bars.

⁷Next to them Melatiah the Gibeonite and Jadon the Meronothite, the men of Gibeon and of Mizpah, made repairs for the official seat (Jerusalem residence) of the governor [of the province] beyond the [Euphrates] River.

⁸Next to them Uzziel the son of Harhaiah, one of the goldsmiths, made repairs. Next to him Hananiah, one of the perfumers, made repairs, and they restored Jerusalem as far as the Broad Wall.

⁹Next to them Rephaiah the son of Hur, official of half the district of Jerusalem, made repairs.

¹⁰Next to them Jedaiah the son of Harumaph made repairs opposite his own house. And next to him Hattush the son of Hashabneiah made repairs.

¹¹Malchijah the son of Harim and Hasshub the son of Pahath-moab repaired another section and the Tower of the Furnaces.

¹²Next to him Shallum the son of Hallohesh, the official of half the district of Jerusalem, made repairs, he and his daughters.

¹³Hanun and the inhabitants of Zanoah repaired the Valley Gate. They built it and set up its doors with its

speak the Word

Thank You, God, for giving me success. I will arise and do whatever You have called me to do.
–ADAPTED FROM NEHEMIAH 2:20

bolts and its bars, and *repaired* a thousand cubits (1,500 ft.) of the wall as far as the Refuse Gate.

14Malchijah the son of Rechab, the official of the district of Beth-haccherem repaired the Refuse Gate. He rebuilt it and set its doors with its bolts and its bars.

15Shallum the son of Col-hozeh, official of the district of Mizpah repaired the Fountain Gate. He rebuilt it and covered it [with a roof], and set up its doors with its bolts and its bars, and [he rebuilt] the wall of the Pool of Shelah (Siloam) by the King's Garden as far as the stairs that descend [the eastern slope] from [the section of Jerusalem known as] the City of David.

16After him Nehemiah the son of Azbuk, official of half the district of Beth-zur, repaired [the wall] as far as [a point] in front of the tombs of David, and as far as the artificial pool and the house of the guards.

17After him the Levites carried out repairs *under* Rehum the son of Bani. Next to him Hashabiah, official of half the district of Keilah, carried out repairs for his district.

18After him their brothers carried out repairs *under* Bavvai the son of Henadad, official of [the other] half of the district of Keilah.

19Next to him Ezer the son of Jeshua, the official of Mizpah, repaired another section [northward] in front of the ascent to the armory at the Angle [in the wall].

20After him Baruch son of Zabbai zealously repaired another section [toward the hill], from the Angle [in the wall] to the door of the house of Eliashib the high priest.

21After him Meremoth the son of Uriah, the son of Hakkoz, repaired another [eastern] section, from the door of Eliashib's house as far as the end of his house.

22After him the priests, the men of the [lower Jordan] valley, carried out repairs.

23After them Benjamin and Hasshub made repairs in front of their house. After them Azariah the son of Maaseiah, the son of Ananiah, carried out repairs beside his own house.

24After him Binnui the son of Henadad repaired another section [of the wall], from the house of Azariah to the Angle [in the wall] and to the corner.

25Palal the son of Uzai *made repairs* in front of the Angle [in the wall] and the tower projecting from the upper house (palace) of the king, which is by the courtyard of the guard. After him Pedaiah the son of Parosh *made repairs.*

26The temple servants were living in Ophel [the hill south of the temple], and they *made repairs* as far as the front of the Water Gate on the east and the projecting tower.

27After them the Tekoites repaired another section in front of the great projecting tower and as far as the wall of Ophel.

28Above the Horse Gate the priests made repairs, each one in front of his own house.

29After them Zadok the son of Immer carried out repairs in front of his house. After him Shemaiah the son of

putting the Word to work

Do you ever struggle with your role in life, thinking others are called to more important or more valuable work? In Nehemiah 3:26–31, some workers were called to repair large portions of the wall, while others were to repair only the section in front of their own house. Be encouraged: All work done for God is significant; and the most important thing is to be obedient to do what God calls you to do.

Shecaniah, keeper of the East Gate, repaired *the wall*.

30After him Hananiah the son of Shelemiah, and Hanun the sixth son of Zalaph, repaired another section. After him Meshullam the son of Berechiah carried out repairs in front of his own quarters.

31After him Malchijah, one of the goldsmiths, carried out repairs as far as the house of the temple servants and of the merchants, in front of the Inspection Gate and as far as the upper room of the corner.

32Between the upper room of the corner and the Sheep Gate the goldsmiths and merchants carried out repairs.

4 BUT WHEN Sanballat heard that we were rebuilding the wall, he became furious, completely enraged, and he ridiculed the Jews. 2He spoke before his brothers and the army of Samaria, "What are these feeble Jews doing? Can they restore it for themselves? Can they offer sacrifices? Can they finish in a day? Can they revive the stones from the heaps of dust *and* rubbish, even the ones that have been burned?"

3Now Tobiah the Ammonite was beside him, and he said, "Even what they are building—if a fox should get up on it, he would break down their stone wall."

4[And Nehemiah prayed] Hear, O our God, how we are despised! Return their taunts on their own heads. Give them up as prey in a land of captivity. 5Do not forgive their wrongdoing and do not let their sin be wiped out

life point

When the enemy is coming against you, the most powerful thing you can do is refuse to let it upset you. Instead, be like Nehemiah in Nehemiah 4:9: intensify your prayers and increase your vigilance.

putting the Word to work

As we live and work for God, opposition will come. Do you find yourself under attack in your ministry? It is vitally important to have people in your life who will be faithfully at your side through prayer and other means of support (see Nehemiah 4:16, 17).

before You, for they have offended the builders [and provoked You].

6So we built the wall and the entire wall was joined together to half its *height*, for the people had a heart to work.

7But when Sanballat, Tobiah, the Arabs, the Ammonites, and the Ashdodites heard that the repair of the walls of Jerusalem went on, and that the breaches were being closed, they were very angry.

8They all conspired together to come and to fight against Jerusalem, and to cause a disturbance in it.

9But we prayed to our God, and because of them we set up a guard against them day and night.

10Then [the leaders of] Judah said,

"The strength of the burden
  bearers is failing,
And there is much rubble;
We ourselves are unable
To rebuild the wall."

11Our enemies said, "They will not know or see us until we are among them, kill them and put a stop to the work."

12When the Jews who lived near them came, they said to us ten times (repeatedly), "From every place you turn, they will come up against us."

13So I stationed *armed men* behind the wall in the lowest places, at the open positions [where it was least protected]; and I stationed the people in families with their swords, spears, and bows.

God will fight evil for you

When people or events come against us to destroy us, as Sanballat and Tobiah tried to destroy Nehemiah and his work, we are to stand firm, confident that everything will work out for the best (see Nehemiah 4:20). Whatever you are going through, remember, "this too shall pass."

When problems arise—and they will—we are not to assume that the Lord will intervene and take care of all our problems without our invitation. We are to pray and ask Him to change our circumstances. Then we are to remain constant and stable as Nehemiah did, and that will be a sign to the enemy of his impending downfall and destruction.

Do you know why our constancy and fearlessness signify to Satan that he will fail? Because he knows that the only way he can overcome a believer is through deception and intimidation. How can he threaten someone who is not afraid of him? How can he deceive someone who recognizes his lies and refuses to believe them? What good does it do him to try to stir up fear or anger or depression in someone who will not be moved by emotions but chooses to stand firmly on the Word of God?

When the devil sees his tactics are not working, he realizes he is failing and will be utterly defeated. God will fight for us as He did for Nehemiah, and we will have the victory.

¹⁴When I saw *their fear,* I stood and said to the nobles and officials and the rest of the people: "Do not be afraid of them; [confidently] remember the Lord who is great and awesome, and [with courage from Him] fight for your brothers, your sons, your daughters, your wives, and for your homes."

¹⁵Now when our enemies heard that we knew about *their plot against us,* and that God had frustrated their plan, we all returned to the wall, each one to his work.

¹⁶From that day on, half of my servants carried on the work while the other half held the spears, shields, bows, and breastplates; and the captains were behind the whole house of Judah.

¹⁷Those who were rebuilding the wall and those who carried burdens loaded themselves *so that everyone* worked with one hand and held a weapon with the other.

¹⁸Every builder *had* his sword secured at his side as he built. And the one who sounded the trumpet [to summon the troops] stood at my side.

¹⁹I said to the nobles, the officials and the rest of the people, "The work is great and extensive, and we are separated on the wall, far from one another.

²⁰"Wherever you hear the sound of the trumpet, gather to us there. Our God will fight for us."

²¹So we carried on with the work with half of them holding spears from dawn until the stars came out.

speak the Word

When my enemies come against me, Lord, I pray that You will frustrate their plans so that I can do as the Israelites and return to the work You have given me.
—ADAPTED FROM NEHEMIAH 4:15

²²At that time I also said to the people, "Let each man with his servant spend the night inside Jerusalem so that they may serve as a guard for us at night and a laborer during the day."

²³So neither I, my brothers (relatives), my servants, nor the men of the guard who followed me, none of us took off our clothes; each took his weapon [even] to the water.

5 NOW THERE was a great outcry of the [poorer] people and their wives against their Jewish brothers [to whom they were deeply in debt].

²For there were some who were saying, "We, *along with* our sons and our daughters, are many; therefore allow us to get grain, so that we may eat and survive."

³There were *others* who were saying, "We are mortgaging our fields, our vineyards, and our houses to buy grain because of the famine."

⁴There were also *others* who were saying, "We have borrowed money on our fields and vineyards for the [Persian] king's [heavy] tax.

⁵"Now our flesh (skin) is the same as that of our brothers (relatives), and our children are like their children, yet here we are forcing (selling) our sons and our daughters to be slaves; and some of our daughters are forced into bondage *already,* and we are powerless [to redeem them] because our fields and vineyards belong to others."

⁶Then I was very angry when I heard their outcry and these words [of accusation].

⁷I thought it over and then challenged the nobles and the rulers. I said to them, "You are exacting usury (excessive interest) from your own brother (relative)." So I held a great assembly to confront them.

⁸I said to them, "According to our ability we have redeemed (purchased back) our Jewish brothers who were

life point

Nehemiah knew how to make the difficult choices that leadership demands. He had to be a leader, not a pal, to the Israelites. Because he related to them not only as a leader but also as a comrade, he was able to confront them successfully in Nehemiah 5:7–10. The great end result of Nehemiah's correction was that the people praised the Lord and said, "We will do exactly as you say" (see Nehemiah 5:12, 13). If we want to be leaders who make a difference in people's lives, we would be wise to follow Nehemiah's example.

sold to the [Gentile] nations; now would you even sell your brothers, that they might be sold to us?" Then they were silent and could not find a [single] word *to say.*

⁹So I said, "What you are doing is not good. Should you not walk in the fear of our God to prevent the taunting by the [pagan] nations, our enemies?

¹⁰"And likewise I, my brothers, and my servants are lending them money and grain. Please, let us stop [charging] this interest. [Ex 22:25]

¹¹"Please, give back to them this very day their fields, their vineyards, their olive groves, and their houses, and also a hundredth part of the money, the grain, the new wine, and the oil that you are lending them."

¹²Then they said, "We will give it back and not require anything from them. We will do exactly as you say." Then I called the priests and took an oath from them that they would act in accordance with this promise.

¹³I also shook out the front of my garment and said, "So may God shake out every man from his house and from his possessions who does not keep this promise; like this may he be shaken out and emptied." And all the assembly said, "Amen!" And they praised the

LORD. Then the people acted in accordance with this promise.

¹⁴Moreover, from the day that I was appointed to be their governor in the land of Judah, from the twentieth year to the thirty-second year of King Artaxerxes, for twelve years, neither I nor my relatives have eaten the governor's food *allowance*.

¹⁵But the former governors who were [in office] before me put heavy burdens on the people and took food and wine from them in addition to forty shekels of silver [as an excessive monthly salary]; even their servants assumed authority over the people. But I did not do so because of the [reverent] fear of God.

¹⁶I also applied myself to the work on this wall; we did not buy any land, and all my servants were gathered together there for the work.

¹⁷Moreover, there were at my table a hundred and fifty Jews and officials, besides those who came to us from the nations that were around us.

¹⁸Now the following were prepared for each day: one ox and six choice sheep; also fowls (poultry) were prepared for me; and in intervals of ten days all sorts of wine *was provided* in abundance. Yet for all this, I did not demand the governor's food *allowance*, because the servitude was heavy on this people.

¹⁹Remember me, O my God, for good, *according to* all I have done for this people. [Heb 6:10]

6 NOW WHEN Sanballat, Tobiah, Geshem the Arab, and the rest of our enemies heard that I had rebuilt the wall, and that there was no breach left in it, although at that time I had not set up doors in the gates,

²Sanballat and Geshem sent *word* to me, saying, "Come, let us meet together at Chephirim in the plain of Ono." But they were planning to harm me.

³So I sent messengers to them, saying, "I am doing a great work and cannot come down. Why should the work stop while I leave to come down to [meet with] you?"

⁴They sent *word* to me four times in this way, and I answered them in the same way.

⁵Then Sanballat sent his servant to me in the same way the fifth time, with an open letter in his hand.

⁶In it was written, "It is reported among the [neighboring] nations, and Gashmu is saying that you and the Jews are planning to revolt, and that is the reason you are rebuilding the wall. And according to these reports, you are to be their king.

⁷"Also [it is reported that] you have appointed prophets to make a proclamation concerning you in Jerusalem, saying, 'There is a king in Judah!' And now these things will be reported to the [Persian] king. So come now, and let us consult together."

putting the Word to work

Are you in a position of leadership or authority? Learn from Nehemiah's example as governor (see Nehemiah 5:14–19). Use your position to serve the people you lead, extend generosity in praise and in provision, and do not use your position for personal gain at the expense of those you lead.

life point

If we need help, we are to confidently ask God for it as Nehemiah did when he cried out to God, "But now, [O God,] strengthen my hands!" (Nehemiah 6:9). Then we are to listen in faith for His answer. The Word explains that when we ask God for something, we must ask in faith with no wavering and no doubting (see James 1:6). God wants us to be totally confident in His desire to manifest His power and love in our lives.

⁸I sent *a message* to him, saying, "Such things as you are saying have not been done; you are inventing them in your own mind."

⁹For they all wanted to frighten us, thinking, "They will become discouraged with the work and it will not be done." But now, [O God,] strengthen my hands.

¹⁰When I went into the house of Shemaiah the son of Delaiah, the son of Mehetabel, who was confined at home, he said, "Let us meet [and take refuge] together in the house of God, within the temple, and let us shut the doors of the temple, because they are coming to kill you, and they are coming to kill you at night."

¹¹But I said, "Should a man like me flee [in fear and hide]? Should someone like me enter the temple [for sanctuary] to save his life? I will not go."

¹²Then I realized that God had not sent him, but he spoke this prophecy against me because Tobiah and Sanballat had hired him.

¹³He was hired for this reason, that I would be frightened and do as he said and sin, so that they would have [grounds to make] a malicious report in order to censure *and* disgrace me.

¹⁴Remember, O My God, Tobiah

finish well

Nehemiah knew how to finish what he started (see Nehemiah 6:15), and God uses people who know how to complete what they have begun. Many of us are good at starting, but not good at finishing. The reason is simple. Emotions motivate us and get us going, but it takes more than emotion to get us to the finish. Let's say we receive an encouraging word from God or someone else, and we are off and running. The question is, how long do we keep running after the emotions wear off? Many of us stop right that minute, as soon as we no longer *feel* anything.

I remember one time early in my Christian walk when I got so excited because of a word the Lord gave me. A guest speaker with the gift of prophecy came to our church, and as he was laying hands on people, praying for them and blessing them, he said to me, "I see you laying hands on multiplied thousands of people, and they are all coming under the power of God."

My emotions were so strong I could hardly contain myself. To me, that word was confirmation of something I believed God had been speaking to me. I got so emotional about it that I think I scared the man! I usually do not respond with such enthusiasm, but I was so excited. After a few years, my emotions were still so strong I could hardly contain myself, but it was for another reason. It was not out of excitement; it was because I was still waiting for it to happen, and I thought, *I don't think I can stand this waiting another moment*. Emotions can be up and they can be down, but we must remember that they are fickle and do not speak truth to us. They can change radically overnight!

The beginning of something new is almost always exciting. But it is not those who start the race in excitement who win; it is those who stick to it and make it across the finish line—when nobody is excited anymore, when nobody is cheering them on, when their emotions are no longer supporting them, when they do not feel they can go on any longer, when it looks as if they will never make it to the end, and when all they have left is that one word from God that got them started in the first place. Those people are called *finishers*, and Nehemiah was certainly a good one!

and Sanballat in regard to these actions of theirs, and also [remember] the prophetess Noadiah and the rest of the prophets who were *trying to* frighten me.

¹⁵So the wall was finished on the twenty-fifth [day] of [the month] Elul, in fifty-two days.

¹⁶When all our enemies heard *about it,* and all the [Gentile] nations around us saw it, they lost their confidence; for they recognized that this work had been accomplished with the help of our God.

¹⁷Moreover, in those days many letters went from the nobles of Judah to Tobiah, and Tobiah's *letters* came to them.

¹⁸For many in Judah were bound by oath to him because he was the son-in-law of Shecaniah the son of Arah, and his son Jehohanan had married the daughter of Meshullam the son of Berechiah.

¹⁹Also, they were speaking about Tobiah's good deeds in my presence,

life point

Nehemiah's enemies had hired someone to tempt him to fear and hide in the temple (see Nehemiah 6:11–13). This was yet another obstacle that Nehemiah refused to accept. In spite of it, he continued to move forward and do what God had called him to do.

Like Nehemiah, God has made a way for us to do everything He has put in our hearts. He does not put dreams and visions in us to frustrate us. We must be like Nehemiah and keep our confidence in God all the way through to the end, not just for a short while. When it looks like the obstacles in front of you are too formidable, do not give up! The completion of your project may be just one or two steps away, as it was for Nehemiah.

life point

Tobiah was trying to frighten Nehemiah (see Nehemiah 6:19), but Nehemiah did not succumb to fear. Fear prevents us from receiving and doing all God has planned for us. Hear God's message to you: "Fear not, for I, the Lord, am with you."

and reporting to him what I said. Then Tobiah sent letters to frighten me.

7 NOW WHEN the wall had been rebuilt and I had set up the doors, and the gatekeepers, singers, and Levites had been appointed,

²I put my brother Hanani, with Hananiah the commander of the fortress, in charge of Jerusalem, for Hananiah was a more faithful and God-fearing man than many [of the others].

³I said to them, "Do not let the gates of Jerusalem be opened until the sun is hot; and while the watchmen are still standing *guard,* have them shut and bar the doors. Appoint guards from the residents of Jerusalem, each at his post [on the wall], and each in front of his own house."

⁴Now the city was spacious and large, but there were few people in it and the houses had not [yet] been built.

⁵Then my God put it into my heart to assemble the nobles, the officials, and the people to be registered by genealogy. Then I found the register of the genealogy of those who came [from Babylon] first, and I found the following record:

⁶These are the sons (descendants, people) of the province who came up from the captivity of the exiles whom Nebuchadnezzar the king of Babylon had deported [to Babylon]; they returned to Jerusalem and to Judah, each to his city,

[7]the ones who came with Zerubbabel, Jeshua, Nehemiah, Azariah, Raamiah, Nahamani, Mordecai, Bilshan, Mispereth, Bigvai, Nehum, and Baanah.

The men of the people of Israel numbered:

[8]the sons of Parosh, 2,172;

[9]the sons of Shephatiah, 372;

[10]the sons of Arah, 652;

[11]the sons of Pahath-moab of the sons of Jeshua and Joab, 2,818;

[12]the sons of Elam, 1,254;

[13]the sons of Zattu, 845;

[14]the sons of Zaccai, 760;

[15]the sons of Binnui, 648;

[16]the sons of Bebai, 628;

[17]the sons of Azgad, 2,322;

[18]the sons of Adonikam, 667;

[19]the sons of Bigvai, 2,067;

[20]the sons of Adin, 655;

[21]the sons of Ater, of Hezekiah, 98;

[22]the sons of Hashum, 328;

[23]the sons of Bezai, 324;

[24]the sons of Hariph, 112;

[25]the sons of Gibeon, 95;

[26]the men of Bethlehem and Netophah, 188;

[27]the men of Anathoth, 128;

[28]the men of Beth-azmaveth, 42;

[29]the men of Kiriath-jearim, Chephirah and Beeroth, 743;

[30]the men of Ramah and Geba, 621;

[31]the men of Michmas, 122;

[32]the men of Bethel and Ai, 123;

[33]the men of the other Nebo, 52;

[34]the sons of the other Elam, 1,254;

[35]the sons of Harim, 320;

[36]the sons of Jericho, 345;

[37]the sons of Lod, Hadid and Ono, 721;

[38]the sons of Senaah, 3,930.

[39]*These are* the priests: the sons of Jedaiah of the house of Jeshua, 973;

[40]the sons of Immer, 1,052;

[41]the sons of Pashhur, 1,247;

[42]the sons of Harim, 1,017.

[43]*These are* the Levites: the sons of Jeshua, of Kadmiel, of the sons of Hodevah, 74.

[44]The singers: the sons of Asaph, 148.

[45]The gatekeepers: the sons of Shallum, the sons of Ater, the sons of Talmon, the sons of Akkub, the sons of Hatita, and the sons of Shobai, 138.

[46]The temple servants: the sons of Ziha, the sons of Hasupha, the sons of Tabbaoth,

[47]the sons of Keros, the sons of Sia, the sons of Padon,

[48]the sons of Lebana, the sons of Hagaba, the sons of Shalmai,

[49]the sons of Hanan, the sons of Giddel, the sons of Gahar,

[50]the sons of Reaiah, the sons of Rezin, the sons of Nekoda,

[51]the sons of Gazzam, the sons of Uzza, the sons of Paseah,

[52]the sons of Besai, the sons of Meunim, the sons of Nephushesim,

[53]the sons of Bakbuk, the sons of Hakupha, the sons of Harhur,

[54]the sons of Bazlith, the sons of Mehida, the sons of Harsha,

[55]the sons of Barkos, the sons of Sisera, the sons of Temah,

[56]the sons of Neziah, the sons of Hatipha.

[57]The sons of Solomon's servants: the sons of Sotai, the sons of Sophereth, the sons of Perida,

[58]the sons of Jaala, the sons of Darkon, the sons of Giddel,

[59]the sons of Shephatiah, the sons of Hattil, the sons of Pochereth-hazzebaim, the sons of Amon.

[60]All the temple servants and the sons of Solomon's servants, *totaled* 392.

[61]And these were the ones who came up from Tel-melah, Tel-harsha, Cherub, Addon and Immer; but they [had no birth records and] could not prove their fathers' houses or their descent, whether they were of Israel:

[62]the sons of Delaiah, the sons of Tobiah, the sons of Nekoda, 642.

[63]Of the priests: the sons of Hobaiah, the sons of Hakkoz, and the sons of

Barzillai, who [was so named because he had] married one of the daughters of Barzillai, the [well-known] Gileadite, and was named after them.

⁶⁴These men searched for their ancestral registration *among* those recorded in the genealogies, but it was not located; so they were *excluded* from the priesthood as [ceremonially] unclean.

⁶⁵The governor told them that they should not eat any of the most holy food until a priest arose with Urim and Thummim [to determine God's will in the matter].

⁶⁶The entire assembly together was 42,360,

⁶⁷besides their male and their female servants, of whom *there were* 7,337; and they had 245 male and female singers.

⁶⁸Their horses were 736; their mules, 245;

⁶⁹*their* camels, 435; *their* donkeys, 6,720.

⁷⁰Some from among the heads of fathers' *households* gave to the work. The governor gave to the treasury 1,000 gold drachmas, 50 basins, 530 priests' garments.

⁷¹Some of the heads of fathers' *households* gave to the treasury for the work 20,000 gold drachmas and 2,200 silver minas.

⁷²And what the rest of the people gave was 20,000 gold drachmas, 2,000 silver minas, and 67 priests' garments.

⁷³So the priests, the Levites, the gatekeepers, the singers, some of the people, the temple servants, along with all Israel, lived in their cities. And when the seventh month came, the sons (descendants) of Israel (Jacob) were in their cities.

8 THEN ALL the people gathered together as one man at the open square in front of the Water Gate; and they asked Ezra the scribe to bring the Book of the Law of Moses which the LORD had given to Israel.

²So Ezra the priest brought the Law before the assembly of men, women and all who *could* listen with understanding, on the first day of the seventh month.

³Then he read from it, in front of the open square which was in front of the Water Gate, from early morning until midday, in the presence of the men and women, those who could understand; and all the people listened carefully to the Book of the Law.

⁴Ezra the scribe stood on a [large] wooden platform which they had constructed for this purpose. And beside him [on the platform] stood Mattithiah, Shema, Anaiah, Uriah, Hilkiah, and Maaseiah on his right; and Pedaiah, Mishael, Malchijah, Hashum, Hashbaddanah, Zechariah, and Meshullam on his left.

⁵Ezra opened the book in the sight of all the people, for he was standing above them; and when he opened it, all the people stood up.

⁶Then Ezra blessed the LORD, the great God. And all the people answered, "Amen, Amen!" while lifting up their hands; and they knelt down and worshiped the LORD with *their* faces toward the ground.

life point

When Ezra opened God's Word, all the people stood (see Nehemiah 8:5). I love this image of honoring the Word because God's Word has the power to change people's lives. I enjoy teaching the Word, and one of my goals in life is to provoke tremendous respect and love for God's Word. If you have not experienced the transforming power of God's Word, I urge you to give it a try—and you will see why it is worthy of honor and respect.

⁷Also Jeshua, Bani, Sherebiah, Jamin, Akkub, Shabbethai, Hodiah, Maaseiah, Kelita, Azariah, Jozabad, Hanan, Pelaiah, and the Levites, explained the Law to the people, and the people *remained* in their places.

⁸So they read from the Book of the Law of God, translating and explaining it so that the people understood the reading.

⁹Then Nehemiah, who was the governor, and Ezra the priest and scribe,

life point

I believe that when we worship God, at least part of the time we need to assume a posture of worship, as the Israelites did in Nehemiah 8:6. We need to bend our knees and bow down before Him because those postures are signs of reverence and humility. They are outward representations of our inner heart attitudes. Satan cannot see what is in our hearts, but he can see our knees bent and our hands uplifted in worship to God.

Why should we make all these outward signs? Isn't what is in our hearts sufficient? As I have already written, the devil cannot see what is in our hearts, but he certainly can see our actions and hear our words. Satan can see the outward manifestation of our uplifted hands, and he knows what is going on when we bow down. That makes him afraid. He knows he cannot deceive and control a true worshiper.

I realize that our posture in worship is an outward form of worship, and outward appearance without a right heart attitude is useless. But both need to work together. Our heart attitude establishes things in the spiritual realm, and our actions and words establish things in the natural realm.

and the Levites who taught the people said to all the people, "This day is holy to the LORD your God; do not mourn or weep." For all the people were weeping when they heard the words of the Law.

¹⁰Then Ezra said to them, "Go [your way], eat the rich festival food, drink the sweet *drink,* and send portions to him for whom nothing is prepared; for this day is holy to our Lord. And do not be worried, for the joy of the LORD is your strength *and* your stronghold."

¹¹So the Levites quieted all the people, saying, "Be still, for the day is holy; do not be worried."

¹²Then all the people went on their way to eat, to drink, to send portions [of food to others] and to celebrate a great festival, because they understood the words which had been communicated to them.

¹³On the second day, all of the heads of fathers' *households* of all the people, the priests, and the Levites, were gathered before Ezra the scribe to gain insight into the words of the Law (divine instruction).

¹⁴They found written in the Law how the LORD had commanded through Moses that the Israelites should live in booths (huts) during the feast of the seventh month.

¹⁵So they proclaimed and published

life point

Isn't it easy to find things to worry about? It is indeed, but if we could learn to laugh a little more, our loads would be much lighter. In the world we live in, there is not a great deal to laugh about, so we will need to look for things to chuckle about on purpose! We need to laugh and have a good time as often as possible. Ask the Lord to help you be joyful and of good cheer. His joy will give you strength (see Nehemiah 8:10).

an announcement in all their cities and in Jerusalem, saying, "Go out to the hills and bring olive branches, wild olive, myrtle, palm, and other leafy branches to make booths, as it is written." [Lev 23:39, 40]

¹⁶So the people went out and brought them and made booths for themselves, each on the roof *of his house,* and in their courtyards and the courtyards of God's house, and in the open square of the Water Gate and in the square of the Gate of Ephraim.

¹⁷The entire assembly of those who had returned from the captivity made booths and lived in them. Indeed since the days of Joshua the son of Nun until that *very* day, the Israelites had not done so. And there was great rejoicing *and* celebration.

¹⁸Every day, from the first day to the last, Ezra read from the Book of the Law of God. They celebrated the feast for seven days; on the eighth day *there was* a [closing] solemn assembly in accordance with the ordinance.

the joy of the Lord is your strength

When the people heard the words of the law they wept because of their sorrow. But Ezra spoke to them and said: "do not be worried, for the joy of the Lord is your strength and your stronghold" (Nehemiah 8:10).

The writer of Proverbs said that a happy heart does us good and acts just like a medicine (17:22). God has given us joy—it is a fruit of the Holy Spirit that belongs to believers, but we must nurture and release it in our lives.

Satan is much more interested in stealing our joy than in stealing our possessions. He knows that if he can sadden us, he can weaken us. He hopes that by causing the washing machine or other things to break down, he can steal our joy. Do not let him do it! No matter what kind of trouble Satan tries to use to distract you, do not pay attention to him.

Each day God gives us is holy and a precious gift from Him. We should enjoy it fully. We should not waste what God gives. Let the devil wear himself out starting fires in your life, but do not spend your time trying to put them out. Put your trust in God, and make a decision to rejoice.

Joy is powerful. Ezra knew that, and that is why he instructed the people to find their strength in God's joy. He also told them to eat, drink, and send portions to those who had nothing. They understood these words and got busy being a blessing and rejoicing. The Bible says it is more blessed to give than to receive (see Acts 20:35). Why? Because when we get something we only get the gift, but when we give we receive the joy of giving. Nothing releases supernatural joy in our lives more than being a blessing to other people.

Selfishness and self-centeredness turn our thoughts toward ourselves and block our joy, but giving does just the opposite. People are happy when they are reaching out to others because they are functioning in the will of God. God has not called us to "in-reach," He has called us to outreach.

Be a blessing and be happy and rejoice on purpose. Satan comes to steal from us, but Jesus came that we might have and enjoy life in abundance (see John 10:10).

9

NOW ON the twenty-fourth day of this month the Israelites assembled with fasting and in sackcloth and with dirt on their heads. ²The descendants of Israel (Jacob) separated themselves from all foreigners, and stood and confessed their sins and the wrongdoings of their fathers. ³While they stood in their places, they read from the Book of the Law of the LORD their God for a fourth of the day and for *another* fourth [of it] they confessed [their sins] and worshiped the LORD their God. ⁴On the platform of the Levites stood Jeshua, Bani, Kadmiel, Shebaniah, Bunni, Sherebiah, Bani, and Chenani, and they called out with a loud voice to the LORD their God. ⁵Then the Levites—Jeshua, Kadmiel, Bani, Hashabneiah, Sherebiah, Hodiah, Shebaniah, and Pethahiah—said, "Stand up and bless (praise, honor) the LORD your God from everlasting to everlasting.

May Your glorious name be
　blessed
And exalted above all blessing and
　praise."
⁶[And Ezra said],
"You are the LORD, You alone;
You have made the heavens,
The heaven of heavens with all
　their host (the heavenly bodies),
The earth and everything that is
　on it,
The seas and everything that is in
　them.
You give life to all of them,
And the heavenly host is bowing
　down [in worship] to You.
⁷"You are the LORD God,
Who chose Abram

And brought him out of Ur of the
　Chaldees,
And gave him the name Abraham.
⁸"You found his heart to be faithful
　before You,
And You made a covenant with
　him
To give him the land of the
　Canaanite,
Of the Hittite, of the Amorite,
Of the Perizzite, the Jebusite, and
　the Girgashite—
To give it to his descendants.
And You have fulfilled Your
　promise,
For You are righteous *and* just.

⁹"You saw our fathers' affliction in
　Egypt,
And You heard their cry by the
　Red Sea (Sea of Reeds).
¹⁰"Then You performed signs and
　wonders against Pharaoh,
Against all his servants and all the
　people of his land;
For You knew that they behaved
　arrogantly toward them (the
　Israelites),

putting the Word to work

Do you ever find yourself doubting God's promises or His ability to act on your behalf? During such times, be sure to remember God's promises and might. Recall and recite the Lord's faithfulness throughout Scripture in your own life, as Ezra and the leaders of Israel did (see Nehemiah 9:5–15), and faith, hope, and confidence in God will well up within you.

speak the Word

God, I will bless Your glorious name. Your name is exalted above all blessing and praise.
—ADAPTED FROM NEHEMIAH 9:5

And You made a name for
   Yourself, as it is to this day.
11 "You divided the sea before them,
So that they passed through the
   midst of the sea on dry land;
You hurled their pursuers into the
   depths,
Like a stone into mighty *and*
   raging waters.
12 "And with a pillar of cloud You led
   them by day,
And with a pillar of fire by night
To light the way for them
In which they were to go.
13 "Then You came down on Mount
   Sinai,
And spoke with them from heaven;
And You gave them fair
   ordinances and true laws,
Good statutes and commandments.
14 "So You made known to them Your
   holy Sabbath,
And gave them commandments,
   statutes, and law,
Through Your servant Moses.
15 "You gave them bread from heaven
   for their hunger,
And brought water for them out of
   a rock for their thirst,
And You told them to enter and
   take possession of
The land that You swore to give
   them. [John 6:31–34]
16 "But they, our fathers, acted
   arrogantly;
They stiffened their necks
   and would not heed Your
   commandments.
17 "They refused to listen *and* obey,
And did not remember Your
   wondrous acts which You had
   performed among them;

So they stiffened their necks and
   [in their rebellion] appointed a
   leader in order to return them to
   slavery in Egypt.
But You are a God of forgiveness,
Gracious and merciful *and*
   compassionate,
Slow to anger and abounding in
   lovingkindness;
And You did not abandon them.
   [Num 14:4]
18 "Even when they had made for
   themselves
A calf of cast metal
And said, 'This is your god
Who brought you up from Egypt,'
And committed great [and
   contemptible] blasphemies,
19 You, in Your great mercy *and*
   compassion,
Did not abandon them in the
   wilderness;
The pillar of the cloud did not
   leave them by day,
To lead them in the way,
Nor the pillar of fire by night,
   to light for them the way they
   should go.
20 "You [also] gave Your good Spirit
   to instruct them,
You did not withhold Your manna
   from their mouth,
And You gave them water for their
   thirst.
21 "Indeed, for forty years You
   sustained them in the
   wilderness; they lacked nothing,
Their clothes did not wear out, and
   their feet did not swell.
22 "You also gave them kingdoms and
   peoples,
And You allotted *the kingdoms* to
   them as a boundary.

speak the Word

Thank You, God, for giving Your good Spirit to instruct me.
—ADAPTED FROM NEHEMIAH 9:20

So they took possession of the land
of Sihon king of Heshbon
And the land of Og king of Bashan.
23 "You made their children as
numerous as the stars of heaven,
And You brought them into the land
Which You told their fathers to
enter and possess.
24 "So their sons (descendants) went in
and took possession of the land;
And You subdued before them
the inhabitants of the land, the
Canaanites,

And You gave them into their
hand, with their kings and the
peoples of the land,
To do with them as they pleased.
25 "They captured fortified cities and
a fertile land.
They took possession of houses
full of all good things,
Hewn cisterns, vineyards, olive
groves,
And fruit trees in abundance.
So they ate and were filled and
became fat,

trusting day by day

In chapter 9 of Nehemiah, Ezra recounted the mighty miracles God had performed
in Israel's past as a way of encouraging the people to believe Him for their present.
In verse 20 he reminded them of God's faithfulness to provide food (manna) for His
people when they were in the wilderness on their way to the Promised Land (see
Exodus 16:15–25). During this time, God provided manna for them every day. He
told them to gather each morning only what they needed for that specific day. He
was teaching them that they were to live by faith, believing that what they needed
each day would be supplied. The only exception to this was the Sabbath. On the day
before the Sabbath, the people were to gather twice as much so they would not
have to work on the day of rest.

There is a great lesson for us here. Have you ever thought that your future would
be secure if you could stockpile God's provision? It is so easy to want to store up
His grace to cover us for today as well as for tomorrow. But God teaches us that His
provision of grace does not work that way. It comes one day at a time. God's grace,
like His provision of manna, cannot be stored up because it doesn't take trust to live
that way.

When you and I start fretting about what we are going to do tomorrow, we are "trying to gather manna for the future." That does not work! God wants us to know we
can trust Him daily. Didn't Jesus teach us to pray, "Give us this day our daily bread"
(Matthew 6:11)? Note that the Lord did not instruct us to ask for tomorrow's bread.
He told us to request *this day's* bread. God wants us to believe that when the time
comes, He will provide what we need.

If you are concerned about what the future holds for you and your loved ones, the
first thing you must do is make a decision not to worry. Believe God will show you
what to do when the time comes. Trust Him to provide for you every day, one day at
a time. If you feel overwhelmed when you think about what may happen tomorrow,
just remember that you do not have tomorrow's grace today, but when tomorrow
comes God's grace will be sufficient for all your needs.

And they reveled *and* were
delighted in Your great goodness.

26 "Yet they were disobedient and
rebelled against You,
And cast Your law behind their
backs
And killed Your prophets who
warned them
To return to You;
And they committed great [and
contemptible] blasphemies.
27 "Therefore You handed them over
to their enemies who oppressed
them.
But when they cried out to You in
the time of their suffering *and*
distress,
You heard them from heaven,
and according to Your great
compassion You gave them
people to rescue *them*.
Who rescued them from the hand
of their enemies.
28 "But as soon as they had rest, they
again did evil before You;
Therefore You abandoned them
into the hand of their enemies,
so that they ruled over them.
Yet when they turned and cried
out again to You, You heard them
from heaven,
And You rescued them many
times in accordance with Your
compassion,
29 And You admonished them *and*
warned them to turn them back
to Your law.
Yet they acted presumptuously
and arrogantly and did not heed
Your commandments, but sinned
against Your ordinances,
Which by keeping, a man will live.

But they turned a stubborn
shoulder, stiffened their neck,
and would not listen.
30 "Yet You were patient with them
for many years,
And admonished them *and* warned
them by Your Spirit through
Your prophets;
Still they would not listen.
Therefore You gave them into the
hand (power) of the peoples of
the lands.
31 "Yet in Your great compassion You
did not utterly destroy them or
abandon them,
For You are a gracious and
merciful God.

32 "Now therefore, our God, the great,
the mighty, and the awesome
God, who keeps the covenant
and lovingkindness,
Do not let all the hardship seem
insignificant before You,
Which has come upon us, our
kings, our princes, our priests,
our prophets, our fathers and on
all Your people,
Since the time of the kings of
Assyria to this day.
33 "However, You are just *and*
righteous in everything that has
come upon us;
For You have dealt faithfully, but
we have acted wickedly.
34 Our kings, our princes, our priests,
and our fathers have not kept
Your law
Or paid attention to Your
commandments and Your
warnings which You have given
them.
35 "But they, in their kingdom,
With Your great goodness which
You gave them,

speak the Word

Thank You, Lord, for being gracious and merciful to me!
−ADAPTED FROM NEHEMIAH 9:31

With the broad and rich land
  which You set before them,
Did not serve You or turn from
  their wicked deeds.
36 "Behold, we are slaves today,
And as for the land which You
  gave our fathers, to eat of its fruit
  and its goodness,
Behold, we are slaves in it.
37 "Its abundant produce is for the
  kings
Whom You have set over us
  because of our sins;
They also rule over our bodies
And over our cattle as they please,
So we are in great distress.
38 "Now because of all this
We are making an agreement in
  writing;
And on the sealed document *are
the names* of our princes, our
Levites, and our priests."

10 NOW *THESE were the names*
on the sealed document: Nehemiah the governor, the
son of Hacaliah. And Zedekiah,
²Seraiah, Azariah, Jeremiah,
³Pashhur, Amariah, Malchijah,
⁴Hattush, Shebaniah, Malluch,
⁵Harim, Meremoth, Obadiah,
⁶Daniel, Ginnethon, Baruch,
⁷Meshullam, Abijah, Mijamin,
⁸Maaziah, Bilgai, Shemaiah—these
were the priests.
⁹And the Levites: Jeshua the son
of Azaniah, Binnui of the sons of
Henadad, Kadmiel,
¹⁰and their brothers: Shebaniah, Hodiah, Kelita, Pelaiah, Hanan,
¹¹Mica, Rehob, Hashabiah,
¹²Zaccur, Sherebiah, Shebaniah,
¹³Hodiah, Bani, Beninu.
¹⁴The leaders of the people: Parosh,
Pahath-moab, Elam, Zattu, Bani,
¹⁵Bunni, Azgad, Bebai,
¹⁶Adonijah, Bigvai, Adin,
¹⁷Ater, Hezekiah, Azzur,
¹⁸Hodiah, Hashum, Bezai,

¹⁹Hariph, Anathoth, Nebai,
²⁰Magpiash, Meshullam, Hezir,
²¹Meshezabel, Zadok, Jaddua,
²²Pelatiah, Hanan, Anaiah,
²³Hoshea, Hananiah, Hasshub,
²⁴Hallohesh, Pilha, Shobek,
²⁵Rehum, Hashabnah, Maaseiah,
²⁶Ahiah, Hanan, Anan,
²⁷Malluch, Harim, Baanah.
²⁸Now the rest of the people—the
priests, the Levites, the gatekeepers,
the singers, the temple servants, and
all those who had separated themselves from the peoples of the lands
to the Law of God, their wives, their
sons, their daughters, all those who
had knowledge and understanding—
²⁹are joining with their fellow Israelites, their nobles, and are taking
on themselves a curse and an oath to
walk in God's Law, which was given
through Moses the servant of God,
and to keep and to observe all the
commandments of GOD our Lord, and
His ordinances and statutes:
³⁰and that we will not give our daughters [as wives] to the peoples of the land
or take their daughters for our sons.
³¹As for the peoples of the land who
bring merchandise or any grain on the
Sabbath day to sell, we will not buy
from them on the Sabbath or on a holy
day; and we will give up *raising crops
during* the seventh year [leaving the
land uncultivated], and *forgive* every
debt. [Ex 23:10, 11; Deut 15:1, 2]
³²Also we pledge ourselves to contribute yearly one third of a shekel for
the service [expenses] of the house of
our God:
³³for the showbread; for the continual grain offerings and the continual
burnt offerings; [for the offerings on]
the Sabbaths, the New Moons, the
[feasts at] appointed times; for the
holy things, for the sin offerings to
make atonement for Israel; and for
all the work of the house of our God.
³⁴We have also cast lots—the priests,

the Levites, and the people—for [contributing] the supply of wood, to bring it to the house of our God, according to our fathers' households, at set times annually, to burn on the altar of the Lord our God, as it is written in the Law;

³⁵and [we obligate ourselves] to bring the first fruits of our ground and the first fruits of all the fruit of every tree to the house of the Lord annually,

³⁶as well as the firstborn of our sons and of our cattle, as is written in the Law, and the firstborn of our herds and flocks, to bring to the house of our God, for the priests who minister in the house of our God.

³⁷We will bring the first [and best] of our dough, our contributions, the fruit of every tree, the new wine and the [olive] oil to the priests, to the chambers of the house of our God, and the tithe of our ground to the Levites, for the Levites are the ones who receive the tithes in all the rural towns.

³⁸The priest, the son of Aaron, shall be with the Levites when they receive tithes, and they shall bring one-tenth of the tithes up to the house of our God, to the chambers of the storehouse.

³⁹For the Israelites and the sons of Levi shall bring the offering of the grain, the new wine, and the oil to the chambers; the utensils of the sanctuary, the priests who are ministering, the gatekeepers, and the singers are there. In this manner, we will not neglect the house of our God.

11 NOW THE leaders of the people lived in Jerusalem; but the rest of the people cast lots to bring one [person] out of ten to live in Jerusalem, the holy city, while nine-tenths *remained* in the *other* cities.

²And the people blessed all the men who volunteered to live in Jerusalem.

³These are the heads of the provinces who lived in Jerusalem, but in the cities of Judah everyone lived on his property in their cities—the Israelites, the priests, the Levites, the temple servants, and the descendants of Solomon's servants.

⁴And some of the sons of Judah and some of the sons of Benjamin lived in Jerusalem. From the sons of Judah: Athaiah the son of Uzziah, the son of Zechariah, the son of Amariah, the son of Shephatiah, the son of Mahalalel, of the sons of Perez;

⁵Maaseiah the son of Baruch, the son of Col-hozeh, the son of Hazaiah, the son of Adaiah, the son of Joiarib, the son of Zechariah, the son of the Shilonite.

⁶All the sons of Perez who lived at Jerusalem were 468 able men.

⁷These are the sons of Benjamin: Sallu the son of Meshullam, the son of Joed, the son of Pedaiah, the son of Kolaiah, the son of Maaseiah, the son of Ithiel, son of Jeshaiah;

⁸and after him Gabbai and Sallai, 928.

⁹Joel the son of Zichri was their overseer, and Judah the son of Hassenuah was second in command of the city.

¹⁰Of the priests: Jedaiah the son of Joiarib, Jachin,

¹¹Seraiah the son of Hilkiah, the son of Meshullam, the son of Zadok, the son of Meraioth, the son of Ahitub, the leader of the house of God,

¹²and their brothers (relatives, fellow workers) who did the work of the house, 822; and Adaiah the son of Jeroham, the son of Pelaliah, the son of Amzi, the son of Zechariah, the son of Pashhur, the son of Malchijah,

¹³and his brothers, heads of fathers' *households*, 242; and Amashsai the son of Azarel, the son of Ahzai, the son of Meshillemoth, the son of Immer,

¹⁴and their brothers, brave men, 128. Their overseer was Zabdiel the son of Haggedolim [one of the great men].

¹⁵Now from the Levites: Shemaiah the son of Hasshub, the son of Azrikam, the son of Hashabiah, the son of Bunni;

¹⁶and Shabbethai and Jozabad, from the leaders of the Levites, who were in charge of the outside work of the house of God;

¹⁷Mattaniah the son of Mica, the son of Zabdi, the son of Asaph, who was the leader to begin the thanksgiving in prayer, and Bakbukiah, second among his brothers; and Abda the son of Shammua, the son of Galal, the son of Jeduthun.

¹⁸All the Levites in the holy city *totaled* 284.

¹⁹The gatekeepers: Akkub, Talmon, and their kinsmen, who kept watch at the gates, *totaled* 172.

²⁰Now the rest of Israel, the priests and the Levites, were in all the cities of Judah, each on his own inheritance.

²¹But the temple servants were living in Ophel; Ziha and Gishpa were in charge of the temple servants.

²²The overseer of the Levites in Jerusalem was Uzzi the son of Bani, the son of Hashabiah, the son of Mattaniah, the son of Mica, from Asaph's sons, who were the singers in regard to the work of the house of God.

²³For *there was* a command from the [Persian] king regarding the singers, *as to their* daily task.

²⁴Pethahiah the son of Meshezabel, of the sons of Zerah the son of Judah, was the king's representative in all matters concerning the people.

²⁵As for the villages with their fields, some sons (descendants) of Judah lived in Kiriath-arba and its towns, Dibon and its towns, and Jekabzeel and its villages,

²⁶in Jeshua, in Moladah, in Beth-pelet,

²⁷in Hazar-shual and in Beersheba and its towns,

²⁸in Ziklag and in Meconah and its towns,

²⁹in En-rimmon, in Zorah, and in Jarmuth,

³⁰Zanoah, Adullam, and their villages, Lachish and its fields, and Azekah and its towns. So they camped from Beersheba as far as the Hinnom Valley.

³¹The sons (descendants) of Benjamin also *lived* from Geba *onward,* at Michmash, Aija, Bethel and its towns,

³²at Anathoth, Nob, Ananiah,

³³Hazor, Ramah, Gittaim,

³⁴Hadid, Zeboim, Neballat,

³⁵Lod, and Ono, the Valley of the Craftsmen.

³⁶And certain divisions of the Levites in Judah belonged to Benjamin.

12 NOW THESE are the priests and Levites who came up with Zerubbabel the son of Shealtiel and with Jeshua: Seraiah, Jeremiah, Ezra,

²Amariah, Malluch, Hattush,

³Shecaniah, Rehum, Meremoth,

⁴Iddo, Ginnethoi, Abijah,

⁵Mijamin, Maadiah, Bilgah,

⁶Shemaiah, Joiarib, Jedaiah,

⁷Sallu, Amok, Hilkiah, and Jedaiah. These were the heads of the priests and their kinsman in the days of Jeshua.

⁸The Levites were Jeshua, Binnui, Kadmiel, Sherebiah, Judah, and Mattaniah who was in charge of the songs of thanksgiving *and* praise, he and his brothers.

⁹Also Bakbukiah and Unni, their brothers, stood opposite them in their divisions of service.

¹⁰Now Jeshua became the father of Joiakim, Joiakim of Eliashib, Eliashib of Joiada,

¹¹and Joiada became the father of Jonathan, and Jonathan of Jaddua.

¹²And in the days of Joiakim, the priests, the heads of fathers' *households* were: of Seraiah, Meraiah; of Jeremiah, Hananiah;

¹³of Ezra, Meshullam; of Amariah, Jehohanan;

¹⁴of Malluchi, Jonathan; of Shebaniah, Joseph;

¹⁵of Harim, Adna; of Meraioth, Helkai;

¹⁶of Iddo, Zechariah; of Ginnethon, Meshullam;

¹⁷of Abijah, Zichri; of Miniamin and of Moadiah, Piltai;

¹⁸of Bilgah, Shammua; of Shemaiah, Jehonathan;

¹⁹of Joiarib, Mattenai; of Jedaiah, Uzzi;

²⁰of Sallai, Kallai; of Amok, Eber;

²¹of Hilkiah, Hashabiah; of Jedaiah, Nethanel.

²²As for the Levites in the days of Eliashib, Joiada, Johanan, and Jaddua, the heads of fathers' *households* were registered; so were the priests, during the reign of Darius the Persian.

²³The sons of Levi, heads of fathers' *households*, were recorded in the Book of the Chronicles until the days of Johanan the son of Eliashib.

²⁴The heads of the Levites were Hashabiah, Sherebiah, and Jeshua the son of Kadmiel, and their brothers opposite them, to praise and to give thanks, as commanded by David the man of God, [one] division [singing] in response to [the men in the opposite] division.

²⁵Mattaniah, Bakbukiah, Obadiah, Meshullam, Talmon, and Akkub were gatekeepers keeping watch at the storehouses of the gates.

²⁶These men *served* in the days of Joiakim the son of Jeshua, the son of Jozadak, and in the days of Nehemiah the governor and Ezra the priest and scribe.

²⁷Now at the dedication of the wall of Jerusalem they sought out the Levites from all their places in order to bring them to Jerusalem to celebrate the dedication with gladness, with hymns of thanksgiving, and with songs *to the accompaniment* of cymbals, harps, and lyres.

²⁸So the sons of the singers gathered together from the district around Jerusalem, and from the villages of the Netophathites,

²⁹from Beth-gilgal and from the

putting the Word to work

When was the last time you celebrated God's goodness and faithfulness in your life? Nehemiah demonstrates the importance of both dedicating our work and accomplishments to the Lord and celebrating what the Lord has done for us. As individuals, families, and as the body of Christ, let's celebrate often the goodness of the Lord!

fields of Geba and Azmaveth, for the singers had built villages for themselves around Jerusalem.

³⁰The priests and the Levites purified themselves; they also purified the people, the gates, and the wall.

³¹Then I had the leaders of Judah come up on the wall, and I appointed two large thanksgiving choirs, the first one proceeding to the right on top of the wall toward the Refuse Gate.

³²Hoshaiah and half of the leaders of Judah followed them,

³³with Azariah, Ezra, Meshullam,

³⁴Judah, Benjamin, Shemaiah, and Jeremiah,

³⁵and some of the priests' sons with trumpets, and Zechariah the son of Jonathan, the son of Shemaiah, the son of Mattaniah, the son of Micaiah, the son of Zaccur, the son of Asaph,

³⁶and his brothers, Shemaiah, Azarel, Milalai, Gilalai, Maai, Nethanel, Judah, and Hanani, with the musical instruments of David the man of God. And Ezra the scribe went in front of them.

³⁷At the Fountain Gate they went directly up the steps of the City of David by the stairway of the wall above David's house to the Water Gate on the east.

³⁸The second choir went to the left; I followed with half of the people on the wall, above the Tower of the Furnaces, to the Broad Wall,

³⁹and above the Gate of Ephraim, and by the Old Gate, by the Fish Gate, by the Tower of Hananel and the Tower of the Hundred, as far as the Sheep Gate; and they stopped at the Gate of the Guard.

⁴⁰Then the two choirs stood in the house of God. So did I, and half of the officials with me;

⁴¹and the priests Eliakim, Maaseiah, Miniamin, Micaiah, Elioenai, Zechariah and Hananiah, with trumpets;

⁴²and Maaseiah, Shemaiah, Eleazar, Uzzi, Jehohanan, Malchijah, Elam, and Ezer. And the singers sang, with Jezrahiah as their leader.

⁴³Also on that day they offered great sacrifices and rejoiced because God had given them great joy; the women and children also rejoiced, so that the joy of Jerusalem was heard from far away.

⁴⁴On that day men were appointed over the chambers for the stores, the contributions, the first fruits, and the tithes, to gather into them from the fields of the cities the portions required by the law for the priests and the Levites; for Judah rejoiced over the priests and Levites who served.

⁴⁵And they performed the worship of their God and the service of purification; so did the singers and gatekeepers, as David and his son Solomon had commanded.

⁴⁶For in the days of David and Asaph, in ancient times, there were leaders of singers, songs of praise and hymns of thanksgiving to God.

⁴⁷So in the days of Zerubbabel and [later of] Nehemiah, all Israel would give the daily portions for the singers and the gatekeepers; and they set apart the consecrated *portion* for the Levites, and the Levites set apart the consecrated *portion* for the sons of Aaron [the priests].

13

ON THAT day they read aloud from the book of Moses so that the people could hear [its words], and in it was found written that no Ammonite or Moabite could ever enter the assembly of God,

²because they did not meet the Israelites with bread and water, but hired Balaam against them to curse them. Yet our God turned the curse into a blessing. [Num 22:3–11; Deut 23:5, 6]

³When the Jews heard the law, they separated from Israel all who were of foreign descent.

⁴Now prior to this, Eliashib the priest, who was appointed over the chambers of the house of our God, and was related to Tobiah [our adversary],

⁵had prepared for Tobiah a large room (chamber) where previously they had put the grain offerings, the frankincense, the utensils, and the tithes of grain, new wine, and [olive] oil which were given by commandment for the Levites, the singers, and gatekeepers, and the contributions for the priests.

⁶But during all this *time* I was not at Jerusalem, for in the thirty-second year of Artaxerxes [Persian] king of Babylon I went to the king. Then after some time I asked for a leave [of absence] from the king,

⁷and I came to Jerusalem. Then I discovered the evil [thing] that Eliashib had done for Tobiah by preparing a room for him in the courtyards of the house of God.

⁸It was very displeasing to me, so I threw all of Tobiah's household furnishings out of the room.

⁹Then I gave an order, and they

speak the Word

Thank You, God, for turning the curses of my life into blessings.
—ADAPTED FROM NEHEMIAH 13:2

cleaned the rooms; and I put back there the utensils of the house of God with the grain offerings and the frankincense.

¹⁰I also discovered that the portions due the Levites had not been given *to them,* so that the Levites and the singers who did the work had gone away, each one back to his own field.

¹¹Then I reprimanded the officials and said, "Why is the house of God neglected?" So I gathered the Levites and singers together and restored them at their posts.

life point

Because Nehemiah was a good leader, he chose faithful and reliable men as treasurers (see Nehemiah 13:13). It does not matter how gifted people are, if they are not faithful, God probably will not use them.

We must understand that God tests faithfulness. It is not enough to say, "Oh, yes, I'm faithful," because God will say, "Well, let's see." Do you know how God tests our faithfulness? He assigns us to do something for a period of time that we do not want to do, something that is not fun or exciting, something that may require us to submit to someone else's authority for a while, and He will speak to our hearts, "Just be faithful."

Faithfulness is not only showing up day after day; it is showing up day after day with a good attitude and an excellent spirit. God will reward that kind of faithfulness. Luke 16:12 tells us that if we are faithful over what belongs to someone else, God will give us our own. If you are being tested in the area of faithfulness, be unwavering in your resolve to be faithful and dependable. You will be glad you did.

¹²Then all Judah brought the tithe of the grain, the new wine, and the oil to the storehouses.

¹³I appointed [as treasurers] over the storehouses: Shelemiah the priest, Zadok the scribe, and Pedaiah of the Levites; assisting them was Hanan son of Zaccur, the son of Mattaniah; for they were considered faithful *and* reliable, and their task was to distribute [supplies] to their brothers (fellow Levites).

¹⁴O my God, remember me concerning this and do not wipe out my loyal deeds *and* kindnesses which I have done for the house of my God and for its services.

¹⁵In those days I saw some in Judah who were treading wine presses on the Sabbath, and bringing in sheaves *or* sacks of grain and loading them on donkeys, as well as wine, grapes, figs, and all kinds of loads, which they brought into Jerusalem on the Sabbath day. So I protested *and* warned them on the day they sold the produce.

¹⁶Also men of Tyre were living there who brought fish and all kinds of merchandise, and they were selling them to the people of Judah on the Sabbath, even in Jerusalem.

¹⁷Then I reprimanded the nobles of Judah, and said to them, "What is this evil thing that you are doing—profaning the Sabbath day?

¹⁸"Did your fathers (ancestors) not do the same, and did our God not bring all this trouble on us and on this city? Yet you are adding to the wrath on Israel by profaning the Sabbath."

¹⁹Now when it began to get dark at the gates of Jerusalem before the Sabbath [began], I commanded that the doors be shut and not be opened until after the Sabbath. Then I stationed some of my servants at the gates so that no load [of merchandise] would enter [Jerusalem] on the Sabbath day.

²⁰So once or twice the merchants and sellers of every kind of merchandise

life point

Nehemiah knew the importance of a Sabbath rest (see Nehemiah 13:19). When Elijah neglected to rest, he grew tired and became discouraged (see 1 Kings 19:1–4). He was depressed, and he wanted to be alone. This is an important lesson for all of us to learn. When we get overly tired and out of balance, depression and discouragement quickly try to come upon us. Whatever you do, remember to rest.

spent the night outside Jerusalem.
²¹But I warned them, saying, "Why do you spend the night by the wall? If you do so again, I will use force against you." From that time on, they did not come on the Sabbath.
²²And I commanded the Levites to purify themselves and come and guard the gates to keep the Sabbath day holy. O my God, remember me *concerning* this also and have compassion on me according to the greatness of Your lovingkindness.
²³In those days I also saw Jews who had married women from Ashdod, Ammon, and Moab.
²⁴As for their children, half spoke in the language of Ashdod, and none of them knew how to speak [Hebrew] the language of Judah, but only the language of his own people.
²⁵So I contended with them and cursed them and struck some of them and pulled out their hair, and made them swear by God, saying, "You shall not give your daughters [in marriage] to their sons, nor take [any of] their daughters for your sons or for yourselves.
²⁶"Did not Solomon king of Israel sin [greatly against God] regarding these things? Yet among the many nations there was no king like him. He was loved by his God, and God made him king over all Israel; nevertheless the foreign women caused even him to sin [by turning to other gods and so, judged by God, he lost his kingdom]. [1 Kin 11:1–11]
²⁷"Do we then hear about you that you have done all this great evil, acting unfaithfully against our God by marrying foreign (pagan) women?"
²⁸One of the sons of Joiada, the son of Eliashib the high priest, was a son-in-law of Sanballat the Horonite, so I chased him away from me.
²⁹O my God, remember them, because they have defiled the priesthood and the covenant of the priesthood and the Levites.
³⁰Thus I cleansed *and* purified them from everything foreign (pagan), and I defined the duties of the priests and Levites, each one in his task;
³¹and *I provided* for the wood offering at appointed times and for the first fruits. O my God, [please] remember me for good [and imprint me on Your heart].

Esther

Author:
Unknown

Date:
Probably before the end of the fifth
century BC

Everyday Life Principles:
Even though you are only one person,
you can make a difference!

In order to fulfill a great calling, you
will need great preparation.

When you do what God asks you to do,
victory is sure.

I believe that the great encouragement the book of Esther offers us is the fact that one person can make a difference. Esther was certainly an unlikely candidate to become the queen of Persia and save the lives of an entire nation. First of all, she was not even Persian, and second, she was an orphan. No natural circumstances facilitated her marrying the king, but God intervened supernaturally and put her in a position of influence so that His purpose for her people, the Jews, would come to pass.

God called and chose Esther to bring deliverance to the Jews when they were marked for destruction. He appointed her for a difficult and dangerous work. Because her call was so significant, she needed thorough preparation. Without proper preparation, she could have faltered in her responsibilities or failed to obey God, but because she was thoroughly prepared and had an obedient heart, she succeeded gloriously. In Esther's case, the preparation included twelve months of beauty treatments and instruction from Hegai, the king's attendant. This type of preparation was necessary to assure that the king would respond favorably to her, which was what she needed in order to save her people.

I believe that God has a great call and purpose for your life, as He did for Esther's. Your assignment may not be the deliverance of a nation, but whatever God has called you to do is extremely significant. Whatever it is, be diligent to embrace the preparation process it requires so you will be well equipped when the time comes for you to act.

1 IT WAS in the days of Ahasuerus (Xerxes) who reigned from India to Ethiopia (Cush) over 127 provinces,

²in those days when King Ahasuerus sat on his royal throne which was at the citadel in Susa [the capital of the Persian Empire],

³in the third year of his reign he held a banquet for all his officials and his attendants. The army *officers* of Persia and Media, the nobles and the officials of the provinces were there in his presence.

⁴And he displayed the riches of his glorious kingdom and the splendor of his great majesty for many days, 180 days *in all*.

⁵When these days were completed, the king held a banquet for all the people who were present at the citadel in Susa [the capital], from the greatest [in importance] to the least, a seven-day feast in the courtyard of the garden of the king's palace.

⁶*There were curtains* (draperies) of fine white and violet linen fastened with cords of fine purple linen to silver rings and marble columns. The couches of gold and silver *rested* on a mosaic floor of porphyry, marble, mother-of-pearl, and precious *colored* stones.

⁷Drinks were served in various kinds of golden goblets, and the royal wine was plentiful, in accordance with the generosity of the king.

⁸The drinking was *carried on* in accordance with the law; no one was compelled [to drink], for the king had directed each official of his household to comply with each guest's wishes.

⁹Queen Vashti also held a [separate] banquet for the women in the palace of King Ahasuerus.

¹⁰On the seventh day, when the king's heart was joyful with wine (in high spirits), he commanded Mehuman, Biztha, Harbona, Bigtha, Abagtha, Zethar, and Carkas, the seven eunuchs who served in the presence of King Ahasuerus [as his attendants],

¹¹to bring Queen Vashti before the king, wearing her royal crown (high turban), to display her beauty before the people and the officials, for she was lovely to see.

¹²But Queen Vashti refused to come at the king's command, which was delivered [to her] by the eunuchs. So the king became extremely angry and burned with rage.

¹³Then the king spoke to the wise men who understood the times [asking for their advice]—for it was the custom of the king *to speak* before all those who were familiar with law and legal matters—

¹⁴and who were close to him [as advisors]: Carshena, Shethar, Admatha, Tarshish, Meres, Marsena, and Memucan, the seven officials of Persia and Media who had access to the king and were ranked highest in the kingdom.

¹⁵[He said,] "According to the law, what is to be done with Queen Vashti because she did not obey the command of King Ahasuerus *which was conveyed* by the eunuchs?"

¹⁶And Memucan answered in the presence of the king and the officials, "Vashti the queen has not only wronged the king but [also] all the officials (royal representatives) and all the peoples who are in all the provinces of King Ahasuerus.

¹⁷"For the queen's conduct will become known to all women, causing them to look on their husbands with contempt (disrespect), since they will say, 'King Ahasuerus commanded Queen Vashti to be brought before him, but she did not come.'

¹⁸"This [very] day the ladies of Persia and Media who have heard of the queen's refusal will speak [in the same way] to all the king's officials, and there will be plenty of contempt and anger.

¹⁹"If it pleases the king, let a royal command be issued by him and let it be written in the laws of the Persians and Medes so that it cannot be repealed *or* modified, that Vashti is no longer to come before King Ahasuerus; and let the king give her royal position to another who is better *and* more worthy than she.

²⁰"So when the king's great decree is proclaimed throughout his [extensive] kingdom, all women will give honor to their husbands, from the great to the insignificant."

²¹This statement (advice) pleased the king and the officials, and the king did what Memucan proposed.

²²So he sent letters to all the royal provinces, to each province in its own script and to each people in their own language, saying that every man should be the master *and* rule in his own home and that he should speak [in the household] in the language of his own people.

2 AFTER THESE things, when the wrath of King Ahasuerus (Xerxes) had subsided, he remembered Vashti and what she had done and what had been decreed against her.

²Then the king's attendants, who served him, said, "Let beautiful young virgins be sought for the king.

³"Let the king appoint administrators in all the provinces of his kingdom, and have them gather all the beautiful young virgins to the citadel in Susa, into the harem, under the custody of Hegai, the king's eunuch, who is in charge of the women; and let their beauty preparations be given *to them*.

⁴"Then let the young woman who pleases the king be queen in place of Vashti." This pleased the king, and he did accordingly.

⁵There was a certain Jew in the citadel of Susa whose name was Mordecai the son of Jair, the son of Shimei, the son of Kish, a Benjamite,

⁶who had been deported from Jerusalem with the captives who had been exiled with Jeconiah king of Judah, whom Nebuchadnezzar the king of Babylon had exiled.

⁷He was the guardian of Hadassah, that is Esther, his uncle's daughter, for she had no father or mother. The young woman was beautiful of form and face; and when her father and mother died, Mordecai took her in as his own daughter.

⁸So it came about when the king's command and his decree were proclaimed and when many young women were gathered together in the citadel of Susa into the custody of Hegai, that Esther was taken to the king's palace [and placed] in the custody of Hegai, who was in charge of the women.

⁹Now the young woman pleased Hegai and found favor with him. So he quickly provided her with beauty preparations and her [portion of] food, and he gave her seven choice maids from the king's palace; then he transferred her and her maids to the best *place* in the harem.

¹⁰Esther did not reveal [the Jewish background of] her people or her family, for Mordecai had instructed her not to do so.

¹¹Every day Mordecai [who was an

putting the Word to work

Often God's assignments for us require preparation, as Esther's did (see Esther 2:12, 13). It may be spiritual preparation, or it may be that certain circumstances must first be in place, such as further training or others to help you. Are you confident that you are prepared for the work the Lord has for you at this time in your life? If not, ask God to show you the further preparation you need and, like Esther, embrace it.

attendant in the king's court] walked back and forth in front of the courtyard of the harem to learn how Esther was getting along and what was happening to her.

¹²Now when it was each young woman's turn to go before King Ahasuerus, after the end of her twelve months under the regulations for the women—for the days of their beautification were completed as follows: six months with oil of myrrh and six months with [sweet] spices *and* perfumes and the beauty preparations for women—

¹³then the young woman would go before the king in this way: anything that she wanted was given her to take with her from the harem into the king's palace.

¹⁴In the evening she would go in and the next morning she would return to the second harem, to the custody of Shaashgaz, the king's eunuch who was in charge of the concubines. She would not return to the king unless he delighted in her and she was summoned by name.

¹⁵Now *as for* Esther, the daughter

putting the Word to work

Do you have a hard time asking for advice? Take a lesson from Esther, who recognized the source of wisdom that the Lord had given her in Hegai (see Esther 2:15). In seeking and heeding his counsel, she found favor that led to great deliverance and victory for her people. Ask the Lord to show you the people who are sources of wisdom and godly counsel in your life.

believe for God's favor

Do you know that there is a verse in the Bible that says God brings one person down and lifts up another (see 1 Samuel 2:7)? In Esther 2:15–17, He raised up Esther from obscurity to become the queen of the entire land. God gave her favor with everyone she met, including the king, because she had favor with Him.

Later in the story, we will see that Esther drew upon that favor to save herself and her people, the Jews, from being murdered by the evil Haman, who was out to destroy them. She was not afraid to go to the king and ask him to intervene on behalf of herself and her people, even though such a bold request of the king could have cost her very life, because she knew that she had favor with God.

If you find yourself in a situation in which you are being harassed, persecuted, or discriminated against; if someone is trying to take something from you that rightfully belongs to you—whether it is your job, your home, your reputation, or anything else in life—do not try to retaliate by seeking natural favor. Instead, believe God for supernatural favor, because despite how hopeless things may look from a human perspective, God can lift you up, and He can bring your enemies down.

Every single day when you go to work, let me encourage you to say, "I believe that I have favor in this place today. I believe that the light of the Lord shines upon me and that I have favor with everyone—with God and with other people."

Do not go through life being afraid that nobody likes you. Do not harbor the fear of rejection. Instead, believe that God is causing everyone you come in contact with to like you, to want to be around you, and to look on you with favor.

of Abihail the uncle of Mordecai who had taken her in as his [own] daughter, when her turn came to go in to the king, she requested nothing except what Hegai the king's eunuch [and attendant] who was in charge of the women, advised. And Esther found favor in the sight of all who saw her.

¹⁶So Esther was taken to King Ahasuerus, to his royal palace in the tenth month, that is, the month of Tebeth (Dec-Jan), in the seventh year of his reign.

¹⁷Now the king loved Esther more than all the *other* women, and she found favor and kindness with him more than all the [other] virgins, so that he set the royal crown on her head and made her queen in the place of Vashti.

¹⁸Then the king held a great banquet, Esther's banquet, for all his officials and his servants; and he made a festival for the provinces and gave gifts in accordance with the resources of the king.

¹⁹And when the virgins were gathered together the second time, Mordecai was sitting at the king's gate.

²⁰Esther had not revealed her family or her people [that is, her Jewish background], just as Mordecai had instructed her; for Esther did what Mordecai told her just as when she was under his care.

²¹In those days, while Mordecai was sitting at the king's gate, Bigthan and Teresh, two of the king's eunuchs who guarded the door, became angry and conspired to attack King Ahasuerus.

²²But the plot became known to Mordecai, who informed Queen Esther, and Esther told the king in Mordecai's name.

life point

Mordecai was a man called and anointed by God to bring deliverance to God's people, just as you and I are called and anointed by God to bring deliverance and help to others in our day.

²³Now when the plot was investigated and found *to be true,* both men were hanged on the gallows. And it was recorded in the Book of the Chronicles in the king's presence.

3 AFTER THESE things King Ahasuerus (Xerxes) promoted Haman, the son of Hammedatha the Agagite, and advanced him and established his authority over all the officials who were with him.

²All the king's servants who were at the king's gate [in royal service] bowed down and honored *and* paid homage to Haman; for this is what the king had commanded in regard to him. But Mordecai [a Jew of the tribe of Benjamin] neither bowed down nor paid homage [to him].

³Then the king's servants who were at the king's gate said to Mordecai, "Why are you disregarding the king's command?"

⁴Now it happened when they had spoken to him day after day and he would not listen to them, that they told Haman to see whether Mordecai's reason [for his behavior] would stand [as valid]; for he had told them that he was a Jew.

⁵When Haman saw that Mordecai neither bowed down nor paid homage to him, he was furious.

speak the Word

God, I pray that You will do for me what You did for Esther, and give me favor in the sight of the people I meet.
–ADAPTED FROM ESTHER 2:17

⁶But he disdained laying hands on Mordecai alone, for they had told him *who* the people of Mordecai were (his nationality); so Haman determined to destroy all the Jews, the people of Mordecai, who *lived* throughout the kingdom of Ahasuerus.

⁷In the first month, the month of Nisan (Mar-Apr), in the twelfth year of King Ahasuerus, Haman cast Pur, that is, the lot, cast before him day after day [to find a lucky day to approach the king], month after month, until the twelfth month, the month of Adar (Feb-Mar).

⁸Then Haman said to King Ahasuerus, "There is a certain people scattered [abroad] and dispersed among the peoples in all the provinces of your kingdom; their laws are different from *those* of all *other* people, and they do not observe the king's laws. Therefore it is not in the king's interest to [tolerate them and] let them stay *here*.

⁹"If it pleases the king, let it be decreed that they be destroyed, and I will pay ten thousand talents of silver into the hands of those who carry out the *king's* business, to put into the king's treasuries."

¹⁰Then the king removed his signet ring from his hand [that is, the special ring which was used to seal his letters] and gave it to Haman, the son of Hammedatha the Agagite, the enemy of the Jews.

¹¹The king said to Haman, "The silver is given to you, and the people *also*, to do with them as you please."

¹²Then the king's scribes (secretaries) were summoned on the thirteenth day of the first month, and it was written just as Haman commanded to the king's satraps (chief rulers), and to the governors who were over each

a better plan

If you are familiar with Esther's story, you know that Esther, the cousin and adopted daughter of a Jew named Mordecai, had been chosen by King Ahasuerus to be elevated to the position of queen of his kingdom. She was taken into the king's harem as a young maiden, and I feel sure that this was not the plan she had for her life. The situation probably frightened her and may even have seemed evil to her at the time. In the harem, her whole purpose was to prepare for a night with the king. Then when the time came, God gave her favor with the king, and he chose her to be his queen (see Esther 2:7–17). Little did she know that God was putting her in position to save a nation (see Esther 3:5, 6).

Often we have a plan in mind for our lives, but something happens to interrupt our plan. We often resist and are not happy about the change, but no matter what we do, this new thing seems to be God's will for us. We cannot imagine how it could turn out well, but God has a plan in mind that is much better than ours. In Esther's case, Mordecai told her that she was called to the kingdom "for such a time as this" (Esther 4:14) because the Jews were in danger of extinction. Her destiny was to save them from destruction, and if she did not do what God was asking her to do, she would perish along with everyone else (see Esther 4:14). She agreed to do whatever needed to be done.

I pray that you and I will be just as courageous as Esther was—even when we are led in a different direction than we had planned.

province and to the officials of each people, each province according to its script (writing), each people according to their own language; being written in the name of King Ahasuerus and sealed with the king's signet ring.

[13]Letters were sent by couriers to all the king's provinces to destroy, to kill and to annihilate all the Jews, both young and old, women and children, in one day, the thirteenth [day] of the twelfth month, which is the month of Adar (March 7, 473 B.C.), and to seize their belongings as plunder.

[14]A copy of the edict to be decreed as law in every province was published to all the peoples, so that they would be ready for this day.

[15]The couriers went out hurriedly by order of the king, and the decree was issued at the citadel in Susa. And while the king and Haman sat down to drink, the city of Susa was perplexed [by the unusual and alarming decree].

4 NOW WHEN Mordecai learned of everything that had been done, he tore his clothes [in mourning], and put on sackcloth and ashes, and went out into the center of the city and cried out loudly and bitterly.

[2]He went [only] as far as the king's gate, because no one was to enter the king's gate dressed in sackcloth.

[3]In each and every province that the decree and law of the king reached, there was great mourning among the

for such a time as this

Queen Esther was asked to do something very difficult in order to help bring deliverance to her people. Most likely, she did not feel like being in the challenging place where God put her. She probably did not want the responsibility, nor did she want to risk the personal harm she knew could come to her. Esther was a young maiden with her whole life ahead of her. Leaving her dreams behind, she was being asked to follow instructions from the Lord that seemed very dangerous. Esther was to go before the king to expose a wicked plot that had been launched against the Jews. No one was allowed to go before the king unless he or she was invited—not even the queen. Esther knew that unless God gave her favor, she would be killed (see Esther 4:16). I would say that Esther put everything on the line in order to obey God's will.

Mordecai, who was speaking to Esther on God's behalf, told her that she must not keep silent. If she did, people would perish. He reminded her that perhaps she had been called to the kingdom for the very task that lay before her.

You, too, may be alive today in order to fulfill the purposes of God in your generation. The timing and place of your birth are not accidental; God intentionally and specifically places us all in certain time frames and places. Many people spend their entire lives never knowing what their purpose is, but perhaps it is because they try to choose their own destiny rather than follow the leading of the Holy Spirit. Following God requires sacrifices and a willingness to be uncomfortable. Esther reached a point of being willing to lay aside all her own thoughts, plans, and ideas. She was even willing to die if she needed to in order to obey God.

Because of Esther's sacrifice and bold step of faith, God did use her to save a nation. She was more blessed in God's will than she could ever have been anywhere else. God's will is not always easy, but it is always worth any sacrifice we need to make.

Jews, with fasting, weeping and wailing; and many lay on sackcloth and ashes.

⁴When Esther's maids and her eunuchs came and told her [what had happened], the queen was seized by great fear. She sent garments to clothe Mordecai so that he would remove his sackcloth, but he did not accept them.

⁵Then Esther summoned Hathach, one of the king's eunuchs, whom the king had appointed to attend her, and ordered him *to go* to Mordecai to find out what this issue was and why it had come about.

⁶So Hathach went out to Mordecai in the [open] square of the city, which was in front of the king's gate.

⁷Mordecai told him everything that had happened to him, and the exact amount of money that Haman had promised to pay to the king's treasuries for the destruction of the Jews.

⁸Mordecai also gave him a copy of the text of the decree which had been issued in Susa for the Jews destruction, so that he might show Esther and explain it to her, and order her to go in to the king to seek his favor and plead with him for [the lives of] her people.

⁹Hathach came back and told Esther what Mordecai had said.

¹⁰Then Esther spoke to Hathach and ordered him *to reply* to Mordecai, saying:

¹¹"All the king's servants and the people of the king's provinces know that for any man or woman who comes to the king to the inner court without being summoned, he has but one law, that he is to be put to death, unless the king holds out to him the golden scepter so that he may live. And as for me,

putting the Word to work

Do you sometimes wonder about your position in life—why you are where you are? Scripture teaches us that God has placed us where we are for His purposes (see Esther 4:14), and Esther is a powerful example of this truth. Look for opportunities around you—in your neighborhood, your workplace, even your home—for ways the Lord wants you to partner with Him in the work of His kingdom.

I have not been summoned to come to the king for these [last] thirty days."

¹²So they told Mordecai what Esther had said.

¹³Then Mordecai told them to reply to Esther, "Do not imagine that you in the king's palace can escape any more than all the Jews.

¹⁴"For if you remain silent at this time, liberation and rescue will arise for the Jews from another place, and you and your father's house will perish [since you did not help when you had the chance]. And who knows whether you have attained royalty for such a time as this [and for this very purpose]?"

¹⁵Then Esther told them to reply to Mordecai,

¹⁶"Go, gather all the Jews that are present in Susa, and observe a fast for me; do not eat or drink for three days, night or day. I and my maids also will fast in the same way. Then I will go in to [see] the king [without being summoned], which is against the law; and if I perish, I perish."

¹⁷So Mordecai went away and did exactly as Esther had commanded him.

speak the Word

God, I pray that You will give me a heart like Esther's, willing to do Your will at any cost.
—ADAPTED FROM ESTHER 4:16

5 ON THE third day [of the fast] Esther put on her royal robes and stood in the inner court of the king's palace opposite his [throne] room. The king was sitting on his royal throne, facing the [main] entrance of the palace.

²When the king saw Esther the queen standing in the court, she found favor in his sight; and the king extended to her the golden scepter which was in his hand. So Esther approached and touched the top of the scepter.

³Then the king said to her, "What is *troubling* you, Queen Esther? What is your request? It shall be given to you, up to half of the kingdom."

⁴Esther said, "If it pleases the king, may the king and Haman come this day to the banquet that I have prepared for him."

⁵Then the king said, "Bring Haman quickly so that we may do as Esther says." So the king and Haman came to the banquet which Esther had prepared.

life point

The Bible contains some radical examples of things people did to obey God. It was radical of Esther to put everything on the line when she went before the king without being summoned. Her motive was right, and she did it in obedience; therefore, God gave her favor, and she was instrumental in saving her nation from disaster.

When we are called upon to make a sacrifice or do something radical for God, we should not feel deprived, but privileged. In the most radical act of human history, Jesus sacrificed His very life for us, and we are to follow in His footsteps. It is time to do what He asks us to do, no matter what the cost.

putting the Word to work

Esther found favor in the sight of the king and received what she asked for (see Esther 5:2–5). Do you ever hesitate to ask Jesus, the King of kings, for what you need or desire? Know that you have favor with God and can approach Him with total confidence because of what Jesus has done on your behalf.

⁶As they drank their wine at the banquet, the king said to Esther, "What is your petition? It shall be granted to you. And what is your request? Even to half of the kingdom it shall be done."

⁷Then Esther replied, "My petition and my request is this:

⁸if I have found favor in the sight of the king, and if it pleases the king to grant my petition and to do as I request, may the king and Haman come to the banquet that I will prepare for them; and tomorrow I will do as the king says [and express my request]."

⁹Haman went away that day joyful and in good spirits. But when he saw Mordecai at the king's gate refusing to stand up or show fear before him, he was filled with rage toward Mordecai.

¹⁰Nevertheless, Haman controlled himself and went home. There he sent for his friends and his wife Zeresh.

¹¹Then Haman recounted to them the glory of his riches, the large number of his sons, and every *instance* in which the king had magnified him and how he had promoted him over the officials and servants of the king.

¹²Haman also said, "Even Queen Esther let no one but me come with the king to the banquet she had prepared; and tomorrow also I am invited by her [together] with the king.

¹³"Yet all of this does not satisfy me as long as I see Mordecai the Jew sitting at the king's gate."

¹⁴Then his wife Zeresh and all his friends said to him, "Have a gallows fifty cubits high made, and in the morning ask the king to have Mordecai hanged on it; then go joyfully to the banquet with the king." And the advice pleased Haman, so he had the gallows made.

6 ON THAT night the king could not sleep; so he ordered that the book of records *and* memorable deeds, the chronicles, be brought, and they were read before the king. ²It was found written there how Mordecai had reported that Bigthana and Teresh, two of the king's eunuchs who were doorkeepers, had planned to attack King Ahasuerus (Xerxes). ³The king said, "What honor or distinction has been given Mordecai for this?" Then the king's servants who attended him said, "Nothing has been done for him."

⁴So the king said, "Who is in the court?" Now Haman had just entered the outer court of the king's palace to ask the king about hanging Mordecai on the gallows which he had prepared for him.

⁵The king's servants said to him, "Look, Haman is standing in the court." And the king said, "Let him come in."

⁶So Haman came in and the king said to him, "What is to be done for the man whom the king desires to honor?" Now Haman thought to himself, "Whom would the king desire to honor more than me?"

⁷So Haman said to the king, "For the man whom the king desires to honor,

⁸let a royal robe be brought which the king has worn, and the horse on which the king has ridden, and on

God does not forget

I would like to share a truth with you. Whatever good thing you and I do, even in secret, God has recorded. He will not forget it. The day will come when our good deeds will be brought out into the open.

Every prayer we have prayed, every time we have submitted to authority when we wanted to rebel, every time we have confessed God's Word when our emotions were screaming at us to say negative things—each act of obedience is recorded and will be rewarded. Every time we have taken our position of faith, worship, and maintaining a good confession, every time we have offered to God the sacrifice of praise, God remembers. He does not forget the things we have done right. He has them recorded in His book of memorable deeds, as we read in Hebrews 6:10: "For God is not unjust so as to forget your work and the love which you have shown for His name in ministering to [the needs of] the saints (God's people), as you do."

Mordecai had been doing some good deeds, but he had not called attention to them. He had simply been doing them in secret, unto the Lord. The Word teaches us that when we do good deeds, we are not to let our left hand know what our right hand is doing (see Matthew 6:3, 4). This means that we should do what we feel God is leading us to do—do it for His glory, then forget it and go on about our business. It means not patting ourselves on the back or telling others what we have done, but simply knowing that our reward will come from God when the time is right. When God's timing was right, He rewarded Mordecai (see Esther 6:1–3), and you can be sure He will do the same for you.

whose head a royal crown has been placed;

⁹and let the robe and the horse be handed over to one of the king's most noble officials. Let him dress the man whom the king delights to honor [in the royal robe] and lead him on horseback through the open square of the city, and proclaim before him, 'This is what shall be done for the man whom the king desires to honor.'"

¹⁰Then the king said to Haman, "Quickly take the royal robe and the horse, as you have said, and do this for Mordecai the Jew, who is sitting at the king's gate. Leave out nothing of all that you have said."

¹¹So Haman took the royal robe and the horse and dressed Mordecai, and led him *on horseback* through the open square of the city, proclaiming before him, "This is what shall be done for the man whom the king desires to honor."

¹²Then Mordecai returned to the king's gate. But Haman hurried to his [own] house, mourning and with his head covered [in sorrow].

¹³Then Haman told Zeresh his wife and all his friends everything that had happened to him. Then his wise counselors and his wife Zeresh said to him, "If Mordecai, before whom you have begun to fall *in status,* is of Jewish heritage, you will not overcome him, but will certainly fall before him."

putting the Word to work

Has there ever been a time in your life when someone else tried to take credit for something you had done? Haman coveted the honor that rightfully belonged to Mordecai. When you do not receive the honor or credit you know is rightfully yours, trust God; He does not forget, and He will be faithful to reward you.

life point

The king, who represents God in this story, was telling Haman, "Every blessing you planned for yourself, you are going to confer on Mordecai. You are going to watch while I bless him" (see Esther 6:7–10). When God decides to bless someone, no person on earth or devil in hell can stop Him.

¹⁴While they were still speaking with him, the king's eunuchs (attendants) arrived and hurriedly brought Haman to the banquet which Esther had prepared.

7 SO THE king and Haman came to drink *wine* with Esther the queen.

²And the king said to Esther on the second day also as they drank their wine, "What is your petition, Queen Esther? It shall be granted to you. And what is your request? Even to half of the kingdom, it shall be done."

³Then Queen Esther replied, "If I have found favor in your sight, O king, and if it pleases the king, let my life be spared as my petition, and my people [be spared] as my request;

⁴for we have been sold, I and my people, to be destroyed, killed and wiped out of existence. Now if we had only been sold as slaves, men and women, I would have remained silent, for our hardship would not be sufficient to burden the king [by even mentioning it]."

⁵Then King Ahasuerus (Xerxes) asked Queen Esther, "Who is he, and where is he, who dares to do such a thing?"

⁶Esther said, "An adversary and an enemy is Haman, this evil man." Then Haman became terrified before the king and queen.

⁷Then in his fury, the king stood

up from drinking wine *and went* into the palace garden [to decide what he should do]; but Haman stayed to plead for his life from Queen Esther, for he saw that harm had been determined against him by the king.

⁸When the king returned from the palace garden to the place where they were drinking wine, Haman was falling on the couch where Esther was. Then the king said, "Will he even *attempt to* assault the queen with me in the palace?" As the king spoke those words, the servants covered Haman's face [in preparation for execution].

⁹Then Harbonah, one of the eunuchs serving the king said, "Now look, there are gallows fifty cubits (75 ft.) high standing at Haman's house, which Haman made for Mordecai, whose good warning saved the king." And the king said, "Hang him on it."

¹⁰So they hanged Haman on the gallows that he had prepared for Mordecai. Then the king's anger subsided.

8 ON THAT day King Ahasuerus (Xerxes) gave the house of Haman, the enemy of the Jews, to Queen Esther; and Mordecai came before the king, because Esther had disclosed what [relation] he was to her.

life point

Esther had worshiped God through her obedience and willingness to stay in a situation that was unpleasant to her. She was willing to lay aside her plan and accept God's plan, even though she did not understand it for a period of time. Each act of obedience is a type of worship that God does not ignore. When we keep our eyes on God, stand firm in faith, continue to worship, and maintain a good confession, we will always see the devil's plan for evil in our lives work for our good and to his demise, just as Esther did.

²The king took off his signet ring which he had taken away from Haman, and gave it to Mordecai. And Esther put Mordecai in charge of the house of Haman.

³Then Esther spoke again to the king and fell down at his feet and wept and implored him to avert the evil *plot* of Haman the Agagite and his plan which he had devised against the Jews [because the decree to annihilate the Jews was still in effect].

⁴Then the king held out to Esther the golden scepter. So Esther arose and stood before the king.

⁵Then she said, "If it pleases the king and if I have found favor before him and the matter is proper in the king's view and I am pleasing in his sight, let it be written to revoke the letters devised by Haman the son of Hammedatha, the Agagite, which he wrote [in order] to destroy the Jews who are in all the king's provinces.

⁶"For how can I endure to see the tragedy that will happen to my people? Or how can I endure to see the destruction of my kindred?"

⁷Then King Ahasuerus said to Queen Esther and to Mordecai the Jew, "Behold, I have given Esther the house of Haman, and they have hanged him on the gallows because he stretched out his hand against the Jews.

⁸"Also, concerning the Jews, write as you see fit, in the king's name, and seal it with the king's signet ring—for a decree which is written in the king's name and sealed with the king's signet ring may not be revoked."

⁹So the king's scribes were called at that time in the third month (that is, the month of Sivan) on the twenty-third day; and it was written in accordance with everything that Mordecai commanded, to the Jews, to the chief rulers (satraps), and the governors and officials of the provinces which *extended* from India to Ethiopia

(Cush), 127 provinces, to every province in its own script (writing), and to every people in their own language and to the Jews according to their script and their language.

¹⁰He wrote [a decree] in the name of King Ahasuerus, and sealed it with the king's ring, and sent letters by couriers on horseback, riding on the royal [mail] relay horses, the offspring of the racing mares.

¹¹In it the king granted the Jews who were in every city *the right* to assemble and to defend their lives; to destroy, to kill, and to annihilate any armed force that might attack them, their little children, and women; and to take the enemies' goods as plunder,

¹²on one day in all the provinces of King Ahasuerus, the thirteenth [day] of the twelfth month (that is, the month of Adar).

¹³A copy of the edict was to be issued as a law in every province and as a proclamation to all peoples, so that the Jews would be ready on that day, to avenge themselves on their enemies.

¹⁴So the couriers, who were mounted on the royal relay horses, left quickly, urged on by the king's command; and the decree was issued at the citadel in Susa [the capital].

¹⁵Then Mordecai departed from the presence of the king in royal apparel of blue and white, with a large crown of gold and with a robe of fine linen and purple wool; and the city of Susa shouted and rejoiced.

¹⁶For [at this time] the Jews had light [a dawn of new hope] and gladness and joy and honor.

¹⁷In each and every province and in each and every city, wherever the king's command and his decree arrived, the Jews *celebrated with* gladness and joy, a feast and a holiday. And many among the peoples of the land became Jews, for the fear of the Jews [and their God] had fallen on them.

9 NOW IN the twelfth month (that is, the month of Adar) on the thirteenth day when the king's command and edict were about to be executed, on the [very] day when the enemies of the Jews had hoped to gain power over them [and slaughter them], it happened the other way around so that the Jews themselves gained power over those who hated them.

²The Jews assembled in their cities throughout the provinces of King Ahasuerus (Xerxes) to apprehend those who wanted to do them harm; and no one could stand before them, for the fear of them [and their God] had fallen on all the peoples.

³Even all the officials of the provinces and the chief rulers (satraps) and the governors and those who attended to the king's business supported the Jews [in defeating their enemies], because the fear of Mordecai [and his God's power] had fallen on them.

⁴For Mordecai was great *and* respected in the king's palace, and his fame spread throughout all the provinces; for the man Mordecai became greater and greater.

⁵So the Jews struck all their enemies with the sword, killing and destroying them; and they did what they pleased to those who hated them.

⁶At the citadel in Susa the Jews killed and destroyed five hundred men,

⁷and [they killed] Parshandatha, Dalphon, Aspatha,

⁸Poratha, Adalia, Aridatha,

⁹Parmashta, Arisai, Aridai, and Vaizatha,

¹⁰the ten sons of Haman the son of Hammedatha, the Jews' enemy; but they did not lay their hands on the plunder.

¹¹On that day the number of those who were killed at the citadel in Susa was reported to the king.

¹²The king said to Queen Esther, "The

Jews have killed and destroyed five hundred men and the ten sons of Haman at the citadel in Susa. What then have they done in the rest of the king's provinces! Now what is your petition? It shall be granted to you. What is your further request? It shall also be done."

¹³Esther replied, "If it pleases the king, let it be granted to the Jews who are in Susa to act tomorrow also in accordance with the decree of today; and let [the dead bodies of] Haman's ten sons be hanged on the gallows." [Esth 9:10]

¹⁴So the king commanded it to be done; the decree was given in Susa, and they hanged [the bodies of] Haman's ten sons.

¹⁵The Jews who were in Susa also gathered together on the fourteenth day of the month of Adar and killed three hundred men in Susa, but they did not lay their hands on the plunder.

¹⁶Now the rest of the Jews who were in the king's provinces assembled, to defend their lives and rid themselves of their enemies, and kill 75,000 of those who hated them; but they did not lay their hands on the plunder.

¹⁷*This was done* on the thirteenth day of the month of Adar, and on the fourteenth day they rested and made it a day of feasting and rejoicing.

¹⁸But the Jews who were in Susa assembled on the thirteenth and on the fourteenth of the same month, and on the fifteenth day they rested and made it a day of feasting and rejoicing.

¹⁹Therefore the Jews of the villages, who live in the rural [unwalled] towns, make the fourteenth day of the month of Adar a holiday for rejoicing and feasting and sending choice portions *of food* to one another.

²⁰Now Mordecai recorded these events, and he sent letters to all the Jews who lived in all the provinces of King Ahasuerus, both near and far,

²¹obliging them to celebrate the fourteenth day of the month of Adar, and the fifteenth day of the same month, annually,

²²because on those days the Jews rid themselves of their enemies, and as the month which was turned for them from grief to joy and from mourning into a holiday; that they should make them days of feasting and rejoicing and sending choice portions *of food* to one another and gifts to the poor.

²³So the Jews undertook what they had started to do, and what Mordecai had written to them.

²⁴For Haman the son of Hammedatha, the Agagite, the enemy of all the Jews, had plotted against the Jews to destroy them and had cast Pur, that is, the lot, [to find the right time] to disturb and destroy them.

²⁵But when it came before the king, he commanded in writing that Haman's wicked scheme which he had devised against the Jews was to return on his own head, and that he and his sons should [endure what he planned for the Jews and] be hanged on the gallows.

²⁶Therefore they called these days

life point

Not only did the Lord turn the tables on Haman so that he had to give Mordecai the honor he had planned for himself (see Esther 6:11, 12), He also turned back on Haman the evil plan he had devised for Mordecai (see Esther 9:25). When Haman went to the dinner that Queen Esther gave for the king and for him, she revealed Haman's wicked plot to kill her and her people. As a result, the king had Haman hanged on the same gallows he had built for Mordecai (see Esther 7:9, 10). When we trust God, the evil that is planned against us will come to ruin and God will give us the ultimate victory.

Purim after the name Pur (lot). And because of all the instructions in this letter, and what they had faced in this regard and what had happened to them,

27the Jews established and made it a custom for themselves and for their descendants and for all who joined them, so that they would not fail to celebrate these two days as it was written and at the appointed time annually.

28So these days were to be remembered and celebrated throughout every generation, every family, every

life point

I wholeheartedly believe that Esther 10:3 is a word in due season for our lives, one that we desperately need right now. Esther and Mordecai did receive honor and position at the end of the story, but first they had to be willing to sacrifice everything to avoid the extinction of their people. They did not seek position for themselves, but unselfishly laid their lives on the line in obedience to God's purpose. They did not give up until their people were saved and the victory was won.

I encourage you to take your position as Mordecai and Esther did. Do not give up. Stand still and trust God. Enter into God's rest. Like Mordecai, seek the welfare of others and speak peace to everyone you meet. Resist the temptation to worry and try to figure out everything that is going on in your life. When you feel you might waver, take your position and see the salvation God has planned for you.

province and every city; and these days of Purim were not to cease from among the Jews, nor their memory fade from their descendants.

29Then Queen Esther, the daughter of Abihail, with Mordecai the Jew, wrote with full power *and* authority to confirm this second letter about Purim.

30He sent letters to all the Jews, to the 127 provinces of the kingdom of Ahasuerus, in words of peace and truth,

31to establish these days of Purim [to be observed] at their appointed times, just as Mordecai the Jew and Queen Esther had established for them, and as they had established for themselves and for their descendants with instructions regarding their times of fasting and their lamentations (expressions of needing help).

32The command of Esther established these customs for Purim, and it was written in the book [of the royal archives].

10 KING AHASUERUS (Xerxes) imposed a tax on the land and on the coastlands of the sea.

2And all the accomplishments of his authority and strength, and the full account of the greatness of Mordecai to which the king had raised him, are they not written in the Book of the Chronicles of the Kings of Media and Persia?

3For Mordecai the Jew was second only to King Ahasuerus, and great among the Jews and in favor with his many fellow people, for he worked for the good of his people and spoke for the welfare *and* peace of his whole nation.

Job

Author:
Uncertain

Date:
Probably written in the second millennium BC, but put in its present written form around the time of Solomon

Everyday Life Principles:
God does allow people to go through difficulties.

God loves us and helps us in the midst of our suffering.

When we suffer, we must be diligent to keep our faith strong and to maintain a good attitude. Faith in God and a positive attitude not only help us endure suffering, but also lead to restoration.

Simply put, the book of Job is about hard times. It teaches us that God does allow His people to suffer at times, but it also reminds us that God is with us in the midst of our suffering and encourages us to cling to Him through it all, no matter what we face in life.

Job endured almost every kind of loss imaginable—the loss of money, possessions, family, health, and the support of his friends. But he did not lose his hope in God. Even when things became so bad that his wife wanted him to "curse God and die!" Job called her foolish and responded: "Shall we indeed accept [only] good from God and not [also] accept adversity and disaster?" (Job 2:9, 10). Verse 10 continues, "In [spite of] all this Job did not sin with [words from] his lips." He remained faithful to God despite devastating and difficult circumstances. In the end, God rewarded Job's faithfulness and restored double what he had lost. I want to repeat that he received *double* what he had lost.

I hope you will remember the lessons of Job when you face suffering in your life. Remember that God loves you, that your Redeemer lives and is working on your behalf, that nothing can steal God's presence from you, that you may have to close your ears to the skeptics in your life, that your persevering faith will ultimately cause you to triumph, and that God is able to restore far more than you have lost or suffered.

1 THERE WAS a man in the land of Uz whose name was Job; and that man was blameless and upright, and one who feared God [with reverence] and abstained from *and* turned away from evil [because he honored God].

²Seven sons and three daughters were born to him.

³He also possessed 7,000 sheep, 3,000 camels, 500 yoke (pairs) of oxen, 500 female donkeys, and a very great number of servants, so that this man was the greatest [and wealthiest and most respected] of all the men of the east (northern Arabia).

⁴His sons used to go [in turn] and feast in the house of each one on his day, and they would send *word* and invite their three sisters to eat and drink with them. [Gen 21:8; 40:20]

⁵When the days of their feasting were over, Job would send [for them] and consecrate them, rising early in the morning and offering burnt offerings *according to* the number of them all; for Job said, "It may be that my sons have sinned and cursed God in their hearts." Job did this at all [such] times.

⁶Now there was a day when the sons of God (angels) came to present themselves before the Lᴏʀᴅ, and Satan (adversary, accuser) also came among them. [Rev 12:10]

⁷The Lᴏʀᴅ said to Satan, "From where have you come?" Then Satan answered the Lᴏʀᴅ, "From roaming around on the earth and from walking around on it."

⁸The Lᴏʀᴅ said to Satan, "Have you considered *and* reflected on My servant Job? For there is none like him on the earth, a blameless and upright man, one who fears God [with reverence] and abstains from *and* turns away from evil [because he honors God]."

⁹Then Satan answered the Lᴏʀᴅ, "Does Job fear God for nothing?

¹⁰"Have You not put a hedge [of protection] around him and his house and all that he has, on every side? You have blessed the work of his hands [and conferred prosperity and happiness upon him], and his possessions have increased in the land.

¹¹"But put forth Your hand now and touch (destroy) all that he has, and he will surely curse You to Your face."

¹²Then the Lᴏʀᴅ said to Satan, "Behold, all that Job has is in your power, only do not put your hand on *the man* himself." So Satan departed from the presence of the Lᴏʀᴅ.

¹³Now there was a day when Job's sons and daughters were eating and drinking wine in their oldest brother's house,

¹⁴and a messenger came to Job and said, "The oxen were plowing and the donkeys were feeding beside them,

¹⁵and the Sabeans attacked *and* swooped down on them and took away the animals. They also killed the servants with the edge of the sword, and I alone have escaped to tell you."

¹⁶While he was still speaking, another [messenger] also came and said, "The fire of God (lightning) has fallen from the heavens and has burned up the sheep and the servants and consumed them, and I alone have escaped to tell you."

¹⁷While he was still speaking, another [messenger] also came and said, "The Chaldeans formed three bands and made a raid on the camels

speak the Word

Help me, God, to be like Job—blameless and upright, fearing You with reverence and abstaining from evil.
–ᴀᴅᴀᴘᴛᴇᴅ ꜰʀᴏᴍ Jᴏʙ 1:1

and have taken them away and have killed the servants with the edge of the sword, and I alone have escaped to tell you."

¹⁸While he was still speaking, another [messenger] also came and said, "Your sons and your daughters were eating and drinking wine in their oldest brother's house,

¹⁹and suddenly, a great wind came from across the desert, and struck the four corners of the house, and it fell on the young people and they died, and I alone have escaped to tell you."

²⁰Then Job got up and tore his robe and shaved his head [in mourning for the children], and he fell to the ground and worshiped [God].

²¹He said,

"Naked (without possessions) I
    came [into this world] from my
    mother's womb,
And naked I will return there.
The Lord gave and the Lord has
    taken away;
Blessed be the name of the Lord."

²²Through all this Job did not sin nor did he blame God.

2 AGAIN THERE was a day when the sons of God (angels) came to present themselves before the Lord, and Satan (adversary, accuser) also came among them to present himself before the Lord.

²The Lord said to Satan, "From where have you come?" Then Satan answered the Lord, "From roaming around on the earth and from walking around on it."

³The Lord said to Satan, "Have you considered and reflected on My servant Job? For there is none like him on the earth, a blameless and upright man,

one who fears God [with reverence] and abstains from and turns away from evil [because he honors God]. And still he maintains and holds tightly to his integrity, although you incited Me against him to destroy him without cause."

⁴Satan answered the Lord, "Skin for skin! Yes, a man will give all he has for his life.

⁵"But put forth Your hand now, and touch his bone and his flesh [and severely afflict him]; and he will curse You to Your face."

⁶So the Lord said to Satan, "Behold, he is in your hand, only spare his life."

⁷So Satan departed from the presence of the Lord and struck Job with loathsome boils and agonizingly painful sores from the sole of his foot to the crown of his head.

⁸And Job took a piece of broken pottery with which to scrape himself, and he sat [down] among the ashes (rubbish heaps).

⁹Then his wife said to him, "Do you still cling to your integrity [and your faith and trust in God, without blaming Him]? Curse God and die!"

¹⁰But he said to her, "You speak as one of the [spiritually] foolish women speaks [ignorant and oblivious to God's will]. Shall we indeed accept [only] good from God and not [also] accept adversity and disaster?" In [spite of] all this Job did not sin with [words from] his lips.

¹¹Now when Job's three friends heard of all this adversity that had come upon him, each one came from his own place, Eliphaz the Temanite, Bildad the Shuhite, and Zophar the Naamathite; for they had made an appointment together to come to sympathize with him and to comfort him.

speak the Word

God, I pray that no matter what I go through, I will not sin nor will I blame You.
– ADAPTED FROM JOB 1:22

12When they looked from a distance and did not recognize him [because of his disfigurement], they raised their voices and wept; and each one tore his robe [in grief] and they threw dust over their heads toward the sky [in sorrow]. 13So they sat down on the ground with Job for seven days and seven nights and no one spoke a word to him, for they saw that his pain was very great.

putting the Word to work

Have you ever struggled to know what to say to someone who is grieving? After seeing Job's profound grief, his friends did not say anything for days, but they did stay with him and share in his grief. Often the best thing to do for those who are grieving is simply to be present in the midst of their pain and pray for them.

3 AFTER THIS, Job opened his mouth and cursed the day of his *birth*. 2And Job said,

3"Let the day on which I was born perish,
And the night which announced: 'There is a man-child conceived.'
4"May that day be darkness;
Let God above not care about it,
Nor light shine on it.
5"Let darkness and gloom claim it for their own;
Let a cloud settle upon it;
Let all that blackens the day terrify it (the day that I was born).
6"As for that night, let darkness seize it;
Let it not rejoice among the days of the year;
Let it not be counted in the number of the months.

7"Behold, let that night be barren [and empty];
Let no joyful voice enter it.
8"Let those curse it who curse the day,
Who are skilled in rousing up Leviathan.
9"Let the stars of its early dawn be dark;
Let *the morning* wait in vain for the light,
Let it not see the eyelids of morning (the day's dawning),
10Because it did not shut the doors of my *mother's* womb,
Nor hide trouble from my eyes.

11"Why did I not die at birth,
Come forth from the womb and expire?
12"Why did the knees receive me?
And why the breasts, that I would nurse?
13"For now I would have lain down and been quiet;
I would have slept then, I would have been at rest [in death],
14With kings and counselors of the earth,
Who built up [now desolate] ruins for themselves;
15Or with princes who had gold,
Who filled their houses with silver.
16"Or like a miscarriage which is hidden *and* put away, I would not exist,
Like infants who never saw light.
17"There [in death] the wicked cease from raging,
And there the weary are at rest.
18"There the prisoners rest together;
They do not hear the taskmaster's voice.
19"The small and the great are there,
And the servant is free from his master. [Jer 20:14–18]
20"Why is the light given to him who is in misery,
And life to the bitter in soul,

21 Who wait for death, but it does not come,
And dig (search) for death more [diligently] than for hidden treasures,
22 Who rejoice exceedingly,
And rejoice when they find the grave?
23 "Why is the light of day given to a man whose way is hidden,
And whom God has hedged in?
24 "For my groaning comes at the sight of my food,
And my cries [of despair] are poured out like water.
25 "For the thing which I greatly fear comes upon me,
And that of which I am afraid has come upon me.

26 "I am not at ease, nor am I quiet,
And I am not at rest, and yet trouble still comes [upon me]."

4 THEN ELIPHAZ the Temanite answered and said,

2 "If we dare to converse with you, will you be impatient [or offended]?
But who can restrain himself from speaking?
3 "Behold, you have admonished and instructed many,
And you have strengthened weak hands.
4 "Your words have helped the one who was stumbling to stand,

understanding misunderstanding

Job's friend Eliphaz gave him wrong advice because he totally misunderstood Job and the cause of his trouble. There are times when, like Job, we are misunderstood by people we thought would understand and comfort us. Sometimes even the people who are the closest to us do not understand our struggles, our dreams, our personality, or our calling from God.

Before my ministry became established, I remember when people misunderstood me because I was too serious for them. They did not like the same things I liked or do things the way I did. Instead, they would ask me, "Why do you act the way you do?"

I look back now and realize that everything I needed to do the work of Joyce Meyer Ministries was already in me. The personality type and qualities that God wanted me to have were already there. God just had to polish me and get me in good working order.

As God is preparing you for His use and as you are discovering exactly what He wants you to do, you might also feel strange and out of place. You may feel that you do not fit into the regular regimen of what is going on around you. If you are already feeling strange, you may be tempted to be confused or bothered when people say things such as, "What's wrong with you? Why do you act the way you do?" Part of your training for leadership is realizing that people will misunderstand you. You have to make up your mind that you are going to stand with God and do what He says even if nobody understands you, agrees with you, or supports you.

I believe God wants to do great things through you, so stick with Him even when others do not understand. Most often, people who do not support you do not mean to hurt you, they simply do not understand.

And you have strengthened feeble knees.
5"But now adversity comes upon you, and you are impatient *and* intolerant;
It touches you, and you are horrified.
6"Is not your fear *of God* your confidence,
And [is not] the integrity *and* uprightness of your ways your hope?

7"Remember now, who, being innocent, ever perished?
Or where [and in what circumstances] were those upright *and* in right standing with God destroyed?
8"As I have seen, those who plow wickedness
And those who sow trouble *and* harm harvest it.
9"By the breath of God they perish,
And by the blast of His anger they are consumed.
10"The roaring of the lion and the voice of the *fierce* lion,
And the teeth of the young lions are broken.
11"The lion perishes for lack of prey,
And the cubs of the lioness are scattered.

12"Now a word was secretly brought to me,
And my ear received a whisper of it.
13"Amid disquieting thoughts from the visions of the night,
When deep sleep falls on men,
14Dread and trembling came upon me,
Which made all my bones shake.
15"Then a spirit passed before my face;
The hair on my skin stood on end!
16"The spirit stood still, but I could not discern its appearance;
A form was before my eyes;

There was silence, and then I heard a voice, saying:
17'Can [mortal] man be just before God *or* be more righteous than He?
Can a man be pure before his Maker *or* be more cleansed than He? [1 John 1:7; Rev 1:5]
18'God puts no trust *or* confidence, even in His [heavenly] servants,
And He charges His angels with error.
19'How much more [will He blame and charge] those who dwell in houses (bodies) of clay,
Whose foundations are in the dust,
Who are crushed like a moth.
20'Between morning and evening they are broken in pieces *and* destroyed;
Unobserved *and* unnoticed, they perish forever.
21'Is not their tent-cord drawn up within them [so that the tent collapses]?
Do they not die, and yet without [acquiring] wisdom?'

5 "CALL NOW—is there anyone who will answer you?
And to which of the holy ones (angels) will you turn?
2"For anger slays the foolish man,
And jealousy kills the simple (naive).
3"I have seen the foolish taking root [and outwardly prospering],
But I cursed his dwelling immediately [for his destruction was certain].
4"His children are far from safety [and included in their father's ruin],
They are oppressed *and* crushed in the [court of justice in the city's] gate,
And there is no one to rescue *them.*
5"The hungry devour his harvest

And take it even [when it grows]
among the thorns;
The trap opens for [his] wealth.
6 "For affliction does not come forth
from the dust,
Nor does trouble spring forth from
the ground.
7 "For man is born for trouble,
[As naturally] as sparks fly
upward.
8 "As for me, I would seek God *and*
inquire of Him,
And I would commit my cause to
God;
9 Who does great and unsearchable
things,
Marvelous things without number.
10 "He gives rain upon the earth
And sends waters upon the fields,
11 So that He sets on high those who
are lowly,
And He lifts to safety those who
mourn.
12 "He frustrates the devices *and*
schemes of the crafty,
So that their hands cannot attain
success *or* achieve anything of
[lasting] worth.
13 "He catches the [so-called] wise in
their own shrewdness,
And the advice of the devious is
quickly thwarted. [1 Cor 3:19, 20]
14 "In the daytime they meet in
darkness,
And at noon they grope as in the
night.
15 "But God saves [the innocent] from
the sword of the mouth of the
devious,
And the poor from the hand of the
mighty.
16 "So the helpless have hope,
And injustice shuts its mouth.
17 "Behold, how happy *and* fortunate
is the man whom God reproves,

So do not despise *or* reject the
discipline of the Almighty
[subjecting you to trial and
suffering].
18 "For He inflicts pain, but He binds
up *and* gives relief;
He wounds, but His hands also
heal.
19 "He will rescue you from six
troubles;
Even in seven, evil will not touch
you.
20 "In famine He will redeem you
from death,
And in war from the power of the
sword.
21 "You will be hidden from the
scourge of the tongue,
And you will not be afraid of
destruction when it comes.
22 "You will laugh at violence and
famine,
And you will not be afraid of the
wild beasts of the earth.
23 "For you will be in harmony with
the stones of the field,

life point

Job 5:22 is one of my favorite passages
on laughter as an expression of joy. It tells
us that we will laugh at destruction and
famine, which is what God would do in a
similar situation. We see God laughing at
His wicked enemies in Psalm 2:4: "He who
sits [enthroned] in the heavens laughs
[at their rebellion]; the [Sovereign] Lord
scoffs at them [and in supreme contempt
He mocks them]." If God can laugh at His
enemies, we can laugh at ours once in a
while. When things come against you, do
not be uptight and sensitive—just stay
godly while you enjoy a good laugh! You
are not laughing about the problem; you
are laughing at the fact that it cannot do
you any permanent harm because God is
on your side.

And the beasts of the field will be at peace with you.
24 "You will know also that your tent is secure *and* at peace,
And you will visit your dwelling and fear no loss [nor find anything amiss].
25 "You will know also that your descendants will be many,
And your offspring as the grass of the earth.
26 "You will come to your grave in old age,
Like the stacking of grain [on the threshing floor] in its season.
27 "Behold this; we have investigated it, *and* it is true.
Hear *and* heed it, and know for yourself [for your own good]."

6 THEN JOB answered and said,

2 "Oh, that my grief could actually be weighed
And placed in the balances together with my tragedy [to see if my grief is the grief of a coward]!
3 "For now it would be heavier than the sand of the sea;
Therefore my words have been incoherent,
4 Because the arrows of the Almighty are within me,
My spirit drinks their poison;
The terrors of God are arrayed against me.
5 "Does the wild donkey bray when he has grass?
Or does the ox low over his fodder?
6 "Can something that has no taste to it be eaten without salt?
Or is there any flavor in the white of an egg?
7 "My soul refuses to touch them;
Such things are like loathsome food to me [sickening and repugnant].

8 "Oh that my request would come to pass,
And that God would grant me the thing that I long for!
9 "I wish that it would please God to crush me,
That He would let loose His hand and cut me off.
10 "Then I would still have consolation,
And I would jump for joy amid unsparing pain,
That I have not denied *or* hidden the words of the Holy One.
11 "What strength do I have left, that I should wait [and hope]?
And what is ahead of me, that I should be patient *and* endure?
12 "Is my strength *and* endurance that of stones,
Or is my flesh made of bronze?
13 "Is it that I have no help within myself,
And that success *and* wisdom have been driven from me?

14 "For the despairing man *there should be* kindness from his friend;
So that he does not abandon (turn away from) the fear of the Almighty.
15 "My brothers have acted deceitfully like a brook,
Like the torrents of brooks that vanish,
16 Which are dull *and* dirty because of ice,
And into which the snow melts *and* hides itself;
17 When it is warm, they are silent *and* cease to flow;
When it is hot, they vanish from their place.
18 "The paths of their course wind along,
They go up into nothing *and* perish.
[Your counsel is as helpful to me as a dry streambed in the heat of summer.]

19 "The caravans of Tema looked [for
water],
The caravans of Sheba waited for
them [in vain].
20 "They were put to shame *and*
disappointed because they had
trusted [that they would find
water];
They came there and were
ashamed.
21 "Indeed, you have now become
like a dried-up stream,
You see a terror [believing me
to be a victim of the wrath
of God] and are afraid [to be
compassionate].
22 "Did I ever say, 'Give me
something,'
Or, 'Pay a bribe for me from your
wealth,'
23 Or, 'Rescue me from the
adversary's hand,'
Or, 'Redeem me from the hand of
the tyrants'?
24 "Teach me, and I will be silent;
And show me how I have erred.
25 "How painful are words of
honesty.
But what does your argument
prove?
26 "Do you intend to reprove my
words [with a convincing
argument],
When the words of one in despair
belong to the wind [and go
ignored]?
27 "You would cast *lots* (gamble) over
the fatherless
And bargain away your friend.
28 "Now please look at me,
And *see* if I lie to your face [for you
know that I would not].
29 "Turn away [from your suspicion],
let there be no injustice;
Turn away, my righteousness *and*
vindication is still in it.
30 "Is there injustice *or* malice on my
tongue?

Can my palate not discern what is
destructive?

7 "IS NOT man forced to labor on
earth?
And are not his days like the
days of a hired man?
2 "As a slave earnestly longs for the
shade,
And as a hired man eagerly awaits
his wages,
3 So am I allotted months of futility
and suffering,
And [long] nights of trouble *and*
misery are appointed to me.
4 "When I lie down I say,
'When shall I arise [and the night
be gone]?'
But the night continues,
And I am continually tossing until
the dawning of day.
5 "My body is clothed with worms
and a crust of dust;
My skin is hardened [and broken
and loathsome], and [breaks out
and] runs.
6 "My days are swifter than a
weaver's shuttle,
And are spent without hope.

7 "Remember that my life is but
breath [a puff of wind, a sigh];
My eye will not see good again.
8 "The eye of him who sees me
[now] will see me no more;
Your eyes *will be* upon me, but I
will not be.
9 "As a cloud vanishes and is gone,
So he who goes down to Sheol (the
nether world, the place of the
dead) does not come up.
10 "He will not return again to his
house,
Nor will his place know about him
anymore.

11 "Therefore I will not restrain my
mouth;
I will speak in the anguish of my
spirit,

I will complain in the bitterness of my soul [O Lord].

12 "Am I the sea, or the sea monster, That You set a guard over me?

13 "When I say, 'My bed will comfort me, My couch will ease my complaint,'

14 Then You frighten me with dreams And terrify me through visions,

15 So that I would choose suffocation, Death rather than my pain.

16 "I waste away and loathe my life; I will not live forever.

Let me alone, for my days are but a breath [futile and without substance].

17 "What is man that You [should] magnify him [and think him important]? And that You are concerned about him? [Ps 8:4]

18 "And that You examine him every morning And try and test him every moment?

19 "Will You never turn Your gaze away from me [it plagues me],

passing the frustration test

I cannot imagine anything more frustrating to Job than suffering as much as he did and never knowing why. We all experience frustration. It usually comes from trying to do something about a situation we cannot do anything about. We get frustrated because it seems things are taking too long, our task is too hard, or no one is willing to help us. We get frustrated because the money we need is not coming in, or the aches, pains, and burdens we have prayed to be removed from us keep going on and on.

I know what frustration is like because I spent a lot of years frustrated. I knew nothing of the grace of God. I have since discovered that when I become frustrated, it is almost always because I am trying to make something happen instead of waiting on the Lord to bring it to pass. My frustration is a sign that I am acting independently.

In order to pass the frustration test, we have to let go and trust God to do what only He can do. We have to let God be God.

Are you frustrated with your spiritual growth? Do you feel that you will never change? Does it seem that the more you pray and seek God, the worse you get? Are you wrestling with some area of your personality that is causing you problems, or are you dealing with some specific bondage in your life? If so, the reason you are getting so frustrated may be that you are trying to change yourself rather than trusting God to change you. The minute you sincerely say, "Lord, I can't do this, so I let it go," you can almost feel the frustration lift right off of you.

God is the only One Who can make things happen for you. He is the only One Who can bring the things you want and desire into your life. He is the only One Who can open doors of ministry for you; trying to knock them down on your own will not do you any good. The more you try to make your own way, the tighter the doors will stay closed. But when you do things God's way, He can open significant doors for you and do it so quickly that you will be amazed. You can end up running, trying just to keep up with God and all the good opportunities He is giving you. So do not give in to frustration. Wait on God, and you will see awesome results.

Nor let me alone until I swallow
my spittle?
²⁰"If I have sinned, what [harm]
have I done to You,
O Watcher of mankind?
Why have You set me as a target
for You,
So that I am a burden to myself?
²¹"Why then do You not pardon my
transgression
And take away my sin *and* guilt?
For now I will lie down in the dust;
And You will seek me [diligently],
but I will not be."

8 THEN BILDAD the
Shuhite answered and said,

²"How long will you say these
things?
And will the words of your mouth
be a mighty wind?
³"Does God pervert justice?
Or does the Almighty pervert
righteousness?
⁴"If your children have sinned
against Him,
Then He has handed them over to
the power of their transgression
and punished them.
⁵"If you would [diligently] seek God
And implore the compassion *and*
favor of the Almighty,
⁶Then, if you are pure and upright,
Surely now He will awaken for you
And restore your righteous place.
⁷"Though your beginning was
insignificant,
Yet your end will greatly increase.

⁸"Inquire, please, of past
generations,
And consider *and* apply yourself to
the things searched out by their
fathers.
⁹"For we are *only* of yesterday and
know nothing,
Because our days on earth are
[like] a shadow [just a breath or
a vapor].

¹⁰"Will they (the fathers) not teach
you *and* tell you,
And utter words from their
hearts [the deepest part of their
nature]?
¹¹"Can the papyrus grow up without
a marsh?
Can the rushes *or* reed grass grow
without water?
¹²"While it is still green (in flower)
and not cut down,
Yet it withers before any *other*
plant [when without water].
¹³"So are the paths of all who forget
God;
And the hope of the godless will
perish,
¹⁴For his confidence is fragile *and*
breaks,
And his trust is [like] a spider's
web.
¹⁵"He trusts in his house, but it does
not stand;
He holds tightly to it, but it does
not endure.
¹⁶"He thrives *and* prospers [like a
green plant] before the sun,
And his branches spread out over
his garden.
¹⁷"His [godless] roots are wrapped
around a pile of rocks,
And he gazes at a house of stones.
¹⁸"If he is snatched from his place
[in the garden],
Then his place will forget him,
saying, 'I have never seen you.'
¹⁹"Behold, this is the joy of His way;
And from out of the dust others
will spring up *and* grow [to take
his place].
²⁰"Behold, God will not reject a *man
of* integrity,
Nor will He strengthen *or* support
evildoers.
²¹"He will yet fill your mouth with
laughter
And your lips with joyful shouting
[if you are found blameless].

22 "Those who hate you will be
    clothed with shame,
And the tents of the wicked will be
    no longer."

9 THEN JOB answered and said,

2 "Yes, I know it is true.
But how can a mortal man be right
    before God?
3 "If one should want to contend *or*
    dispute with Him,
He could not answer Him once in a
    thousand *times*.
4 "*God* is wise in heart and mighty in
    strength;
Who has [ever] defied *or*
    challenged Him and remained
    unharmed?
5 "*It is God* who removes the
    mountains, and they do not
    know it,
When He overturns them in His
    anger;
6 Who shakes the earth out of its
    place,
And its pillars tremble;
7 Who commands the sun, and it
    does not shine;
Who seals up the stars [from
    view];
8 Who alone stretches out the
    heavens
And tramples down the waves of
    the sea;
9 Who made [the constellations] the
    Bear, Orion, and the Pleiades,
And the [vast starry] spaces of the
    south;
10 Who does great things, [beyond
    understanding,] unfathomable,
Yes, marvelous *and* wondrous
    things without number.
11 "Behold, He passes by me, and I do
    not see Him;
He moves past me, but I do not
    perceive Him.
12 "Behold, He snatches away; who
    can restrain *or* turn Him back?

Who will say to Him, 'What are
    You doing?'
13 "God will not turn back His anger;
The [proud] helpers of Rahab [the
    arrogant monster of the sea] bow
    under Him.
14 "How can I answer Him [and plead
    my case],
Choosing my words [to reason]
    with Him?
15 For though I were righteous, I
    could not answer.
I must appeal for mercy to my
    Opponent *and* Judge.
16 "If I called and He answered me,
I could not believe that He was
    listening to my voice.
17 "For He bruises me with a tempest
And multiplies my wounds without
    cause.
18 "He will not allow me to catch my
    breath,
But fills *and* saturates me with
    bitterness.
19 "If it is a matter of strength *and*
    power, behold, *He is* mighty!
And if of justice, who can summon
    and challenge Him?
20 "Though I am innocent *and* in
    the right, my own mouth would
    pronounce me guilty;
Though I am blameless, He would
    denounce me as guilty.
21 "[Though] I am blameless,
I do not care about myself;
I despise my life.
22 "It is *all* one; therefore I say,
'He destroys [both] the blameless
    and the wicked.'
23 "When [His] scourge kills
    suddenly,
He mocks at the despair of the
    innocent.
24 "The earth is given into the hands
    of the wicked;
He covers the faces of its judges
    [so that they are blind to justice].

If it is not He, then who is it
[that is responsible for all this
injustice]?
25 "Now my days are swifter than a
runner;
They vanish, they see no good.
26 "They pass by like the [swift] boats
made of reeds,
Like an eagle that swoops down on
its prey.
27 "If I say, 'I will forget my
complaint,
I will leave off my sad appearance,
and be cheerful and brighten up,'
28 I am afraid of all my pains and
worries [yet to come];
I know that You will not acquit me
and leave me unpunished.
29 "I am accounted wicked and held
guilty;
Why then should I labor in vain [to
appear innocent]?
30 "If I were to wash myself with
snow
And cleanse my hands with lye,
31 You would still plunge me into the
pit,
And my own clothes would hate
me [and refuse to cover my foul
body].
32 "For God is not a [mere] man, as I
am, that I may answer Him,
That we may go to court and
judgment together.
33 "There is no arbitrator between us,

putting the Word to work

In the midst of his trials and difficulties, Job felt as though there was no
one to come to his aid or defense (see
Job 9:32, 33). Have you ever felt this
way? Thankfully, you have an Advocate, Jesus Christ, the one Mediator
between God and man. Trust Him to
intercede for you.

Who could lay his hand upon us
both [would that there were].
[1 Tim 2:5]
34 "Let Him take His rod away from
me,
And let not the dread and fear of
Him terrify me.
35 "Then I would speak [my defense]
and not fear Him;
But I am not like that in myself.

10 "I AM disgusted with my
life and loathe it!
I will give free expression
to my complaint;
I will speak in the bitterness of my
soul.
2 "I will say to God, 'Do not condemn
me [and declare me guilty]!
Show me why You contend and
argue and struggle with me.
3 'Does it indeed seem right to You
to oppress,
To despise and reject the work of
Your hands,
And to look with favor on the
schemes of the wicked?
4 'Do You have eyes of flesh?
Do You see as a man sees?
5 'Are Your days as the days of a
mortal,
Are Your years as man's years,
6 That You seek my guilt
And search for my sin?
7 'Although You know that I am not
guilty or wicked,
Yet there is no one who can rescue
me from Your hand.
8 'Your hands have formed and
made me altogether.
Would You [turn around and]
destroy me?
9 'Remember now, that You have
made me as clay;
So will You turn me into dust
again?
10 'Have You not poured me out like
milk
And curdled me like cheese?

putting the Word to work

Do trials make you wonder if God really cares about you? Even in the midst of his suffering, Job knew he had to remember that it was God Who gave him life and preserved his spirit (see Job 10:12). Ask God to show you ways He is caring for you even in the midst of your difficulty, so you can be strengthened and encouraged.

11 '[You have] clothed me with skin and flesh,
And knit me together with bones and sinews.
12 'You have granted me life and lovingkindness;
And Your providence (divine care, supervision) has preserved my spirit.
13 'Yet these [present evils] You have hidden in Your heart [since my creation]:
I know that this was within You [in Your purpose and thought].
14 'If I sin, then You would take note and observe me,
And You would not acquit me of my guilt.
15 'If I am wicked, woe to me [for judgment comes]!
And if I am righteous, I dare not lift up my head.
For I am sated and filled with disgrace and the sight of my misery.
16 'Should I lift my head up, You would hunt me like a lion;
And again You would show Your marvelous power against me.
17 'You renew Your witnesses against me
And increase Your indignation and anger toward me;
Hardship after hardship is with me [attacking me time after time].

18 'Why then did You bring me out of the womb?
Would that I had perished and no eye had seen me!
19 'I should have been as though I had not existed;
[I should have been] carried from the womb to the grave.'
20 "Would He not let my few days alone,
Withdraw from me that I may have a little cheer
21 Before I go—and I shall not return—
To the land of darkness and the deep shadow [of death],
22 The [sunless] land of utter gloom as darkness itself,
[The land] of the shadow of death, without order,
And [where] it shines as [thick] darkness."

11 THEN ZOPHAR the Naamathite answered and said,

2 "Shall a multitude of words not be answered?
And should a talkative man [making such a long-winded defense] be acquitted?
3 "Should your boasts and babble silence men?
And shall you scoff and no one put you to shame?
4 "For you have said, 'My teaching (doctrine) [that God knowingly afflicts the righteous] is pure,
And I am innocent in your eyes.' [Job 10:7]
5 "But oh, that God would speak,
And open His lips [to speak] against you,
6 And [that He would] show you the secrets of wisdom!
For sound wisdom has two sides.
Know therefore that God forgets a part of your wickedness and guilt.

7 "Can you discover the depths of
  God?
  Can you [by searching] discover
  the limits of the Almighty
  [ascend to His heights, extend to
  His widths, and comprehend His
  infinite perfection]?
8 "*His wisdom* is as high as the
  heights of heaven. What can you
  do?
  It is deeper than Sheol (the nether
  world, the place of the dead).
  What can you know?
9 "It is longer in measure [and
  scope] than the earth,
  And broader than the sea.
10 "If God passes by or arrests,
  Or calls an assembly [of judgment],
  who can restrain Him?
  [If He is against a man, who can
  call Him to account for it?]
11 "For He recognizes *and* knows
  false *and* worthless men,
  And He sees wickedness, will He
  not consider it?
12 "But a hollow (empty-headed) man
  will become intelligent *and* wise
  [Only] when the colt of a wild
  donkey is born as a man.

13 "If you direct your heart [on the
  right path]
  And stretch out your hands to
  Him,
14 If sin is in your hand, put it far
  away [from you],
  And do not let wrongdoing dwell
  in your tents;
15 Then, indeed, you could lift up
  your face [to Him] without *moral*
  defect,
  And you would be firmly
  established *and* secure and not
  fear.
16 "For you would forget your trouble;
  You would remember it as waters
  that have passed by.
17 "And your life would be brighter
  than the noonday;

Darkness [then] would be like the
  morning.
18 "Then you would trust [with
  confidence], because there is
  hope;
  You would look around you and
  rest securely.
19 "You would lie down with no one
  to frighten you,
  And many would entreat *and* seek
  your favor.
20 "But the eyes of the wicked will
  fail,
  And they will not escape [the
  justice of God];
  And their hope is to breathe their
  last [and die]."

12 THEN JOB responded,

2 "No doubt you are the [only wise]
  people [in the world],
  And wisdom will die with you!
3 "But I have intelligence *and*
  understanding as well as you;
  I am not inferior to you.
  Who does not know such things
  as these [of God's wisdom and
  might]?
4 "I am a joke to my friends;
  I, one whom God answered when
  he called upon Him—
  A just and blameless man is a joke
  [and laughed to scorn].
5 "He who is at ease has contempt
  for misfortune,
  But misfortune is ready [and
  anxiously waiting] for those
  whose feet slip.
6 "The tents of the destroyers
  prosper;
  And those who provoke God are
  [apparently] secure,
  Whom God brings into their power.

7 "Now ask the animals, and let
  them teach you [that God does
  not deal with His creatures
  according to their character];

And ask the birds of the air, and let them tell you;
⁸Or speak to the earth [with its many forms of life], and it will teach you;
And let the fish of the sea declare [this truth] to you.
⁹"Who among all these does not recognize [in all these things that good and evil are randomly scattered throughout nature and human life]
That the hand of the LORD has done this,
¹⁰In whose hand is the life of every living thing,
And the breath of all mankind?
¹¹"Does the ear not put words to the test,
Just as the palate tastes its food [distinguishing between the desirable and the undesirable]?
¹²"With the aged [you say] is wisdom,
And with long life is understanding.
¹³"But [only] with Him are [perfect] wisdom and might;
He [alone] has [true] counsel and understanding.
¹⁴"Behold, He tears down, and it cannot be rebuilt;
He imprisons a man, and there can be no release.
¹⁵"Behold, He restrains the waters, and they dry up;
Again, He sends the waters out, and they overwhelm and devastate the earth.

¹⁶"With Him are might and sound wisdom,
The misled and the misleader are His [and in His power].
¹⁷"He makes [great and scheming] counselors walk barefoot
And makes fools of judges.
¹⁸"He loosens the bond of kings
And binds their loins with a loincloth.
¹⁹"He makes priests walk barefoot,
And He overturns men firmly seated and secure.
²⁰"He deprives the trusted ones of speech
And takes away the discernment and discretion of the aged.
²¹"He pours contempt on princes and nobles
And loosens the belt of the strong [disabling them].
²²"He uncovers mysteries [that are difficult to grasp and understand] out of the darkness
And brings black gloom and the shadow of death into light.
²³"He makes nations great, and He destroys them;
He enlarges nations, and leads them away [captive].
²⁴"He removes intelligence and understanding from the leaders of the people of the earth
And makes them wander and move blindly in a pathless waste.
²⁵"They grope in darkness without light,
And He makes them stagger like a drunken man."

speak the Word

Thank You, God, that my life is in Your hand.
—ADAPTED FROM JOB 12:10

God, I declare that perfect wisdom and might are found only in You, and You alone can give me counsel and understanding.
—ADAPTED FROM JOB 12:13

13

[JOB CONTINUED:]
"Behold, my eye has seen all *this*,
My ear has heard and understood it.
2 "What you know I also know;
I am not inferior to you.
3 "But I wish to speak to the Almighty,
And I desire to argue with God.
4 "But you smear me with lies [you defame my character most untruthfully];
You are all worthless physicians *and* have no remedy to offer.
5 "Oh, that you would be completely silent,
And that *silence* would be your wisdom!
6 "Please hear my argument
And listen to the pleadings of my lips.
7 "Will you speak what is unjust for God,
And speak what is deceitful for Him?
8 "Will you show partiality for Him [and be unjust to me so that you may gain favor with Him]?
Will you contend *and* plead for God?
9 "Will it be well for you when He investigates you [and your tactics against me]?
Or will you deceive Him as one deceives a man?
10 "He will surely reprimand you
If you secretly show partiality.
11 "Will not His majesty terrify you,
And will not the dread of Him fall upon you?
12 "Your memorable sayings are [worthless, merely] proverbs of ashes;

Your defenses are defenses of [crumbling] clay.
13 "Be silent before me so that I may speak;
And let happen to me what may.
14 "Why should I take my flesh in my teeth
And put my life in my hands [incurring the wrath of God]?
15 "Even though He kills me;
I will hope in Him.
Nevertheless, I will argue my ways to His face.
16 "This also will be my salvation,
For a godless man may not come before Him.
17 "Listen diligently to my speech,
And let my declaration fill your ears.
18 "Behold now, I have prepared my case;
I know that I will be vindicated.
19 "Who will argue *and* contend with me?
For then I would be silent and die.
20 "Only [O Lord,] do not do two things to me,
And then I will not hide myself from Your face:
21 Withdraw Your hand from me *and* remove this bodily suffering,
And let not the dread of You terrify me.
22 "Then [Lord,] call, and I will answer;
Or let me speak, and then reply to me.
23 "How many are my iniquities and sins [that so much sorrow should come to me]?
Make me recognize *and* understand my transgression and my sin. [Rom 8:1]

speak the Word

God, in the midst of suffering that threatens to defeat me, I will hope in You.
—ADAPTED FROM JOB 13:15

24 "Why do You hide Your face [as if
   offended]
   And consider me Your enemy?
25 "Will You cause a windblown leaf
   to tremble?
   Will You pursue the chaff of the
   dry stubble?
26 "For You write bitter things against
   me [in Your indictment]
   And make me inherit *and* suffer
   for the iniquities of my youth.
27 "You also put my feet in the stocks
   [as punishment]
   And [critically] observe all my
   paths;
   You set a circle *and* limit around
   the soles of my feet [which I must
   not overstep],
28 While I waste away like a rotten
   thing,
   Like a garment that is moth-eaten.

14 "MAN, WHO is born of a
   woman,
   Is short-lived and full of
   turmoil.
2 "Like a flower he comes forth and
   withers;
   He also flees like a shadow and
   does not remain.
3 "You also open Your eyes upon him
   And bring him into judgment with
   Yourself.
4 "Who can make a clean thing out
   of the unclean?
   No one! [Is 1:18; 1 John 1:7]
5 "Since his days are determined,
   The number of his months is with
   You [in Your control],
   And You have made his limits
   so he cannot pass [his allotted
   time].
6 "[O God] turn your gaze from him
   so that he may rest,
   Until he fulfills his day [on earth]
   like a hired man.
7 "For there is hope for a tree,
   If it is cut down, that it will sprout
   again,

And that the shoots of it will not
   cease *nor* fail, [but there is no
   such hope for man].
8 "Though its roots grow old in the
   earth
   And its stump dies in the dry soil,
9 Yet at the scent of water [the stump
   of the tree] will flourish
   And bring forth sprigs *and* shoots
   like a seedling.
10 "But [the brave, strong] man must
   die and lie face down;
   Man breathes his last, and where
   is he?
11 "As water evaporates from the sea,
   And a river drains and dries up,
12 So man lies down and does not
   rise [again].
   Until the heavens are no longer,
   The dead will not awake nor be
   raised from their sleep.

13 "Oh, that You would hide me in
   Sheol (the nether world, the
   place of the dead),
   That You would conceal me until
   Your wrath is past,
   That You would set a definite time
   and then remember me [and in
   Your lovingkindness imprint me
   on your heart]!
14 "If a man dies, will he live again?
   I will wait all the days of my
   struggle
   Until my change *and* release will
   come. [John 5:25; 6:40; 1 Thess
   4:16]
15 "[Then] You will call, and I will
   answer You;
   You will long for [me] the work of
   Your hands.
16 "But now You number [each of] my
   steps;
   You do not observe *nor* take note of
   my sin.
17 "My transgression is sealed up in a
   bag,
   And You cover my wickedness
   [from Your view].

¹⁸"But as a mountain, if it falls,
      crumbles into nothing,
  And as the rock is moved from its
      place,
¹⁹Water wears away the stones,
  Its floods *and* torrents wash away
      the soil of the earth,
  So You [O Lord] destroy the hope
      of man.
²⁰"You prevail forever against him
      and overpower him, and he
      passes on;
  You change his appearance
      and send him away [from the
      presence of the living].
²¹"His sons achieve honor, and he
      does not know it;
  They become insignificant, and he
      is not aware of it.
²²"But his body [lamenting its decay]
      grieves in pain over it,
  And his soul mourns over [the loss
      of] himself."

15 THEN ELIPHAZ the
      Temanite answered [Job]
      and said,

² "Should a wise man [such as
      you] utter such windy *and* vain
      knowledge [as we have just
      heard]
  And fill himself with the east wind
      [of withering, parching, and
      violent accusations]?
³ "Should he rebuke *and* argue with
      useless talk?
  Or with words in which there is no
      benefit?
⁴ "Indeed, you are doing away with
      fear,
  And you are diminishing
      meditation before God.
⁵ "For your guilt teaches your mouth,
  And you choose [to speak] the
      language of the crafty *and*
      cunning.
⁶ "Your own mouth condemns you,
      and not I;

  Yes, your own lips testify against
      you.
⁷ "Were you the first man to be born
      [the original wise man],
  Or were you created before the
      hills?
⁸ "Do you hear the secret counsel of
      God,
  And do you limit [the possession
      of] wisdom to yourself?
⁹ "What do you know that we do not
      know?
  What do you understand that is not
      equally clear to us?
¹⁰"Among us are both the gray-
      haired and the aged,
  Older than your father.
¹¹"Are the consolations of God [as
      we have interpreted them to you]
      too trivial for you,
  [Or] were we too gentle toward
      you [in our first speech] to be
      effective?
¹²"Why does your heart carry
      you away [allowing you to be
      controlled by emotion]?
  And why do your eyes flash [in
      anger or contempt],
¹³That you should turn your spirit
      against God
  And let *such* words [as you have
      spoken] go out of your mouth?
¹⁴"What is man, that he should be
      pure *and* clean,
  Or he who is born of a woman, that
      he should be righteous *and* just?
¹⁵"Behold, God puts no trust in His
      holy ones (angels);
  Indeed, the heavens are not pure
      in His sight—
¹⁶How much less [pure and clean
      is] the one who is repulsive and
      corrupt,
  Man, who drinks unrighteousness
      and injustice like water!

¹⁷"I will tell you, listen to me;
  And what I have seen I will also
      declare;
¹⁸What wise men have [freely] told,

And have not hidden [anything passed on to them] from their fathers,

¹⁹ To whom alone the land was given, And no stranger passed among them [corrupting the truth].

²⁰ "The wicked man writhes with pain all his days, And numbered are the years stored up for him, the ruthless one.

²¹ "A [dreadful] sound of terrors is in his ears; While at peace *and* in a time of prosperity the destroyer comes upon him [the tent of the robber is not at peace].

²² "He does not believe that he will return out of the darkness [for fear of being murdered], And he is destined for the sword [of God's vengeance].

²³ "He wanders about for food, saying, 'Where is it?' He knows that the day of darkness *and* destruction is already at hand.

²⁴ "Distress and anxiety terrify him, They overpower him like a king ready for battle.

²⁵ "Because he has stretched out his hand against God And behaves arrogantly against the Almighty,

²⁶ Running *and* charging headlong against Him With his ornamented *and* massive shield;

²⁷ For he has covered his face with his fat, Adding layers of fat to his thighs [giving himself up to pleasures],

²⁸ And he has lived in desolate [God-forsaken] cities, In houses which no one should inhabit, Which were destined to become heaps [of ruins];

²⁹ He will not become rich, nor will his wealth endure;

And his grain will not bend to the earth *nor* his possessions be extended on the earth.

³⁰ "He will not escape from darkness [fleeing disaster]; The flame [of God's wrath] will wither his branch, And by the blast of His mouth he will go away.

³¹ "Let him not trust in vanity (emptiness, futility) and be led astray; For emptiness will be his reward [for such living].

³² "It will be fulfilled while he still lives, And his branch will not be green [but shall wither away].

³³ "He will fail to bring his grapes to maturity [leaving them to wither unnourished] on the vine, And will cast off blossoms [and fail to bring forth fruit] like the olive tree.

³⁴ "For the company of the godless is barren, And fire consumes the tents of bribery (wrong and injustice).

³⁵ "They conceive mischief and bring forth wickedness, And their inmost soul prepares deceit *and* fraud."

16

THEN JOB answered and said,

² "I have heard many such things; Wearisome *and* miserable comforters are you all.

³ "Is there no end to [your futile] words of wind? Or what plagues you [so much] that you [so boldly] answer [me like this]?

⁴ "I also could speak like you, If you were in my place; I could compose *and* join words together against you And shake my head at you.

⁵"[But instead] I could strengthen
  and encourage you with [the
  words of] my mouth,
And the consolation *and* solace
  of my lips would soothe your
  suffering *and* lessen your
  anguish.
⁶"If I speak [to you miserable
  comforters], my pain is not
  relieved;
And if I refrain [from speaking],
  what [pain or anguish] leaves me?
⁷"But now God has exhausted me.
You [O Lord] have destroyed all
  my family *and* my household.
⁸"You have taken a firm hold on me
  and have shriveled me up,
It has become a witness [against
  me];
And my leanness [and infirmity]
  rises up [as evidence] against me,
It testifies to my face [about my
  guilt].
⁹"His wrath has torn me and hunted
  me down,
He has gnashed at me with his
  teeth;
My adversary sharpens His gaze
  and glares [with piercing eyes]
  at me.
¹⁰"They have gaped at me with their
  mouths,
With contempt they have struck
  me on the cheek;
They massed themselves together
  [and conspired] against me. [Ps
  22:13; 35:21]
¹¹"God hands me over to criminals
And tosses me [headlong] into the
  hands of the wicked.
¹²"I was [living] at ease, but He
  crushed me *and* broke me apart,
And He has seized me by the neck
  and has shaken me to pieces;
He has also set me up as His target.
¹³"His arrows surround me.
He pierces my kidneys (vital
  organs) without mercy;
He pours out my gall on the ground.

¹⁴"He attacks me, making wound
  after wound;
He runs at me like a warrior.
¹⁵"I have sewed sackcloth over my
  skin [as a sign of mourning]
And have defiled my horn (symbol
  of strength) in the dust.
¹⁶"My face is red *and* swollen with
  weeping,
And on my eyelids is the shadow
  of death [my eyes are dimmed],
¹⁷Although there is no violence *or*
  wrongdoing in my hands,
And my prayer is pure.

¹⁸"O earth, do not cover my blood,
And let there be no [resting] place
  for my cry [where it will cease
  being heard].
¹⁹"Even now, behold, my Witness is
  in heaven,
And my Advocate [who vouches
  and testifies for me] is on high.
  [Rom 1:9]
²⁰"My friends are scoffers [who
  ridicule];
My eye pours out tears to God.
²¹"Oh, that a man would mediate *and*
  plead with God [for me]
Just as a man [mediates and
  pleads] with his neighbor *and*
  friend. [1 Tim 2:5]
²²"For when a few years are past,
I shall go the way of no return.

17 "MY SPIRIT is broken, my
  days are extinguished,
  The grave is *ready* for me.
²"Surely there are mockers *and*
  mockery with me,
And my eye gazes on their
  obstinacy *and* provocation.

³"Give me a pledge (guarantee,
  promise) with Yourself
  [acknowledge my innocence
  before my death];
Who is there that will be my
  guarantor *and* give security for
  me?

⁴"But You [Lord] have closed their
   hearts to understanding,
Therefore You will not exalt them
   [by giving a verdict against me].
⁵"He who denounces *and* informs
   against his friends for a share *of
   the spoil,*
The eyes of his children will also
   languish *and* fail.

⁶"But He has made me a byword
   and mockery among the people,
And I have become one in whose
   face people spit.
⁷"My eye has grown dim
   (unexpressive) because of grief,
And all my [body's] members are
   [wasted away] like a shadow.
⁸"The upright will be [astonished
   and] appalled at this,
And the innocent will stir himself
   up against the godless *and*
   polluted.
⁹"Nevertheless the righteous will
   hold to his ways,
And he who has clean hands will
   grow stronger and stronger. [Ps
   24:4]
¹⁰"But as for all of you, come back
   again,
Even though I do not find a wise
   man among you.
¹¹"My days are past, my purposes
   and plans are frustrated *and* torn
   apart;
The wishes of my heart [are
   broken].
¹²"These [thoughts try to] make the
   night into the day;
'The light is near,' *they say* in the
   presence of darkness [but they
   pervert the truth].
¹³"But if I look to Sheol (the nether
   world, the place of the dead) as
   my home,
If I make my bed in the darkness,
¹⁴If I call out to the pit (grave), 'You
   are my father';

And to the worm [that feeds on
   decay], 'You are my mother and
   my sister [because I will soon be
   closest to you],'
¹⁵Where now is my hope?
And who regards *or* considers *or* is
   even concerned about my hope?
¹⁶"Will my hope go down with me
   to Sheol (the nether world, the
   place of the dead)?
Shall we go down together in the
   dust?"

18 THEN BILDAD the Shuhite
   answered and said,

²"How long will you hunt for words
   and continue these speeches?
Do some clear thinking *and* show
   understanding and then we can
   talk.
³"Why are we regarded as beasts,
As if [we are] stupid (senseless) in
   your eyes?
⁴"You who tear yourself apart in
   anger,
Is the earth to be abandoned for
   your sake,
Or the rock to be moved out of its
   place?

⁵"Indeed, the light of the wicked
   will be put out,
And the flame of his fire will not
   shine. [Prov 13:9; 24:20]
⁶"The light will be dark in his tent,
And his lamp beside him will be
   put out. [Ps 18:28]
⁷"The vigorous stride will be
   shortened,
And his own counsel *and* the
   scheme [in which he trusted]
   will bring his downfall.
⁸"For the wicked is thrown into a
   net by his own feet (wickedness),
And he steps on the webbing [of
   the lattice-covered pit].
⁹"A snare catches him by the heel,
And a trap snaps shut on him.

faith over feelings

Job endured many tests and trials, but his patience and faith triumphed in the end, as we will see in chapter 42. God tests us too. One way He does so is by allowing us to go through dry times—times when nothing seems to minister to us or water our souls. We go to church, but we feel no different when we leave. We read the latest book or listen to the latest song, but it does us no good at all.

I have had those times in my life and ministry, and Job certainly had them—in what seems like extreme measure (see Job 19:7–11)! I have gone through mountaintop experiences, and I have been through valleys. I have had dry times in my prayer life and in my praise and worship. I have had times when I would go into a meeting or conference and be able to feel the presence of God, and I have had times when I would go and feel absolutely nothing. I have learned to believe that God is with me whether I feel it or not. There have also been times when I could hear from God so clearly and know that I had heard "a word in season" for me. There have been other times when I have not heard anything at all.

Looking back on my spiritual life, I realize that at times I have gone up and down, up and down. When I was up I felt that I was saved, and when I was down I felt that I was lost. When I felt sure God had called me, I was up, and when I was uncertain of my calling, I was down. When dry times came upon me, I let them affect me. At the time I did not know what was happening to me or why. Now I realize that God was working all the harmful things out of me and getting me to the point where I did not base my faith on my feelings.

I rarely go through those times now. I just love God, and that's it. I worship Him, and that's it. I pray, I believe He hears me, and that's it. I know I am called, and I go out and do what I am called to do, and I do not go through all the ups and downs I used to go through. Why? Because I have learned to stop basing things on my feelings and to live by faith instead. I do not allow my emotions to determine whether I believe God is with me or not. I just choose to believe He is. That does not mean I never experience a rough time or have a bad day, but those times no longer control what I believe.

I do not believe God can allow us to go from one emotional high to another. If He did, we would depend too much on them and would probably start thinking more highly of ourselves than we should. God loves us and protects us from depending on emotions too much so He can continue to use us.

We must learn to trust that God knows what He is doing in us. If we feel something in our emotions, that is fine. If we do not feel anything, that is fine too. We are in this life for the long haul—not just for those times when we feel good, but also for those times when we feel bad or do not feel anything at all. Be patient and stay faithful. God will come through for you, and you will be amazed!

10 "A noose is hidden for him on the ground,
And a trap for him on the path.
11 "Terrors frighten him on every side
And chase at his heels.
12 "The strength [of the wicked] is famished *and* weakened,
And disaster is ready at his side [if he stops].
13 "His skin is devoured by disease;
The firstborn of death [the worst of diseases] consumes his limbs.
14 "He is torn from his tent which he trusted [for safety],
And he is marched *and* brought to the king of terrors (death).
15 "Nothing of his dwells in his tent;
Brimstone (burning sulfur) is scattered over his dwelling [to purify it].
16 "The roots [of the wicked] are dried up below,
And above, his branch is cut off *and* withers.
17 "Memory of him perishes from the earth,
And he has no name on the street.
18 "He is driven *and* propelled from light into darkness,
And chased from the inhabited world.
19 "He has no offspring or prosperity among his people,
Nor any survivor where he sojourned.
20 "Those in the west are astonished *and* appalled at his fate,
And those in the east are seized with horror.
21 "Surely such are the dwellings of the wicked *and* the ungodly,
And such is the place of him who does not know *or* recognize *or* honor God."

19 THEN JOB answered and said,

2 "How long will you torment *and* exasperate me
And crush me with words?

3 "These ten times you have insulted me;
You are not ashamed to wrong me [and harden your hearts against me].
4 "And if it were true that I have erred,
My error would remain with me [and I would be conscious of it].
5 "If indeed you [braggarts] vaunt *and* magnify yourselves over me
And prove my disgrace (humiliation) to me,
6 Know then that God has wronged me *and* overthrown me
And has closed His net around me.

7 "Behold, I cry out, 'Violence!' but I am not heard;
I shout for help, but there is no justice.
8 "He has walled up my way so that I cannot pass,
And He has set darkness upon my paths.
9 "He has stripped me of my honor
And removed the crown from my head.
10 "He breaks me down on every side, and I am gone;
He has uprooted my hope like a tree.
11 "He has also kindled His wrath [like a fire] against me
And He considers *and* counts me as one of His adversaries.
12 "His troops come together
And build up their way *and* siege works against me
And camp around my tent.

13 "He has put my brothers far from me,
And my acquaintances are completely estranged from me.
14 "My relatives have failed [me],
And my intimate friends have forgotten me.
15 "Those who live [temporarily] in my house and my maids consider me a stranger;
I am a foreigner in their sight.

16"I call to my servant, but he does
   not answer;
   I have to implore him with words.
17"My breath is repulsive to my wife,
   And I am loathsome to my own
   brothers.
18"Even young children despise me;
   When I get up, they speak
   against me.
19"All the men of my council hate
   me;
   Those I love have turned
   against me.
20"My bone clings to my skin and to
   my flesh,
   And I have escaped [death] by the
   skin of my teeth.
21"Have pity on me! Have pity on
   me, O you my friends,
   For the hand of God has
   touched me.
22"Why do you persecute me as God
   does?
   Why are you not satisfied with my
   flesh (anguish)?
23"Oh, that the words I now speak
   were written!
   Oh, that they were recorded in a
   scroll!
24"That with an iron stylus and
   [molten] lead
   They were engraved in the rock
   forever!
25"For I know that my Redeemer and
   Vindicator lives,

putting the Word to work

Are you facing great difficulty and
feeling abandoned by all who care
for you? Job certainly did. Like Job,
realize that your Redeemer lives and
that He will never fail nor forsake you
(see Job 19:25). Ask God to surround
you with His presence and to give you
His peace.

life point

God is our Vindicator (see Job 19:25). As
long as we behave properly toward others—even when they come against us or
do not understand us—God will reward
us for being steadfast toward Him.

   And at the last He will take His
   stand upon the earth. [Is 44:6;
   48:12]
26"Even after my [mortal] skin is
   destroyed [by death],
   Yet from my [immortal] flesh I will
   see God,
27Whom I, even I, will see for
   myself,
   And my eyes will see Him and not
   another!
   My heart faints within me.
28"If you say, 'How shall we
   [continue to] persecute him?'
   And 'What pretext for a case
   against him can we find [since
   we claim the root of these
   afflictions is found in him]?'
29"Then beware and be afraid of the
   sword [of divine vengeance] for
   yourselves,
   For wrathful are the punishments
   of that sword,
   So that you may know there is
   judgment."

20 THEN ZOPHAR the
   Naamathite answered and
   said,
2 "Therefore my disquieting
   thoughts make me answer,
   Because of the uneasiness that is
   within me.
3"I have heard the reproof which
   insults me,
   But the spirit of my understanding
   makes me answer.
4"Do you not know this from the old
   days,

Since the time that man was
   placed on the earth,
5 That the triumphing of the wicked
   is short,
And the joy of the godless is only
   for a moment? [Ps 37:35, 36]
6 "Though his pride reaches the
   heavens
And his head touches the clouds,
7 Yet he perishes forever like his
   own refuse;
Those who have seen him will say,
   'Where is he?'
8 "He flies away like a dream and
   cannot be found;
Yes, he is chased away like a vision
   of the night.
9 "The eye which saw him sees him
   no longer,
Neither does his [accustomed]
   place behold him any longer.
10 "His sons favor the poor [and pay
   his obligations],
And his hands give back his [ill-
   gotten] wealth.
11 "His bones are full of youthful
   strength
But it lies down with him in the
   dust.
12 "Though evil and wickedness are
   sweet in his mouth
And he hides it under his tongue,
13 Though he desires it and will not
   let it go
But holds it in his mouth,
14 Yet his food turns [to poison] in his
   stomach;
It is the venom of vipers within
   him.
15 "He swallows [his ill-gotten]
   riches,
But will vomit them up;
God will drive them out of his
   belly.
16 "He sucks the poison of vipers
   [which ill-gotten wealth
   contains];
The viper's tongue slays him.
17 "He does not look at the rivers,

The flowing streams of honey and
   butter [to enjoy his wealth].
18 "He gives back what he has
   labored for and attained
And cannot swallow it [down to
   enjoy it];
As to the riches of his labor,
He cannot even enjoy them.
19 "For he has oppressed and
   neglected the poor;
He has violently taken away
   houses which he did not build.
20 "Because he knew no quietness or
   calm within him [because of his
   greed],
He does not retain anything he
   desires.
21 "There is nothing left of what he
   devoured;
Therefore his prosperity does not
   endure.
22 "In the fullness of his excess (great
   abundance) he will be in trouble;
The hand of everyone who suffers
   will come against him [he is
   miserable on every side].
23 "When he fills his belly,
God will send His fierce anger on
   him
And will rain it upon him while he
   is eating. [Num 11:33; Ps 78:26–
   31]
24 "He may flee from the iron
   weapon,
But the bow of bronze will pierce
   him through.
25 "The arrow is drawn forth and
   it comes out of his back [after
   passing through his body];
Yes, the glittering point comes out
   of his gall.
Terrors march in upon him;
26 Complete darkness (misfortune) is
   held in reserve for his treasures.
An unfanned fire will devour him;
It will consume the survivor in his
   tent.
27 "The heavens will reveal his
   wickedness and guilt,

And the earth will rise up against
  him.
28 "The produce and increase of
  his house will depart [with the
  victors];
His possessions will be dragged
  away in the day of God's wrath.
29 "This is the wicked man's portion
  from God,
And the heritage decreed and
  appointed to him by God."

21

THEN JOB answered and
said,

2 "Listen carefully to my speech,
And let this be the consolation.
3 "Bear with me, and I also will
  speak;
And after I have spoken, you may
  [continue to] mock [me].
4 "As for me, is my complaint to man
  or about him?
And why should I not be impatient
  and my spirit troubled?
5 "Look at me and be astonished *and*
  appalled;
And put your hand over your
  mouth.
6 "Even when I remember, I am
  troubled *and* afraid;
Horror *and* trembling take hold of
  my flesh.
7 "Why do the wicked *still* live,
Become old, and become mighty in
  power?
8 "Their children *and* descendants
  are established with them in
  their sight,
And their offspring before their
  eyes.
9 "Their houses are safe from fear;
And the rod of God is not on them.
10 "His bull breeds and does not fail;
His cow calves and does not
  miscarry.
11 "They send forth their little ones
  like a flock,
And their children skip about.

12 "They lift up their voices *and* sing
  to the tambourine and the lyre
And rejoice to the sound of the
  flute.
13 "They fully enjoy their days in
  prosperity,
And so go down to Sheol (the
  nether world, the place of the
  dead) in a [peaceful] moment.
14 "Yet they say to God, 'Depart from
  us,
For we do not desire the
  knowledge of Your ways.
15 'Who [and what] is the Almighty,
  that we should serve Him?
And what would we gain if we
  plead with Him?' [Ex 5:2]
16 "*But* notice, the prosperity *of the
  wicked* is not in their hand (in
  their power);
The counsel of the wicked [and
  the mystery of God's dealings
  with the ungodly] is far from my
  comprehension.

17 "How often [then] is it that the
  lamp of the wicked is put out,
And that their disaster falls on
  them?
Does God distribute pain *and*
  destruction *and* sorrow [to them]
  in His anger? [Luke 12:46]
18 "Are they like straw before the
  wind,
And like chaff that the storm
  steals *and* carries away?
19 "*You say,* 'God stores away
  [the punishment of] man's
  wickedness for his children.'
Let God repay him so that he may
  know *and* experience it.
20 "Let his own eyes see his
  destruction,
And let him drink of the wrath of
  the Almighty.
21 "For what pleasure does he have in
  his house *and* family after he is
  dead,

When the number of his months [of life] is cut off?

22 "Can anyone teach God knowledge, Seeing that He judges those on high? [Rom 11:34; 1 Cor 2:16]

23 "One dies in his full strength, Being wholly at ease and quiet *and* satisfied;

24 His pails are full of milk [his sides are filled out with fat], And the marrow of his bones is moist,

25 Whereas another dies with a bitter soul, Never even tasting pleasure *or* good fortune.

26 "Together they lie down in the dust, And the worms cover them.

27 "Behold, I know your thoughts, And the plots by which you would wrong me.

28 "For you say, 'Where is the house of the noble man? And where is the tent, the dwelling place of the wicked?'

29 "Have you not asked those who travel this way, And do you not recognize their witness?

30 "That evil men are [now] reserved for the day of disaster *and* destruction, They will be led away on the day of [God's] wrath?

31 "*But* who will confront him with his actions *and* rebuke him face to face, And who will repay him for what he has done?

32 "When he is carried to his grave, *A guard* will keep watch over his tomb.

33 "The [dirt] clods of the valley are sweet to him [and gently cover him], Moreover, all men will follow after him [to a grave],

While countless ones go before him.

34 "How then can you vainly comfort me with empty words, Since your answers remain untrue?"

22

THEN ELIPHAZ the Temanite answered and said,

2 "Can a vigorous man be of use to God, Or a wise man be useful to himself? [Ps 16:2; Luke 17:10]

3 "Is it any pleasure *or* joy to the Almighty that you are righteous? Or is it of benefit to Him that you make your ways perfect? [Is 62:3; Zech 2:8; Mal 3:17; Acts 20:28]

4 "Is it because of your fear of Him that He corrects you, That He enters into judgment against you?

5 "Is not your wickedness great, And your sins without end?

6 "For you have taken pledges of your brothers without cause, And stripped men naked.

7 "You have not given water to the weary to drink, And you have withheld bread from the hungry. [Matt 25:42]

8 "But the land is possessed by the man with power, And the favored *and* honorable man dwells in it.

9 "You have sent widows away empty-handed, And the arms (strength) of the fatherless have been broken.

10 "Therefore snares surround you, And sudden dread terrifies *and* overwhelms you;

11 Or darkness, so that you cannot see, And a flood of water covers you.

12 "Is not God in the height of
      heaven?
   And behold the distant stars, how
      high they are!
13 "You say, 'What does God know
      [about me]?
   Can He judge through the thick
      darkness?
14 'Thick clouds are a hiding place
      for Him, so that He cannot see,
   And He walks on the vault (circle)
      of the heavens.'
15 "Will you keep to the ancient path
   That wicked men walked [in the
      time of Noah], [2 Pet 2:5]
16 Men who were snatched away
      before their time,
   Whose foundations were poured
      out like a river?
17 "They said to God, 'Depart from
      us!
   What can the Almighty do for us *or*
      to us?'
18 "Yet He filled their houses with
      good *things*;
   But the counsel of the wicked *and*
      ungodly is far from me.
19 "The righteous see it and are glad;
   And the innocent mock *and* laugh
      at them, *saying,*
20 'Surely our adversaries are cut off
      and destroyed,
   And fire has consumed their
      abundance.'

21 "Now yield *and* submit yourself
      to Him [agree with God and be
      conformed to His will] and be at
      peace;
   In this way [you will prosper and
      great] good will come to you.
22 "Please receive the law *and*
      instruction from His mouth
   And establish His words in your
      heart *and* keep them. [Ps 119:11]
23 "If you return to the Almighty [and
      submit and humble yourself
      before Him], you will be built up
      [and restored];

life point

There is a nugget of truth in the midst of
the accusations of Job's friend Eliphaz in
Job 22:21. It is true that when we are at
peace, good comes to us. In fact, nothing is worth anything if we do not have
peace.

Money is no good if we do not have
peace. Fame is no good if we do not have
peace. Having the most important, pres-
tigious job in the whole company is not
important if we do not have peace. How
many people will spend their lives trying
to climb the ladder of success, and every
time they go up one more rung they lose
more of their peace because of the pressure? They also lose more of their time to
spend with their family. Everything about
their lives is consumed with the stress
of trying to play the games necessary
to keep that job. They may have a great
position, but they have to worry about
keeping it all the time. Soon their health
is falling apart, and they do not have any
peace of mind. Without peace, our lives
are full of confusion and chaos, but when
we are at peace, we have a good thing
indeed!

   If you remove unrighteousness far
      from your tents,
24 And place your gold in the dust,
   And *the gold of* Ophir among the
      stones of the brooks [considering
      it of little value],
25 And make the Almighty your gold
   And your precious silver,
26 Then you will have delight in the
      Almighty,
   And you will lift up your face to
      God.
27 "You will pray to Him, and He will
      hear you,
   And you will pay your vows.

28 "You will also decide *and* decree a thing, and it will be established for you;
And the light [of God's favor] will shine upon your ways.

29 "When you are cast down *and* humbled, you will speak with confidence,
And the humble person He will lift up *and* save.

30 "He will even rescue the one [for whom you intercede] who is not innocent;
And he will be rescued through the cleanness of your hands." [Job 42:7, 8]

23

THEN JOB answered and said,

2 "Even today my complaint is contentious;
His hand is heavy despite my groaning.

3 "Oh, that I knew where I might find Him,
That I might [even] come to His seat!

4 "I would present my cause before Him
And fill my mouth with arguments.

5 "I would learn the words which He would answer,
And understand what He would say to me.

6 "Would He contend against me with His great power?
No, surely He would give attention to me. [Is 27:4, 5; 57:16]

7 "There the righteous and upright could reason with Him;

So I would be acquitted forever by my Judge.

8 "Behold, I go forward (to the east), but He is not there;
I go backward (to the west), but I cannot perceive Him;

9 To the left (north) He turns, but I cannot behold Him;
He turns to the right hand (south), but I cannot see Him.

10 "But He knows the way that I take [and He pays attention to it].
When He has tried me, I will come forth as [refined] gold [pure and luminous]. [Ps 17:3; 66:10; James 1:12]

11 "My feet have carefully followed His steps;
I have kept His ways and not turned aside.

12 "I have not departed from the commandment of His lips;
I have kept the words of His mouth more than my necessary food.

13 "But He is unique *and* unchangeable, and who can turn Him?
And *what* His soul desires, that He does.

14 "For He performs what is planned (appointed) for me,
And He is mindful of many such things.

15 "Therefore I would be terrified at His presence;
When I consider [all of this], I tremble in dread of Him.

16 "For God has made my heart faint,
And the Almighty has terrified me,

17 But I am not silenced by the darkness [of these woes that fell on me],

speak the Word

God, when I have questions, I want to know Your answers,
and I want to understand what You are saying to me.
—ADAPTED FROM JOB 23:5

Nor by the thick darkness which
covers my face.

24 "WHY DOES the Almighty
not set seasons for
judgment?
Why do those who know Him not
see His days [for punishment of
the wicked]? [Acts 1:7]
2 "Some remove the landmarks;
They [violently] seize and pasture
flocks [appropriating land and
flocks openly].
3 "They drive away the donkeys of
the orphans;
They take the widow's ox for a
pledge.

4 "They crowd the needy off the
road;
The poor of the land all hide
themselves.
5 "Behold, as wild donkeys in the
desert,
The poor go to their work,
diligently seeking food;
As bread for their children in the
desert.
6 "They harvest their fodder in a
field [that is not their own],
And glean the vineyard of the
wicked.
7 "They spend the night naked,
without clothing,
And have no covering against the
cold.

trained to trust

One of the tests we can expect to encounter in our journey with God is the "trust test." Like Job, we must learn to trust God when we do not understand what is going on in our lives.

How many times do we say to God, "What are You doing? What is happening? What is going on in my life? I don't understand this at all." At this point, many people get confused and give up or fail. They fall by the wayside and go back to something that will be quicker and easier for them.

If you are in a place right now where nothing in your life makes any sense, trust God anyway. Say to yourself, "This must be a test."

One lesson I have learned through the years is this: *There is no such thing as trusting God without unanswered questions*. If we have all the answers to all the questions, we have no need to trust because we already know everything.

As long as God is training us to trust, there will always be things in our lives we simply do not understand. That is why we have to learn to say, "God, I don't understand, but I trust You."

Sometimes I start to get frustrated and feel like saying, "Tell me something, Lord." But I have learned that if He does not tell me anything, I need to stay busy doing the last thing He told me to do, whatever it was, and just keep trusting Him. It may be five years before He gives me another direction. If He speaks something different to me, then I will do it. But until He does, I will just go on doing what He has already told me to do.

Without trusting God, life is miserable. So we, like Job, must learn to trust God when we do not understand and when heaven is silent.

8"They are wet from the rain of the mountains
And cling to the rock for lack of shelter.
9"Others snatch the fatherless [infants] from the breast [to sell or make them slaves],
And against the poor they take a pledge [of clothing].
10"They cause the poor to go about naked without clothing,
And they take away the sheaves [of grain] from the hungry.
11"Within the walls [of the wicked] the poor make [olive] oil;
They tread [the grapes in] the wine presses, but thirst.
12"From the [populous and crowded] city men groan,
And the souls of the wounded cry out for help;
Yet God [seemingly] does not pay attention to the wrong [done to them].

13"Others have been with those who rebel against the light;
They do not want to know its ways Nor stay in its paths.
14"The murderer rises at dawn;
He kills the poor and the needy,
And at night he becomes a thief.
15"The eye of the adulterer waits for the twilight,
Saying, 'No eye will see me,'
And he covers his face.
16"In the dark they dig into [the penetrable walls of] houses;
They shut themselves up by day;
They do not know the light [of day].
17"For the morning is the same to him as the thick darkness [of midnight];
For he is familiar with the terrors of thick darkness.
18"They are insignificant on the surface of the water;
Their portion is cursed on the earth;

They do not turn toward the vineyards.
19"Drought and heat consume the snow waters;
So does Sheol (the nether world, the place of the dead) [consume] those who have sinned.
20"A mother will forget him;
The worm feeds on him until he is no longer remembered.
And wickedness will be broken like a tree [which cannot be restored]. [Prov 10:7]
21"He preys on the barren (childless) woman
And does no good for the widow.
22"Yet God draws away the mighty by His power;
He rises, but no one has assurance of life.
23"God gives them security, and they are supported;
And His eyes are on their ways.
24"They are exalted for a little while, and then they are gone;
Moreover, they are brought low and like everything [they are] gathered up and taken out of the way;
Even like the heads of grain they are cut off.
25"And if this is not so, who can prove me a liar
And make my speech worthless?"

25

THEN BILDAD the Shuhite answered and said,

2"Dominion and awe belong to God;
He establishes peace and order in His high places.
3"Is there any number to His [vast celestial] armies?
And upon whom does His light not rise?
4"How then can man be justified and righteous with God?

Or how can he who is born of a
   woman be pure *and* clean? [Ps
   130:3; 143:2]
5 "Behold, even the moon has no
   brightness [compared to God's
   majesty and glory]
And the stars are not pure in His
   sight,
6 How much less man, *that* maggot,
And the son of man, *that* worm!"

26 BUT JOB answered and
said,

2 "What a help you are to the weak
   (powerless)!
How you have saved the arm that
   is without strength!
3 "How you have counseled the one
   who has no wisdom!
And how abundantly you have
   provided sound wisdom *and*
   helpful insight!
4 "To whom have you uttered [these]
   words?
And whose spirit [inspired what]
   came forth from you?

5 "The spirits of the dead tremble
Underneath the waters and their
   inhabitants.
6 "Sheol (the nether world, the place
   of the dead) is naked before God,
And Abaddon (the place of
   destruction) has no covering
   [from His eyes].
7 "*It is* He *who* spreads out the north
   over emptiness
And hangs the earth on nothing.
8 "He wraps the waters in His clouds
   [which otherwise would spill on
   earth all at once],
And the cloud does not burst
   under them.
9 "He covers the face of the full moon
And spreads His cloud over it.
10 "He has inscribed a circular limit
   (the horizon) on the face of the
   waters

putting the Word to work

Do your troubles ever seem so great
that you doubt God's power to act
on your behalf? In the midst of his
trials, Job recalled the greatness of
God and recognized that he saw only
the "fringes of His ways" (Job 26:14).
Be encouraged by the knowledge
that the same God Who is powerful
enough to hang "the earth on nothing" (see Job 26:7) has promised to
act on your behalf!

At the boundary between light and
   darkness.
11 "The pillars of the heavens
   tremble
And are terrified at His rebuke.
12 "He stirred up the sea by His
   power,
And by His understanding He
   smashed [proud] Rahab.
13 "By His breath the heavens are
   cleared;
His hand has pierced the [swiftly]
   fleeing serpent. [Ps 33:6]
14 "Yet these are just the fringes of
   His ways [mere samples of His
   power],
The faintest whisper of His voice!
Who can contemplate the thunder
   of His [full] mighty power?"

27 JOB CONTINUED his discourse and said,

2 "As God lives, who has taken away
   my right *and* denied me justice,
And the Almighty, who has caused
   bitterness *and* grief for my soul,
3 As long as my life is within me,
And the breath of God is [still] in
   my nostrils,
4 My lips will not speak unjustly,
Nor will my tongue utter deceit.

5 "Far be it from me that I should
   admit you are right [in your
   accusations against me];
   Until I die, I will not remove my
   integrity from me.
6 "I hold fast my uprightness *and* my
   right standing with God and I
   will not let them go;
   My heart does not reproach me for
   any of my days.
7 "May my enemy be as the wicked,
   And he who rises up against me be
   as the unrighteous (unjust).
8 "For what is the hope of the
   godless, even though he has
   gained [in this world],
   When God takes his life?
9 "Will God hear his cry
   When trouble *and* distress come
   upon him?
10 "Will he take delight in the
    Almighty?
    Will he call on God at all times?
11 "I will teach you regarding the
    hand (power) of God;
    I will not conceal what is with
    the Almighty [God's actual
    treatment of the wicked].
12 "Behold, all of you have seen it;
    Why then do you act vainly *and*
    foolishly [cherishing worthless
    concepts]?

13 "This [which I am about to explain]
    is the portion of a wicked man
    from God,
    And the inheritance which tyrants
    and oppressors receive from the
    Almighty:
14 "Though his children are many,
    they are destined for the sword;
    And his descendants will not have
    sufficient bread.
15 "Those who survive him will be
    buried because of the plague,
    And [their] widows will not be
    able to weep.
16 "Though he heaps up silver like
    dust
    And piles up clothing like clay,

17 He may prepare it, but the just will
    wear it
    And the innocent will divide the
    silver.
18 "He builds his house like a spider's
    web,
    Like a (temporary) hut which a
    watchman makes.
19 "He lies down rich, but never will
    again;
    He opens his eyes, and it is gone.
20 "Terrors overtake him like a
    [suddenly rising] flood;
    A windstorm steals him away in the
    night.
21 "The east wind lifts him up, and he
    is gone;
    It sweeps him out of his place.
22 "For it will hurl [thunderbolts of
    God's wrath] at him unsparingly
    and without compassion;
    He flees in haste from its power.
23 "People will clap their hands at
    him [to mock and ridicule him]
    And hiss him out of his place.

28 "SURELY THERE is a
    mine for silver,
    And a place where they
    refine gold.
2 "Iron is taken out of the earth,
    And copper is smelted from the
    stone ore.
3 "*Man* puts an end to darkness [by
    bringing in a light],
    And to the farthest bounds he
    searches out
    The rock buried in gloom and deep
    shadow.
4 "He breaks open (mine) shafts far
    away from where people live,
    [In places] forgotten by the
    [human] foot;
    They dangle [in the mines] and
    hang away from men.
5 "[As for] the earth, out of it comes
    food,
    But underneath [its surface, down
    deep] it is turned over as fire.

⁶"Its stones are the bed of sapphires;
It holds dust of gold.
⁷"The path [deep within] no bird of
prey knows,
And the falcon's eye has not
caught sight of it.
⁸"The proud beasts [and their
young] have not walked on it,
Nor has the *fierce* lion passed
over it.
⁹"Man puts his hand on [and tears
apart] the flinty rock;
He overturns the mountains at the
base [looking for treasure].
¹⁰"He cuts out channels *and*
passages among the rocks;
And his eye sees every precious
thing.
¹¹"Man dams up the streams from
flowing [so that they do not
trickle into the mine],
And what is hidden he brings out
to the light.
¹²"But where can wisdom be found?
And where is the place of
understanding?
¹³"Man does not know the value of it;
Nor is it found in the land of the
living.
¹⁴"The deep says, 'It is not in me';
And the sea says, 'It is not with me.'
¹⁵"It cannot be obtained for pure
gold,
Nor can silver be weighed as its
price.
¹⁶"It cannot be valued in [terms of]
the gold of Ophir,

In the precious onyx *or* beryl, or
the sapphire.
¹⁷"Gold and glass cannot equal
wisdom,
Nor can it be exchanged for
articles of fine gold.
¹⁸"No mention of coral and crystal
can be made;
For the possession of wisdom is
even above [that of] rubies *or*
pearls.
¹⁹"The topaz of Ethiopia cannot
compare with it,
Nor can it be valued in pure gold.
²⁰"From where then does wisdom
come?
And where is the place of
understanding?
²¹"It is hidden from the eyes of all the
living
And concealed from the birds of
the heavens.
²²"Abaddon (the place of
destruction) and Death say,
'We have [only] heard a report of it
with our ears.'
²³"God understands the way [to
wisdom]
And He knows its place [for
wisdom is with God alone].
²⁴"For He looks to the ends of the
earth
And sees everything under the
heavens.
²⁵"When He gave weight *and*
pressure to the wind
And allotted the waters by
measure,
²⁶When He made a limit for the rain
And a way for the thunderbolt,
²⁷Then He saw wisdom and declared
it;
He established it and searched it
out.
²⁸"But to man He said, 'Behold, the
reverential *and* worshipful fear
of the Lord—that is wisdom;
And to depart from evil is
understanding.'"

putting the Word to work

Where do you seek wisdom? Do you
understand its value? Job knew that
the value of wisdom is far beyond any
wealth, and that wisdom is found in
fearing the Lord (see Job 28:12–28).
Ask the Lord to teach you what it
means to fear Him and to help you
grow in wisdom.

29

AND JOB again took up his discussion and said,

2 "Oh, that I were as in the months of old,
As in the days when God watched over me, [Eccl 7:10]
3 When His lamp shone upon my head
And by His light I walked through darkness;
4 As I was in the prime of my days,
When the friendship *and* counsel of God were over my tent,
5 When the Almighty was still with me
And my boys were around me,
6 When my steps [through rich pastures] were washed with butter *and* cream [from my livestock],
And the rock poured out for me streams of oil [from my olive groves].
7 "When I went out to the gate of the city,
When I took my seat [as a city father] in the square,
8 The young men saw me and hid themselves,
The aged arose *and* stood [respectfully];
9 The princes stopped talking
And put their hands on their mouths;
10 The voices of the nobles were hushed,
And their tongues stuck to the roof of their mouths.
11 "For when an ear heard [my name mentioned], it called me happy *and* fortunate;
And when an eye saw [me], it testified for me [approvingly],
12 Because I rescued the poor who cried for help,
And the orphan who had no helper.
13 "The blessing of him who was about to perish came upon me,

putting the Word to work

Do you ever struggle with the temptation to boast or brag? Ask the Lord for humility, so you will not have to learn, as Job did, that those who exalt themselves will be humbled.

And I made the widow's heart sing for joy.
14 "I put on righteousness, and it clothed me;
My justice was like a robe and a turban!
15 "I was eyes to the blind
And I was feet to the lame.
16 "I was a father to the needy;
I investigated the case I did not know [and assured justice].
17 "And I smashed the jaws of the wicked
And snatched the prey from his teeth.
18 "Then I said, 'I shall die in my nest,
And I shall multiply my days as the sand.
19 'My root is spread out *and* open to the waters,
And the dew lies all night upon my branch.
20 'My glory *and* honor are fresh in me [being constantly renewed],
And my bow gains [ever] new strength in my hand.'
21 "They listened to me and waited
And kept silent for my counsel.
22 "After I spoke, they did not speak again,
And my speech dropped upon them [like a refreshing shower].
23 "They waited for me [and for my words] as for the rain,
And they opened their mouths as for the spring rain.
24 "I smiled at them when they did not believe,

And they did not diminish the
light of my face.
25 "I chose a way for them and sat as
chief,
And dwelt as a king among his
soldiers,
As one who comforts mourners.

30 "BUT NOW those younger
than I mock *and* laugh at
me,
Whose fathers I refused to put
with the sheepdogs of my flock.
2 "Indeed, how could the strength of
their hands profit me?
Vigor had perished from them.
3 "They are gaunt with want and
famine;
They gnaw the dry *and* barren
ground by night in [the gloom
of] waste and desolation.
4 "They pluck [and eat] saltwort
(mallows) among the bushes,
And their food is the root of the
broom shrub.
5 "They are driven from the
community;
They shout after them as after a
thief.
6 "They must dwell on the slopes of
wadis
And in holes in the ground and in
rocks.
7 "Among the bushes they cry out
[like wild animals];
Beneath the prickly scrub they
gather *and* huddle together.
8 "*They are the* sons of [worthless
and nameless] fools,
They have been driven out of the
land.

9 "And now I have become [the
subject of] their taunting;
Yes, I am a byword *and* a
laughingstock to them.
10 "They hate me, they stand aloof
from me,

And do not refrain from spitting in
my face.
11 "For God has loosed His bowstring
[attacking me] and [He has]
afflicted *and* humbled me;
They have cast off the bridle [of
restraint] before me.
12 "On my right the [rabble] brood
rises;
They push my feet away, and
they build up their ways of
destruction against me [like an
advancing army].
13 "They break up *and* clutter my
path [upsetting my plans],
They profit from my destruction;
No one restrains them.
14 "As *through* a wide breach they
come,
Amid the crash [of falling walls]
they roll on [over me].
15 "Terrors are turned upon me;
They chase away my honor *and*
reputation like the wind,
And my prosperity has passed
away like a cloud.

16 "And now my soul is poured out
within me;
The days of affliction have
seized me.
17 "My bones are pierced [with
aching] in the night season,
And *the pains* that gnaw me take
no rest.
18 "By the great force [of my disease]
my garment (skin) is disfigured
and blemished;
It binds about me [choking me]
like the collar of my coat.
19 "God has cast me into the mire [a
swampland of crisis],
And I have become [worthless]
like dust and ashes.
20 "I cry to You for help, [Lord,] but
You do not answer me;
I stand up, but You [only] gaze
[indifferently] at me.
21 "You have become harsh *and* cruel
to me;

With the might of Your hand
You [keep me alive only to]
persecute me.
22 "You lift me up on the wind and
cause me to ride [upon it];
And You toss me about in the
tempest *and* dissolve me in the
storm.
23 "For I know that You will bring me
to death
And to the house of meeting
[appointed] for all the living.

24 "However, does not one falling in
a heap of ruins stretch out his
hand?
Or in his disaster [will he not]
therefore cry out for help?
25 "Did I not weep for one whose life
was hard *and* filled with trouble?
Was not my heart grieved for the
needy?
26 "When I expected good, then came
evil [to me];
And when I waited for light, then
came darkness.
27 "I am seething within *and* my
heart is troubled and cannot rest;
Days of affliction come to meet me.
28 "I go about mourning without
comfort [my skin blackened by
disease, not by the heat of the
sun];
I stand up in the assembly *and* cry
out for help.
29 "I am a brother to [howling]
jackals,
And a companion to ostriches
[which scream dismally].
30 "My skin falls from me in
blackened flakes,
And my bones are burned with
fever.
31 "Therefore my lyre (harp) is *used*
for [the sound of] mourning,
And my flute for the [sound of the]
voices of those who weep.

31

"I HAVE made a covenant
(agreement) with my eyes;
How then could I gaze
[lustfully] at a virgin?
2 "For what is the portion I would
have from God above,
And what heritage from the
Almighty on high?
3 "Does not tragedy fall [justly] on
the unjust
And disaster to those who work
wickedness?
4 "Does not God see my ways
And count all my steps?

5 "If I have walked with falsehood,
Or if my foot has chased after
deceit,
6 Oh, let Him weigh me with
accurate scales,
And let God know my integrity.
7 "If my step has turned away from
the way [of God],
Or if my heart has [covetously]
followed my eyes,
Or if any spot [of guilt] has stained
my hands,
8 Then let me plant and [let] another
eat [from the results of my labor],
And let my crops be uprooted *and*
ruined.

9 "If my heart has been enticed *and* I
was made a fool by a woman,
Or if I have [covetously] lurked
at my neighbor's door [until his
departure],
10 Let my wife grind [meal, like a
bond slave] for another [man],
And let others kneel down over her.
11 "For *adultery* is a heinous *and*
lustful crime;
Moreover, it would be a sin
punishable by the judges. [Deut
22:22; John 8:5]
12 "For it is a fire which consumes to
Abaddon (destruction, ruin, final
torment);

And [illicit passion] would burn
  and rage *and* uproot all my
  [life's] increase [destroying
  everything].
13 "If I have despised *and* rejected
  the claim of my male or female
  servants
  When they filed a complaint
  against me,
14 What then could I do when God
  arises [to judge me]?
  When He calls me to account, what
  will I answer Him? [Ps 44:21]
15 "Did not He who made me in the
  womb make my servant,
  And did not the same One fashion
  us both in the womb? [Prov
  14:31; 22:2; Mal 2:10]

16 "If I have withheld from the poor
  what *they* desired,
  Or have caused the eyes of the
  widow to look in vain [for relief],
17 Or have eaten my morsel [of food]
  alone,
  And did not share it with the
  orphan
18 (But from my youth the orphan
  grew up with me as with a father,
  And from my mother's womb I
  have been the widow's guide),
19 If I have seen anyone perish for
  lack of clothing,
  Or any poor person without
  covering,
20 If his loins have not thanked *and*
  blessed me [for clothing them],
  And if he was not warmed with the
  fleece of my sheep,
21 If I have lifted my hand against
  the orphan,
  Because I saw [that the judges
  would be] my help at the
  [council] gate,
22 Then let my shoulder fall away
  from its socket,
  And my arm be broken off at the
  elbow.

23 "For tragedy from God is a terror
  to me,
  And because of His majesty *and*
  exaltation I can do nothing [nor
  endure facing Him]. [Is 13:6; Joel
  1:15]
24 "If I have put my trust *and*
  confidence in gold,
  Or have declared fine gold my
  hope *and* assurance,
25 If I gloated *and* rejoiced because
  my wealth was great,
  And because my [powerful] hand
  [alone] had obtained so much,
26 If I beheld the sun [as an object of
  worship] when it shone
  Or the moon going in its splendor,
27 And my heart became secretly
  enticed [by them],
  And my hand threw a kiss from
  my mouth [in respect to them],
28 This also would have been [a
  heinous] sin *calling for* judgment,
  For I would have denied God
  above. [Deut 4:19; 17:2–7]

29 "Have I rejoiced at the destruction
  of the enemy [who hated me],
  Or exulted [in malicious triumph]
  when evil overtook him?
30 "No, I have not allowed my mouth
  to sin
  By cursing my enemy *and* asking
  for his life.
31 "I assure you, the men of my tent
  have said,

putting the Word to work

Have you ever been tempted to consider your wealth as a greater source
of security than God? If so, like Job,
realize that such an attitude denies
God's power and is sinful. Repent and
ask God to increase your faith in His
ability to always provide for you.

'Who can find one [in need] who
   has not been satisfied with his
   meat'?
32 "The stranger has not lodged in
   the street,
   Because I have opened my door to
   the traveler.
33 "Have I concealed my
   transgressions like Adam *or* like
   other men,
   By hiding my wickedness in my
   bosom,
34 Because I feared the great
   multitude,
   And the contempt of families
   terrified me,
   So that I kept silence *and* did not
   acknowledge my sin and did not
   go out of the door?
35 "Oh, that I had one to listen to me!
   Look, here is my signature (mark);
   Let the Almighty answer me!
   Let my adversary write out His
   indictment [and put His vague
   accusations in tangible form].
36 "Surely I would [proudly] bear it
   on my shoulder,
   And bind the scroll around my
   head like a crown.
37 "I would count out to Him the
   number of my steps [with every
   detail of my life],
   Approaching His presence as *if I
   were* a prince.
38 "For if my land has cried out
   against me,
   And its furrows weep together;
39 If I have eaten its fruits without
   paying for them,
   Or have caused its [rightful]
   owners to lose their lives,
40 Let thorns grow instead of wheat,
   And stinkweed *and* cockleburs
   instead of barley."

So the words of Job [with his friends]
are finished.

32 SO THESE three men
   ceased answering Job, because he was righteous in
his own eyes [and could not be persuaded otherwise by them].
2 But Elihu the son of Barachel the
Buzite, of the family of Ram, became
indignant. His indignation was kindled *and* burned *and* he became upset
with Job because he justified himself
rather than God [and even expressed
doubts about God's character].
3 Elihu's anger burned against Job's
three friends because they had found
no answer [and were unable to determine Job's error], and yet they had
condemned Job *and* declared him to
be in the wrong [and responsible for
his own afflictions].
4 Now Elihu had waited to speak to
Job because the others were years
older than he.
5 And when Elihu saw that there
was no answer in the mouths of these
three men, he burned with anger.
6 Then Elihu the son of Barachel the
Buzite said,

   "I am young, and you are aged;
   For that reason I was anxious and
      dared not tell you what I think.
7 "I thought age should speak,

putting the Word to work

Perhaps you have heard the saying
"With age comes wisdom." In some
cases this is true, but not always.
Have you ever dismissed someone's
counsel because they didn't seem to
be old enough or at the proper stage
of life to know what they were talking
about? It is important to recognize,
as Job's friend Elihu did, that it is the
Spirit of the Lord that gives people
understanding and wisdom
(see **Job 32:8**).

And a multitude of years should
teach wisdom.
8 "But there is [a vital force and] a
spirit [of intelligence] in man,
And the breath of the Almighty
gives them understanding. [Prov
2:6]
9 "Those [who are] abundant *in
years* may not [always] be wise,
Nor may the elders [always]
understand justice.
10 "Therefore I say, 'Listen to me;
I also will give you my opinion
[about Job's situation] *and* tell
you plainly what I think.'

11 "You see, I waited for your words,
I listened to your [wise] reasons,
While you pondered *and* searched
out what to say.
12 "I even paid close attention to
[what] you [said],
Indeed, not one of you convinced
Job [nor could you refute him],
Not one of you supplied
[satisfactory] answers to his
words.
13 "Beware if you say,
'We have found wisdom;
God thrusts Job down [justly], not
man [for God alone is dealing
with him].'
14 "Now Job has not directed his
words against me [therefore I
have no reason to be offended],
Nor will I answer him with
arguments like yours. [I speak
for truth, not for revenge.]

15 "They (Job's friends) are dismayed
and embarrassed, they no longer
answer;
The words have moved away *and*
failed them," [says Elihu].
16 "And shall I wait, because they say
nothing,
But stand still and say no more?
17 "I too will give my share of
answers;

life point

In Job 32:17–20, Job said that he was full
of words to the point of feeling as though
he would burst. But, he said, "the spirit
within me constrains me" (Job 32:18).
In the midst of everything he was going
through, Job still exercised self-control.
When you find yourself so hurt, angry, or
stressed that you feel you could burst, be
like Job and exercise self-control!

I too will express my opinion *and*
share my knowledge.
18 "For I am full of words;
The spirit within me
constrains me.
19 "My belly is like unvented wine;
Like new wineskins it is about to
burst.
20 "I must speak so that I may get
relief;
I will open my lips and answer.
21 "I will not [I warn you] be partial to
any man [that is, let my respect
for you mitigate what I say];
Nor flatter any man.
22 "For I do not know how to flatter,
[in an appropriate way, and I
fear that],
My Maker would soon take me
away.

33 "HOWEVER, JOB, please
listen to my words,
And pay attention to
everything I say.
2 "Behold, I have opened my mouth
[to begin my speech];
My tongue in my mouth is going to
speak.
3 "My words will express the
uprightness of my heart,
And my lips will speak what they
know with utter sincerity.
4 "The Spirit of God has made me,
And the breath of the Almighty
gives me life [which inspires me].

5 "Answer me, if you can;
  Set yourselves before me, take
    your stand.
6 "Behold, I belong to God like you;
  I too was formed out of the clay.
7 "Behold, I will not make you afraid
    or terrified of me [for I am only
    mortal and not God],
  Nor should any pressure from me
    weigh heavily upon you.

8 "Surely you have spoken in my
    hearing,
  And I have heard the sound of
    your words, saying:
9 'I am pure, without transgression;
  I am innocent and there is no guilt
    in me.
10 'Behold, God finds pretexts against
    me;
  He counts me as His enemy.
11 'He puts my feet in the stocks [to
    hinder and humiliate me];
  He [suspiciously] watches all my
    paths,' [you say].
12 "Look, let me answer you, in this
    you are not right or just;
  For God is greater and far superior
    to man.

13 "Why do you complain against
    Him?
  That He does not answer [you
    with] all His doings.
14 "For God speaks once,
  And even twice, yet no one notices
    it [including you, Job].
15 "In a dream, a vision of the night
    [one may hear God's voice],
  When deep sleep falls on men
  While slumbering upon the bed,
16 Then He opens the ears of men
  And seals their instruction,
17 That He may turn man aside from
    his conduct,
  And keep him from pride;
18 He holds back his soul from the pit
    [of destruction],

And his life from passing over into
    Sheol (the nether world, the place
    of the dead).

19 "Man is also disciplined with pain
    on his bed,
  And with unceasing complaint in
    his bones,
20 So that his life makes him loathe
    food,
  And his soul [loathe] even his
    favorite dishes.
21 "His flesh is so wasted away that it
    cannot be seen,
  And his bones which were not
    seen now stick out.
22 "Then his soul draws near to the
    pit [of destruction],
  And his life to those who bring
    death (the destroyers).

23 "If there is an angel as a mediator
    for him,
  One out of a thousand,
  To explain to a man what is right
    for him [that is, how to be in
    right standing with God],
24 Then the angel is gracious to him,
    and says,
  'Spare him from going down to the
    pit [of destruction];
  I have found a ransom [a
    consideration, or reason for
    redemption, an atonement]!'
25 "Let his flesh be restored and
    become fresher than in youth;
  Let him return to the days of his
    youthful strength.
26 "He will pray to God, and He shall
    be favorable to him,
  So that he looks at His face with joy;
  For God restores to man His
    righteousness [that is, his right
    standing with God—with its
    joys].
27 "He sings out to other men,
  'I have sinned and perverted that
    which was right,
  And it was not proper for me!

28'God has redeemed my life from
　　going to the pit [of destruction],
　And my life shall see the light.'"

29[Elihu comments,] "Behold, God
　　does all these *things* twice, yes,
　　three times, with a man,
30To bring his life back from the pit
　　[of destruction],
　That he may be enlightened with
　　the light of the living.
31"Pay attention, Job, listen to me;
　Keep silent, and I will speak.
32"If you have anything to say,
　　answer me;
　Speak, for I desire to justify you.
33"If not [and you have nothing to
　　say], listen to me;
　Keep silent, and I will teach you
　　wisdom."

34 ELIHU CONTINUED *his
discourse* and said,

2"Hear my words, you wise men,
　And listen to me, you who have [so
　　much] knowledge.
3"For the ear puts words to the test
　As the palate tastes food.
4"Let us choose for ourselves that
　　which is right;
　Let us know among ourselves what
　　is good.
5"For Job has said, 'I am righteous
　　[and innocent],
　But God has taken away my right;
　　[Job 33:9]
6Although I am right, I am
　　accounted a liar.
　My wound is incurable, *though I
　　am* without transgression.'
7"What man is like Job,
　Who drinks up derision like water,
8Who goes in company with those
　　who do evil
　And walks with wicked men?
9"For he has said, 'It profits a man
　　nothing
　When he takes delight *and* is
　　pleased with God *and* obeys Him.'

10"Therefore hear me, you men of
　　understanding.
　Far be it from God that He would
　　do wickedness,
　And from the Almighty to do
　　wrong.
11"For God pays a man according to
　　his work,
　And He will make every man
　　find [appropriate] *compensation*
　　according to his way.
12"Surely God will not act wickedly,
　Nor will the Almighty pervert
　　justice.
13"Who put God in charge over the
　　earth?
　And who has laid *on Him* the
　　whole world?
14"If God should determine to do so,
　If He should gather to Himself
　　[that is, withdraw from man]
　　His [life-giving] spirit and His
　　breath,
15All flesh would perish together,
　And man would return to dust. [Ps
　　104:29; Eccl 12:7]

16"If *you now have* understanding,
　　hear this;
　Listen to the sound of my words.
17"Shall one who hates justice [and
　　is an enemy of right] govern?
　And will you condemn Him who is
　　just *and* mighty?
18"God who says to a king, 'You are
　　worthless *and* vile,'
　Or to princes *and* nobles, 'You are
　　wicked *and* evil'?
19"Who is not partial to princes,
　Nor does He regard the rich above
　　the poor,
　For they all are the work of His
　　hands.
20"In a moment they die, even at
　　midnight
　The people are shaken and pass
　　away,
　And the powerful are taken away
　　without a [human] hand.

²¹"For God's eyes are on the ways of a
  man,
  And He sees all his steps. [Ps
  34:15; Prov 5:21; Jer 16:17]
²²"There is no darkness nor deep
  shadow
  Where the evildoers may hide
  themselves.
²³"For He sets no appointed time for a
  man,
  That he should appear before Him
  in judgment.
²⁴"He breaks mighty men without
  inquiry,
  And sets others in their place.
  [Dan 2:21]
²⁵"Therefore He knows of their
  works,
  And He overthrows them in the
  night,
  So that they are crushed and
  destroyed.
²⁶"He strikes them like the wicked
  In a public place,
²⁷Because they turned aside from
  following Him
  And would not consider or show
  regard for any of His ways,
  [1 Sam 15:11]
²⁸So that they caused the cry of the
  poor to come to Him,
  And He heard the cry of the
  afflicted. [Ex 22:23; James 5:4]
²⁹"When He keeps quiet, who then
  can condemn?
  When He hides His face
  [withdrawing His favor and
  help], who then can behold Him
  [and make supplication to Him],
  Whether it be a nation or a man by
  himself?—
³⁰So that godless men would not rule
  Nor be snares for the people.

³¹"For has anyone said to God,
  'I have endured my chastisement;
  I will not offend anymore;
³²Teach me what I do not see [in
  regard to how I have sinned];

If I have done wrong (injustice,
  unrighteousness),
I will not do it again'?
³³"Shall God's retribution [for your
  sins] be on your terms, because
  you refuse to accept it?
For you must do the choosing, and
  not I;
Therefore say what you
  [truthfully] know.
³⁴"Men of understanding will tell me,
Indeed, every wise man who hears
  me [will agree],
³⁵'Job speaks without knowledge,
And his words are without wisdom
  and insight.
³⁶'Job ought to be tried to the limit
Because he answers like wicked
  men!
³⁷'For he adds rebellion [in
  his unsubmissive, defiant
  attitude toward God] to his
  [unacknowledged] sin;
He claps his hands among us [in
  open mockery and contempt of
  God],
And he multiplies his words [of
  accusation] against God.'"

35 ELIHU CONTINUED
  speaking [to Job] and said,

²"Do you think this is according to
  [your] justice?
Do you say, 'My righteousness is
  more than God's'?
³"For you say, 'What advantage have
  you [by living a righteous life]?
What profit will I have, more [by
  being righteous] than if I had
  sinned?'
⁴"I will answer you,
And your companions with you.
⁵"Look to the heavens and see;
And behold the skies which are
  [much] higher than you.
⁶"If you have sinned, what do you
  accomplish against Him?

And if your transgressions are
multiplied, what have you done
to Him?

7 "If you are righteous, what do you
give God,
Or what does He receive from your
hand?

8 "Your wickedness *affects only* a
man such as you,
And your righteousness *affects
only* a son of man [but it cannot
affect God, who is sovereign].

9 "Because of the multitudes of
oppressions *the people* cry out;
They cry for help because of the
[violent] arm of the mighty.

10 "But no one says, 'Where is God
my Maker,
Who gives songs [of rejoicing] in
the night, [Acts 16:25]

11 Who teaches us more than the
beasts of the earth
And makes us wiser than the birds
of the heavens?'

12 "The people cry out, but He does
not answer
Because of the pride of evil men.

13 "Surely God will not listen to an
empty cry [which lacks trust],
Nor will the Almighty regard it.

14 "Even though you say that you do
not see Him [when missing His
righteous judgment on earth],
Yet your case is before Him, and
you must wait for Him!

15 "And now, because He has not
[quickly] punished in His anger,
Nor has He acknowledged
transgression *and* arrogance
well [and seems unaware of
the wrong of which a person is
guilty],

16 Job uselessly opens his mouth
And multiplies words without
knowledge [drawing the
worthless conclusion that
the righteous have no more
advantage than the wicked]."

36 ELIHU CONTINUED and said,

2 "Bear with me a little longer, and I
will show you,
That there is yet more to say on
God's behalf.

3 "I will bring my knowledge from
afar,
And will ascribe righteousness to
my Maker.

4 "For truly my words are not false;
He who is perfect in knowledge is
with you.

5 "Behold, God is mighty, and yet
does not despise *anyone* [nor
regard any as trivial];
He is mighty in the strength *and*
power of understanding.

6 "He does not prolong the life of the
wicked,
But gives the afflicted their justice.

7 "He does not withdraw His eyes
from the righteous [those in
right standing with Him];
But with kings upon the throne
He has seated them forever, and
they are exalted.

8 "And if they are bound in bonds [of
adversity],
And held by cords of affliction, [Ps
107:10, 11]

9 Then He declares to them [the true
character of] their deeds
And their transgressions, that
they have acted arrogantly [with
presumption and notions of self-
sufficiency].

10 "He opens their ears to instruction
and discipline,
And commands that they return
from evil.

11 "If they hear and serve *Him,*
They will end their days in
prosperity
And their years in pleasantness
and joy.

12 "But if they do not hear *and* obey,
   they will die by the sword [of
   God's destructive judgments]
And they will die [in ignorance]
   without [true] knowledge.
13 "But the godless in heart store up
   anger [at the divine discipline];
They do not cry [to Him] for help
   when He binds them [with cords
   of affliction]. [Rom 2:5]
14 "They die in youth,
And their life *ends* among the cult
   prostitutes. [Deut 23:17]
15 "He rescues the afflicted in their
   affliction,
And opens their ears [so that they
   pay attention to His voice] in
   times of oppression.
16 "Then indeed, He enticed you
   from the mouth of distress *and*
   confinement,
Into a broad place where there is
   no constraint *or* distress;
And that which was set on your
   table was full of fatness (rich
   food).
17 "But you [Job] were full of
   judgment on the wicked,
Judgment and justice take hold *of*
   you.
18 "Do not let wrath entice you into
   scoffing;
And do not let the greatness *and*
   the extent of the ransom turn
   you aside.
19 "Will your wealth [be sufficient to]
   keep you from [the confinement
   of] distress,
Or will all the force of your
   strength do it?
20 "Do not long for the night,
When people vanish from their
   places.
21 "Take heed *and* be careful, do not
   turn to wickedness,
For you have chosen this [the vice
   of complaining against God]
   rather than [learning from]
   affliction.

22 "Behold, God is exalted in His
   power;
Who is a ruler *or* a teacher like
   Him?
23 "Who has appointed God His way,
And who can say [to Him], 'You
   have done wrong'?
24 "Remember that you should
   magnify God's work,
Of which men have sung.
25 "All men have seen God's work;
Man looks at it from a distance.
26 "Behold, God is exalted, and we do
   not know *Him;*
The number of His years is
   unsearchable. [1 Cor 13:12]
27 "For He draws up the drops of
   water,
They distill rain from the mist,
28 Which the clouds pour down,
They drop abundantly upon
   mankind."
29 "Can anyone understand the
   spreading of the clouds
Or the thundering of His pavilion?
   [Ps 18:11; Is 40:22]
30 "Behold, He spreads His lightning
   around Him [against the dark
   clouds],
And He covers the depths of the
   sea.
31 "For by these [mighty acts] He
   judges the peoples;
He gives food in abundance.
32 "He covers *His* hands with the
   lightning,
And commands it to strike the
   mark.
33 "His thundering voice declares
   [awesomely] His presence;
The cattle also are told of His
   coming storm.

37 "INDEED, AT *His*
   thundering my heart
   trembles
And leaps out of its place.
2 "Listen carefully to the thunder of
   His voice,

And the rumbling that goes out of
His mouth!
3 "He lets it loose under the whole
heaven,
And His lightning to the ends of
the earth.
4 "After it, His voice roars;
He thunders with the voice of His
majesty,
And He does not restrain
His lightning [against His
adversaries] when His voice is
heard.
5 "God thunders marvelously with
His voice;
He does great things which we
cannot comprehend.
6 "For He says to the snow, 'Fall on
the earth';
And [He speaks] to the showers
and to the downpour [of His
mighty rains], 'Be strong.'
7 "God seals (brings to a standstill,
stops) [by severe weather] the
hand of every man,
That all men [whom He has made]
may know His work [that is,
His sovereign power and their
subjection to it].
8 "Then the beast goes into its lair
And remains in its hiding place.
9 "Out of its chamber comes the
storm,
And cold from the north wind.
10 "Ice is made by the breath of God,
And the expanse of the waters is
frozen. [Ps 147:17, 18]
11 "He loads the thick cloud with
moisture;
He disperses the cloud of His
lightning.
12 "Its direction is turned around by
His guidance,
That it may do whatever He
commands it
On the face of the inhabited earth.
13 "Whether [it be] for correction, or
for His earth [generally]

Or for [His] mercy *and*
lovingkindness, He causes it
to happen. [Ex 9:18, 23; 1 Sam
12:18, 19]
14 "Listen to this, Job;
Stand still and consider the
wonders of God.
15 "Do you know how God establishes
and commands them,
And makes the lightning of His
[storm] cloud shine?
16 "Do you know about the layers
of thick clouds [and how they
are balanced and poised in the
heavens],
The wonderful works of Him who
is perfect in knowledge,
17 You whose garments are hot,
When He quiets the earth [in
sultry summer] with the
[oppressive] south wind?
18 "Can you, with Him, spread out the
sky,
Strong as a molten mirror?
19 "Tell us [Job] what words [of man]
shall we say to such a Being;
We cannot state *our case* because
of darkness [that is, our
ignorance in the presence of the
unsearchable God].

life point

Even though Job's friend Elihu was critical
and judgmental of Job, he did offer a
good piece of advice in telling Job to
"stand still" (Job 37:14). Standing still
is action in God's economy. It is spiritual
action. We usually take action in the natural realm and do nothing in the spiritual
realm, but when we wait on God and
stand before Him, we are taking spiritual
action. Do you need God to move in a
circumstance? Take spiritual action by
saying, "Lord, I am going to wait on
You until You do something about this
situation."

20 "So shall it be told Him that I wish
to speak?
Or should a man say that he would
be swallowed up [and destroyed
by God]?
21 "Now people cannot look at the
light when it is bright in the
skies [without being blinded],
When the wind has passed and
cleared them.
22 "Out of the north comes golden
splendor [and people can hardly
look on it];
Around God is awesome splendor
and majesty [far too glorious for
man's eyes].
23 "The Almighty—we cannot find
Him;
He is exalted in power
And He will not do violence to [nor
disregard] justice and abundant
righteousness. [1 Tim 6:16]
24 "Men therefore fear Him;
He does not regard *nor* respect
any who are wise in heart [in
their own under-standing and
conceit]." [Matt 10:28]

38

THEN THE LORD answered
Job out of the whirlwind
and said,

2 "Who is this that darkens counsel
[questioning my authority and
wisdom]
By words without knowledge? [Job
35:16]
3 "Now gird up your loins like a man,
And I will ask you, and you
instruct Me!
4 "Where were you when I laid the
foundation of the earth?
Tell *Me,* if you know *and* have
understanding.
5 "Who determined the
measurements [of the earth], if
you know?
Or who stretched the [measuring]
line on it?

6 "On what were its foundations
fastened?
Or who laid its cornerstone,
7 When the morning stars sang
together
And all the sons of God (angels)
shouted for joy?
8 "Or who enclosed the sea with doors
When it burst forth and went out
of the womb;
9 When I made the clouds its garment
And thick darkness its swaddling
band,
10 And marked for it My [appointed]
boundary
And set bars and doors [defining
the shorelines], [Jer 5:22]
11 And said, 'This far you shall come,
but no farther;
And here your proud waves shall
stop'? [Ps 89:9; 93:4]
12 "*Since* your days began, have you
ever commanded the morning,
And caused the dawn to know its
place,
13 So that light may take hold of the
corners of the earth
And shake the wickedness out of it?
14 "The earth is changed like clay
into which a seal is pressed;
And the things [of the earth]
stand out like a [multi-colored]
garment.
15 "Their light is withheld from the
wicked,
And the uplifted arm is broken.
16 "Have you entered *and* explored
the springs of the sea
Or [have you] walked in the
recesses of the deep?
17 "Have the gates of death been
revealed to you,
Or have you seen the gates of deep
darkness?
18 "Have you understood the expanse
of the earth?
Tell *Me,* if you know all this.

19 "Where is the way *where* light
    dwells?
  And as for darkness, where is its
    place,
20 That you may take it to its territory
  And that you may know the paths
    to its house?
21 "You [must] know, since you were
    born then,
  And because you are so extremely
    old!
22 "Have you entered the storehouses
    of the snow,
  Or have you seen the storehouses
    of the hail,
23 Which I have reserved for the time
    of trouble,
  For the day of battle and war? [Ex
    9:18; Josh 10:11; Is 30:30; Rev
    16:21]
24 "Where is the way that the light is
    distributed,
  Or the east wind scattered over the
    earth?
25 "Who has prepared a channel for
    the torrents of rain *and* for the
    flood,
  Or a path for the thunderbolt,
26 To bring rain on the uninhabited
    land,
  And on the desert where no man
    lives,

life point

When God asked Job where light dwells
and where the place of darkness is (see
Job 38:19), He was making a point about
His limitless knowledge and about the
mystery that surrounds Him. We will
never know everything He knows, nor will
we ever know everything there is to know
about Him. But He knows everything
there is to know about us, and in His awesomeness, He is doing great things for us
and in our lives.

27 To satisfy the barren and desolate
    ground
  And to make the seeds of grass to
    sprout?
28 "Has the rain a father?
  Or who has begotten the drops of
    dew?
29 "Out of whose womb has come the
    ice?
  And the frost of heaven, who has
    given it birth?
30 "Water becomes like stone [and
    hides itself],
  And the surface of the deep is
    frozen *and* imprisoned.
31 "Can you bind the chains of [the
    cluster of stars called] Pleiades,
  Or loose the cords of [the
    constellation] Orion?
32 "Can you lead forth a constellation
    in its season,
  And guide [the stars of] the Bear
    with her sons?
33 "Do you know the ordinances of
    the heavens,
  Or [can you] establish their rule
    over the earth?
34 "Can you lift up your voice to the
    clouds,
  So that an abundance of water will
    cover you?
35 "Can you send forth lightnings that
    they may go
  And say to you, 'Here we are'?
36 "Who has put wisdom in the
    innermost being [of man, or in
    the layers of clouds]
  Or given understanding to the
    mind [of man, or to the heavenly
    display]?
37 "Who can count the clouds by
    [earthly] wisdom,
  Or pour out the water jars of the
    heavens,
38 When the dust hardens into a mass
  And the clods stick together
    [because of the heat]?

³⁹"Can you [Job] hunt the prey for
the lion,
Or satisfy the appetite of the young
lions
⁴⁰When they crouch in their dens
And lie in wait in their lair?
⁴¹"Who provides prey for the raven
When its young cry to God
And wander about without food?

39 "DO YOU know the time
when the wild goats of the
rock give birth [to their
young]?
Do you observe the calving of the
deer?
²"Can you count the months that
they carry offspring,
Or do you know the time when
they give birth?
³"They kneel down, they bring
forth their young,
They cast out their labor pains.
⁴"Their young ones become strong,
they grow up in the open field;
They leave and do not return to
them.
⁵"Who sent out the wild donkey
free [from dependence on man]?
And who has loosed the bonds of
the wild donkey [to survive in
the wild],
⁶To whom I gave the wilderness as
his home
And the salt land as his dwelling
place?
⁷"He scorns the tumult of the city,
And does not hear the shouting of
the taskmaster.
⁸"He explores the mountains as his
pasture
And searches after every green
thing.
⁹"Will the wild ox be willing to
serve you,
Or remain beside your manger at
night?

¹⁰"Can you bind the wild ox with
a harness [to the plow] in the
furrow?
Or will he plow the valleys for
you?
¹¹"Will you trust him because his
strength is great
And leave your labor to him?
¹²"Will you have faith and depend on
him to return your grain
And gather it from your threshing
floor?
¹³"The [flightless] wings of the
ostrich wave joyously;
With the pinion (shackles, fetters)
and plumage of love,
¹⁴For she leaves her eggs on the
ground
And warms them in the dust,
¹⁵Forgetting that a foot may crush
them,
Or that the wild beast may trample
them.
¹⁶"She treats her young cruelly, as if
they were not hers;
Though her labor is in vain
because she is unconcerned [for
the safety of her brood],
¹⁷For God has made her forget
wisdom,
And has not given her a share of
understanding.
¹⁸"Yet when she lifts herself on high,
[So swift is she that] she laughs at
the horse and his rider.
¹⁹"Have you given the horse his
might?
Have you clothed his neck with
quivering and a shaking mane?
²⁰"Have you [Job] made him leap
like a locust?
The majesty of his snorting
[nostrils] is terrible.
²¹"He paws in the valley and rejoices
in his strength;
He goes out to meet the weapons
[of armed men].

22 "He laughs at fear and is not dismayed;
And [in battle] he does not turn back from the sword.
23 "The quiver rattles against him, [As do] the flashing spear and the lance [of his rider].
24 "With fierceness and rage he races to devour the ground,
And he does not stand still at the sound of the [war] trumpet.
25 "As often as the trumpet sounds he says, 'Aha!'
And he smells the battle from far away,
And senses the thunder of the captains and the war cry.
26 "Is it by your understanding that the hawk soars,
Stretching his wings toward the south [as winter approaches]?
27 "Is it at your command that the eagle mounts up
And makes his nest on high [in an inaccessible place]?
28 "On the cliff he dwells and remains [securely],
Upon the point of the rock and the inaccessible stronghold.
29 "From there he spies out the prey; His eyes see it from far away.
30 "His young ones suck up blood; And where the slain are, there is he."

40 THEN THE LORD said to Job,

2 "Will the faultfinder contend with the Almighty?
Let him who disputes with God answer it."

3 Then Job replied to the LORD and said,

4 "Behold, I am of little importance and contemptible; what can I reply to You?

I lay my hand on my mouth. [Ezra 9:6; Ps 51:4]
5 "I have spoken once, but I will not reply again—
Indeed, twice [I have answered], and I will add nothing further."

6 Then the LORD answered Job out of the whirlwind, saying,

7 "Now gird up your loins (prepare yourself) like a man,
And I will ask you, and you instruct Me.
8 "Will you really annul My judgment and set it aside as void?
Will you condemn Me [your God] that you may [appear to] be righteous and justified?
9 "Have you an arm like God,
And can you thunder with a voice like His?
10 "Adorn yourself with eminence and dignity [since you question the Almighty],
And array yourself with honor and majesty.
11 "Pour out the overflowings of your wrath,
And look at everyone who is proud and make him low.
12 Look at everyone who is proud, and humble him,
And [if you are so able] tread down the wicked where they stand.
13 "[Crush and] hide them in the dust together;
Shut them up in the hidden place [the house of death].
14 "[If you can do all this, Job, proving your divine power] then I [God] will also praise you and acknowledge
That your own right hand can save you.
15 "Behold now, Behemoth, which I created as well as you;
He eats grass like an ox.
16 "See now, his strength is in his loins

And his power is in the muscles *and* sinews of his belly.

¹⁷"He sways his tail like a cedar;
The tendons of his thighs are twisted *and* knit together [like a rope].

¹⁸"His bones are tubes of bronze;
His limbs are like bars of iron.

¹⁹"He is the first [in magnitude and power] of the works of God;
[Only] He who made him can bring near His sword [to master him].

²⁰"Surely the mountains bring him food,
And all the wild animals play there.

²¹"He lies down under the lotus plants,
In the hidden shelter of the reeds in the marsh.

²²"The lotus plants cover him with their shade;
The willows of the brook surround him.

²³"If a river rages *and* overflows, he does not tremble;
He is confident, though the Jordan [River] swells and rushes against his mouth.

²⁴"Can anyone capture him when he is on watch,
Or pierce his nose with barbs [to trap him]?

41 "CAN YOU draw out Leviathan with a fishhook?
Or press down his tongue with a cord?

²"Can you put a rope [made] of rushes into his nose
Or pierce his jaw through with a hook?

³"Will he make many supplications to you [begging to be spared]?
Or will he speak soft words to you [to coax you to treat him kindly]?

⁴"Will he make a covenant *or* an arrangement with you?
Will you take him for your servant forever?

⁵"Will you play with him as with a bird?
Or will you bind him [and put him on a leash] for your maidens?

⁶"Will traders bargain over him?
Will they divide him up among the merchants?

⁷"Can you fill his skin with harpoons,
Or his head with fishing spears?

⁸"Lay your hand on him;
Remember the battle [with him]; you will not do such [an ill-advised thing] again!

⁹"Behold, his [assailant's] hope *and* expectation [of defeating Leviathan] is false;
Will not one be overwhelmed even at the sight of him?

¹⁰"No one is so fierce [and foolhardy] that he dares to stir up Leviathan;
Who then is he who can stand before Me [or dares to contend with Me, the beast's creator]?

¹¹"Who has first given to Me that I should repay him?
Whatever is under the whole heaven is Mine. [Who can have a claim against Me who made the unmastered beast?] [Rom 11:35]

¹²"I will not keep silence concerning his limbs,
Nor his mighty strength, nor his orderly frame.

¹³"Who can penetrate *or* strip off his outer armor?
Who can come to his jaws with a double bridle?

¹⁴"Who can open the doors (jaws) of his face?
Around his [open jaws and] teeth there is terror.

¹⁵"His strong scales are his pride,
Bound together as with a tight seal.

¹⁶"One is so near to another

That no air can come between
  them.
¹⁷"They are joined one to another;
  They stick together and cannot be
  separated.
¹⁸"His sneezes flash forth light,
  And his eyes are like the [reddish]
  eyelids of the dawn.
¹⁹"Out of his mouth go burning
  torches,
  And sparks of fire leap out.
²⁰"Out of his nostrils smoke goes
  forth
  As from a boiling pot and [as from]
  burning rushes.
²¹"His breath kindles coals,
  And a flame goes forth from his
  mouth.
²²"In Leviathan's neck resides
  strength,
  And dismay *and* terror dance
  before him.
²³"The folds of his flesh are joined
  together,
  Firm on him and immobile [when
  he moves].
²⁴"His heart is as hard as a stone,
  Indeed, as solid as a lower
  millstone.
²⁵"When he raises himself up, the
  mighty are afraid;
  Because of the crashing they are
  bewildered.

life point

When others have betrayed us or done us wrong, we must pass the test of forgiveness. In Job 42:7–10 we read that Job prayed for his friends. These were the friends who had judged and criticized him. These were the friends who did not stand with him in his pain and suffering when he lost everything. What happened when Job prayed for them and forgave them? He received a double blessing from the Lord. Based on Job's story, I like to say: "If you do things God's way, He will give you double for your trouble."

putting the Word to work

Have you ever been wrongly accused and thus deeply wounded by others? Like Job, pray for those who have hurt you, and forgive them (see Job 42:10). When we forgive, God brings restoration.

²⁶"The sword that reaches him
  cannot avail,
  Nor [does] the spear, the dart, or
  the javelin.
²⁷"He considers iron as straw,
  Bronze as rotten wood.
²⁸"The arrow cannot make him flee;
  Slingstones are treated as stubble
  by him.
²⁹"Clubs [also] are regarded as
  stubble;
  He laughs at the rushing *and* the
  rattling of the javelin.
³⁰"His underparts are like sharp
  pieces of broken pottery;
  He moves across *and* spreads out
  [grooves] like a threshing sledge
  on the mire (muddy river banks).
³¹"He makes the deep water boil like
  a pot;
  He makes the sea like a [foaming]
  pot of ointment.
³²"Behind him he makes a shining
  wake;
  One would think the deep to be
  gray-haired [with foam].
³³"Upon earth there is nothing like
  him—no equal exists,
  A creature made without fear.
³⁴"He looks on everything that is
  high [without terror];
  He is monarch over all the sons
  of pride. [And now, Job, who
  are you who does not dare to
  disturb the beast, yet who dares
  resist Me, the beast's creator?
  Everything under the heavens is
  Mine; therefore, who can have a
  claim against God?]"

42

THEN JOB answered the LORD and said,

2 "I know that You can do all things,
And that no thought *or* purpose of
Yours can be restrained.
3 "[You said to me] 'Who is this that
darkens *and* obscures counsel
[by words] without knowledge?'
Therefore [I now see] I have
[rashly] uttered that which I did
not understand,
Things too wonderful for me,
which I did not know. [Job 38:2]
4 'Hear, please, and I will speak;
I will ask You, and You instruct
[and answer] me.'
5 "I had heard of You [only] by the
hearing of the ear,
But now my [spiritual] eye sees You.
6 "Therefore I retract [my words and
hate myself]
And I repent in dust and ashes."

7 It came about that after the LORD
had spoken these words to Job, that
the LORD said to Eliphaz the Temanite,
"My wrath is kindled against you and
against your two friends, for you have
not spoken of Me what is right, as My
servant Job has.
8 "Now therefore, take for yourselves
seven bulls and seven rams, and go to
My servant Job, and offer up a burnt
offering for yourselves, and My servant Job will pray for you. For I will
accept him [and his prayer] so that
I may not deal with you *according to
your* folly, because you have not spoken of Me the thing that is right, as My
servant Job has."

9 So Eliphaz the Temanite and Bildad
the Shuhite and Zophar the Naamathite
went and did as the LORD told them; and
the LORD accepted Job's prayer.

10 The LORD restored the fortunes of
Job when he prayed for his friends, and
the LORD gave Job twice as much as he
had before. [Deut 30:1–3; Ps 126:1, 2]

11 Then all his brothers and sisters and
all who had known him before came to
him, and they ate bread with him in
his house; and they consoled him and
comforted him over all the [distressing]
adversities that the LORD had brought
on him. And each one gave him a piece
of money, and each a ring of gold.

12 And the LORD blessed the latter
days of Job more than his beginning;
for he had 14,000 sheep, 6,000 camels,
1,000 yoke of oxen, and 1,000 female
donkeys. [Job 1:3]

13 He had seven sons and three
daughters.

14 And he called the name of the first
[daughter] Jemimah, and the name of
the second Keziah, and the name of
the third Keren-happuch.

15 In all the land there were found no
women so fair as the daughters of Job;
and their father gave them an inheritance among their brothers.

16 After this, Job lived 140 years, and
saw his sons and his grandsons, four
generations.

17 So Job died, an old man and full of
days. [James 5:11]

life point

No matter what you are going through,
God still has the same good plan for you
right now that He had the moment you
were born. He has never changed His mind.
From the instant the enemy attacked you,
God has had your restoration in mind.

speak the Word

*God, I know that You can do all things, and that no thought
or purpose of Yours can be restrained.*
–ADAPTED FROM JOB 42:1–2

Psalms

Author:
David, Asaph, the sons of Korah, Moses, and others

Date:
1000 BC–300 BC

Everyday Life Principles:
The Psalms are full of practical advice for you, and they are easy to read and to pray.

When you need encouragement, instruction, or comfort, read the Psalms.

Express your heart to God freely and fully, just as the psalmists did.

The Psalms are a collection of 150 songs and poems written over a period of many years.

Because they were originally intended and used as worship songs for congregations or individuals, many of the psalms address God directly, and they are very easy to read and to pray. They are filled not only with praise and worship to God, but with practical advice and great insight into the various emotions, victories, and struggles people face.

One thing I love about the Psalms is that the writers were very honest with God, and they communicated with Him from their hearts. Whether they were joyful, confident, depressed, angry, lonely, or afraid, they wrote about it. In the midst of expressing themselves freely and fully to Him, they also realized their need for God in fresh new ways and reaffirmed their trust in Him. Every emotion you or I could ever experience seems to be mentioned in the Psalms. No matter what you are going through, God wants to hear your heart.

Many people have a favorite Psalm. For most, it is probably Psalm 23; for others, it is Psalm 91; and for others it is Psalm 100. I would have to say that my personal favorite is Psalm 27.

I encourage you to read the Psalms and read them often. Let them remind you to always tell God what is in your heart and receive comfort, strength, and direction from Him. Let them also remind you to praise and worship God with all your heart.

BOOK ONE

PSALM 1

The Righteous and the Wicked Contrasted.

1 BLESSED [fortunate, prosperous, and favored by God] is the man who does not walk in the counsel of the wicked [following their advice and example],
Nor stand in the path of sinners,
Nor sit [down to rest] in the seat of scoffers (ridiculers).
2 But his delight is in the law of the LORD,
And on His law [His precepts and teachings] he [habitually] meditates day and night. [Rom 13:8–10; Gal 3:1–29; 2 Tim 3:16]
3 And he will be like a tree *firmly* planted [and fed] by streams of water,
Which yields its fruit in its season;
Its leaf does not wither;
And in whatever he does, he prospers [and comes to maturity]. [Jer 17:7, 8]

4 The wicked [those who live in disobedience to God's law] are not so,
But they are like the chaff [worthless and without substance] which the wind blows away.
5 Therefore the wicked will not stand [unpunished] in the judgment,

life point

Psalm 1 promises blessing and God's favor to those who delight in God's law (His precepts and teachings) and who meditate on His Word day and night. In other words, those who give God and His Word first place in their lives can expect to prosper in every way.

Nor sinners in the assembly of the righteous.
6 For the LORD knows *and* fully approves the way of the righteous,
But the way of the wicked shall perish.

PSALM 2

The Reign of the LORD's Anointed.

1 WHY ARE the nations in an uproar [in turmoil against God],
And why do the people devise a vain *and* hopeless plot?
2 The kings of the earth take their stand;
And the rulers take counsel together
Against the LORD and His Anointed (the Davidic King, the Messiah, the Christ), saying, [Acts 4:25–27]
3 "Let us break apart their [divine] bands [of restraint]
And cast away their cords [of control] from us."

4 He who sits [enthroned] in the heavens laughs [at their rebellion];
The [Sovereign] Lord scoffs at them [and in supreme contempt He mocks them].
5 Then He will speak to them in His [profound] anger
And terrify them with His displeasure, saying,
6 "Yet as for Me, I have anointed *and* firmly installed My King
Upon Zion, My holy mountain."

7 "I will declare the decree of the LORD:
He said to Me, 'You are My Son;
This day [I proclaim] I have begotten You. [2 Sam 7:14; Heb 1:5; 3:5, 6; 2 Pet 1:17, 18]
8 'Ask of Me, and I will assuredly give [You] the nations as Your inheritance,

And the ends of the earth as Your
  possession.
9 'You shall break them with a rod of
  iron;
You shall shatter them [in pieces]
  like earthenware.'" [Rev 12:5;
  19:15]

10 Now therefore, O kings, act wisely;
Be instructed *and* take warning,
  O leaders (judges, rulers) of the
  earth.
11 Worship the LORD *and* serve Him
  with reverence [with awe-
  inspired fear and submissive
  wonder];
Rejoice [yet do so] with trembling.
12 Kiss (pay respect to) the Son, so
  that He does not become angry,
  and you perish in the way,
For His wrath may soon be kindled
  and set aflame.

life point

I once saw a movie in which a king
issued a royal decree. He wrote down
his command and then sent forth riders
on horseback throughout the country to
"declare the decree" to the citizens of
that kingdom. In the Scriptures we see
the issuing of such royal decrees in Esther
8:8–14 and in Luke 2:1–3.

In Psalm 2:7, the psalmist wrote that he
would "declare the decree of the LORD."
What decree? The decree in which the
Lord declares that He (Jesus) is God's only
begotten Son (see Hebrews 1:1–5).

The written Word of God is the formal
decree of the Lord, our King. When we
declare God's Word out of our mouths,
with hearts full of faith, those faith-filled
words go forth to establish God's order
in our lives. When the royal decree is pronounced, things begin to change!

How blessed [fortunate, prosperous,
  and favored by God] are all those
  who take refuge in Him!

PSALM 3

Morning Prayer of Trust in God.

A Psalm of David. When he fled
  from Absalom his son.

1 O LORD, how my enemies have
  increased!
Many are rising up against me.
2 Many are saying of me,
"There is no help [no salvation] for
  him in God."   *Selah.*

3 But You, O LORD, are a shield for me,
My glory [and my honor], and the
  One who lifts my head.
4 With my voice I was crying to the
  LORD,
And He answered me from His
  holy mountain.   *Selah.*
5 I lay down and slept [safely];
I awakened, for the LORD
  sustains me.
6 I will not be intimidated *or* afraid
  of the ten thousands
Who have set themselves against
  me all around.

7 Arise, O LORD; save me, O my God!
For You have struck all my
  enemies on the cheek;
You have shattered the teeth of the
  wicked.
8 Salvation belongs to the LORD;
May Your blessing be upon Your
  people.   *Selah.*

PSALM 4

Evening Prayer of Trust in God.

To the Chief Musician; on stringed
  instruments. A Psalm of David.

1 ANSWER ME when I call, O God
  of my righteousness!
You have freed me when I was
  hemmed in *and* relieved me
  when I was in distress;

Be gracious to me and hear [and respond to] my prayer.

[2] O sons of men, how long will my honor *and* glory be [turned into] shame?
How long will you [my enemies] love worthless (vain, futile) things and seek deception *and* lies?   *Selah.*

[3] But know that the LORD has set apart for Himself [and dealt wonderfully with] the godly man [the one of honorable character and moral courage—the one who does right]. The LORD hears *and* responds when I call to Him.

hold your head high

Although there are "downers" in this life, there are also "lifters." In Psalm 3:1–3, the psalmist says that despite his distressing situation, he is not despairing or becoming depressed because his confidence is in the Lord, the One who lifts his head.

When we are depressed, it seems everything around us is falling apart. We lose strength; our heads and hands and hearts all begin to hang down. Even our eyes and our voices are lowered. We become downcast because we are looking at our problems rather than at the Lord.

No matter what is causing us to be downcast, the Lord encourages us throughout His Word to lift our heads and our hands and look to Him. We find one of these many examples in Genesis 13:14 when God told Abraham, who had been shortchanged by his nephew Lot, to "lift up" his eyes and look around him in all directions, for He was giving him all the land as far as he could see for his inheritance. In Psalm 24:7 the psalmist says, "Lift up your heads, O gates, and be lifted up, ancient doors, that the King of glory may come in." In 1 Timothy 2:8, the Apostle Paul encouraged people to pray, "lifting up holy hands."

These instructions are good for us to remember today. When people disappoint us, instead of becoming discouraged and depressed, God wants us to decide to lift up our heads and eyes and look at the possibilities, not the problems, around us, trusting Him to lead us into an even better situation—because He has one for us.

We may be tempted to say, "Oh, what's the use?" and just give up rather than moving in a new direction as Abraham did, but the Lord is constantly exhorting us to lift up our eyes and heads and hearts to take inventory of our blessings and not our problems. He encourages us to look at Him because God has plans to bless and increase us abundantly.

No matter how your life has turned out to this point, you have only two options. One is to give up and quit; the other is to keep going. If you decide to keep going, again you have only two choices. One is to live in depression and misery; the other is to live in hope and joy.

Choosing to live in hope and joy does not mean you will not face any more disappointments or discouraging situations; it just means you have decided not to let them get you down. Instead, you will lift up your eyes and hands and head and heart and look not at your problems, but at the Lord, Who has promised to see you through to abundance and victory.

4 Tremble [with anger or fear], and do not sin;

Meditate in your heart upon your bed and be still [reflect on your sin and repent of your rebellion]. [Eph 4:26]   *Selah.*

5 Offer righteous sacrifices;

Trust [confidently] in the LORD.

6 Many are saying, "Oh, that we might see some good!"

Lift up the light of Your face upon us, O LORD;

7 You have put joy in my heart,

More than [others know] when their wheat and new wine have yielded abundantly.

8 In peace [and with a tranquil heart] I will both lie down and sleep,

For You alone, O LORD, make me dwell in safety *and* confident trust.

PSALM 5

Prayer for Protection from the Wicked.

To the Chief Musician; on wind instruments. A Psalm of David.

1 LISTEN TO my words, O LORD,

Consider my groaning *and* sighing.

2 Heed the sound of my cry for help, my King and my God,

For to You I pray.

3 In the morning, O LORD, You will hear my voice;

In the morning I will prepare [a prayer and a sacrifice] for You and watch *and* wait [for You to speak to my heart].

4 For You are not a God who takes pleasure in wickedness;

No evil [person] dwells with You.

5 The boastful *and* the arrogant will not stand in Your sight;

You hate all who do evil.

6 You destroy those who tell lies;

The LORD detests *and* rejects the bloodthirsty and deceitful man.

7 But as for me, I will enter Your house through the abundance of Your steadfast love *and* tender mercy;

At Your holy temple I will bow [obediently] in reverence for You.

8 O LORD, lead me in Your righteousness because of my enemies;

Make Your way straight (direct, right) before me.

9 For there is nothing trustworthy *or* reliable *or* truthful in what they say;

Their heart is destruction [just a treacherous chasm, a yawning gulf of lies].

Their throat is an open grave;

They [glibly] flatter with their [silken] tongue. [Rom 3:13]

10 Hold them guilty, O God;

Let them fall by their own designs *and* councils!

Cast them out because of the abundance of their transgressions,

For they are mutinous *and* have rebelled against You.

11 But let all who take refuge *and* put their trust in You rejoice,

speak the Word

Thank You, Lord, for hearing and responding to me when I call to You.
—ADAPTED FROM PSALM 4:3

Thank You, God, that I can take refuge in You and put my trust in You.
Thank You for covering me and sheltering me.
—ADAPTED FROM PSALM 5:11

Let them ever sing for joy;
Because You cover *and* shelter them,
Let those who love Your name be
  joyful *and* exult in You.
[12] For You, O LORD, bless the
  righteous man [the one who is in
  right standing with You];
You surround him with favor as
  with a shield.

PSALM 6

Prayer for Mercy in Time of Trouble.

To the Chief Musician; on stringed
  instruments, set [possibly] an
  octave below. A Psalm of David.

[1] O LORD, do not rebuke *or* punish
  me in Your anger,
Nor discipline me in Your wrath.
[2] Have mercy on me *and* be gracious
  to me, O LORD, for I am weak
  (faint, frail);
Heal me, O LORD, for my bones are
  dismayed *and* anguished.
[3] My soul [as well as my body] is
  greatly dismayed.
But as for You, O LORD—how long
  [until You act on my behalf]?

[4] Return, O LORD, rescue my soul;
Save me because of Your [unfailing]
  steadfast love *and* mercy.
[5] For in death there is no mention of
  You;
In Sheol (the nether world, the
  place of the dead) who will
  praise You *and* give You thanks?

[6] I am weary with my groaning;
Every night I soak my bed with
  tears,
I drench my couch with my
  weeping.
[7] My eye grows dim with grief;

It grows old because of all my
  enemies.

[8] Depart from me, all you who do evil,
For the LORD has heard the voice
  of my weeping. [Matt 7:23; Luke
  13:27]
[9] The LORD has heard my
  supplication [my plea for grace];
The LORD receives my prayer.
[10] Let all my enemies be ashamed
  and greatly horrified;
Let them turn back, let them
  suddenly be ashamed [of what
  they have done].

PSALM 7

The LORD Implored to Defend the Psalmist against the Wicked.

An Ode of David, [perhaps in a wild,
  irregular, enthusiastic strain,] which
  he sang to the LORD concerning
  the words of Cush, a Benjamite.

[1] O LORD my God, in You I take
  refuge;
Save me and rescue me from all
  those who pursue me,
[2] So that my enemy will not tear me
  like a lion,
Dragging me away while there is
  no one to rescue [me].

[3] O LORD my God, if I have done this,
If there is injustice in my hands,
[4] If I have done evil to him who was
  at peace with me,
Or without cause robbed him who
  was my enemy,
[5] Let the enemy pursue me and
  overtake me;
And let him trample my life to the
  ground
And lay my honor in the dust.
                                      Selah.

speak the Word

God, I thank You for hearing my supplication and receiving my prayer.
–ADAPTED FROM PSALM 6:9

⁶Arise, O LORD, in Your anger;
  Lift up Yourself against the rage of
    my enemies;
  Rise up for me; You have
    commanded judgment *and*
    vindication.
⁷Let the assembly of the nations be
    gathered around You,
  And return on high over them.

⁸The LORD judges the peoples;
  Judge me, O LORD, *and* grant
    me justice according to my
    righteousness and according to
    the integrity within me.
⁹Oh, let the wickedness of the
    wicked come to an end, but
    establish the righteous [those in
    right standing with You];

when God tests your emotions

In Psalm 7:9 we read that God "tries" our hearts and minds, our emotions (Revelation 2:23 conveys a similar message). What does *the* word *try* mean in this context? It means "to test until purified."

A few years ago, as I was praying, I felt God let me know that He was going to "test my emotions." I had never heard of anything like that, and had not yet discovered the scriptures about this in the Bible.

About six months later, I became an emotional wreck. I cried for no reason. Everything hurt my feelings. There were times when I went to bed praying, feeling as sweet as could be, then I woke up the next morning in a really cranky mood, as if I had stayed up all night eating nails! I thought, *What is the problem here? What's going on?* Then the Lord reminded me of what He had spoken to me earlier: "I am going to test your emotions." As He led me to Psalm 7:9 and Revelation 2:23, He caused me to understand that He was doing a work in my emotional life for my own good. He was going to teach me how to be stable and continue walking in the fruit of the Holy Spirit (see Galatians 5:22, 23) regardless of how I felt.

No matter who you are, there will be periods of time when you feel more emotional than usual. You may wake up one morning and feel like breaking down and crying for no reason. You may feel sad or depressed; you may feel that nobody cares about you; or you might feel sorry for yourself. During those times you must learn how to manage your emotions and not allow them to manage you. At these times your feelings will probably get hurt very easily. The slightest thing might make you angry. Emotions are very fickle! They can be one way one day and entirely different the next day. God has to teach us not to live by our feelings, or we will never enjoy victorious living and we will not give God the glory He deserves.

What should you do when you start feeling that your emotions are being tested? (1) Do not allow yourself to fall under condemnation. (2) Do not even try to figure out what is happening. (3) Instead, simply say, "This is one of those times when my emotions are being tried. I'm going to trust God and learn to control them."

How are you and I ever going to learn to control ourselves emotionally unless God allows us to go through some trying times? Remember, the Bible says that God will never allow any more to come upon us than we are able to bear (see 1 Corinthians 10:13). If the Lord does not allow such testing times to come upon us, we will never grow, and we will never learn how to deal with Satan when he brings things against us—which will happen sooner or later.

Trying times are learning times. They are testing times, and I always say, "Pass your test this time so you will not have to take it again."

For the righteous God tries the
hearts and minds. [Rev 2:23]
¹⁰ My shield *and* my defense depend
on God,
Who saves the upright in heart.
¹¹ God is a righteous judge,
And a God who is indignant every
day.
¹² If a man does not repent, God will
sharpen His sword;
He has strung *and* bent His
[mighty] bow and made it ready.
¹³ He has also prepared [other]
deadly weapons for Himself;
He makes His arrows fiery shafts
[aimed at the unrepentant].
¹⁴ Behold, the [wicked and
irreverent] man is pregnant
with sin,
And he conceives mischief and
gives birth to lies.
¹⁵ He has dug a pit and hollowed it
out,
And has fallen into the [very] pit
which he made [as a trap].
¹⁶ His mischief will return on his
own head,
And his violence will come down on
the top of his head [like loose dirt].
¹⁷ I will give thanks to the LORD
according to His righteousness
and justice,

putting the Word to work

**Have you ever looked into the vast,
starry sky at night and felt very small
in comparison? Consider the greatness
of God as you observe His creation all
around you, and remember that you
are a masterpiece of God's creation,
made in His very image! Take a moment to praise God for His excellence
and thank Him for crowning you with
glory and honor.**

And I will sing praise to the name
of the LORD Most High.

PSALM 8
The LORD's Glory and Man's Dignity.

To the Chief Musician; set to a
Philistine lute [or perhaps to a
particular Hittite tune].
A Psalm of David.

¹ O LORD, our Lord,
How majestic *and* glorious *and*
excellent is Your name in all the
earth!
You have displayed Your splendor
above the heavens.
² Out of the mouths of infants
and nursing babes You have
established strength
Because of Your adversaries,
That You might silence the enemy
and make the revengeful cease.
[Matt 21:15, 16]

³ When I see *and* consider Your
heavens, the work of Your
fingers,
The moon and the stars, which
You have established,
⁴ What is man that You are mindful
of him,
And the son of [earthborn] man
that You care for him?
⁵ Yet You have made him a little
lower than *God,
And You have crowned him with
glory and honor.
⁶ You made him to have dominion
over the works of Your hands;
You have put all things under his
feet, [1 Cor 15:27; Eph 1:22, 23;
Heb 2:6–8]
⁷ All sheep and oxen,
And also the beasts of the field,
⁸ The birds of the air, and the fish of
the sea,

8:5 LXX reads *angels;* Heb *Elohim.*

Whatever passes through the
  paths of the seas.

9 O Lord, our Lord,
How majestic *and* glorious *and*
  excellent is Your name in all the
  earth!

PSALM 9

A Psalm of Thanksgiving
for God's Justice.

To the Chief Musician; on Muth-
  labben. A Psalm of David.

1 I WILL give thanks *and* praise the
  Lord, with all my heart;
I will tell aloud all Your wonders
  and marvelous deeds.
2 I will rejoice and exult in you;
I will sing praise to Your name,
  O Most High.
3 When my enemies turn back,
They stumble and perish before
  You.
4 For You have maintained my right
  and my cause;
You have sat on the throne judging
  righteously.
5 You have rebuked the nations, You
  have destroyed the wicked *and*
  unrepentant;
You have wiped out their name
  forever and ever.
6 The enemy has been cut off *and*
  has vanished in everlasting
  ruins,
You have uprooted their cities;
The very memory of them has
  perished.
7 But the Lord will remain *and* sit
  enthroned forever;

life point

You have been singled out by God, Who
has placed His crown of glory and honor,
or favor and excellence, upon your head,
according to Psalm 8:5. You may not see
your crown, but it is there—just like the
robe of righteousness in which you are
dressed. You may not see with your physical eyes your robe of righteousness or
the crown of God's favor, but they exist
in the spiritual realm (see Isaiah 61:10).
We need to remember that the natural
man cannot perceive the things of God
because they are spiritually discerned
(see 1 Corinthians 2:14).

Even though the Bible *says* we have been
crowned with glory and honor, often we
do not act as though we are. One reason
we do not tap into God's blessings is
that we do not believe we deserve them.
Another reason is that we have not been
taught that God's blessings can be ours
and consequently have not activated our
faith in this area. So we wander through
life, taking whatever the devil throws at
us without ever resisting him and claiming
what is rightfully ours.

If you will reread Psalm 8:6, you will see
that God has put all things under our feet;
He has given us dominion over the works
of His hands. To me, those words do not
indicate that we are supposed to allow
our problems or the devil and his demons
to intimidate, dominate, and oppress us.
If we will receive by faith the blessing of
glory and honor with which the Lord our
God has crowned us, not only will our
faces shine forth with the glory of the
Lord, but we will enjoy respect, esteem,
favor, and a good reputation.

speak the Word

*I will thank You and praise You, Lord, with all my heart, and I will
tell people about the wonderful and marvelous things You have done.
I will rejoice and exult in You.*
—ADAPTED FROM PSALM 9:1, 2

He has prepared *and* established
His throne for judgment. [Heb
1:11]
8And He will judge the world in
righteousness;
He will execute judgment for the
nations with fairness (equity).
[Acts 17:31]
9The LORD also will be a refuge *and*
a stronghold for the oppressed,
A refuge in times of trouble;
10And those who know Your name
[who have experienced Your
precious mercy] will put their
confident trust in You,
For You, O LORD, have not
abandoned those who seek You.
[Ps 42:1]

11Sing praises to the LORD, who
dwells in Zion;
Declare among the peoples His
[great and wondrous] deeds.
12For He who avenges blood
[unjustly shed] remembers them
(His people);
He does not forget the cry of the
afflicted *and* abused.
13Have mercy on me *and* be gracious
to me, O LORD;
See how I am afflicted by those
who hate me,
You who lift me up from the gates
of death,
14That I may tell aloud all Your
praises,
That in the gates of the daughter of
Zion (Jerusalem)
I may rejoice in Your salvation *and*
Your help.
15The nations have sunk down in
the pit which they have made;
In the net which they hid, their
own foot has been caught.
16The LORD has made Himself
known;
He executes judgment;
The wicked are trapped by the
work of their own hands.
                Higgaion (meditation) Selah.

17The wicked will turn to Sheol (the
nether world, the place of the
dead),
Even all the nations who forget God.
18For the poor will not always be
forgotten,
Nor the hope of the burdened
perish forever.
19Arise, O LORD, do not let man
prevail;
Let the nations be judged before
You.
20Put them in [reverent] fear of You,
O LORD,
So that the nations may know they
are but [frail and mortal] men.
                Selah.

PSALM 10

A Prayer for the Overthrow
of the Wicked.

1WHY DO You stand far away,
O LORD?
Why do You hide [Yourself, veiling
Your eyes] in times of trouble?
2In pride *and* arrogance the wicked
hotly pursue *and* persecute the
afflicted;
Let them be caught in the plots
which they have devised.

3For the wicked boasts *and* sings
the praises of his heart's desire,
And the greedy man curses and
spurns [and even despises] the
LORD.
4The wicked, in the haughtiness of
his face, will not seek *nor* inquire
for *Him;*
All his thoughts are, "There
is no God [so there is no
accountability or punishment]."

5His ways prosper at all times;
Your judgments [LORD] are on
high, out of his sight [so he never
thinks about them];
As for all his enemies, he sneers at
them.

6 He says to himself, "I will not be
    moved;
  For throughout all generations
    I will not be in adversity [for
    nothing bad will happen to me]."
7 His mouth is full of curses and
    deceit (fraud) and oppression;
  Under his tongue is mischief and
    wickedness [injustice and sin].
8 He lurks in ambush in the villages;
  In hiding places he kills the
    innocent;
  He lies in wait for the unfortunate
    [the unhappy, the poor, the
    helpless].
9 He lurks in a hiding place like a
    lion in his lair;
  He lies in wait to catch the afflicted;
  He catches the afflicted when he
    draws him into his net.
10 He crushes [his prey] and crouches;
  And the unfortunate fall by his
    mighty *claws*.
11 He says to himself, "God has
    [quite] forgotten;
  He has hidden His face; He will
    never see my deed."

12 Arise, O Lord! O God, lift up Your
    hand [in judgment];
  Do not forget the suffering.
13 Why has the wicked spurned *and*
    shown disrespect to God?
  He has said to himself, "You will
    not require me to account."
14 You have seen it, for You have noted
    mischief and vexation (irritation)
    to take it into Your hand.
  The unfortunate commits *himself*
    to You;
  You are the helper of the
    fatherless.
15 Break the arm of the wicked and
    the evildoer,
  Seek out his wickedness until You
    find no more.

16 The Lord is King forever and ever;
  The nations will perish from His
    land.

17 O Lord, You have heard the desire
    of the humble *and* oppressed;
  You will strengthen their heart,
    You will incline Your ear to hear,
18 To vindicate *and* obtain justice for
    the fatherless and the oppressed,
  So that man who is of the earth
    will no longer terrify them.

PSALM 11

The Lord a Refuge and Defense.

To the Chief Musician. *A Psalm*
of David.

1 IN THE Lord I take refuge [and
    put my trust];
  How can you say to me, "Flee like a
    bird to your mountain;
2 For look, the wicked are bending
    the bow;
  They take aim with their arrow on
    the string
  To shoot [by stealth] in darkness at
    the upright in heart.
3 "If the foundations [of a godly
    society] are destroyed,
  What can the righteous do?"

4 The Lord is in His holy temple; the
    Lord's throne is in heaven.
  His eyes see, His eyelids test the
    children of men. [Acts 7:49; Rev
    4:2]
5 The Lord tests the righteous and
    the wicked,
  And His soul hates the
    [malevolent] one who loves
    violence. [James 1:12]
6 Upon the wicked (godless) He will
    rain coals of fire;
  Fire and brimstone and a dreadful
    scorching wind will be the
    portion of their cup [of doom].
7 For the Lord is [absolutely]
    righteous, He loves
    righteousness (virtue, morality,
    justice);
  The upright shall see His face.

PSALM 12

God, a Helper against the Treacherous.

To the Chief Musician; set an octave below. A Psalm of David.

¹ SAVE *AND* help *and* rescue, LORD,
for godly people cease to be,
For the faithful vanish from
among the sons of men.
² They speak deceitful *and*
worthless words to one another;
With flattering lips and a double
heart they speak.

³ May the LORD cut off all flattering
lips,
The tongue that speaks great
things [in boasting];
⁴ Who have said, "With our tongue
we will prevail;
Our lips are our own; who is lord
and master over us?"
⁵ "Because of the devastation of
the afflicted, because of the
groaning of the needy,
Now I will arise," says the LORD; "I
will place him in the safety for
which he longs."

the importance of faithfulness

In Psalm 12:1 David asked the Lord for help because people were not being godly or faithful. Being faithful is as important today as it was then.

It is hard to find people who will be really faithful—people who will stick with you when they find out you are not perfect. The Bible says, "A friend loves at all times, and a brother is born for adversity" (Proverbs 17:17). In other words, a true friend is a person who is born to stick with you in your hard and not-so-nice times. I believe one of the saddest things in our society today is that we do not have this kind of loyalty and commitment. Many people miss out on so much because they are not faithful to see things through to the finish. Even sadder is that most of them will never even realize what incredible blessings they have missed.

David continues to say in the next verse of this psalm that people were speaking worthless, untrue words with deceitful, double hearts. We need single-minded men and women who can set their hearts on something and stick with it without being double-minded and speaking empty words. Double-hearted people believe one thing one day and something else the next. One day they like you and the next day they do not. They may be for you today, but against you tomorrow.

The Bible gives us many examples of faithful people. One of them was Moses, who was faithful in all the house of God (see Numbers 12:7). That means he was faithful to do exactly the duties God gave him to do day after day, month after month, year after year, even when he did not feel like being faithful. Moses was so faithful that even when his sister and brother, Miriam and Aaron, spoke against him, he loved them and remained faithful to them. He had so much faithfulness in his character that even when the people in his life did not treat him well, he remained the same way.

The Bible tells us that God remains faithful even when we are faithless (see 2 Timothy 2:13). That is the way God wants us to be. If everybody else is faithless, then we remain faithful. If you feel as though you are the only one who is being nice, the only one who apologizes or tries to do the right thing, keep on doing it. Determine in your heart to stay loyal to God and to keep bearing the fruit of faithfulness.

6 The words *and* promises of the
　　Lord are pure words,
　Like silver refined in an
　　earthen furnace, purified
　　seven times.
7 You, O Lord, will preserve *and*
　　keep them;
　You will protect him from this
　　[evil] generation forever.
8 The wicked strut about [in
　　pompous self-importance] on
　　every side,
　As vileness is exalted *and*
　　baseness is prized among the
　　sons of men.

PSALM 13

Prayer for Help in Trouble.

To the Chief Musician. A Psalm
of David.

1 HOW LONG, O Lord? Will You
　　forget me forever?
　How long will You hide Your face
　　from me?
2 How long must I take counsel in
　　my soul,
　Having sorrow in my heart day
　　after day?
　How long will my enemy exalt
　　himself *and* triumph over me?
3 Consider and answer me, O Lord
　　my God;
　Give light (life) to my eyes, or I
　　will sleep the *sleep of* death,
4 And my enemy will say, "I have
　　overcome him,"
　And my adversaries will rejoice
　　when I am shaken.

5 But I have trusted *and* relied
　　on *and* been confident in
　　Your lovingkindness *and*
　　faithfulness;
　My heart shall rejoice *and* delight
　　in Your salvation.
6 I will sing to the Lord,

Because He has dealt bountifully
　　with me.

PSALM 14

Folly and Wickedness of Men.

To the Chief Musician. A Psalm
of David.

1 THE [SPIRITUALLY ignorant]
　　fool has said in his heart, "There
　　is no God."
　They are corrupt, they have
　　committed repulsive *and*
　　unspeakable deeds;
　There is no one who does good.
　　[Rom 3:10]
2 The Lord has looked down from
　　heaven upon the children of men
　To see if there are any who
　　understand (act wisely),
　Who [truly] seek after God,
　　[longing for His wisdom and
　　guidance].
3 They have all turned aside,
　　together they have become
　　corrupt;
　There is no one who does good, not
　　even one. [Rom 3:11, 12]
4 Have all the workers of
　　wickedness *and* injustice no
　　knowledge,
　Who eat up my people as they eat
　　bread,
　And do not call upon the Lord?
5 There they tremble with great fear,
　For God is with the [consistently]
　　righteous generation.
6 You [evildoers] shamefully plan
　　against the poor,
　But the Lord is his safe refuge.

7 Oh, that the salvation of Israel
　　would come out of Zion!
　When the Lord restores His
　　captive people,
　Then Jacob will rejoice, Israel will
　　be glad. [Rom 11:25–27]

PSALM 15

Description of a Citizen of Zion.

A Psalm of David.

1 O LORD, who may lodge [as a
    guest] in Your tent?
Who may dwell [continually] on
    Your holy hill?
2 He who walks with integrity *and*
    strength of character, and works
    righteousness,
And speaks *and* holds truth in his
    heart.
3 He does not slander with his tongue,
Nor does evil to his neighbor,
Nor takes up a reproach against his
    friend;
4 In his eyes an evil person is
    despised,
But he honors those who fear
    the LORD [and obediently
    worship Him with awe-inspired
    reverence and submissive
    wonder].
He keeps his word even to his
    own disadvantage and does not
    change it [for his own benefit];
5 He does not put out his money at
    interest [to a fellow Israelite],
And does not take a bribe against
    the innocent.
He who does these things will
    never be shaken. [Ex 22:25, 26]

PSALM 16

The LORD, the Psalmist's Portion
in Life and Deliverer in Death.

A Mikhtam of David [probably
intended to record memorable
thoughts].

1 KEEP *AND* protect me, O God, for
    in You I have placed my trust
    and found refuge.
2 I said to the LORD, "You are my Lord;
I have no good besides You."
3 As for the saints (godly people)
    who are in the land,

They are the majestic *and* the
    noble *and* the excellent ones in
    whom is all my delight.
4 The sorrows [pain and suffering]
    of those who have chosen
    another *god* will be multiplied
    [because of their idolatry];
I will not pour out their drink
    offerings of blood,
Nor will I take their names upon
    my lips.
5 The LORD is the portion of my
    inheritance, my cup [He is all I
    need];
You support my lot.
6 The [boundary] lines [of the land]
    have fallen for me in pleasant
    places;
Indeed, my heritage is beautiful
    to me.
7 I will bless the LORD who has
    counseled me;
Indeed, my heart (mind) instructs
    me in the night.
8 I have set the LORD continually
    before me;
Because He is at my right hand, I
    will not be shaken.
9 Therefore my heart is glad and
    my glory [my innermost self]
    rejoices;
My body too will dwell
    [confidently] in safety,
10 For You will not abandon me to
    Sheol (the nether world, the
    place of the dead),
Nor will You allow Your Holy One
    to undergo decay. [Acts 13:35]
11 You will show me the path of life;

life point

We must learn to seek God's face and not
just His hand. Seeking God for Who He is,
not just for what He can do for us, assures
us "fullness of joy" (Psalm 16:11) and is
vital to our victory as believers.

In Your presence is fullness of joy;
In Your right hand there are
  pleasures forevermore. [Acts
  2:25–28, 31]

PSALM 17
Prayer for Protection against Oppressors.

A Prayer of David.

¹ HEAR THE just (righteous)
  cause, O LORD; listen to my loud
  [piercing] cry;
Listen to my prayer, that comes
  from guileless lips.
² Let my verdict of vindication come
  from Your presence;
May Your eyes look with equity
  and behold things that are just.
³ You have tried my heart;
You have visited me in the night;
You have tested me and You find
  nothing [evil in me];
I intend that my mouth will not
  transgress.
⁴ Concerning the deeds of men, by
  the word of Your lips
I have kept away from the paths of
  the violent.
⁵ My steps have held closely to Your
  paths;
My feet have not staggered.

⁶ I have called upon You, for You,
  O God, will answer me;
Incline Your ear to me, hear my
  speech.
⁷ Wondrously show Your [marvelous
  and amazing] lovingkindness,
O Savior of those who take refuge
  at Your right hand
From those who rise up *against*
  them.
⁸ Keep me [in Your affectionate
  care, protect me] as the apple of
  Your eye;
Hide me in the [protective]
  shadow of Your wings

⁹ From the wicked who despoil *and*
  deal violently with me,
My deadly enemies who
  surround me.
¹⁰ They have closed their unfeeling
  heart [to kindness and
  compassion];
With their mouths they speak
  proudly *and* make presumptuous
  claims.
¹¹ They track us down *and* have now
  surrounded us in our steps;
They set their eyes to force us to
  the ground,
¹² He is like a lion eager to tear [his
  prey],
And like a young lion lurking in
  hiding places.

¹³ Arise, O LORD, confront him, cast
  him down;
Save my soul from the wicked with
  Your sword,
¹⁴ From men with Your hand, O LORD,
From men of the world [these
  moths of the night] whose
  portion [of enjoyment] is in this
  life—idle and vain,
And whose belly You fill with Your
  treasure;

life point

Psalm 17:15 is one of my favorite verses because it teaches us how to wake up in the morning feeling satisfied in the Lord. Earlier in my life, I had many unhappy days because the minute I awoke each morning, I began to think about the wrong things. But since I have learned the importance of seeking God's presence and not just His presents, I am a different person. I wake up with a thankful heart, and God has taught me to think of others and not just myself. Fellowshipping with God early in the morning is one sure way to begin enjoying every day of your life.

They are satisfied with children,
And they leave what they have left
[of wealth] to their children.
15 As for me, I shall see Your face in
righteousness;
I will be [fully] satisfied when I
awake [to find myself] seeing
Your likeness.

PSALM 18

David Praises the LORD for Rescuing Him.

To the Chief Musician. A Psalm
of David, the servant of the LORD,
who spoke the words of this
song to the LORD on the day
when the LORD rescued him from
the hand of all his enemies and
from the hand of Saul. And he said:

1 "I LOVE You [fervently and
devotedly], O LORD, my strength."
2 The LORD is my rock, my fortress,
and the One who rescues me;
My God, my rock and strength in
whom I trust and take refuge;
My shield, and the horn of my
salvation, my high tower—my
stronghold. [Heb 2:13]
3 I call upon the LORD, who is worthy
to be praised;
And I am saved from my enemies.
[Rev 5:12]

4 The cords of death surrounded me,
And the streams of ungodliness
and torrents of destruction
terrified me.
5 The cords of Sheol (the nether
world, the place of the dead)
surrounded me;

The snares of death
confronted me.
6 In my distress [when I seemed
surrounded] I called upon the
LORD
And cried to my God for help;
He heard my voice from His
temple,
And my cry for help came before
Him, into His very ears.

7 Then the earth shook and quaked,
The foundations of the mountains
trembled;
They were shaken because He was
indignant and angry.
8 Smoke went up from His nostrils,
And fire from His mouth
devoured;
Coals were kindled by it.
9 He bowed the heavens also and
came down;
And thick darkness was under His
feet.
10 And He rode upon a cherub
(storm) and flew;
And He sped on the wings of the
wind.
11 He made darkness His hiding
place (covering); His pavilion
(canopy) around Him,
The darkness of the waters, the
thick clouds of the skies.
12 Out of the brightness before Him
passed His thick clouds,
Hailstones and coals of fire.
13 The LORD also thundered in the
heavens,
And the Most High uttered His
voice,
Hailstones and coals of fire.
14 He sent out His arrows and
scattered them;

speak the Word

*Lord, I declare that You are my Rock and Strength, my Fortress,
and the One who rescues me. You are my Shield, the Horn of my salvation,
and my High Tower—my Stronghold!*
—ADAPTED FROM PSALM 18:2

And *He sent* an abundance of lightning flashes and confused *and* routed them [in defeat].

15 Then the stream beds of the waters appeared,
And the foundations of the world were laid bare
At Your rebuke, O Lord,
At the blast of the breath of Your nostrils.

16 He reached from on high, He took me;
He drew me out of many waters.

17 He rescued me from my strong enemy,
And from those who hated me, for they were too strong for me.

18 They confronted me in the day of my disaster,
But the Lord was my support.

19 He brought me out into a broad place;
He rescued me because He was pleased with me *and* delighted in me.

20 The Lord dealt with me according to my righteousness (moral character, spiritual integrity);
According to the cleanness of my hands He has rewarded me.

21 For I have kept the ways of the Lord,
And have not wickedly departed from my God.

22 For all His ordinances were before me,
And I did not put away His statutes from me.

23 I was blameless before Him,
And I kept myself free from my sin.

24 Therefore the Lord has rewarded me according to my righteousness (moral character, spiritual integrity),
According to the cleanness of my hands in His sight.

25 With the kind (merciful, faithful, loyal) You show Yourself kind,
With the blameless You show Yourself blameless,

26 With the pure You show Yourself pure,
And with the crooked You show Yourself astute.

27 For You save an afflicted *and* humble people,
But bring down those [arrogant fools] with haughty eyes.

28 For You cause my lamp to be lighted *and* to shine;
The Lord my God illumines my darkness.

29 For by You I can crush a troop,
And by my God I can leap over a wall.

30 As for God, His way is blameless.
The word of the Lord is tested [it is perfect, it is faultless];
He is a shield to all who take refuge in Him.

31 For who is God, but the Lord?
Or who is a rock, except our God,

32 The God who encircles me with strength
And makes my way blameless?

33 He makes my feet like hinds' feet [able to stand firmly and tread safely on paths of testing and trouble];
He sets me [securely] upon my high places.

34 He trains my hands for war,

speak the Word

God, I know that Your way is blameless; Your word is tested. It is perfect and faultless. You are a shield to all who take refuge in You.
–adapted from Psalm 18:30

So that my arms can bend a bow of
bronze.
[35] You have also given me the shield
of Your salvation,
And Your right hand upholds *and*
sustains me;
Your gentleness [Your gracious
response when I pray] makes me
great.
[36] You enlarge the path beneath me
and make my steps secure,
So that my feet will not slip.

[37] I pursued my enemies and
overtook them;
And I did not turn back until they
were consumed.
[38] I shattered them so that they were
not able to rise;
They fell [wounded] under my
feet.
[39] For You have encircled me with
strength for the battle;
You have subdued under me those
who rose up against me.
[40] You have also made my enemies
turn their backs to me [in defeat],
And I silenced *and* destroyed those
who hated me.
[41] They cried for help, but there was
no one to save them—
Even to the LORD [they cried], but
He did not answer them.
[42] Then I beat them fine as the dust
before the wind;
I emptied them out as the dirt of
the streets.

[43] You have rescued me from the
contentions of the people;
You have placed me as the head of
the nations;
A people whom I have not known
serve me.
[44] As soon as they hear me, they
respond *and* obey me;
Foreigners feign obedience to me.
[45] Foreigners lose heart,
And come trembling out of their
strongholds.

[46] The LORD lives, blessed be my rock;
And may the God of my salvation
be exalted,
[47] The God who avenges me,
And subdues peoples (nations)
under me.
[48] He rescues me from my enemies;
Yes, You lift me up above those
who rise up against me;
You deliver me from the man of
violence.
[49] Therefore will I give thanks *and*
praise You, O LORD, among the
nations,
And sing praises to Your name.
[Rom 15:9]
[50] He gives great triumphs to His king,
And shows steadfast love *and*
mercy to His anointed,
To David and his descendants
forever. [2 Sam 22:2–51]

PSALM 19

The Works and the Word of God.

To the Chief Musician. A Psalm
of David.

[1] THE HEAVENS are telling of the
glory of God;

putting the Word to work

Our everyday lives are governed
by man-made laws that are for our
benefit—obeying the speed limit,
stopping at red lights, etc. Are you
equally aware of the benefits of living
by God's perfect Law? Wisdom, joy,
righteousness, rewards—all these
things and more are benefits that
come from living according to God's
Law. Spend time studying God's Word
each day, and ask Him to help you live
by it, so you can glorify Him and enjoy
His blessings.

And the expanse [of heaven] is
   declaring the work of His hands.
   [Rom 1:20, 21]
2 Day after day pours forth speech,
   And night after night reveals
   knowledge.
3 There is no speech, nor are there
   [spoken] words [from the stars];
  Their voice is not heard.
4 Yet their voice [in quiet evidence]
   has gone out through all the
   earth,
  Their words to the end of the world.

In them *and* in the heavens He has
   made a tent for the sun, [Rom
   10:18]
5 Which is as a bridegroom coming
   out of his chamber;
It rejoices as a strong man to run
   his course.
6 The sun's rising is from one end of
   the heavens,
And its circuit to the other end of
   them;
And there is nothing hidden from
   its heat.

enjoy God's handiwork

God speaks to everyone through His handiwork. Even people living outside God's will perceive right from wrong and the reality of God, because Psalm 19:1–4 tells us that nature itself testifies of God's power and divine plan.

I encourage you to take time to look at what God has created. The main message God speaks to us through nature is that *He is*. This is an important revelation because the Bible says that before we can get anywhere with God, we must first believe He is: "But without faith it is impossible to [walk with God and] please Him, for whoever comes [near] to God must [necessarily] believe that God exists and that He rewards those who [earnestly and diligently] seek Him" (Hebrews 11:6). We *can* believe God because the Bible says He has given every person a degree of faith to believe in Him (see Romans 12:3).

The very first words of the Bible give our first lesson of faith: "In the beginning God . . ." (Genesis 1:1). Many people acknowledge that God exists, but they have not learned to relate to Him on a day-to-day level. Through grace, God tries to reach us every day, and He places reminders of Himself everywhere. He leaves clues of Himself all around us, clues that bellow out clearly, "I am here. You do not have to live in fear; you do not have to worry, I am here." God wants to be involved in every aspect of your life. If He has taken time to keep all your tears in a bottle and count the very hairs on your head, then surely He cares about everything else.

Jesus said to think about "the lilies and wildflowers of the field" (see Matthew 6:28) and the birds of the air (see Luke 12:24). Meditating on how God adorns the fields and provides for the birds can remind us that He cares even more for us. A nice walk outdoors is a great opportunity to take a short vacation from the pressures of daily living and look at the trees, the birds, the flowers, and the children playing. Let me encourage you to take time to appreciate God's awesome handiwork today and to thank Him that He *is*.

Life is sometimes very complicated, but we can purposefully learn to enjoy the simple yet powerful and beautiful things God has created!

7 The law of the LORD is perfect
  (flawless), restoring *and*
  refreshing the soul;
The statutes of the LORD are
  reliable *and* trustworthy, making
  wise the simple.
8 The precepts of the LORD are right,
  bringing joy to the heart;
The commandment of the LORD is
  pure, enlightening the eyes.
9 The fear of the LORD is clean,
  enduring forever;
The judgments of the LORD
  are true, they are righteous
  altogether.
10 They are more desirable than gold,
  yes, than much fine gold;
Sweeter also than honey and the
  drippings of the honeycomb.
11 Moreover, by them Your servant is
  warned [reminded, illuminated,
  and instructed];
In keeping them there is great
  reward.
12 Who can understand his errors *or*
  omissions? Acquit me of hidden
  (unconscious, unintended) *faults.*
13 Also keep back Your servant
  from presumptuous (deliberate,
  willful) *sins;*
Let them not rule *and* have control
  over me.
Then I will be blameless
  (complete),

life point

In Psalm 19:14, the psalmist prays: "Let
the words of my mouth and the meditation of my heart be acceptable and
pleasing in Your sight, O LORD, my [firm,
immovable] rock and my Redeemer."
Notice that he mentions both the mind
and the mouth. This is because the two
work together. We need to make sure that
meditations (our thoughts) are pleasing
to God so that our words will be acceptable to Him as well.

And I shall be acquitted of great
  transgression.
14 Let the words of my mouth and the
  meditation of my heart
Be acceptable *and* pleasing in Your
  sight,
O LORD, my [firm, immovable] rock
  and my Redeemer.

PSALM 20

Prayer for Victory over Enemies.

To the Chief Musician. A Psalm
of David.

1 MAY THE LORD answer you
  (David) in the day of trouble!
May the name of the God of Jacob
  set you *securely* on high [and
  defend you in battle]!
2 May He send you help from the
  sanctuary (His dwelling place)
And support *and* strengthen you
  from Zion!
3 May He remember all your meal
  offerings
And accept your burnt offering.
                                   Selah.

4 May He grant you your heart's
  desire
And fulfill all your plans.
5 We will sing joyously over your
  victory,
And in the name of our God we
  will set up our banners.
May the LORD fulfill all your
  petitions.

6 Now I know that the LORD saves
  His anointed;
He will answer him from His holy
  heaven
With the saving strength of His
  right hand.
7 Some *trust* in chariots and some in
  horses,
But we will remember *and* trust in
  the name of the LORD our God.
8 They have bowed down and fallen,

But we have risen and stood
   upright.
⁹O Lord, save [the king];
May the King answer us in the day
   we call.

PSALM 21

Praise for Help.

To the Chief Musician. A Psalm
of David.

¹O LORD the king will delight in
   Your strength,
And in Your salvation how greatly
   will he rejoice!
²You have given him his heart's
   desire,
And You have not withheld the
   request of his lips.   *Selah.*
³For You meet him with blessings of
   good things;
You set a crown of pure gold on his
   head.
⁴He asked life of You,
And You gave it to him,
Long life forever and evermore.
⁵His glory is great because of Your
   victory;
Splendor and majesty You bestow
   upon him.
⁶For You make him most blessed
   [and a blessing] forever;
You make him joyful with the joy
   of Your presence. [Gen 12:2]

⁷For the king [confidently] trusts in
   the Lord,
And through the lovingkindness
   (faithfulness, goodness) of the
   Most High he will never be
   shaken.
⁸Your hand will reach out *and*
   defeat all your enemies;
Your right hand will reach those
   who hate you.
⁹You will make them as [if in] a
   blazing oven in the time of your
   anger;

The Lord will swallow them up in
   His wrath,
And the fire will devour them.
¹⁰Their offspring You will destroy
   from the earth,
And their descendants from the
   sons of men.
¹¹For they planned evil against You;
They devised a [malevolent] plot
And they will not succeed.
¹²For You will make them turn their
   backs [in defeat];
You will aim Your bowstring [of
   divine justice] at their faces.
¹³Be exalted, Lord, in Your strength;
We will sing and praise Your
   power.

PSALM 22

A Cry of Anguish and a Song
of Praise.

To the Chief Musician; set
to [the tune of] Aijeleth
Hashshahar (The Doe
of the Dawn). A Psalm of David.

¹MY GOD, my God, why have You
   forsaken me?
Why are You so far from helping
   me, and from the words of my
   groaning? [Matt 27:46]
²O my God, I call out by day, but
   You do not answer;
And by night, but I find no rest *nor*
   quiet.
³But You are holy,
O You who are enthroned in [the
   holy place where] the praises of
   Israel [are offered].
⁴In You our fathers trusted
   [leaned on, relied on, and were
   confident];
They trusted and You rescued
   them.
⁵They cried out to You and were
   delivered;
They trusted in You and were not
   disappointed *or* ashamed.

⁶But I am [treated as] a worm
[insignificant and powerless]
and not a man;
I am the scorn of men and
despised by the people. [Matt
27:39–44]
⁷All who see me laugh at me *and*
mock me;
They [insultingly] open their lips,
they shake their head, *saying,*
[Matt 27:43]
⁸"He trusted *and* committed himself
to the LORD, let Him save him.

life point

God is enthroned in the praises of His
people (see Psalm 22:3). That means He
is comfortable in the midst of our sweet
praises, but He is not comfortable in the
midst of our sour attitudes.

I encourage you to take an inventory of
your inner life because it is the dwelling
place of God. When God dwelled in the
portable tabernacle that the children of
Israel carried through the wilderness,
they understood that the inner court
was a holy place. But now in the mystery
of God's plan, we are like a portable
tabernacle; we move from place to place,
and God dwells inside us. There is still an
outer court, a holy place, and a most holy
place. The outer court is our body, the
holy place is our soul, and the most holy
place is our spirit.

When we examine our inner lives, we are
looking at holy ground where the Spirit
of God wants to make His home. God is
much more interested in our inner lives
than in our outer lives, and we need to be
more concerned about what goes on *inside* us than about our external behavior.
Praise, worship, and honor God in your
inner life. When your "insides" are right,
your "outsides" will follow!

Let Him rescue him, because He
delights in him." [Matt 27:39, 43;
Mark 15:29, 30; Luke 23:35]
⁹Yet You are He who pulled me out
of the womb;
You made me trust when on my
mother's breasts.
¹⁰I was cast upon You from birth;
From my mother's womb You have
been my God.
¹¹Do not be far from me, for trouble
is near;
And there is no one to help.
¹²Many [enemies like] bulls have
surrounded me;
Strong *bulls* of Bashan have
encircled me. [Ezek 39:18;
Amos 4:1]
¹³They open wide their mouths
against me,
Like a ravening and a roaring lion.
¹⁴I am poured out like water,
And all my bones are out of joint.
My heart is like wax;
It is melted [by anguish]
within me.
¹⁵My strength is dried up like a
fragment of clay pottery;
And my [dry] tongue clings to my
jaws;
And You have laid me in the dust
of death. [John 19:28]
¹⁶For [a pack of] dogs have
surrounded me;
A gang of evildoers has encircled
me,
They pierced my hands and my
feet. [Is 53:7; John 19:37]
¹⁷I can count all my bones;
They look, they stare at me. [Luke
23:27, 35]
¹⁸They divide my clothing among
them
And cast lots for my garment.
[John 19:23, 24]
¹⁹But You, O LORD, do not be far
from me;

O You my help, come quickly to my
assistance.
20 Rescue my life from the sword,
My only *life* from the paw of the
dog (the executioner).
21 Save me from the lion's mouth;
From the horns of the wild oxen
You answer me.

22 I will tell of Your name to my
countrymen;
In the midst of the congregation I
will praise You. [John 20:17; Rom
8:29; Heb 2:12]
23 You who fear the LORD [with awe-
inspired reverence], praise Him!
All you descendants of Jacob, honor
Him.
Fear Him [with submissive
wonder], all you descendants of
Israel.
24 For He has not despised nor
detested the suffering of the
afflicted;
Nor has He hidden His face from
him;
But when he cried to Him for help,
He listened.

25 My praise will be of You in the
great assembly.
I will pay my vows [made in the
time of trouble] before those who
[reverently] fear Him.
26 The afflicted will eat and be
satisfied;
Those who [diligently] seek
Him *and* require Him [as their
greatest need] will praise the
LORD.
May your hearts live forever!
27 All the ends of the earth will
remember and turn to the LORD,
And all the families of the nations
will bow down *and* worship
before You,
28 For the kingship *and* the kingdom
are the LORD's
And He rules over the nations.

29 All the prosperous of the earth
will eat and worship;
All those who go down to the dust
(the dead) will bow before Him,
Even he who cannot keep his soul
alive.
30 Posterity will serve Him;
They will tell of the Lord to the
next generation.
31 They will come and declare His
righteousness
To a people yet to be born—that
He has done it [and that it is
finished]. [John 19:30]

PSALM 23

The LORD, the Psalmist's Shepherd.

A Psalm of David.

1 THE LORD is my Shepherd [to
feed, to guide and to shield me],
[Ezek 34:11–31]
I shall not want.

life point

The last part of the beloved Psalm 23
describes the condition in which the Lord
wants us to be continually. He wants us to
be protected, guided, and comforted. He
wants to set a table of blessings before us
in the very face of our enemies. He wants
to anoint us with the oil of joy instead of
mourning. He wants our cup of blessings
to overflow continually in thanksgiving and praise to Him for His goodness,
mercy, and unfailing love toward us. And
He wants us to live, moment by moment,
in His presence.

All these things are part of His good plan
for each of us. Regardless of how far we
may have fallen, He wants to raise us up
and restore us to that right and perfect
plan He has for our lives.

²He lets me lie down in green
  pastures;
He leads me beside the still *and*
  quiet waters. [Rev 7:17]
³He refreshes *and* restores my soul
  (life);
He leads me in the paths of
  righteousness
for His name's sake.

⁴Even though I walk through the
  [sunless] *valley of the shadow
  of death,
I fear no evil, for You are with me;
Your rod [to protect] and Your
  staff [to guide], they comfort *and*
  console me.

23:4 Or *valley of deep darkness.*

putting the Word to work

At some point in our lives, all of us will walk through the valley of the shadow of death, either facing our own death, the death of a loved one or some other extraordinarily difficult time (see Psalm 23:4). Are you or is someone you love walking through that valley right now? Remember, where there is a shadow, there must be light—and the Light of the world, Jesus, has promised to be with you always. Ask Him right now to comfort and guide you, and know that He is walking with you in every situation.

God restores and leads

The twenty-third Psalm is so comforting. In it the psalmist David tells us the Lord leads, feeds, guides, and shields us. He causes us to lie down and rest, and He "refreshes and restores" (Psalm 23:3) our lives. I like the way the Amplified Bible translates this verse, but I also like the way the beautiful old King James Version renders it: "He restoreth my soul." The soul is comprised of the mind, the will, and the emotions.

With our souls, we process our circumstances, we entertain our thoughts, we feel and express emotions, and we make decisions. What a wonderful promise—that God will restore our souls! The word *restore* means "to bring back into existence or use" or "to bring back to an original state or condition." The word is often used in a situation when a dethroned ruler is put back on his throne. *Restore* also means, "to make restitution, to cause to return, or to refresh."

When David says God will restore our souls and our lives, I believe he means that God will return us to the state or condition we were in before we strayed from following the good plan God had predestined for us before our birth, or before Satan attacked us to draw us out of God's plan for our lives.

We can take confidence that God will lead us in the path of righteousness, uprightness, and right standing with Him. I believe David is saying here that God individually leads each of us in the path that is right for us, a path that restores us in every way to the good places God has for us.

God has a path predestined for your restoration. If you will allow Him to do so, He will guide you by His Holy Spirit along the unique way that leads to restoration and to being able to fulfill the great purposes He has for your life.

⁵You prepare a table before me in
the presence of my enemies.
You have anointed *and* refreshed
my head with oil;
My cup overflows.
⁶Surely goodness and mercy *and*
unfailing love shall follow me all
the days of my life,
And I shall dwell forever
[throughout all my days] in the
house *and* in the presence of the
LORD.

PSALM 24

The King of Glory Entering Zion.

A Psalm of David.

¹THE EARTH is the LORD's, and the
fullness of it,
The world, and those who dwell in
it. [1 Cor 10:26]
²For He has founded it upon the seas
And established it upon the
streams *and* the rivers.
³Who may ascend onto the
mountain of the LORD?
And who may stand in His holy
place?
⁴He who has clean hands and a
pure heart,
Who has not lifted up his soul to
what is false,
Nor has sworn [oaths] deceitfully.
[Matt 5:8]
⁵He shall receive a blessing from
the LORD,
And righteousness from the God
of his salvation.
⁶This is the generation (description)
of those who diligently seek Him
and require Him as their greatest
need,

Who seek Your face, even [as did]
Jacob. [Ps 42:1]   *Selah*.
⁷Lift up your heads, O gates,
And be lifted up, ancient doors,
That the King of glory may
come in.
⁸Who is the King of glory?
The LORD strong and mighty,
The LORD mighty in battle.
⁹Lift up your heads, O gates,
And lift them up, ancient doors,
That the King of glory may
come in.
¹⁰Who is [He then] this King of glory?
The LORD of hosts,
He is the King of glory [who
rules over all creation with His
heavenly armies].   *Selah*.

PSALM 25

Prayer for Protection, Guidance and Pardon.

A Psalm of David.

¹TO YOU, O LORD, I lift up my soul.
²O my God, in You I [have
unwavering] trust [and I rely on
You with steadfast confidence],
Do not let me be ashamed *or* my
hope in You be disappointed;
Do not let my enemies triumph
over me.
³Indeed, none of those who
[expectantly] wait for You will
be ashamed;
Those who turn away from what
is right *and* deal treacherously
without cause will be ashamed
(humiliated, embarrassed).
⁴Let me know Your ways, O LORD;
Teach me Your paths.

speak the Word

*God, I pray that You would let me know Your ways and teach me Your paths.
I am asking You to guide me in Your truth. You are my salvation,
and I am waiting expectantly on You.*
—ADAPTED FROM PSALM 25:4, 5

⁵Guide me in Your truth and teach me,
  For You are the God of my salvation;
  For You [and only You] I wait [expectantly] all the day long.
⁶Remember, O LORD, Your [tender] compassion and Your lovingkindnesses,
  For they have been from of old.
⁷Do not remember the sins of my youth or my transgressions;
  According to Your lovingkindness remember me,
  For Your goodness' sake, O LORD.
⁸Good and upright is the LORD;
  Therefore He instructs sinners in the way.
⁹He leads the humble in justice,
  And He teaches the humble His way.
¹⁰All the paths of the LORD are lovingkindness *and* goodness and truth *and* faithfulness

at ease

In order to live victorious lives, we need to be comfortable spiritually. That may sound strange to you, so let me share a story to explain what I mean.

In 1980, I had a job as the pastor's secretary at my church in St. Louis. After working one day, I got fired. Do you know why? Because I was not supposed to be a secretary; therefore, God would not bless me in that job.

You see, my desire to be a secretary was *my* idea, not God's; it was something *I* wanted to do, not something God wanted me to do. The job was not a "fit" for me; it was not comfortable for me, and I did not have grace to do it. It was not part of God's purpose for my life, and He would not allow me to stay in that job because He had other plans for me.

Trying to do things that are not part of God's plan for our lives is like trying to force our feet into shoes that are too small. I have been guilty of wanting to buy shoes that are slightly too tight, but I do not do that anymore. I have learned that tight shoes are not comfortable, and I want my feet to be comfortable.

During those days, I wanted to be comfortable spiritually too. I wanted to be relaxed in spirit; I wanted my inner life to be at ease, as though I were walking around in my most comfortable shoes. I wanted to be relaxed in my relationship with God and to feel at home in His presence. I also wanted to be comfortable around other people and not be afraid of their disapproval. All those things that I wanted I now enjoy because I have learned to follow God's plan rather than my own.

Do you feel the same way? Are you tired of being uncomfortable and being in places that do not fit God's call on your life? Are you tired of being spiritually uncomfortable, insecure, or anxious all the time?

I have good news for you. Psalm 25:12, 13 tell us that we can "dwell in prosperity and goodness," which is another way of saying we can be at ease, if we fear God, worship Him, and do what He has planned for us without trying to force our own agendas or striving to do what *we* want to do. God loves you, and He has awesome plans for your life. Surrender to His plans and His way—and you will find yourself at ease.

To those who keep His covenant
    and His testimonies.
[11]For Your name's sake, O Lord,
    Pardon my wickedness *and* my
    guilt, for they are great.
[12]Who is the man who fears the Lord
    [with awe-inspired reverence
    and worships Him with
    submissive wonder]?
He will teach him [through His
    word] in the way he should
    choose.
[13]His soul will dwell in prosperity
    and goodness,
And his descendants will inherit
    the land.
[14]The secret [of the wise counsel]
    of the Lord is for those who fear
    Him,
And He will let them know His
    covenant *and* reveal to them
    [through His word] its [deep,
    inner] meaning. [John 7:17; 15:15]
[15]My eyes are continually toward the
    Lord,
For He will bring my feet out of the
    net.

[16]Turn to me [Lord] and be gracious
    to me,
For I am alone and afflicted.
[17]The troubles of my heart are
    multiplied;
Bring me out of my distresses.
[18]Look upon my affliction and my
    trouble,
And forgive all my sins.
[19]Look upon my enemies, for they
    are many;
They hate me with cruel *and*
    violent hatred.
[20]Guard my soul and rescue me;
Do not let me be ashamed *or*
    disappointed,
For I have taken refuge in You.
[21]Let integrity and uprightness
    protect me,
For I wait [expectantly] for You.
[22]O God, redeem Israel,
Out of all his troubles.

PSALM 26

Protestation of Integrity and Prayer for Protection.

A Psalm of David.

[1]VINDICATE ME, O Lord, for I
    have walked in my integrity;
I have [relied on and] trusted
    [confidently] in the Lord without
    wavering *and* I shall not slip.
[2]Examine me, O Lord, and try me;
Test my heart and my mind.
[3]For Your lovingkindness is before
    my eyes,
And I have walked [faithfully] in
    Your truth.
[4]I do not sit with deceitful *or*
    unethical *or* worthless men,
Nor seek companionship with
    pretenders (self-righteous
    hypocrites).
[5]I hate the company of evildoers,
And will not sit with the wicked.
[6]I will wash my hands in innocence,
And I will go about Your altar,
    O Lord,
[7]That I may proclaim with the voice
    of thanksgiving
And declare all Your wonders.

[8]O Lord, I love the habitation of
    Your house
And the place where Your glory
    dwells.
[9]Do not sweep my soul away with
    sinners,
Nor [sweep away] my life with
    men of bloodshed,
[10]In whose hands is a wicked
    scheme,
And whose right hand is full of
    bribes.
[11]But as for me, I shall walk in my
    integrity;
Redeem me and be merciful *and*
    gracious to me.
[12]My foot stands on a level place;
In the congregations I will bless the
    Lord.

PSALM 27

A Psalm of Fearless Trust in God.

A Psalm of David.

¹THE LORD is my light and my
    salvation—
Whom shall I fear?
The LORD is the refuge *and* fortress
    of my life—
Whom shall I dread?
²When the wicked came against me
    to eat up my flesh,
My adversaries and my enemies,
    they stumbled and fell.
³Though an army encamp against
    me,
My heart will not fear;

Though war arise against me,
Even in this I am confident.

⁴One thing I have asked of the LORD,
    and that I will seek:
That I may dwell in the house of
    the LORD [in His presence] all the
    days of my life,
To gaze upon the beauty [the
    delightful loveliness and
    majestic grandeur] of the LORD
And to meditate in His temple. [Ps
    16:11; 18:6; 65:4; Luke 2:37]
⁵For in the day of trouble He will
    hide me in His shelter;
In the secret place of His tent He
    will hide me;
He will lift me up on a rock.

seek the "one thing"

If you could ask for only one thing, what would it be? In Psalm 27:4, David said there was only one thing that he sought after—to dwell in God's presence. More than anything else, David wanted to know God, to see God as He really is and to be with Him. Truly, to know God is the highest calling we have.

Unfortunately, we can get so distracted with the busy details of our lives that we neglect the most important thing—spending time with God. Luke 10:38–42 illustrates this point well as it relates the story of busy Martha. When Jesus visited her home, she became preoccupied with serving, but her sister Mary stopped all work and sat at His feet. Jesus told Martha that only one thing was really important, and Mary had chosen it. Mary had decided she was not going to miss the opportunity to listen to the Master. I suppose Martha intended to work Jesus into her schedule somewhere, but Mary was willing to stop what she was doing and work her schedule around Him.

How foolish we are to spend our lives seeking those things that cannot satisfy while we ignore God, the "One Thing" Who can give us great joy, peace, satisfaction, and contentment. The world is filled with empty people who are trying to satisfy the void in their lives with the latest-model car, a promotion at work, a human relationship, a vacation, or some other thing. Their efforts to find fulfillment in those things never work. It is sad that so many people waste their entire lives and never realize it. They never know the joy of seeking the "One Thing" they really need. Each one of us has a God-shaped hole inside, and nothing can fill it except God Himself. No matter what else we try to fill it with, we will remain empty and frustrated.

If God is on your list of things to seek, but not at the top, I encourage you to move everything around and put it all *after* Him. If you will put Him first in everything you do, you will be so blessed. Investing your life in God is the very best thing you can do.

⁶ And now my head will be lifted up
above my enemies around me,
In His tent I will offer sacrifices
with shouts of joy;
I will sing, yes, I will sing praises
to the LORD.
⁷ Hear, O LORD, when I cry aloud;
Be gracious *and* compassionate to
me and answer me.
⁸ *When You said,* "Seek My face [in
prayer, require My presence as
your greatest need]," my heart
said to You,
"Your face, O LORD, I will seek [on
the authority of Your word]."
⁹ Do not hide Your face from me,
Do not turn Your servant away in
anger;
You have been my help;
Do not abandon me nor leave me,
O God of my salvation!

¹⁰ Although my father and my
mother have abandoned me,
Yet the LORD will take me up [adopt
me as His child]. [Ps 22:10]
¹¹ Teach me Your way, O LORD,
And lead me on a level path
Because of my enemies [who lie in
wait].
¹² Do not give me up to the will of my
adversaries,
For false witnesses have come
against me;
They breathe out violence.
¹³ *I would have despaired* had I not
believed that I would see the
goodness of the LORD
In the land of the living.
¹⁴ Wait for *and* confidently expect the
LORD;
Be strong and let your heart take
courage;

the land of the living

In Psalm 27:13, David asked, "What in the world would have happened to me? What kind of condition would I be in? What pit would I be in, had I not believed I would see the Lord's goodness in the land of the living?"

We spend a lot of time talking about what heaven will be like. That is great, but we are here on earth right now. We need to know something good is going to happen to us now. David said that he believed he would see God's goodness while he was alive, not just after he went to heaven.

I am looking forward to heaven, but I do not believe that God put us on earth to try to muddle through life until we get to heaven so we can finally have some joy. In John 10:10, Jesus says, "The thief comes only in order to steal and kill and destroy. I came that they may have and enjoy life, and have it in abundance [to the full, till it overflows]." God wants us to have abundant life right now, and one of the worst things we can do is fail to live lives that we enjoy. I have decided to enjoy my life while I am "in the land of the living." I want to have so much fun that the devil gets frustrated at my joy.

Let me encourage you to be like David and to believe that you will see and experience God's goodness not just in the "sweet by-and-by," but here on earth, every day, in the ordinary activities of your life. No matter what you are going through, put your hope in God's goodness and expect Him to move in your situation. Be brave and of good courage; let your heart be stout and enduring. Wait for and hope for and expect the Lord where you live today—in the land of the living.

Yes, wait for *and* confidently
  expect the LORD.

PSALM 28

A Prayer for Help, and Praise for Its Answer.

A Psalm of David.

1 TO YOU I call, O LORD,
  My rock, do not be deaf to me,
  For if You are silent to me,
  I will become like those who go
    down to the pit (grave).
2 Hear the voice of my supplication
    (specific requests, humble
    entreaties) as I cry to You for help,
  As I lift up my hands *and* heart
    toward Your innermost
    sanctuary (Holy of Holies).
3 Do not drag me away with the
    wicked
  And with those who do evil,
  Who speak peace with their
    neighbors,
  While malice *and* mischief are in
    their hearts.
4 Repay them according to their
    work and according to the evil of
    their practices;
  Repay them according to the deeds
    of their hands;
  Repay them what they deserve.
    [2 Tim 4:14; Rev 18:6]
5 Because they have no regard for
    the works of the LORD
  Nor the deeds of His hands,
  He will tear them down and not
    rebuild them.
6 Blessed be the LORD,
  Because He has heard the voice of
    my supplication.

7 The LORD is my strength and my
    [impenetrable] shield;
  My heart trusts [with unwavering
    confidence] in Him, and I am
    helped;
  Therefore my heart greatly
    rejoices,
  And with my song I shall thank
    Him *and* praise Him.
8 The LORD is their [unyielding]
    strength,
  And He is the fortress of salvation
    to His anointed.
9 Save Your people and bless Your
    inheritance;
  Be their shepherd also, and carry
    them forever.

PSALM 29

The Voice of the LORD in the Storm.

A Psalm of David.

1 ASCRIBE TO the LORD, O sons of
    the mighty,
  Ascribe to the LORD glory and
    strength.
2 Ascribe to the LORD the glory due
    His name;
  Worship the LORD in the beauty
    and majesty of His holiness
    [as the creator and source of
    holiness].
3 The voice of the LORD is upon the
    waters;
  The God of glory thunders;
  The LORD is over many waters.
4 The voice of the LORD is powerful;
  The voice of the LORD is full of
    majesty.
5 The voice of the LORD breaks the
    cedars;

speak the Word

Lord, You are my Strength and my impenetrable Shield.
My heart trusts in You with unwavering confidence.
—ADAPTED FROM PSALM 28:7

Yes, the LORD breaks in pieces the
    cedars of Lebanon.
⁶He makes Lebanon skip like a calf,
And Sirion (Mount Hermon) like a
    young, wild ox.
⁷The voice of the LORD rakes flames
    of fire (lightning).
⁸The voice of the LORD shakes the
    wilderness;
The LORD shakes the wilderness of
    Kadesh.
⁹The voice of the LORD makes the
    doe labor *and* give birth
And strips the forests bare;
And in His temple all are saying,
    "Glory!"

¹⁰The LORD sat *as King* at the flood;
Yes, the LORD sits as King forever.
¹¹The LORD will give [unyielding and
    impenetrable] strength to His
    people;
The LORD will bless His people
    with peace.

PSALM 30

Thanksgiving for Deliverance from Death.

A Psalm; a Song at the Dedication
of the House (Temple). *A Psalm*
of David.

¹I WILL extol *and* praise You,
O LORD, for You have lifted me
    up,
And have not let my enemies
    rejoice over me.
²O LORD my God,
I cried to You for help, and You
    have healed me.

³O LORD, You have brought my life
    up from Sheol (the nether world,
    the place of the dead);
You have kept me alive, so that
    I would not go down to the pit
    (grave).
⁴Sing to the LORD, O you His godly
    ones,
And give thanks at the mention of
    His holy *name*.
⁵For His anger is but for a moment,
His favor is for a lifetime.
Weeping may endure for a night,
But a shout of joy comes in the
    morning. [2 Cor 4:17]

⁶As for me, in my prosperity I said,
    "I shall never be moved."
⁷By Your favor *and* grace, O LORD,
    you have made my mountain
    stand strong;
You hid Your face, and I was
    horrified.
⁸I called to You, O LORD,
And to the Lord I made
    supplication (specific request).
⁹"What profit is there in my blood
    (death), if I go down to the pit
    (grave)?
Will the dust praise You? Will it
    declare Your faithfulness [to
    man]?

¹⁰"Hear, O LORD, be gracious *and*
    show favor to me;
O LORD, be my helper."
¹¹You have turned my mourning
    into dancing for me;
You have taken off my sackcloth
    and clothed me with joy,
¹²That my soul may sing praise to
    You and not be silent.

speak the Word

*Thank You, God, that Your anger lasts but for a moment, but Your favor
is for a lifetime. Thank You that weeping may endure for only a night
and that a shout of joy comes in the morning.*
–ADAPTED FROM PSALM 30:5

O Lᴏʀᴅ my God, I will give thanks to You forever.

PSALM 31

A Psalm of Complaint and of Praise.

To the Chief Musician. A Psalm of David.

¹IN YOU, O Lᴏʀᴅ, I have placed my trust *and* taken refuge;
Let me never be ashamed;
In Your righteousness rescue me.
²Incline Your ear to me, deliver me quickly;
Be my rock of refuge,
And a strong fortress to save me.
³Yes, You are my rock and my fortress;
For Your name's sake You will lead me and guide me.
⁴You will draw me out of the net that they have secretly laid for me,
For You are my strength *and* my stronghold.
⁵Into Your hand I commit my spirit;
You have redeemed me,
O Lᴏʀᴅ, the God of truth *and* faithfulness. [Luke 23:46; Acts 7:59]
⁶I hate those who pay regard to vain (empty, worthless) idols;
But I trust in the Lᴏʀᴅ [and rely on Him with unwavering confidence].
⁷I will rejoice and be glad in Your steadfast love,
Because You have seen my affliction;
You have taken note of my life's distresses,
⁸And You have not given me into the hand of the enemy;
You have set my feet in a broad place.
⁹Be gracious *and* compassionate to me, O Lᴏʀᴅ, for I am in trouble;

My eye is clouded *and* weakened by grief, my soul and my body also.
¹⁰For my life is spent with sorrow
And my years with sighing;
My strength has failed because of my iniquity,
And even my body has wasted away.
¹¹Because of all my enemies I have become a reproach *and* disgrace,
Especially to my neighbors,
And an object of dread to my acquaintances;
Those who see me on the street run from me.
¹²I am forgotten like a dead man, out of mind;
I am like a broken vessel.
¹³For I have heard the slander *and* whispering of many,
Terror is on every side;
While they schemed together against me,
They plotted to take away my life. [Jer 20:10]
¹⁴But as for me, I trust [confidently] in You *and* Your greatness, O Lᴏʀᴅ;
I said, "You are my God."
¹⁵My times are in Your hands;
Rescue me from the hand of my enemies and from those who pursue *and* persecute me.
¹⁶Make Your face shine upon Your servant;
Save me in Your lovingkindness.
¹⁷Let me not be put to shame, O Lᴏʀᴅ, for I call on You;
Let the wicked (godless) be put to shame, let them be silent in Sheol (the nether world, the place of the dead).
¹⁸Let the lying lips be mute,
Which speak insolently *and* arrogantly against the [consistently] righteous
With pride and contempt.

19 How great is Your goodness,
  Which You have stored up for
    those who [reverently] fear You,
  Which You have prepared for
    those who take refuge in You,
  Before the sons of man!
20 In the secret place of Your
    presence You hide them from the
    plots *and* conspiracies of man;
  You keep them secretly in a shelter
    (pavilion) from the strife of
    tongues.
21 Blessed be the LORD,

For He has shown His marvelous
  favor *and* lovingkindness to
  me [when I was assailed] in a
  besieged city.
22 As for me, I said in my alarm,
  "I am cut off from Your eyes."
  Nevertheless You heard the voice
    of my supplications (specific
    requests)
  When I cried to You [for help].

23 O love the LORD, all you His godly
    ones!

everyday Christianity

God is good. All the time! Psalm 31:19 says that He stores up goodness for those who reverently fear Him. Notice also that this verse mentions the importance of trusting God "before the sons of man." This phrase says to me that if I refuse to be what some might call a "closet Christian," but instead be open and live my Christianity before all people, God will store up His goodness for me.

A number of people today profess to be Christians, but they do not want to admit it or live the principles of their faith outside their Christian circles. They are "Sunday morning" Christians, but on Monday morning they act no differently than unbelievers do. I call them "Sunday morning saints and Monday morning sinners."

I was once that way! I used to do all the "right" things in the right Christian circles, but I was not demonstrating vital faith elsewhere. I was on the church board, my husband was an elder in the church, our children went to Christian schools, our social life revolved around church, and we had a set of Christian bumper stickers for our cars. However, in my neighborhood, a person could not tell the difference between my behavior and the behavior of an unsaved person. At work, a person could not tell from my words or behavior that I was any different from my unsaved coworkers. Perhaps there was some difference, but not enough to notice! I was not taking the strong stand that I should have taken for God.

This is true for many of us. Because we are afraid of being rejected, isolated, or laughed at, we are afraid to take a stand and say, "I really don't want to hear a dirty joke. I'm a Christian, and I don't like to hear people take the Lord's name in vain. I'm not really interested in going to movies that leave wrong images in my mind or running to the bar every night after work for happy hour. That's not what I'm about. My life and my relationship with God are too important to me." That is what the Scripture means when it says, "Those who take refuge in You, before the sons of man" will be blessed. We must care more about our reputation in heaven than our reputation among people on earth. Stand strong for God, and never be ashamed or embarrassed to live the Christian life openly and boldly before other people.

The LORD preserves the faithful
   [those with moral and spiritual
   integrity]
And fully repays the [self-
   righteousness of the] arrogant.
24 Be strong and let your hearts take
   courage,
All you who wait for *and*
   confidently expect the LORD.

PSALM 32

Blessedness of Forgiveness and of Trust in God.

A Psalm of David. A skillful song,
or a didactic *or* reflective poem.

1 BLESSED [FORTUNATE,
   prosperous, favored by God]
   is he whose transgression is
   forgiven,
And whose sin is covered.
2 Blessed is the man to whom
   the LORD does not impute
   wickedness,
And in whose spirit there is no
   deceit. [Rom 4:7, 8]

3 When I kept silent *about my sin*,
   my body wasted away
Through my groaning all the day
   long.
4 For day and night Your hand [of
   displeasure] was heavy upon
   me;
My energy (vitality, strength)
   was drained away as with the
   burning heat of summer.   *Selah.*
5 I acknowledged my sin to You,
And I did not hide my wickedness;
I said, "I will confess [all] my
   transgressions to the LORD";
And You forgave the guilt of my
   sin.   *Selah.*
6 Therefore, let everyone who
   is godly pray to You [for
   forgiveness] in a time when You
   [are near and] may be found;

Surely when the great waters
   [of trial and distressing times]
   overflow they will not reach [the
   spirit in] him.
7 You are my hiding place; You,
   LORD, protect me from trouble;
You surround me with songs *and*
   shouts of deliverance.   *Selah.*

8 I will instruct you and teach you in
   the way you should go;
I will counsel you [who are willing
   to learn] with My eye upon you.
9 Do not be like the horse or
   like the mule which have no
   understanding,
Whose trappings include bridle
   and rein to hold them in check,
Otherwise they will not come near
   to you.
10 Many are the sorrows of the
   wicked,
But he who trusts in *and* relies on
   the LORD shall be surrounded
   with compassion *and*
   lovingkindness.

life point

Psalm 32:9 encourages us not to be like
horses or mules, which need bits and
bridles in order to follow their masters.
Either a horse follows the pull of the
bridle, which controls the bit in his mouth,
or he experiences great pain by resisting
it. The same principle applies to us and
to our relationship with the Holy Spirit.
He is our bridle and the bit in our mouths.
He should be controlling the reins of our
lives. If we follow His promptings, we will
end up at the right places and stay out of
the wrong places. But if we do not follow
Him, we will end up with a lot of pain.
Determine today that you will let Him
guide you and that you will not resist His
leading in your life.

11 Be glad in the Lord and rejoice,
   you righteous [who actively seek
   right standing with Him];
Shout for joy, all you upright in
   heart.

PSALM 33

Praise to the Creator and Preserver.

1 REJOICE IN the Lord, you
   righteous ones;
Praise is becoming *and* appropriate
   for those who are upright [in
   heart—those with moral integrity
   and godly character].
2 Give thanks to the Lord with the
   lyre;
Sing praises to Him with the harp
   of ten strings.
3 Sing to Him a new song;
Play skillfully [on the strings] with
   a loud *and* joyful sound.
4 For the word of the Lord is right;
And all His work is done in
   faithfulness.
5 He loves righteousness and justice;
The earth is full of the
   lovingkindness of the Lord.

6 By the word of the Lord were the
   heavens made,
And all their host by the breath of
   His mouth. [Gen 1:1–3; Job 38:4–
   11; Heb 11:3; 2 Pet 3:5]
7 He gathers the waters of the sea
   together as in a wineskin;
He puts the deeps in storehouses.
8 Let all the earth fear *and* worship
   the Lord;
Let all the inhabitants of the world
   stand in awe of Him.
9 For He spoke, and it was done;

He commanded, and it stood fast.
10 The Lord nullifies the counsel of
   the nations;
He makes the thoughts *and* plans
   of the people ineffective.
11 The counsel of the Lord stands
   forever,
The thoughts *and* plans of His
   heart through all generations.
12 Blessed [fortunate, prosperous,
   and favored by God] is the
   nation whose God is the Lord,
The people whom He has chosen
   as His own inheritance. [Deut
   32:8, 9]
13 The Lord looks [down] from
   heaven;
He sees all the sons of man;
14 From His dwelling place He looks
   closely
Upon all the inhabitants of the
   earth—
15 He who fashions the hearts of
   them all,
Who considers *and* understands
   all that they do.
16 The king is not saved by the great
   size of his army;
A warrior is not rescued by his
   great strength.
17 A horse is a false hope for victory;
Nor does it deliver anyone by its
   great strength.
18 Behold, the eye of the Lord is
   upon those who fear Him [and
   worship Him with awe-inspired
   reverence and obedience],
On those who hope [confidently]
   in His compassion *and*
   lovingkindness,
19 To rescue their lives from death
And keep them alive in famine.

speak the Word

*God, I declare that Your word is right and that all
Your work is done in faithfulness.*
—ADAPTED FROM PSALM 33:4

20 We wait [expectantly] for the Lord;
He is our help and our shield.
21 For in Him our heart rejoices,
Because we trust [lean on, rely on,
and are confident] in His holy
name.
22 Let Your [steadfast]
lovingkindness, O Lord, be upon
us,
In proportion as we have hoped in
You.

PSALM 34

The Lord, a Provider and the One Who Rescues Me.

A Psalm of David; when he
pretended to be insane before
Abimelech, who drove him out,
and he went away.

1 I WILL bless the Lord at all times;
His praise shall continually be in
my mouth.
2 My soul makes its boast in the Lord;
The humble *and* downtrodden will
hear it and rejoice.
3 O magnify the Lord with me,
And let us lift up His name
together.

4 I sought the Lord [on the authority
of His word], and He answered
me,
And delivered me from all my
fears. [Ps 73:25; Matt 7:7]
5 They looked to Him and were
radiant;
Their faces will never blush in
shame *or* confusion.

life point

Psalm 34:7 teaches us that "the angel of
the Lord encamps around those who fear
Him" Do you want your angels to go to
work in your life? Then start worshiping
God, because the Bible says that the angel of the Lord camps around those who
revere and worship Him to rescue them.

putting the Word to work

Psalm 34:8 encourages us to "taste
and see" that the Lord is good. Think
for a moment about your favorite
food. Can you imagine how it tastes
and the pleasure it brings? How
infinitely greater is the pleasure of
knowing the goodness of God! Let the
sweetness of His praise be on your lips
continually!

6 This poor man cried, and the Lord
heard him
And saved him from all his troubles.
7 The angel of the Lord encamps
around those who fear Him [with
awe-inspired reverence and
worship Him with obedience],
And He rescues [each of] them.
[2 Kin 6:8–23; Ps 18:1; 145:20]

8 O taste and see that the Lord [our
God] is good;
How blessed [fortunate,
prosperous, and favored by God]
is the man who takes refuge in
Him. [1 Pet 2:2, 3]
9 O [reverently] fear the Lord, you
His saints (believers, holy ones);
For to those who fear Him there is
no want.
10 The young lions lack [food] and
grow hungry,
But they who seek the Lord will
not lack any good thing.
11 Come, you children, listen to me;
I will teach you to fear the Lord
[with awe-inspired reverence
and worship Him with
obedience].
12 Who is the man who desires life
And loves many days, that he may
see good?
13 Keep your tongue from evil
And your lips from speaking deceit.
14 Turn away from evil and do good;
Seek peace and pursue it.

15 The eyes of the LORD are toward
　　the righteous [those with moral
　　courage and spiritual integrity]
　And His ears are open to their cry.
16 The face of the LORD is against
　　those who do evil,

To cut off the memory of them
　　from the earth. [1 Pet 3:10–12]
17 When *the righteous* cry [for help],
　　the LORD hears
　And rescues them from all their
　　distress *and* troubles.

at *all* times

Notice that the psalmist says he will bless the Lord "at all times," not just when it is convenient or it feels good (Psalm 34:1). Let me share with you a story that really emphasized this point for me.

One of my favorite things to do when I have finished a conference is to go to a restaurant, sit down, and have a good meal. I work hard, and that is one way I relax. One time, we called a restaurant and asked for a reservation. They sounded like they had taken our reservation, but when we got there, we found out they had not. The place was jam-packed, and we waited about forty-five minutes for a table. I felt irritation rise in me, but I told myself, *Joyce, you just finished preaching and telling people how to behave in hard times, so just practice what you preach.* (It is amazing how sometimes when you talk about what you believe, Satan will come around and test you on it!)

Finally we were seated and began ordering. The waitress came with our beverages on a large tray. The place was so crowded that she accidentally bumped the tray and dumped all the beverages on my husband, Dave. He had on a very nice suit, and it was soaked in water, coffee, iced tea, and soda pop. At that point he could have blown up. But Dave was so nice to the waitress about the whole ordeal. He said to her, "Don't worry about it. It was a mistake. I understand. I used to work at a restaurant, and one time I dumped malts inside a customer's car. He had on a really nice suit and was taking his date out. I know how you feel. Don't worry about it." Then he went to the manager and said, "I don't want her to get in trouble. The place is overly crowded. She is doing a good job. It was not her fault." He went to the extreme to be nice.

Soon the waitress came back with the second tray of beverages, and it was obvious she had been crying. She said to us, "I feel so bad that I dumped all those drinks on you." Then she looked right at me and said, "I think I'm just nervous because you're here. I watch you on television every day."

In my heart I said, "Oh, thank You, God, thank You, thank You, thank You, that we didn't act badly about this!" What would it have done to her—what would it have said to her about God, about leaders, about television evangelists—if she had heard me preach every day on television and then seen Dave and me throw a fit over her spilling the beverages on him?

Did I feel like blowing up? To be honest, yes. The Bible never says that our temptation to sin dies or goes away. It says that since Christ died for our sin we should consider ourselves dead to sin. And sometimes that means learning to bless Him at *all times*—especially when things are not going our way.

---

18 The LORD is near to the heartbroken
And He saves those who are crushed in spirit (contrite in heart, truly sorry for their sin).

19 Many hardships *and* perplexing circumstances confront the righteous,
But the LORD rescues him from them all.

20 He keeps all his bones;
Not one of them is broken. [John 19:33, 36]

21 Evil will cause the death of the wicked,
And those who hate the righteous will be held guilty *and* will be condemned.

22 The LORD redeems the soul of His servants,
And none of those who take refuge in Him will be condemned.

PSALM 35

Prayer for Rescue from Enemies.

A Psalm of David.

1 CONTEND, O LORD, with those who contend with me;
Fight against those who fight against me.

2 Take hold of shield and buckler (small shield),
And stand up for my help.

3 Draw also the spear and javelin to meet those who pursue me.
Say to my soul, "I am your salvation."

4 Let those be ashamed and dishonored who seek my life;
Let those be turned back [in defeat] and humiliated who plot evil against me.

5 Let them be [blown away] like chaff before the wind [worthless, without substance],
With the angel of the LORD driving them on.

6 Let their way be dark and slippery,
With the angel of the LORD pursuing *and* harassing them.

7 For without cause they hid their net for me;
Without cause they dug a pit [of destruction] for my life.

8 Let destruction come upon my enemy by surprise;
Let the net he hid for me catch him;
Into that very destruction let him fall.

9 Then my soul shall rejoice in the LORD;
It shall rejoice in His salvation.

10 All my bones will say, "LORD, who is like You,
Who rescues the afflicted from him who is too strong for him [to resist alone],
And the afflicted and the needy from him who robs him?"

11 Malicious witnesses rise up;
They ask me of things that I do not know.

12 They repay me evil for good,
To the sorrow of my soul.

13 But as for me, when they were sick, my clothing was sackcloth (mourning garment);
I humbled my soul with fasting,
And I prayed with my head bowed on my chest.

14 I behaved as if grieving for my friend or my brother;
I bowed down in mourning, as one who sorrows for his mother.

15 But in my stumbling they rejoiced and gathered together [against me];
The slanderers whom I did not know gathered against me;
They slandered *and* reviled me without ceasing.

16 Like godless jesters at a feast,
They gnashed at me with their teeth [in malice].

¹⁷Lord, how long will You look on
     [without action]?
Rescue my life from their
     destructions,
My only *life* from the young lions.
¹⁸I will give You thanks in the great
     congregation;
I will praise You among a mighty
     people.
¹⁹Do not let those who are
     wrongfully my enemies rejoice
     over me;
Nor let those who hate me
     without cause wink their eye
     [maliciously]. [John 15:24, 25]
²⁰For they do not speak peace,
But they devise deceitful words
     [half-truths and lies] against
     those who are quiet in the land.
²¹They open their mouths wide
     against me;
They say, "Aha, aha, our eyes have
     seen it!"

²²You have seen this, O Lord; do not
     keep silent.
O Lord, do not be far from me.
²³Wake Yourself up, and arise to my
     right
And to my cause, my God and my
     Lord.
²⁴Judge me, O Lord my God,
     according to Your righteousness
     and justice;
And do not let them rejoice
     over me.
²⁵Do not let them say in their heart,
     "Aha, that is what we wanted!"
Do not let them say, "We have
     swallowed him up *and* destroyed
     him."

²⁶Let those be ashamed and
     humiliated together who rejoice
     at my distress;
Let those be clothed with shame
     and dishonor who magnify
     themselves over me.
²⁷Let them shout for joy and rejoice,
     who favor my vindication *and*
     want what is right for me;
Let them say continually, "Let the
     Lord be magnified, who delights
     and takes pleasure in the
     prosperity of His servant."
²⁸And my tongue shall declare Your
     righteousness (justice),
And Your praise all the day long.

PSALM 36
Wickedness of Men and Lovingkindness of God.

To the Chief Musician. *A Psalm*
of David the servant of the Lord.

¹TRANSGRESSION SPEAKS [like
     an oracle] to the wicked (godless)
     [deep] within his heart;
There is no fear (dread) of God
     before his eyes. [Rom 3:18]
²For he flatters *and* deceives
     himself in his own eyes
Thinking that his sinfulness will
     not be discovered and hated [by
     God].
³The words of his mouth are
     wicked and deceitful;
He has ceased to be wise *and* to do
     good.
⁴He plans wrongdoing on his bed;
He sets himself on a path that is not
     good;
He does not reject *or* despise evil.

speak the Word

Thank You, Lord, that Your loving-kindness and graciousness extend
to the skies and Your faithfulness to the clouds. Your righteousness is like the
mountains and Your judgments are like the great deep.
—adapted from Psalm 36:5, 6

⁵Your lovingkindness *and*
   graciousness, O Lᴏʀᴅ, extend to
   the skies,
   Your faithfulness [reaches] to the
   clouds.
⁶Your righteousness is like the
   mountains of God,
   Your judgments are like the great
   deep.
   O Lᴏʀᴅ, You preserve man and beast.
⁷How precious is Your
   lovingkindness, O God!
   The children of men take refuge in
   the shadow of Your wings.
⁸They drink their fill of the
   abundance of Your house;
   And You allow them to drink from
   the river of Your delights.
⁹For with You is the fountain of
   life [the fountain of life-giving
   water];
   In Your light we see light. [John
   4:10, 14]

¹⁰O continue Your lovingkindness to
   those who know You,
   And Your righteousness (salvation)
   to the upright in heart.
¹¹Do not let the foot of the proud
   [person] overtake me,
   And do not let the hand of the
   wicked drive me away.
¹²There those who [are perverse
   and] do evil have fallen;
   They have been thrust down and
   cannot rise.

PSALM 37

Security of Those Who Trust
in the Lᴏʀᴅ, and Insecurity
of the Wicked.

A Psalm of David.

¹DO NOT worry because of
   evildoers,

Nor be envious toward
   wrongdoers;
²For they will wither quickly like the
   grass,
   And fade like the green herb.
³Trust [rely on and have
   confidence] in the Lᴏʀᴅ and do
   good;
   Dwell in the land and feed
   [securely] on His faithfulness.
⁴Delight yourself in the Lᴏʀᴅ,
   And He will give you the desires
   and petitions of your heart.
⁵Commit your way to the Lᴏʀᴅ;
   Trust in Him also and He will
   do it.
⁶He will make your righteousness
   [your pursuit of right standing
   with God] like the light,
   And your judgment like [the
   shining of] the noonday [sun].

⁷Be still before the Lᴏʀᴅ; wait
   patiently for Him *and* entrust
   yourself to Him;
   Do not fret (whine, agonize)
   because of him who prospers in
   his way,
   Because of the man who carries
   out wicked schemes.
⁸Cease from anger and abandon
   wrath;
   Do not fret; *it leads* only to evil.
⁹For those who do evil will be cut off,
   But those who wait for the Lᴏʀᴅ,
   they will inherit the land. [Is
   57:13c]
¹⁰For yet a little while and the wicked
   one will be gone [forever];
   Though you look carefully where he
   used to be, he will not be [found].
   [Heb 10:36, 37; Rev 21:7, 8]
¹¹But the humble will [at last]
   inherit the land

speak the Word

I declare, God, that with You is the fountain of life. In Your light, I see light.
–ᴀᴅᴀᴘᴛᴇᴅ ꜰʀᴏᴍ Pꜱᴀʟᴍ 36:9

And will delight themselves in
  abundant prosperity *and* peace.
  [Ps 37:29; Matt 5:5]
¹² The wicked plots against the
  righteous
And gnashes at him with his teeth.
¹³ The Lord laughs at him [the
  wicked one—the one who
  oppresses the righteous],
For He sees that his day [of defeat]
  is coming.
¹⁴ The wicked have drawn the sword
  and bent their bow
To cast down the afflicted and the
  needy,
To slaughter those who are upright
  in conduct [those with personal
  integrity and godly character].
¹⁵ The sword [of the ungodly] will
  enter their own heart,
And their bow will be broken.

¹⁶ Better is the little of the righteous
  [who seek the will of God]
Than the abundance (riches) of
  many wicked (godless). [1 Tim
  6:6, 7]
¹⁷ For the arms of the wicked will be
  broken,
But the Lord upholds *and* sustains
  the righteous [who seek Him].
¹⁸ The Lord knows the days of the
  blameless,
And their inheritance will
  continue forever.
¹⁹ They will not be ashamed in the
  time of evil,
And in the days of famine they
  will have plenty *and* be
  satisfied.
²⁰ But the wicked (ungodly) will
  perish,

delight yourself in God

Does a way exist for us to have our desires fulfilled? According to Psalm 37:4, 5, if we delight ourselves in the Lord, He will give us the desires of our hearts. I have learned that letting God give me something is so much better than trying to get it for myself. Most of us struggle greatly in our lives, trying to make things happen that only God can do. He wants us to seek Him, and He promises that He will add the things we desire if and when the time is right.

We are to commit our way unto Him and let Him bring to pass the things that we desire. Jesus said all those who labor and are heavily burdened should come to Him. He promised to renew and refresh their souls (see Matthew 11:28, 29). His ways are higher than our ways, and His thoughts are higher than ours (Isaiah 55:8, 9). In other words, God knows much better than we do what we need to do!

I spent much of my life frustrated and struggling, always trying to do something about things I could not do anything about. I worked really hard at life, but life still was not working for me.

My first Bible was a gift from my mother-in-law, and on the inside cover she wrote: "Commit your way to the Lord" from Psalm 37:5. Little did I know, when she gave me that Bible years ago, just how long it would take for me to let go of my ways and submit to God's.

I do not know why we tend to be so stubborn, but we do. I encourage you to let go of your ways and let God be God in your life. He wants to give you the desires of your heart as you commit your way to Him.

And the enemies of the Lord will be like the glory of the pastures *and* like the fat of lambs [that is consumed in smoke],
They vanish—like smoke they vanish away.
21 The wicked borrows and does not pay back,
But the righteous is gracious *and* kind and gives.
22 For those blessed by God will [at last] inherit the land,
But those cursed by Him will be cut off. [Is 57:13c]

23 The steps of a [good and righteous] man are directed *and* established by the Lord,
And He delights in his way [and blesses his path].
24 When he falls, he will not be hurled down,
Because the Lord is the One who holds his hand *and* sustains him.
25 I have been young and now I am old,
Yet I have not seen the righteous (those in right standing with God) abandoned

life point

God will tell us the way to go (see Psalm 37:23), but we have to do the walking. A walk with God develops by taking one step of obedience at a time. Some people want the entire blueprint for their lives before they will make one decision. God does not usually operate that way; He leads us one step at a time.

By faith, we take the step God has shown us, and then He gives us the next one. At times we may fall down and must get back up; we may stumble, but He always helps us. We continue on by His strength and His grace, knowing that every time we face a fork in the road (a place of decision), God will guide us.

Or his descendants pleading for bread.
26 All day long he is gracious and lends,
And his descendants are a blessing.
27 Depart from evil and do good;
And you will dwell [securely in the land] forever.
28 For the Lord delights in justice
And does not abandon His saints (faithful ones);
They are preserved forever,
But the descendants of the wicked will [in time] be cut off.
29 The righteous will inherit the land
And live in it forever.
30 The mouth of the righteous proclaims wisdom,
And his tongue speaks justice *and* truth.
31 The law of his God is in his heart;
Not one of his steps will slip.
32 The wicked lies in wait for the righteous
And seeks to kill him.
33 The Lord will not leave him in his hand
Or let him be condemned when he is judged.
34 Wait for *and* expect the Lord and keep His way,
And He will exalt you to inherit the land;
[In the end] when the wicked are cut off, you will see it.
35 I have seen a wicked, violent man [with great power]
Spreading *and* flaunting himself like a cedar in its native soil,
36 Yet he passed away, and lo, he was no more;
I sought him, but he could not be found.
37 Mark the blameless man [who is spiritually complete], and behold the upright [who walks in moral integrity];

There is a [good] future for
 the man of peace [because
 a life of honor blesses one's
 descendants].
38 As for transgressors, they will be
 completely destroyed;
 The future of the wicked will be
 cut off.
39 But the salvation of the righteous
 is from the LORD;
 He is their refuge and stronghold
 in the time of trouble.
40 The LORD helps them and rescues
 them;
 He rescues them from the wicked
 and saves them,
 Because they take refuge in Him.

PSALM 38

Prayer in Time of Discipline.

A Psalm of David; to bring
 to remembrance.

1 O LORD, do not rebuke me in Your
 wrath,
 Nor discipline me in Your burning
 anger.
2 For Your arrows have sunk into
 me and penetrate deeply,
 And Your hand has pressed
 down on me and greatly
 disciplined me.
3 There is no soundness in my flesh
 because of Your indignation;
 There is no health in my bones
 because of my sin.
4 For my iniquities have gone over
 my head [like the waves of a
 flood];
 As a heavy burden they weigh too
 much for me.
5 My wounds are loathsome and foul
 Because of my foolishness.
6 I am bent over and greatly bowed
 down;
 I go about mourning all day long.
7 For my sides are filled with
 burning,
 And there is no health in my flesh.

8 I am numb and greatly bruised
 [deadly cold and completely
 worn out];
 I groan because of the disquiet and
 moaning of my heart.
9 Lord, all my desire is before You;
 And my sighing is not hidden from
 You.
10 My heart throbs violently, my
 strength fails me;
 And as for the light of my eyes,
 even that has also gone from me.
11 My loved ones and my friends
 stand aloof from my plague;
 And my neighbors stand far away.
 [Luke 23:49]
12 Those who seek my life lay snares
 for me,
 And those who seek to injure me
 threaten mischievous things and
 destruction;
 They devise treachery all the day
 long.
13 But I, like a deaf man, do not hear;
 I am like a mute man who does not
 open his mouth.
14 Yes, I am like a man who does not
 hear,
 In whose mouth are no arguments.
15 For in You, O LORD, I hope;
 You will answer, O Lord my God.
16 For I pray, "May they not rejoice
 over me,
 Who, when my foot slips, would
 boast against me."
17 For I am ready to fall;
 My sorrow is continually
 before me.
18 For I do confess my guilt and
 iniquity;
 I am filled with anxiety because of
 my sin. [2 Cor 7:9, 10]
19 But my [numerous] enemies are
 vigorous and strong,
 And those who hate me without
 cause are many.
20 They repay evil for good, they
 attack and try to kill me,

Because I follow what is good.
21 Do not abandon me, O LORD;
O my God, do not be far from me.
22 Make haste to help me,
O Lord, my Salvation.

PSALM 39

The Vanity of Life.

To the Chief Musician;
for Jeduthun. A Psalm of David.

1 I SAID, "I will guard my ways
That I may not sin with my tongue;
I will muzzle my mouth
While the wicked are in my
presence."
2 I was mute and silent [before my
enemies],
I refrained even from good,
And my distress grew worse.
3 My heart was hot within me.
While I was musing the fire
burned;
Then I spoke with my tongue:
4 "LORD, let me know my [life's] end
And [to appreciate] the extent of
my days;
Let me know how frail I am [how
transient is my stay here].
5 "Behold, You have made my days
as [short as] hand widths,
And my lifetime is as nothing in
Your sight.
Surely every man at his best is a
mere breath [a wisp of smoke, a
vapor that vanishes]! [Eccl 1:2]
                                    Selah.
6 "Surely every man walks around
like a shadow [in a charade];
Surely they make an uproar for
nothing;

Each one builds up riches, not
knowing who will receive them.
[Eccl 2:18, 19; 1 Cor 7:31; James
4:14]
7 "And now, Lord, for what do I
expectantly wait?
My hope [my confident
expectation] is in You.
8 "Save me from all my transgressions;
Do not make me the scorn and
reproach of the [self-righteous,
arrogant] fool.
9 "I am mute, I do not open my mouth,
Because it is You who has done it.
10 "Remove Your plague from me;
I am wasting away because of the
conflict and opposition of Your
hand.
11 "With rebukes You discipline man
for sin;
You consume like a moth what is
precious to him;
Surely every man is a mere breath
[a wisp of smoke, a vapor that
vanishes].   Selah.

12 "Hear my prayer, O LORD, and
listen to my cry;
Do not be silent at my tears;
For I am Your temporary guest,
A sojourner like all my fathers.
13 "O look away from me, that I may
smile and again know joy
Before I depart and am no more."

PSALM 40

God Sustains His Servant.

To the Chief Musician. A Psalm
of David.

1 I WAITED patiently and
expectantly for the LORD;
And He inclined to me and heard
my cry.

speak the Word

God, all of my hope—my confident expectation—is in You.
—ADAPTED FROM PSALM 39:7

² He brought me up out of a
     horrible pit [of tumult and of
     destruction], out of the miry clay,
And He set my feet upon a rock,
     steadying my footsteps *and*
     establishing my path.
³ He put a new song in my mouth, a
     song of praise to our God;
Many will see and fear [with great
     reverence]

life point

When the Bible speaks of "a horrible pit,"
as it does in Psalm 40:2, I always think of
the depths of depression. The psalmist
David often spoke of feeling as though he
was going down into a pit and calling out
to the Lord to rescue him and set his feet
on solid, level ground.

Like David, nobody wants to be in the pit
of depression. It is a terrible place. I cannot think of a worse place to be. When we
are deeply depressed, we feel bad enough
as it is. Then the devil comes along to
add to our misery by bringing thoughts
of every negative thing imaginable. He
reminds us of every disappointing thing
that has happened to us and tries to make
us believe that nothing good will ever
take place in our lives. His goal is to keep
us so miserable and hopeless that we will
never rise up to cause him any problems
or to fulfill the call of God on our lives.

We must learn to resist descending into
the pit of depression where we are at the
mercy of the tormentor of our souls, who
is determined to totally destroy us and to
damage our witness for Christ. Be like David; cry out to God and allow Him to set
your feet upon a rock and bring stability
to your life.

And will trust confidently in the
     Lord. [Ps 5:11]
⁴ Blessed [fortunate, prosperous,
     and favored by God] is the man
     who makes the Lord his trust,
And does not regard the proud nor
     those who lapse into lies.
⁵ Many, O Lord my God, are the
     wonderful works which You have
     done,
And Your thoughts toward us;
There is none to compare with
     You.
If I would declare and speak of
     your wonders,
They would be too many to count.
⁶ Sacrifice and meal offering You do
     not desire, *nor* do You delight in
     them;
You have opened my ears *and*
     given me the capacity to hear
     [and obey Your word];
Burnt offerings and sin offerings
     You do not require. [Mic 6:6–8]
⁷ Then I said, "Behold, I come [to the
     throne];
In the scroll of the book it is
     written of me.
⁸ "I delight to do Your will, O my
     God;
Your law is within my heart." [Jer
     31:33; Heb 10:5–9]
⁹ I have proclaimed good news of
     righteousness [and the joy that
     comes from obedience to You] in
     the great assembly;
Behold, I will not restrain my
     lips [from proclaiming Your
     righteousness],
As You know, O Lord.
¹⁰ I have not concealed Your
     righteousness within my heart;

speak the Word

God, I delight to do Your will.
–ADAPTED FROM PSALM 40:8

pray and obey

God really wants us to hear and obey Him, and according to Psalm 40:6, He has given us the capacity to do so. In fact, God delights in the atmosphere of our obedience. Naturally, it does not do God any good to talk to us if we are not going to listen and obey!

For many years, I wanted God to talk to me, but I wanted to pick and choose what to obey. Like many others, I had "selective hearing." I wanted to do what God said to do *if* I thought it was a good idea. If I did not want to submit to what I was hearing, I could easily choose to think it was not from God.

God has given us the capacity both to hear Him and to obey Him, and obedience is the greatest sacrifice we can make to Him. Some of what God says to you will be exciting; other things may not be so thrilling to hear. But you can be assured that what God tells you will work out for good if you will just do it His way.

If God convicts you that you were rude to someone and instructs you to apologize, it is pointless to answer back, "Well, that person was rude to me too!" If you talk back with excuses, you may have prayed, and even heard, but you have not obeyed. Instead, go apologize. Say to that person, "I was rude to you, and I'm sorry." *Now* you have obeyed. Now God's anointing can flow through your life because you are obedient.

I was moved by a story about a message given at a pastors' conference by a pastor of a very large church. Hundreds of pastors had gathered from all over the nation to hear this man tell what he did to build his church. He told them simply, "I pray, and I obey. I pray, and I obey." One of the ministers who attended this meeting expressed to me his disappointment in the pastor's message. He said, "I spent all this money and came all this distance to hear this world-renowned leader tell me how his ministry grew to the point it has. For three hours, in various ways, he said the same thing, 'I pray. I obey. I pray. I obey. I pray. I obey. I pray. I obey.' I kept thinking, *Surely there is something else.*"

Looking back over nearly three decades of walking with God, I would have to agree that if I put into words the simplest explanation for all the success we have enjoyed at Joyce Meyer Ministries, we too have learned to pray, hear from God, and then do what God tells us to do. Over the years, I have been seeking God about the call on my life and pressing forward in what I feel He has told me to do. The essence of it all is that I have prayed, and I have obeyed. My obedience has not always been popular with everyone else, but to the best of my ability I have prayed, I have obeyed—and it has worked. God's plan is not hard; *we* make it hard. Like everyone else I have made mistakes, but I have learned from them and have pressed on. Failing does not make you a failure. A person is a failure only if he gives up and refuses to try any longer.

If you want God's will for your life, I can give you the directions in their simplest form: *Pray and obey*. God has given you the capacity to do both.

I have proclaimed Your
faithfulness and Your
salvation.
I have not concealed Your
lovingkindness and Your truth
from the great assembly. [Acts
20:20, 27]

11 Do not withhold Your compassion
and tender mercy from me,
O Lᴏʀᴅ;
Your lovingkindness and
Your truth will continually
preserve me.
12 For innumerable evils have
encompassed me;
My sins have overtaken me, so that
I am not able to see.
They are more numerous than the
hairs of my head,
And my heart has failed me.

13 Be pleased, O Lᴏʀᴅ, to save me;
O Lᴏʀᴅ, make haste to help me.
14 Let those be ashamed and
humiliated together
Who seek my life to destroy it;
Let those be turned back [in
defeat] and dishonored
Who delight in my hurt.
15 Let those be appalled *and* desolate
because of their shame
Who say to me, "Aha, aha
[rejoicing in my misfortune]!"
16 Let all who seek You rejoice and be
glad in You;
Let those who love Your salvation
say continually,
"The Lᴏʀᴅ be magnified!"
17 Even though I am afflicted and
needy,
Still the Lord takes thought *and* is
mindful of me.
You are my help and my rescuer.
O my God, do not delay. [Ps 70:1–5;
1 Pet 5:7]

PSALM 41

The Psalmist in Sickness Complains of Enemies and False Friends.

To the Chief Musician. A Psalm
of David.

1 BLESSED [by God's grace and
compassion] is he who considers
the helpless;
The Lᴏʀᴅ will save him in the day
of trouble.
2 The Lᴏʀᴅ will protect him and
keep him alive;
And he will be called blessed in
the land;
You do not hand him over to the
desire of his enemies.
3 The Lᴏʀᴅ will sustain *and*
strengthen him on his sickbed;
In his illness, You will restore him
to health.

4 As for me, I said, "O Lᴏʀᴅ, be
gracious to me;
Heal my soul, for I have sinned
against You."
5 My enemies speak evil of me,
saying,
"When will he die and his name
perish?"
6 And when one comes to see me, he
speaks empty words,
While his heart gathers malicious
gossip [against me];
When he goes away, he tells it
[everywhere].
7 All who hate me whisper together
about me;
Against me they devise my hurt
[imagining the worst for me],
saying,
8 "A wicked thing is poured out upon
him *and* holds him;
And when he lies down, he will not
rise up again."
9 Even my own close friend in whom
I trusted,
Who ate my bread,

Has lifted up his heel against me
[betraying me]. [John 13:18]

¹⁰ But You, O LORD, be gracious to me
and restore me [to health],
So that I may repay them.

¹¹ By this I know that You favor *and*
delight in me,
Because my enemy does not shout
in triumph over me.

¹² As for me, You uphold me in my
integrity,
And You set me in Your presence
forever.

¹³ Blessed be the LORD, the God of
Israel,
From everlasting to everlasting
[from this age to the next, and
forever].
Amen and Amen (so be it).

BOOK TWO

PSALM 42

Thirsting for God in Trouble and Exile.

To the Chief Musician. A skillful
song, *or* a didactic *or* reflective
poem, of the sons of Korah.

¹ AS THE deer pants [longingly] for
the water brooks,
So my soul pants [longingly] for
You, O God.

putting the Word to work

Psalm 42:1 tells of a deer that longs
for a refreshing stream of water. On
a hot day, *knowing about* water does
nothing to quench your thirst; only
drinking water does. The same is true
of our desire for God. Have you ever
longed for more than just information
about God? God wants you to experience Who He is. Seek Him, and He
will satisfy your desire to know Him
intimately.

life point

In Psalm 42:5, we see David struggling
with depression. I would like for us to
examine how he handled his situation,
because it shows us what to do when we
are feeling depressed.

As we dissect this verse, we see three
distinct responses David gives to his depressed feelings. First, he puts a question
to his own soul and asks himself: "Why
are you in despair, O my soul?" Then he
gives an instruction to his soul: "Hope in
God." Finally, he declares what he is going to do: "I shall again praise Him." We
might say David has a talk with himself.

We must follow this same basic pattern
of action as we confront our feelings of
depression and come out of them and into
victory.

² My soul (my life, my inner self)
thirsts for God, for the living
God.
When will I come and see the face
of God? [Ps 63:1, 2; John 7:37; 1
Thess 1:9, 10]

³ My tears have been my food day
and night,
While they say to me all day long,
"Where is your God?"

⁴ These things I [vividly] remember
as I pour out my soul;
How I used to go along before the
great crowd of people and lead
them in procession to the house
of God [like a choirmaster before
his singers, timing the steps to
the music and the chant of the
song],
With the voice of joy and
thanksgiving, a great crowd
keeping a festival.

⁵ Why are you in despair, O my
soul?

And why have you become restless
   and disturbed within me?
Hope in God *and* wait expectantly
   for Him, for I shall again praise
   Him
For the help of His presence.
6O my God, my soul is in despair
   within me [the burden more than
   I can bear];
Therefore I will [fervently]
   remember You from the land of
   the Jordan

And the peaks of [Mount] Hermon,
   from Mount Mizar.
7Deep calls to deep at the
   [thundering] sound of Your
   waterfalls;
All Your breakers and Your waves
   have rolled over me.
8Yet the Lord will command His
   lovingkindness in the daytime,
And in the night His song will be
   with me,
A prayer to the God of my life.

how to deal with discouragement

In Psalm 42:5, the psalmist is discouraged. Discouragement destroys hope, so naturally the devil always tries to discourage us. Without hope we give up, which is exactly what the devil wants us to do.

The Bible repeatedly tells us not to be discouraged or dismayed. God knows that we will not be victorious if we get discouraged, so He always encourages us as we start out on a project by saying to us, "Do not get discouraged." God wants us to be *en*couraged, not *dis*couraged.

When discouragement or condemnation tries to overtake you, the first thing to do is to examine your thought life. What kind of thoughts have you been thinking? Have they sounded something like this? *I am not going to make it; this is too hard. I always fail; it has always been the same. Nothing ever changes. I am sure other people do not have this much trouble getting their minds renewed. I may as well give up. I'm tired of trying. I pray, but it seems as if God doesn't hear. He probably doesn't answer my prayers because He is so disappointed in the way I act.*

If these examples represent your thoughts, then no wonder you get discouraged or feel condemned! Remember, you become what you think. Think discouraging thoughts, and you will get discouraged. Think condemning thoughts, and you will come under condemnation. Change your thinking and be set free!

Instead of thinking negatively, think more like this: *Well, things are going a little slowly, but, thank God, I am making some progress. I am sure glad I'm on the right path that will lead me to freedom. I had a rough day yesterday. I chose wrong thinking all day long. Father, forgive me, and help me to keep on keeping on. I made a mistake, but at least that is one mistake I won't have to make again. This is a new day. You love me, Lord. Your mercy is new every morning. I refuse to be discouraged. I refuse to be condemned. Father, the Bible says that You do not condemn me. You sent Jesus to die for me. I'll be fine—today will be a great day. I ask You to help me choose right thoughts today.*

I am sure you can already feel the victory in this type of cheerful, positive, godly thinking. Practice this type of thinking today!

⁹I will say to God my rock, "Why
   have You forgotten me?
Why do I go mourning because of
   the oppression of the enemy?"
¹⁰As a crushing of my bones [with a
   sword], my adversaries taunt me,
While they say continually to me,
   "Where is your God?"
¹¹Why are you in despair, O my
   soul?
Why have you become restless *and*
   disquieted within me?
Hope in God *and* wait expectantly
   for Him, for I shall yet praise Him,
The help of my countenance and
   my God.

PSALM 43

Prayer for Rescue.

¹JUDGE *AND* vindicate me, O God;
   plead my case against an ungodly
   nation.
O rescue me from the deceitful
   and unjust man!
²For You are the God of my strength
   [my stronghold—in whom I take
   refuge]; why have You rejected
   me?
Why do I go mourning because of
   the oppression of the enemy?

³O send out Your light and Your
   truth, let them lead me;
Let them bring me to Your holy hill
And to Your dwelling places.
⁴Then I will go to the altar of God,
To God, my exceeding joy;
With the lyre I will praise You,
   O God, my God!

⁵Why are you in despair, O my soul?
And why are you restless *and*
   disturbed within me?

Hope in God *and* wait expectantly
   for Him, for I shall again praise
   Him,
The help of my [sad] countenance
   and my God.

PSALM 44

Former Times of Help and
Present Troubles.

To the Chief Musician. *A Psalm*
of the sons of Korah. A skillful song,
   or a didactic *or* reflective poem.

¹WE HAVE heard with our ears,
   O God,
Our fathers have told us
The work You did in their days,
In the days of old.
²You drove out the [pagan] nations
   with Your own hand;
Then you planted *and* established
   them (Israel);
[It was by Your power that] You
   uprooted the [pagan] peoples,
Then You spread them abroad.
³For our fathers did not possess the
   land [of Canaan] by their own
   sword,
Nor did their own arm save them,
But Your right hand and Your arm
   and the light of Your presence,
Because You favored *and* delighted
   in them.

⁴You are my King, O God;
Command victories *and*
   deliverance for Jacob (Israel).
⁵Through You we will gore our
   enemies [like a bull];
Through Your name we will
   trample down those who rise up
   against us.
⁶For I will not trust in my bow,
Nor will my sword save me.

speak the Word

God, send Your light and Your truth, and let them lead me.
Let them bring me into Your presence.
—ADAPTED FROM PSALM 43:3

7But You have saved us from our
  enemies,
And You have put them to shame
  and humiliated those who
  hate us.
8In God we have boasted all the day
  long,
And we will praise *and* give thanks
  to Your name forever.   *Selah.*

9But now You have rejected us and
  brought us to dishonor,
And You do not go out with our
  armies [to lead us to victory].
10You make us turn back from the
  enemy,
And those who hate us have taken
  spoil for themselves.
11You have made us like sheep to be
  eaten [as mutton]

And have scattered us [in exile]
  among the nations.
12You sell Your people cheaply,
  And have not increased Your
  wealth by their sale.
13You have made us the reproach
  and taunt of our neighbors,
A scoffing and a derision to those
  around us.
14You make us a byword among the
  nations,
A laughingstock among the people.
15My dishonor is before me all day
  long,
And humiliation has covered my
  face,
16Because of the voice of the taunter
  and reviler,
Because of the presence of the
  enemy and the avenger.

be free from shame

In Psalm 44:15 the psalmist writes of "dishonor" and "humiliation." Another way
to express these is to use the word *shame.* Many people are "rooted" in shame.
This means that their shame is so deep it functions as the root of a tree and actually
produces "fruit" in the form of unhealthy thoughts and behaviors.

If you are rooted in shame, then it's important to be aware that shame is different
from guilt. I believe shame is a deeper problem than guilt. We may feel guilty over
something we have done wrong, but shame makes us feel bad about who we are.
There is also a difference between "normal" shame and "rooted" shame.

For example, if I knock over my water glass in a fancy restaurant, I feel ashamed or
embarrassed because I have made a mess in front of everybody. That's normal. But I
soon adjust to the mishap and go on. That incident does not mar my life.

In the Garden of Eden after the Fall, Adam and Eve were ashamed when they realized they were naked, and so they made aprons of fig leaves to cover themselves.
But that too was a normal reaction.

When you and I make mistakes or commit sin, we feel bad about them for a while
until we repent and are forgiven. Then we are able to put them behind us and go on
without any lasting harm.

But when people are rooted in shame, it affects everything about their lives. Their
bad attitudes toward themselves poison everything they try to accomplish. They are
doomed to failure because they have no confidence. Jesus bore our shame for us on
the cross (see Hebrews 12:2). Ask Jesus today to give you understanding of His work
on the cross for you. Ask Him to heal you so that you can live free from shame.

¹⁷All this has come upon us, yet we
   have not forgotten You,
Nor have we been false to Your
   covenant [which You made with
   our fathers].
¹⁸Our heart has not turned back,
Nor have our steps wandered from
   Your path,
¹⁹Yet You have [distressingly]
   crushed us in the place of jackals
And covered us with [the deep
   darkness of] the shadow of
   death.

²⁰If we had forgotten the name of
   our God
Or stretched out our hands to a
   strange god,
²¹Would not God discover this?
For He knows the secrets of the
   heart.
²²But for Your sake we are killed all
   the day long;
We are considered as sheep to be
   slaughtered. [Rom 8:35–39]
²³Awake! Why do You sleep, O Lord?
Awaken, do not reject us forever.
²⁴Why do You hide Your face
And forget our affliction and our
   oppression?
²⁵For our life has melted away into
   the dust;
Our body clings to the ground.
²⁶Rise up! Come be our help,
And ransom us for the sake of
   Your steadfast love.

PSALM 45

A Song Celebrating the King's Marriage.

To the Chief Musician; set
to the [tune of] "Lilies." A Psalm
of the sons of Korah. A skillful
song, *or* a didactic *or* reflective
poem. A Song of Love.

¹MY HEART overflows with a good
   theme;
I address my psalm to the King.

My tongue is like the pen of a
   skillful writer.
²You are fairer than the sons of men;
Graciousness is poured upon Your
   lips;
Therefore God has blessed You
   forever.

³Strap Your sword on *Your* thigh, O
   mighty One,
In Your splendor and Your
   majesty!
⁴And in Your majesty ride on
   triumphantly
For the cause of truth and humility
   and righteousness;
Let Your right hand guide You to
   awesome things.
⁵Your arrows are sharp;
The peoples (nations) fall under
   You;
Your arrows pierce the hearts of
   the King's enemies.

⁶Your throne, O God, is forever and
   ever;
The scepter of uprightness is the
   scepter of Your kingdom.
⁷You have loved righteousness
   (virtue, morality, justice) and
   hated wickedness;
Therefore God, your God, has
   anointed You
Above Your companions with the
   oil of jubilation. [Heb 1:8, 9]
⁸All Your garments are *fragrant
   with* myrrh, aloes *and* cassia;
From ivory palaces stringed
   instruments have made You
   glad.
⁹Kings' daughters are among Your
   noble ladies;
At Your right hand stands the
   queen in gold from Ophir.

¹⁰Hear, O daughter, consider
   and incline your ear [to my
   instruction]:
Forget your people and your
   father's house;

¹¹ Then the King will desire your
　　beauty;
　Because He is your Lord, bow
　　down *and* honor Him.
¹² The daughter of Tyre will come
　　with a gift;
　The rich among the people will
　　seek your favor.
¹³ Glorious is the King's daughter
　　within [the palace];
　Her robe is interwoven with gold.
　　[Rev 19:7, 8]
¹⁴ She will be brought to the King in
　　embroidered garments;
　The virgins, her companions who
　　follow her,
　Will be brought to You.
¹⁵ With gladness and rejoicing will
　　they be led;
　They will enter into the King's
　　palace.
¹⁶ In place of your fathers will be
　　your sons;
　You shall make princes in all the
　　land.
¹⁷ I will make Your name to be
　　remembered in all generations;
　Therefore the peoples will praise
　　and give You thanks forever and
　　ever.

PSALM 46

God the Refuge of His People.

To the Chief Musician. *A
Psalm* of the sons of Korah, set
to soprano voices. A Song.

¹ GOD IS our refuge and strength
　　[mighty and impenetrable],
　A very present *and* well-proved
　　help in trouble.
² Therefore we will not fear, though
　　the earth should change
　And though the mountains be
　　shaken *and* slip into the heart of
　　the seas,
³ Though its waters roar and foam,

life point

What Psalm 45:13 means to me is that
God puts the Holy Spirit inside us to work
on our inner lives; our attitudes, our re-
actions, and our goals. Through His work
in us, our inner lives can be tested and
refined into an environment in which the
Lord is comfortable to reside.

　Though the mountains tremble at
　　its roaring.　　　　　*Selah.*
⁴ There is a river whose streams
　　make glad the city of God,
　The holy dwelling places of the
　　Most High.
⁵ God is in the midst of her [His
　　city], she will not be moved;
　God will help her when the
　　morning dawns.
⁶ The nations made an uproar, the
　　kingdoms tottered *and* were
　　moved;
　He raised His voice, the earth
　　melted.
⁷ The LORD of hosts is with us;
　The God of Jacob is our stronghold
　　[our refuge, our high tower].
　　　　　　　　　　　　Selah.
⁸ Come, behold the works of the
　　LORD,

life point

The Lord encourages us in Psalm 46:10 to
be still and to know that He is God. Often
it is difficult for us to be still or quiet
because our flesh is full of energy and
usually wants to be active doing something. Let me encourage you not to talk to
God only when you want or need something; also spend quiet time with Him just
listening for His voice. He will give you
great revelation and direction if you will
be still before Him and simply listen.

Who has brought desolations *and*
    wonders on the earth.
⁹He makes wars to cease to the end
    of the earth;
He breaks the bow into pieces and
    snaps the spear in two;

He burns the chariots with fire.
¹⁰"Be still and know (recognize,
    understand) that I am God.
I will be exalted among the
    nations! I will be exalted in the
    earth."

express yourself!

The Bible instructs us to dance, to play musical instruments, and to do all kinds of outward things to express worship to the Lord (see Psalms 47:1; 150:3, 4). We need to do this; it brings a release in our lives, it honors God, and it aids in defeating the devil.

It is not enough just to say, "Well, God knows how I feel about Him. I do not have to make a big display." That would be no different from saying, "Well, God knows I believe in Him; therefore, there is no real need for me to be baptized." Or to say, "God knows I am sorry for my sins; therefore, there is no need for me to admit my sins and repent of them." We readily see how foolish this would be, and people from all denominations would agree that we need to be baptized and confess our sins. Yet not all denominations teach people to have outward expression of their praise and worship. Some teach that quiet reverence is the only proper way to worship. We definitely need to be quiet and reverent before the Lord at times, but we also need to express our emotions in worship. I am convinced that God gave us emotions for more purposes than just being enthusiastic at a ball game or about a new car. Surely God wants us to employ our emotions in expressing our love and gratitude to Him.

I am not encouraging unbridled emotion. People who just get "emotional" all the time in worship can be distracting. What we need is balance. I personally believe that if we had a proper emotional release during praise and worship, we might not release emotions at other times in improper ways. Our emotions are just as much a part of us as our body, mind, will, or spirit. God gave us emotions, and they must be cared for, just as the rest of us. We are not to be controlled by emotions because they are known to be fickle or untrustworthy, but neither can we stifle them and not be adversely affected.

I think it is tragic not to allow people the freedom to express their hearts and their love for God in a balanced way. It is wrong to be so afraid of something getting out of balance that we cut it off altogether. It also is a bad idea to do things the same way every time because "that is the way we have always done them." We all must be open to growth, which always involves change. Jesus said that He could not pour new wine into old wineskins, meaning some of the people's old ways had to go (see Matthew 9:17). They had to "let go" of old things and take hold of the new, fresh things. Knowledge and revelation are progressive; if a thing (such as your worship) is not moving forward in your life, it is at the point of dying.

I encourage you to be expressive in your praise and worship. Do this at home if you attend a church where it would be unacceptable to do so in the public services. I also encourage you to pray that everyone will be taught to worship God as He truly deserves to be worshiped.

11 The LORD of hosts is with us;
    The God of Jacob is our stronghold
    [our refuge, our high tower].
                           Selah.

PSALM 47

God the King of the Earth.

To the Chief Musician. A Psalm
of the sons of Korah.

1 O CLAP your hands, all you
    people;
    Shout to God with the voice of
    triumph *and* songs of joy.
2 For the LORD Most High is to be
    feared [and worshiped with
    awe-inspired reverence and
    obedience];
    He is a great King over all the
    earth.
3 He subdues peoples under us
    And nations under our feet.
4 He chooses our inheritance for us,
    The glory *and* excellence of Jacob
    whom He loves. [1 Pet 1:4, 5]
                         Selah.

5 God has ascended amid shouting,
    The LORD with the sound of a
    trumpet.
6 Sing praises to God, sing praises;
    Sing praises to our King, sing
    praises.
7 For God is the King of all the
    earth;
    Sing praises in a skillful psalm *and*
    with understanding.
8 God reigns over the nations;
    God sits on His holy throne.
9 The princes of the people have
    gathered together as the people
    of the God of Abraham,
    For the shields of the earth belong
    to God;
    He is highly exalted.

PSALM 48

The Beauty and Glory of Zion.

A Song; a Psalm of the sons
of Korah.

1 GREAT IS the LORD, and greatly to
    be praised,
    In the city of our God, His holy
    mountain.
2 Fair *and* beautiful in elevation, the
    joy of all the earth,
    Is Mount Zion [the City of David]
    in the far north,
    The city of the great King. [Matt
    5:35]
3 God, in her palaces,
    Has made Himself known as a
    stronghold.

4 For, lo, the kings assembled
    themselves,
    They [came and] passed by
    together.
5 They saw it, then they were amazed;
    They were stricken with terror,
    they fled in alarm.
6 Panic seized them there,
    And pain, as that of a woman in
    childbirth.
7 With the east wind
    You shattered the ships of Tarshish.
8 As we have heard, so have we seen
    In the city of the LORD of hosts, in
    the city of our God:
    God will establish her forever.
                         Selah.

life point

**David frequently wrote of meditating on
all the wonderful works of the Lord—
the mighty acts of God. He said that he
thought about the name of the Lord, the
lovingkindness of God (see Psalm 48:9),
and many other such things. If you and
I will do the same, we will stay encouraged, full of faith, and victorious in our
everyday lives.**

9 We have thought of Your
   lovingkindness, O God,
In the midst of Your temple.
10 As is Your name, O God,
So is Your praise to the ends of the
   earth;
Your right hand is full of
   righteousness (rightness,
   justice).
11 Let Mount Zion be glad,
Let the daughters of Judah rejoice
Because of Your [righteous]
   judgments.
12 Walk about Zion, go all around
   her;
Count her towers,
13 Consider her ramparts,
Go through her palaces,
That you may tell the next
   generation [about her glory].
14 For this is God,
Our God forever and ever;
He will be our guide even until
   death.

PSALM 49

The Folly of Trusting in Riches.

To the Chief Musician. A Psalm
     of the sons of Korah.

1 HEAR THIS, all peoples;
Listen carefully, all inhabitants of
   the world,
2 Both low and high,
Rich and poor together:
3 My mouth will speak wisdom,
And the meditation of my heart
   will be understanding.
4 I will incline my ear and consent to
   a proverb;
On the lyre I will unfold my riddle.

5 Why should I fear in the days of
   evil,
When the wickedness of those
   who would betray me surrounds
   me [on every side],
6 Even those who trust in and rely
   on their wealth

And boast of the abundance of
   their riches?
7 None of them can by any means
   redeem [either himself or] his
   brother,
Nor give to God a ransom for
   him—
8 For the ransom of his soul is too
   costly,
And he should cease trying
   forever—
9 So that he should live on eternally,
That he should never see the pit
   (grave) and undergo decay.

10 For he sees that even wise men die;
The fool and the stupid alike
   perish
And leave their wealth to others.
   [Eccl 2:12–16]
11 Their inward thought is that their
   houses will continue forever,
And their dwelling places to all
   generations;
They have named their lands after
   their own names [ignoring God].
12 But man, with all his [self] honor
   and pomp, will not endure;
He is like the beasts that perish.

13 This is the fate of those who are
   foolishly confident,
And of those after them who
   approve [and are influenced by]
   their words.   Selah.
14 Like sheep they are appointed
   for Sheol (the nether world, the
   place of the dead);
Death will be their shepherd;
And the upright shall rule over
   them in the morning,
And their form and beauty shall be
   for Sheol to consume,
So that they have no dwelling [on
   earth].
15 But God will redeem my life from
   the power of Sheol,
For He will receive me.   Selah.

16 Be not afraid when [an ungodly]
   man becomes rich,

When the wealth *and* glory of his
house are increased;
17 For when he dies he will carry
nothing away;
His glory will not descend after
him.
18 Though while he lives he counts
himself happy *and* prosperous—
And though people praise you
when you do well for yourself—
19 He shall go to the generation of his
fathers;
They shall never again see the light.
20 A man [who is held] in honor,
Yet who lacks [spiritual]
understanding *and* a teachable
heart, is like the beasts that perish.

PSALM 50

God the Judge of the Righteous
and the Wicked.

A Psalm of Asaph

1 THE MIGHTY One, God, the Lord,
has spoken,
And summoned the earth from
the rising of the sun to its setting
[from east to west].
2 Out of Zion, the perfection of beauty,
God has shone forth.
3 May our God come and not keep
silent;
Fire devours before Him,
And around Him a mighty tempest
rages.
4 He summons the heavens above,
And the earth, to judge His people:
5 "Gather My godly ones to Me,
Those who have made a covenant
with Me by sacrifice."
6 And the heavens declare His
righteousness,
For God Himself is judge.   *Selah.*

7 "Hear, O My people, and I will speak;

O Israel, I will testify against you:
I am God, your God.
8 "I do not reprove you for your
sacrifices;
Your burnt offerings are
continually before Me.
9 "I will accept no young bull from
your house
Nor male goat from your folds.
10 "For every beast of the forest is
Mine,
And the cattle on a thousand hills.
11 "I know every bird of the
mountains,
And everything that moves in the
field is Mine.
12 "If I were hungry, I would not tell
you,
For the world and all it contains
are Mine. [1 Cor 10:26]
13 "Shall I eat the flesh of bulls
Or drink the blood of male goats?
14 "Offer to God the sacrifice of
thanksgiving
And pay your vows to the Most High;
15 Call on Me in the day of trouble;
I will rescue you, and you shall
honor *and* glorify Me."

16 But to the wicked God says:
"What right have you to recite My
statutes
Or to take My covenant on your lips?
17 "For you hate instruction *and*
discipline
And cast My words behind you
[discarding them].
18 "When you see a thief, you are
pleased with him *and* condone
his behavior,
And you associate with adulterers.
19 "You give your mouth to evil
And your tongue frames deceit.
20 "You sit and speak against your
brother;
You slander your own mother's son.

speak the Word

Lord, You are not only God, but You are my God.
–ADAPTED FROM PSALM 50:7

21"These things you have done and I
    kept silent;
You thought that I was just like you.
Now I will reprimand *and*
    denounce you and state *the case*
    in order before your eyes.
22"Now consider this, you who forget
    God,
Or I will tear you in pieces, and there
    will be no one to rescue [you].
23"He who offers a sacrifice of praise
    and thanksgiving honors Me;
And to him who orders his way
    rightly [who follows the way that
    I show him],
I shall show the salvation of God."

PSALM 51

A Contrite Sinner's Prayer for Pardon.

To the Chief Musician. A
Psalm of David; when Nathan
the prophet came to him after he
    had sinned with Bathsheba.

1HAVE MERCY on me,
    O God, according to Your
    lovingkindness;
According to the greatness of
    Your compassion blot out my
    transgressions.
2Wash me thoroughly from my
    wickedness *and* guilt
And cleanse me from my sin.
3For I am conscious of my
    transgressions *and* I
    acknowledge them;
My sin is always before me.
4Against You, You only, have I
    sinned
And done that which is evil in Your
    sight,
So that You are justified when You
    speak [Your sentence]
And faultless in Your judgment.
    [Rom 3:4]
5I was brought forth in [a state of]
    wickedness;

life point

In Psalm 51, King David cries out to God
for mercy and forgiveness because the
Lord had been dealing with him about his
sin with Bathsheba and the murder of her
husband. Many people do not realize that
David had done these things one full year
before he wrote this psalm. Apparently,
he never really acknowledged this sin
until long after it happened. He had not
faced the truth, and as long as he refused to face the truth, he could not truly
repent. And as long as he could not truly
repent, he could not receive forgiveness
from God.

Psalm 51:6 conveys a powerful message.
It says that God desires truth "in the innermost being." That means if we want to
receive God's blessings, we must be honest with Him about our sins and ourselves.
Let me encourage you not to let sin linger
in your life. We all sin, and when we do,
we need to be quick to repent.

In sin my mother conceived me
    [and from my beginning I, too,
    was sinful]. [John 3:6; Rom 5:12;
    Eph 2:3]
6Behold, You desire truth in the
    innermost being,
And in the hidden part [of my
    heart] You will make me know
    wisdom.
7Purify me with hyssop, and I will
    be clean;
Wash me, and I will be whiter than
    snow.
8Make me hear joy and gladness
    and be satisfied;
Let the bones which You have
    broken rejoice.
9Hide Your face from my sins
And blot out all my iniquities.
10Create in me a clean heart, O God,
And renew a right *and* steadfast
    spirit within me.

11 Do not cast me away from Your
   presence
   And do not take Your Holy Spirit
   from me.
12 Restore to me the joy of Your
   salvation
   And sustain me with a willing
   spirit.
13 Then I will teach transgressors
   Your ways,
   And sinners shall be converted
   and return to You.

14 Rescue me from bloodguiltiness,
   O God, the God of my salvation;
   Then my tongue will sing joyfully
   of Your righteousness *and* Your
   justice.
15 O Lord, open my lips,
   That my mouth may declare Your
   praise.
16 For You do not delight in sacrifice,
   or else I would give it;
   You are not pleased with burnt
   offering. [1 Sam 15:22]
17 My [only] sacrifice [acceptable] to
   God is a broken spirit;
   A broken and contrite heart
   [broken with sorrow for sin,
   thoroughly penitent], such,
   O God, You will not despise.

18 By Your favor do good to Zion;
   May You rebuild the walls of
   Jerusalem.
19 Then will You delight in the
   sacrifices of righteousness,
   In burnt offering and whole burnt
   offering;
   Then young bulls will be offered
   on Your altar.

PSALM 52

Futility of Boastful Wickedness.

To the Chief Musician. A skillful
song, *or* a didactic *or* reflective
poem. *A Psalm* of David, when
Doeg the Edomite came and told
Saul, "David has come to the house
of Ahimelech."

1 WHY DO you boast of evil,
   O mighty man?
   The lovingkindness of God
   endures all day long.
2 Your tongue devises destruction,
   Like a sharp razor, working
   deceitfully.
3 You love evil more than good,
   And falsehood more than speaking
   what is right.   *Selah.*
4 You love all words that devour,
   O deceitful tongue.

5 But God will break you down
   forever;
   He will take you away and tear you
   away from your tent,
   And uproot you from the land of
   the living.   *Selah.*
6 The righteous will see it and fear,
   And will [scoffingly] laugh, *saying,*
7 "Look, [this is] the man who would
   not make God his strength [his
   stronghold and fortress],
   But trusted in the abundance of his
   riches,
   Taking refuge in his wealth."

8 But as for me, I am like a green
   olive tree in the house of God;
   I trust [confidently] in the
   lovingkindness of God forever
   and ever.

speak the Word

Lord, I will thank You forever because You have rescued me and kept me safe.
I will wait on Your name, for it is good.
–ADAPTED FROM PSALM 52:9

⁹I will thank You forever, because
You have done it, [You have
rescued me and kept me safe].
I will wait on Your name, for it is
good, in the presence of Your
godly ones.

PSALM 53

Folly and Wickedness of Men.

To the Chief Musician; in a
mournful strain. A skillful song,
or didactic *or* reflective poem
of David.

¹THE [empty-headed] fool has said
in his heart, "There is no God."
They are corrupt *and* evil, and
have committed repulsive
injustice;
There is no one who does good.
²God has looked down from heaven
upon the children of men
To see if there is anyone who
understands,
Who seeks after God [who
requires Him, who longs for Him
as essential to life].
³Every one of them has turned
aside *and* fallen away;
Together they have become filthy
and corrupt;
There is no one who does good, no,
not even one. [Rom 3:10–12]

⁴Have workers of wickedness no
knowledge *or* no understanding?
They eat up My people *as though*
they ate bread
And have not called upon God.
⁵There they were, in great terror
and dread, where there had been
no terror *or* dread;
For God scattered the bones of him
who besieged you;

You have put them to shame,
because God has rejected them.
⁶Oh, that the salvation of Israel
would come out of Zion!
When God restores [the fortunes
of] His people,
Let Jacob rejoice, let Israel be glad.

PSALM 54

Prayer for Defense
against Enemies.

To the Chief Musician;
with stringed instruments. A
skillful song, *or* a didactic *or*
reflective poem, of David, when
the Ziphites went and told Saul,
"David is hiding among us."

¹SAVE ME, O God, by Your name;
And vindicate me by Your
[wondrous] power.
²Hear my prayer, O God;
Listen to the words of my mouth.
³For strangers have risen against
me
And violent men have sought my
life;
They have not set God before
them.   *Selah*.

⁴Behold, God is my helper *and* ally;
The Lord is the sustainer of my
soul [my upholder].
⁵He will pay back the evil to my
enemies;
In Your faithfulness destroy them.

⁶With a freewill offering I will
sacrifice to You;
I will give thanks *and* praise Your
name, O Lᴏʀᴅ, for it is good.
⁷For He has rescued me from every
trouble,

speak the Word

Thank You, God, for being my helper and my ally.
–ADAPTED FROM Pꜱᴀʟᴍ 54:4

And my eye has looked *with satisfaction* (triumph) on my enemies.

PSALM 55

Prayer for the Destruction of the Treacherous.

To the Chief Musician; with stringed instruments. A skillful song, *or* a didactic *or* reflective poem, of David.

¹LISTEN TO my prayer, O God,
And do not hide Yourself from my plea.
²Listen to me and answer me;
I am restless *and* distraught in my complaint and distracted
³Because of the voice of the enemy,
Because of the pressure of the wicked;
For they bring down trouble on me,
And in anger they persecute me.

⁴My heart is in anguish within me,
And the terrors of death have fallen upon me.
⁵Fear and trembling have come upon me;
Horror has overwhelmed me.
⁶And I say, "Oh, that I had wings like a dove!
I would fly away and be at rest.
⁷"I would wander far away,
I would lodge in the [peace of the] wilderness.   *Selah*.
⁸"I would hurry to my refuge [my tranquil shelter far away]
From the stormy wind *and* from the tempest."

⁹Confuse [my enemies], O Lord,
divide their tongues [destroying their schemes],

For I have seen violence and strife in the city.
¹⁰Day and night they go around her walls;
Wickedness and mischief are in her midst.
¹¹Destruction is within her;
Oppression and deceit do not depart from her streets *and* market places.

¹²For it is not an enemy who taunts me—
Then I could bear it;
Nor is it one who has hated me who insolently exalts himself against me—
Then I could hide from him.
¹³But it is you, a man my equal *and* my counsel,
My companion and my familiar friend;
¹⁴We who had sweet fellowship together,
Who walked to the house of God in company.
¹⁵Let death come deceitfully upon them;
Let them go down alive to Sheol (the nether world, the place of the dead),
For evil [of every kind] is in their dwelling *and* in their hearts, in their midst.

¹⁶As for me, I shall call upon God,
And the LORD will save me.
¹⁷Evening and morning and at noon I will complain and murmur,
And He will hear my voice.
¹⁸He has redeemed my life in peace from the battle that was against me,
For there were many against me.

speak the Word

God, I thank You that You have redeemed my life in peace from the battle that was against me.
–ADAPTED FROM PSALM 55:18

¹⁹ God will hear and humble them,
  Even He who sits enthroned from
  old—   *Selah.*
  Because in them there has been no
  change [of heart],
  And they do not fear God [at all].
²⁰ He [my companion] has put out his
  hands against those who were at
  peace with him;
  He has broken his covenant [of
  friendship and loyalty].
²¹ The words of his mouth were
  smoother than butter,
  But his heart was hostile;
  His words were softer than oil,
  Yet they were drawn swords.

²² Cast your burden on the LORD
  [release it] and He will sustain
  and uphold you;
  He will never allow the righteous
  to be shaken (slip, fall, fail).
  [1 Pet 5:7]
²³ But You, O God, will bring
  down the wicked to the pit of
  destruction;
  Men of blood and treachery will
  not live out half their days.
  But I will [boldly and
  unwaveringly] trust in You.

PSALM 56

Supplication for Rescue and Grateful Trust in God.

To the Chief Musician; set
to [the tune of] "Silent Dove
Among Those Far Away." A
Mikhtam of David. [A record
of memorable thoughts] when
the Philistines seized him in Gath.

¹ BE GRACIOUS to me, O God, for
  man has trampled on me;
  All day long the adversary
  oppresses *and* torments me.
² My enemies have trampled upon
  me all day long,
  For they are many who fight
  proudly against me.
³ When I am afraid,
  I will put my trust *and* faith in You.
⁴ In God, whose word I praise;
  In God I have put my trust;
  I shall not fear.
  What can mere man do to me?
⁵ All day long they twist my words
  and say hurtful things;
  All their thoughts are against me
  for evil.
⁶ They attack, they hide *and* lurk,
  They watch my steps,
  As they have [expectantly] waited
  to take my life.
⁷ Cast them out because of their
  wickedness.
  In anger bring down the peoples,
  O God!

⁸ You have taken account of my
  wanderings;
  Put my tears in Your bottle.
  Are they not recorded in Your
  book?
⁹ Then my enemies will turn back in
  the day when I call;
  This I know, that God is for me.
  [Rom 8:31]
¹⁰ In God, *whose* word I praise,
  In the LORD, *whose* word I praise,
¹¹ In God have I put my trust *and*
  confident reliance; I will not be
  afraid.
  What can man do to me?

speak the Word

*God, I will cast my burdens on You and release them, knowing
that You will sustain and uphold me. I declare, God, that You will never
allow the righteous to be shaken!*
—ADAPTED FROM PSALM 55:22

¹² Your vows are *binding* upon me,
  O God;
I will give thank offerings to You.
¹³ For You have rescued my soul
  from death,
Yes, and my feet from stumbling,
So that I may walk before God
In the light of life.

PSALM 57

Prayer for Rescue
from Persecutors.

To the Chief Musician; set
to [the tune of] "Do Not Destroy."
A Mikhtam of David. [A
record of memorable thoughts
of David] when he fled from Saul
in the cave.

¹ BE GRACIOUS to me, O God, be
  gracious *and* merciful to me,
For my soul finds shelter *and*
  safety in You,
And in the shadow of Your
  wings I will take refuge *and* be
  confidently secure
Until destruction passes by.
² I will cry to God Most High,
  Who accomplishes *all things* on
  my behalf [for He completes my
  purpose in His plan].
³ He will send from heaven and save
  me;
He calls to account him who
  tramples me down.   *Selah.*
God will send out His
  lovingkindness and His truth.

⁴ My life is among lions;
I must lie among those who
  breathe out fire—
The sons of men whose teeth are
  spears and arrows,
And their tongue a sharp sword.
⁵ Be exalted above the heavens,
  O God;
Let Your glory *and* majesty be over
  all the earth.
⁶ They set a net for my steps;

My very life was bowed down.
They dug a pit before me;
Into the midst of it they themselves
  have fallen.   *Selah.*

⁷ My heart is steadfast, O God, my
  heart is steadfast *and* confident!
I will sing, yes, I will sing praises
  [to You]!
⁸ Awake, my glory!
Awake, harp and lyre!
I will awaken the dawn.
⁹ I will praise *and* give thanks to
  You, O Lord, among the people;
I will sing praises to You among
  the nations.
¹⁰ For Your faithfulness *and*
  lovingkindness are great,
  reaching to the heavens,
And Your truth to the clouds.
¹¹ Be exalted above the heavens,
  O God;
Let Your glory *and* majesty be over
  all the earth.

PSALM 58

Prayer for the Punishment
of the Wicked.

To the Chief Musician; set
to [the tune of] "Do Not Destroy."
A Mikhtam of David. [A record
of memorable thoughts of David.]

¹ DO YOU indeed speak
  righteousness, O gods (heavenly
  beings)?
Do you judge fairly, O sons of men?
  [Ps 82:1, 2]
² No, in your heart you devise
  wrongdoing;
On earth you deal out the violence
  of your hands.
³ The wicked are estranged from the
  womb;
These go astray from birth,
  speaking lies [even twisted
  partial truths].

⁴Their poison is like the venom of a
  serpent;
They are like the deaf horned
  viper that stops up its ear,
⁵So that it does not listen to the
  voice of charmers,
Or of the skillful enchanter casting
  [cunning] spells.

⁶O God, break their teeth in their
  mouth;

Break out the fangs of the young
  lions, O LORD.
⁷Let them flow away like water that
  runs off;
When he aims his arrows, let them
  be as headless shafts.
⁸*Let them be* as a snail which melts
  away (secretes slime) as it goes
  along,
Like the miscarriage of a woman
  which never sees the sun.

steadfast and confident

In Psalm 57:7, we read about a heart that is not only steadfast, but also confident.

I have discovered that staying confident at all times is vital to successful ministry and to an overcoming life. Even while I am in front of an audience teaching and ministering, the devil will try to introduce thoughts into my head to make me lose confidence. For example, there have been times when if I noticed two or three people glance at their watches, the devil whispered to me, "They are so bored they can't wait to get out of here." If a couple of people got up and left to go to the restroom, the devil would say, "They are leaving because they don't like your preaching."

I know that when people are singing or leading worship, it is not uncommon for the devil to tell them, "Nobody likes this. You picked the wrong music. You should have chosen a different song. Your voice sounds lousy. You are singing off-key," and so on and so on.

The mind is a battlefield, and the devil lies to us by putting wrong thoughts in our minds. He is constantly trying to steal our confidence. He does not want us to believe we can hear from God or to believe in the power of prayer. He does not want us to have any confidence concerning God's call on our lives or to be confident that we look nice, that we have any wisdom, or that we know anything at all. He wants us to go around feeling that we are failures. That is why we need to keep our hearts confident within us all the time. I have learned that we do not have to *feel* confident to *be* confident. We can be confident by faith because our confidence should be in Christ, not in ourselves. No matter how I feel, I still believe that I can do whatever I need to do through Christ, Who strengthens me (see Philippians 4:13). If we do not feel confident, then we feel afraid, and I have learned at those times to "do it afraid."

We do not have to drag ourselves out of bed each day in fear or discouragement. Instead, we should get up every morning prepared to keep Satan under our feet. How do we do that? We do it by confidently declaring what the Word says about us, confessing scriptures such as, "I am more than a conqueror through Jesus. I can do all things through Christ Who strengthens me. I am triumphant in every situation because God always causes me to triumph" (see Romans 8:37; Philippians 4:13; 2 Corinthians 2:14). Speaking God's Word not only causes the devil to leave us alone, but it also strengthens our confidence—and confidence is essential if we are going to keep growing and keep going in God.

9 Before your cooking pots can feel the *fire of* thorns [burning under them as fuel],
He will sweep them away with a whirlwind, the green and the burning ones alike.

10 The [unyieldingly] righteous will rejoice when he sees the vengeance [of God];
He will wash his feet in the blood of the wicked.

11 Men will say, "Surely there is a reward for the righteous;
Surely there is a God who judges on the earth."

PSALM 59

Prayer for Rescue from Enemies.

To the Chief Musician; set to [the tune of] "Do Not Destroy."
A Mikhtam of David, [a record of memorable thoughts] when Saul sent men to watch his house in order to kill him.

1 DELIVER ME from my enemies, O my God;
Set me *securely* on an inaccessibly high place away from those who rise up against me.

2 Deliver me from those who practice wrongdoing,
And save me from bloodthirsty men.

3 Look! They lie in wait for my life;
Fierce *and* powerful men [are uniting together to] launch an attack against me,
Not for my wrongdoing nor for any sin of mine, O Lord.

4 They run and set themselves against me though there is no guilt in me;

Stir Yourself to meet *and* help me, and see [what they are doing]!

5 You, O Lord God of hosts, the God of Israel,
Arise to punish all the nations;
Spare no one *and* do not be merciful to any who treacherously plot evil.   *Selah*.

6 They return at evening, they howl *and* snarl like dogs,
And go [prowling] around the city.

7 Look how they belch out [insults] with their mouths;
Swords [of sarcasm, ridicule, slander, and lies] are in their lips,
For *they say,* "Who hears us?"

8 But You, O Lord, will laugh at them [in scorn];
You scoff at *and* deride all the nations.

9 O [God] my strength, I will watch for You;
For God is my stronghold [my refuge, my protector, my high tower].

10 My God in His [steadfast] lovingkindness will meet me;
God will let me look *triumphantly* on my enemies [who lie in wait for me].

11 Do not kill them, or my people will forget;
Scatter them *and* make them wander [endlessly] back and forth by Your power, and bring them down,
O Lord our shield!

12 For the sin of their mouths and the words of their lips,
Let them even be trapped in their pride,

speak the Word

Thank You, God, for always meeting me with steadfast loving-kindness.
—ADAPTED FROM PSALM 59:10

And on account of the curses and
lies which they tell.
¹³ Destroy *them* in wrath, destroy *them*
so that they may be no more;
Let them know that God rules over
Jacob (Israel)
To the ends of the earth.   *Selah.*
¹⁴ They return at evening, they howl
and snarl like dogs,
And go [prowling] around the city.
¹⁵ They wander around for food [to
devour]
And growl all night if they are not
satisfied.

¹⁶ But as for me, I will sing of Your
mighty strength *and* power;
Yes, I will sing joyfully of Your
lovingkindness in the morning;
For You have been my stronghold
And a refuge in the day of my
distress.
¹⁷ To You, O [God] my strength, I will
sing praises;
For God is my stronghold [my
refuge, my protector, my high
tower], the God who shows me
[steadfast] lovingkindness.

PSALM 60

Lament over Defeat in Battle, and
Prayer for Help.

To the Chief Musician;
set to [the tune of] "The
Lily of the Testimony." A
Mikhtam of David [intended
to record memorable thoughts
and] to teach; when he
struggled with the Arameans
of Mesopotamia and
the Arameans of Zobah, and when
Joab returned and struck twelve
thousand Edomites in the Valley
of Salt.

¹ O GOD, You have rejected us *and*
cast us off. You have broken
[down our defenses and
scattered] us;

You have been angry; O restore us
and turn again to us.
² You have made the land quake,
You have split it open;
Heal its rifts, for it shakes *and*
totters.
³ You have made Your people
experience hardship;
You have given us wine to drink
that makes us stagger *and* fall.
⁴ You have set up a banner for those
who fear You [with awe-inspired
reverence and submissive
wonder—a banner to shield them
from attack],
A banner that may be displayed
because of the truth.   *Selah.*
⁵ That Your beloved ones may be
rescued,
Save with Your right hand and
answer us.

⁶ God has spoken in His holiness [in
His promises]:
"I will rejoice, I will divide [the
land of] Shechem and measure
out the Valley of Succoth [west
to east].
⁷ "Gilead is Mine, and Manasseh is
Mine;
Ephraim is My helmet;
Judah is My scepter.
⁸ "Moab is My washbowl;
Over Edom I shall throw My shoe
[in triumph];
Over Philistia I raise the shout [of
victory]."

⁹ Who will bring me into the
besieged city [of Petra]?
Who will lead me to Edom?
¹⁰ Have You not rejected us, O God?
And will You not go out with our
armies?
¹¹ Give us help against the enemy,
For the help of man is worthless
(ineffectual, without purpose).
¹² Through God we will have victory,
For He will trample down our
enemies.

PSALM 61
Confidence in God's Protection.

To the Chief Musician; on stringed instruments. *A Psalm* of David.

¹HEAR MY cry, O God;
Listen to my prayer.
²From the end of the earth I
call to You, when my heart is
overwhelmed *and* weak;
Lead me to the rock that is higher
than I [a rock that is too high to
reach without Your help].
³For You have been a shelter *and* a
refuge for me,
A strong tower against the enemy.
⁴Let me dwell in Your tent forever;
Let me take refuge in the shelter of
Your wings. *Selah.*

⁵For You have heard my vows, O God;
You have given me the inheritance
of those who fear Your name
[with reverence].
⁶You will prolong the king's life
[adding days upon days];
His years will be like many
generations.
⁷He will sit enthroned forever
before [the face of] God;
Appoint lovingkindness and truth
to watch over *and* preserve him.

putting the Word to work

Has life ever seemed so overwhelming that you wanted to run and hide? You can be sure of God's eternal protection and ability to be your refuge (see Psalm 61:3, 4). Whether you need the strength of a strong tower or the comfort of His arms around you, cry out to God; He will answer in your time of need.

speak the Word

God, through You, I will have victory.
—ADAPTED PSALM 60:12

⁸So I will sing praise to Your name
forever,
Paying my vows day by day.

PSALM 62
God Alone a Refuge from Treachery and Oppression.

To the Chief Musician; to Jeduthun [Ethan, the noted musician, founder of an official musical family]. A Psalm of David.

¹FOR GOD alone my soul *waits* in
silence;
From Him comes my salvation.
²He alone is my rock and my
salvation,
My defense *and* my strong
tower; I will not be shaken *or*
disheartened.

³How long will you attack a man
So that you may murder him, all of
you,
Like a leaning wall, like a tottering
fence?
⁴They consult only to throw him
down from his high position [to
dishonor him];
They delight in lies.
They bless with [the words of]
their mouths,
But inwardly they curse. *Selah.*

⁵For God alone my soul waits in
silence *and* quietly submits to
Him,
For my hope is from Him.
⁶He only is my rock and my
salvation;
My fortress *and* my defense, I will
not be shaken *or* discouraged.
⁷On God my salvation and my glory
rest;

stability releases ability

Psalm 62:8 teaches us that we are not to have faith in God just once in a while, but at all times. We need to learn to live from faith to faith (see Romans 1:17), trusting the Lord when things are good and when things are bad.

It is easy to trust God when things are going well. But when things are not going well, we develop character by trusting God in our difficult situations. And the more character we develop, the more our ability can be released. That is why I say that *stability releases ability*. The more stable we become, the more our ability will be released because God will know that He can trust us.

Many people have gifts that can take them to places where their character cannot keep them. Gifts are *given*, but character is *developed*. I have learned this in my own life.

Throughout my childhood, one thing I could do well was talk. In school, I could talk enough to make the teacher think I understood everything she was teaching, when I really knew nothing about it. I have always been a communicator and a convincer. But in order for God to allow me in the pulpit to preach to millions every day, not only did I have to have a gift, I also had to have character so that He could trust me to use my mouth to teach His Word and communicate His heart. Otherwise, He could not allow me to teach that many people, because I might say one thing one day and something else the next day. Or, even worse, I might preach to others what I was unable to do in my own private life.

By disciplining our emotions, our moods, and our mouths, we become stable enough to remain peaceful whatever our situation or circumstances, so that we can walk in the fruit of the Spirit—whether we feel like it or not. The more stable we become, the more ability can be released through us. Desire and pursue stability in every area of your life so that all the ability in you can be released!

He is my rock of [unyielding]
strength, my refuge is in God.
8 Trust [confidently] in Him at all
times, O people;
Pour out your heart before Him.
God is a refuge for us.   *Selah.*

9 Men of low degree are only a
breath (emptiness), and men of
[high] rank are a lie (delusion).
In the balances they go up
[because they have no
measurable weight or value];

They are together lighter than a
breath.
10 Do not trust in oppression,
And do not vainly hope in robbery;
If riches increase, do not set your
heart on them.

11 God has spoken once,
Twice I have heard this:
That power belongs to God.
12 Also to You, O Lord, belong
lovingkindness *and* compassion,

speak the Word

God, I am trusting confidently in You at all times. You are a refuge for me!
–ADAPTED FROM PSALM 62:8

For You compensate every man
according to [the value of] his
work. [Jer 17:10; Rev 22:12]

PSALM 63

The Thirsting Soul Satisfied in God.

A Psalm of David; when he was
in the wilderness of Judah.

¹O GOD, You are my God; with
deepest longing I will seek You;
My soul [my life, my very self]
thirsts for You, my flesh longs
and sighs for You,
In a dry and weary land where
there is no water.
²So I have gazed upon You in the
sanctuary,
To see Your power and Your glory.
[Ps 42:1, 2]

life point

Sacrifice and Christianity have always
been connected. In the Old Testament, the
Law required sacrifices of various kinds.
David speaks of lifting up the hands "as
the evening offering" in Psalm 141:2.

Other scriptures talk about the lifting
up of hands in worship (see Psalm 28:2;
119:48; 134:2; 1 Timothy 2:8). Lifting our
hands to God seems a natural thing to do
when we are in His presence. To me, it is
an expression of adoration, reverence,
and surrender. We should continually
surrender ourselves to God and His plan
for us.

You can lift up your hands and speak a
word of praise all throughout the day.
Even at work, you can go to the restroom
and take a moment to praise God. When
we willingly surrender and worship God
as a sacrifice, He responds.

life point

David spoke frequently about meditating
on God, His goodness, His works, and
His ways. It is tremendously uplifting to
think on the goodness of God and all the
marvelous works of His hands.

I enjoy watching television shows about
nature, animals, ocean life, and other
things in the physical world because they
depict the greatness and the awesomeness of God, His infinite creativity and the
fact that He is upholding all things by His
power (see Hebrews 1:3). Always remember that—and know that He is not only
upholding and maintaining the moon, the
stars, the planets including the earth, the
animals, and all of creation, but that He is
also upholding and maintaining everything about you and your life in the palm
of His hand.

³Because Your lovingkindness is
better than life,
My lips shall praise You.
⁴So will I bless You as long as I live;
I will lift up my hands in Your name.
⁵My soul [my life, my very self] is
satisfied as with marrow and
fatness,
And my mouth offers praises [to
You] with joyful lips.

life point

In Psalm 63:1, David cries out: "O God,
You are my God; with deepest longing I
will seek You" Throughout the Psalms,
David prayed similar prayers, which I call
"seeking prayers." Many times per day,
I find myself whispering in my heart or
even aloud, "Oh, God, I need You." This
is a very simple but very powerful way to
pray. I encourage you to join me in seeking God in this quick and effective way.

⁶When I remember You on my bed,
  I meditate *and* thoughtfully focus
    on You in the night watches,
⁷For You have been my help,
  And in the shadow of Your wings
    [where I am always protected] I
    sing for joy.
⁸My soul [my life, my very self]
    clings to You;
  Your right hand upholds me.

⁹But those who seek my life to
    destroy it
  Will [be destroyed and] go into
    the depths of the earth [into the
    underworld].
¹⁰They will be given over to the
    power of the sword;
  They will be a prey for foxes.
¹¹But the king will rejoice in God;
  Everyone who swears by Him
    [honoring the true God,
    acknowledging His authority
    and majesty] will glory,
  For the mouths of those who speak
    lies will be stopped.

PSALM 64

Prayer for Protection from Secret Enemies.

To the Chief Musician. A Psalm
of David.

¹HEAR MY voice, O God, in my
    complaint;
  Guard my life from the terror of the
    enemy.
²Hide me from the secret counsel
    and conspiracy of the ungodly,
  From the scheming of those who
    do wrong,
³Who have sharpened their
    tongues like a sword.
  They aim venomous words as
    arrows,
⁴To shoot from ambush at the
    blameless [one];
  Suddenly they shoot at him,
    without fear.

⁵They encourage themselves in
    [their pursuit of] an evil agenda;
  They talk of laying snares secretly;
  They say, "Who will discover us?"
⁶They devise acts of injustice,
    saying,
  "We are ready with a well-
    conceived plan."
  For the inward thought and
    the heart of a man are deep
    (mysterious, unsearchable).
⁷But God will shoot them with an
    [unexpected] arrow;
  Suddenly they will be wounded.
⁸So they will be caused to stumble;
  Their own tongue is against them;
  All who gaze at them will shake
    the head [in scorn].
⁹Then all men will fear [God's
    judgment];
  They will declare the work of God,
  And they will consider *and* wisely
    acknowledge what He has done.
¹⁰The righteous will rejoice in the
    Lord and take refuge in Him;
  All the upright in heart will glory
    and offer praise.

PSALM 65

God's Abundant Favor to Earth and Man.

To the Chief Musician. A Psalm
of David. A Song.

¹TO YOU belongs silence
    [the submissive wonder of
    reverence], and [it bursts into]
    praise in Zion, O God;
  And to You the vow shall be
    performed.
²O You who hear prayer,
  To You all mankind comes.
³Wickedness *and* guilt prevail
    against me;
  Yet as for our transgressions,
  You forgive them [removing them
    from Your sight].

⁴Blessed is the one whom You
   choose and bring near
To dwell in Your courts.
We will be filled with the goodness
   of Your house,
Your holy temple.

⁵By awesome *and* wondrous things
   You answer us in righteousness,
O God of our salvation,
You who are the trust *and* hope of
   all the ends of the earth and of
   the farthest sea;
⁶Who creates the mountains by His
   strength,
Being clothed with power,
⁷Who stills the roaring of the seas,
The roaring of their waves,
And the tumult of the peoples,
⁸So they who dwell at the ends *of the
   earth* stand in awe of Your signs
   [the evidence of Your presence].
   [Mark 4:36–41]
You make the dawn and the sunset
   shout for joy.

⁹You visit the earth and make it
   overflow [with water];
You greatly enrich it;
The stream of God is full of water;
You provide their grain, when You
   have prepared the earth.
¹⁰You water its furrows abundantly,
You smooth its ridges;
You soften it with showers,
You bless its growth.
¹¹You crown the year with Your
   bounty,
And Your paths overflow.
¹²The pastures of the wilderness
   drip [with dew],
And the hills are encircled with
   joy.
¹³The meadows are clothed with
   flocks
And the valleys are covered with
   grain;
They shout for joy and they sing.

PSALM 66
Praise for God's Mighty Deeds and for His Answer to Prayer.

To the Chief Musician. A Song.
A Psalm.

¹SHOUT JOYFULLY to God, all the
   earth;
²Sing of the honor *and* glory *and*
   magnificence of His name;
Make His praise glorious.
³Say to God, "How awesome *and*
   fearfully glorious are Your
   works!
Because of the greatness of Your
   power Your enemies will pretend
   to be obedient to You.
⁴"All the earth will [bow down to]
   worship You [in submissive
   wonder],
And will sing praises to You;

life point

In his writings the psalmist often uses the word *selah*, which means "pause, and calmly think of that." This phrase lets the reader know that this is a good place to stop and to slowly digest the meaning of what has just been said. The reader is given the opportunity to do this at the end of Psalm 66:4.

Jeremiah talked about stopping to feed on and digest the words of God. He said, "Your words were found and I ate them, and Your words became a joy to me and the delight of my heart" (Jeremiah 15:16). We must, so to speak, "chew" on the Word of God. Often we read the Bible for *quantity* when we should read for *quality*. Whatever passage you are reading, read in a manner that allows the Word to go down into your innermost being and feed your spirit.

They will praise Your name in
  song."   *Selah.*

⁵Come and see the works of God,
He is awesome in His deeds
  toward the children of men.
⁶He turned the sea into dry land;
They crossed through the river on
  foot;
There we rejoiced in Him. [Ex
  14–15]
⁷Who rules by His might forever,
His eyes keep watch on the
  nations;
Do not let the rebellious exalt
  themselves.   *Selah.*

⁸Bless our God, O peoples,
And make the sound of His praise
  be heard abroad,
⁹Who keeps us among the living,
And does not allow our feet to slip
  or stumble.
¹⁰For You have tested us, O God;
You have refined us as silver is
  refined.
¹¹You brought us into the net;
You laid a heavy burden [of
  servitude] on us.
¹²You made men (charioteers) ride
  over our heads [in defeat];
We went through fire and through
  water,
Yet You brought us out into a
  [broad] *place of* abundance [to
  be refreshed].
¹³I shall come into Your house with
  burnt offerings;
I shall pay You my vows,
¹⁴Which my lips uttered
And my mouth spoke as a promise
  when I was in distress.
¹⁵I shall offer to You burnt offerings
  of fat lambs,

With the [sweet] smoke of rams;
I will offer bulls with male goats.
                                         Selah.

¹⁶Come and hear, all who fear
  God [and worship Him with
  awe-inspired reverence and
  obedience],
And I will tell what He has done
  for me.
¹⁷I cried aloud to Him;
He was highly praised with my
  tongue.
¹⁸If I regard sin *and* baseness in my
  heart [that is, if I know it is there
  and do nothing about it],
The Lord will not hear [me]; [Prov
  15:29; 28:9; Is 1:15; John 9:31;
  James 4:3]
¹⁹But certainly God has heard [me];
He has given heed to the voice of
  my prayer.
²⁰Blessed be God,
Who has not turned away my
  prayer
Nor His lovingkindness from me.

PSALM 67

The Nations Exhorted to Praise God.

To the Chief Musician; on stringed
  instruments. A Psalm. A Song.

¹GOD BE gracious *and* kind-
  hearted to us and bless us,
And make His face shine [with
  favor] on us—   *Selah.*
²That Your way may be known on
  earth,
Your salvation *and* deliverance
  among all nations.
³Let the peoples praise You, O God;
Let all the peoples praise You.

speak the Word

*I bless You, Lord, because You have not turned away my prayer
nor Your loving-kindness from me.*
—ADAPTED FROM PSALM 66:20

⁴Let the nations be glad and sing
   for joy,
For You will judge the people fairly
And guide the nations on earth.
                        Selah.
⁵Let the peoples praise You, O God;
Let all the peoples praise You.
⁶The earth has yielded its harvest
   [as evidence of His approval];
God, our God, blesses us.
⁷God blesses us,
And all the ends of the earth shall
   fear Him [with awe-inspired
   reverence and submissive
   wonder].

putting the Word to work

**God wants all nations and people to
know Him, worship Him, and enjoy
Him. How can you be involved in God's
work in the world?**

PSALM 68

The God of Sinai and
of the Sanctuary.

To the Chief Musician. A Psalm
   of David. A Song.

¹LET GOD arise, and His enemies
   be scattered;
Let those who hate Him flee before
   Him.
²As smoke is driven away, so drive
   them away;
As wax melts before the fire,
So let the wicked *and* guilty perish
   before [the presence of] God.
³But let the righteous be glad; let
   them be in good spirits before
   God,
Yes, let them rejoice with delight.
⁴Sing to God, sing praises to His
   name;
Lift up *a song* for Him who rides
   through the desert—
His name is the Lᴏʀᴅ—be in good
   spirits before Him.

⁵A father of the fatherless and
   a judge *and* protector of the
   widows,
Is God in His holy habitation.
⁶God makes a home for the lonely;
He leads the prisoners into
   prosperity,
Only the stubborn *and* rebellious
   dwell in a parched land.

⁷O God, when You went out before
   Your people,
When You marched through the
   wilderness,   *Selah*.
⁸The earth trembled;
The heavens also poured down
   rain at the presence of God;
Sinai itself trembled at the
   presence of God, the God of
   Israel.
⁹You, O God, sent abroad plentiful
   rain;
You confirmed Your inheritance
   when it was parched *and* weary.
¹⁰Your flock found a dwelling place
   in it;
O God, in Your goodness You
   provided for the poor.

¹¹The Lord gives the command [to
   take Canaan];
The women who proclaim the good
   news are a great host (army);

¹²"The kings of the [enemies']
   armies flee, they flee,
And the beautiful woman who
   remains at home divides the
   spoil [left behind]."
¹³When you lie down [to rest] among
   the sheepfolds,
You [Israel] are like the wings of
   a dove [of victory] overlaid with
   silver,
Its feathers glistening with gold
   [trophies taken from the enemy].
¹⁴When the Almighty scattered [the
   Canaanite] kings in the land of
   Canaan,
It was snowing on Zalmon.

15 A mountain of God is the
    mountain of Bashan;
  A [high] mountain of many
    summits is Mount Bashan
    [rising east of the Jordan].
16 Why do you look with envy,
    mountains with many peaks,
  At the mountain [of the city of
    Zion] which God has desired for
    His dwelling place?
  Yes, the LORD will dwell *there*
    forever.
17 The chariots of God are myriads,
    thousands upon thousands;
  The Lord is among them as He was
    at Sinai, in holiness.
18 You have ascended on high, You
    have led away captive *Your*
    captives;
  You have received gifts among
    men,
  Even from the rebellious also, that
    the LORD God may dwell there.
    [Eph 4:8]

19 Blessed be the Lord, who bears our
    burden day by day,
  The God who is our salvation!
                              Selah.
20 God is to us a God of acts of
    salvation;
  And to GOD the Lord belong
    escapes from death [setting us
    free].
21 Surely God will shatter the head of
    His enemies,
  The hairy scalp of one who goes on
    in his guilty ways.
22 The Lord said, "I will bring your
    enemies back from Bashan;
  I will bring them back from the
    depths of the [Red] Sea,

23 That your foot may crush them in
    blood,
  That the tongue of your dogs
    may have its share from your
    enemies."
24 They have seen Your [solemn]
    procession, O God,
  The procession of my God, my
    King, into the sanctuary [in
    holiness].
25 The singers go in front, the players
    of instruments last;
  Between them the maidens
    playing on tambourines.
26 Bless God in the congregations,
    [give thanks, gratefully praise
    Him],
  The LORD, *you who are* from [Jacob]
    the fountain of Israel.
27 The youngest is there, Benjamin,
    ruling them,
  The princes of Judah and their
    company [the southern tribes],
  The princes of Zebulun and
    the princes of Naphtali [the
    northern tribes].
28 Your God has commanded your
    strength [your power in His
    service and your resistance to
    temptation];
  Show Yourself strong, O God, who
    acted on our behalf.
29 Because of Your temple at
    Jerusalem
  [Pagan] kings will bring gifts to
    You [out of respect].
30 Rebuke the beasts [living] among
    the reeds [in Egypt],
  The herd of bulls (the leaders)
    with the calves of the peoples;
  Trampling underfoot the pieces of
    silver;

speak the Word

Thank You, God, for bearing my burdens day by day.
You are the God of my salvation, Who sets me free.
—ADAPTED FROM PSALM 68:19, 20

He has scattered the peoples who
delight in war.
³¹ Princes *and* envoys shall come
from Egypt;
Ethiopia will quickly stretch out
her hands [with the offerings of
submission] to God.

³² Sing to God, O kingdoms of the
earth,
Sing praises to the Lord!   *Selah.*
³³ To Him who rides in the highest
heavens, the ancient heavens,
Behold, He sends out His voice, a
mighty *and* majestic voice.
³⁴ Ascribe strength to God;
His majesty is over Israel
And His strength is in the skies.
³⁵ O God, *You are* awesome *and*
profoundly majestic from Your
sanctuary;
The God of Israel gives strength
and power to His people.
Blessed be God!

PSALM 69

A Cry of Distress and Imprecation
on Adversaries.

To the Chief Musician; set
to [the tune of] "Lilies." *A Psalm*
of David.

¹ SAVE ME, O God,
For the waters have threatened my
life [they have come up to my
neck].
² I have sunk in deep mire, where
there is no foothold;
I have come into deep waters,
where a flood overwhelms me.
³ I am weary with my crying; my
throat is parched;
My eyes fail while I wait [with
confident expectation] for my
God.
⁴ Those who hate me without cause
are more than the hairs of my
head;

Those who would destroy me are
powerful, being my enemies
wrongfully;
I am forced to restore what I did
not steal. [John 15:25]

⁵ O God, You know my folly;
My wrongs are not hidden from
You.
⁶ Do not let those who wait
[confidently] for You be ashamed
through me, O Lord GOD of hosts;
Do not let those who seek You
[as necessary for life itself] be
dishonored through me, O God
of Israel,
⁷ Because for Your sake I have
borne reproach;
Confusion *and* dishonor have
covered my face.
⁸ I have become estranged from my
brothers
And an alien to my mother's sons.
[John 7:3–5]
⁹ For zeal for Your house has
consumed me,
And the [mocking] insults of those
who insult You have fallen on
me. [John 2:17; Rom 15:3]
¹⁰ When I wept *and* humbled myself
with fasting,
It became my reproach.
¹¹ When I made sackcloth my
clothing [as one in mourning],
I became a byword [a mere object
of scorn] to them.
¹² They who sit in the [city's] gate
talk about me *and* mock me,
And I am the song of the
drunkards.

¹³ But as for me, my prayer is to You,
O LORD, at an acceptable *and*
opportune time;
O God, in the greatness of Your
favor *and* in the abundance of
Your lovingkindness,
Answer me with truth [that is, the
faithfulness of Your salvation].

14 Rescue me from the mire and do
   not let me sink;
Let me be rescued from those
   who hate me and from the deep
   waters.
15 Do not let the floodwater
   overwhelm me,
Nor the deep waters swallow me up,
Nor the pit [of Sheol] shut its
   mouth over me.

16 Answer me, O Lord, for Your
   lovingkindness is sweet *and*
   good *and* comforting;
According to the greatness of Your
   compassion, turn to me.
17 Do not hide Your face from Your
   servant,
For I am in distress; answer me
   quickly.
18 Draw near to my soul and
   redeem it;
Ransom me because of my
   enemies [so that they do not
   delight in my distress].
19 You know my reproach and my
   shame and my dishonor [how I
   am insulted];
My adversaries are all before You
   [each one fully known].

20 Reproach *and* insults have broken
   my heart and I am so sick.
I looked for sympathy, but there
   was none,
And for comforters, but I found
   none.
21 They (self-righteous hypocrites)
   also gave me gall [poisonous and
   bitter] for my food,
And for my thirst they gave me
   vinegar to drink. [Matt 27:34, 48]

22 May their table [with all its
   abundance and luxury] become
   a snare [to them];
And when they are in peace
   [secure at their sacrificial
   feasts], *may it become* a trap.

23 May their eyes be dimmed so that
   they cannot see,
And make their loins shake
   continually [in terror and
   weakness].
24 Pour out Your indignation on
   them,
And let [the fierceness of] Your
   burning anger overtake them.
25 May their encampment be
   desolate;
May no one dwell in their tents.
   [Matt 23:38; Acts 1:20]
26 For they have persecuted him
   whom You have struck,
And they tell of the pain of those
   whom You have pierced *and*
   wounded.
27 Add [unforgiven] iniquity to their
   iniquity [in Your book],
And may they not come into Your
   righteousness.
28 May they be blotted out of the
   book of life [and their lives come
   to an end]
And may they not be recorded
   with the righteous (those in right
   standing with God). [Rev 3:4, 5;
   20:12, 15; 21:27]

29 But I am sorrowful and in pain;
May Your salvation, O God, set me
   [securely] on high.
30 I will praise the name of God with
   song
And magnify Him with
   thanksgiving.
31 And it will please the Lord better
   than an ox
Or a young bull with horns and
   hoofs.
32 The humble have seen it and are
   glad;
You who seek God [requiring
   Him as your greatest need],
   let your heart revive *and* live.
   [Ps 22:26; 42:1]
33 For the Lord hears the needy

And does not despise His *who are* prisoners.

34 Let heaven and earth praise Him,
The seas and everything that
moves in them.
35 For God will save Zion and rebuild
the cities of Judah,
That His servants may remain
there and possess it.
36 The descendants of His servants
will inherit it,
And those who love His name will
dwell in it.

PSALM 70

Prayer for Help
against Persecutors.

To the Chief Musician. *A Psalm*
of David, to bring to remembrance.

1 O GOD, *come quickly* to save me;
O LORD, come quickly to help me!
2 Let those be ashamed and
humiliated
Who seek my life;
Let them be turned back and
humiliated
Who delight in my hurt.
3 Let them be turned back because
of their shame *and* disgrace
Who say, "Aha, aha!"

4 May all those who seek You [as
life's first priority] rejoice and be
glad in You;
May those who love Your salvation
say continually,
"Let God be magnified!"
5 But I am afflicted and needy;
Come quickly to me, O God!
You are my help and my rescuer;
O LORD, do not delay.

PSALM 71

Prayer of an Old Man for Rescue.

1 IN YOU, O LORD, I have put my
trust *and* confidently taken
refuge;
Let me never be put to shame.
2 In Your righteousness deliver me
and rescue me;
Incline Your ear to me and
save me.
3 Be to me a rock of refuge *and* a
sheltering stronghold to which I
may continually come;
You have given the commandment
to save me,
For You are my rock and my
fortress.
4 Rescue me, O my God, from the
hand of the wicked (godless),
From the grasp of the unrighteous
and ruthless man.
5 For You are my hope;
O Lord GOD, *You are* my trust *and*
the source of my confidence
from my youth.
6 Upon You have I relied *and* been
sustained from my birth;
You are He who took me from my
mother's womb *and* You have
been my benefactor from that
day.
My praise is continually of You.

7 I am as a wonder to many,
For You are my strong refuge.
8 My mouth is filled with Your
praise
And with Your glory all day long.
9 Do not cast me off *nor* send me
away in the time of old age;
Do not abandon me when my
strength fails *and* I am weak.

speak the Word

*God, I am seeking You as life's first priority and I am rejoicing in You. I love
Your salvation and I will say continually, "Let God be magnified!"*
—ADAPTED FROM PSALM 70:4

10 For my enemies have spoken
   against me;
   Those who watch for my life have
   consulted together,
11 Saying, "God has abandoned him;
   Pursue and seize him, for there is
   no one to rescue *him.*"

12 O God, do not be far from me;
   O my God, come quickly to help me!
13 Let those who attack my life be
   ashamed and consumed;
   Let them be covered with reproach
   and dishonor, who seek to
   injure me.
14 But as for me, I will wait *and* hope
   continually,
   And will praise You yet more and
   more.
15 My mouth shall tell of Your
   righteousness
   And of Your [deeds of] salvation
   all day long,
   For their number is more than I
   know.
16 I will come with the mighty acts
   of the Lord GOD [and in His
   strength];
   I will make mention of Your
   righteousness, Yours alone.

17 O God, You have taught me from
   my youth,
   And I still declare Your wondrous
   works *and* miraculous deeds.
18 And even when I am old and
   gray-headed, O God, do not
   abandon me,
   Until I declare Your [mighty]
   strength to this generation,
   Your power to all who are to come.
19 Your righteousness, O God,
   reaches to the [height of the]
   heavens,
   You who have done great things;

O God, who is like You, [who is
   Your equal]?
20 You who have shown me many
   troubles and distresses
   Will revive *and* renew me again,
   And will bring me up again from
   the depths of the earth.
21 May You increase my greatness
   (honor)
   And turn to comfort me.

22 I will also praise You with the harp,
   Your truth *and* faithfulness, O my
   God;
   To You I will sing praises with the
   lyre,
   O Holy One of Israel.
23 My lips will shout for joy when I
   sing praises to You,
   And my soul, which You have
   redeemed.
24 My tongue also will speak of Your
   righteousness all day long;
   For they are ashamed, for they are
   humiliated who seek my injury.

PSALM 72

The Reign of the Righteous King.

A Psalm of Solomon.

1 GIVE THE king [knowledge of]
   Your judgments, O God,
   And [the spirit of] Your
   righteousness to the king's son
   [to guide all his ways].
2 May he judge Your people with
   righteousness,
   And Your afflicted with justice.
   [1 Kin 3:1–5]
3 The mountains will bring peace
   and prosperity to the people,
   And the hills, in [the
   establishment of] righteousness.

speak the Word

God, I will wait and hope continually. I will praise You more and more.
−ADAPTED FROM PSALM 71:14

⁴May he bring justice to the poor
among the people,
Save the children of the needy
And crush the oppressor,
⁵Let them fear You [with awe-
inspired reverence and worship
You with obedience] while the
sun endures,
And as long as the moon
[reflects light], throughout all
generations.
⁶May he come down like rain on the
mown grass,
Like showers that water the earth.
⁷In his days may the righteous
flourish,
And peace abound until the moon
is no more. [Is 11:1–9]

⁸May he also rule from sea to sea
And from the River [Euphrates] to
the ends of the earth. [Zech 14:9]
⁹The nomads of the desert will bow
before him,
And his enemies will lick the dust.
¹⁰The kings of Tarshish and of the
islands will bring offerings;
The kings of Sheba and Seba will
offer gifts.
¹¹Yes, all kings will bow down
before him,
All nations will serve him. [Ps 138:4]

¹²For he will rescue the needy when
he cries for help,
The afflicted *and* abused also, and
him who has no helper.
¹³He will have compassion on the
poor and needy,
And he will save the lives of the
needy.
¹⁴He will redeem their life from
oppression *and* fraud and
violence,
And their blood will be precious in
His sight.
¹⁵So may he live, and may the gold of
Sheba be given to him;
And let them pray for him
continually;

Let them bless *and* praise him all
day long.
¹⁶There will be an abundance of
grain in the soil on the top of the
mountains;
Its fruit will wave like [the cedars
of] Lebanon,
And those of the city will flourish
like grass of the earth.
¹⁷May his name endure forever;
May his name continue as long as
the sun;
And let men bless themselves by
him;
Let all nations call him blessed.

¹⁸Blessed be the Lord God, the God
of Israel,
Who alone does wonderful things.
¹⁹Blessed be His glorious name
forever;
And may the whole earth be filled
with His glory.
Amen and Amen.

²⁰The prayers of David son of Jesse
are ended.

BOOK THREE

PSALM 73

The End of the Wicked Contrasted with That of the Righteous.

A Psalm of Asaph.

¹TRULY GOD is good to Israel,
To those who are pure in heart.
²But as for me, my feet came close
to stumbling,
My steps had almost slipped.
³For I was envious of the arrogant
As I saw the prosperity of the
wicked.
⁴For there are no pains in their
death,
Their body is fat *and* pampered.
⁵They are not in trouble *as other* men,
Nor are they plagued like
mankind.

⁶Therefore pride is their necklace;
  Violence covers them like a
    garment [like a long, luxurious
    robe].
⁷Their eye bulges from fatness
    [they have more than the heart
    desires];
  The imaginations of their mind
    run riot [with foolishness].
⁸They mock and wickedly speak of
    oppression;
  They speak loftily [with malice].
⁹They set their mouth against the
    heavens,
  And their tongue swaggers
    through the earth. [Rev 13:6]

¹⁰Therefore his people return to this
    place,
  And waters of abundance [offered
    by the irreverent] are [blindly]
    drunk by them.
¹¹They say, "How does God know?
  Is there knowledge [of us] with the
    Most High?"
¹²Behold, these are the ungodly,
  Who always prosper *and* are at
    ease [in the world]; they have
    increased in wealth.
¹³Surely then in vain I have cleansed
    my heart
  And washed my hands in
    innocence. [Mal 3:14]
¹⁴For all the day long have I been
    stricken,
  And punished every morning.

¹⁵If I had said, "I will say this," [and
    expressed my feelings],
  I would have betrayed the
    generation of Your children.
¹⁶When I considered how to
    understand this,
  It was too great an effort for me
    and too painful
¹⁷Until I came into the sanctuary of
    God;
  Then I understood [for I
    considered] their end.

¹⁸Surely You set the wicked-minded
    and immoral on slippery places;
  You cast them down to destruction.
¹⁹How they are destroyed in a
    moment!
  They are completely swept away
    by sudden terrors!
²⁰Like a dream [which seems real]
    until one awakens,
  O Lord, when stirred, [You observe
    the wicked], You will despise
    their image.

²¹When my heart was embittered
  And I was pierced within [as with
    the fang of an adder],
²²Then I was senseless and ignorant;
  I was like a beast before You.
²³Nevertheless I am continually with
    You;
  You have taken hold of my right
    hand.
²⁴You will guide me with Your
    counsel,
  And afterward receive me to honor
    and glory.

²⁵Whom have I in heaven [but You]?
  And besides You, I desire nothing
    on earth.
²⁶My flesh and my heart may fail,
  But God is the rock *and* strength of
    my heart and my portion forever.
²⁷For behold, those who are far from
    You will perish;
  You have destroyed all those
    who are unfaithful *and* have
    abandoned You.

putting the Word to work

Have you ever wondered who will be
there for you when times are really
tough? Even when you feel as though
you cannot go on, God promises to be
your strength (see Psalm 73:25–28).
Ask God to draw you nearer to Himself, so you can experience His goodness and strength even more fully.

28 But as for me, it is good for me to
draw near to God;
I have made the Lord GOD my refuge
and placed my trust in Him,
That I may tell of all Your works.

PSALM 74

An Appeal against the
Devastation of the Land
by the Enemy.

A skillful song, *or a didactic or*
reflective poem, of Asaph.

1 O GOD, why have You rejected us
forever?
Why does Your anger smoke against
the sheep of Your pasture?
2 Remember Your congregation,
which You have purchased of old,
Which You have redeemed to be
the tribe of Your inheritance;
Remember Mount Zion, where You
have dwelt.
3 Turn your footsteps [quickly]
toward the perpetual ruins;
The enemy has damaged
everything within the sanctuary.
4 In the midst of Your meeting place
Your enemies have roared [with
their battle cry];
They have set up their own
emblems for signs [of victory].
5 It seems as if one had lifted up
An axe in a forest of trees [to set a
record of destruction].
6 And now all the carved work [of
the meeting place]
They smash with hatchets and
hammers.
7 They have burned Your sanctuary
to the ground;
They have profaned the dwelling
place of Your name.
8 They said in their heart, "Let us
completely subdue them."
They have burned all the meeting
places of God in the land.
9 We do not see our symbols;

There is no longer any prophet [to
guide us],
Nor does any among us know for
how long.
10 O God, how long will the adversary
scoff?
Is the enemy to revile Your name
forever?
11 Why do You withdraw Your hand,
even Your right hand [from
judging the enemy]?
Remove Your hand from Your chest,
destroy *them!*

12 Yet God is my King of old,
Working salvation in the midst of
the earth.
13 You divided the [Red] Sea by Your
strength;
You broke the heads of the sea
monsters in the waters. [Ex 14:21]
14 You crushed the heads of
Leviathan (Egypt);
You gave him as food for the
creatures of the wilderness.
[Job 41:1]
15 You broke open fountains and
streams;
You dried up ever-flowing rivers.
[Ex 17:6; Num 20:11; Josh 3:13]
16 The day is Yours, the night also is
Yours;
You have established *and* prepared
the [heavenly] light and the sun.
17 You have defined *and* established
all the borders of the earth [the
divisions of land and sea and of
the nations];
You have made summer and
winter. [Acts 17:26]

18 Remember this, O LORD, the enemy
has scoffed,
And a foolish *and* impious people
has spurned Your name.
19 Oh, do not hand over the soul of
your turtledove to the wild beast;
Do not forget the life of Your
afflicted forever.

²⁰Consider the covenant [You made
   with Abraham],
For the dark places of the land
   are full of the habitations of
   violence.
²¹Let not the oppressed return
   dishonored;
Let the afflicted and needy praise
   Your name.

²²Arise, O God, plead Your own
   cause;
Remember how the foolish man
   scoffs at You all day long.
²³Do not forget the [clamoring]
   voices of Your adversaries,
The uproar of those who rise
   against You, which ascends
   continually [to Your ears].

PSALM 75

God Abases the Proud, but Exalts the Righteous.

To the Chief Musician; set
to [the tune of] "Do Not Destroy."
A Psalm of Asaph. A Song.

¹WE GIVE thanks *and* praise to
   You, O God, we give thanks,
For Your [wonderful works declare
   that Your] name is near;
People declare Your wonders.
²"When I select an appointed time,
I will judge with equity," [says the
   LORD].
³"The earth and all the inhabitants
   of it melt [in tumultuous times].
It is I who will steady its pillars.
                                    Selah.
⁴"I said to the arrogant, 'Do not
   boast;'
And to the wicked, 'Do not lift up
   the horn [of self-glorification].
⁵'Do not lift up your [defiant and
   aggressive] horn on high,
Do not speak with a stiff neck.'"

⁶For not from the east, nor from the
   west,

Nor from the desert comes
   exaltation. [Is 14:13]
⁷But God is the Judge;
He puts down one and lifts up
   another.
⁸For a cup [of His wrath] is in the
   hand of the LORD, and the wine
   foams;
It is well mixed *and* fully spiced,
   and He pours out from it;
And all the wicked of the earth
   must drain it and drink down to
   its dregs. [Ps 60:3; Jer 25:15; Rev
   14:9, 10; 16:19]

⁹But as for me, I will declare it *and*
   rejoice forever;
I will sing praises to the God of
   Jacob.
¹⁰All the horns of the wicked He will
   cut off,
But the horns of the righteous will
   be lifted up.

PSALM 76

The Victorious Power of the God of Jacob.

To the Chief Musician; on stringed
instruments. A Psalm of Asaph.
A Song.

¹GOD IS known in Judah;
His name is great in Israel.
²His tabernacle is in Salem
   (Jerusalem);
His dwelling place is in Zion.
³There He broke the flaming arrows,
The shield, the sword, and the
   weapons of war.   *Selah.*

⁴You are glorious *and* resplendent,
More majestic than the mountains
   of prey.
⁵The stouthearted have been
   stripped of their spoil,
They have slept the sleep [of death];
And none of the warriors could
   use his hands.
⁶At Your rebuke, O God of Jacob,

Both rider and horse were cast into a dead sleep [of death]. [Ex 15:1, 21; Nah 2:13; Zech 12:4]
⁷You, even You, are to be feared [with the submissive wonder of reverence];
Who may stand in Your presence when once You are angry?

⁸You caused judgment to be heard from heaven;
The earth feared and was quiet
⁹When God arose to [establish] judgment,
To save all the humble of the earth.   *Selah*.
¹⁰For the wrath of man shall praise You;
With a remnant of wrath You will clothe *and* arm Yourself.

¹¹Make vows to the Lᴏʀᴅ your God and fulfill them;
Let all who are around Him bring gifts to Him who is to be feared [with awe-inspired reverence].
¹²He will cut off the spirit of princes;
He is awesome *and* feared by the kings of the earth.

PSALM 77

Comfort in Trouble from Recalling God's Mighty Deeds.

To the Chief Musician; according to Jeduthun [one of David's three chief musicians, founder of an official musical family].
A Psalm of Asaph.

¹MY VOICE rises to God, and I will cry aloud;
My voice rises to God, and He will hear me.
²In the day of my trouble I [desperately] sought the Lord;
In the night my hand was stretched out [in prayer] without weariness;
My soul refused to be comforted.

³I remember God; then I am disquieted *and* I groan;
I sigh [in prayer], and my spirit grows faint.   *Selah*.
⁴You have held my eyelids open;
I am so troubled that I cannot speak.
⁵I have considered the ancient days,
The years [of prosperity] of long, long ago.
⁶I will remember my song in the night;
I will meditate with my heart,
And my spirit searches:

⁷Will the Lord reject forever?
And will He never be favorable again?
⁸Has His lovingkindness ceased forever?
Have His promises ended for all time?
⁹Has God forgotten to be gracious?
Or has He in anger withdrawn His compassion?   *Selah*.
¹⁰And I said, "This is my grief,
That the right hand of the Most High has changed [and His lovingkindness is withheld]."

¹¹I will [solemnly] remember the deeds of the Lᴏʀᴅ;
Yes, I will [wholeheartedly] remember Your wonders of old.
¹²I will meditate on all Your works
And thoughtfully consider all Your [great and wondrous] deeds.
¹³Your way, O God, is holy [far from sin and guilt].
What god is great like our God?

life point

In Psalm 77:6, David shows us how he sought God's leading. The next time you have a decision to make, do not try to figure it out with your mind. Go somewhere to get still and let your spirit search diligently for God's voice.

14 You are the [awesome] God who
     works [powerful] wonders;
You have demonstrated Your
     power among the people.
15 You have with Your [great] arm
     redeemed Your people,
The sons of Jacob and Joseph.

                                    Selah.

16 The waters [of the Red Sea] saw
     You, O God;
The waters saw You, they were in
     anguish;
The deeps also trembled.
17 The clouds poured down water;
The skies sent out a sound [of
     rumbling thunder];
Your arrows (lightning) flashed
     here and there.
18 The voice of Your thunder was in
     the whirlwind;
The lightnings illumined the
     world;
The earth trembled and shook.
19 Your way [of escape for Your
     people] was through the sea,
And Your paths through the great
     waters,
And Your footprints were not
     traceable.
20 You led Your people like a flock
By the hand of Moses and Aaron
     [to the promised goal].

PSALM 78

God's Guidance of His People
in Spite of Their Unfaithfulness.

A skillful song, *or* a didactic *or*
     reflective poem, of Asaph.

1 LISTEN, O my people, to my
     teaching;
Incline your ears to the words of
     my mouth [and be willing to
     learn].
2 I will open my mouth in a parable
     [to instruct using examples];

I will utter dark *and* puzzling
     sayings of old [that contain
     important truth]— [Matt 13:34, 35]
3 Which we have heard and known,
And our fathers have told us.
4 We will not hide them from their
     children,
But [we will] tell to the generation
     to come the praiseworthy deeds
     of the LORD,
And [tell of] His great might *and*
     power and the wonderful works
     that He has done.

5 For He established a testimony (a
     specific precept) in Jacob
And appointed a law in Israel,
Which He commanded our fathers
That they should teach to their
     children [the great facts of God's
     transactions with Israel],
6 That the generation to come might
     know them, that the children
     still to be born
May arise and recount them to
     their children,
7 That they should place their
     confidence in God
And not forget the works of God,
But keep His commandments,
8 And not be like their fathers—
A stubborn and rebellious
     generation,
A generation that did not prepare
     its heart to know *and* follow God,
And whose spirit was not faithful
     to God.

9 The sons of Ephraim were armed
     as archers and carrying bows,
Yet they turned back in the day of
     battle.
10 They did not keep the covenant of
     God
And refused to walk according to
     His law;
11 And they forgot His [incredible]
     works
And His miraculous wonders that
     He had shown them.

¹²He did marvelous things in the
  sight of their fathers
In the land of Egypt, in the field of
  Zoan [where Pharaoh resided].
¹³He divided the [Red] Sea and
  allowed them to pass through it,
And He made the waters stand up
  like [water behind] a dam. [Ex
  14:22]

¹⁴In the daytime He led them with a
  cloud
And all the night with a light of
  fire. [Ex 13:21; 14:24]
¹⁵He split rocks in the wilderness
And gave *them* abundant [water to]
  drink like the ocean depths.
¹⁶He brought streams also from the
  rock [at Rephidim and Kadesh]

leave your stubbornness behind

Psalm 78 describes some of the things that happened to the Israelites as they journeyed from Egypt to the Promised Land. Despite God's gracious and miraculous provision for them time and time again, verse 8 tells us that they were very stubborn and rebellious during their years in the wilderness. That is precisely what caused them to die there. They simply would not do what God told them to do! They would cry out to God to get them out of trouble when they got into a mess. They would even respond to His instructions with obedience—until circumstances improved. Then, repeatedly, they would go right back into rebellion.

This same cycle is repeated and recorded so many times in the Old Testament that it is almost unbelievable. And yet, if we are not walking in wisdom, we will spend our lives doing the same thing. As we read about the Israelites and their time in the wilderness, let us learn from their mistakes and not repeat them in our own lives.

I suppose some of us are just by nature a little more strong-willed than others. And then, of course, we must consider our roots and how we got started in life, because that affects us too.

I was born with a strong personality. The years I spent being abused and controlled, plus my already-strong personality, combined to develop in me the mind-set that nobody was going to tell me what to do. Obviously, God had to deal with this bad attitude before He could use me.

The Lord demands that we learn to give up our own way and be pliable and moldable in His hands. As long as we are stubborn and rebellious, He cannot use us.

I describe "stubborn" as obstinate, or difficult to handle or work with; and "rebellious" as resisting control, resisting correction, unruly, or refusing to follow ordinary guidelines. Both these definitions describe me as I used to be! The abuse I had suffered in my early life caused a lot of my out-of-balance attitudes toward authority. But in order to grow as a person and be successful in life, I could not allow my past to become an excuse to stay trapped in stubbornness, rebellion, or anything else.

Victorious living requires prompt and precise obedience to God. We grow in our ability and willingness to lay aside our will and do His. It is vital that we continue to make progress in this area. It is not enough to reach a certain plateau and think, *I have gone as far as I am going to go*. We must be obedient in all things—not holding back anything or keeping any doors in our lives closed to the Lord.

Let Him do a thorough work in you so that you can leave your "wilderness" behind and enter your Promised Land.

And caused waters to run down
   like rivers. [Ex 17:6; Num 20:11]

¹⁷Yet they still continued to sin
   against Him
   By rebelling against the Most High
   in the desert.
¹⁸And in their hearts they put God to
   the test
   By asking for food according to
   their [selfish] appetite.
¹⁹Then they spoke against God;
   They said, "Can God prepare [food
   for] a table in the wilderness?
²⁰"Behold, He struck the rock so that
   waters gushed out
   And the streams overflowed;
   Can He give bread also?
   Or will He provide meat for His
   people?"

²¹Therefore, when the LORD heard,
   He was full of wrath;
   A fire was kindled against Jacob,
   And His anger mounted up against
   Israel,
²²Because they did not believe in
   God [they did not rely on Him,
   they did not adhere to Him],
   And they did not trust in His
   salvation (His power to save).
²³Yet He commanded the clouds
   from above
   And opened the doors of heaven;
²⁴And He rained down manna upon
   them to eat
   And gave them the grain of
   heaven. [Ex 16:14; John 6:31]
²⁵Man ate the bread of angels;
   God sent them provision in
   abundance.
²⁶He caused the east wind to blow in
   the heavens
   And by His [unlimited] power He
   guided the south wind.
²⁷He rained meat upon them like the
   dust,
   And winged birds (quail) like the
   sand of the seas. [Num 11:31]

²⁸And He let them fall in the midst
   of their camp,
   Around their tents.
²⁹So they ate and were well filled,
   He gave them what they craved.
³⁰Before they had satisfied their
   desire,
   And while their food was in their
   mouths, [Num 11:33]
³¹The wrath of God rose against
   them
   And killed some of the strongest of
   them,
   And subdued the choice young
   men of Israel.
³²In spite of all this they still sinned,
   For they did not believe in His
   wonderful *and* extraordinary
   works.
³³Therefore He consumed their days
   like a breath [in emptiness and
   futility]
   And their years in sudden terror.

³⁴When He killed [some of] them,
   then those remaining sought
   Him,
   And they returned [to Him] and
   searched diligently for God [for
   a time].
³⁵And they remembered that God
   was their rock,
   And the Most High God their
   Redeemer.
³⁶Nevertheless they flattered Him
   with their mouths
   And lied to Him with their
   tongues.
³⁷For their heart was not steadfast
   toward Him,
   Nor were they faithful to His
   covenant. [Acts 8:21]
³⁸But He, the source of compassion
   and lovingkindness, forgave
   their wickedness and did not
   destroy them;
   Many times He restrained His
   anger
   And did not stir up all His wrath.

39 For He [graciously] remembered that they were mere [human] flesh,
A wind that goes and does not return.

40 How often they rebelled against Him in the wilderness
And grieved Him in the desert!

41 Again and again they tempted God,
And distressed the Holy One of Israel.

42 They did not remember [the miracles worked by] His [powerful] hand,
Nor the day when He redeemed them from the enemy,

43 How He worked His miracles in Egypt
And His wonders in the field of Zoan [where Pharaoh resided],

44 And turned their rivers into blood,
And their streams, so that they could not drink.

45 He sent among them swarms of flies which devoured them,
And frogs which destroyed them.

46 He also gave their crops to the grasshopper,
And the fruit of their labor to the locust.

47 He destroyed their vines with [great] hailstones
And their sycamore trees with frost.

48 He gave over their cattle also to the hailstones,
And their flocks and herds to thunderbolts. [Ex 9:18–21]

49 He sent upon them His burning anger, [Ex 12:23]
His fury and indignation and distress,
A band of angels of destruction [among them].

50 He leveled a path for His anger [to give it free run];
He did not spare their souls from death,
But turned over their lives to the plague.

51 He killed all the firstborn in Egypt,
The first and best of their strength in the tents [of the land of the sons] of Ham.

52 But God led His own people forward like sheep
And guided them in the wilderness like [a good shepherd with] a flock.

53 He led them safely, so that they did not fear;
But the sea engulfed their enemies. [Ex 14:27, 28]

54 So He brought them to His holy land,
To this mountain [Zion] which His right hand had acquired.

55 He also drove out the nations before the sons of Israel
And allotted *their land* as an inheritance, measured out *and* partitioned;
And He had the tribes of Israel dwell in their tents [the tents of those who had been dispossessed].

56 Yet they tempted and rebelled against the Most High God
And did not keep His testimonies (laws).

57 They turned back and acted unfaithfully like their fathers;
They were twisted like a warped bow [that will not respond to the archer's aim].

58 For they provoked Him to [righteous] anger with their high places [devoted to idol worship]
And moved Him to jealousy with their carved images [by denying Him the love, worship, and obedience that is rightfully and uniquely His].

59 When God heard this, He was filled with [righteous] wrath;
And utterly rejected Israel, [greatly hating her ways],

⁶⁰So that He abandoned the
   tabernacle at Shiloh,
   The tent in which He had dwelled
   among men,
⁶¹And gave up His strength *and*
   power (the ark of the covenant)
   into captivity,
   And His glory into the hand of the
   enemy (the Philistines). [1 Sam
   4:21]
⁶²He also handed His people over to
   the sword,
   And was infuriated with His
   inheritance (Israel). [1 Sam 4:10]
⁶³The fire [of war] devoured His
   young men,
   And His [bereaved] virgins had no
   wedding songs.
⁶⁴His priests [Hophni and Phinehas]
   fell by the sword,
   And His widows could not weep.
   [1 Sam 4:11, 19, 20]

⁶⁵Then the Lord awakened as from
   sleep,
   Like a [mighty] warrior who
   awakens from the sleep of wine
   [fully conscious of his power].
⁶⁶He drove His enemies backward;
   He subjected them to lasting
   shame *and* dishonor.
⁶⁷Moreover, He rejected the tent of
   Joseph,
   And did not choose the tribe
   of Ephraim [in which the
   tabernacle stood].
⁶⁸But He chose the tribe of Judah [as
   Israel's leader],
   Mount Zion, which He loved [to
   replace Shiloh as His capital].
⁶⁹And He built His sanctuary
   [exalted] like the heights [of the
   heavens],
   Like the earth which He has
   established forever.
⁷⁰He also chose David His servant
   And took him from the sheepfolds;
   [1 Sam 16:11, 12]
⁷¹From tending the ewes with
   nursing young He brought him

To shepherd Jacob His people,
And Israel His inheritance. [2 Sam
   7:7, 8]
⁷²So David shepherded them
   according to the integrity of his
   heart;
   And guided them with his skillful
   hands.

PSALM 79

A Lament over the Destruction of Jerusalem, and Prayer for Help.

A Psalm of Asaph.

¹O GOD, the nations have invaded
   [the land of Your people] Your
   inheritance;
   They have defiled Your sacred
   temple;
   They have laid Jerusalem in ruins.
²They have given the dead bodies
   of Your servants as food to the
   birds of the heavens,
   The flesh of Your godly ones to the
   beasts of the earth.
³They have poured out their blood
   like water all around Jerusalem,
   And there was no one to bury
   them.
⁴We have become an object of
   taunting to our neighbors
   [because of our humiliation],
   A derision and mockery to those
   who encircle us.
⁵How long, O LORD? Will You be
   angry forever?
   Will Your jealousy [which cannot
   endure a divided allegiance]
   burn like fire?
⁶Pour out Your wrath on the
   [Gentile] nations that do not
   know You,
   And on the kingdoms that do not
   call on Your name. [2 Thess 1:8]
⁷For they have devoured Jacob
   And made his pasture desolate.

⁸O do not remember against us the
   sins *and* guilt of our forefathers.

Let Your compassion *and* mercy
come quickly to meet us,
For we have been brought very low.
⁹Help us, O God of our salvation, for
the glory of Your name;
Rescue us, forgive us our sins for
Your name's sake.
¹⁰Why should the [Gentile] nations
say, "Where is their God?"
Let there be known [without
delay] among the nations in our
sight [and to this generation],
Your vengeance for the blood of
Your servants which has been
poured out.
¹¹Let the groaning *and* sighing of the
prisoner come before You;
According to the greatness of Your
power keep safe those who are
doomed to die.
¹²And return into the lap of our
neighbors sevenfold
The taunts with which they have
taunted You, O Lord.
¹³So we Your people, the sheep of
Your pasture,
Will give You thanks forever;
We will declare *and* publish
Your praise from generation to
generation.

PSALM 80
God Implored to Rescue His People from Their Calamities.

To the Chief Musician; set
to [the tune of] "Lilies, a
Testimony." A Psalm of Asaph.

¹HEAR US O Shepherd of Israel,
You who lead Joseph like a flock;
You who sit enthroned above
the cherubim [of the ark of the
covenant], shine forth!
²Before Ephraim and Benjamin and
Manasseh, stir up Your power
And come to save us!
³Restore us, O God;

Cause Your face to shine on us
[with favor and approval], and we
will be saved.

⁴O Lord God of hosts,
How long will You be angry with
the prayers of Your people?
⁵You have fed them the bread of
tears,
And You have made them drink
[bitter] tears in abundance.
⁶You make us an object of
contention to our neighbors,
And our enemies laugh [at our
suffering] among themselves.
⁷Restore us, O God of hosts;
And cause Your face to shine on us
[with favor and approval], and
we will be saved.

⁸You uprooted a vine (Israel) from
Egypt;
You drove out the [Canaanite]
nations and planted the vine [in
Canaan].
⁹You cleared away *the ground*
before it,
And it took deep root and filled the
land.
¹⁰The mountains were covered with
its shadow,
And its branches were like the
cedars of God.
¹¹Israel sent out its branches to the
[Mediterranean] Sea,
And its branches to the
[Euphrates] River. [1 Kin 4:21]
¹²Why have You broken down its
walls *and* hedges,
So that all who pass by pick its
fruit?
¹³A boar from the woods eats it away,
And the insects of the field feed
on it.
¹⁴Turn again [in favor to us], O God
of hosts;
Look down from heaven and see,
and take care of this vine,
¹⁵Even the stock which Your right
hand has planted,

And [look down on] the son
that You have reared *and*
strengthened for Yourself.
[16]It is burned with fire, it is cut
down;
They perish at the rebuke of Your
[angry] appearance.
[17]Let Your hand be upon the man of
Your right hand,
Upon the son of man whom You
have made strong for Yourself.
[18]Then we shall not turn back from
You;
Revive us and we will call on Your
name.
[19]Restore us, O LORD God of hosts;
Cause Your face to shine on us
[in favor and approval], and we
shall be saved.

PSALM 81

God's Goodness and Israel's
Waywardness.

To the Chief Musician; set
to the Philistine lute. *A Psalm*
of Asaph.

[1]SING ALOUD to God our strength;
Shout for joy to the God of Jacob
(Israel).
[2]Raise a song, sound the timbrel,
The sweet sounding lyre with the
harp.
[3]Blow the trumpet at the New
Moon,
At the full moon, on our feast day.
[4]For this is a statute for Israel,
An ordinance of the God of Jacob.
[5]He established it for a testimony in
Joseph
When He went throughout the
land of Egypt.
I heard the language [of One
whom] I did not know, *saying,*

[6]"I removed the burden from his
shoulder;
His hands were freed from the
basket.

[7]"You called in [the time of] trouble
and I rescued you;
I answered you in the secret place
of thunder;
I tested you at the waters of
Meribah. [Num 20:3, 13, 24]
Selah.
[8]"Hear, O My people, and I will
admonish you—
O Israel, if you would listen to Me!
[9]"Let there be no strange god
among you,
Nor shall you worship any foreign
god.
[10]"I am the LORD your God,
Who brought you up from the land
of Egypt.
Open your mouth wide and I will
fill it.

[11]"But My people would not listen to
My voice,
And Israel did not [consent to]
obey Me.
[12]"So I gave them up to the
stubbornness of their heart,
To walk in [the path of] their own
counsel. [Acts 7:42, 43; 14:16;
Rom 1:24, 26]
[13]"Oh, that My people would listen to
Me,
That Israel would walk in My
ways!
[14]"Then I would quickly subdue *and*
humble their enemies
And turn My hand against their
adversaries;
[15]Those who hate the LORD would
pretend obedience to Him *and*
cringe before Him,
And their time *of punishment*
would be forever.
[16]"But I would feed Israel with the
finest of the wheat;
And with honey from the rock I
would satisfy you."

PSALM 82

Unjust Judgments Rebuked.

A Psalm of Asaph.

[1]GOD STANDS in the divine
assembly;
He judges among the gods (divine
beings).
[2]How long will you judge unjustly
And show partiality to the wicked?
Selah.
[3]Vindicate the weak and fatherless;
Do justice *and* maintain the rights
of the afflicted and destitute.
[4]Rescue the weak and needy;
Rescue them from the hand of the
wicked.

[5]The rulers do not know nor do
they understand;
They walk on in the darkness [of
complacent satisfaction];
All the foundations of the earth
[the fundamental principles of
the administration of justice] are
shaken.
[6]I said, "You are gods;
Indeed, all of you are sons of the
Most High. [Gen 6:1–4; John
10:34–36; Rom 13:1, 2]
[7]"Nevertheless you will die like
men
And fall like any one of the
princes."
[8]Arise, O God, judge the earth!
For to You belong all the nations.
[Matt 28:18–20; Rev 11:15]

PSALM 83

God Implored to Confound His Enemies.

A Song. A Psalm of Asaph.

[1]DO NOT keep silent, O God;
Do not hold Your peace or be still,
O God.
[2]For behold, Your enemies are in
tumult,

And those who hate You have
raised their heads [in hatred of
You]. [Acts 4:25, 26]
[3]They concoct crafty schemes
against Your people,
And conspire together against
Your hidden *and* precious ones.
[4]They have said, "Come, and let us
wipe them out as a nation;
Let the name of Israel be
remembered no more."
[5]For they have conspired together
with one mind;
Against You they make a
covenant—
[6]The tents of Edom and the
Ishmaelites,
Of Moab and the Hagrites,
[7]Gebal and Ammon and Amalek,
Philistia with the inhabitants of
Tyre.
[8]Assyria also has joined with them;
They have helped the children
of Lot [the Ammonites and the
Moabites] *and* have been an arm
[of strength] to them. *Selah.*

[9]Deal with them as [You did] with
Midian,
As with Sisera and Jabin at the
brook of Kishon, [Judg 4:12–24]
[10]Who were destroyed at En-dor,
Who became like dung for the
earth.
[11]Make their nobles like Oreb and
Zeeb
And all their princes like Zebah
and Zalmunna, [Judg 7:23–25;
8:10–21]
[12]Who said, "Let us possess for
ourselves
The pastures of God."

[13]O my God, make them like
whirling dust,
Like chaff before the wind
[worthless and without
substance].
[14]Like fire consumes the forest,

And like the flame sets the
  mountains on fire,
15 So pursue them with Your tempest
  And terrify them with [the
  violence of] Your storm.
16 Fill their faces with shame *and*
  disgrace,
  That they may [persistently] seek
  Your name, O Lord.
17 Let them be ashamed and
  dismayed forever;
  Yes, let them be humiliated and
  perish,
18 That they may know that You
  alone, whose name is the Lord,
  Are the Most High over all the
  earth.

PSALM 84

Longing for the Temple Worship.

To the Chief Musician;
set to a Philistine lute.
A Psalm of the sons of Korah.

1 HOW LOVELY are Your dwelling
  places,
  O Lord of hosts!
2 My soul (my life, my inner self)
  longs for and greatly desires the
  courts of the Lord;
  My heart and my flesh sing for joy
  to the living God.
3 The bird has found a house,
  And the swallow a nest for herself,
  where she may lay her young—

life point

When our strength is in God, the difficult places in life can be turned into blessings; the valleys of weeping can be turned into springs (see Psalm 84:5, 6). Whenever you face a tough situation or a place of sadness and despair, draw your strength from God. As you do, you will find yourself going "from strength to strength" and "increasing in victorious power," as Psalm 84:7 promises.

putting the Word to work

The Bible teaches us that God is our home. We view our homes as places of rest and comfort, shelters from all the other parts of life. Psalm 84:10 reminds us that dwelling in the presence of God is where the greatest blessing is to be found. Spend time every day with God through prayer, worship, and time in His Word, and you will find there is no place you would rather be than in His presence. When you are with Him, you will feel as though you are at home!

Even Your altars, O Lord of hosts,
  My King and my God.
4 Blessed *and* greatly favored are
  those who dwell in Your house
  and Your presence;
  They will be singing Your praises
  all the day long.   *Selah.*

5 Blessed *and* greatly favored is the
  man whose strength is in You,
  In whose heart are the highways
  to Zion.
6 Passing through the Valley of
  Weeping (Baca), they make it a
  place of springs;
  The early rain also covers it with
  blessings.
7 They go from strength to strength
  [increasing in victorious power];
  Each of them appears before God in
  Zion.

8 O Lord God of hosts, hear my
  prayer;
  Listen, O God of Jacob!   *Selah.*
9 See our shield, O God,
  And look at the face of Your
  anointed [the king as Your
  representative].
10 For a day in Your courts is better
  than a thousand [anywhere
  else];

I would rather stand [as a
  doorkeeper] at the threshold of
  the house of my God
Than to live [at ease] in the tents
  of wickedness.
¹¹For the LORD God is a sun and
  shield;
The LORD bestows grace *and* favor
  and honor;
No good thing will He withhold
  from those who walk uprightly.
¹²O LORD of hosts,
How blessed *and* greatly favored
  is the man who trusts in You
  [believing in You, relying on
  You, and committing himself
  to You with confident hope and
  expectation].

PSALM 85

Prayer for God's Mercy
upon the Nation.

To the Chief Musician. A Psalm
  of the sons of Korah.

¹O LORD, You have [at last] shown
  favor to Your land [of Canaan];
You have restored [from Babylon]
  the captives of Jacob (Israel).
²You have forgiven the wickedness
  of Your people;
You have covered all their sin.
                              Selah.
³You have withdrawn all Your
  wrath,
You have turned away from Your
  burning anger.
⁴Restore us, O God of our salvation,
And cause Your indignation
  toward us to cease.
⁵Will You be angry with us forever?
Will You prolong Your anger to all
  generations?

⁶Will You not revive us *and* bring us
  to life again,
That Your people may rejoice in
  You?
⁷Show us Your lovingkindness,
  O LORD,
And grant us Your salvation.
⁸I will hear [with expectant hope]
  what God the LORD will say,
For He will speak peace to His
  people, to His godly ones—
But let them not turn again to folly.
⁹Surely His salvation is near to
  those who [reverently] fear Him
  [and obey Him with submissive
  wonder],
That glory [the manifest presence
  of God] may dwell in our land.
¹⁰Steadfast love and truth *and*
  faithfulness meet together;
Righteousness and peace kiss each
  other.
¹¹Truth springs from the earth,
And righteousness looks down
  from heaven.
¹²Indeed, the LORD will give what is
  good,
And our land will yield its produce.
¹³Righteousness will go before Him
And will make His footsteps into a
  way [in which to walk].

PSALM 86

A Psalm of Supplication and
Trust.

A Prayer of David.

¹INCLINE YOUR ear, O LORD, and
  answer me,
For I am distressed and needy [I
  long for Your help].

speak the Word

*God, I know that You will give what is good. Righteousness goes before You and
will make Your footsteps into a way in which I can walk.*
–ADAPTED FROM PSALM 85:12, 13

²Protect my life (soul), for I am
godly *and* faithful;
O You my God, save Your
servant, who trusts in You
[believing in You and relying
on You, confidently committing
everything to You].
³Be gracious *and* merciful to me,
O Lord,
For to You I cry out all the day long.
⁴Make Your servant rejoice,
For to You, O Lord, I lift up my soul
[all that I am—in prayer].
⁵For You, O Lord, are good, and
ready to forgive [our sins,
sending them away, completely
letting them go forever and ever];
And abundant in lovingkindness
and overflowing in mercy to all
those who call upon You.
⁶Hear, O Lᴏʀᴅ, my prayer;
And listen attentively to the voice
of my supplications (specific
requests)!
⁷In the day of my trouble I will call
upon You,
For You will answer me.
⁸There is no one like You among
the gods, O Lord,
Nor are there any works [of
wonder and majesty] like Yours.
⁹All nations whom You have made
shall come and kneel down in
worship before You, O Lord,
And they shall glorify Your name.
¹⁰For You are great and do wondrous
works!
You alone are God.
¹¹Teach me Your way, O Lᴏʀᴅ,
I will walk *and* live in Your truth;
Direct my heart to fear Your name
[with awe-inspired reverence
and submissive wonder]. [Ps
5:11; 69:36]

putting the Word to work

Have you ever bent over to let a child whisper something in your ear? God does this for us—He inclines His ear to hear our every cry (see Psalm 86:1–7). If you have ever felt that no one is listening to you, take heart; God hears every one of your prayers, and He will be faithful to answer.

¹²I will give thanks *and* praise You,
O Lord my God, with all my heart;
And will glorify Your name
forevermore.
¹³For great is Your lovingkindness
and graciousness toward me;
And You have rescued my life from
the depths of Sheol [from death].
¹⁴O God, arrogant *and* insolent men
have risen up against me;
A band of violent men have sought
my life,
And they have not set You before
them.
¹⁵But You, O Lord, are a God [who
protects and is] merciful and
gracious,
Slow to anger and abounding in
lovingkindness and truth.
¹⁶Turn to me, and be gracious to me;
Grant Your strength [Your
might and the power to resist
temptation] to Your servant,
And save the son of Your
handmaid.
¹⁷Show me a sign of [Your] goodwill,
That those who hate me may see it
and be ashamed,
Because You, O Lᴏʀᴅ, helped and
comforted me.

speak the Word

Teach me Your way, Lord, that I may walk and live in Your truth. Direct my heart to fear Your name with awe-inspired reverence and submissive wonder.
—ᴀᴅᴀᴘᴛᴇᴅ ꜰʀᴏᴍ Pꜱᴀʟᴍ 86:11

PSALM 87

The Privileges of Citizenship in Zion.

A Psalm of the sons of Korah. A Song.

¹ HIS FOUNDATION is on the holy mountain.
² The LORD loves the gates of Zion
More than all the dwellings of Jacob (Israel).
³ Glorious things are spoken of you,
O city of God [Jerusalem].   *Selah.*
⁴ "I will mention Rahab (Egypt) and Babylon among those who know Me—
Behold, Philistia and Tyre with Ethiopia (Cush)—
'This one was born there.'"
⁵ But of Zion it will be said, "This one and that one were born in her,"
And the Most High Himself will establish her.
⁶ The LORD will count, when He registers the peoples,
"This one was born there."   *Selah.*
⁷ The singers as well as the players of flutes *will say,*
"All my springs *and* sources of joy are in you [Jerusalem, city of God]."

PSALM 88

A Petition to Be Saved from Death.

A Song. A Psalm of the sons of Korah. To the Chief Musician; set to chant mournfully. A didactic or reflective poem of Heman the Ezrahite.

¹ O LORD, the God of my salvation,
I have cried out [for help] by day and in the night before You.
[Luke 18:7]
² Let my prayer come before You *and* enter into Your presence;
Incline Your ear to my cry!

³ For my soul is full of troubles,
And my life draws near the grave (Sheol, the place of the dead).
⁴ I am counted among those who go down to the pit (grave);
I am like a man who has no strength [a mere shadow],
⁵ Cast away [from the living] *and* abandoned among the dead,
Like the slain who lie in a [nameless] grave,
Whom You no longer remember,
And they are cut off from Your hand.
⁶ You have laid me in the lowest pit,
In dark places, in the depths.
⁷ Your wrath has rested heavily upon me,
And You have afflicted me with all Your waves. [Ps 42:7]   *Selah.*
⁸ You have put my friends far from me;
You have made me an object of loathing to them.
I am shut up and I cannot go out.
⁹ My eye grows dim with sorrow.
O LORD, I have called on You every day;
I have spread out my hands to You [in prayer].
¹⁰ Will You perform wonders for the dead?
Shall the departed spirits arise and praise You?   *Selah.*
¹¹ Will Your lovingkindness be declared in the grave
Or Your faithfulness in Abaddon (the underworld)?
¹² Will Your wonders be known in the darkness?
And Your righteousness in the land of forgetfulness [where the dead forget and are forgotten]?

¹³ But I have cried out to You, O LORD, for help;
And in the morning my prayer will come to You.
¹⁴ O LORD, why do You reject me?

Why do You hide Your face from me? [Matt 27:46]

15 I was afflicted and close to death from my youth on;
I suffer Your terrors; I am overcome.

16 Your fierce wrath has swept over me;
Your terrors have destroyed me.

17 They have surrounded me like flood waters all day long;
They have completely encompassed me.

18 Lover and friend You have placed far from me;
My familiar friends are in darkness.

PSALM 89

The Lord's Covenant with David, and Israel's Afflictions.

A skillful song, *or* a didactic *or* reflective poem, of Ethan the Ezrahite.

1 I WILL sing of the goodness *and* lovingkindness of the Lord forever;
With my mouth I will make known Your faithfulness from generation to generation.

2 For I have said, "Goodness *and* lovingkindness will be built up forever;
In the heavens [unchangeable and majestic] You will establish Your faithfulness."

3 [God has said] "I have made a covenant with My chosen one;
I have sworn to David My servant,

4 I will establish your seed forever

And I will build up your throne for all generations." [Is 9:7; Jer 33:14–26; Luke 1:32, 33; Gal 3:16] *Selah*.

5 The heavens (angels) praise Your wonders, O Lord,
Your faithfulness also in the assembly of the holy ones.

6 For who in the heavens can be compared to the Lord?
Who among the divine beings is like the Lord,

7 A God greatly feared *and* reverently worshiped in the council of the holy [angelic] ones,
And awesome above all those who are around Him?

8 O Lord God of hosts, who is like You, O mighty Lord?
Your faithfulness surrounds You [as an intrinsic, unchangeable part of Your very being].

9 You rule the swelling of the sea;
When its waves rise, You still them. [Ps 65:7; 107:29; Mark 4:39]

10 You have crushed Rahab (Egypt) like one who is slain;
You have scattered Your enemies with Your mighty arm.

11 The heavens are Yours, the earth also is Yours;
The world and all that is in it, You have founded *and* established them. [Gen 1:3]

12 The north and the south, You have created them;
Mount Tabor and Mount Hermon shout for joy at Your name.

13 You have a strong arm;
Mighty is Your hand, Your right hand is exalted.

speak the Word

Lord, I will sing of Your goodness and loving-kindness forever. I will tell others of Your faithfulness from generation to generation.
—ADAPTED FROM PSALM 89:1

¹⁴Righteousness and justice are the foundation of Your throne;
Lovingkindness and truth go before You.
¹⁵Blessed *and* happy are the people who know the joyful sound [of the trumpet's blast]!
They walk, O Lord, in the light *and* favor of Your countenance!
¹⁶In Your name they rejoice all the day,
And in Your righteousness they are exalted.
¹⁷For You are the glory of their strength [their proud adornment],
And by Your favor our horn is exalted.
¹⁸For our shield belongs to the Lord,
And our king to the Holy One of Israel.

¹⁹Once You spoke in a vision to Your godly ones,
And said, "I have given help to one who is mighty [giving him the power to be a champion for Israel];
I have exalted one chosen from the people.
²⁰"I have found David My servant;
With My holy oil I have anointed him, [Acts 13:22]
²¹With whom My hand shall be established *and* steadfast;
My arm also shall strengthen him.
²²"The enemy will not outwit him,
Nor will the wicked man afflict *or* humiliate him.
²³"I will crush his adversaries before him,
And strike those who hate him.
²⁴"My faithfulness and My steadfast lovingkindness shall be with him,
And in My name shall his horn be exalted [great power and prosperity shall be conferred upon him].
²⁵"I will also set his hand on the [Mediterranean] sea,

And his right hand on the rivers [the tributaries of the Euphrates].
²⁶"He will cry to Me, 'You are my Father,
My God, and the rock of my salvation.'
²⁷"I will also make him My firstborn (preeminent),
The highest of the kings of the earth. [Rev 1:5]
²⁸"My lovingkindness I will keep for him forevermore,
And My covenant will be confirmed to him.
²⁹"His descendants I will establish forever,
And his throne [will endure] as the days of heaven. [Is 9:7; Jer 33:14–26; Gal 3:16]

³⁰"If his children turn away from My law
And do not walk in My ordinances,
³¹If they break My statutes
And do not keep My commandments,
³²Then I will punish their transgression with the rod [of discipline],
And [correct] their wickedness with stripes. [2 Sam 7:14]
³³"Nevertheless, I will not break off My lovingkindness from him,
Nor allow My faithfulness to fail.
³⁴"My covenant I will not violate,
Nor will I alter the utterance of My lips.
³⁵"Once [for all] I have sworn by My holiness, [My vow which cannot be violated];
I will not lie to David.
³⁶"His descendants shall endure forever
And his throne [will continue] as the sun before Me. [Is 9:7; Jer 33:14–26; Gal 3:16]
³⁷"It shall be established forever like the moon,

And the witness in the heavens
   is ever faithful." [Rev 1:5; 3:14]
                                    Selah.

38 But [in apparent contradiction of
   all this] You [the faithful Lᴏʀᴅ]
   have cast off and rejected;
You have been full of wrath
   against Your anointed.
39 You have spurned *and* repudiated
   the covenant with Your servant;
You have profaned his crown [by
   casting it] in the dust.
40 You have broken down all his [city]
   walls;
You have brought his strongholds
   to ruin.
41 All who pass along the road rob
   him;
He has become the scorn of his
   neighbors.
42 You have exalted the right hand of
   his foes;
You have made all his enemies
   rejoice.
43 Also, You have turned back the
   edge of his sword
And have not made him [strong
   enough] to stand in battle.
44 You have put an end to his
   splendor
And have hurled his throne to the
   ground.
45 You have shortened the days of his
   youth;
You have covered him with shame.
                                    Selah.

46 How long, O Lᴏʀᴅ?
Will You hide Yourself forever?
Will Your wrath burn like fire?
47 Remember how fleeting my
   lifetime is;
For what vanity, [for what
   emptiness, for what futility, for
   what wisp of smoke] You have
   created all the sons of men!
48 What man can live and not see
   death?

Can he rescue his soul from the
   [powerful] hand of Sheol (the
   nether world, the place of the
   dead)?   *Selah.*

49 O Lord, where are Your former
   lovingkindnesses [so abundant
   in the days of David and
   Solomon],
Which You swore to David in Your
   faithfulness?
50 Remember, O Lord, the reproach
   of Your servants [scorned,
   insulted, and disgraced];
How I bear in my heart the
   reproach of all the many peoples,
51 With which Your enemies have
   taunted, O Lᴏʀᴅ,
With which they have mocked the
   footsteps of Your anointed.
52 Blessed be the Lᴏʀᴅ forevermore!
Amen and Amen.

BOOK FOUR

PSALM 90

God's Eternity and Man's Transitoriness.

A Prayer of Moses the man of God.

1 LORD, YOU have been our
   dwelling place [our refuge, our
   sanctuary, our stability] in all
   generations.
2 Before the mountains were born
Or before You had given birth to
   the earth and the world,
Even from everlasting to
   everlasting, You are [the
   eternal] God.

3 You turn man back to dust,
And say, "Return [to the earth], O
   children of [mortal] men!"
4 For a thousand years in Your sight
Are like yesterday when it is past,
Or as a watch in the night. [2 Pet 3:8]

⁵You have swept them away like a flood, they fall asleep [forgotten as soon as they are gone];
In the morning they are like grass which grows anew—
⁶In the morning it flourishes and springs up;
In the evening it wilts and withers away.
⁷For we have been consumed by Your anger
And by Your wrath we have been terrified.
⁸You have placed our wickedness before you,
Our secret *sins* [which we tried to conceal, You have placed] in the [revealing] light of Your presence.
⁹For all our days pass away in Your wrath;
We have finished our years like a whispered sigh. [Num 14:26–35]
¹⁰The days of our life are seventy years—
Or even, if because of strength, eighty years;
Yet their pride [in additional years] is only labor and sorrow,
For it is soon gone and we fly away.
¹¹Who understands the power of Your anger? [Who connects this brevity of life among us with Your judgment of sin?]
And Your wrath, [who connects it] with the [reverent] fear that is due You?
¹²So teach us to number our days,
That we may cultivate *and* bring to You a heart of wisdom.

¹³Turn, O Lᴏʀᴅ [from Your fierce anger]; how long will it be?
Be compassionate toward Your servants—revoke Your sentence.
¹⁴O satisfy us with Your lovingkindness in the morning [now, before we grow older],
That we may rejoice and be glad all our days.
¹⁵Make us glad in proportion to the days You have afflicted us,
And the years we have suffered evil.
¹⁶Let Your work [the signs of Your power] be revealed to Your servants
And Your [glorious] majesty to their children.
¹⁷And let the [gracious] favor of the Lord our God be on us;
Confirm for us the work of our hands—
Yes, confirm the work of our hands.

life point

When you and I feel a tide of emotions beginning to swell within us, we need to return to the secret place of the Most High (see Psalm 91:1), crying out to Him: "Father, help me resist this surge of emotions that threatens to overwhelm me!" If we will do that, the Lord has promised to intervene on our behalf. We need to learn to take refuge under His shadow, where we will be safe and secure, knowing that no power in heaven or on earth can withstand Him.

speak the Word

Lord, teach me to number my days, that I may cultivate and bring to You a heart of wisdom.
—ᴀᴅᴀᴘᴛᴇᴅ ғʀᴏᴍ Psᴀʟᴍ 90:12

God, let Your gracious favor be upon me. Confirm for me the work of my hands.
—ᴀᴅᴀᴘᴛᴇᴅ ғʀᴏᴍ Psᴀʟᴍ 90:17

PSALM 91

Security of the One Who Trusts in the LORD.

¹ HE WHO dwells in the shelter of the Most High
Will remain secure *and* rest in the shadow of the Almighty [whose power no enemy can withstand].
² I will say of the LORD, "He is my refuge and my fortress,
My God, in whom I trust [with great confidence, and on whom I rely]!"
³ For He will save you from the trap of the fowler,
And from the deadly pestilence.
⁴ He will cover you *and* completely protect you with His pinions,
And under His wings you will find refuge;
His faithfulness is a shield and a wall.

⁵ You will not be afraid of the terror of night,
Nor of the arrow that flies by day,
⁶ Nor of the pestilence that stalks in darkness,
Nor of the destruction (sudden death) that lays waste at noon.
⁷ A thousand may fall at your side
And ten thousand at your right hand,
But danger will not come near you.
⁸ You will only [be a spectator as you] look on with your eyes
And witness the [divine] repayment of the wicked [as you watch safely from the shelter of the Most High].
⁹ Because you have made the LORD, [who is] my refuge,
Even the Most High, your dwelling place, [Ps 91:1, 14]
¹⁰ No evil will befall you,
Nor will any plague come near your tent.

what do you say?

David frequently spoke about the goodness and character of God. In Psalm 91:2, David says God is his refuge, his fortress—a God he can really trust. It is interesting to note that David also wrote in this verse, "I will *say* of the LORD . . ." (italics mine). Perhaps we should also regularly ask ourselves, "What am I saying of the Lord?"

We need to *say* right things, not just *think* them. We may think, *I believe all those good things about the Lord*, but are we also *saying* anything that is helping us? Often we claim to believe something, yet the opposite comes out of our mouths.

We need to speak aloud the goodness of God. We need to do it at proper times and in proper places, but we need to be sure we do it. I cannot encourage you strongly enough to make verbal confessions part of your fellowship time with God.

I often take walks in the morning. While I walk, I pray, I sing, and I confess the Word out loud. I say something like, "God is on my side. I can do whatever He assigns me to do." Or "God is good, and He has a good plan for my life. Blessings are chasing me and overflowing in my life." When I speak words like these, I am nullifying the evil plan Satan has for me.

Verbalize your thanksgiving, your praise, and your worship. Say aloud the things that are in your heart about God; sing songs that are filled with praise and worship. Take aggressive action against the enemy by speaking of the goodness of God!

11 For He will command His angels
  in regard to you,
To protect *and* defend *and*
  guard you in all your ways [of
  obedience and service].
12 They will lift you up in their
  hands,
So that you do not [even] strike
  your foot against a stone. [Luke
  4:10, 11; Heb 1:14]
13 You will tread upon the lion and
  cobra;
The young lion and the serpent
  you will trample underfoot.
  [Luke 10:19]

14 "Because he set his love on Me,
  therefore I will save him;
I will set him [securely] on high,
  because he knows My name [he
  confidently trusts and relies
  on Me, knowing I will never
  abandon him, no, never].
15 "He will call upon Me, and I will
  answer him;
I will be with him in trouble;
I will rescue him and honor him.
16 "With a long life I will satisfy him
And I will let him see My
  salvation."

PSALM 92

Praise for the LORD's Goodness.

A Psalm. A Song for the Sabbath
  day.

1 IT IS a good *and* delightful thing to
  give thanks to the LORD,
To sing praises to Your name,
  O Most High,
2 To declare Your lovingkindness in
  the morning
And Your faithfulness by night,
3 With an instrument of ten strings
  and with the harp,
With a solemn sound on the lyre.
4 For You, O LORD, have made me
  glad by Your works;

At the works of Your hands I
  joyfully sing.

5 How great are Your works, O LORD!
Your thoughts are very deep
  [beyond man's understanding].
6 A senseless man [in his crude
  and uncultivated state] knows
  nothing,
Nor does a [self-righteous] fool
  understand this:
7 That though the wicked sprout up
  like grass
And all evildoers flourish,
They will be destroyed forever.
8 But You, LORD, are on high forever.
9 For behold, Your enemies, O LORD,
For behold, Your enemies will
  perish;
All who do evil will be scattered.

10 But my horn [my emblem of
  strength and power] You have
  exalted like that of a wild ox;
I am anointed with fresh oil [for
  Your service].
11 My eye has looked on my foes;
My ears hear of the evildoers who
  rise up against me.
12 The righteous will flourish like the
  date palm [long-lived, upright
  and useful];
They will grow like a cedar in
  Lebanon [majestic and stable].
13 Planted in the house of the LORD,
They will flourish in the courts of
  our God.
14 [Growing in grace] they will still
  thrive *and* bear fruit *and* prosper
  in old age;
They will flourish *and* be vital and
  fresh [rich in trust and love and
  contentment];
15 [They are living memorials] to
  declare that the LORD is upright
  and faithful [to His promises];
He is my rock, and there is no
  unrighteousness in Him.
  [Rom 9:14]

PSALM 93

The Majesty of the Lord.

¹THE LORD reigns, He is clothed
  with majesty *and* splendor;
The LORD has clothed and
  encircled Himself with strength;
the world is firmly established, it
  cannot be moved.
²Your throne is established from of
  old;
You are from everlasting.

³The floods have lifted up, O LORD,
The floods have lifted up their voice;
The floods lift up their pounding
  waves.
⁴More than the sounds of many
  waters,
More than the mighty breakers of
  the sea,
The LORD on high is mighty.
⁵Your precepts are fully confirmed
  and completely reliable;
Holiness adorns Your house,
O LORD, forever.

PSALM 94

The Lord Implored to Avenge His People.

¹O LORD God, You to whom
  vengeance belongs,
O God, You to whom vengeance
  belongs, shine forth [in
  judgment]!
²Rise up, O Judge of the earth;
Give to the proud a fitting
  compensation.
³O LORD, how long will the wicked,
How long will the wicked rejoice in
  triumph?
⁴They pour out *words,* speaking
  arrogant things;
All who do evil boast proudly.
  [Jude 14, 15]
⁵They crush Your people, O LORD,
And afflict *and* abuse Your heritage.

⁶They kill the widow and the alien
And murder the fatherless.
⁷Yet they say, "The LORD does not
  see,
Nor does the God of Jacob (Israel)
  notice it."
⁸Consider thoughtfully, you
  senseless (stupid ones) among
  the people;
And you [dull-minded] fools,
  when will you become wise *and*
  understand?
⁹He who made the ear, does He not
  hear?
He who formed the eye, does He
  not see?
¹⁰He who instructs the nations,
Does He not rebuke *and* punish,
He who teaches man knowledge?
¹¹The LORD knows the thoughts of
  man,
That they are a mere breath (vain,
  empty, futile). [1 Cor 3:20]

life point

In Psalm 94:12–15, God is saying that
He deals with us and disciplines us for a
reason. He wants us to come to the point
where we can keep ourselves calm in the
day of adversity.

In verses 14 and 15, notice the emphasis
on God's faithfulness and justice toward
His children. We can be sure that if we are
being obedient to His Word and His will,
and we are being led by His Holy Spirit, we
have nothing to fear from our enemies,
because the Lord Himself will fight our battles for us (see 2 Chronicles 20:15). Do you
want God's help? If the answer is yes, then
ask for His help and receive it by faith. God
cannot help someone who does not want
to be helped. Decide that you sincerely
want God's help, and He will run to your
aid and move mightily on your behalf.

¹²Blessed [with wisdom and
   prosperity] is the man whom You
   discipline *and* instruct, O LORD,
 And whom You teach from Your
   law,
¹³That You may grant him [power to
   calm himself and find] peace in
   the days of adversity,
 Until the pit is dug for the wicked
   and ungodly.
¹⁴For the LORD will not abandon His
   people,
 Nor will He abandon His
   inheritance.
¹⁵For judgment will again be
   righteous,
 And all the upright in heart will
   follow it.
¹⁶Who will stand up for me against
   the evildoers?
 Who will take a stand for
   me against those who do
   wickedness?

¹⁷If the LORD had not been my help,
 I would soon have dwelt in [the
   land of] silence.
¹⁸If I say, "My foot has slipped,"
 Your compassion *and*
   lovingkindness, O LORD, will hold
   me up.
¹⁹When my anxious thoughts
   multiply within me,
 Your comforts delight me.
²⁰Can a throne of destruction be
   allied with You,
 One which frames *and* devises
   mischief by decree [under the
   sacred name of law]?
²¹They band themselves together
   against the life of the righteous
 And condemn the innocent to death.
²²But the LORD has become my high
   tower *and* defense,
 And my God the rock of my refuge.

²³He has turned back their own
   wickedness upon them
 And will destroy them by means of
   their own evil;
 The LORD our God will wipe them
   out.

PSALM 95

Praise to the LORD, and Warning
   against Unbelief.

¹O COME, let us sing joyfully to the
   LORD;
 Let us shout joyfully to the rock of
   our salvation.
²Let us come before His presence
   with a song of thanksgiving;
 Let us shout joyfully to Him with
   songs.
³For the LORD is a great God
 And a great King above all gods,
⁴In whose hand are the depths of
   the earth;
 The peaks of the mountains are
   His also.
⁵The sea is His, for He made it [by
   His command];
 And His hands formed the dry
   land. [Gen 1:9]

⁶O come, let us worship and bow
   down,
 Let us kneel before the LORD our
   Maker [in reverent praise and
   prayer].
⁷For He is our God
 And we are the people of His
   pasture and the sheep of His
   hand.
 Today, if you will hear His voice,
   [Heb 3:7–11]
⁸Do not harden your hearts *and*
   become spiritually dull as at
   Meribah [the place of strife],

speak the Word

God, when my anxious thoughts multiply within me, Your comforts delight me.
–ADAPTED FROM PSALM 94:19

And as at Massah [the place of testing] in the wilderness, [Ex 17:1–7; Num 20:1–13; Deut 6:16]
9 "When your fathers tested Me, They tried Me, even though they had seen My work [of miracles].
10 "For forty years I was grieved *and* disgusted with that generation, And I said, 'They are a people who err in their heart, And they do not acknowledge *or* regard My ways.'
11 "Therefore I swore [an oath] in My wrath, 'They absolutely shall not enter My rest [the land of promise].'" [Heb 4:3–11]

PSALM 96

A Call to Worship the Lord the Righteous Judge.

1 O SING to the Lord a new song; Sing to the Lord, all the earth!
2 Sing to the Lord, bless His name; Proclaim good news of His salvation from day to day.
3 Declare His glory among the nations, His marvelous works *and* wonderful deeds among all the peoples.
4 For great is the Lord and greatly to be praised; He is to be feared above all gods. [Deut 6:5; Rev 14:7]
5 For all the gods of the peoples are [worthless, lifeless] idols, But the Lord made the heavens.
6 Splendor and majesty are before Him; Strength and beauty are in His sanctuary.
7 Ascribe to the Lord, O families of the peoples, Ascribe to the Lord glory and strength.

8 Ascribe to the Lord the glory of His name; Bring an offering and come into His courts.
9 Worship the Lord in the splendor of holiness; Tremble [in submissive wonder] before Him, all the earth.
10 Say among the nations, "The Lord reigns; Indeed, the world is firmly *and* securely established, it shall not be moved; He will judge *and* rule the people with fairness." [Rev 11:15; 19:6]
11 Let the heavens be glad, and let the earth rejoice; Let the sea roar, and all the things it contains;
12 Let the field be exultant, and all that is in it. Then all the trees of the forest will sing for joy
13 Before the Lord, for He is coming, For He is coming to judge the earth. He will judge the world with righteousness And the peoples in His faithfulness. [1 Chr 16:23–33; Rev 19:11]

PSALM 97

The Lord's Power and Dominion.

1 THE LORD reigns, let the earth rejoice; Let the many islands *and* coastlands be glad.
2 Clouds and thick darkness surround Him [as at Sinai]; Righteousness and justice are the foundation of His throne. [Ex 19:9]
3 Fire goes before Him And burns up His adversaries on all sides.
4 His lightnings have illuminated the world; The earth has seen and trembled.

⁵The mountains melted like wax at
the presence of the Lord,
At the presence of the Lord of the
whole earth.
⁶The heavens declare His
righteousness,
And all the peoples see His glory
and brilliance.
⁷Let all those be [deeply] ashamed
who serve carved images,
Who boast in idols.
Worship Him, all you gods!
[Heb 1:6]
⁸Zion heard this and was glad,
And the daughters (cities) of Judah
rejoiced [in relief]
Because of Your judgments,
O Lord.
⁹For You are the Lord Most High
over all the earth;
You are exalted far above all gods.

¹⁰You who love the Lord, hate evil;
He protects the souls of His godly
ones (believers),
He rescues them from the hand of
the wicked. [Rom 8:13–17]
¹¹Light is sown [like seed] for the
righteous *and* illuminates their
path,
And [irrepressible] joy [is
spread] for the upright in heart
[who delight in His favor and
protection].
¹²Rejoice in the Lord, you righteous
ones [those whose moral and
spiritual integrity places them in
right standing with God],
And praise *and* give thanks at the
remembrance of His holy name.

PSALM 98

A Call to Praise the Lord for His Righteousness.

A Psalm.

¹O SING to the Lord a new song,
For He has done marvelous *and*
wonderful things;
His right hand and His holy arm
have gained the victory for Him.
²The Lord has made known His
salvation;
He has [openly] revealed His
righteousness in the sight of the
nations. [Luke 2:30, 31]
³He has [graciously] remembered
His lovingkindness and His
faithfulness to the house of
Israel;
All the ends of the earth have
witnessed the salvation of our
God. [Acts 13:47; 28:28]

⁴Shout joyfully to the Lord, all the
earth;
Shout [in jubilation] and sing for
joy and sing praises.
⁵Sing praises to the Lord with the
lyre,
With the lyre and the sound of
melody.
⁶With trumpets and the sound of the
horn
Shout with joy before the King, the
Lord.

⁷Let the sea thunder *and* roar, and
all the things it contains,
The world and those who dwell
in it.
⁸Let the rivers clap their hands;

speak the Word

*Thank You, God, that light is sown like seed for the righteous and it illuminates
their path. Thank you for giving irrepressible joy to those who are upright in
heart, for those who delight in Your favor and protection.*
–ADAPTED FROM PSALM 97:11

Let the mountains sing together
  for joy *and* delight
⁹Before the Lᴏʀᴅ, for He is coming
  to judge the earth;
He will judge the world with
  righteousness
And the peoples with fairness.

PSALM 99

Praise to the Lᴏʀᴅ for His Fidelity to Israel.

¹THE LORD reigns, let the peoples
  tremble [with submissive
  wonder]!
He sits enthroned above the
  cherubim, let the earth shake!
²The Lᴏʀᴅ is great in Zion,
And He is exalted *and* magnified
  above all the peoples.
³Let them [reverently] praise Your
  great and awesome name;
Holy is He. [Rev 15:4]
⁴The strength of the King loves
  justice *and* righteous judgment;
You have established fairness;
You have executed justice and
  righteousness in Jacob (Israel).
⁵Exalt the Lᴏʀᴅ our God
And worship at His footstool;
Holy is He.

⁶Moses and Aaron were among His
  priests,
And Samuel was among those who
  called on His name;
They called upon the Lᴏʀᴅ and He
  answered them.
⁷He spoke to them in the pillar of
  cloud;
They kept His testimonies
And the statutes that He gave
  them. [Ps 105:9, 10]
⁸You answered them, O Lᴏʀᴅ our
  God;
You were a forgiving God to them,
And yet an avenger of their *evil*
  practices.
⁹Exalt the Lᴏʀᴅ our God

And worship at His holy hill [Zion,
  the temple mount],
For the Lᴏʀᴅ our God is holy.

PSALM 100

All Men Exhorted to Praise God.

A Psalm of Thanksgiving.

¹SHOUT JOYFULLY to the Lᴏʀᴅ, all
  the earth.
²Serve the Lᴏʀᴅ with gladness *and*
  delight;
Come before His presence with
  joyful singing.
³Know *and* fully recognize with
  gratitude that the Lᴏʀᴅ Himself is
  God;
It is He who has made us, not we
  ourselves [and we are His].
We are His people and the sheep of
  His pasture. [Eph 2:10]

⁴Enter His gates with a song of
  thanksgiving
And His courts with praise.
Be thankful to Him, bless *and*
  praise His name.
⁵For the Lᴏʀᴅ is good;
His mercy *and* lovingkindness are
  everlasting,
His faithfulness [endures] to all
  generations.

life point

When we have the mind of Christ, our thoughts will be filled with praise and thanksgiving. When we complain, we open many doors to the enemy. Complaining—either in thought or word—causes us to live weak, powerless lives and can sometimes bring on physical illness. Do you want to live a powerful life? Take the advice of Psalm 100; be thankful to God and *say* you are thankful. Realize that complaining is a death principle, but being thankful and saying so is a life principle that will bring joy to your everyday life.

PSALM 101

The Psalmist's Profession of Uprightness.

A Psalm of David.

¹I WILL sing of [steadfast] lovingkindness and justice;
To You, O LORD, I will sing praises.
²I will behave wisely *and* follow the way of integrity.
When will You come to me?
I will walk in my house in integrity *and* with a blameless heart.
³I will set no worthless *or* wicked thing before my eyes.
I hate the practice of those who fall away [from the right path];
It will not grasp hold of me.
⁴A perverse heart shall depart from me;
I will not tolerate evil.
⁵Whoever secretly slanders his neighbor, him I will silence;
The one who has a haughty look and a proud (arrogant) heart I will not tolerate.

⁶My eyes will be on the faithful (honorable) of the land, that they may dwell with me;
He who walks blamelessly is the one who will minister to *and* serve me.
⁷He who practices deceit will not dwell in my house;
He who tells lies *and* half-truths will not continue [to remain] in my presence.
⁸Morning after morning I will destroy all the wicked in the land,
That I may cut off from the city of the LORD all those who do evil.

PSALM 102

Prayer of an Afflicted Man for Mercy on Himself and on Zion.

A Prayer of the afflicted; when he is overwhelmed and pours out his complaint to God.

¹HEAR MY prayer, O LORD,
And let my cry for help come to You!
²Do not hide Your face from me in the day of my distress!
Incline Your ear to me;
In the day when I call, answer me quickly.
³For my days have vanished in smoke,
And my bones have been scorched like a hearth.
⁴My heart has been struck like grass and withered,
Indeed, [absorbed by my heartache] I forget to eat my food.
⁵Because of the sound of my groaning [in suffering and trouble]
My bones cling to my flesh.
⁶I am like a [mournful] vulture of the wilderness;
I am like a [desolate] owl of the wasteland.
⁷I am sleepless *and* lie awake [mourning],
I have become like a lonely bird on a housetop.

⁸My enemies taunt me all day long;
Those who ridicule me use my *name* as a curse.
⁹For I have eaten ashes like bread,
And have mingled my drink with tears [Is 44:20]
¹⁰Because of Your indignation and Your wrath,

speak the Word

Lord, I will behave wisely, and I will follow the way of integrity. I will walk within my house in integrity and with a blameless heart.
–ADAPTED FROM PSALM 101:2

For You have lifted me up and
  thrown me away.
11 My days are like an evening
  shadow that lengthens *and*
  vanishes [with the sun];
  And as for me, I wither away like
  grass.

12 But You, O Lord, are enthroned
  forever [ruling eternally as
  sovereign];
  And [the fame and glory of] Your
  name [endures] to all generations.
13 You will arise and have
  compassion on Zion,
  For it is time to be gracious *and*
  show favor to her;
  Yes, the appointed time [the
  moment designated] has come.
  [Ps 12:5; 119:126]
14 For Your servants find
  [melancholy] pleasure in the
  stones [of her ruins]
  And feel pity for her dust.
15 So the nations will fear the name
  of the Lord,
  And all the kings of the earth [will
  recognize] Your glory. [Ps 96:9]
16 For the Lord has built up Zion;
  He has appeared in His glory *and*
  brilliance;
17 He has regarded the prayer of the
  destitute,
  And has not despised their prayer.

18 Let this be recorded for the
  generation to come,
  That a people yet to be created will
  praise the Lord.
19 For He looked down from His holy
  height [of His sanctuary],
  From heaven the Lord gazed on
  the earth,
20 To hear the sighing of the prisoner,

To set free those who were
  doomed to death,
21 So that people may declare the
  name of the Lord in Zion
  And His praise in Jerusalem,
22 When the peoples are gathered
  together,
  And the kingdoms, to serve the Lord.

23 He has exhausted my strength
  [humbling me with sorrow] in
  the way;
  He has shortened my days.
24 I said, "O my God, do not take me
  away in the midst of my days;
  Your years are [eternal]
  throughout all generations.
25 "At the beginning You founded the
  earth;
  The heavens are the work of Your
  hands.
26 "Even they will perish, but You
  endure;
  Yes, all of them will wear out like a
  garment.
  Like clothing You will change
  them and they shall be changed.
27 "But You remain the same,
  And Your years will never end.
  [Heb 1:10–12]
28 "The children of Your servants
  will continue,
  And their descendants will be
  established before You."

PSALM 103

Praise for the Lord's Mercies.

A Psalm of David.

1 BLESS *AND* affectionately praise
  the Lord, O my soul,
  And all that is [deep] within me,
  bless His holy name.

speak the Word

God, I am Your servant. I declare that my descendants
will be established before You.
–ADAPTED FROM PSALM 102:28

2 Bless *and* affectionately praise the
  LORD, O my soul,
And do not forget any of His
  benefits;
3 Who forgives all your sins,
Who heals all your diseases;
4 Who redeems your life from the pit,
Who crowns you [lavishly] with
  lovingkindness and tender mercy;
5 Who satisfies your years with good
  things,
So that your youth is renewed like
  the [soaring] eagle. [Is 40:31]

6 The LORD executes righteousness
And justice for all the oppressed.
7 He made known His ways [of
  righteousness and justice] to
  Moses,
His acts to the children of Israel.
8 The LORD is merciful and gracious,
Slow to anger and abounding in
  compassion *and* lovingkindness.
  [James 5:11]
9 He will not always strive *with us,*
Nor will He keep *His anger* forever.
10 He has not dealt with us according
  to our sins [as we deserve],
Nor rewarded us [with punishment]
  according to our wickedness.
11 For as the heavens are high above
  the earth,
So great is His lovingkindness
  toward those who fear *and*
  worship Him [with awe-filled
  respect and deepest reverence].
12 As far as the east is from the west,
So far has He removed our
  transgressions from us.
13 Just as a father loves his children,
So the LORD loves those who fear
  and worship Him [with awe-filled
  respect and deepest reverence].
14 For He knows our [mortal] frame;
He remembers that we are
  [merely] dust.

15 As for man, his days are like grass;
Like a flower of the field, so he
  flourishes.

16 For the wind passes over it and it
  is no more,
And its place knows it no longer.
17 But the lovingkindness of the LORD is
  from everlasting to everlasting on
  those who [reverently] fear Him,
And His righteousness to
  children's children, [Deut 10:12]
18 To those who honor *and* keep His
  covenant,
And remember to do His
  commandments [imprinting His
  word on their hearts].

19 The LORD has established His
  throne in the heavens,
And His sovereignty rules over all
  [the universe].
20 Bless the LORD, you His angels,
You mighty ones who do His
  commandments,
Obeying the voice of His word!
21 Bless the LORD, all you His hosts,
You who serve Him and do His will.
22 Bless the LORD, all you works
  of His, in all places of His
  dominion;
Bless *and* affectionately praise the
  LORD, O my soul!

PSALM 104

The LORD's Care over All
His Works.

1 BLESS *AND* affectionately praise
  the LORD, O my soul!
O LORD my God, You are very
  great;
You are clothed with splendor and
  majesty,
2 [You are the One] who covers
  Yourself with light as with a
  garment,
Who stretches out the heavens like
  a tent curtain,
3 Who lays the beams of His upper
  chambers in the waters [above
  the firmament],
Who makes the clouds His chariot,

Who walks on the wings of the
  wind,
4 Who makes winds His messengers,
Flames of fire His ministers.
  [Heb 1:7]

5 He established the earth on its
  foundations,
So that it will not be moved forever
  and ever. [Job 38:4, 6]
6 You covered it with the deep as
  with a garment;
The waters were standing above the
  mountains. [Gen 1:2; 2 Pet 3:5]
7 At Your rebuke they fled;
At the sound of Your thunder they
  hurried away.
8 The mountains rose, the valleys
  sank down
To the place which You established
  for them.
9 You set a boundary [for the
  waters] that they may not cross
  over,
So that they will not return to
  cover the earth.

10 You send springs into the valleys;
Their waters flow among the
  mountains.
11 They give drink to every beast of
  the field;
The wild donkeys quench their
  thirst there.
12 Beside them the birds of the
  heavens have their nests;
They lift up their voices and sing
  among the branches. [Matt 13:32]
13 He waters the mountains from His
  upper chambers;
The earth is satisfied with the fruit
  of His works.

14 He causes grass to grow for the
  cattle,
And all that the earth produces for
  cultivation by man,
So that he may bring food from the
  earth—
15 And wine which makes the heart
  of man glad,

So that he may make his face
  glisten with oil,
And bread to sustain and
  strengthen man's heart.
16 The trees of the LORD drink their
  fill,
The cedars of Lebanon which He
  has planted,
17 Where the birds make their nests;
As for the stork, the fir trees are
  her house.

18 The high mountains are for the
  wild goats;
The rocks are a refuge for the
  shephanim.
19 He made the moon for the seasons;
The sun knows the [exact] place of
  its setting.
20 You [O LORD] make darkness and it
  becomes night,
In which prowls about every wild
  beast of the forest.
21 The young lions roar after their
  prey
And seek their food from God.
22 When the sun arises, they
  withdraw
And lie down in their dens.
23 Man goes out to his work
And remains at his labor until
  evening.

24 O LORD, how many and varied are
  Your works!
In wisdom You have made them
  all;
The earth is full of Your riches and
  Your creatures.
25 There is the sea, great and broad,
In which are swarms without
  number,
Creatures both small and great.
26 There the ships [of the sea] sail,
And Leviathan [the sea monster],
  which You have formed to play
  there.

27 They all wait for You
To give them their food in its
  appointed season.

²⁸ You give it to them, they gather it
  up;
  You open Your hand, they are
  filled *and* satisfied with good
  [things].
²⁹ You hide Your face, they are
  dismayed;
  You take away their breath, they
  die
  And return to their dust.
³⁰ You send out Your Spirit, they are
  created;
  You renew the face of the ground.

³¹ May the glory of the Lᴏʀᴅ endure
  forever;
  May the Lᴏʀᴅ rejoice *and* be glad in
  His works—
³² He looks at the earth, and it
  trembles;
  He touches the mountains, and
  they smoke.
³³ I will sing to the Lᴏʀᴅ as long as I
  live;
  I will sing praise to my God while I
  have my being.
³⁴ May my meditation be sweet *and*
  pleasing to Him;
  As for me, I will rejoice *and* be glad
  in the Lᴏʀᴅ.
³⁵ Let sinners be consumed from the
  earth,
  And let the wicked be no more.
  Bless *and* affectionately praise the
  Lᴏʀᴅ, O my soul.
  Praise the Lᴏʀᴅ! (Hallelujah!)

PSALM 105

The Lᴏʀᴅ's Wonderful Works
in Behalf of Israel.

¹ O GIVE thanks to the Lᴏʀᴅ, call
  upon His name;
  Make known His deeds among the
  people.
² Sing to Him, sing praises to Him;
  Speak of all His wonderful acts
  and devoutly praise them.
³ Glory in His holy name;

putting the Word to work

Remembering God's faithfulness to
us is an important means of building
our faith. Psalm 105:5 encourages us
to recall the wonderful things He has
done for us. What are some of your
favorite memories? Regularly take
time to remember God's faithfulness
in your life and what He has done for
you, and thank Him. Share with others
God's goodness to you so they too can
hear what He has done!

  Let the hearts of those who seek
  and require the Lᴏʀᴅ [as their
  most essential need] rejoice.
⁴ Seek *and* deeply long for the Lᴏʀᴅ
  and His strength [His power, His
  might];
  Seek *and* deeply long for His face
  and His presence continually.
⁵ Remember [with awe and
  gratitude] the wonderful things
  which He has done,
  His amazing deeds and the
  judgments uttered by His mouth
  [on His enemies, as in Egypt],
  [Ps 78:43–51]
⁶ O you offspring of Abraham, His
  servant,
  O you sons of Jacob, His chosen
  ones!
⁷ He is the Lᴏʀᴅ our God;
  His judgments are in all the earth.

⁸ He has remembered His covenant
  forever,
  The word which He commanded
  and established to a thousand
  generations,
⁹ *The covenant* which He made with
  Abraham,
  And His sworn oath to Isaac, [Luke
  1:72, 73]
¹⁰ Which He confirmed to Jacob as a
  statute,
  To Israel as an everlasting covenant,

11 Saying, "To you I will give the land
   of Canaan
   As the measured portion of your
   inheritance."
12 When there were only a few men
   in number,
   Very few [in fact], and strangers
   in it;
13 And they wandered from one
   nation to another,
   From one kingdom to another
   people,
14 He allowed no man to oppress them;
   He rebuked kings for their sakes,
   saying, [Gen 12:17; 20:3–7]
15 "Do not touch My anointed ones,

And do My prophets no harm."
   [1 Chr 16:8–22]
16 And He called for a famine upon
   the land [of Egypt];
   He cut off every source of bread.
   [Gen 41:54]
17 He sent a man before them,
   Joseph, who was sold as a slave.
   [Gen 45:5; 50:20, 21]
18 His feet they hurt with shackles;
   He was put in chains of iron,
19 Until the time that his word
   [of prophecy regarding his
   brothers] came true,
   The word of the LORD tested *and*
   refined him.

remember Joseph

Psalm 105 is another wonderful place in the Bible where the writer takes time to recall God's working throughout history. Similar accounts can be found in Nehemiah 9 and in Hebrews 11. Each time a biblical writer recounts stories from the past, our faith can be strengthened and our hearts can be encouraged.

In Psalm 105:17–19, we are reminded of Joseph and of the unjust treatment he received from his brothers. They sold him into slavery and told his father that a wild animal had killed him. Meanwhile, a wealthy man named Potiphar purchased Joseph and took him into his home as a slave. God gave Joseph favor everywhere he went, and soon he found favor with his new master.

Joseph kept getting promoted, but then something unjust happened to him. Potiphar's wife tried to entice him into having an affair, but because he was a man of integrity, he would have nothing to do with her. Lying to her husband, she said Joseph had attacked her, which caused him to be imprisoned for something he had not done!

Joseph tried to help others the entire time he was in prison. He did not complain, and because he had a proper attitude in his suffering, God eventually delivered and promoted him. He ultimately had so much authority in Egypt that no one else in the entire land was above him except Pharaoh himself.

God also vindicated Joseph concerning the situation with his brothers, in that they had to come to Joseph for food when the whole land was in a state of famine. Once again, Joseph displayed a godly attitude by not mistreating them even though they deserved it. He told them what they had meant for his harm, God had worked out for his good—that they were in God's hands, not his, and that he had no right to do anything but bless them (see Genesis 37–45 for the details of this story). We can expect similar results when we stay patient through suffering and keep a positive, forgiving attitude.

20 The king sent and released him,
   The ruler of the peoples [of
   Egypt], and set him free.
21 He made Joseph lord of his house
   And ruler of all his possessions,
   [Gen 41:40]
22 To imprison his princes at his will,
   That he might teach his elders
   wisdom.
23 Israel also came into Egypt;
   Thus Jacob sojourned in the land
   of Ham. [Gen 46:6]
24 There the Lord greatly increased
   [the number of] His people,
   And made them more powerful
   than their enemies.

25 He turned the heart [of the
   Egyptians] to hate His people,
   To deal craftily with His servants.
26 He sent Moses His servant,
   And Aaron, whom He had chosen.
27 They exhibited His wondrous
   signs among them,
   Great miracles in the land of Ham
   (Egypt).
28 He sent [thick, oppressive]
   darkness and made *the land* dark;
   And Moses and Aaron did not rebel
   against His words. [Ex 10:22;
   Ps 99:7]
29 He turned Egypt's waters into blood
   And caused their fish to die. [Ex
   7:20, 21]
30 Their land swarmed with frogs,
   Even in the chambers of their
   kings. [Ex 8:6]
31 He spoke, and there came swarms
   of flies
   And gnats in all their territory. [Ex
   8:17, 24]
32 He gave them hail for rain,
   With flaming fire in their land.
   [Ex 9:23, 25]
33 He struck their vines also and
   their fig trees,
   And shattered the [ice-laden] trees
   of their territory. [Ps 78:47]
34 He spoke, and the [migratory]
   locusts came,

And the young locusts, even
   without number, [Ex 10:4, 13, 14]
35 And ate up all the vegetation in
   their land,
   And devoured the fruit of their
   ground.
36 He also struck down all the
   firstborn in their land,
   The first fruits *and* chief substance
   of all their strength. [Ex 12:29;
   Ps 78:51]

37 He brought the sons of Israel out
   [of Egypt] with silver and gold,
   And among their tribes there was
   not one who stumbled. [Ex 12:35]
38 Egypt was glad when they
   departed,
   For the dread *and* fear of them
   had fallen on the Egyptians.
   [Ex 12:33]
39 The Lord spread a cloud as a
   covering [by day],
   And a fire to illumine the night.
   [Ex 13:21]
40 The Israelites asked, and He
   brought quail,
   And satisfied them with the bread
   of heaven. [Ex 16:12–15]
41 He opened the rock and water
   flowed out;
   It ran in the dry places like a river.
   [Ex 17:6; Num 20:11]
42 For He remembered His holy word
   To Abraham His servant; [Gen
   15:14]
43 He brought out His people with joy,
   And His chosen ones with a joyful
   shout,
44 He gave them the lands of the
   nations [of Canaan],
   So that they would possess *the
   fruits of* those peoples' labor,
   [Deut 6:10, 11]
45 So that they might observe His
   precepts
   And keep His laws [obediently
   accepting and honoring and
   valuing them].
   Praise the Lord! (Hallelujah!)

PSALM 106

Israel's Rebelliousness and the LORD's Deliverances.

1 PRAISE THE LORD! (Hallelujah!)
Oh give thanks to the LORD, for He
  is good;
For His mercy *and* lovingkindness
  endure forever! [1 Chr 16:34]

2 Who can put into words the
  mighty deeds of the LORD?
Or who can proclaim all His praise
  [that is due Him]?
3 Blessed are those who observe
  justice [by honoring God's
  precepts],
Who practice righteousness at all
  times.

be happy

Psalm 106:12–15 reminds us of the Israelites when they became greedy and demanding. It warns us of the dangers of a greedy, lustful heart because such a heart is never satisfied—and that is an unsafe spiritual condition.

Although God had led the Israelites out of bondage in Egypt and had destroyed Pharaoh and his army, who were chasing after them, the Israelites were not satisfied. They continued to gripe and complain every step of the way. No matter how much He provided for them, they always wanted more. They were on the way to the Promised Land, but they were not enjoying the journey. Many times, we have the same problem.

Early in my ministry, I taught twenty-five people every Tuesday evening in my living room. That was all I was mature enough to handle. I had a vision to do what I am doing now, so I grumbled, murmured, pleaded, prayed, fasted, but I never got out of my living room. All my efforts were a waste of time and energy. I could have been relaxing, praising God, laughing, and enjoying my family and my life. But no, I had to be miserable all the time because I was not getting my way.

I finally had an opportunity to teach another Bible study. I was happy with that for a little while, but not for long. Then I went to work for a church where I was associate pastor for five years, but after a while I was not satisfied there anymore. Then I started my own ministry, and before long, I was unhappy with that. No matter what I was doing, I always wanted something else.

If people are not careful, they can waste their entire lives by always wanting what they do not have. They fall in love and cannot wait to get married. Then once they are married, they think about everything that is wrong with their spouse and they are still not happy. They have children and cannot wait for them to grow up and start school. As soon as the children are in school, they cannot wait until they graduate.

On and on it goes. No matter what their place in life, they always want something else. They keep murmuring and grumbling to God about what they want. Then as soon as He gives it to them, they start complaining again because they want something more.

The moral of the story of the Israelites is that they got what they asked for, but they were not really ready to handle it. Ask God to give you a heart that is satisfied and content at every point along your life's journey and to be able to handle increase when it comes. Learn to enjoy where you are on the way to where you are going!

⁴Remember me, O Lᴏʀᴅ, when You
favor Your people.
Visit me with Your salvation [when
You rescue them],
⁵That I may see the prosperity of
Your chosen ones,
That I may rejoice in the gladness
of Your nation,
That I may glory with Your
inheritance.

⁶We have sinned like our fathers;
We have committed iniquity, we
have behaved wickedly. [Lev
26:40–42]
⁷Our fathers in Egypt did not
understand *nor* appreciate Your
miracles;
They did not remember the
abundance of Your mercies *nor*
imprint Your lovingkindnesses
on their hearts,
But they were rebellious at the sea,
at the Red Sea. [Ex 14:21]
⁸Nevertheless He saved them for
His name's sake,
That He might make His
[supreme] power known.
⁹He rebuked the Red Sea, and it
dried up;
And He led them through the
depths as through a pasture.
[Ex 14:21]
¹⁰So He saved them from the hand
of the one that hated them,
And redeemed them from the
hand of the [Egyptian] enemy.
[Ex 14:30]
¹¹And the waters covered their
adversaries;
Not one of them was left. [Ex 14:27,
28; 15:5]
¹²Then Israel believed in [the
validity of] His words;
They sang His praise.

¹³But they quickly forgot His works;
They did not [patiently] wait for
His counsel *and* purpose [to be
revealed regarding them],

¹⁴But lusted intensely in the
wilderness
And tempted God [with their
insistent desires] in the desert.
[Num 11:4]
¹⁵So He gave them their request,
But sent a wasting disease among
them. [Ps 78:29–31]

¹⁶They envied Moses in the camp,
And Aaron [the high priest], the holy
one of the Lᴏʀᴅ, [Num 16:1–32]
¹⁷Therefore the earth opened and
swallowed Dathan,
And engulfed the company of
Abiram. [Num 16:31, 32]
¹⁸And a fire broke out in their
company;
The flame consumed the wicked.
[Num 16:35, 46]

¹⁹They made a calf in Horeb (Sinai)
And worshiped a cast image.
[Ex 32:4]
²⁰Thus they exchanged [the true
God who was] their glory
For the image of an ox that eats
grass.
²¹They forgot God their Savior,
Who had done such great things in
Egypt,
²²Wonders in the land of Ham,
Awesome things at the Red Sea.
²³Therefore He said He would
destroy them,
[And He would have done so]
had not Moses, His chosen one,
stepped into the gap before Him,
To turn away His wrath from
destroying them. [Ex 32:10, 11, 32]
²⁴Then they despised the pleasant
land [of Canaan];
They did not believe in His word
nor rely on it,
²⁵But they sulked *and* complained in
their tents;
They did not listen to the voice of
the Lᴏʀᴅ.
²⁶Therefore He lifted up His hand
[swearing] to them,

That He would cause them to fall
   in the wilderness,
27 And that He would cast out their
   descendants among the nations
   And scatter them in the lands [of
   the earth].

28 They joined themselves also to
   [the idol] Baal of Peor,
   And ate sacrifices offered to the
   dead.
29 Thus they provoked Him to anger
   with their practices,
   And a plague broke out among them.
30 Then Phinehas [the priest] stood
   up and interceded,
   And so the plague was halted.
   [Num 25:7, 8]
31 And that was credited to him for
   righteousness,
   To all generations forever.

32 They provoked Him to anger at the
   waters of Meribah,
   So that it went hard with Moses on
   their account; [Num 20:3–13]
33 Because they were rebellious
   against His Spirit,
   Moses spoke recklessly with his lips.

34 They did not destroy the [pagan]
   peoples [in Canaan],
   As the Lord commanded them,
35 But they mingled with the
   [idolatrous] nations
   And learned their ways,
36 And served their idols,
   Which became a [dreadful] snare
   to them.
37 They even sacrificed their sons
   and their daughters to demons
   [Deut 32:17; 2 Kin 16:3]
38 And shed innocent blood,
   Even the blood of their sons and of
   their daughters,
   Whom they sacrificed to the idols
   of Canaan;
   And the land was polluted with
   their blood.
39 In this way they became unclean
   in their practices;

They played the prostitute in
   their own deeds [by giving their
   worship, which belongs to God
   alone, to other "gods"].

40 Therefore the anger of the Lord
   was kindled against His people
   And He detested His own
   inheritance. [Deut 32:17]
41 He gave them into the hands of the
   nations,
   And those who hated them ruled
   over them.
42 Their enemies also oppressed them,
   And they were subdued under
   the [powerful] hand of their
   enemies.
43 Many times He rescued them;
   But they were rebellious in their
   counsel,
   And sank down in their wickedness.

44 Nevertheless He looked
   [sympathetically] at their distress
   When He heard their cry;
45 And He remembered His covenant
   for their sake,
   And relented [rescinding their
   sentence] according to the
   greatness of His lovingkindness
   [when they cried out to Him],
46 He also made them objects of
   compassion
   Among those who had carried them
   away captive. [2 Kin 25:27–30]

47 Save us, O Lord our God,
   And gather us from among the
   nations,
   That we may give thanks to Your
   holy name
   And glory in praising You.
48 Blessed be the Lord, the God of
   Israel,
   From everlasting even to
   everlasting.
   And let all the people say, "Amen."
   Praise the Lord! (Hallelujah!)
   [1 Chr 16:35, 36]

BOOK FIVE

PSALM 107

The Lord Rescues People from Many Troubles.

¹O GIVE thanks to the Lord, for He
   is good;
For His compassion *and*
   lovingkindness endure forever!
²Let the redeemed of the Lord say so,
   Whom He has redeemed from the
   hand of the adversary,
³And gathered them from the lands,
   From the east and from the west,
   From the north and from the south.

⁴They wandered in the wilderness
   in a [solitary] desert region;
   And did not find a way to an
   inhabited city.
⁵Hungry and thirsty,
   They fainted.
⁶Then they cried out to the Lord in
   their trouble,
   And He rescued them from their
   distresses.
⁷He led them by the straight way,
   To an inhabited city [where they
   could establish their homes].
⁸Let them give thanks to the Lord
   for His lovingkindness,
   And for His wonderful acts to the
   children of men!
⁹For He satisfies the parched throat,
   And fills the hungry appetite with
   what is good.

¹⁰Some dwelt in darkness and in the
   deep (deathly) darkness,
   Prisoners [bound] in misery and
   chains, [Luke 1:79]
¹¹Because they had rebelled against
   the precepts of God
   And spurned the counsel of the
   Most High.
¹²Therefore He humbled their heart
   with hard labor;
   They stumbled and there was no
   one to help.

¹³Then they cried out to the Lord in
   their trouble,
   And He saved them from their
   distresses.
¹⁴He brought them out of darkness
   and the deep (deathly) darkness
   And broke their bonds apart. [Ps
   68:6; Acts 12:7; 16:26]
¹⁵Let them give thanks to the Lord
   for His lovingkindness,
   And for His wonderful acts to the
   children of men!
¹⁶For He has shattered the gates of
   bronze
   And cut the bars of iron apart.

¹⁷Fools, because of their rebellious
   way,
   And because of their sins, were
   afflicted.
¹⁸They detested all kinds of food,
   And they drew near to the gates of
   death.
¹⁹Then they cried out to the Lord in
   their trouble,
   And He saved them from their
   distresses.
²⁰He sent His word and healed them,
   And rescued them from their
   destruction. [2 Kin 20:4, 5;
   Matt 8:8]
²¹Let them give thanks to the Lord
   for His lovingkindness,
   And for His wonderful acts to the
   children of men! [Heb 13:15]
²²And let them offer the sacrifices of
   thanksgiving,
   And speak of His deeds with shouts
   of joy!

²³Those who go down to the sea in
   ships,
   Who do business on great waters;
²⁴They have seen the works of the
   Lord,
   And His wonders in the deep.
²⁵For He spoke and raised up a
   stormy wind,
   Which lifted up the waves of the sea.

26 They went up toward the heavens
  [on the crest of the wave], they
  went down again to the depths
  [of the watery trough];
  Their courage melted away in their
  misery.
27 They staggered and trembled like
  a drunken man,
  And were at their wits' end [all
  their wisdom was useless].
28 Then they cried out to the Lord in
  their trouble,
  And He brought them out of their
  distresses.
29 He hushed the storm to a gentle
  whisper,
  So that the waves of the sea were
  still. [Ps 65:7; 89:9; Matt 8:26]
30 Then they were glad because of the
  calm,
  And He guided them to their
  desired haven (harbor).
31 Let them give thanks to the Lord
  for His lovingkindness,
  And for His wonderful acts to the
  children of men!
32 Let them exalt Him also in the
  congregation of the people,
  And praise Him at the seat of the
  elders.
33 He turns rivers into a wilderness,
  And springs of water into a thirsty
  ground; [1 Kin 17:1, 7]
34 A productive land into a [barren]
  salt waste,
  Because of the wickedness of those
  who dwell in it. [Gen 13:10; 14:3;
  19:25]
35 He turns a wilderness into a pool
  of water
  And a dry land into springs of
  water; [Is 41:18]
36 And there He has the hungry dwell,
  So that they may establish an
  inhabited city,
37 And sow fields and plant
  vineyards,
  And produce an abundant harvest.

38 Also He blesses them so that they
  multiply greatly,
  And He does not let [the number
  of] their cattle decrease.
39 When they are diminished and
  bowed down (humbled)
  Through oppression, misery, and
  sorrow,
40 He pours contempt on princes
  And makes them wander in a
  pathless wasteland.
41 Yet He sets the needy securely on
  high, away from affliction,
  And makes their families like a
  flock.
42 The upright see it and rejoice;
  But all unrighteousness shuts its
  mouth.
43 Who is wise? Let him observe *and*
  heed these things;
  And [thoughtfully] consider the
  lovingkindness of the Lord.

PSALM 108
Praise and Supplication to God
for Victory.

A Song. A Psalm of David.

1 O GOD, my heart is steadfast [with
  confident faith];
  I will sing, I will sing praises, even
  with my soul.
2 Awake, harp and lyre;
  I will awaken the dawn!
3 I will praise *and* give thanks to
  You, O Lord, among the people;
  And I will sing praises to You
  among the nations.
4 For Your lovingkindness is great
  and higher than the heavens;
  Your truth *reaches* to the skies. [Ps
  57:7–11]
5 Be exalted [in majesty], O God,
  above the heavens,
  And Your glory above all the earth.
6 That Your beloved [ones] may be
  rescued,

Save with Your right hand, and
answer me!

7 God has spoken in His holiness:
"I will rejoice, I will portion out
Shechem [as I divide Canaan
among My people],
And measure out the Valley of
Succoth.
8 "Gilead is Mine, Manasseh is Mine;
Ephraim also is the helmet of
My head [My stronghold, My
defense];
Judah is My scepter. [Gen 49:10]
9 "Moab is My washbowl;
Over Edom I will throw My shoe
[to show Edom is Mine];
Over Philistia I will shout [in
triumph]."

10 Who will bring me into the
fortified city [of Petra]?
Who will lead me to Edom?
11 Have You not rejected us, O God?
And will You not go out, O God,
with our armies?
12 Give us help against the adversary,
For deliverance by man is in vain
[a worthless hope].
13 With God we will do valiantly,
For it is He who will trample down
our enemies. [Ps 60:5–12]

PSALM 109

Vengeance Invoked
upon Adversaries.

To the Chief Musician.
A Psalm of David.

1 O GOD of my praise!
Do not keep silent,
2 For the mouth of the wicked and
the mouth of the deceitful are
opened against me;
They have spoken against me with
a lying tongue.
3 They have also surrounded me
with words of hatred,
And have fought against me
without a cause.

4 In return for my love, they attack
me,
But I am in prayer.
5 They have repaid me evil for good,
And hatred for my love.

6 Appoint a wicked man against him,
And let an attacker stand at his
right hand [to kill him].
7 When he enters into dispute, let
wickedness come about.
Let his prayer [for help] result
[only] in sin.
8 Let his days be few;
And let another take his office.
[Acts 1:20]
9 Let his children be fatherless
And his wife a widow.
10 Let his children wander and beg;
Let them seek their food and be
driven far from their ruined
homes. [Gen 4:12]
11 Let the creditor seize all that he has,
And let strangers plunder the
product of his labor.
12 Let there be no one to extend
kindness to him,
Nor let anyone be gracious to his
fatherless children.
13 Let his descendants be cut off,
And in the following generation let
their name be blotted out.

14 Let the wickedness of his fathers
be remembered by the LORD;
And do not let the sin of his
mother be blotted out.
15 Let them be before the LORD
continually,
That He may cut off their memory
from the earth;
16 Because the man did not
remember to show kindness,
But persecuted the suffering and
needy man,
And the brokenhearted, to put
them to death.
17 He also loved cursing, and it came
[back] to him;

He did not delight in blessing, so it
    was far from him.
¹⁸ He clothed himself with cursing as
    with his garment,
    And it seeped into his inner self
    like water
    And like [anointing] oil into his
    bones.
¹⁹ Let it be to him as a robe with
    which he covers himself,
    And as a sash with which he is
    constantly bound.
²⁰ Let this be the reward of my
    attackers from the Lord,
    And of those who speak evil
    against my life.
²¹ But You, O God, the Lord, show
    kindness to me, for Your name's
    sake;

Because Your lovingkindness
    (faithfulness, compassion) is
    good, O rescue me;
²² For I am suffering and needy,
    And my heart is wounded
    within me.
²³ I am vanishing like a shadow
    when it lengthens *and* fades;
    I am shaken off like the locust.
²⁴ My knees are unsteady from
    fasting;
    And my flesh is gaunt and without
    fatness.
²⁵ I also have become a reproach *and*
    an object of taunting to others;
    When they see me, they shake their
    heads [in derision]. [Matt 26:39]

²⁶ Help me, O Lord my God;

healed healers

Psalm 109:22 speaks of a wounded heart. Is it wrong to have a wounded heart? No, a wounded heart is not wrong, but if you have one, I encourage you to receive God's healing and go on with your life.

In Old Testament days if a priest had a wound or a bleeding sore, he could not minister (Leviticus 21:1–16). I think we can learn from that today, because we have a lot of wounded people who are trying to minister and bring healing to others while they themselves still have unhealed wounds from the past. These people are still bleeding and hurting. They are what I call "wounded healers."

Am I saying such people cannot minister? No, but I am saying they need to be healed. Jesus said the blind cannot lead the blind because if they do, they will both fall into a pit (see Matthew 15:14). There is a message in that statement. What is the use of my trying to minister victory to others if I have no victory in my own life? How can I minister emotional healing to others if I am not dealing with my emotional problems from my past? In order to minister properly, we first need to go to God and let Him heal us.

I have found that when I have a relationship problem, when I get wounded or when someone hurts my feelings, I cannot minister properly until I get that situation worked out because it takes away my strength and affects my faith. When I have unresolved problems in my life, I am not as strong as I could be.

God loves to use people who have been hurt or wounded and then healed because nobody can minister to someone else better than a person who has had the same problem or been in the same situation as the person they are trying to help. Ask God to heal you everywhere you hurt so He can use you to help others. Ask Him to make you a healed healer!

Save me according to Your
   lovingkindness—
27 And let them know that this is
   Your hand;
You, LORD, have done it.
28 Let them curse, but You bless.
When adversaries arise, let them
   be ashamed,
But let Your servant rejoice.
29 Let my attackers be clothed with
   dishonor,
And let them cover themselves
   with their own shame as with a
   robe.
30 I will give great praise *and* thanks
   to the LORD with my mouth;
And in the midst of many I will
   praise Him.
31 For He will stand at the right hand
   of the needy,
To save him from those who judge
   his soul.

PSALM 110

The LORD Gives Dominion
to the King.

A Psalm of David.

1 THE LORD (Father) says to my
   Lord (the Messiah, His Son),
"Sit at My right hand
Until I make Your enemies a
   footstool for Your feet [subjugating
   them into complete submission]."
   [Josh 10:24; Matt 26:64; Acts 2:34;
   1 Cor 15:25; Col 3:1; Heb 12:2]
2 The LORD will send the scepter of
   Your strength from Zion, *saying,*
"Rule in the midst of Your
   enemies." [Rom 11:26, 27]
3 Your people will offer themselves
   willingly [to participate in Your
   battle] in the day of Your power;
In the splendor of holiness, from
   the womb of the dawn,

your Provider

Do you need provision in an area of your life, and you are not really sure where it is going to come from? Be encouraged because, in Psalm 111:5, God promises to provide for "those who fear Him [with awe-inspired reverence]." As long as we worship God, we are going to have His provision.

Perhaps you have been told that you are going to lose your job or your housing. Maybe you are elderly and living on a pension or Social Security, and you wonder what is going to happen to you in the future. You see prices on everything rising all the time, and the devil whispers in your ear, "You are not going to have enough to live on." Or maybe the figures just do not add up; your income simply is not enough to support you, and yet you are doing all you know to do.

Whatever the reason for your concern about your provision, mark Psalm 111:5 in your Bible. Meditate on it and even memorize it, because it holds the key to having your needs met. That way when a need arises in your life, you will have hidden the Word of God in your heart, and it will strengthen you and help you remain in faith rather than in fear.

Believe God's Word when He says He gives food and provision to those who reverently fear Him and worship Him. Whatever your situation may be, God will provide for you as you continue to worship and magnify Him.

Worship is actually fun and energizing; worry makes our hearts heavy and causes a loss of joy. Do not worry; worship and see God provide for your every need.

Your young men are to You as the dew.

⁴The LORD has sworn [an oath] and will not change His mind:
"You are a priest forever
According to the order of Melchizedek." [Heb 5:10; 7:11, 15, 21]

⁵The LORD is at Your right hand,
He will crush kings in the day of His wrath.

⁶He will execute judgment [in overwhelming punishment] among the nations;
He will fill them with corpses,
He will crush the chief men over a broad country. [Ezek 38:21, 22; 39:11, 12]

⁷He will drink from the brook by the wayside;
Therefore He will lift up His head [triumphantly].

PSALM 111

The LORD Praised for His Goodness.

¹PRAISE THE LORD! (Hallelujah!)
I will give thanks to the LORD with all my heart,
In the company of the upright and in the congregation.

²Great are the works of the LORD,
Studied by all those who delight in them.

³Splendid and majestic is His work,
And His righteousness endures forever.

⁴He has made His wonderful acts to be remembered;
The LORD is gracious and merciful and full of loving compassion.

⁵He has given food to those who fear Him [with awe-inspired reverence];
He will remember His covenant forever. [Deut 10:12; Ps 96:9]

⁶He has declared and made known to His people the power of His works,

In giving them the heritage of the nations.

⁷The works of His hands are truth and [absolute] justice;
All His precepts are sure (established, reliable, trustworthy).

⁸They are upheld forever and ever;
They are done in [absolute] truth and uprightness.

⁹He has sent redemption to His people;
He has ordained His covenant forever;
Holy and awesome is His name— [inspiring reverence and godly fear].

life point

The Bible says that those who walk in wisdom will be successful and live long lives. They will be exceedingly happy. They will be blessed, so blessed that they will be admired (see Proverbs 3:1–18). But there is no such thing as wisdom without worship. Psalm 111:10 says that reverence for God is the beginning of wisdom. In other words, reverence is foundational to having a fruitful life.

Many people today are seeking knowledge, and knowledge is good, but wisdom is better. Wisdom is the right use of knowledge. Knowledge without wisdom can cause one to be puffed up or filled with pride, which will ultimately ruin his life. A wise person will always be knowledgeable, but not all knowledgeable people are wise.

God's Word tells us to cry out for wisdom, to seek it as we would silver and gold, to make it a vital necessity in life. There is nothing more important than wisdom, and wisdom starts with reverence toward God.

¹⁰ The [reverent] fear of the Lord is
   the beginning (the prerequisite,
   the absolute essential, the
   alphabet) of wisdom;
A good understanding *and* a
   teachable heart are possessed
   by all those who do *the will of the*
   Lord;
His praise endures forever. [Job
   28:28; Prov 1:7; Matt 22:37, 38;
   Rev 14:7]

PSALM 112

Prosperity of the One
Who Fears the Lord.

¹ PRAISE THE Lord! (Hallelujah!)
Blessed [fortunate, prosperous,
   and favored by God] is the man
   who fears the Lord [with awe-
   inspired reverence and worships
   Him with obedience],
Who delights greatly in His
   commandments. [Deut 10:12]
² His descendants will be mighty on
   earth;
The generation of the upright will
   be blessed.
³ Wealth and riches are in his house,
And his righteousness endures
   forever.
⁴ Light arises in the darkness for the
   upright;
He is gracious and compassionate
   and righteous (upright—in right
   standing with God).
⁵ It is well with the man who is
   gracious and lends;
He conducts his affairs with justice.
   [Ps 37:26; Luke 6:35; Col 4:5]
⁶ He will never be shaken;
The righteous will be remembered
   forever. [Prov 10:7]

⁷ He will not fear bad news;
His heart is steadfast, trusting
   [confidently relying on and
   believing] in the Lord.
⁸ His heart is upheld, he will not fear

While he looks [with satisfaction]
   on his adversaries.
⁹ He has given freely to the poor;
His righteousness endures
   forever;
His horn will be exalted in honor.
   [2 Cor 9:9]
¹⁰ The wicked will see it and be
   angered,
He will gnash his teeth and melt
   away [in despair and death];
The desire of the wicked will
   perish *and* come to nothing.

PSALM 113

The Lord Exalts the Humble.

¹ PRAISE THE Lord! (Hallelujah!)
Praise, O servants of the Lord,
Praise the name of the Lord.
² Blessed be the name of the Lord
From this time forth and forever.
³ From the rising of the sun to its
   setting
The name of the Lord is to be
   praised [with awe-inspired
   reverence].
⁴ The Lord is high above all
   nations,
And His glory above the heavens.

⁵ Who is like the Lord our God,
Who is enthroned on high,
⁶ Who humbles Himself to regard
The heavens and the earth? [Ps
   138:6; Is 57:15]
⁷ He raises the poor out of the dust
And lifts the needy from the ash
   heap,
⁸ That He may seat them with
   princes,
With the princes of His people.
⁹ He makes the barren woman live
   in the house
As a joyful mother of children.
Praise the Lord! (Hallelujah!)

PSALM 114

God's Rescue of Israel from Egypt.

¹WHEN ISRAEL came out of Egypt,
The house of Jacob from a people
  of strange language,
²Judah became His sanctuary,
And Israel His dominion. [Ex
  29:45, 46; Deut 27:9]

³The [Red] Sea looked and fled;
The Jordan turned back. [Ex 14:21;
  Josh 3:13, 16; Ps 77:16]
⁴The mountains leaped like rams,
The [little] hills, like lambs.
⁵What ails you, O sea, that you flee?
O Jordan, that you turn back?
⁶O mountains, that you leap like
  rams,
O [little] hills, like lambs?

⁷Tremble, O earth, at the presence
  of the Lord,
At the presence of the God of Jacob
  (Israel),
⁸Who turned the rock into a pool of
  water,
The flint into a fountain of water.
  [Ex 17:6; Num 20:11]

PSALM 115

Pagan Idols Contrasted with the Lord.

¹NOT TO us, O Lord, not to us,
But to Your name give glory
Because of Your lovingkindness,
  because of Your truth and
  faithfulness.
²Why should the nations say,
"Where, now, is their God?"
³But our God is in heaven;
He does whatever He pleases.
⁴The idols [of the nations] are silver
  and gold,
The work of man's hands.
⁵They have mouths, but they
  cannot speak;

They have eyes, but they cannot
  see;
⁶They have ears, but they cannot
  hear;
They have noses, but they cannot
  smell;
⁷They have hands, but they cannot
  feel;
They have feet, but they cannot
  walk;
Nor can they make a sound with
  their throats.
⁸Those who make them will
  become like them,
Everyone who trusts in them. [Ps
  135:15–18]

⁹O Israel, trust and take refuge in
  the Lord! [Be confident in Him,
  cling to Him, rely on His word!]
He is their help and their shield.
¹⁰O house of Aaron, trust in the
  Lord;
He is their help and their shield.
¹¹You who [reverently] fear the Lord,
  trust in Lord;
He is their help and their shield.
¹²The Lord has been mindful of us;
  He will bless,
He will bless the house of Israel;
He will bless the house of Aaron.
¹³He will bless those who fear
  and worship the Lord [with
  awe-inspired reverence and
  submissive wonder],
Both the small and the great. [Ps
  103:11; Rev 11:18; 19:5]
¹⁴May the Lord give you [great]
  increase,
You and your children.
¹⁵May you be blessed of the Lord,
Who made heaven and earth.

¹⁶The heavens are the heavens of the
  Lord,
But the earth He has given to the
  children of men.
¹⁷The dead do not praise the Lord,
Nor do any who go down into
  silence;

18 But as for us, we will bless *and*
affectionately and gratefully
praise the LORD
From this time forth and forever.
Praise the LORD! (Hallelujah!)

PSALM 116

Thanksgiving for Rescue from Death.

1 I LOVE the LORD, because He hears
[and continues to hear]
My voice and my supplications (my
pleas, my cries, my specific needs).
2 Because He has inclined His ear to
me,
Therefore I will call on Him as
long as I live.
3 The cords *and* sorrows of death
encompassed me,
And the terrors of Sheol came
upon me;
I found distress and sorrow.
4 Then I called on the name of the
LORD:
"O LORD, please save my life!"

5 Gracious is the LORD, and
[consistently] righteous;
Yes, our God is compassionate.
6 The LORD protects the simple
(childlike);
I was brought low [humbled and
discouraged], and He saved me.
7 Return to your rest, O my soul,
For the LORD has dealt bountifully
with you. [Matt 11:29]
8 For You have rescued my life from
death,
My eyes from tears,
And my feet from stumbling *and*
falling.
9 I will walk [in submissive wonder]
before the LORD
In the land of the living.
10 I believed [and clung to my God]
when I said,
"I am greatly afflicted." [2 Cor 4:13]
11 I said in my alarm,
"All men are liars."

12 What will I give to the LORD [in
return]
For all His benefits toward me?
[How can I repay Him for His
precious blessings?]
13 I will lift up the cup of salvation
And call on the name of the LORD.
14 I will pay my vows to the LORD,
Yes, in the presence of all His
people.
15 Precious [and of great consequence]
in the sight of the LORD
Is the death of His godly ones [so
He watches over them].
16 O LORD, truly I am Your servant;
I am Your servant, the son of Your
handmaid;
You have unfastened my chains.
17 I will offer to You the sacrifice of
thanksgiving,
And will call on the name of the
LORD.
18 I will pay my vows to the LORD,
Yes, in the presence of all His
people,
19 In the courts of the LORD's house
(temple)—
In the midst of you, O Jerusalem.
Praise the LORD! (Hallelujah!)

life point

Notice that in Psalm 116:17, the psalmist
says that he will "call on the name of the
LORD," but only after he has offered the
sacrifice of thanksgiving.

Many times I have attempted to call on
the power of the Name of Jesus to help
me, while at the same time my life was
filled with complaining—not thankfulness. I have discovered that there is no
positive power in complaining. Complaining is filled with power, but it is negative
(evil) power. If we want God's power to
be released in our lives, we will have to
stop complaining and be thankful.

confess the Word

When we speak what we believe, as the psalmist did in Psalm 116:1, 2, we are making a "confession."

I recommend having a list of confessions—things that can be backed by the Word of God—things that you speak aloud over your life, your family, your circumstances, and your future. You can find a list of Scripture verses to adapt as confessions in the section entitled, "The Word for Your Everyday Life," in the back of this Bible.

Before learning to confess God's Word, I was terribly negative. I was a Christian and active in church work. My husband and I tithed and attended church regularly, but we did not know that we could do anything about any of our circumstances. God began teaching me that I should not think and say negative things. I felt He told me He could not work in my life until I stopped being so negative. I obeyed, and I became happier.

After some time had elapsed, I felt that my circumstances had not improved significantly. I asked the Lord about it, and He said, "You have stopped speaking negatively, but you are not saying anything positive." That was my first lesson in "call[ing] into being that which does not exist" (see Romans 4:17). No one had taught me this principle before; God was teaching me Himself, and it proved to be one of the major breakthroughs in my life. He showed me that confessing His Word helps establish His life-giving truths in our hearts.

I made a list of the things that I had been learning, which were rightfully mine according to the Word of God. I had scriptures to support them. I confessed those truths aloud twice a day for approximately six months. I did this in my house, alone. I was not talking to any human person; I was declaring the Word of God and speaking it into the atmosphere where I lived. To this day, almost twenty years later, when I am praying and confessing the Word, I still hear many of those early confessions come out of my mouth.

I would like to share a few confessions from my list with you:

"I am dead to sin but alive to God" (see Romans 6:11); "I will study the Word of God; I will pray" (see 2 Timothy 2:15; Luke 18:1); "I take every thought captive unto the obedience of Jesus Christ, casting down every imagination, and every exalted and proud thing that exalts itself against the knowledge of God" (see 2 Corinthians 10:5); "No weapon that is formed against me will succeed, but every tongue that rises against me in judgment, I will condemn" (see Isaiah 54:17); "I do not think more highly of myself than I ought to think" (see Romans 12:3); "I intend that my mouth will not transgress. I will speak forth the righteousness and praise of God all the day long" (see Psalm 17:3; 35:28); "I cry to God Most High, Who accomplishes all things on my behalf and completes my purpose in His plan" (see Psalm 57:2). "God has not given me a spirit of fear, but one of power, love, and a sound mind" (see 2 Timothy 1:7).

I can look at my list now, and I am absolutely amazed at how many of the things have come to pass, and how impossible they seemed, naturally speaking, at the time.

I encourage you to make your own list, tailored to your situation. As you begin to confess God's Word, you will notice major changes in your life.

PSALM 117

A Psalm of Praise.

¹O PRAISE the Lord, all you nations!
  Praise Him, all you people! [Rom
  15:11]
²For His lovingkindness prevails
  over us [and we triumph and
  overcome through Him],
And the truth of the Lord endures
  forever.
Praise the Lord! (Hallelujah!)

PSALM 118

Thanksgiving for the Lord's Saving Goodness.

¹O GIVE thanks to the Lord, for He
  is good;
For His lovingkindness endures
  forever.
²Oh let Israel say,
  "His lovingkindness endures
  forever."
³Oh let the house of Aaron say,
  "His lovingkindness endures
  forever."
⁴Oh let those who [reverently] fear
  the Lord, say,
  "His lovingkindness endures
  forever."

⁵Out of my distress I called on the
  Lord;
The Lord answered me and set me
  free.
⁶The Lord is on my side; I will not
  fear.
What can [mere] man do to me?
  [Heb 13:6]
⁷The Lord is on my side, He is
  among those who help me;
Therefore I will look [in triumph]
  on those who hate me.
⁸It is better to take refuge in the
  Lord
Than to trust in man.
⁹It is better to take refuge in the Lord
Than to trust in princes.

¹⁰All nations encompassed me;
  In the name of the Lord I will
  surely cut them off.
¹¹They encompassed me, yes, they
  surrounded me [on every side];
In the name of the Lord I will cut
  them off.
¹²They swarmed around me like
  bees;
They flare up *and* are
  extinguished like a fire of
  thorns;
In the name of the Lord I will
  surely cut them off. [Deut 1:44]
¹³You [my enemy] pushed me
  violently so that I was falling,
But the Lord helped me.
¹⁴The Lord is my strength and song,
  And He has become my salvation.

¹⁵The sound of joyful shouting and
  salvation is in the tents of the
  righteous:
The right hand of the Lord does
  valiantly.
¹⁶The right hand of the Lord is
  exalted;
The right hand of the Lord does
  valiantly.
¹⁷I will not die, but live,
  And declare the works *and* recount
  the illustrious acts of the Lord.
¹⁸The Lord has disciplined me
  severely,
But He has not given me over to
  death. [2 Cor 6:9]

¹⁹Open to me the [temple] gates of
  righteousness;
I shall enter through them, I shall
  give thanks to the Lord.
²⁰This is the gate of the Lord;
  The righteous will enter through
  it. [Ps 24:7]
²¹I will give thanks to You, for You
  have heard *and* answered me;
And You have become my
  salvation [my Rescuer, my
  Savior].

²²The stone which the builders
   rejected
 Has become the chief corner *stone*.
²³This is from the LORD *and* is His
   doing;
 It is marvelous in our eyes. [Matt
   21:42; Acts 4:11; 1 Pet 2:7]
²⁴This [day in which God has saved
   me] is the day which the LORD
   has made;

 Let us rejoice and be glad in it.
²⁵O LORD, save now, we beseech You;
 O LORD, we beseech You, send now
   prosperity *and* give us success!
²⁶Blessed is the one who comes in
   the name of the LORD;
 We have blessed you from the
   house of the LORD [you who come
   into His sanctuary under His
   guardianship]. [Mark 11:9, 10]

the right kind of fear

The psalmist says in Psalm 118:4 that he will reverently fear the Lord by declaring that His loving-kindness endures forever. As he worships God and talks about some of His great attributes, his faith is being strengthened.

Notice something interesting in Psalm 118:5. The psalmist tells how, in his distress, he called upon the Lord. But he did not do that until *after* he had worshiped the Lord and praised Him in verse 4 for the very attributes he was calling upon Him to display in his distressing situation. He continues by declaring: "The LORD is on my side; I will not fear. What can [mere] man do to me?" (Psalm 118:6).

Why should we fear? If Almighty God is for us, *and He is*, then what can mere human beings do to us? We definitely need to realize how big God is and how small our enemies are when compared to Him.

You may be worried about what people are going to do to you. You may be worried that someone is going to take your job away, that someone is not going to give you what you need. A person may treat you unfairly or may reject you. You may be worried about what somebody is going to think or say about you. I encourage you to be more concerned about what God thinks of you than what people think of you.

The Bible tells us that we are not to fear people, but that we are to reverently and worshipfully fear the Lord. When we refuse to fear others, but instead reverently and worshipfully fear God, then He moves on our behalf so that nothing anyone tries to do to us ever harms us permanently. Evil people may come against us one way, but they will have to flee before us "seven ways" (see Deuteronomy 28:7).

For a period of time it may seem as if someone is taking advantage of you. But if you keep your eyes on God and continue to worship Him, keeping your conversation in line with His Word, in the end God will reward you and bring justice because He is a God of justice. He loves justice and hates wrongdoing. God is our Vindicator, and He always makes wrong things right if we keep trusting Him long enough.

We need to retire from self-care and cast our cares upon the Lord. If we place our trust in God, nobody is going to take advantage of us—at least not for long. God has thousands of ways to get His blessings to us. When a door closes, He opens another one. If there are no doors, He makes one!

Do you find yourself in distress or afraid of people? Then do what the psalmist did. First focus on God's loving-kindness, and then encourage yourself with the knowledge that God is on your side.

27 The LORD is God, and He has given
us light [illuminating us with
His grace and freedom and joy].
Bind the festival sacrifices with
cords to the horns of the altar.
28 You are my God, and I give thanks
to You;
[You are] my God, I extol You.
29 O give thanks to the LORD, for He is
good;
For His lovingkindness endures
forever.

PSALM 119

Meditations and Prayers Relating to the Law of God.

א
Aleph.
1 HOW BLESSED *and* favored by God
are those whose way is blameless
[those with personal integrity, the
upright, the guileless],

life point

Psalm 119:1, 2 says that "those whose
way is blameless," who are guided by the
precepts of the Lord, and who keep His
testimonies and seek Him consistently
with all of their hearts can expect God's
blessing and favor. This is true in life's
good times and in its difficult seasons.

When you find yourself in a time of trial, try
not to simply focus on where you are right
now and what is happening to you at the
moment, but see yourself and your circumstances through the eyes of faith. You may
feel as though you are out in the middle of
an ocean with a storm raging around you,
but *you will get to the other side*. There are
blessings waiting for you there, *so do not
jump overboard!* Learn, as the psalmist did,
to walk in a way that is blameless and to
keep seeking God (see Psalm 119:1, 2). You
will be blessed and favored as you do!

Who walk in the law [and who
are guided by the precepts and
revealed will] of the LORD.
2 Blessed *and* favored by God are
those who keep His testimonies,
And who [consistently] seek Him
and long for Him with all their
heart.
3 They do no unrighteousness;
They walk in His ways. [1 John 3:9;
5:18]
4 You have ordained Your precepts,
That we should follow them with
[careful] diligence.
5 Oh, that my ways may be
established
To observe *and* keep Your statutes
[obediently accepting and
honoring them]!
6 Then I will not be ashamed
When I look [with respect] to all
Your commandments [as my
guide].
7 I will give thanks to You with an
upright heart,
When I learn [through discipline]
Your righteous judgments [for
my transgressions].
8 I shall keep Your statutes;
Do not utterly abandon me [when
I fail].

ב
Beth.
9 How can a young man keep his way
pure?
By keeping watch [on himself]
according to Your word
[conforming his life to Your
precepts].

life point

I believe Psalm 119:6 says what we need
to be saying in our hearts every day:
"God, if I will simply read Your Book, respect Your Commandments, and do what
You say, everything in my life will work
out for the best."

10 With all my heart I have sought
   You, [inquiring of You and
   longing for You];
 Do not let me wander from
   Your commandments [neither
   through ignorance nor by willful
   disobedience]. [2 Chr 15:15]
11 Your word I have treasured *and*
   stored in my heart,
 That I may not sin against You.
12 Blessed *and* reverently praised are
   You, O Lord;
 Teach me Your statutes.
13 With my lips I have told of
 All the ordinances of Your mouth.
14 I have rejoiced in the way of Your
   testimonies,
 As much as in all riches.
15 I will meditate on Your precepts
 And [thoughtfully] regard Your
   ways [the path of life established
   by Your precepts]. [Ps 104:34]
16 I will delight in Your statutes;
 I will not forget Your word.

ג
Gimel.

17 Deal bountifully with Your
   servant,
 That I may live and keep Your
   word [treasuring it and being
   guided by it day by day]. [Ps
   119:97–101]
18 Open my eyes [to spiritual truth]
   so that I may behold
 Wonderful things from Your law.
19 I am a stranger on the earth;
 Do not hide Your commandments
   from me. [Gen 47:9; 1 Chr 29:15;
   Ps 39:12; 2 Cor 5:6; Heb 11:13]
20 My soul is crushed with longing
 For Your ordinances at all times.

21 You rebuke the presumptuous *and*
   arrogant, the cursed *ones,*
 Who wander from Your
   commandments.
22 Take reproach and contempt away
   from me,
 For I observe Your testimonies.
23 Even though princes sit and talk to
   one another against me,
 Your servant meditates on Your
   statutes.
24 Your testimonies also are my
   delight
 And my counselors.

ד
Daleth.

25 My earthly life clings to the dust;
 Revive *and* refresh me according
   to Your word. [Ps 143:11]
26 I have told of my ways, and You
   have answered me;
 Teach me Your statutes.
27 Make me understand the way of
   Your precepts,

putting the Word to work

Have you ever been lost? Do you remember the relief you felt when someone was able to give you good directions? The best directions we have for living an abundant life that is pleasing to God are found in the Bible. Hide God's Word in your heart by studying and even memorizing Scripture verses and passages, so you will not sin against Him and will be able to live in His blessings (see Psalm 119:9–11).

speak the Word

Lord, I pray that You would open my eyes to spiritual truth so that I may behold wonderful things in Your Word.
–ADAPTED FROM PSALM 119:18

So that I will meditate (focus my thoughts) on Your wonderful works. [Ps 145:5, 6]

28 My soul dissolves because of grief; Renew *and* strengthen me according to [the promises of] Your word.

29 Remove from me the way of falsehood *and* unfaithfulness, And graciously grant me Your law.

30 I have chosen the faithful way; I have placed Your ordinances *before me*.

31 I cling tightly to Your testimonies; O LORD, do not put me to shame!

32 I will run the way of Your commandments [with purpose], For You will give me a heart that is willing.

ה
He.

33 Teach me, O LORD, the way of Your statutes, And I will [steadfastly] observe it to the end.

34 Give me understanding [a teachable heart and the ability to learn], that I may keep Your law; And observe it with all my heart. [Prov 2:6; James 1:5]

35 Make me walk in the path of Your commandments, For I delight in it.

36 Incline my heart to Your testimonies And not to *dishonest* gain *and* envy. [Ezek 33:31; Mark 7:21, 22; 1 Tim 6:10; Heb 13:5]

37 Turn my eyes away from vanity [all those worldly, meaningless things that distract—let Your priorities be mine], And restore me [with renewed energy] in Your ways.

38 Establish Your word *and* confirm Your promise to Your servant,

As that which produces [awe-inspired] reverence for You. [Deut 10:12; Ps 96:9]

39 Turn away my reproach which I dread, For Your ordinances are good.

40 I long for Your precepts; Renew me through Your righteousness.

ו
Vav.

41 May Your lovingkindness also come to me, O LORD, Your salvation according to Your promise;

42 So I will have an answer for the one who taunts me, For I trust [completely] in Your word [and its reliability].

43 And do not take the word of truth utterly out of my mouth, For I wait for Your ordinances.

44 I will keep Your law continually, Forever and ever [writing Your precepts on my heart].

45 And I will walk at liberty, For I seek *and* deeply long for Your precepts.

46 I will also speak of Your testimonies before kings And shall not be ashamed. [Ps 138:1; Matt 10:18, 19; Acts 26:1, 2]

47 For I shall delight in Your commandments, Which I love.

48 And I shall lift up my hands to Your commandments, Which I love; And I will meditate on Your statutes.

ז
Zayin.

49 Remember [always] the word *and* promise to Your servant, In which You have made me hope.

50 This is my comfort in my affliction,

That Your word has revived me
   and given me life. [Rom 15:4]
[51] The arrogant utterly ridicule me,
   Yet I do not turn away from Your
   law.
[52] I have remembered [carefully]
   Your ancient ordinances, O Lord,
   And I have taken comfort.
[53] Burning indignation has seized me
   because of the wicked,
   Who reject Your law.
[54] Your statutes are my songs
   In the house of my pilgrimage.
[55] O Lord, I remember Your name in
   the night,
   And keep Your law.
[56] This has become mine [as the gift
   of Your grace],
   That I observe Your precepts
   [accepting them with loving
   obedience].

ח
Heth.

[57] The Lord is my portion;
   I have promised to keep Your
   words.
[58] I sought Your favor with all my
   heart;
   Be merciful *and* gracious to me
   according to Your promise.
[59] I considered my ways
   And turned my feet to [follow and
   obey] Your testimonies.
[60] I hurried and did not delay
   To keep Your commandments.
[61] The cords of the wicked have
   encircled *and* ensnared me,
   But I have not forgotten Your law.
[62] At midnight I will rise to give
   thanks to You
   Because of Your righteous
   ordinances.
[63] I am a companion of all who
   [reverently] fear You,
   And of those who keep *and* honor
   Your precepts.
[64] The earth, O Lord, is full of Your
   lovingkindness *and* goodness;
   Teach me Your statutes.

ט
Teth.

[65] You have dealt well with Your
   servant,
   O Lord, according to Your promise.
[66] Teach me good judgment
   (discernment) and knowledge,
   For I have believed *and* trusted *and*
   relied on Your commandments.
[67] Before I was afflicted I went
   astray,
   But now I keep *and* honor Your
   word [with loving obedience].
[68] You are good and do good;
   Teach me Your statutes.
[69] The arrogant have forged a lie
   against me,
   But I will keep Your precepts with
   all my heart.
[70] Their heart is insensitive like fat
   [their minds are dull and brutal],
   But I delight in Your law.
[71] It is good for me that I have been
   afflicted,
   That I may learn Your statutes.
[72] The law from Your mouth is better
   to me
   Than thousands of gold and silver
   pieces.

י
Yodh.

[73] Your hands have made me and
   established me;
   Give me understanding *and* a
   teachable heart, that I may learn
   Your commandments.
[74] May those who [reverently] fear
   You see me and be glad,
   Because I wait for Your word.
[75] I know, O Lord, that Your
   judgments are fair,
   And that in faithfulness You have
   disciplined me. [Heb 12:10]
[76] O may Your lovingkindness *and*
   graciousness comfort me,
   According to Your word (promise)
   to Your servant.

77 Let Your compassion come to me
    that I may live,
For Your law is my delight.
78 Let the arrogant be ashamed *and*
    humiliated, for they sabotage me
    with a lie;
But I will meditate on Your precepts.
79 May those who fear You [with
    submissive wonder] turn to me,
Even those who have known Your
    testimonies.
80 May my heart be blameless in Your
    statutes,
So that I will not be ashamed.

כ

Kaph.

81 My soul languishes *and* grows
    weak for Your salvation;
I wait for Your word.
82 My eyes fail [with longing,
    watching] for [the fulfillment of]
    Your promise,
Saying, "When will You comfort
    me?"
83 For I have become like a wineskin
    [blackened and shriveled] in the
    smoke [in which it hangs],
Yet I do not forget Your statutes.
84 How many are the days of Your
    servant [which he must endure]?
When will You execute judgment
    on those who persecute me?
    [Rev 6:10]
85 The arrogant (godless) have dug
    pits for me,
Men who do not conform to Your law.
86 All Your commandments are
    faithful *and* trustworthy.
They have persecuted me with a
    lie; help me [Lord]!
87 They had almost destroyed me on
    earth,
But as for me, I did not turn away
    from Your precepts.
88 According to Your steadfast love
    refresh me *and* give me life,
So that I may keep *and* obey the
    testimony of Your mouth.

ל

Lamedh.

89 Forever, O Lord,
Your word is settled in heaven
    [standing firm and unchangeable].
    [Ps 89:2; Matt 24:34, 35; 1 Pet 1:25]
90 Your faithfulness *continues* from
    generation to generation;
You have established the earth,
    and it stands [securely].
91 They continue this day according
    to Your ordinances,
For all things [all parts of the
    universe] are Your servants.
    [Jer 33:25]
92 If Your law had not been my
    delight,
Then I would have perished in my
    time of trouble.
93 I will never forget Your precepts,
For by them You have revived me
    and given me life.
94 I am Yours, save me [as Your own];
For I have [diligently] sought Your
    precepts *and* required them [as
    my greatest need]. [Ps 42:1]
95 The wicked wait for me to destroy
    me,
But I will consider Your testimonies.
96 I have seen that all [human]
    perfection has its limits [no
    matter how grand and perfect
    and noble];
Your commandment is exceedingly
    broad *and* extends without limits
    [into eternity]. [Rom 3:10–19]

מ

Mem.

97 Oh, how I love Your law!
It is my meditation all the day.
    [Ps 1:2]
98 Your commandments make me
    wiser than my enemies,
For Your words are always
    with me.

⁹⁹ I have better understanding
   and deeper insight than all
   my teachers [because of Your
   word],
   For Your testimonies are my
   meditation. [2 Tim 3:15]
¹⁰⁰ I understand more than the aged
   [who have not observed Your
   precepts],
   Because I have observed *and* kept
   Your precepts.
¹⁰¹ I have restrained my feet from
   every evil way,
   That I may keep Your word. [Prov
   1:15]
¹⁰² I have not turned aside from Your
   ordinances,
   For You Yourself have taught me.
¹⁰³ How sweet are Your words to my
   taste,
   Sweeter than honey to my mouth!
   [Ps 19:10; Prov 8:11]
¹⁰⁴ From Your precepts I get
   understanding;
   Therefore I hate every false way.

ב

Nun.

¹⁰⁵ Your word is a lamp to my feet
   And a light to my path. [Prov 6:23]
¹⁰⁶ I have sworn [an oath] and have
   confirmed it,
   That I will keep Your righteous
   ordinances. [Neh 10:29]
¹⁰⁷ I am greatly afflicted;

putting the Word to work

Wandering around in the dark can be
scary and frustrating! Do you ever
feel that you are wandering in life, not
sure of which way to go? Learn God's
Word; it is a lamp to your feet and a
light to your path (see Psalm 119:105).
God promises to use His Word to
instruct you in the way you are to go,
one step at a time!

Renew *and* revive me [giving me
   life], O LORD, according to Your
   word.
¹⁰⁸ Accept *and* take pleasure in the
   freewill offerings of my mouth,
   O LORD,
   And teach me Your ordinances.
   [Hos 14:2; Heb 13:15]
¹⁰⁹ My life is continually in my hand,
   Yet I do not forget Your law.
¹¹⁰ The wicked have laid a snare for
   me,
   Yet I do not wander from Your
   precepts.
¹¹¹ I have taken Your testimonies as a
   heritage forever,
   For they are the joy of my heart.
   [Deut 33:4]
¹¹² I have inclined my heart to
   perform Your statutes
   Forever, even to the end.

ס

Samekh.

¹¹³ I hate those who are double-
   minded,
   But I love *and* treasure Your law.
¹¹⁴ You are my hiding place and my
   shield;
   I wait for Your word. [Ps 32:7; 91:1]
¹¹⁵ Leave me, you evildoers,
   That I may keep the
   commandments of my God
   [honoring and obeying them].
   [Ps 6:8; 139:19; Matt 7:23]
¹¹⁶ Uphold me according to Your word
   [of promise], so that I may live;
   And do not let me be ashamed
   of my hope [in Your great
   goodness]. [Ps 25:2; Rom 5:5;
   9:33; 10:11]
¹¹⁷ Uphold me that I may be safe,
   That I may have regard for Your
   statutes continually.
¹¹⁸ You have turned Your back on all
   those who wander from Your
   statutes,
   For their deceitfulness is useless.

119 You have removed all the wicked
   of the earth like dross [for they
   have no value];
   Therefore I love Your testimonies.
120 My flesh trembles in [reverent]
   fear of You,
   And I am afraid *and* in awe of
   Your judgments.

ע
Ayin.

121 I have done justice and
   righteousness;
   Do not leave me to those who
   oppress me.
122 Be the guarantee for Your servant
   for good [as Judah was the
   guarantee for Benjamin];
   Do not let the arrogant oppress
   me. [Gen 43:9]
123 My eyes fail [with longing,
   watching] for [the fulfillment
   of] Your salvation,
   And for [the fulfillment of] Your
   righteous word.
124 Deal with Your servant
   according to Your [gracious]
   lovingkindness,
   And teach me Your statutes.
125 I am Your servant; give me
   understanding [the ability to
   learn and a teachable heart]
   That I may know Your
   testimonies.
126 It is time for the Lord to act;
   They have broken Your law.
127 Therefore I love Your
   commandments more than gold,
   Yes, more than refined gold.
128 Therefore I esteem as right all Your
   precepts concerning everything;
   I hate every false way.

פ
Pe.

129 Your testimonies are wonderful;
   Therefore my soul keeps them.
130 The unfolding of Your [glorious]
   words give light;

life point

According to Psalm 119:130, the unfolding
of God's Word brings light, which is something we all need. We do not always know
or see what we need to do, and many times
we do not recognize our own problems. We
need God's light to understand ourselves
and to see how we need to change and how
we can cooperate with God to make things
better. Reading God's Word is like looking
in a mirror. It enables us to see what needs
to be cleaned up in our lives.

   Their unfolding gives
   understanding to the simple
   (childlike).
131 I opened my mouth and panted
   [with anticipation],
   Because I longed for Your
   commandments.
132 Turn to me and be gracious to me
   and show me favor,
   As is Your way to those who love
   Your name.
133 Establish my footsteps in [the way
   of] Your word;
   Do not let any human weakness
   have power over me [causing
   me to be separated from You].
134 Redeem me from the oppression
   of man;
   That I may keep Your precepts.
   [Luke 1:74]
135 Make Your face shine [with
   pleasure] upon Your servant,
   And teach me Your statutes. [Ps 4:6]
136 My eyes weep streams of water
   Because people do not keep Your
   law.

צ
Tsadhe.

137 Righteous are You, O Lord,
   And upright are Your judgments.
138 You have commanded Your
   testimonies in righteousness
   And in great faithfulness.

¹³⁹ My zeal has [completely] consumed
me,
  Because my enemies have
  forgotten Your words.
¹⁴⁰ Your word is very pure (refined);
  Therefore Your servant loves it.
¹⁴¹ I am small and despised,
  But I do not forget Your precepts.
¹⁴² Your righteousness is an
  everlasting righteousness,
  And Your law is truth. [Ps 19:9;
  John 17:17]
¹⁴³ Trouble and anguish have found
me,
  Yet Your commandments are my
  delight *and* my joy.
¹⁴⁴ Your righteous testimonies are
  everlasting;
  Give me understanding [the
  ability to learn and a teachable
  heart] that I may live.

ק

Qoph.

¹⁴⁵ I cried with all my heart; answer
me, O Lord!
  I will observe Your statutes.
¹⁴⁶ I cried to You; save me
  And I will keep Your testimonies.
¹⁴⁷ I rise before dawn and cry [in
  prayer] for help;
  I wait for Your word.
¹⁴⁸ My eyes anticipate the night
  watches *and* I awake before the
  call of the watchman,
  That I may meditate on Your word.
¹⁴⁹ Hear my voice according to Your
  [steadfast] lovingkindness;
  O Lord, renew *and* refresh me
  according to Your ordinances.
¹⁵⁰ Those who follow after
  wickedness approach;
  They are far from Your law.
¹⁵¹ You are near, O Lord,
  And all Your commandments are
  truth.
¹⁵² Of old I have known from Your
  testimonies
  That You have founded them
  forever. [Luke 21:33]

ר

Resh.

¹⁵³ Look upon my agony and rescue
me,
  For I do not forget Your law.
¹⁵⁴ Plead my cause and redeem me;
  Revive me *and* give me life
  according to [the promise of]
  Your word.
¹⁵⁵ Salvation is far from the wicked,
  For they do not seek Your
  statutes.
¹⁵⁶ Great are Your tender mercies *and*
  steadfast love, O Lord;
  Revive me *and* give me life
  according to Your ordinances.
¹⁵⁷ Many are my persecutors and my
  adversaries,
  Yet I do not turn away from Your
  testimonies.
¹⁵⁸ I see the treacherous and loathe
  them,
  Because they do not respect Your
  law.
¹⁵⁹ Consider how I love Your precepts;
  Revive me *and* give me life,
  O Lord, according to Your
  lovingkindness.
¹⁶⁰ The sum of Your word is truth
  [the full meaning of all Your
  precepts],
  And every one of Your righteous
  ordinances endures forever.

ש

Shin.

¹⁶¹ Princes persecute me without
  cause,
  But my heart stands in [reverent]
  awe of Your words [so I can
  expect You to help me]. [1 Sam
  24:11, 14; 26:18]
¹⁶² I rejoice at Your word,
  As one who finds great treasure.
¹⁶³ I hate and detest falsehood,
  But I love Your law.
¹⁶⁴ Seven times a day I praise You,
  Because of Your righteous
  ordinances.

165 Those who love Your law have
        great peace;
    Nothing makes them stumble.
        [Prov 3:2; Is 32:17]
166 I hope *and* wait [with complete
        confidence] for Your salvation,
        O LORD,
    And I do Your commandments.
        [Gen 49:18]
167 My soul keeps Your testimonies
        [hearing and accepting and
        obeying them];
    I love them greatly.
168 I keep Your precepts and Your
        testimonies,
    For all my ways are [fully known]
        before You.

ת

Tav.

169 Let my [mournful] cry come
        before You, O LORD;
    Give me understanding [the
        ability to learn and a teachable
        heart] according to Your word
        [of promise].
170 Let my supplication come before
        You;
    Deliver me according to Your
        word.
171 Let my lips speak praise [with
        thanksgiving],
    For You teach me Your statutes.
172 Let my tongue sing [praise for the
        fulfillment] of Your word,
    For all Your commandments are
        righteous.
173 Let Your hand be ready to help me,
    For I have chosen Your precepts.
174 I long for Your salvation, O LORD,
    And Your law is my delight.
175 Let my soul live that it may praise
        You,
    And let Your ordinances help me.
176 I have gone astray like a lost sheep;
    Seek Your servant, for I do not
        forget Your commandments. [Is
        53:6; Luke 15:4; 1 Pet 2:25]

PSALM 120

Prayer for Breaking Away
from the Treacherous.

A Song of Ascents.

1 IN MY trouble I cried to the LORD,
    And He answered me.
2 Rescue my soul, O LORD, from lying
        lips,
    And from a deceitful tongue.
3 What shall be given to you, and
        what more shall be done to you,
    You deceitful tongue?—
4 Sharp arrows of the warrior,
    With the burning coals of the
        broom tree.

5 Woe to me, for I sojourn in Meshech,
    and I live among the tents of Kedar
        [among hostile people]! [Gen
        10:2; 25:13; Jer 49:28, 29]
6 Too long my soul has had its
        dwelling
    With those who hate peace.
7 I am for peace, but when I speak,
    They are for war.

PSALM 121

The LORD the Keeper of Israel.

A Song of Ascents.

1 I WILL lift up my eyes to the hills
        [of Jerusalem]—
    From where shall my help come?
        [Jer 3:23]
2 My help comes from the LORD,
    Who made heaven and earth.
3 He will not allow your foot to slip;
    He who keeps you will not
        slumber. [1 Sam 2:9; Ps 127:1;
        Prov 3:23, 26; Is 27:3]
4 Behold, He who keeps Israel
    Will neither slumber [briefly] nor
        sleep [soundly].

5 The LORD is your keeper;
    The LORD is your shade on your
        right hand. [Is 25:4]
6 The sun will not strike you by day,

seek God first

We should be mature enough in our faith that we do not run to somebody else every time we need to know what to do in a certain situation. I am not implying that it is wrong to go to people we feel are wiser than we are to ask for a word of counsel or advice. But I do believe it is wrong, and insulting to God, to go to people too often. Having someone give us advice is not necessarily a problem; the problem comes when we seek man rather than God. God is a jealous God (see James 4:5 and Deuteronomy 4:24), and He wants us to ask for His advice.

It is important to clearly establish in our hearts that we will seek God first, as David did in Psalm 121:1–2. God wants to guide each one of us, every person who truly trusts Him.

I encourage you to seek balance in this area and to wean yourself from seeking other people's opinions if you have a consistent habit of doing so. Discipline yourself to go to God first, and let Him choose whether He wants to speak to you Himself or use the counsel of other believers to clarify things for you.

Nor the moon by night. [Ps 91:5; Is 49:10; Rev 7:16]
7 The LORD will protect you from all evil;
He will keep your life.
8 The LORD will guard your going out and your coming in [everything that you do]
From this time forth and forever. [Deut 28:6; Prov 2:8; 3:6]

PSALM 122

Prayer for the Peace of Jerusalem.

A Song of Ascents. Of David.

1 I WAS glad when they said to me, "Let us go to the house of the LORD." [Is 2:3; Zech 8:21]
2 Our feet are standing
Within your gates, O Jerusalem,
3 Jerusalem, that is built

As a city that is firmly joined together;
4 To which the [twelve] tribes go up, even the tribes of the LORD,
[As was decreed as] an ordinance for Israel,
To give thanks to the name of the LORD.
5 For there the thrones of judgment were set,
The thrones of the house of David.
6 Pray for the peace of Jerusalem: "May they prosper who love you [holy city].
7 "May peace be within your walls
And prosperity within your palaces."
8 For the sake of my brothers and my friends,
I will now say, "May peace be within you."

speak the Word

God, I declare that my help comes from You. You will not allow my foot to slip. You are my keeper and You do not slumber or sleep. You are the shade on my right hand. You will protect me from all evil. You will keep my life and guard my going out and my coming in forever.
—ADAPTED FROM PSALM 121:2–8

⁹For the sake of the house of
the LORD our God [which is
Jerusalem],
I will seek your (the city's) good.

PSALM 123

Prayer for the LORD's Help.

A Song of Ascents.

¹UNTO YOU I lift up my eyes,
O You who are enthroned in the
heavens!
²Behold, as the eyes of servants
look to the hand of their master,
And as the eyes of a maid to the
hand of her mistress,
So our eyes look to the LORD our God,
Until He is gracious *and* favorable
toward us.

³Be gracious to us, O LORD, be
gracious *and* favorable toward us,
For we are greatly filled with
contempt.
⁴Our soul is greatly filled
With the scoffing of those who are
at ease,
And with the contempt of the
proud [who disregard God's law].

PSALM 124

Praise for Rescue from Enemies.

A Song of Ascents. Of David.

¹"IF IT had not been the LORD who
was on our side,"
Let Israel now say,
²"If it had not been the LORD who
was on our side
When men rose up against us,
³Then they would have [quickly]
swallowed us alive,
When their wrath was kindled
against us;
⁴Then the waters would have
engulfed us,
The torrent would have swept over
our soul;
⁵Then the raging waters would
have swept over our soul."

⁶Blessed be the LORD,
Who has not given us as prey to be
torn by their teeth.
⁷We have escaped like a bird from
the snare of the fowlers;
The trap is broken and we have
escaped.
⁸Our help is in the name of the LORD,
Who made heaven and earth.

PSALM 125

The LORD Surrounds His People.

A Song of Ascents.

¹THOSE WHO trust in *and* rely
on the LORD [with confident
expectation]
Are like Mount Zion, which cannot
be moved but remains forever.
²As the mountains surround
Jerusalem,
So the LORD surrounds His people
From this time forth and forever.
³For the scepter of wickedness
shall not rest on the land of the
righteous,
So that the righteous will not reach
out their hands to do wrong.

⁴Do good, O LORD, to those who are
good
And to those who are upright in
their hearts.
⁵But as for those who turn aside
to their crooked ways [in
unresponsiveness to God],
The LORD will lead them away with
those who do evil.
Peace be upon Israel.

life point

God is for us; He is on our side (see Psalm
118:6). The devil has one position: he
is against us. But God is over us, under
us, through us, for us, and He surrounds
us. So like Mount Zion we should not be
moved, because God is all around us
(see Psalm 125:1, 2).

PSALM 126

Thanksgiving for Return from Captivity.

A Song of Ascents.

¹WHEN THE LORD brought back
the captives to Zion (Jerusalem),
We were like those who dream [it
seemed so unreal]. [Ps 53:6; Acts
12:9]
²Then our mouth was filled with
laughter

And our tongue with joyful
shouting;
Then they said among the nations,
"The LORD has done great things
for them."
³The LORD has done great things for
us;
We are glad!

⁴Restore our captivity, O LORD,
As the stream-beds in the South
(the Negev) [are restored by
torrents of rain].

fill your mouth with laughter

Psalm 126:2, 3 speak of laughter and joy. I once watched a Christian television talk show in which the participants were talking about a laughing revival that took place in various parts of the world at one time. Someone asked the host of the show if he thought it was of God.

"Does it offend your mind?" the host asked.

"Yes, it does," answered the person who had raised the question.

"Well, then," responded the host, "it is probably of God."

Have you ever noticed that Jesus offended people who were falsely religious? It sometimes seemed He did it on purpose. In Matthew 15:12 Jesus' disciples said to Him, "Do You know that the Pharisees were offended when they heard You say this?" Jesus' answer to them was: "Leave them alone; they are blind guides [leading blind followers]. If a blind man leads a blind man, both will fall into a pit" (Matthew 15:14). If we are going to follow God, we need to realize that our minds may not always understand everything He does. Stop checking with your mind and start asking if you bear witness in your spirit to what is happening. We often reject things and movements that are genuinely of God simply because we have never seen them and do not understand them in our minds.

We must guard against developing an attitude like the Pharisees' in our hearts and attitudes. If the truth were known, the church today is full of Pharisees. I used to be one of them. In fact, I was a chief Pharisee. I was rigid, legalistic, boring, out to impress others, humorless, critical, and judgmental. I was on my way to heaven, but I was not enjoying the trip.

It is okay for us to relax a bit. Jesus was sent into this world not to bind us up, but to set us free. We need to be free to laugh, enjoy life, love people, and not be afraid to step out and try new things.

Now, I do not mean we are to go through life trying to see how ridiculous we can act. I am not talking about weirdness and fanaticism; I am talking about freedom and joy. I am talking about freely following the leading of the Holy Spirit. Go ahead, laugh a little. God will not be offended; He wants you to be joyful!

⁵They who sow in tears shall reap
   with joyful singing.
⁶He who goes back and forth
   weeping, carrying his bag of
   seed [for planting],
 Will indeed come again with a
   shout of joy, bringing his sheaves
   with him.

PSALM 127

Prosperity Comes from the LORD.

A Song of Ascents. Of Solomon.

¹UNLESS THE LORD builds the
   house,
 They labor in vain who build it;
 Unless the LORD guards the city,
 The watchman keeps awake in
   vain. [Ps 121:1, 3, 5]
²It is vain for you to rise early,
 To retire late,
 To eat the bread of anxious labors—
 For He gives [blessings] to His
   beloved *even in his* sleep.

³Behold, children are a heritage *and*
   gift from the LORD,
 The fruit of the womb a reward.
   [Deut 28:4]
⁴Like arrows in the hand of a
   warrior,
 So are the children of one's youth.
⁵How blessed [happy and
   fortunate] is the man whose
   quiver is filled with them;
 They will not be ashamed

life point

According to Psalm 127:1, unless the Lord
builds the house, those who build it labor
in vain. We may be able to build, but what
we build will not last if God is not involved
in it. He is our Partner in life, and as such,
He desires to be a part of everything we
do. God is interested in every facet of our
lives. Believing that truth is the beginning
of an exciting journey with Him.

When they speak with their enemies
   [in gatherings] at the [city] gate.

PSALM 128

Blessedness of the Fear
of the LORD.

A Song of Ascents.

¹BLESSED [HAPPY and sheltered
   by God's favor] is everyone who
   fears the LORD [and worships
   Him with obedience],
 Who walks in His ways *and*
   lives according to His
   commandments. [Ps 1:1, 2]
²For you shall eat the fruit of [the
   labor of] your hands,
 You will be happy *and* blessed and
   it will be well with you.
³Your wife shall be like a fruitful
   vine
 Within the innermost part of your
   house;
 Your children will be like olive
   plants
 Around your table.
⁴Behold, for so shall the man be
   blessed *and* divinely favored
 Who fears the LORD [and worships
   Him with obedience].

⁵May the LORD bless you from Zion
   [His holy mountain],
 And may you see the prosperity of
   Jerusalem all the days of your life;
⁶Indeed, may you see your [family
   perpetuated in your] children's
   children.
 Peace be upon Israel!

PSALM 129

Prayer for the Overthrow of Zion's
Enemies.

A Song of Ascents.

¹"MANY TIMES they have
   persecuted me (Israel) from my
   youth,"
 Let Israel now say,

2 "Many times they have persecuted
   me from my youth,
   Yet they have not prevailed
   against me.
3 "The [enemies, like] plowers
   plowed on my back;
   They made their furrows [of
   suffering] long [in Israel]."
4 The LORD is righteous;
   He has cut in two the [thick] cords
   of the wicked [which enslaved
   the people of Israel].

5 May all who hate Zion
   Be put to shame and turned
   backward [in defeat].
6 Let them be like the grass on the
   housetops,
   Which withers before it grows up,
7 With which the reaper does not fill
   his hand,
   Nor the binder of sheaves his arms,
8 Nor do those who pass by say,
   "The blessing of the LORD be upon
   you;
   We bless you in the name of the
   LORD."

PSALM 130

Hope in the LORD's Forgiving Love.

A Song of Ascents.

1 OUT OF the depths [of distress] I
   have cried to You, O LORD.
2 Lord, hear my voice!
   Let Your ears be attentive
   To the voice of my supplications.
3 If You, LORD, should keep an
   account of our sins and treat us
   accordingly,
   O Lord, who could stand [before
   you in judgment and claim
   innocence]? [Ps 143:2; Rom 3:20;
   Gal 2:16]

4 But there is forgiveness with You,
   That You may be feared and
   worshiped [with submissive
   wonder]. [Deut 10:12]
5 I wait [patiently] for the LORD, my
   soul [expectantly] waits,
   And in His word do I hope.
6 My soul waits for the Lord
   More than the watchmen for the
   morning;
   More than the watchmen for the
   morning.
7 O Israel, hope in the LORD;
   For with the LORD there is
   lovingkindness,
   And with Him is abundant
   redemption.
8 And He will redeem Israel
   From all his sins.

PSALM 131

Childlike Trust in the LORD.

A Song of Ascents. Of David.

1 LORD, MY heart is not proud, nor
   my eyes haughty;
   Nor do I involve myself in great
   matters,
   Or in things too difficult for me.
2 Surely I have calmed and quieted
   my soul;
   Like a weaned child [resting] with
   his mother,
   My soul is like a weaned child
   within me [composed and freed
   from discontent].
3 O Israel, hope in the LORD
   From this time forth and
   forever.

speak the Word

Lord, I wait patiently for You, and in Your Word my soul expectantly waits.
—ADAPTED FROM PSALM 130:5

PSALM 132

Prayer for the LORD's Blessing Upon the Sanctuary.

A Song of Ascents.

1 O LORD, remember on David's
    behalf
All his hardship *and* affliction;
2 How he swore to the LORD
And vowed to the Mighty One of
    Jacob:
3 "I absolutely will not enter my
    house,
Nor get into my bed—
4 I certainly will not permit my eyes
    to sleep
Nor my eyelids to slumber,
5 Until I find a place for the LORD,
A dwelling place for the Mighty
    One of Jacob (Israel)." [Acts 7:46]

6 Behold, we heard of it at
    Ephrathah;
We found it in the field of Jaar.
    [1 Sam 6:21]
7 Let us go into His tabernacle;
Let us worship at His footstool.
8 Arise, O LORD, to Your resting place,
You and the ark [the symbol] of
    Your strength.
9 Let Your priests be clothed with
    righteousness (right living),
And let Your godly ones shout for
    joy.

10 For the sake of Your servant
    David,
Do not turn away the face of Your
    anointed.
11 The LORD swore to David
A truth from which He will not
    turn back:
"One of your descendants I will
    set upon your throne. [Ps 89:3, 4;
    Luke 1:69; Acts 2:30, 31]
12 "If your children will keep My
    covenant
And My testimony which I will
    teach them,

Their children also shall sit upon
    your throne forever."

13 For the LORD has chosen Zion;
He has desired it for His dwelling
    place:
14 "This is My resting place forever"
    [says the LORD];
"Here will I dwell, for I have
    desired it.
15 "I will abundantly bless her
    provisions;
I will satisfy her poor with bread.
16 "Her priests also I will clothe with
    salvation,
And her godly ones will shout
    aloud for joy.
17 "There I will make the horn
    (strength) of David grow;
I have prepared a lamp for
    My anointed [fulfilling the
    promises]. [1 Kin 11:36; 15:4;
    2 Chr 21:7; Luke 1:69]
18 "His enemies I will clothe with
    shame,
But upon himself shall his crown
    shine."

PSALM 133

The Excellency of Brotherly Unity.

A Song of Ascents. Of David.

1 BEHOLD, HOW good and how
    pleasant it is
For brothers to dwell together in
    unity!
2 It is like the precious oil [of
    consecration] poured on the
    head,
Coming down on the beard,
Even the beard of Aaron,
Coming down upon the edge of his
    [priestly] robes [consecrating
    the whole body]. [Ex 30:25, 30]
3 It is like the dew of [Mount]
    Hermon
Coming down on the hills of Zion;
For there the LORD has commanded
    the blessing: life forevermore.

PSALM 134
Greetings of Night Watchers.
A Song of Ascents.

¹BEHOLD, BLESS *and* praise the LORD, all servants of the LORD (priests, Levites),

Who stand *and* serve by night in the house of the LORD. [1 Chr 9:33]
²Lift up your hands to the sanctuary
And bless the LORD.
³May the LORD bless you from Zion,
He who made heaven and earth.

getting rid of "what-if"

Our oldest son, David, and his wife once needed a place to live temporarily. They had just sold their mobile home, and their newly purchased house would not be ready for a month. Of course, my husband and I invited them to live with us, even though I was a bit wary. My son and I are alike in many ways; we are both strong-willed, which does not always mix well in close quarters. Nothing negative had happened between us, but in anticipation of this move my mind kept coming up with "what-ifs."

My husband and I would be driving down the road, and my mouth would want to start talking about negative things that could take place: "What if there is no hot water left for my shower in the morning after everyone else is finished? What if they leave messes for me to clean up?" David and his wife had not even moved in, and nothing bad had yet happened. But my mouth wanted to declare disaster ahead of time.

The enemy wanted me to prophesy my future. He wanted me to be critical of the situation in advance.

If the devil can get us to be negative, he can provide us with negative circumstances. Often we call for our own problems. We "call into being that which does not exist" (see Romans 4:17), only we do it in the negative sense by sowing negative seeds.

Look at it this way: My blender works regardless of what is placed in it. If I put ice cream and milk in it, I will get a milkshake. If I put in water and dirt, I will get mud. The blender works. It is created to work. It is up to me to decide what I will put in it. What I put in is what I will get out. The same is true with our minds and hearts and mouths. What goes in is what is going to come out—for good or for bad.

Our son and daughter-in-law did live with us for a month, and everything worked out fine. I knew enough biblical principles by then to resist the temptation to complain in advance, and I urge you to beware of this temptation also. When I was tempted to speak negative words, I would choose to say, "This will work out fine. I am sure everyone will cooperate and be sensitive to the needs of the others."

My son and I made a joke about our challenge of getting along for thirty days under the same roof. We both like to be right, so he said, "I'll tell you what, Mom. Let's take turns being right. During the thirty days we are together, you can be right fifteen days, and I will be right fifteen days." We both laughed and had a good time. But the point is that I learned to discard "what-if" and accepted the blessing of pleasant unity in my home (see Psalm 133:1).

PSALM 135

Praise the LORD's Wonderful Works. Vanity of Idols.

¹PRAISE THE LORD! (Hallelujah!)
Praise the name of the LORD;
Praise Him, O servants of the LORD
(priests, Levites),
²You who stand in the house of the
LORD,
In the courts of the house of our
God,
³Praise the LORD, for the LORD is good;
Sing praises to His name, for it is
gracious *and* lovely.
⁴For the LORD has chosen [the
descendants of] Jacob for Himself,
Israel for His own special treasure
and possession. [Deut 7:6]

⁵For I know that the LORD is great
And that our Lord is above all gods.
⁶Whatever the LORD pleases, He does,
In the heavens and on the earth, in
the seas and all deeps—
⁷Who causes the clouds to rise from
the ends of the earth;
Who makes lightning for the rain,
Who brings the wind from His
storehouses;

⁸Who struck the firstborn of Egypt,
Both of man and animal; [Ex 12:12,
29; Ps 78:51; 136:10]
⁹Who sent signs and wonders into
your midst, O Egypt,
Upon Pharaoh and all his servants.
¹⁰Who struck many nations
And killed mighty kings,
¹¹Sihon, king of the Amorites,
Og, king of Bashan,
And all the kingdoms of Canaan;
¹²And He gave their land as a heritage,
A heritage to Israel His people.
¹³Your name, O LORD, endures
forever,
Your fame *and* remembrance,
O LORD, [endures] throughout all
generations.
¹⁴For the LORD will judge His people

And He will have compassion
on His servants [revealing His
mercy]. [Heb 10:30]
¹⁵The idols of the nations are silver
and gold,
The work of men's hands.
¹⁶They have mouths, but they do not
speak;
They have eyes, but they do not see;
¹⁷They have ears, but they do not hear,
Nor is there any breath in their
mouths.
¹⁸Those who make idols are like
them [absolutely worthless—
spiritually blind, deaf, and
powerless];
So is everyone who trusts in *and*
relies on them. [Ps 115:4–8]

¹⁹O house of Israel, bless *and* praise
the LORD [with gratitude];
O house of Aaron, bless the LORD;
²⁰O house of Levi, bless the LORD;
You who fear the LORD [and worship
Him with obedience], bless the
LORD [with grateful praise]! [Deut
6:5; Ps 31:23]
²¹Blessed be the LORD from Zion,
Who dwells [with us] at Jerusalem.
Praise the LORD! (Hallelujah!)

PSALM 136

Thanks for the LORD's Goodness to Israel.

¹GIVE THANKS to the LORD, for He
is good;
For His lovingkindness
(graciousness, mercy,
compassion) endures forever.
²Give thanks to the God of gods,
For His lovingkindness endures
forever.
³Give thanks to the Lord of lords,
For His lovingkindness endures
forever.
⁴To Him who alone does great
wonders,

For His lovingkindness endures forever;

5 To Him who made the heavens with skill,
For His lovingkindness endures forever;

6 To Him who stretched out the earth upon the waters,
For His lovingkindness endures forever;

7 To Him who made the great lights,
For His lovingkindness endures forever;

8 The sun to rule over the day,
For His lovingkindness endures forever;

9 The moon and stars to rule by night,
For His lovingkindness endures forever;

10 To Him who struck the firstborn of Egypt,
For His lovingkindness endures forever; [Ex 12:29]

11 And brought Israel out from among them,
For His lovingkindness endures forever; [Ex 12:51; 13:3, 17]

12 With a strong hand and with an outstretched arm,
For His lovingkindness endures forever;

13 To Him who divided the Red Sea into parts,
For His lovingkindness endures forever; [Ex 14:21, 22]

14 And made Israel pass through the midst of it,
For His lovingkindness endures forever;

15 But tossed Pharaoh and his army into the Red Sea,

For His lovingkindness endures forever;

16 To Him who led His people through the wilderness,
For His lovingkindness endures forever;

17 To Him who struck down great kings,
For His lovingkindness endures forever;

18 And killed mighty kings,
For His lovingkindness endures forever; [Deut 29:7]

19 Sihon, king of the Amorites,
For His lovingkindness endures forever; [Num 21:21–24]

20 And Og, king of Bashan,
For His lovingkindness endures forever; [Num 21:33–35]

21 And gave their land as a heritage,
For His lovingkindness endures forever;

22 Even a heritage to Israel His servant,
For His lovingkindness endures forever; [Josh 12:1]

23 Who [faithfully] remembered us in our lowly condition,
For His lovingkindness endures forever;

24 And has rescued us from our enemies,
For His lovingkindness endures forever;

25 Who gives food to all flesh,
For His lovingkindness endures forever;

26 Give thanks to the God of heaven,
For His lovingkindness (graciousness, mercy, compassion) endures forever.

speak the Word

Thank You, Lord, that Your hand is strong and Your arm is outstretched toward me.
—ADAPTED FROM PSALM 136:12

PSALM 137

An Experience of the Captivity.

¹ BY THE rivers of Babylon,
There we [captives] sat down and
wept,
When we remembered Zion
[the city God imprinted on our
hearts].
² On the willow trees in the midst of
Babylon
We hung our harps.
³ For there they who took us captive
demanded of us a song with
words,
And our tormentors [who made
a mockery of us demanded]
amusement, *saying,*
"Sing us one of the songs of Zion."

⁴ How can we sing the LORD's song
In a strange *and* foreign land?
⁵ If I forget you, O Jerusalem,
Let my right hand forget [her skill
with the harp].
⁶ Let my tongue cling to the roof of
my mouth
If I do not remember you,
If I do not prefer Jerusalem
Above my chief joy. [Ezek 3:26]

⁷ Remember, O LORD, against the
sons of Edom,
The day of [the fall of] Jerusalem,
Who said "Down, down [with her]
To her very foundation."
⁸ O daughter of Babylon, you
devastator,
How blessed will be the one
Who repays you [with destruction]
as you have repaid us. [Is 13:1–22;
Jer 25:12, 13]
⁹ How blessed will be the one who
seizes and dashes your little ones
Against the rock.

PSALM 138

Thanksgiving for the LORD's Favor.

A Psalm of David.

¹ I WILL give You thanks with all my
heart;
I sing praises to You before the
[pagan] gods.
² I will bow down [in worship]
toward Your holy temple
And give thanks to Your name for
Your lovingkindness and Your
truth;
For You have magnified Your word
together with Your name.
³ On the day I called, You answered
me;
And You made me bold *and*
confident with [renewed]
strength in my life.

⁴ All the kings of the land will give
thanks *and* praise You, O LORD,
When they have heard of the
promises of Your mouth [which
were fulfilled].
⁵ Yes, they will sing of the ways of
the LORD [joyfully celebrating
His wonderful acts],
For great is the glory *and* majesty
of the LORD.
⁶ Though the LORD is exalted,
He regards the lowly [and invites
them into His fellowship];
But the proud *and* haughty He
knows from a distance. [Prov
3:34; James 4:6; 1 Pet 5:5]

⁷ Though I walk in the midst of
trouble, You will revive me;
You will stretch out Your hand
against the wrath of my enemies,
And Your right hand will save me.
[Ps 23:3, 4]
⁸ The LORD will accomplish that
which concerns me;

speak the Word

Lord, I declare that You will accomplish that which concerns me!
—ADAPTED FROM PSALM 138:8

Your [unwavering] lovingkindness,
  O Lord, endures forever—
Do not abandon the works of Your
  own hands. [Ps 57:2; Phil 1:6]

PSALM 139

God's Omnipresence and
Omniscience.

To the Chief Musician. A Psalm
  of David.

¹O LORD, you have searched
  me [thoroughly] and have
  known me.
²You know when I sit down and
  when I rise up [my entire life,
  everything I do];

You understand my thought from
  afar. [Matt 9:4; John 2:24, 25]
³You scrutinize my path and my
  lying down,
And You are intimately acquainted
  with all my ways.
⁴Even before there is a word on my
  tongue [still unspoken],
  Behold, O Lord, You know it all.
  [Heb 4:13]
⁵You have enclosed me behind and
  before,
  And [You have] placed Your hand
  upon me.
⁶Such [infinite] knowledge is too
  wonderful for me;
  It is too high [above me], I cannot
  reach it.

God's good plan

God's plan for our lives has been established in the spiritual realm since before the foundation of the earth, and it is a good plan, as we see in Jeremiah 29:11: "'For I know the plans and thoughts that I have for you,' says the Lord, 'plans for peace and well-being and not for disaster to give you a future and a hope.'"

Psalm 139:16 tells us that before we were even born, God had planned our days. However, Satan has worked hard to destroy the Lord's good plan in many of us, and he has had a high success rate.

God sent His Son, Jesus, to redeem us and to restore all things to proper order. He has written down His will for our lives, and as we believe it and confess it, it literally begins to become reality.

Some people believe for a great number of things but see very little manifestation of them. Perhaps the reason is because they are believing but not speaking. They may see some results of their faith, but not the radical results they would experience if they would bring their mouths along with their hearts into God's service (see Romans 10:9, 10).

Some people are trying to live in the blessings of the Lord while still speaking in ungodly ways. We need to avoid making that mistake. We will not see positive results in our daily lives if we speak negative things. We should remember that what we are speaking, we are calling for. We are reaching into the spiritual realm and drawing out *something* according to our words. We can reach into Satan's realm, the realm of curses, and draw out evil, negative things, or we can reach into God's realm, the realm of blessings, and draw out good, positive things. Words are like containers; they carry creative or destructive power.

The choice is up to us.

7 Where can I go from Your Spirit?
Or where can I flee from Your
presence?
8 If I ascend to heaven, You are
there;
If I make my bed in Sheol (the
nether world, the place of the
dead), behold, You are there.
[Rom 11:33]
9 If I take the wings of the dawn,
If I dwell in the remotest part of
the sea,
10 Even there Your hand will lead me,
And Your right hand will take hold
of me.
11 If I say, "Surely the darkness will
cover me,
And the night will be the only light
around me,"
12 Even the darkness is not dark to
You *and* conceals nothing from
You,
But the night shines as bright as
the day;
Darkness and light are alike *to
You*. [Dan 2:22]
13 For You formed my innermost
parts;
You knit me [together] in my
mother's womb.
14 I will give thanks *and* praise to
You, for I am fearfully and
wonderfully made;
Wonderful are Your works,
And my soul knows it very well.
15 My frame was not hidden from
You,
When I was being formed in
secret,
And intricately *and* skillfully
formed [as if embroidered with
many colors] in the depths of the
earth.
16 Your eyes have seen my unformed
substance;
And in Your book were all written
The days that were appointed *for
me,*

When as yet there was not one of
them [even taking shape].
17 How precious also are Your
thoughts to me, O God!
How vast is the sum of them! [Ps
40:5]
18 If I could count them, they would
outnumber the sand.
When I awake, I am still with You.
19 O that You would kill the wicked,
O God;
Go away from me, therefore, men
of bloodshed. [Is 11:4]
20 For they speak against You
wickedly,
Your enemies take *Your name* in
vain. [Jude 15]
21 Do I not hate those who hate You,
O Lord?
And do I not loathe those who rise
up against You?
22 I hate them with perfect *and*
utmost hatred;
They have become my enemies.
23 Search me [thoroughly], O God,
and know my heart;
Test me and know my anxious
thoughts;
24 And see if there is any wicked *or*
hurtful way in me,
And lead me in the everlasting
way.

PSALM 140

Prayer for Protection
against the Wicked.

To the Chief Musician.
A Psalm of David.

1 RESCUE ME, O Lord, from evil
men;
Protect me from violent men.
2 They devise evil things in their
hearts;
They continually [gather together
and] stir up wars.
3 They sharpen their tongues like a
serpent's;

Poison of a viper is under their
lips. [Rom 3:13]   *Selah.*

4 Keep me, O Lᴏʀᴅ, from the hands
of the wicked;
Protect me from violent men
Who intend to trip up my steps.
5 The proud have hidden a trap for
me, and cords;
They have spread a net by the
wayside;
They have set traps for me.   *Selah.*

6 I said to the Lᴏʀᴅ, "You are my
God;
Listen to the voice of my
supplications, O Lᴏʀᴅ.
7 "O Gᴏᴅ the Lord, the strength of
my salvation,
You have covered my head in the
day of battle.
8 "Do not grant, O Lᴏʀᴅ, the desires
of the wicked;
Do not further their evil device,
that they not be exalted.   *Selah.*

9 "Those who surround me raise
their heads;
May the mischief of their own lips
come upon them.
10 "Let burning coals fall upon them;
Let them be thrown into the fire,
Into deep [water] pits from which
they cannot rise.
11 "Do not let a slanderer be
established in the earth;
Let evil quickly hunt the violent
man [to overthrow him and stop
his evil acts]."

12 I know [with confidence] that the
Lᴏʀᴅ will maintain the cause of
the afflicted,
And [will secure] justice for the
poor.
13 Surely the righteous will give
thanks to Your name;
The upright will dwell in Your
presence.

PSALM 141

An Evening Prayer
for Sanctification and Protection.

A Psalm of David.

1 LORD, I call upon You; hurry to me.
Listen to my voice when I call to You.
2 Let my prayer be counted as
incense before You;
The lifting up of my hands as the
evening offering. [1 Tim 2:8;
Rev 8:3, 4]
3 Set a guard, O Lᴏʀᴅ, over my mouth;
Keep watch over the door of my
lips [to keep me from speaking
thoughtlessly].
4 Do not incline my heart to [consent
to or tolerate] any evil thing,
Or to practice deeds of wickedness
With men who plan *and* do evil;
And let me not eat of their delicacies
(be tempted by their gain).

5 Let the righteous [thoughtfully]
strike (correct) me—it is a
kindness [done to encourage my
spiritual maturity].
It is [the choicest anointing] oil on
the head;
Let my head not refuse [to accept
and acknowledge and learn
from] it;
For still my prayer is against their
wicked deeds. [Prov 9:8; 19:25;
25:12; Gal 6:1]

putting the Word to work

Have you ever heard the saying
"Sticks and stones will break my
bones, but words will never hurt me"?
We all know that is not true; in fact,
words can deeply wound us. Heed the
advice of Psalm 141:3 and ask God to
set a guard over your mouth, that your
words will be encouraging and full of
blessing.

⁶Their [wicked, godless] judges are
   thrown down the sides of the
   rocky cliff,
And they [who followed them]
   will hear my words, for they are
   pleasant (just).
⁷As when the one plows and breaks
   open the ground [and the soil
   scatters behind him],

Our bones have been scattered at the
   mouth of Sheol [by the injustices
   of the wicked]. [2 Cor 1:9]

⁸For my eyes are toward You,
   O GOD, the Lord;
In You I take refuge; do not
   pour out my life *nor* leave me
   defenseless.

when your mouth gets you in trouble

I pray Psalm 141:3 often because I know that I need help with my mouth on a daily basis. I want the Holy Spirit to convict me when I am talking too much, when I am saying things I should not say, when I am speaking negatively, when I am complaining, or when I am sounding harsh or engaging in any of the other kinds of "evil speaking."

Anything that offends God in our conversation needs to be eliminated. That is why we need to pray continually: "Set a guard, O LORD, over my mouth; keep watch over the door of my lips [to keep me from speaking thoughtlessly]."

Another scripture on the importance of watching what we say is Psalm 17:3: "I intend that my mouth will not transgress." This says we need to plan to keep our mouths from speaking bad or negative things. We *purpose* not to speak them. Whatever we do in this life of faith, we must do it on purpose. Discipline is a choice. It is not necessarily easy, but it begins with a quality decision. During difficult times when the storm is raging, we will need to purpose to keep our mouths from transgressing.

A third scripture that I pray regularly on this subject is Psalm 19:14: "Let the words of my mouth and the meditation of my heart be acceptable and pleasing in Your sight, O LORD, my [firm, immovable] rock and my Redeemer."

Are you having difficulty with your mouth? Pray the Word. It is God's Word that carries the power of the Holy Spirit. Let the scriptures be the cry of your heart. Be sincere in your desire to gain victory in this area, and as you seek God for His help, you will begin to notice that you are changing. This is what the Lord has done for me, and He can do it for you too; He is not One to show partiality to anyone (see Acts 10:34). All those who follow God-ordained guidelines get God-ordained results.

Pray this prayer of commitment to exercise control over your mouth: "Lord, I pray that You will help me to develop sensitivity to the Holy Spirit concerning everything about my conversation. I do not want to be stubborn like a horse or mule that will not obey without a bridle and bit. I want to move in Your direction with only a gentle nudge from You. Place a guard over my lips and let all the words of my mouth be acceptable in Your sight, O Lord, my Strength and my Redeemer. In Jesus' name I pray. Amen."

⁹Keep me from the jaws of the trap
   which they have set for me,
And from the snares of those who
   do evil.
¹⁰Let the wicked fall into their own
   nets,
While I pass by *and* safely escape
   [from danger].

PSALM 142

Prayer for Help in Trouble.

A skillful song, *or* a didactic *or*
   reflective poem, of David; when he
   was in the cave. A Prayer.

¹I CRY aloud with my voice to the
   LORD;
I make supplication with my voice
   to the LORD.
²I pour out my complaint before
   Him;
I declare my trouble before Him.
³When my spirit was overwhelmed
   and weak within me [wrapped in
   darkness],
You knew my path.
In the way where I walk
They have hidden a trap for me.
⁴Look to the right [the point of
   attack] and see;
For there is no one who has regard
   for me [to act in my favor].
Escape has failed me *and* I have
   nowhere to run;
No one cares about my life.

⁵I cried out to You, O LORD;
I said, "You are my refuge,
My portion in the land of the living.
⁶"Give attention to my cry,
For I am brought very low;
Rescue me from my persecutors,
For they are stronger than I.

⁷"Bring my soul out of prison
   (adversity),
So that I may give thanks *and*
   praise Your name;
The righteous will surround me
   [in triumph],
For You will look after me."

PSALM 143

Prayer for Help and Guidance.

A Psalm of David.

¹HEAR MY prayer, O LORD,
Listen to my supplications!

life point

David's response to his feelings of
depression and gloom was not to meditate on his problem. Instead, he literally
came against the problem by *choosing* to
remember the good times of past days—
pondering the doings of God and the
works of His hands (see Psalm 143:5). In
other words, he thought about something
good, and it helped him overcome his
battle of depression.

Never forget this: *your mind plays an
important role in your victory.*

I know it is the power of the Holy Spirit
working through the Word of God that
brings victory into our lives. But a large
part of the work that needs to be done
is for us to line up our thinking with God
and His Word. If we refuse to do this or
choose to think it is unimportant, we will
never experience victory. But we will win
if we discipline ourselves to meditate on
the good things God has done.

speak the Word

*Thank You, God, for bringing my soul out of adversity so that
I may give thanks and praise Your name.*
—ADAPTED FROM PSALM 142:7

a biblical prescription for depression

Psalm 143:3–10 gives a description of depression and how to overcome it. Let's look at this passage in detail to see the steps we can take to defeat this attack of the enemy:

Psalm 143:3: *Identify the nature and cause of the problem*. The psalmist says he feels that he is dwelling in "dark places, like those who have been long dead." This certainly sounds to me like a description of someone who is depressed. I believe that the source of the depression described here is our enemy, Satan, who attacks the soul.

Psalm 143:4: *Recognize that depression steals life and light*. Depression oppresses a person's spiritual freedom and power. Our spirits (empowered and encouraged by God's Spirit) are powerful and free. Therefore, Satan seeks to oppress our spirits' power and liberty by filling our minds with darkness and gloom. Please realize that it is vital to resist the feeling called "depression" immediately when we begin to sense it. The longer it is allowed to remain, the harder it becomes to resist.

Psalm 143:5: *Remember the good times*. In this verse we see the psalmist's response to his condition. Remembering, meditating, and pondering are all functions of the mind. He obviously knows that his thoughts will affect his feelings, so he gets busy thinking about the kinds of things that will help overcome the attack upon his mind. He thinks about God and the good things He does.

Psalm 143:6: *Praise the Lord in the midst of the problem*. The psalmist knows the importance of praise; he lifts his hands in worship. He declares what his needs truly are: he needs God. Far too often when people get depressed, it is because they are in need of something, and they seek it in the wrong place, which only adds to their problems. God alone can water a thirsty soul. Do not be deceived into thinking that anything else can satisfy you fully and completely. Chasing after the wrong thing will always leave you disappointed, and disappointment opens the door to depression.

Psalm 143:7: *Ask for God's help*. The psalmist asks for help. He is basically saying, "Hurry up, God, because I am not going to be able to hold on very much longer without You."

Psalm 143:8: *Listen to the Lord*. The psalmist knows that he needs to hear from God. He needs to be assured of God's love and kindness. He needs God's attention and direction.

Psalm 143:9: *Pray for deliverance*. Once again the psalmist declares that only God can help him. Please notice that throughout this discourse, he keeps his mind on God and not on the problem.

Psalm 143:10: *Seek God's wisdom, knowledge, and leadership*. Perhaps the psalmist is indicating that he has gotten out of God's will and thus opened the door to the attack on his soul. He wants to be in God's will because he realizes that it is the only safe place to be. Then he asks God to help him be stable. He wants his unsettled emotions to be level—not up and down.

I encourage you to meditate on God's Word and apply its principles to your life. Let it bring you freedom and peace.

Answer me in Your faithfulness,
  and in Your righteousness.
2 And do not enter into judgment
  with Your servant,
  For in Your sight no man living is
  righteous *or* justified. [Ps 130:3;
  Rom 3:20–26; Gal 2:16]
3 For the enemy has persecuted me,
  He has crushed my life down to
  the ground;
  He has made me dwell in dark
  places, like those who have been
  long dead.
4 Therefore my spirit is
  overwhelmed *and* weak within
  me [wrapped in darkness];
  My heart grows numb within me.

life point

What is David doing in Psalm 143:5–8?
He is crying out to God for help. When
you and I feel ourselves sinking into the
pit of depression, we can do what David
did here. We can remember the days of
old. We can meditate on all of the Lord's
doings on our behalf. We can ponder the
mighty works of His hands. We can spread
forth our hands in prayer and supplication
to Him. We can call upon Him to answer
us speedily because we are leaning on
and trusting in Him. We can lift up our
souls, our inner beings, to Him.

All these things constitute an act of faith,
and the Lord has promised to always
respond to faith. If we are under a minor
attack, it may take only a few hours or
days. But if we are under a major attack,
it may take much longer. However long it
may be, we must stand firm and continue
to cry out to God, receiving the help and
encouragement that only He can give. We
need to be confident that the Lord will
deliver us, just as He delivered David from
all his woes.

life point

In the final verses of Psalm 143, David
calls upon the Lord to deliver him from
his enemies because he has run to Him for
help and protection. He asks the Lord to
teach him His will and to let His Spirit lead
him "on level ground" (verse 10).

I believe that what David was asking for
when he spoke of "level ground" was
balanced emotions. Secure in who he was
and in Whose he was, David was able to
place himself into the hands of the Lord.
David allowed God to bring his life out of
trouble, free him from distress, punish his
enemies, and cause him to win the victory
over all those who were afflicting his
soul, because he belonged to the Lord.

You and I are to place ourselves in God's
hands. We need to withstand the devil's
attempts to drag us down into the depths
of depression and despair by allowing
God to move on our behalf to win our
victory.

5 I remember the days of old;
  I meditate on all that You have
    done;
  I ponder the work of Your hands.
6 I reach out my hands to You;
  My throat *thirsts* for You, as a
    parched land [thirsts for water].
                                    Selah.

7 Answer me quickly, O Lord, my
    spirit fails;
  Do not hide Your face from me,
  Or I will become like those who go
    down into the pit (grave).
8 Let me hear Your lovingkindness
    in the morning,
  For I trust in You.
  Teach me the way in which I
    should walk,
  For I lift up my soul to You.

⁹Rescue me, O Lᴏʀᴅ, from my
   enemies;
I take refuge in You.

¹⁰Teach me to do Your will [so that I
   may please You],
For You are my God;
Let Your good Spirit lead me on
   level ground.
¹¹Save my life, O Lᴏʀᴅ, for Your
   name's sake;
In Your righteousness bring my
   life out of trouble.
¹²In your lovingkindness, silence
   and destroy my enemies
And destroy all those who afflict
   my life,
For I am Your servant.

PSALM 144

Prayer for Rescue and Prosperity.

A Psalm of David.

¹BLESSED BE the Lᴏʀᴅ, my Rock
   and my great strength,
Who trains my hands for war
And my fingers for battle;
²My [steadfast] lovingkindness and
   my fortress,
My high tower and my rescuer,
My shield and He in whom I take
   refuge,
Who subdues my people under me.
³Lᴏʀᴅ, what is man that You take
   notice of him?
Or the son of man that You think
   of him? [Job 7:17; Ps 8:4; Heb 2:6]
⁴Man is like a mere breath;
His days are like a shadow that
   passes away.

⁵Bow Your heavens, O Lᴏʀᴅ, and
   come down;
Touch the mountains, and they
   will smoke.
⁶Flash lightning and scatter my
   enemies;

life point

In the opening verses of Psalm 144, David praises the Lord with strong, compelling words—"my Rock and my great strength," "my [steadfast] loving-kindness and my fortress," "my high tower and my rescuer," and more (Psalm 144:1, 2). The Lord subdued his enemies under him, but David also did his part. We must always remember that we are partners with God. God has a part, and we have a part. We cannot do God's part, and He will not do our part. In verse 1, David said the Lord taught his hands to war and his fingers to fight. This is the key to conquering depression. We must do what David did. We must recognize depression, submit it to the Lord, call upon Him for His help, and then fight that depression in the strength and power of the Holy Spirit.

How do we fight depression? By spending time with God, by praying and by speaking His Word. We also fight by lifting our eyes, heads, hands, and hearts and offering the sacrifice of praise and thanksgiving to the Lord, our Rock and our Strength, our High Tower and our Rescuer, our Shield and the One in Whom we take refuge, the One Who subdues our enemies under us.

Send out Your arrows and confuse
   and embarrass *and* frustrate
   them.
⁷Stretch out Your hand from above;
Set me free and rescue me from
   great waters,
Out of the hands of [hostile]
   foreigners [who surround us]
⁸Whose mouths speak deceit
   [without restraint],
And whose right hand is a right
   hand of falsehood.

⁹I will sing a new song to You,
O God;
Upon a harp of ten strings I will
sing praises to You,
¹⁰Who gives salvation to kings,
Who sets David His servant free
from the evil sword.
¹¹Set me free and rescue me from
the hand of [hostile] foreigners,
Whose mouth speaks deceit
[without restraint],
And whose right hand is a right
hand of falsehood.

¹²Let our sons in their youth be like
plants full grown,
And our daughters like corner
pillars fashioned for a palace;
¹³Let our barns be full, supplying
every kind of produce,
And our flocks bring forth
thousands and ten thousands in
our fields;
¹⁴Let our cattle bear
Without mishap and without loss,
And let there be no outcry in our
streets!
¹⁵How blessed *and* favored are the
people in such circumstance;
How blessed [fortunate,
prosperous, and favored] are the
people whose God is the Lord!

PSALM 145

The Lord Extolled for His Goodness.

A Psalm of praise. Of David.

¹I WILL exalt You, my God, O King,
And [with gratitude and
submissive wonder] I will bless
Your name forever and ever.
²Every day I will bless You *and*
lovingly praise You;
Yes, [with awe-inspired reverence]
I will praise Your name forever
and ever.
³Great is the Lord, and highly to be
praised,

And His greatness is [so vast and
profound as to be] unsearchable
[incomprehensible to man]. [Job
5:9; 9:10; Rom 11:33]
⁴One generation shall praise Your
works to another,
And shall declare Your mighty *and*
remarkable acts.
⁵On the glorious splendor of Your
majesty
And on Your wonderful works, I
will meditate.
⁶People will speak of the power of
Your awesome acts,
And [with gratitude and
submissive wonder] I will tell of
Your greatness.
⁷They will overflow [like a
fountain] when they speak
of Your great *and* abundant
goodness
And will sing joyfully of Your
righteousness.

⁸The Lord is gracious and full of
compassion,
Slow to anger and abounding in
lovingkindness.
⁹The Lord is good to all,
And His tender mercies are over
all His works [the entirety of
things created].
¹⁰All Your works shall give thanks to
You *and* praise You, O Lord,
And Your godly ones will bless
You.
¹¹They shall speak of the glory of
Your kingdom
And talk of Your power,
¹²To make known to the sons of men
Your mighty acts
And the glorious majesty of Your
kingdom.
¹³Your kingdom is an everlasting
kingdom,
And Your dominion *endures*
throughout all generations.
[Dan 7:14, 27]

14 The Lord upholds all those [of His own] who fall
And raises up all those who are bowed down.
15 The eyes of all look to You [in hopeful expectation],
And You give them their food in due time.
16 You open Your hand
And satisfy the desire of every living thing.

17 The Lord is [unwaveringly] righteous in all His ways
And gracious *and* kind in all His works.
18 The Lord is near to all who call on Him,
To all who call on Him in truth (without guile).
19 He will fulfill the desire of those who fear *and* worship Him [with awe-inspired reverence and obedience];
He also will hear their cry and will save them.
20 The Lord keeps all who love Him,
But all the wicked He will destroy.
21 My mouth will speak the praise of the Lord,
And all flesh will bless *and* gratefully praise His holy name forever and ever.

PSALM 146

The Lord an Abundant Helper.

1 PRAISE THE Lord! (Hallelujah!)
Praise the Lord, O my soul!
2 While I live I will praise the Lord;
I will sing praises to my God as long as I live.
3 Do not trust in princes,

In mortal man, in whom there is no salvation (help).
4 When his spirit leaves him, he returns to the earth;
In that very day his thoughts *and* plans perish. [1 Cor 2:6]
5 How blessed *and* graciously favored is he whose help is the God of Jacob (Israel),
Whose hope is in the Lord his God, [Gen 32:30]
6 Who made heaven and earth,
The sea, and all that is in them,
Who keeps truth *and* is faithful forever, [Gen 1:3]
7 Who executes justice for the oppressed,
Who gives food to the hungry.
The Lord sets free the prisoners.

8 The Lord opens *the eyes of* the blind;
The Lord lifts up those who are bowed down;
The Lord loves the righteous [the upright in heart]. [Luke 13:13; John 9:7, 32]
9 The Lord protects the strangers;
He supports the fatherless and the widow;
But He makes crooked the way of the wicked.
10 The Lord shall reign forever,
Your God, O Zion, to all generations.
Praise the Lord! (Hallelujah!) [Ps 10:16; Rev 11:15]

PSALM 147

Praise for Jerusalem's Restoration and Prosperity.

1 PRAISE THE Lord!
For it is good to sing praises to our [gracious and majestic] God;

speak the Word

God, I am blessed and graciously favored because
my help and my hope are in You!
—ADAPTED FROM PSALM 146:5

Praise is becoming *and*
appropriate.
²The LORD is building up Jerusalem;
He is gathering [together] the
exiles of Israel.
³He heals the brokenhearted
And binds up their wounds
[healing their pain and
comforting their sorrow]. [Ps
34:18; Is 57:15; 61:1; Luke 4:18]
⁴He counts the number of the stars;
He calls them all by their names.
⁵Great is our [majestic and mighty]
Lord and abundant in strength;
His understanding is inexhaustible
[infinite, boundless].
⁶The LORD lifts up the humble;
He casts the wicked down to the
ground.

⁷Sing to the LORD with thanksgiving;
Sing praises to our God with the
lyre,
⁸Who covers the heavens with clouds,
Who provides rain for the earth,
Who makes grass grow on the
mountains.
⁹He gives to the beast its food,
And to the young ravens that for
which they cry.
¹⁰He does not delight in the strength
(military power) of the horse,
Nor does He take pleasure in the
legs (strength) of a man.
¹¹The LORD favors those who
fear *and* worship Him [with
awe-inspired reverence and
obedience],
Those who wait for His mercy *and*
lovingkindness. [Ps 145:20]

¹²Praise the LORD, O Jerusalem!
Praise your God, O Zion!
¹³For He has strengthened the bars
of your gates,
He has blessed your children
within you.
¹⁴He makes peace in your borders;
He satisfies you with the finest of
the wheat.

¹⁵He sends His command to the earth;
His word runs very swiftly.
¹⁶He gives [to the earth] snow like [a
blanket of] wool;
He scatters the frost like ashes.
¹⁷He casts out His ice like fragments;
Who can stand before His cold?
¹⁸He sends out His word and melts
the ice;
He causes His wind to blow and
the waters to flow.
¹⁹He declares His word to Jacob,
His statutes and His ordinances to
Israel. [Mal 4:4]
²⁰He has not dealt this way with any
[other] nation;
They have not known [understood,
appreciated, heeded, or
cherished] His ordinances.
Praise the LORD! (Hallelujah!)
[Ps 79:6; Jer 10:25]

PSALM 148

The Whole Creation Invoked
to Praise the LORD.

¹PRAISE THE LORD!
Praise the LORD from the heavens;
Praise Him in the heights!
²Praise Him, all His angels;
Praise Him, all His hosts (armies)!
³Praise Him, sun and moon:
Praise Him, all stars of light!
⁴Praise Him, highest heavens,
And the waters above the heavens!
⁵Let them praise the name of the
LORD,
For He commanded and they were
created.
⁶He has also established them
forever and ever;
He has made a decree which shall
not pass away.

⁷Praise the LORD from the earth,
Sea monsters and all deeps;
⁸Lightning and hail, snow and fog;
Stormy wind, fulfilling His orders;
⁹Mountains and all hills;

Fruitful trees and all cedars;
¹⁰Beasts and all cattle;
Creeping things and winged birds;
¹¹Kings of the earth and all people;
Princes and all judges of the earth;
¹²Both young men and virgins;
Old men and children.

¹³Let them praise the name of the
LORD,
For His name alone is exalted *and*
supreme;
His glory *and* majesty are above
earth and heaven.
¹⁴He has lifted up a horn for His
people [giving them strength,
prosperity, dignity, and
preeminence],
Praise for all His godly ones;
For the people of Israel, a people
near to Him.
Praise the LORD! (Hallelujah!) [Ps
75:10; Eph 2:17]

PSALM 149

Israel Invoked to Praise the LORD.

¹PRAISE THE LORD!
Sing to the LORD a new song,
And praise Him in the
congregation of His godly ones
(believers).
²Let Israel rejoice in their Maker;
Let Zion's children rejoice in their
King. [Zech 9:9; Matt 21:5]
³Let them praise His name with
dancing;
Let them sing praises to Him with
the tambourine and lyre.
⁴For the LORD takes pleasure in His
people;
He will beautify the humble with
salvation.

⁵Let the godly ones exult in glory;
Let them sing for joy on their beds.
⁶Let the high praises of God be in
their throats,
And a two-edged sword in their
hands, [Heb 4:12; Rev 1:16]

putting the Word to work

If you have ever been to a professional
sporting event, you have seen and experienced exuberant enthusiasm of the
fans. Do you praise God with that kind
of intensity? While at times you may
praise Him in the quietness of your
heart, the psalmist tells us that we are
also to praise God with instruments,
with dancing, or with shouts of joy! He
is worthy of your exuberant praise.

⁷To execute vengeance on the nations
And punishment on the peoples,
⁸To bind their kings with chains
And their nobles with fetters of
iron,
⁹To execute on them the judgment
written.
This is the honor for all His godly
ones.
Praise the LORD! (Hallelujah!)

PSALM 150

A Psalm of Praise.

¹PRAISE THE LORD!
Praise God in His sanctuary;
Praise Him in His mighty heavens.
²Praise Him for His mighty acts;
Praise Him according to [the
abundance of] His greatness.
[Deut 3:24; Ps 145:5, 6]

³Praise Him with trumpet sound;
Praise Him with harp and lyre.
⁴Praise Him with tambourine and
dancing;
Praise Him with stringed
instruments and flute.
⁵Praise Him with resounding
cymbals;
Praise Him with loud cymbals.
⁶Let everything that has breath *and*
every breath of life praise the
LORD!
Praise the LORD! (Hallelujah!)

Proverbs

Author:
Solomon, with smaller portions by others

Date:
About 950 BC, with portions about 720 BC

Everyday Life Principles:
Whatever you do, seek wisdom.

Walking in wisdom means making decisions today that you will be happy with tomorrow.

Look to Proverbs to find godly, practical advice about many practical matters you face in your everyday life.

Proverbs was written by Solomon, who has been called the wisest man who ever lived, and is a book filled with wisdom and godly common sense about the practical matters of life. One of the most beneficial qualities we can seek in life is wisdom, which I like to define as "decisions you make now that you will be happy with later."

In the pages of Proverbs, you will find sound guidance and advice on a multitude of situations you face on a regular basis, including how to treat people, how to think, how to control your mouth, how to manage finances, how husbands and wives should behave, how to raise children, how children should relate to their parents, how to keep from being foolish and handle those who are, how to be a good friend, how to deal with employees, how to plan for the future, how to deal with offenses, and how to receive correction. It also teaches us that our words are carriers of either life or death, that a happy heart does us good like a medicine, and that the fear of the Lord is the beginning of wisdom.

Because Proverbs has 31 chapters, many people read one chapter of Proverbs per day, each month of the year. Whether you read a chapter per day or the entire book at once, I encourage you to read Proverbs often and let its wisdom saturate your heart and direct your life.

1 THE PROVERBS (truths obscurely expressed, maxims) of Solomon son of David, king of Israel:

2 To know [skillful and godly] wisdom and instruction;
To discern *and* comprehend the words of understanding *and* insight,
3 To receive instruction in wise behavior *and* the discipline of wise thoughtfulness,
Righteousness, justice, and integrity;
4 That prudence (good judgment, astute common sense) may be given to the naive *or* inexperienced [who are easily misled],
And knowledge and discretion (intelligent discernment) to the youth,
5 The wise will hear and increase their learning,
And the person of understanding will acquire wise counsel *and* the skill [to steer his course wisely and lead others to the truth], [Prov 9:9]
6 To understand a proverb and a figure [of speech] *or* an enigma with its interpretation,

life point

Proverbs 1:1–4 says that wisdom involves prudence. *Prudence* means "good management." Prudent people do not operate in extremes. They are balanced and conduct themselves wisely. I encourage you to be prudent in every situation!

speak the Word

And the words of the wise and their riddles [that require reflection].

7 The [reverent] fear of the LORD [that is, worshiping Him and regarding Him as truly awesome] is the beginning *and* the preeminent part of knowledge [its starting point and its essence];
But arrogant fools despise [skillful and godly] wisdom and instruction *and* self-discipline. [Ps 111:10]

8 My son, hear the instruction of your father,
And do not reject the teaching of your mother.
9 For they are a garland of grace on your head,
And chains *and* ornaments [of gold] around your neck.
10 My son, if sinners entice you, Do not consent. [Ps 1:1; Eph 5:11]
11 If they say, "Come with us;
Let us lie in wait to *shed* blood,
Let us ambush the innocent without cause;
12 Let us swallow them alive like Sheol (the place of the dead),
Even whole, as those who go down to the pit [of death];
13 We will find *and* take all kinds of precious possessions,
We will fill our houses with spoil;
14 Throw in your lot with us [they insist];
We will all have one money bag [in common],"
15 My son, do not walk on the road with them;

God, I pray that You will help me to be wise.
Help me to hear and increase in learning, to acquire wise counsel
and the skill to steer my course wisely and lead others to truth.
–ADAPTED FROM PROVERBS 1:5

Keep your foot [far] away from
   their path,
¹⁶For their feet run to evil,
   And they hurry to shed blood.
¹⁷Indeed, it is useless to spread the
   baited net
   In the sight of any bird;
¹⁸But [when these people set a trap
   for others] they lie in wait for
   their own blood;
   They set an ambush for their
   own lives [and rush to their
   destruction].
¹⁹So are the ways of everyone who is
   greedy for gain;
   Greed takes away the lives of its
   possessors. [Prov 15:27; 1 Tim
   6:10]

²⁰Wisdom shouts in the street,
   She raises her voice in the markets;
²¹She calls out at the head of the
   noisy streets [where large
   crowds gather];
   At the entrance of the city gates
   she speaks her words:
²²"How long, O naive ones [you
   who are easily misled], will you
   love being simple-minded *and*
   undiscerning?
   How long will scoffers [who ridicule
   and deride] delight in scoffing,
   How long will fools [who
   obstinately mock truth] hate
   knowledge?
²³"If you will turn *and* pay attention
   to my rebuke,
   Behold, I [Wisdom] will pour out
   my spirit on you;
   I will make my words known to
   you. [Is 11:2; Eph 1:17–20]
²⁴"Because I called and you refused
   [to answer],
   I stretched out my hand and no
   one has paid attention [to my
   offer]; [Is 65:11, 12; 66:4; Jer 7:13,
   14; Zech 7:11–13]
²⁵And you treated all my counsel as
   nothing

life point

Proverbs 1:23 says that wisdom will make
its words known to us if we listen to it
and pay attention to its rebuke. If we
follow wisdom, God will open up wisdom
to us, and we will have more revelation
and understanding than we could ever
imagine.

All we need to do is be obedient to what
God has told us to do. He will reveal to
us treasures hidden in His Word. We have
not even scratched the surface of the
revelation that is in the Word of God. If
we obey Him, He will make His will clearly
known to us. He will speak living words
(His *rhema*) to us, His personal words for
our lives.

   And would not accept my
   reprimand,
²⁶I also will laugh at your disaster;
   I will mock when your dread *and*
   panic come,
²⁷When your dread *and* panic come
   like a storm,
   And your disaster comes like a
   whirlwind,
   When anxiety and distress come
   upon you [as retribution].
²⁸"Then they will call upon me
   (Wisdom), but I will not answer;
   They will seek me eagerly but they
   will not find me, [Job 27:9; 35:12,
   13; Is 1:15, 16; Jer 11:11; Mic 3:4;
   James 4:3]
²⁹Because they hated knowledge
   And did not choose the fear of
   the LORD [that is, obeying Him
   with reverence and awe-filled
   respect], [Prov 8:13]
³⁰They would not accept my counsel,
   And they spurned all my rebuke.
³¹"Therefore they shall eat of the
   fruit of their own [wicked] way
   And be satiated with [the penalty
   of] their own devices.

understanding people

Proverbs 2:1–5 teaches us about the necessity and rewards of understanding. We need to seek understanding—of God's Word and will, of ourselves, and of other people.

I would like to focus for a moment on the importance of really understanding others. In order to minister to them we must have an understanding heart, and how can we do that if we have little understanding of their hurts and struggles?

One way to understand what people are going through is by going through it ourselves. We do not have to experience exactly the same circumstances, but I do not think anyone can understand a hurting person without having been hurt or having gone through a similar situation.

It is amazing how caring and compassionate we are when we have endured a few problems of our own, and how flippant and judgmental we can be if we have not had the same problem ourselves. How easily our answers can be: "Well, now, sister, you just need to believe God." How different it is when we have been hurting for months ourselves, and somebody comes to us with a problem. We throw our arms around that person and say, "Oh, I *understand* how you feel."

We all want understanding. It is one of the things for which we cry out to God when we are going through rough times. We just want to be understood. Jesus understands, as we see in Hebrews 4:15: "For we do not have a High Priest who is unable to sympathize and understand our weaknesses and temptations, but One who has been tempted [knowing exactly how it feels to be human] in every respect as we are, yet without [committing any] sin." Jesus can help us because He knows what we are going through. We can open up to Him without fear of judgment and rejection because He understands.

I am not sure that Jesus ever prayed for anybody until compassion was flowing in His heart. I recall an instance in the Bible in which a man came to Him asking for healing for his son, who was possessed by a demon that caused him terrible suffering. Jesus asked the man, "How long has this been happening to him?" (Mark 9:21). The answer did not affect whether or not Jesus would heal him. I believe Jesus asked the question because He wanted to have even more compassion than He already had for that father and for the boy.

We need to be concerned enough about people to ask them questions about their situations—"How long has this been happening? Where does it hurt? What gives you comfort?"

When some of us ask a person how they are doing and they say that they are having a rough time, we tend to answer, "Well, praise the Lord anyway!" But when we are hurting or in trouble, that is not how we want others to respond to us. We want them to show us some real heartfelt understanding and compassion.

Be a person who seeks understanding and desires to be compassionate—and you will find yourself acting wisely toward others.

32 "For the turning away of the naive
will kill them,
And the careless ease of [self-
righteous] fools will destroy
them. [Is 32:6]
33 "But whoever listens to me
(Wisdom) will live securely *and*
in confident trust
And will be at ease, without fear *or*
dread of evil."

2 MY SON, if you will receive my
words
And treasure my
commandments within you,
2 So that your ear is attentive to
[skillful and godly] wisdom,
And apply your heart to
understanding [seeking it
conscientiously and striving for
it eagerly];
3 Yes, if you cry out for insight,
And lift up your voice for
understanding;
4 If you seek skillful *and* godly
wisdom as you would silver
And search for her as you would
hidden treasures;
5 Then you will understand the
[reverent] fear of the LORD
[that is, worshiping Him and
regarding Him as truly awesome]
And discover the knowledge of
God. [Prov 1:7]
6 For the LORD gives [skillful and
godly] wisdom;
From His mouth come knowledge
and understanding.
7 He stores away sound wisdom for
the righteous [those who are in
right standing with Him];
He is a shield to those who walk
in integrity [those of honorable
character and moral courage],

8 He guards the paths of justice;
And He preserves the way of His
saints (believers). [1 Sam 2:9;
Ps 66:8, 9]
9 Then you will understand
righteousness and justice [in
every circumstance]
And integrity and every good path.
10 For [skillful and godly] wisdom
will enter your heart
And knowledge will be pleasant to
your soul.
11 Discretion will watch over you,
Understanding *and* discernment
will guard you,
12 To keep you from the way of evil
and the evil man,
From the man who speaks
perverse things;
13 From those who leave the paths of
uprightness
To walk in the ways of darkness;
14 Who find joy in doing evil
And delight in the perversity of
evil,
15 Whose paths are crooked,
And who are devious in their ways;
16 To keep you from the immoral
woman;
From the seductress with her
flattering words, [Prov 2:11]
17 Who leaves the companion
(husband) of her youth,
And forgets the covenant of her
God.
18 For her house leads down to death
And her paths lead to the dead;
19 None who go to her return again,
Nor do they regain the paths of
life—
20 So you will walk in the way of good
men [that is, those of personal
integrity, moral courage and
honorable character],

speak the Word

*Thank You, Lord, for giving me skillful and godly
wisdom, knowledge, and understanding.*
—ADAPTED FROM PROVERBS 2:6

And keep to the paths of the righteous.
²¹ For the upright [those who are in right standing with God] will live in the land
And those [of integrity] who are blameless [in God's sight] will remain in it;
²² But the wicked will be cut off from the land
And the treacherous shall be [forcibly] uprooted *and* removed from it.

3 MY SON, do not forget my teaching,
But let your heart keep my commandments;
² For length of days and years of life [worth living]
And tranquility *and* prosperity [the wholeness of life's blessings] they will add to you.
³ Do not let mercy *and* kindness and truth leave you [instead let these qualities define you];

why not ask, "*why?*"

Proverbs 3:5, 6 is basically a passage that encourages us to have faith in God and not in our own thinking or reasoning. People who feel compelled to reason out everything have a hard time with faith because reasoning is not faith, and without faith it is impossible to please God (see Hebrews 11:6).

I can teach on reasoning because I used to be a "class A" chief "reasoner." I was the lady who had to have everything figured out. I had to have a plan. I had to know not only all about my own business but all about other people's business too—even God's. I was continually asking, "Why, God, why? When, God, when?"

In some respects, I had to reason everything out like the religious leaders of Jesus' day. We read about them in Mark 2:6–8: "But some of the scribes were sitting there debating in their hearts [the implication of what He had said], 'Why does this man talk that way? He is blaspheming; who can forgive sins [remove guilt, nullify sin's penalty, and assign righteousness] except God alone?' Immediately Jesus, being fully aware [of their hostility] and knowing in His spirit that they were thinking this, said to them, 'Why are you debating and arguing about these things in your hearts?"

The Amplified Classic version of verse 6 says that the scribes were "holding a dialogue with themselves." Do you ever hold a dialogue with yourself? Realistically, you probably talk to yourself more than you talk to anybody else. I encourage you to examine what you are saying to yourself. These scribes were not saying those unkind things in Mark 2 aloud, but in their hearts. They were asking questions about Jesus within themselves. Immediately, He became aware of their arguing, debating, and reasoning and called it to their attention.

We need to be aware that trying to reason things out by ourselves is a problem. It is a serious matter that we need to deal with, just as Jesus dealt with it in the hearts of those who followed Him. Ask God to help you stop reasoning and begin to live by faith, trusting in and relying on Him, not on your own understanding.

Bind them [securely] around your
neck,
Write them on the tablet of your
heart. [Col 3:9–12]
⁴So find favor and high esteem
In the sight of God and man. [Luke
2:52]
⁵Trust in and rely confidently on
the LORD with all your heart
And do not rely on your own
insight or understanding.
⁶In all your ways know and
acknowledge and recognize Him,
And He will make your paths
straight and smooth [removing
obstacles that block your way].
⁷Do not be wise in your own eyes;
Fear the LORD [with reverent
awe and obedience] and turn
[entirely] away from evil. [Prov
8:13]
⁸It will be health to your body
[your marrow, your nerves, your
sinews, your muscles—all your
inner parts]
And refreshment (physical well-
being) to your bones.
⁹Honor the LORD with your wealth
And with the first fruits of all your
crops (income); [Deut 26:2; Mal
3:10; Luke 14:13, 14]
¹⁰Then your barns will be
abundantly filled
And your vats will overflow with
new wine. [Deut 28:8]
¹¹My son, do not reject or take
lightly the discipline of the LORD
[learn from your mistakes and
the testing that comes from His
correction through discipline];

life point

I believe what God meant when He said,
"Do not be wise in your own eyes" (Proverbs 3:7), was "Do not even think that you
can run your life and do a good job without
My help and direction!" We need His help,
wisdom, and guidance in every situation.

Nor despise His rebuke, [Ps 94:12;
Heb 12:5, 6; Rev 3:19]
¹²For those whom the LORD loves He
corrects,
Even as a father corrects the son in
whom he delights.
¹³Happy [blessed, considered
fortunate, to be admired] is the
man who finds [skillful and
godly] wisdom,
And the man who gains
understanding and insight
[learning from God's word and
life's experiences],
¹⁴For wisdom's profit is better than
the profit of silver,
And her gain is better than fine
gold.
¹⁵She is more precious than rubies;
And nothing you can wish for
compares with her [in value].
[Job 28:12–18]
¹⁶Long life is in her right hand;
In her left hand are riches and
honor. [Prov 8:12–21; 1 Tim 4:8]
¹⁷Her ways are highways of
pleasantness and favor,
And all her paths are peace.
¹⁸She is a tree of life to those who
take hold of her,
And happy [blessed, considered
fortunate, to be admired] is
everyone who holds her tightly.
¹⁹The LORD by His wisdom has
founded the earth;
By His understanding He has
established the heavens. [Col 1:16]
²⁰By His knowledge the deeps were
broken up
And the clouds drip with dew.
²¹My son, let them not escape from
your sight,
But keep sound wisdom and
discretion,
²²And they will be life to your soul
(your inner self)
And a gracious adornment to your
neck (your outer self).

23 Then you will walk on your way
    [of life] securely
  And your foot will not stumble.
    [Ps 91:11, 12; Prov 10:9]
24 When you lie down, you will not be
    afraid;
  When you lie down, your sleep
    will be sweet.
25 Do not be afraid of sudden fear
  Nor of the storm of the wicked
    when it comes [since you will be
    blameless];
26 For the LORD will be your
    confidence, firm *and* strong,
  And will keep your foot from being
    caught [in a trap].

27 Do not withhold good from those
    to whom it is due [its rightful
    recipients],
  When it is in your power to do it.
    [Rom 13:7; Gal 6:10]
28 Do not say to your neighbor, "Go,
    and come back,
  And tomorrow I will give it,"
  When you have it with you. [Lev
    19:13; Deut 24:15]
29 Do not devise evil against your
    neighbor,
  Who lives securely beside you.
30 Do not quarrel with a man without
    cause,

life point

As Christians, we should not place our confidence in our education, our looks, our position, our property, our gifts, our talents, our abilities, our accomplishments, or in other people's opinions. Through Proverbs 3:26, our heavenly Father is basically saying to us, "No more; it is time to let go of all those fleshly things to which you have been holding so firmly for so long. It is time to put your trust and confidence in Me, and Me alone!"

life point

We can have good intentions and still be disobedient. Procrastination is very deceptive and Proverbs 3:27, 28 instructs us not to do it. Often, we do not see putting things off as disobedience because we *intend* to obey God; it is just that we are going to do it *when*—when we have more money, when we are not so busy, as soon as Christmas is over, after school starts next year, when we return from vacation, etc. Remember, the best intentions do not produce results. Ask God to help you take action in a timely manner in every situation.

  If he has done you no harm. [Rom
    12:18]
31 Do not envy a man of violence
  And do not choose any of his ways.
    [Ps 37:1; 73:3; Prov 24:1]
32 For the devious are repulsive to the
    LORD;
  But His private counsel is with
    the upright [those with spiritual
    integrity and moral courage].
    [Ps 25:14]
33 The curse of the LORD is on the
    house of the wicked,
  But He blesses the home of the just
    and righteous. [Ps 37:22; Zech
    5:4; Mal 2:2]
34 Though He scoffs at the scoffers
    and scorns the scorners,
  Yet He gives His grace [His
    undeserved favor] to the
    humble [those who give up self-
    importance]. [James 4:6; 1 Pet 5:5]
35 The wise will inherit honor *and*
    glory,
  But dishonor *and* shame is
    conferred on fools. [Is 32:6]

4 HEAR, O children, the instruction of a father, And pay attention [and be willing to learn] so that you may gain understanding *and* intelligent discernment. ²For I give you good doctrine; Do not turn away from my instruction. ³When I was a son with my father (David),

Tender and the only son in the sight of my mother (Bathsheba), ⁴He taught me and said to me, "Let your heart hold fast my words; Keep my commandments and live. [1 Chr 28:9; Eph 6:4] ⁵"Get [skillful and godly] wisdom! Acquire understanding [actively seek spiritual discernment, mature comprehension, and logical interpretation]!

the benefits of wisdom

Proverbs 4:5 instructs us to gain "understanding and spiritual discernment," which is a way of defining wisdom, and I would like to share some of the results you can expect as you apply wisdom in your life.

Wisdom will always lead you to God's best. Wisdom teaches that you will not keep friends if you try to control and dominate everything that goes on in your life and theirs. You will not keep friends if you talk about them behind their backs or tell their secrets. Wisdom says, "Do not say things about others that you would not want people saying about you."

Wisdom will guide you in money matters. You will not get into debt if you do not spend more money than you make. A lot of people never have fruitful ministries because they think they can run a ministry without good business principles. The Holy Spirit does not need to speak in an audible voice to tell us that we cannot have more money going out than we have coming in. Wisdom tells us that we will get in trouble if we do that.

Wisdom will not let us get overextended in our time commitments if we listen to her. No matter how anxious we may be to accomplish things, wisdom says we need to take time and wait on God to give us peace about what we are to do and not do. It has been very difficult for me over the years to learn to say no to certain speaking opportunities, but I have learned that it is not wise to wear myself out trying to do so much that I end up not doing a quality job.

To God, quality is more important than quantity. Many times wisdom leads us to say no to things to which we would like to say yes. Wisdom may also lead us to say yes to something when we would rather say no. For example, if a friend invites me to do something that is extremely important to her, and I have recently had to say no to her several times, even if I do not really want to accept the invitation, it might be wise for me to do so if I value her friendship and want to keep it.

Wisdom is our friend; it helps us not to live in regret. I think the saddest thing in the world would be to reach old age and look back at my life and feel nothing but regret about what I did or did not do. Wisdom helps us make choices now that we will be happy with later.

Do not forget nor turn away from
the words of my mouth.
6 "Do not turn away from her
(Wisdom) and she will guard and
protect you;
Love her, and she will watch over
you.
7 "The beginning of wisdom is: Get
[skillful and godly] wisdom [it is
preeminent]!
And with all your acquiring, get
understanding [actively seek
spiritual discernment, mature
comprehension, and logical
interpretation]. [James 1:5]
8 "Prize wisdom [and exalt her], and
she will exalt you;
She will honor you if you embrace
her.
9 "She will place on your head a
garland of grace;
She will present you with a crown
of beauty and glory."

10 Hear, my son, and accept my
sayings,
And the years of your life will be
many.
11 I have instructed you in the way of
[skillful and godly] wisdom;
I have led you in upright paths.
12 When you walk, your steps will
not be impeded [for your path
will be clear and open];
And when you run, you will not
stumble.
13 Take hold of instruction; [actively
seek it, grip it firmly and] do not
let go.
Guard her, for she is your life.
14 Do not enter the path of the
wicked,
And do not go the way of evil men.
15 Avoid it, do not travel on it;
Turn away from it and pass on.
16 For the wicked cannot sleep unless
they do evil;
And they are deprived of sleep
unless they make someone
stumble and fall.

17 For they eat the bread of wickedness
And drink the wine of violence.
18 But the path of the just (righteous)
is like the light of dawn,
That shines brighter and brighter
until [it reaches its full strength
and glory in] the perfect day.
[2 Sam 23:4; Matt 5:14; Phil 2:15]
19 The way of the wicked is like
[deep] darkness;
They do not know over what they
stumble. [John 12:35]

20 My son, pay attention to my words
and be willing to learn;
Open your ears to my sayings.

life point

Proverbs 4:18 is so encouraging to me!
This verse says to me that God is not angry with us because we have not yet "arrived." He is pleased that we are pressing
on, that we are staying on the path. If you
and I will just "keep on keeping on," God
will be pleased with our progress.

Keep walking the walk. A walk is something taken one step at a time. This is an
important truth to remember.

If I invited you to take a walk, you would
think I was crazy if I became angry after
the first few steps because we had not yet
arrived at our destination. We can understand ordinary things like this, and yet we
have a difficult time understanding that
God expects our spiritual growth to take
some time.

We do not think there is something wrong
with one-year-old children because they
cannot walk perfectly. They fall down frequently, but we pick them up, love them,
bandage them if necessary, and keep
working with them. Surely our awesome
God can do even more for us than we do
for our children. He is patient and stays
with us until we reach our destination.

21 Do not let them escape from your
    sight;
  Keep them in the center of your
    heart.
22 For they are life to those who find
    them,
  And healing *and* health to all their
    flesh.
23 Watch over your heart with all
    diligence,
  For from it *flow* the springs of life.
24 Put away from you a deceitful
    (lying, misleading) mouth,
  And put devious lips far from you.
25 Let your eyes look directly ahead
    [toward the path of moral
    courage]
  And let your gaze be fixed straight
    in front of you [toward the path
    of integrity].
26 Consider well *and* watch carefully
    the path of your feet,
  And all your ways will be steadfast
    and sure.
27 Do not turn away to the right nor
    to the left [where evil may lurk];
  Turn your foot from [the path of]
    evil.

5 MY SON, be attentive to my
    wisdom [godly wisdom learned
    by costly experience],
  Incline your ear to my
    understanding; [1 Kin 4:29]
2 That you may exercise
    discrimination *and* discretion
    (good judgment),
  And your lips may reserve
    knowledge *and* answer wisely [to
    temptation].
3 For the lips of an immoral woman
    drip honey [like a honeycomb]
  And her speech is smoother than
    oil; [Ezek 20:30; Col 2:8–10;
    2 Pet 2:14–17]
4 But in the end she is bitter like
    [the extract of] wormwood,
  Sharp as a two-edged sword.
5 Her feet go down to death;

life point

Proverbs 4:23 exhorts us to guard our
hearts "with all diligence." Practically,
that means we need to examine our attitudes and our thoughts on a regular basis
and make adjustments as needed.

Many people are deceived into believing
they cannot help what they think, but
we *can* choose our thoughts. We need to
think about what we have been thinking
about. When we do that, it doesn't take
very long to discover the root cause of a
bad attitude.

The enemy will always try to fill our minds
with wrong thinking, but we do not have
to receive everything he tries to give us.
I would not take a spoonful of poison
just because someone offered it to me,
and neither would you. If we are smart
enough not to swallow poison, we should
also be smart enough not to allow Satan
to poison our minds, attitudes, and, ultimately, our lives.

Guard your heart aggressively. Let your
thoughts be good thoughts. Think about
things that are true and honorable (see
Philippians 4:8), and watch your heart
attitude change.

  Her steps take hold of Sheol (the
    nether world, the place of the
    dead),
6 So that she does not think
    [seriously] about the path of life;
  Her ways are aimless *and*
    unstable; you cannot know
    where her path leads.

7 Now then, my sons, listen to me
  And do not depart from (forget)
    the words of my mouth.
8 Let your way [in life] be far from
    her,

And do not go near the door of her house [avoid even being near the places of temptation], [Prov 4:15; Rom 16:17; 1 Thess 5:19–22]

9 Or you will give your honor to others,
And your years to the cruel one,
10 And strangers will be filled with your strength
And your hard-earned wealth will go to the house of a foreigner [who does not know God];
11 And you will groan when your *life is* ending,
When your flesh and your body are consumed;
12 And you say, "How I hated instruction *and* discipline,

life point

As believers, you and I should not hate instruction, as we read about in Proverbs 5:12, but we should be teachable. If we ever reach the point where we think we know everything, then we can be assured that we know nothing! We need to stop hating and despising things—even little things. People use the words *hate* and *despise* quite casually, making comments such as: "I hate going to the grocery store," or "I hate traffic," or "I despise my job." We are not supposed to hate anything but sin.

We all are tempted to hate certain things, just as we are prone to dread certain things. Dread is a close relative of fear. We do not need to dread doing the dishes, getting up, going to work, exercising, or anything else. Satan uses those feelings of dread and our feelings of hatred to deceive us. We simply are not to have hearts that despise anyone or anything. If you have hatred in your heart, repent and then ask God to replace any despising attitude with His love and grace.

And my heart despised correction *and* reproof!
13 "I have not listened to the voice of my teachers,
Nor have I inclined my ear to those who instructed me.
14 "I was almost in total ruin
In the midst of the assembly and congregation."

15 Drink water from your own cistern [of a pure marriage relationship]
And fresh running water from your own well.
16 Should your springs (children) be dispersed,
As streams of water in the streets?
17 [Confine yourself to your own wife.]
Let *your children* be yours alone,
And not *the children* of strangers with you.
18 Let your fountain (wife) be blessed [with the rewards of fidelity],
And rejoice in the wife of your youth. [Song 4:12, 15]
19 *Let her be as* a loving hind and graceful doe,
Let her breasts refresh *and* satisfy you at all times;
Always be exhilarated *and* delight in her love.
20 Why should you, my son, be exhilarated with an immoral woman
And embrace the bosom of an outsider (pagan)?
21 For the ways of man are directly before the eyes of the LORD,
And He carefully watches all of his paths [all of his comings and goings]. [2 Chr 16:9; Job 31:4; 34:21; Prov 15:3; Jer 16:17; Hos 7:2; Heb 4:13]
22 The iniquities done by a wicked man will trap him,
And he will be held with the cords of his sin.
23 He will die for lack of instruction (discipline),

And in the greatness of his foolishness he will go astray *and* be lost.

6 MY SON, if you have become surety (guaranteed a debt or obligation) for your neighbor,
If you have given your pledge for [the debt of] a stranger *or* another [outside your family],
²If you have been snared with the words of your lips,
If you have been trapped by the speech of your mouth,
³Do this now, my son, and release yourself [from the obligation];
Since you have come into the hand of your neighbor,
Go humble yourself, and plead with your neighbor [to pay his debt and release you].
⁴Give no [unnecessary] sleep to your eyes,
Nor slumber to your eyelids;
⁵Tear yourself away like a gazelle from the hand of *the hunter*
And like a bird from the hand of the fowler.

⁶Go to the ant, O lazy one;
Observe her ways and be wise, [Job 12:7]
⁷Which, having no chief, Overseer or ruler,
⁸She prepares her food in the summer
And brings in her provisions [of food for the winter] in the harvest.
⁹How long will you lie down, O lazy one?
When will you arise from your sleep [and learn self-discipline]? [Prov 24:33, 34]
¹⁰"Yet a little sleep, a little slumber,
A little folding of the hands to lie down *and* rest"—

¹¹So your poverty will come like an *approaching* prowler who walks [slowly, but surely]
And your need [will come] like an armed man [making you helpless]. [Prov 10:4; 13:4; 20:4]

¹²A worthless person, a wicked man, Is one who walks with a perverse (corrupt, vulgar) mouth.
¹³Who winks with his eyes [in mockery], who shuffles his feet [to signal],
Who points with his fingers [to give subversive instruction];
¹⁴Who perversely in his heart plots trouble *and* evil continually;
Who spreads discord *and* strife.
¹⁵Therefore [the crushing weight of] his disaster will come suddenly *upon him;*
Instantly he will be broken, and there will be no healing *or* remedy [because he has no heart for God].

¹⁶These six things the LORD hates;
Indeed, seven are repulsive to Him:
¹⁷A proud look [the attitude that makes one overestimate oneself and discount others], a lying tongue,
And hands that shed innocent blood, [Ps 120:2, 3]
¹⁸A heart that creates wicked plans, Feet that run swiftly to evil,
¹⁹A false witness who breathes out lies [even half-truths],
And one who spreads discord (rumors) among brothers.

²⁰My son, be guided by your father's [God-given] commandment (instruction)
And do not reject the teaching of your mother; [Eph 6:1–3]
²¹Bind them continually upon your heart (in your thoughts),
And tie them around your neck. [Prov 3:3; 7:3]

22 When you walk about, they (the godly teachings of your parents) will guide you;
When you sleep, they will keep watch over you;
And when you awake, they will talk to you.
23 For the commandment is a lamp, and the teaching [of the law] is light,
And reproofs (rebukes) for discipline are the way of life, [Ps 19:8; 119:105]
24 To keep you from the evil woman,
From [the flattery of] the smooth tongue of an immoral woman.
25 Do not desire (lust after) her beauty in your heart,
Nor let her capture you with her eyelashes.
26 For on account of a prostitute one is reduced to a piece of bread [to be eaten up],
And the immoral woman hunts [with a hook] the precious life [of a man].
27 Can a man take fire to his chest And his clothes not be burned?
28 Or can a man walk on hot coals And his feet not be scorched?
29 So is the one who goes in to his neighbor's wife;
Whoever touches her will not be found innocent or go unpunished.
30 People do not despise a thief if he steals
To satisfy himself when he is hungry;
31 But when he is found, he must repay seven times [what he stole];
He must give all the property of his house [if necessary to meet his fine].
32 But whoever commits adultery with a woman lacks common sense and sound judgment and an understanding [of moral principles];

He who would destroy his soul does it.
33 Wounds and disgrace he will find, And his reproach (blame) will not be blotted out.
34 For jealousy enrages the [wronged] husband;
He will not spare [the guilty one] on the day of vengeance.
35 He will not accept any ransom [offered to buy him off from demanding full punishment];
Nor will he be satisfied though you offer him many gifts (bribes).

7 MY SON, keep my words And treasure my commandments within you [so they are readily available to guide you].
2 Keep my commandments and live, And keep my teaching and law as the apple of your eye.
3 Bind them [securely] on your fingers;
Write them on the tablet of your heart.
4 Say to [skillful and godly] wisdom, "You are my sister,"
And regard understanding and intelligent insight as your intimate friends;
5 That they may keep you from the immoral woman,
From the foreigner [who does not observe God's laws and] who flatters with her [smooth] words.

6 For at the window of my house I looked out through my lattice.
7 And among the naive [the inexperienced and gullible],
I saw among the youths
A young man lacking [good] sense,
8 Passing through the street near her corner;
And he took the path to her house
9 In the twilight, in the evening;
In the black and dark night.
10 And there a woman met him,

Dressed as a prostitute and sly *and* cunning of heart.
11 She was boisterous and rebellious; She would not stay at home.
12 At times *she was* in the streets, at times in the market places, Lurking *and* setting her ambush at every corner.
13 So she caught him and kissed him And with a brazen *and* impudent face she said to him:
14 "I have peace offerings with me; Today I have paid my vows.
15 "So I came out to meet you [that you might share with me the feast of my offering], Diligently I sought your face and I have found you.
16 "I have spread my couch with coverings *and* cushions of tapestry, With colored fine linen of Egypt.
17 "I have perfumed my bed With myrrh, aloes, and cinnamon.
18 "Come, let us drink our fill of love until morning; Let us console *and* delight ourselves with love.
19 "For my husband is not at home. He has gone on a long journey;
20 He has taken a bag of money with him, And he will come home on the appointed day."
21 With her many persuasions she caused him to yield; With her flattering lips she seduced him.
22 Suddenly he went after her, as an ox goes to the slaughter [not knowing the outcome], Or as one in stocks going to the correction [to be given] to a fool,
23 Until an arrow pierced his liver [with a mortal wound]; Like a bird fluttering straight into the net, He did not know that it *would cost* him his life.

24 Now therefore, my sons, listen to me, And pay attention to the words of my mouth.
25 Do not let your heart turn aside to her ways, Do not stray into her [evil, immoral] paths.
26 For she has cast down many [mortally] wounded; Indeed, all who were killed by her were strong. [Neh 13:26]
27 Her house is the way to Sheol, Descending to the chambers of death. [1 Cor 6:9]

8 DOES NOT wisdom call, And understanding lift up her voice?
2 On the top of the heights beside the way, Where the paths meet, wisdom takes her stand;
3 Beside the gates, at the entrance to the city, At the entrance of the doors, she cries out:
4 "To you, O men, I call, And my voice is directed to the sons of men.
5 "O you naive *or* inexperienced [who are easily misled], understand prudence *and* seek astute common sense; And, O you [closed-minded, self-confident] fools, understand wisdom [seek the insight and self-discipline that leads to godly living]. [Is 32:6]
6 "Listen, for I will speak excellent *and* noble things; And the opening of my lips *will reveal* right things.
7 "For my mouth will utter truth, And wickedness is repulsive *and* loathsome to my lips.
8 "All the words of my mouth are in righteousness (upright, in right standing with God);

There is nothing contrary to truth or perverted (crooked) in them.

9 "They are all straightforward to him who understands [with an open and willing mind], And right to those who find knowledge *and* live by it.

10 "Take my instruction rather than [seeking] silver, And take knowledge rather than choicest gold,

11 "For wisdom is better than rubies; And all desirable things cannot compare with her. [Job 28:15; Ps 19:10; 119:127]

12 "I, [godly] wisdom, reside with prudence [good judgment, moral courage and astute common sense], And I find knowledge and discretion. [James 1:5]

13 "The [reverent] fear *and* worshipful awe of the LORD *includes* the hatred of evil;

life point

Proverbs 8:6–9 describes what should be our confession, our testimony, and our reputation. Our reputation involves not only what we say about ourselves, but also what others say about us.

Unfortunately, many of us have learned to speak in circles, and often when we finish speaking, others do not have the slightest idea what we have just said. We need to learn how to engage in plain, straightforward, honest, truthful communication.

James 3:10 tells us that we should not let both blessings and cursings issue from our mouths. Instead, we ought to be like the virtuous woman in Proverbs 31:26, on whose tongue is the teaching of kindness. As children of God, we need to be excellent in our speech and speak words that are righteous and true.

Pride and arrogance and the evil way, And the perverted mouth, I hate.

14 "Counsel is mine and sound wisdom; I am understanding, power *and* strength are mine.

15 "By me kings reign And rulers decide *and* decree justice. [Dan 2:21; Rom 13:1]

16 "By me princes rule, and nobles, All who judge *and* govern rightly.

17 "I love those who love me; And those who seek me early *and* diligently will find me. [1 Sam 2:30; Ps 91:14; John 14:21; James 1:5]

18 "Riches and honor are with me, Enduring wealth and righteousness (right standing with God). [Prov 3:16; Matt 6:33]

19 "My fruit is better than gold, even pure gold, And my yield is better than choicest silver.

20 "I, [Wisdom, continuously] walk in the way of righteousness, In the midst of the paths of justice,

21 That I may cause those who love me to inherit wealth *and* true riches, And that I may fill their treasuries.

22 "The LORD created *and* possessed me at the beginning of His way, Before His works of old [were accomplished].

23 "From everlasting I was established *and* ordained, From the beginning, before the earth existed, [I, godly wisdom, existed]. [John 1:1; 1 Cor 1:24]

24 "When there were no ocean depths I was born, When there were no fountains *and* springs overflowing with water.

25 "Before the mountains were settled, Before the hills, I was born; [Job 15:7, 8]

26 While He had not yet made the earth and the fields,

Or the first of the dust of the earth.
27 "When He established the
    heavens, I [Wisdom] was there;
When He drew a circle upon the
    face of the deep,
28 When He made firm the skies above,
When the fountains and springs
    of the deep became fixed *and*
    strong,
29 When He set for the sea its
    boundary
So that the waters would not
    transgress [the boundaries set
    by] His command,
When He marked out the
    foundations of the earth— [Job
    38:10, 11; Ps 104:6–9; Jer 5:22]

30 Then I was beside Him, as a
    master craftsman;
And I was daily His delight;
Rejoicing before Him always,
    [Matt 3:17; John 1:2, 18]
31 Rejoicing in the world, His
    inhabited earth,
And having my delight in the sons
    of men. [Ps 16:3]

32 "Now therefore, O sons, listen to me,
For blessed [happy, prosperous, to
    be admired] are they who keep
    my ways. [Ps 119:1, 2; 128:1, 2;
    Luke 11:28]
33 "Heed (pay attention to)
    instruction and be wise,
And do not ignore *or* neglect it.

a little common sense goes a long way

In Proverbs 8:15, 16, wisdom is speaking, and she says that through her, leaders rule. Wisdom brings us to places of leadership, and if we want to be good leaders, we need wisdom and something else with it—common sense!

People often ask me, "How were you able to build a ministry like yours?" I share with them a ministry success principle, one of the most positive aspects of our ministry, the thing that has brought us to where we are today: "Use common sense!"

My husband, Dave, and I use common sense in everything we do in our ministry. You might call it "sanctified common sense." It is not merely reason or logic. The mind of the flesh is sense and reason without the Holy Spirit. Dave and I strive not to walk according to the mind of the flesh, because we are aware that sense and reason alone can cause a lot of trouble. We seek godly, Spirit-filled, sanctified common sense. We believe common sense leads us to present a balanced gospel. We do not buy things we do not have the money to pay for. We do not hire people if we cannot afford to pay their salaries. We know that we cannot try to control our friends if we want to keep them. We have enough common sense to know what to do to stay out of trouble.

Living by common sense really is not difficult; just do what you would want others to do to you. Pay your bills on time; communicate properly; mix encouragement with correction so a person's spirit is not broken—these are just a few examples of good common sense.

As you use more and more common sense, things will get better and better for you. Do not do things that are foolish; do ask God for wisdom. While you are at it, ask Him to help you also use your good, sanctified common sense in every situation.

34 "Blessed [happy, prosperous, to be
   admired] is the man who listens
   to me,
Watching daily at my gates,
Waiting at my doorposts.
35 "For whoever finds me (Wisdom)
   finds life
And obtains favor *and* grace from
   the LORD.
36 "But he who fails to find me *or* sins
   against me injures himself;
All those who hate me love *and*
   court death."

9 WISDOM HAS built her
   [spacious and sufficient] house;
   She has hewn out *and* set up
   her seven pillars.
2 She has prepared her food, she has
   mixed her wine;
She has also set her table. [Matt
   22:2–4]
3 She has sent out her maidens, she
   calls
From the highest places of the city:
4 "Whoever is naive *or* inexperienced,
   let him turn in here!"
As for him who lacks
   understanding, she says,
5 "Come, eat my food
And drink the wine I have mixed
   [and accept my gifts]. [Is 55:1;
   John 6:27]
6 "Leave [behind] your foolishness
   [and the foolish] and live,
And walk in the way of insight *and*
   understanding."
7 He who corrects *and* instructs a
   scoffer gets dishonor for himself,
And he who rebukes a wicked man
   gets insults for himself.
8 Do not correct a scoffer [who
   foolishly ridicules and takes no
   responsibility for his error] or he
   will hate you;
Correct a wise man [who learns
   from his error], and he will love
   you. [Ps 141:5]

life point

We can miss God by being in a hurry to
get what we want. If we do not wait,
especially in important areas, we can
bring trouble into our lives (see Proverbs
8:34–36). I am "fine-tuning" patience in
my life all the time.

I am a natural-born confronter. In the
past, if I wanted a problem solved, I confronted the issue and forced a solution. It
took me years to learn that sometimes it
was not good for me to deal with issues
so directly. I learned that I could make
matters worse, or get in God's way and
end up having to go through the same
situation again because I did not wait for
God's timing. Because I was impatient, I
did not give God a chance to solve things
for me.

I have learned that when I feel overly
anxious to handle something, I should let
it rest for at least twenty-four hours. It is
amazing how we can change our minds
if we will just let things settle for a few
hours. We can save ourselves so much
trouble if we will learn to wait on God.

9 Give *instruction* to a wise man and
   he will become even wiser;
Teach a righteous man and he will
   increase his learning.
10 The [reverent] fear of the LORD
   [that is, worshiping Him and
   regarding Him as truly awesome]
   is the beginning *and* the
   preeminent part of wisdom [its
   starting point and its essence],
And the knowledge of the Holy
   One is understanding *and*
   spiritual insight.
11 For by me (wisdom from God) your
   days will be multiplied,
And years of life shall be
   increased.

¹²If you are wise, you are wise for
yourself [for your own benefit];
If you scoff [thoughtlessly ridicule
and disdain], you alone will pay
the penalty.
¹³The foolish woman is restless *and*
noisy;
She is naive *and* easily misled *and*
thoughtless, and knows nothing
at all [of eternal value].
¹⁴She sits at the doorway of her house,
On a seat by the high *and*
conspicuous places of the city,
¹⁵Calling to those who pass by,
Who are making their paths
straight:
¹⁶"Whoever is naive *or* inexperienced,
let him turn in here!"
And to him who lacks
understanding (common sense),
she says,
¹⁷"Stolen waters (pleasures) are sweet
[because they are forbidden];
And bread *eaten* in secret is
pleasant." [Prov 20:17]
¹⁸But he does not know that the
spirits of the dead are there,
And that her guests are [already]
in the depths of Sheol (the nether
world, the place of the dead).

10 THE PROVERBS of Solomon:

A wise son makes a father glad,
But a foolish [stubborn] son [who
refuses to learn] is a grief to his
mother.
²Treasures of wickedness *and* ill-
gotten gains do not profit,

10:7 Lit *mention.*

But righteousness *and* moral
integrity in daily life rescues
from death.
³The LORD will not allow the
righteous to hunger [God will
meet all his needs],
But He will reject *and* cast away
the craving of the wicked. [Ps
34:9, 10; 37:25]
⁴Poor is he who works with a
negligent *and* idle hand,
But the hand of the diligent makes
him rich.
⁵He who gathers during summer
and takes advantage of his
opportunities is a son who acts
wisely,
But he who sleeps during harvest
and ignores the moment of
opportunity is a son who acts
shamefully.
⁶Blessings are on the head of the
righteous [the upright, those in
right standing with God],
But the mouth of the wicked
conceals violence.
⁷The *memory of the righteous
[person] is a [source of] blessing,
But the name of the wicked will
[be forgotten and] rot [like a
corpse]. [Ps 112:6; 9:5]
⁸The wise in heart [are willing to
learn so they] will accept *and*
obey commands (instruction),
But the babbling fool [who is
arrogant and thinks himself wise]
will come to ruin.
⁹He who walks in integrity *and* with
moral character walks securely,
But he who takes a crooked way
will be discovered *and* punished.

speak the Word

*Thank You, God, that blessings are on the heads of the righteous
and that I am righteous through Your Son!*
—ADAPTED FROM PROVERBS 10:6

¹⁰He who [maliciously] winks
    the eye [of evil intent] causes
    trouble;
  And the babbling fool [who is
    arrogant and thinks himself wise]
    will come to ruin.
¹¹The mouth of the righteous is a
    fountain of life *and* his words of
    wisdom are a source of blessing,
  But the mouth of the wicked
    conceals violence *and* evil.
¹²Hatred stirs up strife,
  But love covers *and* overwhelms
    all transgressions [forgiving and
    overlooking another's faults].
¹³On the lips of the discerning,
    [skillful and godly] wisdom is
    found,
  But discipline *and* the rod are
    for the back of the one who is
    without common sense *and*
    understanding.
¹⁴Wise men store up *and* treasure
    knowledge [in mind and heart],
  But with the mouth of the foolish,
    ruin is at hand.
¹⁵The rich man's wealth is his
    fortress;
  The ruin of the poor is their
    poverty. [Ps 52:7; 1 Tim 6:17]
¹⁶The wages of the righteous [the
    upright, those in right standing
    with God] is [a worthwhile,
    meaningful] life,
  The income of the wicked,
    punishment. [Rom 6:21–23;
    1 Tim 6:10]
¹⁷He who learns from instruction
    and correction is on the [right]
    path of life [and for others
    his example is a path toward
    wisdom and blessing],

  But he who ignores *and* refuses
    correction goes off course [and
    for others his example is a path
    toward sin and ruin].
¹⁸He who hides hatred has lying lips,
  And he who spreads slander is a
    fool. [Prov 26:24–26]
¹⁹When there are many words,
    transgression *and* offense are
    unavoidable,
  But he who controls his lips *and*
    keeps thoughtful silence is wise.
²⁰The tongue of the righteous is like
    precious silver (greatly valued);
  The heart of the wicked is worth
    little.
²¹The lips of the righteous feed *and*
    guide many,
  But fools [who reject God and
    His wisdom] die for lack of
    understanding.
²²The blessing of the Lord brings
    [true] riches,
  And He adds no sorrow to it [for it
    comes as a blessing from God].
²³Engaging in evil is like sport to the
    fool [who refuses wisdom and
    chases sin],
  But to a man of understanding
    [skillful and godly] wisdom
    brings joy.
²⁴What the wicked fears will come
    upon him,
  But the desire of the righteous
    [for the blessings of God] will be
    granted.
²⁵When the whirlwind passes, the
    wicked is no more,
  But the righteous has an
    everlasting foundation. [Ps 125:1;
    Matt 7:24–27]
²⁶Like vinegar to the teeth and
    smoke to the eyes,

speak the Word

Thank You, God, that Your blessing brings true riches
and that You add no sorrow to it.
–ADAPTED FROM PROVERBS 10:22

So is the lazy one to those who
send him *to work*.
27 The [reverent] fear of the Lord
[worshiping, obeying, serving,
and trusting Him with awe-filled
respect] prolongs one's life,
But the years of the wicked will be
shortened.
28 The hope of the righteous [those
of honorable character and
integrity] is joy,
But the expectation of the wicked
[those who oppose God and
ignore His wisdom] comes to
nothing.
29 The way of the Lord is a
stronghold to the upright,
But it is ruin to those who do evil.
30 The [consistently] righteous will
never be shaken,
But the wicked will not inhabit the
earth. [Ps 37:22; 125:1]
31 The mouth of the righteous flows
with [skillful and godly] wisdom,
But the perverted tongue will be
cut out.
32 The lips of the righteous know
(speak) what is acceptable,
But the mouth of the wicked
knows (speaks) what is
perverted (twisted).

11 A FALSE balance *and*
dishonest business
practices are extremely
offensive to the Lord,
But an accurate scale is His delight.
[Lev 19:35, 36; Prov 16:11]
2 When pride comes [boiling up
with an arrogant attitude of
self-importance], then come
dishonor *and* shame,
But with the humble [the teachable
who have been chiseled by
trial and who have learned to
walk humbly with God] there is
wisdom *and* soundness of mind.
3 The integrity *and* moral courage of
the upright will guide them,

But the crookedness of the
treacherous will destroy them.
4 Riches will not provide security in
the day of wrath *and* judgment,
But righteousness rescues from
death. [Prov 10:2; Zeph 1:18]
5 The righteousness of the blameless
will smooth their way *and* keep it
straight,
But the wicked will fall by his own
wickedness.
6 The righteousness of the upright
will rescue them,
But the treacherous will be caught
by their own greed.
7 When the wicked man dies, his
expectation will perish;
And the hope of [godless] strong
men perishes.
8 The righteous is rescued from
trouble,
And the wicked takes his place.
9 With his mouth the godless man
destroys his neighbor,
But through knowledge *and*
discernment the righteous will
be rescued.
10 When it goes well for the
righteous, the city rejoices,
And when the wicked perish,
there are shouts of joy.
11 By the blessing [of the influence]
of the upright the city is exalted,
But by the mouth of the wicked it
is torn down.
12 He who despises his neighbor
lacks sense,
But a man of understanding keeps
silent.
13 He who goes about as a gossip
reveals secrets,
But he who is trustworthy *and*
faithful keeps a matter hidden.
14 Where there is no [wise,
intelligent] guidance, the people
fall [and go off course like a ship
without a helm],
But in the abundance of [wise and
godly] counselors there is victory.

15 He who puts up security *and*
guarantees a debt for an outsider
will surely suffer [for his
foolishness],
But he who hates (declines) being
a guarantor is secure [from its
penalties].
16 A gracious *and* good woman
attains honor,
And ruthless men attain riches
[but not respect].
17 The merciful *and* generous
man benefits his soul [for his
behavior returns to bless him],
But the cruel *and* callous man does
himself harm.
18 The wicked man earns deceptive
wages,
But he who sows righteousness *and*
lives his life with integrity will
have a true reward [that is both
permanent and satisfying]. [Hos
10:12; Gal 6:8, 9; James 3:18]
19 He who is steadfast in
righteousness *attains* life,
But he who pursues evil *attains* his
own death.
20 The perverse in heart are
repulsive *and* shamefully vile to
the Lord,
But those who are blameless *and*
above reproach in their walk are
His delight!

21 Assuredly, the evil man will not go
unpunished,
But the descendants of the
righteous will be freed.
22 As a ring of gold in a swine's snout,
So is a beautiful woman who is
without discretion [her lack of
character mocks her beauty].
23 The desire of the righteous brings
only good,
But the expectation of the wicked
brings wrath.
24 There is the one who [generously]
scatters [abroad], and yet
increases all the more;
And there is the one who withholds
what is justly due, *but it results*
only in want *and* poverty.
25 The generous man [is a source
of blessing and] shall be
prosperous *and* enriched,
And he who waters will himself be
watered [reaping the generosity
he has sown]. [2 Cor 9:6–10]
26 The people curse him who holds
back grain [when the public
needs it],
But a blessing [from God and man]
is upon the head of him who
sells it.
27 He who diligently seeks good
seeks favor *and* grace,
But he who seeks evil, evil will
come to him.
28 He who leans on *and* trusts in *and*
is confident in his riches will fall,
But the righteous [who trust in
God's provision] will flourish like
a *green* leaf.

putting the Word to work

Proverbs 11:14 teaches us that there is safety in a multitude of wise and godly counselors. Do you have wise, godly people who can provide sound counsel in your life? If so, consult them often. Never put them ahead of God, and do not let them make your final decisions, because those should be made between you and God. However, wise counselors are very valuable, and if you do not have such people in your life, ask God to send them.

putting the Word to work

Proverbs 11:25 says that people who are generous will be prosperous and enriched and that when we "water" others, we will be "watered" in return. In what ways can you be generous to someone today?

29 He who troubles (mismanages) his own house will inherit the wind (nothing),
And the foolish will be a servant to the wise-hearted.
30 The fruit of the [consistently] righteous is a tree of life,
And he who is wise captures *and* wins souls [for God—he gathers them for eternity]. [Matt 4:19; 1 Cor 9:19; James 5:20]
31 If the righteous will be rewarded on the earth [with godly blessings],
How much more [will] the wicked and the sinner [be repaid with punishment]!

12

WHOEVER LOVES instruction *and* discipline loves knowledge,
But he who hates reproof *and* correction is stupid.
2 A good man will obtain favor from the Lord,
But He will condemn a man who devises evil.
3 A man will not be established by wickedness,
But the root of the [consistently] righteous will not be moved.
4 A virtuous *and* excellent wife [worthy of honor] is the crown of her husband,
But she who shames him [with her foolishness] is like rottenness in his bones. [Prov 31:23; 1 Cor 11:7]
5 The thoughts *and* purposes of the [consistently] righteous are just (honest, reliable),
But the counsels *and* schemes of the wicked are deceitful.
6 The [malevolent] words of the wicked lie in wait for [innocent] blood [to slander],
But the mouth of the upright will rescue *and* protect them.
7 The wicked are overthrown [by their evil] and are no more,
But the house of the [consistently] righteous will stand [securely].
8 A man will be commended according to his insight *and* sound judgment,
But the one who is of a perverse mind will be despised.
9 Better is he who is lightly esteemed and has a servant,
Than he who [boastfully] honors himself [pretending to be what he is not] and lacks bread.
10 A righteous man has kind regard for the life of his animal,
But even the compassion of the wicked is cruel. [Deut 25:4]
11 He who tills his land will have plenty of bread,
But he who follows worthless *things* lacks common sense *and* good judgment.
12 The wicked desire the plunder of evil men,
But the root of the righteous yields *richer* fruit.
13 An evil man is [dangerously] ensnared by the transgression of his lips,
But the righteous will escape from trouble.
14 A man will be satisfied with good from the fruit of his words,
And the deeds of a man's hands will return to him [as a harvest].
15 The way of the [arrogant] fool [who rejects God's wisdom] is right in his own eyes,
But a wise *and* prudent man is he who listens to counsel. [Prov 3:7; 9:9; 21:2]
16 The [arrogant] fool's anger is quickly known [because he lacks self-control and common sense],
But a prudent man ignores an insult.
17 He who speaks truth [when he testifies] tells what is right,
But a false witness utters deceit [in court].

18 There is one who speaks rashly
  like the thrusts of a sword,
  But the tongue of the wise brings
  healing.
19 Truthful lips will be established
  forever,
  But a lying tongue is [credited]
  only for a moment.
20 Deceit is in the heart of those who
  devise evil,
  But counselors of peace have joy.
21 No harm befalls the righteous,
  But the wicked are filled with
  trouble. [Job 5:19; Ps 91:3; Prov
  12:13; Is 46:4; Jer 1:8; Dan 6:27;
  2 Tim 4:18]
22 Lying lips are extremely
  disgusting to the LORD,

life point

I believe all of us Christians should keep
our hearts light. The King James Version
of Proverbs 12:25 says, "Heaviness in the
heart of man maketh it stoop: but a good
word maketh it glad."

We do not have to go around with
troubled, heavy hearts or with a spirit of
heaviness on us. In John 14:1 Jesus told
His disciples, "Do not let your hearts be
troubled (afraid, cowardly)." Isaiah 61:3
gives a wonderful promise to those who
need the Lord to lift the heaviness from
them. It says that God wants to "grant to
those who mourn in Zion the following:
. . . the oil of joy instead of mourning, the
garment [expressive] of praise instead of
a disheartened spirit . . ."

The Lord does not want us to have heavy
or troubled hearts. The next time things
are not going right for you, remember to
release your burdens and anxieties to the
Lord. He wants you to be lighthearted and
to enjoy life.

But those who deal faithfully are
  His delight. [Prov 6:17; 11:20; Rev
  22:15]
23 A shrewd man is reluctant to
  display his knowledge [until the
  proper time],
  But the heart of [over-confident]
  fools proclaims foolishness. [Is
  32:6]
24 The hand of the diligent will rule,
  But the negligent and lazy will be
  put to forced labor.
25 Anxiety in a man's heart weighs it
  down,
  But a good (encouraging) word
  makes it glad. [Ps 50:4; Prov 15:13]
26 The righteous man is a guide to
  his neighbor,
  But the way of the wicked leads
  them astray.
27 The lazy man does not catch and
  roast his prey,
  But the precious possession of a
  [wise] man is diligence [because
  he recognizes opportunities and
  seizes them].
28 In the way of righteousness is life,
  And in its pathway there is no
  death [but immortality—eternal
  life]. [John 3:36; 4:36; 8:51; 11:26;
  1 Cor 15:54; Gal 6:8]

13 A WISE son heeds and
  accepts [and is the result
  of] his father's discipline
  and instruction,
  But a scoffer does not listen to
  reprimand and does not learn
  from his errors.
2 From the fruit of his mouth a
  [wise] man enjoys good,
  But the desire of the treacherous is
  for violence.
3 The one who guards his mouth
  [thinking before he speaks]
  protects his life;
  The one who opens his lips wide
  [and chatters without thinking]
  comes to ruin.

⁴The soul (appetite) of the lazy
   person craves and gets nothing
   [for lethargy overcomes
   ambition],
But the soul (appetite) of the
   diligent [who works willingly]
   is rich *and* abundantly supplied.
   [Prov 10:4]
⁵A righteous man hates lies,
But a wicked man is loathsome,
   and he acts shamefully.

⁶Righteousness (being in right
   standing with God) guards the
   one whose way is blameless,
But wickedness undermines *and*
   overthrows the sinner.
⁷There is one who pretends to be
   rich, yet has nothing at all;
Another pretends to be poor, yet has
   great wealth. [Prov 12:9; Luke
   12:20, 21]
⁸The ransom for a man's life is his
   wealth,

from disappointment to reappointment

Proverbs 13:12 says that "hope deferred makes the heart sick." What is "hope deferred"? I believe it is what we call disappointment.

We all are disappointed when things do not work out the way we would like. We become disappointed when we have a plan that fails, a hope that does not materialize,
or a goal that we do not reach. We are disappointed by everything from a picnic that
is rained out to the loss of a job. We are disappointed when the new watch we were
given will not keep time correctly, or when the child we had hoped would grow into
a mature adult shows no signs of doing so.

When such things happen, for a certain period of time we experience a letdown,
one that can lead to depression if not handled properly. That is when we have to
make the decision to adapt and adjust, to take a new approach and just keep going
despite our feelings. That is when we must remember that we have the Greater One
residing within us, so that no matter what may happen to frustrate us, or how long
it may take for our dreams and goals to become realities, we are not going to give
up and quit just because of our emotions.

That is when we must remember what God once impressed on me in such a moment:
"When you get disappointed, you can always make the decision to get reappointed!"

Disappointment often leads to discouragement, which is even more of a "downer."
We have all experienced the depressing feeling that comes after we have tried our
very best to do something and either nothing happens or it all falls totally apart.
How disappointing and discouraging it is to see the things we love senselessly destroyed by others or, even worse, by our own neglect or failure. Regardless of how it
may happen or who may be responsible, it is hard to go on when everything we have
counted on falls down around us. That is when those of us who have the creative
power of the Holy Spirit on the inside can get a new vision, a new direction, and a
new goal to help us overcome the frustrating, downward pull of disappointment.
Hope deferred does make the heart sick, but hope can be rekindled, and our hearts
can be made whole again by the power of the Holy Spirit.

But the poor man does not even have to listen to a rebuke *or* threats [from the envious].
⁹The light of the righteous [within him—grows brighter and] rejoices,
But the lamp of the wicked [is a temporary light and] goes out.
¹⁰Through pride *and* presumption come nothing but strife,
But [skillful and godly] wisdom is with those who welcome [well-advised] counsel.
¹¹Wealth *obtained* by fraud dwindles,
But he who gathers gradually by [honest] labor will increase [his riches].
¹²Hope deferred makes the heart sick,
But when desire is fulfilled, it is a tree of life.
¹³Whoever despises the word *and* counsel [of God] brings destruction upon himself,
But he who [reverently] fears *and* respects the commandment [of God] will be rewarded.
¹⁴The teaching of the wise is a fountain *and* source of life,
So that one may avoid the snares of death.
¹⁵Good understanding wins favor [from others],
But the way of the unfaithful is hard [like barren, dry soil].
¹⁶Every prudent *and* self-disciplined man acts with knowledge,
But a [closed-minded] fool [who refuses to learn] displays his foolishness [for all to see].
¹⁷A wicked messenger falls into hardship,
But a faithful ambassador brings healing.
¹⁸Poverty and shame will come to him who refuses instruction *and* discipline,
But he who accepts *and* learns from reproof *or* censure is honored.
¹⁹Desire realized is sweet to the soul;

life point

People who are prudent and self-disciplined are balanced; they avoid extremes in the management of their lives and of their faith. It seems to me, after many years of observation in the kingdom of God, that people have a difficult time with balance. Ideas concerning the power of words, the mouth, confession, calling those things that do not exist as though they do, and speaking things into existence, is one example of an area in which I have seen people move into extremes. It seems that the flesh wants to live in the ditch on one side of the road or the other, but it has a difficult time staying in the middle of the highway between the lines of safety. We should speak positively about our lives and our futures. We should agree with what God says about us in His Word. Our confession does have a lot to do with our possession, but we should not ever think that we can have whatever we want just because we say it. We are to speak forth God's Word, not our carnal desires.

Extremes are actually the devil's playground. If he cannot get believers to totally ignore a truth and live in deception, his next tactic will be to get them so one-sided and out of balance with the truth that they are no better off than they were before. Sometimes they end up even worse off than they were previously.

Wisdom is a central theme of God's Word. As a matter of fact, there is no real victory without it, and we are wise to remain balanced in our everyday lives.

But it is detestable to fools to turn away from evil [which they have planned].
²⁰He who walks [as a companion] with wise men will be wise,

But the companions of [conceited, dull-witted] fools [are fools themselves and] will experience harm. [Is 32:6]

21 Adversity pursues sinners,
But the [consistently] upright will be rewarded with prosperity.

22 A good man leaves an inheritance to his children's children,
And the wealth of the sinner is stored up for [the hands of] the righteous.

23 Abundant food is in the fallow (uncultivated) ground of the poor,
But [without protection] it is swept away by injustice.

24 He who withholds the rod [of discipline] hates his son,
But he who loves him disciplines and trains him diligently and appropriately [with wisdom and love]. [Prov 19:18; 22:15; 23:13; 29:15, 17; Eph 6:4]

25 The [consistently] righteous has enough to satisfy his appetite,
But the stomach of the wicked is in need [of bread].

14 THE WISE woman builds her house [on a foundation of godly precepts, and her household thrives],
But the foolish one [who lacks spiritual insight] tears it down with her own hands [by ignoring godly principles].

2 He who walks in uprightness [reverently] fears the LORD [and obeys and worships Him with profound respect],

But he who is devious in his ways despises Him.

3 In the mouth of the [arrogant] fool [who rejects God] is a rod for his back,
But the lips of the wise [when they speak with godly wisdom] will protect them.

4 Where there are no oxen, the manger is clean,
But much revenue [because of good crops] comes by the strength of the ox.

5 A faithful and trustworthy witness will not lie,
But a false witness speaks lies.

6 A scoffer seeks wisdom and finds none [for his ears are closed to wisdom],
But knowledge is easy for one who understands [because he is willing to learn].

7 Leave the presence of a [shortsighted] fool,
For you will not find knowledge or hear godly wisdom from his lips.

8 The wisdom of the sensible is to understand his way,
But the foolishness of [shortsighted] fools is deceit.

9 Fools mock sin [but sin mocks the fools],
But among the upright there is good will and the favor and blessing of God. [Prov 10:23]

10 The heart knows its own bitterness,
And no stranger shares its joy.

11 The house of the wicked will be overthrown,

speak the Word

Help me, Lord, to speak wisely, because wise words will protect me.
—ADAPTED FROM PROVERBS 14:3

Thank You, God, for making me upright and giving me Your favor and Your blessing.
—ADAPTED FROM PROVERBS 14:9

But the tent of the upright will thrive.

¹²There is a way *which seems* right to a man *and* appears straight before him,
But its end is the way of death.

¹³Even in laughter the heart may be in pain,
And the end of joy may be grief.

¹⁴The backslider in heart will have his fill with his own [rotten] ways,
But a good man will *be satisfied* with his ways [the godly thought and action which his heart pursues and in which he delights].

¹⁵The naive *or* inexperienced person [is easily misled and] believes every word he hears,

free from bitterness

Proverbs 14:10 speaks of bitterness in our hearts. Bitterness (harboring unforgiveness) in our hearts is extremely dangerous because the Bible tells us very plainly that if we will not forgive other people, then God will not forgive us (see Mark 11:26). If we do not forgive others, our faith will not work. And everything that comes from God comes by faith. If our faith does not work, we cannot receive from God and we are in trouble.

When I preach on the subject of forgiveness, I often ask members of the audience to stand if they have been offended and need to forgive someone. I have never seen fewer than 80 percent of the congregation stand.

It does not take a genius to figure out why we are lacking the power we need in the body of Christ. Power comes from love, not from hatred, bitterness, and unforgiveness.

"But you don't know what was done to me," people say when trying to excuse their bitterness, resentment, and unforgiveness. Based on what the Bible says, it really does not matter how great the offense was. We serve a God Who is greater, and if we will handle the offense in the right way, He will bring us justice and recompense if we allow Him to do so.

In Isaiah 61:7 the Lord promises us, "Instead of your [former] shame you will have a double portion." A double portion is a reward. It is a payback for past hurts. It is like workmen's compensation. The Lord once told me, "Joyce, you work for Me, and as long as you do, if you get hurt on the job, I will pay you back."

In Romans 12:19 we are told, "Beloved, never avenge yourselves, but leave the way open for God's wrath [and His judicial righteousness]; for it is written [in Scripture], 'VENGEANCE IS MINE, I WILL REPAY,' says the Lord." Do not try to get people back for what they have done to you. Leave it in God's hands.

Jesus taught us that we are to forgive those who hurt us, bless and show kindness to those who curse us, and pray for those who mistreat us (Luke 6:28). That is hard. But there is something harder: being full of hatred, bitterness, and resentment.

Quite often people do not even know that they have hurt us. Do not spend your life hating someone who is probably out having a good time while you are all upset! Rather, choose to allow God to work forgiveness in you so you can be released from your bitterness and set free to enjoy life.

But the prudent man [is discreet
   and astute and] considers well
   where he is going.
¹⁶ A wise man suspects danger and
   cautiously avoids evil,
But the fool is arrogant and
   careless.
¹⁷ A quick-tempered man acts
   foolishly *and* without self-control,
And a man of wicked schemes is
   hated.
¹⁸ The naive [are unsophisticated
   and easy to exploit and] inherit
   foolishness,
But the sensible [are thoughtful
   and far-sighted and] are
   crowned with knowledge.
¹⁹ The evil will bow down before the
   good,
And the wicked [will bow down] at
   the gates of the righteous.
²⁰ The poor man is hated even by his
   neighbor,
But those who love the rich are
   many.
²¹ He who despises his neighbor
   sins [against God and his fellow
   man],
But happy [blessed and favored by
   God] is he who is gracious *and*
   merciful to the poor.
²² Do they not go astray who devise
   evil *and* wander from the way of
   righteousness?
But kindness and truth will be to
   those who devise good.
²³ In all labor there is profit,
But mere talk leads only to poverty.
²⁴ The crown of the wise is their
   wealth [of wisdom],
But the foolishness of [closed-
   minded] fools is [nothing but]
   folly.

life point

Think of it: a person who has a calm and
undisturbed mind has health for his or her
body. But as we see in Proverbs 14:30,
envy, passion, and anger can actually
destroy the physical body. Keeping these
negative emotions far from you is good
for your health!

²⁵ A truthful witness saves lives,
But he who speaks lies is
   treacherous.
²⁶ In the [reverent] fear of the LORD
   there is strong confidence,
And His children will [always]
   have a place of refuge.
²⁷ The [reverent] fear of the LORD
   [that leads to obedience and
   worship] is a fountain of life,
So that one may avoid the snares
   of death. [John 4:10, 14]
²⁸ In a multitude of people is a king's
   glory,
But in a lack of people is a
   [pretentious] prince's ruin.
²⁹ He who is slow to anger has great
   understanding [and profits from
   his self-control],
But he who is quick-tempered
   exposes *and* exalts his
   foolishness [for all to see]. [Prov
   16:32; James 1:19]
³⁰ A calm *and* peaceful *and* tranquil
   heart is life *and* health to the body,
But passion *and* envy are like
   rottenness to the bones.
³¹ He who oppresses the poor taunts
   and insults his Maker,
But he who is kind *and* merciful
   and gracious to the needy honors
   Him. [Prov 17:5; Matt 25:40, 45]

speak the Word

Thank You, God, that I have strong confidence as I reverently fear You.
In You, I will always have a place of refuge.
—ADAPTED FROM PROVERBS 14:26

life point

The Bible teaches us in Proverbs 15:1 that a "soft and gentle and thoughtful answer turns away wrath." In other words, if someone is angry and yelling, then responding to that person calmly and gently will change the situation and stop an argument. How awesome! The next time angry words seem to be flying around you, respond with soft, gentle words. That's the best way to diffuse a tense conversation.

32 The wicked is overthrown through his wrongdoing,
But the righteous has hope and confidence and a refuge [with God] even in death.
33 Wisdom rests [silently] in the heart of one who has understanding,
But what is in the heart of [shortsighted] fools is made known. [Is 32:6]
34 Righteousness [moral and spiritual integrity and virtuous character] exalts a nation,
But sin is a disgrace to any people.
35 The king's favor and good will are toward a servant who acts wisely and discreetly,
But his anger and wrath are toward him who acts shamefully. [Matt 24:45, 47]

15 A SOFT and gentle and thoughtful answer turns away wrath,
But harsh and painful and careless words stir up anger. [Prov 25:15]
2 The tongue of the wise speaks knowledge that is pleasing and acceptable,
But the [babbling] mouth of fools spouts folly.
3 The eyes of the LORD are in every place,

Watching the evil and the good [in all their endeavors]. [Job 34:21; Prov 5:21; Jer 16:17; 32:19; Heb 4:13]
4 A soothing tongue [speaking words that build up and encourage] is a tree of life,
But a perverse tongue [speaking words that overwhelm and depress] crushes the spirit.
5 A [flippant, arrogant] fool rejects his father's instruction and correction,
But he who [is willing to learn and] regards and keeps in mind a reprimand acquires good sense.
6 Great and priceless treasure is in the house of the [consistently] righteous one [who seeks godly instruction and grows in wisdom],

life point

Throughout the Word of God we are told to be careful how we use our mouths. We are to pay attention to our words. We are never to speak things that will make people want to give up or quit. We are not to pollute one another or ourselves with negative words from our lips.

Proverbs 15:4 tells us that "a perverse tongue [speaking words that overwhelm and depress] crushes the spirit." Notice that the word spirit is spelled with a small s. This verse is not talking about the Holy Spirit; it is referring to our own human spirits. Depression of the human spirit is another problem created and magnified by wrong thoughts and words—our own or those of others.

We are not to use our mouths to hurt, break down, or depress, but rather to heal, restore, and uplift. The tongue has healing power, and we need to use it to bring healing.

But trouble is in the income of the
  wicked one [who rejects the laws
  of God].
7 The lips of the wise spread
  knowledge [sifting it as chaff
  from the grain];
  But the hearts of [shortsighted]
  fools are not so.
8 The sacrifice of the wicked is
  hateful *and* exceedingly offensive
  to the LORD,
  But the prayer of the upright is
  His delight! [Is 1:11; Jer 6:20;
  Amos 5:22]
9 The way [of life] of the wicked
  is hateful *and* exceedingly
  offensive to the LORD,
  But He loves one who pursues
  righteousness [personal
  integrity, moral courage and
  honorable character].
10 There is severe discipline for him
  who turns from the way [of
  righteousness];
  And he who hates correction will
  die.
11 Sheol (the nether world, the
  place of the dead) and Abaddon
  (the abyss, the place of eternal
  punishment) *lie open* before the
  LORD—
  How much more the hearts *and*
  inner motives of the children of
  men. [Job 26:6; Ps 139:8; Rev 9:2;
  20:1, 2]

life point

Those who are wise use their lips to
spread knowledge (see Proverbs 15:7),
but those who are foolish in heart speak
whatever comes to mind. I believe one of
the biggest problems with people is that
they do not use wisdom when they think
and thus do foolish things. Ask God to
help you identify and correct any foolishness in your life and to enable you to use
wisdom in everything to do.

life point

Proverbs 15:13 says that "a heart full
of joy and goodness makes a cheerful
face." In the Amplified Classic version
of the Bible, where I first learned this
verse, it says that a happy heart makes a
"cheerful countenance." The Bible uses
the word *countenance* in many places,
so I think we should pay attention to it.
Your countenance is your face, the way
you look. God is concerned about how
we look because either we are walking advertisements for Jesus or we are
walking advertisements for the enemy.
That is why it is important that we learn
how to have a cheerful countenance and
a pleasant look on our faces.

My husband has a secretary who is always
smiling. Everything he asks her to do, she
does with a smile. I think that is the way
God wants all of us to be. When we smile,
it puts other people at ease. It gives
them freedom and liberty and a sense of
confidence.

It is amazing how much more comfortable
and secure we are when we smile at one
another and how much discomfort and
insecurity we cause one another when we
go around with sour looks on our faces.

Sometimes our problems are not caused
by the devil as we might like to assume;
they are the results of the way we feel
and act. We need to cheer up. When we
relax and smile, it makes us (and everyone
around us) feel better.

12 A scoffer [unlike a wise man]
  resents one who rebukes him
  and tries to teach him;
  Nor will he go to the wise [for
  counsel and instruction].
13 A heart full of joy *and* goodness
  makes a cheerful face,

But when a heart is full of sadness
the spirit is crushed. [Prov 17:22]

14 The mind of the intelligent *and*
discerning seeks knowledge *and*
eagerly inquires after it,
But the mouth of the [stubborn]
fool feeds on foolishness. [Is 32:6]

15 All the days of the afflicted are
bad,
But a glad heart has a continual
feast [regardless of the
circumstances].

16 Better is a little with the [reverent,
worshipful] fear of the LORD
Than great treasure and trouble
with it. [Ps 37:16; Prov 16:8;
1 Tim 6:6]

17 Better is a dinner of vegetables *and*
herbs where love is present
Than a fattened ox served with
hatred. [Prov 17:1]

18 A hot-tempered man stirs up strife,
But he who is slow to anger *and*
patient calms disputes.

19 The way of the lazy is like a hedge
of thorns [it pricks, lacerates,
and entangles him],
But the way [of life] of the upright
is smooth *and* open like a
highway.

20 A wise son makes a father glad,
But a foolish man despises his
mother.

21 Foolishness is joy to him who
is without heart *and* lacks
[intelligent, common] sense,
But a man of understanding walks
uprightly [making his course
straight]. [Eph 5:15]

22 Without consultation *and* wise
advice, plans are frustrated,
But with many counselors they are
established and succeed.

23 A man has joy in giving an
appropriate answer,
And how good *and* delightful
is a word spoken at the right
moment—how good it is!

24 The [chosen] path of life leads
upward for the wise,
That he may keep away from Sheol
(the nether world, the place of the
dead) below. [Phil 3:20; Col 3:1, 2]

25 The LORD will tear down the house
of the proud *and* arrogant (self-
righteous),
But He will establish *and* protect
the boundaries [of the land] of
the [godly] widow.

26 Evil plans *and* thoughts of the
wicked are exceedingly vile *and*
offensive to the LORD,
But pure words are pleasant words
to Him.

27 He who profits unlawfully brings
suffering to his own house,
But he who hates bribes [and does
not receive nor pay them] will
live. [Is 5:8; Jer 17:11]

28 The heart of the righteous thinks
carefully about how to answer
[in a wise and appropriate and
timely way],
But the [babbling] mouth of the
wicked pours out malevolent
things. [1 Pet 3:15]

29 The LORD is far from the wicked
[and distances Himself from
them],
But He hears the prayer of the
[consistently] righteous [that is,
those with spiritual integrity and
moral courage].

30 The light of the eyes rejoices the
hearts of others,
And good news puts fat on the
bones.

31 The ear that listens to *and* learns
from the life-giving rebuke
(reprimand, censure)
Will remain among the wise.

32 He who neglects *and* ignores
instruction *and* discipline
despises himself,
But he who learns from rebuke
acquires understanding [and
grows in wisdom].

33 The [reverent] fear of the LORD
   [that is, worshiping Him and
   regarding Him as truly awesome]
   is the instruction for wisdom [its
   starting point and its essence];
   And before honor comes humility.

16 THE PLANS *and*
   reflections of the heart
   belong to man,
   But the [wise] answer of the
   tongue is from the LORD.
2 All the ways of a man are clean
   and innocent in his own eyes
   [and he may see nothing wrong
   with his actions],
   But the LORD weighs *and* examines
   the motives *and* intents [of the
   heart and knows the truth].
   [1 Sam 16:7; Heb 4:12]
3 Commit your works to the LORD
   [submit and trust them to Him],
   And your plans will succeed [if
   you respond to His will and
   guidance].
4 The LORD has made everything for
   its own purpose,
   Even the wicked [according to
   their role] for the day of evil.
5 Everyone who is proud *and* arrogant
   in heart is disgusting *and*
   exceedingly offensive to the LORD;
   Be assured he will not go
   unpunished. [Prov 8:13; 11:20, 21]
6 By mercy *and* lovingkindness and
   truth [not superficial ritual]
   wickedness is cleansed from the
   heart,
   And by the fear of the LORD one
   avoids evil.
7 When a man's ways please the LORD,
   He makes even his enemies to be
   at peace with him.

life point

Proverbs 16:2 says that all our ways are
"clean and innocent," or pure, in our own
eyes. In other words, most of us do not
see our own faults.

It would do us good to choose about
three of our most trusted friends, sit
down with them several times a year, and
ask them, "How do you see me?" This
is because we see ourselves a whole lot
differently than others see us. Ask this
question of mature, trustworthy, honest
people. Take their answers seriously and
pray about them, asking God to help you
in your weaknesses.

8 Better is a little with righteousness
   Than great income [gained] with
      injustice. [Ps 37:16; Prov 15:16]
9 A man's mind plans his way [as he
      journeys through life],
   But the LORD directs his steps *and*
      establishes them. [Ps 37:23; Prov
      20:24; Jer 10:23]
10 A divine decision [given by God]
      is on the lips of the king [as His
      representative];
   His mouth should not be
      unfaithful *or* unjust in judgment.
      [Deut 17:18–20; 2 Sam 14:17–20;
      1 Kin 3:9–12; Is 11:2]
11 A just balance and [honest] scales
      are the LORD's;
   All the weights of the bag are His
      concern [established by His
      eternal principles].
12 It is repulsive [to God and man] for
      kings to behave wickedly,

speak the Word

*Thank You, God, that as I submit my works to You and trust You,
You will cause my plans to succeed if I respond to Your will and guidance.*
–ADAPTED FROM PROVERBS 16:3

the wise answer of the tongue

Sometimes the Lord gives us "the [wise] answer of the tongue" (Proverbs 16:1) from our very own lips. I learned this truth when I was in a situation where I did not know what to do and my own thoughts left me confused. I was not getting anywhere with my circumstances until I took a walk with a friend.

I was facing a major decision that needed a godly answer, but I could not find God's leading. My friend and I discussed the issue for about an hour as we walked together, enjoying the fresh air and each other's company. That is when I learned that sometimes wisdom comes out of our own mouths as we begin to talk to someone about a situation.

We talked about the circumstance and discussed several different possible solutions and their potential outcomes. We talked about how good it might be if we handled the situation one way and how bad it might be if we handled it another way. Suddenly one particular answer settled in my heart.

What I decided I needed to do was not something I naturally wanted to do. A stubborn mind-set is a great enemy of peace. Some of my struggle was because I wanted to convince God my situation should be dealt with differently from the way He was leading me. His voice was difficult to discern because my mind was already set against His plan.

It's important for us to be willing to lay aside our own desires or we may miss a clear word from God. Our natural inclination is to manipulate things to work the way we want them to work. Some of our best childhood toys taught us that square pegs will not fit into round holes, and we must remember that our plans do not always fit God's ways—no matter how forcefully we try to make the two work together.

While my friend and I considered the situation together, a wise answer came out of my mouth that I knew was from the Lord. It did not come from my mind, but it rose from my inner being. God promises that if we seek Him, He will fill our mouths (see Psalm 81:10), and Jesus promises to give us words and wisdom that none of our "opponents will be able to resist or refute" (Luke 21:15).

For a throne is established on righteousness (right standing with God).

13 Righteous lips are the delight of kings,
And he who speaks right is loved.

14 The wrath of a king is like a messenger of death,
But a wise man will appease it.

15 In the light of the king's face is life,
And his favor is like a cloud bringing the spring rain.

16 How much better it is to get wisdom than gold!
And to get understanding is to be chosen above silver. [Prov 8:10, 19]

17 The highway of the upright turns away *and* departs from evil;
He who guards his way protects his life (soul).

18 Pride goes before destruction,
And a haughty spirit before a fall.

19 It is better to be humble in spirit with the lowly
Than to divide the spoil with the proud (haughty, arrogant).

20 He who pays attention to the word [of God] will find good,

And blessed (happy, prosperous,
to be admired) is he who trusts
[confidently] in the LORD.
²¹ The wise in heart will be called
understanding,
And sweet speech increases
persuasiveness *and* learning [in
both speaker and listener].

²² Understanding (spiritual insight)
is a [refreshing and boundless]
wellspring of life to those who
have it,
But to give instruction *and*
correction to fools is foolishness.
²³ The heart of the wise instructs his
mouth [in wisdom]

humble people are happy people

People who are proud are hard to deal with because they refuse correction and good advice. In fact, Proverbs 16:5 says they are "disgusting and exceedingly offensive to the LORD." They cannot be told anything because they think they already know everything. Since they are so opinionated, they are always on the defensive, which makes it hard for them to receive correction because to them that would seem to be an admission that they are wrong—and that is something they find almost impossible to do.

In my ministry, the Lord uses me to bring correction from His Word. Generally, the flesh does not care for that, but it is what makes us grow up in the Lord. Although I try to do it in a loving way, sometimes it still causes people to react against me because, being proud, they resist the truth. Yet Jesus told us that it is the truth that sets us free (see John 8:32). Remember: free people are happy people.

It was good for me to learn that when the Lord does lead me to correct people, it is not my job to convince them. That is the job of the Holy Spirit. He is the One Who convicts and convinces people of the truth. That means you and I do not have to try to "play God" in other people's lives.

Proud people feel they have to convince others that they are right and everyone else is wrong. They try to tell people how they need to change or what they need to do. As this verse from Proverbs tells us, that kind of domineering, superior approach is not pleasing to God, Who wants His children to walk in kindness and humility, not arrogance and pride.

Proud people are also usually very rigid, which explains why they are often such strict disciplinarians. They have their own way of doings things, and if anyone does not do it their way, they react strongly, sometimes even violently: "This is it! This is the way it has to be done—or else!"

Finally, proud people are often complicated people. Although the Bible calls us to a life of simplicity, proud people feel that they have to make a big deal out of everything, to make a mountain out of every molehill. Part of the reason for this is that they think they have to figure out everything, that they have to know the "ins and outs" of every situation and know the reason behind everything that happens in life. To put it simply, they want to be in control because deep down inside they feel nobody can handle things as well as they can!

All these things help to explain why proud people are usually not very happy people. And unhappy people do not make very many other people happy either. Cultivate humility in your life so you can be happy and bring joy to others.

And adds persuasiveness to his lips.
24 Pleasant words are like a
   honeycomb,
   Sweet *and* delightful to the soul
   and healing to the body.
25 There is a way which seems right
   to a man *and* appears straight
   before him,
   But its end is the way of death.
26 The appetite of a worker works for
   him,
   For his hunger urges him on.
27 A worthless man devises *and* digs
   up evil,
   And the words on his lips are like
   a scorching fire.
28 A perverse man spreads strife,
   And one who gossips separates
   intimate friends. [Prov 17:9]
29 A violent *and* exceedingly covetous
   man entices his neighbor [to sin],
   And leads him in a way that is not
   good.
30 He who [slyly] winks his eyes does
   so to plot perverse things;
   And he who compresses his lips
   [as if in a secret signal] brings
   evil to pass.
31 The silver-haired head is a crown
   of splendor *and* glory;
   It is found in the way of
   righteousness. [Prov 20:29]
32 He who is slow to anger is better
   and more honorable than the
   mighty [soldier],
   And he who rules *and* controls his
   own spirit, than he who captures
   a city.
33 The lot is cast into the lap,
   But its every decision is from the
   Lord.

17 BETTER IS a dry morsel
   [of food served] with
   quietness *and* peace
Than a house full of feasting
   [served] with strife *and*
   contention.

2 A wise servant will rule over
   the [unworthy] son who acts
   shamefully *and* brings disgrace
   [to the family]
   And [the worthy servant] will
   share in the inheritance among
   the brothers.
3 The refining pot is for silver and
   the furnace for gold,
   But the Lord tests hearts. [Ps 26:2;
   Prov 27:21; Jer 17:10; Mal 3:3]
4 An evildoer listens closely to
   wicked lips;
   And a liar pays attention to a
   destructive *and* malicious tongue.
5 Whoever mocks the poor taunts
   his Maker,
   And he who rejoices at [another's]
   disaster will not go unpunished.
   [Job 31:29; Prov 14:31; Obad 12]
6 Grandchildren are the crown of
   aged men,
   And the glory of children is their
   fathers [who live godly lives]. [Ps
   127:3; 128:3]
7 Excellent speech does not benefit a
   fool [who is spiritually blind],
   Much less do lying lips *benefit* a
   prince.
8 A bribe is like a bright, precious
   stone in the eyes of its owner;
   Wherever he turns, he prospers.
9 He who covers *and* forgives an
   offense seeks love,
   But he who repeats *or* gossips
   about a matter separates
   intimate friends.
10 A reprimand goes deeper into one
   who has understanding *and* a
   teachable spirit
   Than a hundred lashes into a fool.
   [Is 32:6]
11 A rebellious man seeks only evil;
   Therefore a cruel messenger will
   be sent against him.
12 Let a man meet a [ferocious] bear
   robbed of her cubs
   Rather than the [angry, narcissistic]
   fool in his folly. [Hos 13:8]

¹³ Whoever returns evil for good,
   Evil will not depart from his
      house. [Ps 109:4, 5; Jer 18:20]
¹⁴ The beginning of strife is like
      letting out water [as from a small
      break in a dam; first it trickles
      and then it gushes];
   Therefore abandon the quarrel
      before it breaks out *and* tempers
      explode.
¹⁵ He who justifies the wicked, and
      he who condemns the righteous
   Are both repulsive to the LORD. [Ex
      23:7; Prov 24:24; Is 5:23]
¹⁶ Why is there money in the hand of
      a fool to buy wisdom,

When he has no common sense *or*
   even a heart for it?
¹⁷ A friend loves at all times,
   And a brother is born for adversity.
¹⁸ A man lacking common sense
   gives a pledge
   And becomes guarantor [for the
      debt of another] in the presence
      of his neighbor.
¹⁹ He who loves transgression loves
      strife *and* is quarrelsome;
   He who [proudly] raises his gate
      seeks destruction [because of his
      arrogant pride].
²⁰ He who has a crooked mind finds no
      good,

people who laugh, last

We need to enjoy life while we work and perform the things we think we are supposed to do each day. Proverbs 17:22 teaches us that happiness in our hearts is like a good medicine.

Because my childhood was stolen from me through abuse, I never learned to be childlike. I never learned to "lighten up" and "live a little." I was so serious that I thought I should not have anything to do with things I considered to be "frivolous." I was always uptight about everything, and I rarely laughed because I was so busy working and taking life seriously. On the other hand, my husband, Dave, is the type who enjoys life regardless of what is going on around him. Although I may never have the ability to be just like he is because of the differences in our personalities, I have learned I can be much happier and more lighthearted than I used to be.

As a minister of the gospel, I have a huge responsibility. I have to work hard at what I have been called to do, and I love it. I really do enjoy my work. But if I am not careful, I can become stressed and burned out. That is why I have to make an effort to apply to my life verses such as Proverbs 17:22 and develop a happy heart and a cheerful mind.

You and I need a balance of fun and responsibility. If we are not emotionally balanced, our entire lives will be affected. I truly believe if we do not learn to laugh more, we will get into trouble because, as the Bible teaches, a happy heart is like medicine. There have been many articles written in recent years stating that medical science now confirms that laughter can be instrumental in bringing healing to the body. Laughter is like internal jogging—it exercises our souls, bringing health to them.

We need to find more humor in our everyday lives. We ought to laugh at ourselves, not take ourselves too seriously. We all need to laugh more—and sometimes we need to do it on purpose. Remember, a happy heart is good medicine!

And he who is perverted in his
language falls into evil. [James
3:8]

²¹ He who becomes the parent of a
fool [who is spiritually blind]
does so to his sorrow,
And the father of a fool [who is
spiritually blind] has no joy.

²² A happy heart is good medicine
and a joyful mind causes
healing,
But a broken spirit dries up the
bones. [Prov 12:25; 15:13, 15]

²³ A wicked man receives a bribe
from the [hidden] pocket
To pervert the ways of justice.

²⁴ [Skillful and godly] wisdom is
in the presence of a person
of understanding [and he
recognizes it],
But the eyes of a [thickheaded]
fool are on the ends of the earth.

²⁵ A foolish son is a grief *and* anguish
to his father
And bitterness to her who gave
birth to him.

²⁶ It is also not good to fine the
righteous,
Nor to strike the noble for their
uprightness.

²⁷ He who has knowledge restrains
and is careful with his words,
And a man of understanding
and wisdom has a cool spirit
(self-control, an even temper).
[James 1:19]

²⁸ Even a [callous, arrogant]
fool, when he keeps silent, is
considered wise;
When he closes his lips he is
regarded as sensible (prudent,
discreet) *and* a man of
understanding.

18
HE WHO [willfully]
separates himself [from
God and man] seeks his
own desire,
He quarrels against all sound
wisdom.

² A [closed-minded] fool does not
delight in understanding,
But only in revealing his personal
opinions [unwittingly displaying
his self-indulgence and his
stupidity].

³ When the wicked man comes [to
the depth of evil], contempt [of
all that is pure and good] also
comes,
And with inner baseness (dishonor)
comes outer shame (scorn).

⁴ The words of a man's mouth are
like deep waters [copious and
difficult to fathom];
The fountain of [mature, godly]
wisdom is like a bubbling stream
[sparkling, fresh, pure, and life-
giving].

⁵ To show respect to the wicked
person is not good,
Nor to push aside *and* deprive the
righteous of justice.

⁶ A fool's lips bring contention *and*
strife,
And his mouth invites a beating.

⁷ A fool's mouth is his ruin,
And his lips are the snare of his
soul.

⁸ The words of a whisperer (gossip)
are like dainty morsels [to be
greedily eaten];
They go down into the innermost
chambers of the body [to be
remembered and mused upon].

⁹ He who is careless in his work
Is a brother to him who destroys.

¹⁰ The name of the Lord is a strong
tower;

speak the Word

God, I declare that Your name is a strong tower. I can run into it and be safe!
—ADAPTED FROM PROVERBS 18:10

The righteous runs to it and is safe
and set on high [far above evil].

¹¹ The rich man's wealth is his strong
city,
And like a high wall [of protection]
in his own imagination *and*
conceit.

¹² Before disaster the heart of a man
is haughty *and* filled with self-
importance,
But humility comes before honor.

¹³ He who answers before he hears
[the facts]—
It is folly and shame to him. [John
7:51]

¹⁴ The spirit of a man sustains him in
sickness,
But as for a broken spirit, who can
bear it?

¹⁵ The mind of the prudent [always]
acquires knowledge,
And the ear of the wise [always]
seeks knowledge.

life point

Proverbs 18:21 teaches us that "death
and life are in the power of the tongue."
I do not believe we can overestimate the
importance of our words, because they
truly can make the difference between
life and death. Determine today to use
the power of your words to speak life
everywhere you go!

¹⁶ A man's gift [given in love or
courtesy] makes room for him
And brings him before great men.
[Gen 32:20; 1 Sam 25:27; Prov
17:8; 21:14]

¹⁷ The first one to plead his case
seems right,
Until another comes and cross-
examines him.

¹⁸ To cast lots puts an end to quarrels

strengthen the weak

Do you realize what Proverbs 18:14 is saying? Regardless of what comes into people's lives, they can bear up under it if they have a strong spirit within to sustain
them in those times of trouble. But if their spirit is weak or wounded, they will have
a hard time bearing anything in life.

Do you know what is wrong with many in the body of Christ today, why they cannot
seem to handle their problems? It is not because their problems are any worse than
those of anybody else. It is because they are weak in spirit. The Bible says that we
are to bear with the weaknesses of people who are not strong (see Romans 15:1).
We are to lift them up and support them.

Romans 12:8 tells us that one of the ministry gifts God gives to the church is that
of the encourager. Such people are usually easy to recognize because every time
we get around them, they make us feel better by the things they say and do. It just
seems to come naturally to them to uplift, encourage, and strengthen others by
their very presence and personality.

If you are like I am and would not call yourself a naturally gifted encourager, then
form a habit of being more encouraging. That is what I have done, and it not only
makes others feel better, it increases my joy level also. We all can give compliments,
and we all can say, "Thank you." We all can refuse to be slanderers. We all can
refuse to allow evil things to come out of our mouths that tear people down. We all
can build up, edify, lift up, and speak life to others.

And decides between powerful contenders.

¹⁹ A brother offended *is harder to win* over than a fortified city,
And contentions [separating families] are like the bars of a castle.

²⁰ A man's stomach will be satisfied with the fruit of his mouth;
He will be satisfied with the consequence of his words.

²¹ Death and life are in the power of the tongue,
And those who love it *and* indulge it will eat its fruit *and* bear the consequences of their words. [Matt 12:37]

life point

Jesus is a friend who sticks closer than a brother (see Proverbs 18:24). Let Him be your best friend. If you do, you will be blessed, and your relationships will be more peaceful and balanced.

²² He who finds a [true and faithful] wife finds a good thing
And obtains favor *and* approval from the Lord. [Prov 19:14; 31:10]

²³ The poor man pleads,
But the rich man answers roughly.

²⁴ The man of *too many* friends [chosen indiscriminately] will be broken in pieces *and* come to ruin,

power in your mouth

Proverbs 18:21 is a verse I have known for years and am very familiar with, but I am blessed every time I read it. I do not think we can read it too often, know it too well, or apply it too much. As you can tell by reading this verse, it teaches us that death and life are in the power of the tongue, and those who indulge in it will eat its fruit, either for death or for life.

Basically, the writer of Proverbs is saying in this verse: "Every time you open your mouth, you are ministering death or life, and whatever you dish out is what you are going to eat."

We have heard the phrase "You're going to have to eat your words," and Proverbs 18:21 confirms this truth. The words we speak have power to influence our lives. In fact, you may be eating your words right now, and that may be why you are not happy with your life. Your mouth may be getting you in trouble with yourself!

Proverbs 18:21 teaches us that words are so awesome. They are containers for power; they carry either a life-giving force or a destructive force.

For example, in my conferences I speak words, and those who hear those words receive life—life in their relationships, in their ministries, in their thoughts, and in all the areas that God uses me to speak to them about.

I have written a book called *Me and My Big Mouth!*, which deals with the words we speak and how to make them work for us instead of against us. The subtitle of the book is "Your Answer Is Right Under Your Nose." Perhaps you are desperately looking for an answer to what is happening in your life. Do you believe it is even remotely possible that your answer could be found in changing the way you talk? Go ahead and try it. I know the truth of Proverbs 18:21 and have experienced it many times in my own life. I believe if you will begin to speak positive, encouraging words of life and blessing, you will see blessing in your life!

But there is a [true, loving] friend who [is reliable and] sticks closer than a brother.

19

BETTER IS a poor man who walks in his integrity Than a [rich] man who is twisted in his speech and is a [shortsighted] fool.

2 Also it is not good for a person to be without knowledge, And he who hurries with his feet [acting impulsively and proceeding without caution or analyzing the consequences] sins (misses the mark).

3 The foolishness of man undermines his way [ruining whatever he undertakes]; Then his heart is resentful *and* rages against the LORD [for, being a fool, he blames the LORD instead of himself].

4 Wealth makes many friends, But a poor man is separated from his friend. [Prov 14:20]

5 A false witness will not go unpunished, And he who breathes out lies will not escape. [Ex 23:1; Deut 19:16–19; Prov 6:19; 21:28]

6 Many will seek the favor of a generous *and* noble man, And everyone is a friend to him who gives gifts.

7 All the brothers of a poor man hate him; How much more do his friends abandon him! He pursues *them with* words, but they are gone.

8 He who gains wisdom *and* good sense loves (preserves) his own soul; He who keeps understanding will find good *and* prosper.

9 A false witness will not go unpunished,

And he who breathes lies will perish.

10 Luxury is not fitting for a fool; Much less for a slave to rule over princes.

11 Good sense *and* discretion make a man slow to anger, And it is his honor *and* glory to overlook a transgression *or* an offense [without seeking revenge and harboring resentment].

12 The king's wrath *terrifies* like the roaring of a lion, But his favor is as [refreshing and nourishing as] dew on the grass. [Hos 14:5]

13 A foolish (ungodly) son is destruction to his father, And the contentions of a [quarrelsome] wife are like a constant dripping [of water].

14 House and wealth are the inheritance from fathers, But a wise, understanding, *and* sensible wife is [a gift and blessing] from the LORD. [Prov 18:22]

15 Laziness casts one into a deep sleep [unmindful of lost opportunity], And the idle person will suffer hunger.

16 He who keeps *and* obeys the commandment [of the LORD] keeps (guards) his own life, But he who is careless of his ways *and* conduct will die. [Prov 13:13; 16:17; Luke 10:28; 11:28]

17 He who is gracious *and* lends a hand to the poor lends to the LORD, And the LORD will repay him for his good deed. [Prov 28:27; Eccl 11:1; Matt 10:42; 25:40; 2 Cor 9:6–8; Heb 6:10]

18 Discipline *and* teach your son while there is hope,

And do not [indulge your anger or resentment by imposing inappropriate punishment nor] desire his destruction.

19 *A man of* great anger will bear the penalty [for his quick temper and lack of self-control];
For if you rescue him [and do not let him learn from the consequences of his action], you will only have to rescue him over and over again.

20 Listen to counsel, receive instruction, *and* accept correction,
That you may be wise in the time to come.

21 Many plans are in a man's mind,
But it is the LORD's purpose for him that will stand (be carried out). [Job 23:13; Ps 33:10, 11; Is 14:26, 27; 46:10; Acts 5:39; Heb 6:17]

22 That which is desirable in a man is his loyalty *and* unfailing love,
But it is better to be a poor man than a [wealthy] liar.

23 The fear of the LORD *leads* to life,
So that one may sleep satisfied, untouched by evil. [Job 5:19; Ps 91:3; Prov 12:13; Is 46:4; Jer 1:8; Dan 6:27; 2 Tim 4:8]

24 The lazy man buries his hand in the [food] dish,
But will not even bring it to his mouth again.

25 Strike a scoffer [for refusing to learn], and the naive may [be warned and] become prudent;
Reprimand one who has understanding *and* a teachable spirit, and he will gain knowledge *and* insight.

26 He who assaults his father and chases away his mother

Is a son who brings shame and disgrace. [1 Tim 5:8]

27 Cease listening, my son, to instruction *and* discipline
And you will stray from the words of knowledge.

28 A wicked *and* worthless witness mocks justice,
And the mouth of the wicked spreads iniquity.

29 Judgments are prepared for scoffers,
And beatings for the backs of [thickheaded] fools. [Is 32:6]

20 WINE IS a mocker, strong drink a riotous brawler;
And whoever is intoxicated by it is not wise. [Prov 23:29, 30; Is 28:7; Hos 4:11]

2 The terror of a king is like the roaring of a lion;
Whoever provokes him to anger forfeits his own life.

3 It is an honor for a man to keep away from strife [by handling situations with thoughtful foresight],
But any fool will [start a] quarrel [without regard for the consequences].

4 The lazy man does not plow when the winter [planting] season arrives;
So he begs at the [next] harvest and has nothing [to reap].

5 A plan (motive, wise counsel) in the heart of a man is like water in a deep well,
But a man of understanding draws it out. [Prov 18:4]

6 Many a man proclaims his own loyalty *and* goodness,

speak the Word

Thank You, Lord, that no matter what plans may be in my mind,
Your purpose for me is what will stand.
—ADAPTED FROM PROVERBS 19:21

But who can find a faithful *and* trustworthy man?

⁷The righteous man who walks in integrity *and* lives life in accord with his [godly] beliefs—
How blessed [happy and spiritually secure] are his children after him [who have his example to follow].

⁸A [discerning] king who sits on the throne of judgment
Sifts all evil [like chaff] with his eyes [and cannot be easily fooled].

⁹Who can say, "I have cleansed my heart,
I am pure from my sin?" [1 Kin 8:46; 2 Chr 6:36; Job 9:30; 14:4; Ps 51:5; 1 John 1:8]

¹⁰Differing weights [one for buying and another for selling] and differing measures,
Both of them are detestable *and* offensive to the Lord. [Deut 25:13; Mic 6:10, 11]

¹¹Even a boy is known *and* distinguished by his acts,
Whether his conduct is pure and right.

¹²The hearing ear and the seeing eye,
The [omnipotent] Lord has made both of them.

¹³Do not love [excessive] sleep, or you will become poor;
Open your eyes [so that you can do your work] and you will be satisfied with bread.

¹⁴"It is [almost] worthless, it is [almost] worthless," says the buyer [as he negotiates the price];
But when he goes his way, then he boasts [about his bargain].

¹⁵There is gold, and an abundance of pearls,
But the lips of knowledge are a vessel of preciousness [the most precious of all]. [Job 28:12, 16–19; Prov 3:15; 8:11]

¹⁶[The judge tells the creditor], "Take the clothes of one who is surety for a stranger;
And hold him in pledge [when he guarantees a loan] for foreigners." [Prov 27:13]

¹⁷Food gained by deceit is sweet to a man,
But afterward his mouth will be filled with gravel [just as sin may be sweet at first, but later its consequences bring despair].

¹⁸Plans are established by counsel;
So make war [only] with wise guidance.

¹⁹He who goes about as a gossip reveals secrets;
Therefore do not associate with a gossip [who talks freely or flatters]. [Rom 16:17, 18]

²⁰Whoever curses his father or his mother,
His lamp [of life] will be extinguished in time of darkness.

²¹An inheritance hastily gained [by greedy, unjust means] at the beginning
Will not be blessed in the end. [Prov 28:20; Hab 2:6]

²²Do not say, "I will repay evil";
Wait [expectantly] for the Lord, and He will rescue *and* save you. [Deut 32:35; 2 Sam 16:12; Rom 12:17–19; 1 Thess 5:15; 1 Pet 3:9]

²³Differing weights are detestable *and* offensive to the Lord,
And fraudulent scales are not good.

²⁴Man's steps are ordered *and* ordained by the Lord.
How then can a man [fully] understand his way?

speak the Word

Lord, I wait expectantly for You. I know that You will rescue and save me.
—ADAPTED FROM PROVERBS 20:22

25 It is a trap for a man to [speak a vow of consecration and] say rashly, "It is holy!" And [not until] afterward consider [whether he can fulfill it].
26 A wise king sifts out the wicked [from among the good] And drives the [threshing] wheel over them [to separate the chaff from the grain].
27 The spirit (conscience) of man is the lamp of the LORD, Searching and examining all the innermost parts of his being. [1 Cor 2:11]
28 Loyalty and mercy, truth and faithfulness, protect the king, And he upholds his throne by lovingkindness.
29 The glory of young men is their [physical] strength, And the honor of aged men is their gray head [representing wisdom and experience].
30 Blows that wound cleanse away evil, And strokes reach to the innermost parts.

21 THE KING'S heart is like channels of water in the hand of the LORD; He turns it whichever way He wishes. [Ex 10:1, 2; Ezra 6:22]
2 Every man's way is right in his own eyes, But the LORD weighs and examines the hearts [of people and their motives]. [Prov 24:12; Luke 16:15]
3 To do righteousness and justice Is more acceptable to the LORD than sacrifice [for wrongs repeatedly committed]. [1 Sam 15:22; Prov 15:8; Is 1:11; Hos 6:6; Mic 6:7, 8]
4 Haughty and arrogant eyes and a proud heart, The lamp of the wicked [their self-centered pride], is sin [in the eyes of God].

5 The plans of the diligent lead surely to abundance and advantage, But everyone who acts in haste comes surely to poverty.
6 Acquiring treasures by a lying tongue Is a fleeting vapor, the seeking and pursuit of death.
7 The violence of the wicked will [return to them and] drag them away [like fish caught in a net], Because they refuse to act with justice.
8 The way of the guilty is [exceedingly] crooked, But as for the pure, his conduct is upright.
9 It is better to live in a corner of the housetop [on the flat roof, exposed to the weather] Than in a house shared with a quarrelsome (contentious) woman.
10 The soul of the wicked desires evil [like an addictive substance]; His neighbor finds no compassion in his eyes. [James 2:16]
11 When the scoffer is punished, the naive [observes the lesson and] becomes wise; But when the wise and teachable person is instructed, he receives knowledge. [Prov 19:25]
12 The righteous one keeps an eye on the house of the wicked— How the wicked are cast down to ruin.
13 Whoever shuts his ears at the cry of the poor Will cry out himself and not be answered. [Matt 18:30–34; James 2:13]
14 A gift in secret subdues anger, And a bribe [hidden] in the pocket, strong wrath.
15 When justice is done, it is a joy to the righteous (the upright, the one in right standing with God), But to the evildoers it is disaster.

16 A man who wanders from the way
    of understanding (godly wisdom)
Will remain in the assembly of the
    dead.
17 He who loves [only selfish]
    pleasure *will become* a poor man;
He who loves *and* is devoted to
    wine and [olive] oil will not
    become rich.
18 The wicked become a ransom for
    the righteous,
And the treacherous in the place
    of the upright [for they fall into
    their own traps].
19 It is better to dwell in a desert land
Than with a contentious and
    troublesome woman.
20 There is precious treasure and oil
    in the house of the wise [who
    prepare for the future],
But a short-sighted *and* foolish
    man swallows it up *and* wastes it.
21 He who earnestly seeks
    righteousness and loyalty
Finds life, righteousness, and
    honor. [Prov 15:9; Matt 5:6]
22 A wise man scales the city [walls]
    of the mighty
And brings down the stronghold in
    which they trust.
23 He who guards his mouth and his
    tongue
Guards himself from troubles.
    [Prov 12:13; 13:3; 18:21; James 3:2]
24 "Proud," "Haughty," "Scoffer," are
    his names
Who acts with overbearing *and*
    insolent pride.
25 The desire of the lazy kills him,
For his hands refuse to labor;
26 He craves all the day long [and
    does no work],

But the righteous [willingly] gives
    and does not withhold [what he
    has]. [2 Cor 9:6–10]
27 The sacrifice of the wicked is
    detestable *and* offensive [to the
    Lord].
How much more [unacceptable
    and insulting can it be] when he
    brings it with evil intention?
28 A false witness will perish,
But a man who listens *to the
    truth* will speak forever *and* go
    unchallenged.
29 A wicked man puts on a bold face,
But as for the upright, he
    considers, directs, *and*
    establishes his way [with the
    confidence of integrity].
30 There is no [human] wisdom or
    understanding
Or counsel [that can prevail]
    against the Lord.
31 The horse is prepared for the day
    of battle,
But deliverance *and* victory belong
    to the Lord.

22 A *GOOD* name [earned by
    honorable behavior, godly
    wisdom, moral courage,
and personal integrity] is more
    desirable than great riches;
And favor is better than silver and
    gold.
2 The rich and poor have a common
    bond;
The Lord is the Maker of them all.
    [Job 31:15; Prov 14:31]
3 A prudent *and* far-sighted *person*
    sees the evil [of sin] and hides
    himself [from it],

speak the Word

*God, I declare that no human wisdom, understanding, or counsel can prevail
against You. Deliverance and victory belong to You alone.*
—ADAPTED FROM PROVERBS 21:30, 31

But the naive continue on and
  are punished [by suffering the
  consequences of sin].
⁴The reward of humility [that is,
  having a realistic view of one's
  importance] and the [reverent,
  worshipful] fear of the LORD
Is riches, honor, and life. [Prov 21:21]
⁵Thorns and snares are in the way
  of the obstinate [for their lack
  of honor and their wrong-doing
  traps them];
He who guards himself [with godly
  wisdom] will be far from them
  and avoid the consequences they
  suffer.
⁶Train up a child in the way he
  should go [teaching him to seek
  God's wisdom and will for his
  abilities and talents],
Even when he is old he will not
  depart from it. [Eph 6:4; 2 Tim
  3:15]
⁷The rich rules over the poor,
And the borrower is servant to the
  lender.
⁸He who sows injustice will reap [a
  harvest of] trouble,
And the rod of his wrath [with
  which he oppresses others] will
  fail.
⁹He who is generous will be blessed,
For he gives some of his food to the
  poor. [2 Cor 9:6–10]
¹⁰Drive out the scoffer, and
  contention will go away;
Even strife and dishonor will cease.
¹¹He who loves purity of heart
And whose speech is gracious will
  have the king as his friend.

putting the Word to work

**Proverbs 22:6 teaches that children
will not depart from good training. If
you are a parent, how can you train
your children in godly ways? Ask God
to help you. He will!**

¹²The eyes of the LORD keep guard
  over knowledge *and* the one who
  has it,
But He overthrows the words of
  the treacherous.
¹³The lazy one [manufactures
  excuses and] says, "There is a
  lion outside!
I will be killed in the streets [if I go
  out to work]!"
¹⁴The mouth of an immoral
  woman is a deep pit [deep and
  inescapable];
He who is cursed by the LORD
  [because of his adulterous sin]
  will fall into it.
¹⁵Foolishness is bound up in the
  heart of a child;
The rod of discipline [correction
  administered with godly wisdom
  and lovingkindness] will remove
  it far from him.
¹⁶He who oppresses *or* exploits the
  poor to get more for himself
Or who gives to the rich [to gain
  influence and favor], will only
  come to poverty.
¹⁷Listen carefully and hear the
  words of the wise,
And apply your mind to my
  knowledge;
¹⁸For it will be pleasant if you keep
  them in mind [incorporating
  them as guiding principles];
Let them be ready on your lips [to
  guide and strengthen yourself
  and others].
¹⁹So that your trust *and* reliance *and*
  confidence may be in the LORD,
I have taught these things to you
  today, even to you.
²⁰Have I not written to you excellent
  things
In counsels and knowledge,
²¹To let you know the certainty of
  the words of truth,
That you may give a correct answer
  to him who sent you? [Luke 1:3, 4]

22 Do not rob the poor because he is
poor [and defenseless],
Nor crush the afflicted [by legal
proceedings] at the gate [where
the city court is held], [Ex 23:6;
Job 31:16, 21]
23 For the LORD will plead their case
And take the life of those who rob
them. [Zech 7:10; Mal 3:5]

24 Do not even associate with a man
given to angry outbursts;
Or go [along] with a hot-tempered
man,
25 Or you will learn his
[undisciplined] ways
And get yourself trapped [in a
situation from which it is hard to
escape].

26 Do not be among those who give
pledges [involving themselves in
others' finances],
Or among those who become
guarantors for *others'* debts.
27 If you have nothing with which
to pay [another's debt when he
defaults],
Why should his creditor take your
bed from under you?

28 Do not move the ancient landmark
[at the boundary of the property]
Which your fathers have set.

29 Do you see a man skillful *and*
experienced in his work?
He will stand [in honor] before
kings;
He will not stand before obscure
men.

23 WHEN YOU sit down to
dine with a ruler,
Consider carefully what is
[set] before you;
2 For you will put a knife to your
throat
If you are a man of *great* appetite.
3 Do not desire his delicacies,

life point

Proverbs 23:7 lets us know how crucial it
is for us to think properly. Thoughts are
powerful, and they have creative ability.
If our thoughts are going to affect what
we become (and they will), then thinking
right thoughts should be a high priority in
our lives.

For it is deceptive food [offered to
you with questionable motives].
4 Do not weary yourself [with the
overwhelming desire] to gain
wealth;
Cease from your own understanding
of it. [Prov 28:20; 1 Tim 6:9, 10]
5 When you set your eyes on wealth,
it is [suddenly] gone.
For *wealth* certainly makes itself
wings
Like an eagle that flies to the
heavens.

6 Do not eat the bread of a selfish
man,
Or desire his delicacies;
7 For as he thinks in his heart, so
is he [in behavior—one who
manipulates].
He says to you, "Eat and drink,"
Yet his heart is not with you [but it
is begrudging the cost].
8 The morsel which you have eaten
you will vomit up,
And you will waste your
compliments.

9 Do not speak in the ears of a fool,
For he will despise the [godly]
wisdom of your words. [Is 32:6]

10 Do not move the ancient landmark
[at the boundary of the property]
And do not go into the fields of the
fatherless [to take what is theirs],
[Deut 19:14; 27:17; Prov 22:28]
11 For their Redeemer is strong *and*
mighty;

He will plead their case against you.
12 Apply your heart to discipline
    And your ears to words of
       knowledge.

13 Do not withhold discipline from
      the child;
   If you swat him with a *reed-like*
      rod [applied with godly wisdom],
      he will not die.
14 You shall swat him with the *reed-like* rod

And rescue his life from Sheol
   (the nether world, the place of
    the dead).

15 My son, if your heart is wise,
   My heart will also be glad;
16 Yes, my heart will rejoice
   When your lips speak right things.

17 Do not let your heart envy sinners
     [who live godless lives and have
      no hope of salvation],

think as God thinks

Proverbs 23:7 teaches us that we become what we think, and I have certainly learned this truth over the years. Indeed, "where the mind goes, the man follows." One of the first principles believers must learn if we intend to walk in real victory is that our minds must be renewed according to the Word of God. We must learn to think like God!

Sadly, we believe many things that simply are not true. For example, some people believe they have no worth and value because people have said they do not or have treated them in a way that made them feel worthless and devalued. However, the Bible makes clear that we are so valuable to God that He sent His only Son, Jesus Christ, to die and suffer in our place in order that we might be redeemed from our sins and have an intimate relationship with Him (see John 3:16, 17).

As we learn to think as God thinks, we exchange depression and hopelessness for joyful expectation. We believe God has a wonderful future planned for us, no matter what our past has been like. We believe God wants to bless us.

When we have negative thoughts, we end up with negative results. But positive thoughts open the door for God to work in our lives. If we think we are unable to do certain things, we will be rendered unable—even though God's Word says that we can do anything God asks us to do because of His ability in us (see Philippians 4:13). Our thoughts are *that* powerful.

If we really want our lives to change, we must first change our way of thinking. Romans 12:2 says we are not to conform to the world and its ways, but that we are to completely renew our minds and attitudes so we can prove for ourselves the good, acceptable, and perfect will of God. In other words, God has good plans for us, but we will not experience them if we cling to old ways of thinking.

It is vital that we cast down wrong thinking and replace it with thinking God approves of. The mind is the battlefield on which our war with Satan is won or lost. Satan is a liar and a deceiver. His lies become our reality only when we believe them. Stop allowing your mind to be a garbage dump for Satan's trash and instead make it available for God's ideas. Then you will enjoy a life worth living and have the testimony of bearing good fruit for God's glory.

But [continue to] live in the [reverent, worshipful] fear of the LORD day by day.
18 Surely there is a future [and a reward],
And your hope *and* expectation will not be cut off.
19 Listen, my son, and be wise,
And direct your heart in the way [of the LORD].
20 Do not associate with heavy drinkers of wine,
Or with gluttonous eaters of meat, [Is 5:22; Luke 21:34; Rom 13:13; Eph 5:18]
21 For the heavy drinker and the glutton will come to poverty,
And the drowsiness [of overindulgence] will clothe one with rags.

22 Listen to your father, who sired you,
And do not despise your mother when she is old.
23 Buy truth, and do not sell it;
Get wisdom and instruction and understanding.

24 The father of the righteous will greatly rejoice,
And he who sires a wise child will have joy in him.
25 Let your father and your mother be glad,
And let her who gave birth to you rejoice [in your wise and godly choices].

26 My son, give me your heart
And let your eyes delight in my ways,
27 For a prostitute is a deep pit,
And an immoral woman is a narrow well.
28 She lurks *and* lies in wait like a robber [who waits for prey],
And she increases the faithless among men.

29 Who has woe? Who has sorrow? Who has strife? Who has complaining?

Who has wounds without cause? Whose eyes are red *and* dim?
30 Those who linger long over wine,
Those who go to taste mixed wine. [Prov 20:1; Eph 5:18]
31 Do not look at wine when it is red,
When it sparkles in the glass,
When it goes down smoothly.
32 At the last it bites like a serpent
And stings like a viper.
33 Your [drunken] eyes will see strange things
And your mind will utter perverse things [untrue things, twisted things].
34 And you will be [as unsteady] as one who lies down in the middle of the sea,
And [as vulnerable to disaster] as one who lies down on the top of a ship's mast, *saying,*
35 "They struck me, but I was not hurt! They beat me, but I did not feel it! When will I wake up?
I will seek more wine."

24 DO NOT be envious of evil men,
Nor desire to be with them;
2 For their minds plot violence,
And their lips talk of trouble [for the innocent].

3 Through [skillful and godly] wisdom a house [a life, a home, a family] is built,
And by understanding it is established [on a sound and good foundation],
4 And by knowledge its rooms are filled
With all precious and pleasant riches.

5 A wise man is strong,
And a man of knowledge strengthens his power; [Prov 21:22; Eccl 9:16]

⁶For by wise guidance you can
  wage your war,
And in an abundance of [wise]
  counselors there is victory *and*
  safety.
⁷Wisdom is too exalted for a
  [hardened, arrogant] fool;
He does not open his mouth in the
  gate [where the city's rulers sit in
  judgment].
⁸He who plans to do evil
Will be called a schemer *or* deviser
  of evil.
⁹The devising of folly is sin,
And the scoffer is repulsive to men.

¹⁰If you are slack (careless) in the
  day of distress,
Your strength is limited.
¹¹Rescue those who are being taken
  away to death,
And those who stagger to the
  slaughter, Oh hold them back
  [from their doom]!
¹²If you [claim ignorance and] say,
  "See, we did not know this,"
Does He not consider it who
  weighs *and* examines the hearts
  and their motives?
And does He not know it who guards
  your life *and* keeps your soul?
And will He not repay [you and]
  every man according to his
  works?

life point

Proverbs 24:10 tells us that our strength is limited if we become careless or slack when we encounter hard times or difficult situations. The Bible never promises that we will not face adversities; it promises us the strength and grace we need in order to overcome those adversities. With God's strength, we never have to become fainthearted or give up, no matter what trials or tribulations come our way.

life point

Have people done you wrong and then later experienced problems in their own lives? Proverbs 24:17, 18 strongly warns us to keep a right heart attitude and not be happy about their afflictions. Basically these verses says that if we rejoice and think they deserve what they are getting, our offense becomes worse than theirs, and we will experience the wrath that would have come against them.

All of us will have to admit that when someone has done us wrong, it takes a lot of "heart work" for us not to be at least a little bit glad to see that person get what is coming to him or her. We may pretend we do not feel this way, but I believe we all have problems with spiteful attitudes from time to time.

We need to see that God is supremely concerned about our heart attitudes. It is so important for us not to be petty and small-minded about offenses against us. We simply need to keep a right heart attitude and let God take care of everybody else. We should always remember, "hurting people hurt people." Those who hurt us are usually hurting themselves, and their pain may be so strong that they are not even aware they are hurting us when they bring pain into our lives.

¹³My son, eat honey, because it is
  good,
And the drippings of the
  honeycomb are sweet to your
  taste.
¹⁴Know that [skillful and godly]
  wisdom is [so very good] for your
  life *and* soul;
If you find wisdom, then there will
  be a future *and* a reward,
And your hope *and* expectation
  will not be cut off.

¹⁵Do not lie in wait, O wicked man,
  against the dwelling of the
  righteous;
Do not destroy his resting place;
¹⁶For a righteous man falls seven
  times, and rises again,
But the wicked stumble in *time of
  disaster and* collapse. [Job 5:19;
  Ps 34:19; 37:24; Mic 7:8]
¹⁷Do not rejoice *and* gloat when your
  enemy falls,
And do not let your heart be glad
  [in self-righteousness] when he
  stumbles,
¹⁸Or the Lᴏʀᴅ will see your gloating
  and be displeased,
And turn His anger away from
  your enemy.
¹⁹Do not get upset because of
  evildoers,
Or be envious of the wicked,
²⁰For there will be no future for the
  evil man;
The lamp of the wicked will be put
  out.
²¹My son, fear the Lᴏʀᴅ and the king;
And do not associate with those who
  are given to change [of allegiance,
  and are revolutionary],
²²For their tragedy will rise
  suddenly,
And who knows the punishment
  that both [the Lᴏʀᴅ and the king]
  will bring on the rebellious?
²³These also are sayings of the wise:
To show partiality in judgment is
  not good.
²⁴He who says to the wicked, "You
  are righteous,"
Peoples will curse him, nations
  will denounce him;
²⁵But to those [honorable judges]
  who rebuke the *wicked,* it will go
  well with them *and* they will find
  delight,
And a good blessing will come
  upon them.

²⁶He kisses the lips [and wins the
  hearts of people]
Who gives a right *and*
  straightforward answer.
²⁷Prepare your work outside
And get it ready for yourself in the
  field;
Afterward build your house *and*
  establish a home.
²⁸Do not be a witness against your
  neighbor without cause,
And do not deceive with your lips
  [speak neither lies nor half-
  truths]. [Eph 4:25]
²⁹Do not say, "I will do to him as he
  has done to me;
I will pay the man back for his
  deed." [Prov 20:22; Matt 5:39, 44;
  Rom 12:17, 19]
³⁰I went by the field of the lazy man,
And by the vineyard of the man
  lacking understanding *and*
  common sense;
³¹And, behold, it was all overgrown
  with thorns,
And nettles were covering its
  surface,
And its stone wall was broken
  down.
³²When I saw, I considered it well;
I looked and received instruction.
³³"Yet a little sleep, a little slumber,
A little folding of the hands to rest
  [and daydream],"
³⁴Then your poverty will come as a
  robber,
And your want like an armed man.

25 THESE ARE also the proverbs of Solomon, which the
men of Hezekiah king of
Judah copied: [1 Kin 4:32]

²It is the glory of God to conceal a
  matter,
But the glory of kings is to search out
  a matter. [Deut 29:29; Rom 11:33]

3 As the heavens for height and the
earth for depth,
So the hearts *and* minds of kings
are unsearchable.
4 Take away the dross from the silver,
And there comes out [the pure metal
for] a vessel for the silversmith [to
shape]. [2 Tim 2:21]
5 Take away the wicked from before
the king,
And his throne will be established
in righteousness.
6 Do not be boastfully ambitious *and*
claim honor in the presence of
the king,
And do not stand in the place of
great men;
7 For it is better that it be said to
you, "Come up here,"
Than for you to be placed lower in
the presence of the prince,
Whom your eyes have seen. [Luke
14:8–10]

8 Do not rush out to argue *your* case
[before magistrates or judges];
Otherwise what will you do in the
end [when your case is lost and]
When your neighbor (opponent)
humiliates you? [Prov 17:14;
Matt 5:25]
9 Argue your case with your
neighbor himself [before you go
to court];
And do not reveal another's secret,
[Matt 18:15]
10 Or he who hears it will shame you
And the rumor about you [and
your action in court] will have
no end.

11 Like apples of gold in settings of
silver
Is a word spoken at the right time.
[Prov 15:23; Is 50:4]
12 Like an earring of gold and an
ornament of fine gold
Is a wise reprover to an ear that
listens *and* learns.

13 Like the cold of snow [brought
from the mountains] in the time
of harvest,
So is a faithful messenger to those
who send him;
For he refreshes the life of his
masters.
14 Like clouds and wind without rain
Is a man who boasts falsely of gifts
[he does not give]. [Jude 12]
15 By patience *and* a calm spirit a
ruler may be persuaded,
And a soft *and* gentle tongue
breaks the bone [of resistance].
[Gen 32:4; 1 Sam 25:24; Prov
15:1; 16:14]
16 Have you found [pleasure sweet
like] honey? Eat only as much as
you need,
Otherwise, being filled excessively,
you vomit it.
17 Let your foot seldom be in your
neighbor's house,
Or he will become tired of you and
hate you.
18 Like a club and a sword and a
piercing arrow
Is a man who testifies falsely
against his neighbor
(acquaintance).
19 Like a broken tooth or an unsteady
foot
Is confidence in an unfaithful man
in time of trouble.
20 Like one who takes off a garment
in cold weather, or like [a
reactive, useless mixture of]
vinegar on soda,

life point

Spending too much time with any one
person or group of people is usually
not a good idea. In fact, Proverbs 25:17
teaches us that people can get tired of
us if we overdo it. We can appreciate one
another more if we stay balanced in our
relationships.

Is he who [thoughtlessly] sings
[joyful] songs to a heavy heart.
[Dan 6:18; Rom 12:15]
²¹ If your enemy is hungry, give him
bread to eat;
And if he is thirsty, give him water
to drink; [Matt 5:44; Rom 12:20]
²² For in doing so, you will heap coals
of fire upon his head,
And the LORD will reward you.
²³ The north wind brings forth rain,
And a backbiting tongue, an angry
countenance.
²⁴ It is better to live in a corner of
the housetop [on the flat roof,
exposed to the weather]
Than in a house shared with
a quarrelsome (contentious)
woman. [Prov 21:9]
²⁵ Like cold water to a thirsty soul,
So is good news from a distant land.
²⁶ Like a muddied fountain and a
polluted spring
Is a righteous man who yields *and*
compromises his integrity before
the wicked.
²⁷ It is not good to eat much honey,
Nor is it glorious to seek one's own
glory.
²⁸ Like a city that is broken down
and without walls [leaving it
unprotected]
Is a man who has no self-control
over his spirit [and sets himself
up for trouble]. [Prov 16:32]

26 LIKE SNOW in summer
and like rain in harvest,
So honor is not fitting for a
[shortsighted] fool. [Is 32:6]
² Like the sparrow in her
wandering, like the swallow in
her flying,
So the curse without cause does
not come *and* alight [on the
undeserving]. [Num 23:8]
³ A whip for the horse, a bridle for
the donkey,

And a rod for the backs of fools
[who refuse to learn].
⁴ Do not answer [nor pretend
to agree with the frivolous
comments of] a [closed-minded]
fool according to his folly,
Otherwise you, even you, will be
like him.
⁵ Answer [and correct the erroneous
concepts of] a fool according to
his folly,
Otherwise he will be wise in his
own eyes [if he thinks you agree
with him]. [Matt 16:1–4; 21:24–27]
⁶ He who sends a message by the
hand of a fool
Cuts off *his own* feet (sabotages
himself) and drinks the violence
[it brings on himself as a
consequence]. [Prov 13:17]
⁷ Like the legs which are useless to
the lame,
So is a proverb in the mouth of a
fool [who cannot learn from its
wisdom].
⁸ Like one who [absurdly] binds
a stone in a sling [making it
impossible to throw],
So is he who [absurdly] gives
honor to a fool.
⁹ Like a thorn that goes [without
being felt] into the hand of a
drunken man,
So is a proverb in the mouth of a
fool [who remains unaffected by
its wisdom].
¹⁰ Like a [careless] archer who
[shoots arrows wildly and]
wounds everyone,
So is he who hires a fool or those
who [by chance just] pass by.
¹¹ Like a dog that returns to his vomit
Is a fool who repeats his
foolishness.
¹² Do you see a man [who is
unteachable and] wise in his
own eyes *and* full of self-conceit?

There is more hope for a fool than for him. [Prov 29:20; Luke 18:11; Rom 12:16; Rev 3:17]

¹³ The lazy person [who is self-indulgent and relies on lame excuses] says, "There is a lion in the road!

A lion is in the open square [and if I go outside to work I will be killed]!" [Prov 22:13]

¹⁴ As the door turns on its hinges, So does the lazy person on his bed [never getting out of it].

¹⁵ The lazy person buries his hand in the dish [losing opportunity after opportunity]; It wearies him to bring it back to his mouth. [Prov 19:24]

¹⁶ The lazy person is wiser in his own eyes Than seven [sensible] men who can give a discreet answer.

¹⁷ Like one who grabs a dog by the ears [and is likely to be bitten] Is he who, passing by, stops to meddle with a dispute that is none of his business.

¹⁸ Like a madman who throws Firebrands, arrows, and death,

¹⁹ So is the man who deceives his neighbor (acquaintance, friend) And then says, "Was I not joking?" [Eph 5:4]

²⁰ For lack of wood the fire goes out, And where there is no whisperer [who gossips], contention quiets down.

²¹ Like charcoal to hot embers and wood to fire, So is a contentious man to kindle strife. [Prov 15:18; 29:22]

²² The words of a whisperer (gossip) are like dainty morsels [to be greedily eaten]; They go down into the innermost chambers of the body [to be remembered and mused upon]. [Prov 18:8]

²³ Like a [common] clay vessel covered with the silver dross [making it appear silver when it has no real value] Are burning lips [murmuring manipulative words] and a wicked heart.

²⁴ He who hates, disguises it with his lips, But he stores up deceit in his heart.

²⁵ When he speaks graciously *and* kindly [to conceal his malice], do not trust him, For seven abominations are in his heart.

²⁶ *Though his* hatred covers itself with guile *and* deceit, His malevolence will be revealed openly before the assembly.

²⁷ Whoever digs a pit [for another man's feet] will fall into it, And he who rolls a stone [up a hill to do mischief], it will come back on him. [Ps 7:15, 16; 9:15; 10:2; 57:6; Prov 28:10; Eccl 10:8]

²⁸ A lying tongue hates those it wounds *and* crushes, And a flattering mouth works ruin.

27

DO NOT boast about tomorrow, For you do not know what a day may bring. [Luke 12:19, 20; James 4:13]

² Let another praise you, and not your own mouth; A stranger, and not your own lips.

³ Stone is heavy and the sand weighty, But a fool's [unreasonable] wrath is heavier *and* more burdensome than both of them.

⁴ Wrath is cruel and anger is an overwhelming flood, But who is able to endure *and* stand before [the sin of] jealousy?

⁵ Better is an open reprimand [of loving correction] Than love that is hidden. [Prov 28:23; Gal 2:14]

⁶Faithful are the wounds of a friend
  [who corrects out of love and
  concern],
  But the kisses of an enemy are
  deceitful [because they serve his
  hidden agenda].
⁷He who is satisfied loathes honey,
  But to the hungry soul any bitter
  thing is sweet.
⁸Like a bird that wanders from her
  nest [with its comfort and safety],
  So is a man who wanders from his
  home.
⁹Oil and perfume make the heart
  glad;
  So does the sweetness of a friend's
  counsel that comes from the
  heart.
¹⁰Do not abandon your own friend
  and your father's friend,
  And do not go to your brother's
  house in the day of your disaster.
  Better is a neighbor who is near
  than a brother who is far away.
¹¹My son, be wise, and make my
  heart glad,
  That I may reply to him who
  reproaches (reprimands,
  criticizes) me. [Prov 10:1; 23:15, 24]
¹²A prudent man sees evil and hides
  himself *and* avoids it,
  But the naive [who are easily
  misled] continue on and are
  punished [by suffering the
  consequences of sin]. [Prov 22:3]
¹³[The judge tells the creditor,] "Take
  the garment of one who is surety
  (guarantees a loan) for a stranger;
  And hold him in pledge when he
  is surety for an immoral woman
  [for it is unlikely the debt will be
  repaid]." [Prov 20:16]
¹⁴He who blesses his neighbor with a
  loud voice early in the morning,
  It will be counted as a curse to him
  [for it will either be annoying or
  his purpose will be suspect].
¹⁵A constant dripping on a day of
  steady rain

And a contentious (quarrelsome)
  woman are alike; [Prov 19:13]
¹⁶Whoever attempts to restrain her
  [criticism] might as well try to
  stop the wind,
  And grasps oil with his right hand.
¹⁷As iron sharpens iron,
  So one man sharpens [and
  influences] another [through
  discussion].
¹⁸He who tends the fig tree will eat
  its fruit,
  And he who faithfully protects
  and cares for his master will be
  honored. [1 Cor 9:7, 13]
¹⁹As in water face *reflects* face,
  So the heart of man reflects man.
²⁰Sheol (the place of the dead) and
  Abaddon (the underworld) are
  never satisfied;
  Nor are the eyes of man ever
  satisfied. [Prov 30:16; Hab 2:5]
²¹The refining pot is for silver and
  the furnace for gold [to separate
  the impurities of the metal],
  And each is tested by the praise
  given to him [and his response
  to it, whether humble or proud].
²²Even though you pound a
  [hardened, arrogant] fool [who
  rejects wisdom] in a mortar with
  a pestle like grain,
  Yet his foolishness will not leave
  him.

²³Be diligent to know the condition
  of your flocks,
  And pay attention to your herds;
²⁴For riches are not forever,
  Nor does a crown *endure* to all
  generations.
²⁵When the grass is gone, the new
  growth is seen,
  And herbs of the mountain are
  gathered in,
²⁶The lambs will *supply wool* for
  your clothing,
  And the goats will bring the price
  of a field.

bold as a lion

If we intend to succeed at being ourselves and truly enjoy our everyday lives, we must reach a point where we allow the Holy Spirit to lead us. Only God, through His Spirit, will lead us to succeed and be all we can be. Other people usually will not, the devil certainly will not, and we are not able to do it ourselves without God.

Being led by the Spirit does not mean we never make mistakes. The Holy Spirit does not make mistakes, but we do. Following the Spirit's leading is a process that can be learned only by doing. We start by stepping out into things we believe God is putting on our hearts, and we learn by wisdom and experience how to hear more clearly and definitely. I always say, "Step out and find out." That is one way to discover if what is in your heart is from God. If it works it is God, and if it doesn't work it is not, and there is no shame in stepping out to find out. Take little baby steps and see if the first one produces good fruit; if it does then take another step. If it does not, then back off and pray some more.

I say that boldness is required to be led by the Spirit because only boldness steps out and only boldness can survive making mistakes. We must remember that the "righteous are bold as a lion" (Proverbs 28:1). When insecure people make mistakes, often they will not try again. Bold people make many mistakes, but their attitude is, "I am going to keep trying until I learn to do this right."

Those who suffer from condemnation usually do not believe they can hear from God. Even if they think they may have heard from God and do step out, a minor failure is a major setback to them. Each time they make a mistake, they come under a new load of guilt and condemnation. They end up spending all their time in the cycle. They make a mistake, feel condemned, make another mistake, feel condemned, and on and on. Finally they become frozen with fear and never fulfill their destinies.

I encourage you to step out in faith and be all that God has called you to be. If you do step out and two weeks later discover you made a mistake, are you going to be bold enough to pray, wise enough to learn from your mistakes, and determined enough to go on—or are you going to feel condemned and go back to wasting your life? There is no point in learning to be led by the Holy Spirit if you do not understand that you will make some mistakes while on the journey.

Be as bold as a lion in your faith. Do not hide behind fears, insecurities, and mistakes any longer. If you have already made major blunders in your life and have been living under condemnation because of them, this is the time to forgive yourself and press on!

In Christ, you can be all God has planned for you to be. Do not be half of it or three-quarters of it, but be *all* that God designed you to be. Do all He wants you to do, and have all He wants you to have. You will not enjoy God's fullness without His boldness. Remember, condemnation destroys boldness, so do not stay under condemnation.

Proverbs 28:1 says that the wicked flee when no one is even pursuing them. The wicked are running all the time. They run from everything. But the uncompromisingly righteous are as bold as a lion. And whether you feel it or not, you are righteous!

27 And *there will be* enough goats' milk for your food,
For the food of your household,
And for the maintenance of your maids.

28 THE WICKED flee when no one pursues them,
But the righteous are as bold as a lion. [Lev 26:17, 36; Ps 53:5]
2 When a land does wrong, it has many princes,
But when the ruler is a man of understanding and knowledge, its stability endures.
3 A poor man who oppresses *and* exploits the lowly
Is like a sweeping rain which leaves no food. [Matt 18:28]
4 Those who set aside the law [of God and man] praise the wicked,
But those who keep the law [of God and man] struggle with them. [Prov 29:18]
5 Evil men do not understand justice,
But they who long for *and* seek the LORD understand it fully. [John 7:17; 1 Cor 2:15; 1 John 2:20, 27]
6 Better is the poor who walks in his integrity
Than he who is crooked *and* two-faced though he is rich. [Prov 19:1]
7 He who keeps the law [of God and man] is a wise *and* discerning son,
But he who is a companion of gluttons humiliates his father [and himself].
8 He who increases his wealth by interest and usury (excessive interest)
Gathers it for him who is gracious to the poor. [Job 27:16, 17; Prov 13:22; Eccl 2:26]
9 He who turns his ear away from listening to the law [of God and man],

Even his prayer is repulsive [to God]. [Ps 66:18; 109:7; Prov 15:8; Zech 7:11]
10 He who leads the upright astray on an evil path
Will himself fall into his own pit,
But the blameless will inherit good.
11 The rich man [who is conceited and relies on his wealth instead of God] is wise in his own eyes,
But the poor man who has understanding [because he relies on God] is able to see through him.
12 When the righteous triumph, there is great glory *and* celebration;
But when the wicked rise [to prominence], men hide themselves.
13 He who conceals his transgressions will not prosper,
But whoever confesses and turns away from his sins will find compassion *and* mercy. [Ps 32:3, 5; 1 John 1:8–10]
14 Blessed *and* favored by God is the man who fears [sin and its consequence] at all times,
But he who hardens his heart [and is determined to sin] will fall into disaster.
15 Like a roaring lion and a charging bear
Is a wicked ruler over a poor people.
16 A leader who is a great oppressor lacks understanding *and* common sense [and his wickedness shortens his days],
But he who hates unjust gain will [be blessed and] prolong his days.
17 A man who is burdened with the guilt of human blood (murder)
Will be a fugitive until death; let no one support him *or* give him refuge.
18 He who walks blamelessly *and* uprightly will be kept safe,
But he who is crooked (perverse) will suddenly fall.

19 He who cultivates his land will
  have plenty of bread,
But he who follows worthless
  people *and* frivolous pursuits
  will have plenty of poverty.
20 A faithful (right-minded) man will
  abound with blessings,
But he who hurries to be rich will
  not go unpunished. [Prov 13:11;
  20:21; 23:4; 1 Tim 6:9]
21 To have regard for one person over
  another *and* to show favoritism is
  not good,
Because for a piece of bread a man
  will transgress.
22 He who has an evil *and* envious
  eye hurries to be rich
And does not know that poverty
  will come upon him. [Prov 21:5;
  28:20]
23 He who [appropriately]
  reprimands a [wise] man will
  afterward find more favor
Than he who flatters with the
  tongue.
24 He who robs his father or his
  mother
And says, "This is no sin,"
Is [not only a thief but also]
  the companion of a man who
  destroys.
25 An arrogant *and* greedy man stirs
  up strife,
But he who trusts in the LORD will
  be blessed *and* prosper.
26 He who trusts confidently
  in his own heart is a [dull,
  thickheaded] fool,
But he who walks in [skillful and
  godly] wisdom will be rescued.
  [James 1:5]

life point

**A life of faithfully serving and obeying
God allows Him to place us in a position
to be consistently blessed. As we learn
from Proverbs 28:20, a person who is
faithful abounds with blessings.**

27 He who gives to the poor will
  never want,
But he who shuts his eyes [from
  their need] will have many curses.
  [Deut 15:7; Prov 19:17; 22:9]
28 When the wicked rise [to power],
  men hide themselves;
But when the wicked perish, the
  [consistently] righteous increase
  and become great. [Prov 28:12]

29 HE WHO hardens his neck
  and refuses instruction
  after being often reproved
  (corrected, criticized),
Will suddenly be broken beyond
  repair.
2 When the righteous are in
  authority *and* become great, the
  people rejoice;
But when the wicked man rules,
  the people groan *and* sigh.
3 A man who loves [skillful and
  godly] wisdom makes his father
  joyful,
But he who associates with
  prostitutes wastes his wealth.
4 The king establishes (stabilizes)
  the land by justice,
But a man who takes bribes
  overthrows it.
5 A man who flatters his neighbor
  [with smooth words intending to
  do harm]
Is spreading a net for his own feet.
6 By his wicked plan an evil man is
  trapped,
But the righteous man sings and
  rejoices [for his plan brings good
  things to him].
7 The righteous man cares for the
  rights of the poor,
But the wicked man has no
  interest in such knowledge. [Job
  29:16; 31:13; Ps 41:1]
8 Scoffers set a city afire [by stirring
  up trouble],

But wise men turn away anger
[and restore order with their
good judgment].
⁹If a wise man has a controversy
with a foolish *and* arrogant man,
The foolish man [ignores logic
and fairness and] only rages or
laughs, and there is no peace
(rest, agreement).
¹⁰The bloodthirsty hate the
blameless [because of his
integrity],
But the upright are concerned for
his life. [Gen 4:5, 8; 1 John 3:12]
¹¹A [shortsighted] fool always loses
his temper *and* displays his anger,
But a wise man [uses self-control
and] holds it back.
¹²If a ruler pays attention to lies [and
encourages corruption],
All his officials *will become* wicked.
¹³The poor man and the oppressor
have this in common:

The LORD gives light to the eyes of
both. [Prov 22:2]
¹⁴If a king faithfully *and* truthfully
judges the poor,
His throne shall be established
forever.
¹⁵The rod and reproof (godly
instruction) give wisdom,
But a child who gets his own way
brings shame to his mother.
¹⁶When the wicked are in authority,
transgression increases,
But the righteous will see the
downfall of the wicked.
¹⁷Correct your son, and he will give
you comfort;
Yes, he will delight your soul.
¹⁸Where there is no vision [no
revelation of God and His word],
the people are unrestrained;
But happy *and* blessed is he who
keeps the law [of God]. [1 Sam
3:1; Amos 8:11, 12]

the importance of vision

People who have a sad past need to be able to believe in a bright future. Proverbs 29:18 says that, "Where there is no vision [no revelation of God and His word], the people are unrestrained."

A vision is something we see in our minds, "a mental sight," as one definition puts it, or even an understanding of God and His Word. It may be something God plants in us supernaturally or something we see on purpose. It often involves the way we think about our past, our future, and ourselves.

Some people are afraid to believe God for a vision. They think they may be setting themselves up for disappointment. They have not realized they will be perpetually disappointed if they do not believe. If I am describing you, remember this truth: *it does not cost anything to believe*. I feel that if I believe for a lot and get even half of it, I am better off than I would be to believe for nothing and get all of nothing.

I challenge you to start believing that something good is going to happen to you. Ask God for a vision to pursue, and believe you can do whatever you need to do in life through Christ (see Philippians 4:13). Do not have a "give-up-easily" attitude. Let your faith soar. Be creative with your thoughts. Take an inventory and ask yourself, "What have I been believing lately?" An honest answer may help you understand why you have not been receiving what you have wanted. Allow God's redemptive revelation to lead you away from the dead ends of your life and give you vision for your future.

19 A servant will not be corrected by words *alone;*
  For though he understands, he will not respond [nor pay attention].
20 Do you see a [conceited] man who speaks quickly [offering his opinions or answering without thinking]?
  There is more hope for a [thickheaded] fool than for him.
21 He who pampers his slave from childhood
  Will find him to be a son in the end.
22 An angry man stirs up strife,
  And a hot-tempered *and* undisciplined man commits many transgressions.
23 A man's pride *and* sense of self-importance will bring him down,
  But he who has a humble spirit will obtain honor. [Prov 15:33; 18:12; Is 66:2; Dan 4:30; Matt 23:12; James 4:6, 10; 1 Pet 5:5]
24 Whoever is partner with a thief hates his own life;
  He hears the curse [when swearing an oath to testify], but discloses nothing [and commits perjury by omission].
25 The fear of man brings a snare,
  But whoever trusts in *and* puts his confidence in the LORD will be exalted *and* safe.
26 Many seek the ruler's favor,
  But justice for man comes from the LORD.
27 An unjust man is repulsive to the righteous,
  And he who is upright in the way [of the LORD] is repulsive to the wicked.

30 THE WORDS of Agur the son of Jakeh, the oracle:
The man says to Ithiel, to Ithiel and to Ucal:

2 Surely I am more brutish *and* stupid than any man,
  And I do not have the understanding of a man [for I do not know what I do not know].
3 I have not learned [skillful and godly] wisdom,
  Nor do I have knowledge of the Holy One [who is the source of wisdom].
4 Who has ascended into heaven and descended?
  Who has gathered the wind in His fists?
  Who has bound the waters in His garment?
  Who has established all the ends of the earth?
  What is His name, and what is His Son's name?
  Certainly you know! [John 3:13; Rev 19:12]

5 Every word of God is tested *and* refined [like silver];
  He is a shield to those who trust *and* take refuge in Him. [Ps 18:30; 84:11; 115:9–11]
6 Do not add to His words,
  Or He will reprove you, and you will be found a liar.

7 Two things I have asked of You;
  Do not deny them to me before I die:
8 Keep deception and lies far from me;
  Give me neither poverty nor riches;
  Feed me with the food that is my portion,

speak the Word

God, every word of Yours is tested and refined like silver;
You are a shield to me because I trust and take refuge in You.
—ADAPTED FROM PROVERBS 30:5

⁹So that I will not be full and deny
  You and say, "Who is the Lᴏʀᴅ?"
Or that I will not be poor and steal,
And so profane the name of my
  God. [Deut 8:12, 14, 17; Neh 9:25,
  26; Job 31:24; Hos 13:6]

¹⁰Do not slander *or* malign a servant
  before his master [stay out of
  another's personal life],
Or he will curse you [for your
  interference], and you will be
  found guilty.

¹¹There is a generation (class of
  people) that curses its father
And does not bless its mother.

¹²There is a generation (class of
  people) that is pure in its own
  eyes,
Yet is not washed from its
  filthiness.

¹³There is a generation (class of
  people)—oh, how lofty are their
  eyes!
And their eyelids are raised *in
  arrogance.*

¹⁴There is a generation (class of
  people) whose teeth are like
  swords
And whose jaw teeth are like
  knives,
To devour the afflicted from the
  earth
And the needy from among men.

¹⁵The leech has two daughters,
  "Give, give!"
There are three things that are
  never satisfied,
Four that do not say, "It is enough":

¹⁶Sheol, and the barren womb,
Earth that is never satisfied with
  water,
And fire that never says, "It is
  enough."

¹⁷The eye that mocks a father
And scorns a mother,
The ravens of the valley will pick
  it out,

And the young vultures will devour
  it. [Lev 20:9; Prov 20:20; 23:22]

¹⁸There are three things which are
  too astounding *and* unexpectedly
  wonderful for me,
Four which I do not understand:

¹⁹The way of an eagle in the air,
The way of a serpent on a rock,
The way of a ship in the middle of
  the sea,
And the way of a man with a maid.

²⁰This is the way of an adulterous
  woman:
She eats and wipes her mouth
And says, "I have done no wrong."

²¹Under three things the earth is
  disquieted *and* quakes,
And under four it cannot bear up:

²²Under a servant when he reigns,
Under a [spiritually blind] fool
  when he is filled with food,

²³Under an unloved woman when
  she gets married,
And *under* a maidservant when
  she supplants her mistress.

²⁴There are four things that are
  small on the earth,
But they are exceedingly wise:

²⁵The ants are not a strong people,
Yet they prepare their food in the
  summer; [Prov 6:6]

²⁶The shephanim are not a mighty
  folk,
Yet they make their houses in the
  rocks; [Ps 104:18]

²⁷The locusts have no king,
Yet all of them go out in groups;

²⁸You may grasp the lizard with your
  hands,
Yet it is in kings' palaces.

²⁹There are three things which are
  stately in step,
Even four which are stately in
  their stride:

³⁰The lion, which is mighty among
  beasts
And does not turn back before any;

31 The strutting rooster, the male
    goat also,
And the king *when his* army is
    with him.

32 If you have foolishly exalted
    yourself,
Or if you have plotted *evil, put your*
    hand on your mouth. [Job 21:5;
    40:4]

33 Surely the churning of milk
    produces butter,
And wringing the nose produces
    blood;
So the churning of anger produces
    strife.

31

THE WORDS of King Lemuel, the oracle, which his mother taught him:

2 What, O my son?
And what, O son of my womb?
And what [shall I advise you], O
    son of my vows?

3 Do not give your [generative]
    strength to women [neither
    foreign wives in marriages of
    alliances, nor concubines],
Nor your ways to that which
    destroys kings.

4 It is not for kings, O Lemuel,
It is not for kings to drink wine,

kindness on your lips

One of my biggest problems as I learned to control my anger and my words was the fact that I had been mistreated and abused in the earlier years of my life. As a result, I ended up with a harsh, hard spirit. I was determined that nobody was ever going to hurt me again, and that attitude influenced the things I said. Although I tried to say things that were right and pleasing to others, by the time my thoughts had passed through my soul and picked up the hardness and bitterness hidden there, my words came out harsh and hard.

No matter how right your heart may be before the Lord, if you have pride or anger or resentment in your spirit, you cannot open your mouth without expressing those negative traits and emotions. Why is that? Because, as Jesus told us, our mouths speak out of whatever fills our hearts (see Matthew 12:34).

I began to realize that the Lord had an important work to do in me. Gentleness became a key issue in my life. Part of what God revealed to me in His Word on this subject was in Proverbs 31, the chapter that speaks of the "spiritual, capable, intelligent, and virtuous" woman (verse 10). In verse 26 the writer says that on her tongue is the "teaching of kindness."

When I read that, I thought, *Oh, God, I've got anything in my mouth but the law of kindness!* It seemed to me that I was so hard inside that whenever I opened my mouth, out came a hammer.

You may relate to that situation. You may have been mistreated and abused as I was so that you are full of hatred, resentment, distrust, anger, and hostility. Instead of kindness and gentleness, you are filled with harshness and hardness.

Ask God to heal you from all the pain of your past and to help you develop the kindness and gentleness He wants you to possess. Let His healing words flow from your mouth and keep kindness on your lips.

Or for rulers to desire strong
   drink, [Eccl 10:17; Hos 4:11]
⁵Otherwise they drink and forget
   the law *and* its decrees,
And pervert the rights *and* justice
   of all the afflicted.
⁶Give strong drink [as medicine] to
   him who is ready to pass away,
And wine to him whose life is
   bitter.
⁷Let him drink and forget his
   poverty
And no longer remember his
   trouble.
⁸Open your mouth for the mute,
For the rights of all who are
   unfortunate *and* defenseless;
   [1 Sam 19:4; Esth 4:16;
   Job 29:15, 16]
⁹Open your mouth, judge
   righteously,
And administer justice for the
   afflicted and needy. [Lev 19:15;
   Deut 1:16; Job 29:12; Is 1:17; Jer
   22:16]

¹⁰An excellent woman [one who is
   spiritual, capable, intelligent,
   and virtuous], who is he who can
   find her?
Her value is more precious than
   jewels *and* her worth is far above
   rubies *or* pearls. [Prov 12:4;
   18:22; 19:14]
¹¹The heart of her husband trusts in
   her [with secure confidence],
And he will have no lack of gain.
¹²She comforts, encourages, *and*
   does him only good and not evil
All the days of her life.
¹³She looks for wool and flax
And works with willing hands in
   delight.
¹⁴She is like the merchant ships
   [abounding with treasure];
She brings her [household's] food
   from far away.
¹⁵She rises also while it is still night
And gives food to her household

And assigns tasks to her maids.
   [Job 23:12]
¹⁶She considers a field before she
   buys *or* accepts it [expanding her
   business prudently];
With her profits she plants fruitful
   vines in her vineyard.
¹⁷She equips herself with strength
   [spiritual, mental, and physical
   fitness for her God-given task]
And makes her arms strong.
¹⁸She sees that her gain is good;
Her lamp does not go out, but
   it burns continually through
   the night [she is prepared for
   whatever lies ahead].
¹⁹She stretches out her hands to the
   distaff,
And her hands hold the spindle
   [as she spins wool into thread for
   clothing].
²⁰She opens *and* extends her hand to
   the poor,
And she reaches out her filled
   hands to the needy.
²¹She does not fear the snow for her
   household,
For all in her household are clothed
   in [expensive] scarlet [wool].
   [Josh 2:18, 19; Heb 9:19–22]
²²She makes for herself coverlets,
   cushions, *and* rugs of tapestry.
Her clothing is linen, pure *and*
   fine, and purple [wool]. [Is 61:10;
   1 Tim 2:9; Rev 3:5; 19:8, 14]
²³Her husband is known in the
   [city's] gates,
When he sits among the elders of
   the land. [Prov 12:4]
²⁴She makes [fine] linen garments
   and sells them;
And supplies sashes to the
   merchants.
²⁵Strength and dignity are her
   clothing *and* her position is
   strong and secure;
And she smiles at the future
   [knowing that she and her
   family are prepared].

26 She opens her mouth in [skillful and godly] wisdom,
And the teaching of kindness is on her tongue [giving counsel and instruction].
27 She looks well to how things go in her household,
And does not eat the bread of idleness. [1 Tim 5:14; Titus 2:5]
28 Her children rise up and call her blessed (happy, prosperous, to be admired);
Her husband also, and he praises her, *saying,*

29 "Many daughters have done nobly, *and* well [with the strength of character that is steadfast in goodness],
But you excel them all."
30 Charm *and* grace are deceptive, and [superficial] beauty is vain,
But a woman who fears the LORD [reverently worshiping, obeying, serving, and trusting Him with awe-filled respect], she shall be praised.
31 Give her of the product of her hands,
And let her own works praise her in the gates [of the city]. [Phil 4:8]

Ecclesiastes

Author:
Traditionally, Solomon

Date:
Traditionally, near Solomon's death
(about 931 BC)

Everyday Life Principles:
We need to accept what God gives us
and be happy with our lives.

Fearing God and keeping His commandments is the solution to every problem
we face in life.

God is the ultimate Judge. We need to
do things His way; and He will reward
us accordingly.

Solomon, the wise king who wrote
Ecclesiastes, had tried everything. After he had exhausted almost
every imaginable worldly pursuit, he
finally realized that everything on
earth is an exercise in vanity if we do
not fear God and obey His Word. He
makes this point in one of my favorite Bible verses, Ecclesiastes 12:13:
"When all has been heard, the end of
the matter is: fear God [worship Him
with awe-filled reverence, knowing
that He is almighty God] and keep
His commandments, for this applies
to every person."

On the way to his conclusion that
everything about our lives comes
down to fearing God and keeping His commandments, Solomon
learned some other lessons that are
important for us. He learned that
being happy in life and in work is
one of the best things we can do.
He learned that there is a time and
a season for everything that needs
to be done. And he learned that God
will bring all of our works, good or
evil, into judgment.

As you read Solomon's words in
Ecclesiastes, remember to take his
advice: enjoy your life, be happy with
your work, fear God, and keep His
Word.

1 THE WORDS of the Preacher, the son of David, king in Jerusalem.

² "Vanity of vanities," says the Preacher.
"Vanity of vanities! All [that is done without God's guidance] is vanity [futile, meaningless—a wisp of smoke, a vapor that vanishes, merely chasing the wind]." [Rom 8:20]

³ What advantage does man have from all his work
Which he does under the sun (while earthbound)?
⁴ One generation goes and another generation comes,
But the earth remains forever. [Ps 119:90]
⁵ Also, the sun rises and the sun sets;
And hurries to the place where it rises again.
⁶ The wind blows toward the south,
Then circles toward the north;
The wind circles *and* swirls endlessly,
And on its circular course the wind returns. [John 3:8]
⁷ All the rivers flow into the sea,
Yet the sea is not full.
To the place where the rivers flow,
There they flow again.
⁸ All things are wearisome *and* all words are frail;
Man cannot express it.
The eye is not satisfied with seeing,
Nor is the ear filled with hearing. [Prov 27:20]
⁹ That which has been is that which will be [again],
And that which has been done is that which will be done again.
So there is nothing new under the sun.
¹⁰ Is there anything of which it can be said,
"See this, it is new"?

It has already existed for [the vast] ages [of time recorded or unrecorded]
Which were before us.
¹¹ There is no remembrance of earlier things,
Nor also of the later things that are to come;
There will be for them no remembrance
By generations who will come after them.

¹² I, the Preacher, have been king over Israel in Jerusalem.
¹³ And I set my mind to seek and explore by [man's] wisdom all [human activity] that has been done under heaven. It is a miserable business *and* a burdensome task which God has given the sons of men with which to be busy *and* distressed.
¹⁴ I have seen all the works which have been done under the sun, and behold, all is vanity, a futile grasping *and* chasing after the wind.
¹⁵ What is crooked cannot be straightened and what is defective *and* lacking cannot be counted.
¹⁶ I spoke with my heart, saying, "Behold, I have acquired great [human] wisdom *and* experience, more than all who were over Jerusalem before me; and my mind has observed a wealth of [moral] wisdom and [scientific] knowledge."
¹⁷ And I set my mind to know [practical] wisdom and to discern [the character of] madness and folly [in which

life point

I like the way Solomon summarized the earthly pursuits so many of us run after. He said that trying to find fulfillment in anything the world has to offer is like chasing the wind (see Ecclesiastes 1:14). No matter how hard we chase after it, it always evades us. No matter how fast we run, we will never catch it.

men seem to find satisfaction]; I realized that this too is a futile grasping *and* chasing after the wind. [1 Thess 5:21]

[18]For in much [human] wisdom there is much displeasure *and* exasperation; increasing knowledge increases sorrow.

2 I SAID to myself, "Come now, I will test you with pleasure *and* gratification; so enjoy yourself *and* have a good time." But behold, this too was vanity (futility, meaninglessness). [Luke 12:19, 20]

[2]I said of laughter, "It is madness," and of pleasure, "What does it accomplish?"

[3]I explored with my mind how to gratify myself with wine while [at the same time] having my mind remain steady *and* guide me wisely; and how to take control of foolishness, until I could see what was good for the sons of men to do under heaven all the days of their lives.

[4]I made great works: I built houses for myself; I planted vineyards for myself;

[5]I made gardens and orchards for myself and I planted in them all kinds of fruit trees;

[6]I made pools of water for myself from which to water the forest *and* make the trees bud.

[7]I bought male and female slaves and had slaves born in my house. I also possessed herds and flocks larger than any who preceded me in Jerusalem.

[8]Also, I collected for myself silver and gold and the treasure of kings and provinces. I provided for myself male singers and female singers, and the delights *and* pleasures of men—many concubines. [1 Kin 9:28; 10:10, 14, 21]

[9]So I became great and excelled more than all who preceded me in Jerusalem. My wisdom also remained with me.

[10]Whatever my eyes looked at with desire I did not refuse them. I did not withhold from my heart any pleasure, for my heart was pleased because of all my labor; and this was my reward for all my labor.

[11]Then I considered all which my hands had done and labored to do, and behold, all was vanity and chasing after the wind and there was no profit (nothing of lasting value) under the sun. [Matt 16:26]

[12]So I turned to consider [secular] wisdom, madness, and folly; for what will the man do who succeeds the king? Nothing *except* what has already been done.

[13]Then I saw that [even secular] wisdom [that brings sorrow] is better than [the pleasures of] folly *and* self-indulgence as light excels darkness.

[14]The wise man's eyes are in his head, but the fool walks in darkness; and yet I know that [in the end] one fate happens to them both. [Prov 17:24]

[15]Then I said to myself, "As it happens to the fool, so death will also happen to me. What use is it then for me to be extremely wise?" Then I said in my heart, "This too is vanity (meaningless)."

[16]For there is no [more] lasting remembrance of the wise man than of the fool, since in the days to come all will be long forgotten. And how does the wise man die? Even as the fool!

[17]So I hated life, for the work which had been done under the sun caused me only great sorrow; because all is futility and chasing after the wind.

[18]So I hated all the fruit (gain) of my labor for which I had labored under the sun, because I must leave it to the man who will succeed me. [Ps 49:10]

[19]And who knows whether he will be a wise man or a fool? Yet he will have control over all the fruit of my labor for which I have labored by acting wisely under the sun. This too is vanity (futility, self-conceit).

[20]So I turned aside and let my heart

despair over all the fruit of my labor for which I had labored under the sun.

²¹For there is a man who has labored with wisdom and knowledge and skill, yet gives his legacy to one who has not labored for it. This too is vanity and a great evil.

²²For what does a man get from all his labor and from the striving *and* sorrow of his heart with which he labors under the sun?

²³For all his days his work is painful and sorrowful; even at night his mind does not rest. This too is vanity (worthless).

²⁴There is nothing better for a man than to eat and drink and assure

putting the Word to work

Ecclesiastes 2:24 tells us that there is nothing better than enjoying what we do. Are you enjoying what you do or are you tired, weary, or bored? Ask God to refresh you and enable you to enjoy your work.

the secret of fulfillment

Solomon writes in Ecclesiastes 2:17, 18: "So I hated life, for the work which had been done under the sun caused me only great sorrow; because all is futility and chasing after the wind. So I hated all the fruit (gain) of my labor for which I had labored under the sun, because I must leave it to the man who will succeed me."

Solomon was a busy man; he tried everything that could be tried and did everything there was to do, but at the end of his experience, he was unfulfilled and bitter. Many people today have this same problem; they try everything they can think of to find satisfaction and joy in life, but in the end, they are exhausted, disappointed, and frustrated.

So what is the secret to happiness and fulfillment in life? I believe it is making sure we are obeying God's will and giving ourselves to what He has called us to do. Will that always be easy? No. Doing God's will is not without challenge. We will struggle at times. We will get tired, but it will be a "good kind of tired" that comes from doing what we are supposed to do.

Let me encourage you today to take a serious inventory of the way you spend your time. Get out the pruning shears and, as God leads you, cut activities and commitments out of your life until you no longer go through every day at such a frantic pace.

Realizing that you cannot do everything, then deciding with God's help what you can and cannot do, will make you more effective at the things you are supposed to do and will greatly increase the level of peace in your life. Peace equals power; without it, you will stay frustrated and weak.

As you evaluate how you are spending your time and what you are doing with your life, use this simple rule: If you have peace about it, keep doing it. If you do not have peace about it, stop. Hearing yourself complaining about it on a regular basis is an indication that you need to make an adjustment.

God does not want you to end up like Solomon, hating your life and being bitter. No, His great desire is for you to enjoy being in His will and to be satisfied and at peace as you fulfill His call on your life.

himself that there is good in his labor. Even this, I have seen, is from the hand of God.

²⁵For who can eat and who can have enjoyment without Him?

²⁶For to the person who pleases Him God gives wisdom, knowledge, and joy; but to the sinner He gives the work of gathering and collecting so that he may give to one who pleases God. This too is vanity and chasing after the wind.

3 THERE IS a season (a time appointed) for everything and a time for every delight *and* event *or* purpose under heaven—

²A time to be born and a time to die;
A time to plant and a time to uproot what is planted. [Heb 9:27]

life point

The enemy offers us two lies: the "forever" lie and the "never" lie. He tells us the negative things in our lives will "never" change and will "forever" be the way they are. He tells us we will "never" get what we want, and we will "never" experience the freedom or healing we desire. He says you will be the way you are right now "forever." The devil is a liar! These lies create fear in our hearts, and they are untrue because sooner or later, everything changes. If we continue to believe God and place our trust in Him, bad things ultimately give way to better things. As Ecclesiastes 3 reminds us, there is a time for everything. The good things you are believing God for are on their way!

speak the Word

³A time to kill and a time to heal;
A time to tear down and a time to build up.
⁴A time to weep and a time to laugh;
A time to mourn and a time to dance.
⁵A time to throw away stones and a time to gather stones;
A time to embrace and a time to refrain from embracing.
⁶A time to search and a time to give up as lost;
A time to keep and a time to throw away.
⁷A time to tear apart and a time to sew together;
A time to keep silent and a time to speak. [Amos 5:13]
⁸A time to love and a time to hate;
A time for war and a time for peace. [Luke 14:26]

⁹What profit is there for the worker from that in which he labors?

¹⁰I have seen the task which God has given to the sons of men with which to occupy themselves.

¹¹He has made everything beautiful *and* appropriate in its time. He has also planted eternity [a sense of divine purpose] in the human heart [a mysterious longing which nothing under the sun can satisfy, except God]—yet man cannot find out (comprehend, grasp) what God has done (His overall plan) from the beginning to the end.

¹²I know that there is nothing better for them than to rejoice and to do good as long as they live;

¹³and also that every man should eat and drink and see *and* enjoy the good of all his labor—it is the gift of God.

¹⁴I know that whatever God does, it endures forever; nothing can be added

God, I want to please You and receive Your wisdom, knowledge, and joy in my life.
—ADAPTED FROM ECCLESIASTES 2:26

to it nor can anything be taken from it, for God does it so that men will fear *and* worship Him [with awe-filled reverence, knowing that He is God]. [Ps 19:9; James 1:17]

¹⁵That which is has already been, and that which will be has already been, for God seeks what has passed by [so that history repeats itself].

¹⁶Moreover, I have seen under the sun that in the place of justice there is wickedness, and in the place of righteousness there is wickedness.

¹⁷I said to myself, "God will judge both the righteous and the wicked," for there is a time [appointed] for every matter and for every deed.

¹⁸I said to myself regarding the sons of men, "God is surely testing them in order for them to see that [by themselves, without God] they are [only] animals."

¹⁹For the [earthly] fate of the sons of men and the fate of animals is the same. As one dies, so dies the other; indeed, they all have the same breath and there is no preeminence *or* advantage for man [in and of himself] over an animal, for all is vanity.

²⁰All go to the same place. All came from the dust and all return to the dust.

²¹Who knows if the spirit of man

putting the Word to work

Ecclesiastes 3:17 declares that there is a time appointed for everything and every purpose. In other words, God has an appointed time in which to do everything He has planned. Are you submitted to His timing in your life, or have you grown impatient waiting for something to happen? I encourage you today to repent for any impatience you have had and to make a fresh surrender to God's perfect timing for everything He wants to do in your life.

ascends upward and the spirit of the animal descends downward to the earth?

²²So I have seen that there is nothing better than that a man should be happy in his own works *and* activities, for that is his portion (share). For who will bring him [back] to see what will happen after he is gone?

4 THEN I looked again *and* considered all the acts of oppression that were being practiced under the sun. And behold *I saw* the tears of the oppressed and they had no one to comfort them; and on the side of their oppressors was power, but they had no one to comfort them.

²So I congratulated *and* thought more fortunate are those who are already dead than the living who are still living.

³But better off than either of them is the one who has not yet been born, who has not seen the evil deeds that are done under the sun.

⁴I have seen that every [effort in] labor and every skill in work *comes from* man's rivalry with his neighbor. This too is vanity (futility, false pride) and chasing after the wind.

⁵The fool folds his hands [together] and consumes his own flesh [destroying himself by idleness and apathy].

⁶One hand full of rest *and* patience is better than two fists full of labor and chasing after the wind.

⁷Then I looked again at vanity under the sun [in one of its peculiar forms].

⁸There was a certain man—without a dependent, having neither a child nor a brother, yet there was no end to all his labor. Indeed, his eyes were not satisfied with riches *and he never asked,* "For whom do I labor and deprive myself of pleasure?" This too is vanity (a wisp of smoke, self-conceit); yes, it is a painful effort *and* an unhappy task. [Prov 27:20; 1 John 2:16]

⁹Two are better than one because

they have a more satisfying return for their labor;

[10] for if either of them falls, the one will lift up his companion. But woe to him who is alone when he falls and does not have another to lift him up.

[11] Again, if two lie down together, then they keep warm; but how can one be warm *alone*?

[12] And though one can overpower him who is alone, two can resist him. A cord of three *strands* is not quickly broken.

[13] A poor yet wise youth is better than an old and foolish king who no longer knows how to receive instruction *and* counsel (friendly reproof, warning) —

[14] for the poor youth has [used his wisdom and] come out of prison to become king, even though he was born poor in his kingdom.

[15] I have seen all the living under the sun join with the second youth (the king's acknowledged successor) who replaces him.

[16] There is no end to all the people; to all who were before them. Yet those who come later will not be happy with him. Surely this also is vanity (emptiness) and chasing after the wind.

5 GUARD YOUR steps *and* focus on what you are doing as you go to the house of God and draw near to listen rather than to offer the [careless or irreverent] sacrifice of fools; for they are too ignorant to know they are doing evil. [Gen 35:1–4; Ex 3:5]

life point

Ecclesiastes 5:1 instructs us to give our minds to what we are doing, and to guard our steps. This means we need to learn to focus on what we are doing. If we do not, we will lose our footing and end up anxious and worried because we will always be mentally dealing with yesterday or tomorrow when we should be living today.

life point

We can be led of the Spirit through internal peace every day of our lives, but we do need to beware of false peace. A strong desire to do something can produce a false peace that actually comes only from excitement. As time passes, this false peace disappears, and God's true will for our lives emerges. For this reason we should never move too quickly on important decisions. A little time of waiting is always wise and prudent. This is why Ecclesiastes 5:2 tells us not to be hasty in what we say or impulsive in our thoughts. Excited emotions are often mistaken for God's will. However, emotions rise and fall, and if our desire and determination rise and fall with them, we will end up in real trouble. I always say, "Let emotions subside and then decide!"

[2] Do not be hasty with your mouth [speaking careless words or vows] or impulsive in thought to bring up a matter before God. For God is in heaven and you are on earth; therefore let your words be few.

[3] For the dream comes through much effort, and the voice of the fool through many words.

life point

Ecclesiastes 5:3 teaches us that we need to put effort into seeing our dreams come true. I hope you have a dream or a vision in your heart for something greater than you are experiencing now. Though you will likely have to work in order to see your dream come to pass, I know that God is for you and He will help you. If you are not dreaming of anything, you are cheating yourself. We all need to think big thoughts, hope big hopes, and dream big dreams!

4When you make a vow *or* a pledge to God, do not put off paying it; for *God takes* no pleasure in fools [who thoughtlessly mock Him]. Pay what you vow. [Ps 50:14; 66:13, 14; 76:11]

5It is better that you should not vow than that you should vow and not pay. [Prov 20:25; Acts 5:4]

6Do not allow your speech to cause you to sin, and do not say before the messenger (priest) *of God* that it was a mistake. Why should God be angry

stay on track

I believe the expression "Guard your steps" in Ecclesiastes 5:1 means "Do not lose your balance or get off track." In other words, it's important to stay focused and not allow our minds to wander.

I used to have a wandering mind, and I had to train it by discipline. It was not easy, and sometimes I still have a relapse. While trying to complete a project, I will suddenly realize that my mind has just wandered off onto something else that has nothing to do with the issue at hand. I have not yet arrived at a place of perfect concentration, but at least I understand how important it is not to allow my mind to go wherever it wishes, whenever it desires.

The word *wander* means "to move about aimlessly; to roam or amble." It implies that a person is taking an irregular course of action at no particular pace and in no particular direction. If you are like I am, you can be sitting in a church service listening to the speaker, really enjoying and benefiting from what is being said, when suddenly your mind begins to wander. After a while you "wake up" to find that you do not remember a thing that has been going on. Even though your body stayed in church, your mind was at the shopping center browsing through the stores or at home cooking dinner.

Remember, in spiritual warfare the mind is the battlefield. That is where the enemy makes his attack. He knows very well that if we cannot keep our minds on what is being taught, we will gain absolutely nothing by being in a church service. The devil knows that we cannot complete a project if we cannot discipline our minds and focus on what we are doing.

This mind-wandering phenomenon also occurs during conversation. There are times when my husband, Dave, is talking to me and I listen for a while; then all of a sudden I realize that I have not heard a thing he has been saying. Why? Because I allowed my mind to wander to something else. My body was standing there appearing to listen, yet in my mind I heard nothing.

For many years, when this sort of thing happened, I would pretend that I knew exactly what Dave was saying. Now I stop and say, "Can you back up and repeat that? I let my mind wander off, and I did not hear a thing you said." This way, I feel that at least I am dealing with the problem.

Confronting issues is the only way to get on the victorious side of them! Staying focused is not only important in our church lives, our professional lives, our social lives, and our relationships; it is also vital in our spiritual lives if we want to overcome the enemy. I encourage you to pay attention to your thoughts and not let your mind wander. Defend your mental battlefield by staying focused!

because of your voice (words) and destroy the work of your hands? [Mal 2:7]

7For in a multitude of dreams and in a flood of words there is worthlessness. Rather [reverently] fear God [and worship Him with awe-filled respect, knowing who He is].

8If you see the oppression of the poor and the denial of justice and righteousness in the province, do not be shocked at the sight [of corruption]; for a higher official watches over another official, and there are higher ones over them [looking out for one another].

9After all, a king who cultivates the field is an advantage to the land.

10He who loves money will not be satisfied with money, nor he who loves abundance *with its* gain. This too is vanity (emptiness).

11When good things increase, those who consume them increase. So what advantage is there to their owners except to see them with their eyes?

12The sleep of a working man is sweet, whether he eats little or much; but the full stomach (greed) of the rich [who hungers for even more] will not let him sleep.

13There is a grievous evil which I have seen under the sun: riches being kept *and* hoarded by their owner to his own misery.

14For when those riches are lost in bad investments and he becomes the father of a son, then there is nothing in his hand [for the support of the child].

15As he came naked from his mother's womb, so he will return as he came; and he will take away nothing from all his labor that he can carry in his hand. [Job 1:21; 1 Tim 6:7]

16This also is a grievous evil—exactly as he was born, so he shall die. So what advantage has he who labors for the wind? [1 Tim 6:6]

17All of his life he also eats in darkness [cheerlessly, without sweetness and light], with great frustration, sickness, and anger.

18Behold, here is what I have seen to be good and fitting: to eat and drink, and to find enjoyment in all the labor in which he labors under the sun

enjoy your journey

Years ago my husband and I enrolled in a nine-month Bible study course because we felt that God's will for us was to begin training for ministry. The course met two or three nights a week, which was quite a commitment, especially for Dave because he worked so hard in the engineering field during the day.

That course seemed like a major undertaking until the Lord gave me a vision about having goals and reaching them. In the vision I saw the horizon ahead of me, which in this case represented graduating from the course. As I began moving toward the horizon in the vision, it faded from sight and another would rise up.

The Lord was showing me that we will always be moving toward some goal or objective in our lives. As soon as we finish one, another will take its place. As believers, we are always extending our faith for something. Whatever we believe God for right now could happen a year from now, but by that time we will be believing God for something else. The Lord was teaching me that since we are going to spend the majority of our lives waiting for something, we should learn to enjoy life as it unfolds. If we do not, life will pass us by, and we will never enjoy where we are right now.

Let me encourage you, as the writer of Ecclesiastes did to enjoy everything you do to the fullest extent, for as long as you live (see Ecclesiastes 5:18)!

during the few days of his life which God gives him—for this is his [allotted] reward. [1 Tim 6:17]

¹⁹Also, every man to whom God has given riches and possessions, He has also given the power *and* ability to enjoy them and to receive [this as] his [allotted] portion and to rejoice in his labor—this is the gift of God [to him].

²⁰For he will not often consider the [troubled] days of his life, because God keeps him occupied *and* focused on the joy of his heart [and the tranquility of God indwells him].

6 THERE IS an evil which I have seen under the sun, and it weighs heavily on men:

²a man to whom God has given riches and wealth and honor, so that he lacks nothing of all that he desires, yet God has not given him the power *or* capacity to enjoy them [all those things which are gifts from God], but a stranger [in whom he has no interest succeeds him and] enjoys them. This is vanity and it is a [cause of] great distress. [Luke 12:20]

³If a man fathers a hundred *children* and lives many years, however many they may be, but his soul is not satisfied with good things and he is not respected *and* is not given a *proper* burial [he is not laid to rest in the sepulcher of his fathers], then I say, "Better the miscarriage than he, [Job 3:16]

⁴for the miscarriage comes in futility (in vain) and passes into obscurity; and its name is covered in obscurity.

⁵"It has not seen the sun nor had any knowledge; yet it has more rest *and* is better off than he.

⁶"Even if the *other* man lives a thousand years twice over and yet has seen no good *and* experienced no enjoyment—do not both go to one place [the grave]?"

⁷All the labor of man is for his mouth [for self-preservation and enjoyment],

and yet the desire [of his soul] is not satisfied. [Prov 16:26]

⁸For what advantage has the wise man over the fool [for being worldly-wise is not the secret to happiness]? What *advantage* has the poor man who has learned how to walk [publicly] among the living [with men's eyes on him; for being poor is not the secret to happiness either]?

⁹What the eyes see [enjoying what is available] is better than [craving] what the soul desires. This too is futility and chasing after the wind.

¹⁰Whatever exists has already been named [long ago], and it is known what [a frail being] man is; for he cannot dispute with Him who is mightier than he.

¹¹For there are many other words that increase futility. What then is the advantage for a man?

¹²For who [limited by human wisdom] knows what is good for man during his lifetime, during the few days of his futile life? He spends them like a shadow [staying busy, but achieving nothing of lasting value]. For who can tell a man what will happen after him [to his work, his treasure, his plans] under the sun [after his life is over]?

7 A GOOD name is better than precious perfume,
  And the day of one's death better than the day of one's birth.
²It is better to go to the house of mourning
  Than to go to the house of feasting,
  For that [day of death] is the end of every man,
  And the living will take it to heart *and* solemnly ponder its meaning.
³Sorrow is better than laughter,
  For when a face is sad (deep in thought) the heart may be happy [because it is growing in wisdom]. [2 Cor 7:10]

⁴The heart of the wise [learns when it] is in the house of mourning,
But the heart of fools is [senseless] in the house of pleasure.
⁵It is better to listen to the rebuke of the wise man *and* pursue wisdom
Than for one to listen to the song of fools *and* pursue stupidity.
⁶For like the crackling of [burning] thorn bushes under a pot,
So is the laughter of the fool;
And this too is vanity (futility).
⁷For oppression makes a wise man foolish,
And a bribe corrupts the [good judgment of the] heart.

⁸The end of a matter is better than its beginning;
Patience of spirit is better than haughtiness of spirit (pride).
⁹Do not be eager in your heart to be angry,
For anger dwells in the heart of fools. [James 1:19, 20]
¹⁰Do not say, "Why were the old days better than these?"
For it is not from wisdom that you ask about this.
¹¹Wisdom along with an inheritance is good
And an [excellent] advantage for those who see the sun.
¹²For wisdom is a protection *even as* money is a protection,

be slow to anger

Ecclesiastes 7:9 exhorts: "Do not be eager in your heart to be angry, for anger dwells in the heart of fools." Not being eager to be angry speaks to me of self-control. We cannot ever develop into victorious, overcoming believers if we do not learn to exercise self-control by managing our emotions, especially the emotion of anger.

Ecclesiastes 7:9 is only one of many Bible verses that address the subject of anger. For example, Proverbs 14:17 says, "A quick-tempered man acts foolishly and without self-control." Proverbs 16:32 reads: "He who is slow to anger is better and more honorable than the mighty [soldier], and he who rules and controls his own spirit, than he who captures a city." Proverbs 19:11 observes: "Good sense and discretion make a man slow to anger"; and James 1:19, 20 reads: "Let everyone be quick to hear [be a careful, thoughtful listener], slow to speak [a speaker of carefully chosen words and], slow to anger [patient, reflective, forgiving]; for the [resentful, deep-seated] anger of man does not produce the righteousness of God [that standard of behavior which He requires of us]."

Notice in James 1:19, 20 that the "anger of man does not produce" righteousness. Part of righteousness, or the right way of being what God wants us to be, is fulfilling our potential—and we cannot do that unless we learn to restrain our anger.

We all want more than we have in various areas of our lives, but we do not always want to operate within the boundaries of self-control. If we really want to grow spiritually, we must keep our passions under control. That does not mean we have to be perfect or that we can never make mistakes. Although the Holy Spirit will give us power to control our emotions, we may still lose our tempers at times. But as soon as we do, we should immediately confess and repent.

A disciplined, self-controlled life not only requires time, determination, and hard work; it also requires self-denial, but the rewards are worth the effort.

But the [excellent] advantage
of knowledge is that wisdom
shields *and* preserves the lives of
its possessors.
¹³Consider the work of God:
Who can make straight what He
has bent?
¹⁴In the day of prosperity be joyful,
But in the day of adversity
consider that
God has made the one as well as the
other,
So that man will not find out
anything *that will be* after him.

¹⁵I have seen everything during my
[fleeting] days of futility; there is a
righteous man who perishes in [spite
of] his righteousness, and there is a
wicked man who lives a long *life* in
[spite of] his wickedness.
¹⁶Do not be excessively righteous
[like those given to self-conceit], and
do not be overly wise (pretentious)—
why should you bring yourself to ruin?
¹⁷Do not be excessively *or* willfully
wicked and do not be a fool. Why
should you die before your time?
¹⁸It is good that you take hold of one
thing (righteousness) and also not let
go of the other (wisdom); for the one
who fears *and* worships God [with
awe-filled reverence] will come forth
with both of them.
¹⁹Wisdom strengthens the wise man
more than ten rulers who are in a city.
[Ps 127:1; 2 Tim 3:15]
²⁰Indeed, there is not a righteous
man on earth who *always* does good
and who never sins. [Is 53:6; Rom 3:23]
²¹Also, do not take seriously everything that is said, so that you will not
hear your servant cursing you,
²²for you also know that you too have
cursed others many times.
²³I have tested all this with wisdom.
I said, "I will be wise [independently
of God]," but true wisdom was far
from me.
²⁴Whatever has been is far off,

deeply remote and exceedingly mysterious. Who can discover it [for it is
beyond the grasp of man]? [Job 28:12–
28; 1 Cor 2:9–16]
²⁵I turned around *and* directed my
heart to know, to investigate and to
seek [skillful and godly] wisdom and
the reason for things, and to know that
wickedness is folly and that foolishness is madness [leading to stupidity
and recklessness].
²⁶And I discovered that [of all irrational sins none has been so destructive
in beguiling one away from God as immoral women for] more bitter than death
is the woman whose heart is [composed
of] snares and nets, and whose hands
are chains. Whoever pleases God will
escape from her, but the sinner will be
taken captive by her [evil].
²⁷"Behold, I have discovered this,"
says the Preacher, "while *adding* one
thing to another to find an explanation,
²⁸which I am still seeking but have
not found. I have found one man
among a thousand [who pleases God],
but I have not found [such] a woman
among all these [a thousand in my
harem]. [1 Kin 11:3]
²⁹"Behold, I have found only this [as
a reason]: God made man upright *and*
uncorrupted, but they [both men and
women] have sought out many devices
[for evil]."

8 WHO IS like the wise man?
And who knows the
interpretation of a matter?
A man's wisdom illumines his face,
And causes his stern face to beam.

²I counsel you to keep the command
of the king because of the oath before
God [by which you swore loyalty to
him]. [2 Sam 21:7]
³Do not be in a hurry to get out of his
presence. Do not join in a malevolent
matter, for the king will do whatever
he pleases.

⁴For the word of a king is
  authoritative *and* powerful,
And who will say to him, "What
  are you doing?"
⁵Whoever keeps *and* observes a
  royal command will experience
  neither trouble *nor* misery;
For a wise heart will know the
  proper time and [appropriate]
  procedure.
⁶For there is a proper time and
  [appropriate] procedure for
  every delight,
Though mankind's misery *and*
  trouble lies heavily upon him
  [who rebels against the king].
⁷For no one knows what will happen;
So who can tell him how *and* when
  it will happen?
⁸There is no man who has power
  and authority over the wind to
  restrain the wind,
Nor does he have authority over
  the day of death;
There is no discharge [from
  service] during time of war,
And evil will not rescue those who
  [actively seek to] practice it.

⁹All this I have seen while applying my mind to every deed that is done under the sun. There is a time in which one man has exercised power over others to their detriment. ¹⁰So then, I have seen the wicked buried, those who used to go in and out of the holy place [but did not thereby escape their doom], and they are [praised in spite of their evil and] soon forgotten in the city where they did such things. This too is futility (vanity, emptiness). ¹¹Because the sentence against an evil act is not executed quickly, the hearts of the sons of men are fully set to do evil. ¹²Though a sinner does evil a hundred *times* and his life [seemingly] is prolonged [in spite of his wickedness], still I know that it will be well with those who [reverently] fear God, who

fear *and* worship Him openly [realizing His omnipresence and His power]. [Ps 37:11, 18, 19; Is 3:10, 11; Matt 25:34] ¹³But it will not be well for the evil man, nor will he lengthen his days like a shadow, because he does not fear God. [Matt 25:41] ¹⁴There is a meaningless *and* futile thing which is done on the earth: that is, there are righteous men whose gain is as though they were evil, and evil men whose gain is as though they were righteous. I say that this too is futility (meaningless, vain). ¹⁵Then I commended pleasure *and* enjoyment, because a man [without God] has no better thing under the sun than to eat and to drink and to be merry, for this will stand by him in his toil through the days of his life which God has given him under the sun. ¹⁶When I applied my mind to know wisdom and to see the activities [of mankind] that take place upon the earth—how some men seem to sleep neither day nor night— ¹⁷and I saw all the work of God, I *concluded* that man cannot discover the work that is done under the sun. Even though man may labor in seeking, he will not discover; and [more than that], though a wise man thinks *and* claims he knows, he will not be able to find it out. [Deut 29:29; Rom 11:33]

life point

If we seek God only when we are desperate, then He will keep us in desperate circumstances because He deeply desires to fellowship with us.

God *will* rescue us and get us out of trouble when we come to Him. But, according to Ecclesiastes 8:12, things will go well for us continually if we fear the Lord with reverence and worship Him in our everyday lives. We must never forget that relationship is built on fellowship.

9 FOR I have taken all this to heart, exploring *and* examining it all, how the righteous (those in right standing with God) and the wise and their deeds are in the hands of God. No man knows whether it will be love or hatred; anything awaits him.

²It is the same for all. There is one fate for the righteous and for the wicked; for the good, for the clean and for the unclean; for the man who offers sacrifices and for the one who does not sacrifice. As the good man is, so is the sinner; as he who swears *an oath* is, so is he who is afraid to swear *an oath*.

³This evil is in all that is done under the sun, that one fate comes to all. Also, the hearts of the sons of men are full of evil, and madness is in their hearts while they live, and afterwards they go to the dead.

⁴[There is no exemption,] but whoever is joined with all the living, has hope; surely a live dog is better than a dead lion.

⁵For the living know that they will die; but the dead know nothing, and they no longer have a reward [here], for the memory of them is forgotten.

⁶Indeed their love, their hatred and their zeal have already perished, and they will no longer have a share [in this age] in anything that is done under the sun.

⁷Go *your way,* eat your bread with joy and drink your wine with a cheerful heart [if you are righteous, wise, and in the hands of God]; for God has already approved *and* accepted your works.

⁸Let your clothes always be white [with purity], and do not let the oil [of gladness] be lacking on your head.

⁹Live joyfully with the wife whom you love all the days of your fleeting life which He has given you under the sun—all the days of vanity *and* futility. For this is your reward in life and in your work in which you have labored under the sun.

¹⁰Whatever your hand finds to do, do it with all your might; for there is no activity or planning or knowledge or wisdom in Sheol (the nether world, the place of the dead) where you are going.

¹¹I again saw under the sun that the race is not to the swift and the battle is not to the strong, and neither is bread to the wise nor riches to those of intelligence *and* understanding nor favor to men of ability; but time and chance overtake them all. [Ps 33:16–19; Rom 9:16]

¹²For man also does not know his time [of death]; like fish caught in a treacherous net, and birds caught in the snare, so the sons of men are ensnared in an evil time when a dark cloud suddenly falls on them.

¹³This [illustration of] wisdom I have also seen under the sun, and great it was to me:

¹⁴There was a little city with few men in it and a great king came against it and besieged it and built great battlements against it.

¹⁵But there was found in it a poor wise man, and by his wisdom he rescued the city. Yet no man [seriously] remembered that poor man.

¹⁶But I say that wisdom is better than strength, though the poor man's wisdom is despised and his words are not heeded.

¹⁷The words of wise men heard in quietness are *better* than the shouting of one who rules among fools.

speak the Word

Thank You, God, that because of Jesus,
You have already approved and accepted my works.
–ADAPTED FROM ECCLESIASTES 9:7

¹⁸Wisdom is better than weapons of war, but one sinner destroys much good.

10 DEAD FLIES make the oil of the perfumer give off a foul odor; so a little foolishness [in one who is esteemed] outweighs wisdom and honor.

²A wise man's heart *turns him* toward the right [which is the way of blessing], but a fool's heart *turns him* toward the left [which is the way of condemnation]. [Matt 25:31–41]

³Even when a fool walks along the road, his [common] sense *and* good judgment fail him and he demonstrates to everyone that he is a fool.

⁴If the temper of the ruler rises against you, do not leave your post [showing resistance], because composure *and* calmness prevent great offenses.

⁵There is an evil I have seen under the sun, like an error which proceeds from the ruler—

⁶folly is set in many exalted places *and* in great dignity while the rich sit in humble places.

⁷I have seen slaves *riding* on horses and princes walking like slaves on the ground.

⁸He who digs a pit [for others] may fall into it, and a serpent may bite him who breaks through a [stone] wall. [Ps 57:6]

⁹He who quarries stones may be hurt with them, and he who splits logs may be endangered by them. [Prov 26:27]

¹⁰If the axe is dull and he does not sharpen its edge, then he must exert more strength; but wisdom [to sharpen the axe] helps him succeed [with less effort].

¹¹If the serpent bites before being charmed, then there is no profit for the charmer.

¹²The words of a wise man's mouth are gracious *and* win him favor, but the lips of a fool consume him;

¹³the beginning of his talking is foolishness and the end of his talk is wicked madness.

¹⁴Yet the fool multiplies words, though no man knows what will happen, and who can tell him what will come after he is gone?

¹⁵The labor of a fool so wearies him [because he is ignorant] that he does not even know how to go to a city.

¹⁶Woe to you, O land, when your king is a child and when your [incompetent] officials *and* princes feast in the morning.

¹⁷Blessed [prosperous and admired] are you, O land, when your king is a man of noble birth, and your princes *and* officials feast at the proper time— for strength and not for drunkenness. [Is 32:8]

¹⁸Through laziness the rafters [of state affairs] decay *and* the roof sags, and through idleness [the roof of] the house leaks.

¹⁹*The officials* make a feast for enjoyment [instead of repairing what is broken], and serve wine to make life merry, and money is the answer to everything.

²⁰Moreover, do not curse the king, even in your bedroom, and in your sleeping rooms do not curse the rich, for a bird of the air will carry the sound and a winged creature will make the matter known. [Ex 22:28]

11 CAST YOUR bread on the surface of the waters, [be diligently active, make thoughtful decisions], for you will find it after many days.

²Give a portion to seven, or even [divide it] to eight, for you do not know what misfortune may occur on the earth.

³If the clouds are full [of rain], they empty themselves on the earth; and if a tree falls toward the south or toward the north, in the place where the tree falls, there it lies.

⁴He who watches the wind [waiting for all conditions to be perfect] will not sow [seed], and he who looks at the clouds will not reap [a harvest].

⁵Just as you do not know the way *and* path of the wind or how the bones *are formed* in the womb of a pregnant woman, even so you do not know the activity of God who makes all things.

⁶Sow your seed in the morning and do not be idle with your hands in the evening, for you do not know whether morning or evening planting will succeed, whether this or that, or whether both alike will be good.

⁷The light is sweet *and* pleasant, and it is good for the eyes to see the sun.

⁸Yes, if a man should live many years, let him rejoice in them all; yet let him remember the days of darkness, for they will be many. All that is to come will be futility.

⁹Rejoice, young man, in your childhood, and let your heart be pleasant in the days of your young manhood. And walk in the ways of your heart and in the desires of your eyes, but know that God will bring you into judgment for all these things.

¹⁰Therefore, remove sorrow and anger from your heart and put away pain from your body, for childhood and the prime of life are fleeting. [2 Cor 7:1; 2 Tim 2:22]

the pitfall of procrastination

In 1993, when God showed my husband, Dave, and me that He wanted our ministry to begin television broadcasts, He said, "I am giving you an opportunity to go on television; but if you procrastinate and do not take the opportunity now, it will never pass by you again." Perhaps, had God not shown us this opportunity was open only for that particular moment, we might have put off pursuing it. After all, we were finally in a position where we could be comfortable and perhaps not have to work as hard as we had in the past.

For nine years, we had been in the process of "birthing" Joyce Meyer Ministries. Now, suddenly, God was giving us an opportunity to reach more people, which is something we wanted with all our hearts. However, in order to do it, we would need to take on new responsibility.

When the Lord asks any of us to do something, we can be tempted to wait for a convenient season, a time when all conditions are perfect, as we read about in Ecclesiastes 11:4. There is always the tendency to hold back until it will not cost anything or be so difficult.

I encourage you to be a person who is not afraid of responsibility and who does not procrastinate when God speaks. If you do only what is easy, you will always remain weak, but as you meet resistance and overcome, you will build your strength.

God expects you and me to be responsible and take care of what He gives us; He wants us to do something with His gifts that will produce good fruit. If we do not use the gifts and talents He has given us when He directs us to do so, then we are not being responsible over what He has entrusted to us.

If you are a procrastinator, I urge you to heed the instruction of Ecclesiastes 11:4. You do not have to wait until everything is perfect to obey God. Do what He says to do, when He says to do it, and you will reap the blessings of obedience.

12 REMEMBER [thought-fully] also your Creator in the days of your youth [for you are not your own, but His], before the evil days come or the years draw near when you will say [of physical pleasures], "I have no enjoyment *and* delight in them"; [2 Sam 19:35]

²before the sun and the light, and the moon and the stars are darkened [by impaired vision], and the clouds [of depression] return after the rain [of tears];

³in the day when the keepers of the house (hands, arms) tremble, and the strong men (feet, knees) bow themselves, and the grinders (molar teeth) cease because they are few, and those (eyes) who look through the windows grow dim;

⁴when the doors (lips) are shut in the streets and the sound of the grinding [of the teeth] is low, and one rises at the sound of a bird *and* the crowing of a rooster, and all the daughters of music (voice, ears) sing softly.

⁵Furthermore, they are afraid of a high place and of dangers on the road; the almond tree (hair) blossoms [white], and the grasshopper (a little thing) is a burden, and the caperberry (desire, appetite) fails. For man goes to his eternal home and the mourners go about the streets *and* market places. [Job 17:13]

⁶*Earnestly remember your Creator* before the silver cord [of life] is broken, or the golden bowl is crushed, or the pitcher at the fountain is shattered and the wheel at the cistern is crushed;

⁷then the dust [out of which God made man's body] will return to the earth as it was, and the spirit will return to God who gave it.

⁸"Vanity of vanities," says the Preacher. "All [that is done without God's guidance] is vanity (futility)." [Eccl 1:2; Rom 8:20]

life point

After a lifetime of trying everything the world had to offer, Solomon finally concluded that the only thing that made any sense at all was God (see Ecclesiastes 12:13). He realized that no one can find any lasting enjoyment apart from Him. Solomon said what he had learned from all his searching was that the best way to spend our lives is to fear God and obey Him. This is our highest purpose and our most noble duty, so I encourage you to make it a priority in your life.

⁹Furthermore, because the Preacher was wise, he still taught the people knowledge; and he pondered and searched out and arranged many proverbs.

¹⁰The Preacher sought to find delightful words, even to write correctly words of truth.

¹¹The words of the wise are like [prodding] goads, and *these* collected sayings are [firmly fixed in the mind] like well-driven nails; they are given by one Shepherd. [Ezek 37:24]

¹²But beyond this my son, [about going further than the words given by one Shepherd], be warned: the writing of many books is endless [so do not believe everything you read], and excessive study *and* devotion *to books* is wearying to the body.

¹³When all has been heard, the end of the matter is: fear God [worship Him with awe-filled reverence, knowing that He is almighty God] and keep His commandments, for this applies to every person.

¹⁴For God will bring every act to judgment, every hidden *and* secret thing, whether it is good or evil. [Matt 12:36; Acts 17:30, 31; Rom 2:16; 1 Cor 4:5]

Song of Solomon

Author:
Attributed to Solomon

Date:
Probably between 970 BC and 930 BC

Everyday Life Principles:
The lessons we learn about love in the Song of Solomon can be applied both spiritually and naturally.

We need to abandon ourselves to those we love in committed, intimate relationships. This is true for believers in relationship with God and for husbands and wives within the marriage covenant.

True love is worth pursuing, and it should be expressed with passion.

Some people believe the Song of Solomon applies only to a physical love relationship between husband and wife; others believe it is entirely symbolic of God's love for His people. I believe its principles and lessons can be applied both naturally and spiritually. It does provide insight and guidance for marriage and for the sexual relationship within marriage, but it also reveals the passion with which God loves us.

This book is a beautiful story about pursuing love, expressing love, and enjoying love. It teaches us to abandon ourselves to the Lover of our souls (God) and to the husbands or wives to whom we are joined in the marriage covenant. It encourages us to love God and our spouses wholeheartedly and passionately, holding nothing back, and it reminds us that God is chasing us, wooing us, pursuing us with the same type of tenderness and zeal as a young man employs when trying to win the heart of the woman he loves.

As you read through the Song of Solomon, I encourage you to learn from it on two levels. First, let it stir your passion for God and inspire your gratitude for His relentless pursuit of you. Second, if you are married or you hope to marry some day, let this book teach you lessons of intimacy that will serve your marriage well. Above all, intensely enjoy and celebrate the beauty and the richness of your love relationship with God and with your mate.

1
THE SONG of Songs [the best of songs], which is Solomon's. [1 Kin 4:32]

(The Shulammite Bride)

2 "May he kiss me with the kisses of his mouth!" [Solomon arrives, she turns to him, saying,]
"For your love is better than wine.
3 "The aroma of your oils is fragrant *and* pleasing;
Your name is perfume poured out;
Therefore the maidens love you.
4 "Draw me away with you *and* let us run *together!*
Let the king bring me into his chambers."

(The Chorus)

"**W**e will rejoice and be glad in you;
We will remember *and* extol your love more [sweet and fragrant] than wine.
Rightly do they love you."

(The Shulammite Bride)

5 "I am deeply tanned but lovely,
O daughters of Jerusalem,
[I am dark] like the tents of [the Bedouins of] Kedar,
Like the [beautiful] curtains of Solomon.
6 "Do not gaze at me because I am deeply tanned,
[I have worked in] the sun; it has left its mark on me.
My mother's sons were angry with me;
They made me keeper of the vineyards,
But my own vineyard (my complexion) I have not kept."
7 "Tell me, O you whom my soul loves,

life point

The maiden portrayed in the Song of Solomon says, "Draw me away with you and let us run together! Let the king bring me into his chambers" (Song of Solomon 1:4). If we look at this as an allegory of our relationship with God, we see that in attempting to have a close intimate relationship with Him, we must first ask Him to draw us by His Holy Spirit. When He knows we want to come to Him and grow in our relationship with Him, He will draw us and we can respond.

Where do you pasture *your flock,*
Where do you make it lie down at noon?
For why should I be like one who is veiled
Beside the flocks of your companions?" [Ps 23:1, 2]

(The Bridegroom)

8 "If you do not know [where your lover is],
O you fairest among women,
Run along, follow the tracks of the flock,
And pasture your young goats
By the tents of the shepherds.

9 "To me, my love, you are like
My [favorite] mare among the chariots of Pharaoh.
10 "Your cheeks are lovely with ornaments,
Your neck with strings of jewels."

(The Chorus)

11 "We will make for you chains *and* ornaments of gold,
[Studded] with beads of silver."

speak the Word

Draw me away with You, Lord, and let us run the race of life together.
—ADAPTED FROM SONG OF SOLOMON 1:4

(The Shulammite Bride)

12 "While the king was at his table,
My perfume (Solomon) sent forth
[his] fragrance [surrounding me].
13 "My beloved is to me like a pouch
of myrrh
Which lies all night between my
breasts.
14 "My beloved is to me a cluster of
henna flowers
In the [fragrant] vineyards of
Engedi."

(The Bridegroom)

15 "Behold, how beautiful you are, my
darling,
Behold, how beautiful you are!
Your eyes are dove's eyes."

(The Shulammite Bride)

16 "Behold, how fair and handsome
you are, my beloved;
And so delightful!
Our arbor is green and luxuriant.
17 "The beams of our houses are
cedars,
Our rafters and panels are
cypresses.

2 "I AM the rose [of the plain] of
Sharon,
The lily of the valleys [that
grows in deep places]."

(The Bridegroom)

2 "Like the lily among the thorns,
So are you, my darling, among the
maidens."

(The Shulammite Bride)

3 "Like an apple tree [rare and
welcome] among the trees of the
forest,
So is my beloved among the young
men!
In his shade I took great delight
and sat down,

And his fruit was sweet and
delicious to my palate.
4 "He has brought me to his
banqueting place,
And his banner over me is love
[waving overhead to protect and
comfort me].
5 "Sustain me with raisin cakes,
Refresh me with apples,
Because I am sick with love.
6 "Let his left hand be under my
head
And his right hand embrace me."
[Deut 33:27; Matt 28:20]

(The Bridegroom)

7 "I command that you take an oath,
O daughters of Jerusalem,
By the gazelles or by the does of
the field [which run free],
That you do not rouse nor awaken
my love
Until she pleases."

life point

Tucked away in the midst of the romance
of the Song of Solomon is an extremely
valuable piece of wisdom for everyday
life: It is "the little foxes" that spoil and
ruin a vineyard (Song of Solomon 2:15).
What this means is that people's lives are
typically not destroyed by what we would
consider "big" issues, but by a series of
smaller, seemingly insignificant choices or
compromises.

Watch the "little foxes" in your life; forgive even the most minor offense so that
your heart stays clean, do not cut corners
in your finances or on the job when you
think no one will notice, do not expose
yourself to ungodly influences, thinking,
It won't hurt me if I do it just this once.
Little things add up to big things, and
before you know it, "little foxes" can ruin
a strong, healthy vine.

(The Shulammite Bride)

8 "Listen! My beloved!
Behold, he comes,
Climbing on the mountains,
Leaping *and* running on the hills!
    [John 10:27]
9 "My beloved is like a gazelle or a
    young stag.
Behold, he is standing behind our
    wall,
He is looking through the windows,
He is gazing through the lattice.

10 "My beloved speaks and says to me,
'Arise, my love, my fair one,
And come away.
11 'For behold, the winter is past,
The rain is over and gone.
12 'The flowers appear on the earth
    once again;
The time for singing has come,
And the voice of the turtledove is
    heard in our land.

13 'The fig tree has budded *and*
    ripens her figs,
And the vines are in blossom and
    give forth their fragrance.
Arise, my love, my fair one,
And come away [to climb the rocky
    steps of the hillside].' "

(The Bridegroom)

14 "O my dove, [here] in the clefts in
    the rock,
In the sheltered *and* secret place of
    the steep pathway,
Let me see your face,
Let me hear your voice;
For your voice is sweet,
And your face is lovely."

(The Chorus)

15 "Catch the foxes for us,
The little foxes that spoil *and* ruin
    the vineyards [of love],
While our vineyards are in
    blossom."

fulfillment in marriage

Solomon uses rich and unusual imagery to portray the love between a man and a woman in marriage. In Song of Solomon 2:16 and in other passages throughout this book, the married couple share a oneness that can be found in no other relationship.

The Bible says that when a man and a woman are married, "they shall become one flesh" (Genesis 2:24). Notice the word *become*. When you and your spouse are married, you are "one" before God as well as legally, but in your relationship you are still in the process of *becoming* one. While you work this process out between you, you should hold your marriage in honor, and esteem your partner as worthy and precious.

Many couples get stumped when trying to work on their marriage because men and women are so different. It helps to understand that God made us different on purpose. An important step of maturity in life and in relationships is to learn not to confuse weaknesses with differences. We are to help build up each other's frailties, but we are not called to change one another's differences. It certainly is not God's plan for us to try to make our partners be like us. But we are in each other's lives to help build each other up to become all that God has in mind for us to be.

I exhort you to treat your spouse as if you were still courting each other because, in effect, you *are* still courting. If you do not work at your marriage, you will not have a good one. Make a fresh commitment today to be diligent in your relationship with your spouse and to keep becoming "one." It will take effort, but the rewards are sweet!

(The Shulammite Bride)

16 "My beloved is mine and I am his;
   He pastures *his flock* among the
      lilies. [Matt 10:32; Acts 4:12]
17 "Until the cool of the day when the
      shadows flee away,
   Return quickly, my beloved, and
      be like a gazelle
   Or a young stag on the mountains
      of Bether [which separate us]."

(The Shulammite Bride)

3 "ON MY bed night after night [I
   dreamed that] I sought the one
   Whom my soul loves;
I sought him but did not find him.
   [Is 26:9]

2 "*I said* 'So I must arise now and go
      out into the city;
   Into the streets and into the
      squares [places I do not know]
   I must seek him whom my soul
      loves.'
   I sought him but I did not find him.
3 "The watchmen who go around the
      city found me,
   And I said, 'Have you seen him
      whom my soul loves?'
4 "Scarcely had I passed them
   When I found him whom my soul
      loves.
   I held on to him and would not let
      him go

first a wedding, then a marriage

Song of Solomon 3:11 mentions Solomon's wedding day and refers to it as "the day of his gladness of heart."

Wedding days are happy indeed, but after every wedding comes a marriage. The Bible says that marriage is a union—such an intimate joining together of two separate entities that they become one. We tend to be somewhat casual in our use of the word *union* today. We know that the Father, Son, and Holy Spirit are in a union known as "the Godhead"; we know that there is supposed to be a union among all believers; and we know that when a man and a woman marry, a union is supposed to take place. But what does this marriage union really mean?

Let me suggest a word picture that may help you understand. Picture an empty glass. Beside that empty glass is a cup of strong coffee and a glass of water. Of course, the coffee is dark and black, while the water is clear. Many times, when two people marry, they are as different as the coffee and the water. Occasionally a husband and a wife are very similar, but typically they are quite different when they first join together.

Now, envision pouring both the coffee and the water into the empty glass. This is a great image of what happens in a marriage. Once you have done that, could you ever possibly separate those two liquids again?

Once the coffee and the water have been poured into the previously empty glass, you cannot even call the substance all-coffee or all-water; it is a mixture of both. It looks and tastes different from 100 percent coffee or 100 percent water—and you would have no idea how to separate one from the other.

When a man and a woman marry, God intends for their lives to blend together in an inseparable way. They become one new person joined together in Christ Jesus. That is the way God planned for our marriages to be. Do everything you can to cultivate a true union in your marriage, and you will enjoy not only your wedding day, but a wonderful life as one with your husband or wife.

Until I had brought him to my
mother's house,
And into the chamber of her who
conceived me." [Rom 8:35;
1 Pet 2:25]

(The Bridegroom)

5 "I command that you take an oath,
O daughters of Jerusalem,
By the gazelles or by the does of
the field,
That you do not rouse nor awaken
my love
Until she pleases."

(The Shulammite Bride)

6 "What is this coming up from the
wilderness
Like [stately] pillars of smoke
Perfumed with myrrh and
frankincense,
With all the fragrant powders of
the merchant?"

(The Chorus)

7 "Behold, it is the couch
(palanquin) of Solomon;
Sixty mighty men around it,
Of the mighty men of Israel.
8 "All of them handle the sword,
All expert in war;
Each man has his sword at his
thigh,
Guarding against the terrors of the
night.
9 "King Solomon has made for
himself a palanquin
From the [cedar] wood of Lebanon.
10 "He made its posts of silver,
Its back of gold,

life point

Just as the woman in Song of Solomon
3:4 who found her beloved and "would
not let him go," we need to do everything
possible to honor the legally and spiritually binding covenant of marriage.

Its seat of purple cloth,
The interior lovingly *and*
intricately wrought
By the daughters of Jerusalem.
11 "Go forth, O daughters of Zion,
And gaze on King Solomon
wearing the crown
With which his mother
[Bathsheba] has crowned him
On the day of his wedding,
On the day of his gladness of heart."

(The Bridegroom)

4 "HOW FAIR *and* beautiful you
are, my darling,
How very beautiful!
Your eyes behind your veil are like
those of a dove;
Your hair is like [the shimmering
black fleece of] a flock of
[Arabian] goats
That have descended from Mount
Gilead [beyond the Jordan].
2 "Your teeth are like a flock of
newly shorn ewes
Which have come up from
washing,
All of which bear twins,
And not one among them has lost
her young.
3 "Your lips are like a ribbon of
scarlet,
And your mouth is lovely.
Your temples are like a slice of the
pomegranate
Behind your veil.
4 "Your neck is like the tower of
David,
Built with rows of [glistening]
stones,
Whereon hang a thousand shields,
All of them shields of warriors.
5 "Your two breasts are like two
fawns,
Twins of a gazelle
Which feed among the lilies.
6 "Until the day breaks
And the shadows flee away,

[In my thoughts] I will go my way
  to the mountain of myrrh
And to the hill of frankincense.

7 "O my love, you are altogether
  beautiful *and* fair.
There is no flaw *nor* blemish in
  you! [John 14:18; Eph 5:27]
8 "*Come away* with me from
  Lebanon, my [promised] bride,
May you come with me from
  Lebanon.
Journey down from the top of
  Amana,
From the summit of Senir and
  Hermon,
From the dens of lions,
From the mountains of leopards.
  [2 Cor 11:2, 3]
9 "You have ravished my heart *and*
  given me courage, my sister, my
  [promised] bride;
You have ravished my heart *and*
  given me courage with a single
  glance of your eyes,
With one jewel of your necklace.
10 "How beautiful is your love, my
  sister, my [promised] bride!
How much better is your love than
  wine,
And the fragrance of your oils
Than all *kinds* of balsam *and*
  spices. [John 15:9; Rom 8:35]
11 "Your lips, my [promised] bride,
  drip honey [as the honeycomb];
Honey and milk are under your
  tongue,

putting the Word to work

The man in Song of Solomon 4:7 is
so in love with his bride that he sees
"no flaw" in her. We know that no
one is perfect, but love does enable
us to overlook people's faults. Is there
anyone for whom you need to "cut
some slack" in your life right now?
Remember to always look for the best
in people.

life point

Marriage is more than a sexual union, and
it is more than a legal institution that binds
the property accumulated by two people
to an equal right of ownership. Marriage is
a promise of companionship and provision
for the need between two people.

And the fragrance of your
  garments is like the fragrance of
  Lebanon.
12 "A garden enclosed is my sister, my
  [promised] bride—
A rock garden locked, a spring
  sealed up.
13 "Your shoots are an orchard of
  pomegranates,
[A paradise] with precious fruits,
  henna with fragrant plants,
  [John 15:5; Eph 5:9]
14 Fragrant plants and saffron,
  calamus and cinnamon,
With all trees of frankincense,
Myrrh and aloes, along with all the
  finest spices.
15 "*You are* a fountain in a garden,
A well of fresh *and* living water,
And streams *flowing* from
  Lebanon." [John 4:10; 7:37, 38]

(The Shulammite Bride)

16 "Awake, O north *wind,*
And come, south *wind* [blow softly
  upon my garden];

life point

Regarding the sexual relationship in
marriage, unless it is perverted outside
marriage, sexuality is to be holy, fun, and
wholesome. It is a stress reliever that
brings two people into a closeness that
cannot be found in any other way except
through a right relationship in a marriage
union. Being single-hearted toward a
person's spouse brings great fulfillment
for both partners in marriage.

Make my garden breathe out
    fragrance, [for the one in whom
    my soul delights],
Let its spices flow forth.
Let my beloved come into his garden
And eat its choicest fruits."

(The Bridegroom)

5 "I HAVE come into my garden,
    my sister, my [promised] bride;
    I have gathered my myrrh
    along with my balsam *and* spice
    [from your sweet words].
I have eaten my honeycomb with
    my honey;
I have drunk my wine with my milk.
Eat, friends;
Drink and drink deeply, O lovers."
    [John 16:33]

(The Shulammite Bride)

2 "I was asleep, but my heart was
    awake.
A voice [in my dream]! My beloved
    was knocking:
'Open to me, my sister, my darling,
My dove, my perfect one!
For my head is drenched with the
    [heavy night] dew;
My hair [is covered] with the
    dampness of the night.' [Job
    11:13–15]
3 "I had taken off my dress,
How can I put it on *again?*
I had washed my feet,
How could I get them dirty *again?*
    [Is 32:9; Heb 3:15]
4 "My beloved extended his hand
    through the opening [of the door],
And my feelings were aroused for
    him.
5 "I arose to open for my beloved;
And my hands dripped with myrrh,
And my fingers with liquid [sweet-
    scented] myrrh,
On the handles of the bolt.
6 "I opened for my beloved,
But my beloved had turned away
    and was gone.

My heart went out *to him* when he
    spoke.
I searched for him, but I could not
    find him;
I called him, but he did not
    answer me.
7 "The watchmen who make the
    rounds in the city found me.
They struck me, they wounded me;
The guardsmen of the walls took
    my shawl from me.
8 "I command that you take an oath,
    O daughters of Jerusalem,
If you find my beloved,
As to what you tell him—
[Say that] I am sick from love [sick
    from being without him]." [Ps 63:1]

(The Chorus)

9 "What is your beloved more than
    another beloved,
O most beautiful among women?
What is your beloved more than
    another beloved,
That you should so command us to
    take an oath?" [John 10:26]

(The Shulammite Bride)

10 "My beloved is exquisitely
    handsome and ruddy,
    Outstanding among ten thousand.
    [Ps 45:2; John 1:14]
11 "His head is *like* [precious] gold,
    pure gold;
His hair is [curly] *like* clusters of
    dates
And black as a raven.
12 "His eyes are like doves
Beside streams of water,
Bathed in milk
And reposed in their setting.
13 "His cheeks are like a bed of balsam,
Banks of sweet, fragrant herbs.
His lips are lilies
Dripping *sweet-scented* myrrh.
14 "His hands are rods of gold
Set with beryl;
His abdomen is a figure of carved
    ivory

Inlaid with sapphires.
15 "His legs are [strong and steady]
    pillars of alabaster
Set upon pedestals of fine gold.
His appearance is like Lebanon,
Stately *and* choice as the cedars.
16 "His mouth is *full of* sweetness;
Yes, he is altogether lovely *and*
    desirable.
This is my beloved and this is my
    friend,
O daughters of Jerusalem." [Ps 92:15;
    Col 1:15]

(The Chorus)

6 "WHERE HAS your beloved
    gone,
O most beautiful among
women?
Where is your beloved hiding
    himself,
That we may seek him with you?"

(The Shulammite Bride)

2 "My beloved has gone down to his
    garden,
To the beds of balsam,
To feed *his flock* in the gardens
And gather lilies.
3 "I am my beloved's and my beloved
    is mine,
He who feeds *his flock* among the
    lilies."

(The Bridegroom)

4 "You are as beautiful as Tirzah, my
    darling,
As lovely as Jerusalem,
As majestic as an army with
    banners!
5 "Turn your [flashing] eyes away
    from me,
For they have confused *and*
    overcome me;

Your hair is like [the shimmering
    black fleece of] a flock of
    [Arabian] goats
That have descended from Mount
    Gilead.
6 "Your teeth are like a flock of ewes
Which have come up from their
    washing,
All of which bear twins,
And not one among them has lost
    her young.
7 "Your temples are like a slice of the
    pomegranate
Behind your veil.
8 "There are sixty queens and eighty
    concubines,
And maidens without number;
9 But my dove, my perfect one,
    stands alone [above them all];
She is her mother's only *daughter*;
She is the pure *child* of the one
    who bore her.
The maidens saw her and called
    her blessed *and* happy,
The queens and the concubines
    also, and they praised her,
    saying, [Col 2:8, 9]

10 'Who is this that looks down like
    the dawn,
Fair *and* beautiful as the full moon,
Clear *and* pure as the sun,
As majestic as an army with
    banners?'
11 "I went down to the orchard of nut
    trees
To see the flowers of the valley,
To see whether the grapevine had
    budded
And the pomegranates were in
    flower.
12 "Before I was aware [of what was
    happening], my desire had
    brought me
Into the area of the princes of my
    people [the king's retinue]."

speak the Word

God, I rejoice that I belong to You. I am Yours and You are mine.
–ADAPTED FROM SONG OF SOLOMON 6:3

(The Chorus)

13 "Return, return, O Shulammite;
Return, return, that we may gaze
at you."

(The Bridegroom)

"Why should you gaze at the
Shulammite,
As at the dance of the two armies?

7 "HOW BEAUTIFUL are your
feet in sandals,
O prince's daughter!
The curves of your hips are like
jewels,
The work of the hands of an artist.
2 "Your navel is a round goblet
Which never lacks mixed wine.
Your belly is like a heap of wheat
Surrounded with lilies.
3 "Your two breasts are like two
fawns,
The twins of a gazelle.
4 "Your neck is like a tower of ivory,
Your eyes the [sparkling] pools of
Heshbon
By the gate of Bath-rabbim.
Your nose is like the tower of
Lebanon
Which looks toward Damascus.
5 "Your head crowns you like Mount
Carmel,
And the flowing hair of your head
like purple threads;
I, the king, am held captive by
your tresses.
6 "How beautiful and how delightful
you are,
My love, with all your delights!
7 "Your stature is like that of a palm
tree
And your breasts like its clusters
[of dates].
8 "I said, 'I will climb the palm tree;
I will grasp its branches.
Let your breasts be like clusters of
the grapevine,
And the fragrance of your breath
like apples,

9 'And your kisses like the best
wine!'"

(The Shulammite Bride)

"It goes down smoothly and
sweetly for my beloved,
Gliding gently over his lips while
he sleeps.

10 "I am my beloved's,
And his desire is for me. [John 10:28]
11 "Come, my beloved, let us go out
into the country,
Let us spend the night in the
villages. [Luke 14:33]
12 "Let us go out early to the vineyards;
Let us see whether the vine has
budded
And its blossoms have opened,
And whether the pomegranates
have flowered.
There I will give you my love.
13 "The mandrakes give forth
fragrance,
And over our doors are all [kinds
of] choice fruits,
Both new and old,
Which I have saved up for you, my
beloved.

8 "OH, THAT you were like a
brother to me,
Who nursed at the breasts of
my mother.
If I found you out of doors, I would
kiss you;
No one would blame me or despise
me, either. [Ps 143:6]
2 "I would lead you and bring you
Into the house of my mother, who
used to instruct me;
I would give you spiced wine
to drink from the juice of my
pomegranates.
3 "Let his left hand be under my head
And his right hand embrace me."
[Ex 19:4; Deut 33:27]

(The Bridegroom)

4 "I command you to take an oath, O
    daughters of Jerusalem,
That you do not rouse nor awaken
    my love
Until she pleases."

(The Chorus)

5 "Who is this coming up from the
    wilderness
Leaning upon her beloved?"

(The Shulammite Bride)

"Under the apple tree I awakened
    you [to my love];
There your mother was in labor
    with you,
There she was in labor and gave
    you birth.

6 "Put me like a seal on your heart,
Like a seal on your arm;
For love is as strong as death,
Jealousy is as severe *and* cruel as
    Sheol (the place of the dead).
Its flashes are flashes of fire,
[A most vehement flame] the very
    flame of the Lord! [Deut 4:24; Is
    49:16; 1 Cor 10:22]

7 "Many waters cannot quench love,
Nor can rivers drown it.
If a man would offer all the riches
    of his house for love,
It would be utterly scorned *and*
    despised."

(The Chorus)

8 "We have a little sister
And she has no breasts.
What shall we do for our sister

On the day when she is spoken for
    [in marriage]?
9 "If she is a wall (discreet, womanly),
We will build on her a turret
    (dowry) of silver;
But if she is a door (bold, flirtatious),
We will enclose her with planks of
    cedar."

(The Shulammite Bride)

10 "I was a wall, and my breasts were
    like the towers.
Then I became in the king's eyes
As one [to be respected and
    allowed] to find peace.
11 "Solomon had a vineyard at Baal-
    hamon;
He entrusted the vineyard to
    caretakers;
Each one was to bring him a
    thousand *shekels* of silver for its
    fruit.
12 "My very own vineyard is at my
    disposal;
The thousand [shekels of silver]
    are for you, O Solomon,
And two hundred are for those
    who tend the fruit."

(The Bridegroom)

13 "O you who sit in the gardens,
My companions are listening for
    your voice—
Let me hear it."

(The Shulammite Bride)

14 "Hurry, my beloved *and* come
    quickly,
Like a gazelle or a young stag
    [taking me home]
On the mountains of spices."

Isaiah

Author:
Isaiah

Date:
Approximately 700 BC–690 BC

Everyday Life Principles:
Sin cannot be tolerated; it must be dealt with. God forgives sin.

God is in the business of redemption and restoration.

God will comfort and guide you.

Isaiah is the first book in a series of books (which make up the remainder of the Old Testament) written by prophets. Prophets are spokespeople for God, and they communicate the things that are on God's heart. They are His mouthpieces, sharing what God wants people to know, informing people of what God intends to do, speaking words of warning and offering encouragement from the Lord. They often prophesy doom and gloom to people who will not obey, and words of comfort, direction, and assurance to those who do obey.

Isaiah's ministry as a prophet included warnings to kings who ignored him, but it also included several prophetic references to Jesus. One such reference is Isaiah 9:6, which declares: "For to us a Child shall be born, to us a Son shall be given; and the government shall be upon His shoulder, and His name shall be called Wonderful Counselor, Mighty God, Everlasting Father, Prince of Peace."

Isaiah's writing is not soft on sin, but it prophetically points to Jesus and gives people clear hope for salvation. This book is loaded with comfort, inspiration, and variety. It speaks of God's love for us, reminds us that He redeems and restores us, encourages us to trust Him, and promises that He will guide us.

Whether you need comfort, strength, hope, peace, or a reminder of God's loving, forgiving heart toward you, you will find it in Isaiah.

1 THE VISION of [the prophet] Isaiah the son of Amoz concerning [the kingdom of] Judah and [its capital] Jerusalem, which he saw [as revealed by God] during the reigns of Uzziah, Jotham, Ahaz, and Hezekiah, kings of Judah.

2 Hear, O heavens, and listen, O earth;
For the Lord has spoken:
"I have reared and brought up sons,
But they have rebelled against Me
and have broken away.
3 "The ox [instinctively] knows its owner,
And the donkey its master's feeding trough,
But Israel does not know [Me as Lord],
My people do not understand."

4 Ah, sinful nation,
A people loaded down with wickedness [with sin, with injustice, with wrongdoing],
Offspring of evildoers,
Sons who behave corruptly!
They have abandoned (rejected) the Lord,
They have despised the Holy One of Israel [provoking Him to anger],
They have turned away from Him.

5 Why should you be stricken *and* punished again [since no change results from it]?
You [only] continue to rebel.
The whole head is sick
And the whole heart is faint *and* sick.
6 From the sole of the foot even to the head
There is nothing healthy in the nation's body,
Only bruises, welts, and raw wounds,
Not pressed out or bandaged,
Nor softened with oil [as a remedy].

7 Your land lies desolate [because of your disobedience],
Your cities are burned with fire,
Your fields—strangers are devouring them in your very presence;
It is desolate, as overthrown by strangers.
8 The Daughter of Zion (Jerusalem) is left like a [deserted] shelter in a vineyard,
Like a watchman's hut in a cucumber field, like a besieged city [isolated, surrounded by devastation].
9 If the Lord of hosts
Had not left us a few survivors,
We would be like Sodom,
We would be like Gomorrah. [Gen 19:24, 25; Rom 9:29]

10 Hear the word of the Lord [rulers of Jerusalem],
You rulers of [another] Sodom,
Listen to the law *and* instruction of our God,
You people of [another] Gomorrah.
11 "What are your multiplied sacrifices to Me [without your repentance]?"
Says the Lord.
"I have had enough of [your] burnt offerings of rams
And the fat of well-fed cattle [without your obedience];
And I take no pleasure in the blood of bulls or lambs or goats [offered without repentance].
12 "When you come to appear before Me,
Who requires this of you, this trampling of My [temple] courts [by your sinful feet]?
13 "Do not bring worthless offerings again,
[Your] incense is repulsive to Me;
[Your] New Moon and Sabbath [observances], the calling of assemblies—

I cannot endure wickedness
[your sin, your injustice, your
wrongdoing] and [the squalor of]
the festive assembly.
14 "I hate [the hypocrisy of] your
New Moon festivals and your
appointed feasts.
They have become a burden to Me;
I am weary of bearing them.
15 "So when you spread out your
hands [in prayer, pleading for
My help],
I will hide My eyes from you;
Yes, even though you offer many
prayers,
I will not be listening.
Your hands are full of blood!

16 "Wash yourselves, make yourselves
clean;
Get your evil deeds out of My sight.
Stop doing evil,
17 Learn to do good.
Seek justice,
Rebuke the ruthless,
Defend the fatherless,
Plead for the [rights of the] widow
[in court].

18 "Come now, and let us reason
together,"
Says the LORD.
"Though your sins are like scarlet,
They shall be as white as snow;
Though they are red like crimson,
They shall be like wool.
19 "If you are willing and obedient,
You shall eat the best of the land;
20 But if you refuse and rebel,
You shall be devoured by the
sword."
For the mouth of the LORD has
spoken.

21 How the faithful city has become a
prostitute [idolatrous, despicable],
She who was full of justice!
Right standing with God once
lodged in her,
But now murderers.

22 Your silver has turned to lead,
Your wine is diluted with water.
23 Your rulers are rebels
And companions of thieves;
Everyone loves bribes
And chases after gifts.
They do not defend the fatherless,
Nor does the widow's cause come
before them [instead they delay
or turn a deaf ear].

24 Therefore the Lord GOD of hosts,
The Mighty One of Israel, declares:
"Ah, I will be freed of My adversaries
And avenge Myself on My enemies.
25 "And I will turn My hand against
you,
And will [thoroughly] purge away
your dross as with lye
And remove all your tin (impurity).
26 "Then I will restore your judges as
at the first,
And your counselors as at the
beginning;
Afterward you will be called the
city of righteousness,
The faithful city."

27 Zion will be redeemed with justice
And her repentant ones with
righteousness.
28 But rebels and sinners will be
crushed and destroyed together,
And those who abandon (turn
away from) the LORD will be
consumed (perish).
29 For you will be ashamed [of the
degradation] of the oaks in which
you took [idolatrous] pleasure,
And you will be ashamed of the
gardens [of passion] which you
have chosen [for pagan worship].
30 For you will be like an oak whose
leaf withers and dies
And like a garden that has no water.
31 The strong man will become tinder,
And his work a spark.
So both will burn together
And there will be none to quench
them.

2 THE WORD [from God] which Isaiah son of Amoz saw [in a vision] concerning [the nation of] Judah and [its capital city] Jerusalem.

2 Now it will come to pass that
In the last days
The mountain of the house of the LORD
Will be [firmly] established as the highest of the mountains,
And will be exalted above the hills;
And all the nations will stream to it.
3 And many peoples shall come and say,
"Come, let us go up to the mountain of the LORD,
To the house (temple) of the God of Jacob;
That He may teach us His ways
And that we may walk in His paths."
For the law will go out from Zion
And the word of the LORD from Jerusalem.
4 And He will judge between the nations,
And will mediate [disputes] for many peoples;
And they will beat their swords into plowshares and their spears into pruning hooks.
Nation will not lift up the sword against nation,
And never again will they learn war. [Mic 4:1–3]
5 O house of Jacob, come, let us walk in the light of the LORD.
6 Most certainly [LORD] You have abandoned your people, the house of Jacob,
Because they are filled with influences from the east,

And they are soothsayers [who foretell] like the Philistines;
Also they strike bargains with the children of foreigners (pagans). [Deut 18:9–12]
7 Their land has also been filled with silver and gold
And there is no end to their treasures;
Their land has also been filled with horses
And there is no end to their chariots. [Deut 17:14–17]
8 Their land has also been filled with idols;
They worship the work of their hands,
That which their own fingers have made.
9 So the common man has been humbled [before idols]
And the man of importance has been degraded,
Therefore do not forgive them [O LORD].
10 Go among the rocks and hide in the dust
From the terror of the LORD and from the splendor of His majesty.
11 The proud look of man will be degraded
And the arrogance of men will be humbled,
And the LORD alone will be exalted in that day.

12 For the LORD of hosts will have a day of reckoning
Against all who are proud and arrogant
And against all who are lifted up,
That they may be degraded. [Zeph 2:3; Mal 4:1]

speak the Word

God, I come to You. Teach me Your ways and help me to walk in Your paths.
−ADAPTED FROM ISAIAH 2:3

when God removes your props

To summarize God's message in Isaiah 2:22, we could say He is basically asking, "Why are you putting your trust in frail people who are only alive for a short time?" Then in the next verse, Isaiah 3:1, God says He is removing from His people their props—the external things on which they depend. The reason? He wants His people to trust Him.

What happens to us when our props are pulled out from under us? We discover what we are leaning on, what we are really rooted and grounded in. Let me give you an example.

My husband and I play golf frequently. On the golf course are little twigs that will someday grow into trees. Those little plants have no strength or roots, and they are so tiny and weak that there are usually sticks set on either side of them as props to hold them up. Without those sticks to hold them up, they would be destroyed when the wind and rain come.

That is the way we are as new believers. When we begin our walk with God we need a prop system, something to help us stand up straight and strong. We need a group of people around us to keep us studying the Bible, praying, and seeking the Lord. If we do not have that support system, then when the storms of life come against us, they will blow us over.

Our support system may take many forms, but whatever it is, sooner or later God is going to start taking it away by removing the props from under us. At first, this is pretty scary because we do not understand it, and we do not like it. Our props may be things from which we derive pleasure and satisfaction—things like singing, playing an instrument, being part of the worship team, or being a recognized leader or pastor in the ministry. Then suddenly, for whatever reason, we lose that position or God requires us to give it up. It is then that we discover how much of our sense of value and worth depends on the things we are doing.

In order for us to grow, God sometimes has to strip away everything we put our security in—everything but Him. This is because He is a God of restoration. He restores our minds, our emotions, our souls, and our health. When we start to restore a beautiful, expensive piece of antique furniture, we have to first strip away the old paint or varnish before we apply a new finish. We have to sand it so the new application will stick. If you are going through that stripping process, do not be upset. Cooperate with God while He does the work.

Do not be like a twig thrashing about in the wind because its props have been taken away. Instead, put down some roots so you can one day stand tall and steady and be a tree of righteousness. And remember that whatever God takes away from you or requires you to give up, He will give you more than you previously had, and everything will be better than before.

¹³ And the wrath of God will be
against all the cedars of Lebanon
[west of the Jordan] that are high
and lifted up,
Against all the oaks of Bashan
[east of the Jordan],
¹⁴ Against all the high mountains,
Against all the hills that are lifted
up,
¹⁵ Against every high tower,
Against every fortified wall,
¹⁶ Against all the ships of Tarshish
And against all the beautiful craft.
¹⁷ Then the pride of man will be
humbled
And the arrogance of men will be
degraded;
The LORD alone shall be exalted in
that day,
¹⁸ And the idols will completely
vanish (be abolished).
¹⁹ They [the stricken, deprived of all
in which they had trusted] will
go into the caves of the rocks
And into the holes of the ground
[fleeing]
From the terror *and* dread of the
LORD
And from the splendor of His
majesty,
When He arises to terrify the
earth. [Luke 23:30]
²⁰ In that day men will throw away to
the moles and to the bats
Their idols of silver and their idols
of gold,
Which they made for themselves
[as objects] to worship,
²¹ To go into the caverns of the rocks
and into the clefts of the [ragged]
cliffs [as they flee]
From the terror *and* dread of the
LORD and the splendor of His
majesty,
When He arises to terrify the earth.
²² Stop regarding man, whose breath
[of life] is in his nostrils [for so
little time];
For why should he be esteemed?

3 LISTEN CAREFULLY, the
Lord GOD of hosts is removing
from Jerusalem and from Judah
Both supply and support, the
whole supply of bread
And the whole supply of water;
² The brave man and the warrior
[He is also removing],
The judge and the prophet,
The diviner and the elder,
³ The captain of fifty and the man of
honor,
The counselor and the expert
artisan,
And the skillful enchanter.
⁴ And I will make *mere* boys their
princes,
And capricious (impulsive,
unpredictable) children will rule
over them.
⁵ And the people will be oppressed,
Each one by another, and each one
by his neighbor;
The boy will be arrogant *and*
insolent toward the elder
And the vulgar (common) toward
the honorable [person of rank].
⁶ When a man takes hold of his
brother in the house of his
father, *saying,*
"You have a robe, you shall be our
judge *and* ruler,
And this pile of ruins will be
under your control,"
⁷ He will protest on that day, saying,
"I will not be a governor;
For in my house there is neither
bread nor clothing;
You should not make me a judge
and ruler of the people."
⁸ For Jerusalem has stumbled and
Judah has fallen,
Because their words and their
actions are against the LORD,
To rebel against His glorious
presence *and* defiantly provoke
Him.
⁹ Their partiality testifies against
them,

They display their sin like Sodom;
They do not even hide it.
Woe (judgment is coming) to them!
For they have brought evil on
   themselves [as a reward].
¹⁰Say to the righteous that *it will go*
   well with them,
For they will eat the fruit of their
   [righteous] actions.
¹¹Woe (judgment is coming) to the
   wicked! *It shall go* badly *with him,*
For what his hand has done shall
   be done to him.
¹²O My people! Children are their
   oppressors,
And women rule over them.
O My people! Your leaders lead you
   astray
And confuse (destroy, swallow up)
   the direction of your paths.

¹³The Lord rises to contend,
And stands to judge the people.
¹⁴The Lord enters into judgment
   with the elders of His people and
   their princes,
"For it is you who have devoured
   the vineyard [with your
   oppression, you have robbed the
   people and ruined the country];
The plunder of the poor is in your
   houses.
¹⁵"What do you mean by crushing
   My people
And grinding the face of the poor?"
Declares the Lord God of hosts.

¹⁶Moreover, the Lord said, "Because
   the daughters of Zion are proud
And walk with outstretched
   necks and seductive (flirtatious,
   alluring) eyes,
And trip along with mincing steps
   and an affected gait
And walk with jingling anklets on
   their feet,
¹⁷Therefore the Lord will afflict
   the crown of the head of the
   daughters of Zion with scabs
   [making them bald],

And the Lord will expose their
   foreheads (send them into
   captivity)."
¹⁸In that day the Lord will take away
the beauty of their anklets, [braided]
caps, crescent [head] ornaments,
¹⁹dangling earrings, bracelets, and
the hanging veils *and* scarves,
²⁰head wraps (turbans), [short, jin-
gling] ankle chains, sashes, perfume
boxes, amulets (charms),
²¹signet [finger] rings, nose rings,
²²festival robes, outer tunics, shawls,
handbags,
²³hand mirrors, [fine linen] undergarments, headbands, and veils [cov-
ering the entire body].

²⁴Now it will come to pass that
   instead of the sweet fragrance of
   spices there will be [the stench
   of] rottenness;
Instead of a belt, a rope;
Instead of well-set hair, baldness;
Instead of fine clothes, a robe of
   sackcloth;
And branding [of captives by
   the scorching heat] instead of
   beauty.
²⁵Your men will fall by the sword
And your mighty men in battle.
²⁶And Jerusalem's gates will lament
   (cry out in grief) and mourn [as
   those who wail for the dead];
And she, being ruined *and* desolate,
   will sit upon the ground.

4 AND IN that day seven women
will take hold of one man, saying,
"We will eat our own food and
wear [and provide] our own clothes;
only let us be called by your name; take
away our shame [of being unmarried]."
²In that day the Branch of the Lord
will be splendid and glorious, and the
fruit of the land will be excellent and
lovely to those of Israel who have survived. [Jer 23:5; 33:15; Zech 3:8; 6:12]
³It will come to pass that he who is

left in Zion and remains in Jerusalem will be called holy (set apart for God) — everyone who is recorded for [eternal] life in Jerusalem. [Joel 3:17; Phil 4:3]

⁴When the Lord has washed away the [moral] filth of the daughters of Zion and has cleansed the bloodstains of Jerusalem from her midst, by the spirit of judgment and by the spirit of burning, ⁵then the LORD will create over the entire site of Mount Zion and over her assemblies, a cloud by day, smoke, and the brightness of a flaming fire by night; for over all the glory *and* brilliance will be a canopy [a defense, a covering of His divine love and protection].

⁶And there will be a pavilion for shade from the heat by day, and a refuge and a shelter from the storm and the rain.

5 NOW LET me sing for my greatly Beloved [LORD] A song of my Beloved about His vineyard (His chosen people).
My greatly Beloved had a vineyard on a very fertile slope (the promised land, Canaan). [Song 6:3; Matt 21:33–40]
²He dug it all around and cleared away its stones,
And planted it with the choicest vine (the people of Judah).
And He built a tower in the center of it;
And also hewed out a wine vat in it.
Then He expected it to produce [the choicest] grapes,
But it produced *only* worthless ones.

³"And now, *says the* LORD, O inhabitants of Jerusalem and men of Judah,
Judge between Me and My vineyard (My people).
⁴"What more could have been done for My vineyard that I have not done in it?

When I expected it to produce *good* grapes, why did it yield worthless ones?
⁵"So now let me tell you what I am going to do to My vineyard:
I will take away its thorn-hedge, and it will be burned up;
I will break down its stone wall and it will be trampled down [by enemies].
⁶"I will turn it into a wasteland;
It will not be pruned or cultivated,
But briars and thorns will come up.
I will also command the clouds not to rain on it."

⁷For the vineyard of the LORD of hosts is the house (nation) of Israel
And the men of Judah are His delightful planting [which He loves].
So He looked for justice, but in fact, [He saw] bloodshed *and* lawlessness;
[He looked] for righteousness, but in fact, [He heard] a cry of distress *and* oppression.

⁸Woe (judgment is coming) to those who join house to house and join field to field [to increase their holdings by depriving others],
Until there is no more room [for others],
So that you have to live alone in the midst of the land!
⁹In my ears the LORD of hosts *said,*
"Be assured that many houses will become desolate,
Even great and beautiful ones will be unoccupied.
¹⁰"For ten acres of vineyard will yield [only] one bath *of wine,*
And a homer (six bushels) of seed will produce [only] one ephah of grain."
¹¹Woe (judgment is coming) to those who rise early in the morning to pursue intoxicating drink,

Who stay up late in the night till wine inflames them!

12 They have lyre and harp, tambourine and flute, and wine at their feasts;
But they do not regard *nor* even pay attention to the deeds of the Lord,
Nor do they consider the work of His hands.

13 Therefore My people go into exile because they lack knowledge [of God];
And their honorable men are famished,
And their common people are parched with thirst.

14 Therefore Sheol (the realm of the dead) has increased its appetite and opened its mouth beyond measure;
And Jerusalem's splendor, her multitude, her [boisterous] uproar and her [drunken] revelers descend *into it*.

15 So the *common* man will be bowed down and the man of *importance* degraded,
And the eyes of the proud (arrogant) will be degraded.

16 But the Lord of hosts will be exalted in justice,
And God, the Holy One, will show Himself holy in righteousness [through His righteous judgments].

17 Then the lambs will graze [among the ruins] as in their own pasture,
And strangers will eat in the desolate places of the [exiled] wealthy.

18 Woe (judgment is coming) to those who drag along wickedness with cords of falsehood,
And sin as if with cart ropes [towing their own punishment];

19 Who say, "Let Him move speedily, let Him expedite His work [His promised vengeance], so that we may see it;
And let the purpose of the Holy One of Israel approach
And come to pass, so that we may know it!"

20 Woe (judgment is coming) to those who call evil good, and good evil;
Who substitute darkness for light and light for darkness;
Who substitute bitter for sweet and sweet for bitter!

21 Woe (judgment is coming) to those who are wise in their own eyes
And clever *and* shrewd in their own sight!

22 Woe (judgment is coming) to those who are heroes at drinking wine
And men of strength in mixing intoxicating drinks,

23 Who justify the wicked *and* acquit the guilty for a bribe,
And take away the rights of those who are in the right!

24 Therefore, as the tongue of fire consumes the stubble [from straw]
And the dry grass collapses into the flame,
So their root will become like rot and their blossom blow away like fine dust;
Because they have rejected the law of the Lord of hosts
And despised *and* discarded the word of the Holy One of Israel.

25 Therefore the anger of the Lord has burned against His people,
And He has stretched out His hand against them and has struck them down.
And the mountains trembled, and their dead bodies lay like rubbish in the middle of the streets.
In *spite of* all this God's anger is not turned away,

But His hand is still stretched out [in judgment].

²⁶He will lift up a flag to [call] the distant nations [to bring His judgment on Judah],
And will whistle for them from the ends of the earth;
And indeed, they will come with great speed swiftly.

²⁷No one among them is weary or stumbles,
No one slumbers or sleeps;
Nor is the belt at their waist undone [as if unprepared for action],
Nor is the strap of their sandal broken.

²⁸Their arrows are sharp and all their bows are strung *and* bent;
Their horses' hoofs seem like flint and their *chariot* wheels like a whirlwind.

²⁹Their roaring is like a lioness, they roar like young lions;
They growl and seize their prey
And carry it off and there is no one to save it.

³⁰And in that day they will roar against them (Judah) like the roaring of the sea.
And if one looks to the land, in fact, there is darkness and distress;
Even the light will be darkened by its clouds.

cleansed, then used

Before God can use us, He needs to cleanse us. In Isaiah 6:1–9, Isaiah realized he had a sinful, unclean mouth that needed to be dealt with. I believe that because Isaiah's heart cried out for change, God sent help.

The coming forward of the seraphim with a coal of fire is recorded in verse 6 as an instantaneous happening, but answers may not always come so quickly with us. We all would prefer miraculous deliverance, but most of the time the Lord puts us through a cleansing process.

Notice that God forgave Isaiah's sin and then issued a call: "Who will go for Us?" (Isaiah 6:8). Isaiah responded, "Here am I. Send me!" (Isaiah 6:8). Isaiah's heart wanted to serve the Lord, and God knew that. God will always look for someone who has a perfect *heart* toward Him, not necessarily someone who has a perfect *performance* before Him. When the Lord has the heart, He can always change the behavior.

This truth should encourage those of us who want to be used by God, but who often feel that we just have too many flaws. God uses "cracked pots," as the saying goes. We come to Him as we are, and He molds and makes us into vessels fit for His use (see 2 Timothy 2:21).

After Isaiah's mouth had been cleansed, God called him, saying, "Go, and tell this people . . ." (Isaiah 6:9). The call, the anointing, and the appointment can occur in different time periods, but no matter how they take place or in what order, the process of preparation is as important to us today as it was to Isaiah long ago. One thing is sure: when God calls us into His presence, He is going to deal with us, and we must let Him do that. He is doing a good work!

6 IN THE year that King Uzziah died, I saw [in a vision] the Lord sitting on a throne, high and exalted, with the train of His royal robe filling the [most holy part of the] temple. [John 12:41]

²Above Him seraphim (heavenly beings) stood; each one had six wings: with two *wings* he covered his face, with two *wings* he covered his feet, and with two *wings* he flew.

³And one called out to another, saying,

"Holy, Holy, Holy is the LORD of hosts;
The whole earth is filled with His glory."

⁴And the foundations of the thresholds trembled at the voice of him who called out, and the temple was filling with smoke.

⁵Then I said,

"Woe is me! For I am ruined,
Because I am a man of [ceremonially] unclean lips,
And I live among a people of unclean lips;
For my eyes have seen the King, the LORD of hosts."

⁶Then one of the seraphim flew to me with a burning coal in his hand, which he had taken from the altar with tongs. ⁷He touched my mouth *with it* and said, "Listen carefully, this has touched your lips; your wickedness [your sin, your injustice, your wrongdoing] is taken away and your sin atoned for *and* forgiven."

⁸Then I heard the voice of the Lord, saying, "Whom shall I send, and who will go for Us?" Then I said, "Here am I. Send me!"

⁹And He said, "Go, and tell this people:

'Keep on listening, but do not understand;
Keep on looking, but do not comprehend.'
¹⁰"Make the heart of this people insensitive,
Their ears dull,
And their eyes dim,
Otherwise they might see with their eyes,
Hear with their ears,
Understand with their hearts,
And return and be healed."

¹¹Then I said, "Lord, how long?" And He answered,

"Until cities are devastated and without inhabitant,
And houses are without people
And the land is utterly desolate,
¹²The LORD has removed [His] people far away,
And there are many deserted places in the midst of the land.
¹³"And though a tenth [of the people] remain in the land,
It will again be *subject* to destruction [consumed and burned],
Like a massive terebinth tree or like an oak
Whose stump remains when it is chopped down.
The holy seed [the elect remnant] is its stump [the substance of Israel]."

speak the Word

God, I declare that You are holy. The whole earth is full of Your glory.
—ADAPTED FROM ISAIAH 6:3

Lord, here I am. Send me wherever You want to send me.
—ADAPTED FROM ISAIAH 6:8

7 NOW IT came to pass in the days of Ahaz the son of Jotham, the son of Uzziah, king of Judah, that Rezin king of Aram (Syria) and Pekah the son of Remaliah, king of Israel, went up to Jerusalem to wage war against it, but they could not conquer it. ²When the house of David (Judah) was told, "Aram is allied with Ephraim (Israel)," the hearts of Ahaz and his people trembled as the trees of the forest tremble in the wind.

³Then the LORD said to Isaiah, "Go out to meet Ahaz [king of Judah], you and your son Shear-jashub, at the end of the aqueduct of the Upper Pool, on the highway to the Fuller's Field;

⁴and say to him, 'Take care and be calm, do not fear and be weak-hearted because of these two stumps of smoldering logs, on account of the fierce anger of [King] Rezin and Aram and of the son of Remaliah (Pekah, usurper of the throne of Israel).

⁵'Because Aram, *along with* Ephraim (Israel) and the son of Remaliah, have planned evil against you (Judah), saying,

⁶"Let us go up against Judah and terrorize it; and let us breach its wall *and* tear it apart [each of us taking a portion] and set up the son of Tabeel over it as its [puppet] king,"

⁷for this is what the Lord GOD says, "It shall not stand nor shall it happen.

⁸"For the head (capital) of Aram is Damascus and the head of Damascus is [King] Rezin (now within sixty-five years Ephraim will be broken to pieces and will no longer be a people).

⁹"And the head (capital) of Ephraim is Samaria, and the head of Samaria is Remaliah's son [King Pekah]. If you will not believe [and trust in God and His message], be assured that you will not be established."' "

¹⁰Then the LORD spoke again to [King] Ahaz, saying,

¹¹"Ask a sign for yourself from the LORD your God [one that will convince you that God has spoken and will keep His word]; make your request as deep as Sheol or as high as heaven."

¹²But Ahaz said, "I will not ask, nor will I test the LORD!"

¹³Then Isaiah said, "Hear then, O house of David! Is it too small a thing for you to try the patience of men, but will you try the patience of my God as well?

¹⁴"Therefore the Lord Himself will give you a sign: Listen carefully, the virgin will conceive and give birth to a son, and she will call his name Immanuel (God with us). [Is 9:6; Jer 31:22; Mic 5:3–5; Matt 1:22, 23]

¹⁵"He will eat curds and honey when he knows *enough* to refuse evil and choose good.

¹⁶"For before the child will know *enough* to refuse evil and choose good, the land (Canaan) whose two kings you dread will be deserted [both Ephraim and Aram]. [Is 7:2]

¹⁷"The LORD will bring on you, on your people, and on your father's house such days as have not come since the day that Ephraim (the ten northern tribes) separated from Judah—[He will call for] the king of Assyria."

¹⁸In that day the LORD will whistle for the fly that is in the mouth of the rivers *and* canals of Egypt and for the bee that is in the land of Assyria.

¹⁹These [armies, like flies and bees] will all come and settle on the steep *and* rugged ravines and in the clefts of the rocks, and on all the thorn bushes and in all the watering places.

²⁰In that day [when foreign armies swarm the land] the Lord will shave with a razor, hired from the regions beyond the Euphrates (*that is,* with the king of Assyria), [that razor will shave] the head and the hair of the legs; and it will also remove the beard [leaving Judah stripped, shamed and scorned]. [2 Kin 16:7, 8; 18:13–16]

²¹Now in that day [because of the

poverty caused by the invaders] a man will keep alive only a young milk cow and two sheep;

²²and because of the abundance of milk produced he will eat curds, for everyone that is left in the land will eat [only] curds and [wild] honey.

²³And it will come to pass in that day, in every place where there used to be a thousand vines, *worth* a thousand silver *shekels,* there will be briars and thorns.

²⁴People will come there [to hunt] with arrows and with bows because all the land will be briars and thorns.

²⁵As for all the hills which used to be cultivated with the pick *and* the hoe, you will no longer go there for fear of briars and thorns; but they will become a place where oxen are pastured and where sheep tread.

8 THEN THE LORD said to me, "Take for yourself a large tablet [for public display] and write on it in ordinary characters: *Belonging* to Maher-shalal-hash-baz.

²"And I will get faithful witnesses to attest [to this prophecy] for me, Uriah the priest and Zechariah the son of Jeberechiah."

³So I approached [my wife] the prophetess, and she conceived and gave birth to a son. Then the LORD said to me, "Name him Maher-shalal-hash-baz [to remind the people of the prophecy];

⁴for before the boy knows how to say, 'My father' or 'My mother,' the riches of Damascus (Aram's capital) and the spoil of Samaria (Israel's capital) will be carried away by the king of Assyria."

⁵Again the LORD spoke to me, saying,

⁶"Because these people (Judah)
    have refused the gently flowing
    waters of Shiloah

speak the Word

And rejoice in Rezin [the king
    of Aram] and Remaliah's son
    [Pekah the king of Israel],
⁷Now therefore, listen carefully, the
    Lord is about to bring on them
    the waters of the [Euphrates]
    River, strong and abundant—
The king of Assyria and all his
    glory;
And it will rise over all its
    channels *and* canals and go far
    beyond its banks. [Is 7:17]
⁸"Then it will sweep on into Judah;
    it will overflow and pass through
    [the hills],
Reaching even to the neck [of
    which Jerusalem is the head],
And its outstretched wings (the
    armies of Assyria) will fill the
    width of Your land, O Immanuel.
    [Num 14:9; Ps 46:7]

⁹"Be broken [in pieces], O peoples,
    and be shattered!
Listen, all you [our enemies from
    the] far countries.
Prepare yourselves [for war], and
    be shattered;
Prepare yourselves [for war], and
    be shattered.
¹⁰"Take counsel together [against
    Judah], but it will come to nothing;
Speak the word, but it will not stand,
For God is with us (Immanuel)."

¹¹For in this way the LORD spoke to me with His strong hand [upon me] and instructed me not to walk in the way of this people [behaving as they do], saying,

¹²"You are not to say, 'It is a
    conspiracy!'
In regard to all that this people call
    a conspiracy,

Thank You, God, for being with me!
–ADAPTED FROM ISAIAH 8:10

And you are not to fear what they fear nor be in dread of it.
13 "It is the LORD of hosts whom you are to regard as holy *and* awesome.
He shall be your [source of] fear,
He shall be your [source of] dread [not man].
14 "Then He shall be a sanctuary [a sacred, indestructible shelter for those who fear and trust Him];
But to both the houses of Israel [both the northern and southern kingdoms—Israel and Judah, He will be] a stone on which to stumble and a rock on which to trip,

A trap and a snare for the inhabitants of Jerusalem. [Is 28:6; Rom 9:33; 1 Pet 2:6–8]
15 "Many [among them] will stumble over them;
Then they will fall and be broken,
They will even be snared and trapped."

16 Bind up the testimony, seal the law *and* the teaching among my (Isaiah's) disciples.
17 And I will wait for the LORD who is hiding His face from the house of Jacob; and I will look eagerly for Him.
18 Listen carefully, I and the children whom the LORD has given me are for

God's government

Isaiah 9:6, 7 reveals so much about the character and nature of Jesus because it lists some of the names by which we know Him. Verse 7 also declares, "There shall be no end to the increase of His government and of peace."

The government that is upon Jesus' shoulders is not a political government; no, this verse refers to the governing of our lives. We are not supposed to be running our own lives. In fact, we are not even capable or qualified to do so. None of us is intelligent enough to know what is best, and that is why we need to be so thankful for God's intervention and His willingness to run our lives for us.

The more God's government increases in my life (the more He directs my thoughts, conversations, decisions, and actions), the more my peace will increase. Peace does not come from success, professional position or promotions, social status, educational achievements, money, or an engaging personality. No, we find peace as we live according to the kingdom of God, which is defined as righteousness, peace, and the joy of the Holy Spirit (see Romans 14:17). Being right with God, knowing we are right with God, and doing right things out of knowing who we are in Christ is a process, but it leads us to peace, and peace leads us to joy.

If we do not have righteousness, peace, and joy, then we are not enjoying the kingdom of God as we should. Occasionally, we may need to take a break from all our other pursuits and simply seek God's kingdom. Matthew 6:33 exhorts us to "*First and most importantly* seek (aim at, strive after) His kingdom and His righteousness [His way of doing and being right—the attitude and character of God], and all these things will be given to you also" (italics mine).

Many times, we work, struggle, and strive for "all these things," such as food, clothing, a relationship we desire, pleasure, and position in society when we should be diligently seeking God's kingdom, loving Jesus, and making sure His government is established in our lives.

signs and wonders [that will occur] in Israel from the LORD of hosts, who dwells on Mount Zion.

¹⁹When the people [instead of trusting God] say to you, "Consult the mediums [who try to talk to the dead] and the soothsayers who chirp *and* whisper and mutter," should not a people consult their God? *Should they consult the dead on behalf of the living?*

²⁰[Direct those people] to the law and to the testimony! If their teachings are not in accord with this word, it is because they have no dawn.

²¹They [who consult mediums and soothsayers] will pass through the land deeply distressed and hungry, and when they are hungry, they will become enraged and will curse their king and their God as they look upward.

²²Then they will look to the earth, they will see only distress and darkness, the gloom of anguish; and *they will be* driven away into darkness *and* overwhelming night.

9 BUT THERE will be no *more* gloom for her who was in anguish [for with judgment comes the promise of salvation]. In earlier times He treated the land of Zebulun and the land of Naphtali with contempt, but later on He will make them honored [by the presence of the Messiah], by the way of the sea, on the other side of Jordan, Galilee of the Gentiles.

²The people who walk in [spiritual] darkness
Will see a great Light;
Those who live in the dark land,
The Light will shine on them.
[Is 42:6; Matt 4:15, 16]

³You [O God] will increase the nation,
You will multiply their joy;
They will rejoice before You
Like the joy *and* jubilation of the harvest,
As men rejoice when they divide the spoil [of victory].
⁴For You will break the yoke of Israel's burden and the staff (goad) on their shoulders,
The rod of their oppressor, as at the battle of Midian. [Judg 7:8–22]
⁵For every boot of the marching warrior in the *battle* tumult,
And [every soldier's] garment rolled in blood, will be *used* for burning, fuel for the fire.
⁶For to us a Child shall be born, to us a Son shall be given;
And the government shall be upon His shoulder,
And His name shall be called Wonderful Counselor, Mighty God,
Everlasting Father, Prince of Peace. [Is 25:1; 40:9–11; Matt 28:18; Luke 2:11]
⁷There shall be no end to the increase of His government and of peace,
[He shall rule] on the throne of David and over his kingdom,
To establish it and to uphold it with justice and righteousness
From that time forward and forevermore.
The zeal of the LORD of hosts will accomplish this. [Dan 2:44; 1 Cor 15:25–28; Heb 1:8]
⁸The Lord sends a word (message) against Jacob,

speak the Word

God, You are my Wonderful Counselor, my Mighty God, my Everlasting Father, and my Prince of Peace.
–ADAPTED FROM ISAIAH 9:6

And it falls on Israel [the ten
northern tribes, the kingdom of
Ephraim].
9 And all the people know it,
That is, Ephraim and the inhabitants
of Samaria [its capital],
Who say in pride and arrogance of
heart:
10 "The bricks have fallen down,
But we will rebuild [all the better]
with ashlar (hewed stones);
The sycamores have been cut
down,
But we will replace them with
[expensive] cedars."
11 Therefore the LORD raises against
Ephraim adversaries from Rezin
[king of Aram]
And spurs their enemies on,
12 The Arameans on the east and the
Philistines on the west;
And they devour Israel with
gaping jaws.
In *spite of* all this, God's anger
does not turn away
But His hand is still stretched out
[in judgment].

13 Yet the people do not turn back [in
repentance] to Him who struck
them,
Nor do they seek the LORD of hosts
[as their most essential need].
14 Therefore the LORD cuts off head
and tail [the highest and the
lowest] from Israel,
Both [the high] palm branch and
[the low] bulrush in one day.
15 The elderly and honorable man, he
is the head;
⸺ And the prophet who teaches lies,
he is the tail.
16 For those who lead this people are
causing *them* to go astray;
And those who are led [astray] by
them are swallowed up.
17 Therefore the Lord does not
rejoice over their young men,
Nor does He have compassion on
their fatherless or their widows;

For every one of them is godless
and an evildoer,
And every mouth is speaking
foolishness.
In *spite of* all this, God's anger
does not turn away
But His hand is still stretched out
[in judgment].

18 For wickedness burns like a fire;
It consumes briars and thorns,
It even sets the forest thickets
ablaze;
And it swirls upward in a column
of smoke.
19 By the wrath of the LORD of hosts
the land is burned up,
And the people are like fuel for the
fire;
No man spares his brother.
20 They slice off [in discord] *what is*
on the right hand but are *still*
hungry,
And they eat *what is* on the left
hand but they are not satisfied;
Each eats the flesh of his own arm.
21 [The tribe of] Manasseh *devours*
[the tribe of his brother]
Ephraim, and Ephraim
Manasseh,
And together they are against
Judah (the southern kingdom, the
house of David).
In *spite of* all this, God's anger
does not turn away
But His hand is still stretched out
[in judgment].

10 WOE (JUDGMENT is
coming) to those [judges]
who issue evil statutes,
And to those [magistrates] who
constantly record unjust *and*
oppressive decisions,
2 So as to deprive the needy of
justice
And rob the poor of My people of
rightful claims,
So that widows may be their spoil

And that they may plunder the
fatherless.
3 Now what will you do in the day of
[God's] punishment,
And in the storm of devastation
which will come from far away?
To whom will you flee for help?
And where will you leave your
wealth [for safekeeping]?
4 Nothing *remains* but to crouch
among the captives
Or fall [dead] among the slain [on
the battlefield].
In *spite of* all this, God's anger
does not turn away,
But His hand is still stretched out
[in judgment].

5 Woe to Assyria, the rod of My
anger [against Israel],
The staff in whose hand is My
indignation *and* fury [against
Israel's disobedience]!
6 I send Assyria against a godless
nation
And commission it against the
people of My wrath
To take the spoil and to seize the
plunder,
And to trample them down like
mud in the streets.
7 Yet it is not Assyria's intention [to
do My will],
Nor does it plan so in its heart,
But instead it is its purpose to
destroy
And to cut off many nations.
8 For Assyria says, "Are not my
princes all kings?
9 "Is not Calno [conquered] like
Carchemish [on the Euphrates]?
Is not Hamath [subdued] like
Arpad [her neighbor]?
Is not Samaria [in Israel] like
Damascus [in Aram]?
10 "As my hand has reached to the
kingdoms of the idols,
Whose carved images were greater
and more feared than those of
Jerusalem and Samaria,

11 Shall I not do to Jerusalem and her
images
Just as I have done to Samaria and
her idols?" [declares Assyria].

12 So when the Lord has completed
all His work [of judgment] on Mount
Zion and on Jerusalem, *He will say,* "I
will punish the fruit [the thoughts, the
declarations, and the actions] of the
arrogant heart of the king of Assyria
and the haughtiness of his pride."
13 For the Assyrian king has said,

"I have done this by the power of my
[own] hand and by my wisdom,
For I have understanding *and* skill.
I have removed the boundaries of
the peoples
And have plundered their treasures;
Like a bull I have brought down
those who sat on thrones.
14 "My hand has found the wealth of
the people like a nest,
And as one gathers eggs that are
abandoned, so I have gathered
all the earth;
And there was not one that
flapped its wing, or that opened
its beak and chirped."

15 Is the axe able to lift itself over the
one who chops with it?
Is the saw able to magnify itself
over the one who wields it?
That would be like a club moving
those who lift it,
Or like a staff raising *him who* is
not [made of] wood [like itself]!
16 Therefore the Lord, the GOD
of hosts, will send a wasting
disease among the stout warriors
of Assyria;
And under his glory a fire will be
kindled like a burning flame.
17 And the Light of Israel will become
a fire and His Holy One a flame,
And it will burn and devour
Assyria's thorns and briars in
a single day. [2 Kin 19:35–37;
Is 31:8, 9; 37:36]

18 The Lord will consume the glory of Assyria's forest and of its fruitful garden, both soul and body,
And it will be as when a sick man wastes away.
19 And the remaining trees of Assyria's forest will be so few in number
That a child could write them down.

20 Now in that day the remnant of Israel, and those of the house of Jacob who have escaped, will never again rely on the one who struck them, but will truly rely on the Lord, the Holy One of Israel.

21 A remnant will return, a remnant of Jacob, to the mighty God.
22 For though your people, O Israel, may be as the sand of the sea,
Only a remnant within them will return;
The destruction is determined [it is decided and destined for completion], overflowing with justice (righteous punishment). [Rom 9:27, 28]

23 For the Lord, the God of hosts, will execute a complete destruction, one that is decreed, in the midst of all the land.
24 Therefore, the Lord God of hosts says this, "O My people who dwell in Zion, do not be afraid of the Assyrian who strikes you with a rod and lifts up his staff against you, as [the king of] Egypt did. [Ex 5]
25 "For yet a very little while and My indignation [against you] will be fulfilled and My anger will be directed toward the destruction of the Assyrian."
26 The Lord of hosts will brandish a whip against them like the slaughter of Midian at the rock of Oreb; and His staff will be over the [Red] Sea and He will lift it up the way He did in [the flight from] Egypt. [Ex 14:26–31; Judg 7:24, 25]
27 So it will be in that day, that the burden of the Assyrian will be removed from your shoulders and his yoke from your neck. The yoke will be broken because of the fat. [Deut 32:15]

28 The Assyrian has come against Aiath [in Judah],
He has passed through Migron [with his army];
At Michmash he stored his equipment.
29 They have gone through the pass, saying,
"Geba will be our lodging place for the night."
Ramah trembles, and Gibeah [the city] of Saul has fled.
30 Cry aloud with your voice [in consternation], O Daughter of Gallim!
Pay attention, Laishah! Answer her, Anathoth!
31 Madmenah has fled;
The inhabitants of Gebim have fled [with their belongings] to safety.
32 Yet today the Assyrian will halt at Nob [the city of priests];
He shakes his fist at the mountain of the Daughter of Zion, at the hill of Jerusalem.

33 Listen carefully, the Lord, the God of hosts, will lop off the [beautiful] boughs with terrifying force;
The tall in stature will be cut down And the lofty will be abased and humiliated.
34 He will cut down the thickets of the forest with an iron axe,
And Lebanon (the Assyrian) will fall by the Mighty One. [Gen 49:24; Is 9:6]

11 THEN A Shoot (the Messiah) will spring from the stock of Jesse [David's father],
And a Branch from his roots will bear fruit. [Is 4:2; Matt 2:23; Rev 5:5; 22:16]

² And the Spirit of the LORD will rest
   on Him—
The Spirit of wisdom and
   understanding,
The Spirit of counsel and strength,
The Spirit of knowledge and of the
   [reverential and obedient] fear
   of the LORD—
³ And He will delight in the fear of
   the LORD,
And He will not judge by what His
   eyes see,
Nor make decisions by what His
   ears hear;
⁴ But with righteousness *and* justice
   He will judge the poor,
And decide with fairness for the
   downtrodden of the earth;
And He shall strike the earth with
   the rod of His mouth,
And with the breath of His lips He
   shall slay the wicked.
⁵ And righteousness will be the belt
   around His loins,
And faithfulness the belt around
   His waist.

⁶ And the wolf will dwell with the
   lamb,
And the leopard will lie down with
   the young goat,
And the calf and the young lion
   and the fatted steer together;
And a little child will lead them.
⁷ And the cow and the bear will
   graze [together],

putting the Word to work

Isaiah 11:2 declares that God's Spirit is
the Spirit of wisdom and understanding, the Spirit of counsel and strength,
the Spirit of knowledge and the reverential and obedient fear of the Lord.
How have you experienced the Holy
Spirit's ministry in each of these ways?
If you have not, ask God to give you
experiences with His Spirit so you will
know Him in these ways.

life point

We see in Isaiah 11:3, 4 that Jesus does
not make decisions by what He sees with
His eyes or hears with His ears, yet the
Spirit of the Lord rests on Him (see Isaiah
11:2) and the Amplified Classic version of
the Bible says that makes Him "of quick
understanding." If we follow His example,
not relying on what we see or hear with
our natural senses, but watching and listening for the Holy Spirit to lead us in our
hearts, we will also understand what we
would otherwise not learn in a lifetime.

Their young will lie down together,
And the lion shall eat straw like
   the ox.
⁸ And the nursing child will [safely]
   play over the hole of the cobra,
And the weaned child will put his
   hand on the viper's den [and not
   be hurt].
⁹ They will not hurt or destroy in all
   My holy mountain,
For the earth will be full of the
   knowledge of the LORD
As the waters cover the sea.

¹⁰ Then in that day
The nations will make
   supplications to the Root of Jesse
Who will stand as a signal for the
   peoples;
And His resting place will be
   glorious. [John 12:32]

¹¹ Then it will happen on that day
   that the Lord
Will again acquire with His hand a
   second time
The remnant of His people, who
   will remain,
From Assyria, from [Lower]
   Egypt, from Pathros, from Cush
   (Ethiopia), from Elam [in Persia],
   from Shinar [Babylonia], from
   Hamath [in Aram],

And from the coastlands
   bordering the [Mediterranean]
   Sea. [Jer 23:5–8]
¹² And He will lift up a signal for the
   nations
And assemble the outcasts of
   Israel,
And will gather the dispersed of
   Judah
From the four corners of the earth.
¹³ Then the jealousy of Ephraim will
   depart,
And those who harass Judah will be
   cut off;
Ephraim will not be jealous of
   Judah,
And Judah will not harass
   Ephraim.
¹⁴ Ephraim and Judah will [unite
   and] swoop down on the slopes
   of the Philistines toward the
   west;
Together they will plunder the
   sons (Arabs) of the east.
They will possess Edom and Moab,
And the sons of Ammon will be
   subject to them.
¹⁵ And the LORD will utterly destroy
The tongue of the Sea of Egypt;
And with His scorching wind
He will wave His hand over the
   River;
He will strike *and* divide it into
   seven channels
And make [it possible for] people
   [to] walk over in sandals.
¹⁶ And there will be a highway from
   Assyria
For the remnant of His people who
   will be left,
Just as there was for Israel
In the day when they came up out
   of the land of Egypt.

12 AND ON that day you will
   say,
   "I will give thanks to You,
O LORD;
For though You were angry with me,
Your anger has turned away,
And You comfort me.
² "Behold, God, my salvation!
I will trust and not be afraid,
For the LORD GOD is my strength
   and song;
Yes, He has become my salvation."
³ Therefore with joy you will draw
   water
From the springs of salvation.
⁴ And in that day you will say,
"Give thanks to the LORD, call on
   His name [in prayer].
Make His deeds known among the
   peoples [of the earth];
Proclaim [to them] that His name
   is exalted!"
⁵ Sing praises to the LORD, for He has
   done excellent *and* glorious things;
Let this be known throughout the
   earth.
⁶ Rejoice and shout for joy, O
   inhabitant of Zion,
For great in your midst is the Holy
   One of Israel.

13 THE [MOURNFUL, in-
   spired] oracle (a burden to
   be carried) concerning Babylon which Isaiah the son of Amoz saw
[in a prophetic vision]:

² Lift up a signal banner on the bare
   mountain,
Summon them [the Medes and
   Persians] with a loud voice,
Wave the [beckoning] hand so that
   they may enter the doorways of
   the [Babylonian] nobles.

speak the Word

God, You are my salvation! I will trust and not be afraid,
for You are my strength and my song.
–ADAPTED FROM ISAIAH 12:2

3 I [the Lord] have commanded My consecrated ones,
I have even called My great warriors,
My proudly exulting ones [the Medes and the Persians who triumph for My honor]—
To *execute* My anger.
4 A sound of tumult on the mountains,
Like that of many people!
A sound of the uproar of the kingdoms,
Of nations gathered together!
The Lord of hosts is mustering an army for battle.
5 They are coming from a distant country,
From the end of heaven [the farthest horizon]—
The Lord and the weapons of His indignation—
To destroy the whole land. [Ps 19:4–6; Is 5:26]
6 Wail, for the day of the Lord is at hand!
It will come as destruction from the Almighty (All Sufficient One—Invincible God)! [Gen 17:1]
7 Therefore all hands will fall limp,
And every man's heart will melt.
8 They [of Babylon] will be shocked *and* terrified,
Pains and anguish will grip them;
They will be in pain like a woman in childbirth.
They will stare aghast *and* horrified at one another,
Their faces aflame [from the effects of the unprecedented warfare].
9 Listen carefully, the day of the Lord is coming,
Cruel, with wrath and raging anger,
To make the land a horror [of devastation];
And He shall exterminate its sinners from it. [Is 2:10–22; Rev 19:11–21]

10 For the stars of heaven and their constellations
Will not flash with their light;
The sun will be dark when it rises,
And the moon will not shed its light.
11 In this way I will punish the world for its evil
And the wicked for their wickedness [their sin, their injustice, their wrongdoing];
I will also put an end to the arrogance of the proud
And will abase the arrogance of the tyrant.
12 I will make mortal man more rare than fine gold,
And mankind [scarcer] than the pure gold of Ophir.
13 Therefore I will make the heavens tremble;
And the earth will be shaken from its place
At the wrath of the Lord of hosts
In the day of His burning anger.
14 And like the hunted gazelle,
Or like sheep that no man gathers,
Each [foreign resident] will turn [and go back] to his own people,
And each one flee to his own land.
15 Anyone who is found will be pierced through,
And anyone who is captured will fall by the sword.
16 Their children also will be smashed to pieces
Before their eyes;
Their houses will be looted
And their wives ravished.

17 Listen carefully, I will put the Medes [in motion] against them,
Who have no regard for silver and do not delight in gold [and therefore cannot be bribed].
18 Their bows will cut down the young men [of Babylon];
They will take no pity on the fruit of the womb,

Their eyes will not look with
   compassion on the children.
¹⁹ And Babylon, the glory of
   kingdoms, the beauty of the
   Chaldeans' pride,
Will be like Sodom and Gomorrah
   when God overthrew them.
²⁰ Babylon will never be inhabited
   or lived in from generation to
   generation;
Nor will the Arab pitch his tent
   there,
Nor will the shepherds let *their*
   sheep lie down there.
²¹ But desert creatures will lie down
   there,
And their houses will be full of
   owls;
Ostriches also will live there, and
   wild goats will dance there.
²² Hyenas will howl in their castles,
And jackals in their luxurious
   palaces.
Babylon's time has nearly come,
And her days will not be prolonged.

14 FOR THE LORD will have
compassion on Jacob (the
captives in Babylon) and
will again choose Israel, and will settle them in their own land. Foreigners
(Gentiles) will join them [as proselytes]
and will attach themselves to the house
of Jacob (Israel). [Esth 8:17]
   ²The peoples will take them along and
bring them to their own place (Judea),
and the house of Israel will possess
them as an inheritance in the land of the
LORD as male and female servants; and
they will take captive those whose captives they have been, and they will rule
over their [former] oppressors. [Ezra 1]
   ³And it will be in the day when the
LORD gives you rest from your pain and
turmoil and from the harsh service in
which you have been enslaved,
   ⁴that you will take up this taunt
against the king of Babylon, and say,

"How the oppressor has ceased
   [his insolence],
And how the fury has ceased!
⁵ "The LORD has broken the staff of
   the wicked,
The scepter of the [tyrant] rulers
⁶ Which used to strike the peoples
   in anger with incessant blows,
Which subdued *and* ruled
   the nations in wrath with
   unrelenting persecution.
⁷ "The whole earth is at rest and is
   quiet;
They break into shouts of joy.
⁸ "Even the cypress trees rejoice
   over you [kings of Babylon], even
   the cedars of Lebanon, *saying,*
'Since you were laid low, no
   woodcutter comes up against us.'
⁹ "Sheol below is excited about you
   to meet you when you come [you
   tyrant of Babylon];
It stirs up the spirits of the dead [to
   greet you], all the leaders of the
   earth;
It raises all the kings of the
   nations from their thrones [in
   astonishment at your fall].
¹⁰ "All of them will respond
   [tauntingly] and say to you,
'You have become as weak as we are.
You have become like us.
¹¹ 'Your pomp and magnificence
   have been brought down to
   Sheol,
Along with the music of your harps;
The maggots [which prey on the
   dead] are spread out under you
   [as a bed]
And worms are your covering
   [Babylonian rulers].'
¹² "How you have fallen from heaven,
O star of the morning [light-
   bringer], son of the dawn!
You have been cut down to the
   ground,
You who have weakened the
   nations [king of Babylon]!
¹³ "But you said in your heart,

'I will ascend to heaven;
I will raise my throne above the
  stars of God;
I will sit on the mount of assembly
In the remote parts of the north.
¹⁴'I will ascend above the heights of
  the clouds;
I will make myself like the Most
  High.'
¹⁵"But [in fact] you will be brought
  down to Sheol,
To the remote recesses of the pit
  (the region of the dead).
¹⁶"Those who see you will gaze at you,
They will consider you, *saying,*
'Is this the man who made the
  earth tremble,
Who shook kingdoms,
¹⁷Who made the world like a
  wilderness
And overthrew its cities,

Who did not permit his prisoners
  to return home?'
¹⁸"All the kings of the nations, all of
  them lie [dead] in glorious array,
Each one in his own sepulcher.
¹⁹"But you [king of Babylon] have
  been cast out of your tomb
  (denied burial)
Like a rejected branch,
Clothed with the slain who are
  pierced by the sword,
Who go down to the stones of the
  pit [into which carcasses are
  thrown],
Like a dead body trampled
  [underfoot].
²⁰"You will not be united with them
  in burial,
Because you have destroyed your
  land,
You have slain your people.

vote against yourself

Notice in Isaiah 14:12–15 that self-will destroyed Lucifer. In exalting himself, he said, "I will" five times. God had an answer for him: "But [in fact] you will be brought down to Sheol, to the remote recesses of the pit (the region of the dead)" (Isaiah 14:15). In other words, "You will be cast down to hell."

We need to guard against self-will by following Jesus' example. Sooner or later God will ask us to do something contrary to our will, and we will need to remember what Jesus said, "My Father, if it is possible [that is, consistent with Your will], let this cup pass from Me; yet not as I will, but as You will" (Matthew 26:39).

Not getting our own way is one of the most painful things we go through in life. When we want something, we really want it, and we do not give up easily. We do not like to vote against our own desires! It takes a lot of work and a lot of humility and brokenness to bring us to the place where we are pliable and moldable in the hands of God, to the point where we can say, "Well, God, I'd rather not do this, but I'm willing to do whatever You want."

The lesson here is that we must be willing to do whatever God says, and not what we think, feel, or want. We must deny ourselves if we are going to follow Him. We need to say, "Your will, God, be done in my life," and really mean it.

We are afraid that we will never get the things we want if we deny ourselves, but God will give us what we desire, and even better, in due time. Do not be afraid to delay gratification and trust God to give you what you really need.

May the descendants of evildoers
   never be named!
²¹"Prepare a slaughtering place for
   his sons
Because of the wickedness
   [the sin, the injustice, the
   wrongdoing] of their fathers.
They must not rise and take
   possession of the earth,
And fill the face of the world with
   cities."

²²"I will rise up against them," says the
Lord of hosts, "and will cut off from
Babylon name and survivors, and son
and grandson," declares the Lord.

²³"I will also make Babylon a posses-
sion of the hedgehog and of swamps
of water, and I will sweep it away with
the broom of destruction," declares
the Lord of hosts.

²⁴The Lord of hosts has sworn [an
oath], saying, "Just as I have intended,
so it has certainly happened, and just
as I have planned, so it will stand—

²⁵to break the Assyrian in My land,
and on My mountains I will trample
him underfoot. Then the Assyrian's
yoke will be removed from them (the
people of Judah) and his burden removed from their shoulder.

²⁶"This is the plan [of God] decided
for the whole earth [regarded as conquered and put under tribute by As-
syria]; and this is the hand [of God] that
is stretched out over all the nations.

²⁷"For the Lord of hosts has decided
and planned, and who can annul it?
His hand is stretched out, and who can
turn it back?"

²⁸In the year that King Ahaz [of Ju-
dah] died this [mournful, inspired]
oracle (a burden to be carried) came:

²⁹"Do not rejoice, O Philistia, any of
   you,
Because the rod [of Judah] that
   struck you is broken;

For out of the serpent's root will
   come a viper [King Hezekiah of
   Judah],
And its offspring will be a flying
   serpent. [2 Kin 18:1, 3, 8]
³⁰"The firstborn of the helpless
   [of Judah] will feed [on My
   meadows],
And the needy will lie down in
   safety;
But I will kill your root with famine,
And your survivors will be put to
   death.
³¹"Howl, O gate; cry, O city!
Melt away, O Philistia, all of you;
For smoke comes out of the north,
And there is no straggler in his
   ranks and no one stands detached
   [in Hezekiah's battalions].
³²"Then what answer will one
   give the messengers of the
   [Philistine] nation?
That the Lord has founded Zion,
And the afflicted of His people will
   seek and find refuge in it."

15

THE [MOURNFUL, inspired]
oracle (a burden to be carried) concerning Moab:

Because in a night Ar of Moab is
   devastated and ruined;
Because in a night Kir of Moab is
   devastated and ruined.
²They have gone up to the temple
   and to Dibon, to the high places
   to weep.
Moab wails over Nebo and over
   Medeba;
Everyone's head is shaved,
   and every beard is cut off [in
   mourning]. [Jer 48:37]
³In their streets they have wrapped
   themselves with sackcloth;
On their [flat] housetops and in
   their open squares
Everyone is wailing, dissolved in
   tears.
⁴Heshbon and Elealeh [cities
   claimed by Moab] cry out;

a person of purpose

Isaiah 14:26, 27 tell us that God is a God of purpose, and that when He purposes something, it *will* come to pass.

Jesus knew His purpose. As we know from John 10:10, He said He came into the world that we might have life. In John 18:37 He told Pilate, "This is why I was born, and for this I have come into the world, to testify to the truth." John wrote that Jesus' purpose was "to destroy the works of the devil" (see 1 John 3:8).

If we do not have a purpose in life, we feel useless, worthless, and frustrated, so it is very important for us to see that God has designed us with a purpose in mind (see Psalm 139:15, 16). Generally, He wants us to enjoy ourselves and to enjoy the life He has given us. But as far as our specific purpose, that varies from individual to individual and from one season of life to the next, so we must seek to discover what it is.

Right now you may be in a time of transition from one season to the next. If so, do not be discouraged. God will show you what He has for you to do next. Sometimes you may have to step out and try a few things until you find what you are comfortable with. But you can be assured that whatever it may be, you do have a purpose, and you will not be fulfilled until you find it and start flowing in it.

Not only do we need to know our purpose, we need to do it "on purpose." This involves making decisions to live right. We need to love on purpose. We do not love because we feel like it; we love because we purpose to do so. Love is not a gooey feeling about people; it is a decision we make about how we relate to people. Giving is also a decision. We do not give only because we feel like giving. We give because we are convinced it is what God wants us to do. We give on purpose and for a purpose.

The same is true of being merciful, being kind, and walking in the Spirit. We do those things not because we necessarily always feel like it, but because we are called to do them. Love, joy, peace, patience, kindness, goodness, and all the other fruit of the Spirit are characteristics of the Holy Spirit that we have within us when we accept Jesus as our Savior (see Galatians 5:22, 23). And we can release them if we do it on purpose. Make a choice to let the good things God has placed in your spirit flow through your soul and body so others may be blessed and God will be glorified.

Our flesh is not going to always agree with us to do these things. But we must choose to love on purpose, give on purpose, and stay at peace on purpose. If we want to have peace, we must purpose to have peace, because the devil will try to steal it.

Everything we do for others, and everything we do in life, needs to be done on purpose. Ask God to help you increasingly become a person of purpose!

Their voice is heard as far as Jahaz.
Therefore the armed men of Moab
cry out;
Moab's soul trembles within him.
5 My heart cries out for Moab;
His fugitives are [fleeing] as far as
Zoar and Eglath-shelishiyah.
For they go up the ascent of Luhith
weeping;
For on the road to Horonaim they
raise a cry of distress over their
destruction. [Jer 48:5]
6 For the waters of Nimrim are
desolate.
Indeed the grass is withered, the
new growth dies;
There is no green thing.
7 Therefore the abundance *which*
they have acquired and stored
away
They carry off over the Brook of
the Willows.
8 For the cry of distress has echoed
around the territory of Moab;
The wailing *goes* as far as Eglaim
and the mournful cry to Beer-
elim.
9 For the waters of Dimon are full of
blood;
Yet I will bring even more *woes* on
Dimon—
A lion upon those of Moab who
escape and upon the remnant of
the land.

16 SEND LAMBS to the ruler
of the land [you Moabites],
From Sela [that is, Petra in
Edom] through the wilderness to
the mountain of the Daughter of
Zion (Jerusalem). [2 Kin 3:4, 5]
2 For like wandering birds or
scattered nestlings,
The daughters of Moab will be at
the fords of the [river] Arnon.
3 [Say to the ruler] "Give us advice,
make a decision [for Moab, king
of Judah];

Cast your shadow [over us] like
night in the midst of noon;
Hide the outcasts, do not betray
the fugitive [to his pursuer].
4 "Let our outcasts of Moab live
among you;
Be a [sheltered] hiding place to
them from the destroyer."
For the extortioner has come to an
end, destruction has ceased,
Oppressors [who trample men]
have completely *disappeared*
from the land,
5 A throne will be established in
lovingkindness,
And One will sit on it in
faithfulness in the tent (dynasty,
family) of David;
Judging *and* seeking justice
And being prompt to do
righteousness. [Ps 96:13; Jer 48:47]
6 We have heard of the pride of
Moab, an excessive pride—
Even of his arrogance, his conceit,
his rage,
His untruthful boasting.
7 Therefore Moab will wail for
Moab; everyone will wail.
You will mourn for the raisin cakes
of Kir-hareseth,
As those who are utterly stricken
and discouraged.
8 For the fields of Heshbon have
languished *and* withered, and
the vines of Sibmah *as well;*
The lords of the nations have
trampled down [Moab's] choice
vine branches,
Which reached as far as Jazer and
wandered into the wilderness;
Its tendrils stretched out, they
passed over [the shores of] the
[Dead] Sea.
9 Therefore I (Isaiah) will weep
bitterly for Jazer, for the vines of
Sibmah.
I will drench you with my tears, O
Heshbon and Elealeh;

For the war-cry [of the enemy] has
  fallen on your summer fruits and
  your harvest.
¹⁰Gladness and joy are taken away
  from the fruitful field;
In the vineyards there will be no
  singing or joyful sound;
No treader treads out wine in the
  presses,
For I (God) put an end to the joyful
  shouting.
¹¹Therefore my heart sounds like a
  harp [in mournful compassion]
  for Moab,
And my inner being *mourns* for
  Kir-hareseth.
¹²So it will come to pass when Moab
  presents himself,
When he wearies himself
  [worshiping] on his high place
  [of idolatry]
And comes to his sanctuary [of
  Chemosh, god of Moab] to pray,
That he will not prevail. [Jer 48:13]

¹³This is the word which the LORD
spoke earlier concerning Moab [when
Moab's pride and resistance to God
were first known].

¹⁴But now the LORD speaks, saying,
"Within three years, as the years of a
hired man [who will not serve longer
than the agreed time], the glory of
Moab will be degraded along with all
the great population, and the remnant
[that survives] will be very small and
of no account."

17 THE [MOURNFUL, in-
spired] oracle (a burden to
be carried) concerning Damascus [capital of Aram (Syria), and
Israel's defense against Assyria].

"Listen carefully, Damascus will
  cease to be a city
And will become a fallen ruin.
²"The cities of Aroer [east of the
  Jordan] are deserted;

They will be [only a refuge] for
  flocks to lie down in,
And there will be no one to make
  them afraid.
³"The fortified city will disappear
  from Ephraim,
And the kingdom from Damascus
And the remnant of Aram (Syria);
They will be like the [departed]
  glory of [her ally] the children of
  Israel,"
Declares the LORD of hosts.

⁴"Now in that day the [former] glory
  of Jacob [Israel—his might, his
  population, his prosperity] will
  fade,
And the fatness of his flesh will
  become lean.
⁵"And it will be like the reaper
  gathering the standing grain,
As his arm harvests the ears of
  grain;
Yes, it will be like one gleaning
  ears of grain
In the [fertile] Valley of Rephaim.
⁶"Yet gleanings will be left in the
  land [of Israel] like the shaking of
  the olive tree,
Two or three olives on the topmost
  branch,
Four or five on the [outermost]
  branches of the fruitful tree,"
Declares the LORD, the God of
  Israel.
⁷In that day man will have regard
  for his Maker,
And his eyes will regard the Holy
  One of Israel [with awe-inspired
  reverence].
⁸And he will not have regard for the
  [idolatrous] altars, the work of
  his hands,
Nor will he look to that which his
  fingers have made,
Neither the Asherim (symbols of
  the goddess Asherah) nor the
  incense altars.

⁹In that day the strong cities of
  Aram and Israel will be like
  deserted places in the forest,
Or like branches which they
  abandoned before the children
  of Israel;
And the land will be a desolation.
¹⁰Because you [Judah] have forgotten
  the God of your salvation
And have not remembered the
  Rock of your Stronghold—
Therefore you plant lovely plants
And set the grounds with vine
  slips of a strange *god,*
¹¹In the day that you plant it you
  carefully fence it in,
And in the morning you bring
  your seed to blossom;
Yet [promising as it is] the harvest
  will be a heap [of ruins that
  passes away]
In the day of sickness and
  incurable pain.

¹²Oh, the uproar of many peoples
Who roar like the roaring of the
  seas,
And the noise of nations
Who roar like the rumbling of
  mighty waters!
¹³The nations roar on like the
  roaring of many waters,
But God will rebuke them and they
  will flee far away,
And be chased like chaff on the
  mountains before the wind,
Or like whirling dust before the
  storm.
¹⁴At evening time, now look, sudden
  terror!
Before morning the Assyrians are
  no more.
This is the portion (fate) of those
  who plunder us,
And the lot of those who pillage us.

18 WOE (JUDGMENT is
  coming) to the land of
  whirring wings
Which is beyond the rivers of
  Cush (Ethiopia),

²Which sends ambassadors by the
  sea,
Even in vessels of papyrus on the
  surface of the waters.
Go, swift messengers, to a nation
  [of people] tall and smooth
  (clean shaven),
To a people feared far and wide,
A powerful and oppressive nation
Whose land the rivers divide.
³All you inhabitants of the world,
  you who dwell on the earth,
When a banner is raised on the
  mountains, you will see it!
When a trumpet is blown, you will
  hear it!

⁴For this is what the LORD has said to
me,

  "I will be quiet and I will look on
    from My dwelling place,
  Like shimmering heat above the
    sunshine,
  Like a cloud of dew in the heat of
    harvest."
⁵For before the harvest, when the
    blossom is over
And the flower becomes a ripening
    grape,
He will cut off the sprigs [without
    buds] with pruning knives,
And [He will] remove and cut
    away the spreading branches.
⁶They (warriors) will be left
    together for the mountain birds
    of prey,
And for the beasts of the earth;
And the birds of prey will [spend
    the] summer *feeding* on them,
And all the beasts of the earth will
    spend harvest time on them.
⁷At that time a gift of homage will
    be brought to the LORD of hosts
From a people tall and smooth
    (clean shaven),
From a people feared far and wide,
A powerful and oppressive nation,
Whose land the rivers divide—

To the place [of worship] of the name of the Lord of hosts, to Mount Zion [in Jerusalem]. [Deut 12:5; 2 Chr 32:23; Is 16:1; 45:14; Zeph 3:10]

19

THE [MOURNFUL, inspired] oracle (a burden to be carried) concerning Egypt:

Listen carefully, the Lord is riding on a swift cloud and is about to come to Egypt;
The idols of Egypt will tremble at His presence,
And the heart of the Egyptians will melt within them.
2 "So I will provoke Egyptians against Egyptians;
And they will fight, each one against his brother and each one against his neighbor,
City against city, kingdom against kingdom.
3 "Then the spirit of the Egyptians will become exhausted within them *and* emptied out;
And I will confuse their strategy,
So that they will consult the idols and the spirits of the dead,
And mediums and soothsayers.
4 "And I will hand over the Egyptians to a hard *and* cruel master,
And a mighty king will rule over them," declares the Lord God of hosts.

5 The waters from the sea will dry up,
And the river will be parched and dry.
6 The canals will become foul-smelling,
The streams of Egypt will thin out and dry up,
The reeds and the rushes will rot away.
7 The meadows by the Nile, by the edge of the Nile,
And all the sown fields of the Nile

Will become dry, be blown away, and be no more.
8 The fishermen will lament (cry out in grief),
And all those who cast a hook into the Nile will mourn,
And those who spread nets upon the waters will languish.
9 Moreover, those who make linen from combed flax
And those who weave white cloth will be ashamed.
10 [Those who are] the pillars *and* foundations *of Egypt* will be crushed;
And all those who work for wages will be grieved in soul.
11 The princes of Zoan are complete fools;
The counsel of the Pharaoh's wisest advisors has become stupid.
How can you say to Pharaoh,
"I am a son of the wise, a son of ancient kings?"
12 Where then are your wise men?
Please let them tell you,
And let them understand what the Lord of hosts
Has purposed against Egypt [if they can].
13 The princes of Zoan have acted like fools,
The princes of Memphis are deluded [and entertain false hope];
Those who are the cornerstone of her tribes
Have led Egypt astray.
14 The Lord has mixed a spirit of distortion within her;
Her leaders have caused Egypt to stagger in all that she does,
As a drunken man staggers in his vomit.
15 There will be no work for Egypt
Which head or tail, [high] palm branch or [low] bulrush, may do.

16 In that day the Egyptians will become like [helpless] women, and they

will tremble and be frightened because of the waving of the hand of the Lord of hosts, which He is going to wave over them.

¹⁷The land of Judah [Assyria's ally] will become a terror to the Egyptians; everyone to whom Judah is mentioned will be in dread of it, because of the purpose of the Lord of hosts which He is planning against Egypt.

¹⁸In that day five cities in the land of Egypt will speak the language of [the Hebrews of] Canaan and swear *allegiance* to the Lord of hosts. One [of them] will be called the City of Destruction.

¹⁹In that day there will be an altar to the Lord in the midst of the land of Egypt, and a memorial stone to the Lord near its border.

²⁰It will become a sign and a witness to the Lord of hosts in the land of Egypt; for they will cry to the Lord because of oppressors, and He will send them a Savior, a [Great] Defender, and He will rescue them. [Judg 2:18; 3:9, 15]

²¹And so the Lord will make Himself known to Egypt, and the Egyptians will know [heed, honor, and cherish] the Lord in that day. They will even worship with sacrifices [of animals] and offerings [of produce]; they will make a vow to the Lord and fulfill it.

²²The Lord will strike Egypt, striking but healing it; so they will return to the Lord, and He will respond to them and heal them.

²³In that day there will be a highway from Egypt to Assyria, and the Assyrians will come into Egypt and the Egyptians into Assyria; and the Egyptians will worship *and* serve [the Lord] with the Assyrians.

²⁴In that day Israel will be the third *party* with Egypt and with Assyria [in a Messianic league], a blessing in the midst of the earth,

²⁵whom the Lord of hosts has blessed, saying, "Blessed is Egypt My people, and Assyria the work of My hands, and Israel My heritage."

20 IN THE year that the Tartan [the Assyrian commander in chief] came to Ashdod [in Philistia], when Sargon king of Assyria sent him and he fought against Ashdod and captured it,

²at that time the Lord spoke through Isaiah the son of Amoz, saying, "Go, untie the sackcloth from your hips and take your sandals off your feet." And he did so, walking around stripped [to his loincloth] and barefoot. [Mic 1:8]

³And the Lord said, "Even as My servant Isaiah has walked stripped and barefoot for three years as a sign and forewarning concerning Egypt and Cush (Ethiopia),

⁴in the same way the king of Assyria will lead away the Egyptian captives and the Cushite exiles, young and old, stripped and barefoot, even with buttocks uncovered—to the shame of Egypt.

⁵"Then they will be dismayed and ashamed because of Cush their hope and Egypt their boast.

⁶"So the inhabitants of this coastland [the Israelites and their neighbors] will say in that day, 'Look what has happened to those in whom we hoped *and* trusted and to whom we fled for help to be spared from the king of Assyria! But we, how will we escape [captivity and exile]?'"

21 THE [MOURNFUL, inspired] oracle (a burden to be carried) concerning the Desert of the Sea (the seasonally flooded plains just south of Babylon):

As windstorms in the Negev (the
    South) sweep through,
So it (God's judgment) comes from
    the desert, from [the hostile
    armies of] a terrifying land.
²A harsh vision has been shown to
    me;
The treacherous one deals
    treacherously, and the destroyer
    destroys.
Go up, Elam! Lay siege, Media!

All the groaning [caused by
  Babylon's ruthless oppressions]
  I [the LORD] have brought to an
  end. [Is 11:11; 13:17]
³Therefore [continues Isaiah] my
  loins are filled with anguish;
Pains have seized me like the
  pains of a woman in childbirth;
I am so bent *and* bewildered that
  I cannot hear, I am so terrified
  that I cannot see.
⁴My mind reels, horror overwhelms
  me;
The twilight I longed for has been
  turned into fear *and* trembling
  for me. [Dan 5:1–4]
⁵They set the table [for the doomed
  banquet], they spread out the
  cloth, they eat, they drink;
"Rise up, captains [of Belshazzar's
  court], oil your shields [for battle,
  for your enemy is at the gates]!"

⁶This is what the Lord says to me,

"Go, station the lookout, let him
  report what he sees.
⁷"When he sees a chariot, horsemen
  in pairs,
A train of donkeys and a train of
  camels,
Let him pay attention *and* listen
  closely, very closely."

⁸And the lookout called *like* a lion,

"O Lord, I stand continually on the
  watchtower by day,
And I am stationed every night at
  my guard post.
⁹"Now look! Here comes a troop of
  riders, horsemen in pairs."
And one said, "Fallen, fallen is
  Babylon;
And all the carved images of
  her gods are shattered on the
  ground."
¹⁰O my threshed *people* [Judah, who
  must be judged and trampled
  down by Babylon], my afflicted
  of the threshing floor.

What I have heard from the LORD
  of hosts,
The God of Israel, I have [joyfully]
  announced to you [that Babylon
  is to fall].

¹¹The [mournful, inspired] oracle
(a burden to be carried) concerning
Dumah (Edom):

Someone keeps calling to me from
  Seir (Edom),
"Watchman, what is left of the
  night [of Assyrian oppression]?
Watchman, what is left of the night?
  [How long until morning?]"
¹²The watchman says,
"The morning comes [only briefly],
  but also [comes] the night [of
  Babylonian oppression].
If you would ask [of me then], ask
  [again, if Edom really wishes to
  know];
Come back again."

¹³The [mournful, inspired] oracle
(a burden to be carried) concerning
Arabia:

In the thickets of Arabia you must
  spend the night,
Caravans of Dedanites.
¹⁴Bring water for the thirsty
  [Dedanites],
O inhabitants of the land of Tema
  [in Arabia];
Meet the fugitive with bread.
¹⁵For they have fled from the swords,
From the drawn sword, from the
  bent bow
And from the press of battle *and*
  grief of war.

¹⁶For the Lord has said this to me,
"Within a year, according to the years
of a hired man [who will work no longer than was agreed], all the splendor
of [the tribe of] Kedar will end;
¹⁷and the remainder of the number
of archers, the mighty men of the sons
of Kedar, will be few; for the LORD, the
God of Israel, has spoken."

22

THE [MOURNFUL, in-spired] oracle (a burden to be carried) concerning the Valley of Vision:

What is the matter with you now, that you have all gone up to the housetops,

2 You [Jerusalem] who were full of noise,
A tumultuous city, a joyous *and* exuberant city;
Your slain were not slain [in a glorious death] with the sword,
Nor did they die in battle.

3 All your leaders have fled together [with your king],
And have been captured without the bow [which they had thrown away];
All of you who were found were taken captive together,
Though they had fled far away.

4 Therefore I say, "Look away from me;
Let me weep bitterly.
Do not try to comfort me over the destruction of the daughter of my people."

5 For the Lord God of hosts has a day of panic *and* of tumult, of trampling, of confusion
In the Valley of Vision,
A [day of] breaking down walls
And a crying [for help] to the mountain.

6 Elam took up the quiver
With the chariots, infantry and horsemen;
And Kir uncovered the shield.

7 And it came to pass that your choicest valleys were full of chariots,
And the horsemen took their fixed positions [in an offensive array] at the gate [of Jerusalem]. [2 Chr 32; Is 36]

8 Then God removed the [protective] covering of Judah;

And in that day you looked to the weapons of the House of the Forest (Solomon's armory). [1 Kin 7:2; 10:17, 21]

9 You saw that the breaches
In the wall of the City of David [the citadel of Zion] were many;
You collected [within the city's walls] the waters of the Lower Pool (Siloam).

10 Then you counted the houses of Jerusalem
And you tore down the houses [to get materials] to fortify the city wall [by extending it].

11 You also made a reservoir between the two walls
For the waters of the Old Pool,
But you did not look to its Maker,
Nor did you recognize Him who planned it long ago.

12 Therefore in that day the Lord God of hosts called you to weeping, to mourning,
To shaving the head and to wearing sackcloth [in humiliation].

13 Instead, there is joy and jubilation,
Killing of oxen and slaughtering of sheep,
Eating meat and drinking wine, *saying,*
"Let us eat and drink, for tomorrow we may die."

14 But the Lord of hosts revealed Himself in my ears,
"This sin absolutely will not be forgiven you
Until you die," says the Lord God of hosts.

15 For the Lord God of hosts says this, "Go to this [contemptible] steward,
To Shebna, who is in charge of the *royal* household [but is building himself a tomb worthy of a king, and say to him],

16 'What business do you have here?
And whom do you have here,

That you have hewn out a tomb
here for yourself,
You who hew a sepulcher on the
height,
You who carve a resting place for
yourself in the rock?
¹⁷'Listen carefully, the Lᴏʀᴅ is about
to hurl you away violently, O man;
And He is about to grasp you firmly
¹⁸And roll you up tightly like a ball
And toss you into a vast country;
There you will die
And there your splendid chariots
will be,
You shame of your master's house.'
¹⁹"I will depose you from your office,
And you will be pulled down from
your position [of importance].
²⁰"Then it will come to pass in that
day
That I will summon My servant
Eliakim the son of Hilkiah.
²¹"And I will clothe him with your
tunic [of distinction]
And tie your sash securely around
him.
I will entrust him with your
authority;
He will become a father to the
inhabitants of Jerusalem and to
the house of Judah.
²²"Then I will set on his shoulder the
key of the house of David;
When he opens no one will shut,
When he shuts no one will open.
²³"I will drive him *like* a peg in a
firm place,
And he will become a throne of
honor *and* glory to his father's
house.

²⁴"So they will hang on him all the
honor *and* glory [the complete respon-
sibility] of his father's house, offspring
and issue [of the family, high and low],
all the least of the articles, from the
bowls to all the jars.
²⁵"In that day," declares the Lᴏʀᴅ
of hosts, "the peg (Eliakim) that was
driven into the firm place will give

way; it will even break off and fall, and
the burden hanging on it will be cut
off, for the Lᴏʀᴅ has spoken."

23
THE [MOURNFUL, in-
spired] oracle (a burden to
be carried) concerning Tyre:
Wail, O ships of Tarshish,
For *Tyre* is destroyed, without
house, without harbor;
It is reported to them from the
land of Cyprus (Kittim).
²Be silent, you inhabitants of the
coastland,
You merchants of Sidon;
Your messengers crossed the sea
³And *they were* on great waters.
The grain of the Shihor, the
harvest of the Nile River, was
Tyre's revenue;
And she was the market of nations.
⁴Be ashamed, O Sidon [mother-
city of Tyre, now like a widow
bereaved of her children];
For the sea speaks, the stronghold
of the sea, saying,
"I have neither labored nor given
birth [to children];
I have neither brought up young
men nor reared virgins."
⁵When the report *reaches* Egypt,
They will be in agony at the report
about Tyre.
⁶Cross over to Tarshish [to seek
safety as exiles];
Wail, O inhabitants of the
coastland [of Tyre].
⁷Is this your jubilant *city*,
Whose origin dates back to
antiquity,
Whose feet used to carry her [far
away] to colonize distant places?

⁸Who has planned this against
Tyre, the bestower of crowns,
Whose merchants were princes,
whose traders were the honored
of the earth?

⁹The LORD of hosts has planned it,
　　to defile the pride of all beauty,
　To bring into contempt *and*
　　humiliation all the honored of
　　the earth.
¹⁰Overflow your land like [the
　　overflow of] the Nile, O
　　Daughter of Tarshish;
　There is no more restraint [on you
　　to make you pay tribute to Tyre].
¹¹He has stretched out His hand
　　over the sea,
　He has shaken the kingdoms;
　The LORD has given a command
　　concerning Canaan to destroy
　　her strongholds *and* her
　　fortresses [like Tyre and Sidon].
¹²He has said, "You shall never again
　　exult [in triumph], O crushed
　　Virgin Daughter of Sidon.
　Arise, cross over to Cyprus; even
　　there you will find no rest."

¹³Now look at the land of the Chaldeans (Babylonia)—this is the people which was not; the Assyrians allocated Tyre for desert creatures—they set up their siege towers, they stripped its palaces, they made it a ruin.

¹⁴Wail, O ships of Tarshish,
　For your stronghold [of Tyre] is
　　destroyed.

¹⁵Now in that day Tyre will be forgotten for seventy years, like the days of one king. At the end of seventy years it will happen to Tyre as in the prostitute's song:

¹⁶Take a harp, walk around the city,
　O forgotten prostitute;
　Play the strings skillfully, sing
　　many songs,
　That you may be remembered.

¹⁷It will come to pass at the end of seventy years that the LORD will remember Tyre. Then she will return to her prostitute's wages and will play the [role of a] prostitute [by trading] with all the kingdoms on the face of the earth. ¹⁸But her commercial gain and her prostitute's wages will be dedicated to the LORD; it will not be treasured or stored up, but her commercial gain will become sufficient food and stately clothing for those who dwell (minister) in the presence of the LORD.

24 BEHOLD, THE LORD lays waste to the earth, devastates it, twists *and* distorts its face and scatters its inhabitants. ²And the people will be like the priest, the servant like his master, the maid like her mistress, the buyer like the seller, the lender like the borrower, the creditor like the debtor [as God's impartial judgment of sin comes on all]. ³The earth will be completely laid waste and utterly pillaged, for the LORD has spoken this word. ⁴The earth dries up and crumbles away, the world dries out and crumbles away, the exalted of the people of the earth fade away.

⁵The earth also is polluted by its inhabitants, because they have transgressed laws, violated statutes, and broken the everlasting covenant. [Gen 9:1–17; Deut 29:20] ⁶Therefore, a curse devours the earth, and those who live on it suffer the punishment of their guilt. Therefore, the inhabitants of the earth are burned [under the curse of God's wrath], and few people are left. [Rom 1:20]

⁷The new wine mourns,
　The vine decays;
　All the merry-hearted sigh *and*
　　groan.
⁸The mirth of the timbrels
　　(tambourines) ceases,
　The noise of those who rejoice ends,
　The joy of the harp ceases.
⁹They do not drink wine with a song;
　Strong drink is bitter to those who
　　drink it.
¹⁰The city of chaos is broken down;
　Every house is shut up so that no
　　one may enter.

11 There is an outcry in the streets
concerning the wine;
All jubilation is darkened,
The joy of the earth is banished.
12 Horrible desolation is left in the city,
And the gate is battered into ruins.
13 For so it will be in the midst of the
earth among the peoples,
As the shaking of an olive tree,
As the gleanings when the grape
harvest is over [and only a little
of the fruit remains].
14 They [who have escaped and
remain] raise their voices, they
shout for joy;
They rejoice from the
[Mediterranean] Sea in the
majesty of the LORD.
15 Therefore honor *and* glorify the
LORD in the east [in the region of
light],
The name of the LORD, the God of
Israel [honor His name],
In the coastlands *and* islands of
the [Mediterranean] Sea.
16 From the ends of the earth we
hear songs, "Glory *and* honor to
the Righteous One,"
But I say, "I waste away, I waste
away. Woe to me!
The treacherous deal treacherously,
Indeed, the treacherous deal very
treacherously."
17 Terror and pit [of destruction] and
snare
Confront you, O inhabitant of the
earth.
18 Then it will be that he who flees at
the sound of terror will fall into
the pit,
And he who comes up out of the pit
will be caught in the snare;

For the windows of heaven are
opened, and the foundations of
the earth tremble.
19 The earth is broken completely
apart,
The earth is split apart,
The earth is shaken violently.
20 The earth reels back and forth like
a drunkard
And sways like a shack;
Its transgression lies heavily upon it,
And it will fall and not rise again.
21 So it will happen in that day
That the LORD will visit *and* punish
the host (fallen angels) of heaven
on high,
And the kings of the earth on the
earth. [1 Cor 15:25; Eph 3:10; 6:12]
22 They will be gathered together
As prisoners [are gathered] in a
dungeon;
They will be shut up in prison,
And after many days they will be
visited *and* punished. [Zech 9:11,
12; 2 Pet 2:4; Jude 6]
23 Then the full moon will be
embarrassed and the sun
ashamed,
For the LORD of hosts will reign on
Mount Zion and in Jerusalem,
And *His* glory *and* brilliance will
shine before His elders.

25 O LORD, You are my God;
I will exalt You, I will
praise *and* give thanks to
Your name;
For You have done miraculous
things,
Plans *formed* long, long ago,
[fulfilled] with perfect
faithfulness.

speak the Word

*God, I declare that You are my God and I exalt You. I praise Your name
because You have done miraculous things planned from long ago for me.
You continue to fulfill those purposes with perfect faithfulness.*
—ADAPTED FROM ISAIAH 25:1

2 For You have made a city into a
heap [of trash],
A fortified city into a ruin;
A palace of foreigners is no longer
a city,
It will never be rebuilt.
3 Therefore a strong people will
honor You;
Cities of terrible and violent
nations will fear You.
4 For You have been a stronghold for
the helpless,
A stronghold for the poor in his
distress,
A shelter from the storm, a shade
from the heat;
For the breath of tyrants
Is like a rainstorm against a wall.
5 Like heat in a dry land, You will
subdue the noise of foreigners
[rejoicing over their enemies];
Like heat in the shadow of a
cloud, the song of the tyrants is
silenced.

6 On this mountain [Zion] the LORD
of hosts will prepare a lavish
banquet for all peoples [to
welcome His reign on earth],
A banquet of aged wines—choice
pieces [flavored] with marrow,
Of refined, aged wines.
7 And on this mountain He will
destroy the covering that is [cast]
over all peoples,
And the veil [of death] that is woven
and spread over all the nations.
8 He will swallow up death [and
abolish it] for all time.
And the Lord GOD will wipe away
tears from all faces,
And He will take away the
disgrace of His people from all
the earth;
For the LORD has spoken. [1 Cor
15:26, 54; 2 Tim 1:10]
9 It will be said in that day,
"Indeed, this is our God for whom
we have waited that He would
save us.

This is the LORD for whom we have
waited;
Let us shout for joy and rejoice in
His salvation."
10 For the hand of the LORD will rest
on this mountain [Zion],
And Moab will be trampled down
in his place
As straw is trampled down in the
[filthy] water of a manure pile.
11 And Moab will spread out his
hands in the middle of the filth
As a swimmer spreads out his
hands to swim,
But the Lord will humiliate his
pride in spite of the [skillful]
movements of his hands.
12 The high fortifications of your
walls He will bring down,
Lay low, and cast to the ground, to
the dust.

26 IN THAT day this song
will be sung in the land of
Judah:

"We have a strong city;
He sets up salvation as walls and
ramparts.
2 "Open the gates, that the righteous
nation may enter,
The one that remains faithful and
trustworthy.
3 "You will keep in perfect and
constant peace the one whose
mind is steadfast [that is,
committed and focused on
You—in both inclination and
character],

putting the Word to work

Isaiah 26:3 promises that God will
keep us in perfect and constant peace
when our minds are steadfast and focused on Him. Are you anxious or worried today? Then turn your thoughts
toward Him so you will experience His
perfect peace.

Because he trusts *and* takes refuge in You [with hope and confident expectation].
4 "Trust [confidently] in the Lord forever [He is your fortress, your shield, your banner],
For the Lord God is an everlasting Rock [the Rock of Ages].
5 "For He has thrown down the [arrogant] ones who dwell on high, the lofty *and* inaccessible city;
He lays it low, He lays it low to the ground, He hurls it to the dust.
6 "The foot will trample it,
Even the feet of the suffering, and the steps of the helpless."

7 The way of the righteous [those in right-standing with God—living in moral and spiritual integrity] is smooth *and* level;
O Upright One, make a level path for the just *and* righteous.
8 Indeed, in the path of Your judgments, O Lord,
We have waited expectantly for You;
Your name, even Your memory, is the desire *and* deep longing of our souls.
9 In the night my soul longs for You [O Lord],
Indeed, my spirit within me seeks You diligently;
For [only] when Your judgments are experienced on the earth
Will the inhabitants of the world learn righteousness.
10 *Though* the wicked is shown compassion *and* favor,
He does not learn righteousness;
In the land of uprightness he deals unjustly,
And refuses to see the majesty of the Lord.

life point

Peace of mind must precede peace in every other area of our lives. Isaiah 26:3 promises perfect and constant peace to those who keep their minds on God. When we allow our minds to wander and when we think too much about everything we do, we push ourselves out of peace and into turmoil; when we think about the future and the responsibilities we will have, we can be overwhelmed. This kind of thinking is called anxiety. Likewise, we grow anxious and lose our peace when we spend today trying to figure out tomorrow or when we try to live tomorrow today in our minds.

We will never enjoy the rich and fruitful lives God intends for us unless we learn to discipline our thoughts and resist anxiety by keeping our minds on God. I repeat what I say often: "Where the mind goes, the man follows." Let your mind lead you into peace!

11 *Though* Your hand is lifted up [to strike], O Lord, the wicked do not see it.
Let them see Your zeal for *Your* people and be put to shame;
Indeed, let the fire reserved for Your enemies consume them.
12 Lord, You will establish peace for us,
Since You have also performed for us all that we have done.
13 O Lord our God, other masters besides You have ruled over us;
But through You alone we confess Your name.
14 The [wicked] dead will not live [again], the spirits of the dead will not rise *and* return;

speak the Word

God, I trust confidently in You. You are my everlasting Rock!
–ADAPTED FROM ISAIAH 26:4

Therefore You have punished and
destroyed them,
And You have wiped out every
memory of them [every trace of
them].
¹⁵You have increased the nation,
O Lord;
You have increased the nation,
You are glorified;
You have extended all the borders
of the land.
¹⁶O Lord, they sought You in distress;
They managed only a prayerful
whisper
When Your discipline was upon
them.
¹⁷As a woman with child approaches
the time to give birth,
She is in pain *and* struggles and
cries out in her labor,
So we were before You, O Lord.
¹⁸We have been with child, we have
twisted *and* struggled *in labor;*
We gave birth, as it seems, *only* to
wind.
We could not accomplish salvation
for the earth,
Nor were inhabitants of the world
born.
¹⁹Your dead will live;
Their dead bodies will rise.
You who lie in the dust, awake and
shout for joy!
For your dew is a dew of [celestial]
light [heavenly, supernatural],
And the earth will give birth to the
spirits of the dead. [Ezek 37:11, 12]

²⁰Come, my people, enter your
chambers
And shut your doors behind you;
Hide for a little while
Until the [Lord's] wrath is past.
²¹Listen carefully, the Lord is about to
come out of His [heavenly] place
To punish the inhabitants of
the earth for their wickedness
[their sin, their injustice, their
wrongdoing];

The earth will reveal the
[innocent] blood shed upon her
And will no longer cover her slain.

27 IN THAT day the Lord
will punish Leviathan the
fleeing serpent
With His fierce and great and
mighty sword [rescuing Israel
from her enemy],
Even Leviathan the twisted serpent;
And He will kill the dragon who
lives in the sea.
²In that day [it will be said of the
redeemed nation of Israel],
"A vineyard of wine, sing in praise
of it!
³"I, the Lord, am its Keeper;
I water it every moment.
So that no one will harm it,
I guard it night and day.
⁴"I have no wrath.
Should anyone give Me briars *and*
thorns in battle,
I would step on them, I would set
them all on fire.
⁵"Or let him (Israel) cling to
My strength *and* rely on My
protection [My stronghold],
Let him make peace with Me,
Let him make peace with Me."
⁶In the generations to come Jacob
will take root;
Israel will blossom and sprout,
And they will fill the surface of
the world with fruit. [Hos 14:1–6;
Rom 11:12]

⁷Like the striking by Him who
has struck them, has He struck
them?
Or like the slaughter of His slain,
have they been slain?
⁸You contended with them by exile,
by driving them away [from
Canaan];
He has expelled them with His
fierce wind on the day of the
east wind.

9 Therefore through this the wickedness [the sin, the injustice, the wrongdoing] of Jacob (Israel) will be atoned for *and* forgiven;
And this will be the full price [that God requires] for taking away his sin:
When Israel makes all the stones of the [pagan] altars like crushed chalk stones;
When the Asherim and the incense altars will not stand.
10 For the fortified city is isolated,
A settlement deserted and abandoned like the desert;
There the calf will graze,
And there it will lie down and feed on its branches.
11 When its branches are dry, they are broken off;
The women come and make a fire with them.
For they are not a people of understanding,
Therefore He who made them will not have compassion on them,
And He who created them will not be gracious to them.

12 In that day the LORD will thresh [out His grain] from the flowing stream of the River [Euphrates] to the Brook of Egypt, and you will be gathered up one by one, O sons of Israel.
13 It will come to pass in that day that a great trumpet will be blown, and those who were lost *and* perishing in the land of Assyria and who were scattered in the land of Egypt will come and worship the LORD on the holy mountain at Jerusalem. [Zech 14:16; Matt 24:31; Rev 11:15]

28 WOE (JUDGMENT is coming) to [Samaria] the splendid crown of the drunkards of Ephraim,
And to the fading flower of its glorious beauty,
Which is at the head of the rich valley
Of those who are overcome with wine!
2 Listen carefully, the Lord has a strong and mighty *agent* [the Assyrian];
Like a tempest of hail, a disastrous storm,
Like a tempest of mighty overflowing waters,
He has cast it down to the earth with *His* hand.
3 The splendid crown of the drunkards of Ephraim is trampled by [the foreigners'] feet.
4 And the fading flower of its glorious beauty,
Which is at the head of the rich valley,
Will be like the early fig before the summer,
Which one sees,
And as soon as it is in his hand
He [greedily] swallows it [and so will the Assyrians rapidly devour Samaria, Israel's capital].
5 In that day the LORD of hosts will become a magnificent crown
And a glorious diadem to the [converted] remnant of His people,
6 A spirit of justice for him who sits in judgment [administering the law],
A strength to those who drive back the battle at the gate.
7 But even these reel with wine and stagger from strong drink:
The priest and the prophet reel with strong drink;
They are confused by wine, they stagger from strong drink;
They reel while seeing visions,
They stagger *when pronouncing* judgment.
8 For all the tables are full of filthy vomit, so that there is no place [that is clean.]

9 *They say* "To whom would He teach knowledge?
And to whom would He explain the message?
Those *just* weaned from milk?
Those *just* taken from the breast?
10 "For *He says,*
'Precept upon precept, precept upon precept,
Rule upon rule, rule upon rule,
Here a little, there a little.' "
11 Indeed, the LORD will teach this people [in a more humiliating way]
By [men with] stammering lips and a foreign tongue,
12 He who said to them, "This is the place of quiet, give rest to the weary,"
And, "This is the resting place," yet they would not listen.
13 Therefore the word of the LORD to them will be [merely monotonous repetitions]:
"Precept upon precept, precept upon precept,
Rule upon rule, rule upon rule,
Here a little, there a little."
That they may go and stumble backward, and be broken, ensnared, and taken captive.
14 Therefore, hear the word of the LORD, you arrogant men
Who rule this people who are in Jerusalem!
15 Because you have said, "We have made a covenant with death,
And with Sheol (the place of the dead) we have made an agreement,
When the overwhelming scourge passes by, it will not reach us,
For we have made lies our refuge and we have concealed ourselves in deception."
16 Therefore the Lord GOD says this,

"Listen carefully, I am laying in Zion a Stone, a tested Stone,
A precious Cornerstone for the [secure] foundation, firmly placed.
He who believes [who trusts in, relies on, and adheres to that Stone] will not be disturbed *or* give way [in sudden panic]. [Ps 118:22; Matt 21:42; Acts 4:11; Rom 9:33; Eph 2:20; 1 Pet 2:4–6]
17 "I will make justice the measuring line
And righteousness the mason's level;
Then hail will sweep away the refuge of lies
And waters will flood over the secret [hiding] place.
18 "Your covenant with death will be annulled,
And your agreement with Sheol (the place of the dead) will not stand;
When the overwhelming scourge passes through,
Then you will become its trampling ground.
19 "As often as it passes through, it will seize you;
For morning after morning it will pass through, by day and by night,
And it will be sheer terror to understand what it means."
20 For the bed is too short to stretch out on,
And the blanket is too narrow to wrap around oneself [and likewise all their preparations are inadequate].
21 For the LORD will rise up as at Mount Perazim,
He will be stirred up as in the Valley of Gibeon,
To do His work, His unusual *and* incredible work,
And to accomplish His work, His extraordinary work. [2 Sam 5:20; 1 Chr 14:16]
22 Now do not carry on as scoffers,
Or the bands which bind you will be made stronger;

For I have heard from the Lord
  God of hosts [a decree]
Of decisive destruction on all the
  earth.

23 Listen and hear my voice;
  Listen carefully and hear my words.
24 Does the farmer plow all day to
  plant seed?
  Does he *continually* dig furrows
  and harrow his ground [after it
  is prepared]?
25 When he has leveled its surface,
  Does he not sow [the seed of] dill
  and scatter cumin,
  And plant wheat in rows,
  And barley in its [intended] place
  and rye within its border?
26 For his God instructs [him correctly]
  and teaches him properly.
27 For dill is not threshed with a
  sharp threshing sledge,
  Nor is a cartwheel rolled over
  cumin;
  But dill is beaten out with a staff,
  and cumin with a rod.
28 Bread *grain* is crushed fine,
  Indeed, the farmer does not
  continue to thresh it forever.
  Because the wheel of his cart and
  his horses *eventually* damage it,
  He does not thresh it longer.
29 This also comes from the Lord of
  hosts,
  Who has made His counsel
  wonderful and His wisdom great.

29

WOE (JUDGMENT is
coming) to Ariel, to Ariel,
the city where David
[once] camped!
Add yet another year; let the feasts
run their course [but only one
year more].
2 Then I will harass Ariel,

And she will be a *city of* mourning
  and lamenting (crying out in grief)
Yet she will be like an Ariel [an
  altar hearth] to Me.
3 I will camp against you and
  encircle you,
  And I will hem you in with siege
  works,
  And I will raise fortifications
  against you.
4 Then you [Jerusalem] will be
  brought low,
  You will speak from the earth,
  And from the dust where you lie
  face down
  Your muffled words *will come*.
  Your voice will also be like that of
  a spirit from the earth [like one
  produced by a medium],
  And your speech will whisper *and*
  squeak from the dust.

5 But the multitude of your enemies
  [that assault you] will become
  like fine dust,
  And the multitude of the tyrants
  like the chaff which blows away;
  And it will happen in an instant,
  suddenly [that your enemy is
  destroyed].
6 You will be punished by the
  Lord of hosts with thunder and
  earthquake and great noise,
  With whirlwind and tempest and
  the flame of a consuming fire.
7 And the multitude of all the
  nations that fight against Ariel
  (Jerusalem),
  Even all who fight against her and
  her stronghold, and who distress
  her,
  Will be like a dream, a vision of
  the night.
8 It will be as when a hungry man
  dreams

speak the Word

God, I declare that You are wonderful in counsel and great in wisdom.
–ADAPTED FROM ISAIAH 28:29

That he is eating,
But when he awakens, his hunger
  is not satisfied;
Or as when a thirsty man dreams
That he is drinking,
But when he awakens, in fact, he
  is faint
And his thirst is not quenched.
So will the multitude of all the
  nations be
Who fight against Mount Zion.

⁹Stop *and* take some time and
  wonder [at this prophecy],
Blind yourselves and be blinded
  [at its fulfillment by your
  spiritual incompetence].
They are drunk, but not from wine;
They stagger, but not from strong
  drink.
¹⁰For the LORD has poured over you a
  spirit of deep sleep.
He has closed your eyes, [you who
  are] the prophets;
And He has covered your heads,
  [you who are] the seers.

¹¹The entire vision [of all these things]
will be to you like the words of a scroll
that is sealed, which they give to one who
can read, saying, "Read this, please," he
shall say, "I cannot, for it is sealed."
¹²Then the book will be given to the
one who cannot read, saying, "Read this,
please." And he will say, "I cannot read."
¹³Then the Lord said,

"Because this nation approaches
  [Me only] with their words
And honors Me [only] with their
  lip service,
But they remove their hearts far
  from Me,
And their reverence for Me is
  a tradition that is learned *by
  rote* [without any regard for its
  meaning],
¹⁴Therefore, listen carefully, I will
  again do marvelous *and* amazing
  things with this people, wonderful
  and astonishing things;

And the wisdom of their wise men
  will perish,
And the understanding of their
  discerning men will be hidden."

¹⁵Woe (judgment is coming) to those
  who [try to] deeply hide their
  plans from the LORD,
Whose deeds are *done* in a dark
  place,
And who say, "Who sees us?" or
  "Who knows us?"
¹⁶You turn *things* upside down [with
  your perversity]!
Shall the potter be considered
  equal with the clay,
That the thing that is made would
  say to its maker, "He did not
  make me";
Or the thing that is formed say to
  him who formed it, "He has no
  understanding"?

¹⁷Is it not yet a very little while
Until Lebanon will be turned into
  a fertile field,
And the fertile field regarded as a
  forest?
¹⁸On that day the deaf will hear the
  words of a book,
And out of *their* gloom and
  darkness the eyes of the blind
  will see [the words of the book].
¹⁹The afflicted also will increase
  their joy in the LORD,
And the needy of mankind will
  rejoice *and* celebrate in the Holy
  One of Israel.
²⁰For the tyrant will come to an end
  and the scorner will be finished,
Indeed all who are intent on doing
  evil will be cut off—
²¹Those who cause a person to be
  condemned with a [false] word,
And lay a trap for him who
  upholds justice at the [city] gate,
And defraud the one in the right
  with meaningless arguments.

²²Therefore, the LORD, who redeemed Abraham [from paganism]

says this, concerning the house of Jacob (Israel):

"Jacob will not be ashamed, nor
  will his face turn pale [with
  disappointment because of his
  children's degenerate behavior];
23 For when he sees his children, the
  work of My hands, in his midst,
They will sanctify My Name;
They will sanctify the Holy One of
  Jacob
And will stand in awe and reverent
  fear of the God of Israel.
24 "Those who err in mind will know
  the truth,
And those who criticize and
  murmur discontentedly will
  accept instruction.

30 "WOE (JUDGMENT is
coming) to the rebellious
children," declares the LORD,
"Who carry out a plan, but not Mine,
And make an alliance [by pouring
  out a libation], but not of My Spirit,

life point

Isaiah 30:1, 2 is another of those "woe" passages we see in the Bible from time to time. In it the Lord pronounces a curse upon those rebellious children who turn from trusting in Him to take counsel of themselves, carry out their own plans, and flee to "the shadow of Egypt," rather than resting under the shadow of the Almighty.

In this case, fleeing to the "shadow of Egypt" refers to turning to the arm of the flesh rather than leaning on the arm of the Lord. In other words, we are not to trust in others, in ourselves, or in the world, but only in the Lord. We are to acknowledge Him in all our ways so that He may direct our paths. We are to find our strength in Him alone.

life point

In Isaiah 30:3–7 the Lord continues to warn against relying on the strength of Egypt—the superpower of that day. I believe the Lord is saying to us, "Do not run away from trusting in Me to trusting in your own plans and devices. They will not work, and you will only end up humiliated and confused. Before you do anything, check with Me to see if it is what you should be doing. Do not look to the world for answers, because it has none to give. The help it has to offer is absolutely worthless. Salvation and deliverance are with Me, and Me alone."

In order to add sin to sin;
2 Who proceed down to Egypt
  Without consulting Me,
To take refuge in the stronghold of
  Pharaoh
And to take shelter in the shadow
  of Egypt!
3 "Therefore the safety and
  protection of Pharaoh will be
  your shame
And the refuge in the shadow of
  Egypt, your humiliation and
  disgrace.
4 "For his princes are at Zoan
And his ambassadors arrive at
  Hanes [in Egypt].
5 "All will be ashamed because of
  a people (the Egyptians) who
  cannot benefit them,
Who are not a help or benefit, but
  a shame and also a disgrace."

6 A [mournful, inspired] oracle (a burden to be carried) concerning the beasts of the Negev (the South):

Through a land of trouble and
  anguish,
From where come lioness and lion,
  viper and [fiery] flying serpent,
They carry their riches on the
  shoulders of young donkeys

And their treasures on the humps
   of camels,
To a people (Egyptians) who
   cannot benefit them.
⁷For Egypt's help is worthless and
   good for nothing.
Therefore, I have called her
"Rahab Who Has Been
   Exterminated."
⁸Now, go, write it on a tablet before
   them
And inscribe it on a scroll,

So that it may serve in the time to
   come
As a witness [against them]
   forevermore.
⁹For this is a rebellious people,
   lying sons,
Sons who refuse to listen to
The law *and* instruction of the Lᴏʀᴅ;
¹⁰Who say to the seers, "You must
   not see *visions from God"*;
And to the prophets, "You must not
   prophesy to us what is right!

from brokenness to blessing

When you and I make our own plans or run to other people instead of trusting in the Lord, we leave a weak spot in our wall of divine protection. At a time when we least expect it, the enemy will break through that weak place. When that happens, we will indeed be like a "crack [in a wall] about to fall, a bulge in a high wall," mentioned in Isaiah 30:13.

God does not want us to have weak spots in our lives, like cracks or bulges in a wall. He wants us to rely on Him and be obedient to Him so our "walls" will remain strong and thick and our lives will be blessed and full.

The more we depend on God, the more He can do through us. But sometimes we go through brokenness before we enter His blessings.

Once, for about a year and a half, I thought I might be going mad. All day long I walked around in my house, praying, "Help me, Lord!" I did not even know what kind of help I needed, or why I needed it. Now as I look back on that experience, I know what was happening. God was breaking off my spirit of independence, and He was bringing me to the point where I knew I could do nothing apart from Him.

I remember one night as I was getting ready to go to sleep, I picked up a little book and started reading it. Suddenly I had a visitation from God. For about forty-five minutes I sat there on the edge of my bed and wept. Finally, the Lord spoke to me and said, "Anything good you do has nothing to do with you. I am the One Who is good. When you see yourself doing anything good, it is only because I have wrestled with you to get your flesh under subjection long enough to allow My glory to shine through it."

Sometimes before God can promote us, He has to remind us of our place. In my own case, my ministry was about to experience a sudden growth spurt. God was preparing me in advance by telling me, "I'm going to do something marvelous in your life and ministry, and when it happens you must remember that it is I and not you who is bringing it to pass."

God was teaching me what He is teaching all of us today: He is the answer to *all* our problems.

Speak to us pleasant things *and*
    smooth words,
Prophesy [deceitful] illusions [that
    we will enjoy].
¹¹ "Get out of the [true] way, turn
    aside from the path [of God],
Stop bothering us with the Holy
    One of Israel."

¹² Therefore, the Holy One of Israel
says this,

"Because you have refused *and*
    rejected this word [of Mine]
And have put your trust in
    oppression and guile, and have
    relied on them,
¹³ Therefore this wickedness
    [this sin, this injustice, this
    wrongdoing] will be to you
Like a crack [in a wall] about to
    fall,
A bulge in a high wall,
Whose collapse comes suddenly in
    an instant,
¹⁴ "Whose collapse is like the
    smashing of a potter's jar,
Crushed so savagely
that there cannot be found among
    its pieces a potsherd [large
    enough]
To take [coals of] fire from a
    fireplace,
Or to scoop water from a cistern."

¹⁵ For the Lord GOD, the Holy One of
Israel has said this,

"In returning [to Me] and rest you
    shall be saved,
In quietness and confident trust is
    your strength."
But you were not willing,
¹⁶ And you said, "No! We will flee on
    horses!"

speak the Word

life point

Isaiah 30:18 is one of my favorite scriptures. If you will meditate on it, it will
begin to bring you great hope.

In this verse, God says that He is actively
looking for someone to be good to.
In fact, He "waits [expectantly]" and
"longs" to be gracious to you! But He
cannot pour out His goodness on anyone
who has a negative attitude. He is looking
for someone who will believe Isaiah 30:18,
someone who is expecting His goodness,
someone who is on the lookout all
the time, someone who is full of faith
and trust, someone who is eagerly anticipating His gracious gifts. He wants to be
good to you, so be expecting an outpouring of His goodness!

Therefore you will flee [from your
    enemies]!
And [you said], "We will ride on
    swift horses!"
Therefore those who pursue you
    shall be swift.
¹⁷ A thousand *of you will flee* at the
    threat of one *man;*
You will flee at the threat of five,
Until you are left like a flag on the
    top of a mountain,
And like a signal on a hill.

¹⁸ Therefore the LORD waits
    [expectantly] *and* longs to be
    gracious to you,
And therefore He waits on high to
    have compassion on you.
For the LORD is a God of justice;

Thank You, God, for saving me as I return to and rest in You.
In quietness and confidence, You give me strength.
–ADAPTED FROM ISAIAH 30:15

Blessed (happy, fortunate) are all those who long for Him [since He will never fail them]. [John 14:3, 27; 2 Cor 12:9; Heb 12:2; 1 John 3:16; Rev 3:5]

¹⁹O people in Zion, inhabitant in Jerusalem, you will weep no longer. He will most certainly be gracious to you at the sound of your cry for help; when He hears it, He will answer you. ²⁰Though the Lord gives you the bread of adversity and the water of oppression, yet your Teacher will no longer hide Himself, but your eyes will [constantly] see your Teacher.

²¹Your ears will hear a word behind you, "This is the way, walk in it," whenever you turn to the right or to the left. ²²And you will defile your carved images overlaid with silver, and your cast images plated with gold. You will scatter them like a bloodstained *cloth,* and will say to them, "Be gone!" ²³Then He will give you rain for the seed with which you sow the ground, and bread [grain] from the produce of the ground, and it will be rich and plentiful. In that day your livestock will graze in large *and* roomy pastures. ²⁴Also the oxen and the young donkeys that work the ground will eat

this is the way

No matter what has happened to you in your lifetime—even if you have been abandoned by your spouse or abused by your parents or hurt by your children or others—if you will stay on the narrow path as God directs you (see Matthew 7:13, 14) and leave all your excess fleshly baggage behind, you will find the peace, joy, and fulfillment you seek. As you walk through this process, you can find comfort in God's promise from Isaiah 30:21 to guide you.

Jesus is the Way, and He has shown us the way in which we are to walk. The Lord has sent upon us His Holy Spirit to lead and guide us in the way we are to go, the narrow way that leads to life and not the broad way that leads to destruction.

Whatever happens, it's necessary for us to keep walking in the ways of the Lord. Galatians 6:9 encourages us: "Let us not grow weary or become discouraged in doing good, for at the proper time we will reap, if we do not give in." The Bible does not promise that when we do right we will reap the rewards immediately. But it does assure us that if we keep doing right, eventually we will be rewarded.

God says that as long as the earth remains, there will be "seedtime and harvest" (Genesis 8:22). We might paraphrase it like this: "As long as the earth remains, there will be *seed, time,* and *harvest.*" When we walk in God's path, we must be patient like the farmer, who plants the seed and expectantly waits for the harvest. He looks forward to reaping the harvest, but he knows that time will elapse between seed planting and harvest. He does not allow that God-ordained process to frustrate him.

God promises in Isaiah 30:21, "Your ears will hear a word behind you, 'This is the way; walk in it.'" If you continue to walk in the way the Lord has prescribed for you in His Word and by His Spirit, you will enjoy great blessing both in this life and in eternity.

So keep walking the narrow path that leads to life—life in all its fullness and abundance!

salted fodder, which has been winnowed with shovel and pitchfork.

25On every lofty mountain and on every high hill there will be streams of water on the day of the great slaughter (the day of the LORD), when the towers fall [and all His enemies are destroyed].

26The light of the full moon will be like the light of the sun, and the light of the sun will be seven times *brighter,* like the light of seven days [concentrated in one], in the day the LORD binds up the fracture of His people and heals the wound He has inflicted [because of their sins].

27Now look, the name of the LORD
  comes from far away,
Burning with His anger, and heavy
  with smoke;
His lips are full of indignation,
And His tongue is like a
  consuming fire.
28His breath is like an overflowing
  river,
Which reaches to the neck,
To sift the nations back and forth
  in a sieve [of disaster],
And *to put* in the jaws of the
  peoples the bridle which leads to
  ruin.
29You will have a song as in the
  night when a holy feast is kept,
And joy of heart as when one
  marches [in procession] with a
  flute,
To go to the [temple on the]
  mountain of the LORD, to the
  Rock of Israel.
30And the LORD will make His
  majestic voice heard,
And show the descending of His
  arm [striking] in [His] fierce
  anger,
And in the flame of a devouring
  fire,
In the crashing sound *of heavy
  rain,* cloudburst, and hailstones.

31For at the voice of the LORD the
  Assyrians will be terrified,
When He strikes [them] with the
  rod.
32And every blow of the rod of
  punishment,
Which the LORD will lay on them,
Will be to *the music of Israel's*
  tambourines and lyres;
And in battles, brandishing
  weapons, He will fight Assyria.
33For Topheth [in Hinnom] has long
  been ready;
Indeed, it has been prepared for
  the [Assyrian] king.
He has made it deep and wide,
A pit of fire with plenty of wood;
The breath of the LORD, like a river
  of brimstone (blazing sulfur),
  kindles *and* fans it. [Jer 7:31, 32;
  Matt 5:22; 25:41]

31 WOE (JUDGMENT is coming) to those who go down to Egypt for help,
Who rely on horses
And trust in chariots because they
  are many,
And in horsemen because they are
  very strong,
But they do not look to the Holy
  One of Israel, nor seek *and*
  consult the LORD!
2Yet He is also wise and will bring
  disaster,
And does not retract His words,
But will arise against the house of
  evildoers
And against the helpers of those
  who do evil.
3Now the Egyptians are men and
  not God,
And their horses are flesh and not
  spirit;
And the LORD will stretch out His
  hand,
And he (Egypt) who helps will
  stumble,

And he (Judah) who is helped will
  fall,
And all of them will perish together.

⁴For so the LORD says to me,

"As the lion or the young lion
  growls over his prey,
And though a large group of
  shepherds is called out against
  him
He will not be terrified at their
  voice nor cringe at their noise,
So the LORD of hosts will come
  down to wage war on Mount
  Zion and on its hill."
⁵Like flying birds, so will the LORD
  of hosts protect Jerusalem;
He will protect and save it,
He will pass over and rescue it.

⁶Return to Him from whom you have
so deeply defected, O sons of Israel.
⁷For in that day every man will reject *and* throw away his idols of silver and his idols of gold [in disgust],
which your own hands have sinfully
made for you.

⁸Then the Assyrian will fall by a
  sword not of man,
And a sword not of man will
  devour him.
And he will flee from the sword [of
  God],
And his young men will become
  forced labor.
⁹"His rock [his stronghold] will
  pass away because of panic,
And his princes will be terrified at
  the [sight of the battle] standard,"
Declares the LORD, whose fire is
  in Zion and whose furnace is in
  Jerusalem.

32 BEHOLD, A King will
   reign in righteousness,
   And princes will rule
with justice.
²Each [one of them] will be like a
  hiding place from the wind

And a shelter from the storm,
Like streams of water in a dry land,
Like the shade of a huge rock in
  a parched *and* weary land [to
  those who turn to them].
³Then the eyes of those who see
  will not be blinded,
And the ears of those who hear
  will listen attentively.
⁴The heart (mind) of those who
  act impulsively will discern the
  truth,
And the tongue of the stammerers
  will hurry to speak clearly.
⁵The fool (the good-for-nothing)
  will no longer be called noble,
Nor the rogue said to be generous.
⁶For the fool speaks nonsense,
And his heart (mind) plans
  wickedness:
To practice ungodliness and to
  speak error concerning the LORD,
To keep the craving of the hungry
  unsatisfied
And to deprive the thirsty of drink.
⁷As for the rogue, his weapons are
  evil;
He conceives wicked plans
To ruin the poor with lies,
Even when the plea of the needy
  one is just *and* right.
⁸But the noble man conceives noble
  and magnificent things;
And he stands by what is noble
  and magnificent.

⁹Rise up, you women who are
  carefree,
And hear my voice,
You confident *and* unsuspecting
  daughters!
Listen to what I am saying.
¹⁰In little more than a year
You will tremble [with anxiety],
  you unsuspecting *and*
  complacent women;
For the vintage has ended,
And the harvest will not come.
¹¹Tremble, you women who are
  carefree;

Tremble with fear, you complacent
    ones!
Strip, undress and wear *sackcloth*
    on your waist [in grief],
¹²Beat your breasts [in mourning]
    for the beautiful fields, for the
    fruitful vine,
¹³For the land of my people growing
    over with thorns and briars—
Yes, [mourn] for all the houses of
    joy in the joyous city.
¹⁴For the palace has been
    abandoned, the populated city
    deserted;
The hill [of the city] and the
    watchtower have become caves
    [for wild animals] forever,
A delight for wild donkeys, a
    pasture for flocks,
¹⁵Until the Spirit is poured out upon
    us from on high,
And the wilderness becomes a
    fertile field,
And the fertile field is valued as a
    forest. [Ps 104:30; Ezek 36:26, 27;
    39:29; Zech 12:10]
¹⁶Then justice will dwell in the
    wilderness,
And righteousness will live in the
    fertile field.
¹⁷And the effect of righteousness
    will be peace,
And the result of righteousness
    will be quietness and confident
    trust forever.
¹⁸Then my people will live in a
    peaceful surrounding,
And in secure dwellings and in
    undisturbed resting places.
¹⁹But it will hail, when the forest
    comes down,
And the [capital] city will fall in
    utter humiliation.

²⁰Blessed (happy, fortunate) are
    you who cast your seed upon all
    waters [when the river overflows
    its banks and irrigates the land],
You who allow the ox and the
    donkey to roam freely.

33 WOE (JUDGMENT
    is coming) to you, O
    destroyer,
You who were not destroyed,
And he who is treacherous, while
    others did not deal treacherously
    with him.
As soon as you finish destroying,
    you will be destroyed;
As soon as you stop dealing
    treacherously, *others* will deal
    treacherously with you.
²O Lᴏʀᴅ, be gracious to us; we have
    waited [expectantly] for You.
Be the arm of Your servants every
    morning [that is, their strength
    and their defense],
Our salvation also in the time of
    trouble.
³At the sound of the tumult, the
    peoples flee;
At the lifting up of Yourself
    nations scatter.
⁴Your spoil [of Israel's foe] is
    gathered [by the people of
    Jerusalem] as the caterpillar
    gathers;
As locusts swarming so people
    swarm on it.
⁵The Lᴏʀᴅ is exalted, for He dwells
    on high;
He has filled Zion with justice and
    righteousness.
⁶And He will be the security *and*
    stability of your times,
A treasure of salvation, wisdom
    and knowledge;

speak the Word

Thank You, God, that the effect of righteousness is peace in my life.
–ADAPTED FROM Iꜱᴀɪᴀʜ 32:17

The fear of the Lord is your treasure.
⁷Now look, their brave men shout
outside;
The ambassadors [seeking a
treaty] of peace weep bitterly.
⁸The highways are deserted, the
traveler has ceased [to appear].
The enemy has broken the
covenant, he has rejected the
cities,
He has no regard for [any] man.
⁹The land mourns and dries out,
Lebanon is shamed and [its lush
foliage] withers;
Sharon is like a desert plain,
And Bashan and [Mount] Carmel
shake off *their leaves*.
¹⁰"Now I will arise," says the Lord.
"Now I will be exalted; now I will
be lifted up.
¹¹"You have conceived dried grass,
you will give birth to stubble;
My breath is a fire that will
consume you.
¹²"The peoples will be burned to lime,
Like thorns cut down which are
burned in the fire.
¹³"You who are far away, hear what I
have done;
And you who are near,
acknowledge My might."
¹⁴The sinners in Zion are terrified;
Trembling has seized the godless.
[They cry] "Who among us can
live with the consuming fire?
Who among us can live with
everlasting burning?"
¹⁵He who walks righteously and
speaks with integrity,
Who rejects gain from fraud *and*
from oppression,
Who shakes his hand free from
the taking of bribes,

Who stops his ears from hearing
about bloodshed
And shuts his eyes to avoid looking
upon evil;
¹⁶He will dwell on the heights,
His place of defense will be the
fortress of rocks,
His bread will be given him;
His water will be permanent.
¹⁷Your eyes will see the King in His
beauty;
They will see a far-distant land.
¹⁸Your mind will meditate on the
terror [asking]:
"Where is he who counts?
Where is he who weighs [the
tribute]?
Where is he who counts the
towers?"
¹⁹You will no longer see the fierce
and insolent people,
A people of unintelligible speech
which no one comprehends,
Of a strange *and* stammering
tongue which no one
understands.
²⁰Look upon Zion, the city of
our appointed feasts *and*
observances;
Your eyes will see Jerusalem, a
undisturbed settlement,
A tent which will not be taken
down;
Not one of its stakes will ever be
pulled up,
Nor any of its ropes be severed.
²¹But there the mighty *and*
magnificent Lord will be for us
A place of broad rivers and streams,
Where no oar-driven boat will go,
And on which no mighty *and*
stately ship will pass.
²²For the Lord is our Judge,

speak the Word

Thank You, God, for the security and stability You bring to my life.
Thank You for the treasure of salvation, wisdom, and knowledge You give me.
—ADAPTED FROM ISAIAH 33:6

The LORD is our Ruler,
The LORD is our King;
He will save us. [Is 2:3, 4; 11:4;
32:1; James 4:12]
23 Your ship's ropes (tackle) hang
loose;
They cannot hold the base of their
mast firmly,
Nor spread out the sail.
Then an abundance of spoil and
plunder will be divided;
Even the lame will take the
plunder.
24 And no inhabitant [of Zion] will
say, "I am sick";
The people who dwell there will
be forgiven their wickedness
[their sin, their injustice, their
wrongdoing].

34

COME NEAR, you nations,
to hear; and listen, O
peoples!
Let the earth and all that is in it
hear, and the world and all that
comes forth from it.
2 For the LORD is angry at all the
nations,
And *His* wrath is against all their
armies;
He has utterly doomed them,
He has given them over to
slaughter.
3 So their slain will be thrown out,
And the stench of their corpses
will rise,
And the mountains will flow with
their blood.
4 All the host of heaven will be
dissolved,
And the skies will be rolled up like
a scroll;
All their hosts [the stars and the
planets] will also wither away
As a leaf withers from the vine,
And as a *fig* withers from the fig
tree. [Rev 6:13, 14]
5 For My sword is satiated [with
blood] in heaven;

Indeed, it will come down for
judgment on Edom
And on the people whom I have
doomed for destruction.
[Obad 8–21]
6 The sword of the LORD is filled
with blood [from sacrifices],
It drips with fat, with the blood of
lambs and goats,
With the fat of the kidneys of rams.
For the LORD has a sacrifice in
Bozrah (Edom's capital city)
And a great slaughter in the land
of Edom.
7 Wild oxen will also fall with them
And the young bulls with the
strong bulls;
And their land will be soaked with
blood,
And their dust made greasy with fat.
8 For the LORD has a day of
vengeance,
A year of retribution for the cause
of Zion.
9 The streams [of Edom] will be
turned into pitch,
And its dust into brimstone,
And its land will become burning
pitch.
10 The burning will not be quenched
night or day;
Its smoke will go up forever.
From generation to generation it
will lie in ruins;
No one will ever again pass
through it. [Rev 19:3]
11 But the pelican and the porcupine
will take possession of it;
The owl and the raven will dwell
in it.
And He will stretch over it (Edom)
the measuring line of desolation
And the plumb line of emptiness.
12 Its nobles—there is no one there
Whom they may proclaim king—
And all its princes will be nothing.
13 Thorns will come up in its fortified
palaces,

Nettles and brambles in its
    fortified cities;
It will be a haunt for jackals,
An abode for ostriches.
14 The creatures of the desert will
    encounter jackals
And the hairy goat will call to its
    kind;
Indeed, Lilith (night demon) will
    settle there
And find herself a place of rest.
15 There the arrow snake will make
    her nest and lay her eggs,
And hatch them and gather *her
    young* under her protection;
Indeed, the birds of prey will be
    gathered there [to breed],
Every one with its own kind.

16 Seek from the book of the Lord,
and read:

Not one of these [creatures] will be
    missing;
None will lack its mate.
For His mouth has commanded,
And His Spirit has gathered them.
17 The Lord has cast the lot for them,
And His hand has divided *and*
    apportioned Edom to the wild
    beasts by measuring-line.
They will possess it forever;
From generation to generation
    they will dwell in it.

35

THE WILDERNESS and
the dry land will be glad;
The Arabah (desert) will
shout in exultation and blossom
Like the autumn crocus.
2 It will blossom abundantly
And rejoice with joy and singing.
The glory of Lebanon will be given
    to it,
The majesty of [Mount] Carmel
    and [the plain] of Sharon.
They will see the glory of the Lord,
The majesty *and* splendor of our
    God.

3 Encourage the exhausted, and
    make staggering knees firm.
    [Heb 12:12]
4 Say to those with an anxious *and*
    panic-stricken heart,
"Be strong, fear not!
Indeed, your God will come with
    vengeance [for the ungodly];
The retribution of God will come,
But He will save you."
5 Then the eyes of the blind will be
    opened
And the ears of the deaf will be
    unstopped.
6 Then the lame will leap like a deer,
And the tongue of the mute will
    shout for joy.
For waters will break forth in the
    wilderness
And streams in the desert. [Matt
    11:5]
7 And the burning sand (mirage)
    will become a pool [of water]
And the thirsty ground springs of
    water;
In the haunt of jackals, where they
    lay resting,
Grass becomes reeds and rushes.
8 A highway will be there, and a
    roadway;
And it will be called the Holy Way.
The unclean will not travel on it,
But it will be for those who walk
    on the way [the redeemed];
And fools will not wander *on it*.
9 No lion will be there,
Nor will any predatory animal
    come up on it;
They will not be found there.
But the redeemed will walk *there*.
10 And the ransomed of the Lord will
    return
And come to Zion with shouts of
    jubilation,
And everlasting joy will be upon
    their heads;
They will find joy and gladness,
And sorrow and sighing will flee
    away.

36

NOW IN the fourteenth year of King Hezekiah, Sennacherib king of Assyria came up against all the fortified cities of Judah and conquered them. [2 Kin 18:13, 17–37; 2 Chr 32:9–19] ²And the king of Assyria sent the Rabshakeh [his military commander] from Lachish [the Judean fortress commanding the road from Egypt] to King Hezekiah at Jerusalem with a large army. And he stood by the canal of the Upper Pool on the highway to the Fuller's Field. ³Then Eliakim the son of Hilkiah, who was in charge of the [royal] household, and Shebna the scribe, and Joah the son of Asaph, the recording historian, came out to [meet] him. ⁴Then the Rabshakeh said to them, "Say to Hezekiah, 'This is what the great king, the king of Assyria says, "What is [the reason for] this confidence that you have? ⁵"I say, 'Your plan and strength for the war are only empty words.' Now in whom do you trust *and* on whom do you rely, that you have rebelled against me? [2 Kin 18:7] ⁶"Listen carefully, you rely on the staff of this broken reed, Egypt, which will pierce the hand of any man who leans on it. So is Pharaoh king of Egypt to all who rely on him. ⁷"But if you say to me, 'We trust in *and* rely on the Lord our God,' is it not He whose high places and whose altars Hezekiah has taken away, saying to Judah and to Jerusalem, 'You shall worship before this altar'? [2 Kin 18:4, 5] ⁸"So now, exchange pledges with my master the king of Assyria and I will give you two thousand horses, if you are able on your part to put riders on them. ⁹"How then can you repulse [the attack of] a single commander of the least of my master's servants, and rely on Egypt for chariots and for horsemen?

¹⁰"Moreover, is it without the Lord that I have now come up against this land to destroy it? The Lord said to me, 'Go up against this land and destroy it.'"'" ¹¹Then Eliakim and Shebna and Joah said to the Rabshakeh, "Please, speak to your servants in Aramaic, because we understand it; and do not speak to us in Judean (Hebrew) in the hearing of the people who are [stationed] on the wall." ¹²But the Rabshakeh said, "Has my master sent me to speak these words *only* to your master and to you, and not to the men sitting on the wall, *doomed* to eat their own dung and drink their own urine with you?" ¹³Then the Rabshakeh stood and called out with a loud voice in Judean (Hebrew): "Hear the words of the great king, the king of Assyria. ¹⁴"This is what the king says, 'Do not let Hezekiah deceive you, for he will not be able to rescue you; ¹⁵nor let Hezekiah make you trust in the Lord, saying, "The Lord will most certainly rescue us; this city will not be given into the hand of the king of Assyria." ¹⁶'Do not listen to Hezekiah,' for this is what the king of Assyria says, 'Make peace with me and come out to me, and each one of you will eat from his own vine and each from his own fig tree and each [one of you] drink from the water of his own cistern, ¹⁷until I come and take you away to a land like your own land, a land of grain and new wine, a land of bread and vineyards. ¹⁸'*Beware* that Hezekiah does not mislead you by saying, "The Lord will rescue us." Has any one of the gods of the nations [ever] rescued his land from the hand of the king of Assyria? ¹⁹'Where are the gods of Hamath and Arpad [in Aram]? Where are the gods of Sepharvaim? And when have they rescued Samaria from my hand?

20'Who among all the gods of these lands have rescued their land from my hand, that [you should think that] the LORD would rescue Jerusalem from my hand?'"

21But they kept silent and did not say a word to him in reply, for King Hezekiah's command was, "Do not answer him."

22Then Eliakim the son of Hilkiah, who was in charge of the household, and Shebna the scribe and Joah the son of Asaph, the recording historian, came to Hezekiah with their clothes torn [in grief], and told him the words of the Rabshakeh [the Assyrian commander].

37 AND WHEN King Hezekiah heard this, he tore his clothes and covered himself with sackcloth and went into the house of the LORD. [2 Kin 19:1–13]

2Then he sent Eliakim, who was in charge of the [royal] household, and Shebna the scribe, and the elders of the priests, covered with sackcloth, to Isaiah the prophet, the son of Amoz.

3They said to him, "This is what Hezekiah says, 'This day is a day of distress, rebuke and disgrace; for children have come to birth, and there is no strength to deliver them.

4'It may be that the LORD your God will hear the words of the Rabshakeh [the commander], whom his master the king of Assyria has sent to taunt *and* defy the living God, and will avenge the words which the LORD your God has heard. Therefore, offer a prayer for the remnant [of His people] that is left.'"

5So the servants of King Hezekiah came to Isaiah.

6Isaiah said to them, "You shall say the following to your master: 'This is what the LORD says, "Do not be afraid because of the words that you have heard, with which the servants of the king of Assyria have blasphemed Me.

7"Listen carefully, I will put a spirit in him so that he will hear a rumor and return to his own land. And I will make him fall by the sword in his own land."'"

8So the Rabshakeh returned and found the king of Assyria fighting against Libnah [a fortified city of Judah], for he had heard that the king had left Lachish.

9And Sennacherib king of Assyria, heard *them* say concerning Tirhakah king of Cush (Ethiopia), "He has come out to fight against you." And when he heard it, he sent messengers to Hezekiah, saying,

10"You shall say to Hezekiah king of Judah, 'Do not let your God in whom you trust deceive you, saying, "Jerusalem will not be given into the hand of the king of Assyria."

11"Listen carefully, you have heard what the kings of Assyria have done to all lands, utterly destroying them. So will you be rescued?

12'Did the gods of the nations which my fathers destroyed rescue them— Gozan, Haran [of Mesopotamia], Rezeph, and the sons of Eden who were in Telassar?

13'Where is the king of Hamath, the king of Arpad [of northern Syria], the king of the city of Sepharvaim, [the king of] Hena, or [the king of] Ivvah?'"

14Then Hezekiah took the letter from the hand of the messengers and read it, and he went up to the house of the LORD and spread it out before the LORD. [2 Kin 19:14–19]

15And Hezekiah prayed to the LORD saying,

16"O LORD of hosts, God of Israel, who is enthroned *above* the cherubim, You are the God, You alone, of all the kingdoms of the earth. You have made heaven and earth.

17"Incline Your ear, O LORD, and hear; open Your eyes, O LORD, and see; and hear all the words of Sennacherib that he has sent to taunt *and* defy the living God.

¹⁸"It is true, O LORD, that the kings of Assyria have laid waste all the countries and their lands,

¹⁹and have cast the gods [of those peoples] into the fire, for they were not gods but the work of men's hands, wood and stone. Therefore they have destroyed them.

²⁰"Now, O LORD our God, save us from his hand so that all the kingdoms of the earth may know *and* fully realize that You alone, LORD, are God."

²¹Then Isaiah son of Amoz sent *word* to Hezekiah, saying, "For the LORD, the God of Israel says this, 'Because you have prayed to Me about Sennacherib king of Assyria, [2 Kin 19:20–37; 2 Chr 32:20, 21]

²²this is the word that the LORD has spoken against him:

> "She has shown contempt for you
>   and mocked you,
> The Virgin Daughter of Zion
>   (Jerusalem);
> She has shaken her head behind
>   you,
> The Daughter of Jerusalem!

²³"Whom have you taunted and
>   blasphemed?
> And against whom have you raised
>   your voice
> And haughtily lifted up your eyes?
> Against the Holy One of Israel!

²⁴"Through your servants you have
>   taunted *and* defied the Lord,
> And you have said, 'With my many
>   chariots I have gone up to the
>   heights of the mountains,
> To the remotest parts of Lebanon.
> I cut down its tallest cedars and its
>   choicest cypress trees;
> And I will go to its remotest height,
>   its most luxuriant *and* thickest
>   forest.

²⁵'I dug *wells* and drank [foreign]
>   waters,

> And with the sole of my feet I
>   dried up
> All the canals [of the Nile] of Egypt.'

²⁶"Have you not heard [says the God
>   of Israel]
> That I did it long ago,
> That I planned it in ancient times?
> Now I have brought it to pass,
> That you [king of Assyria] would
>   [be My instrument to] turn
>   fortified cities into ruinous heaps.

²⁷"Therefore their inhabitants had
>   little power,
> They were terrorized and shamed;
> They were like the grass of the
>   field and the green vegetation,
> Like grass on the housetops *and*
>   like a field [of grain] scorched
>   before it is grown.

²⁸"But I know your sitting down
> And your going out and your coming
>   in [every detail of your life],
> And your raging against Me.

²⁹"Because your raging against Me
> And your arrogance has come up
>   to My ears,
> I will put My hook in your nose
> And My bridle in your mouth,
> And I will turn you back by the
>   way you came.

³⁰"This shall be the sign [of these things] to you [Hezekiah]: you are to eat this year what grows of itself, and in the second year that which springs from the same, and in the third year you are to sow and harvest, and plant vineyards and eat their fruit.

³¹"The surviving remnant of the house of Judah will again take root downward and bear fruit upward.

³²"For out of Jerusalem will come a remnant and from Mount Zion a band of survivors. The zeal of the LORD of hosts will do this."'

³³"Therefore, the LORD says this concerning the king of Assyria, 'He will not come into this city or shoot an arrow there, or come before it with shield, or raise an assault ramp against it.

³⁴'By the way that he came, by the same way he will return, and he will not come into this city,' declares the LORD.

³⁵'For I will defend this city to save it, for My own sake and for the sake of My servant David.'"

³⁶And the angel of the LORD went out and struck 185,000 in the camp of the Assyrians; and when the [surviving] men got up early the next morning, *they saw* all the dead. [2 Kin 19:35]

³⁷So Sennacherib king of Assyria departed and returned and lived at Nineveh.

³⁸It came to pass as he was worshiping in the house of Nisroch his god, that Adrammelech and Sharezer his sons killed him with the sword; and they escaped into the land of Ararat [in Armenia]. And Esarhaddon his son became king in his place.

38

IN THOSE days Hezekiah [king of Judah] became sick and was at the point of death. And Isaiah the prophet, the son of Amoz, came to him and said, "For the LORD says this, 'Set your house in order *and* prepare a will, for you shall die; you will not live.'" [2 Kin 20:1–11; 2 Chr 32:24–26]

²Then Hezekiah turned his face to the wall and prayed to the LORD,

³and said, "Please, O LORD, just remember how I have walked before You in faithfulness *and* truth, and with a whole heart [absolutely devoted to You], and have done what is good in Your sight." And Hezekiah wept greatly.

⁴Then the word of the LORD came to Isaiah, saying,

⁵"Go and say to Hezekiah, 'For the LORD, the God of David your father says this, "I have heard your prayer, I have seen your tears; listen carefully, I will add fifteen years to your life.

⁶"I will rescue you and this city from the hand of the king of Assyria; and I will defend this city [Jerusalem]."'

⁷"This shall be the sign to you from the LORD, that the LORD will do this thing that He has spoken:

⁸"Listen carefully, I will turn the shadow on the stairway [denoting the time of day] ten steps backward, *the shadow* on the stairway (sundial) of Ahaz." And the sunlight went ten steps backward on the stairway where it had [previously] gone down.

⁹*This is the* writing of Hezekiah king of Judah after he had been sick and had recovered from his illness:

¹⁰I said, "In mid-life
  I am to go through the gates of
    Sheol (the place of the dead),
  I am to be summoned, *deprived of*
    the remainder of my years."
¹¹I said, "I will not see the LORD
  The LORD in the land of the living;
  I will no longer see man among the
    inhabitants of the world.
¹²"My dwelling (body) is pulled up
    and removed from me like a
    shepherd's tent;
  I have rolled up my life as a weaver
    [rolls up the finished web].
  He cuts me free from the warp [of
    the loom];
  From day to night You bring me to
    an end.
¹³"I lay down until morning.
  Like a lion, so He breaks all my
    bones;
  From day until night You bring me
    to an end.
¹⁴"Like a swallow, like a crane, so I
    chirp;
  I coo like a dove.

speak the Word

Thank You, God, for hearing my prayer and seeing my tears.
–ADAPTED ISAIAH 38:5

My eyes look wistfully upward;
O Lord, I am oppressed, take my
    side *and* be my security.
¹⁵"What shall I say?
For He has spoken to me, and He
    Himself has done it;
I will wander aimlessly all my
    years because of the bitterness
    of my soul.
¹⁶"O Lord, by *these* things men live,
And in all these is the life of my
    spirit;
Restore me to health and let me live!
¹⁷"Indeed, it was for my own well-
    being that I had such bitterness;
But You have loved back my life
    from the pit of nothingness
    (destruction),
For You have cast all my sins
    behind Your back.
¹⁸"For Sheol cannot praise *or* thank
    You,
Death cannot praise You *and*
    rejoice in You;
Those who go down to the pit
    cannot hope for Your faithfulness.
¹⁹"It is the living who give praise *and*
    thanks to You, as I do today;
A father tells his sons about Your
    faithfulness.
²⁰"The LORD is ready to save me;
Therefore we will play my songs
    on stringed instruments
All the days of our lives at the
    house of the LORD."

²¹Now Isaiah had said, "Have them
take a cake of figs and rub it [as an
ointment] on the inflamed spot, that
he may recover."
²²Hezekiah also had said, "What is
the sign that I will go up to the house
of the LORD?"

39 AT THAT time Merodach-
baladan son of Baladan,
king of Babylon, sent [mes-
sengers with] letters and a present
to Hezekiah, for he had heard that

he had been sick and had recovered.
[2 Kin 20:12–19]
²Hezekiah was pleased and showed
them his treasure house—the silver,
the gold, the spices, the precious oil,
his entire armory and everything that
was found in his treasuries. There was
nothing in his house nor in all his area
of dominion that Hezekiah did not
show them.
³Then Isaiah the prophet came to
King Hezekiah and asked, "What did
these men say? From where have they
come to you?" And Hezekiah said,
"They came to me from a far country,
from Babylon."
⁴Then Isaiah said, "What have they
seen in your house?" And Hezekiah
answered, "They have seen everything that is in my house; there is
nothing among my treasures that I
have not shown them."
⁵Then Isaiah said to Hezekiah,
"Hear the word of the LORD of hosts,
⁶'Listen carefully, the days are coming when everything that is in your
house and everything that your pre-
decessors have stored up until this
day will be carried to Babylon; nothing will be left,' says the LORD.
⁷'And some of your own sons (descendants) who will come from you,
whom you will father, will be taken
away, and they will become officials
in the palace of the king of Babylon.'"
⁸Then said Hezekiah to Isaiah, "The
word of the LORD which you have spoken is good." For he thought, "There
will be peace and faithfulness [to
God's promises to us] in my days."

40 "COMFORT, O comfort My
people," says your God.
²"Speak tenderly to
Jerusalem,
And call out to her, that her time of
    compulsory service in warfare is
    finished,

That her wickedness has
  been taken away [since her
  punishment is sufficient],
That she has received from the
  LORD's hand
Double [punishment] for all her
  sins."

³A voice of one is calling out,
"Clear the way for the LORD in the
  wilderness [remove the obstacles];
Make straight *and* smooth in the
  desert a highway for our God.
  [Mark 1:3]
⁴"Every valley shall be raised,
And every mountain and hill be
  made low;
And let the rough ground become
  a plain,
And the rugged places a broad
  valley.
⁵"And the glory *and* majesty *and*
  splendor of the LORD will be
  revealed,
And all humanity shall see it
  together;
For the mouth of the LORD has
  spoken it." [Luke 3:5, 6]
⁶A voice says, "Call out [prophesy]."
Then he answered, "What shall I
  call out?"
[The voice answered:] All humanity
  is [as frail as] grass, and all that
  makes it attractive [its charm, its
  loveliness] is [momentary] like
  the flower of the field.
⁷The grass withers, the flower fades,
When the breath of the LORD blows
  upon it;
Most certainly [all] the people are
  [like] grass.
⁸The grass withers, the flower fades,
But the word of our God stands
  forever. [James 1:10, 11; 1 Pet
  1:24, 25]

speak the Word

putting the Word to work

We all have "mountaintop" experiences and valleys (low moments) in
our lives; we all have crooked places
that seem confusing, times that are
uneven (up and down), and situations
that are rough and difficult (see Isaiah
40:4). In what ways has God brought
stability and evenness to your life?
How has He made crooked places
straight and given you grace for the
rough spots along your journey?
Remember how He has helped you and
thank Him today.

⁹O Zion, herald of good news,
Get up on a high mountain.
O Jerusalem, herald of good news,
Lift up your voice with strength,
Lift it up, do not fear;
Say to the cities of Judah,
"Here is your God!" [Acts 10:36;
  Rom 10:15]
¹⁰Listen carefully, the Lord GOD will
  come with might,
And His arm will rule for Him.
Most certainly His reward is with
  Him,
And His restitution accompanies
  Him. [Rev 22:7, 12]
¹¹He will protect His flock like a
  shepherd,
He will gather the lambs in His
  arm,
He will carry them in His bosom;
He will gently *and* carefully lead
  those nursing their young.
¹²Who has measured the waters in
  the hollow of His hand,
And marked off the heavens with
  a span [of the hand],

Thank You, God, that Your Word stands forever!
–ADAPTED ISAIAH 40:8

And calculated the dust of the
  earth with a measure,
And weighed the mountains in a
  balance
And the hills in a pair of scales?
13 Who has directed the Spirit of the
  Lord,
Or has taught Him as His
  counselor? [Rom 11:34]
14 With whom did He consult and
  who enlightened Him?
Who taught Him the path of justice
  and taught Him knowledge
And informed Him of the way of
  understanding?
15 In fact, the nations are like a drop
  from a bucket,
And are regarded as a speck of
  dust on the scales;
Now look, He lifts up the islands
  like fine dust.
16 And [the forests of] Lebanon
  cannot supply sufficient *fuel* to
  start a fire,

Nor are its wild beasts enough for
  a burnt offering [worthy of the
  Lord].
17 All the nations are as nothing
  before Him,
They are regarded by Him as less
  than nothing and meaningless.
18 To whom then will you liken God?
  Or with what likeness will you
  compare Him? [Acts 17:29]
19 *As for* the cast image (idol), a
  metalworker casts it,
A goldsmith overlays it with gold
And a silversmith *casts its* silver
  chains.
20 He who is too impoverished for *such*
  an offering [to give to his god]
Chooses a tree that will not rot;
He seeks out for himself a skillful
  craftsman
To [carve and] set up an idol that
  will not totter.
21 Do you [who worship idols] not
  know? Have you not heard?

magnets for His power

Isaiah 40:6, 7 teaches us that the flesh (people, just like you and I) is like grass. We
are here on earth for a very short time; we tend to be fragile, unsure, and shaky
during our relatively brief lifetimes. God knows that and has no problem with it,
because He is willing to work through us and to show Himself strong in our weaknesses. Actually, the Bible teaches that God's strength shows itself most effectively
through our weaknesses (see 2 Corinthians 12:9). Our weaknesses and shortcomings
are like magnets for His power.

God can handle knowing what we lack and knowing that we fail. We, on the other
hand, tend to beat ourselves up over our imperfections. We try to make excuses for
them, try to compensate for them, and try to keep other people from seeing them.
Instead, we need to admit our weaknesses and face them, not feel badly about
them. We need to be honest about what we can do, but we need to be equally honest about what we cannot do, recognizing that those things are great opportunities
for God to work through us.

Let me encourage you to get up every morning, love God, and do your best in every
situation. He will do the rest! Remember that God is not surprised by your inabilities, imperfections, or faults. He has always known about those areas of your life,
even if you are just now discovering them. Only God is perfect; He chose you anyway, and He loves you in spite of all your shortcomings!

Has it not been told to you from
the beginning?
Have you not understood from the
foundations of the earth [the
omnipotence of God and the
stupidity of bowing to idols]?
[Rom 1:20, 21]
²²It is He who sits above the circle of
the earth,
And its inhabitants are like
grasshoppers;
[It is He] who stretches out the
heavens like a veil
And spreads them out like a tent to
dwell in.

life point

I have experienced the truth of Isaiah 40:29, and I honestly believe that being filled with the Holy Spirit actually gives us physical energy.

Many times I have been quickened by the Holy Spirit and have suddenly gone from being extremely tired to feeling as though I could run around the city. This is a good reason to keep ourselves filled with the Holy Spirit; we need all the energy we can get! I firmly believe we can make ourselves feel drained by the way we think and talk. Likewise, we can help ourselves feel energetic by following biblical guidelines for everyday living.

It seems that most people in the world today are tired. Part of their fatigue comes from being too busy, but another large part of it is due to the way they live—how they think, talk, and act toward other people.

The Holy Spirit will not energize us to be mean, hateful, selfish, or self-centered. He will give us strength and energy to do the things God has called us to do and to be kind, loving, diligent, and focused in the process.

²³It is He who reduces dignitaries to
nothing,
Who makes the judges (rulers) of
the earth meaningless (useless).
²⁴Scarcely have they been planted,
Scarcely have they been sown,
Scarcely has their stock taken root
in the earth,
But He merely blows on them, and
they wither,
And a strong wind carries them
away like stubble.
²⁵"To whom then will you compare Me
That I would be his equal?" says
the Holy One.
²⁶Lift up your eyes on high
And see who has created these
heavenly bodies,
The One who brings out their host
by number,
He calls them all by name;
Because of the greatness of His
might and the strength of His
power,
Not one is missing.

²⁷Why, O Jacob, do you say, and
declare, O Israel,
"My way is hidden from the LORD,
And the justice due me escapes the
notice of my God"?
²⁸Do you not know? Have you not
heard?

life point

Quietly waiting on God (spending time alone with Him in prayer, worship, or Bible reading), as Isaiah 40:31 encourages us, does more to restore our bodies, minds, and emotions than anything else we can do. We need to do this regularly. I urge you to insist on quiet time with God; do not let anyone take those consecrated moments from you. In those times, God empowers you to face everything you need to do with renewed physical, emotional, mental, and spiritual strength.

The Everlasting God, the LORD, the
Creator of the ends of the earth
Does not become tired or grow
weary;
There is no searching of His
understanding.
[29] He gives strength to the weary,
And to him who has no might He
increases power. [2 Cor 12:9]
[30] Even youths grow weary and tired,
And vigorous young men stumble
badly,

[31] But those who wait for the LORD
[who expect, look for, and hope
in Him]
Will gain new strength *and* renew
their power;
They will lift up their wings [and
rise up close to God] like eagles
[rising toward the sun];
They will run and not become
weary,
They will walk and not grow tired.
[Heb 12:1–3]

waiting on God

Isaiah 40:31 teaches us that waiting on God is expecting, looking for, and hoping in Him. It is spending time with Him in His Word and in His presence. We do not worry while we wait on God; we do not get frustrated while we wait on God; we do not get upset while we wait on God. We rest.

Sometimes when you start to get nervous and upset, anxious, or worried, you just need to tell yourself, "Sit down." That does not mean just your physical body; it also means your soul—your mind, will, and emotions. It is important to let your entire being rest.

Under the Old Covenant, when the high priest went into the Holy of Holies to make blood sacrifices for the sins of the people, he did not sit down. It seems unlikely that there was a chair in there because the Bible does not mention it, even though it offers detailed descriptions of the Israelites' place of worship. The requirements on the high priest were so stringent that he did what he had to do and left. He could not rest in the presence of God.

I have been told that the high priest wore bells on his robe and had a rope tied to his waist. As he moved around the Holy of Holies, people outside could hear the bells. If the bells stopped ringing, the people knew he had done something wrong and had died, so they pulled him out by the rope.

There is such a lesson in that. It teaches us that people could not rest in God's presence under the Old Covenant. The Old Covenant had many laws and was based on works. But thank God, the New Covenant is based on the work Jesus has accomplished, not on our own merits or works.

Jesus, our High Priest Who went into the Holy of Holies with His own blood, put it on the mercy seat in heaven, and sat down. Now the atonement for the sins of the world is finished.

If you are struggling in your life, take a seat and rest in God's presence. The promise of God's peace is not made to those who work and struggle in their own strength but to those who sit and rest in Christ Jesus. Wait on Him, and your strength will be renewed.

41

"LISTEN TO Me in silence, you islands *and* coastlands,
And let the nations gain their strength;
Let them come near, then let them speak;
Let us come together for judgment [and decide the issue between us concerning the enemy from the east].

2 "Who has stirred up *and* put into action one from the east [the king of Persia, Cyrus the Great]
Whom He calls in righteousness to His service *and* whom victory meets at every step?
The LORD turns nations over to him
And subdues kings.
He makes them like dust with his sword,
Like wind-driven chaff with his bow. [Ezra 1:2]

3 "He (Cyrus) pursues them and passes along safely,
By a way his feet had not traveled before.

4 "Who has performed and done this,
Calling forth [and guiding the destinies of] the generations [of the nations] from the beginning?
'I, the LORD—the first, and with the last [existing before history began, the ever-present, unchanging God]—I am He.'"

5 The islands *and* coastlands have seen and they fear;
The ends of the earth tremble;
They have drawn near and have come.

6 They each help his neighbor
And say to his brother [as he fashions his idols], "Be of good courage!"

7 So the craftsman encourages the goldsmith,
And he who smooths *metal* with the smith's hammer *encourages* him who beats the anvil,
Saying of the soldering (welding), "That is good";
And he fastens the idol with nails,
So that it will not totter *nor* be moved.

8 "But you, Israel, My servant,
Jacob whom I have chosen,
The offspring of Abraham My friend, [Heb 2:16; James 2:23]

9 You whom I [the LORD] have taken from the ends of the earth,
And called from its remotest parts
And said to you, 'You are My servant,
I have chosen you and have not rejected you [even though you are exiled].

10 'Do not fear [anything], for I am with you;
Do not be afraid, for I am your God.
I will strengthen you, be assured I will help you;
I will certainly take hold of you with My righteous right hand [a hand of justice, of power, of victory, of salvation].' [Acts 18:10]

11 "Indeed, all those who are angry with you will be put to shame and humiliated;
Those who strive against you will be as nothing and will perish.

12 "You shall search for those who quarrel with you, but will not find them;
They who war against you will be as nothing, as nothing at all.

life point

If there is something we are supposed to be doing, the Lord will give us the ability to do it. He will not lead us into a situation and then leave us there to face it alone in our own weak, human power. No, because as Isaiah 41:10 reminds us, He is with us. He is our great God; He will help us, and take hold of us with His hand of justice, power, victory, and salvation.

13 "For I the LORD your God keep hold
of your right hand; [I am the
Lord],
Who says to you, 'Do not fear, I
will help you.'
14 "Do not fear, you worm Jacob, you
men of Israel;
I will help you," declares the LORD,
"and your Redeemer is the Holy
One of Israel.
15 "In fact, I have made of you a new,
sharp threshing implement with
sharp edges;
You will thresh the mountains and
crush them,
And make the hills like chaff.
16 "You will winnow them, and the
wind will carry them away,
And a high wind will scatter them;
But you will rejoice in the LORD,
You will glory in the Holy One of
Israel.
17 "The poor and needy are seeking
water, but there is none;
Their tongues are parched with
thirst.
I, the LORD, will answer them
Myself;
I, the God of Israel, will not neglect
them.
18 "I will open rivers on the barren
heights
And springs in the midst of the
valleys;
I will make the wilderness a reed-
pool of water
And the dry land springs of water.
19 "I will put the cedar in the
wilderness,
The acacia, the myrtle and the
olive tree;
I will place the juniper in the desert
Together with the box tree and the
cypress,
20 So that they may see and know,
And consider and understand
together,
That the hand of the LORD has done
this,

That the Holy One of Israel has
created it.
21 "Present your case [for idols made
by men's hands]," says the LORD.
"Produce your evidence [of
divinity],"
Says the king of Jacob.
22 Let them bring forward [their
evidence] and tell us what is
going to happen.
Regarding the former events, tell
what they were,
That we may consider them and
know their outcome;
Or announce to us the things that
are going to come.
23 Tell us the things that are to come
afterward,
That we may know that you are
gods;
Indeed, you should do *something*
good or do evil, that we may be
afraid and fear [you] together [as
we observe the miracle].
24 Hear this! You [idols] are less than
nothing,
And your work is worthless;
The worshiper who chooses you
[as a god] is repulsive. [1 Cor 8:4]
25 "I have stirred up *and* put into
action one from the north [the
king of Persia, Cyrus the Great],
and he has come;
From the rising of the sun he will
call on My Name [in prayer].
And he will trample on [the
Babylonian] officials as on
mortar,
Even as a potter treads clay."
[2 Chr 36:23; Ezra 1:1–3]
26 Who [among the idols] has
declared this from the beginning,
so that we could know?
Or from earlier times, so
that we could say, "*He is*
[unquestionably] right!"?
In fact, there was no one who
declared it,

Indeed, there was no one who
  proclaimed it;
There was no one at all who heard
  you speak [for you pagan gods
  are speechless].
27 "I was first to say to Zion, 'Listen
  carefully, here they are [the Jews
  who will be restored to their own
  land].'
And to Jerusalem, 'I will provide a
  messenger (Isaiah) to bring the
  good news [that Cyrus will be
  stirred up *and* put into action to
  save them].' [Is 40:9; 52:7]
28 "But when I look [on the pagan
  prophets and priests], there is
  no one [who could predict these
  events],
And there is no counselor among
  them,
Who, if I ask, can give an answer.

29 "In fact, all of these [pagan
  prophets and priests] are false;
Their works are worthless,
Their cast images are [merely]
  wind and emptiness.

42 "BEHOLD, MY Servant,
  whom I uphold;
  My Chosen One *in whom*
My soul delights.
I have put My Spirit upon Him;
He will bring forth justice to the
  nations. [Matt 3:16, 17]
2 "He will not call out or shout aloud,
Nor make His voice heard in the
  street.
3 "A broken reed He will not break
  [off]
And a dimly burning wick He will
  not extinguish [He will not harm
  those who are weak and suffering];

God declares new things

In Isaiah 42:9 God speaks to His people and declares new things before they happen. If you are like I am, you may be ready and waiting for some new things in your life. You need some changes, and those changes may be coming soon.

Even though I know the principles I am about to share with you, I too need to be reminded of them occasionally. Sometimes we all need to be "stirred up" in things we already know. That encourages us to begin operating once again in powerful principles that we have let slip away.

If you are tired of the old things, then stop speaking the old things. Do you want some new things? Then start speaking some new things. Spend some time with God. Set aside some special time to study His Word. Find out what His will is for your life. Do not let the devil push you around anymore.

Find out what God's Word promises you, and begin to declare the end from the beginning. Instead of saying, "Nothing will ever change," say, "God is making changes in my life and circumstances every day."

I heard the story of a doctor who was not a believer but who had discovered the power of the principle I am sharing with you. His prescription to his patients was to go home and repeat several times daily: "I am getting better and better every day." He had such marvelous results that people traveled from all over the world to avail themselves of his services. How much better, then, is it when we say God's Word in anticipation of the new thing He says He is going to do. Remember, unlike the words of man, God's Word is eternal and true; it does not return to Him void: "Indeed, the former things have come to pass, now I declare new things" (Isaiah 42:9).

He will faithfully bring forth
justice. [Matt 12:17–21]
4 "He will not be disheartened or
crushed [in spirit];
[He will persevere] until He has
established justice on the earth;
And the coastlands will wait
expectantly for His law." [Rom
8:22–25]

5 This is what God the LORD says,

He who created the heavens and
stretched them out,
Who spread out the earth and its
produce,
Who gives breath to the people on it
And spirit to those who walk on it,
6 "I am the LORD, I have called You
(the Messiah) in righteousness
[for a righteous purpose],
I will also take You by the hand
and keep watch over You,
And I will appoint You as a
covenant to the people [Israel],
As a light to the nations (Gentiles),
7 To open the eyes of the blind,
To bring out prisoners from the
dungeon
And those who sit in darkness
from the prison. [Matt 12:18–21]
8 "I am the LORD, that is My Name;
My glory I will not give to another,
Nor My praise to carved idols.
9 "Indeed, the former things have
come to pass,
Now I declare new things;
Before they spring forth I proclaim
them to you."

10 Sing to the LORD a new song,
Sing His praise from the end of the
earth!
You who go down to the sea, and
all that is in it,
You islands and coastlands, and
those who inhabit them [sing His
praise]!
11 Let the wilderness and its cities lift
up their voices,
The villages where Kedar lives.

Let the inhabitants of Sela shout
for joy,
Let them shout joyfully from the
tops of the mountains.
12 Let them give glory to the LORD
And declare His praise in the
islands and coastlands.
13 The LORD will go forth like a
warrior,
He will stir up His zeal like a man
of war;
He will shout out, yes, He will
raise a war cry.
He will prevail [mightily] against
His enemies.

14 "I [the LORD] have been silent for a
long time,
I have been still and restrained
Myself.
Now I will moan like a woman in
labor,
I will both gasp and pant.
15 "I will lay waste the mountains
and hills
And wither all their vegetation;
I will turn the rivers into
coastlands
And dry up the ponds.
16 "I will lead the blind by a way they
do not know;
I will guide them in paths that they
do not know.
I will make darkness into light
before them
And rugged places into plains.

life point

Many people have 20/20 vision in their
physical eyes, but they are spiritually blind.
If you feel that you are just stumbling
around in the darkness and do not know
what to do, I encourage you to take the
promise from God in Isaiah 42:16 for yourself. God wants to turn your darkness into
light. He has determined to do good for
you, and He will not leave you abandoned.

These things I will do [for them],
And I will not leave them
  abandoned *or* undone."
¹⁷ Those who trust in carved idols
  will be turned back,
And utterly put to shame,
Who say to cast images,
"You are our gods."

¹⁸ Hear, you deaf!
And look, you blind, that you may
  see.
¹⁹ Who is blind but My servant
  [Israel],
Or deaf like My messenger whom I
  send?
Who is blind like the one who is
  at peace *with Me* [in a covenant
  relationship],
Or so blind as the servant of the
  LORD?
²⁰ You have seen many things, but
  you do not observe them;
Your ears are open, but no one
  hears.
²¹ The LORD was pleased for His
  righteousness' sake
To make the law great and prove
  to be glorious.
²² But this is a people despoiled and
  plundered;
All of them are trapped in holes,
Or are hidden away in prisons.
They have become a prey with no
  one to rescue them,
And a spoil, with no one to say,
  "Give them back!" [Luke 19:41–44]

²³ Who among you will listen to this?
Who will listen and pay attention
  in the time to come?
²⁴ Who gave up Jacob [the kingdom
  of Judah] for spoil, and [the
  kingdom of] Israel to the
  plunderers?

Was it not the LORD, He against
  whom we [of Judah] have
  sinned,
And in whose ways they [of Israel]
  were unwilling to walk,
And whose law *and* teaching they
  did not obey?
²⁵ Therefore He poured out on Israel
  the heat of His anger
And the fierceness of battle;
And engulfed him in fire,
Yet he did not recognize [the
  lesson of repentance which the
  Assyrian conquest was intended
  to teach];
It burned him, but he did not take
  it to heart.

43 BUT NOW, this is what
the LORD, your Creator
says, O Jacob,
And He who formed you, O Israel,
"Do not fear, for I have redeemed
  you [from captivity];
I have called you by name; you are
  Mine!
² "When you pass through the
  waters, I will be with you;
And through the rivers, they will
  not overwhelm you.
When you walk through fire, you
  will not be scorched,
Nor will the flame burn you.
³ "For I am the LORD your God,
The Holy One of Israel, your
  Savior;
I have given Egypt [to the
  Babylonians] as your ransom,
Cush (ancient Ethiopia) and Seba
  [its province] in exchange for
  you.
⁴ "Because you are precious in My
  sight,
You are honored and I love you,

speak the Word

Thank You, God, for redeeming me and for calling me by name. I am Yours!
–ADAPTED FROM ISAIAH 43:1

I will give *other* men in return
  for you and *other* peoples in
  exchange for your life.
⁵"Do not fear, for I am with you;
I will bring your offspring
  from the east [where they are
  scattered],
And gather you from the west. [Acts
  18:10]
⁶"I will say to the north, 'Give them
  up!'

And to the south, 'Do not hold them
  back.'
Bring My sons from far way
And My daughters from the ends
  of the earth,
⁷Everyone who is called by My
  Name,
Whom I have created for My glory,
Whom I have formed, even whom
  I have made."

through it all

In Isaiah 43:2, God tells us He will be with us as we go through the water and through the fire. This means we will have to face some tests and trials in our lives; they cannot be avoided. We will have to go through some difficult things.

I do not know what specific form your challenges may take, but I know they are intended to strengthen you, to develop your character, to cause you to persevere, to sanctify you, to purify you, to teach you the unique lessons of suffering, to teach you the benefits and disciplines of sacrifice, and to make you a better person. You may cringe as you think about these things, but if you really want to fulfill your potential, you simply must be prepared to go through them.

I have been through many tests and trials. I have faced loneliness, obstacles, and persecution. There have been times when I wanted to give up, and in the midst of those times, God often put someone in my life I did not particularly like or want to deal with. I now know that He placed those people near me because I needed them. He used them to be the sandpaper that was needed to smooth my rough edges.

Has God put someone or something in your life as sandpaper? That situation may feel like a flood or a fire to you, but it is serving a great purpose, and God is going to take you through the difficulty to the other side. He is going to use it to strengthen you, change you, and advance His purpose for your life.

God must take us through hard things because He must change us in order to use us. We must become like Jesus in our character; we must follow His example and walk in His ways. Gifts are given to us by God, but good fruit and godly character must be developed.

I struggled with the process of change for a long time, but finally realized that I was not going to succeed in getting God to do things my way. He did not want to hear an argument from me; He wanted to hear, "Yes, Lord. Your will be done."

We will always face obstacles and difficulties—"floods and fires"—as God continues to strengthen us and prepare us to be used in His service in greater and greater ways. We would be wise to settle down and deal with the challenges He puts before us. Whatever they are, if we will receive them as His training for us and submit to His will, we will not get stuck, but we will go through to victory.

⁸Bring out the people who are blind,
   even though they have eyes,
And the deaf, even though they
   have ears.
⁹All the nations have gathered
   together
So that the peoples may be
   assembled.
Who among them (the idolaters)
   can predict this [that Judah
   would return from captivity]
And proclaim to us the former
   events?
Let them provide their witnesses
   so that they may be justified,
Or let them hear and say [in
   acknowledgement], "It is the
   truth." [Ps 123:3, 4]
¹⁰"You are My witnesses," declares
   the LORD,
"And My servant whom I have
   chosen,
That you may know and believe Me
And understand that I am He.
Before Me there was no God
   formed,
And there will be none after Me.
¹¹"I, [only] I, am the LORD,
And there is no Savior besides Me.
¹²"I have declared [the future] and
   saved [the nation] and proclaimed
   [that I am God],
And there was no strange (alien)
   god among you;
Therefore you are My witnesses
   [among the pagans]," declares
   the LORD,
"That I am God.
¹³"Even from eternity I am He,
And there is no one who can
   rescue from My hand;
I act, and who can revoke *or*
   reverse it?"

¹⁴This is what the LORD your Redeemer, the Holy One of Israel says,

"For your sake I have sent [one] to
   Babylon,

And I will bring down all of them
   as fugitives,
Even the Chaldeans [who reign
   in Babylon], into the ships over
   which they rejoiced.
¹⁵"I am the LORD, your Holy One,
The Creator of Israel, your King."
¹⁶This is what the LORD says,

He who makes a way through the
   sea
And a path through the mighty
   waters,
¹⁷He who brings out the chariot and
   the horse,
The army and the mighty *warrior,*
(They will lie down together, they
   will not rise again;
They have been extinguished,
   they have been put out like a
   lamp's wick):

life point

Careful consideration of Isaiah 43:18, 19 seems to indicate that you and I can choose to cooperate with God's plan or not. We can even choose to ignore it, for He says, "Will you not be aware of it?"

We can release God's plan for our lives by no longer thinking about the things of the past, believing that God has a good plan for our future. Since what we think about eventually comes out of our mouths, we will never get our mouths straightened out unless we do something about our thoughts.

I believe that if we stop living in the past mentally, we can begin to think in agreement with God. Then once we do that, we can begin to speak in agreement with Him. By so doing we can actually prophesy our own future.

If God can make a road in the wilderness and rivers in the desert, He can make a way for you.

¹⁸"Do not remember the former
things,
Or ponder the things of the past.
¹⁹"Listen carefully, I am about to do
a new thing,
Now it will spring forth;
Will you not be aware of it?
I will even put a road in the
wilderness,
Rivers in the desert.
²⁰"The beasts of the field will honor
Me,
Jackals and ostriches,
Because I have given waters in the
wilderness
And rivers in the desert,
To give drink to My people, My
chosen. [Is 41:17, 18; 48:21]
²¹"The people whom I formed for
Myself
Will make known My praise.

²²"Yet you have not called on Me [in
prayer and worship], O Jacob;
But you have grown weary of Me,
O Israel.
²³"You have not brought Me your
sheep *or* goats for your burnt
offerings,
Nor honored Me with your
sacrifices.
I have not burdened you with
offerings,
Nor wearied you with [demands
for offerings of] incense.
²⁴"You have not bought Me sweet
cane with money,
Nor have you filled Me with the fat
of your sacrifices;
But you have burdened Me with
your sins,
You have wearied Me with your
wickedness.

²⁵"I, *only* I, am He who wipes out your
transgressions for My own sake,
And I will not remember your sins.
²⁶"Remind Me [of your merits with
a thorough report], let us plead
and argue our case together;
State your *position,* that you may
be proved right.
²⁷"Your first father [Jacob] sinned,
And your spokesmen [the
priests and the prophets—your
mediators] have transgressed
against Me.
²⁸"So I will profane the officials of
the sanctuary,
And I will consign Jacob to
destruction and [I will subject]
Israel to defamation *and* abuse.

44 "BUT NOW listen, O
Jacob, My servant,
And Israel, whom I have
chosen:
²This is what the LORD who made
you
And formed you from the womb,
who will help you says,
'Fear not, O Jacob My servant;
And Jeshurun (Israel, the upright
one) whom I have chosen. [Deut
32:15; 33:5, 26]
³'For I will pour out water on him
who is thirsty,
And streams on the dry ground;
I will pour out My Spirit on your
offspring
And My blessing on your
descendants; [Is 32:15; 35:6, 7;
Joel 2:28; John 7:37–39]
⁴And they will spring up among the
grass
Like willows by the streams of
water.'

speak the Word

*Thank You, God, for wiping out my transgressions
and for forgetting my sins completely.*
–ADAPTED FROM ISAIAH 43:25

5"One will say, 'I am the Lord's';
And another will name himself
    after Jacob;
And another will write on his
    hand, 'I am the Lord's,'
And be called by the [honorable]
    name of Israel.

6"For the Lord, the King of Israel and
his Redeemer, the Lord of hosts says
this,

'I am the First and I am the Last;
And there is no God besides Me.
    [Rev 1:17; 2:8; 22:13]
7'Who is like Me? Let him proclaim
    it and declare it;
Yes, let him confront Me,
Since I established the people of
    antiquity.
And let them [those supposed
    gods] tell those people [who
    foolishly follow them] the things
    to come
And the events that are going to
    take place.
8'Do not tremble nor be afraid [of
    the violent upheavals to come];
Have I not long ago proclaimed it
    to you and declared it?
And you are My witnesses.
Is there a God besides Me?
There is no *other* Rock;
I know of none.'"

9All who make carved idols are nothing. Their precious objects are worthless [to them], and their own witnesses
(worshipers) fail to see or know, so
that they will be put to shame.
10Who has made a god or cast an idol
which is profitable for nothing?
11In fact, all his companions will be
put to shame, for the craftsmen themselves are mere men. Let them all assemble, let them stand up, let them be
terrified, let them together be put to
shame.
12The ironsmith shapes iron *and*
uses a chisel and works it over the
coals. He forms the [idol's] core with

hammers and works it with his strong
arm. He also becomes hungry and his
strength fails; he drinks no water and
grows tired.
13The carpenter stretches out a measuring line, he marks out the shape
[of the idol] with red chalk; he works
it with planes and outlines it with the
compass; and he makes it like the form
of a man, like the beauty of man, that
it may sit in a house.
14He cuts cedars for himself, and
takes a cypress or an oak and lets it
grow strong for himself among the
trees of the forest. He plants a fir, and
the rain nourishes it.
15Then it becomes *fuel* for a man
to burn, so he takes one of them and
warms himself; he also kindles a fire
to bake bread. He also makes a god
[from the same wood] and worships
it. He makes it into a carved idol [with
his own hands] and falls down and
worships it!
16He burns half of the wood in the
fire; over this half he [cooks and] eats
meat, he roasts meat and is satisfied.
Also he warms himself and says,
"Aha! I am warm, I have seen the fire."
17But from what is left of the wood
he makes a god, his carved idol. He
falls down before it, he worships it and
prays to it and says, "Save me, for you
are my god."
18They do not know, nor do they understand, for God has muddied their
eyes so that they cannot see, and their
hearts (minds) *as well* so that they
cannot understand.
19No one remembers, nor has knowledge and understanding [enough] to
say [to himself], "I have burned half
of this log in the fire, and also baked
bread on its coals and have roasted
meat and eaten it. Then I make the
rest of it into an repulsive thing [to
God]; I bow down [to worship] before
a block of wood!"
20That kind of man (the idolater)

feeds on ashes [and is satisfied with ashes]! A deceived mind has led him astray, so that he cannot save himself, or ask, "Is this thing [that I am holding] in my right hand not a lie?"

21"Remember [the foolishness of] these things, O Jacob
And Israel, for you are My servant!
I formed you, you are My servant;
O Israel, you will not be forgotten by Me.
22"I have wiped out your transgressions like a thick cloud
And your sins like a heavy mist.
Return to Me, for I have redeemed you."
23Shout for joy, O heavens, for the LORD has done it!
Shout in triumph, you depths of the earth;
Break forth into jubilant rejoicing, you mountains,
O forest, and every tree in it!
For the LORD has redeemed Jacob,
And He shows His glory in Israel.

24For the LORD, your Redeemer, and He who formed you from the womb says this,

"I am the LORD, Maker of all things,
Who alone stretches out the heavens,
Who spreads out the earth by Myself,
25Frustrating the signs and confounding the omens of boasters (false prophets),
Making fools out of fortune-tellers,
Counteracting the wise
And making their knowledge ridiculous, [1 Cor 1:20]
26Confirming the word of His servant
And carrying out the plan of His messengers.
It is I who says of Jerusalem, 'She shall [again] be inhabited!'
And of the cities of Judah, 'They shall [again] be built.'

And I will raise up and restore her ruins.
27"It is I who says to the deep, 'Be dried up!'
And I will make your rivers dry.
28"It is I who says of Cyrus, 'He is My shepherd (ruler),
And he will carry out all that I desire—'
Saying of Jerusalem, 'She shall [again] be built,'
And of the temple, 'Your foundation shall [again] be laid.'"

45 THIS IS what the LORD says to His anointed, to Cyrus [king of Persia],
Whose right hand I have held
To subdue nations before him,
And I will ungird the loins of kings [disarming them];
To open doors before him so that gates will not be shut:
2"I will go before you and level the mountains;
I will shatter the doors of bronze and cut through the bars of iron.
3"I will give you the treasures of darkness [the hoarded treasures]
And the hidden riches of secret places,
So that you may know that it is I,
The LORD, the God of Israel, who calls you (Cyrus the Great) by your name.
4"For the sake of Jacob My servant,
And of Israel My chosen,
I have also called you by your name;
I have given you an honorable name
Though you have not known Me.
5"I am the LORD, and there is no one else;
There is no God except Me.
I will embrace and arm you, though you have not known Me,
6That people may know from the rising to the setting of the sun [the world over]
That there is no one except Me.

I am the Lord, and there is no
other,
7 The One forming light and
creating darkness,
Causing peace and creating disaster;
I am the Lord who does all these
things.

8 "Rain down, O heavens, from above,
Let the clouds pour down
righteousness [all the blessings
of God];
Let the earth open up, let salvation
bear fruit,
And righteousness spring up with it;
I, the Lord, have created it.

9 "Woe (judgment is coming) to him
who quarrels with his Maker—
A [worthless] piece of broken
pottery among other broken
pieces [equally worthless]!
Shall the clay say to the potter,
'What are you doing?'
Or does the thing say, 'He has no
hands'? [Rom 9:20]
10 "Woe (judgment is coming) to him
who says to a father, 'What are
you fathering?'
Or to a woman, 'With what are you
in labor?'"

11 For the Lord, the Holy One of Israel, and its Maker says this,

"Ask Me about the things to come
concerning My sons,
And give Me orders concerning
the work of My hands.
12 "I made the earth and created man
upon it.
My hands, stretched out the
heavens,
And I commanded all their host.
13 "I have stirred up Cyrus and put
him into action in righteousness
[to accomplish My purpose]
And I will make all his ways smooth;
He will build My city and let My
exiles go,

Without any payment or reward,"
says the Lord of hosts.

14 For this is what the Lord says,

"The products of Egypt and the
merchandise of Cush (ancient
Ethiopia)
And the Sabeans, men of stature,
Will come over to you and they
will be yours;
They will walk behind you, in
chains [of subjection to you] they
will come over,
And they will bow down before you;
They will make supplication to you,
[humbly and earnestly] saying,
'Most certainly God is with you,
and there is no other,
No other God [besides Him].'"
[1 Cor 14:25]
15 Truly, You are a God who hides
Himself,
O God of Israel, Savior!
16 They will be put to shame and also
humiliated, all of them;
They who make idols will go away
together in humiliation.
17 Israel has been saved by the Lord
With an everlasting salvation;
You will not be put to shame or
humiliated
for all eternity. [Heb 5:9]

18 For the Lord, who created the heavens (He is God, who formed the earth
and made it; He established it and did
not create it to be a wasteland, but
formed it to be inhabited) says this,

"I am the Lord, and there is no one
else.
19 "I have not spoken in secret,
In a corner of a land of darkness;
I did not say to the descendants of
Jacob,
'Seek Me in vain [with no benefit
for yourselves].'

I, the LORD, speak righteousness
[the truth—trustworthy, a
straightforward correlation
between deeds and words],
Declaring things that are upright.
[John 18:20]

20 "Assemble yourselves and come;
Come together, you survivors of
the nations!
They are ignorant,
Who carry around their wooden
idols [in religious processions or
into battle]
And keep on praying to a god that
cannot save them.
21 "Declare and present *your defense of
idols;*
Indeed, let them consult together.
Who announced this [rise of Cyrus
and his conquests] long before *it
happened?*
Who declared it long ago?
Was it not I, the LORD?
And there is no other God besides
Me,
A [consistently and
uncompromisingly] just *and*
righteous God and a Savior;
There is none except Me.
22 "Turn to Me and be saved, all the
ends of the earth;
For I am God, and there is no other.
23 "I have sworn [an oath] by Myself,
The word is gone out of My mouth
in righteousness
And shall not return,
That to Me every knee shall
bow, every tongue shall swear
[allegiance]. [Rom 14:11; Phil
2:10, 11; Heb 6:13]
24 "It shall be said of Me, 'Only in
the LORD are righteousness and
strength.'
To Him people will come,
And all who were angry at Him will
be put to shame. [1 Cor 1:30, 31]
25 "In the LORD all the offspring of
Israel

Will be justified (declared free of
guilt) and will glory [in God]."

46 BEL HAS bowed down,
Nebo stoops over;
Their idols are on the
beasts [of burden] and on the
cattle.
Your burdens [of idols] are loaded
[on them],
Burdens on the weary *animals.*
2 They stooped over, they have
bowed down together;
They could not rescue the burden
[of their own idols],
But have themselves gone into
captivity.

3 "Listen to Me," [says the LORD], "O
house of Jacob,
And all the remnant of the house
of Israel,
You who have been carried *by Me*
from your birth
And have been carried [in My
arms] from the womb,
4 Even to *your* old age I am He,
And even to *your* advanced old age
I will carry you!
I have made *you,* and I will carry
you;
Be assured I will carry *you* and I
will save *you.*

5 "To whom would you liken Me
And make Me equal and compare
Me,
That we may be alike? [Is 40:18–20]
6 "Those who lavish gold from the
bag
And weigh out silver on the scales
Hire a goldsmith, and he makes it
into a god;
They bow down, indeed they
worship it.
7 "They lift it on their shoulders
[in religious processions or into
battle] and carry it;
They set it in its place and *there* it
remains standing.

It cannot move from its place.
Even if one cries to it [for help],
  the idol cannot answer;
It cannot save him from his
  distress.

8 "Remember this, and take courage;
Take it to heart, you rebellious *and*
  disloyal people.
9 "Remember [carefully] the former
  things [which I did] from ages
  past;
For I am God, and there is no one
  else;
I am God, and there is no one like
  Me,
10 Declaring the end *and* the result
  from the beginning,
And from ancient times the things
  which have not [yet] been done,
Saying, 'My purpose will be
  established,

And I will do all that pleases Me
  and fulfills My purpose,'
11 Calling a bird of prey from the
  east,
From a far country, the man
  (Cyrus) of My purpose.
Truly I have spoken; truly I will
  bring it to pass.
I have planned it, *be assured* I will
  do it.

12 "Listen to Me, you stiff-necked
  people,
You who are far from
  righteousness (right standing
  with God).
13 "I bring near My righteousness [in
  the salvation of Israel], it is not
  far away;
And My salvation will not delay.
And I will grant salvation in Zion,
And My glory for Israel.

life point

In Isaiah 46:9, 10 the Lord says that He is the same God Who has helped us in the past; He is able to declare in the beginning how things will turn out in the end.

The Word says the Lord is the Alpha and Omega, the Beginning and the End (see Revelation 1:8). He is also everything in between. He knows before trouble ever shows up that we can be victorious if we fight the battle His way. His way is not a negative way, but a good and right way. God already has an answer before we have a problem.

Romans 8:37 affirms that we are "more than conquerors . . . through Him who loved us [so much that He died for us]." I believe that means we can know we will win before the battle even begins. Through Him we can see the end from the beginning, and we know that victory is sure.

life point

We learn in Isaiah 46:10 that God knows the beginning from the end of all things. He already knows what our thoughts are, and He already hears every word we will speak. He is acquainted with all our ways (see Psalm 139:1–4). Sometimes we act as though God is shocked to discover that we make mistakes. We need to remember that He is not in heaven wringing His hands, saying, "Oh, no! I had no idea you would act this way when I chose you!" God has a big eraser, and He uses it to keep our records clear and clean. Even with His foreknowledge of our weaknesses and mistakes, He still chose us on purpose and brought us into relationship with Himself through Jesus Christ. When you make a mistake, relax. God knew long ago what you would do and He has provided full forgiveness for you through His Son.

47

"COME DOWN and sit in
the dust,
O virgin daughter of
Babylon;
Sit on the ground [in abject
humiliation]; there is no throne
for you,
O daughter of the Chaldeans,
For you will no longer be called
tender and delicate.
2 "Take millstones [as a female slave
does] and grind meal;
Remove your veil, strip off the skirt,
Uncover the leg, cross the rivers [at
the command of your captors].
3 "Your nakedness will be
uncovered,
Your shame will also be exposed;
I will take vengeance and will
spare no man."
4 Our Redeemer [will do all this],
the Lord of hosts is His name,
The Holy One of Israel.
5 "Sit in silence, and go into
darkness,
O daughter of the Chaldeans;
For you will no longer be called
The queen of kingdoms.
6 "I was angry with My people,
I profaned [Judah] My inheritance
And gave them into your hand
[Babylon].
You showed them no mercy;
You made your yoke very heavy on
the aged.
7 "And you said, 'I shall be a queen
forevermore.'
You did not consider these things,
Nor did you [seriously] remember
the [ultimate] outcome of such
conduct.

8 "Now, then, hear this, you who live
a luxuriant life,
You who dwell safely *and* securely,
Who say in your heart (mind),
'I am [the queen], and there is no
one besides me.
I shall not sit as a widow,
Nor know the loss of children.'

9 "But these two things shall come to
you abruptly, in one day:
Loss of children and widowhood.
They will come on you in full
measure
In spite of your many [claims of
power through your] sorceries,
In spite of the great power of your
enchantments. [Rev 18:7, 8]
10 "For you [Babylon] have trusted
and felt confident in your
wickedness; you have said,
'No one sees me.'
Your wisdom and your knowledge
have led you astray,
And you have said in your heart
(mind),
'I am, and there is no one besides
me.'
11 "Therefore disaster will come on
you;
You will not know how to make it
disappear [with your magic].
And disaster will fall on you
For which you cannot atone [with
all your offerings to your gods];
And destruction about which you
do not know
Will come on you suddenly.

12 "Persist, then, [Babylon] in your
enchantments
And your many sorceries
With which you have labored from
your youth;
Perhaps you will be able to profit
[from them],
Perhaps you may prevail *and* cause
trembling.
13 "You are wearied by your many
counsels.
Just let the astrologers,
The stargazers,
Those who predict by the new
moons [each month]
Stand up and save you from the
things that will come upon you
[Babylon].
14 "In fact, they are like stubble;
Fire burns them.

They cannot save themselves from
the power of the flame [much
less save the nation],
There is no blazing coal for
warming
Nor fire before which to sit!
15 "This is how they have become
to you, those [astrologers and
sorcerers] with whom you have
labored,
Those who have done business
with you from your youth;
Each has wandered in his own way.
There is no one to save you.

48 "HEAR THIS, O house of
Jacob, you who are called
by the name of Israel
And who come from the seed of
Judah,
You who swear [allegiance] by the
name of the LORD
And invoke the God of Israel,
But not in truth (sincerity) nor in
righteousness [with moral and
spiritual integrity].
2 "For they call themselves [citizens
of Jerusalem] after the holy city
And depend on the God of Israel;
The LORD of hosts is His name.
3 "I have declared the former things
[which happened to Israel] in
times past;
They went forth from My mouth
and I proclaimed them;
Suddenly I acted, and they came to
pass.
4 "Because I know that you are
obstinate,
And your neck is an iron tendon
And your brow is bronze [both
unyielding],
5 I have declared them to you long
ago;
Before they came to pass I
announced them to you,
So that you could not say, 'My idol
has done them,

life point

Notice the basic principle of God's method
of operation: first He declares things; then
He does them (see Isaiah 48:3).

This principle explains why God sent
the prophets. They spoke God-inspired,
God-instructed words that brought forth
God's will from the spiritual realm into
the natural realm. Jesus did not come to
earth until first the prophets had spoken
about Him for hundreds of years. God
operates on spiritual laws He has set in
place, and we cannot ignore them.

"Sowing and reaping" is an example of
a law that operates in the natural realm,
but it also operates in the spiritual realm.
We sow material seed, and we reap
material blessings of all kinds. Words are
also seeds. We sow word seeds and reap
according to what we have sown.

God wanted stubborn Israel to know that
it was He Who was doing great works in
their lives, so He announced them ahead
of time. What was the end result? The
things God declared came to pass. His
Word is always true, and He always does
what He says He will do.

And my carved image and my cast
image have commanded them.'
6 "You have heard [these things
foretold]; look at all this [that has
been fulfilled].
And you, will you not declare it?
I proclaim to you [specific] new
things from this time,
Even hidden things which you
have not known.
7 "They are created now [called into
being by the prophetic word]
and not long ago;
And before today you have not
heard of them,

So that you will not say, 'Oh yes! I
    knew them.'
8 "You have not heard, you have not
    known;
Even from long ago your ear has
    not been open.
For I [the LORD] knew that
    you [Israel] would act very
    treacherously;
You have been called a transgressor
    and a rebel from birth.
9 "For the sake of My Name I refrain
    from My wrath,
And for My praise I restrain
    Myself from you,
So that I do not cut you off.
10 "Indeed, I have refined you, but
    not as silver;
I have tested and chosen you in the
    furnace of affliction.
11 "For My own sake, for My own
    sake, I will do it [I refrain and do
    not completely destroy you];
For how can My Name be defiled
    and profaned [as it would if My
    chosen people were completely
    destroyed]?
And I will not give My glory to
    another [by permitting the
    worshipers of idols to triumph
    over you].

12 "Listen to Me, O Jacob, and Israel,
    whom I called;
I am He, I am the First, I am the
    Last. [Is 41:4]
13 "My hand founded and established
    the earth,
And My right hand spread out the
    heavens;
When I call to them, they stand
    together [in obedience to carry
    out My decrees].
14 "Assemble, all of you, and listen!
Who among them [the idols and
    Chaldean astrologers] has
    declared these things?
The LORD loves him (Cyrus of
    Persia); he will do His pleasure
    and purpose against Babylon,

And his arm will be against
    the Chaldeans [who reign in
    Babylon].
15 "I, even I, have spoken; indeed, I
    have called Cyrus;
I have brought him, and will make
    his way successful.
16 "Come near to Me, listen to this:
From the beginning I have not
    spoken in secret,
From the time that it happened, I
    was there.
And now the Lord GOD has sent
    Me, and His [Holy] Spirit."

17 This is what the LORD, your Redeemer, the Holy One of Israel says,

"I am the LORD your God, who
    teaches you to profit (benefit),
Who leads you in the way that you
    should go.
18 "Oh, that you had paid attention to
    My commandments!
Then your peace and prosperity
    would have been like a [flowing]
    river,
And your righteousness [the
    holiness and purity of the
    nation] like the [abundant]
    waves of the sea.
19 "Your offspring would have been
    like the sand,
And your descendants [in number]
    like the grains of sand;

life point

God has an individual plan for each
person. If you will go to Him and submit
to Him, He will come into your heart and
commune with you. He will teach you and
guide you in the way you should go. Do
not try to be someone else. Do not try to
do what someone else does. Just allow
the Lord to show you how to fellowship
with Him. Then follow Him step-by-step as
He directs your life.

Their name would never be cut off
   or destroyed from My presence."
   [Gen 13:16; Jer 33:22; Luke 19:42]

²⁰ Get out of Babylon! Flee from the
   Chaldeans [who reign there]!
Declare with a voice of jubilation,
   proclaim this,
Send it out to the end of the earth;
Say, "The LORD has redeemed His
   servant Jacob."
²¹ They did not thirst when He led
   them through the deserts.
He made the waters flow out of the
   rock for them;
He split the rock and the waters
   flowed.
²² "There is no peace for the wicked,"
   says the LORD.

49 LISTEN TO Me, O islands
   and coastlands,
      And pay attention, you
peoples from far away.
The LORD has called Me from the
   womb;
From the body of My mother He
   has named Me.
² He has made My mouth like a
   sharp sword,
In the shadow of His hand He has
   kept Me hidden;
And He has made Me a sharpened
   arrow,
In His quiver He has hidden Me.
³ And [the LORD] said to Me, "You
   are My Servant, Israel,
In Whom I will show My glory."
   [Gen 32:28; Deut 7:6; 26:18, 19;
   Eph 1:4–6]
⁴ Then I said, "I have labored in vain,
I have spent My strength for
   nothing and vanity (pride,
   uselessness);
However My justice is with the LORD,
And My reward is with My God."

⁵ And now says the LORD, who
   formed Me from the womb to be
   His Servant,

To bring Jacob back to Him and that
   Israel might be gathered to Him,
—For I am honored in the eyes of
   the LORD,
And My God is My strength—
⁶ He says, "It is too trivial a thing
   that You should be My Servant
To raise up the tribes of Jacob and
   to restore the survivors of Israel;
I will also make You a light to the
   nations
That My salvation may reach to the
   end of the earth."
⁷ This is what the LORD, the
   Redeemer of Israel, Israel's Holy
   One says,
To the thoroughly despised One,
To the One hated by the nation
To the Servant of rulers,
"Kings will see and arise,
Princes shall also bow down,
Because of the LORD who is
   faithful, the Holy One of Israel
   who has chosen You."

⁸ This is what the LORD says,
"In a favorable time I have
   answered You,
And in a day of salvation I have
   helped You;
And I will keep watch over You
   and give You for a covenant of
   the people,
To restore the land [from its
   present state of ruin] and
   to apportion *and* give as
   inheritances the deserted
   hereditary lands, [2 Cor 6:2]
⁹ Saying to those who are bound *and*
   captured, 'Go forth,'
And to those who are in [spiritual]
   darkness, 'Show yourselves
   [come into the light of the
   Savior].'
They will feed along the roads [on
   which they travel],
And their pastures will be on all
   the bare heights.
¹⁰ "They will not hunger or thirst,

Nor will the scorching heat or sun
strike them down;
For He who has compassion on
them will lead them,
And He will guide them to springs
of water. [Rev 7:16, 17]
¹¹ "And I will make all My mountains
a roadway,
And My highways will be raised.
¹² "In fact, these will come from far
away;
And, lo, these *shall come* from the
north and from the west,
And these from the land of Aswan
(southern Egypt)."
¹³ Shout for joy, O heavens, and
rejoice, O earth,
And break forth into singing, O
mountains!
For the LORD has comforted His
people
And will have compassion on His
afflicted.

¹⁴ But Zion (Jerusalem in captivity)
said, "The LORD has abandoned
me,
And my Lord has forgotten me."
¹⁵ [The LORD answered] "Can a
woman forget her nursing child
And have no compassion on the
son of her womb?
Even these may forget, but I will
not forget you.
¹⁶ "Indeed, I have inscribed [a
picture of] you on the palms *of
My hands;*
Your city walls [Zion] are
continually before Me.
¹⁷ "Your builders hurry;
Your destroyers and devastators
Will go away from you.

¹⁸ "Lift up your eyes and look around
[at the returning exiles];
All these gather together and they
come to you [to rebuild you].
As I live," declares the LORD,
"You [Zion] will indeed clothe
yourself with all of them as
jewels and tie them on as a bride.
¹⁹ "For your ruins and desolate places
and your land [once the scene] of
destruction—
Certainly now [in the coming
years] will be too cramped for
the inhabitants,
And those who *once* engulfed you
will be far away.
²⁰ "The children of your bereavement
[those born in captivity] will yet
say in your ears,
'The place is too cramped for me';
Make room for me that I may live
here.
²¹ "Then [Zion], you will say in your
heart,
'Who has borne me these *children,*
Since I have been bereaved of my
children
And am barren, an exile and a
wanderer?
And who has reared these?
Indeed, I was left alone;
From where then did these
children come?'"

²² This is what the Lord GOD says,

"Listen carefully, I will lift up My
hand to the [Gentile] nations
And set up My banner to the
peoples;
And they will bring your sons in
the fold of their garments,
And your daughters will be carried
on their shoulders.

speak the Word

Thank You, God, for inscribing a picture of me on Your hands.
That way, I know that You will not forget me!
–ADAPTED FROM ISAIAH 49:16

23 "Kings will be your attendants,
    And their princesses your nurses.
    They will bow down to you with
        their faces to the earth
    And lick the dust of your feet;
    And you shall know [with an
        understanding based on
        personal experience] that I am
        the LORD;
    For they shall not be put to shame
        who wait *and* hope expectantly
        for Me.

24 "Can the spoils of war be taken
        from the mighty man,
    Or the captives of a tyrant be
        rescued?"

25 Indeed, this is what the LORD says,

    "Even the captives of the mighty
        man will be taken away,
    And the tyrant's spoils of war will
        be rescued;
    For I will contend with your
        opponent,
    And I will save your children.
26 "I will make those who oppress
        you consume their own flesh [in
        mutually destructive wars]
    And they will become drunk with
        their own blood as with sweet
        wine;
    And all mankind will know [with a
        knowledge grounded in personal
        experience] that I, the LORD, am
        your Savior
    And your Redeemer, the Mighty
        One of Jacob."

life point

The prophet said that the Lord had given
him the tongue of a disciple—a learner,
one who is taught—so that he would
know how to "sustain the weary with a
word" (Isaiah 50:4).

Do you see weary people in the body
of Christ? While the world has serious
problems that can wear us down, we can
experience joy from God, Who lifts us up.
According to the Bible, the joy of the Lord
is our strength (see Nehemiah 8:10). Joy is
not found in our circumstances; it is found
in Christ, the Mystery of the Ages, Who
dwells within us. You and I are learning
to find our joy in Christ alone. While we
are in the process, speaking a sustaining
word to one another will keep us from
growing weary.

50 THE LORD declares this;
    "Where is the certificate of
        divorce
    By which I have sent your mother
        away, [O Israel]?
    Or to which one of My creditors
        did I sell you [as slaves]?
    In fact, You were sold for your
        wickedness [your sin, your
        injustice, your wrongdoing],
    And for your transgressions your
        mother was sent away.
2 "Why, when I came, was there no
        man [to greet Me]?
    When I called, why was there no
        one to answer?

speak the Word

God, I wait for and hope expectantly for You in my life.
I know that I will not be put to shame.
—ADAPTED FROM ISAIAH 49:23

Thank You, God, for contending with my opponents.
—ADAPTED FROM ISAIAH 49:25

Is My hand really so short that it
  cannot redeem [My servants]?
Or have I no power to rescue?
Listen carefully, with My rebuke I
  dry up the sea,
I make the rivers into a desert;
Their fish stink because there is
  no water
And die of thirst.
3 "I clothe the heavens with the
  blackness [of storm clouds]
And make sackcloth [of mourning]
  their clothing."

4 The Lord GOD has given Me [His
  Servant] the tongue of disciples
  [as One who is taught],
That I may know how to sustain
  the weary with a word.
He awakens *Me* morning by
  morning,
He awakens My ear to listen as a
  disciple [as One who is taught].
5 The Lord GOD has opened My ear,
And I have not been rebellious
Nor have I turned back.
6 I turned My back to those who
  strike *Me*,
And My cheeks to those who pluck
  out the beard;
I did not hide My face from insults
  and spitting. [Matt 26:67; 27:30;
  John 19:1]
7 For the Lord GOD helps Me,
Therefore, I have not been
  ashamed *or* humiliated.
Therefore, I have made My face
  like flint,
And I know that I shall not be put
  to shame. [Luke 9:51; Is 52:13;
  53:10–12]
8 He who declares Me in the right is
  near;
Who will [dare to] contend with
  Me?
Let us stand up to each other;
Who is My adversary?
Let him approach Me. [Rom 8:33–35;
  1 Tim 3:16]
9 In fact, the Lord GOD helps Me;

Who is he who condemns Me [as
  guilty]?
Indeed, they will all wear out like
  a garment;
The moth will eat them. [Heb 1:11,
  12]
10 Who is among you who fears the
  LORD,
Who obeys the voice of His Servant,
Yet who walks in darkness and has
  no light?
Let him trust *and* be confident in
  the name of the LORD and let him
  rely on his God.
11 Listen carefully, all you who
  kindle your own fire [devising
  your own man-made plan of
  salvation],
Who surround yourselves with
  torches,
Walk by the light of your [self-
  made] fire
And among the torches that you
  have set ablaze.
But this you will have from My
  hand:
You will lie down in [a place of]
  torment. [Is 66:24]

51 "LISTEN TO Me, you who
    pursue righteousness
    (right standing with God),
Who seek *and* inquire of the LORD:
Look to the rock from which you
  were cut
And to the excavation of the quarry
  from which you were dug.
2 "Look to Abraham your father
And to Sarah who gave birth to
  you in pain;
For I called him when *he was but*
  one,
Then I blessed him and made him
  many."
3 For the LORD will comfort Zion [in
  her captivity];
He will comfort all her ruins.
And He will make her wilderness
  like Eden,

And her desert like the garden of
the LORD;
Joy and gladness will be found in
her,
Thanksgiving and the voice of a
melody.
4 "Listen carefully to Me [says the
LORD], O My people,
And hear Me, O My nation;
For a [divine] law will go forth
from Me,
And I will quickly *establish* My
justice as a light to the peoples.
5 "My righteousness (justice) is near,
My salvation has gone forth,
And My arms will judge the peoples;
The islands *and* coastlands will
wait for Me,
And they will wait with hope *and*
confident expectation for My arm.
6 "Lift up your eyes to the heavens,
Then look to the earth beneath;
For the heavens will be torn to
pieces *and* vanish like smoke,
And the earth will wear out like a
garment
And its inhabitants will die in like
manner.
But My salvation will be forever,
And My righteousness (justice)
[and faithfully fulfilled promise]
will not be broken. [Matt 24:35;
Heb 1:11; 2 Pet 3:10]
7 "Listen to Me, you who know
righteousness (right standing
with God),
The people in whose heart is My
law *and* instruction;
Do not fear the reproach *and*
taunting of man,
Nor be distressed at their reviling.
8 "For the moth will eat them like a
garment,
And the worm will eat them like
wool.
But My righteousness *and* justice
[faithfully promised] will exist
forever,
And My salvation to all generations."

9 Awake, awake, put on strength *and*
might, O arm of the LORD;
Awake as in the ancient days, as in
the generations of long ago.
Was it not You who cut Rahab
(Egypt) in pieces,
Who pierced the dragon [of
Egypt]? [Is 30:7]
10 Was it not You who dried up the
[Red] Sea,
The waters of the great deep,
Who made the depths of the sea a
pathway
For the redeemed to cross over?
11 So the redeemed of the LORD will
return
And come with joyful shouting to
Zion;
Everlasting joy will be on their
heads.
They will obtain gladness and joy,
And sorrow and sighing will flee
away. [Rev 7:17; 21:1, 4]

12 "I, even I, am He who comforts you.
Who are you that you are afraid of
man who dies
And of a son of man who is made
[as destructible] as grass,
13 That you have forgotten the LORD
your Maker,
Who stretched out the heavens
And laid the foundations of the
earth,
That you continually tremble with
fear all day long because of the
rage of the oppressor,
As he takes aim to destroy?
And where is the rage of the
oppressor?

14 The [captive] exile will soon be set
free, and will not die in the dungeon,
nor will his food be lacking.
15 "For I am the LORD your God, who
stirs up the sea so that its waves roar—
the LORD of hosts is His name.
16 "I have put My words in your
mouth and have covered you with the
shadow of My hand, to establish the

[renewed] heavens and lay the foundations of the [renewed] earth, and to say to Zion (Jerusalem), 'You are My people.'" [Is 65:17; 66:22; Rev 21:1]

17 Wake yourself up! Wake yourself up! Stand up, O Jerusalem,
You who have drunk at the hand of the LORD the cup of His wrath,
You who have drunk the cup of staggering *and* intoxication to the dregs [leaving only sediment].
18 There is no one to guide her among all the sons she has borne,
Nor is there anyone to take her by the hand among all the sons she has reared.
19 These two *tragedies* have befallen you;
Who will show sympathy for you *and* mourn with you?
The desolation and destruction [on the land and city], famine and sword [on the inhabitants];
How shall I comfort you?
20 Your sons have fainted;
They lie *helpless* at the head of every street,
Like an antelope in a net,
Full [from drinking] of the wrath of the LORD,
The rebuke of your God.

21 Therefore, now hear this, you who are afflicted,
Who are drunk, but not with wine [but overwhelmed by the wrath of God].
22 So says your Lord, the LORD, *who is* also your God
Who pleads the cause of His people,
"Listen carefully, I have taken from your hand the cup of staggering *and* intoxication,
The cup of My wrath;
You shall never drink it again.
23 "I will put it into the hands of your tormentors,

Who have said to you, 'Lie down so that we may walk over you.'
You have even made your back like the ground
And like the street for those who walk over it."

52

AWAKE, AWAKE,
Put on your strength, O Zion;
Put on your beautiful garments,
O Jerusalem, the holy city;
For the uncircumcised and the unclean
Will no longer come into you. [Rev 21:27]
2 Shake yourself from the dust, arise,
O captive Jerusalem;
Rid yourself of the chains around your neck,
O captive Daughter of Zion.

3 For the LORD says this, "You were sold for nothing and you will be redeemed, but not with money."
4 For the Lord GOD says this, "My people went down at the first into Egypt to live there; and [many years later Sennacherib] the Assyrian oppressed them without cause.
5 "But now, what do I have here," declares the LORD, "seeing that My people have been taken away without reason? Those who rule over them howl [with taunting and mockery of salvation]," declares the LORD, "and My name is continually blasphemed all day long. [Rom 2:24]
6 "Therefore My people shall know My Name *and* what it means. Therefore in that day I am the One who is speaking, 'Here I am.'" [Ex 3:13, 14]

7 How beautiful *and* delightful on the mountains
Are the feet of him who brings good news,
Who announces peace,
Who brings good news of good [things],

Who announces salvation,
Who says to Zion, "Your God
reigns!" [Acts 10:36; Rom 10:15;
Eph 6:14–16]
⁸Listen! Your watchmen lift up
their voices,
Together they shout for joy;
For they will see face to face
The return of the Lord to Zion.
⁹Break forth, shout joyfully together,
You ruins of Jerusalem;
For the Lord has comforted His
people,
He has redeemed Jerusalem.
¹⁰The Lord has bared His holy arm
(His infinite power)
Before the eyes of all the nations
[revealing Himself as the One by
Whom Israel is redeemed from
captivity],
That all the ends of the earth may
see
The salvation of our God. [Luke
2:29–32; 3:6]

¹¹Depart, depart, go out from there
(the lands of exile),
Touch no unclean thing;
Go out of the midst of her
(Babylon), purify yourselves,
You who carry the articles of the
Lord [on your journey from
there]. [2 Cor 6:16, 17]
¹²For you will not go out in a hurry
[as when you left Egypt],
Nor will you go in flight [fleeing,
as you did from the Egyptians];
For the Lord will go before you,
And the God of Israel will be your
rear guard.

¹³Indeed, My Servant (the Messiah)
will act wisely and prosper;
He will be raised and lifted up and
greatly exalted.

speak the Word

¹⁴Just as many were astonished and
appalled at you, My people,
So His appearance was marred
more than any man
And His form [marred] more than
the sons of men.
¹⁵So He will sprinkle many nations
[with His blood, providing
salvation],
Kings will shut their mouths
because of Him;
For what they had not been told
they will see,
And what they had not heard they
will understand. [Rom 15:21]

53 WHO HAS believed
[confidently trusted in,
relied on, and adhered to]
our message [of salvation]? [Is
52:7, 10]
And to whom [if not us] has the
arm and infinite power of the
Lord been revealed? [John
12:38–41; Rom 10:16]
²For He [the Servant of God] grew
up before Him like a tender shoot
(plant),
And like a root out of dry ground;
He has no stately form or majestic
splendor

life point

Jesus did not seem to let the fact that
He was despised and rejected bother
Him (see Isaiah 53:3). He certainly did
not complain about it. I am sure He felt
intense pain, just as you and I do when
we are rejected, but He did not allow it to
prevent Him from fulfilling His purpose.
Do not let it hinder you either!

Thank You, God, for always going before me and behind me.
I know that I am safe in Your presence!
–ADAPTED FROM ISAIAH 52:12

That we would look at Him,
Nor [handsome] appearance that
we would be attracted to Him.
³He was despised and rejected by
men,
A Man of sorrows *and* pain and
acquainted with grief;
And like One from whom men
hide their faces
He was despised, and we did not
appreciate His worth *or* esteem
Him.

⁴But [in fact] He has borne our
griefs,
And He has carried our sorrows
and pains;
Yet we [ignorantly] assumed that
He was stricken,
Struck down by God and degraded
and humiliated [by Him]. [Matt
8:17]
⁵But He was wounded for our
transgressions,
He was crushed for our
wickedness [our sin, our
injustice, our wrongdoing];
The punishment [required] for our
well-being *fell* on Him,
And by His stripes (wounds) we
are healed.
⁶All of us like sheep have gone astray,
We have turned, each one, to his
own way;
But the LORD has caused the
wickedness of us all [our sin, our
injustice, our wrongdoing]
To fall on Him [instead of us].
[1 Pet 2:24, 25]

⁷He was oppressed and He was
afflicted,

Yet He did not open His mouth [to
complain or defend Himself];
Like a lamb that is led to the
slaughter,
And like a sheep that is silent
before her shearers,
So He did not open His mouth.
⁸After oppression and judgment He
was taken away;
And as for His generation [His
contemporaries], who [among
them] concerned himself *with
the fact*
That He was cut off from the land
of the living [by His death]
For the transgression of my people,
to whom the stroke [of death]
was due?
⁹His grave was assigned with the
wicked,
But He was with a rich man in His
death,
Because He had done no violence,
Nor was there any deceit in His
mouth. [Matt 27:57–60; 1 Pet
2:22, 23]

¹⁰Yet the LORD was willing
To crush Him, causing Him to
suffer;
If He would give Himself as a guilt
offering [an atonement for sin],
He shall see *His* [spiritual]
offspring,
He shall prolong *His* days,
And the will (good pleasure) of the
LORD shall succeed *and* prosper
in His hand.
¹¹As a result of the anguish of His
soul,
He shall see it and be satisfied;

speak the Word

Thank You, Jesus, for bearing my griefs and sicknesses,
for carrying my sorrows and pains, for being wounded for my transgressions.
Thank You for taking the punishment required for my well-being.
I declare today that by Your stripes, I am healed.
–ADAPTED FROM ISAIAH 53:4, 5

condemnation or conviction?

If condemnation is filling our consciences, it is not from God. He sent Jesus to die for us to pay the price for our sins. According to Isaiah 53:3–6 and many passages in the New Testament, Jesus bore our sin and the guilty condemnation that accompanies sin. We should get rid of the sin and not keep the guilt. Once God breaks the yoke of sin from us, He removes the guilt too. He is faithful and just to forgive all of our sins and to continuously cleanse us from all unrighteousness (see 1 John 1:9).

How does condemnation differ from conviction? Let me explain it this way: We need forgiveness every day of our lives. The Holy Spirit sets off the alarm in our consciences so we can recognize sin, and He gives us the power of the blood of Jesus to continuously cleanse us from sin and keep us right before Him. This process is called "conviction," and it is of the Lord, while condemnation is from the enemy.

Often when we are convicted of sin, we become grouchy while God is dealing with us. Until we admit our sin, become ready to turn from it, and ask for forgiveness, we feel a pressure that squeezes out the worst we have in us. As soon as we come into agreement with God, our peace returns and our behavior improves.

The devil knows that condemnation and shame keep us from approaching God in prayer so our needs can be met and we can once again enjoy fellowship with God. Feeling bad about ourselves or thinking God is angry with us separates us from His presence. God does not leave us, but we withdraw from Him because of our guilt or fear.

That is why it is so important to discern the truth and know the difference between conviction and condemnation. Remember, if you heed conviction, it lifts you up and out of sin; condemnation only makes you feel bad about yourself.

When you pray for people to change, the Holy Spirit convicts them of their sin, and many times they will start acting worse than they did before. But do not let that make you believe your prayers are ineffective. Their behavior is actually a good sign that God is indeed working, convicting them of sin and convincing them of their need to change. So keep praying!

As you pray, regularly ask God to convict you of your own sin. Realize that conviction is a blessing, not a problem. If only perfect people could pray and receive answers, nobody would pray. We do not need to be perfect, but we do need to be cleansed of sin. As we begin our prayer time, it is good to ask the heavenly Father to cleanse us of all sin and unrighteousness. When we pray in Jesus' name, we are presenting to our Father all that Jesus is, not all that we are.

Experiencing conviction through the Holy Spirit's work in our lives is necessary for a vital walk with God. Remember that conviction is a gift from God because it leads us to hear from Him. Do not make the mistake of letting it condemn you, as I did for years. Let conviction lift you to a new level in God. Do not resist it; receive it.

By His knowledge [of what He has
  accomplished] the Righteous One,
My Servant, shall justify the
  many [making them righteous—
  upright before God, in right
  standing with Him],
For He shall bear [the
  responsibility for] their sins.
[12] Therefore, I will divide *and* give
  Him a portion with the great
  [kings and rulers],
And He shall divide the spoils
  with the mighty,
Because He [willingly] poured out
  His life to death,
And was counted among the
  transgressors;

Yet He Himself bore *and* took away
  the sin of many,
And interceded [with the Father]
  for the transgressors. [Luke 22:37]

54 "SHOUT FOR joy, O barren
  one, she who has not given
  birth;
Break forth into joyful shouting
  and rejoice, she who has not
  gone into labor [with child]!
For the [spiritual] sons of the
  desolate one *will be* more
  numerous
Than the sons of the married
  woman," says the LORD. [Gal 4:27]

free from shame

Do you have a shame-based nature? Are you rooted or grounded in shame? The curse and power of shame can be broken off of you through the power of God.

We know from Isaiah 54:4 that the Lord has promised to remove shame and dishonor from us so that we remember it no more. In fact, God has promised that in their place He will pour out upon us a twofold blessing. We will possess double what we have lost, and we will have everlasting joy (see Isaiah 61:7).

Take your stand on the Word of God. Become rooted and grounded, not in shame and dishonor, but in the love of Christ, being complete in Him.

Ask the Lord to work a healing miracle in your mind, will, and emotions. Let Him come in and fulfill what He came to do: heal your broken heart, bind up your wounds, proclaim your freedom, give you joy in place of mourning, and clothe you with a garment of praise instead of a disheartened spirit, so you will be called a tree of righteousness, strong and magnificent, and in right standing with God (see Isaiah 61:1–3).

Determine that from this moment on you are going to reject the roots of bitterness, shame, negativism, and perfectionism, and nourish the roots of joy, peace, love, and power.

By faith, draw the bloodline of Jesus Christ across your life and boldly declare that you are healed from the pains and wounds of your past; you have been set free to live a new life of health and wholeness. Continue to praise the Lord and confess His Word over yourself, claiming His forgiveness, cleansing, and healing.

Stop blaming yourself and feeling guilty, unworthy, and unloved. Instead begin to say, "If God is for me, who can be against me? God loves me, and I love myself. Praise the Lord, I am free in Jesus' name. Amen!"

2 "Enlarge the site of your tent [to
  make room for more children];
Stretch out the curtains of your
  dwellings, do not spare them;
Lengthen your tent ropes
And make your pegs (stakes) firm
  [in the ground].
3 "For you will spread out to the
  right and to the left;
And your descendants will take
  possession of nations
And will inhabit deserted cities.

4 "Do not fear, for you will not be put
  to shame,
And do not feel humiliated *or*
  ashamed, for you will not be
  disgraced.
For you will forget the shame of
  your youth,
And you will no longer remember
  the disgrace of your widowhood.
5 "For your husband is your Maker,
The LORD of hosts is His name;
And your Redeemer is the Holy
  One of Israel,
Who is called the God of the whole
  earth.
6 "For the LORD has called you,
Like a wife who has been
  abandoned, grieved in spirit,
And like a wife [married] in
  her youth when she is [later]
  rejected *and* scorned,"
Says your God.
7 "For a brief moment I abandoned
  you,
But with great compassion *and*
  mercy I will gather you [to
  Myself again].
8 "In an outburst of wrath

I hid My face from you for a
  moment,
But with everlasting kindness I
  will have compassion on you,"
Says the LORD your Redeemer.

9 "For this is *like* the waters of Noah
  to Me,
As I swore [an oath] that the
  waters of Noah
Would not flood the earth again;
In the same way I have sworn that
  I will not be angry with you
Nor will I rebuke you.
10 "For the mountains may be
  removed and the hills may
  shake,
But My lovingkindness will not be
  removed from you,
Nor will My covenant of peace be
  shaken,"
Says the LORD who has compassion
  on you.

11 "O you afflicted [city], storm-
  tossed, and not comforted,
Listen carefully, I will set your
  [precious] stones in mortar,
And lay your foundations with
  sapphires.
12 "And I will make your battlements
  of rubies,
And your gates of [shining] beryl
  stones,
And all your [barrier] walls of
  precious stones. [Rev 21:19–21]
13 "And all your [spiritual] sons will
  be disciples [of the LORD],
And great will be the well-being of
  your sons. [John 6:45]

speak the Word

Thank You, God, for being my Husband, my Maker, and my Redeemer.
—ADAPTED FROM ISAIAH 54:5

*God, I declare today that Your loving-kindness will never be removed
from me and that Your covenant of peace will never be shaken.*
—ADAPTED FROM ISAIAH 54:10

14 "You will be firmly established in
   righteousness:
You will be far from [even the
   thought of] oppression, for you
   will not fear,
And from terror, for it will not
   come near you.
15 "If anyone fiercely attacks you it
   will not be from Me.
Whoever attacks you will fall
   because of you.
16 "Listen carefully, I have created
   the smith who blows on the fire
   of coals
And who produces a weapon for its
   purpose;
And I have created the destroyer
   to inflict ruin.
17 "No weapon that is formed against
   you will succeed;
And every tongue that rises
   against you in judgment you will
   condemn.
This [peace, righteousness,
   security, and triumph over
   opposition] is the heritage of the
   servants of the LORD,
And *this is* their vindication from
   Me," says the LORD.

55 "EVERYONE WHO thirsts,
   come to the waters;
   And you who have no
money come, buy grain and eat.
Come, buy wine and milk
Without money and without cost
   [simply accept it as a gift from
   God]. [Rev 21:6, 7; 22:17]
2 "Why do you spend money for that
   which is not bread,
And your earnings for what does
   not satisfy?

Listen carefully to Me, and eat
   what is good,
And let your soul delight in
   abundance. [Jer 31:12–14]
3 "Incline your ear [to listen] and
   come to Me;
Hear, so that your soul may live;
And I will make an everlasting
   covenant with you,
According to the faithful mercies
   [promised and] shown to David.
   [2 Sam 7:8–16; Acts 13:34; Heb
   13:20]
4 "Listen carefully, I have appointed
   him [David, representing the
   Messiah] to be a witness to the
   nations [regarding salvation],
A leader and commander to the
   peoples.
5 "In fact, you [Israel] will call a
   nation that you do not know,
And a nation that does not know
   you will run to you,
Because of the LORD your God,
   even the Holy One of Israel;
For He has glorified you."

6 Seek the LORD while He may be
   found;
Call on Him [for salvation] while
   He is near.
7 Let the wicked leave (behind) his
   way
And the unrighteous man his
   thoughts;
And let him return to the LORD,
And He will have compassion
   (mercy) on him,
And to our God,
For He will abundantly pardon.
8 "For My thoughts are not your
   thoughts,

speak the Word

*I declare today, God, that no weapon formed against me
will succeed and that every tongue that rises against me in judgment
I will condemn. This is my heritage in You!*
–ADAPTED FROM ISAIAH 54:17

Nor are your ways My ways,"
  declares the LORD.
9 "For as the heavens are higher
  than the earth,
So are My ways higher than your
  ways
And My thoughts *higher* than your
  thoughts.
10 "For as the rain and snow come
  down from heaven,
And do not return there without
  watering the earth,
Making it bear and sprout,
And providing seed to the sower
  and bread to the eater, [2 Cor 9:10]

11 So will My word be which goes out
  of My mouth;
"It will not return to Me void
  (useless, without result),
Without accomplishing what I
  desire,
And without succeeding *in the
  matter* for which I sent it.
12 "For you will go out [from exile]
  with joy
And be led forth [by the LORD
  Himself] with peace;
The mountains and the hills will
  break forth into shouts of joy
  before you,

the power of God's Word

God's Word is filled with inherent power. When God speaks, powerful things take place. As we read in Isaiah 55:11, His Word never returns void; it always accomplishes God's desire. When we learn to speak God's Word instead of rehearsing how we feel or declaring what we think, we are also releasing power. The Word of God spoken in faith from a believer's mouth can change circumstances. We may experience negative facts in our lives, but God's Word is truth, and truth is more powerful than facts.

Lazarus was dead; that was a fact. But when Jesus, Who is the Truth, walked up to the tomb and spoke, that truth changed the facts. Throughout the Gospels, we repeatedly read of people who were sick and demon-possessed who went to Jesus. When He spoke, their facts changed. They were healed, delivered, and set free. We must never magnify the facts of our circumstances above God and the power of His Word. When God speaks, things change!

Actually, God has spoken, and all we need to do is believe what He has said. His Word is loaded with promises that are for anyone who will believe them and act accordingly. Just as you may have, I had a set of unpleasant facts in my life. I had been badly abused. I was emotionally wounded and experienced various personality disorders as a result of enduring a very dysfunctional life. I had a sour attitude, a chip on my shoulder, and was filled with bitterness and unforgiveness. But Jesus came into my life, and I learned to believe and speak His Word in faith, and today I am free from all those things that were definitely negative facts years ago.

God compares His Word to seed. When we plant the seed by speaking it, praying it, believing it, and acting upon it, it will yield what it says. God promises us that it will produce! Begin to speak God's Word regularly and believe what it says more than you believe your circumstances. Hold fast your confession of faith in Him (see Hebrews 4:14), and soon you will be sharing your testimony of victory with others.

And all the trees of the field will
  clap their hands.
[13]"Instead of the thorn bush the
  cypress tree will grow,
And instead of the nettle the
  myrtle tree will grow;
And it will be a memorial to the
  LORD,
For an everlasting sign [of His
  mercy] which will not be cut off."

56 THIS IS what the LORD
  says,
  "Maintain justice and do
righteousness,
For My salvation is soon to come,
And My righteousness *and* justice
  is soon to be revealed. [Is 62:1,
  11; Matt 3:2; Luke 21:31; Rom
  13:11, 12]
[2]"Blessed (happy, fortunate) is the
  man who does this,
And the son of man who takes hold
  of it,
Who keeps the Sabbath without
  profaning it,
And keeps his hand from doing any
  evil."

life point

The prophets were mouthpieces for God.
They were called to speak God's words
to people, situations, cities, dry bones,
mountains, or whatever God told them
to speak to. To fulfill their God-ordained
mission, they had to be submitted to the
Lord, and their mouths had to be consecrated to Him.

Those of us who desire to be used by God
need to allow Him to deal with us concerning our mouths and the things we say.
If you want Him to use you, be prepared
for Him to deal with you concerning your
words so you are able to represent Him
well with your mouth when the time
comes for you to speak His Word.

life point

Under the Old Covenant, the temple was
the house of God, the place of prayer for
His people. Under the New Covenant, *we*
are now God's house because He dwells
within us (see 1 Corinthians 3:16; 6:19). We
may still be under construction, but none-
theless we are His house, His tabernacle,
His dwelling place. Therefore, we should
consider ourselves "houses of prayer."

Ephesians 6:18 gives some practical
instruction on how to be a true house of
prayer. It lets us know that we can pray
anywhere at any time about anything,
and that we should be watchful to do so:
"With all prayer and petition pray [with
specific requests] at all times [on every
occasion and in every season] in the
Spirit, and with this in view, stay alert
with all perseverance and petition [inter-
ceding in prayer] for all God's people."
Believing and practicing Ephesians 6:18
can be life-changing. This kind of continual communion with God helps us truly
become the living "house[s] of prayer"
the Bible mentions in Isaiah 56:7.

[3]Do not let the foreigner who has
  joined himself to the LORD say,
"The LORD will most certainly
  separate me from His people."
And do not let the eunuch say,
  "Look, I am a dry tree."
[4]This is what the LORD says,

"To the eunuchs who keep My
  Sabbaths
And choose what pleases Me,
And hold firmly to My covenant,
[5]To them I will give in My house
  and within My walls a memorial,
And a name better than that of
  sons and daughters;
I will give them an everlasting
  name which will not be cut off.

⁶"Also the foreigners who join
  themselves to the LORD,
To minister to Him, and to love the
  name of the LORD,
To be His servants, everyone
  who keeps the Sabbath without
  profaning it
And holds fast to My covenant [by
  conscientious obedience];
⁷All these I will bring to My holy
  mountain
And make them joyful in My
  house of prayer.
Their burnt offerings and their
  sacrifices will be accepted on My
  altar;
For My house will be called a
  house of prayer for all the
  peoples."
⁸The Lord GOD, who gathers the
  dispersed of Israel, declares:
"I will gather yet *others* to them
  (Israel), to those [already]
  gathered."

⁹All you beasts of the field,
All you beasts (hostile nations) in
  the forest,
Come to eat.
¹⁰Israel's watchmen are blind,
They are all without knowledge.
They are all mute dogs, they cannot
  bark;
Panting, lying down, they love to
  slumber.
¹¹And the dogs are greedy; they
  never have enough.
They are shepherds who have no
  understanding;
They have all turned to their own
  way,
Each one to his unlawful gain,
  without exception.
¹²"Come," [they say,] "let us get wine,
  and let us fill ourselves with
  strong drink;
And tomorrow will be like today,
  very great indeed."

57 THE RIGHTEOUS man
  perishes [at the hand of
  evil], and no one takes it to
heart;
Faithful *and* devout men are taken
  away, while no one understands
That the righteous person is
  taken away [to be spared] from
  disaster *and* evil.
²He enters into peace [through
  death];
They rest in their beds (graves),
Each one who walked uprightly
  [following God's will, living with
  integrity].
³"But come here, you sons of a
  sorceress [raised in deception
  and superstition],
Offspring of an adulterer and a
  prostitute.
⁴"Of whom do you make fun?
Against whom do you open wide
  your mouth
And stick out your tongue?
Are you not children of rebellion
  (sin),
Offspring of deceit,
⁵Who inflame yourselves [with lust
  in pagan rites] among the oaks
  (terebinth trees),
Under every green *and* leafy tree,
Who slaughter the children [in
  sacrifice] in the ravines
Under the clefts of the rocks?
⁶"Among the smooth *stones* of the
  ravine
Is your portion, they (the idols) are
  your lot;
Even to them you have poured out
  a drink offering,
You have offered a grain offering.
Should I be quiet concerning
  these things [leaving them
  unpunished—bearing them with
  patience]?
⁷"Upon a high and lofty mountain
You have [openly and shamelessly]
  made your [idolatrous and
  adulterous] bed;

Even there you went up to offer
sacrifice [to idols, in spiritual
unfaithfulness to Me].
8 "Behind the door and the doorpost
You have set up your [pagan]
symbol;
Indeed, far removed from Me, you
have uncovered yourself,
And have gone up and made your
bed wide.
And you have made a [new]
agreement for yourself with the
adulterers,
You have loved their bed,
You have looked [with passion] on
their manhood. [Deut 6:5, 6, 9;
11:18, 20]
9 "You have gone to the king [of a
pagan land] with oil
And increased your perfumes;
You have sent your messengers a
great distance
And made *them* go down to Sheol
(the realm of the dead).
10 "You were wearied by the length of
your road,
Yet you did not say, 'It is no use.'
You found renewed strength,
Therefore you did not grow weak.
11 "About whom were you worried
and fearful
That you lied and did not
remember Me,
Nor give Me a thought?
Was I not silent even for a long time

putting the Word to work

Isaiah 57:15 tells us that God dwells in
a high and holy place, but that He also
dwells with those who are contrite
and humble in spirit. Do you have a
contrite and humble spirit? Are you
struggling with stubbornness or pride
in any area of your life? If so, repent
and ask God to forgive you. Then He
will revive your heart, as He promises
in this verse.

And [as a result] you do not fear
Me?
12 "I will declare your [hypocritical]
righteousness and your deeds,
But they will not benefit you.
13 "When you cry out [for help], let
your [ridiculous] collection *of
idols* save you.
But the wind will carry them all
away,
A [mere] breath will take them.
But he who takes refuge in Me will
possess the land [Judea]
And will inherit My holy
mountain." [Ps 37:9, 11; 69:35, 36;
Is 49:8; Matt 5:5; Heb 12:22]
14 And it will be said,
"Build up, build up, clear the way.
Remove the stumbling block out of
the way [of the spiritual return]
of My people."
15 For the high and exalted One
He who inhabits eternity, Whose
name is Holy says this,
"I dwell on the high and holy place,
But *also* with the contrite and
humble in spirit
In order to revive the spirit of the
humble
And to revive the heart of the
contrite [overcome with sorrow
for sin]. [Matt 5:3]
16 "For I will not contend forever,
Nor will I always be angry;
For [if I did stay angry] the spirit
[of man] would grow weak
before Me,
And the breath *of those whom* I
have created.
17 "Because of the wickedness of
his unjust gain I was angry and
struck him;
I hid *My face* and was angry,
And he went on turning away *and*
backsliding, in the way of his
[own willful] heart.
18 "I have seen his [willful] ways, but
I will heal him;

I will lead him [also] and will restore comfort to him and to those who mourn for him, [Is 61:1, 2; 66:10]
19 As I create the praise of his lips,
Peace, peace, to him who is far away [both Jew and Gentile] and to him who is near!"
Says the LORD;
"And I will heal him [making his lips blossom anew with thankful praise]." [Acts 2:39; Eph 2:13–17, 18; Heb 13:15]
20 But the wicked are like the tossing sea,
For it cannot be quiet,
And its waters toss up mire and mud.
21 "There is no peace," says my God, "for the wicked."

58 "CRY ALOUD, do not hold back;
Lift up your voice like a trumpet,
And declare to My people their transgression
And to the house of Jacob their sins.
2 "Yet they seek Me day by day and delight [superficially] to know My ways,
As [if they were in reality] a nation that has done righteousness
And has not abandoned (turned away from) the ordinance of their God.
They ask of Me righteous judgments,
They delight in the nearness of God.
3 'Why have we fasted,' they say, 'and You do not see it?
Why have we humbled ourselves and You do not notice?'
Hear this [O Israel], on the day of your fast [when you should be grieving for your sins] you find something you desire [to do],
And you force your hired servants to work [instead of stopping all work, as the law teaches]. [Lev 16:29]

life point

The scene we read about in Isaiah 58:5 is an exchange between the Israelites and God. The people had been fasting, and they felt God had not noticed. He told them that they were fasting with the wrong motives, and that they had things in their lives that needed to be dealt with.

True fasting is for the purpose of breaking the power of the flesh in our lives. It is supposed to be a special, consecrated time of prayer in which God's people seek Him seriously and sacrificially for themselves or for others. True fasting, with right motives, *is* effective.

4 "The facts are that you fast *only* for strife and brawling and to strike with the fist of wickedness.
You do not fast as *you do* today to make your voice heard on high.
5 "Is a fast such as this what I have chosen, a day for a man to humble himself [with sorrow in his soul]?
Is it *only* to bow down his head like a reed
And to make sackcloth and ashes as a bed [pretending to have a repentant heart]?
Do you call this a fast and a day pleasing to the LORD?
6 "[Rather] is this not the fast which I choose,
To undo the bonds of wickedness,
To tear to pieces the ropes of the yoke,
To let the oppressed go free
And break apart every [enslaving] yoke? [Acts 8:23]
7 "Is it not to divide your bread with the hungry
And bring the homeless poor into the house;
When you see the naked, that you cover him,

And not to hide yourself from [the needs of] your own flesh *and* blood?

8 "Then your light will break out like the dawn,
And your healing (restoration, new life) will quickly spring forth;
Your righteousness will go before you [leading you to peace and prosperity],
The glory of the Lord will be your rear guard. [Ex 14:19, 20; Is 52:12]

9 "Then you will call, and the Lord will answer;
You will cry for help, and He will say, 'Here I am.'
If you take away from your midst the yoke [of oppression],
The finger pointed in scorn [toward the oppressed or the godly], and [every form of] wicked (sinful, unjust) speech, [Ex 3:14]

10 And if you offer yourself to [assist] the hungry
And satisfy the need of the afflicted,
Then your light will rise in darkness
And your gloom *will become* like midday.

11 "And the Lord will continually guide you,
And satisfy your soul in scorched *and* dry places,
And give strength to your bones;
And you will be like a watered garden,
And like a spring of water whose waters do not fail.

12 "And your people will rebuild the ancient ruins;
You will raise up *and* restore the age-old foundations [of buildings that have been laid waste];

first things first

Some people become so involved in ministry that they overlook their own family members and friends, but the Lord makes clear in Isaiah 58:7 that we are not to neglect one in order to attend to the other.

In this verse, God tells us that we are not only to meet the needs of those around us in the world (the poor, needy, and disadvantaged), but that we are also to meet the needs of our immediate and extended families.

I have a widowed aunt to whom I minister quite often. I once thought I was too busy to help her, but God showed me that she is my "flesh and blood." She is part of my family, and I am responsible to minister to her needs just as I am responsible to minister to thousands of people in arenas all over the world. If I ignore my responsibilities toward my relatives, I will pay the price of losing an aspect of God's anointing in other areas of my life.

We must also obey what we read in God's Word. And in Isaiah 58:7, the Word says that we should not only feed the hungry and clothe the naked, but that we must also not hide ourselves from the needs of our own flesh and blood. After we have done these things, then Isaiah 58:8 will work for us: our light will breakout like the dawn, our healing (our restoration and the power of a new life) will spring forth quickly, our righteousness will go before us, leading us to peace and prosperity, and God's glory will guard us from behind. Those are awesome promises, and I encourage you to do what is necessary for you to be in position to receive them in your life.

You will be called Repairer of the
   Breach,
Restorer of Streets with Dwellings.
13 "If you turn back your foot from
   [unnecessary travel on] the
   Sabbath,
From doing your own pleasure on
   My holy day,
And call the Sabbath a [spiritual]
   delight, and the holy day of the
   Lord honorable,
And honor it, not going your own
   way
Or engaging in your own pleasure
Or speaking your own [idle] words,
14 Then you will take pleasure in the
   Lord,
And I will make you ride on the
   high places of the earth,
And I will feed you with the
   [promised] heritage of Jacob
   your father;
For the mouth of the Lord has
   spoken." [Gen 27:28, 29; 28:13–15]

59 BEHOLD, THE Lord's hand
   is not so short
      That it cannot save,
Nor His ear so impaired
That it cannot hear.
2 But your wickedness has separated
   you from your God,
And your sins have hidden *His* face
   from you so that He does not hear.

life point

What wonderful promises we find in
Isaiah 58:10–12! When can we expect
these blessings of the Lord to come upon
us? When we stop judging others and
put away every form of vain, false, harsh,
unjust, and wicked speaking. We should
not expect God's blessings when our
mouths are speaking curses, but when we
begin to speak blessings to others from
a sincere heart, blessings begin to flow
toward us.

3 For your hands are defiled with
   blood
And your fingers with wickedness
   [with sin, with injustice, with
   wrongdoing];
Your lips have spoken lies,
Your tongue mutters wickedness.
4 No one sues righteously [but
   for the sake of doing injury to
   others—to take some undue
   advantage], and no one pleads
   [his case] in truth; [but rather]
They trust in empty *arguments* and
   speak lies;
They conceive trouble and bring
   forth injustice.
5 They hatch vipers' eggs and weave
   the spider's webs;
He who eats of their eggs dies,
And *from an egg* which is crushed
   a viper breaks out.
6 Their webs will not serve as
   clothing,
Nor will they cover themselves
   with what they make;
Their works are works of
   wickedness [of sin, of injustice,
   of wrongdoing],
And the act of violence is in their
   hands.
7 Their feet run to evil,
And they rush to shed innocent
   blood.
Their thoughts are thoughts of
   wickedness [of sin, of injustice,
   of wrongdoing];
Devastation and destruction are in
   their highways.
8 They do not know the way of
   peace,
And there is no justice in their
   tracks.
They have made them into crooked
   paths;
Whoever walks on them does not
   know peace. [Rom 3:15–18]

9 Therefore justice is far from us,
And righteousness does not
   overtake us.

We [expectantly] hope for light,
   but only see darkness;
We hope for gleam of light, *but* we
   walk in darkness *and* gloom.
[10] We grope for a wall like the blind,
   We grope like those who have no
   eyes.
We stumble at midday as in the
   twilight;
Among those who are healthy *we
   are* like dead men.
[11] We all groan *and* growl like bears,
And coo sadly like doves;
We hope for justice, but there is
   none,
For salvation, but it is far from us.
[12] For our transgressions are
   multiplied before You [O LORD],
And our sins testify against us;
For our transgressions are with us,
And we know *and* recognize
   our wickedness [our sin, our
   injustice, our wrongdoing]:
[13] Rebelling against and denying the
   LORD,
Turning away from [following] our
   God,
Speaking oppression and revolt,
Conceiving and muttering from
   the heart lying words.
[14] Justice is pushed back,
And righteous behavior stands far
   away;
For truth has fallen in the city
   square,
And integrity cannot enter.
[15] Yes, truth is missing;
And he who turns away from evil
   makes himself a prey.

Now the LORD saw it,
And it displeased Him that there
   was no justice.
[16] He saw that there was no man,
And was amazed that there was
   no one to intercede [on behalf of
   truth and right];
Therefore His own arm brought
   salvation to Him,

And His own righteousness
   sustained Him. [Is 53:11; Col 2:9;
   1 John 2:1, 2]
[17] For He [the LORD] put on
   righteousness like a coat of armor,
And salvation like a helmet on His
   head;
He put on garments of vengeance
   for clothing
And covered Himself with zeal
   [and great love for His people] as
   a cloak. [Eph 6:14, 17; 1 Thess 5:8]
[18] As their deeds deserve, so He will
   repay:
Wrath to His adversaries,
   retribution to His enemies;
To the islands *and* coastlands He
   will repay.
[19] So they will fear the name of the
   LORD from the west
And His glory from the rising of
   the sun.
For He will come in like a narrow,
   rushing stream
Which the breath of the LORD
   drives [overwhelming the
   enemy]. [Matt 8:11; Luke 13:29]
[20] "A Redeemer (Messiah) will come to
   Zion,
And to those in Jacob (Israel) who
   turn from transgression (sin),"
   declares the LORD.

[21] "As for Me, this is My covenant
with them," says the LORD: "My Spirit
which is upon you [writing the law
of God on the heart], and My words
which I have put in your mouth shall
not depart from your mouth, nor from
the mouths of your [true, spiritual]
children, nor from the mouth of your
children's children," says the LORD,
"from now and forever." [Jer 31:33;
Rom 11:26, 27; Gal 3:29; Heb 12:22–24]

60

"ARISE [from spiritual
depression to a new life],
shine [be radiant with the
glory *and* brilliance of the LORD];
for your light has come,

And the glory *and* brilliance of the LORD has risen upon you. [Zech 8:23]

2 "For in fact, darkness will cover the earth

And deep darkness *will cover* the peoples;

But the LORD will rise upon you [Jerusalem]

And His glory *and* brilliance will be seen on you. [Is 60:19–22; Mal 4:2; Rev 21:2, 3]

3 "Nations will come to your light,

And kings to the brightness of your rising. [Is 2:2, 3; Jer 3:17]

4 "Lift up your eyes around you and see;

They all gather together, they come to you.

Your sons will come from far away,

And your daughters will be looked after at *their* side.

5 "Then you will see and be radiant,

And your heart will tremble [with joy] and rejoice

Because the abundant wealth of the seas will be brought to you,

The wealth of the nations will come to you. [Ps 119:32]

6 "A multitude of camels [from the eastern trading tribes] will cover you [Jerusalem],

The young camels of Midian and Ephah;

All those from Sheba [who once came to trade] will come

Bringing gold and frankincense

And proclaiming the praises of the LORD. [Matt 2:11]

7 "All the flocks of Kedar will be gathered to you [as the eastern pastoral tribes join the trading tribes],

The rams of Nebaioth will serve you;

They will go up with acceptance [as sacrifices] on My altar,

And I will glorify the house of My honor *and* splendor.

8 "Who are these who fly like a cloud And like doves to their windows?

9 "The islands *and* coastlands will confidently wait for Me;

And the ships of Tarshish *will come* first,

To bring your sons from far away,

Their silver and gold with them,

For the name of the LORD your God,

For the Holy One of Israel because He has glorified you.

10 "Foreigners will build up your walls,

And their kings will serve you;

For in My [righteous] wrath I struck you,

But in My favor *and* grace I have had compassion on you.

11 "Your gates will be open continually;

They shall not be shut day or night,

So that people may bring to you the wealth of the nations—

With their kings led in procession. [Rev 21:24–27]

12 "For the nation or the kingdom which will not serve you [Jerusalem] shall perish,

And the nations [that refuse to serve] shall be utterly ruined.

13 "The glory of Lebanon will come to you,

The cypress, the juniper, and the cedar together,

To beautify the place of My sanctuary;

And I will honor *and* make the place of My feet glorious.

14 "The sons of those who oppressed you will come bowing down to you [in submission],

And all those who despised you *and* treated you disrespectfully will bow down at the soles of your feet,

And they will call you the City of the LORD,

The Zion of the Holy One of Israel. [Rev 3:9]

15 "Whereas you [Jerusalem] have
  been abandoned and hated
With no one passing through,
I will make you an object of pride
  forever,
A joy from generation to generation.
16 "You will suck the milk of the
  [Gentile] nations
And suck the breast (abundance)
  of kings;
Then you will recognize *and* know
  that I, the LORD, am your Savior
And your Redeemer, the Mighty
  One of Jacob.
17 "Instead of bronze I will bring gold,
And instead of iron I will bring
  silver,
And instead of wood, bronze,
And instead of stones, iron.
And [instead of the tyranny of the
  present] I will appoint peace as
  your officers,
And righteousness your rulers.
18 "Violence will not be heard again
  in your land,
Nor devastation or destruction
  within your borders;
But you will call your walls
  Salvation, and your gates Praise
  [to God].
19 "The sun will no longer be your
  light by day,
Nor shall the bright glow of the
  moon give light to you,
But the LORD will be an everlasting
  light for you;
And your God will be your glory *and*
  splendor. [Jer 9:23, 24; Rev 21:23]
20 "Your sun will no longer set,
Nor will your moon wane;
For the LORD will be your
  everlasting light,
And the days of your mourning
  will be over.

21 "Then all your people will
  be [uncompromisingly and
  consistently] righteous;
They will possess the land forever,
The branch of My planting,
The work of My hands,
That I may be glorified.
22 "The smallest one will become a
  thousand (a clan),
And the least one a mighty nation.
I, the LORD, will quicken it in its
  [appointed] time."

61 THE SPIRIT of the Lord
  GOD is upon me,
  Because the LORD has
anointed *and* commissioned me
To bring good news to the humble
  and afflicted;
He has sent me to bind up [the
  wounds of] the brokenhearted,
To proclaim release [from
  confinement and condemnation]
  to the [physical and spiritual]
  captives
And freedom to prisoners, [Rom
  10:15]
2 To proclaim the favorable year of
  the LORD,

life point

In Luke 4:18 Jesus stood up in the temple to read the prophetic passage from Isaiah 61:1, and after doing so He said, "Today this Scripture has been fulfilled" (Luke 4:21). One of the things said in Isaiah 61:1 is that Jesus has come to open prison doors and set captives free. I believe this refers to the prison of sin, guilt, and condemnation. Jesus died so our sins could be forgiven and completely removed along with any sense of guilt and condemnation.

speak the Word

God, You are an everlasting light to me. You are my glory and my splendor.
–ADAPTED ISAIAH 60:19

And the day of vengeance *and*
  retribution of our God,
To comfort all who mourn, [Matt
  11:2–6; Luke 4:18, 19; 7:22]
3 To grant to those who mourn in
  Zion *the following:*
To give them a turban instead of
  dust [on their heads, a sign of
  mourning],
The oil of joy instead of mourning,
The garment [expressive] of praise
  instead of a disheartened spirit.
So they will be called the trees
  of righteousness [strong and
  magnificent, distinguished
  for integrity, justice, and right
  standing with God],

The planting of the LORD, that He
  may be glorified.
4 Then they will rebuild the ancient
  ruins,
They will raise up *and* restore the
  former desolations;
And they will renew the ruined
  cities,
The desolations (deserted
  settlements) of many generations.
5 Strangers will stand and feed your
  flocks,
And foreigners will be your
  farmers and your vinedressers.
6 But you shall be called the priests
  of the LORD;

healing in every way

Jesus can heal us everywhere we hurt! He wants to help us mentally and emotionally, as well as spiritually and physically. For a long time, I did not know that, and my lack of knowledge caused me to live a dysfunctional life. Abuse and rejection had left me emotionally wounded until I discovered that Jesus wanted to give me—and all of us—"the oil of joy instead of mourning" and "the garment [expressive] of praise instead of a disheartened spirit" (Isaiah 61:3).

When we accept Jesus as Savior and Lord, a great exchange takes place in the spirit realm. He gives us everything He has and is—and we are supposed to give Him not only everything we are, but even what we are not. He takes our weakness and gives us His strength. He takes our sickness and gives us His health and healing. We give Him our sin, and He gives us His righteousness. He will give us joy instead of mourning, as long as we are willing to give up our sadness. We cannot live in the past and press into the future at the same time. I had to let go of what was behind me and choose to start enjoying the new life that Jesus had for me. I encourage you to do the same because that will be the path to blessing in your life.

When I married my husband in 1967, I had no automobile, but he did, so suddenly I had one too. My poverty was swallowed up in his abundance. Similarly, when we accept Jesus, our sin-filled, miserable, hopeless lives are swallowed up in His goodness, mercy, and grace. If you have problems, you are just the person Jesus died for. He came for the sick and needy, not for those who need nothing. There is no shame in being needy. The greatest need that most people have is to admit they have a need!

It is time for you to enjoy God's favor. That means He will bless you even though you do not deserve it if you place your faith in Him. God wants you to enjoy yourself and your life. He wants to heal you everywhere you hurt! He wants to heal you spiritually, mentally, emotionally, physically, financially, and socially. Do not close off any part of your life to His healing touch. Invite Jesus into every area and ask Him to make you whole.

double for your trouble

When Isaiah says that the Lord will give us a "double portion" for our former shame and humiliation (Isaiah 61:7), he means that God will make up for all the hurts we have experienced in life.

One of the greatest mistakes we make is trying to avenge ourselves, to get even, to bring the scales of justice into balance rather than trusting God to do that for us. If we try to do this ourselves, we only wind up making a huge mess. The Bible says, "Beloved, never avenge yourselves, but leave the way open for God's wrath [and His judicial righteousness]; for it is written [in Scripture], 'VENGEANCE IS MINE, I WILL REPAY,' says the Lord" (Romans 12:19).

When the Bible talks about recompense or justice, it simply means that you and I will get what is right for us, what is coming to us. Now, as blood-bought children of God, we know that as long as we trust in the Lord and are obedient to Him and repentant of our sins and failures, we will not get what is coming to us in the form of punishment for our sins, but we will get rewards for our righteousness. Jesus took our punishment, and we receive His inheritance.

The Bible says in Psalm 37:1, 2, "Do not worry because of evildoers, nor be envious toward wrongdoers; for they will wither quickly like the grass, and fade like the green herb." We should not want anyone to "wither quickly," even those people who have harmed us. Instead, we need to allow God's love to be "poured out within our hearts through the Holy Spirit Who was given to us" (Romans 5:5).

In my own life, I thank God I have come to the place of not wanting to see my tormentors have miserable lives. But what God has promised us who belong to Him and follow Him is that those who have hurt us will one day pay for their transgressions against us, unless they come to a place of repentance. Yet God will make it up to us if we trust Him to do so.

Too often believers do not seem to realize they are not to take matters into their own hands. Many of them are angry at what has been done to them—and that anger manifests itself in many destructive ways.

Part of the problem is that we as Christians have not yet learned that everybody experiences difficulties in life. The Bible says, "Many hardships and perplexing circumstances confront the righteous" (Psalm 34:19). We fail to realize that even though we are God's children, not everything will go just the way we want, and not everyone will treat us as we would like to be treated. However, the Bible teaches that if we continue to trust God no matter what happens to us, if we keep our eyes on Him and have faith and confidence in Him, He will balance out the scales. The second half of Psalm 34:19 says a person may have problems, "but the LORD rescues him from them all."

The time will come when everything will be set straight. Our enemies will be repaid for all they have done to us, and we will be paid back double for all we have lost and suffered. True justice is worth waiting for.

People will speak of you as the
  ministers of our God.
You will eat the wealth of nations,
And you will boast of their riches.
  [Ex 19:6; 1 Pet 2:5; Rev 1:6; 5:10;
  20:6]
⁷Instead of your [former] shame
  you will have a double *portion;*

life point

If we consistently believe God's Word, He
will turn circumstances from negative to
positive, as Isaiah 61:1–3 describes, in His
perfect timing.

A lot of negative things have happened
to me, and Satan used them to sour my
attitude toward life and people. I was
trapped in my past because I did not believe I had a future. As soon as I believed
in Jesus Christ, I was released from the
past and began making progress toward
the good things God had in mind for me.
It did not all come to me immediately in
manifested form, but believing in God
gave me renewed hope that kept me
going from day to day. Slowly but surely
I began to see changes take place in my
life, and each change encouraged me to
believe God more.

Believing God is the key to receiving from
Him. No matter what has happened to
you in the past, if you believe, you can receive blessings instead of the difficult or
painful things from your past too. You can
begin to enjoy the good future that is set
aside for you in Jesus Christ, Who came to
do the will of His Father in heaven.

And *instead of* humiliation your
  people will shout for joy over
  their portion.
Therefore in their land they will
  possess double [what they had
  forfeited];
Everlasting joy will be theirs.
⁸For I, the Lord, love justice;
I hate robbery with a burnt
  offering.
And I will faithfully reward them,
And make an everlasting covenant
  with them.
⁹Then their offspring will be
  known among the nations,
And their descendants among the
  peoples.
All who see them [in their
  prosperity] will recognize *and*
  acknowledge them
That they are the people whom the
  Lord has blessed.
¹⁰I will rejoice greatly in the Lord,
My soul will exult in my God;
For He has clothed me with
  garments of salvation,
He has covered me with a robe of
  righteousness,
As a bridegroom puts on a turban,
And as a bride adorns herself with
  her jewels.
¹¹For as the earth brings forth its
  sprouts,
And as a garden causes what is
  sown in it to spring up,
So the Lord God will [most
  certainly] cause righteousness
  and justice and praise
To spring up before all the nations
  [through the power of His word].

speak the Word

*God, I will greatly rejoice in You. My soul will exult in You because You have
clothed me with garments of salvation and with a robe of righteousness.*
—ADAPTED FROM ISAIAH 61:10

62

FOR ZION'S sake I (Isaiah) will not be silent, And for Jerusalem's sake I will not keep quiet, Until her righteousness *and* vindication go forth as brightness, And her salvation goes forth like a burning torch.
2 The nations will see your righteousness *and* vindication [by God], And all kings [will see] your glory; And you will be called by a new name Which the mouth of the Lord will designate. [Rev 2:17]
3 You will also be [considered] a crown of glory *and* splendor in the hand of the Lord, And a royal diadem [exceedingly beautiful] in the hand of your God.
4 It will no longer be said of you [Judah], "Azubah (Abandoned)," Nor will it any longer be said of your land, "Shemamah (Desolate)"; But you will be called, "Hephzibah (My Delight is in Her)," And your land, "Married"; For the Lord delights in you, And *to Him* your land will be married [owned and protected by the Lord].
5 For as a young man marries a virgin [O Jerusalem], So your sons will marry you; And as the bridegroom rejoices over the bride, So your God will rejoice over you.
6 On your walls, O Jerusalem, I have appointed *and* stationed watchmen (prophets), Who will never keep silent day or night; You who profess the Lord, take no rest for yourselves,

7 And give Him no rest [from your prayers] until He establishes Jerusalem And makes her a praise on the earth.
8 The Lord has sworn [an oath] by His right hand and by His mighty arm, "I will never again give your grain as food for your enemies, Nor will [the invading] foreigners drink your new wine for which you have labored."
9 But they who have harvested it will eat it and praise the Lord, And they who have gathered it will drink it [at the feasts celebrated] in the courtyards of My sanctuary.
10 Go through, go through the gates, Clear the way for the people; Build up, build up the highway, Remove the stones, lift up a banner over the peoples.
11 Listen carefully, the Lord has proclaimed to the end of the earth, Say to the Daughter of Zion, "Look now, your salvation is coming [in the Lord]; Indeed, His reward is with Him, and His restitution accompanies Him." [Is 40:10]
12 And they will call them "The Holy People, The Redeemed of the Lord"; And you will be called "Sought Out, A City Not Deserted."

63

WHO IS this who comes from Edom, With crimson-stained garments from Bozrah [in Edom], This One (the Messiah) who is majestic in His apparel, Marching in the greatness of His might?

"It is I, [the One] who speaks in righteousness [proclaiming vindication], mighty to save."
2 Why is Your apparel red,
And Your garments like the one who treads in the wine press?
3 "I have trodden the wine trough alone,
And of the peoples there was no one with Me.
I also trod them in My anger
And trampled them in My wrath;
And their lifeblood is sprinkled on My garments,
And I stained all My clothes.
4 "For the day of vengeance [against ungodliness] was in My heart,
And My year of redemption [of those who put their trust in Me—the year of My redeemed] has come.
5 "I looked, but there was no one to help,
And I was amazed *and* appalled that there was no one to uphold [truth and right].
So My own arm brought salvation to Me,
And My wrath sustained Me.
6 "I trampled the peoples in My anger
And made them drunk with [the cup of] My wrath,
And I spilled their lifeblood on the earth."

7 I will tell of the lovingkindnesses of the LORD, and the praiseworthy deeds of the LORD,
According to all that the LORD has done for us,
And *His* great goodness toward the house of Israel,
Which He has shown them according to His compassion
And according to the abundance of His lovingkindnesses.
8 For He said, "Be assured, they are My people,
Sons who will not be faithless."
So He became their Savior [in all their distresses].

9 In all their distress He was distressed,
And the angel of His presence saved them,
In His love and in His compassion He redeemed them;
And He lifted them up and carried them all the days of old. [Ex 23:20–23; 33:14, 15; Deut 1:31; 32:10–12]
10 But they rebelled
And grieved His Holy Spirit;
Therefore He changed into their enemy,
And He fought against them.
11 Then His people remembered the days of old, of Moses [and they said],
Where is He who brought our fathers up out of the [Red] Sea, with the shepherds of His flock [Moses and Aaron]?
Where is He who put His Holy Spirit in their midst,
12 Who caused His glorious arm *and* infinite power to go at the right hand of Moses,
Dividing the waters before them to make for Himself an everlasting name,
13 Who led them through the depths [of the Red Sea],
Like a horse in the wilderness, [so that] they did not stumble?
14 Like the cattle that go down into the valley [to find better pasture and rest],
The Spirit of the LORD gave them rest.
So You led Your people [O LORD]
To make for Yourself a beautiful *and* glorious name [preparing the way for the acknowledgment of Your name by all nations].

15 Look down from heaven and see from Your lofty dwelling place, holy and glorious.

Where are Your zeal and Your
  mighty acts [Your miracles
  which you did for Your people]?
The stirring of Your heart and
  Your compassion are restrained
  and withheld from me.
¹⁶For [most certainly] You are our
  Father, even though Abraham
  [our ancestor] does not know us
And Israel does not
  acknowledge us.
You, O Lᴏʀᴅ, are [still] our Father,
Our Redeemer from everlasting is
  Your name.
¹⁷O Lᴏʀᴅ, why do You cause us to
  stray from Your ways
And harden our heart from fearing
  You [with reverence and awe]?
Return for Your servants' sake, the
  tribes of Your heritage.
¹⁸Your holy people possessed Your
  sanctuary for [only] a little while;
Our adversaries have trampled it
  down.
¹⁹We have become *like* those over
  whom You have never ruled,
Like those who were not called by
  Your name.

64 OH, THAT You would
  tear open the heavens and
  come down,
That the mountains might quake
  at Your presence—
²As [sure as] fire kindles the
  brushwood, as fire causes water
  to boil—
To make Your name known to
  Your adversaries,
That the nations may tremble at
  Your presence!
³When You did awesome *and*
  amazing things which we did not
  expect,
You came down [at Sinai]; the
  mountains quaked at Your
  presence.
⁴For from days of old no one has
  heard, nor has ear perceived,

Nor has the eye seen a God besides
  You,
Who works *and* acts in behalf of the
  one who [gladly] waits for Him.
⁵You meet him who rejoices in
  doing that which is morally right,
Who remembers You in Your ways.
Indeed, You were angry, for we
  sinned;
We have long *continued* in our sins
  [prolonging Your anger].
And shall we be saved [under such
  circumstances]?
⁶For we all have become like one
  who is [ceremonially] unclean
  [like a leper],
And all our deeds of righteousness
  are like filthy rags;
We all wither *and* decay like a leaf,
And our wickedness [our sin, our
  injustice, our wrongdoing], like
  the wind, takes us away [carrying
  us far from God's favor, toward
  destruction]. [Lev 13:45, 46]
⁷There is no one who calls on Your
  name,
Who awakens *and* causes himself
  to take hold of You;
For You have hidden Your face
  from us
And have handed us over to the
  [consuming and destructive]
  power of our wickedness
  [our sin, our injustice, our
  wrongdoing]. [Rom 1:21–24]

⁸Yet, O Lᴏʀᴅ, You are our Father;
We are the clay, and You our
  Potter,
And we all are the work of Your
  hand.
⁹Do not be angry beyond measure,
  O Lᴏʀᴅ,
Do not remember our wickedness
  [our sin, our injustice, our
  wrongdoing] forever.
Now look, consider, for we are all
  Your people.
¹⁰Your holy cities have become a
  wilderness,

Zion has become a wilderness,
Jerusalem a desolation.
11 Our holy and beautiful house [the
    temple built by Solomon],
Where our fathers praised You,
Has been burned by fire;
And all our precious objects are in
    ruins.
12 Considering these [tragedies], will
    You restrain Yourself, O LORD
    [and not help us]?
Will You keep silent and humiliate
    and oppress us beyond measure?

65 "I LET Myself be sought
    by those who did not ask
    for Me;
I let Myself be found by those who
    did not seek Me.
I said, 'Here am I, here am I,'
To the nation [Israel] which did not
    call on My Name. [Ex 3:14; Is 58:9]
2 "I have spread out My hands all
    the day long to a rebellious *and*
    stubborn people,
Who walk in the way that is not
    good, [following] after their own
    thoughts *and* intentions,
3 The people who continually
    provoke Me to My face,
Sacrificing [to idols] in gardens
    and making offerings with
    incense on bricks [instead of at
    the designated altar];
4 Who sit among the graves [trying
    to conjure up evil spirits] and
    spend the night in the secret
    places [where spirits are thought
    to dwell];
Who eat swine's flesh,
And their pots *hold* the broth of
    unclean meat;
5 Who say, 'Keep to yourself, do not
    come near me,
For I am too holy for you [and you
    might defile me]!'
These [people] are smoke in My
    nostrils,
A fire that burns all the day.

6 "Indeed, it is written before Me,
I will not keep silent, but I will
    repay;
I will even repay it [directly] into
    their arms,
7 Both your own wickedness and the
    wickedness of your fathers," says
    the LORD.
"Since they *too* have made
    offerings with incense on the
    mountains
And scorned *and* taunted Me on
    the hills,
I therefore will measure
    [punishment for] their former
    work [directly] into their arms."

8 This is what the LORD says,

"As the new wine is found in the
    cluster,
And one says, 'Do not destroy it,
    for there is a blessing *and* benefit
    in it,'
So I will do for the sake of My
    servants
In order not to destroy all of them.
9 "I will bring forth descendants
    from Jacob,
And an heir of My mountains from
    Judah;
Even My chosen ones shall inherit it,
And My servants will live there.
10 "And [the plain of] Sharon will be
    a place for flocks to graze,
And the Valley of Achor a resting
    place for herds,
For My people who seek Me [who
    long for Me and require My
    presence in their lives].
11 "But you who abandon (turn away
    from) the LORD,
Who forget *and* ignore My holy
    mountain (Zion),
Who set a table for Gad [the
    Babylonian god of fortune],
And who fill a jug of mixed wine
    for Meni [the god of fate],
12 I will destine you for the sword,
    [says the LORD],

And all of you will bow down to
   the slaughter,
Because when I called, you did not
   answer;
When I spoke, you did not listen or
   obey.
But you did [what was] evil in My
   sight
And chose that in which I did not
   delight."

¹³Therefore, the Lord GOD says this,

"Listen carefully, My servants will
   eat, but you will be hungry;
Indeed, My servants will drink,
   but you will be thirsty;
Indeed, My servants will rejoice,
   but you will be put to shame.
¹⁴"Indeed, My servants will shout for
   joy from a happy heart,
But you will cry out with a heavy
   heart,
And you shall wail and howl from
   a broken spirit.
¹⁵"And you will leave your name
   behind to My chosen ones [who
   will use it] as a curse,
And the Lord GOD will put you to
   death,
But He will call His servants by
   another name [a much greater
   name, just as the name Israel
   was greater than the name
   Jacob]. [Gen 32:28; Jer 29:22]
¹⁶"Because he who blesses himself
   on the earth
Will bless himself by the God of
   truth and faithfulness;
And he who swears [an oath] on
   the earth
Will swear by the God of truth and
   faithfulness;
Because the former troubles are
   forgotten,
And because they are hidden from
   My sight. [2 Cor 1:20; Rev 3:14]
¹⁷"Behold, I am creating new
   heavens and a new earth;

And the former things [of life]
   will not be remembered or come
   to mind. [Is 66:22; 2 Pet 3:13;
   Rev 21:1]
¹⁸"But be glad and rejoice forever
   over what I create;
Behold, I am creating Jerusalem to
   be a source of rejoicing
And her people a joy.
¹⁹"I will also rejoice in Jerusalem
   and be glad in My people;
And there will no longer be heard
   in her
The voice of weeping and the
   sound of crying.
²⁰"No longer shall there be in it an
   infant who lives only a few days,
Or an old man who does not finish
   his days;
For the youth who dies at the age
   of a hundred,
And the one who does not reach
   the age of a hundred
Will be thought of as accursed.
²¹"They will build houses and live in
   them;
They will plant vineyards and eat
   the fruit.
²²"They will not build and another
   occupy;
They will not plant and another
   eat [the fruit].
For as the lifetime of a tree, so will
   be the days of My people,
And My chosen [people] will fully
   enjoy [and long make use of] the
   work of their hands.
²³"They will not labor in vain,
Or bear children for disaster;
For they are the descendants of
   those blessed by the LORD,
And their offspring with them.

²⁴"It shall also come to pass that before
they call, I will answer; and while they
are still speaking, I will hear. [Is 30:19;
58:9; Matt 6:8]
²⁵"The wolf and the lamb will graze
together, and the lion will eat straw
like the ox [there will no longer be

predator and prey]; and dust will be the serpent's food. They will do no evil or harm in all My holy mountain (Zion)," says the Lord.

66 THIS IS what the Lord says,
"Heaven is My throne and the earth is My footstool.
Where, then, is a house that you could build for Me?
And where will My resting place be? [Acts 17:24]
2 "For all these things My hand has made,
So all these things came into being [by and for Me]," declares the Lord.
"But to this one I will look [graciously],
To him who is humble and contrite in spirit, and who [reverently] trembles at My word *and* honors My commands. [John 4:24]

3 "He who kills an ox [for pagan sacrifice] is [as guilty] as one who kills a man;
He who sacrifices a lamb, as one who breaks a dog's neck;
He who offers a grain offering, *as one who offers* swine's blood;
He who offers incense, as one who blesses an idol.
Such people have chosen their own ways,
And their soul delights in their repulsive acts;
4 So I will choose their punishments,
And will bring the things they dread upon them
Because I called, but no one answered;
I spoke, but they did not listen *or* obey.
But they did evil in My sight
And chose that in which I did not delight."

5 Hear the word of the Lord, you who tremble [with awe-filled reverence] at His word:
"Your brothers who hate you, who exclude you for My Name's sake,
Have said, 'Let the Lord be glorified, that we may see your joy.'
But they will be put to shame.
6 "The sound of an uproar from the city! A voice from the temple!
The voice of the Lord, providing retribution to His enemies.

7 "Before she (Zion) was in labor, she gave birth;
Before her labor pain came, she gave birth to a boy.
8 "Who has heard of such a thing? Who has seen such things?
Can a land be born in one day?
Or can a nation be brought forth in a moment?
As soon as Zion was in labor, she also brought forth her sons.
9 "Shall I bring to the moment of birth and not give delivery?" says the Lord.
"Or shall I who gives delivery shut *the womb?*" says your God.
10 "Rejoice with Jerusalem and be glad for her, all you who love her;
Rejoice greatly with her, all you who mourn over her,
11 That you may nurse and be satisfied with her comforting breasts,
That you may drink deeply and be delighted with her bountiful bosom."
12 For the Lord says this, "Behold, I extend peace to her (Jerusalem) like a river,
And the glory of the nations like an overflowing stream;
And you will be nursed, you will be carried on *her* hip and [playfully] rocked on *her* knees.
13 "As one whom his mother comforts, so I will comfort you;
And you will be comforted in Jerusalem."

14 When you see this, your heart will
   rejoice;
   Your bones will flourish like new
   grass.
   And the [powerful] hand of the
   Lord will be revealed to His
   servants,
   But His indignation will be toward
   His enemies.
15 For indeed, the Lord will come in
   fire
   And His chariots will be like the
   stormy wind,
   To render His anger with rage,
   And His rebuke with flames of fire.
16 For the Lord will execute judgment
   by fire
   And by His sword on all mankind,
   And those slain by the Lord will be
   many.
17 "Those who [vainly attempt to]
   sanctify and cleanse themselves
   to go to the gardens [to sacrifice
   to idols],
   Following after one in the center,
   Who eat swine's flesh, detestable
   things and mice,
   Will come to an end together," says
   the Lord.

18 "For I know their works and their
thoughts. *The time* is coming to gather
all nations and languages, and they
will come and see My glory.
19 "I will set up a [miraculous] sign
among them, and from them I will
send survivors to the nations: Tarshish, Pul (Put), Lud, Meshech, Tubal
and Javan, to the distant islands *and*
coastlands that have not heard of My
fame nor seen My glory. And they will
declare *and* proclaim My glory among
the nations.
20 "Then they shall bring all your
countrymen (children of Israel) from
all the nations as a grain offering to
the Lord—on horses, in chariots, in lit-
ters, on mules and on camels—to My
holy mountain Jerusalem," says the
Lord, "just as the sons of Israel bring
their grain offering in a clean vessel
to the house of the Lord.
21 "I will also take some of them as
priests and Levites," says the Lord.

22 "For just as the new heavens and
   the new earth
   Which I make will remain *and*
   endure before Me," declares the
   Lord,
   "So your offspring and your name
   will remain *and* endure.
23 "And it shall be that from New
   Moon to New Moon
   And from Sabbath to Sabbath,
   All mankind will come to bow
   down *and* worship before Me,"
   says the Lord.
24 "Then they will go forth and look
   Upon the dead bodies of the
   [rebellious] men
   Who have transgressed against Me;
   For their worm (maggot) will not die,
   And their fire will not go out;
   And they will be an abhorrence to
   all mankind."

Jeremiah

Author:
Jeremiah

Date:
626 BC–586 BC

Everyday Life Principles:
Remember that you were born with a God-given purpose. Stay focused on Him, even amid opposition, and you will prevail in fulfilling your purpose.

Trust God with all your heart.

Make a priority of seeking God above and before everything else.

Have you ever met someone you considered "a born leader," "a born athlete," or "a born salesman"? Well, Jeremiah was truly "a born prophet." God called him in his mother's womb, before he ever breathed his first breath, for the specific purpose of delivering His message to the people of Judah. Jeremiah enjoyed good times during the reign of a good king, Josiah; he also endured persecution and hostility when he had to speak difficult messages and warnings to bad kings. Even though he did not quickly embrace his call as a prophet in his younger days, he did obey God and stayed faithful to Him.

Some of Jeremiah's key themes include: obeying God's call, trusting God, putting faith in God instead of people, staying faithful to a covenant relationship with God, seeking God wholeheartedly, continuing to obey God in the face of opposition, and remembering that God loves us with an everlasting love. In addition to these great themes, Jeremiah also includes some beloved Bible verses, such as Jeremiah 29:11: "'For I know the plans and thoughts that I have for you,' says the LORD, 'plans for peace and well-being and not for disaster, to give you a future and a hope.'"

I hope you will read the book of Jeremiah and be encouraged in God's purpose for your life as you continue to trust and seek Him.

1 THE WORDS of Jeremiah the son of Hilkiah, [one] of the priests who were in Anathoth in the land of Benjamin,

²to whom the word of the LORD came during the thirteenth year (627 B.C.) of the reign of Josiah the son of Amon, king of Judah.

³It came [to Jeremiah] also in the days of Jehoiakim the son of Josiah, king of Judah, [continuing] until the end of the eleventh year of Zedekiah the son of Josiah, king of Judah, [and continuing] until the exile of [the people of] Jerusalem in the fifth month (July-August, 586 B.C.). [2 Kin 25:8–11]

⁴Now the word of the LORD came to me, saying,

⁵"Before I formed you in the womb
  I knew you [and approved of you
  as My chosen instrument],
And before you were born I
  consecrated you [to Myself as My
  own];
I have appointed you as a prophet
  to the nations." [Ex 33:12; Is 49:1,
  5; Rom 8:29]
⁶Then I said, "Ah, Lord GOD!
Behold, I do not know how to speak,
For I am [only] a young man." [Ex
  4:10; 6:12, 30; 1 Kin 3:7]
⁷But the LORD said to me,
"Do not say, 'I am [only] a young
  man,'
Because everywhere I send you,
  you shall go,

approved!

God told Jeremiah that He knew him and approved of him before he was formed in his mother's womb (see Jeremiah 1:5). When God said He "knew" Jeremiah, He was not speaking of a casual acquaintance, but of the deepest, most intimate knowledge possible. God knows us the same way. He knows everything about us, even things we will never discover about ourselves. He knows every mistake we will ever make—and He loves us and approves of us anyway.

God does not always approve of our behavior and choices, but He does approve of us as His chosen instruments. There is a big difference between *who* we are and *what* we do. Jeremiah was a child of God, and God knew his heart. He did not do everything right. For example, he was afraid of what people would think of him. The fear of man displeases God. He wants us to realize that when He is on our side, it does not matter who is against us. It's important for us to strive to be God-pleasers, not people-pleasers.

If we live with the sense that God disapproves of us, we will always have the wrong kind of fear of Him, and that will hinder us from enjoying an intimate relationship and rich fellowship with Him. God wants us to have a reverential fear and awe of Him, but He does not want us to be afraid of Him in a wrong way. He wants us to come confidently and without fear to His throne of grace and ask Him to meet our needs and help us in every situation we face (see Hebrews 4:16). Ephesians 3:12 teaches us that our faith gives us boldness to approach Him with freedom and openness.

Do not shrink back in fear, but press forward in faith. Without faith we cannot please God (see Hebrews 11:6), and without fear we cannot please Satan. Whom do you want to please? I am sure it is God, so begin right now by living in the freedom of realizing that God *knows* you and approves of you as His chosen instrument.

And whatever I command you, you
shall speak.
8 "Do not be afraid of them [or their
hostile faces],
For I am with you [always] to
protect you *and* deliver you,"
says the LORD.

9 Then the LORD stretched out His hand
and touched my mouth, and the LORD
said to me,

"Behold (hear Me), I have put My
words in your mouth.
10 "See, I have appointed you this day
over the nations and over the
kingdoms,
To uproot and break down,
To destroy and to overthrow,
To build and to plant."

11 The word of the LORD came to me,
saying, "Jeremiah, what do you see?"
And I said, "I see the branch of an almond tree."
12 Then the LORD said to me, "You have
seen well, for I am [actively] watching
over My word to fulfill it."
13 The word of the LORD came to me a
second time, saying, "What do you see?"
And I said, "I see a boiling pot, tilting
away from the north [its mouth about to
pour out on the south, on Judea]."
14 Then the LORD said to me, "Out of
the north the evil [which the prophets
foretold as the result of national sin]
will reveal itself *and* spill out on all the
people of the land.
15 "For, behold, I will call all the tribes
of the kingdoms of the north," says the

you are chosen

We all want other people to like us and approve of us. However, our desire for
approval can only truly be met by receiving God's acceptance and approval of us.
God told Jeremiah that before He formed him in his mother's womb, He knew him
and approved of him as His chosen instrument (see Jeremiah 1:5). When God says He
knows us, He means He really *knows* us. This is a knowing that leaves out nothing.

I am amazed that God chose me. I do not think I would have chosen myself. But God's
tool chest has some interesting things in it. He works with and uses for His purpose
things that are seemingly insignificant and worthless (see 1 Corinthians 1:27, 28).

Yes, God chooses and uses what the world would reject! Was Jeremiah perfect? Absolutely not! Jeremiah was fearful, and God had to correct him concerning his fear
of people. Jeremiah was afraid of being rejected and disapproved of. God corrected
him about speaking negatively and encouraged him to go forward and not give up.

It is interesting to note that God actually told Jeremiah in Jeremiah 1:8 not to be
afraid of people's faces. Why is that? We tend to watch people's faces to see if they
approve or disapprove of everything about us—what we are wearing, our hair, our
performance, et cetera. We pay too much attention to how people respond to us.

Yes, Jeremiah had problems just as we do. When God saw Jeremiah, He did not see
perfection, but He obviously did see someone with a right heart who believed in
Him. He saw in Jeremiah two main ingredients essential to pleasing God: (1) faith
in God, and (2) a deep desire to please Him. Although Jeremiah was not perfect, he
did submit to the call of God on his life. Jeremiah, despite criticism, unpopularity,
and attacks against him, faithfully delivered God's message to the nation of Judah.
By doing so, he honored God, demonstrated faith and courage, and chose obedience
over his personal preferences. I encourage you to do likewise!

LORD; "and they will come and each one will set his throne at the entrance of the gates of Jerusalem, and against all its surrounding walls, and against all the cities of Judah [as My judicial act, the consequence of Judah's deliberate disobedience].

16"I will speak My judgments against them for all the wickedness of those who have abandoned (rejected) Me, offered sacrifices *or* burned incense to other gods, and worshiped the [idolatrous] works of their own hands.

17"But you [Jeremiah], gird up your loins [in preparation]! Get up and tell them all which I command you. Do not be distraught *and* break down at the sight of their [hostile] faces, or I will bewilder you before them *and* allow you to be overcome.

18"Now behold, I have made you today like a fortified city and like an iron pillar and like bronze walls against the whole land—against the [successive] kings of Judah, against its leaders, against its priests, and against the people of the land [giving you divine strength which no hostile power can overcome]. [Is 50:7; 54:17; Jer 6:27; 15:20; Luke 21:15; Acts 6:10]

19"They will fight against you, but they will not [ultimately] prevail over you, for I am with you [always] to protect you *and* deliver you," says the LORD.

2 NOW THE word of the LORD came to me saying, 2"Go and proclaim in the ears of Jerusalem, saying, 'Thus says the LORD,

"I remember [earnestly] the
    lovingkindness *and* devotion of
    your youth,
Your time of betrothal [like that of
    a bride during the early years in
    Egypt and again at Sinai],
When you followed Me in the
    wilderness,
Through a land not sown.

3"Israel was holy [something set
    apart from ordinary purposes,
    consecrated] to the LORD,
The first fruits of His harvest [in
    which no outsider was allowed to
    share].
All who ate of it [injuring Israel]
    became guilty;
Evil came on them," says the LORD.'"

4Hear the word of the LORD, O house of Jacob, and all the families of the house of Israel.

5Thus says the LORD,

"What injustice *or*
    unrighteousness did your fathers
    find in Me,
That they have wandered far from
    Me
And [habitually] walked after
    emptiness *and* futility and
    became empty?
6"They did not say, 'Where is the
    LORD
Who brought us up from the land
    of Egypt,
Who led us through the wilderness,
Through a land of deserts and of
    pits,
Through a land of drought and
    of the deep darkness [of the
    shadow of death],
Through a land that no man
    passed through
And where no man lived?'
7"I brought you into a plentiful land
To eat its fruit and [enjoy] its good
    things.
But you came and defiled My land
And you made My inheritance
    repulsive.
8"[Even] the priests did not say,
    'Where is the LORD?'
And those who deal with the
    law [given to Moses] did not
    know Me.
The rulers *and* shepherds also
    transgressed against Me,

And the prophets prophesied by [the authority and in the name of] Baal
And walked after [idolatrous] things that did not benefit [them].

⁹"Therefore I will still contend (struggle) with you [by bringing judgment on you]," says the LORD,
"And I will contend with your children's children."
¹⁰"For cross over to the coasts of Kittim (Cyprus) [to the west] and see,
Send also to Kedar (Arabia) [to the east] and carefully observe *and* consider
And see whether there has been such [a thing] as this!
¹¹"Has a nation [ever] changed gods

Even though they were not gods [but merely man-made objects]?
But My people have exchanged their Glory (the true God)
For that [man-made idol] which does not benefit [them].
¹²"Be appalled, O heavens, at this;
Be shocked *and* shudder with horror [at the behavior of the people]," says the LORD.
¹³"For My people have committed two evils:
They have abandoned (rejected) Me,
The fountain of living water,
And they have carved out their own cisterns,
Broken cisterns
That cannot hold water.
¹⁴"Is Israel a servant? Is he a slave by birth?

make your work succeed

The people in Jeremiah 2:13 worked hard to dig wells for themselves, but their wells could not hold water. I am sure they were very disappointed when they did not get the result they wanted after working so hard. I know what it is like to work hard with no results. I have spent many years of my life digging "empty wells," and that frustrated and discouraged me. It took me a long time to realize that "Unless the LORD builds the house, they labor in vain who build it" (Psalm 127:1).

You may be digging an empty well right now. You may be working on something or somebody. You may have your own little project going on, but you are doing it your way. You may be following your own little plan, trying to make things happen in your own strength and ability. If so, and you have left God out of your plan, it is not going to work.

There is nothing more frustrating than trying to do something about something you cannot do anything about. It is similar to having your car stuck in the mud and continuing to press the accelerator down, spinning your wheels until you burn up the engine. We often burn out from weariness due to works of the flesh, which are works that do not work!

Many times, we make a plan and then pray for it to work. God wants us to pray *first* and ask Him for His plan. After we have His plan, then He wants us to trust Him to bring it to pass.

Activity birthed out of the flesh actually prevents God from showing Himself strong in our lives. That is not the way to live the higher life that God has prepared for us. Ask God to help you and lead you as you work so your efforts will be productive.

Why has he become a captive *and*
    a prey?
15 "The young lions have roared at
    him,
They have made their voices heard
    and roared loudly.
And they have made his land a
    waste;
His cities have been destroyed
    and are burned ruins, without
    inhabitant.
16 "Moreover, the men of Memphis
    and Tahpanhes [as powerful
    enemies]
Have shaved the crown of your
    head [to degrade you].
17 "Have you not brought this on
    yourself
By abandoning (rejecting) the
    LORD your God
When He led you in the way?
18 "Now what are you doing by going
    to Egypt [in search of an ally],
To drink the [muddy] waters of the
    Nile?
Or what are you doing by going to
    Assyria [in search of an ally],
To drink the [muddy] waters of the
    Euphrates?
19 "Your own wickedness will
    discipline you,
And your desertion of the faith
    will punish you.
Know therefore that it is an evil
    and bitter thing
For you to abandon (reject) the
    LORD your God,
And for you to be indifferent to Me
    and dismiss the [reverent] fear of
    Me," says the Lord GOD of hosts.
20 "For long ago you broke your yoke
    [in deliberate disobedience]
And tore off your bonds [of the law
    that I gave you];
You said, 'I will not serve *and* obey
    You!'
For on every high hill
And under every green tree

You have lain down [in idolatrous
    worship] like a [compliant]
    prostitute.
21 "Yet I had planted you [O house of
    Israel as] a choice vine,
A completely faithful seed.
How then have you turned against
    Me
Into degenerate shoots of a foreign
    and wild vine [alien to Me]?
22 "For though you wash yourself
    with lye
And use much soap,
The stain of your guilt is [still]
    before Me [and you are soiled
    and dirty]," says the Lord GOD.
23 "How can you say, 'I am not defiled,
I have not gone after [man-made
    gods like] the Baals'?
Look at your way in the valley;
Know [without any doubt] what
    you have done!
You are a swift *and* restless young
    [female] camel [in the heat of her
    passion] running here and there,
24 Or [you have the untamed and
    reckless nature of] a wild donkey
    accustomed to the wilderness,
That sniffs the wind in her passion
    [for the scent of a mate].
In her mating season who can
    restrain her?
No males seeking her need to
    weary themselves;
In her month they will find her
    [looking for them].
25 "[Cease your mad running after
    idols to]
Keep your feet from becoming bare
And your throat from becoming dry;
But you said, 'It is hopeless!
For I have loved strangers *and*
    foreign gods,
And I will walk after them.'
26 "As the thief is shamed when he is
    caught,
So the house of Israel is shamed—
They, their kings, their leaders,
Their priests, and their prophets—

27 Who say to a tree, 'You are my
    father,'
And to a stone, 'You gave me birth.'
For they have turned their backs
    to Me,
And not their faces;
But in the time of their trouble
    they will say,
'Arise [O Lord] and save us.'
28 "But where are your gods
Which you made for yourself?
Let them get up, if they can save you
In the time of your trouble!
For [as many as] the number of
    your cities
Are your gods, O Judah. [Why do
    not your many man-made idols
    run to help you?]

29 "Why do you complain and
    contend with Me?
You have all rebelled
    (transgressed) against Me," says
    the Lord.
30 "In vain I have punished your
    people [with the consequences of
    their disobedience];
They received no insight from
    correction [and refused to
    change].
Your [own] sword has devoured
    your prophets
Like a destroying lion.
31 "O generation [that you are],
    consider and regard carefully the
    word of the Lord.
Have I been a wilderness to Israel
    [like a land without food],
A land of thick and deep darkness
    [like a path without light]?
Why do My people say, 'We [have
    broken loose and we] are free to
    roam [at will];
We will no longer come to You'?
32 "Can a virgin forget [to wear] her
    ornaments,
Or a bride her attire [that identifies
    her as a married woman]?
Yet My people have forgotten Me
Days without number.

33 "How well you prepare your path
To seek and obtain [adulterous]
    love!
Even the most wicked of women
Have learned [indecent] ways
    from you.
34 "Also on your skirts is found
The lifeblood of the innocent poor;
You did not find them breaking in
    [a house].
But in spite of all these things
    [your disobedience, your
    love of idolatry, your lack of
    compassion]—
35 Yet you keep saying, 'I am innocent;
Surely His anger has turned away
    from me.'
Behold (listen very carefully), I
    will bring you to judgment and
    will plead my case against you
Because you say, 'I have not sinned.'
36 "Why do you go around and
    wander so much
Changing your way?
Also, you will be shamed by Egypt
As you were shamed by Assyria.
37 "From Egypt also you will come
    away [as captives]
With your hands on your head;
For the Lord has rejected those in
    whom you trust (confide),
And you will not be successful
    with them."

3 THAT IS to say, "If a man
    divorces his wife
And she goes [away] from him
And becomes another man's [wife],
Will he return to her again? [Of
    course not!]
Will not that land [where such a
    thing happened] be completely
    desecrated?
But you [rebelled against Me and
    you] are a prostitute with many
    lovers;
Yet you turn to Me." says the Lord.
2 "Lift up your eyes to the barren
    heights and see;

Where have you not been violated?
You sat by the road waiting [eagerly]
    for them [those man-made gods]
Like an Arab [tribesman who
    waits to attack] in the desert,
And you have desecrated the land
With your [vile] prostitution and
    your wickedness (disobedience
    to God).
³"Therefore the showers have been
    withheld,
And there has been no spring rain.
Yet you have the forehead
    (appearance) of a prostitute;
You refuse to be ashamed.
⁴"Will you not just now call out to Me,
'My Father, you were the guide *and*
    companion of my youth?
⁵'Will He be angry forever?
Will He be indignant to the end?'
Behold, you have spoken,
And you have done all the evil
    things [you could],
And you have had your way
and have carried out your
    wickedness."

⁶Moreover, the LORD said to me in
the days of Josiah the king [of Judah],
"Have you seen what that faithless Israel has done—how she went up on
every high hill and under every green
tree, and there she was a prostitute?
⁷"I thought, 'After she has done all
these things she will return to Me'; but
she did not return, and her treacherous (faithless) sister Judah saw it.
⁸"And I saw [that even though Judah
knew] that for all the acts of adultery
(idolatry) of faithless Israel, I [the
LORD] had sent her away and given her
a certificate of divorce, yet her treacherous sister Judah was not afraid; but
she went and was a prostitute also
[following after idols].
⁹"Because of the thoughtlessness of
Israel's prostitution [her immorality
mattered little to her], she desecrated
the land and committed adultery with
[idols of] stones and trees.

¹⁰"Yet in spite of all this her treacherous sister Judah did not return to
Me with her whole heart, but rather
in [blatant] deception [she merely
pretended obedience to King Josiah's
reforms]," declares the LORD. [2 Chr
34:33; Hos 7:13, 14]
¹¹And the LORD said to me, "Faithless
Israel has proved herself less guilty
than treacherous Judah [a land of ren-
egades].
¹²"Go and proclaim these words toward the north [where the ten tribes
have been taken as captives] and say,

'Return, faithless Israel,' says the
    LORD;
'I will not look on you in anger.
For I am gracious *and* merciful,'
    says the LORD;
'I will not be angry forever.
¹³'Only understand fully *and*
    acknowledge your wickedness
    and guilt,
That you have rebelled
    (transgressed) against the LORD
    your God
And have scattered your favors
    among strangers under every
    green tree,
And you have not obeyed My
    voice,' says the LORD.
¹⁴'Return, O faithless children [of
    the twelve tribes],' says the LORD,
'For I am a master *and* husband to
    you,
And I will take you [not as a
    nation, but individually]—one
    from a city and two from a
    [tribal] family—

putting the Word to work

**Do you have a "spiritual shepherd" (a
spiritual leader) who has God's heart,
as mentioned in Jeremiah 3:15? If so,
thank God for that person. If not, ask
God to give you such a leader.**

And I will bring you to Zion.'
[Luke 15:20–22]

15"Then [in the final time] I will give you [spiritual] shepherds after My own heart, who will feed you with knowledge and [true] understanding. 16"It will be in those days when you have [repented and] multiplied and increased in the land," says the LORD, "they will no longer say, 'The ark of the covenant of the LORD.' It will not come to mind, nor will they [seriously] remember it, nor will they miss it, nor will it be made again [for instead of the ark, which symbolized My presence, I will be present]. [Is 65:17; Rev 21:3, 22, 23] 17"At that time they will call Jerusalem 'The Throne of the LORD,' and all the nations will be gathered to it, to Jerusalem, for the name (renown) of the LORD; and they will not walk anymore after the stubbornness of their [own] evil heart. 18"In those days the house of Judah will walk with the house of Israel, and they will come together from the land of the north to the land that I gave your fathers as an inheritance. 19"Then I said,

'How [gloriously and honorably] I
  would set you among My children
And give you a pleasant land—a
  wonderful heritage,
The most beautiful inheritance of
  the nations!'
And I said, 'You shall call Me, My
  Father
And not turn away from following
  Me.'
20"Surely, as a wife treacherously
  (unfaithfully) leaves her husband,
So you have dealt treacherously
  with Me,
O house of Israel," says the LORD.

21A voice is heard on the barren
  heights,
The weeping and pleading of the
  children of Israel,

Because they have lost their way,
They have [deliberately] forgotten
  the LORD their God.
22"Return, O faithless sons," [says
  the LORD],
"I will heal your unfaithfulness."
[They answer] "Behold, we come
  to You,
For You are the LORD our God.
23"Truly, [the hope of salvation
  from] the hill [where idols are
  worshiped] is a deception,
A tumult and noisy multitude on
  the mountains;
Truly in the LORD our God
Is the salvation of Israel.

24"But the shameful act [of idolatry] has consumed the labor of our fathers since our youth—their flocks and their herds, their sons and their daughters. 25"Let us lie down in our shame, and let our dishonor and humiliation cover us; for we have sinned against the LORD our God, we and our fathers; from our youth even to this day we have not obeyed the voice of the LORD our God."

4 "IF YOU will return, O Israel,"
  says the LORD,
  "If you will return to Me,
And if you will put away your
  detestable things and remove
  your man-made gods from My
  sight,
And not stray or waver,
2And if you swear [your oaths], 'As
  the LORD lives,'
In truth, in justice, and in
  righteousness,
Then the nations will bless
  themselves in Him,
And in Him they will glory."

3For this is what the LORD says to the men of Judah and to Jerusalem,

"Plow your uncultivated ground
  [for a season],
And do not sow among thorns.

⁴"Circumcise (dedicate, sanctify)
  yourselves to the LORD
And remove the foreskin [sins] of
  your heart,
Men of Judah and inhabitants of
  Jerusalem,
Or else My wrath will go forth like
  fire [consuming all that gets in
  its way]
And burn and there will be no one
  to quench it,
Because of the evil of your acts."

⁵Declare in Judah and proclaim in
  Jerusalem, and say,
"Blow the trumpet in the land;
Cry aloud and say,
'Assemble yourselves, and let us go
Into the fortified cities.'
⁶"Raise a banner toward Zion [to
  mark the way for those seeking
  safety inside Jerusalem's walls]!
Seek refuge, do not stand
  [immobile],
For I am bringing evil from the
  north (the army of Babylon),
And great destruction.
⁷"A lion has left his lair,
And a destroyer of nations is on
  his way.
He has gone out from his place
To desolate your land;
Your cities will be in ruins
Without an inhabitant.
⁸"For this reason, put on sackcloth
  [for mourning],
Lament (mourn with expressions
  of grief for the dead) and wail,
For the fierce anger of the LORD
Has not turned back from us."

⁹"It shall come about in that day," says
the LORD, "that the heart and courage
of the king will fail (be paralyzed),
and also the heart of the princes; the
priests will be appalled and the prophets will be astounded and horrified."
¹⁰Then I said, "Alas, Lord GOD! Surely
You have completely deceived and misled this people and Jerusalem, [for the

prophets represented You as] saying [to
Your people], 'You will have peace,' but
[in fact] a sword reaches to their throat."
¹¹In that time it will be said to this
people and to Jerusalem, "A scorching
wind from the barren heights in the
wilderness [comes at My command]
against the daughter of My people—not
[a wind] to winnow and not to cleanse
[from chaff, as when threshing, but]
¹²a wind too strong and full for this
comes at My word. Now I will also
speak judgment against My people."

¹³"Behold, the enemy comes up like
  clouds,
His chariots like the whirlwind;
His horses are swifter than eagles.
Woe (judgment is coming) to us,
  for we are ruined!"

¹⁴O Jerusalem, wash your heart from
  wickedness,
That you may be saved.
How long will your wicked and
  immoral thoughts
Lodge within you?
¹⁵For a voice declares from Dan [far
  in the north],
And proclaims evil from Mount
  Ephraim.
¹⁶"Warn the [neighboring] nations
  now [that our enemy is coming]!
Announce to Jerusalem,
'Besiegers are coming from a far
  country,
And they lift their voices and shout
  against the cities of Judah.
¹⁷'Like watchmen of a field they are
  against her on all sides,
Because she has rebelled against
  Me,' says the LORD.
¹⁸"Your ways and your deeds
Have brought these things on you.
This is your tragedy and doom; how
  bitter,
How it has touched your heart!"

¹⁹My soul, my soul! I writhe in
  anguish and pain! Oh, the walls
  of my heart!

My heart is pounding *and*
  throbbing within me;
I cannot be silent,
For you have heard, O my soul,
The sound of the trumpet,
The alarm of war.
20 News of one [terrible] disaster
  comes close after another,
For the whole land is devastated;
Suddenly my tents are spoiled *and*
  destroyed,
My [tent] curtains [ruined] in a
  moment.
21 How long [O Lord] must I see the
  banner [marking the way for
  flight]
And hear the sound of the trumpet
  [urging the people to run for
  safety]?
22 "For My people are stupid *and*
  foolish," [says the Lord to
  Jeremiah];
"They do not know Me;
They are foolish children
And have no understanding.
They are shrewd [enough] to do
  evil,
But they do not know [how] to do
  good."

23 I looked at the earth [in my vision],
  and behold, it was [as at the time
  of creation] formless and void;
And to the heavens, and they had
  no light.
24 I looked at the mountains, and
  behold, they were trembling,
And all the hills moved back and
  forth.
25 I looked, and behold, there was no
  man,
And all the birds of the air had
  fled.
26 I looked, and behold, the fertile
  land was a wilderness,
And all its cities were pulled down
Before the [presence of the] Lord,
  before His fierce anger.

27 Therefore says the Lord,

"The whole land shall be a
  desolation,
Yet I will not cause total destruction.
  [Jer 5:10, 18; 30:11; 46:28]
28 "For this reason the earth shall
  mourn
And the heavens above shall
  become dark,
Because I have spoken, I have
  decided,
And I will not change my mind
  (relent), nor will I turn back
  from it."
29 Every city runs away at the sound
  of the horsemen and archers.
They go into the thickets and
  climb among the rocks;
Every city is deserted,
And no man lives in them.
30 And you, O desolate one, what will
  you do?
Though you clothe yourself in
  scarlet,
Though you adorn *yourself with*
  ornaments of gold,
Though you enlarge your eyes
  with paint,
You make yourself beautiful in
  vain.
Your lovers (allies) despise you;
They seek your life.
31 For I heard a cry like a woman in
  labor,
The anguish as of one giving birth
  to her first child,
The cry of the Daughter of Zion
  (Jerusalem), who gasps for breath,
Who stretches out her hands,
  saying,
"Woe is me [my judgment comes]!
  I faint [in fear] before the
  murderers."

5 "ROAM BACK and forth through
  the streets of Jerusalem,
  And look now and take note.
And look in her open squares
To see if you can find a man [as
  Abraham sought in Sodom],

One who is just, who [has integrity
and moral courage and] seeks
truth (faithfulness);
Then I will pardon Jerusalem—
[for the sake of one
uncompromisingly righteous
person]. [Gen 18:22–32]
2 "And though they say, 'As the Lord
lives,'
Surely they swear [their oaths]
falsely."
3 O Lord, do not Your eyes look for
truth?
You [have seen their faithless
heart and] have stricken them,
But they did not weaken;
You have consumed them,
But they refused to take correction
or instruction.
They have made their faces harder
than rock;
They have refused to repent and
return to You.

4 Then I said, "[Surely] these are
only the poor (uneducated);
They are [sinfully] foolish
and have no [spiritual]
understanding,
For they do not know the way of
the Lord
Or the ordinance of their God [and
the requirements of His just and
righteous law].
5 "I will go to the great [men]
And speak to them,
For they [must] know the way of
the Lord,
The ordinance of their God."
But [I found the reverse to be
true, that] they too had all alike
broken the yoke [of God's law]
And had burst the bonds [of
obedience to Him].
6 Therefore a lion from the forest
will kill them,
A wolf of the deserts will destroy
them,
A leopard is watching their cities.

Everyone who goes out of them
shall be torn in pieces,
Because their transgressions are
many,
Their desertions of faith are
countless.

7 "Why should I [overlook these
offenses and] forgive you?
Your children have abandoned
(rejected) Me
And sworn [their oaths] by those
who are not gods.
When I had fed them until they
were full [and bound them to Me
by a promise],
They committed [spiritual]
adultery,
Assembling in troops at the houses
of prostitutes (idols).
8 "They were like well-fed, lusty
stallions,
Each one neighing after his
neighbor's wife.
9 "Shall I not punish them [for these
things]?" says the Lord;
"Shall I not avenge Myself
On a nation such as this?"

10 "Go up through the rows of
Jerusalem's vineyards and
destroy [them],
But do not completely destroy
everything.
Strip away her branches and the
tendrils [of her vines],
For they are not the Lord's.
11 "For the house of Israel and the
house of Judah
Have dealt very treacherously
(faithlessly) with Me," declares
the Lord.
12 They have lied about and denied
the Lord
By saying, "It is not He [who
speaks through His prophets];
Misfortune and evil shall not come
on us,
Nor will we see war or famine.

13 "The prophets are like the wind
   [their prophecy will not come to
   pass],
And the word [of God] is not in
   them.
In this manner it will be done to
   them [as they prophesied, not to
   us]."

14 Therefore, thus says the LORD God
   of hosts,
"Because you [people] have
   spoken this word,
Behold, I am making My words a
   fire in your mouth [Jeremiah]

And this people wood, and My
   words will consume them.
15 "Behold, I am bringing a nation
   against you from far away, O
   house of Israel," says the LORD.
"It is a mighty *and* enduring
   nation,
It is an ancient nation,
A nation whose language you do
   not know,
Whose words you do not
   comprehend.
16 "Their quiver is [filled with the
   dead] like an open grave;

words of fire

In Jeremiah 5:14, we see that God was calling Jeremiah to a new level where his words would be mighty and powerful, like fire.

God is also calling you and me to experience a higher level of His power and blessing, and we need to realize that with every new level comes new opposition. In the face of that opposition, we should choose our words carefully. We must realize that wrong words can open doors for the enemy that we do not want to open.

For years, God spoke to me about not opening doors to Satan. Then one day He said, "Joyce, forget about doors; Satan is looking for any tiny crack he can crawl through in your life." God was actually telling me I would need to live more carefully than ever before.

Whatever Jeremiah had been doing previously was not as aggressive against the kingdom of darkness as what God had planned. I believe the same thing holds true in your life and mine. Things that God was patient with in the past, He will have to deal with now. We cannot walk in the flesh until it is time to exercise our ministry gifts and then quickly try to get in the Spirit. There will be no power, no anointing, released through such a life.

Remember that God told Jeremiah He would make His words like fire in his mouth, and that He would make the people like wood. I have read books that spoke of past revivals and explained how the anointing of the Lord was so strong on the preaching at times that hundreds of people fell out of their chairs onto the floor and began crying out for deliverance and salvation. I believe that is a manifestation of God, making the words of the speakers' mouths like fire and the people like wood. But we will not see such signs and wonders as long as we intentionally allow a mixture in our lives and in the words of our mouths. We may never experience complete perfection in this area, but it is time to deal with this issue seriously.

When I speak God's Word, I want it to have a dramatic effect on people, changing them radically. Let me encourage you to do likewise. Ask God to put His fire in your mouth so that your words will be life changing for those who hear them.

They are all mighty men [heroes
of their nation].
17 "They will consume your harvest
and [eat up] your bread;
They will consume your sons and
your daughters;
They will consume your flocks and
your herds;
They will consume your vines and
your fig trees.
With the sword they will break
down and demolish your fortified
cities in which you trust.

18 "But even in those days," says the
LORD, "I will not totally destroy you.
19 "It will come about when your people say, 'Why has the LORD our God
done all these things to us?' then you
shall answer them, 'As you have abandoned (rejected) Me,' [says the LORD,]
'and have served strange and foreign
gods in your land, so you will serve
strangers in a land that is not yours.'

20 "Declare this in the house of Jacob
And proclaim it in Judah, saying:
21 'Now hear this, O foolish people
without heart,
Who have eyes but do not see,
Who have ears but do not hear.
[Is 6:9, 10; Matt 13:10–15;
Mark 8:17, 18]
22 'Do you not fear Me?' says the LORD.
'Do you not tremble [in awe] in My
presence?
For I have placed the sand as a
boundary for the sea,
An eternal decree and a perpetual
barrier beyond which it cannot
pass.
Though the waves [of the sea]
toss and break, yet they cannot
prevail [against the sand
ordained to hold them back];
Though the waves and the billows
roar, yet they cannot cross over
[the barrier].
[Is not such a God to be feared?]

23 'But this people has a stubborn
heart and a rebellious will [that
draws them away from Me];
They have turned away and have
gone [into idolatry].
24 'They do not say in their heart,
"Let us now fear and worship the
LORD our God [with profound
awe and reverence],
Who gives rain in its season,
Both the autumn and the spring
rain,
Who keeps for us
The appointed weeks of the
harvest."
25 'Your wickedness has turned these
[blessings] away,
And your sins have withheld good
[harvests] from you.
26 'For wicked men are found among
My people,
They watch like fowlers who lie in
wait;
They set a trap,
They catch men.
27 'As a cage is full of birds,
So are their houses full of deceit
and treachery;
Therefore they have become
influential and rich.
28 'They are fat and they are sleek
(prosperous),
They *excel in acts of wickedness;
They do not plead the cause,
The cause of the orphan, so that
they [the wicked] may prosper,
And they do not defend the rights
of the poor.
29 'Shall I not punish them [for these
things]?' says the LORD.
'Shall I not avenge Myself
On such a nation as this?'

30 "An appalling and horrible
thing [bringing desolation and
destruction]
Has come to pass in the land:
31 The prophets prophesy falsely,

5:28 Lit pass over, or, overlook deeds.

And the priests rule on their own
authority;
And My people love [to have] it so!
But what will you do when the end
comes?

6 "RUN FOR safety, you children
of Benjamin,
Out of the midst of Jerusalem!
And blow a trumpet in Tekoa [in
Judah]
And raise a signal-fire in Beth-
haccherem [near Jerusalem];
For evil is looking down [with eager
anticipation] from the north,
And great destruction.
²"I will destroy the Daughter of
Zion (Jerusalem), the lovely and
delicate one [so like a luxurious
pasture].
³"Shepherds with their flocks will
come against her;
They will pitch their tents all
around her;
They will pasture, each one in
his place [eating up all her rich
grasses].
⁴"[They shout], 'Prepare for war
against her;
Arise, let us [take her by surprise
and] attack her at noon.
But alas, the daylight pales,
The evening shadows grow long.
⁵'Arise, let us [awaken to] attack her
at night
And destroy her [fortified] palaces!'"

⁶For the Lord of hosts has said,

"Cut down her trees
And build a siege [mound] against
Jerusalem.
This is the city which must be
punished;
There is nothing but oppression
inside her [walls].
⁷"As a fountain springs up *and*
pours out its fresh waters,
So she [continually] pours out her
fresh wickedness.

life point

In Jeremiah 6, the Lord told Jeremiah
to warn His children of the impending
destruction of the city that was full of
oppression. God wants to protect and
provide for His people, and it is so tragic
when they cannot hear His voice because
they have closed their ears to Him (see
Jeremiah 6:10). Ask God to make your
ears open and sensitive to His voice.

Violence and destruction are
heard inside her [walls];
Sickness and wounds are always
before Me.
⁸"Be wise *and* be warned,
O Jerusalem,
Or I will be alienated from you,
And make you a desolation,
An uninhabited land."

⁹Thus says the Lord of hosts,
"They will thoroughly gather like
[fruit on] a vine what is left of
Israel;
Pass your hand [over the vine]
again *and* again [Babylon, tool of
destruction] like a grape gatherer,
Over the branches [stripping the
tendrils off the vine]."
¹⁰To whom shall I (Jeremiah) speak
and give warning
That they may hear?
Behold, their ears are closed
[absolutely deaf to God]
And they cannot listen.
Behold, the word of the Lord has
become a reprimand *and* an
object of scorn to them;
They have no delight in it. [Acts 7:51]
¹¹But I am full of the wrath
(judgment) of the Lord;
I am tired of restraining it.
"[I will] pour it out on the children
in the street
And on the young men gathered
together;

For both the husband and wife
  shall be taken,
The aged and the very old [though
  full of days they are not exempt
  from judgment].
¹²"Their houses shall be turned over
  to others,
Their fields and their wives
  together;
For I will stretch out My hand
Against the inhabitants of the
  land," says the LORD.
¹³"For from the least of them even to
  the greatest of them,
Everyone is greedy for [unfair]
  gain;
And from the prophet even to the
  priest
Everyone deals deceitfully.
¹⁴"They have treated superficially
  the [bloody] broken wound of My
  people,
Saying, 'Peace, peace,'
When there is no peace.
¹⁵"Were they ashamed because they
  had committed disgusting *and*
  vile things?
No, they were not at all ashamed;
They did not even know how to
  blush [at their idolatry].
Therefore they will fall among
  those who fall;
At the time that I punish them
They will be overthrown," says the
  LORD.

¹⁶Thus says the LORD,
  "Stand by the roads and look; ask
    for the ancient paths,
Where the good way is; then walk
  in it,
And you will find rest for your souls.
But they said, 'We will not walk in
  it!' [Matt 11:29]
¹⁷"I have set watchmen (prophets)
  over you,
Saying, 'Listen *and* pay attention
  to the [warning] sound of the
  trumpet!'
But they said, 'We will not listen.'

¹⁸"Therefore hear, O [Gentile]
  nations,
And see, O congregation, what
  [vengeful act] is to be done to
  them.
¹⁹"Hear, O earth: behold, I am
  bringing disaster on this people,
The fruit of their schemes,
Because they have not listened *and*
  paid attention to My words,
And as for My law, they have
  rejected it also.
²⁰"For what purpose does
  frankincense come to Me from
  Sheba
And the sweet cane from a distant
  land?
Your burnt offerings are not
  acceptable
And your sacrifices are not sweet
  and pleasing to Me."

²¹Therefore, thus says the LORD,

  "Behold, I am laying stumbling
    blocks before this people.
The fathers and the sons together
Will stumble against them;
The neighbor and his friend will
  perish."

²²Thus says the LORD,
  "Behold, a people is coming from
    the north country,
And a great nation shall be stirred
  up *and* put into action from the
  remote parts of the earth.
²³"They seize bow and spear;
They are cruel *and* inhuman and
  have no mercy.
Their voice sounds like the roaring
  sea;
They ride [in formation] on horses,
Arrayed as a man for battle
Against you, O Daughter of Zion
  (Jerusalem)!"
²⁴We have heard the report of it;
Our hands become limp *and*
  helpless.
Anguish has gripped us,

Pain like that of a woman in
childbirth.
²⁵ Do not go out into the field
Nor walk on the road,
For the enemy is armed with the
sword;
Terror is on every side.
²⁶ O daughter of my people [says
Jeremiah],
Clothe yourself in sackcloth and
wallow in ashes;
Mourn [aloud] as for an only son,
A most bitter cry [of sorrow and
regret],
For suddenly the destroyer will
come upon us [on both prophet
and people].
²⁷ "I [the LORD] have set you as an
assayer [O Jeremiah] and as a
tester [of the ore] of My people,
That you may know and analyze
their acts."
²⁸ They are all the worst [kind] of
[stiff-necked, godless] rebels,
Going around spreading slander.
They are [not gold and silver ore,
but] bronze and iron;
They are all corrupt.
²⁹ The bellows blow fiercely,
The lead is consumed by the fire;
In vain they continue refining,
But the wicked are not separated
and removed.
³⁰ They call them rejected silver
[only dross, without value],
Because the LORD has rejected them.

7 THE WORD that came to Jeremiah from the LORD, saying,
²"Stand in the gate of the LORD's
house and proclaim there this word
and say, 'Hear the word of the LORD, all
you of Judah who enter by these gates
to worship the LORD.'"
³Thus says the LORD of hosts, the
God of Israel, "Change your ways and
your behavior, and I will let you live
in this place.
⁴"Do not trust in the deceptive and

lying words [of the false prophets who
claim that Jerusalem will be protected
by God because of the temple], saying,
'This is the temple of the LORD, the temple of the LORD, the temple of the LORD.'
⁵"For if you thoroughly change your
ways and your behavior, if you thoroughly and honestly practice justice
between a man and his neighbor,
⁶if you do not oppress the transient
and the foreigner, the orphan, or the
widow, and do not shed innocent blood
[by oppression and by unjust judicial
murders] in Jerusalem, nor follow after other gods to your own ruin,
⁷then I will let you live in this place,
in the land that I gave to your fathers
[to live in] forever and ever.
⁸"Behold, you are trusting in deceptive and useless words that bring no
benefit.
⁹"Will you steal, murder, commit
adultery, swear [oaths] falsely, offer
sacrifices or burn incense to Baal, and
follow after other gods that you have
not known,
¹⁰and [then dare to] come and stand
before Me in this house, which is
called by My Name, and say, 'We are
protected and set free [by this act of
religious ritual]!'—only to go on with
this wickedness and these disgusting
and loathsome things?
¹¹"Has this house, which is called by
My Name, become a den of robbers in
your eyes [a place of retreat for you
between acts of violence]? Behold, I
Myself have seen it," says the LORD.
¹²"But go now to My place which was
in Shiloh [in Ephraim], where I first
set My Name, and see what I did to it
because of the wickedness of My people Israel. [1 Sam 4:10–18]
¹³"And now, because you have done
all these things," says the LORD, "and I
spoke [persistently] to you, even rising up early and speaking, but you did
not listen, and I called you but you did
not answer,

¹⁴therefore, I will do to this house (the temple) which is called by My Name, in which you trust, and to the place which I gave you and your fathers, just as I did to Shiloh.

¹⁵"I will cast you out of My sight, as I have cast out all your brothers (relatives through Jacob), all the descendants of Ephraim.

¹⁶"Therefore, do not pray for this people [of Judah] or lift up a cry or entreaty for them or make intercession to Me, for I do not hear you.

¹⁷"Do you not see what they are doing in the cities of Judah and in the streets of Jerusalem?

¹⁸"The children gather wood, the fathers kindle the fire, and the women knead the dough to make cakes for the queen of heaven; and they pour out drink offerings to other gods that they may offend *and* provoke Me to anger.

¹⁹"Do they offend *and* provoke Me to anger?" says the LORD. "Is it not themselves [they offend], to their own shame?"

²⁰Therefore thus says the Lord GOD, "Behold, My anger and My wrath will be poured out on this place, on man and beast, on the trees of the field and the fruit of the ground; and it will burn and [the fire will] not be quenched."

²¹Thus says the LORD of hosts, the God of Israel, "Add your burnt offerings to your sacrifices and eat the meat.

²²"For in the day that I brought them out of the land of Egypt, I did not speak to your fathers or command them concerning burnt offerings or sacrifices.

²³"But this thing I did command them: 'Listen to *and* obey My voice, and I will be your God, and you shall be My people; and you will walk in all the way which I command you, so that it may be well with you.'

²⁴"But they did not obey Me or bend their ear [to hear Me], but followed the counsels and the stubbornness of their [own] evil heart (mind), and

[they turned and] went backward instead of forward.

²⁵"Since the day that your fathers came out of the land of Egypt until this day, I have [persistently] sent you all My servants the prophets, sending them daily, early [and late].

²⁶"Yet they did not listen to Me *and* obey Me or bend their ear [to hear Me], but stiffened their neck; they did more evil *and* behaved worse than their fathers.

²⁷"You shall speak all these words to them, but they will not listen to you; and you shall [also] call to them, but they will not answer you.

²⁸"You shall say to them, 'This is the nation that did not obey the voice of the LORD their God or accept correction *and* warning; truth *and* faithfulness have perished and have completely vanished from their mouths.

²⁹'Cut off your hair [your crown,
    O Jerusalem] and throw it away,
And take up a mournful cry on the
    barren heights,
For the LORD has rejected and
    abandoned
The generation of His wrath.'

³⁰"For the children of Judah have done evil in My sight," says the LORD; "they have set their disgusting *and* shamefully vile things in the house which is called by My Name, to defile it.

³¹"They have built the high places of Topheth, which is in the Valley of Ben-hinnom (son of Hinnom), to burn their sons and their daughters in the fire [to honor Molech, the fire god]—which I did not command, nor did it come into My heart (mind). [Lev 18:21; Josh 15:8; 2 Kin 16:2, 3; 21:1, 6; Is 30:33]

³²"Therefore, behold, the days are coming," declares the LORD, "when it will no longer be called Topheth or the Valley of Ben-hinnom, but the Valley of the Slaughter, for [in bloody warfare] they will bury [the dead] in

Topheth until there is no more room.
[Jer 19:6]

[33] "And the dead bodies of this people will be food for the birds of the air and for the beasts of the earth and no one will frighten them away.

[34] "Then I will cause the voices of joy and gladness, and the voices of the bridegroom and the bride to vanish from the cities of Judah and from the streets of Jerusalem; for the land will become a ruin—a wasteland.

8 "AT THAT time," says the LORD, "they [the Babylonian army] will bring out from their graves the bones of the kings of Judah, the bones of its princes, the bones of the priests, the bones of the prophets, and the bones of the inhabitants of Jerusalem.

[2] "They will [carelessly scatter and] spread them out before the sun and the moon and all the host of heaven, which the dead have loved and which they have served, and which they have walked after and which they have sought, and which they have worshiped. They will not be gathered or be buried; they will be like dung on the face of the earth.

[3] "And death will be chosen rather than life by all the remnant of those who remain of this evil family (nation), who remain in all the places to which I have driven them," says the LORD of hosts.

[4] "Moreover [Jeremiah], you shall say to them, 'Thus says the LORD,

"Do men fall and not rise up again?
Does one turn away [from God] and
   not repent and return [to Him]?
[5] "Why then has this people of
   Jerusalem
Turned away with a perpetual
   turning away [from Me]?
They hold tightly to deceit
   (idolatry);
They refuse to repent and return
   [to God].

[6] "I have listened and heard,
But they have spoken what is not
   right;
No man repented of his wickedness,
Saying, 'What have I done?'
Everyone turns to his [individual]
   course,
As the horse rushes like a torrent
   into battle.
[7] "Even the stork in the sky
Knows her seasons [of migration],
And the turtledove, the swallow
   and the crane
Observe the time of their return.
But My people do not know
The law of the LORD.

[8] "How can you say, 'We are wise,
And the law of the LORD is with
   us [and we are learned in its
   language and teachings]'?
Behold, [the truth is that] the lying
   pen of the scribes
Has made the law into a lie [a mere
   code of ceremonial observances].
   [Mark 7:13]
[9] "The wise men are shamed,
They are dismayed and caught.
Behold, they have [manipulated
   and] rejected the [truth in the]
   word of the LORD,
And what kind of wisdom and
   insight do they have?
[10] "Therefore I will give their wives
   to others
And their fields to new owners;
Because from the least even to the
   greatest
Everyone is greedy for [unjust]
   gain;
From the prophet even to the priest
Everyone practices deceit and
   deals in corruption.
[11] "For they have treated the
   brokenness of the daughter of
   My people superficially,
Saying, 'Peace, peace,'
When there is no peace.

12 "Were they ashamed because of the extremely disgusting *and* shamefully vile things they had done?
They were not at all ashamed,
And they did not know how to blush.
Therefore, they shall fall among those who fall;
At the time of their punishment they shall be overthrown,"
Says the LORD. [Jer 6:12–15]

13 "I will gather *and* snatch them away [utterly consuming them],"
says the LORD.
"There will be no grapes on the vine,
Nor figs on the fig tree,
And even the leaf will wither;
And the things that I have given them will pass away [by the hand of those whom I have appointed]." ' " [Matt 21:18, 19]
14 Why are we sitting still [the people wonder]?
Assemble yourselves, and let us enter the fortified cities
And let us die there,
For the LORD our God has decreed our ruin
And given us bitter *and* poisonous water to drink,
Because we have sinned against the LORD.
15 We waited for peace *and* salvation, but no good came,
And for a time of healing, but behold, terror!
16 The snorting of [Nebuchadnezzar's] horses is heard from Dan [on Palestine's northern border].
At the sound of the neighing of his strong stallions
The whole land quakes;
For they come and devour the land and all that is in it,
The city and those who live in it.
17 "For behold, I am sending serpents among you,

Vipers which cannot be charmed,
And they will bite you," says the LORD.
18 Oh, that I (Jeremiah) could find comfort from my sorrow [for my grief is beyond healing],
My heart is sick *and* faint *within me!*
19 Behold, [hear the sound of] the cry of the daughter of my people from the distant land [of Babylon]:
"Is not the LORD in Zion? Is not her King within her?"
[But the LORD answers] "Why have they provoked Me to anger with their carved images and with foreign idols?"
20 "The harvest is past, the summer has ended *and* the gathering of fruit is over,
But we are not saved," [comes the voice of the people again].
21 For the brokenness of the daughter of my people I (Jeremiah) am broken;
I mourn, anxiety has gripped me.
22 Is there no balm in Gilead?
Is there no physician there?
Why then has not the [spiritual] health of the daughter of my people been restored?

9 OH THAT my head were waters
And my eyes a fountain of tears,
That I might weep day and night
For the slain of the daughter of my people!
2 Oh that I had in the wilderness
A lodging place (a mere shelter) for wayfaring men,
That I might leave my people
And go away from them!
For they are all adulterers [worshiping idols instead of the LORD],
[They are] an assembly of treacherous men [of weak character, men without integrity].

3 "They bend their tongue like their
    bow;
[Their] lies and not truth prevail
    and grow strong in the land;
For they proceed from evil to evil,
And they do not know and
    understand and acknowledge
    Me," says the LORD.
4 "Let everyone beware of his
    neighbor
And do not trust any brother.
For every brother is a supplanter
    [like Jacob, a deceiver, ready to
    grab his brother's heel],
And every neighbor goes around
    as a slanderer. [Gen 25:26]
5 "Everyone deceives and mocks his
    neighbor
And does not speak the truth.
They have taught their tongue to
    speak lies;
They exhaust themselves with sin
    and cruelty.
6 "Your dwelling is in the midst
    of deceit [oppression upon
    oppression and deceit upon
    deceit];
Through deceit they refuse to know
    (understand) Me," says the LORD.

7 Therefore thus says the LORD of
hosts,

"Behold, I will refine them [through
    suffering] and test them;
For how else should I deal with the
    daughter of My people?
8 "Their tongue is a murderous
    arrow;
It speaks deceit;
With his mouth one speaks peace
    to his neighbor,
But in his heart he lays traps and
    waits in ambush for him.
9 "Shall I not punish them for these
    things?" says the LORD.
"Shall I not avenge Myself
On such a nation as this?

10 "I will take up a weeping and
    wailing for the mountains,

And a [funeral] dirge for the
    pastures of the wilderness,
Because they are burned up and
    desolated so that no one passes
    through [them];
Nor can anyone hear the lowing of
    cattle.
Both the birds of the air and the
    beasts have fled; they are gone.
11 "I will make Jerusalem a heap of
    ruins,
A haunt and dwelling place of
    jackals;
And I will make the cities of Judah
    a desolation, without inhabitant."

12 Who is the wise man who may understand this [without any doubt]? To
whom has the mouth of the LORD spoken, so that he may declare it? Why is
the land ruined, laid waste like a wilderness, so that no one passes through?
13 The LORD said, "Because they have
turned away from My law which I set
before them, and have not listened to
and obeyed My voice nor walked in
accordance with it, 14 but have walked stubbornly after
their [own] heart and after the Baals,
as their fathers taught them," 15 therefore thus says the LORD of
hosts, the God of Israel, "behold,
I will feed them, this people, with
wormwood and give them bitter and
poisonous water to drink. 16 "I will [also] scatter them among
nations that neither they nor their fa-
thers have known, and I will send the
sword after them until I have annihilated them."
17 Thus says the LORD of hosts,

"Consider and call for the
    mourning women to come;
Send for the wailing women to
    come.
18 "Let them hurry and take up a
    wailing for us,
That our eyes may shed tears
And our eyelids flow with water.

¹⁹"For a sound of wailing is heard
   [coming] from Zion:
'How we are ruined!
We are greatly perplexed *and*
   utterly shamed,
Because we have left the land,
Because they have torn down our
   dwellings.'"
²⁰Now hear the word of the Lord, O
   you women,
And let your ear hear the word of
   His mouth;
Teach your daughters a song of
   mourning,
And each one [teach] her neighbor
   a dirge.
²¹For death has come up through
   our windows;
It has entered our palaces,
Cutting off the children from the
   streets
And the young men from the town
   squares.
²²Speak, "Thus says the Lord,
'The dead bodies of men will fall
   like dung on the open field,
And like sheaves [of grain] behind
   the reaper,
And no one will gather them.'"
   [Jer 8:2]

²³Thus says the Lord, "Let not the
one who is wise *and* skillful boast
in his insight; let not the one who
is mighty *and* powerful boast in his
strength; let not the one who is rich
boast in his [temporal satisfactions
and earthly] abundance;
²⁴but let the one who boasts boast in
this, that he understands and knows
Me [and acknowledges Me and honors Me as God and recognizes without any doubt], that I am the Lord who
practices lovingkindness, justice and

righteousness on the earth, for in these
things I delight," says the Lord. [1 Cor
1:31; 2 Cor 10:17]
²⁵"Behold, the days are coming,"
says the Lord, "when I will punish
all who are circumcised [physically]
and yet uncircumcised [spiritually]—
[Rom 2:25–29]
²⁶Egypt and Judah, and Edom and
the sons of Ammon, and Moab and
all those who live in the desert who
clip off the hair on their temples; for
all these nations are uncircumcised
(sinful, impure), and all the house of
Israel are uncircumcised in heart."

10 HEAR THE word which the
Lord speaks to you, O house
of Israel.
²Thus says the Lord,

"Do not learn the way of the
   [pagan] nations,
And do not be terrified *and*
   distressed by the signs of the
   heavens
Although the pagans are terrified
   by them;
³For the customs *and* decrees of
   the peoples are [mere] delusion
   [exercises in futility];
It is only wood which one cuts
   from the forest [to make a god],
The work of the hands of the
   craftsman with the axe *or*
   cutting tool.
⁴"They adorn the idol with silver
   and with gold;
They fasten it with hammers and
   nails
So that it will not fall apart.
⁵"They are like scarecrows in a
   cucumber field;
They cannot speak;

speak the Word

God, I glory only in the fact that I know You and that I understand
You are the Lord Who practices loving-kindness, justice, and righteousness.
—ADAPTED FROM JEREMIAH 9:24

They have to be carried,
Because they cannot walk!
Do not be afraid of them,
For they can do no harm *or* evil,
Nor can they do any good."

⁶There is none like You, O LORD;
You are great, and great is Your
mighty *and* powerful name.
⁷Who would not fear You, O King of
the nations?
For it is appropriate *and* it is Your
due!
For among all the wise men of the
nations
And in all their kingdoms,
There is none like You.
⁸But they are altogether irrational
and stupid and foolish
In their discipline of delusion—
their idol is [only] wood [it
is ridiculous, empty and
worthless]!
⁹Silver *that has been* beaten [into
plates] is brought from Tarshish,
And gold from Uphaz,
The work of the craftsman and of
the hand of the goldsmith;
Violet and purple are their clothing;
They are all the work of skilled
men.
¹⁰But the LORD is the true God *and*
the God who is Truth;
He is the living God and the
everlasting King.
The earth quakes *and* shudders at
His wrath,
And the nations are not able to
endure His indignation.

¹¹In this manner you shall say to
them, "The gods that did not make the
heavens and the earth will perish from
the earth and from under the heavens."

¹²God made the earth by His power;
He established the world by His
wisdom
And by His understanding *and* skill
He has stretched out the heavens.

¹³When He utters His voice, *there
is* a tumult of waters in the
heavens,
And He causes the clouds *and* the
mist to ascend from the end of
the earth;
He makes lightning for the rain,
And brings out the wind from
His treasuries *and* from His
storehouses.
¹⁴Every man has become [like a
brute] irrational *and* stupid,
without knowledge [of God];
Every goldsmith is shamed by his
carved idols;
For his molten images are frauds
and lies,
And there is no breath in them.
¹⁵They are worthless *and* devoid of
promise, a work of delusion *and*
mockery;
In their time of [trial and]
punishment they will perish
[without hope].
¹⁶The Portion of Jacob [the true God
on whom Israel has a claim] is
not like these;
For He is the Designer *and* Maker
of all things,
And Israel is the tribe of His
inheritance [and He will not fail
them]—
The LORD of hosts is His name.

¹⁷Gather up your bundle [of goods]
from the ground,
You who live under siege.

¹⁸For thus says the LORD;

"Behold, I am slinging out at this
time the people of this land,
And will cause them [great]
distress,
That they may find it [to be as I
have said]."

¹⁹"Woe to me because of my [spiritual]
brokenness!" [says Jeremiah,
speaking for the nation.]
"My wound is incurable."

But I said, "Surely this sickness
  and suffering *and* grief are mine,
And I must bear it."
²⁰ My tent is destroyed,
And all my [tent] cords are broken;
My children have been taken from
  me [as captives] and are no more.
There is no one to stretch out my
  tent again
And to set up my [tent] curtains.
²¹ For the shepherds [of the people]
  have become [like brutes,]
  irrational *and* stupid,
And have not searched for the
  LORD *or* asked about Him *or*
  realized their need for Him;
Therefore they have not been wise
  and have not prospered,
And all their flocks are scattered.
²² The sound of a report! Behold, [the
  invader] comes—
A great commotion from
  the country of the north
  (Babylonia)—
To make the cities of Judah
A desolation, a haunt *and* dwelling
  place of jackals.
²³ O LORD, I know that the path of
  [life of] a man is not in himself;
It is not within [the limited ability
  of] man [even one at his best] to
  choose *and* direct his steps [in
  life]. [Ps 37:23; Prov 20:24]

life point

Life would be so much easier if we would
believe God's Word and act accordingly,
but most of us have to find out the hard
way what works and what does not work.
God's Word says in Jeremiah 10:23 that
we do not have it in us to run our own
lives, but we still try. Let me encourage
you to give up trying to control your own
life or someone else's. God is in control,
so relax and let Him direct your steps.

²⁴ O LORD, correct me [along with
  Your people], but with mercy *and*
  in just measure—
Not in Your anger, or You will crush
  me *and* bring me to nothing.
²⁵ Pour out Your wrath on the nations
  that do not know *nor* recognize
  You
And on the families that do not call
  Your name.
For they have devoured Jacob;
They have devoured him and
  consumed him
And made his land a desolate waste.

11 THE WORD that came to
Jeremiah from the LORD,
² "Hear the words of this
[solemn] covenant, and speak to the
men of Judah and to the people of Jerusalem.

³ "Say to them, 'Thus says the LORD,
the God of Israel, "Cursed is the man
who does not heed the words of this
covenant

⁴ which I commanded your fathers at
the time that I brought them out of the
land of Egypt, from the iron furnace,
saying, 'Listen to My voice and do according to all that I command you. So
you shall be My people, and I will be
your God,'

⁵ that I may complete the oath which
I swore to your fathers, to give them
a land [of plenty] flowing with milk
and honey, as it is this day.' " " Then I
answered, "Amen (so be it), O LORD."

⁶ And the LORD said to me, "Proclaim
all these words in the cities of Judah
and in the streets of Jerusalem: 'Hear
the words of this [solemn] covenant
and do them.

⁷ 'For I solemnly warned your fa-
thers at the time that I brought them
up from the land of Egypt, even to this
day, warning them persistently, saying, "Obey My voice."

⁸ 'Yet they did not obey or incline
their ear [to listen to Me], but everyone

walked in the stubborn way of his [own] evil heart. Therefore I brought on them all [the suffering threatened in] the words of this covenant, which I commanded them to do, but they did not.'"

⁹Then the LORD said to me, "A conspiracy has been found among the men of Judah and among the people of Jerusalem.

¹⁰"They have returned to the wickedness of their ancestors who refused to hear My words; they have followed other gods [in order] to serve them. The house of Israel and the house of Judah have broken My [solemn] covenant which I made with their fathers."

¹¹Therefore thus says the LORD, "Behold I am bringing disaster *and* suffering on them which they will not be able to escape; though they cry to Me, I will not listen to them.

¹²"Then the cities of Judah and the people of Jerusalem will go and cry to the [man-made] gods to whom they burn incense, but they cannot save them in the time of their disaster.

¹³"For [as many as] the number of your cities are your gods, O Judah; and [as many as] the number of the streets of Jerusalem are the altars you have set up to the shameful thing, altars to burn incense to Baal.

¹⁴"Therefore do not pray for this people, nor lift up a cry or prayer for them, for I shall not listen when they cry to Me in the time of their disaster.

¹⁵"What right has My beloved [to be] in My house
  When she has done many vile
    things *and* acted treacherously
    [over and over again]?
  Can vows *and* the meat of
    your sacrifices remove your
    wickedness from you *and* cancel
    the consequences of your sin,
  So that you can [escape your
    judgment and] rejoice?"

¹⁶The LORD [acknowledged you
    once as worthy and] called your
    name,
  "A green olive tree, fair *and*
    beautiful in fruit and form";
  But with the roar of a great
    tempest
  He has set fire to it,
  And its branches are worthless.
    [Ps 52:8; Jer 21:14]

¹⁷For the LORD of hosts, who planted you, has pronounced evil *and* horror against you because of the evil of the house of Israel and of the house of Judah, which they have done to provoke Me [to anger] by offering sacrifices *and* burning incense to Baal.

¹⁸Then the LORD gave me knowledge
    [of their plot], and I knew it;
  So You [O LORD] revealed their
    deeds to me.
¹⁹But I was like a gentle *and* tame
    lamb brought to the slaughter;
  And I did not know that they
    had devised plots *and* schemes
    against me, saying,
  "Let us destroy the tree with its
    fruit;
  Let us cut him off from the land of
    the living,
  That his name be remembered no
    longer."
²⁰But, O LORD of hosts, who judges
    righteously,
  Who tests the feelings and the
    heart (mind),

life point

Every time God gives us a test, we can tell how far we have come and how far we still have to go by how we react during it. Attitudes of the heart that we did not know we had often reveal themselves through tests and trials. Embrace your tests as opportunities for growth and development.

Let me see Your vengeance on them,
For to You I have committed my
cause.

²¹Therefore thus says the LORD regarding the men of Anathoth, who seek your life, saying, "Do not prophesy in the name of the LORD, so that you will not die by our hand."

²²Therefore, thus says the LORD of hosts, "Behold, I am about to punish them. Their young men will die by the sword, their sons and their daughters will die by famine;

²³and there will be no remnant [of the conspirators] left, for I will bring disaster *and* horror on the men of

how to pass life's tests

Jeremiah 11:20 tells us that God tests our minds and emotions.

When we want to test something, how do we do it? We put pressure on it to see if it will do what it says it will do; we look to see if it will hold up under the stress. God does the same with us. When we pray, asking Him to use us and to put us into positions of leadership, His answer is, "Let Me try you out first. Let Me put you to the test."

I am saddened when I realize how many people never make it past the trying point. They never pass the test. They spend their whole lives going around and around the same proverbial mountains. But in God's school we do not flunk; we get to keep taking the test again and again until we pass it.

To test something means to prove its truth or genuineness by an experiment, a trial, or an examination. It also means to compare something against a standard. One of the ways God tests us is by requiring us to manifest what we say we know. Head knowledge alone is not enough. If we cannot produce the goods, head knowledge means nothing.

Deuteronomy 8:2 says that God led the Israelites in the wilderness for forty years to humble them, to test them, and to see if they would keep His commandments. Tests usually do not come in good times. They come in hard times because not everything God asks us to do is going to be easy. That is why He tests us to see if we are ready and able before He promotes us to a higher level of responsibility.

So many things come our way every day that are nothing more than tests. For example, sometimes when we have to wait to be seated at a table in a restaurant and then we get a bad meal, it is a test. Sometimes when we are going to pull into a parking space and someone zooms in and takes it, it is a test. Sometimes when our boss tells us to do something we do not want to do, it is a test.

James 1:2–4 says that tests bring out what is in us. In times of trial we become best acquainted with ourselves and with what we are capable of doing. Peter did not think he would ever deny Jesus, but when he was put to the test, that is exactly what he did (see Luke 22:61, 62). God is not impressed with what we say we will do; He is impressed with what we prove we will do under pressure. We do not get promoted in ministry because we have our Bibles underlined in two colors. We are raised up in life and ministry because we have been tested and tried, and we have passed our tests.

Anathoth in the year of their punishment."

12

YOU, O LORD are [uncompromisingly] righteous *and* consistently just when I plead my case with You;

Yet let me discuss issues of justice with You:

Why has the way of the wicked prospered?

Why are those who deal in treachery (deceit) at ease *and* thriving?

2 You have planted them, they have also taken root;

They grow, they have even produced fruit.

You are honored by their [hypocritical] lips

But [You are] far from their heart *and* mind.

3 But You, O LORD, know me [and understand my devotion to You];

You see me;

And You examine *the attitude of* my heart toward You.

Drag out the faithless like sheep for the slaughter [O LORD]

And set them apart for the day of slaughter.

4 How long must the land mourn

And the grass of the countryside wither?

Because of the wickedness *and* hypocrisy of those who live in it,

The beasts and the birds are consumed *and* are swept away [by the drought],

Because men [mocking me] have said, "He will not [live long enough to] see [what happens at] our final end."

5 [The LORD rebukes Jeremiah for his impatience, saying] "If you have raced with men on foot and they have tired you out,

Then how can you compete with horses?

If you fall down in a land of peace [where you feel secure],

Then how will you do [among the lions] in the [flooded] thicket beside the Jordan?

6 "For even your [tribal] brothers and the household of your father,

Even they have dealt treacherously (unfaithfully) with you;

Indeed they are [like a pack of hounds] howling after you.

Do not believe them, although they may say kind words *and* promise you good things."

7 "I have abandoned My house,

I have given up My [precious] inheritance (Judah);

I have given the [dearly] beloved of My life

Into the hands of her enemies.

8 "My inheritance has become to Me

Like a lion in the forest;

She has raised her voice *and* roared against Me;

So I have come to [treat her as if I] hate her.

9 "Is My inheritance like a speckled bird of prey to Me [unlike the others]?

Are the birds of prey (enemies) surrounding her on every side?

Go, gather all the [wild] beasts of the field;

Bring them to devour [her]!

10 "Many shepherds (invaders) have destroyed My vineyard (Judah),

They have trampled My field underfoot;

They have made My pleasant field A desolate wilderness.

11 "They have made it a wasteland,

Desolate, it mourns before Me;

The whole land has been made a wasteland,

Because no man takes it to heart.

12 "Destroyers have come

On all the caravan roads in the desert,

For the sword of the Lord
   (Babylon) is devouring
From one end of the land even to
   the other;
No one has peace *or* a way of escape.
[13]"They have planted wheat but
   have reaped thorns;
They have exhausted themselves
   but without profit.
So be ashamed of your harvest
Because of the fierce *and* raging
   anger of the Lord."

[14]Thus says the Lord regarding all My evil neighbors (Gentile nations) who strike at the inheritance which I have granted to My people Israel, "Behold, I will uproot them from their land and I will uproot the house of Judah from among them.

[15]"And it shall come about that after I have uprooted them, I will return *and* have compassion on them; and I will bring them back again, each one to his inheritance and each one to his land.

[16]"And if these [neighboring nations] will diligently learn the ways of My people, to swear by My Name, saying, 'As the Lord lives'—even as they taught My people to swear by Baal, then they will be built up among My people.

[17]"But if [any nation] will not listen *and* obey, I will [completely] uproot and destroy that nation, says the Lord."

13 THUS THE Lord said to me, "Go and buy yourself a linen waistband and put it on your loins, but do not put it in water."

[2]So I bought the waistband according to the word of the Lord and put it on my loins.

[3]Then the word of the Lord came to me a second time, saying,

[4]"Get up and take the waistband that you have bought, which is [wrapped] around your loins, and go to the [river] Euphrates and hide it there in a crevice of the rock."

[5]So I went and hid it by the Euphrates, as the Lord had commanded me.

[6]And after many days the Lord said to me, "Get up, go to the Euphrates and get the waistband which I commanded you to hide there."

[7]Then I went to the Euphrates and dug, and I took the waistband from the place where I had hidden it. And behold, the waistband was decayed *and* ruined; it was completely worthless.

[8]Then the word of the Lord came to me, saying,

[9]"Thus says the Lord, 'In this same way I shall destroy the pride of Judah and the great pride of Jerusalem.

[10]'These wicked *and* malevolent people, who refuse to listen to My words, who walk in the stubborn way of their heart and have followed other gods [which are nothing—just man-made carvings] to serve them and to worship them, let them be just like this waistband which is completely worthless.

[11]'For as the waistband clings to the body of a man, so I caused the whole house of Israel and the whole house of Judah to cling to Me,' says the Lord, 'that they might be for Me a people, a name, a praise, and a glory; but they did not listen *and* obey.'

[12]"Therefore you are to speak this word to them, 'Thus says the Lord, the God of Israel, "Every jar should be filled with wine."' The people will say to you, 'Do we not already know that every jar should be filled with wine?'

[13]"Then say to them, 'Thus says the Lord, "Behold, I am about to fill with drunkenness all the people of this land, even the kings who sit on David's throne, the priests, the prophets and all the people of Jerusalem.

[14]"I will smash them one against another, both the fathers and the sons together," says the Lord. "I shall destroy them [nothing will restrain Me]; I will not show pity nor be sorry nor have compassion."'"

¹⁵ Listen and pay close attention,
   do not be haughty *and*
   overconfident,
For the LORD has spoken [says
   Jeremiah].
¹⁶ Give glory to the LORD your God,
   Before He brings darkness
   And before your feet stumble
   On the dark *and* shadowy
   mountains,
   And while you are longing for light
He turns it into the shadow of
   death,
   And makes it into thick darkness.
¹⁷ But if you will not listen *and* obey,
   My soul will weep in secret for
   your pride;
   My eyes will weep bitterly
   And flow with tears,
Because the LORD's flock has been
   taken captive.
¹⁸ Say to the king and the queen
   mother,
   "Humble yourselves *and* take a
   lowly seat,
For your beautiful crown [the
   crown of your glory]
Has come down from your head."
¹⁹ The cities of the South (the Negev)
   have been closed up,
   And there is no one to open them;
All Judah has been carried into
   exile,
Completely carried away into exile.

²⁰ "Lift up your eyes and see
   Those coming from the north.
   Where is the flock that was given
   to you [to shepherd],
   Your beautiful flock?
²¹ "What will you say [O Jerusalem]
   when the LORD appoints [foreign
   nations to rule] over you—
   Those former friends and allies
   whom you have encouraged [to
   be your companions]—
Will not pain seize you
Like [that of] a woman in
   childbirth?

²² "And if you [wonder and] say in
   your heart,
   'Why have these things happened
   to me?'
It is because of the greatness *and*
   nature of your sin
That your skirts have been pulled
   away [subjecting you to public
   disgrace]
And [like a barefoot slave] your
   heels have been wounded.
²³ "Can the Ethiopian change his skin
   Or the leopard his spots?
Then you also can do good
Who are accustomed to evil *and*
   even trained to do it.
²⁴ "Therefore I will scatter you like
   drifting straw
[Driven away] by the desert wind.
²⁵ "This is your destiny, the portion
   [of judgment] measured to you
From Me," says the LORD,
"Because you have forgotten Me
And trusted in [pagan] lies
   [the counterfeit gods, and the
   pretense of alliance]."
²⁶ "So I Myself will throw your skirts
   up over your face,
That your shame may be exposed
   [publicly].
²⁷ "I have seen your vile *and*
   detestable acts,
Even your adulteries and your
   lustful neighings [after idols],
And the lewdness of your
   prostitution
On the hills in the fields.
Woe (judgment is coming) to you,
   O Jerusalem!
How long will you remain unclean
   [by ignoring My precepts]?"

14 THE WORD of the LORD that
   came to Jeremiah concerning the drought:

² "Judah mourns
And her gates languish;
Her people sit on the ground in
   mourning *clothes*

And the cry of Jerusalem has
  gone up.
³"Their nobles have sent their
  servants for water;
They have come to the cisterns
  and found no water.
They have returned with empty
  vessels;
They have been shamed and
  humiliated,
And they cover their heads.
⁴"The ground is cracked
Because there has been no rain on
  the land;
The farmers are distressed,
And they have covered their heads
  [in shame].
⁵"The doe in the field has given
  birth only to abandon *her young*
Because there is no grass.
⁶"And the wild donkeys stand on
  the barren heights;
They pant for air like jackals,
Their eyesight fails
Because there is no grass.
⁷"O Lord, though our many sins
  testify against us" [prays
  Jeremiah],
"Act now [for us and] for Your
  name's sake [so that the faithless
  may witness Your faithfulness]!
For our backslidings are countless;
We have sinned against You.
⁸"O Hope of Israel,
Her Savior in time of distress *and*
  trouble,
Why should You be like a
  sojourner (temporary resident)
  in the land
Or like a traveler who turns aside
  and spreads his tent to linger
  [only] for a night?
⁹"Why should You be [hesitant and
  inactive] like a man astounded
  and perplexed,
Like a mighty man unable to save?
Yet You, O Lord, are among us,
And we are called by Your name;
Do not leave us!"

¹⁰Thus says the Lord to this people
[Judah], "In the manner *and* to the degree [already pointed out] they have
loved to wander; they have not restrained their feet. Therefore the Lord
does not accept them; He will now remember [in detail] their wickedness
and punish them for their sins."
¹¹So the Lord said to me, "Do not
pray for good things for this people.
¹²"Though they fast, I will not hear
their cry; and though they offer burnt
offerings and grain offerings, I will
not accept them [because they are
done as obligations, and not as acts of
loving obedience]. Instead I will consume them by the sword, by famine,
and by pestilence."
¹³But I said, "Alas, Lord God! Behold,
the [false] prophets are telling them,
'You will not see the sword nor will
you have famine, but I [the Lord] will
give you lasting peace in this place.' "
¹⁴Then the Lord said to me, "The
[counterfeit] prophets are prophesying lies in My Name. I have neither
sent them nor authorized them nor
spoken to them. They are prophesying
to you made-up visions [pretending to
call forth responses from handmade
gods], a worthless divination and the
deceit of their own mind.
¹⁵"Therefore, thus says the Lord concerning the [false] prophets who are
prophesying in My Name, although I
did not send them—yet they keep saying, 'Sword and famine shall not be in
this land': by sword and famine those
prophets shall meet their end *and* be
consumed.
¹⁶"And the people to whom they
are prophesying will be thrown out
into the streets of Jerusalem, victims
of famine and sword; and they will
have no one to bury them—neither
them, nor their wives, nor their sons,
nor their daughters. For I will pour
out their [own] wickedness on them
[and not only on the imposters posing

as prophets, for the people could not have been deceived without their own consent].

17 "Therefore [Jeremiah] you will say this word to them,
'Let my eyes flow with tears night and day,
And let them never cease;
For the virgin daughter of my people has been crushed with a great blow,
With a very serious *and* severely infected wound.
18 'If I go out into the field,
Then I gaze on those slaughtered with the sword!
And if I enter the city,
Then I gaze on [those tormented with] the diseases of famine!
For both prophet and priest [who should have guided the people]
Go about [bewildered and exiled] in a land (Babylon) that they do not know *or* understand.' "

19 Have You [O Lord] completely rejected Judah?
Do You loathe Zion?
Why have You stricken us so that there is no healing for us?
We looked for peace *and* completeness, but nothing good came;
And [we hoped] for a time of healing, but behold, terror!
20 We know *and* acknowledge,
O Lord,
Our wickedness and the iniquity of our fathers; for we have sinned against You.
21 Do not treat us with contempt *and* condemn us, for Your own name's sake;
Do not disgrace Your glorious throne;
Remember [with consideration] and do not break Your [solemn] covenant with us.

22 Are there any among the idols of the nations who can send rain?
Or can the heavens [of their own will] give showers?
Is it not You, O Lord our God?
Therefore we will wait *and* hope [confidently] in You,
For You are the one who has made all these things [the heavens and the rain].

15 THEN THE Lord said to me, "Even though Moses and Samuel were to stand before Me [interceding for them], My heart would still not be [turned with favor] toward this people [Judah]. Send them away from My presence *and* out of My sight and let them go! 2 "And it shall be that when they say to you, 'Where should we go?' then tell them, 'Thus says the Lord:

"Those [destined] for death, to death;
Those for the sword, to the sword;
Those for famine, to famine;
Those for captivity, to captivity." '

3 "I will appoint four kinds of destroyers over them," says the Lord, "the sword to slay, the dogs to tear *and* drag away, and the birds of the air and the beasts of the earth to devour and to destroy. 4 "I will make them an object of horror to all nations of the earth because of Manasseh [the despicable] son of Hezekiah, king of Judah, for the [evil and detestable] things which he did in Jerusalem. [2 Kin 21:1–18]

5 "For who will have pity on you, O Jerusalem,
Or who will mourn for you,
Or who will turn aside to ask about your welfare?
6 "You have abandoned (rejected) Me," says the Lord.
"You keep going backward.
Therefore I shall stretch out My hand against you and destroy you;

I am tired of delaying [your
   punishment]!
7 "I will winnow (sort, separate)
   them with a winnowing fork
At the gates of the land;
I will deprive them of children, I
   will destroy My people;
They did not repent *and* turn from
   their [evil] ways.
8 "I will make their widows more
   numerous before Me
Than the sand of the seas;
I will bring against them, against
   the mother of the young men,
A destroyer at noonday;
I will suddenly cause anguish and
   terror
To fall on her.
9 "She who has borne seven [sons]
   languishes;
She has breathed out her soul.
Her sun has set while it was still
   day;
She has been shamed and
   humiliated.
So I will hand over [the rest of] the
   survivors to the sword
Before their enemies," says the Lord.

10 Woe to me, my mother, that you
   have given birth to me
To be a man of strife and a man of
   contention to all the earth!
I have not loaned, nor have men
   lent money to me,
Yet everyone curses me. [Jer 1:18, 19]
11 The Lord said, "Surely [it will
   go well for Judah's obedient
   remnant for] I will set you free
   for good *purposes;*
Surely [Jeremiah] I will [intercede
   for you with the enemy and I
   will] cause the enemy to plead
   with you [for help]

In a time of disaster and a time of
   distress. [Jer 21:1, 2; 37:3; 42:2;
   Rom 8:28]

12 "Can anyone crush iron,
   The iron from the north, or bronze?
13 "Your [nation's] riches and your
   treasures
I will give as plunder without price
   [to the Babylonians],
Because of all your sins
And within all your territories.
14 "Then I will make your enemies
   bring [you along with] your
   possessions
Into a land which you do not know
   [for there you will serve your
   conquerors];
For a fire has been kindled in My
   anger,
Which will burn upon you."

15 O Lord, You know *and* understand;
Remember me [thoughtfully], take
   notice of me,
take vengeance for me on my
   persecutors.
Do not, in view of Your patience,
   take me away;
Know that for Your sake I endure
   [continual] rebuke *and* dishonor.
16 Your words were found and I ate
   them,
And Your words became a joy to
   me and the delight of my heart;
For I have been called by Your
   name,
O Lord God of hosts.
17 I did not sit with the group of those
   who celebrate,
Nor did I rejoice;
I sat alone because Your
   [powerful] hand was *upon me,*
For You had filled me with
   indignation [at their sin].

speak the Word

*God, to me Your words are a joy and the delight my heart,
because I belong to You and am called by Your name.*
—ADAPTED FROM JEREMIAH 15:16

18 Why has my pain been perpetual
　And my wound incurable, refusing
　　to be healed?
　Will you indeed be to me like a
　　deceptive *brook*
　With water that is unreliable?
19 Therefore, thus says the LORD [to
　　Jeremiah],
　"If you repent [and give up this
　　mistaken attitude of despair and
　　self-pity], then I will restore you
　　[to a state of inner peace]
　So that you may stand before Me
　　[as My obedient representative];
　And if you separate the precious
　　from the worthless [examining
　　yourself and cleansing your
　　heart from unwarranted doubt
　　concerning My faithfulness],
　You will become My spokesman.
　Let the people turn to you [and
　　learn to value My values]—
　But you, you must not turn to them
　　[with regard for their idolatry
　　and wickedness].
20 "And I will make you to this people
　A fortified wall of bronze;
　They will fight against you,
　But they will not prevail over you,
　For I am with you [always] to save
　　you
　And protect you," says the LORD.
21 "So I will rescue you out of the
　　hand of the wicked,
　And I will redeem you from the
　　[grasping] palm of the terrible
　　and ruthless [tyrant]."

16 THE WORD of the LORD also
came to me, saying,
2 "You shall not take a wife or
have sons and daughters in this place
(Jerusalem)."
3 For thus says the LORD concerning
the sons and daughters who are born
in this place, and concerning the mothers who give birth to them, and the fathers who father them in this land:
4 "They will die of deadly diseases.

They will not be mourned or buried;
they will be like dung on the surface
of the ground and come to an end by
sword and famine, and their dead
bodies will be food for the birds of the
air and for the beasts of the earth."
5 For thus says the LORD, "Do not
enter a house of mourning, nor go to
lament (express grief) or bemoan [the
dead], for I have taken My peace away
from this people," says the LORD, "even
My lovingkindness and compassion.
6 "Both great men and small will die
in this land; they will not be buried, nor
will they be lamented (mourned over
with expressions of grief in death), nor
will anyone cut himself or shave his
head for them [in mourning].
7 "*People* will not offer food to the
mourners, to comfort anyone [as they
grieve] for the dead, nor give them a
cup of consolation to drink for anyone's father or mother.
8 "And you [Jeremiah] shall not go
into a house of feasting to sit with
them to eat and drink."
9 For thus says the LORD of hosts, the
God of Israel, "Behold, I will remove
from this place, before your very eyes
and in your time, the sound of joy and
the shout of gladness, the voice of the
bridegroom and the voice of the bride.
10 "Now when you tell these people all
these words and they ask you, 'Why
has the LORD decreed all this great
tragedy against us? And what is our
iniquity, what is the sin which we have
committed against the LORD our God?'
11 "Then you are to say to them, 'It is
because your fathers have abandoned
(rejected) Me,' says the LORD, 'and
have walked after other gods and have
served them and bowed down to the
handmade idols and have abandoned
(rejected) Me and have not kept My law,
12 and because you have done worse
[things] than your fathers. Just look,
every one of you walks in the stubbornness of his own evil heart, so that
you do not listen [obediently] to Me.

13"Therefore I will hurl you out of this land [of Judah] into the land [of the Babylonians] which neither you nor your fathers have known, and there you will serve other gods day and night, for I will show you no compassion.'

14"Therefore behold, the days are coming," says the Lord, "when it will no longer be said, 'As the Lord lives, who brought up the sons of Israel out of the land of Egypt,'

15but, 'As the Lord lives, who brought up the sons of Israel from the land of the north and from all the countries to which He had driven them.' And I will bring them back to their land which I gave to their fathers.

16"Behold (listen carefully), I will send for many fishermen," says the Lord, "and they will fish for them; and afterward I will send for many hunters, and they will hunt them from every mountain and from every hill and out of the clefts of the rocks.

17"For My eyes are on all their ways; they are not hidden from My face, nor is their wickedness concealed from My eyes.

18"I will first doubly repay and punish them for their wickedness and their sin [before I return them to their land], because they have profaned My land; they have filled My inheritance with the carcasses of their detestable idols and with their abominations."

19[Then said Jeremiah] "O Lord, my
   Strength and my Stronghold,
And my Refuge in the day of
   distress and need,
The nations will come to You
From the ends of the earth and say,
'Our fathers have inherited
   nothing but lies and illusion,
[Worthless] things in which there
   is no benefit!'
20"Can a man make gods for himself?
Such [things] are not gods!
21"Therefore," [says the Lord]
   "behold, I will make them know—

This time I will make them know
My power and My might;
And they will know and recognize
   [without any doubt] that My
   Name is the Lord."

17 THE SIN of Judah is
written down with an iron
stylus;
With a diamond point it is engraved
   upon the tablet of their heart
And on the horns of their altars.
2As they remember their children,
So they remember [in detail] their
   [pagan] altars and their Asherim
Beside green trees on the high hills.
3O [Jerusalem] My mountain in the
   countryside,
I will give [to the Babylonians,
   as the cost of your sin] your
   wealth and all your treasures as
   plunder,
And throughout your territory,
   your high places of sin.
4And you will, through your own
   fault, let go of your [grip on your]
   inheritance
That I gave you;
And I will make you serve your
   enemies
In a land which you do not know;
For you have kindled a fire in My
   anger
Which will burn forever.
5Thus says the Lord,
"Cursed is the man who trusts in
   and relies on mankind,
Making [weak, faulty human]
   flesh his strength,
And whose mind and heart turn
   away from the Lord.
6"For he will be like a shrub in the
   [parched] desert;
And shall not see prosperity when
   it comes,
But shall live in the rocky places of
   the wilderness,
In an uninhabited salt land.

7"Blessed [with spiritual security] is the man who believes *and* trusts in *and* relies on the Lord
And whose hope *and* confident expectation is the Lord.
8"For he will be [nourished] like a tree planted by the waters,
That spreads out its roots by the river;
And will not fear the heat when it comes;
But its leaves will be green *and* moist.
And it will not be anxious *and* concerned in a year of drought
Nor stop bearing fruit.

9"The heart is deceitful above all things
And it is extremely sick;
Who can understand it fully *and* know its secret motives? [Matt 13:15–17; Mark 7:21–23; Eph 4:20–24]
10"I, the Lord, search *and* examine the mind,
I test the heart,
To give to each man according to his ways,
According to the results of his deeds.
11"Like the partridge that hatches eggs which she has not laid,

live deeper

Jeremiah 17:9 teaches us that our hearts are "deceitful above all things." Self-deception is one of the easiest traps of the enemy that we can fall into. The self always helps the self get whatever it wants. When we have a strong desire for something, we can easily deceive ourselves by telling ourselves whatever we want to hear. If my will wants a thing, my mind will give me a variety of reasons I should have it, and my emotions will certainly produce ample feelings that agree with my will's wants!

We must learn to live deeper than the shallowness of our own minds, wills, and feelings. Deeper living means we go beyond what we want, what we think, and how we feel and live by the Word of God. We must bow our knees in humility to God's Word and His will because that is where we find true blessings.

I encourage you to have regular times of waiting in God's presence, asking Him to reveal any impure motives you might have. Pray against deception, for Satan is the great deceiver. When we believe something that is not true, we are deceived. Satan also seeks to lead us astray through reasoning that is contrary to the truth.

When you believe a lie, it becomes truth to you even though it is not actually truth at all. Do not trust yourself too much. Realize that not everything you want is best for you. Ask God for what you want, but always be willing to change if you discover that you are not in agreement with God's will. If what you ask God for is His will, it will come in due time. If it does not come, then believe He has something better in mind for you.

Above all, hold your peace and remain at rest. God can easily lead the believer who is not frustrated and anxious. Say as David did in Psalm 51:6: "Behold, You desire truth in the innermost being, and in the hidden part [of my heart] You will make me know wisdom." The more you truly know God's wisdom in your heart, the less likely you are to be deceived.

So is he who makes a fortune in
   ways that are unjust.
It will be lost to him before his
   days are over,
And in the end he will be [nothing
   but] a fool."
¹²A glorious throne, set on high from
   the beginning,
Is the place of our sanctuary (the
   temple).
¹³O LORD, the hope of Israel,
All who abandon You will be
   shamed.
Those who turn away on earth will
   be written down,
Because they have abandoned the
   LORD, the fountain of living waters.
¹⁴Heal me, O LORD, and I will be
   healed;
Save me and I will be saved,
For You are my praise.
¹⁵Behold, they keep saying to me,
"Where is the word of the LORD
   [that is, the disaster that you
   prophesied]?
Let it come now!"
¹⁶But as for me, I have not tried to
   escape from being a shepherd
   [walking] after You,
Nor have I longed for the woeful
   day [of judgment];
You know that, whatever I said
Was [spoken] in Your presence
   and was from You.
¹⁷Do not be a terror to me;
You are my refuge and my hope in
   the day of disaster.
¹⁸Let those who persecute me be
   shamed, but as for me, protect
   me from shame;
Let them lose courage, but let me
   be undaunted.
Bring on them a day of tragedy,

And destroy them with double
   destruction!

¹⁹Thus the LORD said to me, "Go
and stand in the public gate, through
which the kings of Judah come in and
go out, and [stand] also in all the gates
of Jerusalem;
²⁰and say to them, 'Listen to the
word of the LORD, kings of Judah, and
all Judah, and all the people of Jerusalem who enter through these gates.
²¹'Thus says the LORD, "Pay attention
for your own good, [and for the sake of
your future] do not carry any load on
the Sabbath day or bring anything in
through the gates of Jerusalem.
²²"You shall not carry a load out of
your houses on the Sabbath day nor
do any work, but keep the Sabbath day
holy [by setting it apart as a day of wor-
ship], as I commanded your fathers.
²³"Yet they would not listen and obey
and control their behavior; but they
were stiff-necked in order not to hear
and take instruction.
²⁴"But it will come about, if you listen diligently to Me," says the LORD, "to
bring no load in through the gates of
this city on the Sabbath day, but keep
the Sabbath day holy by doing no work
on it,
²⁵then kings and princes who will
sit on the throne of David will enter
through the gates of this city, riding
in chariots and on horses—the kings
and their princes, the men of Judah
and the inhabitants of Jerusalem; and
this city will be inhabited and endure
throughout the ages.
²⁶"People will come from the cities of
Judah and the places all around Jerusalem, from the land of Benjamin, from
the lowland, from the hill country and

speak the Word

*Lord, heal me and I will be healed; save me
and I will be saved. You are my praise.*
−ADAPTED FROM JEREMIAH 17:14

from the South (the Negev), bringing burnt offerings and sacrifices, grain offerings and incense, and bringing sacrifices of thanksgiving to the house of the LORD.

27"But if you will not listen to Me and keep the Sabbath day holy by not carrying a load as you come in the gates of Jerusalem on the Sabbath day, then I will kindle a fire in her gates that cannot be extinguished, and it will devour the palaces of Jerusalem."'"

18 THE WORD which came to Jeremiah from the LORD: 2"Arise and go down to the potter's house, and there I will make you hear My words."

3Then I went down to the potter's house, and saw that he was working at the wheel.

4But the vessel that he was making from clay was spoiled by the potter's hand; so he made it over, reworking it and making it into another pot that seemed good to him.

5Then the word of the LORD came to me:

6"O house of Israel, can I not do with you as this potter does?" says the LORD. "Look carefully, as the clay is in the potter's hand, so are you in My hand, O house of Israel.

7"At one moment I might [suddenly] speak concerning a nation or kingdom, that I will uproot and break down and destroy;

8if that nation against which I have spoken turns from its evil, I will *relent *and* reverse My decision concerning the devastation that I intended to do.

9"Or at another time I might [suddenly] speak about a nation or kingdom that I will build up or establish;

10and if they do evil in My sight by not obeying My voice, then I will reverse My decision concerning the

18:8 Lit *repent of.*

life point

In Jeremiah 18:1–4 we read of the potter who had to remake his vessel because it had been marred. That is a picture of us in the hands of the Lord, the Master Potter.

When we enter into a relationship with Christ, the Bible tells us that we become new creatures (see 2 Corinthians 5:17). Old things have passed away, and we are given an opportunity for a new beginning. We become new spiritual clay for the Holy Spirit to work with. I believe He is shaping you into a beautiful vessel, perfectly designed for the great purposes He has for your life.

good with which I had promised to bless them.

11"Now then, say to the men of Judah and to the citizens of Jerusalem, 'Thus says the LORD, "Behold, I am shaping a disaster and working out a plan against you. Turn back, each of you from his evil way; correct your habits and change your actions for the better."'

12"But they will say, 'That is hopeless! For we are going to follow our own plans, and each of us will act in accordance with the stubbornness of his evil heart.'

13"Therefore thus says the LORD,
'Ask now among the nations,
Who has heard of such things?
The virgin Israel
Has done a very vile *and* horrible thing.
14'Will the snow of [Mount] Lebanon melt *and* vanish from its rocks [which tower above Israel]?
Will the cold, rushing waters of foreign *lands* [that flow down from the distant land] be dried up?
15'Yet My people have forgotten Me;

They burn incense to worthless
gods,
They have stumbled from their
ways
From the ancient roads,
To walk in pathways,
Not on a highway,
[16] Making their land a desolation *and*
a horror,
A thing to be hissed at perpetually;
Everyone who passes by will be
astounded
And shake his head [in scorn].
[17] 'I will scatter them like an east wind
Before the enemy;
I will show them My back and not
My face
In the day of their disaster [says
the Lord].'"

[18] Then [my enemies] said, "Come
and let us work out schemes against
Jeremiah. Surely the law is not going
to be lost to the priest [as Jeremiah
predicts], nor the counsel from the
wise, nor the word from the prophet.
Come and let us strike him with our
tongue [by making charges against
him before the king], and let us ignore
anything he says."

[19] Pay attention to me, O Lord [and
intercede];
Listen to what my adversaries are
saying [and are plotting against
me]—
[20] Should good be repaid with evil?
Yet they have dug a pit for me.
Remember [with compassion] that
I stood before You
To speak good on their behalf,
To turn Your anger away from them.
[21] Therefore, give their children over
to the famine;
Give them over to the power of the
sword.
And let their wives become
childless and widowed;
Let their men meet death [by
virulent disease],

Their young men be struck down
by the sword in battle.
[22] Let an outcry be heard from their
houses
When You suddenly bring [a troop
of] raiders upon them,
For they have dug a pit to capture
me
And have hidden snares for my
feet.
[23] Yet You, O Lord, know
All their deadly plotting against me;
Do not forgive their wickedness
Or blot out their sin from Your sight.
But let them be overthrown before
You;
Deal with them in the time of Your
anger.

19 THUS SAYS the Lord, "Go
and buy a potter's earthenware jar, and take some of
the elders of the people and some of
the senior priests
[2] and go out to the Valley of Ben-
hinnom (son of Hinnom), which is
near the entrance of the Potsherd
Gate; and proclaim there the words
that I tell you,
[3] and say, 'Hear the word of the Lord,
O kings of Judah and inhabitants of Jerusalem. Thus says the Lord of hosts,
the God of Israel, "Behold (listen carefully), I am going to bring such disaster
on this place that the ears of everyone
who hears about it will tingle [in shock].
[4] "Because the people [of Jerusalem]
have abandoned (rejected) Me and
have made this an alien *and* profaned
place by burning sacrifices *and* incense
in it to other gods, that neither they nor
their fathers nor the kings of Judah ever
knew, and because they have filled this
place with the blood of the innocent
[5] and have built the high places of
Baal to burn their sons in the fire as
burnt offerings to Baal, which I never
commanded or spoke of, nor did it
ever enter My mind (heart);

⁶therefore, listen very closely, the days are coming," says the Lord, "when this place shall no longer be called Topheth or the Valley of Ben-hinnom, but the Valley of Slaughter. [Jer 7:31–32]

⁷"I will pour out *and* nullify the counsel (plans) of [the men of] Judah and Jerusalem in this place, and I will make their people fall by the sword before their enemies and by the hand of those who seek their lives; and I will give their dead bodies as food for the birds of the air and for the beasts of the earth.

⁸"I will make this city a desolation and an *object of* hissing; everyone who passes by it will be amazed and will hiss [in scorn] because of all its plagues *and* disasters.

⁹"And I will make them eat the flesh of their sons and their daughters, and each one will eat one another's flesh during the siege and distress brought by their enemies and those who seek their lives."'

¹⁰"Then you are to break the jar in the sight of the men who accompany you,

¹¹and say to them, 'Thus says the Lord of hosts, "This is the way I will break this people and this city as one breaks a potter's vessel, so that it cannot be mended. They will bury [corpses] in Topheth until there is no more room left [in that place] to bury [the dead].

¹²"This I will do to this place," says the Lord, "and to its inhabitants; and I will even make this city like Topheth.

¹³"The houses of Jerusalem and the houses of the kings of Judah will be defiled like this place, Topheth, all the houses on whose rooftops incense has been burned to all the host of heaven (sun, moon, stars), and where drink offerings have been poured out to other gods."'" [Acts 7:42, 43]

¹⁴Then Jeremiah came from Topheth, where the Lord had sent him to prophesy; and he stood in the court of the Lord's house and said to all the people:

¹⁵"Thus says the Lord of hosts, the God of Israel, 'Behold, I am going to bring on this city and on all its towns, all the devastation that I have declared against it, because they have become stiff-necked and refused to hear *and* obey My words.'"

20 NOW PASHHUR the son of Immer, the priest, who was [also] chief officer in the house of the Lord, heard Jeremiah prophesying these things.

²Then Pashhur beat Jeremiah the prophet and put him in the stocks that were at the upper Benjamin Gate by the house of the Lord. [Jer 1:19; 15:15]

³And the next day Pashhur brought Jeremiah out of the stocks. Then Jeremiah said to him, "The Lord does not call your name Pashhur, but Magor-missabib (terror on every side).

⁴"For thus says the Lord, 'Behold, I will make you a terror to yourself and to all your friends; they will fall by the sword of their enemies while you look on. And I will give all Judah into the hand of the king of Babylon; he will carry them away to Babylon as captives and will slaughter them with the sword.

⁵'Moreover, I will hand over all the riches of this city, all the result of its labor, all its precious things; even all the treasures of the kings of Judah I will hand over to their enemies, and they will plunder them, and take them away and carry them to Babylon.

⁶'And you, Pashhur, and all who live in your house will go into captivity; you will go to Babylon, and there you will die and be buried, you and all your friends to whom you have falsely prophesied.'"

⁷[Jeremiah said,] O Lord, You
    have persuaded me and I was
    deceived;
You are stronger than I and You
    have prevailed.
I am a laughingstock all day long;
Everyone mocks me.

8 For whenever I speak, I must shout
    out;
I shout violence and destruction,
Because the word of the Lord has
    become to me
A reprimand and a mockery *and* has
    brought me insult all day long.
9 If I say, "I will not remember Him
Or speak His name anymore,"
Then my heart becomes a burning
    fire
Shut up in my bones.
And I am weary of enduring *and*
    holding it in;
I cannot endure it [nor contain it
    any longer].
10 For I have heard the whispering
    and defaming words of many,
"Terror on every side!
Denounce him! Let us denounce
    him!"
All my familiar *and* trusted friends,
[Those who are] watching for my
    fall, say,
"Perhaps he will be persuaded *and*
    deceived; then we will overcome
    him,
And take our revenge on him."
11 But the Lord is with me as a dread
    champion [one to be greatly
    feared];
Therefore my persecutors will
    stumble and not overcome [me].
They will be completely shamed,
    for they have not acted wisely *and*
    have failed [in their schemes];
Their eternal dishonor will never
    be forgotten.
12 But, O Lord of hosts, You who
    examine the righteous,
Who see the heart and the mind,
Let me see Your vengeance on
    them;
For to You I have committed my
    cause.
13 Sing to the Lord! Praise the Lord!
For He has rescued the life of the
    needy one
From the hand of evildoers.

14 Cursed be the day on which I was
    born;
Do not bless the day on which my
    mother gave birth to me!
15 Cursed be the man who brought
    the news
To my father, saying,
"A son has been born to you!"
Making him very glad.
16 And let that man be like the cities
Which the Lord overthrew without
    regret.
Let him hear an outcry in the
    morning
And a shout of alarm at noon;
17 Because he did not kill me before
    my birth,
So that my mother might have
    been my grave,
And her womb always pregnant.
18 Why did I come out of the womb
To see trouble and sorrow,
So that my days have been filled
    with shame?

21 THE WORD which came
to Jeremiah from the Lord
when King Zedekiah sent
to him Pashhur the son of Malchijah,
and Zephaniah the priest the son of
Maaseiah, saying,
2 "Please inquire of the Lord for us,
because Nebuchadnezzar king of Babylon is making war against us. Perhaps
the Lord will deal [favorably] with us
according to all His wonderful works
and force him to withdraw from us."
3 Then Jeremiah said to them, "Say
this to Zedekiah:
4 'Thus says the Lord, the God of Israel, "Behold, I will turn back *and* dull
the edge of the weapons of war that are
in your hands, [those] with which you
fight against the king of Babylon and
the Chaldeans who are besieging you
outside the walls; and I will bring them
into the center of this city (Jerusalem).
5 "I Myself will fight against you
with an outstretched hand and with

a strong arm in anger, in fury, and in great indignation *and* wrath.

⁶"I will also strike the inhabitants of this city, both man and beast; they will die of a great virulent disease.

⁷"Then afterward," says the LORD, "I will hand over Zedekiah king of Judah and his servants and the people in this city who survive the virulent disease, the sword, and the famine, to Nebuchadnezzar king of Babylon, and into the hand of their enemy, into the hand of those who seek their lives. And he will strike them with the edge of the sword; he will not spare them nor have mercy and compassion on them."'

⁸"And to this people you (Jeremiah) shall also say, 'Thus says the LORD, "Behold, I set before you the way of life and the way of death.

⁹"He who remains in this city [of Jerusalem] will die by the sword and by famine and by virulent disease. But he who goes outside and surrenders to the Chaldeans who are besieging you will live, and his life will be like a prize of war to him.

¹⁰"For I have set My face against this city to do harm and not good," says the LORD. "It shall be given into the hand of the king of Babylon and he will burn it with fire."'

¹¹"And concerning the royal house of the king of Judah [you shall say], 'Hear the word of the LORD,

¹²O house of David, thus says the LORD:

"Administer justice in the morning,
And rescue the one who has been
  robbed from the hand of his
  oppressor,
That My wrath will not roar up
  like fire
And burn so [hotly] that none can
  extinguish it,
Because of the evil of their deeds.

¹³"Understand this, I am against
  you, O inhabitant of the valley,

O rock of the plain," says the LORD—
"You who say, 'Who will come
  down against us?
Or who will enter into our dwelling
  places?'
¹⁴"But I will punish you in
  accordance with the [appropriate]
  consequences of your decisions
  and your actions," says the LORD.
"I will kindle a fire in your forest,
And it will devour all that is
  around you."'"

22 THUS SAYS the LORD, "Go down to the house of the king of Judah and speak this word there:

²'Hear the word of the LORD, O king of Judah, you who sit on the throne of David—you and your servants and your people who enter by these gates.

³'Thus says the LORD, "Execute justice and righteousness, and rescue the one who has been robbed from the hand of his oppressor. And do no wrong; do no violence to the stranger, the fatherless, or the widow, nor shed innocent blood in this place.

⁴"For if you will indeed obey this word, then kings will enter through the gates of this palace, sitting in David's place on his throne, riding in chariots and on horses, *even the king* himself and his servants and his people.

⁵"But if you will not hear *and* obey these words, I swear [an oath] by Myself," says the LORD, "that this house will become a desolation."'"

⁶For thus says the LORD in regard to the house of the king of Judah:

"You are [as valuable] to Me as [the
  green pastures of] Gilead [east of
  the Jordan]
Or as the [plentiful] summit of
  Lebanon [west of the Jordan],
Yet most certainly [if you will not
  listen to Me] I will make you a
  wilderness,
And uninhabited cities.

7"For I will prepare *and* appoint
  destroyers [to execute My
  judgments] against you,
Each with his weapons;
And they will cut down your
  [palaces built of] choicest cedars
And throw them in the fire.

8"Many nations will pass by this
city; and each man will say to another,
'Why has the LORD done this to this
great city?'
9"Then they will answer, 'Because
the people ignored *and* abandoned
the [solemn] covenant with the LORD
their God and worshiped other gods
and served them.'"

10Do not weep for the dead or mourn
  for him;
But weep bitterly for the one who
  goes away [into exile],
For he will never return
And see his native country [again].

11For thus says the LORD in regard
to Shallum (Jehoahaz) the [third] son
of Josiah, king of Judah, who reigned
instead of Josiah his father and who
went from this place, "Shallum will
not return here anymore;
12he will die in the place where they
led him captive and not see this land
again.

13"Woe (judgment is coming) to him
  who builds his house by [acts of]
  unrighteousness
And his upper chambers by
  injustice,
Who uses his neighbor's service
  without pay
And does not give him wages [for
  his work],
14Who says, 'I will build myself a
  spacious house
With large upper rooms,
And cut out its [wide] windows,
And panel it with cedar and paint
  it vermilion.'

15"Do you think that you become
  a king because you have much
  more cedar [in your palace than
  Solomon]?
Did not your father [Josiah], as he
  ate and drank,
Do just and righteous acts [being
  upright and in right standing
  with God]?
Then all was well with him.
16"He defended the cause of the
  afflicted and needy;
Then all was well.
Is that not what it means to know
  Me?"
Says the LORD.
17"But your eyes and your heart
Are only intent on your own
  dishonest gain,
On shedding innocent blood,
On oppression and extortion *and*
  violence."

18Therefore thus says the LORD in
regard to Jehoiakim the [second] son
of Josiah, king of Judah,

"The relatives will not lament
  (mourn over with expressions of
  grief) for him:
'Alas, my brother!' or, 'Alas, sister,'
  [how great our loss]!
The subjects will not lament for
  him:
'Alas, master!' or 'Alas, majesty
  [how great was his glory]!'
19"He shall be buried with the burial
  of a donkey—
Dragged off and thrown out
  beyond the gates of Jerusalem.
20"Go up [north] to Lebanon and cry
  out,
And raise your voice in [the hills
  of] Bashan [across the Jordan];
Cry out also from Abarim,
For all your lovers (allies) have
  been destroyed. [Jer 27:6, 7]
21"I spoke to you in your [times of]
  prosperity,
But you said, 'I will not listen!'

This has been your attitude *and* practice from your youth;
You have not obeyed My voice.
²²"The wind [of adversity] will carry away all your shepherds (rulers, statesmen),
And your lovers (allies) will go into exile.
Surely then you will be ashamed and humiliated *and* disgraced
Because of all your wickedness.
²³"O inhabitant of [Jerusalem, whose palaces are made from the cedars of] Lebanon,
You who nest in the cedars,
How you will groan *and* how miserable you will be when pains come on you,
Pain like a woman in childbirth!
     [1 Kin 7:2]

²⁴"As I live," says the Lord, "though Coniah the son of Jehoiakim king of Judah were the signet [ring] on My right hand, yet would I pull you (Coniah) off. ²⁵"And I will place you in the hand of those who seek your life and in the hand of those whom you fear, even into the hand of Nebuchadnezzar king of Babylon and into the hand of the Chaldeans. ²⁶"I will hurl you and the mother who gave you birth into another country where you were not born, and there you will die. ²⁷"But as for the land to which they long to return, they will not return to it.

²⁸"Is this man [King] Coniah a despised, broken jar?
Is he a vessel in which no one takes pleasure?
Why are he and his [royal] descendants hurled out
And cast into a land which they do not know *or* understand?
²⁹"O land, land, land,
Hear the word of the Lord!

³⁰"Thus says the Lord,

'Write this man [Coniah] down as childless,

A man who will not prosper (succeed) in his lifetime;
For not one of his descendants will succeed
In sitting on the throne of David
Or ruling again in Judah.'"

23 "WOE TO the shepherds (civil leaders, rulers) who are destroying and scattering the sheep of My pasture!" says the Lord. ²Therefore thus says the Lord, the God of Israel, in regard to the shepherds who care for *and* feed My people: "You have scattered My flock and driven them away, and have not attended to them; hear this, I am about to visit *and* attend to you for the evil of your deeds," says the Lord. ³"Then I will gather the remnant of My flock out of all the countries to which I have driven them and bring them back to their folds *and* pastures; and they will be fruitful and multiply. ⁴"I will set up shepherds over them who will feed them. And they will not be afraid any longer, nor be terrified, nor will any be missing," says the Lord.

⁵"Behold (listen closely), the days are coming," says the Lord,
"When I will raise up for David a righteous Branch;
And He will reign as King and act wisely
And will do [those things that accomplish] justice and righteousness in the land.
⁶"In His days Judah will be saved,
And Israel will dwell safely;
Now this is His name by which He will be called;
'The Lord Our Righteousness.'
     [Matt 1:21–23; Rom 3:22]

⁷"Therefore behold, the days are coming," says the Lord, "when they will no longer say, 'As the Lord lives, who brought up the children of Israel from the land of Egypt,'

⁸but [they will say], 'As the Lᴏʀᴅ lives, who brought up and led back the descendants of the house of Israel from the north country and from all the countries to which I had driven them.' Then they will live in their own land." [Jer 16:14, 15]

⁹Concerning the prophets:
My heart [says Jeremiah] is broken within me,
All my bones shake;
I have become like a drunken man,
A man whom wine has overcome,
Because of the Lᴏʀᴅ
And because of His holy words [declared against unfaithful leaders].
¹⁰For the land is full of adulterers (unfaithful to God);
The land mourns because of the curse [of God upon it].
The pastures of the wilderness have dried up.
The course of action [of the false prophets] is evil *and* they rush into wickedness;
And their power is not right.
¹¹"For both [false] prophet and priest are ungodly (profane, polluted);
Even in My house I have found their wickedness," says the Lᴏʀᴅ.
¹²"Therefore their way will be to them like slippery paths
In the dark; they will be pushed and fall into them;
For I will bring disaster on them,
In the year of their punishment," says the Lᴏʀᴅ.

¹³"And I have seen a foolish *and* an offensive thing in the prophets of Samaria:
They prophesied by Baal and caused My people Israel to go astray.
¹⁴"Also I have seen a horrible thing in the prophets of Jerusalem:
They commit adultery and walk in lies;

They encourage *and* strengthen the hands of evildoers,
So that no one has turned back from his wickedness.
All of them have become like Sodom to Me,
And her inhabitants like Gomorrah.

¹⁵"Therefore thus says the Lᴏʀᴅ of hosts in regard to the prophets,

'Behold, I am going to feed them [the bitterness of] wormwood
And make them drink the poisonous water [of gall],
For from the [counterfeit] prophets of Jerusalem
Profaneness *and* ungodliness have spread into all the land.'"

¹⁶Thus says the Lᴏʀᴅ of hosts,
"Do not listen to the words of the [false] prophets who prophesy to you.
They are teaching you worthless things *and* are leading you into futility;
They speak a vision of their own mind *and* imagination
And not [truth] from the mouth of the Lᴏʀᴅ.
¹⁷"They are continually saying to those who despise Me [and My word],
'The Lord has said, "You will have peace"';
And they say to everyone who walks after the stubbornness of his own heart,
'No evil will come on you.'
¹⁸"But who [among them] has stood in the council of the Lᴏʀᴅ,
That he would perceive and hear His word?
Who has marked His word [noticing and observing and paying attention to it] and has [actually] heard it?
¹⁹"Behold, the tempest of the Lᴏʀᴅ has gone forth in wrath,
A whirling tempest;

It will whirl *and* burst on the heads of the wicked.

20"The anger of the LORD will not turn back
Until He has set in motion and accomplished the thoughts *and* intentions of His heart;
In the last days you will clearly understand it.
21"I did not send [these counterfeit] prophets,
Yet they ran;
I did not speak to them,
Yet they prophesied.
22"But if they had stood in My council,
Then they would have caused My people to hear My words,
Then they would have turned My people from their evil way
And from the evil of their decisions *and* deeds.
23"Am I a God who is at hand," says the LORD,
"And not a God far away?"
24"Can anyone hide himself in secret places
So that I cannot see him?" says the LORD.
"Do I not fill heaven and earth?" says the LORD.

25"I have heard what the prophets have said who prophesy lies in My Name, saying, 'I have dreamed, I have dreamed [visions when on my bed at night].'
26"How long [shall this state of affairs continue]? Is there anything in the hearts of the prophets who prophesy falsehood, even these prophets of the deception of their own heart,
27who think that they can make My people forget My Name by their [contrived] dreams which each one tells another, just as their fathers forgot My Name because of Baal?
28"The prophet who has a dream may tell his dream; but he who has My word, let him speak My word faithfully. What has straw in common with wheat [for nourishment]?" says the LORD.
29"Is not My word like fire [that consumes all that cannot endure the test]?" says the LORD, "and like a hammer that breaks the [most stubborn] rock [in pieces]?
30"Therefore behold (hear this), I am against the [counterfeit] prophets," says the LORD, "[I am descending on them with punishment, these prophets] who steal My words from one another [imitating the words of the true prophets].
31"Hear this, I am against the prophets," says the LORD, "who use their [own deceitful] tongues and say, 'Thus says *the Lord.*'
32"Hear this, I am against those who have prophesied false *and* made-up dreams," says the LORD, "and have told them and have made My people err *and* go astray by their lies and by their reckless boasting; yet I did not send them or command them nor do they benefit *and* enhance [the life of] these people in the slightest way," says the LORD.
33"Now when this people or a prophet or a priest asks you [in jest], 'What is the oracle of the LORD [the burden to be lifted up and carried]?' Then you shall say to them, 'What oracle [besides the one that declares you people to be the burden]!' The LORD says, 'I will unburden Myself *and* I will abandon you.'
34"And as for the prophet, the priest, or [any of] the people, whoever says, 'The oracle of the LORD,' [as if he

speak the Word

God, I declare that I do have Your word and I ask you to help me to speak it faithfully.
—ADAPTED FROM JEREMIAH 23:28

knows God's will], I will punish that man and his household.

35"[For the future, in speaking of the words of the LORD] thus each of you shall say to his neighbor and to his brother, 'What has the LORD answered?' or, 'What has the LORD spoken?'

36"For you will no longer remember the oracle of the LORD, because every man's own word will become the oracle, [for as they mockingly call all prophecies oracles, whether good or bad, so will it prove to be to them; God will take them at their own word]; and you have perverted the words [not of a lifeless idol, but] of the living God, the LORD of hosts, our God.

37"Thus you will [reverently] say to the prophet, 'What has the LORD answered you?' and, 'What has the LORD spoken?'

38"For if you say, 'The oracle of the LORD!' surely thus says the LORD, 'Because you said this word, "The oracle of the LORD!" when I have also sent to you, saying, "You shall not say, 'The oracle of the LORD!'"'

39"Therefore behold, I, even I, will assuredly forget you and send you away from My presence, you and the city (Jerusalem) which I gave to you and to your fathers.

40"And I will bring an everlasting disgrace on you and a perpetual humiliation (shame) which will not be forgotten."

24 AFTER NEBUCHADNEZZAR king of Babylon had taken Jeconiah [who was also called Coniah and Jehoiachin] the son of Jehoiakim, king of Judah, and the princes of Judah [along] with the craftsmen and smiths into exile from Jerusalem to Babylon, the LORD showed me [in a vision] two baskets of figs set before the temple of the LORD.

2One basket had very good figs, like the figs that are the first to ripen; but the other basket had very bad figs, so rotten that they could not be eaten.

3Then the LORD said to me, "What do you see, Jeremiah?" And I said, "Figs, the good figs, very good; and the bad figs, very bad, so rotten that they cannot be eaten."

4Again the word of the LORD came to me, saying,

5"Thus says the LORD, the God of Israel, 'Like these good figs, so I will regard as good the captives of Judah, whom I have sent from this place into the land of the Chaldeans.

6'For I will set My eyes on them for good, and I will bring them again to this land; and I will build them up and not overwhelm them, and I will plant them and not uproot them.

7'I will give them a heart to know Me, [understanding fully] that I am the LORD; and they will be My people, and I will be their God, for they will return to Me with their whole heart.

8'And as for the bad figs, which are so rotten that they cannot be eaten,' surely thus says the LORD, 'so I will abandon Zedekiah king of Judah and his princes, and the remnant of Jerusalem who remain in this land and those who live in the land of Egypt.

9'I will make them a focus of ridicule and disappointment [tossed back and forth] among all the kingdoms of the earth, a [notorious] disgrace, a byword, a taunt and a curse in all places where I will scatter them.

speak the Word

Thank You, God, for setting Your eyes upon me for good and building me up.
Thank You for giving me a heart to know You and for being my God.
—ADAPTED FROM JEREMIAH 24:6, 7

¹⁰'I will send the sword, famine and virulent disease among them until they are consumed from the land which I gave to them and to their fathers.'"

25 THE WORD that came to Jeremiah in regard to all the people of Judah in the fourth year of the reign of Jehoiakim the son of Josiah, king of Judah (that was the first year of the reign of Nebuchadnezzar king of Babylon),

²which Jeremiah the prophet spoke to all the people of Judah and to all the inhabitants of Jerusalem, saying,

³"For these twenty-three years—from the thirteenth year of Josiah the son of Amon, king of Judah, even to this day—the word of the LORD has come to me and I have spoken to you over and over again, but you have not listened.

⁴"Although the LORD has persistently sent to you all His servants the prophets, you have not listened nor [even] inclined your ear to hear [His message],

⁵saying, 'Turn now everyone from his evil way and the evil of your actions [that you may not forfeit the right to] live in the land that the LORD has given to you and your forefathers forever and ever;

⁶and do not go after other gods to serve them and to worship them, and do not provoke Me to anger with the work of your hands, and I will do you no harm.'

⁷"Yet you have not listened to Me," says the LORD, "so that you have provoked Me to anger with the work (idols) of your hands to your own harm.

⁸"Therefore thus says the LORD of hosts, 'Because you have not obeyed My words,

⁹behold (hear this), I will send for all the families of the north,' says the LORD, 'and I will send for Nebuchadnezzar king of Babylon, My servant [to enact My plan], and I will bring

them against this land and against its inhabitants and against all these surrounding nations; and I will utterly destroy them and make them a horror and a hissing [that is, an object of warning and ridicule] and an everlasting desolation.

¹⁰'Moreover, I will take from them the voice of joy and the voice of gladness, the voice of the bridegroom and the voice of the bride, the sound of the millstones [grinding meal] and the light of the lamp [to light the night]. [Jer 7:34]

¹¹'This whole land will be a waste and a horror, and these nations will serve the king of Babylon seventy years. [2 Chr 36:20–23; Jer 4:27; 12:11, 12; Dan 9:2]

¹²'Then when seventy years are completed, I will punish the king of Babylon and that nation, the land of the Chaldeans (Babylonia),' says the LORD, 'for their wickedness, and will make the land [of the Chaldeans] a perpetual waste. [Jer 29:10]

¹³'I will bring on that land all My words which I have pronounced against it, all that is written in this book which Jeremiah has prophesied against all the nations.

¹⁴'(For many nations and great kings will make slaves of them, even the Chaldeans [who enslaved other nations]; and I will repay [all of] them according to their deeds and according to the work of their [own] hands.)'"

¹⁵For thus says the LORD, the God of Israel, to me, "Take this cup of the wine of wrath from My hand and cause all the nations to whom I send you to drink it.

¹⁶"They will drink and stagger and go mad because of the sword that I will send among them."

¹⁷Then I (Jeremiah) took the cup from the LORD's hand and made all the nations to whom the LORD had sent me drink it:

¹⁸Jerusalem and the cities of Judah

[being most guilty because their privileges were greatest], its kings and princes, to make them a horror, a ruin, a hissing and a curse, as it is to this day; [1 Pet 4:17]

¹⁹Pharaoh king of Egypt, his servants, his princes, all his people,

²⁰and all the foreign (mixed) population, all the kings of the land of Uz, and all the kings of the land of the Philistines (and [their cities of] Ashkelon, Gaza, Ekron, and the remnant of Ashdod);

²¹Edom, Moab, and the children of Ammon;

²²all the kings of Tyre, all the kings of Sidon, and the kings of the islands *and* the coastlands across the [Mediterranean] Sea;

²³Dedan, Tema, Buz [the neighboring tribes north of Arabia], and all who clip off the side-growth *of their hair;* [Lev 19:27; Jer 9:26]

²⁴all the kings of Arabia and all the kings of the foreign population who live in the desert;

²⁵all the kings of Zimri, all the kings of Elam (Persia), and all the kings of Media;

²⁶all the kings of the north, far and near, one after another—and all the kingdoms of the world which are on the face of the earth. And the king of Sheshach (Babylon) shall drink after them.

²⁷"Then you shall say to them, 'Thus says the LORD of hosts, the God of Israel, "Drink, be drunk, vomit, and fall to rise no more because of the sword which I will send among you."'

²⁸"And if they refuse to take the cup from your hand to drink, then you will say to them, 'Thus says the LORD of hosts, "You shall surely drink!

²⁹"For behold, I am beginning to work disaster in the city which is called by My Name, and shall you go unpunished? You will not be exempt from punishment, for I am calling for a sword against all the inhabitants of the earth," says the LORD of hosts.' [Jer 7:10]

³⁰"Therefore prophesy all these words against them and say to them:

'The LORD will roar from on high
And utter His voice from His holy
　dwelling;
He will roar mightily against His
　fold *and* pasture.
He will jubilantly shout like those
　who tread *the grapes* [in the wine
　press],
Against all the inhabitants of the
　earth.

³¹'A noise has come to the end of the
　earth,
For the LORD has a controversy
　with *and* an indictment against
　the nations.
He is entering into judgment with
　all mankind;
As for the wicked, He has given
　them to the sword,' says the LORD."

³²Thus says the LORD of hosts,
"Behold, evil is going forth
From nation to nation,
And a great whirling tempest is
　rising
From the remotest part of the
　earth.

³³"And those slain by the LORD on that day will be from one end of the earth to the other end of the earth. They will not be lamented (mourned over with expressions of grief) or gathered or buried; they will be like dung on the ground. [Jer 8:2; 16:4]

³⁴"Wail, you shepherds, and cry;
And roll in ashes, you masters of
　the flock.
For the days of your slaughter and
　of your dispersions have come
　in full,
And you will fall *and* be broken
　into pieces like a choice vessel.
³⁵"The shepherds will have no way
　to flee,

Nor the masters of the flock any
    [way of] escape.
³⁶"A voice! The cry of the shepherds
    And the wailing of the masters of
      the flock!
    For the Lord is destroying their
      pasture,
³⁷"And the peaceful folds are
    devastated *and* made silent
    Because of the fierce anger of the
      Lord.
³⁸"He has left His lair like the lion;
    For their land has become a horror
    Because of the fierceness of the
      oppressor
    And because of the Lord's fierce
      anger."

26 IN THE beginning of the reign of Jehoiakim the son of Josiah, king of Judah, this word came from the Lord, saying,

²"Thus says the Lord, 'Stand in the court of the Lord's house [Jeremiah], and speak to all [the people of] the cities of Judah who have come to worship in the Lord's house all the words that I have commanded you to speak to them. Do not omit a word!

³'It may be that they will listen and everyone will turn from his wickedness, so that I may relent *and* reverse [My decision concerning] the disaster which I am planning to do to them because of their malevolent deeds.'

⁴"And you will say to them, 'Thus says the Lord, "If you will not listen to Me and obey My law which I have set before you,

⁵and listen *and* follow [carefully] the words of My servants the prophets, whom I have been sending to you repeatedly—though you have not listened—

⁶then I will make this house [the temple] like Shiloh, and I will make this city [subject to] the curse of all nations of the earth [because it will be so vile in their sight]." ' " [1 Sam 4; Jer 7:12]

⁷The priests and the [false] prophets and all the people heard Jeremiah speaking these words in the house of the Lord.

⁸Now when Jeremiah finished proclaiming everything that the Lord had commanded him to speak to all the people, the priests and the [false] prophets and all the people seized him, saying, "You must die!

⁹"Why have you prophesied in the name of the Lord saying, 'This house will be like Shiloh [after the ark of the Lord had been taken by our enemies] and this city [Jerusalem] will be desolate, without inhabitant'?" And all the people were gathered around Jeremiah in the [outer area of the] house of the Lord.

¹⁰When the princes (court officials) of Judah heard these things, they came up from the king's house to the house of the Lord and sat in the entrance of the New Gate of the house of the Lord.

¹¹Then the priests and the [false] prophets said to the princes and to all the people, "This man is deserving of death, for he has prophesied against this city as you have heard with your own ears."

¹²Then Jeremiah spoke to all the princes and to all the people, saying, "The Lord sent me to prophesy against this house and against this city all the words that you have heard.

¹³"Therefore, now change your ways and your deeds and obey the voice of the Lord your God; then the Lord will relent *and* reverse His decision concerning the misfortune which He has pronounced against you.

¹⁴"As for me, behold, I am in your hands; do with me as seems good and suitable to you.

¹⁵"But know for certain that if you put me to death, you will bring innocent blood on yourselves and on this city and on its inhabitants, for in truth

the LORD has sent me to you to speak all these words in your hearing."

¹⁶Then the princes and all the people said to the priests and to the [false] prophets, "This man is not deserving of death, for he has spoken to us in the name of the LORD our God."

¹⁷Then some of the elders of the land stood up and spoke to all the assembly of the people, saying,

¹⁸"Micah of Moresheth prophesied in the days of Hezekiah king of Judah; and he spoke to all the people of Judah, saying, 'Thus says the LORD of hosts,

"Zion will be plowed like a field,
And Jerusalem will become [heaps of] ruins,
And the mountain of the house [of the LORD—Mount Moriah, on which stands the temple, shall become covered not with buildings, but] like a densely wooded height." ' [Mic 3:12]

¹⁹"Did Hezekiah king of Judah and all Judah put Micah to death? Did he not [reverently] fear the LORD and entreat the favor of the LORD? And did not the LORD relent *and* reverse His decision concerning the misfortune which He had pronounced against them? But [here] we are [thinking of] committing a great evil against ourselves."

²⁰And there was also a man who prophesied in the name of the LORD, Uriah the son of Shemaiah of Kiriath-jearim, who prophesied against this city and against this land in words similar to all those of Jeremiah.

²¹And when Jehoiakim the king, with all his mighty men and all the princes, heard his words, the king sought to put Uriah to death; but when Uriah heard of it, he was afraid and fled and escaped to Egypt.

²²Then Jehoiakim the king sent men to Egypt: Elnathan the son of Achbor and certain [other] men with him [went] to Egypt.

²³And they brought Uriah [God's spokesman] from Egypt and led him to King Jehoiakim, who executed him with a sword and threw his dead body among the graves of the common people.

²⁴But the hand of Ahikam the son of Shaphan was with Jeremiah, so that he was not given into the hands of the people to put him to death.

27 IN THE beginning of the reign of Zedekiah the son of Josiah, king of Judah, this word came to Jeremiah from the LORD:

²Thus says the LORD to me, "Make for yourself bonds and yokes and put them on your neck,

³and send word to the king of Edom, to the king of Moab, to the king of the sons of Ammon, to the king of Tyre, and to the king of Sidon by the messengers who come to Jerusalem to Zedekiah king of Judah.

⁴"Command them to go to their masters, saying, 'Thus says the LORD of hosts, the God of Israel, you shall say this to your masters:

⁵"I have made the earth, the men and the animals that are on the face of the earth by My great power and by My outstretched arm, and I will give it to whomever pleases Me.

⁶"Now I have given all these lands into the hand of Nebuchadnezzar king of Babylon, My servant *and* instrument, and I have also given the wild animals of the field to serve him.

⁷"All nations shall serve him and his son and his grandson until the [appointed] time [of punishment] for his own land comes; then many nations and great kings shall make him their servant.

⁸"But any nation or kingdom that will not serve this same Nebuchadnezzar king of Babylon and put its neck under the yoke of the king of Babylon, that nation I will punish," says the LORD, "with the sword, with

famine and with pestilence (virulent disease), until I have destroyed it by Nebuchadnezzar's hand.

9"And as for you, do not listen to your [counterfeit] prophets, your diviners, your dreams *and* dreamers, your soothsayers or your sorcerers, who say to you, 'You will not serve the king of Babylon.'

10"For they prophesy a lie to you which will cause you to be removed far from your land; and I will drive you out and you will perish.

11"But the nation which will bow its neck under the yoke of the king of Babylon and serve him, that nation I will let remain on its own land," says the LORD, "to cultivate it and live in it."'"

12I spoke to Zedekiah king of Judah in the same way, saying, "Bring your necks under the yoke of the king of Babylon and serve him and his people, and live!

13"Why will you die, you and your people, by the sword, by famine and by virulent disease, as the LORD has spoken to any nation which will not serve the king of Babylon?

14"Do not listen to *and* believe the words of the [false] prophets who are saying to you, 'You will not serve the king of Babylon,' for they prophesy a lie to you;

15for I have not sent them," says the LORD, "but they are prophesying falsely in My Name, in order that I may drive you out and that you may perish, you [together] with the [false] prophets who prophesy to you."

16Then I said to the priests and to all these people, saying, "Thus says the LORD: Do not listen to the words of your [false] prophets who are prophesying to you, saying, 'Behold, the articles of the LORD's house will now shortly be brought back from Babylon'; for they are prophesying a lie to you.

17"Do not listen to them; serve the king of Babylon, and live! Why should this city become a ruin?

18"But if they are [true] prophets, and if the word of the LORD is [really spoken] by them, let them now entreat the LORD of hosts that the articles which are [still] left in the house of the LORD, in the house of the king of Judah and in Jerusalem may not go to Babylon.

19"For thus says the LORD of hosts concerning the [bronze] pillars, the [bronze] Sea, the [bronze] bases [of the ten basins in Solomon's temple used for washing sacrificial animals], and the rest of the articles that are left in this city (Jerusalem), [1 Kin 7:23–37; 2 Chr 4:6; Jer 52:17]

20which Nebuchadnezzar king of Babylon did not take when he carried Jeconiah the son of Jehoiakim, king of Judah, into exile from Jerusalem to Babylon, along with all the nobles of Judah and Jerusalem.

21"Yes, thus says the LORD of hosts, the God of Israel, concerning the articles which remain in the house of the LORD, in the house of the king of Judah and in Jerusalem,

22"They will be carried to Babylon and they will be there until the day that I visit them [with My favor],' says the LORD. 'Then I will bring them back and restore them to this place.'"

28 IN THE same year, in the beginning of the reign of Zedekiah king of Judah, in the fourth year and the fifth month, the [false] prophet Hananiah the son of Azzur, who was from Gibeon [one of the priests' cities], spoke [without godly authority] to me in the house of the LORD in the presence of the priests and all the people, saying:

2"Thus says the LORD of hosts, the God of Israel, 'I have broken the yoke of the king of Babylon.

3'Within two years I am going to bring back to this place all the articles of the LORD's house, which Nebuchadnezzar king of Babylon took away from this place and carried to Babylon.

⁴"And I will also bring back to this place Jeconiah the son of Jehoiakim, king of Judah, along with all the exiles from Judah who went to Babylon,' says the Lord, 'for I will break the yoke of the king of Babylon.'" [Jer 22:10, 24–27; 52:34]

⁵Then the prophet Jeremiah spoke to the prophet Hananiah in the presence of the priests and all the people who stood in the house of the Lord,

⁶and the prophet Jeremiah said, "Amen! May the Lord do so; may the Lord confirm *and* fulfill your words which you have prophesied to bring back the articles of the Lord's house and all the captives, from Babylon to this place.

⁷"Nevertheless, listen now to this word which I am about to speak in your hearing and in the hearing of all the people!

⁸"The prophets who were before me and before you from ancient times prophesied against many lands and against great kingdoms, of war and of disaster and of virulent disease.

⁹"But as for the prophet who [on the contrary] prophesies of peace, when that prophet's word comes to pass, [only] then will it be known that the Lord has truly sent him."

¹⁰Then Hananiah the [false] prophet took the yoke off the neck of the prophet Jeremiah and smashed it.

¹¹Hananiah spoke in the presence of all the people, saying, "Thus says the Lord, 'Even so within two full years I will break the yoke of Nebuchadnezzar king of Babylon from the neck of all the nations.'" Then the prophet Jeremiah went his way.

¹²The word of the Lord came to Jeremiah [some time] after Hananiah the prophet had broken the yoke off the neck of the prophet Jeremiah, saying,

¹³"Go and tell Hananiah, 'The Lord says this, "You have broken yokes of wood, but you have made in their place bars of iron."

¹⁴"For thus says the Lord of hosts, the God of Israel, "I have put the iron yoke [of servitude] on the neck of all these nations, that they may serve Nebuchadnezzar king of Babylon; and they will serve him. And I have even given him the beasts of the field."'" [Jer 27:6, 7]

¹⁵Then the prophet Jeremiah said to Hananiah the prophet, "Listen now, Hananiah, the Lord has not sent you, and you have made this people trust in a lie.

¹⁶"Therefore thus says the Lord, 'Behold, I am about to send you away from the face of the earth. This year you will die, because you have spoken *and* counseled rebellion against the Lord.'"

¹⁷So Hananiah the [false] prophet died [two months later], the same year, in the seventh month.

29 NOW THESE are the words of the letter which Jeremiah the prophet sent from Jerusalem to the rest of the elders in exile and to the priests, the prophets and all the people whom Nebuchadnezzar had taken into captivity from Jerusalem to Babylon.

²(This was after King Jeconiah and the queen mother, the eunuchs, the princes (court officials) of Judah and Jerusalem, the craftsmen and the smiths had departed from Jerusalem.)

³*The letter was* hand-carried by Elasah the son of Shaphan and Gemariah the son of Hilkiah, whom Zedekiah king of Judah sent to Babylon to Nebuchadnezzar king of Babylon, saying,

⁴"So says the Lord of hosts, the God of Israel, to all the captives whom I have sent into exile from Jerusalem to Babylon,

⁵'Build houses and live *in them*; plant gardens and eat their fruit.

⁶'Take wives and have sons and

daughters; take wives for your sons and give your daughters in marriage, that they may bear sons and daughters; multiply there and do not decrease [in number].

⁷"Seek peace *and* well-being for the city where I have sent you into exile, and pray to the LORD on its behalf; for in its peace (well-being) you will have peace."

⁸"For thus says the LORD of hosts, the God of Israel, 'Do not let your [false] prophets who are among you and your diviners deceive you; pay no attention *and* attach no significance to the dreams which they dream *or* to yours,

⁹for they prophesy falsely to you in My Name. I have not sent them,' says the LORD.

¹⁰"For thus says the LORD, 'When seventy years [of exile] have been completed for Babylon, I will visit (inspect) you and keep My good promise to you, to bring you back to this place.

¹¹'For I know the plans *and* thoughts that I have for you,' says the LORD, 'plans for peace *and* well-being and not for disaster, to give you a future and a hope.

life point

The Lord sees not only what you are right now, but also what you can become. He knows the plans He has for you, and, according to Jeremiah 29:11, they are good plans for peace and well-being, not for disaster. Let me encourage you to give God everything about yourself. He will be patient with you as He works His good plans in you.

God's good plan

According to Jeremiah 29:11, God has a plan for each of us, a plan that should give us great hope for our future. It is our destiny. But that plan is a possibility, not a "positively."

If someone prophesies over us wonderful things in the name of the Lord, what they say to us may express the heart, the will, and the desire of God for us. But that does not mean it is positively going to happen just as it is prophesied. This is because it cannot and will not come to pass if we choose not to cooperate with God or to stray away from His will.

God does have a plan for our lives, but we need to participate in that plan for it to come true. God is not likely to do anything in our lives without our cooperation.

We need to cooperate with God every single day of our lives in order for our potential to be developed. Every day we ought to learn something. Every day we ought to grow. Every day we ought to discover something. Every day we ought to be a bit further along than we were the day before. We should be "lifetime learners."

We must understand that no other human being on the face of the earth can develop our potential for us. It is vital for each of us to discover our own God-given gifts and talents and what we are truly capable of, then put ourselves to the task of developing those gifts, talents, and capabilities to their fullest extent.

God has a plan for each of us. It is a good plan, an uncommon plan, a great plan; it is not an average, mediocre plan. I encourage you to seek that plan and cooperate with God so it will be wonderfully fulfilled in your life.

¹²'Then you will call on Me and you will come and pray to Me, and I will hear [your voice] *and* I will listen to you.

¹³'Then [with a deep longing] you will seek Me *and* require Me [as a vital necessity] and [you will] find Me when you search for Me with all your heart. [Deut 4:29, 30]

¹⁴'I will be found by you,' says the Lᴏʀᴅ, 'and I will restore your fortunes and I will [free you and] gather you from all the nations and from all the places where I have driven you,' says the Lᴏʀᴅ, 'and I will bring you back to the place from where I sent you into exile.'

¹⁵"Because you [who have remained in Jerusalem] have said, 'The Lᴏʀᴅ has raised up prophets for us in Babylon,'

life point

Jeremiah 29:13 is an awesome promise; God says, "Then [with a deep longing] you will seek Me and require Me [as a vital necessity] and [you will] find Me when you search for Me with all your heart." Notice that we are to require God "as a vital necessity." In other words, the wonderful life Jesus died for us to have depends on our personal relationship with God. We need Him just as we need food, water, and air to breathe.

When you spend time with God, everyone knows that you become calmer; you are easier to get along with; you do not lose control of your emotions as quickly. Your patience increases, wisdom is manifested through you, and your heart soon understands what God likes and what offends Him. As with any friend, the more time you spend with God, the more you become like Him. Spend time with God today. Make it a priority. Your life depends on it because He is your vital necessity.

¹⁶thus says the Lᴏʀᴅ concerning the king who sits on the throne of David, and concerning all the people who live in this city, your brothers (fellow people of Judah) who did not go with you into captivity—

¹⁷thus says the Lᴏʀᴅ of hosts, 'Behold (listen very carefully), I am sending the sword, famine, and virulent disease (pestilence) on them, and I will make them like rotten figs that are so bad they cannot be eaten.

¹⁸'I will pursue them with the sword, with famine and with virulent disease; and I will make them a terror (warning) to all the kingdoms of the earth, to be a curse, a horror, a hissing, and a disgrace among all the nations to which I have driven them,

¹⁹because they have not listened to *and* honored My words,' says the Lᴏʀᴅ, 'which I sent to them again and again by My servants the prophets. Moreover, you [exiles] did not listen [either],' says the Lᴏʀᴅ. [Ezek 2:5, 7]

²⁰"Hear, therefore, the word of the Lᴏʀᴅ, all you exiles whom I have sent away from Jerusalem to Babylon.

²¹"Thus says the Lᴏʀᴅ of hosts, the God of Israel, concerning Ahab the son of Kolaiah and concerning Zedekiah the son of Maaseiah, who are prophesying lies to you in My Name, 'Behold, I will hand them over to Nebuchadnezzar king of Babylon, and he will slaughter them before your eyes [yes, all the false prophets in Babylon whom you follow shall die]! [Jer 29:15]

²²'Because of them, this curse shall be taken up *and* used by all the exiles from Judah who are in Babylon, saying, "May the Lᴏʀᴅ make you like Zedekiah and like Ahab, whom the king of Babylon roasted in the fire,

²³because they have acted foolishly in Israel and have committed adultery with their neighbors' wives and in My Name have spoken false *and* concocted words, which I did not command them.

I am He who knows and I am a witness," says the LORD.'"

²⁴Also you shall speak to Shemaiah of Nehelam [among the exiles in Babylon], saying,

²⁵"Thus says the LORD of hosts, the God of Israel, 'Because you have sent letters in your own name to all the people who are in Jerusalem, and to Zephaniah the son of Maaseiah, the priest, and to all the priests, saying,

²⁶"The LORD has made you [Zephaniah] priest instead of Jehoiada the [deputy] priest, to be the overseer in the house of the LORD over every madman who prophesies, to put him in the stocks and in the iron collar,

²⁷now therefore [continued the letter from Shemaiah in Babylon to Zephaniah in Jerusalem], why have you not rebuked Jeremiah of Anathoth, who prophesies to you?

²⁸"For he has sent *word* to us in Babylon, saying, *'This captivity* [of yours] will be long; build houses and live *in them* and plant gardens and eat their fruit.'"'"

²⁹Zephaniah the priest read this letter to Jeremiah the prophet.

³⁰Then came the word of the LORD to Jeremiah, saying,

³¹"Send [this message] to all the exiles, saying, 'Thus says the LORD concerning Shemaiah of Nehelam, "Because Shemaiah has prophesied to you, although I did not send him, and he has made you trust in a lie,"

³²therefore thus says the LORD, "Behold, I am about to punish Shemaiah of Nehelam and his descendants. He will not have anyone [born] to live among this people, nor will he see the good that I am about to do to My people," says the LORD, "because he has spoken *and* preached rebellion against the LORD."'"

30

THE WORD which came to Jeremiah from the LORD:
²"Thus says the LORD God of Israel, 'Write in a book all the words which I have spoken to you.

³'For behold (hear this), the days are coming,' says the LORD, 'when I will restore the fortunes of My people Israel and Judah,' says the LORD, 'and I will return them to the land that I gave to their forefathers and they will take possession of it.'"

⁴Now these are the words the LORD spoke concerning Israel and Judah:

⁵"Thus says the LORD,

'We have heard a terrified voice
Of panic *and* dread, and there is no
   peace.
⁶'Ask now, and see
Whether a man can give birth [to
   a child].
Why then do I see every man
With his hands on his loins, as a
   woman in labor?
Why have all faces turned pale?
⁷'Alas! for that day is great,
There is none like it;
It is the time of Jacob's
   [unequaled] trouble,
But he will be saved from it. [Matt
   24:29, 30; Rev 7:14]

⁸'It shall come about on that day,' says the LORD of hosts, 'that I will break the yoke off your neck and I will tear off your bonds *and* force apart your shackles; and strangers will no longer make slaves of the people [of Israel].

⁹'But they shall serve the LORD their God and [the descendant of] David their King, whom I will raise up for them. [Jer 23:5]

¹⁰'Fear not, O Jacob My servant,' says
   the LORD,
'Nor be dismayed *or* downcast,
   O Israel;
For behold, I will save you from a
   distant land [of exile]

And your descendants from the
    land of their captivity.
Jacob will return and will be quiet
    and at ease,
And no one will make him afraid.
¹¹'For I am with you,' says the LORD,
    'to save you;
For I will destroy completely
    all the nations where I have
    scattered you,
But I will not destroy you
    completely.
But I will judge *and* discipline you
    fairly
And will by no means regard
    you as guiltless *and* leave you
    unpunished.'
¹²"For thus says the LORD,
    'Your wound is incurable
And your injury is beyond healing.
¹³'There is no one to plead your
    cause;
No [device to close and allow the]
    healing of your wound,
No recovery for you.
¹⁴'All your lovers (allies) have
    forgotten you;
They do not seek *and* long for you.
For I have injured you with the
    wound of an enemy,
With the punishment of a cruel
    and merciless foe,
Because your guilt is great
And your sins are glaring *and*
    innumerable.
¹⁵'Why do you cry out over your
    injury [since it is the natural
    result of your sin]?
Your pain is incurable (deadly).
Because your guilt is great
And your sins are glaring *and*
    innumerable,
I have done these things to you.

¹⁶'Therefore all who devour you will
    be devoured;
And all your adversaries, every
    one of them, will go into
    captivity.
And they who plunder you will
    become plunder,
And all who prey upon you I will
    give for prey.
¹⁷'For I will restore health to you
And I will heal your wounds,' says
    the LORD,
'Because they have called you an
    outcast, saying:
"This is Zion; no one seeks her *and*
    no one cares for her."'
¹⁸"Thus says the LORD,
    'Behold (hear this), I will restore
    the fortunes of the tents of Jacob
And have mercy on his dwelling
    places;
The city will be rebuilt on its [old,
    mound-like] ruin,
And the palace will stand on its
    rightful place.
¹⁹'From them (city, palace) will come
    [songs of] thanksgiving
And the voices of those who dance
    and celebrate.
And I will multiply them and
    they will not be diminished [in
    number];
I will also honor them and they
    will not be insignificant.
²⁰'Their children too will be as in
    former times,
And their congregation will be
    established before Me;
And I will punish all their
    oppressors.
²¹'Their prince will be one of them,
And their ruler will come forward
    from among them.

speak the Word

Thank You, God, for restoring health to me and for healing my wounds.
—ADAPTED FROM JEREMIAH 30:17

I will bring him near and he shall
approach Me,
For who is he who would have the
boldness *and* would dare [on his
own initiative] to risk his life to
approach Me?' says the LORD.
22 'Then you shall be My people,
And I will be your God.'" [Jer 7:23]

23 Behold, the tempest of the LORD!
Wrath has gone forth,
A sweeping *and* gathering tempest;
It will burst on the head of the
wicked.
24 The fierce (righteous) anger of the
LORD will not turn back
Until He has fulfilled and until He
has accomplished
The intent of His heart (mind);
In the latter days you will
understand this.

31
"AT THAT time," says the
LORD, "I will be the God of
all the families of Israel,
and they shall be My people."
2 Thus says the LORD,
"The people who survived the sword
Found grace in the wilderness [of
exile]—
Israel (the Northern Kingdom),
when it went to find its rest."
3 The LORD appeared to me (Israel)
from ages past, *saying,*
"I have loved you with an
everlasting love;
Therefore with lovingkindness I
have drawn you *and* continued
My faithfulness to you. [Deut 7:8]
4 "Again I will build you and you
will be rebuilt,
O Virgin Israel!
You will again be adorned with
your tambourines *and* timbrels

And go out to the dances of those
who celebrate. [Is 37:22; Jer 18:13]
5 "Again you will plant vineyards
On the mountains of Samaria;
The planters will plant
And enjoy the [abundant] fruit [in
peace].
6 "For there will be a day when the
watchmen
On the hills of Ephraim cry out,
'Arise, and let us go up to Zion,
To the LORD our God.'"

7 For thus says the LORD,
"Sing aloud with gladness for Jacob,
And shout for the first *and*
foremost of the nations [the
chosen people, Israel];
Proclaim, give praise and say,
'O LORD save Your people,
The remnant of Israel!'
8 "Behold, I am bringing them from
the north country,
And I will gather them from the
remote parts of the earth,
Among them [will be] the blind
and the lame,
The woman with child and
she who labors in childbirth,
together;
A great company, they will return
here [to Jerusalem].
9 "They will come with weeping [in
repentance and for joy],
And by [their] prayer [for the
future] I will lead them;
I will make them walk by streams
of waters,
On a straight path in which they
will not stumble,
For I am a Father to Israel,
And Ephraim (Israel) is My
firstborn."

speak the Word

*Thank You, Lord, for loving me with an everlasting love, for drawing me
with Your loving-kindness, and for continuing Your faithfulness to me.*
—ADAPTED FROM JEREMIAH 31:3

¹⁰Hear the word of the Lord, O you nations,
And declare it in the isles *and* coastlands far away,
And say, "He who scattered Israel will gather him
And will keep him as a shepherd keeps his flock."
¹¹For the Lord has ransomed Jacob
And has redeemed him from the hand of him who was stronger than he.
¹²"They will come and sing aloud *and* shout for joy on the height of Zion,
And will be radiant [with joy] over the goodness of the Lord—
For the grain, for the new wine, for the oil,
And for the young of the flock and the herd.
And their life will be like a watered garden,
And they shall never sorrow *or* languish again.
¹³"Then the virgin will rejoice in the dance,
And the young men and old, together,
For I will turn their mourning into joy
And will comfort them and make them rejoice after their sorrow.
¹⁴"I will fully satisfy the soul of the priests with abundance,
And My people will be satisfied with My goodness," says the Lord.
¹⁵Thus says the Lord,
"A voice is heard in Ramah,
Lamentation (songs of mourning) and bitter weeping.
Rachel (Israel) is weeping for her children;
She refuses to be comforted for her children,
Because they are gone." [Matt 2:18]
¹⁶Thus says the Lord,
"Restrain your voice from weeping
And your eyes from tears,
For your work will be rewarded," says the Lord;
"And your children will return from the enemy's land.
¹⁷"There is [confident] hope for your future," says the Lord;
"Your children will come back to their own country.
¹⁸"I have surely heard Ephraim (Israel) moaning *and* grieving,
'You have chastised me, and I was chastised,
Like a bull unaccustomed to the yoke *or* an untrained calf;
Bring me back that I may be restored,
For You are the Lord my God.
¹⁹'After I turned away [from You], I repented;
After I was instructed, I struck my thigh [in remorse];
I was ashamed and even humiliated
Because I carried the disgrace of my youth [as a nation].'
²⁰"Is Ephraim My dear son?
Is he a darling *and* beloved child?
For as often as I have spoken against him,

speak the Word

Thank You, God, for turning my mourning into joy, for comforting me, and for making me rejoice after my sorrow.
—ADAPTED FROM Jeremiah 31:13

God, I declare today I have confident hope for my future!
—ADAPTED FROM Jeremiah 31:17

I certainly still remember him.
Therefore My affection is renewed
   and My heart longs for him;
I will surely have mercy on him,"
   says the LORD.

21 "Place for yourself road signs
   [toward Canaan],
Make for yourself guideposts;
Turn your thought *and* attention to
   the highway,
To the way by which you went [into
   exile].
Retrace your steps, O virgin of
   Israel,
Return to these your cities.
22 "How long will you hesitate [to
   return],
O you faithless *and* renegade
   daughter?
For the LORD has created a new
   thing in the land [of Israel]:
A woman will encompass (tenderly
   love) a man."

23 Thus says the LORD of hosts, the
God of Israel, "Once more they will
speak these words in the land of Judah (the Southern Kingdom) and in
her cities when I restore their fortunes
and release them from exile,

   'The LORD bless you, O habitation
      of justice *and* righteousness,
   O holy mountain!'

24 "And [the people of] Judah and all
its cities will live there together—the
farmer and they who wander about
with flocks.
25 "For I [fully] satisfy the weary soul,
and I replenish every languishing *and*
sorrowful person."
26 At this I (Jeremiah) awoke and
looked, and my [trancelike] sleep was
sweet [in the assurance it gave] to me.
27 "Behold (listen carefully), the days

are coming," says the LORD, "when I
will sow the house of Israel and the
house of Judah with the seed of man
and with the seed of beast.
28 "It will be that as I have watched
over them to uproot and to break
down, to overthrow, destroy, and
afflict with disaster, so I will watch
over them to build and to plant [with
good]," says the LORD.
29 "In those days they will not say
   again,
   'The fathers have eaten sour grapes,
   And the children's teeth are set on
      edge.' [Ezek 18:2]
30 "But everyone will die [only] for his
own wickedness; every man who eats
sour grapes—his [own] teeth shall be
set on edge.
31 "Behold, the days are coming,"
says the LORD, "when I will make a
new covenant with the house of Israel
(the Northern Kingdom) and with the
house of Judah (the Southern Kingdom), [Luke 22:20; 1 Cor 11:25]
32 not like the covenant which I made
with their fathers in the day when I
took them by the hand to bring them
out of the land of Egypt, My covenant
which they broke, although I was a
husband to them," says the LORD.
33 "But this is the covenant which I
will make with the house of Israel after those days," says the LORD, "I will
put My law within them, and I will
write it on their hearts; and I will be
their God, and they will be My people.
34 "And each man will no longer teach
his neighbor and his brother, saying,
'Know the LORD,' for they will all know
Me [through personal experience],
from the least of them to the greatest," says the LORD. "For I will forgive

speak the Word

God, You fully satisfy my weary soul, and You replenish me.
—ADAPTED FROM JEREMIAH 31:25

their wickedness, and I will no longer remember their sin." [Heb 8:8–12; 10:16, 17]

35 Thus says the LORD,
Who gives the sun for light by day
And the fixed order of the moon
    and of the stars for light by
    night,
Who stirs up the sea's roaring
    billows *or* stills the waves when
    they roar;
The LORD of hosts is His name:
36 "If this fixed order departs
From before Me," says the LORD,
"Then the descendants of Israel
    also will cease
From being a nation before Me
    forever."

37 Thus says the LORD,

"If the heavens above can be
    measured

And the foundations of the earth
    searched out below,
Then I will also cast off *and*
    abandon all the descendants of
    Israel
For all that they have done," says
    the LORD.

38 "Behold, the days are coming," says the LORD, "when the city [of Jerusalem] will be rebuilt for the LORD from the Tower of Hananel to the Corner Gate. 39 "The measuring line will go out farther straight ahead to the hill Gareb; then it will turn to Goah. 40 "And the whole valley (Hinnom) of the dead bodies and [the hill] of the ashes [long dumped there from the temple sacrifices], and all the fields as far as the brook Kidron, to the corner of the Horse Gate toward the east, shall be holy to the LORD. It (the city)

"I will remember your sin no more"

No matter what your problem is or how badly you feel about yourself as a result of it, God loves you. In Jesus Christ He has given you a new life. He will provide new friends to love, accept, appreciate, and uphold you. You are okay, and you are going to make it because of the One Who lives inside you and cares for you.

Regardless of what you may have done, you need a deeper revelation of what God means when He says in Jeremiah 31:34, "I will no longer remember their sin." Once you have confessed your sins and asked for God's forgiveness, if you continue to bring them up every time you go to Him in prayer, you are reminding Him of something He has promised to forget—something He has removed from you as far as the east is from the west (see Psalm 103:12). You need to realize that once you have confessed your sins to God and asked Him to forgive you of them, He has not only *forgiven* them, but He has actually *forgotten* them.

You may have to look at yourself in the mirror and confess your deepest failure. You may need to say to God something like, "I had an abortion." Or, "I committed adultery. I did that, Lord, and it is a marvel to me to realize that I can stand here and look myself in the eye. But I can do so because I know that even though I did something so wrong, You have put my sins as far away from me as the east is from the west, and You remember them no more!"

Whatever your sin or failure, it's crucial to confess it to God and then let it go. Stop punishing yourself for something that is in the past. Refuse to remember something God has chosen to forget.

will not be uprooted or overthrown anymore to the end of the age." [Zech 14:10, 11]

32 THE WORD that came to Jeremiah from the LORD in the tenth year of Zedekiah king of Judah, which was the eighteenth year of Nebuchadnezzar.

²Now at that time the army of the king of Babylon was besieging Jerusalem, and Jeremiah the prophet was shut up in the court of the guard, which was in the house of the king of Judah.

³For Zedekiah [the last] king of Judah had locked him up, saying, "Why do you prophesy [disaster] and say, 'Thus says the LORD, "Behold, I am giving this city into the hand of the king of Babylon, and he shall take it;

⁴and Zedekiah king of Judah will not escape from the hand of the Chaldeans, but he will surely be given into the hand of the king of Babylon, and he will speak with him face to face and see him eye to eye;

⁵and he will lead Zedekiah to Babylon, and he will be there until I visit him [for evaluation and judgment]," says the LORD. "If you fight against the Chaldeans, you will not succeed"'?" [Jer 21:3–7; 34:2–5; 37:17; 52:7–14]

⁶And Jeremiah [answered King Zedekiah and] said, "The word of the LORD came to me, saying,

⁷'Behold (listen carefully), Hanamel the son of Shallum your uncle is coming to you, saying, "Buy my field that is in Anathoth, for you have the right of redemption to buy it [in accordance with the law]."'

⁸"Then Hanamel my uncle's son came to me in the court of the guard in accordance with the word of the LORD, and he said to me, 'Please buy my field that is at Anathoth, which is in the land of Benjamin, for you have the right of inheritance and the redemption is yours; buy it for yourself.'

Then I knew that this was the word of the LORD.

⁹"I bought the field that was at Anathoth from Hanamel my uncle's son, and weighed out the money for him, seventeen shekels of silver.

¹⁰"I signed the deed and sealed it, and called in witnesses, and weighed out the money on the scales.

¹¹"So I took the deeds of the purchase, both the sealed *copy containing* the terms and conditions, and the unsealed copy;

¹²and I gave the purchase deed to Baruch the son of Neriah, the son of Mahseiah, in the sight of Hanamel my uncle's son and in sight of the witnesses who signed the purchase deed, in the presence of all the Jews who were sitting in the court of the guard.

¹³"And I commanded Baruch in their presence, saying,

¹⁴'Thus says the LORD of hosts, the God of Israel, "Take these deeds, both this purchase deed which is sealed and this unsealed deed, and put them in an earthen jar, that they may last a long time."

¹⁵'For thus says the LORD of hosts, the God of Israel, "Houses and fields and vineyards will again be purchased in this land."'

¹⁶"Now when I had delivered the purchase deed to Baruch the son of Neriah, I prayed to the LORD, saying,

¹⁷'Ah Lord GOD! Behold, You have made the heavens and the earth by Your great power and by Your outstretched arm! There is nothing too difficult *or* too wonderful for You—

¹⁸You who show lovingkindness to thousands, but repay the wickedness (sin, guilt) of the fathers into the bosom of their children after them [that is, calling the children to account for the sins of their fathers], O great and mighty God; the LORD of hosts is His name;

¹⁹great [are You] in counsel and mighty in deed, whose eyes are open

to all the ways of the sons of men, to reward *or* repay each one according to his ways and according to the fruit of his deeds;

²⁰who set signs and wonders in the land of Egypt, and even to this day [continues to do so] both in Israel and among mankind; and You have made a name for Yourself, as at this day.

²¹'You brought Your people Israel out of the land of Egypt with signs and wonders, with a strong hand and with an outstretched arm and with great terror;

²²and gave them this land, which You swore to their forefathers to give them, a land [of plenty] flowing with milk and honey.

²³'They entered and took possession of it, but they did not obey Your voice or walk in Your law; they have done nothing of all that You commanded them to do. Therefore You have caused all this disaster *and* suffering to come upon them.

²⁴'See the siege ramps [of mounded earth that the enemy has built against the walls]; they have come up to the city to capture it. And the city is given into the hand of the Chaldeans [of Babylon] who fight against it, because of the sword, the famine and the virulent disease [that have overcome the people]. What You have spoken has come to pass, and behold, You see it.

²⁵'Yet, O Lord God, You said to me, "Buy the field with money and get witnesses," even though the city is given into the hands of the Chaldeans.'"

²⁶Then came the word of the Lord to Jeremiah, saying,

²⁷"Behold, I am the Lord, the God of all flesh; is there anything too difficult for Me?"

²⁸Therefore thus says the Lord, "Behold, I am about to give this city into the hand of the Chaldeans and into the hand of Nebuchadnezzar king of Babylon, and he will take it.

²⁹"The Chaldeans who are fighting against this city will come in and set this city on fire and burn it, along with the houses on whose roofs incense has been offered to Baal and drink offerings have been poured out to other gods to provoke Me to anger. [Jer 19:13]

³⁰"For the children of Israel and the children of Judah have done only evil in My sight from their youth; for the children of Israel have been provoking Me to anger by the [idols that are the] work of their hands," says the Lord.

³¹"From the day that they built it [during the reign of Solomon], even to this day, this city has been such *a provocation of* My anger and My wrath, that I must remove it from My sight, [1 Kin 11:1–13]

³²because of all the evil of the children of Israel and of the children of Judah which they have done to provoke Me to anger—they, their kings, their princes, their priests, their prophets, the men of Judah and the inhabitants of Jerusalem.

³³"They have turned their back to Me and not their face; though I taught them repeatedly, yet they would not listen and receive instruction.

³⁴"But they put their detestable things (idols) in the house which is called by My Name, to defile it.

³⁵"They built the high places [for worship] of Baal in the Valley of Ben-hinnom (son of Hinnom) to make their sons and their daughters pass through *the fire* to [worship and honor] Molech—which I had not commanded them nor had it entered My mind that they should do this repulsive thing, to cause Judah to sin. [Jer 7:30, 31]

³⁶"Now therefore thus says the Lord God of Israel concerning this city of which you say, 'It is given into the hand of the king of Babylon by sword and by famine and by virulent disease.'

³⁷"Behold, I will gather them out of

all countries to which I have driven them in My anger, in My wrath and in great indignation; and I will bring them back to this place and make them live in safety.

³⁸"They will be My people, and I will be their God;

³⁹and I will give them one heart and one way, that they may [reverently] fear Me forever, for their own good and for the good of their children after them.

⁴⁰"I will make an everlasting covenant with them that I will do them good and not turn away from them; and I will put in their heart a fear *and* reverential awe of Me, so that they will not turn away from Me. [Jer 31:31–34]

⁴¹"I will rejoice over them to do them good, and I will faithfully plant them in this land with all My heart and with all My soul.

⁴²"For thus says the LORD, 'Just as I have brought all this great disaster on this people, so I am going to bring on them all the good that I am promising them.

⁴³'Fields will be bought in this land of which you say, "It is desolate, without man or animal; it is given into the hands of the Chaldeans."

⁴⁴'People will buy fields for money, sign deeds, seal them, and call in witnesses in the land of Benjamin, in the places around Jerusalem, in the cities of Judah, in the cities of the hill country, in the cities of the lowland, and in the cities of the South (the Negev); for I will restore their fortunes *and* release them from exile,' says the LORD."

33 THEN THE word of the LORD came to Jeremiah the second time, while he was still confined in the court of the guard, saying,

²"Thus says the LORD who made *the earth,* the LORD who formed it to establish it—the LORD is His name,

³'Call to Me and I will answer you, and tell you [and even show you] great

and mighty things, [things which have been confined and hidden], which you do not know *and* understand *and* cannot distinguish.'

⁴"For thus says the LORD, the God of Israel, concerning the houses of this city and the houses of the kings of Judah which are torn down *to make a defense* against the siege ramps and against the sword, [Is 22:10; Jer 6:6]

⁵'While they (the besieged Jews) are coming to fight against the Chaldeans and to fill the houses with the dead bodies of men whom I have slain in My anger and in My wrath, for I have hidden My face [in disgust] from this city because of all their wickedness.

⁶'Behold, [in the restored Jerusalem] I will bring to it health and healing, and I will heal them; and I will reveal to them an abundance of peace (prosperity, security, stability) and truth.

⁷'I will restore the fortunes of Judah and the fortunes of Israel and will rebuild them as they were at first.

⁸'I will cleanse them from all their wickedness (guilt) by which they have sinned against Me, and I will pardon (forgive) all their sins by which they rebelled against Me.

⁹'Jerusalem will be to Me a name of joy, praise and glory before all the nations of the earth which will hear of all the good that I do for it, and they shall fear and tremble because of all the good and all the peace (prosperity, security, stability) that I provide for it.'

¹⁰"Thus says the LORD, 'Yet again there will be heard in this place of which you say, "It is a [desolate] waste, without man and without animal"— even in the cities of Judah and in the streets of Jerusalem that are desolate, without man and without inhabitant and without animal—

¹¹the [sound of the] voice of joy and the voice of gladness, the voice of the bridegroom and the voice of the bride, the [song-filled] voice of those who say,

"Give praise *and* thanks to the
  Lord of hosts,
For the Lord is good;
For His [steadfast] lovingkindness
  (mercy) endures forever";

and of those who bring a thank offering into the house of the Lord. For I will restore the fortunes of the land as they were at first,' says the Lord.

¹²"Thus says the Lord of hosts, 'There will again be in this desolate place—[a place] without man or animal—and in all its cities, pastures for shepherds who rest their flocks.

¹³'In the cities of the hill country, in the cities of the lowland, in the cities of the South (the Negev), in the land of Benjamin, in the places around Jerusalem and in the cities of Judah, the flocks will again pass under the hand of the one who counts them,' says the Lord.

¹⁴'Behold, the days are coming,' says the Lord, 'when I will fulfill the good word *and* promise which I have made regarding the house of Israel and the house of Judah.

¹⁵'In those days and at that time I will cause a righteous Branch of David to spring forth; and He (the Messiah) shall execute justice and righteousness on the earth. [Is 4:2; Jer 23:5; Zech 3:8; 6:12]

¹⁶'In those days Judah will be saved and [the people of] Jerusalem will live in safety; and this is *the name* by which she will be called: the Lord Our Righteousness (Justice).'

¹⁷"For thus says the Lord, 'David shall never lack a man (descendant) to sit on the throne of the house of Israel;

¹⁸and the Levitical priests shall never lack a man (descendant) to offer burnt offerings before Me and to burn grain offerings and to prepare sacrifices all day long.'"

¹⁹The word of the Lord came to Jeremiah, saying,

²⁰"Thus says the Lord, 'If you can break My covenant for the day and My covenant for the night, so that day and night do not take place at their appointed times,

²¹then My covenant may also be broken with David My servant so that he will not have a son to reign on his throne, and [My covenant may also be broken] with the Levitical priests, My ministers.

²²'As the host of [the stars of] heaven cannot be counted and the sand of the sea cannot be measured, so I will multiply the descendants of David My servant and the Levites who minister to Me.'"

²³And the word of the Lord came to Jeremiah, saying,

²⁴"Have you not noticed what this people have spoken, saying, 'The two families [Israel the northern kingdom, and Judah the southern kingdom] which the Lord chose, He has rejected'? Thus they despise My [chosen] people, no longer are they [considered] as a nation in their sight.

²⁵"Thus says the Lord, 'If My covenant with day and night does not stand, and if I have not established the fixed patterns of heaven and earth, [the whole order of nature,]

²⁶then I would [also] reject the descendants of Jacob and David My servant, not taking from his descendants rulers over the descendants of Abraham, Isaac, and Jacob. But I will restore their fortunes, and will have mercy on them.'" [Gen 49:10]

speak the Word

Thank You, God, that a time is coming when You will fulfill every good promise You have made to me.
—ADAPTED FROM JEREMIAH 33:14

34

THE WORD that came to Jeremiah from the LORD when Nebuchadnezzar king of Babylon and all his army, with all the kingdoms of the earth that were under his sovereignty and all the peoples, were fighting against Jerusalem and against all of its cities: ²"Thus says the LORD God of Israel, 'Go and speak to Zedekiah king of Judah and tell him: "Thus says the LORD, 'Behold, I am giving this city into the hand of the king of Babylon, and he will set it on fire *and* burn it down.

³'You will not escape from his hand, for you will definitely be captured and handed over to him; you will see the king of Babylon eye to eye, and he will speak with you face to face; and you will go to Babylon.' " '

⁴"Yet hear the word of the LORD, O Zedekiah king of Judah! Thus says the LORD concerning you, 'You will not die by the sword.

⁵'You will die in peace; and as *spices* were burned for [the memory and honor of] your fathers, the former kings who reigned before you, so shall a [ceremonial] burning be made for you; and people will lament (grieve) for you, saying, "Alas, lord (master)!" ' For I have spoken the word," says the LORD.

⁶Then Jeremiah the prophet spoke all these words to Zedekiah king of Judah in Jerusalem

⁷when the army of the king of Babylon was fighting against Jerusalem and against all the remaining cities of Judah, against Lachish and Azekah, for these were the [only] fortified cities among the cities of Judah.

⁸The word came to Jeremiah from the LORD after King Zedekiah had made a covenant (solemn pledge) with all the [Hebrew] people who were [slaves] in Jerusalem to proclaim liberty to them:

⁹that every man should let his Hebrew slaves, male and female, go free, so that no one should make a slave of a Jew, his brother.

¹⁰So all the princes and all the people who had entered into the covenant agreed that everyone would let his male servant and his female servant go free, and that no one would keep them in bondage any longer; they obeyed, and set *them free*.

¹¹But afterward they backed out [of the covenant] and made the male servants and the female servants whom they had set free return [to them], and brought the male servants and the female servants again into servitude.

¹²Therefore the word of the LORD came to Jeremiah from the LORD, saying,

¹³"Thus says the LORD, the God of Israel, 'I made a covenant (solemn pledge) with your forefathers in the day that I brought them out of the land of Egypt, out of the house of bondage, saying,

¹⁴"At the end of seven years each of you shall set free his Hebrew brother who has sold himself [into servitude] *or* who has been sold to you and has served you six years, you shall release him from [serving] you; but your forefathers did not listen [submissively] to Me or obey Me. [Deut 15:12]

¹⁵"So then you recently turned *and* repented, doing what was right in My sight, each man proclaiming release [from servitude] to his countryman [who was his bond servant]; and you had made a covenant before Me in the house which is called by My Name.

¹⁶"Yet you backed out [of the covenant] and profaned My Name, and each man took back his servants, male and female, whom had been set free in accordance with their desire, and you brought them into servitude [again] to be your male servants and your female servants." '

¹⁷"Therefore says the LORD, 'You have not obeyed Me; you have not proclaimed liberty to your brother and your countryman. Behold (listen very

carefully), I am proclaiming liberty to you—[liberty to be put] to the sword, [liberty] to [be ravaged by] the virulent disease, and [liberty] to [be decimated by] famine,' says the LORD; 'and I will make you a horror *and* a warning to all the kingdoms of the earth.

18'The men who have violated My covenant, who have not kept the terms of the solemn pledge which they made before Me when they split the [sacrificial] calf in half, and then afterwards walked between its separated pieces [sealing their pledge to Me by placing a curse on themselves should they violate the covenant—those men I will make like the calf]! [Gen 15:9, 10, 17]

19'The princes of Judah, the princes

proclaim release

I encourage you to give the gift of freedom and proclaim release to your family, friends, neighbors, and coworkers. People will love you for it. In the Amplified Classic version, Jeremiah 34:15 says to "proclaim liberty," which is the same as freedom or release. Obviously, this does not mean letting others do whatever they want to do. But it does mean that you stop trying to control people and situations and let God be God.

For years, I tried desperately to control and remold my husband and children, until I finally realized that my efforts were acts of selfishness, not love. I told myself that I simply wanted God's best for them; however, I had decided what His best was and was trying to force it upon them.

Unknowingly, I was ignoring scriptures that shed light on the proper attitude parents should have toward their children. Proverbs 22:6 tells us that we are to train up our children in the way they should go, and when they are old, they will not depart from it. Ephesians 6:4 tells us that we are not to provoke our children or exasperate them to resentment, but to "bring them up [tenderly, with lovingkindness] in the discipline and instruction of the Lord." Quite frequently, we have plans for our children. We have our own ideas about what they should do with their lives, and we pressure them to go in the direction we desire for them.

At one point in my life, I wanted all my children to preach, just as I do. That did not happen, and, actually, I now realize that was not even what would have blessed me after all. Each of my grown children performs a different function that fulfills a great need for me in the ministry, and I would really be missing something if I had gotten my way with them. God is in control, and I am glad. Trying to control others is hard work, and it *does not work*!

Make sure the atmosphere in your home and your business is free and relaxed, not one that makes people feel that if they do not please you all the time, tension will fill the air and tempers will explode. When people make mistakes, do not make them feel rejected, but go the extra mile to make them feel forgiven and accepted. Treat others the way you want to be treated.

Relax. Loosen up a bit. Proclaim release as Jeremiah 34:15 instructs, and give everyone around you the gift of freedom.

of Jerusalem, the high officials, the priests, and all the people of the land who passed between the parts of the calf,

²⁰I will give into the hand of their enemies and into the hand of those who seek their lives. And [like the body of the calf] their dead bodies will be food for the birds of the sky and the beasts of the earth.

²¹"Zedekiah king of Judah and his princes I will place into the hand of their enemies and into the hand of those who seek their life, and into the hand of the army of the king of Babylon which has withdrawn from you.

²²'Behold, I am going to command [the Chaldeans who rule Babylon],' says the LORD, 'and I will bring them back to this city; and they will fight against it and take it and set it on fire. I will make the cities of Judah a desolation without inhabitant.'"

35 THE WORD that came to Jeremiah from the LORD in the days of Jehoiakim the son of Josiah, king of Judah:

²"Go to the house of the Rechabites and speak to them, and bring them into the house of the LORD, into one of the [side] chambers; then give them [who are pledged not to drink wine] some wine to drink."

³So I took Jaazaniah the son of Jeremiah, the son of Habazziniah, and his brothers and all his sons and the whole house of the Rechabites,

⁴and I brought them into the house of the LORD, into the chamber of the sons of Hanan the son of Igdaliah, the man of God, which was near the chamber of the princes, above the chamber of Maaseiah the son of Shallum the doorkeeper.

⁵Then I set before the men of the house of the Rechabites pitchers full of wine, and cups, and I said to them, "Drink wine."

⁶But they said, "We will not drink wine, for Jonadab the son of Rechab, our father, commanded us: 'You shall not drink wine, neither you nor your sons, forever.

⁷'Nor shall you build a house or sow seed or plant a vineyard or own one; but you shall live in tents all your days, that you may live many days in the land where you are sojourners (temporary residents).'

⁸"We have obeyed the words of Jonadab the son of Rechab, our father, in all that he commanded us, in all our days we have never drunk wine, nor have our wives, our sons, or our daughters,

⁹nor have we built ourselves houses to live in; nor do we have vineyards or fields or seed.

¹⁰"We have lived only in tents, and have obeyed and done [everything] according to all that Jonadab our father commanded us.

¹¹"But when Nebuchadnezzar king of Babylon came up against the land, we said, 'Come and let us go to Jerusalem for fear of the army of the Chaldeans [who rule Babylon] and for fear of the army of the Arameans.' So we have lived in Jerusalem."

¹²Then came the word of the LORD to Jeremiah, saying,

¹³"Thus says the LORD of hosts, the God of Israel, 'Go and say to the men of Judah and the inhabitants of Jerusalem, "Will you not receive instruction by listening to My words *and* honoring them?" says the LORD.

¹⁴"The command which Jonadab the son of Rechab gave to his sons not to drink wine has been observed [as a custom for more than two hundred years]. To this day they do not drink *wine,* for they have obeyed their father's command. But I have repeatedly spoken to you, yet you have not listened to Me.

¹⁵"I have also sent to you all My servants the prophets, sending them

repeatedly, saying, 'Let every one of you turn now from his evil way and alter your behavior, and do not follow other gods to worship *and* serve them; and then you will live in the land which I have given to you and to your forefathers. But you have not submitted or listened to Me.

¹⁶'Indeed, the sons of Jonadab the son of Rechab have observed the command of their father which he gave them, but this people has not listened to Me.' " '

¹⁷"Therefore thus says the Lord God of hosts, the God of Israel, 'Behold (hear this), I am bringing on Judah and all the inhabitants of Jerusalem all the disaster that I have pronounced against them, because I have spoken to them, but they have not listened, and I have called to them, but they have not answered.' "

¹⁸Then Jeremiah said to the house of the Rechabites, "Thus says the Lord of hosts, the God of Israel, 'Because you have obeyed the command of Jonadab your father and have kept all his commands and have done according to all that he commanded you,

¹⁹therefore thus says the Lord of hosts, the God of Israel, "Jonadab the son of Rechab shall never fail to have a man (descendant) to stand before Me always." ' "

36 IN THE fourth year of Jehoiakim the son of Josiah, king of Judah, this word came to Jeremiah from the Lord, saying,

²"Take a scroll [of parchment] and write on it all the words which I have spoken to you concerning Israel and Judah, and all the nations, from the day I [first] spoke to you in the days of [King] Josiah until this day.

³"It may be that the house of Judah will hear all the disaster which I plan to bring on them, so that each one will turn from his evil way, that I may forgive their wickedness and their sin." [Jer 18:7–10; 26:3]

⁴Then Jeremiah called Baruch the son of Neriah, and Baruch wrote on the scroll of the book all the words which Jeremiah dictated, [words] which the Lord had spoken to him.

⁵Jeremiah commanded Baruch, saying, "I am [in hiding, virtually] restrained; I cannot go into the house of the Lord.

⁶"So you go to the Lord's house on a day of fasting and read from the scroll the words of the Lord to the people which you have written as I dictated. And also you shall read them to all *the people of* Judah who come from their cities.

⁷"It may be that their supplication [for mercy] will come before the Lord, and everyone will turn from his evil way, for great is the anger and the wrath that the Lord has pronounced against this people."

⁸Baruch the son of Neriah did everything that Jeremiah the prophet commanded him, reading from [Jeremiah's scroll] the words of the Lord in the Lord's house.

⁹Now in the fifth year of Jehoiakim the son of Josiah, king of Judah, in the ninth month, a fast was proclaimed before the Lord for all the people in Jerusalem and all the people who came to Jerusalem from the cities of Judah.

¹⁰Then Baruch read to all the people the words of Jeremiah from the scroll of the book in the house of the Lord, in the chamber of Gemariah the son of Shaphan the scribe, in the upper court, at the entry of the New Gate of the Lord's house.

¹¹When Micaiah the son of Gemariah, the son of Shaphan, had heard all the words of the Lord from the scroll,

¹²he went down to the king's house, into the scribe's chamber; and behold, all the princes were sitting there: Elishama the scribe, Delaiah the son of Shemaiah, Elnathan the son of Achbor, Gemariah the son of Shaphan,

do it again!

Even though Jeremiah was in prison, he still received prophecies from the Lord and recorded them, according to Jeremiah 36. God would give him a message, and he would record it on parchment that was rolled up into a scroll. Then one of his servants would carry the message throughout the land, since Jeremiah was unable to go personally. From this we see that God is not put off by inconveniences; He always finds a way to get the job done.

The people of those days did not have computers and printers, typewriters, or even ballpoint pens and pads of paper, so imagine how tedious their job of writing was! Everything had to be taken down by a quill and ink on a scroll. If more than one copy was needed, then it had to be made by hand from the original, which was a long, tiresome, painstaking process.

In Jeremiah 36:1, 2, God gave Jeremiah a specific prophecy about Israel and Judah, and He told him to record it on a scroll. Jeremiah called his secretary, Baruch, who wrote while Jeremiah dictated (see Jeremiah 36:4). When the king heard about the scroll, he ordered it to be brought to the royal palace and read to him. As his attendant Jehudi was reading it to him, the king would take a few columns that had been read, cut them off the scroll with a knife, and then burn them in a fire (see Jeremiah 36:22, 23).

It was wintertime. Maybe the king was sitting there by the fire, warming his toes and eating an apple. Whatever the case, the king did not like what Jehudi was reading because he liked his unrighteous lifestyle and did not want to change it. So he cut up and burned section after section from the scroll until he burned up all Jeremiah's prophecies.

Can you imagine how Jeremiah must have felt when he learned that all of his hard work had been burned up? Can you relate to that experience? Have you ever worked on something for a long time and struggled and tried and done everything you knew how to do and somehow the devil got in and destroyed it all? The word to you is: *Do it again!*

That is what Jeremiah did. God's answer to Jeremiah's terrible dilemma and discouragement was: "Take another scroll and write on it all the former words that were on the first scroll" (Jeremiah 36:28). God said, basically, "Jeremiah, go get yourself another scroll and write it all over again."

In other words, *do it again*.

If you and I want to be strong and victorious in the kingdom of God, we must be willing to do it—and then do it again and again and again, if necessary—until we get a breakthrough to complete what God has called us to do.

Zedekiah the son of Hananiah, and all the [other] princes.

¹³Then Micaiah declared to them all the words that he had heard when Baruch read from the scroll to all the people.

¹⁴Therefore all the princes sent Jehudi the son of Nethaniah, the son of Shelemiah, the son of Cushi, to Baruch, saying, "Take in your hand the scroll from which you have read to the people and come [to us]." So Baruch the son of Neriah took the scroll in his hand and went to them.

¹⁵And they said to him, "Sit down now and read it to us." So Baruch read it to them.

¹⁶Now when they had heard all the words, they turned one to another in fear and said to Baruch, "We must surely report all these words to the king."

¹⁷And they asked Baruch, "Tell us now, how did you write all these words? At his (Jeremiah's) dictation?"

¹⁸Then Baruch answered them, "He dictated all these words to me, and I wrote them with ink on the scroll."

¹⁹Then the princes said to Baruch, "Go and hide, you and Jeremiah, and do not let anyone know where you are."

²⁰Then they went into the court to the king, but they [first] put the scroll in the chamber of Elishama the scribe; then they reported all the words to the king.

²¹So the king sent Jehudi to get the scroll, and he took it out of the chamber of Elishama the scribe. And Jehudi read it to the king and all the princes who stood beside the king.

²²Now it was the ninth month, and the king was sitting in the winter house, with *a fire* burning there in the brazier before him.

²³And after Jehudi had read three or four columns [of the scroll], *King Jehoiakim* would cut off *that portion* with a scribe's knife and throw it into the fire that was in the brazier, until

the [entire] scroll was consumed by the fire.

²⁴Yet the king and all his servants who heard all these words were not afraid, nor did they tear their clothes.

²⁵Even though Elnathan and Delaiah and Gemariah pleaded with the king not to burn the scroll, he would not listen to them.

²⁶And the king commanded Jerahmeel the king's son, Seraiah the son of Azriel, and Shelemiah the son of Abdeel to seize Baruch the scribe and Jeremiah the prophet, but the LORD hid them.

²⁷Then the word of the LORD came to Jeremiah after the king had burned the scroll containing the words which Baruch had written at the dictation of Jeremiah:

²⁸"Take another scroll and write on it all the former words that were on the first scroll which Jehoiakim the king of Judah burned.

²⁹"And concerning Jehoiakim king of Judah you shall say, 'Thus says the LORD, "You have burned this scroll, saying, 'Why have you written on it that the king of Babylon will certainly come and destroy this land, and will cut off man and beast from it?'"

³⁰'Therefore thus says the LORD concerning Jehoiakim king of Judah, "He shall have no heir to sit on the throne of David, and his dead body shall be thrown out to the heat of the day and to the frost of the night.

³¹"I will also punish him and his descendants and his servants for their wickedness, and I will bring on them and the inhabitants of Jerusalem and the men of Judah all the destruction that I have declared against them—but they would not listen."'"

³²Then Jeremiah took another scroll and gave it to Baruch the scribe, the son of Neriah, who wrote on it at the dictation of Jeremiah all the words of the scroll which Jehoiakim king of Judah

had burned in the fire; and many similar words were added to them.

37 NOW NEBUCHADNEZ-ZAR king of Babylon made Zedekiah the son of Josiah king in the land of Judah so he reigned as king instead of Coniah (also called Jeconiah and Jehoiachin) the son of Jehoiakim.

²But neither he nor his servants nor the people of the land listened to the words of the LORD which He spoke through the prophet Jeremiah.

³Yet King Zedekiah sent Jehucal the son of Shelemiah [along] with Zephaniah the son of Maaseiah, the priest, to the prophet Jeremiah, saying, "Please pray [now] to the LORD our God for us."

⁴Now Jeremiah was coming and going among the people, for they had not [yet] put him in prison.

⁵Meanwhile, Pharaoh's army had set out from Egypt; and when the Chaldeans who were besieging Jerusalem heard the news about them, they withdrew from Jerusalem.

⁶Then the word of the LORD came to the prophet Jeremiah:

⁷"Thus says the LORD, the God of Israel, 'This is what you are to say to the king of Judah, who sent you to Me to inquire of Me: "Behold, Pharaoh's army, which has come out to help you, will return to Egypt, to their own land.

⁸"And the Chaldeans [of Babylon] will come again and fight against this city, and they will capture it and set it on fire."'

⁹"Thus says the LORD, 'Do not deceive yourselves, saying, "The Chaldeans will certainly stay away from us," for they will not stay away.

¹⁰"For even if you had defeated the whole army of the Chaldeans who fight against you, and there remained only the wounded men among them, yet they would rise up, every man confined in his tent, and burn down this city with fire.'"

¹¹Now it happened when the army of the Chaldeans departed from Jerusalem for fear of Pharaoh's [approaching] army,

¹²that Jeremiah left Jerusalem [during the withdrawal of the Chaldean invaders] to go to [Anathoth, his hometown, in] the land of Benjamin to take possession of [the title to] the land [which he had purchased] there among the people. [Jer 32:6–12]

¹³When he was at the Gate of Benjamin, a captain of the guard whose name was Irijah, the son of Shelemiah the son of Hananiah was there; and he seized *and* arrested Jeremiah the prophet, saying, "You are deserting to join the Chaldeans [of Babylon]!"

¹⁴But Jeremiah said, "That is a lie! I am not deserting to join the Chaldeans." But the guard would not listen to him. So Irijah took Jeremiah and brought him to the princes (court officials).

¹⁵The princes were enraged with Jeremiah and beat him and put him in prison in the house of Jonathan the scribe—for they had made that the prison.

¹⁶When Jeremiah had come into the vaulted cell in the dungeon and had remained there many days,

¹⁷Zedekiah the king sent and brought him out; and in his palace the king secretly asked him, "Is there any word from the LORD?" And Jeremiah said, "There is!" Then he said, "You will be handed over to the king of Babylon."

¹⁸Moreover, Jeremiah said to King Zedekiah, "In what way have I sinned against you, or against your servants, or against this people, that you have put me in prison?

¹⁹"Where then are your prophets who prophesied to you, saying, 'The king of Babylon will not come against you or against this land?'

²⁰"Therefore now, please listen, O my lord the king; please let my petition come before you *and* be acceptable and do not make me return to

the house of Jonathan the scribe, that I may not die there."

²¹Then King Zedekiah commanded, and they committed Jeremiah to the court of the guardhouse, and a [round] loaf of bread from the bakers' street was given to him daily, until all the bread in the city was gone. So Jeremiah remained [imprisoned] in the court of the guardhouse.

38 NOW SHEPHATIAH the son of Mattan, and Gedaliah the son of Pashhur, and Jucal (also called Jehucal) the son of Shelemiah, and Pashhur the son of Malchijah heard the words that Jeremiah was speaking to all the people, saying,

²"So says the Lord, 'He who remains in this city will die by the sword, by famine, and by virulent disease (pestilence), but he who goes out to the Chaldeans [of Babylon] will live and have his [own] life as a reward and stay alive.' [Jer 21:9]

³"Thus says the Lord, 'This city will certainly be given into the hand of the army of the king of Babylon and he will take it.'"

⁴Therefore the princes (court officials) said to the king, "Please [we implore you] let this man [Jeremiah] be put to death; for [speaking] in this way he discourages *and* weakens [the will of] the soldiers who remain in this city and he discourages *and* weakens [the will of] all the people by speaking such words to them; for this man is not seeking the well-being of these people, but rather their harm."

⁵Then King Zedekiah [fearing the princes] said, "Listen, he is in your hand; for the king is in no position to do anything against you."

⁶So they took Jeremiah and threw him into the cistern of Malchijah the king's son, which was in the court of the guardhouse; and they let Jeremiah down [into the cistern] with ropes.

Now there was no water in the cistern but only mud, and Jeremiah sank in the mud.

⁷Now Ebed-melech the Ethiopian (Cushite), one of the eunuchs who was in the king's palace, heard that they had put Jeremiah in the cistern, and while the king was sitting in the Gate of Benjamin,

⁸Ebed-melech went out of the king's palace and spoke to the king, saying,

⁹"My lord the king, these men have acted wickedly in all that they have done to Jeremiah the prophet whom they have thrown into the cistern; and he will die [of hunger] where he is because of the famine, for there is no more bread in the city."

¹⁰Then the king commanded Ebed-melech the Ethiopian, saying, "Take thirty men from here with you and lift Jeremiah the prophet out of the cistern before he dies."

¹¹So Ebed-melech took the men with him and went into the palace of the king to *a place* under the storeroom and took from there old rags and worn-out clothes and let them down by ropes into the cistern to Jeremiah.

¹²Then Ebed-melech the Ethiopian said to Jeremiah, "Now put these old rags and worn-out clothes under your armpits, then place the ropes under the padding"; and Jeremiah did so.

¹³So they pulled Jeremiah up with the ropes and took him up out of the cistern; and Jeremiah remained in the court of the guardhouse.

¹⁴Then King Zedekiah sent and had Jeremiah the prophet brought to him at the third entrance that is in the house of the Lord. And the king said to Jeremiah, "I am going to ask you something; hide nothing from me."

¹⁵Then Jeremiah said to Zedekiah, "If I tell you, will you not certainly put me to death? Even if I do give you advice, you will not listen to me."

¹⁶But King Zedekiah swore secretly to

Jeremiah, "As the Lord lives, who made our lives, be assured that I will not put you to death or put you into the hand of these men who are seeking your life."

¹⁷Then Jeremiah said to Zedekiah, "Thus says the Lord God of hosts, the God of Israel, 'If you will go out *and* surrender to the officers of the king of Babylon, then you will live and this city will not be burned with fire; and you and your household will live.

¹⁸'But if you will not go out to the officers of the king of Babylon, then this city will be given into the hand of the Chaldeans [of Babylon] and they will set it on fire; and you yourself will not escape from their hand.'"

¹⁹Then King Zedekiah said to Jeremiah, "I am afraid of the Jews [my former subjects] who have deserted to join the Chaldeans, for the enemy may put me into their hand and they will mock me *and* abuse me."

²⁰But Jeremiah said, "They will not hand you over [to them]. Please obey [the voice of] the Lord [who speaks to you through me] in what I am saying to you. Then it will go well with you and you will live.

²¹"But if you keep refusing to go out *and* surrender to them, this is the word [and the vision] which the Lord has shown me:

²²"Then behold, all the women who are left in the palace of the king of Judah will be brought out to the officers of the king of Babylon and those women will say [to you, King Zedekiah],

"Your close friends
Have prevailed against your better
   judgment *and* have overpowered
   and deceived you;
While your feet were sunk in the
   mire [of trouble],
They turned back."

²³'Also, all your wives and your children will be brought out to the Chaldeans; and you yourself will not escape

from their hand, but you will be seized by the king of Babylon, and this city [Jerusalem] will be burned down with fire.'"

²⁴Then Zedekiah said to Jeremiah, "Let no man know about this conversation and you will not die.

²⁵"But if the princes (court officials) hear that I have talked with you, and they come to you and say, 'Tell us now what you said to the king and what he said to you; do not hide it from us and we will not execute you,'

²⁶then you are to say to them, 'I was presenting my [humble] petition *and* plea to the king so that he would not send me back to Jonathan's house to die there.'"

²⁷Then all the princes (court officials) came to Jeremiah and asked him [just what King Zedekiah had anticipated they would ask], and he reported to them in accordance with all that the king had commanded. So they stopped questioning him, since the conversation [with the king] had not been overheard.

²⁸So Jeremiah remained in the court of the guardhouse until the day that Jerusalem was captured [by the Chaldeans of Babylon].

39 NOW REGARDING the capture of Jerusalem: In the ninth year of [the reign of] Zedekiah king of Judah, in the tenth month, Nebuchadnezzar king of Babylon and all his army came against Jerusalem and besieged it; [Jer 52:4–27]

²and in the eleventh year of Zedekiah, in the fourth month, on the ninth day of the month, they breached the wall *and* broke into the city.

³Then all the officials of the king of Babylon came in and sat in the Middle Gate [establishing both military control of the city and their authority to judge the captives]: Nergal-sarezer, Samgar-nebu, Sar-sekim the

Rab-saris (chief of the eunuchs), and Nergal-sar-ezer the Rab-mag (chief of the magicians), with all the rest of the officials of the king of Babylon.

⁴When Zedekiah the king of Judah and all the men of war saw them, they fled and escaped from the city at night by way of the king's garden, through the gate between the two walls; and the king went out toward the Arabah (Jordan Valley).

⁵But the Chaldean (Babylonian) army pursued them and overtook Zedekiah in the plains of Jericho. When they had seized him, they brought him up to Neb-uchadnezzar king of Babylon at Rib-lah in the [Aramean] land of Hamath, where he passed sentence on him.

⁶Then at Riblah the king of Babylon killed the sons of Zedekiah before his eyes; the king of Babylon also killed all the nobles of Judah.

⁷Moreover, he blinded Zedekiah and bound him with bronze shackles to take him to Babylon. [Ezek 12:13]

⁸The Chaldeans also burned down the king's palace and the houses of the people, and they broke down the walls of Jerusalem.

⁹Then Nebuzaradan the [chief executioner and] captain of the bodyguard took the rest of the people who remained in the city, along with those who had deserted and surrendered to him, and the rest of the [so-called better class of] people who were left and carried them into exile in Babylon.

¹⁰But Nebuzaradan the [Babylonian] captain of the bodyguard left behind in the land of Judah some of the poor people who had nothing, and gave them vineyards and fields at that time.

¹¹Now Nebuchadnezzar king of Babylon gave orders concerning Jeremiah through Nebuzaradan the captain of the bodyguard, saying,

¹²"Take him and look after him; do nothing to harm him, but rather deal with him just as he asks of you."

¹³So Nebuzaradan the captain of the bodyguard sent word, along with Nebushazban the Rab-saris (chief of the high officials), and Nergal-sar-ezer the Rab-mag (chief of the magicians), and all the leading officers of the king of Babylon;

¹⁴they even sent and took Jeremiah out of the court of the guardhouse and entrusted him to Gedaliah [a prominent citizen], the son of Ahikam [who had once saved Jeremiah's life], the son of Shaphan, to take him home [with him to Mizpah]. So Jeremiah [was released and] lived among the people. [Jer 26:24]

¹⁵Now the word of the LORD had come to Jeremiah while he was [still] confined in the court of the guardhouse, saying,

¹⁶"Go and speak to Ebed-melech the Ethiopian, saying, 'Thus says the LORD of hosts, the God of Israel, "Behold, I am about to bring My words [of judgment] against this city through disaster and not for good; and they will take place before you on that day.

¹⁷"But I will protect you [Ebed-melech] on that day," says the LORD, "and you will not be handed over to the men of whom you are afraid. [Jer 38:7–13]

¹⁸"For I will certainly rescue you; and you will not fall by the sword, but you will have your [own] life as a reward of battle, because you have placed your trust in Me," says the LORD.'"

40 THE WORD which came to Jeremiah from the LORD after Nebuzaradan the captain of the bodyguard had released him from Ramah, when he had taken him bound in chains among all the captives of Jerusalem and Judah who were being taken as exiles to Babylon.

²And the captain of the bodyguard had taken Jeremiah and said to him, "The LORD your God promised this disaster on this place.

³"Now the LORD has brought it about and has done just as He promised. Because you [people of Judah] have sinned against the LORD and did not listen to *and* honor His voice, therefore this thing has happened to you.

⁴"But now, listen carefully, [because of your innocence] I am freeing you today from the chains which are on your hands. If you would prefer to come with me to Babylon, come, and I will look after you [carefully]; but if you would prefer not to come with me to Babylon, then do not do so. Look, all the land is before you; go wherever it seems good and right (convenient) for you to go."

⁵While Jeremiah was still hesitating, the captain of the bodyguard said, "Go on back then to Gedaliah the son of Ahikam, the son of Shaphan, whom the king of Babylon has appointed [governor] over the cities of Judah, and stay with him among the people; or else go wherever it seems right for you to go." So the captain of the bodyguard gave him an allowance of food and a gift and let him go.

⁶Then Jeremiah went to Gedaliah the son of Ahikam at Mizpah and stayed with him among the people who were left in the land.

⁷Now when all the commanders of the forces that were [scattered] in the open country [of Judah] and their men heard that the king of Babylon had made Gedaliah the son of Ahikam governor in the land [of Judah] and had put him in charge of the men, women, and children, those of the poorest of the land who had not been exiled to Babylon,

⁸they went to Gedaliah at Mizpah—Ishmael the son of Nethaniah, Johanan and Jonathan the sons of Kareah, Seraiah the son of Tanhumeth, the sons of Ephai the Netophathite, and Jezaniah the son of the Maacathite, they and their men.

⁹Then Gedaliah the son of Ahikam, the son of Shaphan, swore to them and their men, saying, "Do not be afraid to serve the Chaldeans; stay in this land and serve the king of Babylon, that it may go well with you.

¹⁰"As for me, I am going to stay at Mizpah to stand [for you] before the Chaldeans who come to us [ministering to them and looking after the king's interests]; but as for you, gather in wine, summer fruit and oil and store them in your utensils [designed for such purposes], and live in your cities that you have taken over."

¹¹Likewise, when all the Jews who were in Moab and among the people of Ammon and in Edom and who were in all the [other] countries heard that the king of Babylon had left a remnant [of the people] in Judah and had appointed Gedaliah the son of Ahikam, the son of Shaphan over them [as governor],

¹²then all the Jews returned from all the places to which they had been driven and came back to the land of Judah, to Gedaliah at Mizpah, and gathered a great abundance of wine and summer fruits.

¹³Moreover, Johanan the son of Kareah and all the commanders of the forces that were [scattered] in the open country came to Gedaliah at Mizpah

¹⁴and said to him, "Do you know that Baalis the king of the Ammonites has sent Ishmael the son of Nethaniah to take your life?" But Gedaliah the son of Ahikam did not believe them.

¹⁵Then Johanan the son of Kareah spoke secretly to Gedaliah in Mizpah, saying, "Let me go and kill Ishmael the son of Nethaniah, and not a man will know [who is responsible]. Why should he kill you and cause all the Jews who are gathered near you to be scattered and the remnant of Judah to perish?"

¹⁶But Gedaliah the son of Ahikam

said to Johanan the son of Kareah, "Do not do this thing, for you are lying about Ishmael."

41 NOW IN the seventh month Ishmael the son of Nethaniah, the son of Elishama, of the royal family [of David] and one of the princes of the king, came [at the instigation of the Ammonites] with ten men to Gedaliah the son of Ahikam in Mizpah. As they were eating a meal together there in Mizpah,

²Ishmael the son of Nethaniah and the ten men who were with him got up and struck down Gedaliah the son of Ahikam, the son of Shaphan, with the sword and killed the one whom the king of Babylon had appointed [governor] over the land. [2 Kin 25:25]

³Ishmael also killed all the Jews who were [at the banquet] with Gedaliah at Mizpah, in addition to the Chaldean soldiers who were there.

⁴Now it happened on the second day after the killing of Gedaliah, before anyone knew about it,

⁵that eighty men came from Shechem, from Shiloh, and from Samaria with their beards shaved off and their clothes torn and their bodies cut, carrying in their hands grain offerings and incense to present at the [site of the] house of the LORD [in Jerusalem].

⁶Then Ishmael the son of Nethaniah went out from Mizpah to meet them, weeping [false tears] as he went. As he met them, he said to them, "Come to Gedaliah the son of Ahikam!"

⁷Yet when they came into the city, Ishmael the son of Nethaniah and the men who were with him slaughtered them *and threw them* into the cistern (underground water reservoir).

⁸But ten men who were among them said to Ishmael, "Do not kill us! We have stores of wheat and barley and oil and honey hidden in the field." So

he stopped and did not kill them along with their companions.

⁹Now the cistern into which Ishmael had thrown all the corpses of the men whom he had killed along with Gedaliah was the one which King Asa [of Judah] had made [about three hundred years earlier] on account of King Baasha of Israel [believing that Baasha would lay siege to Mizpah]. Ishmael the son of Nethaniah filled it with [the bodies of] those who were killed.

¹⁰Then Ishmael took captive all the rest of the people who were in Mizpah—even the king's daughters (ladies of the court) and all the people who remained in Mizpah, whom Nebuzaradan the captain of the bodyguard had put under the charge of Gedaliah the son of Ahikam. Ishmael the son of Nethaniah took them captive and crossed over [the Jordan] to [meet his allies] the Ammonites.

¹¹But when Johanan the son of Kareah and all the commanders of the forces that were with him heard of the murderous behavior of Ishmael the son of Nethaniah,

¹²they took all their men and went to fight with Ishmael the son of Nethaniah and found him by the great pool in Gibeon.

¹³Now when all the [captive] people who were with Ishmael saw Johanan the son of Kareah and all the commanders of the forces that were with him, they were glad.

¹⁴So all the people whom Ishmael had taken captive from Mizpah turned around and came back, and joined Johanan the son of Kareah.

¹⁵But Ishmael the son of Nethaniah escaped from Johanan with eight men and went to join the Ammonites.

¹⁶Then Johanan the son of Kareah and all the commanders of the forces that were with him took from Mizpah all the people whom he had rescued from Ishmael the son of Nethaniah,

after Ishmael had killed Gedaliah the son of Ahikam: the soldiers, the women, the children, and the high officials whom Johanan had brought back from Gibeon.

¹⁷And they went and stayed in Geruth [the lodging place of] Chimham, which is near Bethlehem, intending to go to Egypt

¹⁸because of the Chaldeans; for they were afraid of them because Ishmael the son of Nethaniah had killed Gedaliah the son of Ahikam, whom the king of Babylon had appointed [governor] over the land [and whose death the king might avenge].

42 THEN ALL the commanders of the forces, and Johanan the son of Kareah and Jezaniah (Azariah) the son of Hoshaiah, and all the people from the least to the greatest approached

²and said to Jeremiah the prophet, "Please let our petition be presented before you, and pray to the Lord your God for us, *that is,* for all this remnant [of the people of Judah]; for we were once many, but now [only] a few of us are left, as you see with your own eyes, [so please pray]

³that the Lord your God may show us the way in which we should walk and the thing that we should do."

⁴Then Jeremiah the prophet said to them, "I have heard you. Now hear me, I will pray to the Lord your God in accordance with your words; and I will declare to you whatever message the Lord answers; I will keep nothing back from you."

⁵Then they said to Jeremiah, "May the Lord be a true and faithful witness

against us if we fail to act in accordance with all the things that the Lord your God sends you to tell us.

⁶"Whether it is pleasant or unpleasant, we will listen to *and* honor the voice of the Lord our God to whom we are sending you, so that it may go well with us when we listen to the voice of the Lord our God."

⁷Now after ten days [of prayer] had passed the word of the Lord came to Jeremiah.

⁸Then he called for Johanan the son of Kareah and all the commanders of the forces that were with him and all the people from the least to the greatest,

⁹and said to them, "Thus says the Lord, the God of Israel, to whom you sent me to present your petition before Him:

¹⁰'If you will indeed remain in this land, then I will build you up and not tear you down, and I will plant you and not uproot you; for I will relent *and* be satisfied concerning the disaster that I have inflicted on you [as discipline, and I will replace judgment with compassion]. [Jer 31:4, 28]

¹¹'Do not be afraid of the king of Babylon, whom you now fear [as if he were deity]; do not be afraid of him,' says the Lord, 'for [he is a mere man, but I am the living, omniscient God and] I am with you [always] to protect you and to deliver you from his hand.

¹²'And I will show you compassion, so that he will have compassion on you and restore you to your own land.

¹³'But if you are going to say, "We will not stay in this land," and [in so doing] do not listen to the voice of the Lord your God,

¹⁴saying, "No, but we will go to the

speak the Word

God, I pray that You would show me the way in which I should walk and the things that I should do.
—ADAPTED FROM JEREMIAH 42:3

land of Egypt, where we will not see war or hear the sound of the [warrior's] trumpet or hunger for bread, and we will stay there,"

¹⁵then in that case listen to the word of the Lord, O remnant of Judah. Thus says the Lord of hosts, the God of Israel, "If you are really determined to go to Egypt and to reside there [temporarily],

¹⁶then the sword, of which you are afraid, will overtake you there in the land of Egypt; and the famine of which you are afraid will follow closely after you in Egypt, and you will die there.

¹⁷"So all the men who set their mind to go to Egypt to reside there [temporarily] will die by the sword, by famine and by virulent disease; none of them will remain or survive the disaster that I am going to bring on them."'"

¹⁸For thus says the Lord of hosts, the God of Israel, "As My anger and My wrath have been poured out on the inhabitants of Jerusalem, so My wrath will be poured out on you when you enter Egypt. You will become detested, an object of horror, a curse and a people scorned; and you will no longer see this place."

¹⁹The Lord has spoken to you, O remnant of Judah, "Do not go into Egypt!" Know with certainty that I [Jeremiah] have warned you *and* testified to you this day

²⁰that you have deceived yourselves; for you sent me to the Lord your God, saying, "Pray for us to the Lord our God; and whatever the Lord our God says, declare it to us and we will do it."

²¹And so I have told you today, but you have not listened to the voice of the Lord your God, in anything that He has sent me to tell you.

²²Now therefore know for certain that you will die by the sword, by famine, and by virulent disease in the land [of Egypt] where you wish to reside [temporarily].

43

NOW IT happened when Jeremiah, whom the Lord their God had sent, had finished telling all the people all the words of the Lord their God—that is, all these words—

²Azariah the son of Hoshaiah and Johanan the son of Kareah and all the proud *and* insolent men said to Jeremiah, "You are not telling the truth! The Lord our God has not sent you to say, 'Do not go into Egypt to live there.'

³"But Baruch the son of Neriah is inciting you against us to hand us over to the Chaldeans, so they may [either] put us to death or exile us to Babylon."

⁴So Johanan the son of Kareah and all the commanders of the forces and all the people disobeyed the voice of the Lord [which told them] to stay in the land of Judah.

⁵But Johanan the son of Kareah and all the commanders of the forces took all the remnant of Judah who had returned to live in the land of Judah from all the nations to which they had been driven—

⁶the men, women, and children, the king's daughters (ladies of the court), and every person whom Nebuzaradan the captain of the bodyguard had left with Gedaliah the son of Ahikam, the son of Shaphan; he also took Jeremiah the prophet and Baruch the son of Neriah.

⁷So they entered the land of Egypt (for they did not obey the voice of the Lord) and they went in as far as Tahpanhes.

⁸Then came the word of the Lord to Jeremiah in Tahpanhes, saying,

⁹"Take some large stones in your hands and hide them in the mortar in the brickwork [of the terrace] which is at the entrance of Pharaoh's house in Tahpanhes, in the sight of some of the *men of* Judah;

¹⁰and say to them, 'Thus says the Lord of hosts, the God of Israel, "Behold, I am

going to send and get Nebuchadnezzar the king of Babylon, My servant, and I am going to set his throne over these stones that I have hidden; and his [majestic, royal] canopy will be spread over them. [Ezek 29:19, 20]

¹¹"He will also come and strike the land of Egypt, giving those who are [destined] for death, to death, and those who are [destined] for captivity, to captivity, and those who are [destined] for the sword, to the sword.

¹²"And [through him] I will set fire to the temples of the gods of Egypt, and he will burn them and take them (Egyptian idols) captive. He will wrap himself with the land of Egypt as a shepherd wraps himself with his garment, and he will go away from there safely.

¹³"Nebuchadnezzar will also break the images *and* shatter the obelisks of Heliopolis in the land of Egypt; and he will burn down the temples of the gods of Egypt."'"

44 THE WORD that came to Jeremiah concerning all the Jews who were living in the land of Egypt—at Migdol, at Tahpanhes, at Memphis, and in the land of Pathros, saying,

²"Thus says the Lord of hosts, the God of Israel, 'You have seen all the disaster that I have brought on Jerusalem and on all the cities of Judah; and see, this day they are desolated and no one lives in them

³because of the wickedness which they committed, provoking Me to anger by continuing to burn sacrifices *and* incense to serve other gods that they had not known, *neither* they, nor you, nor your fathers.

⁴'Yet I sent to you all My servants the prophets, again and again, saying, "Oh, do not do this shamefully vile thing which I hate."

⁵'But they did not listen or turn [obediently] from their wickedness, and

stop burning sacrifices *and* incense to other gods.

⁶'Therefore My wrath and My anger were poured out and burned in the cities of Judah and in the streets of Jerusalem; so they have become a ruin and a desolation, as it is this day.

⁷'Therefore now thus says the Lord God of hosts, the God of Israel, "Why did you commit this great evil against yourselves [bringing disaster] that will cut off from you man and woman, child and infant, out of Judah, leaving yourselves without a remnant?

⁸"Why do you [deliberately] provoke Me to anger with the works (idols) of your hands, burning sacrifices *and* incense to [make-believe] gods in the land of Egypt, where you [of your own accord] have come to live [as temporary residents], that you might be cut off and become a curse and a disgrace [an object of taunts] among all the nations of the earth?

⁹"Have you forgotten the wickedness of your fathers, the wickedness of the kings of Judah, the wickedness of their wives [who served their foreign gods], your own wickedness, and the wickedness of your wives [who imitated the sin of the queens], which they committed in the land of Judah and in the streets of Jerusalem?

¹⁰"They have not become apologetic [for their guilt and sin] even to this day; they have not feared [Me with reverence] nor walked in My law or My statutes, which I have set before you and before your fathers."' [Jer 6:15; 26:4–6; 44:23]

¹¹"Therefore thus says the Lord of hosts, the God of Israel, 'Behold, I am going to set My face against you for woe—even to cut off (destroy) all Judah [from the land].

¹²'And I will take the remnant of Judah who have decided to go into the land of Egypt to live there [instead of surrendering to the Chaldeans as directed],

and they will all fall and die in the land of Egypt; they will fall by the sword or perish by famine. From the least to the greatest, they will die by the sword or by famine; and they will become detestable, an object of horror, a curse, and a disgrace.

¹³'For I will punish all the inhabitants of the land of Egypt, as I have punished Jerusalem, with the sword, with famine, and with virulent disease;

¹⁴so none of the survivors from the remnant of Judah who have entered the land of Egypt to live there will survive, even though they lift up their souls in longing to return to the land of Judah, [the place] to which they long to return to live; none will return except a few refugees.'"

¹⁵Then all the men who knew that their wives were burning sacrifices to other gods, and all the women who were standing by, a large group, including all the people who were living in Pathros in the land of Egypt, answered Jeremiah, saying,

¹⁶"As for the word (message) that you have spoken to us in the name of the Lord, we are not going to listen to you.

¹⁷"But rather we will certainly perform every word of the vows we have made: to burn sacrifices to the queen of heaven (Ishtar) and to pour out drink offerings to her, just as we ourselves and our forefathers, our kings and our princes did in the cities of Judah and in the streets of Jerusalem; for [then] we had plenty of food and were prosperous and saw no misfortune.

¹⁸"But since we stopped burning sacrifices to the queen of heaven and pouring out drink offerings to her, we have lacked everything and have been consumed by the sword and by famine."

¹⁹And said the wives, "When we were burning sacrifices to the queen of heaven and were pouring out drink offerings to her, was it without [the knowledge and approval of] our husbands that we made cakes [in the shape of a star] to represent her and pour out drink offerings to her?"

²⁰Then Jeremiah said to all the people, to the men and to the women and to all the people who had given him that answer,

²¹"The smoking sacrifices (incense) that you burned in the cities of Judah and in the streets of Jerusalem—you and your forefathers, your kings and your princes, and the people of the land—did not the Lord remember [in detail your idolatry] and did it not all come into His mind?

²²"The Lord could no longer endure it, because of the evil of your acts and the repulsive acts which you have committed; because of them your land has become a ruin, an object of horror and a curse, without inhabitant, as it is this day.

²³"Because you have burned sacrifices [to idols] and because you have sinned against the Lord and have not obeyed the voice of the Lord or walked in His law and in His statutes and in His testimonies, therefore this tragedy has fallen on you, as it has this day."

²⁴Then Jeremiah said to all the people, including all the women, "Hear the word of the Lord, all [you of] Judah who are in the land of Egypt,

²⁵thus says the Lord of hosts, the God of Israel, as follows: 'You and your wives have both declared with your mouth and fulfilled it with your hand, saying, "We will certainly perform our vows that we have vowed, to burn sacrifices to the queen of heaven (Ishtar) and to pour out drink offerings to her." Surely then confirm your vows and go ahead and perform your vows! [If you intend to defy all My warnings, proceed!]'

²⁶"Therefore hear the word of the Lord, all [you people of] Judah who are living in the land of Egypt, 'Behold, I

have sworn [an oath] by My great Name,'
says the Lord, 'that My Name shall never
again be invoked by the mouth of any
man of Judah in all the land of Egypt,
saying, "As the Lord God lives."'

27'Behold, I am watching over them for
harm and not for good; and all the men
of Judah who are in the land of Egypt
shall be consumed by the sword and by
famine until they are all destroyed.

28'Yet a small number [of My choos-
ing] who escape the sword will return
from the land of Egypt to the land of
Judah; and all the remnant of Judah
who have gone to the land of Egypt to
reside there will know whose words
will stand, Mine or theirs.

29'And this will be the sign to you,'
says the Lord, 'that I am going to punish you in this place, so that you may
know that My words will surely stand
against you for harm.'

30"Thus says the Lord, 'Behold, I will
give Pharaoh Hophra king of Egypt
into the hand of his enemies and into
the hand of those who seek his life,
just as I gave Zedekiah king of Judah
into the hand of Nebuchadnezzar king
of Babylon, who was his enemy and
was seeking his life.'"

45 THE WORD that Jeremiah
the prophet spoke to Bar-
uch the son of Neriah, when
he had written these words in a book at
the dictation of Jeremiah, in the fourth
year of Jehoiakim the son of Josiah,
king of Judah, saying,

2"Thus says the Lord, the God of Israel, to you, O Baruch:

3'You said, "Woe is me! For the Lord
has added sorrow to my pain; I am
weary with my groaning and sighing
and I find no rest."'

4"Say this to him, 'The Lord speaks
in this way, "Behold, what I have built
I will break down, and that which I
have planted I will uproot, that is, the
whole land."

5'And do you seek great things for
yourself? Do not seek them; for behold, I will bring disaster on all flesh,'
says the Lord, 'but I will give your life
to you [as your only reward and] as a
prize of war wherever you go.'"

46 THE WORD of the Lord
that came to Jeremiah the
prophet concerning the
[Gentile] nations.

2Concerning Egypt, against the
army of Pharaoh Neco king of Egypt,
which was by the river Euphrates at
Carchemish, which Nebuchadnezzar
king of Babylon defeated [decisively]
in the fourth year of Jehoiakim son of
Josiah, king of Judah: [Is 19–20; Ezek
29–32; Zech 14:18, 19]

3"Line up the buckler (small shield)
    and [large] shield,
  And advance for battle!
4"Harness the horses,
  And mount, you riders!
  Take your stand with your helmets!
  Polish the spears,
  Put on the coats of mail!
5"Why have I seen it?
  They are terrified
  And have turned back,
  And their warriors are beaten down.
  They take flight in haste
  Without looking back;
  Terror is on every side!"
  Says the Lord. [Ps 31:13; Jer 6:25;
    20:3, 10; 49:29]
6Do not let the swift man run,
  Nor the mighty man escape;
  In the north by the river Euphrates
  They have stumbled and fallen.
7Who is this that rises up like the
    Nile [River],
  Like the rivers [in the delta of
    Egypt] whose waters surge about?
8Egypt rises like the Nile,
  Even like the rivers whose waters
    surge about.

And He has said, "I will rise, I will cover that land;
I will certainly destroy the city and its inhabitants."
⁹Charge, you horses,
And drive like madmen, you chariots!
Let the warriors go forward:
Ethiopia and Put (Libya) who handle the shield,
And the Lydians who handle and bend the bow.
¹⁰For that day belongs to the Lord GOD of hosts,
A day of vengeance, that He may avenge Himself on His adversaries.
And the sword will devour and be satiated
And drink its fill of their blood;
For the Lord GOD of hosts has a sacrifice [like that of a great sin offering]
In the north country by the river Euphrates.
¹¹Go up to Gilead and obtain [healing] balm,
O Virgin Daughter of Egypt!
In vain you use many medicines;
For you there is no healing or remedy.
¹²The nations have heard of your disgrace and shame,
And your cry [of distress] has filled the earth.
For warrior has stumbled against warrior,
And both of them have fallen together.

¹³The word that the LORD spoke to Jeremiah the prophet concerning the coming of Nebuchadnezzar king of Babylon to strike the land of Egypt:

¹⁴"Declare in Egypt and proclaim in Migdol,
And proclaim in Memphis and in Tahpanhes;

Say, 'Take your stand and get yourself ready,
For the sword has devoured those around you.'
¹⁵"Why have your strong ones been cut down?
They do not stand because the LORD drove them away.
¹⁶"He will make many stumble and fall;
Yes, they have fallen one on another.
Then they said, 'Arise, and let us go back
To our own people and to the land of our birth,
Away from the sword of the oppressor.'
¹⁷"They cried there, 'Pharaoh king of Egypt is destroyed and is merely a loud noise;
He has let the appointed time [of opportunity] pass by!'
¹⁸"As I live," says the King,
Whose name is the LORD of hosts,
"Surely like Tabor among the mountains
Or like Carmel by the sea,
So shall he [the great king of Babylon] come.
¹⁹"O you daughter who dwells in Egypt and you who dwell with her,
Prepare yourselves [with all you will need] to go into exile,
For Memphis will become desolate;
It will even be burned down and without inhabitant.
²⁰"Egypt is a very pretty heifer,
But a horsefly (Babylonia) is coming [against her] out of the north!
²¹"Also her mercenaries in her army
Are like fattened calves,
For they too have turned back and have fled together;
They did not stand [their ground],
Because the day of their disaster has come upon them,
The time of their punishment.

22 "The sound [of Egypt fleeing from
the enemy] is like [the rustling
of] an escaping serpent,
For her foes advance with a mighty
army
And come against her like
woodcutters with axes.
23 "They have cut down her forest,"
says the LORD;
"Certainly it will no longer be found,
Because they (the invaders) are
more numerous than locusts
And cannot be counted.
24 "The Daughter of Egypt has been
shamed,
Given over to the power of
the people of the north [the
Chaldeans of Babylonia]."

25 The LORD of hosts, the God of Israel, says, "Behold, I am going to punish Amon [chief god of the sacred city]
of Thebes [the capital of Upper Egypt],
and Pharaoh, and Egypt along with
her gods and her kings—even Pharaoh
and those who put their trust in him
[as a shield against Babylon].
26 "I will put them into the hand of
those who seek their lives, and into the
hand of Nebuchadnezzar king of Babylon and into the hand of his servants.
Afterward Egypt will be inhabited as
in the days of old," says the LORD.

27 "But as for you, do not fear, O My
servant Jacob,
Nor be dismayed, O Israel!
For behold, I will save you from
[your captivity in] a distant land,
And your descendants from the
land of their exile;
And Jacob will return and be quiet
and secure,
And no one will make him afraid.

28 "Do not fear, O Jacob My servant,"
says the LORD,
"For I am with you.
For I will make a full and complete
end of all the nations
To which I have driven you;
Yet I will not make a full end of you.
But I will discipline and correct
you appropriately
And by no means will I declare
you guiltless or leave you
unpunished."

47 THE WORD of the LORD
that came to Jeremiah the
prophet concerning the
Philistines before Pharaoh attacked
and conquered [the Philistine city
of] Gaza. [Is 14:29–31; Ezek 25:15–17;
Amos 1:6–8; Zeph 2:4–7; Zech 9:5–7]
2 Thus says the LORD:

"Behold, waters are going to rise
out of the north (Babylonia)
And become an overflowing stream
And overflow the land and all that
is in it,
The city and those who live in it.
Then the people will cry out,
And all the inhabitants of the land
[of Philistia] will wail.
3 "Because of the noise of the
stamping of the hoofs of the war-
horses [of the Babylonian king],
The rattling of his chariots, and
the rumbling of his wheels,
The fathers have not looked and
turned back for their children,
So weak are their hands [with
terror]
4 Because of the day that is coming
To destroy all the Philistines
And to cut off from Tyre and Sidon
Every ally who remains.

speak the Word

God, I will not fear, because You are with me.
—ADAPTED FROM JEREMIAH 46:28

For the LORD is going to destroy the
    Philistines,
The remnant [still surviving] of the
    coastland of Caphtor. [Amos 9:7]
5 "Baldness [as a sign of mourning]
    will come on Gaza;
Ashkelon will be cut off *and* ruined.
O remnant of their valley,
How long will you gash yourselves
    [as a sign of mourning]?
6 "O you sword of the LORD,
How long will it be before you are
    quiet?
Put yourself into your sheath;
Rest and be still.
7 "How can His sword be quiet
When the LORD has given it an
    order?
Against Ashkelon and against the
    [whole Philistine] seashore
There He has assigned it."

48 CONCERNING MOAB.

Thus says the LORD of
hosts, the God of Israel,
"Woe (judgment is coming) to [the
    city of] Nebo, for it has been
    destroyed!
Kiriathaim has been shamed, it
    has been captured;
Misgab [the high fortress] has
    been shamed, broken down *and*
    crushed. [Is 15–16; 25:10–12;
    Ezek 25:8–11; Amos 2:1–3; Zeph
    2:8–11]
2 "The glory of Moab is no more;
In Heshbon they planned evil
    against her,
Saying, 'Come, let us cut her off
    from being a nation!'
You also, O [city of] Madmen, shall
    be silenced;
The sword will pursue you.
3 "The sound of an outcry from
    Horonaim,
'Desolation and great destruction!'
4 "Moab is destroyed;

Her little ones have called out a
    cry *of distress* [to be heard as far
    as Zoar].
5 "For the Ascent of Luhith
Will be climbed by [successive
    groups of] fugitives with
    continual weeping;
For on the descent of Horonaim
They have heard the distress of
    the cry of destruction.
6 "Run! Save your lives,
That you may be like a juniper in
    the wilderness.
7 "For because you have trusted in
    your works [your hand-made
    idols] and in your treasures
    [instead of in God],
Even you yourself will be
    captured;
And Chemosh [your disgusting
    god cannot rescue you, but] will
    go away into exile [along with
    the fugitives]
Together with his priests and his
    princes.
8 "And the destroyer will come upon
    every city;
No city will escape.
The [Jordan] valley also will be
    ruined
And the plain will be devastated,
As the LORD has said.
9 "Give a gravestone to Moab,
For she will fall into ruins;
Her cities (pastures, farms) will be
    desolate,
Without anyone to live in them.
10 "Cursed is the one who does the
    work of the LORD negligently,
And cursed is the one who
    restrains his sword from blood
    [in executing the judgment of
    the LORD].

11 "Moab has been at ease from his
    youth;
He has also been undisturbed, and
    settled like wine on his dregs,
And he has not been emptied from
    one vessel to another,

Nor has he gone into exile.
Therefore his flavor remains in
  him,
And his scent has not changed.

12"Therefore behold, the days are coming," says the LORD, "when I will send to Moab those who will tip him over and who will empty his vessels and break his [earthenware] jars in pieces. 13"And Moab shall be ashamed of Chemosh [his worthless, disgusting god], as the house of Israel was ashamed of Bethel, their [misplaced] confidence. [1 Kin 12:28, 29]

14"How can you say, 'We are great
  warriors
And valiant men in war?'
15"Moab has been made desolate and
  his cities have gone up [in smoke
  and flame];
And his chosen young men have
  gone down to the slaughter,"
Says the King, whose name is the
  LORD of hosts.
16"The destruction of Moab will
  come soon,
And his disaster hurries quickly.
17"Show sympathy for him, all you
  [nations] who are around him,
And all you [distant nations] who
  know his name;
Say, 'How has the mighty scepter
  [of national power] been broken,
And the splendid staff [of glory]!'
18"Come down from your glory,
O Daughter living in Dibon,
And sit on the parched ground
  [among the thirsty]!
For the destroyer of Moab has
  advanced against you;
He has destroyed your
  strongholds.
19"O inhabitant of Aroer,
Stand by the road and keep watch!
Ask [of] him who flees and [ask
  of] her who escapes,
Saying, 'What has happened?'

20"Moab is shamed, for she has been
  broken down and shattered.
Wail and cry out!
Tell by [the banks of] the Arnon
That Moab has been destroyed.

21"Judgment has come on [the land of] the plain—upon Holon, Jahzah, and against Mephaath, 22against Dibon, Nebo, and Beth-diblathaim, 23against Kiriathaim, Beth-gamul, and Beth-meon, 24against Kerioth, Bozrah and all the cities of the land of Moab, far and near. 25"The horn (strength) of Moab has been cut off and his arm [of authority] is shattered," says the LORD. 26"Make him drunk, for he has become arrogant and magnified himself against the LORD [by denying Reuben's occupation of the land the LORD had assigned him]. Moab also will wallow in his vomit, and he too shall become a laughingstock. [Num 22:1–7] 27"For was not Israel a laughingstock to you? Was he caught among thieves? For whenever you speak of him you shake your head in scorn.

28"You inhabitants of Moab,
Leave the cities and live among the
  rocks,
And be like the dove that makes
  her nest
In the walls of the yawning ravine.
29"We have heard of the [giddy]
  pride of Moab, the extremely
  proud one—
His haughtiness, his arrogance, his
  conceit, and his self-exaltation.
30"I know his [insolent] wrath," says
  the LORD,
"But it is futile;
His idle boasts [in his deeds] have
  accomplished nothing.
31"Therefore I will wail over Moab,
And I will cry out for all Moab.

I will sigh *and* mourn over the men of Kir-heres (Kir-hareseth). [Is 15:1; 16:7, 11]

³²"O vines of Sibmah, I will weep for you

More than the weeping of Jazer [over its ruins and wasted vineyards].

Your tendrils [of influence] stretched across the sea,

Reaching [even] to the sea of Jazer.

The destroyer has fallen

On your summer fruits and your [season's] crop of grapes.

³³"So joy and gladness are taken away From the fruitful field and from the land of Moab.

And I have made the wine cease from the wine presses;

No one treads *the grapes* with shouting.

Their shouting is not joyful shouting [but is instead, a battle cry].

³⁴"From the outcry at Heshbon even to Elealeh, even to Jahaz they have raised their voice, from Zoar even to Horonaim and Eglath-shelishiyah; for even the waters of Nimrim will become desolations.

³⁵"Moreover, I will cause to cease in Moab," says the Lᴏʀᴅ, "the one who ascends *and* offers sacrifice in the high place and the one who burns incense to his gods.

³⁶"Therefore My heart moans *and* sighs for Moab like flutes, and My heart moans *and* sighs like flutes for the men of Kir-heres (Kir-hareseth); therefore [the remnant of] the abundant riches they gained has perished.

³⁷"For every head is [shaven] bald and every beard cut off; there are cuts (slashes) on all the hands and sackcloth on the loins [all expressions of mourning]. [Is 15:2, 3]

³⁸"On all the housetops of Moab and in its streets there is lamentation (expressions of grief for the dead) everywhere, for I have broken Moab like a vessel in which there is no pleasure," says the Lᴏʀᴅ.

³⁹"How it is broken down! How they have wailed! How Moab has turned his back in shame! So Moab will become a laughingstock and a [horrifying] terror to all who are around him."

⁴⁰For thus says the Lᴏʀᴅ:

"Behold, one (Nebuchadnezzar of Babylon) will fly swiftly like an eagle

And spread out his wings against Moab. [Ezek 17:3]

⁴¹"Kerioth [and the cities] has been taken

And the strongholds seized;

And the hearts of the warriors of Moab in that day

Shall be like the heart of a woman in childbirth.

⁴²"Moab will be destroyed from being a nation (people)

Because he has become arrogant *and* magnified himself against the Lᴏʀᴅ.

⁴³"Terror and pit and snare are before you,

O inhabitant of Moab," says the Lᴏʀᴅ. [Is 24:7]

⁴⁴"The one who flees from the terror

Will fall into the pit,

And the one who gets up out of the pit

Will be taken *and* caught in the trap;

For I shall bring upon it, even upon Moab,

The year of their punishment," says the Lᴏʀᴅ.

⁴⁵"In the shadow of Heshbon

The fugitives stand powerless [helpless and without strength],

For a fire has gone out from Heshbon,

A flame from the midst of Sihon;

It has destroyed the forehead of Moab

And the crowns of the heads of
  [the arrogant Moabites] the ones
  in tumult.
46 "Woe (judgment is coming) to you,
  O Moab!
The people of [the pagan god
  called] Chemosh have perished;
For your sons have been taken
  away captive
And your daughters into captivity.
47 "Yet I will return the captives and
  restore the fortunes of Moab
In the latter days," says the Lord.

Thus far is the judgment on Moab.

49 CONCERNING THE sons
  (descendants) of Ammon.

Thus says the Lord:
"Does Israel have no sons
  [to reclaim Gad from the
  Ammonites]?
Has he no heir?
Why then has Malcam taken
  possession of Gad
And [why do] his people live in the
  cities [of Gad]?
2 "Therefore behold, the days are
  coming," says the Lord,
"When I will cause an alarm of
  war to be heard
Against Rabbah of the Ammonites;
And it [along with the high ground
  on which it stands] will become
  a desolate heap,
And its villages will be set on fire.
Then will Israel take possession of
  his possessors,"
Says the Lord. [Ezek 21:28–32; 25:1–
  7, 11; Amos 1:13–15; Zeph 2:8–11]
3 "Wail, O Heshbon, for Ai [in
  Ammon] has been destroyed!
Cry out, O daughters of Rabbah!
Wrap yourselves with sackcloth
  and lament (cry out in grief),
And rush back and forth inside the
  enclosures;

For Malcam [your powerless god]
  will go into exile
Together with his priests and his
  princes.
4 "Why do you boast of your valleys?
Your valley is flowing away,
[O Ammon] rebellious and
  faithless daughter
Who trusts in her treasures, saying,
'Who will come against me?'
5 "Behold, I am going to bring terror
  on you,"
Says the Lord God of hosts,
"From all who are around you;
And each of you will be driven out
  headlong,
And there will be no one to gather
  the fugitives together.
6 "But afterward I will reverse
The captivity of the children
  of Ammon and restore their
  fortunes,"
Says the Lord.

7 Concerning Edom.
Thus says the Lord of hosts,
"Is there no longer any wisdom in
  Teman?
Has good counsel vanished from
  the intelligent and prudent?
Has their wisdom decayed? [Is 34;
  63:1–6; Ezek 25:12–14; 35; Amos
  1:11, 12; Obad 1–16; Mal 1:2–5]
8 "Flee, turn back, dwell in the
  depths [of the desert to escape
  the judgment of Edom],
O inhabitants of Dedan,
For I will bring the destruction of
  Esau (Edom) upon him
When I inspect and punish him.
9 "If grape gatherers came to you,
Would they not leave some
  ungleaned grapes [on the vines]?
If thieves came by night,
Would they not destroy [only]
  what is enough [for them]?
10 "But I have stripped Esau (Edom)
  bare;
I have uncovered his hiding places
And he cannot hide himself.

His descendants have been
   destroyed along with his brothers
   (relatives) and his neighbors;
And he is no more.
11 "Leave your orphans behind; I will
   [do what is needed to] keep them
   alive.
And let [those who are] your
   widows trust *and* confide in Me."

12 For thus says the Lord, "Behold,
those (Israel) who were not sentenced
to drink the cup [of wrath] shall certainly drink it, and are you to remain
unpunished? You will not be acquitted
and go unpunished, but you will certainly drink [from the cup of wrath
and judgment]. [Jer 25:28, 29]
13 "For I have sworn [an oath] by
Myself," says the Lord, "that Bozrah
will become an object of horror, a reproach, a ruin, and a curse; and all its
cities will become perpetual ruins."

14 I have heard a report from the
   Lord,
And a messenger has been sent to
   the nations, saying,
"Gather together and come against
   her,
And rise up for the battle."
15 "For behold, [Edom] I have made
   you small among the nations
And despised among men. [Ezek
   35:9]
16 "As for Your terror,
The pride *and* arrogance of your
   heart have deceived you,
O you who live in the clefts of the
   rock (Sela also called Petra),
Who hold *and* occupy the height of
   the hill.
Though you make your nest as
   high as the eagle's,
I will bring you down from there,"
   says the Lord.

17 "Edom will become an object of
horror; everyone who goes by it will
be astonished and shall hiss [scorn-
fully] at all its plagues *and* disasters.

18 "As [it was] in the overthrow of
Sodom and Gomorrah with their neighboring cities," says the Lord, "no man
will live there, nor will a son of man
dwell in it.
19 "See, one will come like a lion from
the thicket of the Jordan against the
enduring habitation [of Edom] *and* its
watered pastures; for in an instant I
will make him (Edom) run from his
land. I will appoint over him the one
whom I choose. For who is like Me,
and who will summon Me [into court]
and prosecute Me [for this]? Who is
the [earthly] shepherd who can stand
[defiantly] before Me?"
20 Therefore hear the plan of the
Lord which He has devised against
Edom, and [hear] what He has purposed against the inhabitants of
Teman: surely they will be dragged
away, even the little ones of the flock;
surely He will make their dwelling
place desolate because of them.
21 The earth has quaked at the noise
of their downfall. There is an outcry!
The sound of its noise has been heard
at the Red Sea.
22 Behold, He will mount up and fly
swiftly like an eagle and spread His
wings against [the city of] Bozrah;
and in that day the heart of the mighty
warriors of Edom will be like the heart
of a woman in childbirth. [Jer 48:41]
23 Concerning Damascus [in Syria].

"Hamath and Arpad are perplexed
   and shamed,
For they have heard bad news;
They are disheartened;
Troubled *and* anxious like a
   [storm-tossed] sea
Which cannot be calmed.
24 "Damascus has become helpless;
She has turned away to flee,
Terror (panic) has seized her;
Anguish and distress have gripped
   her
Like a woman in childbirth.

25 "Why has the renowned city not
    been deserted,
The city of My joy!
26 "Therefore, her young men will
    fall in her streets,
And all her men of war will be
    destroyed in that day," says the
    Lord of hosts. [Is 17:1–3; Amos
    1:3–5; Zech 9:1]
27 "I will set fire to the wall of
    Damascus,
And it will consume the palaces of
    Ben-hadad."

28 Concerning Kedar and concerning
the kingdoms of Hazor, which Nebuchadnezzar king of Babylon defeated.
Thus says the Lord,

"Arise, go up against Kedar
And destroy the men of the east.
29 "They (the Babylonians) will take
    away their tents and their flocks;
They will carry off for themselves
Their tent curtains, all their goods
    and their camels,
And they will call out to one
    another, 'Terror on every side!'
    [Ps 31:13; Jer 6:25; 20:3, 10; 46:5]
30 "Flee, run far away! Dwell in the
    depths [of the desert],
O inhabitants of Hazor," says the
    Lord,
"For Nebuchadnezzar king of
    Babylon has planned a course of
    action against you
And devised a scheme against you.
31 "Arise [Nebuchadnezzar], go up
    against a nation which is at ease,
Which lives securely," says the
    Lord,
"A nation which has neither gates
    nor bars;
They dwell apart and alone.
32 "Their camels will become plunder,
And their herds of cattle a spoil;
And I will scatter to all the [four]
    winds those who cut the corners
    of their hair [as evidence of their
    idolatry],

And I will bring their disaster
    from every side," says the Lord.
    [Lev 19:27]
33 "Hazor will become a haunt and
    dwelling place of jackals,
A desolation forever;
No one will live there,
Nor will a son of man reside in it."

34 The word of the Lord that came
to Jeremiah the prophet concerning
Elam, in the beginning of the reign of
Zedekiah king of Judah, saying:

35 "Thus says the Lord of hosts,
'Behold (listen carefully), I am
    going to break the bow of Elam,
The finest [weapon] of their
    strength.
36 'And I will bring upon Elam the
    four winds
From the four corners of heaven;
And I will scatter them toward all
    those winds,
And there will be no nation
To which the outcasts of Elam will
    not go.
37 'So I will cause Elam to be
    shattered (dismayed) before
    their enemies
And before those who seek their
    lives;
And I will bring disaster on them,
Even My fierce anger,' says the
    Lord.
'And I will send the sword after
    them
Until I have consumed them.
38 'Then I will set My throne [of
    judgment] in Elam
And I will destroy from there the
    king and princes,'
Says the Lord. [Neh 1:1; Esth 1:2;
    Dan 8:1, 2]
39 'But it will be in the last days (the
    end of days)
That I will reverse the captivity
    and restore the fortunes of
    Elam,'"
Says the Lord.

50

THE WORD that the LORD spoke concerning Babylon and concerning the land of the Chaldeans through Jeremiah the prophet: [Is 13:1–14:23; 47; Hab 1:1, 2]

2 "Declare among the nations.
Lift up a signal [to spread the news]—publish *and* proclaim it,
Do not conceal it; say,
'Babylon has been taken,
Bel [the patron god] has been shamed, Marduk (Bel) has been shattered.
Babylon's images have been shamed, her [worthless] idols have been thrown down.'

3 "For out of the north a nation (Media) has come against her which will make her land desolate, and no one will live there. They have fled, they have gone away—both man and animal.

4 "In those days and at that time," says the LORD, "the children of Israel will come, they and the children of Judah together; they will come up weeping [in repentance] as they come and seek the LORD their God [inquiring for and of Him].

5 "They will ask the way to Zion, with their faces in that direction, saying, 'Come, let us join ourselves to the LORD in an everlasting covenant that will not be forgotten.'

6 "My people have become lost sheep;
Their shepherds have led them astray.
They have made them turn aside [to the seductive places of idolatry] on the mountains.
They have gone along [from one sin to another] from mountain to hill;
They have forgotten their [own] resting place. [Is 53:6; 1 Pet 2:25]
7 "All who found them have devoured them;
And their adversaries have said, 'We are not guilty,

Because they have sinned against the LORD [and are no longer holy to Him], their [true] habitation of righteousness *and* justice,
Even the LORD, the [confident] hope of their fathers.'
8 "Wander away from the midst of Babylon
And go out of the land of the Chaldeans;
Be like the male goats [who serve as leaders] at the head of the flocks. [Jer 51:6, 9, 45; 2 Cor 6:17; Rev 18:4]
9 "For behold, I will stir up and bring up against Babylon
An assembly of great nations from the north country.
They will equip themselves *and* set up the battle lines against her;
From there she will be taken captive.
Their arrows will be like an expert warrior
Who will not return empty-handed.
10 "Chaldea will become plunder;
All who plunder her will be satisfied," says the LORD.

11 "Though you are glad, though you rejoice,
O you who plunder My heritage,
Though you are wanton *and* skip about like a heifer in the grass
And neigh like stallions,
12 Your mother [Babylon] shall be greatly shamed;
She who gave you birth will be ashamed.
Behold, *she will be* the least of the nations,
A wilderness, a parched land and a desert.
13 "Because of the wrath of the LORD she will not be inhabited
But she will be completely desolate;
Everyone who goes by Babylon will be appalled

And will hiss (mock) at all her
wounds *and* plagues.
14 "Set yourselves in battle formation
against Babylon on every side,
All you archers.
Shoot at her! Do not spare the
arrows,
For she has sinned against the LORD.
15 "Raise the battle cry against her on
every side!
She has given her hand
[in agreement] *and* has
surrendered; her pillars have
fallen,
Her walls have been torn down.
For this is the vengeance of the
LORD:
Take vengeance on her;
As she has done [to others], do to
her.
16 "Cut off the sower from Babylon
And the one who handles the
sickle at the time of harvest.
For fear of the sword of the
oppressor
Everyone will return to his own
people
And everyone will flee to his own
land.
17 "Israel is a hunted *and* scattered
flock [driven here and there as prey];
the lions have chased *them away*. First
the king of Assyria devoured him, and
now at last Nebuchadnezzar king of
Babylon has broken (gnawed) his
bones.
18 "Therefore thus says the LORD of
hosts, the God of Israel, 'Behold, I will
visit (inspect, examine) *and* punish
the king of Babylon and his land, just
as I visited *and* punished the king of
Assyria.
19 'And I will bring Israel [home]
again to his pasture and he will graze
on [the most fertile lands of] Carmel
[in the west] and Bashan [in the east],
and his soul will be satisfied on the
hills of Ephraim and Gilead.
20 'In those days and at that time,'

says the LORD, 'a search will be made
for the wickedness of Israel, but there
will be none and for the sins of Judah,
but none will be found, for I will pardon those whom I leave as a remnant.'
[Is 1:9; 43:25; Jer 31:34; 33:8; Rom 9:27]

21 "Go against [Babylon] the land of
Merathaim (Double Rebellion),
Go up against it and against the
people of Pekod (Punishment).
Kill and utterly destroy them," says
the LORD,
"And do everything that I have
commanded you."
22 "The noise of battle is in the land,
And [the noise of] great
destruction.
23 "How the hammer of the whole
earth
Is crushed and broken!
How Babylon has become
A horror [of desolation] among the
nations!
24 "I set a trap for you and you also
were caught, O Babylon,
And you did not know it;
You have been found and also
seized
Because you have struggled
against the LORD."
25 The LORD has opened His armory
And has brought out [the nations
who unknowingly are] the
weapons of His indignation
(wrath),
For it is a work of the Lord GOD of
hosts
In the land of the Chaldeans.
26 Come against her from the farthest
border.
Open her storehouses;
Pile it up like heaps of rubbish.
Burn *and* destroy her completely;
Let nothing be left of her.
27 Kill all her young bulls [her
strength—her young men];
Let them go down to the slaughter!
Woe (judgment is coming) to the
Chaldeans, for their day has come,

The time of their punishment.

²⁸Listen to the voice of the refugees
who flee and escape from the
land of Babylon,
Proclaiming in Zion the vengeance
of the Lᴏʀᴅ our God,
The vengeance [of the Lᴏʀᴅ against
the Chaldeans] for [plundering
and destroying] His temple.

²⁹"Call together many [archers]
against Babylon,
All those who bend the bow.
Encamp against her on every side;
Let no one from there escape.
Repay her according to her actions;
Just as she has done, do to her.
For she has been proudly defiant
and presumptuous against the
Lᴏʀᴅ,
Against the Holy One of Israel.

³⁰"Therefore her young men will fall
in her streets,
And all her soldiers will be
destroyed on that day," says the
Lᴏʀᴅ.

³¹"Behold, I am against you, [O
Babylon, you] arrogant one, [you
who are pride and presumption
personified],"
Says the Lord Gᴏᴅ of hosts,
"For your day has come,
The time when I will punish you.

³²"The arrogant (proud) one will
stumble and fall
With no one to raise him up;
And I will set fire to his cities
And it will devour all who are
around him."

³³Thus says the Lᴏʀᴅ of hosts,
"The children of Israel are
oppressed,
And the children of Judah as well;
And all who took them captive
have held them tightly,
They have refused to let them go.

³⁴"Their Redeemer is strong; the
Lᴏʀᴅ of hosts is His name.

He will most certainly plead their
case and defend their cause
So that He may bring rest to their
land,
But turmoil to the inhabitants of
Babylon.

³⁵"A sword against the Chaldeans,"
says the Lᴏʀᴅ,
"And against the inhabitants of
Babylon
And against her princes (officials,
civic rulers) and against her wise
men (astrologers, religious rulers)!

³⁶"A sword against the oracle priests
(the babbling liars), and they
will become fools!
A sword against her mighty
warriors, and they will be
shattered and destroyed!

³⁷"A sword against their horses and
against their chariots
And against all the foreign troops
that are in her midst,
And they will become [as weak
and defenseless as] women!
A sword against her treasures, and
they will be plundered!

³⁸"A drought on her waters, and they
will dry up!
For it is a land of [worthless] idols,
And they are mad over fearsome
idols [those objects of terror in
which they foolishly trust].

³⁹"Therefore wild beasts of the desert
will live there [in Babylon] with
the jackals;
The ostriches also will live there,
And it will never again be
inhabited [with people]
Or lived in from generation to
generation. [Is 13:20–22]

⁴⁰"As when God overthrew Sodom
And Gomorrah and their
neighboring cities," says the Lᴏʀᴅ,
"So no man will live there;
Nor shall any son of man live
there." [Jer 49:18]

⁴¹"Behold, a people is coming from
the north,

And a great nation and many kings
Will be stirring from the remote
parts of the earth.
42 "They seize their bow and spear;
They are cruel and have no
compassion.
They sound like the roaring of the
sea;
They ride on horses,
Every man equipped like a man
[ready] for the battle
Against you, O Daughter of
Babylon.
43 "The king of Babylon has heard
the report about them,
And his hands fall limp *and*
helpless;
Anguish has seized him,
And agony like that of a woman in
childbirth.

44 "See, one will come up like a lion
from the thicket of the Jordan against
the enduring habitation [of Babylon]
and its watered pastures; for in an instant I will make Babylon run from his
land. I will appoint over Babylon the
one whom I choose. For who is like Me,
and who will summon Me [into court]
and prosecute Me [for this]? Who is
the [earthly] shepherd who can stand
[defiantly] before Me?" [Jer 49:19]

45 Therefore hear the plan of the LORD
which He has devised against Babylon, and hear what He has purposed
against [the inhabitants of the land
of] the Chaldeans: surely they will be
dragged away, [even] the little ones of
the flock; surely He will make their
habitation desolate because of them.

46 At the shout, "Babylon has been
seized!" the earth quakes, and an outcry is heard among the nations.

51

THUS SAYS the LORD:

"Behold, I am going to stir
up *and* put into action [a fury]
against Babylon

And against the [rebellious]
people of Leb-kamai (Chaldea)
A destroying wind *and* hostile
spirit;
2 "And I will send foreigners to
Babylon that they may winnow
her
And may devastate *and* empty her
land;
For in the day of destruction
They will be against her on every
side.
3 "Do not let him (the Chaldean
defender) who bends his bow
bend it,
Nor let him rise up in his coat of
armor.
So do not spare her young men;
Devote her entire army to
destruction.
4 "They shall fall down dead in the
land of the Chaldeans,
And wounded in her streets."

5 For neither Israel nor Judah has
been abandoned
By his God, the LORD of hosts,
Though their land is full of sin *and*
guilt
Before the Holy One of Israel.
6 Flee out of Babylon,
Let every one of you save his life!
Do not be destroyed in her
punishment,
For this is the time of the LORD's
vengeance;
He is going to pay her what she
has earned. [Jer 50:28; 2 Cor 6:17;
Rev 18:4]
7 Babylon has been a golden cup in
the LORD's hand,
Intoxicating all the earth.
The nations drank her wine;
Therefore the nations have gone
mad. [Rev 14:8; 17:4]
8 Babylon has suddenly fallen and is
shattered!
Wail for her [if you care to]!
Get balm for her [incurable] pain;
Perhaps she may be healed. [Jer
25:15; Rev 14:8–10; 16:19; 18:2, 3]

9 We would have healed Babylon,
   but she was not to be healed.
Abandon her and let each [captive]
   return to his own country,
For her guilt *and* judgment have
   reached to heaven
And are lifted up to the very skies.
   [Gen 18:20, 21]
10 The LORD has brought about our
   vindication *and* has revealed the
   righteousness of our cause;
Come and let us proclaim in Zion
The work of the LORD our God!

11 Sharpen the arrows, take up the
   shields [and cover yourselves]!
The LORD has stirred up the spirit
   of the kings of the Medes,
Because His purpose concerning
   Babylon is to destroy it;
For that is the vengeance of the
   LORD, vengeance [on Babylon] for
   [plundering and destroying] His
   temple.
12 Set up a signal on the walls of
   Babylon [to spread the news];
Post a strong blockade,
Station the guards,
Prepare the men for ambush!
For the LORD has both purposed
   and done
That which He spoke against the
   people of Babylon.
13 [O Babylon] you who live by many
   waters,
Rich in treasures,
Your end has come,
And the line measuring your life is
   cut. [Rev 17:1–6]
14 The LORD of hosts has sworn [an
   oath] by Himself, saying,
"Surely I will fill you with men, as
   with [a swarm of] locusts [who
   strip the land clean],
And they will lift up a song *and*
   shout of victory over you."

15 He made the earth by His power;
He established the world by His
   wisdom
And stretched out the heavens by
   His understanding.
16 When He utters His voice, *there
   is* a tumult of waters in the
   heavens,
And He causes the clouds to ascend
   from the ends of the earth.
He makes lightnings for the rain
And brings out the wind from His
   storehouses.
17 Every man has become stupid *and*
   brutelike, without knowledge [of
   God];
Every goldsmith is shamed by the
   cast images he has made;
For his molten idols are a lie,
And there is no breath [of life] *or*
   spirit in them.
18 They are worthless (empty, false,
   futile), a work of delusion *and*
   worthy of derision;
In the time of their inspection *and*
   punishment they will perish.
19 The Portion of Jacob [the true
   God of Israel] is not like these
   [handmade gods];
For He is the Maker of all *and* the
   One who formed *and* fashioned
   all things,
And Israel is the tribe of His
   inheritance—
The LORD of hosts is His name. [Jer
   10:12–16]
20 "You [Cyrus of Persia, soon to
   conquer Babylon] are My battle-
   axe and weapon of war—
For with you I shatter nations,
With you I destroy kingdoms.
21 "With you I shatter the horse and
   his rider,
With you I shatter the chariot and
   its driver,
22 With you I shatter man and woman,
With you I shatter old man and
   youth,
With you I shatter young man and
   virgin,
23 With you I shatter the shepherd
   and his flock,

With you I shatter the farmer and
　his yoke of oxen,
And with you I shatter governors
　and commanders.

24"And I will [completely] repay
Babylon and all the people of Chaldea for all the evil that they have done
in Zion—before your very eyes [I will
do it]," says the LORD.

25"Behold, I am against you,
　O destroying mountain [conqueror
　　of nations],
Who destroys the whole earth,"
　declares the LORD,
"I will stretch out My hand against
　you,
And roll you down from the
　[rugged] cliffs,
And will make you a burnt
　mountain (extinct volcano).
26"They will not take from you
　[even] a stone for a cornerstone
Nor any rock for a foundation,
But you will be desolate forever,"
　says the LORD.

27Lift up a signal in the land [to
　spread the news]!
Blow the trumpet among the
　nations!
Dedicate the nations [for war]
　against her;
Call against her the kingdoms of
　Ararat, Minni, and Ashkenaz.
Appoint a marshal against her;
Cause the horses to come up like
　bristly locusts [with their wings
　not yet released from their
　cases].
28Prepare and dedicate the nations
　for war against her—
The kings of Media,
With their governors and
　commanders,
And every land of their dominion.
29The land trembles and writhes [in
　pain and sorrow],
For the purposes of the LORD
　against Babylon stand,

To make the land of Babylon
A desolation without inhabitants.
30The mighty warriors of Babylon
　have ceased to fight;
They remain in their strongholds.
Their strength and power have
　failed;
They are becoming [weak and
　helpless] like women.
Their dwelling places are set on
　fire;
The bars on her gates are broken.
31One courier runs to meet another,
And one messenger to meet
　another,
To tell the king of Babylon
That his city has been captured
　from end to end;
32And that the fords [across the
　Euphrates] have been blocked
　and [the ferries] seized,
And they have set the [great]
　marshes on fire,
And the men of war are terrified.

33For thus says the LORD of hosts, the
God of Israel:

"The Daughter of Babylon is like a
　threshing floor
At the time it is being trampled
　and prepared;
Yet in a little while the time of
　harvest will come for her."

34"Nebuchadnezzar king of Babylon
　has devoured me, he has
　crushed me,
He has set me down like an empty
　vessel.
Like a monster he has swallowed
　me up,
He has filled his belly with my
　delicacies;
He has spit me out and washed me
　away.
35"May the violence done to me and
　to my flesh and blood be upon
　Babylon,"
The inhabitant of Zion will say;

And, "May my blood be upon the inhabitants of Chaldea,"
Jerusalem will say.

36 Therefore thus says the Lord,

"Behold, I will plead your case
And take full vengeance for you;
I will dry up her sea *and* great reservoir
And make her fountain dry.
37 "Babylon will become a heap [of ruins], a haunt *and* dwelling place of jackals,
An object of horror (an astonishing desolation) and a hissing [of scorn and amazement], without inhabitants.
38 "They (the Chaldean lords) will be roaring together [before their sudden capture] like young lions [roaring over their prey],
They (the princes) will be growling like lions' cubs.
39 "When they are inflamed [with wine and lust during their drinking bouts], I will prepare them a feast [of My wrath]
And make them drunk, that they may rejoice
And may sleep a perpetual sleep
And not wake up," declares the Lord.
40 "I will bring them down like lambs to the slaughter,
Like rams together with male goats.

41 "How Sheshak (Babylon) has been captured,
And the praise of the whole earth been seized!
How Babylon has become an astonishing desolation *and* an object of horror among the nations!
42 "The sea has come up over Babylon;
She has been engulfed with its tumultuous waves.
43 "Her cities have become an astonishing desolation *and* an object of horror,

A parched land and a desert,
A land in which no one lives,
And through which no son of man passes.
44 "I will punish *and* judge Bel [the handmade god] in Babylon
And take out of his mouth what he has swallowed up [the stolen sacred articles and the captives of Judah and elsewhere].
The nations will no longer flow to him.
Yes, the wall of Babylon has fallen down!

45 "Come out of her midst, My people,
And each of you [escape and] save yourself
From the fierce anger of the Lord. [Jer 50:8; 2 Cor 6:17; Rev 18:4]
46 "Now *beware* so that you do not lose heart,
And so that you are not afraid at the rumor that will be heard in the land—
For the rumor shall come one year,
And after that another rumor in another year,
And violence *shall be* in the land,
Ruler against ruler—
47 "Therefore behold (listen carefully), the days are coming
When I will judge *and* punish the idols of Babylon;
Her whole land will be perplexed *and* shamed,
And all her slain will fall in her midst.
48 "Then heaven and earth and all that is in them
Will shout *and* sing for joy over Babylon,
For the destroyers will come against her from the north,"
Says the Lord. [Is 44:23; Jer 51:11; Rev 12:12; 18:20]

49 Indeed Babylon is to fall for the slain of Israel,

As also for Babylon the slain of all
the earth have fallen.
50 You who have escaped the sword,
Go away! Do not stay!
Remember the LORD from far away,
And let [desolate] Jerusalem come
into your mind.
51 We are perplexed *and* ashamed,
for we have heard reproach;
Disgrace has covered our faces,
For foreigners [from Babylon]
have come
Into the [most] sacred parts of
the sanctuary of the LORD [even
those places forbidden to all but
the appointed priest].
52 "Therefore behold, the days are
coming," says the LORD,
"When I will judge *and* punish the
idols [of Babylon],
And throughout her land the
mortally wounded will groan."
53 "Though Babylon should ascend to
the heavens,
And though she should fortify her
lofty stronghold,
Yet destroyers will come on her
from Me," says the LORD.
54 The sound of an outcry [comes]
from Babylon,
And [the sound] of great destruction
from the land of the Chaldeans!
55 For the LORD is going to destroy
Babylon *and* make her a ruin,
And He will still her great voice
[that hums with city life].
And the waves [of her conquerors]
roar like great waters,
The noise of their voices is raised up
[like the marching of an army].
56 For the destroyer is coming against
her, against Babylon;
And her mighty warriors will be
captured,
Their bows are shattered;
For the LORD is a God of [just]
restitution;
He will fully repay.

57 "I will make her princes and her
wise men drunk,
Her governors and her
commanders and her mighty
warriors;
They will sleep a perpetual sleep
and not wake up,"
Says the King—the LORD of hosts is
His name.
58 Thus says the LORD of hosts,
"The broad wall of Babylon will be
completely overthrown *and* the
foundations razed
And her high gates will be set on
fire;
The peoples will labor in vain,
And the nations become exhausted
[only] for fire [that will destroy
their work]." [Hab 2:13]

59 The message which Jeremiah the
prophet commanded Seraiah the son
of Neriah, the grandson of Mahseiah,
when he went with Zedekiah the king
of Judah to Babylon in the fourth year
of his reign. Now this Seraiah was
chief chamberlain *or* quartermaster
[and brother of Baruch].
60 So Jeremiah wrote in a single scroll
all the disaster which would come
on Babylon, [that is] all these words
which have been written concerning
Babylon.
61 Then Jeremiah said to Seraiah,
"When you come to Babylon, see to it
that you read all these words aloud,
62 and say, 'You, O LORD, have promised concerning this place to cut it off
and destroy it, so that there shall be
nothing living in it, neither man nor
animal, but it will be perpetually desolate.'
63 "And as soon as you finish reading this scroll, you shall tie a stone to
it and throw it into the middle of the
Euphrates.
64 "Then say, 'In the same way Babylon will sink down and not rise because of the disaster that I will bring

on her; and the Babylonians will become [hopelessly] exhausted.'" Thus the words of Jeremiah are completed. [Rev 18:21]

52 ZEDEKIAH WAS twenty-one years old when he became king, and he reigned eleven years in Jerusalem; and his mother's name was Hamutal the daughter of Jeremiah of Libnah. [2 Kin 24:18–25:21]

²He did that which was evil in the sight of the LORD like all that Jehoiakim had done.

³For all this came about in Jerusalem and Judah because of the anger of the LORD, and [in the end] He cast them from His presence. And Zedekiah rebelled against the king of Babylon.

⁴Now it came about in the ninth year of his reign, in the tenth month, on the tenth day, Nebuchadnezzar king of Babylon came, he and all his army, against Jerusalem; and they camped against it and built moveable towers *and* siege mounds all around it. [Jer 39:1–10]

⁵So the city was besieged until the eleventh year of King Zedekiah. [2 Chr 36:11–13]

⁶In the fourth month, on the ninth day of the month, the famine was so severe in the city that there was no food for the people of the land.

⁷Then the city was broken into, and all the soldiers fled. They left the city at night [as Ezekiel prophesied] passing through the gate between the two walls by the king's garden, though the Chaldeans were all around the city. They fled by way of the Arabah (the Jordan Valley). [Ezek 12:12]

⁸But the army of the Chaldeans pursued the king and overtook Zedekiah in the plains of Jericho; and his entire army was scattered from him.

⁹Then they seized the king and brought him to the king of Babylon at Riblah in the [Syrian] land of Hamath [on the northern border of Israel], where he pronounced sentence on him.

¹⁰The king of Babylon killed the sons of Zedekiah before his eyes; he also killed all the princes of Judah at Riblah.

¹¹Then the king of Babylon blinded Zedekiah, bound him with bronze shackles and took him to Babylon and there he put him in prison [in a mill] until the day of his death. [Ezek 12:13]

¹²Now in the fifth month, on the tenth day, which was the nineteenth year of Nebuchadnezzar king of Babylon, Nebuzaradan captain of the guard, who served the king of Babylon, came to Jerusalem.

¹³He burned down the house of the LORD and the king's palace and all the houses of Jerusalem; every great house *or* important structure he set on fire.

¹⁴So all the army of the Chaldeans who were with the captain of the guard broke down all the walls around Jerusalem.

¹⁵Then Nebuzaradan the captain of the guard took away into exile some of the poorest of the people, those who were left in the city [at the time it was captured], along with those who deserted to join the king of Babylon [during the siege] and the rest of the artisans.

¹⁶But Nebuzaradan the captain of the guard left some of the poorest of the land to be vinedressers and farmers.

¹⁷Now the Chaldeans broke into pieces the pillars of bronze which belonged to the house of the LORD, and the bronze pedestals [which supported the ten basins] and the [enormous] bronze Sea, which were in the house of the LORD, and carried all the bronze to Babylon.

¹⁸They also took away the pots [for carrying away ashes] and the shovels and the snuffers and the bowls and the spoons and all the bronze articles used in the *temple* service.

¹⁹The captain of the guard also took away the [small] bowls and the fire-pans and the basins and the pots and the lampstands and the incense cups and the bowls for the drink offerings—whatever was made of fine gold and whatever was made of fine silver.

²⁰The two pillars, the one [enormous] Sea (basin), and the twelve bronze bulls under the Sea, and the stands, which King Solomon had made for the house of the LORD—the bronze of all these things was beyond weighing.

²¹Concerning the pillars, the height of each pillar was eighteen cubits (twenty-seven feet), and a line [an ornamental molding] of twelve cubits (eighteen feet) went around its circumference; it was four fingers thick, and [the pillar was] hollow.

²²A capital of bronze was on [top of] it. The height of each capital was five cubits (seven and one-half feet), with a lattice-work and pomegranates around it, all of bronze. The second pillar also, with its pomegranates, was similar to these.

²³There were ninety-six pomegranates on the sides; and a hundred pomegranates were on the lattice-work all around.

²⁴Then the captain of the guard took [as prisoners] Seraiah the chief priest and Zephaniah the second priest and the three doorkeepers.

²⁵He also took out of the city one official who was overseer of the soldiers, and seven of the king's advisers who were found in the city, and the scribe of the commander of the army who mustered the people of the land, and sixty men who were still in the city.

²⁶Nebuzaradan the captain of the guard took them and brought them to the king of Babylon at Riblah.

²⁷Then the king of Babylon struck them down and put them to death at Riblah in the land of Hamath. So Judah was led away into exile from its own land.

²⁸This is the number of people whom Nebuchadnezzar took captive and exiled: in the seventh year, 3,023 Jews;

²⁹in the eighteenth year of Nebuchadnezzar, [he took captive] 832 persons from Jerusalem;

³⁰in the twenty-third year of Nebuchadnezzar, Nebuzaradan the captain of the [Babylonian] guard took captive 745 Jewish people; there were 4,600 persons in all.

³¹Now it came about in the thirty-seventh year of the exile of Jehoiachin [also called Coniah and Jeconiah] king of Judah, in the twelfth month, on the twenty-fifth of the month, Evil-merodach king of Babylon, in the first year of his reign, showed favor to Jehoiachin king of Judah and brought him out of prison. [2 Kin 25:27–30]

³²He spoke kindly to him and gave him a throne above the thrones of the kings who were [captives] with him in Babylon.

³³Jehoiachin changed his prison clothes, and he dined regularly at the king's table all the days of his life.

³⁴And his allowance, a regular allowance was given to him by the king of Babylon, a daily portion [according to his needs] until the day of his death, all the days of his life.

Lamentations

Author:
Traditionally, Jeremiah

Date:
587 BC

Everyday Life Principles:
Bad things—even devastating things—happen. When they do, run to God and find comfort.

Even when we know we do not deserve God's mercy, we can still call upon Him. Because of His great compassion, He will hear us and help us.

Never stop hoping in God's mercy.

To "lament" is to feel intense sorrow, sadness, or grief, even to cry or to wail. This book, entitled Lamentations, focuses on suffering, loss, and hopelessness. It acknowledges the reality of pain, grief, and tragedy, not only in Old Testament times (pain and grief resulting from Israel's turning away from God), but in our lives today. Even though some of the circumstances of our suffering may be different from the Israelites' experience, the pain of suffering is just as real.

Against the dismal backdrop of Lamentations, a ray of hope begins to shine. Having written extensively about destruction at the beginning of Lamentations, the writer admits in Lamentations 3:17, "I have forgotten happiness." But then he begins to come out of his misery, saying: "But this I call to mind, therefore have I hope" (Lamentations 3:21). He then moves into one of the best-known, best-loved scriptures I know of: "It is because of the LORD's lovingkindnesses that we are not consumed, because His [tender] compassions never fail. They are new every morning; great and beyond measure is Your faithfulness" (Lamentations 3:22, 23).

No matter what you are facing today, let Lamentations remind you of God's faithfulness to you. Recall God's mercy in every situation, and let it give you hope and expectation!

1 HOW SOLITARY *and* lonely
sits the city [Jerusalem]
That was [once] full of people!
How like a widow she has become.
She who was great among the
nations!
The princess among the provinces,
Has become a forced laborer!
2 She weeps bitterly in the night
And her tears are [constantly] on
her cheeks;
Among all her lovers (political allies)
She has no one to comfort her.
All her friends have dealt
treacherously with her;
They have become her enemies.
[Jer 3:1; 4:30]
3 Judah has gone into exile under
affliction
And under harsh servitude;
She dwells among the [pagan]
nations,
But she has found no rest;
All her pursuers have overtaken her
In the midst of [her] distress.
4 The roads to Zion are in mourning
Because no one comes to the
appointed feasts.
All her gates are desolate;
Her priests are groaning,
Her virgins are grieved *and*
suffering,
And she suffers bitterly.
5 Her adversaries have become her
masters,
Her enemies prosper;
For the LORD has caused her grief
Because of the multitude of her
transgressions;
Her young children have gone
Into captivity before the enemy.
[Jer 30:14, 15; 52:28; Dan 9:7–14]
6 All her beauty *and* majesty
Have departed from the Daughter
of Zion (Jerusalem).
Her princes have become like deer
That have found no pasture;
They have fled without strength
Before the pursuer.

7 In the days of her affliction and
homelessness
Jerusalem remembers all her
precious things
That she had from the days of old,
When her people fell into the hand
of the adversary,
And no one helped her,
The enemy saw her,
They mocked at her downfall.
8 Jerusalem sinned greatly;
Therefore she has become an
unclean thing [and has been
removed].
All who honored her [now]
despise her
Because they have seen her
nakedness;
Even she herself groans and turns
[her face] away.
9 Her (ceremonial) uncleanness was
on her skirts;
She did not [seriously] consider
her future.
Therefore she has come down
[from throne to slavery] in an
astonishing manner;
She has no comforter.
"O LORD" [cries Jerusalem], "look at
my affliction,
For the enemy has magnified
himself [in triumph]!"
10 The adversary has spread out his
hand
Over all her precious *and* desirable
things;
For she has seen the [Gentile]
nations enter her sanctuary (the
Jerusalem temple)—
The ones whom You commanded
That they should not enter into
Your congregation [not even in
the outer courts]. [Deut 23:3; Jer
51:51; Ezek 44:7, 9]
11 All her people groan, seeking bread;
They have exchanged their
desirable *and* precious things for
food
To restore their lives.

"See, O Lord, and consider
How despised *and* repulsive I have
become!"
¹²"Is it nothing to you, all you who
pass this way?
Look and see if there is any pain
like my pain
Which was severely dealt out to
me,
Which the Lord has inflicted [on
me] on the day of His fierce
anger.
¹³"From on high He sent fire into my
bones,
And it prevailed *over them*.
He has spread a net for my feet;
He has turned me back.
He has made me desolate *and*
hopelessly miserable,
Faint all the day long.
¹⁴"The yoke of my transgressions is
bound;
By His hand they are knit *and*
woven together.
They have come upon my neck.
He has made my strength fail;
The Lord has put me into the hand
Of *those against whom* I cannot
stand. [Deut 28:48]
¹⁵"The Lord has rejected all the
strong men
In my midst;
He has proclaimed an established
time against me
To crush my young men.
The Lord has trampled down as in
a wine press
The Virgin Daughter of Judah.
¹⁶"I weep for these things;
My eyes overflow with tears,
Because a comforter,
One who could restore my soul, is
far away from me.
My children are desolate *and*
perishing,
For the enemy has prevailed."
[Lam 1:21]
¹⁷Zion stretches out her hands,
But there is no comforter for her.

The Lord has commanded
concerning Jacob
That his neighbors should be his
enemies;
Jerusalem has become a filthy
thing [an object of contempt]
among them.
¹⁸"The Lord is righteous *and* just;
For I have rebelled against His
commandment (His word).
Hear now, all you peoples,
And look at my pain;
My virgins and my young men
Have gone into captivity.
¹⁹"I [Jerusalem] called to my lovers
(political allies), but they
deceived me.
My priests and my elders perished
in the city
While they looked for food to
restore their strength.
²⁰"See, O Lord, how distressed I am!
My spirit is deeply disturbed;
My heart is overturned within me
and cannot rest,
For I have been very rebellious.
In the street the sword kills *and*
bereaves;
In the house there is [famine,
disease and] death!
²¹"People have heard that I groan,
That I have no comforter [in You].
All my enemies have heard of my
desperation;
They are delighted [O Lord] that
You have done it.
Oh, that You would bring the day
[of judgment] which You have
proclaimed
So that they will become like me.
[Is 14:5, 6; Jer 30:16]
²²"Let all their wickedness come
before You;
And deal with them as You have
dealt with me
Because of all my transgressions;
For my groans are many and my
heart is faint."

2 HOW THE Lord has covered
the Daughter of Zion
(Jerusalem)
With a cloud in His anger!
He has cast down from heaven to
the earth
The glory *and* splendor of Israel
And has not remembered His
footstool
In the day of His anger.
² The Lord has swallowed up; He
has not spared
All the country places of Jacob.
In His wrath He has thrown down
The strongholds of the Daughter of
Judah (Jerusalem).
He has brought them down to the
ground [in disgrace];
He has debased the kingdom and
its princes.
³ In fierce anger He has cut off *and*
destroyed
Every horn of Israel.
He has withdrawn His right hand
From the presence of the enemy.
And He has burned in Jacob like a
flaming fire
Consuming all around.
⁴ He has bent His bow like an enemy;
He has set His right hand like an
adversary
And slain all that were delightful
and pleasing to the eye;
In the tent of the Daughter of Zion
He has poured out His wrath like
fire.
⁵ The Lord has become like an
enemy;
He has swallowed up Israel.
He has swallowed up all its
palaces;
He has destroyed its strongholds
And multiplied in the Daughter of
Judah
Mourning and lamentation
(expressions of grief).
⁶ And He has violently broken down
His temple like a [fragile] garden
hedge;

He has destroyed His appointed
meeting place.
The Lord has caused the appointed
feast and Sabbath
To be forgotten in Zion
And has despised *and* rejected the
king and the priest
In the indignation of His anger.
⁷ The Lord has rejected His altar;
He has abandoned His sanctuary.
He has given into the hand of the
enemy
The walls of her palaces;
They have made a noise in the
house of the Lord
As on a day of an appointed feast.
⁸ The Lord determined to lay in ruins
The [city] wall of the Daughter of
Zion.
He has stretched out a line,
He has not stopped His hand from
destroying.
He has caused the rampart and the
wall to lament (mourn in grief);
They have languished together.
⁹ Her gates have sunk into the
ground;
He has destroyed and broken her
bars.
Her king and her princes are
[exiled] among the nations;
The law is no more.
Also, her prophets no longer find
Vision from the Lord.
¹⁰ The elders of the Daughter of Zion
Sit on the ground keeping silent;
They have thrown dust on their
heads,
They have covered themselves
with sackcloth.
The virgins of Jerusalem
Have bowed their heads to the
ground.
¹¹ My eyes fail because of tears
[mourns Jeremiah],
My spirit is deeply disturbed;
My heart is poured out on the
earth [in grief]

Because of the destruction of
   the daughter of my people
   [Jerusalem],
When little ones and infants faint
In the streets of the city.
12 They cry to their mothers,
   "Where is grain and wine?"
As they faint like a wounded man
In the streets of the city,
As their life [slips away and] is
   poured out
In their mothers' arms.
13 How shall I console you?
   To what shall I compare you,
O Daughter of Jerusalem?
With what shall I compare you, so
   that I may comfort you,
O Virgin Daughter of Zion?
For your ruin is as vast as the sea;
Who can heal you? [Lam 1:12;
   Dan 9:12]
14 Your prophets have seen
   (imagined) for you
False and foolish *visions;*
And they have not exposed your
   wickedness
To restore you from captivity [by
   teaching you to repent],
But they have seen (imagined)
   and declared to you false and
   misleading oracles.
15 All who pass along the way
   Clap their hands *in derision* at you;
They scoff and shake their heads
At the Daughter of Jerusalem,
   saying,
"Is this the city that was called
'The perfection of beauty,
The joy of all the earth'?"
16 All your enemies
   Have opened their mouths wide
   against you;

They [scornfully] hiss and gnash
   their teeth.
They say, "We have swallowed
   her up!
Certainly this is the day for which
   we waited;
We have reached it, we have
   seen it!"
17 The LORD has done what He
   planned;
He has accomplished His word
Which He commanded from days
   of old.
He has demolished without
   sparing,
And He has caused the enemy to
   rejoice over you;
He has exalted the power of your
   enemies. [Lev 26:14–39; Deut
   28:15–68]
18 Their hearts cried out to the Lord.
   "O wall of the Daughter of Zion,
Let your tears run down like a
   river day and night;
Give yourself no relief,
Let your eyes have no rest.
19 "Arise, cry aloud in the night,
At the beginning of the night
   watches;
Pour out your heart like water
Before the presence of the Lord;
Lift up your hands to Him
For the life of your little ones
Who are faint from hunger
At the head of every street." [Ps 62:8]
20 See, O LORD, and look!
With whom have You dealt this way?
Should women eat their offspring,
The little ones *who were born*
   healthy and beautiful?
Should priest and prophet be killed
In the sanctuary of the Lord?
21 The young and the old

speak the Word

Lord, I will pour out my heart like water before Your presence.
I will freely and fully express my feelings to You.
   –ADAPTED FROM LAMENTATIONS 2:19

Lie on the ground in the streets;
My virgins and my young men
Have fallen by the sword.
You have killed them in the day of
    Your anger,
You have slaughtered, not sparing.
22 You [LORD] called as in the day of
    an appointed feast
My terrors (dangers) on every
    side;
And there was no one who escaped
    or survived
In the day of the LORD's anger.
Those I have cared for and
    brought up with tenderness,
My enemy annihilated them.

3 I AM [Jeremiah] the man who
    has seen affliction
    Because of the rod of His
    wrath.
2 He has led me and made me walk
In darkness and not in light.
3 Surely He has turned His hand
    against me
Repeatedly all the day.
4 He has caused my flesh and my
    skin to waste away;
He has shattered my bones.
5 He has besieged and surrounded
    me with bitterness and hardship.
6 He has made me live in dark places
Like those who have long been
    dead.
7 He walled me in so that I cannot
    get out;
He has weighted down my chain.
8 Even when I cry out and shout for
    help,
He shuts out my prayer.
9 He has blocked my ways with cut
    stone;
He has made my paths crooked.
10 He is to me like a bear lying in wait,
And like a lion [hiding] in secret
    places.
11 He has turned aside my ways and
    torn me in pieces;
He has made me desolate.

life point

In Lamentations 3:19, 20, we read about
the writer of this book, who has his mind
on all his problems and whose soul is
bowed down within him with affliction.
However, he declares in Lamentations
3:21: "But this I call to mind, therefore
have I hope." Now he makes a turn. He
says, "Okay, I am going to get something
else in my mind that gives me hope and
the expectation of good." The thing that
he begins to think about pulls him out
of this pit. Then in verses 22–24 he talks
about the Lord's loving-kindness, compassion, and faithfulness.

The writer's positive thoughts about
God brought him out of the depressed,
miserable state he was in. When we think
about our problems, we sink lower and
lower, but thoughts about God's goodness, mercy, kindness, and faithfulness
give us hope.

12 He has bent His bow
And set me as a target for the
    arrow.
13 He has caused the arrows of His
    quiver
To enter my inner parts.
14 I have become the [object of]
    ridicule to all my people,
And [the subject of] their *mocking*
    song all the day.
15 He has filled me with bitterness;
He has made me drunk with
    wormwood (bitterness).
16 He has broken my teeth with
    gravel;
He has [covered me with ashes
    and] made me cower in the dust.
17 My soul has been cast far away
    from peace;
I have forgotten happiness.
18 So I say, "My strength has perished

And so has my hope *and* expectation from the LORD."

¹⁹Remember [O LORD] my affliction and my wandering, the wormwood and the gall (bitterness).
²⁰My soul *continually* remembers them
And is bowed down within me.

²¹But this I call to mind,
Therefore I have hope.
²²It is because of the LORD's lovingkindnesses that we are not consumed,
Because His [tender] compassions never fail. [Mal 3:6]
²³They are new every morning;
Great *and* beyond measure is Your faithfulness. [Is 33:2]

new every morning

Perhaps you learned Lamentations 3:22, 23 the way I did in the Amplified Classic version, that "It is because of the Lord's mercy and loving-kindness that we are not consumed, because His [tender] compassions fail not. They are new every morning; great and abundant is Your stability and faithfulness." Thank God for His great and abundant mercy (compassion)! His mercies are new every morning (see Lamentations 3:22, 23). Surely we would live miserable, defeated lives separated from God's presence, if not for His compassion and willingness to forgive us.

When we meditate on God's mercy and loving-kindness and truly realize how willingly He forgives us, we can much more easily show mercy to others. Good relationships are impossible unless we are generous with compassion and forgiveness. Being merciful simply means that we are good to those who do not deserve goodness. We have received unmerited blessings from God, and He expects us to give to others what we have received from Him. Let the goodness of God flow through you, because He has created you to be blessed and to be a blessing.

Jesus said that we are to forgive our enemies (see Luke 6:27–37) and be kind, doing favors in such a way that people derive benefit from them. In this way we show ourselves to be like our Father in heaven, for He is merciful, kind, and good. He promised that we would lose nothing and our reward would be great. God is our Vindicator, and we will always come out on top when we do things His way.

God's mercies and compassions are new every morning, and I am glad—because I am sure I use my allotted portion every day. I am grateful for a new, fresh start each day. God desires mercy, not sacrifice. When we make mistakes, He does not want our sacrifice. Jesus is the only sacrifice ever needed. He wants us to admit our mistakes, repent, and receive forgiveness and mercy. When others make mistakes and hurt or offend us, He wants us to give them mercy and not require sacrifices from them. What this means is that we are not to try to make people feel guilty or pay for their errors, but to give them the gift of mercy instead, just as we receive that gift from God.

We are wise to give mercy today because none of us knows how much mercy and loving-kindness we will need tomorrow. Learn to give and receive mercy regularly. Let mercy become a way of life for you.

24 "The LORD is my portion *and* my
  inheritance," says my soul;
  "Therefore I have hope in Him *and*
  wait expectantly for Him." [Num
  18:20]
25 The LORD is good to those who wait
  [confidently] for Him,
  To those who seek Him [on the
  authority of God's word].
26 It is good that one waits quietly
  For the salvation of the LORD.
27 It is good for a man that he should
  bear
  The yoke [of godly discipline] in
  his youth.
28 Let him sit alone [in hope] and
  keep quiet,
  Because God has laid it on him [for
  his benefit]. [Rom 8:28]
29 Let him put his mouth in the
  dust [in recognition of his
  unworthiness];
  There may yet be hope. [Mic 7:17]
30 Let him give his cheek to the one
  who strikes him;
  Let him be filled with reproach.
31 For the Lord will not reject forever,
  [Ps 94:14]
32 For if He causes grief,
  Then He will have compassion
  According to His abundant
  lovingkindness *and* tender
  mercy.

life point

Lamentations 3:25 says that God is good
to those who wait confidently for Him.
I believe this means they expect Him to
be good to them. We do not deserve His
goodness, but it is available to all who are
confident in it.

speak the Word

putting the Word to work

In Lamentations 3:40, the people
decide to "test and examine" their
ways, and return to the Lord. Have you
examined your ways lately? Ask God
to show you whether or not you have
strayed from Him in any area of your
life. Then turn back to Him through repentance and receive His great mercy.

33 For He does not afflict willingly
  and from His heart
  Or grieve the children of men.
  [Ezek 18:23, 32; Hos 11:8; Heb
  12:5–10; 2 Pet 3:9]
34 To trample *and* crush under His
  feet
  All the prisoners of the land,
35 To deprive a man of justice
  In the presence of the Most High,
36 To defraud a man in his lawsuit—
  The Lord does not approve of
  these things.
37 Who is there who speaks and it
  comes to pass,
  Unless the Lord has authorized
  and commanded it?
38 Is it not from the mouth of the Most
  High
  That both adversity (misfortune)
  and good (prosperity, happiness)
  proceed?
39 Why should any living mortal, or
  any man,
  Complain [of punishment] in view
  of his sins?
40 Let us test and examine our ways,
  And let us return to the LORD.

Thank You, God, that You have compassion according to
Your abundant loving-kindness and tender compassion.
–ADAPTED FROM LAMENTATIONS 3:32

41 Let us lift up our hearts and our hands [in prayer]
Toward God in heaven;
42 We have transgressed and rebelled,
You have not pardoned.
43 You have covered *Yourself* with anger
And pursued us;
You have slain [without pity] and have not spared.
44 You have covered Yourself with a cloud
So that no prayer can pass through.
45 You have made us scum and refuse
Among the peoples (Gentile nations).
46 All our enemies have gaped at us.
47 Panic and pitfall (traps, danger) have come on us,
Devastation and destruction.
48 My eyes overflow with streams of tears
Because of the destruction of the daughter of my people (Jerusalem).
49 My eyes overflow unceasingly,
Without stopping,
50 Until the LORD looks down
And sees from heaven.
51 My eyes [see things that] bring pain to my soul
Because of all the daughters of my city.
52 Without cause my enemies
Hunted me down like a bird;
53 They silenced me in the pit
And placed a stone over me. [Jer 38]
54 The waters ran down on my head;
I said, "I am cut off (destroyed)!"

55 I called on Your name, O LORD,
Out of the lowest pit. [Jer 38:6]
56 You have heard my voice,
"Do not hide Your ear from my *prayer* for relief,
From my cry for help."
57 You drew near on the day I called to You;
You said, "Do not fear." [James 4:8]
58 O Lord, You have pleaded my soul's cause [You have guided my way and protected me];
You have rescued *and* redeemed my life.
59 O LORD, You have seen the wrong [done to me];
Judge my case.
60 You have seen all their vengeance,
All their schemes against me.
61 You have heard their reproach, O LORD,
And all their schemes against me.
62 The lips and whispering of my assailants
Are against me all day long.
63 Look at their sitting and their rising [their actions and secret counsels];
I am their mocking song [the subject of their ridicule]. [Ps 139:2; Is 37:28]
64 You will repay them, O LORD,
According to the work of their hands.
65 You will harden their hearts;
Your curse will be upon them.
66 You will pursue them in anger and destroy them
From under the heavens of the LORD.

speak the Word

Lord, I will lift up my heart and my hands to You in prayer.
–ADAPTED FROM LAMENTATIONS 3:41

Thank You, God, for drawing near when I call to You and for pleading my soul's cause—guiding my way and protecting me.
You have rescued and redeemed my life!
–ADAPTED FROM LAMENTATIONS 3:57, 58

4 HOW DARK *and* dim the gold
    has become,
    How the pure gold has
changed!
The sacred stones [of the temple]
    are poured out *and* scattered
At the head of every street.
² The [noble and] precious sons of
    Zion,
[Once] worth their weight in fine
    gold,
How they are regarded [merely] as
    earthen jars,
The work of a potter's hands! [Is
    30:14; Jer 19:11; 2 Cor 4:7]
³ Even the jackals offer the breast,
They nurse their young;
But the daughter of my people has
    become cruel
Like ostriches in the wilderness
    [that desert their young].
⁴ The tongue of the infant clings
To the roof of its mouth because of
    thirst;
The little ones ask for food,
But no one gives it to them.
⁵ Those who feasted on delicacies
Are perishing in the streets;
Those reared in purple [as nobles]
Embrace ash heaps.
⁶ For the [punishment of the]
    wickedness of the daughter of
    my people [Jerusalem]
Is greater than the [punishment
    for the] sin of Sodom,
Which was overthrown in a
    moment,
And no hands were turned toward
    her [to offer help]. [Gen 19:25]
⁷ Her princes were purer than snow,
They were whiter than milk [in
    appearance];
They were more ruddy in body
    than rubies,
Their polishing was like lapis
    lazuli (sapphire).
⁸ Their appearance is [now] blacker
    than soot [because of the
    prolonged famine];

They are not recognized in the
    streets;
Their skin clings to their bones;
It is withered, and it has become
    [dry] like wood.
⁹ Those killed with the sword
Are more fortunate than those
    killed with hunger;
For the hungry pine *and* ebb away,
For the lack of the fruits of the
    field.
¹⁰ The hands of compassionate
    women
Boiled their own children;
They became food for them
Because of the destruction of the
    daughter of my people [Judah].
¹¹ The LORD has fulfilled His wrath;
He has poured out His fierce anger
And has kindled a fire in Zion
That has consumed her
    foundations.
¹² The kings of the earth did not
    believe,
Nor did any of the inhabitants of
    the earth,
That the adversary (oppressor)
    and enemy
Could enter the gates of Jerusalem.
¹³ Because of the sins of her
    [counterfeit] prophets
And the wickedness of her
    [unfaithful] priests,
Who have shed in her midst
The blood of the just *and*
    righteous;
¹⁴ They wandered, blind, in the
    streets;
They were defiled with blood
So that no one could touch their
    garments.
¹⁵ People cried to them, "Go away!
    Unclean!
Depart! Depart! Do not touch!"
So they fled, then they wandered
    [as fugitives];
People among the nations said,
"They shall not stay here any
    longer *with us*."

[16] The presence of the LORD scattered
them [among the nations];
He will not continue to look after
them.
They did not honor the priests;
They did not favor the elders.
[17] [And as for us,] yet our eyes failed,
Looking in vain for help.
Watching [from the towers] we
watched
For a nation that could not save.
[Ezek 29:16]
[18] The enemy hunted our steps,
So that we could not walk in our
streets;
Our end drew near,
Our days were finished
For our end had come.
[19] Our pursuers were swifter
Than the eagles of the sky;
They pursued us on the mountains,
They waited in ambush for us in
the wilderness.
[20] The breath of our nostrils, the
anointed of the LORD [our king],
Was captured in their snares,
He of whom we had said, "Under
his shadow
We shall live among the nations."
[21] Rejoice and be glad, O Daughter of
Edom,
Who lives in the land of Uz.
But the cup [of the wine of God's
wrath] will pass to you as well;
You will become drunk and make
yourself naked. [Jer 25:17]
[22] *The punishment* of your sin has been
completed, O Daughter of Zion;
The LORD will no longer send you
into exile.
But He will punish your sin, O
Daughter of Edom;
He will expose your sins. [Ps 137:7]

5 O LORD, remember what has
come upon us;
Look, and see our reproach
(national disgrace)!
[2] Our inheritance has been turned
over to strangers,

Our houses to foreigners.
[3] We have become orphans without
a father;
Our mothers are like widows.
[4] We have to pay for our drinking
water;
Our wood comes to us at a price.
[5] Our pursuers are at our necks;
We are worn out, there is no rest
for us.
[6] We have given the hand [as
a pledge of fidelity and
submission] to Egypt and
Assyria to get enough bread.
[7] Our fathers sinned, and are no
more;
It is we who have carried their sin.
[Is 65:7; Jer 16:11, 12; 31:29; Ezek
18:2–4]
[8] Servants rule over us;
There is no one to rescue us out of
their hand. [Neh 5:15]
[9] We get our bread at the risk of our
lives
Because of the sword [of the
Arabs] in the wilderness [who
may attack if we go out to
harvest the crop].
[10] Our skin is as hot as [the heat of]
an oven
Because of the burning heat of
[the fever of] famine.
[11] They ravished the women in Zion,
The virgins in the cities of Judah.
[12] Princes were hung by their hands;
Elders were not respected.
[13] Young men worked at the grinding
mill,
And boys fell [staggering] under
loads of wood.
[14] Elders are gone from the gate;
Young men from their music.
[15] The joy of our hearts has ended;
Our dancing has been turned into
mourning.
[16] The crown has fallen from our head
[our honor is covered with dust]!
Woe to us, for we have sinned!
[17] Because of this our heart is faint,

Because of these things our eyes
are dim.
18 As for Mount Zion, which lies
desolate,
Foxes *and* the jackals prowl over it.

19 But You, O LORD, reign forever;
Your throne endures from
generation to [all] generations.

20 Why do You forget us forever?
Why do You forsake us so long?
21 Return us to You, O LORD, so that
we may be restored;
Renew our days as of old,
22 Unless You have utterly rejected us
And are exceedingly angry
with us.

Ezekiel

Author:
Ezekiel

Date:
593 BC–571 BC

Everyday Life Principles:
Hope and restoration are always available in God.

Hard, stony hearts can be made soft and tender again by the touch of the Holy Spirit.

"Dry bones," things that seem to be dead in your life, can live again!

The name Ezekiel means "God is strong," and throughout the book that bears Ezekiel's name, we see the strength of God. Ezekiel was a righteous man, called by God to be a preacher of righteousness in a pagan culture. In the midst of idolatry and sin, he trumpeted a prophetic message of God's unending, unbreakable covenant with His people. He called them to return to God and be changed and restored.

Though Ezekiel's message was intended for an entire nation, it can be applied in very personal ways. I believe one of the most hopeful, personal promises we find in the Bible is found in Ezekiel 11:19: "And I will give them one heart [a new heart], and put a new spirit within them. I will take from them the heart of stone, and will give them a heart of flesh [that is responsive to My touch]." Similarly, God promises in Ezekiel 36:26: "I will give you a new heart and put a new spirit within you, and I will remove the heart of stone from your flesh and give you a heart of flesh."

As you read through Ezekiel, you will find fascinating stories and interesting prophetic content. More than anything, I hope this book will encourage and remind you that, as a believer, you are in covenant with God. His hope and restoration are always near to you!

1

NOW IT came about [when I was] in my thirtieth year [of life], on the fifth day of the fourth month, while I was among the exiles beside the River Chebar [in Babylonia], the heavens were opened and I saw visions of God.

²(On the fifth of the month, which was in the fifth year of King Jehoiachin's captivity, [2 Kin 24:12–14]

³the word of the LORD came expressly to Ezekiel the priest, the son of Buzi, in the land of the Chaldeans by the River Chebar; and the hand of the LORD came upon him there.) [1 Kin 18:46; 2 Kin 3:15]

⁴As I looked, I saw a stormy wind coming out of the north, a great cloud with fire flashing continually from it; and a brightness was around it, and in its core [there was] something like glowing [amber-colored] metal in the midst of the fire.

⁵Within it there were figures resembling four living beings. And this was their appearance: they had human form.

⁶Each one had four faces and four wings.

⁷Their legs were straight and the soles of their feet were like a calf's hoof, and they sparkled *and* gleamed like shiny bronze.

⁸Under their wings on their four sides they had human hands. As for the faces and wings of the four of them,

⁹their wings touched one another; *their faces* did not turn when they moved, each went straight forward.

¹⁰Regarding the form *and* appearance of their faces: they [each] had the face of a man [in front], and each had the face of a lion on the right side, and the face of an ox on the left side; all four also had the face of an eagle [at the back of their heads]. [Rev 4:7]

¹¹Such were their faces. Their wings were stretched out upward; two [wings] of each one were touching another [the wings of the beings on either side of it], and [the remaining] two [wings of each being] were covering their bodies.

¹²And each went straight forward; wherever the spirit was about to go, they would go, without turning as they went.

¹³Among the living beings there was something that looked like burning coals of fire, like torches moving back and forth among the living beings. The fire was bright, and lightning was flashing from the fire.

¹⁴And the living beings moved rapidly back and forth like flashes of lightning.

¹⁵Now as I looked at the living beings, I saw one wheel on the ground beside the living beings, for each of the four of them.

¹⁶Regarding the appearance of the wheels and their construction: they gleamed like chrysolite (beryl, olivine); and the four were made alike. Their appearance and construction were a wheel [set at a right angle] within a wheel.

¹⁷Whenever they moved, they went in any [one] of their four directions without turning as they moved.

¹⁸Regarding their rims: they were so high that they were awesome *and* dreadful, and the rims of all four of them were full of eyes all around.

¹⁹Whenever the living beings moved, the wheels moved with them; and when the living beings rose from the earth, the wheels rose also.

²⁰Wherever the spirit went, the beings went in that direction. And the wheels rose along with them; for the spirit *or* life of the living beings was in the wheels.

²¹Whenever those went, these went; and whenever those came to a stop, these came to a stop; and whenever those rose from the earth, the wheels rose close beside them, for the spirit of the living beings was in the wheels.

²²Now stretched over the heads of the

living beings *there was* something like an expanse, looking like the terrible *and* awesome shimmer of icy crystal.

²³Under the expanse their wings *were stretched out* straight, one toward another. Every living being had two wings which covered its body on one side and on the other side.

²⁴As they moved, I also heard the sound of their wings like the sound of great [rushing] waters, like the voice of the Almighty, the sound of tumult like the noise of an army camp. Whenever they came to a stop, they lowered their wings.

²⁵And there was a voice above the expanse that was over their heads; whenever they stopped, they lowered their wings.

²⁶Now above the expanse that was over their heads there was something resembling a throne, it appeared like [it was made of] sapphire *or* lapis lazuli; and [seated] on that which looked like a throne, high up, was a figure with the appearance of a man. [Phil 2:5–8]

²⁷Now upward, from that which appeared to be His waist, I saw something like glowing metal that looked like it was filled with fire all around it; and downward, from that which appeared to be His waist, I saw something like fire; and *there was* a brightness *and* a remarkable radiance [like a halo] around Him.

²⁸As the appearance of the rainbow in the clouds on a rainy day, so was the appearance of the surrounding radiance. This was the appearance of the likeness of the glory *and* brilliance of the Lord. And when I saw it, I fell face downward and I heard a voice of One speaking. [Rev 4:3]

2 THEN HE said to me, "Son of man, stand on your feet and I will speak to you."

²Then as He spoke to me the Spirit entered me and set me on my feet; and I heard Him speaking to me.

³And He said to me, "I am sending you, son of man, to the children of Israel, to a rebellious people [in both the north and the south] that have rebelled against Me; they and their fathers have sinned *and* revolted against Me to this very day.

⁴"I am sending you to them who are stubborn and obstinate children, and you shall say to them, 'Thus says the Lord God.'

⁵"As for them, whether they listen or refuse [to listen]—for they are a rebellious house—yet they will know *and* be fully aware of the fact that there has been a prophet among them.

⁶"And you, son of man, neither fear them nor fear their words; though briars and thorns are all around you and you sit among scorpions, neither fear their words nor be dismayed at their presence, for they are a rebellious house.

⁷"But you shall speak My words to them whether they will listen or refuse [to listen], for they are [most] rebellious.

⁸"As for you, son of man, listen to what I say to you; do not be rebellious like that rebellious house; open your mouth and eat what I am giving you."

⁹Then I looked, and I saw a hand stretched out toward me; and behold, a scroll of a book was in it.

¹⁰And He spread it before me, and it was written on the front and on the back, and written on it were [words of] lamentation (funeral songs) and mourning and woe.

speak the Word

Lord, I pray that I will be like Ezekiel and hear You when You speak to me.
—ADAPTED FROM EZEKIEL 2:2

3 HE SAID to me, "Son of man, eat what you find [in this book]; eat this scroll, then go, speak to the house of Israel."

²So I opened my mouth, and He fed me the scroll.

³He said to me, "Son of man, eat this scroll that I am giving you and fill your stomach with it." So I ate it, and it was as sweet as honey in my mouth.

⁴Then He said to me, "Son of man, go to the house of Israel and speak My words to them.

⁵"For you are not being sent to a people of unintelligible speech or difficult language, but to the house of Israel,

⁶not to many peoples of unintelligible speech or difficult language, whose words you cannot understand. But I have sent you to them who should listen to you *and* pay attention to My message;

⁷yet the house of Israel will not be willing to listen to you *and* obey you, since they are not willing to listen to Me *and* obey Me, for the entire house of Israel is stubborn and obstinate.

⁸"Behold, I have made your face as hard as their faces and your forehead as hard as their foreheads.

⁹"I have made your forehead like emery (diamond), harder than flint. Do not be afraid of them or be dismayed before them, though they are a rebellious house." [Is 50:7; Jer 1:18; 15:20; Mic 3:8]

¹⁰Moreover, He said to me, "Son of man, receive into your heart all My words which I will speak to you and hear with your ears (listen closely).

¹¹"Go to the [Jewish] exiles [in Babylon], to the children of your people, and speak to them, whether they listen or not, and tell them, 'Thus says the Lord God.'"

¹²Then the Spirit lifted me up, and I heard a great rushing sound behind me, "Blessed be the glory of the Lord in His place [above the expanse]."

¹³And then I *heard* the sound of the wings of the living beings as they touched one another and [I heard] the sound of the wheels beside them, a great rushing sound.

¹⁴So the Spirit lifted me up and took me away, and I went embittered [by the sins of Israel] in the rage of my spirit; and the hand of the Lord was strong on me.

¹⁵Then I came to the exiles who lived beside the River Chebar at Tel Abib. I sat there for seven days [in the place] where they were living, overwhelmed with astonishment [by my vision and the work before me].

¹⁶At the end of seven days the word of the Lord came to me, saying,

¹⁷"Son of man, I have appointed you as a watchman to the house of Israel; whenever you hear a word from My mouth, warn them from Me. [Is 52:8; 56:10; 62:6; Jer 6:17]

¹⁸"When I say to the wicked, 'You will certainly die,' and you do not warn him or speak out to tell him to turn from his wicked way to save his life, that same evil man will die in his sin, but you will be responsible for his blood.

¹⁹"However, if you have warned the wicked and he does not turn from his wickedness or from his wicked way, he will die in his sin; but you have freed yourself [from responsibility].

²⁰"Again, when a righteous man turns from his righteousness (right standing with God) and sins, and I

speak the Word

God, every word that You speak to me I will not only hear with my ears, but I will also receive in my heart.
–ADAPTED FROM EZEKIEL 3:10

place an obstacle before him, he will die; since you have not warned him, he will die in his sin, and the righteous deeds which he has done will not be remembered; but you will be responsible for his blood.

²¹"However, if you have warned the righteous man not to sin and he does not sin, he will surely live because he took warning; also you have freed yourself [from responsibility]."

²²The hand of the Lord was on me there, and He said to me, "Arise, go out to the plain, and I will speak to you."

²³So I got up and went out to the plain; and behold, the glory and brilliance of the Lord was standing there, like the glory I had seen by the River Chebar, and I fell face downward.

²⁴Then the Spirit entered me and made me stand on my feet; He spoke and said to me, "Go, shut yourself up in your house.

²⁵"As for you, son of man, they will put ropes on you and bind you with them so that you cannot go out among them.

²⁶"And I will make your tongue stick to the roof of your mouth so that you cannot talk and you cannot be a man who rebukes the people, for they are a rebellious house.

²⁷"But when I speak with you, I will open your mouth and you will say to them, 'Thus says the Lord God.' He who hears, let him hear; and he who refuses [to hear], let him refuse; for they are a rebellious house.

4 "NOW YOU, son of man, take a brick, place it before you and inscribe on it [a diagram of] the city of Jerusalem.

²"Then lay siege against it, build a siege wall, raise a ramp against it; set up [enemy] camps and place battering rams all around it.

³"Further, take an iron plate and place it as an iron wall between you and the city, and set your face toward it so that it is under siege, and besiege it. This is a sign to the house of Israel.

⁴"Then lie down on your left side (toward the north) to bear [symbolically] the wickedness and punishment of the house of Israel. You shall bear their wickedness and punishment for the number of days that you lie on your side.

⁵"For I have assigned you the years of their wickedness and punishment, according to the number of the days, three hundred and ninety days [representing three hundred and ninety years]; in this way you shall bear [symbolically] the wickedness and punishment of the house of Israel.

⁶"When you have completed these [days for Israel], lie down again, but on your right side (toward the south), and you shall bear the wickedness and punishment of the house of Judah forty days. I have assigned you one day for each year.

⁷"Then you shall set your face toward the siege of Jerusalem with your arm bared and prophesy against it.

⁸"Now behold, I will put ropes on you so that you cannot turn from one side to the other until you have completed the days of your siege.

⁹"But as for you, take wheat, barley, beans, lentils, millet, and spelt, and put them into one vessel and make them into bread for yourself. You shall eat it according to the number of the days that you lie on your side, three hundred and ninety days.

¹⁰"The food you eat each day shall be [measured] by weight, twenty shekels, to be eaten daily at a set time.

¹¹"You shall drink water by measure also, the sixth part of a hin; you shall drink daily at a set time.

¹²"You shall eat your food as barley cakes, having baked it in their sight over human dung."

¹³Then the Lord said, "Thus the children of Israel will eat their bread

unclean *and* defiled among the nations where I will banish them." [Hos 9:3]

¹⁴But I said, "Ah, Lord God! Behold (hear me), I have never been defiled; for from my youth until now I have never eaten what died on its own or was torn by beasts, nor has any unclean meat ever entered my mouth." [Acts 10:14]

¹⁵Then He said to me, "See, I will let you use cow's dung instead of human dung over which you shall prepare your food."

¹⁶Moreover, He said to me, "Son of man, behold (listen carefully), I am going to break the staff of bread [that supports life] in Jerusalem; and they shall eat bread [rationed] by weight and [eat it] with anxiety *and* fear, and drink water by measure and [drink it] in horror [of the impending starvation], [Lev 26:26; Ps 105:16; Is 3:1]

¹⁷because bread and water will be scarce; and they will look at one another in dismay and waste away [in punishment] for their wickedness.

5 "AND YOU [Ezekiel], son of man, take a sharp sword and use it as a barber's razor and shave your head and your beard. Then take scales for weighing and divide the hair [into three parts].

²"You shall burn one third with fire in the center of the city, when the days of the siege are completed. Then you shall take one third and strike it with the sword all around the city, and one third you shall scatter to the wind; and I will unsheathe a sword behind them.

³"Also take some of them and bind them in the edges of your robes.

⁴"Again take some hair and throw them into the fire and burn them in the fire; from it a fire will spread to all the house of Israel.

⁵"Thus says the Lord God, 'This is Jerusalem; I have set her in the center of the nations, and countries are around her.

⁶'And she has rebelled against My ordinances more wickedly than the [pagan] nations and against My statutes more than the countries that are around her; for Israel has rejected My ordinances and has not walked in My statutes.' [Rom 2:14, 15]

⁷"Therefore, thus says the Lord God, 'Because you have more turmoil than the nations which surround you and have not walked in My statutes, nor kept My ordinances, nor observed the ordinances of the nations which surround you,' [Deut 7:2–6; Josh 23:7; Judg 2:2]

⁸therefore, thus says the Lord God, 'Behold, I, I Myself, am against you, and I will execute judgments among you in the sight of the nations.

⁹'And because of all your abominations, I will do among you that which I have not done, and the like of which I will not do again. [Lam 4:6; Dan 9:12; Amos 3:2]

¹⁰'Therefore, fathers will eat their sons among you, and sons will eat their fathers; and I will execute judgments on you and I will scatter to all the winds the remnant of you. [Lev 26:33; Deut 28:64; Ezek 12:14; Zech 2:6]

¹¹'So, as I live,' says the Lord God, 'surely, because you have defiled My sanctuary with all your detestable idols and with all your abominations, therefore I will also diminish you *and* withdraw, and My eye will have no pity and I will not spare [you].

¹²'One third of you will die of virulent disease or be consumed by famine among you; one third will fall by the sword around you; and one third I will scatter to all the winds, and I will unsheathe a sword behind them.

¹³'Thus My anger will come to an end and I will satisfy My wrath on them, and I will be appeased; then they will know [without any doubt] that I the Lord have spoken in My zeal when I have spent My wrath on them. [Ezek 36:6; 38:19]

¹⁴'Moreover, I will make you a desolation and a disgrace among the nations which surround you and in the sight of all who pass by. [Lev 26:31, 32; Neh 2:17]

¹⁵'So it will be a disgrace, a taunt, a warning and an object of horror to the [pagan] nations who surround you when I execute judgments against you in anger and in wrath and in raging reprimands—I, the Lᴏʀᴅ, have spoken. [Deut 28:37; Ps 79:4; Jer 24:9]

¹⁶'When I send against them the deadly arrows of hunger which were for the destruction of those whom I will send to destroy you, then I will increase the famine upon you and break your staff of bread.

¹⁷'Further, I will send against you hunger and wild beasts, and they will bereave you of children; virulent disease and bloodshed also will pass through you, and I will bring the sword on you. I, the Lᴏʀᴅ, have spoken.'"

6 AND THE word of the Lᴏʀᴅ came to me, saying,
²"Son of man, set your face against the mountains of Israel and prophesy against them,

³and say, 'You mountains of Israel, hear the word of the Lord Gᴏᴅ! Thus says the Lord Gᴏᴅ to the mountains and the hills, to the ravines and the valleys: "Behold, I Myself am going to bring a sword on you, and I will destroy your high places [of idolatrous worship],

⁴and your altars will become deserted and your pillars for sun-worship will be smashed in pieces; and I will throw down your slain in front of your idols [that cannot bring them back to life]. [Lev 26:30]

⁵"I will also lay the dead bodies of the children of Israel in front of their [Canaanite] idols; and I will scatter your bones all around your altars.

⁶"Everywhere you live, the cities will become waste and the high places will become deserted, so that your altars may bear their guilt *and* become deserted, your idols may be broken and destroyed, your incense altars [for sun-worship] may be cut down, and your works may be blotted out.

⁷"The slain will fall among you, then you shall know [without any doubt] that I am the Lᴏʀᴅ.

⁸"Yet I will leave some of you alive [a remnant], for you will have some who escaped the sword among the nations when you are scattered throughout the countries.

⁹"Then those of you who escape will remember Me among the nations to which they will be exiled, how I have been broken by their lewdness *and* their adulterous hearts which have turned away from Me, and by their eyes which lust after their idols; and they will loathe themselves for the evils which they have committed, for all their repulsive acts.

¹⁰"Then they will know [without any doubt] that I am the Lᴏʀᴅ; I have not said in vain that I would bring this disaster [as punishment] on them."'

¹¹"Thus says the Lord Gᴏᴅ, 'Strike with your fist, stamp with your foot and say, "Alas, because of all the evil atrocities of the house of Israel, which will fall by sword, by famine, and by virulent disease!

¹²"He who is far away will die of the virulent disease, and he who is near will fall by the sword, and he who remains and is besieged will die by the famine. Thus I will spend My wrath on them.

¹³"Then you will know [without any doubt] that I am the Lᴏʀᴅ, when their slain are among their idols around their altars, on every high hill, on all the tops of the mountains, under every leafy tree and under every oak with thick branches, the places where they offered sweet incense *and* a soothing aroma to all their idols.

¹⁴"And I will stretch out My hand

against them and make the land a more desolate waste than the wilderness toward Diblah [the Moabite city], throughout all the places where they live; and they will know [without any doubt] that I am the LORD.'''

7 MOREOVER, THE word of the LORD came to me, saying, ²"Also, son of man, thus says the Lord GOD to the land of Israel, 'An end! The end is coming on the four corners of the land. [Ezek 11:13; Amos 8:2]

³'Now the end is upon you, and I will send My anger against you and will judge you in accordance with your ways and I will bring [retribution for] all your abominations upon you.

⁴'For My eye will have no pity on you, nor will I spare you, but I will repay you for your evil ways, while your abominations are among you; and you will know (recognize, understand) [without any doubt] that I am the LORD.'

⁵"Thus says the Lord GOD, 'A disaster is coming, [one so destructive and injurious, so sudden and violent, that it stands alone,] a unique disaster, look it is coming!

⁶'An end is coming; the end has come! It has awakened against you. Look, it has come!

⁷'Your doom has come to you, O inhabitant of the land; the time has come, the day is near—tumult rather than joyful shouting on the mountains.

⁸'Now I will soon pour out My wrath on you and spend My anger against you, and I will judge you in accordance with your ways and will repay you [with punishment] for all your outrageous acts.

⁹'My eye will show no pity nor will I spare [you]. I will repay you in accordance with your ways, while your abominations are in your midst; then you will know and understand that it is I, the LORD, who strikes you.

¹⁰"Behold, the day! Behold, it is coming! Your doom has gone forth, the rod has blossomed, arrogance has sprouted.

¹¹"Violence has grown into a rod of wickedness; none of them (Israel) will remain, none of their people, none of their wealth, nor anything eminent among them.

¹²"The time has come, the day has arrived. Let not the buyer rejoice nor the seller mourn, for wrath is against all their multitude [of people].

¹³"For the seller will not regain and return to what he sold, even were they yet alive; for the vision [of punishment] regarding all the multitude [of people] will not be turned back, nor will any one of them sustain his life because of his sin.

¹⁴"They have blown the trumpet and have made everything ready, but no one is going to the battle, for My wrath is against all their multitude [of people].

¹⁵"The sword is outside and virulent disease and famine are within. He who is in the field will die by the sword, and famine and disease will devour those in the city.

¹⁶"Even when their survivors escape, they will be on the mountains like doves of the valleys, all of them moaning, each over his [punishment for] sin.

¹⁷"All hands will hang limp and all knees will be as weak as water. [Is 13:7; Jer 6:24; Ezek 21:7]

¹⁸"They will also cover themselves with sackcloth; horror will overwhelm them, and shame will be on all faces and baldness on all their heads [as evidence of grief].

¹⁹"They will fling their silver into the streets and their gold will be [discarded] like something unclean; their silver and their gold shall not be able to save them in the day of the wrath of the LORD. These [things] cannot satisfy their soul nor fill their stomachs, for they have become their stumbling

block *and* source of sin. [Prov 11:4; Zeph 1:18]

²⁰'As for the beauty of [gold for] ornaments, they turned it to pride and from it made the images of their repulsive things (idols) and of their vile things. Therefore I will make it an unclean thing to them.

²¹'I will give it into the hands of strangers (Babylonians) as plunder and to the wicked of the earth as spoil, and they shall profane it.

²²'I will also turn My face away from them, and they will desecrate My secret treasure (the Jerusalem temple); and robbers will enter [irreverently] into it (the Holy of Holies) and violate it.

²³'Prepare the chain [for imprisonment], for the land is full of bloody crimes [murders committed under the pretense of civil justice] and the city is full of violence.

²⁴'Therefore, I will bring the worst of the [Gentile] nations, and they will take possession of their houses [those of the people of Judah]; I will also silence their pride, and their holy places will be profaned.

²⁵'When anguish comes, they [of Judah] shall seek peace, but there will be none.

²⁶'Disaster will come upon disaster and rumor will be *heaped* on rumor; they will seek a vision from a prophet, but the law *and* guidance will be lost from the priest and [wise] counsel [will cease] from the elders. [Ps 74:9; Lam 2:9]

²⁷'The king [of Judah] will mourn and the prince (Zedekiah) will be clothed with [garments of] despair *and* anguish, and the hands of the people of the land shall tremble [in terror]. I will deal with them in accordance with their conduct, and by their judgments I will judge them. And they will know [without any doubt] that I am the Lord.'"

8 IT CAME about in the sixth year [of the captivity of King Jehoiachin], on the fifth day of the sixth month, as I sat in my house [near Babylon] with the elders of Judah sitting before me, that the hand of the Lord God fell on me there.

²Then I looked, and behold, a likeness [of a man] with the appearance of fire; from His loins downward He was like fire, and from His loins upward He had the appearance of brightness, like gleaming metal (bronze).

³He stretched out the form of a hand and took me by a lock of hair on my head; and the Spirit lifted me up between earth and heaven and brought me in the visions of God to Jerusalem, to the entrance of the north gate of the inner *courtyard,* where the seat of the idol (image) of jealousy, which provokes to jealousy, was *located.* [2 Kin 16:10–16; 21:4, 5]

⁴And behold, the glory *and* brilliance of the God of Israel [who had loved and chosen them] was there, like the vision which I saw in the plain. [Ezek 1:28; 3:22, 23]

⁵Then He said to me, "Son of man, now raise your eyes toward the north." So I looked toward the north, and behold, to the north of the altar gate was this idol (image) of jealousy at the entrance.

⁶Furthermore, He said to me, "Son of man, do you see what they are doing, the great repulsive acts which the house of Israel is committing here, to drive Me far away from My sanctuary? But you will again see greater repulsive acts."

⁷Then He brought me to the entrance of the courtyard; and when I looked, behold, [there was] a hole in the wall.

⁸He said to me, "Son of man, now dig into the wall." And when I had dug into the wall, behold, there was an entrance.

⁹And He said to me, "Go in and see

the wicked, repulsive acts that they are committing here."

¹⁰So I entered and looked, and saw every kind of creeping things and beasts and loathsome things, and all the idols of the house of Israel, carved all around on the wall.

¹¹Standing before these [images] were seventy elders of the house of Israel, and among them stood Jaazaniah the son of Shaphan [the scribe], each man with his censer in his hand and a thick *and* fragrant cloud of incense was rising [as they prayed to these gods].

¹²Then He said to me, "Son of man, do you see what the elders of the house of Israel do in the dark, each man in his [secret] room of carved images? For they say, 'The Lord does not see us; the Lord has abandoned the land.'"

¹³He also said to me, "Yet again you will see even greater repulsive acts which they are committing."

¹⁴Then He brought me to the entrance of the north gate of the Lord's house; and behold, women were sitting there weeping for Tammuz.

¹⁵He said to me, "Do you see this, son of man? Yet you will see still greater repulsive acts than these [that they are committing]."

¹⁶So He brought me to the inner court of the Lord's house. And behold, at the entrance to the temple of the Lord, between the porch (vestibule, portico) and the [bronze] altar, were about twenty-five men with their backs to the temple of the Lord and their faces toward the east; and they were bowing down toward the east *and* worshiping the sun.

¹⁷He said to me, "Do you see this, son of man? Is it too slight a thing for the house of Judah to commit the repulsive acts which they have committed here, that they have filled the land with violence and repeatedly provoked Me to anger? And behold, they are putting the branch to their nose.

¹⁸"Therefore, I indeed will deal in wrath. My eye will have no pity nor will I spare [them]; and though they cry loudly in My ears, yet I will not listen to them." [Prov 1:28; Is 1:15; Jer 11:11; 14:12; Mic 3:4; Zech 7:13]

9 THEN [in my vision] I heard Him cry out with a thunderous voice, saying, "Approach now, executioners of the city, each with his weapon of destruction in his hand."

²Behold, six men [angelic beings] came from the direction of the Upper Gate, which faces north, each with his battle-axe in his hand; and among them was a certain man clothed in linen, with a scribe's writing case at his side. They entered and stood beside the bronze altar.

³Then the [Shekinah] glory *and* brilliance of the God of Israel (the cloud) went up from the cherubim on which it had rested, to [stand above] the threshold of the [Lord's] temple. And the Lord called to the man clothed with linen, who had the scribe's writing case at his side.

⁴The Lord said to him, "Go through the midst of the city, throughout all of Jerusalem, and put a mark on the foreheads of the men who sigh [in distress] and grieve over all the repulsive acts which are being committed in it."

⁵But to the others I heard Him say, "Follow him [the man with the scribe's writing case] throughout the city and strike; do not let your eyes have pity and do not spare [anyone].

⁶"Utterly slay old men, young men, maidens, little children, and women; but do not touch *or* go near anyone on whom is the mark. Begin at My sanctuary." So they began with the old men who were in front of the temple [who did not have the Lord's mark on their foreheads]. [1 Pet 4:17]

⁷And He said to the executioners, "Defile the temple and fill its courtyards with the dead. Go out!" So they

went out and struck down *the people* in the city.

⁸As they were executing them and I *alone* was left, I fell face downward and cried out, "Alas, Lord GOD! Will You destroy all that is left of Israel [the whole remnant] by pouring out Your wrath *and* indignation on Jerusalem?"

⁹Then He said to me, "The wickedness (guilt) of the house of Israel and Judah is extremely great; the land is full of blood and the city is full of perversion *and* injustice; for they say, 'The LORD has abandoned the land; the LORD does not see [what we are doing].'

¹⁰"But as for Me, My eye will have no pity, nor will I spare, but I will bring their [wicked] conduct upon their [own] heads."

¹¹Then behold, the man clothed in linen, who had the scribe's writing case at his side, reported, "I have done just as You have commanded me."

10 THEN I looked, and behold, in the expanse (firmament) that was over the heads of the cherubim there appeared something [glorious and brilliant] above them looking like a [huge] sapphire stone, formed to resemble a throne.

²And the LORD spoke to the man (seventh angel) clothed in linen and said, "Go between the whirling wheels under the cherubim; fill your hands with coals of fire from between the cherubim and scatter them over the city." And he entered as I watched. [Rev 8:5]

³Now the cherubim were standing on the right side of the temple when the man entered; and a cloud [the Shekinah glory of God] filled the inner courtyard.

⁴Then the glory *and* brilliance of the LORD moved upward from the cherubim to [rest over] the threshold of the temple; and the temple was filled with the cloud and the courtyard was filled with the brightness of the LORD's glory. [1 Kin 8:10, 11; Ezek 43:5]

⁵And the sound of the wings of the cherubim was heard [even] as far as the outer courtyard, like the voice of God Almighty when He speaks. [Ps 29:3, 4]

⁶It came about when He commanded the man clothed in linen, saying, "Take fire from between the whirling wheels, from between the cherubim," the man entered and stood beside a wheel.

⁷Then a cherub stretched out his hand from between the cherubim to the fire that was between [the four of] them, and took some [of it] and put it into the hands of the man clothed in linen, who took it and departed.

⁸Beneath their wings the cherubim seemed to have [something in] the form of a man's hand.

⁹Then I looked and behold, [there were] four wheels beside the cherubim, one wheel beside one cherub and another wheel beside each other cherub; and the appearance of the wheels was like a sparkling Tarshish stone (beryl).

¹⁰As for their appearance, all four looked alike, as if one wheel were within another wheel.

¹¹When they moved, they went in any of their four directions without turning as they went; but they followed in the direction which they faced, without turning as they went.

¹²Their whole body, their backs, their hands, their wings, and the wheels were full of eyes all around, even the wheels belonging to all four of them.

¹³Regarding the wheels [attached to them], I heard them called, "the whirling (rolling, revolving) wheels."

¹⁴And each one had four faces: the first face was the face of the cherub, the second the face of a man, the third the face of a lion, and the fourth the face of an eagle.

¹⁵Then the cherubim rose upward. They are the [same four] living beings [regarded as one] that I saw by the River Chebar [in Babylonia]. [Ezek 1:5]

¹⁶Now when the cherubim moved, the wheels would go beside them; and when the cherubim lifted up their wings to rise from the earth, the wheels would remain beside them.

¹⁷When the cherubim stood still, the wheels would stand still; and when they rose upward, the wheels would rise with them, for the spirit of the living beings was in these [wheels]. [Ezek 1:21]

¹⁸Then the [Shekinah] glory of the Lord departed from the threshold of the temple and rested over the cherubim.

¹⁹As I looked at them, the cherubim lifted up their wings and rose up from the earth, they departed with the wheels beside them; and they stood still at the entrance of the east gate of the house of the Lord, and the glory *and* brilliance of the God of Israel hovered over them.

²⁰These are the living beings that I saw beneath the God of Israel by the River Chebar; and I knew that they were cherubim.

²¹Each one had four faces and each one had four wings, and beneath their wings was the form of human hands.

²²As for the likeness of their faces, they were the same faces whose appearance I had seen by the River Chebar. Each one went straight forward.

11 MOREOVER, THE Spirit lifted me up and brought me to the gate of the Lord's house, which faced eastward. And behold, at the entrance of the gate *there were* twenty-five men; and I saw among them Jaazaniah the son of Azzur and Pelatiah the son of Benaiah, princes of the people.

²Then the Spirit said to me, "Son of man, these are the men who devise evil and give wicked advice in this city,

³who say, 'Is not *the time* near to build houses? This *city* is [secure just like] the pot and we are the meat [in it].'

⁴"Therefore, prophesy against them; prophesy, son of man!"

⁵Then the Spirit of the Lord fell upon me, and He said to me, "Say, 'Thus says the Lord, "This is what you think, house of Israel, for I know your thoughts.

⁶"You have multiplied your slain in this city, and you have filled its streets with the corpses [of righteous men]."

⁷'Therefore, thus says the Lord God, "Your dead whom you have laid in the midst of your city are the meat and this city is the pot; but I shall force you out of [the security of] it.

⁸"You have feared the sword; so I will bring a sword upon you," says the Lord God.

⁹"And I will bring you out of the midst of the city and hand you over to strangers and execute judgment against you.

¹⁰"You will fall by the sword; I will judge *and* punish you [in front of your neighbors] at the border of [the land of] Israel; and you will know [without any doubt] that I am the Lord.

¹¹"This *city* will not be a pot for you, nor will you be meat [safe] in it, but I will judge you at the border of Israel.

¹²"And you will know [without any doubt] that I am the Lord; for you have not walked in My statutes nor have you executed My ordinances, but you have acted in accordance with the ordinances of the nations around you."'"

¹³Now it came about while I was prophesying, that Pelatiah the son of Benaiah died. Then I fell face downward and cried out loudly, "Alas, Lord God! Will You bring the remnant of Israel to a complete end?"

¹⁴Then the word of the Lord came to me, saying,

¹⁵"Son of man, your brothers, your relatives, your fellow exiles and the whole house of Israel, all of them, are those to whom the [present] inhabitants of Jerusalem have said, 'Go

far away from the Lord; this land has been given to us as a possession.'

¹⁶"Therefore say, 'Thus says the Lord God, "Though I had removed Israel far away among the nations and though I had scattered them among the countries, yet I have been a sanctuary for them for a little while in the countries to which they had gone."'

¹⁷"Therefore say, 'Thus says the Lord God, "I will gather you from the peoples and assemble you out of the countries where you have been scattered, and I will give [back] to you the land of Israel."'

¹⁸"When they return there, they will remove from it all [traces of] its detestable things and all its repulsive things (remnants of paganism).

¹⁹"And I will give them one heart [a new heart], and put a new spirit within them. I will take from them the heart

the cure for hard-heartedness

I believe the secret to being happy is to walk in love. And walking in love is impossible unless we allow the Holy Spirit to tenderize our hearts. As Ezekiel 11:19 indicates, it is not His will for us to be hard-hearted.

I had a hard heart because I had been abused as a child and abandoned by people who said they loved me. It seemed that all my life, people had taken advantage of me and used me for their own selfish purposes. My response was to become hard-hearted in an attempt to block further emotional pain.

Once our hearts become hard, it is nearly impossible to change them by decision alone. That type of change requires a supernatural working of the Holy Spirit. He is the only One Who can get inside our souls and heal the wounds and bruises there. He alone can restore us to the condition we were in prior to our injuries. He is the One Who sheds God's love abroad in our hearts. He is also the One Who teaches us, convicting us of wrong conduct when we mistreat others, and He works in us to give us tender hearts.

When I realized that I grieved the Holy Spirit when I was sharp, angry, or hateful toward someone, I began to take that kind of behavior more seriously. I loved God, and I certainly did not want to grieve His Spirit.

When you and I do grieve the Holy Spirit, we also feel grieved. Even though we may not realize what is wrong with us, we know that we feel sad or depressed, or that something is just not right.

I have come to believe that much of the sadness, depression, and heaviness we experience is most likely linked to our behavior toward other people. Galatians 6:7 says that whatever we sow, we will reap. If we sow words and actions that sadden others, we will reap sadness. But if we sow happiness in the lives of others, we will reap happiness in our own lives.

Do not ever allow yourself to remain hard-hearted. Pray for God to soften your heart and to give you a tender conscience, one that is responsive to His touch. Ask Him to allow you to feel what He feels and to work His character in you. Learn how to walk in love with a heart that is open to God and sensitive to the needs of others.

of stone, and will give them a heart of flesh [that is responsive to My touch], [Ezek 18:31; 36:26; 2 Cor 3:3]

²⁰that they may walk in My statutes and keep My ordinances and do them. Then they shall be My people, and I will be their God.

²¹"But as for those whose heart longs for *and* follows after their detestable things and their repulsive things [associated with idolatry], on their own head I will repay [them in full for] their [vile] conduct," says the Lord GOD.

²²Then the cherubim lifted up their wings with the wheels beside them, and the [Shekinah] glory of the God of Israel hovered over them.

²³Then the glory *and* brilliance of the LORD went up from the midst of the city and paused over the mountain, [the Mount of Olives] which is east of the city.

²⁴And the Spirit lifted me up and brought me in a vision by the Spirit of God to the exiles in Chaldea (Babylonia). Then the vision that I had seen left me.

²⁵Then I told the exiles everything that the LORD had shown me.

12 THE WORD of the LORD also came to me, saying, ²"Son of man, you live among a rebellious house, who have eyes to see but do not see, who have ears to hear but do not hear; for they are a rebellious people. [Mark 8:18]

³"Therefore, son of man, prepare your belongings for exile, and move into exile during the day when they will see you; even go into exile from your place to another place as they watch. Perhaps they will understand even though they are a rebellious people.

⁴"Bring your provisions *and* supplies out during the day as they watch, as provisions *and* supplies for [going into] exile. Then you shall go out at evening as they watch, as those going into exile.

life point

In Ezekiel 11:19, God says He will replace the stony hearts in His people with new hearts that are sensitive to His touch.

When we give our lives to God, He puts a sense of right and wrong deep within our consciences. But if we rebel against our consciences too many times, we can become hard-hearted. If that happens, we need to let God soften our hearts so we can be spiritually sensitive to the leadership of the Holy Spirit.

I was very hard-hearted before I began really fellowshipping with God. Being in His presence regularly developed the new heart in me, the new heart that Jesus died to give me. Without a heart sensitive to God's touch, we will not recognize many of the times He is speaking to us. He speaks gently, in a still, small voice, or with gentle conviction about a matter.

Those who are hard-hearted and busy "doing their own thing" will not be sensitive to God's voice. I am grateful that He has softened my heart with His Word, because a hardened heart cannot receive the blessings He wants to give.

⁵"Dig through the wall as they watch and go out through the hole.

⁶"As they look on, load *the provisions and supplies* on your shoulder and carry it out in the dark. You shall cover your face so that you cannot see the land, for I have set you as a sign to the house of Israel."

⁷I did as I had been commanded. I brought out my provisions *and* supplies during the day, like the provisions *and* supplies of an exile, and in the evening I dug through the wall with my hands. I brought out *my provisions and supplies* in the dark, carrying it on my shoulder as they watched.

8In the morning the word of the LORD came to me, saying,

9"Son of man, has not the house of Israel, the rebellious house, asked you, 'What you are doing?'

10"Say to them, 'Thus says the Lord GOD, "This oracle (a burden to be carried) concerns the prince (Zedekiah) in Jerusalem as well as all the house of Israel who are there."'

11"Say, 'I am a sign to you. As I have done, so it will be done to them; they will go into exile, into captivity.'

12"The prince who is among them will load *his provisions and supplies* on his shoulder in the dark and go out. They will dig a hole through the wall to go out. He will cover his face so that he cannot see the land with his eyes.

13"I will also spread My net over him, and he will be caught in My snare. And I will bring him to Babylon, to the land of the Chaldeans; yet he will not see it, though he will die there. [2 Kin 25:1–7; Jer 39:5; 52:7–11]

14"I will scatter to every wind all who are around him, his helpers and all his troops; and I will draw out a sword after them.

15"So they will know *and* understand fully that I am the LORD when I scatter them among the nations and disperse them among the [pagan] countries.

16"But I will leave a few [survivors] who will escape the sword, the famine, and the virulent disease, that they may confess all their repulsive (idolatrous) acts among the nations where they go, and may know [without any doubt] that I am the LORD."

17Moreover, the word of the LORD came to me, saying,

18"Son of man, eat your bread with anxiety, and drink your water with trembling and with fear.

19"Then say to the people of the land, 'Thus says the Lord GOD concerning the inhabitants of Jerusalem in the land of Israel, "They will eat their bread with anxiety and drink their water with horror, because their land will be stripped *and* looted of its fullness because of the violence of all those who live in it.

20"The cities that are inhabited will be in ruins and the land will be deserted; and you will know [without any doubt] that I am the LORD."'"

21Then the word of the LORD came to me, saying,

22"Son of man, what is this proverb that you have in the land of Israel, saying, 'The days are long and every vision fails'?

23"Therefore tell them, 'Thus says the Lord GOD, "I will put an end to this proverb, and they will no longer use it as a proverb in Israel." But say to them, "The days draw near as well as the fulfillment of every vision.

24"For there will no longer be any false *and* empty vision or flattering divination within the house of Israel.

25"For I the LORD will speak, and whatever word I speak will be accomplished. It will no longer be delayed, for in your days, O rebellious house, I will speak the word and I will fulfill it," says the Lord GOD.'"

26Again the word of the LORD came to me, saying,

27"Son of man, behold, the house of Israel is saying, 'The vision that Ezekiel sees is for many years *from now,* and he prophesies of the times that are far off.'

28"Therefore say to them, 'Thus says the Lord GOD, "None of My words will be delayed any longer. Whatever word I speak will be fulfilled completely,"'" says the Lord God.

13 AND THE word of the LORD came to me saying,

2"Son of man, prophesy against the prophets of Israel who prophesy, and say to those who prophesy from their own inspiration, 'Hear the word of the LORD!

[3]"Thus says the Lord God, "Woe (judgment is coming) to the foolish prophets who are following their own spirit [claiming to have seen things] but have [in fact] seen nothing.

[4]"O Israel, your prophets have been like foxes among the ruins.

[5]"You have not gone up into the gaps *or* breaches, nor built the wall around the house of Israel that it might stand in the battle on the day of the Lord.

[6]"They have seen falsehood and lying divination, saying, 'The Lord says,' but the Lord has not sent them. Yet they hope *and* make men to hope for the confirmation of their word.

[7]"Did you not see (make up) a false vision and speak a lying divination when you said, 'The Lord declares,' but it is not I who have spoken?"'"

[8]Therefore, thus says the Lord God, "Because you have spoken empty *and* delusive words and have seen lies, therefore behold, I am against you," says the Lord God.

[9]"So My hand will be against the [counterfeit] prophets who see (make up) empty *and* delusive visions and who give lying prophecies. They will have no place in the [secret] council of My people, nor will they be recorded in the register of the house of Israel, nor will they enter into the land of Israel, that you may know [without any doubt] that I am the Lord God.

[10]"It is definitely because they have seduced My people, saying, 'Peace,' when there is no peace, and because when one builds a [flimsy] wall, behold, these [lying] prophets plaster it over with whitewash;

[11]so tell those who plaster it with whitewash, that it will fall! A flooding rain [of judgment] will come, and you, O [great] hailstones, will fall; and a violent wind will tear the wall apart.

[12]"Behold, when the wall has fallen, will you not be asked, 'Where is the coating with which you [prophets] plastered it?'"

[13]"Therefore, thus says the Lord God, "I will make a violent wind break out in My wrath, and there will be in My anger an overwhelming rain and great hailstones to destroy [that wall] in wrath.

[14]"So I will tear down the wall which you have plastered with whitewash and bring it down to the ground, so that its foundations will be exposed; when it falls, you will perish in its midst. And you shall know *and* understand fully that I am the Lord.

[15]"Thus I will expend My wrath on the wall and on those who have plastered it with whitewash and I will say to you, 'The wall is gone and its plasterers are gone,

[16]*along with* the [false] prophets of Israel who prophesy [deceitfully] to Jerusalem, and who see [false] visions of peace for her when there is no peace,' says the Lord God.

[17]"Now you, son of man, set your face against the daughters of your people who are prophesying out of [the wishful thinking of] their own mind (inspiration). Prophesy against them

[18]and say, 'Thus says the Lord God, "Woe to the women who fasten *magic* (protective) charms on all wrists and make veils for the heads of those of every stature to capture [human] lives! Will you capture the lives of My people but keep your own?

[19]"You have profaned Me among My people [in payment] for handfuls of barley and for pieces of bread, killing people who should not die and giving [a guarantee of] life to those who should not live, because of your lies to My people who pay attention to lies."'"

[20]Therefore, thus says the Lord God, "Behold, I am against your *magic* bands [and veils] by which you hunt [human] lives as birds and I will tear them from your arms; and I will let the lives you hunt go free, even those lives whom you hunt as birds.

[21]"I will also tear off your [pagan] veils and rescue My people from your

hands, and they will no longer be in your grip to be hunted *and* trapped. Then you will know [without any doubt] that I am the LORD.

²²"Because you disheartened the righteous with falsehood when I did not cause him grief, but have encouraged the wicked not to turn from his wicked way and preserve his life,

²³therefore, you women will no longer see false visions or practice divinations, and I will rescue My people from your hand. Then you will know [without any doubt] that I am the LORD."

14 THEN CERTAIN of the elders of Israel came to me [seeking an oracle from God] and sat down before me.

²And the word of the LORD came to me, saying,

³"Son of man, these men have set up [and honored] their idols in their hearts and have put right before their faces the [vile] stumbling block of their wickedness *and* guilt; should I [permit Myself to] be consulted by them at all?

⁴"Therefore speak to them and say to them, 'Thus says the Lord GOD, "Any man of the house of Israel who takes his idols [of rebellion] into his heart, and puts the [vile] stumbling block of his wickedness *and* guilt [images of silver and gold] before his face, and yet comes to the prophet [to ask of him], I the LORD will answer him, [but I will answer him] in accordance with the number of his idols,

⁵in order that I may take hold of the heart (mind) of the house of Israel who are all estranged from Me because of their idols."'

⁶"Therefore say to the house of Israel, 'Thus says the Lord GOD, "Repent and turn away from your idols and turn your faces away from all your disgusting *and* vile acts.

⁷"For anyone of the house of Israel or among the strangers who immigrate

putting the Word to work

In Ezekiel 14:6, God calls Israel to repent and turn away from idols. An idol is anything we worship by giving it too much attention or anything that is more important to us than God. Do you have any idols—social status, money, your job, your house or car, your children? Obey God's Word and ask Him to forgive you and to help you put Him in first place in your life. He will gladly do it!

to Israel who separates himself from Me, taking his idols into his heart, and puts right before his face the [vile] stumbling block of his wickedness *and* guilt, and [then] comes to the prophet to ask of Me for himself, I the LORD will answer him Myself.

⁸"I will set My face against that man [that hypocrite] and will make him a sign and a proverb, and I will cut him off from among My people; and you will know [without any doubt] that I am the LORD.

⁹"But if the prophet [who speaks without My authority] is enticed to speak a word [of his own], it is I the LORD who have caused that prophet [to speak falsely to please the inquirer, thus allowing himself to be a party to the inquirer's sin], and I will stretch out My hand against him and destroy him from among My people Israel.

¹⁰"They [both] will bear *the punishment* of their wickedness; the sin of the [counterfeit] prophet will be the same as the sin of the [hypocritical] inquirer,

¹¹so that the house of Israel may no longer drift away from Me and no longer defile themselves with all their transgressions, but they will be My people, and I will be their God,"' says the Lord GOD."

¹²The word of the LORD came [again] to me, saying,

¹³"Son of man, if a land sins against Me by committing unfaithfulness, and I stretch out My hand against it and destroy its source of bread and send famine on it and cut off from it both man and animal,

¹⁴even if these three men, Noah, Daniel, and Job were in that land, by their own righteousness (right standing with God) they could only save (deliver) themselves," says the Lord GOD.

¹⁵"If I were to cause predatory beasts to pass through the land and they ravaged it *and* depopulated it of children, and it became desolate so that no one would pass through because of the predators,

¹⁶*though* these three men were in the land, as I live," says the Lord GOD, "they could not save either their sons or their daughters. They alone would be saved, but the land would be desolate (ruined, deserted).

¹⁷"Or if I were to bring a sword on that land and say, 'Let a sword go through the land and cut off man and animal from it,'

¹⁸even *though* these three men were in the land, as I live," says the Lord GOD, "they could not save either their sons or their daughters, but they alone would be saved.

¹⁹"Or if I should send a virulent disease into that land and pour out My wrath in blood on it to cut off man and animal from it,

²⁰even though Noah, Daniel, and Job were in the land, as I live," says the Lord GOD, "they could not save either their son or their daughter; they would save only themselves by their righteousness [that is, their right-standing with God— their moral and spiritual integrity]."

²¹For thus says the Lord GOD, "How much more when I send My four severe judgments against Jerusalem— sword, famine, predatory beasts, and virulent disease—to cut off man and animal from it! [Lev 26:21–33]

²²"Yet, behold, survivors will be left in it [escaping the judgments], both sons and daughters. Listen carefully, they are going to come out to you [in Babylon] and you will see their [wicked] conduct and [despicable] actions; then you will be at peace in regard to the disaster which I have brought against Jerusalem for everything which I have brought on it [has been deserved].

²³"Then they will reassure you [in regard to the appropriateness of the judgments] when you see their [heinous] conduct and actions, for you will know that I have not done without cause whatever I did to it," declares the Lord GOD.

15 AND THE word of the LORD came to me, saying, ²"Son of man, how is the wood of the grapevine (Israel) better than any wood of a branch which is among the trees of the forest? [Ps 80:8–13; Jer 2:21]

³"Can wood be taken from it to make any object? Or can men take a peg from it on which to hang any vessel?

⁴"If it has been thrown into the fire for fuel, and the fire has consumed both of its ends and the middle section has been charred, is it suitable *or* useful for anything?

⁵"Notice this, even when it was complete, it was not useful *and* was not made into anything. How much less, after the fire has burned [part of] it and [the remainder of] it is charred, can it still be made into anything?

⁶"Therefore, thus says the Lord GOD, 'Like the wood of the grapevine among the trees of the forest, which I have given to the fire for fuel, so have I given up the people of Jerusalem;

⁷and I set My face against them. *Though* they have come out of the fire, yet the fire will consume them. Then you will know [without any doubt] that I am the LORD, when I set My face against them.

8'I will make the land desolate (ruined, deserted), because they have acted unfaithfully [through their idolatry],' says the Lord God."

16 AGAIN THE word of the Lord came to me, saying, 2"Son of man, make Jerusalem understand [the heinous and vile nature of] her repulsive (idolatrous) acts

3and say, 'Thus says the Lord God to Jerusalem (all of Israel), "Your [spiritual] origin and your birth are from the land of the Canaanite; your [spiritual] father was an Amorite and your [spiritual] mother a Hittite. [Ezek 16:45; John 8:44]

4"And as for your birth, on the day you were born your navel cord was not cut, nor were you washed with water for cleansing, nor were you rubbed with salt or even wrapped in cloths.

5"No eye looked with pity on you to do any of these things for you, to have compassion on you; but you were thrown out in the open field, for you were loathed on the day that you were born.

6"When I passed by you and saw you squirming in your [newborn] blood, I said to you while you were there in your blood, 'Live!' Yes, I said to you while you were there in your blood, 'Live!'

7"I made you (Israel) multiply like plants [which grow] in the field, and you grew up and became tall and you reached the age for [wearing] fine jewelry; your breasts were formed and your hair had grown, yet you were naked and bare.

8"Then I passed by you [again] and looked on you; behold, you were maturing *and* at the time for love, and I spread My skirt over you and covered your nakedness. Yes, I swore [an oath] to you and entered into a covenant with you," says the Lord God, "and you became Mine."

9"Then I washed you with water; yes, I [thoroughly] washed away from you the [clinging] blood and anointed you with oil.

10"I also clothed you with embroidered cloth and put sandals of porpoise skin on your feet; and I wrapped you with fine linen and covered you with silk.

11"I adorned you with ornaments and I put bracelets on your wrists and a necklace around your neck.

12"I also put a ring in your nostril and earrings in your ears and a beautiful crown on your head.

13"Thus you were adorned with gold and silver, and your dress was [made] of fine linen and silk and embroidered cloth. You ate fine flour and honey and oil; so you were extremely beautiful and you advanced *and* prospered into royalty.

14"Then your fame went out among the nations on account of your beauty, for it was perfect because of My majesty *and* splendor which I bestowed on you," says the Lord God.

15"But you trusted in *and* relied on your beauty and prostituted yourself [in idolatry and its debauched rituals] because of your fame, and you poured out your immoralities on every [willing] passer-by and your beauty was his [as you worshiped the idols of the Gentile nations].

16"You took some of your clothes and made for yourself [decorated] high places *and* shrines of various colors and prostituted yourself on them— things which should never have come about and taken place.

17"You also took your beautiful jewels *and* beautiful vessels made of My gold and My silver, which I had given you, and made for yourself images of men so that you could prostitute yourself with them;

18and you took your embroidered clothing and covered them, and offered My oil and My incense before them.

¹⁹"Also My bread which I gave you, [made from the] fine flour and oil and honey with which I fed you, you even offered it before idols [no better than cow dung] as a sweet *and* soothing aroma; so it happened," says the Lord GOD.

²⁰"Moreover, you took your sons and your daughters whom you had borne to Me, and you destroyed them as sacrifices [to your man-made gods]. Were your gross immoralities so small a matter?

²¹"You slaughtered My children and offered them up to [worthless] idols, forcing them to pass through the [hideousness of the] fire.

²²"And in all your repulsive acts and prostitutions (idolatrous immoralities) you did not [pause to] remember the days of your youth, when you were naked and bare, squirming in your [newborn] blood.

²³"Then it came about after all your wickedness ('Woe, woe to you!' says the Lord GOD),

²⁴that you built yourself an altar for prostitution and made yourself a high place [for ritual prostitution] in every square [of Jerusalem].

²⁵"At the beginning of every street you built your high place and made your beauty repulsive; and you offered your body to every passer-by and multiplied your obscene immorality.

²⁶"You also prostituted yourself with the Egyptians, your lustful neighbors [by embracing their pagan rituals], and you multiplied your obscene immorality to provoke Me to anger.

²⁷"Behold now [listen very carefully], I have stretched out My hand against you, reduced your portion, and handed you over to the desire of those who hate you, the daughters of the Philistines, who are ashamed of your infamous behavior.

²⁸"You prostituted yourself with the Assyrians because you were not satisfied; you prostituted yourself with them and still were not satisfied.

²⁹"Moreover, you increased your obscene immorality with the land of tradesmen, Chaldea (Babylonia), and yet even with this you were not satisfied."'"

³⁰"How weakened by longing *and* lust is your heart (mind)," says the Lord GOD, "while you do all these things, the actions of a bold *and* brazen prostitute.

³¹"When you built your shrine altar for prostitution at the beginning of every street and made your high place in every public square, you were not like a prostitute because you refused payment.

³²"You adulterous wife, who welcomes *and* receives strangers instead of her husband!

³³"Men give gifts to all prostitutes, but you give your gifts to all your lovers, bribing the pagan nations to come to you [as allies] from every direction for your obscene immoralities.

³⁴"And you are different from other [unfaithful] women in your promiscuity, in that no one follows you to lure you into prostitution, and because you give money and no money is given you; in this way you are different."

³⁵Therefore, O prostitute [Israel], hear the word of the LORD.

³⁶Thus says the Lord GOD, "Because your lewdness was poured out and your nakedness uncovered through your obscene immoralities with your lovers (pagan allies), and with all your [repulsive] idols, and because of the blood of your sons that you gave to them,

³⁷therefore, listen, I will gather all your lovers (pagan allies) with whom you took pleasure, and all those whom you loved with all those whom you hated; I will even gather them against you from every direction and will expose your nakedness to them that they may see all your nakedness [making you, Israel, an object of loathing and of mockery, a spectacle among the nations].

³⁸"And I [the Lord GOD] will judge you like women who commit adultery or shed blood are judged; and I will

bring on you the blood of wrath and jealousy. [Num 5:18]

³⁹"I will also hand you over to your lovers, and they will tear down your shrines, demolish your high places, strip you of your clothing, take away your jewels, and they will leave you naked and bare.

⁴⁰"They will also incite a crowd against you and they will stone you and slaughter you with their swords.

⁴¹"They will burn down your houses with fire and execute judgments on you in the sight of many women (Gentile nations). Then I will make you cease your prostitution, and you will no longer hire your lovers.

⁴²"So I will calm My wrath toward you and My jealousy [resulting from being denied what is rightfully and uniquely mine] will turn away from you; I will be pacified and no longer angry.

⁴³"Because you have not remembered the days of your youth but have enraged Me with all these things, therefore, I in turn will bring your conduct down on your own head," says the Lord GOD, "so that you will not commit this lewdness on top of all your other repulsive acts.

⁴⁴"Behold, everyone who uses proverbs will use this proverb against you: 'Like mother, like daughter.'

⁴⁵"You are the daughter of your mother, who loathed her husband and her children. You are the sister of your sisters, who loathed their husbands and their children. Your [spiritual] mother was a Hittite and your [spiritual] father an Amorite.

the sin of ignoring the needy

Sodom and Gomorrah are usually known for their sexual sin, but we see in Ezekiel 16:49 that God actually considered another sin to be the root of all Sodom's problems. First of all, they had such an overabundance of everything that their hearts became arrogant. This still happens today; when people do not have any needs, they frequently turn away from God in pride.

According to Ezekiel 16:49, life was too easy for the people in Sodom. The city had many problems, but one of the worst was that its people did not help the poor and needy.

God's Word explicitly teaches us to help those less fortunate than we are. He instructs us to share some of what we have with those who are in need. When we do not share, we may invite a curse into our lives. God is always giving. Something good is always flowing out of Him to those in need—and as His children, He expects us to be giving too.

Pure religion that is unblemished in God's sight is to visit and help and care for the orphans and widows in their distress and need (see James 1:27). This simply means we should be involved in helping people who are hurting and needy. Our religion is worthless if we are not.

God has not called the church to "in-reach;" He has called us to "out-reach." I frequently find that I cannot solve my own problems, but I can always reach out and help someone else. When I do, I am sowing seeds for the harvest I need in my own life. Proverbs 11 teaches us that when we are merciful to the poor and needy we benefit ourselves (see Proverbs 11:17, 25). Do not be like Sodom and become proud in your abundance. Instead, make giving and helping others in need part of your daily life.

⁴⁶"Now your older sister is Samaria, she with her daughters (outlying cities) who live north of you; and your younger sister is Sodom, she with her daughters who live south of you.

⁴⁷"Yet you have not merely walked in their ways or behaved in accordance with their pagan practices; but, as if that were too little, you [soon] acted more corruptly in all your ways than they. [Matt 11:20–24]

⁴⁸"As I live," says the Lord GOD, "Sodom, your sister and her daughters have not done as you and your daughters have done.

⁴⁹"Behold, this was the sin of your sister Sodom: she and her daughters (outlying cities) had arrogance, abundant food, and careless ease, but she did not help the poor and needy.

⁵⁰"They were haughty and committed repulsive acts before Me; therefore I removed them when I saw it. [Gen 13:13; 18:20; 19:5]

⁵¹"Furthermore, Samaria did not commit half of your sins, but you have greatly increased your repulsive acts more than they. So you have made your [wicked] sisters [Samaria and Sodom] appear righteous *and* justified by [comparison to] all the disgusting things which you have done.

⁵²"Also bear your disgrace [as punishment], having made judgment favorable for your sisters, for [you virtually absolved them] because of your sins in which you behaved more repulsively than they; they are more in the right than you. Yes, be ashamed and bear your disgrace, for you made your [pagan] sisters seem righteous.

⁵³"Nevertheless, I will restore them [again] from their captivity, the captivity of Sodom and her daughters (outlying cities), the captivity of Samaria and her daughters, and along with them [I will restore you from] your own captivity [in the day of the Lord GOD], [Is 1:9]

⁵⁴"so that you [Judah] will bear your humiliation *and* disgrace, and be [thoroughly] ashamed for all [the wickedness] that you have done to console *and* comfort them.

⁵⁵"Your sisters, Sodom and her daughters and Samaria and her daughters will return to their former state; and you and your daughters will return to your former state.

⁵⁶"For [the name of] your sister Sodom was not mentioned by you [except as a byword] in the day of your pride [when David ruled],

⁵⁷before your [own] wickedness was uncovered. Now you have become an object of reproach *and* a byword for the daughters of Aram *and* of Edom and all who are around her, and for the daughters of the Philistines—those surrounding you who despise you.

⁵⁸"You have borne [the penalty of] your lewdness and your repulsive acts," says the LORD.

⁵⁹"Yes, thus says the Lord GOD, "I will also deal with you as you have done, you who have despised the oath by breaking the covenant.

⁶⁰"Nevertheless, I will remember [with compassion] My covenant with you in the days of your youth, and I will establish an everlasting covenant with you. [Ps 106:45]

⁶¹"Then you will remember your ways and be ashamed when you receive your sisters, both your older and your younger; I will give them to you as daughters, but not because of your covenant [with Me]. [John 10:16]

⁶²"And I will establish My covenant with you, and you will know [without any doubt] that I am the LORD, [Hos 2:19, 20]

speak the Word

Thank You, God, for establishing Your covenant with me and helping me know, without any doubt that You are the Lord.

–ADAPTED FROM EZEKIEL 16:62

63so that you may remember [in detail] and be ashamed and never open your mouth again because of your humiliation, when I have forgiven you for all that you have done," says the Lord GOD.

17 NOW THE word of the LORD came to me, saying, 2"Son of man, ask a riddle and tell a parable to the house of Israel,

3saying, 'Thus says the Lord GOD, "A great eagle (Nebuchadnezzar) with great wings, long pinions and a rich plumage of many colors came to Lebanon (Jerusalem) and took away the top of the cedar (Judah).

4"He broke off the topmost of its young twigs (young King Jehoiachin) and carried it to a land of traders (Babylonia); he set it in a city of merchants (Babylon).

5"He also took some of the seed of the land (Zedekiah, of the royal family) and planted it in fertile soil *and* a fruitful field; he placed it beside abundant waters and set it like a willow tree.

6"Then it sprouted *and* grew and became a low, spreading vine whose branches turned [in submission] toward him, but its roots remained under it. So it became a vine and yielded shoots and sent out branches.

7"There was [also] another great eagle with great wings and many feathers; and behold, this vine (Zedekiah) bent its roots toward him and sent out its branches toward him, away from the beds where it was planted, for him to water.

8"It was planted in good soil where water was plentiful for it to produce leaves *and* branches and to bear fruit, so that it might become a splendid vine."'

9"Thus says the Lord GOD, 'Ask, "Will it thrive? Will he (Nebuchadnezzar) not uproot it and strip off its fruit so that all its sprouting leaves will wither? It will not take a strong arm or many people to uproot it [ending Israel's national existence]. [2 Kin 25:1–7]

10"Though it is planted, will it thrive *and* grow? Will it not completely wither when the east wind touches it? It will wither in the beds where it grew." '" [Hos 13:9–12, 15]

11Moreover, the word of the LORD came to me, saying,

12"Say now to the rebellious house, 'Do you not know (realize) what these things *mean?*' Tell them, 'Hear this, the king of Babylon came to Jerusalem and took its king [Jehoiachin] and its princes and brought them with him to Babylon. [2 Kin 24:11–16]

13'And he took a member of the royal family [the king's uncle, Zedekiah] and made a covenant with him, putting him under oath. He also took the important leaders of the land, [2 Kin 24:17]

14so that the kingdom would be in subjection, unable to restore itself *and* rise again, but that by keeping his covenant it might continue.

15'But Zedekiah rebelled against Nebuchadnezzar by sending his ambassadors to Egypt so that they might give him horses and many troops. Will he succeed? Will he who does such things escape? Can he indeed break the covenant [with Babylon] and [still] escape?

16'As I live,' says the Lord GOD, 'surely in the country of the king (Nebuchadnezzar) who made Zedekiah [the vassal] king, whose oath he despised and whose covenant he broke, in Babylon Zedekiah shall die.

17'Pharaoh with his mighty army and great company will not help him in the war, when they (the Babylonians) put up ramps and build siege walls to destroy many lives.

18'Now Zedekiah dishonored the oath by breaking the covenant, and behold, he gave his hand *and* pledged his allegiance, yet did all these things; he shall not escape.'"

19Therefore, thus says the Lord GOD, "As I live, I will bring down on his own head My oath [made on My behalf by Nebuchadnezzar] which Zedekiah dishonored and My covenant which he broke.

20"I will spread My net over him, and he will be caught in My snare; and I will bring him to Babylon and will enter into judgment with him there for his treason which he has committed against Me.

21"All the choice men [from Judah] in all his troops will fall by the sword, and those that survive will be scattered to every wind; and you will know [without any doubt] that I the LORD have spoken."

22Thus says the Lord GOD, "I Myself will take *a twig* from the lofty top of the cedar and will set it out; I will crop off from the topmost of its young twigs a tender one and I will plant it on a high and lofty mountain. [Is 11:1, 10; 53:2; Jer 23:5; Zech 3:8]

23"I will plant it on the mountain heights of Israel, that it may grow boughs and bear fruit and be a noble *and* stately cedar. And birds of every kind will live under it; they will nest [securely] in the shade of its branches.

24"All the trees of the field will know that I the LORD bring down the tall tree, exalt the low tree, dry up the green tree, and make the dry tree flourish. I am the LORD; I have spoken, and I will fulfill it."

18 THE WORD of the LORD came to me again, saying, 2"What do you mean by using this proverb concerning the land of Israel,

'The fathers eat sour grapes [they sin],
But the children's teeth are set on edge'?

3"As I live," says the Lord GOD, "you are certainly not going to use this proverb [as an excuse] in Israel anymore.

4"Behold (pay close attention), all souls are Mine; the soul of the father as well as the soul of the son is Mine. The soul who sins will die. [Rom 6:23]

5"But if a man is righteous (keeps the law) and practices justice and righteousness,

6and does not eat [at the pagan shrines] on the mountains or raise his eyes to the idols of the house of Israel, or defile his neighbor's wife or approach a woman during her [monthly] time of impurity—

7if a man does not oppress anyone, but restores to the debtor his pledge, does not commit robbery, but gives his bread to the hungry and covers the naked with clothing,

8if he does not charge interest or take *a percentage of* increase [on what he lends in compassion], if he keeps his hand from sin and executes true justice between man and man,

9if he walks in My statutes and [keeps] My ordinances so as to act with integrity; [then] he is [truly] righteous and shall certainly live," says the Lord GOD. [Ezek 20:11; Amos 5:4]

10"If he is the father of a violent son who sheds blood, and who does any of these things to a brother

11(though the father did not do any of these things), that is, the son even eats [the food set before idols] at the mountain *shrines,* and defiles his neighbor's wife,

12oppresses the poor and needy, commits robbery, does not restore [to the debtor] his pledge, but raises his eyes to the idols, and commits repulsive acts,

13and charges interest and takes [a percentage of] increase on what he has loaned; will he then live? He will not live! He has done all these disgusting things, he shall surely be put to death; his blood will be on his own head.

14"Now behold, if this [wicked] man has a son who has observed all the sins which his father committed, and considers [thoughtfully what he has observed] and does not do like his father:

¹⁵"He does not eat [food set before idols] at the mountain *shrines* or raise his eyes to the idols of the house of Israel, or defile his neighbor's wife,

¹⁶or oppress anyone, or take anything in pledge, or commit robbery, but he gives his bread to the hungry and covers the naked with clothing,

¹⁷he keeps his hand from [oppressing] the poor, does not receive interest or increase [from the needy], but executes My ordinances and walks in My statutes; he shall not die for the sin (guilt) of his father; he shall certainly live.

¹⁸"As for his father, because he practiced extortion, robbed his brother, and did that which is not good among his people, behold, he shall die for his sin.

¹⁹"Yet do you say, 'Why should the son not bear the punishment for the father's sin?' When the son has practiced justice and righteousness and has kept all My statutes and has done them, he shall certainly live.

²⁰"The person who sins [is the one that] will die. The son will not bear the punishment for the sin of the father, nor will the father bear the punishment for the sin of the son; the righteousness of the righteous shall be on himself, and the wickedness of the wicked shall be on himself.

²¹"But if the wicked man turns [away] from all his sins which he has committed and keeps all My statutes and practices justice and righteousness, he shall certainly live; he shall not die.

²²"All of his transgressions which he has committed will not be remembered against him; because of his righteousness which he has practiced [for his moral and spiritual integrity in every area and relationship], he will live.

²³"Do I take any pleasure in the death of the wicked," says the Lord GOD, "rather than that he should turn [away] from his [malevolent] acts and live?

²⁴"But when the righteous man turns away from his righteousness and commits sin and acts in accordance with all the repulsive things that the wicked man does, will he live? All of his righteous deeds which he has done will not be remembered because of the treachery that he has committed and for his sin which he has committed; for them he shall die.

²⁵"Yet you say, 'The way of the Lord is not right.' Hear now, O house of Israel! Is My way not right? Is it not your ways that are not right?

²⁶"When a righteous man turns away from his righteousness, and commits sin and dies because of it, it is for his sin which he has committed that he dies.

²⁷"Again, when a wicked man turns away from his wickedness which he has committed and practices justice and righteousness, he will save his life.

²⁸"Because he considered and turned away from all the transgressions which he had committed, he shall certainly live; he shall not die.

²⁹"Yet the house of Israel says, 'The way of the Lord is not right!' O house of Israel, are My ways not right? Is it not your ways that are not right?

³⁰"Therefore I will judge you, O house of Israel, each one in accordance with his conduct," says the Lord GOD. "Repent (change your way of thinking) and turn away from all your transgressions, so that sin may not become a stumbling block to you. [Matt 3:2; Rev 2:5]

³¹"Cast away from you all your transgressions which you have committed [against Me], and make yourselves a new heart and a new spirit! For why should you die, O house of Israel? [Eph 4:22, 23]

³²"For I have no pleasure in the death of anyone who dies," says the Lord GOD. "Therefore, repent and live!"

19

"AS FOR you, take up a dirge (funeral poem to be sung) for the princes of Israel ²and say,

'What was your mother [Jerusalem and Judah]?
A lioness among lions!
She lay down among young lions,
She reared her cubs.
³'When she [the royal mother-city] brought up [Jehoahaz] one of her cubs,
He became a [young] lion,
And he learned to catch *and* tear the prey;
He devoured men. [2 Kin 23:30, 32]
⁴'The nations heard about him;
He was captured in their pit,
And they brought him with hooks
To the land of Egypt. [2 Chr 36:1, 4]
⁵'When she saw, as she waited,
That her hope was lost,
She took another of her cubs
And made him a young lion. [2 Kin 23:34; 24:1, 6]
⁶'And he moved among the lions;
He became a young lion,
He learned to tear the prey;
He devoured men.
⁷'He destroyed their palaces
And he flattened their cities;
And the land and all who were in it were appalled
By the sound of his roaring.
⁸'Then the nations set against him (the king)
On every side from the provinces,
And they spread their net over him;
He was captured in their pit. [2 Kin 24:8–15]
⁹'They put him in a cage with hooks *and* chains
And brought him to the king of Babylon;
They brought him in hunting nets
So that his voice would be heard no more
On the mountains of Israel.

¹⁰'Your mother [Jerusalem] was like a vine in your vineyard,
Planted by the waters;
It was fruitful and full of branches
Because of abundant water. [2 Kin 24:17; Ezek 17:7]
¹¹'And it had strong branches for the scepters of rulers,
And its height was raised above the thick branches *and* into the clouds
So that it was seen [easily] in its height with the mass of its branches.
¹²'But the vine was uprooted in [godly] wrath [by His representative]
And it was thrown down to the ground;
The east wind dried up its fruit.
Its strong branch was broken off
So that it withered;
The fire [of God's judgment] consumed it.
¹³'And now it is transplanted in the wilderness,
In a dry and thirsty land [of Babylon].
¹⁴'And the fire [of Zedekiah's rebellion] has gone out from its branch;
It has consumed the vine's shoots and fruit,
So that it has in it no [longer a] strong branch
As a scepter to rule.'"

This is a dirge (funeral poem to be sung), and has become a dirge.

20

IN THE seventh year, in the fifth *month,* on the tenth of the month [after the beginning of the exile in Babylon], certain of the elders of Israel came to inquire of the LORD and sat down before me. [Jer 25:11; 29:10] ²Then came the word of the LORD to me, saying, ³"Son of man, speak to the elders of

Israel and say to them, 'Thus says the Lord GOD, "Have you come to inquire of Me? As I live," says the Lord GOD, "I will not be inquired of by you."'

⁴"Will you judge them, son of man, will you judge them? Then make them know [accurately] *and* understand fully the repulsive acts of their fathers; [Matt 23:29–33; Acts 7:51, 52]

⁵and say to them, 'Thus says the Lord GOD, "On the day when I chose Israel and lifted up My hand *and* swore to the descendants of the house of Jacob and made Myself known to them in the land of Egypt, when I swore to them, saying, I am the LORD your God,

⁶on that day I swore to them to bring them out of the land of Egypt into a land that I had selected for them, [plentiful and] flowing with milk and honey, [a land] which is an ornament *and* a glory to all lands.

⁷"Then I said to them, 'Let every man throw away the detestable things on which he feasts his eyes, and do not defile yourselves with the idols of Egypt; I am the LORD your God.'

⁸"But they rebelled against Me and were not willing to listen to Me; they did not throw away the detestable things on which they feasted their eyes, nor did they give up the idols of Egypt.

"Then I decided to pour out My wrath on them and finish My anger against them in the land of Egypt.

⁹"But I acted for My Name's sake, that it would not be profaned in the sight of the [pagan] nations among whom they lived, in whose sight I made Myself known to them by bringing them out of the land of Egypt.

¹⁰"So I made them leave the land of Egypt and brought them into the wilderness.

¹¹"I gave them My statutes and explained My ordinances to them, which, if a man keeps, he will live.

¹²"Also I gave them My Sabbaths to be a sign between Me and them, that they might know [without any doubt] that I am the LORD who sanctifies them (separates and sets them apart).

¹³"But the house of Israel rebelled against Me in the wilderness. They did not walk in My statutes and they despised *and* rejected My ordinances, which, if a man keeps, he will live; and they greatly profaned My Sabbaths. Then I decided to pour out My wrath on them in the wilderness, to annihilate them.

¹⁴"But I acted for My Name's sake, that it would not be profaned in the sight of the [pagan] nations in whose sight I had brought them out [of slavery].

¹⁵"I also swore to them in the wilderness that I would not bring them into the land which I had given them, [a land of plenty] flowing with milk and honey, which is the ornament *and* glory of all lands,

¹⁶because they rejected My ordinances, and as for My statutes, they did not walk in them; they even profaned My Sabbaths, for their heart continually went after their [worthless] idols.

¹⁷"Yet My eye [looked on them with compassion and] spared them instead of destroying them, and I did not annihilate them in the wilderness.

¹⁸"But I said to their children in the wilderness, 'Do not walk in the statutes

speak the Word

Thank You, God, for the gift of the Sabbath. Help me to live a balanced life, not wearing myself out or overworking, but knowing without any doubt that You are the Lord and regularly observing the times of rest and refreshment You provide.
—ADAPTED FROM EZEKIEL 20:12

of your fathers nor observe their ordinances nor defile yourselves with their idols.

¹⁹'I am the LORD your God; walk in My statutes and keep My ordinances and observe them.

²⁰'Sanctify My Sabbaths *and* keep them holy; and they shall be a sign between Me and you, that you may know [without any doubt] that I am the LORD your God.'

²¹"Yet the children rebelled against Me; they did not walk in My statutes, nor were they careful to observe My ordinances, which, if a man keeps, he will live; they profaned My Sabbaths. Then I decided to pour out My wrath on them and finish My anger against them in the wilderness.

²²"Yet I withdrew My hand and acted for My Name's sake, that it would not be profaned in the sight of the [pagan] nations in whose sight I had brought them out [of slavery].

²³"Moreover, I swore to them in the wilderness that I would scatter them among the [Gentile] nations and disperse them among the countries,

²⁴because they had not observed My ordinances, but had [dishonored and] rejected My statutes and had profaned My Sabbaths, and set their eyes on the [man-made] idols of their fathers.

²⁵"[Therefore] I also gave them statutes that were not good and ordinances by which they could not live; [Ps 81:12; Is 66:4; Rom 1:21–25, 28]

²⁶and I pronounced them unclean because of their offerings [to their idols], in that they made all their firstborn pass through *the fire* [as pagan sacrifices], so that I might make them desolate, in order that they might know [without any doubt] that I am the LORD." ' [Lev 20:2–5]

²⁷"Therefore, son of man, speak to the house of Israel and say to them, 'Thus says the Lord GOD, "Again in this your fathers have blasphemed Me, in that they acted faithlessly *and* treacherously against Me.

²⁸"For when I had brought them into the land which I swore to give to them, they saw every high hill and every dark *and* leafy tree [as a place for idol worship], and there they offered their sacrifices and there they presented their offering that provoked My anger; there also they made their sweet-smelling aroma and there poured out their drink offerings.

²⁹"Then I said to them, 'What is the high place to which you go?' So the name of it is called Bamah (High Place) to this day." '

³⁰"Therefore, say to the house of Israel, 'Thus says the Lord GOD, "Will you [exiles] defile yourselves in the same manner as your fathers? And will you prostitute yourselves before their loathsome *and* heinous things?

³¹"When you offer your gifts, when you make your sons pass through the fire, you are defiling yourselves with all your idols to this day. And shall I be asked by you [for an oracle], O house of Israel? As I live," says the Lord GOD, "I will not be inquired of by you.

³²"What comes into your mind will never happen, when you say, 'We will be like the [pagan] nations, like the tribes of the [Gentile] countries, serving [idols made of] wood and stone.'

³³"As I live," says the Lord GOD, "most certainly with a mighty hand and an outstretched arm and with wrath poured out, I shall be King over you.

³⁴"I will bring you out from the peoples and will gather you from the countries in which you are scattered, with a mighty hand and with an outstretched arm, and with wrath poured out;

³⁵and I will bring you into the wilderness of the peoples, and there I will enter into judgment with you *and* contend with you face to face.

³⁶"As I entered into judgment with your fathers in the wilderness of the

land of Egypt, so I will enter into judgment *and* contend with you," says the Lord GOD. [Num 11; Ps 106:15; 1 Cor 10:5–10]

³⁷"I will make you pass under the rod [as the shepherd does with his sheep when he counts them, and I will count you as Mine and constrain you] and bring you into the bond of the covenant [to which you are permanently bound]. [Lev 27:32]

³⁸"And I will separate from you the rebels and those who transgress against Me; I will bring them out of the land where they temporarily live, but they will not enter the land of Israel. Thus you will know [without any doubt] that I am the LORD. [Heb 4:2, 3]

³⁹"As for you, O house of Israel," thus says the Lord GOD, "Go, let everyone serve his idols; but later you shall most certainly listen to Me, and you shall no longer profane My holy name with your gifts and with your idols.

⁴⁰"For on My holy mountain, on the high mountain of Israel (Zion)," says the Lord GOD, "there the whole house of Israel, all of them in the land, shall serve Me. There I will [graciously] accept them, and there I will seek (require) your offerings and the choicest of your gifts, with all your holy *and* sacred things.

⁴¹"I will accept you [graciously] as a pleasant *and* soothing aroma when I bring you out from the peoples and

put God first

Ezekiel 20:40 says we should bring to the Lord the choicest selections of all our offerings. To stay in perfect peace, we should give God the best of our time and our goods. We must be honest with ourselves about what our priorities are and start making changes that will enable us to keep God in first place.

Being too busy is not an acceptable excuse for not staying focused on what is truly important. Everyone sets his or her own schedule. We need to establish boundaries, and we need to learn to say no when people ask us to do something that leads us away from peace.

Be honest with yourself as you examine how you spend your time. Do not give God your leftovers; do not give Him the part of your day when you are worn out and you cannot think straight or keep your eyes open. Give God the firstfruits of your attention. Give Him the best part of your day.

God needs to be your priority in *everything* you do. From getting dressed to setting your schedule, you can ask God for wisdom to make choices that will glorify Him. You can intermingle your time with God into everything you do to such a degree that you can pray without ceasing by praying your way through your day. As you become aware of His presence, it will not be possible to separate secular activities from sacred ones. Even ordinary events will become sacred because He is involved in them.

You can simply talk to God as you go about your day, asking Him to direct you in the choices you are making and to empower you for the jobs you need to get done. As you acknowledge that God is always with you, you will keep Him first in everything you set out to do, and He will show you a direct path that will lead you to peace. You will experience great pleasure in your life, knowing you are keeping God first and thereby partnering with Him in everything you do.

gather you from the lands in which you have been scattered; and I will prove Myself holy *and* manifest My holiness among you in the sight of the nations. [Eph 5:2; Phil 4:18]

42"And you will know [without any doubt] that I am the Lord, when I bring you into the land of Israel, into the land which I swore to give to your fathers.

43"There you will remember your ways and all your deeds with which you have defiled yourselves; and you will loathe yourselves in your own sight because of all your evil deeds which you have done.

44"And you will know [without any doubt] that I am the Lord when I have dealt with you for My Name's sake, not in accordance with your evil ways nor with your corrupt conduct, O house of Israel," says the Lord God.'"

45Now the word of the Lord came to me, saying,

46"Son of man, set your face toward Teman, and speak out against the south and prophesy against the forest land of the Negev (the South),

47and say to the forest of the Negev, 'Hear the word of the Lord: thus says the Lord God, "Behold, I am about to kindle a fire in you, and it will devour every one of your green trees, as well as every one of your dry trees. The blazing flame will not be quenched and the whole surface from the south to the north will be burned by it.

48"All flesh will see that I the Lord have kindled it; it will not be quenched."'"

49Then I said, "Ah, Lord God! They are saying of me, 'Is he not [just] speaking in parables *and* making allegories?'"

21 AND THE word of the Lord came to me, saying, 2"Son of man, set your face toward Jerusalem, and direct your [prophetic] word against the sanctuaries; prophesy against the land of Israel 3and say to the land of Israel, 'Thus says the Lord, "Behold, I am against you and will draw My sword out of its sheath and I will cut off from you both the righteous and the wicked.

4"Because I will cut off from you both the righteous and the wicked, therefore My sword will go from its sheath against all flesh from south to north,

5and all living will know [without any doubt] that I the Lord have drawn My sword out of its sheath; it will not be sheathed again."'

6"As for you, son of man, groan with breaking heart and bitter grief, groan in their sight.

7"And when they say to you, 'Why do you sigh *and* groan?' you shall answer, 'Because of the news that is coming; and every heart will melt and all hands will be frail, and every spirit will faint and all knees will be weak as water. Behold, it comes and it will happen,' says the Lord God."

8Again the word of the Lord came to me, saying,

9"Son of man, prophesy and say, 'Thus says the Lord.' Say,

'A sword, a sword [from Babylon] is sharpened
And also polished!
10'It is sharpened to make a slaughter, Polished to flash *and* glimmer like lightning!'

Shall we then rejoice [when such a disaster approaches]? But it rejects *and* views with contempt the scepter of My son [Judah]. [Gen 49:9, 10; 2 Sam 7:23]

11"The sword [of Babylon] is ready to be polished so that it may be handled *and* put to use; the sword is sharpened and polished to be put in the hand of the slayer (Nebuchadnezzar).

12"Cry out and wail, son of man, for it is against My people; it is against all the princes of Israel. They are thrown to the sword along with My [terrified] people. Therefore strike your thigh *and* strike your chest [in grief].

¹³"For this sword has been tested [on others]; and what if it views with contempt the scepter [of Judah]? The scepter shall be no more [but shall be swept away]," says the Lord GOD.

¹⁴"Therefore, son of man, prophesy and strike your hands together; and let the sword be doubled the third time [in intensity], the sword for the slain. It is the sword for the great slaughter which surrounds them [so that no one can escape, even by hiding in their inner rooms],

¹⁵so that hearts may melt, and many will fall at their gates. I have given the glittering sword. Ah! It is made [to flash] like lightning; it is pointed *and* sharpened for slaughter.

¹⁶"Turn O sword and cut right or cut left, whichever way your thirst for blood *and* your edge direct you.

¹⁷"I will also strike My hands together, and I will cause My wrath to rest. I the LORD have spoken."

¹⁸The word of the LORD came to me, saying,

¹⁹"As for you, son of man, mark out two ways for the sword of the king of Babylon to come, both starting from the same land. And make a signpost; place it at the head of the way to the city.

²⁰"You shall point out a way for the [Babylonian] sword to come to Rabbah [the capital] of the sons of Ammon, and to Judah into fortified Jerusalem.

²¹"For the king of Babylon stands at the parting of the way, at the fork of the two ways, to use divination. He shakes the arrows, he consults the teraphim (household idols), he looks at the liver [of an animal for an omen].

²²"In his right hand is the lot marked for Jerusalem: to set battering rams, to open the mouth calling for destruction, to lift up the voice with a war cry, to set battering rams against the gates, to put up assault ramps, and to build siege walls.

²³"It will seem like a false divination in their eyes, those who have sworn solemn oaths [of allegiance to Nebuchadnezzar]. But he will remind them of their guilt [by rebelling and violating their oath], that they may be caught. [2 Chr 36:10, 13; Ezek 17:15, 18–21]

²⁴"Therefore, thus says the Lord GOD, 'Because you have caused your guilt to be remembered, in that your rebellion is uncovered, so that your sins appear in everything that you do—because you have come to mind, you will be seized with the hand [of the enemy].

²⁵'And you, O dishonored and wicked one [Zedekiah], the prince of Israel, whose day has come, whose time of final punishment is here,'

²⁶thus says the Lord GOD, 'Remove the turban and take off the crown; things shall not remain as they have been. Exalt that which is low and abase the high.

²⁷'A ruin, a ruin, I will make it a ruin! It shall no longer exist until He comes whose right it is [to reign], and I will give it *to Him.*' [Gen 49:10; Is 9:6, 7; 11:1–4; Dan 7:14; Luke 1:31–33]

²⁸"And you, son of man, prophesy and say, 'Thus says the Lord GOD concerning the sons of Ammon and concerning their reproach (disgrace),' and say: 'A sword, a sword is drawn for the slaughter; it is sharpened *and* polished to put an end [to everything], and to flash like lightning,

²⁹while they (Ammonite prophets) see false visions [of peace] for you, while they divine lies [of escape] for you—to place you [of Ammon] on the headless bodies of the wicked who are slain, whose day has come, whose time of the final punishment is here.

³⁰'Return the sword to its sheath. In the place where you were created, in the land of your origin (birth), I will judge you.

³¹'I will pour out My indignation on you [sons of Ammon]; I will blow on you with the fire of My wrath, and I

will place you in the hand of brutal men, skilled in destruction.

³²'You will be fuel for the fire; your blood will be in the midst of the land. You will not be remembered, for I the LORD have spoken.'" [Jer 49:1–6; Ezek 25:1–7; Amos 1:13–15; Zeph 2:8–11]

22 THEN THE word of the LORD came to me, saying, ²"And you, son of man [Ezekiel], will you judge, will you judge the city of bloodshed? Then make her recognize all her repulsive acts.

³"You shall say, 'Thus says the Lord GOD, "A city that sheds blood in her midst, so that her time [of doom] will come, and makes idols to defile her, contrary to her *interest!*

⁴"You have become guilty by the blood which you have shed, and you are defiled by the idols which you have made. Thus you have caused your day [of judgment and punishment] to approach and have arrived at [the completion of] your years; therefore, I have made you an object of scorn to the [pagan] nations and a thing to be mocked by all countries.

⁵"Those who are near and those who are far from you will mock you, you [infamous one] of ill repute, full of turmoil.

⁶"Behold, the princes of Israel, every one according to his power, have been intending to shed blood in you.

⁷"In you they have treated father and mother lightly. They have oppressed the stranger among you; and in your presence they have wronged the fatherless and the widow.

⁸"You have despised *and* scorned My sacred things and have profaned My Sabbaths.

⁹"In you are men who slander for the purpose of shedding blood, and in your presence they have eaten [food offered to idols] at the mountain shrines; in your midst they have committed acts of lewdness.

¹⁰"In you men have uncovered their fathers' nakedness [the nakedness of mother or stepmother]; in you they have violated women who are [set apart as ceremonially] unclean during their menstrual impurity [or after childbirth].

¹¹"In you one has committed a shameful act with his neighbor's wife, another has lewdly defiled his daughter-in-law, and another has violated his sister, his father's daughter.

¹²"In you they have accepted bribes to shed blood; you have taken [forbidden] interest and [a percentage of] profits, and you have injured your neighbors for gain by oppression *and* extortion, and you have forgotten Me," says the Lord GOD.

¹³"Behold, therefore, I strike My hands [together] at your dishonest gain which you have acquired and at the bloodshed which is among you.

¹⁴"Can your heart (courage) endure, or can your hands be strong in the days that I will deal with you? I the LORD have spoken, and will act.

¹⁵"I will scatter you among the nations and disperse you through the countries, and I will destroy your filthiness.

¹⁶"You will defile yourself in the sight of the [Gentile] nations, and you will know [without any doubt] that I am the LORD."'"

¹⁷And the word of the LORD came to me, saying,

¹⁸"Son of man, the house of Israel has become dross (metallic waste) to Me. All of them are (useless) bronze, tin, iron, and lead in the furnace; they are the dross of silver.

¹⁹"Therefore, thus says the Lord GOD, 'Because you have all become dross, therefore, behold, I will gather you [O Israel] into the midst of Jerusalem.

²⁰'As they gather silver and bronze and iron and lead and tin into the furnace to blow fire on it in order to melt it, so I will gather you in My anger and

in My wrath, and I will put you there and melt you.

²¹'I will gather you and blow on you with the fire of My wrath, and you will be melted in the midst of it.

²²'As silver is melted in the furnace, so will you be melted in the midst of it; and you will know [without any doubt] that I the LORD have poured out My wrath on you [O Israel].'"

²³And the word of the LORD came to me, saying,

²⁴"Son of man, say to her, 'You [Israel] are a land that is not pronounced clean or rained on in the day of indignation.'

²⁵"There is a conspiracy of her [false] prophets in her midst, like a roaring lion tearing the prey. They have devoured [human] life; they have taken [in their greed] treasure and precious things; they have made many widows among her.

²⁶"Her priests have done violence to My law and have profaned My holy

stand in the gap

God is looking for people today who will "stand in the gap" for others, just as He was in Ezekiel's time (Ezekiel 22:30). If there is a gap in a person's relationship with God due to a particular sin in his life, we have the privilege of placing ourselves in that breach and praying for him. If he has needs, we can intercede for him and expect to see him comforted and encouraged while he waits. We can also expect a timely breakthrough in terms of needs being met for this person.

I do not know what I would do if people did not intercede for me. Literally thousands of people have told me over the years that they pray for me. I actually ask God for intercessors. I petition Him to give me people to intercede for me and for the fulfillment of the ministry to which He has called me.

If our prayers are filled with only petitions for the things we want and are void of intercession, that makes a statement about our character—just as when petition outweighs praise and thanksgiving in our prayer lives. I have discovered that the more I am delivered from selfishness, the more I pray for others.

Praying for others is equivalent to sowing seed. We all know we must sow seed if we are to reap a harvest (see Galatians 6:7). Sowing seed into the lives of other people is one sure way to reap a harvest in our own lives. Each time we pray for someone else, we are assuring our own success.

If you want to succeed as a believer, I highly recommend that you include ample intercession for others in your prayer life. Give away what you need or want.

If you want to be a success, help someone else succeed by praying for them. If you want your ministry to succeed, pray for someone else's ministry. If you want your business to succeed, pray for someone else's business. If you need a breakthrough over some bad habit that is hindering you and holding you back, pray for someone who has a need in a similar area.

Remember, we are often tempted to judge others, and that only holds us in bondage. Give people *prayer* instead of *judgment*, and stand in the gap for them as often and as fervently as you possibly can. Then you will be a blessing to them, and you will make much faster progress toward the fulfillment of your destiny.

things. They have made no distinction between the holy (sacred) and the profane (secular), they have not taught [people] the difference between the unclean and the clean; and they hide their eyes from My Sabbaths, and I am profaned among them.

27"Her princes within her are like wolves tearing *and* devouring the prey, shedding blood and destroying lives in order to get dishonest gain.

28"Her prophets have smeared whitewash for them, seeing false visions and divining lies for them, saying, 'Thus says the Lord GOD'—when the LORD has not spoken.

29"The people of the land have practiced oppression *and* extortion and have committed robbery; they have wronged the poor and needy and they have oppressed the stranger without justice.

30"I searched for a man among them who would build up the wall and stand in the gap before Me for [the sake of] the land, that I would not destroy it, but I found no one [not even one].

31"Therefore I have poured out My indignation on them; I have consumed them with the fire of My wrath; I have repaid their way [by bringing it] upon their own heads," says the Lord GOD.

23 THE WORD of the LORD came to me again, saying, 2"Son of man, there were two women (Israel and Judah), the daughters of one mother (the united kingdom);

3and they prostituted themselves in Egypt. From their youth they were grossly immoral; in that place their breasts were embraced and their virgin bosom was grasped.

4"Their names were Oholah the elder and Oholibah her sister, and they became Mine and they gave birth to sons and daughters. And as for [the identity of] their names, Oholah is Samaria (capital city of Israel) and Oholibah is Jerusalem (capital city of Judah).

5"Oholah played the prostitute while she was Mine; and she adored *and* lusted after her lovers (allies), the Assyrians, her neighbors,

6who were clothed in purple, governors and officials, all of them attractive young men, horsemen riding on horses.

7"She bestowed [freely] her immoralities on them, the choicest men of Assyria, all of them; and with all whom she adored *and* lusted after, she defiled herself with their idols.

8"She did not give up the acts of prostitution that originated *during her time in* Egypt; for in her youth men had lain with her, and they handled her virgin bosom and poured out their depravity on her.

9"Therefore, I placed her in the hand of her lovers (allies), into the hand of the Assyrians whom she adored.

10"They uncovered her nakedness; they took her sons and her daughters and they killed her with the sword. So she became notorious among women, and they executed judgments on her.

11"Now her sister Oholibah saw this, yet she was more corrupt in her lust than she, and her acts of prostitution were more [wanton] than the immoralities of her sister.

12"She lusted after the Assyrians—governors and officials, her neighbors, magnificently clothed, horsemen riding on horses, all of them desirable young men.

13"I saw that she had defiled herself; they both *behaved* the same way.

14"But Oholibah carried her depravity further, for she saw men pictured on the wall, the images of the Chaldeans (Babylonians) sketched *and* portrayed in vermilion (bright red pigment),

15girded with belts on their loins, with flowing turbans on their heads, all of them looking like officers, like the Babylonian men whose native land was Chaldea.

16"When she saw [the sketches of] them, she lusted after them and sent messengers to them in Chaldea.

17"The Babylonians came to her to the bed of love and they defiled her with their evil desire; and when she had been defiled by them, she (Jerusalem) broke the relationship *and* pushed them away from her in disgust.

18"So she flaunted her acts of prostitution and exposed her nakedness; then I became disgusted with her [and turned away], as I had become disgusted with her sister [and turned away].

19"Yet she multiplied her depravities, remembering the days of her youth, when she was actively immoral in the land of Egypt.

20"For she lusted after her lovers [there], whose flesh is like the flesh of donkeys and whose issue is like the issue of horses.

21"Thus you longed for the lewdness *and* vulgarity of your youth, when the Egyptians handled your bosom on account of the breasts of your youth.

22"Therefore, O Oholibah, thus says the Lord God, 'Behold, I will stir up your lovers (allies) against you, from whom you turned away in disgust, and I will bring them against you from every side:

23the Babylonians and all the Chaldeans, Pekod and Shoa and Koa, and all the Assyrians with them, desirable young men, governors and officials all of them, princes, officers and men of renown, all of them riding on horses.

24'They will come against you with weapons, chariots, and wagons, and with a company of people (infantry) who will array themselves against you on every side with large shield and small, and helmet; and I will commit the judgment *and* the punishment to them, and they will judge *and* punish you in accordance with their [pagan] customs.

25'I will set My jealous indignation against you [demanding what is rightfully and uniquely mine], and they will deal with you in fury. They will remove your nose and your ears, and your survivors will fall by the sword. They will take your sons and your daughters; and the survivors will be devoured by the fire.

26'They will also strip you (Judah) of your clothes and take away your beautiful jewels.

27'Thus I will put an end to your lewdness and your prostitution *brought* from the land of Egypt, so that you will not lift up your eyes to them or remember Egypt [with longing] anymore.'

28"For thus says the Lord God, 'Behold, I will place you into the hands of those whom you hate, into the hands of those from whom you turned away in disgust.

29'They will deal with you in hatred, take all your property, and leave you naked and bare. And the nakedness of your depravity will be uncovered, both your lewdness and your obscene practices.

30'These things will be done to you because you have prostituted yourself with the [Gentile] nations, because you have defiled yourself with their idols.

31'You have walked in the way of your sister (Samaria); therefore I will give her cup [of judgment] into your hand.'

32"Thus says the Lord God,

'You will drink your sister's cup,
Which is deep and wide [and filled
     to the brim].
You shall be laughed at and
     derided;
It contains much [too much to
     endure].
33'You shall be filled with
     drunkenness and sorrow,
With the cup of horror and
     desolation,

With the cup of your sister
   Samaria.
34'You will drink it and drain it,
   Then you will gnaw its fragments
   And tear your breasts;

for I have spoken,' says the Lord God.
35"Therefore, thus says the Lord God, 'Because you have forgotten Me and cast Me behind your back, therefore bear now [the consequences of] your lewdness and prostitution.'"
36Moreover, the Lord said to me, "Son of man, will you judge Oholah (Samaria, capital of Israel) and Oholibah (Jerusalem, capital of Judah)? Then inform them of their atrocities [the detestable and vile things they do].
37"For they have committed adultery, and blood is on their hands. They have committed adultery [against Me] with their idols and have even forced their sons, whom they bore to Me, to pass through the fire as [an offering of] food to them (idols).
38"Moreover, they have done this to Me: they have defiled My sanctuary on the same day [of their idolatries] and have profaned My Sabbaths.
39"For when they had killed their children [as offerings] to their idols, then they came the same day to My sanctuary to profane it [by daring to offer a sacrifice there also]. And behold, this they did within My house.
40"Furthermore, you have even sent a messenger for men to come from far away; and behold, they came—those for whom you bathed, painted your eyes, and decorated yourself with ornaments;
41and you sat on a splendid couch with a table arranged before it on which you had set My incense and My oil.
42"The sound of a carefree crowd was with her; and drunkards were brought from the wilderness with men of a common sort, who put bracelets on the hands of the women (both sisters) and beautiful crowns on their heads.

43"Then I said concerning the one (Oholah) worn out by adulteries, 'Will they now commit adultery with her when she is like this?'
44"But they committed adultery with her as they would with a prostitute. So they went in to Oholah (Israel) and to Oholibah (Judah), the lewd women.
45"And they, righteous men, will judge and condemn them with the judgment (punishment) of adulteresses and with the judgment of women who shed blood, because they are adulteresses and blood is on their hands.
46"For thus says the Lord God, 'Bring up a horde (mob) against them and hand them over to terror and plunder.
47'And the horde will stone them with stones and cut them down with their swords; they will kill their sons and their daughters and burn down their houses with fire.
48'Thus I will make lewdness cease from the land, that all women may be admonished and taught not to commit immoral acts as you have done.
49'Thus your lewdness will be repaid to you, and you will suffer the penalty for your [sinful] idolatry; and you will know [without any doubt] that I am the Lord God.'"

24 AGAIN IN the ninth year [of King Jehoiachin's captivity by Nebuchadnezzar of Babylon], in the tenth month, on the tenth [day] of the month, the word of the Lord came to me, saying,
2"Son of man, record the name of the day, this very day. The king of Babylon has laid siege to Jerusalem this very day.
3"Speak a parable against the rebellious house [of Judah] and say to them, 'Thus says the Lord God,

  "Put on a pot; put it on and also
    pour water into it;
4"Put in it the pieces [of meat],

Every good piece (the people of
Jerusalem), the thigh and the
shoulder;
Fill it with choice bones.
⁵"Take the choicest of the flock,
And also pile wood under the pot.
Make it boil vigorously
And boil its bones in the pot."

⁶'Therefore, thus says the Lord God,
"Woe (judgment is coming) to the
bloody city,
To the pot in which there is rust
And whose rust has not gone out
of it!
Take out of it piece by piece,
Without making any choice.
⁷"For her blood [that she has shed]
remains in her midst;
She put it on the bare rock;
She did not pour it on the ground
To cover it with dust.
⁸"That it may cause wrath to come
up to take vengeance,
I have put her blood [guilt for her
children sacrificed to Molech] on
the bare rock,
That it may not be covered."

⁹'Therefore, thus says the Lord God,

"Woe to the bloody city!
I will also make the pile [of wood]
high.
¹⁰"Heap on wood, kindle the fire,
Boil the meat well [done]
And mix in the spices,
And let the bones be burned.
¹¹"Then set the empty pot
(Jerusalem) back on the coals
So that it may be hot
And its bronze may glow
And its filthiness may be melted
And its rust (scum) may be
consumed.
¹²"She has wearied Me with toil,
Yet her great rust has not left her;
Her thick rust and filth will not be
burned away by fire [no matter
how hot the flame].

¹³"In your filthiness are lewdness
and outrage.
Therefore I would have cleansed
you,
Yet you were not [willing to be]
cleansed,
You will not be cleansed from your
filthiness again
Until I have satisfied My wrath
against you.

¹⁴"I the Lord have spoken; it is coming
and I will act. I will not relent, and I
will not have compassion and I will
not be sorry; in accordance with your
ways and in accordance with your
deeds I will judge and punish you,"
says the Lord God.'"
¹⁵Also the word of the Lord came to
me, saying,
¹⁶"Son of man, listen carefully, I am
about to take away from you the desire of your eyes [your wife] with a
single stroke. Yet you shall not mourn
and you shall not weep, and your tears
shall not flow.
¹⁷"Sigh and groan in silence; do not
mourn for the dead. Bind on your turban and put your sandals on your feet,
and do not cover your mustache or eat
the bread of [mourners furnished by
other] men."
¹⁸So I spoke to the people in the
morning, and in the evening my wife
died. And the next morning I did as I
was commanded.
¹⁹The people said to me, "These
things that you are doing—tell us,
what do they mean for us?"
²⁰Then I answered them, "The word
of the Lord came to me, saying,
²¹'Speak to the house of Israel, "Thus
says the Lord God, 'Behold, I will profane My sanctuary, the pride of your
strength, the desire of your eyes, and
the delight of your soul; and your sons
and your daughters whom you have
left behind [in Jerusalem] will fall by
the sword.
²²'You will do as I [Ezekiel] have done;

you shall not cover your mustache nor eat the bread of [mourning brought to you by other] men.

²³'Your turbans will be on your heads and your sandals on your feet. You will not mourn or weep, but you will rot away in your sins and you will groan to one another. [Lev 26:39]

²⁴'So Ezekiel will be a sign to you; in accordance with all that he has done you will do. And when this [destruction of the temple] comes, then you will know [without any doubt] that I am the Lord GOD.'"

²⁵'As for you, son of man, on the day when I take their strength *and* their stronghold from them, their joy and their glory, the desire of their eyes and their heart's [chief] delight (the temple), and I also take their sons and their daughters,

²⁶that on that day a survivor will come to you to let you hear [of the destruction of Jerusalem] with your [own] ears.

²⁷'On that day your mouth will be opened to him who escaped, and you will speak and no longer be mute. In this way you shall be a sign to them, and they will know [without any doubt] that I am the Lord.'"

25

THE WORD of the Lord came to me again, saying, ²"Son of man, set your face toward the Ammonites and prophesy against them.

³"And say to the Ammonites, 'Hear the word of the Lord GOD, for thus says the Lord GOD, "Because you said, 'Aha!' against My sanctuary when it was profaned and against the land of Israel when it was made desolate and against the house of Judah when they went into exile,

⁴therefore, behold, I am going to give you to the people of the East as a possession, and they will set their encampments among you and make

their dwellings among you; they will eat your fruit and drink your milk.

⁵"I will make Rabbah [your chief city] a pasture for camels and [the cities of] the Ammonites a resting place for flocks [of sheep]. And you will know [without any doubt] that I am the Lord."

⁶'For thus says the Lord GOD, "Because you have clapped your hands and stamped your feet and rejoiced with all the contempt, *and* malice, *and* spite of your soul against the land of Israel,

⁷therefore, behold, I have stretched out My hand against you and will hand you over as prey *and* spoil to the nations. And I will cut you off from the peoples and will cause you to perish from the countries; I will destroy you. Then you shall know [without any doubt] that I am the Lord." [Jer 49:1–6; Ezek 21:28–32; Amos 1:13–15; Zeph 2:8–11]

⁸'Thus says the Lord GOD, "Because Moab and Seir (Edom) say, 'Behold, the house of Judah is like all the [pagan] nations,'

⁹therefore, behold, I will deprive the flank of Moab of its cities which are on its frontiers, the glory of the land, Bethjeshimoth, Baal-meon and Kiriathaim.

¹⁰"I will give it, along with the children of Ammon, to the people of the East as a possession, so that the children of Ammon will not be remembered among the nations [any longer].

¹¹"Thus I will execute judgment *and* punishment on Moab, and they will know [without any doubt] that I am the Lord." [Is 15, 16; Jer 48; Amos 2:1–3; Zeph 2:8–11]

¹²'Thus says the Lord GOD, "Because Edom has acted against the house of Judah by taking vengeance, and has greatly offended *and* has incurred grievous guilt by taking revenge on them,"

¹³therefore thus says the Lord GOD, "I will also stretch out My hand against

Edom and I will cut off *and* destroy man and beast. I will make it desolate; from Teman even to Dedan they will fall by the sword.

¹⁴"I will take My vengeance on Edom by the hand of My people Israel. Therefore, they will act in Edom in accordance with My anger and My wrath, and they will know *and* experience My vengeance," says the Lord GOD. [Is 34; Ezek 35; Amos 1:11, 12; Obad]

¹⁵'Thus says the Lord GOD, "Because the Philistines have acted revengefully and have taken vengeance [contemptuously] with malice in their hearts to destroy with everlasting hostility *and* hatred,"

¹⁶therefore thus says the Lord GOD, "Behold, I will stretch out My hand against the Philistines, and I will cut off the Cherethites and destroy the remnant of the seacoast.

¹⁷"I will execute great vengeance on them with wrathful rebukes *and* chastisements and they will know [without any doubt] that I am the LORD when I lay My vengeance on them."'" [Is 14:29–31; Jer 47; Amos 1:6–8; Zeph 2:4–7; Zech 9:5–7]

26 NOW IN the eleventh year, on the first [day] of the month [after the capture of King Jehoiachin], the word of the LORD came to me, saying,

²"Son of man, because Tyre has said against Jerusalem, 'Aha! The gateway of the people is broken; she is open to me. I will be filled, *now that* she is a desolate waste,'

³therefore, thus says the Lord GOD, 'Behold, I am against you, O Tyre, and I will cause many nations to come up against you, as the sea makes its waves crest.

⁴'They will destroy the walls of Tyre and break down her towers; and I will scrape her dust *and* debris from her and make her as bare as [the top of] a rock.

life point

Basically, God was saying in Ezekiel 25:15–17 that He would take vengeance on the Philistines because they had taken vengeance upon their enemies with hostility and hatred in their hearts. When people hurt us, we are wise not to take our own vengeance upon them; instead, we need to turn them over to God. Waiting on God to make things right is an act of trust, and it is also the smartest response we can give.

⁵'Her island in the midst of the sea will become a dry place to spread nets, for I have spoken,' says the Lord GOD, 'and she will become a prey *and* a spoil for the nations.

⁶'Also Tyre's daughters (towns, villages) on the mainland will be killed by the sword, and they will know [without any doubt] that I am the LORD.'"

⁷For thus says the Lord GOD, "Behold, I will bring upon Tyre from the north Nebuchadnezzar the king of Babylon, king of kings, with horses and chariots and with horsemen and a great army.

⁸"He will kill your daughters on the mainland with the sword, and he shall make siege walls against you and build a siege ramp against you and raise [a roof of] large shields [as a defense] against you.

⁹"He will direct the [shocking] blow of his battering rams against your walls, and he will tear down your towers with his crowbars.

¹⁰"Because of the great number of his horses, their dust will cover you; your walls [O Tyre] will shake from the noise of the horsemen and the wagons and the chariots when he enters your gates as men enter a city that is breached.

¹¹"With the hoofs of his horses Nebuchadnezzar will trample all your

streets; with the sword he will kill your people, and your strong pillars (obelisks) will fall to the ground.

¹²"Also they will take your riches as spoil and plunder your merchandise, and tear down your walls and your pleasant houses, and throw your stones and your timber and the debris [from your city] out in the water.

¹³"So I will silence your songs, and the sound of your lyres will no longer be heard.

¹⁴"I will make you [Tyre] a bare rock; you will be a dry place on which to spread nets. You will never be rebuilt, for I the LORD have spoken," says the Lord GOD.

¹⁵Thus says the Lord GOD to Tyre, "Shall not the coastlands shake at the sound of your fall when the wounded groan, when the slaughter occurs in your midst?

¹⁶"Then all the princes of the sea will go down from their thrones and remove their robes and take off their embroidered garments. They will clothe themselves with trembling; they will sit on the ground, tremble again and again, and be appalled at you.

¹⁷"They will take up a dirge (funeral poem to be sung) for you and say to you,

'How you have perished *and*
  vanished, O renowned city,
From the seas, O renowned city,
Which was mighty on the sea,
She and her inhabitants,
Who imposed her terror
On all who lived there!
¹⁸'Now the coastlands will tremble
On the day of your fall;
Yes, the coastlands which are by
  the sea
Will be terrified at your
  departure.'"

¹⁹For thus says the Lord GOD, "When I make you a desolate city, like the cities which are not inhabited, when I bring up the deep over you and great waters cover you,

²⁰then I will bring you down with those who descend into the pit (the place of the dead), to the people of old, and I will make you [Tyre] live in the depths of the earth, like the ancient ruins, with those who go down to the pit, so that you will not be inhabited; but I will set glory *and* splendor in the land of the living.

²¹"I will bring terrors on you and you will be no more. Though you will be sought, yet you will never be found again," says the Lord GOD.

27 THE WORD of the LORD came to me again, saying, ²"Now you, son of man, take up a dirge (funeral poem to be sung) for Tyre,

³and say to Tyre, who lives at the entrance to the sea, merchant of the peoples to many coastlands, 'Thus says the Lord GOD,

"O Tyre, you have said, 'I am
  perfect in beauty.'
⁴"Your borders are in the heart of
  the seas;
Your builders have perfected your
  beauty.
⁵"They have made all your planks
  of fir trees from Senir;
They have taken a cedar from
  Lebanon to make a mast for you.
⁶"Of the oaks of Bashan they have
  made your oars;
They have made your deck of
  boxwood from the coastlands of
  Cyprus, inlaid with ivory.
⁷"Your sail was of fine embroidered
  linen from Egypt
So that it became your
  distinguishing mark (insignia);
Your [ship's] awning [which
  covered you] was blue and
  purple from the coasts of Elishah
  [of Asia Minor].

8"The inhabitants of Sidon and
   [the island] of Arvad were your
   oarsmen;
Your skilled *and* wise men, O Tyre,
   were with you; they were your
   pilots.
9"The elders of Gebal and its skilled
   and wise men were with you,
   repairing your leaks;
All the ships of the sea with their
   mariners were with you to deal
   in your merchandise.

10"Persia and Lud and Put (Libya)
were in your army as your men of war.
They hung the shield and the helmet
on you; they gave you splendor.
11"The men of Arvad with your army
were upon your walls, all around, and
the Gammadim (men of valor) were in
your towers. They hung their shields
on your walls, all around; they perfected your beauty.
12"Tarshish [in Spain] was your customer *and* traded with you because of
the abundance of your riches of all
kinds; with silver, iron, tin, and lead
they paid for your wares.
13"Javan (Greece), Tubal and
Meshech (Asia Minor) traded with
you; with the lives of men [taken as
slaves] and vessels of bronze they paid
for your merchandise.
14"Those from Beth-togarmah (Arme-
nia) traded for your wares with [char-
iot] horses, war horses, and mules.
15"The men of Dedan were your
traders. Many coastlands were your
markets; ivory tusks and ebony they
brought to you in payment *or* as gifts.
16"Aram traded with you because of
the abundance of the goods you made.
They paid for your merchandise with
emeralds, purple, embroidered work,
fine linen, coral, and rubies.
17"Judah and the land of Israel, they
were your traders; with the wheat of
Minnith [in Ammon], cakes, honey,
oil, and balm they paid for your goods.
18"Damascus traded with you because

of the abundance of your handiworks
and the immense wealth of every kind,
with the wine of Helbon [Aleppo] and
the white wool [of Sachar in Syria].
19"Vedan and Javan traded with yarn
from Uzal [in Arabia] for your wares;
wrought iron, cassia, and sweet cane
were among your merchandise.
20"Dedan traded with you in saddle
blankets for riding.
21"Arabia and all the princes of Kedar,
they were your customers for lambs,
rams, and goats [favored by you]; for
these they were your customers.
22"The merchants of Sheba and
Raamah [in Arabia], they traded with
you; they paid for your wares with the
choicest of all kinds of spices and all
kinds of precious stones and gold.
23"Haran and Canneh and Eden
[in Mesopotamia], the merchants of
Sheba [on the Euphrates], Asshur and
Chilmad traded with you.
24"They traded with you in choice
fabrics *and* garments, in clothes of
blue *or* violet and embroidered work,
and in [treasures of] multi-colored
damask *and* knotted carpets bound
with tightly wound cords, *which were*
among your merchandise.
25"The ships of Tarshish were the
caravans for your merchandise,

And you [Tyre] were replenished
   and very glorious [heavily laden
   with an imposing fleet]
In the heart of the seas.

26"Your rowers have brought you
   Into great *and* deep waters;
   The east wind has broken *and*
      shipwrecked you
   In the heart of the seas.
27"Your riches, your wares, your
      merchandise
   Your oarsmen and your pilots,
   Your caulkers, your dealers in
      merchandise,
   And all your men of war who are
      with you,

With all your company that is in
  your midst,
Will sink in the heart of the seas
On the day of your ruin.
28 "The pasture lands *and* the
  countryside will shake
At the [piercing] sound of the
  [hopeless, wailing] cry of your
  pilots.
29 "All who handle the oar,
The mariners and all the pilots of
  the sea
Will come down from their ships;
They will stand on the shore,
30 And they will make their voice
  heard [as they wail loudly] over
  you
And they will cry bitterly.
They will throw dust on their
  heads;
They will wallow in ashes.
31 "And they will make themselves
  [completely] bald for you
And wrap themselves in sackcloth;
And in bitterness of soul they will
  weep for you
With bitter mourning *and* wailing.
32 "In their wailing they will take up
  a dirge (funeral poem to be sung)
  for you
And sing a dirge for you:
'Who is like Tyre,
Like her who is silent [destroyed]
  in the midst of the sea?
33 'When your wares went out to the
  sea,
You met the desire, *and* the
  demand, *and* the necessities of
  many people;
You enriched the kings of the earth
With your abundant wealth and
  merchandise.
34 'Now you are shattered by the seas
In the depths of the waters;
Your merchandise and all your
  crew
Have gone down with you.
35 'All the inhabitants of the
  coastlands

Are aghast *and* appalled at you,
And their kings are horribly
  frightened *and* shudder;
Their faces twitch *and* pale.
36 'The merchants among the people
  hiss at you [with malicious joy];
You have become a horror *and* a
  source of terrors.
You will cease to be forever.' " ' "

28 THE WORD of the Lord
came again to me, saying,
2 "Son of man, say to the
prince of Tyre, 'Thus says the Lord God,

"Because your heart is lifted up
And you have said *and* thought, 'I
  am a god,
I sit in the seat of the gods
In the heart of the seas';
Yet you are [only] a man [weak,
  feeble, made of earth] and not
  God,
Though you [imagine yourself to
  be more than mortal and] think
  your mind is as [wise as] the
  mind of God—
3 Behold, you are [imagining
  yourself] wiser than Daniel;
There is no secret [you think] that
  is hidden from you;
4 With your [own] wisdom and with
  your [own] understanding
You have acquired your riches *and*
  power
And have brought gold and silver
  into your treasuries;
5 By your great wisdom and by your
  trade
You have increased your riches
  and power,
And your heart is proud *and*
  arrogant because of your wealth;

6 Therefore thus says the Lord God,

'Because you have imagined your
  mind [to be]
Like the mind of God [having
  thoughts and plans like God
  Himself], [Obad 3]

7Therefore, behold, I will bring
   strangers (Babylonians) upon you,
  The most ruthless *and* violent of
   the nations.
  And they will draw their swords
  Against the beauty of your wisdom
   [O Tyre]
  And defile your splendor.
8'They will bring you down to the
   pit [of destruction],
  And you will die the death of all
   those who die
  In the heart of the seas.
9'Will you still say, "I am a god,"
  In the presence of him who kills
   you?
  But you are [only] a man [made of
   earth] and not God,
  In the hands of those who wound
   and profane you.
10'You will die the death of the
   uncircumcised [barbarian]
  By the hand of strangers,
  For I have spoken!' says the Lord
   GOD."'"

11Again the word of the LORD came
to me, saying, 12"Son of man, take up a dirge (funeral poem to be sung) for the king of Tyre and say to him, 'Thus says the Lord GOD,

  "You had the full measure of
   perfection *and* the finishing
   touch [of completeness],
  Full of wisdom and perfect in
   beauty.
13"You were in Eden, the garden of
   God;
  Every precious stone was your
   covering:
  The ruby, the topaz, and the
   diamond;
  The beryl, the onyx, and the jasper;
  The lapis lazuli, the turquoise, and
   the emerald;
  And the gold, the workmanship of
   your settings and your sockets,
  Was in you.

  They were prepared
  On the day that you were created.
   [Gen 3:14, 15; Is 14:12–15; Matt
   16:23]
14"You were the anointed cherub
   who covers *and* protects,
  And I placed you there.
  You were on the holy mountain of
   God;
  You walked in the midst of the
   stones of fire [sparkling jewels].
   [Ex 24:10]
15"You were blameless in your ways
  From the day you were created
  Until unrighteousness *and* evil
   were found in you.
16"Through the abundance of your
   commerce
  You were internally filled with
   lawlessness *and* violence,
  And you sinned;
  Therefore I have cast you out as a
   profane *and* unholy thing
  From the mountain of God.
  And I have destroyed you, O
   covering cherub,
  From the midst of the stones of fire.
17"Your heart was proud *and*
   arrogant because of your beauty;
  You destroyed your wisdom for the
   sake of your splendor.
  I cast you to the ground;
  I lay you before kings,
  That they might look at you.
18"You profaned your sanctuaries
  By the great quantity of your sins
   and the enormity of your guilt,
  By the unrighteousness of your
   trade.
  Therefore I have brought forth a
   fire from your midst;
  It has consumed you,
  And I have reduced you to ashes
   on the earth
  In the sight of all who look at you.
19"All the peoples (nations) who
   knew you
  Are appalled at you;

You have come to a horrible *and*
   terrifying end
And will forever cease to be." ' "
   [Is 23; Joel 3:4–8; Amos 1:9, 10;
   Zech 9:3, 4]

20Again the word of the Lord came
to me, saying,
   21"Son of man, set your face toward
Sidon, and prophesy against her
   22and say, 'Thus says the Lord God,

"Behold, I am against you, O Sidon,
And I will show My glory *and* be
   glorified in your midst.
Then they will know [by personal
   experience] that I am the Lord
   when I bring judgment *and*
   punishment on her,
And I will manifest My holiness in
   her.
23"For I will send virulent disease to
   her
And blood into her streets,
And the wounded will fall in her
   midst
By the sword upon her from every
   side,
And they shall know [without any
   doubt] that I am the Lord.

24"And there will no longer be a briar
or a painful thorn to prick the house
of Israel from all those around them
who treated them with contempt; then
they will know [with clarity] that I am
the Lord God."
   25'Thus says the Lord God, "When I
gather the house of Israel from the nations among whom they are scattered,
and I manifest my Holiness in them in
the sight of the nations, then they will
live in their own land which I gave to
My servant Jacob.
   26"They shall live in it securely; and
they will build houses, plant vineyards and live securely when I execute
judgment on all those around them
who despise them. Then they will
know [with clarity and confidence]
that I am the Lord their God." ' "

29 IN THE tenth year [of the
captivity of King Jehoiachin
by the king of Babylon], in
the tenth *month,* on the twelfth of the
month, the word of the Lord came to
me, saying,
   2"Son of man, set your face toward
Pharaoh king of Egypt, and prophesy
against him and against all Egypt.
   3"Speak and say, 'Thus says the Lord
God,

"Behold, I am against you, Pharaoh
   king of Egypt,
The great monster that lies in the
   midst of his rivers,
[Boastfully] declaring, 'My Nile is
   my own, and I have made it for
   myself.'
4"I will put hooks in your jaws
And [I will] make the fish of your
   rivers stick to your scales.
And I will pull you up from the
   midst of your rivers,
And all the fish of your rivers will
   stick to your scales.
5"I will abandon you to the
   wilderness, you and all the fish
   of your rivers;
You will fall on the open field; and
   you will not be gathered up or
   buried.
I have given you as food to the
   [wild] animals of the earth and
   the birds of the sky.
6"And all the inhabitants of Egypt
   will know [without any doubt]
   that I am the Lord,
Because they have been [only] a
   staff made of [fragile] reeds to
   the house of Israel.
7"When they (Israel) grasped you
   (Egypt) by the hand,
You broke and tore apart their
   hands;
When they leaned on you,
You broke and strained their backs."

8'Therefore thus says the Lord God,
"Behold, I am going to bring a sword

on you and cut off (destroy) both man and animal,

⁹and the land of Egypt will be a desolation and a wasteland. And they will know [without any doubt] that I am the Lord.

"Because you said, 'The Nile is mine and I have made it,'

¹⁰behold (hear this), therefore, I am against you and against your rivers (the Nile, its tributaries), and I will make the land of Egypt a complete waste and a desolation, from [northern] Migdol to [southern] Syene, even as far as the border of Ethiopia (Cush).

¹¹"No man's foot will pass through it, no animal's foot will pass through it, and it will not be inhabited for forty years.

¹²"So I will make the land of Egypt a desolation [plundered and ruined] among desolated lands; and her cities, among cities that are laid waste, will be desolate forty years. I will scatter the Egyptians among the nations and [I will] disperse them through the lands."

¹³'For thus says the Lord God, "At the end of forty years I will gather the Egyptians from the nations among whom they were scattered. [Jer 46:25, 26]

¹⁴"I will reverse the fortunes of Egypt [as I will that of Israel] and cause them to return to the land of Pathros, the land of their origin, and there they will be a lowly kingdom.

¹⁵"It will be the lowliest of the kingdoms, and it will never again exalt itself above the nations; I will diminish the Egyptians so they will never again rule over the nations.

¹⁶"And Egypt will never again have the confidence of the house of Israel; their wickedness will be remembered whenever Israel looks toward them [for help]. Then they will know [without any doubt] that I am the Lord God."'"

¹⁷In the twenty-seventh year [after King Jehoiachin was taken to Babylon], in the first *month,* on the first of the month, the word of the Lord came to me, saying,

¹⁸"Son of man, Nebuchadnezzar king of Babylon made his army work hard [at My command] against Tyre; every [soldier's] head became bald and every shoulder was worn *and* peeled [from carrying loads of dirt and stones for siege works]. Yet he had no wages from Tyre [in proportion to the time and labor expended during the siege], either for himself or his army, for the work that he had done against it [for Me]."

¹⁹Therefore thus says the Lord God, "Behold, I will give the land of Egypt to Nebuchadnezzar king of Babylon. And he will carry off her wealth and capture her spoil and seize her plunder; and it shall be the wages for his army.

²⁰"I have given him the land of Egypt for the hard work which he did [against Tyre], because they did it for Me," says the Lord God.

²¹"In that day I will make a horn sprout for the house of Israel, and I will open your mouth among them, and they will know [without any doubt] that I am the Lord [when I renew their strength]."

30 THE WORD of the Lord came again to me, saying, ²"Son of man, prophesy and say, 'Thus says the Lord God,

"Wail, 'Alas for the day!'
³"For the day is near,
Even the day of the Lord is near,
It will be a cloudy day;
A time *of doom* for the nations.
⁴"A sword will come upon Egypt,
And anguish *and* trembling will be in Ethiopia (Cush),
When the slain fall in Egypt
And they [of Babylon] carry away her great mass of people *and* her riches
And her foundations are torn down.

5"Ethiopia (Cush), Put, Lud, all Arabia, Libya (Cub) and the people of the land of the covenant [the Jews who had taken refuge in Egypt] will fall with the Egyptians by the sword."

6'Thus says the LORD,
  "Those who uphold *and* support
    Egypt will fall
  And the pride of her power will
    come down;
  From Migdol [in the north] to
    Syene [in the south]
  They will fall within her by the
    sword,"
  Says the Lord GOD.
7"And they will be desolate
  In the midst of countries that are
    desolated;
  And her cities will be
  Among cities that are devastated
    [by plunder and slavery].
8"And they will know [without any
    doubt] that I am the LORD,
  When I have set a fire in Egypt
  And all her helpers are shattered
    and destroyed.

9"On that day [swift] messengers will go from Me in ships to frighten the careless *and* unsuspecting Ethiopians, and there will be anguish *and* trembling in them as in the day of [judgment for] Egypt; for behold, it is coming!"
  10'Thus says the Lord GOD,

  "I will also make the great people
    of Egypt cease
  By the hand of Nebuchadnezzar
    king of Babylon.
11"He and his people with him,
  The most violent *and* ruthless of
    the nations,
  Will be brought in to destroy the
    land,
  And they will draw their swords
    against Egypt
  And fill the land with the slain.
12"And I will make the rivers [of the
    Nile delta] dry

And sell the land into the hands of
    evil men;
  I will make the land desolate
  And all that is in it,
  By the hand of strangers. I the
    LORD have spoken."

13'Thus says the Lord GOD,
  "I will also destroy the idols
  And I will put an end to the images
    in Memphis;
  There will no longer be a prince of
    the land of Egypt.
  And I will put fear in the land of
    Egypt.
14"I will make Pathros desolate,
  Set fire to Zoan
  And execute judgments *and*
    punishments on Thebes.
15"I will pour out My wrath on
    Pelusium,
  The stronghold of Egypt,
  And I will cut off (destroy) the
    population of Thebes.
16"I will set fire to Egypt;
  Pelusium will writhe in [great]
    anguish,
  Thebes shall be torn open
  And Memphis shall be in daily
    distress.
17"The young men of On (Aven) and
    of Pi-beseth
  Will fall by the sword,
  And the women [and children]
    will go into captivity.
18"In Tehaphnehes the day will be
    dark
  When I break the yoke bars *and*
    dominion of Egypt there.
  Then the pride of her power will
    come to an end;
  A cloud [of disasters] will cover
    her,
  And her daughters will go into
    captivity.
19"In this way I will bring judgment
    and punishment on Egypt.
  Then they shall know [without any
    doubt] that I am the LORD."'"

²⁰In the eleventh year [after King Jehoiachin was taken to Babylon], in the first *month,* on the seventh of the month, the word of the Lord came to me, saying,

²¹"Son of man, I have broken the arm of Pharaoh king of Egypt; and behold, it has not been bound up to heal or wrapped with a bandage, so that it may be strong to hold *and* wield the sword.

²²"Therefore thus says the Lord God, 'Behold, I am against Pharaoh king of Egypt and will break his arms, both the strong one and the broken, and I will make the sword fall from his hand.

²³'I will scatter the Egyptians among the nations and will disperse them throughout the lands.

²⁴'I will strengthen the arms of the king of Babylon and put My sword in his hand; but I will break Pharaoh's arms and he will groan before him (Nebuchadnezzar) with the groanings of a [mortally] wounded man.

²⁵'But I will strengthen *and* hold up the arms of the king of Babylon and the arms of Pharaoh will fall down. Then the people [of Egypt] will know that I am the Lord, when I put My sword into the hand of the king of Babylon and he stretches it out against the land of Egypt.

²⁶'When I scatter the Egyptians among the nations and disperse them through the lands, then they will know [without any doubt] that I am the Lord.'"

31 IN THE eleventh year [after King Jehoiachin was taken captive to Babylon], in the third *month,* on the first of the month, the word of the Lord came to me, saying,

²"Son of man, say to Pharaoh king of Egypt and to his hordes,

'Whom are you like in your greatness?
³'Behold (listen carefully), Assyria was a cedar in Lebanon

With beautiful branches and with forest shade,
And of high stature,
With its top among the clouds.
⁴'The waters nourished it, the deep [underground waters] made it grow tall.
Its rivers ran all around the place where it was planted,
Sending out its streams to all the trees (other nations) of the field.
⁵'Therefore it towered higher than all the trees of the forest
And its boughs multiplied and its branches grew long;
Because there was so much water they spread outward.
⁶'All the birds of the sky made their nests in its twigs,
And under its branches all the animals of the field gave birth [to their young],
And all of the great nations lived under its shadow.
⁷'So it was beautiful in its greatness, in the length of its branches;
For its roots extended [downward] to great waters.
⁸'The cedars in the garden of God could not hide *or* rival it;
The cypress trees did not have boughs like it,
And the plane trees did not have branches like it.
No tree in the garden of God was like it in its beauty.
⁹'I made it beautiful with the great mass of its branches,
So that all the trees of Eden which were in the garden of God were jealous of it (Assyria).

¹⁰Therefore thus says the Lord God, "Because it is high in stature and has set its top among the thick boughs *and* the clouds, and its heart is proud of its height, [2 Kin 18:31–35]

¹¹I will hand it over to a mighty one *and* a mighty one of the nations; he will most certainly deal with it. I have

driven it away in accordance with its wickedness.

¹²"Alien tyrants of the nations have cut it down and left it; its foliage has fallen on the mountains and in all the valleys and its branches have been broken in all the ravines of the land. And all the nations of the earth have come from under its shade and have left it.

¹³"All the birds of the sky will nest in its ruins, and all the animals of the field will rest on its *fallen* branches

¹⁴so that none of the trees by the waters may exalt themselves because of their height, nor set their top among the clouds, nor their well-watered mighty ones stand [arrogantly] in their height. For they have all been handed over to death, to the earth beneath, among the sons of men, with those who go down to the pit (the grave)."

¹⁵'Thus says the Lord God, "On the day when Assyria went down to Sheol (the place of the dead) I caused mourning; I closed the deep [subterranean waters] over it and restrained its rivers. And the many waters [that contributed to its prosperity] were held back; and I made [the heart of] Lebanon mourn for it, and all the trees of the field wilted away because of it.

¹⁶"I made the nations quake at the sound of its fall when I cast it down to Sheol with those who descend into the pit; and all the well-watered trees of Eden, the choicest and the best of Lebanon, will be comforted in the earth beneath [at Assyria's downfall].

¹⁷"They also went down to Sheol with it to those who were slain by the sword; those who were its strength lived under its shade among the nations.

¹⁸"Which among the trees of Eden do you equal in glory and in greatness [O Egypt]? Yet you [also] will be brought down with the trees of Eden to the earth beneath (nether world). You will lie among the uncircumcised (the barbaric, the boorish, the crude) with those who were slain by the sword. This is *how it shall be* with Pharaoh and all his hordes!"' says the Lord God." [Ezek 28:10; 32:19]

32

IN THE twelfth year [after King Jehoiachin of Judah was taken into exile by the king of Babylon], in the twelfth month, on the first of the month, the word of the Lord came to me, saying,

²"Son of man, take up a dirge (funeral poem to be sung) over Pharaoh king of Egypt and say to him,

'You have compared yourself to a
     young lion among the nations,
But you are like a monster in the
     seas;
You burst into your rivers
And disturbed *and* muddied the
     waters with your feet
And fouled their rivers [the source
     of their prosperity].'"

³Thus says the Lord God,

"I will spread out My net over you
With a company of many nations,
And they will bring you up in My
     net.
⁴"Then I will leave you (Egypt) on
     the land;
I will hurl you on the open field.
And I will make all the birds of the
     sky dwell on you,
And I will satisfy the animals of all
     the earth with you.
⁵"And I will scatter your flesh on
     the mountains
And fill the valleys with your debris
     [your corpses and their worms].
⁶"I will also water the land with
     your flowing blood
As far as the mountains,
And the ravines will be full of you.
⁷"And when I extinguish you,
I will cover the heavens [of Egypt]
     and darken their stars;
I will cover the sun with a cloud

And the moon will not give its
light.
[8]"All the bright lights in the heavens
I will darken over you
And I will place darkness on your
land,"
Says the Lord GOD.

[9]"I will also put fear into the hearts of
many peoples when I bring your destruction [and captivity] among the
nations, into countries which you have
not known.
[10]"I will make many peoples appalled at you [at your judgment and
your defeat], and their kings will be
horribly afraid of you when I brandish
My sword [of judgment] before them;
they will tremble and shudder every
moment, every man for his own life,
on the day of your downfall."
[11]For thus says the Lord GOD, "The
sword of the king of Babylon will come
on you.
[12]"I will make your horde [of people]
fall by the swords of the mighty—all of
them are tyrants among the nations,

And they will devastate the pride
and presumption of Egypt,
And all its hordes will be
destroyed.
[13]"I will also destroy all its cattle
from beside its great waters;
And the foot of man will not
muddy them anymore
Nor will the hoofs of the animals
muddy them.
[14]"Then I will make their waters
quiet and clear;
I will make their rivers run [slowly
and smoothly] like oil,"
Says the Lord GOD.
[15]"When I make the land of Egypt
desolate,
And the country is stripped and
deprived of all that which filled it,
When I strike all those who live
in it,

Then they will know [without any
doubt] that I am the LORD.

[16]"This is the dirge (funeral poem to be
sung) and they shall sing it [for her].
The daughters of the nations shall
sing it; for Egypt and for all her hordes
they shall sing it," says the Lord GOD.

[17]In the twelfth year [after King Jehoiachin of Judah was taken into ex-
ile], on the fifteenth of the month, the
word of the LORD came to me, saying,
[18]"Son of man, wail over the hordes
of Egypt and cast them down, both her
and the daughters of the powerful and
majestic nations, to the nether world
(the place of the dead), with those who
go down to the pit;

[19]'Whom [among them] do you
surpass in beauty?
Go down and make your bed with
the uncircumcised (the barbaric,
the boorish, the crude).'

[20]"They will fall among those who
are slain by the sword. She (Egypt) is
handed over to the sword; they have
drawn her and all her hordes away [to
judgment].
[21]"The strong among the mighty rulers will say of him (Pharaoh) and his allies from the midst of Sheol, 'They have
gone down [defeated]; they lie still, the
uncircumcised, slain by the sword.'
[22]"Assyria is there with all her warriors; their graves are all around her.
All of them are slain, fallen by the
sword,
[23]whose graves are set in the remotest parts of the pit and her army
is all around her grave. All of them are
slain, fallen by the sword, who spread
terror in the land of the living.
[24]"Elam [a conquest of Assyria] is
there and all her hordes around her
grave; all of them slain, fallen by the
sword, who have gone down uncircumcised to the lower parts of the
earth, who made their terror spread
in the land of the living and bore their

shame *and* defeat with those who went down to the pit.

²⁵"They have made a bed for her among the slain with all her hordes. Her graves are around it; they are all uncircumcised (barbaric, boorish, crude), slain by the sword (for their terror had been spread in the land of the living), and they bore their disgrace with those who go down to the pit; they were laid among the slain.

²⁶"Meshech, Tubal, and all their hordes are there; their graves surround them. All of them uncircumcised, slain by the sword, for they spread their terror in the land of the living.

²⁷"Nor do they lie beside the fallen heroes of the uncircumcised, who went down to Sheol with their weapons of war, whose swords were laid [with honors] under their heads. The punishment for their sins rested on their bones, for the terror of these heroes *was once* in the land of the living.

²⁸"But you will be broken in the midst of the uncircumcised and you will lie [without honors] with those who are slain by the sword.

²⁹"Edom is there also, her kings and all her princes, who for all their power *and* strength are laid with those who were slain by the sword; they will lie [in shame and defeat] with the uncircumcised and with those who go down to the pit.

³⁰"The princes of the north are there also, all of them, and all the Sidonians, who in spite of the terror resulting from their power, have gone down in shame with the slain. So they lay down uncircumcised with those slain by the sword and bore their disgrace with those who go down to the pit.

³¹"Pharaoh will see them, and he will be comforted for all his hordes slain by the sword—Pharaoh and all his army," says the Lord GOD.

³²"Though I instilled a terror of him in the land of the living, yet he will be made to lie down among the uncircumcised along with those slain by the sword, even Pharaoh and all his hordes," says the Lord GOD. [Is 19; Jer 46; Zech 14:18, 19]

33

AND THE word of the LORD came to me, saying, ²"Son of man, speak to the sons of your people [who are exiled in Babylon] and say to them, 'If I bring a sword on a land, and the people of the land take one man from among them and make him their watchman,

³and he sees the sword coming on the land, and he blows the trumpet and warns the people,

⁴then whoever hears the sound of the trumpet and does not take warning, and a sword comes and takes him away, his blood will be on his [own] head.

⁵'He heard the sound of the trumpet but did not take warning; his blood shall be on himself. But if he had taken warning, he would have saved his life.

⁶'But if the watchman sees the sword coming and does not blow the trumpet and the people are not warned, and the sword comes and takes any one of them, he is taken away because of his corruption *and* sin; but I will require his blood from the watchman's hand.'

⁷"Now as for you, son of man, I have made you a watchman for the house of Israel; so you shall hear a message from My mouth and give them a warning from Me.

⁸"When I say to the wicked, 'O wicked man, you will certainly die,' and you do not speak to warn the wicked from his way, that wicked man will die because of his sin; but I will require his blood from your hand.

⁹"But if you on your part warn the wicked man to turn from his [evil] way and he does not turn from his [evil] way, he will die in his sin; but you have saved your life.

¹⁰"Now as for you, son of man, say to the house of Israel, 'Thus you have said, "Truly our transgressions and our sins are on us, and we are rotting away because of them; how then can we live?"'

¹¹"Say to them, 'As I live,' says the Lord GOD, 'I take no pleasure in the death of the wicked, but rather that the wicked turn from his way and live. Turn back (change your way of thinking), turn back [in repentance] from your evil ways! For why should you die, O house of Israel?'

¹²"And you, son of man, say to the sons of your people, 'The righteousness of the righteous man will not save him in the day of his transgression; and as for the wickedness of the wicked, he will not stagger because of it in the day that he turns from his wickedness, whereas a righteous man will not be able to live because of his [previous acts of] righteousness on the day when he commits sin.'

¹³"When I say to the righteous that he will most certainly live, and he trusts in his [previous acts of] righteousness [to save him] and commits injustice, none of his righteous deeds will be remembered; but he will die for his injustice that he committed.

¹⁴"But when I say to the wicked, 'You will certainly die,' and he turns from his sin and practices that which is just (fair) and right—

¹⁵if a wicked man returns [what he took as] a pledge, pays back what he had taken by robbery, walks in the statutes which ensure life, without committing injustice, he will certainly live; he will not die.

¹⁶"None of his sins that he has committed will be remembered against him. He has practiced that which is just (fair) and right; he will most certainly live.

¹⁷"Yet your people [who are in exile in Babylon] say, 'The way of the Lord is not right;' but as for them, it is their own way that is not right.

¹⁸"When the righteous turns back from his righteousness and commits injustice, he will also die because of it.

¹⁹"But when a wicked man turns back from his wickedness and practices what is just (fair) and right, he will live because of it.

²⁰"Yet you say, 'The way of the Lord is not right.' O house of Israel, I will judge you, every one [of you] in accordance with his own ways!"

²¹In the twelfth year of our exile [in Babylon], on the fifth of the tenth month, a survivor from Jerusalem came to me, saying, "The city has been captured."

²²Now the hand of the LORD had been upon me in the evening, before the survivor came. And He opened my mouth at the time he came to me in the morning; so my mouth was opened [in readiness] and I was no longer mute.

²³Then the word of the LORD came to me, saying,

²⁴"Son of man, those [back in Palestine] who inhabit these ruins in the land of Israel are saying, 'Abraham was [only] one man and he took possession of the land, but we are many; the land has [most certainly] been given to us [to possess] as property.'

²⁵"Therefore say to them, 'Thus says the Lord GOD, "You eat meat with the blood *in it* and raise your eyes to your idols and shed blood. Should you take possession of the land? [Gen 9:4; Lev 3:17; 7:27; Acts 15:28, 29]

²⁶"You rely on your sword [as your security]; you commit outrageous *and* disgraceful acts and each of you defiles his neighbor's wife. Should you then take possession of the land?"'

²⁷"You shall say this to them, 'Thus says the Lord GOD, "As I live, those who are in the ruins certainly will fall by the sword, and I will give whoever is in the open field to the [predatory]

animals to be devoured, and those who are in strongholds and in caves will die of virulent diseases.

²⁸"And I will make the land [of Israel] a desolation and a ruin, and her pride in her power will be brought to an end; and the mountains of Israel will be so deserted that no one will pass through.

²⁹"Then they will know [without any doubt] that I am the Lord, when I make the land a desolation and a ruin because of all the atrocities which they have committed."'

³⁰"But as for you, son of man, your people who talk about you by the walls and in the doorways of the houses say one to another, every one to his brother, 'Come now and hear what the message is that comes from the Lord.'

³¹"They come to you as people come, and they sit before you as My people, and they hear your words, but they do not practice them; for with their mouth they *express* loving devotion, but their heart goes after their (unlawful) gain.

³²"Behold, you are to them like a love song by one who has a pleasant voice and plays well on a stringed instrument [merely to entertain them]; for they hear your words but do not practice them.

³³"So when it comes to pass—as it most certainly will—then they will know [without any doubt] that a prophet has been among them."

34

AND THE word of the Lord came to me, saying,

²"Son of man, prophesy against the shepherds of Israel. Prophesy and say to them, the [spiritual] shepherds, 'Thus says the Lord God, "Woe (judgment is coming) to the [spiritual] shepherds of Israel who have been feeding themselves! Should not the shepherds feed the flock?

³"You eat the fat [the choicest of

meat], and clothe yourselves with the wool, you slaughter the best of the livestock, but you do not feed the flock.

⁴"You have not strengthened those who are weak, you have not healed the sick, you have not bandaged the crippled, you have not brought back those gone astray, you have not looked for the lost; but you have ruled them with force and violence.

⁵"They were scattered because there was no shepherd, and when they were scattered they became food for all the predators of the field.

⁶"My flock wandered through all the mountains and on every high hill; My flock was scattered over all the face of the earth and no one searched or sought them."'" [Matt 9:36]

⁷Therefore, you [spiritual] shepherds, hear the word of the Lord:

⁸"As I live," says the Lord God, "certainly because My flock has become prey, My flock has even become food for every predator of the field for lack of a shepherd, and My shepherds did not search for My flock, but *rather* the shepherds fed themselves and did not feed My flock;

⁹therefore, you [spiritual] shepherds, hear the word of the Lord:

¹⁰"Thus says the Lord God, "Behold, I am against the shepherds, and I will demand My flock from them and make them stop tending the flock, so that the shepherds cannot feed themselves anymore. I will rescue My flock from their mouth, so that they will not be food for them."'"

¹¹"For thus says the Lord God, "Behold, I Myself will search for My flock and seek them out.

¹²"As a shepherd cares for his sheep on the day that he is among his scattered flock, so I will care for My sheep; and I will rescue them from all the places to which they were scattered on a cloudy and gloomy day.

¹³"I will bring them out from the nations and gather them from the countries and bring them to their own land; and I will feed them on the mountains of Israel, by the streams, and in all the inhabited places of the land.

¹⁴"I will feed them in a good pasture, and their grazing ground will be on the mountain heights of Israel. There they will lie down on good grazing ground and feed in rich pasture on the mountains of Israel.

¹⁵"I will feed My flock and I will let them lie down [to rest]," says the Lord God.

¹⁶"I will seek the lost, bring back the scattered, bandage the crippled, and strengthen the weak *and* the sick; but I will destroy the fat and the strong [who have become hard-hearted and perverse]. I will feed them with judgment *and* punishment. [Luke 19:10]

¹⁷"And as for you, My flock, thus says the Lord God, 'Behold, I judge between one sheep and another, between the rams and the male goats [between the righteous and the unrighteous].

¹⁸'Is it too little a thing for you that you [unrighteous ones who are well-fed] feed in the best pasture, yet you must trample down with your feet [of wickedness] the rest of your pastures? Or that you drink clear [still] water, yet you must muddy with your feet [of wickedness] the rest [of the water]?

¹⁹'As for My flock (the righteous), they must feed on what you trample with your feet and drink what you muddy with your feet!' "

²⁰Therefore thus says the Lord God to them, "Behold, I Myself will judge between the [well-fed] fat sheep and the lean sheep.

²¹"Because you push with side and shoulder, and gore with your horns all those that have become weak *and* sick until you have scattered them away,

²²therefore, I will rescue My flock, and they shall no longer be prey; and I will judge between one sheep [ungodly] and another [godly].

²³"Then I will appoint over them one shepherd and he will feed them, [a ruler like] My servant David; he will feed them and be their shepherd. [Ezek 37:24; John 10:14–18]

²⁴"And I the Lord will be their God, and My servant David will be a prince among them; I the Lord have spoken.

²⁵"I will make a covenant of peace with them and will eliminate the predatory animals from the land so that they may live securely in the wilderness and sleep [safely] in the woods. [Ps 127:2; Is 11:6–9; John 14:27; 16:33]

²⁶"I will make them and the places around My hill (Jerusalem, Zion) a blessing. And I will make showers come down in their season; there will be [abundant] showers of blessing (divine favor).

²⁷"Also the tree of the field will yield its fruit and the earth will yield its produce; and My people will be secure on their land. Then they will know [with confidence] that I am the Lord, when I have broken the bars of their yoke and have rescued them from the hand of those who made them slaves.

²⁸"They will no longer be prey to the nations, and the predators of the earth will not devour them; but they will live safely, and no one will make them afraid [in the day of the Messiah's reign]. [Is 60:21; 61:3]

speak the Word

Thank You, God, for seeking what is lost and bringing back what has been scattered in my life. Thank You for bandaging my hurts and strengthening me.
—ADAPTED FROM Ezekiel 34:16

²⁹"I will prepare for them a place renowned for planting [crops], and they will not again be victims of famine in the land, and they will not endure the insults of the nations any longer.

³⁰"Then they will know [with assurance] that I the LORD their God, am with them and that they, the house of Israel, are My people," says the Lord GOD.

³¹"As for you, My flock, the flock of My pasture, you are men, and I am your God," says the Lord GOD.

35

MOREOVER, THE word of the LORD came to me, saying,

²"Son of man, set your face against Mount Seir (Edom), and prophesy against it

³and say to it, 'Thus says the Lord GOD,

"Behold, Mount Seir, I am against you,
And I will stretch out My hand against you
And make you completely desolate.
⁴"I will destroy your cities
And you will become a wasteland.
Then you shall know [without any doubt] that I am the LORD.

⁵"Because you [descendants of Esau] have had an everlasting hatred [for Jacob (Israel)] and you handed over the sons of Israel to the power of the sword at the time of their tragedy, at the time of their final punishment [the Babylonian conquest], [Ezek 25:12–14; 36:5]

⁶therefore, as I live," says the Lord GOD, "I will hand you over to bloodshed, and bloodshed will pursue you since you have not hated bloodshed, bloodshed will pursue you.

⁷"I will make Mount Seir (Edom) a ruin and a desolate wasteland and I will cut off from it the one who passes through it and the one who returns.

⁸"I will fill its mountains with its slain; those killed by the sword will fall on your hills, and in your valleys, and in all your ravines.

⁹"I will make you an everlasting desolation and your cities will not be inhabited. Then you will know [without any doubt] that I am the LORD.

¹⁰"Because you [descendants of Esau] have said, 'These two nations [Israel and Judah] and these two lands shall be mine, and we will take possession of them,' although the LORD was there,

¹¹therefore, as I live," says the Lord GOD, "I will deal with you in accordance with the anger and envy you showed because of your hatred for them; and I will make Myself known among them [as Judge] when I judge *and* punish you.

¹²"Then you will know [without any doubt] that I am the LORD, and that I have heard all your scornful speeches which you have spoken against the mountains of Israel, saying, 'They have been made a wasteland; they have been given to us as food.'

¹³"So you have boasted *and* spoken arrogantly against Me, and have multiplied your words against Me; I have heard it."

¹⁴'Thus says the Lord GOD, "While the whole earth rejoices, I will make you a wasteland.

¹⁵"As you rejoiced over the inheritance of the house of Israel because it was desolate, so I will do to you; you will be a desolate waste, O Mount Seir, and all Edom, all of it. Then they will know [without any doubt] that I am the LORD."'

36

"AND YOU, son of man, prophesy to the mountains of Israel and say, 'You mountains of Israel, hear the word of the LORD.

²'Thus says the Lord GOD, "Because the enemy has said of you, 'Aha!' and, 'The ancient heights have become our property,'

³therefore prophesy and say, 'Thus says the Lord God, "For good reason they have made you a desolation, and they crushed you from every side so that you would become a possession of the rest of the nations and you have become the talk and the whispering of the people." ' "

⁴'Therefore, O mountains of Israel, hear the word of the Lord God. Thus says the Lord God to the mountains and to the hills, to the ravines and to the valleys, to the desolate ruins and to the deserted cities which have become prey and a mockery to the rest of the nations which surround you,

⁵therefore thus says the Lord God, "Most certainly in the fire of My jealousy (love for that which is Mine) I have spoken against the rest of the nations and against all Edom, who appropriated My land for themselves as a possession with wholehearted joy and with uttermost contempt, so that they might empty it out [and possess it] as prey."

⁶'Therefore prophesy concerning the land of Israel and say to the mountains and to the hills, to the ravines and to the valleys, "Thus says the Lord God, 'Behold, I have spoken in My jealousy (love for that which is Mine) and in My wrath because you have endured the [shameful] insults of the nations.'

⁷"Therefore thus says the Lord God, 'I have lifted up My hand *and* sworn [an oath] that the nations that are around you will themselves endure their [shameful] insults.

⁸'But you, O mountains of Israel, will put out your branches and bear your fruit to My people Israel; for they will soon come [home].

⁹'For, behold, I am for you, and I will turn to you [in favor], and you shall be cultivated and sown.

¹⁰'I will multiply people on you, all the house of Israel, [indeed] all of it; the cities shall be inhabited and the ruins will be rebuilt.

¹¹'I will multiply on you man and animal; and they will increase and be fruitful. And I will cause you to be inhabited as you were formerly, and I will do better [things] for you than at your beginning. Then you will know [with great confidence] that I am the Lord.

¹²'Yes, [O mountains of Israel] I will cause men—My people Israel—to walk on you and take possession of you, so that you will become their inheritance and never again bereave them of children.'

¹³"Thus says the Lord God, 'Because they say to you, "You [O land] are a devourer of people and have bereaved your nation of children,"

¹⁴therefore you will no longer devour people, and no longer bereave your nation of children,' says the Lord God.

¹⁵"I will not let you hear insults from the nations anymore, nor will you bear disgrace from the peoples any longer, nor will you cause your nation to stumble [through idolatry] any longer," says the Lord God.' "

¹⁶Moreover, the word of the Lord came to me, saying,

¹⁷"Son of man, when the house of Israel was living in their own land, they defiled it by their [own] behavior and by their [idolatrous] actions. Their conduct before Me was like the uncleanness of a woman during her [physical] impurity.

¹⁸"So I poured out My wrath on them for the blood which they had shed on the land and because they had defiled it with their idols.

speak the Word

Thank You, God, that You turn to me in favor!
—ADAPTED FROM EZEKIEL 36:9

¹⁹"Also I scattered them among the nations and they were dispersed throughout the countries. I judged *and* punished them in accordance with their conduct and their [idolatrous] behavior.

²⁰"When they came to the nations wherever they went, they profaned My holy name, because it was said of them, 'These are the people of the LORD; yet they have come out of His land.'

²¹"But I had concern for My holy name, which the house of Israel had profaned among the nations where they went.

²²"Therefore say to the house of Israel, 'Thus says the Lord GOD, "It is not for your sake, O house of Israel, that I am about to act, but for My holy name, which you have profaned among the nations where you went.

²³"I will vindicate the holiness of My great name which has been profaned among the nations, which you have profaned among them. Then the nations will know [without any doubt] that I am the LORD," says the Lord GOD, "when I prove Myself holy among you in their sight.

²⁴"For I will take you from the nations and gather you from all the countries and bring you into your own land.

²⁵"Then I will sprinkle clean water on you, and you will be clean; I will cleanse you from all your uncleanness and from all your idols.

²⁶"Moreover, I will give you a new heart and put a new spirit within you, and I will remove the heart of stone from your flesh and give you a heart of flesh.

²⁷"I will put my Spirit within you and cause you to walk in My statutes, and you will keep My ordinances and do them.

²⁸"You will live in the land that I gave to your fathers; and you will be My people, and I will be your God.

²⁹"I will also save you from all your uncleanness, and I will call for the

life point

Ezekiel 36:26, 27 contain God's promise that the day would come when He would give people a new heart and put His Spirit *within* them. Under the Old Covenant, the Holy Spirit was with people and came *upon* people for special purposes, but He did not live inside them. God dwelt in a tabernacle made with human hands during that dispensation. But under the New Covenant, signed and sealed in the blood of Jesus Christ, He no longer dwells in a tabernacle made by human hands (see Acts 7:48), but in the hearts of people who have committed their lives to Him.

grain and make it abundant, and I will not bring famine on you.

³⁰"I will multiply the fruit of the tree and the produce of the field, so that you will not suffer again the disgrace of famine among the nations.

³¹"Then you will remember [clearly] your [own] evil ways and your deeds that were not good, and you will loathe yourselves in your own sight for your sins and for your outrageous atrocities.

³²"I am not doing this for your sake," says the Lord GOD. "Let that be known to you. Be ashamed and humiliated for your [wicked] ways, O house of Israel!"

³³'Thus says the Lord GOD, "On the day that I cleanse you from all your sins I will also cause the cities [of Israel] to be inhabited, and the ruins will be rebuilt.

³⁴"The desolate land will be cultivated instead of being a desolation in the sight of everyone who passes by.

³⁵"Then they will say, 'This land that was deserted *and* desolate has become like the garden of Eden; and the waste, desolate, and ruined cities are fortified and inhabited.'

³⁶"Then the nations that are left

around you will know that I the LORD have rebuilt the ruined places and planted that which was desolate. I the LORD have spoken, and will do it."

37 "Thus says the Lord GOD, "This too I will let the house of Israel ask Me to do for them: I will increase their people like a flock.

38 "Like the flock for sacrifices, like the flock at Jerusalem during her appointed feasts, so will the desolate cities be filled with flocks of people. Then they will know [with confident assurance] that I am the LORD." ' "

37

THE HAND of the LORD was upon me, and He brought me out in the Spirit of the LORD and set me down in the middle of the valley; and it was full of bones.

²He caused me to pass all around them, and behold, *there were* very many [human bones] in the open valley; and lo, *they were* very dry.

³And He said to me, "Son of man, can these bones live?" And I answered, "O Lord GOD, You know." [1 Cor 15:35]

⁴Again He said to me, "Prophesy to these bones and say to them, 'O dry

an exchange of hearts

You and I may have similar backgrounds. I had lived a hard life, and my heart was hardened because of it. I suffered many years of abuse. I built invisible walls around myself and decided that nobody could hurt me if I did not let them into my life.

When we receive Jesus as our Savior, He takes our old hard hearts and gives us His heart instead (see Ezekiel 36:26, 27). The new heart God gives is one that desires to love and be involved with people. It usually takes time, and we go through a process of change before our actions and behavior catch up with our new hearts, but God does give us new desires. He gives us a heart to obey Him and, for this reason, we can no longer be comfortable with sin. We still sin, but we do not want to. Our consciences are bothered when we go against God and His Word. Our new spirits war against the flesh; the two are continually antagonistic toward each other. But thank God, we submit areas of our lives to Him little by little, and as we do, He changes our behavior to match our new hearts.

God gives us His Spirit, and only because of His Spirit within us can we obey God and His Word. The Holy Spirit Who dwells in us strengthens us and enables us to do God's will. We must learn to lean on Him and not be independent, trying to do things in our own strength.

Galatians 3:3 teaches us a wonderful lesson. It asks: "Having begun [your new life by faith] with the Spirit, are you now being perfected and reaching spiritual maturity by the flesh?" In other words, why do we think we can perfect ourselves by our own effort? We need to learn to "let go and let God be God," and that is one of the biggest challenges we face. Jesus said that we can do absolutely nothing apart from Him (see John 15:5). Our job is to believe, and God's job is to perform. If we were called to achieve we would be called achievers, not believers. God said, "I will put my Spirit within you and cause you to walk in My statutes" (Ezekiel 36:27). Learn to depend more on the Holy Spirit within you and less on yourself. If you do, you will love the results. Your peace and joy will greatly increase, and your progress will be apparent to you and to everyone around you.

bones, hear the word of the Lord.' [John 5:28]

5"Thus says the Lord God to these bones, 'Behold, I will make *breath enter you so that you may come to life.

6'I will put sinews on you, make flesh grow back on you, cover you with skin, and I will put breath in you so that you may come alive; and you will know that I am the Lord.'"

7So I prophesied as I was commanded; and as I prophesied, there was a [thundering] noise, and behold, a rattling; and the bones came together, bone to its bone.

8And I looked, and behold, there were sinews on the bones, and flesh grew and skin covered them; but there was no breath in them.

9Then He said to me, "Prophesy to the breath, son of man, and say to the breath, 'Thus says the Lord God, "Come from the four winds, O breath, and breathe on these slain, that they may live."'"

10So I prophesied as He commanded me, and the breath came into them, and they came to life and stood up on their feet, an exceedingly great army. [Rev 11:11]

11Then He said to me, "Son of man, these bones are the whole house of Israel. Behold, they say, 'Our bones are dried up and our hope is lost. We are completely cut off.'

12"Therefore prophesy and say to them, 'Thus says the Lord God, "Behold, I will open your graves and make you come up out of your graves, My people; and I will bring you [back home] to the land of Israel. [Hos 13:14]

13"Then you will know [with confidence] that I am the Lord, when I have

life point

You may feel as if your life is no better than the dead, dry bones described by the prophet in Ezekiel 37:1–4. Your circumstances may be so dead they stink. Your hope may seem lost, but God has a way out.

As this passage continues, the prophet does as God instructs, and he sees God totally revive and bring breath and spirit back into what once were dead, dry bones (see Ezekiel 37:5–10). The same can happen to you. God can revive things that have been dry, brittle, and dead in your life.

opened your graves and made you come up out of your graves, My people.

14"I will put My *Spirit in you and you will come to life, and I will place you in your own land. Then you will know that I the Lord have spoken, and fulfilled it," says the Lord.'"

15The word of the Lord came again to me, saying,

16"And you, son of man, take a stick and write on it, 'For Judah and for the children of Israel, his companions'; then take another stick and write on it, 'For Joseph, the stick of Ephraim and all the house of Israel, his companions.'

17Then join them together into one stick, so that they may become one in your hand.

18"When your people say to you, 'Will you not tell us what you mean by these?'

19say to them, 'Thus says the Lord God, "Behold, I am going to take the stick of Joseph, which is in the hand of

37:5 Or spirit, and so throughout the chapter.   37:14 Or breath.

speak the Word

Thank You, God, for putting Your Spirit in me!
–ADAPTED FROM EZEKIEL 37:14

Ephraim, and the tribes of Israel, his companions; and I will join the stick of Judah with it and make them one stick, and they will be one in My hand."'

20"The sticks on which you write shall be in your hand before their eyes. 21"Say to them, 'Thus says the Lord GOD, "Behold, I am going to take the children of Israel from among the nations where they have gone, and I will gather them from every side and bring them into their own land;

22and I will make them one nation in the land, on the mountains of Israel; and one king will be king over all of them; and they will no longer be two

hear the word of the Lord

I am sure that at one time or another in your life, you have felt that everywhere you looked you saw a pile of dead, dry bones, such as the scene in Ezekiel 37:1–4.

God showed a pile of such brittle bones to Ezekiel and asked him, "Can these bones live?" (Ezekiel 37:3). In other words, He was asking, "Can anything be done with this mess? Can this situation change?"

Then He told Ezekiel to speak to the bones and say to them, "O dry bones, hear the word of the LORD" (Ezekiel 37:4).

If you have a big mess in your life and you are trying to run the devil off your property and keep him under your feet, you can do it with words. You can say, "Listen, you big mountain, hear the word of the Lord. Listen, you big mess, hear the word of the Lord. Listen, poverty, hear the word of the Lord. Listen, sickness and disease, hear the word of the Lord. Listen, you tormenting spirit, hear the word of the Lord."

As you read the remainder of the story in Ezekiel chapter 37, you will find that after Ezekiel had done what God told him to do and prophesied to those dry bones, they came together, sinews and flesh came upon them, and skin covered them.

Then, in Ezekiel 37:9, the Lord told Ezekiel to prophesy and command breath and spirit to come into them. In verse 10 Ezekiel said, "So I prophesied as He commanded me, and the breath came into them, and they came to life and stood up on their feet, an exceedingly great army." All of that happened because one man prophesied God's Word over a situation that needed to be changed.

Let me ask you: What are you saying to the dead, dry circumstances in your life? Are you prophesying to your dead bones? Or is what you are saying making them deader and dryer?

Maybe this sounds familiar to you: "Nothing in my life is ever going to change. Every time I get a dollar the devil takes it away from me. It never fails; every time I think something good is going to happen, I get attacked." If that is what you are saying, then you are just asking for more trouble. Every time you speak that way, you are giving the devil the right to use his power. Instead, learn how to speak God's Word and neutralize Satan's power.

Do not talk about how you feel or what you think; do not look at your life and what you do not have. Open your mouth and talk about what God has promised you! Once you change your words, it's all over for the devil. There is nothing he can do against God's Word. The victory belongs to you!

nations, and will no longer be divided into two kingdoms. [Jer 50:4]

²³"They will no longer defile themselves with their idols, or with their detestable things, or with any of their transgressions; but I will save them from all their transgressions in which they have sinned, and I will cleanse them. So they will be My people, and I will be their God.

²⁴"My servant David will be king over them, and they all will have one shepherd. They will also walk in My ordinances and keep My statutes and observe them.

²⁵"They will live in the land where your fathers lived, [the land] that I gave to My servant Jacob, and they will live there, they and their children and their children's children, forever; and My servant David will be their leader forever. [Is 60:21; Joel 3:20; Amos 9:15]

²⁶"I will make a covenant of peace with them; it will be an everlasting covenant with them. And I will place them and multiply them, and will put My sanctuary in their midst forever.

²⁷"My dwelling place also will be with them; and I will be their God, and they will be My people.

²⁸"Then the nations will know [without any doubt] that I am the Lord who sets apart and sanctifies Israel [for holy use], when My sanctuary is in their midst forever."'"

38 AND THE word of the Lord came to me, saying, ²"Son of man, set your face against Gog of the land of Magog, the chief ruler of Meshech and Tubal, and prophesy against him,

³and say, 'Thus says the Lord God, "Behold, I am against you, O Gog, chief ruler of Meshech and Tubal.

⁴"I will turn you around and put hooks into your jaws, and I will bring you out, and all your army, horses and horsemen, all of them magnificently

clothed in full armor, a great horde with buckler (small shield) and [large] shield, all of them wielding swords;

⁵Persia (Iran), Cush (Ethiopia), and Put (Libya, N. Africa) with them, all of them with shield and helmet;

⁶Gomer and all its troops; Beth-togarmah from the remote parts of the north and all its troops—many peoples with you.

⁷"You [Gog] be prepared; prepare yourself, you and all your hordes that are assembled around you, and be a guard and a lookout for them.

⁸"After many days you will be summoned [for service]; in the latter years you shall come into the land that is restored from [the ravages of] the sword, where people have been gathered out of many nations to the mountains of Israel, which had been a continual wasteland; but its people were brought out of the nations, and they are living securely, all of them. [Is 24:22]

⁹"You will go up [against them], you will come like a storm; you shall be like a cloud covering the land, you and all your troops, and many peoples with you."

¹⁰'Thus says the Lord God, "It will come about on that day that thoughts will come into your mind, and you will devise an evil plan,

¹¹and you will say, 'I will go up against an open country; I will come against those who are at rest and peaceful, who live securely, all of them living without walls and having neither bars nor gates,

¹²to take spoil and seize plunder, to turn your hand against the ruins which are now inhabited, and against the people who are gathered from the nations, who have acquired cattle and goods, who live at the center of the world [Israel].'

¹³"Sheba and Dedan and the merchants of Tarshish (southern Spain), with all its young lions (villages) will

say to you, 'Have you come to take spoil? Have you assembled your hordes [of fighting men] to seize plunder, to carry away silver and gold, to take away cattle and goods, to take great spoil?'"'

¹⁴"Therefore, son of man, prophesy and say to Gog, 'Thus says the Lord God, "On that day when My people Israel live securely, will you not become aware of it [and become active]?

¹⁵"You will come from your place in the remote parts of the north, you and many nations with you, all of them riding horses, a great horde, and a mighty army;

¹⁶and you will go up against My people Israel like a cloud to cover the land. In the last days it will come about that I will bring you against My land, so that the nations may know Me when I show Myself holy through you before their eyes, O Gog."

¹⁷'Thus says the Lord God, "Are you the one of whom I spoke in former days through My servants, the prophets of Israel, who prophesied in those days for many years that I would bring you (Gog) against them?

¹⁸"It will come about on that day, when Gog comes against the land of Israel," says the Lord God, "that My wrath will rise and show on My face.

¹⁹"In My zeal and in My blazing rage I declare that on that day there will most certainly be a great earthquake in the land of Israel,

²⁰so that the fishes of the sea, the birds of the sky, the animals of the field, all the creatures that crawl on the earth, and all the men that are on the face of the earth will tremble *and* shake at My presence; the mountains will crumble, the steep places will fall, and every wall will fall to the ground.

²¹"I will call for a sword against Gog throughout all My mountains," says the Lord God. "Every man's (invading soldier's) sword will be against his brother (ally) [in panic and confusion].

²²"With pestilence and with bloodshed I will enter into judgment with Gog; and I will rain on him torrents of rain with [great] hailstones, fire and brimstone on his hordes and on the many nations that are with him. [Ps 11:6]

²³"Thus I shall magnify Myself *and* demonstrate My greatness and sanctify Myself, and I will be recognized *and* will make Myself known in the sight of many nations; they will know [without any doubt] that I am the Lord."'

39 "AND YOU, son of man, prophesy against Gog, 'Thus says the Lord God, "Behold, I am against you, O Gog, chief prince (ruler) of Meshech and Tubal;

²and I will turn you around and lead you along, and bring you up from the remotest parts of the north, and I will bring you against the mountains of Israel.

³"I will strike your bow from your left hand and make your arrows to fall out of your right hand.

⁴"You will fall [dead] on the mountains of Israel, you and all your troops and the nations who are with you. I will give you to every kind of predatory bird and animal of the field as food.

⁵"You will fall in the open field, for I have spoken," says the Lord God.

⁶"I will also send fire on Magog and on those who live securely in the coastlands; and they will know [without any doubt] that I am the Lord.

⁷"I will make My holy name known in the midst of My people Israel, and I will not let them profane My holy name anymore; and the nations will know that I am the Lord, the Holy One of Israel.

⁸"Behold, it is coming and it will be done," says the Lord God. "That is the day of which I have spoken.

⁹"And [when you, Gog, no longer exist] those who live in the cities of

Israel will go out and make fires with the weapons and burn them, both the [large] shields and the bucklers (small shields), the bows and the arrows, the war clubs and the spears; and for seven years they will burn them.

¹⁰"They will not take any wood from the field or cut down *and* gather [any] firewood from the forests, because they will make their fires using the weapons. And they will take the spoil from those who despoiled them and seize the plunder of those who plundered them," says the Lord GOD.

¹¹"And on that day I will give Gog a place for burial there in Israel, the valley of those who pass through east of the sea, and it will block the way of those who would pass through. So they will bury Gog there with all his hordes, and they will call it the Valley of Hamon-gog (the multitude of Gog).

¹²"For seven months the house of Israel will be burying them in order to cleanse the land.

¹³"Yes, all the people of the land will bury them; and it will be to their renown on the day that I appear in My glory *and* brilliance," says the Lord GOD.

¹⁴"They will elect men who will constantly go through the land, [men commissioned] to bury those who were passing through, those bodies that lie unburied on the surface of the ground, in order to cleanse it. At the end of seven months they will do a search.

¹⁵"As those who pass through the land pass through and anyone sees a human bone, he will set up a marker beside it, until the buriers have buried it in the Valley of Hamon-gog.

¹⁶"And even the name of the city will be Hamonah. In this manner they shall cleanse the land."'

¹⁷"As for you, son of man, thus says the Lord GOD, 'Say to every kind of bird and to every animal of the field, "Assemble and come, gather from every side to My sacrifice that I am slaughtering for you, as a great sacrificial feast on the mountains of Israel, and you will eat flesh and drink blood.

¹⁸"You will eat the flesh of mighty men and drink the blood of the princes of the earth, *as though they were* rams, lambs, goats, and bulls, all of them fatlings of Bashan [east of the Jordan].

¹⁹"So you will eat fat until you are filled and drink blood till you are drunk, at the sacrificial feast which I have prepared for you.

²⁰"You will eat your fill at My table with horses and riders, with mighty men, and with all the men of war," says the Lord GOD.

²¹"And I will bring [and manifest] My glory among the nations; and all the nations will see My judgment *and* justice [in the punishment] which I have executed and My hand which I have laid on them.

²²"So the house of Israel will know [with absolute confidence] that I am the LORD their God from that day forward.

²³"And the nations will know [without any doubt] that the house of Israel went into exile for their great sin, because they acted treacherously against Me; and I hid My face (favor, blessing) from them. So I gave them into the hand of their enemies, and they all fell [into captivity or were killed] by [the power of] the sword. [Deut 31:17]

²⁴"I dealt with them in accordance with their uncleanness and their transgressions, and I hid My face from them."'"

²⁵Therefore thus says the Lord GOD, "Now I will restore the fortunes of Jacob (Israel) and have mercy on the whole house of Israel; and I will be jealous for My holy name [demanding what is rightfully and uniquely mine].

²⁶"They will forget their disgrace and all their treachery (unfaithfulness) which they perpetuated against Me, when they live securely in their own land and there is no one who makes them afraid.

²⁷"When I bring them back from the nations and gather them out of their enemies' lands, then I shall show Myself holy [and My justice and holiness will be vindicated] through them in the sight of many nations. ²⁸"Then they will know [without any doubt] that I am the Lord their God because I made them go into exile among the nations, and then gathered them to their own land. I will leave none of them there [among the nations] any longer. ²⁹"I will not hide My face from them any longer, because I will have poured out My Spirit on the house of Israel," says the Lord God.

40 IN THE twenty-fifth year of our exile [in Babylon], in the beginning of the year, on the tenth [day] of the month, in the fourteenth year after the city [of Jerusalem] was taken, on that [very] same day the hand of the Lord was upon me and He brought me there. ²In the visions of God He brought me to the land of Israel and set me down on a very high mountain, on the south side of which *there was* what seemed to be a structure of a city. ³So He brought me there; and behold, there was a man [an angel] whose appearance was like bronze, with a line of flax and a measuring rod in his hand; and he was standing in the gateway. ⁴The man said to me, "Son of man, look with your eyes and hear with your ears and set your heart on all that I am going to show you; for you have been brought here that I may show it to you. Declare to the house of Israel all that you see."

⁵And behold, there was a wall all around the outside [area] of the temple (house) [of the Lord], and in the man's hand a measuring rod six cubits long (10.2 ft.), each cubit being longer than the standard one by a hand width. So he measured the thickness of the wall, one rod; and the height, one rod. ⁶Then he went to the gate which faced the east and went up its [seven] steps and measured the threshold of the gate, one rod in width; and the other threshold [of the gate inside the thick wall] was one rod in width. ⁷The guardroom was one rod long and one rod wide, and [the space] between the guardrooms was five cubits. And the threshold of the gate by the porch (portico) of the gate facing inward was one rod. ⁸He also measured the porch of the gate facing inward [toward the temple of the Lord], one rod. ⁹Then he measured the porch of the gate, eight cubits, and its side pillars, two cubits. The porch of the gate faced inward [toward the temple of the Lord]. ¹⁰There were three guardrooms on each side of the gate toward the east; the three were the same size, and the side pillars on each side measured the same. ¹¹And he measured the width of the gateway, ten cubits, and the length of the gate, thirteen cubits. ¹²On each side a border (barrier wall) one cubit wide stood in front of the guardrooms on each side; and the guardrooms were six cubits *square* on each side. ¹³He measured the gate from the roof of one guardroom to the roof of the other, a width of twenty-five cubits from one door to the opposite door.

speak the Word

Help me, Lord, to look with my eyes, hear with my ears, and to set my heart on all that You are going to show me.
—ADAPTED FROM EZEKIEL 40:4

¹⁴He made [the measurement of] the side pillars sixty cubits *high;* the gate *extended* all around to the side pillar of the courtyard.

¹⁵From the front of the entrance gate [on the outside] to the front of the inner porch (portico) of the gate [the distance] was fifty cubits.

¹⁶*There were* shuttered windows *looking* toward the guardrooms, and toward their side pillars within the gate all around, and likewise for the porches. And windows were all around inside; and palm tree decorations were on each side pillar.

¹⁷Then he brought me into the outer courtyard, and behold, *there were* chambers and a pavement made for the courtyard all around; thirty chambers faced the pavement.

¹⁸The pavement (*that is,* the lower pavement) was by the side of the gates, corresponding to the length of the gates.

¹⁹Then he measured the width from the front of the lower gate to the front of the exterior of the inner court, a hundred cubits [both] on the east and on the north.

²⁰And as for the gate of the outer courtyard which faced the north he measured [both] its length and its width.

²¹Its guardrooms, three on each side, and its side pillars and its porches had the same measurement as the first gate. Its length was fifty cubits and the width was twenty-five cubits.

²²Its windows and its porches and its palm tree decorations had the same measurements as the gate that faced toward the east. It was reached by going up seven steps, and its porch was in front of them.

²³The inner courtyard had a gate opposite the gate on the north as well as *the gate* on the east; and he measured a hundred cubits from gate to gate.

²⁴Then he led me toward the south, and behold, there was a gate toward the south; and he measured its side pillars and its porches, and they measured the same as the others.

²⁵The gate and its porches had windows all around like those windows [in the other gateways]; the length was fifty cubits and the width was twenty-five cubits.

²⁶*There were* seven steps going up to the gate, and its porches were in front of them; and it had palm tree decorations [carved] on its side pillars, one on each side.

²⁷The inner courtyard had a gate toward the south; and he measured from gate to gate toward the south, a hundred cubits.

²⁸Then the man (angel) brought me to the inner courtyard by the south gate; and he measured the south gate according to those same measurements.

²⁹Its guardrooms also, its side pillars and its porches measured the same as the others. And the gate and its porches had windows all around; the length was fifty cubits and the width was twenty-five cubits.

³⁰*There were* porches all around, twenty-five cubits long and five cubits wide.

³¹Its porches faced the outer courtyard; and palm tree decorations were [carved] on its side pillars, and its stairway had eight steps.

³²He brought me into the inner courtyard toward the east, and he measured the gate; it measured the same as the others.

³³Its guardrooms also, its side pillars and its porches measured the same as the others. The gate and its porches had windows all around; it was fifty cubits long and twenty-five cubits wide.

³⁴Its porches faced the outer courtyard; and palm tree decorations were [carved] on either side of its side pillars, and its stairway had eight steps.

³⁵Then he brought me to the north

gate and he measured it; the measurements were the same as those of the other gates,

36with its guardrooms, its side pillars, its porches; and the gate had windows all around. The length was fifty cubits and the width was twenty-five cubits.

37Its side pillars faced the outer courtyard, and palm tree decorations were [carved] on them on either side. And its stairway had eight steps.

38A chamber with its doorway was by the side pillars of the gates; there the burnt offering was to be washed.

39In the porch (portico) of the gate were two tables on each side, on which to slaughter the burnt offering, the sin offering and the guilt offering.

40On the outer side, as one went up to the gateway toward the north, were two tables; and on the other side of the porch of the gate were two tables.

41Four tables were on each side next to the gate; [a total of] eight tables on which they slaughter sacrifices.

42Moreover, there were four tables of hewn stone (ashlar) for the burnt offering, a cubit and a half long, a cubit and a half wide, and one cubit high, on which they lay the instruments with which they slaughter the burnt offering and the sacrifice.

43The double hooks, one hand width in length were installed in the house all around. The meat of the offering was [to be placed] on the tables.

44From the outside to the inner gate were chambers for the singers in the inner courtyard, one of which was beside the north gate, with its front toward the south, and one beside the south gate facing toward the north.

45He [who was guiding me] said to me, "This is the chamber which faces toward the south; it is for the priests who have the responsibility and take care of the temple;

46but the chamber which faces toward the north is for the priests who have the responsibility and take care of the altar. These are the sons of Zadok, who [alone] from the sons of Levi come near to the LORD to minister to Him."

47He measured the courtyard, a hundred cubits long and a hundred cubits wide, a perfect square; and the altar was in front of the temple.

48Then he brought me to the porch of the temple, and he measured each side pillar of the porch, five cubits on each side; and the width of the gate was three cubits on each side.

49The length of the porch was twenty cubits and the width eleven cubits; and at the stairway by which it was ascended, there were [two] columns beside the side pillars, one on each side [of the entrance].

41 THEN HE (the angel) brought me to the nave (outer sanctuary) and measured the side pillars; six cubits wide on each side was the width of the side pillar.

2The width of the entrance was ten cubits and the sides of the entrance were five cubits on each side; and he measured its length, forty cubits, and its width, twenty cubits.

3Then he went inside [the inner sanctuary] and measured each side pillar of the doorway, two cubits, and the doorway, six cubits [high], and the width of the doorway, seven cubits. [Heb 9:6, 7; 10:19–25]

4He measured the length [of the interior of the inner sanctuary], twenty cubits, and the width, twenty cubits, opposite the nave (outer sanctuary); and he said to me, "This is the Most Holy Place."

5Then he measured the wall of the temple, six cubits [thick, to accommodate side chambers]; and the width of every side chamber, four cubits, all around the temple on every side.

6The side chambers were three stories

[high], one above another, and thirty chambers in each story; and the side chambers extended to the wall which stood on their inward side all around, so that they would be attached, but not attached to the wall of the temple *itself.*

⁷The side chambers became wider at each successive level as they encompassed the temple. Because the structure surrounding the temple went higher by stages on all sides of the temple, for that reason the width of the temple *increased* as it went higher; and thus one went up from the lowest *story* to the highest one by way of the second *story.*

⁸I also saw that the temple (house) had a raised platform all around it; the foundations of the side chambers *measured* a full rod of six long cubits *in height.*

⁹The thickness of the outer wall of the side chambers was five cubits. But the free space between the side chambers belonging to the temple

¹⁰and the *outer* chambers was a width of twenty cubits all around the temple on every side.

¹¹The doorways of the side chambers toward the free space were one doorway toward the north and another doorway toward the south; and the width of the free space was five cubits all around.

¹²The building that was in front of the separate area on the side toward the west was seventy cubits wide; and the wall of the building was five cubits thick all around, and its length was ninety cubits.

¹³Then he measured the temple, a hundred cubits long; the separate area and the building with its walls were also a hundred cubits long.

¹⁴Also the width of the front of the temple and the separate areas along the east *side totaled* a hundred cubits.

¹⁵He (the angel) measured the length of the building along the front of the separate area behind it, with a gallery on each side, a hundred cubits; he also *measured* the inner sanctuary and the porches (porticoes) of the courtyard.

¹⁶The thresholds, the latticed windows, and the galleries all around their three stories, opposite the threshold, were paneled with wood all around, and from the ground to the windows (but the windows were covered),

¹⁷over the entrance, and to the inner room, and on the outside, and on all the wall all around inside and outside, by measurement.

¹⁸It was carved with [figures of] cherubim and palm trees; so that a palm decoration was between cherub and cherub, and every cherub had two faces,

¹⁹so that the face of a man was toward the palm decoration on the one side, and the face of a young lion toward the palm decoration on the other side. It was carved [this way] on the entire house (temple) all around.

²⁰From the floor to [the space] above the entrance cherubim and palm decorations were carved, and also on the wall of the nave [the Holy Place].

²¹The doorposts of the nave were square; as for the front of the sanctuary, the appearance of one doorpost was like that of the other.

²²The altar was of wood, three cubits high and two cubits long; and its corners, its base, and its sides were wood. And he said to me, "This is the table that is before the LORD."

²³The nave (Holy Place) and the sanctuary (Holy of Holies) each had a double door.

²⁴Each of the doors had two leaves, two swinging (folding) leaves; two *leaves* for the one door and two leaves for the other.

²⁵And there were carved on them, on the doors of the nave, cherubim and palm decorations like those carved on the walls; and *there was* a threshold of wood on the front of the porch outside.

²⁶*There were* latticed windows and palm decorations on one side and on the other, on the sides of the porch. Thus were the side chambers and the thresholds of the house.

42 THEN HE (the angel) brought me out into the outer courtyard, toward the north; and he led me to the [attached] chamber which was opposite the separate area and opposite the building to the north.

²Along the length, one hundred cubits, was the north door; and the width was fifty cubits.

³Opposite the twenty *cubits* which belonged to the inner courtyard, and opposite the pavement which belonged to the outer courtyard, was gallery (balcony) corresponding to gallery in three stories.

⁴In front of the [attached] chambers was an inner walkway ten cubits wide and one *hundred* cubits long; and their entrances were on the north.

⁵Now the upper chambers were smaller because the galleries took away more *space* from them than from the chambers on the lower and middle stories of the building;

⁶for they were in three stories and did not have pillars like the pillars of the [outer] courtyards; therefore *the upper chambers* were set back from the ground more than the lower and the middle ones.

⁷And the outer wall, by the side of the chambers, toward the outer courtyard facing the chambers, was fifty cubits long.

⁸For the length of the chambers which were in the outer courtyard was fifty cubits, while *the length of* those facing the temple was a hundred cubits.

⁹Below these chambers was the entrance on the east side, as one enters them from the outer courtyard.

¹⁰In the width of the wall of the courtyard toward the east, facing the separate area and facing the building, were chambers;

¹¹and a passage in front of them was like the appearance of the [attached] chambers on the north, *and* they had the same length and width, and all their exits were like both their arrangements and their entrances.

¹²And like the entrances of the chambers that were toward the south there was an entrance at the head of the walkway, the walkway in front of the dividing wall toward the east, as one enters them.

¹³Then he (the angel) said to me, "The north chambers and the south chambers, which are opposite the separate area, are the holy chambers where the priests who are close to the LORD shall eat the most holy *offerings*. There they shall place the most holy things—the grain offering, the sin offering, and the guilt offering—for the place is holy.

¹⁴"When the priests enter [the Holy Place], they shall not go out from the sanctuary into the outer court unless they lay there their garments in which they minister, for these are holy (set apart). They shall put on other garments before they approach that which is for the people."

¹⁵Now when he had finished measuring the inner temple, he brought me out toward the gate which faced east and measured the outer area all around.

¹⁶He measured the east side with the measuring rod, five hundred rods by the measuring rod.

¹⁷He measured the north side, five hundred rods by the measuring rod.

¹⁸He measured the south side, five hundred rods by the measuring rod.

¹⁹He turned about to the west side and measured five hundred rods by the measuring rod.

²⁰He measured it on the four sides; it

had a wall all around, the length five hundred and the width five hundred, to make a separation between that which was holy [the temple proper] and that which was common [the outer area].

43 THEN HE (the angel) led me to the gate, the gate that faces toward the east. ²And behold, the glory *and* brilliance of the God of Israel was coming from the way of the east; and His voice was like the sound of many waters, and the earth shone with His glory. [Rev 1:15; 14:2] ³And it was like the appearance of the vision which I saw, like the vision I saw when He came to destroy the city. And the visions were like the vision I saw beside the River Chebar [near Babylon]; and I fell face downward. [Ezek 1:4; 3:23; 10:15, 22] ⁴And the glory *and* brilliance of the LORD entered the temple by way of the gate facing toward the east. ⁵Then the Spirit lifted me up and brought me into the inner courtyard; and behold, the glory *and* brilliance of the LORD filled the temple. ⁶And I heard One speaking to me from the temple, while a man was standing beside me. ⁷And He [the LORD] said to me, "Son of man, *this is* the place of My throne and the place of the soles of My feet, where I will dwell in the midst of the sons (descendants) of Israel forever. And the house of Israel will not again defile My holy name, neither they nor their kings, by their [idolatrous] prostitution and by the corpses *and* monuments of their kings in their graves, ⁸by setting their threshold by My threshold and their doorpost beside My doorpost, with [only] the wall between Me and them. They have defiled *and* desecrated My holy name by the vile atrocities which they have committed. So I have consumed them in My anger.

⁹"Now let them put far away from Me their [idolatrous] prostitution and the corpses *and* monuments of their kings, and I will dwell in their midst forever. ¹⁰"As for you, son of man, describe the temple to the house of Israel, so that they will be ashamed of their sins; and let them measure its plan [in detail]. ¹¹"If they are ashamed of all that they have done, make known to them the design of the temple (house), its layout, its exits, its entrances, all its designs, all its statutes, and all its laws. And write it down in their sight, so that they may keep its whole design and all its statutes and do them. ¹²"This is the law of the temple: Its entire area all around on the top of the mountain (Mount Moriah) *shall be* most holy. Behold, this is the law of the temple. ¹³"And these are the measurements of the altar [of burnt offering] in cubits (the cubit being a [long] cubit [the length of a forearm] and a hand width): the base *shall be* a cubit [long] and a cubit wide, with its border on its edge all around it of a span [in width]. And this *shall be the height of* the base of the altar. ¹⁴"From the base on the ground to the lower ledge *shall be* two cubits and the width one cubit; and from the smaller ledge to the larger ledge *shall be* four cubits and the width one cubit. ¹⁵"The altar hearth *shall be* four cubits high, and from the altar hearth shall extend upwards four horns [one from each corner, each one cubit high]. ¹⁶"Now the altar hearth *shall be* twelve *cubits* long by twelve wide, square in its four sides. ¹⁷"The ledge *shall be* fourteen *cubits* long by fourteen wide on its four sides, and the border around it *shall be* half a cubit; and its base *shall be* a cubit all around, and its steps shall face the east." [Ex 20:26] ¹⁸And He [the LORD] said to me, "Son of man, thus says the Lord GOD, 'These

are the statutes *and* regulations for [the use of] the altar on the day that it is built, to offer burnt offerings on it and to sprinkle blood on it.

¹⁹'You shall give to the priests, the Levites who are from the descendants of Zadok, who are close to Me to minister to Me,' says the Lord GOD, 'a young bull for a sin offering [as a memorial to Christ's sacrifice].

²⁰'And you shall take some of its blood and put it on the four horns [of the altar of burnt offering] and on the four corners of the ledge and on the border all around; thus you shall cleanse it (from sin) and make atonement for it.

²¹'You shall also take the bull for the sin offering, and it shall be burned in the appointed place of the temple, outside the sanctuary. [Heb 13:11]

²²'On the second day you shall offer a male goat without blemish for a sin offering, and they shall cleanse the altar as they cleansed it with the bull.

²³'When you have finished cleansing it, you shall offer a young bull without blemish and a ram from the flock without blemish.

²⁴'You shall present them before the LORD, and the priests shall throw salt on them, and they shall offer them up as a burnt offering to the LORD.

²⁵'For seven days you shall prepare daily a goat for a sin offering; also a young bull and a ram from the flock, without blemish, shall be prepared.

²⁶'For seven days they shall make atonement for the altar and purify it; so the priests shall consecrate it [to receive offerings]. [Ex 29:37]

²⁷'When they have completed these days, on the eighth day and from then onward, the priests shall offer your burnt offerings on the altar, and your peace offerings; and I will accept you,' says the Lord GOD." [Rom 12:1; 1 Pet 2:5]

44

THEN HE brought me back by the way of the outer gate of the sanctuary, which faces the east; and it was shut.

²Then the LORD said to me, "This gate shall be shut; it shall not be opened, and no one shall enter by it, for the LORD, the God of Israel, has entered by it; therefore it shall be shut.

³"As for the prince, he shall sit in it as prince to eat bread before the LORD; he shall enter by way of the porch (portico) of the gate and shall go out the same way."

⁴Then He brought me by way of the north gate to the front of the house; I looked, and behold, the glory *and* brilliance of the LORD filled the house of the LORD, and I fell face downward. [Rev 15:8]

⁵The LORD said to me, "Son of man, pay careful attention, see with your eyes and hear with your ears all that I say to you concerning all the statutes of the house of the LORD and all its laws; and pay careful attention to the entering of the house [by people], with all the departures *from* the sanctuary [of people, those who are allowed to enter the temple and all those who are excluded from the sanctuary].

⁶"You shall say to the rebellious ones, to the house of Israel, 'Thus says the Lord GOD, "Enough of all your repulsive acts, O house of Israel!

⁷"In that you brought in foreigners, uncircumcised in heart and uncircumcised in flesh, to be in My sanctuary to pollute *and* profane it—My house—when you offered My bread, the fat, and the blood; and they made My covenant void —*this* in addition to all your *other* repulsive acts.

⁸"And you have not kept charge of My holy things yourselves, but you have chosen *foreigners* [to please yourselves] and have set them in charge of My sanctuary."

9"Thus says the Lord God, "No foreigner uncircumcised in heart and flesh, of all the foreigners who are among the sons of Israel, shall enter My sanctuary.

10"But the Levites who went far away from Me when Israel went astray, who went astray from Me after their idols, they shall bear *the punishment for* their sin *and* guilt.

11"Yet they shall minister in My sanctuary, having oversight [as guards] at the gates of the temple and ministering in the temple. They shall slaughter the burnt offering and the sacrifice for the people, and they shall stand before them to minister to them.

12"Because the priests ministered to them before their idols and became a stumbling block of sin to the house of Israel, therefore I have lifted up My hand *and* have sworn [an oath] against them," says the Lord God, "that they shall bear *the punishment for* their sin *and* guilt.

13"And they shall not come near to Me to serve as priests to Me, nor come near to any of My holy things, to the things that are most holy; but they shall bear their shame *and* their disgrace and [the consequences of] their repulsive acts which they have committed.

14"Yet I will appoint them as caretakers of the temple, for all its service and for all that shall be done in it.

15"But the Levitical priests, the sons of Zadok, who performed the duty of My sanctuary when the children (descendants) of Israel went astray from Me, shall come near to Me to minister to Me; and they shall stand before Me to offer to Me the fat and the blood," declares the Lord God.

16"They shall enter into My sanctuary; and they shall come near to My table to minister to Me and they shall perform [the priestly] duty to me.

17"It shall be that when they enter the gates of the inner courtyard, they shall be clothed in linen garments; no wool shall be on them while they minister at the gates of the inner courtyard and within the temple (house).

18"They shall have linen turbans on their heads and linen undergarments on their loins; they shall not dress themselves with *anything which makes them* sweat.

19"When they go out into the outer court, into the outer courtyard to the people, they shall take off the garments in which they have been ministering and leave them in the holy chambers; then they shall put on other clothing so that they will not transmit holiness to the people with their [ceremonial] garments.

20"Also they shall not shave their heads, yet they shall not allow their hair to grow long; they shall only cut short *or* trim their hair.

21"Nor shall any priest drink wine when he enters the inner courtyard.

22"And they shall not marry a widow or a divorced woman; but they shall marry virgins of the descendants of the house of Israel, or a widow who was previously married to a priest.

23"The priests shall teach My people *the difference* between the holy and the common, and teach them to distinguish between the (ceremonially) unclean and the clean.

24"In a controversy they shall take their stand to act as judges; they shall judge it in accordance with My

speak the Word

God, I pray that You would help me to know how to distinguish between the holy and the common, between the unclean and the clean. I want to live a life that is holy and clean before You.
—ADAPTED FROM Ezekiel 44:23

ordinances. They shall also keep My laws and My statutes in all My appointed feasts and sanctify My Sabbaths.

25"They shall not go to a dead person to defile *themselves;* except for father or for mother, for son or for daughter, for brother or for sister who has had no husband; they may defile themselves. [Lev 21:1, 2]

26"After he is cleansed [from the defilement of a corpse], seven days more shall elapse for him [before returning to the temple].

27"On the day that he goes into the sanctuary, into the inner courtyard to minister in the sanctuary, he shall offer his sin offering," says the Lord God.

28"It [their ministry to Me] shall be as an inheritance to them, for I am their inheritance; and you shall give them no property (land) in Israel, for I am their possession. [Josh 13:14, 33]

29"They shall eat the grain offering, the sin offering and the guilt offering; and every devoted thing (offering) in Israel [dedicated by a solemn vow to God] shall be theirs.

30"The first of all the first fruits of every kind, and every contribution *and* offering of every kind, from all your contributions *and* offerings, shall belong to the priests. You shall also give to the priest the first of your coarse meal *and* bread dough, so that a blessing may rest on your house.

31"The priests shall not eat any bird or animal that has died a natural death or has been torn to pieces.

45 "MOREOVER, WHEN you divide the land by lot for inheritance, you shall [set apart and] offer an allotment (contribution) to the Lord, a holy portion of the land [to be used for sacred purposes]. The length shall be 25,000 *cubits,* and the width shall be 20,000 *cubits.* It shall be holy (set apart for sacred use) within its every area. [Ezek 48:9, 12, 13]

2"Of this there shall be a square plot five hundred by five hundred *cubits* in perimeter for the holy place, and fifty cubits for the open space around it.

3"And in this area you shall measure off a portion 25,000 *cubits* in length and 10,000 *cubits* in width. And in it shall be the sanctuary which is most holy.

4"It shall be the holy portion of the land; it shall be for the priests, the ministers of the sanctuary, who come near to minister to the Lord, and it shall be a place for their houses and a holy place for the sanctuary.

5"And *another portion of land* 25,000 *cubits* long and 10,000 cubits wide shall be for the Levites, the ministers of the temple (house), and they shall possess it as a place in which to live.

6"You shall give the city possession of *an area* 5,000 *cubits* wide and 25,000 *cubits* long, alongside the portion set aside as a holy section. It shall belong to the whole house of Israel.

7"The prince shall have *land* on either side of the portion set aside as a holy section and the property of the city, adjacent to the holy section and the property of the city, on the west side toward the west and on the east side toward the east, and in length comparable to one of the portions, from the west border to the east border.

8"This shall be his land for a possession in Israel; so My princes shall no longer oppress My people, but they shall give *the rest of* the land to the house of Israel according to their tribes."

9"Thus says the Lord God, "Enough, O princes of Israel! Put away violence and destruction, and practice justice and righteousness. Stop your forceful seizure of property from My people," says the Lord God.

10"You shall have just balances *and* weights [on your scales and just measures], a just ephah [dry volume measure] and a just bath [liquid measure].

11"The ephah and the bath [measures]

shall be the same quantity, the bath containing one tenth of a homer and the ephah one tenth of a homer; their standard [measure] shall be according to the homer.

¹²"The shekel shall be twenty gerahs; twenty shekels, twenty-five shekels, and fifteen shekels [added together, a total of sixty] shall be your maneh (mina).

¹³"This is the offering that you shall offer: a sixth of an ephah from a homer of wheat; a sixth of an ephah from a homer of barley;

¹⁴and the prescribed portion of oil, (namely, the bath of oil), a tenth part of a bath [of oil] from each kor (which is ten baths or a homer, for ten baths make a homer);

¹⁵and [you shall offer] one sheep out of every flock of two hundred from the watering places of Israel—for a grain offering, for a burnt offering, and for peace offerings to make atonement for [those who brought] them," says the Lord God.

¹⁶"All the people of the land shall give to this offering for the prince in Israel.

¹⁷"It shall be the prince's responsibility to provide the burnt offerings, the grain offerings, and the drink offerings at the feasts, on the New Moons and on the Sabbaths, at all the appointed feasts of the house of Israel. He shall prepare and provide the sin offering, the grain offering, the burnt offering and the peace offerings, to make atonement for the house of Israel."

¹⁸'Thus says the Lord God, "In the first month, on the first of the month, you shall take a young bull without blemish and cleanse the sanctuary (from sin).

¹⁹"The priest shall take some of the blood of the sin offering and put it on the door posts of the temple, on the four corners of the ledge of the altar, and on the posts of the gate of the inner courtyard.

²⁰"You shall do this on the seventh [day] of the month for everyone who goes astray [and sins through error or ignorance] and for him who is naive; so shall you make atonement for the temple (house).

²¹"In the first month, on the fourteenth day of the month, you shall have the Passover, a feast of seven days; unleavened bread shall be eaten.

²²"On that day the prince shall provide for himself and for all the people of the land a bull for a sin offering.

²³"And for the seven days of the feast he shall provide as a burnt offering to the Lord seven bulls and seven rams without blemish on every day for the seven days, and a male goat daily for a sin offering.

²⁴"He shall provide as a grain offering [to be offered] with each bull an ephah [of grain], an ephah with each ram, and a hin of oil with each ephah [of grain].

²⁵"In the seventh month, on the fifteenth day of the month at the feast, he shall provide [offerings] like these for the seven days, as the sin offering, the burnt offering, the grain offering, and the oil."

46 'THUS SAYS the Lord God, "The gate of the inner courtyard that faces east shall be shut during the six working days, but it shall be opened on the Sabbath day and opened on the day of the New Moon.

²"The prince shall enter by the porch (portico) of the gate from outside and stand by the post of the gate. The priests shall prepare and provide his burnt offering and his peace offerings, and he shall worship at the threshold of the gate and then go out; but the gate shall not be shut until evening.

³"The people of the land shall also worship at the entrance of that gate before the Lord on the Sabbaths and on the New Moons.

⁴"The burnt offering which the prince shall offer to the Lord on the Sabbath day shall be six lambs without blemish and a ram without blemish.

⁵"The grain offering shall be an ephah with the ram, and the grain offering with the lambs as much as he is able to give, and a hin of oil with an ephah.

⁶"On the day of the New Moon *he shall offer* a young bull without blemish, also six lambs and a ram, without blemish.

⁷"And he shall provide a grain offering, an ephah with the bull and an ephah with the ram, and with the lambs as much as he is able, and a hin of oil with an ephah.

⁸"When the prince enters, he shall enter by way of the porch of the gate and go out by the same way.

⁹"But when the people of the land come before the Lord at the appointed feasts, he who enters by way of the north gate to worship shall go out by way of the south gate. And he who enters by way of the south gate shall go out by way of the north gate. No one shall return by way of the gate through which he entered, but shall go out straight ahead [through the opposite gate]. [Phil 3:13]

¹⁰"When they go in, the prince shall go in among them; and when they go out, he shall go out.

¹¹"At the feasts and the appointed festivals the grain offering shall be an ephah with a bull and an ephah with a ram, and with the lambs as much as one is able to give, and a hin of oil with an ephah.

¹²"When the prince provides a freewill offering, a burnt offering, or peace offerings voluntarily to the Lord, the gate that faces east shall be opened for him, and he shall provide his burnt offering and his peace offerings as he does on the Sabbath day. Then he shall go out, and after he goes out the gate shall be shut.

¹³"And you [priests] shall provide a lamb a year old without blemish as a burnt offering to the Lord each day; morning by morning you shall provide it.

¹⁴"Also you shall provide a grain offering with it morning by morning, one-sixth of an ephah with one-third of a hin of oil to sprinkle on the finely-milled flour. This is a perpetual ordinance for a continual grain offering to the Lord.

¹⁵"Thus they shall provide the lamb, the grain offering and the oil every morning as a continual burnt offering."

¹⁶'Thus says the Lord God, "If the prince gives a gift to any of his sons from his inheritance, it shall belong to his sons [permanently]; it is their possession by inheritance.

¹⁷"But if he gives a gift from his inheritance to one of his servants, then it shall be his until the year of liberty [the Year of Jubilee]; after that it shall be returned to the prince. His inheritance *shall be* only his sons' [permanently]; it shall belong to them.

¹⁸"Moreover, the prince shall not take from the people's inheritance by oppression *and* by evicting them from their property; he shall give his sons an inheritance from his own possession, so that My people will not be scattered, anyone from his possession."'"

¹⁹Then he [my guide] brought me through the entrance, which was at the side of the gate, into the holy chambers for the priests, which faced the north; and behold, a place was there at their extreme westward end.

²⁰He said to me, "This is the place where the priests shall boil (cook) the guilt offering and the sin offering, and where they shall bake the grain offering, so that they do not bring them out into the outer courtyard to transmit holiness to the people."

²¹Then he brought me out into the outer courtyard and led me across to

the four corners of the courtyard; and behold, in every corner of the courtyard *there was a small* courtyard.

²²In the four corners of the courtyard *there were* enclosed courtyards, forty *cubits* long and thirty wide; these four in the corners were the same size.

²³*There was* a row *of masonry* all around inside them, around [each of] the four courtyards, and it was made with cooking hearths under the rows all around.

²⁴Then he said to me, "These are the kitchens of the cooks, where the ministers (Levites) of the temple shall boil (cook) the sacrifices of the people."

47 THEN HE [my guide] brought me back to the door of the house [the temple of the Lord]; and behold, water was flowing from under the threshold of the house (temple) toward the east, for the front of the temple was facing east. And the water was flowing down from under, from the right side of the house, from south of the altar.

²Then he brought me out by way of the north gate and led me around on the outside to the outer gate by the way of *the gate* that faces east. And behold, water was spurting out from the south side [of the gate]. [Zech 14:8; Rev 22:1, 2]

³When the man went out toward the east with a measuring line in his hand, he measured a thousand cubits, and he led me through the water, water that was ankle-deep.

⁴Again he measured a thousand [cubits] and led me through the water, water that was knee-deep. Again he measured a thousand [cubits] and led me through *the water,* water *reaching* the hips.

⁵Again he measured a thousand [cubits]; *and it was* a river that I could not pass through, for the water had risen, *enough* water to swim in, a river that could not be crossed [by wading].

⁶And he said to me, "Son of man, have you seen this?" Then he brought me back to the bank of the river.

⁷Now when I had returned, behold, on the bank of the river were very many trees on the one side and on the other.

⁸Then he said to me, "These waters go out toward the eastern region and go down into the Arabah (the Jordan Valley); then they go toward the sea, being made to flow into the sea, and the waters *of the Dead Sea* shall be healed *and* become fresh.

⁹"It will come about that every living creature which swarms in every place where the river goes, will live. And there will be a very great number of fish, because these waters go there so that the waters of the sea are healed *and* become fresh; so everything will live wherever the river goes.

¹⁰"And it will come about that fishermen will stand beside it [at the banks of the Dead Sea]; from Engedi to Eneglaim there will be dry places to spread nets. Their fish will be of very many kinds, like the fish of the Great [Mediterranean] Sea.

¹¹"But its swamps and marshes will not become fresh [and wholesome for animal life]; they will [as the river subsides] be left encrusted with salt.

¹²"By the river on its bank, on one side and on the other, will grow all *kinds of* trees for food. Their leaves will not wither and their fruit will not fail. They shall bear every month because their water flows from the sanctuary, and their fruit will be for food and their leaves for healing." [Rev 22:2]

¹³Thus says the Lord God, "This *shall be* the boundary by which you shall divide the land as an inheritance among the twelve tribes of Israel; Joseph *shall have* two portions.

¹⁴"You shall divide it as an inheritance, each one equally with the other. I lifted up My hand *and* swore to give it

to your fathers, and this land shall fall to you as an inheritance.

¹⁵"And this shall be the boundary of the land on the north side: from the Great [Mediterranean] Sea by way of Hethlon to the entrance of Zedad,

¹⁶Hamath, Berothah, Sibraim, which is between the border of Damascus and the border of Hamath; [as far as] Hazer-hatticon, which is on the border of Hauran.

¹⁷"So the boundary will extend from the [Mediterranean] Sea to Hazar-enan at the border of Damascus, and on the north, northward, is the border of Hamath. This is the north side.

¹⁸"The east side, from between Hauran, Damascus, Gilead, and the land of Israel, *shall be* the Jordan; from the *north* border to the eastern sea you shall measure. This is the east side.

¹⁹"The south side, southward, from Tamar [near the Dead Sea] *shall extend* as far as the waters of Meribath-kadesh, to the Brook of Egypt and to the Great [Mediterranean] Sea. This is the south side toward the south.

²⁰"The west side *shall be* the Great [Mediterranean] Sea, from the *south* border to a point opposite Lebo-hamath [north of Mount Hermon]. This is the west side.

²¹"So you shall divide this land among yourselves according to the tribes of Israel.

²²"You shall divide it by lot as an inheritance among yourselves and among the foreigners who stay among you, who give birth to sons among you. They shall be to you as the native-born [in the country] among the children (descendants) of Israel; they shall be allotted an inheritance with you among the tribes of Israel.

²³"In whatever tribe the foreigner resides, there shall you give him his inheritance," says the Lord GOD.

48 "NOW THESE are the names of the tribes: from the north end, beside the way of Hethlon to Lebo-hamath, as far as Hazar-enan, which is on the northern border of Damascus, beside Hamath, and running from the east to the west, Dan, one *portion*.

²"Beside the border of Dan, from the east side to the west side, Asher, one *portion*.

³"Beside the border of Asher, from the east side to the west side, Naphtali, one *portion*.

⁴"Beside the border of Naphtali, from the east side to the west side, Manasseh, one *portion*.

⁵"Beside the border of Manasseh, from the east side to the west side, Ephraim, one *portion*.

⁶"Beside the border of Ephraim, from the east side to the west side, Reuben, one *portion*.

⁷"Beside the border of Reuben, from the east side to the west side, Judah, one *portion*.

⁸"And beside the border of Judah, from the east side to the west side, shall be the allotment *and* contribution of land which you shall set apart *and* offer, 25,000 *cubits* in width, and in length like one of the [tribal] portions, from the east side to the west side; and the sanctuary shall be in the midst of it.

⁹"The allotment [of land] that you shall set apart *and* offer to the LORD *shall be* 25,000 *cubits* in length and 10,000 in width.

¹⁰"The holy allotment shall be for these, *namely* for the priests, toward the north 25,000 *cubits in length,* and toward the west 10,000 in width, and toward the east 10,000 in width, and toward the south 25,000 in length; and the sanctuary of the LORD shall be in the midst of it.

¹¹*"It shall be* for the priests who are sanctified of the sons of Zadok, who

have kept My charge, and who did not go astray when the children (descendants) of Israel went astray as the [other] Levites did.

¹²"And this [land offering] shall be an allotment to them from the allotment of the land, a most holy portion beside the border of the [other] Levites.

¹³"Alongside the border of the priests, the [other] Levites *shall have* 25,000 *cubits* in length and 10,000 in width. The whole length *shall be* 25,000 *cubits* and the width 10,000.

¹⁴"And they shall not sell any of it or exchange it, or allow this choice *portion* of land to pass *to others;* for it is holy to the LORD.

¹⁵"The remaining [strip of] 5,000 *cubits* in width and 25,000 in length shall be for the city's common (secular) use, for a place in which to live and for open country. The city shall be in the midst of it.

¹⁶"These *shall be* the measurements of it: the north side 4,500 *cubits,* the south side 4,500, the east side 4,500, and the west side 4,500. [Rev 21:16]

¹⁷"The city shall have open country: toward the north 250 *cubits,* and toward the south 250, toward the east 250, and toward the west 250.

¹⁸"The remainder of the length alongside the holy allotment shall be 10,000 *cubits* to the east and 10,000 to the west; and it shall be beside the holy allotment. The produce from it shall be food for the workers of the city.

¹⁹"The workers of the city, from all the tribes of Israel shall cultivate it.

²⁰"The whole allotment *shall be* 25,000 by 25,000 *cubits;* you shall set apart the holy allotment, a square, with the property of the city.

²¹"The remainder, on both sides of the holy allotment and of the property possessed by the city, *shall belong* to the prince. In front of the 25,000 cu-

bits of the allotment toward the east border and westward in front of the 25,000 toward the west border, alongside the [tribal] portions, *it shall be* for the prince. The holy allotment with the sanctuary of the temple shall be in the midst of it.

²²Exclusive of the property of the Levites and of the property of the city, which are in the middle of that which belongs to the prince, *everything* between the border of Judah and the border of Benjamin shall be for the prince.

²³"As for the rest of the tribes: from the east side to the west side, Benjamin, one *portion.*

²⁴"Beside the border of Benjamin, from the east side to the west side, Simeon, one *portion.*

²⁵"Beside the border of Simeon, from the east side to the west side, Issachar, one *portion.*

²⁶"Beside the border of Issachar, from the east side to the west side, Zebulun, one *portion.*

²⁷"Beside the border of Zebulun, from the east side to the west side, Gad, one *portion.*

²⁸"And beside the border of Gad, at the south side, southward, the border shall extend from Tamar to the waters of Meribath-kadesh, to the Brook [of Egypt], to the Great [Mediterranean] Sea.

²⁹"This is the land which you shall divide by lot among the tribes of Israel as their inheritance, and these are their *several* portions," says the Lord GOD.

³⁰"These are the exits of the city: on the north side, [which is to extend] 4,500 *cubits* by measurement,

³¹there shall also be gates of the city, *named* after the names of the tribes of Israel, three gates toward the north: one gate of Reuben, one gate of Judah, one gate of Levi.

³²"On the east side, 4,500 *cubits,* also

three gates: one gate of Joseph, one gate of Benjamin, one gate of Dan.

33"On the south side, 4,500 *cubits,* by measurement, also three gates: one gate of Simeon, one gate of Issachar, one gate of Zebulun.

34"On the west side, 4,500 *cubits,* three gates: one gate of Gad, one gate of Asher, one gate of Naphtali.

35"The distance around the city shall be 18,000 (4 x 4,500) *cubits;* and the name of the city from that day [and ever after] *shall be,* 'The LORD is There.'" [Rev 21:12, 13, 16]

Daniel

Author:
Daniel

Date:
Late sixth century BC

Everyday Life Principles:
Like Daniel, we must determine in our hearts that we will not defile ourselves, but that we will stay faithful to the Lord.

An excellent spirit is one of the best character qualities a person can have.

We must refuse to compromise or to allow the world's influence to cause us to turn from God.

Daniel is one of several biblical books that teach their lessons through a person's life. Two of the great lessons we learn from Daniel are excellence and courage. Daniel 5:12 and Daniel 6:3 both tell us that Daniel had an "extraordinary spirit." Other Bible translations render this an "excellent spirit." Throughout the book of Daniel, we see Daniel making excellent choices, and we read that he did things in an excellent way. But his choices and his actions were "fruits," not roots. The fruit of excellent decisions and behavior was rooted in his excellent spirit. As believers, you and I have God's Spirit living in us and we, like Daniel, can live with excellence because God is an excellent God!

Daniel also teaches us about courage. He was always willing to stand up to the authorities in Babylon, who did not share his devotion to God. He was willing to suffer and even to die for his beliefs. His courageous refusal to compromise landed him in a den of hungry lions, but God delivered him! Daniel ended up in a high government position—and the king of Babylon forsook his old ways, turned to God, and required his subjects to believe in God as well.

As you read the book of Daniel, I pray that you will be inspired to higher levels of excellence in everything you do and that your courage will be stirred. As we learn from Daniel, one uncompromising and brave person can change a nation!

1 IN THE third year of the reign of Jehoiakim king of Judah, Nebuchadnezzar king of Babylon came to Jerusalem and besieged it.

²The Lord gave Jehoiakim king of Judah into his hand, along with some of the articles of the house of God; and he brought them into the land of Shinar, to the house of his god, and brought the articles into the treasury of his god. [2 Chr 36:5–7; Jer 27:19, 20; Dan 5:1–3]

³And the [Babylonian] king told Ashpenaz, the chief of his *officials, to bring in some of the sons of Israel, including some from the royal family and from the nobles, [2 Kin 20:17, 18]

⁴young men without blemish and handsome in appearance, skillful in all wisdom, endowed with intelligence *and* discernment, and quick to understand, competent to stand [in the presence of the king] *and* able to serve in the king's palace. He also *ordered Ashpenaz* to teach them the literature and language of the Chaldeans.

life point

After the fall of Judah to Babylon, Nebuchadnezzar, the king of Babylon at that time, decided to train some young Hebrew men as his attendants. His purpose was for them to conform to the lifestyle of his court.

But Daniel, one of the devout young men of Judah who loved the Lord, was determined to be a God-pleaser and not a people-pleaser. He refused to conform to what the king and others thought he should do and be.

Daniel stood his ground and won favor with the king and his court. As a result of his fearless stand, God ended up using him in a powerful way.

1:3 Or *eunuchs,* and so throughout.

putting the Word to work

Daniel had the opportunity to eat "the king's finest food" (Daniel 1:8), but he was determined not to defile himself with those delicacies. You and I have similar opportunities to defile ourselves today, especially in the area of entertainment. We can be defiled by the ungodly influences of the television shows or movies we watch or the music we listen to. We can also defile ourselves by compromising and going along with friends who are making wrong choices. Are you willing to be like Daniel and to be determined not to defile yourself? Ask God to help you make godly choices and stay faithful to Him.

⁵The king assigned a daily ration for them from his finest food and from the wine which he drank. They were to be educated *and* nourished this way for three years so that at the end of that time they were [prepared] to enter the king's service.

⁶Among them from the sons of Judah were: Daniel, Hananiah, Mishael, and Azariah.

⁷The commander of the officials gave them [Babylonian] names: Daniel he named Belteshazzar, Hananiah *he named* Shadrach, Mishael *he named* Meshach, and Azariah *he named* Abed-nego.

⁸But Daniel made up his mind that he would not defile (taint, dishonor) himself with the king's finest food or with the wine which the king drank; so he asked the commander of the officials that he might [be excused so that he would] not defile himself. [Num 6:1–4; 1 Cor 10:21]

⁹Now God granted Daniel favor and compassion in the sight of the commander of the officials,

the blessings of wholehearted commitment

Because of their sins against the Lord, the nation of Judah was carried away into captivity in Babylon. There, some of the most promising young men, including Daniel and three of his friends, were chosen to become attendants to the Babylonian king. As part of their three-year period of training and preparation, these young men were supposed to follow a diet of rich meat and wine provided from the king's table. However, Daniel and his friends had apparently made a previous commitment to God concerning their diet, and they determined they would not defile themselves by eating the king's food and drinking his wine (see Daniel 1:8). Instead, Daniel asked the eunuch who oversaw them if it would be possible for them to follow their own diet of vegetables and water.

The Bible tells us that the Lord gave Daniel favor and compassion with the eunuch, who agreed to allow them to follow their diet as long as it did not harm them. Of course, not only did it not harm them, it made them stronger and healthier than all the other young men in training as royal attendants. In fact, the king was so impressed by their wisdom that he chose them out of all the young men to enter his personal service (see Daniel 1:10–20).

God's favor rested on Daniel and his friends so strongly that eventually Daniel rose to become the chief governor of Babylon, the world's greatest power at that time, and the other three were made high officials in the Babylonian kingdom.

What was the key to Daniel's success? He followed God with his whole heart and refused to compromise, and, as a result, God gave him wisdom, skill, and favor.

¹⁰and the commander of the officials said to Daniel, "I am afraid of my lord the king, who has prearranged your food and your drink; for why should he see your faces looking more haggard than the young men who are your own age? Then you would make me forfeit my head to the king."

¹¹But Daniel said to the overseer whom the commander of the officials had appointed over Daniel, Hananiah, Mishael, and Azariah,

¹²"Please, test your servants for ten days, and let us be given some vegetables to eat and water to drink.

¹³"Then let our appearance and the appearance of the young men who eat the king's finest food be observed *and* compared by you, and deal with your servants in accordance with what you see."

¹⁴So the man listened to them in this matter and tested them for ten days.

¹⁵At the end of ten days it seemed that they were looking better and healthier than all the young men who ate the king's finest food.

¹⁶So the overseer continued to withhold their fine food and the wine they were to drink, and kept giving them vegetables.

¹⁷As for these four young men, God gave them knowledge and skill in all *kinds of* literature and wisdom; Daniel

speak the Word

God, I pray that You would give me knowledge and skill in all the things I need to know.
–ADAPTED FROM DANIEL 1:17

also understood all *kinds of* visions and dreams. [Luke 21:15; James 1:5–7]

¹⁸At the end of the time set by the king to bring all the young men in [before him], the commander of the officials presented them to Nebuchadnezzar.

¹⁹The king spoke with them, and among them all not one was found like Daniel, Hananiah, Mishael, and Azariah; so they were [selected and] assigned to stand before the king *and* enter his personal service.

²⁰In every matter of wisdom and understanding about which the king consulted them, he found them ten times better than all the [learned] magicians and enchanters (Magi) in his whole realm.

²¹And Daniel remained there until the first year of [the reign of] King Cyrus [over Babylon; now this was at the end of the seventy-year exile of Judah (the Southern Kingdom) in Babylonia, as foretold by Jeremiah]. [Ezra 1:1–3; Jer 25:11, 12; 29:10]

2 IN THE second year (604 B.C.) of the reign of Nebuchadnezzar, Nebuchadnezzar had dreams which troubled *and* disturbed his spirit and [interfered with] his ability to sleep.

²Then the king gave a command to call the magicians, the enchanters, the sorcerers, and the Chaldeans to tell the king his dreams. So they came in and stood before the king.

³The king said to them, "I had a dream, and my spirit is troubled *and* anxious to know the [content and meaning of the] dream."

⁴Then the Chaldeans said to the king in Aramaic, "O king, live forever! Tell the dream to your servants, and we will declare the interpretation."

⁵The king replied to the Chaldeans, "My command is firm *and* unchangeable: if you do not reveal to me the [content of the] dream along with its interpretation, you shall be cut into pieces and your houses shall be made a heap of rubbish.

⁶"But if you tell [me] the [content of the] dream along with its interpretation, you shall receive from me gifts and rewards and great honor. So tell me the dream and its interpretation."

⁷They answered again, "Let the king tell the dream to his servants, and we will explain its interpretation [to you]."

⁸The king replied, "I know for certain that you are bargaining for time, because you have seen that my command [to you] is firm *and* irrevocable.

⁹"If you will not reveal to me the [content of the] dream, there is but one sentence for you; for you have [already] prepared lying and corrupt words [and you have agreed together] to speak [them] before me [hoping to delay your execution] until the situation is changed. Therefore, tell me the dream [first], and then I will know [with confidence] that you can give me its interpretation."

¹⁰The Chaldeans answered the king and said, "There is not a man on earth who can tell the king this matter, for no king, lord or ruler has ever asked such a thing as this of any magician or enchanter or Chaldean.

¹¹"Furthermore, what the king demands is an unusual *and* difficult thing indeed! No one except the gods can reveal it to the king, and their dwelling is not with [mortal] flesh."

¹²Because of this the king was indignant and extremely furious and gave a command to destroy all the wise men of Babylon.

¹³So the decree went out that the wise men were to be killed; and they looked for Daniel and his companions to put them to death.

¹⁴Then Daniel replied with discretion and wisdom to Arioch, the captain of the king's bodyguard, who had gone out to execute the wise men of Babylon;

¹⁵he said to Arioch, the king's captain, "Why is the decree from the king so harsh *and* urgent?" Then Arioch explained the matter to Daniel.

¹⁶So Daniel went in and asked the king to appoint a date *and* give him time, so that he might reveal to the king the interpretation *of the dream*.

¹⁷Then Daniel returned to his house and discussed the matter with Hananiah, Mishael, and Azariah, his companions,

¹⁸in order that they might seek compassion from the God of heaven regarding this secret, so that Daniel and his companions would not be executed with the rest of the wise men of Babylon.

¹⁹Then the secret was revealed to Daniel in a vision of the night, and Daniel blessed the God of heaven.

²⁰Daniel answered,

"Blessed be the name of God
    forever and ever,
For wisdom and power belong to
    Him.
²¹"It is He who changes the times
    and the seasons;
He removes kings and establishes
    kings.
He gives wisdom to the wise
And [greater] knowledge to those
    who have understanding!
    [Dan 4:35]
²²"It is He who reveals the profound
    and hidden things;
He knows what is in the darkness,
And the light dwells with Him.
    [Job 15:8; Ps 25:14; Matt 6:6]
²³"I thank You and praise You,
    O God of my fathers,
For You have given me wisdom
    and power;
Even now You have made known
    to me what we requested of You,
For You have made known to
    us [the solution to] the king's
    matter."

²⁴So Daniel went to Arioch, whom the king had appointed to destroy the wise men of Babylon; he went and said this to him: "Do not execute the wise men of Babylon! Bring me before the king, and I will reveal to the king the interpretation [of his dream]."

²⁵Then Arioch hurriedly brought Daniel before the king and said this to him: "I have found a man among the exiles of Judah who can explain to the king the interpretation [of the dream]."

²⁶The king said to Daniel, whose [Babylonian] name was Belteshazzar, "Are you able to reveal to me the [content of the] dream which I have seen and its interpretation?"

²⁷Daniel answered the king and said, "Regarding the mystery about which the king has inquired, neither the wise men, enchanters, magicians, nor astrologers are able to answer the king,

²⁸but there is a God in heaven who reveals secrets, and He has shown King Nebuchadnezzar what will take place in the latter days (end of days). This was your dream and the vision [that appeared] in your mind while on your bed.

²⁹"As for you, O king, as you were lying on your bed thoughts came into your mind about what will take place in the future; and He who reveals secrets has shown you what will occur.

³⁰"But as for me, this secret has not

putting the Word to work

Daniel 2:21 tells us that God "changes the times and the seasons." This is true not only in the natural world, but in our lives. His timing and His ways are always perfect. Are you fully trusting Him to bring the changes you need in your life at the time that is right? He is doing a good work in you, so I encourage you to cooperate with the changes He brings. You'll be glad you did.

been revealed to me because my wisdom is greater than that of any other living man, but in order to make the interpretation known to the king, and so that you may understand [fully] the thoughts of your mind.

31"You, O king, were looking, and behold, [there was] a single great statue; this image, which was large and of unsurpassed splendor, stood before you, and its appearance was awesome *and* terrifying.

32"As for this statue, its head *was made* of fine gold, its breast and its arms of silver, its belly and its thighs of bronze,

33its legs of iron, its feet partly of iron and partly of clay [pottery].

34"As you were looking, a stone was cut out without [human] hands, and it struck the statue on its feet of iron and clay and crushed them. [1 Pet 2:3–8]

35"Then the iron, the clay, the bronze, the silver, and the gold were crushed together and became like the chaff from the summer threshing floors; and the wind carried them away so that not a trace of them could be found. And the stone that struck the statue became a great mountain and filled the whole earth.

36"This was the dream; now we will tell the king its interpretation.

37"You, O king, are the king of [earthly] kings, to whom the God of heaven has given the kingdom, the power, the strength and the glory; [Jer 25:9; 27:6; 28:14]

38and wherever the sons of men dwell, and the beasts of the field, and the birds of the heavens, He has given them into your hand and has made you ruler over them all. You [king of Babylon] are the head of gold.

39"After you will arise another kingdom (Medo-Persia) inferior to you, and then a third kingdom of bronze (Greece under Alexander the Great), which will rule over all the earth.

40"Then a fourth kingdom (Rome) will be strong as iron, for iron breaks to pieces and shatters all things; and like iron which crushes things in pieces, it will break and crush all these [others]. [Dan 7:7, 23]

41"And as you saw the feet and toes, partly of potter's clay and partly of iron, it will be a divided kingdom; but there will be in it some of the durability *and* strength of iron, just as you saw the iron mixed with common clay.

42"As the [ten] toes of the feet were partly of iron and partly of clay, so some of the kingdom will be strong, and *another* part of it will be brittle.

43"And as you saw the iron mixed with common clay, so they will combine with one another in the seed of men; but they will not merge [for such diverse things or ideologies cannot unite], even as iron does not mix with clay.

44"In the days of those [final ten] kings the God of heaven will set up a kingdom that will never be destroyed, nor will its sovereignty be left for another people; but it will crush and put an end to all these kingdoms, and it will stand forever. [Dan 7:14–17; Luke 1:31–33; Rev 11:15]

45"Just as you saw that a stone was cut out of the mountain without hands and that it crushed the iron, the bronze, the clay, the silver and the gold, the great God has revealed to the king what will take place in the future; so the dream is true and its interpretation is trustworthy."

46Then King Nebuchadnezzar fell face downward and paid respect to Daniel [as a great prophet of the highest God], and gave orders for an offering and fragrant incense to be presented to him [in honor of his God].

47The king answered Daniel and said, "Most certainly your God is the God of gods and the Lord of kings and a revealer of mysteries, since you have

been able to reveal this mystery!"
[Prov 3:32; Rev 19:16]

⁴⁸Then the king promoted Daniel [to an exalted position] and gave him many great gifts, and he made him ruler over the entire province of Babylon and chief governor over all the wise men of Babylon.

⁴⁹And Daniel made a request of the king, and he appointed Shadrach, Meshach, and Abed-nego over the affairs of the province of Babylon, while Daniel was at the court of the king.

3 NEBUCHADNEZZAR THE king made a gold [-plated] image, whose height [including the pedestal] was sixty cubits (ninety feet) and its width six cubits (nine feet). He set it up on the plain of Dura in the province of Babylon.

²Then Nebuchadnezzar the king sent *word* to assemble the satraps, the prefects and the governors, the counselors, the treasurers, the judges, the magistrates *and* lawyers and all the chief officials of the provinces to come to the dedication of the image that King Nebuchadnezzar had set up.

³Then the satraps, the prefects, the governors, the counselors, the treasurers, the judges, the magistrates *and* lawyers, and all the chief officials of the provinces gathered together for the dedication of the image that King Nebuchadnezzar had set up; and they stood before it.

⁴Then the herald loudly proclaimed,

refuse to conform

Daniel went through a period of testing and trial, but, in the end, the same king who tried to get him to conform had such respect for him that he exalted him to a high position in the kingdom (see Daniel 2:48).

The same thing happened to me years ago in the work world. My boss wanted me to help him steal some money in a roundabout way. I was a bookkeeper, and he wanted me to write off a customer's credit balance. The customer had paid a bill twice, and my employer did not want that fact reflected on the client's statement.

I refused.

Several years later, I ended up having great favor in that company. I was made second-in-command in charge of the office, the warehouse, all of the inventory, and all the truck drivers. I was called upon to solve problems I did not even understand, and God gave me the wisdom I needed to do the job well.

As a young woman, I had a major position of leadership in the company. I did not really have the education or even the training for the position. How did that happen? It came about because, like Daniel, I refused to conform to a lower standard. I was respected in the company and was exalted to a higher position of honor.

Those who try to get you to conform will not respect you if you do conform. In fact, they will despise your weakness. They will know they are controlling you and that what they are doing is wrong. But if you will stand your ground, you will be the one who ends up with the respect. For a while they may treat you as though you were the lowest creature on earth. But when all is said and done, you will gain their respect. Integrity and godly convictions lead to blessing and favor.

"You are commanded, O peoples, nations, and *speakers of every* language,

⁵that at the moment you hear the sound of the horn, pipe, lyre, trigon (four-stringed harp), dulcimer, bagpipe, and all kinds of music, you are to fall down and worship the golden image that King Nebuchadnezzar has set up.

⁶"Whoever does not fall down and worship shall immediately be thrown into the midst of a furnace of blazing fire."

⁷So when the people heard the sound of the horn, pipe, lyre, trigon, dulcimer, bagpipe and all kinds of music, all the peoples, nations, and *speakers of every* language fell down and worshiped the golden image that Nebuchadnezzar the king had set up.

⁸At that time certain Chaldeans

life point

King Nebuchadnezzar set up a huge golden image in Babylon and required everyone to bow down before it and worship it (see Daniel 3:6). Anyone who refused to do so would be thrown into a fiery furnace.

Shadrach, Meshach, and Abed-nego, three of Daniel's close friends, refused to bow down (see Daniel 3:14). They had the same excellent, godly spirit Daniel had, so they refused. The king basically said to them, "If you do not do as I say, I am going to burn you alive" (see Daniel 3:15).

Isn't that what the world often says to you and me? If we refuse to conform to its standards, the world threatens us by saying, "If you do not bow down and do what we want you to do, if you do not fit into our mold, we are going hurt you in some way." The world may threaten us, but with God, we will always emerge victorious.

came forward and brought [malicious] accusations against the Jews.

⁹They said to King Nebuchadnezzar, "O king, live forever!

¹⁰"You, O king, have made a decree that everyone who hears the sound of the horn, pipe, lyre, trigon, harp, dulcimer, bagpipe, and all kinds of music is to fall down and worship the golden image.

¹¹"Whoever does not fall down and worship shall be thrown into the midst of a furnace of blazing fire.

¹²"There are certain Jews whom you have appointed over the administration of the province of Babylon, *namely* Shadrach, Meshach, and Abed-nego. These men, O king, pay no attention to you; they do not serve your gods or worship the golden image which you have set up."

¹³Then Nebuchadnezzar in a furious rage gave a command to bring Shadrach, Meshach, and Abed-nego; and these men were brought before the king.

¹⁴Nebuchadnezzar said to them, "Is it true, Shadrach, Meshach, and Abed-nego, that you do not serve my gods or worship the golden image which I have set up?

¹⁵"Now if you are ready, when you hear the sound of the horn, pipe, lyre, trigon, harp, dulcimer, and all kinds of music, to fall down and worship the image which I have made, very good. But if you do not worship, you shall be thrown at once into the midst of a furnace of blazing fire; and what god is there who can rescue you out of my hands?"

¹⁶Shadrach, Meshach, and Abed-nego answered the king, "O Nebuchadnezzar, we do not need to answer you on this point.

¹⁷"If it be so, our God whom we serve is able to rescue us from the furnace of blazing fire, and He will rescue us from your hand, O king.

¹⁸"But even if *He does* not, let it be

known to you, O king, that we are not going to serve your gods or worship the golden image that you have set up!" [Job 13:15; Acts 4:19, 20]

¹⁹Then Nebuchadnezzar was filled with fury, and his facial expression changed toward Shadrach, Meshach, and Abed-nego. Then he gave a command that the furnace was to be heated seven times hotter than usual.

²⁰He commanded certain strong men in his army to tie up Shadrach, Meshach, and Abed-nego and to throw them into the furnace of blazing fire.

²¹Then these [three] men were tied up in their trousers, their coats, their turbans, and their other clothes, and were thrown into the midst of the furnace of blazing fire.

²²Because the king's command was urgent and the furnace was extremely hot, the flame of the fire killed the men who carried up Shadrach, Meshach, and Abed-nego.

²³But these three men, Shadrach, Meshach, and Abed-nego, fell into the midst of the furnace of blazing fire *still* tied up.

life point

Do you know what I like about Shadrach, Meshach, and Abed-nego? Their absolute refusal to be frightened or intimidated. They told the king: "We believe God is going to deliver us, but even if He *does not*, we will not conform to what you think we ought to do. We are going to do what God is telling us to do. You can do what you want to with your furnace. But whatever happens to us, we will have peace" (see Daniel 3:17, 18).

This is the attitude we should have toward those who would try to pressure us into disobeying what we know to be God's will for us. Pray for that kind of courage and faith in your life.

life point

Shadrach, Meshach, and Abed-nego experienced affliction when they remained firm in their commitment to the one true God. When they refused the command of the wicked king Nebuchadnezzar to worship the golden image he had set up, Nebuchadnezzar cast them into the fiery furnace, which he heated seven times hotter than usual (see Daniel 3:19)!

Nebuchadnezzar was "astounded" to see that Shadrach, Meshach, and Abed-nego met a fourth man in their fiery furnace—one who was, according to the King James Version, "like the Son of God" (Daniel 3:25). Not only did the three come out of the fiery furnace loosed from their bonds and totally unharmed, they did not even smell of smoke!

Just as God was with these men in their furnace of affliction, He will be with you in whatever situation you may have to face in life.

²⁴Then Nebuchadnezzar the king [looked and] was astounded, and he jumped up and said to his counselors, "Did we not throw three men who were tied up into the midst of the fire?" They replied to the king, "Certainly, O king."

²⁵He answered, "Look! I see four men untied, walking around in the midst of the fire, and they are not hurt! And the appearance of the fourth is like a son of the gods!" [Phil 2:5–8]

²⁶Then Nebuchadnezzar approached the door of the blazing furnace and said, "Shadrach, Meshach, and Abed-nego, servants of the Most High God, come out [of there]! Come here!" Then Shadrach, Meshach, and Abed-nego came out of the midst of the fire.

²⁷The satraps, the prefects, the

governors and the king's counselors gathered around them and saw that in regard to these men the fire had no effect on their bodies—their hair was not singed, their clothes were not scorched *or* damaged, even the smell of smoke was not on them.

²⁸Nebuchadnezzar responded and said, "Blessed be the God of Shadrach, Meshach, and Abed-nego, who has sent His angel and rescued His servants who believed in, trusted in, *and* relied on Him! They violated the king's command and surrendered their bodies rather than serve or worship any god except their own God.

²⁹"Therefore I make a decree that any people, nation, or language that speaks anything offensive against the God of Shadrach, Meshach, and Abednego shall be cut into pieces and their houses be made a heap of rubbish, for there is no other god who is able to save in this way!"

³⁰Then the king caused Shadrach, Meshach, and Abed-nego to prosper in the province of Babylon.

4 NEBUCHADNEZZAR THE king, to all the peoples, nations, and *speakers of every* language that live in all the earth: "May your peace abound!

²"It has seemed good to me to declare the signs and wonders which the Most High God has done for me.

³"How great are His signs
And how mighty are His wonders!
His kingdom is an everlasting kingdom
And His dominion is from generation to generation. [Dan 7:13, 14; Luke 1:31–33]

⁴"I, Nebuchadnezzar, was at rest in my house and prospering in my palace.

⁵"I saw a dream and it made me afraid; and the fantasies *and* thoughts

and the visions [that appeared] in my mind *as I lay* on my bed kept alarming me.

⁶"So I gave orders to bring in before me all the wise men of Babylon, so that they might make known to me the interpretation of the dream.

⁷"Then the magicians, the enchanters (Magi), the Chaldeans [who were the master astrologers] and the diviners came in, and I told them the dream, but they could not interpret it *and* make known its meaning to me.

⁸"But at last Daniel came in before me, whose name is Belteshazzar, after the name of my god, and in whom is *a spirit of the holy gods; and I told the dream to him, *saying,*

⁹'O Belteshazzar, chief of the magicians, because I know that a spirit of the holy gods is in you and no mystery baffles *or* troubles you, tell me the visions of my dream which I have seen, along with its interpretation.

¹⁰'The visions that passed through my mind as I lay on my bed were these: I was looking, and behold, *there was* a tree in the middle of the earth, and its height was great.

¹¹'The tree grew large and became strong
And its height reached to heaven,
And it was visible to the end of the earth.
¹²'Its leaves were beautiful and its fruit abundant,
And in it was food for all.
The beasts of the field found shade under it,
And the birds of the sky nested in its branches,
And all living creatures fed themselves from it.

¹³'And behold, I saw in the visions of my mind *as I lay* on my bed, an *angelic* watcher, a holy one, descended from heaven.

4:8 Or possibly *the Spirit of the holy God,* and so throughout the chapter.

¹⁴'He shouted aloud and said this:
"Cut down the tree and cut off its
branches;
Shake off its leaves and scatter its
fruit;
Let the living creatures run from
under it
And the birds fly from its branches.
¹⁵"Nevertheless leave the stump
with its roots in the ground,
Bound with a band of iron and
bronze
In the new grass of the field;
And let him be wet with the dew of
heaven,
And let him feed with the animals
in the grass of the earth.
¹⁶"Let his mind *and* nature be
changed from a man's
And let an animal's mind *and*
nature be given to him,
And let seven periods of time pass
over him.
¹⁷"This sentence is by the decree of
the *angelic* watchers
And the decision is a command of
the holy ones,
So that the living may know
[without any doubt]
That the Most High [God] rules
over the kingdom of mankind
And He bestows it on whomever
He desires
And sets over it the humblest *and*
lowliest of men." [Dan 2:21; 5:21]

¹⁸'This is the dream which I, King
Nebuchadnezzar, have seen. Now
you, Belteshazzar, explain its meaning, since none of the wise men of my
kingdom are able to reveal its interpretation to me; but you are able, for a
spirit of the holy gods is in you.'

¹⁹"Then Daniel, whose [Babylonian]
name was Belteshazzar, was appalled
and speechless for a while [because he
was deeply concerned about the destiny
of the king], and his thoughts alarmed
him. The king said, 'Belteshazzar, do
not let the dream or its interpretation

frighten you.' Belteshazzar answered,
'My lord, may the dream be [meant] for
those who hate you and its message for
your enemies!

²⁰"The tree that you saw, which became great and grew strong, whose
height reached to heaven and which
was visible to all the earth,
²¹whose foliage was beautiful and its
fruit abundant, and on which was food
for all, under which the beasts of the
field lived, and in whose branches the
birds of the sky nested—
²²it is you, O king, who have become
great and grown strong; your greatness has increased and it reaches to
heaven, and your dominion [reaches]
to the ends of the earth.

²³'In that the king saw an *angelic*
watcher, a holy one, descending from
heaven and saying, "Cut the tree down
and destroy it; but leave the stump with
its roots in the earth, but with a band
of iron and bronze *around it* in the new
grass of the field, and let him be wet
with the dew of heaven, and let him
feed with the beasts of the field until
seven periods of time pass over him,"
²⁴this is the interpretation, O king: It
is the decree of the Most High [God],
which has come upon my lord the king:
²⁵that you shall be driven from mankind and your dwelling place shall be
with the beasts of the field; and that
you be given grass to eat like the cattle
and be wet with the dew of heaven;
and seven periods of time shall pass
over you, until you know [without any
doubt] that the Most High [God] rules
over the kingdom of mankind and He
bestows it to whomever He desires.
²⁶'And in that it was commanded to
leave the stump with the roots of the
tree [in the earth], your kingdom shall
be restored to you after you recognize
(understand fully) that Heaven rules.
²⁷'Therefore, O king, let my advice to
you be [considered and found] acceptable; break away now from your sins

and exhibit your repentance by doing what is right, and from your wickedness by showing mercy to the poor, so that [if you repent] there may possibly be a continuance of your prosperity *and* tranquility *and* a healing of your error.'

28"All this happened to Nebuchadnezzar the king.

29"Twelve months later he was walking on the upper level of the royal palace of Babylon.

30"The king said thoughtfully, 'Is not this the great Babylon which I myself have built as the royal residence *and* seat of government by the might of my power and for the honor *and* glory of my majesty?'

31"While the words were still in the king's mouth, a voice came [as if falling] from heaven, *saying*, 'O King Nebuchadnezzar, to you it is declared: "The kingdom has been removed from you,

32and you will be driven away from mankind, and your dwelling place will be with the animals of the field. You will be given grass to eat like the cattle, and seven periods of time will pass over you until you know [without any doubt] that the Most High God rules over the kingdom of mankind and He bestows it on whomever He desires."'

33"Immediately the word concerning Nebuchadnezzar was fulfilled. He was driven away from mankind and began eating grass like cattle, and his body was wet with the dew of heaven until his hair had grown like eagles' *feathers* and his nails were like birds' *claws*.

34"But at the end of the days [that is, at the seven periods of time], I, Nebuchadnezzar, raised my eyes toward heaven, and my understanding *and* reason returned to me; and I blessed the Most High [God] and I praised and honored *and* glorified Him who lives forever,

For His dominion is an everlasting dominion;
And His kingdom *endures* from generation to generation.
35"All the inhabitants of the earth are regarded as nothing.
But He does according to His will in the host of heaven
And among the inhabitants of the earth;
And no one can hold back His hand
Or say to Him, 'What have You done?'

36"Now at the same time my reason returned to me; and for the glory of my kingdom, my majesty and splendor were returned to me, and my counselors and my nobles began seeking me out; so I was re-established in my kingdom, and still more greatness [than before] was added to me.

37"Now I, Nebuchadnezzar, praise and exalt and honor the King of heaven, for all His works are true *and* faithful and His ways are just, and He is able to humiliate *and* humble those who walk in [self-centered, self-righteous] pride."

5 BELSHAZZAR THE king [who was a descendant of Nebuchadnezzar] gave a great feast for a thousand of his nobles, and he was drinking his wine in the presence of the thousand [guests].

2Belshazzar, as he tasted the wine, gave a command to bring in the gold and silver vessels which his father

speak the Word

God, I declare like Nebuchadnezzar that all Your works are true and faithful. All Your ways are just!
–ADAPTED FROM DANIEL 4:37

Nebuchadnezzar had taken out of the temple which was in Jerusalem, so that the king and his nobles, his wives and his concubines might drink from them.

³Then they brought in the gold *and* silver vessels that had been taken out of the temple, the house of God which was in Jerusalem; and the king and his nobles, his wives and his concubines drank from them.

⁴They drank the wine and praised the gods of gold and silver, of bronze, iron, wood and stone.

⁵Suddenly the fingers of a man's hand appeared and began writing opposite the lampstand on [a well-lit area of] the plaster of the wall of the king's palace, and the king saw the part of the hand that did the writing.

⁶Then the king's face grew pale, and his thoughts alarmed him; the joints *and* muscles of his hips *and* back weakened and his knees began knocking together.

⁷The king called aloud to bring in the enchanters (Magi), the Chaldeans [who were master astrologers] and the diviners. The king said to the wise men of Babylon, "Whoever can read this writing and explain its interpretation to me shall be clothed with purple and have a chain of gold put around his neck, and have authority as the third *ruler* in the kingdom."

⁸Then all the king's wise men came in, but they could not read the writing or reveal to the king its interpretation.

⁹Then King Belshazzar was greatly perplexed, his face became even paler, and his nobles were bewildered *and* alarmed.

¹⁰Now the queen [mother], over-hearing the [excited] words of the king and his nobles, came into the banquet area. The queen [mother] spoke and said, "O king, live forever! Do not be alarmed at your thoughts or let your face be changed.

¹¹"There is a man in your kingdom in

life point

Daniel 5:12 tells us that "an extraordinary spirit" was found in Daniel. Other Bible translations render this "an excellent spirit." We must make up our minds and get into agreement with God that we, like Daniel, are going to be excellent, not mediocre. We must take an inventory of our lives and prune anything that entangles us or simply steals our time. We must be determined, work hard, and refuse to quit or give up—drawing strength from God and not depending on ourselves. If we will do these things persistently and with an excellent spirit, we will eventually be victorious.

whom is a spirit of the holy gods; and in the days of your father, illumination, understanding and wisdom like the wisdom of the gods were found in him. And King Nebuchadnezzar, your father—your father the king, appointed him chief of the magicians, enchanters, Chaldeans and diviners.

¹²"It was because an extraordinary spirit, knowledge and insight, the ability to interpret dreams, clarify riddles, and solve complex problems were found in this Daniel, whom the king named Belteshazzar. Now let Daniel be called and he will give the interpretation."

¹³Then Daniel was brought in before the king. And the king said to Daniel, "Are you that Daniel who is one of the sons of the exiles of Judah, whom my father the king brought from Judah?

¹⁴"I have heard of you, that a spirit of the gods is in you, and that illumination, insight, and extraordinary wisdom have been found in you.

¹⁵"Now the wise men and the enchanters, were brought in before me so that they might read this writing and reveal its meaning to me, but they

could not give the interpretation of the message.

¹⁶"But I personally have heard about you, that you are able to make interpretations and solve complex problems. Now if you are able to read the writing and reveal its interpretation to me, you shall be clothed with purple and have a chain of gold put around your neck, and you shall have authority as the third *ruler* in the kingdom."

¹⁷Then Daniel answered and said before the king, "Keep your gifts for yourself and give your rewards to someone else; however, I will read the writing to the king and reveal the interpretation to him.

¹⁸"O king, the Most High God gave Nebuchadnezzar your father a kingdom and greatness and glory and majesty;

¹⁹and because of the greatness that He gave him, all the peoples, nations, and *speakers of every* language trembled and feared him. Whomever he wished he killed, and whomever he wished he kept alive; whomever he wished he promoted and whomever he wished he humbled.

²⁰"But when his heart was lifted up and his spirit became so proud that he behaved arrogantly, he was deposed from his royal throne and his glory was taken away from him.

²¹"He was also driven from mankind, and his mind was made like that of an animal, and his dwelling place was with the wild donkeys. He was given grass to eat like cattle, and his body was wet with the dew of heaven until he came to know [without any doubt] that the Most High God rules over the kingdom of mankind and He appoints it to whomever He wills.

²²"And you, his son, O Belshazzar, have not humbled your heart (mind), even though you knew all this.

²³"And you have exalted yourself against the Lord of heaven, and

the vessels of His house have been brought before you, and you and your nobles, your wives and your concubines have been drinking wine from them; and you have praised the gods of silver and gold, of bronze, iron, wood and stone, which do not see or hear or understand. But the God who holds in His hand your breath of life and your ways you have not honored *and* glorified [but have dishonored and defied].

²⁴"Then the hand was sent from the presence [of the Most High God], and this inscription was written:

²⁵"This is the inscription that was written, 'MENE, MENE, TEKEL, UPHARSIN [numbered, numbered, weighed, and divided].'

²⁶"This is the interpretation of the message: 'MENE'—God has numbered the days of your kingdom and put an end to it;

²⁷'TEKEL'—you have been weighed on the scales [of righteousness] and found deficient;

²⁸'PERES'—your kingdom has been divided and given over to the Medes and Persians."

²⁹Then Belshazzar gave the command, and Daniel was clothed with purple and a chain of gold was put around his neck, and a proclamation concerning him was issued [declaring] that he now had authority as the third *ruler* in the kingdom.

³⁰During that same night Belshazzar the [last] Chaldean king was slain [by troops of the invading army].

³¹So Darius the Mede received the kingdom; he was about the age of sixty-two.

6 IT SEEMED good to Darius [who became king after Belshazzar] to appoint over the kingdom 120 satraps who would be in charge throughout the kingdom,

²and over them three chief commissioners (of whom Daniel was one), that

these satraps might be accountable to them, so that the king would have no loss [from disloyalty or mismanagement].

³Then this Daniel, because of the extraordinary spirit within him, began distinguishing himself among the commissioners and the satraps, and the king planned to appoint him over the entire realm.

⁴Then the [other two] commissioners and the satraps began trying to find a reason to bring a complaint against Daniel concerning the [administration of the] kingdom; but they could find no reason for an accusation or *evidence of* corruption, because he was faithful [a man of high moral character and personal integrity], and no negligence or corruption [of any kind] was found in him.

⁵Then these men said, "We will not find any basis for an accusation against this Daniel unless we find something against him in connection with the law of his God." [Acts 24:13–21; 1 Pet 4:12–16]

⁶Then these commissioners and satraps agreed to approach the king and said to him, "King Darius, live forever!

be excellent!

Daniel was a man of excellence, and, because of that, the king promoted him to a position of great influence and authority (see Daniel 6:3). Daniel was also a man who refused to compromise. Even if his choices endangered his life, he would not compromise. He believed strongly in keeping his commitments, promises, and vows, and he was willing to endure personal discomfort to do so. The Bible says we should swear to our own hurt and sin not (see Psalm 15:4). In other words, we should do what we say we are going to do even if it is hard or hurts us.

Ecclesiastes 5:4, 5 says: "When you make a vow or a pledge to God, do not put off paying it; for God takes no pleasure in fools [who thoughtlessly mock Him]. Pay what you vow. It is better that you should not vow than that you should vow and not pay."

In Daniel 1, we see that Daniel requested not to have to eat the king's rich food because he felt it would defile him. Obviously, he had made a commitment not to eat that type of food. Because of his convictions, God caused Daniel to find favor with the man in charge, and no harm came to him.

In Daniel 6, the king signed a decree stating that anyone who asked a petition of any god or person besides the king for thirty days would be cast into a den of lions. Daniel refused to stop praying to God and was indeed sent into the lions' den; however, no harm came to him because God miraculously shut the lions' mouths. The king was so impressed with Daniel's decision and the miraculous way God took care of him that he issued a decree that all the people had to fear and tremble before Daniel's God, because He was indeed the living God. After this, Daniel prospered during the reign of King Darius and during the reign of King Cyrus.

Our God is an excellent God, and He has called us to be excellent too. To be excellent is a decision we can make, and it means we always go the extra mile to do things the very best way they can be done. We strive to do what we believe God would do in a situation similar to the one we are in. Make a decision today to be excellent!

⁷"All the commissioners of the kingdom, the prefects and the satraps, the counselors and the governors have consulted *and* agreed together that the king should establish a *royal* statute and enforce an injunction that anyone who petitions (prays to) any god or man besides you, O king, during the next thirty days, shall be thrown into the den of lions.

⁸"Now, O king, establish the injunction and sign the document so that it may not be changed, in accordance with the law of the Medes and Persians, which [insures that it] may not be altered *or* revoked."

⁹So King Darius signed the document, that is, the injunction.

¹⁰Now when Daniel knew that the document was signed, he went into his house (now in his roof chamber his windows were open toward Jerusalem); he continued to get down on his knees three times a day, praying and giving thanks before his God, as he had been doing previously. [Ps 5:7]

¹¹Then, by agreement, these men came [together] and found Daniel praying and making requests before his God.

¹²Then they approached and spoke before the king regarding his injunction, "Have you not signed an injunction that anyone who petitions (prays to) any god or man except you, O king, within the *designated* thirty days, is to be thrown into the den of lions?" The king answered, "The statement

uncompromising worship

Daniel's enemies were jealous of him and of his high position in the kingdom. Because Daniel was a righteous man, they knew there was no way to bring a true accusation against him because of any wrong behavior. Therefore, they sought to find a way to stop his worship and devotion to God through fear of harm.

Daniel's enemies knew that his habit was to go into his room three times a day, open the windows toward Jerusalem, and kneel down to pray and worship God (see Daniel 6:10). With this in mind, they persuaded the king to issue a decree that for a thirty-day period, no one would be allowed to petition any god or man other than the king. Anyone caught disobeying this order would be thrown into a den of lions.

Daniel continued to worship after the decree had been issued. I love the part of this story that says he prayed with his windows open, as he had done previously. In other words, he was not trying to keep his worship a secret. His reverential fear and awe of God far exceeded any fear of man.

Because Daniel refused to compromise his worship, his enemies brought him before the king for not honoring the decree (see Daniel 6:13). The king had no choice but to have him thrown into the den of lions. The king spent a sleepless night and in the morning cried out in front of the den, "O Daniel, servant of the living God, has your God, whom you constantly serve, been able to rescue you from the lions?" (Daniel 6:20). Daniel came out of that lions' den in triumph, totally unharmed and refreshed in his faith because God had shut the mouths of the lions. Afterward, Daniel's enemies were thrown into the same den and were all destroyed by the hungry lions.

If you and I will trust God and worship Him when our enemies conspire to bring harm to us, then, like Daniel, we can count on God's protection.

is true, in accordance with the law of the Medes and Persians, which may not be altered *or* revoked."

¹³Then they answered and said before the king, "Daniel, who is one of the exiles from Judah, does not pay any attention to you, O king, or to the injunction which you have signed, but keeps praying [to his God] three times a day."

¹⁴Then, as soon as the king heard these words, he was deeply distressed [over what he had done] and set his mind on rescuing Daniel; and he struggled until the sun went down [trying to work out a way] to save him.

¹⁵Then, by agreement, these same men came to the king and said, "Know, O king, that it is a law of the Medes and Persians that no injunction or statute which the king establishes may be altered *or* revoked."

¹⁶Then the king gave a command, and Daniel was brought and thrown into the den of lions. The king said to Daniel, "May your God, whom you constantly serve, rescue you Himself!" [Ps 34:7, 19; 37:39, 40; 50:15]

¹⁷A stone was brought and laid over the mouth of the den; and the king sealed it with his own signet ring and with the signet rings of his nobles, so that nothing would be changed concerning Daniel.

¹⁸Then the king returned to his palace and spent the night fasting; and no music or entertainment was brought before him, and he remained unable to sleep.

¹⁹Then the king arose at dawn, at the break of day, and hurried to the den of lions.

²⁰When he had come near the den,

life point

We know by reading Daniel 6:10 that Daniel believed in the importance of prayer. The king had issued a royal decree saying that for thirty days anyone asking a petition of any god or man other than the king would be cast into a den of lions.

Daniel continued to pray as he always had. He apparently knew that God's protection could render men's threats totally null and void. If we believe we are doing God's will and then run into opposition, we need to be like Daniel and boldly continue to do as God has instructed us, trusting Him to protect us.

he called out to Daniel with a troubled voice. The king said to Daniel, "O Daniel, servant of the living God, has your God, whom you constantly serve, been able to rescue you from the lions?"

²¹Then Daniel spoke to the king, "O king, live forever!

²²"My God has sent His angel and has shut the mouths of the lions so that they have not hurt me, because I was found innocent before Him; and also before you, O king, I have committed no crime." [2 Tim 4:17]

²³Then the king was greatly pleased and ordered that Daniel be taken out of the den. So Daniel was taken out of the den, and no injury whatever was found on him, because he believed in *and* relied on *and* trusted in his God.

²⁴The king then gave a command, and those men who had maliciously accused Daniel were brought and thrown into the den of lions, they, their children and their wives; and

speak the Word

God, I pray that I will constantly serve You, as Daniel did, and that You will rescue me from harm.
–ADAPTED FROM DANIEL 6:16

before they reached the bottom of the den, the lions overpowered them and crushed all their bones.

²⁵Then Darius the king wrote to all the peoples, nations, and *speakers of every* language who were living in all the land: "May peace abound to you!

²⁶"I issue a decree that in all the dominion of my kingdom men are to [reverently] fear and tremble before the God of Daniel,

For He is the living God, enduring
and steadfast forever,
And His kingdom is one which will
not be destroyed,
And His dominion will be forever.
²⁷"He rescues and saves and
performs signs and wonders
In heaven and on earth—
He who has rescued Daniel from
the power of the lions."

²⁸So this [man] Daniel prospered *and* enjoyed success in the reign of Darius and in the reign of Cyrus the Persian.

7 IN THE first year of Belshazzar king of Babylon Daniel had a dream and visions appeared in his mind *as he lay* on his bed; then he wrote the dream down and related a summary of it.

²Daniel said, "I saw in my vision by night, and behold, the four winds of heaven were stirring up the great sea (the nations).

³"And four great beasts, each different from the other, were coming up out of the sea [in succession].

⁴"The first (the Babylonian Empire under Nebuchadnezzar) was like a lion and had the wings of an eagle. I kept looking until its wings were plucked, and it was lifted up from the ground and made to stand on two feet like a man; a human mind was given to it. [Dan 2:37, 38]

⁵"And behold, another beast, a second

life point

Daniel's life was characterized by pressure to conform to what others wanted him to do and be. He refused to yield to that pressure. After a period of trial and tribulation, God exalted him, and he was put in charge of the entire kingdom.

Have the courage to be different. It will change your life, and God will exalt you in the process.

one (the Medo-Persian Empire), was like a bear, and it was raised up on one side (domain), and three ribs were in its mouth between its teeth; and it was told, 'Arise, devour much meat.'

⁶"After this I kept looking, and behold, another one (the Greek Empire of Alexander the Great), like a leopard, which had on its back four wings like those of a bird; the beast also had four heads (Alexander's generals, his successors), and power to rule was given to it. [Dan 2:39; 8:20–22]

⁷"After this I kept looking in the night visions, and behold, [I saw] a fourth beast (the Roman Empire), terrible and extremely strong; and it had huge iron teeth. It devoured and crushed and trampled down what was left with its feet. It was different from all the beasts that came before it, and it had ten horns (ten kings). [Dan 2:40–43; 7:23]

⁸"While I was considering the horns, behold, there came up among them another horn, a little one, and three of the first horns were pulled up by the roots before it; and behold, in this horn were eyes like the eyes of a man and a mouth boasting of great things.

⁹"I kept looking
Until thrones were set up,
And the Ancient of Days (God)
took His seat;
His garment was white as snow

And the hair of His head like pure
   wool.
His throne was flames of fire;
Its wheels were a burning fire.
   [1 Kin 22:19; Ps 90:2; Ezek 1:26–28;
   Dan 7:13, 22; Matt 19:28; Rev 20:4]
10"A river of fire was flowing
And coming out from before Him;
A thousand thousands were
   attending Him,
And ten thousand times ten
   thousand were standing before
   Him;
The court was seated,
And the books were opened.

11"Then I kept looking because of the
sound of the great *and* boastful words
which the horn was speaking. I kept
looking until the beast was slain, and
its body destroyed and given to be
burned with fire.

12"As for the rest of the beasts, their
power was taken away; yet their lives
were prolonged [for the length of their
lives was fixed] for a predetermined
time.

13"I kept looking in the night visions,
And behold, on the clouds of
   heaven
One like a Son of Man was coming,
And He came up to the Ancient of
   Days
And was presented before Him.
14"And to Him (the Messiah) was
   given dominion (supreme
   authority),
Glory and a kingdom,
That all the peoples, nations, and
   speakers of every language
Should serve *and* worship Him.
His dominion is an everlasting
   dominion
Which will not pass away;
And His kingdom is one
Which will not be destroyed.
   [Rev 5:1–10]

15"As for me, Daniel, my spirit was
distressed *and* anxious within me,
and the visions [that appeared] in my
mind kept alarming (agitating) me.

16"I approached one of those who
stood by and began asking him the
exact meaning of all this. So he told
me and explained to me the interpretation of the things:

17"These four great beasts are four
kings who will arise from the earth.

18"But the saints (believers) of the
Most High [God] will receive the kingdom and possess the kingdom forever,
for all ages to come.' [Rom 8:17; 1 Pet
2:9; Rev 3:21]

19"Then I wished to know the exact
meaning of the fourth beast, which
was different from all the others, extremely dreadful, with teeth of iron
and claws of bronze, which devoured,
crushed and trampled down what was
left with its feet,

20and *the meaning* of the ten horns

life point

Daniel 7:21 speaks of the king who made
"war with the saints." Daniel 7 continues
and in verse 25 tells us that in the end
times Satan will "wear down the saints."
But it also tells us in verse 27 what happens after that: "Then the kingdom and
the dominion and the greatness of all the
kingdoms under the whole heaven will be
given to the people of the saints (believers) of the Most High."

Even though Satan is releasing an attack
of weariness against the saints, Jesus
came to give us victory over the attacks
of Satan and "to destroy the works of the
devil" (1 John 3:8).

Let this truth sink in: *Jesus came to destroy
the works of the devil.* Even though Satan
will try to attack those of us who have
received Jesus, "He who is in you is greater
than he (Satan) who is in the world"
(1 John 4:4). Always remember that!

how to resist satan

Satan works diligently to cause trouble in virtually every area of our lives. He does not attack every area at one time, but eventually he gets to everything. He will bring inconvenience of every kind. Problems never come when we feel ready to deal with them.

Daniel 7:25 says that Satan seeks to wear down the saints of the Most High God. How does this wearing down take place? Often Satan's work is barely noticeable because he tries to wear us down gradually—a little here and a little there. Satan knows it takes more than one attack to wear us out, so he relentlessly comes again and again. One way Satan seeks to wear us out is by stealing our time, forcing us to deal with trouble he starts. He would like us to spend our lives trying to put out the little fires he builds.

What is the answer? James 4:7 says we are to submit ourselves to God's authority, resist the devil, and he will flee. We see that we have to *resist* the devil. But when should we resist him, how long should we wait, how much should we put up with before coming against him? While the Bible teaches Christians to be patient with one another, we are not to be patient with the devil. First Peter 5:9 shares a wonderful and most important principle: "But resist him, be firm in your faith [against his attack—rooted, established, immovable]." The Amplified Classic version of this verse says we are to resist the devil at "his onset."

When Satan attacks, we should immediately begin to praise God; in this way, we resist Satan. When he speaks lies, we should speak truth. The instant we sense an attack, we should draw near to God, be alert, and pray. Several times the Word of God instructs us to "watch and pray." This means to watch for things going wrong in our own lives or the lives of others and to pray immediately. As I like to say: "Do not delay, *pray right away!*"

Another way to resist Satan is to apply the blood of Jesus by faith to the situation. Just as the Israelites were delivered from death by putting the blood of the lamb on the lintels and doorframes of their homes during Passover (see Exodus 12:1–13), so we can apply the blood of our Passover Lamb, Jesus, by faith and be protected.

When Satan begins to attack you, remind him of the cross on which Jesus totally defeated him; remind him that he is already a defeated foe and that you will not be deceived or deluded in any way. Let Satan know that you recognize it is he who is coming against you and that you will not blame people, God, or life for what he is doing.

Satan wants us weak and worn-down; that way we have no power to resist him. He knows that if he gains a foothold, he can get a stronghold. I remind you that it is so important for us to *resist the devil at his onset!* Be aggressive; do not wait to see what will happen. If you wait, you will not like it. Stir yourself up in the Holy Spirit, fan the embers of your inner fire, and do not let them go out during times of trouble. Remember that Jesus, the Victor, lives inside you. You have the victory!

(kings) that were on its head and the other *horn* which came up later, and before which three of the horns fell, specifically, that horn which had eyes and a mouth that boasted great *things* and which looked larger than the others.

21"As I kept looking, that horn was making war with the saints (believers) and overpowering them [Rev 13:7–9]

22until the Ancient of Days came and judgment was passed in favor of the saints of the Most High [God], and the time arrived when the saints (believers) took possession of the kingdom.

23"Thus the angel said, 'The fourth beast shall be a fourth kingdom on earth, which will be different from all other kingdoms and will devour the whole earth and tread it down, and crush it.

24'As for the ten horns, out of this kingdom ten kings will arise; and another will arise after them, and he will be different from the former ones, and he will subdue three kings.

25'He will speak words against the Most High [God] and wear down the saints of the Most High, and he will intend to change the times and the law; and they will be given into his hand for a time, [two] times, and half a time [three and one-half years]. [Rev 13:1–6]

26'But the court [of the Most High] will sit *in judgment,* and his dominion will be taken away, [first to be] consumed [gradually] and [then] to be destroyed forever.

27"Then the kingdom and the dominion and the greatness of all the kingdoms under the whole heaven will be given to the people of the saints (believers) of the Most High; His kingdom will be an everlasting kingdom, and all the dominions will serve and obey Him.'

28"This is the end of the matter. As for me, Daniel, my [waking] thoughts were extremely troubling and alarming and my face grew pale; but I kept the matter [of the vision and the angel's explanation] to myself."

8 IN THE third year of the reign of King Belshazzar a [second] vision appeared to me, Daniel, [this was two years] after the one that first appeared to me.

2I looked in the vision and it seemed that I was at the citadel of Susa, [the capital of Persia], which is in the province of Elam; and I looked in the vision and I saw myself by the Ulai Canal.

3Then I raised my eyes and looked, and behold, there in front of the canal stood a [lone] ram (the Medo-Persian Empire) which had two horns. The two horns were high, but one (Persia) was higher than the other (Media), and the higher one came up last.

4I saw the ram (Medo-Persia) charging westward and northward and southward; no beast could stand before him, nor was there anyone who could rescue [anything] from his power, but he did as he pleased and magnified *himself.* [Dan 8:20]

5As I was observing [this], behold, a male goat (Greece) was coming from the west [rushing] across the face of the whole earth without touching the ground; and the goat had a conspicuous *and* remarkable horn (Alexander the Great) between his eyes. [Dan 8:21]

6He came up to the ram that had the two horns, which I had seen standing in front of the canal, and charged at him in [the fury of] his power *and* wrath.

7[In my vision] I saw him come close to the ram (Medo-Persia), and he was filled with rage toward him; and the goat (Greece) struck the ram and shattered his two horns, and the ram had no strength to stand before him. So the goat threw him to the ground and trampled on him, and there was no one who could rescue the ram from his power.

8Then the male goat magnified himself exceedingly, and when he was [young and] strong, the great horn (Alexander) was [suddenly] broken; and in its place there came up four prominent *horns* [among whom the kingdom was divided, one] toward [each of] the four winds of heaven.

⁹Out of one of them (Antiochus IV Epiphanes) came forth a rather small horn [but one of irreverent presumption and profane pride] which grew exceedingly powerful toward the south, toward the east, and toward the Beautiful *Land* (Israel). [Dan 8:23]

¹⁰And [in my vision] this horn grew up to the host of heaven, and caused some of the host and some of the stars to fall to the earth, and it trampled on them.

¹¹Indeed, it magnified itself to be equal with the Commander of the host [of heaven]; and it took away from Him the daily sacrifice (burnt offering), and the place of His sanctuary was thrown down (profaned).

¹²Because of the transgression [of God's people—their irreverence and ungodliness] the host will be given over *to the wicked horn,* along with the regular sacrifice; and righteousness *and* truth will be flung to the ground, and the horn will do as it pleases [by divine permission] and prosper.

¹³Then I heard a holy one (angel) speaking, and another holy one said to the one who was speaking, "How much time will be required to complete the vision regarding the regular sacrifice, the transgression that brings horror, and the trampling underfoot of both the sanctuary and the host [of the people]?" [Luke 21:24]

¹⁴He said to me, "For 2,300 evenings and mornings; then the sanctuary will be cleansed *and* properly restored."

¹⁵When I, Daniel, had seen the vision, I sought to understand it; then behold, standing before me was one who looked like a man.

¹⁶And I heard the voice of a man between *the banks of* the Ulai, which called out and said, "Gabriel, give this man (Daniel) an understanding of the vision." [Dan 9:21; Luke 1:19, 26]

¹⁷So he came near where I was standing, and when he came I was frightened and fell face downward; but he said to me, "Understand, son of man, that the [fulfillment of the] vision pertains to [events that will occur in] the time of the end."

¹⁸Now as he (Gabriel) was speaking with me, I drifted into a deep sleep (unconsciousness) with my face to the ground; but he touched me and made me stand [where I had stood before].

¹⁹He said, "Behold, I am going to let you know what will happen during the final time of the indignation *and* wrath [of God upon the ungodly], for it concerns the appointed time of the end.

²⁰"The ram which you saw with the two horns represents the kings of Media and Persia.

²¹"The shaggy (rough-coated) male goat *represents* the kingdom of Greece, and the great horn between his eyes is the first king.

²²"*Regarding* the shattered *horn* and the four *others that* arose in its place, four kingdoms will rise from *his* (Alexander's) nation, although not with his power *and* heritage.

²³"At the latter period of their reign,
When the transgressors have finished,
A king will arise
Insolent and skilled in intrigue *and* cunning.

²⁴"His power will be mighty, but not by his own power;
And he will corrupt *and* destroy in an astonishing manner
And [he will] prosper and do exactly as he wills;
He shall corrupt *and* destroy mighty men and the holy people.
[Dan 8:9–12; 2 Thess 2:3–10; Rev 13:4–10]

25"And through his shrewdness
  He will cause deceit to succeed by
    his hand (influence);
  He will magnify himself in his
    mind,
  He will corrupt *and* destroy many
    who enjoy a false sense of
    security.
  He will also stand up *and* oppose
    the Prince of princes,
  But he will be broken, and that by
    no human hand [but by the hand
    of God]. [Rev 19:19, 20]
26"The vision of the evenings and
    the mornings
  Which has been told [to you] is
    true.
  But keep the vision a secret,
  For it has to do with many days *in
    the now distant future.*"

27And I, Daniel, was exhausted and
was sick for [several] days. Afterward
I got up and continued with the king's
business; but I was astounded at the
vision, and there was no one who
could explain it.

9 IN THE first year of Darius the
  son of Ahasuerus, of Median descent, who was made king over
the realm of the Chaldeans—
  2in the first year of his reign, I, Daniel, understood from the books the
number of years which, according to
the word of the LORD to Jeremiah the
prophet, must pass before the desolations [which had been] pronounced
on Jerusalem would end; and it was
seventy years. [Jer 25:11, 12; 29:10]
  3So I directed my attention to the
Lord God to seek Him by prayer and
supplications, with fasting, sackcloth
and ashes.
  4I prayed to the LORD my God and

confessed and said, "O Lord, the great
and awesome God, who keeps His
covenant and extends lovingkindness
toward those who love Him and keep
His commandments,
  5we have sinned and committed
wrong, and have behaved wickedly
and have rebelled, turning away from
Your commandments and ordinances.
  6"Further, we have not listened to *and*
heeded Your servants the prophets,
who spoke in Your name to our kings,
our princes and our fathers, and to all
the people of the land.
  7"Righteousness belongs to You,
O Lord, but to us confusion *and* open
shame, as it is this day—to the men
of Judah, to the inhabitants of Jerusalem, and to all Israel, those who are
nearby and those who are far away, in
all the countries to which You have
driven them, because of the [treacher-
ous] acts of unfaithfulness which they
have committed against You.
  8"O LORD, to us belong confusion
and open shame—to our kings, to our
princes, and to our fathers—because
we have sinned against You.
  9"To the Lord our God *belong* mercy
and lovingkindness and forgiveness,
for we have rebelled against Him;
  10and we have not obeyed the voice
of the LORD our God by walking in His
laws which He set before us through
His servants the prophets.
  11"Yes, all Israel has transgressed
Your law, even turning aside, not
obeying Your voice; so the curse has
been poured out on us and the oath
which is written in the Law of Moses
the servant of God, because we have
sinned against Him. [Lev 26:14–45;
Deut 28:15–68]
  12"And He has carried out completely

speak the Word

God, to You belong mercy and loving-kindness and forgiveness!
–ADAPTED FROM DANIEL 9:9

His [threatening] words which He had spoken against us and against our rulers [the kings, princes, and judges] who ruled us, to bring on us a great tragedy; for under the whole heaven there has not been done anything [so dreadful] like that which [He commanded and] was done to Jerusalem.

¹³"Just as it is written in the Law of Moses, all this tragedy has come on us. Yet we have not wholeheartedly begged for forgiveness *and* sought the favor of the Lord our God by turning from our wickedness and paying attention to *and* placing value in Your truth. [Deut 4:29; 28:15ff]

¹⁴"Therefore the Lord has kept the tragedy ready and has brought it on us, for the Lord our God is [uncompromisingly] righteous *and* openly just in all His works which He does—He keeps His word; and we have not obeyed His voice.

¹⁵"And now, O Lord our God, who brought Your people out of the land of Egypt with a mighty hand and who made for Yourself a name, as it is today—we have sinned, we have been wicked.

¹⁶"O Lord, in accordance with all Your righteous *and* just acts, please let Your anger and Your wrath turn away from Your city Jerusalem, Your holy mountain. Because of our sins and the wickedness of our fathers, Jerusalem and Your people *have become* an object of scorn *and* a contemptuous byword to all who are around us.

¹⁷"Now therefore, our God, listen to (heed) the prayer of Your servant (Daniel) and his supplications, and for Your own sake let Your face shine on Your desolate sanctuary.

¹⁸"O my God, incline Your ear and hear; open Your eyes and look at our desolations and the city which is called by Your name; for we are not presenting our supplications before You because of our own merits *and* righteousness, but because of Your great mercy *and* compassion.

¹⁹"O Lord, hear! O Lord, forgive! O Lord, listen and take action! Do not delay, for Your own sake, O my God, because Your city and Your people are called by Your name."

²⁰While I was still speaking and praying, and confessing my sin and the sin of my people Israel, and presenting my supplication before the Lord my God in behalf of the holy mountain of my God,

²¹while I was still speaking in prayer and extremely exhausted, the man Gabriel, whom I had seen in the earlier vision, came to me about the time of the evening sacrifice. [Dan 8:16]

²²He instructed me and he talked with me and said, "O Daniel, I have now come to give you insight *and* wisdom and understanding.

²³"At the beginning of your supplications, the command [to give you an answer] was issued, and I have come to tell you, for you are highly regarded *and* greatly beloved. Therefore consider the message and begin to understand the [meaning of the] vision.

²⁴"Seventy weeks [of years, or 490 years] have been decreed for your people and for your holy city (Jerusalem), to finish the transgression, to make an end of sins, to make atonement (reconciliation) for wickedness, to bring in everlasting righteousness (right-standing with God), to seal up

speak the Word

God, I declare that You are uncompromisingly righteous and openly just in all Your works and that You always keep Your word.
—ADAPTED FROM DANIEL 9:14

vision and prophecy *and* prophet, and to anoint the Most Holy *Place.*

²⁵"So you are to know and understand that from the issuance of the command to restore and rebuild Jerusalem until [the coming of] the Messiah (the Anointed One), the Prince, *there will be* seven weeks [of years] and sixty-two weeks [of years]; it will be built again, with [a city] plaza and moat, even in times of trouble.

²⁶"Then after the sixty-two weeks [of years] the Anointed One will be cut off [and denied His Messianic kingdom] and have nothing [and no one to defend Him], and the people of the [other] prince who is to come will destroy the city and the sanctuary. Its end *will come* with a flood; even to the end there will be war; desolations are determined. [Is 53:7–9; Nah 1:8; Matt 24:6–14]

²⁷"And he will enter into a binding *and* irrevocable covenant with the many for one week (seven years), but in the middle of the week he will stop the sacrifice and grain offering [for the remaining three and one-half years]; and on the wing of abominations *will come* one who makes desolate, even until the complete destruction, one that is decreed, is poured out on the one who causes the horror."

10 IN THE third year of Cyrus king of Persia a message was revealed to Daniel, who was named Belteshazzar; and the message was true and it referred to great conflict (warfare, misery). And he understood the message and had an understanding of the vision. [Dan 8:26; Rev 19:9]

²In those days I, Daniel, had been mourning for three entire weeks.

³I ate no tasty food, nor did any meat or wine enter my mouth; and I did not anoint (refresh, groom) myself at all for the full three weeks.

⁴On the twenty-fourth day of the first month, as I was on the bank of the great river Hiddekel [which is the Tigris],

⁵I raised my eyes and looked, and behold, there was a certain man dressed in linen, whose loins were girded with [a belt of] pure gold of Uphaz.

⁶His body also was like beryl [with a golden luster], his face had the appearance of lightning, his eyes were like flaming torches, his arms and his feet like the gleam of burnished bronze, and the sound of his words was like the noise of a multitude [of people or the roaring of the sea]. [Rev 1:12–16; 19:6]

⁷And I, Daniel, alone saw the vision [of this heavenly being], for the men who were with me did not see the vision; nevertheless, a great panic overwhelmed them, so they ran away to hide themselves.

⁸So I was left alone and saw this great vision; yet no strength was left in me, for my normal appearance turned to a deathly pale, and I grew weak *and* faint [with fright].

⁹Then I heard the sound of his words; and when I heard the sound of his words, I fell on my face in a deep sleep, with my face toward the ground.

¹⁰Then behold, a hand touched me and set me unsteadily on my hands and knees.

¹¹So he said to me, "O Daniel, you highly regarded *and* greatly beloved man, understand the words that I am about to say to you and stand upright, for I have now been sent to you." And while he was saying this word to me, I stood up trembling.

¹²Then he said to me, "Do not be afraid, Daniel, for from the first day that you set your heart on understanding this and on humbling yourself before your God, your words were heard, and I have come in response to your words.

¹³"But the prince of the kingdom of Persia was standing in opposition to

me for twenty-one days. Then, behold, Michael, one of the chief [of the celestial] princes, came to help me, for I had been left there with the kings of Persia.

¹⁴"Now I have come to make you understand what will happen to your people in the latter days, for the vision is in regard to the days yet to come."

¹⁵When he had spoken to me according to these words, I turned my face toward the ground and was speechless.

¹⁶And behold, one who resembled the sons of men touched my lips. Then I opened my mouth and spoke and said to him who was standing before me, "O my lord, because of the vision anguish has come upon me, and I have retained no strength.

¹⁷"For how can such a [weakened] servant of my lord talk with such [a being] as my lord? For now there remains no strength in me, nor has any breath been left in me."

¹⁸Then the one (Gabriel) whose appearance was like that of a man touched me again, and he strengthened me.

¹⁹He said, "O man, highly regarded and greatly beloved, do not be afraid. Peace be to you; take courage and be strong." Now when he had spoken to me, I was strengthened and said, "Let my lord speak, for you have strengthened me."

²⁰Then he said, "Do you understand [fully] why I came to you? Now I shall return to fight against the [hostile] prince of Persia; and when I have gone, behold, the prince of Greece is about to come.

²¹"But I (Gabriel) will tell you what is inscribed in the writing of truth. There is no one who stands firmly with me and strengthens himself against these [hostile spirit forces] except Michael, your prince [the guardian of your nation].

11 "ALSO I, in the first year of Darius the Mede, I (Gabriel) arose to be an encouragement and a protection for him.

²"And now I will tell you the truth. Behold, three more kings are going to arise in Persia. Then a fourth will become far richer than all of them. When he becomes strong through his riches he will stir up the whole *empire* against the realm of Greece.

³"Then a mighty [warlike, threatening] king will arise who will rule with great authority and do as he pleases.

⁴"But as soon as he (Alexander) has risen, his kingdom will be broken [by his death] and divided toward the four winds of heaven [the north, south, east, and west], but not to his descendants, nor according to the [Grecian] authority with which he ruled, for his kingdom will be torn out *and* uprooted and given to others (his four generals) to the exclusion of these.

⁵"Then the king of the South (Egypt) will be strong, along with one of his princes who will be stronger than he and have dominance over him; his domain will be a great dominion.

⁶"After some years the Syrian king of the North and the Egyptian king of the South will make an alliance; the daughter (Berenice) of the king of the South will come to the king of the North to make an equitable *and* peaceful agreement (marriage); but she will not retain the power of her position, nor will he retain his power. She will be handed over with her attendants and her father as well as he who supported her in those times.

⁷"But out of a branch of her [familial] roots will one (her brother, Ptolemy III Euergetes I) arise in his place, and he will come against the [Syrian] army and enter the fortress of the king of the North, and he will deal with them and will prevail.

⁸"Also he will carry off to Egypt their

[Syrian] gods with their cast images and their precious *and* costly treasure of silver and of gold, and he will refrain from waging war against the king of the North for some years.

⁹"And the king of the North will come into the realm of the king of the South, but he will retreat to his own country [badly defeated].

¹⁰"His sons will prepare for battle and assemble a multitude of great forces; which will keep on coming and overflow [the land], and pass through, so that they may again wage war as far as his fortress.

¹¹"The king of the South (Ptolemy IV Philopator of Egypt) will be enraged and go out and fight with the king of the North (Antiochus III the Great); and the Syrian king will raise a great multitude (army), but the multitude shall be given into the hand of the *Egyptian king.*

¹²"When the multitude (army) is captured *and* carried away, the heart of the *Egyptian king* will be proud (arrogant), and he will cause tens of thousands to fall, but he will not prevail.

¹³"For the king of the North will again raise a multitude (army) greater than the one before, and after several years he will advance with a great army and substantial equipment.

¹⁴"In those times many will rise up against the king of the South (Egypt); also the violent men among your own people will arise in order to fulfill the [earlier] visions, but they will fail.

¹⁵"Then the king of the North (Syria) will come and build up siege ramps and capture a well-fortified city. The forces of the South will not stand *their ground,* not even the finest troops, for there will be no strength to stand [against the Syrian king].

¹⁶"But he (Syria) who comes against him (Egypt) will do exactly as he pleases, and no one will be able to stand against him; he (Antiochus III

the Great) will also stay for a time in the Beautiful *and* Glorious Land [of Israel], with destruction in his hand.

¹⁷"He will be determined to come with the power of his entire kingdom, and propose equitable conditions *and* terms of peace, which he will put into effect [by making an agreement with the king of the South]. He will also give him his daughter (Cleopatra I), *in an attempt* to overthrow the kingdom, but it will not succeed or be to his advantage.

¹⁸"After this, he (Antiochus III the Great, King of Syria) will turn his attention to the islands *and* coastlands and capture many [of them]. But a commander (Lucius Scipio Asiaticus of Rome) will put an end to his aggression [toward Rome's territorial interests]; in fact, he will repay his insolence *and* turn his audacity back upon him.

¹⁹"Then he will turn back toward the fortresses of his own land [of Syria], but he will stumble and fall and not be found.

²⁰"Then in his place one (his eldest son, Seleucus IV Philopator) will arise who will send an oppressor through the Jewel of his kingdom; yet within a few days he will be shattered, though not in anger nor in battle.

²¹"And in his place [in Syria] will arise a despicable *and* despised person, to whom royal majesty *and* the honor of kingship have not been conferred, but he will come [without warning] in a time of tranquility and seize the kingdom by intrigue. [Dan 8:9–12, 23–25]

²²"The overwhelming forces [of the invading armies of Egypt] will be flooded away before him *and* smashed; and also the prince of the covenant [will be smashed].

²³"After an alliance is made with him he will work deceitfully, and he will go up and gain power with a small *force of* people.

²⁴"In a time of tranquility, [without warning] he will enter the most

productive *and* richest parts of the kingdom [of Egypt], and he will accomplish that which his fathers never did, nor his fathers' fathers; he will distribute plunder, spoil and goods among them. He will devise plans against strongholds, but only for a time [decreed by God].

²⁵"He will stir up his strength and courage against [his former Egyptian ally] the king of the South (Ptolemy VI) with a great army; so the king of the South will prepare an extremely great and powerful army to wage war, but he will not stand, for schemes will be devised against him.

²⁶"Yes, those who eat his fine food will betray *and* destroy him (Ptolemy VI), and his army will be swept away, and many will fall down slain.

²⁷"And as for both of these kings, their hearts will be set on doing evil; they will speak lies over the same table, but it will not succeed, for the end is yet to come at the appointed time.

²⁸"Then he (Antiochus IV Epiphanes) will return to his land with great treasure (plunder); and his heart will be set against the holy covenant, and he will take action and return to his own land (Syria).

²⁹"At the time appointed [by God] he will return and come into the South, but this last time will not be successful as were the previous invasions [of Egypt].

³⁰"For ships of Cyprus [in Roman hands] will come against him; therefore he will be discouraged and turn back [to Israel] and carry out his rage against the holy covenant and take action; so he will return and show favoritism toward those [Jews] who abandon (break) the holy covenant [with God].

³¹"Armed forces of his will arise [in Jerusalem] and defile *and* desecrate the sanctuary, the [spiritual] stronghold, and will do away with the regular sacrifice [that is, the daily burnt

offering]; and they will set up [a pagan altar in the sanctuary which is] the abomination of desolation.

³²"With smooth *words* [of flattery and praise] he will turn to godlessness those who [are willing to] disregard the [Mosaic] covenant, but the people who [are spiritually mature and] know their God will display strength and take action [to resist].

³³"They who are wise *and* have spiritual insight among the people will instruct many *and* help them understand; yet for many days some [of them and their followers] will fall by the sword and by flame, by captivity and by plunder.

³⁴"Now when they fall they will receive a little help, and many will join with them in hypocrisy.

³⁵"Some of those who are [spiritually] wise *and* have insight will fall [as martyrs] in order to refine, to purge and to make those among God's people pure, until the end time; because it is yet to come at the time appointed [by God].

³⁶"Then the king (the Antichrist) will do exactly as he pleases; he will exalt himself and magnify himself above every god and will speak astounding *and* disgusting things against the God of gods and he will prosper until the indignation is finished, for that which is determined [by God] will be done.

³⁷"He will have no regard for the gods of his fathers or for the desire of women, nor will he have regard for any *other* god, for he shall magnify himself above them all.

³⁸"Instead, he will honor a god of fortresses, a god whom his fathers did not know; he will honor him with gold and silver, with precious stones and with expensive things.

³⁹"He will act against the strongest fortresses with *the help of* a foreign god; he will give great honor to those

who acknowledge him and he will cause them to rule over the many, and will parcel out land for a price.

⁴⁰"At the end time the king of the South will push *and* attack him (the Antichrist), and the king of the North will storm against him with chariots and horsemen and with many ships; and he will enter countries, overwhelm them and pass through.

⁴¹"He shall also enter the Beautiful *and* Glorious Land (Israel), and many countries will fall, but these will be rescued out of his hand: Edom, Moab, and the foremost [core] of the people of Ammon.

⁴²"Then he will stretch out his hand against other countries, but Egypt will not be among the ones which escape.

⁴³"He will have power over the treasures of gold and silver and over all the precious things of Egypt, and the Libyans and the Ethiopians *will follow* in his footsteps.

⁴⁴"But rumors from the east and from the north will alarm *and* disturb him, and he will set out with great fury to destroy and to annihilate many.

⁴⁵"He will pitch his palatial tents between the seas and the glorious Holy Mountain (Zion); yet he will come to his end with no one to help him [in his final battle with God]. [2 Thess 2:4; Rev 13:5–8]

12 "NOW AT that [end] time Michael, the great [angelic] prince who stands *guard* over the children of your people, will arise. And there will be a time of distress such as never occurred since there was a nation until that time; but at that time your people, everyone who is found written in the Book [of Life], will be rescued.

²"Many of those who sleep in the dust of the ground will awake (resurrect), these to everlasting life, but some to disgrace and everlasting contempt (abhorrence). [John 5:29]

³"Those who are [spiritually] wise will shine brightly like the brightness of the expanse of heaven, and those who lead many to righteousness, [will shine] like the stars forever and ever. [Matt 13:43]

⁴"But as for you, Daniel, conceal these words and seal up the scroll until the end of time. Many will go back and forth *and* search anxiously [through the scroll], and knowledge [of the purpose of God as revealed by His prophets] will [greatly] increase." [Amos 8:12]

⁵Then I, Daniel, looked, and behold, there stood two others, the one [angel] on this bank of the river and the other [angel] on that bank of the river.

⁶And one said to the man dressed in linen, who was above the waters of the river, "How long *will it be* until the end of these wonders?" [Dan 10:5]

⁷And I heard the man dressed in linen, who was above the waters of the river, as he held up his right hand and his left hand toward heaven, and swore by Him who lives forever that it would be for a time, times, and a half a time (three and a half years); and as soon as they finish shattering *and* crushing the power of the holy people, all these things will be finished.

⁸As for me, I heard, but I did not understand; so I said, "My lord, what will be the outcome of these things?"

⁹And the angel said, "Go *your way,* Daniel, for the words are concealed and sealed up until the end of time.

¹⁰"Many will be purged, purified (made white) and refined, but the wicked will behave wickedly. None of the wicked shall understand, but those who are [spiritually] wise will understand. [Dan 11:33–35]

¹¹"From the time that the regular sacrifice [that is, the daily burnt offering] is taken away and the abomination of

desolation is set up [ruining the temple for worship of the true God], *there will be* 1,290 days. [Dan 11:31]

¹²"How blessed [happy, fortunate, spiritually prosperous] *and* beloved is he who waits expectantly [enduring without wavering for the period of tribulation] and comes to the 1,335 days!

¹³"But as for you (Daniel), go *your way* until the end [of your life]; for you will rest and rise *again* for your allotted inheritance at the end of the age." [Heb 11:32–40]

Hosea

Author:
Hosea

Date:
About 750 BC

Everyday Life Principles:
God loves us unconditionally.

God is faithful, even when we are faithless.

God's love and mercy never stop reaching out to us. We can always have a new beginning in Him, no matter what we have done.

Sometimes people who are prophets of God must live the messages they preach. That was certainly the case with Hosea. God had called Hosea, whose name means "salvation" or "deliverance," to proclaim His love and faithfulness to the people of Israel, who had turned their backs on Him, forgotten His goodness, and forsaken Him as a man forsakes his wife for a prostitute. In fact, God said through Hosea that Israel had "played the prostitute" (Hosea 2:5).

In order to understand and demonstrate God's love for backsliding Israel, God required Hosea to marry a prostitute named Gomer, who continually turned her back on him and lived as a harlot. Hosea, in response, repeatedly rescued Gomer from her sinful, low-class living, took her back home, and loved and cared for her. But after a while, she would leave him again and return to prostitution. The cycle of her unfaithfulness and Hosea's unconditional love continues throughout this book to show God's people that He never, ever gives up on us. It also teaches us that love cannot be bought; it must be received as a gift, for God says in Hosea 14:4, "I will love them freely."

As you read the book of Hosea, let it remind you of God's unconditional love and unfailing mercy. He will never leave you or let you down, no matter how you may have sinned or turned away from Him. In God, you can always have a fresh start.

1 THE WORD of the LORD that came to Hosea the son of Beeri in the days of Uzziah, Jotham, Ahaz and Hezekiah, kings of Judah, and in the days of Jeroboam the son of Joash king of Israel.

²When the LORD first spoke through Hosea, the LORD said to him, "Go, take for yourself a wife of prostitution and have children of [her] prostitution; for the land commits great acts of prostitution by not following the LORD."

³So he went and took Gomer the daughter of Diblaim, and she conceived and bore him a son.

⁴And the LORD said to him, "Name him Jezreel; for yet in a little while I will avenge the blood [that was shed in the Valley] of Jezreel *and* inflict the punishment for it on the house of Jehu, and I will put an end to the kingdom of the house of Israel. [2 Kin 10:1–11]

⁵"On that day I will break the bow [of the military power] of Israel in the Valley of Jezreel."

⁶Then Gomer conceived again and gave birth to a daughter. And the LORD said to Hosea, "Name her Lo-Ruhamah (not shown mercy), for I will no longer have mercy on the house of Israel, that I would ever forgive them.

⁷"But I will have mercy on the house of Judah and will rescue them by the LORD their God, and will not rescue them by bow, sword, war, horses, or horsemen." [Is 31:8; 37:33–35]

⁸Now when Gomer had weaned Lo-Ruhamah, she conceived and gave birth to a son.

⁹And the LORD said, "Name him Lo-Ammi (not my people), for you are not My people and I am not your God."

¹⁰Yet the number of the sons of
  Israel
 Shall be like the sand of the sea,
 Which cannot be measured or
  numbered;
 And in the place
 Where it is said to them,

"You are not My people,"
It will be said to them,
"*You are* the sons of the living
 God." [Gen 22:17; Rom 9:26]
¹¹Then the sons of Judah and the
 sons of Israel shall be gathered
 together,
And they will appoint for
 themselves one leader,
And they will go up from the land,
For great *and* glorious will be the
 day of Jezreel. [Is 11:12, 13; Ezek
 37:15–28]

2 "[HOSEA,] SAY to your brothers, 'Ammi (you are my people),' and to your sisters, 'Ruhamah (you have been pitied and have obtained mercy).'

²"Contend with your mother
 (nation); contend,
For she is not my wife and I am not
 her husband;
And have her remove her [marks
 of] prostitution from her face
And her adultery from between
 her breasts [Is 50:1]
³Or I will strip her naked
And expose her as on the day she
 was born,
And make her like a wilderness
And make her like a parched land
And slay her with thirst.
⁴"Also, I will have no mercy on her
 children,
Because they are the children of
 prostitution.
⁵"For their mother has played the
 prostitute;
She who conceived them has acted
 shamefully,
For she said, 'I will pursue my
 lovers
Who give me my food and my water,
My wool and my flax, my oil and
 my [refreshing] drinks.'
⁶"Therefore, behold, I [the LORD
 God] will hedge up her way with
 thorns;

And I will build a wall against her
　[shutting off her way] so that she
　cannot find her paths.
7 "She will [passionately] pursue her
　lovers, but she will not overtake
　them;
And she will seek them, but will
　not find them.
Then she will say, 'Let me go and
　return to my first husband,
For it was better for me then than
　now!'

8 "For she (Israel) has not noticed
　nor understood *nor* realized that
　it was I [the LORD God] who gave
　her the grain and the new wine
　and the oil,
And lavished on her silver and gold,
Which they used for Baal *and*
　made into his image.
9 "Therefore, I will return *and* take
　back My grain at harvest time
And My new wine in its season.
I will also take away My wool and
　My flax
Given to cover her nakedness.
10 "And now I will uncover her
　lewdness *and* shame
In the sight of her lovers,
And no one will rescue her from
　My hand.
11 "I will also put an end to all her
　rejoicing,
Her feasts, her New Moons, her
　Sabbaths,
And all her festivals.
12 "I will destroy her vines and her
　fig trees
Of which she has said, 'These are
　my wages
Which my lovers have given me.'
And I will make them a forest,

And the animals of the open
　country will devour them.
13 "And I will punish her for the
　[feast] days of the Baals,
When she used to offer sacrifices
　and burn incense to them
And adorn herself with her
　earrings *and* nose rings and her
　jewelry,
And follow her lovers, so that she
　forgot Me," says the LORD.

14 "Therefore, behold, I will allure
　Israel
And bring her into the wilderness,
And I will speak tenderly to her [to
　reconcile her to Me].
15 "Then I will give her her vineyards
　from there,
And make the Valley of Achor a
　door of hope *and* expectation
　[anticipating the time when I
　will restore My favor on her].
And she will sing there *and*
　respond as in the days of her
　youth
As in the day when she came up
　from the land of Egypt. [Ex 15:2;
　Josh 7:24–26]
16 "It shall come about in that day,"
　says the LORD,
"That you will call Me Ishi (my
　husband)
And will no longer call Me Baali
　(my Baal).
17 "For I will remove the names of
　the Baals from her mouth,
So that they will no longer be
　mentioned *or* remembered by
　their names. [Ex 23:13]
18 "And in that day I will make a
　covenant for Israel
With the animals of the open
　country

speak the Word

*Thank You, Lord, for speaking tenderly to me and for making my trouble a
door of hope, expectation, and restored favor.*
–ADAPTED FROM HOSEA 2:14, 15

And with the birds of the heavens
And with the creeping things of
the ground.
And I will abolish the bow and the
sword and [banish] war from the
land
And will make them lie down in
safety.
¹⁹"And I will betroth you (Israel) to
Me forever;
Yes, I will betroth you to Me in
righteousness and in justice,
In lovingkindness *and* loyalty, and
in compassion.
²⁰"I will betroth you to Me in
stability *and* in faithfulness.
Then you will know (recognize,
appreciate) the LORD
[and respond with loving
faithfulness].
²¹"It will come about in that day that
I will respond," says the LORD.
"I will respond to the heavens
[which ask for rain to pour on the
earth], and they will respond to
the earth [which begs for the rain],
²²And the earth shall respond to the
grain and the new wine and the
oil [which beg it to bring them
forth],
And they will respond to Jezreel [My
Israel, who will now be restored].
²³"I will sow her for Myself in the land.
I will also have mercy on her who
had not obtained mercy;
And I will say to those who were
not My people,
'You are My people,'
And they will say, *'You are* my
God!'" [1 Pet 2:9, 10]

speak the Word

3 THEN THE LORD said to me, "Go
again, love a woman (Gomer)
who is beloved by her husband
and yet is an adulteress, even as the
LORD loves the children of Israel,
though they turn to other gods and
love the raisin cakes [used in the feasts
in pagan worship]."
²So I bought her for myself for fifteen
pieces of silver and a homer and a half
of barley [the price of a common slave].
³And I said to her, "You shall stay
with me for many days. You shall not
play the prostitute nor shall you have a
man; so I will also be toward you [until
you have proved your faithfulness]."
⁴For the sons of Israel will remain
for many days without king or prince,
without sacrifice or [idolatrous] pillar, and without ephod or teraphim
(household idols).
⁵Afterward the sons of Israel will
return [in deep repentance] and seek
the LORD their God and [seek from the
line of] David their king [the King of
kings—the Messiah]; and they will
come trembling to the LORD and to His
goodness *and* blessing in the last days.
[Jer 30:9; Ezek 34:24]

4 HEAR THE word of the LORD,
you children of Israel,
For the LORD has a [legal] case
with the inhabitants of the land,
Because there is no faithfulness [no
steadfast love, no dependability]
or loyalty *or* kindness
Or knowledge of God [from
personal experience with Him]
in the land.

Thank You, Lord, for betrothing me to You forever in righteousness
and justice, in loving-kindness, loyalty, and compassion, and in stability
and faithfulness. I will know, recognize, and appreciate You and
respond with loving faithfulness.
—ADAPTED FROM HOSEA 2:19, 20

2 There is [false] swearing *of
  oaths*, deception (broken faith),
  murder, stealing, and adultery;
They employ violence, so that one
  [act of] bloodshed follows closely
  on another.
3 Therefore the land [continually]
  mourns,
And everyone who lives in it
  languishes [in tragic suffering]
Together with the animals of the
  open country and the birds of
  the heavens;
Even the fish of the sea disappear.

4 Yet let no one find fault, nor let any
  rebuke [others];
For your people are like those who
  contend with the priest.
5 So you will stumble in the
  daytime,
And the [false] prophet will also
  stumble with you in the night;
And I will destroy your mother
  (Israel). [Ex 19:6]
6 My people are destroyed for lack
  of knowledge [of My law, where I
  reveal My will].
Because you [the priestly nation]
  have rejected knowledge,
I will also reject you from being
  My priest.
Since you have forgotten the law of
  your God,
I will also forget your children.

putting the Word to work

**Can you think of a specific situation in
which not knowing something about
a person or a situation was hurtful
or detrimental to you? Ask God to
continually give you knowledge and
revelation so that lack of knowledge
will not destroy you (see Hosea 4:6).**

7 The more they multiplied [in
  numbers and increased in
  power], the more they sinned
  against Me;
I will change their glory into
  shame.
8 They (the priests) feed on the sin
  offering of My people
And set their heart on their
  wickedness. [Lev 7:7, 8]
9 And it shall be: like people, like
  priest [both are wicked and both
  will be judged];
So I will punish them for their
  ways
And repay them for their deeds.
10 They will eat, but not have
  enough;
They will play the prostitute, but
  not increase [their descendants],
Because they have stopped giving
  heed to the LORD.

11 Prostitution, wine, and new wine
  take away the mind *and* the
  [spiritual] understanding.
12 My people consult their [lifeless]
  wooden idol, and their [diviner's]
  wand gives them oracles.
For a spirit of prostitution has
  led them astray [morally and
  spiritually],
And they have played the
  prostitute, *withdrawing
  themselves* from their God.
13 They sacrifice on the tops of the
  mountains
And burn incense on the hills,
Under oaks, poplars, and
  terebinths,
Because the shade is pleasant
  there.
Therefore your daughters play the
  prostitute
And your brides commit adultery.
14 I will not punish your daughters
  when they play the prostitute
Or your brides when they commit
  adultery,

For the men themselves slip away
    with prostitutes,
And they offer sacrifices with
    temple prostitutes [who give
    their bodies in honor of the idol].
So the people without
    understanding [stumble and fall
    and] come to ruin.

15 Though you, Israel, play the
    prostitute [by worshiping idols],
Do not let Judah become guilty [of
    the same thing];

And do not go to Gilgal [where
    idols are worshiped],
Or go up to Beth-aven (House of
    Wickedness),
Nor swear [oaths in idolatrous
    worship, saying],
"As the LORD lives!"
16 For Israel is stubborn,
Like a stubborn heifer.
Can the LORD now pasture them
Like a lamb in a large field?
17 Ephraim is joined to idols,
So let him alone [to suffer the
    consequences].

when we know right, we can choose to do right

We cannot do what is right if we do not know what is right. This is why it is vital for us to learn God's Word and, by it, learn His will and His ways. Righteousness is, first of all, a position given to us by Jesus Christ when we accept Him as our Savior. It is then to be worked out in our lives and is said to be "conforming to the will of God in thought, word, and deed" (see 1 John 2:29 AMPC).

We learn from Hosea 4:6 that people are destroyed through a lack of knowledge. Satan is the great deceiver. When people do not know better, they believe Satan's lies and live miserable lives. Satan comes only to kill, steal, and destroy; but Jesus came that we might enjoy our lives in abundance (see John 10:10). For many years Satan stole from me while I blamed other people; sometimes I even blamed God.

As a child I was filled with fear and torment. I did not know that Satan was the source of all my problems. I did not know that even though people had hurt me, Satan himself was actually inflicting the pain as he worked through them. I was unaware that although I had a painful past, I could have a wonderful future. There was so much I did not know! I had a genuine lack of knowledge and I was perishing—living in darkness and bondage—because of it.

In 1976, God gave me a strong desire to study and understand His Word, and my life has been changing for the better ever since. Once I knew that God loved me and wanted me to have a good life, my outlook on everything changed. Prior to knowing truth, I felt hopeless and trapped; I was very bitter. I blamed everyone for my pain except Satan, the real culprit. Yes, people had hurt me, and they were responsible too, but I learned that "hurting people, hurt people." The people who hurt me had done so because someone had hurt them. This knowledge helped me forgive my enemies, and my healing began.

When you take time and make the effort to gain knowledge, you not only help yourself but all your descendants too. My children have better lives than I did because of the knowledge I have. We never know so much that we do not need to keep learning. Make a decision to be a "lifetime learner" so that a lack of knowledge will not cause you or anyone around you to suffer.

18 When their liquor is gone [and
their drinking parties are over],
They habitually go to play the
prostitute;
Ephraim's rulers continue to
dearly love shame [more than
her glory which is the LORD,
Israel's God].
19 The wind [of God's relentless
wrath] has wrapped up Israel in
its wings,
And [in captivity] they will be
ashamed because of their
sacrifices [to calves, to sun, to
moon, to stars, and to pagan
gods].

5 HEAR THIS *and* pay close
attention, O priests!
Give heed, O house of Israel!
Listen, O house of the king!
For the [pronounced] judgment
pertains to you *and* is meant for
you to hear,
Because you have been a snare at
Mizpah
And a net spread out over Tabor
(military strongholds on either
side of the Jordan River).
2 The revolters have gone deep into
depravity,
But I [the LORD God] will chastise
them all.
3 I know Ephraim, and Israel is not
hidden from Me;
For now, O Ephraim, you have
played the prostitute *and* have
worshiped idols;
Israel has defiled itself.
4 Their [immoral] practices will not
permit them
To return to their God,
For the spirit of prostitution is
within them
And they do not know the
LORD [they do not recognize,
appreciate, heed or cherish Him].
5 But the pride *and* self-reliance of
Israel testifies against him.

life point

The Bible is filled with scriptures inviting us
to seek God in whatever circumstances we
find ourselves. Hosea 5:15; 6:1 encourages
us to seek Him when we need forgiveness
and healing from the distress of our guilt.

Exactly how do we seek God? One way is
to think about Him and to consider what
matters to Him and what He says about
certain situations. When we seek Him, we
find much more than His answers to our
problems. We also find joy, peace, love,
wisdom, and everything else we need. Let
me urge you to seek Him in every area of
your life today.

Therefore Israel, and [especially]
Ephraim, stumble *and* fall in
their wickedness *and* guilt;
Judah also has stumbled with them.
6 They will go with their flocks and
with their herds
To seek the LORD [diligently
searching for Him], but they will
not find Him;
He has withdrawn from them
[refusing to hear the prayers of
the unrepentant].
7 They have dealt treacherously
against the LORD,
For they have borne illegitimate
(pagan) children.
Now the New Moon will devour
them along with their land
[bringing judgment and
captivity].

8 Blow the horn in Gibeah,
The trumpet in Ramah [the lofty
hills on Benjamin's northern
border].
Sound the alarm at Beth-aven:
"Behind you *and* coming after you
[is the enemy], O Benjamin [be
on guard]!"
9 Ephraim will become a desolation
in the day of rebuke;

Among the tribes of Israel I
declare what is certain.
10 The princes of Judah are like those
who move a boundary *marker;*
I will pour out My wrath on them
like [an unrestrained flood of]
water. [Deut 19:14; Prov 22:28]
11 Ephraim is oppressed; he is
broken *and* crushed by [divine]
judgment,
Because he was determined to
follow *man's* command (vanities,
filth, secular precepts).
12 Therefore I am like a moth to
Ephraim
And like dry rot to the house of
Judah [in My judgment against
them].
13 When Ephraim saw his sickness,
And Judah his wound,
Then Ephraim went to Assyria
[instead of the LORD]
And sent to [Assyria's] great King
Jareb [for help].
But he cannot heal you
Nor will he cure you of your
wound [received in judgment].
14 For I *will be* like a lion to Ephraim
And like a young lion to the house
of Judah.
I, even I, will tear to pieces and go
on [tearing];
I will carry off [the prey] and there
will be no one to rescue *them.*
15 I will go away and return to My
place [on high]
Until they acknowledge their
offense *and* bear their guilt and
seek My face;
In their distress they will earnestly
seek Me, *saying,*

6 "COME AND let us return [in
repentance] to the LORD,
For He has torn us, but He will
heal us;
He has wounded us, but He will
bandage us.
2 "After two days He will revive us;
On the third day He will raise us up
That we may live before Him. [Is
26:19; Ezek 37:1–10]
3 "So let us know *and* become
personally acquainted with
Him; let us press on to know *and*
understand fully the [greatness
of the] LORD [to honor, heed, and
deeply cherish Him].
His appearing is prepared *and* is
as certain as the dawn,
And He will come to us [in
salvation] like the [heavy] rain,
Like the spring rain watering the
earth."

life point

Hosea 6:1 contains one of God's promises
to heal us. Unless we receive a miracle,
all healing is a process that takes time,
especially emotional healing. Healing does
not come easily and can be quite painful.
Sometimes we have emotional wounds
that are still infected, and before we can
be thoroughly healed, those wounds must
be opened and the infection removed. Only
God knows how to do this properly. As
you seek God for healing from your hurts,
there are two main things you can do to
facilitate the process: spend time with
God in His Word and wait in His presence. I
guarantee you will find healing there!

speak the Word

*God, let Your people know and become personally acquainted with You. Let
us press on to understand fully Your greatness and to honor, heed, and deeply
cherish You. For Your appearing is prepared and is as certain as the dawn,
and You will come to us in salvation like the heavy rain.*
—ADAPTED FROM HOSEA 6:3

4 O Ephraim, what shall I do with
    you?
O Judah, what shall I do with you?
For your [wavering] loyalty *and*
    kindness are [transient] like the
    morning cloud
And like the dew that goes away
    early.
5 Therefore, I have hewn them in
    pieces by [the words of] the
    prophets;
I have slain them by the words of
    My mouth;
My judgments [pronounced upon
    them by the prophets] are
    like the light that shines forth
    [obvious to all].
6 For I desire *and* delight in
    [steadfast] loyalty [faithfulness
    in the covenant relationship],
    rather than sacrifice,
And in the knowledge of God more
    than burnt offerings. [Matt 9:13;
    12:7]
7 But they, like Adam, have
    transgressed the covenant;
There they have dealt
    treacherously against Me.
8 Gilead is a city of wrongdoers;
It is tracked with bloody *footprints.*
9 And as bands of robbers [lie in]
    wait for a man,
So a band of priests murder on the
    road toward Shechem [covering
    their crimes in that city of
    refuge];
Certainly they have committed
    crimes *and* outrages.
10 I have seen a horrible thing [sins
    of every kind] in the house of
    Israel!
Ephraim's prostitution (idolatry) is
    there; Israel has defiled itself.
11 Also, O Judah, there is a harvest
    [of divine judgment] appointed
    for you,
When I restore the fortunes of My
    people [who have been slaves to
    the misery of sin].

7 WHEN I would heal Israel,
    The sin (guilt) of Ephraim is
    uncovered,
And the wickedness of Samaria,
Because they practice false
    dealing;
The thief enters,
Bandits ravage *and* raid outside.
2 But they do not consider in their
    hearts (minds)
That I remember [always] all their
    wickedness.
Now their deeds surround *and*
    entangle them;
They are before My face.
3 They make the king glad with
    their wickedness,
And the princes with their lies.
4 They are all adulterers;
Like the heat of an oven
When the baker ceases to stir *the
    fire,* [their passion smolders]
From the kneading of the dough
    until it is leavened.
5 On the [special] day of our king,
    the princes became sick with the
    heat of wine;
The king stretched out his hand
    [in association] with scoffers
    (lawless people).
6 As they approach their plotting,
Their mind burns [with intrigue]
    like an oven [while they lie in
    wait].
Their anger smolders all night;
In the morning it blazes like a
    flaming fire.
7 They are all hot like an oven
And they consume their judges
    (rulers);
All their kings have fallen.
There is no one among them who
    calls to Me.

8 Ephraim mixes himself with the
    [Gentile] nations [seeking favor
    with one country, then another];
Ephraim is a cake not turned
    [worthless; ready to be thrown
    away].

⁹Strangers have devoured his
 strength,
Yet he does not know it;
Gray hairs are sprinkled on him,
Yet he does not know.
¹⁰Though the pride of Israel testifies
 against him,
Yet they do not return [in
 repentance] to the Lᴏʀᴅ their God,
Nor seek *nor* search for *nor* desire
 Him [as essential] in spite of all
 this.
¹¹Ephraim also is like a silly dove,
 without heart *or* good sense;
They call to Egypt [for help], they
 go to Assyria.
¹²When they go, I will spread My net
 over them;
I will bring them down like birds
 of the heavens [into Assyrian
 captivity].
I will chastise them in accordance
 with the proclamation
 (prophecy) to their congregation.
 [Lev 26:14–39; Deut 28:15–68]
¹³Woe (judgment is coming) to them,
 for they have wandered away
 from Me!
Devastation is theirs, because they
 have rebelled *and* trespassed
 against Me!
I would redeem them, but they
 speak lies against Me.
¹⁴They do not cry out to Me from
 their heart
When they wail on their beds [in
 unbelieving despair];
For the sake of grain and new wine
 they assemble themselves [as if
 worshiping Baal];
They rebel against Me.
¹⁵Although I trained and
 strengthened their arms [for
 victory over their enemies],
Yet they devise evil against Me.
¹⁶They turn, but they do not turn
 upward to the Most High.
They are like a poorly crafted bow
 [that misses the mark];

Their princes shall fall by the sword
Because of the insolence of their
 tongue.
This *will be* cause for their
 mockery *and* disdain in the land
 of Egypt.

8 SET THE trumpet to your
 lips [announcing impending
 judgment]!
Like a [great] vulture *the enemy
 comes* against the house of the
 Lᴏʀᴅ,
Because they have broken My
 covenant
And transgressed *and* rebelled
 against My law.
²Then they will cry out to Me,
"My God, we of Israel know You!"
³Israel has rejected the good;
The enemy shall pursue him.
⁴They set up kings, but not from Me
 [therefore without My blessing];
They have appointed princes, but I
 did not know it.
With their silver and their gold
 they made idols for themselves,
That they might be cut off.
⁵He has rejected your [pagan] calf,
 O Samaria, *saying,*
"My wrath burns against them."
How long will they be incapable of
 innocence?
⁶For even this [loathsome calf] is
 from Israel.
A craftsman made it, so it is not
 God;
Surely the calf of Samaria will be
 broken to pieces *and* go up in
 flames.
⁷For they sow the wind [in evil]
And they reap the whirlwind [in
 disaster].
The standing grain has no growth;
It yields no grain.
If it were to yield, strangers would
 swallow it up.

⁸Israel is [as if] swallowed up [by
enemies];
They are now among the nations
Like a vessel [of cheap, coarse
pottery] that is useless.
⁹For they have gone up to Assyria,
Like a wild donkey wandering
alone *and* taking her own way;
Ephraim has hired lovers (pagan
allies).
¹⁰Yes, even though [with presents]
they hire *allies* among the
nations,
Now I will gather them up;
And [in a little while] they will
begin to grow weak *and* diminish
Because of the burden imposed by
the king of princes [the king of
Assyria].

¹¹For Ephraim has constructed
many altars for sin;
They are altars intended for sinning
[which multiply his guilt].
¹²I wrote for him the ten thousand
precepts of My law,
But they are regarded as a strange
thing [which does not concern
him].
¹³As for My sacrificial offerings,
They sacrifice the meat [as a mere
formality] and eat it,
But the LORD is not pleased with
them *and* does not accept them.
Now He will remember *and* take
into account their wickedness
and guilt,
And punish them for their sins.
They will return [in captivity]
to [another] Egypt [that is,
Assyria]. [Deut 28:68]
¹⁴For Israel has forgotten his Maker
and built palaces [and pagan
temples],
And Judah has built many fortified
cities;
But I will send a fire upon their
cities so that it may consume
their palaces *and* fortresses.
[Amos 1:4, 7, 10, 12, 14; 2:2, 5]

9 DO NOT rejoice, O Israel, with
exultation as do the [pagan]
peoples,
For you have played the prostitute,
turning away from your God.
You have loved *prostitutes'*
earnings on every threshing
floor [attributing the harvest to
the Baals instead of to God].
²The threshing floor and the wine
press will no longer feed them,
And the new wine will fail them
[because they failed to honor the
God who provides].
³They will not remain in the land of
the LORD,
But Ephraim will return to
[another] Egypt [in bondage]
And they will eat [ceremonially]
unclean *food* in Assyria. [2 Kin
25:26; Ezek 4:13]
⁴They will not pour out drink
offerings of wine to the LORD;
Their sacrifices will not please
Him.
Their bread will be like mourners'
bread [eaten at funerals];
All who eat it will be
[ceremonially] unclean,
For their bread will be for
themselves;
It will not enter the house of the
LORD [to be consecrated].
⁵What will you do on the day of the
appointed festival
And on the day of the feast of the
LORD [when you are in exile]?
⁶For behold, they will go away
because of devastation *and*
destruction;
Egypt will gather them up,
Memphis will bury them.
Weeds will take over their
treasures of silver;
Thorns *will grow* in their tents.

⁷The days of punishment have
come;
The days of retribution are at hand;
Let Israel know this!

The prophet is [considered] a fool;
The man [of God] who is inspired
is [treated as if] demented,
Because of the abundance of your
wickedness *and* guilt,
And *because* your deep antagonism
[toward God and the prophets] is
so great. [Luke 21:22]
⁸Ephraim was a watchman with my
God, a [true] prophet [to warn
the nation];
But the snare of a bird catcher was
laid in all his paths.
And there is *only* deep hostility in
the house of his God (the land of
Israel).
⁹They have deeply corrupted
(perverted) themselves
As in the days of Gibeah.
The Lord will remember their
wickedness *and* guilt;
He will punish their sins. [Judg 20]

¹⁰I found Israel like grapes in the
wilderness [an unexpected and
refreshing delight];
I saw your fathers (ancestors) as
the first ripe fruit on the fig tree
in its first *season,*
But they came to Baal-peor and
consecrated themselves to
shamefulness [the worship of
Baal],
And [because of their spiritual and
physical adultery] they became
as detestable *and* loathsome as
the thing they loved.
¹¹As for Ephraim, their glory will fly
away like a bird;
No birth, no pregnancy, and
[because of their impurity] no
conception.
¹²Even though they bring up their
children,
Yet I will bereave them until not one
is left.
Indeed, woe (judgment is coming)
to them when I look away *and*
withdraw [My blessing from
them!

¹³Ephraim, as I have seen,
Is planted in a pleasant [and
prosperous] meadow like Tyre;
But Ephraim will bring out his
children to the executioner [for
slaughter].
¹⁴Give them [the punishment they
deserve], O Lord! What will You
give?
Give them a miscarrying womb
and dry breasts.

¹⁵All their wickedness [says the
Lord] is focused in Gilgal;
Indeed, I came to hate them there!
Because of the wickedness of their
[idolatrous] practices
I will drive them out of My house
(the land of Israel)!
I will love them no longer;
All their princes are rebels. [Hos
4:15; 12:11]
¹⁶Ephraim is stricken, their root is
dried up,
They will bear no fruit.
Even though they give birth,
I will slay the precious children of
their womb.
¹⁷My God will reject them *and* cast
them away
Because they did not listen to Him;
And they will be wanderers
(fugitives) among the nations.

10 ISRAEL IS a luxuriant *and*
prolific vine;
He produces fruit for
himself.
The more his fruit,
The more altars he made [to Baal];
The richer his land,
The better he made the
[idolatrous] pillars.
²Their heart is divided (faithless);
Now they must bear their guilt *and*
punishment.
The Lord will break down [the
horns of] their altars;
He will destroy their *idolatrous*
pillars.

3 Surely now they will say [in
  despair], "We have no [true] king,
For we do not revere the LORD;
And as for the king, what can he
  do for us [to rescue us]?"
4 They have spoken *empty
  (disingenuous)* words,
Swearing falsely to make
  covenants [they intend to break];
Therefore, judgment springs up
  like poisonous weeds in the
  furrows of the field.
5 The people of Samaria will fear
  and tremble
For the [idolatrous] calf of Beth-
  aven (House of Wickedness).
Indeed, its people will mourn over it
And its idolatrous priests will cry
  out *and* wail over it,
Over its glory, because the glory
  [of their calf god] has departed
  from it.
6 The golden calf itself will be
  carried to Assyria
As tribute to King Jareb;
Ephraim will be seized with shame
And Israel will be ashamed of his
  own counsel [to worship the calf
  and separate Israel from Judah].
7 As for Samaria, her king will be
  cut off *and* float away
Like a twig on the surface of the
  water.
8 Also the high places of Aven (Beth-
  aven), the sin of Israel, will be
  destroyed;
The thorn and the thistle will grow
  on their [pagan] altars,
And [in despair] they will say to
  the mountains,
"Cover us!" And to the hills, "Fall
  on us!" [Luke 23:30; Rev 6:16; 9:6]

9 O Israel, you have [willfully]
  sinned since the days of Gibeah;
There they (Israel) stand!
Will not the battle against the sons
  of wickedness overtake them at
  Gibeah? [Judg 20]
10 When it is my desire [to defend My
  righteousness], I will chastise
  them;
And [hostile] peoples will be
  gathered against them
When they are bound *and*
  punished for their double guilt
  [their revolt against the LORD and
  their worship of idols]. [Jer 2:13;
  Lam 3:31–33]

11 Ephraim is a trained heifer that
  loves to tread out the grain,
But I will come over her fair neck
  with a heavy yoke [for hard field
  work].
I will harness Ephraim;
Judah will plow and Jacob will
  harrow *and* rake for himself.
12 Sow with a view to righteousness
  [that righteousness, like seed,
  may germinate];
Reap in accordance with mercy
  and lovingkindness.
Break up your uncultivated
  ground,
For it is time to seek *and* search
  diligently for the LORD [and to
  long for His blessing]
Until He comes to rain
  righteousness *and* His gift of
  salvation on you. [2 Cor 9:10]
13 You have plowed *and* planted
  wickedness, you have reaped the
  [willful] injustice [of oppressors],
You have eaten the fruit of lies.

speak the Word

*God, I will sow with a view to righteousness and reap in accordance with
mercy and loving-kindness. I will break up the uncultivated ground in my
heart, for it is time to seek and search diligently for You.*
—ADAPTED FROM HOSEA 10:12

Because you have trusted in your
own way *and* your chariots, and
in your many warriors,
¹⁴Therefore an uproar will arise
among your people,
And all your fortresses will be
destroyed,
As Shalman destroyed Beth-arbel
on the day of battle,
When mothers were dashed in
pieces with their children. [2 Kin
17:3]
¹⁵In this way it will be done to you
at [idolatrous] Bethel because of
your great wickedness;
At daybreak the king of Israel will
be completely cut off.

11 WHEN ISRAEL was a
child [a young nation], I
loved him,
And I called My son out of Egypt.
[Matt 2:15]
²The more they [the prophets]
called them [to repentance and
obedience],
The more they went away from
them;
They kept sacrificing to the Baals
And burning incense to the carved
images.
³Yet it is I who taught Ephraim to
walk,
Taking them in My arms
[nurturing the young nation];
But they did not know that I healed
them.
⁴I led them *gently* with cords of a
man, with bonds of love [guiding
them],
And I was to them as one who lifts
up *and* eases the yoke [of the
law] over their jaws;
And I bent down to them and fed
them.

⁵They will not return to the land of
Egypt,
But Assyria will be their king
[bringing them into captivity]

Because they refused to return
to Me.
⁶The sword will whirl against *and*
fall on their cities,
And will demolish the bars of their
gates *and* fortifications
And will consume them because of
their counsels.
⁷My people are bent on turning
from Me;
Though the prophets call them to
the One on high,
None at all exalts *Him*.

⁸How can I give you up, O Ephraim?
How can I surrender you, O Israel?
How can I make you like Admah?
How can I treat you like Zeboiim?
My heart recoils within Me;
All My compassions are kindled
together [for My nation of Israel].
[Deut 29:23]
⁹I will not execute the fierceness of
My anger;
I will not return to Ephraim to
destroy him again.
For I am God and not man, the
Holy One in your midst [who will
not revoke My covenant],
And I will not come in wrath *or*
enter the city [in judgment].
¹⁰They will walk after the Lᴏʀᴅ [in
obedience and worship],
Who will roar like a lion;
He will roar [summoning them]
And *His* sons will come trembling
from the west.
¹¹They will come trembling *and*
hurriedly like birds from Egypt
And like doves from the land of
Assyria;
And I will settle them in their
houses [in the land of their
inheritance], declares the Lᴏʀᴅ.

¹²Ephraim surrounds Me with lies
And the house of Israel with deceit;
Judah is also unruly against God,
Even against the faithful Holy One.

12

EPHRAIM FEEDS on the
[emptiness of the] wind
And [continually] pursues
the [parching] east wind [which
brings destruction];
Every day he multiplies lies and
violence.
Further, he makes a covenant with
Assyria
And (olive) oil is carried to Egypt
[to seek alliances]. [Is 30:6, 7]
²The Lord also has a dispute
[a legal complaint and an
indictment] with Judah,
And He will punish Jacob in
accordance with his ways;
He will repay him in accordance
with his deeds.
³In *their mother's* womb he took his
brother by the heel,
And in his maturity he contended
with God. [Gen 25:26; 27:36]
⁴He wrestled with the angel and
prevailed;
He wept [in repentance] and
sought His favor.
He met Him at Bethel
And there God spoke with [him
and through him with] us—
[Gen 28:12–19; 32:28; 35:1–15]
⁵Even the Lord, the God of hosts,
The name of Him [who spoke with
Jacob] is the Lord.
⁶Therefore, return [in repentance]
to your God,
Observe *and* highly regard
kindness and justice,
And wait [expectantly] for your
God continually.
⁷A merchant, in whose hand are
false *and* fraudulent balances;
He loves to oppress *and* exploit.
⁸Ephraim said, "I have indeed
become rich [and powerful as a
nation];
I have found wealth for myself.
In all my labors they will not find
in me

life point

Hosea 12:6 teaches us to wait expectantly
for the Lord. Waiting for God means
spending time with Him in His Word and
in His presence. When we wait expectantly for God, we are anticipating something good from our time with Him.

Any wickedness that *would be* sin."
[Rev 3:17]
⁹But I *have been* the Lord your God
since [you became a nation in]
the land of Egypt;
I will make you live in tents again,
As in the days of the appointed *and*
solemn festival. [Lev 23:39–43]
¹⁰I have also spoken to [you
through] the prophets,
And I gave [them] many visions [to
make My will known],
And through the prophets I gave
parables [to appeal to your sense
of right and wrong].
¹¹Is there wickedness (idolatry) in
Gilead?
Surely the people there are
worthless.
In Gilgal [they defy Me when] they
sacrifice bulls,
Yes, [after My judgment] their
[pagan] altars are like the stone
heaps
In the furrows of the fields.

¹²Now Jacob (Israel) fled into the
open country of Aram (Paddan-
aram), [Gen 28:2, 5]
And [there] Israel (Jacob) worked
and served for a wife,
And for a wife he kept *sheep*. [Gen
29:18–20; 30:31; 31:38–41]
¹³And by a prophet (Moses) the Lord
brought Israel up from Egypt,
And by a prophet Israel was
preserved.
¹⁴Ephraim has provoked most bitter
anger;

So his Lord will leave his bloodguilt
on him [invoking punishment]
And bring back to him his shame
and dishonor.

13

WHEN EPHRAIM spoke,
there was trembling *and*
terror.
He exalted himself [above the
other tribes] in Israel;
But through [the worship of]
Baal he became guilty and died
[spiritually, and then came ruin,
sealing Israel's doom as a nation].
2 And now they sin more and more,
And make for themselves molten
images,
Idols skillfully made from their
silver [as it pleased them],
All of them the work of the
craftsmen.
They say of these [very works of
their hands], "Let those who
sacrifice kiss *and* show respect to
the calves [as if they were living
gods]!"
3 Therefore they will be [swiftly
dissipated] like the morning
cloud
Or like dew which soon disappears,
Like chaff which swirls with the
whirlwind from the threshing
floor,
And like smoke from the
chimney *or* through the
window [worthless and without
substance —they will vanish].

4 Yet I *have been* the Lord your God
Since [the time you became a
nation in] the land of Egypt;
And you were not to know any god
except Me,
For there is no savior besides Me.

5 I knew *and* regarded you *and* cared
for you in the wilderness,
In the land of drought.
6 When *they had* their pasture, they
became satisfied,
And being satisfied, their heart
became proud (self-centered);
Therefore they forgot Me.
7 So I will be like a lion to them;
Like a leopard I will watch *and* lie
in wait [ready to attack] by the
road [to Assyria].
8 I will encounter them like a bear
robbed of her cubs,
And I will tear open their chests;
There I will also devour them like
a lioness,
As a wild beast would tear them.

9 It is your destruction, O Israel,
Because *you are* against Me, [and
have rebelled] against your help.
10 Where now is your king
That he may save you [when you
are attacked] in all your cities?
And your judges of whom you
asked,
"Give me a king and princes"?
11 I gave you a king in My anger,
And I took him away in My wrath
[as punishment].
12 The wickedness of Ephraim
[which is not yet completely
punished] is bound up [as in a
bag];
His sin is stored up [for judgment
and destruction].
13 The pains of childbirth come on
him;
But he is not a wise son,
For it is not the time to delay [his
chance at a new birth] as the
womb opens [but he ignores the
opportunity to change].

speak the Word

Lord, I declare that there is no Savior besides You.
–ADAPTED FROM HOSEA 13:4

14 Shall I ransom them from the power of Sheol (the place of the dead)?
Shall I redeem them from death?
O death, where are your thorns?
O Sheol, where is your sting?
Compassion is hidden from My eyes [because of their failure to repent]. [1 Cor 15:55]

15 For though he flourishes among the reeds (his fellow tribes),
An east wind (Assyria) will come,
The breath of the Lord rising from the desert;
And Ephraim's spring will become dry
And his fountain will be dried up.

Assyria will plunder his treasury of every precious object.
16 Samaria will be found guilty [and become desolate],
Because she rebelled against her God;
They will fall by the sword,
Their infants will be dashed in pieces,
And their pregnant women will be ripped open.

14 O ISRAEL, return [in repentance] to the Lord your God,
For you have stumbled *and* fallen [visited by tragedy], because of your sin.

God loves you freely

Do you ever wonder how God can love us, as imperfect as we are? He can because He *wants to;* it pleases Him. Hosea 14:4 tells us that God wants to heal our faithlessness and love us freely.

God's Word is full of verses about His love. Ephesians 1:5 teaches: "He predestined and lovingly planned for us to be adopted to Himself as [His own] children through Jesus Christ, in accordance with the kind intention and good pleasure of His will."

God loves because love is His nature; God is love (see 1 John 4:8). If He were otherwise, He would not be Who He is.

God always loves us! He may not always love everything we do, but He does love us. His love is unconditional. It is love based on Him, not on us; we receive God's love without deserving it. God's unconditional love is the power that forgives our sins, heals our emotional wounds, and mends our broken hearts (see Psalm 147:3).

Once you realize that you are loved by God, not because of anything you are or anything you have done, then you can quit trying to deserve or earn His love and simply receive and enjoy it. Remember, He loves you freely—without requiring or asking anything of you.

If you struggle to believe or accept God's unconditional love for you, start by confessing that God loves you. Say, "God loves me," aloud several times a day when you are alone. Speak it out into the atmosphere and become accustomed to hearing it. Get comfortable with the thought of it. Bask in His love, soak in it, and let it saturate your thinking and your emotions. Imagine how awesome it is: *"God loves me!"*

Once your heart is filled with the knowledge of God's awesome, unconditional love, you can begin to love Him in return and to express His love to others.

²Take the words [confessing your guilt] with you and return to the LORD.
Say to Him, "Take away all our wickedness;
Accept what is good *and* receive us graciously,
So that we may present the fruit of our lips (gratitude). [Heb 13:15]
³"Assyria will not save us;
We will not ride on horses [relying on military might],
Nor will we say again to [the idols who are] the work of our hands,
'You are our gods.'
For in You [O LORD] the orphan finds love *and* compassion *and* mercy."

⁴I will heal their apostasy *and* faithlessness;
I will love them freely,
For My anger has turned away from Israel.
⁵I shall be like the dew to Israel;
He will blossom like the lily,
And he will take root like *the cedars of* Lebanon.
⁶His shoots will sprout,
And his beauty will be like the olive tree
And his fragrance like *the cedars of* Lebanon.
⁷Those who live in his shadow

putting the Word to work

In what ways has God shown you love, compassion, and mercy (see Hosea 14:3)? How has He healed you and loved you (see Hosea 14:4)? Thank Him today!

Will again raise grain,
And they will blossom like the vine.
His renown *will be* like the wine of Lebanon.

⁸O Ephraim, what more have I to do with idols?
It is I who have answered and will care for you *and* watch over you.
I am like a luxuriant cypress tree;
With Me your fruit is found [which is to nourish you].

⁹Whoever is [spiritually] wise, let him understand these things;
Whoever is [spiritually] discerning *and* understanding, let him know them.
For the ways of the LORD are right,
And the righteous will walk in them,
But transgressors will stumble *and* fall in them. [Ps 107:43; Is 26:7; Jer 9:12; Dan 12:10]

Joel

Author:
Joel

Date:
Traditional view is about 830 BC

Everyday Life Principles:
Sin requires repentance.

Continual sin and lack of repentance lead to God's judgment.

God does execute judgment, but He also brings restoration.

In modern-day language, the basic message of the book of Joel is: "Straighten up!" Joel wrote during difficult days, a time when the entire land of Judah suffered under a massive locust plague, in which crops failed, livestock died, and people perished. Joel interpreted this destruction as God's judgment and declared that to the people. Joel went on to urge the people to repent and to encourage them by telling them God wanted to bring restoration to their devastation.

Perhaps the most familiar passage in Joel is God's promise of restoration in Joel 2:25, 26: "And I will compensate you for the years that the swarming locust has eaten, the creeping locust, the stripping locust, and the gnawing locust—My great army which I sent among you. You will have plenty to eat and be satisfied and praise the name of the LORD, your God who has dealt wondrously with you: and My people shall never be put to shame."

Whatever has been lost in your life, I pray that the book of Joel will remind you that God is a God of restoration. He is able to restore what has been lost or stolen from you. He wants to make the words of Joel 2:26 a reality in your life so you are able to declare that the Lord your God "has dealt wondrously with you."

1 THE WORD of the LORD that
came to Joel, the son of Pethuel.
² Hear this, O elders,
Listen closely, all inhabitants of
the land!
Has *such a thing as* this occurred
in your days,
Or even in the days of your fathers?
³ Tell your children about it,
And let your children tell their
children,
And their children the next
generation.

⁴ What the gnawing locust has left,
the swarming locust has eaten;
And what the swarming locust
has left, the creeping locust has
eaten;
And what the creeping locust has
left, the stripping locust has
eaten [in judgment of Judah].
⁵ Awake [from your intoxication],
you drunkards, and weep;
Wail, all you drinkers of wine,
Because of the [fresh] sweet wine
That is cut off from your mouth.
⁶ For a [pagan and hostile] nation
has invaded My land [like
locusts],
Mighty and without number;
Its teeth are the teeth of a lion,
And it has the fangs of a lioness.
[Rev 9:7, 8]
⁷ It has made My vine (My people) a
waste *and* object of horror,
And splintered *and* broken My fig
tree.
It has stripped them completely
bare and thrown them away;
Their branches have become
white. [Is 5:5, 6]
⁸ Wail like a virgin [bride] clothed
with sackcloth
For the bridegroom of her youth
[who has died].
⁹ The [daily] grain offering and the
drink offering are cut off
From the house of the LORD;

The priests mourn
Who minister to the LORD.
¹⁰ The field is ruined,
The ground mourns;
For the grain is ruined,
The new wine is dried up,
The fresh oil fails.
¹¹ Be ashamed, O farmers;
Wail, O vinedressers,
For the wheat and for the barley,
Because the harvest of the field
has perished.
¹² The vine dries up
And the fig tree fails;
The pomegranate, the palm also,
and the apple tree,
All the trees of the field dry up,
Indeed, joy dries up *and* withdraws
From the sons of men.

¹³ Clothe yourselves *with sackcloth*
And lament (cry out in grief), O
priests;
Wail, O ministers of the altar!
Come, spend the night in sackcloth
[and pray without ceasing],
O ministers of my God,
For the grain offering and the
drink offering
Are withheld from the house of
your God.
¹⁴ Consecrate a fast,
Proclaim a solemn assembly,
Gather the elders
And all the inhabitants of the land
To the house of the LORD your God,
And cry out to the LORD [in
penitent pleadings].
¹⁵ Alas for the day!
For the [judgment] day of the LORD
is at hand,
And it will come [upon the nation]
as a destruction from the
Almighty. [Zeph 1:14–18]
¹⁶ Has not the food been cut off
before our eyes,
Joy and gladness from the house of
our God?
¹⁷ The seeds [of grain] shrivel under
the clods,

The storehouses are desolate *and*
  empty,
The barns are in ruins
Because the grain is dried up.
¹⁸How the animals groan!
  The herds of cattle are bewildered
  and wander aimlessly
Because they have no pasture;
Even the flocks of sheep suffer.
¹⁹O Lord, I cry out to You,
  For fire has devoured the pastures
  of the wilderness,
And the flame has burned up all
  the trees of the field.
²⁰Even the wild animals pant [in
  longing] for You;
For the water brooks are dried up
And fire has consumed the
  pastures of the wilderness.

2 BLOW THE trumpet in
  Zion [warning of impending
  judgment],
Sound an alarm on My holy
  mountain [Zion]!
Let all the inhabitants of the land
  tremble *and* shudder in fear,
For the [judgment] day of the Lord
  is coming;
It is close at hand, [Ezek 7:2–4;
  Amos 5:16–20]
²A day of darkness and gloom,
A day of clouds and of thick [dark]
  mist,
Like the dawn spread over the
  mountains;
There is a [pagan, hostile] people
  numerous and mighty,
The like of which has never been
  before
Nor will be again afterward
Even for years of many generations.
³Before them a fire devours,
And behind them a flame burns;
Before them the land is like the
  Garden of Eden,
But behind them a desolate
  wilderness;
And nothing at all escapes them.

⁴Their appearance is like the
  appearance of horses,
And they run like war horses.
⁵Like the noise of chariots
They leap on the tops of the
  mountains,
Like the crackling of a flame of
  fire devouring the stubble,
Like a mighty people set in battle
  formation. [Rev 9:7, 9]
⁶Before them the people are in
  anguish;
All faces become pale [with terror].
⁷They run like warriors;
They climb the wall like soldiers.
They each march [straight ahead]
  in line,
And they do not deviate from their
  paths.
⁸They do not crowd each other;
Each one marches in his path.
When they burst through the
  defenses (weapons),
They do not break ranks.
⁹They rush over the city,
They run on the wall;
They climb up into the houses,
They enter at the windows like a
  thief.
¹⁰The earth quakes before them,
The heavens tremble,
The sun and the moon grow dark
And the stars lose their brightness.
  [Rev 9:2–4; 16:14]
¹¹The Lord utters His voice before
  His army,
For His camp is very great,
Because strong *and* powerful is he
  who [obediently] carries out His
  word.
For the day of the Lord is indeed
  great and very terrible [causing
  dread];
Who can endure it? [Is 26:20, 21;
  34:1–4, 8; Rev 6:16, 17]
¹²"Even now," says the Lord,
  "Turn *and* come to Me with all your
  heart [in genuine repentance],

With fasting and weeping and
mourning [until every barrier
is removed and the broken
fellowship is restored];
¹³ Rip your heart to pieces [in sorrow
and contrition] and not your
garments."
Now return [in repentance] to the
LORD your God,
For He is gracious and
compassionate,
Slow to anger, abounding in
lovingkindness [faithful to His
covenant with His people];
And He relents [His sentence of]
evil [when His people genuinely
repent].
¹⁴ Who knows whether He will relent
[and revoke your sentence],
And leave a blessing behind Him,
Even a grain offering and a drink
offering [from the bounty He
provides you]
For the LORD your God?
¹⁵ Blow a trumpet in Zion [warning
of impending judgment],

putting the Word to work

**Have you ever received a halfhearted
apology? Repentance is not simply a
matter of going through the motions;
it is contrite confession and a conscious decision to return to following
God. I encourage you not ever to take
for granted God's grace, kindness, and
mercy, but recognize your sin and be
wholehearted and sincere in asking
for forgiveness. God will have compassion on you (see Joel 2:13)!**

Dedicate a fast [as a day of
restraint and humility], call a
solemn assembly.
¹⁶ Gather the people, sanctify the
congregation,
Assemble the elders,
Gather the children and the
nursing infants.
Let the bridegroom come out of his
room
And the bride out of her bridal
chamber. [No one is excused
from the assembly.]
¹⁷ Let the priests, the ministers of the
LORD,
Weep between the porch and the
altar,
And let them say, "Have
compassion *and* spare Your
people, O LORD,
And do not make Your inheritance
(Israel) an object of ridicule,
Or a [humiliating] byword among
the [Gentile] nations.
Why should they say among the
peoples,
'Where is their God?'"
¹⁸ Then the LORD will be jealous for
His land [ready to defend it since
it is rightfully and uniquely His]
And will have compassion on His
people [and will spare them].
¹⁹ The LORD will answer and say to
His people,
"Behold, I am going to send you
grain and new wine and oil,
And you will be satisfied *in full*
with them;
And I will never again make you
an object of ridicule among the
[Gentile] nations.
²⁰ "But I will remove the northern
army far away from you,

speak the Word

*When I sin, I repent and return to You, my God, for You are gracious and
compassionate, slow to anger, and abounding in loving-kindness.*
—ADAPTED FROM JOEL 2:13

And I will drive it into a parched
  and desolate land,
With its forward guard into the
  eastern sea (Dead Sea)
And with its rear guard into the
  western sea (Mediterranean Sea).
And its stench will arise and its foul
  odor of decay will come up [this
  is the fate of the northern army in
  the final day of the LORD],
For He has done great things."
  [Is 34:1–4, 8; Amos 4:10]

²¹ Do not fear, O land; be glad and
  rejoice,
For the LORD has done great
  things! [Zech 12:8–10]
²² Do not be afraid, you animals of the
  field,
For the pastures of the wilderness
  have turned green;
The tree has produced its fruit,
And the fig tree and the vine have
  yielded in full.
²³ So rejoice, O children of Zion,
And delight in the LORD, your God;
For He has given you the early
  [autumn] rain in vindication
And He has poured down the rain
  for you,
The early [autumn] rain and the
  late [spring] rain, as before.

putting the Word to work

All of us have experienced the consequences of sin. Is there an area in
your life where you are still feeling
the ramifications of your sin? Be
encouraged; God can bring healing
and restoration (see Joel 2:25–27).
Remember to thank Him for His grace
and mercy.

life point

Joel 2:28 states that in the last days the
old men shall dream dreams, and the
young men shall see visions.

Dreams are certainly one of the valid
ways God speaks, but they also represent
an area in which people can easily get
out of balance. This is because dreaming
is common to all of us and not all dreams
are from God. If you want to know
whether or not a dream is from God, use
discernment, wisdom, and balance, and I
believe you will have confirmation in your
heart if God is trying to speak to you or
show you something.

²⁴ And the threshing floors shall be
    full of grain,
And the vats shall overflow with
    new wine and oil.
²⁵ "And I will compensate you for the
    years
That the swarming locust has
    eaten,
The creeping locust, the stripping
    locust, and the gnawing locust—
My great army which I sent among
    you.
²⁶ "You will have plenty to eat and be
    satisfied

putting the Word to work

Have you ever been discriminated
against because of your age, gender,
or situation in life? God does not
discriminate, and He continues to pour
out His Spirit. Ask God today for a
fresh outpouring of His Spirit in your
life (see Joel 2:28, 29).

speak the Word

God, I will not fear. I will be glad and rejoice, for You have done great things.
—ADAPTED FROM JOEL 2:21

And praise the name of the LORD
your God
Who has dealt wondrously with
you;
And My people shall never be put
to shame.
27 "And you shall know [without any
doubt] that I am in the midst of
Israel [to protect and bless you],
And that I am the LORD your God,
And there is no other;
My people will never be put to
shame.

28 "It shall come about after this
That I shall pour out My Spirit on
all mankind;
And your sons and your daughters
will prophesy,
Your old men will dream dreams,
Your young men will see visions.
29 "Even on the male and female
servants
I will pour out My Spirit in those
days.
30 "I will show signs *and* wonders
[displaying My power] in the
heavens and on the earth,

rejoice!

Joel 2:23 instructs us to rejoice because God has done great things. Joy is one of the most powerful weapons we have against the devil. He has evil intentions to destroy our lives, but joy is a great source of strength that God has given us to interrupt Satan's plan. The devil wants us to feel down because he knows if we lose our joy, we will lose our strength, and if we lose our strength, he will be able to walk all over us. But the Lord wants to lift us up, and He does that through His joy, which is our strength (see Nehemiah 8:10).

The Bible says to be "rejoice always" (1 Thessalonians 5:16). It is not godly to be joyless all the time. Instead, I believe we need to aim to be joyful on a regular, ongoing basis. Let me urge you not to wait to feel joyful, but to be joyful on purpose. Think about right things; smile and laugh as often as possible. Believing releases joy. Believe in God, believe His promises, and believe He really wants you to enjoy your life.

I was not raised in a joyful atmosphere. I was made to feel that if I was having fun, I was doing something wrong, so I was frequently discouraged and sad. I worked hard and was a responsible person, but I did not really enjoy my life.

Satan robbed me of many things through my ignorance of God's Word (see Hosea 4:6). Because I lacked proper spiritual knowledge, for a while Satan deceived me and stole the victorious, joy-filled life Jesus had already provided in His plan for me. Now I live a life of joy because the Lord has helped me.

The next time you feel you have lost your joy, I encourage you to remember that joy is a fruit of the Holy Spirit (see Galatians 5:22, 23). However, it is released only by making a decision not to allow adverse circumstances to rule your emotional and mental attitudes.

Through joy, you can receive strength to do things that would otherwise be impossible. Through joy, you can overcome problems the devil will tell you cannot be overcome. You can be defeated only if you lose your joy. No matter what happens in your life, remember this: You have the ability to maintain and release joy in your life, and there is nothing Satan can do to stop you when your heart is full of joy. So, take Joel's advice and rejoice in the Lord your God!

Blood and fire and columns of
　　smoke.
31 "The sun will be turned into
　　darkness
And the moon into blood
Before the great and terrible day
　　of the LORD comes. [Is 13:6, 9–11;
　　24:21–23; Ezek 32:7–10; Matt
　　24:29, 30; Rev 6:12–17]
32 "And it shall come about that
　　whoever calls on the name of the
　　LORD

Will be saved [from the coming
　　judgment]
For on Mount Zion and in
　　Jerusalem
There will be those who escape,
As the LORD has said,
Even among the remnant [of
　　survivors] whom the LORD calls.
　　[Acts 2:17–21; Rom 10:13]

3 "FOR BEHOLD, in those
[climactic] days and at that time,
When I restore the fortunes of
Judah and Jerusalem,
2 I will gather together all the
　　[Gentile] nations [that were
　　hostile to My people]
And bring them down into the
　　Valley of Jehoshaphat (the LORD
　　has judged).
And there I will deal with them
　　and enter into judgment with
　　them there

putting the Word to work

**Have you ever called on someone for
help and that person was either too
busy to lend a hand or could not provide the help you needed? No matter
how desperate your situation, God's
promise is sure: He will save whoever
calls on Him (see Joel 2:32).**

God of restoration

Joel 2:25 teaches us that God will compensate for things we have lost. Other translations of the Bible say He will "restore." God is a God of restoration (see Joel 2:25, 26).
He makes worn-out and destroyed things brand-new. In fact, many words that begin
with "re" describe actions of God: He re-news, re-wards, re-deems, re-fines, brings
re-compense, re-surrects, re-stores, re-vives, re-leases, and He teaches us to re-pent.

The *pent*house is the highest place in an apartment building or hotel. When we *repent*, God takes us back to the highest place, where we belong and from which we
have fallen through sin. God is the God of mercy, Who continues to work with us as
long as we desire change in our lives. He never gives up on us. He is not a harsh taskmaster Who is angry and impatient. Actually, God is just the opposite. He is merciful,
gracious, kind, patient, slow to anger, compassionate, good, faithful, and every
other wonderful thing.

When something has been lost or stolen from us, we can become bitter unless we
know there is hope of restoration. God not only gives back what was lost, but also
promises us "double for our trouble." Isaiah 61:7, 8 say that for our former shame He
will give us a "a double portion." Instead of suffering with humiliation, God promises we will shout for joy over our portion, for He loves justice.

Job went through a very difficult time, but he remained faithful to God—and God
restored to him twice as much as he had lost. How can a person be bitter about his or
her past when God promises such a bright future? Forget what lies behind, remember
that God loves to restore, and press on toward the new things He has for you.

For [their treatment of] My people,
   My inheritance, Israel,
Whom they have scattered among
   the nations,
And [because] they have
   encroached on My land *and*
   divided it up.
³"They have also cast lots for My
   people,
And have traded a boy for a
   prostitute
And have sold a girl for wine that
   they may drink.

⁴"Moreover, what are you to Me, O
Tyre and Sidon and all the [five small]
regions of Philistia? Will you pay Me
back for something [I have supposedly
done to you]? Even if you do pay Me
back, I will swiftly and speedily return your deed [of retaliation] on your
own head. [Is 23; Ezek 26:1–18; Amos
1:6–10; Zeph 2:4–7; Zech 9:2–7]
   ⁵"Because you have taken My silver and My gold and have carried My
precious treasures to your temples *and*
palaces,
   ⁶and have sold the children of Judah
and the children of Jerusalem to the
Greeks, so that you may send them far
away from their territory,
   ⁷behold, I am going to stir them up
from the place where you have sold
them [and return them to their land],
and I shall return your action [of re-
taliation] on your own head.
   ⁸"Also I will sell your sons and your
daughters into the hand of the children of Judah, and they will sell them
to the Sabeans, to a distant nation," for
the LORD has spoken. [Is 14:2; 60:14]

   ⁹Proclaim this among the [pagan]
nations:

speak the Word

putting the Word to work

**Do you remember the day you decided
to follow Jesus? Perhaps it was a quick
decision, or perhaps you spent months
or even years thinking about it. Joel's
message is both timely and urgent
for today: as you once were, there are
countless people still in the "valley
of decision" (Joel 3:14), weighing
whether or not to follow God. Pray
earnestly both for those you know
personally and for those you do not
know who are in the valley, that they
will decide to follow Him.**

Prepare a war! Stir up the mighty
   men!
Let all the men of war come near,
   let them come up!
¹⁰Beat your plowshares into swords
And your pruning hooks into
   spears;
Let the weak say, "I am strong!"
   [Is 2:4; Mic 4:3]
¹¹Hurry and come, all you
   surrounding nations,
And gather yourselves there;
Bring down, O LORD, Your mighty
   ones (Your warriors).
¹²Let the nations be stirred [to
   action]
And come up to the Valley of
   Jehoshaphat,
For there I will sit to judge *and*
   punish
All the surrounding nations.
¹³Put in the sickle [of judgment], for
   the harvest is ripe;
Come, tread [the grapes], for the
   wine press is full;

Lord, I declare that in You I am strong!
–ADAPTED FROM JOEL 3:10

The vats overflow, for the
   wickedness [of the people] is great.
   [Mark 4:29; Rev 14:15, 18–20]
¹⁴Multitudes, multitudes in the
   valley of decision (judgment)!
   For the day of the Lᴏʀᴅ is near in the
   valley of decision [when judgment
   is executed]. [Zech 14:1–9]
¹⁵The sun and the moon grow dark
   And the stars lose their brightness.
¹⁶The Lᴏʀᴅ thunders and roars from
   Zion
   And utters His voice from
   Jerusalem [in judgment of His
   enemies],
   And the heavens and the earth
   tremble and shudder;
   But the Lᴏʀᴅ is a refuge for His
   people
   And a stronghold [of protection]
   to the children of Israel. [Amos
   9:11–15; Mic 4:1–3; 5:2; Zeph
   3:13–20; Zech 6:12, 13; 12:8, 9]
¹⁷Then you will know and
   understand fully that I am the
   Lᴏʀᴅ your God,
   Dwelling in Zion, My holy
   mountain.
   Then Jerusalem will be holy,

And strangers [who do not belong]
   will no longer pass through it.
¹⁸And in that day
   The mountains will drip with sweet
   wine
   And the hills will flow with milk;
   And all the brooks and riverbeds
   of Judah will flow with water,
   And a fountain will go out from
   the house of the Lᴏʀᴅ
   To water the [desert] Valley of
   Shittim. [Ezek 47:1–12; Amos
   9:13; Zech 14:8]
¹⁹Egypt will become a waste,
   And Edom will become a desolate
   wilderness,
   Because of their violence against
   the children of Judah,
   In whose land they have shed
   innocent blood. [Ex 1:16;
   Amos 1:11]
²⁰But Judah shall be inhabited
   forever
   And Jerusalem from generation to
   generation.
²¹And I shall avenge their blood
   which I have not avenged,
   For the Lᴏʀᴅ dwells in Zion.

speak the Word

Lord, You are a refuge and a stronghold of protection for me.
—ADAPTED FROM Joel 3:16

Amos

Author:
Amos

Date:
760 BC–750 BC

Everyday Life Principles:
Guard your heart during good or prosperous times so you do not forget God.

Continue to seek the Lord in the midst of blessing, when everything seems to be wonderful and you may not feel a need for God.

True life is not found in prosperity or ease, but in seeking and finding the Lord.

A mos prophesied during a time of great prosperity in Israel and Judah. The nations were powerful politically, economically, and militarily—and everything appeared to be going better than ever. Because the people enjoyed such power, wealth, and material abundance, they assumed that God was pleased with them and that their prosperity was a sign of His blessing.

The truth was that in the midst of seemingly good times, there was much corruption, idolatry, injustice, and immorality. God sent Amos into this situation to declare to His people that their prosperity did not indicate His pleasure. Instead, He was displeased with their hearts and their behavior, and judgment was inevitable unless they changed their ways and began to seek Him again.

Amos teaches us that God will judge corruption and immorality in a society. He is not looking for cities or nations that will be merely "religious," but for those who value and practice righteousness and justice, and for people who will love one another, stand up for the oppressed, and seek Him.

Remember as you read the book of Amos that material prosperity is not always a sign of God's blessing and can cause people to think they do not need God. Let this book remind you of your desperate need to seek Him, because, as Amos 5 repeatedly affirms, we live not by material abundance, but by truly seeking the Lord.

1 THE WORDS of Amos, who was among the sheepherders of Te-koa, which he saw [in a divine revelation] concerning Israel in the days of Uzziah king of Judah, and in the days of Jeroboam the son of Joash, king of Israel, two years before the earthquake. [Zech 14:5]

2 And he said,
"The LORD thunders and roars from Zion [in judgment]
And utters His voice from Jerusalem;
Then the pastures of the shepherds mourn,
And the summit of [Mount] Carmel dries up [because of God's judgment]." [Is 42:13; Jer 25:30; Joel 3:16]

3 Thus says the LORD,
"For three transgressions of Damascus and for four (multiplied delinquencies)
I shall not reverse its punishment or revoke My word concerning it,
Because they have threshed Gilead [east of the Jordan River] with sharp iron sledges [having spikes that crushed and shredded]. [2 Kin 10:32, 33]
4 "So I will send a fire [of war, conquest, and destruction] upon the house of Hazael,

---

putting the Word to work

The name Amos means "Bur-den-Bearer." Do you know the meaning of your name? If you are a follower of Jesus, "Christian" is one of your names, and it means "one belonging to or resembling Christ." Like Amos, seek to serve the Lord your God with all your heart.

And it shall devour the palaces and strongholds of Ben-hadad (Hazael's son).
5 "I also will break the bar [of the gate] of Damascus,
And cut off and destroy the inhabitant from the Valley of Aven (Wickedness),
And the ruler who holds the scepter, from Beth-eden (Damascus);
And the people of Aram [conquered by the Assyrians] will go into exile to Kir,"
Says the LORD. [Ezek 30:17]

6 Thus says the LORD,
"For three transgressions of Gaza [in Philistia] and for four (multiplied delinquencies)
I will not reverse its punishment or revoke My word concerning it,
Because [as slave traders] they took captive the entire [Jewish] population [of defenseless Judean border villages, of which none was spared]
And deported them to Edom [for the slave trade]. [Joel 3:6]

7 "So I will send a fire [of war, conquest, and destruction] on the wall of Gaza
And it shall consume her citadels.
8 "And I will cut off and destroy the inhabitants from Ashdod,
And the ruler who holds the scepter, from Ashkelon;
And I will unleash My power and turn My hand [in judgment] against Ekron,
And the rest of the Philistines [in Gath and the towns dependent on these four Philistine cities] shall die,"
Says the Lord GOD. [Josh 13:3]

9 Thus says the LORD,
"For three transgressions of Tyre and for four (multiplied delinquencies)

I will not reverse its punishment
　　or revoke My word concerning it,
Because they [as middlemen]
　　deported an entire [Jewish]
　　population to Edom
And did not [seriously] remember
　　their covenant of brotherhood.
　　[1 Kin 5:1, 12; 9:12, 13]
10 "So I will send a fire [of war,
　　conquest, and destruction] on
　　the wall of Tyre,
And it shall consume her citadels."

11 Thus says the LORD,
　　"For three transgressions of
　　Edom [the descendants of
　　Esau] and for four (multiplied
　　delinquencies)
I will not reverse its punishment
　　or revoke My word concerning it,
Because he pursued his brother
　　Jacob (Israel) with the sword,
Corrupting *and* stifling his
　　compassions *and* casting off all
　　mercy;
His destructive anger raged
　　continually,
And he maintained [and nurtured]
　　his wrath forever.
12 "So I will send a fire [of war,
　　conquest, and destruction] upon
　　Teman,
And it shall consume the citadels
　　of Bozrah [in Edom]."

13 Thus says the LORD,
　　"For three transgressions of the
　　children of Ammon and for four
　　(multiplied delinquencies)
I will not reverse its punishment
　　or revoke My word concerning it,
Because the Ammonites have
　　ripped open the pregnant
　　women of Gilead,
That they might enlarge their
　　border.
14 "So I will kindle a fire [of war,
　　conquest, and destruction] on
　　the wall of Rabbah [in Ammon]
And it shall devour its strongholds

putting the Word to work

**The people of Judah rejected God's
Word and did not keep His commandments (see Amos 2:4). Most of
us would be quick to say we do not
despise God's Word, but do you know
that the word *despise* also means "to
regard as unimportant"? Know that
living by God's Word is important in
every area of your life, and make every effort to keep His commandments.**

Amid war cries *and* shouts of
　　alarm on the day of battle,
And a tempest on the day of the
　　whirlwind [when the enemy
　　captures the city].
15 "Their king shall go into exile,
He and his princes together," says
　　the LORD.

2　THUS SAYS the LORD,
　　"For three transgressions of
　　Moab and for four (multiplied
　　delinquencies)
I will not reverse its punishment
　　or revoke My word concerning it,
Because he burned the bones
　　of the king of Edom [Esau's
　　descendant] into lime [and used
　　it to plaster a Moabite house].
2 "So I will send a fire [of war,
　　conquest, and destruction] upon
　　Moab
And it shall devour the
　　strongholds of Kerioth;
And Moab shall die amid tumult
　　and uproar,
With war cries *and* shouts of alarm
　　and the sound of the trumpet.
3 "I will also cut off *and* destroy the
　　ruler from its midst
And slay all the princes with him,"
　　says the LORD.

4 Thus says the LORD,

"For three transgressions of
Judah and for four (multiplied
delinquencies)
I will not reverse its punishment
or revoke My word concerning it,
Because they have rejected the
law of the LORD [the sum of God's
instruction to His people]
And have not kept His
commandments;
But their lies [and their idols],
after which their fathers walked,
Caused them to go astray.
⁵"So I will send a fire [of war,
conquest, and destruction by the
Babylonians] upon Judah
And it will devour the strongholds
of Jerusalem."

⁶Thus says the LORD,
"For three transgressions of
Israel and for four (multiplied
delinquencies)
I will not reverse its punishment
or revoke My word concerning it,
Because they sell the righteous
and innocent for silver
And the needy for the price of a
pair of sandals.
⁷"These who pant after (long to see)
the dust of the earth on the head
of the helpless [as sign of their
grief and distress]
Also turn aside the way of the
humble;
And a man and his father will go
to the same girl
So that My holy name is profaned.
⁸"They stretch out beside every
[pagan] altar on clothes taken
in pledge [to secure a loan,
disregarding God's command],
And in the house of their God
[in contempt of Him] they
frivolously drink the wine
[which has been] taken from
those who have been fined. [Ex
22:26; Deut 24:12, 13]

⁹"Yet it was I [not the false gods]
who destroyed the Amorite
before them,
Though his height was like the
height of the cedars,
And he was as strong as the oaks;
I even destroyed his fruit above
and his root below.
¹⁰"Also it was I who brought you up
out of the land of Egypt,
And I led you forty years through
the wilderness
That you might possess the land of
the Amorite.
¹¹"Then I raised up some of your sons
to be prophets [who gave you My
revelation],
And some of your young men to be
Nazirites (dedicated ones).
Is this not true, O you children of
Israel?" says the LORD.
[Num 6:1–8]
¹²"But you gave the Nazirites wine to
drink [despite their vows]
And commanded the prophets,
saying, 'You shall not prophesy!'
¹³"Behold, I am weighted down
beneath you
As a cart that is weighted down
when it is full of sheaves.
¹⁴"Flight will be lost to the swift [so
they will be unable to escape],
And the strong shall not
strengthen *nor* maintain his
power,
Nor shall the mighty man save his
own life.
¹⁵"He who handles the bow will not
stand *his ground,*
The one who is swift of foot will
not escape,
Nor will he who rides the horse
save his life [from the invading
army].
¹⁶"Even the bravest among the
warriors shall flee naked on that
day," says the LORD.

3 HEAR THIS word that the Lord has spoken against you, O children of Israel, against the whole family which I brought up from the land of Egypt:

2 "I have known [chosen, cared for, and loved] only you of all the families of the earth;
Therefore I shall punish you for all your wickedness."
3 Do two men walk together unless they have made an appointment?
4 Does a lion roar in the forest when he has no prey?
Does a young lion growl from his den if he has not captured *something*?
5 Does a bird fall into a trap on the ground when there is no bait in it?
Does a trap spring up from the ground when it has caught nothing at all? [Of course not! So it is that Israel has earned her impending judgment.]
6 If a trumpet is blown in a city [warning of danger] will not the people tremble?
If a disaster *or* misfortune occurs in a city has not the Lord caused it?
7 Surely the Lord God does nothing Without revealing His secret plan [of the judgment to come] To His servants the prophets. [Rev 10:7]
8 The lion has roared! Who will not fear?
The Lord God has spoken [to the prophets]! Who can but prophesy? [Acts 4:20; 5:20, 29; 1 Cor 9:16]

9 Proclaim on the fortresses in Ashdod (Philistia) and on the citadels in the land of Egypt, and say, "Assemble yourselves on the mountains of Samaria, and see the great confusion within her and the oppressions *and* abuse of authority in her midst.
10 "For they do not know how to do

life point

In Amos 3:3 we read, "Do two men walk together unless they have made an appointment?" In the Amplified Classic version, this verse reads: "Do two walk together except they make an appointment *and have agreed?*" (italics mine). To walk with God, we must agree with God. This means agreeing with His Word, with His heart, and with His character. We need to agree with everything He says, everything He does, and everything He is. As we do, we will be empowered to live victorious, blessed, overcoming lives.

right," says the Lord, "these who store up violence and devastation [like treasures] in their strongholds."
11 Therefore, thus says the Lord God,

"An adversary (Assyria), even one surrounding the land,
Shall pull down your strength from you
And your fortresses will be looted."
12 Thus says the Lord,
"Just as the shepherd snatches from the mouth of the lion a couple of legs or a piece of the [sheep's] ear [to prove to the owner that he has not stolen the animal],
So will the [remaining] children of Israel living in Samaria be snatched away
With the corner of a bed and [part of] the damask covering of a couch.
13 "Hear and testify against the house of Jacob,"
Says the Lord God, the God of hosts,
14 "On that day when I punish Israel's transgressions,
I shall also punish the altars of Bethel [with their golden calves];
And the horns of the altar shall be cut off
And fall to the ground.

15"And I shall tear down the winter
  house with the summer house;
And the houses of ivory shall also
  perish
And the great houses shall come to
  an end,"
Says the LORD.

4 HEAR THIS word, you [well-
  fed, pampered] cows (women)
  of Bashan who are on the
mountain of Samaria,
Who oppress the poor, who crush
  the needy,
Who say to their husbands, "Bring
  [the wine] now, and let us
  drink!" [Ps 22:12; Ezek 39:18]
2The Lord GOD has sworn [an oath]
  by His holiness
That, "Behold, the days are coming
  upon you
When they shall take you away
  with meat hooks,
And the last of you with fish
  hooks. [Ps 89:35]
3"And you shall go out through the
  breaches [made in the city wall],
Every woman straight before her
  [unable to turn aside],
And you shall be cast to Harmon,"
Says the LORD.

4"Come to Bethel [where the golden
  calf is] and transgress;
In Gilgal [where idols are
  worshiped] multiply
  transgression;
Bring your sacrifices every
  morning,
Your tithes every three days!
5"Offer [by burning] a sacrifice of
  thanksgiving of that which is
  leavened,
And [boastfully] proclaim freewill
  offerings, announce them.
For this you so love to do, O
  children of Israel!"
Says the Lord GOD.

6"I also gave you cleanness of teeth
  [because of the famine] in all
  your cities
And lack of bread in all your places,
Yet you have not returned to Me
  [in repentance]," says the LORD.
7"Furthermore, I withheld the rain
  from you
When there were still three months
  until the harvest.
Then I would send rain on one city,
And on another city I would not
  send rain;
One piece of ground was rained on,
While the part not rained on
  would dry up.
8"So [the people of] two or three
  cities would stagger into one city
  to drink water,
But would not be satisfied;
Yet you have not returned to Me
  [in repentance]," says the LORD.
9"I wounded you with blight [from
  the hot, blasting east wind] and
  with mildew;
And the caterpillar devoured
Your many gardens and vineyards,
  your fig trees and your olive
  trees;
Yet you have not returned to Me
  [in repentance]," says the LORD.
10"I sent a plague among you like
  [those of] Egypt;
I killed your young men with the
  sword and I captured your horses,
I made the stench of your camp
  rise up into your nostrils;
Yet you have not returned to Me
  [in repentance]," says the LORD.
  [2 Kin 8:12; 13:3, 7]
11"I overthrew and destroyed
  [some among] you, as [I, your]
  God overthrew Sodom and
  Gomorrah,
And you were [rescued] like a log
  pulled out of the flame;
Yet you have not returned to Me
  [in repentance]," says the LORD.
  [Gen 19:24, 25; Is 13:19; Jer 49:18]

12 "Therefore this is what I shall do
   to you, O Israel;
Because I will do this to you,
Prepare to meet your God [in
   judgment], O Israel!"
13 For behold, He who forms the
   mountains and creates the wind
And declares to man what are His
   thoughts,
He who makes the dawn into
   darkness
And treads on the heights of the
   earth—
The Lord God of hosts is His name.
   [Ps 139:2; Dan 2:28]

5 HEAR THIS word which I take
   up for you as a funeral song, O
   house of Israel:

2 She has fallen, she will not rise
   again—
The virgin Israel.
She lies neglected on her land;
There is no one to raise her up.
3 For thus says the Lord God,
"The city which goes forth a
   thousand *strong*
Will have a hundred left,
And the one which goes forth a
   hundred *strong*
Will have ten left to the house of
   Israel."

4 For thus says the Lord to the house
of Israel,

"Seek Me [search diligently for Me
   and regard Me as more essential
   than food] so that you may live.
   [2 Chr 15:2; Jer 29:13]
5 "But do not resort to Bethel [to
   worship the golden calf]
Nor enter [idolatrous] Gilgal,

Nor cross over to Beersheba [and
   its idols];
For Gilgal will certainly go into
   captivity *and* exile,
And Bethel will come to nothing.
6 "Seek the Lord [search diligently
   for Him and long for Him as your
   most essential need] so that you
   may live,
Or He will rush down like a
   [devouring] fire, O house of
   Joseph,
And there will be no one to quench
   the flame for [idolatrous] Bethel,
7 "For those [shall be consumed]
   who turn justice into wormwood
   (bitterness)
And cast righteousness down to
   the earth."

8 He who made the [cluster of
   stars called] Pleiades and [the
   constellation] Orion,
Who turns deep darkness into the
   morning
And darkens the day into night,
Who calls for the waters of the sea
And pours them out on the surface
   of the earth,
The Lord is His name.
9 It is He who causes [sudden]
   destruction to flash forth on the
   strong
So that destruction comes on the
   fortress.

10 They hate the one who reprimands
   [the unrighteous] in the [court
   held at the city] gate [regarding
   him as unreasonable and
   rejecting his reprimand],
And they detest him who speaks
   [the truth] with integrity *and*
   honesty.

speak the Word

*God, I know that as I seek You, search diligently for You, and regard
You as more essential than food, I will live.*
—adapted from Amos 5:4

11 Therefore, because you impose
   heavy rent on the poor
And demand a tribute (food-tax) of
   grain from them,
Though you have built [luxurious]
   houses of square stone,
You will not live in them;
You have planted beautiful
   vineyards, but you will not drink
   their wine.
12 For I know your transgressions
   are many and your sins are great
   (shocking, innumerable),
You who distress the righteous and
   take bribes,
And turn away from the poor
   in the [court of the city] gate
   [depriving them of justice].

13 Therefore, he who is prudent *and*
   has insight will keep silent at such
   a [corrupt and evil] time, for it is
   an evil time [when people will not
   listen to truth and will disregard
   those of good character].

14 Seek (long for, require) good and
   not evil, that you may live;
And so may the LORD God of hosts
   be with you,
Just as you have said!
15 Hate evil and love good,
And establish justice in the [court
   of the city] gate.
Perhaps the LORD God of hosts
Will be gracious to the remnant
   of Joseph [that is, those who
   remain after God's judgment].

a healthy kind of anger

Amos 5:15 tells us to hate what is evil and love what is good. Since the devil is
the source of all evil, being angry with him and the devastation he causes can be
healthy—if that anger is expressed in a biblical manner. In Ephesians 6:12 we are
told that we war "against the world forces of this [present] darkness, against the
spirit forces of wickedness in the heavenly (supernatural) places." So we see that
our war is definitely not against God or against people, but against the enemy of
our souls. How can anger at the devil be effectively expressed? Let me give you an
example from my own life.

For many years, I was angry with Satan because of the fifteen years of child abuse I
had endured, but I was venting my anger the wrong way. I became hard-hearted and
harsh in dealing with others. I have since learned that we defeat and overcome evil
with good (see Romans 12:21).

I was angry at the devil because he had stolen my childhood from me, but being bitter and resentful was not repaying him for my loss. Now I am preaching the gospel,
helping people who are hurting, and seeing countless lives restored. As I do these
things I am overcoming the evil Satan did to me by being good to others through
bringing the good news of God to them. This is the way to get back at the devil!

When you have been hurt, you will be better off if you help someone else. Reaching
out to other hurting people helps you forget about your own pain.

The only way to repay the devil for hurt and devastation in your personal life is to
aggressively and vehemently do the work of Jesus. Hate evil, and be angry at the
devil, who causes it; just express that anger in a godly, productive way.

[16]Therefore, thus says the Lord God of hosts, the Lord,

"There is wailing in all the public plazas,
And in all the streets they say, 'Alas! Alas!'
And they call the farmers to mourning [for those who have died]
And professional mourners to wailing.
[17]"And in all vineyards *there is* wailing,
For I will pass through your midst [in judgment]," says the Lord. [Ex 12:12]
[18]Woe (judgment is coming) to you who desire the day of the Lord [expecting rescue from the Gentiles]!
Why would you want the day of the Lord?
It is darkness (judgment) and not light [and rescue and prosperity];
[19]It is as if a man runs from a lion [escaping one danger]
And a bear meets him [so he dies anyway],
Or goes home, and leans with his hand against the wall
And a snake bites him.
[20]Will not the day of the Lord be darkness, instead of light,
Even very dark with no brightness in it?

[21]"I hate, I despise *and* reject your [sacred] feasts,
And I do not take delight in your solemn assemblies.

[22]"Even though you offer Me your burnt offerings and your grain offerings,
I will not accept them;
And I will not even look at the peace offerings of your fattened animals.
[23]"Take the noise of your songs away from Me [they are an irritation]!
I shall not even listen to the melody of your harps.
[24]"But let justice run down like waters
And righteousness like an ever-flowing stream [flowing abundantly].

[25]"Did you bring Me sacrifices and grain offerings during those forty years in the wilderness, O house of Israel? [Certainly not!]
[26]"You carried along your king Sikkuth and Kayyun [your man-made gods of Saturn], your images of your star-god which you made for yourselves [but you brought Me none of the appointed sacrifices].
[27]"Therefore, I will send you to go into exile far beyond Damascus," says the Lord, whose name is the God of hosts. [Acts 7:42, 43]

6 WOE (JUDGMENT is coming) to those who are at ease *and* carefree in Zion (Judah)
And to those on the mountain of Samaria who feel secure,
The distinguished men of the foremost of nations,
To whom the house of Israel comes. [Luke 6:24, 25]
[2]Go over to Calneh [in Babylonia] and look,

speak the Word

God, I pray that as Your Word says, justice will run down like waters, and righteousness like an ever-flowing stream.
—ADAPTED FROM AMOS 5:24

And from there go [north of
　Damascus] to the great city of
　Hamath;
Then go down to Gath of the
　Philistines.
Are they better than these
　kingdoms [of yours],
Or is their territory greater than
　yours?
³Do you put off the day of
　punishment,
Yet cause the seat of violence to
　come near?

⁴Those who lie on [luxurious] beds
　of ivory
And lounge around out on their
　couches,
And eat lambs from the flock
And calves from the midst of the
　stall,
⁵Who improvise to the sound of the
　harp—
Like David they have composed
　songs for themselves— [1 Chr
　23:5]
⁶Who drink wine from sacrificial
　bowls
And anoint themselves with the
　finest oils [reflecting their
　unrestrained celebration];
Yet they are not grieved over the
　ruin of Joseph (Israel). [Gen
　49:22, 23]
⁷Therefore, they will now go
　into exile with the first of the
　captives,
And the cultic revelry *and*
　banqueting of those who lounge
　around [on their luxurious
　couches] will pass away.

⁸The Lord GOD has sworn [an oath]
　by Himself—the LORD God of
　hosts, says:
"I loathe *and* reject the [self-
　centered] arrogance of Jacob
　(Israel),
And I hate his palaces *and* citadels;

life point

Amos 6:8 tells us that God hates arrogance and pride (per AMPC). Pride is a hideous monster that prevents us from asking for help. We want to be self-sufficient and independent. However, God created us in such a way that although we do have strengths, we also have weaknesses and will always need help. He knows how much we need Him, and He wants us to recognize our need for Him. When we are proud, we do not acknowledge our need for Him, and that keeps Him from blessing us. This is one reason God hates pride.

Therefore, I shall hand over the
　[idolatrous] city [of Samaria]
　with all that it contains [to the
　Assyrian invaders]."

⁹And it shall come to pass that if there remain ten men in one house, they shall die [by the pestilence that comes with war].
¹⁰Then one's uncle, or his undertaker, shall come to bring the [disease-infected] body out of the house, [to cremate it], and he will say to another in the farthest part of the house, "Is there anyone else with you?" And that one will say, "No one." Then he will respond, "Hush! Keep quiet! For the name of the LORD is not to be mentioned [even casually, for fear that we might invoke even more punishment]." [1 Sam 31:12]
¹¹For behold, the LORD is going to command that the great house be smashed to pieces and the small house to fragments.

¹²Do horses run on rocks?
Do men plow rocks with oxen? [Of
　course not!]
Yet you have turned justice into
　poison
And the fruit of righteousness into
　wormwood (bitterness),

¹³ You who [self-confidently] rejoice
     in Lo-debar (Nothing),
Who say, "Have we not by our
     own strength taken Karnaim
     (Strength) for ourselves?"
¹⁴ "For behold, I am going to stir up a
     nation against you,
O house of Israel," says the LORD,
     the God of hosts,
"And they will afflict *and* torment
     you [to the entire limits of Israel]
     from the entrance of Hamath [in
     the north]
To the brook of the Arabah [in the
     south]."

7 THUS THE Lord GOD showed me
[a vision], and behold, He was
forming a swarm of locusts when
the spring crop began to sprout. And
behold, the spring crop was after the
king's mowing.
     ²And when the locusts had finished
eating the plants of the land, then I said,

"O Lord GOD, please forgive!
How can Jacob stand,
For he is so small [that he cannot
     endure this]?"
³ The LORD revoked this sentence.
"It shall not take place," said the
     LORD.

     ⁴Thus the Lord GOD showed me, and
behold, the Lord GOD called for punishment with fire, and it devoured the

putting the Word to work

A plumb line provides a true measure
for a vertical line or for depth. Amos
is telling the Israelites that God is
going to measure them by His standard (see Amos 7:7–9). How do you
measure your life? I encourage you
to spend time in God's Word so you
can learn about His standards and His
promises for your life.

great deep [underground sources of
water] and began to consume the land.
     ⁵Then I said,

"O Lord GOD, please stop!
How can Jacob stand,
For he is so small [that he cannot
     endure this]?"
⁶ The LORD revoked this sentence.
"This also shall not be," said the
     Lord GOD.

     ⁷Thus He showed me [a vision],
and behold, the Lord was standing
by a vertical wall with a plumb line
in His hand [to determine if the wall
was straight or if it needed to be de-
stroyed]. [2 Kin 21:13; Is 34:11]
     ⁸The LORD said to me, "Amos, what
do you see?" And I said, "A plumb
line." Then the Lord said,

"Behold, I am setting a plumb line
     [as a standard]
Among My people Israel [showing
     the defectiveness of the nation,
     requiring judgment].
I shall not spare them any longer.
     [The door of mercy is shut.]
⁹ "And the [idolatrous] high
     places of Isaac (Israel) will be
     devastated *and* deserted,
And the sanctuaries of Israel will
     be in ruins.
Then I shall rise up against the
     house of Jeroboam with the sword
     [and destroy the monarchy]."

     ¹⁰Then Amaziah, the priest of Bethel
[site of the golden calf shrine], sent
word to Jeroboam king of Israel, saying, "Amos has conspired against you
in the midst of the house of Israel; the
land is unable to endure all his words.
[1 Kin 12:31, 32]
     ¹¹"For in this way Amos has said,
'Jeroboam will die by the sword and
Israel will certainly go from its land
into exile.'"
     ¹²Then Amaziah said to Amos, "Go,
you seer, run for your life [from Is-
rael] to the land of Judah [your own

country] and eat bread and live as a prophet there!

¹³"But do not prophesy any longer at Bethel, for it is the king's sanctuary and a royal residence." [Luke 10:10–12]

¹⁴Then Amos replied to Amaziah, "I am not a prophet [by profession], nor am I a prophet's son; I am a herdsman and a grower of sycamore figs.

¹⁵"But the LORD took me as I followed the flock and the LORD said to me, 'Go, prophesy to My people Israel.'

¹⁶"Now therefore, listen to the word of the LORD: You say, 'You shall not prophesy against Israel nor shall you speak against the house of Isaac.'

¹⁷"Therefore, thus says the LORD, 'Your wife shall become a prostitute in the city [when the Assyrians capture Samaria] and your sons and your daughters shall fall by the sword, and your land shall be divided by a measuring line; you yourself shall die in an unclean *and* defiled [pagan] land, and Israel shall certainly go from its land into exile.'"

8 THUS THE Lord GOD showed me [a vision], and behold, *there was* a basket of [overripe] summer fruit.

²And He said, "Amos, what do you see?" And I said, "A basket of summer fruit." Then the LORD said to me, "The end has come for My people Israel. I will spare them no longer [for the nation is ripe for judgment].

³"In that day, the songs of the palace shall turn to wailing," says the Lord GOD. "There will be many dead bodies; in [sacred] silence they will throw them everywhere."

⁴Hear this, you who trample down the needy, and do away with the poor of the land,

⁵saying,

"When will the New Moon
  [festival] be over
So that we may sell grain,

putting the Word to work

Do you ever feel you are not important enough to do great things for God? Imagine Amos's surprise when God told him, a shepherd with no "prophetic qualifications," to prophesy to Israel (see Amos 7:14, 15)! Ask God to show you what He would like you to do, and, like Amos, be confident that as you are obedient to God's call, He will equip you to do it.

And the Sabbath ended so that we
  may open the wheat *market,*
Making the ephah [measure]
  smaller and the shekel bigger [that
  is, selling less for a higher price]
And to cheat by falsifying the
  scales,
⁶So that we may buy the poor [as
  slaves] for silver [since they are
  unable to support themselves]
And the needy for a pair of
  sandals,
And that we may sell the leftovers
  of the wheat [as if it were a good
  grade of grain]?"

⁷The LORD has sworn [an oath] by
  the pride of Jacob,
"Surely I shall never forget [nor
  leave unpunished] any of their
  [rebellious] acts.
⁸"Because of this [coming judgment]
  will the land not quake
And everyone mourn who dwells
  in it?
Indeed, all of it shall rise up like
  the Nile,
And it will be tossed around [from
  the impact of judgment]
And [afterward] subside again like
  the Nile of Egypt.
⁹"It shall come about in that day,"
  says the Lord GOD,
"That I shall cause the sun to go
  down at noon,

And I shall darken the earth in
broad daylight. [Ezek 32:7–10]
10 "And I shall turn your festivals *and*
feasts into mourning
And all your songs into dirges
(funeral poems to be sung);
And I shall cause sackcloth to be
put on everyone's loins
And baldness on every head
[shaved for mourning].
And I shall make that time like *a
time of* mourning for an only son
[who has died],
And the end of it shall be like a
bitter day.
11 "Behold, the days are coming,"
says the Lord GOD,
"When I will send hunger over the
land,
Not hunger for bread or a thirst for
water,
But rather [a hunger] for hearing
the words of the LORD.
12 "People shall stagger from sea to
sea [to the very ends of the earth]
And from the north even to the east;
They will roam here and there
to seek the word of the LORD
[longing for it as essential for life],
But they will not find it.
13 "In that day the beautiful virgins
And [even the vigorous] young
men shall faint from thirst.
14 "Those who swear [their oaths]
by the sin (guilt) of Samaria *or*
Ashimah (a pagan goddess),
Who say, 'By the life of your god
[the golden calf], O Dan!'
And [swear], 'By the life of the
way of [idolatrous] Beersheba,'
They shall fall and not rise again."

9 I SAW [in a vision] the Lord
standing at the altar, and He said,

"Destroy the capitals (tops) of the
pillars so that the thresholds will
shake,

And break them on the heads of all
of the people!
Then I will kill the rest of them
with the sword;
They will not have a fugitive who
will get away,
Or a survivor who will escape.
2 "Though they dig into Sheol [to
hide in the deepest pit],
From there My hand will take
them [for judgment];
And though they climb up to
heaven [to hide in the realm of
light],
From there will I bring them down
[for judgment].
3 "Though they hide on the summit
of [Mount] Carmel,
I will track them down and take
them from there;
And though they hide from My
sight on the floor of the sea,
From there I shall command the
serpent and it will bite them.
4 "And though they go into captivity
before their enemies,
From there I shall command the
sword to kill them,
And I will set My eyes against
them for evil (judgment,
punishment) and not for good
[that is, not for correction
leading to restoration]."

5 The Lord GOD of hosts [the
Omnipotent Ruler],
It is He who touches the earth [in
judgment] and it melts,
And all who dwell on it mourn [in
despair and fear],
And all of it rises up like the Nile
And subsides like the Nile of Egypt;
6 It is He who builds His upper
chambers in the heavens
And has established His vaulted
dome (the firmament of heaven)
over the earth,
He who calls to the waters of the sea
And pours them out on the face of
the earth—

The LORD is His name.

7 "Are you [degenerate ones] not as the [despised] sons of Ethiopia to Me,
O sons of Israel?" says the LORD.
"Have I not brought up Israel from the land of Egypt,
And the Philistines from Caphtor and the Arameans (Syrians) from Kir?
8 "Behold, the eyes of the Lord GOD are on the sinful [northern] kingdom [of Israel's ten tribes]
And I shall destroy it from the face of the earth;
But I shall not totally destroy the house of Jacob [that is, the entire nation of Israel],"
Says the LORD.
9 "For behold, I am commanding,
And I shall shake *and* sift the house of Israel among all nations [and cause it to tremble]
Like *grain* is shaken in a sieve [removing the chaff],
But not a kernel [of the faithful remnant] shall fall to the ground *and* be lost [from My sight]. [Lev 26:33; Deut 28:64; Hos 9:17]
10 "All the sinners among My people will die by the sword,
Those who say [defiantly], 'The disaster will not overtake or confront us.'

11 "In that day I shall raise up *and* restore the fallen tabernacle (booth) of David,
And wall up its breaches [in the city walls];

I will also raise up *and* restore its ruins
And rebuild it as it was in the days of old,
12 That they may possess the remnant of Edom (ancient enemies)
And all the nations that are called by My name,"
Says the LORD who does this. [Acts 15:15–17]

13 "Behold, the days are coming," says the LORD,
"When the plowman shall overtake the one who gathers the harvest,
And the one who treads the grapes [shall overtake] him who sows the seed [for the harvest continues until planting time];
When the mountains will drip sweet wine
And all the hills shall melt [that is, everything that was once barren will overflow with streams of blessing]. [Lev 26:5; Joel 3:18]
14 "Also I shall bring back the exiles of My people Israel,
And they will rebuild the deserted *and* ruined cities and inhabit them;
They will also plant vineyards and drink their wine,
And make gardens and eat their fruit.
15 "I will also plant them on their land,
And they shall never again be uprooted from their land
Which I have given them,"
Says the LORD your God.

Obadiah

Author:
Obadiah

Date:
Between the ninth century and the fourth century BC

Everyday Life Principles:
The pride of our hearts does deceive us.

Pride will cause us to mistreat other people.

Judgment comes as a result of mistreating others.

Obadiah is the shortest book in the Old Testament, but it conveys a powerful message that is as valid today as it was when the prophet Obadiah, whose name means "servant of the Lord," wrote it centuries ago. Obadiah prophesied God's judgment against the kingdom of Edom, which was formed by the descendants of Esau. The Edomites were strong people who were enemies of God's people Israel, just as their founder, Esau, had been opposed to his brother, the Israelite patriarch Jacob. The rivalry between the two brothers extended to their descendants, and the Edomites seemed to take great pleasure in invading and plundering Jerusalem.

Simply put, the Edomites had a problem with pride, just as many nations and individuals do today. Obadiah declared God's warning of destruction to Edom, saying, "Behold [Edom], I shall [humiliate you and] make you small among the nations; you are greatly despised. The pride and arrogance of your heart have deceived you" (Obadiah 2, 3).

In the end, the Edomites' pride did lead to their destruction. God did execute His judgment against them, and these people are never mentioned in Scripture again after the fall of Jerusalem in AD 70.

I hope the message of Obadiah will remind us that pride is deadly. God wants us to live before Him and before others with a humble, tender heart. Pride, whether it is in a nation or in an individual, will not escape God's judgment, but humility brings His blessing and favor.

¹THE VISION of Obadiah.

Thus says the Lord GOD
concerning Edom—
We have heard a report from the
LORD,
And an ambassador has been sent
among the nations, *saying,*
"Arise, and let us rise up against
Edom for battle [with the LORD
as commander]!" [Ps 137:7; Is
34:1–15; 63:1–6; Jer 49:7–22; Ezek
25:12–14]
²"Behold [Edom], I shall [humiliate
you and] make you small among
the nations;
You are greatly despised. [Ezek 35]
³"The pride *and* arrogance of your
heart have deceived you,
You who live in the clefts *and* lofty
security of the rock (Sela),
Whose dwelling place is high,
Who say [boastfully] in your heart,
'Who will bring me down to
earth?'
⁴"Though you build [your nest] on
high like the eagle,
Though you set your nest among the
stars,
I will bring you down from there,"
says the LORD.
⁵"If thieves came to you,
If robbers by night—
How you will be ruined!—
Would they not steal only until
they had enough?
If grape gatherers came to you,
Would they not leave some grapes
for gleaning? [Jer 49:9]
⁶"How Esau (Edom) shall be
ransacked [by men who come to
ravage with divine approval]!
How his hidden treasures shall be
searched out!
⁷"All the men allied with you
Shall send you on your way to the
border;
The men who were at peace with
you

life point

The pride spoken of in Obadiah 3 says,
"Who will bring me down to earth?" This
kind of pride says, "I am better than you; I
am smarter than you. My opinion matters;
yours does not. Everything I do is better."

Did you know that "me, myself, and I" are
the greatest problems we have? We spend
our time and energy admiring ourselves
and simply being full of ourselves, when in
reality we are supposed to be full of God
and empty of ourselves—totally empty.

God can use only humble men and women.
I have heard it said that it is yet to be
seen what God can do through a man or a
woman who will give Him all the glory.

Pride and love do not mix. Love is not
proud and haughty. It is not boastful or
vainglorious. It is not puffed up. Love
does not look down on others; it does
not see others as little and insignificant.
Because love values every individual,
everyone who comes in contact with a
person full of love will be inspired to feel
special, valuable, and encouraged.

Do you want God to use you? Ask Him to
deal with your pride and give you love for
people. Look to your example, Jesus, Who
humbled Himself and gave Himself for you.

Shall deceive you and overpower
you;
Those who eat your bread [those
you trust]
Shall set a hostile ambush for you.
(There is no understanding of it.)
⁸"Will I not on that day," says the
LORD,
"Destroy the wise men from Edom
[removing all wisdom]
And understanding from the
mountain of Esau?

9"And your mighty men shall be
    dismayed *and* demoralized,
    O Teman,
So that everyone from the
    mountain of Esau may be cut off
    in the slaughter.
10"Because of the violence you did
    against your brother Jacob,
Shame shall cover you
    [completely],
And you shall be cut off forever.
11"On the day that [Jerusalem was
    destroyed] you stood aloof [from
    your brother Jacob]—

On the day that strangers took his
    forces captive *and* carried off his
    wealth,
And foreigners entered his gates
And cast lots for Jerusalem
    [dividing the city for plunder]—
You too were like one of them
    [collaborating with the enemy].
    [Num 20:18–20; Amos 1:11, 12]
12"Do not gaze *and* gloat [in triumph]
    over your brother's day,
The day when his misfortune came.
Do not rejoice over the sons of
    Judah
In the day of their destruction;
Do not speak arrogantly [jeering
    and maliciously mocking]
In the day of their distress.
13"Do not enter the gate of My people
In the day of their disaster;
Yes, you, do not look [with delight]
    on their misery
In the day of their ruin,
And do not loot treasures
In the day of their ruin.
14"Do not stand at the crossroad

putting the Word to work

Have you ever been tempted to be
glad about someone else's hardship?
Clearly this is displeasing to God.
When people around you are facing
adversity, extend the same mercy and
compassion to them that God extends
to you.

who, me?

Pride is a difficult problem for us to deal with because it hides. As Obadiah 3 says, it deceives us and causes us to think we do not have it. It hides in our thinking, in the deepest recesses of our minds. It will not admit that it is present because it is too proud to do so!

For years, Joyce Meyer Ministries has had teaching resources available on the subject of pride. They were not our best sellers! I believe that is because those people who need them are too proud to admit it and begin getting the help they need. After all, someone might see them or hear about it and wonder if they have a problem with pride!

Luke 18:9–14 describes someone who was full of pride, and I doubt he even realized it. He was a religious leader who looked down on a tax collector he considered to be lowly and unworthy of God. If we are not careful, the spirit of pride can deceive us that same way.

Satan wants our minds and attitudes to be filled with pride so he can bring destruction into our lives. Ask God to show you anywhere pride may be hiding in your life and also to help you develop the humble attitude He wants you to have.

To cut down those [of Judah] who
   escaped;
And do not hand over [to the
   enemy] those [of Judah] who
   survive
In the day of their distress.

15 "For the [judgment] day of the
   LORD draws near on all the
   nations.
As you have done, it shall be done
   to you [in retribution];
Your [evil] dealings will return on
   your own head. [Ps 137:7–9; Is
   2:10–22; Zeph 3:8–20; Zech 12:1–
   14; Rev 19:11–21]
16 "Because just as you [Edom]
   drank on My holy mountain
   [desecrating it in the revelry of
   the destroyers],
So shall all the nations drink
   continually [one by one, of My
   wrath];
Yes, they shall drink and swallow
   [the full measure of punishment]
And become as though they had
   never existed. [Rev 16:14–16]
17 "But on Mount Zion [in Jerusalem]
   there shall be [deliverance for]
   those who escape,
And it shall be holy [no pagan will
   defile it];
And the house of Jacob shall
   possess their [former]
   possessions. [Ezek 36; Joel 2:32]
18 "Then the house of Jacob shall be a
   fire
And the house of Joseph a flame
   [in executing God's wrath];

life point

In Obadiah 17, God expresses through the
prophet His desire for His people to be
holy—and that comes by the Holy Spirit.
The Holy Spirit is in the conviction business. He is the Agent of sanctification. He
works out the process of holiness in us.
Ask Him to help you with that today.

putting the Word to work

Most of us struggle with loss and
brokenness in our lives. Has your
enemy the devil robbed you of joy?
Has he turned your peace into doubt
or insecurity? Do you know that God
wants to bring healing and restoration
to you? Ask God to come into those
broken places in your life, and trust
Him in His perfect ways and timing to
bring wholeness again.

But the house of Esau will be like
   stubble.
They (Jacob) shall set them on
   fire and consume them (the
   Edomites),
So that there shall be no survivor
   of the house of Esau,"
For the LORD has spoken. [Ezek
   25:12–14]
19 Then those of the Negev shall
   possess the mountain of Esau,
And those of the Shephelah [shall
   possess] the Philistine plain;
Also, [they shall] possess the fields
   of Ephraim and the fields of
   Samaria,
And Benjamin will possess Gilead
   [across the Jordan River]. [Amos
   9:12; Zeph 2:7]
20 And the exiles of this host of the
   sons (descendants) of Israel
Who are among the Canaanites as
   far as Zarephath,
And the exiles of Jerusalem who
   are in Sepharad
Shall possess the cities of the
   Negev.
21 The deliverers shall go up on
   Mount Zion
To rule and judge the mountain of
   Esau,
And the kingdom and the kingship
   shall be the LORD's. [Zech 12:8, 9;
   Mal 1:2–5; Matt 24:27–30; Luke
   1:31–33; Acts 15:14–17]

Jonah

Author:
Jonah or an unnamed narrator

Date:
About 760 BC or after 612 BC

Everyday Life Principles:
Whatever God sends you to do, do it without delay.

Remember that you cannot successfully run from God or from His call.

God loves everyone and desires to be merciful and compassionate to every person, city, and nation on earth.

The message of the book of Jonah centers on obedience. God specifically called the prophet Jonah to go and call the people of Nineveh to repentance and announce that God's mercy would follow their repentance. The problem was that Jonah was a devout patriot of Israel, and Nineveh belonged to the Assyrians, who were dreaded and despised enemies of Israel. Jonah was bullish on Israel and did not want to tell the Ninevites that God wanted to be compassionate and merciful to them, so he tried to run away.

You will read in the book of Jonah that the prophet had to endure all kinds of unpleasant circumstances and hardships as a result of his disobedience. In the end, he finally obeyed God and went to Nineveh. The Ninevites did repent, and God was merciful to them, proving to Jonah that God loves everyone, not just particular races or nationalities.

Let the story of Jonah remind you that God requires obedience. He can wait patiently for us to do as He asks, but we are wise to respond promptly. We can try to run away, but in the end we must obey, or we will be miserable. When God calls us to do something, He is serious. We may not want to do it, but no matter how we resist, He will not change His mind. When He calls you, be quick to obey.

1 NOW THE word of the LORD came to Jonah the son of Amittai, saying,

²"Go to Nineveh, that great city, and proclaim [judgment] against it, for their wickedness has come up before Me." [Gen 10:11, 12]

³But Jonah ran away to Tarshish to escape from the presence of the LORD [and his duty as His prophet]. He went down to Joppa and found a ship going to Tarshish [the most remote of the Phoenician trading cities]. So he paid the fare and went down into the ship to go with them to Tarshish away from the presence of the LORD. [Gen 4:16; Job 1:12; 2:7]

⁴But the LORD hurled a great wind toward the sea, and there was a violent tempest on the sea so that the ship was about to break up. [Ps 107:23–27]

⁵Then the sailors were afraid, and each man cried out to his god; and to lighten the ship [and diminish the danger] they threw the ship's cargo into the sea. But Jonah had gone below into the hold of the ship and had lain down and was sound asleep.

⁶So the captain came up to him and said, "How can you stay asleep? Get up! Call on your god! Perhaps your god will give a thought to us so that we will not perish."

⁷And they said to another, "Come, let us cast lots, so we may learn who is to

life point

In Jonah 1:1–3 we read that God told Jonah to go to Nineveh and preach repentance to the people there. But Jonah did not want to go, so he ran away to Tarshish, a city in the opposite direction from Nineveh. Running from God does not help us to be at peace with Him. If God gives you an assignment, embrace it. If you do not want to do it or if you find it exceedingly difficult, ask Him to help you have the right attitude about it and give you strength to fulfill it.

putting the Word to work

Have you ever been tempted to think that disobeying God will not affect anyone but you? Jonah's story paints a very different picture (see Jonah 1:10–15)! By not obeying God, he put the lives of others in jeopardy. In contrast, his obedience was a blessing to a whole city! When you are tempted to disobey God, remember that you, and others as well, will face consequences. Ask God to help you to obey Him, so that you, like Jonah, can be a blessing to many.

blame for this disaster." So they cast lots and the lot fell on Jonah.

⁸Then they said to him, "Now tell us! Who is to blame for this disaster? What is your occupation? Where do you come from? What is your country?"

⁹So he said to them, "I am a Hebrew, and I [reverently] fear *and* worship the LORD, the God of heaven, who made the sea and the dry land."

¹⁰Then the men became extremely frightened and said to him, "How could you do this?" For the men knew that he was running from the presence of the LORD, because he had told them.

¹¹Then they said to him, "What should we do to you, so that the sea will become calm for us?"—for the sea was becoming more and more violent.

¹²Jonah said to them, "Pick me up and throw me into the sea. Then the sea will become calm for you, for I know that it is because of me that this great storm *has come* upon you."

¹³Nevertheless, the men rowed hard [breaking through the waves] to return to land, but they could not, because the sea became even more violent [surging higher] against them.

¹⁴Then they called on the LORD and said, "Please, O LORD, do not let us perish because of taking this man's life,

and do not make us accountable for innocent blood; for You, O Lord, have done as You pleased."

¹⁵So they picked up Jonah and threw him into the sea, and the sea stopped its raging.

¹⁶Then the men greatly feared the Lord, and they offered a sacrifice to the Lord and made vows.

¹⁷Now the Lord had prepared (appointed, destined) a great fish to swallow Jonah. And Jonah was in the stomach of the fish three days and three nights. [Matt 12:40]

2 THEN JONAH prayed to the Lord his God from the stomach of the fish,
²and said,

"I called out of my trouble *and* distress to the Lord,
And He answered me;
Out of the belly of Sheol I cried for help,
And You heard my voice. [Ps 120:1; 130:1; 142:1; Lam 3:55–58]
³"For You cast me into the deep,
Into the [deep] heart of the seas,
And the currents surrounded *and* engulfed me;
All Your breakers and billowing waves passed over me. [Ps 42:7]
⁴"Then I said, 'I have been cast out of Your sight.
Nevertheless I will look again toward Your holy temple.' [Ps 31:22]
⁵"The waters surrounded me, to the point of death.

speak the Word

*Thank You, God, for hearing me in my trouble and distress.
I know You hear my voice, no matter where I am.*
–ADAPTED FROM JONAH 2:2

*God, You have brought up my life from the pit. When my soul
was fainting within me, I remembered You and You heard my prayer.*
–ADAPTED FROM JONAH 2:6, 7

putting the Word to work

Are you currently in unusual or difficult circumstances? No doubt Jonah felt that way in the belly of the whale, yet God was using those circumstances to get his attention. No matter how desperate or hopeless your situation, no matter how far away God seems, know that God hears your prayer and will help you.

The great deep engulfed me,
Seaweed was wrapped around my head. [Ps 69:1; Lam 3:54]
⁶"I descended to the [very] roots of the mountains.
The earth with its bars closed behind me [bolting me in] forever,
Yet You have brought up my life from the pit (death), O Lord my God.
⁷"When my soul was fainting within me,
I remembered the Lord,
And my prayer came to You,
Into Your holy temple.
⁸"Those who regard *and* follow worthless idols
Turn away from their [living source of] mercy *and* lovingkindness.
⁹"But [as for me], I will sacrifice to You
With the voice of thanksgiving;
I shall pay that which I have vowed.
Salvation is from the Lord!"

¹⁰So the Lord commanded the fish, and it vomited Jonah up onto the dry land.

3 NOW THE word of the LORD came to Jonah the second time, saying, ²"Go to Nineveh the great city and declare to it the message which I am going to tell you."

³So Jonah went to Nineveh in accordance with the word of the LORD. Now Nineveh was an exceedingly great city, a three days' walk [about sixty miles in circumference].

⁴Then on the first day's walk, Jonah began to go through the city, and he called out and said, "Forty days more [remain] and [then] Nineveh will be overthrown!"

putting the Word to work

Have you ever needed a second chance? God went to great lengths to give Jonah a second chance, and when Jonah availed himself of the opportunity God gave him, lives were changed for eternity (see Jonah 3:1–5). God is still the God of second chances today! Ask Him for yours, and then do everything you can do to be faithful to follow through on it.

never too late

What happens when we go in the opposite direction from where God has directed us? What happened to Jonah? Jonah chapter 1 tells us that when he boarded a ship and headed in his own direction, a storm arose. Many of the storms we face in life are the results of our own stubbornness, nothing else. We may try to blame them on other things and people, but the truth is that in many instances, we have been disobedient to the voice and leadership of God.

The violent storm that came upon Jonah frightened the men on the ship, and they knew they would all die if something did not change. They cast lots to see who was causing the trouble, and the lot fell on Jonah. They asked Jonah what he had done that made God so angry. He knew he had disobeyed God, so he told the men to throw him overboard in order to deliver them from danger. They did as he requested; the storm stopped, and a great fish swallowed Jonah. From the fish's belly (not a pleasant place), he cried out to God for deliverance and repented of his stubborn ways.

Even though Jonah was in a bad place—seaweed was wrapped around his head and the "abyss" surrounded him—he turned to the Lord.

Jonah did the right thing. He did not say to himself, "Well, I've really blown it now. I've disobeyed God so much that there is no turning back." Instead, Jonah turned to the Lord, praised Him, and expressed faith in His delivering power.

It is never too late for us to pray to God, even when we may have run in the opposite direction from Him. God is a God of mercy and grace. He heard Jonah's prayer and spoke to the fish to vomit him out on dry land. While this was not pleasant for Jonah, his life was spared. His story speaks to us that we can never stray so far from God that He cannot hear us. He will respond when we cry out to Him. We will be able to say, as Jonah: "I called out of my trouble and distress to the LORD, and He answered me" (Jonah 2:2).

⁵The people of Nineveh believed *and* trusted in God; and they proclaimed a fast and put on sackcloth [in penitent mourning], from the greatest even to the least of them.

⁶When word reached the king of Nineveh [of Jonah's message from God], he rose from his throne, took off his robe, covered himself with sackcloth and sat in the dust [in repentance].

⁷He issued a proclamation and it said, "In Nineveh, by the decree of the king and his nobles: No man, animal, herd, or flock is to taste anything. They are not to eat or drink water.

the God of the second chance

In Jonah 3:1, 2 we see that the word of the Lord came to Jonah a second time, and it was no different from the first time (see Jonah 1:2). God told him to go to Nineveh and preach to the people there. God gave Jonah a second chance.

No matter how long we avoid God's instruction, it is still there for us to deal with when we stop running. Eventually we see that being *in* God's will, not *out* of His will, is what brings us peace and joy. We have to surrender our own wills because walking in our self-centered ways keeps us unhappy.

Running from difficult things never works in the long-term. I know a woman who ran from everything that was difficult in her life. She ignored things she needed to deal with, including abuse in her home. She lived in fear and had a very miserable life. She ultimately carried so much turmoil she had a complete mental and emotional breakdown. Pretending her problems did not exist did not make them go away. They were there, pressuring her all the time. God was trying to lead her to deal with her conflicts, but she would not trust Him enough to do so.

God never leads us anywhere He cannot keep us. If God is leading you to deal with an unpleasant situation in your life, do not run from it. He promises to be with you at all times and never to leave you or forsake you.

Surrendering to God can be frightening when we first begin to practice it because we do not know what the outcome will be if we yield ourselves to God's will. However, once we have surrendered and begin to experience God's faithfulness and the peace that passes understanding (see Philippians 4:7), we learn quickly that God's way is better than any plan we could ever devise.

Not knowing exactly what will happen in the future, but trusting God to take care of us and enjoying peace is far better than erroneously thinking we have life all figured out while continuing to live in fear and anxiety. To enjoy peace with God, we must become comfortable with not always knowing what the future holds.

There is no such thing as trust without unanswered questions. If God is leading you to do something difficult, just begin to take baby steps of faith, and after each one He will show you what to do next. We do not have to have an entire blueprint for the future; we do not need to have all the answers. All we need is to know the One Who knows, and that is Jesus Himself.

putting the Word to work

When you share your faith with people, do you ever feel your words are falling on deaf ears? Ask God for what you are to say to people when you talk with them, and then pray that they will have hearts ready to respond to God as wholeheartedly as the Ninevites did (see Jonah 3:5–10).

⁸"But both man and animal must be covered with sackcloth; and every one is to call on God earnestly *and* forcefully that each may turn from his wicked way and from the violence that is in his hands.

⁹"Who knows, God may turn [in compassion] and relent and withdraw His burning anger (judgment) so that we will not perish." [Joel 2:13, 14]

¹⁰When God saw their deeds, that they turned from their wicked way, then God [had compassion and] relented concerning the disaster which He had declared that He would bring upon them. And He did not do it.

4 BUT IT greatly displeased Jonah and he became angry.

²He prayed to the LORD and said, "O LORD, is this not what I said when I was still in my country? That is why I ran to Tarshish, because I knew that You are a gracious and compassionate God, slow to anger and great in lovingkindness, and [when sinners turn to You] You revoke the [sentence of] disaster [against them]. [Ex 34:6]

³"Therefore now, O LORD, just take my life from me, for it is better for me to die than to live."

⁴Then the LORD said, "Do you have a good reason to be angry?"

⁵Then Jonah went out of the city and sat east of it. There he made himself a shelter and sat under its shade so that he could see what would happen in the city.

⁶So the LORD God prepared a plant and it grew up over Jonah, to be a shade over his head to spare him from discomfort. And Jonah was extremely happy about [the protection of] the plant.

⁷But God prepared a worm when morning dawned the next day, and it attacked the plant and it withered.

⁸When the sun came up God prepared a scorching east wind, and the sun beat down on Jonah's head so that he fainted and he wished to die, and said, "It is better for me to die than to live."

⁹Then God said to Jonah, "Do you have a good reason to be angry about [the loss of] the plant?" And he said, "I have a [very] good reason to be angry, angry enough to die!"

¹⁰Then the LORD said, "You had compassion on the plant for which you did not work and which you did not cause to grow, which came up overnight and perished overnight.

¹¹"Should I not have compassion on Nineveh, the great city in which there are more than 120,000 [innocent] persons, who do not know *the difference* between their right and left hand [and are not yet accountable for sin], as well as many [blameless] animals?"

life point

As Jonah noted in Jonah 4:2, one of God's awesome character traits is compassion. Compassion chooses to be kind and good to people who deserve to be punished. Always remember that God is a compassionate God and that, according to Lamentations 3:22, 23, His compassions are new every morning. We may deserve to be punished, but God has extended His compassion through Jesus Christ, and it never runs out!

Micah

Author:
Micah

Date:
Between 704 BC and 696 BC

Everyday Life Principles:
Leaders must practice what they preach.

God does not require strict adherence to rules and regulations; He requires us to practice justice, to be kind and merciful to others, and to live in humility.

Waiting on God is always worth it.

Micah, whose name means "who is like the Lord?" declares in his prophecy that God has no equal, especially when it comes to His compassion and faithfulness. Against that backdrop, Micah calls attention to the poor leadership that prevailed in his day among not only civic authorities, but also among priests and prophets. These leaders did not do as they commanded the people to do, and they failed to honor God as they carried out their responsibilities. Their disregard for God and lack of holiness demanded judgment, but Micah continually contrasts their sin with God's mercy.

Though God's mercy and the importance of good leadership are prevailing themes in Micah, this book also stresses holiness, not tolerating injustice, the importance of practicing what we preach, and the rewards of waiting on God. It also emphasizes God's promise of restoration, reminding us that there are no dead ends in God; there is always hope.

Perhaps the best-known verse in this book is Micah 6:8, which says: "He has told you, O man, what is good; and what does the LORD require of you except to be just, and to love [and to diligently practice] kindness (compassion), and to walk humbly with your God [setting aside any overblown sense of importance or self-righteousness]?"

I hope you will learn from the various lessons of the book of Micah. Above all, remember to act justly, to love kindness and compassion, and to walk humbly before God and others.

1 THE WORD of the Lord that came to Micah of Moresheth in the days of Jotham, Ahaz, and Hezekiah, kings of Judah, which he saw [through divine revelation] concerning Samaria and Jerusalem.

2 Hear, O peoples, all of you;
Listen closely, O earth and all that is in it,
And let the Lord God be witness [giving a testimony of the judgment] against you,
The Lord from His holy temple [in the heavens]. [1 Kin 22:28]
3 For behold, the Lord is coming down from His place
He shall come down and tread [in judgment] on the high places of the earth. [Zech 14:3, 4; Mal 4:2, 3; Matt 24:27–30; Rev 1:7; 19:11–16]
4 The mountains shall melt under Him
And the valleys shall be split
Like wax before the fire,
Like waters poured down a steep place.
5 All this is because of the rebellion and apostasy of Jacob
And for the sins of the house of Israel (the Northern Kingdom).
What is the rebellion and apostasy of Jacob?
Is it not [the abandonment of God in order to worship the idols of] Samaria?
What are the high places [of idolatry] in Judah (the Southern Kingdom)?
Are they not Jerusalem [the capital and center of corruption]?
6 Therefore I [the Lord] shall make Samaria a heap of ruins [and of stones and arable land] in the open country,
A place for planting vineyards;
And I will pour her stones down into the ravine
And lay bare her foundations.
[2 Kin 19:25; Ezek 13:14]

7 All her idols shall be broken in pieces,
All her earnings [from her idolatry] shall be burned with fire,
And all her images I shall make desolate;
For from the earnings of a prostitute she collected them,
And to the earnings of a prostitute they shall return.

8 Because of this I [Micah] must lament (mourn over with expressions of grief) and wail,
I must go barefoot and naked [without outer garments as if robbed];
I must wail like the jackals
And lament [with a loud, mournful cry] like the ostriches.
9 For Samaria's wound is incurable,
For it has come to Judah;
The enemy has reached the gate of my people,
Even to Jerusalem.
10 Announce it not in Gath [in Philistia],
Weep not at all [and in this way betray your grief to Gentiles];
In Beth-le-aphrah (House of Dust) roll in the dust [among your own people].
11 Go on your way [into exile— stripped of beauty, disarmed], inhabitants of Shaphir (Beautiful), in shameful nakedness.
The inhabitant of Zaanan (Go Out) does not go out [of the house];
The wailing of Beth-ezel (House of Removal) will take away from you its support.
12 For the inhabitant of Maroth (Bitterness)
Writhes in pain [at its losses] and waits anxiously for good,
Because a catastrophe has come down from the Lord
To the gate of Jerusalem.

13 Harness the chariot to the team of
   horses [to escape the invasion],
O inhabitant of Lachish—
She was the beginning of sin
To the Daughter of Zion
   (Jerusalem)—
Because in you were found
The rebellious acts of Israel.
14 Therefore you will give parting
   gifts
On behalf of Moresheth-gath
   (Micah's home);
The houses of Achzib (Place of
   Deceit) will become a deception
To the kings of Israel.
15 Moreover, I will bring on you
The one who takes possession,
O inhabitant of Mareshah
   (Prominent Place).
The glory (nobility) of Israel will
   enter Adullam [seeking refuge].
   [1 Sam 22:1]
16 Make yourself bald [in
   mourning]—shave off your hair
For the children of your delight;
Remain as bald as the eagle,
For your children will be taken
   from you into exile.

2 WOE (JUDGMENT is
   coming) to those who devise
   wickedness
And plot evil on their beds!
When morning comes, they
   practice evil
Because it is in the power of their
   hands.
2 They covet fields and seize them,
And houses, and take them away.
They oppress and rob a man and
   his house,
A man and his inheritance. [Is 5:8;
   Ex 20:17; Lev 25:23ff.]

3 Therefore, thus says the LORD,

"Behold, I am planning against
   this family a disaster (exile)
[Like a noose] from which you
   cannot remove your necks;

Nor will you be able to walk
   haughtily and erect,
For it will be an evil time [of
   subjugation to the invaders].
4 "On that day they shall take up
   a [taunting, deriding] parable
   against you
And wail with a doleful and bitter
   song of mourning and say,
'We are completely destroyed!
God exchanges the inheritance of
   my people;
How He removes it from me!
He divides our fields to the
   rebellious [our captors].'
5 "Therefore, you will have no one
   stretching a measuring line
   [dividing the common land]
For you by lot in the assembly of
   the LORD. [Rev 21:27]

6 'Do not speak out,' so they speak
   out.
But if they do not speak out
   concerning these things,
Reproaches will not be turned back.
7 "Is it being said, O house of Jacob:
'Is the Spirit of the LORD impatient?
Or are these [prophesied
   judgments] His doings?'
Do not My words do good
To the one walking uprightly?
8 "But lately My people have stood
   up as an enemy [and have made
   Me their antagonist].
You strip the ornaments off the
   garment
Of those unsuspecting passers-by,
Like those returned from war.
9 "You evict the women (widows) of
   My people,
Each one from her pleasant house;
From her [young, fatherless]
   children you take away My
   splendor and blessing forever [by
   putting them among the pagans,
   away from Me].
10 "Arise and depart [because the
   captivity is inevitable],

For this [land] is not the place of
   rest
Because of the defilement that
   brings destruction,
A painful *and* terrible destruction.
11 "If a man walking in a false spirit
   [spouting deception]
Should lie and say,
'I will prophesy to you [O Israel] of
   wine and liquor (greed, sensual
   pleasure),'
He would be the acceptable
   spokesman of this people.
   [Jer 5:31]

12 "I shall most certainly assemble all
   of you, O Jacob;
I shall surely gather the remnant
   of Israel.
I shall bring them together like
   sheep in the fold [multiplying
   the nation];
Like a flock in the midst of its
   pasture.
The place will swarm with many
   people *and* hum loudly with
   noise.
13 "The breaker [the Messiah, who
   opens the way] shall go up
   before them [liberating them].
They will break out, pass through
   the gate and go out;
So their King goes on before them,
The LORD at their head." [Ex 23:20,
   21; 33:14; Is 63:8, 9; Hos 3:5;
   Amos 9:11]

3 AND I said,
   "Hear now, heads of Jacob
   And rulers of the house of Israel.
Is it not for you to know *and*
   administer justice?
2 "You who hate good and love evil,
Who tear the skin off my people
And their flesh from their bones;
3 You who eat the flesh of my people,
Strip off their skin from them,
Break their bones
And chop them in pieces as for
   the pot,

life point

Micah 3:8 teaches us that we can be full
of power by the Holy Spirit. I believe any
common, ordinary, everyday person can
be mightily used by God. I believe we can
do great things, things that will totally
amaze us, if we believe God can use us
and if we are daring enough to have
uncommon goals and visions. By "uncommon," I mean things we could never do
without divine help. Our vision does not
always make sense to the mind, but it can
be solidly planted in our hearts.

Ephesians 3:20 teaches us that God is able
to "do superabundantly more than all that
we dare ask or think [infinitely beyond
our greatest prayers, hopes, or dreams],
according to His power that is at work
within us." God does it, but He does it
through us, so we need to cooperate with
Him. That means we need to be daring in
our faith and in our prayers.

Some of us do not believe for enough. We
need to stretch our faith into new realms.
We need to be people with uncommon
goals because we are full of power by the
Spirit of the Lord.

   Like meat in a kettle."
4 Then they will cry to the LORD,
But He will not answer them;
Instead, He will even hide His
   face from them at that time
   [withholding His mercy]
Because they have practiced *and*
   tolerated *and* ignored evil acts.
   [Is 1:15]

5 Thus says the LORD concerning the
[false] prophets who lead my people
astray;

   When they have *something good* to
   bite with their teeth,
   They call out, "Peace,"

But against the one who gives
  them nothing to eat,
They declare a holy war.
⁶Therefore *it will* be night (tragedy)
  for you—without vision,
And darkness (cataclysm) for
  you—without foresight.
The sun shall go down on the
  [false] prophets,
And the day shall become dark *and*
  black over them.
⁷The seers shall be ashamed
And the diviners discredited *and*
  embarrassed;
Indeed, they shall all cover their
  mouths [in shame]
Because there is no answer from
  God.
⁸But in fact, I am filled with power,
With the Spirit of the Lord,
And with justice and might,
To declare to Jacob his
  transgression
And to Israel his sin.
⁹Now hear this, you heads of the
  house of Jacob
And rulers of the house of Israel,
Who hate *and* reject justice
And twist everything that is
  straight,
¹⁰Who build Zion with blood [and
  extortion and murder]
And Jerusalem with violent
  injustice.
¹¹Her leaders pronounce judgment
  for a bribe,
Her priests teach for a fee,
And her prophets foretell for money;
Yet they lean on the Lord, saying,
"Is not the Lord among us?
No tragedy *or* distress will come
  on us." [Is 1:10–15]
¹²Therefore, on account of you
Zion shall be plowed like a field,
Jerusalem shall become a heap of
  ruins,
And the mountain of the house
  [of the Lord] *shall become* like a
  densely wooded hill. [Jer 26:17–19]

4 BUT IT shall come about in the
  last days
    That the mountain of the
  house of the Lord
Shall be established as the highest
  and chief of the mountains;
It shall be above the hills,
And peoples shall flow [like a
  river] to it.
²And many nations shall come and
  say,
"Come, let us go up to the
  mountain of the Lord,
To the house of the God of Jacob,
That He may teach us about His
  ways
And that we may walk in His paths."
For the law shall go forward from
  Zion,
And the word of the Lord [the
  revelation about Him and His
  truth] from Jerusalem.
³And He will judge between many
  peoples
And render decisions for strong
  and distant nations.
Then they shall hammer their
  swords into plowshares
And their spears into pruning
  hooks [so that the implements
  of war may become the tools of
  agriculture];
Nation shall not lift up sword
  against nation,
Nor shall they ever again train for
  war. [Is 2:2–4; Joel 3:10]

putting the Word to work

Do you sometimes dread watching the
news because of the overwhelming
amount of evil we see played out before us? Micah 4:1–4 reminds us that
a day is coming when the kingdom
of God will be fully established, and
injustice, violence, and war will cease.
Pray for the nations of the world as
you wait for this day.

4 Each of them shall sit [in security
   and peace] under his vine
And under his fig tree,
With no one to make them afraid,
For the mouth of the [omnipotent]
   Lord of hosts has spoken it.
   [Zech 3:10]
5 For all the peoples [now] walk
Each in the name of his god [in a
   transient relationship],
As for us, we shall walk [securely]
In the name of the Lord our [true]
   God forever and ever.

6 "In that day," says the Lord,
"I shall assemble the lame,
And gather the outcasts [from
   foreign captivity],
Even those whom I have caused
   pain.
7 "I shall make the lame a [godly]
   remnant
And the outcasts a strong nation;
And the Lord shall reign over
   them in Mount Zion
From this time on and forever.
8 "As for you [Jerusalem], tower of
   the flock [of Israel],
Hill and stronghold of the Daughter
   of Zion (Jerusalem's inhabitants),
To you the former dominion shall
   come,
The kingdom of the Daughter of
   Jerusalem [when the Messiah
   reigns in Jerusalem, and the
   times of the Gentiles are
   fulfilled]. [Luke 21:24]

9 "Now, why do you cry out loudly?
Is there no king among you?
Has your counselor perished?
For agony has gripped you like a
   woman in childbirth.
10 "Writhe in pain and labor to give
   birth,
O Daughter of Zion,
Like a woman in childbirth;
For now you shall go out of the city,
Live in the field,
And go to Babylon.

There you will be rescued;
There the Lord shall redeem you
From the hand of your enemies.
11 "Now many [conquering] nations
   are assembled against you,
Who say, 'Let her be profaned
   [through Gentile presence and
   the temple's destruction],
And let our eyes gaze on and gloat
   over Zion.'
12 "But they (Gentile nations) do not
   know the thoughts of the Lord,
Nor do they understand His
   purpose and plan;
For He has gathered them
   (Gentiles) like sheaves to the
   threshing floor [for destruction].
13 "Arise and thresh, O Daughter of
   Zion!
For I will make your horn iron
And I will make your hoofs
   bronze;
That you may beat many peoples
   in pieces [trampling down your
   enemies],
That you may devote to the
   Lord their unjust gain (pagan
   possessions)
And their wealth to the Lord of all
   the earth. [Zech 12:1–8; 14:14]

5 "NOW GATHER yourself in
troops, O daughter of troops;
A state of siege has been placed
against us.
They shall strike the ruler of Israel
   on the cheek with a rod (scepter).
2 "But as for you, Bethlehem
   Ephrathah,
Too little to be among the clans of
   Judah;
From you One shall come forth for
   Me [who is] to be Ruler in Israel,
His goings forth (appearances) are
   from long ago,
From ancient days." [Gen 49:10;
   Matt 2:5–12; John 7:42]
3 Therefore, He will give them up
   until the time

When she who is in labor has
given birth to a child.
Then what is left of His kinsmen
Shall return to the children of
Israel.
⁴And He shall stand and shepherd
and guide *His flock*
In the strength of the LORD,
In the majesty of the name of the
LORD His God;
And they shall dwell [secure in
undisturbed peace],
Because at that time He shall be
great [extending His authority]
[Even] to the ends of the earth. [Ps
72:8; Is 40:11; Zech 9:10; Luke
1:32, 33]
⁵This One [the Messiah] shall be
our peace.

When the Assyrian invades our
land
And tramples on our citadels *and*
in our palaces,
Then shall we raise against him
Seven shepherds and eight princes
[an overpowering force] among
men. [Is 9:6; Eph 2:14]
⁶They shall devastate the land of
Assyria with the sword and
The land of Nimrod within her
[own] gates.
And He (the Messiah) shall rescue
us from the Assyrian (all enemy
nations)
When he attacks our land
And when he tramples our territory.

⁷Then the remnant of Jacob
Shall be among many peoples
Like dew from the LORD,
Like showers on the grass [a
source of blessing]
Which [come suddenly and] do not
wait for man

Nor delay for the sons of men.
[Ps 72:6; 110:3]
⁸The remnant of Jacob
Shall be among the nations,
In the midst of many peoples
Like a lion among the beasts of the
forest,
Like a young lion [suddenly
appearing] among the flocks of
sheep
Which, if he passes through,
Tramples down and tears into
pieces [the nations in judgment],
And there is no one to rescue.
⁹Your hand will be lifted up against
your adversaries,
And all your enemies shall be cut
off *and* destroyed.

¹⁰"And in that day," says the LORD,
"I will cut off your horses from
among you
And destroy your chariots [on
which you depend]. [Ps 20:7, 8;
Zech 9:10]
¹¹"I will cut off the cities of your land
And tear down all your
fortifications.
¹²"I will cut off witchcrafts *and*
sorceries from your hand,
And you shall have no more
fortune-tellers.
¹³"I will also cut off your carved
images
And your *sacred* pillars from
among you,
So that you will no longer worship
and bow down
To the work of your hands.
¹⁴"I will root out your Asherim
(symbols of the goddess
Asherah) from among you
And destroy your cities [which are
the centers of pagan worship].
[Deut 16:21]

speak the Word

Thank You, God, that Jesus, the prophesied Messiah, is my peace.
—ADAPTED FROM MICAH 5:5

15 "And in anger and wrath I shall
   execute vengeance
On the nations which have not
   obeyed [such vengeance as they
   have not known before]."

6 HEAR NOW what the Lord is
   saying,
   "Arise, plead your case before
the mountains,
And let the hills [as witnesses]
   hear your voice.
2 "Hear, O mountains, the
   indictment of the Lord,
And you enduring foundations of
   the earth,
For the Lord has a case (a legal
   complaint) against His people,
And He will dispute (challenge)
   Israel.
3 "O My people, what have I done to
   you [since you have turned away
   from Me]?
And how have I wearied you?
   Answer Me.
4 "For I brought you up from the
   land of Egypt
And ransomed you from the house
   of slavery,
And I sent before you Moses [to
   lead you], Aaron [the high priest],
   and Miriam [the prophetess].
5 "My people, remember now
What Balak king of Moab devised
   [with his evil plan against Israel]
And what Balaam the son of Beor
   answered him [turning the curse
   into blessing for Israel],
[Remember what the Lord did for
   you] from Shittim to Gilgal,

So that you may know the righteous
   and saving acts [displaying the
   power] of the Lord." [Num 23:7–
   24; 24:3–24; Josh 3:1; 4:19]
6 With what shall I come before the
   Lord [to honor Him]
And bow myself before God on
   high?
Shall I come before Him with
   burnt offerings,
With yearling calves?
7 Will the Lord be delighted with
   thousands of rams,
Or with ten thousand rivers of oil?
Shall I present my firstborn for my
   acts of rebellion,
The fruit of my body for the sin of
   my soul?
8 He has told you, O man, what is
   good;
And what does the Lord require
   of you
Except to be just, and to love [and
   to diligently practice] kindness
   (compassion),
And to walk humbly with your God
   [setting aside any overblown
   sense of importance or self-
   righteousness]? [Deut 10:12, 13]

9 The voice of the Lord shall call to
   the city [of Jerusalem]—
And it is sound wisdom to heed
   [solemnly] and fear Your name
   [with awe-filled reverence];
"Hear, O tribe [the rod of
   punishment]. Who has
   appointed its time?
10 "Are there not still treasures
   gained by wickedness
In the house of the wicked,
And a short (inaccurate) measure
   [for grain] that is cursed? [Deut
   25:14–16]

speak the Word

*God, I know what is good and what You require of me: to be just,
to love kindness and compassion, and to walk humbly with You.*
—ADAPTED FROM MICAH 6:8

11"Can I [be guiltless and] justify
  deceptive scales
And a bag of dishonest weights?
  [1 Thess 4:6]
12"For the rich men of the city are
  full of violence [of every kind];
Her inhabitants speak lies
And their tongue is deceitful in
  their mouth.
13"So also I will make you sick,
  striking you down,
Desolating *and* devastating you,
  because of your sins.

14"You shall eat, but you will not be
  satisfied,
And your emptiness shall be among
  you;
You will [try to] remove [your goods
  and those you love] *for safekeeping*
But you will fail to save *anything*,
And what you do save I shall give
  to the sword.
15"You shall sow but you shall not
  reap;
You shall tread olives, but shall not
  anoint yourself with oil,

God's requirements

What we think God requires of us and what He actually requires can often be very different. We might think God requires us to do a lot of church work or a certain number of good deeds. We might think He requires extreme sacrifices or perfection from us. We might even think He requires us to read the Bible from Genesis to Revelation every year and spend hours each day in prayer and meditation. Although all of these things can be good and have their place, we may do them and still miss what God considers to be important.

His requirements have a lot to do with how we treat people. According to Micah 6:8, we are to be just, love kindness, and walk humbly with our God. God is just, which means that He is always fair and that He works to make wrong things right. We should treat people justly and work to see that justice is done in their lives. Many people have been terribly mistreated and abused, and we have the opportunity as God's representatives to help them enjoy what Jesus died for them to have. We can help restore them to the knowledge of God and His love for them, as well as bringing practical aid and help in areas where it is needed.

God also requires us to love mercy and kindness. We certainly need more kindness and compassion in the world! People do not need to be pressured to perform perfectly; they need to be loved and accepted. It is the kindness of God—not the judgment of God—that leads people to repentance (see Romans 2:4). Our job is not to be faultfinders, but to be dispensers of God's mercy and kindness. God is kind and compassionate toward us, and He expects us to give to others what we have received from Him.

Finally, as shown in Micah 6:8, humility is the attitude of heart and mind God requires of us. We should never view ourselves as better than or above other people. According to Proverbs 6:17 a proud person overestimates himself and discounts others. If we think more highly of ourselves than we should, having an exaggerated opinion of our own importance, we will see others as beneath us. This can cause us to have a disrespectful attitude and harsh behavior toward other people, even our family and friends. Strive to give God what He truly requires, which is to do justly, love kindness, and walk humbly with Him.

And [you will extract juice from]
the grapes, but you shall not
drink the wine.

16 "For [you have kept] the statutes of
Omri [the idolatrous king],
And all the works of the [wicked]
house (dynasty) of Ahab;
And you walk in their counsels
and policies.
Therefore, I shall hand you over
for destruction *and* horror
And your [city's] inhabitants for
ridicule,
And you shall bear the rebuke *and*
scorn of My people."

7 WOE IS me (judgment is
coming)! For I am
Like one who gathers the
summer fruits, like one who
gleans the vintage grapes.
There is not a cluster of grapes to
eat,
No first-ripe fig which my appetite
craves.

2 The godly person [who is faithful
and loyal to God] has perished
from the earth,
And there is no upright *person*
[one with good character and
moral integrity] among men.
They all lie in wait to shed blood;

outlast the devil

Your enemy, Satan, may come against you, but when you fall, you will rise (see Micah 7:7, 8). I encourage you to make the decision to endure whatever comes against you. That literally means you will outlast the devil. Greater is He Who is in you than he who is in the world (see 1 John 4:4). You are more than a conqueror through Jesus Christ (see Romans 8:37).

Even during times of intense trouble, believers should live with expectancy. Expect God to work something good out of your situation, and expect Him to bless you even in the presence of your enemies. David said in Psalm 23:5, "You prepare a table before me in the presence of my enemies. You have anointed and refreshed my head with oil; my cup overflows." In the midst of trouble, keep a positive attitude and talk about the possibilities, not the problem.

Being positive is important because it leads to progress or forward motion. We cannot go forward or overcome negative situations unless we choose to be positive. I believe there is something good in everything that happens to us; we just need to look for it. If you are stuck in traffic and in a hurry, you may become frustrated or angry, but the delay might have caused you to avoid being involved in an accident. God may have saved your life!

God hears us when we pray in faith. Put your confidence in Him and expect something good to happen to you. Expect your situation to change for the better, and know that in the meantime, God will use whatever you are going through to help you be a better person in the end. You can choose to let every trial you encounter make you bitter or better. Trials and tribulations are a part of life, and the way we handle them reveals our level of spiritual maturity. Be stable and do not let Satan intimidate you. This will be a sign to him of his impending destruction. Satan cannot do any real harm to a person he cannot manipulate and control. God has a good plan for your life, and He never changes His mind about it. Make the decision right now that you will never give up; once you do, your victory is sure.

Each hunts the other with a net.
³Concerning evil, both of their
   hands pursue it and do it
   diligently *and* thoroughly;
The prince asks, also the judge, for
   a bribe,
And a great man speaks the [evil]
   desire of his soul.
So they twist the course of justice
   between them.
⁴The best of them is [injurious] like
   a briar;
The most upright is [prickly] like a
   thorn hedge.
The day of your watchmen [that
   is, the time predicted by the
   prophets]
And your punishment comes;
Now shall be their confusion.
⁵Do not trust in a neighbor
   [because of the moral corruption
   in the land];
Do not have confidence in a friend.
Guard the doors of your mouth
From her who lies in your bosom.
   [Luke 12:51–53]
⁶For the son dishonors the father
   and treats him contemptuously,
The daughter rises up [in hostility]
   against her mother,
The daughter-in-law against her
   mother-in-law—
A man's enemies are the
   men (members) of his own
   household. [Matt 10:21, 35, 36;
   Mark 13:12, 13]

⁷But as for me, I will look
   expectantly for the Lord *and*
   with confidence in Him I will
   keep watch;
I will wait [with confident
   expectation] for the God of my
   salvation.

putting the Word to work

Micah 7:7 teaches us how to wait.
Whether sitting in traffic, waiting for
an appointment, or standing in line at
the grocery store, waiting is a part of
everyday life for most of us. Is it hard
for you to wait? When you wait on
God, you can wait with hopeful expectation that He hears your every prayer
and is working for your good.

My God will hear me.
⁸Do not rejoice over me [amid my
   tragedies], O my enemy!
Though I fall, I will rise;
Though I sit in the darkness [of
   distress], the Lord is a light for me.

⁹I will bear the indignation *and*
   wrath of the Lord
Because I have sinned against Him,
Until He pleads my case and
   executes judgment for me.
He will bring me out to the light,
And I will behold His [amazing]
   righteousness *and* His
   remarkable deliverance. [Rom
   10:1–4; 11:23–27]
¹⁰Then my enemy [all the pagan
   nations] shall see it,
And shame [for despising the Lord]
   will cover her who said to me,
"Where is the Lord your God?"
My eyes will look on her [with
   satisfaction at her judgment];
Now she (unbelievers) will be
   trampled down
Like mud of the streets.
¹¹*It shall be* a day for building your
   walls,

speak the Word

God, I will look expectantly for You. With confidence in You,
I will keep watch. I will wait with confident expectation for the God
of my salvation. I know that You will hear me. When I fall I will rise;
when I sit in darkness You will be a light to me.
—ADAPTED FROM MICAH 7:7, 8

On that day the boundary [of Israel] shall be [greatly] extended. [Is 33:17; Amos 9:11]
¹²It *shall be* a day when the Gentiles will come to you
From Assyria and from the cities of Egypt,
And from Egypt even to the river Euphrates,
From sea to sea and from mountain to mountain.
¹³Yet the earth [beyond the land of Israel] shall become desolate because of those who dwell in it,
Because of the fruit of their deeds.

¹⁴Shepherd *and* rule Your people with Your scepter [of blessing],
The flock of Your inheritance *and* Your possession
Which dwells alone [separate and secure from attack] in the forest,
In the midst of a garden land.
Let them feed in Bashan and Gilead
As in the days of old [the days of Moses and Elijah].
¹⁵"As in the days when you came out from the land of Egypt,
I shall show you marvelous *and* miraculous things."
¹⁶The [pagan] nations shall see [God's omnipotence in delivering Israel] and be ashamed
Of all their might [which cannot be compared to His].
They shall put their hand on their mouth [in silent astonishment];
Their ears shall be deaf.
¹⁷They shall lick the dust like a serpent;
Like crawling things of the earth
They shall come trembling out of their fortresses *and* hiding places.

putting the Word to work

Do you ever have a hard time forgiving someone? When it is hard to forgive, focus on God's forgiveness and remember His mercy and loving-kindness toward you (see Micah 7:18–20). Ask Him to help you let go of your anger, and to extend compassion and forgiveness to those who have wronged you. You may not be able to quickly forget the wrong or hurt you have experienced, but you can quickly forgive, as God does.

They shall turn *and* come with fear *and* dread to the Lord our God
And they shall be afraid *and* stand in awe before You [O Lord]. [Jer 33:9]
¹⁸Who is a God like You, who forgives wickedness
And passes over the rebellious acts of the remnant of His possession?
He does not retain His anger forever,
Because He [constantly] delights in mercy *and* lovingkindness.
¹⁹He shall again have compassion on us;
He will subdue *and* tread underfoot our wickedness [destroying sin's power].
Yes, You will cast all our sins
Into the depths of the sea. [Ps 103:12]
²⁰You shall give truth to Jacob
And lovingkindness *and* mercy to Abraham,
As You have sworn to our forefathers
From the days of old. [Luke 1:54, 55]

speak the Word

Thank You, God, that You do not retain Your anger forever, because You constantly delight in mercy and loving-kindness.
—ADAPTED FROM MICAH 7:18

Nahum

Author:
Nahum

Date:
Shortly before 612 BC

Everyday Life Principles:
God will not tolerate evil forever.

Trouble comes to every life.

God never gives us more than we can bear with His help.

The message of Nahum is that even though evil may seem to prevail for a period of time, God will not tolerate it forever. As we read in Psalm 37:2, evildoers will "wither quickly like the grass." Sin is extremely serious; it is not something God ignores or takes lightly, even if it seems to go unpunished for a season. Nahum 1:3 teaches us that the Lord is slow to anger, but He is also great in power. When He does execute His judgment, it is so fierce that nothing can stand against it.

The primary theme of Nahum is God's judgment on the Assyrian city of Nineveh, but it also contains a message of great comfort to the people of Judah. This is appropriate, since it was written by a man whose name, Nahum, means "consolation" or "comfort."

One of the verses of comfort in Nahum is Nahum 1:7: "The LORD is good, a strength and stronghold in the day of trouble; He knows [He recognizes, cares for, and understand fully] those who take refuge and trust in Him." Even when our enemies seem to prevail and a "day of trouble comes," God will intervene, and He will not give us more than we can bear.

I encourage you to remember that God is your strength and your stronghold when trouble comes, and He knows you intimately if you have put your trust in Him.

1 THE ORACLE (a burdensome message—a pronouncement from God) concerning Nineveh [the capital city of Assyria]. The book of the vision of Nahum of Elkosh [which he saw in spirit and prophesied].

2 The Lord is a jealous and avenging God [protecting and demanding what is rightfully and uniquely His];
The Lord avenges and He is full of wrath.
The Lord takes vengeance on His adversaries,
And He reserves wrath for His enemies. [Ex 20:5]
3 The Lord is slow to anger and great in power
And He will by no means leave *the guilty* unpunished.

putting the Word to work

Do you know someone, perhaps even yourself, with a quick temper? Those bursts of temper can be frightening, but they are nothing compared to the anger of God as described in Nahum 1:2–6. It is important to recognize that God has been slow to anger in your life, reaching out to you with His mercy, grace, and compassion through Jesus Christ. Although God is merciful and long-suffering, justice ultimately must be satisfied. If we continue in willful sin, God's judgment will eventually come into our lives, but if we admit we are sinners, ask God to forgive us, and receive Jesus Christ as our Savior, we can be spared and enjoy the abundant life He has promised.

life point

Nahum 1:7 reminds us that God is good. Goodness is one of His many wonderful character traits. When something is part of an individual's character, we can expect him to always respond in ways that are consistent with that trait. God is good all the time—not just some of the time, *all* the time.

The Lord has His way in the whirlwind and in the storm,
And the clouds are the dust beneath His feet. [Ex 34:6, 7]
4 He rebukes the sea and dries it up;
He dries up all the rivers [illustrating His judgment].
Bashan [on the east] and [Mount] Carmel [on the west] wither,
And [in the north] the blossoms of Lebanon fade.
5 The mountains quake before Him
And the hills melt away;
Indeed the earth is shaken by His presence—

putting the Word to work

Have you ever seen or visited a castle and been impressed by the strength of its fortifications? Although the city of Nineveh had remarkable protection— immense walls, moats, armed guards, and more—in the face of God's wrath, those defenses drastically failed (see Nahum 1:8). No matter how great the trouble or calamity you face, as one who trusts in God, you are protected by the ultimate stronghold—the Lord Himself (see Nahum 1:7). His protection will never fail you.

speak the Word

Lord, I thank You that You are slow to anger and great in power.
—ADAPTED FROM NAHUM 1:3

Yes, the world and all that dwell
   in it.
⁶Who can stand before His
   indignation [His great wrath]?
And who can stand up *and* endure
   the fierceness of His anger?
His wrath is poured out like fire
And the rocks are destroyed by
   Him.
⁷The LORD is good,
A strength *and* stronghold in the
   day of trouble;
He knows [He recognizes, cares for,
   and understands fully] those who
   take refuge *and* trust in Him. [Ps
   1:6; Hos 13:5; John 10:14, 27]
⁸But with an overwhelming flood
   [of judgment through invading
   armies]

He will make a complete
   destruction of its site
And will pursue His enemies into
   darkness.

⁹Whatever [plot] you [Assyrians]
   devise against the LORD,
He will make a complete end of it;
Affliction [of God's people by the
   hand of Assyria] will not occur
   twice.
¹⁰Like tangled thorn branches
   [gathered for fuel],
And like those drowned in
   drunkenness,
The people of Nineveh are
   consumed [through fire]
Like stubble completely withered
   and dry [in the day of the LORD's
   wrath]. [Mal 4:1]

in the day of trouble

What will you do in the "day of trouble" (Nahum 1:7)? I believe we are wise to make up our minds ahead of time concerning what we will do when trouble comes. Let me encourage you to decide to be stable before trouble ever comes. Decide to stay in faith and remain thankful for what God is doing in your life. When difficulties arise, keep praising Him, and do not ever give up.

Do not be surprised by trouble. Jesus said that in the world we would have tribulation and suffering (see John 16:33), but we know that He will also strengthen us and enable us to do whatever we need to do in life (see Philippians 4:13). God is our Strength, our Refuge, and our Stronghold in the day of trouble.

God knows those who trust Him, and He already has a plan for our deliverance before our trouble ever begins. The Bible teaches us that we are more than conquerors through Christ, Who loves us (see Romans 8:37). I have thought a lot about what that means, and I believe one way to explain it is to say, "In Christ, we have won the battle before it ever begins." Therefore, we have no reason to be afraid of anything that comes our way.

You may be tempted to think God will not help you in your times of trouble if you have made mistakes or been less than perfect, but that is not true. James 1:5 tells us that if we ask for wisdom in our times of trial, He will help us without blaming us. Yes, the Lord is good, and, thankfully, our weaknesses cannot change that. He loves us unconditionally and looks for a heart that trusts and loves Him, not for perfect performance. Trust in the Lord with all your heart, and do not rely on your own understanding (see Proverbs 3:5). You may not know how your problem will be solved, but as long as you know God and He knows you, then you know all you really need to know.

11 From you [O Nineveh],
  One has gone forth who plotted
    evil against the LORD,
  A malevolent counselor [the king
    of Assyria]. [2 Kin 19:20–23; Is
    10:5–7; 36:15–20]

12 This is what the LORD says,

  "Though they are at full *strength*
    and many in number,
  Even so, they will be cut off and
    pass away.
  Though I have afflicted you *and*
    caused you grief [O Jerusalem],
  I will afflict you no longer. [2 Kin
    19:35–37; John 5:14]
13 "Now, I will break his yoke [of
    taxation] off you,
  And I will tear off your shackles."
    [Is 14:25]

14 The LORD has given a command
    concerning you [O king of
    Nineveh]:
  "Your name will no longer be
    perpetuated.
  I will cut off the carved idols and
    cast images
  From the temple of your gods;
  I will prepare your grave,
  For you are vile *and* unworthy."
    [Is 37:38; Ezek 32:22, 23]

putting the Word to work

Do you remember the last time you received good news? Just as the bearer of good news in Nahum 1:15 brought word of deliverance from the tyranny of the enemy, the good news of the gospel of Jesus Christ was delivered to you. You too have been set free from the enemy! Ask God to show you someone to whom you can deliver this good news, that they too might enjoy freedom from the enemy and new life in Christ!

15 Behold, on the mountains the feet
    of him who brings good news
    [telling of Assyria's destruction],
  Who announces peace *and*
    prosperity!
  Celebrate your feasts, O Judah;
  Perform your vows.
  For the wicked one [the king of
    Assyria] will never again pass
    through you;
  He is completely cut off. [Is 52:7;
    Rom 10:15]

2 THE ONE who scatters has
    come up against you [Nineveh].
  Man the fortress *and* ramparts,
    watch the road;
  Strengthen your back [prepare
    for battle], summon all your
    strength.
2 For the LORD will restore the
    splendor *and* majesty of Jacob
  Like the splendor of [ancient and
    united] Israel,
  Even though destroyers have
    destroyed them
  And ruined their vine branches.
    [Is 10:12]

3 The shields of his soldiers [of Media
    and Babylon] are colored red;
  The warriors are dressed in scarlet.
  The chariots blaze with fire of
    [flashing] steel
  When he is prepared *to march,*
  And the cypress *spears* are
    brandished [for battle].
4 The chariots race madly in the
    streets;
  They rush wildly in the broad
    plazas.
  Their appearance is like torches;
  They rush in various directions
    like forked lightning.
5 He remembers *and* summons his
    nobles;
  They stumble in their march
    [terrified because of the attack].
  They hurry to the city wall,

And the mantelet is prepared *and* firmly set up.
⁶The gates of the rivers [surrounding Nineveh] are opened
And the palace [of sun-dried brick] is dissolved [by the torrents].
⁷It is decreed:
Nineveh is stripped, and she is carried away,
And her handmaids are moaning like the sound of doves,
Beating on their breasts [in sorrow].

⁸Though Nineveh was like a pool of water throughout her days,
Now her inhabitants are fleeing;
"Stop! Stop!" [a few cry,]
But no one turns back.
⁹Plunder the silver!
Plunder the gold!
For there is no end to the treasure—
Wealth from every precious object.
¹⁰She is emptied! She is desolate and waste!
Hearts melting [in fear] and knees knocking!
Anguish is in the whole body,
And the faces of all grow pale!
[Is 13:7, 8]
¹¹Where is the den of the lions (Assyria)
And the feeding place of the young lions,
Where the lion, lioness, and lion's cub prowled
With nothing to fear?
¹²The lion [of Assyria] tore enough for his cubs (Assyrian citizens),
Killed [enough prey] for his lionesses,
And filled his lairs with prey
And his dens with torn flesh.

¹³"Behold, I am against you [Nineveh]," declares the LORD of hosts, "and I will burn your chariots in the smoke, and the sword will devour your young lions. I will cut off your prey from the land, and the voice of your messengers will no longer be heard."

3 WOE (JUDGMENT is coming) to the city of blood [guilty of murder and mayhem], completely full of lies and pillage;
Her prey never departs [alive].
[Ezek 24:6, 9, 10; Hab 2:12]
²The noise of the [cracking of the] whip,
The noise of the rattling of the wheel,
Galloping horses
And rumbling *and* bounding chariots [in the assault of Nineveh]!
³Horsemen charging,
Swords flashing, spears gleaming,
Many slain, a mass of corpses,
No end of corpses—
The horsemen stumble over the corpses!
⁴All because of the many acts of prostitution of [Nineveh] the prostitute,
The charming *and* well-favored one, the mistress of sorceries,
Who betrays nations by her acts of prostitution (idolatry)
And families by her sorceries.
⁵"Behold, I am against you," declares the LORD of hosts,
"And I will lift up your skirts over your face,
And I will let the nations look at your nakedness [O Nineveh]
And the kingdoms at your disgrace.
⁶"I will throw filth on you
And make you vile *and* treat you with contempt,
And set you up as a spectacle.
⁷"And it will come about that all who see you
Will shrink back *and* run from you and say,
'Nineveh is completely ruined!
Who will grieve for her?'
Where will I seek comforters for you?"

⁸Are you better than Thebes,
Which was situated by the waters of the Nile,

With water surrounding her,
Whose defense was the sea (the
  Nile),
Whose wall *consisted* of the sea?
9 Ethiopia was her strength,
And Egypt too, without limits.
Put and Lubim were among her
  helpers.
10 Yet she became an exile;
She went into captivity.
Her young children were dashed
  to pieces
At the head of every street;
They cast lots for her honorable
  men,
And all her great men were bound
  with chains.
11 You too [Nineveh] will become
  drunk [with the cup of God's
  wrath];
You will be hidden.
You too [Nineveh] will search
  [in vain] for a refuge from the
  enemy.
12 All your fortresses are [nothing
  but] fig trees with ripe figs—
When shaken they fall into the
  mouth of the eater.
13 Behold, your people are [as weak
  and helpless as] women in your
  midst!
The gates of your land are opened
  wide to your enemies;
Fire consumes the bars across
  your gates.
14 Draw water for a [long, continued]
  siege!
Strengthen your fortresses!
Go down to the clay pits, trample
  the mortar!

Prepare the brick kiln [to burn
  bricks for the rampart]!
15 But there [in the very midst of
  these preparations] the fire will
  devour you;
The sword will cut you down;
It will devour you as the locust does.
Multiply yourself like the creeping
  locusts;
Multiply yourself like the
  swarming locusts.
16 You have increased your traders
  more than the [visible] stars of
  heaven—
The creeping locust strips *and*
  destroys and then flies away.
17 Your guardsmen are like the
  swarming locusts.
Your marshals are like the hordes
  of grasshoppers
Settling in the stone walls on a
  cold day.
When the sun rises, they fly away,
And no one knows the place where
  they are.
18 Your shepherds are asleep, O king
  of Assyria;
Your nobles are lying down [in
  death].
Your people are scattered on the
  mountains
And there is no one to gather them.
19 There is no relief *and* healing for
  your hurt;
Your wound is incurable.
All who hear the news about you
Clap their hands over [what has
  happened to] you.
For on whom has your [unceasing]
  evil not come continually?

Habakkuk

Author:
Habakkuk

Date:
Probably between 612 BC and 586 BC

Everyday Life Principles:
Remember that righteous people live by faith.

God always does what is right.

God will give us opportunities to grow.

The book of Habakkuk was written as a dialogue, or conversation, between God and the prophet Habakkuk. In the beginning of this book, Habakkuk is overwhelmed by the devastation that surrounds him. He cannot seem to get his focus off his circumstances and the bad things that are happening in his country.

In Habakkuk 2, God tells Habakkuk that righteous people live by faith and that even in the midst of suffering, oppression, and destruction, the righteous know and trust that God is doing what is right.

One verse many people know from Habakkuk is 3:19, which says: "The Lord GOD is my strength [my source of courage, my invincible army]; He has made my feet [steady and sure] like hinds' feet and makes me walk [forward with spiritual confidence] on my high places [of challenge and responsibility]."

As you read the book of Habakkuk, be reminded that God is your very own invincible army and that He is helping you make spiritual progress by giving you opportunities to grow, which may include trouble, suffering, or responsibility, but which are designed to make you stronger. No matter what happens around you or in your own life, live by faith and trust God to do what is right.

1 THE ORACLE (a burdensome message—a pronouncement from God) which Habakkuk the prophet saw.

2 O Lord, how long will I call for help
And You will not hear?
I cry out to You, "Violence!"
Yet You do not save.
3 Why do You make me see iniquity,
And cause me to look on
wickedness?
For destruction and violence are
before me;
Strife continues and contention
arises.
4 Therefore, the law is ineffective
and ignored
And justice is never upheld,
For the wicked surround the
righteous;
Therefore, justice becomes
perverted.

5 [The Lord replied,] "Look among
the nations! See!
Be astonished! Wonder!
For I am doing something in your
days—
You would not believe it if you
were told. [Acts 13:40, 41]
6 "For behold, I am raising up
the Chaldeans [who rule in
Babylon],
That fierce and impetuous nation
Who march throughout the earth
To take possession of dwelling
places that do not belong to them.
[2 Kin 24:2]
7 "The Chaldeans are dreaded and
feared;
Their justice and authority
originate with themselves *and*
are defined only by their decree.
8 "Their horses are swifter than
leopards
And keener than [hungry] wolves
in the evening,
Their horsemen come galloping,

putting the Word to work

When you see evidence of violence and injustice in the world, do you ever wonder why God does not put a stop to such evils? Habakkuk asked God such questions, and found that God answered him in unexpected ways (see Habakkuk 1:2–6). God wants us to bring our questions to Him, but we may not always get the answers we expect. We can, however, always trust that God's ways are best, even when we do not fully understand them.

Their horsemen come from far
away;
They fly like an eagle swooping
down to devour.
9 "They all come for violence;
Their horde of faces moves
[eagerly] forward,
They gather prisoners like sand.
10 "They make fun of kings
And rulers are a laughing matter
to them.
They ridicule every stronghold
And heap up rubble [for earth
mounds] and capture it.
11 "Then they will sweep by like the
wind and pass on.
But they will be held guilty,
They [and all men] whose own
power *and* strength is their god."
12 Are You not from everlasting,
O Lord, my God, My Holy One?
We will not die.
O Lord, You have appointed the
Chaldeans [who rule in Babylon]
to execute [Your] judgment,
And You, O Rock, have established
them to correct *and* chastise.
[Deut 32:4]
13 Your eyes are too pure to approve
evil,
And You cannot look *favorably* on
wickedness.
Why then do You look favorably

On those who act treacherously?
Why are you silent when the
  wicked (Chaldean oppressors)
  destroy
Those more righteous than they?
[14] Why do You make men like the
  fish of the sea,
Like reptiles *and* creeping things
  that have no ruler [and are
  helpless against their enemies]?
[15] *The Chaldeans* bring all of them up
  with a hook,
And drag them away with a net,
And gather them together in their
  fishing net;
So they rejoice and are glad.
[16] Therefore, they offer sacrifices to
  their net
And burn incense to their fishing
  net;
Because through these things
  their catch is large *and* they live
  luxuriously,
And their food is plentiful.
[17] Will they continue to empty their
  net
And [mercilessly] go on destroying
  nations without sparing?

2 I WILL stand at my guard post
  And station myself on the
  tower;
And I will keep watch to see what
  He will say to me,
And what answer I will give [as
  His spokesman] when I am
  reproved.
[2] Then the LORD answered me and
  said,

"Write the vision
And engrave it plainly on [clay]
  tablets
So that the one who reads it will
  run.
[3] "For the vision is yet for the
  appointed [future] time
It hurries toward the goal [of
  fulfillment]; it will not fail.
Even though it delays, wait
  [patiently] for it,
Because it will certainly come; it
  will not delay. [Heb 10:37, 38]

[4] "Look at the proud one,
His soul is not right within him,
But the righteous will live by his
  faith [in the true God]. [Rom
  1:17; Gal 3:11]
[5] "Moreover, wine is treacherous
  and betrays the arrogant man,
So that he does not stay at home.
His appetite is large like Sheol,
And he is like death, never satisfied.

putting the Word to work

Habakkuk fully expected that God would respond to his questions, and he waited in a position of watchful expectation (see Habakkuk 2:1–3). Do you believe God will answer you? Like Habakkuk, learn to wait for God's reply. Ask God to help you recognize when you are seeing His answer to you. Keeping a journal of God's responses to your prayers is a wonderful testimony to His faithfulness.

speak the Word

*God, I know that Your eyes are too pure to approve evil
and that You cannot look favorably on wickedness.*
—ADAPTED FROM HABAKKUK 1:13

*Thank You, God, that the righteous shall live by faith in the true God.
I declare that I am righteous in Christ; therefore, I live by faith in You.*
—ADAPTED FROM HABAKKUK 2:4

He gathers to himself all nations
And collects to himself all peoples
  [as if he owned them].

6 "Will all these [victims of his
  greed] not take up a taunting
  song against him,
And in mocking derision against
  him
Say, 'Woe (judgment is coming) to
  him who increases that which is
  not his—
How long [will he possess it]?
And [woe to him who] makes
  himself wealthy with loans.'

7 "Will your creditors not rise up
  suddenly,
And those who collect from you
  awaken?
Then you will become plunder for
  them.
8 "Because you [king of Babylon]
  have looted many nations,
All peoples who are left will loot
  you—
Because of human bloodshed and
  for the violence done to the
  land,
To the city and all its inhabitants.

discovering your vision

Do you know what God's will is for you? Do you have a vision? Do you know what you are going to do with your life? You should! Having a vision for your life is very important, as God's Word declares in Habakkuk 2:2, 3.

When young people start out in life, they may not know what their future is going to hold. There is nothing wrong with that, because many times God unfolds His plan as we start to move in a direction and trust Him to lead. What young people need to do is to seek God's plan for their lives and then write down what they believe God is saying to them. As they begin to move in a certain direction, what they are sup-posed to do with their lives will become increasingly clear.

People who are older should have figured out their purpose in life. However, many of them still do not know what they want to be when they "grow up" because issues in their lives have blocked the formation of their vision.

Too many people concentrate on what they cannot do. They focus on everything they do wrong and never on what they do right. They get so caught up in their mis-takes and inabilities that they lose sight of the fact that we serve a great God. If this is you, I encourage you to study Hebrews 12:2. This verse tells you to look away from the things that distract you and focus on Jesus. Even if you are being sidetracked by your own inabilities and weaknesses, stop looking at those things and start looking up at Jesus. If you believe you can do only one thing, make up your mind that you are going to do that one thing well. Decide that you are going to be the best you can be at that one thing.

Take an inventory of your life and decide what you have that you can use to fulfill God's purpose for you. What are you doing with your time, your energy, and your abilities? Stop looking at what you do not have and begin using what you do have.

Be a person of purpose. Know why you are doing what you are doing. Make sure you do not lose sight of your goals. In order to do that, you may need to heed the advice of Habakkuk: write your vision and make it plain!

9 "Woe (judgment is coming) to him
   who obtains wicked gain for his
   house [and thinks by so doing]
To set his nest on high,
That he may be rescued from the
   hand of evil.
10 "You have devised a shameful
   thing for your house
By cutting off *and* putting an end
   to many peoples;
So you are sinning against your
   own life *and* forfeiting it.
11 "For the stone will cry out from the
   wall [to accuse you—built in sin!]
And the rafter will answer it out of
   the woodwork.

12 "Woe (judgment is coming) to him
   who builds a city with bloodshed
And establishes a town by
   violence!
13 "Is it not indeed from the LORD of
   hosts
That peoples labor [only] for the
   fire [that will destroy their work],

life point

Habakkuk 2:3 speaks of an "appointed
[future] time" for a vision to come to
pass. "Appointed time" simply means the
time God knows is right. We must humble
ourselves and our ideas under His wisdom
and power; and we must trust Him when
He says He will not be late.

"Appointed time" also means a time already established and decided for certain
reasons. It is like having an appointment.
We cannot have access to a doctor, a
dentist, or a mechanic until our appointment time has come. Similarly, God has
"appointments" for specific things in our
lives. Those things will happen at their appointed times; they will not be early, but
they will not be even one minute late. Be
encouraged. God will keep the appointments He has for you!

putting the Word to work

Have you ever been tempted to cheat
on your taxes or to not be completely
honest in your business practices (see
Habakkuk 2:9, 10)? While such actions
may bring short-term gain, they lead
to shame and seriously damage your
relationships with others and God. Be
intentional about acting with integrity
and honesty in your business dealings.

And nations grow weary for
   nothing [that is, things which
   have no lasting value]?
14 "But [the time is coming when] the
   earth shall be filled
With the knowledge of the glory of
   the LORD,
As the waters cover the sea. [Is 11:9]

15 "Woe (judgment is coming) to you
   who make your neighbors drink,
Who mix in your venom to make
   them drunk
So that you may look at their
   nakedness!
16 "You will be filled with disgrace
   instead of honor.
Now drink and expose your own
   nakedness!
The cup [of wrath] in the LORD's
   right hand will come around to
   you [O destroyer],
And utter disgrace will be on your
   own glory. [Rev 16:19]
17 "For the violence done to Lebanon
   will overwhelm you;
The destruction of the animals
   will terrify you
On account of human bloodshed
   and the violence done to the land,
To the city and all its inhabitants.

18 "What profit is the carved image
   when its maker has formed it?
It is only a cast image, and a
   teacher of lies.

For its maker trusts in his own
   creation [as his god]
When he makes speechless idols.
19 "Woe (judgment is coming) to him
   who says to the wooden image,
   'Awake!'
And to the speechless stone, 'Arise!'
And that is your teacher?
Look, it is overlaid with gold and
   silver,
And there is no breath at all
   inside it.
20 "But the LORD is in His holy temple.
Let all the earth hush *and* be silent
   before Him." [Zeph 1:7; Zech 2:13]

3 A PRAYER of Habakkuk the
prophet, set to wild *and* enthusiastic music.

2 O LORD, I have heard the report
   about You and I fear.
O LORD, revive Your work in the
   midst of the years,
In the midst of the years make it
   known;
In wrath [earnestly] remember
   compassion *and* love.

3 God [approaching from Sinai]
   comes from Teman (Edom),
And the Holy One from Mount
   Paran.
Selah (pause, and calmly think of that).
His splendor *and* majesty covers
   the heavens

life point

Habakkuk 2:20 instructs us to "be silent"
before the Lord. I believe that sitting
silently in God's presence is a type of
prayer and is one aspect of what we define as "waiting on God." Waiting is a vital part of prayer, and learning to wait on
the Lord is extremely important. Prayer is
not talking to God all the time—it is also
listening to Him, which may require waiting. Take time today to be quiet before
God and to wait on Him to speak to you.

life point

In Habakkuk 3:2, the prophet prays for
God to remember compassion and love in
the midst of His wrath.

Some people cannot appreciate God's
mercy until they have experienced a bit of
His wrath. It is important for us to understand that God is never wrathful against
His people personally; He directs His anger toward the sin in their lives. He hates
sin, and we must learn to hate it also. Like
God, we must hate sin but love the sinner.

If we do not receive God's mercy for our
sins and failures, we will not have any
mercy to give to others when they fail
or disappoint us. We cannot lead people
into powerful relationships with the Lord
through harshness, hardness, rigidity,
and legalism. We must show them that
the God we serve is merciful, patient,
and long-suffering. In His wrath, He does
remember mercy.

And the earth is full of His praise.
4 His brightness is like the sunlight;
He has [bright] rays *flashing* from
   His hand,
And there [in the sunlike
   splendor] is the hiding place of
   His power.
5 Before Him goes the pestilence [of
   judgment as in Egypt],
And [the burning] plague [of
   condemnation] follows at His
   feet [as in Sennacherib's army].
   [Ex 7:2–4; 2 Kin 19:32–35]
6 He stood and measured the earth;
He looked and startled the nations,
Yes, the eternal mountains were
   shattered,
The ancient hills bowed low *and*
   collapsed.
His ways are eternal.

⁷I [Habakkuk, in my vision] saw the
  tents of Cushan under distress;
The tent curtains of the land of
  Midian were trembling.

⁸Did the LORD rage against the rivers,
  Or was Your anger against the
  rivers,
Or was Your wrath against the
  [Red] Sea,
That You rode on Your horses,
On Your chariots of salvation?
⁹Your bow was made bare;
The rods of chastisement were
  sworn.
  Selah (pause, calmly think of that).
You split the earth with rivers
  [bringing waters to dry places].
  [Ex 17:6; Num 20:11]

¹⁰The mountains saw You and [they]
  trembled *and* writhed [as if in
  pain];
The downpour of waters swept by
  [as a deluge].
The deep uttered its voice *and*
  raged,
It lifted its hands high.
¹¹The sun and moon stood in their
  places [as before Joshua];
They went away at the light of
  Your [swift] arrows,
At the radiance *and* gleam of Your
  glittering spear. [Josh 10:12, 13]
¹²In indignation You marched
  through the earth;
In anger You trampled *and*
  threshed the nations.

the Lord is your strength

What should we do when everything in life seems to be going wrong? What if we have several problems all at one time, like the situation mentioned in Habakkuk 3:17? Perhaps you are having problems in any number of areas: your children, your marriage, your finances, your health, your job, your neighbors, or your mind and emotions. If so, I am sure you need to be encouraged.

God promises to be your Strength. He is the God of our salvation. That means He delivers us and provides a way out of the troubles in which we find ourselves. It is important to keep rejoicing even in times of trouble, because the joy of the Lord is our Strength (see Nehemiah 8:10). Depression, discouragement, and despair only weaken us, but being positive and finding something to rejoice about adds energy to our lives. Even if you cannot find "something" to rejoice about, you can rejoice over your relationship with the Lord. *He* is our joy, not our circumstances.

When we trust in God, He enables us to make spiritual progress even during times of trouble. Through Him we can keep on walking forward. I have said in the past, "Keep on walking when the devil is stalking." Satan's favorite tool to use against God's children is fear. Fear immobilizes us if we let it, and it prevents us from making progress. But thank God that in Him we can still make progress even in times that are hard to endure.

We tend to think the highest place to be is on the mountaintop with no problems and everything going our way, but that is not true according to God's Word. He says that our high places are trouble, suffering, and responsibility, and He promises that He will give us "hinds' feet." A hind is a type of mountain goat that can leap about freely on the rocky, difficult slopes. Hinds climb mountains with seemingly no effort at all because of the way God has made them.

Look to God as your Strength, and trust Him to help you make progress during trouble.

13 You went forth for the salvation of
　　Your people,
　For the salvation *and* rescue of
　　Your anointed [people Israel].
　You struck the head from the
　　house of the wicked
　To lay him open from the thigh to
　　the neck.
　Selah (pause, and calmly think of that).
14 With the enemy's own spears, You
　　pierced
　The head of his hordes.
　They stormed out to scatter us,
　Rejoicing like those
　Who secretly devour the
　　oppressed [of Israel].
15 You have trampled on the sea with
　　Your horses,
　On the surge of many waters.
　　[Ex 15:8]
16 I heard and my whole inner self
　　trembled;
　My lips quivered at the sound.
　Decay *and* rottenness enter my
　　bones,
　And I tremble in my place.
　Because I must wait quietly for the
　　day of distress,
　For the people to arise who will
　　invade *and* attack us.

life point

The prophet proclaims in Habakkuk 3:18
that he *will* rejoice in God. Similarly, the
psalmist David said, "This [day in which
God has saved me] is the day which the
LORD has made; let us rejoice and be glad
in it" (Psalm 118:24). I believe David had
chosen to rejoice, and he was establishing
this attitude not only for himself but also
for everyone who wanted to listen.

Joy is not just a feeling; it is a decision.
We can decide to declare: "God has given
me this day. And if He has decided to let
me breathe another day, then I am going
to enjoy it." Choose today, like Habakkuk
and David, to rejoice!

life point

Whatever obstacles you may have right
now in your life, I encourage you to go
through them and not give up!

Habakkuk 3:19 says that we need to allow
our difficulties to help us develop "hinds'
feet." What is a hind? It is an animal that
can climb mountains swiftly. When we
have hinds' feet, we will not stand still in
terror in the face of our problems. Instead,
we will walk and make progress through
our trouble, suffering, responsibility, or
whatever is trying to hold us back.

It is easy to quit in hard times; it takes
faith to go through those hard times.
Know that God wants to be with you
to help you make spiritual progress. He
wants to strengthen you and encourage
you to "keep on keeping on" through the
storms of your life.

17 Though the fig tree does not
　　blossom
　And there is no fruit on the vines,
　Though the yield of the olive fails
　And the fields produce no food,
　Though the flock is cut off from
　　the fold
　And there are no cattle in the stalls,
18 Yet I will [choose to] rejoice in the
　　LORD;
　I will [choose to] shout in
　　exultation in the [victorious]
　　God of my salvation! [Rom 8:37]
19 The Lord GOD is my strength [my
　　source of courage, my invincible
　　army];
　He has made my feet [steady and
　　sure] like hinds' feet
　And makes me walk [forward
　　with spiritual confidence] on my
　　high places [of challenge and
　　responsibility].

For the choir director, on my stringed
instruments.

Zephaniah

Author:
Zephaniah

Date:
About 630 BC

Everyday Life Principles:
God is the God of history.

After repentance comes restoration.

God is singing over you.

One of Zephaniah's key themes is that God is the God of history—and that He has always been and will always be deeply involved in human affairs. Like other Old Testament prophets, Zephaniah recognized the sin that surrounded him. Specifically, his prophecy was a message of impending judgment against Judah, Jerusalem, and surrounding nations. He urged repentance, knowing that sin demands judgment, and He knew that God was merciful and eager to forgive. He believed God would always have a remnant of faithful people who would seek Him, who would go after Him with all their might. Zephaniah knew that God's wrath is severe; but he also knew that God's love is awesome.

Zephaniah gives us a beloved Old Testament verse, one that has encouraged people in God's love for generations: "The LORD your God is in your midst, a Warrior who saves. He will rejoice over you with joy; He will be quiet in His love [making no mention of your past sins], He will rejoice over you with shouts of joy" (Zephaniah 3:17).

I urge you to learn from Zephaniah that repentance is the only appropriate response to sin and that restoration follows. I also encourage you to remember that no matter what happens in life, God loves you and is always singing over you.

1 THE WORD of the Lord which came to Zephaniah the son of Cushi, the son of Gedaliah, the son of Amariah, the son of Hezekiah, in the days of Josiah the son of Amon, king of Judah:

2 "I will completely consume *and* sweep away all *things*
From the face of the earth [in judgment]," says the Lord.
3 "I will consume *and* sweep away man and beast;
I will consume *and* sweep away the birds of the air
And the fish of the sea,
And the stumbling blocks (idols) along with the wicked;
And I will cut off *and* destroy man from the face of the earth," declares the Lord.
4 "I will also stretch out My hand [in judgment] against Judah
And against all the inhabitants of Jerusalem.
And I will cut off *and* destroy the remnant of Baal from this place,
And the names *and* remembrance of the idolatrous priests along with the [false] priests,
5 And those who bow down *and* worship the host of heaven [the sun, the moon, and the stars] on their housetops
And those who bow down and swear [oaths] to [and pretend to worship] the Lord and [yet also] swear by [the pagan god called] Milcom [god of the Ammonites],
6 And those who have turned back from following the Lord,
And those who have not sought the Lord [as their most important need] or inquired of Him."

7 [Hush!] Be silent before the Lord God [there is no acceptable excuse to offer]!
For the day [of the vengeance] of the Lord is near,

putting the Word to work

Have you ever heard someone say, "All religions are alike; it doesn't really matter what you believe," or something like that? The truth is that it does matter whom you believe in, and Zephaniah 1:5, 6 illustrate that following and worshiping God alone is what is acceptable.

For the Lord has prepared a sacrifice (Judah),
He has set apart [for His use] those who have accepted His invitation [the Chaldeans who rule Babylon]. [Hab 2:20]
8 "Then it will come about on the day of the Lord's sacrifice
That I will punish the princes and the king's sons
And all who are clothed in [lavish] foreign apparel [reflecting their paganism]. [Num 15:38, 39]
9 "On that day I will also punish all those who leap over the *temple* threshold,
Who fill their [pagan] lord's temple with violence and deceit.
10 "On that day," declares the Lord,
"There will be the sound of crying from the Fish (Damascus) Gate [in the northern wall of Jerusalem where invaders enter]
And wailing from the Second Quarter [of the city],
And a loud crash from the hills.
11 "Wail [in anguish], you inhabitants of the Mortar (Valley of Siloam),
For all the merchants of Canaan will be silenced *and* destroyed;
All who weigh out silver will be cut off.
12 "It will come about at that time
That I will search Jerusalem with lamps
And I will punish the men

Who [like old wine] are stagnant in
spirit,
Who say in their hearts,
'The LORD will not do good, nor
will He do evil.'
13 "Furthermore, their wealth will
become plunder
And their houses a desolation.
Yes, they will build houses but not
live in them,
And plant vineyards but not drink
their wine." [Deut 28:30, 39;
Amos 5:11, 12]

14 The great [judgment] day of the
LORD is near,
Near and coming very quickly.
Listen! The [voice of the] day of the
LORD!
The warrior cries out bitterly
[unable to fight or to flee].
15 That day is a day of [the outpouring
of the] wrath [of God],
A day of trouble and distress,
A day of destruction and
devastation,
A day of darkness and gloom,
A day of clouds and thick
darkness, [Jer 30:7; Joel 2:11;
Amos 5:18]
16 A day of trumpet and the battle cry
[of invaders]
Against the fortified cities
And against the high corner
towers (battlements).
17 I will bring distress on men

putting the Word to work

Although we do not know the specific
time, the day of God's judgment is
coming, and Zephaniah 1:14, 15 help
us understand how terrible that day
will be. Do you regularly pray for
people who do not yet know God and
have not yet found salvation in Jesus
Christ? Let me encourage you to do so.

putting the Word to work

Many people are driven by the pursuit
of money, convinced that it is both
necessary for fulfillment in life and
also the ultimate protection against
calamity, but that is not true (see
Zephaniah 1:18). Do you invest more
time and effort in pursuing money or
intimacy with God? While making a
living is admirable, remember that it is
your relationship with God that brings
the greatest reward and the ultimate
security.

So that they will walk like the blind
[unable to find a way of escape],
Because they have sinned against
the LORD;
Their blood will be poured out like
dust [and trampled underfoot],
And their flesh like dung.
18 Neither their silver nor their gold
Will be able to rescue them
On the day of the LORD's
indignation and wrath.
And the whole earth will be
consumed
In the fire of His jealous wrath,
For He shall make a full and
complete end,
Indeed a terrifying one,
Of all the inhabitants of the earth.
[Luke 21:35, 36; 2 Pet 3:10–13]

2 GATHER YOURSELVES
together [in repentance], yes,
gather [in submission],
O nation without shame,
2 Before the decree takes effect [and
the time for repentance is lost]—
The day passes like the chaff
[whirled by the wind]—
Before the burning and fierce anger
of the LORD comes upon you,
Before the day of the wrath of the
LORD comes upon you.

³ Seek the Lord [search diligently
for Him and regard Him as the
foremost necessity of your life],
All you humble of the land
Who have practiced His
ordinances *and* have kept His
commandments;
Seek righteousness, seek humility
[regard them as vital].
Perhaps you will be hidden [and
pardoned and rescued]
In the day of the Lord's anger.

⁴ For [this is the fate of the
Philistines:] Gaza will be
abandoned
And Ashkelon a desolation;
[The people of] Ashdod will be
driven out at noon [in broad
daylight]
And Ekron will be uprooted *and*
destroyed.
⁵ Woe (judgment is coming) to the
inhabitants of the seacoast,
The nation of the Cherethites [in
Philistia]!
The word of the Lord is against you,
O Canaan, land of the Philistines;
I will destroy you
So that no inhabitant will be left.
⁶ So the [depopulated] seacoast
shall be pastures,
With [deserted] meadows for
shepherds and folds for flocks.
⁷ The seacoast will belong
To the remnant of the house of
Judah;
They will pasture [their flocks] on it.
In the [deserted] houses of
Ashkelon [in Philistia] they [of
Judah] will lie down *and* rest in
the evening,
For the Lord their God will care for
them;

And restore their fortune
[permitting them to occupy the
land]. [Is 14:29–31; Amos 1:6–8]

⁸ "I have heard the taunting of Moab
And the revilings of the sons of
Ammon,
With which they have taunted My
people
And become arrogant against their
territory [by violating Israel's
boundary and trying to seize its
land].
⁹ "Therefore, as I live," declares the
Lord of hosts,
The God of Israel,
"Moab will in fact become like
Sodom
And the sons of Ammon like
Gomorrah,
A land possessed by nettles and
salt pits,
And a perpetual desolation.
The remnant of My people will
plunder them
And what is left of My nation will
inherit them [as their own]."

¹⁰ This they shall have in return for
their pride, because they have taunted
and become arrogant against the peo-
ple of the Lord of hosts. ¹¹ The Lord will be terrifying *and*
awesome to them, for He will starve all
the gods of the earth; and all the coastlands of the nations will bow down *and*
worship Him, everyone from his own
place. [Joel 2:11; Zeph 1:4; 3:9]

¹² "You also, O Ethiopians, will be
slain by My sword." [Is 18]
¹³ And the Lord will stretch out His
hand against the north
And destroy Assyria,

speak the Word

*Lord, I seek You. I search diligently for you
and regard You as the foremost necessity in my life.*
—ADAPTED FROM ZEPHANIAH 2:3

And He will make Nineveh a
desolation [a wasteland],
Parched as the desert. [Is 10:12;
Nah 1:1]
14 Flocks will lie down in her midst,
All the animals which range in
herds;
Both the pelican and the short-
eared owl
Will roost on the top of Nineveh's
pillars.
Birds will sing in the window,
Desolation will be on the threshold;
For He has uncovered the cedar
paneling.
15 This is the joyous city
Which dwells carelessly [feeling
so secure],
Who says in her heart,
"I am, and there is no one besides
me."
What a desolation she has become,
A lair for [wild] animals!
Everyone who passes by her will
hiss [in scorn]
And wave his hand in contempt. [Is
10:5–34; 47:8, 10]

3 WOE (JUDGMENT is coming)
to her who is rebellious and
defiled,
The tyrannical city [Jerusalem]!
2 She did not listen and heed the
voice [of God];
She accepted no correction.
She did not trust in the LORD [but
trusted her own power];
She did not draw near to her God
[but to the pagan gods of Baal or
Molech].
3 Her officials within her are roaring
lions;

Her judges are [as hungry as] the
wolves at evening,
They leave nothing for the
morning.
4 Her prophets are reckless and
treacherous men;
Her priests have profaned the
sanctuary;
They have done violence to the
law [by pretending their word
is God's word]. [Jer 23:11; Ezek
22:26; Hos 9:7]
5 The LORD is righteous within her;
He will do no injustice.
Every morning He brings His
justice to light;
He does not fail.
But the unjust person knows no
shame.
6 "I [the LORD] have cut off and
destroyed nations [as a warning
to Judah];
Their corner towers (battlements)
are in ruins.
I have made their streets desolate
So that no one passes by;
Their cities are destroyed
So that there is no man, there is no
inhabitant.
7 "I said, 'Most certainly you will
[reverently] fear Me;
Accept correction.'
So Jerusalem's dwelling will not be
cut off
In accordance with all that I have
appointed concerning her
[punishment],
But they were eager [even rising
early] to make all their deeds
corrupt. [Jer 7:13]
8 "Therefore [you of the godly
remnant of Judah, patiently] wait
for Me," declares the LORD,

speak the Word

*Thank You, God, that You are righteous.
Every morning You bring Your justice to light. You never fail me.*
–ADAPTED FROM ZEPHANIAH 3:5

"[Wait] for the day when I rise up
   as a witness [against the nations].
For it is My decision *and* My right
   to gather the nations,
To assemble kingdoms,
To pour out on them My
   indignation,
All [the heat of] My burning anger;
For [in that day] all the earth shall
   be consumed
By the fire of My zeal.
⁹"Then I will give to the peoples
   [clear and pure speech from]
   purified lips [which reflect their
   purified hearts],
That all of them may call on the
   name of the Lord,
To serve Him shoulder to shoulder
   (united).
¹⁰"From beyond the rivers of Ethiopia
My worshipers, [the descendants
   of] My dispersed ones,
Will bring My offerings.
¹¹"On that day you [Israel] will feel
   no shame
Because of all your acts
By which you have rebelled *and*
   sinned against Me;
Then I will remove from among you
Your rejoicing ones who delight in
   their pride;
And you will never again behave
   arrogantly
On My holy mountain [Mount Zion].

putting the Word to work

Do you ever wonder how much God
really loves you? Zephaniah 3:17, in
Hebrew, gives us the image that God
literally "spins around" with joy over
you and that He sings and shouts over
you with joy! God has not only saved
you from His wrath through Jesus, but
He delights in you! Thank God for His
great love for you, and ask Him to help
you more fully understand the depths
of His love for you.

life point

Zephaniah 3:19 says that God wants to
bless those who would appear to be outcasts, those with "limps" in their lives. He
has determined to gather and bless those
who are imperfect—and that includes all
of us. He promises to cast out the enemy,
which is in many cases shame, blame,
or disgrace. God does not want you to
"limp" through life anymore. He wants
you to have peace and enjoy your life.

¹²"But I will leave among you
   A humble and lowly people,
   And they will take refuge *and* trust
     confidently in the name of the
     Lord.
¹³"The remnant of Israel will do no
     wrong
   Nor speak lies,
   Nor will a deceitful tongue
   Be found in their mouths;
   For they will eat and lie down
   With no one to make them tremble
     and feel afraid."

¹⁴Shout for joy, O Daughter of Zion!
   Shout *in triumph,* O Israel!
   Rejoice, be in high spirits *and* glory
     with all your heart,
   O Daughter of Jerusalem [in that
     day]!
¹⁵The Lord has taken away the
     judgments against you;
   He has cleared away your enemies.
   The King of Israel, even the Lord
     [Himself], is in your midst;
   You will no longer fear disaster.
¹⁶In that day it will be said to
     Jerusalem:
   "Do not be afraid, O Zion;
   Do not let your hands fall limp.
¹⁷"The Lord your God is in your
     midst,
   A Warrior who saves.
   He will rejoice over you with joy;

He will be quiet in His love
   [making no mention of your past
   sins],
He will rejoice over you with shouts
   of joy.
18 "I will gather those [Israelites in
   captivity] who grieve about the
   appointed feasts—
They came from you, [O Zion];
On whom the reproach [of exile] is
   a burden.
19 "Behold, at that time I am going to
   deal
With all your oppressors;
I will save the lame

And gather the scattered,
And I will turn their shame into
   praise and renown
In every land [where they have
   suffered]. [Mic 4:6, 7]
20 "At that time I will bring you in,
Yes, at the time I gather you
   together;
For I will make you a name and a
   praise
Among all the peoples of the earth
When I restore your fortunes [and
   freedom] before your eyes,"
Says the LORD.

Haggai

Author:
Haggai

Date:
520 BC

Everyday Life Principles:
We can be deceived into thinking we are obeying God simply because we have good intentions to do so.

Good intentions do not equal obedience.

We need to obey God quickly.

After the Jews returned to Jerusalem from exile, much restoration was needed in the city. The prophet Haggai, along with Zechariah, realized the importance of having a place to worship and encouraged the Jews to rebuild the temple, as God had directed them. The Jews were slow to obey God, and after He told them to rebuild the temple, they spent eighteen years rebuilding their own homes and ignoring God's house. They had good intentions of rebuilding the temple, but they had not done it. They thought their good intentions and plans to rebuild the temple would satisfy God's request; they thought they were being obedient to Him because they knew they would eventually get around to doing what He had told them to do. But after eighteen years of putting off obedience to God, they began to suffer drought, crop failure, and all kinds of discomfort and trouble because of their procrastination (see Haggai 1:6, 10, 11).

Haggai knew the people were struggling because they had not obeyed God promptly. They had put their own desire for comfortable homes ahead of their desire to complete the task God had assigned to them.

We must learn from the Jews' mistake to prioritize God's work and respond quickly to the assignments He gives us. Good intentions will not get the job done; we must act. Let the book of Haggai remind you to obey without delay when God asks you to do something for Him.

1 IN THE second year of Darius the king [of Persia], on the first day of the sixth month (Aug 29, 520 B.C.), the word of the LORD came by Haggai the prophet to Zerubbabel the son of Shealtiel, governor of Judah, and to Joshua the son of Jehozadak, the high priest, saying,

²"Thus says the LORD of hosts: 'These people say, "The time has not come that the LORD's house (temple) should be rebuilt."'" [Ezra 1:1–6; 4:1–6, 24; 5:1–3]

³Then the word of the LORD came by Haggai the prophet, saying,

⁴"Is it time for you yourselves to live in your [expensive] paneled houses while this house [of the LORD] lies in ruins?"

⁵Now therefore, thus says the LORD of hosts, "Consider your ways *and* thoughtfully reflect on your conduct!

⁶"You have planted much, but you harvest little; you eat, but you do not have *enough*; you drink, but you do not have *enough* to be intoxicated; you

putting the Word to work

Some people believe the Bible is simply a collection of stories and legends. Others view it solely as a historical document. Yet in Haggai 1:1–4 we see that Scripture is set in history and also that God is actively involved in human affairs, speaking to His people. How do you view God's Word? As you read the Bible, ask God to reveal Himself to you more fully through His living Word.

clothe yourselves, but no one is warm *enough;* and he who earns wages earns them *just to put* them in a bag with holes in it [because God has withheld His blessing]."

⁷Thus says the LORD of hosts, "Consider your ways *and* thoughtfully reflect on your conduct!

⁸"Go up to the hill country, bring lumber and rebuild My house (temple), that I may be pleased with it and

consider your ways

The first chapter of Haggai introduces us to a group of people who had ignored an instruction from God. He had told them to rebuild the temple eighteen years earlier, but they told themselves it was not the right time to do it. Instead of rebuilding God's house, they built their own houses during those eighteen years and experienced fruitlessness and frustration as a result. They found themselves in desperate circumstances. They never had enough money. Things were not working out for them. Whatever they did gain, they quickly lost.

God spoke to them through the prophet Haggai and said, "Consider your ways" (Haggai 1:7). In other words, "Look at your situation and ask yourselves why you are in such dire straits; it is because you are trying to take care of yourselves instead of obeying Me and working together to provide something for everyone. It will not work!"

Selfishness did not work for the people of Haggai's day, and it will not work for us today. It stops up every avenue of blessing that would otherwise flow into our lives.

Selfish people are quite miserable and usually think if they could just get what they want, they would feel better. Satan has them on a treadmill of striving to make themselves happy and never succeeding.

be glorified," says the LORD [accepting it as done for My glory].

⁹"You look for much [harvest], but it comes to little; and even when you bring that home, I blow it *away*. Why?" says the LORD of hosts. "Because of My house, which lies in ruins while each of you runs to his own house [eager to enjoy it].

¹⁰"Therefore, because of you [that is, your sin and disobedience] the heavens withhold the dew and the earth withholds its produce.

¹¹"I called for a drought on the land and the hill country, on the grain, on the new wine, on the oil, on what the ground produces, on men, on cattle, and on all the labor of your hands."

¹²Then Zerubbabel the son of Shealtiel and Joshua the son of Jehozadak, the high priest, with all the remnant of the people [who had returned from exile], listened carefully *and* obeyed the voice of the LORD their God and the words of Haggai the prophet, since the LORD their God had sent him. And the people [reverently] feared the LORD.

putting the Word to work

Have you ever heard the saying "You have to look out for number one?" Our culture emphasizes putting self over anything or anyone else. Yet God, through Haggai, told the people that as they trusted Him and gave to Him of their time and money, He would see to their needs. "Consider your ways," as Haggai 1:7 instructs, and ask God to show you areas in your life where you still need to put Him first. You will be blessed as you honor and trust Him.

putting the Word to work

Haggai 2:3, 4 are verses about dealing with change. When changes come in the life of a church, some people are unhappy. They will say, "I wish we could go back to the way we did it before," or, "I liked the old way better." How do you handle change in your church? Pray for your church leaders, that they will have wisdom in making decisions concerning the church, and continue to be actively involved in the life and ministry of the church, remembering that God is with you.

¹³Then Haggai, the LORD's messenger, spoke the LORD's message to the people saying, " 'I am with you,' declares the LORD."

¹⁴So the LORD stirred up the spirit of Zerubbabel the son of Shealtiel, governor of Judah, and the spirit of Joshua the son of Jehozadak, the high priest, and the spirit of all the remnant of the people; and they came and worked on the house of the LORD of hosts, their God,

¹⁵on the twenty-fourth day of the sixth month (Sept 21, 520 B.C.) in the second year of Darius the king.

2 ON THE twenty-first day of the seventh month (Oct 17, 520 B.C., the second year of Darius king of Persia), the word of the LORD came by the prophet Haggai, saying,

²"Speak now to Zerubbabel the son of Shealtiel, governor of Judah, and to Joshua the son of Jehozadak, the high priest, and to the remnant of the people, saying,

³'Who is left among you who saw this

speak the Word

God, I will be courageous because You are with me.
–ADAPTED FROM HAGGAI 2:4

house (temple) in its former glory? And how do you see it now? Does it not seem to you like nothing in comparison?

⁴'But now be courageous, Zerubbabel,' declares the LORD, 'be courageous also, Joshua the son of Jehozadak, the high priest, and be courageous, all you people of the land,' declares the LORD, 'and work; for I am with you,' declares the LORD of hosts.

⁵As for the promise which I made with you when you came out of Egypt,

more and more glory

In Haggai 2:9, God promises that the glory of the latter house will be greater than the glory of the former temple.

Do you know that you and I are the temple of God today (see 2 Corinthians 6:16) and that God's glory (His manifest excellence) is on us? Just as the temple in Haggai would increase in glory, so you and I also increase in glory as we grow in God. The glory we had in the past (the former glory) is not as great as what we have today or will have tomorrow.

In 2 Corinthians 3:18, Paul states that God changes us from one degree of glory to another. In other words, the changes in us personally, as well as in our circumstances, take place in degrees.

If you are born again, then you are somewhere on the path of the righteous—somewhere in the glory—right now. You may not be as far along as you would like to be, but thank God, you are on the path. There was a time when you were totally outside covenant relationship with God through unbelief (see Ephesians 2:11, 12). But now you belong to the household of God and are being transformed by Him day by day. Enjoy the glory you have right now, and do not feel jealous of where others may be. They may have already passed through the place where you are now.

We have a strong tendency to compare our glory with everybody else's, but this is fleshly thinking. The devil arranges for us to think that way, but it is not God's way. God wants us to realize that each of us is a unique individual and that He has a unique plan for every one of us. Satan wants to make sure we never enjoy where we are at the moment. He wants us in competition with one another, always wanting what someone else has. When we do not know how to enjoy the glory we are in right now, all we do is slow down the maturity process. I do not believe we pass into the next degree of glory until we have learned to enjoy the one we are in at the moment.

In this sense, a "glory" is simply a place that is better than the previous one. I had so many flaws in my personality and character that even after five years of trying to walk with the Lord, I still felt that I had made practically no progress. Yet, all that time I was gradually becoming a little more "glorious."

We are usually too hard on ourselves. We would grow faster if we relaxed more. We cannot live by our feelings in these matters. Satan makes sure we frequently "feel" that we are an unredeemable mess or that God is not working in our lives. We must learn to live by God's Word and not by how we feel. His Word states that as long as we believe, He is working in us! Your latter glory will be greater than your former!

My Spirit stands [firm and immovable] *and* continues with you; do not fear!'

⁶"For thus says the Lᴏʀᴅ of hosts, 'Once more, in a little while, I am going to shake the heavens and the earth, the sea and the dry land. [Heb 12:26]

⁷'I will shake all the nations; and they will come with the desirable *and* precious things of all nations, and I will fill this house with glory *and* splendor,' says the Lᴏʀᴅ of hosts. [Is 60:5; Matt 2:1–12]

⁸'The silver is Mine and the gold is Mine,' declares the Lᴏʀᴅ of hosts.

⁹'The latter glory of this house will be greater than the former,' says the Lᴏʀᴅ of hosts, 'and in this place I shall give [the ultimate] peace *and* prosperity,' declares the Lᴏʀᴅ of hosts."

¹⁰On the twenty-fourth day of the ninth month (Dec 18, 520 B.C.), in the second year of Darius, the word of the Lᴏʀᴅ came to Haggai the prophet, saying,

¹¹"Thus says the Lᴏʀᴅ of hosts, 'Ask the priests for a ruling:

¹²'If a man carries meat that is holy [because it has been offered in sacrifice to God] in the fold of his garment, and he touches bread, or cooked food, or wine, or oil, or any [kind of] food

life point

As we see in Haggai 2:11–13, unholiness is infectious; holiness is not. This means that when you and I associate with someone who is living a sinful life, that individual's sinfulness can rub off on us. We can catch it like a disease. But holiness is not like that. It cannot be picked up by contact or exposure; it has to be chosen on purpose. Choose to be holy today!

speak the Word

putting the Word to work

Haggai 2:15–19 illustrates the importance of making God's purposes for your life your top priority. Without priorities, it is difficult to live with any sense of purpose or to accomplish much. What are your priorities in your life?

with this fold, does what he touches become holy [dedicated exclusively to God's service]?'" And the priests answered, "No!" [Holiness is not transferrable.]

¹³Then Haggai said, "If one who is [ceremonially] unclean because of [contact with] a corpse touches any of these [articles of food], will it be unclean?" And the priests answered, "It will be unclean." [Ceremonial uncleanness, like sin, is infectious.]

¹⁴Then Haggai answered, " 'So is this people. And so is this nation before Me,' declares the Lᴏʀᴅ, 'and so is every work of their hands; and what they offer there [on the altar] is unclean [because they who offer it are unclean].

¹⁵'But now, do consider [what will happen] from this day forward: before one stone was placed on another in the temple of the Lᴏʀᴅ,

¹⁶from that time when one came to a *grain* heap *expecting* twenty *measures,* there would be only ten; and when one came to the wine vat to draw out fifty measures, there would be only twenty.

¹⁷'I struck you and the work of your hands with scorching wind, mildew, and hail; yet you did not come back to Me,' declares the Lᴏʀᴅ.

¹⁸'Do consider from this day forward, from the twenty-fourth day of the ninth

Thank You, God, for giving me peace and prosperity.
–ᴀᴅᴀᴘᴛᴇᴅ ꜰʀᴏᴍ Hᴀɢɢᴀɪ 2:9

month; from the day when the temple of the LORD was founded, consider:

¹⁹Is the seed still in the barn? As to the vine, the fig tree, the pomegranate, and the olive tree—they have not produced. Yet from this day on I will bless you [in the harvest of your crops].' "

²⁰And again the word of the LORD came to Haggai on the twenty-fourth day of the month (Dec 18, 520 B.C.), saying,

²¹"Speak to Zerubbabel governor of Judah, saying, 'I am going to shake the heavens and the earth. [Hag 2:6; Matt 1:12, 13]

²²'I will [in the distant future] overthrow the thrones of kingdoms and destroy the power of the kingdoms of the [ungodly] nations; and I will overthrow the chariots and those who ride in them, and the horses and their riders will go down, every one by the sword of his brother [annihilating one another]. [Dan 2:34, 35, 44, 45; Rev 19:11–21]

²³'On that day,' declares the LORD of hosts, 'I will take you, Zerubbabel, the son of Shealtiel, My servant,' declares the LORD, 'and I will make you [through the Messiah, your descendant] like a signet ring, for I have chosen you [as the one with whom to renew My covenant to David's line],' " declares the LORD of hosts. [2 Sam 7:12, 16]

speak the Word

Thank You, God, that You are blessing me today and from this day on.
—ADAPTED FROM HAGGAI 2:19

Zechariah

Author:
Zechariah

Date:
580 BC—possibly after 480 BC

Everyday Life Principles:
The only way to overcome the enemy is by God's Spirit.

Rely on God's grace and on the power of the Holy Spirit to overcome obstacles.

We make progress little by little.

Zechariah is a book of encouragement to Jews who were rebuilding the temple after their return to Jerusalem from exile. Zechariah's encouragement is as relevant to us today as it was to them centuries ago. Whatever work you have set your hand to, these truths from Zechariah 4 will serve you well.

First, the only way to defeat an enemy or accomplish God's purpose is through His Spirit (see Zechariah 4:6). One of the biggest mistakes we make is trying to obey God in our own strength rather than by His Spirit. We will fail if we try to achieve anything by human effort, but when we work by His Spirit, we always succeed.

Second, we will encounter obstacles as we seek to obey God, and we need God's grace in order to overcome them. As we rely on the Holy Spirit to help us, those mountain-sized obstacles become as molehills.

Third, we make progress step-by-step. We are not to despise small things (see Zechariah 4:10) or look upon seemingly minor accomplishments as insignificant. Everything big has to start small, and in fact comprises many, many small parts.

As you read Zechariah's words, I hope you will be encouraged in the work God has given you to do. Just as He encouraged the Jews in the rebuilding of the temple through the prophet, He is encouraging you today by His Spirit. Just as He brought about the restoration of the temple in their day, He wants to bring restoration to every area of your life today.

1 IN THE eighth month of the second year [of the reign] of Darius [the king of Persia], the word of the LORD came to Zechariah (the LORD remembers) the son of Berechiah, the son of Iddo, the prophet, saying, [Ezra 5:1]

²"The LORD was extremely angry with your fathers.

³"Therefore say to the Jews, 'Thus says the LORD of hosts (armies), "Return to Me," declares the LORD of hosts, "and I shall return to you.

⁴"Do not be like your fathers, to whom the former prophets proclaimed, 'Thus says the LORD of hosts, "Repent [that is, change your way of thinking] and return now from your evil way [of life] and from your evil deeds."' But they did not listen or pay attention to Me," declares the LORD. [2 Kin 17:13; Is 45:22; Jer 18:11; Ezek 33:11]

⁵"Your fathers, where are they? And the prophets, do they live forever?

⁶"But did not My words (warnings) and My statutes, which I commanded My servants the prophets, overtake your fathers? Then they repented and said, 'As the LORD of hosts planned to do to us [in discipline and punishment], in accordance with our ways and our deeds, so has He dealt with us.'"'

⁷On the twenty-fourth day of the eleventh month (Feb 15, 519 B.C.), which is the month of Shebat, in the second year of [the reign of] Darius, the word of the LORD came to Zechariah the prophet, the son of Berechiah, the son of Iddo, as follows:

⁸In the night I saw [a vision] and behold, a Man was riding on a red horse, and it stood among the myrtle trees that were in the ravine; and behind Him were horses: red, sorrel (reddish-brown), and white.

⁹Then I said, "O my lord, what are these?" And the angel who was speaking with me said, "I will show you what these are."

¹⁰And the Man who stood among the myrtle trees answered and said, "These are the ones whom the LORD has sent to go throughout the earth and patrol it."

¹¹And the men on the horses answered the Angel of the LORD who stood among the myrtle trees and said, "We have gone throughout the earth [patrolling it] and behold, all the earth sits at rest [in peace and free from war]."

¹²Then the Angel of the LORD said, "O LORD of hosts, how long will You withhold mercy and compassion from Jerusalem and the cities of Judah, against which You have had indignation and anger these seventy years [of the Babylonian captivity]?"

¹³And the LORD answered the angel who was speaking with me with gracious and comforting words.

¹⁴So the angel who was speaking with me said to me, "Proclaim, 'Thus says the LORD of hosts, "I am jealous [with a burning, fiery passion] for Jerusalem and for Zion [demanding what is rightfully and uniquely mine] with a great jealousy.

¹⁵"But I am very angry with the nations who are at ease and feel secure; for while I was only a little angry, they furthered the disaster [against the people of Israel]."

¹⁶'Therefore, thus says the LORD, "I have returned to Jerusalem with mercy and compassion. My house shall be built in it," says the LORD of hosts, "and a measuring line shall be stretched out over Jerusalem."'

¹⁷"Proclaim again, 'Thus says the LORD of hosts, "My cities shall again overflow with prosperity, and the LORD shall again comfort Zion and again choose Jerusalem."'"

¹⁸Then I looked up, and saw four horns (powers)!

¹⁹So I asked the angel who was speaking with me, "What are these?" And he answered me, "These are the

horns [the powerful Gentile nations] that have scattered Judah (the Southern Kingdom), Israel (the Northern Kingdom), and Jerusalem (capital city of Judah)."

²⁰Then the LORD showed me four craftsmen.

²¹I asked, "What are these [horns and craftsmen] coming to do?" And he said, "These are the horns (powers) that have scattered Judah so that no man raised up his head [because of the suffering inflicted by the Gentile nations]. But these *craftsmen* have come to terrify them *and* make them panic, and throw down the horns of the nations who have lifted up their horns against the land of Judah in order to scatter it."

2 AND I looked up, and saw a man with a measuring line in his hand.

²So I said, "Where are you going?" And he said to me, "To measure Jerusalem, to see how wide it is and how long it is."

³And behold, the angel who was speaking with me was going out, and another angel was coming out to meet him,

⁴and he said to the second angel, "Run, speak to that young man, saying, 'Jerusalem will be inhabited [like villages] without walls [spreading out into the open country] because of the great number of people and livestock in it.

⁵'For I,' declares the LORD, 'will be a wall of fire around her [protecting her from enemies], and I will be the glory in her midst.'"

⁶"Hear this! Flee from [Babylon] the land of the north [which shall come under judgment]," declares the LORD, "for I have scattered you like the four winds of the heavens," declares the LORD.

⁷"Hear, Zion (Jerusalem)! Escape, you who are living with the daughter of Babylon!"

⁸For thus says the LORD of hosts, "After glory He has sent Me against the nations which plunder you—for he who touches you, touches the apple of His eye.

⁹"Behold, I will wave my hand over them and they shall become plunder for their own slaves. Then you shall know (recognize, understand fully) that the LORD of hosts has sent Me.

¹⁰"Sing for joy and rejoice, O Daughter of Zion; for behold, I am coming, and I will dwell in your midst," declares the LORD.

¹¹"Many nations shall join themselves to the LORD in that day and shall be My people. And I will dwell in your midst, and you shall know (recognize, understand fully) that the LORD of hosts has sent Me to you. [Is 2:3; Mic 4:2]

¹²"The LORD will take possession of Judah as His portion in the holy land and will again choose Jerusalem.

¹³"Be still before the LORD, all mankind; for He is roused (raised up) from His holy habitation [in response to His persecuted people]." [Hab 2:20; Zeph 1:7]

3 THEN THE guiding angel showed me Joshua the high priest [representing disobedient, sinful Israel] standing before the Angel of the LORD, and Satan standing at Joshua's right hand to be his adversary *and* to accuse him.

speak the Word

God, I know that anyone who comes against me
comes against the apple of Your eye.
—ADAPTED FROM ZECHARIAH 2:8

²And the LORD said to Satan, "The LORD rebuke you, Satan! Even the LORD, who [now and ever] has chosen Jerusalem, rebuke you! Is this not a log snatched *and* rescued from the fire?" [Jude 9]

³Now Joshua was clothed with filthy (nauseatingly vile) garments and was standing before the Angel [of the LORD].

⁴He spoke to those who stood before Him, saying, "Remove the filthy garments from him." And He said to Joshua, "See, I have caused your wickedness to be taken away from you, and I will clothe *and* beautify you with rich robes [of forgiveness]."

⁵And I (Zechariah) said, "Let them put a clean turban on his head." So they put a clean turban on his head and clothed him with [rich] garments. And the Angel of the LORD stood by.

⁶And the Angel of the LORD [solemnly and earnestly] admonished Joshua, saying,

⁷"Thus says the LORD of hosts, 'If you will walk in My ways [that is, remain faithful] and perform My service, then you will also govern My house and

putting the Word to work

Zechariah 3:3–5 is a brief illustration of God's power and desire to cleanse us from sin. Have you ever had a piece of clothing ruined by a stain that would not come out? Our lives are stained by sin, and there is nothing we can do on our own to cleanse the stain. Yet God removed the stain of sin in our lives through the sacrifice of His Son, Jesus. If you have not already done so, acknowledge that your life is stained by sin, and ask God for forgiveness. Rejoice that He will remove the stain of sin and clothe you with righteousness!

life point

Are you facing a difficult obstacle in your life? Like the Israelites, you cannot overcome any situation by determination alone. You do need to be determined, but as Zechariah 4:6 teaches, be determined *in the Holy Spirit*—not in the effort of your own flesh. The Holy Spirit is your Helper; seek His help. Lean on Him. You cannot make it alone. You need Him.

have charge of My courts, and I will give you free access [to My presence] among these who are standing here.

⁸'Now listen, Joshua, the high priest, you and your colleagues who are sitting in front of you—indeed they are men who are a symbol [of what is to come]—for behold, I am going to bring in My servant the Branch [in Messianic glory]. [Is 4:2; Jer 23:5; 33:15; Zech 6:12]

⁹'For behold, the stone which I have set before Joshua; on that one stone are seven eyes (symbolizing infinite intelligence, omniscience). Behold, I will engrave an inscription on it,' declares the LORD of hosts, 'and I will remove the wickedness *and* guilt of this land in a single day. [2 Chr 16:9; Jer 50:20; Zech 4:10]

¹⁰'In that day,' declares the LORD of hosts, 'every one of you will invite his neighbor to sit under his vine and his fig tree [enjoying peace and prosperity in the kingdom].'" [Mic 4:1–4]

4 AND THE angel who was speaking with me came back and awakened me, like a man who is awakened out of his sleep.

²He said to me, "What do you see?" I said, "I see, and behold, a lampstand all of gold, with its bowl [for oil] on the top of it and its seven lamps on it with seven spouts belonging to each of the lamps which are on the top of

it. [Matt 5:14, 16; Luke 12:35; Phil 2:15; Rev 1:20]

³"And there are two olive trees by it, one on the right side of the bowl and the other on its left side [supplying it continuously with oil]." [Rev 11:4–13]

⁴So I asked the angel who was speaking with me, "What are these, my lord?"

⁵Then the angel who was speaking with me answered me, "Do you not know what these are?" And I said, "No, my lord."

⁶Then he said to me, "This [continuous supply of oil] is the word of the LORD to Zerubbabel [prince of Judah], saying, 'Not by might, nor by power, but by My Spirit [of whom the oil is a symbol],' says the LORD of hosts.

⁷'What are you, O great mountain [of obstacles]? Before Zerubbabel [who will rebuild the temple] *you will become* a plain (insignificant)! And he will bring out the capstone [of the new temple] with loud shouts of "Grace, grace to it!"'" [Ezra 4:1–5, 24; Is 40:4]

⁸Also the word of the LORD came to me, saying,

⁹"The hands of Zerubbabel have laid the foundations of this house, and his hands will finish it. Then you will know (recognize, understand fully) that the LORD of hosts has sent me [as His messenger] to you.

by His Spirit

Have you ever been frustrated because you were doing everything right that you knew to do in a situation, but no matter what you did, nothing worked? I have certainly had times like that, and I believe everyone else has too. After many years of being frustrated most of the time, I finally learned I was placing too much trust in myself and my own efforts and not trusting God enough.

God's Word refers to us as "believers," and our job is to believe. We usually think we should be doing or achieving something, but if that were the case we would be called "achievers" instead of "believers." We are certainly responsible to do certain things, but most of us go far beyond our God-given responsibility and try to do things only God can do.

What needs to be accomplished in our lives and circumstances is not going to happen by might or power on our part, but it will be done by the Spirit of God as we place our trust in Him (see Zechariah 4:6). God gives us the Holy Spirit as our divine Helper. He enables us to do what we need to do, and He does what we cannot do. We are partners with God; He has a part and we have a part. Our part is to trust God and do whatever He leads us to do, and His part is to accomplish what needs to be done in our lives and work in our behalf. God will not do our part, and we cannot do His part. This is one of the most important lessons we must learn in life unless we want to be frustrated most of the time.

When I begin to feel frustrated, I know I have slipped over into trying to make things happen by my own efforts and have stopped fully trusting God. As soon as I get my trust back where it belongs, which is in God and not in myself, I start to feel relaxed again. Jesus said if we are weary and overburdened, we should come to Him (see Matthew 11:28). He put it very simply, and we need to simply do what He said. What needs to be done in our lives will not be done by might or power, but by the Holy Spirit.

¹⁰"Who [with reason] despises the day of small things (beginnings)? For these seven [eyes] shall rejoice when they see the plumb line in the hand of Zerubbabel. They are the eyes of the LORD which roam throughout the earth." [Rev 5:6]

¹¹Then I said to him [who was speaking with me], "What are these two olive trees on the right side of the lampstand and on its left?"

¹²And a second time I said to him, "What are these two olive branches which are beside the two golden pipes by which the golden oil is emptied?"

¹³And he answered me, "Do you not know what these are?" And I said, "No, my lord."

¹⁴Then he said, "These are the two sons of fresh oil [Joshua the high priest and Zerubbabel the prince of Judah] who are standing by the Lord of the whole earth [as His anointed ones]." [Rev 11:4]

life point

In Zechariah 4:7, the Lord tells Zechariah that the problem facing the Israelites, although it may appear to be a mountain, is actually a molehill. How would you like for all your mountains to become molehills? They can, if you will do what God is saying here and look not at the problems, but at the Lord and His power.

If God has told you to do something, it certainly is His will that you begin it. But it is also His will that you finish it. You will never complete your God-given task if you do not understand grace—the power of the Holy Spirit—and shout, "Grace, Grace!" to the obstacles in front of you.

Remember, it is not by power or by might, but by the Spirit that we win the victory over our enemy. We overcome through faith, by grace.

life point

Zechariah 4:10 instructs us not to despise "the day of small things (beginnings)." When we despise something, we take it lightly; we disregard it and count it as nothing.

When we are believing God for something "big," we need to remember that great things start small. We need to appreciate "the day of small things," because the little things will grow if we recognize them, appreciate them, and honor them as gifts from God and indicators of greater things to come.

5 AGAIN I looked up, and I saw a scroll flying *in the air!*

²And the angel said to me, "What do you see?" And I answered, "I see a flying scroll; its length is twenty cubits (thirty feet) and its width is ten cubits (fifteen feet)."

³Then he said to me, "This is the curse that is going out over the face of the whole land; for everyone who steals will be cut off according to the writing on one side, and everyone who swears [oaths falsely] shall be cut off according to the writing on the other side. [Is 24:6; Mal 3:8, 9]

⁴"I will send the curse out," declares the LORD of hosts, "and it will enter the house of the thief and the house of the one who swears falsely by My name; and it will spend the night in that house and consume it, both its timber and its stones."

⁵Then the angel who was speaking with me came forward and said to me, "Now look up and see what this is going forth."

⁶And I said, "What is it?" And he said, "This is the ephah (grain basket) going forth. This," he continued, "is their appearance throughout the land [Amos 8:5]

⁷(and behold, a [round, flat] lead cover was lifted up); and there sat a woman inside the ephah."

⁸Then he said, "This is Wickedness (Godlessness)!" And he threw her back down into the middle of the ephah and threw the lead cover on its opening.

⁹Then I looked up, and there were two women coming out with the wind in their wings; and they had wings like the wings of a stork, and they lifted up the ephah between the earth and the heavens.

¹⁰I said to the angel who was speaking with me, "Where are they taking the ephah?"

small things lead to big things

As I look back on the early days of my ministry, I can remember "the day of small things (beginnings)" (Zechariah 4:10), which would have been so easy to despise! When I first started out, my meetings drew only a handful of people, maybe fifty at the most. It is just as hard to preach to fifty as it is to preach to five thousand, so I had to put the same amount of time and effort into my lessons then as I do now.

When my ministry team started traveling, we needed a vehicle to transport all our equipment and us. The first van we bought cost twenty-six hundred dollars. It had bald tires and rust spots on it. We would leave our hometown and drive to a little town several hours away, where there would be from seventy to one hundred twenty-five people in attendance at our meeting.

Since we did not have enough money to spend the night in a motel, we would drive back home that same evening after the services had ended. We would usually get back about three o'clock in the morning. On the way home we would get so tired we would have to pull off on the side of the road and get ten or fifteen minutes of sleep before driving on.

Those days frustrated me while I was living them, but now I can see their value. They were important because they were times of preparation for the greater days the Lord knew lay ahead. I sincerely believe Joyce Meyer Ministries would not have grown to the point of reaching the number of people it does today had we not been faithful enough to press through those early hardships. We need to remember that God anointed David to be king long before he actually became king, and David was tested in many ways while he waited. Patience must be tested, humility must be manifested, and faith must grow. Only after we pass our tests do we get promoted to the next level of what God has in mind for us.

I'm always saddened when I see people give up in the hard times and never get to enjoy the fruit of all their labors. Starting an endeavor is easy, but finishing it is much harder. In the beginning, we are excited, and usually people give us all kinds of enthusiastic support. But as the days go by and the "great and glorious cause" becomes a matter of daily, consistent hard work, often we are left with nobody to urge us on except God and ourselves.

That is when we have to decide if we are going to see it through to the finish. That is when we have to realize everything we are going through at the moment will one day pass and we will enjoy the fruit of our labors. In the meantime, we need to enjoy where we are while we are on the way to where we are going and be sure to appreciate the small things.

¹¹And he said to me, "To the land of Shinar (Babylon) to build a temple for her; and when it is prepared, she shall be set there on her own pedestal."

6 NOW AGAIN I looked up, and four chariots were coming out from between two mountains; and the mountains were mountains of [firm, immovable] bronze (divine judgment).

²The first chariot had red horses (war, bloodshed), the second chariot had black horses (famine, death), [Rev 6:4–6]

³the third chariot had white horses (victory), and the fourth chariot had strong dappled horses (death through judgment). [Rev 6:2, 8]

⁴Then I said to the angel who was speaking with me, "What are these, my lord?"

⁵The angel answered me, "These are the four spirits of the heavens, which go out after presenting themselves before the Lord of all the earth, [Ps 104:4; Matt 24:31]

⁶with the chariot with the black horses going toward the north country; then the one with the white horses follows after them [because there are two northern powers to overcome], and the chariot with the dappled horses goes toward the south country."

⁷When the strong horses went out, they were eager to patrol the earth. And the Lord said, "Go, patrol the earth." So they patrolled the earth [watching and protecting it].

⁸Then He called out to me and said to me, "See, those who are going to the north country have quieted My Spirit [of wrath] in the north country."

⁹The word of the Lord also came to me, saying,

¹⁰"Take an offering from the exiles, from Heldai, from Tobijah, and from Jedaiah [as representatives]; and you go the same day and enter the house of Josiah the son of Zephaniah, where they have arrived from Babylon.

¹¹"Take silver and gold [from them], and make an ornate crown and set it on the head of Joshua the son of Jehozadak, the high priest.

¹²"Then say to Joshua, 'Thus says the Lord of hosts, "Behold (look, keep in sight, watch), a Man (Messiah) whose name is Branch, for He shall branch out from His place (Israel, the Davidic line); and He shall build the [ultimate] temple of the Lord. [Is 4:2; Jer 23:5; 33:15; Zech 3:8]

¹³"Yes, [you are to build a temple of the Lord, but] it is He who shall build the [ultimate] temple of the Lord, and He shall bear the honor and majesty [as the only begotten of the Father] and sit and rule on His throne. And He shall be a Priest on His throne, and the counsel of peace shall be between the two offices [Priest and King]."' [John 1:14; 17:5; Heb 2:9]

¹⁴"Now the crown shall become a reminder in the temple of the Lord to Helem, Tobijah, Jedaiah, and Hen the son of Zephaniah. [Matt 10:41]

¹⁵"And those who are far away will come and [help] build the temple of the Lord." Then you shall know [without any doubt] that the Lord of hosts sent me (Zechariah) to you. And it will come about if you will diligently obey the [voice of the] Lord your God.

7 IN THE fourth year of [the reign of] King Darius [of Persia], the word of the Lord came to Zechariah on the fourth day of the ninth month, which is Chislev (Dec 7, 518 B.C.).

²Now the people of Bethel had sent Sharezer and Regem-melech and their men to seek the favor of the Lord,

³speaking to the priests who belong to the house of the Lord of hosts and to the prophets, saying, "[Now that I am returned from exile] shall I weep in the fifth month [mourning the destruction

of the temple], and fast as I have done these many years [in Babylon]?"

⁴Then the word of the Lord of hosts came to me (Zechariah), saying,

⁵"Speak to all the people of the land and to the priests, saying, 'When you fasted and mourned in the fifth and seventh months these seventy years [that you were in exile], was it actually for Me that you fasted?

⁶'When you eat and when you drink, do you not eat for yourselves and do you not drink for yourselves [to satisfy your own needs]?

⁷'Should you not hear the words which the Lord proclaimed by the former prophets, when Jerusalem was inhabited and prosperous along with her cities around her, and the South (the Negev) and the foothills were inhabited?'"

⁸Then the word of the Lord came to Zechariah, saying,

⁹"Thus has the Lord of hosts said, 'Dispense true justice and practice kindness and compassion, to each other;

¹⁰and do not oppress *or* exploit the widow or the fatherless, the stranger or the poor; and do not devise *or* even imagine evil in your hearts against one another.'

¹¹"But they refused to listen *and* pay attention and turned a stubborn shoulder [stiffening themselves in resistance] and stopped up their ears.

¹²"They made their hearts [hard] like flint, so that they could not hear the law and the words which the Lord of hosts had sent by His Spirit through the former prophets. Therefore great wrath came from the Lord of hosts.

¹³"And just as He called and they would not listen, so they called and I would not listen," says the Lord of hosts;

¹⁴"but I scattered them with a storm wind among all the nations whom they have not known. Thus the land was desolate after they had gone, so that no one passed through or returned, for they [by their sins] had made the pleasant land desolate *and* deserted."

8 THEN THE word of the Lord of hosts came [to me], saying,

²"Thus says the Lord of hosts, 'I am jealous for Zion with great jealousy [demanding what is rightfully and uniquely mine], and I am jealous for her with great wrath [against her enemies].'

³"Thus says the Lord, 'I shall return to Zion and will dwell in the midst of Jerusalem, and Jerusalem shall be called the [faithful] City of Truth, and the mountain of the Lord of hosts will be called the Holy Mountain.'

⁴"Thus says the Lord of hosts, 'Old men and old women will again sit in the streets (public places) of Jerusalem, each man with his staff in his hand because of his advanced age.

⁵'And the streets of the city will be filled with boys and girls playing in its streets.'

⁶"Thus says the Lord of hosts, 'If it is difficult in the eyes of the remnant of this people in those days [in which this comes to pass], will it also be difficult in My sight?' declares the Lord of hosts. [Gen 18:14; Jer 32:17, 27; Luke 18:27]

⁷"Thus says the Lord of hosts, 'Behold, I am going to save My people from the east country and from the west, [Is 43:5, 6]

⁸and I will bring them home and they will live in the midst of Jerusalem; and they shall be My people, and I will be their God in truth (faithfulness) and in righteousness.'

⁹"Thus says the Lord of hosts, 'Let your hands be strong, you who in these days hear these words from the mouths of the prophets who, on the day that the foundation of the house of the Lord of hosts was laid, foretold that the temple might be rebuilt.

¹⁰'For before those days there were no wages for man or animal; nor was there any peace *or* success for him who went out or came in because of his enemies, for I set all men against one another.

¹¹'But now [in this time since you began to build] I will not treat the remnant of this people as in the former days,' declares the Lord of hosts.

¹²'For there the seed will produce peace *and* prosperity; the vine will yield its fruit, and the ground will produce its increase, and the heavens will give their dew. And I will cause the remnant of this people to inherit *and* possess all these things.

¹³'And as you have been a curse among the nations, O house of Judah (Southern Kingdom) and house of Israel (Northern Kingdom), so I will save you, that you may be a blessing. Fear not; let your hands be strong.' [Jer 22:8, 9]

¹⁴'For thus says the Lord of hosts, 'Just as I planned to do harm to you when your fathers provoked Me to wrath,' says the Lord of hosts, 'and I did not relent,

¹⁵so I have again planned in these days to do good to Jerusalem and to the house of Judah. Do not fear!

¹⁶'These are the things which you should do: speak the truth with one another; judge with truth and pronounce the judgment that brings

putting the Word to work

Clearly, acting with integrity and peace and for the good of others is important to God (see Zechariah 8:16, 17). Let me encourage you to take an opportunity to reach out to someone with a word of encouragement or an act of kindness. Ask God to show you how to be good to others, and pray for those around you to be blessed.

peace in [the courts at] your gates. [Eph 4:25]

¹⁷'And let none of you devise *or* even imagine evil in your heart against another, and do not love lying *or* half-truths; for all these things I hate,' declares the Lord."

¹⁸Then the word of the Lord of hosts came to me (Zechariah), saying,

¹⁹"Thus says the Lord of hosts, 'The fast of the fourth [month to mourn the breaching of Jerusalem's walls], the fast of the fifth [month to mourn the temple's destruction], the fast of the seventh [month to mourn Gedaliah's assassination], and the fast of the tenth [month to mourn the siege of Jerusalem] will become times of joy and gladness and cheerful feasts for the house of Judah; so [to bring this about] love truth and peace.' [Jer 39:2; 2 Kin 25:1, 2, 8, 25]

²⁰"Thus says the Lord of hosts, 'It will come to pass that peoples and the inhabitants of many cities will come [to Jerusalem].

²¹'The inhabitants of one [city] will go to another, saying, "Let us go at once to ask the favor of the Lord and to seek the Lord of hosts. I will go also."

²²'So many peoples and powerful nations will come to seek the Lord of hosts in Jerusalem and to ask the Lord for His favor.'

²³"Thus says the Lord of hosts, 'In those days ten men [as representatives] from all the nations will grasp the robe of a Jew, saying, "Let us go with you, for we have heard that God is with you."''

9 THE ORACLE (a burdensome message) of the word of the Lord is against the land of Hadrach [in Syria], with Damascus as its resting place (for the eyes of men, especially of all the tribes of Israel, are toward the Lord), [Nah 1:1]

2 And Hamath also, which borders
   on it (Damascus),
Tyre and Sidon, though they are
   very wise.
3 For Tyre built herself an
   [impregnable] stronghold [on an
   island offshore],
And she has heaped up silver like
   dust
And gold like the mire of the streets.
4 Behold, the Lord will dispossess
   her
And throw her wealth into the sea;
And Tyre will be devoured by fire.
5 Ashkelon will see it and fear;
Gaza will writhe in pain,
And Ekron, for her hope and
   expectation, has been ruined.
The king will perish from Gaza,
And Ashkelon will not be
   inhabited.
6 And a mongrel race will live in
   Ashdod,
And I will put an end to the pride
   and arrogance of the Philistines.
7 I will take the blood from their
   mouths
And their detestable things from
   between their teeth [those
   repulsive, idolatrous sacrifices
   eaten with the blood].
Then they too will be a remnant
   for our God,
And be like a clan in Judah,
And Ekron will be like one of the
   Jebusites.

life point

As "prisoners who have the hope" (Zechariah 9:12), it is so important for us to
be filled with hope—to think hope and
speak hope all the time. When you face a
seemingly hopeless situation and you feel
captive in it, remember that in God, you
are a prisoner who has hope; there is no
way to get away from the hope that is in
Him.

8 Then I will camp around My house
   [as a guard] because of an army,
Because of him who passes by and
   returns;
And no oppressor will again
   overrun them (Israel),
For now My eyes are upon them
   [providentially protecting them].
9 Rejoice greatly, O Daughter of Zion!
Shout aloud, O Daughter of
   Jerusalem!
Behold, your King (Messianic
   King) is coming to you;
He is righteous and endowed with
   salvation,
Humble and unassuming [in
   submission to the will of the
   Father] and riding on a donkey,
Upon a colt, the foal of a donkey.
10 I will cut off the [war] chariot from
   Ephraim
And the [war] horse from
   Jerusalem,
And the bow of war will be cut off.
And He will speak [words of]
   peace to the nations,
And His dominion shall be from
   sea to sea [absolutely endless],
And from the River [Euphrates] to
   the ends of the earth. [Ps 72:8]

11 As for you also, because of the
   blood of My covenant with you
   [My chosen people, the covenant
   that was sealed with blood]
I have freed your prisoners from
   the waterless pit. [Gen 37:24; Ex
   24:4–8; Heb 9:16]
12 Return to the stronghold [of
   security and prosperity], O
   prisoners who have the hope;
Even today I am declaring that I
   will restore double [your former
   prosperity] to you [as firstborn
   among nations]. [Ps 40:2; Is 40:2]
13 For I will bend Judah as My bow,
I will fit the bow with Ephraim [as
   My arrow].
And I will stir up your sons, O Zion,
   against your sons, O Greece,

And will make you [Israel] like the
sword of a warrior.
14 Then the LORD will be seen
[hovering] over them [protecting
His people],
And His arrow will go forth like
lightning;
And the Lord GOD will blow the
trumpet
And will march in the windstorms
of the south.
15 The LORD of hosts shall defend and
protect them;
And they will devour [the
enemy] and trample down the
slingstones [that have missed
their mark],
And they will drink [of victory]
and be boisterous as with wine;

And they shall be filled like
sacrificial bowls [used to catch
the blood],
Drenched like the corners of the
[sacrificial] altar.
16 And the LORD their God shall save
them on that day
As the flock of His people;
For they are like the [precious]
jewels of a crown,
Displayed *and* glittering in His
land.
17 For how great is God's goodness
and how great is His beauty!
And how great [He will make
Israel's] goodliness and [Israel's]
beauty!
Grain and new wine will make the
young men and virgins flourish.

prisoners of hope

What is a prisoner who has the hope (see Zechariah 9:12)? It is someone who refuses
to stop hoping in God, no matter how bad his or her circumstances are. Abraham
was such a man. We learn from God's Word that all human reason for hope being
gone, Abraham hoped on in faith that God's promise would come to pass in his life
(see Romans 4:18).

Godly hope is not the same as what the world calls "hope." It has a different
quality. Usually when we hear people say they are "hoping" something will or will
not happen, they are vaguely hoping, but clearly doubting. They speak negatively
and complain about almost everything and then wonder why nothing works out for
them. True biblical hope is a solid foundation; it is a springboard for our faith to take
off from and actually take hold of the promises of God.

I know this may sound simple, but I think we can say real hope is a constant positive attitude that no matter what is happening currently, things will change for the
better. Satan cannot defeat a person who refuses to stop hoping in God. Abraham
refused to give up hope, and just as God had told him, he did become a father when
he was far too old to father children. Hope is powerful. It opens the door for the
impossible to become possible. All things are possible with God, but we must cooperate with Him by being hopeful and full of faith.

God promises that He will restore double what we have lost or had stolen if we
will stay hopeful. It does no good at all to be hopeless. It only makes us unhappy,
critical, and grouchy. Hopelessness leads to depression and many other problems.
Become a prisoner who has hope. Be the kind of person who absolutely refuses to
be negative, and get ready to receive a blessing.

10 ASK *FOR* rain from the Lord at the time of the spring rain.
It is the Lord who makes the thunder clouds;
And He will give them showers of rain, grass in the field to everyone.
2 For the teraphim (household idols) speak wickedness (emptiness, worthlessness),
And the diviners see lying visions
And tell false dreams;
They comfort in vain.
Therefore the people wander like sheep,
They are afflicted *and* suffer because there is no shepherd.
3 "My anger is kindled against the shepherds [who are not true shepherds],
And I shall punish the male goats (leaders);
For the Lord of hosts has visited His flock, the house of Judah (the Southern Kingdom),
And will make them like His beautiful *and* majestic horse in the battle. [Ezek 34:1–10]
4 "From them (Judah) shall come the Cornerstone,
From them the tent peg,
From them the bow of battle,
From them every ruler, all of them together. [Jer 30:21]
5 "They will be like mighty men
Trampling down *their enemies* in the mire of the streets in the battle;
And they will fight because the Lord is with them,
And the [enemies'] riders on horses will be shamed.
6 "I will strengthen the house of Judah [making it superior],
And I will save the house of Joseph.
I will bring them back [and allow them to live securely],

Because I have had compassion on them.
They will be as though I had not rejected them,
For I am the Lord their God, and I will listen *and* answer them.
7 "Then Ephraim will be like a mighty warrior,
And their heart will rejoice as if from wine;
Yes, their children will see it and rejoice;
Their heart will rejoice *and* shout triumphantly in the Lord.
8 "I will whistle for them and gather them together,
For I have redeemed them;
And they will increase [again] as they have increased before [in Egypt]. [Ezek 36:10, 11]
9 "When I scatter them among the nations,
They will remember Me in far countries,
And with their children they will live and come back [to Me and the land I gave them].
10 "I will bring them (all Israel) back home again from the land of Egypt
And gather them from Assyria,
And I will bring them into the land of Gilead and Lebanon [the land on the east and on the west of the Jordan]
Until no room can be found for them.
11 "And they will pass through the sea of distress *and* anxiety [with the Lord leading His people, as at the Red Sea]
And He will strike the waves in the sea,
So that all the depths of the Nile will dry up;
And the pride of Assyria will be brought down
And the scepter [of the taskmasters] of Egypt will pass away.

¹²"And I will strengthen Israel in the LORD,
And they will walk [and glory] in
His name," declares the LORD.

11 OPEN YOUR doors,
O Lebanon,
That fire may devour your
cedars.
²Wail, O cypress, for the cedar has
fallen,
Because the magnificent trees
have been destroyed;
Wail, O oaks of Bashan,
For the inaccessible forest [on the
steep mountainside] has come
down.
³There is a sound of the shepherds'
wail,
For their splendor (grazing land) is
ruined;
There is a sound of the young
lions' roar,
For the pride of the Jordan is ruined.

⁴Thus says the LORD my God, "Pasture the flock *doomed* for slaughter,
⁵whose buyers slay them and go unpunished, and those who sell them say, 'Blessed be the LORD, for I have become rich!' And their own shepherds have no pity on them *nor* protect them [from the wolves].
⁶"For I will no longer have pity on the inhabitants of the land," declares the LORD; "but behold, I will cause the men to fall, each into the hand of another and into the hands of his [foreign] king. And the enemy will strike the land, and I will not rescue the people from their hand."
⁷So I [Zechariah] pastured the flock *doomed* for slaughter, truly [as the name implies] the most miserable of

sheep. And I took two [shepherd's] staffs, the one I called Favor (Grace) and the other I called Union (Bonds); so I pastured the flock.
⁸Then I eliminated the three [incompetent, unfit] shepherds [the civil rulers, the priests, and the prophets] in one month, for I was impatient with them, and they also were tired of me *and* despised me. [Jer 2:8, 26; 18:18]
⁹So I said, "I will not pasture you. What is to die, let it die, and what is to be destroyed, let it be destroyed; and let the survivors devour one another's flesh."
¹⁰I took my staff, Favor, and broke it in pieces, breaking the covenant which I had made with all the peoples.
¹¹So the covenant was broken on that day, and thus the most wretched of the flock who were watching me realized that it was the word of the LORD.
¹²I said to them, "If it seems good to you, give me my wages; but if not, do not." So they weighed out thirty pieces of silver as my wages.
¹³Then the LORD said to me, "Throw it to the potter [as if to the dogs]—that *magnificent* sum at which I am valued by them!" So I took the thirty pieces of silver and threw them to the potter in the house of the LORD. [Matt 26:14, 15; 27:3–10]
¹⁴Then I broke my second staff, Union, into pieces to break the brotherhood between Judah (the Southern Kingdom) and Israel (the Northern Kingdom).
¹⁵The LORD said to me, "Take again for yourself the equipment [of a shepherd, but this time] of a foolish shepherd. [Ezek 34:2–6]
¹⁶"For behold, I am going to raise

speak the Word

Thank You, Lord, that I am being strengthened in You.
I will walk and glory in Your name.
−ADAPTED FROM ZECHARIAH 10:12

up a [false] shepherd in the land who will not care for the perishing, seek the scattered, heal the broken, or feed the healthy; but will eat the flesh of the fat ones and tear off their hoofs [to consume everything].

¹⁷"Woe (judgment is coming) to the
    worthless *and* foolish shepherd
Who deserts the flock!
The sword will strike his arm
And his right eye!
His arm shall be totally withered
And his right eye completely
    blinded." [Jer 23:1; John 10:12, 13]

12 THE ORACLE (a burdensome message) of the word of the Lord concerning Israel. **T**hus declares the Lord who stretches out the heavens and lays the foundation of the earth and forms the spirit of man within him:

²"Behold, I am going to make Jerusalem a cup that causes reeling (staggering) to all the surrounding peoples; and when the siege is against Jerusalem, it will also be against Judah.

³"And in that day I will make Jerusalem a heavy stone for all the peoples; all who lift it will be severely injured. And all the nations of the earth will come *and* be gathered against it.

⁴"In that day," declares the Lord, "I will strike every horse with panic and his rider with madness; but I will open My eyes *and* watch over the house of Judah, and will strike every horse of the [opposing] nations with blindness.

⁵"Then the clans of Judah will say in

the Spirit of grace and supplication

In Zechariah 12:1–10 God is saying to His people that He will destroy all their enemies and give them a great victory by pouring out upon them His Spirit of grace (or unmerited favor) and supplication.

There is no way to live in victory without an understanding of the Spirit of grace and supplication. These two words, *grace* and *supplication*, go together because the Spirit of supplication is the Holy Spirit. That means He is the Spirit of prayer. Each time we sense a desire to pray, the Holy Spirit is giving us that desire.

We may not realize when a person or situation comes to mind that the Holy Spirit is leading us to pray for them. We may wonder why we are thinking of them so much, but we neglect to pray for them. We do not grasp the fact that the Holy Spirit is at work in our thoughts.

Recognizing when we are being led by the Holy Spirit to pray is often a lesson that takes a long time to learn. We attribute too many things to coincidence or chance rather than understanding that God is attempting to lead us by His Spirit.

It is important that we realize the Spirit of supplication and grace accomplishes what we cannot do in our flesh if we will trust God's leading. We can relax and let God intercede through us as we pray. I believe what God is saying in Zechariah 12:10 is: "When the Spirit of supplication comes upon you and you begin to pray in faith, then My Spirit of grace will come flooding into your life. Through that channel of prayer I will, by My power, accomplish in your life what needs to be done, that which you cannot do alone."

their hearts, 'The inhabitants of Jerusalem are our strength in the LORD of hosts, their God.'

⁶"In that day I will make the clans of Judah like a firepot in a woodpile, and like a flaming torch among sheaves [of grain]. They will devour all the surrounding peoples on the right hand and on the left; and the people of Jerusalem will again live [securely] in their own place, in Jerusalem.

⁷"The LORD shall save the tents of Judah first, so that the glory of the house of David and the glory of the inhabitants of Jerusalem will not be magnified above Judah.

⁸"In that day the LORD will defend the people of Jerusalem, and the one who is impaired among them in that day [of persecution] will become [strong and noble] like David; and the house of David will be like God, like the Angel of the LORD [who is] before them.

⁹"And in that day I will seek to destroy all the nations that come against Jerusalem.

¹⁰"I will pour out on the house of David and on the people of Jerusalem, the Spirit of grace (unmerited favor) and supplication. And they will look at Me whom they have pierced; and they will mourn for Him as one mourns for an only son, and they will weep bitterly over Him as one who weeps bitterly over a firstborn. [John 19:37; Rev 1:7]

¹¹"In that day there shall be a great

life point

The Holy Spirit not only leads us to pray, He also helps us pray. He shows us how to pray when we do not know what to pray for (see Romans 8:26, 27). Welcome the Spirit of supplication into your life and allow the ministry of prayer to be fulfilled through you. It is quite wonderful to watch the miraculous things that take place in response to prayer.

mourning in Jerusalem, like the mourning of [the city of] Hadadrimmon in the Valley of Megiddo [over beloved King Josiah]. [2 Chr 35:22–25]

¹²"The land will mourn, every family by itself; the [royal] family of the house of David by itself and their wives by themselves; the family of the house of Nathan [David's son] by itself and their wives by themselves;

¹³the [priestly] family of the house of Levi by itself and their wives by themselves; the family of Shimei [grandson of Levi] by itself and their wives by themselves;

¹⁴all the families that remain, each by itself, and their wives by themselves [each with an overwhelming individual regret for having blindly rejected their Messiah].

13 "IN THAT day a fountain shall be opened for the house of David and for the people of Jerusalem for [cleansing from] sin and impurity.

²"In that day," declares the LORD of hosts, "I will cut off the names of the idols from the land, and they will no longer be remembered. I will also remove the [false] prophets and the unclean spirit from the land.

³"And if anyone still [appears as a prophet and falsely] prophesies, then his father and his mother who gave birth to him will say to him, 'You shall not live, for you have spoken lies in the name of the LORD'; and his father and his mother who gave birth to him shall pierce him through when he prophesies.

⁴"And in that day the [false] prophets will each be ashamed of his vision when he prophesies, and they will not wear a hairy robe [of true prophets] in order to deceive,

⁵but he will [deny his identity and] say, 'I am no prophet. I work the ground, because a man sold me as a slave in my youth.'

⁶"And one will say to him, 'What are these wounds between your arms?' Then he will answer, 'Those wounds I received in the house of my friends.'

⁷"Awake, O sword, against My
    Shepherd,
And against the Man, My Associate,"
Declares the LORD of hosts.
"Strike the Shepherd so that the
    sheep [of the flock] may be
    scattered;
And I will turn My hand *and* stretch
    it out against the little ones [of the
    flock]. [Matt 26:31, 32]
⁸"It will come about in all the land,"
Declares the LORD,
"Two parts in it will be cut off and
    perish,
But the third will be left alive.
    [Hos 2:23; Rom 11:5]
⁹"And I will bring the third part
    through the fire,
Refine them as silver is refined,
And test them as gold is tested.
They will call on My name,
And I will listen *and* answer them;
I will say, 'They are My people,'
And they will say, 'The LORD is my
    God.'"

putting the Word to work

Have you ever heard the phrase "trial by fire"? God says He tests us by fire to refine us, to remove the impurities of sin (see Zechariah 13:9). If you are in a season of testing or trials in your life, call upon God. He has promised to answer you. Trust Him as He refines you, and know that He is at work to accomplish His purposes in you.

speak the Word

14 BEHOLD, A day is coming for the LORD when the spoil taken from you (Jerusalem) will be divided in your midst.

²For I will gather all nations against Jerusalem to battle, and the city will be captured and the houses plundered and the women ravished; and half of the city will be exiled, but the rest of the people will not be cut off from the city. ³Then the LORD will go forth and fight against those nations, as when He fights on a day of battle. ⁴In that day His feet shall stand on the Mount of Olives, which lies before Jerusalem on the east; and the Mount of Olives will be split in half from the east to the west by a very large valley, and half of the mountain will move toward the north and half of it toward the south. [Is 64:1, 2] ⁵You will flee by the valley of My mountains, for the valley of the mountains will reach to Azel; and you will flee just as you fled from the earthquake in the days of Uzziah king of Judah. Then the LORD my God will come, and all the holy ones (believers, angels) with Him. [Amos 1:1; Col 3:4; 1 Thess 4:14; Jude 14, 15] ⁶In that day there will be no light; the glorious ones (heavenly bodies) shall be darkened. ⁷But it will be a unique day which is known to the LORD—not day and not night, but at evening time there will be light. ⁸And in that day living waters will flow out from Jerusalem, half of them to the eastern sea (Dead Sea) and half of them to the western sea (the Mediterranean); it will be in summer as well as in winter.

Thank You, God, that You listen to me and answer me when I call upon Your name. You say that I am Yours, and I say that You are my God.
—ADAPTED FROM ZECHARIAH 13:9

⁹And the LORD shall be king over all the earth; in that day the LORD shall be *the only* one [worshiped], and His name *the only* one.

¹⁰All the land will be changed into a plain from Geba to Rimmon, [the Rimmon that is] south of Jerusalem; but Jerusalem will rise and remain [lifted up] on its site from Benjamin's Gate to the place of the First Gate to the Corner Gate, and from the Tower of Hananel to the king's wine presses.

¹¹It will be inhabited, for there will no longer be a curse, for Jerusalem will dwell in security. [Rev 22:3]

¹²Now this will be the plague with which the LORD shall strike all the peoples that have warred against Jerusalem: Their flesh will rot while they stand on their feet, and their eyes will rot in their sockets, and their tongue will rot in their mouth.

¹³In that day a great panic *and* dismay from the LORD will fall on them; and they will seize one another's hand, and the hand of the one will be raised against the hand of the other.

¹⁴Judah also will fight at Jerusalem; and the wealth of all the surrounding nations will be gathered together— gold and silver and garments in great abundance.

¹⁵So like this plague [on men] there will be the plague on the horses, mules, camels, donkeys, and all the livestock in those camps.

¹⁶Then everyone who is left of all the nations that went against Jerusalem will go up from year to year to worship the King, the LORD of hosts, and celebrate the Feast of Booths (Tabernacles).

¹⁷And it will be that whichever of the families of the earth does not go up to Jerusalem to worship the King, the LORD of hosts, there will be no rain on them.

¹⁸If the family of Egypt does not go up [to Jerusalem] and present themselves, then no *rain will fall* on them. It will be the plague with which the LORD will strike the nations who do not go up to celebrate the Feast of Booths (Tabernacles).

¹⁹This will be the [consequent] punishment [for the sin] of Egypt, and the [consequent] punishment [for the sin] of all the nations that do not go up to celebrate the Feast of Booths (Tabernacles).

²⁰In that day there will *be written* on the little bells on the horses, "HOLY TO THE LORD." And the cooking pots in the LORD's house will be [holy to the LORD] like the bowls before the altar.

²¹Every cooking pot in [all the houses in] Jerusalem and in Judah will be holy to the LORD of hosts, and all who sacrifice will come and take them and boil [their sacrifices] in them. And in that day there will no longer be a Canaanite [that is, any godless or spiritually unclean person, whether Jew or Gentile] in the house of the LORD of hosts. [Eph 2:19–22]

Malachi

Author:
Malachi

Date:
About 450 BC

Everyday Life Principles:
Even when we regularly attend a place of worship, it is still vitally important for us to have hearts that worship and honor God.

Christian leaders must live holy lives, not causing others to sin but setting worthy examples for them to follow.

Christianity is about relationship, not religion.

The name Malachi means "my messenger," and indeed Malachi was God's messenger to the Jews in the years following the rebuilding of the temple. Even though the temple had finally been rebuilt, the people were not worshiping and relating to God as they should have been. Some had turned to idolatry, some had disobeyed God by marrying foreigners, and some were neglecting to pay their tithes. These practices and others combined to create a general dishonor toward God and disregard for the things of God—and these attitudes demand judgment unless people repent.

Malachi does rebuke the people for their attitudes and behavior, but he also addresses leaders extensively, rebuking the priests for causing the people to stumble and for not living holy lives. He promises that God will come "like a refiner's fire" and "like launderer's soap" (Malachi 3:2) to purify the priests and restore them to a place of being able to serve Him in righteousness, with right heart attitudes and right actions.

As you read the book of Malachi, remember that being a Christian is not about religion, but about relationship. It is not about going to a "temple," which in today's society would be equal to going to church, but about developing and maintaining the heart attitudes that keep you in close relationship with God.

1

THE ORACLE (burdensome message) of the word of the LORD to Israel through [My messenger] Malachi.

²"I have loved you," says the LORD. But you say, "How *and* in what way have You loved us?" "Was not Esau Jacob's brother?" declares the LORD. "Yet I loved Jacob (Israel);

³but [in comparison with My love for Jacob] I have hated Esau (Edom), and I have made his mountains a wasteland, and *have given* his inheritance to the jackals of the wilderness." [Rom 9:13, 16]

⁴Though [impoverished] Edom says, "We have been beaten down, but we will return and build up the ruins." Thus says the LORD of hosts, "They may build, but I will tear down; and men will call them the Wicked Territory, the people against whom the LORD is indignant forever."

⁵Your own eyes will see this and you will say, "The LORD is great *and* shall be magnified beyond the border of Israel!" [Is 34; 63:1–6; Jer 49:7–22; Ezek 25:12–14; Obad 1]

⁶" 'A son honors his father, and a servant his master. Then if I am a Father, where is My honor? And if I am a Master, where is the [reverent] fear *and* respect due Me?' says the LORD of hosts to you, O priests, who despise My name. But you say, 'How *and* in what way have we despised Your name?'

⁷"You are presenting defiled food upon My altar. But you say, 'How have we defiled You?' By thinking that the table of the LORD is contemptible *and* may be despised.

⁸"When you [priests] present the blind [animals] for sacrifice, is it not evil? And when you present the lame and the sick, is it not evil? Offer such a thing [as a blind or lame or sick animal] to your governor [as a gift or as payment for your taxes]. Would he be pleased with you? Or would he receive you graciously?" says the LORD of hosts.

⁹"But now will you not entreat God's favor, that He may be gracious to us? With such an offering from your hand [as an imperfect animal for sacrifice], will He show favor to any of you?" says the LORD of hosts.

¹⁰"Oh, that there were even one among you [whose duty it is to minister to Me] who would shut the gates, so that you would not kindle *fire on* My altar uselessly [with an empty, worthless pretense]! I am not pleased with you," says the LORD of hosts, "nor will I accept an offering from your hand.

¹¹"For from the rising of the sun, even to its setting, My name shall be great among the nations. In every place incense is going to be offered to My name, and a grain offering that is pure; for My name shall be great among the nations," says the LORD of hosts.

¹²"But you [priests] profane it when you say, 'The table of the Lord is defiled, and as for its fruit, its food is to be despised.'

putting the Word to work

Many things in life—our studies, our work, our relationships—demand or expect our best. Do you give your best to God in worship? I encourage you to commit to worshiping Him wholeheartedly and always doing your very best for Him (see Malachi 1:11–14).

speak the Word

God, You are my Father and my Master. I honor You and I reverently fear and respect You.
–ADAPTED FROM MALACHI 1:6

¹³"You also say, 'How tiresome this is!' And you disdainfully sniff at it," says the LORD of hosts, "and you bring what was taken by robbery, and the lame or the sick [animals]; this you bring as an offering! Should I receive it with pleasure from your hand?" says the LORD. [Lev 1:3; Deut 15:21]

¹⁴"But cursed is the swindler who has a male in his flock and vows [to offer] it, but sacrifices to the Lord a blemished *or* diseased thing! For I am a great King," says the LORD of hosts, "and My name is to be [reverently and greatly] feared among the nations."

2 "NOW, O priests, this commandment is for you.
²"If you do not listen, and if you do not take it to heart to honor My name," says the LORD of hosts, "then I will send the curse upon you and I will curse your blessings [on the people]. Indeed, I have cursed them already, because you are not taking it to heart.

³"Behold, I am going to rebuke your seed, and I will spread the refuse on your faces, the refuse from the festival offerings; and you will be taken away with it [in disgrace].

⁴"Then you will know [without any doubt] that I have sent this [new] commandment to you (priests), that My covenant may continue with Levi [the priestly tribe]," says the LORD of hosts.

⁵"My covenant with Levi was [one of] life and peace, and I gave them to him as an object of reverence; so he [and the priests] feared Me and stood in reverent awe of My name.

life point

There is power in the name of the Lord, and His name is to be reverently feared (see Malachi 1:14). You and I need to have such reverence for the Lord and for His name that we are afraid to speak His holy name casually or without purpose.

life point

Malachi 2:5–7 deals with priests and the way they are supposed to speak. Since I am a minister of the gospel, this subject naturally interests me. But in reality, according to Revelation 1:6, all believers are kings and priests because Jesus Christ has "formed us into a kingdom [as His subjects], priests to His God and Father."

Notice that in Malachi 2:5, God says He has made a covenant with His priest. In the Bible, whenever there is a covenant between two individuals, each has a part to play in that agreement or contract. In our covenant with the Lord, He has a part to play, and we have a part to play. He covenants to give us life and peace; our part is to give Him reverence and worshipful fear, to revere Him, and to stand in awe of His name.

If we have reverential and worshipful fear of the Lord—if we revere Him and stand in awe of His name—then we will not use our mouths to speak evil against His people, whom we serve as His priests and ministers.

⁶"True instruction was in Levi's mouth and injustice was not found on his lips. He walked with Me in peace and uprightness, and he turned many from wickedness.

⁷"For the lips of the priest should guard *and* preserve knowledge [of My law], and the people should seek instruction from his mouth; for he is the messenger of the LORD of hosts.

⁸"But as for you [priests], you have turned from the way and you have caused many to stumble by your instruction [in the law]. You have violated the covenant of Levi," says the LORD of hosts.

⁹"So I have also made you despised and abased before all the people, just

as you are not keeping My ways but are showing partiality [to people] in [your administration of] the law."

¹⁰Do we not all have one Father? Has not one God created us? Why do we deal treacherously with one another, profaning the covenant of our fathers [with God]?

¹¹Judah has been treacherous (disloyal), and an repulsive act has been committed in Israel and in Jerusalem; for Judah has profaned the sanctuary of the LORD which He loves, and has married the daughter of a foreign god. [Ezra 9:2; Jer 2:3]

¹²As for the man who does this, may the LORD cut off from the tents of Jacob to the last man those who do this [evil thing], awake and aware, even the one who brings an offering to the LORD of hosts.

¹³This is another thing you do: you cover the altar of the LORD with tears, with [your own] weeping and sighing, because the LORD no longer regards your offering or accepts it with favor from your hand.

¹⁴But you say, "Why [does He reject

life point

In Malachi 2:14–16, the prophet is addressing the issue of marriage. In Malachi 2:16, he writes: "Keep watch on your spirit, so that you do not deal treacherously [with your wife]." We cannot expect anything to go well for us or in our marriages if we do not allow ourselves to be controlled by God's Spirit. But if we will listen to God and be diligent to obey, our lives and our marriages can be wonderful.

it]?" Because the LORD has been a witness between you and the wife of your youth, against whom you have dealt treacherously. Yet she is your marriage companion and the wife of your covenant [made by your vows].

¹⁵But not one has done so who has a remnant of the Spirit. And what did that one do while seeking a godly offspring? Take heed then to your spirit, and let no one deal treacherously against the wife of your youth.

¹⁶"For I hate divorce," says the LORD, the God of Israel, "and him who covers

the refiner's fire

God desires to consume everything in our lives that does not bring Him glory. He sends the Holy Spirit to live inside us believers, to be in close fellowship with us, and to bring conviction of our every wrong thought, word, or action. We must all go through the "refiner's fire" (Malachi 3:2).

What does that mean? It means God will deal with us. He will change our attitudes, desires, ways, thoughts, and conversations. Those of us who go through the fire instead of running from it are the ones who will bring great glory to God.

Going through fire sounds frightening. It reminds us of pain and even death. However, in Romans 8:17 Paul said that if we want to share Christ's inheritance, we must also share His suffering. Because of that truth, it is important for us to think about how Jesus suffered. We know He suffered horribly on the cross, so are we expected to go to the cross also? The answer is yes and no. We do not have to physically go to a cross and be nailed to it for our sins, but in Mark 8:34 Jesus did teach us to take up our cross and follow Him. What does that mean? Taking up our cross means laying aside a selfish, self-centered lifestyle. Believe me, getting rid of selfishness takes some fire (difficult times)—and usually a lot of it—but it is worth it in the end.

his garment with wrong *and* violence," says the LORD of hosts. "Therefore keep watch on your spirit, so that you do not deal treacherously [with your wife]."

¹⁷You have wearied the LORD with your words. But you say, "In what way have we wearied Him?" In that you say, "Everyone who does evil is good in the sight of the LORD, and He delights in them," or [by asking], "Where is the God of justice?"

3 "BEHOLD, I am going to send My messenger, and he will prepare *and* clear the way before Me. And the Lord [the Messiah], whom you seek, will suddenly come to His temple; the Messenger of the covenant, in whom you delight, behold, He is coming," says the LORD of hosts. [Matt 11:10; Luke 1:13–17, 76]

²"But who can endure the day of His coming? And who can stand when He appears? For He is like a refiner's fire and like launderer's soap [which removes impurities and uncleanness]. [Rev 6:12–17]

³He will sit as a refiner and purifier of silver, and He will purify the sons of Levi [the priests], and refine them like gold and silver, so that they may

life point

In our daily relationship with God, one thing we appreciate most about Him is the fact that we can count on Him not to change.

We love God and can trust Him because He never changes. He says in Malachi 3:6, basically, "This is the way I have always been, and this is the way I'm always going to be." If you can count on anything, you can count on Jesus never changing. He can change anything else that needs to be changed, but He always remains constant, steady, and eternal. Hallelujah!

life point

Verses 10–12 of Malachi chapter 3, a chapter known for its teaching on tithing and giving, describe the blessings God tells Israel tithing will bring them: God will rebuke the devourer for the tithers' sake. The fruit of their ground will not be destroyed, and all nations will call them happy and blessed. By obeying God's directions rather than following the world's system, they will be blessed.

The Lord wants His people to bring their tithes to the storehouse to prove Him. When we bring tithes in obedience to His Word, He promises to pour out a blessing so enormous that there will not be enough room to contain it.

present to the LORD [grain] offerings in righteousness.

⁴"Then the offering of Judah and Jerusalem will be pleasing to the LORD as in the days of old and as in ancient years.

⁵"Then I will come near you for judgment; I will be a swift witness against sorcerers, against adulterers, against perjurers, and against those who oppress the laborer in his wages and widows and the fatherless, and *against* those who turn away the alien [from his right], and those who do not fear Me [with awe-filled reverence]," says the LORD of hosts. [Deut 24:17]

⁶"For I am the LORD, I do not change [but remain faithful to My covenant with you]; that is why you, O sons of Jacob, have not come to an end.

⁷"Yet from the days of your fathers you have turned away from My statutes *and* ordinances and have not kept them. Return to Me, and I will return to you," says the LORD of hosts. "But you say, 'How shall we return?'

⁸"Will a man rob God? Yet you are robbing Me! But you say, 'In what way

have we robbed You?' In tithes and offerings [you have withheld].

⁹"You are cursed with a curse, for you are robbing Me, this whole nation! [Lev 26:14–17]

¹⁰"Bring all the tithes (the tenth) into the storehouse, so that there may be food in My house, and test Me now in this," says the LORD of hosts, "if I will not open for you the windows of heaven and pour out for you [so great] a blessing until there is no more room to receive it. [Mal 2:2]

¹¹"Then I will rebuke the devourer

are you angry with God?

Many times people blame God for their unhappiness. They develop bitterness and resentment toward God, especially if they have had a lot of disappointments in their lives.

The devil wants us to blame God if we are not happy. He wants to create a rift between God and us so we will lose our joy. In Malachi 3:13–15, we read about people who were angry with God and spoke harshly against Him. Similarly, we may become angry with God and if so, then we need to take steps to get rid of that anger.

Sometimes we try to get things we want from God by imitating what we have seen others do. Then we get upset when He does not answer the way we think He should. But by copying others' actions, we may be doing things God never told us to do. Do not be angry with God for not blessing something He did not tell you to do. And do not blame Him for the things the devil has brought into your life.

This may sound odd to you, but if you are angry with God, you need to "forgive" Him. God does not need your forgiveness—He has done nothing wrong—but you need to be released from the harsh results of the unforgiveness and bitterness you may have directed toward God. If you have unforgiveness in your heart against God, give it up and let it go. God is your friend, not your enemy. Let faith and joy fill that place where unforgiveness once was.

You will not be disappointed with God if you wait in faith to hear from Him. Romans 10:17 teaches: "So faith comes from hearing [what is told], and what is heard comes by the [preaching of the] message concerning Christ." If you want joy in your life, it's necessary to believe that God is good and that He rewards those who seek Him earnestly and diligently (see Hebrews 11:6). Joy will fill you when you quit demanding answers to your questions about why bad things have happened to you. Trust God's ways and His timing, and remember that trust always requires some unanswered questions.

God wants to bless every person. No matter what is going on in your life right now, no matter how badly it hurts, do not blame God. You may not always understand what is happening, but God is perfect. He is good, and He is right. Fault and error are either caused by people or instigated by the devil.

If you have been upset with God, I encourage you to release your anger to Him. Pray with me, "God, I have held anger against You. I know You have done nothing wrong, and I am in need of *Your* forgiveness. But I believe that my saying, 'I forgive You,' will help me let go of unforgiveness that I have misdirected toward You. I forgive You. My problems are not Your fault. You are my *answer*."

(insects, plague) for your sake and he will not destroy the fruits of the ground, nor will your vine in the field drop *its grapes* [before harvest]," says the LORD of hosts.

¹²"All nations shall call you happy *and* blessed, for you shall be a land of delight," says the LORD of hosts.

¹³"Your words have been harsh against Me," says the LORD. "But you say, 'What have we spoken against You?'

¹⁴"You have said, 'It is useless to serve God. What profit is it if we keep His ordinances, and walk around like mourners before the LORD of hosts?

¹⁵'So now we call the arrogant happy *and* blessed. Evildoers are exalted *and*

prosper; and when they test God, they escape [unpunished].'"

¹⁶Then those who feared the LORD [with awe-filled reverence] spoke to one another; and the LORD paid attention and heard it, and a book of remembrance was written before Him of those who fear the LORD [with an attitude of reverence and respect] and who esteem His name.

¹⁷"They will be Mine," says the LORD of hosts, "on that day when I publicly recognize them *and* openly declare them to be My own possession [that is, My very special treasure]. And I will have compassion on them *and* spare them as a man spares his own son who serves him."

a book of remembrance

The Lord listens to every conversation we have. A greater awareness of that fact would probably cause us to change some of our conversations. When our conversations please Him, He records them in a book called a "book of remembrance" (Malachi 3:16).

I keep a book of remembrance, and I believe keeping such a book is a good habit for anyone to form. In my book, which is more like a journal, I record things God has done for me, special things that clearly remind me that His favor and love are upon me. Writing them down helps me to remember them. We are to be thankful and to give God praise at all times. Keeping a record of God's awesome deeds is beneficial to us because we can read them anytime we want to and bring to our minds how good He is to us.

Why would God keep a book of remembrance of the things we say in conversation to others? I believe He does so because our words come from our hearts. Words are very important; they are containers for power. Our words can bless or they can curse; they can build up or tear down. Obviously our words are extremely important to God, they are important enough for Him to record the good ones. I wonder if He also reads over His book of remembrance and gets pleasure when He thinks of His children who have sat at lunch having conversations that included praise and a grateful attitude or loving and kind words for others.

God actually indicates that a day will come when He will openly and publicly declare that type of person to be His special treasure, or His jewel. All righteous deeds bring a reward in due time, and all unrighteous deeds bring a curse in due time. We reap what we sow. Start today guarding your conversations, and let the words of your mouth be filled with good things so God can record them in His special book of remembrance.

¹⁸Then you will again distinguish between the righteous and the wicked, between the one who serves God and the one who does not serve Him.

4 "FOR BEHOLD, the day is coming, burning like a furnace, and all the arrogant (proud, self-righteous, haughty), and every evildoer shall be stubble; and the day that is coming shall set them on fire," says the LORD of hosts, "so that it will leave them neither root nor branch. [Is 5:21–25; Matt 3:12]

²"But for you who fear My name [with awe-filled reverence] the sun of righteousness will rise with healing in its wings. And you will go forward and leap [joyfully] like calves [released] from the stall.

³"You will trample the wicked, for

putting the Word to work

Do you ever wonder if faithfully serving God is really worth it, as people did in Malachi 3:14? Sometimes it may seem as though it really does not make a difference. But be encouraged! Know that God sees your faithfulness and remembers. Ask God to help you to trust that He is always at work in you and through you for your good and for His purposes.

putting the Word to work

All of us have areas of brokenness in our lives or wounded hearts. These wounds may be from a broken relationship, a difficult experience, or a disappointment. Is there a particular area in your life where you need healing? God promises to bring healing (see Malachi 4:2); ask Him to cover you with His wings of healing and to bring restoration and wholeness to your life.

they will be ashes under the soles of your feet on the day that I do this," says the LORD of hosts.

⁴"Remember [with thoughtful concern] the Law of Moses My servant, the statutes and the ordinances which I commanded him on [Mount] Horeb [to give] to all Israel.

⁵"Behold, I am going to send you Elijah the prophet before the coming of the great and terrible day of the LORD. [Matt 11:14; 17:10–13]

⁶"He will turn the hearts of the fathers to their children, and the hearts of the children to their fathers [a reconciliation produced by repentance], so that I will not come and strike the land with a curse [of complete destruction]." [Luke 1:17]

New Testament

Matthew

Author:
Attributed to Matthew

Date:
Probably shortly before AD 70

Everyday Life Principles:
Jesus' teachings in the book of Matthew and in the other Gospels are as relevant and as important to your life today as they were while He lived on earth.

Jesus taught with words, with stories, and by personal example. I strongly encourage you to study His teachings and to imitate His attitudes and actions.

One way to be blessed is to cultivate the heart attitudes and character qualities Jesus taught in The Beatitudes and throughout the book of Matthew.

The book of Matthew begins the New Testament and is the first of the four Gospels—accounts of Jesus' life and ministry, which include stories He told (called parables), lessons He taught, and miracles He worked. The Gospels also include the teachings, insights, and instructions Jesus gave to the people who followed Him so many centuries ago—and to those who follow Him today.

Matthew focuses on Jesus as the fulfillment of the Old Testament law, on Jesus as the Messiah who was prophesied so long ago, and on the kingdom of heaven. There are so many treasures in Matthew; it is especially rich with Jesus' practical instructions for our lives. This book emphasizes Jesus' teaching ministry, and as we read it we see Jesus teaching people both through the spoken word and by example how to live, how to think, how to treat people, how to pray, and how to be wise and godly in everyday life.

In Matthew chapters 5—7, we find a collection of teachings called The Sermon on the Mount. In this great sermon are "The Beatitudes" (a list of heart attitudes and character qualities that bring blessing to our lives, found in 5:1–12) and "The Lord's Prayer" (6:9–13).

I hope you will take time to read, meditate on, and apply to your life the teachings and truths in Matthew. As you do, you will be blessed.

1

THE RECORD of the genealogy of Jesus the Messiah, the son (descendant) of David, the son (descendant) of Abraham: [Ps 132:11; Is 11:1]

²Abraham was the father of Isaac, Isaac the father of Jacob, and Jacob the father of Judah and his brothers [who became the twelve tribes of Israel].

³Judah was the father of Perez and Zerah by Tamar, Perez was the father of Hezron, and Hezron the father of Ram.

⁴Ram was the father of Aminadab, Aminadab the father of Nahshon, and Nahshon the father of Salmon.

⁵Salmon was the father of Boaz by Rahab, Boaz was the father of Obed by Ruth, and Obed the father of Jesse.

⁶Jesse was the father of David the king.

David was the father of Solomon by *Bathsheba who had been the wife of Uriah. [Ruth 4:18–22; 1 Chr 2:13–15]

⁷Solomon was the father of Rehoboam, Rehoboam the father of Abijah, and Abijah the father of Asa.

⁸Asa was the father of Jehoshaphat, Jehoshaphat the father of Joram, and Joram the father of Uzziah.

⁹Uzziah was the father of Jotham, Jotham the father of Ahaz, and Ahaz the father of Hezekiah.

¹⁰Hezekiah was the father of Manasseh, Manasseh the father of Amon, and Amon the father of Josiah.

¹¹Josiah became the father of Jeconiah [also called Coniah and Jehoiachin] and his brothers, at the time of the deportation (exile) to Babylon. [2 Kin 24:14; 1 Chr 3:15, 16]

¹²After the deportation to Babylon: Jeconiah became the father of Shealtiel, and Shealtiel the father of Zerubbabel.

¹³Zerubbabel was the father of Abihud, Abihud the father of Eliakim, and Eliakim the father of Azor.

¹⁴Azor was the father of Zadok, Zadok the father of Achim, and Achim the father of Eliud.

¹⁵Eliud was the father of Eleazar, Eleazar the father of Matthan, and Matthan the father of Jacob.

¹⁶Jacob was the father of Joseph the husband of Mary, by whom Jesus was born, who is called the Messiah (Christ).

¹⁷So all the generations from Abraham to David are fourteen; from David to the Babylonian deportation (exile), fourteen generations; and from the Babylonian deportation to the Messiah, fourteen generations.

¹⁸Now the birth of Jesus Christ was as follows: when His mother Mary had been betrothed to Joseph, before they came together she was found to be with child by [the power of] the Holy Spirit.

¹⁹And Joseph her [promised] husband, being a just *and* righteous man and not wanting to expose her publicly to shame, planned to send her away *and* divorce her quietly.

²⁰But after he had considered this, an angel of the Lord appeared to him in a dream, saying, "Joseph, descendant of David, do not be afraid to take Mary as your wife, for the Child who has been *conceived in her is of the Holy Spirit.

²¹"She will give birth to a Son, and you shall name Him Jesus (The LORD is salvation), for He will save His people from their sins."

²²All this happened in order to fulfill what the Lord had spoken through the prophet [Isaiah]:

²³"BEHOLD, THE VIRGIN SHALL BE WITH CHILD AND GIVE BIRTH TO A SON, AND THEY SHALL CALL HIS NAME IMMANUEL"—which, when translated, means, "GOD WITH US." [Is 7:14]

²⁴Then Joseph awoke from his sleep and did as the angel of the Lord had commanded him, and he took *Mary* [to his home] as his wife,

1:6 Lit *her of Uriah.* 1:20 Lit *begotten.*

²⁵but he kept her a virgin until she had given birth to a Son [her firstborn child]; and he named Him Jesus (The LORD is salvation).

2 NOW WHEN Jesus was born in Bethlehem of Judea in the days of Herod the king (Herod the Great), magi (wise men) from the east came to Jerusalem, asking,

²"Where is He who has been born King of the Jews? For we have seen His star in the east and have come to worship Him." [Num 24:17; Jer 23:5; Zech 9:9]

³When Herod the king heard this, he was disturbed, and all Jerusalem with him.

⁴So he called together all the chief priests and scribes of the people and [anxiously] asked them where the Christ (the Messiah, the Anointed) was to be born.

⁵They replied to him, "In Bethlehem of Judea, for this is what has been written by the prophet [Micah]:

⁶'AND YOU, BETHLEHEM, IN THE
LAND OF JUDAH,
ARE NOT IN ANY WAY LEAST AMONG
THE LEADERS OF JUDAH;
FOR FROM YOU SHALL COME A
RULER
WHO WILL SHEPHERD MY PEOPLE
ISRAEL.' " [Mic 5:2]

⁷Then Herod secretly sent for the magi and learned from them the [exact] time the star [had first] appeared.

⁸Then he sent them to Bethlehem, saying, "Go and search carefully for the Child; and when you have found Him, report to me, so that I too may come and worship Him."

⁹After hearing the king, they went their way; and behold, the star, which they had seen in the east, went on before them [continually leading the way] until it came and stood over *the place* where the young Child was.

¹⁰When they saw the star, they rejoiced exceedingly with great joy.

¹¹And after entering the house, they saw the Child with Mary His mother; and they fell down and worshiped Him. Then, after opening their treasure chests, they presented to Him gifts [fit for a king, gifts] of gold, frankincense, and myrrh.

¹²And having been warned [by God] in a dream not to go back to Herod, the magi left for their own country by another way.

¹³Now when they had gone, an angel of the Lord appeared to Joseph in a dream and said, "Get up! Take the Child and His mother and flee to Egypt, and remain there until I tell you; for Herod intends to search for the Child in order to destroy Him."

¹⁴So Joseph got up and took the Child and His mother while it was still night, and left for Egypt.

life point

Satan is always out to kill things in their infancy, which is why he planted in Herod's mind the idea of ordering every male child in Bethlehem, two years old and under, put to death. Because Herod was frightened of the newborn Christ Child—the "King of the Jews" Whom the wise men sought—he wanted to kill Him (see Matthew 2:1–16).

I find it interesting that Satan was afraid of a child, and that a child was the King of the Jews. Kings rule, and perhaps one lesson here is that if we desire to rule and reign as kings in life (see Romans 5:17), we must also become like little children. When we become childlike (humble, trusting, and forgiving), we frighten the devil just as the Christ Child frightened Herod. If you want to be a threat to the enemy, one way to do it is to be childlike in your faith.

¹⁵He remained there until the death of Herod. *This was* to fulfill what the Lord had spoken by the prophet [Hosea]: "OUT OF EGYPT I CALLED MY SON." [Hos 11:1]

¹⁶Then Herod, when he realized that he had been tricked by the magi, was extremely angry, and he sent [soldiers] and put to death all the male children in Bethlehem and in all that area who were two years old and under, according to the date which he had learned from the magi.

¹⁷Then what had been spoken through Jeremiah the prophet was fulfilled:

¹⁸"A VOICE WAS HEARD IN RAMAH,
WEEPING AND GREAT MOURNING,
RACHEL WEEPING FOR HER
   CHILDREN;
SHE REFUSED TO BE COMFORTED,
BECAUSE THEY WERE NO MORE."
   [Jer 31:15]

¹⁹But when Herod died, an angel of the Lord appeared in a dream to Joseph in Egypt, and said,

²⁰"Get up! Take the Child and His mother, and go to the land of Israel; for those who sought the Child's life are dead."

²¹Then Joseph got up, and took the Child and His mother, and came into the land of Israel.

²²But when he heard that Archelaus was ruling over Judea in place of his father Herod [the Great], he was afraid to go there. Then being warned *by God* in a dream, he left for the region of Galilee,

²³and went and settled in a city called Nazareth. *This was* to fulfill what was spoken through the prophets: "He shall be called a Nazarene."

3 IN THOSE days John the Baptist appeared, preaching in the Wilderness of Judea [along the western side of the Dead Sea] and saying,

²"Repent [change your inner self—your old way of thinking, regret past sins, live your life in a way that proves repentance; seek God's purpose for your life], for the kingdom of heaven is at hand."

³This is the one who was mentioned by the prophet Isaiah when he said,

"THE VOICE OF ONE SHOUTING IN THE
   WILDERNESS,
'PREPARE THE ROAD FOR THE LORD,
MAKE HIS HIGHWAYS STRAIGHT
   (level, direct)!'" [Is 40:3]

⁴Now this same John had clothing made of camel's hair and a [wide] leather band around his waist; and his food was locusts and wild honey. [Lev 11:22; 2 Kin 1:8; Zech 13:4]

⁵At that time Jerusalem was going out to him, and all Judea and all the district around the Jordan;

⁶and they were being baptized by him in the Jordan River, as they confessed their sins.

⁷But when he saw many of the Pharisees and Sadducees coming for baptism, he said to them, "You brood of vipers, who warned you to flee from the [divine] wrath *and* judgment to come?

⁸"So produce fruit that is consistent with repentance [demonstrating new behavior that proves a change of heart, and a conscious decision to turn away from sin];

⁹and do not presume to say to yourselves [as a defense], 'We have Abraham for our father [so our inheritance assures us of salvation]'; for I say to you that from these stones God is able

speak the Word

God, I pray that my life will bring forth fruit consistent with the change of heart You have worked in me.
–ADAPTED FROM MATTHEW 3:8

to raise up children (descendants) for Abraham. [Luke 3:8]

¹⁰"And already the axe [of God's judgment] is swinging toward the root of the trees; therefore every tree that does not bear good fruit is cut down and thrown into the fire.

¹¹"As for me, I baptize you with water because of [your] repentance [that is, because you are willing to change your inner self—your old way of thinking, regret your sin and live a changed life], but He (the Messiah) who is coming after me is mightier [more powerful, more noble] than I, whose sandals I am not worthy to remove [even as His slave]; He will baptize you [who truly repent] with the Holy Spirit and [you who remain unrepentant] with fire (judgment). [Luke 3:16]

¹²"His winnowing fork is in His hand, and He will thoroughly clear out His threshing floor; and He will gather His wheat (believers) into His barn (kingdom), but He will burn up the chaff (the unrepentant) with unquenchable fire."

¹³Then Jesus came from Galilee to John at the Jordan [River], to be baptized by him. [Mark 1:9–11; Luke 3:21, 22; John 1:32]

¹⁴But John tried to prevent Him [vigorously protesting], saying, "It is I who need to be baptized by You, and do You come to me?"

¹⁵But Jesus replied to him, "Permit it just now; for this is the fitting way for us to fulfill all righteousness." Then John permitted [it and baptized] Him.

¹⁶After Jesus was baptized, He came up immediately out of the water; and behold, the heavens were opened, and he (John) saw the Spirit of God descending as a dove and lighting on Him (Jesus), [John 1:32]

¹⁷and behold, a voice from heaven said, "This is My beloved Son, in whom I am well-pleased *and* delighted!" [Ps 2:7; Is 42:1]

putting the Word to work

Do you ever struggle with wondering if you do enough to please God? When Jesus was baptized, He had not yet taught publicly, performed miracles, or done any sort of ministry. Yet God called Him "My beloved Son, in whom I am well-pleased and delighted!" (Matthew 3:17). Likewise, God is delighted with you because you are His child. That pleases Him far more than anything you can do. Ask Him to show you more and more how delighted He is in you.

4 THEN JESUS was led by the [Holy] Spirit into the wilderness to be tempted by the devil. [Luke 4:1–13]

²After He had gone without food for forty days and forty nights, He became hungry. [Ex 34:28; 1 Kin 19:8]

³And the tempter came and said to Him, "If You are the Son of God, command that these stones become bread."

⁴But Jesus replied, "It is written *and* forever remains written, 'MAN SHALL NOT LIVE BY BREAD ALONE, BUT BY EVERY WORD THAT COMES OUT OF THE MOUTH OF GOD.' " [Deut 8:3]

⁵Then the devil took Him into the holy city [Jerusalem] and placed Him on the pinnacle (highest point) of the temple. [Neh 11:1; Dan 9:24]

⁶And he said [mockingly] to Him, "If You are the Son of God, throw Yourself down; for it is written,

'HE WILL COMMAND HIS ANGELS
    CONCERNING YOU [to serve, care
    for, protect and watch over You]';
and

'THEY WILL LIFT YOU UP ON *their*
    HANDS,

So that You will not strike Your foot against a stone.'" [Ps 91:11, 12]

[7]Jesus said to him, "On the other hand, it is written *and* forever remains written, 'You shall not test the Lord your God.'" [Deut 6:16]

[8]Again, the devil took Him up on a very high mountain and showed Him all the kingdoms of the world and the glory [splendor, magnificence, and excellence] of them;

[9]and he said to Him, "All these things I will give You, if You fall down and worship me."

[10]Then Jesus said to him, "Go away, Satan! For it is written *and* forever remains written, 'You shall worship the Lord your God, and serve Him only.'" [Deut 6:13]

[11]Then the devil left Him; and angels came and ministered to Him [bringing Him food and serving Him].

[12]Now when Jesus heard that John [the Baptist] had been arrested *and* put in prison, He left for Galilee.

[13]And leaving Nazareth, He went and settled in Capernaum, which is by the sea, in the country of Zebulun and Naphtali. [Mark 2:1]

[14]*This was* to fulfill what was spoken by the prophet Isaiah:

putting the Word to work

We should not be surprised when temptation comes. Satan deliberately tried to tempt Jesus, and he tries to tempt us. How do you respond to temptation? Every time Jesus was tempted, He responded with the Word of God (see Matthew 4:1–11). Be diligent to study God's Word, so that when temptation comes, you too will know what action to take in order to resist and overcome it.

[15]"The land of Zebulun and the land of Naphtali,
By the way of the sea, beyond the Jordan, Galilee [in the district] of the Gentiles—
[16]"The people who were sitting (living) in [spiritual] darkness have seen a great Light,
And for those who were sitting (living) in the land and shadow of [spiritual and moral] death,
Upon them a Light has dawned." [Is 9:1, 2]

[17]From that time Jesus began to preach and say, "Repent [change your inner self—your old way of thinking, regret past sins, live your life in a way that proves repentance; seek God's purpose for your life], for the kingdom of heaven is at hand."

[18]As Jesus was walking by the Sea of Galilee, He noticed two brothers, Simon who was called Peter, and Andrew his brother, casting a net into the sea; for they were fishermen.

[19]And He said to them, "Follow Me [as My disciples, accepting Me as your Master and Teacher and walking the same path of life that I walk], and I will make you fishers of men."

[20]Immediately they left their nets and followed Him [becoming His disciples, believing and trusting in Him and following His example].

[21]And going on [further] from there He noticed two other brothers, James the *son* of Zebedee, and his brother John, in the boat with their father Zebedee, mending their nets; and He called them [to follow Him as His disciples].

[22]Immediately they left the boat and their father, and followed Him [becoming His disciples, believing and trusting in Him and following His example].

[23]And He went throughout all Galilee, teaching in their synagogues and preaching the good news (gospel) of the kingdom, and healing every kind

of disease and every kind of sickness among the people [demonstrating and revealing that He was indeed the promised Messiah].

²⁴So the news about Him spread throughout all Syria; and they brought to Him all who were sick, those suffering with various diseases and pains, those under the power of demons, and epileptics, paralytics; and He healed them.

²⁵Large crowds followed Him from Galilee and the Decapolis and Jerusalem and Judea and the other side of the Jordan.

5 WHEN JESUS saw the crowds, He went up on the mountain; and when He was seated, His disciples came to Him.

²Then He *began* to teach them, saying,

³"Blessed [spiritually prosperous, happy, to be admired] are the poor in spirit [those devoid of spiritual arrogance, those who regard themselves as insignificant], for theirs is the kingdom of heaven [both now and forever]. [Luke 6:20–23]

⁴"Blessed [forgiven, refreshed by God's grace] are those who mourn [over their sins and repent], for they will be comforted [when the burden of sin is lifted]. [Is 61:2]

⁵"Blessed [inwardly peaceful, spiritually secure, worthy of respect] are the *gentle [the kind-hearted, the sweet-spirited, the self-controlled], for they will inherit the earth. [Ps 37:11]

⁶"Blessed [joyful, nourished by God's goodness] are those who hunger and thirst for righteousness [those who actively seek right standing with God], for they will be [completely] satisfied. [Is 55:1, 2]

⁷"Blessed [content, sheltered by God's promises] are the merciful, for they will receive mercy.

⁸"Blessed [anticipating God's presence, spiritually mature] are the pure in heart [those with integrity, moral courage, and godly character], for they will see God. [Ps 24:3, 4]

⁹"Blessed [spiritually calm with life-joy in God's favor] are the makers *and* maintainers of peace, for they will [express His character and] be called the sons of God. [Heb 12:14]

¹⁰"Blessed [comforted by inner peace and God's love] are those who are persecuted for *doing that which is morally right, for theirs is the kingdom of heaven [both now and forever].

¹¹"Blessed [morally courageous and spiritually alive with life-joy in God's goodness] are you when *people* insult you and persecute you, and falsely say all kinds of evil things against you because of [your association with] Me.

¹²"Be glad and exceedingly joyful, for your reward in heaven is great [absolutely inexhaustible]; for in this same way they persecuted the prophets who were before you. [2 Chr 36:16]

¹³"You are the salt of the earth; but if the salt has lost its taste (purpose), how can it be made salty? It is no longer good for anything, but to be thrown

life point

In Matthew 5:4, Jesus said that those who mourn are blessed and that they will be comforted. The comfort of God, which is administered by His Holy Spirit, is so awesome that it is almost worth having a problem just to be able to experience it. As with most of the things of God, it goes far beyond any kind of ordinary comfort.

Let God be your source of comfort. When you are hurting, just ask Him to comfort you. Then wait in His presence while He works in your heart and emotions. He will not fail you.

5:5 Or *humble, meek.* **5:10** Lit *the sake of righteousness.*

out and walked on by people [when the walkways are wet and slippery].

¹⁴"You are the light of [Christ to] the world. A city set on a hill cannot be hidden;

¹⁵nor does *anyone* light a lamp and put it under a basket, but on a lamp-stand, and it gives light to all who are in the house. [Mark 4:21; Luke 8:16; 11:33]

¹⁶"Let your light shine before men in such a way that they may see your good deeds *and* moral excellence, and [recognize and honor and] glorify your Father who is in heaven.

¹⁷"Do not think that I came to do away with *or* undo the Law [of Moses] or the [writings of the] Prophets; I did not come to destroy but to fulfill.

¹⁸"For I assure you *and* most solemnly say to you, until heaven and earth pass away, not the smallest letter or stroke [of the pen] will pass from the Law until all things [which it fore-shadows] are accomplished.

¹⁹"So whoever breaks one of the least [important] of these commandments, and teaches others to do the same, will be called least [important] in the king-dom of heaven; but whoever practices and teaches them, he will be called great in the kingdom of heaven.

²⁰"For I say to you that unless your righteousness (uprightness, moral essence) is more than that of the scribes and Pharisees, you will never enter the kingdom of heaven.

²¹"You have heard that it was said to the men of old, 'YOU SHALL NOT MUR-DER,' and 'Whoever murders shall be *guilty before the court.' [Ex 20:13; Deut 5:17; 16:18]

²²"But I say to you that everyone who continues to be angry with his brother

pure-hearted and powerful

God is seeking people who are "pure in heart" (Matthew 5:8). A person who has a pure heart, who is wholeheartedly serving God, is truly powerful. In Psalm 51:6, David tells us that having a pure heart means having truth in our "innermost being," which is who we really are deep in our hearts. Having a pure heart starts with paying attention to our thoughts, because from our thoughts come our words, our emotions, our attitudes, and our motives.

It took me a long time to realize that God will not bless actions based in wrong motives or an impure heart.

Purity of heart is not a natural trait; it is something most of us must work on. This is a challenge that every believer should be excited about accepting, but we do not have to face it alone.

God has created us to be dependent upon Him, to bring Him our challenges and to allow Him to help us with them. Only He knows what is in our hearts, and He is an expert at removing the worthless things from us while retaining the valuable.

There is a price to pay to have a pure heart, but there is also a reward for it. We do not have to be afraid to make the commitment to allow God to do a deep purifying work in us. We may not always feel comfortable about the truth He brings us, but if we do our part—facing it, accepting it, and allowing it to change us—He will make sure we are blessed.

5:21 Or *liable to.*

or harbors malice against him shall be guilty before the court; and whoever speaks [contemptuously and insultingly] to his brother, 'Raca (You empty-headed idiot)!' shall be guilty before the supreme court (Sanhedrin); and whoever says, 'You fool!' shall be in danger of the *fiery hell.

23"So if you are presenting your offering at the altar, and *while* there you remember that your brother has something [such as a grievance or legitimate complaint] against you,

24leave your offering there at the altar and go. First make peace with your brother, and then come and present your offering.

life point

In Matthew 5:13, Jesus tells us we are the salt of the earth, but if salt loses its flavor it is not good for anything.

I say that all of life is tasteless without love. Even acts of generosity that are done out of obligation, but without sincere love, leave us empty. Love represents the salt; it is the energy and the flavor of our lives.

Every day can be exciting if we see ourselves as God's secret agents, waiting in the shadows to sprinkle some salt on the bland lives of the people we encounter. For example, behind a counter in a fast food restaurant we might see a woman who looks unhappy, tired, and angry. A simple comment such as, "Your hair is really pretty," can add flavor to her day.

Love is an effort, and sometimes we allow ourselves to become lazy in dispersing this gift. I hope you will actively express God's love everywhere you go, sprinkling "salt" on everyone you meet because God has placed you where you are for that very purpose.

5:22 Lit *Gehenna of fire.*

25"Come to terms quickly [at the earliest opportunity] with your opponent at law while you are with him on the way [to court], so that your opponent does not hand you over to the judge, and the judge to the guard, and you are thrown into prison. [Luke 12:58, 59]

26"I assure you *and* most solemnly say to you, you will not come out of there until you have paid the last cent.

27"You have heard that it was said, 'YOU SHALL NOT COMMIT ADULTERY'; [Ex 20:14; Deut 5:18]

28but I say to you that everyone who [so much as] looks at a woman with lust for her has already committed adultery with her in his heart.

29"If your right eye makes you stumble *and* leads you to sin, tear it out and throw it away [that is, remove yourself from the source of temptation]; for it is better for you to lose one of the parts of your body, than for your whole body to be thrown into hell.

30"If your right hand makes you stumble *and* leads you to sin, cut it off and throw it away [that is, remove yourself from the source of temptation]; for it is better for you to lose one of the parts of your body than for your whole body to go into hell.

31"It has also been said, 'WHOEVER DIVORCES HIS WIFE IS TO GIVE HER A CERTIFICATE OF DIVORCE';

32but I say to you that whoever divorces his wife, except on grounds of sexual immorality, causes her to commit adultery; and whoever marries a woman who has been divorced commits adultery. [Deut 24:1–4; Luke 16:18]

33"Again, you have heard that it was said to the men of old, 'YOU SHALL NOT MAKE FALSE VOWS, BUT YOU SHALL FULFILL YOUR VOWS TO THE LORD [as a religious duty].'

34"But I say to you, do not make an oath at all, either by heaven, for it is the throne of God;

³⁵or by the earth, for it is the footstool of His feet; or by Jerusalem, for it is THE CITY OF THE GREAT KING. [Ps 48:2; Is 66:1]

³⁶"Nor shall you make an oath by your head, for you are not able to make a single hair white or black.

³⁷"But let your statement be, 'Yes, yes' or 'No, no' [a firm yes or no]; anything more than that comes from the evil one. [Lev 19:12; Num 30:2; Deut 23:21]

³⁸"You have heard that it was said, 'AN EYE FOR AN EYE, AND A TOOTH FOR A TOOTH [punishment that fits the offense].' [Ex 21:24; Lev 24:20; Deut 19:21]

³⁹"But I say to you, do not resist an evil person [who insults you or violates your rights]; but whoever slaps you on the right cheek, turn the other toward him also [simply ignore insignificant insults or trivial losses and do not bother to retaliate—maintain your

secret goodness

In Matthew 6:1, Jesus warns us against trying to impress people with our good deeds and encourages us to wait for our reward from God. God really brought this point home for me once through something that happened in my life.

I was having my nails done in a shop where I went regularly, and I happened to be wearing a rhinestone "Jesus" pin. God prompted me to give it to a nurse, who was sitting nearby talking about ministering to cancer patients in the hospital where she worked. She said that she was not allowed to preach to them openly, but wanted to be able to minister to them somehow.

I felt the Lord was leading me to give her my pin so that when she wore it on her lapel as she bent over her patients, the name of Jesus would minister to them. I hesitated because I felt the Lord wanted me to do that privately, but saw no way to do so because of the girl who was doing my nails.

Suddenly the manicurist stopped and said, "Oh, I ran out of something. I have to run next door to get some more. I will be right back."

I knew God was making a way for me to give the nurse my pin discreetly and without any fanfare, but my flesh wanted some credit. So instead of doing what God wanted me to do the way He wanted me to do it, I kept putting it off, reasoning to myself, *I think it would really bless this manicurist to see my generosity.*

I waited until the girl came back. Then I took off the pin and made a big deal about giving it to the nurse. Just as I envisioned, the ladies expounded on my generosity, going on and on about how kind it was of me to give away my pin. As I left the shop thinking about how generous I had been, the Holy Spirit spoke to my heart and said, "Well, I hope you enjoyed that because it is all the reward you are going to get. Whatever reward you would have had from Me, you just traded for those compliments."

I often wonder what God would have done for me had I obeyed what He told me to do, letting Him have all the glory and credit. Let me urge you not to make the same mistake I did. Obey God and do what He wants you to do, when He wants you to do it, the way He wants you to do it.

dignity, your self-respect, your poise]. [Luke 6:29, 30; Rom 12:17–21]

⁴⁰"If anyone wants to sue you and take your shirt, let him have your coat also [for the Lord repays the offender].

⁴¹"And whoever forces you to go one mile, go with him two.

⁴²"Give to him who asks of you, and do not turn away from him who wants to borrow from you. [Deut 15:8; Prov 24:29]

⁴³"You have heard that it was said, 'YOU SHALL LOVE YOUR NEIGHBOR (fellow man) and hate your enemy.' [Lev 19:18; Ps 139:21, 22]

⁴⁴"But I say to you, love [that is, unselfishly seek the best or higher good for] your enemies and pray for those who persecute you, [Prov 25:21, 22]

⁴⁵so that you may [show yourselves to] be the children of your Father who is in heaven; for He makes His sun rise on those who are evil and on those who are good, and makes the rain fall on the righteous [those who are morally upright] and the unrighteous [the unrepentant, those who oppose Him].

⁴⁶"For if you love [only] those who love you, what reward do you have? Do not even the tax collectors do that?

⁴⁷"And if you greet only your brothers [wishing them God's blessing and peace], what more [than others] are you doing? Do not even the Gentiles [who do not know the Lord] do that?

⁴⁸"You, therefore, will be perfect [growing into spiritual maturity both in mind and character, actively integrating godly values into your daily life], as your heavenly Father is perfect. [Lev 19:2]

6 "BE [VERY] careful not to do your good deeds publicly, to be seen by men; otherwise you will have no reward [prepared and awaiting you] with your Father who is in heaven.

²"So whenever you give to the poor and do acts of kindness, do not blow a trumpet before you [to advertise it], as the hypocrites do [like actors acting out a role] in the synagogues and in the streets, so that they may be honored and recognized and praised by men. I assure you and most solemnly say to you, they [already] have their reward in full.

³"But when you give to the poor and do acts of kindness, do not let your left hand know what your right hand is doing [give in complete secrecy],

life point

Pharisees and hypocrites want to be "honored and recognized and praised" by the people around them, according to Matthew 6:2. I call this kind of desire "approval addiction."

Many people never receive God's best for them because they are addicted to the approval of others. Even if they know God's will for them, they will not walk in it because they are afraid their friends may not understand or agree.

Not everyone approves of the way God moves in our lives. In fact, almost everyone I knew rejected me when I began following His will for my life. It was hard to stand alone against so much disapproval, but during that time I learned that other people's opinions do not really matter; it is what God thinks that is important.

In Galatians 1:10, Paul wrote, "Am I now trying to win the favor and approval of men, or of God? Or am I seeking to please someone? If I were still trying to be popular with men, I would not be a bond-servant of Christ" (the Messiah).

Do not be addicted to approval. Follow your heart. Do what you believe God is telling you to do, and stand firm in Him and Him alone.

⁴so that your charitable acts will be done in secret; and your Father who sees [what is done] in secret will reward you.

⁵"Also, when you pray, do not be like the hypocrites; for they love to pray [publicly] standing in the synagogues and on the corners of the streets so that they may be seen by men. I assure you *and* most solemnly say to you, they [already] have their reward in full.

⁶"But when you pray, go into your most private room, close the door and pray to your Father who is in secret, and

life point

Although some prayers are meant to be public prayers or group prayers, most of our prayer lives should be conducted in secret. In other words, we do not have to broadcast how much we pray and everything we pray about. Jesus encourages us in Matthew 6:5, 6 to practice "secret prayer."

"Secret prayer" means a number of things. It means that we do not tell everyone our personal experiences in prayer. We pray about the things and people God places on our hearts, and we keep our prayers between Him and us unless we have a good reason to do otherwise.

There is nothing wrong with saying to a friend, "I have been praying for the youth of our nation a lot lately," or, "I have been praying for people to enter into a more serious relationship with God." Sharing of this type is simply a part of friendship, but some things God places on our heart to pray about we should keep to ourselves.

"Secret prayer" means that we do not make a display of our prayers to impress people. True secret prayer from a humble, fervent heart results in awesome answers from God.

your Father who sees [what is done] in secret will reward you.

⁷"And when you pray, do not use meaningless repetition as the Gentiles do, for they think they will be heard because of their many words. [1 Kin 18:25–29]

⁸"So do not be like them [praying as they do]; for your Father knows what you need before you ask Him.

⁹"Pray, then, in this way:

'Our Father, who is in heaven,
  Hallowed be Your name. [Luke 11:2–4]
¹⁰'Your kingdom come,
  Your will be done
  On earth as it is in heaven.
¹¹'Give us this day our daily bread.
¹²'And forgive us our debts, as
  we have forgiven our debtors
  [letting go of both the wrong and the resentment].
¹³'And do not lead us into
  temptation, but deliver us from
  evil. [For Yours is the kingdom
  and the power and the glory
  forever. Amen.]' [Luke 11:2–4]

¹⁴"For if you forgive others their trespasses [their reckless and willful sins], your heavenly Father will also forgive you.

¹⁵"But if you do not forgive others [nurturing your hurt and anger with the result that it interferes with your relationship with God], then your Father will not forgive your trespasses.

¹⁶"And whenever you are fasting, do not look gloomy like the hypocrites, for they put on a sad and dismal face [like actors, discoloring their faces with ashes or dirt] so that their fasting may be seen by men. I assure you *and* most solemnly say to you, they [already] have their reward in full. [Is 58:5]

¹⁷"But when you fast, put oil on your head [as you normally would to groom your hair] and wash your face

¹⁸so that your fasting will not be noticed by people, but by your Father who is in secret; and your Father who sees [what is done] in secret will reward you.

¹⁹"Do not store up for yourselves [material] treasures on earth, where moth and rust destroy, and where thieves break in and steal.

²⁰"But store up for yourselves treasures in heaven, where neither moth nor rust destroys, and where thieves do not break in and steal;

²¹for where your treasure is, there your heart [your wishes, your desires; that on which your life centers] will be also.

putting the Word to work

Do you have a savings account or a financial portfolio? Even if you do not, you are probably very aware of your financial situation. It is wise to plan and be financially responsible. Being greedy, however, is a different story. Do not let the pursuit of money or material possessions keep you from pursuing the treasures of God's Kingdom, which have far greater worth and eternal value than anything on earth (see Matthew 6:19–21).

short and simple

I believe God has instructed me to make my requests of Him with as few words as possible. As I follow this practice, I understand more and more why He has asked me to pray this way. I find if I can keep my requests simple and not confuse the issue by trying to come up with too many words, my prayers actually are more clear and powerful.

We need to spend our energy releasing our faith, not repeating phrases over and over when they only serve to make our prayers long and involved.

I am not advocating praying only for a short period of time, but I am suggesting that each prayer be simple, direct, to the point, and filled with faith. Let me give you an example. If I need forgiveness, I can pray, "Lord, I lost my temper, and I am sorry. I ask You to forgive me. I receive Your forgiveness, and I thank You for it, in Jesus' name. Amen."

Keeping my prayers short and simple was difficult when I first began praying that way. Then I realized the reason I struggled was that I lacked faith to believe my prayer would get to God if it was short, simple, and to the point. I fell into the same trap that many people do—"the-longer-the-better" mentality. However, after praying long, complicated prayers, most of the time I felt confused and unsure, as though I still had not gotten the job done.

Now as I follow God's direction to keep it simple and make my request without unnecessary and excessive words, I experience a much greater release of my faith, and I know that God has heard me and will answer.

Confidence in prayer is vital to our lives as believers. Be honest with yourself about your prayer life and make adjustments where needed. If you are not praying enough, pray more. If your prayers are complicated, simplify them. God wants to hear what you have to say through prayer and He wants to answer. I encourage you to become more effective in prayer by keeping it short and simple.

²²"The eye is the lamp of the body; so if your eye is clear [spiritually perceptive], your whole body will be full of light [benefiting from God's precepts].

²³"But if your eye is bad [spiritually blind], your whole body will be full of darkness [devoid of God's precepts]. So if the [very] light inside you [your inner self, your heart, your conscience] is darkness, how great *and* terrible is that darkness!

²⁴"No one can serve two masters; for either he will hate the one and love the other, or he will be devoted to the one and despise the other. You cannot serve God and mammon [money, possessions, fame, status, or whatever is valued more than the Lord].

²⁵"Therefore I tell you, stop being worried *or* anxious (perpetually uneasy, distracted) about your life, as to what you will eat or what you will drink; nor about your body, as to what you will wear. Is life not more than food, and the body more than clothing? [Luke 12:22–31]

²⁶"Look at the birds of the air; they neither sow [seed] nor reap [the harvest] nor gather [the crops] into barns, and yet your heavenly Father keeps feeding them. Are you not worth much more than they?

²⁷"And who of you by worrying can add one hour to [the length of] his life? [Ps 39:5–7]

²⁸"And why are you worried about clothes? See how the lilies *and* wildflowers of the field grow; they do not labor nor do they spin [wool to make clothing],

²⁹yet I say to you that not even Solomon in all his glory *and* splendor dressed himself like one of these. [1 Kin 10:4–7]

³⁰"But if God so clothes the grass of the field, which is alive *and* green today and tomorrow is [cut and] thrown [as fuel] into the furnace, *will He* not much more *clothe* you? You of little faith!

putting the Word to work

Are you worried about something right now? Jesus understood how burdensome and destructive worry can be in our lives, and He commands us not to worry (see Matthew 6:25–31, 34). Instead, He calls us to look to God's sure and faithful provision as the antidote to our worry (see Matthew 6:33). Encourage yourself by remembering the times when God has provided for you and ask Him to help you trust Him for your every need instead of worrying.

³¹"Therefore do not worry *or* be anxious (perpetually uneasy, distracted), saying, 'What are we going to eat?' or 'What are we going to drink?' or 'What are we going to wear?'

³²"For the [pagan] Gentiles eagerly seek all these things; [but do not worry,] for your heavenly Father knows that you need them.

³³"But first *and* most importantly seek (aim at, strive after) His kingdom and His righteousness [His way of doing and being right—the attitude and character of God], and all these things will be given to you also.

³⁴"So do not worry about tomorrow; for tomorrow will worry about itself. Each day has enough trouble of its own.

life point

God gives us enough grace for one day at a time, and to avoid fatigue and burnout, weariness and fainting in our minds, we must learn to live one day at a time. That is why Jesus teaches us in Matthew 6:34 to meet each day's challenges as they come and not to borrow trouble from tomorrow. If we will do that, then at the appointed time God's grace will be available to us in sufficient supply to help us face and overcome whatever may occur in our lives.

first place

Simply put, I believe Matthew 6:33 teaches that, "the main thing is to keep the main thing the main thing." We must know what the most important thing in our lives is and keep our priorities in line. In our society today we see a huge emphasis on commerce and material things, but we must remember that things are not most important to God. He wants us to have and enjoy nice things, but He demands first place in our lives. We are taught to seek the kingdom of God and His way of being and doing before we seek anything else.

The word *seek* is a very strong word. It means "to pursue," "to crave," and "to go after with all your might." When we seek something, we think about it often; we talk about it; and we are willing to pay a price to have it. Some people even fall into the trap of seeking God so He will give them the things they want. When they do that, their motives are wrong and God usually withholds what they want.

We must form a habit of seeking God's face and not His hand. In other words, we are to seek His "presence," not His "presents." I urge you to seek Him for who He is, not for what He can do for you.

God is pleased immensely when we want to spend time with Him just because we love Him. He is also pleased when we praise and worship Him because of Who He is. Everyone enjoys having their "being" celebrated, not just their "doing." I do not want friends who are only interested in what I can do for them; I want them to be interested in who I am and to like me for me. I am sure you feel the same way—and so does God.

When we put Him first, keep Him there, and seek to do things His way, we are showing that we delight in Him. Then He gives us the desires of our hearts (see Psalm 37:4).

7 "DO NOT judge *and* criticize *and* condemn [others unfairly with an attitude of self-righteous superiority as though assuming the office of a judge], so that you will not be judged [unfairly].
²"For just as you [hypocritically] judge others [when you are sinful and unrepentant], so will you be judged; and in accordance with your standard of measure [used to pass out judgment], judgment will be measured to you.
³"Why do you look at the [insignificant] speck that is in your brother's eye, but do not notice *and* acknowledge the [egregious] log that is in your own eye?

life point

Matthew 7:1, 2 plainly tells us we will reap what we sow (see Galatians 6:7). Sowing and reaping do not apply solely to the agricultural and financial realms, they also apply to the mental realm. We can sow and reap an attitude as well as a crop or an investment.

One pastor wisely says that when he hears that someone has talked about him in an unkind or judgmental way, he asks himself, "Are they sowing, or am I reaping?" Many times we are reaping in our lives what we have previously sown into someone else's life. Be sure you sow good seeds!

4"Or how can you say to your brother, 'Let me get the speck out of your eye,' when there is a log in your own eye?

5"You hypocrite (play-actor, pretender), first get the log out of your own eye, and then you will see clearly to take the speck out of your brother's eye.

6"Do not give that which is holy to dogs, and do not throw your pearls before pigs, for they will trample them under their feet, and turn and tear you to pieces.

7"Ask *and* keep on asking and it will be given to you; seek *and* keep on seeking and you will find; knock *and* keep on knocking and the door will be opened to you. [Luke 11:9–13]

8"For everyone who keeps on asking receives, and he who keeps on seeking finds, and to him who keeps on knocking, it will be opened.

9"Or what man is there among you who, if his son asks for bread, will [instead] give him a stone?

life point

The devil loves to keep us busy, identifying and judging the faults of others in our minds. That way, we never see or deal with what is wrong with us!

When we focus our thoughts and conversations on the shortcomings of others, we are usually being deceived about our own conduct. Therefore, Jesus commanded that we not concern ourselves with the wrongs of others when we have so much wrong with ourselves (see Matthew 7:3–5).

We cannot change others; only God can. We cannot change ourselves either, but we can cooperate with the Holy Spirit and allow Him to do the work. Allow God to deal with you first, and then you will be able to humbly, lovingly, and effectively help others.

10"Or if he asks for a fish, will [instead] give him a snake?

11"If you then, evil (sinful by nature) as you are, know how to give good *and* advantageous gifts to your children, how much more will your Father who is in heaven [perfect as He is] give what is good *and* advantageous to those who keep on asking Him.

12"So then, in everything treat others the same way you want them to treat you, for this is [the essence of] the Law and the [writings of the] Prophets.

13"Enter through the narrow gate. For wide is the gate and broad *and* easy to travel is the path that leads the way to destruction *and* eternal loss, and there are many who enter through it.

14"But small is the gate and narrow *and* difficult to travel is the path that leads the way to [everlasting] life, and there are few who find it. [Deut 30:19; Jer 21:8]

15"Beware of the false prophets, [teachers] who come to you dressed as sheep [appearing gentle and innocent], but inwardly are ravenous wolves. [Ezek 22:27]

16"By their fruit you will recognize them [that is, by their contrived doctrine and self-focus]. Do people pick grapes from thorn bushes or figs from thistles? [Luke 6:43, 44]

17"Even so, every healthy tree bears good fruit, but the unhealthy tree bears bad fruit.

18"A good tree cannot bear bad fruit, nor can a bad tree bear good fruit.

19"Every tree that does not bear good fruit is cut down and thrown into the fire.

20"Therefore, by their fruit you will recognize them [as false prophets].

21"Not everyone who says to Me, 'Lord, Lord,' will enter the kingdom of heaven, but only he who does the will of My Father who is in heaven.

²²"Many will say to Me on that day [when I judge them], 'Lord, Lord, have we not prophesied in Your name, and driven out demons in Your name, and done many miracles in Your name?' ²³"And then I will declare to them publicly, 'I never knew you; DEPART FROM ME [you are banished from My presence], YOU WHO ACT WICKEDLY [disregarding My commands].' [Ps 6:8]

do not judge

I believe Matthew 7:6 refers to our God-given ability to love each other. If we have the ability to love others and know that God has commanded us to love them, but we judge and criticize them instead, we have taken the holy thing (love) and cast it before dogs and pigs (evil spirits). We have opened a door for those spirits to trample on holy things and turn and tear us to pieces.

When I became pregnant with our fourth child, I was a Christian, baptized in the Holy Spirit, called into ministry, and a diligent Bible student. I had learned about exercising my faith for healing. Yet, during the first three months of the pregnancy, I was very, very sick. I lost weight and energy. I spent most of my time lying on the couch, so nauseated and tired I could barely move.

This situation was really confusing to me since I had felt wonderful during my other three pregnancies. I was also sincerely trusting God that I would not be sick during this fourth pregnancy.

One day as I lay in bed listening to my husband and children having a good time in the backyard, I aggressively asked God, "What in the world is wrong with me? Why am I so sick? And why am I not getting well?"

The Holy Spirit prompted me to read Matthew 7, and as I did, He reminded me of an event that had happened a couple of years earlier.

As I lay in my bed that day, I recalled that a Christian friend and I had talked about, judged, and criticized another Christian friend who was pregnant and had stopped attending our weekly Bible study because she felt so bad. We believed her problem was that she was unwilling to "press though" her circumstances and come to Bible study. We never offered to help her in any way. We decided that she was a weakling and was using her pregnancy as an excuse to be lazy and self-indulgent.

Now, I was in the same circumstance that woman had been in. God showed me that although I was healthy during my first three pregnancies, my judgment and criticism had opened a huge door for the devil. I took my pearls, the holy things (my ability to love the woman), threw them before the dogs and pigs, and now they were turned and tearing me to pieces. I can tell you, I was quick to repent. As soon as I did, my health was completely restored.

From this incident I learned an important lesson about the dangers of judging and criticizing others. Jesus tells us not to judge others for our own good; He does not want us to be judged in return. Resist the temptation to criticize and judge, and thereby enable yourself and others to enjoy blessings instead of judgment.

²⁴"So everyone who hears these words of Mine and acts on them, will be like a wise man [a far-sighted, practical, and sensible man] who built his house on the rock. [Luke 6:47–49]

²⁵"And the rain fell, and the floods *and* torrents came, and the winds blew and slammed against that house; yet it did not fall, because it had been founded on the rock.

²⁶"And everyone who hears these words of Mine and does not do them, will be like a foolish (stupid) man who built his house on the sand.

²⁷"And the rain fell, and the floods *and* torrents came, and the winds blew and slammed against that house; and it fell— and great *and* complete was its fall."

²⁸When Jesus had finished [speaking] these words [on the mountain],

persistent, not repetitious

It is difficult to lay down strict rules on the subject of how often to pray about the same situation. I have heard some people say, "Pray repeatedly until you see the breakthrough." I have heard others say, "If you pray more than once for something, then you do not believe you got it the first time."

I do not believe we can make any strict rules, but I do think there are some guidelines we can apply to help us have more confidence in the power of prayer.

If my children told me their shoes were worn out and asked me to get them some new ones, I would probably respond, "Okay, I will get them as soon as I can."

What I would want from my children is trust. I would want them to trust me to do what they asked me to do. I would not mind, and might even like it, if they occasionally said, "Mom, I am sure looking forward to those new shoes," or, "I am excited about my new shoes, Mom; I will be glad when I get them and can wear them." Both of those statements would declare to me that they believed I would do as I promised. They would actually be reminding me of my promise, but in a way that would not question my integrity.

On the other hand, if they came back to me an hour later and made the same request again, I might be irritated. If they said, "Mom, my shoes are worn out, and I am asking you to get me some new ones," I would think, "I heard you the first time, and I told you I would get them as soon as I can."

I believe that, sometimes, asking God for the same thing repeatedly is a sign of doubt and unbelief, not of faith and persistence.

When I ask the Lord for something, and that thing comes to my mind or heart again later, I talk to Him about it again. But when I do, I try to refrain from asking Him the same thing as if I think He did not hear me the first time. I believe we honor God when we demonstrate faith and persistence by thanking Him for hearing and answering us.

Jesus said in Matthew 7:7: "Keep on asking . . . keep on seeking . . . keep on knocking." We should be persistent, but not repetitious in prayer. Keep pressing on and do not give up, and keep expressing your faith and gratitude to God for answering you.

the crowds were astonished *and* overwhelmed at His teaching;

²⁹for He was teaching them as one who had authority [to teach entirely of His own volition], and not as their scribes [who relied on others to confirm their authority].

8 WHEN JESUS came down from the mountain, large crowds followed Him.

²And a leper came up to Him and bowed down before Him, saying, "Lord, if You are willing, You are able to make me clean (well)." [Mark 1:40–44; Luke 5:12–14]

³Jesus reached out His hand and touched him, saying, "I am willing; be cleansed." Immediately his leprosy was cleansed.

⁴And Jesus said to him, "See that you tell no one [about this]; but go, show yourself to the priest [for inspection]

life point

In Matthew 7:13, 14, Jesus speaks of two different paths we can take in our lives: the broad way that leads to destruction and the narrow way that leads to life.

As I meditated on this passage, the Lord quickened it to me by saying, "Joyce, on the broad way there is room for all kinds of fleshly things like bitterness, unforgiveness, resentment, and vindictiveness. But on the narrow way there is only room for the Spirit."

In the flesh it is easy to take the broad path, but the end result is destruction. It is much harder to take the narrow path, but in the end it leads to life.

Emotions tempt us to take the easy way, to do what feels good for the moment. Wisdom moves us to take the way that seems hard at first, but later on we find that it leads to life.

and present the offering that Moses commanded, as a testimony (evidence) to them [of your healing]." [Lev 14:2]

⁵As Jesus went into Capernaum, a centurion came up to Him, begging Him [for help], [Luke 7:1–10]

⁶and saying, "Lord, my servant is lying at home paralyzed, with intense *and* terrible, tormenting pain."

⁷Jesus said to him, "I will come and heal him."

⁸But the centurion replied to Him, "Lord, I am not worthy to have You come under my roof, but only say the word, and my servant will be healed.

⁹"For I also am a man subject to authority [of a higher rank], with soldiers subject to me; and I say to one, 'Go!' and he goes, and to another, 'Come!' and he comes, and to my slave, 'Do this!' and he does it."

¹⁰When Jesus heard this, He was amazed and said to those who were following Him, "I tell you truthfully, I have not found such great faith [as this] with anyone in Israel.

¹¹"I say to you that many [Gentiles] will come from east and west, and will sit down [to feast at the table, and enjoy God's promises] with Abraham, Isaac, and Jacob in the kingdom of heaven [because they accepted Me as Savior],

¹²while the sons *and* heirs of the kingdom [the descendants of Abraham who will not recognize Me as Messiah] will be thrown out into the outer darkness; in that place [which is farthest removed from the kingdom] there will be weeping [in sorrow and pain] and grinding of teeth [in distress and anger]." [Ps 107:2, 3; Is 49:12; 59:19; Mal 1:11]

¹³Then Jesus said to the centurion, "Go; it will be done for you as you have believed." And the servant was restored to health at that very hour.

¹⁴When Jesus went into Peter's house [in Capernaum], He saw Peter's

mother-in-law lying sick in bed with a fever. [Mark 1:29–34; Luke 4:38–41]

¹⁵He touched her hand and the fever left her; and she got up and served Him.

¹⁶When evening came, they brought to Him many who were under the power of demons; and He cast out the *evil* spirits with a word, and restored to health all who were sick [exhibiting His authority as Messiah],

¹⁷so that He fulfilled what was spoken by the prophet Isaiah: "HE HIMSELF TOOK OUR INFIRMITIES [upon Himself] AND CARRIED AWAY OUR DISEASES." [Is 53:4]

¹⁸Now when Jesus saw a crowd around Him, He gave orders to cast off for the other side *of the Sea of Galilee*.

¹⁹Then [on His way to board the boat] a scribe [who was a respected and authoritative interpreter of the Law] came and said to Him, "Master, I will accompany You [as Your student] wherever You go." [Luke 9:57–60]

²⁰Jesus replied to him, "Foxes have

known by our fruit

One time my husband and I were in Florida, and I saw a tree that I thought was very attractive. I asked, "What kind of tree is that?" Before anyone could answer, I saw oranges beginning to blossom on the branches, and I realized that it was an orange tree. I knew it by its fruit.

Jesus teaches in Matthew 7:20 that we will know people by their fruit. Let me encourage you to examine your fruit to see if it is good. I did that in my own life and discovered that I was like an apple tree that sat all day long and yelled, "I am an apple tree! I am an apple tree!" but never produced any apples.

Believers often carry outward signs of their Christianity in an attempt to share their faith. Bumper stickers on automobiles are a good example. These signs say that the drivers are Christians, but what kind of fruit do the people bear in traffic? Are they obeying the speed limit or are they speeding? How do they react to other drivers, especially to those who cut them off in traffic? Their actions are true signs of what they are.

You and I can carry big Bibles, wear Christian jewelry, and display large collections of Christian books in our homes—and still not be producing any good fruit. We must be concerned about producing the fruit of the Holy Spirit, because the Holy Spirit is concerned with it. One of His main purposes in making us His home is to continually work His fruit in us and display it through us.

In John 15, Jesus compares our relationship with Him to that of a living plant. He is the Vine; we are the branches. Although it is not stated in John 15, we could also say the Holy Spirit is the Gardener who prunes us and keeps the weeds in us from choking the fruit.

God has planted a garden in each of us (see 1 Corinthians 3:9) and He has assigned the Holy Spirit the job of Gardener. A gardener aids in the production of fruit. That is what the Holy Spirit was sent to do in us—help us bear good fruit.

Examine your own fruit regularly. If any of it is diseased or rotten, ask the Gardener to help you get rid of it and produce a new crop. He will gladly do it!

holes and the birds of the air have nests, but the Son of Man has nowhere to lay His head." [Dan 7:13; Mark 8:31, 38; Luke 12:8; John 1:51; Acts 7:56]

²¹Another of the disciples said to Him, "Lord, let me first go and bury my father (collect my inheritance)." [Luke 9:59, 60]

²²But Jesus said to him, "Follow Me [believing in Me as Master and Teacher],

as you have believed

In Matthew 8:13, Jesus told the centurion that the healing he requested would be done as he believed. The centurion had a positive, believing attitude and Jesus did what he asked Him to do.

Do you know that positive minds produce positive lives? Negative minds produce negative lives. Positive thoughts are always full of faith and hope. Negative thoughts are always full of fear and doubt.

Some people are afraid to hope because they have been hurt so much in their lives. They experience so many disappointments that they do not think they can face the pain of another one. Therefore, they refuse to hope so they will not be disappointed in case things do not work out as they would like.

Disappointment hurts! But this type of behavior sets up a negative lifestyle. Everything becomes negative because the thoughts are negative. Remember, Proverbs 23:7 says, "For as he thinks in his heart, so is he . . ."

Many years ago, I was extremely negative. I often say that if I thought two positive thoughts in a row my mind would cramp. My whole philosophy was this: "If you do not expect anything good to happen, then you will not be disappointed when it does not."

I thought my avoidance of hope would protect me from being hurt. I had encountered so many disappointments in life—so many devastating things had happened to me—that I was afraid to believe that anything good might happen. I had a terribly negative outlook on everything. Since my thoughts were all negative, so were my words and therefore, so was my life.

When I really began to study God's Word and to trust Him to restore me, one of the first things I realized was that the negativism had to go. I began to see the truth of Matthew 8:13—that it will be done for me as I have believed.

I do not mean to imply that you and I can get anything we want by simply thinking about it. God has a perfect plan for each of us, and we cannot control Him with our thoughts and words. But, we must think and speak in agreement with His will and plan for us.

If you do not have any idea what God's will is for you at this point, at least begin by thinking, "I may not know God's plan for me, but I know He loves me. Whatever He does will be good, and I will be blessed."

Begin to think positively about your life; practice being positive in each situation that arises. Even if whatever is taking place in your life at the moment is not so good, expect God to bring good out of it, as He has promised in His Word.

and allow the [spiritually] dead to bury their own dead."

²³When He got into the boat, His disciples followed Him. [Mark 4:36–41; Luke 8:22–25]

²⁴And suddenly a violent storm arose on the sea, so that the boat was being covered by the waves; but Jesus was sleeping.

²⁵And the disciples went and woke Him, saying, "Lord, save us, we are going to die!"

²⁶He said to them, "Why are you afraid, you men of little faith?" Then He got up and rebuked the winds and the sea, and there was [at once] a great *and* wonderful calm [a perfect peacefulness].

²⁷The men wondered in amazement, saying, "What kind of man is this, that even the winds and the sea obey Him?"

²⁸When He arrived at the other side in the country of the Gadarenes, two demon-possessed men coming out of the tombs met Him. *They were* so extremely fierce *and* violent that no one could pass by that way. [Mark 5:1–17; Luke 8:26–37]

²⁹And they screamed out, "What business do we have [in common] with each other, Son of God? Have You come to torment us before the appointed time [of judgment]?" [Judg 11:12; 2 Sam 16:10; Matt 25:41; Mark 5:7; Luke 4:34; Rev 20:10]

³⁰Some distance from them a large herd of pigs was grazing.

³¹The demons *began* begging Him, "If You drive us out, send us into the herd of pigs."

³²And He said to them, "Go!" So they came out [of the men] and went into the pigs, and the whole herd rushed down the steep bank into the sea and died in the water.

³³The herdsmen ran away, and went to the city and reported everything, including what had happened to the men under the power of demons.

³⁴And the whole city came out to meet Jesus; and as soon as they saw Him, they begged Him to leave their region.

9 AND JESUS, getting into a boat, crossed over *the Sea of Galilee* and came to [Capernaum] His own city.

²They brought to Him a man who was paralyzed, lying on a stretcher. Seeing their [active] faith [springing from confidence in Him], Jesus said to the paralytic, "Do not be afraid, son; your sins are forgiven [the penalty is paid, the guilt removed, and you are declared to be in right standing with God]." [Mark 2:3–12; Luke 5:18–26]

³And some of the scribes said to themselves, "This *man* blasphemes [by claiming the rights and prerogatives of God]!"

⁴But Jesus, knowing their thoughts, said, "Why do you think evil in your hearts?

⁵"For which is easier, to say, 'Your sins are forgiven *and* the penalty paid,' or to say, 'Get up and walk'? [Both are possible for God; both are impossible for man.]

⁶"But so that you may know that the Son of Man has authority *and* the power on earth to forgive sins"—then He said to the paralytic, "Get up, pick up your stretcher and go home."

⁷And he got up and went home [healed and forgiven].

⁸When the crowds saw this, they were awestruck, and glorified God *and* praised Him, who had given such authority *and* power to men.

⁹As Jesus went on from there, He saw a man named Matthew (Levi) sitting in the tax collector's booth; and He said to him, "Follow Me [as My disciple, accepting Me as your Master and Teacher and walking the same path of life that I walk]." And Matthew got up and followed Him. [Mark 2:14–22; Luke 5:27–39]

[10]Then as Jesus was reclining *at the table* in *Matthew's* house, many tax collectors and sinners [including non-observant Jews] came and ate with Him and His disciples.

[11]When the Pharisees saw this, they asked His disciples, "Why does your Master eat with tax collectors and sinners?"

[12]But when Jesus heard *this,* He said, "Those who are healthy have no need for a physician, but [only] those who are sick.

[13]"Go and learn what this [Scripture] means: 'I DESIRE COMPASSION [for those in distress], AND NOT [animal] SACRIFICE,' for I did not come to call [to repentance] the [self-proclaimed] righteous [who see no need to change], but sinners [those who recognize their sin and actively seek forgiveness]." [Hos 6:6; Mark 2:17; Luke 5:32]

[14]Then the disciples of John [the Baptist] came to Jesus, asking, "Why do we and the Pharisees often fast [as a religious exercise], but Your disciples do not fast?"

[15]And Jesus replied to them, "Can the guests of the bridegroom mourn while the bridegroom is with them? The days will come when the bridegroom is taken away from them, and then they will fast.

[16]"But no one puts a piece of unshrunk (new) cloth on an old garment; for the patch pulls away from the garment, and a worse tear results.

[17]"Nor is new wine put into old wineskins [that have lost their elasticity]; otherwise the wineskins burst, and the [fermenting] wine spills and the wineskins are ruined. But new wine is put into fresh wineskins, so both are preserved."

[18]While He was saying these things to them, a ruler (synagogue official) entered [the house] and kneeled down *and* worshiped Him, saying, "My daughter has just now died; but come and lay Your hand on her, and she will live." [Mark 5:22–43; Luke 8:41–56]

[19]Jesus got up and *began* to accompany the ruler, with His disciples.

[20]Then a woman who had suffered from a hemorrhage for twelve years came up behind Him and touched the [tassel] fringe of His outer robe; [Matt 14:36]

[21]for she had been saying to herself, "If I only touch His outer robe, I will be healed."

[22]But Jesus turning and seeing her said, "Take courage, daughter; your [personal trust and confident] faith [in Me] has made you well." And at once the woman was [completely] healed.

[23]When Jesus came to the ruler's house, and saw the flute players [who were professional, hired mourners] and the [grieving] crowd making an uproar,

[24]He said, "Go away; for the girl is not dead, but is sleeping." And they laughed *and* jeered at Him.

[25]But when the crowd had been sent outside, Jesus went in and took her by the hand, and the girl got up.

[26]And the news about this spread throughout all that district.

[27]As Jesus went on from there, two blind men followed Him, screaming loudly, "Have mercy *and* compassion on us, Son of David (Messiah)!"

[28]When He went into the house, the blind men came up to Him, and Jesus said to them, "Do you believe [with a deep, abiding trust] that I am able to do this?" They said to Him, "Yes, Lord."

[29]Then He touched their eyes, saying, "According to your faith [your trust and confidence in My power and My ability to heal] it will be done to you."

[30]And their eyes were opened. And Jesus sternly warned them: "See that no one knows this!"

[31]But they went out and spread the news about Him throughout that whole district.

³²While they were going away, a mute, demon-possessed man was brought to Jesus.

³³And when the demon was driven out [by Jesus], the mute man spoke; and the crowds wondered in amazement, saying, "Never before has anything like this [miracle] been seen in Israel."

³⁴But the Pharisees were saying, "He casts out the demons by [the power of] the ruler of demons."

³⁵Jesus went throughout all the cities

treasure mercy

As a young woman, born again, filled with the Spirit, and in ministry, I had no idea I had a problem with mercy. I had probably preached messages on mercy, but God was impressing upon me that I needed to experience the truth of Matthew 9:13. In my heart, I could hear Him say over and over again: "Go and learn what this means: *I desire mercy.*" Maybe that's because I first learned Matthew 9:13 in the Amplified Classic version of the Bible. There, Jesus said, "Go and learn what this means: I desire mercy . . . and not sacrifice." In the 2015 Amplified version, He says, "I desire compassion." Mercy and compassion are very similar.

Mercy and compassion result in kindness. It took a long time for me to understand what I am sharing with you, but slowly I discovered two things about myself: I was not a merciful person, and I was not compassionate to others because I was raised in an atmosphere in which I had not experienced much compassion in my own life.

I became very legalistic and rigid. I had a way I wanted things done and that was the way I wanted them done. I was not very willing to give an inch in either direction. If I did not get something the way I wanted it, although the other person did their best and really could not give me what I wanted, I became upset with him or her. I was not compassionate. I refused to give people any room for error.

Although I reached a place where I wanted with all my heart to be merciful and compassionate, I was not able to be. I grew angry at times because I saw other people show that type of kindness, and I wanted to do the same. Then God showed me that there are two sides to mercy. We have to learn how to *receive* it from God before we can *give* it to others.

I had a hard time being compassionate because I would not receive compassion. I was very legalistic with myself, and therefore, very legalistic with everyone else. The Bible says you are to love your neighbor as you love yourself (see Matthew 22:39). It is important to look at how you treat yourself because sometimes you try to give something to someone that you yourself do not have.

If you do not receive God's love and then love yourself in a balanced way, how can that love flow through you to anyone else? If you do not receive God's mercy when you make mistakes, you do not have a reservoir of mercy from which to draw for others.

I have learned to be a compassionate person, and I enjoy the compassion of God every day in my own life. When I sin, I receive mercy and forgiveness immediately. I am sorry for the mistakes I make, but I refuse to live under condemnation (see Romans 8:1). We should admit our sins so we can repent, ask God to forgive us, receive His mercy and compassion, and press forward.

and villages [in Galilee], teaching in their synagogues and proclaiming the good news (gospel) of the kingdom, and healing every kind of disease and every kind of sickness [His words and His works reflecting His Messiahship].

³⁶When He saw the crowds, He was moved with compassion *and* pity for them, because they were dispirited and distressed, like sheep without a shepherd. [Zech 10:2]

³⁷Then He said to His disciples, "The harvest is [indeed] plentiful, but the workers are few.

³⁸"So pray to the Lord of the harvest to send out workers into His harvest."

10 JESUS SUMMONED His twelve disciples and gave them authority *and* power over unclean spirits, to cast them out, and to heal every kind of disease and every kind of sickness. [Mark 6:7; Luke 9:1]

²Now these are the names of the twelve apostles (special messengers, personally chosen representatives): first, Simon, who is called Peter, and Andrew, his brother; James the son of Zebedee, and John his brother; [Mark 3:16–19; Luke 6:13–16]

³Philip and Bartholomew (Nathanael); Thomas and Matthew (Levi) the tax collector; James the son of Alphaeus, and Thaddaeus (Judas, not Iscariot);

⁴Simon the Cananaean (Zealot), and Judas Iscariot, the one who betrayed Him.

⁵Jesus sent out these twelve, instructing them: "Do not go among the Gentiles, and do not go into a city of the Samaritans;

⁶but rather go to the lost sheep of the house of Israel.

⁷"And as you go, preach, saying, 'The kingdom of heaven is at hand.'

⁸"Heal the sick, raise the dead, cleanse the lepers, cast out demons. Freely you have received, freely give.

⁹"Do not take gold, or silver, or [even] copper money in your money belt,

¹⁰or a provision bag for your journey, or even two tunics, or sandals, or a staff; for the worker deserves his support.

¹¹"Whatever city or village you enter, ask who in it is worthy [who welcomes you and your message], and stay at his house until you leave [that city].

¹²"As you go into the house, give it your greeting [that is, 'Peace be to this house'].

¹³"If [the family living in] the house is worthy [welcoming you and your message], give it your [blessing of] peace [that is, a blessing of well-being and prosperity, the favor of God]. But if it is not worthy, take back your *blessing of* peace.

¹⁴"Whoever does not welcome you, nor listen to your message, as you leave that house or city, shake the dust [of it] off your feet [in contempt, breaking all ties]. [Mark 6:11; Acts 13:51]

¹⁵"I assure you *and* most solemnly say to you, it will be more tolerable on the day of judgment for the land of Sodom and Gomorrah than for that city [since it rejected the Messiah's messenger].

¹⁶"Listen carefully: I am sending you out like sheep among wolves; so be wise as serpents, and innocent as doves [have no self-serving agenda]. [Gen 3:1]

¹⁷"Beware of men [whose nature is to act in opposition to God], for they will hand you over to the courts and flog you in their synagogues;

speak the Word

God, I pray that You will teach me how to be as wise as a serpent and as innocent as a dove.
–ADAPTED FROM MATTHEW 10:16

¹⁸and you will be brought before governors and kings for My sake, as witnesses to them and to the Gentiles.

¹⁹"But when they hand you over, do not worry about how or what you are to say; for what you are to say will be given you within that [very] hour; [Mark 13:11–13; Luke 21:12–19]

²⁰for it is not you speaking, but the Spirit of your Father speaking through you.

²¹"Brother will betray brother to death, and the father his child; and children will rise up *and* rebel against their parents and cause them to be put death.

²²"And you will be hated by everyone because of [your association with] My name, but it is the one who has patiently persevered *and* endured to the end who will be saved.

²³"When they persecute you in one city [because of your faith in Me], flee to the next; for I assure you *and* most solemnly say to you, you will not finish *going through* all the cities of Israel before the Son of Man comes.

²⁴"A disciple is not above his teacher, nor is a bond-servant above his master.

²⁵"It is enough for the disciple to be like his teacher, and the bond-servant like his master. If they have called the head of the house Beelzebul (Satan), how much more [will they speak evil of] the members of his household. [2 Kin 1:2]

²⁶"So do not be afraid of them, for nothing is hidden that will not be revealed [at the judgment], or kept secret that will not be made known [at the judgment]. [Mark 4:22; Luke 12:2–9]

²⁷"What I say to you in the dark (privately), tell in the light (publicly); and what you hear *whispered* in your ear, proclaim from the housetops [to many people].

²⁸"Do not be afraid of those who kill the body but cannot kill the soul; but rather be afraid of Him who can destroy both soul and body in hell.

²⁹"Are not two little sparrows sold for a copper coin? And yet not one of them falls to the ground apart from your Father's will.

³⁰"But even the very hairs of your head are all numbered [for the Father is sovereign and has complete knowledge].

³¹"So do not fear; you are more valuable than many sparrows.

³²"Therefore, the one who confesses *and* acknowledges Me before men [as Lord and Savior, affirming a state of oneness with Me], that one I will also confess *and* acknowledge before My Father who is in heaven.

³³"But the one who denies *and* rejects Me before men, that one I will also deny *and* reject before My Father who is in heaven.

³⁴"Do not think that I have come to bring peace on the earth; I have not come to bring peace, but a sword [of division between belief and unbelief]. [Luke 12:51–53]

³⁵"For I have come to SET A MAN AGAINST HIS FATHER, AND A DAUGHTER AGAINST HER MOTHER, AND A DAUGHTER-IN-LAW AGAINST HER MOTHER-IN-LAW;

³⁶and A MAN'S ENEMIES WILL BE THE MEMBERS OF HIS [own] HOUSEHOLD [when one believes and another does not]. [Mic 7:6]

³⁷"He who loves father or mother more than Me is not worthy of Me; and he who loves son or daughter more than Me is not worthy of Me. [Luke 14:26]

³⁸"And he who does not take his cross [expressing a willingness to endure whatever may come] and follow Me [believing in Me, conforming to My example in living and, if need be, suffering or perhaps dying because of faith in Me] is not worthy of Me.

³⁹"Whoever finds his life [in this world] will [eventually] lose it [through

death], and whoever loses his life [in this world] for My sake will find it [that is, life with Me for all eternity]. [Matt 16:25; Mark 8:35; Luke 9:24; 17:33; John 12:25]

40"He who receives *and* welcomes you receives Me, and he who receives Me receives Him who sent Me. [Mark 9:37; Luke 10:16; John 13:20]

41"He who receives *and* welcomes a prophet because he is a prophet will receive a prophet's reward; and he who receives a righteous (honorable) man because he is a righteous man will receive a righteous man's reward.

42"And whoever gives to one of these little ones [these who are humble in rank or influence] even a cup of cold water to drink because he is my disciple, truly I say to you, he will not lose his reward."

11 WHEN JESUS had finished giving instructions to His twelve disciples, He went on from there to teach and to preach in their [Galilean] cities.

2Now when John [the Baptist] in prison heard about the activities of Christ, he sent *word* by his disciples [Luke 7:18–35]

3and asked Him, "Are You the Expected One (the Messiah), or should we look for someone else [who will be

putting the Word to work

The Bible tells us that we love because God first loved us. Who do you love most? Your love for God should exceed even the strongest love you have for another person. As a follower of Jesus, you demonstrate your love for Him by placing His purposes before your own interests. Ask God to show you what it means to pick up your cross to follow Him (see Matthew 10:38).

the promised One]?" [Gen 49:10; Num 24:17; Ps 40:7; 118:26; Is 59:20]

4Jesus answered, "Go and report to John what you hear and see:

5the BLIND RECEIVE [their] SIGHT and the lame walk, the lepers are cleansed [by healing] and the deaf hear, the dead are raised, and the POOR HAVE THE GOSPEL PREACHED TO THEM. [Is 35:5, 6; 61:1]

6"And blessed [joyful, favored by God] is he who does not take offense at Me [accepting Me as the Messiah and trusting confidently in My message of salvation]." [Luke 7:23]

7As these men were going away, Jesus began to speak to the crowds about John: "What did you go out in the wilderness to see? A reed shaken by the wind [which is commonplace]?

8"What did you go out to see? A man dressed in soft *clothing* [entirely unsuited for the harsh desert]? Those who wear soft *clothing* are in the palaces of kings!

9"But what did you [really] go out to see? A prophet? Yes, I tell you, and one [more eminent, more remarkable, and] far more than a prophet [who foretells the future].

10"This is the one of whom it is written [by the prophet Malachi],

'BEHOLD, I SEND MY MESSENGER
    AHEAD OF YOU,
WHO WILL PREPARE YOUR WAY
    BEFORE YOU.' [Mal 3:1]

11"I assure you *and* most solemnly say to you, among those born of women there has not risen *anyone* greater than John the Baptist; yet the one who is least in the kingdom of heaven is greater [in privilege] than he.

12"From the days of John the Baptist until now the kingdom of heaven suffers violent assault, and violent men seize it by force [as a precious prize].

13"For all the prophets and the Law prophesied up until John.

¹⁴"And if you are willing to accept it, John himself is [the fulfillment of] Elijah [as the messenger] who was to come [before the kingdom]. [Mal 4:5]

¹⁵"He who has ears to hear, let him hear *and* heed My words.

¹⁶"But to what shall I compare this generation? It is like little children sitting in the market places, who call to the others,

¹⁷and say 'We piped the flute for you [playing wedding], and you did not dance; we wailed sad dirges [playing funeral], and you did not mourn *and* cry aloud.'

¹⁸"For John came neither eating nor drinking [with others], and they say, 'He has a demon!'

¹⁹"The Son of Man came eating and drinking [with others], and they say, 'Look! A glutton and a drunkard, a friend of tax collectors and sinners [including non-observant Jews]!' Yet wisdom is justified *and* vindicated by her deeds [in the lives of those who respond to Me]."

²⁰Then He began to denounce [the people in] the cities in which most of His miracles were done, because they did not repent [and change their hearts and lives].

²¹"Woe (judgment is coming) to you, Chorazin! Woe to you, Bethsaida! For if the miracles done in you had been done in Tyre and Sidon [cities of the Gentiles], they would have repented

lighten your load

God will give you the power and the strength you need to serve Him. Matthew 11:28–30 teaches us that Jesus is not a hard taskmaster.

In this passage, Jesus is saying that He is good and His system is good, not burdensome or difficult. Religious rules and regulations can be harsh and pressing, and you can easily get overburdened if you do not know how to do everything you feel is expected of you. But Jesus is saying here: "I am not that way. My ways are not like that. They are not hard, harsh, sharp, and pressing, but they are comfortable, gracious, gentle, and pleasant" (see Matthew 11:30, AMPC).

God not only tells us what to do, He gives us the strength and wisdom to do it. If God did not give me the power to run Joyce Meyer Ministries, I would be burdened and in way over my head. But it is not hard for me. I am comfortable doing what God has equipped me to do. I would not be equipped with any power to get it done if I tried to serve God from the standpoint of mere rules and regulations, and I would be miserable. But I serve Him because I deeply love Him; therefore, I find joy in what I do.

Jesus leads us to a place that is comfortable, gracious, and pleasant. I believe that serving God is easy if we learn to hear from Him and simply obey rather than struggle to do things He never asked us to do for Him.

Take time and seek God about whether your works are His works. Is He leading you to do them? If you discover that you are involved in works of the flesh and that God has not given you the grace to do them, do not be afraid to put them aside and seek His will for your life. Remember, it will not always be easy, but there will be comfort, grace, and pleasure associated with doing what He has for you to do. Jesus wants to lighten the load you have been carrying all by yourself and give you rest.

long ago in sackcloth and ashes [their hearts would have been changed and they would have expressed sorrow for their sin and rebellion against God].

²²"Nevertheless I say to you, it will be more tolerable for [the pagan cities of] Tyre and Sidon on the day of judgment than for you.

²³"And you, Capernaum, are you to be exalted to heaven [for your apathy and unresponsiveness]? You will descend to Hades (the realm of the dead); for if the miracles done in you had been done in Sodom, it would have remained until this day.

²⁴"But I say to you, it will be more tolerable for the land of Sodom on the day of judgment, than for you."

²⁵At that time Jesus said, "I praise You, Father, Lord of heaven and earth [I openly and joyfully acknowledge Your great wisdom], that You have hidden these things [these spiritual truths] from the wise and intelligent and revealed them to infants [to new believers, to those seeking God's will and purpose].

²⁶"Yes, Father, for this way was well-pleasing in Your sight.

²⁷"All things have been handed over to Me by My Father; and no one fully knows *and* accurately understands the Son except the Father; and no one fully knows *and* accurately understands the Father except the Son, and anyone to whom the Son [deliberately] wills to reveal *Him*.

²⁸"Come to Me, all who are weary and heavily burdened [by religious rituals that provide no peace], and I will give you rest [refreshing your souls with salvation].

²⁹"Take My yoke upon you and learn from Me [following Me as My disciple], for I am gentle and humble in heart, and YOU WILL FIND REST (renewal, blessed quiet) FOR YOUR SOULS. [Jer 6:16]

³⁰"For My yoke is easy [to bear] and My burden is light."

12

AT THAT particular time Jesus went through the grainfields on the Sabbath, and His disciples were hungry and began to pick the heads of grain and eat them. [Deut 23:25; Mark 2:23–28; Luke 6:1–5]

²But when the Pharisees saw this, they said to Him, "Look! Your disciples are doing what is unlawful on the Sabbath." [Ex 20:10; 23:12; Deut 5:14]

³He said to them, "Have you not read [in the Scriptures] what David did when he was hungry, he and those who accompanied him— [Lev 24:9; 1 Sam 21:1–6]

⁴how he went into the house of God, and they ate the consecrated bread, which was not lawful for him to eat nor for those with him, but for the priests only?

⁵"Or have you not read in the Law, that on the Sabbath the priests in the temple break [the sanctity of] the Sabbath and yet are innocent? [Num 28:9, 10]

⁶"But I tell you that something greater than the temple is here.

⁷"And if you had only known what this statement means, 'I DESIRE COMPASSION [for those in distress], AND NOT [animal] SACRIFICE,' you would not have condemned the innocent. [Hos 6:6; Matt 9:13]

speak the Word

Thank You, Jesus, that You will give me rest and refresh my soul with salvation when I am weary. Thank You that I can take Your yoke on myself and learn from You, because You are gentle and humble in heart and you will give me rest, renewal, and blessed quiet for my soul. Your yoke is easy and Your burden is light.
–ADAPTED FROM MATTHEW 11:28–30

[8]"For the Son of Man is Lord of the Sabbath."

[9]Leaving there, He went into their synagogue. [Mark 3:1–6; Luke 6:6–11]

[10]A man *was there* whose hand was withered. And they asked Jesus, "Is it lawful *and* permissible to heal on the Sabbath?"—*they asked this* so that they might accuse Him *and* bring charges into court.

[11]But He said to them, "What man is there among you who, if he has only one sheep and it falls into a pit on the Sabbath, will not take hold of it and lift it out?

[12]"How much more valuable then is a man than a sheep! So it is lawful *and* permissible to do good on the Sabbath."

[13]Then He said to the man, "Reach out your hand!" The man reached out and it was restored, as normal *and* healthy as the other.

[14]But the Pharisees went out and conspired against Him, *discussing* how they could destroy Him.

[15]Being aware of this, Jesus left there. Many followed Him, and He healed all of them [who were sick],

[16]and warned them not to tell [publicly] who He was.

[17]*This was* to fulfill what was spoken by the prophet Isaiah;

[18]"BEHOLD, MY SERVANT WHOM
  I HAVE CHOSEN;
MY BELOVED IN WHOM MY SOUL
  IS WELL-PLEASED;
I WILL PUT MY SPIRIT UPON HIM,
AND HE WILL PROCLAIM JUSTICE
  TO THE NATIONS.
[19]"HE WILL NOT QUARREL, NOR CRY
  OUT LOUDLY;
NOR WILL ANYONE HEAR HIS VOICE
  IN THE STREETS.
[20]"A BATTERED REED HE WILL NOT
  BREAK,
AND A SMOLDERING WICK HE WILL
  NOT EXTINGUISH,
UNTIL HE LEADS JUSTICE TO
  VICTORY.
[21]"AND IN HIS NAME THE GENTILES
  (all the nations of the world)
  WILL HOPE [with confidence]."
  [Is 42:1–4]

[22]Then a demon-possessed man who was blind and mute was brought to Jesus, and He healed him, so that the mute man both spoke and saw. [Mark 3:22–27; Luke 11:14, 15]

[23]All the people wondered in amazement, and said, "Could this be the Son of David (the Messiah)?"

[24]But the Pharisees heard it and said, "This man casts out demons only by [the help of] Beelzebul (Satan) the prince of the demons."

[25]Knowing their thoughts Jesus said to them, "Any kingdom that is divided against itself is being laid waste; and no city or house divided against itself will [continue to] stand.

[26]"If Satan casts out Satan [that is, his demons], he has become divided against himself *and* disunited; how then will his kingdom stand?

[27]"If I cast out the demons by [the help of] Beelzebul (Satan), by whom do your sons drive them out? For this reason they will be your judges.

[28]"But if it is by the Spirit of God that I cast out the demons, then the kingdom of God has come upon you [before you expected it].

[29]"Or how can anyone go into a strong man's house and steal his property unless he first overpowers *and* ties up the strong man? Then he will ransack *and* rob his house. [Is 49:24, 25; Mark 3:27]

[30]"He who is not with Me [once and for all on My side] is against Me; and he who does not [unequivocally] gather with Me scatters. [Luke 9:50; 11:23]

[31]"Therefore I say to you, every sin and blasphemy [every evil, abusive, injurious speaking, or indignity against sacred things] will be forgiven people, but blasphemy against the [Holy] Spirit will not be forgiven.

³²"Whoever speaks a word against the Son of Man will be forgiven; but whoever speaks against the Holy Spirit [by attributing the miracles done by Me to Satan] will not be forgiven, either in this age or in the *age* to come. [Mark 3:29; Luke 12:10]

³³"Either make the tree good and its fruit good, or make the tree bad and its fruit bad; for the tree is recognized *and* judged by its fruit.

³⁴"You brood of vipers, how can you speak good things when you are evil? For the mouth speaks out of that which fills the heart.

³⁵"The good man, from his [inner] good treasure, brings out good things; and the evil man, from his [inner] evil treasure, brings out evil things.

³⁶"But I tell you, on the day of judgment people will have to give an accounting for every careless *or* useless word they speak.

³⁷"For by your words [reflecting your spiritual condition] you will be justified *and* acquitted of the guilt of sin; and by your words [rejecting Me] you will be condemned *and* sentenced."

³⁸Then some of the scribes and Pharisees said to Him, "Teacher, we want to see a sign (attesting miracle)

life point

Matthew 12:33 says that a tree is recognized by its fruit. The same is true in our lives. Thoughts bear fruit. If we think good thoughts, the fruit in our lives will be good. If we think bad thoughts, the fruit in our lives will be bad.

We can look at a person's attitude and know what kind of thinking is prevalent in his or her life. A sweet, kind person does not have mean, vindictive thoughts. By the same token, a truly evil person does not have good, loving thoughts. Your thoughts determine your results in life, so think good thoughts and bear good fruit!

life point

Matthew 12:34 teaches us that "the mouth speaks out of that which fills the heart." If we permit wrong thoughts to dwell in our hearts, we will ultimately speak them. Whatever is hidden in our hearts will sooner or later be expressed openly through our mouths.

from You [proving that You are what You claim to be]."

³⁹But He replied and said to them, "An evil and adulterous generation [that is morally unfaithful to God] craves *and* demands a [miraculous] sign; but no sign will be given to it except the sign of the prophet Jonah; [Luke 11:29–32]

⁴⁰for just as JONAH WAS THREE DAYS AND THREE NIGHTS IN THE BELLY OF THE SEA MONSTER, so will the Son of Man be three days and three nights in the heart of the earth. [Jon 1:17]

⁴¹"The men of Nineveh will stand up [as witnesses] at the judgment against this generation, and will condemn it because they repented at the preaching of Jonah; and now, something greater than Jonah is here. [Jon 3:5]

life point

As parents, employers, friends, husbands, wives, and children—all of us need to make a commitment to love with our words and to build confidence in others. Every word we speak can be a brick to build with or a bulldozer to destroy.

Choose your words carefully because according to Matthew 12:36, you will have to account for the careless or useless things you say. Remember, words are seeds; they are containers for power. They carry creative or destructive power and they produce a good harvest or a bad harvest in your life and in the lives of those you love.

⁴²"The Queen of the South (Sheba) will stand up [as a witness] at the judgment against this generation, and will condemn it because she came from the ends of the earth to listen to the wisdom of Solomon; and now, something greater than Solomon is here. [1 Kin 10:1; 2 Chr 9:1]

⁴³"Now when the unclean spirit has gone out of a man, it roams through waterless (dry, arid) places in search of rest, but it does not find it.

⁴⁴"Then it says, 'I will return to my house from which I came.' And when it arrives, it finds *the place* unoccupied, swept, and put in order.

⁴⁵"Then it goes and brings with it seven other spirits more wicked than itself, and they go in and make their home there. And the last condition of that man becomes worse than the first. So will it also be with this wicked generation."

⁴⁶While He was still talking to the crowds, it happened that His mother and brothers stood outside, asking to speak to Him. [Mark 3:31–35; Luke 8:19–21]

⁴⁷Someone said to Him, "Look! Your mother and Your brothers are standing outside asking to speak to You."

⁴⁸But Jesus replied to the one who told Him, "Who is My mother and who are My brothers?"

⁴⁹And stretching out His hand toward His disciples [and all His other followers], He said, "Here are My mother and My brothers!

⁵⁰"For whoever does the will of My Father who is in heaven [by believing in Me, and following Me] is My brother and sister and mother."

13

THAT SAME day Jesus went out of the house and was sitting beside the sea [of Galilee]. [Mark 4:1–20; Luke 8:4–15]

²But such large crowds gathered around Him that He got into a boat and sat there [positioning Himself as a teacher], while the whole crowd stood on the shore.

³He told them many things in parables, saying, "Listen carefully: a sower went out to sow [seed in his field];

⁴and as he sowed, some *seed* fell beside the road [between the fields], and the birds came and ate it.

⁵"Other seed fell on rocky ground, where they did not have much soil; and at once they sprang up because they had no depth of soil.

⁶"But when the sun rose, they were scorched; and because they had no root, they withered away.

⁷"Other seed fell among thorns, and thorns came up and choked them out.

⁸"Other seed fell on good soil and yielded grain, some a hundred times as much [as was sown], some sixty [times as much], and some thirty.

⁹"He who has ears [to hear], let him hear *and* heed My words."

¹⁰Then the disciples came to Him and asked, "Why do You speak to the crowds in parables?"

¹¹Jesus replied to them, "To you it has been granted to know the mysteries of the kingdom of heaven, but to them it has not been granted. [Mark 4:11]

¹²"For whoever has [spiritual wisdom because he is receptive to God's word], to him *more* will be given, and he will be richly *and* abundantly supplied; but whoever does not have [spiritual wisdom because he has devalued God's word], even what he has will be taken away from him. [Matt 25:29; Mark 4:25; Luke 8:18]

¹³"This is the reason I speak to the crowds in parables: because while [having the power of] seeing they do not see, and while [having the power of] hearing they do not hear, nor do they understand *and* grasp [spiritual things].

¹⁴"In them the prophecy of Isaiah is being fulfilled, which says,

'YOU WILL HEAR *and* KEEP
ON HEARING, BUT NEVER
UNDERSTAND;
AND YOU WILL LOOK *and* KEEP
ON LOOKING, BUT NEVER
COMPREHEND;
¹⁵FOR THIS NATION'S HEART HAS
GROWN HARD,
AND WITH THEIR EARS THEY
HARDLY HEAR,
AND THEY HAVE [tightly] CLOSED
THEIR EYES,
OTHERWISE THEY WOULD SEE WITH
THEIR EYES,
AND HEAR WITH THEIR EARS,
AND UNDERSTAND WITH THEIR
HEART, AND TURN [to Me]
AND I WOULD HEAL THEM
[spiritually].' [Is 6:9]

¹⁶"But blessed [spiritually aware, and favored by God] are your eyes, because they see; and your ears, because they hear. [Luke 10:23, 24] ¹⁷"I assure you *and* most solemnly say to you, many prophets and righteous men [who were honorable and in right standing with God] longed to see what you see, and did not see it, and to hear what you hear, and did not hear it. ¹⁸"Listen then to the [meaning of the] parable of the sower: [Mark 4:2–20; Luke 8:4–15] ¹⁹"When anyone hears the word of the kingdom [regarding salvation] and does not understand *and* grasp it, the evil one comes and snatches away what was sown in his heart. This is the one on whom seed was sown beside the road. ²⁰"The one on whom seed was sown on rocky ground, this is the one who hears the word and at once welcomes it with joy;

²¹yet he has no [substantial] root in himself, but is only temporary, and when pressure or persecution comes because of the word, immediately he stumbles *and* falls away [abandoning the One who is the source of salvation]. ²²"And the one on whom seed was sown among thorns, this is the one who hears the word, but the worries *and* distractions of the world and the deceitfulness [the superficial pleasures and delight] of riches choke the word, and it yields no fruit. ²³"And the one on whom seed was sown on the good soil, this is the one who hears the word and understands *and* grasps it; he indeed bears fruit and yields, some a hundred times [as much as was sown], some sixty [times as much], and some thirty." [Mark 4:2–20; Luke 8:4–15] ²⁴Jesus gave them another parable [to consider], saying, "The kingdom of heaven is like a man who sowed good seed in his field. ²⁵"But while his men were sleeping, his enemy came and sowed *weeds [resembling wheat] among the wheat, and went away. ²⁶"So when the plants sprouted and formed grain, the weeds appeared also. ²⁷"The servants of the owner came to him and said, 'Sir, did you not sow good seed in your field? Then how does it have weeds in it?' ²⁸"He replied to them, 'An enemy has done this.' The servants asked him, 'Then do you want us to go and pull them out?' ²⁹"But he said, 'No; because as you pull out the weeds, you may uproot the wheat with them.

speak the Word

God, I pray that I will be one who hears the Word, understands it, and grasps it. As the Word takes root in my heart, I pray that I will bear fruit.
–ADAPTED FROM MATTHEW 13:23

13:25 Lit *tares.*

³⁰"Let them grow together until the harvest; and at harvest time I will tell the reapers, "First gather the weeds and tie them in bundles to be burned; but gather the wheat into my barn."'"

³¹He gave them another parable [to consider], saying, "The kingdom of heaven is like a mustard seed, which a man took and sowed in his field; [Mark 4:30–32; Luke 13:18, 19]

³²and of all the seeds [planted in the region] it is the smallest, but when it has grown it is the largest of the garden herbs and becomes a tree, so that THE BIRDS OF THE AIR FIND SHELTER IN ITS BRANCHES." [Ezek 17:23]

³³He told them another parable, "The kingdom of heaven is like leaven, which a woman took and worked into three measures of flour until all of it was leavened." [Gen 18:6; Luke 13:21]

³⁴All these things Jesus said to the crowds in parables, and He said nothing to them without [using] a parable.

³⁵This was to fulfill what was spoken by the prophet:

"I WILL OPEN MY MOUTH IN
 PARABLES;
 I WILL UTTER THINGS [unknown
 and unattainable] THAT HAVE
 BEEN HIDDEN [from mankind]
 SINCE THE FOUNDATION OF THE
 WORLD." [Ps 78:2]

³⁶Then He left the crowds and went into the house. And His disciples came to Him saying, "Explain [clearly] to us the parable of the weeds in the field."

³⁷He answered, "The one who sows the good seed is the Son of Man,

³⁸and the field is the world; and [as for] the good seed, these are the sons of the kingdom; and the weeds are the sons of the evil one;

³⁹and the enemy who sowed them is the devil, and the harvest is the end of the age; and the reapers are angels.

⁴⁰"So just as the weeds are gathered up and burned in the fire, so will it be at the end of the age.

⁴¹"The Son of Man will send out His angels, and they will gather out of His kingdom all things that offend [those things by which people are led into sin], and all who practice evil [leading others into sin],

⁴²and will throw them into the furnace of fire; in that place there will be weeping [over sorrow and pain] and grinding of teeth [over distress and anger].

⁴³"Then THE RIGHTEOUS [those who seek the will of God] WILL SHINE FORTH [radiating the new life] LIKE THE SUN in the kingdom of their Father. He who has ears [to hear], let him hear and heed My words. [Dan 12:3]

⁴⁴"The kingdom of heaven is like a [very precious] treasure hidden in a field, which a man found and hid again; then in his joy he goes and sells all he has and buys that field [securing the treasure for himself].

⁴⁵"Again, the kingdom of heaven is like a merchant in search of fine pearls,

⁴⁶and upon finding a single pearl of great value, he went and sold all that he had and bought it.

⁴⁷"Again, the kingdom of heaven is like a dragnet which was lowered into the sea, and gathered fish of every kind,

⁴⁸and when it was full, they dragged it up on the beach; and they sat down and sorted out the good fish into baskets, but the worthless ones they threw away.

⁴⁹"So it will be at the end of the age; the angels will come and separate the wicked from the righteous

⁵⁰and throw the wicked into the furnace of fire; in that place there will be weeping [over sorrow and pain] and grinding of teeth [over distress and anger].

⁵¹"Have you understood all these things [in the lessons of the parables]?" They said to Jesus, "Yes."

⁵²He said to them, "Therefore every scribe who has become a disciple of the

kingdom of heaven is like the head of a household, who brings out of his treasure things that are new *and* fresh and things that are old *and* familiar."

⁵³When Jesus had finished these parables, He left there.

⁵⁴And after coming to [Nazareth] His hometown, He *began* teaching them in their synagogue, and they were astonished, and said, "Where did this Man get this wisdom and these miraculous powers [what is the source of His authority]? [Mark 6:1–6; Luke 4:16, 23]

⁵⁵"Is not this the carpenter's son? Is not His mother called Mary? And are not His brothers, James and Joseph and Simon and Judas?

⁵⁶"And His sisters, are they not [living here] among us? Where then did this Man get all this [wisdom and power]?"

⁵⁷And they took offense at Him [refusing to believe in Him]. But Jesus said to them, "A prophet is not without honor except in his hometown and in his own household."

⁵⁸And He did not do many miracles there [in Nazareth] because of their unbelief.

14 AT THAT time Herod [Antipas], the tetrarch [who governed a portion of Palestine including Galilee and Perea], heard the reports about Jesus, [Luke 9:7–9]

²and said to his attendants, "This is John the Baptist; he has been raised from the dead, and that is why the miraculous powers are at work in him."

³For Herod had John arrested and bound him and put him in prison [at the fortress of Machaerus, east of the Jordan, to keep him away] because of Herodias, the wife of his brother Philip, [Mark 6:17; Luke 3:19]

⁴for John had said to him, "It is not lawful (morally right) for you to have her [living with you as your wife]." [Lev 18:16; 20:21]

⁵Although Herod wished to have him put to death, he feared the people, for they regarded John as a prophet.

⁶But when Herod's birthday came, [his niece Salome], the daughter of Herodias danced [immodestly] before them and pleased *and* fascinated Herod,

⁷so much that he promised with an oath to give her whatever she asked.

⁸She, being coached by her mother [Herodias], said, "Give me here on a platter the head of John the Baptist."

⁹The king was distressed, but because of his oaths, and because of his dinner guests, he ordered it to be given her.

¹⁰He sent and had John beheaded in the prison.

¹¹His head was brought on a platter and given to the girl, and she brought it to her mother [Herodias].

¹²And John's disciples came and took away the body and buried it. Then they went and told Jesus.

¹³When Jesus heard *about John,* He left there privately in a boat and went to a secluded place. But when the crowds heard of this, they followed Him on foot from the cities. [Mark 6:32–44; Luke 9:10–17; John 6:1–13]

¹⁴When He went ashore, He saw a large crowd, and felt [profound] compassion for them and healed their sick.

¹⁵When evening came, the disciples came to Him and said, "This is an isolated place and the hour is already late; send the crowds away so that they may go into the villages and buy food for themselves."

¹⁶But Jesus said to them, "They do not need to go away; you give them *something* to eat!"

¹⁷They replied, "We have nothing here except five loaves and two fish."

¹⁸He said, "Bring them here to Me."

¹⁹Then He ordered the crowds to sit down on the grass, and He took the five loaves and the two fish and, looking up toward heaven, He blessed and broke

the loaves and gave them to the disciples, and the disciples *gave them* to the people,

²⁰and they all ate and were satisfied. They picked up twelve full baskets of the leftover broken pieces.

²¹There were about 5,000 men who ate, besides women and children.

²²Immediately He directed the disciples to get into the boat and go ahead of Him to the other side [of the Sea of Galilee], while He sent the crowds away. [Mark 6:45–52; John 6:15–21]

²³After He had dismissed the crowds, He went up on the mountain by Himself to pray. When it was evening, He was there alone.

²⁴But the boat [by this time] was already a *long distance from land, tossed *and* battered by the waves; for the wind was against them.

²⁵And in the fourth watch of the night (3:00–6:00 a.m.) Jesus came to them, walking on the sea. [Mark 6:48; John 6:19]

²⁶When the disciples saw Him walking on the sea, they were terrified, and said, "It is a ghost!" And they cried out in fear.

²⁷But immediately He spoke to them, saying, "Take courage, it is I! Do not be afraid!" [Ex 3:14]

²⁸Peter replied to Him, "Lord, if it is [really] You, command me to come to You on the water."

²⁹He said, "Come!" So Peter got out of the boat, and walked on the water and came toward Jesus.

³⁰But when he saw [the effects of] the wind, he was frightened, and he began to sink, and he cried out, "Lord, save me!"

³¹Immediately Jesus extended His hand and caught him, saying to him, "O you of little faith, why did you doubt?"

³²And when they got into the boat, the wind ceased.

³³Then those in the boat worshiped Him [with awe-inspired reverence], saying, "Truly You are the Son of God!"

³⁴When they had crossed over [the sea], they went ashore at Gennesaret.

³⁵And when the men of that place recognized Him, they sent *word* throughout all the surrounding district and brought to Him all who were sick;

³⁶and they begged Him to let them merely touch the fringe of His robe; and all who touched it were perfectly restored. [Matt 9:20]

15 THEN SOME Pharisees and scribes from Jerusalem came to Jesus and said,

²"Why do Your disciples violate the tradition (religious laws) handed down by the [Jewish] elders? For Your disciples do not [ceremonially] wash their hands before they eat."

³He replied to them, "Why also do you violate the commandment of God for the sake of your tradition [handed down by the elders]?

⁴"For God said [through Moses], 'HONOR YOUR FATHER AND MOTHER,' and, 'HE WHO SPEAKS EVIL OF *or* INSULTS *or* TREATS IMPROPERLY FATHER OR MOTHER IS TO BE PUT TO DEATH.' [Ex 20:12; 21:17; Lev 20:9; Deut 5:16]

⁵"But you say, 'If anyone says to his father or mother, "Whatever [money or resource that] I have that would help you is [already dedicated and] given *to God*,"

⁶he is not to honor his father or his mother [by helping them with their need].' So by this you have invalidated the word of God [depriving it of force and authority and making it of no effect] for the sake of your tradition [handed down by the elders].

⁷"You hypocrites (play-actors, pretenders), rightly did Isaiah prophesy of you when he said,

14:24 Lit *many stadia*; a stadion being about an eighth of a mile or 192 meters.

8'THIS PEOPLE HONORS ME WITH
  THEIR LIPS,
BUT THEIR HEART IS FAR AWAY
  FROM ME.
9'BUT IN VAIN DO THEY WORSHIP ME,
FOR THEY TEACH AS DOCTRINES THE
  PRECEPTS OF MEN.'" [Is 29:13]

¹⁰After Jesus called the crowd to Him, He said, "Listen and understand *this:*
¹¹It is not what goes into the mouth of a man that defiles *and* dishonors him, but what comes out of the mouth, this defiles *and* dishonors him."
¹²Then the disciples came and said to Jesus, "Do You know that the Pharisees were offended when they heard *you say* this?"
¹³He answered, "Every plant which My heavenly Father did not plant will be torn up by the roots. [Is 60:21]
¹⁴"Leave them alone; they are blind guides [leading blind followers]. If a blind man leads a blind man, both will fall into a pit."
¹⁵Peter asked Him, "Explain this parable [about what defiles a person] to us."
¹⁶And He said, "Are you still so dull [and unable to put things together]?
¹⁷"Do you not understand that whatever goes into the mouth passes into the stomach, and is eliminated?
¹⁸"But whatever [word] comes out of the mouth comes from the heart, and this is what defiles *and* dishonors the man.
¹⁹"For out of the heart come evil thoughts *and* plans, murders, adulteries, sexual immoralities, thefts, false testimonies, slanders (verbal abuse, irreverent speech, blaspheming).
²⁰"These are the things which defile *and* dishonor the man; but eating with [ceremonially] unwashed hands does not defile the man."
²¹After leaving there, Jesus withdrew to the district of Tyre and Sidon. [Mark 7:24–30]
²²And a Canaanite woman from that district came out and *began* to cry out

[urgently], saying, "Have mercy on me, O Lord, Son of David (Messiah); my daughter is cruelly possessed by a demon."
²³But He did not say a word in answer to her. And His disciples came and asked Him [repeatedly], "Send her away, because she keeps shouting out after us."
²⁴He answered, "I was commissioned by God *and* sent only to the lost sheep of the house of Israel."
²⁵But she came and *began* to kneel down before Him, saying, "Lord, help me!"
²⁶And He replied, "It is not good (appropriate, fair) to take the children's bread and throw it to the pet dogs."
²⁷She said, "Yes, Lord; but even the pet dogs eat the crumbs that fall from their [young] masters' table."
²⁸Then Jesus answered her, "Woman, your faith [your personal trust and confidence in My power] is great; it will be done for you as you wish." And her daughter was healed from that moment.
²⁹Jesus went on from there and passed along by [the eastern shore of] the Sea of Galilee. Then He went up on the hillside and was sitting there.
³⁰And great crowds came to Him, bringing with them the lame, crippled, blind, mute, and many others, and they put them down at His feet; and He healed them.
³¹So the crowd was amazed when they saw the mute speaking, the crippled restored, the lame walking, and the blind seeing; and they praised *and* glorified the God of Israel.
³²Then Jesus called His disciples to Him, and said, "I feel compassion for the crowd, because they have been with Me now three days and have nothing [left] to eat; and I do not want to send them away hungry, because they might faint [from exhaustion] on the way [home]." [Mark 8:1–21]

³³The disciples said to Him, "Where are we to get enough bread in this isolated place to feed so large a crowd?"

³⁴And Jesus asked them, "How many loaves [of bread] do you have?" They replied, "Seven, and a few small fish."

³⁵He directed the crowd to sit down on the ground,

³⁶and He took the seven loaves and the fish; and when He had given thanks, He broke them and started giving them to the disciples, and the disciples [gave them] to the people.

³⁷And they all ate and were satisfied, and they gathered up seven full baskets of the broken pieces that were left over.

³⁸[Among] those who ate were 4,000 men, not counting women and children.

³⁹Then Jesus sent the crowds away, got into the boat and went to the district of Magadan.

16 NOW THE Pharisees and Sadducees came up, and testing Jesus [to get something to use against Him], they asked Him to show them a sign from heaven [which would support His divine authority].

²But He replied to them, "When it is evening, you say, 'It will be fair weather, for the sky is red.'

³"And in the morning, 'It will be stormy today, for the sky is red and has a threatening look.' You know how to interpret the appearance of the sky, but cannot interpret the signs of the times?

⁴"An evil and [morally] unfaithful generation craves a [miraculous] sign; but no sign will be given to it, except the sign of [the prophet] Jonah." Then He left them and went away. [Jon 3:4, 5]

⁵When the disciples reached the other side *of the sea*, they realized that they had forgotten to bring bread.

⁶Jesus said to them, "Watch out and be on your guard against the leaven of the Pharisees and Sadducees."

⁷They began to discuss this among themselves, saying, "*He said that* because we did not bring bread."

⁸But Jesus, aware of this, said, "You men of little faith, why are you discussing among yourselves that you have no bread?

⁹"Do you still not understand or remember the five loaves for the five thousand, and how many baskets you picked up?

¹⁰"Or the seven loaves for the four thousand, and how many large baskets you picked up?

¹¹"How is it that you fail to understand that I was not talking to you about bread? But beware of the leaven of the Pharisees and Sadducees."

¹²Then they understood that He did not tell them to beware of the leaven of bread, but of the [false] teaching of the Pharisees and Sadducees.

¹³Now when Jesus went into the region of Caesarea Philippi, He asked His disciples, "Who do people say that the Son of Man is?" [Mark 8:27–29; Luke 9:18–20]

¹⁴And they answered, "Some say John the Baptist; others, Elijah; and still others, Jeremiah, or [just] one of the prophets."

¹⁵He said to them, "But who do you say that I am?"

¹⁶Simon Peter replied, "You are the Christ (the Messiah, the Anointed), the Son of the living God."

¹⁷Then Jesus answered him, "Blessed [happy, spiritually secure, favored by God] are you, Simon son of Jonah, because flesh and blood (mortal man) did not reveal this to you, but My Father who is in heaven.

¹⁸"And I say to you that you are Peter, and on this rock I will build My church; and the gates of Hades (death) will not overpower it [by preventing the resurrection of the Christ]. [Eph 1:22; 4:15; 5:23; Col 1:18]

¹⁹"I will give you the keys (authority)

of the kingdom of heaven; and whatever you bind [forbid, declare to be improper and unlawful] on earth will have [already] been bound in heaven, and whatever you loose [permit, declare lawful] on earth will have [already] been loosed in heaven." [Is 22:22; Matt 18:18]

²⁰Then He gave the disciples strict orders to tell no one that He was the Christ (the Messiah, the Anointed).

²¹From that time on Jesus began to show His disciples [clearly] that He must go to Jerusalem, and endure many things at the hands of the elders and the chief priests and scribes (Sanhedrin, Jewish High Court), and be killed, and be raised [from death to life] on the third day. [Mark 8:31–9:1; Luke 9:22–27]

²²Peter took Him aside [to speak to Him privately] and began to reprimand Him, saying, "May God forbid it! This will never happen to You."

²³But Jesus turned and said to Peter, "Get behind Me, Satan! You are a stumbling block to Me; for you are not setting your mind on things of God, but on things of man."

²⁴Then Jesus said to His disciples, "If anyone wishes to follow Me [as My disciple], he must deny himself [set aside selfish interests], and take up his cross [expressing a willingness to endure whatever may come] and follow Me [believing in Me, conforming to My example in living and, if need

be, suffering or perhaps dying because of faith in Me].

²⁵"For whoever wishes to save his life [in this world] will [eventually] lose it [through death], but whoever loses his life [in this world] for My sake will find it [that is, life with Me for all eternity].

²⁶"For what will it profit a man if he gains the whole world [wealth, fame, success], but forfeits his soul? Or what will a man give in exchange for his soul?

²⁷"For the Son of Man is going to come in the glory *and* majesty of His Father with His angels, and THEN HE WILL REPAY EACH ONE IN ACCORDANCE WITH WHAT HE HAS DONE. [Ps 62:12]

²⁸"I assure you *and* most solemnly say to you, there are some of those standing here who will not taste death before they see the Son of Man coming in His kingdom."

17 SIX DAYS later Jesus took with Him Peter and James and John the brother of James, and led them up on a high mountain by themselves. [Mark 9:2–8; Luke 9:28–36]

²And His appearance changed dramatically in their presence; and His face shone [with heavenly glory, clear and bright] like the sun, and His clothing became as white as light.

life point

What rock is Jesus talking about in Matthew 16:17, 18? He is talking about the rock of faith. He tells Simon Peter that on the faith he has just displayed He will build His Church, and "the gates of hell shall not prevail against it" (KJV). That means that the powers of hell will not prevail against the person who walks in faith.

life point

Matthew 16:19 teaches us that we have authority as believers to bring heaven's will to earth by acting in partnership with God. He is in heaven, and we are on earth. Because His Spirit is in us, and because we have His Word, we can know His will. We have authority on earth to bring heaven's will into action. What God binds or looses in heaven—what He allows or disallows— is all we can allow or disallow here in the earth.

³And behold, Moses and Elijah appeared to them, talking with Jesus.

⁴Then Peter began to speak and said to Jesus, "Lord, it is good *and* delightful *and* auspicious that we are here; if You wish, I will put up three [sacred] tents here—one for You, one for Moses, and one for Elijah."

⁵While he was still speaking, behold, a bright cloud overshadowed them, and a voice from the cloud said, "This is My beloved Son, with whom I am well-pleased *and* delighted! Listen to Him!" [Ps 2:7; Is 42:1]

⁶When the disciples heard it, they fell on their faces and were terrified.

"not me!"

In Matthew 16:22, Peter reprimanded Jesus. Anyone who rebukes Jesus has a problem with pride, and Peter had a big pride problem. He was full of himself. He thought he had a better idea than Jesus did.

Jesus had just said He was going to Jerusalem to be killed and to be raised from the dead. Peter's response was something like, "Oh, no Jesus. You must not go. No, that is not the thing to do." How did Jesus respond to Peter's remark? He said in Matthew 16:23, "Get behind Me, Satan! You are a stumbling block to Me."

Later Jesus told Peter that Satan would try to sift him like grain and that Peter would deny His Lord three times. Jesus told Peter He had prayed for him that his faith would not fail (see Luke 22:31–34). Peter did not believe that, nor did he say, "Oh, thank You, Jesus. Please pray for me." He essentially said, "Oh, I would never deny You. No, not me."

Have you ever said, "I will never do that!"? It is amazing the number of things we think we will never do, yet we end up doing them.

It is interesting that when Jesus was being accused, Peter was the only disciple recognized as having been with Him. Others were present, but the spotlight shined on Peter. Peter vehemently denied this and started cursing to prove he did not know Jesus (see Matthew 26:69–74). I believe God arranged for Peter to be recognized because Peter needed to be humbled. God had a plan for Peter's life.

Peter loved Jesus, but he was still full of himself. He argued with Jesus on these occasions. I do not think he did it maliciously, but that happens when someone has a spirit of pride. They think they know more than others do and will always argue, attempting to prove they are right.

Jesus knew Peter was useable material, but he needed some work. You might say Peter was a diamond in the rough. Peter needed some polishing; he needed some time on the Potter's wheel—but he was blind to his own faults and weaknesses, just as we usually are. Jesus had to teach him a lesson, and teach him He did. Peter ended up very meek, very repentant, and very submissive after his humbling experience.

God has a plan for your life and He will deal with every bad attitude and character flaw in you in order to prepare you to fulfill and enjoy the great purpose He has for your life, just as He did with Peter.

⁷But Jesus came and touched them and said, "Get up, and do not be afraid."

⁸And when they looked up, they saw no one except Jesus Himself alone.

⁹And as they were going down the mountain, Jesus commanded them, "Do not tell anyone what you have seen until the Son of Man has been raised from the dead."

¹⁰The disciples asked Him, "Then why do the scribes say that Elijah must come first?"

¹¹He answered and said, "Elijah is coming and will restore all things;

¹²but I say to you that Elijah has come already, and they did not recognize him, but did to him as they wished. The Son of Man is also going to suffer at their hands."

¹³Then the disciples understood that He had spoken to them about John the Baptist. [Mal 4:5]

¹⁴When they approached the crowd, a man came up to Jesus, kneeling before Him and saying, [Mark 9:14–27; Luke 9:37–42]

¹⁵"Lord, have mercy on my son, for he is a lunatic (moonstruck) and suffers terribly; for he often falls into the fire and often into the water.

¹⁶And I brought him to Your disciples, and they were not able to heal him."

¹⁷And Jesus answered, "You unbelieving and perverted generation, how long shall I be with you? How long shall I put up with you? Bring him here to Me."

¹⁸Jesus rebuked the demon, and it came out of him, and the boy was healed at once.

¹⁹Then the disciples came to Jesus privately and asked, "Why could we not drive it out?"

²⁰He answered, "Because of your little faith [your lack of trust and confidence in the power of God]; for I assure you and most solemnly say to you, if you have [living] faith the size of a mustard seed, you will say to this mountain, 'Move from here to there,' and [if it is God's will] it will move; and nothing will be impossible for you. [Mark 11:23; Luke 17:6; 1 John 5:14]

²¹[But this kind of demon does not go out except by prayer and fasting.]"

²²When they were gathering together in Galilee, Jesus said to them, "The Son of Man is going to be betrayed and handed over to men [who are His enemies];

²³and they will kill Him, and He will be raised [from death to life] on the third day." And they were deeply grieved and distressed.

²⁴When they arrived in Capernaum, the collectors of the half-shekel [temple tax] went up to Peter and said, "Does not your teacher pay the half-shekel?" [Ex 30:13; 38:26]

²⁵Peter answered, "Yes." And when he came home, Jesus spoke to him first, saying, "What do you think, Simon? From whom do earthly rulers collect duties or taxes, from their sons or from strangers?"

²⁶When Peter said, "From strangers," Jesus said to him, "Then the sons are exempt [from taxation].

²⁷However, so that we do not offend them, go to the sea and throw in a hook, and take the first fish that comes up; and when you open its mouth, you will find a shekel. Take it and give it to them [to pay the temple tax] for you and Me."

18 AT THAT time the disciples came to Jesus and asked, "Who is greatest in the kingdom of heaven?" [Mark 9:33–37; Luke 9:46–48]

²He called a little child and set him before them,

³and said, "I assure you and most solemnly say to you, unless you repent [that is, change your inner self—your old way of thinking, live changed lives]

and become like children [trusting, humble, and forgiving], you will never enter the kingdom of heaven.

⁴"Therefore, whoever humbles himself like this child is greatest in the kingdom of heaven.

⁵"Whoever receives *and* welcomes one child like this in My name receives Me;

⁶but whoever causes one of these little ones who believe in Me to stumble *and* sin [by leading him away from My teaching], it would be better for him to have a heavy millstone [as large as one turned by a donkey] hung around his neck and to be drowned in the depth of the sea. [Mark 9:42; Luke 17:2]

⁷"Woe (judgment is coming) to the world because of stumbling blocks *and* temptations to sin! It is inevitable that stumbling blocks come; but woe to the person on whose account *or* through whom the stumbling block comes! [Luke 17:1]

⁸"If your hand or your foot causes you to stumble *and* sin, cut it off and throw it away from you [that is, remove yourself from the source of temptation]; it is better for you to enter life crippled or lame, than to have two hands or two feet and be thrown into everlasting fire.

⁹"If your eye causes you to stumble *and* sin, pluck it out and throw it away from you [that is, remove yourself from the source of temptation]; it is better for you to enter life with only one eye, than to have two eyes and be thrown into the fiery hell.

¹⁰"See that you do not despise *or* think less of one of these little ones, for I say to you that their angels in heaven [are in the presence of and] continually look upon the face of My Father who is in heaven. [Acts 12:15; Heb 1:14]

¹¹"[For the Son of Man has come to save that which was lost.]

¹²"What do you think? If a man has a hundred sheep, and one of them gets lost, will he not leave the ninety-nine on the mountain and go in search of the one that is lost? [Luke 15:4–7]

¹³"And if it turns out that he finds it, I assure you *and* most solemnly say to you, he rejoices over it more than over the ninety-nine that did not get lost.

¹⁴"So it is not the will of your Father who is in heaven that one of these little ones be lost.

¹⁵"If your brother sins, go and show him his fault in private; if he listens *and* pays attention to you, you have won back your brother.

¹⁶"But if he does not listen, take along with you one or two others, so that EVERY WORD MAY BE CONFIRMED BY THE TESTIMONY OF TWO OR THREE WITNESSES.

¹⁷"If he pays no attention to them [refusing to listen and obey], tell it to the church; and if he refuses to listen even to the church, let him be to you as a Gentile (unbeliever) and a tax collector. [Lev 19:17; Deut 19:15]

¹⁸"I assure you *and* most solemnly say to you, whatever you bind [forbid, declare to be improper and unlawful] on earth shall have [already] been bound in heaven, and whatever you loose [permit, declare lawful] on earth shall have [already] been loosed in heaven. [Matt 16:19]

putting the Word to work

When another Christian wrongs or offends you, what do you do? Your first inclination may be to run and tell someone else all about it or to let anger or hurt build up inside of you. However, Jesus teaches us the appropriate method for bringing correction and reconciliation in Matthew 18:15–17. The next time you are hurt or wronged by another believer, be sure to go to that person first. Ask God to help you forgive.

life point

The Amplified Bible makes clear in Matthew 18:18, 19 that God gives us authority in order to bring His will to earth, not to bring our own will to pass.

As believers, we have spiritual authority and we should exercise it. One way to do that is through prayer. God desires to use His surrendered servants to pray His will down from heaven to earth, as Jesus taught us to pray: "Your will be done on earth as it is in heaven" (Matthew 6:10).

What an awesome privilege. Our prayers can affect our own lives as well as the lives of other people. God can use us to help them experience the fullness of all He has planned for them.

¹⁹"Again I say to you, that if two *believers on earth agree [that is, are of one mind, in harmony] about anything that they ask [within the will of God], it will be done for them by My Father in heaven. [1 John 5:14] ²⁰"For where two or three are gathered in My name [meeting together as My followers], I am there among them." [Ex 3:14] ²¹Then Peter came to Him and asked, "Lord, how many times will my brother sin against me and I forgive him *and* let it go? Up to seven times?" ²²Jesus answered him, "I say to you, not up to seven times, but seventy times seven. ²³"Therefore the kingdom of heaven is like a king who wished to settle accounts with his slaves. ²⁴"When he began the accounting, one who owed him 10,000 talents was brought to him. ²⁵"But because he could not repay, his master ordered him to be sold, with his wife and his children and

18:19 Lit *of you.*

everything that he possessed, and payment to be made. ²⁶"So the slave fell on his knees and begged him, saying, 'Have patience with me and I will repay you everything.' ²⁷"And his master's heart was moved with compassion and he released him and forgave him [canceling] the debt. ²⁸"But that same slave went out and found one of his fellow slaves who owed him a hundred denarii; and he seized him and *began* choking him, saying, 'Pay what you owe!' ²⁹"So his fellow slave fell on his knees and begged him earnestly, 'Have patience with me and I will repay you.' ³⁰"But he was unwilling and he went and had him thrown in prison until he paid back the debt. ³¹"When his fellow slaves saw what had happened, they were deeply grieved and they went and reported to their master [with clarity and in detail] everything that had taken place. ³²"Then his master called him and said to him, 'You wicked *and* contemptible slave, I forgave all that [great] debt of yours because you begged me. ³³'Should you not have had mercy on your fellow slave [who owed you little by comparison], as I had mercy on you?'

putting the Word to work

Sometimes forgiving someone can be very difficult, especially if that person has repeatedly hurt or offended us. Is there someone in your life you are having a hard time forgiving? Remember the gracious gift of God's forgiveness to you. As you have received forgiveness, you are called to extend forgiveness to others (see Matthew 18:21–35). Ask God to help you forgive as you have been forgiven.

³⁴"And in wrath his master turned him over to the torturers (jailers) until he paid all that he owed.

³⁵"My heavenly Father will also do the same to [every one of] you, if each of you does not forgive his brother from your heart."

19 NOW WHEN Jesus had finished saying these things, He left Galilee and went into the part of Judea that is beyond the Jordan; ²and large crowds followed Him, and He healed them there.

³And Pharisees came to Jesus, testing Him and asking, "Is it lawful for a man to divorce his wife for just any reason?"

⁴He replied, "Have you never read that He who created them from the beginning MADE THEM MALE AND FEMALE,

⁵and said, 'FOR THIS REASON A MAN SHALL LEAVE HIS FATHER AND MOTHER AND SHALL BE JOINED INSEPARABLY TO HIS WIFE, AND THE TWO SHALL BECOME ONE FLESH'? [Gen 1:27; 2:24; Mark 10:7]

how many times?

As believers, we will never experience joy-filled, victorious lives unless we are ready to forgive people. This is something we will have to do frequently, and according to Matthew 18:21, 22, even repeatedly. The Lord tells us plainly in the Bible that if we will not forgive other people for the wrong things they have done against us, then God will not forgive us for the wrong things we have done against Him (see Matthew 6:14, 15).

What kind of condition would we be in if God refused to forgive us? We could not possibly have a proper relationship with Him. Everything in our lives would be stopped up. We like to think we can stay angry with other people and yet go to God and receive forgiveness for our sins. But the Lord tells us in the Bible that this is not so.

Jesus taught us to pray, "And forgive us our debts, as we have forgiven our debtors [letting go of both the wrong and the resentment]" (Matthew 6:12). God is a God of mercy, and this issue of forgiveness is very important to Him. He tells us repeatedly in His Word that if we want mercy, we have to give mercy.

In Matthew 18:21, 22, Peter asked Jesus how many times he had to forgive his brother: "Up to seven times?" Jesus' answer was not seven times, but seventy times that many.

I do not know about you, but I am glad God does not put a limit on how many times He will forgive us. How many of us have done the same wrong thing at least seventy times seven, and God has still forgiven us for it? We are willing to keep taking and taking forgiveness from God, but it is amazing how little we want to extend forgiveness to others. We freely accept mercy, yet it is surprising how rigid, legalistic, and merciless we can be toward others, especially if they have wronged us in some way. Yet the Bible says the debt we owe God is much greater than any debt anyone may owe us. Always remember how great God's generosity is, especially in the area of forgiveness. Aim to forgive others as quickly, as often, and as generously as God forgives you.

⁶"So they are no longer two, but one flesh. Therefore, what God has joined together, let no one separate."

⁷The Pharisees said to Him, "Why then did Moses command us to GIVE HER A CERTIFICATE OF DIVORCE AND SEND HER AWAY?" [Deut 24:1–4]

⁸He said to them, "Because your hearts were hard *and* stubborn Moses permitted you to divorce your wives; but from the beginning it has not been this way.

⁹"I say to you, whoever divorces his wife, except for sexual immorality, and marries another woman commits adultery."

¹⁰The disciples said to Jesus, "If the relationship of a man with his wife is like this, it is better not to marry."

¹¹But He said to them, "Not all men can accept this statement, but *only* those to whom [the capacity to receive] it has been given.

¹²"For there are eunuchs who have been born that way from their mother's womb [making them incapable of consummating a marriage]; and there are eunuchs who have been made eunuchs by men [for royal service]; and there are eunuchs who have made themselves so for the sake of the kingdom of heaven. He who is able to accept this, let him accept it."

¹³Then children were brought to Jesus so that He might place His hands on them [for a blessing] and pray; but the disciples reprimanded them.

¹⁴But He said, "Leave the children alone, and do not forbid them from coming to Me; for the kingdom of heaven belongs to such as these."

¹⁵After placing His hands on them [for a blessing], He went on from there.

¹⁶And someone came to Him and said, "Teacher, what [essentially] good thing shall I do to obtain eternal life [that is, eternal salvation in the Messiah's kingdom]?" [Lev 18:5; Mark 10:17–30; Luke 18:18–30]

¹⁷Jesus answered, "Why are you asking Me about what is [essentially] good? There is *only* One who is [essentially] good; but if you wish to enter into *eternal* life, keep the commandments." [Luke 10:28]

¹⁸He said to Jesus, "Which commandments?" And Jesus answered, "YOU SHALL NOT COMMIT MURDER; YOU SHALL NOT COMMIT ADULTERY; YOU SHALL NOT STEAL; YOU SHALL NOT GIVE FALSE TESTIMONY; [Ex 20:12–16; Deut 5:16–20]

¹⁹HONOR YOUR FATHER AND MOTHER; and LOVE YOUR NEIGHBOR AS YOURSELF" [that is, unselfishly seek the best or higher good for others]. [Lev 19:18; Matt 22:39]

²⁰The young man said to Him, "I have kept all these things [from my youth]; what do I still lack?" [Luke 18:21]

²¹Jesus answered him, "If you wish to be perfect [that is, have the spiritual maturity that accompanies godly character with no moral or ethical deficiencies], go and sell what you have and give [the money] to the poor, and you will have treasure in heaven; and come, follow Me [becoming My disciple, believing and trusting in Me and walking the same path of life that I walk]."

²²But when the young man heard this, he left grieving *and* distressed, for he owned much property *and* had many possessions [which he treasured more than his relationship with God].

²³Jesus said to His disciples, "I assure you *and* most solemnly say to you, it is difficult for a rich man [who clings to possessions and status as security] to enter the kingdom of heaven.

²⁴"Again I tell you, it is easier for a camel to go through the eye of a needle, than for a rich man [who places his faith in wealth and status] to enter the kingdom of God."

²⁵When the disciples heard this, they were completely astonished *and* bewildered, saying, "Then who can be saved [from the wrath of God]?"

26But Jesus looked at them and said, "With people [as far as it depends on them] it is impossible, but with God all things are possible." [Gen 18:14; Job 42:2]

27Then Peter answered Him, saying, "Look, we have given up everything and followed You [becoming Your disciples and accepting You as Teacher and Lord]; what then will there be for us?"

28Jesus said to them, "I assure you *and* most solemnly say to you, in the renewal [that is, the Messianic restoration and regeneration of all things] when the Son of Man sits on His glorious throne, you [who have followed Me, becoming My disciples] will also sit on twelve thrones, judging the twelve tribes of Israel.

29"And everyone who has left houses or brothers or sisters or father or mother or children or farms for My name's sake will receive many times as much, and will inherit eternal life.

30"But many *who are* first [in this world] will be last [in the world to come]; and the last, first.

love yourself

One of the greatest problems many people have today is that they do not think well of themselves. They need to know that God's Word teaches them to love themselves!

Since the Lord commands us to love our neighbors as we love ourselves (see Matthew 19:19, AMPC), He must think that loving ourselves is as important as loving others. But it is not enough simply to love ourselves; we must also *like* ourselves.

I learned this truth several years ago when I was having a terrible time getting along with other people. I discovered the reason I had so much trouble getting along with others was that I was not getting along with myself.

If you do not like yourself, you will have a hard time liking anyone else. You may pretend you do, but pretense does not alter fact. Sooner or later, the truth will come out.

Every one of us is supposed to be a powerhouse for God, living in balance and harmony within ourselves and with others. In order to do that, we must not only have the right attitude toward others but also the right attitude toward ourselves. We need to be at peace with our past, content with our present, and sure about our future, knowing it is all in God's hands. We need to be stable, rooted, and grounded in the love of God as expressed in His Son Jesus Christ.

Because we are rooted and grounded in love, we can be relaxed and at ease, knowing that our acceptance is not based on our performance or our perfect behavior. We can be secure in the knowledge that our value and worth are not dependent on who we are or what we think or say or do. They are based on who we are in Christ Jesus and what He has done for us.

Secure in our knowledge of who we are in Him, we can give up our masks and facades. We do not have to pretend anymore. We do not have to be phony. Instead, we are free to simply be ourselves—just as we are. We are also free to love ourselves, and that will enable us to love others too.

20 "FOR THE kingdom of heaven is like the owner of an estate who went out in the morning at dawn to hire workmen for his vineyard.

²"When he had agreed with the laborers for a denarius for the day, he sent them into his vineyard.

³"And he went out about the third hour (9:00 a.m.) and saw others standing idle in the market place;

⁴and he said to them, 'You also go into the vineyard, and I will pay you whatever is right (an appropriate wage).' And they went.

⁵"He went out about the sixth hour (noon) and the ninth hour (3:00 p.m.), and did the same thing.

⁶"And about the eleventh hour (5:00 p.m.) he went out and found others standing *around,* and he said to them, 'Why have you been standing here idle all day?'

⁷"They answered him, 'Because no one hired us.' He told them, 'You go into the vineyard also.'

all things are possible

It is exciting to know that "with God all things are possible" (Matthew 19:26). In our human thinking we hit brick walls, so to speak, when we come up against something that is impossible for us. We feel frustrated and hopeless. But with God, that never has to happen. When we put our trust in Him another world opens up to us, a world of possibilities we would have never thought possible, given our natural abilities.

You may have practically worn yourself out trying to accomplish something and, when you finally gave up and turned it over to God, you saw Him do with ease what you had struggled with for a long time. That has happened to me over and over again.

I am so glad we serve a God of possibilities. Even the word *impossible* makes me feel hopeless and frustrated. I always like to believe there is hope, no matter how bad things may look.

If God can take a hard, sinful, hateful, bitter heart, and make it soft, holy, loving, and forgiving then, as far as I am concerned, He can do anything. I think that sometimes we do not realize what a miracle our salvation is. We become completely new creatures and are given a brand-new start in life by accepting Jesus Christ as our Savior (see 2 Corinthians 5:17). How much more awesome could anything be? No wonder the gospel is called the "good news"!

God can change hearts, heal a sick body, rekindle a marriage, or restore finances. He can feed five thousand people with a little boy's lunch, walk on water, read men's hearts, and anything else He wants to do. Nothing is impossible with God. Do not ever look at a situation and think or say, "This is impossible." It may be impossible from a human standpoint, but with God all things are possible.

If we keep praying and believing, God can keep working, but if we give up, we close the door on the miracle God has in mind for us. You may say, "You just don't realize what a mess I have in my life." My advice to you is to ask God to take your mess and turn it into your greatest miracle. He can work it out for your good and you will have a testimony that encourages others. With God, all things *are* possible.

8"When evening came, the owner of the vineyard said to his manager, 'Call the workers and pay them their wages, beginning with the last [to be hired] and ending with the first [to be hired].' [Lev 19:13; Deut 24:15]

9"Those who had been *hired* at the eleventh hour (5:00 p.m.) came and received a denarius each [a day's wage].

10"Now when the first [to be hired] came, they thought they would get more; but each of them also received a denarius.

11"When they received it, they protested *and* grumbled at the owner of the estate,

12saying, 'These men who came last worked [only] one hour, and yet you have made them equal [in wages] to us who have carried [most of] the burden and [worked in] the scorching heat of the day.'

13"But the owner of the estate replied to one of them, 'Friend, I am doing you no injustice. Did you not agree with me for a denarius?

14'Take what belongs to you and go, but I choose to give to this last man [hired] the same as I give to you.

15'Am I not lawfully permitted to do what I choose with what is mine? Or is your eye *envious because I am generous?'

16"So those who are last [in this world] shall be first [in the world to come], and those who are first, last."

17As Jesus was going up to Jerusalem, He took the twelve [disciples] aside, and along the way He said to them,

18"Listen carefully: we are going up to Jerusalem; and the Son of Man will be handed over to the chief priests and scribes (Sanhedrin, Jewish High Court), and they will [judicially] condemn Him *and* sentence Him to death,

19and will hand Him over to the Gentiles (Roman authorities) to be mocked and scourged and crucified, and He will be raised [to life] on the third day."

20Then [Salome] the mother of Zebedee's children [James and John] came up to Jesus with her sons and, kneeling down [in respect], asked a favor of Him. [Mark 10:35–45]

21And He said to her, "What do you wish?" She answered Him, "Command that in Your kingdom these two sons of mine may sit [in positions of honor and authority] one on Your right and one on Your left."

22But Jesus replied, "You do not realize what you are asking. Are you able to drink the cup [of suffering] that I am about to drink?" They answered, "We are able."

23He said to them, "You will drink My cup [of suffering]; but to sit on My right and on My left this is not Mine to give, but it is for those for whom it has been prepared by My Father."

24And when the [other] ten heard this, they were resentful *and* angry with the two brothers.

25But Jesus called them to Himself and said, "You know that the rulers of the Gentiles have absolute power *and* lord it over them, and their great men exercise authority over them [tyrannizing them]. [Mark 10:42–45; Luke 22:25–27]

26"It is not this way among you, but whoever wishes to become great among you shall be your servant,

27and whoever wishes to be first among you shall be your [willing and humble] slave;

28just as the Son of Man did not come to be served, but to serve, and to give His life as a ransom for many [paying the price to set them free from the penalty of sin]."

29As they were leaving Jericho, a large crowd followed Him. [Mark 10:46–52; Luke 18:35–43]

20:15 Lit *evil because I am good?*

[30]And two blind men were sitting by the road, and when they heard that Jesus was passing by, they cried out, "Lord, have mercy on us, Son of David (Messiah)!"

[31]The crowd sternly told them to be quiet, but they cried out all the more, "Lord, Son of David (Messiah) have mercy on us!"

[32]Jesus stopped and called them, and asked, "What do you want Me to do for you?"

[33]They answered Him, "Lord, *we want* our eyes to be opened."

[34]Moved with compassion, Jesus touched their eyes; and immediately they regained their sight and followed Him [as His disciples].

21 WHEN THEY approached Jerusalem and had reached Bethphage, at the Mount of Olives, Jesus sent two disciples [ahead], [Mark 11:1–10; Luke 19:29–38; John 12:12–15]

[2]saying to them, "Go into the village opposite you, and at once you will find a donkey tied, and a colt with her; untie them and bring them to Me.

[3]"If anyone says anything to you, you should say, 'The Lord needs them,' and without delay the owner will send them [with you]."

[4]This happened so that what was spoken by the prophet would be fulfilled, saying:

[5]"TELL THE DAUGHTER OF ZION (the people of Jerusalem),
'BEHOLD, YOUR KING IS COMING TO YOU,
GENTLE AND MOUNTED ON A DONKEY,
EVEN ON A COLT, THE FOAL OF A BEAST OF BURDEN.'" [Is 62:11; Zech 9:9]

[6]Then the disciples went and did as Jesus had instructed them,

[7]and they brought the donkey and the colt, and placed their coats on them; and Jesus sat on the coats.

[8]Most of the crowd spread their coats on the road [as before a king], while others were cutting branches from the trees and spreading them on the road.

[9]The crowds that went ahead of Him, and those that followed Him, were shouting [in praise and adoration],

"Hosanna to the Son of David (Messiah);
BLESSED [praised, glorified] IS HE WHO COMES IN THE NAME OF THE LORD;
Hosanna in the highest [heaven]!" [Ps 118:26]

[10]When He entered Jerusalem, all the city was trembling [with excitement], saying, "Who is this?"

[11]And the crowds were saying, "This is the prophet Jesus, from Nazareth in Galilee."

[12]And Jesus entered the temple [grounds] and drove out [with force] all who were buying and selling [birds and animals for sacrifice] in the temple *area*, and He turned over the tables of the moneychangers [who made a profit exchanging foreign money for temple coinage] and the chairs of those who were selling doves [for sacrifice]. [Mark 11:15–18; Luke 19:45–47; John 2:14–16]

[13]Jesus said to them, "It is written [in Scripture], 'MY HOUSE SHALL BE CALLED A HOUSE OF PRAYER'; but you are making it a ROBBERS' DEN." [Is 56:7; Jer 7:11]

[14]And the blind and the lame came to Him in [the porticoes and courts of] the temple *area*, and He healed them.

[15]But when the chief priests and the scribes saw the wonderful *and* miraculous things that Jesus had done, and *heard* the boys who were shouting in [the porticoes and courts of] the temple [in praise and adoration], "Hosanna to the Son of David (the Messiah)," they became indignant

¹⁶and they said to Him, "Do You hear what these *children* are saying?" And Jesus replied to them, "Yes; have you never read [in the Scripture], 'OUT OF THE MOUTHS OF INFANTS AND NURSING BABIES YOU HAVE PREPARED *and* PROVIDED PRAISE FOR YOURSELF'?" [Ps 8:2]

¹⁷Then He left them and went out of the city to Bethany, and spent the night there.

¹⁸Now early in the morning, as Jesus was coming back to the city, He was hungry. [Mark 11:12–14, 20–24]

¹⁹Seeing a lone fig tree at the roadside, He went to it and found nothing but leaves on it; and He said to it, "Never again will fruit come from you." And at once the fig tree withered.

²⁰When the disciples saw it, they were astonished and asked, "How is it that the fig tree has withered away all at once?"

²¹Jesus replied to them, "I assure you *and* most solemnly say to you, if you have faith [personal trust and confidence in Me] and do not doubt *or* allow yourself to be drawn in two directions, you will not only do what was done to the fig tree, but even if you say to this mountain, 'Be taken up and thrown into the sea,' it will happen [if God wills it]. [1 John 5:14]

²²"And whatever you ask for in prayer, believing, you will receive."

²³When He entered the temple *area,* the chief priests and elders of the people came to Him as He was teaching and said, "By what [kind of] authority are You doing these things, and who gave You this authority [to exercise this power]?" [Mark 11:27–33; Luke 20:1–8]

²⁴Jesus replied to them, "I will also ask you a question, and if you tell Me the answer, then I will tell you by what authority I do these things.

²⁵"The baptism of John—from where did it come? From heaven [that is, ordained by God] or from men?" And they *began* debating among themselves

[considering the implications of their answer], saying, "If we say, 'From heaven,' He will say to us, 'Then why did you not believe John?'

²⁶"But if we say, 'From men,' we are afraid of the [response of the] crowd; for they all regard John as a prophet."

²⁷So they answered Jesus, "We do not know." And He said to them, "Neither will I tell you by what [kind of] authority I do these things."

²⁸"What do you think? There was a man who had two sons, and he came to the first and said, 'Son, go and work in the vineyard today.'

²⁹"And he answered, 'I will not'; but afterward he regretted it *and* changed his mind and went.

³⁰"Then the man came to the second son and said the same thing; and he replied, 'I *will,* sir'; but he did not go.

³¹"Which of the two did the will of the father?" The chief priests and elders replied, "The first one." Jesus said to them, "I assure you *and* most solemnly say to you that the tax collectors and the prostitutes will get into the kingdom of God before you.

³²"For John came to you [walking] in the way of righteousness and you did not believe him; but the tax collectors and the prostitutes did believe him; and you, seeing this, did not even change your mind afterward and believe him [accepting what he proclaimed to you].

³³"Listen to another parable. There was a landowner who PLANTED A VINEYARD AND PUT A WALL AROUND IT AND DUG A WINE PRESS IN IT, AND BUILT A TOWER, and rented it out to tenant farmers and went on a journey [to another country]. [Is 5:1–7; Mark 12:1–12; Luke 20:9–19]

³⁴"When the harvest time approached, he sent his servants to the tenants to get his [share of the] fruit.

³⁵"But the tenants took his servants and beat one, and killed another, and stoned a third.

36"Again he sent other servants, more than the first time; and they treated them the same way.

37"Finally he sent his own son to them, saying, 'They will respect my son *and* have regard for him.'

38"But when the tenants saw the son, they said to themselves, 'This [man] is the heir; come on, let us kill him and seize his inheritance.'

39"So they took the son and threw him out of the vineyard, and killed him.

40"Now when the owner of the vineyard comes back, what will he do to those tenants?"

41They said to Him, "He will put those despicable men to a miserable end, and rent out the vineyard to other tenants [of good character] who will pay him the proceeds at the *proper* seasons."

42Jesus asked them, "Have you never read in the Scriptures:

'THE [very] STONE WHICH THE
  BUILDERS REJECTED *and* THREW
  AWAY,
HAS BECOME THE CHIEF
  CORNERSTONE;
THIS IS THE LORD'S DOING,
AND IT IS MARVELOUS *and*
  WONDERFUL IN OUR EYES'?
[Ps 118:22, 23]

43"Therefore I tell you, the kingdom of God will be taken away from you and given to [another] people who will produce the fruit of it.

44"And he who falls on this Stone will be broken to pieces; but he on whom it falls will be crushed." [Is 8:14, 15; Dan 2:34, 35]

45When the chief priests and the Pharisees heard His parables, they understood that He was talking about them.

46And although they were trying to arrest Him, they feared the people, because they regarded Jesus as a prophet.

22 JESUS SPOKE to them again in parables, saying, 2"The kingdom of heaven may be compared to a king who gave a wedding feast for his son.

3"And he sent his servants to call those who had [previously] been invited to the wedding feast, but they refused to come.

4"Then he sent out some other servants, saying, 'Tell those who have been invited, "Look, I have prepared my dinner; my oxen and fattened calves are butchered and everything is ready; come to the wedding feast."'

5"But they paid no attention [they disregarded the invitation, treating it with contempt] and went away, one to his farm, another to his business.

6"The rest [of the invited guests] seized his servants and mistreated them [insulting and humiliating them] and killed them.

7"The king was enraged [when he heard this], and sent his soldiers and destroyed those murderers and burned their city.

8"Then he said to his servants, 'The wedding [feast] is ready, but those who were invited were not worthy.

9"So go to the main highways that lead out of the city, and invite to the wedding feast as many as you find.'

10"Those servants went out into the streets and gathered together all *the people* they could find, both bad and good; so the wedding hall was filled with dinner guests [sitting at the banquet table].

11"But when the king came in to see the dinner guests, he saw a man there who was not dressed [appropriately] in wedding clothes,

12and he said, 'Friend, how did you come in here without wearing the wedding clothes [that were provided for you]?' And the man was speechless *and* without excuse.

13"Then the king said to the attendants,

'Tie him hand and foot, and throw him into the darkness outside; in that place there will be weeping [over sorrow and pain] and grinding of teeth [over distress and anger].'

¹⁴"For many are called (invited, summoned), but few are chosen."

¹⁵Then the Pharisees went and conspired together plotting how to trap Him by [distorting] what He said. [Mark 12:13–17; Luke 20:20–26]

¹⁶They sent their disciples to Him, along with the Herodians, saying, "Teacher, we know that You are sincere and that You teach the way of God truthfully, without concerning Yourself about [what] anyone [thinks or says of Your teachings]; for You are impartial *and* do not seek anyone's favor [and You treat all people alike, regardless of status].

¹⁷"Tell us then, what do You think? Is it permissible [according to Jewish law and tradition] to pay a poll-tax to Caesar, or not?"

¹⁸But Jesus, aware of their malice, asked, "Why are you testing Me, you hypocrites?

¹⁹"Show me the coin used for the poll-tax." And they brought Him a denarius [a day's wage].

²⁰And Jesus said to them, "Whose likeness and inscription is this?"

²¹They said, "[The Emperor Tiberius] Caesar's." Then He said to them, "Then pay to Caesar the things that are

life point

I once heard a Bible teacher say that Matthew 22:14 means many are called or given an opportunity to do something for the Lord, but few are willing to take the responsibility to answer that call. God's call does come with responsibility, but it also comes with rewards. I believe you are called for a very special purpose. I hope you will say yes to Him!

Caesar's; and to God the things that are God's."

²²When they heard this, they were caught off guard, and they left Him and went away.

²³On that day some Sadducees, who say that there is no resurrection [of the dead], came to Him and asked Him a question, [Mark 12:18–27; Luke 20:27–40]

²⁴saying, "Teacher, Moses said, 'IF A MAN DIES, LEAVING NO CHILDREN, HIS BROTHER AS NEXT OF KIN SHALL MARRY HIS WIDOW, AND RAISE CHILDREN FOR HIS BROTHER.' [Deut 25:5]

²⁵"Now there were seven brothers among us; the first married and died, and having no children left his wife to his brother.

²⁶"The second also [died childless], and the third, down to the seventh.

²⁷"Last of all, the woman died.

²⁸"So in the resurrection, whose wife of the seven will she be? For they all had *married* her."

²⁹But Jesus replied to them, "You are all wrong because you know neither the Scriptures [which teach the resurrection] nor the power of God [for He is able to raise the dead].

³⁰"For in the resurrection neither do *men* marry nor are *women* given in marriage, but they are like angels in heaven [who do not marry nor produce children].

³¹"But as to the resurrection of the dead—have you not read [in the Scripture] what God said to you:

³²'I AM THE GOD OF ABRAHAM, AND THE GOD OF ISAAC, AND THE GOD OF JACOB'? He is not the God of the dead, but of the living." [Ex 3:6]

³³When the crowds heard this, they were astonished at His teaching.

³⁴Now when the Pharisees heard that He had silenced (muzzled) the Sadducees, they gathered together. [Mark 12:28–31; Luke 10:25–28]

³⁵One of them, a lawyer [an expert in

Mosaic Law], asked Jesus *a question,* to test Him:

[36]"Teacher, which is the greatest commandment in the Law?" [Mark 12:28]

[37]And Jesus replied to him, " 'YOU SHALL LOVE THE LORD YOUR GOD WITH ALL YOUR HEART, AND WITH ALL YOUR SOUL, AND WITH ALL YOUR MIND.' [Deut 6:5]

[38]"This is the first and greatest commandment.

[39]"The second is like it, 'YOU SHALL LOVE YOUR NEIGHBOR AS YOURSELF [that is, unselfishly seek the best or higher good for others].' [Lev 19:18; Matt 19:19]

[40]"The whole Law and the [writings of the] Prophets depend on these two commandments."

[41]Now while the Pharisees were [still] gathered together, Jesus asked them a question: [Mark 12:35–37; Luke 20:41–44]

[42]"What do you [Pharisees] think of the Christ (the Messiah, the Anointed)? Whose Son is He?" They said to Him, "*The son* of David."

[43]Jesus asked them, "How is it then that David by the inspiration of the Spirit, calls Him 'Lord,' saying,

[44]'THE LORD (the Father) SAID TO MY
    LORD (the Son, the Messiah),
 "SIT AT MY RIGHT HAND,
 UNTIL I PUT YOUR ENEMIES UNDER
    YOUR FEET" '? [Ps 110:1]

[45]"So then, if David calls Him (the Son, the Messiah) 'Lord,' how is He David's son?"

[46]No one was able to say a word to Him in answer, nor from that day on did anyone dare to question Him again.

23 THEN JESUS spoke to the crowds and to His disciples, [2]saying: "The scribes and Pharisees have seated themselves in Moses' chair [of authority as teachers of the Law];

[3]so practice and observe everything they tell you, but do not do as they do; for they preach [things], but do not practice *them.*

[4]"The scribes and Pharisees tie up heavy loads [that are hard to bear] and place them on men's shoulders, but they themselves will not lift a finger [to make them lighter].

[5]"They do all their deeds to be seen by men; for they make their phylacteries (tefillin) wide [to make them more conspicuous] and make their tassels long. [Ex 13:9; Num 15:38; Deut 6:8]

[6]"They love the place of distinction *and* honor at feasts and the best seats in the synagogues [those on the platform near the scrolls of the Law, facing the congregation],

[7]and to be greeted [with respect] in the market places *and* public forums, and to have people call them Rabbi.

[8]"But do not be called Rabbi (Teacher); for One is your Teacher, and you are all [equally] brothers.

[9]"Do not call *anyone* on earth [who guides you spiritually] your father; for One is your Father, He who is in heaven.

[10]"Do not *let yourselves* be called leaders *or* teachers; for One is your Leader (Teacher), the Christ.

[11]"But the greatest among you will be your servant.

[12]"Whoever exalts himself shall be humbled; and whoever humbles himself shall be raised to honor.

[13]"But woe (judgment is coming) to you, [self-righteous] scribes and Pharisees, hypocrites, because you shut off the kingdom of heaven in front of people; for you do not enter yourselves, nor do you allow those who are [in the process of] entering to do so. [Luke 11:52]

[14]"[Woe to you, scribes and Pharisees, hypocrites, because you swallow up widows' houses, and to cover it up you make long prayers; therefore you

will receive the greater condemnation.]

¹⁵"Woe to you, [self-righteous] scribes and Pharisees, hypocrites, because you travel over sea and land to make a single proselyte (convert to Judaism), and when he becomes a convert, you make him twice as much a son of hell as you are.

¹⁶"Woe to you, blind guides, who say, 'Whoever swears [an oath] by the sanctuary of the temple, that is nothing (non-binding); but whoever swears [an oath] by the gold of the temple is obligated [as a debtor to fulfill his vow and keep his promise].'

¹⁷"You fools and blind men! Which is more important, the gold or the sanctuary of the temple that sanctified the gold? [Ex 30:29]

¹⁸"And [you scribes and Pharisees say], 'Whoever swears [an oath] by the altar, that is nothing (non-binding), but whoever swears [an oath] by the offering on it, he is obligated [as a debtor to fulfill his vow and keep his promise].'

¹⁹"You [spiritually] blind men, which is more important, the offering, or the altar that sanctifies the offering?

²⁰"Therefore, whoever swears [an oath] by the altar, swears both by it and by everything [offered] on it.

²¹"And whoever swears [an oath] by the sanctuary of the temple, swears by it and by Him who dwells within it. [1 Kin 8:13; Ps 26:8]

²²"And whoever swears [an oath] by heaven, swears both by the throne of God and by Him who sits upon it.

²³"Woe to you, [self-righteous] scribes and Pharisees, hypocrites! For you give a tenth (tithe) of your mint and dill and cumin [focusing on minor matters], and have neglected the weightier [more important moral and spiritual] provisions of the Law: justice and mercy and faithfulness; but these are the [primary] things you ought to have done without neglecting the others.

²⁴"You [spiritually] blind guides, who strain out a gnat [consuming yourselves with miniscule matters] and swallow a camel [ignoring and violating God's precepts]! [Lev 11:24; 27:30; Mic 6:8]

²⁵"Woe to you, [self-righteous] scribes and Pharisees, hypocrites! For you clean the outside of the cup and of the plate, but inside they are full of extortion *and* robbery and self-indulgence (unrestrained greed).

²⁶"You [spiritually] blind Pharisee, first clean the inside of the cup and of the plate [examine and change your inner self to conform to God's precepts], so that the outside [your public life and deeds] may be clean also.

²⁷"Woe to you, [self-righteous] scribes and Pharisees, hypocrites! For you are like whitewashed tombs which look beautiful on the outside, but inside are full of dead men's bones and everything unclean.

²⁸"So you, also, outwardly seem to be just *and* upright to men, but inwardly you are full of hypocrisy and lawlessness. [Ps 5:9]

²⁹"Woe to you, [self-righteous] scribes and Pharisees, hypocrites! For you build tombs for the prophets and decorate *and* adorn the monuments of the righteous,

³⁰and you say, 'If we had been *living* in the days of our fathers, we would not have joined them in *shedding* the blood of the prophets.'

³¹"So you testify against yourselves that you are the descendants of those who murdered the prophets.

³²"Fill up, then, the [allotted] measure *of the guilt* of your fathers' *sins*.

³³"You serpents, you spawn of vipers, how can you escape the penalty of hell?

³⁴"Therefore, take notice, I am sending you prophets and wise men [interpreters, teachers] and scribes [men educated in the Mosaic Law and the

writings of the prophets]; some of them you will kill and *even* crucify, and some you will flog in your synagogues, and pursue *and* persecute from city to city,

³⁵so that on you will come *the guilt of* all the blood of the righteous shed on earth, from the blood of righteous Abel to the blood of Zechariah [the priest], the son of Berechiah, whom you murdered between the temple and the altar. [Gen 4:8; 2 Chr 24:21; Luke 11:51]

³⁶"I assure you *and* most solemnly say to you, [the judgment for] all these things [these vile and murderous deeds] will come on this generation. [2 Chr 36:15, 16]

³⁷"O Jerusalem, Jerusalem, who murders the prophets and stones [to death] those [messengers] who are sent to her [by God]! How often I wanted to gather your children together [around Me], as a hen gathers her chicks under her wings, and you were unwilling. [Luke 13:34, 35]

³⁸"Listen carefully: your house is being left to you desolate [completely abandoned by God and destitute of His protection]! [1 Kin 9:6, 7; Jer 22:5]

³⁹"For I say to you, you will not see Me again [ministering to you publicly] until you say, 'BLESSED [to be celebrated with praise] IS HE WHO COMES IN THE NAME OF THE LORD!'" [Ps 118:26]

24 JESUS LEFT the temple *area* and was going on His way when His disciples came up to Him to call His attention to the [magnificent and massive] buildings of the temple. [Mark 13; Luke 21:5–36]

²And He said to them, "Do you see all these things? I assure you *and* most solemnly say to you, not one stone here will be left on another, which will not be torn down."

³While Jesus was seated on the Mount of Olives, the disciples came to Him privately, and said, "Tell us, when will this [destruction of the temple] take place, and what will be the sign of Your coming, and of the end (completion, consummation) of the age?"

⁴Jesus answered, "Be careful that no one misleads you [deceiving you and leading you into error].

⁵"For many will come in My name [misusing it, and appropriating the strength of the name which belongs to Me], saying, 'I am the Christ (the Messiah, the Anointed),' and they will mislead many.

⁶"You will *continually* hear of wars and rumors of wars. See that you are not frightened, for *those things* must take place, but that is not yet the end [of the age].

⁷"For nation will rise against nation, and kingdom against kingdom, and there will be famines and earthquakes in various places.

⁸"But all these things are *merely* the beginning of birth pangs [of the intolerable anguish and the time of unprecedented trouble].

⁹"Then they will hand you over to [endure] tribulation, and will put you to death, and you will be hated by all nations because of My name.

¹⁰"At that time many will be offended *and* repelled [by their association with Me] *and* will fall away [from the One whom they should trust] and will betray one another [handing over believers to their persecutors] and will hate one another.

¹¹"Many false prophets will appear and mislead many.

¹²"Because lawlessness is increased, the love of most people will grow cold.

¹³"But the one who endures *and* bears up [under suffering] to the end will be saved.

¹⁴"This good news of the kingdom [the gospel] will be preached throughout the whole world as a testimony to all the nations, and then the end [of the age] will come.

¹⁵"So when you see the ABOMINA-TION OF DESOLATION [the appalling sacrilege that astonishes and makes desolate], spoken of by the prophet Daniel, standing in the Holy Place (let the reader understand), [Dan 9:27; 11:31; 12:11]

¹⁶then let those who are in Judea flee to the mountains [for refuge].

¹⁷"Whoever is on the housetop must not go down to get the things that are in his house [because there will not be enough time].

¹⁸"Whoever is in the field must not turn back to get his coat.

¹⁹"And woe to those who are pregnant and to those who are nursing babies in those days!

²⁰"Pray that your flight [from persecution and suffering] will not be in winter, or on a Sabbath [when Jewish laws prohibit travel].

²¹"For at that time there will be a great tribulation (pressure, distress, oppression), such as has not occurred since the beginning of the world until

keep love from growing cold

The twenty-fourth chapter of Matthew deals with signs of the end times. Most of them we are familiar with—wars and rumors of wars, earthquakes, famines, and widespread deception. But there is another sign of the end times. Matthew 24:12 says, "the love of most people will grow cold" due to the lawlessness and wickedness in the land.

The phrase "most people" refers to the church, not the world. The pressure of rampant evil, difficult circumstances, and even the stress of our modern-day lifestyle produces an atmosphere so supercharged with problems that most people totally ignore their love walk with God. Instead they concentrate on themselves, look out for themselves, and try to solve their own problems.

This is something God never told us to do. If we tend to His business, He will tend to ours. We are to concentrate on representing Him properly, and that is impossible unless we are walking in love. As we do represent Him well, He gives us wisdom to deal with our problems and brings deliverance from our foes.

Have you ever noticed that God does not always give us the ability to solve our own problems, yet when we are powerless to solve our own, He enables us to solve someone else's?

At one point in my own life, I realized I was spinning my wheels, so to speak. I was trying to solve all my problems, thinking that when my life got straightened out I could go forward in ministry to others. The fact is I had it backwards, as do so many others. I needed to cast my care on the Lord. I needed to do what He showed me concerning my situations in life without getting entangled in them. I needed to sow seeds in other people's lives by helping them, and then God would bring a harvest in my own life.

Refuse to let your love grow cold. Stir up the love in your life—toward your spouse, family members, friends, neighbors, and coworkers. Reach out to others who are hurting and in need. Pray for people and bless them. Grow to the point that one of your first thoughts each morning is about how you can bless someone else that day.

now, nor ever will [again]. [Dan 12:1; Joel 2:2]

²²"And if those days [of tribulation] had not been cut short, no human life would be saved; but for the sake of the elect (God's chosen ones) those days will be shortened.

²³"Then if anyone says to you [during the great tribulation], 'Look! Here is the Christ,' or 'There *He is,*' do not believe *it.*

²⁴"For false Christs and false prophets will appear and they will provide great signs and wonders, so as to deceive, if possible, even the elect (God's chosen ones).

²⁵"Listen carefully, I have told you in advance.

²⁶"So if they say to you, 'Look! He is in the wilderness,' do not go out there, or, 'Look! He is in the inner rooms [of a house],' do not believe it.

²⁷"For just as the lightning comes from the east and flashes as far as the west, so will be the coming [in glory] of the Son of Man [everyone will see Him clearly].

²⁸"Wherever the corpse is, there the vultures will flock together. [Job 39:30]

²⁹"Immediately after the tribulation of those days THE SUN WILL BE DARKENED, AND THE MOON WILL NOT PROVIDE ITS LIGHT, AND THE STARS WILL FALL from the sky, and the powers of the heavens will be shaken. [Is 13:10; 34:4; Joel 2:10, 11; Zeph 1:15]

³⁰"And at that time the sign of the Son of Man [coming in His glory] will appear in the sky, and then all the tribes of the earth [and especially Israel] will mourn [regretting their rebellion and rejection of the Messiah], and they will see the SON OF MAN COMING ON THE CLOUDS OF HEAVEN with power and great glory [in brilliance and splendor]. [Dan 7:13; Rev 1:7]

³¹"And He will send His angels with A LOUD TRUMPET and THEY WILL GATHER TOGETHER His elect (God's chosen ones) from the four winds, from one end of the heavens to the other. [Is 27:13; Zech 9:14]

³²"Now learn this lesson from the fig tree: As soon as its young shoots become tender and it puts out its leaves, you know that summer is near; [Mark 13:28, 29; Luke 21:29–31]

³³so you, too, when you see all these things [taking place], know for certain that He is near, right at the door.

³⁴"I assure you *and* most solemnly say to you, this generation [the people living when these signs and events begin] will not pass away until all these things take place.

³⁵"Heaven and earth [as now known] will pass away, but My words will not pass away.

³⁶"But of that [exact] day and hour no one knows, not even the angels of heaven, nor the Son [in His humanity], but the Father alone.

³⁷"For the coming of the Son of Man (the Messiah) will be just like the days of Noah.

³⁸"For as in those days before the flood they were eating and drinking, marrying and giving in marriage, until the [very] day when Noah entered the ark,

³⁹and they did not know *or* understand until the flood came and swept them all away; so will the coming of the Son of Man be [unexpected judgment]. [Gen 6:5–8; 7:6–24]

⁴⁰"At that time two men will be in the field; one will be taken [for judgment] and one will be left.

⁴¹"Two women *will be* grinding at the mill; one will be taken [for judgment] and one will be left.

⁴²"So be alert [give strict attention, be cautious and active in faith], for you do not know which day [whether near or far] your Lord is coming.

⁴³"But understand this: If the head of the house had known what time of the night the thief was coming, he would

have been on the alert and would not have allowed his house to be broken into. [Luke 12:39, 40]

⁴⁴"Therefore, you [who follow Me] must also be ready; because the Son of Man is coming at an hour when you do not expect Him.

⁴⁵"Who then is the faithful and wise servant whom his master has put in charge of his household to give the others [in the house] their food *and* supplies at the proper time? [Luke 12:42–46]

⁴⁶"Blessed is that [faithful] servant when his master returns and finds him doing so.

⁴⁷"I assure you *and* most solemnly say to you that he will put him in charge of all his possessions.

⁴⁸"But if that servant is evil and says in his heart, 'My master is taking his time [he will not return for a long while],'

⁴⁹and begins to beat his fellow servants and to eat and drink with drunkards;

⁵⁰the master of that servant will come on a day when he does not expect him and at an hour of which he is not aware,

⁵¹and will cut him in two and put him with the hypocrites; in that place there will be weeping [over sorrow and pain] and grinding of teeth [over distress and anger].

25 "THEN THE kingdom of heaven will be like ten virgins, who took their lamps and went to meet the bridegroom.

²"Five of them were foolish [thoughtless, silly, and careless], and five were wise [far-sighted, practical, and sensible].

³"For when the foolish took their lamps, they did not take any [extra] oil with them,

⁴but the wise took flasks of oil along with their lamps.

⁵"Now while the bridegroom was delayed, they all began to nod off, and they fell asleep.

⁶"But at midnight there was a shout, 'Look! The bridegroom [is coming]! Go out to meet *him.*'

⁷"Then all those virgins got up and put their own lamps in order [trimmed the wicks and added oil and lit them].

⁸"But the foolish *virgins* said to the wise, 'Give us some of your oil, because our lamps are going out.'

⁹"But the wise replied, 'No, otherwise there will not be enough for us and for you, *too*; go instead to the dealers and buy *oil* for yourselves.'

¹⁰"But while they were going away to buy *oil,* the bridegroom came, and those who were ready went in with him to the wedding feast; and the door was shut *and* locked.

¹¹"Later the others also came, and said, 'Lord, Lord, open [the door] for us.'

¹²"But He replied, 'I assure you *and* most solemnly say to you, I do not know you [we have no relationship].'

¹³"Therefore, be on the alert [be prepared and ready], for you do not know the day nor the hour [when the Son of Man will come].

¹⁴"For it is just like a man who was *about* to take a journey, and he called his servants together and entrusted them with his possessions. [Luke 19:12–27]

¹⁵"To one he gave five talents, to another, two, and to another, one, each according to his own ability; and then he went on his journey.

¹⁶"The one who had received the five talents went at once and traded with them, and he [made a profit and] gained five more.

¹⁷"Likewise the one who had two [made a profit and] gained two more.

¹⁸"But the one who had received the one went and dug *a hole* in the ground and hid his master's money.

¹⁹"Now after a long time the master

of those servants returned and settled accounts with them.

²⁰"And the one who had received the five talents came and brought him five more, saying, 'Master, you entrusted to me five talents. See, I have [made a profit and] gained five more talents.'

²¹"His master said to him, 'Well done, good and faithful servant. You have

life point

All ten virgins in Matthew 25:1–10 had the same opportunity, but only half of them were prepared to take it.

In a society where people needed oil to provide light, five virgins were wise and had extra oil on hand; the other five were foolish and lost out because they did not keep their lamps filled with oil. When the bridegroom came, the five virgins without the oil missed their opportunity to go with him because they were lazy when they should have been working and were out trying to buy more oil for their lamps at the wrong time.

God is an "equal-opportunity employer." It does not matter to Him what kind of background we come from, what kind of parents or family life we have, what color or gender we are, what kind of education we received, or what our physical handicaps may be. None of those things make any difference to Him. In Him, we all have equal opportunity. Anyone who will follow His guidelines and do as He tells them to do can be blessed and used by Him. All ten virgins had the same opportunity, but only five were willing to do their part.

God puts potential in all of us and if we are willing to develop it, we will see wonderful things take place in our lives. Do your part and don't be left out as the five foolish virgins were.

been faithful *and* trustworthy over a little, I will put you in charge of many things; share in the joy of your master.'

²²"Also the one who had the two talents came forward, saying, 'Master, you entrusted two talents to me. See, I have [made a profit and] gained two more talents.'

²³"His master said to him, 'Well done, good and faithful servant. You have been faithful *and* trustworthy over a little, I will put you in charge of many things; share in the joy of your master.'

²⁴"The one who had received one talent also came forward, saying, 'Master, I knew you to be a harsh *and* demanding man, reaping [the harvest] where you did not sow and gathering where you did not scatter *seed*.

²⁵'So I was afraid [to lose the talent], and I went and hid your talent in the ground. See, you have what is your own.'

²⁶"But his master answered him, 'You wicked, lazy servant, you knew that I reap [the harvest] where I did not sow and gather where I did not scatter *seed*.

²⁷'Then you ought to have put my money with the bankers, and at my return I would have received my *money* back with interest.

²⁸'So take the talent away from him, and give it to the one who has the ten talents.'

²⁹"For to everyone who has [and values his blessings and gifts from God, and has used them wisely], more will be given, and [he will be richly supplied so that] he will have an abundance; but from the one who does not have [because he has ignored or disregarded his blessings and gifts from God], even what he does have will be taken away. [Matt 13:12; Luke 19:26]

³⁰"And throw out the worthless servant into the outer darkness; in that place [of grief and torment] there will be weeping [over sorrow and pain]

and grinding of teeth [over distress and anger].

³¹"But when the Son of Man comes in His glory *and* majesty and all the angels with Him, then He will sit on the throne of His glory. [Rev 20:4–6]

³²"All the nations will be gathered before Him [for judgment]; and He will separate them from one another, as a shepherd separates his sheep from the goats; [Ezek 34:17]

³³and He will put the sheep on His right [the place of honor], and the goats on His left [the place of rejection].

³⁴"Then the King will say to those on His right, 'Come, you blessed of My Father [you favored of God, appointed to

use it or lose it

In Matthew 25:14, 15, Jesus tells the story of a man going on a long journey. He called his servants together and gave them different amounts of money to handle, according to their abilities.

No, we do not all have the same talents and abilities. We cannot all do the same things, but we can all be what God has called us individually to be. I cannot be what you are, and you cannot be what I am, but we can each be all God wants us to be.

Many people are frustrated and miserable because they do not feel fulfilled. They are not being all they can be and are not doing all they know they are supposed to be doing. They are letting the devil or other people talk them out of their callings and their blessings.

This is what happened to one of the servants in Matthew 25. The man who was going on the journey gave talents to three of his servants before he left. While he was gone, one servant invested what he was given and received it back with interest. When the man returned and found out what the servant did with the talent, he said, "Well done, good and faithful servant. You have been faithful and trustworthy over a little, I will put you in charge of many things" (Matthew 25:21). The second servant did the same, and the man spoke the same words to him (see Matthew 25:22, 23). But the third servant buried his talent in the ground because he was afraid. When the man found out what that servant did, he was so upset with him that he took away his talent and gave it to the servant who had the ten talents (see Matthew 25:24–28).

Many people are like that third servant. They hide their talents because they are afraid—afraid of responsibility, afraid of judgment, afraid of what people will think. They are afraid to step out; afraid they might fail, afraid of criticism, afraid of other people's opinions, afraid of being misunderstood. They are afraid of sacrifice and hard work.

I do not want you to be afraid to take the talent God gave you and use it for His glory. I do not want you to end up unhappy, unfulfilled, and dissatisfied because you are compromising what He has placed in you. Let me encourage you to use your talents to the greatest possible extent and to do your best in every area of your life. Then you will hear your Master say, "Well done!"

eternal salvation], inherit the kingdom prepared for you from the foundation of the world.

³⁵'For I was hungry, and you gave Me something to eat; I was thirsty, and you gave Me *something* to drink; I was a stranger, and you invited Me in;

³⁶*I was* naked, and you clothed Me; I was sick, and you visited Me [with help and ministering care]; I was in prison, and you came to Me [ignoring personal danger].' [Is 58:7]

³⁷"Then the righteous will answer Him, 'Lord, when did we see You hungry, and feed You, or thirsty, and give You something to drink?

³⁸'And when did we see You as a stranger, and invite You in, or naked, and clothe You?

³⁹'And when did we see You sick, or in prison, and come to You?'

⁴⁰"The King will answer and say to them, 'I assure you *and* most solemnly say to you, to the extent that you did it for one of these brothers of Mine, *even* the least *of them,* you did it for Me.' [Prov 19:17]

⁴¹"Then He will say to those on His left, 'Leave Me, you cursed ones, into the eternal fire which has been prepared for the devil and his angels (demons);

⁴²for I was hungry, and you gave Me *nothing* to eat; I was thirsty, and you gave Me nothing to drink;

⁴³I was a stranger, and you did not invite Me in; naked, and you did not clothe Me; sick, and in prison, and you did not visit Me [with help and ministering care].'

⁴⁴"Then they also [in their turn] will answer, 'Lord, when did we see You hungry, or thirsty, or as a stranger, or naked, or sick, or in prison, and did not minister to You?'

⁴⁵"Then He will reply to them, 'I assure you *and* most solemnly say to you, to the extent that you did not do it for one of the least of these [my followers],

you did not do it for Me.' [Prov 14:31; 17:5]

⁴⁶"Then these [unbelieving people] will go away into eternal (unending) punishment, but those who are righteous *and* in right standing with God [will go, by His remarkable grace] into eternal (unending) life." [Dan 12:2]

26 WHEN JESUS had finished this discourse, He said to His disciples,

²"You know that the Passover is coming in two days, and the Son of Man is to be betrayed *and* handed over for crucifixion." [Mark 14:1, 2; Luke 22:1, 2]

³Then the chief priests and the elders of the people gathered in the courtyard of the [elegant home of the Jewish] high priest, whose name was Caiaphas,

⁴and plotted together to arrest Jesus by stealth and kill Him.

⁵But they said, "It must not be during the festival (Passover), otherwise there might be a riot among the people."

⁶Now when Jesus was [back] in Bethany, at the home of Simon the leper, [Mark 14:3–9; John 12:1–8]

⁷a woman came to Him with an alabaster vial of very expensive perfume and she poured it on Jesus' head as He reclined *at the table.*

⁸But when the disciples saw it they were indignant *and* angry, saying, "Why all this waste [of money]?

⁹"For this *perfume* might have been sold at a high price and *the money* given to the poor."

¹⁰But Jesus, aware [of the malice] of this [remark], said to them, "Why are you bothering the woman? She has done a good thing to Me.

¹¹"For you always have the poor with you; but you will not always have Me. [Deut 15:11; Mark 14:7]

¹²"When she poured this perfume on My body, she did it to prepare Me for burial.

¹³"I assure you *and* most solemnly say to you, wherever this gospel [of salvation] is preached in the whole world, what this woman has done will also be told in memory of her [for her act of love and devotion]."

¹⁴Then one of the twelve [disciples], who was called Judas Iscariot, went to the chief priests

¹⁵and said, "What are you willing to give me if I hand Jesus over to you?" And they weighed out thirty pieces of silver. [Ex 21:32; Zech 11:12]

¹⁶And from that moment Judas *began* looking for an opportune time to betray Jesus. [Mark 14:10, 11; Luke 22:3–6; John 6:71]

¹⁷Now on the first day of Unleavened Bread (Passover Week) the disciples came to Jesus and asked, "Where do You want us to prepare for You to eat the Passover?" [Mark 14:12–16; Luke 22:7–13]

¹⁸He said, "Go into the city to a certain man, and say to him, 'The Teacher says, "My time [to suffer and atone for sin] is near; I *am to* keep the Passover at your house with My disciples."'"

¹⁹[Accordingly] the disciples did as Jesus had directed them, and they prepared the Passover. [Deut 16:5–8]

²⁰When evening came, Jesus was reclining *at the table* with the twelve disciples. [Mark 14:17–21]

²¹And as they were eating, He said, "I assure you *and* most solemnly say to you that one of you will betray Me."

²²Being deeply grieved *and* extremely distressed, each one of them began to say to Him, "Surely not I, Lord?"

²³Jesus answered, "He who has dipped his hand in the bowl with Me [as a pretense of friendship] will betray Me.

²⁴"The Son of Man is to go [to the cross], just as it is written [in Scripture] of Him; but woe (judgment is coming) to that man by whom the Son of Man is betrayed! It would have been good for

that man if he had never been born." [Ps 41:9]

²⁵And Judas, the betrayer, said, "Surely it is not I, Rabbi?" Jesus said to him, "You have said it yourself."

²⁶Now as they were eating Jesus took bread, and after blessing it, He broke it and gave it to the disciples, and said, "Take, eat; this is My body." [Mark 14:22–25; Luke 22:17–20; 1 Cor 11:23–25]

²⁷And when He had taken a cup and given thanks, He gave it to them, saying, "Drink from it, all of you;

²⁸for this is My blood of the [new and better] covenant, which [ratifies the agreement and] is being poured out for many [as a substitutionary atonement] for the forgiveness of sins. [Ex 24:6–8]

²⁹"But I say to you, I will not drink of this fruit of the vine from now on until that day when I drink it new with you in My Father's kingdom."

³⁰After singing a hymn, they went out to the Mount of Olives.

³¹Then Jesus said to them, "You will all fall away because of Me this night [disillusioned about Me, confused, and some even ashamed of Me], for it is written [in the Scriptures], 'I WILL STRIKE THE SHEPHERD, AND THE SHEEP OF THE FLOCK WILL BE SCATTERED.' [Zech 13:7]

³²"But after I am raised [to life], I will go ahead of you [leading the way] to Galilee."

³³Peter replied to Him, "Though they all fall away because of You [and doubt and disown You], I will never fall away!" [Mark 14:29–31; Luke 22:33, 34; John 13:37, 38]

³⁴Jesus said to him, "I assure you *and* most solemnly say to you, this night, before a rooster crows, you will [completely] deny Me three times."

³⁵Peter said to Jesus, "Even if I have to die with You, I will not deny You!" And all the disciples said the same thing.

³⁶Then Jesus came with them to a place called Gethsemane (olive-press),

and He told His disciples, "Sit here while I go over there and pray." [Mark 14:32–42; Luke 22:40–46]

³⁷And taking with Him Peter and the two sons of Zebedee [James and John], He began to be grieved and greatly distressed.

³⁸Then He said to them, "My soul is deeply grieved, so that I am almost dying *of sorrow*. Stay here and stay awake *and* keep watch with Me."

³⁹And after going a little farther, He fell face down and prayed, saying, "My Father, if it is possible [that is, consistent with Your will], let this cup pass from Me; yet not as I will, but as You will."

⁴⁰And He came to the disciples and found them sleeping, and said to Peter, "So, you *men* could not stay awake *and* keep watch with Me for one hour?

⁴¹"Keep *actively* watching and praying that you may not come into temptation; the spirit is willing, but the body is weak."

⁴²He went away a second time and prayed, saying, "My Father, if this cannot pass away unless I drink it, Your will be done."

⁴³Again He came and found them sleeping, for their eyes were heavy.

⁴⁴So, leaving them again, He went away and prayed for the third time, saying the same words once more.

⁴⁵Then He returned to the disciples and said to them, "Are you still sleeping and resting? Listen, the hour [of My sacrifice] is at hand and the Son of Man is being betrayed into the hands

life point

We need to apply Jesus' admonition to "keep actively watching and praying" (Matthew 26:41) to our lives. Watch for the attacks of the enemy in your life and then pray immediately. Come against Satan when he is trying to get a foothold, and he will never get a stronghold!

of sinners [whose way and nature is to oppose God].

⁴⁶"Get up, let us go. Look, My betrayer is near!"

⁴⁷As Jesus was still speaking, Judas [Iscariot], one of the twelve [disciples], came up accompanied by a large crowd with swords and clubs, [who came as representatives] from the chief priests and elders of the people. [Mark 14:43–50; Luke 22:47–53; John 18:3–11]

⁴⁸Now the betrayer had given them a sign, saying, "Whomever I kiss, He is the one; seize Him."

⁴⁹Immediately Judas went to Jesus and said, "Greetings (rejoice), Rabbi!" And he kissed Him [in a deliberate act of betrayal].

⁵⁰Jesus said to Judas, "Friend, do what you came for." Then they came and seized Jesus and arrested Him.

⁵¹And one of those who were with Jesus reached out and drew his sword, and struck [Malchus] the slave of the high priest and cut off his ear. [Mark 14:47; Luke 22:50; John 18:10]

⁵²Then Jesus said to him, "Put your sword back in its place; for all those who *habitually* draw the sword will die by the sword. [Gen 9:6]

⁵³"Do you think that I cannot appeal to My Father, and He will immediately provide Me with more than twelve legions of angels?

⁵⁴"How then will the Scriptures be fulfilled, that it must happen this way?"

⁵⁵At that moment Jesus said to the crowds, "Have you come out with swords and clubs to arrest Me as *you would* against a robber? Day after day I used to sit in the porches *and* courts of the temple teaching, and you did not arrest Me.

⁵⁶"But all this has taken place so that the Scriptures of the prophets would be fulfilled." Then all the disciples deserted Him and fled.

⁵⁷Those who had seized Jesus led Him away to Caiaphas, the high priest, where the scribes and the elders (Sanhedrin, Jewish High Court) had gathered [illegally] together. [Mark 14:53–65; Luke 22:66–71; John 18:12f, 19–24]

⁵⁸But Peter followed Him at a distance as far as the courtyard of the [elegant home of the Jewish] high priest, and went inside, and sat with the guards to see the outcome.

⁵⁹Now the chief priests and the whole Council (Sanhedrin, Jewish High Court) tried to get false witnesses to testify against Jesus, so that they might [have a reason to] put Him to death.

⁶⁰They found none, even though many false witnesses came forward. At last two came forward,

⁶¹and testified, "This man said, 'I am able to tear down the temple of God and rebuild it in three days.'"

⁶²The high priest stood up and said to Jesus, "Have You no answer to give? What is it that these men are testifying against You?"

⁶³But Jesus kept silent. And the high priest said to Him, "I call on You to swear a binding oath by the living God, that you tell us whether You are the Christ, the Son of God."

⁶⁴Jesus said to him, "You have [in fact] said it; but more than that I tell you [regardless of what you do with Me now], in the future you will see [Me revealed as] THE SON OF MAN SEATED AT THE RIGHT HAND OF POWER, and COMING ON THE CLOUDS OF HEAVEN." [Ps 110:1; Dan 7:13]

⁶⁵Then the high priest tore his robes [in mock horror] and exclaimed, "He has blasphemed [by making Himself God's equal]! What further need have we of witnesses or evidence? See, you have now heard the blasphemy. [Lev 24:16; Num 14:6]

⁶⁶"What do you think?" They answered, "He deserves to be put to death."

⁶⁷Then they spat in His face and struck Him with their fists; and some slapped Him, [Is 50:6]

⁶⁸saying, "Prophesy to us, You Christ (Messiah, Anointed); who was it that struck You?"

⁶⁹Now Peter was sitting outside in the courtyard, and a servant-girl came up to him and said, "You too were with Jesus the Galilean." [Mark 14:66–72; Luke 22:55–62; John 18:16–18, 25–27]

⁷⁰But he denied it before them all, saying, "I do not know what you are talking about."

⁷¹And when he had gone out to the gateway, another *servant-girl* saw him and she said to the bystanders, "This man was with Jesus the Nazarene."

⁷²And again he denied it with an oath, "I do not know the man."

⁷³After a little while the bystanders came up and said to Peter, "Surely you are one of them too; for even your [Galilean] accent gives you away."

⁷⁴Then he began to curse [that is, to invoke God's judgment on himself] and swear [an oath], "I do not know the man!" And at that moment a rooster crowed.

⁷⁵And Peter remembered the [prophetic] words of Jesus, when He had said, "Before a rooster crows, you will deny Me three times." And he went outside and wept bitterly [in repentance].

27 WHEN IT was morning, all the chief priests and the elders of the people (Sanhedrin, Jewish High Court) conferred together against Jesus, [plotting how] to put Him to death [since under Roman rule they had no power to execute anyone];

²so they bound Him, and led Him away and handed Him over to Pilate the governor [of Judea, who had the authority to condemn prisoners to death].

³When Judas, His betrayer, saw that Jesus was condemned, he was gripped

with remorse and returned the thirty pieces of silver to the chief priests and the elders, [Ex 21:32]

⁴saying, "I have sinned by betraying innocent blood." They replied, "What is that to us? See to that yourself!"

⁵And throwing the pieces of silver into the temple sanctuary, he left; and went away and hanged himself.

⁶The chief priests, picking up the pieces of silver, said, "It is not lawful to put these in the treasury [of the temple], because it is the price of blood."

⁷So after consultation they used the money to buy the Potter's Field as a burial place for strangers.

⁸Therefore that piece of ground has been called the Field of Blood to this day.

⁹Then the words spoken by Jeremiah the prophet were fulfilled: "AND THEY TOOK THE THIRTY PIECES OF SILVER, THE PRICE OF HIM ON WHOM A PRICE HAD BEEN SET by the sons of Israel; [Jer 18:1, 2; 19:1–15; 32:6–9]

¹⁰AND THEY GAVE THEM FOR THE POTTER'S FIELD, AS THE LORD DIRECTED ME." [Zech 11:13]

¹¹Now Jesus stood before [Pilate] the governor, and the governor asked Him, "Are you the King of the Jews?" [In affirmation] Jesus said to him, "*It is as* you say." [Mark 15:2–5; Luke 23:2, 3; John 18:29–37]

¹²But when the charges were brought against Him by the chief priests and elders, He did not answer. [Is 53:7]

¹³Then Pilate said to Him, "Do You not hear how many things they are testifying against You?"

¹⁴But Jesus did not reply to him, not even to a single accusation, so that the governor was greatly astonished.

¹⁵Now at the feast [of the Passover] the governor was in the habit of setting free any one prisoner whom the people chose. [Mark 15:6–15; Luke 23:18–25; John 18:39–19:16]

¹⁶And at that time they were holding a notorious prisoner [guilty of insurrection and murder], called Barabbas.

¹⁷So when they had assembled [for this purpose], Pilate said to them, "Whom do you want me to set free for you? Barabbas, or Jesus who is called Christ?"

¹⁸For Pilate knew that it was because of jealousy that the chief priests and elders had handed Jesus over to him.

¹⁹While he was seated on the judgment seat, his wife sent him *a message,* saying, "Have nothing to do with that righteous *and* innocent Man; for last night I suffered greatly in a dream because of Him."

²⁰But the chief priests and the elders persuaded the crowds to ask for Barabbas and to put Jesus to death.

²¹The governor said to them, "Which of the two do you wish me to set free for you?" And they said, "Barabbas."

²²Pilate said to them, "Then what shall I do with Jesus who is called Christ?" They all replied, "Let Him be crucified!"

²³And he said, "Why, what has He done that is evil?" But they continued shouting all the louder, "Let Him be crucified!" [Mark 15:14; Luke 23:4, 14, 22; John 18:39; 19:4, 6]

²⁴So when Pilate saw that he was getting nowhere, but rather that a riot was breaking out, he took water and washed his hands [to ceremonially cleanse himself of guilt] in the presence of the crowd, saying, "I am innocent of this [righteous] Man's blood; see *to that* yourselves." [Deut 21:6–9; Ps 26:6]

²⁵And all the people answered, "Let [the responsibility for] His blood be on us and on our children!" [Josh 2:19]

²⁶So he set Barabbas free for them; but after having Jesus severely whipped (scourged), he handed Him over to be crucified.

²⁷Then the governor's soldiers took Jesus into the Praetorium, and they gathered the whole Roman cohort

around Him. [Mark 15:16–20; John 19:1–3]

²⁸They stripped him and put a scarlet robe on Him [as a king's robe].

²⁹And after twisting together a crown of thorns, they put it on His head, and put a reed in His right hand [as a scepter]. Kneeling before Him, they ridiculed Him, saying, "Hail (rejoice), King of the Jews!"

³⁰They spat on Him, and took the reed and struck Him *repeatedly* on the head.

³¹After they finished ridiculing Him, they stripped Him of the *scarlet* robe and put His own clothes on Him, and led Him away to crucify Him.

³²Now as they were coming out, they found a man of Cyrene named Simon, whom they forced into service to carry the cross of Jesus. [Mark 15:21; Luke 23:26]

³³And when they came to a place called Golgotha, which means Place of a Skull, [Mark 15:22–32; Luke 23:33–43; John 19:17–24]

³⁴they offered Him wine mixed with gall (myrrh, a bitter-tasting narcotic) to drink; but after tasting it, He refused to drink it.

³⁵And when they had crucified Him, they divided His clothes among them by casting lots. [Ps 22:18]

³⁶Then sitting down there, they *began* to keep watch over Him [to guard against any rescue attempt].

³⁷And above His head they put the accusation against Him which read, "THIS IS JESUS THE KING OF THE JEWS."

³⁸At the same time two robbers were crucified with Jesus, one on the right and one on the left.

³⁹Those who passed by were hurling abuse at Him *and* jeering at Him, wagging their heads [in scorn and ridicule], [Ps 22:7, 8; 109:25]

⁴⁰and they said [tauntingly], "You who would destroy the temple and rebuild it in three days, save Yourself [from death]! If You are the Son of God, come down from the cross."

⁴¹In the same way the chief priests also, along with the scribes and elders, mocked Him, saying,

⁴²"He saved others [from death]; He cannot save Himself. He is the King of Israel; let Him now come down from the cross, and we will believe in Him *and* acknowledge Him.

⁴³"HE TRUSTS IN GOD; LET GOD RESCUE *Him* now, IF HE DELIGHTS IN HIM; for He said, 'I am the Son of God.'" [Ps 22:8]

⁴⁴The robbers who had been crucified with Him also began to insult Him in the same way.

⁴⁵Now from the sixth hour (noon) there was darkness over all the land until the ninth hour (3:00 p.m.). [Mark 15:33–41; Luke 23:44–49]

⁴⁶About the ninth hour Jesus cried out with a loud [agonized] voice, "ELI, ELI, LAMA SABACHTHANI?" that is, "MY GOD, MY GOD, WHY HAVE YOU FORSAKEN ME?" [Ps 22:1]

⁴⁷When some of the bystanders there heard it, they *began* saying, "This man is calling for Elijah."

⁴⁸Immediately one of them ran, and took a sponge, soaked it with sour wine and put it on a reed, and gave Him a drink. [Ps 69:21; Mark 15:36f; Luke 23:36; John 19:29, 30]

⁴⁹But the rest said, "Let us see whether Elijah will come to save Him [from death]."

⁵⁰And Jesus cried out again with a loud [agonized] voice, and gave up His spirit [voluntarily, sovereignly dismissing and releasing His spirit from His body in submission to His Father's plan]. [John 10:18]

⁵¹And [at once] the veil [of the Holy of Holies] of the temple was torn in two from top to bottom; the earth shook and the rocks were split apart. [Ex 26:31–35]

⁵²The tombs were opened, and many bodies of the saints (God's people)

who had fallen asleep [in death] were raised [to life];

⁵³and coming out of the tombs after His resurrection, they entered the holy city (Jerusalem) and appeared to many people.

⁵⁴Now the centurion, and those who were with him keeping guard over Jesus, when they saw the earthquake and the things that were happening, they were terribly frightened *and* filled with awe, and said, "Truly this was the Son of God!"

⁵⁵There were also many women there looking on from a distance, who had accompanied Jesus from Galilee, ministering to Him.

⁵⁶Among them was Mary Magdalene, and Mary the mother of James and Joseph, and [Salome] the mother of Zebedee's sons [James and John].

⁵⁷When it was evening, there came a rich man from Arimathea, named Joseph, who was also a disciple of Jesus. [Mark 15:42–47; Luke 23:50–56; John 19:38–42]

⁵⁸He went to Pilate and asked for the body of Jesus [so that he might bury Him], and Pilate ordered that it be given *to him.*

⁵⁹And Joseph took the body and wrapped it in a clean linen cloth (burial wrapping),

⁶⁰and laid it in his own new tomb, which he had cut in the rock; and he rolled a large stone over the entrance of the tomb and went away.

⁶¹And Mary Magdalene was there, and the other Mary, sitting opposite the tomb.

⁶²The next day, that is, *the day* after the [day of] preparation [for the Sabbath], the chief priests and the Pharisees assembled before Pilate,

⁶³and said, "Sir, we have remembered that when He was still alive that deceiver said, 'After three days I will rise [from the dead].'

⁶⁴"Therefore, give orders to have the tomb made secure *and* safeguarded until the third day, otherwise His disciples may come and steal Him *away* and tell the people, 'He has risen from the dead,' and the last deception [the reporting of His resurrection] will be worse than the first [the reporting that He is the Messiah]."

⁶⁵Pilate said to them, "You have a guard [of soldiers]; go [with them], make the tomb as secure as you know how."

⁶⁶So they went and made the tomb secure, and along with [stationing] a guard of soldiers [to be on watch] they set a seal on the stone.

28 NOW AFTER the Sabbath, near dawn of the first *day* of the week, Mary Magdalene and the other Mary went to look at the tomb. [Mark 16:1–8; Luke 24:1–10, John 20:1–8]

²And a great earthquake had occurred, for an angel of the Lord descended from heaven and came and rolled away the stone [from the opening of the tomb], and sat on it.

³The angel's appearance was like lightning, and his clothes were as white as snow.

⁴The guards shook, paralyzed with fear [at the sight] of him and became like dead men [pale and immobile].

⁵But the angel said to the women, "Do not be afraid; for I know that you are looking for Jesus who has been crucified.

⁶"He is not here, for He has risen, just as He said [He would]. Come! See the place where He was lying.

speak the Word

Thank You, Jesus, that You rose from the dead, just as You said You would!
—ADAPTED FROM MATTHEW 28:6

7"Then go quickly and tell His disciples that He has risen from the dead; and behold, He is going ahead of you into Galilee [as He promised]. There you will see Him; behold, I have told you."

8So the women left the tomb quickly with fear and great joy, and ran to tell [the good news to] the disciples.

9And *as they went,* suddenly, Jesus met them, saying, "Rejoice!" And they went to Him and took hold of His feet [in homage] and worshiped Him [as the Messiah].

10Then Jesus said to them, "Do not be afraid; go and tell My brothers to leave for Galilee, and there they will see Me [just as I promised]."

11While they were on their way, some of the [Roman] guards went into the city and reported to the chief priests everything that had happened.

12And when the chief priests had gathered with the elders and had consulted together [to develop a plan of deception], they gave a sufficient sum of money [as a bribe] to the soldiers,

13and said, "You say this, 'His disciples came at night and stole Him while we were sleeping.'

14"And if the governor (Pilate) hears about it, we will calm him down and keep you out of trouble."

15So they took the money [they were paid for lying] and did as they were instructed; and this [fabricated] story was widely spread among the Jews, and is to the present day.

16Now the eleven disciples went to Galilee, to the mountain which Jesus had designated.

17And when they saw Him, they worshiped *Him;* but some doubted [that it was really He].

18Jesus came up and said to them, "All authority (all power of absolute rule) in heaven and on earth has been given to Me.

19"Go therefore and make disciples of all the nations [help the people to learn of Me, believe in Me, and obey My words], baptizing them in the name of the Father and of the Son and of the Holy Spirit,

20teaching them to observe everything that I have commanded you; and lo, I am with you always [remaining with you perpetually—regardless of circumstance, and on every occasion], even to the end of the age."

putting the Word to work

Have you ever wondered about your purpose in life? Know that you have been called by God to teach others about Who He is and what it means to follow Him. God gave you the authority to do so, and has promised to not leave you on your own, but to be with you always (see Matthew 28:18–20). Ask God to show you where He wants you to go—to someone in your office, in your neighborhood, perhaps even in your own family—so you can help others follow Him too.

Mark

Author:
Mark

Date:
possibly AD 55–65

Everyday Life Principles:
In order to follow Jesus, we must deny ourselves and lose sight of our own interests.

We must continually and steadfastly cling to Jesus in every aspect of our lives.

The only way to experience true joy is to allow God to work through you to bless others.

Mark is the shortest of the four Gospels and tells the story of Jesus in a style that is simple and concise, yet detailed. It focuses on facts more than themes and on actions more than attitudes. Because of Mark's straightforward and unadorned approach, many believe this book gives a much more vivid account of Jesus' life and ministry than the other Gospels.

Scholars believe Mark's Gospel was written during a time when Christians were viciously persecuted and killed for their faith. This may be the reason for the sense of urgency we feel in Mark's writing and for its emphasis on the cost of following Jesus. Mark 8:34 records Jesus' words: "If anyone wishes to follow Me [as My disciple], he must deny himself [set aside selfish interests], and take up his cross [expressing a willingness to endure whatever may come] and follow Me [believing in Me, conforming to My example in living and, if need be, suffering or perhaps dying because of faith in Me]."

I do not believe the "cross" we are to carry is a burden of disaster, disease, and misery, but is a sacrificial life of allowing God to work through us to bless others. This kind of cross is the only way to truly experience the joy that Jesus gives.

As you read Mark's vivid presentation of Jesus' life and ministry, I pray that you will see Him more clearly and follow Him more faithfully.

1

THE BEGINNING of the [facts regarding the] good news of Jesus Christ, the Son of God. ²As it is written *and* forever remains in the [writings of the] prophet Isaiah:

"BEHOLD, I SEND MY MESSENGER
AHEAD OF YOU,
WHO WILL PREPARE YOUR WAY—
[Mal 3:1]
³A VOICE OF ONE SHOUTING IN THE
WILDERNESS,
'PREPARE THE WAY OF THE LORD,
MAKE HIS PATHS STRAIGHT!'"
[Is 40:3]

⁴John the Baptist appeared in the wilderness preaching a baptism of repentance for the forgiveness of sins [that is, requiring a change of one's old way of thinking, turning away from sin and seeking God and His righteousness].

⁵And all the country of Judea and all the people of Jerusalem were *continually* going out to him; and they were being baptized by him in the Jordan River, as they confessed their sins.

⁶John wore clothing made of camel's hair and had a [wide] leather band around his waist, and he ate locusts and wild honey. [Lev 11:22; 2 Kin 1:8]

⁷And he was preaching, saying, "After me comes He who is mightier [more powerful, more noble] than I, and I am not worthy to stoop down and untie the straps of His sandals [even as His slave].

⁸"As for me, I baptized you [who came to me] with water [only]; but He will baptize you [who truly repent] with the Holy Spirit."

⁹In those days Jesus came from Nazareth of Galilee and was baptized by John in the Jordan. [Matt 3:13–17; Luke 3:21, 22; John 1:32]

¹⁰Immediately coming up out of the water, he (John) saw the heavens torn open, and the Spirit like a dove descending on Him (Jesus);

¹¹and a voice came out of heaven saying: "You are My beloved Son, in You I am well-pleased *and* delighted!" [Ps 2:7; Is 42:1]

¹²Immediately the [Holy] Spirit forced Him out into the wilderness.

¹³He was in the wilderness forty days being tempted [to do evil] by Satan; and He was with the wild animals, and the angels ministered *continually* to Him.

¹⁴Now after John [the Baptist] was arrested *and* taken into custody, Jesus went to Galilee, preaching the good news of [the kingdom of] God,

¹⁵and saying, "The [appointed period of] time is fulfilled, and the kingdom of God is at hand; repent [change your inner self—your old way of thinking, regret past sins, live your life in a way that proves repentance; seek God's purpose for your life] and believe [with a deep, abiding trust] in the good news [regarding salvation]."

¹⁶As Jesus was walking by the shore of the Sea of Galilee, He saw Simon [Peter] and Simon's brother, Andrew, casting a net in the sea; for they were fishermen.

¹⁷And Jesus said to them, "Follow Me [as My disciples, accepting Me as your Master and Teacher and walking the

life point

Before Jesus' public ministry began, He was immersed in water and anointed with the Holy Spirit and with power (see Mark 1:10). This enabled Him to do the task His Father sent Him to do. Similarly, when we are filled with the Holy Spirit, we are equipped for service in God's kingdom because we are able to draw on the power of the Holy Spirit we received when He came upon us to be His witnesses. His power can be defined as the ability, efficiency, and might that enable us to be who God wants us to be as witnesses for Him.

same path of life that I walk], and I will make you fishers of men."

[18]Immediately they left their nets and followed Him [becoming His disciples, believing and trusting in Him and following His example].

[19]Going on a little farther, He saw James the son of Zebedee, and his brother John, who were also in the boat mending *and* cleaning the nets.

[20]Immediately Jesus called to them; and they left their father Zebedee in the boat with the hired workers, and went away to follow Him [becoming His disciples, believing and trusting in Him and following His example].

[21]They went into Capernaum, and immediately on the Sabbath Jesus went into the synagogue and *began* to teach. [Luke 4:31–37]

[22]They were completely amazed at His teaching; because He was teaching them as one having [God-given] authority, and not as the scribes.

[23]Just then there was a man in their synagogue with an unclean spirit; and he cried out [terribly from the depths of his throat],

putting the Word to work

Several of Jesus' disciples were fishermen by trade (see Mark 1:16–20). Have you ever been fishing? Even if you have not, you probably know that people use many different types of bait to catch a fish. As a "fisher" of men and women, God asks you to demonstrate through your life, words, and actions the blessing of following Him. Some people will respond to the bait of hearing about God, others will respond to your actions that demonstrate His love and grace, and still others to seeing the joy and peace you have in your life. Remember, every day brings opportunities to fish!

[24]saying, "What business do You have with us, Jesus of Nazareth? Have You come to destroy us? I know who You are—the Holy One of God!"

[25]Jesus rebuked him, saying, "Be quiet (muzzled, silenced), and come out of him!"

[26]The unclean spirit threw the man into convulsions, and screeching with a loud voice, came out of him.

[27]They were all so amazed that they debated *and* questioned each other, saying, "What is this? A new teaching with authority! He commands even the unclean spirits (demons), and they obey Him."

[28]Immediately the news about Him spread everywhere throughout the district surrounding Galilee.

[29]And immediately they left the synagogue and went into the house of Simon [Peter] and Andrew, accompanied by James and John. [Matt 8:14–17; Luke 4:38–41]

[30]Now Simon's mother-in-law was lying sick with a fever; and immediately they told Him about her.

[31]Jesus went to her, and taking her by the hand, raised her up; and the fever left her, and she *began* to serve them [as her guests].

[32]Now when evening came, after the sun had set [and the Sabbath Day had ended, in a steady stream] they were bringing to Him all who were sick and those who were under the power of demons,

[33]until the whole city had gathered together at the door.

[34]And Jesus healed many who were suffering with various diseases; and He drove out many demons, but would not allow the demons to speak, because they knew Him [recognizing Him as the Son of God].

[35]Early in the morning, while it was still dark, Jesus got up, left [the house], and went out to a secluded place, and was praying there.

life point

Surely prayer was important to Jesus; otherwise, He might have stayed in bed! Most of us do not get up early for anything unless it is important.

But, Jesus did not make a big display of prayer. In Mark 1:35, He went to a private place, where the Bible simply says, He "was praying." Prayer is vital and powerful, but needs to be kept simple in our lives.

³⁶Simon [Peter] and his companions searched [everywhere, looking anxiously] for Him,
³⁷and they found Him and said, "Everybody is looking for You!"
³⁸He replied, "Let us go on to the neighboring towns, so I may preach there also; that is why I came [from the Father]."
³⁹So He went throughout Galilee, preaching [the gospel] in their synagogues and casting out demons.
⁴⁰And a leper came to Him, begging Him and falling on his knees before Him, saying, "If You are willing, You are able to make me clean." [Matt 8:2–4; Luke 5:12–14]
⁴¹Moved with compassion [for his suffering], Jesus reached out with His hand and touched him, and said to him, "I am willing; be cleansed."
⁴²The leprosy left him immediately and he was cleansed [completely healed and restored to health].
⁴³And Jesus [deeply moved] admonished him sternly and sent him away immediately,
⁴⁴saying to him, "See that you tell no one anything [about this]; but go, show yourself to the priest and offer for your purification what Moses commanded, as proof to them [that you are really healed]." [Lev 13:45; 14:2–32]
⁴⁵But he went out and began to proclaim it freely and to spread the news [of his healing], to such an extent that

Jesus could no longer openly enter a city [where He was known], but stayed out in the unpopulated places; yet people were still coming to Him from everywhere.

2 JESUS RETURNED to Capernaum, and a few days later the news went out that He was at home. [Matt 4:13]
²So many people gathered together that there was no longer room [for them], not even near the door; and Jesus was discussing with them the word [of God].
³Then they came, bringing to Him a paralyzed man, who was being carried by four men. [Matt 9:2–8; Luke 5:18–26]
⁴When they were unable to get to Him because of the crowd, they removed the roof above Jesus; and when they had dug out an opening, they let down the mat on which the paralyzed man was lying.
⁵When Jesus saw their [active] faith [springing from confidence in Him], He said to the paralyzed man, "Son, your sins are forgiven."
⁶But some of the scribes were sitting there debating in their hearts [the implication of what He had said],
⁷"Why does this man talk that way? He is blaspheming; who can forgive sins [remove guilt, nullify sin's penalty, and assign righteousness] except God alone?"

putting the Word to work

Some people have a hard time coming to Jesus, just as the man mentioned in Mark 2:1–4. They may be "paralyzed" by their doubts, their questions, or even their fears. Is there anyone in your life like this? Make a commitment to do whatever it takes to help this person see Jesus. Ask the Holy Spirit to break through their walls of unbelief.

8Immediately Jesus, being fully aware [of their hostility] *and* knowing in His spirit that they were thinking this, said to them, "Why are you debating *and* arguing about these things in your hearts?

9"Which is easier, to say to the paralyzed man, 'Your sins are forgiven'; or to say, 'Get up, and pick up your mat and walk'?

10"But so that you may know that the Son of Man has the authority *and* power on earth to forgive sins"—He said to the paralyzed man,

11"I say to you, get up, pick up your mat and go home."

12And he got up and immediately picked up the mat and went out before them all, so that they all were astonished and they glorified *and* praised

life point

Do you ever hold a negative dialogue with yourself, as the scribes were doing in Mark 2:6 when they were "debating in their hearts"? The fact is that you probably talk to yourself more than you talk to anybody else. The question is, what are you saying to yourself?

These scribes were questioning Jesus' authority to be God's Son by asking, "Who does this Man think He is?" They did not speak those words aloud, but deep within their hearts.

Without a word being spoken, Jesus picked up right away that they were debating and reasoning within themselves. As believers we need to avoid this kind of negative self-talk. It is a serious matter that we need to deal with in our lives, just as Jesus dealt with it in the scribes. We need to learn to have simple faith, to be discerning, and to be led by the Spirit instead of by our own divisive thoughts and reasoning.

God, saying, "We have never seen anything like this!"

13Jesus went out again along the [Galilean] seashore; and all the people were coming to Him, and He was teaching them.

14As He was passing by, He saw Levi (Matthew) the son of Alphaeus sitting in the tax collector's booth, and He said to him, "Follow Me [as My disciple, accepting Me as your Master and Teacher and walking the same path of life that I walk]." And he got up and followed Him [becoming His disciple, believing and trusting in Him and following His example]. [Matt 9:9–17; Luke 5:27–39]

15And it happened that Jesus was reclining *at the table* in Levi's house, and many tax collectors and sinners [including non-observant Jews] were eating with Him and His disciples; for there were many of them and they were following Him.

16When the scribes [belonging to the sect] of the Pharisees saw that Jesus was eating with the sinners [including non-observant Jews] and tax collectors, they asked His disciples, "Why does He eat and drink with tax collectors and sinners?"

17When Jesus heard this, He said to them, "Those who are healthy have no need of a physician, but [only] those who are sick; I did not come to call the righteous, but sinners [who recognize their sin and humbly seek forgiveness]."

18Now John's disciples and the Pharisees were fasting [as a ritual]; and they came and asked Jesus, "Why are John's disciples and the disciples of the Pharisees fasting, but Your disciples are not doing so?"

19Jesus answered, "The attendants of the bridegroom cannot fast while the bridegroom is [still] with them, can they? As long as they have the bridegroom with them, they cannot fast.

²⁰"But the days will come when the bridegroom is [forcefully] taken away from them, and they will fast at that time.

²¹"No one sews a patch of unshrunk (new) cloth on an old garment; otherwise the patch pulls away from it, the new from the old, and the tear becomes worse.

²²"No one puts new wine into old wineskins; otherwise the [fermenting] wine will [expand and] burst the skins, and the wine is lost as well as the wineskins. But new wine must be put into new wineskins."

²³One Sabbath He was walking along [with His disciples] through the grainfields, and as they went along, His disciples began picking the heads of grain. [Deut 23:25; Matt 12:1–8; Luke 6:1–5]

²⁴The Pharisees said to Him, "Look, why are they doing what is unlawful on the Sabbath?"

²⁵Jesus said to them, "Have you never read [in the Scriptures] what David did when he was in need and was hungry, he and his companions; [1 Sam 21:1–6]

²⁶how he went into the house of God in the time of Abiathar the high priest, and ate the sacred bread, which is not lawful for anyone but the priests to eat, and how he also gave it to the men who were with him?" [1 Sam 21:1–6]

²⁷Jesus said to them, "The Sabbath was made for man, not man for the Sabbath. [Ex 23:12; Deut 5:14]

²⁸"So the Son of Man is Lord even of the Sabbath [and He has authority over it]."

3 AGAIN JESUS went into a synagogue; and a man was there whose hand was withered. [Matt 12:9–14; Luke 6:6–11]

²The Pharisees were watching Jesus *closely to see* if He would heal him on the Sabbath, so that they might accuse Him [in the Jewish high court].

³He said to the man whose hand was withered, "Get up and come forward!"

⁴He asked them, "Is it lawful on the Sabbath to do good or to do evil, to save a life or to kill?" But they kept silent.

⁵After looking around at them with anger, grieved at the hardness *and* arrogance of their hearts, He told the man, "Hold out your hand." And he held it out, and his hand was [completely] restored.

⁶Then the Pharisees went out and immediately *began* conspiring with the Herodians [to plot] against Him, as to how they might [fabricate some legal grounds to] put Him to death.

⁷Jesus withdrew to the sea with His disciples; and a large crowd from Galilee followed Him; and *also people* from Judea,

⁸and from Jerusalem, and from Idumea, and [from the region] beyond the Jordan, and around Tyre and Sidon; a vast number of people came to Him because they were hearing about all [the things] that He was doing.

⁹And He told His disciples to have a small boat stand ready for Him because of the many people, so that they would not crowd Him;

¹⁰for He had healed many, and as a result all who had diseases pressed around Him to touch Him.

¹¹Whenever the unclean spirits saw Him, they fell down before Him and screamed out, "You are the Son of God!"

¹²Jesus sternly warned them [again and again] not to tell who He was.

¹³He went up on the hillside and called those whom He Himself wanted *and* chose; and they came to Him.

¹⁴And He appointed twelve [disciples], so that they would be with Him [for instruction] and so that He could send them out to preach [the gospel as apostles—that is, as His special messengers, personally chosen representatives],

¹⁵and to have authority *and* power to cast out demons.

¹⁶He appointed the twelve: Simon (to whom He gave the name Peter), [Matt 10:2–4; Luke 6:13–16]

¹⁷and James, the son of Zebedee, and John the brother of James (to them He gave the name Boanerges, that is, "Sons of Thunder");

¹⁸and [He also appointed] Andrew, and Philip, and Bartholomew (Nathanael), and Matthew (Levi the tax collector), and Thomas, and James the son of Alphaeus, and Thaddaeus (Judas the son of James), and Simon the Zealot;

¹⁹and Judas Iscariot, who betrayed Him.

²⁰Then He came to a house [in Capernaum], and a crowd formed again, so [many people] that Jesus and His disciples could not even eat a meal [together].

²¹When His own family heard this they went to take custody of Him; for they were saying, "He is out of His mind."

²²The scribes who came down from Jerusalem were saying, "He is possessed by Beelzebul (Satan)," and "He is driving out the demons by the [power of the] ruler of the demons." [Matt 12:22–37; Luke 11:14–28]

²³So He called them to Himself and spoke to them in parables, "How can Satan drive out Satan?

²⁴"If a kingdom is divided [split into factions and rebelling] against itself, that kingdom cannot stand.

²⁵"And if a house is divided against itself, that house cannot stand.

²⁶"And if Satan has risen up against himself and is divided, he cannot stand, but is coming to an end.

²⁷"But no one can go into a strong man's house and steal his property unless he first overpowers *and* ties up the strong man, and then he will ransack *and* rob his house. [Is 49:24, 25; Matt 12:29]

²⁸"I assure you *and* most solemnly say to you, all sins will be forgiven the sons of men, and all the abusive *and* blasphemous things they say;

²⁹but whoever blasphemes against the Holy Spirit *and* His power [by attributing the miracles done by Me to Satan] never has forgiveness, but is guilty of an everlasting sin [a sin which is unforgivable in this present age as well as in the age to come]"— [Matt 12:32; Luke 12:10]

³⁰[Jesus said this] because the scribes and Pharisees were [attributing His miracles to Satan by] saying, "He has an unclean spirit."

³¹Then His mother and His brothers arrived, and standing outside they sent *word* to Him and called for Him. [Matt 12:46–50; Luke 8:19–21]

³²A crowd was sitting around Him, and they said to Him, "Look! Your mother and Your brothers are outside asking for You."

³³And He replied, "Who are My mother and My brothers?"

³⁴Looking at those who were sitting in a circle around Him, He said, "Here are My mother and My brothers!

³⁵For whoever does the will of God [by believing in Me, and following Me], he is My brother and sister and mother."

4 AGAIN JESUS began to teach beside the sea [of Galilee]. And a very large crowd gathered around Him, so He got into a boat [anchoring it a short distance out] on

life point

Jesus teaches us in Mark 3:27 that we must bind the strong man if we want to plunder his house. The strong man represents the devil. I urge you not to ever become passive as a Christian and forget that Jesus instructs us to take authority over and bind the enemy.

the sea and sat down; and the whole crowd was by the sea on the shore. [Matt 13:1–15; Luke 8:4–15]

²And He taught them many things in parables, and in His teaching He said to them,

³"Listen! A sower went out to sow *seed;*

⁴and as he was sowing, some *seed* fell by the road, and the birds came and ate it up.

⁵"Other *seed* fell on rocks where there was not much soil; and immediately a plant sprang up because the soil had no depth.

⁶"And when the sun came up, the plant was scorched; and because it had no root, it dried up *and* withered away.

⁷"Other *seed* fell among thorns, and the thorns came up and choked it, and it yielded no grain.

⁸"And other *seed* fell into good soil, and as the plants grew and increased, they yielded a crop and produced thirty, sixty, and a hundred times [as much as had been sown]."

⁹And He said, "He who has ears to hear, let him hear *and* heed My words."

¹⁰As soon as He was alone, those who were around Him, together with the twelve [disciples], *began* asking Him about [the interpretation of] the parables.

¹¹He said to them, "The mystery of the kingdom of God has been given to you [who have teachable hearts], but those who are outside [the unbelievers, the spiritually blind] get everything in parables,

¹²so that THEY WILL CONTINUALLY LOOK BUT NOT SEE, AND THEY WILL CONTINUALLY HEAR BUT NOT UNDERSTAND, OTHERWISE THEY MIGHT TURN [from their rejection of the truth] AND BE FORGIVEN." [Is 6:9, 10; Matt 13:11–15]

¹³Then He said to them, "Do you not understand this parable? How will you understand *and* grasp the meaning of all the parables? [Matt 13:18–23; Luke 8:11–15]

¹⁴"The sower sows the word [of God, the good news regarding the way of salvation].

¹⁵"These [in the first group] are the ones along the road where the word is sown; but when they hear, Satan immediately comes and takes away the word which has been sown in them.

¹⁶"In a similar way these [in the second group] are the ones on whom seed was sown on rocky ground, who, when they hear the word, immediately receive it with joy [but accept it only superficially];

¹⁷and they have no real root in themselves, so they endure only for a little while; then, when trouble or persecution comes because of the word, immediately they [are offended and displeased at being associated with Me and] stumble *and* fall away.

¹⁸"And others are the ones on whom seed was sown among the thorns; these are the ones who have heard the word,

¹⁹but the worries *and* cares of the world [the distractions of this age with its worldly pleasures], and the deceitfulness [and the false security or glamour] of wealth [or fame], and the passionate desires for all the other things creep in and choke out the word, and it becomes unfruitful.

²⁰"And those [in the last group] are the ones on whom seed was sown on the good soil; and they hear the word [of God, the good news regarding the way of salvation] and accept it and bear fruit—thirty, sixty, and a hundred times as much [as was sown]."

²¹He said to them, "A lamp is not brought in to be put under a basket or under a bed, is it? Is it not [brought in] to be put on the lampstand? [Matt 5:15; Luke 8:16; 11:33]

²²"For nothing is hidden, except to be revealed; nor has anything been kept secret, but that it would come to light [that is, things are hidden only

temporarily, until the appropriate time comes for them to be known]. [Matt 10:26–33; Luke 12:2–9]

23"If anyone has ears to hear, let him hear *and* heed My words."

24Then He said to them, "Pay attention to what you hear. By your own standard of measurement [that is, to the extent that you study spiritual truth and apply godly wisdom] it will be measured to you [and you will be given even greater ability to respond]—and more will be given to you besides.

25"For whoever has [a teachable heart], to him *more* [understanding] will be given; and whoever does not have [a yearning for truth], even what he has will be taken away from him." [Matt 13:12; 25:29; Luke 8:18]

26Then He said, "The kingdom of God is like a man who throws seed on the ground;

27and he goes to bed at night and gets up every day, and [in the meantime]

the seed sprouts and grows; how [it does this], he does not know.

28"The earth produces crops by itself; first the blade, then the head [of grain], then the mature grain in the head.

29"But when the crop ripens, he immediately puts in the sickle [to reap], because [the time for] the harvest has come."

life point

Mark 4:24 is a great scripture! It tells us that the more time we spend thinking about the Word we read and hear, the more power and ability we will have to obey it—the more revelation knowledge we will have about what we have read or heard. Basically this tells us that we will get out of God's Word what we put into it. I want you to receive maximum benefit from God's awesome Word, so be diligent to read it, study it, and apply it to your life.

when your breakthrough is delayed

I discovered a long time ago that when I became impatient, frustrated, and fretful it was because I tried to make something happen that only God could make happen. I was caught up in works of the flesh, which I define as "human energy attempting to do God's job."

Sometimes when we pray and believe for a breakthrough, it seems like nothing happens. If we really want to know how to act during those times, we can receive much help from the story of the patient farmer Jesus spoke of in Mark 4:26–29.

The farmer sows his seed in the ground and then goes on his way, sleeping and rising. Eventually, the ground brings forth its yield on its own. The farmer does not know how the harvest will come or exactly when it will come, but his job is to get up in the morning, do his work, and go to bed at night. He keeps up his patient vigil over the seed he has sown until he receives the harvest.

Jesus was telling us that this is the way we should respond to God. Our problem is that we are often impatient. We continually ask God, "How are You going to do this? When are You going to do that?"

A farmer never knows exactly when his crop will come in. He just keeps sleeping and rising, does what he can to enrich his soil and cultivate his crops, but leaves the rest in the hands of the Creator. Let me encourage you to do likewise.

³⁰And He said, "How shall we *picture the kingdom of God, or what parable shall we use to illustrate *and* explain it? [Matt 13:31, 32; Luke 13:18, 19] ³¹"It is like a mustard seed, which, when it is sown on the ground, even though it is smaller than all the [other] seeds that are [sown] on the soil, ³²yet when it is sown, it grows up and becomes larger than all the garden

what to do on a sinking boat

It is always exciting when Jesus says to us, "Let's do a new thing." To me the phrase, "Let us go over to the other side" (Mark 4:35), is equivalent to saying, "Promotion is coming," or "Blessings are on their way," or "Come up higher," or any variety of phrases God uses to communicate to us that it is time for a change.

I am sure the disciples were excited to see what would happen on "the other side." What they did not expect or foresee was a raging storm on the way!

The disciples probably were not nearly as excited in the middle of their voyage as they may have been in the beginning.

Although God often calls us to launch out to a new destination, He usually does not let us know what is going to happen on the way. We leave the security of where we are and start out for the blessings of the other side, but it is often in the middle that we encounter the storms. The middle is often a place of testing.

The storm the disciples experienced was no little "April shower" or harmless summer squall, but a storm of hurricane proportions. The waves were not gently rolling and tossing; they were beating the boat with such fury that it quickly filled with water. That would be enough to frighten anyone.

The storm was in full force, and Jesus was asleep! Does that sound familiar? Have you ever had times when you felt you were sinking fast, and Jesus was asleep? You prayed and prayed and heard nothing from God. You spent time with Him and tried to sense His presence, and yet you felt nothing. You searched for an answer, but no matter how hard you struggled against the wind and waves, the storm raged on and you did not know what to do about it.

We sometimes refer to those seasons as "the midnight hour" or "the dark night of the soul."

At times like these, when it looks like the boat is sinking with us in it, we must use our faith. Jesus simply wanted His disciples to believe Him. He said, "Let us go over to the other side." He expected them to believe that if He said it, it would happen. But, like us, they were afraid. Jesus calmed the storm, but He rebuked the disciples for their lack of faith.

It is vital to our future that we grow in faith, which shows confidence and trust in God. We must learn to conquer our fear and press on to the other side. We must also learn to have peace and joy in the midst of the storm, not only when it has passed.

4:30 Lit *compare*.

herbs; and it puts out large branches, so that THE BIRDS OF THE SKY are able to MAKE NESTS *and* LIVE UNDER ITS SHADE." [Ps 104:12; Ezek 17:23; 31:6]

³³With many such parables, Jesus spoke the word to them, as they were able to hear *and* understand it;

³⁴and He did not say *anything* to them without [using] a parable; He did, however, explain everything privately to His own disciples.

³⁵On that [same] day, when evening had come, He said to them, "Let us go over to the other side [of the Sea of Galilee]."

³⁶So leaving the crowd, they took Him with them, just as He was, in the boat. And other boats were with Him. [Matt 8:23–27; Luke 8:22–25]

³⁷And a fierce windstorm began to blow, and waves were breaking over the boat, so that it was already being swamped.

³⁸But Jesus was in the stern, asleep [with His head] on the [sailor's leather] cushion. And they woke Him and said to Him, "Teacher, do You not care that we are about to die?"

³⁹And He got up and [sternly] rebuked the wind and said to the sea, "Hush, be still (muzzled)!" And the

life point

When Jesus and the disciples were crossing the lake and a storm arose, the disciples panicked, but Jesus was able to stand up in the boat and rebuke the storm (see Mark 4:39).

You cannot rebuke the storms in your life if you have a storm on the inside of yourself. The disciples could not rebuke the storm because they lost their peace and were as "stormy" as the storm. But when Jesus spoke out of His reservoir of peace for the wind and waves to be still, immediately there was calm.

wind died down [as if it had grown weary] and there was [at once] a great calm [a perfect peacefulness].

⁴⁰Jesus said to them, "Why are you afraid? Do you still have no faith *and* confidence [in Me]?"

⁴¹They were filled with great fear, and said to each other, "Who then is this, that even the wind and the sea obey Him?"

5 THEY CAME to the other side of the sea, to the region of the Gerasenes. [Matt 8:28–34; Luke 8:26–37]

²When Jesus got out of the boat, immediately a man from the tombs with an unclean spirit met Him,

³and the man lived in the tombs, and no one could bind him anymore, not even with chains.

⁴For he had often been bound with shackles [for the feet] and with chains, and he tore apart the chains and broke the shackles into pieces, and no one was strong enough to subdue *and* tame him.

⁵Night and day he was constantly screaming *and* shrieking among the tombs and on the mountains, and cutting himself with [sharp] stones.

⁶Seeing Jesus from a distance, he ran up and bowed down before Him [in homage];

⁷and screaming with a loud voice, he said, "What business do we have in common with each other, Jesus, Son of the Most High God? I implore you by God [swear to me], do not torment me!" [Matt 8:29; Luke 4:34]

⁸For Jesus had been saying to him, "Come out of the man, you unclean spirit!"

⁹He was asking him, "What is your name?" And he replied, "My name is Legion; for we are many."

¹⁰And he *began* begging Him repeatedly not to send them out of the region.

11Now there was a large herd of pigs grazing there on the mountain.

12And the demons begged Him, saying, "Send us to the pigs so that we may go into them!"

13Jesus gave them permission. And the unclean spirits came out [of the man] and entered the pigs. The herd, numbering about two thousand, rushed down the steep bank into the sea; and they were drowned [one after the other] in the sea.

14The herdsmen [tending the pigs] ran away and reported it in the city and in the country. And the people came to see what had happened.

15They came to Jesus and saw the man who had been demon-possessed sitting down, clothed and in his right mind, the man who had [previously] had the "legion" [of demons]; and they were frightened.

16Those who had seen it described [in detail] to the people what had happened to the demon-possessed man, and [told them all] about the pigs.

17So the people began to beg with Jesus to leave their region.

18As He was stepping into the boat, the [Gentile] man who had been demon-possessed was begging with Him [asking] that he might go with Him [as a disciple].

19Jesus did not let him [come], but [instead] He said to him, "Go home to your family and tell them all the great things that the Lord has done for you, and how He has had mercy on you."

20So he [obeyed and] went away and began to publicly proclaim in Decapolis [the region of the ten Hellenistic cities] all the great things that Jesus had done for him; and all the people were astonished.

21When Jesus had again crossed over in the boat to the other side [of the sea], a large crowd gathered around Him; and so He stayed by the seashore.

22One of the synagogue officials named Jairus came up; and seeing Him, fell at His feet [Matt 9:18–26; Luke 8:41–56]

23and begged anxiously with Him, saying, "My little daughter is at the point of death; [please] come and lay Your hands on her, so that she will be healed and live."

24And Jesus went with him; and a large crowd followed Him and pressed in around Him [from all sides].

25A woman [in the crowd] had [suffered from] a hemorrhage for twelve years,

26and had endured much [suffering] at the hands of many physicians. She had spent all that she had and was not helped at all, but instead had become worse.

27She had heard [reports] about Jesus, and she came up behind Him in the crowd and touched His outer robe.

28For she thought, "If I just touch His clothing, I will get well."

29Immediately her flow of blood was dried up; and she felt in her body [and

life point

The woman with the issue of blood, whose story is told in Mark 5:25–29, had the same problem for twelve years. She had suffered greatly, and no one was able to help her.

Surely this woman was attacked with thoughts of hopelessness. When she thought about going to Jesus, surely she must have heard, "What's the use?" But she pressed on past the crowd, which was so thick on all sides that it was suffocating. As she touched the hem of Jesus' garment, His healing virtue flowed to her and she was made well.

Whatever you are facing today—no matter how long you have struggled with it—let me encourage you to press on. Whatever it takes, reach out and touch Jesus!

knew without any doubt] that she was healed of her suffering.

³⁰Immediately Jesus, recognizing in Himself that power had gone out from Him, turned around in the crowd and asked, "Who touched My clothes?"

³¹His disciples said to Him, "You see the crowd pressing in around You [from all sides], and You ask, 'Who touched Me?'"

³²Still He kept looking around to see the woman who had done it.

³³And the woman, though she was afraid and trembling, aware of what had happened to her, came and fell down before Him and told Him the whole truth.

³⁴Then He said to her, "Daughter, your faith [your personal trust and confidence in Me] has restored you to health; go in peace and be [permanently] healed from your suffering."

³⁵While He was still speaking, some people came from the synagogue official's house, saying [to Jairus], "Your daughter has died; why bother the Teacher any longer?"

³⁶Overhearing what was being said, Jesus said to the synagogue official, "Do not be afraid; only keep on believing [in Me and my power]."

³⁷And He allowed no one to go with Him [as witnesses], except Peter and James and John the brother of James.

³⁸They came to the house of the synagogue official; and He looked [with understanding] at the uproar *and* commotion, and people loudly weeping and wailing [in mourning].

³⁹When He had gone in, He said to them, "Why make a commotion and weep? The child has not died, but is sleeping."

⁴⁰They *began* laughing [scornfully] at Him [because they knew the child was dead]. But He made them all go outside, and took along the child's father and mother and His own [three] companions, and entered *the room* where the child was.

⁴¹Taking the child's hand, He said [tenderly] to her, "Talitha kum!"—which translated [from Aramaic] means, "Little girl, I say to you, get up!"

⁴²The little girl immediately got up and *began* to walk, for she was twelve years old. And immediately they [who witnessed the child's resurrection] were overcome with great wonder *and* utter amazement.

⁴³He gave strict orders that no one should know about this, and He told them to give her *something* to eat.

6 JESUS LEFT there and came to His hometown [Nazareth]; and His disciples followed Him. [Matt 13:54–58; Luke 4:16, 23]

²When the Sabbath came, He began to teach in the synagogue; and many who listened to Him were astonished, saying, "Where did this man get these things [this knowledge and spiritual insight]? What is this wisdom [this confident understanding of the Scripture] that has been given to Him, and such miracles as these performed by His hands?

³"Is this not the carpenter, the son of Mary, and the brother of James and Joses and Judas and Simon? Are His sisters not here with us?" And they were [deeply] offended by Him [and their disapproval blinded them to the fact that He was anointed by God as the Messiah].

speak the Word

God, when I am tempted to be afraid, may I remember Jesus' words to the ruler of the synagogue: "Do not be afraid; only keep on believing" in You and in Your power.
–ADAPTED FROM MARK 5:36

⁴Jesus said to them, "A prophet is not without honor (respect) except in his hometown and among his relatives and in his own household."

⁵And He could not do a miracle there at all [because of their unbelief] except that He laid His hands on a few sick people and healed them.

⁶He wondered at their unbelief.

And He was going around in the villages teaching.

⁷And He called the twelve [disciples] and began to send them out [as His special messengers] two by two, and gave them authority *and* power over the unclean spirits.

⁸He told them to take nothing for the journey except a mere walking stick—no bread, no [traveler's] bag, no money in their belts—

⁹but to wear sandals; and [He told them] not to wear two tunics.

¹⁰And He told them, "Wherever you go into a house, stay there until you leave that town.

¹¹"Any place that does not welcome you or listen to you, when you leave there, shake the dust off the soles of your feet as a testimony against them [breaking all ties with them because they rejected My message]." [Matt 10:14; Acts 13:51]

¹²So they went out and preached that men should repent [that is, think differently, recognize sin, turn away from it, and live changed lives].

¹³And they were casting out many demons and were anointing with oil many who were sick, and healing them.

¹⁴King Herod [Antipas] heard about this, for Jesus' name *and* reputation had become well known. People were saying, "John the Baptist has been raised

shake off rejection

Mark 6:11 speaks of rejection. When I first started preaching, I was extremely insecure and often felt rejected. If a few people got up and walked out of a service, the devil told me they were leaving because they did not like to see a woman preaching. That did happen a few times in churches whose pastors warned me ahead of time that they had never had a woman in their pulpit and were not sure how their congregations would react. When it did happen, I was always embarrassed and I felt bad.

Then God gave me this scripture from Luke 10:16: "The one who listens to you listens to Me; and the one who rejects you rejects Me; and the one who rejects Me rejects Him [My heavenly Father] who sent Me."

The Lord simply told me, "I am the One who called you. Do not worry about what people think. If you do, you are going to worry all your life because the devil will never stop finding people who will think something unkind about you."

In Mark 6:7–11 when Jesus sent His disciples out into the towns to preach, He told them what to do if people rejected them. He did not tell them to stand around and cry and be wounded, hurt, bleeding, and embarrassed. He told them to "shake it off!"

You and I need to take Jesus' advice and learn to shake off our troubles, problems, disappointments, and rejections. If there is a call on your life, and one person or group of people rejects you, there will be others who will accept you.

Just shake off the rejection and move on.

from the dead, and that is why these miraculous powers are at work in Him."

¹⁵But others were saying, "He is Elijah!" And others were saying, "It is a prophet, like one of the prophets [of old]."

¹⁶But when Herod heard [of it], he kept saying, "John, whom I beheaded, has risen [from the dead]!"

¹⁷For Herod himself had sent [guards] and had John arrested and shackled in prison because of Herodias, the wife of his [half-] brother Philip, because he (Herod) had married her. [Matt 14:3; Luke 3:19]

¹⁸For John had been saying to Herod, "It is not lawful [under Mosaic Law] for you to have your brother's wife." [Lev 18:16; 20:21]

¹⁹Herodias had a grudge against John and wanted to kill him, but she could not,

²⁰because Herod feared John, knowing that he was a righteous and holy man, and he *continually* kept him safe. When he heard John [speak], he was very perplexed; but he enjoyed listening to him.

²¹But an opportune time [finally] came [for Herodias]. Herod on his birthday gave a banquet for his officials (nobles, courtiers) and military commanders and the leading men of Galilee.

²²Now [Salome] the daughter of Herodias came in and danced [for the men]. She pleased *and* beguiled Herod and his dinner guests; and the king said to the girl, "Ask me for whatever you want and I will give it to you."

²³And he swore to her, "Whatever you ask me, I will give it to you; up to half of my kingdom." [Esth 5:3, 6]

²⁴She went out and said to her mother, "What shall I ask for?" And Herodias replied, "The head of John the Baptist!"

²⁵And she rushed back to the king and asked, saying, "I want you to give me right now the head of John the Baptist on a platter!"

²⁶The king was deeply grieved, but because of his oaths and his dinner guests [who might have regarded him as weak], he was unwilling to [break his word and] refuse her.

²⁷So the king immediately sent for an executioner and commanded him to bring back John's head. And he went and had John beheaded in the prison,

²⁸and brought back his head on a platter, and gave it to the girl; and the girl gave it to her mother.

²⁹When his disciples heard *about this,* they came and took away John's body and laid it in a tomb.

³⁰The apostles [who had been sent out on a mission] gathered together with Jesus and told Him everything that they had done and taught.

³¹He said to them, "Come away by yourselves to a secluded place and rest a little while"—for there were many [people who were continually] coming and going, and they could not even find time to eat.

³²And they went away by themselves in the boat to a secluded place. [Matt 14:13–21; Luke 9:10–17; John 6:1–13]

³³Many [people] saw them leaving, and recognized *them* and ran there together on foot from all the [surrounding] cities, and got there ahead of them.

³⁴When Jesus went ashore, He saw a large crowd [waiting], and He was moved with compassion for them because they were like sheep without a shepherd [lacking guidance]; and He began to teach them many things.

³⁵When the day was nearly gone, His disciples came to Him and said, "This is an isolated place, and it is already late;

³⁶send the crowds away so that they may go into the surrounding countryside and villages and buy themselves something to eat."

³⁷But He replied, "You give them something to eat!" And they asked

Him, "Shall we go and buy 200 denarii worth of bread and give it to them to eat?" [2 Kin 4:42–44]

[38]He said to them, "How many loaves do you have? Go look!" And when they found out, they said, "Five [loaves], and two fish."

[39]Then Jesus commanded them all to sit down by groups on the green grass.

[40]They sat down in groups of hundreds and of fifties [so that the crowd resembled an orderly arrangement of colorful garden plots].

[41]Taking the five loaves and two fish, He looked up to heaven and said a blessing [of praise and thanksgiving to the Father]. Then He broke the loaves and [repeatedly] gave them to the disciples to set before the people; and He divided up the two fish among them all.

[42]They all ate and were satisfied.

[43]And the disciples picked up twelve full baskets of the broken pieces [of the loaves], and of the fish.

[44]Those who ate the loaves were five thousand men [not counting the women and children].

[45]Jesus immediately insisted that His disciples get into the boat and go ahead [of Him] to the other side to Bethsaida, while He was dismissing the crowd. [Matt 14:22–32; John 6:15–21]

[46]And after He said goodbye to them, He went to the mountain to pray.

[47]Now when evening had come, the boat was in the middle of the sea, and Jesus was alone on the land.

[48]Seeing the disciples straining at the oars, because the wind was against them, at about the fourth watch of the night (3:00–6:00 a.m.) He came to them, walking on the sea. And [acted as if] He intended to pass by them. [Matt 14:25; John 6:19]

[49]But when they saw Him walking on the sea, they thought it was a ghost, and cried out [in horror];

[50]for they all saw Him and were shaken *and* terrified. But He immediately spoke with them and said, "Take courage! It is I (I AM)! Stop being afraid." [Ex 3:14]

[51]Then He got into the boat with them, and the wind ceased [as if exhausted by its own activity]; and they were completely overwhelmed,

[52]because they had not understood [the miracle of] the loaves [how it revealed the power and deity of Jesus]; but [in fact] their heart was hardened [being oblivious and indifferent to His amazing works].

[53]When they had crossed over [the sea], they reached the land of Gennesaret and anchored at the shore.

[54]They got out of the boat and immediately *people* recognized Him,

[55]and ran throughout that surrounding countryside and began to carry around on their mats those who were sick, to any place where they heard He was.

[56]And wherever He came into villages, or cities, or the countryside, they were laying the sick in the market places and pleading with Him [to allow them] just to touch the fringe (tassel with a blue cord) of His robe; and all who touched it were healed.

putting the Word to work

Do you ever feel you do not have much to offer in ministry? As you willingly offer Jesus what you do have, He will bless and multiply it to meet the needs of others, as He did in the story in Mark 6:30–44. What may seem to you like a small contribution of time, treasure, or talent, can become an enormous blessing when you put it in God's hands.

7 NOW THE Pharisees and some of the scribes came from Jerusalem and gathered around Him,

[2]and they had seen that some of His disciples ate their bread with

[ceremonially] impure hands, that is, unwashed [and defiled according to Jewish religious ritual].

³(For the Pharisees and all of the Jews do not eat unless they carefully wash their hands, holding firmly to the traditions of the elders;

⁴and *when they come* from the market place, they do not eat unless they cleanse themselves [completely according to ritual]; and there are many other things [oral, man-made laws and traditions handed down to them] which they follow diligently, such as the washing of cups and pitchers and copper utensils.)

⁵So the Pharisees and scribes asked Jesus, "Why do Your disciples not live

the lonely leader

In Mark 6:45–47, we see that Jesus sent the disciples and the crowds away and ended up by Himself. Apparently Jesus chose to have a few moments of solitude. All leaders need solitude at times, but there will also be times when we face loneliness. That is part of leadership. I do not know what you think about people who are "at the top" in leadership, but let me share a little secret with you: Sometimes it can get pretty lonely up there.

The relationship between a Christian leader and those who work with him or her is similar to an employer/employee relationship. There may be some exceptions, but usually it is not a workable situation for the boss or leader to become extremely close to those under his or her authority. Sometimes employees do not realize this fact and think their employers separate themselves from them because they think they are better than their employees.

The fact is that usually, if spiritual leaders try to be chummy with the people who work for them, they frequently develop a spirit of familiarity that causes them to take liberties they should not take with a boss or employer and to assume things they should not assume about the relationship. Through years of experience I have learned that I simply cannot become close buddies with most of my employees because it inevitably causes problems. As I said earlier, there are exceptions, but they are rare.

When you are in a position of leadership, people tend to look up to you. They may even develop expectations of you that are not realistic. They know you are only human, as they are, but they really do not want to see your human flaws and weaknesses. For example, they do not want to ever see you lose your temper or say anything negative about anything or anybody. The first time something like that happens, the devil whispers in their ear, "How can you receive ministry from someone who acts like that?"

Whatever position of leadership you may fill, realize that you must depend upon God to bring what I call "divine connections" into your life. By that I mean people who are right for you, people with whom you can develop close relationships, people who understand your call and know how they should relate to you and your ministry.

One of the things to understand about leadership is that if you really want to be a key leader, then you will probably experience some loneliness.

their lives according to the tradition of the elders, but [instead] eat their bread with [ceremonially] unwashed hands?"

⁶He replied, "Rightly did Isaiah prophesy about you hypocrites (play-actors, pretenders), as it is written [in Scripture],

'THESE PEOPLE HONOR ME WITH
  THEIR LIPS,
BUT THEIR HEART IS FAR FROM ME.
⁷'THEY WORSHIP ME IN VAIN [their
  worship is meaningless and
  worthless, a pretense],
TEACHING THE PRECEPTS OF MEN
  AS DOCTRINES [giving their
  traditions equal weight with
  the Scriptures].' [Is 29:13]

⁸"You disregard *and* neglect the commandment of God, and cling [faithfully] to the tradition of men."

⁹He was also saying to them, "You are experts at setting aside *and* nullifying the commandment of God in order to keep your [man-made] tradition *and* regulations.

¹⁰"For Moses said, 'HONOR YOUR FATHER AND YOUR MOTHER [with respect and gratitude]'; and, 'HE WHO SPEAKS EVIL OF HIS FATHER OR MOTHER MUST BE PUT TO DEATH'; [Ex 20:12; 21:17; Lev 20:9; Deut 5:16]

¹¹but you [Pharisees and scribes] say, 'If a man tells his father or mother, "Whatever I have that would help you is Corban, (that is to say, *already* a gift to God),"'

¹²then you no longer let him do anything for his father or mother [since helping them would violate his vow of Corban];

¹³so you nullify the [authority of the] word of God [acting as if it did not apply] because of your tradition which you have handed down [through the elders]. And you do many things such as that."

¹⁴After He called the people to Him again, He *began* saying to them, "Listen [carefully] to Me, all of you, [hear] and understand [what I am saying]:

¹⁵there is nothing outside a man [such as food] which by going into him can defile him [morally or spiritually]; but the things which come out of [the heart of] a man are what defile *and* dishonor him.

¹⁶["If anyone has ears to hear, let him hear."]

¹⁷When Jesus had left the crowd and gone into the house, His disciples asked Him about the parable.

¹⁸And He said to them, "Are you, too, so foolish *and* lacking in understanding? Do you not understand that whatever goes into the man from outside cannot defile *and* dishonor him,

¹⁹since it does not enter his heart, but [only] his stomach, and [from there it] is eliminated?" (*By this, He* declared all foods ceremonially clean.)

²⁰And He said, "Whatever comes from [the heart of] a man, that is what defiles *and* dishonors him.

²¹"For from within, [that is] out the heart of men, come base *and* malevolent thoughts *and* schemes, acts of sexual immorality, thefts, murders, adulteries,

²²acts of greed *and* covetousness, wickedness, deceit, unrestrained conduct, envy *and* jealousy, slander *and* profanity, arrogance *and* self-righteousness and foolishness (poor judgment).

²³"All these evil things [schemes and desires] come from within and defile *and* dishonor the man."

²⁴Jesus got up and left there and went to the region of Tyre [and Sidon, the coastal area of Phoenicia]. He entered a house and did not want anyone to know *about it;* but it was impossible for Him to be hidden [from the public]. [Matt 15:21–28]

²⁵Instead, after hearing about Him, a woman whose little daughter had an unclean spirit immediately came and fell at His feet.

²⁶Now the woman was a Gentile (Greek), a Syrophoenician by nationality. And she kept pleading with Him to drive the demon out of her daughter.

²⁷He was saying to her, "First let the children [of Israel] be fed, for it is not right to take the children's bread and throw it to the pet dogs (non-Jews)."

²⁸But she replied, "Yes, Lord, but even the pet dogs under the table eat the children's crumbs."

²⁹And He said to her, "Because of this answer [reflecting your humility and faith], go [knowing that your request is granted]; the demon has left your daughter [permanently]."

³⁰And returning to her home, she found the child lying on the couch [relaxed and resting], the demon having gone.

³¹Soon after this Jesus left the region of Tyre, and passed through Sidon to the Sea of Galilee, through the region of Decapolis [the ten Hellenistic cities].

³²They brought to Him a man who was deaf and had difficulty speaking, and they begged Jesus to place His hand on him.

³³Jesus, taking him aside by himself, away from the crowd, put His fingers into the man's ears, and after spitting, He touched the man's tongue [with the saliva];

³⁴and looking up to heaven, He sighed deeply and said to the man, "Ephphatha," which [in Aramaic] means, "Be opened and released!"

³⁵And his ears were opened, his tongue was released, and he began speaking plainly.

³⁶Jesus commanded them not to tell anyone; but the more He ordered them, the more widely they continued to proclaim it.

³⁷They were thoroughly astounded and completely overwhelmed, saying, "He has done everything well! He even makes the deaf hear and the mute speak!"

8 IN THOSE days, when there was again a large crowd [gathered before Him] and they had nothing to eat, Jesus called His disciples and told them, [Matt 15:32–39]

²"I feel compassion for the crowd; they have been with Me now for three days and have nothing [left] to eat.

³"If I send them away to their homes hungry, they will faint [from exhaustion] on the road; because some of them have come a long way."

⁴His disciples replied to Him, "Where will anyone be able to find enough bread here in this isolated place to feed these people?"

⁵He asked them, "How many loaves [of bread] do you have?" They said, "Seven."

⁶He directed the people to sit down on the ground; and taking the seven loaves, He gave thanks and broke them, and [repeatedly] gave them to His disciples to set before them, and they served the crowd.

⁷They also had a few small fish; and when Jesus had blessed them [and given thanks], He ordered these [fish] to be set before them as well.

⁸And the people ate and were satisfied; and they picked up seven large baskets full of the broken pieces that were left over.

⁹About four thousand [men] were there [besides women and children]; and He sent them away.

¹⁰Then immediately He got into the boat with His disciples and went to the district of Dalmanutha.

¹¹The Pharisees came out and began to argue [contentiously and debate] with Him, demanding from Him a sign from heaven, to test Him [because of their unbelief].

¹²He groaned and sighed deeply in His spirit and said, "Why does this generation demand a sign? I assure you and most solemnly say to you, no sign will be given to this generation!"

reasoning robs your peace

In Mark 8:14–17, as in other Bible passages, we see that Jesus was able to discern what was going on among the disciples, who did not always act wisely. They were reasoning and talking with one another, trying to figure out what to do because they had no bread. They needed revelation, not reasoning.

For all their reasoning, they failed, as we often do, to understand what the Lord was saying to them. Jesus was not talking about literal bread; He was talking about spiritual leaven—the legalistic teachings and practices of the Pharisees. He warned His disciples to stay away from hypocritical attitudes that say, "Do what I say, not what I do." Jesus knew that a person is poisoned when he does not practice the good things he preaches and hides behind a legalistic front.

But the disciples did not understand what Jesus meant, so they "reasoned with one another" (AMPC) about it. Notice in verse 17, in the Amplified Classic version of the Bible, that Jesus' response was, "Why are you reasoning . . . Do you not yet discern or understand?"

That is what I used to do. I used to have a lot of problems with reasoning. I was always trying to figure things out. Then one day the Lord said something interesting to me: "As long as you continue to reason, you will never have discernment."

Discernment starts in the heart and enlightens the mind. As long as my mind was so busy reasoning, God could not get through to me, just as Jesus could not get through to His disciples.

This is an important issue. Reasoning is a huge problem because reasoning is not faith. Romans 8:6 in the Amplified Classic Version of the Bible says that the mind of the flesh is "sense and reason" without the Holy Spirit. It goes on to say that those operating in the mind of the flesh will experience a miserable life, but those who flow in the mind of the Holy Spirit will have life and peace. Reasoning belongs to the mind of the flesh and does not produce good fruit.

The "reasoning" I refer to is reasoning that is contrary to the truth of God's Word. God wants us to use common sense. There is nothing wrong with using our minds in an attempt to understand something. However, when we reason to the point of becoming confused we need to recognize that we have gone too far. At that point we need to pray for discernment and wait on God to reveal to us what we need to know.

You cannot have peace of mind and heart if you reason without God's truth to enlighten you. If you lack peace in your life, it may be that you are trying to figure out too many things. Stop asking, "Why, God, why?" Just say, "Lord, You know, and I need to be satisfied with that. When You are ready to show me, do so. Until then, with Your help, I am going to enjoy my life, trusting that You are in charge and that You will take care of everything that concerns me."

¹³Leaving them, He again boarded the boat and left for the other side.

¹⁴Now the disciples had forgotten to bring bread, and they had only one loaf with them in the boat.

¹⁵Jesus repeatedly ordered them, saying, "Watch out! Beware of the leaven of the Pharisees and the leaven of Herod."

¹⁶They *began* discussing this with one another, saying, "It is because we have no bread [that He said this]."

¹⁷Jesus, aware of this [discussion], said to them, "Why are you discussing [the fact] that you have no bread? Do you still not see or understand? Are your hearts hardened? [Is 6:9, 10]

¹⁸"THOUGH YOU HAVE EYES, DO YOU NOT SEE? AND THOUGH YOU HAVE EARS, DO YOU NOT HEAR *and* LISTEN [to what I have said]? And do you not remember, [Jer 5:21]

¹⁹when I broke the five loaves for the five thousand, how many baskets full of broken pieces you picked up?" They answered, "Twelve."

²⁰"And [when I broke] the seven [loaves] for the four thousand, how many large baskets full of broken pieces did you pick up?" And they answered, "Seven."

²¹And He was saying to them, "Do you still not understand?"

²²Then they came to Bethsaida; and some people brought a blind man to Jesus and begged Him to touch him.

²³Taking the blind man by the hand, He led him out of the village; and after spitting on his eyes and laying His hands on him, He asked him, "Do you see anything?"

²⁴And he looked up and said, "I see people, but [they look] like trees, walking around."

²⁵Then again Jesus laid His hands on his eyes; and the man stared intently and [his sight] was [completely] restored, and he *began* to see everything clearly.

²⁶And He sent him to his home, saying, "Do not even enter the village."

²⁷Then Jesus and His disciples went out to the villages of Caesarea Philippi; and on the way He asked His disciples, "Who do people say that I am?" [Matt 16:13–16; Luke 9:18–20]

²⁸They answered Him, "John the Baptist; and others say Elijah; but others, one of the prophets."

²⁹And He asked them, "But who do you say that I am?" Peter replied to Him, "You [in contrast to the others] are the Christ (the Messiah, the Anointed)."

³⁰Then Jesus strictly warned them not to tell anyone about Him.

³¹And He began to teach them that the Son of Man must [of necessity] suffer many things and be rejected [as the

life point

Jesus heard clearly from His Father that He needed to go to the cross. In Mark 8:31, Jesus told the disciples it was necessary for Him to suffer many things, be rejected by the elders and the chief priests and scribes, and be put to death. But, after three days, He said, He would rise again from the dead. In response, Peter "took Him aside and began to reprimand Him" (Mark 8:32). But Jesus disregarded Peter's comments and rebuked him. Jesus honored whatever His Father said, no matter what it cost. He was a God-pleaser, not a people-pleaser.

Sometimes we only listen to God if what He says will not cost us anything, or if He tells us what we want to hear. Most of the time, if we receive a discomforting word, we act like Peter and say, "Oh no, this cannot be God!" We cannot have what I call "selective hearing," only paying attention to those things that please us. We must hear and obey all of what God says to us through His Word.

Messiah] by the elders and the chief priests and the scribes, and must be put to death, and after three days rise [from death to life]. [Matt 16:21–28; Luke 9:22–27]

³²He was stating the matter plainly [not holding anything back]. Then Peter took Him aside and began to reprimand Him.

³³But turning around [with His back to Peter] and seeing His disciples, He rebuked Peter, saying, "Get behind Me, Satan; for your mind is not set on God's will or His values and purposes, but on what pleases man."

³⁴Jesus called the crowd together with His disciples, and said to them, "If anyone wishes to follow Me [as My disciple], he must deny himself [set aside selfish interests], and take up his cross [expressing a willingness to endure whatever may come] and follow Me [believing in Me, conforming to My example in living and, if need be, suffering or perhaps dying because of faith in Me].

³⁵"For whoever wishes to save his life [in this world] will [eventually] lose it [through death], but whoever loses his life [in this world] for My sake and

the cross we bear

Jesus died on the cross for us and said that those of us who want to follow Him will also have to carry a cross in life (see Mark 8:34). What is the cross we are expected to bear as believers in Jesus Christ? It's not disasters, disease, devastation, or any other miserable thing we can think of. Some people like to make Christianity seem like a burden to bear rather than a relationship to enjoy.

We do carry a cross, but Jesus said our cross is to live unselfish lives. He encouraged us to forget about ourselves, losing sight of our own interests. That literally means we must live for God and other people. We must lay our lives down and do what is for the good of other people and the kingdom of God. When we think of the choice to live an unselfish life, something deep within us cries out, "What about me?" The good news is that God takes care of us if we do what He asks us to do. Each act of obedience to God's will is a seed that reaps an abundant harvest of peace, joy, and blessing in our lives.

We can spend our lives trying to take care of ourselves and we will end up needy and unhappy. God has not called us to take care of ourselves. He has not called us to "in-reach," but to "out-reach." Reach out to others, and God will reach into your life and take care of all of your needs.

God's ways sometimes seem to be upside-down from what we think. He says that the first will be last (see Matthew 20:16) and that the greatest of all is the servant of all (see Matthew 23:11). Paul indicates in 2 Corinthians 9:6 that the way to get more money is to give away some of what you have. None of these statements seems to make sense to the natural mind, but they do work. God's ways always work.

Do not be afraid to trust God with yourself. Give yourself away, sow yourself as a seed, and get ready for a great life. Jesus said that unless the grain of wheat falls into the ground and dies, it would remain alone, but if it dies, it will produce a harvest (see John 12:24).

the gospel's will save it [from the consequences of sin and separation from God]. [Matt 10:39; Luke 17:33; John 12:25]

³⁶"For what does it benefit a man to gain the whole world [with all its pleasures], and forfeit his soul?

³⁷"For what will a man give in exchange for his soul *and* eternal life [in God's kingdom]?

³⁸"For whoever is ashamed [here and now] of Me and My words in this adulterous and sinful generation, the Son of Man will also be ashamed of him when He comes in the glory of His Father with the holy angels."

9 AND JESUS said to them, "I assure you *and* most solemnly say to you, there are some of those who are standing here who will not taste (experience) death before they see the kingdom of God after it has come with power."

²Six days later, Jesus took with Him Peter and James and John, and led them up on a high mountain by themselves. And He was transfigured (changed in form) before them [and began to shine brightly with divine and regal glory]; [Matt 17:1–8; Luke 9:28–36]

³and His clothes became radiant *and* dazzling, intensely white, as no launderer on earth can whiten them.

⁴Elijah appeared to them along with Moses, and they were having a conversation with Jesus.

⁵Peter responded and said to Jesus, "Rabbi (Master), it is good for us to be here; let us make three [sacred] tents—one for You, and one for Moses, and one for Elijah."

⁶For he did not [really] know what to say because they were terrified [and stunned by the miraculous sight].

⁷Then a cloud formed, overshadowing them, and a voice came out of the cloud, "This is My beloved Son. Listen to Him *and* obey Him!"

⁸Suddenly they looked around and no longer saw anyone with them, except Jesus alone.

⁹As they were coming down from the mountain, Jesus expressly ordered them not to tell anyone what they had seen, until the Son of Man had risen from the dead.

¹⁰So they [carefully and faithfully] kept the matter to themselves, discussing *and* questioning [with one another] what it meant to rise from the dead.

¹¹They asked Him, saying, "Why do the scribes say that Elijah must come first [before the Messiah comes]?" [Mal 4:5, 6]

¹²He answered them, "Elijah does come first and restores *and* reestablishes all things. And yet how is it written of the Son of Man that He will suffer many things [grief and physical distress] and be treated with contempt [utterly despised and rejected]? [Is 53:3]

¹³"But I say to you that Elijah has in fact come [already], and they did to him whatever they wished, just as it is written [in Scripture] of him."

¹⁴When they came [back] to the [other nine] disciples, they saw a large crowd around them, and scribes questioning *and* arguing with them. [Matt 17:14–18; Luke 9:37–42]

¹⁵Immediately, when the entire crowd saw Jesus, they were startled and *began* running up to greet Him.

¹⁶He asked them, "What are you discussing with them?"

¹⁷One of the crowd replied to Him, "Teacher, I brought You my son, possessed with a spirit which makes him unable to speak;

¹⁸and whenever it seizes him [intending to do harm], it throws him down, and he foams [at the mouth], and grinds his teeth and becomes stiff. I told Your disciples to drive it out, and they could not do it."

[19]He replied, "O unbelieving (faithless) generation, how long shall I be with you? How long shall I put up with you? Bring him to Me!"

[20]They brought the boy to Him. When the [demonic] spirit saw Him, immediately it threw the boy into a convulsion, and falling to the ground he *began* rolling around and foaming *at the mouth*.

[21]Jesus asked his father, "How long has this been happening to him?" And he answered, "Since childhood.

[22]"The demon has often thrown him both into fire and into water, intending to kill him. But if You can do anything, take pity on us and help us!"

[23]Jesus said to him, "[You say to Me,] 'If You can?' All things are possible for the one who believes *and* trusts [in Me]!"

[24]Immediately the father of the boy cried out [with a desperate, piercing cry], saying, "I do believe; help [me overcome] my unbelief."

[25]When Jesus saw that a crowd was rapidly gathering [around them], He rebuked the unclean spirit, saying to it, "You deaf and mute spirit, I command you, come out of him and never enter him again!"

[26]After screaming out and throwing him into a terrible convulsion, it came out. The boy looked so much like

putting the Word to work

Most of us can relate to this man who asked Jesus, "help [me overcome] my unbelief!" in Mark 9:24. The man's honesty is so refreshing, and Jesus immediately acts on his behalf. Is there an area of your life where you need more faith? Be honest with God and know that He is compassionate and will meet you where you are. Ask Him to increase your faith daily so you will know with certainty that all things are possible when we believe.

life point

Mark 9:23 teaches us that "All things are possible for the one who believes and trusts [in Me]!" Spiritually speaking, when you and I believe something, we receive it into our hearts. If a physical manifestation is needed, it will come after we have believed, not before. In the world we are taught to believe what we see. In God's kingdom, we believe first, and then in due time we will see manifested what we have believed.

a corpse [so still and pale] that many [of the spectators] said, "He is dead!"

[27]But Jesus took him by the hand and raised him; and he stood up.

[28]When He had gone indoors, His disciples *began* asking Him privately, "Why were we unable to drive it out?"

[29]He replied to them, "This kind [of unclean spirit] cannot come out by anything but prayer [to the Father]."

[30]They went on from there and *began* to go through Galilee. Jesus did not want anyone to know it,

[31]because He was teaching His disciples [and preparing them for the future]. He told them, "The Son of Man is to be betrayed *and* handed over to men [who are His enemies], and they will kill Him; and when He has been killed, He will rise [from the dead] three days later."

[32]But they did not understand this statement, and they were afraid to ask Him [what He meant].

[33]They arrived at Capernaum; and when He was in the house, He asked them, "What were you discussing *and* arguing about on the road?" [Matt 18:1–5; Luke 9:46–48]

[34]But they kept quiet, because on the road they had discussed *and* debated with one another which one [of them] was the greatest.

[35]Sitting down [to teach], He called

the twelve [disciples] and said to them, "If anyone wants to be first, he must be last of all [in importance] and a servant of all."

³⁶Taking a child, He set him before them; and taking him in His arms, He said to them,

³⁷"Whoever receives *and* welcomes one child such as this in My name receives Me; and whoever receives Me receives not [only] Me, but Him who sent Me." [Matt 10:40; Luke 10:16; John 13:20]

³⁸John said to Him, "Teacher, we saw someone casting out demons in Your name, and we tried to stop him because he was not accompanying us [as Your disciple]." [Luke 9:49, 50]

³⁹But Jesus said, "Do not stop him; for there is no one who will perform a miracle in My name, and be able soon afterward to speak evil of Me.

⁴⁰"For he who is not against us is for us. [Num 11:27–29]

⁴¹"For whoever gives you a cup of water to drink because of your name as followers of Christ, I assure you *and* most solemnly say to you, he will not lose his reward.

⁴²"But whoever causes one of these little ones who believe *and* trust in Me to stumble [that is, to sin or lose faith], it would be better for him if a heavy millstone [one requiring a donkey's strength to turn it] were hung around his neck and he were thrown into the sea. [Matt 18:6; Luke 17:2]

⁴³"If your hand causes you to stumble *and* sin, cut it off [that is, remove yourself from the source of temptation]! It is better for you to enter life crippled, than to have two hands and go into hell, into the unquenchable fire,

⁴⁴[where THEIR WORM DOES NOT DIE, AND THE FIRE IS NOT PUT OUT.] [Is 66:24]

⁴⁵"If your foot causes you to stumble *and* sin, cut it off [that is, remove yourself from the source of temptation]! It

would be better for you to enter life lame than to have two feet and be thrown into hell,

⁴⁶[where THEIR WORM DOES NOT DIE, AND THE FIRE IS NOT PUT OUT.] [Is 66:24]

⁴⁷"If your eye causes you to stumble *and* sin, throw it out [that is, remove yourself from the source of temptation]! It would be better for you to enter the kingdom of God with one eye, than to have two eyes and be thrown into hell,

⁴⁸where THEIR WORM [that feeds on the dead] DOES NOT DIE, AND THE FIRE IS NOT PUT OUT. [Is 66:24]

⁴⁹"For everyone will be salted with fire.

⁵⁰"Salt is good *and* useful; but if salt has lost its saltiness (purpose), how will you make it salty? Have salt within yourselves *continually,* and be at peace with one another."

10 GETTING UP, He left there (Capernaum) and went to the region of Judea and beyond the Jordan; and crowds gathered around Him again *and* accompanied Him, and as was His custom, He once more *began* to teach them.

²Pharisees came to Jesus to test Him [intending to trick Him into saying something wrong], and asked Him, "Is it lawful [according to Scripture] for a man to divorce his wife *and* send her away?"

³He replied to them, "What did Moses command you?"

⁴They said, "Moses allowed *a man* TO WRITE A CERTIFICATE OF DIVORCE AND TO SEND HER AWAY." [Deut 24:1–4]

⁵But Jesus said to them, "Because of your hardness of hearts [your callousness and insensitivity toward your wives and the provision of God] he wrote you this precept.

⁶"But from the beginning of creation *God* MADE THEM MALE AND FEMALE. [Gen 1:27; 5:2]

7"FOR THIS REASON A MAN SHALL LEAVE HIS FATHER AND HIS MOTHER [to establish a home with his wife], [Matt 19:5]

8AND THE TWO SHALL BECOME ONE FLESH; so that they are no longer two, but [are united as] one flesh. [Gen 2:24]

9"Therefore, what God has united *and* joined together, man must not separate [by divorce]."

10In the house the disciples *began* questioning Him again about this.

11And He said to them, "Whoever divorces his wife and marries another woman commits adultery against her;

12and if a woman divorces her husband and marries another man, she commits adultery."

13People were bringing children to Him so that He would touch *and* bless them, but the disciples reprimanded them *and* discouraged them [from coming].

14But when Jesus saw this, He was indignant and He said to them, "Allow the children to come to Me; do not forbid them; for the kingdom of God belongs to such as these.

15"I assure you *and* most solemnly say to you, whoever does not receive *and* welcome the kingdom of God like a child will not enter it at all."

16And He took the children [one by one] in His arms and blessed them [with kind, encouraging words], placing His hands on them.

17As He was leaving on His journey, a man ran up and knelt before Him and asked Him, "Good Teacher [You who are essentially good and morally perfect], what shall I do to inherit eternal life [that is, eternal salvation in the Messiah's kingdom]?" [Matt 19:16–29; Luke 18:18–30]

18Jesus said to him, "Why do you call Me good? No one is [essentially] good [by nature] except God alone.

19"You know the commandments: 'DO NOT MURDER, DO NOT COMMIT ADULTERY, DO NOT STEAL, DO NOT TESTIFY FALSELY, Do not defraud, HONOR YOUR FATHER AND MOTHER.'" [Ex 20:12–16; Deut 5:16–20]

20And he replied to Him, "Teacher, I have [carefully] kept all these [commandments] since my youth."

21Looking at him, Jesus felt a love (high regard, compassion) for him, and He said to him, "You lack one thing: go and sell all your property and give [the money] to the poor, and you will have [abundant] treasure in heaven; and come, follow Me [becoming My disciple, believing and trusting in Me and walking the same path of life that I walk]."

22But the man was saddened at Jesus' words, and he left grieving, because he owned much property *and* had many possessions [which he treasured more than his relationship with God].

23Jesus looked around and said to His disciples, "How difficult it will be for those who are wealthy [and cling to possessions and status as security] to enter the kingdom of God!"

24The disciples were amazed *and* bewildered by His words. But Jesus said to them again, "Children, how difficult it is [for those who place their hope and confidence in riches] to enter the kingdom of God!

25"It is easier for a camel to go through the eye of a needle than for a rich man [who places his faith in wealth or status] to enter the kingdom of God."

26They were completely *and* utterly astonished, and said to Him, "Then who can be saved [from the wrath of God]?"

speak the Word

God, I declare that there are things that are impossible with people, but that all things are possible with You!
—ADAPTED FROM MARK 10:27

²⁷Looking at them, Jesus said, "With people [as far as it depends on them] it is impossible, but not with God; for all things are possible with God."

²⁸Peter started saying to Him, "Look, we have given up everything and followed You [becoming Your disciples and accepting You as Teacher and Lord]."

²⁹Jesus said, "I assure you *and* most solemnly say to you, there is no one who has given up a house or brothers or sisters or mother or father or children or farms, for My sake and for the gospel's sake,

³⁰who will not receive a hundred times as much now in the present age—houses and brothers and sisters and mothers and children and farms— along with persecutions; and in the age to come, eternal life.

³¹"But many *who are* first will be last, and the last, first."

³²Now they were on the road going up to Jerusalem, and Jesus was walking on ahead of them; and they were perplexed [at what Jesus had said], and those who were following were alarmed *and* afraid. And again He took the twelve [disciples] aside and began telling them what was going to happen to Him,

³³*saying*, "Listen very carefully: we are going up to Jerusalem, and the Son of Man will be betrayed *and* handed over to the chief priests and the scribes; and they will condemn Him to death and hand Him over to the Gentiles (Romans).

³⁴"They will mock *and* ridicule Him and spit on Him, and whip (scourge) Him and kill *Him,* and three days later He will rise [from the dead]."

³⁵James and John, the two sons of Zebedee, came to Him, saying, "Teacher, we want You to do for us whatever we ask of You." [Matt 20:20, 21]

when obedience means sacrifice

Several years ago, our ministry needed two couples to go to Australia and manage our office there. In order to move that distance, they basically had to give up everything they owned and start over. It was too expensive to ship a lot of personal belongings that far.

The two couples who responded to God's call to go to Australia took a big step of obedience. In stepping out, they made huge personal sacrifices. They sold their cars and furniture, left behind family and friends, and separated themselves from churches where they were deeply rooted. They left everything and everyone they loved in order to obey God and move to a faraway place. Despite their love for God and their desire to do His will, it was a difficult transition.

When we go to a new place, often we feel that everything and everyone around us is strange. We are lonely and do not feel comfortable or "at home." But that kind of radical obedience pays great dividends—not only in terms of the personal happiness and contentment that come from knowing we are in God's will, but also in terms of the material blessings God provides according to the promises of His Word.

When we take steps of faith and obedience and give up important things for the sake of the gospel, we will find the promise of Mark 10:29, 30 to be true. We will experience great rewards now and for eternity.

36And He replied to them, "What do you want Me to do for you?"

37They said to Him, "Grant that we may sit [with You], one on Your right and one on *Your* left, in Your glory [Your majesty and splendor in Your kingdom]."

38But Jesus said to them, "You do not know what you are asking. Are you able to drink the cup that I drink, or to be baptized with the baptism [of suffering and death] with which I am baptized?"

39And they replied to Him, "We are able." Jesus told them, "The cup that I drink you will drink, and you will be baptized with the baptism with which I am baptized.

40"But to sit on My right or left, this is not Mine to give; but it is for those for whom it has been prepared [by My Father]."

41Hearing this, the [other] ten became indignant with James and John.

42Calling them to Himself, Jesus said to them, "You know that those who are recognized as rulers of the Gentiles lord it over them; and their powerful men exercise authority over them [tyrannizing them].

43"But this is not how it is among you; instead, whoever wishes to become great among you must be your servant,

44and whoever wishes to be first *and* most important among you must be slave of all.

45"For even the Son of Man did not come to be served, but to serve, and to give His life as a ransom for many."

46Then they came to Jericho. And as He was leaving Jericho with His disciples and a large crowd, a blind beggar, Bartimaeus, the son of Timaeus, was sitting beside the road [as was his custom]. [Matt 20:29–34; Luke 18:35–43]

47When Bartimaeus heard that it was Jesus of Nazareth, he began to shout and say, "Jesus, Son of David (Messiah), have mercy on me!"

48Many sternly rebuked him, telling

putting the Word to work

If God asked you today, "What do you want me to do for you?" how would you respond? James and John wanted positions of honor for themselves (see Mark 10:35–37). Bartimaeus, however, wanted to *see* and the first thing he saw was Jesus Himself (see Mark 10:46–52). What do you want God to do for you? Ask God to help you to see—more of Him, His purposes for your life, and what you are to do as you follow Him.

him to keep still *and* be quiet; but he kept on shouting out all the more, "Son of David (Messiah), have mercy on me!"

49Jesus stopped and said, "Call him." So they called the blind man, telling him, "Take courage, get up! He is calling for you."

50Throwing his cloak aside, he jumped up and came to Jesus.

51And Jesus said, "What do you want Me to do for you?" The blind man said to Him, "Rabboni (my Master), let me regain my sight."

52Jesus said to him, "Go; your faith [and confident trust in My power] has made you well." Immediately he regained his sight and *began* following Jesus on the road. [Is 42:6, 7]

11 WHEN THEY were nearing Jerusalem, at Bethphage and Bethany near the Mount of Olives, Jesus sent two of His disciples, [Matt 21:1–9; Luke 19:29–38; John 12:12–15]

2saying to them, "Go into the village in front of you, and immediately as you enter it, you will find a [donkey's] colt tied, which has never been ridden by anyone; untie it and bring it here.

3"If anyone asks you, 'Why are you doing this?' say, 'The Lord needs it'; and immediately he will send it here."

⁴So they went away [to the village] and found a colt tied outside at a gate in the street, and they untied it.

⁵Some of the people who were standing there said to them, "What are you doing, untying the colt?"

⁶They replied to them just as Jesus had directed, and they allowed them to go.

⁷They brought the colt to Jesus and put their coats on it, and He sat on it.

⁸And many [of the people] spread their coats on the road [as an act of tribute and homage before a new king], and others [scattered a layer of] leafy branches which they had cut from the fields [honoring Him as Messiah]. [2 Kin 9:13]

putting the Word to work

When world leaders or other famous dignitaries gather, there is often a great deal of pomp and pageantry involved. Most people in Jesus' day would expect a king to arrive in Jerusalem on a great horse with a large entourage, surrounded by evidence of military might and wealth. Jesus entered the city on the back of a colt (see Mark 11:1–11). Does God always work in your life in ways you expect? Ask God to help you recognize Him at work in your life, and enjoy His presence even when He works in unexpected ways.

Jesus loves to be merciful

Mercy precedes healing. My favorite story about mercy and healing is the story of blind Bartimaeus in Mark 10:46–52. In this passage, Bartimaeus cried out to Jesus, "Jesus, Son of David (Messiah), have mercy on me!" (Mark 10:47).

I can imagine the scene. Jesus was on His way somewhere and this guy shouted out, "Jesus! Have mercy on me." The crowd urged the blind man, "Shut up. Quit bothering Him. He does not want to be bothered with you." But this made Bartimaeus all the more determined for Jesus to hear him, so he continued to cry out for Jesus' mercy. What did Jesus do? He stopped. He could have listened to the crowd and ignored the man, but He responded to the man's plea for mercy. Jesus healed blind Bartimaeus.

We do not cry out for God's mercy enough. We spend too much time trying to deserve God's goodness. In Luke 17:12–19, lepers cried out for mercy, and they all received healing, but only one came back to give Jesus thanks. In Matthew 15:22–28, a woman from the Canaanite district said with a loud and urgent cry, "Have mercy on me, O Lord, Son of David (Messiah); my daughter is cruelly possessed by a demon." Her daughter was delivered. In Matthew 17:15, we see a man whose son had a tormenting problem, and he came to Jesus and said, "Lord, have mercy on my son, for he is a lunatic (moonstruck) and suffers terribly; for he often falls into the fire and often into the water." Jesus stopped and cured the boy.

It seems wherever Jesus traveled, somebody asked Him for mercy. In response to them, He stopped, talked to them, and met their needs.

Let me assure you that Jesus will listen to and respond to your cry for mercy, just as He did for blind Bartimaeus and many others.

⁹Those who went in front and those who were following [Him] were shouting [in joy and praise],

"Hosanna (Save, I pray)!
BLESSED (praised, glorified) IS HE WHO COMES IN THE NAME OF THE LORD! [Ps 118:26]

¹⁰"Blessed is the coming kingdom of our father David!
Hosanna in the highest [heaven]!"

¹¹Jesus entered Jerusalem and went to the temple [enclosure]; and after looking around at everything, He left for Bethany with the twelve

walk the talk

In Mark 11:13, 14, when the hungry Jesus saw that the fig tree did not have any figs on it, He said to it, "No one will ever eat fruit from you again!" Mark 11:20 tells us that the next morning the fig tree had completely withered.

I did not understand what happened in this story and why when I first read it, but I later learned that *the fruit of the fig tree appears at the same time as the leaves*. Then the story made sense to me.

With most fruit trees, if there are leaves, there is fruit under the leaves. When Jesus saw that the fig tree had leaves but no fruit, He cursed it because it was a phony. Where there are leaves, there is supposed to be fruit also!

If our lives revolve around the church but we have no fruit, we are not living our faith. We can put Christian bumper stickers on our cars, wear Jesus pins, carry our Bibles around, spend our lunch break sitting alone reading our Bibles, hang plaques listing the fruit of the Spirit on our walls, and listen to teaching tapes and say, "Praise the Lord! Hallelujah," but if we do not have time to help anybody else or even show kindness, we are like the fig tree with leaves but no fruit.

If a friend calls and says, "Could you do me a favor and watch my children for half an hour? I have a problem and need to run somewhere quickly," and we respond, "I would like to help you, but I just can't right now. I have plans. I'm sorry. I hope you understand." If we could have changed our plans but were simply too selfish to do so, we are like that phony fig tree.

People with a spiritual outward appearance but no fruit are hard to get along with and never allow themselves to be inconvenienced by anybody else. I know because I used to be that way! But I decided a long time ago that I am not going to be a phony Christian.

I want people to see that Christians are genuine. I want them to see that our ministry is real and what we do behind the scenes is the same as what we preach outwardly. If we have leaves, we need to also have fruit.

Many people who are searching for God will be watching us. They will want to know Jesus like we do when they see that our fruit is real and that we are not pretenders that only look good on the outside. We will be the ambassadors Christ intends us to be for Him.

[disciples], because it was already late [in the day].

¹²On the next day, when they had left Bethany, He was hungry. [Matt 21:18–22]

¹³Seeing at a distance a fig tree in leaf, He went to see if He would find anything on it. But He found nothing but leaves, for it was not the season for figs.

¹⁴He said to it, "No one will ever eat fruit from you again!" And His disciples were listening [to what He said].

¹⁵Then they came to Jerusalem. And He entered the temple [grounds] and began driving out [with force] the people who were selling and buying [animals for sacrifice] in the temple area, and overturned the tables of the moneychangers [who made a profit exchanging foreign money for temple coinage] and the seats of those who were selling doves; [Matt 21:12–16; Luke 19:45–47; John 2:13–16]

¹⁶and He would not permit anyone to carry merchandise *or* household wares through the temple [grounds, using the temple area irreverently as a shortcut].

¹⁷He *began* to teach and say to them, "Is it not written, 'MY HOUSE SHALL BE CALLED A HOUSE OF PRAYER FOR ALL THE NATIONS'? But you have made it a ROBBERS' DEN." [Is 56:7; Jer 7:11]

¹⁸The chief priests and the scribes heard this and *began* searching for a way to destroy Him; for they were afraid of Him, since the entire crowd was struck with astonishment at His teaching.

¹⁹When evening came, Jesus and His disciples would leave the city.

²⁰In the morning, as they were passing by, the disciples saw that the fig tree had withered away from the roots up.

²¹And remembering, Peter said to Him, "Rabbi (Master), look! The fig tree which You cursed has withered!"

²²Jesus replied, "Have faith in God [constantly].

²³"I assure you *and* most solemnly say to you, whoever says to this mountain, 'Be lifted up and thrown into the sea!' and does not doubt in his heart [in God's unlimited power], but believes that what he says is going to take place, it will be done for him [in accordance with God's will]. [Matt 17:20; Luke 17:6; 1 John 5:14]

²⁴"For this reason I am telling you, whatever things you ask for in prayer [in accordance with God's will], believe [with confident trust] that you have received them, and they will be *given* to you.

²⁵"Whenever you stand praying, if you have anything against anyone, forgive him [drop the issue, let it go], so that your Father who is in heaven will also forgive you your transgressions *and* wrongdoings [against Him and others].

²⁶["But if you do not forgive, neither will your Father in heaven forgive your transgressions."]

²⁷They came again to Jerusalem. And as Jesus was walking in the [courts and porches of the] temple, the chief priests, the scribes, and the

life point

Notice in Mark 11:22 that the first thing Jesus tells us to do is to have faith in God constantly. We must beware of putting our faith in anything other than God Himself and His Word. There was a time in my life when I had my faith in my faith. I relied on my ability to believe God rather than relying on God Himself. Then I read in God's Word that even when we are faithless He remains faithful (see 2 Timothy 2:13). None of us has perfect faith. Although we should strive to have faith in God constantly, there will be times when we allow doubt to creep in. I am comforted by the knowledge that even in those times God is still God and He does not change. He is always faithful!

elders came to Him, [Matt 21:23–27; Luke 20:1–8] [28]and *began* saying to Him, "By what authority are You doing these things, or who gave You this authority to do these things?"

[29]Jesus said to them, "I will ask you one question, and you answer Me, and then I will tell you by what authority I do these things.

[30]"Was the baptism of John [the Baptist] from heaven [that is, ordained by God] or from men? Answer Me."

[31]They *began* discussing it with each other, saying, "If we say, 'From heaven,' He will say, 'Then why did you not believe him?'

[32]"But *shall we say, 'From men?'"—they were afraid [to answer because] of the crowd, for everyone considered John to have been a real prophet.

[33]So they replied to Jesus, "We do not know." And Jesus said to them, "Neither will I tell you by what authority I do these things."

12 JESUS BEGAN to speak to them [the chief priests, scribes and elders who were questioning Him] in parables: "A man

what to do with your mountain

Usually when we have mountains in our lives we talk *about* them, but God's Word instructs us to talk *to* them, as we see in Mark 11:22, 23.

When Jesus said that we are to speak to our mountains in faith, commanding them to be lifted up and thrown into the sea, He made a radical statement and one that deserves some thought.

First of all, what do we say to the mountains in our lives? It is obvious that we should not hurl our will at them; we are to hurl God's will at them—and His will is His Word.

Speaking the Word of God is powerful and absolutely necessary in conquering our mountains. However, it is only the beginning. Obedience is equally important. If people think they can live in disobedience, but speak God's Word to their mountains and get results, they will be sadly disappointed, as Jesus clearly stated in this passage.

Mark 11:22–26 must be considered as a whole. In verse 22 Jesus said to constantly have faith in God. In verse 23 He talked about releasing faith by speaking to mountains. In verse 24 He spoke of prayer and the importance of praying believing prayers. In verse 25 He gave a command to forgive. And in verse 26 He stated plainly that if we do not forgive, neither will our Father in heaven forgive us our failings and shortcomings.

There is no power in speaking to a mountain if our hearts are full of unforgiveness. Yet the problem of unforgiveness is rampant among God's children. Multitudes of people who have accepted Christ as their personal Savior fall into the deception of trying to operate under one of God's principles while completely ignoring another.

Ask God to help you understand the whole counsel of His Word so you can live a balanced, victorious life as a believer.

11:32 Or *if we say.*

PLANTED A VINEYARD AND PUT A WALL AROUND IT, AND DUG A PIT FOR THE WINE PRESS AND BUILT A TOWER; and he rented it out to tenant farmers and left the country. [Is 5:1, 2; Matt 21:33–46; Luke 20:9–19]

²"When the *harvest* season came he sent a servant to the tenants, in order to collect from them some of the fruit of the vineyard.

³"They took him and beat him and sent him away empty-handed.

⁴"Again he sent them another servant, and they [threw stones and] wounded him in the head, and treated him disgracefully.

⁵"And he sent another, and that one they killed; then many others—some they beat and some they killed.

⁶"He still had one man left *to send,* a beloved son; he sent him last of all to them, saying, 'They will respect my son.'

⁷"But those tenants said to each other, 'This *man* is the heir! Come on, let us kill him [and destroy the evidence], and his inheritance will be ours!'

⁸"So they took him and killed him, and threw his body outside the vineyard.

⁹"What will the owner of the vineyard do? He will come and destroy the tenants, and will give the vineyard to others.

¹⁰"Have you not even read this Scripture:

'THE STONE WHICH THE BUILDERS
  REGARDED AS UNWORTHY *and*
  REJECTED,
THIS [very stone] HAS BECOME
  THE CHIEF CORNERSTONE
¹¹THIS CAME ABOUT FROM THE LORD,
AND IT IS MARVELOUS *and*
  WONDERFUL IN OUR EYES'?"
  [Ps 118:22, 23]

¹²And they were looking for a way to seize Him, but they were afraid of the crowd; for they knew that He spoke this parable in reference to [and as a charge against] them. And so they left Him and went away.

¹³Then they sent some of the Pharisees and Herodians to Jesus in order to trap Him into *making* a statement [that they could use against Him]. [Matt 22:15–22; Luke 20:20–26]

¹⁴They came and said to Him, "Teacher, we know that You are truthful and have no personal bias toward anyone; for You are not influenced by outward appearances *or* social status, but in truth You teach the way of God. Is it lawful [according to Jewish law and tradition] to pay the poll-tax to [Tiberius] Caesar, or not?

¹⁵"Should we pay [the tax] or should we not pay?" But knowing their hypocrisy, He asked them, "Why are you testing Me? Bring Me a coin (denarius) to look at."

¹⁶So they brought one. Then He asked them, "Whose image and inscription is this?" They said to Him, "Caesar's."

¹⁷Jesus said to them, "Pay to Caesar the things that are Caesar's, and to God the things that are God's." And they were greatly amazed at Him.

¹⁸Some Sadducees (who say that there is no resurrection) came to Him, and *began* questioning Him, saying, [Matt 22:23–33; Luke 20:27–38]

¹⁹"Teacher, Moses wrote for us [a law] that IF A MAN'S BROTHER DIES and leaves a wife BUT LEAVES NO CHILD, HIS BROTHER IS TO MARRY THE WIDOW AND RAISE UP CHILDREN FOR HIS BROTHER. [Deut 25:5]

²⁰"There were seven brothers; the first [one] took a wife, and died leaving no children.

²¹"The second brother married her, and died leaving no children; and the third likewise;

²²and so all seven [married her and died, and] left no children. Last of all the woman died also.

23"In the resurrection, whose wife will she be? For all seven [brothers] were married to her."

24Jesus said to them, "Is this not why you are wrong, because you know neither the Scriptures [that teach the resurrection] nor the power of God [who is able to raise the dead]?

25"For when they rise from the dead, they do not marry nor are they given in marriage, but are like angels in heaven.

26"But concerning the raising of the dead, have you not read in the book of Moses, in the *passage* about the *burning* bush, how God spoke to him, saying, 'I AM THE GOD OF ABRAHAM, AND THE GOD OF ISAAC, AND THE GOD OF JACOB'? [Ex 3:2–6]

27"He is not the God of the dead, but of the living; you are greatly mistaken *and* you are deceiving yourselves!"

28Then one of the scribes [an expert in Mosaic Law] came up and listened to them arguing [with one another], and noticing that Jesus answered them well, asked Him, "Which commandment is first *and* most important of all?" [Matt 22:34–40; Luke 10:25–28]

29Jesus answered, "The first *and* most important *one* is: 'HEAR, O ISRAEL, THE LORD OUR GOD IS ONE LORD;

30AND YOU SHALL LOVE THE LORD YOUR GOD WITH ALL YOUR HEART, AND WITH ALL YOUR SOUL (life), AND WITH ALL YOUR MIND (thought, understanding), AND WITH ALL YOUR STRENGTH.' [Deut 6:4, 5]

31"This is the second: 'YOU SHALL [unselfishly] LOVE YOUR NEIGHBOR AS YOURSELF.' There is no other commandment greater than these." [Lev 19:18]

32The scribe said to Him, "Admirably answered, Teacher; You truthfully

stated that HE IS ONE, AND THERE IS NO OTHER BUT HIM;

33AND TO LOVE HIM WITH ALL THE HEART AND WITH ALL THE UNDERSTANDING AND WITH ALL THE STRENGTH, AND TO [unselfishly] LOVE ONE'S NEIGHBOR AS ONESELF, is much more than all burnt offerings and sacrifices." [1 Sam 15:22; Hos 6:6; Mic 6:6–8; Heb 10:8]

34When Jesus saw that he answered thoughtfully *and* intelligently, He said to him, "You are not far from the kingdom of God." And after that, no one would dare to ask Him any more questions.

35Jesus *began* to say, as He taught in [a portico or court of] the temple, "How can the scribes say that the Christ is the son of David? [Matt 22:41–46; Luke 20:41–44]

36"David himself said [when inspired] by the Holy Spirit,

'THE LORD (the Father) SAID TO MY LORD (the Son, the Messiah),
"SIT AT MY RIGHT HAND,
UNTIL I PUT YOUR ENEMIES UNDER YOUR FEET."' [Ps 110:1]

37"David himself calls Him (the Son, the Messiah) 'Lord'; so how can it be that He is David's Son?" The large crowd enjoyed hearing Jesus *and* listened to Him with delight.

38In [the course of] His teaching He was saying, "Beware of the scribes, who like to walk around in long robes [displaying their prominence], and *like to receive* respectful greetings in the market places,

39and [they love] the chief seats in the synagogues and the places of distinction *and* honor at banquets,

40[these scribes] who devour (confiscate) widows' houses, and offer long

speak the Word

Help me, Lord, to love You with all of my heart, soul, mind, and strength and to truly love my neighbor as I love myself.
–ADAPTED FROM MARK 12:30, 31

prayers for appearance's sake [to impress others]. These men will receive greater condemnation."

⁴¹And He sat down opposite the [temple] treasury, and *began* watching how the people were putting money into the treasury. And many rich people were putting in large sums. [Luke 21:1–4]

⁴²A poor widow came and put in two small copper coins, which amount to a mite.

⁴³Calling His disciples to Him, He said to them, "I assure you *and* most solemnly say to you, this poor widow put in [proportionally] more than all the contributors to the treasury.

⁴⁴"For they all contributed from their surplus, but she, from her poverty, put in all she had, all she had to live on."

13 AS HE was coming out of the temple [grounds], one of His disciples said to Him, "Teacher, look what *wonderful stones and what wonderful buildings!" [Matt 24; Luke 21:5–36]

²Jesus replied to him, "You see these great buildings? Not one stone will be left on another which will not be torn down!"

³As He was sitting on the Mount of Olives opposite the temple, Peter and James and John and Andrew asked Him privately,

⁴"Tell us, when will these things happen, and what will be the sign when all these things are about to be fulfilled?"

⁵Jesus began to say to them, "Be careful *and* see to it that no one misleads you.

⁶"Many will come in My name [misusing My name or claiming to be the Messiah], saying, 'I am *He!* ' and will deceive *and* mislead many.

⁷"When you hear of wars and rumors of wars, do not be alarmed (frightened, troubled); *these things* must take place, but the end is not yet.

⁸"For nation will rise up against nation, and kingdom against kingdom; there will be earthquakes in various places; there will be famines. These things are the beginning of the birth pangs [the intolerable anguish and suffering].

⁹"But be on your guard; they will turn you over to courts, and you will be beaten in synagogues, and you will stand [as accused] before governors and kings for My sake, as a testimony to them.

¹⁰"The gospel [that is, the good news regarding the way of salvation] must first be preached to all the [Gentile] nations. [Col 1:6, 23]

¹¹"When they take you and turn you over [to the court], do not worry beforehand about what to say, but say whatever is given to you [by God] in that hour; for it is not you who speak, but it is the Holy Spirit [who will speak through you].

¹²"Brother will betray brother to [be put to] death, and a father [will hand over] his child; and children will rise up *and* take a stand against parents and have them put to death.

¹³"You will be hated by everyone because of [your association with] My name, but the one who [patiently perseveres empowered by the Holy Spirit and] endures to the end, he will be saved.

¹⁴"But when you see the ABOMINATION OF DESOLATION standing [in the temple sanctuary] where it ought not to be (let the reader understand) then those who are in Judea must flee to the mountains. [Dan 9:27; 11:31; 12:11]

¹⁵"Whoever is on the housetop must not go down [to enter the house], or go inside to take anything out of his house;

¹⁶whoever is in the field must not turn back to get his coat.

¹⁷"And woe to those women who are

13:1 Lit *how great.*

pregnant and to those who are nursing babies in those days!

18"Pray that it will not occur in winter,

19for at that time there will be such tribulation as has not occurred, from the beginning of the creation which God made, until now—and never will [be again].

20"And if the Lord had not shortened the days, no human life would have been saved; but for the sake of the elect, whom He chose [for Himself], He shortened the days. [Dan 12:1]

21"Then if anyone says to you, 'Look, here is the Christ (the Messiah, the Anointed)!' or, 'Look, *He is* there!' do not believe it;

22for false Christs and false prophets will arise, and they will provide signs and wonders in order to deceive, if [such a thing were] possible, even the elect [those God has chosen for Himself].

23"But be on your guard; I have told you everything in advance.

24"But in those days, after [the suffering and distress of] that tribulation, THE SUN WILL BE DARKENED, AND THE MOON WILL NOT GIVE ITS LIGHT, [Is 13:10]

25AND THE STARS WILL BE FALLING from the sky, and the powers that are in the heavens will be shaken. [Is 34:4]

26"Then they will see THE SON OF MAN COMING IN CLOUDS with great power and glory [in royal majesty and splendor]. [Dan 7:13, 14]

27"And then He will send out the angels, and will gather together His elect [those He has chosen for Himself] from the four winds, from the farthest end of the earth to the farthest end of heaven.

28"Now learn this lesson from the fig tree: as soon as its branch becomes tender and it puts out its leaves, you recognize that summer is near. [Matt 24:32, 33; Luke 21:29–31]

29"Even so, you too, when you see these things happening, know [for certain] that He is near, *right* at the door.

30"I assure you *and* most solemnly say to you, this generation [the people living when these signs and events begin] will not pass away until all these things take place.

31"Heaven and earth [as now known] will pass away, but My words will not pass away.

32"But of that [exact] day or hour no one knows, not even the angels in heaven, nor the Son [in His humanity], but the Father *alone*.

33"Be on guard and stay constantly alert **[and pray]**; for you do not know when the *appointed* time will come.

34"It is like a man away on a journey, *who* when he left home put his servants in charge, each with his *particular* task, and also ordered the doorkeeper to be *continually* alert.

35"Therefore, be *continually* on the alert—for you do not know when the master of the house is coming, whether in the evening, or at midnight, or when the rooster crows, or in the morning—

36[stay alert,] in case he should come suddenly *and* unexpectedly and find you asleep *and* unprepared.

37"What I say to you I say to everyone, 'Be on the alert [stay awake and be continually cautious]!'"

putting the Word to work

When your boss is away from the office, what do you spend your time doing? As a good employee, you should spend your time working diligently to continue the work you were assigned to do. The same principle applies as you wait for Jesus' return. Do not waste time speculating about when He is coming back, but serve Him wholeheartedly every day, as Mark 13:33 instructs.

14 IT WAS now two days before the Passover and [the festival of] Unleavened Bread, and the chief priests and the scribes were searching for a deceitful way to arrest Jesus and kill *Him;* [Matt 26:2–5; Luke 22:1, 2]

²but they were saying, "Not during the festival, for the people might riot."

³While He was in Bethany [as a guest] at the home of Simon the leper, and reclining *at the table,* a woman came with an alabaster vial of very costly *and* precious perfume of pure nard; and she broke the vial and poured the perfume over His head.

⁴But there were some who were indignantly *remarking* to one another, "Why has this perfume been wasted?

⁵"For this perfume might have been sold for more than three hundred denarii [a laborer's wages for almost a year], and *the money* given to the poor." And they scolded her.

⁶But Jesus said, "Let her alone; why are you bothering her *and* causing trouble? She has done a good *and* beautiful thing to Me.

⁷"For you always have the poor with you, and whenever you wish you can do something good to them; but you will not always have Me. [Deut 15:11]

⁸"She has done what she could; she has anointed My body beforehand for the burial.

⁹"I assure you *and* most solemnly say to you, wherever the good news [regarding salvation] is proclaimed throughout the world, what she has done will be told in memory of her."

¹⁰Then Judas Iscariot, who was one of the twelve [disciples], went to the chief priests to betray Jesus to them. [Matt 26:14–16; Luke 22:3–6; John 6:71]

¹¹When they heard this they were delighted, and promised to give him money. And he *began* looking for an opportune time to betray Jesus.

¹²On the first day [of the festival] of Unleavened Bread, when [as was customary] they sacrificed the Passover lamb, His disciples asked Him, "Where do You want us to go and prepare for You to eat the Passover?" [Matt 26:17–19; Luke 22:7–13]

¹³And He sent two of His disciples, saying to them, "Go into the city, and a man carrying a jar of water will meet you; follow him;

¹⁴and say to the owner of the *house* he enters, 'The Teacher asks, "Where is My guest room in which I may eat the Passover with My disciples?"'

¹⁵"He will show you a large upstairs room, furnished and ready [with carpets and dining couches]; prepare [the supper] for us there."

¹⁶The disciples left and went to the city and found everything just as He had told them, and they prepared the Passover.

¹⁷When it was evening, He came with the twelve [disciples]. [Matt 26:20–25]

¹⁸While they were reclining *at the table,* Jesus said, "I assure you *and* most solemnly say to you that one of you will betray Me—one who is eating with Me." [Ps 41:9]

¹⁹They began to be grieved *and* deeply distressed and to say to Him one by one, "Surely not I?"

²⁰And He replied, "It is one of the twelve [disciples], one who is dipping *bread* in the bowl with Me.

²¹"For the Son of Man goes [to the cross] just as it is written [in Scripture] of Him; but woe to that man by whom the Son of Man is betrayed! *It would have been* good for that man if he had not been born."

²²While they were eating, Jesus took bread and blessed it [giving thanks and praise], and He broke it, and gave it to them and said, "Take it. This is My body." [Matt 26:26–29; Luke 22:17–20; 1 Cor 11:23–25]

²³And when He had taken a cup [of wine] and given thanks, He gave it to

them, and they all drank from it. [Ex 24:8]

²⁴And He said to them, "This is My blood of the [new] covenant, [My blood] which is being poured out for many [for the forgiveness of sins].

²⁵"I assure you *and* most solemnly say to you, I will not drink again of the fruit of the vine until that day when I drink it new in the kingdom of God."

²⁶After they had sung a hymn, they went out to the Mount of Olives.

²⁷Jesus said to them, "You will all fall away [and be ashamed and be afraid to be associated with Me as disciples], because it is written, 'I WILL STRIKE THE SHEPHERD, AND THE SHEEP WILL BE SCATTERED.' [Zech 13:7]

²⁸"But after I have been raised [from the dead], I will go ahead of you to Galilee."

the meaning of communion

The scene in Mark 14:22–24 is what we commonly refer to as "The Last Supper." Jesus wanted to eat a final meal with His disciples and be strengthened in their fellowship before facing the agony that was ahead. During this last meal He spoke prophetically, instructing them to partake of His broken body and shed blood by eating and drinking the bread and wine. In Mark 14:24 He made clear that His blood would seal and validate the New Covenant they were to have with Almighty God. Today we remember Jesus' shed blood and broken body through our taking of Communion.

Like many others, I received and participated in Communion services for years without truly understanding what I was doing. I knew the bread and juice represented the body and blood of the Lord Jesus. I knew He instructed that we eat it and drink it in remembrance of Him. But Communion has a much deeper and more glorious meaning.

Holy Communion was never intended to be an empty ritual with little or no meaning to those participating in it. First, we take the bread: Jesus is the Bread of Life, He is the Word made flesh (John 1:14; 6:35). As we partake of the bread, we take Him as our Living Bread, the only source that can truly satisfy our hunger in life. We remember what He has done for us. Then we take Him as our Living Drink, the only source that can satisfy our thirst. As we drink of the cup, it is the equivalent of "sprinkling blood" or "shedding blood" on the sacrifice of His body. It is important that we take both the bread and the cup. If people attempt to remove the blood, they are removing the power of the gospel.

Communion can and should be a fresh dedication of our lives to the Lord, a reminder of the blood covenant we have with God because Jesus stood in our place. In His great love for us, He took our sins upon Himself and remembers them no more. His sacrifice on the cross made it possible for us to receive His salvation, mercy, grace, and favor.

When you take Communion, realize that Jesus has given you His best. Remember that He shed His blood and gave His life for you. Communion is a time to examine your life and ask for forgiveness in areas where it is needed. It is also a good time to release your faith and ask God for healing in your physical body, as well as in every other area of your life.

²⁹But Peter said to Him, "Even if they all fall away [and desert You, ashamed and afraid of being associated with You], yet I will not [do so]!"

³⁰Jesus said to him, "I assure you *and* most solemnly say to you, this very night, before a rooster crows twice, you will deny [that you even know] Me three times." [Matt 26:34; John 13:38]

³¹But Peter kept saying insistently, "If I have to die with You, I will not deny You!" And they all were saying the same thing as well.

³²Then they went to a place called Gethsemane; and Jesus said to His disciples, "Sit down here until I have prayed." [Matt 26:36–46; Luke 22:40–46]

³³He took Peter and James and John with Him, and He began to be deeply distressed and troubled [extremely anguished at the prospect of what was to come].

³⁴And He said to them, "My soul is deeply grieved *and* overwhelmed with sorrow, to the point of death; remain here and keep watch."

³⁵After going a little farther, He fell to the ground [distressed by the weight of His spiritual burden] and *began* to pray that if it were possible [in the Father's will], the hour [of suffering and death for the sins of mankind] might pass from Him.

³⁶He was saying, "Abba, Father! All things are possible for You; take this cup [of judgment] away from Me; but not what I will, but what You will."

³⁷And He came back and found them sleeping, and He said to Peter, "Simon, are you asleep? Were you unable to keep watch for one hour?

³⁸"Keep [actively] watching and praying so that you do not come into temptation; the spirit is willing, but the body is weak."

³⁹He went away again and prayed, saying the same words.

⁴⁰And again He came back and found them sleeping, because their eyes were very heavy; and they did not know how to answer Him.

⁴¹He came back a third time and said to them, "Are you still sleeping and resting? Enough [of that]! The hour has come. Look, the Son of Man is being betrayed into the hands of sinners.

⁴²"Get up, let us go. Look, my betrayer is near!"

⁴³And at once, while He was still speaking, Judas [Iscariot], one of the

life point

Those of us who are leaders on any level at all may encounter what I call the "Judas-kiss test," that is, the test of being betrayed by friends, as happened to Jesus in Mark 14:43–46.

Years ago I talked with a person who went through something that was emotionally hard because it involved rejection and betrayal by people this individual considered close trusted friends. I told this person the same thing I share with you now.

There were certain things Jesus did for us that we should not have to go through. For example, He bore our sins so we do not have to bear them. But there are other things that Jesus went through and that He endured as an example for us, things we will have to follow in His footsteps and go through. Betrayal is one of them.

Frankly, I do not know many key leaders, people who have been in positions of leadership for very long, who have not at one time or another been betrayed by someone they really loved, respected, and trusted. If and when that happens to you, do as Jesus did and stay focused on your purpose. Forgive the offender and do not allow him or her to cause you to fail or delay in doing what God has called you to do.

twelve [disciples], came up, and with him a crowd of men with swords and clubs, *who came* from the chief priests, the scribes, and the elders [of the Sanhedrin]. [Matt 26:47–56; Luke 22:47–53; John 18:3–11]

⁴⁴Now the betrayer had given them a signal, saying, "Whomever I kiss, He is the one; seize Him and lead Him away safely [under guard]."

⁴⁵When Judas came, immediately he went up to Jesus and said, "Rabbi (Master)!" and he kissed Him [forcefully].

⁴⁶They laid hands on Him and seized Him.

⁴⁷But one of the bystanders [Simon Peter] drew his sword and struck [Malchus] the slave of the high priest and cut off his ear. [Matt 26:51; Luke 22:50; John 18:10]

⁴⁸Jesus said to them, "Have you come out with swords and clubs to arrest Me, as *you would* against a robber?

⁴⁹"Day after day I was with you, teaching in the [courts and porches of the] temple, and you did not seize Me; but *this has happened* so that the Scriptures would be fulfilled."

⁵⁰Then all of His disciples abandoned Him and fled.

⁵¹A young man was following Him, wearing [only] a linen sheet over *his* naked *body;* and some men seized him.

⁵²But pulling free of the linen sheet, he escaped [from them] naked.

⁵³They led Jesus away to the high priest, and all the chief priests and the elders and the scribes (Sanhedrin, Jewish High Court) gathered together. [Matt 26:57–68; Luke 22:66–71; John 18:12f, 19–24]

⁵⁴Peter had followed Him at a distance, right into the courtyard of the high priest; and he was sitting with the officers [guards and servants] and warming himself at the fire.

⁵⁵Now the chief priests and the entire Council (Sanhedrin, Jewish High Court) were trying to obtain testimony against Jesus [which they could use] to have Him [condemned and] executed, but they were not finding any.

⁵⁶For many [people] were giving false testimony against Him, but their testimonies were not consistent.

⁵⁷Some stood up and *began* to give false testimony against Him, saying,

⁵⁸"We heard Him say, 'I will destroy this temple (sanctuary) that was made with hands, and in three days I will build another made without hands.'" [John 2:19–21]

⁵⁹Not even in this respect was their testimony consistent.

⁶⁰The high priest stood up and came forward and asked Jesus, "Have You no answer to give [in response] to what these men are testifying against You?"

⁶¹But Jesus kept silent and gave no answer at all. Again the high priest was questioning Him, and saying to Him, "Are You the Christ (the Messiah, the Anointed), the Son of the Blessed One?"

⁶²Jesus said, "I am; and you will [all] see THE SON OF MAN SEATED [with authority] AT THE RIGHT HAND OF POWER (the Father), and COMING WITH THE CLOUDS OF HEAVEN." [Ps 110:1; Dan 7:13]

⁶³Then tearing his robe [to express his indignation], the high priest said, "What further need do we have of witnesses? [Num 14:6]

⁶⁴"You have heard the blasphemy [that is, His claim to be the Son of God]. What is your decision?" And they all condemned Him to be [guilty and] deserving of death. [Lev 24:16]

⁶⁵And some began to spit on Him, and to blindfold Him, and to beat Him with their fists, and to say to Him, "Prophesy [by telling us who hit you]!" Then the officers took custody of Him and struck him in the face.

⁶⁶While Peter was down below in the courtyard, one of the servant-girls of the high priest came, [Matt 26:69–75; Luke 22:55–62; John 18:16–18, 25–27]

⁶⁷and when she saw Peter warming himself, she looked intently at him and said, "You were with Jesus the Nazarene, too."

⁶⁸But he denied it, saying, "I neither know nor understand what you are talking about." Then he went out [of the courtyard] to the porch, [and a rooster crowed.]

⁶⁹The servant-girl saw him, and began once more to tell the bystanders, "This [man] is *one* of them."

⁷⁰But again he denied it. After a little while, the bystanders again said to Peter, "You are in fact *one* of them, for [it is clear from your accent, that] you are a Galilean, too."

⁷¹But he began to invoke a curse [on himself] and to swear [an oath], "I do not know this man you are talking about!"

⁷²Immediately a rooster crowed the second time. And Peter remembered what Jesus said to him: "Before a rooster crows twice, you will deny Me three times." And thinking of this, he began weeping [in anguish].

15 EARLY IN the morning the chief priests, with the elders and scribes and the whole Council (Sanhedrin, Jewish High Court), immediately consulted together; and they bound Jesus, they took Him away [violently] and handed Him over to Pilate. [Is 53:8]

²Pilate questioned Him, "Are You the King of the Jews?" And He replied to him, "It is as you say." [Matt 27:11–14; Luke 23:2, 3; John 18:29–37]

³The chief priests *began* accusing Him of many things.

⁴Then Pilate again asked Him, "Have You no answer [to give]? See how many charges they are bringing against You!"

⁵But Jesus gave no further answer; so Pilate was perplexed. [Is 53:7]

⁶Now at the [Passover] feast Pilate used to set free for them any one prisoner whom they requested. [Matt 27:15–26; Luke 23:18–25; John 18:39–19:16]

⁷The man called Barabbas was imprisoned with the insurrectionists (revolutionaries) who had committed murder in the civil rebellion.

⁸The crowd came up and began asking Pilate to do as he usually did for them.

⁹Pilate answered them, saying, "Do you want me to set free for you the King of the Jews?"

¹⁰For he was aware that the chief priests had turned Jesus over to him because of envy *and* resentment.

¹¹But the chief priests stirred up the crowd to get him to release Barabbas for them instead.

¹²Again Pilate answered, "Then what shall I do with Him whom you call the King of the Jews?"

¹³They screamed back, "Crucify Him!"

¹⁴But Pilate asked them, "Why, what has He done that is evil?" But they screamed all the more, "Crucify Him!"

¹⁵So Pilate, wishing to satisfy the crowd, set Barabbas free for them; and after having Jesus scourged, he handed Him over [to his soldiers] to be crucified. [Is 53:5]

¹⁶The soldiers led Him away into the palace (that is, the Praetorium), and they called together the entire [Roman] battalion [of 600 soldiers]. [Matt 27:27–31]

¹⁷They dressed Him up in [a ranking Roman officer's robe of] purple, and after twisting [together] a crown of thorns, they placed it on Him;

¹⁸and they began saluting *and* mocking Him: "Hail, King of the Jews!"

¹⁹They kept beating Him on the head with a reed and spitting on Him, and kneeling and bowing in [mock] homage to Him. [Is 50:6]

²⁰After they had mocked Him, they

took off the purple robe and put His own clothes on Him. And they led Him out [of the city] to crucify Him.

²¹They forced into service a passer-by coming in from the countryside, Simon of Cyrene (the father of Alexander and Rufus), to carry His cross. [Matt 27:32; Luke 23:26]

²²Then they brought Him to the place [called] Golgotha, which is translated, Place of a Skull. [Matt 27:33–44; Luke 23:33–43; John 19:17–24]

²³They tried to give Him wine mixed with myrrh [to dull the pain], but He would not take it.

²⁴And they crucified Him, and divided up His clothes among themselves, casting lots for them to see who should take what. [Ps 22:18]

²⁵It was the third hour (9:00 a.m.) when they crucified Him. [Ps 22:14–16]

²⁶The inscription of the accusation against Him had been written [above Him]: "THE KING OF THE JEWS."

²⁷They crucified two robbers with Him, one on His right and one on His left.

²⁸[And the Scripture was fulfilled which says, "He was counted with the transgressors."] [Is 53:12]

²⁹Those who were passing by were insulting Him with abusive and insolent language, wagging their heads [as a sign of contempt], and saying, "Ha! You who would destroy the temple and rebuild it in [only] three days, [John 2:19]

³⁰save Yourself by coming down from the cross!"

³¹In the same way the chief priests also, along with the scribes, were ridiculing and mocking Him among themselves and saying, "He saved others [from death]; He cannot save Himself! [Ps 22:7, 8]

³²"Let the Christ (the Messiah, the Anointed), the King of Israel, now come down from the cross, so that we may see and believe and trust [in Him]!" Those who were crucified with Him were also insulting Him.

³³When the sixth hour (noon) came, darkness covered the whole land until the ninth hour (3:00 p.m.). [Matt 27:45–56; Luke 23:44–49]

³⁴And at the ninth hour Jesus cried out with a loud voice, "ELOI, ELOI, LAMA SABACHTHANI?"—which is translated, "MY GOD, MY GOD, WHY HAVE YOU FORSAKEN ME?" [Ps 22:1]

³⁵Some of the bystanders heard Him and said, "Look! He is calling for Elijah!"

³⁶Someone ran and filled a sponge with sour wine, put it on a reed and gave Him a drink, saying, "Let us see whether Elijah is coming to take Him down." [Ps 69:21; Matt 27:48, 50; Luke 23:36; John 19:29, 30]

³⁷But Jesus uttered a loud cry, and breathed out His last [voluntarily, sovereignly dismissing and releasing His

life point

When Jesus died, the veil that separated the Holy Place from the Most Holy Place in the temple was torn from the top to the bottom (see Mark 15:37, 38). That opened the way for anyone to go into God's presence. Prior to Jesus' death, only the high priest could go into God's presence, and then only once a year with the blood of slain animals to cover and atone for his sins and the sins of the people.

It is significant that the tear in the veil of the temple was from top to bottom. The veil or curtain was so high and thick that no human could have torn it. It was torn supernaturally by the power of God, showing that He was opening a new and living way for His people to approach Him.

spirit from His body in submission to His Father's plan].

³⁸And the veil [of the Holy of Holies] of the temple was torn in two from top to bottom.

³⁹When the centurion, who was standing opposite Him, saw the way He breathed His last [being fully in control], he said, "Truly this man was the Son of God!"

⁴⁰Now some women also were watching from a distance, among whom were Mary Magdalene, and Mary the mother of James the Less and of Joses, and Salome. [John 19:25]

⁴¹When Jesus was in Galilee, they used to accompany him and minister to Him; and *there were* also many other women who came up with Him to Jerusalem.

⁴²When evening had already come, because it was the preparation day, that is, the day before the Sabbath, [Deut 21:22, 23; Matt 27:57–61; Luke 23:50–56; John 19:38–42]

⁴³Joseph of Arimathea came, a prominent *and* respected member of the Council (Sanhedrin, Jewish High Court), who was himself waiting for the kingdom of God—and he courageously dared to go in before Pilate, and asked for the body of Jesus.

⁴⁴Pilate wondered if He was dead by this time [only six hours after being crucified], and he summoned the centurion and asked him whether He was already dead.

⁴⁵And when he learned from the centurion [that Jesus was in fact dead], he gave the body to Joseph [by granting him permission to remove it].

⁴⁶So Joseph purchased a [fine] linen cloth [for wrapping the body], and after taking Jesus down [from the cross], he wrapped Him in the linen cloth and placed Him in a tomb which had been cut out of rock. Then he rolled a [large, wheel-shaped] stone against the entrance of the tomb. [Is 53:9]

⁴⁷Mary Magdalene and Mary the *mother* of Joses were [carefully] watching to see where He was laid.

16

WHEN THE Sabbath was over, Mary Magdalene, Mary the *mother* of James, and Salome purchased [sweet-smelling] spices, so that they might go and anoint Him. [Matt 28:1–8; Luke 24:1–10; John 20:1–8]

²Very early on the first day of the week, they came to the tomb when the sun had risen.

³And they were saying to one another, "Who will roll back the stone for us from the entrance of the tomb?"

⁴Looking up, they saw that the stone had been rolled away, though it was extremely large.

⁵Entering the tomb, they saw a young man sitting on the right, wearing a [long, stately] white robe; and they were amazed *and* bewildered.

⁶And he said to them, "Do not be amazed; you are looking for Jesus the Nazarene, who was crucified. He has risen; He is not here. See, [here is] the place where they laid Him. [Ps 16:10]

⁷"But go, tell His disciples and Peter, 'He is going ahead of you to Galilee; you will see Him there, just as He told you.'" [Mark 14:28]

⁸They went out and fled from the tomb, for they were seized with trembling and astonishment; and they said nothing [about it] to anyone, because they were afraid.

⁹[Now Jesus, having risen [from death] early on the first day of the week, appeared first to Mary Magdalene, from whom He had cast out seven demons.

¹⁰She went and reported it to those who had been with Him, while they were mourning and weeping.

¹¹When they heard that He was alive and had been seen by her, they did not believe it.

¹²After that, He appeared in a different form to two of them as they were walking along the way to the country. [Luke 24:13–35]

¹³They returned [to Jerusalem] and told the others, but they did not believe them either.

¹⁴Later, Jesus appeared to the eleven [disciples] themselves as they were reclining *at the table;* and He called them to account for their unbelief and hardness of heart, because they had not believed those who had seen Him after He had risen [from death].

¹⁵And He said to them, "Go into all the world and preach the gospel to all creation.

¹⁶"He who has believed [in Me] and has been baptized will be saved [from the penalty of God's wrath and judgment]; but he who has not believed will be condemned.

¹⁷"These signs will accompany those who have believed: in My name they will cast out demons, they will speak in new tongues;

¹⁸they will pick up serpents, and if they drink anything deadly, it will not hurt them; they will lay hands on the sick, and they will get well."

¹⁹So then, when the Lord Jesus had spoken to them, He was taken up into heaven and sat down at the right hand of God. [Ps 110:1]

²⁰And they went out and preached everywhere, while the Lord was working with them and confirming the word by the signs that followed.]

life point

Mark 16:15 records what we commonly call the Great Commission: "And He said to them, 'Go into all the world and preach the gospel to all creation.'" People from every Christian church accept and attempt to carry out this verse. Yet two verses later, in Mark 16:17, 18, Jesus says believers will cast out demons, speak in new tongues, and lay hands on the sick. Some churches do not practice these things, and many teach against them.

I believe a few moments of sincere thought will reveal to the seeking soul that if Jesus meant for us to carry out Mark 16:15, then He intended for us to carry out verses 17 and 18 as well. It is dangerous business to pick and choose among scriptures. If we are going to follow the full gospel, we cannot take the scriptures we are comfortable with and ignore the rest. We need the whole counsel of God's Word, not just bits and pieces of it.

life point

Mark 16:20 says the apostles went everywhere preaching the Word, and God confirmed the Word with "signs that followed."

I always believed those signs and wonders to be miraculous healings until God began showing me to believe not only for miraculous healings to confirm the Word preached, but also to believe for and expect miraculous breakthroughs and abundant fruit in the area in which I was ministering.

Whatever you do to serve the Lord, whether it is at home taking care of your family, as an employee of a corporation, as a public servant, as a volunteer at a hospital or nursing home—whatever you do, wherever you do it—believe God for miraculous breakthroughs to follow the things you do to serve Him. Jesus heals us everywhere we hurt! When we are about His business, we can expect signs and wonders to follow us.

Luke

Author:
Luke

Date:
Around AD 60

Everyday Life Principles:
As you read Luke and see its emphasis on the ministry of the Holy Spirit, remember that He wants to be actively involved in every aspect of your life today.

Nothing is impossible with God.

Do not let the devil intimidate you. Talk back to him, using the Word of God.

Each of the four Gospels is unique. These books are written in different styles, to different audiences, from different points of view, and with different emphases on certain aspects of Jesus' life and ministry. Luke's Gospel is the longest of the four Gospels and presents Jesus as the Savior of the world; it highlights the ministry of the Holy Spirit; and it pays particular attention to women, children, the poor, and the oppressed.

Luke contains many wonderful stories and lessons, including one of the greatest and most important truths for any Christian's life: "For with God nothing [is or ever] shall be impossible" (Luke 1:37). No matter how difficult our situations are, God can always bring change and restoration.

In Luke 4, we learn another critical lesson. We see the devil tempting Jesus in the wilderness and every time the devil says something, Jesus immediately responds, "It is written and forever remains written," and fights back with a verse or passage of Scripture. This teaches us that we too must know the Word and use it as our weapon against the enemy. Jesus overcame him that way, and so will we.

As you read the book of Luke, I pray you will remember that nothing is impossible with God, that the Holy Spirit is always there to help you, and that you can have victory over the enemy as you use the weapon of the Word against him.

1 SINCE [AS is well known] many have undertaken to compile an orderly account of the things which have been fulfilled among us [by God],

²exactly as they were handed down to us by those [with personal experience] who from the beginning [of Christ's ministry] were eyewitnesses and ministers of the word [that is, of the teaching concerning salvation through faith in Christ],

³it seemed fitting for me as well, [and so I have decided] after having carefully searched out *and* investigated all the events accurately, from the *very* beginning, to write an orderly account for you, most excellent Theophilus; [Acts 1:1]

⁴so that you may know the exact truth about the things you have been taught [that is, the history and doctrine of the faith].

⁵In the days of Herod [the Great], king of Judea, there was a certain priest whose name was Zacharias, of the division of Abijah. His wife was* a descendant of Aaron [the first high priest of Israel], and her name was Elizabeth.

⁶They both were righteous (approved) in the sight of God, walking blamelessly in all the commandments and requirements of the Lord.

⁷But they were childless, because Elizabeth was barren, and they were both far advanced in years.

⁸Now it happened while Zacharias was serving as priest before God in the *appointed* order of his priestly division,

⁹as was the custom of the priesthood, he was chosen by lot to enter [the sanctuary of] the temple of the Lord and burn incense [on the altar of incense]. [Ex 30:7]

¹⁰And all the congregation was praying outside [in the court of the temple] at the hour of the incense offering.

¹¹And an angel of the Lord appeared to him, standing to the right of the altar of incense.

¹²When Zacharias saw *the angel,* he was troubled and overcome with fear.

¹³But the angel said to him, "Do not be afraid, Zacharias, because your petition [in prayer] was heard, and your wife Elizabeth will bear you a son, and you will name him John.

¹⁴"You will have great joy and delight, and many will rejoice over his birth,

¹⁵for he will be great *and* distinguished in the sight of the Lord; and will never drink wine or liquor, and he will be filled with *and* empowered to act by the Holy Spirit while still in his mother's womb. [Num 6:3]

¹⁶"He will turn many of the sons of Israel back [from sin] to [love and serve] the Lord their God.

¹⁷"It is he who will go *as a forerunner* before Him in the spirit and power of Elijah, TO TURN THE HEARTS OF THE FATHERS BACK TO THE CHILDREN, and the disobedient to the attitude of the righteous [which is to seek and submit to the will of God]—in order to make ready a people [perfectly] prepared [spiritually and morally] for the Lord." [Is 40:3; Mal 4:5, 6]

¹⁸And Zacharias said to the angel, "How will I be certain of this? For I am an old man and my wife is advanced in age."

¹⁹The angel replied and said to him, "I am Gabriel; I stand *and* minister in the [very] presence of God, and I have been sent [by Him] to speak to you and to bring you this good news. [Dan 8:16; 9:21]

²⁰"Listen carefully, you will be *continually* silent and unable to speak until the day when these things take place, because you did not believe what I told you; but my words will be fulfilled at their proper time."

1:5 Lit *from the daughters of.*

²¹The people [outside in the court] were waiting for Zacharias, and were wondering about his *long* delay in the temple.

²²But when he did come out, he was unable to speak to them. They realized that he had seen a vision in the temple; and he kept making signs to them, and remained mute.

²³When his time of priestly service was finished, he returned to his home.

²⁴Now after this his wife Elizabeth became pregnant, and for five months she secluded herself completely, saying,

²⁵"This is how the Lord has dealt with me in the days when He looked with favor on *me,* to take away my disgrace among men." [Gen 30:23; Is 4:1]

²⁶Now in the sixth month [of Elizabeth's pregnancy] the angel Gabriel was sent from God to a city in Galilee called Nazareth,

²⁷to a virgin betrothed to a man whose name was Joseph, a descendant of the house of David; and the virgin's name was Mary.

²⁸And coming to her, the angel said, "Greetings, favored one! The Lord is with you."

²⁹But she was greatly perplexed at what he said, and kept carefully considering what kind of greeting this was.

³⁰The angel said to her, "Do not be afraid, Mary, for you have found favor with God.

³¹"Listen carefully: you will conceive in your womb and give birth to a son, and you shall name Him Jesus.

³²"He will be great *and* eminent and will be called the Son of the Most High; and the Lord God will give Him the throne of His father David;

³³and He will reign over the house of

putting the Word to work

Has God ever asked you to do something you never expected to do? No doubt, Mary was very surprised when the angel told her she would give birth to the Son of God (see Luke 1:26–35). Mary's trust in God and her obedience to God's plans and purposes is a great example to follow. Allow God to work in you as He wants to, and know that all His plans for you are for your good. When unexpected things happen, keep trusting Him!

Jacob (Israel) forever, and of His kingdom there shall be no end." [Is 9:6, 7; Dan 2:44]

³⁴Mary said to the angel, "How will this be, since I am a virgin *and* have no intimacy with any man?"

³⁵Then the angel replied to her, "The Holy Spirit will come upon you, and the power of the Most High will overshadow you [like a cloud]; for that reason the holy (pure, sinless) Child shall be called the Son of God. [Ex 40:34; Is 7:14]

³⁶"And listen, even your relative Elizabeth has also conceived a son in her old age; and she who was called barren is now in her sixth month.

³⁷"For with God nothing [is or ever] shall be impossible."

³⁸Then Mary said, "Behold, *I am* the servant of the Lord; may it be done to me according to your word." And the angel left her.

³⁹Now at this time Mary arose and hurried to the hill country, to a city of Judah (Judea),

⁴⁰and she entered the house of Zacharias and greeted Elizabeth.

⁴¹When Elizabeth heard Mary's

speak the Word

Lord, I know that with You, nothing is or ever shall be impossible.
–ADAPTED FROM LUKE 1:37

greeting, her baby leaped in her womb; and Elizabeth was filled with the Holy Spirit *and* empowered by Him.

⁴²And she exclaimed loudly, "Blessed [worthy to be praised] are you among women, and blessed is the fruit of your womb!

⁴³"And how has it *happened* to me, that the mother of my Lord would come to me?

⁴⁴"For behold, when the sound of your greeting reached my ears, the baby in my womb leaped for joy.

⁴⁵"And blessed [spiritually fortunate and favored by God] is she who believed *and* confidently trusted that there would be a fulfillment of the things that were spoken to her [by the angel sent] from the Lord."

⁴⁶And Mary said,

"My soul magnifies *and* exalts the Lord,
⁴⁷And my spirit has rejoiced in God my Savior.
⁴⁸"For He has looked [with loving care] on the humble state of His maidservant;
For behold, from now on all generations will count me blessed *and* happy *and* favored by God!
⁴⁹"For He who is mighty has done great things for me;
And holy is His name [to be worshiped in His purity, majesty, and glory].
⁵⁰"AND HIS MERCY IS UPON GENERATION AFTER GENERATION
TOWARD THOSE WHO [stand in great awe of God and] FEAR HIM. [Ps 103:17]
⁵¹"He has done mighty deeds with His [powerful] arm;
He has scattered *those who were* proud in the thoughts of their heart.
⁵²"He has brought down rulers from *their* thrones,

And exalted those who were humble.
⁵³"HE HAS FILLED THE HUNGRY WITH GOOD THINGS;
And sent the rich away empty-handed.
⁵⁴"He has helped His servant Israel,
In remembrance of His mercy,
⁵⁵Just as He promised to our fathers,
To Abraham and to his descendants forever." [Gen 17:7; 18:18; 22:17; 1 Sam 2:1–10; Mic 7:20]

⁵⁶And Mary stayed with Elizabeth for about three months, and then returned to her home.

⁵⁷Now the time had come for Elizabeth to give birth, and she gave birth to a son.

⁵⁸Her neighbors and relatives heard that the Lord had shown His great mercy toward her, and they were rejoicing with her.

⁵⁹It happened that on the eighth day they came to circumcise the child [as required by the Law], and they intended to name him Zacharias, after his father; [Gen 17:12; Lev 12:3]

⁶⁰but his mother answered, "No indeed; instead he will be called John."

⁶¹And they said to her, "None of your relatives is called by that name."

⁶²Then they made signs to his father, as to what he wanted him called.

⁶³And he asked for a *writing* tablet and wrote as follows, "His name is John." And they were all astonished.

⁶⁴At once Zacharias' mouth was opened and his tongue *freed,* and he *began* speaking, praising *and* blessing *and* thanking God.

⁶⁵Then fear came on all their neighbors; and all these things were discussed throughout the hill country of Judea.

⁶⁶All who heard these things kept them in mind, saying, "What then will this little boy *turn out to* be?" For the

hand of the Lord was certainly with him [to bring about his birth].

⁶⁷Now Zacharias his father was filled with the Holy Spirit *and* empowered by Him, and he prophesied, saying,

⁶⁸"Blessed (praised, glorified) be
the Lord, the God of Israel,
Because He has visited us and
brought redemption to His
people,
⁶⁹And He has raised up a horn of
salvation [a mighty and valiant
Savior] for us
In the house of David His
servant—
⁷⁰Just as He promised by the mouth
of His holy prophets from the
most ancient times—
⁷¹Salvation FROM OUR ENEMIES,
And FROM THE HAND OF ALL WHO
HATE US; [Ps 106:10]
⁷²To show mercy [as He promised]
to our fathers,
And to remember His holy
covenant [the promised
blessing],
⁷³The oath which He swore to
Abraham our father,
⁷⁴To grant us that we, being rescued
from the hand of our enemies,
Might serve Him without fear,
⁷⁵In holiness [being set apart] and
righteousness [being upright]
before Him all our days.
⁷⁶"And you, child, will be called a
prophet of the Most High;
For you will go on BEFORE THE
LORD (the Messiah) TO PREPARE
HIS WAYS; [Is 40:3; Mal 4:5]
⁷⁷To give His people the knowledge
of salvation
By the forgiveness of their sins,
⁷⁸Because of the tender mercy of
our God,
With which the Sunrise (the
Messiah) from on high will
dawn *and* visit us, [Mal 4:2]

⁷⁹TO SHINE UPON THOSE WHO SIT IN
DARKNESS AND IN THE SHADOW
OF DEATH,
To guide our feet [in a straight
line] into the way of peace *and*
serenity." [Is 9:2]

⁸⁰The child continued to grow and to become strong in spirit, and he lived in the deserts until the day of his public appearance to Israel [as John the Baptist, the forerunner of the Messiah].

2 NOW IN those days a decree went out from [the emperor] Caesar Augustus, that all the inhabited world (the Roman Empire) should be registered [in a census]. ²This was the first census taken while Quirinius was governor of Syria. ³And everyone went to register for the census, each to his own city. ⁴So Joseph also went up from Galilee, from the city of Nazareth, to Judea, to the city of David which is called Bethlehem, because he was of the house and family of David, ⁵in order to register with Mary, who was betrothed to him, and was with child. [Matt 1:18–25] ⁶While they were there [in Bethlehem], the time came for her to give birth, ⁷and she gave birth to her Son, her firstborn; and she wrapped Him in [swaddling] cloths and laid Him in a manger, because there was no [private] room for them in the inn. ⁸In the same region there were shepherds staying out in the fields, keeping watch over their flock by night. ⁹And an angel of the Lord suddenly stood before them, and the glory of the Lord flashed *and* shone around them, and they were terribly frightened. ¹⁰But the angel said to them, "Do not be afraid; for behold, I bring you good news of great joy which will be for all the people. ¹¹"For this day in the city of David

there has been born for you a Savior, who is Christ the Lord (the Messiah). [Mic 5:2]

¹²"And this will be a sign for you [by which you will recognize Him]: you will find a Baby wrapped in [swaddling] cloths and lying in a manger." [1 Sam 2:34; 2 Kin 19:29; Is 7:14]

¹³Then suddenly there appeared with the angel a multitude of the heavenly host (angelic army) praising God and saying,

¹⁴"Glory to God in the highest [heaven],
And on earth peace among men with whom He is well-pleased."

¹⁵When the angels had gone away from them into heaven, the shepherds *began* saying one to another, "Let us go straight to Bethlehem, and see this [wonderful] thing that has happened which the Lord has made known to us."

¹⁶So they went in a hurry and found their way to Mary and Joseph, and the Baby as He lay in the manger.

¹⁷And when they had seen this, they made known what had been told them about this Child.

¹⁸and all who heard it were astounded *and* wondered at what the shepherds told them.

¹⁹But Mary treasured all these things, giving careful thought to them *and* pondering them in her heart.

²⁰The shepherds returned, glorifying and praising God for all that they had heard and seen, just as it had been told them.

²¹At the end of eight days, when He was to be circumcised, He was named Jesus, the name given [to Him] by the angel [Gabriel] before He was conceived in the womb.

²²And when the time for their purification came [that is, the mother's purification and the baby's dedication] according to the Law of Moses, they brought Him up to Jerusalem to present Him to the Lord [set apart as the Firstborn] [Lev 12:1–4]

²³(as it is written in the Law of the Lord, "EVERY *firstborn* MALE THAT OPENS THE WOMB SHALL BE CALLED HOLY [set apart and dedicated] TO THE LORD)" [Ex 13:1, 2, 12; Num 8:17]

²⁴and [they came also] to offer a sacrifice according to what is said in the Law of the Lord [to be appropriate for a family of modest means], "A PAIR OF TURTLEDOVES OR TWO YOUNG PIGEONS." [Lev 12:6–8]

²⁵Now there was a man in Jerusalem whose name was Simeon; and this man was righteous and devout [carefully observing the divine Law], and looking for the Consolation of Israel; and the Holy Spirit was upon him.

²⁶It had been revealed to him by the Holy Spirit that he would not die before he had seen the Lord's Christ (the Messiah, the Anointed).

²⁷Prompted by the Spirit, he came into the temple [enclosure]; and when the parents brought in the child Jesus, to do for Him the custom required by the Law,

²⁸Simeon took Him into his arms, and blessed *and* praised *and* thanked God, and said,

²⁹"Now, Lord, You are releasing Your bond-servant to leave [this world] in peace,
According to Your word;
³⁰For my eyes have seen Your Salvation, [Is 52:10]
³¹Which You have prepared in the presence of all peoples,
³²A LIGHT FOR REVELATION TO THE GENTILES [to disclose what was previously unknown],
And [to bring] the praise *and* honor *and* glory of Your people Israel." [Is 42:6; 49:6]

³³And His [legal] father and His mother were amazed at what was said about Him.

when *not* to speak

Mary had some pretty serious things happen in her life. She was a sweet, ordinary girl who loved God when an angel of the Lord appeared to her and told her she was going to become the mother of the Son of God.

She must have thought about Joseph, the man she was engaged to marry. Surely she wondered how to tell him this news and how he would react. She had to have questioned whether her parents and friends would believe her story.

Then time passed and the birth took place. By then, an angel had explained the situation to Joseph. When the baby was born, the angels appeared to the shepherds and told them to come to the stable and worship the Christ Child. The shepherds told Mary, Joseph, and everyone else about the angel who appeared to them as they were watching their flocks that dark night and what he had said to them. These are the things that Mary did not speak of. She kept them in her heart and pondered them, according to Luke 2:19.

Whatever Mary may have thought or felt, she controlled it because she said to the angel who first brought the news, "may it be done to me according to your word" (Luke 1:38).

I believe that when God speaks something to us, many times we need to keep it to ourselves. He gives us the faith to believe what He has said to us, but if we try to tell it to others, they may wonder if we are thinking correctly.

You should have heard some of the things people said to me when I told them that God spoke to my heart and called me into the ministry. Knowing my background and the condition I was in at the time, they were not encouraging at all.

That is one of the problems with sharing too much with others; we become discouraged instead of encouraged. Other people do not always have the faith to believe what God has told us.

When God calls you to do something, He also gives you the faith to do it. You do not have to live in fear all the time, thinking you are not able to do what He has given you to do. When you have a gift of faith, certain things seem easy to you. But to someone without that gift of faith, these things seem impossible.

When God spoke to Mary through the angel, there was a gift of faith that came with that word to her from the Lord, so she was able to say, "May it be done." But she was also wise enough not to go around knocking on doors saying, "I just had a visitation from an angel who told me I am going to give birth to the Son of God. I am going to get pregnant by the Holy Spirit, and the Child I will bear will be the Savior of the world." Mary knew how to keep her mouth shut and her heart open. What a good example for us all!

³⁴Simeon blessed them and said to Mary His mother, "Listen carefully: this *Child* is appointed *and* destined for the fall and rise of many in Israel, and for a sign that is to be opposed— [Is 8:14, 15]

³⁵and a sword [of deep sorrow] will pierce through your own soul—so that the thoughts of many hearts may be revealed."

³⁶There was a prophetess, Anna, the daughter of Phanuel, of the tribe of Asher. She was very old, and had lived with her husband for seven years after her marriage, [Josh 19:24]

³⁷and then as a widow to the age of eighty-four. She did not leave the [area of the] temple, but was serving *and* worshiping night and day with fastings and prayers.

³⁸She, too, came up at that very moment and *began* praising *and* giving thanks to God, and continued to speak of Him to all who were looking for the redemption *and* deliverance of Jerusalem.

³⁹And when they had done everything [in connection with Jesus' birth] according to the Law of the Lord, they went back to Galilee, to their own city, Nazareth.

⁴⁰And the Child continued to grow and become strong [in spirit], filled with wisdom; and the grace (favor, spiritual blessing) of God was upon Him. [Judg 13:24]

⁴¹Now His parents went to Jerusalem every year for the Passover Feast. [Deut 16:1–8; Ex 23:15]

⁴²And when He was twelve years old, they went up *to Jerusalem,* according to the custom of the Feast;

⁴³and as they were returning [to Nazareth], after spending the required number of days [at the Feast], the boy Jesus remained behind in Jerusalem. Now His parents did not know this,

⁴⁴but supposed Him to be in the caravan, and traveled a day's journey;

and [then] they *began* searching [anxiously] for Him among their relatives and acquaintances.

⁴⁵When they did not find Him, they went back to Jerusalem looking for Him [everywhere].

⁴⁶Three days later they found Him in the [court of the] temple, sitting among the teachers, both listening to them and asking them questions.

⁴⁷All who heard Him were amazed by His intelligence *and* His understanding and His answers.

⁴⁸When they saw Him, they were overwhelmed; and His mother said to Him, "Son, why have You treated us like this? Listen, Your father and I have been [greatly distressed and] anxiously looking for You."

⁴⁹And He answered, "Why did you have to look for Me? Did you not know that I had to be in My Father's *house?*"

⁵⁰But they did not understand what He had said to them.

⁵¹He went down to Nazareth with them, and was continually submissive *and* obedient to them; and His mother treasured all these things in her heart.

⁵²And Jesus kept increasing in wisdom and in stature, and in favor with God and men. [1 Sam 2:26]

3 NOW IN the fifteenth year of [Emperor] Tiberius Caesar's reign—when Pontius Pilate was

putting the Word to work

Throughout the Bible, we see that children hold a special place in God's heart. Think for a moment about a child who is important to you. Do you pray regularly for him or her? Praying for children as they grow up is one of the greatest gifts you can give to them. Pray that he or she, like Jesus, will increase in wisdom and in stature and in favor with God and with people (see Luke 2:52).

governor of Judea, and Herod [Antipas] was tetrarch of Galilee, and his brother Philip was tetrarch of the region of Ituraea and Trachonitis, and Lysanias was tetrarch of Abilene—

²in the high priesthood of Annas and Caiaphas [his son-in-law], the word of God came to John, the son of Zacharias, in the wilderness.

³And he went into all the country around the Jordan, preaching a baptism of repentance for the forgiveness of sin;

⁴as it is written *and* forever remains written in the book of the words of Isaiah the prophet,

"THE VOICE OF ONE SHOUTING IN
    THE WILDERNESS,
'PREPARE THE WAY OF THE LORD,
MAKE HIS PATHS STRAIGHT.
⁵'EVERY RAVINE SHALL BE FILLED UP,
AND EVERY MOUNTAIN AND HILL
    SHALL BE LEVELED;
AND THE CROOKED [places] SHALL
    BE MADE STRAIGHT,
AND THE ROUGH ROADS SMOOTH;
⁶AND ALL MANKIND SHALL SEE THE
    SALVATION OF GOD.'" [Is 40:3–5]

⁷So he *began* saying to the crowds who were coming out to be baptized by him, "You brood of vipers, who warned you to flee from the wrath [of God that is] to come?

⁸"Therefore produce fruit that is worthy of [and consistent with your] repentance [that is, live changed lives, turn from sin and seek God and His righteousness]. And do not *even* begin to say to yourselves [as a defense], 'We have Abraham for our father [and so our heritage assures us of salvation]'; for I say to you that from these stones God is able to raise up children (descendants) for Abraham [for God can replace the unrepentant, regardless of their heritage, with those who are obedient]. [Matt 3:9]

⁹"Even now the axe [of God's judgment] is swinging toward the root of the trees; so every tree that does not produce good fruit is being cut down and thrown into the fire."

¹⁰The crowds asked him, "Then what are we to do?"

¹¹And John replied, "The man who has two tunics is to share with him who has none; and he who has food is to do the same."

¹²Even *some* tax collectors came to be baptized, and they asked, "Teacher, what are we to do?"

¹³And he told them, "Collect no more than the *fixed amount* you have been ordered to [collect]."

¹⁴*Some* soldiers asked him, "And *what about* us, what are we to do?" And he replied to them, "Do not extort money from anyone or harass *or* blackmail *anyone,* and be satisfied with your wages."

¹⁵Now the people were in a state of expectation, and all were wondering in their hearts about John, as to whether he was the Christ (the Messiah, the Anointed).

¹⁶John answered them all by saying, "As for me, I baptize you [only] with water; but One who is mightier [more powerful, more noble] than I is coming, and I am not fit to untie the strap of His sandals [even as His slave]. He will baptize you [who truly repent] with the Holy Spirit and [you who remain unrepentant] with fire. [Matt 3:11]

¹⁷"His winnowing fork is in His hand to thoroughly clear His threshing floor, and to gather the wheat (believers) into His barn (kingdom); but He will burn up the chaff (the unrepentant) with unquenchable fire."

¹⁸So with many other appeals *and* various admonitions John preached the good news (gospel) to the people.

¹⁹But when Herod [Antipas] the tetrarch was *repeatedly* reprimanded [and convicted by John's disapproval] for having Herodias, his brother's wife [as his own], and for all the wicked

things that Herod had done, [Matt 14:3; Mark 6:17]

²⁰he also added this to them all: he locked up John in prison.

²¹Now when all the people were baptized, Jesus was also baptized, and while He was praying, the [visible] heaven was opened, [Matt 3:13–17; Mark 1:9–11; John 1:32]

²²and the Holy Spirit descended on Him in bodily form like a dove, and a voice came from heaven, "You are My Son, My Beloved, in You I am well-pleased *and* delighted!" [Ps 2:7; Is 42:1]

²³When He began His ministry, Jesus Himself was about thirty years of age, being, as was supposed, the son of Joseph, the son [by marriage] of Eli,

²⁴the son of Matthat, the son of Levi, the son of Melchi, the son of Jannai, the son of Joseph,

²⁵the son of Mattathias, the son of Amos, the son of Nahum, the son of Hesli, the son of Naggai,

²⁶the son of Maath, the son of Mattathias, the son of Semein, the son of Josech, the son of Joda,

²⁷the son of Joanan, the son of Rhesa, the son of Zerubbabel, the son of Shealtiel, the son of Neri,

²⁸the son of Melchi, the son of Addi, the son of Cosam, the son of Elmadam, the son of Er,

²⁹the son of Joshua, the son of Eliezer, the son of Jorim, the son of Matthat, the son of Levi,

³⁰the son of Simeon, the son of Judah, the son of Joseph, the son of Jonam, the son of Eliakim,

³¹the son of Melea, the son of Menna, the son of Mattatha, the son of Nathan, the son of David,

³²the son of Jesse, the son of Obed, the son of Boaz, the son of Salmon, the son of Nahshon,

³³the son of Amminadab, the son of Admin, the son of Ram, the son of Hezron, the son of Perez, the son of Judah,

³⁴the son of Jacob, the son of Isaac, the son of Abraham, the son of Terah, the son of Nahor,

³⁵the son of Serug, the son of Reu, the son of Peleg, the son of Heber, the son of Shelah,

³⁶the son of Cainan, the son of Arphaxad, the son of Shem, the son of Noah, the son of Lamech,

³⁷the son of Methuselah, the son of Enoch, the son of Jared, the son of Mahalaleel, the son of Cainan,

³⁸the son of Enosh, the son of Seth, the son of Adam, the son of God. [Gen 5:3–32; 11:10–26; Ruth 4:18–22; 1 Chr 1:1–4, 24–28; 2:1–15]

4 NOW JESUS, full of [and in perfect communication with] the Holy Spirit, returned from the Jordan and was led by the Spirit in the wilderness [Matt 4:1–11]

²for forty days, being tempted by the devil. And He ate nothing during those days, and when they ended, He was hungry. [Deut 9:9; 1 Kin 19:8]

³Then the devil said to Him, "If You are the Son of God, command this stone to turn into bread."

⁴Jesus replied to him, "It is written *and* forever remains written, 'MAN SHALL NOT LIVE BY BREAD ALONE.'" [Deut 8:3]

⁵Then he led Jesus up [to a high mountain] and displayed before Him all the kingdoms of the inhabited earth [and their magnificence] in the twinkling of an eye.

speak the Word

God, I believe by faith that because I am in Christ,
You say to me as You said to Him: "You are . . . My Beloved,
in You I am well-pleased and delighted!"
—ADAPTED FROM LUKE 3:22

⁶And the devil said to Him, "I will give You all this realm and its glory [its power, its renown]; because it has been handed over to me, and I give it to whomever I wish.

⁷"Therefore if You worship before me, it will all be Yours."

⁸Jesus replied to him, "It is written *and* forever remains written, 'YOU SHALL WORSHIP THE LORD YOUR GOD AND SERVE ONLY HIM.'" [Deut 6:13; 10:20]

⁹Then he led Jesus to Jerusalem and had Him stand on the pinnacle (highest point) of the temple, and said [mockingly] to Him, "If You are the Son of God, throw Yourself down from here;

¹⁰for it is written *and* forever remains written,

'HE WILL COMMAND HIS ANGELS
    CONCERNING YOU TO GUARD *and*
    PROTECT YOU,'

¹¹and,

'THEY WILL LIFT YOU UP ON *their*
    HANDS,
SO THAT YOU DO NOT STRIKE YOUR
    FOOT AGAINST A STONE.'"
    [Ps 91:11, 12]

¹²Jesus replied to him, "It is said [in Scripture], 'YOU SHALL NOT TEMPT THE LORD YOUR GOD [to prove Himself to you].'" [Deut 6:16; Matt 4:7]

¹³When the devil had finished every temptation, he [temporarily] left Him until a more opportune time.

¹⁴Then Jesus went back to Galilee in the power of the Spirit, and the news about Him spread through the entire region.

¹⁵And He *began* teaching in their synagogues and was praised *and* glorified *and* honored by all.

¹⁶So He came to Nazareth, where He had been brought up; and as was His custom, He entered the synagogue on the Sabbath, and stood up to read.

¹⁷The scroll of the prophet Isaiah was handed to Him. He unrolled the scroll and found the place where it was written, [Is 61:1, 2]

¹⁸"THE SPIRIT OF THE LORD IS UPON
    ME (the Messiah),
BECAUSE HE HAS ANOINTED ME TO
    PREACH THE GOOD NEWS TO THE
    POOR.
HE HAS SENT ME TO ANNOUNCE
    RELEASE (pardon, forgiveness)
    TO THE CAPTIVES,
AND RECOVERY OF SIGHT TO THE
    BLIND,
TO SET FREE THOSE WHO ARE
    OPPRESSED (downtrodden,
    bruised, crushed by tragedy),

life point

Jesus answered every temptation the devil used against Him with God's Word. Throughout Luke 4:1–12, we read that He repeatedly said, "It is written and forever remains written" and then quoted scriptures that directly addressed the enemy's lies and tempting schemes.

We may start to fight the devil with the Word, but when we do not see quick results, many times we stop speaking the Word and begin talking about our feelings or our circumstances.

Let me encourage you to be persistent as you wage war against the enemy by speaking the Word. A stonecutter may strike a rock ninety-nine times without even making a crack in it. But the hundredth strike may split the rock in two. Each blow weakened the rock, even though there were no outward signs of it.

Persistence is vital to victory in our lives just as it is in the stonecutter's work. Do not relent in speaking the Word against the enemy. The next time you do, it may deal him a deathblow!

[19] TO PROCLAIM THE FAVORABLE YEAR OF THE LORD [the day when salvation and the favor of God abound greatly]." [Is 61:1, 2]

[20] Then He rolled up the scroll [having stopped in the middle of the verse], gave it back to the attendant and sat down [to teach]; and the eyes of all those in the synagogue were [attentively] fixed on Him.

[21] He began speaking to them: "Today this Scripture has been fulfilled in your hearing *and* in your presence."

[22] And [as He continued on] they all were speaking well of Him, and were in awe *and* were wondering about the words of grace which were coming from His lips; and they were saying, "Is this not Joseph's son?"

[23] So He said to them, "You will no doubt quote this proverb to Me, 'Physician, heal Yourself! Whatever [miracles] that we heard were done [by You] in Capernaum, do here in Your hometown as well.'"

[24] Then He said, "I assure you *and* most solemnly say to you, no prophet is welcome in his hometown.

[25] "But in truth I say to you, there were many widows in Israel in the days of Elijah, when the sky was closed up for three years and six months, when a great famine came over all the land;

[26] and yet Elijah was not sent [by the Lord] to a single one of them, but only to Zarephath *in the land* of Sidon, to a woman who was a widow. [1 Kin 17:1, 8–16; 18:1]

[27] "And there were many lepers in Israel in the time of Elisha the prophet; and not one of them was cleansed [by being healed] except Naaman the Syrian." [2 Kin 5:1–14]

[28] As they heard these things [about God's grace to these two Gentiles], *the people* in the synagogue were filled with a great rage;

[29] and they got up and drove Him out of the city, and led Him to the crest of the hill on which their city had been built, in order to hurl Him down the cliff.

[30] But passing [miraculously] through the crowd, He went on His way.

[31] Then He came down [from the hills of Nazareth] to Capernaum, a city of Galilee [on the shore of the sea], and He was teaching them on the Sabbath; [Mark 1:21–28]

[32] and they were surprised [almost overwhelmed] at His teaching, because His message was [given] with authority *and* power *and* great ability.

[33] There was a man in the synagogue who was possessed by the spirit of an unclean demon; and he cried out with a loud *and* terrible voice,

[34] "Let us alone! What business do we have [in common] with each other, Jesus of Nazareth? Have You come to destroy us? I know who You are—the Holy One of God!"

[35] But Jesus rebuked him, saying, "Be silent (muzzled, gagged) and come out of him!" And when the demon had thrown the man down among them, he came out of him without injuring him in any way.

[36] They were all astonished *and* in awe, and *began* saying to one another, "What is this message? For with authority and power He commands the unclean spirits and they come out!"

[37] And the news about Him spread into every place in the surrounding district (Galilee).

[38] Then Jesus got up and left the synagogue and went to Simon's (Peter's) house. Now Simon's mother-in-law was suffering from a high fever, and they asked Him to help her. [Matt 8:14–17; Mark 1:29–34]

[39] Standing over her, He rebuked the fever, and it left her; and immediately she got up and *began* serving them [as her guests].

[40] While the sun was setting [marking the end of the Sabbath day], all those

who had any *who were* sick with various diseases brought them to Jesus; and laying His hands on each one of them, He was healing them [exhibiting His authority as Messiah]. [Matt 8:16, 17; Mark 1:32–34]

⁴¹Demons also were coming out of many people, shouting, "You are the Son of God!" But He rebuked them and would not allow them to speak, because they knew that He was the Christ (the Messiah, the Anointed).

⁴²When daybreak came, Jesus left [Simon Peter's house] and went to a secluded place; and the crowds were searching for Him, and [they] came to Him and tried to keep Him from leaving them.

⁴³But He said, "I must preach [the good news of] the kingdom of God to the other cities also, because I was sent for this purpose."

⁴⁴So He continued preaching in the synagogues of Judea [the country of the Jews, including Galilee].

5 NOW IT happened that while Jesus was standing by the Lake of Gennesaret (Sea of Galilee), with the people crowding all around Him and listening to the word of God;

²that He saw two boats lying at the edge of the lake, but the fishermen had gotten out of them and were washing their nets.

³He got into one of the boats, which was Simon's, and asked him to put out a little distance from the shore. And He sat down and *began* teaching the crowds from the boat.

⁴When He had finished speaking, He said to Simon [Peter], "Put out into the deep water and lower your nets for a catch [of fish]."

⁵Simon replied, "Master, we worked hard all night [to the point of exhaustion] and caught nothing [in our nets], but at Your word I will [do as you say and] lower the nets [again]."

⁶When they had done this, they caught a great number of fish, and their nets were [at the point of] breaking;

⁷so they signaled to their partners in the other boat to come and help them. And they came and filled both of the boats [with fish], so that they began to sink.

⁸But when Simon Peter saw this, he fell down at Jesus' knees, saying, "Go away from me, for I am a sinful man, O Lord!"

⁹For he and all his companions were completely astounded at the catch of fish which they had taken;

¹⁰and so were James and John, sons of Zebedee, who were partners with Simon [Peter]. Jesus said to Simon, "Have no fear; from now on you will be catching men!"

¹¹After they had brought their boats to land, they left everything and followed Him [becoming His disciples, believing and trusting in Him and following His example].

¹²While Jesus was in one of the cities, there came a man covered with [an advanced case of] leprosy; and when he saw Jesus, he fell on his face and begged Him, saying, "Lord, if You are willing, You can make me clean *and* well." [Matt 8:2–4; Mark 1:40–44]

¹³And Jesus reached out His hand and touched him, saying, "I am willing; be cleansed." And immediately the leprosy left him.

¹⁴Jesus ordered him to tell no one [that he might happen to meet], "But go and show yourself to the priest, and make an offering for your purification, just as Moses commanded, as a testimony (witness) to them [that this is a work of Messiah]." [Lev 13:49; 14:2–32]

¹⁵But the news about Him was spreading farther, and large crowds kept gathering to hear Him and to be healed of their illnesses.

¹⁶But Jesus Himself would often slip

away to the wilderness and pray [in seclusion].

17One day as He was teaching, there were Pharisees and teachers of the Law sitting there who had come from every village of Galilee and Judea and from Jerusalem. And the power of the Lord was *present* with Him to heal.

18*Some* men came carrying on a stretcher a man who was paralyzed, and they tried to bring him in and lay him down in front of Jesus. [Matt 9:2–8; Mark 2:3–12]

19But finding no way to bring him in because of the crowd, they went up on the roof [and removed some tiles to make an opening] and lowered him through the tiles with his stretcher, into the middle *of the crowd,* in front of Jesus.

20When Jesus saw their [active] faith [springing from confidence in Him], He said, "Man, your sins are forgiven."

21The scribes and the Pharisees began to consider *and* question [the implications of what He had said], saying, "Who is this man who speaks blasphemies [by claiming the rights and prerogatives of God]? Who can forgive sins [that is, remove guilt, nullify sin's

step out and find out

The only way we ever fulfill our destinies and succeed at being our true selves is to take many, many steps of faith. Stepping out into the unknown and launching out into the deep water, as we read about in Luke 5:4, can be frightening.

Because of feelings of fear, many people never *step out*; therefore they never *find out* what they are capable of.

Each of us needs to obey God when He wants us to step out into something new or challenging. We are living in the dispensation of grace and many doors of opportunity are open to share the gospel of Jesus Christ with others. Make the decision that you will not miss any opportunity God gives you. Do what God asks you to do even if you must "do it afraid." Feel the fear and do it anyway!

Many people miss God's will for their lives because they play it safe. I do not want to come to the end of my life and say, "I was safe, but I am sorry."

"Better safe than sorry" does not always work in God's economy. If I tried to be safe all the time, I am sure I would not be where I am today. I would never have sown the seeds of obedience that produced the harvest I now enjoy in my ministry and in many other areas of my life. Nothing feels better than knowing you are in the will of God—and nothing feels worse than knowing you are not.

I am not suggesting we all start doing things that are unwise, but I know for a fact that not everything God wants us to do makes sense to the natural mind. You and I must learn to be led by discernment in the inner man (the spirit) and not by our own carnal minds or by what other people suggest to us. When we step out, we should do all we can do to be sure we respond in faith and obedience to God's leadership—and not act on some wild thought we have or on a lie that Satan uses to lure us into destruction. I encourage you to be willing to go into deep waters for God. Ask Him to make clear what He wants you to do and then obey.

penalty, and assign righteousness] except God alone?"

²²But Jesus, knowing their [hostile] thoughts, answered them, "Why are you questioning [these things] in your hearts?

²³"Which is easier, to say, 'Your sins are forgiven you,' or to say, 'Get up and walk'?

²⁴"But, in order that you may know that the Son of Man (the Messiah) has authority *and* power on earth to forgive sins"—He said to the paralyzed man, "I say to you, get up, pick up your stretcher and go home."

²⁵He immediately stood up before them, picked up his stretcher, and went home glorifying *and* praising God.

²⁶They were all astonished, and they *began* glorifying God; and they were filled with [reverential] fear and kept saying, "We have seen wonderful *and* incredible things today!"

²⁷After this Jesus went out and noticed a tax collector named Levi (Matthew) sitting at the tax booth; and He said to him, "Follow Me [as My disciple, accepting Me as your Master and Teacher and walking the same path of life that I walk]." [Matt 9:9–17; Mark 2:14–22]

²⁸And he left everything behind and got up and *began* to follow Jesus [as His disciple].

²⁹Levi (Matthew) gave a great banquet for Him at his house; and there was a large crowd of tax collectors and others who were reclining *at the table* with them.

³⁰The Pharisees and their scribes

life point

Jesus made sure He had seasons of peace and time alone (see Luke 5:15, 16). He ministered to the people, but He slipped away regularly from the crowds to be alone and pray. Surely if Jesus needed this type of lifestyle, we do also.

[seeing those with whom He was associating] *began* murmuring in discontent to His disciples, asking, "Why are you eating and drinking with the tax collectors and sinners [including non-observant Jews]?"

³¹And Jesus replied to them, "It is not those who are healthy who need a physician, but [only] those who are sick.

³²"I did not come to call the [self-proclaimed] righteous [who see no need to repent], but sinners to repentance [to change their old way of thinking, to turn from sin and to seek God and His righteousness]."

³³Then they said to Him, "The disciples of John [the Baptist] often practice fasting and offer prayers [of special petition], and so do the *disciples* of the Pharisees; but Yours eat and drink."

³⁴Jesus said to them, "Can you make the wedding guests of the bridegroom fast while he is with them?

³⁵"But days [for mourning] will come when the bridegroom is [forcefully] taken away from them. They will fast in those days."

³⁶He also told them a parable: "No one tears a piece of cloth from a new garment and puts it on an old one; otherwise he will both tear the new, and the piece from the new will not match the old.

³⁷"And no one puts new wine into old wineskins; otherwise the new [fermenting] wine will [expand and] burst the skins and it will be spilled out, and the skins will be ruined.

³⁸"But new wine must be put into fresh wineskins.

³⁹"And no one, after drinking old *wine,* wishes for new; for he says, 'The old is fine.'"

6 ONE SABBATH while Jesus was passing through fields of standing grain, it happened that His disciples were picking the heads of grain, rubbing them in their hands, and eating them. [Deut 23:25; Matt 12:1–8; Mark 2:23–28]

²But some of the Pharisees said, "Why are you doing what is unlawful on the Sabbath?" [Ex 20:10; 23:12; Deut 5:14]

³Jesus replied to them, "Have you not even read [in the Scriptures] what David did when he was hungry, he and those who were with him— [1 Sam 21:1–6]

⁴how he went into the house of God, and took and ate the *consecrated bread, which is not lawful [for anyone] to eat except the priests alone, and [how he also] gave it to the men who were with him?" [Lev 24:9]

⁵Jesus was saying to them, "The Son of Man (the Messiah) is Lord [even] of the Sabbath."

⁶On another Sabbath He went into the synagogue and taught, and a man was present whose right hand was withered. [Matt 12:9–14; Mark 3:1–6]

give Jesus all you are not

If you are needy, you are just the person that Jesus died for (see Luke 5:31). Often we feel we must hide our weaknesses and pretend we are strong and in need of nothing, but that attitude only closes the door to God's help. He said, "Ask and keep on asking, and it will be given to you" (see Luke 11:9). Do not be ashamed of yourself or your needs.

I suggest that when people receive Jesus Christ as their Savior, they give Him not only all they are, but especially all they are not. We try to impress God and other people with what we are while we hide what we are not. I do not believe people can become all God wants them to be until they face what they are not and no longer have a problem with it.

I am a teacher, but I am not a singer, or a musician. I tried for a period of time to learn to play the guitar and sing, but I simply did not have the ability. I struggled and wasted time—precious time I could have spent developing the gift of teaching that I do have. Many people never fulfill their God-ordained destinies because they keep trying to be something or somebody they were never meant to be. All God wants us to be is who we are!

We do not have to compare ourselves with others or compete with them. We *all* have weaknesses and inabilities. Satan would like for you to think you are the only one with the problem or weakness you have, but that simply is not true. If we were all perfect, Jesus would not have needed to come to earth. According to Luke 5:31, He came for those who were sick (needy) not those who were healthy (not needy).

When the Apostle Paul finally saw this truth, he stopped struggling with his weaknesses and said he would "all the more gladly boast" in them from that point on (2 Corinthians 12:7–10). God's strength is made perfect in our weaknesses. Whatever we are not, He is, and He is what He is, for us.

Go ahead and be needy. Tell God everything you need. He already knows anyway and is waiting for you to ask for help.

6:4 Or *showbread;* lit *bread of presentation.*

[7]The scribes and the Pharisees were watching Him closely [with malicious intent], to see if He would [actually] heal [someone] on the Sabbath, so that they might find *a reason* to accuse Him.

[8]But He was aware of their thoughts, and He said to the man with the withered hand, "Get up and come forward." So he got up and stood *there*.

[9]Then Jesus said to them, "I ask you directly: Is it lawful to do good on the Sabbath or to do evil, to save a life or to destroy it?"

[10]After looking around at them all, He said to the man, "Stretch out your hand!" And he did, and his hand was [fully] restored.

[11]But the scribes and Pharisees were filled with senseless rage [and lacked spiritual insight], and discussed with one another what they might do to Jesus.

[12]Now at this time Jesus went off to the mountain to pray, and He spent the whole night in prayer to God.

[13]When day came, He called His disciples and selected twelve of them, whom He also named apostles (special messengers, personally chosen representatives): [Matt 10:2–4; Mark 3:16–19]

[14]Simon, whom He also named Peter, and his brother Andrew; and [the brothers] James and John; and Philip, and Bartholomew [also called Nathanael];

[15]and Matthew (Levi, the tax collector) and Thomas; and James *the son* of Alphaeus, and Simon who was called the Zealot;

[16]Judas [also called Thaddaeus] *the son* of James, and Judas Iscariot, who became a traitor [to the Lord].

[17]Then Jesus came down with them and stood on a level place; and *there was* a large crowd of His disciples, and a vast multitude of people from all over Judea and Jerusalem and the coastal region of Tyre and Sidon,

[18]who had come to listen to Him and to be healed of their diseases. Even those who were troubled by unclean spirits (demons) were being healed.

[19]All the people were trying to touch Him, because [healing] power was coming from Him and healing them all.

[20]And looking toward His disciples, He began speaking: "Blessed [spiritually prosperous, happy, to be admired] are you *who are* poor [in spirit, those devoid of spiritual arrogance, those who regard themselves as insignificant], for the kingdom of God is yours [both now and forever]. [Matt 5:3–12]

[21]"Blessed [joyful, nourished by God's goodness] are you who hunger now [for righteousness, actively seeking right standing with God], for you will be [completely] satisfied. Blessed [forgiven, refreshed by God's grace] are you who weep now [over your sins and repent], for you will laugh [when the burden of sin is lifted].

[22]"Blessed [morally courageous and spiritually alive with life-joy in God's goodness] are you when people hate you, and exclude you [from their fellowship], and insult you, and scorn your name as evil because of [your association with] the Son of Man.

[23]"Rejoice on that day and leap for joy, for your reward in heaven is great [absolutely inexhaustible]; for their fathers used to treat the prophets in the same way.

[24]"But woe (judgment is coming) to you who are rich [and place your faith in possessions while remaining spiritually impoverished], for you are [already] receiving your comfort in full [and there is nothing left to be awarded to you].

[25]"Woe to you who are well-fed (gorged, satiated) now, for you will be hungry. Woe *to you* who laugh now [enjoying a life of self-indulgence], for you will mourn and weep [and deeply long for God].

²⁶"Woe *to you* when all the people speak well of you *and* praise you, for their fathers used to treat the false prophets in the same way.

²⁷"But I say to you who hear [Me and pay attention to My words]: Love [that is, unselfishly seek the best or higher good for] your enemies, [make it a practice to] do good to those who hate you,

further than forgiveness

Luke 6:27, 28 teaches us how to deal with our enemies. Something is missing when we say we forgive those who have hurt or offended us, and then go no further.

Let me share with you a lesson I learned from ministering on the subject of forgiveness. I once asked the Lord, "Father, why is it that people come to our meetings and pray for the ability to forgive, and yet in just a short time they are right back again still having the same problems with being bitter, angry, and offended, and asking for help?"

The first thing the Lord told me is that these types of people are not doing what He instructs in His Word.

You see, though God tells us in His Word to *forgive* others, He does not stop there. He goes on to instruct us to *bless* them. In this context, the word *bless* means "to speak well of." So one of our problems is that even though we pray and try to forgive those who offend us, we turn right around and curse them with our tongues or we rehash the offense again and again with others.

This will not work!

To work through the process of forgiveness and enjoy the peace we seek, we must do what God tells us to do, which is not only to forgive but also to bless.

One reason we find it so hard to pray for those who hurt us and mistreat us is that we tend to think we are asking God to bless them physically or materially. The truth is that we are not praying for them to make more money or have more possessions; we are praying for them to be blessed spiritually. What we are doing is asking God to bring them truth and revelation about their attitude and behavior so they will be willing to repent and be free from their sins.

It is not enough to merely say we forgive others; we also need to be careful not to curse them or speak evil of them, even if we think they deserve it. Instead, we must do as Jesus did and pray for them, bless them, and speak well of them. Why? Because by doing so, we bless not only them, but ourselves too. Hating those who hurt you is like taking poison and hoping your enemy will die. Obviously, anyone who did that would only be hurting himself. Why spend your life angry with people who probably do not even know or care that you are angry? These people are thoroughly enjoying their lives while you are miserable. Release them, let the offense go, drop it, and have the same attitude toward them that Jesus had toward His enemies. By doing this, you will experience wonderful freedom and God will show Himself strong as your Vindicator.

[28]bless *and* show kindness to those who curse you, pray for those who mistreat you.

[29]"Whoever strikes you on the cheek, offer him the other one also [simply ignore insignificant insults or losses and do not bother to retaliate—maintain your dignity]. Whoever takes away your coat, do not withhold your shirt from him either. [Matt 5:39–42]

[30]"Give to everyone who asks of you. Whoever takes away what is yours, do not demand it back.

[31]"Treat others the same way you want them to treat you.

[32]"If you [only] love those who love you, what credit is that to you? For even sinners love those who love them.

[33]"If you do good to those who do good to you, what credit is that to you? For even sinners do the same.

[34]"If you lend [money] to those from whom you expect to receive [it back], what credit is that to you? Even sinners lend to sinners expecting to receive back the same *amount.*

[35]"But love [that is, unselfishly seek the best or higher good for] your enemies, and do good, and lend, expecting nothing in return; for your reward will be great (rich, abundant), and you will be sons of the Most High; because He Himself is kind *and* gracious *and* good to the ungrateful and the wicked.

[36]"Be merciful (responsive, compassionate, tender) just as your [heavenly] Father is merciful.

[37]"Do not judge [others self-righteously], and you will not be judged; do not condemn [others when you are guilty and unrepentant], and you will not be condemned [for your hypocrisy]; pardon [others when they truly repent and change], and you will

speak the Word

life point

The blind cannot lead the blind—if they try to do so, they will both fall into a hole in the ground (see Luke 6:39). Think of it another way: trying to help others while ignoring our own problems never helps anyone.

be pardoned [when you truly repent and change]. [Matt 7:1–5]

[38]"Give, and it will be given to you. They will pour into your lap a good measure—pressed down, shaken together, and running over [with no space left for more]. For with the standard of measurement you use [when you do good to others], it will be measured to you in return."

[39]He also told them a parable: "Can a blind man guide [another] blind man? Will they not both fall into a hole in the ground?

[40]"A student is not superior to his teacher; but everyone, after he has been completely trained, will be like his teacher.

[41]"Why do you look at the speck that is in your brother's eye, but do not notice *or* consider the log that is in your own eye?

[42]"How can you say to your brother, 'Brother, allow me to take out the speck that is in your eye,' when you yourself do not see the log that is in your own eye? You hypocrite (play actor, pretender), first take the log out of your own eye, and then you will see clearly to take out the speck that is in your brother's eye.

[43]"For there is no good tree which produces bad fruit, nor, on the other hand, a bad tree which produces good fruit. [Matt 7:16, 18]

Help me, God, to be merciful—responsive, compassionate, and tender—to others, just as You are all of these to me.
—ADAPTED FROM LUKE 6:36

putting the Word to work

Luke 6:43–45 teaches us that our actions reflect what is in our hearts. Does any of your behavior indicate a need for a change in your heart? Ask God to continue to transform you more and more into His image, so your actions will reflect His work and His presence in your heart.

⁴⁴"For each tree is known *and* identified by its own fruit. For figs are not picked from thorn bushes, nor is a cluster of grapes picked from a briar bush.
⁴⁵"The [intrinsically] good man produces what is good *and* honorable *and* moral out of the good treasure [stored] in his heart; and the [intrinsically] evil *man* produces what is wicked *and* depraved out of the evil [in his heart]; for his mouth speaks from the overflow of his heart.
⁴⁶"Why do you call Me, 'Lord, Lord,' and do not practice what I tell you?
⁴⁷"Everyone who comes to Me and listens to My words and obeys them, I will show you whom he is like: [Matt 7:24–27]
⁴⁸he is like a [far-sighted, practical, and sensible] man building a house, who dug deep and laid a foundation on the rock; and when a flood occurred, the torrent burst against that house and yet could not shake it, because it had been securely built *and* founded on the rock.
⁴⁹"But the one who has [merely] heard and has not practiced [what I say], is like a [foolish] man who built a house on the ground without *any* foundation,

the root of unhealthy attitudes

Jesus said that every tree is known and identified by its fruit (see Luke 6:44). Imagine looking at a fruit tree that depicts all the bad things produced in the life of someone who is unhealthy emotionally. If you look at the roots of that person's life you will see things like rejection, abuse, guilt, negativism, shame, and others.

If you have a problem with unhealthy attitudes in your life, they are the bitter fruit of what has rooted into your thinking. You may be the product of improper mirroring and imaging of your parents and others. You may suffer from bad examples to which you were exposed in your earlier years.

If parents, teachers, or other authority figures told you over and over during your youth that you were no good, that there was something wrong with you, that you could not do anything right, that you were worthless and would never amount to anything, you may actually believe it. Satan reinforces that message by repeating it in your mind again and again until it becomes such a part of your self-image that you actually become on the outside what you envision yourself to be on the inside.

It has been proven that if people believe something about themselves strongly enough, they will actually begin to behave as they perceive themselves. But I have good news: Your mind can be renewed by the Word of God (see Romans 12:2). This does not happen instantly, but it is possible with the help of the Holy Spirit. God wants you to bear good fruit, and He will help you do so by replacing bad roots with good roots as you meditate on His Word. Jesus invites us to be rooted and grounded in Him and in His love (see Ephesians 3:17; Colossians 2:7).

and the torrent burst against it; and it immediately collapsed, and the ruin of that house was great."

putting the Word to work

What do you think is the most important part of a house? It's the foundation, of course, as we learn from Luke 6:47–49. Without a firm foundation, a house is constantly in danger of collapsing. The same is true in your life as a Christian. Knowing God's Word and obeying it is the foundation of the Christian life. Ask God to teach you His Word and to obey Him in every area of your life so you can stand strong in all circumstances.

7 AFTER HE had finished all that He had to say in the hearing of the people, He went to Capernaum. [Matt 8:5–13]

²Now a [Roman] centurion's slave, who was highly regarded by him, was sick and on the verge of death.

³When the centurion heard about Jesus, he sent some Jewish elders to Him, asking Him to come and save the life of his slave.

⁴When they reached Jesus, they pleaded with Him earnestly [to come], saying, "He is worthy for You to do this for him,

⁵because he loves our nation and he built us our synagogue [at his own expense]."

⁶And Jesus went with them. But when He was near the house, the centurion sent friends to Him, saying, "Lord, do not trouble Yourself further, for I am not worthy for You to come under my roof.

⁷"Therefore I did not even consider myself worthy to come to You. But just speak a word, and my slave will be healed.

⁸"For I also am a man subject to authority, with soldiers under me; and I say to this one, 'Go,' and he goes, and to another, 'Come,' and he comes, and to my slave, 'Do this,' and he does it."

⁹Now when Jesus heard this, He was amazed at him, and turned and said to the crowd that was following Him, "I say to you, not even in Israel have I found such great faith [as this man's]."

¹⁰When the messengers who had been sent returned to the house, they found the slave in good health.

¹¹Soon afterward Jesus went to a city called Nain [near Nazareth], and His disciples and a large crowd accompanied Him.

¹²Now as He approached the city gate, a dead man was being carried out—the only son of his mother, and she was a widow. And a large crowd from the city was with her [in the funeral procession].

¹³When the Lord saw her, He felt [great] compassion for her, and said to her, "Do not weep."

¹⁴And He came up and touched the bier [on which the body rested], and the pallbearers stood still. And He said, "Young man, I say to you, arise [from death]!"

¹⁵The man who was dead sat up and began to speak. And *Jesus* gave him back to his mother.

¹⁶Fear *and* profound awe gripped them all, and they *began* glorifying *and* honoring *and* praising God, saying, "A great prophet has arisen among us!" and, "God has visited His people [to help and care for and provide for them]!"

¹⁷This news about Him spread through all of Judea and in all the surrounding countryside. [1 Kin 17:17–24; 2 Kin 4:32–37]

¹⁸John's disciples brought word to him [in prison] of all these things. [Matt 11:2–19]

¹⁹John called two of his disciples and

sent them to the Lord, saying, "Are You the Expected One (the Messiah), or should we look for someone else?"

²⁰So the men came to Jesus and said, "John the Baptist sent us to You to ask, 'Are You the Expected One (the Messiah), or should we look for someone else?'"

²¹At that very hour Jesus healed many *people* of sicknesses and infirmities and evil spirits; and He gave [the gracious gift of] sight to many *who were* blind.

²²So He replied to them, "Go and tell John about everything you have seen and heard: the BLIND RECEIVE SIGHT, the lame walk, the lepers are cleansed, the deaf hear, the dead are raised up, and the POOR HAVE THE GOOD NEWS (gospel) PREACHED TO THEM. [Is 29:18, 19; 35:5, 6; 61:1]

²³"Blessed [joyful, spiritually favored] is he who does not take offense at Me."

²⁴When John's messengers left, Jesus began speaking to the crowds about John: "What did you go out to the wilderness to see? A reed shaken by the wind?

²⁵"But what did you go out to see? A man dressed in soft clothing [entirely unsuited for the harsh wilderness]? Those who wear splendid clothing and live in luxury are in royal palaces!

²⁶"But what did you [really] go out to see? A prophet? Yes, I say to you, and one far more [eminent and remarkable] than a prophet [who foretells the future].

²⁷"This is the one of whom it is written [by the prophet Malachi],

'BEHOLD, I SEND MY MESSENGER
    AHEAD OF YOU,
WHO WILL PREPARE YOUR WAY
    BEFORE YOU.' [Mal 3:1]

²⁸"I tell you, among those born of women there is no one greater than John; yet he who is least in the kingdom of God is greater [in privilege] than he."

²⁹All the people and the tax collectors who heard Jesus, acknowledged [the validity of] God's justice, having been baptized with the baptism of John.

³⁰But the Pharisees and the lawyers [who were experts in the Mosaic Law] annulled *and* set aside God's purpose for themselves, not having been baptized by John.

³¹"To what then shall I compare the people of this generation [who set aside God's plan], and what are they like?

³²"They are like children sitting in the market place and calling to one another, and saying, 'We played the flute for you [pretending to be at a wedding], and you did not dance; we sang a dirge [pretending to be at a funeral], and you did not weep [so nothing we did appealed to you].'

³³"For John the Baptist has come neither eating bread nor drinking wine, and you say, 'He has a demon!'

³⁴"The Son of Man has come eating and drinking, and you say, 'Look, a man who is a glutton and a [heavy] wine-drinker, a friend of tax collectors and sinners [including non-observant Jews].'

³⁵"Yet wisdom is vindicated *and* shown to be right by all her children [by the lifestyle, moral character, and good deeds of her followers]."

³⁶One of the Pharisees asked Jesus to eat with him, and He went into the Pharisee's house [in the region of Galilee] and reclined *at the table*.

³⁷Now there was a woman in the city who was [known as] a sinner; and when she found out that He was reclining *at the table* in the Pharisee's house, she brought an alabaster vial of perfume;

³⁸and standing behind Him at His feet, weeping, she began wetting His

feet with her tears, and wiped them with the hair of her head, and [respectfully] kissed His feet [as an act signifying both affection and submission] and anointed them with the perfume.

³⁹Now when [Simon] the Pharisee who had invited Him saw this, he said to himself, "If this Man were a prophet He would know who and what sort of woman this is who is touching Him, that she is a [notorious] sinner [an outcast, devoted to sin]."

⁴⁰Jesus, answering, said to the Pharisee, "Simon, I have something to say to you." And he replied, "Teacher, say it."

⁴¹"A certain moneylender had two debtors: one owed him five hundred denarii, and the other fifty.

⁴²"When they had no means of repaying [the debts], he freely forgave them both. So which of them will love him more?"

⁴³Simon answered, "The one, I take it, for whom he forgave more." Jesus said to him, "You have decided correctly."

⁴⁴Then turning toward the woman, He said to Simon, "Do you see this woman? I came into your house [but you failed to extend to Me the usual courtesies shown to a guest]; you gave Me no water for My feet, but she has wet My feet with her tears and wiped them with her hair [demonstrating her love].

⁴⁵"You gave Me no [welcoming] kiss, but from the moment I came in, she has not ceased to kiss My feet.

⁴⁶"You did not [even] anoint My head with [ordinary] oil, but she has anointed My feet with [costly and rare] perfume.

a woman with a past

The woman mentioned in Luke 7:37 was a woman with a past. She sold her love by the hour; she was a prostitute. The Pharisee called her "a [notorious] sinner" (Luke 7:39). I believe her presence in the Bible and in Jesus' life shows us that God does not always call people with wonderful pasts to serve Him, but He does call them to a powerful, blessed future. Just because you did not have a good beginning in life does not mean you cannot have a great finish.

In Luke 7:38, we see the account of the woman anointing Jesus' feet with a bottle of very expensive perfume, washing them with her tears, and drying them with her hair. Since she was a prostitute, the perfume was probably either a gift from one of her clients or purchased with money she earned from her profession. Other people probably viewed her act of love as erotic because of her past, but Jesus knew it was an act of pure love.

When we have an unpleasant past, people often misjudge our actions, and we find ourselves caught up in the approval game, trying to convince others that we are acceptable. People do not forget our past as easily as God does. The Pharisee could not understand why Jesus allowed the woman to even touch Him (see Luke 7:39). But Jesus responded to this by saying those who have been forgiven much will love much (see Luke 7:47).

This woman knew her past well; she loved Jesus greatly because He forgave her greatly for her sins. She wanted to give Him the most expensive thing she owned; she wanted to serve Him. He saw her heart, not her past. This is what He sees in you too.

⁴⁷"Therefore I say to you, her sins, which are many, are forgiven, for she loved much; but he who is forgiven little, loves little."

⁴⁸Then He said to her, "Your sins are forgiven."

⁴⁹Those who were reclining *at the table* with Him began saying among themselves, "Who is this who even forgives sins?"

⁵⁰Jesus said to the woman, "Your faith [in Me] has saved you; go in peace [free from the distress experienced because of sin]."

8 SOON AFTERWARD, Jesus *began* going around from one city and village to another, preaching and proclaiming *the good news of* the kingdom of God. The twelve [disciples] were with Him,

²and *also* some women who had been healed of evil spirits and diseases: Mary, called Magdalene [from the city of Magdala in Galilee], from whom seven demons had come out,

³and Joanna, the wife of Chuza, Herod's household steward, and Susanna, and many others who were contributing to their support out of their private means [as was the custom for a rabbi's disciples].

⁴When a large crowd was gathering together, and people from city after city were coming to Him, He spoke [to them] using a parable: [Matt 13:2–9; Mark 4:1–9]

⁵"The sower went out to sow his seed; and as he sowed, some fell beside the road and it was trampled underfoot, and the birds of the sky ate it up.

⁶"And some *seed* fell on [shallow soil covering] the rocks, and as soon as it sprouted, it withered away, because it had no moisture.

⁷"Other *seed* fell among the thorns, and the thorns grew up with it and choked it out.

⁸"And some fell into good soil, and grew up and produced a crop a hundred times as great." As He said these things, He called out, "He who has ears to hear, let him hear *and* heed My words."

⁹Now His disciples *began* asking Him what this parable meant.

¹⁰And He said, "To you [who have been chosen] it has been granted to know *and* recognize the mysteries of the kingdom of God, but to the rest it is in parables, so that *though* SEEING THEY MAY NOT SEE, AND HEARING THEY MAY NOT UNDERSTAND. [Is 6:9, 10; Jer 5:21; Ezek 12:2]

¹¹"Now [the meaning of] the parable is this: The seed is the word of God [concerning eternal salvation].

¹²"Those beside the road are the people who have heard; then the devil comes and takes the message [of God] away from their hearts, so that they will not believe [in Me as the Messiah] and be saved.

¹³"Those on the rocky *soil are* the people who, when they hear, receive *and* welcome the word with joy; but these have no *firmly grounded* root. They believe for a while, and in time of trial *and* temptation they fall away [from Me and abandon their faith].

¹⁴"The *seed* which fell among the thorns, these are the ones who have heard, but as they go on their way they are suffocated with the anxieties and riches and pleasures of this life, and they bring no fruit to maturity.

¹⁵"But as for that *seed* in the good soil, these are the ones who have heard the word with a good and noble heart, and hold on to it tightly, and bear fruit with patience.

¹⁶"Now no one lights a lamp and then covers it with a container [to hide it], or puts it under a bed; instead, he puts it on a lampstand, so that those who come in may see the light. [Matt 5:15; Mark 4:21; Luke 11:33]

¹⁷"For there is nothing hidden that

will not become evident, nor *anything* secret that will not be known and come out into the open.

¹⁸"So be careful how you listen; for whoever has [a teachable heart], to him *more* [understanding] will be given; and whoever does not have [a longing for truth], even what he thinks he has will be taken away from him." [Matt 13:12; 25:29; Mark 4:25]

¹⁹Then Jesus' mother and His brothers came up toward Him, but they could not reach Him because of the crowd. [Matt 12:46–50; Mark 3:31–35]

²⁰And He was told, "Your mother and Your brothers are standing outside, asking to see You."

²¹But He answered, "My mother and My brothers are these who listen to the word of God and do it!"

²²Now on one of *those* days Jesus and His disciples got into a boat, and He said to them, "Let us cross over to the other side of the lake (Sea of Galilee)." So they set out. [Matt 8:23–27; Mark 4:36–41]

²³But as they were sailing, He fell asleep. And a fierce gale of wind swept down [as if through a wind tunnel] on the lake, and they *began* to be swamped, and were in great danger.

²⁴They came to Jesus and woke Him, saying, "Master, Master, we are about to die!" He got up and rebuked the wind and the raging, violent waves, and they ceased, and it became calm [a perfect peacefulness].

²⁵And He said to them, "Where is your faith [your confidence in Me]?" They were afraid and astonished, saying to one another, "Who then is this, that He commands even the winds and the sea, and they obey Him?"

²⁶Then they sailed to the country of the Gerasenes, which is east of Galilee. [Matt 8:28–34; Mark 5:1–17]

²⁷Now when Jesus stepped out on land, He was met by a man from the city [of Gerasa] who was possessed with demons. For a long time he had worn no clothes, and was not living in a house, but among the tombs.

²⁸Seeing Jesus, he cried out [with a terrible voice from the depths of his throat] and fell down before Him [in dread and terror], and shouted loudly, "What business do we have [in common] with each other, Jesus, Son of the Most High God? I beg You, do not torment me [before the appointed time of judgment]!"

²⁹Now He was [already] commanding the unclean spirit to come out of the man. For it had seized him [violently] many times; and he was kept under guard and bound with chains and shackles, but he would break the bonds and be driven by the demon into the desert.

³⁰Then Jesus asked him, "What is your name?" And he answered, "Legion"; because many demons had entered him.

³¹They *continually* begged Him not to command them to go into the abyss. [Rev 9:1]

³²Now a large herd of pigs was feeding there on the mountain. *The demons* begged Jesus to allow them to enter the pigs, and He gave them permission.

³³Then the demons came out of the man and entered the pigs; and the herd rushed down the steep bank into the lake and was drowned.

³⁴When the herdsmen saw what had happened, they ran away and told it in the city and out in the country.

³⁵*And people* came out to see what had happened. They came to Jesus, and found the man from whom the demons had gone out, sitting at Jesus' feet, clothed and in his right mind (mentally healthy); and they were frightened.

³⁶Those who had seen it told them how the man who had been demon-possessed had been healed.

³⁷Then all the people of the country

of the Gerasenes and the surrounding district asked Him to leave them, because they were overwhelmed with fear. So Jesus got into the boat and returned [to the west side of the Sea of Galilee].

38But the man from whom the demons had gone out kept begging Him, pleading to go with Him; but Jesus sent him away, saying,

39"Return home and tell [about] all the great things God has done for you." So the man went away, proclaiming throughout the whole city what great things Jesus had done for him.

40Now as Jesus was returning [to Galilee], the people welcomed Him, for they had all been expecting Him.

41Now a man named Jairus, a synagogue official, came [to Him]; and he fell at Jesus' feet and *began* begging Him to come to his house; [Matt 9:18–26; Mark 5:22–43]

42for he had an only daughter, about twelve years old, and she was dying. But as Jesus went, the people were crowding against Him [almost crushing Him].

43And a woman who had [suffered from] a hemorrhage for twelve years [and had spent all her money on physicians], and could not be healed by anyone,

44came up behind Him and touched the fringe of His outer robe, and immediately her bleeding stopped.

45Jesus said, "Who touched Me?" While they all were denying it, Peter [and those who were with him] said, "Master, the people are crowding and pushing against You!"

46But Jesus said, "Someone did touch Me, because I was aware that power [to heal] had gone out of Me."

47When the woman saw that she had not escaped notice, she came up trembling and fell down before Him. She declared in the presence of all the people the reason why she had touched Him, and how she had been immediately healed.

48He said to her, "Daughter, your faith [your personal trust and confidence in Me] has made you well. Go in peace (untroubled, undisturbed well-being)."

49While He was still speaking, someone from the synagogue official's house came and said [to Jairus], "Your daughter is dead; do not inconvenience the Teacher any further."

50But Jesus, hearing this, answered him, "Do not be afraid *any longer*; only believe *and* trust [in Me and have faith in My ability to do this], and she will be made well."

51When He came to the house, He allowed no one to enter with Him, except Peter and John and James, and the girl's father and mother.

52Now they were all weeping loudly and mourning for her; but He said, "Do not weep, for she is not dead, but is sleeping."

53Then they *began* laughing scornfully at Him *and* ridiculing Him, knowing [without any doubt] that she was dead.

54But Jesus took hold of her hand and spoke, saying, "Child, arise!"

55And her spirit returned, and she got up immediately; and He ordered that she be given *something* to eat.

56Her parents were greatly astonished [by the miracle]; but He instructed them to tell no one what had happened.

9 NOW JESUS called together the twelve [disciples] and gave them [the right to exercise] power and authority over all the demons and to heal diseases.

2Then He sent them out [on a brief journey] to preach the kingdom of God and to perform healing. [Matt 10:5]

3And He said to them, "Take nothing for *your* journey [that might encumber you]—neither a walking stick, nor bag, nor bread, nor money; and do not *even* have two tunics apiece.

⁴"Whatever house you enter, stay there until you leave that city [to go to another].

⁵"And as for all those who do not welcome you, when you leave that city, shake the dust off your feet [breaking all ties with them] as a testimony against them [that they rejected My message]."

⁶So they *began* going from village to village, preaching the gospel and healing *the sick* everywhere.

⁷Now Herod [Antipas] the tetrarch [who governed a portion of Palestine including Galilee and Perea] heard about all that was being done [by Jesus], and he was thoroughly perplexed, because it was said by some that John [the Baptist whom he had ordered beheaded] had been raised from the dead, [Matt 14:1, 2]

⁸and by others that Elijah had appeared, and by others that one of the [other] prophets of old had been resurrected.

⁹Herod said, "I personally had John beheaded. Who is this man about whom I hear such things?" And he kept trying to see Jesus.

¹⁰When the apostles returned, they told Him all that they had done. He took them with Him and He privately withdrew [across the Jordan] to a city called Bethsaida. [Matt 14:13–21; Mark 6:32–44; John 6:5–13]

¹¹But when the crowds learned of it, they followed Him; and He welcomed them and He *began* talking to them about the kingdom of God, and healing those who needed to be healed.

¹²Now the day was ending, and the twelve [disciples] came and said to Him, "Send the crowd away, so that they may go into the surrounding villages and countryside and find lodging, and get provisions; because here we are in an isolated place."

¹³But He said to them, "You give them *something* to eat." They said, "We have no more than five loaves and two fish—unless perhaps we go and buy food for all these people." [2 Kin 4:42–44]

¹⁴(For there were about 5,000 men.) And He said to His disciples, "Have them sit down *to eat* in groups of about fifty each."

¹⁵They did so, and had them all sit down.

¹⁶Then He took the five loaves and the two fish, and He looked up to heaven [and gave thanks] and blessed them, and broke *them* and kept giving *them* to the disciples to set before the crowd.

¹⁷They all ate and were [completely] satisfied; and the broken pieces which they had left over were [abundant and were] picked up—twelve baskets full.

¹⁸Now it happened that as Jesus was praying privately, the disciples were with Him, and He asked them, "Who do the crowds say that I am?" [Matt 16:13–16; Mark 8:27–29]

¹⁹They answered, "John the Baptist, and some say, Elijah; but others, that one of the ancient prophets has come back to life."

²⁰And He said to them, "But who do you say that I am?" Peter replied, "The Christ (the Messiah, the Anointed) of God!"

²¹But He strictly warned and admonished them not to tell this to anyone,

²²saying, "The Son of Man must suffer many things and be rejected [as the Messiah] by the elders and chief priests and scribes (Sanhedrin, Jewish High Court), and be put to death, and on the third day be raised up [from death to life]." [Matt 16:21–28; Mark 8:31–9:1]

²³And He was saying to them all, "If anyone wishes to follow Me [as My disciple], he must deny himself [set aside selfish interests], and take up his cross daily [expressing a willingness to endure whatever may come]

and follow Me [believing in Me, conforming to My example in living and, if need be, suffering or perhaps dying because of faith in Me].

²⁴"For whoever wishes to save his life [in this world] will [eventually] lose it [through death], but whoever loses his life [in this world] for My sake, he is the one who will save it [from the consequences of sin and separation from God].

²⁵"For what does it profit a man if he gains the whole world [wealth, fame, success], and loses or forfeits himself?

²⁶"For whoever is ashamed [here and now] of Me and My words, the Son of Man will be ashamed of him when He comes in His glory and *the glory* of the [heavenly] Father and of the holy angels.

²⁷"But I tell you truthfully, there are some among those standing here who will not taste death before they see the kingdom of God."

²⁸Now about eight days after these teachings, He took along Peter and John and James and went up on the mountain to pray. [Matt 17:1–8; Mark 9:2–8]

²⁹As He was praying, the appearance of His face became different [actually transformed], and His clothing *became* white *and* flashing with the brilliance of lightning.

³⁰And behold, two men were talking with Him; and they were Moses and Elijah,

³¹who appeared in glory, and were speaking of His departure [from earthly life], which He was about to bring to fulfillment at Jerusalem.

³²Now Peter and those who were with him had been overcome with sleep; but when they were fully awake, they saw His glory *and* splendor *and* majesty, and the two men who were standing with Him.

³³And as these [men, Moses and Elijah] were leaving Him, Peter said to Jesus, "Master, it is delightful *and* good

for us to be here; we should make three [sacred] tents; one for You, one for Moses, and one for Elijah"—not realizing what he was saying.

³⁴But even as he was saying this, a cloud formed and *began* to overshadow them; and they were [greatly] afraid as they entered the cloud.

³⁵Then a voice came out of the cloud, saying, "This is My beloved Son, My Chosen One; listen *and* obey *and* yield to Him!"

³⁶When the voice had ceased, Jesus was found *there* alone. And they kept silent, and told no one at that time any of the things which they had seen [concerning the divine manifestation]. [2 Pet 1:16–19]

³⁷On the next day, when they came down from the mountain, a large crowd met Him. [Matt 17:14–18; Mark 9:14–27]

³⁸And a man from the crowd shouted for help, "Teacher, I beg You to look at my son, because he is my only child;

³⁹and a spirit seizes him, and suddenly he cries out, and it throws him into a convulsion so that he foams *at the mouth;* and only with [great] difficulty does it leave him, mauling *and* bruising him *as it leaves.*

⁴⁰"I begged Your disciples to cast it out, but they could not."

⁴¹Jesus answered, "You unbelieving and perverted generation! How long shall I be with you and put up with you? Bring your son here [to Me]."

⁴²Even while the boy was coming, the demon slammed him down and threw him into a [violent] convulsion. But Jesus rebuked the unclean spirit, and healed the boy and gave him back to his father.

⁴³They were all amazed [practically overwhelmed] at the [evidence of the] greatness of God *and* His majesty *and* His wondrous work. [Mark 9:30–32]

But while they were still awed by everything Jesus was doing, He said to His disciples,

⁴⁴"Let these words sink into your ears: the Son of Man is going to be betrayed *and* handed over to men [who are His enemies]."

⁴⁵However, they did not understand this statement. Its meaning was kept hidden from them so that they would not grasp it; and they were afraid to ask Him about it.

⁴⁶An argument started among them as to which of them might be the greatest [surpassing the others in esteem and authority]. [Matt 18:1–5; Mark 9:33–37]

⁴⁷But Jesus, knowing what they were thinking in their heart, took a child and had him stand beside Him,

⁴⁸and He told them, "Whoever welcomes this child in My name welcomes Me; and whoever welcomes Me [also] welcomes Him who sent Me; for the one who is least among all of you [that is, the one who is genuinely humble— the one with a realistic self-view]—he is the one who is [truly] great."

⁴⁹John replied, "Master, we saw someone driving out demons in Your name; and we tried to stop him because he does not follow along with us." [Mark 9:38–40]

⁵⁰But Jesus told him, "Do not stop *him;* for he who is not against you is for you." [Matt 12:30]

⁵¹Now when the time was approaching for Him to be taken up [to heaven], He was determined to go to Jerusalem [to fulfill His purpose].

⁵²He sent messengers on ahead of Him, and they went into a Samaritan village to make arrangements for Him;

⁵³but the people would not welcome Him, because He was traveling toward Jerusalem.

⁵⁴When His disciples James and John saw this, they said, "Lord, do You want us to command fire to come down from heaven and destroy them?" [2 Kin 1:9–16]

⁵⁵But He turned and rebuked them

[and He said, "You do not know what kind of spirit you are;

⁵⁶for the Son of Man did not come to destroy men's lives, but to save them."] And they journeyed on to another village.

⁵⁷As they were going along the road, someone said to Him, "I will follow You wherever You go." [Matt 8:19–22]

⁵⁸And Jesus told him, "Foxes have holes and the birds of the air have nests, but the Son of Man has no place to lay His head."

⁵⁹He said to another, "Follow Me [accepting Me as Master and Teacher]." But he said, "Lord, allow me first to go and bury my father." [Matt 8:21, 22]

⁶⁰But He said to him, "Allow the [spiritually] dead to bury their own dead; but as for you, go and spread the news about the kingdom of God."

⁶¹Another also said, "I will follow You, Lord [as Your disciple]; but first let me say goodbye to those at my home."

⁶²But Jesus said to him, "No one who puts his hand to the plow and looks back [to the things left behind] is fit for the kingdom of God."

10 NOW AFTER this the Lord appointed seventy others, and sent them out ahead of Him, two by two, into every city and place where He was about to go.

²He was saying to them, "The harvest is abundant [for there are many who need to hear the good news about salvation], but the workers [those available to proclaim the message of salvation] are few. Therefore, [prayerfully] ask the Lord of the harvest to send out workers into His harvest.

³"Go your way; listen carefully: I am sending you out like lambs among wolves.

⁴"Do not carry a money belt, a provision bag, or [extra] sandals; and do not greet anyone along the way [who would delay you].

5"Whatever house you enter, first say, 'Peace [that is, a blessing of well-being and prosperity, the favor of God] to this house.'

6"And if anyone of peace is there [someone who is sweet-spirited and hospitable], your [blessing of] peace will rest on him; but if not, it will return to you.

7"Stay in that house, eating and

intimacy with Jesus

We know from Luke 10:1 that Jesus appointed at least seventy people to travel ahead of Him to every place He went. We know that He chose twelve disciples to share a deeper level of intimacy with Him than the others, and out of the twelve there were three—Peter, James, and John—He took into situations none of the others shared (see Matthew 17:1, 2). But of these three, who was closest to Jesus? Only John felt comfortable enough to rest his head on Jesus' chest (an act of intimacy) as he listened to the Lord talk at the Passover Feast (see John 13:23). When Jesus was dying on the cross, he told John to take care of His mother. He knew John loved Him enough to do whatever He asked of him.

Jesus had seventy acquaintances, twelve disciples, three close friends, and one who loved Him even more deeply than all the others. Jesus loved them all, and they all loved Jesus, but there were few willing to make the same level of commitment as those who entered into a more intimate relationship with Him.

Not everyone is willing to obey God and pay the price required to be close to Him. Intimacy with God requires an investment of time and not everyone is willing to invest the same amount of it.

God does not ask for all of our time, but He does ask to be kept in first place at all times (see 1 John 5:21). Some people think the only way to be close to God is to do nothing but spiritual things. However, God designed us with a body, a soul, and a spirit; and He expects us to take care of each area of our being. If we keep God first, then everything we do can be *spiritual.* Even something like cooking breakfast can be an act of worship if we do it unto the Lord and for His glory.

However, I believe the main issue of intimacy with God involves how we *prioritize* our time.

We may say we do not have time to seek God, but we take time to do the things that are most important to us. "I am busy" can be an excuse. We all have to fight distractions every day to protect our time to seek God. He is the most important requirement in our lives, so why does He not have that place of importance in our time? Perhaps it is because when we start making a spiritual investment, we want instant gratification. But to seek God means to *continue* craving, pursuing, and going after Him.

We will not experience instant gratification when we seek God. We sow before we reap; we invest before we get a return. In other words, we lose before we gain; we give up time for ourselves before we can experience intimacy with God.

drinking what they provide, for the laborer is worthy of his wages. Do not move from house to house. [Deut 24:15]

⁸"Whenever you go into a city and they welcome you, eat what is set before you;

⁹and heal those in it who are sick

life point

When Jesus sent His followers out two by two to do His kingdom work (see Luke 10:1–11), He said to them, basically, "Go and find a house and say, 'Peace be unto you.' And if your peace settles on that house, then you can stay there. If it does not, shake the dust off your feet and go on" (see Luke 10:5–11; Matthew 10:12–14).

One time God kept leading me to these scriptures, and I did not know what He was trying to get across to me. Then finally I saw it. He was trying to help me understand the same thing that Jesus was saying to His disciples: "I want you to minister with My power and anointing, Joyce, but to do that you need to live in peace."

In Luke 10:5–7, Jesus was essentially saying, "Once you find a peaceful place, it can be your base of operations, and you can go out and come back, go out and come back. If it is not peaceful, you need to do whatever you can to gain and maintain a peaceful atmosphere because strife and confusion adversely affect the anointing and power of God that rest on your life."

Let me encourage you to do all you can do to ensure peace in your "home base." That way, everyone who lives and works from that place will do so in God's power and with His anointing—and they will have success.

[authenticating your message], and say to them, 'The kingdom of God has come near to you.'

¹⁰"But whatever city you enter and they do not welcome you, go out into its streets and say,

¹¹'Even the dust of your city which clings to our feet we wipe off *in protest* against you [breaking all ties]; yet understand this, that the kingdom of God has come near [and you rejected it].'

¹²"I tell you, it will be more bearable in that day [of judgment] for Sodom than for that city. [Gen 19:24–28]

¹³"Woe (judgment is coming) to you, Chorazin! Woe to you, Bethsaida! For if the miracles performed in you had been performed in Tyre and Sidon, they would have repented *and* changed their minds long ago, sitting in sackcloth and ashes [to show deep regret for sin].

¹⁴"However, it will be more tolerable for Tyre and Sidon in the judgment than for you.

¹⁵"And you, Capernaum, will not be exalted to heaven, will you? You will descend to Hades (the realm of the dead).

¹⁶"The one who listens to you listens to Me; and the one who rejects you rejects Me; and the one who rejects Me rejects Him [My heavenly Father] who sent Me."

¹⁷The seventy returned with joy, saying, "Lord, even the demons are subject to us in Your name."

¹⁸He said to them, "I watched Satan fall from heaven like [a flash of] lightning.

¹⁹"Listen carefully: I have given you authority [that you now possess] to tread on serpents and scorpions, and [the ability to exercise authority] over all the power of the enemy (Satan); and nothing will [in any way] harm you.

²⁰"Nevertheless do not rejoice at this, that the spirits are subject to you, but

rejoice that your names are recorded in heaven." [Ex 32:32; Ps 69:28; Dan 12:1; Rev 3:5]

²¹In that very hour He was overjoyed *and* rejoiced greatly in the Holy Spirit, and He said, "I praise You, O Father, Lord of heaven and earth, that You have hidden these things [relating to salvation] from the wise and intelligent, and have revealed them to infants [the childlike and untaught]. Yes, Father, for this way was [Your gracious will and choice, and was] well-pleasing in Your sight.

²²"All things have been transferred *and* turned over to Me by My Father and no one knows who the Son is except the Father, or who the Father is except the Son, and anyone to whom the Son wishes to reveal Him."

²³Then turning to His disciples, Jesus said privately, "Blessed [joyful, spiritually enlightened, and favored by God] are the eyes which see what you see, [Matt 13:16, 17]

²⁴for I say to you that many prophets and kings longed to see what you see, and they did not see it; and to hear what you hear, and did not hear it."

²⁵And a certain lawyer [an expert in Mosaic Law] stood up to test Him, saying, "Teacher, what must I do to inherit eternal life?" [Matt 22:34–40; Mark 12:28–31]

²⁶Jesus said to him, "What is written in the Law? How do you read it?"

²⁷And he replied, "YOU SHALL LOVE THE LORD YOUR GOD WITH ALL YOUR HEART, AND WITH ALL YOUR SOUL, AND WITH ALL YOUR STRENGTH, AND WITH ALL YOUR MIND; AND YOUR NEIGHBOR AS YOURSELF." [Lev 19:18; Deut 6:5]

²⁸Jesus said to him, "You have answered correctly; DO THIS *habitually*

putting the Word to work

When you see people in need, do you know how to help? The parable of the Good Samaritan in Luke 10:30–37 provides some valuable insight. First, it is necessary to draw near to people in difficulty to be able to offer comfort and assess their needs. Second, be aware that you may not be able to meet all of their needs, and that you may need others to help. Pray that God will help you see the needs of those around you and give you wisdom regarding who to help and how best to care for them.

AND YOU WILL LIVE." [Lev 18:5; Ezek 20:11; Matt 19:17]

²⁹But he, wishing to justify *and* vindicate himself, asked Jesus, "And who is my neighbor?"

³⁰Jesus replied, "A man was going down from Jerusalem to Jericho, and he encountered robbers, who stripped him of his clothes [and belongings], beat him, and went their way [unconcerned], leaving him half dead.

³¹"Now by coincidence a priest was going down that road, and when he saw him, he passed by on the other side.

³²"Likewise a Levite also came down to the place and saw him, and passed by on the other side [of the road].

³³"But a Samaritan (foreigner), who was traveling, came upon him; and when he saw him, he was deeply moved with compassion [for him],

³⁴and went to him and bandaged up his wounds, pouring oil and wine on *them* [to sooth and disinfect the injuries]; and he put him on his own

speak the Word

Jesus, help me be like Mary and choose to put anxieties aside, seating myself at Your feet and continually listening to Your teaching.
—ADAPTED FROM LUKE 10:39

pack-animal, and brought him to an inn and took care of him.

³⁵"On the next day he took out two denarii (two days' wages) and gave them to the innkeeper, and said, 'Take care of him; and whatever more you spend, I will repay you when I return.'

³⁶"Which of these three do you think proved himself a neighbor to the man who encountered the robbers?"

³⁷He answered, "The one who showed compassion *and* mercy to him." Then Jesus said to him, "Go and *constantly* do the same."

³⁸Now while they were on their way, Jesus entered a village [called Bethany], and a woman named Martha welcomed Him into her home. [John 11:1]

³⁹She had a sister named Mary, who seated herself at the Lord's feet and was *continually* listening to His teaching.

⁴⁰But Martha was very busy *and* distracted with all of her serving responsibilities; and she approached Him and said, "Lord, is it of no concern to You that my sister has left me to do the serving alone? Tell her to help me *and* do her part."

take time to enjoy Jesus

Are you too busy? It seems almost everyone is these days. Quite often I run into people I have not seen for a long time and when I ask them how they have been they reply, "Busy." I think that is a shame and a problem. Martha was also busy (see Luke 10:40). She was too busy to take time to enjoy Jesus when He came to her home. She was busy working and trying to impress Jesus and everyone else. She wanted everything to be just right and everything was just right—except her motives.

Mary, on the other hand, seized the opportunity to sit at the feet of Jesus and learn (see Luke 10:39). She knew the work would always be there, but Jesus would not. It's vital to spend regular, quality time with God. Do not make the mistake of trying to work Him into your schedule, but make a decision to put Him first and work the rest of your schedule around your time with Him.

Not spending time with God is the biggest mistake we make in our spiritual lives. Isaiah 40:31 tells us that "those who wait for the LORD [who expect, look for, and hope in Him] will gain new strength and renew their power; they will lift up their wings [and rise up close to God] like eagles [rising toward the sun]; they will run and not become weary, they will walk and not grow tired." Spending time studying God's Word, praying, and fellowshiping with Him changes us and makes us strong enough to endure whatever challenges come our way. The truth of the matter is that we really cannot get along well at all unless we do this one thing that Jesus told Martha was so important. He told her there was need of only one thing and "Mary has chosen the good part" (Luke 10:42).

Nobody on a deathbed has ever said, "I wish I spent more time working at the office." Most people wish they spent more time in relationships. If we make right decisions now, we will not live in the agony of regret later in life. Learn to recognize the time of your visitation, those special times when God calls you to come and spend time with Him. When Jesus knocks at the door of your heart, do not answer with, "I'm busy. Come back another time." Welcome Him in and enjoy His presence.

⁴¹But the Lord replied to her, "Martha, Martha, you are worried and bothered *and* anxious about so many things;

⁴²but *only* one thing is necessary, for Mary has chosen the good part [that which is to her advantage], which will not be taken away from her."

life point

In Luke 10:41, Jesus implied more than we sometimes realize when He spoke, "Martha, Martha." Martha was too busy for relationships; she chose work and worry over intimacy. As a result, she misused her time and missed what was vital to her.

Mary operated in wisdom; she took advantage of the moment. She could spend the rest of her life cleaning, but Jesus was there and she wanted Him to feel welcome. He came to see her and Martha, not their clean house. This does not mean that a clean house is not important, but there is a time for everything—and this was not the time for tidying up or sweeping the floor. Let us use wisdom and not miss God's presence when it is available.

11 IT HAPPENED that while Jesus was praying in a certain place, after He finished, one of His disciples said to Him, "Lord, teach us to pray just as John also taught his disciples."
²He said to them,

"When you pray, say:
'Father, hallowed be Your name.
Your kingdom come.
³'Give us each day our daily bread.
⁴'And forgive us our sins,
For we ourselves also forgive everyone who is indebted to us [who has offended or wronged us].

putting the Word to work

Do you ever struggle with how to pray or what to pray for? You are not alone—even the disciples needed to learn how to pray (see Luke 11:1–4). Although there is no one "right way" to pray, the prayer that Jesus taught His disciples is an excellent model.

Worship, intercession, repentance, surrender, praise, and petition are all important elements of prayer. Even as the disciples did, ask God to teach you about prayer and be sure to spend time with Him in prayer daily.

And lead us not into temptation [but rescue us from evil].'"
⁵Then He said to them, "Suppose one of you has a friend, and goes to him at midnight and says, 'Friend, lend me three loaves [of bread];
⁶for a friend of mine who is on a journey has just come to *visit* me, and I have nothing to serve him';
⁷and from inside he answers, 'Do not bother me; the door has already been shut and my children and I are in bed; I cannot get up and give you *anything*.'
⁸"I tell you, even though he will not get up and give him *anything just* because he is his friend, yet because of his persistence *and* boldness he will get up and give him whatever he needs.
⁹"So I say to you, ask *and* keep on asking, and it will be given to you; seek *and* keep on seeking, and you will find; knock *and* keep on knocking, and the door will be opened to you. [Matt 7:7–11]
¹⁰"For everyone who keeps on asking [persistently], receives; and he who keeps on seeking [persistently], finds; and to him who keeps on knocking [persistently], the door will be opened.

life point

Our asking, seeking, and knocking (see Luke 11:9) needs to be sincere and we should always be ready to make a deeper commitment to God. When this happens, He will move and send His Holy Spirit to touch each of us in a special way. Ask and believe by faith that God will do something wonderful. While you wait for Him to do it, keep thanking Him and offering Him praise.

¹¹"What father among you, if his son asks for a fish, will give him a snake instead of a fish?

¹²"Or if he asks for an egg, will give him a scorpion?

¹³"If you, then, being evil [that is, sinful by nature], know how to give good gifts to your children, how much more will your heavenly Father give the Holy Spirit to those who ask *and* continue to ask Him!"

¹⁴And [at another time] Jesus was casting out a demon, and it was [controlling a man so as to make him] mute; when the demon had gone out, the mute man spoke. And the crowds were awed. [Matt 12:22–24]

¹⁵But some of them said, "He drives out demons by [the power of] Beelzebul (Satan), the ruler of the demons."

¹⁶Others, trying to test Him, were demanding of Him a sign from heaven.

¹⁷But He, *well* aware of their thoughts *and* purpose, said to them, "Every kingdom divided against itself is doomed to destruction; and a house *divided* against itself falls.

¹⁸"If Satan also is divided against himself, how will his kingdom stand *and* continue to survive? For you are saying that I drive out demons by [the power of] Beelzebul.

¹⁹"Now if I drive out the demons by Beelzebul, by whom do your sons [the Jewish exorcists] drive them out? For this reason they will be your judges.

²⁰"But if I drive out the demons by the finger of God, then the kingdom of God has already come upon you.

²¹"When the strong man, fully armed, guards his own house, his belongings are undisturbed *and* secure.

²²"But when someone stronger than he attacks and overpowers him, he robs him of all his armor on which he had relied and divides his [goods as] spoil.

²³"He who is not with Me [believing in Me as Lord and Savior] is against Me [there is no impartial position]; and he who does not gather with Me [assisting in My ministry], scatters.

²⁴"When the unclean spirit comes out of a person, it roams through waterless places in search [of a place] of rest; and not finding any, it says, 'I will go back to my house (person) from which I came.'

²⁵"And when it comes, it finds the place swept and put in order.

²⁶"Then it goes and brings seven other spirits more evil than itself, and they go in [the person] and live there; and the last state of that person becomes worse than the first."

²⁷Now while Jesus was saying these things, one of the women in the crowd raised her voice and said to Him, "Blessed (happy, favored by God) is the womb that gave birth to You and the breasts at which You nursed!"

²⁸But He said, "On the contrary,

speak the Word

God, I know that You are faithful and that if I ask and keep on asking, I will receive from You. If I seek and keep on seeking, I will find. If I knock and keep on knocking, the door will be opened.
—ADAPTED FROM LUKE 11:10

blessed (happy, favored by God) are those who hear the word of God and continually observe it."

²⁹Now as the crowds were increasing [in number], He began to say, "This [present] generation is a wicked generation; it seeks a sign (attesting miracle), but no sign will be given to it except the sign of Jonah [the prophet]. [Matt 12:39–42]

³⁰"For just as Jonah became a sign to the people of Nineveh, so will the Son of Man also be [a sign] to this generation. [Jon 3:4–10]

³¹"The Queen of the South (the king-dom of Sheba) will rise up in the judgment with the men of this generation and condemn them, because she came from the ends of the earth to listen to the wisdom of Solomon, and look, something greater than Solomon is here. [1 Kin 10:1–13; 2 Chr 9:1–12]

³²"The men of Nineveh will stand up [as witnesses] at the judgment with this generation and condemn it, be-cause they repented at the preaching of Jonah, and look, something greater than Jonah is here. [Jon 3:5]

³³"No one lights a lamp and then puts it in a cellar nor under a basket [hiding

ask, seek, knock

Luke 11:9–13 encourages us to keep on asking, seeking, and knocking, on a continual basis, day in and day out, 365 days a year, so we may keep receiving what we need.

How many times do we stay awake all night wrestling with our problems and losing sleep over them, instead of simply casting our cares on the Lord and asking Him to meet our needs—then trusting Him to do so?

How often do we try to make something happen in our lives without asking God for help? How often do we try to prosper in some area without asking God for prosperity? And how often do we try to handle our own problems without asking God to work them out for us?

Our mistake is failing to ask and seek and knock—failing to trust God, our loving heavenly Father, to give us all the good things we ask of Him. We struggle and frustrate ourselves with works of the flesh when we should humble ourselves under God's mighty hand knowing that at the appropriate time He will bring to pass what is right for us (see I Peter 5:6).

In Matthew 7:11, Jesus says, "If you then, evil (sinful by nature) as you are, know how to give good and advantageous gifts to your children, how much more will your Father who is in heaven [perfect as He is] give what is *good and advantageous* to those who keep on asking Him." (emphasis mine). In Luke 11:13, Jesus says, "how much more will your heavenly Father give *the Holy Spirit* to those who ask and continue to ask Him!" (emphasis mine).

Notice that both passages say that if we who are evil know how to bless our children with good gifts, how much more will our heavenly Father who is perfect be willing to bless His children with good things. The most important of those "good things" that God wants to give us is His own Holy Spirit. This is a truly awesome gift.

the light], but [instead it is put] on the lampstand, so that those who come in may see the light. [Matt 5:15; Mark 4:21; Luke 8:16]

³⁴"The eye is the lamp of your body. When your eye is clear [spiritually perceptive, focused on God], your whole body also is full of light [benefiting from God's precepts]. But when it is bad [spiritually blind], your body also is full of darkness [devoid of God's word].

³⁵"Be careful, therefore, that the light that is in you is not darkness.

³⁶"So if your whole body is illuminated, with no dark part, it will be entirely bright [with light], as when the lamp gives you light with its bright rays."

³⁷Now after Jesus had spoken, a Pharisee asked Him to have lunch with him. He went in [the Pharisee's home] and reclined *at the table* [without ceremonially washing His hands].

³⁸The Pharisee noticed this and was surprised that Jesus did not first ceremonially wash before the meal.

³⁹But the Lord said to him, "Now you Pharisees clean the outside of the cup and plate [as required by tradition]; but inside you are full of greed and wickedness.

⁴⁰"You foolish ones [acting without reflection or intelligence]! Did not He who made the outside make the inside also?

⁴¹"But give that which is within as charity [that is, acts of mercy and compassion, not as a public display, but as an expression of your faithfulness to God], and then indeed all things are clean for you.

⁴²"But woe (judgment is coming) to you Pharisees, because you [self-righteously] tithe mint and rue and every [little] garden herb [tending to all the minutiae], and yet disregard *and* neglect justice and the love of God; but these are the things you should have done, without neglecting the others. [Lev 27:30; Mic 6:8]

⁴³"Woe to you Pharisees, because you love the best seats in the synagogues and to be respectfully greeted in the market places.

⁴⁴"Woe to you! For you are like graves which are unmarked, and people walk over them without being aware of it [and are ceremonially unclean]."

⁴⁵One of the lawyers [an expert in the Mosaic Law] answered Him, "Teacher, by saying this, You insult us too!"

⁴⁶But He said, "Woe to you lawyers as well, because you weigh men down with burdens [man-made rules, unreasonable requirements] which are hard to bear, and you yourselves will not even touch the burdens with one of your fingers [to lighten the load].

⁴⁷"Woe to you! For you repair *or* build tombs for the prophets, and it was your fathers who killed them.

⁴⁸"So you are witnesses and approve the deeds of your fathers, because they [actually] killed them, and you repair *or* build their tombs.

⁴⁹"For this reason also the wisdom of God said [in the Scriptures], 'I will send them prophets and apostles, some of whom they will put to death and some they will persecute,

⁵⁰so that charges may be brought against this generation [holding them responsible] for the blood of all the prophets shed since the foundation of the world,

⁵¹from the blood of Abel to the blood of Zechariah [the priest], who was murdered between the altar and the house *of God*. Yes, I tell you, charges will be brought against this generation.' [Gen 4:8; 2 Chr 24:20, 21; Zech 1:1; Matt 23:35]

⁵²"Woe to you lawyers, because you have taken away the key to knowledge (scriptural truth). You yourselves did not enter, and you held back those who were entering [by your flawed

interpretation of God's word and your man-made tradition]." [Matt 23:13]

⁵³When He left there, the scribes and the Pharisees began to be very hostile [toward Him] and to interrogate Him on many subjects,

⁵⁴plotting against Him to catch *Him* in something He might say.

12 IN THE meantime, after so many thousands of the people had gathered that they were stepping on one another, Jesus began speaking first *of all* to His disciples, "Be *continually* on your guard against the leaven of the Pharisees [that is, their pervasive, corrupting influence and teaching], which is hypocrisy [producing self-righteousness].

²"But there is nothing [so carefully] concealed that it will not be revealed, nor so hidden that it will not be made known. [Matt 10:26–33; Mark 4:22]

³"For that reason, whatever you have said in the dark will be heard in the light, and what you have whispered behind closed doors will be proclaimed on the housetops.

⁴"I say to you, My friends, do not be afraid of those who kill the body and after that have nothing more that they can do.

⁵"But I will point out to you whom you should fear: fear the One who, after He has killed, has authority *and* power to hurl [you] into hell; yes, I say to you, [stand in great awe of God and] fear Him!

⁶"Are not five sparrows sold for two copper coins? Yet not one of them has [ever] been forgotten in the presence of God.

⁷"Indeed the very hairs of your head are all numbered. Do not be afraid; you are far more valuable than many sparrows.

uncovering the treasures in God's Word

God's Word contains incredible hidden treasures, powerful life-giving secrets God wants to reveal to us, and Luke 12:2 confirms that whatever is hidden to us will be revealed. How does this happen? These treasures are disclosed to those who meditate, ponder, study, think about, mentally practice, and declare the Word of God.

As a teacher of God's Word, I know personally the truth of this principle. It seems there is no end to what God can show me out of one verse from His Word. I will study it one time and gain an understanding, and later I will see something new that I did not even notice before.

The Lord reveals His secrets to those who are diligent to study and meditate on the Word. Do not be the kind of person who always wants to live off someone else's revelation. Study the Word for yourself and allow the Holy Spirit to bless your life with truth. Love God's Word and give it a place of priority in your daily life and you will walk in wisdom and power.

Meditating on God's Word is one of the most important things you and I can learn to do. As you go about your daily life, ask the Holy Spirit to remind you of certain scriptures so you can meditate on them. You will be amazed at how much power will be released into your life through this practice. The more you meditate on the Word of God, the more you can readily draw upon its strength in times of trouble. The power to obey the Word comes from the practice of meditating on it (see Joshua 1:8).

⁸"I say to you, whoever declares openly *and* confesses Me before men [speaking freely of Me as his Lord], the Son of Man also will declare openly *and* confess him [as one of His own] before the angels of God.

⁹"But he who denies Me before men will be denied in the presence of the angels of God.

¹⁰"And everyone who speaks a word against the Son of Man, it will be forgiven him; but he who blasphemes against the Holy Spirit [that is, whoever intentionally discredits the Holy Spirit by attributing the authenticating miracles done by Me to Satan], it will not be forgiven him [for him there is no forgiveness]. [Matt 12:31; Mark 3:28–30]

¹¹"When they bring you before the synagogues and the magistrates and the authorities, do not be worried about how you are to defend yourselves or what you are to say;

¹²for the Holy Spirit will teach you in that very hour what you ought to say."

¹³Someone from the crowd said to Him, "Teacher, tell my brother to divide the *family* inheritance with me."

¹⁴But He said to him, "Man, who appointed Me a judge or an arbitrator over [the two of] you?"

¹⁵Then He said to them, "Watch out and guard yourselves against every form of greed; for not even when one has an overflowing abundance does his life consist of *nor* is it derived from his possessions."

¹⁶Then He told them a parable, saying, "There was a rich man whose land was very fertile *and* productive.

¹⁷"And he began thinking to himself, 'What shall I do, since I have no place [large enough in which] to store my crops?'

¹⁸Then he said, 'This is what I will do: I will tear down my storehouses and build larger ones, and I will store all my grain and my goods there.

¹⁹'And I will say to my soul, "Soul, you have many good things stored up, [enough] for many years; rest *and* relax, eat, drink and be merry (celebrate continually)."'

²⁰"But God said to him, 'You fool! This *very* night your soul is required of you; and *now* who will own all the things you have prepared?' [Job 27:8; Jer 17:11]

²¹"So it is for the one who continues to store up *and* hoard possessions for himself, and is not rich [in his relationship] toward God."

²²Jesus said to His disciples, "For this reason I tell you, do not worry about your life, as to what you will eat; or about your body, as to what you will wear. [Matt 6:25–33]

²³"For life is more than food, and the body more than clothes.

²⁴"Consider the ravens, for they neither sow [seed] nor reap [the crop]; they have no storehouse or barn, and yet God feeds them. How much more valuable are you than the birds!

²⁵"And which of you by worrying can add one hour to his life's span?

²⁶"So if you are not even able to do a very little thing [such as that], why are you worried about the rest?

²⁷"Consider the lilies *and* wildflowers, how they grow [in the open field]. They neither labor nor spin [wool to make clothing]; yet I tell you, not even Solomon in all his glory *and* splendor dressed himself like one of these. [1 Kin 10:4–7]

²⁸"But if this is how God clothes the grass which is in the field today and

speak the Word

God, I will not be worried about my life, because I know that I am very valuable to You and that You will take care of me.
—ADAPTED FROM LUKE 12:22–24

tomorrow is thrown into the furnace, how much more *will He clothe* you? You of little faith!

29"So as for you, do not seek what you will eat and what you will drink; nor have an anxious *and* unsettled mind.

30For all the [pagan] nations of the world greedily seek these things; and your [heavenly] Father [already] knows that you need them.

31"But [strive for and actively] seek His kingdom, and these things will be given to you as well.

32"Do not be afraid *and* anxious, little flock, for it is your Father's good pleasure to give you the kingdom.

33"Sell your possessions (show compassion) and give [donations] to the poor. Provide money belts for yourselves that do not wear out, an unfailing *and* inexhaustible treasure in the heavens, where no thief comes near and no moth destroys.

34"For where your treasure is, there your heart will be also.

35"Be dressed and ready for active service, and keep your lamps continuously burning.

36"Be like men who are waiting for their master when he returns from the wedding feast, so that when he comes and knocks they may immediately open *the door* for him.

37"Blessed (happy, prosperous, to be admired) are those servants whom the master finds awake *and* watching when he arrives. I assure you *and* most solemnly say to you, he will prepare himself *to serve,* and will have them

life point

God's children are not to be like the world. The world seeks things, but we are to seek the Lord and His kingdom. He promises that if we will do that, He will add to us everything else He knows we need (see Luke 12:31).

recline *at the table,* and will come and wait on them.

38"Whether he comes in the second watch (before midnight), or even in the third (after midnight), and finds them so [prepared and ready], blessed are those *servants.*

39"But be sure of this, that if the head of the house had known at what time the thief was coming, he [would have been awake and alert, and] would not have allowed his house to be broken into. [Matt 24:43, 44]

40"You too, be *continually* ready; because the Son of Man is coming at an hour that you do not expect."

41Peter said, "Lord, are You addressing this parable to us [disciples], or to everyone else as well?"

42The Lord said, "Who then is the faithful and wise steward [of the estate], whom his master will put in charge over his household, to give *his* servants their portion of food at the proper time? [Matt 24:45–51]

43"Blessed (happy, prosperous, to be admired) is that servant whom his master finds so doing when he arrives.

44"I assure you *and* most solemnly say to you, he will put him in charge of all his possessions.

45"But if that servant says in his heart, 'My master is taking his time in coming,' and begins to beat the servants, both men and women, and to eat and drink and get drunk,

46the master of that servant will come on a day when he does not expect him and at an hour he does not know, and will cut him in pieces, and assign him a place with the unbelievers.

47"And that servant who knew his master's will, and yet did not get ready or act in accord with his will, will be beaten with many lashes [of the whip],

48but the one who did not know it and did things worthy of a beating, will receive only a few [lashes]. From everyone to whom much has been given, much will be required; and to whom they entrusted much, of him they will ask all the more. [Num 15:29, 30; Deut 25:2, 3]

⁴⁹"I have come to cast fire (judgment) on the earth; and how I wish that it were already kindled!

⁵⁰"I have a baptism [of great suffering] with which to be baptized, and how [greatly] I am distressed until it is accomplished!

⁵¹"Do you suppose that I came to grant peace on earth? No, I tell you, but rather division [between believers and unbelievers]; [Matt 10:34–36]

⁵²for from now on five in one household will be divided [over Me], three against two and two against three.

⁵³"They will be divided, father against son and son against father, mother against daughter and daughter against mother, mother-in-law against daughter-in-law and daughter-in-law against mother-in-law." [Mic 7:6]

⁵⁴He also said to the crowds, "When you see a cloud rising in the west, you immediately say, 'It is going to rain,' and that is how it turns out.

⁵⁵"And when [you see that] a south wind is blowing, you say, 'It will be a hot day,' and it happens.

⁵⁶"You hypocrites (play-actors, pretenders)! You know how to analyze and intelligently interpret the appearance of the earth and sky [to forecast the weather], but why do you not intelligently interpret this present time?

⁵⁷"And why do you not even on your own initiative judge what is right?

⁵⁸"For while you are going with your opponent [at law] to appear before a magistrate, on the way make an effort to settle, so that he does not drag you before the judge, and the judge does not [rule against you and] turn you over to the officer, and the officer does not throw you into prison. [Matt 5:25, 26]

⁵⁹"I say to you, you [absolutely] will not get out of there until you have paid the very last cent."

13 JUST AT that time some people came who told Jesus about the Galileans whose blood Pilate [the governor] had mixed with their sacrifices.

²Jesus replied to them, "Do you think that these Galileans were worse sinners than all other Galileans because they have suffered in this way?

³"I tell you, no; but unless you repent [change your old way of thinking, turn from your sinful ways and live changed lives], you will all likewise perish.

⁴"Or do you assume that those eighteen on whom the tower in Siloam fell and killed were worse sinners than all the others who live in Jerusalem?

⁵"I tell you, no; but unless you repent [change your old way of thinking, turn from your sinful ways and live changed lives], you will all likewise perish."

⁶Then He began telling them this parable: "A certain man had a fig tree that had been planted in his vineyard; and he came looking for fruit on it, but did not find any;

⁷so he said to the vineyard-keeper, 'For three years I have come looking for fruit on this fig tree and have found none. Cut it down! Why does it even use up the ground [depleting the soil and blocking the sunlight]?'

⁸"But he replied to him, 'Let it alone, sir, [just] one more year until I dig around it and put in fertilizer;

⁹and if it bears fruit after this, fine; but if not, cut it down.'"

¹⁰Now Jesus was teaching in one of the synagogues on the Sabbath.

¹¹And there was a woman who for eighteen years had had an illness caused by a spirit (demon). She was bent double, and could not straighten up at all.

¹²When Jesus saw her, He called her over and said to her, "Woman, you are released from your illness."

¹³Then He laid His hands on her; and immediately she stood erect again and she *began* glorifying *and* praising God.

¹⁴But the leader of the synagogue, indignant because Jesus had healed on the Sabbath, *began* saying to the crowd in response, "There are six days in which work ought to be done; so come on those days and be healed, and not on the Sabbath day." [Ex 20:9, 10]

¹⁵But the Lord replied to him, "You hypocrites (play-actors, pretenders)! Does not each one of you on the Sabbath untie his ox or his donkey from the stall and lead it away to water it?

¹⁶"And this woman, a daughter (descendant) of Abraham whom Satan has bound for eighteen long years, should she not have been released from this bond on the Sabbath day?"

¹⁷As He was saying this, all His opponents were being humiliated; and the entire crowd was rejoicing over all the glorious things that were being done by Him.

¹⁸So this led Him to say, "What is the kingdom of God like? And to what shall I compare it? [Matt 13:31, 32; Mark 4:30–32]

¹⁹"It is like a mustard seed, which a man took and planted in his own garden; and it grew and became a tree, and THE BIRDS OF THE SKY FOUND SHELTER *and* NESTED IN ITS BRANCHES." [Ezek 17:23; Dan 4:12]

²⁰And again He said, "To what shall I compare the kingdom of God?

²¹"It is like leaven, which a woman took and hid in three peck measures of flour until it was all leavened." [Matt 13:33]

²²Jesus journeyed on through cities and villages, teaching and making His way toward Jerusalem.

²³And someone asked Him, "Lord, will only a few be saved [from the penalties of the last judgment]?" And He said to them,

²⁴"Strive to enter through the narrow door [force aside unbelief and the attractions of sin]; for many, I tell you, will try to enter [by their own works] and will not be able.

²⁵"Once the head of the house gets up and closes the door, and you begin to stand outside and knock on the door [again and again], saying, 'Lord, open to us!' then He will answer you, 'I do not know where you are from [for you are not of My household].'

²⁶"Then you will begin to say, 'We ate and drank in Your presence, and You taught in our streets';

²⁷but He will say to you, 'I do not know where you are from; DEPART FROM ME, ALL YOU EVILDOERS!' [Ps 6:8]

²⁸"In that place there will be weeping [in sorrow and pain] and grinding of teeth [in distress and anger] when you see Abraham and Isaac and Jacob and all the prophets in the kingdom of God, but yourselves being thrown out *and* driven away.

²⁹"And *people* will come from east and west, and from north and south, and they will sit down [and feast at the table] in the kingdom of God.

³⁰"And behold, *some* are last who will be first, and *some* are first who will be last."

³¹At that very hour some Pharisees came up and said to Him, "Leave and go away from here, because Herod [Antipas] wants to kill You."

³²And He said to them, "Go and tell that fox [that sly, cowardly man], 'Listen carefully: I cast out demons and perform healings today and tomorrow, and on the third *day* I reach My goal.'

³³"Nevertheless I must travel on today and tomorrow and the *day* after that—for it cannot be that a prophet would die outside of Jerusalem.

[34]"O Jerusalem, Jerusalem, who kills the prophets and stones [to death] those [messengers] who are sent to her [by God]! How often I have wanted to gather your children together [around Me], just as a hen *gathers* her young under her wings, but you were not willing! [Matt 23:37–39]

[35]"Listen carefully: your house is left to you desolate [abandoned by God and destitute of His protection]; and I say to you, you will not see Me until *the time* comes when you say, 'BLESSED [to be celebrated with praise] IS HE WHO COMES IN THE NAME OF THE LORD!'" [Ps 118:26; Jer 22:5]

14 IT HAPPENED one Sabbath, when He went for a meal at the house of one of the ruling Pharisees, that they were watching Him closely *and* carefully [hoping to entrap Him].

[2]And there in front of Him was a man who had dropsy (extreme swelling).

[3]And Jesus asked the lawyers and the Pharisees, "Is it lawful to heal on the Sabbath, or not?"

[4]But they kept silent. Then He took hold of the man and healed him, and sent him on his way.

[5]Then He said to them, "Which one of you, having a son or an ox that falls into a well, will not immediately pull him out on the Sabbath day?"

[6]And they were unable to reply to this.

[7]Now Jesus *began* telling a parable to the invited guests when He noticed how they had been selecting the places of honor *at the table,* saying to them,

[8]"When you are invited by someone to a wedding feast, do not sit down [to eat] at the place of honor, since a more distinguished person than you may have been invited by the host, [Prov 25:6, 7]

[9]and he who invited both of you will come and say to you, 'Give this man your place,' and then, in disgrace you proceed to take the last place.

[10]"But when you are invited, go and sit down [to eat] at the last place, so that when your host comes, he will say to you, 'Friend, move up higher'; and then you will be honored in the presence of all who are at the table with you.

[11]"For everyone who exalts himself will be humbled [before others], and he who *habitually* humbles himself (keeps a realistic self-view) will be exalted."

[12]Jesus also went on to say to the one who had invited Him, "When you give a luncheon or a dinner, do not invite your friends or your brothers or your relatives or wealthy neighbors, otherwise they may also invite you in return and that will be your repayment.

[13]"But when you give a banquet *or* a reception, invite the poor, the disabled, the lame, and the blind,

[14]and you will be blessed because they cannot repay you; for you will be repaid at the resurrection of the righteous (the just, the upright)."

[15]When one of those who were reclining *at the table* with Him heard this, he said to Him, "Blessed (happy, prosperous, to be admired) is he who will eat bread in the kingdom of God!"

[16]But Jesus said to him, "A man was giving a big dinner, and he invited many *guests;*

[17]and at the dinner hour he sent his servant to tell those who had been invited, 'Come, because everything is ready now.'

[18]"But they all alike began to make excuses. The first one said to him, 'I have purchased a piece of land and I have to go out and see it; please consider me excused.'

[19]"Another one said, 'I have purchased five yoke of oxen, and I am going to try them out; please consider me excused.'

²⁰"And another said, 'I have [recently] married a wife, and for that reason I am unable to come.' [Deut 24:5]

²¹"So the servant came back and reported this to his master. Then [his master,] the head of the household, became angry [at the rejections of his invitation] and said to his servant, 'Go out quickly into the streets and the lanes of the city and bring in here the poor and the disabled and the blind and the lame.'

²²"And the servant [after returning] said, 'Sir, what you commanded has been done, and still there is room.'

²³"Then the master told the servant, 'Go out into the highways and along the hedges, and compel them to come in, so that my house may be filled [with guests].

²⁴'For I tell you, not one of those who were invited [and declined] will taste my dinner.'"

²⁵Now large crowds were going along with Jesus; and He turned and said to them,

²⁶"If anyone comes to Me, and does not hate his own father and mother and wife and children and brothers and sisters, yes, and even his own life [in the sense of indifference to or relative disregard for them in comparison with his attitude toward God]—he cannot be My disciple.

²⁷"Whoever does not carry his own cross [expressing a willingness to endure whatever may come] and follow after Me [believing in Me, conforming to My example in living and, if need be, suffering or perhaps dying because of faith in Me] cannot be My disciple.

²⁸"For which one of you, when he wants to build a watchtower [for his guards], does not first sit down and calculate the cost, to see if he has enough to finish it?

²⁹"Otherwise, when he has laid a foundation and is unable to finish [the building], all who see it will begin to ridicule him,

³⁰saying, 'This man began to build and was not able to finish!'

³¹"Or what king, when he sets out to meet another king in battle, will not first sit down and consider whether he is strong enough with ten thousand men to encounter the one who is coming against him with twenty thousand?

³²"Or else [if he feels he is not powerful enough], while the other [king] is still a far distance away, he sends an envoy and asks for terms of peace.

³³"So then, none of you can be My disciple who does not [carefully consider the cost and then for My sake] give up all his own possessions.

³⁴"Therefore, salt is good; but if salt has become tasteless, with what will it be seasoned?

³⁵"It is fit neither for the soil nor for the manure pile; it is thrown away. He who has ears to hear, let him hear *and* heed My words."

15 NOW ALL the tax collectors and sinners [including non-observant Jews] were coming near Jesus to listen to Him.

²Both the Pharisees and the scribes *began* muttering *and* complaining, saying, "This man accepts *and* welcomes sinners and eats with them."

³So He told them this parable:

⁴"What man among you, if he has a hundred sheep and loses one of them, does not leave the ninety-nine in the wilderness and go after the one which is lost, [searching] until he finds it? [Matt 18:12–14]

⁵"And when he has found it, he lays it on his shoulders, rejoicing.

⁶"And when he gets home, he calls together his friends and his neighbors, saying to them, 'Rejoice with me, because I have found my lost sheep!'

⁷"I tell you, in the same way there will be more joy in heaven over one

sinner who repents than over ninety-nine righteous people who have no need of repentance.

⁸"Or what woman, if she has ten silver coins [each one equal to a day's wages] and loses one coin, does not light a lamp and sweep the house and search carefully until she finds it?

⁹"And when she has found it, she calls together her [women] friends and neighbors, saying, 'Rejoice with me, because I found the lost coin!'

¹⁰"In the same way, I tell you, there is joy in the presence of the angels of God over one sinner who repents [that is, changes his inner self—his old way of thinking, regrets past sins, lives his life in a way that proves repentance; and seeks God's purpose for his life]."

¹¹Then He said, "A certain man had two sons.

¹²"The younger of them [inappropriately] said to his father, 'Father, give me the share of the property that falls to me.' So he divided the estate between them. [Deut 21:15–17]

¹³"A few days later, the younger son gathered together everything [that he

putting the Word to work

Have you ever lost something of great value, like the man and the woman Jesus talks about in Luke 15:1–10? If so, you probably spent some frenzied moments searching and retracing your steps, and you may have even asked others to help you look for your lost valuable. Do you remember the joy you experienced when you found what was lost? That joy pales in comparison to the joy in heaven when even one sinner repents. If there is someone in your life who does not yet know God, pray often that he or she will soon come to know Jesus as Savior and Lord.

had] and traveled to a distant country, and there he wasted his fortune in reckless *and* immoral living.

¹⁴"Now when he had spent everything, a severe famine occurred in that country, and he began to do without *and* be in need.

¹⁵"So he went and forced himself on one of the citizens of that country, who sent him into his fields to feed pigs.

¹⁶"He would have gladly eaten the [carob] pods that the pigs were eating [but they could not satisfy his hunger], and no one was giving *anything* to him. [Jer 30:14]

¹⁷"But when he [finally] came to his senses, he said, 'How many of my father's hired men have more than enough food, while I am dying here of hunger!

¹⁸'I will get up and go to my father, and I will say to him, "Father, I have sinned against heaven and in your sight.

¹⁹'I am no longer worthy to be called your son; [just] treat me like one of your hired men."'

²⁰"So he got up and came to his father. But while he was still a long way off, his father saw him and was moved with compassion *for him*, and ran and embraced him and kissed him.

²¹"And the son said to him, 'Father, I have sinned against heaven and in your sight; I am no longer worthy to be called your son.'

²²"But the father said to his servants, 'Quickly bring out the best robe [for the guest of honor] and put it on him; and give him a ring for his hand, and sandals for his feet. [Gen 41:42; Zech 3:4]

²³'And bring the fattened calf and slaughter it, and let us [invite everyone and] feast and celebrate;

²⁴for this son of mine was [as good as] dead and is alive again; he was lost and has been found.' So they began to celebrate.

25"Now his older son was in the field; and when he returned and approached the house, he heard music and dancing.

26"So he summoned one of the servants and *began* asking what this [celebration] meant.

27"And he said to him, 'Your brother has come, and your father has killed the fattened calf because he has received him back safe and sound.'

28"But the elder brother became angry *and* deeply resentful and was not willing to go in; and his father came out and *began* pleading with him.

29"But he said to his father, 'Look! These many years I have served you, and I have never neglected *or* disobeyed your command. Yet you have never given me [so much as] a young goat, so that I might celebrate with my friends;

30but when this [other] son of yours arrived, who has devoured your estate with immoral women, you slaughtered that fattened calf for him!'

31"The father said to him, 'Son, you are always with me, and all that is mine is yours.

32'But it was fitting to celebrate and rejoice, for this brother of yours was [as good as] dead and *has begun* to live. He was lost and has been found.'"

16 NOW JESUS was also saying to the disciples, "There was a certain rich man who had a manager [of his estate], and accusations [against this man] were brought to him, that this man was squandering his [master's] possessions.

2"So he called him and said to him, 'What is this I hear about you? Give an accounting of your management [of my affairs], for you can no longer be [my] manager.'

3"The manager [of the estate] said to himself, 'What will I do, since my master is taking the management away from me? I am not strong enough to dig [for a living], and I am ashamed to beg.

4'I know what I will do, so that when I am removed from the management, people [who are my master's debtors] will welcome me into their homes.'

5"So he summoned his master's debtors one by one, and he said to the first, 'How much do you owe my master?'

6"He said, 'A hundred measures of [olive] oil.' And he said to him, 'Take your bill, and sit down quickly and write fifty.'

7"Then he said to another, 'And how much do you owe?' He said, 'A hundred measures of wheat.' He said to him, 'Take your bill, and write eighty.'

8"And his master commended the unjust manager [not for his misdeeds, but] because he had acted shrewdly [by preparing for his future unemployment]; for the sons of this age [the non-believers] are shrewder in relation to their own kind [that is, to the ways of the secular world] than are the sons of light [the believers].

9"And I tell you [learn from this], make friends for yourselves [for eternity] by means of the wealth of unrighteousness [that is, use material resources as a way to further the work of God], so that when it runs out, they will welcome you into the eternal dwellings.

10"He who is faithful in a very little thing is also faithful in much; and he who is dishonest in a very little thing is also dishonest in much.

11"Therefore if you have not been faithful in the *use of* earthly wealth, who will entrust the true *riches* to you?

12"And if you have not been faithful in *the use of* that [earthly wealth] which belongs to another [whether God or man, and of which you are a trustee], who will give you that which is your own?

13"No servant can serve two masters; for either he will hate the one and love

the problem with a double purpose

In Luke 16:13, Jesus talked about not serving "two masters." Let me give you an example from a time in my life when I wrestled with this truth.

Years ago I served at a church as an associate pastor. I loved this ministry and the people of the church, but I knew the Lord was leading me to leave my job there and start my own ministry.

I also knew that when the Lord calls you to do something, it's vital that you do it. If you do not move forward to answer that call, everything else in your life will dry up.

In addition, I recognized that I no longer enjoyed what I was doing and eventually realized the reason was that God was finished with it. And when God gets finished, we may as well get finished too or we will end up essentially miserable trying to serve "two masters." The job I once thoroughly enjoyed, I now dreaded, simply because God was calling me to something new.

Even though I knew all this, I stayed in that position for another year. During that time I experienced all kinds of things I did not like. I was not happy at all, and I did not know why. Nothing seemed to be right any longer.

Finally, the Lord spoke to me and said, "Take your ministry and go north, south, east, and west." I obeyed that direction, but for three years I felt deeply the loss of what I left behind. I experienced excitement about the future and sorrow over the past at the same time. I could not understand why I felt the sadness and sorrow, since I thought I had heard from God and was doing His will. My pastor felt the same way I did and we kept trying to work out ways I could have my own ministry but still work at the church and be heavily involved in everything they were doing.

Through all of this, God really dealt with me. Finally, He said to me, "Joyce, I cannot do anything else in your ministry until you set your heart fully and completely on what I have called you to do." I came to realize that I had "soul ties" to that old job. I had invested five years of my life there. God told me to move on, but my soul (mind, will, and emotions) was still tied to the place I left behind. My basic problem was that I tried to serve two masters. As long as I was torn between my past and my future, I could not find peace of mind. I made the same mistake that multitudes of others make. I tried to press into the future while holding on to the past.

This is why, when God called Abraham, He told him to get away from his country, his family, his relatives, and everything he knew, and go to a place God would show him (see Genesis 12:1). This does not mean we must all leave our family members behind to serve God. However, some scholars believe that many of Abraham's relatives were idol worshipers and for that reason, God did not want anything from the past influencing him. Paul said we must let go of what lies behind and press on to what lies ahead (see Philippians 3:13–14). The Lord told Israel through the prophet Isaiah, "Do not remember the former things, or ponder the things of the past. Listen carefully, I am about to do a new thing" (Isaiah 43:18, 19).

Our problem is that when we want to hold on to the past and still go into the future, we are double-minded and serving "two masters." Let me encourage you today to let go of the past and embrace the good things God has ahead for you!

the other, or he will stand devotedly by the one and despise the other. You cannot serve *both* God and mammon [that is, your earthly possessions or anything else you trust in and rely on instead of God]."

¹⁴Now the Pharisees, who were lovers of money, were listening to all these things and were sneering *and* ridiculing Him.

¹⁵So He said to them, "You are the ones who declare yourselves just *and* upright in the sight of men, but God knows your hearts [your thoughts, your desires, your secrets]; for that which is highly esteemed among men is detestable in the sight of God. [1 Sam 16:7; Prov 21:2]

¹⁶"The Law and the [writings of the] Prophets were proclaimed until John; since then the gospel of the kingdom of God has been *and* continues to be preached, and everyone tries forcefully to go into it.

¹⁷"Yet it is easier for heaven and earth to pass away than for a single stroke of a letter of the Law to fail *and* become void.

¹⁸"Whoever divorces his wife and marries another commits adultery, and he who marries one who is divorced from her husband commits adultery. [Matt 5:31, 32]

¹⁹"Now there was a certain rich man who was habitually dressed in expensive purple and fine linen, and celebrated *and* lived joyously in splendor every day.

²⁰"And a poor man named Lazarus, was laid at his gate, covered with sores.

²¹"He [eagerly] longed to eat the *crumbs* which fell from the rich man's table. Besides, even the dogs were coming and licking his sores.

²²"Now it happened that the poor man died and his spirit was carried away by the angels to Abraham's bosom (paradise); and the rich man also died and was buried.

²³"In Hades (the realm of the dead), being in torment, he looked up and saw Abraham far away and Lazarus in his bosom (paradise).

²⁴"And he cried out, 'Father Abraham, have mercy on me, and send Lazarus so that he may dip the tip of his finger in water and cool my tongue, because I am in severe agony in this flame.'

²⁵"But Abraham said, 'Son, remember that in your lifetime you received your good things [all the comforts and delights], and Lazarus likewise bad things [all the discomforts and distresses]; but now he is comforted here [in paradise], while you are in severe agony.

²⁶'And besides all this, between us and you [people] a great chasm has been fixed, so that those who want to come over from here to you will not be able, and none may cross over from there to us.'

²⁷"So the rich man said, 'Then, father [Abraham], I beg you to send Lazarus to my father's house—

²⁸for I have five brothers—in order that he may *solemnly* warn them *and* witness to them, so that they too will not come to this place of torment.'

²⁹"But Abraham said, 'They have [the Scriptures given by] Moses and the [writings of the] Prophets; let them listen to them.'

³⁰"He replied, 'No, father Abraham, but if someone from the dead goes to them, they will repent [they will change their old way of thinking and seek God and His righteousness].'

³¹"And he said to him, 'If they do not listen to [the messages of] Moses and the Prophets, they will not be persuaded even if someone rises from the dead.'"

17 JESUS SAID to His disciples, "Stumbling blocks [temptations and traps set to lure one to sin] are sure to come,

but woe (judgment is coming) to him through whom they come! [Matt 18:7]

²"It would be better for him if a millstone [as large as one turned by a donkey] were hung around his neck and he were hurled into the sea, than for him to cause one of these little ones to stumble [in sin and lose faith]. [Matt 18:6; Mark 9:42]

³"Pay attention *and* always be on guard [looking out for one another]! If your brother sins *and* disregards God's precepts, solemnly warn him; and if he repents *and* changes, forgive him.

⁴"Even if he sins against you seven times a day, and returns to you seven times and says, 'I repent,' you must forgive him [that is, give up resentment and consider the offense recalled and annulled]."

⁵The apostles said to the Lord, "Increase our faith [our ability to confidently trust in God and in His power]."

⁶And the Lord said, "If you have [confident, abiding] faith in God [even as small] as a mustard seed, you could say to this mulberry tree [which has very strong roots], 'Be pulled up by the roots and be planted in the sea'; and [if the request was in agreement with the will of God] it would have obeyed you. [Matt 17:20; Mark 11:23; 1 John 5:14]

⁷"Which of you who has a servant plowing or tending sheep will say to him when he comes in from the field, 'Come at once and sit down to eat?'

⁸"Will he not instead say to him, 'Prepare something for me to eat, and *appropriately* clothe yourself [for service] and serve me while I eat and drink; then afterward you may eat and drink?'

⁹"He does not thank the servant just because he did what he was ordered to do, does he?

¹⁰"So you too, when you have done everything that was assigned *and* commanded you, say, 'We are unworthy servants [undeserving of praise or a reward, for we have not gone beyond our obligation]; we have *merely* done what we ought to do.'"

how to increase your faith

People often pray for "great faith," yet they do not understand that faith grows through challenges like stepping out to do things they do not fully understand or have experience with. I do not believe anyone is automatically a person of great faith; faith becomes great through experience. It develops as it is used.

In Luke 17:5 the apostles said to the Lord, "Increase our faith." Jesus responded in the next verse by encouraging them to have faith like a small mustard seed; then they could say to a mulberry tree, "Be pulled up by the roots and be planted in the sea" (Luke 17:6), and the tree would obey them. I believe what Jesus meant was that if we have any faith, we will plant it by doing something. One way we release our faith is by doing something God asks of us. Faith often requires us to take action. The apostles were doing nothing in this situation, yet they wanted great faith.

I am not saying to take action without God's leading. There are times when God does not want us to take action because He wants us to wait for Him to take action for us. However, we need to understand that trust is active rather than passive. It includes being active in prayer, praise, and confession of God's Word. We should actively trust God, pray, and confess His Word in our situation while we wait for Him to act on our behalf. As we do, our faith will increase.

¹¹While Jesus was on the way to Jerusalem, He was passing [along the border] between Samaria and Galilee.

¹²As He entered a village, He was met by ten lepers who stood at a distance;

¹³and they raised their voices and called out, "Jesus, Master, have mercy on us!"

¹⁴When He saw them, He said to them, "Go and show yourselves to the priests." And as they went, they were [miraculously] healed *and* made clean. [Lev 14:2–32]

¹⁵One of them, when he saw that he was healed, turned back, glorifying *and* praising *and* honoring God with a loud voice;

¹⁶and he lay face downward at Jesus' feet, thanking Him [over and over]. He was a Samaritan.

¹⁷Then Jesus asked, "Were not ten [of you] cleansed? Where are the [other] nine?

¹⁸"Was there no one found to return and to give thanks *and* praise to God, except this foreigner?"

¹⁹Jesus said to him, "Get up and go [on your way]. Your faith [your personal trust in Me and your confidence in God's power] has restored you to health."

²⁰Now having been asked by the Pharisees when the kingdom of God would come, He replied, "The kingdom

putting the Word to work

When was the last time you thanked God for working in your life? Even if you have not seen your breakthrough yet, it is important to cultivate an attitude of gratitude for all God has done and is doing for you. Be like the leper in Luke 17:11–19 and be sure to take time to thank God for His work in your life, for His unfailing love and grace, and for all He means to you.

of God is not coming with signs to be observed *or* with a visible display;

²¹nor will people say, 'Look! Here it is!' or, 'There it is!' For the kingdom of God is among you [because of My presence]."

²²Then He said to the disciples, "The time will come when you will long to see [even] one of the days of the Son of Man, and you will not see it.

²³"They will say to you, 'Look [the Messiah is] there!' or 'Look [He is] here!' Do not go away [to see Him], and do not run after *them*.

²⁴"For just like the lightning, when it flashes out of one part of the sky, gives light to the other part of the sky, so [visible] will the Son of Man be in His day.

²⁵"But first He must suffer many things and be repudiated *and* rejected *and* considered unfit [to be the Messiah] by this [unbelieving] generation.

²⁶"And just as it was in the days of Noah, so it will be in the time of [the second coming of] the Son of Man:

²⁷the people were eating, they were drinking, they were marrying, they were being given in marriage, [they were indifferent to God] until the day that Noah went into the ark, and the flood came and destroyed them all. [Gen 6:5–8; 7:6–24]

²⁸"It was the same as it was in the days of Lot. People were eating, they were drinking, they were buying, they were selling, they were planting, they were building [carrying on business as usual, without regard for their sins];

²⁹but on the [very] day that Lot left Sodom it rained fire and brimstone (burning sulfur) from heaven and destroyed them all.

³⁰"It will be just the same on the day that the Son of Man is revealed. [Gen 18:20–33; 19:24, 25]

³¹"On that day, whoever is on the housetop, with his belongings in the house, must not come down [and go

inside] to take them out; and likewise whoever is in the field must not turn back.

³²"Remember [what happened to] Lot's wife [when she looked back]! [Gen 19:26]

³³"Whoever seeks to save his life will [eventually] lose it [through death], and whoever loses *his life* [in this world] will keep it [from the consequences of sin and separation from God]. [Matt 10:39; 16:25; Mark 8:35; Luke 9:24; John 12:25]

³⁴"I tell you, on that night [when Messiah comes again] there will be two [sleeping] in one bed; the one (the non-believer) will be taken [away in judgment] and the other (the believer) will be left.

³⁵"There will be two women grinding [at the mill] together; the one (the non-believer) will be taken [away in judgment] and the other (the believer) will be left.

³⁶["Two men will be in the field; one will be taken and the other will be left."]

³⁷And they asked Him, "Where, Lord?" He answered, "Where the corpse is, there the vultures will be gathered."

18 NOW JESUS was telling the disciples a parable to make the point that at all times they ought to pray and not give up *and* lose heart,

²saying, "In a certain city there was a judge who did not fear God and had no respect for man.

³"There was a [desperate] widow in that city and she kept coming to him and saying, 'Give me justice *and* legal protection from my adversary.'

⁴"For a time he would not; but later he said to himself, 'Even though I do not fear God nor respect man,

⁵yet because this widow *continues* to bother me, I will give her justice *and*

legal protection; otherwise by continually coming she [will be an intolerable annoyance and she] will wear me out.'"

⁶Then the Lord said, "Listen to what the unjust judge says!

⁷"And will not [our just] God defend *and* avenge His elect [His chosen ones] who cry out to Him day and night? Will He delay [in providing justice] on their behalf?

⁸"I tell you that He will defend *and* avenge them quickly. However, when the Son of Man comes, will He find [this kind of persistent] faith on the earth?"

⁹He also told this parable to some people who trusted in themselves *and* were confident that they were righteous [posing outwardly as upright and in right standing with God], and who viewed others with contempt:

¹⁰"Two men went up into the temple [enclosure] to pray, one a Pharisee and the other a tax collector.

¹¹"The Pharisee stood [ostentatiously] and began praying to himself [in a self-righteous way, saying]: 'God, I thank You that I am not like the rest of men—swindlers, unjust (dishonest), adulterers—or even like this tax collector.

¹²'I fast twice a week; I pay tithes of all that I get.'

¹³"But the tax collector, standing at a distance, would not even raise his eyes toward heaven, but was striking his chest [in humility and repentance],

life point

In Luke 18:8, Jesus asks whether He will find faith on the earth when He returns. We need to remember that God is pleased with us as long as we believe. We need to maintain a high level of confidence in Him. We need to deal sternly with our flesh and not allow it to rule, remembering that Jesus wants to find us full of faith.

saying, 'God, be merciful *and* gracious to me, the [especially wicked] sinner [that I am]!'

¹⁴"I tell you, this man went to his home justified [forgiven of the guilt of sin and placed in right standing with God] rather than the other man; for everyone who exalts himself will be

the trap of trusting yourself

In Luke 18:9–14, Jesus speaks a parable to people who trusted in themselves. This means they were proud; they felt confident they were righteous, upright, and in right standing with God because of their own works.

The parable describes two people who came to the temple to pray. One was a Pharisee and one was a tax collector. The Pharisees were revered because they were religious, and the tax collectors were hated because many of them extorted money from their own people. Tax collectors were considered very wicked.

The Amplified Bible depicts this Pharisee in such a way that I can almost picture him: "The Pharisee stood [ostentatiously] and began praying to himself [in a self-righteous way]" (Luke 18:11). Do you see that? The Pharisee was not even talking to God; he was talking to himself. This portion of Scripture helped me realize there were times in my own life when I also prayed publicly but was not truly talking to God. My only concern was how I sounded in front of people. Now when I lead a prayer in front of other people, I always try to keep my attention fully on God, not on what the people think about how I sound.

The Pharisee continued his monologue with himself. He favorably compared himself to others he considered lowly—robbers, swindlers, and adulterers—or even "this tax collector." Ouch! This Pharisee was saying, "Thank You God that I am not like he is; thank You that I am so holy."

I have never prayed that prayer, but that does not mean I never thought it. You may have a friend in your life right now to whom you consider yourself spiritually superior. This could be a Christian friend who does not practice his or her spirituality the way you do. You attend early-morning prayer meetings three times a week and this person does not. Your tithe even includes money you received as a birthday gift and you are sure theirs does not.

Those Pharisees were such good little tithers. They gave ten percent of every little mint and leaf, every little grain of spice. They would not miss giving their tithes, but they were rotten to the core. Jesus referred to them as a bunch of whitewashed tombs full of dead men's bones. Jesus had a problem with the Pharisees because they put on a good show, but they had rotten hearts (see Matthew 23:23–27). God tells us to give a tithe of all of our increase, but He does not tell us to presume we know what others are doing.

It is so easy to develop an "I'm-better-than-you" attitude when we compare ourselves to others. Guard your heart against self-righteous attitudes. Be like the man in this parable who trusted in the mercy of God—not in himself or his own goodness.

humbled, but he who humbles himself [forsaking self-righteous pride] will be exalted."

¹⁵Now they were also bringing their babies to Him, so that He would touch *and* bless them, and when the disciples noticed it, they *began* reprimanding them.

¹⁶But Jesus called them to Himself, saying [to the apostles], "Allow the children to come to Me, and do not forbid them, for the kingdom of God belongs to such as these.

¹⁷"I assure you *and* most solemnly say to you, whoever does not receive the kingdom of God [with faith and humility] like a child will not enter it at all."

¹⁸A certain ruler asked Him, "Good Teacher [You who are essentially and morally good], what shall I do to inherit eternal life [that is, eternal salvation in the Messiah's kingdom]?" [Matt 19:16–29; Mark 10:17–30]

¹⁹Jesus said to him, "Why do you call Me good? No one is [essentially and morally] good except God alone.

²⁰"You know the commandments: 'DO NOT COMMIT ADULTERY, DO NOT MURDER, DO NOT STEAL, DO NOT TESTIFY FALSELY, HONOR YOUR FATHER AND YOUR MOTHER.'" [Ex 20:12–16; Deut 5:16–20]

²¹He replied, "I have kept all these things from my youth."

²²When Jesus heard this, He said to him, "You still lack one thing; sell everything that you have and distribute the money to the poor, and you will have [abundant] treasure in heaven; and come, follow Me [becoming My disciple, believing and trusting in Me and walking the same path of life that I walk]."

²³But when he heard these things, he became very sad, for he was extremely rich.

²⁴Jesus looked at him and said, "How difficult it is for those who are wealthy to enter the kingdom of God!

²⁵"For it is easier for a camel to go through the eye of a needle than for a rich man [who places his faith in wealth or status] to enter the kingdom of God."

²⁶And those who heard it said, "Then who can be saved?"

²⁷But He said, "The things that are impossible with people are possible with God." [Gen 18:14; Jer 32:17]

²⁸Peter said, "Look, we have left all [things—homes, families, businesses] and followed You."

²⁹And He said to them, "I assure you *and* most solemnly say to you, there is no one who has left house or wife or

life point

In Luke 18:17, Jesus stressed the importance of being childlike in our faith. What are children like? Matthew 18:3 states they are "trusting, humble, and forgiving." Oh, how much more would we enjoy our lives if we only operated in these three virtues! I encourage you to develop them in your life.

life point

Do you have a miserable past? Are your current circumstances negative and depressing? Do you face situations that are so bad it seems you have no real reason to hope? I say to you boldly, *your future is not determined by your past or your present!*

Let me encourage you today to believe that with God all things are possible (see Luke 18:27). Humanly speaking, some things may be impossible, but we serve a God who created everything we see out of nothing (see Hebrews 11:3). Give Him your nothingness and watch Him go to work. All He needs is your faith in Him. He needs you to believe, and He will do the rest.

brothers or parents or children for the sake of the kingdom of God,

³⁰who will not receive many times as much in this present age and in the age to come, eternal life."

³¹Then taking the twelve [disciples] aside, He said to them, "Listen carefully: we are going up to Jerusalem, and all things that have been written through the prophets about the Son of Man will be fulfilled *and* completed. [Is 53:1–12]

³²"He will be betrayed *and* handed over to the Gentiles (Roman authorities), and will be mocked *and* ridiculed and insulted *and* abused and spit on, [Is 50:6]

³³and after they have scourged Him, they will kill Him; and on the third day He will rise [from the dead]." [Ps 16:10]

³⁴But the disciples understood none of these things [about the approaching death and resurrection of Jesus]. This statement was hidden from them, and they did not grasp the [meaning of the] things that were said [by Jesus].

³⁵As He was approaching Jericho [on His way to Jerusalem], it happened that a blind man was sitting beside the road begging. [Matt 20:29–34; Mark 10:46–52]

³⁶Now when he heard a crowd going by, he *began* to ask what this was [about].

³⁷They told him, "Jesus of Nazareth is passing by."

³⁸So he shouted out, saying, "Jesus, Son of David (Messiah), have mercy on me!"

³⁹Those who were leading the way were sternly telling him to keep quiet; but he screamed all the more, "Son of David, have mercy on me!"

⁴⁰Then Jesus stopped and ordered that the blind man be led to Him; and when he came near, Jesus asked him,

⁴¹"What do you want Me to do for you?" He said, "Lord, let me regain my sight!"

⁴²Jesus said to him, "Regain your sight; your [personal trust and confident] faith [in Me] has made you well."

⁴³Immediately he regained his sight and *began* following Jesus, glorifying *and* praising *and* honoring God. And all the people, when they saw it, praised God.

19 JESUS ENTERED Jericho and was passing through. ²And there was a man called Zaccheus; he was a chief tax collector [a superintendent to whom others reported], and he was rich.

³Zaccheus was trying to see who Jesus was, but he could not see because of the crowd, for he was short in stature.

⁴So he ran on ahead [of the crowd] and climbed up in a sycamore tree in order to see Him, for He was about to pass through that way.

⁵When Jesus reached the place, He looked up and said to him, "Zaccheus, hurry and come down, for today I must stay at your house."

⁶So Zaccheus hurried and came down, and welcomed Jesus with joy.

⁷When the people saw it, they all *began* muttering [in discontent], "He has gone to be the guest of a man who is a [notorious] sinner."

⁸Zaccheus stopped and said to the Lord, "See, Lord, I am [now] giving half of my possessions to the poor, and if I have cheated anyone out of anything, I will give back four times as much." [Ex 22:1; Lev 6:5; Num 5:6, 7]

⁹Jesus said to him, "Today salvation has come to this household, because he, too, is a [spiritual] son of Abraham;

¹⁰for the Son of Man has come to seek and to save that which was lost."

¹¹While they were listening to these things, Jesus went on to tell a parable, because He was near Jerusalem, and they assumed that the kingdom of God was going to appear immediately [as soon as He reached the city].

¹²So He said, "A nobleman went to a distant country to obtain for himself a kingdom, and [then] to return.

¹³"So he called ten of his servants, and gave them ten minas [one apiece, each equal to about a hundred days' wages] and said to them, 'Do business [with this] until I return.'

¹⁴"But his citizens [the residents of his new kingdom] hated him and sent a delegation after him, saying, 'We do not want this man to be a king over us.'

¹⁵"When he returned, after receiving the kingdom, he ordered that these servants, to whom he had given the money, be called to him, that he might find out what business they had done.

¹⁶"The first one came before him and said, 'Lord, your mina has made ten more minas.'

¹⁷"And he said to him, 'Well done, good servant! Because you proved yourself faithful *and* trustworthy in a very little thing, you shall [now] have authority over ten cities [in my kingdom].'

¹⁸"The second one came and said, 'Lord, your mina has made five minas.'

¹⁹"And he said to him also, 'And you shall take charge over five cities.'

²⁰"Then another came and said, 'Lord, here is your mina, which I have kept laid up in a handkerchief [for safekeeping].

life point

Notice that Luke 19:10 says "that which," not "those who." In the previous verse we see that the chief tax collector, Zaccheus, and his household received salvation. They were lost and were now saved, but their salvation was not going to end there. The statement Jesus made about coming to save that which was lost tells me He intends to save us not only from our sins, but also from everything Satan tries to do to ruin our lives.

²¹'I was [always] afraid of you, because you are a stern man; you pick up what you did not lay down and you reap what you did not sow.'

²²"He said to the servant, 'I will judge *and* condemn you by your own words, you worthless servant! Did you [really] know that I was a stern man, picking up what I did not lay down and reaping what I did not sow?

²³'Then why did you not [at the very least] put my money in a bank? Then on my return, I would have collected it with interest.'

²⁴"Then he said to the bystanders, 'Take the mina away from him and give it to the one who has the ten minas.'

²⁵"And they said to him, 'Lord, he has ten minas *already!*'

²⁶"[Jesus explained,] 'I tell you that to everyone who has [because he valued his gifts from God and has used them wisely], *more* will be given; but from the one who does not have [because he disregarded his gifts from God], even what he has will be taken away.'

²⁷"[The king ended by saying,] 'But as for these enemies of mine who did not want me to be king over them, bring them here and kill them in my presence.'"

²⁸After saying these things, Jesus went on ahead [of them], going up to Jerusalem.

²⁹When He approached Bethphage and Bethany, at the mount that is called Olivet, He sent two of the disciples, [Matt 21:1–9; Mark 11:1–10; John 12:12–15]

³⁰saying, "Go into the village ahead of you; there, as you enter, you will find a [donkey's] colt tied, on which no one has ever sat. Untie it and bring it here.

³¹"If anybody asks you, 'Why are you untying the colt?' you will say, 'The Lord needs it.'"

³²So those who were sent left and found the colt just as He had told them.

³³As they were untying the colt, its owners asked them, "Why are you untying the colt?"

³⁴They said, "The Lord needs it."

³⁵They brought it to Jesus, and they threw their robes over the colt and put Jesus on it. [Zech 9:9]

³⁶As He rode along, people were spreading their coats on the road [as an act of homage before a king]. [2 Kin 9:13]

³⁷As soon as He was approaching [Jerusalem], near the descent of the Mount of Olives, the entire multitude of the disciples [all those who were or claimed to be His followers] began praising God [adoring Him enthusiastically and] joyfully with loud voices for all the miracles *and* works of power that they had seen,

³⁸shouting,

"BLESSED (celebrated, praised)
   IS THE KING WHO COMES IN THE
   NAME OF THE LORD!
Peace in heaven and glory
   (majesty, splendor) in the
   highest [heaven]!" [Ps 118:26]

³⁹Some of the Pharisees from the crowd said to Him, "Teacher, rebuke Your disciples [for shouting these Messianic praises]."

⁴⁰Jesus replied, "I tell you, if these [people] keep silent, the stones will cry out [in praise]!" [Hab 2:11]

⁴¹As He approached *Jerusalem,* He saw the city and wept over it [and the spiritual ignorance of its people],

⁴²saying, "If [only] you had known on this day [of salvation], even you, the things which make for peace [and on which peace depends]! But now they have been hidden from your eyes.

⁴³"For a time [of siege] is coming when your enemies will put up a barricade [with pointed stakes] against you, and surround you [with armies] and hem you in on every side, [Is 29:3; Jer 6:6; Ezek 4:2]

⁴⁴and they will level you to the ground, you [Jerusalem] and your children within you. They will not leave in you one stone on another, all because you did not [come progressively to] recognize [from observation and personal experience] the time of your visitation [when God was gracious toward you and offered you salvation]."

⁴⁵Jesus went into the temple [enclosure] and began driving out those who were selling, [Matt 21:12, 13; Mark 11:15–17; John 2:13–16]

⁴⁶saying to them, "It is written, 'MY HOUSE SHALL BE A HOUSE OF PRAYER'; but you have made it a ROBBERS' DEN." [Is 56:7; Jer 7:11]

⁴⁷He was teaching day after day in the temple [porches and courts]; but the chief priests and scribes and the leading men among the people were seeking [a way] to put Him to death,

⁴⁸and they could not find anything that they could do, for all the people [stayed close to Him and] were hanging on to every word He said.

20 ON ONE of the days, as Jesus was instructing the people in the temple [area] and preaching the good news (gospel), the chief priests and the scribes along with the elders confronted *Him,* [Matt 21:23–27; Mark 11:27–33]

²and said to Him, "Tell us by what *kind of* authority You are doing these things? Or who is the one who gave You this authority?"

³Jesus replied, "I will also ask you a question. You tell Me:

⁴"The baptism of John [the Baptist]— was it from heaven [that is, ordained by God] or from men?"

⁵They discussed *and* debated it among themselves, saying, "If we say, 'From heaven,' He will say, 'Why did you not believe him?'

⁶"But if we say, 'From men,' all the people will stone us to death, for they

are *firmly* convinced that John was a prophet."

⁷So they replied that they did not know from where *it came.*

⁸Then Jesus said to them, "Nor am I telling you by what [kind of] authority I do these things."

⁹Then He began to tell the people this parable: "A man planted a vineyard and leased it to tenant farmers, and went on a journey for a long time [to another country]. [Is 5:1–7; Matt 21:33–46; Mark 12:1–12]

¹⁰"At *harvest* time he sent a servant [as his representative] to the tenants, so that they would give him *his share* of the fruit of the vineyard; but the tenants beat the servant and sent him away empty-handed.

¹¹"So he again sent another servant; they also beat him and dishonored *and* treated him disgracefully and sent him away empty-handed.

¹²"And he sent yet a third; and this one too they wounded and threw out [of the vineyard].

¹³"Then the owner of the vineyard said, 'What shall I do? I will send my beloved son; perhaps they will have respect for him.'

¹⁴"But when the tenants saw him, they discussed it among themselves, saying, 'This [man] is the heir; let us kill him so that the inheritance will be ours.'

¹⁵"So they threw the son out of the vineyard and killed him. What, then, will the owner of the vineyard do to them?

¹⁶"He will come and put these tenants to death and will give the vineyard to others." When the chief priests, the scribes, and the elders heard this, they said, "May it never be!"

¹⁷But Jesus looked at them and said, "What then is [the meaning of] this that is written:

'THE [very] STONE WHICH THE BUILDERS REJECTED,

THIS BECAME THE CHIEF CORNERSTONE'? [Ps 118:22, 23]

¹⁸"Everyone who falls on that stone will be broken *and* shattered in pieces; and on whomever it falls, it will crush him." [Is 8:14, 15; Dan 2:34, 35]

¹⁹The scribes and the chief priests tried to [find a way to] arrest Him at that very hour, but they were afraid of the people; because they understood that He spoke this parable against them.

²⁰So they watched [for a chance to trap] Him. They sent spies who pretended to be upright *and* sincere, in order that they might catch Him in some statement [that they could distort and use against Him], so that they could turn Him over to the control and authority of [Pilate] the governor. [Matt 22:15–22; Mark 12:13–17]

²¹They asked Him, "Teacher, we know that You speak and teach correctly, and that You show no partiality to anyone, but teach the way of God truthfully.

²²"Is it lawful [according to Jewish law and tradition] for us to pay taxes (tribute money) to Caesar or not?"

²³But He saw through their trickery and said to them,

²⁴"Show Me a [Roman] denarius. Whose image and inscription does the coin have?" They answered, "[the Emperor Tiberius] Caesar's."

²⁵He said to them, "Then pay to Caesar the things that are Caesar's, and to God the things that are God's."

²⁶They were not able to seize on anything He said in the presence of the people; and being unnerved at His reply, they were silent.

²⁷Now some of the Sadducees (who say that there is no resurrection) came to Him [Matt 22:23–33; Mark 12:18–27]

²⁸and they questioned Him, saying, "Teacher, Moses wrote for us [a law that] IF A MAN'S BROTHER DIES, leaving a wife AND NO CHILDREN, HIS BROTHER

SHOULD MARRY THE WIFE AND RAISE CHILDREN FOR HIS BROTHER. [Deut 25:5, 6]

²⁹"Now there were seven brothers; and the first took a wife and died childless.

³⁰"And the second,

³¹and the third married her, and in the same way all seven died, leaving no children.

³²"Finally the woman also died.

³³"So in the [life after] resurrection, whose wife does she become? For all seven had married her."

³⁴Jesus said to them, "The sons of this [world and present] age marry and [the women] are given in marriage;

³⁵but those who are considered worthy to gain that [other world and that future] age and the resurrection from the dead, neither marry nor are given in marriage;

³⁶and they cannot die again, because they are [immortal] like the angels (equal to, angel-like). And they are children of God, being participants in the resurrection.

³⁷"But [as for the fact] that the dead are raised [from death], even Moses showed, in the *passage about the burning* bush, when he calls the Lord THE GOD OF ABRAHAM, THE GOD OF ISAAC, AND THE GOD OF JACOB. [Ex 3:6]

³⁸"Now He is not the God of the dead, but of the living [so these forefathers will be among the resurrected]; for all live [in a definite relationship] to Him."

³⁹Some of the scribes replied, "Teacher, you have spoken well [so that there is no room for blame]."

⁴⁰And they did not dare to question Him further about anything [because of the wisdom He displayed in His answers].

⁴¹Then He said to them, "How *is it that* people say that the Christ (the Messiah, the Anointed) is David's son? [Matt 22:41–46; Mark 12:35–37]

⁴²"For David himself says in the book of Psalms,

'THE LORD (the Father) SAID TO MY LORD (the Son, the Messiah), "SIT AT MY RIGHT HAND,
⁴³ UNTIL I MAKE YOUR ENEMIES A FOOTSTOOL FOR YOUR FEET."' [Ps 110:1]

⁴⁴"So David calls Him (the Son) 'Lord,' and how *then* is He David's son?"

⁴⁵And with all the people listening, He said to His disciples,

⁴⁶"Beware of the scribes, who like to walk around in long robes [displaying their prominence], and love respectful greetings in the [crowded] market places, and chief seats in the synagogues and places of honor at banquets.

⁴⁷"These [men] who confiscate *and* devour widows' houses, and for a pretense [to appear devout] offer long prayers. These [men] will receive the greater [sentence of] condemnation."

21

LOOKING UP, He saw the rich people putting their gifts into the treasury. [Mark 12:41–44]

²And He saw a poor widow putting in two small copper coins.

³He said, "Truly I say to you, this poor widow has put in [proportionally] more than all *of them;*

⁴for they all put in gifts from their abundance; but she out of her poverty put in all she had to live on."

⁵As some were talking about the temple, that it was decorated with beautiful stones and consecrated offerings [of magnificent gifts of gold which were displayed on the walls and hung in the porticoes], He said, [Matt 24; Mark 13]

⁶"As for all these things which you see, the time will come when there will not be one stone left on another that will not be torn down."

⁷They asked Him, "Teacher, when will these things happen? And what

will be the sign when these things are about to happen?"

⁸He said, "Be careful *and* see to it that you are not misled; for many will come in My name [appropriating for themselves the name Messiah which belongs to Me alone], saying, 'I am *He,*' and, 'The time is near!' Do not follow them.

⁹"When you hear of wars and disturbances [civil unrest, revolts, uprisings], do not panic; for these things must take place first, but the end will not *come* immediately."

¹⁰Then Jesus told them, "Nation will rise against nation and kingdom against kingdom. [2 Chr 15:6; Is 19:2]

¹¹"There will be violent earthquakes, and in various places famines and [deadly and devastating] pestilences (plagues, epidemics); and there will be terrible sights and great signs from heaven.

¹²"But before all these things, they will lay their hands on you and will persecute you, turning you over to the synagogues and prisons, and bringing you before kings and governors for My name's sake. [Matt 10:19–22; Mark 13:11–13]

¹³"This will be a time *and* an opportunity for you to testify [about Me].

¹⁴"So make up your minds not to prepare beforehand to defend yourselves;

¹⁵for I will give you [skillful] words and wisdom which none of your opponents will be able to resist or refute.

¹⁶"But you will be betrayed *and* handed over even by parents and brothers and relatives and friends, and they will put *some* of you to death,

¹⁷and you will be *continually* hated by everyone because of [your association with] My name.

¹⁸"But not a hair of your head will perish. [1 Sam 14:45]

¹⁹"By your [patient] endurance [empowered by the Holy Spirit] you will gain your souls.

²⁰"But when you see Jerusalem surrounded by [hostile] armies, then understand [with confident assurance] that her complete destruction is near.

²¹"At that time, those who are in Judea must flee to the mountains, and those who are inside the city (Jerusalem) must get out, and those who are [out] in the country must not enter the city;

²²for these are days of vengeance [of rendering full justice or satisfaction], so that all things which are written will be fulfilled.

²³"Woe to those women who are pregnant and to those who are nursing babies in those days! For great trouble *and* anguish will be on the land, and wrath *and* retribution on this people [Israel].

²⁴"And they will fall by the edge of the sword, and will be led captive into all nations; and Jerusalem will be trampled underfoot by the Gentiles until the times of the Gentiles are fulfilled (completed). [Is 63:18; Dan 8:13]

²⁵"There will be signs (attesting miracles) in the sun and moon and stars; and on the earth [there will be] distress *and* anguish among nations, in perplexity at the roaring *and* tossing of the sea and the waves, [Is 13:10; Joel 2:10; Zeph 1:15]

²⁶people fainting from fear and expectation of the [dreadful] things coming on the world; for the [very] powers of the heavens will be shaken.

²⁷"Then they will see THE SON OF MAN COMING IN A CLOUD with [transcendent, overwhelming] power [subduing the nations] and with great glory. [Dan 7:13, 14]

²⁸"Now when these things begin to occur, stand tall and lift up your heads [in joy], because [suffering ends as] your redemption is drawing near."

²⁹Then He told them a parable: "Look at the fig tree and all the trees; [Matt 24:32, 33; Mark 13:28, 29]

³⁰as soon as they put out leaves, you see it and know for yourselves that summer is near.

³¹"So you too, when you see these things happening, know [without any doubt] that the kingdom of God is near.

³²"I assure you *and* most solemnly say to you, this generation [those living at that definite period of time preceding the second coming] will not pass away until everything takes place.

³³"Heaven and earth will pass away, but My words will not pass away.

³⁴"But be on guard, so that your hearts are not weighed down *and* depressed with the giddiness of debauchery and the nausea of self-indulgence and the worldly worries of life, and then that day [when the Messiah returns] will not come on you suddenly like a trap;

³⁵for it will come upon all those who live on the face of all the earth.

³⁶"But keep alert at all times [be attentive and ready], praying that you may have the strength *and* ability [to be found worthy and] to escape all these things that are going to take place, and to stand in the presence of the Son of Man [at His coming]."

³⁷Now in the daytime Jesus was teaching in [the porches and courts of] the temple, but at night He would go out and spend the night on the mount that is called Olivet.

³⁸And early in the morning all the people would come to Him in the temple to listen to Him.

22 NOW THE Festival of Unleavened Bread, which is called the Passover, was approaching. [Lev 23:4, 5; Ezek 45:21; Matt 26:2–5; Mark 14:1, 2]

²The chief priests and the scribes were looking for a way to put Him to death; for they were afraid of the people [who listened devotedly to His teaching, and who respected His spiritual wisdom].

³Then Satan entered Judas, the one called Iscariot, who was one of the twelve [disciples].

⁴And he went away and discussed with the chief priests and officers how he might betray Him *and* hand Him over to them.

⁵They were delighted and agreed with him to give him money.

⁶So he consented, and *began* looking for a good opportunity to betray Jesus to them [at a time when He was] separated from the crowd [because the people might riot or stop them from seizing Him].

⁷Then came the *preparation* day of

life point

Judas was one of Jesus' twelve disciples, yet we read that Satan entered into him (see Luke 22:3). It's important for us to understand that Satan can work through anyone, even those close to us. That is why it is dangerous to expect too much of the people around us. When we expect them never to hurt us, we set ourselves up for severe disappointment.

That does not mean we should adopt a sour, bitter, cynical attitude toward everyone and say, "Well, a person cannot trust anybody these days." I am not saying that at all. I like people, and I trust people. I do not go through life being suspicious of everyone I meet. At the same time, I also do not go through life expecting never to be hurt by anyone because I know that other people are flesh and blood, just as I am. I realize that they are going to fail just as I fail. Therefore, I put my trust not in people but in Jesus, the Friend who sticks closer than a brother (see Proverbs 18:24). I encourage you to do the same. He will never disappoint you!

Unleavened Bread on which the Passover *lamb* had to be sacrificed. [Ex 12:18–20; Deut 16:5–8; Matt 26:17–19; Mark 14:12–16]

⁸So Jesus sent Peter and John, saying, "Go and prepare the Passover meal for us, so that we may eat it."

⁹They asked Him, "Where do You want us to prepare it?"

¹⁰He replied, "When you have entered the city, a man carrying an *earthen* jar of water will meet you; follow him into the house that he enters.

¹¹"And say to the owner of the house, 'The Teacher asks, "Where is the guest room in which I may eat the Passover with My disciples?"'

¹²"Then he will show you a large upstairs room, furnished [with carpets and dining couches]; prepare the meal there."

¹³They left and found it just as He had told them; and they prepared the Passover.

¹⁴When the hour [for the meal] had come, Jesus reclined *at the table,* and the apostles with Him.

¹⁵He said to them, "I have earnestly wanted to eat this Passover with you before I suffer;

¹⁶for I say to you, I will not eat it again until it is fulfilled in the kingdom of God."

¹⁷And when He had taken a cup and given thanks, He said, "Take this and share it among yourselves; [Matt 26:26–29; Mark 14:22–25; 1 Cor 11:23–25]

¹⁸for I say to you, I will not drink of the fruit of the vine from now on until the kingdom of God comes."

¹⁹And when He had taken bread and given thanks, He broke it and gave it to them, saying, "This is My body which is given for you; do this in remembrance of Me."

²⁰And in the same way *He took* the cup after they had eaten, saying, "This cup, which is poured out for you, is the new covenant [ratified] in My blood.

²¹"But listen, the hand of the one betraying Me is with Mine on the table. [Ps 41:9]

²²"For indeed, the Son of Man is going as it has been determined; but woe (judgment is coming) to that man by whom He is betrayed *and* handed over!"

²³And they began to discuss among themselves which one of them it might be who was going to do this.

²⁴Now a dispute also arose among them as to which of them was regarded to be the greatest.

²⁵Jesus said to them, "The kings of the Gentiles have absolute power *and* lord it over them; and those in authority over them are called 'Benefactors.' [Matt 20:25–28; Mark 10:42–45]

²⁶"But it is not to be this way with you; on the contrary, the one who is the greatest among you must become like the youngest [and least privileged], and the [one who is the] leader, like the servant.

²⁷"For who is the greater, the one who reclines *at the table* or the one who serves? Is it not the one who reclines *at the table?* But I am among you as the one who serves.

²⁸"You are those who have remained *and* have stood by Me in My trials;

²⁹and just as My Father has granted Me a kingdom, I grant you [the privilege]

³⁰that you may eat and drink at My table in My kingdom, and you will sit on thrones judging the twelve tribes of Israel.

³¹"Simon, Simon (Peter), listen! Satan has demanded *permission* to sift [all of] you like grain; [Job 1:6–12; Amos 9:9]

³²but I have prayed [especially] for you [Peter], that your faith [and confidence in Me] may not fail; and you, once you have turned back again [to Me], strengthen *and* support your brothers [in the faith]."

33And Peter said to Him, "Lord, I am ready to go with You both to prison and to death!" [Matt 26:33–35; Mark 14:29–31; John 13:37, 38]

34Jesus said, "I say to you, Peter, before the rooster crows today, you will [utterly] deny three times that you know Me."

35And He said to them, "When I sent you out without a money belt and [provision] bag and [extra] sandals, did you lack anything?" They answered, "Nothing."

36Then He said to them, "But now, he who has a money belt is to take it along, and also his [provision] bag, and he who has no sword is to sell his coat and buy one.

37"For I tell you that this [Scripture] which is written must be completed and fulfilled in Me: 'AND HE WAS COUNTED WITH THE CRIMINALS'; for that which refers to Me has its fulfillment [and is settled]." [Is 53:12]

38They said, "Lord, look, here are two swords." And He said to them, "It is enough."

39And He came out and went, as was His habit, to the Mount of Olives; and the disciples followed Him.

40When He arrived at the place [called Gethsemane], He said to them, "Pray continually that you may not fall into temptation." [Matt 26:36–46; Mark 14:32–42]

41And He withdrew from them about a stone's throw, and knelt down and prayed,

42saying, "Father, if You are willing, remove this cup [of divine wrath] from Me; yet not My will, but [always] Yours be done."

who is the greatest?

Early in my life, I struggled with jealousy and envy as I compared myself to other people. This is a common habit of the insecure. If we are not secure concerning our worth and value as unique individuals, we will find ourselves competing with anyone who appears to be successful and doing well.

Learning that I was an individual with a God-ordained, unique, personal plan for my life has indeed been one of the most valuable and precious freedoms the Lord has granted me. I am assured that I do not need to compare myself, or my ministry, to anyone.

I am always encouraged that there is hope for me when I look at Jesus' disciples and realize that they struggled with many of the same things I do. In Luke 22:24 we find the disciples arguing over which of them was the greatest. Jesus responded to them by saying that the greatest was actually the one who was willing to be considered the least or the one who was willing to be a servant (see Luke 22:26). Our Lord spent a great deal of His time trying to teach His disciples that life in the kingdom of God is usually the direct opposite of the way of the world or the flesh.

Jesus taught His disciples great principles like these: Many who are first will be last, and the last will be first (see Mark 10:31); rejoice with the lost who have been found (see Luke 15:6, 32); love your enemies and pray for people who persecute you (see Matthew 5:44). It is more blessed to give than to receive (see Acts 20:35). The world says these things are foolishness—but Jesus says they are true power. Be a disciple and determine to live your life by Jesus' kingdom principles.

putting the Word to work

Jesus struggled when faced with the reality of going to the cross, yet He chose God's will over His own (see Luke 22:39–42). How will you respond when God asks you to choose His will over what you want to do? You may never be asked to sacrifice your life for your faith; yet in every sacrifice, great or small, ask God for the strength to do His will, His way.

43Now an angel appeared to Him from heaven, strengthening Him.

44And being in agony [deeply distressed and anguished; almost to the point of death], He prayed more intently; and His sweat became like drops of blood, falling down on the ground. [Heb 5:7]

45When He rose from prayer, He came to the disciples and found them sleeping from sorrow,

46and He said to them, "Why are you sleeping? Get up and pray that you may not fall into temptation."

47While He was still speaking, a crowd came, and the man called Judas, one of the twelve [disciples], was leading the way for them. He approached Jesus to kiss Him. [Matt 26:47–56; Mark 14:43–50; John 18:3–11]

48And Jesus said to him, "Judas, are you betraying the Son of Man with a kiss?"

49When those who were around Him saw what was about to happen, they said, "Lord, should we strike with the sword?"

50And one of them struck the slave of the high priest and cut off his right ear. [Matt 26:51; Mark 14:47; John 18:10]

51But Jesus replied, "Stop! No more of this." And He touched the ear and healed him.

52Then Jesus said to the chief priests and officers of the temple and elders [of the Sanhedrin] who had come out against Him, "Have you come out with swords and clubs as you would against a robber?

53"Day after day when I was with you in the temple, you did not lay hands on Me; but this hour and the power and authority of darkness are yours."

54Then they seized Him, and led Him away and brought Him to the [elegant] house of the [Jewish] high priest. And Peter was following at a [safe] distance.

55After they had kindled a fire in the middle of the courtyard and had sat down together, Peter sat among them. [Matt 26:69–75; Mark 14:66–72; John 18:16–18, 25–27]

56And a servant-girl, seeing him as he sat in the firelight and looking intently at him, said, "This man was with Him too."

57But Peter denied it, saying, "Woman, I do not know Him!"

58A little later someone else saw him and said, "You are one of them too." But Peter said, "Man, I am not!"

59After about an hour had passed, another man began to insist, "This man was with Him, for he is a Galilean too."

60But Peter said, "Man, I do not know what you are talking about." Immediately, while he was still speaking, a rooster crowed.

61The Lord turned and looked at Peter. And Peter remembered the word of the Lord, how He had told him, "Before a rooster crows today, you will deny Me three times."

62And he went out and wept bitterly [deeply grieved and distressed].

speak the Word

Help me, Jesus, to never deny You.
–ADAPTED FROM LUKE 22:61

⁶³Now the men who were holding Jesus in custody were mocking *and* ridiculing Him [and treating Him with contempt] and beating Him.

⁶⁴They blindfolded Him and asked, "Prophesy, who is it that struck You?"

⁶⁵And they were saying many other [evil and slanderous] things against Him, blaspheming [speaking sacrilegiously and abusively about] Him.

⁶⁶When day came, the Council of the elders of the people (Sanhedrin, Jewish High Court) assembled, both chief priests and scribes; and they led Jesus away to the council *chamber,* saying,

⁶⁷"If You are the Christ (the Messiah, the Anointed), tell us." But He said to them, "If I tell you, you will not believe [what I say],

⁶⁸and if I ask a question, you will not answer.

⁶⁹"But from now on, THE SON OF MAN WILL BE SEATED AT THE RIGHT HAND of the power OF GOD." [Ps 110:1]

⁷⁰And they all said, "Are You the Son of God, then?" He replied, *"It is just as* you say."

⁷¹Then they asked, "What further need of testimony do we have? For we ourselves have heard it from His own mouth."

23 THEN THE whole assembly got up and brought Him before Pilate.

²They began to accuse Jesus, asserting, "We found this Man misleading *and* perverting our nation and forbidding us to pay taxes to Caesar, and claiming that He Himself is Christ (the Messiah, the Anointed), a King." [Matt 27:11–14; Mark 15:2–5; John 18:29–37]

³So Pilate asked Him, "Are You the King of the Jews?" And He answered him, *"It is just as* you say."

⁴Then Pilate said to the chief priests and the crowds, "I find no guilt in this Man."

⁵But they were insistent and said, "He stirs up the people [to rebel], teaching throughout Judea, starting from Galilee even as far as here [in Jerusalem]."

⁶When Pilate heard it, he asked whether the man was a Galilean.

⁷And when he learned that He belonged to the jurisdiction of Herod [Antipas, the tetrarch of Galilee], he sent Him to Herod, who was also in Jerusalem at that time.

⁸When Herod saw Jesus, he was exceedingly pleased. He had wanted to see Him for a long time because of what he had heard about Him, and was hoping to see some [miraculous] sign [even something spectacular] done by Him.

⁹And he questioned Him at some length, but Jesus made no reply. [Is 53:7]

¹⁰The chief priests and the scribes were standing there, *continually* accusing Him heatedly.

¹¹And Herod with his soldiers, after treating Him with contempt and mocking *and* ridiculing Him, dressed Him in a gorgeous robe and sent Him back to Pilate. [Is 53:8]

¹²Now that very day Herod and Pilate became friends with each other—before this they had been enemies.

¹³Pilate summoned the chief priests and the rulers and the people,

¹⁴and said to them, "You brought this man before me as one who corrupts *and* incites the people to rebellion. After examining Him before you, I have found no guilt in this Man regarding the charges which you make against Him.

¹⁵"No, nor has Herod, for he sent Him back to us; and indeed, He has done nothing to deserve death.

¹⁶"Therefore I will punish Him [to teach Him a lesson] and release Him."

¹⁷[Now he was obligated to release to them one prisoner at the Feast.]

¹⁸But they [loudly] shouted out all together, saying, "Away with this Man, and release Barabbas to us!" [Matt 27:15–26; Mark 15:6–15; John 18:39–19:16]

¹⁹(He was one who had been thrown into prison for an insurrection that happened in the city, and for murder.)

²⁰Pilate addressed them again, wanting to release Jesus,

²¹but they kept shouting out, "Crucify, crucify Him!"

²²A third time he said to them, "Why, what wrong has He done? I have found no guilt [no crime, no offense] in Him *demanding* death; therefore I will punish Him [to teach Him a lesson] and release Him."

²³But they were insistent *and* unrelenting, demanding with loud voices that Jesus be crucified. And their voices *began* to prevail *and* accomplish their purpose.

²⁴Pilate pronounced sentence that their demand be granted.

²⁵And he released the man they were asking for who had been thrown into prison for insurrection and murder, but he handed over Jesus to their will.

²⁶When they led Him away, they seized a man, Simon of Cyrene, who was coming in [to the city] from the country, and placed on him the cross to carry behind Jesus. [Matt 27:32; Mark 15:21]

²⁷Following Him was a large crowd of the people, including women who were mourning and wailing for Him.

²⁸But Jesus, turning toward them, said, "Daughters of Jerusalem, do not weep for Me, but weep for yourselves and for your children.

²⁹"For behold, the days are coming when they will say, 'Blessed are the barren, and the wombs that have not given birth, and the breasts that have never nursed.'

³⁰"Then they will begin TO SAY TO THE MOUNTAINS, 'FALL ON US!' AND TO THE HILLS, 'COVER US!' [Is 2:19, 20; Hos 10:8; Rev 6:16]

³¹"For if they do these things when the tree is green, what will happen when it is dry?"

³²Two others also, who were criminals, were being led away to be executed with Him. [Is 53:12]

³³When they came to the place called The Skull, there they crucified Him and the criminals, one on the right and one on the left. [Matt 27:33–44; Mark 15:22–32; John 19:17–24]

³⁴And Jesus was saying, "Father, forgive them; for they do not know what they are doing." And they cast lots, dividing His clothes among themselves. [Ps 22:18]

³⁵Now the people stood by, watching; but even the rulers ridiculed *and* sneered at Him, saying, "He saved others [from death]; let Him save Himself if He is the Christ (the Messiah, the Anointed) of God, His Chosen One."

³⁶The soldiers also mocked Him, coming up to Him and [cruelly] offering Him sour wine, [Ps 69:21; Matt 27:48; Mark 15:36f; John 19:29, 30]

³⁷and sarcastically saying, "If you are [really] the King of the Jews, save Yourself [from death]!"

³⁸Now there was also an inscription above Him: "THIS IS THE KING OF THE JEWS."

³⁹One of the criminals who had been hanged [on a cross beside Him] kept hurling abuse at Him, saying, "Are You not the Christ? Save Yourself and us [from death]!"

⁴⁰But the other one rebuked him, saying, "Do you not even fear God, since you are under the same sentence of condemnation?

⁴¹"We *are suffering* justly, because we are getting what we deserve for what we have done; but this Man has done nothing wrong."

⁴²And he was saying, "Jesus, [please]

remember me when You come into Your kingdom!"

⁴³Jesus said to him, "I assure you *and* most solemnly say to you, today you will be with Me in Paradise." [2 Cor 12:4; Rev 2:7]

⁴⁴It was now about the sixth hour (noon), and darkness came over the whole land until the ninth hour (3:00 p.m.), [Matt 27:45–56; Mark 15:33–41; John 19:14]

⁴⁵because the sun was obscured; and the veil [of the Holy of Holies] of the temple was torn in two [from top to bottom]. [Ex 26:31–35]

⁴⁶And Jesus, crying out with a loud voice, said, "Father, INTO YOUR HANDS I COMMIT MY SPIRIT!" Having said this, He breathed His last. [Ps 31:5]

⁴⁷Now when the centurion saw what had taken place, he *began* praising *and* honoring God, saying, "Certainly this Man was innocent."

⁴⁸All the crowds who had gathered for this spectacle, when they saw what had happened, *began* to return [to their homes], beating their breasts [as a sign of mourning or repentance].

⁴⁹And all His acquaintances and the women who had accompanied Him from Galilee were standing at a distance, watching these things.

⁵⁰A man named Joseph, who was a member of the Council (Sanhedrin, Jewish High Court), a good and honorable man [Matt 27:57–61; Mark 15:42–47; John 19:38–42]

putting the Word to work

Do you ever struggle with feeling you need to earn God's love and favor? Take a lesson from the criminal in Luke 23:39–43: there is nothing you can do to make God love you any more, and there is nothing you have done that makes God love you any less.

⁵¹(he had not consented to the Council's plan and action) *a man* from Arimathea, a city of the Jews, who was waiting for *and* expecting the kingdom of God;

⁵²this man went to Pilate and asked for the body of Jesus.

⁵³And [after receiving permission] he took it down and wrapped it in a linen [burial] cloth and laid Him in a tomb cut into the rock, where no one had yet been laid.

⁵⁴It was the day of preparation [for the Sabbath], and the Sabbath was dawning.

⁵⁵Now the women who had come with Him from Galilee followed [closely], and saw the tomb and how His body was laid.

⁵⁶Then they went back and prepared spices and ointments *and* sweet-smelling herbs.

And on the Sabbath they rested in accordance with the commandment [forbidding work]. [Ex 12:16; 20:10]

24 BUT ON the first day of the week, at early dawn, the women went to the tomb bringing the spices which they had prepared [to finish anointing the body]. [Matt 28:1–8; Mark 16:1–8; John 20:1–8]

²And they found the [large, circular] stone rolled back from the tomb,

³but when they went inside, they did not find the body of the Lord Jesus.

⁴While they were perplexed *and* wondering about this, suddenly, two men in dazzling clothing stood near them;

⁵and as the women were terrified and were bowing their faces to the ground, the men said to them, "Why are you looking for the living One among the dead?

⁶"He is not here, but has risen. Remember how He told you, while He was still in Galilee,

⁷saying that the Son of Man must

be handed over to sinful men, and be crucified, and on the third day rise [from death to life]." [Ps 16:10]

⁸And they remembered His words,

⁹and after returning from the tomb, they reported all these things to the eleven [apostles] and to all the rest.

¹⁰Now they were Mary Magdalene and Joanna [the wife of Chuza, Herod's steward] and Mary the *mother* of James; also the other women with them were telling these things to the apostles.

¹¹But their report seemed to them like idle talk *and* nonsense, and they would not believe them.

¹²But Peter got up and ran to the tomb. Stooping [at the small entrance] and looking in, he saw only the linen wrappings; and he went away, wondering about what had happened. [John 20:3–6]

¹³And then, that very day two of them were going to a village called Emmaus, which was about *seven miles from Jerusalem. [Mark 16:12]

¹⁴And they were talking with each other about all these things which had taken place.

¹⁵While they were talking and discussing it, Jesus Himself came up and *began* walking with them.

¹⁶But their eyes were [miraculously] prevented from recognizing Him.

¹⁷Then Jesus asked them, "What are you discussing with one another as you walk along?" And they stood still, looking brokenhearted.

¹⁸One *of them,* named Cleopas, answered Him, "Are you the only stranger visiting Jerusalem who is unaware of the things which have happened here in these [recent] days?"

¹⁹He asked, "What things?" And they replied, "The things about Jesus of Nazareth, who was a prophet powerful in deed and word in the sight of God and all the people,

²⁰and how the chief priests and our rulers handed Him over to be sentenced to death, and crucified Him.

²¹"But we were hoping that it was He who was going to redeem Israel *and* set our nation free. Indeed, besides all this, it is the third day since these things happened.

²²"And also some of the women among us shocked us. They were at the tomb early in the morning,

²³and they did not find His body. Then they came back, saying that they had even seen a vision of angels who said that He was alive!

²⁴"Some of those who were with us went to the tomb and found it just exactly as the women had said, but they did not see Him."

²⁵Then Jesus said to them, "O foolish men, and slow of heart to trust *and* believe in everything that the prophets have spoken!

²⁶"Was it not necessary for the Christ to suffer these things and [only then to] enter His glory?"

²⁷Then beginning with Moses and [throughout] all the [writings of the] prophets, He explained *and* interpreted for them the things referring to Himself [found] in all the Scriptures.

²⁸Then they approached the village where they were going, and He acted as if He were going farther.

²⁹But they urged Him [not to go on], saying, "Stay with us, because it is almost evening, and the day has just about ended." So He went inside to stay with them.

³⁰And it happened that as He reclined *at the table* with them, He took the bread and blessed it, and breaking it, He *began* giving it to them.

³¹Then their eyes were [suddenly] opened [by God] and they [clearly] recognized Him; and He vanished from their sight.

³²They said to one another, "Were not

24:13 Lit *sixty stadia,* a Roman measurement.

our hearts burning within us while He was talking with us on the road and opening the Scriptures to us?"

33They got up that very hour and went back to Jerusalem, and found the eleven [apostles] gathered together and those who were with them,

34saying, "The Lord has really risen and has appeared to Simon [Peter]!"

35They *began* describing in detail what had happened on the road, and how Jesus was recognized by them when He broke the bread.

36While they were talking about this, Jesus Himself [suddenly] stood among them and said to them, "Peace be to you."

37But they were startled and terrified and thought that they were seeing a spirit.

38And He said, "Why are you troubled, and why are doubts rising in your hearts?

39"Look at [the marks in] My hands and My feet, [and see] that it is I Myself. Touch Me and see; a spirit does not have flesh and bones, as you see that I have." [John 20:20–27]

40After saying this, He showed them His hands and His feet.

41While they still did not believe it because of their joy and amazement, He asked them, "Do you have anything here to eat?"

42They gave Him a piece of broiled fish,

43and He took it and ate it in front of them. [Acts 10:40, 41]

44Then He said to them, "This is what I told you while I was still with you, everything which has been written about Me in the Law of Moses and the [writings of the] Prophets and the Psalms must be fulfilled."

45Then He opened their minds to [help them] understand the Scriptures,

46and said, "And so it is written, that the Christ (the Messiah, the Anointed) would suffer and rise from the dead on the third day, [Hos 6:2]

47and that repentance [necessary] for forgiveness of sins would be preached in His name to all the nations, beginning from Jerusalem.

48"You are witnesses of these things.

49"Listen carefully: I am sending the Promise of My Father [the Holy Spirit] upon you; but you are to remain in the city [of Jerusalem] until you are clothed (fully equipped) with power from on high." [John 14:26; Acts 1:4]

50Then He led them out as far as Bethany, and lifted up His hands and blessed them. [Matt 21:17; Acts 1:9–12]

51While He was blessing them, He left them and was taken up into heaven.

52And they worshiped Him and returned to Jerusalem with great joy [fully understanding that He lives and that He is the Son of God];

53and they were continually in the temple blessing *and* praising God.

John

Author:
Apostle John

Date:
Near the close of the first century

Everyday Life Principles:
We live under a new commandment—
to love one another. This is essential.

Apart from Jesus, we can do nothing.

The Holy Spirit is our Comforter, our
Counselor, our Helper, and our Teacher.
He is also the Spirit of Truth.

While Matthew, Mark, and Luke differ in several ways, they are similar in that they include many of the same teachings and parables of Jesus in sequential order. John, on the other hand, does not take such a chronological approach, but tells about Jesus in terms of themes and topics.

One of the great themes in John is love—loving God, receiving His love, and loving others. In John 13:34, Jesus says: "I am giving you a new commandment, that you love one another. Just as I have loved you, so you too are to love one another." This is one of the most important principles of our faith and is vital to our lives as believers.

Another important theme in John is the necessity of abiding in Jesus. In John 15:5, He tells us: "apart from Me [that is, cut off from vital union with Me] you can do nothing." We are wise to stay as close to Jesus as we possibly can. As we do, we are blessed and our lives bear much fruit.

John also gives us great insight into the ministry of the Holy Spirit (see chapters 14—16), Who is our Teacher, our Comforter, our Helper, our Counselor, and the Spirit of Truth.

As you read John, be reminded of God's love for you and of the necessity of staying intimately connected to Jesus. Allow the Holy Spirit to minister to you in every area of your life.

1 IN THE beginning [before all time] was the Word (Christ), and the Word was with God, and the Word was God Himself. [Gen 1:1; Is 9:6]

²He was [continually existing] in the beginning [co-eternally] with God.

³All things were made *and* came into existence through Him; and without Him not even one thing was made that has come into being.

⁴In Him was life [and the power to bestow life], and the life was the Light of men.

⁵The Light shines on in the darkness, and the darkness did not understand it *or* overpower it *or* appropriate it *or* absorb it [and is unreceptive to it]. [Gen 1:3]

⁶There came a man commissioned *and* sent from God, whose name was John. [Mal 3:1]

⁷This man came as a witness, to testify about the Light, so that all might believe [in Christ, the Light] through him.

⁸John was not the Light, but came to testify about the Light.

⁹There it was—the true Light [the genuine, perfect, steadfast Light] which, coming into the world, enlightens everyone. [Is 49:6]

¹⁰He (Christ) was in the world, and though the world was made through Him, the world did not recognize Him.

¹¹He came to that which was His own [that which belonged to Him—His world, His creation, His possession], and those who were His own [people—the Jewish nation] did not receive *and* welcome Him.

¹²But to as many as did receive *and* welcome Him, He gave the right [the authority, the privilege] to become children of God, *that is,* to those who believe in (adhere to, trust in, and rely on) His name— [Is 56:5]

¹³who were born, not of blood [natural conception], nor of the will of the flesh [physical impulse], nor of the will of man [that of a natural father], but of God [that is, a divine and supernatural birth—they are born of God—spiritually transformed, renewed, sanctified].

¹⁴And the Word (Christ) became flesh, and lived among us; and we [actually] saw His glory, glory as belongs to the [One and] only begotten *Son* of the Father, [the Son who is truly unique, the only One of His kind, who is] full of grace and truth (absolutely free of deception). [Is 40:5]

¹⁵John testified [repeatedly] about Him and has cried out [testifying officially for the record, with validity and relevance], "This was He of whom I said, 'He who comes after me has a higher rank than I *and* has priority over me, for He existed before me.'"

¹⁶For out of His fullness [the superabundance of His grace and truth] we have all received grace upon grace [spiritual blessing upon spiritual blessing, favor upon favor, and gift heaped upon gift].

¹⁷For the Law was given through Moses, but grace [the unearned, undeserved favor of God] and truth came through Jesus Christ. [Ex 20:1]

¹⁸No one has seen God [His essence, His divine nature] at any time; the [One and] only begotten God [that is, the unique Son] who is in the intimate presence of the Father, He has explained Him [and interpreted and revealed the awesome wonder of the Father]. [Prov 8:30]

¹⁹This is the testimony of John [the

speak the Word

Thank You, Jesus, that because I have received You, You have given me the right to become a child of God, because I believe in and rely on Your name.
–ADAPTED FROM JOHN 1:12

Baptist] when the Jews sent priests and Levites to him from Jerusalem to ask him, "Who are you?"

²⁰And he confessed [truthfully] and did not deny [that he was only a man], but acknowledged, "I am not the Christ (the Messiah, the Anointed)!"

²¹They asked him, "What then? Are you Elijah?" And he said, "I am not." "Are you the [promised] Prophet?" And he answered, "No." [Deut 18:15, 18; Mal 4:5]

²²Then they said to him, "Who are you? *Tell us,* so that we may give an answer to those who sent us. What do you say about yourself?"

²³He said, "I am THE VOICE OF ONE SHOUTING IN THE WILDERNESS, 'MAKE STRAIGHT THE WAY OF THE LORD,' as the prophet Isaiah said." [Is 40:3]

²⁴Now they had been sent from the Pharisees.

²⁵They asked him, "Why then are you baptizing, if you are not the Christ, nor Elijah, nor the Prophet?"

²⁶John answered them, "I baptize [only] in water, but among you there stands One whom you do not recognize *and* of whom you know nothing. [Mal 3:1]

²⁷"It is He [the preeminent One] who comes after me, the strap of whose sandal I am not worthy to untie [even as His slave]."

²⁸These things occurred in Bethany across the Jordan [at the Jordan River crossing], where John was baptizing.

²⁹The next day he saw Jesus coming to him and said, "Look! The Lamb of God who takes away the sin of the world! [Ex 12:3; Is 53:7]

³⁰"This is He on behalf of whom I said, 'After me comes a Man who has a higher rank than I *and* has priority over me, for He existed before me.'

³¹"I did not recognize Him [as the Messiah]; but I came baptizing in water so that He would be [publicly] revealed to Israel."

³²John gave [further] evidence [testifying officially for the record, with validity and relevance], saying, "I have seen the Spirit descending as a dove out of heaven, and He remained upon Him. [Matt 3:13–17; Mark 1:9–11; Luke 3:22, 23]

³³"I did not recognize Him [as the Messiah], but He who sent me to baptize in water said to me, 'He upon whom you see the Spirit descend and remain, this One is He who baptizes with the Holy Spirit.'

³⁴"I myself have [actually] seen [that happen], and my testimony is that this is the Son of God!"

³⁵Again the next day John was standing with two of his disciples,

³⁶and he looked at Jesus as He walked along, and said, "Look! The Lamb of God!"

³⁷The two disciples heard him say this, and they followed Jesus.

³⁸And Jesus turned and saw them following Him, and asked them, "What do you want?" They answered Him, "Rabbi (which translated means Teacher), where are You staying?"

³⁹He said to them, "Come, and you will see." So they went [with Him] and saw where He was staying; and they stayed with Him that day, for it was about the tenth hour.

⁴⁰One of the two who heard what John said and [as a result] followed Jesus was Andrew, Simon Peter's brother.

⁴¹He first looked for *and* found his own brother Simon and told him, "We have found the Messiah" (which translated means the Christ).

⁴²Andrew brought Simon to Jesus. Jesus looked at him and said, "You are Simon the son of John. You shall be called Cephas (which is translated Peter)."

⁴³The next day Jesus decided to go into Galilee, and He found Philip and said to him, "Follow Me [as My disciple, accepting Me as your Master and

Teacher, and walking the same path of life that I walk]."

⁴⁴Now Philip was from Bethsaida, the city of Andrew and Peter.

⁴⁵Philip found Nathanael and told him, "We have found the One Moses in the Law and also the Prophets wrote about—Jesus from Nazareth, the son of Joseph [according to public record]."

⁴⁶Nathanael answered him, "Can anything good come out of Nazareth?" Philip replied, "Come and see."

⁴⁷Jesus saw Nathanael coming toward Him, and said of him, "Here is an Israelite indeed [a true descendant of Jacob], in whom there is no guile *nor* deceit *nor* duplicity!"

⁴⁸Nathanael said to Jesus, "How do You know [these things about] me?" Jesus answered, "Before Philip called you, when you were still under the fig tree, I saw you."

⁴⁹Nathanael answered, "Rabbi (Teacher), You are the Son of God; You are the King of Israel."

⁵⁰Jesus replied, "Because I said to you that I saw you under the fig tree, do you believe [in Me]? You will see greater things than this."

⁵¹Then He said to him, "I assure you *and* most solemnly say to you, you will see heaven opened and the angels of God ascending and descending on the Son of Man [the bridge between heaven and earth]." [Gen 28:12; Dan 7:13]

2 ON THE third day there was a wedding at Cana of Galilee, and the mother of Jesus was there; ²and both Jesus and His disciples were invited to the wedding. ³When the wine was all gone, the mother of Jesus said to Him, "They have no *more* wine."

dealing with prejudice

For years, I did not understand John 1:45–47. Nathanael seemed to make a negative statement when he said, "Can anything good come out of Nazareth?" Yet in the next verse Jesus seemed to compliment Nathanael saying, "Here is an Israelite indeed [a true descendent of Jacob], in whom there is no guile nor deceit nor duplicity!"

Then one day I saw it. Nathanael had a negative opinion of Nazareth because the prevailing sentiment of his day was that nothing good ever happened there. So when he heard that Jesus was from Nazareth, Nathanael was initially closed to the idea that Jesus was the true Messiah, simply because of where He came from.

So often we are like Nathanael. We decide a person cannot be any good because of where he lives or where he comes from. We can be so biased and opinionated, often without even realizing it. We have prejudices that have been placed in us by others through the things they have said to us. This is why we have to carefully examine our hearts to see if they are truly open.

What Jesus seemed to like about Nathanael was that although he appeared convinced that nothing good could come out of Nazareth, he was willing to check it out. Even though he had a strong opinion, he had an open heart. Let me encourage you to have an open heart toward everyone you meet. Think of it. Had Nathanael been unwilling to open his heart to Jesus, he would have missed the best blessing of his life—a great relationship with the Lord. I believe God has blessings in store for you through relationships too, so keep your heart open.

[4]Jesus said to her, "[Dear] woman, what is that to you and to Me? My time [to act and to be revealed] has not yet come." [Eccl 3:1]

[5]His mother said to the servants, "Whatever He says to you, do it."

[6]Now there were six stone waterpots set there for the Jewish custom of purification (ceremonial washing), containing twenty or thirty gallons each.

[7]Jesus said to the servants, "Fill the waterpots with water." So they filled them up to the brim.

[8]Then He said to them, "Draw *some* out now and take it to the headwaiter [of the banquet]." So they took it *to him*.

[9]And when the headwaiter tasted the water which had turned into wine, not knowing where it came from (though the servants who had drawn the water knew) he called the bridegroom,

[10]and said to him, "Everyone else serves his best wine first, and when *people* have drunk freely, *then he serves* that which is not so good; but you have kept back the good wine until now."

[11]This, the first of His signs (attesting miracles), Jesus did in Cana of Galilee, and revealed His glory [displaying His deity and His great power openly], and

putting the Word to work

Has God ever asked you to do something that did not seem to make much sense? No doubt the servants wondered why Jesus asked them to fill pots with water when it was the wine that ran out. To their credit, they obeyed—and they witnessed Jesus' first miracle. Even when you don't understand why God asks you to do something, heed Mary's advice and do whatever God tells you to do. You will be blessed because of your obedience.

His disciples believed [confidently] in Him [as the Messiah—they adhered to, trusted in, and relied on Him]. [Deut 5:24; Ps 72:19]

[12]After this He went down to Capernaum, He and His mother and brothers and His disciples; and they stayed there a few days.

[13]Now the Passover of the Jews was approaching, so Jesus went up to Jerusalem.

[14]And in the temple [enclosure] He found the people who were selling oxen and sheep and doves, and the money changers sitting *at their tables*. [Matt 21:12ff; Mark 11:15, 17]

[15]He made a whip of cords, and drove them all out of the temple, with the sheep and the oxen; and He scattered the coins of the money changers and overturned their tables;

[16]then to those who sold the doves He said, "Take these things away! Stop making My Father's house a place of commerce!" [Ps 93:5]

[17]His disciples remembered that it is written [in the Scriptures], "ZEAL (love, concern) FOR YOUR HOUSE [and its honor] WILL CONSUME ME." [Ps 69:9]

[18]Then the Jews retorted, "What sign (attesting miracle) can You show us as [proof of] your authority for doing these things?"

[19]Jesus answered them, "Destroy this temple, and in three days I will raise it up."

[20]Then the Jews replied, "It took forty-six years to build this temple, and You will raise it up in three days?"

[21]But He was speaking of the temple which was His body.

[22]So when He had risen from the dead, His disciples remembered what He had said. And they believed *and* trusted in *and* relied on the Scripture and the words that Jesus had spoken. [Ps 16:10]

[23]Now when He was in Jerusalem at the Passover feast, many believed

in His name [identifying themselves with Him] after seeing His signs (attesting miracles) which He was doing.

24But Jesus, for His part, did not entrust Himself to them, because He knew all *people* [and understood the superficiality and fickleness of human nature],

25and He did not need anyone to testify concerning man [and human nature], for He Himself knew what was in man [in their hearts—in the very core of their being]. [1 Sam 16:7]

3 NOW THERE was a certain man among the Pharisees named Nicodemus, a ruler (member of the Sanhedrin) among the Jews,

2who came to Jesus at night and said to Him, "Rabbi (Teacher), we know [without any doubt] that You have come from God as a teacher; for no one can do these signs [these wonders, these attesting miracles] that You do unless God is with him."

3Jesus answered him, "I assure you *and* most solemnly say to you, unless

people aren't perfect

Having unrealistic expectations of people sets us up to be disappointed. Am I saying that we should not be expectant? Of course not! We should expect the best from people, but at the same time we should remember they are human beings with imperfections.

When Jesus' disciples disappointed Him, He was not devastated because He already knew and fully understood human nature, as we learn from John 2:25. Jesus expected His disciples to do their best, but He knew even their best would still be imperfect.

I have come to realize that we tend to look for the perfect spouse, perfect friend, perfect job, perfect neighborhood, perfect church, and the truth is, it does not exist! As long as we live in earthly bodies we will manifest imperfection. God must have known that to be true, because in His Word He gave us instructions about how to handle people who irritate or disappoint us.

People are not perfect, and to expect them to be flawless is frustrating for everyone involved. We can learn to be generous with mercy and to sow seeds of mercy so we can reap mercy when we need it.

We all like to plan ahead for our lives and have people cooperate with us. We want situations to go exactly as we plan, but that rarely happens. This isn't negative; it is truth. As believers, we have the power of the Holy Spirit to help us do difficult things and deal with human imperfections—not to make our lives so easy that we never need to use our faith.

I urge you to expect good things to happen in your life. I also urge you to be realistic and realize that we all have to deal with circumstances that are unpleasant and people who are disagreeable. Your attitude in these trying situations greatly affects your enjoyment of life. You can be realistic, walk in truth, and still have a positive attitude as you deal with your own imperfections and those of the people around you.

a person is born again [reborn from above—spiritually transformed, renewed, sanctified], he cannot [ever] see *and* experience the kingdom of God."

⁴Nicodemus said to Him, "How can a man be born when he is old? He cannot enter his mother's womb a second time and be born, can he?"

⁵Jesus answered, "I assure you *and* most solemnly say to you, unless one is born of water and the Spirit he cannot [ever] enter the kingdom of God. [Ezek 36:25–27]

⁶"That which is born of the flesh is flesh [the physical is merely physical], and that which is born of the Spirit is spirit.

⁷"Do not be surprised that I have told you, 'You must be born again [reborn from above—spiritually transformed, renewed, sanctified].'

⁸"The wind blows where it wishes and you hear its sound, but you do not know where it is coming from and where it is going; so it is with everyone who is born of the Spirit."

⁹Nicodemus said to Him, "How can these things be *possible*?"

¹⁰Jesus replied, "You are the [great and well-known] teacher of Israel, and yet you do not know *nor* understand these things [from Scripture]?

¹¹"I assure you *and* most solemnly say to you, we speak only of what we [absolutely] know and testify about what we have [actually] seen [as eyewitnesses]; and [still] you [reject our evidence and] do not accept our testimony.

¹²"If I told you earthly things [that is, things that happen right here on earth] and you do not believe, how will you believe *and* trust Me if I tell you heavenly things?

¹³"No one has gone up into heaven, but there is One who came down from heaven, the Son of Man [Himself—whose home is in heaven].

¹⁴"Just as Moses lifted up the [bronze] serpent in the desert [on a pole], so must the Son of Man be lifted up [on the cross], [Num 21:9]

¹⁵so that whoever believes will in Him have eternal life [after physical death, and will actually live forever].

¹⁶"For God so [greatly] loved *and* dearly prized the world, that He [even] gave His [One and] only begotten Son, so that whoever believes *and* trusts in Him [as Savior] shall not perish, but have eternal life.

¹⁷"For God did not send the Son into the world to judge *and* condemn the world [that is, to initiate the final judgment of the world], but that the world might be saved through Him.

¹⁸"Whoever believes *and* has decided to trust in Him [as personal Savior and Lord] is not judged [for this one, there is no judgment, no rejection, no condemnation]; but the one who does not believe [and has decided to reject Him as personal Savior and Lord] is judged already [that one has been convicted and sentenced], because he has not believed *and* trusted in the name of the [One and] only begotten Son of God [the One who is truly unique, the only One of His kind, the One who alone can save him].

¹⁹"This is the judgment [that is, the cause for indictment, the test by which people are judged, the basis for the

speak the Word

Thank You, God, for loving me so much that You even gave Your only Son, so that if I believe and trust in Him, I will not perish, but have eternal life. I know that You did not send Your Son to condemn or judge me, but that I might be saved through Him.
—ADAPTED FROM JOHN 3:16, 17

sentence]: the Light has come into the world, and people loved the darkness rather than the Light, for their deeds were evil. [Is 5:20]

20"For every wrongdoer hates the Light, and does not come to the Light [but shrinks from it] for fear that his [sinful, worthless] activities will be exposed *and* condemned.

21"But whoever practices truth [and does what is right—morally, ethically, spiritually] comes to the Light, so that his works may be plainly shown to be what they are—accomplished in God [divinely prompted, done with God's help, in dependence on Him]."

22After these things Jesus and His disciples went into the land of Judea, and there He spent time with them and baptized. [John 4:1, 2]

23Now John was also baptizing at Aenon near Salim, because there was an abundance of water there; and *people* were coming and were being baptized—

24for John had not yet been thrown into prison.

25Therefore there arose a controversy between John's disciples and a Jew in regard to purification (ceremonial washing).

26So they came to John and said to him, "Rabbi (Teacher), the Man who was with you on the other side of the Jordan [at the Jordan River crossing]—and to whom you have testified—look, He is baptizing too, and everyone is going to Him!"

27John replied, "A man can receive nothing [he can claim nothing at all] unless it has been granted to him from heaven [for there is no other source than the sovereign will of God].

28"You yourselves are my witnesses that I stated, 'I am not the Christ (the Messiah, the Anointed),' but, 'I have [only] been sent ahead of Him [as His appointed forerunner and messenger to announce and proclaim His coming].' [Mal 3:1]

29"He who has the bride is the bridegroom; but the friend of the bridegroom, who stands by and listens to him, rejoices greatly because of the bridegroom's voice. So this pleasure *and* joy of mine is now complete. [Song 5:1]

30"He must increase [in prominence], but I must decrease. [Is 9:7]

31"He who comes from [heaven] above is above all *others;* he who is of the earth is from the earth and speaks [about things] of the earth [his viewpoint and experience are earthly]. He who comes from heaven is above all.

32"What He has [actually] seen and heard, of that He testifies; and yet no one accepts His testimony [as true].

33"Whoever receives His testimony has set his seal [of approval] to this: God is true [and he knows that God cannot lie].

34"For He whom God has sent speaks the words of God [proclaiming the Father's own message]; for God gives the [gift of the] Spirit without measure [generously and boundlessly]! [Deut 18:18]

35"The Father loves the Son and has given *and* entrusted all things into His hand. [Dan 7:14]

36"He who believes *and* trusts in the Son *and* accepts Him [as Savior] has eternal life [that is, already possesses it]; but he who does not believe the Son *and* chooses to reject Him, [disobeying Him and denying Him as Savior] will not see [eternal] life, but [instead] the wrath of God hangs over him *continually.*" [Heb 3:18]

speak the Word

God, I pray that You will increase and I will decrease more and more.
—ADAPTED FROM JOHN 3:30

4 SO WHEN the Lord learned that the Pharisees had been told that Jesus was making and baptizing more disciples than John

[2](although Jesus Himself was not baptizing, but His disciples were),

[3]He left Judea and returned again to Galilee.

[4]Now He had to go through Samaria.

[5]So He arrived at a Samaritan town called Sychar, near the tract of land that Jacob gave to his son Joseph;

[6]and Jacob's well was there. So Jesus, tired as He was from His journey, sat down by the well. It was then about the sixth hour (noon).

[7]Then a woman from Samaria came to draw water. Jesus said to her, "Give Me a drink"—

[8]For His disciples had gone off into the city to buy food—

[9]The Samaritan woman asked Him, "How is it that You, being a Jew, ask me, a Samaritan woman, for a drink?" (For Jews have nothing to do with Samaritans.)

[10]Jesus answered her, "If you knew [about] God's gift [of eternal life], and who it is who says, 'Give Me a drink,' you would have asked Him [instead], and He would have given you living water (eternal life)."

[11]She said to Him, "Sir, You have nothing to draw with [no bucket and rope] and the well is deep. Where then do You get that living water?

[12]"Are You greater than our father Jacob, who gave us the well, and who used to drink from it himself, and his sons and his cattle also?"

[13]Jesus answered her, "Everyone who drinks this water will be thirsty again.

[14]"But whoever drinks the water that I give him will never be thirsty again.

But the water that I give him will become in him a spring of water [satisfying his thirst for God] welling up [continually flowing, bubbling within him] to eternal life."

[15]The woman said to Him, "Sir, give me this water, so that I will not get thirsty nor [have to continually] come all the way here to draw."

[16]At this, Jesus said, "Go, call your husband and come back."

[17]The woman answered, "I do not have a husband." Jesus said to her, "You have correctly said, 'I do not have a husband';

[18]for you have had five husbands, and the man you are now living with is not your husband. You have said this truthfully."

[19]The woman said to Him, "Sir, I see that You are a prophet.

[20]"Our fathers worshiped on this mountain, but you *Jews* say that the place where one ought to worship is in Jerusalem [at the temple]."

[21]Jesus replied, "Woman, believe Me, a time is coming [when God's kingdom comes] when you will worship the Father neither on this mountain nor in Jerusalem.

[22]"You [Samaritans] do not know what you worship; we [Jews] do know what we worship, for salvation is from the Jews.

[23]"But a time is coming and is already here when the true worshipers will worship the Father in spirit [from the heart, the inner self] and in truth; for the Father seeks such people to be His worshipers.

[24]"God is spirit [the Source of life, yet invisible to mankind], and those who worship Him must worship in spirit and truth."

[25]The woman said to Him, "I know

speak the Word

Help me, God, to worship You in spirit and in truth.
—ADAPTED FROM JOHN 4:24

that Messiah is coming (He who is called Christ—the Anointed); when that One comes, He will tell us everything [we need to know]."

²⁶Jesus said to her, "I who speak to you, am *He* (the Messiah)."

²⁷Just then His disciples came, and they were surprised to find Him talking with a woman. However, no one said, "What are You asking about?" or, "Why are You talking to her?"

²⁸Then the woman left her water jar, and went into the city and began telling the people,

²⁹"Come, see a man who told me all the things that I have done! Can this be the Christ (the Messiah, the Anointed)?"

³⁰So the people left the city and were coming to Him.

³¹Meanwhile, the disciples were urging Jesus [to have a meal], saying, "Rabbi (Teacher), eat."

³²But He told them, "I have food to eat that you do not know about."

³³So the disciples said to one another, "Has anyone brought Him *something* to eat?"

³⁴Jesus said to them, "My food is to do the will of Him who sent Me and to completely finish His work.

³⁵"Do you not say, 'It is still four months until the harvest comes?' Look, I say to you, raise your eyes and look at the fields *and* see, they are white for harvest.

³⁶"Already the reaper is receiving *his* wages and he is gathering fruit for eternal life; so that he who plants and he who reaps may rejoice together.

³⁷"For in this *case* the saying is true, 'One [person] sows and another reaps.'

³⁸"I sent you to reap [a crop] for which you have not worked. Others have worked and you have been privileged to reap the results of their work."

³⁹Now many Samaritans from that city believed in Him *and* trusted Him [as Savior] because of what the woman said when she testified, "He told me all the things that I have done."

⁴⁰So when the Samaritans came to Jesus, they asked Him to remain with them; and He stayed there two days.

⁴¹Many more believed in Him [with a deep, abiding trust] because of His word [His personal message to them];

⁴²and they told the woman, "We no longer believe *just* because of what you said; for [now] we have heard *Him* for ourselves and know [with confident assurance] that this One is truly the Savior of [all] the world."

⁴³After the two days He went on from there into Galilee.

⁴⁴For Jesus Himself declared that a prophet has no honor in his own country.

⁴⁵So when He arrived in Galilee, the Galileans welcomed Him, since they had seen all the things that He did in Jerusalem at the feast; for they too came to the feast.

⁴⁶So Jesus came again to Cana of Galilee, where He had turned the water into wine. And there was a certain royal official whose son was sick in Capernaum.

⁴⁷Having heard that Jesus had come back from Judea to Galilee, he went to *meet* Him and began asking Him to come down and heal his son; for he was at the point of death.

⁴⁸Then Jesus said to him, "Unless you [people] see [miraculous] signs and wonders, you [simply] will not believe."

⁴⁹The royal official pleaded with Him, "Sir, do come down [at once] before my child dies!"

⁵⁰Jesus said to him, "Go; your son lives!" The man believed what Jesus said to him and started home.

⁵¹As he was already going down [the road], his servants met him and reported that his son was living [and was healthy].

⁵²So he asked them at what time he

began to get better. They said, "Yesterday during the seventh hour the fever left him."

⁵³Then the father realized that it was at that *very* hour when Jesus had said to him, "Your son lives"; and he and his entire household believed *and* confidently trusted [in Him as Savior].

⁵⁴This is the second sign (attesting miracle) that Jesus performed [in Cana] after He had come from Judea to Galilee [revealing that He is the Messiah].

5 LATER ON there was a Jewish feast (festival), and Jesus went up to Jerusalem.

²Now in Jerusalem, near the Sheep Gate, there is a pool, which is called in Hebrew (Jewish Aramaic) Bethesda, having five porticoes (alcoves, colonnades).

³In these *porticoes* lay a great number of people who were sick, blind, lame, withered, [waiting for the stirring of the water;

⁴for an angel of the Lord went down into the pool at appointed seasons and stirred up the water; the first one to go in after the water was stirred was healed of his disease.]

⁵There was a certain man there who had been ill for thirty-eight years.

⁶When Jesus noticed him lying there [helpless], knowing that he had been

be pitiful or be powerful

Why was this man we read about in John 5:1–9 lying beside the pool for thirty-eight years? Not only was he sick in his body, he was also sick in his soul. Sicknesses of the soul are much worse, and sometimes harder to deal with, than sicknesses of the body. I believe the condition of his body and soul stole his confidence and caused him to give up in a gradual, passive kind of way.

Notice that when Jesus asked the sick man if he wanted to get well, he said he had no one to help him get into the pool where he could be healed. Jesus did not stand there and pity the man. Instead, He gave a specific instruction: "Get up; pick up your pallet and walk." In other words, "Don't just lie there, do something!"

Jesus knew self-pity would not deliver the man, so He did not feel sorry for him. He had compassion on him, and that is different from emotional pity. Jesus was not being harsh, hard, or mean. He was trying to set the man free!

Self-pity is a major problem. I know, because I lived in it for many years. It affected me, my family, and the plan of God for my life. God finally told me that I could be pitiful or I could be powerful, but I could not be both. If I wanted to be powerful, I had to give up self-pity.

Being sexually abused for approximately fifteen years and growing up in a dysfunctional home left me lacking confidence and filled with shame. I wanted to have good things in my life, but I was stuck in emotional torment and despair.

Like the man in John 5, Jesus did not give me pity either. Jesus was actually very firm with me and He applied a lot of tough love, but His refusal to let me wallow in self-pity was a turning point in my life. I now have a great life. If you will reject self-pity, actively look to God, and do what He instructs you to do, you can have a great life too.

in that condition a long time, He said to him, "Do you want to get well?"

⁷The invalid answered, "Sir, I have no one to put me in the pool when the water is stirred up, and while I am coming [to get into it myself], someone else steps down ahead of me."

⁸Jesus said to him, "Get up; pick up your pallet and walk."

⁹Immediately the man was healed *and* recovered his strength, and picked up his pallet and walked.

Now that day was the Sabbath. ¹⁰So the Jews kept saying to the man who had been healed, "It is the Sabbath, and you are not permitted to pick up your pallet [because it is unlawful]."

¹¹He answered them, "The Man who healed me *and* gave me back my strength was the One who said to me, 'Pick up your pallet and walk.'"

¹²They asked him, "Who is the Man who told you, 'Pick up *your pallet* and walk'?"

¹³Now the man who had been healed did not know who it was, for Jesus had slipped away [unnoticed] since there was a crowd in that place.

¹⁴Afterward, Jesus found him in the temple and said to him, "See, you are well! Stop sinning or something worse may happen to you."

¹⁵The man went away and told the Jews that it was Jesus who had made him well.

¹⁶For this reason the Jews began to persecute Jesus *continually* because He was doing these things on the Sabbath.

¹⁷But Jesus answered them, "My Father has been working until now [He has never ceased working], and I too am working."

¹⁸This made the Jews more determined than ever to kill Him, for not only was He breaking the Sabbath [from their viewpoint], but He was also calling God His own Father, making Himself equal with God.

¹⁹So Jesus answered them by saying, "I assure you *and* most solemnly say to you, the Son can do nothing of Himself [of His own accord], unless it is something He sees the Father doing; for whatever things the Father does, the Son [in His turn] also does in the same way.

²⁰"For the Father *dearly* loves the Son and shows Him everything that He Himself is doing; and *the Father* will show Him greater works than these, so that you will be filled with wonder.

²¹"Just as the Father raises the dead and gives them life [and allows them to live on], even so the Son also gives life to whom He wishes.

²²"For the Father judges no one, but has given all judgment [that is, the prerogative of judging] to the Son [placing it entirely into His hands],

²³so that all will give honor (reverence, homage) to the Son just as they give honor to the Father. [In fact] the one who does not honor the Son does not honor the Father who has sent Him.

²⁴"I assure you *and* most solemnly say to you, the person who hears My word [the one who heeds My message], and believes *and* trusts in Him who sent Me, has (possesses now) eternal life [that is, eternal life actually begins—the believer is transformed], and does not come into judgment *and*

life point

John 5:19 teaches us that Jesus was always obedient to the Father and showed it by refraining from doing anything He did not first see the Father do. None of us is at that level yet, but it should certainly be our goal.

I believe the world will take notice if we as the body of Jesus Christ on earth will wage war against selfishness, walk in love, and do what we see the Father doing.

condemnation, but has passed [over] from death into life.

25"I assure you *and* most solemnly say to you, a time is coming and is [here] now, when the dead will hear the voice of the Son of God, and those who hear it will live.

26"For just as the Father has life in Himself [and is self-existent], even so He has given to the Son to have life in Himself [and be self-existent].

27"And He has given Him authority to execute judgment, because He is a Son of Man [sinless humanity, qualifying Him to sit in judgment over mankind]. [Dan 7:13, 14]

28"Do not be surprised at this; for a time is coming when all those who are in the tombs will hear His voice,

29and they will come out—those who did good things [will come out] to a resurrection of [new] life, but those who did evil things [will come out] to a resurrection of judgment [that is, to be sentenced]. [Dan 12:2; Rev 20:11–15]

30"I can do nothing on my own initiative *or* authority. Just as I hear, I judge; and My judgment is just (fair, righteous, unbiased), because I do not seek My own will, but only the will of Him who sent Me.

31"If I *alone* testify about Myself, My testimony is not valid.

32"There is another [My Father] who testifies about Me, and I know [without any doubt] that His testimony on My behalf is true *and* valid.

33"You have sent [an inquiry] to John [the Baptist] and he has testified [as an eyewitness] to the truth.

34"But the testimony I receive is not from man [a merely human witness]; but I say these things so that you may be saved [that is, have eternal life].

35"John was the lamp that kept on burning and shining [to show you the way], and you were willing for a while to rejoice in his light. [John 1:23–25]

36"But the testimony which I have is far greater than *the testimony of* John; for the works that the Father has given Me to finish—the very same works [that is, the miracles and proofs of My deity] that I am [now] doing—testify about Me, [by providing evidence] that the Father has sent Me.

37"And the Father who sent Me has Himself testified about Me. You have never heard His voice nor seen His form [His majesty and greatness—what He is like].

38"You do not have His word (Scripture) abiding in you [actually living in your hearts and minds], because you do not believe in Him whom He has sent.

39"You search *and* keep on searching *and* examining the Scriptures because you think that in them you have eternal life; and yet it is those [very Scriptures] that testify about Me;

40and still you are unwilling to come to Me so that you may have life.

41"I do not receive glory *and* approval from men;

42but I know you *and* recognize that you do not have the love of God in yourselves.

43"I have come in My Father's name *and* with His power, and you do not receive Me [because your minds are

life point

In John 5:38 Jesus chastised some people because they were not keeping His Word alive in their hearts. They weren't trusting God and clinging to Him and His Word. Jesus said that if we really believe in Him, we will keep His Word alive in our hearts. We can accomplish this by studying and meditating on it. God's Word represents His thoughts and when we give His Word first place in our lives, His thoughts become our thoughts and we will experience the good plans He has for us.

closed]; but if another comes in his own name *and* with no authority or power except his own, you will receive him *and* give your approval to an imposter.

⁴⁴"How can you believe [in Me], when you [seek and] receive glory *and* approval from one another, and yet you do not seek the glory *and* approval which comes from the *one and* only God?

⁴⁵"Do not think that I [am the One who] will accuse you before the Father. There [already] is one who accuses you: Moses, [the very one] in whom you have placed your hope [for salvation].

⁴⁶"For if you believed *and* relied on [the Scriptures written by] Moses, you would believe Me, for he wrote about Me [personally]. [Gen 3:15; 22:18; 49:10; Num 24:17; Deut 18:15]

⁴⁷"But if you do not believe his writings, how will you believe My words?"

6 AFTER THIS, Jesus went to the other side of the Sea of Galilee (or Sea of Tiberias). [Matt 14:13–21; Mark 6:32–44; Luke 9:10–17; John 6:23; 21:1]

²A large crowd was following Him because they had seen the signs (attesting miracles) which He *continually* performed on those who were sick.

³And Jesus went up on the mountainside and sat down there with His disciples.

⁴Now the Passover, the feast of the Jews, was approaching. [Ex 12:1–36]

⁵Jesus looked up and saw that a large crowd was coming toward Him, and He said to Philip, "Where will we buy bread for these *people* to eat?"

⁶But He said this to test Philip, because He knew what He was about to do.

⁷Philip answered, "Two hundred denarii (200 days' wages) worth of bread is not enough for each one to receive even a little."

⁸One of His disciples, Andrew, Simon Peter's brother, said to Him,

⁹"There is a little boy here who has five barley loaves and two fish; but what are these for so many people?"

¹⁰Jesus said, "Have the people sit down [to eat]." Now [the ground] there was [covered with] an abundance of grass, so the men sat down, about 5,000 in number.

¹¹Then Jesus took the loaves, and when He had given thanks, He distributed them to those who were seated; the same also with the fish, as much as they wanted.

¹²When they had eaten enough, He said to His disciples, "Gather up the leftover pieces so that nothing will be lost."

¹³So they gathered them up, and they filled twelve large baskets with pieces from the five barley loaves which were left over by those who had eaten.

¹⁴When the people saw the sign (attesting miracle) that He had done, they *began* saying, "This is without a doubt the promised Prophet who is to come into the world!" [Deut 18:15, 18; John 1:21; Acts 3:22]

¹⁵Then Jesus, knowing that they were going to come and take Him by force to make Him king, withdrew again to the mountainside by Himself.

¹⁶When evening came, His disciples went down to the sea,

¹⁷and they got into a boat and started to cross the sea to Capernaum. It was already dark, and Jesus had still not come [back] to them.

¹⁸The sea was getting rough *and* rising high because a strong wind was blowing.

¹⁹Then, when they had rowed three or four miles [and were near the center of the sea], they saw Jesus walking on the sea and approaching the boat; and they were [terribly] frightened.

²⁰But Jesus said to them, "It is I (I AM); do not be afraid." [Matt 14:27; John 8:58]

²¹Then they were willing to take Him on board the boat, and immediately the boat reached the [shore of the] land to which they were going.

²²The next day the crowd that stood on the other side of the sea realized that there had been only one small boat there, and that Jesus had not boarded the boat with His disciples, but that His disciples had gone away alone.

²³[Now some] other small boats from Tiberias had come in near the place where they ate the bread after the Lord had given thanks.

²⁴So when the crowd saw that neither Jesus nor His disciples were there, they boarded the small boats themselves and came to Capernaum looking for Jesus.

²⁵And when they found Him on the other side of the sea, they asked Him, "Rabbi, when did You get here?"

²⁶Jesus answered, "I assure you *and* most solemnly say to you, you have been searching for Me, not because you saw the signs (attesting miracles), but because you ate the loaves and were filled.

²⁷"Do not work for food that perishes, but for food that endures [and leads] to eternal life, which the Son of Man will give you; for God the Father has authorized Him *and* put His seal on Him."

²⁸Then they asked Him, "What are we to do, so that we may *habitually* be doing the works of God?"

²⁹Jesus answered, "This is the work of God: that you believe [adhere to, trust

believe to achieve

Many times I have said to the Lord, "Father, what do You want me to do? If You will just show me what to do, I will gladly do it."

I was a doer. All anybody had to do was show me what needed to be done, and I did it—and I did my best to do it right. But what frustrated and confused me was when I did something right and it still did not work. I had not yet learned that "unless the LORD builds the house, they labor in vain who build it" (Psalm 127:1).

The people in John 6:28 wanted to know what they needed to do to please God. They wanted to know what to do in order to work the works of God. What was Jesus' answer to them? "This is the work of God: that you believe [adhere to, trust in, rely on, and have faith] in the One whom He has sent." (John 6:29).

When the Lord first revealed this passage to me, I thought He was going to show me how to finally be successful in doing His works. And in a sense He did.

He told me, "Believe."

You and I think we are supposed to be achievers, and we are. But the way we achieve is to first believe. That frees us from worry and reasoning and enables us to live victorious, blessed lives. God has works for us to do, but faith must come first and works will follow. When done in faith, works are easy and God gets the credit instead of us. Faith without works is dead, but we must be careful not to get "the cart before the horse." When we do that, we struggle and make every effort, yet we see no progress. We are called "believers," not "achievers." Our first and foremost work is always to believe!

life point

God is pleased when we believe in His Son, Jesus, and He is not pleased when we do not. We can do many good and benevolent works, yet if we have no faith in Jesus, God is still not pleased with us. But if we simply believe and trust in God, He is pleased.

in, rely on, and have faith] in the One whom He has sent."

³⁰So they said to Him, "What sign (attesting miracle) will You do that we may see it and believe You? What [supernatural] work will You do [as proof]?

³¹"Our fathers ate the manna in the wilderness; as it is written [in Scripture], 'HE GAVE THEM BREAD OUT OF HEAVEN TO EAT.'" [Ex 16:15; Neh 9:15; Ps 78:24]

³²Then Jesus said to them, "I assure you *and* most solemnly say to you, it is not Moses who has given you the bread out of heaven, but it is My Father who gives you the true bread out of heaven.

³³"For the Bread of God is He who comes down out of heaven, and gives life to the world."

³⁴Then they said to Him, "Lord, always give us this bread."

³⁵Jesus replied to them, "I am the Bread of Life. The one who comes to Me will never be hungry, and the one who believes in Me [as Savior] will never be thirsty [for that one will be sustained spiritually].

³⁶"But as I told you, you have seen Me and still you do not believe.

³⁷"All that My Father gives Me will come to Me; and the one who comes to Me I will most certainly not cast out [I will never, never reject anyone who follows Me].

³⁸"For I have come down from heaven, not to do My own will, but to do the will of Him who sent Me.

³⁹"This is the will of Him who sent Me, that of all that He has given Me I lose nothing, but that I [give new life and] raise it up at the last day.

⁴⁰"For this is My Father's will *and* purpose, that everyone who sees the Son and believes in Him [as Savior] will have eternal life, and I will raise him up [from the dead] on the last day."

⁴¹Now the Jews murmured *and* found fault with Him because He said, "I am the Bread that came down out of heaven."

⁴²They kept saying, "Is this not Jesus, the son of Joseph, whose father and mother we know? How does He now [have the arrogance to] say, 'I have come down out of heaven'?"

⁴³So Jesus answered, "Stop murmuring among yourselves.

⁴⁴"No one can come to Me unless the Father who sent Me draws him [giving him the desire to come to Me]; and I will raise him up [from the dead] on the last day.

⁴⁵"It is written in the prophets, 'AND THEY WILL ALL BE TAUGHT OF GOD.' Everyone who has listened to and learned from the Father, comes to Me. [Is 54:13]

⁴⁶"Not that anyone has seen the Father, except He [who was with the Father and] who is from God; He [alone] has seen the Father.

⁴⁷"I assure you *and* most solemnly say to you, he who believes [in Me as Savior—whoever adheres to, trusts in,

putting the Word to work

Your body lets you know when you are hungry. Your stomach growls; you may get cranky or feel a little light-headed. Did you know your spirit can also get hungry? Just as you feed your body daily, it is necessary to daily feed on the Bread of Life by spending time with God and in His Word.

relies on, and has faith in Me—already] has eternal life [that is, now possesses it].

48"I am the Bread of Life [the Living Bread which gives and sustains life].

49"Your fathers ate the manna in the wilderness, and they died.

50"This is the Bread that comes down out of heaven, so that one may eat of it and not die.

51"I am the Living Bread that came down out of heaven. If anyone eats of this Bread [believes in Me, accepts Me as Savior], he will live forever. And the Bread that I will give for the life of the world is My flesh (body)."

52Then the Jews *began* to argue with one another, saying, "How can this man give us His flesh to eat?"

53And Jesus said to them, "I assure you *and* most solemnly say to you, unless you eat the flesh of the Son of Man and drink His blood [unless you believe in Me as Savior and believe in the saving power of My blood which will be shed for you], you do not have life in yourselves.

54"The one who eats My flesh and drinks My blood [believes in Me, accepts Me as Savior] has eternal life [that is, now possesses it], and I will raise him up [from the dead] on the last day.

55"For My flesh is true [spiritual] food, and My blood is true [spiritual] drink.

56"He who eats My flesh and drinks My blood [believes in Me, accepts Me as Savior] remains in Me, and I [in the same way remain] in him.

57"Just as the living Father sent Me, and I live because of the Father, even so the one who feeds on Me [believes in Me, accepts Me as Savior] will also live because of Me.

58"This is the Bread which came down out of heaven. It is not like [the manna that] our fathers ate and they [eventually] died; the one who eats this Bread [believes in Me, accepts Me as Savior] will live forever."

59He said these things in a synagogue while He was teaching in Capernaum.

60When many of His disciples heard *this,* they said, "This is a difficult *and* harsh *and* offensive statement. Who can [be expected to] listen to it?"

61But Jesus, aware that His disciples were complaining about it, asked them, "Does this cause you to stumble *and* take offense?

62"*What* then [will you think] if you see the Son of Man ascending to [the realm] where He was before?

63"It is the Spirit who gives life; the flesh conveys no benefit [it is of no account]. The words I have spoken to you are spirit and life [providing eternal life].

64"But [still] there are some of you who do not believe *and* have faith." For Jesus knew from the beginning who did not believe, and who would betray Him.

65And He was saying, "This is the reason why I have told you that no one can come to Me unless it has been granted him [that is, unless he is enabled to do so] by the Father."

66As a result of this many of His disciples abandoned Him, and no longer walked with Him.

67So Jesus said to the twelve [disciples], "You do not want to leave too, do you?"

68Simon Peter answered, "Lord, to whom shall we go? You [alone] have the words of eternal life [you are our only hope].

69"We have believed *and* confidently trusted, and [even more] we have come to know [by personal observation and experience] that You are the Holy One of God [the Christ, the Son of the living God]."

70Jesus answered them, "Did I not choose you, the twelve [disciples]?

And yet one of you is a devil (ally of Satan)."

⁷¹Now He was speaking of Judas, *the son* of Simon Iscariot; for he, one of the twelve [disciples], was about to betray Him.

7 AFTER THIS, Jesus walked [from place to place] in Galilee, for He would not walk in Judea because the Jews were seeking to kill Him.

²Now the Jewish Feast of Tabernacles (Booths) was approaching.

³So His brothers said to Him, "Leave here and go to Judea, so that Your disciples [there] may also see the works that You do.

⁴"No one does anything in secret when he wants to be *known* publicly. If You [must] do these things, show Yourself openly to the world *and* make Yourself known!"

⁵For not even His brothers believed in Him.

⁶So Jesus said to them, "My time has not yet come; but any time is right for you.

⁷"The world cannot hate you [since you are part of it], but it does hate Me because I denounce it *and* testify that its deeds are evil.

⁸"Go up to the feast yourselves. I am not going up to this feast because My time has not yet fully come."

⁹Having said these things to them, He stayed behind in Galilee.

¹⁰But [afterward], when His brothers had gone up to the feast, He went up too, not publicly [with a caravan], but quietly [because He did not want to be noticed].

¹¹So the Jews kept looking for Him at the feast and asking, "Where is He?"

¹²There was a lot of whispered discussion *and* murmuring among the crowds about Him. Some were saying, "He is a good man"; others said, "No, on the contrary, He misleads the people [giving them false ideas]."

¹³Yet no one was speaking out openly *and* freely about Him for fear of [the leaders of] the Jews.

¹⁴When the feast was already half over, Jesus went up into the temple [court] and *began to* teach.

¹⁵Then the Jews were perplexed. They said, "How did this man become learned [so versed in the Scriptures and theology] without formal training?"

¹⁶Jesus answered them by saying, "My teaching is not My own, but His who sent Me.

¹⁷"If anyone is willing to do His will, he will know whether the teaching is of God or whether I speak on My own accord *and* by My own authority.

¹⁸"He who speaks on his own accord seeks glory *and* honor for himself. But He who seeks the glory *and* the honor of the One who sent Him, He is true, and there is no unrighteousness *or* deception in Him.

¹⁹"Did not Moses give you the Law? And yet not one of you keeps the Law. Why do you want to kill Me [for not keeping it]?"

²⁰The crowd answered, "You have a demon [You are out of Your mind]! Who wants to kill You?"

²¹Jesus replied, "I did one work, and you are all astounded. [John 5:1–9]

²²"For this reason Moses has given you [God's law regarding] circumcision (not that it originated with Moses, but with the patriarchs) and you circumcise a man [even] on the Sabbath.

²³"If, to avoid breaking the Law of Moses, a man undergoes circumcision on the Sabbath, why are you angry with Me for making a man's whole body well on the Sabbath?

²⁴"Do not judge by appearance [superficially and arrogantly], but judge fairly *and* righteously."

²⁵Then some of the people of Jerusalem said, "Is this not the Man they want to kill?

²⁶"Look, He is speaking publicly, and

they say nothing to Him! Is it possible that the rulers really know that this is the Christ?

²⁷"But we know where this Man is from; whenever the Christ comes, no one will know where He is from."

²⁸Then Jesus called out as He taught in the temple, "You know Me and know where I am from; and I have not come on my own initiative [as self-appointed], but He who sent Me is true, and Him you do not know.

²⁹"I know Him Myself because I am from Him [I came from His very presence] and it was He [personally] who sent Me."

³⁰So they were eager to arrest Him; but no one laid a hand on Him, because His time had not yet come.

³¹But many from the crowd believed in Him. And they kept saying, "When the Christ comes, will He do more signs *and* exhibit more proofs than this Man?"

³²The Pharisees heard the crowd muttering these things [under their breath] about Him, and the chief priests and Pharisees sent guards to arrest Him.

³³Therefore Jesus said, "For a little while longer I am [still] with you, and then I go to Him who sent Me.

³⁴"You will look for Me, and will not [be able to] find Me; and where I am, you cannot come."

³⁵Then the Jews said among themselves, "Where does this Man intend to go that we will not find Him? Does He intend to go to the Dispersion [of Jews scattered and living] among the Greeks, and teach the Greeks?

³⁶"What does this statement of His mean, 'You will look for Me, and will not [be able to] find Me; and where I am, you cannot come'?"

³⁷Now on the last and most important day of the feast, Jesus stood and called out [in a loud voice], "If anyone is thirsty, let him come to Me and drink!

³⁸"He who believes in Me [who adheres to, trusts in, and relies on Me], as the Scripture has said, 'From his innermost being will flow *continually* rivers of living water.'" [Is 58:11; John 4:14]

³⁹But He was speaking of the [Holy] Spirit, whom those who believed in Him [as Savior] were to receive *afterward.* The Spirit had not yet been given, because Jesus was not yet glorified (raised to honor).

⁴⁰Listening to these words, some of the people said, "This is certainly the Prophet!" [Deut 18:15, 18; John 1:21; 6:14; Acts 3:22]

⁴¹Others said, "This is the Christ (the Messiah, the Anointed)!" But others said, "Surely the Christ is not going to come out of Galilee, is He?

⁴²"Does the Scripture not say that the Christ comes from the descendants of David, and from Bethlehem, the village where David lived?" [Ps 89:3, 4; Mic 5:2]

life point

Notice in John 7:37–39 that Jesus did not say that rivers of living water will flow from those who believe in Him *once in a while.* He said these rivers of living water will flow *continually.* That living water is the Holy Spirit.

In this passage, Jesus talks about the outpouring of the Holy Spirit, which we have received if we have accepted Jesus as Lord and Savior—the Person and the power of the Holy Spirit in us.

The river of living water flows within you and me. It is not supposed to be stopped up, but it is to bubble up within us and flow out of us. And we can release the power of that living water in an even greater measure by receiving the fullness of the Holy Spirit. Ask Him to fill you today and every day.

⁴³So the crowd was divided because of Him.

⁴⁴Some of them wanted to arrest Him, but no one laid hands on Him.

⁴⁵Then the guards went [back] to the chief priests and Pharisees, who asked them, "Why did you not bring Him [here with you]?"

⁴⁶The guards replied, "Never [at any time] has a man talked the way this Man talks!"

⁴⁷Then the Pharisees said to them, "Have you also been deluded *and* swept off your feet?

⁴⁸"Has any of the rulers or Pharisees believed in Him?

⁴⁹"But this [ignorant, contemptible] crowd that does not know the Law is accursed *and* doomed!"

⁵⁰Nicodemus (the one who came to Jesus before and was one of them) asked,

⁵¹"Does our Law convict someone without first giving him a hearing and finding out what he is [accused of] doing?"

⁵²They responded, "Are you also from Galilee? Search [and read the Scriptures], and see [for yourself] that no prophet comes from Galilee!"

⁵³[And everyone went to his own house.

8 BUT JESUS went to the Mount of Olives.

²Early in the morning He came back into the temple [court], and all the people were coming to Him. He sat down and *began* teaching them.

³Now the scribes and Pharisees

finding your true identity

Our identity is established as a result of who and what we choose to identify with. If we identify with people and what they say about us, we will end up in trouble; but if we identify with Jesus and His opinion of us, we will not have an identity crisis.

Jesus knew who He was. John 8:14 tells us Jesus knew who He was because He knew where He came from and where He was going. This infuriated many of the Pharisees, the religious leaders of the day; they thought Jesus was blaspheming by claiming to be the Son of God. They were angry at His confidence in Who He was. But no matter what people said about Jesus, He did not identify with it. He identified with what His heavenly Father said about Him. He identified with God!

Identification with Christ is a doctrinal foundation of the Christian faith. It's not taught as frequently and fully as it should be. Some religious organizations spend far too much time telling people what they need to do, and not enough time telling them who they are in Christ. We need to be taught to identify with Jesus, not with people.

You belong to God! Knowing that truth will give you confidence to walk in this world with your head held high. You will be able to follow your heart and avoid adverse effects when people do not agree with you or your choices. You will have greater confidence, which will enable you to do more for God.

From now on, when people say something unkind about you, respond by saying to yourself, or to them if appropriate: "I do not identify with that."

See yourself as complete in Christ.

brought a woman who had been caught in adultery. They made her stand in the center *of the court,*

⁴and they said to Him, "Teacher, this woman has been caught in the very act of adultery.

⁵"Now in the Law Moses commanded us to stone such women [to death]. So what do You say [to do with her—what is Your sentence]?" [Deut 22:22–24]

⁶They said this to test Him, hoping that they would have grounds for accusing Him. But Jesus stooped down and began writing on the ground with His finger.

⁷However, when they persisted in questioning Him, He straightened up and said, "He who is without [any] sin among you, let him be the first to throw a stone at her." [Deut 17:7]

⁸Then He stooped down again and started writing on the ground.

⁹They listened [to His reply], and they *began* to go out one by one, starting with the oldest ones, until He was left alone, with the woman [standing there before Him] in the center *of the court.*

¹⁰Straightening up, Jesus said to her, "Woman, where are they? Did no one condemn you?"

¹¹She answered, "No one, Lord!" And Jesus said, "I do not condemn you either. Go. From now on sin no more."]

¹²Once more Jesus addressed the crowd. He said, "I am the Light of the world. He who follows Me will not walk in the darkness, but will have the Light of life."

¹³Then the Pharisees told Him, "You are testifying on Your own behalf; Your testimony is not valid."

¹⁴Jesus replied, "Even if I do testify on My own behalf, My testimony is valid, because I know where I came from and where I am going; but you do not know where I come from or where I am going.

¹⁵"You judge according to human standards [just by what you see]. I do not judge anyone.

¹⁶"But even if I do judge, My judgment is true *and* My decision is right; for I am not alone [in making it], but I and the Father who sent Me [make the same judgment].

¹⁷"Even in your own law it is written that the testimony of two persons is true [valid and admissible]. [Deut 19:15]

¹⁸"I am One [of the Two] who testifies about Myself, and My Father who sent Me testifies about Me."

¹⁹Then the Pharisees said to Him, "Where is this Father of Yours?" Jesus answered, "You know neither Me nor My Father; if you knew Me, you would know My Father also."

²⁰Jesus said these things in the treasury, as He taught in the temple [courtyard]; and no one seized Him, because His time had not yet come.

²¹Then He said again to them, "I am going away, and you will look for Me, and you will die [unforgiven and condemned] in your sin. Where I am going, you cannot come."

²²So the Jews were asking [among themselves], "Will He kill Himself? Is that why He says, 'Where I am going, you cannot come'?"

²³He said to them, "You are from below, I am from above; you are of this world, I am not of this world.

²⁴"That is why I told you that you will die [unforgiven and condemned] in your sins; for if you do not believe that I am *the One* [I claim to be], you will die in your sins." [Ex 3:14; Matt 24:5; Mark 13:6; Luke 21:8]

²⁵So they said to Him, "Who are You [anyway]?" Jesus replied, "What have I been saying to you from the beginning?

²⁶"I have many things to say and judge concerning you, but He who sent Me is true; and I say to the world [only] the things that I have heard from Him."

²⁷They did not realize [or have the

spiritual insight to understand] that He was speaking to them about the Father.

²⁸So Jesus said, "When you lift up the Son of Man [on the cross], you will know then [without any doubt] that I am *He,* and that I do nothing on My own authority, but I say these things just as My Father taught Me.

²⁹"And He who sent Me is [always] with Me; He has not left Me alone, because I always do what pleases Him."

³⁰As He said these things, many believed in Him.

³¹So Jesus was saying to the Jews who had believed Him, "If you abide in My word [continually obeying My teachings and living in accordance with them, then] you are truly My disciples.

³²"And you will know the truth [regarding salvation], and the truth will set you free [from the penalty of sin]."

³³They answered Him, "We are Abraham's descendants and have never been enslaved to anyone. What do You mean by saying, 'You will be set free'?"

³⁴Jesus answered, "I assure you *and* most solemnly say to you, everyone who practices sin *habitually* is a slave of sin.

³⁵"Now the slave does not remain in a household forever; the son [of the master] does remain forever.

³⁶"So if the Son makes you free, then you are unquestionably free.

³⁷"I know that you are Abraham's descendants; yet you plan to kill Me, because My word has no place [to grow] in you [and it makes no change in your heart].

³⁸"I tell the things that I have seen at My Father's side [in His very presence]; so you also do the things that you heard from your father."

³⁹They answered, "Abraham is our father." Jesus said to them, "If you are

[truly] Abraham's children, then do the works of Abraham *and* follow his example.

⁴⁰"But as it is, you want to kill Me, a Man who has told you the truth, which I heard from God. This is not the way Abraham acted.

⁴¹"You are doing the works of your [own] father." They said to Him, "We are not illegitimate children; we have one [spiritual] Father: God."

⁴²Jesus said to them, "If God were your Father [but He is not], you would love *and* recognize Me, for I came from God [out of His very presence] and have arrived *here*. For I have not even come on My own initiative [as self-appointed], but He [is the One who] sent Me.

⁴³"Why do you misunderstand what I am saying? It is because [your spiritual ears are deaf and] you are unable to hear [the truth of] My word.

⁴⁴"You are of *your* father the devil, and it is your will to practice the desires [which are characteristic] of your father. He was a murderer from the beginning, and does not stand in the truth because there is no truth in him. When he lies, he speaks what it natural to him, for he is a liar and the father of lies *and* half-truths.

⁴⁵"But because I speak the truth, you do not believe Me [and continue in your unbelief].

⁴⁶"Which one of you [has proof and] convicts Me of sin? If I speak truth, why do you not believe Me?

⁴⁷"Whoever is of God *and* belongs to Him hears [the truth of] God's words; for this reason you do not hear them: because you are not of God *and* you are not in fellowship with Him."

⁴⁸The Jews answered Him, "Are we not right when we say You are a

speak the Word

Help me, God, to know the truth because only the truth will set me free!
—ADAPTED FROM JOHN 8:32

Samaritan and [that You] have a demon [and are under its power]?"

⁴⁹Jesus answered, "I do not have a demon. On the contrary, I honor My Father, and you dishonor Me.

⁵⁰"However, I am not seeking glory for Myself. There is One who seeks [glory for Me] and judges [those who dishonor Me].

⁵¹"I assure you *and* most solemnly say to you, if anyone keeps My word [by living in accordance with My message] he will indeed never, ever see *and* experience death."

⁵²The Jews said to Him, "Now we know that You have a demon [and are under its power]. Abraham died, and also the prophets; yet You say, 'If anyone keeps My word, he will never, ever taste of death.'

⁵³"Are You greater than our father Abraham, who died? The prophets died too! Whom do You make Yourself out to be?"

⁵⁴Jesus answered, "If I glorify Myself, My glory is [worth] nothing. It is My Father who glorifies Me, of whom you say, 'He is our God.'

⁵⁵Yet you do not know Him, but I know Him fully. If I said I did not know Him, I would be a liar like you. But I do know Him and keep His word.

⁵⁶"Your father Abraham [greatly] rejoiced to see My day (My incarnation). He saw it and was delighted." [Heb 11:13]

⁵⁷Then the Jews said to Him, "You are not even fifty years old, and You [claim to] have seen Abraham?"

⁵⁸Jesus replied, "I assure you *and* most solemnly say to you, before Abraham was born, I Am." [Ex 3:14]

⁵⁹So they picked up stones to throw at Him, but Jesus concealed Himself and left the temple.

9 WHILE HE was passing by, He noticed a man [who had been] blind from birth.

²His disciples asked Him, "Rabbi (Teacher), who sinned, this man or his parents, that he would be born blind?"

³Jesus answered, "Neither this man nor his parents sinned, but it was so that the works of God might be displayed *and* illustrated in him.

⁴"We must work the works of Him who sent Me while it is day; night is coming when no one can work.

⁵"As long as I am in the world, I am the Light of the world [giving guidance through My word and works]."

⁶When He had said this, He spat on the ground and made mud with His saliva, and He spread the mud [like an ointment] on the man's eyes.

⁷And He said to him, "Go, wash in the pool of Siloam" (which is translated, Sent). So he went away and washed, and came back seeing.

⁸So the neighbors, and those who used to know him as a beggar, said, "Is not this the man who used to sit and beg?"

⁹Some said, "It is he." Still others said, "No, but he looks like him." But he kept saying, "I am the man."

¹⁰So they said to him, "How were your eyes opened?"

¹¹He replied, "The Man called Jesus made mud and smeared it on my eyes and told me, 'Go to Siloam and wash.' So I went and washed, and I received my sight!"

¹²They asked him, "Where is He?" He said, "I do not know."

¹³Then they brought the man who was formerly blind to the Pharisees.

¹⁴Now it was on a Sabbath day that Jesus made the mud and opened the man's eyes.

¹⁵So the Pharisees asked him again how he received his sight. And he said to them, "He smeared mud on my eyes, and I washed, and now I see."

¹⁶Then some of the Pharisees said, "This Man [Jesus] is not from God, because He does not keep the Sabbath."

But others said, "How can a man who is a sinner (a non-observant Jew) do such signs *and* miracles?" So there was a difference of opinion among them.

[17]Accordingly they said to the blind man again, "What do you say about Him, since He opened your eyes?" And he said, "[It must be that] He is a prophet!"

[18]However, the Jews did not believe that he had been blind and had received his sight until they called the man's parents.

[19]They asked them, "Is this your son, who you say was born blind? Then how does he now see?"

[20]His parents answered, "We know that this is our son, and that he was born blind;

[21]but as to how he now sees, we do not know; or who has opened his eyes, we do not know. Ask him [and stop asking us]; he is of age, he will speak for himself *and* give his own account of it."

[22]His parents said this because they were afraid of [the leaders of] the Jews; for the Jews had already agreed that if anyone acknowledged Jesus to be the Christ, he would be put out of the synagogue (excommunicated).

[23]Because of this his parents said, "He is of age; ask him."

[24]So a second time they called the man who had been [born] blind, and said to him, "Give God glory *and* praise [for your sight]! We know this Man [Jesus] is a sinner [separated from God]."

[25]Then he answered, "I do not know whether He is a sinner [separated from God]; but one thing I do know, that though I was blind, now I see."

[26]So they said to him, "What did He [actually] do to you? How did He open your eyes?"

[27]He answered, "I already told you and you did not listen. Why do you want to hear it again *and* again? Do you want to become His disciples, too?"

[28]And [at that remark] they stormed at him and jeered, "You are His disciple, but we are disciples of Moses!

[29]"We know [for certain] that God has spoken to Moses, but as for this Man, we do not know where He is from."

[30]The man replied, "Well, this is astonishing! You do not know where He comes from, and yet He opened my eyes!

[31]"We know [according to your tradition] that God does not hear sinners; but if anyone fears God and does His will, He hears him.

[32]"Since the beginning of time it has never been heard that anyone opened the eyes of a person born blind.

[33]"If this Man were not from God, He would not be able to do anything [like this because God would not hear His prayer]."

[34]They answered him, "You were born entirely in sins [from head to foot], and you [presume to] teach us?" Then they threw him out [of the synagogue].

[35]Jesus heard that they had put him out [of the synagogue], and finding him, He asked, "Do you believe in the Son of Man?"

[36]He answered, "Who is He, Sir? Tell me so that I may believe in Him."

[37]Jesus said to him, "You have both seen Him, and [in fact] He is the one who is talking with you."

[38]And he said, "Lord, I believe [in You and Your word]!" And he worshiped Him [with reverence and awe].

[39]Then Jesus said, "I came into this world for judgment [to separate those who believe in Me from those who reject Me—to declare judgment on those who choose to be separated from God], so that the sightless would see, and those who see would become blind."

[40]Some Pharisees who were with Him heard these things and said to Him, "Are we also blind?"

[41]Jesus said to them, "If you were blind [to spiritual things], you would

have no sin [and would not be blamed for your unbelief]; but since you claim to have [spiritual] sight, [you have no excuse so] your sin *and* guilt remain. [Prov 26:12]

10 "I ASSURE you *and* most solemnly say to you, he who does not enter by the door into the sheepfold, but climbs up from some other place [on the stone wall], that one is a thief and a robber.

²"But he who enters by the door is the shepherd of the sheep [the protector and provider].

³"The doorkeeper opens [the gate] for this man, and the sheep hear his voice *and* pay attention to it. And [knowing that they listen] he calls his own sheep by name and leads them out [to pasture].

⁴"When he has brought all his own *sheep* outside, he walks on ahead of them, and the sheep follow him because they know his voice *and* recognize his call.

⁵"They will never follow a stranger, but will run away from him, because they do not know the voice of strangers."

⁶Jesus used this figure of speech with them, but they did not understand what He was talking about.

⁷So Jesus said again, "I assure you *and* most solemnly say to you, I am the Door for the sheep [leading to life].

⁸"All who came before Me [as false messiahs and self-appointed leaders] are thieves and robbers, but the [true] sheep did not hear them.

⁹"I am the Door; anyone who enters through Me will be saved [and will live forever], and will go in and out [freely], and find pasture (spiritual security).

¹⁰"The thief comes only in order to steal and kill and destroy. I came that they may have *and* enjoy life, and have

discerning God's voice

People ask, "How can I be sure I am hearing from God?" As believers, hearing God speak to us is our right and our privilege. The Word says we can *know* His voice and distinguish it from others; He gives us discernment to identify His voice over voices of deception. In John 10:3–5, He parallels this discernment with the instinctive nature of sheep that recognize the voice of their shepherd.

We can discern the difference between God's voice and the voice of deception if we truly know God's character, nature and the history of how He has led others before us. We will know that what we have heard is consistent with His nature. We will also know that what He has said does not contradict His Word, wisdom, or common sense.

If we truly belong to God, He will give us discernment to know if what we are hearing is truly from Him or not. He will enable us to distinguish His voice from the deceptive spirit of error. Then we can have confidence that we are following God's direction, whether He is leading us to go forward or telling us to wait.

To hear God and avoid the spirit of error, it is important to look into God's Word and spend time with Him there. The more we study and learn the Word, the more we will let its power flow through our lives and the better we will be able to hear, discern, and obey God's voice.

it in abundance [to the full, till it over-flows].

¹¹"I am the Good Shepherd. The Good Shepherd lays down His [own] life for the sheep. [Ps 23; Is 40:11]

¹²"But the hired man [who merely serves for wages], who is neither the shepherd nor the owner of the sheep, when he sees the wolf coming, deserts the flock and runs away; and the wolf snatches the sheep and scatters *them*.

¹³"The *man runs* because he is a hired hand [who serves only for wages] and is not concerned about the [safety of the] sheep.

¹⁴"I am the Good Shepherd, and I know [without any doubt those who are] My own and My own know Me [and have a deep, personal relationship with Me]—

¹⁵even as the Father knows Me and I know the Father—and I lay down My [very own] life [sacrificing it] for *the benefit of* the sheep.

¹⁶"I have other sheep [beside these] that are not of this fold. I must bring those also, and they will listen to My voice *and* pay attention to My call, and

putting the Word to work

Have you ever had anything stolen from you? Even if you replaced the article that was stolen, it was probably a trying experience. As difficult as that might have felt, however, Satan—the thief—wants to do even more damage in your life. He does not want to steal your bicycle or your stereo or even your car—he wants to rob you of the joy, the peace, and the hope you have found in God. But be encouraged: Jesus, your Good Shepherd, has saved you and gives you abundant life. Ask Him to restore anything Satan has robbed from you and to teach you how to walk in the abundant life He has promised you.

they will become one flock with one Shepherd. [Ezek 34:23; Eph 2:13–18]

¹⁷"For this reason the Father loves Me, because I lay down My [own] life so that I may take it back.

¹⁸"No one takes it away from Me, but I lay it down voluntarily. I am authorized *and* have power to lay it down *and* to give it up, and I am authorized *and* have power to take it back. This command I have received from My Father."

¹⁹A division [of opinion] occurred again among the Jews because of these words [of His].

²⁰Many of them said, "He has a demon and He is mad [insane—He raves and rambles]. Why listen to Him?"

²¹Others were saying, "These are not the words *and* thoughts of one possessed by a demon. Can a demon open the eyes of the blind?"

²²At that time the Feast of Dedication took place at Jerusalem.

²³It was winter, and Jesus was walking in the temple [area] in Solomon's portico.

²⁴So the Jews surrounded Him and began saying to Him, "How long are You going to keep us in suspense? If You are [really] the Christ (the Messiah, the Anointed), tell us so plainly *and* openly."

²⁵Jesus answered them, "I have told you so, yet you do not believe. The works that I do in My Father's name testify concerning Me [they are My credentials and the evidence declaring who I am].

²⁶"But you do not believe Me [so you do not trust and follow Me] because you are not My sheep.

²⁷"The sheep that are My own hear My voice *and* listen to Me; I know them, and they follow Me.

²⁸"And I give them eternal life, and they will never, ever [by any means] perish; and no one will ever snatch them out of My hand.

²⁹"My Father, who has given *them* to

Me, is greater *and* mightier than all; and no one is able to snatch *them* out of the Father's hand.

³⁰"I and the Father are One [in essence and nature]."

³¹Again the Jews picked up stones to stone Him.

³²Jesus answered them, "I showed you many good works [and many acts of mercy] from the Father; for which of them are you stoning Me?"

³³The Jews answered Him, "We are not going to stone You for a good work, but for blasphemy, because You, a *mere* man, make Yourself out to be God."

³⁴Jesus answered them, "Is it not written in your Law, 'I SAID, YOU ARE GODS [human judges representing God, not divine beings]'? [Ps 82:6]

³⁵"If He called them gods, men to whom the word of God came (and the Scripture cannot be undone *or* annulled *or* broken),

³⁶[if that is true] then do you say of Him whom the Father sanctified *and* set apart *for Himself* and sent into the world, 'You are blaspheming,' because I said, 'I am the Son of God'?

³⁷"If I do not do the works of My Father [that is, the miracles that only

enjoying everyday life

Satan has one goal and that is destruction. He comes only to kill, steal, and destroy everything good that God has in mind for us. Jesus said He came that we might have life and enjoy our lives.

Are you enjoying life? Are you enjoying every facet of life or just what you consider to be the "fun" parts? I truly believe that through the power of the Holy Spirit we can enjoy everything. We can enjoy our work and times of waiting. We can enjoy the journey and not just the destination. Life is really all about the journey. Even when a train arrives at the station for which it is headed, it soon leaves again for another station. We spend more time in life waiting than we do arriving. God created us to be goal-oriented. Once we reach one goal, it is not long before we find ourselves setting another one. We need to learn to enjoy where we are on the way to where we are going.

One way Satan steals from us is by making us think we can only enjoy certain things and not others. But the truth is that we can get a new mindset and decide to enjoy everything in life. I used to spend a lot of time waiting in airports. Sometimes flights were cancelled or delayed and I let that steal my joy. I often became very aggravated, frustrated, and upset—but that did not change my circumstances; it only stole my joy and peace. I finally learned that when circumstances change, I do not have to change with them. I can refuse to allow Satan to get me upset. When Satan steals from you or aggravates you, he really does not want your goods, he wants your joy!

Making the decision to enjoy my life was an important one for me and it may be for you too. Life is wasted if we allow ourselves to be miserable all the time. Jesus said in John 14:27 that He has left us His peace and we are to stop allowing ourselves to be upset. He has given us gifts and responsibilities. We are partners with God. His part is to provide peace and joy and our part is not to let the devil steal it. Decide today to start enjoying everyday life!

God could perform], then do not believe Me.

³⁸"But if I am doing them, even if you do not believe Me *or* have faith in Me, [at least] believe the works [that I do—admit that they are the works of God], so that you may know and keep on knowing [clearly—without any doubt] that the Father is in Me, and I am in the Father [that is, I am One with Him]."

³⁹So they tried again to seize Him, but He eluded their grasp.

⁴⁰He went back again across the Jordan to the place where John was first baptizing, and He was staying there.

⁴¹Many came to Him, and they were saying, "John did not perform a single sign (attesting miracle), but everything John said about this Man was true *and* accurate."

⁴²And many there believed *and* confidently trusted in Him [accepting Him as Savior, and following His teaching].

11 NOW A certain man named Lazarus was sick. He was from Bethany, the village where Mary and her sister Martha lived.

²It was the Mary who anointed the Lord with perfume and wiped His feet with her hair, whose brother Lazarus was sick. [John 12:3]

³So the sisters sent *word* to Him, saying, "Lord, he [our brother and Your friend] whom You love is sick."

⁴When Jesus heard this, He said, "This sickness will not end in death; but [on the contrary it is] for the glory *and* honor of God, so that the Son of God may be glorified by it."

⁵Now Jesus loved *and* was concerned about Martha and her sister and Lazarus [and considered them dear friends].

⁶So [even] when He heard that Lazarus was sick, He stayed in the same place two more days.

⁷Then He said to His disciples, "Let us go back to Judea."

⁸The disciples said to Him, "Rabbi (Teacher), the Jews were only recently going to stone You, and You are [thinking of] going back there again?"

⁹Jesus answered, "Are there not twelve hours [of light] in the day? Anyone who walks in the daytime does not stumble, because he sees [by] the light of this world.

¹⁰"But if anyone walks in the night, he stumbles, because there is no light in him."

¹¹He said this, and after that said, "Our friend Lazarus has fallen asleep; but I am going *there* to wake him."

¹²The disciples answered, "Lord, if he has fallen asleep, he will recover."

¹³However, Jesus had spoken of his death, but they thought that He was referring to natural sleep.

¹⁴So then Jesus told them plainly, "Lazarus is dead.

¹⁵"And for your sake I am glad that I was not there, so that you may believe. But let us go to him."

¹⁶Then Thomas, who was called Didymus (the twin), said to his fellow disciples, "Let us go too, that we may die with Him."

¹⁷So when Jesus arrived, He found that Lazarus had already been in the tomb four days.

¹⁸Bethany was near Jerusalem, about two miles away;

¹⁹and many of the Jews had come to see Martha and Mary, to comfort them concerning [the loss of] their brother.

²⁰So when Martha heard that Jesus was coming, she went to meet Him, while Mary remained sitting in the house.

²¹Then Martha said to Jesus, "Lord, if You had been here, my brother would not have died.

²²"Even now I know that whatever You ask of God, God will give to You."

²³Jesus told her, "Your brother will rise [from the dead]."

²⁴Martha replied, "I know that he will rise [from the dead] in the resurrection on the last day."

²⁵Jesus said to her, "I am the Resurrection and the Life. Whoever believes in (adheres to, trusts in, relies on) Me [as Savior] will live even if he dies;

²⁶and everyone who lives and believes in Me [as Savior] will never die. Do you believe this?"

²⁷She said to Him, "Yes, Lord; I have believed *and* continue to believe that You are the Christ (the Messiah, the Anointed), the Son of God, He who was [destined and promised] to come into the world [and it is for You that the world has waited]."

²⁸After she had said this, she left and called her sister Mary, privately whispering [to her], "The Teacher is here and is asking for you."

²⁹And when she heard this, she got up quickly and went to Him.

³⁰Now Jesus had not yet entered the village, but was still at the place where Martha had met Him.

³¹So when the Jews who were with her in the house comforting her, saw how quickly Mary got up and left, they followed her, assuming that she was going to the tomb to weep there.

³²When Mary came [to the place] where Jesus was and saw Him, she fell at His feet, saying to Him, "Lord, if You had been here, my brother would not have died."

³³When Jesus saw her sobbing, and the Jews who had come with her also sobbing, He was deeply moved in spirit [to the point of anger at the sorrow caused by death] and was troubled,

³⁴and said, "Where have you laid him?" They said, "Lord, come and see."

³⁵Jesus wept.

³⁶So the Jews were saying, "See how He loved him [as a close friend]!"

³⁷But some of them said, "Could not this Man, who opened the blind man's eyes, have kept this man from dying?"

³⁸So Jesus, again deeply moved within [to the point of anger], approached the tomb. It was a cave, and a boulder was lying against it [to cover the entrance].

³⁹Jesus said, "Take away the stone." Martha, the sister of the dead man, said to Him, "Lord, by this time there will be an offensive odor, for he has been *dead* four days! [It is hopeless!]"

⁴⁰Jesus said to her, "Did I not say to you that if you believe [in Me], you will see the glory of God [the expression of His excellence]?"

⁴¹So they took away the stone. And Jesus raised His eyes [toward heaven] and said, "Father, I thank You that You have heard Me.

⁴²"I knew that You always hear Me *and* listen to Me; but I have said this because of the people standing around, so that they may believe that You have sent Me [and that You have made Me Your representative]."

putting the Word to work

Many people are afraid of death. Are you? Martha had just buried her brother, yet she took Jesus at His word and believed that He was the Son of God and that her brother would live again. As a believer in Jesus, you do not need to fear death. As Martha discovered, you too can know that Jesus has defeated the power of death. Although your body will one day die, your spirit will live forever with God.

life point

In John 11:41 we see a good example of Jesus giving thanks to God. When you pray, I encourage you to end your prayer, as Jesus did here, by saying, "Father, I thank You that You have heard me."

⁴³When He had said this, He shouted with a loud voice, "Lazarus, come out!"

⁴⁴Out came the man who had been dead, his hands and feet *tightly* wrapped in burial cloths (linen strips), and with a [burial] cloth wrapped around his face. Jesus said to them, "Unwrap him and release him."

⁴⁵So then, many of the Jews who had come to [be with] Mary and who were eyewitnesses to what Jesus had done, believed in Him.

⁴⁶But some of them went back to the Pharisees and told them what Jesus had done.

⁴⁷So the chief priests and Pharisees convened a council [of the leaders in Israel], and said, "What are we doing? For this man performs many signs (attesting miracles).

⁴⁸"If we let Him go on like this, everyone will believe in Him, and the Romans will come and take away both our [holy] place (the temple) and our nation."

⁴⁹But one of them, Caiaphas, who was the high priest that year [the year of Christ's crucifixion], said to them, "You know nothing at all!

⁵⁰"Nor do you understand that it is expedient *and* politically advantageous for you that one man die for the people, and that the whole nation not perish."

⁵¹Now he did not say this [simply] on his own initiative; but being the high priest that year, he [was unknowingly used by God and] prophesied that Jesus was going to die for the nation, [Is 53:8]

⁵²and not only for the nation, but also for the purpose of gathering together into one body the children of God who have been scattered abroad. [Is 49:6]

⁵³So from that day on they planned together to kill Him.

⁵⁴For that reason Jesus no longer walked openly among the Jews, but left there *and* went to the district that borders on the uninhabited wilderness, to a town called Ephraim; and He stayed there with the disciples.

⁵⁵Now the Passover of the Jews was approaching, and many from the country went up to Jerusalem before Passover to purify themselves [ceremonially, so that they would be able to participate in the feast].

⁵⁶So they were looking for Jesus as they stood in the temple [area], and saying among themselves, "What do you think? Will He not come to the feast at all?"

⁵⁷Now the chief priests and Pharisees had given orders that if anyone knew where He was, he was to report it so that they might arrest Him.

12 SIX DAYS before the Passover, Jesus went to Bethany, where Lazarus was, whom He had raised from the dead. [Matt 26:6–13; Mark 14:3–9]

²So they gave a supper for Him there. Martha was serving, and Lazarus was one of those reclining *at the table* with Him.

³Then Mary took a pound of very expensive perfume of pure nard, and she poured it on Jesus' feet and wiped His feet with her hair; and the house was filled with the fragrance of the perfume.

⁴But Judas Iscariot, one of His disciples, the one who was going to betray Him, said,

⁵"Why was this perfume not sold for three hundred denarii and [the money] given to the poor?"

⁶Now he said this, not because he cared about the poor [for he had never cared about them], but because he was a thief; and since he had the money box [serving as treasurer for the twelve disciples], he used to pilfer what was put into it.

⁷So Jesus said, "Let her alone, so that she may keep [the rest of] it for the day of My burial.

[8]"You always have the poor with you, but you do not always have Me."

[9]A large crowd of Jews learned that He was there [at Bethany]; and they came, not only because of Jesus, but also to see Lazarus, whom He had raised from the dead.

[10]So the chief priests planned to kill Lazarus also,

[11]because on account of him many of the Jews were going away [from the teaching and traditions of the Jewish leaders] and believing in Jesus [following Him as Savior and Messiah].

[12]The next day, when the large crowd who had come to the *Passover* feast heard that Jesus was coming to Jerusalem, [Matt 21:4–9; Mark 11:7–10; Luke 19:35–38]

[13]they took branches of palm trees [in homage to Him as King] and went out to meet Him, and they *began* shouting *and* kept shouting "Hosanna! BLESSED (celebrated, praised) IS HE WHO COMES IN THE NAME OF THE LORD, even the King of Israel!" [Ps 118:26]

[14]And Jesus, finding a young donkey, sat on it; just as it is written [in Scripture],

[15]"DO NOT FEAR, DAUGHTER OF ZION; BEHOLD, YOUR KING IS COMING, SEATED ON A DONKEY'S COLT." [Zech 9:9]

[16]His disciples did not understand [the meaning of] these things at first; but when Jesus was glorified *and* exalted, they remembered that these things had been written about Him and had been done to Him.

[17]So the people, who were with Him when He called Lazarus out of the tomb and raised him from the dead, continued to tell others *about Him.*

[18]For this reason the crowd went to meet Him, because they heard that He had performed this [miraculous] sign.

[19]Then the Pharisees [argued and] said to one another, "You see that your efforts are futile. Look! The whole world has gone [running] after Him!"

[20]Now there were some Greeks (Gentiles) among those who were going up to worship at the feast;

[21]these came to Philip, who was from Bethsaida in Galilee, with a request, saying, "Sir, we wish to see Jesus."

[22]Philip came and told Andrew; then Andrew and Philip went and told Jesus.

[23]And Jesus answered them, "The hour has come for the Son of Man to be glorified *and* exalted.

[24]"I assure you *and* most solemnly say to you, unless a grain of wheat falls into the earth and dies, it remains alone [just one grain, never more]. But if it dies, it produces much grain *and* yields a harvest.

[25]"The one who loves his life [eventually] loses it [through death], but the one who hates his life in this world [and is concerned with pleasing God] will keep it for life eternal.

[26]"If anyone serves Me, he must [continue to faithfully] follow Me [without hesitation, holding steadfastly to Me, conforming to My example in living and, if need be, suffering or perhaps dying because of faith in Me]; and wherever I am [in heaven's glory], there will My servant be also. If anyone serves Me, the Father will honor him.

[27]"Now My soul is troubled *and* deeply distressed; what shall I say? 'Father, save Me from this hour [of trial and agony]'? But it is for this [very] purpose

speak the Word

Jesus, I will serve You and continue to faithfully follow You.
I will conform to Your example in living, and if need be, in dying.
Wherever You are, I will be also.
−ADAPTED FROM JOHN 12:26

that I have come to this hour [this time and place].

28"[Rather, I will say,] 'Father, glorify (honor, extol) Your name!'" Then a voice came from heaven saying, "I have both glorified it, and will glorify it again."

29The crowd *of people* who stood nearby and heard the voice said that it had thundered; others said, "An angel has spoken to Him!"

30Jesus answered, "This voice has come for your sake, not for mine.

31"Now judgment is upon this world [the sentence is being passed]. Now the ruler of this world (Satan) will be cast out.

32"And I, if *and* when I am lifted up from the earth [on the cross], will draw all *people* to Myself [Gentiles, as well as Jews]."

33He said this to indicate the kind of death by which He was to die.

34At this the crowd answered Him, "We have heard from the Law that the Christ is to remain forever; how then can You say, 'The Son of Man must be lifted up'? Who is this Son of Man?" [Ps 110:4]

35So Jesus said to them, "The Light is among you [only] a little while longer. Walk while you have the Light [keep on living by it], so that darkness will not overtake you. He who walks in the darkness does not know where he is going [he is drifting aimlessly].

36"While you have the Light, believe *and* trust in the Light [have faith in it, hold on to it, rely on it], so that you may become sons of Light [being filled with Light as followers of God]."

Jesus said these things, and then He left and hid Himself from them.

37Even though He had done so many signs (attesting miracles) right before them, yet they still did not believe *and* failed to trust Him—

38*This was* to fulfill what Isaiah the prophet said: "LORD, WHO HAS BELIEVED OUR MESSAGE? AND TO WHOM HAS THE ARM (the power) OF THE LORD BEEN SHOWN (unveiled, revealed)?" [Is 53:1]

39Therefore they could not believe, for Isaiah said again,

40"HE HAS BLINDED THEIR EYES AND HE HARDENED THEIR HEART, TO KEEP THEM FROM SEEING WITH THEIR EYES AND UNDERSTANDING WITH THEIR HEART AND BEING CONVERTED; OTHERWISE, I [their God] WOULD HEAL THEM."

41Isaiah said these things because he saw His glory and spoke about Him. [Is 6:9, 10]

42Nevertheless, even many of the leading men believed in Him [as Savior and Messiah], but because of the Pharisees they would not confess it, for fear that [if they acknowledged Him openly] they would be put out of the synagogue (excommunicated);

43for they loved the approval of men more than the approval of God.

44But Jesus loudly declared, "The one who believes *and* trusts in Me does not believe [only] in Me but [also believes] in Him who sent Me.

45"And whoever sees Me sees the One who sent Me.

46"I have come as Light into the world, so that everyone who believes *and* trusts in Me [as Savior—all those who anchor their hope in Me and rely on the truth of My message] will not continue to live in darkness.

47"If anyone hears My words and does not keep them, I do not judge him; for I did not come to judge *and* condemn the world [that is, to initiate the final judgment of the world], but to save the world.

48"Whoever rejects Me and refuses to accept My teachings, has one who judges him; the *very* word that I spoke will judge *and* condemn him on the last day.

49"For I have never spoken on My own initiative *or* authority, but the Father Himself who sent Me has given

Me a commandment *regarding* what to say and what to speak. [Deut 18:18, 19]

⁵⁰"I know that His commandment is eternal life. So the things I speak, I speak [in accordance with His exact instruction,] just as the Father has told Me."

13 NOW BEFORE the Passover Feast, Jesus knew that His hour had come [and it was time] for Him to leave this world *and* return to the Father. Having [greatly] loved His own who were in the world, He loved them [and continuously loves them with His perfect love] to the end (eternally).

²It was during supper, when the devil had already put [the thought of] betraying Jesus into the heart of Judas Iscariot, Simon's son,

³that Jesus, knowing that the Father had put everything into His hands, and that He had come from God and was [now] returning to God,

⁴got up from supper, took off His [outer] robe, and taking a [servant's] towel, He tied it around His waist.

⁵Then He poured water into the basin and began washing the disciples' feet and wiping them with the towel which was tied around His waist.

⁶When He came to Simon Peter, he said to Him, "Lord, are You going to wash my feet?"

⁷Jesus replied to him, "You do not realize now what I am doing, but you will [fully] understand it later."

⁸Peter said to Him, "You will never wash my feet!" Jesus answered, "Unless I wash you, you have no part with Me [we can have nothing to do with each other]."

⁹Simon Peter said to Him, "Lord, [in that case, wash] not only my feet, but also my hands and my head!"

¹⁰Jesus said to him, "Anyone who has bathed needs only to wash his feet, and is completely clean. And you [My disciples] are clean, but not all *of you*."

¹¹For He knew who was going to betray Him; for that reason He said, "Not all of you are clean."

¹²So when He had washed their feet and put on His [outer] robe and reclined *at the table* again, He said to them, "Do you understand what I have done for you?

¹³"You call Me Teacher and Lord, and you are right in doing so, for *that is who* I am.

¹⁴"So if I, the Lord and the Teacher, washed your feet, you ought to wash one another's feet as well.

¹⁵"For I gave you [this as] an example, so that you should do [in turn] as I did to you.

¹⁶"I assure you *and* most solemnly say to you, a slave is not greater than his master, nor is one who is sent greater than the one who sent him.

¹⁷"If you know these things, you are blessed [happy and favored by God] if you put them into practice [and faithfully do them].

¹⁸"I am not speaking of all of you. I know whom I have chosen; but [this has happened] in order that the Scripture may be fulfilled: 'HE WHO EATS MY BREAD HAS RAISED UP HIS HEEL AGAINST ME [as My enemy].' [Ps 41:9]

¹⁹"From now on I am telling you [what will happen] before it occurs, so that when it does take place you may believe that I am *He* [who I say I am—the Christ, the Anointed, the Messiah].

²⁰"I assure you *and* most solemnly say to you, the one who receives *and* welcomes whomever I send receives Me; and the one who receives Me receives Him who sent Me [in that same way]."

²¹After Jesus had said these things, He was troubled in spirit, and testified and said, "I assure you *and* most solemnly say to you, one of you will betray Me *and* hand Me over."

²²The disciples *began* looking at one another, puzzled *and* disturbed as to whom He could mean.

²³One of His disciples, whom Jesus loved (esteemed), was leaning against Jesus' chest.

²⁴So Simon Peter motioned to him (John) and [quietly] asked [him to ask Jesus] of whom He was speaking.

²⁵Then leaning back against Jesus' chest, he (John) asked Him [privately], "Lord, who is it?"

²⁶Jesus answered, "It is the one to whom I am going to give this piece [of bread] after I have dipped it." So when He had dipped the piece of bread [into the dish], He gave it to Judas, *son* of Simon Iscariot.

²⁷After [Judas had taken] the piece of bread, Satan entered him. Then Jesus said to him, "What you are going to do, do quickly [without delay]."

²⁸But no one reclining *at the table* knew why He said *this* to him.

²⁹Some thought that, since Judas [as the treasurer of the group] had the money box, Jesus was telling him, "Buy what we need for the feast," or that he was to give something to the poor.

³⁰After taking the piece of bread, he went out immediately; and it was night.

³¹So when Judas had left, Jesus said, "Now is [the time for] the Son of Man [to be] glorified, and God is glorified in Him;

great people serve

Pride never kept the Lord from showing His love. John 13:5–15 tells the story of how Jesus washed the feet of His disciples in an act of servanthood to show them how very much He loved them.

In a culture where people's sandals did not protect their feet from the dirt of the roads, servants—not masters—were supposed to wash feet. But Jesus, fully knowing Who He was—the Greatest of all—became the Servant of all.

When the Lord came to Simon Peter to wash his feet, Peter resisted Him saying, "Lord, are You going to wash my feet?" (John 13:6). Imagine for a moment how you would feel if Jesus told you that He wanted to wash your feet. You probably would feel hesitant, as Peter did, thinking you should be the one washing the Lord's feet, instead of Him washing yours. How did Jesus respond to Peter's rash vow of never letting Jesus wash his feet? Jesus said that unless Peter let Him do this, he would have no part in Him (see John 13:7, 8).

After Jesus completed washing all of His disciples' feet, He told them they needed to follow His example as their Lord and Teacher and wash one another's feet (see John 13:14). I believe Jesus was saying that unless we are willing to serve one another, we have no true part in Him or in each other. If we love someone to the highest degree, we will be willing to serve that person.

In our relationship with Him, Jesus calls us to sacrifice our self-will. We are not to be served, but to serve. We are to be sensitive to other people's needs, even in little things. We, like Jesus, should seek to serve others rather than merely letting them serve us. When we have people in our lives who serve us in various ways, we should always treat them with the utmost respect and be good to them.

³²[if God is glorified in Him,] God will also glorify Him (the Son) in Himself, and will glorify Him at once.

³³"Little children, I am with you [only] a little longer. You will look for Me and, as I told the Jews, so I tell you now, 'Where I am going, you are not able to come.' [John 8:21]

³⁴"I am giving you a new commandment, that you love one another. Just as I have loved you, so you too are to love one another.

³⁵"By this everyone will know that you are My disciples, if you have love *and* unselfish concern for one another."

³⁶Simon Peter said to Him, "Lord, where are You going?" Jesus answered, "Where I am going, you cannot follow Me now; but you will be able to follow later."

³⁷Peter said to Him, "Lord, why cannot I follow You now? I will lay down my life for You!" [Matt 26:33–35; Mark 14:29–31; Luke 22:33, 34]

³⁸Jesus answered, "Will you [really] lay down your life for Me? I assure you

major in love

Is love the main theme of your life? If not, it's probably time to make a change. Often we spend time seeking things we think are important, but they aren't important to God at all. I did that for a long time. I tried to build a worldwide ministry, tried to change myself and my husband and children, and tried to prosper and succeed. I tried a lot of things, but I ignored the one thing Jesus told us was important.

Do not major in what Jesus considers to be minor. In other words, don't spend your time and effort on things that have no lasting value and don't add to the kingdom of God. We should all take a regular and honest inventory of our love walk. Do you study love? Do you purposefully walk in love? Do you even really know what love is? It is certainly more than theory or speech. The Bible says love is seen in our behavior toward one another. It is by our love that the world will know we are Jesus' disciples (see John 13:35).

The world will not be impressed with anything other than seeing a consistent love walk among Christians. That will impress them because it is rarely seen and it is impossible for anyone to maintain without Jesus Christ in their lives. Talk is easy, but the world needs to see action. God is love; so when people see real love, they see God.

Love can be described quite eloquently, but I believe the real power of love is seen in how we treat one another. Are we patient, kind, humble, ready to believe the best at all times, not easily provoked or offended, and ready to lay aside our rights for other people? Are we ready to quickly and frequently forgive, and to never keep records of wrongs that we have suffered? Will we endure everything without weakening and bear with the failings of the weak? The willingness to do these things is what love is all about. Love is an effort and it always costs us something. Most people today are looking for the easy road, but that is one that leads to destruction. I encourage you to take the narrow road—the one on which you'll find people who are willing to treat others as they want to be treated.

and most solemnly say to you, before a rooster crows you will deny *and* completely disown Me three times.

putting the Word to work

Have you ever wondered what the best way to tell someone about Jesus is? The answer is, "Love them." Live out the selfless, sacrificial love you have received from Jesus. Extend that love to those who have not yet trusted Him as Lord and Savior, and your actions will speak loudly about who Jesus is and what He is all about.

14 "DO NOT let your heart be troubled (afraid, cowardly). Believe [confidently] in God *and* trust in Him, [have faith, hold on to it, rely on it, keep going and] believe also in Me.

²"In My Father's house are many dwelling places. If it were not so, I would have told you, because I am going there to prepare a place for you.

³"And if I go and prepare a place for you, I will come back again and I will take you to Myself, so that where I am you may be also.

⁴"And [to the place] where I am going, you know the way."

⁵Thomas said to Him, "Lord, we do not know where You are going; so how can we know the way?"

⁶Jesus said to him, "I am the [only] Way [to God] and the [real] Truth and the [real] Life; no one comes to the Father but through Me.

⁷"If you had [really] known Me, you would also have known My Father. From now on you know Him, and have seen Him."

⁸Philip said to Him, "Lord, show us the Father and then we will be satisfied."

⁹Jesus said to him, "Have I been with you for so long a time, and you do not know Me yet, Philip, *nor* recognize clearly who I am? Anyone who has seen Me has seen the Father. How can you say, 'Show us the Father?'

¹⁰"Do you not believe that I am in the Father, and the Father is in Me? The words I say to you I do not say on My own initiative *or* authority, but the Father, abiding *continually* in Me, does His works [His attesting miracles and acts of power].

¹¹"Believe Me that I am in the Father and the Father is in Me; otherwise believe [Me] because of the [very] works themselves [which you have witnessed].

¹²"I assure you *and* most solemnly say to you, anyone who believes in Me [as Savior] will also do the things that I do; and he will do even greater things than these [in extent and outreach], because I am going to the Father.

¹³"And I will do whatever you ask in My name [as My representative], this I will do, so that the Father may be glorified *and* celebrated in the Son. [Ex 3:14]

¹⁴"If you ask Me anything in My name [as My representative], I will do it.

¹⁵"If you [really] love Me, you will keep *and* obey My commandments.

putting the Word to work

Have you ever been in a car with someone who doesn't know where he is going and refuses to ask for directions? Some people think there are many ways to God, and they search for truth in different places, ignoring the directions that God gave us. However, the reality is that there is only one way to God, and it is through Jesus Christ. As you follow Jesus, Who is the Way, He will lead you in truth and you will experience fullness of life. Pray for those who do not yet know Jesus, that they, too, will find life and truth in Him.

life point

To whatever degree we love God, to that same degree we obey Him. The degree to which we obey Him is the measure of our love for Him. As our love for Jesus grows, so will our obedience.

16"And I will ask the Father, and He will give you another Helper (Comforter, Advocate, Intercessor—Counselor, Strengthener, Standby), to be with you forever—

17the Spirit of Truth, whom the world cannot receive [and take to its heart] because it does not see Him or know Him, *but* you know Him because He (the Holy Spirit) remains with you *continually* and will be in you.

18"I will not leave you as orphans [comfortless, bereaved, and helpless]; I will come [back] to you.

19"After a little while the world will no longer see Me, but you will see Me; because I live, you will live also.

20"On that day [when that time comes] you will know for yourselves that I am in My Father, and you *are* in Me, and I *am* in you.

21"The person who has My commandments and keeps them is the one who [really] loves Me; and whoever [really] loves Me will be loved by My

life point

Things get hard when we try to do them independently without leaning and relying on God's grace. If everything in life were easy, we wouldn't need the power of the Holy Spirit to help us.

One way the Bible refers to the Holy Spirit is as our "Helper." He is in us and with us all the time to *help* us, to enable us to do what we cannot do—and, I might add, to do with ease what would be difficult without Him.

Father, and I will love him and reveal Myself to him [I will make Myself real to him]."

22Judas (not Iscariot) asked Him, "Lord, what has happened that You are going to reveal Yourself to us and not to the world?"

23Jesus answered, "If anyone [really] loves Me, he will keep My word (teaching); and My Father will love him, and We will come to him and make Our dwelling place with him.

24"One who does not [really] love Me does not keep My words. And the word (teaching) which you hear is not Mine, but is the Father's who sent Me.

25"I have told you these things while I am still with you.

26"But the Helper (Comforter, Advocate, Intercessor—Counselor, Strengthener, Standby), the Holy Spirit, whom the Father will send in My name [in My place, to represent Me and act on My behalf], He will teach you all things. And He will help you remember everything that I have told you. [Matt 5:7, 13, 24, 25; Luke 24:49; John 14:16; Acts 1:4]

27"Peace I leave with you; My [perfect] peace I give to you; not as the world gives do I give to you. Do not let your heart be troubled, nor let it be afraid. [Let My perfect peace calm you in every circumstance and give you courage and strength for every challenge.]

28"You heard Me tell you, 'I am going away, and I am coming *back* to you.' If you [really] loved Me, you would have rejoiced, because I am going [back] to

life point

John 14:17 calls the Holy Spirit the "Spirit of Truth." He works continually in and with believers to bring us into new levels of truth awareness. Entering a new level always means leaving an old one behind, but we have nothing to fear because He promises to be with us. Always.

life point

We see plainly from John 14:27 that Jesus has provided us peace, but we must appropriate it and not allow our hearts to be troubled or afraid. We cannot just passively wait to feel peaceful. We are to pursue God's peace and refuse to live without it.

the Father, for the Father is greater than I.

²⁹"I have told you now before it happens, so that when it does take place, you may believe *and* have faith [in Me].

³⁰"I will not speak with you much longer, for the ruler of the world (Satan) is coming. And he has no claim on Me [no power over Me nor anything that he can use against Me];

³¹but so that the world may know [without any doubt] that I love the Father, I do exactly as the Father has commanded Me [and act in full agreement with Him]. Get up, let us go from here.

15 "I AM the true Vine, and My Father is the vinedresser. ²"Every branch in Me that does not bear fruit, He takes away; and every *branch* that continues to bear fruit, He [repeatedly] prunes, so that it will bear more fruit [even richer and finer fruit].

³"You are already clean because of the word which I have given you [the teachings which I have discussed with you].

⁴"Remain in Me, and I [will remain] in you. Just as no branch can bear fruit by itself without remaining in the vine, neither can you [bear fruit, producing evidence of your faith] unless you remain in Me.

⁵"I am the Vine; you are the branches. The one who remains in Me and I in him bears much fruit, for [otherwise] apart from Me [that is, cut off from vital union with Me] you can do nothing.

putting the Word to work

Have you ever seen fruit grow apart from the vine, tree, or plant to which it was attached? Of course not! As a disciple of Jesus, the same is true for you. Unless you stay in His presence, you will not grow or bear fruit. The word *abide* means "to dwell; to take up residence." Allow Jesus to take up residence in your life. Just as the vine is the source of nourishment and health for the fruit, Jesus is your source of life. Cultivate an ever-growing relationship with Him by spending time with Him in prayer and reading and studying God's Word.

⁶"If anyone does not remain in Me, he is thrown out like a [broken off] branch, and withers *and* dies; and they gather such branches and throw them into the fire, and they are burned.

⁷"If you remain in Me and My words remain in you [that is, if we are vitally united and My message lives in your heart], ask whatever you wish and it will be done for you.

⁸"My Father is glorified *and* honored by this, when you bear much fruit, and prove yourselves to be My [true] disciples.

life point

John 15:1-8 tells us that God prunes us and cuts away things that no longer bear the kind of fruit He desires us to show. This "cutting away" is often painful and not immediately understood, but it is necessary for us to grow into the fruit-bearing believers in Jesus Christ that He wants us to be. We need to understand that God is progressive, and sometimes He needs to prune us as He leads us to higher places.

"help, Lord"

God wants us to depend entirely on Him. He wants us to lean on, trust in, and rely on Him. Actually, that is part of the definition of faith. We are partners with God, and that means we both have responsibility. But we must lean on Him in order to do the things that are our part. God called me into the ministry and He anointed (enabled) and gifted me to do what I need to do, but I still have to trust Him and remember how much I need Him at all times.

Sometimes we may think we don't need God's help with things we have done over and over again successfully. Why would we need help with something we already know we can do? It is dangerous to become self-reliant. The book of Proverbs speaks frequently of the self-confident fool. People who think they are self-sufficient and can take care of themselves are being foolish—and eventually that will be proven to everyone including them.

An independent attitude is part of the baby stage of Christianity. Mature Christians know they can do nothing of any real value apart from Jesus. Of course, we can do things, but that doesn't mean they will be done right, that we will enjoy them, or that they will produce any real lasting fruit.

When the Lord says we can do nothing apart from Him, He means things will not work properly in our lives unless we invite Him into everything. His presence can eliminate much of the struggle we experience in life. It makes impossible things possible, hard things easy, and frustrating things peaceful. Do not ever be afraid to say, "Help, Lord. I can't do this without You."

⁹"I have loved you just as the Father has loved Me; remain in My love [and do not doubt My love for you].

¹⁰"If you keep My commandments *and* obey My teaching, you will remain in My love, just as I have kept My Father's commandments and remain in His love.

¹¹"I have told you these things so that My joy *and* delight may be in you, and that your joy may be made full *and* complete *and* overflowing.

¹²"This is My commandment, that you love *and* unselfishly seek the best for one another, just as I have loved you.

¹³"No one has greater love [nor stronger commitment] than to lay down his own life for his friends.

¹⁴"You are my friends if you keep on doing what I command you.

¹⁵"I do not call you servants any longer, for the servant does not know what his master is doing; but I have called you [My] friends, because I have revealed to you everything that I have heard from My Father.

¹⁶"You have not chosen Me, but I have chosen you and I have appointed *and* placed *and* purposefully planted you, so that you would go and bear fruit *and*

speak the Word

Thank You, Jesus, for calling me Your friend.
—ADAPTED FROM JOHN 15:15

keep on bearing, and that your fruit will remain *and* be lasting, so that whatever you ask of the Father in My name [as My representative] He may give to you.

[17]"This [is what] I command you: that you love *and* unselfishly seek the best for one another.

[18]"If the world hates you [and it does], know that it has hated Me before *it hated* you.

[19]"If you belonged to the world, the world would love [you as] its own *and* would treat you with affection. But you are not of the world [you no longer belong to it], but I have chosen you out of the world. And because of this the world hates you.

[20]"Remember [and continue to remember] that I told you, 'A servant is not greater than his master.' If they persecuted Me, they will also persecute you. If they kept My word, they will keep yours also.

[21]"But they will do all these [hurtful] things to you for My name's sake [because you bear My name and are identified with Me], for they do not know the One who sent Me.

[22]"If I had not come and spoken to them, they would not have [the guilt of their] sin; but now they have no excuse for their sin.

[23]"The one who hates Me also hates My Father.

[24]"If I had not done among them the works (attesting miracles) which no one else [ever] did, they would not have [the guilt of their] sin; but now [the fact is that] they have both seen [these works] and have hated Me [and continue to hate Me] and My Father as well.

[25]"But [this is so] that the word which has been written in their Law would be fulfilled, 'THEY HATED ME WITHOUT A CAUSE.' [Ps 35:19; 69:4]

[26]"But when the Helper (Comforter, Advocate, Intercessor—Counselor, Strengthener, Standby) comes, whom I will send to you from the Father, *that is* the Spirit of Truth who comes from the Father, He will testify *and* bear witness about Me.

[27]"But you will testify also *and* be My witnesses, because you have been with Me from the beginning.

16

"I HAVE told you these things so that you will not stumble or be caught off guard *and* fall away.

[2]"They will put you out of the synagogues *and* make you outcasts. And a time is coming when whoever kills you will think that he is offering service to God.

[3]"And they will do these things because they have not known the Father or Me.

[4]"I have told you these things [now], so that when their time comes, you will remember that I told you about them. I did not say these things to you at the beginning, because I was with you.

[5]"But now I am going to Him who sent Me; and none of you asks Me, 'Where are You going?'

[6]"But because I have said these things to you, sorrow has filled your hearts [and taken complete possession of them].

[7]"But I tell you the truth, it is to your advantage that I go away; for if I do not go away, the Helper (Comforter, Advocate, Intercessor—Counselor, Strengthener, Standby) will not come to you; but if I go, I will send Him (the Holy Spirit) to you [to be in close fellowship with you].

[8]"And He, when He comes, will convict the world about [the guilt of] sin [and the need for a Savior], and about righteousness, and about judgment:

[9]about sin [and the true nature of it], because they do not believe in Me [and My message];

[10]about righteousness [personal

integrity and godly character], because I am going to My Father and you will no longer see Me;

¹¹about judgment [the certainty of it], because the ruler of this world (Satan) has been judged *and* condemned.

¹²"I have many more things to say to you, but you cannot bear [to hear] them now.

¹³"But when He, the Spirit of Truth, comes, He will guide you into all the truth [full and complete truth]. For He will not speak on His own initiative, but He will speak whatever He hears [from the Father—the message regarding the Son], and He will disclose to you what is to come [in the future].

¹⁴"He will glorify *and* honor Me, because He (the Holy Spirit) will take from what is Mine and will disclose it to you.

¹⁵"All things that the Father has are Mine. Because of this I said that He [the Spirit] will take from what is Mine and will reveal it to you.

¹⁶"A little while, and you will no longer see Me; and again a little while, and you will see Me."

¹⁷Some of His disciples said to one another, "What does He mean when He

welcome the Holy Spirit's work

In John 16:7, 8, Jesus told the disciples that when the Holy Spirit came, He would have close fellowship with them and would convict them of sin.

The Holy Spirit guides believers into all the truth (see John 16:13), and He is the agent in the process of sanctification in their lives. This is partially accomplished by His convicting work. Every time we get off track or go in a wrong direction, the Holy Spirit convicts us that our behavior or decision is wrong. This is accomplished by a "knowing" in our spirit that what we are doing is not right.

When you and I feel convicted, we should repent and change our direction. No more and no less is required or acceptable. If we are willing to cooperate with the Holy Spirit, we can move on to spiritual maturity and release all the planned blessings of God in our lives. If, however, we ignore the Holy Spirit's conviction and go our own way, we will find it very difficult. Our lives will not be blessed and as a result, they won't bear fruit.

Satan does not want us to be convicted by the Holy Spirit, nor does he even want us to understand when we are under conviction. He always has a counterfeit for the good things God offers—something that appears to be similar to what God offers, but which, if received, brings destruction instead of blessing.

I believe Satan's counterfeit for true godly conviction is condemnation. Condemnation always produces feelings of guilt. It makes us feel "down" in every way. When we are condemned, we feel "under" something heavy, which is where Satan wants us.

God, on the other hand, sent Jesus to set us free and to give us righteousness, peace, and joy (see Romans 14:17). Our spirits should be light and carefree, not oppressed and heavy with burdens we are unable to bear. We cannot bear our sins; Jesus came to bear them. He alone is able and willing to do it for us.

life point

John 16:8–11 tells us that the Holy Spirit speaks to our conscience to convict us of sin and convince us of righteousness. His conviction is intended to convince us to repent, which means to turn and go in the right direction rather than the wrong one in which we are currently headed.

Learning that conviction is different from condemnation took a long time for me. Erroneously, I condemned myself each time the Holy Spirit convicted me of something that was not God's will in my life. Godly conviction is meant to lift us out of something, to help us move up higher in God's will and plan for our lives. Condemnation, on the other hand, presses us down and puts us under a burden of guilt.

It is healthy and normal to feel guilty when we are initially convicted of sin; but to keep the guilty feeling after we have repented of the sin is not healthy, nor is it God's will.

tells us, 'A little while, and you will not see Me; and again a little while, and you will see Me'; and, 'because I am going to My Father'?"

¹⁸So they were saying, "What does He mean when He says, 'A little while'? We do not know what He is talking about."

¹⁹Jesus knew that they wanted to ask Him, so He said to them, "Are you wondering among yourselves about what I meant when I said, 'A little while, and you will not see Me, and again a little while, and you will see Me'?

²⁰"I assure you *and* most solemnly say to you, that you will weep and grieve [in great mourning], but the world will rejoice. You will be sorrowful, but your sorrow will be turned into joy.

²¹"A woman, when she is in labor, has pain because her time [to give birth] has come; but when she has given birth to the child, she no longer remembers the anguish because of her joy that a child has come into the world.

²²"So for now you are in grief; but I will see you again, and [then] your hearts will rejoice, and no one will take away from you your [great] joy.

²³"In that day you will not [need to] ask Me about anything. I assure you *and* most solemnly say to you, whatever you ask the Father in My name [as My representative], He will give you.

²⁴"Until now you have not asked [the Father] for anything in My name; but

life point

Truth is one of the most powerful weapons a believer has against the kingdom of darkness. Truth is light, and the Bible says that the darkness has never overpowered the light, and it never will (see John 1:5).

Jesus said that truth will set us free (see John 8:32). Truth is revealed by the Spirit of Truth.

Jesus could have showed His disciples all the truth, but John 16:12, 13 reveals that He knew they were not ready for it. He told them they needed to wait until the Holy Spirit came down from heaven to abide with them and to dwell in them. We know that after Jesus ascended into heaven, He did indeed send the Holy Spirit (see Luke 24:49; Acts 2:1-18).

How can we have the Holy Spirit work in our lives if we do not face truth? He is called "the Spirit of Truth" (John 16:13). A major facet of His ministry to you and me is to help us face truth—to bring us to a place of truth, because only the truth will set us free.

now ask *and* keep on asking and you will receive, so that your joy may be full *and* complete.

²⁵"I have told you these things in figurative language (veiled language, proverbs); the hour is now coming when I will no longer speak to you in figures of speech, but I will tell you plainly about the Father.

²⁶"In that day you will ask in My name, and I am not saying to you that I will ask the Father on your behalf [because it will be unnecessary];

²⁷for the Father Himself [tenderly] loves you, because you have loved Me and have believed that I came from the Father.

²⁸"I came from the Father and have come into the world; again, I am leaving the world and going to the Father."

²⁹His disciples said, "Ah, now You are speaking plainly to us and not in figures of speech!

³⁰"Now we know that You know all things, and have no need for anyone to question You; because of this we believe [without any doubt] that you came from God."

³¹Jesus answered them, "Do you now [at last] believe?

³²"Take careful notice: an hour is coming, and has arrived, when you will all be scattered, each to his own *home,* leaving Me alone; and yet I am not alone, because the Father is with Me.

the Spirit of Truth

In John 16:12, 13, Jesus told His disciples He had many things to say to them that they were unable to bear. But He promised that the Holy Spirit would come and lead them into all truth and continue to teach them (see also John 14:26).

When Jesus spoke these words, He was talking to men with whom He had spent the previous three years. They were with Him day and night, yet He indicated that He had more to teach them. We might think that if Jesus were with us personally for three years, day and night, we would have learned all there is to know. I think that if I had one uninterrupted month with people, I could tell them everything I know. But Jesus said to expect more because He will always have things to teach us and something to say to us about new situations we are facing.

Jesus always knew the right thing to do because He only did what He saw His Father do. As our Lord, we can trust Him to personally lead us on the right path every day. Jesus said, "It is written in the prophets, 'And they will all be taught of God.' Everyone who has listened to and learned from the Father, comes to Me" (John 6:45).

God knew we needed help understanding His plan for us, so He sent the Holy Spirit to dwell inside every Christian. He is our Guide, our Teacher of truth, our Counselor, and our Helper. He is also our Comforter.

Jesus said it was good for us that He went away, because if He did not go, the Holy Spirit would not come to us (see John 16:7). Jesus was confined to a body just as we are and could be only at one place at a time. But the Holy Spirit can be in each of us everywhere we go, all the time, individually leading and guiding us. If we learn to *listen* to the Holy Spirit and follow His lead, we can live the abundant life God wants us to live.

33"I have told you these things, so that in Me you may have [perfect] peace. In the world you have tribulation *and* distress *and* suffering, but be courageous [be confident, be undaunted, be filled with joy]; I have overcome the world." [My conquest is accomplished, My victory abiding.]

17 WHEN JESUS had spoken these things, He raised His eyes to heaven [in prayer] and said, "Father, the hour has come. Glorify Your Son, so that Your Son may glorify You.

2"Just as You have given Him power *and* authority over all mankind, [now glorify Him] so that He may give eternal life to all whom You have given Him [to be His—permanently and forever].

3"Now this is eternal life: that they may know You, the only true [supreme and sovereign] God, and [in the same manner know] Jesus [as the] Christ whom You have sent.

4"I have glorified You [down here] on the earth by completing the work that You gave Me to do.

5"Now, Father, glorify Me together with Yourself, with the glory *and* majesty that I had with You before the world existed.

6"I have manifested Your name [and revealed Your very self, Your real self] to the people whom You have given Me out of the world; they were Yours and You gave them to Me, and they have kept *and* obeyed Your word.

7"Now [at last] they know [with confident assurance] that all You have given Me is from You [it is really and truly Yours].

8"For the words which You gave Me I have given them; and they received *and* accepted them and truly understood [with confident assurance] that I came from You [from Your presence], and they believed [without any doubt] that You sent Me.

9"I pray for them; I do not pray for the world, but for those You have given Me, because they belong to You;

10and all things that are Mine are Yours, and [all things that are] Yours are Mine; and I am glorified in them.

11"I am no longer in the world; yet they are still in the world, and I am coming to You. Holy Father, keep them in Your name, *the name* which You have given Me, so that they may be one just as We are.

12"While I was with them, I was keeping them in Your name which You have given Me; and I guarded them *and* protected them, and not one of them was lost except the son of destruction, so that the Scripture would be fulfilled. [Ps 41:9; John 6:70]

13"But now I am coming to You; and I say these things [while I am still] in the world so that they may experience My joy made full *and* complete *and* perfect within them [filling their hearts with My delight].

14"I have given to them Your word [the message You gave Me]; and the world has hated them because they are not of the world *and* do not belong to the world, just as I am not of the world *and* do not belong to it.

15"I do not ask You to take them out of the world, but that You keep them *and* protect them from the evil one.

16"They are not of the world, just as I am not of the world.

17"Sanctify them in the truth [set them apart for Your purposes, make them holy]; Your word is truth.

speak the Word

Sanctify me, Lord. Set me apart for Your purposes and make me holy in the truth. Your Word is truth.
—ADAPTED FROM JOHN 17:17

¹⁸"Just as You commissioned *and* sent Me into the world, I also have commissioned *and* sent them (believers) into the world.

¹⁹"For their sake I sanctify Myself [to do Your will], so that they also may be sanctified [set apart, dedicated, made holy] in [Your] truth.

²⁰"I do not pray for these alone [it is not for their sake only that I make this request], but also for [all] those who [will ever] believe *and* trust in Me through their message,

²¹that they all may be one; just as You, Father, are in Me and I in You, that they also may be one in Us, so that the world may believe [without any doubt] that You sent Me.

²²"I have given to them the glory *and* honor which You have given Me, that they may be one, just as We are one;

²³I in them and You in Me, that they may be perfected *and* completed into one, so that the world may know [without any doubt] that You sent Me, and [that You] have loved them, just as You have loved Me.

²⁴"Father, I desire that they also, whom You have given to Me [as Your gift to Me], may be with Me where I am, so that they may see My glory which You have given Me, because You loved Me before the foundation of the world.

²⁵"O just *and* righteous Father, although the world has not known You *and* has never acknowledged You [and the revelation of Your mercy], yet I have *always* known You; and these [believers] know [without any doubt] that You sent Me;

²⁶and I have made Your name known to them, and will *continue to* make it known, so that the love with which You have loved Me may be in them [overwhelming their heart], and I [may be] in them."

18 HAVING SAID these things, Jesus left with His disciples and went across the ravine of the Kidron. There was a garden there, which He and His disciples entered.

²Now Judas, who was betraying Him, knew the place, because Jesus had often met there with His disciples.

³So Judas, having obtained the *Roman* cohort and some officers from the high priests and the Pharisees, came there with lanterns and torches and weapons. [Matt 26:47–56; Mark 14:43–50; Luke 22:47–53]

⁴Then Jesus, knowing all that was about to happen to Him, went to them and asked, "Whom do you want?"

⁵They answered Him, "Jesus the Nazarene." Jesus said, "I am *He*." And Judas, who was betraying Him, was also standing with them.

⁶When Jesus said, "I am *He*," they drew back and fell to the ground.

⁷Again He asked them, "Whom do you want?" And they said, "Jesus the Nazarene."

⁸Jesus answered, "I told you that I am *He*; so if you want Me, let these men go on their way."

⁹*This was* to fulfill *and* verify the words He had spoken, "Of those whom You have given Me, I have not lost even one." [John 6:39; 17:12]

putting the Word to work

Is your church affiliated with any particular denomination? While denominations can provide helpful structure and teaching and tools for ministry, there is not one "right" denomination that renders all the others "wrong." Throughout Scripture, followers of God are called to unity. Be committed to the unity of the Church; pray for other churches in your neighborhood and for Christians of every denomination to be blessed and effective in ministry.

[10]Then Simon Peter, who had a sword, drew it and struck the high priest's servant, cutting off his right ear. The servant's name was Malchus. [11]So Jesus said to Peter, "Put the sword [back] in its sheath! Shall I not drink the cup which My Father has given Me?" [12]So the cohort and their commander and the officers of the Jews arrested Jesus and bound Him, [13]and led Him to Annas first; for he was the father-in-law of Caiaphas, who was high priest that year. [14]It was Caiaphas who had advised the Jews that it was expedient for one man to die on behalf of the people. [John 11:49, 50] [15]Simon Peter and another disciple were following Jesus. Now that disciple was known to the high priest, so he went with Jesus into the courtyard of the [residence of the] high priest; [16]but Peter was standing outside at the door. So the other disciple (John), who was known to the high priest, went out and spoke to the doorkeeper, and brought Peter inside. [Matt 26:69–75; Mark 14:66–72; Luke 22:55–62] [17]Then the servant girl who kept the door said to Peter, 'You are not one of this Man's disciples, are you?" He said, "I am not." [18]Now the servants and the officers had made a fire of coals, because it was cold, and they were standing and warming themselves. And Peter was with them, standing and warming himself. [19]Then the high priest questioned Jesus about His disciples and about His teaching. [Matt 26:59–68; Mark 14:55–65; Luke 22:63–71] [20]Jesus answered him, "I have spoken openly to the world. I always taught in a synagogue and in the temple [area], where all the Jews *habitually* congregate; and I said nothing in secret. [21]"Why question Me? Question those who have heard what I said to them. They know what I said." [22]But when He said this, one of the officers who was standing nearby struck Jesus [in the face], saying, "Is that how You answer the high priest?" [23]Jesus replied, "If I have said *anything* wrong, make a formal statement about the wrong; but if [I spoke] properly, why did you strike Me?" [24]So Annas sent Him bound to Caiaphas the high priest. [25]Now Simon Peter was [still] standing and warming himself. So they said to him, "You are not one of His disciples, are you?" He denied it and said, "I am not." [Matt 26:71–75; Mark 14:69–72; Luke 22:58–62] [26]One of the high priest's servants, a relative of the one whose ear Peter cut off, said, "Did I not see you with Him in the garden?" [27]So Peter denied it again, and immediately a rooster crowed. [28]Then the Jews led Jesus from Caiaphas to the Praetorium (governor's palace). Now it was early and the Jews did not enter the Praetorium so that they would not be [ceremonially] unclean, but might [be able to] eat [and participate in the Feast of Unleavened Bread which began after] the Passover [supper]. [29]So Pilate came out to them and asked, "What accusation do you bring against this Man?" [Matt 27:11–14; Mark 15:2–5; Luke 23:2, 3] [30]They answered, "If He were not a criminal, we would not have handed Him over to you [for judgment]." [31]Then Pilate said to them, "Take Him yourselves and judge Him according to your own law." The Jews said, "We are not permitted to put anyone to death." [32]*This was* to fulfill the word which Jesus had spoken to indicate by what manner of death He was going to die. [John 12:32–34]

³³So Pilate went into the Praetorium again, and called Jesus and asked Him, "Are You the King of the Jews?"

³⁴Jesus replied, "Are you saying this on your own initiative, or did others tell you about Me?"

³⁵Pilate answered, "I am not a Jew, am I? Your own people and their chief priests have handed You over to me. What have You done [that is worthy of death]?"

³⁶Jesus replied, "My kingdom is not of this world [nor does it have its origin in this world]. If My kingdom were of this world, My servants would be fighting [hard] to keep Me from being handed over to the Jews; but as it is, My kingdom is not of this world."

³⁷So Pilate said to Him, "Then You are a King?" Jesus answered, "You say [correctly] that I am a King. This is why I was born, and for this I have come into the world, to testify to the truth. Everyone who is of the truth [who is a friend of the truth and belongs to the truth] hears *and* listens carefully to My voice." [Dan 7:13, 14; Luke 1:32, 33]

³⁸Pilate said to Him [scornfully], "What is truth?"

And when he had said this, he went out to the Jews again and told them, "I find no guilt in Him [no crime, no cause for an accusation].

³⁹"But you have a custom that I release someone for you at the Passover. So shall I release for you the King of the Jews?" [Matt 27:15–26; Mark 15:6–15; Luke 23:18–25]

⁴⁰Then they all shouted back again, "Not this Man, but Barabbas!" Now Barabbas was a robber.

19

SO THEN Pilate took Jesus and had Him scourged (flogged, whipped). ²And the soldiers twisted together a crown of thorns and put it on His head, and put a purple robe around Him; [Matt 27:27–30; Mark 15:16–19]

³and they kept coming up to Him, saying [mockingly], "Hail, King of the Jews [Good health! Peace! Long life to you, King of the Jews]!" And they slapped Him *in the face.* [Is 53:3, 5, 7]

⁴Then Pilate came out again and said to them, "Look, I am bringing Him out to you so that you may know that I find no guilt in Him [no crime, no cause for an accusation]."

⁵So Jesus came out, wearing the crown of thorns and the purple robe, and *Pilate* said to them, "Look! The Man!"

⁶When the chief priests and officers saw Him, they shouted, "Crucify [Him]! Crucify [Him]!" Pilate said to them, "Take Him yourselves and crucify Him, for I find no guilt in Him [no crime, no cause for an accusation]." [Luke 23:4, 14, 22; John 18:38; 19:4]

⁷The Jews answered him, "We have a law [regarding blasphemy], and according to that law He should die, because He made Himself out to be the Son of God." [Lev 24:16]

⁸So when Pilate heard this said, he was [even] more alarmed *and* afraid.

⁹He went into the Praetorium again and said to Jesus, "Where are You from?" But Jesus did not answer him. [Is 53:7]

¹⁰So Pilate said to Him, "You do not speak to me? Do You not know that I have authority to release You, and I have authority to crucify You?"

¹¹Jesus answered, "You would have no authority over Me at all if it had not been given to you from above. For this reason the sin *and* guilt of the one who handed Me over to you is greater [than your own]."

¹²As a result of this, Pilate kept making efforts to release Him, but the Jews kept screaming, "If you release this Man, you are no friend of Caesar! Anyone who makes himself out [to be] a king opposes Caesar [and rebels against the emperor]!"

¹³When Pilate heard this, he brought Jesus out, and sat down on the judgment seat at a place called The Pavement, but in Hebrew, Gabbatha.

¹⁴Now it was the day of Preparation for the Passover [week], and it was about the sixth hour. He said to the Jews, "Look, your King!"

¹⁵But they shouted, "Away with *Him,* away with *Him,* crucify Him!" Pilate said to them, "Shall I crucify your King?" The chief priests answered, "We have no king but Caesar!"

¹⁶Then he handed Him over to them to be crucified.

¹⁷So they took Jesus, and He went out, bearing His own cross, to the place called the Place of the Skull, which is called in Hebrew, Golgotha. [Matt 27:33–44; Mark 15:22–32; Luke 23:33–43]

¹⁸There they crucified Him, and with Him two others, one on either side, and Jesus between them. [Is 53:12]

¹⁹Pilate also wrote an inscription [on a placard] and put it on the cross. And it was written: "JESUS THE NAZARENE, THE KING OF THE JEWS." [Matt 27:33–44; Mark 15:22–32; Luke 23:33–43]

²⁰And many of the Jews read this inscription, for the place where Jesus was crucified was near the city; and it was written in Hebrew, in Latin, and in Greek.

²¹Then the chief priests of the Jews said to Pilate, "Do not write, 'The King of the Jews'; but, 'He said, "I am King of the Jews."'"

²²Pilate replied, "What I have written I have written [and it remains written]."

²³Then the soldiers, when they had crucified Jesus, took His outer clothes and made four parts, a part for each soldier, and also the tunic. But the tunic was seamless, woven [in one piece] from the top throughout. [Matt 27:35; Mark 15:24; Luke 23:34]

²⁴So they said to one another, "Let us not tear it, but cast lots for it, *to decide* whose it will be." *This was* to fulfill the Scripture, "THEY DIVIDED MY OUTER CLOTHING AMONG THEM, AND FOR MY CLOTHING THEY CAST LOTS." [Ps 22:18]

²⁵So the soldiers did these things.

But standing by the cross of Jesus were His mother, His mother's sister [Salome], Mary the *wife* of Clopas, and Mary Magdalene. [Mark 15:40]

²⁶So Jesus, seeing His mother, and the disciple whom He loved (esteemed) standing near, said to His mother, "[Dear] woman, look, [here is] your son!"

²⁷Then He said to the disciple (John), "Look! [here is] your mother [protect and provide for her]!" From that hour the disciple took her into his own *home.*

²⁸After this, Jesus, knowing that all was now finished, said in fulfillment of the Scripture, "I am thirsty." [Ps 69:21]

²⁹A jar full of sour wine was placed there; so they put a sponge soaked in the sour wine on [a branch of] hyssop and held it to His mouth. [Matt 27:48, 50; Mark 15:36f; Luke 23:36]

³⁰When Jesus had received the sour wine, He said, "It is finished!" And He bowed His head and [voluntarily] gave up His spirit.

³¹Since it was the day of Preparation [for the Sabbath], in order to prevent the bodies from hanging on the cross on the Sabbath (for that Sabbath was a high holy day) the Jews asked Pilate to have their legs broken [to hasten death] and the bodies taken away.

³²So the soldiers came and broke the legs of the first man, and of the other who had been crucified with Him.

³³But when they came to Jesus and saw that He was already dead, they did not break His legs.

³⁴But one of the soldiers pierced His side with a spear, and immediately blood and water came [flowing] out.

³⁵And he (John, the eyewitness) who

has seen it has testified, and his testimony is true; and he knows that he is telling the truth, so that you also [who read this] may believe.

³⁶For these things took place to fulfill the Scripture, "NOT A BONE OF HIS SHALL BE BROKEN." [Ex 12:46; Num 9:12; Ps 34:20]

³⁷And again another Scripture says, "THEY SHALL LOOK AT HIM WHOM THEY HAVE PIERCED." [Zech 12:10]

³⁸And after this, Joseph of Arimathea—a disciple of Jesus, but secretly for fear of the Jews—asked Pilate to let him take away the body of Jesus; and Pilate gave him permission. So he came and took away His body. [Matt 27:57–61; Mark 15:42–47; Luke 23:50–56]

³⁹Nicodemus, who had first come to Him at night, also came bringing a mixture of myrrh and aloes, [weighing] about a hundred [Roman] pounds.

⁴⁰So they took Jesus' body and bound it in linen wrappings with the fragrant spices, as is the burial custom of the Jews.

⁴¹Now there was a garden at the place where He was crucified, and in the garden a new tomb [cut out of solid rock] in which no one had yet been laid.

⁴²Therefore, because of the Jewish day of Preparation, and since the tomb was nearby, they laid Jesus there.

20 NOW ON the first day of the week Mary Magdalene came to the tomb early, while it was still dark, and saw the stone [already] removed from the [groove across the entrance of the] tomb. [Matt 28:1–8; Mark 16:1–8; Luke 24:1–10]

²So she ran and went to Simon Peter and to the other disciple (John), whom Jesus loved (esteemed), and said to them, "They have taken away the Lord out of the tomb, and we do not know where they have laid Him!"

³So Peter and the other disciple left, and they were going to the tomb. [Luke 24:12]

⁴And the two were running together, but the other disciple outran Peter and arrived at the tomb first.

⁵Stooping down and looking in, he saw the linen wrappings [neatly] lying *there;* but he did not go in.

⁶Then Simon Peter came up, following him, and went into the tomb and saw the linen wrappings [neatly] lying *there;*

⁷and the [burial] face-cloth which had been on Jesus' head, not lying with the [other] linen wrappings, but rolled up in a place by itself.

⁸So the other disciple, who had reached the tomb first, went in too; and he saw [the wrappings and the face-cloth] and believed [without any doubt that Jesus had risen from the dead].

⁹For as yet they did not understand the Scripture, that He must rise from the dead. [Ps 16:10]

¹⁰Then the disciples went back again to their own homes.

¹¹But Mary [who had returned] was standing outside the tomb sobbing; and so, as she wept, she stooped down and looked into the tomb;

¹²and she saw two angels in white sitting *there,* one at the head and one at the feet, where the body of Jesus had lain.

¹³And they said to her, "Woman, why are you crying?" She told them, "Because they have taken away my Lord, and I do not know where they have laid Him."

¹⁴After saying this, she turned around and saw Jesus standing *there,* but she did not know that it was Jesus.

¹⁵Jesus said to her, "Woman, why are you crying? For whom are you looking?" Supposing that He was the gardener, she replied, "Sir, if you are the one who has carried Him away *from here,* tell me where you have put Him, and I will take Him away."

¹⁶Jesus said to her, "Mary!" She turned and said to Him in Hebrew, "Rabboni!" (which means, Teacher).

¹⁷Jesus said to her, "Do not hold Me, for I have not yet ascended to the Father; but go to My brothers and tell them, 'I am ascending to My Father and your Father, and to My God and your God.'"

¹⁸Mary Magdalene came, reporting to the disciples that she had seen the Lord and that He had said these things to her.

¹⁹So when it was evening on that *same* day, the first day of the week, though the disciples were [meeting] behind barred doors for fear of the Jews, Jesus came and stood among them, and said, "Peace to you."

²⁰After He said this, He showed them His hands and His side. When the disciples saw the Lord, they were filled with great joy.

²¹Then Jesus said to them again, "Peace to you; as the Father has sent Me, I also send you [as My representatives]."

²²And when He said this, He breathed on them and said to them, "Receive the Holy Spirit. [Acts 1:8; 2:1–3]

putting the Word to work

You have probably heard the saying, "It's not what you know, but who you know that is important." As a Christian, you are most likely learning that this is true. Are you searching for something more in your life? Jesus did not ask Mary "what" she was looking for, He asked her "whom" she was looking for, and that made all the difference. Knowing about Jesus is important, but it is the act of knowing Jesus, the Risen Savior, that is most valuable and important in our lives. Ask Him to help you know Him more fully.

putting the Word to work

As a Christian, you have been sent into the world to do the work that Jesus began. Do you ever get tired or discouraged as you do so? Ask God on a regular basis for a fresh filling of the Holy Spirit so you will be empowered to do all He has called you to do.

²³"If you forgive the sins of anyone they are forgiven [because of their faith]; if you retain *the sins* of anyone, they are retained [and remain unforgiven because of their unbelief]."

²⁴But Thomas, one of the twelve [disciples], who was called Didymus (the twin), was not with them when Jesus came.

²⁵So the other disciples kept telling him, "We have seen the Lord!" But he said to them, "Unless I see in His hands the marks of the nails, and put my finger into the nail prints, and put my hand into His side, I will never believe."

²⁶Eight days later His disciples were again inside *the house*, and Thomas was with them. Jesus came, though the doors had been barred, and stood among them and said, "Peace to you."

²⁷Then He said to Thomas, "Reach here with your finger, and see My hands; and put out your hand and place it in My side. Do not be unbelieving, but [stop doubting and] believe." [Luke 24:39]

²⁸Thomas answered Him, "My Lord and my God!"

²⁹Jesus said to him, "Because you have seen Me, do you now believe? Blessed [happy, spiritually secure, and favored by God] are they who did not see [Me] and yet believed [in Me]."

³⁰There are also many other signs (attesting miracles) that Jesus performed in the presence of the disciples, which are not written in this book;

³¹but these have been written so that you may believe [with a deep,

abiding trust] that Jesus is the Christ (the Messiah, the Anointed), the Son of God; and that by believing [and trusting in and relying on Him] you may have life in His name. [Ps 2:7, 12]

21 AFTER THIS Jesus revealed Himself again to the disciples at the Sea of Tiberias (Galilee). And He did it in this way:

²Simon Peter, and Thomas who is called Didymus (the twin), and Nathanael from Cana of Galilee, as well as [John and James] the sons of Zebedee, and two others of His disciples were together.

³Simon Peter said to them, "I am going fishing." They said, "And we are

putting the Word to work

Have you ever doubted God? If you are like most Christians, you probably have, and you may have even felt guilty about doubting Him. Jesus welcomes you to bring your doubts to Him.

Like Thomas, be honest with Jesus about your doubts. He will meet you where you are. Ask Him to show you that He is who He says He is and to help you believe He can do what He says He can do. He will be faithful to do so, and like Thomas, your faith will increase.

forgiveness and the Holy Spirit

I believe the number one rule in forgiving sins is to do as Jesus commanded in John 20:22 and receive the Holy Spirit, Who provides the strength and ability to forgive. None of us can do that on our own.

I believe that when Jesus breathed on the disciples and they received the Holy Spirit, they were born again, at that very moment. The next thing He said to them was whatever sins they forgave were forgiven and whatever sins they retained were retained (see John 20:23).

The forgiving of sins seems to be the first power conferred upon people when they are born again. If that is so, then the forgiving of sins is our first duty as believers. But although we have the power to forgive sins, it is not always easy to do it.

Whenever someone does something to me and I need to forgive that person for it, I pray, "Holy Spirit, breathe on me and give me the strength to forgive this person." I do that because my emotions are screaming inside of me, "You have hurt me—and that is not fair!"

At that point I have to remember to let go and allow the God of justice to work out everything. I have to remind myself that my job is to pray; His job is to be my Vindicator. When we trust God He always makes wrong things right at the appropriate time.

When someone does something hurtful to you, go to the Lord and receive from Him the strength to place your will on the altar and say, "Lord, I forgive this person. I loose him; I let him go." Once you have done that, let it drop. Don't think or talk about it anymore.

coming with you." So they went out and got into the boat; and that night they caught nothing.

⁴As morning was breaking, Jesus [came and] stood on the beach; however, the disciples did not know that it was Jesus.

⁵So Jesus said to them, "Children, do you have any fish [to eat along with your bread]?" They answered, "No."

⁶And He said to them, "Cast the net on the right-hand side of the boat (starboard) and you will find some." So they cast [the net], and then they were not able to haul it in because of the great catch of fish.

⁷Then that disciple (John) whom Jesus loved (esteemed) said to Peter, "It is the Lord!" So when Simon Peter heard that it was the Lord, he put on his outer tunic (for he was stripped *for work*) and threw himself into the sea [and swam ashore].

⁸But the other disciples came in the small boat, for they were not far from shore, only about a hundred yards away, dragging the net full of fish.

⁹So when they got out on the beach, they saw a charcoal fire set up and fish on it *cooking,* and bread.

¹⁰Jesus said to them, "Bring some of the fish which you have just caught."

¹¹So Simon Peter went aboard and hauled the net to land, full of large fish, a hundred and fifty-three [of them]; and although there were so many, the net was not torn.

¹²Jesus said to them, "Come *and* have breakfast." None of the disciples dared to ask Him, "Who are You?" They knew [without any doubt] that it was the Lord.

¹³Jesus came and took the bread and gave it to them, and likewise the fish.

¹⁴This was now the third time that Jesus appeared to the disciples, after He had risen from the dead.

¹⁵So when they had finished breakfast, Jesus said to Simon Peter, "Simon, *son* of John, do you love Me more than

these [others do—with total commitment and devotion]?" He said to Him, "Yes, Lord; You know that I love You [with a deep, personal affection, as for a close friend]." Jesus said to him, "Feed My lambs."

¹⁶Again He said to him a second time, "Simon, *son* of John, do you love Me [with total commitment and devotion]?" He said to Him, "Yes, Lord; You know that I love You [with a deep, personal affection, as for a close friend]." Jesus said to him, "Shepherd My sheep."

¹⁷He said to him the third time, "Simon, *son* of John, do you love Me [with a deep, personal affection for Me, as for a close friend]?" Peter was grieved that He asked him the third time, "Do you [really] love Me [with a deep, personal affection, as for a close friend]?" And he said to Him, "Lord, You know everything; You know that I love You [with a deep, personal affection, as for a close friend]." Jesus said to him, "Feed My sheep.

¹⁸"I assure you *and* most solemnly say to you, when you were younger you dressed yourself and walked wherever you wished; but when you grow old, you will stretch out your hands *and* arms, and someone else will dress you, and carry you where you do not wish to go."

¹⁹Now He said this to indicate the kind of death by which Peter would glorify God. And after saying this, He said to him, "Follow Me [walk the same path of life that I have walked]!"

²⁰Peter turned and saw the disciple whom Jesus loved following them; the one who also had leaned back on His chest at the supper and had said, "Lord, who is it that is going to betray You?"

²¹So when Peter saw him, he asked Jesus, "Lord, and what about this man [what is in his future]?"

²²Jesus said to him, "If I want him to stay alive until I come [again], what *is that* to you? You follow Me!"

life point

In John 21:18, Jesus told Peter about the hardships he would endure in order to serve and glorify Him. As soon as Jesus said these things to him, Peter turned, saw John, and immediately asked Jesus what His will was for that disciple. Peter wanted to make sure that if he was going to have rough times ahead, so would John.

In response, Jesus politely told Peter to mind his own business. When you are tempted to compare yourself with others or to be jealous, remember this advice!

²³So this word went out among the brothers that this disciple (John) was not going to die; yet Jesus did not say to him that he was not going to die, but *only,* "If I want him to stay alive until I come [again], what *is that* to you?"

²⁴This is the *same* disciple who is testifying to these things and has recorded them; and we know [without any doubt] that his testimony is true.

²⁵And there are also many other things which Jesus did, which if they were recorded one by one, I suppose that even the world itself could not contain the books that would be written.

Acts

Author:
Attributed to Luke.

Date:
About AD 62.

Everyday Life Principles:
We desperately need the power of the Holy Spirit in our lives today, and thank God, it is readily available to us!

Christianity is not a religious activity; it is a way of life.

The Holy Spirit wants to be involved in every area of your life, every day.

The book of Acts basically picks up where the Gospels end. Before His death and resurrection, Jesus told His disciples that it was to their advantage for Him to go away, because if He did not, the Holy Spirit would not come to them (see John 16:7). In Acts, we see that the Holy Spirit did come and we learn that He is still on earth today teaching, guiding, helping, and empowering us to do the things God calls us to do.

Acts gives us a clear and vivid picture of how the church should operate. It shows us that we need unity and the power of the Holy Spirit and reveals the importance of constantly reaching out to others and helping people. In this book, we see that when the Holy Spirit is given free rein in our lives and in the church, tremendous growth in the kingdom of God and in our lives as individuals takes place.

As you read Acts, I pray you will see that Christianity is so much more than going to church, but also allowing the Holy Spirit to guide us in all the affairs of our lives. He came to help and empower us in *every* area of our lives, not just the parts we call "spiritual." We are not to divide our lives into secular and sacred; everything about us belongs to God, and He wants to be involved in all of it.

1 THE FIRST account I made, Theophilus, was [a continuous report] about all the things that Jesus began to do and to teach [Luke 1:1–4]

²until the day when He ascended *to heaven,* after He had by the Holy Spirit given instruction to the apostles (special messengers) whom He had chosen.

³To these [men] He also showed Himself alive after His suffering [in Gethsemane and on the cross], by [a series of] many infallible proofs *and* unquestionable demonstrations, appearing to them over *a period of* forty days and talking to them about the things concerning the kingdom of God.

⁴While being together *and* eating with them, He commanded them not to leave Jerusalem, but to wait for what the Father had promised, "Of which," *He said,* "you have heard Me speak. [John 14:16, 26; 15:26]

⁵"For John baptized with water, but

life point

Jesus told His disciples in Acts 1:4 to wait for what the Father promised them. He was referring to the power they would receive "when the Holy Spirit comes upon you" (Acts 1:8). Jesus was saying, "Do not try to do any mighty works until you have received that power from on high." The disciples knew that if they did not wait, they would not have any power. They did as He instructed and waited for the coming of the Holy Spirit.

Jesus' instruction to wait was not only for His disciples centuries ago. It is a truth that applies to us today. I encourage you to actively wait for God's promises by listening for what He is telling you to do instead of running ahead of Him and doing something in the flesh. Wait for the Word of God and for His promises.

you will be baptized *and* empowered *and* united with the Holy Spirit, not long from now."

⁶So when they had come together, they asked Him *repeatedly,* "Lord, are You at this time reestablishing the kingdom *and* restoring it to Israel?"

⁷He said to them, "It is not for you to know the times or epochs which the Father has fixed by His own authority.

⁸"But you will receive power *and* ability when the Holy Spirit comes upon you; and you will be My witnesses [to tell people about Me] both in Jerusalem and in all Judea, and Samaria, and even to the ends of the earth."

⁹And after He said these things, He was caught up as they looked on, and a cloud took Him up out of their sight.

¹⁰While they were looking intently into the sky as He was going, two men in white clothing suddenly stood beside them,

¹¹who said, "Men of Galilee, why do you stand looking into the sky? This [same] Jesus, who has been taken up from you into heaven, will return in just the same way as you have watched Him go into heaven."

¹²Then the disciples returned to Jerusalem from the mount called Olivet (Olive Grove), which is near Jerusalem, [only] a Sabbath day's journey (less than one mile) away.

¹³When they had entered *the city,* they went upstairs to the upper room where they were staying [indefinitely]; that is, Peter, and John and [his brother] James, and Andrew, Philip and Thomas, Bartholomew (Nathanael) and Matthew, James *the son of* Alphaeus, and Simon the Zealot, and Judas (Thaddaeus) the son of James.

¹⁴All these with one mind *and* one purpose were continually devoting themselves to prayer, [waiting together] along with the women, and Mary the mother of Jesus, and with His brothers.

¹⁵Now on one of these days Peter stood up among the brothers and sisters (a gathering of about a hundred and twenty believers was there) and he said,

¹⁶"Brothers and sisters, it was necessary that the Scripture be fulfilled, which the Holy Spirit foretold by the lips of David [king of Israel] about Judas [Iscariot], who acted as guide to those who arrested Jesus.

¹⁷"For he (Judas) was counted among us and received his share [by divine allotment] in this ministry."

¹⁸(Now Judas Iscariot acquired a piece of land [indirectly] with the [money paid him as a] reward for his treachery, and falling headlong, his body burst open in the middle and all his intestines poured out.

¹⁹All the people in Jerusalem learned about this, so in their own dialect—Aramaic—they called the piece of land Hakeldama, that is, Field of Blood.)

"you shall receive power"

We all need and want power, and Jesus promised in Acts 1:8 that "you will receive power and ability when the Holy Spirit comes upon you." I do not know of anyone who hopes and prays for weakness and inability. God desires for us to be powerful and live and enjoy power-packed lives—lives that include victory over Satan and all his wicked plots and schemes.

The Holy Spirit is the enabling power of God, and when He comes into our lives we become more powerful. We might even say that our power level is dependent on the level to which we surrender to Him. Have you surrendered every room in your heart to the Holy Spirit? Have you invited Him into every area of your life, or do you reserve certain areas for yourself—areas where you want no interference from anyone, not even God?

Spiritual maturity is a process. We release areas of our lives to the Lord little by little. The more we release to Him, the better our lives become. We often cling to the very things that make us miserable, and yet we are afraid to let go of them. Trust God and know for certain that everything He asks you to do is for your good and will make your life better.

The power of the Holy Spirit enables us to be what God wants us to be. I noticed years ago that Acts 1:8 states that the people received power to "be" witnesses, not power to "do" witnessing. God wants us to become what He has in mind for us, and then out of who we are we will begin to do what He wants us to do. "Doing" witnessing is good, but it's also important to "be" witnesses for Christ in our everyday lives. We can show up at church and do good deeds, but God's deepest desire for each of us is that we become like Christ in all of our thoughts, attitudes, words, and deeds.

We often make the mistake of being overly concerned about what is happening in our circumstances when our priority should be what is happening in our hearts. God is more interested in changing us than He is in changing our circumstances. Invite the Lord to have His way in you and your life, and you will experience an increase of the Holy Spirit's power.

²⁰"For in the book of Psalms it is written,

'LET HIS PLACE OF RESIDENCE
  BECOME DESOLATE,
AND LET THERE BE NO ONE TO LIVE
  IN IT';

and [again],

'LET ANOTHER TAKE HIS POSITION
  AS OVERSEER.' [Ps 69:25; 109:8]

²¹"So of the men who have accompanied us during all the time that the Lord Jesus spent with us,

²²beginning with the baptism by John [at the outset of Jesus' ministry]

until the day when He was taken up from us—one of these men *must* become a witness with us [to testify] of His resurrection."

²³And they put forward two men, Joseph, the one called Barsabbas (who was surnamed Justus), and Matthias.

²⁴They prayed and said, "You, Lord, who know all hearts [their thoughts, motives, desires], show us which one of these two You have chosen

²⁵to occupy this ministry and apostleship which Judas left to go to his own place [of evil]."

²⁶And they cast lots for them, and

wait for God

I believe the key word in Acts 1:13 is *indefinitely*. The disciples went into the upper room with a mindset that said, "We are not coming out of here until God shows up." They did not go in there to wait ten minutes. They did not go in there to wait two days. They did not go in there to wait three months. No, they went in there saying, "We cannot do all that God wants us to do without His full power in our lives. Like those who entered the upper room to wait for the promised outpouring of the Holy Spirit, our attitude should be, "I am waiting on You, Lord, *indefinitely until I receive power from on high*!"

Waiting for God indefinitely is hard for us to do. We have so much energy and zeal in our flesh that even if we ever get around to waiting, we pause only for short periods of time and then the energy of our flesh takes over again.

If God does not do something as quickly as we want Him to do it, then our bright ideas overtake us again, and we turn right back to our fleshly strength. We constantly cover the same ground again and again. We make some progress, and then we become impatient and lose it. We gain a little ground, and then we lose it. We have to "gain and maintain." It is important that we learn to stand firm in the liberty God has given us and not subject ourselves again to a burden of bondage once we have broken free from it (see Galatians 5:1). Even when we do not see something or feel that God is working, He is moving mightily on our behalf. We inherit the promises of God through patient endurance (see Hebrews 10:36).

The mindset we need to have is this: "God, I have come to the end of myself. I have tried this, and I have tried that. I have tried everything I can possibly think of for all these years. Now it is obvious that I cannot do what needs to be done by myself. God, I need You. Only You can do it. So I am waiting on You."

Be willing to wait indefinitely for God—as long as it takes.

the lot fell to Matthias; and he was added to the eleven apostles.

2 WHEN THE day of Pentecost had come, they were all together in one place, [2]and suddenly a sound came from heaven like a rushing violent wind, and it filled the whole house where they were sitting. [3]There appeared to them tongues resembling fire, which were being distributed [among them], and they rested on each one of them [as each person received the Holy Spirit]. [4]And they were all filled [that is, diffused throughout their being] with the Holy Spirit and began to speak in other *tongues (different languages), as the Spirit was giving them the ability to speak out [clearly and appropriately]. [5]Now there were Jews living in Jerusalem, devout and God-fearing men from every nation under heaven. [6]And when this sound was heard, a crowd gathered, and they were bewildered because each one was hearing those in the upper room speaking in his own language or dialect. [7]They were completely astonished, saying, "Look! Are not all of these who are speaking Galileans? [8]"Then how is it that each of us hears in our own language or native dialect? [9]"[Among us there are] Parthians, Medes and Elamites, and people of Mesopotamia, Judea and Cappadocia, Pontus and Asia [Minor], [10]Phrygia and Pamphylia, Egypt and the districts of Libya around Cyrene, and the visitors from Rome, both Jews and proselytes (Gentile converts to Judaism), [11]Cretans and Arabs—we all hear them speaking in our [native] tongues about the mighty works of God!" [12]And they were beside themselves with amazement and were greatly perplexed, saying one to another, "What could this mean?"

[13]But others were laughing and joking and ridiculing them, saying, "They are full of sweet wine and are drunk!"

[14]But Peter, standing with the eleven, raised his voice and addressed them: "Men of Judea and all you who live in Jerusalem, let this be explained to you; listen closely and pay attention to what I have to say.

[15]"These people are not drunk, as you assume, since it is [only] the third hour of the day (9:00 a.m.);

[16]but this is [the beginning of] what was spoken of through the prophet Joel:

[17]'AND IT SHALL BE IN THE LAST DAYS,'
   says God,
'THAT I WILL POUR OUT MY SPIRIT
   UPON ALL MANKIND;
AND YOUR SONS AND YOUR
   DAUGHTERS SHALL PROPHESY,
AND YOUR YOUNG MEN SHALL SEE
   [divinely prompted] VISIONS,
AND YOUR OLD MEN SHALL DREAM
   [divinely prompted] DREAMS;
[18]EVEN ON MY BOND-SERVANTS, BOTH
   MEN AND WOMEN,
I WILL IN THOSE DAYS POUR OUT MY
   SPIRIT
And they shall prophesy.
[19]'AND I WILL BRING ABOUT WONDERS
   IN THE SKY ABOVE

life point

Not only do you need God, God needs you! Do not discount yourself by thinking God could not possibly use you. Note that in Acts 2:17, 18, God speaks of pouring out His Spirit on "all mankind"—sons and daughters, men and women (emphasis mine). Joel 2:28, 29 first prophesied these words, and Peter repeats them here in Acts. This prophetic word from the Lord definitely includes you and me!

2:4 Or languages, the Greek can have either meaning.

AND SIGNS (attesting miracles)
    ON THE EARTH BELOW,
BLOOD AND FIRE AND SMOKING
    VAPOR.
20 'THE SUN SHALL BE TURNED INTO
    DARKNESS
AND THE MOON INTO BLOOD,
BEFORE THE GREAT AND GLORIOUS
    DAY OF THE LORD COMES.
21 'AND IT SHALL BE THAT EVERYONE
    WHO CALLS UPON THE NAME OF
    THE LORD [invoking, adoring,
    and worshiping the Lord
    Jesus] SHALL BE SAVED (rescued
    spiritually).' [Joel 2:28–32]

22"Men of Israel, listen to these words: Jesus of Nazareth, a Man accredited *and* pointed out *and* attested to you by God with [the power to perform] miracles and wonders and signs which God worked through Him in your [very] midst, just as you yourselves know—

23this *Man,* when handed over [to the Roman authorities] according to the predetermined decision and foreknowledge of God, you nailed to a cross and put to death by the hands of lawless *and* godless men.

24"But God raised Him up, releasing Him *and* bringing an end to the agony of death, since it was impossible for Him to be held in death's power.

25"For David says of Him,

the power of Jesus' name

I want to share a story with you about the power of Jesus' name (see Acts 2:21). A person I know was driving through an intersection one day and his little three- or four-year-old son was in the car with him. He did not realize that the car door on the passenger side was not secured tightly, and he made a sharp turn. This happened before seat belt laws were passed, and the child was not wearing one. The car door flew open, and the little boy rolled out of the vehicle right into the middle of traffic coming from four ways! The last thing my friend saw was a set of car wheels about to roll over his son. This car was moving at a very fast rate of speed. All my friend knew to do was cry out, "JESUS!"

As soon as he could bring his car to a halt, he jumped out and ran to his son, who was perfectly all right. But the man driving the car that almost hit the child was absolutely hysterical. My friend went over to him and started trying to comfort him.

"Man, don't be upset!" he said. "My son is all right. He's okay. Don't be concerned about it. Just thank God you were able to stop!"

"You don't understand!" the man responded. "I never touched my brakes!"

This was a crisis situation. There was no time for anyone to do anything, no time to think, plan, or reason. Although there was nothing either man could do, the name of Jesus prevailed. Miracle-working power came on the scene, and the boy's life was spared.

I believe we need more confidence in the name of Jesus and less confidence in ourselves or anyone else to solve our problems.

There is power in the name of Jesus!

'I SAW THE LORD CONSTANTLY
　BEFORE ME;
FOR HE IS AT MY RIGHT HAND, SO
　THAT I WILL NOT BE SHAKEN
　[from my state of security].
26 'THEREFORE MY HEART REJOICED
　AND MY TONGUE EXULTED
　EXCEEDINGLY;
　MOREOVER MY FLESH ALSO WILL
　LIVE IN HOPE [that is, will
　encamp in anticipation of
　the resurrection];
27 'FOR YOU WILL NOT FORSAKE ME *and*
　ABANDON MY SOUL TO HADES (the
　realm of the dead),
　NOR LET YOUR HOLY ONE UNDERGO
　DECAY [after death].
28 'YOU HAVE MADE KNOWN TO ME THE
　WAYS OF LIFE;
　YOU WILL FILL ME [infusing my soul]
　WITH JOY WITH YOUR PRESENCE.'
　[Ps 16:8–11]

29 "Brothers, I may confidently *and*
freely say to you regarding the patriarch David that he both died and was
buried, and his tomb is with us to this
day.
30 "And so, being a prophet and
knowing fully that GOD HAD SWORN
TO HIM WITH AN OATH THAT HE WOULD
SEAT *one* OF HIS DESCENDANTS ON HIS
THRONE, [2 Sam 7:12–16; Ps 132:11]
31 he foresaw and spoke [propheti-
cally] of the resurrection of the Christ
(the Messiah, the Anointed), that HE
WAS NOT ABANDONED [in death] TO HA-
DES (the realm of the dead), NOR DID
His body UNDERGO DECAY. [Ps 16:10]
32 "God raised this Jesus [bodily from
the dead], and of that [fact] we are all
witnesses.
33 "Therefore having been exalted
to the right hand of God, and having
received from the Father the promise
of the Holy Spirit, He has poured out
this [blessing] which you both see and
hear.
34 "For David did not ascend into the
heavens, yet he himself says,

'THE LORD [the Father] SAID TO
　MY LORD [the Son],
"SIT AT MY RIGHT HAND,
35 UNTIL I MAKE YOUR ENEMIES A
　FOOTSTOOL FOR YOUR FEET."'
　[Ps 110:1]

36 "Therefore let all the house of Israel
recognize beyond all doubt that God
has made Him both Lord and Christ
(Messiah, Anointed)—this Jesus
whom you crucified."
37 Now when they heard this, they
were cut to the heart [with remorse
and anxiety], and they said to Peter
and the rest of the apostles, "Brothers,
what are we to do?"
38 And Peter said to them, "Repent
[change your old way of thinking,
turn from your sinful ways, accept
and follow Jesus as the Messiah] and
be baptized, each of you, in the name
of Jesus Christ because of the forgiveness of your sins; and you will receive
the gift of the Holy Spirit.
39 "For the promise [of the Holy
Spirit] is for you and your children and
for all who are far away [including the
Gentiles], as many as the Lord our God
calls to Himself." [Is 57:19; Joel 2:32]
40 And Peter solemnly testified and
continued to admonish *and* urge them
with many more words, saying, "Be
saved from this crooked *and* unjust
generation!"
41 So then, those who accepted his
message were baptized; and on that

speak the Word

*Thank You, Lord, that the promise of the Holy Spirit is for me
and for my children, and for all You call to Yourself.*
–ADAPTED FROM ACTS 2:39

day about 3,000 souls were added [to the body of believers].

⁴²They were continually *and* faithfully devoting themselves to the instruction of the apostles, and to fellowship, to eating meals together and to prayers.

⁴³A sense of awe was felt by everyone, and many wonders and signs (attesting miracles) were taking place through the apostles.

⁴⁴And all those who had believed [in Jesus as Savior] were together and had all things in common [considering their possessions to belong to the group as a whole].

⁴⁵And they *began* selling their property and possessions and were sharing the proceeds with all [the other believers], as anyone had need.

⁴⁶Day after day they met in the temple [area] continuing with one mind, and breaking bread in various private homes. They were eating their meals together with joy and generous hearts,

⁴⁷praising God *continually*, and having favor with all the people. And the Lord kept adding to their number daily those who were being saved.

3 NOW PETER and John were going up to the temple at the hour of prayer, the ninth hour (3:00 p.m.), ²and a man who had been unable to walk from birth was being carried along, whom they used to set down every day at that gate of the temple which is called Beautiful, so that he could beg alms from those entering the temple.

³So when he saw Peter and John about to go into the temple, he *began* asking [them] for coins.

putting the Word to work

Acts 2:42–47 gives us a snapshot of life for the believers in the early church. Being part of a local church is one of the great joys and responsibilities of every believer. However, it involves more than showing up on Sunday. How do you participate in the life of your church? While you experience different levels of involvement in a church during different seasons of your life, be sure to consistently avail yourself of opportunities to fellowship, worship, serve, and receive teaching of the Word.

⁴But Peter, along with John, stared at him intently and said, "Look at us!"

⁵And the man *began* to pay attention to them, eagerly expecting to receive something from them.

⁶But Peter said, "Silver and gold I do not have; but what I do have I give to you: In the name (authority, power) of Jesus Christ the Nazarene—[begin now to] walk *and* go on walking!"

⁷Then he seized the man's right hand with a firm grip and raised him up. And at once his feet and ankles became strong *and* steady,

⁸and with a leap he stood up and *began* to walk; and he went into the temple with them, walking and leaping and praising God.

⁹All the people saw him walking and praising God;

¹⁰and they recognized him as the very man who usually sat *begging* for coins at the Beautiful Gate of the temple, and they were filled with wonder

speak the Word

Father, help me be like Peter
and freely use the name of Jesus to bless those in need around me.
–ADAPTED FROM ACTS 3:6

and amazement *and* were mystified at what had happened to him.

¹¹Now while he was still holding on to Peter and John, all the people, utterly amazed, ran together *and* crowded around them at the covered porch called Solomon's portico.

¹²And Peter, seeing this, said to the people, "You men of Israel, why are you amazed at this? Why are you staring at us, as though by our own power or godliness we had made this man walk?

¹³"The God of Abraham, Isaac, and Jacob, the God of our fathers, has glorified His Servant *and* Son Jesus [doing Him this honor], *the One* whom you handed over and disowned *and* rejected before Pilate, when he had decided to release Him. [Ex 3:6; Is 52:13]

¹⁴"But you disowned *and* denied the Holy and Righteous One and asked for [the pardon of] a murderer to be granted to you.

¹⁵"But you killed the Prince (Author, Originator, Source) of life, whom God raised [bodily] from the dead. To this [fact] we are witnesses [for we have seen the risen Christ].

¹⁶"And on the basis of faith in His name, it is the name of Jesus which has strengthened this man whom you see and know; and the faith which *comes* through Him has given him this perfect health *and* complete wholeness in your presence.

¹⁷"Now, brothers, I know that you acted in ignorance [not fully aware of what you were doing], just as your rulers did also.

¹⁸"And so God has fulfilled what He foretold by the mouth of all the prophets, that His Christ (Messiah, Anointed) would suffer.

¹⁹"So repent [change your inner self—your old way of thinking, regret past sins] and return [to God—seek His purpose for your life], so that your sins may be wiped away [blotted out, completely erased], so that times of

refreshing may come from the presence of the Lord [restoring you like a cool wind on a hot day];

²⁰and that He may send [to you] Jesus, the Christ, who has been appointed for you,

²¹whom heaven must keep until the time for the [complete] restoration of all things about which God promised through the mouth of His holy prophets from ancient time.

²²"Moses said, 'THE LORD GOD WILL RAISE UP FOR YOU A PROPHET LIKE ME FROM YOUR COUNTRYMEN; YOU SHALL LISTEN TO HIM *and* OBEY everything He tells you.

²³'And it will be that every person that does not listen to *and* heed that Prophet will be utterly destroyed from among the people.' [Deut 18:15–19]

²⁴"Indeed, all the prophets who have spoken, from Samuel and those who came after him, also announced these days.

²⁵"You are the sons (descendants) of the prophets and [heirs] of the covenant which God made with your fathers, saying to Abraham, 'AND IN YOUR SEED (descendant) ALL THE FAMILIES OF THE EARTH SHALL BE BLESSED.' [Gen 22:18; Gal 3:16]

²⁶"*It was* for you first *of all that* God raised up His Servant *and* Son [Jesus], and sent Him to bless you by turning every one *of you* from your wicked ways." [Acts 2:24; 3:22]

4 AND WHILE Peter and John were talking to the people, the priests and the captain [who was in charge of the temple area and] of the temple *guard* and the Sadducees came up to them,

²being extremely disturbed *and* thoroughly annoyed because they were teaching the people and proclaiming in [the case of] Jesus the resurrection of the dead.

³So they arrested them and put them

in jail until the next day, because it was evening.

⁴But many of those who heard the message [of salvation] believed [in Jesus and accepted Him as the Christ]. And the number of the men came to be about 5,000.

⁵On the next day, their magistrates and elders and scribes (Sanhedrin, Jewish High Court) were gathered together in Jerusalem;

⁶and Annas the high priest *was there,* and Caiaphas and John and Alexander, and all others who were of high-priestly descent.

⁷When they had put the men in front of them, they repeatedly asked, "By what sort of power, or in what name [that is, by what kind of authority], did you do this [healing]?"

⁸Then Peter, filled with [the power of] the Holy Spirit, said to them, "Rulers and elders of the people [members of the Sanhedrin, the Jewish High Court],

⁹if we are being put on trial today [to interrogate us] for a good deed done to [benefit] a disabled man, as to how this man has been restored to health,

¹⁰let it be known *and* clearly understood by all of you, and by all the

His presence refreshes

Acts 3:19 teaches us that "times of refreshing" come to us when we spend time in God's presence. Until we come to the place where we want God's presence more than anything else, the devil will have an edge over us. Once we see God's truth, the devil loses his advantage, and we begin making radical progress in our relationship and fellowship with God.

Most of us will try almost everything else before we finally learn that what we need is not what God can *give* us, but God *Himself*. These times often represent years of frustration and misery, but thank God, His Holy Spirit who lives in us also teaches us, and reveals truth to us as we continue to study, read, and listen to the Word of God.

If you are diligent to seek God, you will know Him in a deeper, more intimate way; God will reveal Himself to you; He will be found by you (see Jeremiah 29:13). When God wants to manifest Himself, He will. You do not need to get frustrated trying to find God. Just learn to wait on Him and pray, "God, reveal Yourself to me. Manifest Your presence to me."

God manifests His presence in many ways. Sometimes we cannot see Him but, like the wind, we can see the work He does in us. If I am weary, tired, worn out, frustrated, or bothered about something, and I become refreshed after spending time with God, then I know that the wind of the Lord has blown upon me.

God wants to bring a refreshing into your life, like a mighty wind. Do not be poverty-stricken in your soul when the answer is so close. If you are too busy to spend time with God, then make some adjustments to your lifestyle. Do not get burned out, upset, weary, and stressed out when times of refreshing are available to you.

Learn to separate yourself from the busyness of life to spend time with God as Jesus did. I tell people, "You had better come apart and spend time with God before you fall apart." I encourage you to take those words personally and act on them.

people of Israel, that in the name of Jesus Christ the Nazarene, whom you [demanded be] crucified [by the Romans and], whom God raised from the dead—in this name [that is, by the authority and power of Jesus] this man stands here before you in good health.

11"This Jesus is the STONE WHICH WAS DESPISED *and* REJECTED by you, THE BUILDERS, *but* WHICH BECAME THE CHIEF CORNERSTONE. [Ps 118:22]

12"And there is salvation in no one else; for there is no other name under heaven that has been given among people by which we must be saved [for God has provided the world no alternative for salvation]."

13Now when the men of the Sanhedrin (Jewish High Court) saw the confidence *and* boldness of Peter and John, and grasped the fact that they were uneducated and untrained [ordinary] men, they were astounded, and *began* to recognize that they had been with Jesus.

14And seeing the man who had been healed standing *there* with them, they had nothing to say in reply.

putting the Word to work

Do you ever feel inadequate sharing about God with other people because you have not received much formal Christian education or training, like Peter and John in Acts 4:13? The best schooling is what I call "the school of the Holy Spirit." Ask Him to teach you through the Word, as you spend time in prayer and as you rely on His grace. We learn through the Word of God and our experiences in life. Experience itself is a good teacher. God's Spirit leads us through many situations and will teach us as we go through them if we are open to learning. Enroll in the "school of the Holy Spirit" and you will get an education that far exceeds anything you can learn from a traditional classroom.

life point

In the Gospels, Jesus does miracles, but in Acts, ordinary people do miracles by the power of the Holy Spirit (see Acts 4:16). Believe that God can use you in mighty ways!

15But after ordering them to step out of the Council [chamber], they *began* to confer among themselves,

16saying, "What are we to do with these men? For the fact that an extraordinary miracle has taken place through them is public knowledge *and* clearly evident to all the residents of Jerusalem, and we cannot deny it.

17"But to keep it from spreading further among the people *and* the nation, let us [sternly] warn them not to speak again to anyone in this name."

18So they sent for them, and commanded them not to speak [as His representatives] or teach at all in the name of Jesus [using Him as their authority].

19But Peter and John replied to them, "Whether it is right in the sight of God to listen to you *and* obey you rather than God, you must judge [for yourselves];

20for we, on our part, cannot stop telling [people] about what we have seen and heard."

21When the rulers and Council members had threatened them further, they let them go, finding no way to punish them because [of their fear] of the people, for they were all praising *and* glorifying *and* honoring God for what had happened;

22for the man to whom this sign (attesting miracle) of healing had happened was more than forty years old.

23After Peter and John were released, they returned to their own [people] and reported everything that the chief priests and elders had said to them.

24And when they heard it, they raised

their voices together to God and said, "O Sovereign Lord [having complete power and authority], it is You who MADE THE HEAVEN AND THE EARTH AND THE SEA, AND EVERYTHING THAT IS IN THEM, [Ex 20:11; Ps 146:6] [25]who by the Holy Spirit, *through* the mouth of our father David, Your servant, said,

'WHY DID THE NATIONS (Gentiles) BECOME ARROGANT *and* RAGE, AND THE PEOPLES DEVISE FUTILE THINGS [against the Lord]? [26]'THE KINGS OF THE EARTH TOOK THEIR STAND [to attack], AND THE RULERS WERE ASSEMBLED TOGETHER AGAINST THE LORD AND AGAINST HIS ANOINTED (the Christ, the Messiah).' [Ps 2:1, 2]

[27]"For in this city there were gathered together against Your holy Servant Jesus, whom You anointed, both Herod and Pontius Pilate, along with the Gentiles and the peoples of Israel, [28]to do whatever Your hand and Your purpose predestined [before the creation of the world] to occur [and so without knowing it, they served Your own purpose]. [29]"And now, Lord, observe their threats [take them into account] and grant that Your bond-servants may declare Your message [of salvation] with great confidence, [30]while You extend Your hand to heal, and signs and wonders (attesting miracles) take place through the name [and the authority and power] of Your holy Servant *and* Son Jesus." [31]And when they had prayed, the place where they were meeting together was shaken [a sign of God's

presence]; and they were all filled with the Holy Spirit and *began* to speak the word of God with boldness *and* courage. [32]Now the company of believers was of one heart and soul, and not one [of them] claimed that anything belonging to him was [exclusively] his own, but everything was common property *and* for the use of all. [33]And with great ability *and* power the apostles were *continuously* testifying to the resurrection of the Lord Jesus, and great grace [God's remarkable lovingkindness and favor and goodwill] rested richly upon them all. [34]There was not a needy person among them, because those who were owners of land or houses were selling them, and bringing the proceeds of the sales [35]and placing *the money* down at the apostles' feet. Then it was distributed to each as anyone had need. [36]Now Joseph, a Levite and native of Cyprus, who was surnamed Barnabas by the apostles (which translated means Son of Encouragement), [37]sold a field belonging to him and brought the money and set it at the apostles' feet.

5 NOW A man named Ananias, with his wife Sapphira, sold a piece of property, [2]and with his wife's full knowledge [and complicity] he kept back some of the proceeds, bringing only a portion of it, and set it at the apostles' feet. [3]But Peter said, "Ananias, why has Satan filled your heart to lie to the Holy Spirit and [secretly] keep back for yourself some of the proceeds [from the sale] of the land? [4]"As long as it remained [unsold], did

speak the Word

God, help me live and do business in perfect integrity, never attempting to deceive Your Holy Spirit.
–ADAPTED FROM ACTS 5:1–3

it not remain your own [to do with as you pleased]? And after it was sold, was the money not under your control? Why is it that you have conceived this act [of hypocrisy and deceit] in your heart? You have not [simply] lied to people, but to God."

⁵And hearing these words, Ananias fell down suddenly and died; and great fear *and* awe gripped those who heard of it.

⁶And the young men [in the congregation] got up and wrapped up the body, and carried it out and buried it.

⁷Now after an interval of about three hours his wife came in, not knowing what had happened.

⁸Peter asked her, "Tell me whether you sold your land for so much?" And she said, "Yes, for so much."

⁹Then Peter said to her, "How could you two have agreed together to put the Spirit of the Lord to the test? Look! The feet of those who have buried your husband are at the door, and they will carry you out also."

¹⁰And at once she fell down at his feet and died; and the young men came in and found her dead, and they carried her out and buried her beside her husband.

¹¹And great fear *and* awe gripped the whole church, and all who heard about these things.

¹²At the hands of the apostles many signs and wonders (attesting miracles) were *continually* taking place among the people. And by common consent they all met together [at the temple] in [the covered porch called] Solomon's portico.

¹³But none of the rest [of the people, the non-believers] dared to associate with them; however, the people were holding them in high esteem *and* were speaking highly of them.

¹⁴More *and* more believers in the Lord, crowds of men and women, were constantly being added to *their number,*

¹⁵to such an extent that they even carried their sick out into the streets and put them on cots and sleeping pads, so that when Peter came by at least his shadow might fall on one of them [with healing power].

¹⁶And the people from the towns in the vicinity of Jerusalem were coming together, bringing the sick and those who were tormented by unclean spirits, and they were all being healed.

¹⁷But the high priest stood up, along with all his associates (that is, the sect of the Sadducees), and they were filled with jealousy *and* resentment.

¹⁸They arrested the apostles and put them in a public jail.

¹⁹But during the night an angel of the Lord opened the prison doors, and leading them out, he said,

²⁰"Go, stand and *continue* to tell the people in the temple [courtyards] the whole message of this Life [the eternal life revealed by Christ and found through faith in Him]."

²¹When they heard this, they went into the temple [courtyards] about daybreak and *began* teaching.

Now when the high priest and his associates arrived, they called together the Council (Sanhedrin, Jewish High Court), even all the council of elders of the sons of Israel, and sent word to the prison for the apostles to be brought [before them].

²²But when the officers arrived, they did not find them in the prison; and they came back and reported,

²³"We found the prison securely locked and the guards standing at the doors, but when we opened [the doors], we found no one inside."

²⁴Now when the captain of the temple *guard* and the chief priests heard these things, they were greatly perplexed, wondering what would come of this.

²⁵But someone came and told them, "The men whom you put in prison are

standing [right here] in the temple [area], teaching the people!"

²⁶Then the captain went with the officers and brought them back, without hurting them (because they were afraid of the people, worried that they might be stoned).

²⁷So they brought them and presented them before the Council (Sanhedrin, Jewish High Court). The high priest questioned them,

²⁸saying, "We gave you strict orders not to continue teaching in this name, and yet you have filled Jerusalem with your teaching and you intend to bring this Man's blood on us [by accusing us as His murderers]."

²⁹Then Peter and the apostles replied, "We must obey God rather than men [we have no other choice].

³⁰"The God of our fathers raised up Jesus, whom you had put to death by hanging Him on a cross [and you are responsible]. [Deut 21:22, 23]

³¹"God exalted Him to His right hand as Prince and Savior and Deliverer, in order to grant repentance to Israel, and [to grant] forgiveness of sins.

³²"And we are witnesses of these things; and so is the Holy Spirit, whom God has bestowed on those who obey Him."

³³Now when they heard this, they were infuriated and they intended to kill the apostles.

³⁴But a Pharisee named Gamaliel, a teacher of the Law [of Moses], highly esteemed by all the people, stood up in the Council (Sanhedrin, Jewish High Court) and ordered that the men be taken outside for a little while.

³⁵Then he said to the Council, "Men of Israel, be careful in regard to what you propose to do to these men.

³⁶"For some time ago Theudas rose up, claiming to be somebody [of importance], and a group of about four hundred men allied themselves with him. But he was killed, and all who

followed him were scattered and came to nothing.

³⁷"After this man, Judas the Galilean rose up, [and led an uprising] during the time of the census, and drew people after him; he was also killed, and all his followers were scattered.

³⁸"So in the present case, I say to you, stay away from these men and let them alone, for if this plan or action is of men [merely human in origin], it will fail and be destroyed;

³⁹but if it is of God [and it appears that it is], you will not be able to stop them; or else you may even be found fighting against God!"

⁴⁰The Council (Sanhedrin, Jewish High Court) took his advice; and after summoning the apostles, they flogged them and ordered them not to speak in the name of Jesus, and released them.

⁴¹So they left the Council, rejoicing that they had been considered worthy [dignified by indignity] to suffer shame for [the sake of] His name.

⁴²And every single day, in the temple [area] and in homes, they did not stop teaching and telling the good news of Jesus as the Christ (the Messiah, the Anointed).

6 NOW ABOUT this time, when the number of disciples was increasing, a complaint was made by the Hellenists (Greek-speaking Jews) against the [native] Hebrews, because their widows were being overlooked in the daily serving of food.

²So the Twelve called the disciples together and said, "It is not appropriate for us to neglect [teaching] the word of God in order to serve tables and manage the distribution of food.

³"Therefore, brothers, choose from among you seven men with good reputations [men of godly character and moral integrity], full of the Spirit and of wisdom, whom we may put in charge of this task.

⁴"But we will [continue to] devote ourselves [steadfastly] to prayer and to the ministry of the word."

⁵The suggestion pleased the whole congregation; and they selected Stephen, a man full of faith [in Christ Jesus], and [filled with and led by] the Holy Spirit, and Philip, Prochorus, Nicanor, Timon, Parmenas, and Nicolas (Nikolaos), a proselyte (Gentile convert) from Antioch.

⁶They brought these men before the apostles; and after praying, they laid their hands on them [to dedicate and commission them for this service].

⁷And the message of God kept on growing *and* spreading, and the number of disciples continued to increase greatly in Jerusalem; and a large number of the priests were becoming obedient to the faith [accepting Jesus as Messiah and acknowledging Him as the Source of eternal salvation].

⁸Now Stephen, full of grace (divine blessing, favor) and power, was doing great wonders and signs (attesting miracles) among the people.

⁹However, some men from what was called the Synagogue of the Freedmen (freed Jewish slaves), both Cyrenians and Alexandrians, and some from Cilicia and [the province of] Asia, rose up and questioned *and* argued with Stephen.

¹⁰But they were not able to successfully withstand *and* cope with the

choose your battles

Acts 6:2–4 teaches us that it is not wise to be involved in everything going on around us. Instead, we should select our activities carefully so we can remain calm, cool, and steady in life. I often refer to this as "choosing your battles carefully."

There are many things I could do at my office that I have learned to just stay out of and let another qualified person handle. Previously, I wanted to be part of everything that happened, especially the problems. I learned the hard way that I simply cannot be involved in everything; too much is going on for me to do that. I pick my battles now, and that has greatly increased my level of peace.

I firmly believe that God provides for whatever He assigns to us. He will make sure we have all the people we need to help us, but it is not their fault if we will not rely on them.

If you find yourself trying to do something and you do not have the help you need, you might need to ask yourself if you are doing the right thing. Why would God ask you to do something, then sit by and watch you be frustrated and miserable because the burden is too much? God meets all of our needs, including the people we need to work alongside us.

Acts 6:2–4 gives an example of this act of wisdom. Had the apostles not recognized their need for help, their priorities would have remained out of line and their true assignment unfulfilled. They would have ended up frustrated, and just like the people they were trying to serve, they could have lost their peace, and therefore, their power. It is quite possible that the loss of peace was what triggered their decision to ask for help. This is an excellent example for us to follow.

wisdom *and* the intelligence [and the power and inspiration] of the Spirit by whom he was speaking.

¹¹Then [to attack him another way] they secretly instructed men to say, "We have heard this man [Stephen] speak blasphemous (slanderous, sacrilegious, abusive) words against Moses and *against* God."

¹²And they provoked *and* incited the people, as well as the elders and the scribes, and they came up to Stephen and seized him and brought him before the Council (Sanhedrin, Jewish High Court).

¹³They presented false witnesses who said, "This man never stops speaking against this holy place and the Law [of Moses];

¹⁴for we have heard him say that this Jesus the Nazarene will tear down this place and will change the traditions *and* customs which Moses handed down to us."

¹⁵Then all those who were sitting in the Council, stared [intently] at him, and they saw that Stephen's face was like the face of an angel.

7 NOW THE high priest asked [Stephen], "Are these charges true?"

²And he answered, "Brothers and fathers, listen to me! The God of glory [the Shekinah, the radiance of God] appeared to our father Abraham when he was in Mesopotamia, before he lived in Haran, [Gen 11:31; 15:7; Ps 29:3]

³and He said to him, 'LEAVE YOUR COUNTRY AND YOUR RELATIVES, AND COME TO THE LAND THAT I WILL SHOW YOU.' [Gen 12:1]

⁴"Then he left the land of the Chaldeans and settled in Haran. And from there, after his father died, *God* sent him to this country in which you now live. [Gen 11:31; 12:5; 15:7]

⁵"But He did not give him inheritable property, not even enough ground to take a step on, yet He promised that HE WOULD GIVE IT TO HIM AS A POSSESSION, AND TO HIS DESCENDANTS AFTER HIM. [Gen 12:7; 17:8; Deut 2:5]

⁶"And this is, in effect, what God spoke [to him]: That his DESCENDANTS WOULD BE ALIENS (strangers) IN A FOREIGN LAND, AND THAT THEY WOULD BE ENSLAVED AND MISTREATED FOR FOUR HUNDRED YEARS.

⁷" 'AND I WILL JUDGE ANY NATION TO WHOM THEY WILL BE IN BONDAGE,' said God, 'AND AFTER THAT THEY WILL COME OUT AND SERVE ME [in worship] IN THIS PLACE.' [Gen 15:13, 14; Ex 3:12]

⁸"And God gave Abraham a covenant [a formal agreement to be strictly observed] of [which] circumcision [was the sign]; and so [under these circumstances] Abraham became the father of Isaac, and circumcised him on the eighth day; and Isaac [became the father] of Jacob, and Jacob [became the father] of the twelve patriarchs. [Gen 17:10–14; 21:2–4; 25:26; 29:31–35; 30:1–24; 35:16–26]

⁹"The [ten elder] patriarchs, *overwhelmed* with jealousy, sold [their younger brother] Joseph into [slavery in] Egypt; but God was with him, [Gen 37:11, 28; 45:4]

¹⁰and He rescued him from all his suffering, and gave him favor and wisdom in the sight of Pharaoh, king of Egypt, and he made Joseph governor over Egypt and over his entire household. [Gen 39:2, 3, 21; 41:40–46; Ps 105:21]

¹¹"Now a famine came over all Egypt and Canaan, bringing great distress and our fathers could not find food [for their households and livestock]. [Gen 41:54, 55; 42:5]

¹²"But when Jacob heard that there was grain in Egypt, he sent our fathers *there* the first time. [Gen 42:2]

¹³"And on the second *visit* Joseph identified himself to his brothers, and

Joseph's family *and* background were revealed to Pharaoh. [Gen 45:1–4]

14"Then Joseph sent and invited Jacob his father and all his relatives to come to him, seventy-five persons in all. [Gen 45:9, 10]

15"And Jacob (Israel) went down into Egypt, and there he died, as did our fathers; [Gen 49:33]

16and [from Egypt] their bodies were taken back to Shechem and placed in the tomb which Abraham had purchased for a sum of money from the sons of Hamor in Shechem. [Gen 50:13; Josh 24:32]

17"But as the time [for the fulfillment] of the promise which God had made to Abraham was approaching, the [Hebrew] people increased and multiplied in Egypt, [Deut 10:22]

18until [the time when] THERE AROSE ANOTHER KING OVER EGYPT WHO DID NOT KNOW JOSEPH [nor his history and the merit of his service to Egypt]. [Ex 1:7, 8]

19"He shrewdly exploited our race and mistreated our fathers, forcing them to expose their [male] babies so that they would die. [Ex 1:7–11, 15–22]

20"It was at this [critical] time that Moses was born; and he was lovely in the sight of God, and for three months he was nourished in his father's house. [Ex 2:2]

21"Then when he was set outside [to die], Pharaoh's daughter rescued him *and* claimed him for herself, and cared for him as her own son. [Ex 2:5, 6, 10]

22"So Moses was educated in all the wisdom *and* culture of the Egyptians, and he was a man of power in words and deeds.

23"But when he reached the age of forty, it came into his heart to visit his brothers, the sons of Israel.

24"And when he saw one [of them] being treated unfairly, he defended the oppressed man and avenged him by striking *and* killing the Egyptian.

25"He expected his countrymen to understand that God was granting them freedom through him [assuming that they would accept him], but they did not understand.

26"Then on the next day he suddenly appeared to two of them as they were fighting, and he tried to reconcile them, saying, 'Men, you are brothers; why do you wrong one another?'

27"But the man who was injuring his neighbor pushed Moses away, saying, 'WHO APPOINTED YOU RULER AND JUDGE OVER US?

28'DO YOU INTEND TO KILL ME AS YOU KILLED THE EGYPTIAN YESTERDAY?'

29"At this remark MOSES FLED AND BECAME AN EXILE IN THE LAND OF MIDIAN, where he fathered two sons. [Ex 2:11–15, 22; 18:3, 4]

30"After forty years had passed, AN ANGEL APPEARED TO HIM IN THE WILDERNESS OF MOUNT Sinai, IN THE FLAME OF A BURNING THORN BUSH.

31"When Moses saw it, he was astonished at the sight; but as he went near to look more closely, the voice of the Lord came [to him, saying]:

32'I AM THE GOD OF YOUR FATHERS, THE GOD OF ABRAHAM AND OF ISAAC AND OF JACOB.' Moses trembled with fear and did not dare to look.

33"THEN THE LORD SAID TO HIM, 'REMOVE THE SANDALS FROM YOUR FEET, FOR THE PLACE WHERE YOU ARE STANDING IS HOLY GROUND [worthy of reverence and respect].

34'I HAVE MOST CERTAINLY SEEN THE OPPRESSION OF MY PEOPLE IN EGYPT AND HAVE HEARD THEIR GROANING, AND I HAVE COME DOWN TO RESCUE THEM. NOW COME, AND I WILL SEND YOU TO EGYPT [as My messenger].' [Ex 3:1–10]

35"This Moses whom they rejected, saying, 'WHO MADE YOU A RULER AND A JUDGE?' is the very one whom God sent to be both a ruler and a deliverer, with the [protecting and helping] hand of the Angel who appeared to him in the thorn bush. [Ex 2:14]

³⁶"This man led them out [of Egypt] after performing wonders and signs in the land of Egypt and at the Red Sea and in the wilderness for forty years. [Ex 7:3; 14:21; Num 14:33]

³⁷"This is the Moses who said to the children of Israel, 'GOD WILL RAISE UP FOR YOU A PROPHET LIKE ME FROM YOUR COUNTRYMEN.' [Deut 18:15, 18]

³⁸"This is the one who was in the congregation in the wilderness together with the Angel who spoke to him on Mount Sinai, and *who was* with our fathers; and he received living oracles [divine words that still live] to be handed down to you. [Ex 19]

³⁹"Our fathers were unwilling to be subject to him [and refused to listen to him]. They rejected him, and in their hearts turned back to Egypt. [Num 14:3, 4]

⁴⁰"THEY SAID TO AARON, 'MAKE FOR US GODS WHO WILL GO BEFORE US; FOR THIS MOSES WHO LED US OUT OF THE LAND OF EGYPT, WE DO NOT KNOW WHAT HAS HAPPENED TO HIM.' [Ex 32:1, 23]

⁴¹"In those days they made a calf and brought a sacrifice to the idol, and rejoiced *and* celebrated over the works of their hands. [Ex 32:4, 6]

⁴²"But God turned away [from them] and handed them over to serve the host of heaven. As it is written *and* forever remains written in the book of the prophets, 'IT WAS NOT [really] TO ME THAT YOU OFFERED VICTIMS AND SACRIFICES FOR FORTY YEARS IN THE WILDERNESS, WAS IT, O HOUSE OF ISRAEL? [Jer 19:13]

⁴³'YOU ALSO TOOK ALONG THE TABERNACLE (portable temple) OF MOLOCH AND THE STAR OF THE GOD ROMPHA, THE IMAGES WHICH YOU MADE TO WORSHIP; AND I WILL REMOVE YOU BEYOND BABYLON [carrying you away into exile].' [Amos 5:25–27]

⁴⁴"Our fathers had the tabernacle of testimony in the wilderness, just as God directed Moses to make it according to the pattern which he had seen. [Ex 25:9–40]

⁴⁵"Our fathers also brought it in [with them into the land] with Joshua when they dispossessed the nations whom God drove out before our fathers, [and so it remained here] until the time of David, [Deut 32:49; Josh 3:14–17]

⁴⁶who found favor (grace, spiritual blessing) in the sight of God and asked that he might [be allowed to] find a dwelling place for the God of Jacob. [2 Sam 7:8–16; Ps 132:1–5]

⁴⁷"But it was Solomon who built a house for Him. [1 Kin 6]

⁴⁸"However, the Most High [the One infinitely exalted above humanity] does not dwell in *houses* made by human hands; as the prophet [Isaiah] says, [1 Kin 8:27]

⁴⁹'HEAVEN IS MY THRONE,
AND THE EARTH IS THE FOOTSTOOL FOR MY FEET;
WHAT KIND OF HOUSE WILL YOU BUILD FOR ME?' says the Lord,
'OR WHAT PLACE IS THERE FOR MY REST?
⁵⁰'WAS IT NOT MY HAND THAT MADE ALL THESE THINGS?' [Is 66:1, 2]

⁵¹"You stiff-necked *and* stubborn people, uncircumcised in heart and ears, you are always actively resisting the Holy Spirit. You are doing just as your fathers did. [Ex 33:3, 5; Num 27:14; Is 63:10; Jer 6:10; 9:26]

⁵²"Which one of the prophets did your fathers not persecute? They killed those who proclaimed beforehand the coming of the Righteous One, whose betrayers and murderers you have now become;

⁵³you who received the law as ordained *and* delivered to you by angels, and yet you did not obey it!"

⁵⁴Now when they heard this [accusation and understood its implication], they were cut to the heart, and they

began grinding their teeth [in rage] at him.

⁵⁵But he, being full of the Holy Spirit *and* led by Him, gazed into heaven and saw the glory [the great splendor and majesty] of God, and Jesus standing at the right hand of God;

⁵⁶and he said, "Look! I see the heavens opened up [in welcome] and the Son of Man standing at the right hand of God!"

⁵⁷But they shouted with loud voices, and covered their ears and together rushed at him [considering him guilty of blasphemy].

⁵⁸Then they drove him out of the city and *began* stoning him; and the

life point

Have you ever wondered what it means to be "uncircumcised in heart" (Acts 7:51)? To "circumcise" is to cut off. When a person has an uncircumcised heart and something wicked comes into it, he does not cut it off. Instead, he lets the evil stay there. But a person with a circumcised heart will immediately cut off any wrong attitude that comes into his mind and heart.

Remember, the enemy will come at us with wrong heart attitudes at every opportunity, but taking his bait never helps us. It only hinders our growth and development. If we want to have a circumcised heart, we must immediately get rid of anger, hatred, jealousy, envy, or any other kind of wrong attitude when it first comes into our mind. If we let that wrong thing stay in our heart, we are not being what God has called us to be. We are not living our lives before Him with an uncircumcised heart. A victorious believer maintains a circumcised heart by saying "no" to anything that will keep him or her from being a person whose heart is right before God.

witnesses placed their outer robes at the feet of a young man named Saul. [Acts 22:20]

⁵⁹They continued stoning Stephen as he called on *the Lord* and said, "Lord Jesus, receive *and* accept *and* welcome my spirit!"

⁶⁰Then falling on his knees [in worship], he cried out loudly, "Lord, do not hold this sin against them [do not charge them]!" When he had said this, he fell asleep [in death].

8 SAUL WHOLEHEARTEDLY approved of Stephen's death.

And on that day a great *and* relentless persecution broke out against the church in Jerusalem; and the believers were all scattered throughout the regions of Judea and Samaria, except for the apostles.

²Some devout men buried Stephen, and mourned greatly over him [expressing a personal sense of loss].

³But Saul *began* ravaging the church [and assaulting believers]; entering house after house and dragging off men and women, putting them in prison.

⁴Now those [believers] who had been scattered went from place to place preaching the word [the good news of salvation through Christ].

⁵Philip [the evangelist] went down to the city of Samaria and *began* proclaiming Christ (the Messiah, the Anointed) to them. [Acts 6:5]

⁶The crowds gathered and were paying close attention to everything Philip said, as they heard [the message] and saw the [miraculous] signs which he was doing [validating his message].

⁷For unclean spirits (demons), shouting loudly, were coming out of many who were possessed; and many who had been paralyzed and lame were healed.

⁸So there was great rejoicing in that city.

⁹Now there was a man named Simon,

who previously practiced magic in the city and amazed the people of Samaria, claiming to be someone great. ¹⁰They all paid [a great deal of] attention to him, from the least to the greatest, saying, "This man is what is called the Great Power of God!" ¹¹They were paying attention to him because for a long time he had mystified *and* dazzled them with his magic. ¹²But when they believed Philip as he preached the good news about the kingdom of God and the name of Jesus Christ, they were being baptized, both men and women. ¹³Even Simon believed [Philip's message of salvation]; and after being baptized, he continued on with Philip, and as he watched the *attesting* signs and great miracles taking place, he was constantly amazed.

¹⁴When the apostles in Jerusalem heard that [the people of] Samaria had accepted the word of God, they sent Peter and John to them. ¹⁵They came down and prayed for them that they might receive the Holy Spirit; ¹⁶for He had not yet fallen on any of them; they had simply been baptized in the name of the Lord Jesus [as His possession]. ¹⁷Then Peter and John laid their hands on them [one by one], and they received the Holy Spirit. ¹⁸Now when Simon saw that the Spirit was given through the laying on of the apostles' hands, he offered them money, ¹⁹saying, "Give me this authority *and* power too, so that anyone on whom I lay my hands may receive the Holy Spirit." ²⁰But Peter said to him, "May your money be destroyed along with you, because you thought you could buy the [free] gift of God with money! ²¹"You have no part or share in this matter, because your heart (motive, purpose) is not right before God. [Ps 78:37]

²²"So repent of this wickedness of yours, and pray to the Lord that, if possible, this thought of your heart may be forgiven you. ²³"For I see that you are provoked by bitterness and bound by sin." [Deut 29:18; Is 58:6] ²⁴But Simon answered, "Pray to the Lord for me both of you, so that nothing of what you have said will come upon me."

²⁵So, when Peter and John had given their testimony and preached the word of the Lord, they started back to Jerusalem, preaching the good news [about salvation] in many Samaritan villages [along the way]. ²⁶But an angel of the Lord said to Philip, "Get up and go south to the road that runs from Jerusalem down to Gaza." (This is a desert road). ²⁷So he got up and went; and there was an Ethiopian eunuch [a man of great authority], a court official of Candace, queen of the Ethiopians, who was in charge of all her treasure. He had come to Jerusalem to worship, ²⁸and he was returning, and sitting in his chariot he was reading [the scroll of] the prophet Isaiah. ²⁹Then the [Holy] Spirit said to Philip, "Go up and join this chariot." ³⁰Philip ran up and heard the man reading the prophet Isaiah, and asked, "Do you understand what you are reading?" ³¹And he said, "Well, how could I [understand] unless someone guides me [correctly]?" And he invited Philip to come up and sit with him. ³²Now this was the passage of Scripture which he was reading:

"LIKE A SHEEP HE WAS LED TO THE
    SLAUGHTER;
AND AS A LAMB BEFORE ITS SHEARER
    IS SILENT,
SO HE DOES NOT OPEN HIS MOUTH.

Do you always understand what you read in Scripture? Acts 8:26–31 reminds us that there is no shame in asking for help to understand; it is actually wise to do so. Always ask the Holy Spirit, your Teacher, to help you understand, and also ask God to place around you trusted people who can help you personally apply God's Word in your life.

[33] "IN HUMILIATION HIS JUDGMENT
  WAS TAKEN AWAY [justice was
  denied Him].
WHO WILL DESCRIBE HIS
  GENERATION?
FOR HIS LIFE IS TAKEN FROM THE
  EARTH." [Is 53:7, 8]

[34]The eunuch replied to Philip, "Please *tell me*, about whom does the prophet say this? About himself or about someone else?"
[35]Then Philip spoke and beginning with this Scripture he preached Jesus to him [explaining that He is the promised Messiah and the source of salvation].
[36]As they continued along the road, they came to some water; and the eunuch exclaimed, "Look! Water! What forbids me from being baptized?"
[37][Philip said to him, "If you believe with all your heart, you may." And he replied, "I do believe that Jesus Christ is the Son of God."]
[38]And he ordered that the chariot be stopped; and both Philip and the eunuch went down into the water, and Philip baptized him.
[39]When they came up out of the water, the Spirit of the Lord [suddenly] took Philip [and carried him] away [to a different place]; and the eunuch no longer saw him, but he went on his way rejoicing.

[40]But Philip found himself at Azotus, and as he passed through he preached the good news [of salvation] to all the cities, until he came to Caesarea [Maritima].

9 NOW SAUL, still breathing threats and murder against the disciples of the Lord [and relentless in his search for believers], went to the high priest,
[2]and he asked for letters [of authority] from him to the synagogues at Damascus, so that if he found any men or women there belonging to the Way [believers, followers of Jesus the Messiah], men and women alike, he could arrest them *and* bring them bound [with chains] to Jerusalem.
[3]As he traveled he approached Damascus, and suddenly a light from heaven flashed around him [displaying the glory and majesty of Christ];
[4]and he fell to the ground and heard a voice [from heaven] saying to him, "Saul, Saul, why are you persecuting *and* oppressing Me?"
[5]And Saul said, "Who are You, Lord?" And He *answered*, "I am Jesus whom you are persecuting,
[6]now get up and go into the city, and you will be told what you must do."
[7]The men who were traveling with him [were terrified and] stood speechless, hearing the voice but seeing no one.
[8]Saul got up from the ground, but though his eyes were open, he could see nothing; so they led him by the hand and brought him into Damascus.
[9]And he was unable to see for three days, and he neither ate nor drank.
[10]Now in Damascus there was a disciple named Ananias; and the Lord said to him in a vision, "Ananias." And he answered, "Here I am, Lord."
[11]And the Lord said to him, "Get up and go to the street called Straight, and ask at the house of Judas for a man from

Tarsus named Saul; for he is praying [there],

¹²and in a vision he has seen a man named Ananias come in and place his hands on him, so that he may regain his sight."

¹³But Ananias answered, "Lord, I have heard from many people about this man, especially how much suffering *and* evil he has brought on Your saints (God's people) at Jerusalem;

¹⁴and here [in Damascus] he has authority from the high priests to put in chains all who call on Your name [confessing You as Savior]."

¹⁵But the Lord said to him, "Go, for this man is a [deliberately] chosen instrument of Mine, to bear My name before the Gentiles and kings and the sons of Israel;

¹⁶for I will make clear to him how much he must suffer *and* endure for My name's sake."

¹⁷So Ananias left and entered the house, and he laid his hands on Saul and said, "Brother Saul, the Lord Jesus, who appeared to you on the road as you came [to Damascus], has sent me so that you may regain your sight and be filled with the Holy Spirit [in order to proclaim Christ to both Jews and Gentiles]."

¹⁸Immediately something like scales fell from Saul's eyes, and he regained his sight. Then he got up and was baptized;

¹⁹and he took some food and was strengthened.

For several days [afterward] Saul remained with the disciples who were at Damascus.

²⁰And immediately he *began* proclaiming Jesus in the synagogues, saying, "This Man is the Son of God [the promised Messiah]!"

²¹All those who heard him continued to be amazed and said, "Is this not the man who in Jerusalem attacked those who called on this name [of Jesus],

and had come here [to Damascus] for the express purpose of bringing them bound [with chains] before the chief priests?"

²²But Saul increased in strength more and more, and continued to perplex the Jews who lived in Damascus by examining [theological evidence] *and* proving [with Scripture] that this *Jesus* is the Christ (the Messiah, the Anointed).

²³After considerable time had passed [about three years or so], the Jews plotted together to kill him,

²⁴but their plot became known to Saul. They were also watching the city's gates day and night so they could kill him;

²⁵but his disciples took him at night and let him down through *an opening in* the wall, lowering him in a large basket.

²⁶When he arrived in Jerusalem, he tried to join the disciples; but they were all afraid of him, not believing that he really was a disciple.

²⁷However, Barnabas took him and brought him to the apostles, and described to them how Saul had seen the Lord on the road [to Damascus], and how He had spoken to him, and how at Damascus Saul had preached openly *and* spoken confidently in the name of Jesus.

²⁸So he was with them, moving around freely [as one among them] in Jerusalem, speaking out boldly in the name of the Lord.

²⁹He was talking and arguing with the Hellenists (Greek-speaking Jews); but they were attempting to kill him.

³⁰When the brothers found out [about the plot], they brought him down to Caesarea [Maritima] and sent him off to Tarsus [his home town].

³¹So the church throughout Judea and Galilee and Samaria enjoyed peace [without persecution], being built up [in wisdom, virtue, and faith];

how Paul was filled with the Holy Spirit

Some people say that believers receive everything they will ever get or ever need when they accept Jesus as Savior. That may be the case with some believers, but certainly not with all. Different people have different experiences. I do not deny that some may be born again and baptized in the Holy Spirit at the same time; but others are not, and Paul was one of them (see Acts 9:17, 18).

Chapter nine of Acts tells the story of how Paul was saved and filled with the Holy Spirit. As you probably know, Paul was formerly called Saul and had been a zealous but misguided religious Pharisee (see Acts 23:6). He persecuted Christians and believed he did God a service by doing so (see Philippians 3:5, 6).

As Saul was on the way to bring believers back to Jerusalem for trial and punishment, a light from heaven shone around him, and he fell to the ground. He heard a voice say, "Saul, Saul, why are you persecuting and oppressing Me?" (Acts 9:4). Saul asked, "Who are You, Lord?" Jesus answered, "I am Jesus whom you are persecuting" (Acts 9:5). Then Jesus went on to tell Saul to get up, go into the city, and await instructions for what he was to do next (see Acts 9:6). This was the moment of Saul's conversion, the time of his surrender and acknowledging Jesus as "Lord."

Saul was blinded during this experience. For three days he could not see and did not eat or drink anything. In a vision, the Lord spoke to a disciple named Ananias in Damascus and told him where he would find Saul, noting that he would be praying. At the same time, Saul had a vision and saw a man named Ananias enter and place his hands on him so he would regain his sight.

Because Ananias knew of Saul and how much evil he had brought on the saints, he was reluctant to go. But the Lord said to Ananias, "Go," so he went. The Lord told Ananias that Saul was a chosen instrument of His to bear His name before the Gentiles and the descendants of Israel (see Acts 9:10–15).

In Acts 9:17 we see that Ananias laid his hands on Saul, calling him "Brother Saul." The fact that he called him a brother is another proof of Saul's conversion. Ananias said the Lord sent him to Saul and that he would recover his sight and be "filled with the Holy Spirit" (Acts 9:17). After Saul miraculously and instantly received his sight, he arose and was baptized (see Acts 9:18).

This seems to be quite clear. Saul was converted first; then, three days later, he was filled with the Holy Spirit and baptized in water. If Saul, who became the Apostle Paul, needed to be completely filled with the Holy Spirit, then I believe we need to be also. When we are born again (accept Jesus as our Savior) we receive the Holy Spirit, but we need to be completely filled with the Holy Spirit. As I said, this occurs for different people at different times. As a believer in Jesus you have the Holy Spirit, but does the Holy Spirit have you? And, if He does, how much of you does He have? It may be time for a *complete* surrender in your life. Ask God to completely fill you with His Spirit and keep you "constantly guided by Him" (see Ephesians 5:18).

and walking in the fear of the Lord and in the comfort *and* encouragement of the Holy Spirit, it continued to grow [in numbers].

³²Now as Peter was traveling throughout *the land,* he went down to [visit] the saints (God's people) who lived at Lydda.

³³There he found a man named Aeneas, who had been bedridden for eight years and was paralyzed.

³⁴Peter said to him, "Aeneas, Jesus Christ heals you. Get up and make your bed." Immediately Aeneas got up.

³⁵Then all who lived at Lydda and *the plain of* Sharon saw [what had happened to] him, and they turned to the Lord.

³⁶Now in Joppa there was a disciple named Tabitha, (which translated *into Greek* means Dorcas). She was rich in acts of kindness and charity which she continually did.

³⁷During that time it happened that she became sick and died; and when they had washed her body, they laid it in an upstairs room.

³⁸Since Lydda was near Joppa, the disciples, hearing that Peter was there, sent two men to him, urging him, "Come to us without delay."

³⁹So Peter got up [at once] and went with them. When he arrived, they brought him into the upstairs room; and all the widows stood beside him, weeping and showing [him] all the *tunics and robes that Dorcas used to make while she was with them.

⁴⁰But Peter sent them all out [of the room] and knelt down and prayed; then turning to the body he said, "Tabitha, arise!" And she opened her eyes, and when she saw Peter, she sat up.

⁴¹And he gave her his hand and helped her up; and then he called in the saints (God's people) and the widows, and he presented her [to them] alive.

9:39 Or *inner garments.*

⁴²This became known all over Joppa, and many came to believe in the Lord [that is, to adhere to and trust in and rely on Jesus as Christ and Savior].

⁴³And so it was that Peter stayed in Joppa for many days with Simon, a tanner.

putting the Word to work

God can use even the most unexpected people in extraordinary ways to further His kingdom purposes. Is there someone in your life who seems so far away from God that he or she will never become a believer? Be encouraged; God's transforming power changed Paul from a great persecutor of the church to one of the church's greatest advocates (see Acts 9:20–22). Pray for the unsaved people in your life, that they, like Paul, will receive salvation and live for God.

10 NOW AT Caesarea [Maritima] *there was* a man named Cornelius, a centurion of what was known as the Italian Regiment,

²a devout man and one who, along with all his household, feared God. He made many charitable donations to the *Jewish* people, and prayed to God always.

³About the ninth hour (3:00 p.m.) of the day he clearly saw in a vision an angel of God who had come to him and said, "Cornelius!"

⁴Cornelius was frightened and stared intently at him and said, "What is it, lord (sir)?" And the angel said to him, "Your prayers and gifts of charity have ascended as a memorial offering before God [an offering made in remembrance of His past blessings].

⁵"Now send men to Joppa and have them call for a man *named* Simon,

who is also called Peter [and invite him here];

⁶he is staying with Simon the tanner, whose house is by the sea."

⁷When the angel who was speaking to him had gone, Cornelius called two of his servants and a devout soldier from among his own personal attendants;

⁸and after explaining everything to them, he sent them to Joppa.

⁹The next day, as they were on their way and were approaching the city, Peter went up on the roof of the house about the sixth hour (noon) to pray,

¹⁰but he became hungry and wanted something to eat. While the meal was being prepared he fell into a trance;

¹¹and he saw the sky opened up, and an *object like a great sheet descending, lowered by its four corners to the earth,

¹²and it contained all *kinds of* four-footed animals and crawling creatures of the earth and birds of the air.

¹³A voice came to him, "Get up, Peter, kill and eat!"

¹⁴But Peter said, "Not at all, Lord, for I have never eaten anything that is common (unholy) and [ceremonially] unclean."

¹⁵And the voice came to him a second time, "What God has cleansed *and* pronounced clean, no longer consider common (unholy)."

¹⁶This happened three times, and then immediately the object was taken up into heaven.

¹⁷Now Peter was still perplexed *and* completely at a loss as to what his vision could mean when the men who had been sent by Cornelius, having asked directions to Simon's house, arrived at the gate.

¹⁸And they called out to ask whether Simon, who was also called Peter, was staying there.

¹⁹While Peter was thoughtfully considering the vision, the Spirit said to him, "Now listen, three men are looking for you.

²⁰"Get up, go downstairs and go with them without hesitating *or* doubting, because I have sent them Myself."

²¹Peter went down to the men and said, "I am the one you are looking for. For what reason have you come?"

²²They said, "Cornelius, a centurion, an upright and God-fearing man well spoken of by all the Jewish people, was *divinely* instructed by a holy angel to send for you *to come* to his house and hear what you have to say."

²³So Peter invited them in and gave them lodging [for the night].

The next day Peter got up and left with them, and some of the brothers from Joppa went with him.

²⁴On the following day he [and the others] entered Caesarea. Cornelius was waiting for them, and had called together his relatives and close friends.

²⁵When Peter arrived, Cornelius met him, and fell down at his feet and worshiped *him*.

²⁶But Peter raised him up, saying, "Stand up; I too am only a man."

²⁷As Peter talked with him, he entered [the house] and found a large group of people assembled.

²⁸He said to them, "You know that it is unlawful for a Jewish man to associate with *or* befriend a Gentile, or to visit him; and yet God has shown me that I am not to call anyone common or [ceremonially] unclean.

²⁹"Therefore when I was sent for, I came without raising an objection. So I ask for what reason have you sent for me?"

³⁰Cornelius said, "Four days ago to this hour, I was praying in my house during the ninth hour (3:00–4:00 p.m.); and a man [dressed] in bright, dazzling clothing suddenly stood before me,

³¹and he said, 'Cornelius, your prayer

10:11 Or *vessel*.

God has no favorites

Acts 10:34 tells us that God shows no partiality. This means He has no favorites. If we want to love as God loves, then we must not show partiality either.

This does not mean that we cannot have special friends or that we cannot be involved more with certain people than others. It does mean that we cannot treat some people one way and other people differently. We cannot be kind to those who are good friends with us, and not care how we treat those who are of no interest or importance to us.

I know many people with whom I am not interested in having a deep personal relationship, because I know that, for one reason or another, it would not be fruitful for either of us. This does not mean these people are bad; it just means a casual relationship between us is better than a close relationship.

All of us need certain things from our close friends, and not all people are able to give them to us. God has what I call "divine connections" for all of us—people who are just right for us.

God has given me several people like that in my life, and I appreciate them very much. But He has also taught me to treat everyone with respect, to make them feel valued, to listen to them when they are talking to me, and not to judge them in a critical way.

Our love walk with God is readily seen by how we treat people who cannot do us any good. If we truly want to love as God loves, we will treat everyone impartially, with equal honor and respect.

has been heard, and your acts of charity have been remembered before God [so that He is about to help you].

³²'Therefore send *word* to Joppa and invite Simon, who is also called Peter, to come to you. He is staying at the house of Simon the tanner by the sea.'

³³"So I sent for you at once, and you have been kind enough to come. Now then, we are all here present before God to listen to everything that you have been instructed by the Lord [to say]."

³⁴Opening his mouth, Peter said: "Most certainly I understand now that God is not one to show partiality [to people as though Gentiles were excluded from God's blessing],

³⁵but in every nation the person who fears God and does what is right [by seeking Him] is acceptable *and* welcomed by Him.

³⁶"You know the message which He sent to the sons of Israel, announcing the good news of peace through Jesus Christ, who is Lord of all—

³⁷you know the things that have taken place throughout Judea, starting in Galilee after the baptism preached by John—

speak the Word

Thank you, God, that You are not One to show partiality.
–ADAPTED FROM ACTS 10:34

³⁸how God anointed Jesus of Nazareth with the Holy Spirit and with great power; and He went around doing good and healing all who were oppressed by the devil, because God was with Him. [Is 61:1–3; Luke 4:18–21]

³⁹"We are [personally] eyewitnesses of everything that He did both in the land of the Jews and in Jerusalem [in particular]. They also put Him to death by hanging Him on a cross;

⁴⁰God raised Him [to life] on the third day and caused Him to be plainly seen,

⁴¹not to all the people, but to witnesses who were chosen *and* designated beforehand by God, *that is,* to us who ate and drank together with Him after He rose from the dead. [Luke 24:42, 43; John 21:12–15]

⁴²"He commanded us to preach to the people [both Jew and Gentile], and to solemnly testify that He is the One who has been appointed *and* ordained by God as Judge of the living and the dead.

⁴³"All the prophets testify about Him, that through His name everyone who believes in Him [whoever trusts in and relies on Him, accepting Him as Savior and Messiah] receives forgiveness of sins."

⁴⁴While Peter was still speaking these words, the Holy Spirit fell on all those who were listening to the message [confirming God's acceptance of Gentiles].

⁴⁵All the circumcised believers who came with Peter were amazed, because the gift of the Holy Spirit had been poured out even on the Gentiles.

be filled with the Holy Spirit

The Word of God teaches that though some people received the Holy Spirit through the laying on of hands, other times the Holy Spirit was simply poured out upon people. Acts 10:44 says that while Peter preached to the people, the Holy Spirit fell on all who listened. The following verses in Acts 10 tell us that the believers who came with Peter were amazed because they witnessed how freely the gift of the Holy Spirit was poured out on the crowd as evidenced by their speaking in unknown tongues.

You can ask God to fill you and baptize you in the Holy Spirit right now, right where you are, by simply praying. Here is a prayer you may want to use:

Father, in Jesus' name, I ask You to baptize me in the Holy Spirit with the evidence of speaking in tongues. Grant me boldness as You did those who were filled on the Day of Pentecost, and give me any other spiritual gifts You desire for me to have.

Now you may want to confirm your faith by saying out loud, "I believe I have received the baptism in the Holy Spirit, and I will never be the same again."

If you have prayed that prayer, wait on God quietly and believe you have received that for which you asked. If you do not believe you have received, then even if you have received, it will be as if you have not. You cannot act upon something you do not believe you have.

I want to stress the importance of "believing by faith" that you have received, and not making your decision based on feelings. Believe and keep believing!

⁴⁶For they heard them talking in [unknown] tongues (languages) and exalting *and* magnifying *and* praising God. Then Peter said,

⁴⁷"Can anyone refuse water for these people to be baptized, since they have received the Holy Spirit just as we did?"

⁴⁸And he ordered that they be baptized in the name of Jesus Christ. Then they asked him to stay there for a few days.

11 NOW THE apostles and the believers who were throughout Judea heard [with astonishment] that the Gentiles also had received *and* accepted the word of God [the message concerning salvation through Christ].

²So when Peter went up to Jerusalem, those of the circumcision [certain Jewish believers who followed the Law] took issue with him [for violating Jewish customs],

³saying, "You went to uncircumcised men and [even] ate with them!"

⁴But Peter began [at the beginning] and explained [the events] to them step by step, saying,

⁵"I was in the city of Joppa praying; and in a trance I saw a vision of an object coming down from heaven, like a huge sheet being lowered by the four corners; and [it descended until] it came right down to me,

⁶and looking closely at it, I saw *all kinds of* the four-footed animals of the earth and the wild beasts and the crawling creatures and the birds of the air [both clean and unclean according to the Law],

⁷and I also heard a voice saying to me, 'Get up, Peter; kill and eat.'

⁸"But I said, 'Not at all, Lord; for nothing common (unholy) or [ceremonially] unclean has ever entered my mouth.'

⁹"But the voice from heaven answered a second time, 'What God has cleansed *and* pronounced clean, no longer consider common (unholy).'

¹⁰"This happened three times, and everything was drawn up again into heaven.

¹¹"And right then the three men who had been sent to me from Caesarea arrived at the house where we were *staying.*

¹²"The Spirit told me to go with them without the slightest hesitation. So these six brothers also went with me and we went to the man's house.

¹³"And Cornelius told us how he had seen the angel standing in his house, saying, 'Send *word* to Joppa and have Simon, who is also called Peter, brought here;

¹⁴he will bring a message to you by which you will be saved [and granted eternal life], you and all your household.'

¹⁵"When I began to speak, the Holy Spirit fell on them just as *He did* on us at the beginning [at Pentecost]. [Acts 2:1–4]

¹⁶"Then I remembered the word of the Lord, how He used to say, 'John baptized with water, but you will be baptized with the Holy Spirit.'

¹⁷"So, if God gave Gentiles the same gift [equally] as He gave us after we accepted *and* believed *and* trusted in the Lord Jesus Christ [as Savior], who was I to interfere *or* stand in God's way?"

¹⁸When they heard this, they quieted down and glorified *and* praised God, saying, "Then God has also granted to the Gentiles repentance *that leads* to *eternal* life [that is, real life after earthly death]."

¹⁹So then [since they were unaware of these developments] those who were scattered because of the persecution that occurred in connection with [the stoning of] Stephen traveled as far as Phoenicia and Cyprus and Antioch, without telling the message [of

salvation through Christ] to anyone except Jews.

20But there were some of them, men of Cyprus and Cyrene, who came to Antioch and *began* speaking to the Greeks as well, proclaiming [to them] the good news about the Lord Jesus.

21And the hand (the power and presence) of the Lord was with them, and a great number who believed turned to the Lord [for salvation, accepting and drawing near to Jesus as Messiah and Savior].

22The news of this reached the ears of the church in Jerusalem, and they sent Barnabas to Antioch.

23When he arrived and saw the grace of God [that was bestowed on them], he rejoiced and *began* to encourage them all with an unwavering heart to stay true *and* devoted to the Lord.

24For Barnabas was a good man [privately and publicly—his godly character benefited both himself and others] and *he was* full of the Holy Spirit and full of faith [in Jesus the Messiah, through whom believers have everlasting life]. And a great number of people were brought to the Lord.

25And Barnabas left for Tarsus to search for Saul;

putting the Word to work

Encouragement is a powerful gift. It is not flattery or empty praise, but heartening words that inspire us with hope and confidence meant to build us up in our relationships with God and others. Barnabas was an encourager, and God sent him to edify and build up the people in Antioch (see Acts 11:19–24). Do you have a "Barnabas" in your life? Thank God for that person. Are you a "Barnabas" in someone else's life? Ask God to help you be an encouragement to others.

26and when he found him, he brought him back to Antioch. For an entire year they met [with others] in the church and instructed large numbers; and it was in Antioch that the disciples were first called Christians. [Acts 26:28; 1 Pet 4:16]

27Now at this time some prophets came down from Jerusalem to Antioch.

28One of them named Agabus stood up and prophesied through the [Holy] Spirit that a severe famine would come on the entire world. And this did happen during the reign of Claudius.

29So the disciples decided to send *a contribution,* each according to his individual ability, to the believers who lived in Judea.

30And this they did, sending the contribution to the elders by Barnabas and Saul.

12 NOW AT that time Herod [Agrippa I] the king [of the Jews] arrested some who belonged to the church, intending to harm them.

2And he had James the brother of John put to death with a sword;

3and when he saw that it pleased the Jews, he proceeded to have Peter arrested as well. This was during the days of Unleavened Bread [the Passover week].

4When he had seized Peter, he put him in prison, turning him over to four squads of soldiers of four each to guard him [in rotation throughout the night], planning after the Passover to bring him out before the people [for execution].

5So Peter was kept in prison, but fervent *and* persistent prayer for him was being made to God by the church.

6The very night before Herod was to bring him forward, Peter was sleeping between two soldiers, bound with two chains, and sentries were in front of the door guarding the prison.

⁷Suddenly, an angel of the Lord appeared [beside him] and a light shone in the cell. The angel struck Peter's side and awakened him, saying, "Get up quickly!" And the chains fell off his hands.

⁸The angel said to him, "Prepare yourself and strap on your sandals [to get ready for whatever may happen]." And he did so. Then the angel told him, "Put on your robe and follow me."

⁹And Peter went out following *the angel*. He did not realize that what was being done by the angel was real, but thought he was seeing a vision.

¹⁰When they had passed the first guard and the second, they came to the iron gate that leads into the city. Of its own accord it swung open for them; and they went out and went along one street, and at once the angel left him.

¹¹When Peter came to his senses, he said, "Now I know for certain that the Lord has sent His angel and has rescued me from the hand of Herod and from all that the Jewish people were expecting [to do to me]."

¹²When he realized what had happened, he went to the house of Mary the mother of John, who was also called Mark, where many [believers] were gathered together and were praying *continually* [and had been praying all night].

¹³When he knocked at the door of the gateway, a servant-girl named Rhoda came to answer.

¹⁴Recognizing Peter's voice, in her joy she failed to open the gate, but ran in and announced that Peter was standing in front of the gateway.

¹⁵They said to her, "You are out of your mind!" But she kept insisting that it was so. They kept saying, "It is his angel!" [Matt 18:10; Heb 1:14]

¹⁶But [meanwhile] Peter continued knocking; and when they opened *the*

door and saw him, they were completely amazed.

¹⁷But motioning to them with his hand to be quiet *and* listen, he described how the Lord had led him out of the prison. And he said, "Report these things to James and the brothers and sisters." Then he left and went to another place.

¹⁸Now when day came, there was no small disturbance among the soldiers over what had become of Peter.

¹⁹When Herod had searched for him and could not find him, he interrogated the guards and commanded that they be led away *to execution*. Then he went down from Judea to Caesarea [Maritima] and spent some time there.

²⁰Now Herod [Agrippa I] was extremely angry with the people of Tyre and Sidon; and their delegates came to him in a united group, and after persuading Blastus, the king's chamberlain [to support their cause], they asked for peace, because their country was fed by [imports of grain and other goods from] the king's country.

²¹On an appointed day Herod dressed himself in his royal robes, sat on his throne (tribunal, rostrum) and *began* delivering a speech to the people.

²²The assembled people kept shouting, "It is the voice of a god and not of a man!"

²³And at once an angel of the Lord struck him down because he did not give God the glory [and instead permitted himself to be worshiped], and he was eaten by worms and died [five days later].

²⁴But the word of the Lord [the good news about salvation through Christ] continued to grow and spread [increasing in effectiveness].

²⁵Barnabas and Saul came back from Jerusalem when they had completed their mission, bringing with them John, who was also called Mark. [Acts 11:28–30]

13

NOW IN the church at Antioch there were prophets [who spoke a new message of God to the people] and teachers: Barnabas, Simeon who was called Niger, Lucius of Cyrene, Manaen who had been brought up with Herod [Antipas] the tetrarch, and Saul. ²While they were serving the Lord and fasting, the Holy Spirit said, "Set apart for Me Barnabas and Saul (Paul) for the work to which I have called them." ³Then after fasting and praying, they laid their hands on them [in approval and dedication] and sent them away [on their first journey].

⁴So then, being sent out by the Holy Spirit, they went down to Seleucia, and from there they sailed to Cyprus. ⁵When Barnabas and Saul arrived at Salamis, they *began* to preach the word of God [proclaiming the message of eternal salvation through faith in Christ] in the synagogues of the Jews; and they also had John [Mark] as their assistant. ⁶When they had traveled through the entire island [of Cyprus] as far as Paphos, they found a sorcerer, a Jewish false prophet named Bar-Jesus, ⁷who was [closely associated] with the proconsul [of the province], Sergius Paulus, an intelligent *and* sensible man. He called for Barnabas and Saul and wanted to hear the word of God [concerning eternal salvation through faith in Christ]. ⁸But Elymas the sorcerer (for that is how his name is translated) opposed them, trying to turn the proconsul away from *accepting* the faith. ⁹But Saul, who was also *known as* Paul, filled with the Holy Spirit *and* led by Him, looked steadily at Elymas, ¹⁰and said, "You [Elymas] who are full of every [kind of] deceit, and every [kind of] fraud, you son of the devil, enemy of everything that is right *and*

good, will you never stop perverting the straight paths of the Lord? [Hos 14:9] ¹¹"Now, watch! The hand of the Lord is on you, and you will be blind, [so blind that you will be] unable to see the sun for a time." Immediately a mist and darkness fell upon him, and he groped around, seeking people to lead him by the hand.

¹²The proconsul believed [the message of salvation] when he saw what had happened, being astonished at the teaching concerning the Lord.

¹³Now Paul and his companions sailed from Paphos and came to Perga in Pamphylia; but John [Mark] left them and went back to Jerusalem. ¹⁴Now they went on from Perga and arrived at Antioch in Pisidia, and on the Sabbath day they went into the synagogue and sat down. ¹⁵After the reading of the Law and the [writings of the] Prophets, the officials of the synagogue sent *word* to them, saying, "Brothers (kinsmen), if you have any word of encouragement for the people, say it."

¹⁶So Paul stood up, and motioning with his hand, he said,

"**M**en of Israel, and you who fear God, listen! ¹⁷"The God of this people Israel chose our fathers and made the people great *and* numerous during their stay [as foreigners] in the land of Egypt, and then with an uplifted arm He led them out of there. [Ex 6:1, 6] ¹⁸"For a period of about forty years He put up with their behavior in the wilderness. [Deut 1:31] ¹⁹"When He had destroyed seven nations in the land of Canaan, He gave their land [to our ancestors] as an inheritance—this took about four hundred and fifty years. [Deut 7:1; Josh 14:1, 2] ²⁰"After this, He gave *them* judges until the prophet Samuel.

[21]"Then they asked for a king, and God gave them Saul the son of Kish, a man of the tribe of Benjamin, for forty years.

[22]"And when He had removed him, He raised up David to be their king: of him He testified and said, 'I HAVE FOUND DAVID the son of Jesse, A MAN AFTER MY OWN HEART [conforming to My will and purposes], who will do all My will.' [1 Sam 13:14; Ps 89:20; Is 44:28]

[23]"From this man's descendants God has brought to Israel a Savior, [in the person of] Jesus, according to His promise.

[24]"Before His coming John [the Baptist] had preached a baptism of repentance to all the people of Israel.

[25]"And as John was finishing his course [of ministry], he kept saying, 'What or who do you think that I am? I am not He [the Christ]; but be aware, One is coming after me whose sandals I am not worthy to untie [even as His slave]!'

[26]"Brothers, sons of Abraham's family, and those among you who fear God, to us has been sent the message of this salvation [obtained through faith in Jesus Christ]. [Ps 107:20]

[27]"For those who live in Jerusalem, and their rulers, who failed to recognize or understand both Jesus and the voices of the prophets which are read every Sabbath, have fulfilled these [very prophecies] by condemning Him.

[28]"And though they found no cause or charge deserving death, they asked Pilate to have Him executed.

[29]"And when they had finished carrying out everything that was written [in Scripture] about Him, they took Him down from the cross and laid Him in a tomb.

[30]"But God raised Him from the dead;

[31]and for many days (forty) He appeared to those who came up with Him from Galilee to Jerusalem, the very ones who are now His witnesses to the people.

[32]"And we are bringing you the good news of the promise made to our fathers (ancestors),

[33]that God has *completely* fulfilled this *promise* to our children by raising up Jesus, as it is also written in the second Psalm, 'YOU ARE MY SON; TODAY I HAVE BEGOTTEN (fathered) YOU.' [Ps 2:7]

[34]"And [as for the fact] that He raised Him from the dead, never again to return to decay [in the grave], He has spoken in this way: 'I WILL GIVE YOU THE HOLY AND SURE *blessings* OF DAVID [those blessings and mercies that were promised to him].' [Is 55:3]

[35]"For this reason He also says in another *Psalm,* 'YOU WILL NOT ALLOW YOUR HOLY ONE TO SEE DECAY.' [Ps 16:10]

[36]"For David, after he had served the purpose of God in his own generation, fell asleep and was buried among his fathers and experienced decay [in the grave];

[37]but He whom God raised [to life] did not experience decay [in the grave].

[38]"So let it be clearly known by you, brothers, that through Him forgiveness of sins is being proclaimed to you;

[39]and through Him everyone who believes [who acknowledges Jesus as Lord and Savior and follows Him] is justified *and* declared free of guilt from all things, from which you could not be justified *and* freed of guilt through the Law of Moses.

[40]"Therefore be careful, so that the thing spoken of in the [writings of the] Prophets does not come upon you:

[41]'LOOK, YOU MOCKERS, AND MARVEL,
  AND PERISH *and* VANISH AWAY;
FOR I AM DOING A WORK IN YOUR
  DAYS,
A WORK WHICH YOU WILL NEVER
  BELIEVE, even IF SOMEONE
  DESCRIBES IT TO YOU [telling you
  about it in detail].'" [Hab 1:5]

⁴²As Paul and Barnabas were leaving [the synagogue], the people kept begging that these things might be spoken to them on the next Sabbath. ⁴³When the congregation of the synagogue had been dismissed, many of the Jews and the devout converts to Judaism followed Paul and Barnabas, who, talking to them were urging them to continue in the grace of God. ⁴⁴On the next Sabbath almost the entire city gathered together to hear the word of the Lord [about salvation through faith in Christ]. ⁴⁵But when the Jews saw the crowds, they were filled with jealousy and *began* contradicting the things said by Paul, and were slandering him. ⁴⁶And [at the same time] Paul and Barnabas spoke out boldly *and* confidently, saying, "It was necessary that God's message [of salvation through faith in Christ] be spoken to you [Jews] first. Since you repudiate it and judge yourselves unworthy of eternal life, now we turn to the Gentiles. ⁴⁷"For that is what the Lord has commanded us, saying,

'I HAVE PLACED YOU AS A LIGHT
  FOR THE GENTILES,
SO THAT YOU MAY BRING [the
  message of eternal] SALVATION
  TO THE END OF THE EARTH.'"
  [Is 49:6]

⁴⁸When the Gentiles heard this, they *began* rejoicing and glorifying [praising and giving thanks for] the word of the Lord; and all those who had been appointed (designated, ordained) to eternal life [by God] believed [in Jesus as the Christ and their Savior]. ⁴⁹And so the word of the Lord [regarding salvation] was being spread through the entire region. ⁵⁰But the Jews incited the devout, prominent women and the leading men of the city, and instigated persecution against Paul and Barnabas, and drove them forcibly out of their district. ⁵¹But they shook its dust from their feet *in protest* against them and went to Iconium. [Matt 10:14; Mark 6:11] ⁵²And the disciples were continually filled [throughout their hearts and souls] with joy and with the Holy Spirit.

14 NOW IN Iconium Paul and Barnabas went into the Jewish synagogue together and spoke in such a way [with such power and boldness] that a large number of Jews as well as Greeks believed [and confidently accepted Jesus as Savior]; ²but the unbelieving Jews [who rejected Jesus as Messiah] stirred up and embittered the minds of the Gentiles against the believers. ³So Paul and Barnabas stayed for a long time, speaking boldly *and* confidently for the Lord, who continued to testify to the word of His grace, granting that signs and wonders (attesting miracles) be done by them. ⁴But the people of the city were divided; some were *siding* with the Jews, and some with the apostles. ⁵When there was an attempt by both the Gentiles and the Jews, together with their rulers, to shamefully mistreat and to stone them, ⁶they, aware of the situation, escaped to Lystra and Derbe, [taking refuge in the] cities of Lycaonia, and the neighboring region; ⁷and there they continued to preach the good news. ⁸Now at Lystra a man sat who was unable to use his feet, for he was crippled from birth and had never walked. ⁹This man was listening to Paul as he spoke, and Paul looked intently at him and saw that he had faith to be healed, ¹⁰and said with a loud voice, "Stand up on your feet." And he jumped up and *began* to walk.

[11]And the crowds, when they saw what Paul had done, raised their voices, shouting in the Lycaonian language, "The gods have come down to us in human form!"

[12]They began calling Barnabas, Zeus [chief of the Greek gods], and Paul, Hermes [messenger of the Greek gods], since he took the lead in speaking.

[13]The priest of Zeus, whose *temple* was at the entrance of the city, brought bulls and garlands to the city gates, and wanted to offer sacrifices with the crowds.

[14]But when the apostles Barnabas and Paul heard about it, they tore their robes and rushed out into the crowd, shouting,

[15]"Men, why are you doing these things? We too are only men of the same nature as you, bringing the good news to you, so that you turn from these useless *and* meaningless things to the living God, WHO MADE THE HEAVEN AND THE EARTH AND THE SEA AND EVERYTHING THAT IS IN THEM. [Ex 20:11; Ps 146:6]

[16]"In generations past He permitted all the nations to go their own ways;

[17]yet He did not leave Himself without some witness [as evidence of Himself], in that He kept constantly doing good things *and* showing you kindness, and giving you rains from heaven and productive seasons, filling your hearts with food and happiness."

[18]Even saying these words, with difficulty they prevented the people from offering sacrifices to them.

[19]But Jews arrived from Antioch and Iconium, and having won over the crowds, they stoned Paul and dragged him out of the city, thinking he was dead. [2 Cor 11:25; 2 Tim 3:11]

[20]But the disciples formed a circle around him, and he got up and went back into the city; and the next day he went on with Barnabas to Derbe.

[21]They preached the good news to that city and made many disciples, then they returned to Lystra and to Iconium and to Antioch,

[22]strengthening *and* establishing the hearts of the disciples; encouraging them to remain firm in the faith, saying, "It is through many tribulations *and* hardships that we must enter the kingdom of God."

[23]When they had appointed elders for them in every church, having prayed with fasting, they entrusted them to the Lord in whom they believed [and joyfully accepted as the Messiah].

[24]Then they passed through Pisidia and came to Pamphylia.

[25]When they had spoken the word [of salvation through faith in Christ] in Perga, they went down to Attalia.

[26]From there they sailed back to Antioch, where they had been entrusted to the grace of God for the work which they had now completed.

[27]Arriving *there,* they gathered the church together and *began* to report [in great detail] everything that God had done with them and how He had opened to the Gentiles a door of faith [in Jesus as the Messiah and Savior].

[28]And they stayed there a long time with the disciples.

15 SOME MEN came down from Judea and *began* teaching the brothers, "Unless you are circumcised in accordance with the custom of Moses, you cannot be saved." [Gen 17:9–14]

[2]Paul and Barnabas disagreed greatly and debated with them, so it was determined that Paul and Barnabas and some of the others from their group would go up to Jerusalem to the apostles and the elders [and confer with them] concerning this issue.

[3]So, after being supplied *and* sent on their way by the church, they went through both Phoenicia and Samaria telling in detail the conversion of the

Gentiles, and they brought great joy to all the believers.

⁴When they arrived in Jerusalem, they were received warmly by the church and the apostles and the elders, and they reported to them all the things that God had accomplished through them.

⁵But some from the sect of the Pharisees who had believed [in Jesus as the Messiah] stood up and said, "It is necessary to circumcise the Gentile converts and to direct them to observe the Law of Moses."

⁶The apostles and the elders came together to consider this matter.

⁷After a long debate, Peter got up and said to them, "Brothers, you know that in the early days God made a choice among you, that by my mouth the Gentiles would hear the message of the gospel and believe.

⁸"And God, who knows *and* understands the heart, testified to them, giving them the Holy Spirit, just as He also did to us;

⁹and He made no distinction between us and them, cleansing their hearts by faith [in Jesus].

¹⁰"Now then, why are you testing God by placing a yoke on the neck of the disciples which neither our fathers nor we have been able to endure?

¹¹"But we believe that we are saved through the [precious, undeserved] grace of the Lord Jesus [which makes us free of the guilt of sin and grants us eternal life], in just the same way as they are."

¹²All the people remained silent, and they listened [attentively] to Barnabas and Paul as they described all the signs and wonders (attesting miracles) that God had done through them among the Gentiles.

¹³When they had finished speaking, James replied, "Brothers, listen to me.

¹⁴"Simeon (Simon Peter) has described how God first concerned Himself about taking from among the Gentiles a people for His name [to honor Him and be identified with Him].

¹⁵"The words of the Prophets agree with this, just as it is written [in Scripture],

¹⁶'AFTER THESE THINGS I will return,
AND I WILL REBUILD THE TENT OF
    DAVID WHICH HAS FALLEN;
I WILL REBUILD ITS RUINS,
AND I WILL RESTORE IT,
¹⁷ SO THAT THE REST OF MANKIND MAY
    SEEK THE LORD,
AND ALL THE GENTILES UPON WHOM
    MY NAME HAS BEEN INVOKED,'
¹⁸ SAYS THE LORD,
WHO HAS BEEN MAKING THESE
    THINGS KNOWN FROM LONG AGO.
    [Is 45:21; Jer 12:15; Amos 9:11, 12]

¹⁹"Therefore it is my judgment that we do not trouble *and* make it difficult for those who are turning to God among the Gentiles [by putting obstacles in their way],

²⁰but that we write to them that they are to abstain from anything that has been contaminated by [being offered to] idols and from sexual impurity and from [eating the meat of] what has been strangled and from [the consumption of] blood.

²¹"For from ancient generations [the writing of] Moses has been preached in every city, since he is read *aloud* in the synagogues every Sabbath."

²²Then the apostles and the elders, together with the whole church, decided to select some of their men to go to Antioch with Paul and Barnabas—Judas, who was called Barsabbas, and Silas

speak the Word

Thank You, God, that You know and understand my heart.
–ADAPTED FROM ACTS 15:8

[also called Silvanus, both], leading men among the brothers. ²³With them they sent the following letter:

"The apostles and the brothers who are the elders, to the brothers and sisters who are from the Gentiles in Antioch, Syria, and Cilicia, Greetings. ²⁴"Since we have heard that some of our men have troubled you with *their* teachings, causing distress *and* confusion—men to whom we gave no *such* orders *or* instructions— ²⁵it has been decided by us, having met together, to select men and send them to you with our beloved Barnabas and Paul, ²⁶men who have risked their lives for the name of our Lord Jesus Christ. ²⁷"So we have sent Judas and Silas, who will report by word of mouth the same things [that we decided in our meeting]. ²⁸"For it seemed good to the Holy Spirit and to us not to place on you any greater burden than these essentials: ²⁹that you abstain from things sacrificed to idols, and from [consuming] blood, and from [eating the meat of] things that have been strangled, and from sexual impurity. If you keep yourselves from these things, you will do well. Farewell."

³⁰So when they were sent off, they went down to Antioch; and after assembling the congregation, they delivered the letter. ³¹And when they had read it, the people rejoiced greatly at the encouragement *and* comfort [it brought them]. ³²Judas and Silas, who were themselves prophets (divinely inspired spokesmen), encouraged and strengthened the believers with many words.

³³After spending some time there, they were sent back by the brothers with [the greeting of] peace to those who had sent them. ³⁴[However, Silas decided to stay there.] ³⁵But Paul and Barnabas remained in Antioch, and with many others also continued teaching and proclaiming the good news, the word of the Lord [concerning eternal salvation through faith in Christ].

³⁶After some time Paul said to Barnabas, "Let us go back and visit the brothers and sisters (believers) in every city where we preached the message of the Lord, and see how they are doing." ³⁷Now Barnabas wanted to take [his cousin] John, who was called Mark, along with them. ³⁸But Paul kept insisting that they should not take along with them the one who had quit *and* deserted them in Pamphylia and had not gone on with them to the work. ³⁹And it became such a sharp disagreement that they separated from one another, and Barnabas took [John] Mark with him and sailed away to Cyprus. ⁴⁰But Paul chose Silas [who was again in Antioch] and set out [on his second journey], commended by the brothers to the grace *and* favor of the Lord. ⁴¹And he traveled through Syria and Cilicia, strengthening the churches.

16 NOW PAUL traveled to Derbe and also to Lystra. A disciple named Timothy was there, the son of a Jewish woman who was a believer [in Christ], however, his father was a Greek. ²Timothy was well spoken of by the brothers and sisters who were in Lystra and Iconium. ³Paul wanted Timothy to go with him [as a missionary]; and he took him and circumcised him because of the Jews

who were in those places, since they all knew that his father was a Greek.

⁴As they traveled from town to town, they delivered the decrees decided on by the apostles and elders who were in Jerusalem, for the churches to observe.

⁵So the churches were strengthened in the faith, and they *continually* increased in number day after day.

⁶Now they passed through the territory of Phrygia and Galatia, after being forbidden by the Holy Spirit to speak the word in [the west coast province of] Asia [Minor];

⁷and after they came to Mysia, they tried to go into Bithynia, but the Spirit of Jesus did not permit them;

⁸so passing by Mysia, they went down to Troas.

⁹Then a vision appeared to Paul in the night: a man from [the Roman province of] Macedonia was standing and pleading with him, saying, "Come over to Macedonia and help us!"

¹⁰And when he had seen the vision, we (including Luke) tried to go on into Macedonia at once, concluding that God had called us to preach the gospel to them.

¹¹So setting sail from Troas, we ran a direct course to Samothrace, and the next day [went on] to Neapolis;

¹²and from there [we came] to Philippi, which is a leading city of the district of Macedonia, a *Roman* colony. We stayed on in this city for several days;

¹³and on the Sabbath day we went outside the city gate to the bank of the [Gangites] river, where we thought there would be a place of prayer, and we sat down and began speaking to the women who had come there.

¹⁴A woman named Lydia, from the city of Thyatira, a dealer in purple fabrics who was [already] a worshiper of God, listened to us; and the Lord opened her heart to pay attention *and* to respond to the things said by Paul.

¹⁵And when she was baptized, along with her household, she pleaded with us, saying, "If you have judged me *and* decided that I am faithful to the Lord [a true believer], come to my house and stay." And she persuaded us.

¹⁶It happened that as we were on our way to the place of prayer, we were met by a slave-girl who had *a spirit of divination [that is, a demonic spirit claiming to foretell the future and discover hidden knowledge], and she brought her owners a good profit by fortune-telling.

¹⁷She followed after Paul and us and kept screaming *and* shouting, "These men are servants of the Most High God! They are proclaiming to you the way of salvation!"

¹⁸She continued doing this for several days. Then Paul, being greatly annoyed *and* worn out, turned and said to the spirit [inside her], "I command you in the name of Jesus Christ [as His representative] to come out of her!" And it came out at that very moment.

¹⁹But when her owners saw that their hope of profit was gone, they seized Paul and Silas and dragged them before the authorities in the market place [where trials were held],

²⁰and when they had brought them before the chief magistrates, they said, "These men, who are Jews, are throwing our city into confusion *and* causing trouble.

²¹"They are publicly teaching customs which are unlawful for us, as Romans, to accept or observe."

²²The crowd also joined in the attack against them, and the chief magistrates tore their robes off them and ordered that Paul and Silas be beaten with rods. [2 Cor 11:25]

²³After striking them many times

16:16 Lit *a python spirit*. In Greek mythology, Python the earth-dragon (serpent goddess), was associated with the oracle at Delphi.

open your heart

In the city of Philippi, where God directed Paul and those traveling with him, a group of women gathered together for prayer on the bank of a river (see Acts 16:13). Paul began speaking to these women, telling them some things they had never heard before. They were accustomed to living under the Jewish Law, and Paul delivered a message of grace. One of the women named Lydia "opened her heart" to receive what Paul said (Acts 16:14).

We, like Lydia, need to open our hearts to the things of God. The reason an open heart is so important is that without it, we will not listen to new things—not strange, off-the-wall things—but different things God wants to do in our lives. I am amazed when I hear about great promises in the Bible that people refuse to believe because they are not part of what they have been taught in the past. Why can't our believing be progressive? Why can't we accept that there may be a few things we do not know?

I am not saying we should be so open that we believe anything we are told or anything the devil wants to dump on us, but I am saying we should avoid being so narrow-minded that we reject great, new things from God. We should not be afraid to listen to what is being said and check it out for ourselves by reading the Bible and talking to God about it to see if it is really true.

We are supposed to be single-minded, not narrow-minded. I get concerned about people who think there is only one way to do things, and it is their way. People like that are very difficult to work with. They often have so much pride they will not listen to anything anybody tells them. In contrast, a humble believer's heart is open to the truth.

We need to have open hearts. God's Word and our hearts will affirm truth to us when we hear truth. Our minds may be closed, but our hearts must be open to God to allow Him to do new things in our everyday lives.

[with the rods], they threw them into prison, commanding the jailer to guard them securely.

²⁴He, having received such a [strict] command, threw them into the inner prison (dungeon) and fastened their feet in the stocks [in an agonizing position].

²⁵But about midnight when Paul and Silas were praying and singing hymns of praise to God, and the prisoners were listening to them;

²⁶suddenly there was a great earthquake, so [powerful] that the very foundations of the prison were shaken and at once all the doors were opened

and everyone's chains were unfastened.

²⁷When the jailer, shaken out of sleep, saw the prison doors open, he drew his sword and was about to kill himself, thinking that the prisoners had escaped.

²⁸But Paul shouted, saying, "Do not hurt yourself, we are all here!"

²⁹Then the jailer called for torches and rushed in, and trembling with fear he fell down before Paul and Silas,

³⁰and after he brought them out [of the inner prison], he said, "Sirs, what must I do to be saved?"

³¹And they answered, "Believe in the

life point

Acts 16:22–26 relates an incident in the lives of Paul and Silas and how their joy preceded and precipitated a "sudden" breakthrough.

These men of God exercised the power of joy in the midst of very difficult circumstances. Their clothes were torn off, they were beaten with rods and thrown into jail, and yet they did nothing wrong. In that depressing situation, they expressed a supernatural joy evidenced by their praying and singing. Their joy could not have been a natural response, because there was nothing in the natural realm to be joyful about.

As a result of seeing firsthand the supernatural joy of Paul and Silas, the jailer was saved (see Acts 16:27–34). I believe more people in the world will receive the salvation that waits for them when Christians truly begin to express the joy of their own salvation.

Lord Jesus [as your personal Savior and entrust yourself to Him] and you will be saved, you and your household [if they also believe]."

³²And they spoke the word of the Lord [concerning eternal salvation through faith in Christ] to him and to all who were in his house.

³³And he took them that *very* hour of the night and washed their *bloody* wounds, and immediately he was baptized, he and all his *household.*

³⁴Then he brought them into his house and set food before them, and rejoiced greatly, since he had believed in God with his entire family [accepting with joy what had been made known to them about the Christ].

³⁵Now when day came, the chief magistrates sent their officers, saying, "Release those men."

³⁶And the jailer repeated the words to Paul, *saying,* "The chief magistrates have sent *word* to release you; so come out now and go in peace."

³⁷But Paul said to them, "They have beaten us in public without a trial, men who are Romans, and have thrown us into prison; and now they are sending us out secretly? No! Let them come here themselves and bring us out!"

³⁸The officers reported this message to the chief magistrates, and when they heard that the prisoners were Romans, they were frightened;

³⁹so they came [to the prison] and appealed to them [with apologies], and when they brought them out, they kept begging them to leave the city.

⁴⁰So they left the prison and went to Lydia's *house;* and when they had seen the brothers and sisters, they encouraged *and* comforted them, and left.

17 NOW AFTER Paul and Silas had traveled through Amphipolis and Apollonia, they came to Thessalonica, where there was a synagogue of the Jews.

²And Paul entered the synagogue, as was his custom, and for three Sabbaths he engaged in discussion *and* friendly debate with them from the Scriptures,

³explaining and pointing out [scriptural evidence] that it was necessary for the Christ to suffer and rise from the dead, and *saying,* "This Jesus, whom I am proclaiming to you, is the Christ (the Messiah, the Anointed)."

⁴And some of them were persuaded *to believe* and joined Paul and Silas, along with a large number of the God-fearing Greeks and many of the leading women.

⁵But the [unbelieving] Jews became jealous, and taking along some thugs from [the lowlifes in] the market place, they formed a mob and set the city in an uproar; and then attacking Jason's

house tried to bring Paul and Silas out to the people.

⁶But when they failed to find them, they dragged Jason and some brothers before the city authorities, shouting, "These men who have turned the world upside down have come here too;

⁷and Jason has welcomed them [into his house and protected them]! And they all are saying things contrary to the decrees of Caesar, [actually] claiming that there is another king, Jesus."

⁸They stirred up the crowd and the city authorities who heard these things.

⁹And when they had taken security (bail) from Jason and the others, they let them go.

¹⁰The brothers immediately sent Paul and Silas away by night to Berea; and when they arrived, they entered the Jewish synagogue.

¹¹Now these people were more noble *and* open-minded than those in Thessalonica, so they received the message [of salvation through faith in the Christ] with great eagerness, examining the Scriptures daily to see if these things were so.

¹²As a result many of them became believers, together with a number of prominent Greek women and men.

¹³But when the Jews of Thessalonica learned that the word of God [concerning eternal salvation through faith in Christ] had also been preached by Paul at Berea, they came there too, agitating and disturbing the crowds.

¹⁴So at that time the brothers immediately sent Paul away to go as far as the sea; but Silas and Timothy remained there [at Berea].

¹⁵Those who escorted Paul brought him to Athens; and [after] receiving instructions [from Paul] for Silas and Timothy to join him as soon as possible, they left.

¹⁶Now while Paul was waiting for them at Athens, his spirit was greatly

angered when he saw that the city was full of idols.

¹⁷So he had discussions in the synagogue with the Jews and the God-fearing *Gentiles*, and in the market place day after day with any who happened to be there.

¹⁸And some of the Epicurean and Stoic philosophers began to engage in conversation with him. And some said, "What could this idle babbler [with his eclectic, scrap-heap learning] have in mind to say?" Others said, "He seems to be a proclaimer of strange deities"— because he was preaching the good news about Jesus and the resurrection.

¹⁹They took him and brought him to the Areopagus (Hill of Ares, the Greek god of war), saying, "May we know what this [strange] new teaching is which you are proclaiming?

²⁰"For you are bringing some startling *and* strange things to our ears; so we want to know what they mean."

²¹(Now all the Athenians and the foreigners visiting there used to spend their [leisure] time in nothing other than telling or hearing something new.)

²²So Paul, standing in the center of the Areopagus, said: "Men of Athens, I observe [with every turn I make throughout the city] that you are very religious *and* devout in all respects.

²³"Now as I was going along and carefully looking at your objects of worship, I came to an altar with this inscription:

putting the Word to work

Receiving good teaching from pastors, teachers, and ministers is a blessing, but it is equally important to study Scripture for yourself (see Acts 17:11). Do you regularly set aside time each day to read the Word of God? If not, ask Him to help you have a hunger to read and study His Word, and make every effort to do so daily.

'TO AN UNKNOWN GOD.' Therefore what you already worship as unknown, this I proclaim to you.

24"The God who created the world and everything in it, since He is Lord of heaven and earth, does not dwell in temples made with hands;

25nor is He served by human hands, as though He needed anything, because it is He who gives to all [people] life and breath and all things. [Is 42:5]

26"And He made from one *man* every nation of mankind to live on the face of the earth, having determined their appointed times and the boundaries of their lands *and* territories.

27"This was so that they would seek God, if perhaps they might grasp for Him and find Him, though He is not far from each one of us.

28"For in Him we live and move and exist [that is, in Him we actually have our being], as even some of your own poets have said, 'For we also are His children.'

29"So then, being God's children, we should not think that the Divine Nature (deity) is like gold or silver or stone, an image formed by the art and imagination *or* skill of man.

30"Therefore God overlooked *and* disregarded the *former* ages of ignorance; *but* now He commands all *people* everywhere to repent [that is, to change their old way of thinking, to regret their past sins, and to seek God's purpose for their lives],

31because He has set a day when He will judge the *inhabited* world in righteousness by a Man whom He has appointed *and* destined for that task, and He has provided credible proof to everyone by raising Him from the dead." [Ps 9:8; 96:13; 98:9]

32Now when they heard [the term] resurrection from the dead, some mocked *and* sneered; but others said, "We will hear from you again about this matter."

33So Paul left them.

34But some men joined him and believed; among them were Dionysius, [a judge] of the *Council of* Areopagus, and a woman named Damaris, and others with them.

18 AFTER THIS Paul left Athens and went to Corinth. 2There he met a Jew named Aquila, a native of Pontus, who had recently come from Italy with his wife, Priscilla, because [the Roman Emperor] Claudius had issued an edict that all the Jews were to leave Rome. Paul went to see them,

3and because he was of the same trade, he stayed with them; and they worked *together* for they were tentmakers.

4And he reasoned *and* debated in the synagogue every Sabbath, trying to persuade Jews and Greeks;

5but when Silas and Timothy came down from Macedonia (northern Greece), Paul *began* devoting himself completely to [preaching] the word, and solemnly testifying to the Jews that Jesus is the Christ (the Messiah, the Anointed).

6But since the Jews kept resisting *and* opposing him, and blaspheming [God], he shook out his robe and said to them, "Your blood (damnation) be on your own heads! I am innocent of it. From now on I will go to the Gentiles." [Acts 13:46]

7Then he moved on from there and went to the house of a man named Titius Justus, who worshiped God and whose house was next door to the synagogue.

8Crispus, the leader of the synagogue, believed in the Lord together with his entire household [joyfully acknowledging Him as Messiah and Savior]; and many of the Corinthians who heard [Paul's message] were believing and being baptized.

⁹One night the Lord said to Paul in a vision, "Do not be afraid anymore, but go on speaking and do not be silent; ¹⁰for I am with you, and no one will attack you in order to hurt you, because I have many people in this city." [Is 43:5; Jer 1:8] ¹¹So he settled *there* for a year and six months, teaching them the word of God [concerning eternal salvation through faith in Christ].

¹²But when Gallio was proconsul of Achaia (southern Greece), the Jews made a united attack on Paul and brought him before the judgment seat, ¹³declaring, "This man is persuading people to worship God in violation of the law [of Moses]."

"in Christ"

The phrases "in Christ," "in Him," or "in Whom," which are found in many books of the New Testament, are vitally important. If we do not understand these terms, we will never have proper insight concerning our "who" and we will be frustrated as we spend our lives trying to improve our "do."

Acts 17:28 says, "For in Him we live and move and exist." When we receive Jesus Christ as Savior, we are considered to be "in Him." What He earned and deserves is ours through inheritance. Examining the relationship with our natural children may better help us understand this subject.

I have four children who were originally "in me." Many aspects of their appearances and personalities result from the fact that they began their lives "in me." They received my physical makeup, my nature, my temperament, and so forth. Now that they are grown, they are free to go about life "doing" things that will make me proud of them—but, it must never be forgotten that they began "in me." That relationship will last forever.

A saving relationship with Jesus is referred to in John 3:3, 4 as being "born again." Nicodemus asked Jesus, "How can a man be born when he is old? He cannot enter his mother's womb a second time and be born, can he?" Nicodemus failed to see that Jesus spoke of a spiritual birth, a birth where we are taken out of a worldly way of living and placed "into Christ" and into a new way of thinking, speaking, and acting.

Each of us must know who we are "in Christ." That is our beginning, the place where we begin the new life. Without a deep understanding of this truth, we will ramble around in life and even in Christianity believing the lie that our acceptance by God is based on our performance.

The truth is that our acceptance by God is based on Jesus' performance, not ours. When He died on the cross, we died with Him. When He was buried, we were buried with Him. When He was resurrected, we were resurrected with Him. That is the way God chooses to see all of us who sincerely believe in Jesus as our substitutionary sacrifice and the payment for all our sins. That is what it means to be "in Him." When we know who we are "in Him," our behavior will change and we will progressively behave more and more in ways that are Christlike.

¹⁴But when Paul was about to reply, Gallio said to the Jews, "If it were a matter of some misdemeanor or serious crime, O Jews, I would have reason to put up with you;

¹⁵but since it is merely a question [of doctrine within your religion] about words and names and your own law, see to it yourselves; I am unwilling to judge these matters."

¹⁶And he drove them away from the judgment seat.

¹⁷Then the Greeks all seized Sosthenes, the leader of the synagogue, and *began* beating him right in front of the judgment seat; but Gallio paid no attention to any of this. [1 Cor 1:1]

¹⁸Paul stayed for a while longer, and then told the brothers and sisters goodbye and sailed for Syria; and he was accompanied by Priscilla and Aquila. At Cenchrea [the southeastern port of Corinth] he had his hair cut, because he was keeping a [Nazirite] vow [of abstention].

¹⁹Then they arrived in Ephesus, and he left the others there; but he entered the synagogue and reasoned *and* debated with the Jews.

²⁰When they asked him to stay for a longer time, he refused;

²¹but after telling them goodbye and saying, "I will return again if God is willing," he set sail from Ephesus.

²²When he had landed at Caesarea, he went up and greeted the church [at Jerusalem], and then went down to Antioch.

²³After spending some time *there,* he left and traveled through the territory of Galatia and Phrygia, strengthening *and* encouraging all the disciples.

²⁴Now a Jew named Apollos, a native of Alexandria, came to Ephesus. He was an eloquent *and* cultured man, and well versed in the [Hebrew] Scriptures.

²⁵This man had been instructed in the way of the Lord, and being spiritually impassioned, he was speaking and teaching accurately the things about Jesus, though he knew only the baptism of John;

²⁶and he began to speak boldly *and* fearlessly in the synagogue. But when Priscilla and Aquila heard him, they took him aside and explained more accurately to him the way of God [and the full story of the life of Christ].

²⁷And when Apollos wanted to go across to Achaia (southern Greece), the brothers encouraged him and wrote to the disciples, [urging them] to welcome him gladly. When he arrived, he was a great help to those who, through grace, had believed *and* had followed Jesus as Lord and Savior,

²⁸for he powerfully refuted the Jews in public *discussions,* proving by the Scriptures that Jesus is the Christ (the Messiah, the Anointed).

19 IT HAPPENED that while Apollos was in Corinth, Paul went through the upper [inland] districts and came down to Ephesus, and found some disciples.

²He asked them, "Did you receive the Holy Spirit when you believed [in Jesus as the Christ]?" And they said, "No, we have not even heard that there is a Holy Spirit."

³And he asked, "Into what then were you baptized?" They said, "Into John's baptism."

⁴Paul said, "John performed a baptism of repentance, *continually* telling the people to believe in Him who was coming after him, that is, [to confidently accept and joyfully believe] in Jesus [the Messiah and Savior]."

⁵After hearing this, they were baptized [again, this time] in the name of the Lord Jesus.

⁶And when Paul laid his hands on them, the Holy Spirit came on them, and they *began* speaking in [unknown] tongues (languages) and prophesying.

⁷There were about twelve men in all.

⁸And he went into the synagogue and for three months spoke boldly, reasoning *and* arguing and persuading *them* about the kingdom of God.

⁹But when some were becoming hardened and disobedient [to the word of God], discrediting *and* speaking evil of the Way (Jesus, Christianity) before the congregation, Paul left them, taking the disciples with him, and went on holding daily discussions in the lecture hall of Tyrannus [instead of in the synagogue].

¹⁰This continued for two years, so that all the inhabitants of [the west coast province of] Asia [Minor], Jews as well as Greeks, heard the word of the Lord [concerning eternal salvation through faith in Christ].

¹¹God was doing extraordinary *and* unusual miracles by the hands of Paul,

¹²so that even handkerchiefs *or* face-towels or aprons that had touched his skin were brought to the sick, and their diseases left them and the evil spirits came out [of them].

¹³Then some of the traveling Jewish exorcists also attempted to call the name of the Lord Jesus over those who had evil spirits, saying, "I implore you *and* solemnly command you by the Jesus whom Paul preaches!"

¹⁴Seven sons of one [named] Sceva, a Jewish chief priest, were doing this.

¹⁵But the evil spirit retorted, "I know *and* recognize *and* acknowledge Jesus, and I know about Paul, but as for you, who are you?"

¹⁶Then the man, in whom was the evil spirit, leaped on them and subdued all of them and overpowered them, so that they ran out of that house [in terror, stripped] naked and wounded.

¹⁷This became known to all who lived in Ephesus, both Jews and Greeks. And fear fell upon them all, and the name of the Lord Jesus was magnified *and* exalted.

¹⁸Many of those who had become believers were coming, confessing and disclosing their [former sinful] practices.

¹⁹And many of those who had practiced magical arts collected their books and [throwing book after book on the pile] began burning them in front of everyone. They calculated their value and found it to be 50,000 pieces of silver.

²⁰So the word of the Lord [concerning eternal salvation through faith in Christ] was growing greatly and prevailing.

²¹Now after these events, Paul determined in the Spirit that he would travel through Macedonia and Achaia (most of the Greek mainland), and go to Jerusalem, saying, "After I have been there, I must also see Rome [and preach the good news of salvation]."

²²And after sending two of his assistants, Timothy and Erastus, to Macedonia [ahead of him], he stayed on in [the west coast province of] Asia [Minor] for a while.

²³About that time there occurred no small disturbance concerning the Way (Jesus, Christianity).

²⁴Now a man named Demetrius, a silversmith, who made silver shrines of [the goddess] Artemis (Diana), was bringing no small profit to the craftsmen.

²⁵These [craftsmen] he called together, along with the workmen of similar *trades,* and said, "Men, you are well aware that we make a good living from this business.

²⁶You see and hear that not only at Ephesus, but almost all over [the province of] Asia, this Paul has persuaded [people to believe his teaching] and has misled a large number of people, claiming that gods made by [human] hands are not *really* gods *at all.*

²⁷Not only is there danger that this trade of ours will be discredited, but also that the [magnificent] temple of the great goddess Artemis will be

discredited, and that she whom all Asia and the world worship will even be dethroned *and* lose her glorious magnificence."

28When they heard this, they were filled with rage, and they *began* shouting, "Great is Artemis of the Ephesians!"

29Then the city was filled with confusion; and people rushed together [as a group] into the amphitheater, dragging along with them Gaius and Aristarchus, Macedonians who were Paul's traveling companions.

30Paul wanted to go into the [pagan] assembly, but the disciples would not let him.

31Even some of the Asiarchs (officials) who were his friends sent *word* to him and repeatedly warned him not to venture into the amphitheater.

32Now some shouted one thing and some another, for the gathering was in confusion and most of the people did not know why they had come together.

33Some of the crowd advised Alexander [to speak], since the Jews had pushed him forward; and Alexander motioned with his hand [for attention] and intended to make a defense to the people.

34But when they realized that he was a Jew, a single outcry went up from the crowd as they shouted for about two hours, "Great is Artemis of the Ephesians!"

35After the town clerk had quieted the crowd, he said, "Men of Ephesus, what person is there who does not know that the city of the Ephesians is the guardian of the temple of the great Artemis and of that [sacred stone image of her] which fell from the sky?

36"So, since these things cannot be denied, you ought to be quiet *and* stay calm and not do anything rash.

37"For you have brought these men here who are neither temple robbers nor blasphemers of our goddess.

38"So then, if Demetrius and the craftsmen who are with him have a complaint against anyone, the courts are in session and proconsuls are *available;* let them bring charges against one another there.

39"But if you want anything beyond this, it will be settled in the lawful assembly.

40"For we are running the risk of being accused of rioting in regard to today's events, and since there is no reason for it, we will be unable to give an account *and* justify this disorderly gathering."

41And when he had said these things, he dismissed the assembly.

20 AFTER THE uproar had ended, Paul sent for the disciples, and when he had encouraged them he told them goodbye, and set off to go to Macedonia.

2After he had gone through those districts and had encouraged the believers, he came to Greece.

3And he stayed three months, and when a plot was formed against him by the Jews as he was about to set sail for Syria, he decided to return through Macedonia (northern Greece).

4He was accompanied by Sopater of Berea, *the son* of Pyrrhus, and by Aristarchus and Secundus of the Thessalonians, and by Gaius of Derbe, and Timothy, and Tychicus and Trophimus of Asia.

5These men went on ahead and were waiting for us (including Luke) at Troas.

6We sailed from Philippi after the days of Unleavened Bread (Passover week), and within five days we reached them at Troas, where we stayed for seven days.

7Now on the first day of the week (Sunday), when we were gathered together to break bread (share communion), Paul *began* talking with them, intending to leave the next day; and he kept on with his message until midnight.

⁸Now there were many lamps in the upper room where we were assembled, ⁹and there was a young man named Eutychus ("Lucky") sitting on the window sill. He was sinking into a deep sleep, and as Paul kept on talking longer and longer, he was completely overcome by sleep and fell down from the third story; and he was picked up dead.

¹⁰But Paul went down and threw himself on him and embraced him, and said [to those standing around him], "Do not be troubled, because he is alive."

¹¹When Paul had gone back upstairs and had broken the bread and eaten, he talked [informally and confidentially] with them for a long time—until daybreak [in fact]—and then he left. ¹²They took the boy [Eutychus] home alive, and were greatly comforted *and* encouraged.

¹³But we went on ahead to the ship and set sail for Assos, intending to take Paul on board there; for that was what he had arranged, intending himself to go [a shorter route] by land. ¹⁴So when he met us at Assos, we took him on board and sailed on to Mitylene. ¹⁵Sailing from there, we arrived the next day [at a point] opposite Chios; the following day we crossed over to Samos, and the next day we arrived at Miletus [about 30 miles south of Ephesus]. ¹⁶Paul had decided to sail on past Ephesus so that he would not end up spending time [unnecessarily] in [the province of] Asia (modern Turkey); for he was in a hurry to be in Jerusalem, if possible, on the day of Pentecost. ¹⁷However, from Miletus he sent *word* to Ephesus and summoned the elders of the church [to meet him there].

¹⁸And when they arrived he said to them:

"You know well how I [lived when I] was with you, from the first day that I set foot in Asia [until now], ¹⁹serving the Lord with all humility and with tears and trials which came on me because of the plots of the Jews [against me]; ²⁰[you know] how I did not shrink back in fear from telling you anything that was for your benefit, or from teaching you in public meetings, and from house to house, ²¹solemnly [and wholeheartedly] testifying to both Jews and Greeks, urging them to turn in repentance to God and [to have] faith in our Lord Jesus Christ [for salvation]. ²²"And now, compelled by the Spirit *and* obligated by my convictions, I am going to Jerusalem, not knowing what will happen to me there, ²³except that the Holy Spirit solemnly [and emphatically] affirms to me in city after city that imprisonment and suffering await me. ²⁴"But I do not consider my life as something of value *or* dear to me, so that I may [with joy] finish my course and the ministry which I received from the Lord Jesus, to testify faithfully of the good news of God's [precious, undeserved] grace [which makes us free of the guilt of sin and grants us eternal life]. ²⁵"And now, listen carefully: I know that none of you, among whom I went

life point

Whatever your present station in life, whatever you are called to do, wherever you are called to go, enjoy the journey, so you can do as Acts 20:24 encourages and finish your course with joy. Do not waste one day of the precious life God has given you!

about preaching the kingdom, will see me again.

²⁶"For that reason I testify to you on this [our parting] day that I am innocent of the blood of all people.

²⁷"For I did not shrink from declaring to you the whole purpose *and* plan of God.

²⁸"Take care *and* be on guard for yourselves and for the whole flock over which the Holy Spirit has appointed you as overseers, to shepherd (tend, feed, guide) the church of God which He bought with His own blood.

²⁹"I know that after I am gone, [false teachers like] ferocious wolves will come in among you, not sparing the flock;

³⁰even from among your own selves men will arise, speaking perverse *and* distorted things, to draw away the disciples after themselves [as their followers].

³¹"Therefore be *continually* alert, remembering that for three years, night or day, I did not stop admonishing *and* advising each one [of you] with tears.

³²"And now I commend you to God [placing you in His protective, loving care] and [I commend you] to the word of His grace [the counsel and promises of His unmerited favor]. His grace is able to build you up and to give you the [rightful] inheritance among all those who are sanctified [that is, among those who are set apart for God's purpose—all believers].

³³"I had no desire for anyone's silver or gold or [expensive] clothes.

³⁴"You know personally that these hands ministered to my own needs [working in manual labor] and to [those of] the people who were with me.

³⁵"In everything I showed you [by example] that by working hard in this way you must help the weak and remember the words of the Lord Jesus, that He Himself said, 'It is more blessed [and brings greater joy] to give than to receive.'"

³⁶When he had said these things, he knelt down and prayed with them all.

³⁷And they *began* to weep openly and threw their arms around Paul's neck, and repeatedly kissed him,

³⁸grieving *and* distressed especially over the word which he had spoken, that they would not see him again. And they accompanied him to the ship.

21 WHEN WE had torn ourselves away from them and set sail, we ran a straight course and came to Cos, and on the next day to Rhodes, and from there to Patara;

²and after finding a ship crossing over to Phoenicia, we went on board and set sail.

³After we came in sight of Cyprus, leaving it on our left (port side), we sailed on to Syria and put in at Tyre; for there the ship was to unload her cargo.

⁴After looking up the disciples [in Tyre], we stayed there [with them] seven days; and they kept telling Paul through the [Holy] Spirit not to set foot in Jerusalem.

⁵When our days there came to an end, we left and proceeded on our journey, while all of the disciples, with their wives and children, escorted us on our way until *we were* outside the city. After kneeling down on the beach and praying, we told one another goodbye.

⁶Then we boarded the ship, and they returned to their homes.

⁷When we had completed the voyage from Tyre, we landed [twenty miles to the south] at Ptolemais, and after greeting the believers, we stayed with them for one day.

⁸On the next day we left and came to Caesarea, and we went to the house of Philip the evangelist, who was one of the seven [deacons], and stayed with him. [Acts 6:3–6]

⁹He had four virgin daughters who had the gift of prophecy.

¹⁰As we were staying there for some time, a prophet named Agabus came down from Judea.

¹¹And coming to [see] us, he took Paul's [wide] band (belt, sash) and bound his own feet and hands, and said, "This is what the Holy Spirit says: 'In this same way the Jews in Jerusalem will bind the man who owns this band, and they will hand him over to the Gentiles (pagans).'"

¹²Now when we had heard this, both we and the local residents *began* pleading with Paul trying to persuade him not to go up to Jerusalem.

¹³Then Paul replied, "What are you doing, weeping and breaking my heart [like this]? For I am ready not only to be bound *and* imprisoned, but even to die at Jerusalem for the name of the Lord Jesus."

¹⁴And since he would not be dissuaded, we stopped pleading *and* fell silent, saying, "The Lord's will be done!"

¹⁵After this we got ready and started on our way up to Jerusalem.

¹⁶Some of the disciples from Caesarea also came with us, taking us to [the house of] Mnason, a man from Cyprus, a disciple of long standing with whom we were to lodge.

¹⁷When we arrived in Jerusalem, the brothers and sisters welcomed us gladly.

¹⁸On the next day Paul went with us to [see] James, and all the elders *of the church* were present.

¹⁹After greeting them, Paul *began* to give a detailed account of the things that God had done among the Gentiles through his ministry.

²⁰And when they heard it, they *began* glorifying *and* praising God; and they said to him, "You see, brother, how many thousands of believers there are among the Jews, and they are all

enthusiastic supporters of the Law [of Moses].

²¹"Now they have been told about you, that you are teaching all the Jews who are *living* among the Gentiles to turn away from [the Law of] Moses, advising them not to circumcise their children or to live according to the [Mosaic] customs.

²²"What then should be done? They will certainly hear that you have arrived.

²³"Therefore do just what we tell you. We have four men who have taken a vow;

²⁴take these men and purify yourself along with them, and pay their expenses [for the temple offerings] so that they may shave their heads. Then everyone will know that there is nothing to the things they have been told about you, but that you yourself also follow and keep the Law.

²⁵"But with regard to the Gentiles who have believed [in Christ], we have sent them a letter with our decision that they should abstain from meat sacrificed to idols and from [consuming] blood and from [the meat of] what has been strangled and from sexual immorality."

²⁶Then Paul took the [four] men, and the next day he purified himself along with them [by submitting to the ritual]. He went into the temple to give notice of [the time] when the days of purification [ending each vow] would be fulfilled and the usual offering could be presented on behalf of each one.

²⁷When the seven days [required to complete the ritual] were almost over, [some] Jews from [the province of] Asia [Minor], caught sight of him in the temple, and *began* to stir up the crowd, and they seized him,

²⁸shouting, "Men of Israel, help us! This is the man who teaches all men everywhere against our people and

the Law and this place. And besides, he has brought Greeks into the temple and has defiled this holy place."

²⁹For they had previously seen Trophimus the Ephesian in the city with Paul, and they assumed that he had brought the man into the temple [beyond the court of the Gentiles].

³⁰Then the whole city was provoked *and* confused, and the people rushed together. They seized Paul and dragged him out of the temple, and immediately the gates were closed.

³¹Now while they were trying to kill him, word came to the commander of the [Roman] garrison that all Jerusalem was in a state of upheaval.

³²So he immediately took soldiers and centurions and ran down among them. When the people saw the commander and the soldiers, they stopped beating Paul.

³³Then the commander came up and arrested Paul, and ordered that he be bound with two chains. Then he asked who he was and what he had done.

³⁴But some in the crowd were shouting one thing and others something else; and since he could not determine the facts because of the uproar, he ordered that Paul be taken to the barracks [in the tower of Antonia].

³⁵When Paul got to the steps, he was carried by the soldiers because of the violence of the mob;

³⁶for the majority of the people kept following them, shouting, "Away with him! [Kill him!]"

³⁷Just as Paul was about to be taken into the barracks, he asked the commander, "May I say something to you?" And the man replied, "Do you know Greek?

³⁸"Then you are not [as I assumed] the Egyptian who some time ago stirred up a rebellion and led those 4,000 men of the Assassins out into the wilderness?"

³⁹Paul said, "I am a Jew from Tarsus in Cilicia (Mersin Province, Turkey), a citizen of no insignificant city; and I beg you, allow me to speak to the people."

⁴⁰When the commander had given him permission, Paul, standing on the steps, gestured with his hand to the people; and when there was a great hush, he spoke to them in the Hebrew dialect (Jewish Aramaic), saying,

22 "BRETHREN AND fathers (kinsmen), hear my defense which I now offer to you."

²When they heard that he was addressing them in the Hebrew dialect, they became even more quiet. And he continued,

³"I am a Jew, born in Tarsus of Cilicia, but brought up in this city, educated at the feet of Gamaliel according to the strictness of the law of our fathers, being ardent *and* passionate for God just as all of you are today.

⁴"I persecuted *and* pursued the followers of this Way to the death, binding them with chains and putting [followers of Jesus] both men and women into prisons,

⁵as the high priest and all the Council of the elders (Sanhedrin, Jewish High Court) can testify; because from them I received letters to the brothers, and I was on my way to Damascus in order to bring those [believers] who were there to Jerusalem in chains to be punished.

⁶"But as I was on my way, approaching Damascus about noontime, a great blaze of light suddenly flashed from heaven *and* shone around me.

⁷"And I fell to the ground and heard a voice saying to me, 'Saul, Saul, why are you persecuting Me?'

⁸"And I replied, 'Who are You, Lord?' And He said to me, 'I am Jesus the Nazarene, whom you are persecuting.'

⁹"Now those who were with me saw the light, but did not understand the

voice of the One who was speaking to me.

¹⁰"And I asked, 'What shall I do, Lord?' And the Lord answered me, 'Get up and go into Damascus. There you will be told all that is appointed *and* destined for you to do.'

¹¹"But since I could not see because of the [glorious intensity and dazzling] brightness of that light, I was led by the hand by those who were with me and came into Damascus.

¹²"And one Ananias, a devout man according to the standard of the Law, and well spoken of by all the Jews who lived there,

¹³came to [see] me, and standing near, he said to me, 'Brother Saul, receive your sight!' And at that very moment I [recovered my sight and] looked up at him.

¹⁴"And he said, 'The God of our fathers has appointed you to know His will, [and to progressively understand His plan with clarity and power] and to see the Righteous One [Jesus Christ, the Messiah] and to hear a message from His [own] mouth.

¹⁵'For you will be His witness to all men *testifying* of what you have seen and heard.

¹⁶'Now, why do you delay? Get up and be baptized, and wash away your sins by calling on His name [for salvation].'

¹⁷"Then it happened when I had returned to Jerusalem and was praying in the temple [enclosure], that I fell into a trance (vision);

¹⁸and I saw Him saying to me, 'Hurry and get out of Jerusalem quickly, because they will not accept your testimony about Me.'

¹⁹"And I said, 'Lord, they themselves know [without any doubt] that in one synagogue after another I used to imprison and beat those who believed in You [and Your message of salvation].

²⁰'And when the blood of Your witness Stephen was being shed, I also was standing nearby approving *and* consenting [to his death], and guarding the coats of those who were killing him.'

²¹"And the Lord said to me, 'Go, I will send you far away to the Gentiles.'"

²²They listened to Paul until [he made] this [last] statement, but now they raised their voices and shouted, "Away with such a man from the earth! He is not fit to live!"

²³And as they were shouting and throwing off their coats [getting ready to stone Paul] and tossing dust into the air [expressing their anger],

²⁴the commander ordered him to be brought into the barracks, stating that he was to be interrogated with a whip in order to learn why the people were shouting against him that way.

²⁵But when they had stretched him out with the *leather* straps [in preparation for the whip], Paul said to the centurion who was standing by, "Is it legal for you to whip a man who is a Roman *citizen* and uncondemned [without a trial]?"

²⁶When the centurion heard *this,* he went to the commander and said to him, "What are you about to do? This man is a Roman!"

²⁷So the commander came and asked Paul, "Tell me, are you a Roman?" And he said, "Yes."

²⁸The commander replied, "I purchased this citizenship [of mine] for a large sum of money [so how did you acquire yours?]." Paul said, "But I was actually born a *citizen.*"

²⁹So those who were about to interrogate him *by torture* immediately let him go; and the commander was also afraid when he realized that Paul was a Roman and he had put him in chains.

³⁰But on the next day, wanting to know the real reason why Paul was being accused by the Jews, he released him and ordered the chief priests and the whole Council (Sanhedrin, Jewish

High Court) to assemble; and brought Paul down and presented him before them.

23

THEN PAUL, looking intently at the Council (Sanhedrin, Jewish High Court), said, "Kinsmen, I have lived my life before God with a perfectly good conscience until this very day."

²[At this] the high priest Ananias ordered those who stood beside him to strike Paul on the mouth.

³Then Paul said to him, "God is going to strike you, you whitewashed wall! Do you actually sit to judge me according to the Law, and yet in violation of the Law order me to be struck?"

⁴But those who stood near Paul said, "Are you insulting the high priest of God?"

⁵Paul said, "I was not aware, brothers, that he was high priest; for it is written, 'YOU SHALL NOT SPEAK EVIL OF A RULER OF YOUR PEOPLE.'" [Ex 22:28]

⁶But recognizing that one group were Sadducees and the other Pharisees, Paul *began* affirming loudly in the Council *chamber*, "Kinsmen, I am a Pharisee, a son of Pharisees; I am on trial for the hope and resurrection of the dead!"

⁷When he said this, an angry dispute erupted between the Pharisees and the Sadducees, and the [whole crowded] assembly was divided [into two factions].

⁸For the Sadducees say that there is no [such thing as a] resurrection, nor an angel, nor a spirit, but the Pharisees [speak out freely and] acknowledge [their belief in] them all.

⁹Then a great uproar occurred, and some of the scribes of the Pharisees' party stood up and *began* to argue heatedly [in Paul's favor], saying, "We find nothing wrong with this man; suppose a spirit or an angel has [really] spoken to him?"

¹⁰And as the dissension became even greater, the commander, fearing that Paul would be torn to pieces by them, ordered the troops to go down and forcibly take him from them, and bring him to the barracks.

¹¹On the following night the Lord stood near Paul and said, "Be brave; for as you have solemnly *and* faithfully witnessed about Me at Jerusalem, so you must also testify at Rome."

¹²Now when day came, the Jews formed a conspiracy and bound themselves under an oath (curse), saying that they would not eat or drink until they had killed Paul.

¹³There were more than forty [men] who formed this plot [and swore this oath].

¹⁴They went to the chief priests and elders and said, "We have bound ourselves under a solemn oath not to taste anything [neither food nor drink] until we have killed Paul.

¹⁵"So now you, along with the Council (Sanhedrin, Jewish High Court), notify the commander to bring Paul down to you, as if you were going to investigate his case more thoroughly. But we are ready to kill him before he comes near [the place]."

¹⁶But the son of Paul's sister heard of their [planned] ambush, and he went to the barracks and told Paul.

¹⁷Then Paul, calling in one of the centurions, said, "Take this young man to the commander, for he has something to tell him."

¹⁸So he took him and led him to the commander and said, "Paul the prisoner called for me and asked me to bring this young man to you, because he has something to tell you."

¹⁹The commander took him by the hand and stepping aside, *began* to ask him privately, "What is it that you have to tell me?"

²⁰And he said, "The Jews have agreed to ask you to bring Paul down to the

Council (Sanhedrin, Jewish High Court) tomorrow, as if they were going to interrogate him more thoroughly.

[21]"But do not listen to them, for more than forty of them are lying in wait for him, and they have bound themselves with an oath not to eat or drink until they have killed him. Even now they are ready, just waiting for your promise."

[22]So the commander let the young man leave, instructing him, "Do not tell anyone that you have given me this information."

[23]Then summoning two of the centurions, he said, "Have two hundred soldiers ready by the third hour of the night (9:00 p.m.) to go as far as Caesarea, with seventy horsemen and two hundred spearmen;

[24]also provide mounts for Paul to ride, and bring him safely to Felix the governor."

[25]And [after instructing the centurions] he wrote a letter to this effect:

[26]"Claudius Lysias, to the most excellent governor Felix, greetings.

[27]"This man was seized [as a prisoner] by the Jews and was about to be killed by them, when I came upon him with the troops and rescued him, having learned that he was a Roman citizen.

[28]"And wanting to know the *exact* charge which they were making against him, I brought him down to their Council (Sanhedrin, Jewish High Court);

[29]and I discovered that he was accused in regard to questions *and* issues in their Law, but [he was] under no accusation that would call for the penalty of death or [even] for imprisonment.

[30]"When I was told that there would be a plot against the man, I sent him to you immediately, also directing his accusers to bring their charges against him before you."

[31]So the soldiers, in compliance with their orders, took Paul and brought him to Antipatris during the night.

[32]And the next day, leaving the horsemen to go on with him, they returned to the barracks.

[33]When these [horsemen] reached Caesarea, they delivered the letter to the governor, and also presented Paul to him.

[34]After reading the letter, he asked which province Paul was from, and when he learned that he was from Cilicia [an imperial province],

[35]he said, "I will hear your case when your accusers have arrived," giving orders that Paul be kept under guard in Herod's Praetorium (the governor's official residence).

24 FIVE DAYS later, the high priest Ananias came down [from Jerusalem to Caesarea] with some elders and an attorney *named* Tertullus [acting as spokesman and counsel]. They presented to the governor their [formal] charges against Paul.

[2]After Paul had been summoned, Tertullus began the complaint [against him], saying *to the governor:*

"Since through you we have attained great peace, and since by your foresight reforms are being carried out for this nation,

[3]in every way and in every place, most excellent Felix, we acknowledge this with all gratitude.

[4]"But so that I do not weary you further, I beg you to grant us, by your kindness, a brief hearing.

[5]"For we have found this man to be a public menace and one who instigates dissension among all the Jews throughout the world, and a ringleader of the [heretical] sect of the Nazarenes.

⁶"He even tried to desecrate the temple, but we took him into custody [and we intended to judge him by our Law,

⁷but Lysias the commander came, and with great force took him out of our hands,

⁸and ordered his accusers to come before you.] By interrogating him yourself concerning all these matters you will be able to determine [the truth about] these things with which we charge him."

⁹The Jews also joined in the attack, declaring *and* insisting that these things were so.

¹⁰When the governor nodded for him to speak, Paul answered,

"**K**nowing that for many years you have been a judge over this nation, I make my defense cheerfully *and* with good courage.

¹¹As you can easily verify, it has been no more than twelve days since I went up to Jerusalem to worship.

¹²"Neither in the temple, nor in the synagogues, nor *elsewhere* in the city did they find me carrying on a discussion *or* disputing with anybody or causing a crowd to gather.

¹³"Nor can they present evidence to you to prove what they now bring against me.

¹⁴"But I confess this to you, that according to the Way, which they call a [divisive and heretical] sect, I do worship *and* serve the God of our fathers, [confidently] believing everything that is in accordance with the Law [of Moses] and that is written in the Prophets;

¹⁵having [the same] hope in God which these men cherish themselves, that there shall certainly be a resurrection of [the dead], both of the righteous and of the wicked.

¹⁶"In view of this, I also do my best *and* strive always to have a clear conscience before God and before men.

¹⁷"Now after several years I came [to Jerusalem] to bring to my people charitable contributions and offerings.

¹⁸"They found me in the temple presenting these *offerings*, after I had undergone [the rites of] purification, without any crowd or uproar. But *there were* some Jews from [the west coast province of] Asia [Minor],

¹⁹who ought to have been here before you to present their charges, if they have anything against me.

²⁰"Or else let these men tell what crime they found [me guilty of] when I stood before the Council (Sanhedrin, Jewish High Court),

²¹other than for this one statement which I had shouted out as I stood among them, 'For the resurrection of the dead I am on trial before you today.'"

²²But Felix, having a rather accurate understanding about the Way, put them off, saying, "When Lysias the commander comes down, I will decide your case."

²³Then he ordered the centurion to keep Paul in custody, but to let him have some freedom, and [he told the centurion] not to stop any of his friends from providing for his needs.

²⁴Several days later Felix came with his wife Drusilla, who was a Jewess. He sent for Paul and listened to him talk about faith in Christ Jesus.

²⁵But as he was discussing righteousness, self-control [honorable behavior, personal integrity], and the judgment to come, Felix became frightened and said, "Go away for now, and when I find [a convenient] time I will send for you."

²⁶At the same time he was also hoping to get money from Paul [as a bribe]; so he continued to send for him quite often and talked with him.

²⁷But after two years had passed, Felix was succeeded [in office] by Porcius Festus; and wishing to do the Jews a favor, Felix left Paul imprisoned.

25 NOW FESTUS arrived in the province, and three days later he went up to Jerusalem from Caesarea [Maritima].

²And [there in Jerusalem] the chief priests and the leading men of the Jews brought charges against Paul [before Festus], and they repeatedly pleaded with him,

³asking as a concession against Paul, that he would have him brought to Jerusalem; (meanwhile planning an ambush to kill him on the way).

⁴Festus answered that Paul was being held in custody in Caesarea [Maritima] and that he himself was about to leave shortly.

⁵"So," he said, "let those who are in a position of authority among you go there with me, and if there is anything criminal about the man, let them bring charges against him."

⁶Now after Festus had spent no more than eight or ten days among them, he went down to Caesarea, and on the next day he took his seat on the tribunal (the judicial bench), and ordered Paul to be brought [before him].

⁷After Paul arrived, the Jews who had come down from Jerusalem stood around him, bringing many serious charges against him which they were not able to prove,

⁸while Paul declared in his own defense, "I have done no wrong and committed no offense either against the Law of the Jews or against the temple or against Caesar."

⁹But Festus, wishing to do the Jews a favor, answered Paul, "Are you willing to go up to Jerusalem and stand trial there in my presence [before the Jewish Sanhedrin] on these charges?"

¹⁰Paul said, "I am standing before Caesar's tribunal, where I ought to be tried. I have done nothing wrong to the Jews, as you also very well know.

¹¹"Therefore, if I am guilty and have committed anything worthy of death, I do not try to escape death; but if there is nothing to the accusations which these men are bringing against me, no one can hand me over to them. I appeal to Caesar (Emperor Nero)."

¹²Then Festus, after conferring with [the men who formed] his council, answered, "You have appealed to Caesar; to Caesar you shall go."

¹³Now several days later, Agrippa [II] the king and Bernice [his sister] arrived at Caesarea and paid their respects to Festus [the new governor].

¹⁴While they were spending many days there, Festus laid Paul's case before the king, saying, "There is a man here who was left as a prisoner by Felix.

¹⁵"When I was at Jerusalem, the chief priests and the elders of the Jews [told me about him and] brought charges against him, petitioning for a sentence of condemnation against him.

¹⁶"I told them that it was not the custom of the Romans to hand over any man [for punishment] before the accused meets his accusers face to face and has the opportunity to defend himself against the charges.

¹⁷"So after they arrived together here, I did not delay, but on the next day took my place on the tribunal and ordered that the man be brought before me.

¹⁸"When his accusers stood up, they brought no charges against him of crimes that I was expecting [neither civil nor criminal actions],

¹⁹instead they had some points of disagreement with him about their own religion and about one Jesus, a man who had died, but whom Paul kept asserting and insisting [over and over] to be alive.

²⁰"And I, being at a loss as to how to investigate these things, asked whether he was willing to go to Jerusalem and be tried there regarding these matters.

²¹"But when Paul appealed to be held in custody for a decision by the Emperor [Nero], I ordered him to be kept in custody until I *could* send him to Caesar."

²²Then Agrippa said to Festus, "I would like to hear the man myself." "Tomorrow," Festus replied, "you will hear him."

²³So the next day Agrippa and [his sister] Bernice came with great pageantry, and they went into the auditorium accompanied by the military commanders and the prominent men of the city. At the command of Festus, Paul was brought in.

²⁴Then Festus said, "King Agrippa and all you gentlemen present with us, you see this man [Paul] about whom all the Jewish people appealed to me, both at Jerusalem and here, loudly insisting that he ought not to live any longer.

²⁵"But I found that he had done nothing worthy of death; however, since he appealed to the Emperor [Nero], I decided to send him [to Rome].

²⁶"But I have nothing specific about him to write to my lord. So I have brought him before *all of* you, and especially before you, King Agrippa, so that after the investigation has taken place, I will have something to put in writing.

²⁷"For it seems absurd *and* unreasonable to me to send a prisoner [to Rome] without indicating the charges against him."

26 THEN AGRIPPA said to Paul, "You are [now] permitted to speak on your own behalf." At that, Paul stretched out his hand [as an orator] and made his defense [as follows]:

²"I consider myself fortunate, King Agrippa, since it is before you that I am to make my defense today regarding all the charges brought against me by the Jews,

³especially because you are an expert [fully knowledgeable, experienced and unusually conversant] in all the Jewish customs and controversial issues; therefore, I beg you to listen to me patiently.

⁴"So then, all the Jews know my manner of life from my youth up, which from the beginning was spent among my own nation [the Jewish people], and in Jerusalem.

⁵"They have known me for a long time, if they are willing to testify to it, that according to the strictest sect of our religion, I have lived as a Pharisee.

⁶"And now I am standing trial for the hope of the promise made by God to our fathers. [Acts 13:32, 33]

⁷"Which hope [of the Messiah and the resurrection] our twelve tribes [confidently] expect to realize as they serve *and* worship *God* in earnest night and day. And for this hope, O King, I am being accused by Jews!

⁸"Why is it thought incredible by [any of] you that God raises the dead?

⁹"So then, I [once] thought to myself that it was my duty to do many things in opposition to the name of Jesus of Nazareth.

¹⁰"And this is just what I did in Jerusalem; I not only locked up many of the saints (God's people) in prison after receiving authority from the chief priests, but also when they were being condemned to death, I cast my vote against them.

¹¹"And I often punished them [making them suffer] in all the synagogues and tried to force them to blaspheme; and in my extreme rage at them, I kept hunting them even to foreign cities [harassing and persecuting them].

¹²"While so engaged, as I was traveling to Damascus with the authority and commission *and* full power of the chief priests,

¹³at midday, O King, I saw on the way a light from heaven surpassing

the brightness of the sun, shining all around me and those who were traveling with me.

¹⁴"And when we all had fallen to the ground, I heard a voice in the Hebrew dialect (Jewish Aramaic) saying to me, 'Saul, Saul, why are you persecuting Me? It is hard for you to kick [repeatedly] against the goads [offering pointless resistance].'

¹⁵"And I said, 'Who are You, Lord?' And the Lord said, 'I am Jesus whom you are persecuting.

¹⁶'Get up and stand on your feet. I have appeared to you for this purpose, to appoint you [to serve] as a minister and as a witness [to testify, with authority,] not only to the things which you have seen, but also to the things in which I will appear to you,

¹⁷[choosing you for Myself and] rescuing you from the *Jewish* people and from the Gentiles, to whom I am sending you, [Ezek 2:1, 3]

¹⁸to open their [spiritual] eyes so that they may turn from darkness to light and from the power of Satan to God, that they may receive forgiveness *and* release from their sins and an inheritance among those who have been sanctified (set apart, made holy) by faith in Me.' [Is 42:7, 16]

¹⁹"So, King Agrippa, I was not disobedient to the heavenly vision,

²⁰but I openly proclaimed first to those at Damascus, then at Jerusalem and throughout the region of Judea, and *even* to the Gentiles, that they should repent [change their inner self—their old way of thinking] and turn to God, doing deeds *and* living lives which are consistent with repentance.

²¹"Because of this *some* Jews seized me in the temple and tried to kill me.

²²"But I have had help from God to this day, and I stand [before people] testifying to small and great alike, stating nothing except what the Prophets and Moses said would come to pass—

²³that the Christ (the Messiah, the Anointed) was to suffer, and that He by being the first to rise from the dead [with an incorruptible body] would proclaim light (salvation) both to the *Jewish* people and to the Gentiles."

²⁴While Paul was making this defense, Festus said loudly, "Paul, you are out of your mind! Your great education is turning you toward madness."

²⁵But Paul replied, "I am not out of my mind, most excellent *and* noble Festus, but [with a sound mind] I am uttering rational words of truth *and* reason.

²⁶"For [your majesty] the king understands these things, and [therefore] I am also speaking to him with confidence *and* boldness, since I am convinced that none of these things escape his notice; for this has not been done in a corner [hidden from view, in secret].

²⁷"King Agrippa, do you believe the [writings of the] Prophets [their messages and words]? I know that you do."

²⁸Then Agrippa said to Paul, "In a short time [and with so little effort] you [almost] persuade me to become a Christian."

²⁹And Paul replied, "Whether in a short time or long, I wish to God that not only you, but also all who hear me today, might become such as I am, except for these chains."

³⁰Then the king stood up, and [with him] the governor and Bernice, and those who were sitting with them;

³¹and after they had gone out, they *began* saying to one another, "This man is not doing anything worthy of death or [even] of imprisonment."

³²And Agrippa said to Festus, "This man could have been set free if he had not appealed to Caesar (Emperor Nero)."

27

NOW WHEN it was deter-mined that we (including Luke) would sail for Italy, they turned Paul and some other prisoners over to a centurion of the Augustan Regiment named Julius.

²And going aboard a ship from Adramyttian which was about to sail for the ports along the [west] coast [province] of Asia [Minor], we put out to sea; and Aristarchus, a Macedonian from Thessalonica, accompanied us.

³The next day we landed at Sidon; and Julius, treating Paul with [thought-ful] consideration, allowed him to go to his friends *there* and be cared for *and* refreshed.

⁴From there we put out to sea and sailed to the leeward (sheltered) side of Cyprus [for protection from weather] because the winds were against us.

⁵When we had sailed across the sea along the coasts of Cilicia and Pam-phylia, we landed at Myra in Lycia [on the south coast of Asia Minor].

⁶There the centurion [Julius] found an Alexandrian ship [a grain ship of the Roman fleet] sailing for Italy, and he put us aboard it.

⁷For a number of days we sailed slowly and arrived with difficulty off Cnidus; then, because the wind did not allow us to go farther, we sailed under the leeward (sheltered) side of Crete, off Salmone;

⁸and hugging the shore with diffi-culty, we came to a place called Fair Havens, near the city of Lasea [on the south side of Crete].

⁹Now much time had been lost, and navigation was dangerous, because even [the time for] the fast (Day of Atonement) was already over, so Paul *began* to strongly warn them,

¹⁰saying, "Men, I sense [after care-ful thought and observation] that this voyage will certainly be a disaster and with great loss, not only of the cargo and the ship, but also of our lives."

¹¹However, the centurion [Julius, ranking officer on board] was per-suaded by the pilot and the owner of the ship rather than by what Paul said.

¹²Because the harbor was not well situated for wintering, the majority [of the sailors] decided to put to sea from there, hoping somehow to reach Phoe-nix, a harbor of Crete facing southwest and northwest, and spend the winter *there*.

¹³So when the south wind blew softly, thinking that they had obtained their goal, they weighed anchor and sailed along Crete, hugging the coast.

¹⁴But soon afterward a violent wind, called Euraquilo [a northeaster, a tem-pestuous windstorm like a typhoon], came rushing down from the island;

¹⁵and when the ship was caught in it and could not head against the wind [to gain stability], we gave up and [let-ting her drift] were driven along.

¹⁶We ran under the shelter of a small island [twenty-five miles south of Crete] called Clauda, and with great difficulty we were able to get the *ship's* skiff on the deck *and* secure it.

¹⁷After hoisting the skiff [on board], they used support lines [for frapping] to undergird *and* brace the ship's hull; and fearing that they might run aground on *the shallows of* Syrtis [off the north coast of Africa], they let down the sea anchor *and* lowered the sails and were driven along [back-wards with the bow into the wind].

¹⁸On the next day, as we were being violently tossed about by the storm [and taking on water], they began to jettison the cargo;

¹⁹and on the third day they threw the ship's tackle (spare lines, blocks, mis-cellaneous equipment) overboard with their own hands [to further reduce the weight].

²⁰Since neither sun nor stars ap-peared for many days, and no small storm kept raging about us, from then

on all hope of our being saved was [growing worse and worse and] gradually abandoned.

²¹After they had gone a long time without food [because of seasickness and stress], Paul stood up before them and said, "Men, you should have followed my advice and should not have set sail from Crete, and brought on this damage and loss.

²²"But *even* now I urge you to keep up your courage *and* be in good spirits, because there will be no loss of life among you, but *only loss* of the ship.

²³"For this very night an angel of the God to whom I belong and whom I serve stood before me,

²⁴and said, 'Stop being afraid, Paul. You must stand before Caesar; and behold, God has given you [the lives of] all those who are sailing with you.'

²⁵"So keep up your courage, men, for I believe God *and* have complete confidence in Him that it will turn out exactly as I have been told;

²⁶but we must run [the ship] aground on some island."

²⁷The fourteenth night had come and we were drifting *and* being driven about in the Adriatic Sea, when about midnight the sailors *began* to suspect that they were approaching some land.

²⁸So they took soundings [using a weighted line] and found [the depth to be] twenty fathoms (120 feet); and a little farther on they sounded again and found [the depth to be] fifteen fathoms (90 feet).

²⁹Then fearing that we might run aground somewhere on the rocks, they dropped four anchors from the stern [to slow the ship] and kept wishing for daybreak to come.

³⁰But as the sailors were trying to escape [secretly] from the ship and had let down the skiff into the sea, pretending that they were going to lay out anchors from the bow,

³¹Paul said to the centurion and the soldiers, "Unless these men remain on the ship, you cannot be saved."

³²Then the soldiers cut away the ropes that held the skiff and let it fall *and* drift away.

³³While they waited for the day to dawn, Paul encouraged them all [and told them] to have some food, saying, "This is the fourteenth day that you have been constantly on watch and going without food, having eaten nothing.

³⁴"So I urge you to eat some food, for this is for your survival; for not a hair from the head of any of you will perish."

³⁵Having said this, he took bread and gave thanks to God in front of them all, and he broke it and began to eat.

³⁶Then all of them were encouraged *and* their spirits improved, and they also ate some food.

³⁷All told there were two hundred and seventy-six of us aboard the ship.

³⁸After they had eaten enough, they *began* to lighten the ship by throwing the wheat [from Egypt] overboard into the sea.

³⁹When day came, they did not recognize the land, but they noticed a bay with a beach, and they decided to run the ship ashore there if they could.

⁴⁰So they cut the cables *and* severed the anchors and left them in the sea while at the same time unlashing the ropes of the rudders; and after hoisting the foresail to the wind, they headed steadily for the beach.

⁴¹But striking a reef with waves breaking in on either side, they ran the ship aground. The prow (forward point) stuck fast and remained immovable, while the stern *began* to break up under the [violent] force *of the waves.*

⁴²The soldiers' plan was to kill the prisoners, so that none of them would dive overboard *and* swim [to land] and escape;

⁴³but the centurion, wanting to save Paul, kept them from [carrying out] their plan. He commanded those who

could swim to jump overboard first and get to the shore;

⁴⁴and [he commanded] the rest *to follow*, some on [floating] planks, and others on various things from the ship. And so it was that all of them were brought safely to land.

28 AFTER WE were safe [on land], we found out that the island was called Malta.

²And the natives showed us extraordinary kindness *and* hospitality; for they kindled a fire and welcomed us all, since it had begun to rain and was cold.

³But when Paul had gathered a bundle of sticks and laid them on the fire, a viper crawled out because of the heat and fastened itself on his hand.

⁴When the natives saw the creature hanging from his hand, they *began* saying to one another, "Undoubtedly this man is a murderer, and though he has been saved from the sea, Justice [the avenging goddess] has not permitted him to live."

⁵Then Paul [simply] shook the creature off into the fire and suffered no ill effects.

⁶But they stood watching *and* expecting him to swell up or suddenly drop dead. But after they had waited a long time and had seen nothing unusual happen to him, they changed their minds and *began* saying that he was a god.

⁷In the vicinity of that place there were estates belonging to the leading man of the island, named Publius, who welcomed and entertained us hospitably for three days.

⁸And it happened that the father of Publius was sick [in bed] with recurring attacks of fever and dysentery; and Paul went to him, and after he had prayed, he laid his hands on him and healed him.

⁹After this occurred, the rest of the people on the island who had diseases were coming to him and being healed.

¹⁰They also gave us many honors [gifts and courtesies expressing respect]; and when we were setting sail, they supplied us with all the things we needed.

¹¹At the end of three months we set sail on a ship which had wintered at the island, an Alexandrian ship with the Twin Brothers [Castor and Pollux] as its figurehead.

¹²We landed at Syracuse [on Sicily] and stayed there three days.

¹³From there we sailed around and arrived at Rhegium [on Italy's southern tip]; and a day later a south wind came up, and on the second day we arrived at Puteoli.

¹⁴There we found some believers and were invited to stay with them for seven days. And so we came to Rome.

¹⁵And the brothers and sisters, having heard news about us, came from as far away as the Forum of Appius and Three Inns to meet us. When Paul saw them, he thanked God and was encouraged.

life point

Acts 28:1–5 tells the story of Paul and his traveling companions when they were shipwrecked on the island of Malta. Paul was busy gathering sticks to make a fire and dry his clothes when a poisonous snake, driven out of the flames, suddenly bit Paul's hand. The Bible says Paul simply shook it off into the fire and "suffered no ill effects" (Acts 28:5). You and I should do the same when things try to "bite" us—we too should be bold inwardly and shake it off!

Whatever may trouble you from the past, *shake it off!* God has a great future planned for you. The dreams of the future have no room for the snakebites of the past!

¹⁶When we entered Rome, Paul was allowed to stay by himself [in rented quarters] with the soldier who was guarding him.

¹⁷Three days later he called together the leaders of the Jews; and when they had gathered, he said to them, "Kinsmen, though I have done nothing against our people or against the customs of our fathers, yet I was turned over as a prisoner from Jerusalem into the hands of the Romans.

¹⁸"After they had interrogated me, they were ready to release me because I was not guilty of any offense deserving death.

¹⁹"But when the Jews objected [to my release], I was forced to appeal to Caesar (Emperor Nero), not because I had any charge to make against my nation.

²⁰"For this reason I have asked to see you and talk with you, since it is for the sake of the hope of Israel (the Messiah, the resurrection) that I am bound with this chain."

²¹They said to him, "We have not received [any] letters about you from Judea, nor have any of the [Jewish] brothers come here and reported or said anything bad about you.

²²"But we would like to hear from you what your views are [that is, exactly what you believe]; for in regard to this sect (Christianity), we are fully aware that it is denounced everywhere."

²³When they had set a day for Paul, they came to his lodging in large numbers. And he carefully explained [Christianity] to them from morning until evening, solemnly testifying about the kingdom of God and trying to persuade them concerning Jesus, both from the Law of Moses and from the [writings of the] Prophets.

²⁴Some were persuaded by what he said, but others would not believe.

²⁵They disagreed among themselves and they *began* to leave after Paul had made one *last* statement: "The Holy Spirit rightly spoke through Isaiah the prophet to your fathers, saying,

²⁶'GO TO THIS PEOPLE AND SAY,

"YOU WILL KEEP ON HEARING,
    BUT WILL NOT UNDERSTAND,
YOU WILL KEEP ON SEEING, BUT
    WILL NOT PERCEIVE;
²⁷"FOR THE HEART (the
    understanding, the soul) OF
    THIS PEOPLE HAS BECOME DULL
    (calloused),
AND WITH THEIR EARS THEY
    SCARCELY HEAR,
AND THEY HAVE SHUT THEIR EYES
    [to the truth];
OTHERWISE THEY MIGHT SEE WITH
    THEIR EYES,
AND HEAR WITH THEIR EARS,
AND UNDERSTAND WITH THEIR
    HEART AND RETURN [to Me],
AND I WOULD HEAL THEM."'
    [Is 6:9, 10]

²⁸"Therefore let it be known to you that [this message of] the salvation of God has been sent to the Gentiles; they indeed will listen!" [Ps 67:2]

²⁹[And when he had said these things, the Jews left, arguing among themselves.]

³⁰And Paul lived there for two full years [at his own expense] in his own rented lodging and welcomed all who came to him,

³¹preaching *and* proclaiming the kingdom of God and teaching about the Lord Jesus Christ with all openness *and* boldness, unhindered *and* unrestrained.

Romans

Author:
Paul

Date:
About AD 57.

Everyday Life Principles:
Separate your "who" from your "do."
You may do things that God is not
pleased with, but He is always pleased
with who you are because you are in
Christ.

We cannot do anything to earn or
deserve God's love; we receive it
as a gift from Him.

Jesus has made us righteous and
because of His death on the cross,
we are in right relationship with God.

The book of Romans contains many
vital truths that are essential to a
proper understanding of Christianity.
I personally feel that people who do
not know and understand Romans
will struggle to truly comprehend
what it means to have new life in
Christ and may fail to enjoy much of
the blessed life God has for His people.

I like to talk about the difference
between our "who" and our "do."
Though Paul did not use those
terms, much of the book of Romans
addresses that very issue with clarity
and detail. Paul understood so well
that the things we *do* are separate
from *who* we are. He teaches that
once we know who we are in Christ,
our behavior (our "do") will change,
but trying to just change behavior
will never work. He knows that
transformation comes to our "do"
as we understand our "who" from
God's perspective.

Many of Christianity's basic truths
are found in Romans: we cannot
earn God's love, but we must receive
it as a gift; everyone sins; sin requires
death; Jesus' death paid the price for
our sin; in Christ, we are made righteous; we do not have to live under
guilt and condemnation; *nothing* can
separate us from God's love.

As you read the book of Romans,
remember the truths on which our
faith is built. Remember especially
that you are righteous because of
Jesus (see Romans 3:26) and that
nothing can ever separate you from
the love of God (see Romans 8:35–39).

1 PAUL, A bond-servant of Christ Jesus, called as an apostle (special messenger, personally chosen representative), set apart for [preaching] the gospel of God [the good news of salvation],

²which He promised beforehand through His prophets in the sacred Scriptures—

³[the good news] regarding His Son, who, as to the flesh [His human nature], was born a descendant of David [to fulfill the covenant promises],

⁴and [as to His divine nature] according to the Spirit of holiness was openly designated to be the Son of God with power [in a triumphant and miraculous way] by *His* resurrection from the dead: Jesus Christ our Lord.

⁵It is through Him that we have received grace and [our] apostleship to promote obedience to the faith *and* make disciples for His name's sake among all the Gentiles,

⁶and you also are among those who are called of Jesus Christ to belong to Him;

⁷[I am writing] to all who are beloved of God in Rome, called to be saints (God's people) *and* set apart for a sanctified life, [that is, set apart for God and His purpose]: Grace to you and peace [inner calm and spiritual well-being] from God our Father and from the Lord Jesus Christ.

⁸First, I thank my God through Jesus Christ for all of you, because your faith [your trust and confidence in His power, wisdom, and goodness] is being proclaimed in all the world.

⁹For God, whom I serve with my spirit by *preaching* the gospel of His Son, is my witness as to how continuously I mention you

¹⁰in my prayers; always pleading that somehow, by God's will, I may now at last come to you.

¹¹For I long to see you so that I may share with you some spiritual gift, to strengthen *and* establish you;

¹²that is, that we may be mutually encouraged *and* comforted by each other's faith, both yours and mine.

¹³I do not want you to be unaware, brothers and sisters, that many times I have planned to come to you, (and have been prevented so far) so that I may have some fruit [of my labors] among you, even as *I have* among the rest of the Gentiles.

¹⁴I have a duty to perform *and* a debt to pay both to Greeks and to barbarians [the cultured and the uncultured], both to the wise and to the foolish.

¹⁵So, for my part, I am ready *and* eager to preach the gospel also to you who are in Rome.

¹⁶I am not ashamed of the gospel, for it is the power of God for salvation [from His wrath and punishment] to everyone who believes [in Christ as Savior], to the Jew first and also to the Greek.

¹⁷For in the gospel the righteousness of God is revealed, *both springing* from faith *and leading* to faith [disclosed in a way that awakens more faith]. As it is written *and* forever remains written, "THE JUST *and* UPRIGHT SHALL LIVE BY FAITH." [Hab 2:4]

¹⁸For [God does not overlook sin and] the wrath of God is revealed from heaven against all ungodliness and unrighteousness of men who in their wickedness suppress *and* stifle the truth,

¹⁹because that which is known about God is evident within them [in their inner consciousness], for God made it evident to them.

speak the Word

God, I declare that I am not ashamed of the Gospel of Jesus Christ, because it is Your power for salvation for everyone who believes.
—ADAPTED FROM ROMANS 1:16

²⁰For ever since the creation of the world His invisible attributes, His eternal power and divine nature, have been clearly seen, being understood through His workmanship [all His creation, the wonderful things that He has made], so that they [who fail to believe and trust in Him] are without excuse *and* without defense. [Ps 19:1–4; Eph 2:10]

²¹For even though they knew God [as the Creator], they did not *honor Him as God or give thanks [for His wondrous creation]. On the contrary, they became worthless in their thinking [godless, with pointless reasonings, and silly speculations], and their foolish heart was darkened.

²²Claiming to be wise, they became fools,

²³and exchanged the glory *and* majesty *and* excellence of the immortal God for an image [worthless idols] in the shape of mortal man and birds and four-footed animals and reptiles.

²⁴Therefore God gave them over in the lusts of their own hearts to [sexual] impurity, so that their bodies would be dishonored among them

consistent, confident faith

Romans 1:17 teaches us that people who are just and upright "shall live by faith." Faith is confidence in God. It is important that we learn to be *consistently* confident, not *occasionally* confident. Let me give you an example to illustrate what I mean.

In ministry, I learned to remain confident in God when someone got up and walked out while I was preaching. In the beginning of my ministry, that type of occurrence brought out all of my insecurities and practically destroyed my confidence. In addition, due to a lack of properly understanding God's Word, some of our friends and family members told me that a woman should not preach the Word of God. I also knew that some people, particularly men, had difficulty receiving the Word from a woman. This was confusing to me because I knew God called me and anointed me to preach His Word. I could not have done it otherwise, but people's rejection still affected me because I lacked confidence. I had to grow in confidence to the place where people's opinions and their acceptance or rejection did not alter my confidence level. My confidence had to be in God, not in people.

When the growth and progress of my ministry seemed painfully slow, I had to practice being consistently confident. It is easier to remain confident when we see progress, but during times of waiting the devil attacks our confidence and attempts to destroy it. But we can resist him, and we need to do so.

Romans 1:17 speaks about the whole issue of faith. It says that we will live by faith. The King James Version of this verse says the righteousness of God is revealed "from faith to faith." I spent many years going from faith to doubt to unbelief and then back to faith. I lost a lot of precious time until I became consistent in my faith walk. Since then, I have tried to practice being confident in all things with God's help.

You can have consistent and confident faith too. Ask God to help you resist the enemy's attack when he tries to rob you of that faith. Learn to go from "faith to faith" with overcoming confidence.

1:21 Lit *glorify*.

[abandoning them to the degrading power of sin],

²⁵because [by choice] they exchanged the truth of God for a lie, and worshiped and served the creature rather than the Creator, who is blessed forever! Amen. [Jer 2:11]

²⁶For this reason God gave them over to degrading *and* vile passions; for their women exchanged the natural function for that which is unnatural [a function contrary to nature],

²⁷and in the same way also the men turned away from the natural function of the woman and were consumed with their desire toward one another, men with men committing shameful acts and in return receiving in their own bodies the inevitable *and* appropriate penalty for their wrongdoing.

²⁸And since they did not see fit to acknowledge God *or* consider Him worth knowing [as their Creator], God gave them over to a depraved mind, to do things which are improper *and* repulsive,

²⁹until they were filled (permeated, saturated) with every kind of unrighteousness, wickedness, greed, evil; full of envy, murder, strife, deceit, malice *and* mean-spiritedness. They are gossips [spreading rumors],

³⁰slanderers, haters of God, insolent, arrogant, boastful, inventors [of new forms] of evil, disobedient *and* disrespectful to parents,

³¹without understanding, untrustworthy, unloving, unmerciful [without pity].

³²Although they know God's righteous decree *and* His judgment, that those who do such things deserve death, yet they not only do them, but they even [enthusiastically] approve *and* tolerate others who practice them.

2 THEREFORE YOU have no excuse *or* justification, everyone of you who [hypocritically] judges

and condemns others; for in passing judgment on another person, you condemn yourself, because you who judge [from a position of arrogance or self-righteousness] are *habitually* practicing the very same things [which you denounce].

²And we know that the judgment of God falls justly *and* in accordance with truth on those who practice such things.

³But do you think this, O man, when you judge *and* condemn those who practice such things, and yet do the

life point

Romans 2:1 teaches us that the things we judge in other people are the very things we do ourselves.

The Lord once gave me a good example to help me understand this principle. I was pondering why we would do something ourselves, thinking it was perfectly all right, but then judge someone else for doing it. He showed me that I was looking at myself through rose-colored glasses, but at everyone else through a magnifying glass.

We make excuses for our own behavior, but when someone else behaves exactly the same way, we are often merciless. Treating others as we want them to treat us (see Matthew 7:12) is a good life principle to follow, one that prevents us from indulging in judgment and criticism.

Judgmental thoughts come from a negative mind—a mind that thinks about what is wrong with someone instead of what is right.

I encourage you to learn to be positive and not negative. Others will appreciate your upbeat attitude, but you will benefit more than anyone.

same yourself, that you will escape God's judgment *and* elude His verdict?

⁴Or do you have no regard for the wealth of His kindness and tolerance and patience [in withholding His wrath]? Are you [actually] unaware *or* ignorant [of the fact] that God's kindness leads you to repentance [that is, to change your inner self, your old way of thinking—seek His purpose for your life]?

⁵But because of your callous stubbornness and unrepentant heart you are [deliberately] storing up wrath for yourself on the day of wrath when God's righteous judgment will be revealed.

⁶He WILL PAY BACK TO EACH PERSON ACCORDING TO HIS DEEDS [justly, as his deeds deserve]: [Ps 62:12; Prov 24:12] ⁷to those who by persistence in doing good seek [unseen but certain heavenly] glory, honor, and immortality, [He will give the gift of] eternal life.

⁸But for those who are selfishly ambitious *and* self-seeking and disobedient to the truth but responsive to wickedness, [there will be] wrath and indignation.

⁹*There will be* tribulation and anguish [torturing confinement] for every human soul who does [or permits] evil, to the Jew first and also to the Greek,

¹⁰but glory and honor and *inner* peace [will be given] to everyone who *habitually* does good, to the Jew first and also to the Greek.

¹¹For God shows no partiality [no arbitrary favoritism; with Him one person is not more important than another]. [Deut 10:17; 2 Chr 19:7]

¹²For all who have sinned without the Law will also perish without [regard to] the Law, and all who have sinned under the Law will be judged *and* condemned by the Law.

¹³For it is not those who merely hear the Law [as it is read aloud] who are just *or* righteous before God, but it is those who [actually] obey the Law who will be justified [pronounced free of the guilt of sin and declared acceptable to Him].

¹⁴When Gentiles, who do not have the Law [since it was given only to Jews], do instinctively the things the Law requires [guided only by their conscience], they are a law to themselves, though they do not have the Law.

¹⁵They show that the essential requirements of the Law are written in their hearts; and their conscience [their sense of right and wrong, their moral choices] bearing witness and their thoughts alternately accusing or perhaps defending them

¹⁶on that day when, as my gospel proclaims, God will judge the secrets [all the hidden thoughts and concealed sins] of men through Christ Jesus. [Eccl 12:14]

¹⁷But if you bear the name "Jew" and rely on the Law [for your salvation] and boast in [your special relationship to] God,

¹⁸and [if you claim to] know His will and approve the things that are essential *or* have a sense of what is excellent, based on your instruction from the Law,

¹⁹and [if you] are confident that you are a [qualified] guide to the blind [those untaught in theology], a light to those who are in darkness,

²⁰and [that you are] a corrector of the foolish, a teacher of the [spiritually] childish, having in the Law the

speak the Word

Thank you, God, that You show no partiality or favoritism.
With You, one person is not more important than another.
—ADAPTED FROM ROMANS 2:11

embodiment of knowledge and of the truth—

²¹well then, you who teach others, do you not teach yourself? You who preach against stealing, do you steal [in ways that are discrete, but just as sinful]?

²²You who say that one must not commit adultery, do you commit adultery? You who detest idols, do you rob [pagan] temples [of valuable idols and offerings]? [Deut 7:25; Acts 19:37]

²³You who boast in the Law, do you [repeatedly] dishonor God by breaking the Law?

²⁴For, "THE NAME OF GOD IS BLAS-PHEMED AMONG THE GENTILES BECAUSE OF YOU," just as it is written [in Scripture]. [Is 52:5; Ezek 36:20]

²⁵Circumcision [the sign of the covenant of Abraham] is indeed of value if you practice the Law; but if you *habitually* break the Law, your circumcision has become uncircumcision [it is meaningless in God's sight].

²⁶So if the uncircumcised man keeps the requirements of the Law, will not his uncircumcision be regarded [by God] as circumcision?

²⁷Then he who is physically uncircumcised but keeps [the spirit of] the Law will judge you who, even though you have the written code and circumcision, break the Law.

²⁸For he is not a [real] Jew who is only one outwardly, nor is [true] circumcision something external and physical.

²⁹But he is a Jew who is one inwardly; and [true] circumcision is *circumcision* of the heart, by the Spirit, not by [the fulfillment of] the letter [of the Law]. His praise is not from men, but from God.

3 THEN WHAT is the advantage of the Jew? Or what is the benefit of circumcision?

²Great in every respect. To begin with, the Jews were entrusted with the oracles of God [His very words]. [Ps 147:19]

³What then? If some did not believe *or* were unfaithful [to God], their lack of belief will not nullify *and* make invalid the faithfulness of God *and* His word, will it?

⁴Certainly not! Let God be found true [as He will be], though every person *be found* a liar, just as it is written [in Scripture],

"THAT YOU MAY BE JUSTIFIED
 IN YOUR WORDS,
AND PREVAIL WHEN YOU ARE
 JUDGED [by sinful men]." [Ps 51:4]

⁵But if our unrighteousness demonstrates the righteousness of God, what shall we say? God is not wrong to inflict His wrath [on us], is He? (I am speaking in purely human terms.)

⁶Certainly not! For *otherwise,* how will God judge the world?

⁷But [as you might say] if through my lie God's truth was magnified *and* abounded to His glory, why am I still being judged as a sinner?

⁸And why not say, (as some slanderously report and claim that we teach) "Let us do evil so that good may come of it"? Their condemnation [by God] is just.

⁹Well then, are we [Jews] better off than they? Not at all; for we have already charged that both Jews and Greeks (Gentiles) are under the control of sin *and* subject to its power.

¹⁰As it is written *and* forever remains written,

"THERE IS NONE RIGHTEOUS [none
 that meets God's standard], NOT
 EVEN ONE. [Ps 14:3]
¹¹"THERE IS NONE WHO UNDERSTANDS,
THERE IS NONE WHO SEEKS FOR GOD.
 [Ps 14:2]
¹²"ALL HAVE TURNED ASIDE, TOGETHER
 THEY HAVE BECOME USELESS;
THERE IS NONE WHO DOES GOOD, NO,
 NOT ONE." [Ps 53:1–3]

¹³ "THEIR THROAT IS AN OPEN GRAVE;
THEY [habitually] DECEIVE WITH
THEIR TONGUES."
"THE VENOM OF ASPS IS BENEATH
THEIR LIPS." [Ps 5:9; 140:3]

¹⁴ "THEIR MOUTH IS FULL OF CURSING
AND BITTERNESS." [Ps 10:7]

¹⁵ "THEIR FEET ARE SWIFT TO SHED
BLOOD,

¹⁶ DESTRUCTION AND MISERY ARE IN
THEIR PATHS,

¹⁷ AND THEY HAVE NOT KNOWN THE
PATH OF PEACE." [Is 59:7, 8]

¹⁸ "THERE IS NO FEAR OF GOD [and
His awesome power] BEFORE
THEIR EYES." [Ps 36:1]

¹⁹Now we know that whatever the
Law [of Moses] says, it speaks to those
who are under the Law, so that [the excuses of] every mouth may be silenced
[from protesting] and that all the world
may be held accountable to God [and
subject to His judgment].

²⁰For no person will be justified [freed
of guilt and declared righteous] in His
sight by [trying to do] the works of the
Law. For through the Law we become
conscious of sin [and the recognition of
sin directs us toward repentance, but
provides no remedy for sin].

²¹But now the righteousness of
God has been clearly revealed [inde-
pendently and completely] apart from
the Law, though it is [actually] confirmed by the Law and the [words and
writings of the] Prophets.

²²This righteousness of God comes
through faith in Jesus Christ for all
those [Jew or Gentile] who believe [and
trust in Him and acknowledge Him as
God's Son]. There is no distinction,
[1 Cor 12:13; Gal 3:28]

life point

Romans 3:17 describes how my life used
to be. I had no experience with enjoying
a peaceful life; I did not even know how
to begin. I grew up in an atmosphere of
strife, and that was all I ever knew. I had
to learn an entirely new way of living.

Now I am addicted to peace. As soon as
my peace disappears, I ask myself how I
lost it and start looking for ways to get it
back.

I believe you can become so hungry for
peace with God, peace with yourself, and
peace with others that you will be willing
to make any adjustment you need to make
in order to have it. Let me encourage
you to begin to follow peace at all times
because peace will lead you into God's
perfect will for your life.

²³since all have sinned and *continually* fall short of the glory of God,

²⁴and are being justified [declared
free of the guilt of sin, made acceptable to God, and granted eternal life]
as a gift by His [precious, undeserved]
grace, through the redemption [the
payment for our sin] which is [pro-
vided] in Christ Jesus,

²⁵whom God displayed publicly [be-
fore the eyes of the world] as a [life-
giving] sacrifice of atonement *and*
reconciliation (propitiation) by His
blood [to be received] through faith.
This was to demonstrate His righteousness [which demands punishment for
sin], because in His forbearance [His
deliberate restraint] He passed over

speak the Word

Thank You, Lord, that I am justified and made acceptable to You
through the gift of Your grace and through the redemption
You have provided for me in Christ Jesus.
—ADAPTED FROM ROMANS 3:24

the sins previously committed [before Jesus' crucifixion].

^{26}*It was* to demonstrate His righteousness at the present time, so that He would be just and the One who justifies those who have faith in Jesus [and rely confidently on Him as Savior].

^{27}Then what becomes of [our] boasting? It is excluded [entirely ruled out, banished]. On what principle? On [the principle of good] works? No, but on the principle of faith.

^{28}For we maintain that an individual is justified by faith distinctly apart from works of the Law [the observance of which has nothing to do with justification, that is, being declared free of the guilt of sin and made acceptable to God].

life point

If we truly desire to succeed at being ourselves, we need a thorough understanding of what justifies us and makes us right with God. Romans 3:28 gives us great news! It tells us we are justified by faith in Christ alone and not by our works (see also Ephesians 2:8, 9).

If we have real faith, we will do good works, but our dependence will not be on works. Our works will be done as acts of love for God—in obedience to Him—rather than as works of the flesh by which we hope to gain right standing and acceptance with Him.

all have sinned

We sometimes fall into the trap of thinking we are the worst person on the face of the earth and that nobody does as many wrong things as we do. But Romans 3:23 says that *"all* have sinned and continually fall short of the glory of God" (emphasis mine). Every man, woman, or child who was ever born, or ever will be, has a problem with sin. But the good news is that God has provided an answer to our dilemma.

Just as all have sinned, all are justified and made righteous through the redemption provided in Christ Jesus. That means that, as believers in Him, we now have "rightness" instead of "wrongness." For much of my life I felt all wrong. I had a recording playing in my head over and over again: "What is wrong with me?"

Satan wants us to feel wrong, worthless, and like a hopeless mess. He knows that without confidence we will never step out in faith to fulfill our God-ordained destiny. He knows if he can keep us in the prison of self-hatred, self-rejection, or just plain not liking ourselves that he will prevent us from making progress or ever being a threat to him and to the kingdom of darkness.

We must believe we have been made righteous in God's sight before we will behave rightly. We cannot produce the fruit of something for which no seed has been sown. Jesus Himself is the Righteous Seed sown in death and resurrected in power, so we can say along with the Apostle Paul, "He made Christ who knew no sin to [judicially] be sin on our behalf, so that in Him we would become the righteousness of God [that is, we would be made acceptable to Him and placed in a right relationship with Him by His gracious lovingkindness]" (2 Corinthians 5:21).

²⁹Or is God *the God* of Jews only? Is He not also *the God* of Gentiles [who were not given the Law]? Yes, of Gentiles also,

³⁰since indeed it is one [and the same] God who will justify the circumcised by faith [which began with Abraham] and the uncircumcised through [their newly acquired] faith.

³¹Do we then nullify the Law by this faith [making the Law of no effect, overthrowing it]? Certainly not! On the contrary, we confirm *and* establish *and* uphold the Law [since it convicts us all of sin, pointing to the need for salvation].

4 WHAT THEN shall we say that Abraham, our forefather humanly speaking, has found? [Has he obtained a favored standing?] ²For if Abraham was justified [that is, acquitted from the guilt of his sins] by works [those things he did that were good], he has something to boast about, but not before God.

³For what does the Scripture say? "ABRAHAM BELIEVED IN (trusted, relied on) GOD, AND IT WAS CREDITED TO HIS ACCOUNT AS RIGHTEOUSNESS (right living, right standing with God)." [Gen 15:6]

⁴Now to a laborer, his wages are not credited as a favor *or* a gift, but as an obligation [something owed to him].

⁵But to the one who does not work [that is, the one who does not try to earn his salvation by doing good], but believes *and* completely trusts in Him who justifies the ungodly, his faith is credited to him as righteousness (right standing with God).

⁶And in this same way David speaks of the blessing on the one to whom God credits righteousness apart from works:

⁷"BLESSED *and* HAPPY *and* FAVORED ARE THOSE WHOSE LAWLESS ACTS HAVE BEEN FORGIVEN, AND WHOSE SINS HAVE BEEN COVERED UP *and* COMPLETELY BURIED.

⁸"BLESSED *and* HAPPY *and* FAVORED IS THE MAN WHOSE SIN THE LORD WILL NOT TAKE INTO ACCOUNT *nor* CHARGE AGAINST HIM." [Ps 32:1, 2]

⁹Is this blessing only for the circumcised, or also for the uncircumcised? For we say, "FAITH WAS CREDITED TO ABRAHAM AS RIGHTEOUSNESS."

¹⁰How then was it credited [to him]? Was it after he had been circumcised, or before? Not after, but while [he was] uncircumcised.

¹¹He received the sign of circumcision, a seal *or* confirmation of the righteousness which he had by faith while [he was still] uncircumcised—this was so that he would be the [spiritual] father of all who believe without being circumcised—so that righteousness would be credited to them,

¹²and [that he would be] the [spiritual] father of those circumcised who are not only circumcised, but who also walk in the steps of the faith of our father Abraham which he had before he was circumcised.

¹³For the promise to Abraham or to his descendants that he would be heir of the world was not through [observing the requirements of] the Law, but through the righteousness of faith. [Gen 17:4–6; 22:16–18]

¹⁴If those who are [followers] of the Law are [the true] heirs [of Abraham], then faith [leading to salvation] is of no effect *and* void, and the promise [of God] is nullified.

¹⁵For the Law results in [God's] wrath [against sin], but where there is no law, there is no violation [of it either].

¹⁶Therefore, [inheriting] the promise depends entirely on faith [that is, confident trust in the unseen God], in order that *it may be given* as an act of grace [His unmerited favor and mercy], so that the promise will be [legally]

life point

I encourage you to take a positive look at the possibilities of the future and call "into being that which does not exist" (Romans 4:17). Think and speak about your future in a positive way according to what God has placed in your heart—not according to what you have seen in the past or are seeing even now in the present. He has a great future for you. Believe it and confess it!

guaranteed to all the descendants [of Abraham]—not only for those [Jewish believers] who keep the Law, but also for those [Gentile believers] who share the faith of Abraham, who is the [spiritual] father of us all—

¹⁷(as it is written [in Scripture], "I HAVE MADE YOU A FATHER OF MANY NATIONS") in the sight of Him in whom he believed, that is, God who gives life to the dead and calls into being that which does not exist. [Gen 17:5]

¹⁸In hope against hope Abraham believed that he would become a father

life point

Look beyond where you are and see with the eyes of faith, believing God for even the impossible! Romans 4:18 says that Abraham had no reason at all to hope, but he hoped in faith that God's promise to him would be fulfilled (see Genesis 15:5). A hopeful mind and attitude leads to peace and joy, while fear and discouragement steal peace and joy.

It costs nothing to be positive and believe God can change you and your life. Jump-start your blessings by saying you love your life, and be thankful in all things, no matter what the circumstances may be.

of many nations, as he had been promised [by God]: "SO [numberless] SHALL YOUR DESCENDANTS BE." [Gen 15:5]

¹⁹Without becoming weak in faith he considered his own body, now as good as dead [for producing children] since he was about a hundred years old, and [he considered] the deadness of Sarah's womb. [Gen 17:17; 18:11]

²⁰But he did not doubt *or* waver in unbelief concerning the promise of God, but he grew strong *and* empowered by faith, giving glory to God,

²¹being fully convinced that God had the power to do what He had promised.

life point

Romans 4:18–21 reminds us that God promised Abraham he would have an heir from his own body (see Genesis 15:1–6). Many years came and went, and still there was no child as a result of Abraham and Sarah's relationship. Abraham still stood in faith, believing that what God had said would come to pass. As he stood, he was attacked with thoughts of doubt, and the spirit of unbelief pressed him to disobey God.

Disobedience in a situation like this can simply mean giving up when God prompts us to press on. Disobedience is disregarding the voice of the Lord, or whatever God is speaking to us personally, not just transgressing the Ten Commandments or a specific Bible verse.

Romans 4:20 states that Abraham did not doubt God's promises. In fact, he waited on God, he became stronger and more empowered in his faith and kept giving glory to God. He felt confident that God would keep His word. Take Abraham's example and keep your heart filled with faith and your actions filled with obedience.

faith for fulfillment

When I am in a battle, knowing what God has promised but still experiencing attacks of doubt and unbelief, I like to meditate on Romans 4:18–21.

When God tells us something or asks us to do something, the faith to believe or do it comes with that word from Him. It is ridiculous to think God would expect us to do something without giving us the ability to believe we can do it. Satan knows how dangerous we are when our hearts are full of faith, so he attacks us with doubt and unbelief.

It isn't that we do not have faith; it is just that Satan tries to destroy our faith with lies.

Let me give you an example concerning the time I received my call to the ministry. It was an ordinary morning like any other, except that I had just finished listening to my first Christian teaching tape. I was stirred in my heart and amazed that anyone could teach from one scripture for a whole hour, and that all of his teaching would be interesting. I suddenly felt an intense desire to teach God's Word well up in me. Then the voice of the Lord came to me saying, "You will go all over the place and teach My Word, and you will have a large teaching tape ministry." I did not hear God's audible voice, but I did hear a still small voice deep inside of me.

There would have been no natural reason at all for me to believe that God actually spoke to me, or that I could or ever would do what I thought I heard. I had many problems within myself. I did not look like "ministry material," but God chooses the weak and foolish things of the world to put the wise to shame (see 1 Corinthians 1:27). He looks on the heart of man and not the outward appearance (see 1 Samuel 16:7). If a person's inner heart is right, God can change the outside.

Although there was nothing in the natural realm to indicate that I should believe when the desire for a teaching ministry came over me, I was filled with faith that I could do what the Lord wanted me to do. When God calls, He gives desire, faith, and ability to do the job. But, I also want to tell you that during the years I spent in training and waiting, the devil regularly attacked me with doubt and unbelief.

God places dreams and visions in the hearts of His people; they begin as little "seeds." Just as a woman has a seed planted into her womb when she becomes pregnant, so we become "pregnant," so to speak, with the things God speaks and promises. During the "pregnancy," Satan works hard to try and get us to "abort" our dreams. One of the tools he uses is doubt; another is unbelief. Both of these work against the mind.

Faith is a product of the spirit; it is a spiritual force. The enemy does not want your mind to agree with your spirit. He knows that if God places in you the faith to do something, and you develop a positive attitude and start consistently believing you can actually do it, then you will do considerable damage to his kingdom.

I encourage you to be assured in your faith that God will follow through on what He has promised you by His Word. Get His promises into your mind; think about them; speak of them; and let your faith increase.

putting the Word to work

Have you ever wondered if God can really do what He has promised? Abraham had good reason to doubt—God promised him a child even though he and his wife were far beyond childbearing years. Yet God's Word tells us that Abraham's faith grew stronger as he waited for the fulfillment of God's promise (see Romans 4:20). When you are tempted to doubt God's promises, ask God to give you growing faith like Abraham's so you too will be convinced that what God promises, He will fulfill in your life.

²²Therefore his faith WAS CREDITED TO HIM AS RIGHTEOUSNESS (right standing with God). [Gen 15:6]

²³Now not for his sake alone was it written that it was credited to him,

²⁴but for our sake also—to whom righteousness will be credited, as those who believe in Him who raised Jesus our Lord from the dead—

²⁵who was betrayed *and* crucified because of our sins, and was raised [from the dead] because of our justification [our acquittal—absolving us of all sin before God].

5 THEREFORE, SINCE we have been justified [that is, acquitted of sin, declared blameless before God] by faith, [let us grasp the fact that] we have peace with God [and the joy of reconciliation with Him] through our Lord Jesus Christ (the Messiah, the Anointed).

²Through Him we also have access by faith into this [remarkable state of] grace in which we [firmly and safely and securely] stand. Let us rejoice in our hope *and* the confident assurance of [experiencing and enjoying] the glory of [our great] God [the manifestation of His excellence and power].

³And not only *this,* but [with joy] let us exult in our sufferings *and* rejoice in our hardships, knowing that hardship (distress, pressure, trouble) produces patient endurance;

⁴and endurance, proven character (spiritual maturity); and proven character, hope *and* confident assurance [of eternal salvation].

⁵Such hope [in God's promises] never disappoints *us,* because God's love has been abundantly poured out within our hearts through the Holy Spirit who was given to us.

⁶While we were still helpless [powerless to provide for our salvation], at the right time Christ died [as a substitute] for the ungodly.

⁷Now it is an extraordinary thing for one to willingly give his life even for an upright man, though perhaps for a good man [one who is noble and selfless and worthy] someone might even dare to die.

⁸But God clearly shows *and* proves His own love for us, by the fact that while we were still sinners, Christ died for us.

⁹Therefore, since we have now been justified [declared free of the guilt of sin] by His blood, [how much more certain is it that] we will be saved from the wrath *of God* through Him.

¹⁰For if while we were enemies we were reconciled to God through the death of His Son, *it is* much more *certain,* having been reconciled, that we will be saved [from the consequences of sin] by His life [that is, we will be saved because Christ lives today].

¹¹Not only that, but we also rejoice in God [rejoicing in His love and perfection] through our Lord Jesus Christ, through whom we have now received *and* enjoy our reconciliation [with God]. [Jer 9:24]

¹²Therefore, just as sin came into

you are loved

Romans 5:5 says that the love of God is poured out in our hearts through the Holy Spirit, Whom He gave to us. This simply means that when the Lord, in the form of the Holy Spirit, comes to dwell in our hearts through our faith in His Son Jesus Christ, He brings love with Him, because God is love (see 1 John 4:8).

We all need to ask ourselves what we are doing with the love of God that has been given freely to us. Do we reject it because we don't think we are valuable enough to be loved? Do we believe God is like other people who have rejected and hurt us? Or do we receive His love by faith, believing He is greater than our failures and weaknesses?

What kind of relationship do you have with God, with yourself, and ultimately with others?

For a long time, I did not know I had a relationship with myself. It was something I never thought of until God began teaching me in this area. I now realize that I spend more time with myself than with anyone else, and it is vital that I get along well with myself. Of course, the same is true for you too.

We all know how agonizing it is to work day after day with someone we do not get along with, but at least we do not have to take that person home with us at night. But we are with ourselves all the time, day and night. We never have one minute away from ourselves, not even one second—therefore, it is of the utmost importance that we have peace with ourselves and accept God's love in our hearts. I encourage you to receive God's love in a fresh way today.

the world through one man, and death through sin, so death spread to all people [no one being able to stop it or escape its power], because they all sinned.

¹³Sin was [committed] in the world before the Law [was given], but sin is not charged [against anyone] when there is no law [against it].

¹⁴Yet death ruled [over mankind] from Adam to Moses [the Lawgiver], even over those who had not sinned as Adam did. Adam is a type of Him (Christ) who was to come [but in reverse—Adam brought destruction, Christ brought salvation]. [Gen 5:5; 7:22; Deut 34:5]

¹⁵But the free gift [of God] is not like the trespass [because the gift of grace overwhelms the fall of man]. For if many died by one man's trespass [Adam's sin], much more [abundantly] did God's grace and the gift [that comes] by the grace of the one Man, Jesus Christ, overflow to [benefit] the many.

¹⁶Nor is the gift [of grace] like *that which came* through the one who sinned. For on the one hand the judgment

putting the Word to work

Would you give your life for someone who despised you? That is exactly what Jesus did, according to Romans 5:6–8. God loved you so much that even before you loved Him, when you were against Him, He sent Jesus to die for you. Thank God for His awesome love today!

[following the sin] *resulted* from one trespass and brought condemnation, but on the other hand the free gift *resulted* from many trespasses and brought justification [the release from sin's penalty for those who believe].

¹⁷For if by the trespass of the one (Adam), death reigned through the one (Adam), much more *surely* will those who receive the abundance of grace and the free gift of righteousness reign in [eternal] life through the One, Jesus Christ.

life point

What do you believe about yourself? Do you believe you must have approval from people in order to be happy? If so, you will never be happy when anyone disapproves of you. Do you believe that you are all wrong? If you do, you will continue to produce wrong behavior. Your life will bear fruit on the outside of what you believe about yourself on the inside.

God wants us to behave correctly, so He gives us what we need in order to do that. God never requires us to do something without giving us what we need to do it. God gives us the gift of righteousness so we can become righteous in what we think, say, and do! Although we sin, God's free gift of righteousness cannot even be compared to our sin. Our sin is great, but His free gift of righteousness is greater. Our sin is swallowed up in His righteousness. Our righteousness is not found in what people think of us, it is found in Christ. Romans 5:17 says that God's free gift of righteousness is ours through Jesus Christ.

Let that truth sink into your heart and mind. Jesus Christ is your righteousness. You are righteous in Him, and because of that God is pleased with you.

¹⁸So then as through one trespass [Adam's sin] there resulted condemnation for all men, even so through one act of righteousness there resulted justification of life to all men.

¹⁹For just as through one man's disobedience [his failure to hear, his carelessness] the many were made sinners, so through the obedience of the one Man the many will be made righteous *and* acceptable to God *and* brought into right standing with Him.

²⁰But the Law came to increase *and* expand [the awareness of] the trespass [by defining and unmasking sin]. But where sin increased, [God's remarkable, gracious gift of] grace [His unmerited favor] has surpassed it *and* increased all the more,

²¹so that, as sin reigned in death, so also grace would reign through righteousness which brings eternal life through Jesus Christ our Lord.

6 WHAT SHALL we say [to all this]? Should we continue in sin *and* practice sin as a habit so that [God's gift of] grace may increase *and* overflow?

²Certainly not! How can we, the very ones who died to sin, *continue to* live in it any longer?

³Or are you ignorant of the fact that all of us who have been baptized into Christ Jesus were baptized into His death?

⁴We have therefore been buried with Him through baptism into death, so that just as Christ was raised from the dead through the glory *and* power of the Father, we too might walk *habitually* in newness of life [abandoning our old ways].

⁵For if we have become one with Him [permanently united] in the likeness of His death, we will also certainly be [one with Him and share fully] *in the likeness* of His resurrection.

⁶We know that our old self [our

the power of obedience

Romans 5:19 teaches us that our choices to obey or not to obey not only affect us, but many other people too. We see an example of this in Scripture when the Israelites experienced the fruit of their disobedience after their exodus from Egypt. Had they promptly obeyed God, their lives would have been so much better (see Hebrews 3:8–11)! Many of them and their children died in the wilderness because they would not submit to God's ways. Their children were affected by their decisions, and so are ours.

Recently, my oldest son said, "Mom, I have something to tell you, and I may cry, but hear me out. I have been thinking about you and Dad and the years you have put into this ministry, and all the times you chose to obey God and how it has not always been easy for you. I realize, Mom, that you and Dad have gone through things that nobody knows about, and I want you to know that this morning God made me aware that I am benefiting greatly from your obedience, and I appreciate it."

What he said meant a lot to me, and it reminded me of Romans 5:19.

Your decision to obey God affects other people, and when you decide to disobey God, that also affects others too. You may disobey God and choose to stay in the wilderness, but please keep in mind that if you now have children or ever will have children, your decisions will keep them in the wilderness with you. They may manage to get themselves out when they are grown, but I can assure you that they will pay a price for your disobedience.

Obedience is a far-reaching choice; it closes the gates of hell and opens the windows of heaven, and it has the power to affect many people. Just think of it: Because of Jesus' willingness to be obedient, countless multitudes will be brought into right standing with God.

Your life might be in better shape now had someone in your past obeyed God. If there is a cycle of disobedience in your family or among your friends, why not break it by refusing to be disobedient in your life? Tell God you want to obey and ask Him to help you. That way, you will set up yourself and your children for great blessings!

human nature without the Holy Spirit] was nailed to the cross with *Him,* in order that our body of sin might be done away with, so that we would no longer be slaves to sin.

⁷For the person who has died [with Christ] has been freed from [the power of] sin.

⁸Now if we have died with Christ, we believe that we will also live [together] with Him,

⁹because we know [the self-evident truth] that Christ, having been raised from the dead, will never die again; death no longer has power over Him.

¹⁰For the death that He died, He died to sin [ending its power and paying the sinner's debt] once and for all; and the life that He lives, He lives to [glorify] God [in unbroken fellowship with Him].

¹¹Even so, consider yourselves to be dead to sin [and your relationship to it broken], but alive to God [in unbroken fellowship with Him] in Christ Jesus.

¹²Therefore do not let sin reign in your mortal body so that you obey its lusts *and* passions.

¹³Do not go on offering members of your body to sin as instruments of wickedness. But offer yourselves to God [in a decisive act] as those alive [raised] from the dead [to a new life], and your members [all of your abilities—sanctified, set apart] as instruments of righteousness [yielded] to God.

¹⁴For sin will no longer be a master over you, since you are not under Law [as slaves], but under [unmerited] grace [as recipients of God's favor and mercy].

¹⁵What then [are we to conclude]? Shall we sin because we are not under Law, but under [God's] grace? Certainly not!

¹⁶Do you not know that when you *continually* offer yourselves to someone to do his will, you are the slaves of the one whom you obey, either [slaves] of sin, which leads to death, or of obedience, which leads to righteousness (right standing with God)?

¹⁷But thank God that though you were slaves of sin, you became obedient with all your heart to the standard of teaching in which you were instructed *and* to which you were committed.

¹⁸And having been set free from sin, you have become the slaves of righteousness [of conformity to God's will and purpose].

¹⁹I am speaking in [familiar] human terms because of your natural limitations [your spiritual immaturity]. For just as you presented your bodily members as slaves to impurity and to [moral] lawlessness, leading to further lawlessness, so now offer your members [your abilities, your talents] as slaves to righteousness, leading to sanctification [that is, being set apart for God's purpose].

putting the Word to work

Romans 6:15 says that the fact that we know we will receive forgiveness does not mean we are free to sin! Grace is not meant to encourage sin. Rather, we are to live in obedience. Is there an area of sin in your life that you struggle with? Do not treat it casually because you know you will be forgiven, but ask God to strengthen you and to help you break free from it.

²⁰When you were slaves of sin, you were free in regard to righteousness [you had no desire to conform to God's will].

²¹So what benefit did you get at that time from the things of which you are now ashamed? [None!] For the outcome of those things is death!

²²But now since you have been set free from sin and have become [willing] slaves to God, you have your benefit, resulting in sanctification [being made holy and set apart for God's purpose], and the outcome [of this] is eternal life.

²³For the wages of sin is death, but the free gift of God [that is, His remarkable, overwhelming gift of grace to believers] is eternal life in Christ Jesus our Lord.

7 OR DO you not know, brothers and sisters (for I am speaking to those who know the Law), that the Law has jurisdiction [to rule] over a person as long as he lives?

²For the married woman [as an example] is bound *and* remains bound by law to her husband while he lives; but if her husband dies, she is released *and* exempt from the law concerning her husband.

³Accordingly, she will be designated as an adulteress if she unites herself to another man while her husband is

alive. But if her husband dies, she is free from the law [regarding marriage], so that she is not an adulteress if she marries another man.

⁴Therefore, my fellow believers, you too died to the Law through the [crucified] body of Christ, so that you may belong to another, to Him who was raised from the dead, in order that we may bear fruit for God.

⁵When we were *living* in the flesh [trapped by sin], the sinful passions,

enjoy your freedom

Romans 6:18 affirms that those of us who are Christians have been set free from sin. As children of God, we should experience the glorious freedom and liberty Jesus died to give us—freedom to enjoy all God has given to us through His Son.

But Satan tries to rob us of enjoying our lives. He accuses us, condemns us, and makes us feel insecure because he knows we cannot simultaneously enjoy life and have negative feelings about ourselves. Thank God, we can break out of his trap and start enjoying our blood-bought freedom and liberty.

Jesus talked about our right to be free in John 8:31, 32: "If you abide in My word . . . you are truly My disciples. And you will know the truth [regarding salvation], and the truth will set you free [from the penalty of sin]" (see also John 8:36).

Are you enjoying spiritual freedom in Jesus, or are you sacrificing your joy because you are trapped in the legalistic, rigid mind-set of believing you have to do it all? If you live an inflexible life, you will not have an enjoyable life. I know. The time came when I faced the fact that I was legalistic and rigid in my life, and though this truth was hard on me emotionally, God used it to set me free.

Jesus came that we might have and enjoy life to the fullest, until it overflows (see John 10:10). Following a legalistic lifestyle will lead us into works—futile efforts that cause us to struggle and live in frustration. Remember, there is no bondage or burden in God. His rules (His ways for us to do things) are fulfilling and liberating. Jesus came to set us free!

Feeling guilty and condemned most of the time is not freedom. Being in mental and emotional turmoil is not freedom. Being sad and depressed is not freedom.

Have you reached the point where you are tired of trying to be in control of everything? Are you willing to give up and ask God to help you? If so, pray this prayer:

"Lord, I am tired of being legalistic and complicated. I just want to have some peace and enjoy my life. So, Lord, give me the desire to do what is right in Your eyes. If You do not do what needs to be done, then it is not going to get done. I completely surrender, and I place my trust in You."

I encourage you to lay aside the limitations and defeat of legalism and do your best, beginning right now, to enjoy the life of freedom God makes available to you in Jesus Christ.

putting the Word to work

What is the difference between a paycheck and a gift? You earn a paycheck, but you receive a gift. In Romans 6:23, Paul teaches that the payment, the unavoidable consequence we earned because of our sin, is death. What a relief that God offers to every individual the gift—something we cannot earn—of eternal life in Jesus Christ. If you have received this gift, thank God for His generosity and grace! If you have not yet received God's gift of eternal life, I encourage you to ask Him for it. He will gladly give it to you!

which were awakened by [that which] the Law [identifies as sin], were at work in our body to bear fruit for death [since the willingness to sin led to death and separation from God].

⁶But now we have been released from the Law *and* its penalty, having died [through Christ] to that by which we were held captive, so that we serve [God] in the newness of the Spirit and not in the oldness of the letter [of the Law].

⁷What shall we say then? Is the Law sin? Certainly not! On the contrary, if it had not been for the Law, I would not have recognized sin. For I would not have known [for example] about coveting [what belongs to another, and would have had no sense of guilt] if the Law had not [repeatedly] said, "YOU SHALL NOT COVET." [Ex 20:17; Deut 5:21]

⁸But sin, finding an opportunity through the commandment [to express itself] produced in me every kind of coveting *and* selfish desire. For without the Law sin is dead [the recognition of sin is inactive].

⁹I was once alive without [knowledge of] the Law; but when the commandment came [and I understood its meaning], sin became alive and I died

[since the Law sentenced me to death]. [Ps 73:22]

¹⁰And the *very* commandment which was intended to bring life, actually proved to bring death for me. [Lev 18:5]

¹¹For sin, seizing its opportunity through the commandment, beguiled *and* completely deceived me, and using it as a weapon killed me [separating me from God].

¹²So then, the Law is holy, and the commandment is holy and righteous and good.

¹³Did that which is good [the Law], then become death to me? Certainly not! But sin, in order that it might be revealed as sin, was producing death in me by [using] this good thing [as a weapon], so that through the commandment sin would become exceedingly sinful.

¹⁴We know that the Law is spiritual, but I am *a creature* of the flesh [worldly, self-reliant—carnal and unspiritual], sold into slavery to sin [and serving under its control].

¹⁵For I do not understand my own actions [I am baffled and bewildered by them]. I do not practice what I want *to do,* but I am doing the very thing I hate [and yielding to my human nature, my worldliness—my sinful capacity].

¹⁶Now if I *habitually* do what I do not want to do, [that means] I agree with the Law, *confessing* that it is good (morally excellent).

¹⁷So now [if that is the case, then] it is no longer I who do it [the disobedient thing which I despise], but the sin [nature] which lives in me.

¹⁸For I know that nothing good lives in me, that is, in my flesh [my human nature, my worldliness—my sinful capacity]. For the willingness [to do good] is present in me, but the doing of good is not.

¹⁹For the good that I want to do, I do not do, but I practice the very evil that I do not want.

newness of life

The Old Covenant is finished and has been replaced with a new and better covenant. God's Law no longer comes to us on stone tablets, but is written in our hearts (see 2 Corinthians 3:3). We no longer live under the Law, which *tells* us God's will; we now live under grace, which enables us to *do* God's will because we want to and not merely because it is the Law. The Law ministers death, but grace ministers life.

Grace is the power of the Holy Spirit in our lives enabling us to do whatever God instructs us to do. It is by grace (God's power) through faith that we are saved and made partakers of Christ's salvation.

We are to be led by the inner promptings of the Holy Spirit. The Holy Spirit lives in us and wants us to willingly allow Him to lead, guide, and direct us. When we submit to His promptings, we experience newness of life. The law only gives us rules and regulations, and we feel guilty and condemned when we do not follow them. But the Spirit gives us not only the desire to do what is right, but also the ability and a fresh zeal to do it. He enables us to serve God with enthusiasm, not out of a sense of obligation.

Learning to be led by the Holy Spirit should be a primary goal of every believer in Jesus Christ. Only the Holy Spirit knows the mind of God concerning our lives and our circumstances. He will reveal God's will to us and lead us into its fullness as we diligently follow His promptings.

To *prompt* means "to remind" or "to give a cue." It does not indicate force, control, or manipulation. When someone reminds us to do something we have forgotten or are in danger of forgetting, we can still choose whether or not we will act on that reminder. The Holy Spirit is a gentleman and will never force Himself or God's will on us. God sets before each of us life and death and encourages us to choose life so that we and our descendants may have the life He has carefully planned for us (see Deuteronomy 30:19).

I encourage you to learn all you can about how to be led by the Holy Spirit because doing so is a blessing, a privilege, and an act of obedience for Christians.

20But if I am doing the very thing I do not want to do, I am no longer the one doing it [that is, it is not me that acts], but the sin [nature] which lives in me.

21So I find *it to be* the law [of my inner self], that evil is present in me, the one who wants to do good.

22For I joyfully delight in the law of God in my inner self [with my new nature], [Ps 1:2]

23but I see a different law *and* rule of action in the members of my body [in its appetites and desires], waging war against the law of my mind *and* subduing me and making me a prisoner of the law of sin which is within my members.

24Wretched *and* miserable man that I am! Who will [rescue me and] set me free from this body of death [this corrupt, mortal existence]?

25Thanks be to God [for my deliverance] through Jesus Christ our Lord! So then, on the one hand I myself with my mind serve the law of God, but on the other, with my flesh [my human nature, my worldliness, my sinful capacity—I serve] the law of sin.

8 THEREFORE THERE is now no condemnation [no guilty verdict, no punishment] for those who are in Christ Jesus [who believe in Him as personal Lord and Savior]. [John 3:18] ²For the law of the Spirit of life [which is] in Christ Jesus [the law of our new being] has set you free from the law of sin and of death.

³For what the Law could not do [that is, overcome sin and remove its penalty, its power] being weakened by the flesh [man's nature without the Holy Spirit], God did: He sent His own Son in the likeness of sinful man as an offering for sin. And He condemned

no condemnation in Christ

Even though Romans 8:1 teaches us that there is no condemnation for those who are in Christ, many believers still struggle greatly with guilt and condemnation. Because of our love for God we want to do what is right, yet there are times we walk in the flesh instead of in the Spirit and we make mistakes. We sin and make wrong choices. When we realize we have sinned we should quickly and thoroughly repent, being willing to turn away from the sin and do what is right with God's help. Once we have repented and asked God to forgive us we are not to continue carrying a heavy burden of condemnation. Jesus delivered us from both iniquity and guilt. When we repent and ask God to forgive us He not only forgives, but He forgets and removes our sin as far as the east is from the west (see Psalm 103:12; Hebrews 10:17, 18).

Jesus died as the perfect sacrifice for sin—and no other sacrifice is or will ever be needed (see Hebrews 10:11, 12). The guilt we feel when we sin is often our way of "sacrificing" to pay for the sins we have committed. Somehow we think that if we are miserable and do not allow ourselves to enjoy life, our feelings of condemnation help balance the scales of justice. That kind of thinking is wrong!

Guilt is an invisible burden that wears us out and does no good at all. It actually prevents progress and renders us incapable of proper fellowship with God because we must approach Him in faith and with boldness, not with fear and guilt.

Some people are literally addicted to guilt. They do not feel right unless they feel wrong! I was like that for many years, and God taught me to use my faith to live free from guilt and condemnation. We either believe that Jesus paid for our sins in full, or we believe we must add our sacrifice to His, which, of course, is incorrect.

Romans 8:1–14 encourages us to walk after the Spirit, and not the flesh. One way we do that is by handling our sins the way the Holy Spirit tells us to, which is definitely not to repent and then feel guilty. God promises that He is faithful to forgive our sins and cleanse us from them if we will repent and admit them (see 1 John 1:9). God never does anything halfway. Jesus' work on the cross is finished, so start enjoying the freedom from guilt and condemnation that is available to you. Do not believe your feelings more than you believe God's Word!

sin in the flesh [subdued it and overcame it in the person of His own Son], [Lev 7:37]

⁴so that the [righteous and just] requirement of the Law might be fulfilled in us who do not live our lives in the ways of the flesh [guided by worldliness and our sinful nature], but [live our lives] in the ways of the Spirit [guided by His power].

⁵For those who are *living* according to the flesh set their minds on the things of the flesh [which gratify the body], but those who are *living* according to the Spirit, [set their minds on] the things of the Spirit [His will and purpose].

⁶Now the mind of the flesh is death [both now and forever—because it pursues sin]; but the mind of the Spirit is life and peace [the spiritual wellbeing that comes from walking with God—both now and forever];

⁷the mind of the flesh [with its sinful pursuits] is actively hostile to God.

life point

When condemnation comes against you, let me encourage you to quote Romans 8:1 as a "Word weapon." Remind Satan and yourself that you do not walk after the flesh but after the Spirit. Walking after the flesh is depending on yourself; walking after the Spirit is depending on God.

When you fail (which you will), that does not mean that you are a failure. It simply means that you do not do everything right. We all have to accept the fact that we have strengths along with weaknesses. Let Christ be strong in your weaknesses; let Him be your strength on your weak days. If you are waiting for the victory in an area and you have not seen it, rather than being condemned about it, be patient. Do not receive condemnation; walk in the Spirit.

It does not submit itself to God's law, since it cannot,

⁸and those who are in the flesh [living a life that caters to sinful appetites and impulses] cannot please God.

⁹However, you are not [living] in the flesh [controlled by the sinful nature] but in the Spirit, if in fact the Spirit of God lives in you [directing and guiding you]. But if anyone does not have the Spirit of Christ, he does not belong to Him [and is not a child of God]. [Rom 8:14]

¹⁰If Christ lives in you, though your [natural] body is dead because of sin, your spirit is alive because of righteousness [which He provides].

life point

When the deceiver speaks to us, he cannot give peace. When we try to solve things with our own reasoning, we cannot find peace, because according to Romans 8:6, the mind of the flesh is death, but the mind of the Holy Spirit is life and peace.

Do you have to make a decision? Lay it on the "peace scale" and do not proceed if peace cannot hold its weight against the guidance you have heard. You do not have to explain to others why you do not have peace about it; sometimes you will not know why yourself. You can say simply, "It's not wise for me to do this, because I don't have peace about it."

Even when you believe God has spoken to you, you should wait to act until peace fills your soul to do what He has instructed you to do. In this way you are assured that your timing is right.

I often say, "Let emotions subside and then decide." If we wait for God's true peace, we will be obedient with faith. Peace is true confirmation that we are hearing from God.

life point

Romans 8:6–14 helps us understand the differences between following our fleshly desires and allowing God's Spirit to lead us. Any time our flesh wants to do one thing and the Spirit of God wants us to do something else, by choosing to follow the Spirit of God we need to know that our flesh will suffer. We do not like that, but the Bible says that if we want to share Christ's glory, we have to be willing to share His suffering (see 1 Peter 4:13).

I like to encourage those who are just beginning to walk with God that once the fleshly appetite is no longer in control they will get to the point where it is easy to obey God. Even if obedience is difficult they will get to the place where they actually *enjoy* doing it. If you are new to the Christian faith, be encouraged!

¹¹And if the Spirit of Him who raised Jesus from the dead lives in you, He who raised Christ Jesus from the dead will also give life to your mortal bodies through His Spirit, who lives in you. ¹²So then, brothers and sisters, we have an obligation, but not to our flesh [our human nature, our worldliness, our sinful capacity], to live according to the [impulses of the] flesh [our nature without the Holy Spirit]— ¹³for if you are living according to the [impulses of the] flesh, you are going to die. But if [you are living] by the [power of the Holy] Spirit you are *habitually* putting to death the *sinful* deeds of the body, you will [really] live *forever.* ¹⁴For all who are *allowing themselves to* be led by the Spirit of God are sons of God. ¹⁵For you have not received a spirit of slavery leading again to fear [of God's judgment], but you have received the Spirit of adoption as sons [the Spirit

life point

Romans 8:15 teaches us that the Holy Spirit is the Spirit of adoption. Here, the word *adoption* means that we have been brought into God's family even though we were previously outsiders, unrelated to Him in any way. We were sinners who served Satan, but God in His great mercy redeemed us and purchased us with the blood of His own Son. Think of yourself as a child of God—loved, accepted, and empowered by His unconditional love for you.

producing sonship] by which we [joyfully] cry, "Abba! Father!" ¹⁶The Spirit Himself testifies *and* confirms together with our spirit [assuring us] that we [believers] are children of God. ¹⁷And if [we are His] children, [then we are His] heirs also: heirs of God and fellow heirs with Christ [sharing His spiritual blessing and inheritance], if indeed we share in His suffering so that we may also share in His glory. [John 17:24; Gal 3:29; 4:7; Eph 1:3, 11; 3:6; Heb 6:12] ¹⁸For I consider [from the standpoint

putting the Word to work

Paul suffered greatly during his lifetime—shipwrecks, beatings that left him near death, abandonment of friends, imprisonment, and eventually, execution (see 2 Corinthians 11:23–28). Scripture teaches that all of us face various forms of suffering in our lives (see John 16:33). How can you withstand suffering? One way is to ask God to help you have Paul's attitude of confidence that earthly sufferings cannot come close to comparing to the glory you will one day see (see Romans 8:18).

of faith] that the sufferings of the present life are not worthy to be compared with the glory that is about to be revealed to us *and* in us!

¹⁹For [even the whole] creation [all nature] waits eagerly for the children of God to be revealed.

²⁰For the creation was subjected to frustration *and* futility, not willingly [because of some intentional fault on its part], but by the will of Him who subjected it, in hope [Eccl 1:2]

²¹that the creation itself will also be freed from its bondage to decay [and gain entrance] into the glorious freedom of the children of God.

²²For we know that the whole creation has been moaning together as in the pains of childbirth until now. [Jer 12:4, 11]

safe or obedient?

Even when we are in a place of obedience to God, we often have no natural way of knowing for sure whether we are right or wrong. We have nothing more than faith to help us take that first step. We may not be certain that what we are doing is the right thing until after we have done it and then look back to see if God's grace was there to cause our efforts to bear good fruit.

Sometimes we may be wrong. That thought seems frightening, so we think, *I had better just stay here where it is safe.* But if we do that, we will soon be miserable if God truly told us to move forward.

If our hearts are right, and we do our best when we hear from Him, God will redeem us and honor our steps of obedience. If we move in childlike trust to obey what we believe in our hearts He has told us to do, even if that decision is wrong, God will take that mistake and work it out for our good. I know this is true because Romans 8:28 says that all things work together in God's plan for good for those of us who are called according to His purpose.

Many people are afraid to act because they think that if they make a mistake, God will be angry with them. But this is where trusting His character is so vital to walking in faith. People who are too afraid to obey are so miserable anyway that they cannot get any worse off by stepping out and trying to do what God is telling them to do.

I once held a ministry position at our home church. I loved it, but felt God was leading me to step out into something new. I did leave, but not because I wanted to. I left because God's anointing and power for me to be there had lifted, and I became miserable until I obeyed Him. I realized I would only find peace if I left my "safety zone" and tested what I believed He told me to do. That was the only way to find out if I was right or wrong about hearing His voice. I had to step out to find out!

I exhort you with this truth: Do not spend all your life playing it safe! Safety is very comfortable, but it may keep you from God's perfect plan for your life. Trust His Word and keep your heart willing and ready to obey. You will find throughout your life that God regularly calls us out of our comfort zone and into new places of faith and growth in Him.

²³And not only this, but we too, who have the first fruits of the Spirit [a joyful indication of the blessings to come], even we groan inwardly, as we wait eagerly for [the sign of] our adoption as sons—the redemption *and* transformation of our body [at the resurrection]. [2 Cor 5:2, 4; Eph 4:30]

²⁴For in this hope we were saved [by faith]. But hope [the object of] which is seen is not hope. For who hopes for what he already sees?

²⁵But if we hope for what we do not see, we wait eagerly for it with patience *and* composure.

²⁶In the same way the Spirit [comes to us and] helps us in our weakness. We do not know what prayer to offer *or* how to offer it as we should, but the Spirit Himself [knows our need and at the right time] intercedes on our behalf with sighs *and* groanings too deep for words.

²⁷And He who searches the hearts knows what the mind of the Spirit is, because the Spirit intercedes [before God] on behalf of God's people in accordance with God's will. [Ps 139:1, 2]

²⁸And we know [with great confidence] that God [who is deeply concerned about us] causes all things to work together [as a plan] for good for those who love God, to those who are called according to His plan *and* purpose.

²⁹For those whom He foreknew [and loved and chose beforehand], He also predestined to be conformed to the image of His Son [and ultimately share

in His complete sanctification], so that He would be the firstborn [the most beloved and honored] among many believers.

³⁰And those whom He predestined, He also called; and those whom He called, He also justified [declared free of the guilt of sin]; and those whom He justified, He also glorified [raising them to a heavenly dignity].

³¹What then shall we say to all these things? If God is for us, who can be [successful] against us? [Ps 118:6]

³²He who did not spare [even] His own Son, but gave Him up for us all, how will He not also, along with Him, graciously give us all things?

³³Who will bring any charge against God's elect (His chosen ones)? It is God who justifies us [declaring us blameless and putting us in a right relationship with Himself].

³⁴Who is the one who condemns us? Christ Jesus is the One who died [to pay our penalty], and more *than that,* who was raised [from the dead], and who is at the right hand of God interceding [with the Father] for us.

³⁵Who shall ever separate us from the love of Christ? Will tribulation, or distress, or persecution, or famine, or nakedness, or danger, or sword?

³⁶Just as it is written *and* forever remains written,

"FOR YOUR SAKE WE ARE PUT TO
  DEATH ALL DAY LONG;
WE ARE REGARDED AS SHEEP FOR
  THE SLAUGHTER." [Ps 44:22]

life point

God did not create us for failure. We may fail at some things on our way to success, but if we trust Him, He will take even our errors and work them out for our good (see Romans 8:28). God can take our mistakes and turn them into miracles if we continue to trust confidently in Him.

life point

God approved of you before anybody else ever got a chance to disapprove. If God approves of you and accepts you as you are, why worry about what anyone else thinks? If God is for you—and He is, according to Romans 8:31—who can be successful against you?

³⁷Yet in all these things we are more than conquerors *and* gain an overwhelming victory through Him who loved us [so much that He died for us]. ³⁸For I am convinced [and continue to be convinced—beyond any doubt] that neither death, nor life, nor angels, nor principalities, nor things present *and* threatening, nor things to come, nor powers, ³⁹nor height, nor depth, nor any other created thing, will be able to separate us from the [unlimited] love of God, which is in Christ Jesus our Lord.

God is for you

Romans 8:31 tells us clearly that God is for us. We also know that Satan is against us. That leaves us with the question: Are we going to agree with God or with the devil? You know the answer. Stop opposing yourself and mentally beating yourself up just because Satan is against you!

Sad to say, sometimes we discover people are also against us. Satan does not always work alone in the spiritual realm; he also works through people in the natural realm. He attacks our confidence through the things people say or do not say. He can cause us to feel unworthy or rejected because of another person's words or actions.

How important are people's opinions of us? Are we thinking for ourselves, or are we always agreeing with everyone else's opinion? If people's opinions, judgments, and attitudes toward us are sometimes inspired by the devil, then we must resist what people think and say instead of agreeing with it.

If we know God is for us, then how we feel or what other people think of us should not matter. As the Bible says in Romans 8:31, who can be successful against us if God is for us? If He is on our side, then what can others do to us? Hebrews 13:6 makes a similar point: "So we take comfort and are encouraged and confidently say, 'The Lord is my Helper [in time of need], I will not be afraid. What will man do to me?'"

Most of us, to some extent, need to be delivered from the fear of people and from caring too much about what others think. People who always need the approval of others desperately want everyone to look at them from head to toe and say, "Perfect." When they do any kind of a job, they want everybody to say, "Perfect." In everything they do—the way they look, the things they say, every action they take—they want people to say, "Perfect."

If we try to be perfect, we will be disappointed. It will not work because you and I are imperfect human beings. Even if we could manifest perfection, some people would still not be satisfied simply because they are unhappy individuals who will not ever be content with anything until they change their own attitudes.

We need to be confident that God accepts us with our imperfections. Even though He continues to work in us to make us more Christlike, we do not have to struggle to win His approval or the approval of others. If God is for us—and He is—we do not need to fear anyone who is against us.

life point

All that Jesus asks of the Father, God answers. So whatever He prays for me, whatever He prays for you, we will receive. Jesus never stops praying for us. This means we can relax, because Romans 8:34 promises that Jesus sits at the right hand of the Father and intercedes for us. Think of it! Jesus is praying for you.

9 I AM telling the truth in Christ, I am not lying, my conscience testifies with me [enlightened and prompted] by the Holy Spirit,

²that I have great sorrow and unceasing anguish in my heart.

³For [if it were possible] I would wish that I myself were accursed, [separated, banished] from Christ for the sake [of the salvation] of my brothers, my natural kinsmen, [Ex 32:32]

⁴who are Israelites, to whom belongs the adoption as sons, the glory (Shekinah), the [special] covenants [with Abraham, Moses, and David], the giving of the Law, the [system of temple] worship, and the [original] promises. [Ex 4:22; Hos 11:1]

⁵To them belong the patriarchs, and from them, according to His natural descent, *came* the Christ (the Messiah, the Anointed), He who is exalted *and*

putting the Word to work

Do your circumstances ever cause you to question God's love for you? The truth is, even in the midst of the most difficult of circumstances, God's love is real and active in your life. Nothing can ever separate you from His love; nothing can ever cause Him to love you less (see Romans 8:35–39).

In the midst of difficulty, cling to God's love for you, and ask Him to keep revealing His love to you.

supreme over all, God blessed forever. Amen.

⁶However, it is not as though God's word has failed [coming to nothing]. For not all who are descended from Israel (Jacob) are [the true] Israel;

⁷and they are not all the children of Abraham because they are his descendants [by blood], but [the promise was]: "YOUR DESCENDANTS WILL BE NAMED THROUGH ISAAC" [though Abraham had other sons]. [Gen 21:9–12]

⁸That is, it is not the children of the body [Abraham's natural descendants] who are God's children, but it is the children of the promise who are counted as [Abraham's true] descendants.

⁹For this is what the promise said: "ABOUT THIS TIME [next year] I WILL COME, AND SARAH SHALL HAVE A SON." [Gen 18:10]

¹⁰And not only that, but this too: Rebekah conceived *twin sons* by one man [under the same circumstances], by our father Isaac;

life point

The Apostle Paul said in Romans 9:1 that he knew he was doing the right thing, not because his reasoning said it was right, but because it bore witness in his spirit.

The mind does aid the spirit at times. The mind and the spirit work together, but the spirit should always be honored above the mind.

If you know in your spirit that something is wrong, you should not allow reasoning to talk you into it. Also, if you know something is right, do not allow reasoning to talk you out of it. Do as Romans 9:1 instructs and allow the Holy Spirit to testify to you concerning whether something is right or wrong. Let your conscience always be enlightened and prompted by the Holy Spirit.

¹¹and though *the twins* were not yet born and had not done anything *either* good or bad, so that God's purpose [His choice, His election] would stand, not because of works [done by either child], but because of [the plan of] Him who calls them,

¹²it was said to her, "THE OLDER (Esau) WILL SERVE THE YOUNGER (Jacob)." [Gen 25:21–23]

¹³As it is written *and* forever remains written, "JACOB I LOVED (chose, protected, blessed), BUT ESAU I HATED (held in disregard compared to Jacob)." [Mal 1:2, 3]

¹⁴What shall we say then? Is there injustice with God? Certainly not!

¹⁵For He says to Moses, "I WILL HAVE MERCY ON WHOMEVER I HAVE MERCY, AND I WILL HAVE COMPASSION ON WHOMEVER I HAVE COMPASSION." [Ex 33:19]

¹⁶So then God's choice is not dependent on human will, nor on human effort [the totality of human striving], but on God who shows mercy [to whomever He chooses—it is His sovereign gift].

¹⁷For the Scripture says to Pharaoh, "I RAISED YOU UP FOR THIS VERY PURPOSE, TO DISPLAY MY POWER IN [dealing with] YOU, AND SO THAT MY NAME WOULD BE PROCLAIMED IN ALL THE EARTH." [Ex 9:16]

¹⁸So then, He has mercy on whom He wills (chooses), and He hardens [the heart of] whom He wills.

¹⁹You will say to me then, "Why does He still blame me [for sinning]? For who [including myself] has [ever] resisted His will *and* purpose?"

²⁰On the contrary, who are you, O man, who answers [arrogantly] back to God *and* dares to defy Him? Will the thing which is formed say to him who formed it, "Why have you made me like this?" [Is 29:16; 45:9]

²¹Does the potter not have the right over the clay, to make from the same lump [of clay] one object for honorable use [something beautiful or distinctive] and another for common use [something ordinary or menial]?

²²What if God, although willing to show His [terrible] wrath and to make His power known, has tolerated with great patience the objects of His wrath [which are] prepared for destruction? [Prov 16:4]

²³And what if He has done so to make known the riches of His glory to the objects of His mercy, which He has prepared beforehand for glory,

²⁴*including* us, whom He also called, not only from among the Jews, but also from among the Gentiles?

²⁵Just as He says in [the writings of the prophet] Hosea:

"I WILL CALL THOSE WHO WERE NOT
    MY PEOPLE, 'MY PEOPLE,'
AND [I will call] HER WHO WAS NOT
    BELOVED, 'BELOVED.'" [Hos 2:23]
²⁶"AND IT SHALL BE THAT IN THE
    PLACE WHERE IT WAS SAID TO
    THEM, 'YOU ARE NOT MY PEOPLE,'
THERE THEY SHALL BE CALLED SONS
    OF THE LIVING GOD." [Hos 1:10]

²⁷And Isaiah calls out concerning Israel: "THOUGH THE NUMBER OF THE SONS OF ISRAEL BE LIKE THE SAND OF THE SEA, IT IS ONLY THE REMNANT [a small believing minority] THAT WILL BE SAVED [from God's judgment];

²⁸FOR THE LORD WILL EXECUTE HIS WORD UPON THE EARTH [He will conclude His dealings with mankind] COMPLETELY AND WITHOUT DELAY." [Is 10:22, 23]

²⁹It is as Isaiah foretold,

"IF THE LORD OF HOSTS HAD NOT
    LEFT US SEED [future generations
    from which a believing remnant
    of Israelites came],
WE WOULD HAVE BECOME LIKE
    SODOM, AND WOULD HAVE
    RESEMBLED GOMORRAH [totally
    rejected and destroyed]!" [Is 1:9]

³⁰What shall we say then? That Gentiles, who did not pursue righteousness [who did not seek salvation and a right relationship with God, nevertheless] obtained righteousness, that is, the righteousness which is produced by faith;

³¹whereas Israel, [though always] pursuing the law of righteousness, did not succeed in fulfilling the law. [Is 51:1]

³²And why not? Because it was not by faith [that they pursued it], but as though it were by works [relying on the merit of their works instead of their faith]. They stumbled over the stumbling Stone [Jesus Christ]. [Is 8:14; 28:16]

³³As it is written *and* forever remains written,

"BEHOLD I AM LAYING IN ZION
    A STONE OF STUMBLING AND A
    ROCK OF OFFENSE;
AND HE WHO BELIEVES IN HIM
    [whoever adheres to, trusts
    in, and relies on Him] WILL
    NOT BE DISAPPOINTED [in his
    expectations]." [Is 28:16]

10 BROTHERS AND sisters, my heart's desire and my prayer to God for Israel is for their salvation.

²For I testify about them that they have a certain enthusiasm for God, but not in accordance with [correct and vital] knowledge [about Him and His purposes].

³For not knowing about God's righteousness [which is based on faith], and seeking to establish their own [righteousness based on works], they did not submit to God's righteousness.

⁴For Christ is the end of the law [it leads to Him and its purpose is fulfilled in Him], for [granting] righteousness to everyone who believes [in Him as Savior].

⁵For Moses writes that the man who practices the righteousness which is based on law [with all its intricate demands] shall live by it. [Lev 18:5]

⁶But the righteousness based on faith [which produces a right relationship with Him] says the following: "DO NOT SAY IN YOUR HEART, 'WHO WILL ASCEND INTO HEAVEN?' that is, to bring Christ down;

⁷or, 'WHO WILL DESCEND INTO THE ABYSS?' that is, to bring Christ up from the dead [as if we had to be saved by our own efforts, doing the impossible]." [Deut 30:12, 13]

⁸But what does it say? "THE WORD IS NEAR YOU, IN YOUR MOUTH AND IN YOUR HEART"—that is, the word [the message, the basis] of faith which we preach— [Deut 30:14]

⁹because if you acknowledge *and* confess with your mouth that Jesus is Lord [recognizing His power, authority, and majesty as God], and believe in your heart that God raised Him from the dead, you will be saved.

¹⁰For with the heart a person believes [in Christ as Savior] resulting in his justification [that is, being made righteous—being freed of the guilt of sin and made acceptable to God]; and with the mouth he acknowledges *and* confesses [his faith openly], resulting in *and* confirming [his] salvation.

¹¹For the Scripture says, "WHOEVER BELIEVES IN HIM [whoever adheres to, trusts in, and relies on Him] WILL NOT BE DISAPPOINTED [in his expectations]." [Is 28:16]

speak the Word

Thank You, Jesus, for fulfilling the purpose of the Law so I can be in right relationship with God because I believe in You as Savior.
—ADAPTED FROM ROMANS 10:4

¹²For there is no distinction between Jew and Gentile; for the same *Lord* is Lord over all [of us], and [He is] abounding in riches (blessings) for all who call on Him [in faith and prayer].

¹³For "WHOEVER CALLS ON THE NAME OF THE LORD [in prayer] WILL BE SAVED." [Joel 2:32]

¹⁴But how will people call on Him in whom they have not believed? And how will they believe in Him of whom they have not heard? And how will they hear without a preacher (messenger)?

¹⁵And how will they preach unless they are commissioned *and* sent [for that purpose]? Just as it is written *and* forever remains written, "HOW BEAUTIFUL ARE THE FEET OF THOSE WHO BRING GOOD NEWS OF GOOD THINGS!" [Is 52:7]

¹⁶But they did not all pay attention to the good news [of salvation]; for Isaiah says, "LORD, WHO HAS BELIEVED OUR REPORT?" [Is 53:1]

¹⁷So faith *comes* from hearing [what is told], and what is heard *comes* by the [preaching of the] message concerning Christ.

¹⁸But I say, did they not hear? Indeed they have;

putting the Word to work

Romans 10:14, 15 remind us that we need to tell people about God and His love for them. Many people may have heard of God, and maybe even believe that He is a loving God, but they have not heard about His love for them personally. Do you remember the first person who shared with you the good news of God's love for you? Take a moment and thank God for that person and ask Him to show you someone with whom you can share the good news about His love!

life point

When the Word is heard, faith is imparted to believe it (see Romans 10:17). Once we have heard the Word and believe it, we should continue believing. God invites us to live from faith to faith. As believers, one of our most important jobs is to simply believe. Jesus said, "If you believe [in Me], you will see the glory of God" (John 11:40).

"THEIR VOICE [that of creation
    bearing God's message] HAS
    GONE OUT TO ALL THE EARTH,
AND THEIR WORDS TO THE [farthest]
    ENDS OF THE WORLD." [Ps 19:4,
    7–11]

¹⁹But I say, did Israel fail to understand [that the gospel was to go also to the Gentiles]? First Moses says,

"I WILL MAKE YOU JEALOUS OF
    THOSE WHO ARE NOT A NATION
    (Gentiles);
WITH A NATION THAT LACKS
    UNDERSTANDING I WILL MAKE
    YOU ANGRY." [Deut 32:21]

²⁰Then Isaiah is very bold and says,

"I HAVE BEEN FOUND BY THOSE WHO
    DID NOT SEEK ME;
I HAVE SHOWN MYSELF TO THOSE
    WHO DID NOT [consciously] ASK
    FOR ME." [Is 65:1]

²¹But of Israel he says, "ALL DAY LONG I HAVE STRETCHED OUT MY HANDS [in compassion] TO A DISOBEDIENT AND OBSTINATE PEOPLE." [Is 65:2]

11 I SAY then, has God rejected *and* disowned His people? Certainly not! For I too am an Israelite, a descendant of Abraham, of the tribe of Benjamin. [1 Sam 12:22; Jer 31:37; 33:24–26; Phil 3:5]

²God has not rejected His [chosen] people whom He foreknew. Or do you

not know what the Scripture says of Elijah, how he pleads with God against Israel? [Ps 94:14; 1 Kin 19]

[3]"Lord, THEY HAVE KILLED YOUR PROPHETS, THEY HAVE TORN DOWN YOUR ALTARS, AND I ALONE AM LEFT [of the prophets], AND THEY ARE SEEKING MY LIFE."

[4]But what is God's response to him? "I HAVE KEPT for Myself SEVEN THOUSAND MEN WHO HAVE NOT BOWED THE KNEE TO BAAL." [1 Kin 19:18]

[5]So too then, at the present time there has come to be a remnant [a small believing minority] according to *God's* gracious choice.

[6]But if it is by grace [God's unmerited favor], it is no longer on the basis of works, otherwise grace is no longer grace [it would not be a gift but a reward for works].

[7]What then? Israel failed to obtain what it was seeking [that is, God's favor by obedience to the Law], but the

life point

What the Apostle Paul tells us in Romans 11:6 is simply this: grace and works are diametrically opposed to one another. They cannot fellowship together or have anything to do with each other.

Stated another way, grace and works of the flesh are mutually exclusive. Where one exists, the other cannot exist.

If you and I are into our own works, then we are out of grace. If we are in grace, then we are out of works. Any time we get into works, the grace of God ceases to operate on our behalf. God has no choice but to back off and wait until we have finished trying to handle things ourselves. I encourage you to take your hands off of the situations, circumstances, and relationships that concern you—and let God's grace go to work for you!

elect [those chosen few] obtained it, while the rest of them became hardened *and* callously indifferent;

[8]just as it is written [in Scripture],

"GOD GAVE THEM A SPIRIT OF
    STUPOR,
EYES THAT DO NOT SEE AND EARS
    THAT DO NOT HEAR,
[a spiritual apathy that has
    continued] TO THIS VERY DAY."
    [Deut 29:4; Is 29:10]

[9]And David says,

"LET THEIR TABLE (abundance)
    BECOME A SNARE AND A TRAP,
A STUMBLING BLOCK AND A
    RETRIBUTION TO THEM. [Ps 69:22]
[10]"LET THEIR EYES BE DARKENED SO
    THAT THEY DO NOT SEE,
AND MAKE THEIR BACKS BEND
    [under their burden] FOREVER."
    [Ps 69:23]

[11]So I say, have they stumbled so as to fall [to spiritual ruin]? Certainly not! But by their transgression [their rejection of the Messiah] salvation *has come* to the Gentiles, to make Israel jealous [when they realize what they have forfeited].

[12]Now if Israel's transgression means riches for the world [at large] and their failure means riches for the Gentiles, how much more will their fulfillment *and* reinstatement be!

[13]But *now* I am speaking to you who are Gentiles. Inasmuch then as I am an apostle to the Gentiles, I magnify my ministry,

[14]in the hope of somehow making my fellow countrymen jealous [by stirring them up so that they will seek the truth] and *perhaps* save some of them.

[15]For if their [present] rejection [of salvation] is for the reconciliation of the world [to God], what will their acceptance [of salvation] be but [nothing less than] life from the dead?

[16]If the first portion [of dough offered as the first fruits] is holy, so is the *whole*

batch; and if the root (Abraham, the patriarchs) is holy, so are the branches (the Israelites). [Num 15:19–21]

¹⁷But if some of the branches were broken off, and you [Gentiles], being like a wild olive shoot, were grafted in among them to share with them the rich root of the olive tree,

¹⁸do not boast over the [broken] branches *and* exalt yourself at their expense. If you do boast *and* feel superior, *remember that* it is not you who supports the root, but the root that *supports* you.

¹⁹You will say then, "Branches were broken off so that I might be grafted in."

²⁰That is true. They were broken off because of their unbelief, but you stand by your faith [as believers understanding the truth of Christ's deity]. Do not be conceited, but [rather stand in great awe of God and] fear [Him];

²¹for if God did not spare the natural branches [because of unbelief], He will not spare you either.

²²Then appreciate the gracious kindness and the severity of God: to those who fell [into spiritual ruin], severity, but to you, God's *gracious* kindness—if you continue in His kindness [by faith and obedience to Him]; otherwise you too will be cut off.

²³And even they [the unbelieving Jews], if they do not continue in their unbelief, will be grafted in; for God has the power to graft them in again.

²⁴For if you were cut off from what is by nature a wild olive tree, and against nature were grafted into a cultivated olive tree, how much easier will it be to graft these who are the natural *branches* back into [the original parent stock of] their own olive tree?

²⁵I do not want you, believers, to be unaware of this mystery [God's previously hidden plan]—so that you will not be wise in your own opinion—that a partial hardening has [temporarily] happened to Israel [to last] until the full number of the Gentiles has come in;

²⁶and so [at that time] all Israel [that is, all Jews who have a personal faith in Jesus as Messiah] will be saved; just as it is written [in Scripture],

"THE DELIVERER (Messiah) WILL
    COME FROM ZION,
HE WILL REMOVE UNGODLINESS
    FROM JACOB." [Is 59:20, 21]
²⁷"THIS IS MY COVENANT WITH THEM,
WHEN I TAKE AWAY THEIR SINS."
    [Is 27:9; Jer 31:33]

²⁸From the standpoint of the gospel, the Jews [at present] are enemies [of God] for your sake [which is for your benefit], but from the standpoint of God's choice [of the Jews as His people], they are still loved by Him for the sake of the fathers.

²⁹For the gifts and the calling of God are irrevocable [for He does not withdraw what He has given, nor does

life point

We need to realize that God is smarter than we are (see Romans 11:34). His plan really is better. No matter what you or I may think, God's way is better than ours.

I look back now at many of the frustrating times I went through in my life as I tried to make things happen according to my timing and how I grew frustrated when none of my efforts worked and I had to wait. I realize now that I really was not ready for those things.

God knew I was not ready, but I thought I was. I spent so much of my time asking, "Why, God, why?" and "When, God, when?" I asked questions only God could answer, and He had no intention of answering me.

Remember, God wants our trust, not our questions. God does not need our counsel in order to work; He needs our faith.

He change His mind about those to whom He gives His grace or to whom He sends His call].

³⁰Just as you once were disobedient *and* failed to listen to God, but have now obtained mercy because of their disobedience,

³¹so they too have now become disobedient so that they too may one day receive mercy because of the mercy shown to you.

³²For God has imprisoned all in disobedience so that He may show mercy to all [Jew and Gentile alike].

³³Oh, the depth of the riches and wisdom and knowledge of God! How unsearchable are His judgments *and* decisions and how unfathomable *and* untraceable are His ways!

³⁴For WHO HAS KNOWN THE MIND OF THE LORD, OR WHO HAS BEEN HIS COUNSELOR? [Is 40:13, 14]

³⁵Or WHO HAS FIRST GIVEN TO HIM THAT IT WOULD BE PAID BACK TO HIM?

³⁶For from Him [all things originate] and through Him [all things live and exist] and to Him are all things [directed]. To Him be glory *and* honor forever! Amen.

12 THEREFORE I urge you, brothers and sisters, by the mercies of God, to present your bodies [dedicating all of yourselves, set apart] as a living sacrifice, holy and well-pleasing to God, *which is* your rational (logical, intelligent) act of worship.

²And do not be conformed to this world [any longer with its superficial values and customs], but be transformed *and* progressively changed [as you mature spiritually] by the renewing of your mind [focusing on godly values and ethical attitudes], so that you may prove [for yourselves] what the will of God is, that which is good and acceptable and perfect [in His plan and purpose for you].

³For by the grace [of God] given to me I say to everyone of you not to think more highly of himself [and of his importance and ability] than he ought to think; but to think so as to have sound judgment, as God has apportioned to each a degree of faith [and a purpose designed for service].

⁴For just as in one [physical] body we have many parts, and these parts do not all have the same function *or* special use,

⁵so we, who are many, are [nevertheless just] one body in Christ, and individually [we are] parts one of another [mutually dependent on each other].

⁶Since we have gifts that differ according to the grace given to us, *each*

life point

Do you know what Paul is telling us in Romans 12:1? He says we are to dedicate everything about ourselves to God—not just our possessions, money, time, energy, and efforts, but also our bodies, heads, hands, tongues, and even our minds, emotions, and attitudes.

We are to dedicate everything about ourselves to God as a "living sacrifice," holy, devoted, consecrated, and pleasing to Him. This is our rational, logical, intelligent act of worship.

Often we get the impression that to totally serve and worship God means to involve our body and spirit, but there is more. Here Paul says that we are to serve and worship Him with our minds and emotions also. Invite God to think and speak through you. Let Him touch people through you. You can even serve God with your face by smiling and being friendly to other people. Allow God to use all of you. The more of yourself you release to Him the more you will be fulfilled and experience His peace and joy.

life point

Romans 12:2 informs us that God has a plan in mind for us. His will toward us is good and acceptable and perfect, but we must completely renew our minds before we will ever experience the good things He has planned. We renew our minds and get new attitudes and new ideals by studying God's Word. His Word is truth (see John 17:17)

of us is to use them accordingly: if [someone has the gift of] prophecy, [let him speak a new message from God to His people] in proportion to the faith *possessed;*

[7]if service, in the act of serving; or he who teaches, in the act of teaching;

[8]or he who encourages, in the act of encouragement; he who gives, with generosity; he who leads, with diligence; he who shows mercy [in caring for others], with cheerfulness.

[9]Love is to be sincere *and* active [the real thing—without guile and hypocrisy]. Hate what is evil [detest all ungodliness, do not tolerate wickedness]; hold on tightly to what is good.

[10]Be devoted to one another with [authentic] brotherly affection [as

putting the Word to work

Can you imagine a church where everyone did the same thing and had the same gifts? It would not be very exciting or effective, would it? The Word of God teaches us that there are different gifts and functions within the church, and Romans 12:4–8 reminds us that we should graciously use the gifts we have been given, united as one body in Christ. Ask God to reveal your gifts to you and teach you how you can make your unique contribution as a member of the body of Christ.

putting the Word to work

Have you ever heard the saying, "If you talk the talk, you have to walk the walk?" As a Christian, it is important to live by the principles found in the Word of God. Romans 12:9–21 includes practical principles for living the Christian life. As you read this passage, identify areas in your life where you need to put some of these principles into practice. Be intentional about making these principles a lifestyle, and ask the Holy Spirit to help you do so. You will see for yourself how by living this way, good will overcome evil.

members of one family], give preference to one another in honor;

[11]never lagging behind in diligence; aglow in the Spirit, *enthusiastically* serving the Lord;

[12]*constantly* rejoicing in hope [because of our confidence in Christ], steadfast *and* patient in distress, devoted to prayer [continually seeking wisdom, guidance, and strength],

[13]contributing to the needs of God's people, pursuing [the practice of] hospitality.

[14]Bless those who persecute you [who cause you harm or hardship]; bless and do not curse [them]. [Matt 5:44; Luke 6:28]

[15]Rejoice with those who rejoice [sharing others' joy], and weep with those who weep [sharing others' grief].

[16]Live in harmony with one another; do not be haughty [conceited, self-important, exclusive], but associate with humble people [those with a realistic self-view]. Do not overestimate yourself. [Prov 3:7]

[17]Never repay anyone evil for evil. Take thought for what is right *and* gracious *and* proper in the sight of everyone. [Prov 20:22]

how to stay on fire for God

Romans 12:11 instructs us to be "aglow in the Spirit" as we serve the Lord with enthusiasm. In order to do this, we have to stay on fire.

How do we stay on fire? I have discovered that the Word of God coming out of my own mouth in the form of prayer, praise, preaching, or confession is the best way I can fan the flames. It stirs up the gift within me, keeps the fire aflame, and prevents my spirit from sinking within me. Staying thankful also keeps me enthusiastic.

The writer of Ecclesiastes tells us, "Whatever your hand finds to do, do it with all your might; for there is no activity or planning or knowledge or wisdom in Sheol (the nether world, the place of the dead), where you are going" (Ecclesiastes 9:10). Stay active; there is no point in putting off doing things until later. That is an expression of passivity, and it is one of the greatest tools Satan uses against God's people. The more passive we are, the more our flame diminishes. Procrastination and laziness are the cousins of passivity, and they usually attack in a group. Passive people wait to be moved by an outside force before they take action. But we are to be motivated and led by the Holy Spirit within us, not by outside forces. The best way to be on guard against the spirit of passivity is to do what we need to do now, and do it with all our might.

Remember, everything we do is to be done unto the Lord and for His glory (see 1 Corinthians 10:31). We should do it through Him, to Him, for Him, by Him, and with Him. And we should do it willingly, with our whole heart stirred up, on fire, and aglow within us.

¹⁸If possible, as far as it depends on you, live at peace with everyone.

¹⁹Beloved, never avenge yourselves, but leave the way open for God's wrath [and His judicial righteousness]; for it is written [in Scripture], "VENGEANCE IS MINE, I WILL REPAY," says the Lord. [Deut 32:35]

²⁰"BUT IF YOUR ENEMY IS HUNGRY, FEED HIM; IF HE IS THIRSTY, GIVE HIM A DRINK; FOR BY DOING THIS YOU WILL HEAP BURNING COALS ON HIS HEAD." [Prov 25:21, 22]

²¹Do not be overcome *and* conquered by evil, but overcome evil with good.

life point

Some people are basically impossible to get along with, but I love Romans 12:18, which essentially says do as much as you can to live at peace with everyone if at all possible. You cannot do *their* part, but you can do *your* part to maintain peace with others.

I challenge you to be a maker and maintainer of peace today and every day of your life.

13 LET EVERY person be subject to the governing authorities. For there is no authority except from God [granted by His permission and sanction], and those which exist have been put in place by God. [Prov 8:15]

²Therefore whoever resists [governmental] authority resists the ordinance

life point

Romans 12:19 encourages us not to try to get people back for what they have done to us. Whatever the situation is, you can leave it in God's hands and trust Him to do what is right.

of God. And those who have resisted it will bring judgment (civil penalty) on themselves.

³For [civil] authorities are not a source of fear for [people of] good behavior, but for [those who do] evil. Do you want to be unafraid of authority? Do what is good and you will receive approval *and* commendation.

⁴For he is God's servant to you for good. But if you do wrong, [you should] be afraid; for he does not carry the [executioner's] sword for nothing. He is God's servant, an avenger who brings punishment on the wrongdoer.

⁵Therefore one must be subject [to civil authorities], not only to escape the punishment [that comes with wrongdoing], but also as a matter of principle [knowing what is right before God].

⁶For this same reason you pay taxes, for *civil authorities* are God's servants, devoting themselves to governance.

⁷Pay to all what is due: tax to whom tax *is due,* customs to whom customs, respect to whom respect, honor to whom honor.

⁸Owe nothing to anyone except to love *and* seek the best for one another; for he who [unselfishly] loves his

life point

The Bible tells us that the way to defeat evil is by overcoming it with good (see Romans 12:21). But that takes effort and determination. It will not just happen; you have to decide to do it. Start where you are, and God will take you where you need to end up.

neighbor has fulfilled the [essence of the] law [relating to one's fellowman]. [Matt 22:36–40]

⁹The commandments, "YOU SHALL NOT COMMIT ADULTERY, YOU SHALL NOT MURDER, YOU SHALL NOT STEAL, YOU SHALL NOT COVET," and any other commandment are summed up in this statement: "YOU SHALL LOVE YOUR NEIGHBOR AS YOURSELF." [Ex 20:13–17; Lev 19:18]

¹⁰Love does no wrong to a neighbor [it never hurts anyone]. Therefore [unselfish] love is the fulfillment of the Law.

¹¹Do this, knowing that this is a critical time. It is already the hour for you to awaken from your sleep [of spiritual complacency]; for our salvation is nearer to us now than when we first believed [in Christ].

¹²The night [this present evil age] is almost gone and the day [of Christ's return] is almost here. So let us fling away the works of darkness and put on the [full] armor of light.

¹³Let us conduct ourselves properly *and* honorably as in the [light of] day, not in carousing and drunkenness, not in sexual promiscuity and irresponsibility, not in quarreling and jealousy.

¹⁴But clothe yourselves with the Lord Jesus Christ, and make no provision for [nor even think about gratifying] the flesh in regard to its improper desires.

14 AS FOR the one whose faith is weak, accept him [into your fellowship], but not for [the purpose of] quarreling over his opinions.

²One man's faith permits him to eat everything, while the weak *believer* eats *only* vegetables [to avoid eating ritually unclean meat or something previously considered unclean].

³The one who eats [everything] is not to look down on the one who does

not eat, and the one who does not eat must not criticize *or* pass judgment on the one who eats [everything], for God has accepted him.

⁴Who are you to judge the servant of another? Before his own master he stands [approved] or falls [out of favor]. And he [who serves the Master—the Lord] will stand, for the Lord is able to make him stand.

⁵One person regards one day as better [or more important] than another, while another regards every day [the same as any other]. Let everyone be fully convinced (assured, satisfied) in his own mind.

⁶He who observes the day, observes it for the Lord. He who eats, eats for the Lord, since he gives thanks to God; while he who abstains, abstains for the Lord and gives thanks to God.

⁷None of us lives for himself [for his own benefit, but for the Lord], and none of us dies for himself [but for the Lord].

⁸If we live, we live for the Lord, and if we die, we die for the Lord. So then, whether we live or die, we are the Lord's.

⁹For Christ died and lived again for this reason, that He might be Lord of both the dead and the living.

¹⁰But you, why do you criticize your brother? Or you again, why do you look down on your [believing] brother *or* regard him with contempt? For we will all stand before the judgment seat of God [who alone is judge].

¹¹For it is written [in Scripture],

"AS I LIVE, SAYS THE LORD, EVERY
   KNEE SHALL BOW TO ME,
AND EVERY TONGUE SHALL GIVE
   PRAISE TO GOD." [Is 45:23]

¹²So then, each of us will give an account of himself to God.

¹³Then let us not criticize one another anymore, but rather determine this—not to put an obstacle or a stumbling block *or* a source of temptation in another believer's way.

¹⁴I know and am convinced [as one] in the Lord Jesus that nothing is unclean [ritually defiled, and unholy] in itself; but [nonetheless] it is unclean to anyone who thinks it is unclean.

¹⁵If your brother is being hurt *or* offended because of food [that you insist on eating], you are no longer walking in love [toward him]. Do not let what you eat destroy *and* spiritually harm one for whom Christ died.

¹⁶Therefore do not let what is a good thing for you [because of your freedom to choose] be spoken of as evil [by someone else];

¹⁷for the kingdom of God is not *a matter of* eating and drinking [what one likes], but of righteousness and peace and joy in the Holy Spirit.

¹⁸For the one who serves Christ in this way [recognizing that food choice is secondary] is acceptable to God and is approved by men.

¹⁹So then, let us pursue [with enthusiasm] the things which make for peace and the building up of one another [things which lead to spiritual growth].

²⁰Do not, for the sake of food, tear down the work of God. All things indeed are [ceremonially] clean, but they are wrong for the person who eats and offends [another's conscience in the process].

²¹It is good [to do the right thing and] not eat meat or drink wine, or do anything that offends your brother *and* weakens him spiritually.

life point

Confronting the criticism and judgment of other people becomes easier when we remember that ultimately it is before our Master that we stand or fall. In the end we will answer to God alone (see Romans 14:12).

²²The faith which you have [that gives you freedom of choice], have as your own conviction before God [just keep it between yourself and God, seeking His will]. Happy is he who has no reason to condemn himself for what he approves.

²³But he who is uncertain [about eating a particular thing] is condemned if he eats, because he is not *acting* from faith. Whatever is not from faith is sin [whatever is done with doubt is sinful].

15 NOW WE who are strong [in our convictions and faith] ought to [patiently] put up with the weaknesses of those who are not strong, and not just please ourselves.

²Let each one of us [make it a practice to] please his neighbor for his good, to build him up spiritually.

³For even Christ did not please Himself; but as it is written [in Scripture], "THE REPROACHES OF THOSE WHO REPROACHED YOU (the Father) FELL ON ME (the Son)." [Ps 69:9]

⁴For whatever was written in earlier times was written for our instruction, so that through endurance and the encouragement of the Scriptures we might have hope *and* overflow with confidence in His promises.

⁵Now may the God who gives endurance and who supplies encouragement grant that you be of the same mind with one another according to Christ Jesus,

⁶so that with one accord you may with one voice glorify *and* praise *and* honor the God and Father of our Lord Jesus Christ.

⁷Therefore, [continue to] accept *and* welcome one another, just as Christ has accepted *and* welcomed us to the glory of [our great] God.

⁸For I tell you that Christ has become a servant *and* a minister to the circumcision (Jews) on behalf of God's truth, to confirm *and* verify the promises made to the fathers,

⁹and for the Gentiles to glorify God for His mercy [to them, since God had no covenant with them]. As it is written *and* forever remains written,

"THEREFORE I PRAISE YOU AMONG THE GENTILES,
AND SING PRAISES TO YOUR NAME."
[Ps 18:49]

¹⁰Again it says,

"REJOICE *and* CELEBRATE, O GENTILES, ALONG WITH HIS PEOPLE." [Deut 32:43]

¹¹And again,

"PRAISE THE LORD ALL YOU GENTILES,
AND LET ALL THE PEOPLES PRAISE HIM!" [Ps 117:1]

¹²Again Isaiah says,

"THERE SHALL BE A ROOT OF JESSE,
HE WHO ARISES TO RULE [as King] OVER THE GENTILES,
IN HIM SHALL THE GENTILES HOPE."
[Is 11:1, 10; Rev 5:5; 22:16]

¹³May the God of hope fill you with all joy and peace in believing [through the experience of your faith] that by the power of the Holy Spirit you will abound in hope *and* overflow with confidence in His promises.

¹⁴Personally I am convinced about you, my brothers and sisters, that you yourselves are full of goodness, amply filled with all [spiritual] knowledge, and competent to admonish *and* counsel *and* instruct one another.

¹⁵Still, on some points I have written to you very boldly *and* without reservation to remind you [about them] again, because of the grace that was given to me from God,

¹⁶to be a minister of Christ Jesus to the Gentiles. I minister as a priest the gospel of God, in order that my offering

pleasing God, pleasing others

Wanting to please and be acceptable is a natural trait. We might even say it is godly. God wants us to be good to people and strive to accommodate them. Romans 15:2, 3 teach us to make a practice of pleasing our neighbors. But there is balance in that.

Above all, we are to be God-pleasers, not self-pleasers or people-pleasers. If we seek and love the approval of others, we are probably people-pleasers. We usually discover in our experience that if we do not please people, they do not approve of us; therefore, if we have an out-of-balance need for approval, we will be people-pleasers.

The Apostle Paul said in Galatians that he did not seek popularity with man, yet in 1 Corinthians he stated that he tried to please people and accommodate himself to their opinions and desires in order that they might be saved. Let's read and compare these two scriptures:

"Am I now trying to win the favor and approval of men, or of God? Or am I seeking to please someone? If I were still trying to be popular with men, I should not be a bond-servant of Christ" (Galatians 1:10).

"Just as I please everyone in all things [as much as possible adapting myself to the interests of others], not seeking my own benefit but that of the many, so that they [will be open to the message of salvation and] may be saved" (1 Corinthians 10:33).

When we consider these two verses, they almost seem to oppose one another; yet if we understand the heart behind them, we see that they are not contradictory.

Paul wanted to please people. He wanted to maintain good relationships with people, especially for the purpose of leading them to accept Jesus as their Savior. He also wanted to please God and fulfill the call on his life. Paul knew how to maintain balance in this area. He tried to please people, as long as pleasing them did not cause him to displease the Lord. The Bible also says in Acts 5:29, "We must obey God rather than men."

Pleasing people is good, but it is not good to become "people-pleasers." I define people-pleasers as those who try to please people even if they have to compromise their conscience to do so. People-pleasers are those who need approval so desperately that they allow others to control, manipulate, and use them. They are not led by the Holy Spirit, as God's Word instructs us to be (see Romans 8:14).

People-pleasers are fear-based individuals. They fear rejection, judgment, what people think and say, and especially anger or disapproval. God-pleasers are grace-based individuals who do not seek approval out of insecurity or fear. They strive to follow God with all their heart, but they also seek to please and minister to others without compromise or fear of rejection.

of the Gentiles may become acceptable [to Him], sanctified [made holy and set apart for His purpose] by the Holy Spirit.

[17]In Christ Jesus, then, I have found [legitimate] reason for boasting in things related [to my service] to God. [18]For I will not [even] presume to

life point

One night I felt miserable. I was just walking around my house doing what I needed to do, but I was not happy, not enjoying life.

"What is the matter with me, Lord?" I asked. "What is my problem?"

A sense of heaviness engulfed me, something that drained the joy out of me. As I wandered around the house, I began looking at a box of Bible verses I kept on my desk. I flipped it open to Romans 15:13, and the Holy Spirit within me instantly confirmed the truth that I saw in this verse.

I recognized immediately that a large part of my problem was simply that I was doubting instead of believing—and believing is what brings joy and peace (see Romans 15:13). I was doubting the call of God on my life, wondering if He would meet our financial needs, questioning my decisions and actions, etc.

I became negative instead of positive. I doubted instead of believing.

Doubt is an attitude that can easily creep up on us, which is why it's so important that we be on guard against it and not to permit it to do so.

Doubt may certainly knock at the door of your heart. When it does, answer with a believing heart, and you will always maintain victory. Doubt steals your joy, but believing releases it.

speak of anything except what Christ has done through me [as an instrument in His hands], resulting in the obedience of the Gentiles [to the gospel], by word and deed,

19with the power of signs and won-ders, [and all of it] in the power of the Spirit. So [starting] from Jerusalem and as far *away* as Illyricum, I have fully preached the gospel [faithfully preaching the good news] of Christ [where it had not before been preached].

20Accordingly I set a goal to preach the gospel, not where Christ's name was already known, so that I would not build on another man's foundation;

21but [instead I would act on this goal] as it is written [in Scripture],

"THEY WHO HAD NO NEWS OF HIM
    SHALL SEE,
AND THEY WHO HAVE NOT HEARD
    [of Him] SHALL UNDERSTAND."
    [Is 52:15]

22This [goal—my commitment to this principle] is the reason why I have often been prevented from coming to you [in Rome].

23But now, with no further place for work in these regions, and since I have longed for many years to come to you—

24whenever I go [on my trip] to Spain—I hope to see you as I pass through [Rome], and to be helped on my journey there by you, after I have first enjoyed your company for a little while.

25But for now, I am going to Jerusalem to serve the saints (Jewish believers).

26For [Gentile believers in] Macedonia and Achaia have been pleased to make a contribution for the poor among the saints (Jewish believers) in Jerusalem.

27They were pleased to do it, and they are indebted to them. For if the Gentiles have come to share in their spiritual things, then they are indebted to serve them also in [tangible] material things.

28Therefore, when I have finished this [mission] and have safely given to them what has been raised, I will go on by way of you to Spain.

²⁹I know that when I do come to you, I will come in the abundant blessing of Christ.

³⁰I urge you, believers, by our Lord Jesus Christ and by the love of the Spirit, to join together with me in your prayers to God in my behalf,

³¹[and pray] that I may be rescued from the unbelievers in Judea, and that my service for Jerusalem may be acceptable to the saints (Jewish believers) *there*;

³²so that by God's will I may come to you with joy and find rest in your company.

³³May the God of peace be with you all! Amen.

16 NOW I introduce *and* commend to you our sister Phoebe, a deaconess (servant) of the church at Cenchrea,

²that you may receive her in the Lord [with love and hospitality], as God's people ought to receive one another. And that you may help her in whatever matter she may require assistance from you, for she has been a helper of many, including myself.

³Greet Prisca and Aquila, my fellow workers in Christ Jesus,

⁴who risked their own necks [endangering their very lives] for my life. To them not only do I give thanks, but also all the churches of the Gentiles.

⁵Also *greet* the church that meets in their house. Greet my beloved Epaenetus, who is the first convert to Christ from [the west coast province of] Asia [Minor].

⁶Greet Mary, who has worked so hard for you.

⁷Greet Andronicus and Junias, my kinsmen and [once] my fellow prisoners, who are held in high esteem in *the estimation of* the apostles, and who were [believers] in Christ before me.

⁸Greet Ampliatus, my beloved in the Lord.

⁹Greet Urbanus, our fellow worker in Christ, and my beloved Stachys.

¹⁰Greet Apelles, the one tested *and* approved in Christ. Greet those who belong to the *household* of Aristobulus.

¹¹Greet my kinsman Herodion. Greet those of the *household* of Narcissus, who are in the Lord.

¹²Greet those workers in the Lord, Tryphaena and Tryphosa. Greet my beloved Persis, who has worked hard in the Lord.

¹³Greet Rufus, an eminent *and* choice man in the Lord, also his mother [who has been] a mother to me as well.

¹⁴Greet Asyncritus, Phlegon, Hermes, Patrobas, Hermas, and the brothers who are with them.

¹⁵Greet Philologus and Julia, Nereus and his sister, and Olympas, and all God's people who are with them.

¹⁶Greet one another with a holy kiss. All the churches of Christ greet you.

¹⁷I urge you, brothers and sisters, to keep your eyes on those who cause dissensions and create obstacles *or* introduce temptations [for others] to commit sin, [acting in ways] contrary to the doctrine which you have learned. Turn away from them.

¹⁸For such people do not serve our Lord Christ, but their own appetites and base desires. By smooth and flattering speech they deceive the hearts of the unsuspecting [the innocent and the naive].

speak the Word

Thank You, Lord, that You are the God of peace! I receive Your peace today.
—ADAPTED FROM ROMANS 15:33

¹⁹For *the report of* your obedience has reached everyone, so that I rejoice over you, but I want you to be wise in what is good and innocent in what is evil.

²⁰The God of peace will soon crush Satan under your feet.

The [wonderful] grace of our Lord Jesus be with you.

²¹Timothy, my fellow worker, sends his greetings to you, as do Lucius, Jason and Sosipater, my kinsmen.

²²I, Tertius, the writer (scribe) of this letter, greet you in the Lord.

²³Gaius, who is host to me and to the whole church here, greets you. Erastus, the city treasurer, and our brother Quartus, greet you.

²⁴[The grace of our Lord Jesus Christ be with you all. Amen.]

²⁵Now to Him who is able to establish *and* strengthen you [in the faith] according to my gospel and the preaching of Jesus Christ, according to the revelation of the mystery [of the plan of salvation] which has been kept secret for long ages past,

²⁶but now has been disclosed and through the prophetic Scriptures has been made known to all the nations, according to the commandment of the eternal God, *leading them* to obedience to the faith,

²⁷to the only wise God, through Jesus Christ, be the glory forevermore! Amen.

First Corinthians

Author:
Paul

Date:
About AD 55.

Everyday Life Principles:
Our motives and behavior are extremely important to God.

If you want to walk in love, read 1 Corinthians 13 and apply its principles to your life.

Let everything you do be done in love.

First Corinthians covers a variety of subjects and is full of practical information for everyday life, but if I had to reduce the main theme to its simplest form, I would say that this book is about our motives and behavior as believers—and both are very important to God. This letter was written by the Apostle Paul and addressed to the Christians in Corinth, a wealthy city on the Mediterranean Sea, where people from various cultures and religions often converged. Their diverse backgrounds and religious experiences often caused problems in the church and created a need for Paul to write this letter.

First Corinthians deals with everything from spiritual issues such as the gifts of the Holy Spirit, the importance of unity among believers, and confidence in God to practical matters such as how to behave in church. It also gives us advice on practical matters, such as healthy eating and taking care of our bodies and handling money and possessions. Perhaps most important, this book gives us the Bible's most extensive and vivid definition of love and teaches us how to walk in love (see chapter 13); without it we are "nothing" (1 Corinthians 13:2).

As you read 1 Corinthians, I pray you will apply its excellent and varied teachings to your life and that you will take the great advice of 1 Corinthians 16:14 and, "Let everything you do be done in love."

1 PAUL, CALLED as an apostle (special messenger, personally chosen representative) of Jesus Christ by the will of God, and our brother Sosthenes,

²To the church of God in Corinth, to those sanctified (set apart, made holy) in Christ Jesus, who are selected *and* called as saints (God's people), together with all those who in every place call on *and* honor the name of our Lord Jesus Christ, their *Lord* and ours:

³Grace to you and peace [inner calm and spiritual well-being] from God our Father and the Lord Jesus Christ.

⁴I thank my God always for you because of the grace of God which was given you in Christ Jesus,

⁵so that in everything you were [exceedingly] enriched in Him, in all speech [empowered by the spiritual gifts] and in all knowledge [with insight into the faith].

⁶In this way our testimony about Christ was confirmed *and* established in you,

⁷so that you are not lacking in any *spiritual* gift [which comes from the Holy Spirit], as you eagerly wait [with confident trust] for the revelation of our Lord Jesus Christ [when He returns].

⁸And He will also confirm you to the end [keeping you strong and free of any accusation, so that you will be] blameless *and* beyond reproach in the day [of the return] of our Lord Jesus Christ.

⁹God is faithful [He is reliable, trustworthy and ever true to His promise—He can be depended on], and through Him you were called into fellowship with His Son, Jesus Christ our Lord.

¹⁰But I urge you, believers, by the

putting the Word to work

Do you ever look around and notice the competition in our society today, even among Christians? It happens, and that is sad because there is simply no room for rivalry in the body of Christ; we are called to be one in Him (see 1 Corinthians 1:10–17). Pray for and do all you can to promote unity and harmony everywhere you go.

name of our Lord Jesus Christ, that all of you be in full agreement in what you say, and that there be no divisions *or* factions among you, but that you be perfectly united in your way of thinking and in your judgment [about matters of the faith].

¹¹For I have been informed about you, my brothers and sisters, by those of Chloe's *household,* that there are quarrels *and* factions among you.

¹²Now I mean this, that each one of you says, "I am [a disciple] of Paul," or "I am [a disciple] of Apollos," or "I am [a disciple] of Cephas (Peter)," or "I am [a disciple] of Christ."

¹³Has Christ been divided [into different parts]? Was Paul crucified for you? Or were you baptized into the name of Paul? [Certainly not!]

¹⁴I thank God that I did not baptize any of you except Crispus and Gaius, [Acts 18:8; Rom 16:23]

¹⁵so that no one would say that you were baptized into my name.

¹⁶Now I also baptized the household of Stephanas; beyond that, I do not know if I baptized anyone else.

¹⁷For Christ did not send me [as an apostle] to baptize, but [commissioned and empowered me] to preach the good

speak the Word

God, I declare that in You, I am not lacking in any spiritual gift as I eagerly wait for the revelation and return of our Lord Jesus Christ.
—ADAPTED FROM 1 CORINTHIANS 1:7, 8

news [of salvation]—not with clever *and* eloquent speech [as an orator], so that the cross of Christ would not be made ineffective [deprived of its saving power].

¹⁸For the message of the cross is foolishness [absurd and illogical] to those who are perishing *and* spiritually dead [because they reject it], but to us who are being saved [by God's grace] it is [the manifestation of] the power of God.

¹⁹For it is written *and* forever remains written,

"I WILL DESTROY THE WISDOM OF
  THE WISE [the philosophy of the
  philosophers],
AND THE CLEVERNESS OF THE
  CLEVER [who do not know Me]
  I WILL NULLIFY." [Is 29:14]

²⁰Where is the wise man (philosopher)? Where is the scribe (scholar)? Where is the debater (logician, orator) of this age? Has God not exposed the foolishness of this world's wisdom?

²¹For since the world through all its [earthly] wisdom failed to recognize God, God in His wisdom was well-pleased through the foolishness of the message preached [regarding salvation] to save those who believe [in Christ and welcome Him as Savior].

²²For Jews demand signs (attesting miracles), and Greeks pursue [worldly] wisdom *and* philosophy,

²³but we preach Christ crucified, [a message which is] to Jews a stumbling block [that provokes their opposition], and to Gentiles foolishness [just utter nonsense],

²⁴but to those who are the called, both Jews and Greeks (Gentiles), Christ is the power of God and the wisdom of God. [Rom 8:28]

²⁵[This is] because the foolishness of God [is not foolishness at all and] is wiser than men [far beyond human comprehension], and the weakness of

God is stronger than men [far beyond the limits of human effort].

²⁶Just look at your own calling, believers; not many [of you were considered] wise according to human standards, not many powerful *or* influential, not many of high *and* noble birth.

²⁷But God has selected [for His purpose] the foolish things of the world to shame the wise [revealing their ignorance], and God has selected [for His purpose] the weak things of the world to shame the things which are strong [revealing their frailty].

²⁸God has selected [for His purpose] the insignificant (base) things of the world, and the things that are despised

life point

God works through imperfect people, or what I often call "jars of clay" or "cracked pots" (see 1 Corinthians 1:27–29). This means that we are all flawed, so when people look at us and see amazing things happening, they know God must be at work because without Him, we certainly could not achieve or accomplish what we do. I believe anyone who really knows me has no difficulty realizing the work I am doing today certainly must be God at work in and through me. They give Him the glory, not me, because they see my imperfections and know my limitations. God indeed chooses the "foolish" and "weak" on purpose so no human being can have pretense for boasting in His presence.

Imagine a clay pot with a lamp in it and a lid on it. Even though it may be filled with light, no one can see the light within it. Yet if the pot is cracked, the light will shine through the cracks. In this same way, God works through our imperfections. Ask Him to work through you, in spite of your imperfections. You will be amazed at what He can accomplish through you!

and treated with contempt, [even] the things that are nothing, so that He might reduce to nothing the things that are,

²⁹so that no one may [be able to] boast in the presence of God.

³⁰But it is from Him that you are in Christ Jesus, who became to us wisdom from God [revealing His plan of salvation], and righteousness [making us acceptable to God], and sanctification [making us holy and setting us apart for God], and redemption [providing our ransom from the penalty for sin],

³¹so then, as it is written [in Scripture], "HE WHO BOASTS *and* GLORIES, LET HIM BOAST *and* GLORY IN THE LORD." [Jer 9:24]

2 AND WHEN I came to you, brothers and sisters, proclaiming to you the testimony of God [concerning salvation through Christ], I did not come with superiority of speech or of wisdom [no lofty words of eloquence or of philosophy as a Greek orator might do];

²for I made the decision to know nothing [that is, to forego philosophical or theological discussions regarding inconsequential things and opinions while] among you except Jesus Christ, and Him crucified [and the meaning of His redemptive, substitutionary death and His resurrection].

putting the Word to work

Do you sometimes hesitate to share about God because you are not sure what to say? Even Paul, a great evangelist and teacher, did not count on flowery speech or his ability to persuade people; he depended on the Holy Spirit to speak through him (see 1 Corinthians 2:1–5). Ask the Holy Spirit to speak through you too and believe that He will.

³I came to you in [a state of] weakness and fear and great trembling.

⁴And my message and my preaching were not in persuasive words of wisdom [using clever rhetoric], but [they were delivered] in demonstration of the [Holy] Spirit [operating through me] and of [His] power [stirring the minds of the listeners and persuading them],

⁵so that your faith would not rest on the wisdom *and* rhetoric of men, but on the power of God.

⁶Yet we do speak wisdom among those *spiritually* mature [believers who have teachable hearts and a greater understanding]; but [it is a higher] wisdom not [the wisdom] of this *present* age nor of the rulers *and* leaders of this age, who are passing away;

⁷but we speak God's wisdom in a mystery, the *wisdom* once hidden [from man, but now revealed to us by God, that wisdom] which God predestined before the ages to our glory [to lift us into the glory of His presence].

⁸None of the rulers of this age recognized *and* understood this *wisdom*; for if they had, they would not have crucified the Lord of glory;

life point

First Corinthians 2:5 teaches us not to put our faith in human wisdom or philosophy, but in the power of God. Verse 11 of this same chapter says that no one knows the thoughts of God except the Spirit of God. Since the Holy Spirit knows the secret counsel of God, it is a vital necessity for us to know how to hear what He wants to say to us. The Holy Spirit helps us realize, comprehend, and appreciate the gifts of divine favor and blessing God bestows on us. Human wisdom does not teach us this truth; it comes from the Holy Spirit, Who gives us the mind of Christ (see 1 Corinthians 2:12–16). Ask Him to give you the mind of Christ today.

9but just as it is written [in Scripture],

"THINGS WHICH THE EYE HAS NOT
  SEEN AND THE EAR HAS NOT
  HEARD,
AND WHICH HAVE NOT ENTERED
  THE HEART OF MAN,
ALL THAT GOD HAS PREPARED FOR
  THOSE WHO LOVE HIM [who hold
  Him in affectionate reverence,
  who obey Him, and who
  gratefully recognize the benefits
  that He has bestowed]." [Is 64:4;
  65:17]

10For God has unveiled them *and* revealed *them* to us through the [Holy] Spirit; for the Spirit searches all things [diligently], even [sounding and measuring] the [profound] depths of God [the divine counsels and things far beyond human understanding].
11For what person knows the thoughts and motives of a man except the man's spirit within him? So also no one knows the *thoughts* of God except the Spirit of God.
12Now we have received, not the spirit of the world, but the [Holy] Spirit who is from God, so that we may know *and* understand the [wonderful] things freely given to us by God.
13We also speak of these things, not in words taught *or* supplied by human wisdom, but in those taught by the Spirit, combining *and* interpreting spiritual *thoughts* with spiritual *words* [for those being guided by the Holy Spirit].
14But the natural [unbelieving] man does not accept the things [the teachings and revelations] of the Spirit of God, for they are foolishness [absurd

life point

First Corinthians 2:14 explains that a natural person cannot understand spiritual things because they must be spiritually discerned. This means that spiritual things take place in the regenerated (born-again) spirit of the inner person, not in the natural mind.

I am very grateful for discernment and spiritual understanding. I appreciate the fact that you and I, as believers in Jesus Christ, filled with His Spirit, can make decisions courageously because we can trust what is in our hearts.

and illogical] to him; and he is incapable of understanding them, because they are spiritually discerned *and* appreciated, [and he is unqualified to judge spiritual matters].
15But the spiritual man [the spiritually mature Christian] judges all things [questions, examines and applies what the Holy Spirit reveals], yet is himself judged by no one [the unbeliever cannot judge and understand the believer's spiritual nature].
16For WHO HAS KNOWN THE MIND *and* PURPOSES OF THE LORD, SO AS TO INSTRUCT HIM? But we have the mind of Christ [to be guided by His thoughts and purposes]. [Is 40:13]

3 HOWEVER, BROTHERS and sisters, I could not talk to you as to spiritual people, but [only] as to worldly people [dominated by human nature], *mere* infants [in the new life] in Christ!

speak the Word

Thank You, God, for preparing for me things my eyes have not seen, my ears have not heard, and my heart has not thought of—things that can only be revealed to me by Your Spirit.
—ADAPTED FROM 1 CORINTHIANS 2:9, 10

the difference between knowing and *really* knowing

The natural man does not understand the spiritual man (see 1 Corinthians 2:14). Some of the choices and decisions a spiritual person makes do not make sense at all to a non-spiritual person. Those who are natural or non-spiritual try to understand everything with their minds, but those who are spiritual discern things by the spirit. They live out of their new hearts and out of the attitudes God gives them. Recently I told someone something I believed and they said, "That makes no sense at all." I responded by saying, "I know it. I believe a lot of things that do not make sense to my mind." Carnal or natural people want to know things in their minds and with their intellect, but spiritual people know things by the spirit. When they need answers they look to their hearts, not their heads.

There is a difference in "knowing" and "really knowing." Someone who has met me might say, "I know Joyce Meyer," when in reality that person does not really know much about me at all. But, when my husband says, "I know Joyce Meyer," he really knows me thoroughly and completely. He has seen me in every kind of situation and often knows how I will respond to certain circumstances before I even have a chance to respond.

The spiritual realm is just as real to the spiritual person as the natural world is to the natural person. Just because we cannot see something does not mean it does not exist. We depend entirely too much on what we see, feel, and understand. Satan sends lies to your mind and you can either believe what he says or you can ask yourself, "Now, what do I know in my heart about this?"

Spiritual people are hard to understand mentally. Sometimes they might even seem a bit odd to non-spiritual people. They live by discernment. They look into things with their spirit, not only with their natural eyes. They live by what they know and truly feel in their spirit, not what they see or feel. Faith has nothing to do with feelings and sight—and that is exactly how the spiritual person lives. He lives by faith! He is saved by faith, justified by faith, made right with God by faith—and he walks by faith. The spiritual life is definitely misunderstood by natural, non-spiritual people, but it is a wonderful, fulfilling, exciting life.

²I fed you with milk, not solid food; for you were not yet able *to receive it.* Even now you are still not ready.

³You are still worldly [controlled by ordinary impulses, the sinful capacity]. For as long as there is jealousy and strife *and* discord among you, are you not unspiritual, and are you not walking like ordinary men [unchanged by faith]?

⁴For when one *of you* says, "I am [a disciple] of Paul," and another, "I am [a disciple] of Apollos," are you not [proving yourselves unchanged, just] *ordinary* people?

⁵What then is Apollos? And what is Paul? Just servants through whom you believed [in Christ], even as the Lord appointed to each his task.

⁶I planted, Apollos watered, but God [all the while] was causing the growth.

⁷So neither is the one who plants nor the one who waters anything, but [only] God who causes the growth.

⁸He who plants and he who waters are one [in importance and esteem,

life point

Envy and jealousy cause us to strive for things God will give us in His timing, if it is His will for us to have them. A jealous, envious heart never blesses God and is a characteristic of a worldly, unspiritual person (see 1 Corinthians 3:3). We are not to envy what other people have.

working toward the same purpose]; but each will receive his own reward according to his own labor.

⁹For we are God's fellow workers [His servants working together]; you are God's cultivated field [His garden, His vineyard], God's building. [Is 61:3]

¹⁰According to the [remarkable] grace of God which was given to me [to prepare me for my task], like a skillful master builder I laid a foundation, and now another is building on it. But each one must be careful how he builds on it,

¹¹for no one can lay a foundation other than the one which is [already] laid, which is Jesus Christ.

jealousy prevents blessing

First Corinthians 3:3 teaches us that envy comes from fleshly impulses.

Years ago I discovered that the best way to get over envy or jealousy is to admit it. When you feel jealous or envious, be honest with God and ask Him to help you live free from it. Anything we hide has power over us, so bringing hidden things into the light not only exposes them, but also weakens their power over us.

I must admit, there are times when I hear about a blessing that someone receives, and I start to think, *When is that going to happen to me?* When that thought enters my mind, I immediately open my mouth and say, "I am happy for him. If God can do it for him, He can do it for me too."

If a young woman is unmarried and prays and asks God to give her a husband, she may have difficulty being truly happy for her friends when they get married.

In similar situations, instead of being unhappy or jealous or envious, we all need to learn to be happy for others and let their blessings be encouraging to us. We can believe that what God did for them, He can do for us. If He did it once, He can do it again!

We should learn to pray for other people to be blessed. We should pray for God to do for them what we want Him to do for us. What we sow into others through our prayers, God can make happen for us.

We should also bless others and not be afraid they will get ahead of us. We must not envy anyone else's appearance, possessions, education, social standing, marital status, gifts and talents, job, or anything else because that will only hinder our own blessing.

Being jealous and envious of others is a total waste of time. We all have gifts that God gives us; they do not come from any other source. We must be content with what heaven sends us. God has a unique plan for each of our lives, and the gifts He gives us are part of that plan. We can trust Him; He knows His business. What He does for others is actually none of our business. Our business is to walk in love.

putting the Word to work

First Corinthians 3:10, 11 teach us about foundations. People try to build their lives on many things—money, education, job titles, possessions and other resources. However, these are all faulty foundations. Let me ask you: Who or what is the foundation of your life? Jesus Christ is the only sure foundation on which you can build your life. Ask God to help you build your life wisely upon the firm foundation of Jesus.

¹²But if anyone builds on the foundation with gold, silver, precious stones, wood, hay, straw,
¹³each one's work will be clearly shown [for what it is]; for the day [of judgment] will disclose it, because it is to be revealed with fire, and the fire will test the quality *and* character *and* worth of each person's work. [2 Cor 5:10]
¹⁴If any person's work which he has built [on this foundation, that is, any outcome of his effort] remains [and survives this test], he will receive a reward.
¹⁵But if any person's work is burned up [by the test], he will suffer the loss [of his reward]; yet he himself will be saved, but only as [one who has barely escaped] through fire. [Job 23:10]
¹⁶Do you not know *and* understand that you [the church] are the temple of God, and that the Spirit of God dwells [permanently] in you [collectively and individually]?
¹⁷If anyone destroys the temple of God [corrupting it with false doctrine], God will destroy the destroyer; for the temple of God is holy (sacred), and that is what you are.
¹⁸Let no one deceive himself. If anyone among you thinks that he is wise in this age, let him become a fool [discarding his worldly pretensions and

acknowledging his lack of wisdom], so that he may become [truly] wise. [Is 5:21]
¹⁹For the wisdom of this world is foolishness (absurdity, stupidity) before God; for it is written [in Scripture], "[He is] THE ONE WHO CATCHES THE WISE *and* CLEVER IN THEIR CRAFTINESS;" [Job 5:13]
²⁰and again, "THE LORD KNOWS THE THOUGHTS of the [humanly] wise, THAT THEY ARE USELESS." [Ps 94:11]
²¹So let no one boast in men [about their wisdom, or of having this or that one as a leader]. For all things are yours,
²²whether Paul or Apollos or Cephas (Peter) or the world or life or death or things present or things to come; all things are yours,
²³and you belong to Christ; and Christ belongs to God.

4 SO THEN, let us [who minister] be regarded as servants of Christ and stewards (trustees, administrators) of the mysteries of God [that He chooses to reveal].
²In this case, moreover, it is required [as essential and demanded] of stewards that one be found faithful *and* trustworthy.
³But [as for me personally] it matters very little to me that I may be judged by you or *any* human court [on this point]; in fact, I do not even judge myself.

life point

When we accept Christ, the Holy Spirit comes to dwell in us. God chooses to move into our spirit—into the center core of our lives—where He can be closer to us than any other living thing. When God's Holy Spirit moves into our human spirit, our spirit is prepared as a dwelling place for God and is made holy because God is there (see 1 Corinthians 3:16, 17).

[4]I am aware of nothing against myself *and* I feel blameless, but I am not by this acquitted [before God]. It is the Lord who judges me.

[5]So do not go on passing judgment before the appointed time, *but wait* until the Lord comes, for He will both bring to light the [secret] things that are hidden in darkness and disclose the motives of the hearts. Then each one's praise will come from God.

[6]Now I have applied these things [that is, the analogies about factions] to myself and Apollos for your benefit, believers, so that you may learn from us not to go beyond what is written [in Scripture], so that none of you will become arrogant *and* boast in favor of one [minister or teacher] against the other.

[7]For who regards you as superior *or* what sets you apart as special? What do you have that you did not receive [from another]? And if in fact you received it [from God or someone else], why do you boast as if you had not received it [but had gained it by yourself]?

[8][You behave as if] you are already filled [with spiritual wisdom and in need of nothing more]. Already you have become rich [in spiritual gifts]! You [in your conceit] have ascended your thrones *and* become kings without us; and how I wish [that it were true and] that you did reign as kings, so that we might reign with you.

[9]For, I think, God has exhibited us apostles at the end of the line, like men sentenced to death [and paraded as prisoners in a procession], because we have become a spectacle to the world [a show in the world's amphitheater], both to angels and to men.

[10]We are [regarded as] fools for Christ, but you are so wise in Christ; we are weak, but you are strong; you are highly esteemed, but we are dishonored.

[11]To this present hour we are both hungry and thirsty; we are *continually* poorly dressed, and we are roughly treated, and wander homeless.

[12]We work [for our living], working *hard* with our own hands. When we are reviled *and* verbally abused, we bless. When we are persecuted, we take it patiently *and* endure.

[13]When we are slandered, we *try to be* conciliatory *and* answer softly. We have become like the scum of the world, the dregs of all things, even until now.

[14]I do not write these things to shame you, but to warn *and* advise you as my beloved children.

[15]For even if you were to have ten thousand teachers [to guide you] in Christ, yet you would not have many fathers [who led you to Christ and assumed responsibility for you], for I became your father in Christ Jesus through the good news [of salvation].

[16]So I urge you, be imitators of me [just as a child imitates his father].

[17]For this reason I have sent Timothy to you, who is my beloved and faithful child in the Lord, and he will remind you of my way of life in Christ [my conduct and my precepts for godly living], just as I teach everywhere in every church.

[18]Now some of you have become arrogant *and* pretentious, as though I were not coming to see you.

[19]But I will come to you soon, if the Lord is willing, and I will find out not just the talk of these arrogant people, but [evaluate] their [spiritual] power [whether they live up to their own claims].

[20]For the kingdom of God is not based on talk but on power.

speak the Word

Thank You, God, that Your kingdom is not based on talk, but on power.
−ADAPTED FROM 1 CORINTHIANS 4:20

a father's heart

Paul had a father's heart toward the believers in the church at Corinth (see 1 Corinthians 4:15).

A father's heart is that tender, nurturing, training, teaching, stick-to-it kind of attitude that does not give up on people just because they do not learn quickly.

A father delights in teaching his children how to walk or to play ball. He does not become angry with them because they do not master the steps the first time. He keeps working and working with them until they learn how to do it. A good father does not give up on his children. He is committed to them all of their lives.

Paul said the church is full of instructors, full of teachers, full of people who can preach a sermon and tell others what to do. But he also said there are not enough fathers in the church.

If you want to be a leader in the body of Christ, especially if you want to be a pastor, it is vital to have the heart of a father.

Perhaps you feel unqualified to "father" someone in the spiritual life. Perhaps you did not have a father who was a good role model to you. Perhaps you do not know how to be "fatherlike." The truth is that we all have had less-than-perfect fathers here on earth. Realize that God is a good heavenly Father. He can nurture you as your loving Father, and He can show you how to treat others the same way. Ask Him to help you. He will.

²¹Which do you prefer? Shall I come to you with a rod [of discipline and correction], or with love and a gentle spirit?

5 IT IS actually reported [everywhere] that there is sexual immorality among you, a kind of immorality that is condemned even among the [unbelieving] Gentiles: that someone has [an intimate relationship with] his father's wife. [Deut 22:30; 27:20]

²And you are proud and arrogant! You should have mourned in shame so that the man who has done this [disgraceful] thing would be removed from your fellowship!

³For I, though absent [from you] in body but present in spirit, have already passed judgment on him who has committed this [act], as if I were present.

⁴In the name of our Lord Jesus, when you are assembled, and I am with you in spirit, with the power of our Lord Jesus,

⁵you are to hand over this man to Satan for the destruction of his body, so that his spirit may be saved in the day of the Lord Jesus.

⁶Your boasting [over the supposed spirituality of your church] is not good [indeed, it is vulgar and inappropriate]. Do you not know that [just] a little leaven ferments the whole batch [of dough, just as a little sin corrupts a person or an entire church]?

⁷Clean out the old leaven so that you may be a new batch, just as you are, still unleavened. For Christ our Passover Lamb has been sacrificed.

⁸Therefore, let us celebrate the feast, not with old leaven, nor with leaven of vice and malice and wickedness, but

with the unleavened bread of sincerity and [untainted] truth. [Ex 12:19; 13:7; Deut 16:3]

⁹I wrote you in my [previous] letter not to associate with [sexually] immoral people—

¹⁰not meaning the immoral people of this world, or the greedy ones and swindlers, or idolaters, for then you would have to get out of the world *and* human society altogether!

¹¹But actually, I have written to you not to associate with any so-called [Christian] brother if he is sexually immoral or greedy, or is an idolater [devoted to anything that takes the place of God], or is a reviler [who insults or slanders or otherwise verbally abuses others], or is a drunkard or a swindler—you must not so much as eat with such a person. [2 Thess 3:6]

¹²For what business is it of mine to judge outsiders (non-believers)? Do you not judge those who are within *the church* [to protect the church as the situation requires]?

¹³God *alone* sits in judgment on those who are outside [the faith]. REMOVE THE WICKED ONE FROM AMONG YOU [expel him from your church]. [Deut 17:7]

6 DOES ANY one of you, when he has a complaint (civil dispute) with another [believer], dare to go to law before unrighteous men (non-believers) instead of [placing the issue] before the saints (God's people)?

²Do you not know that the saints (God's people) will [one day] judge the world? If the world is to be judged by you, are you not competent to try trivial (insignificant, petty) cases?

³Do you not know that we [believers] will judge angels? How much more then [as to] matters of this life?

⁴So if you have lawsuits dealing with matters of this life, are you appointing those as judges [to hear disputes] who are of no account in the church?

⁵I say this to your shame. Can it be that there is not one wise man among you who [is governed by integrity and] will be able *and* competent to decide [private disputes] between his fellow believers,

⁶but *instead,* brother goes to law against brother, and that before [judges who are] unbelievers?

⁷Why, the very fact that you have lawsuits with one another is already a defeat. Why not rather be wronged? Why not rather be defrauded?

⁸On the contrary, it is you who wrong and defraud, and you do this even to your brothers and sisters.

⁹Do you not know that the unrighteous will not inherit *or* have any share in the kingdom of God? Do not be deceived; neither the sexually immoral, nor idolaters, nor adulterers, nor effeminate [by perversion], nor those who participate in homosexuality,

¹⁰nor thieves, nor the greedy, nor drunkards, nor revilers [whose words are used as weapons to abuse, insult, humiliate, intimidate, or slander], nor swindlers will inherit *or* have any share in the kingdom of God.

¹¹And such were some of you [before you believed]. But you were washed [by the atoning sacrifice of Christ], you were sanctified [set apart for God, and made holy], you were justified [declared free of guilt] in the name of the Lord Jesus Christ and in the [Holy] Spirit of our God [the source of the believer's new life and changed behavior].

¹²Everything is permissible for me, but not all things are beneficial. Everything is permissible for me, but I will not be enslaved by anything [and brought under its power, allowing it to control me].

¹³Food is for the stomach and the stomach for food, but God will do away with both of them. The body is not intended for sexual immorality, but for the Lord, and the Lord is for the body

life point

The Apostle Paul wrote that even if something is permissible for him, at the same time it may not be helpful or beneficial for him (see 1 Corinthians 6:12). There are many things we *could* do, and God will not say a thing about them. We refer to this as God's "permissive will." He is not likely to give us a divine word about every single move we make, but He will always give us wisdom if we ask for it. Walk in wisdom and you will not live in regret.

[to save, sanctify, and raise it again because of the sacrifice of the cross].

¹⁴And God has not only raised the Lord [to life], but will also raise us up by His power.

¹⁵Do you not know that your bodies are members of Christ? Am I therefore to take the members of Christ and make them part of a prostitute? Certainly not!

¹⁶Do you not know that the one who joins himself to a prostitute is one body *with her?* For He says, "THE TWO SHALL BE ONE FLESH." [Gen 2:24]

¹⁷But the one who is united *and* joined to the Lord is one spirit *with Him.*

¹⁸Run away from sexual immorality [in any form, whether thought or behavior, whether visual or written]. Every *other* sin that a man commits is outside the body, but the one who is sexually immoral sins against his own body.

¹⁹Do you not know that your body is a temple of the Holy Spirit who is within you, whom you have [received as a gift] from God, and that you are not your own [property]?

speak the Word

²⁰You were bought with a price [you were actually purchased with the precious blood of Jesus and made His own]. So then, honor *and* glorify God with your body.

putting the Word to work

Some people think being a Christian only has to do with "spiritual" things and not "physical" things. However, Paul is very clear that your physical body, along with your spirit, were bought at a great price: the blood of Jesus (see 1 Corinthians 6:20). Once you become a Christian, your body is where the Holy Spirit lives. How do you treat your body? Remember that good health and sexual purity are integral parts of glorifying God with your body.

7 NOW AS to the matters of which you wrote: It is good (beneficial, advantageous) for a man not to touch a woman [outside marriage].

²But because of [the temptation to participate in] sexual immorality, let each man have his own wife, and let each woman have her own husband.

³The husband must fulfill his [marital] duty to his wife [with good will and kindness], and likewise the wife to her husband.

⁴The wife does not have [exclusive] authority over her own body, but the husband *shares with her;* and likewise the husband does not have [exclusive] authority over his body, but the wife *shares with him.*

Thank You, Lord, for living in me by the Holy Spirit. I know that I am not my own, but that You have bought me with a price, the blood of Your Son. I will honor and glorify You with my body.
—ADAPTED FROM 1 CORINTHIANS 6:19, 20

⁵Do not deprive each other [of marital rights], except perhaps by mutual consent for a time, so that you may devote yourselves [unhindered] to prayer, but come together again so that Satan will not tempt you [to sin] because of your lack of self-control.

⁶But I am saying this as a concession, not as a command.

⁷I wish that all the people were as I am; but each person has his own gift from God, one of this kind and one of that.

⁸But I say to the unmarried and to the widows, [that as a practical matter] it is good if they remain [single and entirely devoted to the Lord] as I am.

⁹But if they do not have [sufficient] self-control, they should marry; for it is better to marry than to burn *with passion*.

¹⁰But to the married [believers] I give instructions—not I, but the Lord—that the wife is not to separate from her husband,

¹¹(but even if she does leave him, let her remain single or else be reconciled to her husband) and that the husband should not leave his wife.

¹²To the rest I declare—I, not the Lord [since Jesus did not discuss this]—that if any [believing] brother has a wife who does not believe [in Christ], and she consents to live with him, he must not leave her.

¹³And if any [believing] woman has an unbelieving husband, and he consents to live with her, she must not leave him.

¹⁴For the unbelieving husband is sanctified [that is, he receives the blessings granted] through his [Christian] wife, and the unbelieving wife is sanctified through her believing husband. Otherwise your children would be [ceremonially] unclean, but as it is they are holy.

¹⁵But if the unbelieving partner leaves, let him leave. In such cases the [remaining] brother or sister is not [spiritually or morally] bound. But God has called us to peace.

¹⁶For how do you know, wife, whether you will save your husband [by leading him to Christ]? Or how do you know, husband, whether you will save your wife [by leading her to Christ]?

¹⁷Only, let each one live the life which the Lord has assigned him, and to which God has called him [for each person is unique and is accountable for his choices and conduct, let him walk in this way]. This is the rule I make in all the churches.

¹⁸Was anyone at the time of his calling [from God already] circumcised? He is not to become uncircumcised. Has anyone been called while uncircumcised? He is not to be circumcised. [Gal 5:1–3]

¹⁹Circumcision is nothing, and uncircumcision is nothing, but *what matters is* keeping the commandments of God.

²⁰Each one should remain in the condition in which he was [when he was] called.

²¹Were you a slave when you were called? Do not worry about that [since your status as a believer is equal to that of a freeborn believer]; but if you are able to gain your freedom, do that.

²²For he who was a slave when he was called in the Lord is a freedman of the Lord, likewise he who was free when he was called is a slave of Christ.

²³You were bought with a price [a precious price paid by Christ]; do not become slaves to men [but to Christ].

²⁴Brothers, let each one remain with God in that *condition* in which he was [when he was] called.

²⁵Now concerning the virgins [of marriageable age] I have no command of the Lord, but I give my opinion as one who by the Lord's mercy is trustworthy.

²⁶I think then that because of the impending distress [that is, the pressure

of the current trouble], it is good for a man to remain as he is.

²⁷Are you bound to a wife? Do not seek to be released. Are you unmarried? Do not seek a wife.

²⁸But if you do marry, you have not sinned [in doing so]; and if a virgin marries, she has not sinned [in doing so]. Yet those [who marry] will have troubles (special challenges) in this life, and I am trying to spare you that.

²⁹But I say this, believers: the time has been shortened, so that from now on even those who have wives should be as though they did not;

³⁰and those who weep, as though they did not weep; and those who rejoice, as though they did not rejoice; and those who buy, as though they did not possess [anything];

³¹and those who use the world [taking advantage of its opportunities], as though they did not make full use of it. For the outward form of this world [its present social and material nature] is passing away.

³²But I want you to be free from concern. The unmarried man is concerned about the things of the Lord, how he may please the Lord;

³³but the married man is concerned about worldly things, how he may please his wife,

³⁴and *his interests* are divided. The unmarried woman or the virgin is concerned about the matters of the Lord, how to be holy *and* set apart both in body and in spirit; but a married woman is concerned about worldly things, how she may please her husband.

³⁵Now I say this for your own benefit; not to restrict you, but to promote what is appropriate and secure undistracted devotion to the Lord.

³⁶But if any man thinks that he is not acting properly *and* honorably toward his virgin *daughter,* [by not permitting her to marry], if she is past her youth,

and it must be so, let him do as he wishes, he does not sin; let her marry.

³⁷But the man who stands firmly committed in his heart, having no compulsion [to yield to his daughter's request], and has authority over his own will, and has decided in his own heart to keep his own virgin [daughter from being married], he will do well.

³⁸So then both the father who gives his virgin *daughter* in marriage does well, and he who does not give her in marriage will do better.

³⁹A wife is bound [to her husband by law] as long as he lives. But if her husband dies, she is free to marry whomever she wishes, only [provided that he too is] in the Lord.

⁴⁰But in my opinion a widow is happier if she stays as she is. And I think that I also have the Spirit of God [in this matter].

8 NOW ABOUT food sacrificed to idols, we know that we all have knowledge [concerning this]. Knowledge [alone] makes [people self-righteously] arrogant, but love [that unselfishly seeks the best for others] builds up *and* encourages others to grow [in wisdom].

²If anyone imagines that he knows *and* understands anything [of divine matters, without love], he has not yet known as he ought to know.

³But if anyone loves God [with awe-filled reverence, obedience and gratitude], he is known by Him [as His very own and is greatly loved].

⁴In this matter, then, of eating food offered to idols, we know that an idol is nothing in the world [it has no real existence], and that there is no God but one. [Deut 6:4]

⁵For even if there are so-called gods, whether in heaven or on earth, as indeed there are many gods and many lords,

⁶yet for us there is but one God, the

life point

In 1 Corinthians 8:1, Paul said that knowledge makes people arrogant (what some versions of the Bible call "puffed up"), but love builds up. If we seek to walk in real love more than we seek to know things we are much better off. Pride makes us think we do not need God. Pride always comes before destruction. Beware of pride and seek love. Love is humble, not puffed up or inflated with pride or arrogance. Instead of being anxious to tell others what we know, let's do our best to edify them and build them up. We do not need to try to impress other people; we need to humble ourselves and let God exalt us in His timing.

Father, who is the source of all things, and we *exist* for Him; and one Lord, Jesus Christ, by whom are all things [that have been created], and we [believers exist and have life and have been redeemed] through Him. [Mal 2:10]

[7]However, not all [believers] have this knowledge. But some, being accustomed [throughout their lives] to [thinking of] the idol until now [as real and living], still eat food as if it were sacrificed to an idol; and because their conscience is weak, it is defiled (guilty, ashamed).

[8]Now food will not commend us to God *nor* bring us close to Him; we are no worse off if we do not eat, nor are we better if we do eat.

[9]Only be careful that this liberty of yours [this power to choose] does not somehow become a stumbling block [that is, a temptation to sin] to the weak [in conscience].

[10]For if someone sees you, a person having knowledge, eating in an idol's temple, then if he is weak, will he not be encouraged to eat things sacrificed to idols [and violate his own convictions]?

[11]For through your knowledge (spiritual maturity) this weak man is ruined [that is, he suffers in his spiritual life], the brother for whom Christ died.

[12]And when you sin against the brothers and sisters in this way and wound their weak conscience [by confusing them], you sin against Christ.

[13]Therefore, if [my eating a certain] food causes my brother to stumble (sin), I will not eat [such] meat ever again, so that I will not cause my brother to stumble.

9 AM I not free [unrestrained and exempt from any obligation]? Am I not an apostle? Have I not seen Jesus our [risen] Lord [in person]? Are you not [the result and proof of] my work in the Lord?

[2]If I am not [considered] an apostle to others, at least I am one to you; for you are the seal *and* the certificate *and* the living evidence of my apostleship in the Lord [confirming and authenticating it].

[3]This is my defense to those who would put me on trial *and* interrogate me [concerning my authority as an apostle]:

[4]Have we not the right to our food and drink [at the expense of the churches]?

[5]Have we not the right to take along with us a believing wife, as do the rest

speak the Word

God, I declare that You are the only God. You are the source of all things, and I am living for You. I declare that Jesus Christ is the only Lord. By Him, all things exist, including me!
–ADAPTED FROM 1 CORINTHIANS 8:6

of the apostles and the Lord's brothers and Cephas (Peter)?

⁶Or is it only Barnabas and I who have no right to stop doing manual labor [in order to support our ministry]? ⁷[Consider this:] Who at any time serves as a soldier at his own expense? Who plants a vineyard and does not eat its fruit? Or who tends a flock and does not use the milk of the flock?

⁸Do I say these things only from a man's perspective? Does the Law not endorse the same principles? ⁹For it is written in the Law of Moses, "YOU SHALL NOT MUZZLE AN OX WHILE IT IS TREADING OUT THE GRAIN [to keep it from eating the grain]." Is it [only] for oxen that God cares? [Deut 25:4] ¹⁰Or does He speak entirely for our sake? Yes, it was written for our sake: The plowman ought to plow in hope, and the thresher to thresh in hope of sharing the harvest. ¹¹If we have sown [the good seed of] spiritual things in you, is it too much if we reap material things from you? ¹²If others share in this rightful claim over you, do not we even more? However, we did not exercise this right, but we put up with everything so that we will not hinder [the spread of] the good news of Christ.

¹³Do you not know that those who officiate in the sacred services of the temple eat from the temple [offerings of meat and bread] and those who regularly attend the altar have their share from the [offerings brought to the] altar? [Deut 18:1] ¹⁴So also [on the same principle] the Lord directed those who preach the gospel to get their living from the gospel.

¹⁵But I have used none of these privileges, nor am I writing this [to suggest] that any such provision be made for me now. For it would be better for me to die than to have anyone deprive me of my boast [in this matter of financial support].

¹⁶For if I [merely] preach the gospel, I have nothing to boast about, for I am compelled [that is, absolutely obligated to do it]. Woe to me if I do not preach the good news [of salvation]! ¹⁷For if I do this work of my own free will, then I have a reward; but if it is not of my will [but by God's choosing], I have been entrusted with a [sacred] stewardship. ¹⁸What then is my reward? [Just this:] that, when I preach the gospel, I may offer the gospel without charge [to everyone], so as not to take advantage of my rights [as a preacher and apostle] in [preaching] the gospel.

¹⁹For though I am free from all men, I have made myself a slave to everyone, so that I may win more [for Christ]. ²⁰To the Jews I became as a Jew, so that I might win Jews [for Christ]; to men under the Law, [I became] as one under the Law, though not being under the Law myself, so that I might win those who are under the Law. ²¹To those who are without (outside) the Law, [I became] as one without the Law, though [I am] not without the law of God, but under the law of Christ, so that I might win those who are without law.

putting the Word to work

When you tithe, do you know how all of your offering is used? Probably not, but most likely a portion of it goes to pay the pastors and staff at your church. It is scriptural for us to give to those who take care of us spiritually (see 1 Corinthians 9:14). That is God's will and His plan for their support, and it is one of the ways we show appreciation for what they have done for us. Always give with a cheerful heart because doing so glorifies God.

²²To the weak I became [as the] weak, to win the weak. I have become all things to all men, so that I may by all means [in any and every way] save some [by leading them to faith in Jesus Christ].

²³And I do all this for the sake of the gospel, so that I may share in its blessings along with you.

²⁴Do you not know that in a race all the runners run [their very best to win], but only one receives the prize? Run [your race] in such a way that you may seize the prize *and* make it yours!

²⁵Now every athlete who [goes into training and] competes in the games is disciplined *and* exercises self-control in all things. They do it to win a crown that withers, but we [do it to receive] an imperishable [crown that cannot wither].

²⁶Therefore I do not run without a

life point

Those of us who intend to run the race to win must conduct ourselves with discipline in all things (see 1 Corinthians 9:24–27). We cannot expect someone else to make us do what is right. We must listen to the Holy Spirit and take action ourselves.

Paul said he disciplined his body strictly. He means that he disciplined it because he did not want to preach to others, tell them what they should do, while failing to do it himself. Paul was running the race to win! He knew he could not develop his potential without bringing his body, mind, and emotions under control.

Self-discipline is essential to the Christian life. Unless we discipline our minds, our mouths, and our emotions, life will be extremely difficult for us. Unless we learn to rule our temper, we can never achieve the successes that rightfully belong to us.

definite goal; I do not flail around like one beating the air [just shadow boxing].

²⁷But [like a boxer] I strictly discipline my body and make it my slave, so that, after I have preached [the gospel] to others, I myself will not somehow be disqualified [as unfit for service].

10 FOR I do not want you to be unaware, believers, that our fathers were all under the cloud [in which God's presence went before them] and they all passed [miraculously and safely] through the [Red] Sea; [Ex 13:21; 14:22, 29]

²And all [of them] were baptized into Moses [into his safekeeping as their leader] in the cloud and in the sea;

³and all [of them] ate the same spiritual food; [Ex 16:4, 35]

⁴and all [of them] drank the same spiritual drink, for they were drinking from a spiritual rock which followed them; and the rock was Christ. [Ex 17:6; Num 20:11]

⁵Nevertheless, God was not well-pleased with most of them, for they were scattered along the ground in the wilderness [because their lack of self-control led to disobedience which led to death]. [Num 14:29, 30]

⁶Now these things [the warnings and admonitions] took place as examples for us, so that we would not crave evil things as they did. [Num 11:4, 34]

⁷Do not be worshipers of handmade gods, as some of them were; just as it is written [in Scripture], "THE PEOPLE SAT DOWN TO EAT AND DRINK [after sacrificing to the golden calf at Horeb], AND STOOD UP TO PLAY [indulging in immoral activities]." [Ex 32:6]

⁸We must not indulge in [nor tolerate] sexual immorality, as some of them did, and twenty-three thousand [suddenly] fell [dead] in a single day! [Num 25:1–18]

⁹We must not tempt the Lord [that

is, test His patience, question His purpose or exploit His goodness], as some of them did—and they were killed by serpents. [Num 21:5, 6]

¹⁰And do not murmur [in unwarranted discontent], as some of them did—and were destroyed by the destroyer. [Num 16:41, 49]

¹¹Now these things happened to them as an example *and* warning [to us]; they were written for our instruction [to admonish and equip us], upon whom the ends of the ages have come.

¹²Therefore let the one who thinks he stands firm [immune to temptation, being overconfident and self-righteous], take care that he does not fall [into sin and condemnation].

¹³No temptation [regardless of its source] has overtaken *or* enticed you that is not common to human experience [nor is any temptation unusual or beyond human resistance]; but God is faithful [to His word—He is compassionate and trustworthy], and He will not let you be tempted beyond your ability [to resist], but along with the temptation He [has in the past and is now and] will [always] provide the way out as well, so that you will be able to endure it [without yielding, and will overcome temptation with joy].

¹⁴Therefore, my beloved, run [keep far, far away] from [any sort of] idolatry [and that includes loving anything more than God, or participating in

life point

First Corinthians 10:13 promises us that God will not allow us to be tempted beyond what we can bear, but with every temptation He will also provide the way out—the means of escape. The end result will be that we will be able to endure whatever negative circumstances we face without yielding to them and to overcome the temptation with joy.

anything that leads to sin and enslaves the soul].

¹⁵I am speaking as to wise *and* sensible people; judge [carefully and thoughtfully consider] for yourselves what I say.

¹⁶Is the cup of blessing which we bless [at the Lord's Supper] not a sharing in the blood of Christ? [Indeed it is.] Is the bread which we break not a sharing in the body of Christ? [Indeed it is.]

¹⁷Since there is one bread, we [believers] who are many are [united into] one body; for we all partake of the one bread [which represents the body of Christ].

¹⁸Consider the people of Israel; are those who eat the sacrifices not partners of the altar [united in their worship of the same God]? [Indeed they are.] [Lev 7:6]

¹⁹What do I mean then? That a thing offered to idols is anything [special or changed simply because it is offered], or that an idol is anything?

²⁰On the contrary, the things which the Gentiles (pagans) sacrifice, they sacrifice to demons [in effect], and not to God; and I do not want you to become partners with demons [by eating at feasts in pagan temples]. [Deut 32:17]

²¹You cannot drink [both] the Lord's cup and the cup of demons. You cannot share in both the Lord's table and the table of demons [thereby becoming partners with them].

²²Do we [really] provoke the Lord to jealousy [when we eat food sacrificed to handmade "gods" at pagan feasts]? Are we [spiritually] stronger than He? [Certainly not! He knows that the idols are nothing. But we deeply offend Him.] [Deut 32:21; Eccl 6:10; Is 45:9]

²³All things are lawful [that is, morally legitimate, permissible], but not all things are beneficial *or* advantageous. All things are lawful, but not all

things are constructive [to character] *and* edifying [to spiritual life].

²⁴Let no one seek [only] his own good, but [also] that of the other person.

²⁵[Regarding meat offered to idols:] Eat anything that is sold in the meat market without asking any questions for the sake of your conscience,

²⁶FOR THE [whole] EARTH IS THE LORD'S, AND EVERYTHING THAT IS IN IT. [Ps 24:1; 50:12]

²⁷If one of the unbelievers invites you [to a meal at his home] and you want to go, eat whatever is served to you without asking questions [about its source] for the sake of your conscience.

²⁸But if anyone says to you, "This meat has been offered in sacrifice to an idol," do not eat it, out of consideration for the one who told you, and for conscience's sake—

²⁹and by conscience I mean for the

life point

Real joy comes from being an empty vessel for God's use and glory, letting Him choose where He takes you, what He does with you, when He does it—and not resisting it. Be willing to do everything for the honor and glory of God, as 1 Corinthians 10:31 instructs, and you will have great contentment and joy in your life.

sake of the other *man's,* not yours. For why is my freedom [of choice] judged by another's conscience [another's ethics—another's sense of right and wrong]?

³⁰If I take my share [of food] with thankfulness, why am I accused because of something for which I give thanks?

³¹So then, whether you eat or drink or whatever you do, do all to the glory of [our great] God.

the spiritual in the natural

It is true that there are earthly things we must tend to on earth. We cannot be "spiritual" all the time. But, if any person has what I call a "religious spirit" about him, he will either ignore the natural things he should take care of, or he will not enjoy the earthly things he does handle. He will always rush through those mundane things, trying to get back to some spiritual activity, thinking that is the only way he can feel good about himself. He only feels God's approval when he does what he considers "spiritual" things.

It's important for us to understand that we can communicate with God while doing the laundry as well as on bended knee. I personally believe God prefers a person who talks to Him intermittently throughout the day to a person who sets a clock for a certain amount of time to spend with Him. The instant the time is up, he cuts off communication with God until the next day.

The Lord is ever present and always available for fellowship when we pray and study His Word. But, in order to enjoy our entire life, we need to learn that He is willing to be involved in everything we do.

According to 1 Corinthians 10:31, we should do everything to the glory of God. This includes the everyday things we do in the secular realm as well as our spiritual pursuits in the spiritual realm.

³²Do not offend Jews or Greeks or even the church of God [but live to honor Him];

³³just as I please everyone in all things [as much as possible adapting myself to the interests of others], not seeking my own benefit but that of the many, so that they [will be open to the message of salvation and] may be saved.

11 IMITATE ME, just as I *imitate* Christ. ²I praise *and* appreciate you because you remember me in everything and you firmly hold to the traditions [the substance of my instructions], just as I have passed them on to you.

³But I want you to understand that Christ is the head (authority over) of every man, and man is the head of woman, and God is the head of Christ.

⁴Every man who prays or prophesies with *something* on his head dishonors his head [and the One who is his head].

⁵And every woman who prays or prophesies when she has her head uncovered disgraces her head; for she is one and the same as the woman whose head is shaved [in disgrace].

⁶If a woman does not cover her head, she should have her hair cut off; and if it is disgraceful for a woman to have her hair cut off or her head shaved, she should cover her head.

⁷A man ought not have his head covered [during worship], since he is the image and [reflected] glory of God; but the woman is [the expression of] man's glory. [Gen 1:26]

⁸For man does not originate from woman, but woman from man; [Gen 2:21–23]

⁹for indeed man was not created for the sake of woman, but woman for the sake of man. [Gen 2:18]

¹⁰Therefore the woman ought to have a *sign of* authority on her head, for the sake of the angels [so as not to offend them].

¹¹Nevertheless, woman is not independent of man, nor is man independent of woman.

¹²For as the woman originates from the man, so also man is born through the woman; and all things [whether male or female] originate from God [as their Creator].

¹³Judge for yourselves; is it proper for a woman to offer prayer to God [publicly] with her head uncovered?

¹⁴Does not common sense itself teach you that if a man has long hair, it is a dishonor to him,

¹⁵but if a woman has long hair, it is her ornament *and* glory? For her long hair is given to her as a covering.

¹⁶Now if anyone is inclined to be contentious [about this], we have no other practice [in worship than this], nor do the churches of God [in general].

¹⁷But in giving this next instruction, I do not praise you, because when you meet together it is not for the better but for the worse.

¹⁸For, in the first place, when you meet together in church, I hear that there are divisions among you; and in part I believe it,

¹⁹for [doubtless] there have to be factions among you, so that those who are of approved character may be clearly recognized among you.

²⁰So when you meet together, it is not to eat the Lord's Supper,

²¹for when you eat, each one hurries to get his own supper first [not waiting for others or the poor]. So one goes hungry while another gets drunk.

²²What! Do you not have houses in which to eat and drink? Or do you show contempt for the church of God and humiliate those [impoverished believers] who have nothing? What will I say to you? Shall I praise you for this? In this I will not praise you!

[23]For I received from the Lord Himself that [instruction] which I passed on to you, that the Lord Jesus on the night in which He was betrayed took bread;

[24]and when He had given thanks, He broke it and said, "This is (represents) My body, which is [offered as a sacrifice] for you. Do this in [affectionate] remembrance of Me."

[25]In the same way, after supper *He took* the cup, saying, "This cup is the new covenant [ratified and established] in My blood; do this, as often as you drink it, in [affectionate] remembrance of Me."

[26]For every time you eat this bread and drink this cup, you are [symbolically] proclaiming [the fact of] the Lord's death until He comes [again].

[27]So then whoever eats the bread or drinks the cup of the Lord in a way that is unworthy [of Him] will be guilty of [profaning and sinning against] the body and blood of the Lord.

[28]But a person must [prayerfully] examine himself [and his relationship to Christ], and only when he has done so should he eat of the bread and drink of the cup.

[29]For anyone who eats and drinks [without solemn reverence and heartfelt gratitude for the sacrifice of Christ], eats and drinks a judgment on

putting the Word to work

What do you think about when you receive the Lord's Supper? The next time you partake of this special meal, remember that Jesus' body was broken for you and His blood was shed for you (see 1 Corinthians 11:23–25) and celebrate that your sins are forgiven. Rejoice that one day He will come back. Receive the healing, restoration, and strength He purchased for you with His body and blood.

himself if he does not recognize the body [of Christ].

[30]That [careless and unworthy participation] is the reason why many among you are weak and sick, and a number sleep [in death].

[31]But if we evaluated *and* judged ourselves honestly [recognizing our shortcomings and correcting our behavior], we would not be judged.

[32]But when we [fall short and] are judged by the Lord, we are disciplined [by undergoing His correction] so that we will not be condemned [to eternal punishment] along with the world.

[33]So then, my brothers and sisters, when you come together to eat [the Lord's Supper], wait for one another [and see to it that no one is left out].

[34]If anyone is too hungry [to wait], let him eat at home, so that you will not come together for judgment [on yourselves]. About the remaining matters [of which I was informed], I will take care of them when I come.

12 NOW ABOUT the spiritual *gifts* [the special endowments given by the Holy Spirit], brothers and sisters, I do not want you to be uninformed.

[2]You know that when you were pagans, *you were* led off after speechless idols; however you were led off [whether by impulse or habit].

[3]Therefore I want you to know that no one speaking by the [power and influence of the] Spirit of God can say, "Jesus be cursed," and no one can say, "Jesus is [my] Lord," except by [the power and influence of] the Holy Spirit.

[4]Now there are [distinctive] varieties of *spiritual* gifts [special abilities given by the grace and extraordinary power of the Holy Spirit operating in believers], but it is the same Spirit [who grants them and empowers believers].

[5]And there are [distinctive] varieties

of ministries *and* service, but it is the same Lord [who is served].

⁶And there are [distinctive] ways of working [to accomplish things], but it is the same God who produces all things in all *believers* [inspiring, energizing, and empowering them].

⁷But to each one is given the manifestation of the Spirit [the spiritual illumination and the enabling of the Holy Spirit] for the common good.

⁸To one is given through the [Holy] Spirit [the power to speak] the message of wisdom, and to another [the power to express] the word of knowledge *and* understanding according to the same Spirit;

⁹to another [wonder-working] faith [is given] by the same [Holy] Spirit, and to another the [extraordinary] gifts of healings by the one Spirit;

¹⁰and to another the working of miracles, and to another prophecy [foretelling the future, speaking a new message from God to the people], and to another discernment of spirits [the ability to distinguish sound, godly doctrine from the deceptive doctrine of man-made

religions and cults], to another *various* kinds of [unknown] tongues, and to another interpretation of tongues.

¹¹All these things [the gifts, the achievements, the abilities, the empowering] are brought about by one and the same [Holy] Spirit, distributing to each one individually just as He chooses.

¹²For just as the body is one and yet has many parts, and all the parts, though many, form [only] one body, so it is with Christ.

¹³For by one [Holy] Spirit we were all baptized into one body, [spiritually transformed—united together] whether Jews or Greeks (Gentiles), slaves or free, and we were all made to drink of one [Holy] Spirit [since the same Holy Spirit fills each life]. [Rom 3:22; Gal 3:28]

¹⁴For the [human] body does not

life point

I believe there are certain individuals to whom God gives the gift of faith (see 1 Corinthians 12:9) for specific occasions such as a dangerous missionary trip or a challenging situation. When this gift operates in people, they are able to comfortably believe God for something other people would see as impossible. They have total faith for something that terrifies others.

People operating under a gift of faith must be careful to avoid thinking those who do not have this gift are faithless or cowards. They need to understand that when the gift of faith operates in a person, God gives that individual an unusual portion of faith to ensure that His purpose on the earth is accomplished.

Every person is given a certain degree of faith (see Romans 12:3). We can be assured that God will always give us enough faith to receive His grace for the fulfillment of every task He gives us.

putting the Word to work

Do you know that the Holy Spirit gives you spiritual gifts to use (see 1 Corinthians 12:4–11)? Every believer—including you—has been given at least one spiritual gift, and usually more than one. If you do not know what your spiritual gifts are, pray for the Holy Spirit to reveal them to you. Inquire at your church about taking a class on spiritual gifts, or seek information about a spiritual gifts test you can take. These tests often help people understand themselves and give them confidence to begin functioning in their gifts. Thank the Holy Spirit for giving you the gifts He has chosen, and ask Him for wisdom in using them.

the gift of discernment

I believe the discernment of spirits mentioned as a gift of the Holy Spirit in 1 Corinthians 12:10 is an extremely valuable gift, and I encourage you to desire and develop it.

I also encourage you not to be limited in your understanding of what this gift is. The discernment of spirits gives people supernatural insight into the spirit realm when God allows it. It is not exclusively the discerning of evil or demon spirits, as when Paul identified the spirit of divination in a girl who told fortunes at Philippi (see Acts 16:16–18); it is also the discerning of divine spirits, as when Moses looked into the spirit realm and saw the "back" of God (see Exodus 33:18–23), or when John was in exile on the isle of Patmos and saw a vision of the resurrected Jesus (see Revelation 1:9–18).

The discernment of spirits also helps us know the true nature of those we deal with, whether they are good or evil. In other words, it helps us know the motivation behind a person or the true nature of a situation. For example, someone may appear to do a good thing, yet we may feel wrong about that person inside. That is often God's way of warning us that the person's intention is evil. Satan himself uses such people to deceive Christians and demolish their godly endeavors.

I have prayed a lot for discernment in my years in ministry and I rely on it a great deal. Let me encourage you to pray for this gift as well, because it can help you as you deal with many of the people and situations in your life.

consist of one part, but of many [limbs and organs].

¹⁵If the foot says, "Because I am not a hand, I am not *a part* of the body," is it not on the contrary still *a part* of the body?

¹⁶If the ear says, "Because I am not an eye, I am not *a part* of the body," is it not on the contrary still *a part* of the body?

¹⁷If the whole body were an eye, where would the hearing be? If the whole [body] were an ear, where would the sense of smell be?

¹⁸But now [as things really are], God has placed *and* arranged the parts in the body, each one of them, just as He willed *and* saw fit [with the best balance of function].

¹⁹If they all were a single *organ,* where would [the rest of] the body be?

²⁰But now [as things really are] there are many parts [different limbs and organs], but a single body.

²¹The eye cannot say to the hand, "I have no need of you," nor again the head to the feet, "I have no need of you."

²²But quite the contrary, the parts of the body that seem to be weaker are [absolutely] necessary;

²³and as for those *parts* of the body

putting the Word to work

Do you ever feel your spiritual gifts are not as important as someone else's? That's like saying your eyes are not as important as your ears. The truth is, every gift is necessary for the body of Christ to function as God intends (see 1 Corinthians 12:20–25). Recognize and celebrate the importance of each person's gifts, including yours. However, be sure not to think more highly of your gifts than of someone else's.

which we consider less honorable, these we treat with greater honor; and our less presentable parts are treated with greater modesty,

[24]while our more presentable parts do not require it. But God has combined the [whole] body, giving greater honor to that part which lacks it,

[25]so that there would be no division *or* discord in the body [that is, lack of adaptation of the parts to each other], but that the parts may have the same concern for one another.

[26]And if one member suffers, all the parts share the suffering; if one member is honored, all rejoice with it.

[27]Now you [collectively] are Christ's body, and individually [you are] members of it [each with his own special purpose and function].

[28]So God has appointed *and* placed in the church [for His own use]: first apostles [chosen by Christ], second prophets [those who foretell the future, those who speak a new message from God to the people], third teachers, then those who work miracles, then those with the gifts of healings, the helpers, the administrators, and speakers in *various* kinds of [unknown] tongues.

[29]Are all apostles? Are all prophets? Are all teachers? Are all workers of miracles?

[30]Do all have gifts of healing? Do all speak with tongues? Do all interpret?

[31]But earnestly desire *and* strive for the greater gifts [if acquiring them is going to be your goal].

And yet I will show you a still more excellent way [one of the choicest graces and the highest of them all: unselfish love].

love above all

Love is the greatest thing in the world. First Corinthians 12:31 teaches us that love should be number one on our spiritual priority list. We should study love, pray about love, and develop the fruit of love by practicing loving others. We learn in Galatians 5:22, 23 that love is one of the nine fruit of the Spirit available to those in whom God's Holy Spirit lives.

First John 4:8 says, "God is love," so when we walk in His love we abide in Him. Because we walk in God's love by receiving and expressing it, we should not deceive ourselves into thinking we can love God while we hate other people (see 1 John 4:20).

We seek many things during our lifetime hoping to find fulfillment in them. But without love, these things fall short of the desired goal. When we put our time and energy into things that do not fulfill us, we feel frustrated.

Love is the best thing we can commit our life to. It took me about forty-five years to realize that my priorities were mixed up and that love was not the main thing in my life. It was not my first priority, but it needed to be. The commitment to learn how to walk in love has been the single best decision I have ever made as a Christian.

Love not only blesses others; it also blesses the one doing the loving. Concentrating on being a blessing to others has brought me joy. I find it exciting.

All of us need to become students of love, excelling in the most important quality of all—love.

13

IF I speak with the tongues of men and of angels, but have not love [for others growing out of God's love for me], then I have become only a noisy gong or a clanging cymbal [just an annoying distraction].

²And if I have *the gift of* prophecy [and speak a new message from God to the people], and understand all mysteries, and [possess] all knowledge; and if I have all [sufficient] faith so that I can remove mountains, but do not have love [reaching out to others], I am nothing.

³If I give all my possessions to feed *the poor,* and if I surrender my body to be burned, but do not have love, it does me no good at all.

⁴Love endures with patience *and* serenity, love is kind *and* thoughtful, and is not jealous *or* envious; love does not brag and is not proud *or* arrogant.

⁵It is not rude; it is not self-seeking, it is not provoked [nor overly sensitive and easily angered]; it does not take into account a wrong *endured.*

⁶It does not rejoice at injustice, but rejoices with the truth [when right and truth prevail].

life point

First Corinthians 13:1–3 begins a discourse on love. It tells us clearly that no matter how many gifts of the Spirit we may operate in, if we are not operating in love, all other gifts are useless. If we speak in tongues, but do not love, we simply make a big noise. If we have prophetic power, and power to understand and interpret secrets and mysteries, if we have all knowledge and so much faith we can move mountains, but have no love, according to the Apostle Paul, we are useless nobodies. Even if we give away all that we have to feed the poor and surrender our very lives, but do it with wrong motives and not out of love, we gain nothing.

⁷Love bears all things [regardless of what comes], believes all things [looking for the best in each one], hopes all things [remaining steadfast during difficult times], endures all things [without weakening].

⁸Love never fails [it never fades nor ends]. But as for prophecies, they will pass away; as for tongues, they will cease; as for the gift of special knowledge, it will pass away.

⁹For we know in part, and we prophesy in part [for our knowledge is fragmentary and incomplete].

¹⁰But when that which is complete *and* perfect comes, that which is incomplete *and* partial will pass away.

¹¹When I was a child, I talked like a child, I thought like a child, I reasoned like a child; when I became a man, I did away with childish things.

¹²For now [in this time of imperfection]

life point

Love is the greatest thing in life (see 1 Corinthians 13:13), and walking in love should be our main focus. God is love, and He wants us to love one another (see 1 John 4:8, 11). We can only truly love others by receiving and expressing God's love. In order to do so, we need to understand that He loves us and accept His love. When we do, we begin a love walk that causes us to live in a new way—a new way of thinking, a new way of speaking, and a new way of acting.

Love is expressed in many different ways, but one factor is always the same: love gives.

I pray that you will become addicted to walking in love and blessing people. Give Satan a nervous breakdown—become radical in your love walk by joining me in praying as I often do: *Lord, reduce me to love!*

we see in a mirror dimly [a blurred reflection, a riddle, an enigma], but then
[when the time of perfection comes
we will see reality] face to face. Now I
know in part [just in fragments], but
then I will know fully, just as I have
been fully known [by God].

¹³And now there remain: faith
[abiding trust in God and His prom-
ises], hope [confident expectation
of eternal salvation], love [unselfish
love for others growing out of God's
love for me], these three [the choicest graces]; but the greatest of these
is love.

14 PURSUE [THIS] love [with
eagerness, make it your goal],
yet earnestly desire and cultivate the spiritual gifts [to be used by
believers for the benefit of the church],
but especially that you may prophesy
[to foretell the future, to speak a new
message from God to the people].

²For one who speaks in an unknown
tongue does not speak to people but to
God; for no one understands him or
catches his meaning, but by the Spirit
he speaks mysteries [secret truths,
hidden things].

³But [on the other hand] the one who

the most important thing

First Corinthians 13:13 says love is the greatest thing. Faith and hope are vitally
necessary, but as important as they are, they are not more important than love.
Jesus gave us one new commandment, which is to love one another as He loved us
(see John 13:34). He said that this would be the way the world knows we are His
disciples (see John 13:35).

Love is not theory or talk, but action. It is revealed in the way we talk to people,
how we treat them, and what we do or don't do for them. Love has many practical
facets and can be seen in a variety of ways. For example, love is patient. When people
are walking in love they are longsuffering with the weaknesses and faults of others.
Instead of believing the worst, love always believes the best of every person.

Love is not rude. It actually strives to have good manners and that is something we
desperately need in society today. Love takes time to say "please" and "thank you."
Love takes time to really listen when others are talking. It is genuinely interested in
others. Love builds people up; it edifies. Love does not find fault and criticize.

One of the facets of love that I enjoy thinking about is that "Love covers a multitude
of sins" (1 Peter 4:8). Love does not expose people's faults. Instead it actually covers
them unless, of course, something really needs to be exposed and then love handles
the situation appropriately and with wisdom. Often we rush to tell every negative
thing we hear or know about anybody, but real love does not behave that way. Love
treats other people the way it wants to be treated. Ask yourself, "Would I want
someone to spread rumors about me and be a talebearer, or would I want them
to cover my faults and pray for me?" Of course, we know the answer, but still we
often follow the flesh and do what we know we should not do.

Be hopeful at all times and walk in faith, but above all seek love and walk in it. God
is love, and when we walk in love we show Him to those with whom we come in
contact.

prophesies speaks to people for edification [to promote their spiritual growth] and [speaks words of] encouragement [to uphold and advise them concerning the matters of God] and [speaks words of] consolation [to compassionately comfort them].

⁴One who speaks in a tongue edifies himself; but one who prophesies edifies the church [promotes growth in spiritual wisdom, devotion, holiness, and joy].

⁵Now I wish that all of you spoke in *unknown* tongues, but *even* more [I wish] that you would prophesy. The one who prophesies is greater [and more useful] than the one who speaks in tongues, unless he translates *or* explains [what he says], so that the church may be edified [instructed, improved, strengthened].

⁶Now, believers, if I come to you speaking in *unknown* tongues, how will I benefit you unless I also speak to you [clearly] either by revelation [revealing God's mystery], or by knowledge [teaching about God], or by prophecy [foretelling the future, speaking a new message from God to the people], or by instruction [teaching precepts that develop spiritual maturity]?

⁷Yet *even* lifeless things, whether flute or harp, when producing a sound, if they do not produce distinct [musical] tones, how will anyone [listening] know what is piped or played?

⁸And if the [war] bugle produces an indistinct sound, who will prepare himself for battle?

⁹So it is with you, if you speak words

life point

First Corinthians 14:3 tells us that prophecy builds people up. It does not tear people down; rather it constructively aids their spiritual progress and offers them encouragement and consolation in the process.

[in an unknown tongue] that are not intelligible *and* clear, how will anyone understand what you are saying? You will be talking into the air [wasting your breath]!

¹⁰There are, I suppose, a great many kinds of languages in the world [unknown to us], and none is lacking in meaning.

¹¹But if I do not know the meaning of the language, I will [appear to] be a foreigner to the one who is speaking [since he knows exactly what he is saying], and the one who is speaking will [appear to] be a foreigner to me.

¹²So it is with you, since you are so very eager to have spiritual gifts *and* manifestations of the Spirit, strive to excel in ways that will build up the church [spiritually].

¹³Therefore let one who speaks in a tongue pray that he may [be gifted to] translate *or* explain [what he says].

¹⁴For if I pray in a tongue, my spirit prays, but my mind is unproductive [because it does not understand what my spirit is praying].

¹⁵Then what am I to do? I will pray with the spirit [by the Holy Spirit that is within me] and I will pray with the mind [using words I understand]; I will sing with the spirit [by the Holy Spirit that is within me] and I will sing with the mind [using words I understand].

¹⁶Otherwise if you bless [and give thanks to God] in the spirit only, how will any outsider *or* someone who is not gifted [in spiritual matters] say the "Amen" [of agreement] to your thanksgiving, since he does not know what you are saying? [1 Chr 16:36; Ps 106:48]

¹⁷You are giving thanks well enough [in a way that God is glorified], but the other person [who does not understand you] is not edified [and spiritually strengthened since he cannot join in your thanksgiving].

¹⁸I thank God that I speak in [unknown] tongues more than all of you;

¹⁹nevertheless, in public worship I would rather say five *understandable* words in order to instruct others, than ten thousand words in a tongue [which others cannot understand].

²⁰Brothers and sisters, do not be children [immature, childlike] in your thinking; be infants in [matters of] evil [completely innocent and inexperienced], but in your minds be mature [adults].

²¹It is written in the Law, "BY MEN OF STRANGE TONGUES AND BY THE LIPS OF FOREIGNERS I WILL SPEAK TO THIS

a word about personal prophecy

First Corinthians 14:1, 3, 4 help us understand prophecy and prophetic ministry. Prophecy must be in line with the Word of God, and a personal word of prophecy should confirm something that is already in your heart. It is nice when that happens, because you know that the person giving you that word did not know anything about what God was saying to you. But if somebody tells you to go to the mission field, or to Bible college, do not quit your job and go unless *you know* God has spoken to your heart this same word. I have seen people get into horrendous messes by trying to run their lives based on what other people have told them was a "prophetic message from God."

If the prophecy does not bear witness in your heart, do not worry about it. There are a lot of well-meaning people who think they hear from God for others, but they do not. If someone prophesies to you something that is not already in your heart, then I suggest you write down the words that are spoken over you and simply wait for the Lord to reveal to you whether or not the words are from Him.

If a word of prophecy is truly from God, He will make it happen in His own time. Lay aside the prophecy and wait to see if God brings it to pass. He will speak to you in other ways to confirm it, if it is really from Him.

I know of situations in which five to ten years passed before something happened to prove that a prophecy was truly from God. So even when we have clear direction from God, we need to let Him fulfill His promises without trying to manipulate their manifestation. When a promise does come to pass, the Holy Spirit will help us recall that word we received years before to let us know we are indeed walking in God's perfect plan.

If prayerful godly believers have spoken a good word over you, then opposition can be one of the greatest signs that their message was truly from God. Refer to the spoken or written message when the enemy tells you that you are not called, or you will never do what is in your heart to do, or you are never going to prosper, or you'll never get a breakthrough in your situation, or whatever the case may be. One of your weapons against his attacks will be the word that has been prophesied to you.

Remember, what has been said through the gift of prophecy will help you remain steadfast in faith when the devil wages war against your calling or purpose. If the prophecy is truly from God, the enemy will eventually try to discourage you from believing the truth, and you will be able to stand firm in faith because you know what the Lord has said about you.

PEOPLE, AND NOT EVEN THEN WILL THEY LISTEN TO ME," says the Lord. [Is 28:11, 12]

²²Therefore, [unknown] tongues are [meant] for a [supernatural] sign, not to believers but to unbelievers [who might be receptive]; while prophecy [foretelling the future, speaking a new message from God to the people] is not for unbelievers but for believers.

²³So then, if the whole church gathers together and all of you speak in [unknown] tongues, and outsiders *or* those who are not gifted [in spiritual matters] or unbelievers come in, will they not say that you are out of your mind?

²⁴But if all prophesy [foretelling the future, speaking a new message from God to the people], and an unbeliever or outsider comes in, he is convicted [of his sins] by all, and he is called to account by all [because he can understand what is being said];

²⁵the secrets of his heart are laid bare. And so, falling on his face, he will worship God, declaring that God is really among you.

²⁶What then is *the right course,* believers? When you meet together, each one has a psalm, a teaching, a revelation (disclosure of special knowledge), a tongue, *or* an interpretation. Let everything be constructive *and* edifying *and* done for the good of all the church.

²⁷If anyone speaks in a tongue, *it should be limited* to two or at the most three, and *each one speaking* in turn, and one must interpret [what is said].

²⁸But if there is no one to interpret, the one [who wishes to speak in a tongue] must keep silent in church; let him speak to himself and to God.

²⁹Let two or three prophets speak [as inspired by the Holy Spirit], while the rest pay attention *and* weigh carefully what is said.

³⁰But if an inspired revelation is made to another who is seated, then the first one must be silent.

³¹For [in this way] you can all prophesy one by one, so that everyone may be instructed and everyone may be encouraged;

³²for the spirits of prophets are subject to the prophets [the prophecy is under the speaker's control, and he can stop speaking];

³³for God [who is the source of their prophesying] is not *a God* of confusion *and* disorder but of peace *and* order.

As [is the practice] in all the churches of the saints (God's people),

³⁴the women should be silent in the churches, for they are not authorized to speak, but are to take a subordinate place, as the Law says.

³⁵If there is anything they want to learn [that is, if they have questions about anything being said or taught], they are to ask their own husbands at home; for it is improper for a woman to talk in church.

³⁶Did the word of the Lord originate from you [Corinthians], or has it come to you only [so that you know best what God requires]?

³⁷If anyone thinks *and* claims that he is a prophet [a true spokesman for God] or spiritually astute [filled with and energized by the Holy Spirit], let him recognize that the things which I write to you are the Lord's commandment.

³⁸If anyone does not recognize this [that it is a command of the Lord], he is not recognized [by God].

³⁹Therefore, believers, desire earnestly to prophesy [to foretell the future, to speak a new message from God to the people], and do not forbid speaking in *unknown* tongues.

⁴⁰But all things must be done appropriately and in an orderly manner.

15
NOW BROTHERS and sisters, let me remind you [once again] of the good news [of salvation] which I preached to you,

which you welcomed *and* accepted and on which you stand [by faith].

²By this *faith* you are saved [reborn from above—spiritually transformed, renewed, and set apart for His purpose], if you hold firmly to the word which I preached to you, unless you believed in vain [just superficially and without complete commitment].

³For I passed on to you as of first importance what I also received, that Christ died for our sins according to [that which] the Scriptures [foretold], [Is 53:5–12]

⁴and that He was buried, and that He was [bodily] raised on the third day according to [that which] the Scriptures [foretold], [Ps 16:9, 10]

⁵and that He appeared to Cephas (Peter), then to the Twelve.

⁶After that He appeared to more than five hundred brothers and sisters at one time, the majority of whom are still alive, but some have fallen asleep [in death].

⁷Then He was seen by James, then by all the apostles,

⁸and last of all, as to one untimely (prematurely, traumatically) born, He appeared to me also. [Acts 9:1–9]

⁹For I am the least [worthy] of the apostles, and not fit to be called an apostle, because I [at one time] fiercely oppressed *and* violently persecuted the church of God.

¹⁰But by the [remarkable] grace of God I am what I am, and His grace toward me was not without effect. In fact, I worked harder than all of the apostles, though it was not I, but the grace of God [His unmerited favor and blessing which was] with me.

¹¹So whether it was I or they, this is what we preach, and this is what you believed *and* trusted in *and* relied on with confidence.

¹²Now if Christ is preached as raised from the dead, how is it that some among you say that there is no resurrection of the dead?

¹³But if there is no resurrection of the dead, then not even Christ has been raised;

¹⁴and if Christ has not been raised, then our preaching is vain [useless, amounting to nothing], and your faith is also vain [imaginary, unfounded, devoid of value and benefit—not based on truth].

¹⁵We are even discovered to be false witnesses [misrepresenting] God, because we testified concerning Him that He raised Christ, whom He did not raise, if in fact the dead are not raised.

¹⁶For if the dead are not raised, then Christ has not been raised, either;

¹⁷and if Christ has not been raised, your faith is worthless *and* powerless [mere delusion]; you are still in your sins [and under the control and penalty of sin].

¹⁸Then those also who have fallen asleep in Christ are lost.

¹⁹If we who are [abiding] in Christ have hoped only in this life [and this is all there is], then we are of all people most miserable *and* to be pitied.

²⁰But now [as things really are] Christ has *in fact* been raised from the dead, [and He became] the first fruits [that is, the first to be resurrected with an incorruptible, immortal body, foreshadowing the resurrection] of those who have fallen asleep [in death]. [Col 1:18]

²¹For since [it was] by a man that death *came* [into the world], it is also by a Man that the resurrection of the dead *has come.*

speak the Word

Thank You, God, that I am what I am by Your grace and that Your grace was not without effect.
–ADAPTED FROM 1 CORINTHIANS 15:10

²²For just as in Adam all die, so also in Christ all will be made alive.

²³But each in his own order: Christ the first fruits, then those who are Christ's [own will be resurrected with incorruptible, immortal bodies] at His coming.

²⁴After that comes the end (completion), when He hands over the kingdom to God the Father, after He has made inoperative *and* abolished every ruler and every authority and power.

²⁵For Christ must reign [as King] until He has put all His enemies under His feet. [Ps 110:1]

²⁶The last enemy to be abolished *and* put to an end is death.

²⁷For HE (the Father) HAS PUT ALL THINGS IN SUBJECTION UNDER HIS (Christ's) FEET. But when He says, "All things have been put in subjection [under Christ]," it is clear that He (the Father) who put all things in subjection to Him (Christ) is excepted [since the Father is not in subjection to His own Son]. [Ps 8:6]

²⁸However, when all things are subjected to Him (Christ), then the Son Himself will also be subjected to the One (the Father) who put all things under Him, so that God may be all in all [manifesting His glory without any opposition, the supreme indwelling and controlling factor of life].

²⁹Otherwise, what will those do who are being baptized for the dead? If the dead are not raised at all, why are people even baptized for them?

³⁰[For that matter] why are we [running such risks and putting ourselves] in danger [nearly] every hour [if there is no resurrection]?

³¹I assure you, believers, by the pride which I have in you in [your union with] Christ Jesus our Lord, I die daily [I face death and die to self].

³²What good has it done me if, [merely] from a human point of view, I fought with wild animals at Ephesus?

If the dead are not raised [at all], LET US EAT AND DRINK [enjoying ourselves now], FOR TOMORROW WE DIE. [Is 22:13; 2 Cor 1:8, 9]

³³Do not be deceived: "Bad company corrupts good morals."

³⁴Be sober-minded [be sensible, wake up from your spiritual stupor] as you ought, and stop sinning; for some [of you] have no knowledge of God [you are disgracefully ignorant of Him, and ignore His truths]. I say this to your shame.

³⁵But someone will say, "How are the dead raised? And with what kind of body will they come?"

³⁶You fool! Every time you plant *seed* you sow something that does not come to life [germinating, springing up and growing] unless it *first* dies.

³⁷The seed you sow is not the body (the plant) which it is going to become, but it is a bare seed, perhaps of wheat or some other grain.

³⁸But God gives it a body just as He planned, and to each kind of seed a body of its own [is given]. [Gen 1:11]

³⁹All flesh is not the same. There is one kind for humans, another for animals, another for birds, and another for fish.

⁴⁰There are also heavenly bodies [sun, moon and stars] and earthly

putting the Word to work

First Corinthians 15:33 teaches us that "Bad company corrupts good morals." It is not realistic to think you will always be surrounded by other Christians, and God's Word teaches that you are to be light in a dark world. However, it is important to remember that you are to be a godly influence on the lives of those around you and to stay on guard against evil influences. Be sure when you are around evil or ungodly people that you affect them and they do not infect you.

bodies [humans, animals, and plants], but the glory *and* beauty of the heavenly is one kind, and the *glory* of the earthly is another.

[41]There is a glory *and* beauty of the sun, another glory of the moon, and yet another [distinctive] glory of the stars; and one star differs from another in glory *and* brilliance.

[42]So it is with the resurrection of the dead. The [human] body that is sown is perishable *and* mortal, it is raised imperishable *and* immortal. [Dan 12:3]

[43]It is sown in dishonor, it is raised in glory; it is sown in weakness, it is raised in strength;

[44]it is sown a natural body [mortal, suited to earth], it is raised a spiritual body [immortal, suited to heaven]. As surely as there is a physical body, there is also a spiritual *body*.

[45]So it is written [in Scripture], "The first MAN, Adam, BECAME A LIVING SOUL (an individual);" the last Adam (Christ) *became* a life-giving spirit [restoring the dead to life]. [Gen 2:7]

[46]However, the spiritual [the immortal life] is not first, but the physical [the mortal life]; then the spiritual.

different is okay

We are all different. Like the sun, the moon, and the stars (see 1 Corinthians 15:41), God created us to be different from one another, and He did so on purpose. Each of us meets a need, and we are all part of God's overall plan. When we struggle to be like others, not only do we lose ourselves, but we also grieve the Holy Spirit. God wants us to fit into His plan, not to feel pressured to try and fit into everyone else's plans. Different is okay; it is all right to be different.

We are all born with different temperaments, different physical features, different fingerprints, different gifts and abilities, etc. Our goal is to discover what we are supposed to be as individuals, and then succeed at that.

Romans 12 teaches us that we are to give ourselves to our gifts. In other words, we are to find out what we are good at and then throw ourselves wholeheartedly into exercising our gifts.

I discovered that I enjoy doing what I am good at doing. Some people feel they are not good at anything, but that is not true. When we make an effort to do what others are good at doing, we often fail because we are not gifted for those things; but that does not mean we are good for nothing. We should look for what we are good at and function in it.

We all have limitations, and we must accept them. That is not bad; it is just a fact. It is wonderful to be free to be different, not to feel that something is wrong with us because we are different.

We should be free to love and accept one another, as well as ourselves, without feeling pressure to compare or compete. Secure people who know God loves them and has a plan for them are not threatened by the abilities of others. I encourage you to be secure enough to enjoy what other people can do and to enjoy what you can do. Say positive things about yourself instead of negative things because that will help release the gifts God has placed in you.

⁴⁷The first man [Adam] is from the earth, earthy [made of dust]; the second Man [Christ, the Lord] is from heaven. [Gen 2:7]
⁴⁸As is the earthly man [the man of dust], so are those who are of earth; and as is the heavenly [Man], so are those who are of heaven.
⁴⁹Just as we have borne the image of the earthly [the man of dust], we will also bear the image of the heavenly [the Man of heaven].
⁵⁰Now I say this, believers, that flesh and blood cannot inherit *nor* be part of the kingdom of God; nor does the perishable (mortal) inherit the imperishable (immortal).
⁵¹Listen very carefully, I tell you a mystery [a secret truth decreed by God and previously hidden, but now revealed]; we will not all sleep [in death], but we will all be [completely] changed [wondrously transformed],
⁵²in a moment, in the twinkling of an eye, at [the sound of] the last trumpet call. For a trumpet will sound, and the dead [who believed in Christ] will be raised imperishable, and we will be [completely] changed [wondrously transformed].
⁵³For this perishable [part of us] must put on the imperishable [nature], and this mortal [part of us that is capable of dying] must put on immortality [which is freedom from death].
⁵⁴And when this perishable puts on the imperishable, and this mortal puts on immortality, then the Scripture will be fulfilled that says, "DEATH IS SWALLOWED UP in victory (vanquished forever). [Is 25:8]
⁵⁵"O DEATH, WHERE IS YOUR VICTORY? O DEATH, WHERE IS YOUR STING?" [Hos 13:14]
⁵⁶The sting of death is sin, and the power of sin [by which it brings death] is the law;
⁵⁷but thanks be to God, who gives us the victory [as conquerors] through our Lord Jesus Christ.
⁵⁸Therefore, my beloved brothers and sisters, be steadfast, immovable, always excelling in the work of the Lord [always doing your best and doing more than is needed], being *continually* aware that your labor [even to the point of exhaustion] in the Lord is not futile *nor* wasted [it is never without purpose].

16 NOW CONCERNING the money collected for [the relief of] the saints [in Jerusalem], you are to do the same as I directed the churches of Galatia *to do*.
²On the first day of every week each one of you is to put something aside, in proportion to his prosperity, and save

putting the Word to work

The loss of a loved one through death is very painful. Are you mourning such a loss right now? Ask God to comfort you with His presence and with the assurance that for believers in Jesus the sting of death is swallowed up by the victory of Jesus Christ and His resurrection (see 1 Corinthians 15:50–57). Death is not the end, because in Christ we live forever. Pray for those in your life who do not yet know Jesus that they too will believe in Him and enjoy eternal life.

putting the Word to work

Do you ever feel your work for God is not making a difference? Be encouraged by 1 Corinthians 15:58. This verse promises that even if you cannot always see the results, your work is not futile or wasted. Ask God to make you steadfast and to strengthen you daily for the work that He has called you to. God sees your labor for Him and He will reward you.

it so that no collections [will need to] be made when I come.

³When I arrive, I will send whomever you approve with letters [of authorization] to take your gift [of charity and love] to Jerusalem;

⁴and if it is fitting for me to go too, they will accompany me.

⁵I will visit you after I go through Macedonia, for I am only passing through Macedonia;

⁶but it may be that I will stay with you [for a while], or even spend the winter, so that you may send me on my way to wherever I may go *afterward*.

⁷For I do not wish to see you right now *just* in passing, but I hope to remain with you for some time [later on], if the Lord permits.

⁸But I will stay in Ephesus until Pentecost,

⁹because a wide door for effective service has opened to me [in Ephesus, a very promising opportunity], and there are many adversaries. [Acts 19:23–41]

¹⁰If Timothy comes, see to it that [you put him at ease, so that] he has nothing to fear in regard to you, for he is [devotedly] doing the Lord's work, just as I am.

¹¹So allow no one to treat him with disdain [as if he were inconsequential]. But send him off [cordially, and speed him on his way] in peace, so that he may come to me, for I am expecting him [to come along] with the *other* brothers.

¹²As for our brother Apollos, I have strongly encouraged him to visit you with the other brothers. It was not at all his desire to come now, but he will come when he has the opportunity.

¹³Be on guard; stand firm in your faith [in God, respecting His precepts and keeping your doctrine sound]. Act like [mature] men *and* be courageous; be strong. [Ps 31:24]

¹⁴Let everything you do be done in love [motivated and inspired by God's love for us].

¹⁵Brothers and sisters, you know that *those of* the household of Stephanas were the first converts in Achaia, and that they have devoted themselves for ministry to *God's people—now I urge you

¹⁶to be subject to such leaders [treating them with courtesy and respect], and to everyone who helps in the work and labors [for the benefit of yourselves and the church].

¹⁷I rejoice because Stephanas and Fortunatus and Achaicus have arrived, for they have made up for your absence.

¹⁸They have refreshed my spirit as well as yours. So fully acknowledge such men *and* deeply appreciate them.

¹⁹The churches of Asia send you their greetings. Aquila and Prisca, together with the church [that meets] in their house, send you their warm greetings in the Lord.

²⁰All the believers greet you. Greet one another with a holy kiss.

²¹This greeting is in my own hand—Paul.

²²If anyone does not love the Lord [does not obey and respect and believe in Jesus Christ and His message], he is to be accursed. Maranatha (O our Lord, come)!

²³The grace of our Lord Jesus [His unmerited favor, His spiritual blessing, His profound mercy] be with you.

²⁴My love be with all of you in Christ Jesus. Amen.

speak the Word

Father, I pray that everything I do will be done in love.
–ADAPTED FROM 1 CORINTHIANS 16:14

16:15 Lit *the saints*.

Second Corinthians

Author:
Paul

Date:
About AD 55, seemingly a few months after 1 Corinthians was written.

Everyday Life Principles:
In Christ, you are a new creation. Your past is finished and you are made new.

Because of Jesus, you are righteous, which means you are in a right relationship with God.

You are an ambassador for Jesus Christ everywhere you go.

Second Corinthians is perhaps the most personal of all letters from the Apostle Paul. Obviously, it is his second letter to the believers in Corinth, probably because their problems continued after his first letter. Into their situation of strife and conflict, Paul sends this letter to thank and encourage those who have been faithful to God and loyal to him, to share some personal insights and struggles, and to encourage people in the church.

One of the great themes in 2 Corinthians is that a believer in Jesus Christ is a new creation, one who has right standing with God and is an ambassador for Him. When we receive Jesus as Savior and Lord, our past is completely washed away. We do not have to feel guilty about it anymore because we are forgiven, nor do we have to allow past behaviors or thoughts to influence us anymore. Instead, we are made new in our hearts and we are continually to renew our minds in the Word of God, which further strengthens us and grounds us in the realities of our faith.

As you read 2 Corinthians, I hope you will become increasingly aware that your old life has passed away and that you are a new creation in Jesus Christ. You are in right relationship with God and you are His representative to the people around you. These are extremely important aspects of your Christian faith and they will lead you to victory in your everyday life.

1 PAUL, AN apostle (special messenger, personally chosen representative) of Christ Jesus (the Messiah) by the will of God, and Timothy *our* brother,

To the church of God which is at Corinth, and to all the saints (God's people) throughout Achaia (southern Greece):

²Grace to you and peace [inner calm and spiritual well-being] from God our Father and the Lord Jesus Christ.

³Blessed [gratefully praised and adored] be the God and Father of our Lord Jesus Christ, the Father of mercies and the God of all comfort,

⁴who comforts *and* encourages us in every trouble so that we will be able to comfort *and* encourage those who are in any kind of trouble, with the comfort with which we ourselves are comforted by God.

⁵For just as Christ's sufferings are ours in abundance [as they overflow to His followers], so also our comfort [our reassurance, our encouragement, our consolation] is abundant through Christ [it is truly more than enough to endure what we must].

⁶But if we are troubled *and* distressed, it is for your comfort and salvation; or if we are comforted *and* encouraged, it is for your comfort, which works [in you] when you patiently endure the same sufferings which we experience.

⁷And our hope for you [our confident expectation of good for you] is firmly grounded [assured and unshaken], since we know that just as you share

find comfort in God

Have you been disappointed, hurt, or mistreated? Have you had changes in your life or are you experiencing loss of some kind? Have you failed in some way? Are you simply tired? What is your trouble today? Second Corinthians 1:3, 4 says that God wants to help you by comforting you when you need it.

The Holy Spirit is actually called the Comforter, among other descriptive names (see John 14:26). His various names describe His character. They reveal what He does and what He desires to do for believers. He is willing to do so much for us if we are willing to receive His help.

For many years I regularly became angry with my husband Dave because he would not comfort me when I felt I needed it. I am sure he was trying, but now I realize that God would not allow Dave to give me the comfort I should have been seeking from Him. God was longing to give me that comfort by the Holy Spirit, if only I had asked!

God will only allow people to do a certain amount for us, and no more. Even those people who are extremely close to us cannot give us everything we need all the time. When we expect others to do for us what only God can do, our expectations are in the wrong place, and we will always be disappointed.

No comfort is as good as the comfort God provides. People can never give us what we really need, unless God Himself uses other people to reach us, which He often does. Whether He uses another person to comfort you or He comforts you Himself by the Holy Spirit, let me remind you that He is the Comforter. Ask for and receive His comfort whenever you need it.

putting the Word to work

Times of suffering and trials are a part of everyone's life. Is this a time of suffering in your life? Ask God to surround you with His comfort and to help you experience it in tangible ways. He is able to comfort you no matter what the trial. Although it may not help much right now, know that someday you will be able to comfort someone else as God comforts you (see 2 Corinthians 1:3–5).

as partners in our sufferings, so also you share *as partners* in our comfort.

⁸For we do not want you to be uninformed, brothers and sisters, about our trouble in [the west coast province of] Asia [Minor], how we were utterly weighed down, beyond our strength, so that we despaired even of life [itself].

⁹Indeed, we felt within ourselves that we had received the sentence of death [and were convinced that we would die, but this happened] so that we would not trust in ourselves, but in God who raises the dead.

¹⁰He rescued us from so great a *threat of* death, and will *continue to* rescue us. On Him we have set our hope. And He will again rescue us [from danger and draw us near],

¹¹while you join in helping us by your prayers. Then thanks will be given by many persons on our behalf for the gracious gift [of deliverance] granted to us through *the prayers of* many [believers].

¹²This is our [reason for] proud confidence: our conscience testifies that we have conducted ourselves in the world [in general], and especially toward you, with pure motives and godly sincerity, not in human wisdom, but in the grace of God [that is, His gracious lovingkindness that leads people to Christ and spiritual maturity].

¹³For we write you nothing other than what you read and understand [there is no double meaning in what we say]. And I hope you will [accurately] understand [divine things] until the end;

¹⁴just as you have [already] partially understood us, [and one day will recognize] that you can be proud of us just as we are of you, in the day of our Lord Jesus.

¹⁵It was with this confidence that I planned at first to visit you, so that you might receive twice a token of grace;

¹⁶that is, [I wanted] to visit you on my way to Macedonia, and [then] to come back to you [on my return] from Macedonia, and have you send me on my way to Judea.

¹⁷So then, was I indecisive *or* capricious when I was [originally] planning this? Or the things I plan, do I plan in a self-serving way like a worldly man, ready to say, "Yes, yes" and "No, no" [at the same time]?

¹⁸But [as surely as] God is faithful *and* means what He says, our message to you is not "Yes" and "No" [at the same time].

¹⁹For the Son of God, Jesus Christ, who was preached among you by us, by me, Silvanus, and Timothy, was not "Yes" and "No," but has proved to be "Yes" in Him [true and faithful, the divine "Yes" affirming God's promises].

²⁰For as many as are the promises of God, in Christ they are [all answered] "Yes." So through Him we say our "Amen" to the glory of God.

putting the Word to work

Do you know that all of the promises of God are for you (see 2 Corinthians 1:20)? As you spend time in the Word, look for the promises of God. Ask Him to show you how He has already fulfilled certain promises and to fill you with expectation that He will fulfill others.

life point

If we pray in the Holy Spirit, we can be assured that all things will work out for good (see Romans 8:27, 28). God is great and mighty; there is no situation He cannot use for good as we pray and trust Him. We dare not pray the way we want to, but as we are led by the Holy Spirit. I believe Spirit-filled prayers receive a "yes" and "amen" from God, as we read about in 2 Corinthians 1:20.

²¹Now it is God who establishes *and* confirms us [in joint fellowship] with you in Christ, and who has anointed us [empowering us with the gifts of the Spirit];
²²it is He who has also put His seal on us [that is, He has appropriated us and certified us as His] and has given us the [Holy] Spirit in our hearts as a pledge [like a security deposit to guarantee the fulfillment of His promise of eternal life].
²³But I call on God as my soul's witness, that it was to spare you [pain and discouragement] that I did not come again to Corinth—
²⁴not that we rule [like dictators] over your faith, but *rather* we work with you for [the increase of] your joy; for in your faith you stand firm [in your strong conviction that Jesus of Nazareth—the Messiah—is the Son of God, through whom we obtain eternal salvation].

2 BUT I made up my mind not to grieve you with another painful visit.
²For if I cause you grief [by a well-deserved rebuke], who then provides me enjoyment but the very one whom I have made sad?
³And I wrote this same thing to you, so that when I came, I would not be filled with sorrow by those who ought

to make me glad, for I trusted in you *and* felt confident that my joy would be shared by all of you.
⁴For I wrote to you out of great distress and with an anguished heart, and with many tears, not to cause you sorrow but to make you realize the [overflowing] love which I have especially for you.
⁵But if someone has caused [all this] sorrow, he has caused it not to me, but in some degree—not to put it too severely—[he has distressed and grieved] all of you.
⁶For such a one this punishment by the majority is sufficient,
⁷so instead [of further rebuke, now] you should rather [graciously] forgive and comfort *and* encourage him, to keep him from being overwhelmed by excessive sorrow.
⁸Therefore I urge you to reinstate him in your affections *and* reaffirm your love for him.
⁹For this was my purpose in writing, to see if you would stand the test, whether you are obedient *and* committed to following my instruction in all things.
¹⁰If you forgive anyone anything, I too forgive [that one]; and what I have forgiven, if I have forgiven anything,

life point

Second Corinthians 2:10, 11 teach us that we are to forgive in order to keep Satan from taking advantage of us. When we forgive others, we not only do them a favor, we do ourselves an even greater favor.

The reason we do ourselves such a favor is that unforgiveness fills us with resentment and produces a root of bitterness that poisons our entire system.

Bitterness always belongs to bondage. Forgiveness releases bitter bondage.

has been for your sake in the presence of [and with the approval of] Christ,

¹¹to keep Satan from taking advantage of us; for we are not ignorant of his schemes.

¹²Now when I arrived at Troas to *preach* the good news of Christ, even though a door [of opportunity] opened for me in the Lord,

¹³my spirit could not rest because I did not find my brother Titus *there;* so saying goodbye to them, I left for Macedonia.

¹⁴But thanks be to God, who always leads us in triumph in Christ, and through us spreads *and* makes evident everywhere the sweet fragrance of the knowledge of Him.

¹⁵For we are the *sweet* fragrance of Christ [which ascends] to God, [discernible both] among those who are being saved and among those who are perishing;

¹⁶to the *latter* one an aroma from death to death [a fatal, offensive odor], but to the other an aroma from life to life [a vital fragrance, living and fresh]. And who is adequate *and* sufficiently qualified for these things?

¹⁷For we are not like many, [acting like merchants] peddling God's word [shortchanging and adulterating God's message]; but from pure [uncompromised] motives, as [commissioned and sent] from God, we speak [His message] in Christ in the sight of God.

3 ARE WE starting to commend ourselves again? Or do we need, like some [false teachers], letters of recommendation to you or from you? [No!]

²You are our letter [of recommendation], written in our hearts, recognized and read by everyone.

³You show that you are a letter from Christ, delivered by us, written not with ink but with the Spirit of the living God, not on tablets of stone but on tablets of human hearts. [Ex 24:12; 31:18; 32:15, 16; Jer 31:33]

⁴Such is the confidence *and* steadfast reliance *and* absolute trust that we have through Christ toward God.

⁵Not that we are sufficiently qualified in ourselves to claim anything as *coming* from us, but our sufficiency *and* qualifications come from God.

⁶He has qualified us [making us sufficient] as ministers of a new covenant [of salvation through Christ], not of the letter [of a written code] but of the Spirit; for the letter [of the Law] kills [by revealing sin and demanding obedience], but the Spirit gives life. [Jer 31:31]

life point

God always energizes us to do what He leads us to do. It is only when we go beyond His will to follow our own will (or other people's desires) that we are likely to get exhausted. Second Corinthians 2:14 says that God "always leads us in triumph." His will is not for us to live weak, defeated lives; He wants us to be "more than conquerors" (see Romans 8:37). His will for us is strength, not weakness; victory, not defeat.

putting the Word to work

Many cultures today place a high value on self-sufficiency. Do you believe you are self-sufficient? The truth is that no one is sufficient in himself. Second Corinthians 3:5 says our only sufficiency is from God. Whether you recognize it or not, your ability to do anything, including minister to others, comes from God alone. Thank Him that you do not have to depend on yourself, but can rely on His strength and power for everything you do!

⁷Now if the ministry of death, engraved in letters on stones [the covenant of the Law which led to death because of sin], came with such glory *and* splendor that the Israelites were not able to look steadily at the face of Moses because of its glory, [a brilliance] that was fading, [Ex 34:29–35]

⁸how will the ministry of the Spirit [the new covenant which allows us to be Spirit-filled] fail to be even more glorious *and* splendid?

⁹For if the ministry that brings condemnation [the old covenant, the Law] has glory, how much more does glory overflow in the ministry that brings righteousness [the new covenant which declares believers free of guilt and sets them apart for God's special purpose]!

relationship, not "religion"

I feel sometimes that "religion" is killing people. In 2 Corinthians 3:6, Paul said, "The letter [of the Law] kills [by revealing sin and demanding obedience], but the Spirit gives life."

There are so many precious people who seek a relationship with God, and the religious community continues to tell them they need to "do" something else in order to be acceptable to Him.

Do not be offended by my use of the word *religion*. I realize it has been a popular, spiritual-sounding word for centuries. I am only trying to present a clear difference between an impersonal set of rules and regulations and a personal relationship with the living God.

Jesus spoke of His personal relationship with the Father, and the religious leaders of His day persecuted Him. I am amazed when I encounter certain people who are opposed to hearing others talk about God in a personal way or about feeling empowered by Him. Obviously, Satan hates a personal relationship with God and the power it makes available in a believer's life.

In certain religious circles, if you and I were to talk about God as though we know Him personally, we would be judged and criticized. People would ask, "Who do you think you are?" Religion wants us to picture God as being far away—somewhere up in the sky—not approachable by anyone except the "elite" of the Church. Furthermore, they want us to believe we can only reach Him through rule-keeping and good behavior.

This "religious spirit" was alive in Jesus' day, and even though He died to put an end to it and bring people into a close personal relationship with Himself, the Father, and the Holy Spirit. That same religious spirit still torments people to this day if they do not know the truth.

The Law was given in order to show people their need for a Savior. We try to keep it until we realize that we absolutely cannot, and then hopefully we humble ourselves and ask God to help us, which He did in the person of Jesus Christ and continues to do through the Holy Spirit. As you walk with God, remember to keep your relationship with Him at the center and to keep "religion" far from you.

¹⁰Indeed, what had glory [the Law], in this case no longer has glory because of the glory that surpasses it [the gospel].

¹¹For if that [Law] which fades away *came* with glory, *how* much more *must* that [gospel] which remains *and* is permanent abide in glory *and* splendor!

¹²Since we have such a [glorious] hope *and* confident expectation, we speak with great courage,

¹³and we are not like Moses, *who* used to put a veil over his face so that the Israelites would not gaze at the end of the glory which was fading away.

¹⁴But [in fact] their minds were hardened [for they had lost the ability to understand]; for until this very day at the reading of the old covenant the same veil remains unlifted, because it is removed [only] in Christ.

¹⁵But to this day whenever Moses is read, a veil [of blindness] lies over their heart;

¹⁶but whenever a person turns [in repentance and faith] to the Lord, the veil is taken away.

life point

In 2 Corinthians 3:13–15 we learn that when the Law is read, a veil lies over the hearts and minds of the people. A veil is a separation.

As long as we read the Bible as Law, a separation will exist between God and us and it will prevent proper relationship. Even though the Old Covenant is now void and done away with, if we are legalistic, we will read legalism into everything the Bible says.

Remember, a legalist is someone who is overly concerned with keeping rules. He exalts rules above relationship. Do not be a legalist, hiding behind a veil of regulations, but come to God just as you are with an open heart and unveiled face.

life point

Second Corinthians 3:17 affirms that God wants us to live in liberty and not legalism. In the same verse liberty is defined as "emancipation from bondage; true freedom." We read in John 8:36, "If the Son makes you free, then you are unquestionably free."

You may ask, "What am I free from?" You are:

Free from the power of sin!

Free from manipulation and control!

Free from fear of what others think of you!

Free from comparing yourself with everybody else!

Free from competition with others!

Free from selfishness!

Free from legalism!

Free to be an individual!

Free to be you!

Free! Free! Free!

¹⁷Now the Lord is the Spirit, and where the Spirit of the Lord is, *there* is liberty [emancipation from bondage, true freedom]. [Is 61:1, 2]

life point

We change gradually, little by little, or as 2 Corinthians 3:18 states, "From [one degree of] glory to [even more] glory." While these changes take place, we still make mistakes, and God's forgiveness is always available to us through Jesus Christ. Receiving this forgiveness actually strengthens us and enables us to keep pressing toward new levels of holiness or better behavior.

18And we all, with unveiled face, *continually* seeing as in a mirror the glory of the Lord, are *progressively* being transformed into His image from [one degree of] glory to [even more] glory, which comes from the Lord, [who is] the Spirit.

4 THEREFORE, SINCE we have this ministry, just as we received mercy [from God, granting us salvation, opportunities, and blessings], we do not get discouraged *nor* lose our motivation.

2But we have renounced the disgraceful things hidden because of shame; not walking in trickery or adulterating the word of God, but by stating the truth [openly and plainly], we commend ourselves to everyone's conscience in the sight of God.

3But even if our gospel is [in some

free to be

In 2 Corinthians 3:18 we read that we must come "with unveiled face" in order to receive the benefit God wants us to have from the New Covenant.

To me, this means that when I stop being religious and legalistic and simply come to Jesus, when I lay aside all "my" works and begin to see Him, when I allow Him to remove the veil from my eyes, then He and I can enter into personal relationship that will ultimately change me into His image.

If we want to grow in our relationships with Him, it's so important that we learn to "be" and not always feel that we must "do."

In Christian circles today there is a big emphasis on spending personal time with the Lord, and rightly so. More than anything else, we need His presence. He is the only One Who can bring any good and lasting change into our lives. Unfortunately, many people are frustrated by this emphasis in teaching. They want to spend time with God, but feel uncomfortable; or, they do not know what to do during these times.

Others express that they never sense God's presence. They find prayer and fellowship to be a dry experience. I believe one reason this happens is that people live under the Law instead of under grace. Grace is not the freedom to sin; it is the power to live a holy life.

But grace also sees when our hearts are right toward God and even though our performance may not always be perfect, grace forgives and helps us get from where we are to where we need to be.

The Law condemns. Grace removes the condemnation and sets us free—free *from* and free *to*. Free *from* condemnation, self-hatred, self-rejection, fear of God, and many other negative traps. And free *to* serve God without pressure, free *to* use the life and energy we are given to behave better, rather than to fight condemnation.

When you spend time with God, do not try to be or sound "religious," just be yourself. Talk to Him and listen to hear what He will speak to your heart. Read His Word and other Christian books that will edify and help you grow as a believer in Jesus Christ. Do not make your time with Him complicated, keep it simple and trust Him to teach you in all areas of life.

sense] hidden [behind a veil], it is hidden [only] to those who are perishing;

4among them the god of this world [Satan] has blinded the minds of the unbelieving to prevent them from seeing the illuminating light of the gospel of the glory of Christ, who is the image of God.

5For we do not preach ourselves, but Jesus Christ as Lord, and ourselves [merely] as your bond-servants for Jesus' sake.

6For God, who said, "Let light shine out of darkness," is the One who has shone in our hearts to give us the Light of the knowledge of the glory *and* majesty of God [clearly revealed] in the face of Christ. [Gen 1:3]

7But we have this *precious* treasure [the good news about salvation] in [unworthy] earthen vessels [of human frailty], so that the grandeur *and* surpassing greatness of the power will be [shown to be] from God [His sufficiency] and not from ourselves.

8We are pressured in every way [hedged in], but not crushed; perplexed [unsure of finding a way out], but not driven to despair;

9hunted down *and* persecuted, but not deserted [to stand alone]; struck down, but never destroyed;

10always carrying around in the body the dying of Jesus, so that the [resurrection] life of Jesus also may be shown in our body.

11For we who live are constantly [experiencing the threat of] being handed over to death for Jesus' sake, so that the [resurrection] life of Jesus also may be evidenced in our mortal body [which is subject to death].

12So *physical* death is [actively] at work in us, but [spiritual] life [is actively at work] in you.

13Yet we have the same spirit of faith as he had, who wrote *in Scripture,* "I BELIEVED, THEREFORE I SPOKE." We also believe, therefore we also speak, [Ps 116:10]

14knowing that He who raised the Lord Jesus will also raise us with Jesus and will present us [along] with you in His presence.

15For all [these] things are for your sake, so that as [God's remarkable, undeserved] grace reaches to more and more people it may increase thanksgiving, to the glory of [our great] God.

16Therefore we do not become discouraged [spiritless, disappointed, or afraid]. Though our outer self is [progressively] wasting away, yet our inner *self* is being [progressively] renewed day by day.

17For our momentary, light distress [this passing trouble] is producing for us an eternal weight of glory [a fullness] beyond all measure [surpassing all comparisons, a transcendent splendor and an endless blessedness]!

18So we look not at the things which are seen, but at the things which are unseen; for the things which are visible are temporal [just brief and fleeting], but the things which are invisible are everlasting *and* imperishable.

5 FOR WE know that if the earthly tent [our physical body] which is our house is torn down [through death], we have a building from God, a house not made with hands, eternal in the heavens.

speak the Word

Thank You, God, for allowing me to possess the precious treasure of salvation in my frail human vessel so everyone will know that the power in my life comes from You, not from me.
—ADAPTED FROM 2 CORINTHIANS 4:7

this too shall pass

When I face difficult times, I tell myself, "This can't last forever. This, too, shall pass."

You can probably look back at your life and see many difficult things you endured even though at the time you thought, *I cannot stand this for another day.* The devil probably tempted you every five minutes to believe the trial was going to last forever.

As you consider how many times you have already made it to the other side of pain, you can be confident you will make it again through Christ, Who strengthens you (see Philippians 4:13). And on the other side of trials, you will see how God turned those experiences into good for your life (see Romans 8:28).

If you have had a problem for more than six months, you probably feel as though your problem has lasted for an eternity. But our years on earth are only a little drop of nothing compared to forever.

Paul said in 2 Corinthians 4:17, 18 that the seasons of trials pass. Going through trials is tough, but Paul learned to keep his eyes on the prize of heaven and trusted God to prepare him so that God's glory was revealed through his life.

When you are tempted to become discontented, remember: "This, too, shall pass." Your afflictions are "momentary and light" from the perspective of eternity. No matter how bad your current situation may look, God loves you. Never let go of the truth that God loves you, no matter what happens in your life. You can trust that everything will work out because of His great love for you.

²For indeed in this *house* we groan, longing to be clothed with our [immortal, eternal] celestial dwelling,

³so that by putting it on we will not be found naked.

⁴For while we are in this tent, we groan, being burdened [often weighed down, oppressed], not that we want to be unclothed [separated by death from the body], but to be clothed, so that what is mortal [the body] will be swallowed up by life [after the resurrection].

⁵Now He who has made us *and* prepared us for this very purpose is God, who gave us the [Holy] Spirit as a pledge [a guarantee, a down payment on the fulfillment of His promise].

⁶So then, being always filled with good courage *and* confident hope, and knowing that while we are at home in the body we are absent from the Lord—

⁷for we walk by faith, not by sight [living our lives in a manner consistent with our confident belief in God's promises]—

⁸we are [as I was saying] of good

putting the Word to work

Are you facing some physical challenges at this time in your life? It can be discouraging to know that your body cannot do everything it used to be able to do (see 2 Corinthians 5:1–4). Ask God for strength to face those physical challenges, and be encouraged, knowing that your eternal body will always be perfect and strong, and that you will live with Him forever (see 2 Corinthians 5:5–8).

fickle feelings

Second Corinthians 5:7 says we walk by faith and not by sight; we do not make decisions according to what we see or feel. We have to search our hearts, where faith abides, and live from there. The kingdom of God is *within* us, and we should follow those inner promptings that lead to righteousness, peace, and joy in the Holy Spirit.

Feelings can mislead us and steal our faith more than any other single influence. The problem with feelings is that they change constantly. We can feel one thousand different ways about the same thing in thirty days. One minute we may feel like doing something, and the next minute we do not. Feelings also provoke us to say things that are unwise, and we talk a lot about how we feel!

Do you believe the god of your feelings or the God of the Bible? This is a question we would be wise to consider. More than anything, people who come to me for help and counsel tell me how they feel. We should tell each other what the Word of God says, not just how we feel.

Our feelings do not convey truth to us; Satan uses them to deceive and lead us astray. Emotions are unreliable; do not believe them or trust them. Respond with your heart, where the Spirit of God abides, and always be sure you have peace. Check with your heart, not your emotions, before making a decision. Learn to walk by faith, not by things you can see, touch, or feel.

courage *and* confident hope, and prefer rather to be absent from the body and to be at home with the Lord.

⁹Therefore, whether we are at home [on earth] or away from home [and with Him], it is our [constant] ambition to be pleasing to Him.

¹⁰For we [believers will be called to account and] must all appear before the judgment seat of Christ, so that each one may be repaid for what has been done in the body, whether good or bad [that is, each will be held responsible for his actions, purposes, goals, motives—the use or misuse of his time, opportunities and abilities].

¹¹Therefore, since we know the fear of the Lord [and understand the importance of obedience and worship], we persuade people [to be reconciled to Him]. But we are plainly known to God [He knows everything about us]; and I hope that we are plainly known also in your consciences [your God-given discernment].

¹²We are not commending ourselves to you again, but are giving you an occasion to be [rightfully] proud of us, so that you will have *an answer* for those who take pride in [outward] appearances [the virtues they pretend to have] rather than what is [actually] in heart.

¹³If we are out of our mind [just unstable fanatics as some critics say], it is for God; if we are in our right mind, it is for your benefit.

speak the Word

Thank You, God, for giving me the Holy Spirit as a pledge and guarantee of the fulfillment of Your promise in my life.
    –ADAPTED FROM 2 CORINTHIANS 5:5

life point

The more we love Jesus, the more we operate in self-control. It is easier for us to say no to selfish desires and yes to God, because "the love of Christ" (2 Corinthians 5:14) urges us to do so.

As our love for God grows, we will not want to offend Him. We will not want to grieve the Holy Spirit. We will want to do what God wants us to do, and obedience will give us great joy in our everyday lives.

Our walk with God is progressive and we do get better and better in every way as we continue in His Word. Do not be discouraged with yourself. You may not be where you want to be, but thank God you are not where you used to be!

life point

As "a new creature," you do not have to allow the old things that happened to you to affect your new life in Christ. You are a new creation with a new life in Christ (see 2 Corinthians 5:17). You can have your mind renewed according to the Word of God. Good things will happen to you. Rejoice! It is a new day!

¹⁴For the love of Christ controls *and* compels us, because we have concluded this, that One died for all, therefore all died;
¹⁵and He died for all, so that all those who live would no longer live for themselves, but for Him who died and was raised for their sake.
¹⁶So from now on we regard no one

God's ambassadors

Do you understand from 2 Corinthians 5:18–20 that God wants us—and through us, everyone on earth—to be in favor with Him? Do you also understand from what we have said that the devil steals that favor through deceit and delusion? Jesus came to restore favor to God's people—and through us to everyone everywhere.

Part of our inheritance is to have and enjoy favor. Part of our ministry is to act as Christ's ambassadors by drawing others to receive God's wonderful gift of forgiveness and reconciliation and to share in His marvelous grace, His unmerited favor.

God wants to restore us to favor with Him so we may act as His ambassadors on the earth. This is how we need to look upon ourselves, as emissaries from a foreign land. The Bible says we are aliens and strangers here, that this earth is not our home, we are merely passing through (see 1 Peter 2:11). Through us God makes His appeal to others to receive His forgiveness, grace, and favor.

Now think for a moment: how are foreign ambassadors treated? Are they not treated royally? That is the way we should expect to be treated, and that is the way we should treat others to whom we are sent by the Lord for the sake of His kingdom.

The Bible tells us that not only are we ambassadors for Christ, but that we are kings and priests unto our God (see Revelation 1:6, KJV). That is why we need a different attitude toward ourselves and others. We need to act like royal ambassadors, like divine diplomats, because we are God's representatives on earth.

from a human point of view [according to worldly standards and values]. Though we have known Christ from a human point of view, now we no longer know Him *in this way.*

¹⁷Therefore if anyone is in Christ [that is, grafted in, joined to Him by faith in Him as Savior], *he is* a new creature [reborn and renewed by the Holy Spirit]; the old things [the previous moral and spiritual condition] have passed away. Behold, new things have come [because spiritual awakening brings a new life].

¹⁸But all *these* things are from God, who reconciled us to Himself through Christ [making us acceptable to Him] and gave us the ministry of reconciliation [so that by our example we might bring others to Him],

¹⁹that is, that God was in Christ reconciling the world to Himself, not counting people's sins against them [but canceling them]. And He has committed to us the message of reconciliation [that is, restoration to favor with God].

²⁰So we are ambassadors for Christ, as though God were making His appeal through us; we [as Christ's representatives] plead with you on behalf of Christ to be reconciled to God.

²¹He made Christ who knew no sin to [judicially] be sin on our behalf, so that in Him we would become the

life point

According to 2 Corinthians 5:20 we are God's ambassadors, His personal representatives. And God makes His appeal to mankind to be saved through us as believers in Jesus Christ. This is a very big responsibility, one we should take seriously. We need to display the character of Jesus through our love for one another and through the good fruit He has produced in our lives, so others will be drawn to Him.

putting the Word to work

Do you know that you are Christ's ambassador (see 2 Corinthians 5:20)? Just as you were reconciled to God through Jesus, He now entrusts you to tell others that they too can be reconciled to God, and have a loving, personal relationship with Him. Think of someone to whom you can be Christ's ambassador and pray for an opportunity to share God's love with that person.

life point

Many believers are tormented by negative thinking about themselves. They think about how God must be so displeased with them because of all their weaknesses and failures.

How much time do you waste living under guilt and condemnation? Notice that I asked how much time is *wasted*, because that is exactly what that kind of thinking is—a waste of time!

Do not think about how terrible you were before you came to Christ. Instead, think about the fact that you have been made the righteousness of God in Him. Remember: thoughts turn into actions. If you ever want to behave better, you have to change your thinking first. Keep thinking about how terrible you are, and you will only act worse. Every time a negative, condemning thought comes to your mind, remind yourself that God loves you and you have been made the righteousness of God in Christ.

You are changing for the better all the time. Every day you grow spiritually. God has a glorious plan for your life. These are the truths you must think about.

righteousness of God [that is, we would be made acceptable to Him and placed in a right relationship with Him by His gracious lovingkindness].

6 WORKING TOGETHER *with Him,* we strongly urge you not to receive God's grace in vain [by turning away from sound doctrine and His merciful kindness].

²For He says,

"AT THE ACCEPTABLE TIME (the time of grace) I LISTENED TO YOU,

AND I HELPED YOU ON THE DAY OF SALVATION."

Behold, now is "THE ACCEPTABLE TIME," behold, now is "THE DAY OF SALVATION"— [Is 49:8]

³we put no obstruction in anyone's path, so that the ministry will not be discredited,

⁴but we commend ourselves in every way as servants of God: in great endurance, in sufferings, in hardships, in distresses,

⁵in beatings, in imprisonments, in

right with God

Being made right with God and being acceptable to Him through Jesus Christ is a wonderful privilege and blessing (see 2 Corinthians 5:21). Just think of it! We no longer have to fear or feel ashamed and condemned when we try to pray or fellowship with God. We can approach the throne of God boldly, unreservedly, and as often as we choose. God loves us and welcomes us with open arms. He loves to hear our requests and work with us to bring us into the fullness of His will for us.

Most people feel wrong about themselves, not right. Prior to accepting Jesus as Savior, we cannot do anything but feel wrong because many things about us are wrong. We say wrong things, make wrong choices, do wrong things and behave in wrong ways toward other people. But through Christ we are made right with God and we become acceptable to Him. We still do things that are wrong, but justice is satisfied in Jesus Christ, Who paid the debt we owed and became the final sacrifice for our sins.

We place our faith in Jesus and we give Him everything we have, everything we are, and especially everything we are not. In exchange He gives us everything He has and is. That is the best deal anyone will find anywhere.

When I married my husband Dave, he had a car. I did not have a car while I was single, but when we married I suddenly had a car. Everything Dave had became mine after I made a full commitment of my life to Dave. His car was not legally mine as long as we were dating, but as soon as we were married everything he had was legally mine and everything I had was his. Dave had money and I did not, so suddenly I had some money. He had a large loving family and mine was rather dysfunctional, so suddenly I had a good family too. Dave had a lot more than I did, which reminds me of my relationship with Jesus.

We have sin and Jesus has righteousness, so when we make a full commitment to Him we give Him our sin and He gives us His righteousness. Exchange your sin consciousness for a righteousness consciousness and you will start seeing wonderful changes in your life and behavior.

riots, in labors, in sleepless nights, in hunger,

⁶in purity *and* sincerity, in knowledge *and* spiritual insight, in patience, in kindness, in the Holy Spirit, in genuine love,

⁷in [speaking] the word of truth, in the power of God; by the weapons of righteousness for the right hand [like holding the sword to attack] and for the left [like holding the shield to defend],

⁸amid glory and dishonor; by evil report and good report; *branded* as deceivers and yet [vindicated as] truthful;

⁹as unknown [to the world], yet well-known [by God and His people]; as dying, yet we live; as punished, yet not killed;

¹⁰as sorrowful, yet always rejoicing; as poor, yet bestowing riches on many; as having nothing, yet possessing all things.

¹¹We are speaking freely to you, Corinthians [we are keeping nothing back], and our heart is opened wide. [Is 60:5; Ezek 33:22]

¹²There is no limit to our affection for you, but you are limited in your own affection [for us].

¹³Now in the same way as a fair exchange [for our love toward you]—I am speaking as [I would] to children— open wide [your hearts] *to us* also.

¹⁴Do not be unequally bound together with unbelievers [do not make mismatched alliances with them, inconsistent with your faith]. For what partnership can righteousness have with lawlessness? Or what fellowship can light have with darkness?

¹⁵What harmony can there be between Christ and Belial (Satan)? Or

putting the Word to work

Relationships are an important part of life, and close relationships that are healthy and godly can be great blessings in our lives. However, 2 Corinthians 6:14–18 warns against being in a close relationship with anyone who causes you to stray from God's purposes and will. Are you in any relationships that cause you to compromise your faith? Ask God to help you know how to eliminate wrong, ungodly relationships, to give you wisdom in your relationships, and to provide you with healthy, godly friendships.

what does a believer have in common with an unbeliever?

¹⁶What agreement is there between the temple of God and idols? For we are the temple of the living God; just as God said:

"I WILL DWELL AMONG THEM AND
  WALK AMONG THEM;
AND I WILL BE THEIR GOD, AND
  THEY SHALL BE MY PEOPLE. [EX
  25:8; 29:45; Lev 26:12; Jer 31:1;
  Ezek 37:27]
¹⁷"SO COME OUT FROM AMONG
  UNBELIEVERS AND BE SEPARATE,"
  says the Lord,
"AND DO NOT TOUCH WHAT IS
  UNCLEAN;
And I will graciously receive you
  and welcome you [with favor],
  [Is 52:11]
¹⁸And I will be a Father to you,
And you will be My sons and
  daughters,"
Says the Lord Almighty. [Is 43:6;
  Hos 1:10]

speak the Word

Thank You, God, for being my Father.
—ADAPTED FROM 2 CORINTHIANS 6:18

7 THEREFORE, SINCE we have these [great and wonderful] promises, beloved, let us cleanse ourselves from everything that contaminates body and spirit, completing holiness [living a consecrated life—a life set apart for God's purpose] in the fear of God.

²Make room for us *in your hearts;* we have wronged no one, we have corrupted no one, we have cheated no one.

³I do not say *this* to condemn *you,* for I have said before that you are [nested] in our hearts [and you will remain there] to die together and to live together [with us].

⁴Great is my confidence in you; great is my pride *and* boasting on your behalf. I am filled [to the brim] with comfort; I am overflowing with joy in spite of all our trouble.

⁵For even when we arrived in Macedonia our bodies had no rest, but we were oppressed at every turn— conflicts *and* disputes without, fears *and* dread within.

⁶But God, who comforts *and* encourages the depressed *and* the disquieted, comforted us by the arrival of Titus.

⁷And not only by his arrival, but also by [his account of] the encouragement which he received in regard to you. He told us about your longing [for us], your mourning [over sin], *and* how eagerly you took my part and supported me, so that I rejoiced even more.

⁸For even though I did grieve you with my letter, I do not regret it [now]; though I did regret it —for I see that the letter hurt you, though only for a little while—

⁹yet I am glad now, not because you were hurt *and* made sorry, but because your sorrow led to repentance [and you turned back to God]; for you felt a grief such as God meant you to feel, so that you might not suffer loss in anything on our account.

¹⁰For [godly] sorrow that is in accord with *the will of* God produces a repentance without regret, *leading* to salvation; but worldly sorrow [the hopeless sorrow of those who do not believe] produces death.

¹¹For [you can look back and] see what an earnestness *and* authentic concern this godly sorrow has produced in you: what vindication of yourselves [against charges that you tolerate sin], what indignation [at sin], what fear [of offending God], what longing [for righteousness and justice], what passion [to do what is right], what readiness to punish [those who sin and those who tolerate sin]! At every point you have proved yourselves to be innocent in the matter.

¹²So even though I wrote to you [as I did], it was not for the sake of the offender nor for the sake of the one offended, but in order to make evident to you before God how earnestly you do care for us [and your willingness to accept our authority].

¹³It is for this reason that we are comforted *and* encouraged.

And in addition to our comfort, we were especially delighted at the joy of Titus, because you have refreshed his spirit.

¹⁴For if I have boasted to him at all concerning you, I was not disappointed. But just as everything we ever said to you was true, so our boasting [about you] to Titus has proved true also.

¹⁵His affection is greater than ever as he remembers the obedience [to his guidance] that all of you exhibited, and how you received him with the greatest respect.

¹⁶I rejoice that in everything I have [perfect] confidence in you.

8 NOW, BROTHERS and sisters, we want to tell you about the grace of God which has been evident in

the churches of Macedonia [awakening in them a longing to contribute];

²for during an ordeal of severe distress, their abundant joy and their deep poverty [together] overflowed in the wealth of their lavish generosity.

³For I testify that according to their ability, and beyond their ability, *they gave* voluntarily,

⁴begging us insistently for the privilege of participating in the service for [the support of] the saints [in Jerusalem].

⁵Not only [did they give materially] as we had hoped, but first they gave themselves to the Lord and to us [as His representatives] by the will of God [disregarding their personal interests and giving as much as they possibly could].

⁶So we urged Titus that, as he began it, he should also complete this gracious work among you as well.

⁷But just as you excel in everything, [and lead the way] in faith, in speech, in knowledge, in genuine concern, and in your love for us, see that you excel in this gracious work [of giving] also.

⁸I am not saying *this* as a command [to dictate to you], but to prove, by [pointing out] the enthusiasm of others, the sincerity of your love as well.

⁹For you are recognizing [more clearly] the grace of our Lord Jesus Christ [His astonishing kindness, His generosity, His gracious favor], that though He was rich, yet for your sake He became poor, so that by His poverty you might become rich (abundantly blessed).

¹⁰I give you *my* opinion in this matter: this is to your advantage, who were the first to begin a year ago not only to take action [to help the believers in Jerusalem], but also [the first] to desire *to do it.*

¹¹So now finish this, so that your eagerness in desiring it may be equaled by your completion of it, according to your ability.

¹²For if the eagerness [to give] is there, it is acceptable according to what one has, not according to what he does not have.

¹³For it is not [intended] that others be relieved [of their responsibility] and that you be burdened [unfairly], but that there be equality [in sharing the burden]—

¹⁴at this present time your surplus [over necessities] *is going* to *supply* their need, so that [at some other time] their surplus may be *given* to *supply* your need, that there may be equality;

¹⁵as it is written [in Scripture], "HE WHO *gathered* MUCH DID NOT HAVE TOO MUCH, AND HE WHO *gathered* LITTLE DID NOT LACK." [Ex 16:18]

¹⁶But thanks be to God who puts the same genuine concern for you in the heart of Titus.

¹⁷For Titus not only accepted our appeal, but was so very interested in you that he has gone to *visit* you of his own accord.

¹⁸And we have sent along with him the brother who is praised in the gospel [ministry] throughout all the churches;

¹⁹and not only *this,* but he has also been appointed by the churches to travel with us in regard to this gracious offering which we are administering for the glory of the Lord Himself, and *to show* our eagerness [as believers to help one another].

speak the Word

*Thank You, God, that I am recognizing more clearly
the grace of my Lord Jesus Christ—His astonishing kindness,
His generosity, and His gracious favor.*
–ADAPTED FROM 2 CORINTHIANS 8:9

²⁰We are taking precaution so that no one will [find anything with which to] discredit us in our administration of this generous gift. ²¹For we have regard for what is honorable [and above suspicion], not only in the sight of the Lord, but also in the sight of men. ²²We have sent with them our brother, whom we have often tested and found to be diligent in many things, but who is now even more diligent [than ever] because of his great confidence in you. ²³As for Titus, *he is* my partner and fellow worker in your service; and as for the [other two] brothers, *they are* [special] messengers of the churches, a glory *and* credit to Christ. ²⁴Therefore, show these men, in the sight of the churches, the proof of your love and our reason for being proud of you.

9 NOW IT is unnecessary for me to write to you about the offering [that is to be made] for the saints [in Jerusalem]; ²for I know your eagerness [to promote this cause], and I have [proudly] boasted to the people of Macedonia about it, telling them that Achaia has been prepared since last year [for this contribution], and your enthusiasm has inspired the majority of them [to respond]. ³Still, I am sending the brothers [on to you], so that our pride in you may not be an empty boast in this case, and so that you may be prepared, just as I told them you would be; ⁴otherwise, if any Macedonians come with me and find you unprepared, we—to say nothing of yourselves—will be humiliated for being so confident. ⁵That is why I thought it necessary to urge these brothers to go to you [before I come] and make arrangements in advance for this generous, previously promised gift of yours, so that it would be ready, not as something extorted [or wrung out of you], but as a [voluntary and] generous gift. ⁶Now [remember] this: he who sows sparingly will also reap sparingly, and he who sows generously [that blessings may come to others] will also reap generously [and be blessed]. ⁷Let each one give [thoughtfully and with purpose] just as he has decided in his heart, not grudgingly or under compulsion, for God loves a cheerful giver [and delights in the one whose heart is in his gift]. [Prov 22:9] ⁸And God is able to make all grace [every favor and earthly blessing] come in abundance to you, so that you may always [under all circumstances, regardless of the need] have complete sufficiency in everything [being completely self-sufficient in Him], and have an abundance for every good work *and* act of charity. ⁹As it is written *and* forever remains written,

"HE [the benevolent and generous person] SCATTERED ABROAD, HE GAVE TO THE POOR,

putting the Word to work

Have you ever thought about not tithing in order to save money or to use that money for something else? I think we have all been tempted to use our tithe for something else, but that is a temptation we should aggressively resist. The tithe does not even belong to us; it belongs to God. He says in Malachi 3 that if we withhold it we are robbing Him. Second Corinthians 9:6–8 is both a warning and a wonderful promise. God is a God of abundance, not scarcity. Ask God to give you a cheerful heart as you give, and to increase your faith to see abundance for every good work.

HIS RIGHTEOUSNESS ENDURES FOREVER!" [Ps 112:9]

[10]Now He who provides seed for the sower and bread for food will provide and multiply your seed for sowing [that is, your resources] and increase the harvest of your righteousness [which shows itself in active goodness, kindness, and love]. [Is 55:10; Hos 10:12]

[11]You will be enriched in every way so that you may be generous, and this [generosity, administered] through us is producing thanksgiving to God [from those who benefit].

[12]For the ministry of this service (offering) is not only supplying the needs of the saints (God's people), but is also overflowing through many expressions of thanksgiving to God.

[13]Because of this act of ministry, they will glorify God for your obedience to the gospel of Christ which you confess, as well as for your generous participation [in this gift] for them and for all [the other believers in need],

[14]and they also long for you while they pray on your behalf, because of the surpassing measure of God's grace [His undeserved favor, mercy, and blessing which is revealed] in you.

[15]Now thanks be to God for His indescribable gift [which is precious beyond words]!

10 NOW I, Paul, urge you by the gentleness and graciousness of Christ—I who am meek [so they say] when with you face to face, but bold [outspoken and fearless] toward you when absent!

[2]I ask that when I do come I will not be driven to the boldness that I intend to show toward those few who regard us as if we walked according to the flesh [like men without the Spirit].

[3]For though we walk in the flesh [as mortal men], we are not carrying on our [spiritual] warfare according to the flesh *and* using the weapons of man.

[4]The weapons of our warfare are not physical [weapons of flesh and blood]. Our weapons are divinely powerful for the destruction of fortresses.

[5]*We are* destroying sophisticated arguments and every exalted *and* proud thing that sets itself up against the [true] knowledge of God, and *we are* taking every thought *and* purpose captive to the obedience of Christ,

[6]being ready to punish every act of disobedience, when your own obedience [as a church] is complete.

[7]You are looking [only] at the outward appearance of things. If anyone is confident that he is Christ's, he should reflect *and* consider this, that just as he is Christ's, so too are we.

[8]For even though I boast rather freely about the authority the Lord gave us for building you up and not for destroying you, I will not be ashamed [of the truth],

[9]nor do I want to seem to be trying to frighten you with my letters;

[10]for they say, "His letters are weighty and forceful *and* impressive, but his personal presence is unimpressive and his speech contemptible [of no account]."

[11]Let such people realize that what we say by word in letters when we are absent, is the same as what *we are* in action when present.

[12]We do not have the audacity to put

speak the Word

Thank You, God, for providing seed for the sower and for multiplying my resources for sowing and increasing the harvest of my righteousness. Thank You that I am enriched in every way so that I may be generous.
—ADAPTED FROM 2 CORINTHIANS 9:10, 11

the mind is the battlefield

Our thoughts get us into trouble more than anything else. This is because our thoughts are the roots of every word and deed.

In Isaiah 55:8, the Lord says, "For My thoughts are not your thoughts, nor are your ways My ways." No matter what you or I may think, God has written His thoughts for us in His book, the Bible. We must choose to examine our thoughts in light of the Word of God, always being willing to submit our thoughts to His thoughts, knowing His are best.

This is exactly the point of 2 Corinthians 10:4, 5. Through careful strategy and cunning deceit, Satan attempts to set up "fortresses" in our minds. Many of us, like me, learned these verses in another Bible translation and refer to them as "strongholds." A stronghold is an area in which we are held in bondage due to a wrong way of thinking. Examine what is in your mind. If it does not agree with God's thoughts (the Bible), then cast down your own thoughts and think God's thoughts instead. In order to do this, you must know God's Word well enough to compare your thoughts with what is in the mind of God.

People living in the vanity of their own minds not only destroy themselves, but far too often, they bring destruction to others around them. Those who live by God's truth, on the other hand, are blessed and bring blessings to others.

The mind is the battlefield!

On the battleground of the mind you will either win or lose the war that Satan has launched against you. My heartfelt prayer is that you will cast down imaginations and every high and lofty thing that exalts itself against the knowledge of God, bringing *every* thought into captivity, into obedience to Jesus Christ so you can live in victory, joy, and peace.

ourselves in the same class or compare ourselves with some who [supply testimonials to] commend themselves. When they measure themselves by themselves and compare themselves with themselves, they lack wisdom *and* behave like fools.

¹³We, on the other hand, will not boast beyond our proper limit, but [will keep] within the limits of our commission (territory, authority) which God has granted to us as a measure, which reaches *and* includes even you.

¹⁴We are not overstepping the limits of our province, as if we did not [legitimately] reach to you, for we were the

life point

I believe one of the biggest mistakes we make is comparing ourselves with other people and our gifts with their gifts.

God is not going to help me be anyone but myself and, likewise, He will not help you be anyone but yourself. He is not calling us to compete with others, but to love and help them. We should use our gifts to enhance other people's gifts, never allowing ourselves to fall prey to the spirit of jealousy that is so prevalent in our society.

[very] first to come even as far as you with the good news of Christ.

¹⁵We do not go beyond our proper limit, boasting in the work of other men, but we have the hope that as your faith [in Christ and His divine power] continues to grow, our field among you may be greatly expanded [but still within the limits of our commission],

¹⁶so that *we may* preach the gospel even in the lands beyond you, but not to boast in work already accomplished in another one's field of activity.

¹⁷However, "LET HIM WHO BOASTS BOAST IN THE LORD." [Jer 9:24]

¹⁸For it is not he who commends *and* praises himself who is approved [by God], but it is the one whom the Lord commends *and* praises.

11 I WISH you would bear with me [while I indulge] in a little foolishness; but indeed you are bearing with me [as you read this].

²I am jealous for you with a godly jealousy because I have promised you to one husband, to present you as a pure virgin to Christ. [Hos 2:19, 20]

³But I am afraid that, even as the serpent beguiled Eve by his cunning, your minds may be corrupted *and* led away from the simplicity of [your sincere and] pure devotion to Christ. [Gen 3:4]

⁴For [you seem willing to allow it] if one comes and preaches another Jesus whom we have not preached, or if you receive a different spirit from

the beauty of simplicity

In 2 Corinthians 11:3, Paul warns the people not to let their minds be corrupted from "the simplicity of [your sincere and] pure devotion to Christ." I especially like the way the King James Version renders that phrase: the "simplicity that is in Christ."

Learn to keep life as simple as possible. It is fine to have a plan for your life and for your everyday activities, but be open to following God's plan if He wants you to go in another direction. We can block God's plan by following our own fleshly desires and plans without consulting Him.

God's plan for us is actually so simple that many times we miss it. We tend to look for something more complicated—something more difficult, something we think we are expected to do to please God.

Jesus told us what to do to follow God's plan: Believe! My life is an example of the magnitude of God's ability to fulfill His plan in our lives, no matter how unlikely the possibility may seem, when we simply believe.

Think about the simple, uncomplicated approach a child has to life. A few things children seem to have in common are these: They are going to enjoy themselves if at all possible. They are carefree and completely without concern. They believe what they are told. Their nature is to trust unless they have had an experience that has taught them otherwise. They are simple, and they approach life with simplicity.

We need to develop these aspects of childlikeness as we relate to God and as we go about our lives.

the one you received, or a different gospel from the one you accepted. You tolerate all this beautifully [welcoming the deception].

⁵Yet I consider myself in no way inferior to the [so-called] super-apostles. ⁶But even if I am unskilled in speaking, yet I am not [untrained] in knowledge [I know what I am talking about]; but we have made this evident to you in every way, in all things.

⁷Or did I [perhaps] sin by humbling myself so that you might be exalted *and* honored, because I preached God's gospel to you free of charge? ⁸I robbed other churches by accepting [more than their share of] financial support for my ministry to you. ⁹And when I was with you and ran short [financially], I did not burden any of you; for what I needed was fully supplied by the brothers (Silas and Timothy) who came from Macedonia (the church at Philippi). So I kept myself from being a burden to you in any way, and will continue to do so. [Phil 4:15, 16] ¹⁰As the truth of Christ is in me, my boast [of independence] will not be silenced in the regions of Achaia (southern Greece). ¹¹Why? Because I do not love you [or wish you well, or have regard for your welfare]? God knows [that I do]!

¹²But what I am doing I will keep doing, [for I am determined to keep this independence] in order to cut off the claim of those who want an opportunity to be regarded just as we are in the things they brag about. ¹³For such men are counterfeit apostles, deceitful workers, masquerading as apostles of Christ. ¹⁴And no wonder, since Satan himself masquerades as an angel of light. ¹⁵So it is no great surprise if his servants also masquerade as servants of righteousness, but their end will correspond with their deeds.

¹⁶I repeat then, let no one think that I am foolish; but even if you do, at least accept me as foolish, so that I too may boast a little. ¹⁷What I say in this confident boasting, I say not as the Lord would [with His authority], but foolishly. ¹⁸Since many boast [of worldly things and brag] about human accomplishments, I will boast too. ¹⁹For you, being so wise, gladly tolerate *and* accept the foolish [like me]! ²⁰For you tolerate it if anyone makes you his slave; or devours you *and* your possessions; or takes advantage of you; or acts presumptuously; or hits you in the face. ²¹To my shame, I must say, we have been too weak [in comparison to those pseudo-apostles who take advantage of you].

But in whatever anyone else dares to boast—I am speaking foolishly—I also dare to boast. ²²Are they Hebrews? So am I. Are they Israelites? So am I. Are they descendants of Abraham? So am I. ²³Are they [self-proclaimed] servants of Christ?—I am speaking as if I were out of my mind—I am more so [for I exceed them]; with far more labors, with far more imprisonments, beaten times without number, and often in danger of death. ²⁴Five times I received from the Jews thirty-nine *lashes*. [Deut 25:3] ²⁵Three times I was beaten with rods, once I was stoned. Three times I was shipwrecked, a night and a day I have spent *adrift* on the sea; ²⁶many times on journeys, [exposed to] danger from rivers, danger from bandits, danger from my own countrymen, danger from the Gentiles, danger in the city, danger in the wilderness, danger on the sea, danger among those posing as believers; ²⁷in labor and hardship, often unable to sleep, in hunger and thirst, often [driven to] fasting [for lack of food], in cold and exposure [without adequate clothing].

²⁸Besides those external things, there is the daily [inescapable] pressure of my concern for all the churches.

²⁹Who is weak, and I do not feel [his] weakness? Who is made to sin, and I am not on fire [with sorrow and concern]?

³⁰If I must boast, I will boast of the things that reveal my weakness [the things by which I am made weak in the eyes of my opponents].

³¹The God and Father of the Lord Jesus, He who is blessed *and* to be praised forevermore, knows that I am not lying.

³²In Damascus the governor (ethnarch) under King Aretas guarded the city of Damascus in order to arrest me,

³³and I was [actually] let down in a basket through a window in the wall, and slipped through his fingers.

12 IT IS necessary to boast, though nothing is gained by it; but I will go on to visions and revelations of the Lord.

²I know a man in Christ who fourteen years ago—whether in the body I do not know, or out of the body I do not know, [only] God knows—such a man was caught up to the third heaven. [Luke 23:43]

³And I know that such a man—whether in the body or out of the body I do not know, [only] God knows—

⁴was caught up into Paradise and heard inexpressible words which man is not permitted to speak [words too sacred to tell].

⁵On behalf of such a man [and his experiences] I will boast; but in my own behalf I will not boast, except in regard to my weaknesses.

⁶If I wish to boast, I will not be foolish, because I will be speaking the truth. But I abstain [from it], so that

no one will credit me with more than [is justified by what] he sees in me or hears from me.

⁷Because of the surpassing greatness *and* extraordinary nature of the revelations [which I received from God], for this reason, to keep me from thinking of myself as important, a thorn in the flesh was given to me, a messenger of Satan, to torment *and* harass me—to keep me from exalting myself! [Job 2:6]

⁸Concerning this I pleaded with the Lord three times that it might leave me;

⁹but He has said to me, "My grace is sufficient for you [My lovingkindness and My mercy are more than enough—always available—regardless of the situation]; for [My] power is being perfected [and is completed and shows itself most effectively] in [your] weakness." Therefore, I will all the more gladly boast in my weaknesses, so that the power of Christ [may completely enfold me and] may dwell in me.

¹⁰So I am well pleased with weaknesses, with insults, with distresses, with persecutions, and with difficulties, for the sake of Christ; for when I am weak [in human strength], then I am strong [truly able, truly powerful, truly drawing from God's strength].

¹¹Now I have become foolish; you have forced me [by questioning my apostleship]. Actually I should have been commended by you [instead of

life point

Jesus told Paul that His grace is sufficient for us; that His power shows itself most effectively in our weaknesses (see 2 Corinthians 12:9). We become frustrated when we try to achieve by *works* a life that God not only brought into being, but designed to be received by *grace*. Grace is the power of God to meet our needs and solve our problems.

putting the Word to work

Weakness is not very popular. Most people do not advertise their limitations. However, in 2 Corinthians 12:9, Paul says he boasts in his weaknesses. Why? Because he knows that God's strength is great in the midst of his infirmity. Is there an area in your life where you feel weak? Do not try to rely on your own strength; ask God to be strong in your weakness. When you admit your frailty, God pours out His strength. Know that His grace is more than sufficient and thank God for His power, which is made perfect in your weakness.

being treated disdainfully], for I was not inferior to those super-apostles, even if I am nobody.

¹²The signs that indicate a genuine apostle were performed among you fully *and* most patiently—signs and wonders and miracles.

¹³For in what respect were you treated as inferior to the rest of the churches, except [for the fact] that I did not burden you [with my financial support]? Forgive me [for doing you] this injustice!

¹⁴Now for the third time I am ready to visit you. I will not burden you [financially], because I do not want what is yours [not your money or your possessions], but you. For children are not responsible to save up for their parents, but parents for their children.

¹⁵But I will very gladly spend [my own resources] and be utterly spent for your souls. If I love you greatly, am I to be loved less [by you]?

¹⁶But be that as it may, I did not burden you [with my support]. But [some say that] I was sly and took you by trickery.

¹⁷Did I take advantage of you *or* make any money off you through any of the messengers I sent you? [Certainly not!]

¹⁸I urged Titus to go, and I sent the brother with him. Titus did not take advantage of you, did he? [No!] Did we not conduct ourselves in the same spirit and walk in the same steps? [Of course!]

¹⁹All this time you have been thinking that we are [merely] defending ourselves to you. It is in the sight of God that we have been speaking [as one] in Christ; and everything, dearly beloved, is to strengthen you [spiritually].

²⁰For I am afraid that perhaps when I come I may find you not to be as I wish, and that you may find me not as you wish—that perhaps *there may be* strife, jealousy, angry tempers, disputes, slander, gossip, arrogance and disorder;

²¹I am afraid that when I come again my God may humiliate me before you, and I may mourn over many of those who have sinned in the past and not repented of the impurity, sexual immorality and decadence which they formerly practiced.

13 THIS IS the third time that I am visiting you. EVERY FACT SHALL BE SUSTAINED *and* CONFIRMED BY THE TESTIMONY OF TWO OR THREE WITNESSES. [Deut 19:15]

²I have already warned those who have sinned in the past and all the rest *as well,* and I warn them now even though I am absent [from you] as I did when I was with you the second time, that if I come back I will not spare *anyone,*

³since you seek [forensic] proof that Christ is speaking in *and* through me. He is not weak *or* ineffective in dealing with you, but powerful within you.

⁴For even though He was crucified in weakness [yielding Himself], yet He lives [resurrected] by the power of God [His Father]. For we too are weak

life point

Second Corinthians 13:5 tells us to "test and evaluate" ourselves, and I wholeheartedly agree that we need to do so. We should examine ourselves to see if we have sin in our lives or in our hearts, and if we do, we should sincerely repent, then move on to live without that sin in our lives.

There is a great difference between examination and condemnation. Examination shows us what is wrong in our behavior so we can admit it, ask for forgiveness, and go in a new direction. Allowing the Holy Spirit to guide us in proper self-examination will deliver us and set us free. Condemnation keeps us mired in the very sin for which we feel condemned. Condemnation does not deliver us; it traps us! It weakens us and saps all our spiritual strength. We give our energy toward feeling condemned rather than living righteously.

in Him [as He was humanly weak], yet we are alive *and* well [in fellowship] with Him because of the power of God *directed* toward you.

⁵Test *and* evaluate yourselves *to see* whether you are in the faith *and* living your lives as [committed] believers. Examine yourselves [not me]! Or do you not recognize this about yourselves [by an ongoing experience] that Jesus Christ is in you—unless indeed you fail the test *and* are rejected as counterfeit?

13:13 Lit *the saints*.

⁶But I hope you will acknowledge that we do not fail the test *nor* are we to be rejected.

⁷But I pray to God that you may do nothing wrong. Not so that we [and our teaching] may appear to be approved, but that you may continue doing what is right, even though we [by comparison] may seem to have failed.

⁸For we can do nothing against the truth, but only for the truth [and the gospel—the good news of salvation].

⁹We are glad when we are weak [since God's power comes freely through us], but you [by comparison] are strong. We also pray for this, that you be made complete [fully restored, growing and maturing in godly character and spirit—pleasing your heavenly Father by the life you live].

¹⁰For this reason I am writing these things while absent from you, so that when I come, I will not need to deal severely [with you], in my use of the authority which the Lord has given me [to be used] for building you up and not for tearing you down.

¹¹Finally, believers, rejoice! Be made complete [be what you should be], be comforted, be like-minded, live in peace [enjoy the spiritual well-being experienced by believers who walk closely with God]; and the God of love and peace [the source of lovingkindness] will be with you.

¹²Greet one another with a holy kiss.

¹³All *God's people greet you.

¹⁴The grace of the Lord Jesus Christ and the love of God, and the fellowship of the Holy Spirit be with you all.

Galatians

Author:
Paul

Date:
Approximately AD 53–57

Everyday Life Principles:
We approach God through grace, not through the Law.

Believers are to reject legalism and embrace God's grace in every area of life.

Walk in the Spirit, not in the flesh.

In Galatians, Paul emphasizes a subject that is very important to me and should be to all believers: the grace of God. Many people tend to approach God through the Law, which simply means doing what is right and obeying the "rules" of Christianity. This is called legalism. Galatians teaches us that we approach God through grace—which is simply God's power at work in us, causing us to want to obey Him and enabling us to do so. Legalism teaches that we obey God out of obligation; grace teaches that we obey out of love. Legalism urges us to "act right" through works of the flesh, while grace enables us to "be right" by the power of the Holy Spirit.

Throughout the short but life-changing letter of Galatians, you will find encouragement to live and walk "in the Spirit." Only as you invite the Holy Spirit into your life and ask Him to help you in every situation will you truly be able to live in a way that pleases God. Without the Holy Spirit's help and enablement, all of us are left to live as best we can in our own strength. With His help, we can relax, stop striving, and enjoy life.

As you read Galatians, I pray that God's awesome grace becomes more and more real to you and that you will be able to live in His grace and walk in the power of the Holy Spirit for the rest of your life.

1 PAUL, AN apostle (not commissioned *and* sent from men nor through the agency of man, but through Jesus Christ—the Messiah—and God the Father, who raised Him from the dead),

²and all the brothers who are with me,

To the churches of Galatia:

³Grace to you and peace [inner calm and spiritual well-being] from God our Father and the Lord Jesus Christ,

⁴who gave Himself [as a sacrifice to atone] for our sins [to save and sanctify us] so that He might rescue us from this present evil age, in accordance with the will *and* purpose *and* plan of our God and Father—

⁵to Him be [ascribed all] the glory through the ages of the ages. Amen.

⁶I am astonished *and* extremely irritated that you are so quickly shifting your allegiance *and* deserting Him who called you by the grace of Christ, for a different [even contrary] gospel;

⁷which is really not another [gospel]; but there are [obviously] some [people masquerading as teachers] who are disturbing *and* confusing you [with a misleading, counterfeit teaching] and want to distort the gospel of Christ [twisting it into something which it absolutely is not].

⁸But even if we, or an angel from heaven, should preach to you a gospel contrary to that which we [originally] preached to you, let him be condemned to destruction!

⁹As we have said before, so I now say again, if anyone is preaching to you a gospel different from that which you received [from us], let him be condemned to destruction!

¹⁰Am I now trying to win the favor *and* approval of men, or of God? Or am I seeking to please someone? If I were still trying to be popular with men, I would not be a bond-servant of Christ.

¹¹For I want you to know, believers,

putting the Word to work

Have you ever thought God could not or would not use you because of your past? No one was more likely to feel that way than the Apostle Paul, who tried to destroy the early church. However, Paul received God's forgiveness and recognized that it was God who gave him his ministry and his authority (see Galatians 1:1). No matter what your past may be, God wants to use you too.

that the gospel which was preached by me is not man's gospel [it is not a human invention, patterned after any human concept].

¹²For indeed I did not receive it from man, nor was I taught it, but *I received it* through a [direct] revelation of Jesus Christ.

¹³You have heard of my career *and* former manner of life in Judaism, how I used to hunt down *and* persecute the church of God extensively and [with fanatical zeal] tried [my best] to destroy it.

¹⁴And [you have heard how] I surpassed many of my contemporaries among my countrymen in [my advanced study of the laws of] Judaism, as I was extremely loyal to the traditions of my ancestors.

¹⁵But when God, who had chosen me *and* set me apart before I was born,

life point

The Apostle Paul said in Galatians 1:10 that if he wanted to be popular with people, he would not be a servant of Jesus Christ. Basically, Paul is saying that an excessive need for people's approval can steal our destiny. We cannot always be God-pleasers and people-pleasers at the same time.

and called me through His grace, was pleased [Is 49:1; Jer 1:5]

[16]to reveal His Son in me so that I might preach Him among the Gentiles [as the good news—the way of salvation], I did not immediately consult with anyone [for guidance regarding God's call and His revelation to me].

[17]Nor did I [even] go up to Jerusalem to those who were apostles before me; but I went to Arabia *and* stayed awhile, and afterward returned once more to Damascus.

[18]Then three years later I did go up to Jerusalem to get acquainted with Cephas (Peter), and I stayed with him fifteen days.

[19]But I did not see any other apostle except James, the [half] brother of the Lord.

[20](Now in what I am writing to you, I assure you as if I were standing before God that I am not lying.)

[21]Then I went into the regions of Syria and Cilicia.

[22]And I was still unknown by sight to the churches which were in Christ in Judea (Jerusalem and the surrounding region);

[23]they only kept hearing, "He who used to persecute us is now preaching the [good news of the] faith which he once was trying to destroy."

[24]And they were glorifying God [as the Author and Source of what had taken place and all that had been accomplished] in me.

2 THEN AFTER a period of fourteen years I again went up to Jerusalem, [this time] with Barnabas, taking Titus along also.

[2]I went up [to Jerusalem] because of a [divine] revelation, and I put before them the gospel which I preach among the Gentiles. But *I did so* in private before those of reputation, for fear that I might be running or had run [the course of my ministry] in vain.

[3]But [all went well, for] not even Titus, who was with me, was compelled [as some had anticipated] to be circumcised, despite the fact that he was a Greek.

[4]My concern was because of the false brothers [those people masquerading as Christians] who had been secretly smuggled in [to the community of believers]. They had slipped in to spy on the freedom which we have in Christ Jesus, in order to bring us back into bondage [under the Law of Moses].

[5]But we did not yield to them even for a moment, so that the truth of the gospel would continue to remain with you [in its purity].

[6]But from those who were of high

life point

Paul says in Galatians 1:15, 16 that when God called him to preach the gospel to the Gentiles, he did not discuss the matter with anyone else.

Many times when we receive a message from God, we confer too much with flesh and blood. We look for someone to assure us that we are doing the right thing. What we need to do is believe John 14:17, which tells us that we have the Holy Spirit, the Spirit of Truth, within us. But since we have invited the Spirit of Truth to guide us, should we always shun advice from others? No, the writer of Proverbs says, "In the abundance of [wise and godly] counselors there is victory" (Proverbs 11:14). Like many areas of life, knowing who to talk to and when—and who not to talk to—is an area in which we need balance. We can and should be open to receive advice from those who are wiser and more experienced than we are in certain matters, but we should not depend so much on what people say that we fail to listen to God Himself.

how to handle God's call

Paul said he kept the news of his calling to himself; he did not check it out with "the big guys" who were supposed to hear from God (see Galatians 1:15–19). He knew what God did in his life on the road to Damascus and how it changed him forever (see Acts 9:3–9). He knew that the Son of God was unveiled and disclosed on the inside of him, and that he could never go back to the life he once lived. And he knew that for the rest of his life he would preach the gospel and remain faithful to what he heard Jesus say to him.

But Paul also had the wisdom to know that people would find his calling unbelievable. So he waited on God. He did not go running around checking with the other apostles, saying, "Hey guys, I saw a light on the road and fell down, and this happened and that happened. What do you all think?" Instead, he went to Arabia, and then came back to Damascus. Three years after that, he traveled to Jerusalem to become acquainted with Peter, but did not see any of the other apostles except James.

Paul kept God's Word in his heart and let it grow and manifest on its own. Then he started doing what he was called to do. Soon others recognized that the calling on his life must have been from God. What was the result? Galatians 1:24 tells us that the people glorified God as the "Author and Source" of what had taken place in Paul.

Has God called you to serve Him? As you stay in His Word and wait on Him, you will see growth in your life and receptivity to your message.

reputation (whatever they were—in terms of individual importance—makes no difference to me; God shows no partiality—He is not impressed with the positions that people hold nor does He recognize distinctions such as fame or power)—well, those who were of reputation contributed nothing to me [that is, they had nothing to add to my gospel message nor did they impose any new requirements on me]. [Deut 10:17]

⁷But on the contrary, they saw that I had been entrusted with the gospel to the uncircumcised (Gentiles), just as Peter *had been* [entrusted to proclaim the gospel] to the circumcised (Jews);

⁸(for He who worked effectively for Peter *and* empowered him in his ministry to the Jews also worked effectively for me *and* empowered me in my ministry to the Gentiles).

⁹And recognizing the grace [that God had] bestowed on me, James and Cephas (Peter) and John, who were reputed to be pillars [of the Jerusalem church], gave to me and Barnabas the right hand of fellowship, so that we could go to the Gentiles [with their blessing] and they to the circumcised (Jews).

¹⁰*They asked* only [one thing], that we remember the poor, the very thing I was also eager to do.

¹¹Now when Cephas (Peter) came to Antioch, I opposed him face to face [about his conduct there], because he stood condemned [by his own actions].

¹²Before certain men came from James, he used to eat [his meals] with the Gentiles; but when the men [from Jerusalem] arrived, he *began* to withdraw and separate himself [from the Gentile believers], because he was afraid of those from the circumcision.

¹³The rest of the Jews joined him in this hypocrisy [ignoring their knowledge that Jewish and Gentile Christians

were united, under the new covenant, into one faith], with the result that even Barnabas was carried away by their hypocrisy.

¹⁴But when I saw that they were not being straightforward about the truth of the gospel, I told Cephas (Peter) in front of everyone, "If you, being a Jew, live [as you have been living] like a Gentile and not like a Jew, how is it that you are [now virtually] forcing the Gentiles to live like Jews [if they want to eat with you]?"

¹⁵[I went on to say] "We are Jews by birth and not sinners from among the Gentiles;

¹⁶yet we know that a man is not justified [and placed in right standing with God] by works of the Law, but [only] through faith in [God's beloved Son,] Christ Jesus. And even we [as Jews] have believed in Christ Jesus, so that we may be justified by faith in Christ and not by works of the Law. By observing the Law no one will ever be justified [declared free of the guilt of sin and its penalty]. [Ps 143:2]

¹⁷"But if, while we seek to be justified in Christ [by faith], we ourselves are found to be sinners, does that make Christ an advocate *or* promoter of our sin? Certainly not!

¹⁸"For if I [or anyone else should] rebuild [through word or by practice] what I once tore down [the belief that observing the Law is essential for salvation], I prove myself to be a transgressor.

¹⁹"For through the Law I died to the Law *and* its demands on me [because salvation is provided through the death and resurrection of Christ], so that I might [from now on] live to God.

²⁰"I have been crucified with Christ [that is, in Him I have shared His crucifixion]; it is no longer I who live, but Christ lives in me. The *life* I now live in the body I live by faith [by adhering to, relying on, and completely trusting] in the Son of God, who loved me and gave Himself up for me.

life point

In Galatians 3:2–4, Paul asked the Galatians why they were trying to reach perfection by depending upon the flesh. He urged them to remember that their entire new spiritual life was given birth because of faith and leaning on the Holy Spirit. Therefore, he asked, why did they need to try to reach spiritual maturity through the works of their flesh?

He concluded by telling them that if they did not stop this type of legalistic behavior, everything they had suffered would be in vain and accomplish no purpose.

I don't know about you, but I have come too far and gone through too much to mess it all up now. I want to know the right way to approach God, and as far as I can see in His Word, that is through faith in what Jesus has done, not through faith in what I can do.

We cannot live as victorious Christians without knowing these truths. We cannot succeed without stepping out in *faith*, not *works*. If we believe our acceptance is based on our doing, we will always feel rejected when we fail to do the right thing. But if we see that our acceptance is based on what God has done, we will be truly free.

speak the Word

Thank You, God, that I am not justified or placed in right standing with You by works of the Law, but only through faith in Your beloved Son, Christ Jesus.
—ADAPTED FROM GALATIANS 2:16

²¹"I do not ignore *or* nullify the [gracious gift of the] grace of God [His amazing, unmerited favor], for if righteousness *comes* through [observing] the Law, then Christ died needlessly. [His suffering and death would have had no purpose whatsoever.]"

3 O YOU foolish *and* thoughtless *and* superficial Galatians, who has bewitched you [that you would act like this], to whom—right before your very eyes—Jesus Christ was publicly portrayed as crucified [in the gospel message]?

²This is all I want to ask of you: did you receive the [Holy] Spirit as the result of obeying [the requirements of] the Law, or was it the result of hearing [the message of salvation and] with faith [believing it]?

³Are you so foolish *and* senseless? Having begun [your new life by faith] with the Spirit, are you now being perfected *and* reaching spiritual maturity by the flesh [that is, by your own works and efforts to keep the Law]?

⁴Have you suffered so many things *and* experienced so much all for nothing—if indeed it was all for nothing?

⁵So then, does He who supplies you with His [marvelous Holy] Spirit and

do your part

Before we can enjoy any real victory over sin and experience change in our behavior we must learn that only God can change us (see Galatians 3:2–5). We cannot perfect ourselves and when we try to do so, we only become frustrated. God has called us to perfection and has given us a perfect heart (see Matthew 5:48), but the working out of it is a process that takes faith, patience, and time. As we face truth, admit our faults, and place our faith in God to change us we will see results, but we must trust His timing. Things do not always happen when we think they should.

We are partners with God and we do have a part to play. Our part is to believe and obey any specific instruction God might give us; His part is to work the good thing He has placed inside of us to bring it to the outside of us where it can be seen and enjoyed by others and ourselves. When we get into "works of the flesh" (using our energy to try to do God's job) we get frustrated. God Himself opposes us until we humble ourselves and lean entirely on Him (see 1 Peter 5:5). It took a long time, but I finally learned that every time I felt frustrated I had stopped trusting God and started trusting myself to accomplish what needed to be done at the time.

We received Christ totally by faith, so we need to live our lives totally by faith. We realize that we need to change and frequently become very disappointed with ourselves—even condemned—when we do not. We are much better off to put all the energy we use trying to change ourselves into prayer and to trust God to do what He needs to do.

By faith God is working in you and you will see wonderful changes, but you must turn the project of your perfection over to Him entirely. Let God be God in your life! Instead of saying, "I'll never change," say, "God is working in me as I trust Him and I believe I am getting better and better every day. God is strengthening me in my weaknesses and helping me overcome bad habits."

works miracles among you, do it as a result of the works of the Law [which you perform], or because you [believe confidently in the message which you] heard with faith?

⁶Just as Abraham BELIEVED GOD, AND IT WAS CREDITED TO HIM AS RIGHTEOUS-NESS, [as conformity to God's will and purpose—so it is with you also]. [Gen 15:6]

⁷So understand that it is the people who live by faith [with confidence in the power and goodness of God] who are [the true] sons of Abraham.

⁸The Scripture, foreseeing that God would justify the Gentiles by faith, proclaimed the good news [of the Savior] to Abraham in advance [with this promise], *saying,* "IN YOU SHALL ALL THE NATIONS BE BLESSED." [Gen 12:3]

⁹So then those who are people of faith [whether Jew or Gentile] are blessed *and* favored by God [and declared free of the guilt of sin and its penalty, and placed in right standing with Him] along with Abraham, the believer.

¹⁰For all who depend on the Law [seeking justification and salvation by obedience to the Law and the observance of rituals] are under a curse; for it is written, "CURSED (condemned to destruction) IS EVERYONE WHO DOES NOT ABIDE BY ALL THINGS WRITTEN IN THE BOOK OF THE LAW, SO AS TO PRACTICE THEM." [Deut 27:26]

¹¹Now it is clear that no one is justified [that is, declared free of the guilt of sin and its penalty, and placed in right standing] before God by the Law, for "THE RIGHTEOUS (the just, the upright) SHALL LIVE BY FAITH." [Hab 2:4]

¹²But the Law does not rest on *or* require faith [it has nothing to do with faith], but [instead, the Law] *says,*

"HE WHO PRACTICES THEM [the things prescribed by the Law] SHALL LIVE BY THEM [instead of faith]." [Lev 18:5]

¹³Christ purchased our freedom *and* redeemed us from the curse of the Law *and* its condemnation by becoming a curse for us—for it is written, "CURSED IS EVERYONE WHO HANGS [crucified] ON A TREE (cross)"— [Deut 21:23]

¹⁴in order that in Christ Jesus the blessing of Abraham might also come to the Gentiles, so that we would all receive [the realization of] the promise of the [Holy] Spirit through faith.

¹⁵Brothers and sisters, I speak in terms of human relations: even though a last will and testament is just a human covenant, yet when it has been signed *and* made legally binding, no one sets it aside or adds to it [modifying it in some way].

¹⁶Now the promises [in the covenants] were decreed to Abraham and to his seed. God does not say, "And to seeds (descendants, heirs)," as if [referring] to many [persons], but as to one, "And to your Seed," who is [none other than] Christ. [Gen 13:15; 17:8]

¹⁷This is what I mean: the Law, which came into existence four hundred and thirty years later [after the covenant concerning the coming Messiah], does not *and* cannot invalidate the covenant previously established by God, so as to abolish the promise. [Ex 12:40]

¹⁸For if the inheritance [of what was promised] is based on [observing] the Law [as these false teachers claim], it is no longer based on a promise; however, God granted it to Abraham [as a gift] by virtue of His promise.

¹⁹Why, then, the Law [what was its purpose]? It was added [after the promise to Abraham, to reveal to

speak the Word

Thank You, Jesus, for purchasing my freedom and redeeming me from the curse of the Law and its condemnation by becoming a curse for me.
—ADAPTED FROM GALATIANS 3:13

life point

Galatians 3:16 refers to Jesus Christ as the "Seed." I like that, because if I have a seed, I can have a harvest.

Jesus is the Seed of everything good that God desires us to have. God plants the seed, but it must be cultivated, nurtured, watered, and cared for. The ground in which it is planted must be kept plowed and weed-free.

Our hearts and lives are the ground. Everything that needs to be changed or removed in us is not taken care of all at once. There is a great work to be done, and only the Holy Spirit knows the proper "when and how." As He deals with us about certain issues, we are to submit to Him our wills, which means submitting the flesh to the leadership of the Spirit. It is not easy, but it is definitely worth it. Going through change is hard, but staying in bondage is even more difficult.

people their guilt] because of transgressions [that is, to make people conscious of the sinfulness of sin], and [the Law] was ordained through angels *and* delivered to Israel by the hand of a mediator [Moses, the mediator between God and Israel, to be in effect] until the Seed would come to whom the promise had been made. [20]Now the mediator *or* go-between [in a transaction] is not [needed] for just one *party;* whereas God is *only* one [and was the only One giving the promise to Abraham, but the Law was a contract between two, God and Israel; its validity depended on both]. [21]Is the Law then contrary to the promises of God? Certainly not! For if a *system of* law had been given which could impart life, then righteousness (right standing with God) would actually have been based on law.

[22]But the Scripture has imprisoned everyone [everything—the entire world] under sin, so that [the inheritance, the blessing of salvation] which was promised through faith in Jesus Christ might be given to those who believe [in Him and acknowledge Him as God's precious Son].
[23]Now before faith came, we were kept in custody under the Law, [perpetually] imprisoned [in preparation] for the faith that was destined to be revealed,
[24]with the result that the Law has become our tutor *and* our disciplinarian *to guide us* to Christ, so that we may be justified [that is, declared free of the guilt of sin and its penalty, and placed in right standing with God] by faith.
[25]But now that faith has come, we are no longer under [the control and authority of] a tutor *and* disciplinarian.
[26]For you [who are born-again have been reborn from above—spiritually transformed, renewed, sanctified and] are all children of God [set apart for His purpose with full rights and privileges] through faith in Christ Jesus.
[27]For all of you who were baptized into Christ [into a spiritual union with the Christ, the Anointed] have clothed yourselves with Christ [that is, you have taken on His characteristics and values].
[28]There is [now no distinction in

putting the Word to work

Have you ever been discriminated against? It is a painful experience. There is no room for discrimination in the body of Christ; rather, we are called to unity in Christ Jesus (see Galatians 3:28). Ask God to reveal to you any prejudice that may linger in your heart or mind. Repent of it, and ask God to help you bring unity where there is division around you.

life point

Galatians 3:28 teaches that we "are all one in Christ Jesus." But, as long as time has existed, Satan has breathed life into the poisonous practice of one race or group of people being prejudiced against another. Most wars are birthed out of prejudice and hatred. The Holocaust came from that same poison, as did slavery.

Hatred has existed since the beginning of humanity. Adam's son, Cain, hated his brother Abel so much that he killed him (see Genesis 4:2–8), and it seems hatred has never stopped since then. Hating people is hard work, and it kills everything good in life. Even various religious sects have hated one another and allowed the spirit of pride to fill their hearts.

You and I may not agree with everything another person believes or does, but we have no right to hate him or her because of it, and we certainly should not mistreat that person.

God hates sin, but He loves every sinner. He hates stubbornness and rebellion, but still loves the person who is stubborn and rebellious. He has not told us we have to approve of everyone's beliefs, choices, and actions, but He has told us to love everyone (see John 13:34).

regard to salvation] neither Jew nor Greek, there is neither slave nor free, there is neither male nor female; for you [who believe] are all one in Christ Jesus [no one can claim a spiritual superiority]. [Rom 3:22; 1 Cor 12:13]

speak the Word

²⁹And if you belong to Christ [if you are in Him], then you are Abraham's descendants, and [spiritual] heirs according to [God's] promise.

4 NOW WHAT I mean [when I talk about children and their guardians] is this: as long as the heir is a child, he does not differ at all from a slave even though he is the [future owner and] master of all [the estate];
²but he is under [the authority of] guardians and household administrators *or* managers until the date set by his father [when he is of legal age].
³So also we [whether Jews or Gentiles], when we were children (spiritually immature), were kept like slaves under the elementary [man-made religious or philosophical] teachings of the world.
⁴But when [in God's plan] the proper time had fully come, God sent His Son, born of a woman, born under the [regulations of the] Law,
⁵so that He might redeem *and* liberate those who were under the Law, that we [who believe] might be adopted as sons [as God's children with all rights as fully grown members of a family]. [Rom 11:17–24]
⁶And because you [really] are [His] sons, God has sent the Spirit of His Son into our hearts, crying out, "Abba! Father!"
⁷Therefore you are no longer a slave (bond-servant), but a son; and if a son, then also an heir through [the gracious act of] God [through Christ].
⁸But at that time, when you did not know [the true] God *and* were unacquainted with Him, you [Gentiles] were slaves to those [pagan] things

Thank You, God, for making me Your child
and sending the Holy Spirit into my heart to cry out, "Father"
and to help me understand what it means to belong to You.
—ADAPTED FROM GALATIANS 4:5–7

which by [their very] nature were not *and* could not be gods *at all*.

⁹Now, however, since you have come to know [the true] God [through personal experience], or rather to be known by God, how is it that you are turning back again to the weak and worthless elemental principles [of religions and philosophies], to which you want to be enslaved all over again?

¹⁰[For example,] you observe [particular] days and months and seasons and years.

¹¹I fear for you, that perhaps I have labored [to the point of exhaustion] over you in vain.

¹²Believers, I beg of you, become as I am [free from the bondage of Jewish ritualism and ordinances], for I *have become* as you are [a Gentile]. You did me no wrong [when I first came to you; do not do it now].

¹³On the contrary, you know that it was because of a physical illness that I [remained and] preached the gospel to you the first time;

¹⁴and even though my physical condition was a trial to you, you did not regard it with contempt, or scorn *and* reject me; but you received me as an angel of God, even as Christ Jesus *Himself*.

¹⁵What then has become of that sense of blessing *and* the joy that you once had [from your salvation and your relationship with Christ]? For I testify of you that, if possible, you would have torn out your own eyes and given them to me [to replace mine].

¹⁶So have I become your enemy by telling you the truth?

¹⁷These men [the Judaizers] eagerly seek you [to entrap you with honeyed words and attention, to win you over to their philosophy], not honorably [for their purpose is not honorable or worthy of consideration]. They want to isolate you [from us who oppose them] so that you will seek them.

¹⁸Now it is always pleasant to be eagerly sought after [provided that it is] for a good purpose, and not just when I am with you [seeking you myself—but beware of the others doing it].

¹⁹My little children, for whom I am again in [the pains of] labor until Christ is [completely and permanently] formed within you—

²⁰how I wish that I were with you now and could change my tone, because I am perplexed in regard to you.

²¹Tell me, you who are bent on being under the Law, do you not listen to [what] the Law [really says]?

²²For it is written that Abraham had two sons, one by the slave woman [Hagar] and one by the free woman [Sarah]. [Gen 16:15; 21:2, 9]

²³But the child of the slave woman was born according to the flesh *and* had an ordinary birth, while the son of the free woman was born in fulfillment of the promise.

²⁴Now these facts are about to be used [by me] as an allegory [that is, I will illustrate by using them]: for these *women* can represent two covenants: one [covenant originated] from Mount Sinai [where the Law was given] that bears children [destined] for slavery; she is Hagar.

²⁵Now Hagar is (represents) Mount Sinai in Arabia and she corresponds to the present Jerusalem, for she is in slavery with her children.

²⁶But the Jerusalem above [that is, the way of faith, represented by Sarah] is free; she is our mother.

²⁷For it is written [in the Scriptures],

"REJOICE, O BARREN WOMAN WHO
    HAS NOT GIVEN BIRTH;
BREAK FORTH INTO A [joyful]
    SHOUT, YOU WHO ARE NOT IN
    LABOR;
FOR THE DESOLATE WOMAN HAS
    MANY MORE CHILDREN
THAN SHE WHO HAS A HUSBAND."
    [Is 54:1]

²⁸And we, [believing] brothers and sisters, like Isaac, are children [not merely of physical descent, like Ishmael, but are children born] of promise [born miraculously].

²⁹But as at that time the child [of ordinary birth] born according to the flesh persecuted the son *who was born* according to [the promise and working of] the Spirit, so it is now also. [Gen 21:9]

³⁰But what does the Scripture say?

"CAST OUT THE BONDWOMAN [Hagar] AND HER SON [Ishmael], FOR NEVER SHALL THE SON OF THE BONDWOMAN BE HEIR *and* SHARE THE INHERITANCE WITH THE SON OF THE FREE WOMAN." [Gen 21:10]

³¹So then, believers, we [who are born again—reborn from above—spiritually transformed, renewed, and set apart

life point

In Galatians 4:24–31, the Bible speaks about two covenants, describing two ways in which we can live.

The first way we choose to live is by works of our own flesh. We take care of ourselves; make our own plans and struggle to make things happen our way, in our timing. This describes the natural way, the "normal" way most people live. It is a way that produces every kind of misery. We struggle, become frustrated, fail, and end up weary and worn-out most of the time. We are confused and defeated, and have no peace or joy.

The second way we can live is supernaturally, by the power of God. We live by faith, trusting God to do what needs to be done in our lives. This way is described in the Bible as a "new and living way" (Hebrews 10:20). This new way produces peace, joy, ease, and success.

for His purpose] are not children of a slave woman [the natural], but of the free woman [the supernatural].

5 IT WAS for this freedom that Christ set us free [completely liberating us]; therefore keep standing firm and do not be subject again to a yoke of slavery [which you once removed].

²Notice, it is I, Paul, who tells you that if you receive circumcision [as a supposed requirement of salvation], Christ will be of no benefit to you [for you will lack the faith in Christ that is necessary for salvation].

³Once more I solemnly affirm to every man who receives circumcision [as a supposed requirement of salvation], that he is under obligation *and* required to keep the whole Law.

⁴You have been severed from Christ, if you seek to be justified [that is, declared free of the guilt of sin and its penalty, and placed in right standing with God] through the Law; you have fallen from grace [for you have lost your grasp on God's unmerited favor and blessing].

⁵For we [not relying on the Law but] through the [strength and power of the Holy] Spirit, by faith, are waiting [confidently] for the hope of righteousness [the completion of our salvation].

⁶For [if we are] in Christ Jesus neither circumcision nor uncircumcision means anything, but only faith activated *and* expressed *and* working through love.

⁷You were running [the race] well; who has interfered *and* prevented you from obeying the truth?

⁸This [deceptive] persuasion is not from Him who called you [to freedom in Christ].

⁹A little leaven [a slight inclination to error, or a few false teachers] leavens the whole batch [it perverts

the concept of faith and misleads the church].

¹⁰I have confidence in you in the Lord that you will adopt no other view [contrary to mine on the matter]; but the one who is disturbing you, whoever he is, will have to bear the penalty.

¹¹But as for me, brothers, if I am still preaching circumcision [as I had done before I met Christ; and as some accuse me of doing now, as necessary for salvation], why am I still being persecuted [by Jews]? In that case the stumbling block of the cross [to unbelieving Jews] has been abolished.

¹²I wish that those who are troubling you [by teaching that circumcision is

putting the Word to work

There is great freedom in belonging to God. What does this freedom mean to you? God's Word teaches us that this freedom is not the absence of morality, but a freedom to serve others in love (see Galatians 5:13, 14). Thank God for setting you free from the bondage of sin, and ask Him to help you experience even more deeply the joy of serving others and seeking the best for them.

necessary for salvation] would even [go all the way and] castrate themselves!

choose life in the Spirit

Paul said we should choose to walk habitually in the Spirit, and by making that choice, we will not fulfill the lusts of the flesh that continually tempt us (see Galatians 5:16).

There are many things available to lead us—people, the devil and his demons, the flesh (our own body, mind, will, emotions), and the Holy Spirit. There are many voices in the world that speak to us, often several at the same time. It is imperative that we learn to be led by the Holy Spirit, to "seek Him and be responsive to His guidance," as Galatians 5:16 says. Remember: The Holy Spirit is the One Who knows the will of God and Who is sent to dwell in each of us to aid us in being all God has designed us to be and to give us all God wants us to have.

It is important for us to see that the Holy Spirit lives in each of us to help us. When we allow the Holy Spirit to lead us, He becomes involved in every decision we make—major and minor. He leads us by peace and by wisdom, as well as by the Word of God. He speaks in a still, small voice in our hearts, or what we often call "the inward witness." Those of us who want to be led by the Holy Spirit must learn to follow the inward witness and to respond quickly.

For example, if we are engaged in a conversation, and we begin feeling uncomfortable inside, that inner discomfort may be the Holy Spirit signaling that we need to turn the conversation in another direction or be quiet. If we are about to purchase something, and we feel uncomfortable inside, we should wait and discern why we are uncomfortable. Perhaps we do not need the item, or we may find it on sale somewhere else, or we may be trying to purchase it at the wrong time. Remember, we do not always have to know why; we just need to obey the Spirit's leading to find peace and contentment in our daily living.

¹³For you, my brothers, were called to freedom; only do not let your freedom *become* an opportunity for the sinful nature (worldliness, selfishness), but through love serve *and* seek the best for one another.

¹⁴For the whole Law [concerning human relationships] is fulfilled in one precept, "YOU SHALL LOVE YOUR NEIGHBOR AS YOURSELF [that is, you shall have an unselfish concern for others and do things for their benefit]." [Lev 19:18]

¹⁵But if you bite and devour one another [in bickering and strife], watch out that you [along with your entire fellowship] are not consumed by one another.

¹⁶But I say, walk *habitually* in the [Holy] Spirit [seek Him and be responsive to His guidance], and then you will certainly not carry out the desire of the sinful nature [which responds impulsively without regard for God and His precepts].

¹⁷For the sinful nature has its desire which is opposed to the Spirit, and the [desire of the] Spirit opposes the sinful nature; for these [two, the sinful nature and the Spirit] are in direct opposition to each other [continually in conflict], so that you [as believers] do not [always] do whatever [good things] you want to do.

¹⁸But if you are guided *and* led by the Spirit, you are not subject to the Law.

¹⁹Now the practices of the sinful nature are *clearly* evident: they are sexual immorality, impurity, sensuality (total irresponsibility, lack of self-control),

²⁰idolatry, sorcery, hostility, strife, jealousy, fits of anger, disputes, dissensions, factions [that promote heresies],

life point

Galatians 5:19–23 gives us a list of sins of the flesh and a list of the fruit of the Spirit, or as verse 22 says, "the result of His presence within us." I really like that way of saying it. The fruit of the Holy Spirit are qualities we see in Jesus Himself: love, joy, peace, patience, kindness, goodness, faithfulness, gentleness, and self-control. This is the goal of the Holy One living within us, to produce or accomplish this fruit in our lives—big, luscious fruit for everyone to see and admire.

Love is the everlasting fruit that will not fade away. To bear fruit we must abide in God's love, meaning to stay alert to His love for us, dwell in His love by loving others, and endure testing by responding to trials with love.

²¹envy, drunkenness, riotous behavior, and *other* things like these. I warn you beforehand, just as I did previously, that those who practice such things will not inherit the kingdom of God.

²²But the fruit of the Spirit [the result of His presence within us] is love [unselfish concern for others], joy, [inner] peace, patience [not the ability to wait, but how we act while waiting], kindness, goodness, faithfulness,

²³gentleness, self-control. Against such things there is no law.

²⁴And those who belong to Christ Jesus have crucified the sinful nature together with its passions and appetites.

²⁵If we [claim to] live by the [Holy] Spirit, we must also walk by the Spirit

speak the Word

Help me, Lord, to walk habitually in the Holy Spirit,
being responsive to and led by the Spirit in every situation
so I will not carry out the desire of the sinful nature.
–ADAPTED FROM GALATIANS 5:16

[with personal integrity, godly character, and moral courage—our conduct
empowered by the Holy Spirit].
²⁶We must not become conceited,
challenging *or* provoking one another,
envying one another.

6 BROTHERS, IF anyone is caught
in any sin, you who are spiritual
[that is, you who are responsive

life point

Galatians 6:1–3 quickly reveals how
we should respond to the weaknesses
we observe in others. It sets forth the
mental attitude we are to maintain within
ourselves. We are to have a "holy fear"
of pride and be very careful of judging
others or of being critical of them.

true love

We can move into the blessed, exceptional type of life we truly desire through developing the character qualities of the fruit of the Spirit listed in Galatians 5:22, 23.
When we as Christians know what God has available for us and are open to receiving from Him, His Spirit gives us the power we need to develop the fruit and live the
type of life God wants for us.

God gives us various gifts to use, but He gives us the fruit of the Spirit to develop.
When the Holy Spirit lives inside us, we have everything He has. His fruit is in us.
The seed is planted. In order to use the gifts in the most powerful way God desires,
we need to allow the seed of the fruit to grow up and mature in us by cultivating it.
The gifts of the Spirit must be accompanied by the fruit of the Spirit to get the best
results.

We can cultivate all the fruit by focusing on love, the first in the list of the nine fruit,
and self-control, the last in the list. Love and self-control are like bookends that hold
the others in place. All of the fruit issue from love and actually are a form of love,
but they are kept in place by self-control.

If you concentrate on developing the fruit of love as you walk through your day you
will not become impatient with people. You will not be anything but kind. You will
be good to people, supportive and faithful instead of being haughty or trying to
appear better than others.

If you are not motivated by love, you will find that operating in the fruit is very difficult. But even when you are motivated to express God's love as a lifestyle, there will
be times (*many* times when you first begin developing the fruit) when you will not
feel like being patient, joyful, peaceful, or even kind! Those are the times you need
self-control so you can continue to respond with the fruit of the Spirit even though
you do not feel like it.

If you need to develop this fruit of self-control, begin by simply making little choices
throughout the day to respond with the fruit to situations you encounter. Remember, love, self-control, and all the other fruit of the Spirit grow when you allow the
Holy Spirit's presence within you to accomplish His work.

to the guidance of the Spirit] are to restore such a person in a spirit of gentleness [not with a sense of superiority or self-righteousness], keeping a watchful eye on yourself, so that you are not tempted as well.

2Carry one another's burdens and in this way you will fulfill the requirements of the law of Christ [that is, the law of Christian love]. [John 13:34]

3For if anyone thinks he is something [special] when [in fact] he is nothing [special except in his own eyes], he deceives himself.

life point

Galatians 6:2 indicates that we should learn to get along with each other. When we deal with others, we will have to learn to put up with some things we do not like. Not everybody is going to think and speak and act the way we want them to. But forgiving them is part of what we are called to do as members of the body of Christ. Not everyone is going to be or do what we want, but we can forgive them and love them.

patience, not pride

I have personally read and meditated on Galatians 6:1–3 hundreds of times. My natural temperament avoids humility, so I need all the scriptural help I can get. I do want to please God, and I am willing to do things His way, no matter how difficult it is. Reading this passage reminds me that while misconduct should be confronted in a loving way, I will also have times of needing simply to bear and endure the troublesome faults that others have.

Humility allows us to be patient with other peoples' mistakes. As we walk in love and pray for people, God will intervene and deal with their faults. We reap what we sow: If we sow mercy, we will reap mercy when we need it.

Even though we find it difficult at times to bear with the weaknesses of others, the Word of God actually strengthens and enables us to do God's will. When you are tempted to be prideful, study and meditate on the Word, asking the Holy Spirit to do through you what you cannot do by sheer willpower. Remember, pride is a sin and it is the root of many broken relationships.

The signs of pride include an unwillingness to admit fault or a reluctance to take responsibility for one's actions. Pride wants to do all the talking, and none of the listening. Pride does not make peace. Pride is stubborn; it does not want to be instructed, it wants to instruct others.

Pride was Lucifer's sin; he said he would lift himself and his throne above God's! Therefore, we see that pride manifests when a person esteems himself above the value of another, but God says we are all equal in His eyes. Lucifer, of course, never was equal with God, but as far as human relationships are concerned, no one person is better than another. Remember that, and you will be well on your way to avoiding pride. Do not deceive yourself into thinking pride will get you where you want to go. Rather, allow the truth of Galatians 6:1–3 to sink deep in your heart and change you from the inside out.

putting the Word to work

We are not meant to bear life's burdens alone. God's Word teaches us to love one another as He loves us, and it is out of this love that we are to carry one another's burdens (see Galatians 6:2). Is there someone in your life who needs your help bearing a burden? As you seek to help that person, remember that Jesus is your burden-bearer, and He will help you help that person.

⁴But each one must carefully scrutinize his own work [examining his actions, attitudes, and behavior], and then he can have the personal satisfaction and inner joy of doing something commendable without comparing himself to another. ⁵For every person will have to bear [with patience] his own burden [of faults and shortcomings for which he alone is responsible]. ⁶The one who is taught the word [of God] is to share all good things with his teacher [contributing to his spiritual and material support]. ⁷Do not be deceived, God is not mocked [He will not allow Himself to be ridiculed, nor treated with contempt nor allow His precepts to be scornfully set aside]; for whatever a man sows, this *and* this only is what he will reap.

putting the Word to work

Are you ever tempted to compare yourself to someone else? The Word of God warns against such behavior because it can lead to self-conceit (see Galatians 6:3, 4). Rather, Jesus' life and teachings are the standard by which we measure our lives. Ask God to help you honestly assess the areas in your life that need improvement and thank Him for bringing transformation to other areas.

⁸For the one who sows to his flesh [his sinful capacity, his worldliness, his disgraceful impulses] will reap from the flesh ruin *and* destruction, but the one who sows to the Spirit will from the Spirit reap eternal life. ⁹Let us not grow weary *or* become discouraged in doing good, for at the proper time we will reap, if we do not give in. ¹⁰So then, while we [as individual believers] have the opportunity, let us do good to all people [not only being helpful, but also doing that which promotes their spiritual well-being], and especially [be a blessing] to those of the household of faith (born-again believers). ¹¹See with what large letters I am writing to you with my own hand. ¹²Those who want to make a good impression in public [before the Jews] try to compel you to be circumcised, just so they will escape being persecuted for [faithfulness to] the cross of Christ.

life point

The "proper time" as mentioned in Galatians 6:9 is God's season, not ours. We are often in a hurry, but God is not. He takes time to do things right; He lays a solid foundation before He attempts to build a building. We are God's buildings under construction. He is the Master Builder, and He knows what He is doing. We may not know what He is doing, but He does. We may not always know all the answers, but we can be satisfied to know the One Who knows.

God's timing seems to be His own little secret. The Bible promises us that He will never be late, but I have also discovered that He is usually not early. It seems He takes every available opportunity to develop the fruit of patience in us.

13For even the circumcised [Jews] themselves do not [really] keep the Law, but they want to have you circumcised so that they may boast in your flesh [that is, in the fact that they convinced you to be circumcised].

14But far be it from me to boast [in anything or anyone], except in the cross of our Lord Jesus Christ, through whom the world has been crucified to me, and I to the world.

15For neither is circumcision anything [of any importance], nor uncircumcision, but [only] a new creation [which is the result of a new birth—a spiritual transformation—a new nature in Christ Jesus].

16Peace and mercy be upon all who walk by this rule [who discipline themselves and conduct their lives by this principle], and upon the [true] Israel of God (Jewish believers). [Ps 125:5]

17From now on let no one trouble me [by making it necessary for me to justify my authority as an apostle, and the absolute truth of the gospel], for I bear on my body the branding-marks of Jesus [the wounds, scars, and other outward evidence of persecutions—these testify to His ownership of me].

18The grace of our Lord Jesus Christ be with your spirit, my brothers and sisters. Amen.

life point

In Galatians 6:14 the Apostle Paul makes clear that he did not boast in anything or anyone, because the world was crucified to him and he to the world. He kept all things—including people, places, and positions—in proper balance in his life. He was not dependent upon anyone or anything for his joy and peace and victory except the Lord. Let me encourage you to be the same way!

Ephesians

Author:
Paul

Date:
About AD 60

Everyday Life Principles:
God loves you.

You are totally accepted in Christ.

God has a great plan for your life.

Though Ephesians is literally filled with wisdom, encouragement, and great teaching about what it means to be a Christian and how the church should operate, I believe one of the most important messages in this letter is that you and I are unconditionally loved and totally accepted in Christ. Indeed, one of the key points in this book is that *God loves you* and you can receive and enjoy that love and become increasingly rooted and grounded in it.

In addition, this book addresses: the spiritual blessings that belong to us in Christ; our position of authority in Christ; the mysteries of God; the need to walk in love and in the light; the importance of unity among believers; proper order in families and relationships; how to deal with anger and how to war against the powers and principalities in the spiritual realm.

As you spend time in Ephesians, I hope that its many rich teachings take root in your heart and that you will apply them in your everyday life. I especially hope and pray that through this book, you experience God's love and acceptance in a deeply personal way and are filled with a sense of purpose as you read about how He feels about you. God has great things for you, things He ordained before the foundation of the world. Ask Him to reveal them and enable you to do them by the power of the Holy Spirit.

1 PAUL, AN apostle (special messenger, personally chosen representative) of Christ Jesus (the Messiah, the Anointed), by the will of God [that is, by His purpose and choice],

To the saints (God's people) who are at Ephesus and are faithful *and* loyal *and* steadfast in Christ Jesus:

²Grace to you and peace [inner calm and spiritual well-being] from God our Father and the Lord Jesus Christ.

³Blessed *and* worthy of praise be the God and Father of our Lord Jesus Christ, who has blessed us with every spiritual blessing in the heavenly realms in Christ,

⁴just as [in His love] He chose us in Christ [actually selected us for Himself as His own] before the foundation

life point

Ephesians 1:4 is a wonderful scripture! In it the Lord tells us we are His, and He sets forth what He wants for us—that we should know we are loved, chosen, and selected as His very own.

Naturally, we should do what we can do to live holy lives. But thank God, when we do make mistakes, we can be forgiven. We do not lose our God-given position of holiness, and we remain blameless and above reproach—all "in Christ."

of the world, so that we would be holy [that is, consecrated, set apart for Him, purpose-driven] and blameless in His sight. In love

you have been chosen

Three of the strongest desires human beings have are to be loved, to be accepted, and to feel that we belong. We want a sense of connection and belonging to something or someone. We want to feel valuable. We cannot be guaranteed of always getting that in our dealings with people, but we can get it from God. Even though God knows everything about us—and I do mean everything—He still chooses us on purpose. According to Ephesians 1:4, He actually picked us out on purpose to be His own and to belong to Him. I encourage you to say aloud right now, "I belong to God."

God set us apart for Himself and made provision in Jesus for us to be holy, blameless, and consecrated. We can live before Him in love without reproach. This means we do not have to feel guilty about all of our weaknesses and faults. You and I are no surprise to God. He knew exactly what He was getting when He chose us. God did not choose us and then become disappointed because of our inabilities. God has hope for us, and He believes in us and is working in us to help us be all He has planned for us.

I encourage you to relax in God's love. Learn to receive God's love. Think about it, thank Him for it, and watch for it to manifest in your daily life. God shows His love for us in many ways, but we often are unaware of it. He loves us first so we can love Him and other people. God never expects us to give away something He has not first given us. His love is poured into our hearts by the Holy Spirit and He wants us to live before Him in love.

Let love in and let it out. You are destined to be a channel for God to flow through, and not a reservoir that merely sits and collects things. You are special and God has a special plan for you. Get excited about that and rejoice!

⁵He predestined *and* lovingly planned for us to be adopted to Himself as [His own] children through Jesus Christ, in accordance with the kind intention *and* good pleasure of His will—

⁶to the praise of His glorious grace *and* favor, which He so freely bestowed on us in the Beloved [His Son, Jesus Christ].

⁷In Him we have redemption [that is, our deliverance and salvation] through His blood, [which paid the penalty for our sin and resulted in] the forgiveness *and* complete pardon of our sin, in accordance with the riches of His grace

⁸which He lavished on us. In all wisdom and understanding [with practical insight]

⁹He made known to us the mystery of His will according to His good pleasure, which He purposed in Christ,

¹⁰with regard to the fulfillment of the times [that is, the end of history, the climax of the ages]—to bring all things together in Christ, [both] things in the heavens and things on the earth.

¹¹In Him also we have received an inheritance [a destiny—we were claimed by God as His own], having been predestined (chosen, appointed beforehand) according to the purpose of Him who works everything in agreement with the counsel *and* design of His will,

¹²so that we who were the first to hope in Christ [who first put our confidence in Him as our Lord and Savior] would exist to the praise of His glory.

¹³In Him, you also, when you heard the word of truth, the good news of your salvation, and [as a result] believed in Him, were stamped with the seal of the promised Holy Spirit [the One promised by Christ] as owned *and* protected [by God]. [John 7:39; Acts 2:33]

¹⁴The Spirit is the guarantee [the first installment, the pledge, a foretaste] of our inheritance until the redemption of *God's own* [purchased] possession [His believers], to the praise of His glory.

¹⁵For this reason, because I have heard of your faith in the Lord Jesus and your love for all God's people,

¹⁶I do not cease to give thanks for you, remembering you in my prayers;

¹⁷[I always pray] that the God of our Lord Jesus Christ, the Father of glory, may grant you a spirit of wisdom and of revelation [that gives you a deep and personal and intimate insight] into the true knowledge of Him [for we know the Father through the Son].

¹⁸And [I pray] that the eyes of your heart [the very center and core of your being] may be enlightened [flooded with light by the Holy Spirit], so that you will know *and* cherish the hope [the divine guarantee, the confident expectation] to which He has called you, the riches of His glorious inheritance in the saints (God's people),

¹⁹and [so that you will begin to know] what the immeasurable *and* unlimited

speak the Word

Thank You, God, that You predestined and lovingly planned to adopt me as Your own child through Jesus Christ, so I could be to the praise of Your glorious grace and favor, which You so freely bestowed on me in the Beloved, Your Son Jesus Christ.
—ADAPTED FROM EPHESIANS 1:5, 6

Thank You, Jesus, that in You I have redemption, deliverance, and salvation through Your blood, the forgiveness and complete pardon of my sins, in accordance with the riches of Your grace, which You have lavished upon me.
—ADAPTED FROM EPHESIANS 1:7, 8

and surpassing greatness of His [active, spiritual] power is in us who believe. These are in accordance with the working of His mighty strength

²⁰which He produced in Christ when He raised Him from the dead and seated Him at His own right hand in the heavenly *places,*

²¹far above all rule and authority and power and dominion [whether angelic or human], and [far above] every name that is named [above every title that can be conferred], not only in this age *and* world but also in the one to come.

²²And He put all things [in every realm] in subjection under Christ's feet, and appointed Him as [supreme and authoritative] head over all things in the church, [Ps 8:6; Col 1:18]

²³which is His body, the fullness of Him who fills *and* completes all things in all [believers].

2 AND YOU [He made alive when you] were [spiritually] dead *and* separated from Him because of your transgressions and sins,

²in which you once walked. You were following the ways of this world [influenced by this present age], in accordance with the prince of the power of the air (Satan), the spirit who is now at work in the disobedient [the unbelieving, who fight against the purposes of God].

³Among these [unbelievers] we all once lived in the passions of our flesh [our behavior governed by the sinful self], indulging the desires of human nature [without the Holy Spirit] and [the impulses] of the [sinful] mind. We were, by nature, children [under the sentence] of [God's] wrath, just like the rest [of mankind].

⁴But God, being [so very] rich in mercy, because of His great *and* wonderful love with which He loved us,

⁵even when we were [spiritually] dead *and* separated from Him be-

putting the Word to work

Can you imagine trying to earn your way into God's favor? That would be an impossible task. No amount of good works would ever be enough. Take a moment and reflect on the riches of God's grace and mercy, and thank Him for His love and kindness toward you (see Ephesians 2:4–7).

cause of our sins, He made us [spiritually] alive together with Christ (for by His grace—His undeserved favor and mercy—you have been saved from God's judgment). [Rom 6:1–10]

⁶And He raised us up together with Him [when we believed], and seated us with Him in the heavenly *places,* [because we are] in Christ Jesus,

⁷[and He did this] so that in the ages to come He might [clearly] show the immeasurable *and* unsurpassed riches of His grace in [His] kindness toward us in Christ Jesus [by providing for our redemption].

⁸For it is by grace [God's remarkable compassion and favor drawing you to Christ] that you have been saved [actually delivered from judgment and given eternal life] through faith. And this [salvation] is not of yourselves [not

life point

Grace is a wonderful thing. It is God's unmerited favor and remarkable compassion by which we are saved through faith in Jesus Christ, as Paul tells us in Ephesians 2:8.

The Holy Spirit ministers grace to us from God the Father. It can be said that grace is the Holy Spirit's power flowing out from God's throne to save us; it enables us to live holy lives and to accomplish the will of God.

seated in heavenly places

The Bible depicts Jesus after His resurrection as seated in heavenly places at the right hand of God. Being "seated" refers to being in the rest of God. God wants each of us to enter His rest. He wants us to be relaxed, not worried or anxious, and to enjoy life while we wait for Him to make all our enemies a footstool for our feet. Our part is to believe and rest in Him and His part is to work on our behalf.

According to Scripture, we died with Christ when He died, we were buried with Him, resurrected with Him, and we are now seated with Him in the heavenly places (see Ephesians 2:6). How can we be seated with Him in heaven when we can clearly see that we are here on earth? Simply because each of us is a spirit, we have a soul, and we live in a body. Physically we are on earth, but simultaneously we can be spiritually seated with Christ in heaven. That belief gives us the ability to enter His rest. The work of Christ is finished and we can enjoy its results. His kingdom offers "righteousness and peace and joy in the Holy Spirit" (see Romans 14:17), and it is available to us right now, not just when we go to heaven. God wants us to enjoy the life that Jesus died to give us starting the moment we accept Him as Savior and Lord.

Have you entered God's rest? Have you trusted Him entirely to do what needs to be done in you and in your life? Are you perhaps still working in the flesh trying to do what only God can do and the result is frustration and disappointment? Perhaps you just need to sit down! I do not mean physically, but spiritually. We can sit in a chair and still be worried, fearful, and anxious. God is not calling us to rest *from* our work, but *in* our work. As we go about our daily business, we can do it all while seated in Christ. He is our Refuge and our Hiding Place.

Be zealous and exert yourself and strive diligently to enter that place of rest. It is available today, so do not let it pass you by. Release all your frustrations and worries—and have a seat in Christ.

through your own effort], but it is the [undeserved, gracious] gift of God;

9not as a result of [your] works [nor your attempts to keep the Law], so that no one will [be able to] boast *or* take credit in any way [for his salvation].

10For we are His workmanship [His own master work, a work of art], created in Christ Jesus [reborn from above—spiritually transformed, renewed, ready to be used] for good works, which God prepared [for us] beforehand [taking paths which He set], so that we would walk in them [living the good life which He prearranged and made ready for us]. [Rom 1:20]

life point

Ephesians 2:10 tells us that we are God's workmanship. He created us with His own hands. We human beings got messed up along the way, so we were recreated in Christ Jesus. We had to be born-again spiritually so we could go ahead and do the good works God preplanned for us before Satan tried to ruin us.

Just because you and I make mistakes or have trouble in our lives, that does not mean God's plan has changed. It is still in effect. All we have to do is get back in it by trusting and obeying Him.

¹¹Therefore, remember that at one time you Gentiles by birth, who are called "Uncircumcision" by those who called themselves "Circumcision," [itself a mere mark] *which is* made in the flesh by human hands—

¹²*remember* that at that time you were separated from Christ [excluded from any relationship with Him], alienated from the commonwealth of Israel, and strangers to the covenants of promise [with no share in the sacred Messianic promise and without knowledge of God's agreements], having no hope [in

God has a good plan

God had a good plan laid out for each one of us long before we made our appearance on this planet (see Ephesians 2:10). It is not a plan of failure, misery, poverty, sickness, disaster, and disease. God's plan is a good plan, a plan for life, health, happiness, and fulfillment. Other scriptures affirm this truth.

In Jeremiah 29:11 we read, "'For I know the plans and thoughts that I have for you,' says the Lord, 'plans for peace and well-being and not for disaster to give you a future and a hope.'"

In John 10:10 Jesus said, "The thief comes only in order to steal and kill and destroy. I came that they may have and enjoy life, and have it in abundance [to the full, till it overflows]."

In 3 John 2 we read, "Beloved, I pray that in every way you may succeed and prosper and be in good health [physically], just as [I know] your soul prospers [spiritually]."

We will benefit greatly if we say to ourselves several times a day, "God has a good plan for my life." Why should we do that? We need to be firmly convinced of this truth to keep us from being affected by our changing circumstances and emotions.

You may ask, "If God has such a wonderful plan for my life, why am I not living in it?"

I understand why you ask that question. It does seem strange that if God loves us so much and has such good plans for us, we still suffer as we sometimes do. What's important to remember is that we have an enemy who is out to disrupt God's wonderful plan and to destroy the good things God has in mind for us. This happened to me. Though God had a good plan for my life, I grew up in an abusive environment because the devil came and tried to disrupt that good plan.

But there is something else, something really awesome we need to understand about God. God does not like it when someone hurts us and tries to undermine His plan for us. He always has a plan for our healing and restoration. While He is making us "lie down in green pastures" to restore our souls (see Psalm 23:2), He is getting up to do something about our situation!

God is on our side and it should be a great comfort to us to know that what we cannot do for ourselves, the Lord will do for us—if we entrust ourselves to Him. Only He has the power to restore what was lost to us, whether that loss was our own fault or the fault of our enemy.

His promise] and [living] in the world without God.

¹³But now [at this very moment] in Christ Jesus you who once were [so very] far away [from God] have been brought near by the blood of Christ.

¹⁴For He Himself is our peace *and* our bond of unity. He who made both *groups*—[Jews and Gentiles]—*into* one body and broke down the barrier, the dividing wall [of spiritual antagonism between us],

¹⁵by abolishing in His [own crucified] flesh the hostility *caused by* the Law with its commandments *contained* in ordinances [which He satisfied]; so that in Himself He might make the two into one new man, thereby establishing peace.

¹⁶And [that He] might reconcile them both [Jew and Gentile, united] in one body to God through the cross, thereby putting to death the hostility.

¹⁷AND HE CAME AND PREACHED THE GOOD NEWS OF PEACE TO YOU [Gentiles] WHO WERE FAR AWAY, AND PEACE TO THOSE [Jews] WHO WERE NEAR. [Is 57:19]

¹⁸For it is through Him that we both have a [direct] way of approach in one Spirit to the Father.

¹⁹So then you are no longer strangers and aliens [outsiders without rights of citizenship], but you are fellow citizens with the saints (God's people), and are [members] of God's household,

²⁰having been built on the foundation of the apostles and prophets, with Christ Jesus Himself as the [chief] Cornerstone,

²¹in whom the whole structure is joined together, and it continues [to increase] growing into a holy temple in the Lord [a sanctuary dedicated, set apart, and sacred to the presence of the Lord].

²²In Him [and in fellowship with one another] you also are being built together into a dwelling place of God in the Spirit.

3 FOR THIS reason [because I preach that you and believing Jews are joint heirs] I, Paul, am the prisoner of Christ Jesus on behalf of you Gentiles—

²assuming that you have heard of the stewardship of God's grace that was entrusted to me [to share with you] for your benefit;

³and that by [divine] revelation the mystery was made known to me, as I have already written in brief. [Eph 1:9]

⁴By referring to this, when you read it you can understand my insight into the mystery of Christ,

⁵which in other generations was not disclosed to mankind, as it has now been revealed to His holy apostles and prophets by the [Holy] Spirit;

⁶[it is this:] that the Gentiles are now joint heirs [with the Jews] and members of the same body, and joint partakers [sharing] in the [same divine] promise in Christ Jesus through [their faith in] the good news [of salvation].

⁷Of this [gospel] I was made a minister by the gift of God's grace given me through the working of His power.

⁸To me, [though I am] the very least of all the saints (God's people), this grace [which is undeserved] was graciously given, to proclaim to the Gentiles the good news of the incomprehensible riches of Christ [that spiritual wealth which no one can fully understand],

⁹and to make plain [to everyone] the plan of the mystery [regarding the uniting of believing Jews and Gentiles into one body] which [until now] was

speak the Word

Thank You, Jesus, for being my peace.
—ADAPTED FROM EPHESIANS 2:14

putting the Word to work

How many times have you heard someone say, "God loves you"? Hopefully, a lot! But do you really understand the depths of God's love for you? Paul fervently prayed that the Ephesians would understand the width, length, depth, and height of God's love for them, and that they would be rooted and grounded in that boundless love. Take time to meditate on Ephesians 3:14–19. Ask God to reveal to you more and more of His love and to expand your capacity to receive this awesome love and all the fullness of God.

kept hidden through the ages in [the mind of] God who created all things.

¹⁰So now through the church the multifaceted wisdom of God [in all its countless aspects] might now be made known [revealing the mystery] to the [angelic] rulers and authorities in the heavenly *places*.

¹¹*This is* in accordance with [the terms of] the eternal purpose which He carried out in Christ Jesus our Lord,

¹²in whom we have boldness and confident access through faith in Him [that is, our faith gives us sufficient courage to freely and openly approach God through Christ].

¹³So I ask you not to lose heart at my sufferings on your behalf, for they are your glory *and* honor.

¹⁴For this reason [grasping the greatness of this plan by which Jews and Gentiles are joined together in Christ] I bow my knees [in reverence] before the Father [of our Lord Jesus Christ],

life point

Ephesians 3:20 teaches us that God is able to do "superabundantly more than all that we dare ask or think . . . according to His power that is at work within us." It is God's power, but it is done through us, so we need to cooperate with Him. This means we need to be daring in our faith and in our prayers. I encourage you to stretch your faith into new realms "infinitely beyond our greatest prayers, hopes, or dreams."

¹⁵from whom every family in heaven and on earth derives its name [God—the first and ultimate Father].

¹⁶May He grant you out of the riches of His glory, to be strengthened *and* spiritually energized with power through His Spirit in your inner self, [indwelling your innermost being and personality],

¹⁷so that Christ may dwell in your hearts through your faith. And may you, having been [deeply] rooted and [securely] grounded in love,

¹⁸be fully capable of comprehending with all the saints (God's people) the width and length and height and depth of His love [fully experiencing that amazing, endless love];

¹⁹and [that you may come] to know [practically, through personal experience] the love of Christ which far surpasses [mere] knowledge [without experience], that you may be filled up [throughout your being] to all the fullness of God [so that you may have the richest experience of God's presence in your lives, completely filled and flooded with God Himself].

²⁰Now to Him who is able to [carry

speak the Word

Thank You, God, for strengthening me with power through Your Holy Spirit in my inner self. Thank You that Christ dwells in my heart through faith.
—ADAPTED FROM EPHESIANS 3:16, 17

be filled!

Just imagine having your personality filled with the Holy Spirit of the living God and having "the richest experience of God's presence" in your life, "completely filled and flooded with God Himself" (Ephesians 3:16–19)! The Apostle Paul was a person filled with the Holy Spirit; he was also a person who forsook everything to follow Jesus. Any area of our lives that we hold back from God is an area where we cannot be filled with His Spirit. I encourage you to open and surrender every room in your heart to God. Your time is His; your money is His, as are your gifts and talents, your family, career, thoughts, attitudes, and desires. He wants to be involved in every area of your life: how you dress, the friends you choose, what you do for entertainment, what you eat, and so on.

After conversion, Jesus is our Savior, but is He our Lord? Any area we claim as our own is one we have not surrendered to the lordship of Jesus Christ.

I lived a defeated life for many years simply because I was not fully surrendered. I accepted Jesus as Savior; I had enough of Jesus to stay out of hell, but I had not accepted Him as my Lord in every area of my life; I had not accepted enough of Him to walk in victory—and there is a difference.

The blessedness of being filled with the Spirit is clearly visible in the change in the people's lives after Pentecost. Peter, for example, who displayed great fear in not being willing to even admit that he knew Jesus, became a bold apostle who stood in the streets of Jerusalem and preached the gospel so fervently that about three thousand souls were added to the "body of believers" in one day (see Acts 2:40, 41).

Complete surrender to God brings good change into our lives. Surrendering to Him actually opens the door to the things we desire, and yet we waste our own energy trying to access them our own way. I encourage you today to surrender every area of your life to God so you may be filled to overflowing with His Spirit in every way.

out His purpose and] do superabundantly more than all that we dare ask or think [infinitely beyond our greatest prayers, hopes, or dreams], according to His power that is at work within us,

²¹to Him be the glory in the church and in Christ Jesus throughout all generations forever and ever. Amen.

4 SO I, the prisoner for the Lord, appeal to you to live a life worthy of the calling to which you have been called [that is, to live a life that exhibits godly character, moral courage, personal integrity, and mature behavior—a life that expresses gratitude to God for your salvation],

²with all humility [forsaking self-righteousness], and gentleness [maintaining self-control], with patience, bearing with one another in [unselfish] love.

³Make every effort to keep the oneness of the Spirit in the bond of peace [each individual working together to make the whole successful].

⁴*There is* one body [of believers] and one Spirit—just as you were called to one hope when called [to salvation]—

⁵one Lord, one faith, one baptism,

⁶one God and Father of us all who

believe big

In the natural realm or in our natural strength, many things are impossible. But in the supernatural realm with God, nothing is impossible. God wants us to believe for great things, make big plans, and expect Him to do things so great that we are left with our mouths hanging open in awe. James 4:2 tells us we do not have because we do not ask! We can be bold in our asking, and Ephesians 3:20 challenges us to ask for big things.

When our desires seem overwhelmingly big and we do not see the way to accomplish them, we should remember even though we do not know the way, we know the Waymaker!

God has a way for us to do everything He places in our hearts. He does not put dreams and visions in us to frustrate us. We must keep our confidence in God all the way through to the end, not just for a little bit and then give up when it looks like the mountain is too big!

It is untold what people can do—even people who do not appear to be able to do anything. God does not usually call people who are capable; if He did, He would not get the glory when they accomplish great things. He frequently chooses those who, naturally speaking, feel they are in completely over their heads but who are ready to stand up on the inside and take bold steps of faith as they receive direction from God.

We usually want to wait until we "feel ready" before we step out, but if we feel ready, then we tend to lean on ourselves instead of on God.

Know your weaknesses and know God—know His strength and faithfulness. Remember that He is able to do "superabundantly more" than anything you could ever dare to ask or think!

is [sovereign] over all and [working] through all and [living] in all.

⁷Yet grace [God's undeserved favor] was given to each one of us [not indiscriminately, but in different ways] in proportion to the measure of Christ's [rich and abundant] gift.

⁸Therefore it says,

"WHEN HE ASCENDED ON HIGH,
HE LED CAPTIVITY CAPTIVE,
AND HE BESTOWED GIFTS ON MEN."
　[Ps 68:18]

⁹(Now this *expression,* "He ascended," what does it mean except that He also had *previously* descended [from the heights of heaven] into the lower parts of the earth?

¹⁰He who descended is the *very* same as He who also has ascended high above all the heavens, that He [His presence] might fill all things [that is, the whole universe]).

¹¹And [His gifts to the church were varied and] He Himself appointed some as apostles [special messengers, representatives], some as prophets [who speak a new message from God to the people], some as evangelists [who spread the good news of salvation], and some as pastors and teachers [to shepherd and guide and instruct],

¹²[and He did this] to fully equip *and* perfect the saints (God's people) for works of service, to build up the body of Christ [the church];

¹³until we all reach oneness in the faith and in the knowledge of the Son of God, [growing spiritually] to become a mature believer, reaching to the measure of the fullness of Christ [manifesting His spiritual completeness and exercising our spiritual gifts in unity].

¹⁴So that we are no longer children [spiritually immature], tossed back and forth [like ships on a stormy sea] and carried about by every wind of [shifting] doctrine, by the cunning *and* trickery of [unscrupulous] men, by the deceitful scheming of people ready to do anything [for personal profit].

¹⁵But speaking the truth in love [in all things—both our speech and our lives expressing His truth], let us grow up in all *things* into Him [following His example] who is the Head—Christ.

¹⁶From Him the whole body [the church, in all its various parts], joined and knitted *firmly* together by what every joint supplies, when each part is working properly, causes the body to grow *and* mature, building itself up in [unselfish] love.

¹⁷So this I say, and solemnly affirm together with the Lord [as in His presence], that you must no longer live as the [unbelieving] Gentiles live, in the futility of their minds [and in the foolishness and emptiness of their souls],

¹⁸for their [moral] understanding is darkened *and* their reasoning is clouded; [they are] alienated *and* self-banished from the life of God [with no share in it; this is] because of the [willful] ignorance *and* spiritual blindness that is [deep-seated] within them, because of the hardness *and* insensitivity of their heart.

¹⁹And they, [the ungodly in their spiritual apathy], having become callous *and* unfeeling, have given themselves over [as prey] to unbridled sensuality, eagerly craving the practice of every kind of impurity [that their desires may demand].

life point

Ephesians 4:17–19 says unbelievers can be so callous and hard that they become unfeeling. The same verse says they live by their feelings in unbridled sensuality and carnality. As I meditated on what appears to be a paradox here, the Lord showed me that such people are past doing what they should be doing with their feelings.

God gives people feelings for a specific purpose and use in their walk with Him. But people who have alienated themselves from God are hardened to the point that they are beyond using their feelings for the right purpose. Satan moves them into an area where they live riotous lives, doing whatever they feel like doing.

What is the world's philosophy today? "If it feels good, do it!" You and I are not to live that way, but to make the truth of God's Word our standard and to obey it by the power of the Holy Spirit.

²⁰But you did not learn Christ in this way!

²¹If in fact you have [really] heard Him and have been taught by Him, just as truth is in Jesus [revealed in His life and personified in Him],

²²that, regarding your previous way of life, you put off your old self [completely discard your former nature], which is being corrupted through deceitful desires,

²³and be *continually* renewed in the spirit of your mind [having a fresh, untarnished mental and spiritual attitude],

²⁴and put on the new self [the regenerated and renewed nature], created in God's image, [godlike] in the righteousness and holiness of the truth [living in a way that expresses to God your gratitude for your salvation].

²⁵Therefore, rejecting all falsehood

[whether lying, defrauding, telling half-truths, spreading rumors, any such as these], SPEAK TRUTH EACH ONE WITH HIS NEIGHBOR, for we are all parts of one another [and we are all parts of the body of Christ]. [Zech 8:16]

²⁶BE ANGRY [at sin—at immorality, at injustice, at ungodly behavior], YET DO NOT SIN; do not let your anger [cause you shame, nor allow it to] last until the sun goes down. [Ps 4:4]

life point

In Ephesians 4:23 we read that we are to be "continually renewed in the spirit" of our minds, "having a fresh, untarnished mental and spiritual attitude." Attitudes begin in the mind. Our minds are renewed by the Word of God. Reading the Word daily renews our minds and changes our attitudes. Renew your mind in the Word today!

how to really change

Ephesians 4:22–24 teaches us about the connection between our thoughts and our actions. Verse 22 says we should strip ourselves of our former nature and discard our old unrenewed self. Verse 24 continues the thought and tells us to put on the new nature created in God's image "in the righteousness and holiness of the truth."

So we see that verse 22 basically tells us to stop acting improperly, and verse 24 tells us to begin acting properly. But verse 23 is what I call "the bridge scripture." It tells us how to get from verse 22 (wrong actions) to verse 24 (right actions): "And be continually renewed in the spirit of your mind [having a fresh, untarnished mental and spiritual attitude]."

It is impossible to get from wrong behavior to right behavior without first changing our thoughts. A passive person may want to do the right thing, but he will never do so unless he purposely activates his mind and lines it up with God's Word and His will.

An example that comes to mind involves a man who once got into the prayer line at one of my seminars. He had a problem with lust. He really loved his wife and did not want their marriage to be destroyed, but his problem needed a solution or he would surely ruin his marriage.

"Joyce, I have a problem with lust," he said. "I just cannot seem to stay away from other women. Will you pray for my deliverance? I have been prayed for many times, but I never seem to make any progress."

This is what the Holy Spirit prompted me to tell him, "Yes, I will pray for you, but you must be accountable for what you are allowing to show on the picture screen of your mind. You cannot visualize pornographic pictures in your thinking or imagine yourself with these other women if you ever want to enjoy freedom."

Like this man, others realize why they are not experiencing a breakthrough even though they want to be free: they want to change their behavior, but not their thinking. If you desire to act differently, you will have to start by thinking differently because your behavior starts with your thoughts. Wrong thoughts lead to wrong actions, but right thoughts lead to right actions.

27And do not give the devil an opportunity [to lead you into sin by holding a grudge, or nurturing anger, or harboring resentment, or cultivating bitterness].

28The thief [who has become a believer] must no longer steal, but instead he must work hard [making an honest living], producing that which is good with his own hands, so that he will have *something* to share with those in need.

29Do not let unwholesome [foul, profane, worthless, vulgar] words ever come out of your mouth, but only such *speech* as is good for building up others, according to the need *and* the

life point

Ephesians 4:26, 27 basically tell us to let go of our anger before bedtime. There is only one problem: What happens when we become good and angry just before bedtime? If we become angry in the morning, at least we have all day to get over it. But when we become angry close to bedtime, we have to make a quick decision about what to do with our anger.

Why is it so unwise for us to go to bed angry? I think it is because while we sleep, what we are angry about has time to take root in us. But the Word admonishes us not to leave room for the devil to gain a foothold through our anger. If we refuse to get over our anger by bedtime, we open a door for the devil and give him a foothold. Once Satan gains a foothold in our lives, he sees an opportunity to move on to a stronghold.

I encourage you today to deal with your anger quickly and decisively so the devil sees no opportunity to take advantage of the situation. No matter how you feel, you can *choose* to forgive and walk in love.

occasion, so that it will be a blessing to those who hear [you speak].

30And do not grieve the Holy Spirit of God [but seek to please Him], by whom you were sealed *and* marked [branded as God's own] for the day of redemption [the final deliverance from the consequences of sin]. [Eph 1:13, 14; Phil 3:20, 21]

31Let all bitterness and wrath and anger and clamor [perpetual animosity, resentment, strife, fault-finding] and slander be put away from you, along with every kind of malice [all spitefulness, verbal abuse, malevolence].

32Be kind *and* helpful to one another, tender-hearted [compassionate, understanding], forgiving one another [readily and freely], just as God in Christ also forgave you.

5 THEREFORE BECOME imitators of God [copy Him and follow His example], as well-beloved children [imitate their father];

2and walk *continually* in love [that is, value one another—practice empathy and compassion, unselfishly seeking the best for others], just as Christ also loved you and gave Himself up for us, an offering and sacrifice to God [slain for you, so that it became] a sweet fragrance. [Ezek 20:41]

3But sexual immorality and all [moral] impurity [indecent, offensive behavior] or greed must not even be hinted at among you, as is proper among saints [for as believers our way of life, whether in public or in private, reflects the validity of our faith].

4Let there be no filthiness and silly talk, or coarse [obscene or vulgar] joking, *because* such things are not appropriate [for believers]; but instead speak of your thankfulness [to God].

5For be sure of this: no immoral, impure, or greedy person—for that one is [in effect] an idolater—has any inheritance in the kingdom of Christ and God

a tender conscience

Having a tender heart (see Ephesians 4:32) is equivalent to having a tender conscience, and tenderness of conscience is vital to being used by God.

In 1 Timothy 4:1, 2 Paul wrote, "But the [Holy] Spirit explicitly and unmistakably declares that in later times some will turn away from the faith, paying attention instead to deceitful and seductive spirits and doctrines of demons, [misled] by the hypocrisy of liars whose consciences are seared as with a branding iron [leaving them incapable of ethical functioning]."

It is dangerous to become hard-hearted and to develop a seared conscience. If we do, we cannot really tell if we are doing anything wrong or not. One way we develop a tender conscience is by being quick to repent and avoid excuses when God convicts us of something.

When God shows us we did something wrong, we need to say, "You are right Lord, I am wrong. There is no excuse, so please forgive me and help me not do this again."

It is amazing how much that will help us develop a tender conscience toward God. But as soon as we start trying to reason things out and make excuses for our wrongs, we start getting a little callous in our conscience. It becomes just a little bit harder for us to feel than it was the time before.

For example, if I mistreat someone and do not repent, my conscience begins to become callous. The next time I do it, my conscience gets a little more callous. Soon, though I go around presenting myself as a person who loves God, He cannot use me anymore because I am mistreating people in my words and actions toward them. The worst thing is that I do not even realize how I am treating them because I no longer have a tender heart and a tender conscience toward God.

We must remember that God's main interest is not how gifted or talented we are; His primary concern is our heart attitude. If we have a willing heart, a stirred-up heart, a wise heart, a perfect heart, and a tender conscience, the devil's plan for destruction is destroyed because then nothing can stop us from being used by God.

[for such a person places a higher value on something other than God].

⁶Let no one deceive you with empty arguments [that encourage you to sin], for because of these things the wrath of God comes upon the sons of disobedience [those who habitually sin]. [Lev 18:24, 25]

⁷So do not participate *or* even associate with them [in the rebelliousness of sin].

⁸For once you were darkness, but now you are light in the Lord; walk as children of Light [live as those who are native-born to the Light]

⁹(for the fruit [the effect, the result] of the Light consists in all goodness and righteousness and truth),

¹⁰trying to learn [by experience] what is pleasing to the Lord [and letting your lifestyles be examples of what is most acceptable to Him—your behavior expressing gratitude to God for your salvation].

putting the Word to work

Is there someone in your life you admire so much that you try to be like that person? It is not bad to have godly role models. Ephesians 5:1, 2 tell us that our best role model is God and that we are to imitate Him. One of the best ways to do that is to walk in love. Ask God often to show you how to walk in His love, how to receive it from Him, and then how to extend it to others.

putting the Word to work

Time is a very valuable commodity. Have you ever found yourself wishing there were more than twenty-four hours in a day? Ask God to teach you to live wisely (see Ephesians 5:15–17). Pay attention to the way you spend your time and make the most of every opportunity.

---

[11]Do not participate in the worthless *and* unproductive deeds of darkness, but instead expose them [by exemplifying personal integrity, moral courage, and godly character];
[12]for it is disgraceful even to mention the things that such people practice in secret.
[13]But all things become visible when they are exposed by the light [of God's precepts], for it is light that makes everything visible.
[14]For this reason He says,

"Awake, sleeper,
And arise from the dead,
And Christ will shine [as dawn]
    upon you *and* give you light."
[Is 26:19; 51:17; 52:1; 60:1, 2]

[15]Therefore see that you walk carefully [living life with honor, purpose, and courage; shunning those who tolerate and enable evil], not as the unwise, but as wise [sensible, intelligent, discerning people],

[16]making the very most of your time [on earth, recognizing and taking advantage of each opportunity and using it with wisdom and diligence], because the days are [filled with] evil.
[17]Therefore do not be foolish *and* thoughtless, but understand *and* firmly grasp what the will of the Lord is.
[18]Do not get drunk with wine, for that is wickedness (corruption, stupidity), but be filled with the [Holy] Spirit *and* constantly guided by Him. [Prov 23:20]
[19]Speak to one another in psalms and hymns and spiritual songs, [offering praise by] singing and making melody with your heart to the Lord;
[20]always giving thanks to God the Father for all things, in the name of our Lord Jesus Christ;
[21]being subject to one another out of reverence for Christ.
[22]Wives, be *subject* to your own husbands, as [a service] to the Lord.
[23]For the husband is head of the wife, as Christ is head of the church, Himself *being* the Savior of the body.
[24]But as the church is subject to Christ, so also wives should be subject to their husbands in everything

speak the Word

Father, I pray that I learn what is pleasing to You and that my lifestyle will be an example of what is most acceptable to You.
—ADAPTED FROM EPHESIANS 5:10

God, I give thanks to You for all things in the name of my Lord Jesus Christ.
—ADAPTED FROM EPHESIANS 5:20

[respecting both their position as protector and their responsibility to God as head of the house].

²⁵Husbands, love your wives [seek the highest good for her and surround her with a caring, unselfish love], just as Christ also loved the church and gave Himself up for her,

²⁶so that He might sanctify the church, having cleansed her by the washing of water with the word [of God],

²⁷so that [in turn] He might present the church to Himself in glorious splendor, without spot or wrinkle or any such thing; but that she would be holy [set apart for God] and blameless.

²⁸Even so husbands should *and* are morally obligated to love their own wives as [being in a sense] their own bodies. He who loves his own wife loves himself.

²⁹For no one ever hated his own body, but [instead] he nourishes *and* protects and cherishes it, just as Christ does the church,

³⁰because we are members (parts) of His body.

³¹FOR THIS REASON A MAN SHALL LEAVE HIS FATHER AND HIS MOTHER AND SHALL BE JOINED [and be faithfully devoted] TO HIS WIFE, AND THE TWO SHALL BECOME ONE FLESH. [Gen 2:24]

³²This mystery [of two becoming one] is great; but I am speaking with reference to [the relationship of] Christ and the church.

³³However, each man among you [without exception] is to love his wife as his very own self [with behavior worthy of respect and esteem, always seeking the best for her with an attitude of lovingkindness], and the wife [must see to it] that she respects *and* delights in her husband [that she notices him and prefers him and treats him with loving concern, treasuring him, honoring him, and holding him dear]. [1 Pet 3:2]

life point

Ephesians 5:18–20 is such a powerful passage! How can we obey it and stay filled with the Holy Spirit? We can do it by speaking to ourselves (through our thoughts) or to others (through our words) in "psalms and hymns and spiritual songs." We need to keep our thoughts and words full of God's Word by continuously offering praise and giving thanks to Him.

6 CHILDREN, OBEY your parents in the Lord [that is, accept their guidance and discipline as His representatives], for this is right [for obedience teaches wisdom and self-discipline].

²HONOR [esteem, value as precious] YOUR FATHER AND YOUR MOTHER [and be respectful to them]—this is the first commandment with a promise—

³SO THAT IT MAY BE WELL WITH YOU, AND THAT YOU MAY HAVE A LONG LIFE ON THE EARTH. [Ex 20:12]

⁴Fathers, do not provoke your children to anger [do not exasperate them to the point of resentment with demands that are trivial or unreasonable or humiliating or abusive; nor by showing favoritism or indifference to any of them], but bring them up [tenderly, with lovingkindness] in the discipline and instruction of the Lord.

⁵Slaves, be obedient to those who are your earthly masters, with respect

putting the Word to work

Some of the most rewarding and most challenging relationships can be those with family members, but Ephesians 6:1–4 helps us know how to live with our families in a godly way. If your parents are still living, how can you honor them, even as an adult? If you are a parent, how can you raise your children according to God's principles?

for authority, and with a sincere heart [seeking to please them], as [service] to Christ—

⁶not in the way of eye-service [working only when someone is watching you and only] to please men, but as slaves of Christ, doing the will of God from your heart;

⁷rendering service with goodwill, as to the Lord, and not [only] to men,

⁸knowing that whatever good thing each one does, he will receive this back from the Lord, whether [he is] slave or free.

⁹You masters, do the same [showing goodwill] toward them, and give up threatening *and* abusive words, knowing that [He who is] both their true Master and yours is in heaven, and that there is no partiality with Him [regardless of one's earthly status].

life point

Many of us fight battles in the realm of our emotions, but as Ephesians 6:11–18 teaches, our battle is not just with our emotions, but with the spiritual forces that play on our emotions.

In the King James Version of Ephesians 6:12 we are told that we do not war with "flesh and blood, but against principalities, against powers, against the rulers of the darkness of this world, against spiritual wickedness in high places." This means we war against strong spiritual entities.

It is important for us to see we that cannot fight darkness with darkness. I believe the best way to resist and overcome our powerful spiritual enemy is not by venting our anger and frustration in some fleshly manner. Rather, we need to put on our spiritual armor as described in Ephesians 6:13–17 and yield ourselves to the power and presence of the Holy Spirit within us as we pray (see Ephesians 6:18).

¹⁰In conclusion, be strong in the Lord [draw your strength from Him and be empowered through your union with Him] and in the power of His [boundless] might.

¹¹Put on the full armor of God [for His precepts are like the splendid armor of a heavily-armed soldier], so that you may be able to [successfully] stand up against all the schemes *and* the strategies *and* the deceits of the devil.

¹²For our struggle is not against flesh and blood [contending only with physical opponents], but against the rulers, against the powers, against the world forces of this [present] darkness, against the spiritual *forces* of wickedness in the heavenly (supernatural) *places*.

¹³Therefore, put on the complete armor of God, so that you will be able to [successfully] resist *and* stand your ground in the evil day [of danger], and having done everything [that the crisis demands], to stand firm [in your place, fully prepared, immovable, victorious].

¹⁴So stand firm *and* hold your ground, HAVING TIGHTENED THE WIDE BAND OF TRUTH (personal integrity, moral courage) AROUND YOUR WAIST and HAVING PUT ON THE BREASTPLATE

life point

Ephesians 6:12 gives us insight into the spiritual war that all believers are in. Our enemies are not natural, but spiritual. We can never win our battles if we fight against the wrong source in a wrong way. We tend to think that people or circumstances are our problem, but the source of many of our troubles is Satan and his demons. We cannot fight him with carnal (natural) weapons, but only with supernatural ones that God gives us for the destruction of the fortresses Satan builds in our minds (see 2 Corinthians 10:4, 5).

OF RIGHTEOUSNESS (an upright heart), [Is 11:5]

¹⁵and having strapped on YOUR FEET THE GOSPEL OF PEACE IN PREPARATION [to face the enemy with firm-footed stability and the readiness produced by the good news]. [Is 52:7]

¹⁶Above all, lift up the [protective] shield of faith with which you can extinguish all the flaming arrows of the evil *one*.

¹⁷And take THE HELMET OF SALVATION, and the sword of the Spirit, which is the Word of God. [Is 59:17]

¹⁸With all prayer and petition pray [with specific requests] at all times [on every occasion and in every season] in the Spirit, and with this in view, stay alert with all perseverance and petition [interceding in prayer] for all God's people.

¹⁹And *pray* for me, that words may be given to me when I open my mouth, to proclaim boldly the mystery of the good news [of salvation],

²⁰for which I am an ambassador in chains. And *pray* that in *proclaiming* it I may speak boldly *and* courageously, as I should.

²¹Now, so that you may know how I am and what I am doing, Tychicus, the beloved brother and faithful minister in the Lord, will tell you everything.

²²I have sent him to you for this very purpose, so that you may know how we are, and that he may comfort *and* encourage *and* strengthen your hearts.

²³Peace be to the brothers and sisters, and love joined with faith, from God the Father and the Lord Jesus Christ.

²⁴Grace be with all who love our Lord Jesus Christ with undying *and* incorruptible *love*.

putting the Word to work

Would you ever leave your house half-dressed? Of course not! However, many of us often forget to put on our spiritual clothing. Every day the forces of Satan wage war against you, and it is important to be protected. With this spiritual protection and authority, you can stand against evil forces. Learn about your spiritual armor (see Ephesians 6:10–18), and as you put your clothes on each day, also put on your armor and pick up your sword. For example, walking in peace is equivalent to putting on your shoes of peace, or walking in righteousness is equivalent to putting on your breastplate of righteousness, which protects your heart from condemnation. God supplies the armor we need to defeat all the attacks of the devil, but we must put it on.

Philippians

Author:
Paul

Date:
About AD 61

Everyday Life Principles:
Strength comes from the joy of the Lord.

Rejoice in all things and cultivate real joy in your life.

Joy is more than emotional happiness; it can be anything from extreme hilarity to calm delight. Practice calm delight in every area of your life.

Philippians is full of truths and principles for living a victorious Christian life; it contains much practical advice for everyday life; and it is a book of great joy. Even though Paul wrote this book from a prison cell, undoubtedly in very bad conditions, he had real joy in his heart and he encouraged his readers to do the same. He knew that the joy of the Lord is so important because it is our strength (see Nehemiah 8:10). He knew that the enemy always wants to steal our joy so he can sap our strength. His words are as true today as they were when he wrote them, and you and I need to develop and maintain our joy just as Paul did so long ago.

I define joy as "anything from extreme hilarity to calm delight, a feeling of pleasure." We all enjoy extreme hilarity from time to time, but what we want in everyday life is calm delight—that steadfast sense of peace, pleasure, and well-being we can only find through a personal relationship with God.

Whatever you are facing as you read Philippians, let me urge you to rejoice. Even in the midst of difficulties or sadness, the joy of the Lord is available to you and it is your strength. Do learn the many practical lessons that Philippians teaches, but above all, learn to live in the strength that comes from rejoicing in God in every situation. Remember that happiness is based on what happens, but joy is a fruit of the Holy Spirit Who dwells in us as believers in Jesus Christ.

1 PAUL AND Timothy, bond-servants of Christ Jesus (the Messiah, the Anointed),

To all the saints (God's people) in Christ Jesus who are at Philippi, including the overseers and deacons:

²Grace to you and peace [inner calm and spiritual well-being] from God our Father and the Lord Jesus Christ.

³I thank my God in every remembrance of you,

⁴always offering every prayer of mine with joy [and with specific requests] for all of you,

⁵[thanking God] for your participation *and* partnership [both your comforting fellowship and gracious contributions] in [advancing] the good news [regarding salvation] from the first day [you heard it] until now.

⁶I am convinced *and* confident of

life point

Do not be discouraged with yourself just because you have not yet arrived at a place of perfection in your thoughts and behavior. God would not be angry with you if He came back today and found you just as you are, as long as He sees that you have the right attitude and are cooperating with the work He is doing in you. He knows you are a work in progress— and you will be for as long as you live (see Philippians 1:6). Enjoy where you are on the way to where you are going!

this very thing, that He who has begun a good work in you will [continue to] perfect *and* complete it until the day of Christ Jesus [the time of His return]. [Rom 14:10]

God will finish the work

God always finishes what He starts. He has called us unto Himself and started a good work in us and He will finish it (see Philippians 1:6). That is a promise. Of course, we have a part to play, which is to keep believing Him and cooperating with the sanctifying work of the Holy Spirit in our lives. I know it is frustrating sometimes to feel we are in the middle of something and do not know how to go forward, but to also know we cannot go back. We love Jesus and want to go all the way through to the finish with Him, but sometimes it becomes difficult. Jesus understands that.

Jesus lived in a fleshly body while He was here on earth and He understands what temptation is like. You may experience temptation to sin or even just to quit and give up, but God will strengthen you to go all the way to the finish with Him if you ask Him. Keep your eyes on the prize. It may be uncomfortable now, but you will be pleased in the end if you allow God to do whatever He wants to do in you.

So many people today start things they never finish and that is not pleasing to God. In fact, it's not even a good representation of someone who desires to walk in integrity. It is easy to start something because our emotions are excited about something new. But character is seen in what people do when their feelings are no longer supporting them and perhaps they are left alone with just God and a lot of hard work. God's character is to always finish what He starts. What about you? Before you begin anything, count the cost and make a decision before you begin that you will finish.

God has promised to finish the work He started in you. Will you make a similar commitment to Him to finish whatever He gives you to do in this life?

7It is right for me to feel this way about you, because [you have me in your heart as] I have you in my heart, since both in my imprisonment and in the defense and confirmation of the good news [regarding salvation], all of you share in [His matchless] grace with me.

8For God is my witness, how I long for all of you with the affection of Christ Jesus [whose great love fills me].

9And this I pray, that your love may abound more and more [displaying itself in greater depth] in real knowledge and in practical insight,

10so that you may learn to recognize *and* treasure what is excellent [identifying the best, and distinguishing moral differences], and that you may be pure and blameless until the day of Christ [actually living lives that lead others away from sin];

11filled with the fruit of righteousness which comes through Jesus Christ, to the glory and praise of God [so that His glory may be both revealed and recognized].

12Now I want you to know, believers, that what has happened to me [this imprisonment that was meant to stop me] has actually served to advance [the spread of] the good news [regarding salvation].

13My imprisonment in [the cause of] Christ has become common knowledge throughout the whole praetorian (imperial) guard and to everyone else.

14Because of my chains [seeing that I am doing well and that God is accomplishing great things], most of the brothers have renewed confidence in the Lord, and have far more courage to speak the word of God [concerning salvation] without fear [of the

speak the Word

putting the Word to work

Sometimes it is hard to stay positive in difficult circumstances. Is this a challenging time in your life? Know that God can work through you in any circumstance to further the gospel and His purposes, just as He did for Paul in Philippians 1:12–14. Ask Him to help you see Him at work even in ways you will not expect.

consequences, seeing that God can work His good in all circumstances].

15Some, it is true, are [actually] preaching Christ out of envy and rivalry [toward me—for no better reason than a competitive spirit or misguided ambition], but others out of goodwill *and* a loyal spirit [toward me].

16The latter [preach Christ] out of love, because they know that I have been put here [by God on purpose] for the defense of the gospel;

17but the former preach Christ [insincerely] out of selfish ambition [just self-promotion], thinking that they are causing me distress in my imprisonment.

18What then [does it matter]? So long as in every way, whether in pretense [for self-promotion] or in all honesty [to spread the truth], Christ is being preached; and in this I rejoice.

Yes, and I will rejoice [later as well],

19for I know [with confidence] that this will turn out for my deliverance *and* spiritual well-being, through your prayers and the [superabundant] supply of the Spirit of Jesus Christ [which upholds me].

20It is my own eager expectation and hope, that [looking toward the

God, I pray that my love may abound more and more in real knowledge and practical insight, that it may display itself in greater depth.
—ADAPTED FROM PHILIPPIANS 1:9

future] I will not disgrace myself *nor* be ashamed in anything, but that with courage *and* the utmost freedom of speech, even now as always, Christ will be magnified *and* exalted in my body, whether by life or by death.

²¹For to me, to live is Christ [He is my source of joy, my reason to live] and to die is gain [for I will be with Him in eternity].

²²If, however, it is to be life here *and* I am to go on living, this *will mean* useful *and* productive service for me; so I do not know which to choose [if I am given that choice].

²³But I am hard-pressed between the two. I have the desire to leave [this world] and be with Christ, for that is far, far better;

²⁴yet to remain in my body is more necessary *and* essential for your sake.

²⁵Since I am convinced of this, I know that I will remain and continue with all of you for your progress and joy in the faith,

²⁶so that your rejoicing for me may overflow in Christ Jesus through my coming to you again.

²⁷Only [be sure to] lead your lives in a manner [that will be] worthy of the gospel of Christ, so that whether I do come and see you or remain absent, I will hear about you that you are standing firm in one spirit [and one purpose], with one mind striving side by side [as if in combat] for the faith of the gospel.

²⁸And in no way be alarmed *or* intimidated [in anything] by your opponents, for such [constancy and fearlessness on your part] is a [clear] sign [a proof and a seal] for them of

constant and fearless

Notice the two words *constancy* and *fearlessness* in the amplification of Philippians 1:28. They describe the rock-like temperament you and I should display in the face of attacks and onslaughts by our opponents and adversaries—both physical and spiritual.

When people or events come against us to destroy us, we should stand firm and confident that everything is going to work out for the best. We are not to change, but we must remain constant and let God do the changing of the circumstances.

When problems arise—and they will from time to time—we are not to assume that the Lord will intervene and take care of all our problems for us without our invitation. We are to pray and ask Him to change our circumstances. Then we are to remain constant and unchanging, which is a sign to the enemy of his impending downfall and destruction.

Do you know why our constancy and fearlessness are signs to Satan that he will fail? Because he knows the only way he can overcome a believer is through deception and intimidation. How can he threaten someone who has no fear of him? How can he deceive someone who recognizes his lies and refuses to believe them? What good does it do him to try to stir up fear or anger or depression in someone who will not be moved by emotions, but chooses to stand firmly on the Word of God?

When the devil sees his tactics are not working, he realizes he is failing and will be utterly defeated. Stay constant and fearless and you will overcome the enemy in your life.

[their impending] destruction, but [a clear sign] for you of deliverance *and* salvation, and that *too,* from God. ²⁹For you have been granted [the privilege] for Christ's sake, not only to believe *and* confidently trust in Him, but also to suffer for His sake, ³⁰[and so you are] experiencing the same [kind of] conflict which you saw me endure, and which you hear to be mine now.

2 THEREFORE IF there is any encouragement *and* comfort in Christ [as there certainly is in abundance], if there is any consolation of love, if there is any fellowship [that we share] in the Spirit, if [there is] any [great depth of] affection and compassion, ²make my joy complete by being of the same mind, having the same love [toward one another], knit together in spirit, intent on one purpose [and living a life that reflects your faith and spreads the gospel—the good news regarding salvation through faith in Christ]. ³Do nothing from selfishness or empty conceit [through factional motives, or strife], but with [an attitude of] humility [being neither arrogant nor self-righteous], regard others as more important than yourselves. ⁴Do not *merely* look out for your own personal interests, but also for the interests of others. ⁵Have this same attitude in yourselves which was in Christ Jesus [look to Him as your example in selfless humility], ⁶who, although He existed in the form *and* unchanging essence of God [as One with Him, possessing the fullness of all the divine attributes—the entire nature of deity], did not regard equality with God a thing to be grasped *or* asserted [as if He did not already possess it, or was afraid of losing it];

life point

Inspired by the Holy Spirit, the Apostle Paul tells us in Philippians 2:3, 4 how to avoid strife through the true spirit of humility by regarding others as "more important" than ourselves. That is a difficult challenge because our flesh wants to shout, "But what about me?"

Yet, this passage clearly exhorts us to be of the same humble mind Jesus displayed: to think of others as better than ourselves, to be more concerned for their interests and welfare than for our own, and to do nothing from conceit or empty arrogance. If we are obedient to this instruction, if we humble ourselves and are willing to serve others, we will live in harmony and therefore be pleasing to God.

⁷but emptied Himself [without renouncing or diminishing His deity, but only temporarily giving up the outward expression of divine equality and His rightful dignity] by assuming the form of a bond-servant, and being made in the likeness of men [He became completely human but was without sin, being fully God and fully man]. ⁸After He was found in [terms of His] outward appearance as a man [for a divinely-appointed time], He humbled Himself [still further] by becoming obedient [to the Father] to the point of death, even death on a cross. ⁹For this reason also [because He obeyed and so completely humbled Himself], God has highly exalted Him

life point

Jesus set the example for obedience, as we see in Philippians 2:5–8. I want to encourage you to come up to a higher level of obedience. Be quick to obey and radical in your obedience.

and bestowed on Him the name which is above every name,

¹⁰so that at the name of Jesus EVERY KNEE SHALL BOW [in submission], of those who are in heaven and on earth and under the earth, [Is 45:23]

¹¹and that every tongue will confess *and* openly acknowledge that Jesus Christ is Lord (sovereign God), to the glory of God the Father.

¹²So then, my dear ones, just as you have always obeyed [my instructions with enthusiasm], not only in my presence, but now much more in my absence, continue to work out your salvation [that is, cultivate it, bring it to full effect, actively pursue spiritual maturity] with awe-inspired fear and trembling [using serious caution and critical self-evaluation to avoid anything that might offend God or discredit the name of Christ].

¹³For it is [not your strength, but it is] God who is effectively at work in you, both to will and to work [that is, strengthening, energizing, and creating in you the longing and the ability to fulfill your purpose] for His good pleasure.

¹⁴Do everything without murmuring or questioning [the providence of God],

¹⁵so that you may prove yourselves to be blameless *and* guileless, innocent *and* uncontaminated, children of God without blemish in the midst of a [morally] crooked and [spiritually] perverted generation, among whom you are seen as bright lights [beacons shining out clearly] in the world [of darkness],

putting the Word to work

Do you ever wonder if your life as a Christian makes a difference to those around you? The Bible teaches that it certainly does! In Philippians 2:14, 15, Paul says that just as beacons brightly shine against the dark of night, so our lives as Christians shine like bright lights in the spiritual darkness of the world. Ask God to help you shine brightly with His love and joy to those around you.

¹⁶holding out *and* offering to everyone the word of life, so that in the day of Christ I will have reason to rejoice greatly because I did not run [my race] in vain nor labor without result.

¹⁷But even if I am being poured out as a drink offering on the sacrifice and service of your faith [for preaching the message of salvation], still I rejoice and share my joy with you all. [Num 28:7; 2 Tim 4:6]

¹⁸You too, rejoice in the same way and share your joy with me.

¹⁹But I hope in the Lord Jesus to send Timothy to you soon, so that I may also be encouraged by learning news about you.

²⁰For I have no one else [like him who is] so kindred a spirit who will be genuinely concerned for your [spiritual] welfare.

²¹For the others [who deserted me after my arrest] all seek [to advance] their own interests, not those of Jesus Christ.

²²But you know of Timothy's tested worth *and* his proven character, that he

speak the Word

*Thank You, God, that You are effectively at work in me
both to will and to work for Your good pleasure.*
–ADAPTED FROM PHILIPPIANS 2:13

Lord, I delight in You and I will continue to rejoice because I am in You!
–ADAPTED FROM PHILIPPIANS 3:1

has served with me to advance the gospel like a son *serving* with his father.

²³Therefore, I hope [that it is His will] to send him immediately, just as soon as I see how my case turns out;

²⁴and I trust [confidently] in the Lord that soon I also will be coming *to you.*

²⁵However, I thought it necessary to send *back* to you Epaphroditus, [who has been] my brother and companion and fellow soldier, who was also *sent as* your messenger to take care of my needs.

²⁶For he has been longing for all of you and was distressed because you had heard that he was sick.

²⁷He certainly was sick and close to death. But God had mercy on him, and not only on him but also on me, so that I would not have sorrow upon sorrow.

²⁸So I have sent him all the more eagerly so that when you see him again you may rejoice and I may be less concerned *about you.*

²⁹Welcome him *home* in the Lord with great joy, and appreciate *and* honor men like him;

³⁰because he came close to death for the work of Christ, risking his life to complete what was lacking in your service to me [which distance prevented you from rendering personally].

3 FINALLY, MY fellow believers, continue to rejoice *and* delight in the LORD. To write the same

the spiritual and the natural

In Philippians 2:25–30 we find a man named Epaphroditus who was sick due to overwork in the ministry. He was emotionally distressed and homesick. He probably was away from home a long time and possibly lonely. He became so ill he almost died. But the Apostle Paul tells us God had compassion on him and spared his life. In this passage, Paul writes to the Philippians to tell them he was sending Epaphroditus home to rest and recuperate.

I find it interesting that though God healed this man, he still needed time off to rest.

This same principle is evident in the story of Jesus' raising of a young girl from death. In the eighth chapter of Luke, we read that a Jewish religious leader named Jairus asked Jesus to come to his house and heal his twelve-year-old daughter who was dying. By the time they got to Jairus' home, the girl had already died. But Jesus raised her from the dead. As soon as she got up from her bed, the first thing Jesus told her parents was to give her something to eat (see Luke 8:55).

From those two stories I learned that there is a spiritual side to life and there is also a natural side, and both of them must be kept in balance. Jesus took care of the spiritual side of this young girl's life, but then He instructed her parents to tend to the natural side of her life.

God expects us to use common sense with our spirituality. I encourage you to live a balanced life, obeying both spiritual principles and natural laws. Even though Epaphroditus worked for the Lord, he still became ill because he did not take care of himself. We cannot break God's laws of health and expect to have no adverse consequences. Remember to stay in balance and it will help you keep the enemy out of your life.

things again is no trouble for me, and it is a safeguard for you.

²Look out for the dogs [the Judaizers, the legalists], look out for the trouble-makers, look out for the false circumcision [those who claim circumcision is necessary for salvation];

³for we [who are born-again have been reborn from above—spiritually transformed, renewed, set apart for His purpose and] are the *true* circumcision, who worship in the Spirit of God and glory *and* take pride *and* exult in Christ Jesus and place no confidence [in what we have or who we are] in the flesh—

⁴though I myself might have [some grounds for] confidence in the flesh [if I were pursuing salvation by works]. If anyone else thinks that he has reason to be confident in the flesh [that is, in his own efforts to achieve salvation], I *have* far more:

⁵circumcised when I was eight days old, of the nation of Israel, of the tribe of Benjamin, a Hebrew of Hebrews [an exemplary Hebrew]; as to the [observance of the] Law, a Pharisee;

⁶as to my zeal [for Jewish tradition], a persecutor of the church; and as to righteousness [supposed right living] which [my fellow Jews believe] is in the Law, I proved myself blameless.

⁷But whatever *former* things were gains to me [as I thought then], these things [once regarded as advancements in merit] I have come to consider as loss [absolutely worthless] for the sake of Christ [and the purpose which He has given my life].

⁸But more than that, I count everything as loss compared to the priceless privilege *and* supreme advantage of knowing Christ Jesus my Lord [and of growing more deeply and thoroughly acquainted with Him—a joy unequaled]. For His sake I have lost everything, and I consider it all garbage, so that I may gain Christ,

life point

We are not to put confidence in the flesh (see Philippians 3:3)—ours or anybody else's. Where does God want our confidence to be placed? In Him alone.

God despises independence. He wants us to be totally reliant upon Him. He wants us to be as dependent upon Him as a branch is on a vine; the branch withers quickly if it is detached from the vine (see John 15:5, 6). He wants us to lean on Him for everything in our lives and to be confident in His love and provision.

⁹and may be found in Him [believing and relying on Him], not having any righteousness of my own derived from [my obedience to] the Law *and* its rituals, but [possessing] that [genuine righteousness] which comes through faith in Christ, the righteousness which comes from God on the basis of faith.

¹⁰*And this, so* that I may know Him [experientially, becoming more thoroughly acquainted with Him, understanding the remarkable wonders of His Person more completely] and [in that same way experience] the power of His resurrection [which overflows and is active in believers], and [that I may share] the fellowship of His sufferings, by being *continually* conformed [inwardly into His likeness even] to His death [dying as He did];

¹¹so that I may attain to the resurrection [that will raise me] from the dead.

¹²Not that I have already obtained it [this goal of being Christlike] or have already been made perfect, but I actively press on so that I may take hold of that [perfection] for which Christ Jesus took hold of me *and* made me His own. [1 Cor 9:24; 1 Tim 6:12]

¹³Brothers and sisters, I do not consider that I have made it my own yet; but one thing *I do:* forgetting what *lies*

take the pressure off

In Philippians 3:9 Paul says he wants to achieve one thing in life—to be found in Christ.

This needs to be our attitude also. We cannot always manifest perfect behavior, but with God's help we can keep pressing toward the goal.

Do you know why God never allows us to achieve perfect behavior? If we ever did, we would derive our sense of worth from our perfection and performance rather than from His love and grace.

If you and I behaved perfectly all the time, we would think God owed us an answer to our prayers because of our obedience to all the rules and regulations. So do you know what God does? He leaves us some weaknesses so we have to go to Him constantly to ask for His help. Our weaknesses keep us dependent on Him whether we like it or not.

God will not let us work our way into a sense of peace and fulfillment. But He will allow us to work ourselves into a fit and frenzy. Why? So we realize that works of the flesh produce nothing but misery and frustration (see Romans 3:20).

If that is so, what are we supposed to do? Trust God, relax, and enjoy life. We need to learn to enjoy God more. That will not only help us, it will also take the pressure off the people around us. We need to quit demanding perfection from ourselves and from everyone around us. We need to start enjoying people just as they are.

In essence Paul said he wanted to stand before God and say, "Well, here I am, Lord, and though I do not have a perfect record, I do believe in Jesus. My righteousness is in Him, not in my ability to perform." I encourage you to make that your goal, too!

behind and reaching forward to what *lies* ahead,

¹⁴I press on toward the goal to win the [heavenly] prize of the upward call of God in Christ Jesus.

¹⁵All of us who are mature [pursuing spiritual perfection] should have this attitude. And if in any respect you

putting the Word to work

Do you know your purpose in life? Paul indicates in Philippians 3:12 that there is a specific, unique purpose in life for which Christ took hold of you. Ask God to continue revealing to you what your purpose is so you can lay hold of all God has for you!

have a different attitude, that too God will make clear to you.

¹⁶Only let us stay true to what we have already attained.

¹⁷Brothers and sisters, together follow my example and observe those who live by the pattern we gave you.

¹⁸For there are many, of whom I have often told you, and now tell you even with tears, who live as enemies of the cross of Christ [rejecting and opposing His way of salvation],

¹⁹whose fate is destruction, whose god is *their* belly [their worldly appetite, their sensuality, their vanity], and *whose* glory is in their shame—who focus their mind on earthly *and* temporal things.

²⁰But [we are different, because] our

life point

The devil wants each of us to concentrate on how far we have fallen, rather than how far we have risen. Satan wants us to focus on our past instead of our future and on how far we still have to go, rather than how far we have come. He wants us to think about how many times we fail, rather than how many times we succeed.

But God wants us to focus on our strengths and not our weaknesses, our victories and not our losses, our joys and not our problems. Philippians 3:13, 14 tell us that God wants us to press forward and respond to His upward call and forget "what lies behind" us. Pay attention to what you focus on and magnify the works of the Lord. Do not believe the lies of the devil.

citizenship is in heaven. And from there we eagerly await [the coming of] the Savior, the Lord Jesus Christ; [21]who, by exerting that power which enables Him even to subject everything to Himself, will [not only] transform [but completely refashion] our *earthly* bodies so that they will be like His glorious *resurrected* body.

4 THEREFORE, MY fellow believers, whom I love and long for, my delight and crown [my wreath of victory], in this way stand firm in the Lord, my beloved.
[2]I urge Euodia and I urge Syntyche to agree *and* to work in harmony in the Lord.
[3]Indeed, I ask you too, my true companion, to help these women [to keep on cooperating], for they have shared my struggle in the [cause of the] gospel, together with Clement and the rest of my fellow workers, whose names are in the Book of Life. [Dan 12:1; Mal 3:16, 17; Rev 3:5; 21:27]
[4]Rejoice in the Lord always [delight,

putting the Word to work

Have you ever thought it would be neat to be mentioned in the Bible? Imagine being known in God's Word, as Euodia and Syntyche are in Philippians 4:2, 3 for arguing! When you disagree with others, ask God to give you a gracious spirit and do all you can to resolve conflicts when they happen.

take pleasure in Him]; again I will say, rejoice! [Ps 37:4]
[5]Let your gentle *spirit* [your graciousness, unselfishness, mercy, tolerance, and patience] be known to all people. The Lord is near.
[6]Do not be anxious *or* worried about anything, but in everything [every circumstance and situation] by prayer and petition with thanksgiving, continue to make your [specific] requests known to God.
[7]And the peace of God [that peace which reassures the heart, that peace] which transcends all understanding,

life point

In Philippians 4:6 the Apostle Paul teaches us how to solve our problems. He instructs us to pray "with thanksgiving" in every circumstance.

The Lord taught the same principle to me this way: "Joyce, why should I give you anything else, if you are not thankful for what you already have? Why should I give you something else to complain about?"

If we cannot offer our current prayer requests from the foundation of a life that is currently filled with thanksgiving, we will not get a favorable response. The Word does not instruct us to pray with complaining, it says to pray with thanksgiving.

[that peace which] stands guard over your hearts and your minds in Christ Jesus [is yours]. [John 14:27]

⁸Finally, believers, whatever is true, whatever is honorable *and* worthy of respect, whatever is right *and* confirmed by God's word, whatever is pure *and* wholesome, whatever is lovely *and* brings peace, whatever is admirable *and* of good repute; if there is any excellence, if there is anything worthy of praise, think *continually* on these things [center your mind on them, and implant them in your heart].

⁹The things which you have learned

putting the Word to work

You probably spend a lot of time thinking. Do you ever think about what you are thinking about? If you are not careful, your thought life can lead you into problems. It is important to think before you act, and if you concentrate on things that are true, honorable, worthy of respect, right, pure and wholesome, lovely, admirable, and excellent (see Philippians 4:8), your actions will reflect God's character and heart.

think about what you're thinking about

The Bible presents detailed instruction concerning the kinds of things we should think about. You can see from Philippians 4:8 that we are instructed to think on good things, things that will build us up and not tear us down.

Our thoughts certainly affect our attitudes and moods. Everything the Lord tells us is for our own good. He knows what makes us happy and what makes us miserable. When people are full of wrong thoughts, they are miserable, and I have learned from personal experience that miserable people usually end up making others miserable also.

Take a personal inventory on a regular basis and ask yourself, "What have I been thinking about?" Spend some time examining your thought life.

Thinking about what you are thinking about is very valuable because Satan usually deceives people into thinking the source of their misery or trouble is something other than it really is. He wants them to think they are unhappy due to what is going on around them (their circumstances), but the misery is actually due to what is going on *inside* them (their thoughts).

For many years I believed I was unhappy because of things other people were doing or not doing. I blamed my misery on my husband and my children. I thought I would be happy if they were different, if they were more attentive to my needs, or if they helped around the house more. It was one thing and then another for years. I finally faced the truth, which was that none of these things made me unhappy if I chose to have the right attitude. My thoughts were making me miserable.

I urge you to *think about what you are thinking about*. When you change the things you allow your mind to dwell on, you are on your way to greater freedom, wholeness, and victory.

and received and heard and seen in me, practice these things [in daily life], and the God [who is the source] of peace *and* well-being will be with you.

¹⁰I rejoiced greatly in the Lord, that now at last you have renewed your concern for me; indeed, you were concerned about me *before*, but you had no opportunity to show it.

¹¹Not that I speak from [any personal] need, for I have learned to be content [and self-sufficient through Christ, satisfied to the point where I am not disturbed or uneasy] regardless of my circumstances.

¹²I know how to get along and live humbly [in difficult times], and I also know how to enjoy abundance *and* live in prosperity. In any and every circumstance I have learned the secret [of facing life], whether well-fed or going hungry, whether having an abundance or being in need.

¹³I can do all things [which He has called me to do] through Him who strengthens *and* empowers me [to fulfill His purpose—I am self-sufficient in Christ's sufficiency; I am ready for anything and equal to anything through Him who infuses me with inner strength and confident peace.]

¹⁴Nevertheless, it was right of you to share [with me] in my difficulties.

¹⁵And you Philippians know that in the early days of preaching the gospel, after I left Macedonia, no church shared with me in the matter of giving and receiving except you alone;

¹⁶for even in Thessalonica you sent *a gift* more than once for my needs.

¹⁷Not that I seek the gift itself, but I do seek the profit which increases to

life point

Philippians 4:13 is frequently quoted, especially from the King James version: "I can do all things . . . " I believe sometimes this verse is taken out of context. It does not mean I can do anything I *want* to do, or that I can do anything someone else does. It means I am able to do whatever God assigns me.

In this context the Apostle Paul refers to the ability to "get along and live humbly [in difficult times]" or how to "enjoy abundance and live in prosperity" and to be content either way (Philippians 4:12). He knew that whatever state he was in, it was God's will for him at that moment, and he also knew God would strengthen him to do what He was calling him to do. Paul believed that even unpleasant things would ultimately work out for his good (Romans 8:28).

This understanding of Philippians 4:13 helps me a great deal to deal with difficulties and remain positive in my everyday life, and it helps me in my ministry. It teaches me to remain within the boundaries of what the Lord has called and equipped me to do and not try to undertake things that are not within my God-given talents and abilities to accomplish. This attitude takes pressure off of me and it will do the same for you.

your [heavenly] account [the blessing which is accumulating for you].

¹⁸But I have received everything in

speak the Word

I declare, Lord, that I can do all the things You have called me to do through Him who strengthens and empowers me. I am ready for anything and equal to anything through Him who infuses me with inner strength and confident peace.
–ADAPTED FROM PHILIPPIANS 4:13

full and more; I am amply supplied, having received from Epaphroditus the gifts you sent me. They are the fragrant aroma of an offering, an acceptable sacrifice which God welcomes *and* in which He delights.

¹⁹And my God will liberally supply (fill until full) your every need according to His riches in glory in Christ Jesus.

²⁰To our God and Father be the glory forever and ever. Amen.

²¹Remember me to every saint in Christ Jesus. The brothers who are with me greet you.

putting the Word to work

All of us have daily needs and wants. Do you realize that sometimes what you want might not be what you need? Thank God that He knows exactly what you need and He will be faithful to provide (see Philippians 4:19).

²²All God's people wish to be remembered to you, especially those of Caesar's household.

²³The grace of the Lord Jesus Christ be with your spirit.

Colossians

Author:
Paul

Date:
About AD 61

Everyday Life Principles:
Whatever you do, keep Jesus first.

Do everything you do as though you are working for God.

Remember that you are complete and fully forgiven in Christ.

Paul's message in his letter to the Colossians is all about Jesus. In this book, Paul addresses a popular false teaching that undermined the sufficiency and lordship of Jesus Christ and was prevalent in the city of Colossae. In response, Paul wrote throughout Colossians of Jesus' power and preeminence and of His superiority over worldly thinking, legalism, and carnal Christianity. His loyalty and passion for Jesus is seen throughout this letter, and I hope his zeal inspires you today.

Among all the great teaching in Colossians, Paul continually urges us to keep Jesus first in our lives. He tells us that Christ is in us as the hope of glory (see Colossians 1:27) and reminds us that we are complete and forgiven in Him (see Colossians 2:10, 13). He also exhorts us to do everything as though we are doing it for God and not for other people (see Colossians 3:23).

As you read Colossians, my prayer for you is the same as Paul's prayer in Colossians 1:9–11: that you are filled with the knowledge of God's will, that you have spiritual wisdom and understanding, that you walk in a manner worthy of the Lord, that your life bears fruit in good works, that you steadily grow and increase in the knowledge of God, and that you are strengthened with all power and patience with joy. I also pray that you see Jesus in ways you never have before and that His presence and power will increase daily in your life.

1 PAUL, AN apostle (special messenger, personally chosen representative) of Christ Jesus (the Messiah, the Anointed) by the will of God, and Timothy our brother,

²To the saints and faithful believers in Christ [who are] at Colossae: Grace to you and peace [inner calm and spiritual well-being] from God our Father.

³We give thanks to God, the Father of our Lord Jesus Christ, as we pray always for you,

⁴for we have heard of your faith in Christ Jesus [how you lean on Him with absolute confidence in His power, wisdom, and goodness], and of the [unselfish] love which you have for all the saints (God's people);

⁵because of the [confident] hope [of experiencing that] which is reserved *and* waiting for you in heaven. You previously heard of this *hope* in the message of truth, the gospel [regarding salvation]

⁶which has come to you. Indeed, just as in the whole world *the gospel* is constantly bearing fruit and spreading [by God's power], just as *it has been doing* among you ever since the day you first heard *of it* and understood the grace of God in truth [becoming thoroughly and deeply acquainted with it].

life point

According to Colossians 1:4, faith is leaning on God in absolute trust and confidence in His power, wisdom, and goodness.

Do you know what this says to me? It says that my faith is manifested as I lean on God totally, taking all the weight off myself and placing everything on Him, trusting in: 1) His power and ability to do *what* needs to be done; 2) His wisdom and knowledge to do it *when* it needs to be done; and 3) His goodness and love to do it the *way* it needs to be done.

putting the Word to work

What kind of prayers do you pray for yourself and for others? Colossians 1:9–11 is an awesome prayer to pray. Ask God to fill you "with the knowledge of His will in all spiritual wisdom" and understanding so you can live a life worthy of Him and bear fruit. Ask Him also to strengthen you with power.

⁷You learned it from [our representative] Epaphras, our beloved fellow bond-servant, who is a faithful minister of Christ on our behalf

⁸and he also has told us of your love [well-grounded and nurtured] in the [Holy] Spirit.

⁹For this reason, since the day we heard about it, we have not stopped praying for you, asking [specifically] that you may be filled with the knowledge of His will in all spiritual wisdom [with insight into His purposes], and in understanding [of spiritual things],

¹⁰so that you will walk in a manner worthy of the Lord [displaying admirable character, moral courage, and personal integrity], to [fully] please *Him* in all things, bearing fruit in every good work and steadily growing

life point

Paul prayed that the Colossians would endure "with joy" (Colossians 1:11). Why with joy? Joy enables us to enjoy our journey in life whether we are in adverse circumstances or not. Joy is also our strength and a weapon of spiritual warfare. In addition, joy is a fruit of the Holy Spirit.

We will never experience the joy Jesus intended for us to have if we wait until every circumstance is perfect in our lives. No matter what we endure, we can pray for one another to experience God's joy. I encourage you to pray for and live in that joy.

strengthened with joy

We learn a good lesson by examining the prayers of the Apostle Paul. It seems to me that he never prayed for deliverance from difficult situations, but for the strength to endure those challenges with joy. He certainly prayed that way for the church at Colossae, as we see in Colossians 1:11.

In thirty years of ministry, I never had anyone ask me to pray for them to endure with joy, but people frequently ask me to pray for deliverance from difficult circumstances. I believe we can learn a valuable lesson from Paul's prayer.

God is more interested in changing us than He is in changing our circumstances. He does not delight in watching us suffer or have a hard time, but He does delight in our spiritual growth. If we are honest with ourselves we must admit that most of our spiritual maturity develops during the hard times in our lives, not during the easy times.

Opposition stretches us. It stretches our faith, teaches us not to trust in ourselves to solve our problems, and gives us compassion for other people who go through difficulties. The Apostle James said that our trials will eventually bring out patience or endurance, and the result of that patient endurance will be that we will lack nothing (see James 1:4). He even states that we should be exceedingly joyful in various trials and tribulations because of what they are producing in us (see James 1:2, 3).

I want to encourage you to pray as Paul prayed in Colossians 1:11. Ask for strength to endure with joy rather than wanting to avoid everything that is difficult, and remember that anything God allows will ultimately work out for your good if you trust Him and keep on praying.

in the knowledge of God [with deeper faith, clearer insight and fervent love for His precepts];

[11] [we pray that you may be] strengthened *and* invigorated with all power, according to His glorious might, to attain every kind of endurance and patience with joy;

[12] giving thanks to the Father, who has qualified us to share in the inheritance of the saints (God's people) in the Light.

[13] For He has rescued us *and* has drawn us to Himself from the dominion of darkness, and has transferred us to the kingdom of His beloved Son,

[14] in whom we have redemption [because of His sacrifice, resulting in] the forgiveness of our sins [and the cancellation of sins' penalty].

[15] He is the exact living image [the essential manifestation] of the unseen God [the visible representation of the invisible], the firstborn [the

speak the Word

Thank You, Lord, for rescuing me and drawing me to Yourself out of the dominion of darkness and transferring me into the kingdom of Your beloved Son, in Whom I have redemption and the forgiveness of sins.
—ADAPTED FROM COLOSSIANS 1:13, 14

preeminent one, the sovereign, and the originator] of all creation.

¹⁶For by Him all things were created in heaven and on earth, [things] visible and invisible, whether thrones or dominions or rulers or authorities; all things were created *and* exist through Him [that is, by His activity] and for Him.

¹⁷And He Himself existed *and* is before all things, and in Him all things hold together. [His is the controlling, cohesive force of the universe.] [Prov 8:22–31]

¹⁸He is also the head [the life-source and leader] of the body, the church; and He is the beginning, the firstborn from the dead, so that He Himself will occupy the first place [He will stand supreme and be preeminent] in everything. [1 Cor 15:20]

¹⁹For it pleased the *Father* for all the fullness [of deity—the sum total of His essence, all His perfection, powers, and attributes] to dwell [permanently] in Him (the Son),

²⁰and through [the intervention of] the Son to reconcile all things to Himself, making peace [with believers] through the blood of His cross; through Him, [I say,] whether things on earth or things in heaven.

²¹And although you were at one time estranged *and* alienated and hostile-minded [toward Him], *participating* in evil things,

first priority

When setting our priorities, it is important to understand that Jesus is the holding power of all that is good in our lives, according to Colossians 1:17. He should always be our first priority because He holds everything together.

A couple cannot have a good marriage if Jesus is not holding it together. In fact, people have difficulty having good personal relationships with *anybody* if Jesus is not leading and influencing individuals to love each other. Our finances are usually a mess without Jesus. Our thoughts are clouded and confused without Jesus. Our emotions are out of control without Him.

Colossians 1:18 tells us that Jesus is the head of the church body; therefore, He alone, in every respect, should occupy the chief place in our lives. If Jesus is not first in our lives, then we need to rearrange our priorities. Matthew 6:33 says if we "first and most importantly seek (aim at, strive after)" the kingdom of God and His righteousness, other things will be added to our lives. Righteousness is defined in the same verse as "His way of doing and being right—the attitude and character of God."

Seeking the kingdom means finding out how God wants things done; finding out how He wants us to treat people, how He wants us to act in situations and circumstances, what He wants us to do with our money, what kind of attitude we should have, even finding out what kind of entertainment Jesus approves of.

Our lives will not be blessed if we keep God in a little Sunday-morning box and let Him have our attention for only forty-five minutes, once a week during a church service. As long as we are here in this world, we will have to resist becoming like the world. Life in our world can be a daily battle, but the key to victory is to remember that Jesus holds everything together and that we need to keep Him first in our lives.

²²yet Christ has now reconciled you [to God] in His physical body through death, in order to present you before the Father holy and blameless and beyond reproach—

²³[and He will do this] if you continue in the faith, well-grounded and steadfast, and not shifting away from the [confident] hope [that is a result] of the gospel that you have heard, which was proclaimed in all creation under heaven, and of which [gospel] I, Paul, was made a minister.

²⁴Now I rejoice in my sufferings on your behalf. And with my own body I supplement whatever is lacking [on our part] of Christ's afflictions, on behalf of His body, which is the church.

²⁵In *this church* I was made a minister according to the stewardship which God entrusted to me for your sake, so that I might make the word of God fully known [among you]—

²⁶*that is,* the mystery which was hidden [from angels and mankind] for ages and generations, but has now been revealed to His saints (God's people).

²⁷God [in His eternal plan] chose to make known to them how great for the Gentiles are the riches of the glory of this mystery, which is Christ in *and* among you, the hope *and* guarantee of [realizing the] glory.

²⁸We proclaim Him, warning and instructing everyone in all wisdom [that is, with comprehensive insight into the word and purposes of God], so that we may present every person complete in Christ [mature, fully trained, and perfect in Him—the Anointed].

²⁹For this I labor [often to the point of exhaustion], striving with His power

the hope of glory

Colossians 1:26, 27 tells us that Christ "in and among" us is the Hope of glory. You and I can only realize and experience the glory of God in our lives because Christ is in us. He is our hope of seeing better things.

The glory of God is His manifested excellence. As the children of God, we have a blood-bought right to experience the best God has planned for us. Satan furiously fights the plan of God in each of our lives, and his primary weapon is deception. When we are deceived, we believe something that is not true. Even though it is not true, it seems true for us because that is what we believe.

Much of the time we feel defeated as we look at ourselves and our lack of ability. What we need to do is remember that Christ in us is our "hope and guarantee of [realizing the] glory." He keeps us encouraged enough to press on toward better things. We limit ourselves when we look to ourselves alone and fail to see Jesus.

In John 11:40 Jesus said to Martha, "Did I not say to you that if you believe [in Me], you will see the glory of God [the expression of His excellence]?" The Lord has destined His church for glory. Glory is manifested excellence and goodness. He is coming back for a glorious church (see Ephesians 5:27). We can be excellent people with excellent attitudes, excellent thoughts, and excellent words. God's glory can be manifested in us and among us only if we believe it is possible.

God is looking for someone who will believe and receive. Start expecting more of His glory in your life. He is waiting to manifest His glory to you and through you!

life point

Glory is the manifestation of God's excellence and goodness. We all want glory, but we can only hope to experience it because of God's presence in our lives as believers in Jesus Christ. That is what Paul talks about in Colossians 1:27.

Christ must live in us; otherwise there is no hope of our ever experiencing the glory of God. We can look forward to new realms of glory on a continual basis because of His grace and favor, which He gives to those who believe. Rejoice in the hope and guarantee of the glory, which is Christ in you.

and energy, which so greatly works within me.

2 FOR I want you to know how great a struggle I have for you and for those [believers] at Laodicea, and for all who [like yourselves] have never seen me face to face.
²[For my hope is] that their hearts may be encouraged as they are knit together in [unselfish] love, so that they may have all the riches that come from the full assurance of understanding [the joy of salvation], resulting in a true [and more intimate] knowledge of the mystery of God, *that is,* Christ,
³in whom are hidden all the treasures of wisdom and knowledge [regarding the word and purposes of God].
⁴I say this so that no one will deceive you with persuasive [but thoroughly deceptive] arguments.
⁵For even though I am absent [from you] in body, nevertheless I am with you in spirit, delighted to see your good discipline [as you stand shoulder to shoulder and form a solid front] and to see the stability of your faith in Christ [your steadfast reliance on Him and your unwavering confidence in His power, wisdom, and goodness].
⁶Therefore as you have received Christ Jesus the Lord, walk in [union with] Him [reflecting His character in the things you do and say—living lives that lead others away from sin],
⁷having been deeply rooted [in Him] and *now* being *continually* built up in Him and [becoming increasingly more] established *in your faith, just as you were taught, and overflowing in it with gratitude.
⁸See to it that no one takes you captive through philosophy and empty deception [pseudo-intellectual babble], according to the tradition [and musings] of *mere* men, following the elementary principles of this world, rather than following [the truth—the teachings of] Christ.
⁹For in Him all the fullness of Deity (the Godhead) dwells in bodily form [completely expressing the divine essence of God].

speak the Word

Thank You, Jesus, that all the treasures of wisdom and knowledge regarding the word and purposes of God are hidden in You. I ask You to reveal them to me.
—ADAPTED FROM COLOSSIANS 2:3

God, I pray that I would be deeply rooted and continually built up in You, becoming increasingly more established in my faith.
—ADAPTED FROM COLOSSIANS 2:7

2:7 Or *by.*

¹⁰And in Him you have been made complete [achieving spiritual stature through Christ], and He is the head over all rule and authority [of every angelic and earthly power].

¹¹In Him you were also circumcised with a circumcision not made with hands, but by the [spiritual] circumcision of Christ in the stripping off of the body of the flesh [the sinful carnal nature],

¹²having been buried with Him in baptism and raised with Him [to a new life] through [your] faith in the working of God, [as displayed] when He raised Christ from the dead.

¹³When you were dead in your sins and in the uncircumcision of your flesh (worldliness, manner of life), God made you alive together with Christ, having [freely] forgiven us all our sins,

¹⁴having canceled out the certificate of debt consisting of legal demands [which were in force] against us and which were hostile to us. And this certificate He has set aside *and* completely removed by nailing it to the cross.

¹⁵When He had disarmed the rulers and authorities [those supernatural forces of evil operating against us], He made a public example of them [exhibiting them as captives in His triumphal procession], having triumphed over them through the cross.

¹⁶Therefore let no one judge you in regard to food and drink or in regard to [the observance of] a festival or a new moon or a Sabbath day.

¹⁷Such things are only a shadow of what is to come *and* they have only symbolic value; but the substance [the reality of what is foreshadowed] belongs to Christ.

¹⁸Let no one defraud you of your prize [your freedom in Christ and your salvation] by insisting on mock humility and the worship of angels, going into detail about *visions* [he claims] he has seen [to justify his authority], puffed up [in conceit] by his unspiritual mind,

¹⁹and not holding fast to the head [of the body, Jesus Christ], from whom the entire body, supplied and knit together by its joints and ligaments, grows with the growth [that can come only] from God.

²⁰If you have died with Christ to the elementary principles of the world, why, as if you were still living in the world, do you submit to rules *and* regulations, such as,

²¹"Do not handle [this], do not taste [that], do not [even] touch!"?

²²(these things all perish with use)—in accordance with the commandments and teachings of men. [Is 29:13]

²³These practices indeed have the appearance [that popularly passes as that] of wisdom in self-made religion and mock humility and severe treatment of the body (asceticism), but are of no value against sinful indulgence [because they do not honor God].

3 THEREFORE IF you have been raised with Christ [to a new life, sharing in His resurrection from the dead], keep seeking the things that are above, where Christ is, seated at the right hand of God. [Ps 110:1]

²Set your mind *and* keep focused *habitually* on the things above [the heavenly things], not on things that are on the earth [which have only temporal value].

speak the Word

Thank You, Jesus, for disarming the supernatural forces of evil operating against me and making a public example of them by triumphing over them at the cross.
– ADAPTED FROM COLOSSIANS 2:15

³For you died [to this world], and your [new, real] life is hidden with Christ in God.

⁴When Christ, who is our life, appears, then you also will appear with Him in glory.

⁵So put to death *and* deprive of power the evil longings of your earthly body [with its sensual, self-centered instincts] immorality, impurity, *sinful* passion, evil desire, and greed, which is [a kind of] idolatry [because it replaces your devotion to God].

⁶Because of these [sinful] things the [divine] wrath of God is coming on the

life point

If you want to live the resurrection life that Jesus provides, then seek that new, powerful life by setting your mind and keeping it set on things above, not on things on the earth.

The Apostle Paul is simply saying in Colossians 3:1, 2 that if you and I want the good life, then we must keep our minds on good things.

Many believers want the good life, but they passively sit around wishing for something good to happen. Often, they are jealous of others who live in victory and are resentful that their own lives are so difficult.

If you desire victory over your problems, if you truly want to live the resurrection life, you'll need to have a backbone and not just a wishbone. You must be *determined* to have victory and refuse to settle for anything less than the best that God has for you. You must be active, not passive. Right action begins with right thinking. Do not be passive in your mind. Start today by choosing right thoughts. Set your mind on the things that are above and keep it there.

putting the Word to work

Think about your life before you became a Christian. How is your life different now? Most likely Colossians 3:5–11 describes some of the changes you have made in your life. Ask God to continue to help you put off the "old self" and put on the "new self" created in His image. Be intentional about pursuing righteousness in every area of your life.

sons of disobedience [those who fail to listen and who routinely and obstinately disregard God's precepts],

⁷and in these [sinful things] you also once walked, when you were *habitually* living in them [without the knowledge of Christ].

⁸But now rid yourselves [completely] of all these things: anger, rage, malice, slander, and obscene (abusive, filthy, vulgar) language from your mouth.

⁹Do not lie to one another, for you have stripped off the old self with its *evil* practices,

¹⁰and have put on the new [spiritual] self who is being *continually* renewed in true knowledge in the image of Him who created the new self— [Gen 1:26]

¹¹*a renewal* in which there is no [distinction between] Greek and Jew, circumcised and uncircumcised, [nor between nations whether] barbarian or Scythian, [nor in status whether] slave or free, but Christ is all, and in all [so believers are equal in Christ, without distinction].

life point

I turn to Colossians 3:12 often to remind me of what kind of behavior I should display in all situations. I remind myself that patience is not my ability to wait, but my ability to keep a good attitude while I wait. I encourage you too to exercise patience in every circumstance.

let peace be your umpire

For years, I have quoted and taught the first part of Colossians 3:15 from the Amplified Classic version of the Bible: "And let the peace (soul harmony which comes) from Christ rule (act as umpire continually) in your hearts."

The umpire in a ball game decides if a player is "in" or "out." Peace is to be the umpire that decides if something in your life should be in or out.

Many people do not enjoy peace because they are out of the will of God. They follow their own will rather than His will. They do what they feel like doing or what they think is right rather than follow God's Word and to be led by peace.

Quite often something comes up that I want to do. It sounds good, feels good, and can even be good. However, if I do not have peace about it, I have learned to leave it alone. Occasionally I am offered an opportunity for a speaking engagement that I want to take, but I do not have peace about it. I do not know why, but sometimes the peace is just not there. I have learned that if I take the opportunity anyway, I always find out later the reason that I should have followed peace and declined the offer.

One engagement I remember was when I first started traveling. I received an invitation to speak at a church in Texas. I was so excited that I immediately said I would go. As my emotions calmed down, I got a gnawing feeling on my insides every time I thought about it. It got stronger and stronger. I plainly had no peace about going, and yet God gave me no reason for the unrest. I waited and waited. Finally, I knew I had to call them and ask for a release from the commitment. I told them I would come if they could not find a suitable replacement, but for some reason, I had no peace about going. They released me from the commitment.

A few weeks later I found out that my home church was dedicating their new building the weekend I would have been in Texas. I was an associate pastor in that church for quite some time, and it was important for me to be with them on that occasion.

Why didn't the Lord just tell me what was going on? For some reason, He chose not to. His Word says to be led by peace. Many times that is all He will give you to let you know if you are in or out of His will. Later you may know why, or you may never know why.

Be led by peace. Do not buy something, especially a major purchase, if you do not have peace about it. No matter how much you want it, you will be sorry if you go against the leading of the Holy Spirit. Take time to acknowledge God in all your ways and He will direct your path (see Proverbs 3:6).

Enjoying a peaceful life is not possible if you disobey God's leading and follow your own will. If you do obey His guidance and follow peace, you will be blessed.

¹²So, as God's own chosen people, who are holy [set apart, sanctified for His purpose] and well-beloved [by God Himself], put on a heart of compassion, kindness, humility, gentleness, and patience [which has the power to endure whatever injustice or unpleasantness comes, with good temper];

¹³bearing graciously with one another, and willingly forgiving each other if one has a cause for complaint against another; just as the Lord has forgiven you, so should you forgive.

¹⁴Beyond all these things put on *and* wrap yourselves in [unselfish] love, which is the perfect bond of unity [for everything is bound together in agreement when each one seeks the best for others].

¹⁵Let the peace of Christ [the inner calm of one who walks daily with Him] be the controlling factor in your hearts [deciding and settling questions that arise]. To this *peace* indeed you were called as members in one body [of believers]. And be thankful [to God always].

¹⁶Let the [spoken] word of Christ have its home within you [dwelling in your heart and mind—permeating every aspect of your being] as you teach [spiritual things] and admonish *and* train one another with all wisdom, singing psalms and hymns and spiritual songs with thankfulness in your hearts to God.

¹⁷Whatever you do [no matter what it is] in word or deed, do everything in the name of the Lord Jesus [and in dependence on Him], giving thanks to God the Father through Him.

life point

If you let the Word have its home in your heart and mind, it will give you insight and intelligence and wisdom. Let God's Word dwell in you (see Colossians 3:16), and you will see a difference in your life!

life point

Colossians 3:22 tells us that we are to be good employees. We are to do our jobs well and with a good attitude. We are not to be two-faced, showing our employers what we think they want to see and then showing something different when they are not around. We need to be real, sincere, honest, and trustworthy all the time.

I think it is sad when those of us who have jobs grumble about them when there are so many people who do not have jobs. We should be grateful for our work and thankful we are able to do it. Thank God today for the work He has given you to do!

¹⁸Wives, be subject to your husbands [out of respect for their position as protector, and their accountability to God], as is proper *and* fitting in the Lord.

¹⁹Husbands, love your wives [with an affectionate, sympathetic, selfless love that always seeks the best for them] and do not be embittered *or* resentful toward them [because of the responsibilities of marriage].

²⁰Children, obey your parents [as God's representatives] in all things, for this [attitude of respect and obedience] is well-pleasing to the Lord [and will bring you God's promised blessings].

²¹Fathers, do not provoke *or* irritate *or* exasperate your children [with demands that are trivial or unreasonable or humiliating or abusive; nor by favoritism or indifference; treat them tenderly with lovingkindness], so they will not lose heart *and* become discouraged *or* unmotivated [with their spirits broken].

²²Servants, in everything obey those who are your masters on earth, not only with external service, as those who merely please people, but with sincerity of heart because of your fear of the Lord.

²³Whatever you do [whatever your task may be], work from the soul [that is, put in your very best effort], as [something done] for the Lord and not for men,

²⁴knowing [with all certainty] that it is from the Lord [not from men] that you will receive the inheritance which is your [greatest] reward. It is the Lord Christ whom you [actually] serve.

²⁵For he who does wrong will be punished for his wrongdoing, and [with God] there is no partiality [no special treatment based on a person's position in life].

4 MASTERS, [ON your part] deal with your slaves justly and fairly, knowing that you also have a Master in heaven. [Lev 25:43, 53]

²Be persistent *and* devoted to prayer, being alert *and* focused in your prayer life with *an attitude of* thanksgiving.

³At the same time pray for us, too, that God will open a door [of opportunity] to us for the word, to proclaim the mystery of Christ, for which I have been imprisoned;

⁴that I may make it clear [and speak boldly and unfold the mystery] in the way I should.

⁵Conduct yourself with wisdom in your interactions with outsiders (nonbelievers), make the most of each opportunity [treating it as something precious].

⁶Let your speech at all times be gracious *and* pleasant, seasoned with salt, so that you will know how to answer each one [who questions you].

⁷As to all my affairs, Tychicus, who is a much-loved brother and faithful assistant and fellow bond-servant in

speak the Word

putting the Word to work

Colossians 4:6 gives us good instruction about our speech. Do you always think before you speak? If not, you may experience trouble you could avoid. Very often we are not sensitive to other people when we open our mouth and speak. We might give correction at a time when a person needs edification or we may tell them something that causes them to worry at a time when they have many other situations they are dealing with. Not only do we need to use wisdom with our words, but timing is very important. We may need to discuss a matter with someone, but if we do it at the wrong time we will only create more problems. Ask God to give you wisdom to know when to speak, to whom to speak, and what to say.

the Lord, will give you all the information. [Eph 6:21]

⁸I have sent him to you for this very purpose, that you may know how we are doing and that he may encourage your hearts;

⁹and with him is Onesimus, our faithful and beloved brother, who is one of you. They will let you know everything about the situation here [in Rome].

¹⁰Aristarchus, my fellow prisoner, wishes to be remembered to you; as does Mark, the cousin of Barnabas (about whom you received instructions; if he comes to you, welcome him);

¹¹and from Jesus, who is called Justus. These are the only fellow workers for the kingdom of God who are from

God, I pray that You will help me be persistent and devoted to prayer, being alert and focused in my prayer life with thanksgiving.
–ADAPTED FROM COLOSSIANS 4:2

the circumcision (Jewish Christians), and they have proved to be an encouragement *and* a comfort to me.

¹²Epaphras, who is one of you and a bond-servant of Christ Jesus, sends you greetings. [He is] always striving for you in his prayers, praying with genuine concern, [pleading] that you may [as people of character and courage] stand firm, [spiritually mature] and fully assured in all the will of God.

¹³For I testify for him that he has worked strenuously for you and for the believers in Laodicea and those in Hierapolis.

¹⁴Luke, the beloved physician, and Demas greet you.

¹⁵Give my greetings to the brothers and sisters at Laodicea, and to Nympha and the church that meets in her house.

¹⁶When this letter has been read among you, see that it is read in the church of the Laodiceans; and also that you in turn read my letter [that is coming to you] from Laodicea.

¹⁷And say to Archippus, "See to it that you fulfill [carefully the duties of] the ministry which you have received in the Lord."

¹⁸I, Paul, write this greeting with my own hand. Remember my chains. May grace (God's unmerited favor and blessing) be with you.

First Thessalonians

Author:
Paul

Date:
Probably AD 51

Everyday Life Principles:
As you wait for Christ's return, honor Him and represent Him well in your everyday life.

When you suffer persecution, do so with courage and steadfast faith.

Remember the instructions in 1 Thessalonians 5:14–22 and incorporate them into your daily activities.

In every chapter of 1 Thessalonians, Paul mentions the second coming of Jesus Christ. This is a topic that has sparked interest, speculation, excitement, and controversy for years. I do not believe that trying to figure out when Jesus will return is a good use of time or energy. Instead, I believe we need to live with an awareness of His return and to conduct our everyday lives in ways that honor Him and represent Him well—treating other people as we want to be treated, keeping God first in our lives, obeying Him, and seeking to do good—while we wait.

Also in this book, Paul commends the Thessalonians' courage and steadfast faith in the midst of persecution. Their conduct serves as an example and an encouragement to us today when we are persecuted or ridiculed.

As you read 1 Thessalonians, I hope you will pay attention to all the important insights in this book, especially to 1 Thessalonians 5:14–22, which is a wonderful list of instructions for everyday life. I also want to encourage you, as Paul did the Thessalonians, to always remember that "Faithful and absolutely trustworthy is He who is calling you [to Himself for your salvation], and He will do it [He will fulfill His call by making you holy, guarding you, watching over you, and protecting you as His own]" (1 Thessalonians 5:24).

1 PAUL, SILVANUS (Silas), and Timothy,

To the church of the Thessalonians in God the Father and the Lord Jesus Christ: Grace to you and peace [inner calm and spiritual well-being from God].

²We give thanks to God always for all of you, *continually* mentioning you in our prayers;

³recalling unceasingly before our God and Father your work energized by faith, and your service motivated by love and unwavering hope in [the return of] our Lord Jesus Christ. [1 Thess 1:10]

⁴Brothers and sisters beloved by God, we know that He has chosen you;

⁵for our good news [regarding salvation] came to you not only in word, but also in [its inherent] power and in the Holy Spirit and with great conviction [on our part]. You know what kind of men we proved to be among you for your benefit.

⁶You became imitators of us and [through us] of the Lord, after you welcomed our message in [a time of] great trouble with the joy supplied by the Holy Spirit;

⁷so that you became an example to all the believers in Macedonia and in Achaia.

⁸For the word of the Lord has resounded from you *and* has echoed [like thunder], not only in Macedonia and Achaia, but in every place [the news of] your [great] faith in God has spread, so that we never need to say anything about it.

⁹For they themselves report about us, *telling* what kind of reception we had among you, and how you turned to God from idols to serve the living and true God,

¹⁰and to [look forward and confidently] wait for [the coming of] His Son from heaven, whom He raised from the dead—Jesus, who [personally] rescues us from the coming wrath [and draws us to Himself, granting us all the privileges and rewards of a new life with Him].

2 FOR YOU know, brothers and sisters, that our coming to you has not been ineffective (fruitless, in vain),

²but after we had already suffered and been outrageously treated in Philippi, as you know, yet in [the strength of] our God we summoned the courage to proclaim boldly to you the good news of God [regarding salvation] amid great opposition.

³For our appeal does not *come* from delusion or impure motives, nor [is it motivated] by deceit [our message is complete, accurate, and based on the truth—it does not change].

⁴But just as we have been approved by God to be entrusted with the gospel [that tells the good news of salvation through faith in Christ], so we speak, not as [if we were trying] to please people [to gain power and popularity], but *to please* God who examines our hearts [expecting our best].

⁵For as you well know, we never came with words of flattery nor with a pretext for greed—God is our witness—

⁶nor did we seek glory *and* honor from people, neither from you nor from anyone else, though as apostles of Christ we had the power to assert our authority.

⁷But we behaved gently when we

speak the Word

*Thank You, Lord, that I am beloved by You
and that You have chosen and selected me.*
–ADAPTED FROM 1 THESSALONIANS 1:4

were among you, like a devoted *mother* tenderly caring for her own children.

⁸Having such a deep affection for you, we were delighted to share with you not only God's good news but also our own lives, because you had become so very dear to us.

⁹For you remember, believers, our labor and hardship. We worked night and day [practicing our trade] in order not to be a [financial] burden to any of you while we proclaimed the gospel of God to you.

¹⁰You are witnesses, and so is God, how unworldly and just and blameless was our behavior toward you who believe [in our Lord Jesus Christ].

¹¹For you know how we were exhorting and encouraging and imploring each one of you just as a father does [in dealing with] his own children, [guiding you]

¹²to live lives [of honor, moral courage, and personal integrity] worthy of the God who [saves you and] calls you into His own kingdom and glory.

¹³And we also thank God continually for this, that when you received the word of God [concerning salvation] which you heard from us, you welcomed it not as the word of [mere] men, but as it truly is, the word of God, which is effectually at work in you who believe [exercising its inherent, supernatural power in those of faith].

¹⁴For you, brothers and sisters, became imitators of the churches of God in Christ Jesus that are in Judea,

life point

According to 1 Thessalonians 2:13, God is at work in your life right this very minute, whether you know it or not. I encourage you to say every day, "God is working in me right now. He is changing me!" Speak from your mouth what the Word says, not what you feel.

because you too suffered the same [kind of] persecution from your own countrymen, as they did from the Jews,

¹⁵who killed both the Lord Jesus and the prophets, and harassed *and* drove us out; and [they] continue to be highly displeasing to God and [to show themselves] hostile to all people,

¹⁶forbidding us from speaking to the Gentiles (non-Jews) so that they may be saved. So, as always, they fill up [to the brim] the measure of their sins [allotted to them by God]. But [God's] wrath has come upon them at last [completely and forever]. [Gen 15:16]

¹⁷But since we were taken away from you, believers, for a little while—in person, but not in heart—we endeavored, with great longing to see you face to face.

¹⁸For we wanted to come to you—I, Paul, again and again [wanted to come], but Satan hindered us.

¹⁹For who is [the object of] our hope or joy or our victor's wreath of triumphant celebration [when we stand] in the presence of our Lord Jesus at His coming? Is it not you?

²⁰For you are [indeed] our glory and our joy!

3 THEREFORE, WHEN we could no longer endure our separation [from you], we thought it best to be left behind, alone at Athens,

²and so we sent Timothy, our brother and God's servant in [spreading] the good news of Christ, to strengthen and encourage you [exhorting, comforting, and establishing you] in regard to your faith,

³so that no one would be unsettled by these difficulties [to which I have referred]. For you know that we have been destined for this [as something unavoidable in our position].

⁴For even when we were with you, we warned you plainly in advance that we were going to experience

persecution; and so, as you know, it has come to pass.

⁵For this reason, when I could no longer endure the suspense, I sent *someone* to find out about your faith [how you were holding up under pressure], for fear that somehow the tempter had tempted you and our work [among you] would prove to be ineffective.

⁶But now that Timothy has come back to us from [his visit with] you, and has brought us good news of your [steadfast] faith and [the warmth of your] love, and [reported] that you always think kindly of us *and* treasure your memories of us, longing to see us just as we long to see you,

⁷for this reason, brothers and sisters, during all our distress and suffering we have been comforted *and* greatly encouraged about you because of your faith [your unwavering trust in God—placing yourselves completely in His loving hands];

⁸because now we *really* live [in spite of everything], if you stand firm in the Lord.

⁹For what [adequate] thanks can we offer to God for you in return for all the joy *and* delight we have before our God on your account?

¹⁰We continue to pray night and day most earnestly that we may see you face to face, and may complete whatever may be imperfect *and* lacking in your faith.

¹¹Now may our God and Father Himself, and Jesus our Lord guide our steps to you [by removing the obstacles that stand in our way].

¹²And may the Lord cause you to increase and excel *and* overflow in love for one another, and for all people, just as we also do for you;

¹³so that He may strengthen *and* establish your hearts without blame in holiness in the sight of our God and Father at the coming of our Lord Jesus with all His saints (God's people).

4 FINALLY, BELIEVERS, we ask and admonish you in the Lord Jesus, that you follow the *instruction* that you received from us about how you ought to walk and please God (just as you are actually doing) and that you excel even more and more [pursuing a life of purpose and living in a way that expresses gratitude to God for your salvation].

putting the Word to work

Have you ever heard the saying, "You've got to look out for number one"? This means to live for yourself, because that is what everyone else is trying to do. However, as a Christian, you are called to live a life that is pleasing to God (see 1 Thessalonians 4:1). Ask Him to continually show you how to live to please Him.

²For you know what commandments *and* precepts we gave you by the *authority of* the Lord Jesus.

³For this is the will of God, that you be sanctified [separated and set apart from sin]: that you abstain *and* back away from sexual immorality;

⁴that each of you know how to control his own body in holiness and honor [being available for God's purpose and separated from things profane],

speak the Word

Lord, I pray that You would make me increase, excel, and overflow in love for my fellow believers and for all people and that You would strengthen and establish my heart in holiness in Your sight.
—ADAPTED FROM 1 THESSALONIANS 3:12, 13

putting the Word to work

Do you know that God is concerned about your body as well as your soul? God commands you to abstain from sexual immorality (see 1 Thessalonians 4:3–6) because engaging in sexual activity outside of marriage will keep you from living a holy life. Avoid situations that may tempt you or stir up lust in you. Practice fidelity in marriage and chastity in singleness.

[5]not [to be used] in lustful passion, like the Gentiles who do not know God *and* are ignorant of His will;

[6]and that [in this matter of sexual misconduct] no man *shall* transgress and defraud his brother because the Lord is the avenger in all these things, just as we have told you before and solemnly warned you.

[7]For God has not called us to impurity, but to holiness [to be dedicated, and set apart by behavior that pleases Him, whether in public or in private].

[8]So whoever rejects *and* disregards this is not [merely] rejecting man but the God who gives His Holy Spirit to you [to dwell in you and empower you to overcome temptation].

[9]Now concerning brotherly love, you have no need for *anyone* to write you, for you have been [personally] taught by God to love one another [that is, to have an unselfish concern for others and to do things for their benefit]. [Lev 19:18; John 13:34]

[10]For indeed you already do practice it toward all the believers throughout Macedonia [by actively displaying your love and concern for them]. But

life point

Did you know the Bible specifically tells us to mind our own business (see 1 Thessalonians 4:11)?

Minding our own business is a principle we need to follow, and we will discover that we enjoy life so much more when we apply it. Many times we get involved in situations that were really none of our business to begin with, and those very things end up making us miserable.

God does not give us an anointing to handle someone else's business; He gives us anointing for our "own affairs." This is why things become so messy when we get involved where we should not. There is obviously a time to help people in need, but there is also a balance that should be honored. Ask God to help you know when to get involved in a situation and when to mind your own business.

we urge you, brothers and sisters, that you excel [in this matter] more and more,

[11]and to make it your ambition to live quietly *and* peacefully, and to mind your own affairs and work with your hands, just as we directed you,

[12]so that you will behave properly toward outsiders [exhibiting good character, personal integrity, and moral courage worthy of the respect of the outside world], and be dependent on no one *and* in need of nothing [be self-supporting].

[13]Now we do not want you to be uninformed, believers, about those who are asleep [in death], so that you will not grieve [for them] as the others do

speak the Word

Thank You, Father, that You have called me to holiness—dedicated and set apart behavior that pleases You, both in public and in private.
—ADAPTED FROM 1 THESSALONIANS 4:7

who have no hope [beyond this present life].

¹⁴For if we believe that Jesus died and rose again [as in fact He did], even so God [in this same way—by raising them from the dead] will bring with Him those [believers] who have fallen asleep in Jesus.

¹⁵For we say this to you by the Lord's [own] word, that we who are still alive and remain until the coming of the Lord, will in no way precede [into His presence] those [believers] who have fallen asleep [in death].

¹⁶For the Lord Himself will come down from heaven with a shout of command, with the voice of the archangel and with the [blast of the] trumpet of God, and the dead in Christ will rise first.

¹⁷Then we who are alive and remain [on the earth] will *simultaneously* be caught up (raptured) together with them [the resurrected ones] in the clouds to meet the Lord in the air, and so we will always be with the Lord! [John 14:3; 1 Cor 15:52; 2 Cor 5:8; Phil 1:23; Col 3:4]

¹⁸Therefore comfort *and* encourage one another with these words [concerning our reunion with believers who have died].

5 NOW AS to the times and dates, brothers and sisters, you have no need for anything to be written to you.

²For you yourselves know perfectly well that the day of the [return of the] Lord is coming just as a thief [comes unexpectedly and suddenly] in the night.

³While they are saying, "Peace and safety [all is well and secure!]" then [in a moment unforeseen] destruction will come upon them suddenly like labor pains on a woman with child, and they will absolutely not escape [for there will be no way to escape the judgment of the Lord].

⁴But you, believers, [all you who believe in Christ as Savior and acknowledge Him as God's Son] are not in *spiritual* darkness [nor held by its power], that the day [of judgment] would overtake you [by surprise] like a thief;

⁵for you are all sons of light and sons of day. We do not belong to the night nor to darkness.

⁶So then let us not sleep [in spiritual indifference] as the rest [of the world does], but let us keep wide awake [alert and cautious] and let us be sober [self-controlled, calm, and wise].

⁷For those who sleep, sleep at night, and those who are drunk get drunk at night.

⁸But since we [believers] belong to the day, let us be sober, having put on the breastplate of faith and love, and as a helmet, the hope *and* confident assurance of salvation.

⁹For God has not destined us to [incur His] wrath [that is, He did not select us to condemn us], but to obtain salvation through our Lord Jesus Christ,

¹⁰who died [willingly] for us, so that whether we are awake (alive) or asleep (dead) [at Christ's appearing], we will live together with Him [sharing eternal life].

¹¹Therefore encourage *and* comfort one another and build up one another, just as you are doing.

speak the Word

Thank You, God, that You have not destined me to wrath, but to obtain salvation through Jesus Christ, Who died for me so I might live with Him and share His eternal life.
–ADAPTED FROM 1 THESSALONIANS 5:9, 10

¹²Now we ask you, brothers and sisters, to appreciate those who diligently work among you [recognize, acknowledge, and respect your leaders], who are in charge over you in the Lord and who give you instruction,

¹³and [we ask that you appreciate them and] hold them in the highest

putting the Word to work

The Bible is full of practical instructions for everyday life, and 1 Thessalonians 5:12–22 is an excellent list of exhortations for us. How can you apply these instructions practically in your everyday life?

pray without ceasing

The King James Version of 1 Thessalonians 5:17 says, "Pray without ceasing." I used to read those words and wonder, "Lord, how can I ever get to the place that I am able to pray without ceasing?" To me, the phrase, "without ceasing" meant nonstop, without ever quitting. I could not see how that type of prayer was possible.

Now I have a better understanding of Paul's instruction. He meant that prayer should be like breathing, something we do continually but often unconsciously, without being totally aware of it.

You and I live by breathing. Our physical lives require that we inhale and exhale; and the air we breathe sustains our bodies. In the same way, our spiritual lives are designed to be nurtured and sustained by prayer.

Religious thinking sometimes gives us the mistaken idea that if we do not keep up a certain schedule of prayer we miss the mark. We have become too "clock-oriented" concerning prayer. But just as we breathe all day long but never spend time counting our breaths, so we are to pray all day long without keeping track of our prayers.

I have never carried a clock around with me for reminding me to breathe every so many seconds. I have never come home from work at night and written in a journal how many times I breathed that day. I just breathe when I need to, continually and continuously, without even being aware I am doing it.

That is the way we are to be about our prayers.

I do not know how many times I pray a day; I just know I pray all throughout the day. I start praying when I get up in the morning, and I pray many times until I go to sleep at night. I also enjoy special "set apart" times for prayer, but I do not pray for only thirty minutes in the morning and then forget about God the rest of the day. As an intercessor once said, "I never pray very long at one time, but I never go very long without praying."

Does all this mean I am always thinking about prayer and spiritual things? No, there are periods when I give myself to other things, just as we all must do. But as we grow in spiritual maturity and endeavor to deepen our prayer lives, it is important for us to realize that we can pray at all times on every occasion and in every season (see Ephesians 6:18) just as naturally as we breathe. Let me encourage you to pray that way!

esteem in love because of their work [on your behalf]. Live in peace with one another.

¹⁴We [earnestly] urge you, believers, admonish those who are out of line [the undisciplined, the unruly, the disorderly], encourage the timid [who lack spiritual courage], help the [spiritually] weak, be very patient with everyone [always controlling your temper]. [Is 35:4]

¹⁵See that no one repays another with evil for evil, but always seek that which is good for one another and for all people.

¹⁶Rejoice always *and* delight in your faith;

¹⁷be unceasing *and* persistent in prayer;

¹⁸in every situation [no matter what the circumstances] be thankful *and* continually give thanks *to God;* for this is the will of God for you in Christ Jesus.

¹⁹Do not quench [subdue, or be unresponsive to the working and guidance of] the [Holy] Spirit.

give thanks

Having a thankful heart is very important. We are to be "thankful" and to "continually give thanks" (see 1 Thessalonians 5:18). We need to express our gratitude to God and to the people He uses to help and bless us. Be thankful for small things as well as big things. I often thank God for hot water in which to take a bath. I think of all the people in the world who do not even have clean water, let alone hot water, and I am reminded of how blessed I am to go to a faucet anytime I desire and get clean hot and cold water.

Voicing our thanks helps because when we do, we also remind ourselves afresh of how blessed we are. It is easy to fall into the trap of looking at what we do not have and complaining about it, but God looks for people who are thankful and give thanks in all circumstances. There is something good in everything if we will search for it.

I remember a time when I asked God to give me something I desired. He showed me that until I stopped complaining about what I already had there was no point in His giving me anything else because I would ultimately complain about that too. Why should God give us more if we complain about what we already have? Complaining grieves and quenches the Holy Spirit.

Giving thanks in all things is God's will for us, according to 1 Thessalonians 5:18. If we will not submit to His will in something like being thankful and saying so, how can we expect to be led into His will for greater things? Many people want to know what God's specific will is for their lives, but they have not yet fulfilled His general will (what His Word says to all of us) for them. We see His will throughout the Bible in instructions to be thankful, to walk in love, to give, to repent of our sins, to stay peaceful, and others. As we strive to obey God in these ways He reveals and leads us into His specific calling and will for each of us.

I encourage you to take some time every day and choose to think of all the things and people God has blessed you with and to *voice* your thankfulness to Him. Also form a habit of expressing gratitude to those who help you and make your life better. This way, you can be certain that you are fulfilling the will of God.

²⁰Do not scorn *or* reject gifts of prophecy *or* prophecies [spoken revelations— words of instruction or exhortation or warning].

²¹But test all things carefully [so you can recognize what is good]. Hold firmly to that which is good.

²²Abstain from every form of evil [withdraw and keep away from it].

²³Now may the God of peace Himself sanctify you through and through [that is, separate you from profane and vulgar things, make you pure and whole and undamaged—consecrated to Him—set apart for His purpose]; and may your spirit and soul and body be kept complete and [be found] blameless at the coming of our Lord Jesus Christ.

²⁴Faithful *and* absolutely trustworthy is He who is calling you [to Himself for your salvation], and He will do it [He will fulfill His call by making you holy, guarding you, watching over you, and protecting you as His own].

do not despise prophecy

Following the instruction in 1 Thessalonians 5:19 not to quench the Holy Spirit, we have an instruction not to despise prophesying, we are not to "scorn or reject gifts of prophecy or prophecies" (see 1 Thessalonians 5:20).

In both the Old and New Testaments, prophets were valuable vessels for God.

In the Old Testament, God spoke to His people using prophets as His mouthpieces. Wise kings listened and obeyed these prophetic words; unwise kings who refused to listen brought themselves and their kingdoms into eventual ruin. In the New Testament, we see that among the gifts God gave to the church were people who functioned as prophets (see Ephesians 4:11; 1 Corinthians 12:28). First Corinthians 14:3 describes the New Testament prophet as one who "speaks to people for edification" and who speaks to people "to uphold and advise them concerning the matters of God."

There are, of course, modern-day prophets gifted by God to foretell future events, but not everyone who prophesies is called to stand in the office of a prophet. First Corinthians 12:10 states that prophecy is "foretelling the future, speaking a new message from God to the people." I believe anointed teachers of God's Word prophesy every time they teach. They interpret, or tell forth, the divine will and counsel of God.

What does the Bible mean when it says if we despise prophesying we will quench the Holy Spirit?

First, I believe it means we must love the preaching of God's Word, or we will quench the progress the Holy Spirit desires for us to make. It is impossible to grow spiritually without God's Word. His Word is to our spirit what food is to our body; we must have it regularly to be healthy.

Second, I believe it means we should not have a judgmental or otherwise bad attitude toward the gift of prophecy or any of the other gifts of the Spirit. We should have respect for all the ways God chooses to work through people. We should cherish His gifts and honor those through whom they flow. Their gifts were given to them by the Holy Spirit for our benefit, to help us grow and mature.

life point

After encouraging us to thank God in everything, the Bible says not to "quench [subdue, or be unresponsive to the working and guidance of] the [Holy] Spirit" (1 Thessalonians 5:18, 19).

I believe one way we quench the Holy Spirit is through complaining. The truth is, we *need* the Holy Spirit to work in our lives, and the more thankful we are, the more freedom the Holy Spirit has to work in our circumstances. Our natural tendency is to complain, but to give thanks when we are tested and tried by life's circumstances is supernatural.

²⁵Brothers and sisters, pray for us.
²⁶Greet all the believers with a holy kiss [as brothers and sisters in God's family].
²⁷I solemnly charge you by the Lord

life point

Many people do not understand that we are three-part beings: spirit, soul, and body. We *are* a spirit, we *have* a soul (composed of our mind, will, and emotions), and we *live in* a body. Our new birth begins in our spirit, is carried out through our soul, and is finally visible to other people through a demonstration of God's glory in our physical lives.

Many Christians make the mistake of thinking that God cares only about the spirit. But He wants us to be whole in soul and body, too. Be blessed in the knowledge that God is faithful and will sanctify you in body, soul, and spirit.

to have this letter read before all the *congregation.
²⁸The grace of our Lord Jesus Christ be with you.

speak the Word

Lord, I declare that You are faithful and absolutely trustworthy. You will fulfill Your call by making me holy, guarding me, watching over me, and protecting me as your own.
–ADAPTED FROM 1 THESSALONIANS 5:24

5:27 Lit *brethren*.

Second Thessalonians

Author:
Paul

Date:
Probably AD 51

Everyday Life Principles:
Remember that no one knows exactly when Jesus will return. Keep a proper perspective on life as you wait.

Remember that rebellion and lawlessness are two of the characteristics of the end times. Be careful to stay submitted to the authority God has placed in your life.

Use your time wisely and spend your life doing the things you know Jesus wants you to do.

Because the people in Thessalonica did not properly understand some of the things Paul wrote to them in his first letter, he soon had to write them a second time. In this letter, he addressed the fact that some people overreacted to his comments on Jesus' return to earth. They thought the second coming of Christ was so imminent that they lost their proper perspective on life.

Like the Thessalonian believers centuries ago, you and I also wait for the return of Christ. We do not know when it will happen, but Paul's advice in this letter to them also applies to us. He tells them to watch for the signs preceding Christ's second coming: lawlessness, apostasy, rebellion against authority, and counterfeit signs and wonders, among other things (see 2 Thessalonians 2:1–9). He also encourages them to hold fast to their faith and to the truth of God and reminds them that "the Lord is faithful, and He will strengthen you [setting you on a firm foundation] and will protect and guard you from the evil one" (2 Thessalonians 3:3).

Let 2 Thessalonians encourage you to live every day as though Jesus is coming back at any minute. Do the things you want to be found doing if He were to suddenly appear. Stay at peace; keep your joy; use your time wisely; submit to authority; love God and love other people. Regardless of when He returns, Jesus will be pleased with these things in your life.

1
PAUL, SILVANUS (Silas), and Timothy,

To the church of the Thessalonians in God our Father and the Lord Jesus Christ:

²Grace to you and peace [inner calm and spiritual well-being] from God the Father and the Lord Jesus Christ.

³We ought always *and* indeed are morally obligated [as those in debt] to give thanks to God for you, brothers and sisters, as is fitting, because your faith is growing ever greater, and the [unselfish] love of each one of you toward one another is continually increasing.

⁴Therefore, we speak of you with pride among the churches of God for your steadfastness [your unflinching endurance, and patience] and your firm faith in the midst of all the persecution and [crushing] distress which you endure.

⁵*This is* a positive proof of the righteous judgment of God [a sign of His fair verdict], so that you will be considered worthy of His kingdom, for which indeed you are suffering.

⁶For after all it is *only* just for God to repay with distress those who distress you,

⁷and to *give* relief to you who are so distressed and to us as well when the Lord Jesus is revealed from heaven with His mighty angels in a flame of fire,

⁸dealing out [full and complete] vengeance to those who do not [seek to]

speak the Word

putting the Word to work

Do you know that there are Christians in the world today who cannot worship freely and have been disowned by their families, imprisoned, or even killed for their faith? I encourage you to remember and pray regularly for persecuted believers around the world. Pray they will have strength to withstand the persecution they face and remain strong in their faith, and that the name of Jesus will be glorified in and through their lives (see 2 Thessalonians 1:11, 12).

know God and to those who ignore *and* refuse to obey the gospel of our Lord Jesus [by choosing not to respond to Him].

⁹These people will pay the penalty *and* endure the punishment of everlasting destruction, banished from the presence of the Lord and from the glory of His power,

¹⁰when He comes to be glorified in His saints on that day [that is, glorified through the changed lives of those who have accepted Him as Savior and have been set apart for His purpose], and to be marveled at among all who have believed, because our testimony to you was believed *and* trusted [and confirmed in your lives].

¹¹With this in view, we constantly pray for you, that our God will count you worthy of your calling [to faith]

God, I pray that my faith will grow ever greater and that my love for others will continually increase.
–ADAPTED FROM 2 THESSALONIANS 1:3

Father, I pray that You count me worthy of my calling, and that with Your power You will fulfill every desire for goodness and complete my every work of faith, so the name of the Lord Jesus will be glorified in me, and I in Him, according to Your grace.
–ADAPTED FROM 2 THESSALONIANS 1:11, 12

and with [His] power fulfill every desire for goodness, and complete [your] every work of faith,

¹²so that the name of our Lord Jesus will be glorified in you [by what you do], and you in Him, according to the [precious] grace of our God and the Lord Jesus Christ.

2 NOW IN regard to the coming of our Lord Jesus Christ and our gathering together to *meet* Him, we ask you, brothers and sisters, [Mark 13:27; 1 Thess 2:19; 4:15–17]

²not to be quickly unsettled or alarmed either by a [so-called prophetic revelation of a] spirit or a message or a letter [alleged to be] from us, to the effect that the day of the Lord has [already] come.

³Let no one in any way deceive *or* entrap you, for *that day will not come* unless the apostasy comes first [that is, the great rebellion, the abandonment of the faith by professed Christians], and the man of lawlessness is revealed, the son of destruction [the Antichrist, the one who is destined to be destroyed], [Dan 7:25; 8:25; 1 Tim 4:1]

⁴who opposes and exalts himself [so proudly and so insolently] above every so-called god or object of worship, so that he [actually enters and] takes his seat in the temple of God, publicly proclaiming that he himself is God. [Ezek 28:2; Dan 11:36, 37]

⁵Do you not remember that when I was still with you, I was telling you these things?

⁶And you know what restrains him now [from being revealed]; it is so that he will be revealed at his own [appointed] time.

⁷For the mystery of lawlessness [rebellion against divine authority and the coming reign of lawlessness] is already at work; [but it is restrained] only until he who now restrains it is taken out of the way.

⁸Then the lawless one [the Antichrist] will be revealed and the Lord Jesus will slay him with the breath of His mouth and bring him to an end by the appearance of His coming. [Is 11:4]

⁹The coming of the [Antichrist, the lawless] one is through the activity of Satan, [attended] with great power [all kinds of counterfeit miracles] and [deceptive] signs and false wonders [all of them lies],

¹⁰and by unlimited seduction to evil *and* with all the deception of wickedness for those who are perishing, because they did not welcome the love of the truth [of the gospel] so as to be saved [they were spiritually blind, and rejected the truth that would have saved them].

¹¹Because of this God will send upon them a misleading influence, [an activity of error and deception] so they will believe the lie,

¹²in order that all may be judged *and* condemned who did not believe the truth [about their sin, and the need for salvation through Christ], but *instead* took pleasure in unrighteousness.

¹³But we should *and* are [morally] obligated [as debtors] always to give thanks to God for you, believers beloved by the Lord, because God has chosen you from the beginning for salvation through the sanctifying work of the Spirit [that sets you apart for God's purpose] and by your faith in the truth [of God's word that leads you to spiritual maturity].

speak the Word

God, I pray that You would comfort, encourage, and strengthen my heart, keeping it steadfast and on course in every good work and word.
–ADAPTED FROM 2 THESSALONIANS 2:16, 17

putting the Word to work

Encouragement is a powerful and valuable gift. Who do you receive encouragement from? When you need encouragement, remember that God Himself is always ready to encourage you (see 2 Thessalonians 2:16, 17), to bring comfort to you, and to strengthen you.

¹⁴It was to this end that He called you through our gospel [the good news of Jesus' death, burial, and resurrection], so that you may obtain *and* share in the glory of our Lord Jesus Christ.

¹⁵So then, brothers and sisters, stand firm and hold [tightly] to the traditions which you were taught, whether by word *of mouth* or by letter from us.

life point

In 2 Thessalonians 2:17, Paul prays that God will encourage the Thessalonians, "[keeping them steadfast and on course] in every good work and word." What an awesome thing it is to be good to people!

The Bible says that God anointed Jesus with the Holy Spirit and with strength, ability and power, and that Jesus went about doing good because God was with Him (see Acts 10:38). Jesus spent His days being good to all people. He helped and encouraged people everywhere He went.

We are anointed to bless people as Jesus did. God gives us the strength, ability, and power to do awesome works in His name. Take the advice of 2 Thessalonians 2:17, and strengthen your heart "in every good work and word."

speak the Word

¹⁶Now may our Lord Jesus Christ Himself and God our Father, who has loved us and given us everlasting comfort *and* encouragement and the good [well-founded] hope [of salvation] by *His* grace,

¹⁷comfort *and* encourage and strengthen your hearts [keeping them steadfast and on course] in every good work and word.

3 FINALLY, BROTHERS and sisters, pray *continually* for us that the word of the Lord will spread rapidly and be honored [triumphantly celebrated and glorified], just as it was with you;

²and [pray] that we will be rescued from perverse and evil men; for not everyone has the faith.

³But the Lord is faithful, and He will strengthen you [setting you on a firm foundation] and will protect *and* guard you from the evil *one*.

⁴We have confidence in the Lord concerning you, that you are doing and will *continue* to do the things [which] we command.

⁵May the Lord direct your hearts into the love of God and into the steadfastness *and* patience of Christ.

⁶Now we command you, believers, in the name of our Lord Jesus Christ *and*

putting the Word to work

Do you regularly pray for your pastor and other church leaders? It is important to do so (see 2 Thessalonians 3:1, 2). Pray that they are wise and effective in their ministries and that the Word of God goes forth in power. Pray also for their protection and for their families.

Thank You, Lord, that You are faithful, and that You strengthen me, set me on a firm foundation, and guard me from the evil one.
—ADAPTED FROM 2 THESSALONIANS 3:3

enjoy the wait!

In 2 Thessalonians 3:5, Paul prays for his readers to realize that God wants to work several important character traits in them. One of these qualities is patience. I have learned that patience is not my *ability* to wait; it is how I *act* while I am waiting. I need to learn to wait with a good attitude.

Waiting is a fact of life. We are going to wait no matter what we do. We actually spend more time waiting than we do receiving. Our attitudes and actions during the wait determine whether we enjoy the trip and also help determine the length of the wait.

There is a good reason we need to be patient. We must deal with attitudes that hinder us, such as: being jealous of others who already have what we are waiting for; regularly having our own "pity parties;" riding an emotional roller coaster; giving birth to "Ishmaels" in our own strength (see Genesis 16), and displaying other kinds of bad attitudes. These ways of thinking and feeling need to be worked out of us, and that's the reason we need to wait. Preparation is a process that requires time— and any length of time requires a wait.

Even when we are more mature and ready for some of God's best, we may be waiting for God to deal with the other people who will be involved with us.

God's work is intricate and multifaceted. You will be better off if you just let God work. Let God be God in your life and learn patience while He works unhealthy attitudes out of you. You will enjoy your wait so much more if you do.

by His authority, that you withdraw *and* keep away from every brother or sister who leads an undisciplined life and does not live in accordance with the tradition *and* teaching that you have received from us.

[7]For you yourselves know how you ought to follow our example, because we did not act in an undisciplined *or* inappropriate manner when we were with you [we were never idle or lazy, nor did we avoid our duties],

[8]nor did we eat anyone's bread without paying for it, but with labor and hardship we worked night and day [to pay our own way] so that we would not be a *financial* burden on any of you [for our support];

[9]not because we do not have a right *to such support,* but [we provided our own financial support] to offer ourselves as a model for you, so that you would follow our example.

life point

The Bible instructs us in 2 Thessalonians 3:10–12 to work. Why is that?

I believe people are happier and experience more joy and peace in life when they work and use their resources. We all have a built-in knowledge that it is right to make progress and wrong to sit idle and watch life pass us by.

People who do nothing are often jealous of those who prosper. I encourage you not to be jealous of what others have if you are not willing to do what they did to get it.

God expects us to manage the resources He gives us and to use them wisely so they will increase. When we follow God's instruction to work, it may be hard at times, but we will reap blessings and fulfillment in life that idle people do not possess.

¹⁰For even while we were with you, we used to give you this order: if anyone is not willing to work, then he is not to eat, either.

¹¹Indeed, we hear that some among you are leading an undisciplined *and* inappropriate life, doing no work at all, but acting like busybodies [meddling in other people's business].

¹²Now such people we command and exhort in the Lord Jesus Christ to settle down *and* work quietly and earn their own food *and* other necessities [supporting themselves instead of depending on the hospitality of others].

¹³And as for [the rest of] you, believers, do not grow tired *or* lose heart in doing good [but continue doing what is right without weakening].

¹⁴Now if anyone [in the church] does not obey what we say in this letter, take special note of that person and do not associate with him, so that he will be ashamed *and* repent.

¹⁵Do not regard him as an enemy, but keep admonishing him as a [believing] brother.

¹⁶Now may the Lord of peace Himself grant you His peace at all times *and* in every way [that peace and spiritual

do the right thing

Doing what is right occasionally or for a short while will not bring the breakthroughs we need in life. Second Thessalonians 3:13 exhorts us to continue doing the right thing without losing heart. We must do it over and over and over, and when we feel ourselves becoming weary we should go to God and wait on Him to give us fresh strength so we are enabled by His grace to press through to the completion of His will.

Doing what is right when we do not seem to be getting right results is difficult, but it must be done. When a farmer plants seed in the ground, he must keep his patient vigil over it until it finally sprouts and produces a harvest. It is a process that takes time and effort. If the farmer gives up on his garden and stops caring for it, he will miss the joy of harvest.

One of Satan's favorite things to do to us is to try to get us to give up. However, God teaches us to endure, persist, continue, and finish. He teaches us to be long-suffering, patient, determined, and steadfast.

My experience has taught me that I often have to treat other people rightly for a long time before they begin to treat me the same way. I have to do the right thing with a right attitude for a long time before I start getting right results. Just as natural seed finally takes root and the beginning of a plant breaks through the ground, we also will see breakthrough if we continue to do the right thing, regardless of what others do.

People frequently give up too easily. When their feelings quit on them, they quit too. I have learned that I can feel wrong and still choose to do what is right. One sign of spiritual maturity is the ability to live beyond our feelings. People who are spiritually mature live by decisions made based on God's Word, not on how they feel. When we advance to this stage of growth we are well on our way to a wonderful harvest that will leave us amazed.

Let me encourage you today: Do not give up; keep on keeping on!

well-being that comes to those who walk with Him, regardless of life's circumstances]. The Lord be with you all. [John 14:27]

¹⁷I, Paul, write you this final greeting with my own hand. This is the distinguishing mark in every letter [of mine, that shows it is genuine]. It is the way I write [my handwriting and signature].

¹⁸The grace of our Lord Jesus Christ be with all of you.

speak the Word

Lord, I pray that You would grant me Your peace—the peace and spiritual well-being that comes to those who walk with You, regardless of life's circumstances—at all times and in every way.
—ADAPTED FROM 2 THESSALONIANS 3:16

First Timothy

Author:
Paul

Date:
Possibly AD 63–65

Everyday Life Principles:
Pray for people, especially for those in positions of authority over you.

Pursue righteousness, godliness, faith, love, steadfastness, and gentleness in your everyday life.

Do not give up or be discouraged in your Christian walk, but fight the good fight of faith.

First Timothy is the first of two letters the Apostle Paul wrote to a young minister, his "true son in the faith," named Timothy (1 Timothy 1:2). This letter is relevant to all of us, but it is especially helpful to leaders and ministers because it includes instructions on how to lead God's people and how to deal with problems in the church.

In 1 Timothy, Paul emphasizes the importance of praying for people, especially those who are in authority. He writes, "First of all, then, I urge that petitions (specific requests), prayers, intercessions (prayers for others) and thanksgivings be offered on behalf of all people, for kings and all who are in [positions of] high authority . . ." (1 Timothy 2:1, 2). This is an instruction I take seriously, and I hope you will too.

Also in 1 Timothy, we find the qualifications and characteristics needed in church leaders, instruction on proper behavior in church services, insight on dealing with doctrinal error, and exhortation to honor widows, elders, and people in authority.

As you read 1 Timothy, I hope you will apply all of its lessons to your life. I also want to encourage you as Paul did Timothy: " . . . aim at and pursue righteousness [true goodness, moral conformity to the character of God], godliness [the fear of God], faith, love, steadfastness, and gentleness. Fight the good fight of the faith . . ." (1 Timothy 6:11, 12).

1 PAUL, AN apostle (special messenger, personally chosen representative) of Christ Jesus by the commandment of God our Savior, and of Christ Jesus (the Messiah, the Anointed) our Hope [the fulfillment of our salvation],

²to Timothy, my true son in the faith: Grace, mercy, and peace [inner calm and spiritual well-being] from God the Father and Christ Jesus our Lord.

³As I urged you when I was on my way to Macedonia, stay on at Ephesus so that you may instruct certain individuals not to teach any different doctrines,

⁴nor to pay attention to legends (fables, myths) and endless genealogies, which give rise to useless speculation *and* meaningless arguments rather than advancing God's program *of instruction* which is grounded in faith [and requires surrendering the entire self to God in absolute trust and confidence].

⁵But the goal of our instruction is love [which springs] from a pure heart and a good conscience and a sincere faith.

⁶Some individuals have wandered away from these things into empty arguments *and* useless discussions,

⁷wanting to be teachers of the Law [of Moses], even though they do not understand the terms they use or the subjects about which they make [such] confident declarations.

⁸Now we know [without any doubt] that the Law is good, if one uses it lawfully *and* appropriately,

⁹understanding the fact that law is not enacted for the righteous person [the one in right standing with God], but for lawless and rebellious people, for the ungodly and sinful, for the irreverent and profane, for those who kill their fathers or mothers, for murderers,

¹⁰for sexually immoral persons, for homosexuals, for kidnappers *and* slave traders, for liars, for perjurers—and for whatever else is contrary to sound doctrine,

¹¹according to the glorious gospel of the blessed God, with which I have been entrusted.

¹²I thank Christ Jesus our Lord, who has granted me [the needed] strength *and* made me able for this, because He considered me faithful *and* trustworthy, putting me into service [for this ministry],

¹³even though I was formerly a blasphemer [of our Lord] and a persecutor [of His church] and a shameful *and* outrageous *and* violent aggressor [toward believers]. Yet I was shown mercy because I acted out of ignorance in unbelief.

¹⁴The grace of our Lord [His amazing, unmerited favor and blessing] flowed out in superabundance [for me, together] with the faith and love which are [realized] in Christ Jesus.

¹⁵This is a faithful *and* trustworthy statement, deserving full acceptance *and* approval, that Christ Jesus came into the world to save sinners, among whom I am foremost.

¹⁶Yet for this reason I found mercy, so that in me as the foremost [of sinners], Jesus Christ might demonstrate His perfect patience as an example *or* pattern for those who would believe in Him for eternal life.

¹⁷Now to the King of the ages [eternal], immortal, invisible, the only God, be honor and glory forever and ever. Amen.

speak the Word

Thank You, Lord, that You give me all the strength and ability I need in order to do what You have called me to do.
—ADAPTED FROM 1 TIMOTHY 1:12

¹⁸This command I entrust to you, Timothy, my son, in accordance with the prophecies previously made concerning you, so that [inspired and aided] by them you may fight the good fight [in contending with false teachers],

¹⁹keeping your faith [leaning completely on God with absolute trust and confidence in His guidance] and

life point

All disobedience is sin and is the root cause of unhappiness. Our sin and disobedience grieve the Holy Spirit, especially when we know that our behavior is going against God's commands.

There are times in our lives when we disobey God, but we do it ignorantly. The Apostle Paul is an example of a person who did not know he was disobeying God before his conversion to Christ. Paul once persecuted Christians zealously and thought he was doing God a favor. He was a very religious man who sincerely believed that Christians were evil. The Lord confronted him, and Paul immediately converted to Christ and was baptized (see Acts 9:1–22). He writes in 1 Timothy 1:13 that he received mercy from God because he acted in ignorance and unbelief. Notice that he says God bestowed *superabundant* grace upon him, a chief sinner, and that he received God's mercy so Jesus Christ might be seen in him as an example to those who believe (see 1 Timothy 1:14–16).

All of our sin, whether known or unknown, must be dealt with at the cross of Jesus Christ. We do receive great mercy when we sin unintentionally, and we stand in need of God's mercy all the time. Anyone who wishes to live a life filled with the peace and joy of God's grace needs to be obedient to God.

having a good conscience; for some [people] have rejected [their moral compass] and have made a shipwreck of their faith.

²⁰Among these are Hymenaeus and Alexander, whom I have handed over to Satan, so that they will be disciplined *and* taught not to blaspheme.

2 FIRST OF all, then, I urge that petitions (specific requests), prayers, intercessions (prayers for others) and thanksgivings be offered on behalf of all people,

²for kings and all who are in [positions of] high authority, so that we may live a peaceful and quiet life in all godliness and dignity.

³This [kind of praying] is good and acceptable *and* pleasing in the sight of God our Savior,

life point

When the Apostle Paul exhorts us in 1 Timothy 2:1 to make "petitions (specific requests), prayers, intercessions (prayers for others) and thanksgivings" on behalf of all people, I believe he means we are to pray for all people everywhere. To intercede for someone is to pray for him and plead his case before the throne of God.

Jesus and the Holy Spirit are our examples; they intercede for us. Hebrews 7:25 speaks of Christ when it says: "He always lives to intercede and intervene on their behalf [with God]." In Romans 8:27, Paul teaches us that: ". . . the Spirit intercedes [before God] on behalf of God's people in accordance with God's will."

Intercession is one of the most important ways we carry on the ministry of Jesus Christ. Obey the instruction of 1 Timothy 2:1 and pray for others often. God will lead you as you pray, and blessing will be the fruit of your prayers.

putting the Word to work

Have you ever complained about the government of your country? Scripture teaches that if we want to enjoy the blessing of good government, we are to pray for all those in authority over us (see 1 Timothy 2:1, 2). Commit to pray for government officials on local, state, and national levels. Be sure to include prayers of thanksgiving for their leadership, for wisdom as they govern, and prayers for the salvation of those who do not know Jesus.

⁴who wishes all people to be saved and to come to the knowledge *and* recognition of the [divine] truth.

⁵For there is [only] one God, and [only] one Mediator between God and mankind, the Man Christ Jesus,

⁶who gave Himself as a ransom [a substitutionary sacrifice to atone] for all, the testimony given at the right *and* proper time.

⁷And for this matter I was appointed a preacher and an apostle—I am telling the truth, I am not lying [when I say this]—a teacher of the Gentiles in faith and truth.

⁸Therefore I want the men in every place to pray, lifting up holy hands, without anger and disputing *or* quarreling *or* doubt [in their mind].

⁹Likewise, *I want* women to adorn themselves modestly *and* appropriately and discreetly in proper clothing, not with [elaborately] braided hair and gold or pearls or expensive clothes,

¹⁰but instead *adorned* by good deeds [helping others], as is proper for women who profess to worship God.

be found faithful

The third chapter of 1 Timothy gives an extensive list of character qualities people need to develop if they want to lead in the body of Christ. All these requirements point to one overall qualification as a leader: We must be *faithful*. Just as God tested the Israelites in the wilderness, we must learn how to be faithful in the wilderness, faithful in the hard times. We must be faithful to keep on doing what is right, even when everything around us is wrong.

God works through and blesses faithful people, those who are faithful in the wilderness as well as in the Promised Land. Being faithful means being devoted, supportive, and loyal. Faithful people are worthy of trust or belief; they are reliable, consistent, constant, steady, and steadfast, meaning that they will stay wherever God places them and be true to those with whom God has given them to work. There is a reward for such people.

If we want to exercise authority, we must also know how to submit to authority. We must learn to be faithful and stay wherever God has placed us until He moves us. We must respect and obey those in authority over us. We also need to do the right thing simply because it is right, even though we may never understand why—which is a real test of our faithfulness and obedience.

If you want to be a spiritual leader, you desire a good thing. Expect to be tested in your faithfulness and obedience as God works these qualities in you so you will develop the faithfulness necessary for a good leader to possess.

¹¹A woman must quietly receive instruction with all submissiveness.

¹²I do not allow a woman to teach or exercise authority over a man, but to remain quiet [in the congregation].

¹³For Adam was formed first [by God from the earth], then Eve; [Gen 2:7, 21, 22]

¹⁴and it was not Adam who was deceived, but the woman who was led astray and fell into sin. [Gen 3:1–6]

¹⁵But *women* will be preserved (saved) through [the pain and dangers of] the bearing of children if they continue in faith and love and holiness with self-control *and* discretion.

3 THIS IS a faithful *and* trustworthy saying: if any man [eagerly] seeks the office of overseer (bishop, superintendent), he desires an excellent task.

²Now an overseer must be blameless *and* beyond reproach, the husband of one wife, self-controlled, sensible, respectable, hospitable, able to teach,

³not addicted to wine, not a bully *nor* quick-tempered *and* hot-headed, but gentle *and* considerate, free from the love of money [not greedy for wealth and its inherent power—financially ethical].

⁴*He must* manage his own household well, keeping his children under control with all dignity [keeping them respectful and well-behaved]

⁵(for if a man does not know how to manage his own household, how will he take care of the church of God?).

⁶and *He must* not be a new convert, so that he will not [behave stupidly and] become conceited [by appointment to this high office] and fall into the [same] condemnation incurred by

the well-rounded leader

First Timothy 3:2 tells us that spiritual leaders are to live their lives in such a way that no one has grounds to accuse them; they must be above reproach. In other words, they must behave so well that people cannot find any reason to blame them for wrongdoing.

Notice that leaders are to be self-controlled, respectable, hospitable, able to teach, and *sensible*. I love that! The biggest problem with many people, including some in the body of Christ, is that they can be just plain goofy. They do not always use common sense in decision-making. Sometimes it seems that when people become born again and filled with the Holy Spirit, or filled with God's power and ability to fulfill His will for their life, some think they have to throw all common sense out the window in order to be "spiritual." Just the opposite is true. Anyone who is going to build a ministry is also going to need a lot of plain old common sense. Notice also that leaders must be well behaved and dignified, leading orderly and disciplined lives.

Leaders need to be hospitable and friendly, especially to foreigners or those who are outsiders. For example, at social gatherings good leaders will go out of their way to make people outside their circle of family and friends feel comfortable and accepted.

Leaders must also be capable and qualified teachers. This involves teaching by example. People want to see Christians who live good, clean lives. They want to be able to trust someone, and it is our job to set good examples and pass along the principles of godly living to others.

life point

Paul asks a very important question in 1 Timothy 3:4, 5: How can a person manage the church if he does not know how to manage his own household? Paul is not talking here about dictatorial, controlling, or iron-fisted managing. The successful leader is capable of guiding, leading, and nurturing his household with godly wisdom, love, and understanding.

the devil [for his arrogance and pride]. [Is 14:12–14]

⁷And he must have a good reputation *and* be well thought of by those outside *the church,* so that he will not be discredited and fall into the devil's trap.

⁸Deacons likewise *must be* men worthy of respect [honorable, financially ethical, of good character], not double-tongued [speakers of half-truths], not addicted to wine, not greedy for dishonest gain,

⁹but upholding *and* fully understanding the mystery [that is, the true doctrine] of the [Christian] faith with a clear conscience [resulting from behavior consistent with spiritual maturity].

¹⁰These men must first be tested; then if they are found to be blameless *and* beyond reproach [in their Christian lives], let them serve as deacons.

¹¹Women must likewise be worthy of respect, not malicious gossips, but self-controlled, [thoroughly] trustworthy in all things.

¹²Deacons must be husbands of *only* one wife, and good managers of *their* children and their own households.

¹³For those who have served well as deacons gain a high standing [having a good reputation among the congregation], and great confidence in the faith which is [founded on and centered] in Christ Jesus.

¹⁴I hope to come to you before long,

life point

In 1 Timothy 3:10, Paul warns against putting people into leadership positions too quickly. Before they lead, they need to be prepared; they need to be "tested . . . found to be blameless and beyond reproach [in their Christian lives]."

Preparation for ministry involves going through some tests and some hard, dry places. Hard times change us. They can make us bitter or make us better. Hopefully they develop our character; they mature us; and they force us to look to God instead of to ourselves, to other people, or to things. We have a choice to make about how we will respond to hard times. I encourage you to make choices that will help prepare you for the great future God has planned for you.

but I am writing these instructions to you

¹⁵in case I am delayed, so that you will know how people ought to conduct themselves in the household of God, which is the church of the living God, the pillar and foundation of the truth.

¹⁶And great, we confess, is the mystery [the hidden truth] of godliness:

He (Jesus Christ) who was
　revealed in human flesh,
Was justified *and* vindicated in
　the Spirit,
Seen by angels,
Preached among the nations,
Believed on in the world,
Taken up in glory.

4 BUT THE [Holy] Spirit explicitly *and* unmistakably declares that in later times some will turn away from the faith, paying attention instead to deceitful *and* seductive spirits and doctrines of demons,

²[misled] by the hypocrisy of liars whose consciences are seared as with

putting the Word to work

To see another Christian stray from faith in Christ is sad and distressing. Yet 1 Timothy 4:1, 2 warns that before Christ comes again, there will be those who turn away from the faith. Do you know anyone who questions his or her faith? Pray that these people will not fall into deception and become hardened to spiritual truth. Guard yourself against deceptive doctrine through diligent study of the Word of God.

putting the Word to work

Do you remember when you turned sixteen? How about twenty-one? In many cultures, turning a particular age has special significance and such milestones often bring increased privileges and responsibilities. In the Christian life, however, your age is not as important as your conduct. No matter how young, you are called to live a life that is an example—in speech, conduct, love, faith, and purity—to other believers (see 1 Timothy 4:12).

a branding iron [leaving them incapable of ethical functioning],

³who forbid marriage and *advocate* abstaining from [certain kinds of] foods which God has created to be gratefully shared by those who believe and have [a clear] knowledge of the truth.

⁴For everything God has created is good, and nothing is to be rejected if it is received with gratitude;

⁵for it is sanctified [set apart, dedicated to God] by means of the word of God and prayer.

⁶If you point out these instructions to the brothers and sisters, you will be a good servant of Christ Jesus, *constantly* nourished [through study] on the words of the faith and of the good [Christian] doctrine which you have closely followed.

⁷But have nothing to do with irreverent folklore *and* silly myths. On the other hand, discipline yourself for the purpose of godliness [keeping yourself spiritually fit].

⁸For physical training is of some value, but godliness (spiritual training) is of value in everything *and* in every

way, since it holds promise for the present life and for the life to come.

⁹This is a faithful *and* trustworthy saying worthy of full acceptance *and* approval.

¹⁰It is for this that we labor and strive [often called to account], because we have fixed our [confident] hope on the living God, who is the Savior of all people, especially of those who believe [in Him, recognize Him as the Son of God, and accept Him as Savior and Lord].

¹¹Keep commanding and teaching these things.

¹²Let no one look down on [you because of] your youth, but be an example *and* set a pattern for the believers in speech, in conduct, in love, in faith, and in [moral] purity.

¹³Until I come, devote yourself to public reading [of Scripture], to preaching and to teaching [the sound doctrine of God's word].

¹⁴Do not neglect the spiritual gift within you, [that special endowment] which was intentionally bestowed on you [by the Holy Spirit] through prophetic utterance when the elders laid

speak the Word

Help me, Lord, to nourish myself on the words of the faith and of good Christian doctrine.
–ADAPTED FROM 1 TIMOTHY 4:6

their hands on you [at your ordination].

[15]Practice *and* work hard on these things; be absorbed in them [completely occupied in your ministry], so that your progress will be evident to all.

[16]Pay close attention to yourself [concentrate on your personal development] and to your teaching; persevere in these things [hold to them], for as you do this you will ensure salvation both for yourself and for those who hear you.

5 DO NOT sharply reprimand an older man, but appeal to him as [you would to] a father, to younger men as brothers,

[2]to older women as mothers, to younger women as sisters, in all purity [being careful to maintain appropriate relationships].

a Christian duty

Are you helping take care of and provide for your relatives who are unable to take care of themselves, especially parents and grandparents? Did you know that doing so is God's will and our Christian duty (see 1 Timothy 5:4)?

I was abused during my childhood and as a result, my attitude toward this biblical instruction was that I was exempt from this expectation because of how I was treated. After all, how could God expect me to take care of people who never did anything for me but hurt me? Perhaps your parents have hurt you and now you ignore them. This is understandable, but not acceptable. We must realize that "hurting people hurt people," so we must develop a merciful, forgiving attitude toward those who have wounded us. When we have truly forgiven we are then willing to help those who may not deserve to be helped. We do not deserve God's help, but He helps us anyway and He expects us to do the same for others.

Although it was difficult, there came a time when I made the decision to take care of my elderly parents and I have seen God's favor and blessing as a result. We may do other "good works," or "church work," but if we ignore this duty, we are not doing what is right. If a believer fails to provide for his relatives he is worse than an unbeliever who does perform his obligation in this matter (see 1 Timothy 5:8).

Maybe you were not ever mistreated by your parents, but are now too busy to call them, your grandparents, and your other relatives. Perhaps your schedule is too full to attend family functions. Most of our schedules are too full of things that are not even important. They are filled with things we want to do, not with things we should do. Although God wants us to be blessed and have our desires met, He first and foremost wants us to fulfill our duty as believers in Jesus Christ. If we do not care for our own families, God is not pleased.

God's Word teaches us not to hide ourselves from the needs of our own flesh and blood (see Isaiah 58:7). The instruction is followed by a promise of blessing. "Then your light will break out like the dawn, and your healing (restoration, new life) will quickly spring forth . . ." (Isaiah 58:8). Blessings do follow obedience. Let me encourage you specifically to obey 1 Timothy 5:4–8. I believe you will experience blessings as you do.

³Honor *and* help those widows who are truly widowed [alone, and without support].

⁴But if a widow has children or grandchildren [who are adults], see to it that these first learn to show great respect to their own family [as their religious duty and natural obligation], and to compensate their parents *or* grandparents [for their upbringing]; for this is acceptable *and* pleasing in the sight of God.

⁵Now a woman who is really a widow and has been left [entirely] alone [without adequate income] trusts in God and continues in supplications and prayers night and day.

⁶Whereas she who lives for pleasure *and* self-indulgence is *spiritually* dead even while she *still* lives.

⁷Keep instructing [the people to do] these things as well, so that they may be blameless *and* beyond reproach.

⁸If anyone fails to provide for his own, and especially for those of his own family, he has denied the faith [by disregarding its precepts] and is worse than an unbeliever [who fulfills his obligation in these matters].

⁹A widow is to be put on the list [to receive regular assistance] only if she is over sixty years of age, [having been] the wife of one man,

¹⁰and has a reputation for good deeds; [she is eligible] if she has brought up children, if she has shown hospitality to strangers, if she has washed the feet of the saints (God's people), if she has assisted the distressed, and has devoted herself to doing good in every way.

¹¹But refuse [to enroll the] younger widows, for when they feel their natural desires in disregard of Christ, they wish to marry *again,*

¹²and so they incur condemnation for having set aside their previous pledge.

¹³Now at the same time, they also learn to be idle as they go from house to house; and not only idle, but also

life point

First Timothy 5:8 teaches us that we have a responsibility to care for our families. We have a duty not only to care for our spouses and our children, but if we have elderly parents or grandparents, we need to provide for them as well. This is a duty for us to perform whether we feel like it or not.

You may have dependent elderly parents who never really took proper care of you. They may have even abused you. Is it really your duty to take care of them now? Yes, it is. If you cannot do it for *them*, do it for *God* with a good attitude. As you do, you will demonstrate the kind of fruit that accompanies obedient faith.

gossips and busybodies [meddlers in things that do not concern them], talking about things they should not *mention.*

¹⁴So I want younger *widows* to get married, have children, manage their households, and not give opponents of the faith any occasion for slander.

¹⁵Some [widows] have already turned away [from the faith] to follow Satan.

¹⁶If any believing woman has [dependent] widows [in her household], she must assist them [according to her ability]; and the church must not be burdened [with them], so that it may assist those who are truly widows [those who are all alone and are dependent].

¹⁷The elders who perform their leadership duties well are to be considered worthy of double honor (financial support), especially those who work hard at preaching and teaching [the word of God concerning eternal salvation through Christ].

¹⁸For the Scripture says, "YOU SHALL NOT MUZZLE THE OX WHILE IT IS TREADING OUT THE GRAIN [to keep it from

eating]," and, "The worker is worthy of his wages [he deserves fair compensation]." [Deut 25:4; Luke 10:7]

¹⁹Do not accept an accusation against an elder unless it is based on [the testimony of at least] two or three witnesses. [Deut 19:15]

²⁰As for those [elders] who continue in sin, reprimand them in the presence of all [the congregation], so that the rest will be warned.

²¹I solemnly charge you in the presence of God and of Christ Jesus and of His chosen angels that you guard *and* keep these rules without bias, doing nothing out of favoritism.

²²Do not hurry to lay hands on anyone [ordaining and approving someone for ministry or an office in the church, or in reinstating expelled offenders],

and thereby share in the sins of others; keep yourself free from sin.

²³No longer continue drinking [only] water, but use a little wine for the sake of your stomach and your frequent illnesses.

²⁴The sins of some people are conspicuous, leading the way for them into judgment [so that they are clearly not qualified for ministry]; but the sins of others appear later [for they are hidden and follow behind them].

²⁵Likewise, good deeds are quite evident, and those which are otherwise cannot be hidden [indefinitely].

6 ALL WHO are under the yoke as bond-servants (slaves) are to regard their own masters as worthy of honor *and* respect so that the name

the secret of true contentment

You may not realize it yet, but contentment is worth more than all the material possessions you can possibly accumulate in a lifetime. Nothing you have or will ever obtain is worth anything if you are not satisfied inside. The Apostle Paul referenced this when he wrote 1 Timothy 6:6.

Paul also talks about finding contentment in the fourth chapter of Philippians. He says, "I have learned to be content [and self-sufficient through Christ, satisfied to the point where I am not disturbed or uneasy] regardless of my circumstances. I know how to get along and live humbly [in difficult times], and I also know how to enjoy abundance and live in prosperity. In any and every circumstance I have learned the secret [of facing life], whether well-fed or going hungry, whether having an abundance or being in need." (Philippians 4:11, 12).

We usually do not learn contentment until we give up seeking it our own way. What usually happens is that we live discontented lives for a long time and then finally pray, "Lord, I do not want to live this way any longer. Getting this thing or having that thing is not worth it. I do not want to be miserable anymore. Just give me what You want me to have because unless You want me to have it, I do not want it. From now on I'm not going to compare myself with anyone else. I'm not going to be envious of anyone. I'm not going to be jealous of people who receive a promotion at work. I do not want what anyone else has. Lord, I want only what You want me to have and I want to be content with that."

Saying to God, "Lord, I want only what You want me to have," and meaning it, is the secret to finding peace, happiness, and contentment in life.

of God and the teaching [about Him] will not be spoken against.

²Those who have believing masters are not to be disrespectful toward them because they are brothers [in Christ], but they should serve them even better, because those who benefit from their kindly service are believers and beloved. Teach and urge these [duties and principles].

³If anyone teaches a different doctrine and does not agree with the sound words of our Lord Jesus Christ, and with the doctrine *and* teaching which is in agreement with godliness (personal integrity, upright behavior),

⁴he is conceited and woefully ignorant [understanding nothing]. He has a morbid interest in controversial questions and disputes about words, which produces envy, quarrels, verbal abuse, evil suspicions,

⁵and perpetual friction between men who are corrupted in mind and deprived of the truth, who think that godliness is a source of profit [a lucrative, money-making business—withdraw from them].

⁶But godliness *actually* is a source of great gain when accompanied by contentment [that contentment which comes from a sense of inner confidence based on the sufficiency of God].

⁷For we have brought nothing into

putting the Word to work

Are you ever tempted to think you would be more content if you had more money? This is certainly a common idea in our society, but 1 Timothy 6:6–10 warns that striving to be rich and the love of money are dangerous snares that lead to destruction, not to contentment. Ask God to help you be content in His provision for you, knowing He knows everything you need and is faithful to provide.

life point

The kingdom of God offers great benefits. As we see in 1 Timothy 6:6, one benefit is the privilege of being content and satisfied even when circumstances in our lives do not suit us.

First Timothy 6:8 says it is possible for us to be content if we have only food and clothing. Most of us have at least that, but we still have much discontentment. This verse is not saying that food and clothing are all God wants us to have, but it does say that we do not need extra things to make us happy. We are wise to be content with the basic necessities in life because we realize life does not consist of the abundance of things we possess. We may have things, but our joy and contentment cannot be in them.

the world, so [it is clear that] we cannot take anything out of it, either.

⁸But if we have food and clothing, with these we will be content.

⁹But those who [are not financially ethical and] crave to get rich [with a compulsive, greedy longing for wealth] fall into temptation and a trap and into many foolish and harmful desires that plunge people into ruin and destruction [leading to personal misery].

¹⁰For the love of money [that is, the greedy desire for it and the willingness to gain it unethically] is a root of all sorts of evil, and some by longing for it have wandered away from the faith and pierced themselves [through and through] with many sorrows.

¹¹But as for you, O man of God, flee from these things; aim at *and* pursue righteousness [true goodness, moral conformity to the character of God], godliness [the fear of God], faith, love, steadfastness, and gentleness. [2 Tim 3:17]

¹²Fight the good fight of the faith [in

the conflict with evil]; take hold of the eternal life to which you were called, and [for which] you made the good confession [of faith] in the presence of many witnesses.

[13]I *solemnly* charge you in the presence of God, who gives life to all things, and [in the presence] of Christ Jesus, who made the good confession [in His testimony] before Pontius Pilate,

[14]to keep all His precepts without stain or reproach until the appearing of our Lord Jesus Christ,

[15]which He will bring about in His own time—He who is the blessed and only Sovereign [the absolute Ruler], the King of those who reign as kings and Lord of those who rule as lords,

[16]He alone possesses immortality [absolute exemption from death] and lives in unapproachable light, whom

life point

Keeping our thoughts pure and in the will of God is a lifetime battle. We must "fight the good fight of the faith [in the conflict with evil]," according to 1 Timothy 6:12.

The mind is the battlefield on which we fight. Satan wages war in the realm of our thoughts because he knows that if he controls our thoughts, he controls us and our destinies. As we live our lives and pursue our destinies, there will be times of fighting the good fight of faith, and if we win enough battles, we will win the war.

no man has ever seen or can see. To Him be honor and eternal power *and* dominion! Amen.

[17]As for the rich in this present world,

fight the good fight

To be aggressive is to be a fighter. Just as the Apostle Paul said he fought the good fight of faith (see also 2 Timothy 4:7), so he instructed his young disciple Timothy to "fight the good fight" in 1 Timothy 6:12. In the same way, we should fight the good fight of faith in our daily lives as we struggle against spiritual enemies in high places and in our own minds and hearts.

One part of fighting the good fight of faith is the ability to recognize our enemy. As long as we are passive, Satan will torment us. Nothing is going to change about our situation if all we do is sit and wish things were different. We have to take action. Too often we do not move against the enemy when he comes against us with discouragement, fear, doubt, or guilt. We just draw back into a corner somewhere and let him beat us up. We believe his lies when we should stand against them with the truth of God's Word.

You and I are not supposed to be punching bags for the devil; instead, we are called to be fighters and respond aggressively to his attacks.

The devil tries to trick us into fighting with others around us. But God wants us to forget all the junk Satan stirs up within us to cause us to be offended toward other people. Instead, He wants us to fight against the spiritual enemies who try to war over our lives and who try to steal our peace and joy.

Take Paul's words to heart. Lay hold of the eternal life you have been called to receive and fight the good fight of faith.

instruct them not to be conceited *and* arrogant, nor to set their hope on the uncertainty of riches, but on God, who richly *and* ceaselessly provides us with everything for our enjoyment.

[18]*Instruct them* to do good, to be rich in good works, to be generous, willing to share [with others].

[19]In this way storing up for themselves the *enduring* riches of a good foundation for the future, so that they may take hold of that which is truly life.

[20]O Timothy, guard *and* keep safe the deposit [of godly truth] entrusted to you, turn away from worldly and godless chatter [with its profane, empty words], and the contradictions of what is falsely called "knowledge"—

speak the Word

putting the Word to work

If you had lots of money, would you be more secure in life? Worldly riches are uncertain (see 1 Timothy 6:17–19); true security is found in trusting God Who gives generously. If you are wealthy, you have a great responsibility to honor God with your wealth, and to be a faithful steward of it, doing good works and being eager to share your resources with others.

[21]which some have professed and by doing so have erred (missed the mark) *and* strayed from the faith.

Grace be with you.

Thank You, Lord, for richly and ceaselessly giving me everything for my enjoyment. Help me to do good, to be rich in good works, and to be generous and willing to share with others.
—ADAPTED FROM 1 TIMOTHY 6:17, 18

Second Timothy

Author:
Paul

Date:
AD 66–67

Everyday Life Principles:
Hold fast to the teachings of your Christian faith, being diligent to know, honor, and obey God's Word.

Be a good "first class" soldier of Christ Jesus.

Finish your race on earth having kept the faith.

Second Timothy is filled with encouragement, perhaps because the young man Timothy really needed it! Many scholars believe Paul wrote this letter shortly before his death, while he was suffering a much more harsh imprisonment than he previously endured. For that reason, this is quite a personal letter from the older Apostle to his spiritual son—like Paul's final instructions before he finished his course on earth.

We find many practical instructions for living the Christian life in 2 Timothy, exhortations we need to apply to our lives today. For example, we are encouraged to boldly testify of the Lord and not be ashamed of our faith; to hold fast to the teaching of the gospel; to be diligent and hardworking; to be strong in the grace that is found in Jesus; to avoid trivial disagreements that lead to strife and to endure hardship "like a good soldier of Christ Jesus" (2 Timothy 2:3); to know, honor, and obey the truth of God's Word and to fulfill God's calling on our lives.

I pray that you apply the instructions and exhortations of 2 Timothy to your life so when the time draws near for the end of your earthly life, you will be able to say, as Paul did: "I have fought the good and worthy and noble fight, I have finished the race, I have kept the faith [firmly guarding the gospel against error]" (2 Timothy 4:7).

1 PAUL, AN apostle (special messenger, personally chosen representative) of Christ Jesus (the Messiah, the Anointed) by the will of God, according to the promise of life that is in Christ Jesus,

²to Timothy, my beloved son: Grace, mercy, and peace [inner calm and spiritual well-being] from God the Father and Christ Jesus our Lord.

³I thank God, whom I worship *and* serve with a clear conscience the way my forefathers did, as I constantly remember you in my prayers night and day,

⁴and as I recall your tears, I long to see you so that I may be filled with joy.

⁵I remember your sincere *and* unqualified faith [the surrendering of your entire self to God in Christ with confident trust in His power, wisdom and goodness, a faith] which first lived in [the heart of] your grandmother Lois and your mother Eunice, and I am confident that it is in you as well.

⁶That is why I remind you to fan into flame the gracious gift of God, [that inner fire—the special endowment] which is in you through the laying on of my hands [with those of the elders at your ordination].

⁷For God did not give us a spirit of timidity *or* cowardice *or* fear, but [He has given us a spirit] of power and of love and of sound judgment *and* personal discipline [abilities that result in a calm, well-balanced mind and self-control].

⁸So do not be ashamed to testify about our Lord or about me His prisoner, but with me take your share of suffering for the gospel [continue to preach regardless of the circumstances],

life point

It appears that Timothy was becoming fearful, weary, and unsure of his call. His spirit was sinking, so Paul came in with a strong word to revive him. In 2 Timothy 1:5, 6, Paul reminded him of his faith and how it came to him. He told him in essence, "I remember your grandmother's faith. I remember your mother's faith. I remember when I laid my hands on you and we prayed for you to receive the gifts that are in you." Then he said, "Now fan the flame of the gift within you" (see 2 Timothy 1:6).

Nobody can stir up your gift or fan the flame within you the way you can. Other people can stir you up, but as soon as you are alone, you can grow cold again. That is when you have to stir up yourself. Pray, worship, and praise God. Remember what He has spoken to you. Preach to yourself if you have to. Just do whatever it takes for you to stay stirred up in God!

in accordance with the power of God [for His power is invincible],

⁹for He delivered us *and* saved us and called us with a holy calling [a calling that leads to a consecrated life—a life set apart—a life of purpose], not because of our works [or because of any personal merit—we could do nothing to earn this], but because of His own purpose and grace [His amazing, undeserved favor] which was granted to us in Christ Jesus before the world began [eternal ages ago],

¹⁰but now [that extraordinary purpose and grace] has been fully disclosed *and* realized by us through the

speak the Word

Father, I declare that You have not given me a spirit of fear.
You have given me a spirit of power and of love
and of sound judgment and personal discipline.
—ADAPTED FROM 2 TIMOTHY 1:7

power, love, and discipline

Second Timothy 1:7 tells us that "timidity," which is the same as "fear," is not from God and that God gives us power, love, sound judgment, and personal discipline.

I am going to tell you a little secret: fear will never stop coming against us. We must learn to do what God tells us to do whether we feel fear or not. We must "do it afraid" if necessary, but that is what courage does; it feels the fear and does what it should anyway.

I always thought that as long as I felt fear, I was a coward, but I have learned differently. When God told Joshua repeatedly not to fear (see Joshua 1:9; 10:8), He let him know that fear would attack him, but that he must walk in obedience to what God spoke.

We are not cowards because we feel fear. We are cowards only if we let fear rule our decisions.

Fear is a spirit that produces physical and emotional symptoms. When fear attacks us, we may feel shaky and weak or find ourselves sweating. It may take everything we can muster just to speak or move. None of that means we are cowards. The Word of God does not say "do not sweat, do not shake, do not tremble." The Word says, many times, "do not fear." The way to conquer fear is to press on through it and get to the other side of it—the side of freedom, which is the side of power.

appearing of our Savior Christ Jesus who [through His incarnation and earthly ministry] abolished death [making it null and void] and brought life and immortality to light through the gospel,

¹¹for which I was appointed a preacher and an apostle and a teacher [of this good news regarding salvation].

¹²This is why I suffer as I do. Still, I am not ashamed; for I know Him [and I am personally acquainted with Him] whom I have believed [with absolute trust and confidence in Him and in the truth of His deity], and I am persuaded [beyond any doubt] that He is able to guard that which I have entrusted to Him until that day [when I stand before Him]. [1 Cor 1:8, 3:13; Phil 1:6]

¹³Keep *and* follow the pattern of sound teaching (doctrine) which you have heard from me, in the faith and love which are in Christ Jesus.

¹⁴Guard [with greatest care] *and* keep unchanged, the treasure [that precious truth] which has been entrusted to you [that is, the good news about salvation through personal faith in Christ Jesus], through [the help of] the Holy Spirit who dwells in us.

¹⁵You are aware of the fact that all who are in [the province of] Asia turned away *and* deserted me, Phygelus and Hermogenes among them.

speak the Word

Help me, God, to guard with greatest care
and keep unchanged the precious truth that has been entrusted to me
by the help of the Holy Spirit Who dwells in me.
–ADAPTED FROM 2 TIMOTHY 1:14

¹⁶The Lord grant mercy to the family of Onesiphorus, because he often refreshed me *and* showed me kindness [comforting and reviving me like fresh air] and he was not ashamed of my chains [for Christ's sake];

¹⁷but [instead] when he reached Rome, he eagerly searched for me and found me—

¹⁸the Lord grant to him that he may find mercy from the Lord on that [great] day. You know very well how many things he did for me *and* what a help he was at Ephesus [you know better than I can tell you].

2 SO YOU, my son, be strong [constantly strengthened] *and* empowered in the grace that is [to be found only] in Christ Jesus.

²The things [the doctrine, the precepts, the admonitions, the sum of my ministry] which you have heard me teach in the presence of many witnesses, entrust [as a treasure] to reliable *and* faithful men who will also be capable *and* qualified to teach others.

³Take with me your share of hardship [passing through the difficulties which you are called to endure], like a good soldier of Christ Jesus.

⁴No soldier in active service gets entangled in the [ordinary business] affairs of civilian life; [he avoids them] so that he may please the one who enlisted him to serve.

⁵And if anyone competes as an athlete [in competitive games], he is not crowned [with the wreath of victory] unless he competes according to the rules.

⁶The hard-working farmer [who labors to produce crops] ought to be the first to receive his share of the crops.

⁷Think over the things I am saying [grasp their application], for the Lord will grant you insight *and* understanding in everything.

⁸Remember Jesus Christ [the everliving Lord who has] risen from the dead, [as the prophesied King] descended from David [king of Israel], according to my gospel [the good news that I preach], [Ps 16:10]

⁹for that [gospel] I am suffering even to [the point of] wearing chains like a criminal; but the word of God is not chained *or* imprisoned!

¹⁰For this reason I [am ready to] patiently endure all things for the sake of those who are the elect (God's chosen ones), so that they too may obtain the salvation which is in Christ Jesus and with it the reward of eternal glory.

¹¹This is a faithful *and* trustworthy saying:

If we died with Him, we will also
    live with Him;
¹²If we endure, we will also reign
    with Him;
If we deny Him, He will also deny
    us;
¹³If we are faithless, He remains
    faithful [true to His word and
    His righteous character], for He
    cannot deny Himself.

¹⁴Remind *the people* of these facts, and solemnly charge *them* in the presence of God to avoid petty controversy over words, which does no good, and [upsets and undermines and] ruins [the faith of] those who listen.

¹⁵Study *and* do your best to present yourself to God approved, a workman [tested by trial] who has no reason to be ashamed, accurately handling *and* skillfully teaching the word of truth.

speak the Word

Lord, I pray that I would be constantly strengthened and empowered in the grace found only in Christ Jesus.
—ADAPTED FROM 2 TIMOTHY 2:1

¹⁶But avoid all irreverent babble and godless chatter [with its profane, empty words], for it will lead to further ungodliness,

¹⁷and their teaching will spread like gangrene. So it is with Hymenaeus and Philetus,

¹⁸who have deviated from the truth. They claim that the resurrection has already taken place, and they undermine the faith of some.

¹⁹Nevertheless, the firm foundation of God [which He has laid] stands [sure and unshaken despite attacks], bearing this seal: "The Lord knows those who are His," and, "Let everyone who names the name of the Lord stand apart from wickedness *and* withdraw from wrongdoing." [Num 16:5; Is 26:13]

²⁰Now in a large house there are not only vessels *and* objects of gold and silver, but also vessels *and* objects of wood and of earthenware, and some are for honorable (noble, good) use and some for dishonorable (ignoble, common).

²¹Therefore, if anyone cleanses himself from these *things* [which are dishonorable—disobedient, sinful], he will be a vessel for honor, sanctified [set apart for a special purpose and], useful to the Master, prepared for every good work.

²²Run away from youthful lusts—pursue righteousness, faith, love, and peace with those [believers] who call on the Lord out of a pure heart.

²³But have nothing to do with foolish and ignorant speculations [useless disputes over unedifying, stupid controversies], since you know that they produce strife *and* give birth to quarrels.

speak the Word

life point

Second Timothy 2:16 instructs us to "avoid all irreverent babble and godless chatter [with its profane, empty words]." Instead, we need to learn to speak as God speaks. It is the Word of God spoken in truth and love from our lips that will return to Him after accomplishing His will and purpose. But in order to speak that Word in truth and love, our hearts must be right before the Lord because "the mouth speaks out of that which fills the heart," for good or for evil (Matthew 12:34).

You are bound by your words and by your declaration. You are also judged by them. That is why it is so important to place a guard upon your lips so that what issues forth from them is not only truthful, but also kind, positive, edifying, and in line with the will of God.

You can change your action and behavior, but in order to do so you must first change your thoughts and words. To do that, you need the help of the indwelling Spirit of God. Ask Him to help you. He will!

²⁴The servant of the Lord must not participate in quarrels, but must be kind to everyone [even-tempered, preserving peace, and he must be], skilled in teaching, patient *and* tolerant when wronged.

²⁵He must correct those who are in opposition with courtesy *and* gentleness in the hope that God may grant that they will repent and be led to the knowledge of the truth [accurately understanding and welcoming it],

God, I pray that You will help me study and present myself to You approved, a workman tested by trials, who has no reason to be ashamed, accurately handling and skillfully teaching the Word of truth.
—ADAPTED FROM 2 TIMOTHY 2:15

life point

In 2 Timothy 2:24 the Apostle Paul teaches us that the servants of the Lord must not "participate in quarrels." Instead, we need to be kind and good to everyone. We are to live as peacemakers, not troublemakers.

²⁶and that they may come to their senses and *escape* from the trap of the devil, having been held captive by him to do his will.

3 BUT UNDERSTAND this, that in the last days dangerous times [of great stress and trouble] will come [difficult days that will be hard to bear].

²For people will be lovers of self [narcissistic, self-focused], lovers of money [impelled by greed], boastful, arrogant, revilers, disobedient to parents, ungrateful, unholy *and* profane,

³[and they will be] unloving [devoid of natural human affection, calloused

special people for special purposes

God's Word instructs us in 2 Timothy 2:20, 21 to "be vessels for honor, sanctified, useful to the Master, prepared for every good work." To be sanctified is to be set apart for a special use.

To God, we are precious treasures. According to His great plan, we are vessels He sets aside for a special purpose. God wants to show His glory through us and to use us to bring others to Himself. We are His representatives, His ambassadors here on earth. God makes His appeal to the world through us (see 2 Corinthians 5:20).

The meaning of the word *sanctify* is very similar to the meaning of the word *dedicate*; it means to give, to offer to another, or to set aside for a purpose. If I say that a room in my house is dedicated to prayer, I mean that I want that particular room used primarily for the purpose of prayer and not for other things.

I own some dresses that I wear for fancy parties. I have set them aside in a certain place in my closet and keep them inside garment bags for protection. This makes them special; they are not used for ordinary occasions, but are set apart for special purposes. This is the way God views us; we are not meant for the world's purposes, but for God's. We are in the world, yet Jesus tells us we are not "of" the world (see John 15:19). So let me encourage you to resist the temptation to be worldly, adopting the world's ways and methods.

Even after we dedicate ourselves to God, we should regularly rededicate ourselves to our real purpose, as Romans 12:1 encourages: "Therefore I urge you, brothers and sisters, by the mercies of God, to present your bodies [dedicating all of yourselves, set apart] as a living sacrifice, holy and well-pleasing to God, which is your rational (logical, intelligent) act of worship."

It is not too much for God to ask us to dedicate every facet of our being to Him. In fact, that is actually our worship and spiritual service. Under Old Covenant law, God required animal sacrifices to atone for sin. He no longer wants dead sacrifices; He wants us offering ourselves as living sacrifices unto Him for His purpose and use. Sanctify yourself to God and be set apart and prepared for any good work!

avoid strife at all costs

Those who serve the Lord must be makers and maintainers of peace (see 2 Timothy 2:23, 24). They are not to engage in strife. Strife is bickering, arguing, heated disagreement, and an angry undercurrent. It is dangerous and destructive, like a deadly, contagious disease. It spreads rapidly unless it is confronted and stopped.

Strife destroys marriages, friendships, businesses, and churches. It is a tool Satan uses to stop the will of God. Strife or contention comes only by pride (see Proverbs 13:10). Servants of the Lord must be willing to humble themselves and go the extra mile to maintain peace. Paul told the Philippians they would complete his joy if they lived in harmony (see Philippians 2:2). Paul knew the power believers have if they commit to live in unity and agreement (see Matthew 18:19). We must pursue peace, crave it, and seek it with all of our heart and soul. Without peace we are without power!

I urge you not to get involved in conversations that lead to strife. Avoid controversies over things that really do not even matter and refuse to be involved in gossip and talebearing, which are ungodly and unnecessary. Do not spread rumors or tell other people's secrets. These things cause an angry undercurrent and they hinder or eliminate God's power and blessing. Many homes cannot prosper and be blessed because everyone is in strife. Mom and Dad bicker and argue, the siblings argue and resent one another, and nobody is happy but the devil.

I want to repeat that strife is very dangerous and that as servants of the Lord we must not be part of it. It is good and pleasant when brothers dwell together in unity. Unity releases anointing (God's presence and power) and it is also where God commands a blessing to be released (see Psalm 133).

God instructed Dave and me to stay out of strife when we began our ministry. He showed us that He could not bless us and we would not succeed if we allowed strife in our marriage, home, or ministry. We have worked diligently over the years to keep strife out of our lives. It requires willingness to constantly communicate and confront issues. Strife will not go away if it is ignored; it must be dealt with. I encourage you to ask for the Holy Spirit's help to be a person who avoids strife and restores peace everywhere you go.

and inhumane], irreconcilable, malicious gossips, devoid of self-control [intemperate, immoral], brutal, haters of good,

⁴traitors, reckless, conceited, lovers of [sensual] pleasure rather than lovers of God,

⁵holding to a form of [outward] godliness (religion), although they have denied its power [for their conduct nullifies their claim of faith]. Avoid

life point

Just as Paul predicted long ago when he wrote 2 Timothy 3:1, 2, we live in an ungrateful generation. It seems the more people have, the less they appreciate.

As believers, we are in the world, but we must strive not to be like the world. The more others around us complain, the more we should express gratitude to God.

putting the Word to work

Does it seem to you that we are living in perilous times? Think of the world around you as you read 2 Timothy 3:1–5; you probably see evidence of many of the vices described. In times such as these, it's necessary for believers to stand strong in the truth of God's Word and have nothing to do with people who seem religious but do not exhibit true godliness or spiritual power.

such people *and* keep far away from them.

⁶For among them are those who worm their way into homes and captivate *morally* weak *and* spiritually-dwarfed women weighed down by [the burden of their] sins, easily swayed by various impulses,

⁷always learning *and* listening to anybody who will teach them, but never able to come to the knowledge of the truth.

⁸Just as Jannes and Jambres [the court magicians of Egypt] opposed Moses, so these *men* also oppose the truth, men of depraved mind, unqualified *and* worthless [as teachers] in regard to the faith. [Ex 7:11]

⁹But they will not get very far, for their meaningless nonsense *and* ignorance will become obvious to everyone, as was that of Jannes and Jambres.

¹⁰Now you have diligently followed [my example, that is] my teaching, conduct, purpose, faith, patience, love, steadfastness,

¹¹persecutions, and sufferings—such as happened to me at Antioch, at Iconium, and at Lystra; what persecutions I endured, but the Lord rescued me from them all! [2 Cor 12:10]

¹²Indeed, all who delight in pursuing righteousness *and* are determined to live godly lives in Christ Jesus will be hunted *and* persecuted [because of their faith].

life point

Second Timothy 3:12 tells us that we will suffer persecution as believers. Satan brings opposition, trouble, trials, and tribulations in the hope of driving us away from God. If we intend to succeed at being victorious believers and being all God wants us to be, we must be prepared to stand strong in times of persecution.

If we will stay standing on the inside, God will take care of the outside. If we do what we can do, God will do what we cannot do.

¹³But evil men and impostors will go on from bad to worse, deceiving and being deceived.

¹⁴But as for you, continue in the things that you have learned and of which you are convinced [holding tightly to the truths], knowing from whom you learned *them,*

¹⁵and how from childhood you have known the sacred writings (Hebrew Scriptures) which are able to give you the wisdom that leads to salvation through faith which is in Christ Jesus [surrendering your entire self to Him and having absolute confidence in His wisdom, power and goodness].

¹⁶All Scripture is God-breathed [given by divine inspiration] and is profitable for instruction, for conviction [of sin], for correction [of error and restoration to obedience], for training

putting the Word to work

Though written by men, all of Scripture is divinely inspired (literally, God-breathed), and it is our authority and rule for faith and life (see 2 Timothy 3:16). What can you do to become a more serious student of God's Word, the Bible, so you can be complete and equipped "for every good work" (see 2 Timothy 3:17)?

in righteousness [learning to live in conformity to God's will, both publicly and privately—behaving honorably with personal integrity and moral courage];

¹⁷so that the man of God may be complete *and* proficient, outfitted *and* thoroughly equipped for every good work.

4 I SOLEMNLY charge you in the presence of God and of Christ Jesus, who is to judge the living and the dead, and by His appearing and His kingdom:

²preach the word [as an official messenger]; be ready when the time is right and *even* when it is not [keep your sense of urgency, whether the opportunity seems favorable or unfavorable, whether convenient or inconvenient, whether welcome or unwelcome]; correct [those who err in doctrine or behavior], warn [those who sin], exhort *and* encourage [those who are growing toward spiritual maturity], with inexhaustible patience and [faithful] teaching.

³For the time will come when people will not tolerate sound doctrine *and* accurate instruction [that challenges them with God's truth]; but *wanting* to have their ears tickled [with something pleasing], they will accumulate for themselves [many] teachers [one after another, chosen] to satisfy their own desires *and* to support the errors they hold,

⁴and will turn their ears away from the truth and will wander off into myths *and* man-made fictions [and will accept the unacceptable].

⁵But as for you, be clear-headed in every situation [stay calm and cool and steady], endure every hardship [without flinching], do the work of an evangelist, fulfill [the duties of] your ministry.

⁶For I am already being poured out as a drink offering, and the time of my departure [from this world] is at hand *and* I will soon go free. [Num 15:1–12; 28:7; Phil 2:17]

⁷I have fought the good *and* worthy *and* noble fight, I have finished the race, I have kept the faith [firmly guarding the gospel against error].

⁸In the future there is reserved for me the [victor's] crown of righteousness [for being right with God and doing right], which the Lord, the righteous Judge, will award to me on that [great] day—and not to me only, but also to all those who have loved *and* longed for *and* welcomed His appearing.

⁹Make every effort to come to me soon;

¹⁰for Demas, having loved [the pleasures of] this present world, has

putting the Word to work

Have you ever waited for the "perfect time" to share your faith with someone? The truth of the matter is that there may not always be the perfectly right time to share, but it is important to be ready to take advantage of every opportunity God gives to share your faith and to proclaim and teach His Word. Pray that God will help you recognize every opportunity and give you boldness to share!

life point

In 2 Timothy 4:5, Paul gives Timothy some helpful instructions on how to handle his ministry. What he says is good advice for all of us. If we are calm, cool, and steady, people know they can depend on us. God can depend on us. No one has to wonder what we might be like one day from the next. When our unsaved friends see the calm and steady faith we have, they will be open to our testimony of the gospel. Stability is a necessary trait in every believer's life, one that brings personal blessings and peace that attracts others.

deserted me and gone to Thessalonica; Crescens *has gone* to Galatia, Titus to Dalmatia.

¹¹Only Luke is with me. Get Mark and bring him with you, for he is very helpful to me for the ministry.

¹²But Tychicus I have sent to Ephesus.

¹³When you come bring the coat that I left at Troas with Carpus, and the books, especially the parchments.

¹⁴Alexander the coppersmith did me great harm; [but that is no concern of mine, for] the Lord will repay him according to his actions.

¹⁵Be on guard against him yourself, because he vigorously opposed our message.

¹⁶At my first trial no one supported me [as an advocate] *or* stood with me, but they all deserted me. May it not be counted against them [by God].

¹⁷But the Lord stood by me and strengthened *and* empowered me, so that through me the [gospel] message might be fully proclaimed, and that all the Gentiles might hear it; and I was rescued from the mouth of the lion.

¹⁸The Lord will rescue me from every evil assault, and He will bring me safely into His heavenly kingdom; to Him be the glory forever and ever. Amen.

¹⁹Give my greetings to Prisca and Aquila, and to the household of Onesiphorus.

²⁰Erastus stayed on at Corinth, but I left Trophimus sick at Miletus.

²¹Try your best to come [to me] before winter. Eubulus wishes to be remembered to you, as do Pudens and Linus and Claudia and all the brothers and sisters.

²²The Lord be with your spirit. Grace be with you.

the heart of a hero

Paul experienced a lot to bring the gospel to the early world. He was persecuted, beaten, and thrown in prison for preaching the Good News. Many times he suffered because of opposition, as he describes in 2 Timothy 4:14–16.

In this passage, Paul says, "Alexander the coppersmith did me great harm; [but that is no concern of mine, for] the Lord will repay him according to his actions."

How much better our lives would be if we took that attitude toward many things, if we would simply cast our cares on the Lord and allow Him to handle them for us.

In verse 16, Paul says that no one supported him at his trial. I wonder how we would feel if we suffered everything Paul went through to bless so many others only to end up without a single soul to stand up for us in our time of greatest need. Paul risked his very life for others, yet they were not willing to be associated with him for fear they might be punished too.

What was Paul's response to their abandonment? He prayed that their failure would not be laid to their charge. That shows us his heart.

We can go through the Bible and look at the great men and women of God, and we can quickly see why they were called "heroes of the faith" (see Hebrews 11). It was not because they were smarter than everybody else or because they had more going for them in the natural realm than others. It was simply because they had great hearts. Ask God to give you the heart of a hero too.

Titus

Author:
Paul

Date:
Probably between AD 63–65

Everyday Life Principles:
Good Christian doctrine should lead to good Christian living.

Be diligent and enthusiastic about doing good works in order to demonstrate your love for Jesus.

Make sure your good works are led and empowered by the Holy Spirit.

Titus, like Timothy, was a young minister who followed Paul's leadership and received oversight of the church in Crete. This church seems unorganized and full of people who needed much instruction and correction. To help Titus, Paul wrote this letter, which addresses several subjects he also wrote about in 1 Timothy. In Titus, Paul emphasizes the proper structure of the church, solid doctrine, and godly living, especially in the form of good works.

In fact, Paul writes in Titus 2:14 that Jesus, "gave Himself [to be crucified] on our behalf to redeem us and purchase our freedom from all wickedness, and to purify for Himself a chosen and very special people to be His own possession, who are enthusiastic for doing what is good." We must remember that people know us as believers by our fruit; we reveal our love for Jesus more through what we do than through any other means.

As you read the book of Titus, I pray you will remember how important it is to be in a good church and to submit to godly spiritual leadership. I also hope you will remember to demonstrate your faith by good works and by living a holy life. Remember that good works and holiness for the sake of good works and holiness will result in legalism, but when these endeavors are led and empowered by the Holy Spirit, they will bring life to you and to others.

1 PAUL, A bond-servant of God and an apostle (special messenger, personally chosen representative) of Jesus Christ, for the faith of God's chosen ones and [to lead and encourage them to recognize and pursue] the knowledge of the truth which leads to godliness,

²based on the hope *and* divine guarantee of eternal life, [the life] which God, who is ever truthful *and* without deceit, promised before the ages of time began,

³and at the appointed time has made known His word *and* revealed it as His message, through preaching, which was entrusted to me according to the command of God our Savior—

⁴To Titus, my true child in a common faith: Grace and peace [inner calm and spiritual well-being] from God the Father and Christ Jesus our Savior.

⁵For this reason I left you *behind* in Crete, so that you would set right what remains *unfinished,* and appoint elders in every city as I directed you,

⁶*namely,* a man of unquestionable integrity, the husband of one wife, having children who believe, not accused of being immoral or rebellious.

⁷For the overseer, as God's steward, must be blameless, not self-willed, not quick-tempered, not addicted to wine, not violent, not greedy for dishonest gain [but financially ethical].

⁸And *he must be* hospitable [to believers, as well as strangers], a lover of what is good, sensible (upright), fair, devout, self-disciplined [above reproach—whether in public or in private].

life point

In many of Paul's epistles, he greets his readers with a message of "grace and peace," just as he does in Titus 1:4. We cannot enjoy peace unless we understand and receive grace. Ask God to help you receive grace so you can be at peace.

⁹He must hold firmly to the trustworthy word [of God] as it was taught to him, so that he will be able both to give accurate instruction in sound [reliable, error-free] doctrine and to refute those who contradict [it by explaining their error].

¹⁰For there are many rebellious men who are empty talkers [just windbags] and deceivers; especially those of the circumcision [those Jews who insist that Gentile believers must be circumcised and keep the Law in order to be saved].

¹¹They must be silenced, because they are upsetting whole families by teaching things they should not teach for the purpose of dishonest *financial* gain.

¹²One of them [Epimenides, a Cretan], a prophet of their own, said, "Cretans are always liars, evil beasts, lazy gluttons."

¹³This description is true. So rebuke them sharply so that they will be sound in the faith *and* free from doctrinal error,

¹⁴not paying attention to Jewish myths and the commandments *and* rules of men who turn their backs on the truth.

¹⁵To the pure, all things are pure; but to the corrupt and unbelieving, nothing is pure; both their mind and their conscience are corrupted.

putting the Word to work

Having godly church leaders is so important. Paul specifically addresses the character and responsibilities of church leaders called elders in Titus 1:5–16. Do you know who the various leaders of your church are? Be sure to pray for them often, and ask God to continue to build in them the character, spiritual maturity, and abilities necessary to be wise and faithful church leaders.

¹⁶They profess to know God [to recognize and be acquainted with Him], but by *their* actions they deny *and* disown Him. They are detestable and disobedient and worthless for good work of any kind.

2 BUT AS for you, teach the things which are in agreement with sound doctrine [which produces men and women of good character whose lifestyle identifies them as true Christians].

²Older men are to be temperate, dignified, sensible, sound in faith, in love, in steadfastness [Christlike in character].

³Older women similarly are to be reverent in their behavior, not malicious gossips nor addicted to much wine, teaching what is right *and* good,

⁴so that they may encourage the young women to tenderly love their husbands and their children,

⁵to be sensible, pure, makers of a home [where God is honored], good-natured, being subject to their own husbands, so that the word of God will not be dishonored.

⁶In a similar way urge the young men

walk the talk

Paul instructed Titus to teach good sound doctrine and to teach people to live right so they might be identified as true Christians (see Titus 2:1). One of the greatest needs of the church today is credibility. The reputation of Christianity has been terribly hurt by people who tell others what to do but do not do it themselves. They are people who call themselves Christians but do not conduct their lives as Christians should; in other words, they do not "walk the talk." Those of us chosen by God to live at this point in history have an opportunity to repair the damage done by others who have gone before us. We must each choose an excellent lifestyle that displays the true attributes of Jesus Christ.

The way you live your life is very important! When you put a Christian bumper sticker on your car, wear jewelry with the cross on it or shirts with scriptures, and go to church, people watch you—and they look for authenticity.

Wearing a bracelet with the letters "WWJD" became a fad at one time. The initials stood for "What would Jesus do?" Wearing a bracelet is nice, but what is inside a person should match what he or she promotes on the outside. How would you like it if you saw a grocery store sign and when you went inside you found hardware? You would be aggravated because what was advertised was not what was offered. I believe the world feels the same way about people who advertise Christianity through bumper stickers, jewelry, T-shirts, and church attendance but do not live the life they should.

The Bible is filled with instructions on how to live. It teaches us how to think, talk, and act, as well as who to associate with and how to manage our money. It also teaches us not to be lazy or out of balance in any area. What good does it do to have a "Jesus loves you" bumper sticker on our car and then break the speed limit, refuse to wear a seat belt, and park in handicapped parking spaces when we are not handicapped? I encourage you to examine your life regularly and make sure the way you live accurately represents what you say you believe. Be authentic!

how to live the good life

In Titus 2:14, Paul writes that Jesus gave His life so that we could be people who are "enthusiastic for doing what is good."

We are not to spend our lives moping around, depressed, discouraged, and despondent. We are also not to spend so much time thinking about all of our faults that we lose our hope and enthusiasm about living a good life.

God is not honored by people who have bad attitudes toward themselves; in fact, that is insulting to Him. If you loved and valued a group of people so much that you were willing to suffer horribly and die for them so they could enjoy themselves and their lives, how would you feel if they refused your gift? I pray you see what I am trying to say.

Paul said that he knew he was not perfect, but he pressed on to lay hold of that for which Christ Jesus laid hold of him and made him His own (see Philippians 3:12). He was speaking of the quality of life Jesus wanted him to have. Paul knew he did not deserve it, but for Jesus' sake he was determined to have it. Likewise, we do not deserve "the good life," but Jesus died to give it to us, so we honor Him when we receive it with eagerness and enthusiasm.

If you struggle with negative attitudes that hold you back from the good things of God in your life, I urge you to make a change today. Choose a new attitude toward yourself. Paul had to make that choice, I had to make it, and you'll need to make it also if you want to glorify God with your life.

to be sensible *and* self-controlled *and* to behave wisely [taking life seriously].

⁷And in all things show yourself to be an example of good works, with purity in doctrine [having the strictest regard for integrity and truth], dignified,

⁸sound *and* beyond reproach in instruction, so that the opponent [of the faith] will be shamed, having nothing bad to say about us.

⁹Urge bond-servants to be subject to their own masters in everything, to be pleasing and not talk back,

¹⁰not stealing [things, regardless of value], but proving themselves trustworthy, so that in every respect they will adorn *and* do credit to the teaching of God our Savior.

¹¹For the [remarkable, undeserved] grace of God that brings salvation has appeared to all men.

¹²It teaches us to reject ungodliness and worldly (immoral) desires, and to live sensible, upright, and godly lives [lives with a purpose that reflect spiritual maturity] in this present age,

¹³awaiting *and* confidently expecting the [fulfillment of our] blessed hope

speak the Word

Lord, in all things let my life be to others an example of good works.
—ADAPTED FROM TITUS 2:7

Thank You, Lord, for Your remarkable, undeserved grace, which brings salvation to everyone.
—ADAPTED FROM TITUS 2:11

putting the Word to work

Most people are familiar with the term VIP – Very Important Person. Do you know that Jesus gave Himself for you in order to make you His own special person (see Titus 2:14)? He redeemed you from evil and made you holy. He has also given you a desire to do good works. Ask God to show you each day the good works He has prepared for you to do and then be eager to do them!

and the glorious appearing of our great God and Savior, Christ Jesus, [14]who [willingly] gave Himself [to be crucified] on our behalf to redeem us *and* purchase our freedom from all wickedness, and to purify for Himself a chosen *and* very special people to be His own possession, *who are* enthusiastic for doing what is good. [Deut 14:2; Ps 130:8; Ezek 37:23]

[15]Tell *them* these things. Encourage and rebuke with full authority. Let no one disregard *or* despise you [conduct yourself and your teaching so as to command respect].

prepare to prosper

God does not do anything without first being ready for it; neither will He allow us to do His work without adequate preparation.

In Titus 3:1, Paul writes, "Be ready and willing to do good" And in 2 Timothy 2:15 he instructs his young disciple: "Study and do your best to present yourself to God approved, a workman [tested by trial] who has no reason to be ashamed, accurately handling and skillfully teaching the word of truth."

Your process of becoming ready may mean going to Bible college or getting some other kind of formal training, or it may mean spending a few years working under someone else's authority so you know how to handle your life in the future. It could mean working at a job you do not particularly like for a boss of whom you are not very fond. It could also mean spending some years in which your basic needs are met, but you are definitely not living in abundance because you are learning how to believe God for prosperity and how to handle it when it comes.

Many people desire to prosper, but not all want to prepare to prosper.

Preparation can take place in a lot of different settings and has many different phases. Each phase we go through in our preparation is important. There is something to be learned at every step. It is all part of our preparation. We must "graduate," so to speak, from each phase or level into the next one, and this comes after we prove ourselves on the current level. Between all of these stages of preparation, there is a lot of waiting.

Unless we learn to wait well, we will be miserable. Miserable people are usually grouchy, critical, and generally hard to get along with. Miserable people usually make other people miserable.

Enjoy the trip! Being miserable will not make it any shorter, but it can make it longer. Realize that you are in training and becoming equipped for something great in the kingdom. Prepare to prosper.

life point

Titus 3:1 encourages us to be submissive to our authorities. If you are not in a position of leadership in your job or in your church, it's important for you to have a healthy attitude toward the people who are. With God, the attitude of the heart is everything. We can do what our bosses tell us to do while murmuring and grumbling behind their backs, but if we do that, we are not the kind of employees the Bible tells us to be. We may seem to get away with this attitude for a while, but we will not be rewarded.

Our reward comes from obeying the specific calling God places on our lives, not from trying to be like someone else or managing to accomplish great things. God rewards those who follow an obedient lifestyle, which includes submission to authority. If we will simply do what God asks us to do and be who He made us to be, His rewards will chase us down and flood our lives.

3 REMIND PEOPLE to be subject to rulers and authorities, to be obedient, to be ready *and* willing to do good,

²to slander *or* abuse no one, to be kind *and* conciliatory and gentle, showing unqualified consideration *and* courtesy toward everyone.

³For we too once were foolish, disobedient, deceived, enslaved to various *sinful* desires and pleasures, spending *and* wasting our life in malice and envy, hateful, hating one another.

speak the Word

Thank You, Lord, for saving me not because of any work of righteousness that I have done, but because of Your compassion and mercy, which you poured out so richly through Jesus Christ my Savior.
—ADAPTED FROM TITUS 3:5

putting the Word to work

What country do you live in? As a Christian, you are a citizen of God's kingdom and you are also a citizen of your earthly country. You submit to God, and you should also be obedient to civil laws and authorities (see Titus 3:1). As you respect those in authority and obey the laws of the land, you have an opportunity to demonstrate principles of the kingdom of God as you do so peaceably, in humility, without speaking evil of anyone, and being considerate and courteous toward everyone (see Titus 3:1, 2). You will bless others and honor God as you do so.

⁴But when the goodness *and* kindness of God our Savior and *His* love for mankind appeared [in human form as the Man, Jesus Christ],

⁵He saved us, not because of any works of righteousness that we have done, but because of His own compassion *and* mercy, by the cleansing of the new birth (spiritual transformation, regeneration) and renewing by the Holy Spirit,

⁶whom He poured out richly upon us through Jesus Christ our Savior,

⁷so that we would be justified [made free of the guilt of sin] by His [compassionate, undeserved] grace, and that we would be [acknowledged as acceptable to Him and] made heirs of eternal life [actually experiencing it] according to our hope (His guarantee).

⁸This is a faithful *and* trustworthy saying; and concerning these things I want you to speak with great confidence,

so that those who have believed God [that is, those who have trusted in, relied on, and accepted Christ Jesus as Savior,] will be careful to participate in doing good *and* honorable things. These things are excellent [in themselves] and profitable for the people. ⁹But avoid foolish *and* ill-informed *and* stupid controversies and genealogies and dissensions and quarrels about the Law, for they are unprofitable and useless.

putting the Word to work

Do you know someone who argues incessantly? Not only can this be frustrating, but the Word of God warns that there is no room for division in the life of the church, and that a person who brings division is sinning (see Titus 3:9–11). Pray and work for unity in your church and in the entire body of Christ.

¹⁰After a first and second warning reject a divisive man [who promotes heresy and causes dissension—ban him from your fellowship and have nothing more to do with him], ¹¹well aware that such a person is twisted and is sinning; he is convicted *and* self-condemned [and is gratified by causing confusion among believers]. ¹²When I send Artemas or [perhaps] Tychicus to you, make every effort to come to me at Nicopolis, for I have decided to spend the winter there. ¹³Do your best to help Zenas the lawyer and Apollos on their way; see that they are supplied *and* lack nothing. ¹⁴Our people must learn to do good deeds to meet necessary demands [whatever the occasion may require], so that they will not be unproductive. ¹⁵All who are with me greet you. Greet those who love us in the faith.

Grace be with all of you.

Philemon

Author:
Paul

Date:
AD 60–61

Everyday Life Principles:
There may come a time when you need to "go to bat" for fellow believers. If so, be sure to handle the matter in an orderly fashion.

If you find yourself in a tense situation involving other believers, remember that humility and genuine love never fail.

As a believer in Jesus Christ, do everything you can as the Holy Spirit leads you to bring mutual respect, unity, and reconciliation among the Christians in your life.

Philemon is a very short book with a very important message. From prison, Paul wrote this letter to his friend, a prominent and wealthy Christian man named Philemon. According to the customs of his time, Philemon was a slave-owner. His slave, Onesimus, escaped, went to Rome, became converted, and met Paul. When Paul realized what happened, he decided to write Philemon and encourage reconciliation and forgiveness between the two men.

Paul handled this matter very well, in an orderly fashion. Relationships among Christians are not perfect, and there are times when a third party needs to be involved. When this happens, interactions must take place in order and with the right heart attitudes.

Paul opens his letter by addressing Philemon as "our dearly beloved friend," making sure to show respect and affection for a fellow believer (Philemon 1). He then affirms Philemon's work and ministry before confronting Philemon with the need to take Onesimus back not as his slave but to receive him as a Christian brother. Throughout this letter, there is a tone of friendship and unity in Christ. Paul's humility and genuine love for both Philemon and Onesimus are evident and allow him to make a bold request for their reconciliation.

Let Paul's letter to Philemon serve as an example for handling relationships in an orderly way, and let it encourage you to handle all of your relationships properly, with a humble heart. Seek to bring love, forgiveness, and restoration everywhere you go.

¹PAUL, A prisoner [for the sake] of Christ Jesus (the Messiah, the Anointed), and our brother Timothy,

To Philemon our dearly beloved friend and fellow worker,

²and to [your wife] Apphia our sister, and to Archippus our fellow soldier [in ministry], and to the church that meets in your house:

³Grace to you and peace [inner calm and spiritual well-being] from God our Father and the Lord Jesus Christ.

⁴I thank my God always, making mention of you in my prayers,

⁵because I hear of your love and of your faith which you have toward the Lord Jesus and toward all the saints (God's people).

⁶I pray that the sharing of your faith may become effective *and* powerful because of your *accurate* knowledge of every good thing which is ours in Christ.

putting the Word to work

Do you thank God for the people He has placed in your life? Paul did, and we read about his prayers for Philemon in Philemon 4–6. Be sure to thank God often for the people He blesses you with and let them know you are praying for them.

⁷For I have had great joy and comfort *and* encouragement from your love, because the hearts of the saints (God's people) have been refreshed through you, my brother.

⁸Therefore [on the basis of these facts], though I have enough confidence in Christ to order you to do what is appropriate,

⁹yet for love's sake I prefer to appeal *to you*—since I am such a person as Paul, an old man, and now also a prisoner [for the sake] of Christ Jesus—

speak the Word

life point

The sharing of our faith becomes effective and powerful because of our "accurate knowledge of every good thing which is ours *in Christ*" (Philemon 6, emphasis mine), not by acknowledging everything that is wrong with *us*.

The devil wants us to acknowledge every bad thing we see in ourselves. He is known as the "accuser of our [believing] brothers" (Revelation 12:10), and he continually tries to redirect our focus from who we are in Christ back onto our shortcomings. He bombards us with opportunities to think negative thoughts about ourselves so we will return to that pattern of thinking, which many of us learned growing up. We will fall again into the deception that our worth is based on our performance, and because of our faults, we are worthless.

One reason it is so important to avoid speaking negatively about ourselves is that we believe what we say more than what anybody else says. But once we truly understand who we are in Christ and see how much He did for us through shedding His blood to make us worthy, we will realize we actually insult our heavenly Father by excessively meditating on our faults, flaws, and failures.

Rather than dwell on your inadequacies, focus on every good thing that is yours through your identification with Jesus Christ.

¹⁰I appeal to you for my [own spiritual] child Onesimus, whom I have fathered [in the faith] while a captive in these chains.

Thank You, God, for giving me grace and peace—inner calm and spiritual well-being.
−ADAPTED FROM PHILEMON 3

life point

In Philemon 8–21, Paul encourages Philemon to forgive Onesimus. Forgiveness is extending love and mercy to someone who has wronged or hurt you. It is not saying that what was done was acceptable, or that it did not matter; it is a choice to release the person from the burden of guilt for what they have done wrong and not allow that offense to affect your relationship. Have you ever wronged someone and received forgiveness from them? If so, you know that forgiveness clears the way for reconciliation. If there is someone you need to receive forgiveness from or extend forgiveness to, do not procrastinate. Seek the restoration of your relationship through forgiveness.

¹¹Once he was useless to you, but now he is indeed useful to you as well as to me.

¹²I have sent him back to you in person, that is, *like sending* my very heart.

¹³I would have chosen to keep him with me, so that he might minister to me on your behalf during my imprisonment for the gospel;

¹⁴but I did not want to do anything without first getting your consent, so that your goodness would not be, in effect, by compulsion but of your own free will.

¹⁵Perhaps it was for this reason that he was separated from you for a while, so that you would have him back forever,

¹⁶no longer as a slave, but [as someone] more than a slave, as a brother [in Christ], especially dear to me, but how

putting the Word to work

God's Word encourages us to be hospitable (see Philemon 22). Extending hospitality is a great way to show appreciation for traveling ministers or missionaries or to people who are lonely. In what ways can you show hospitality to visitors, newcomers, or people who need a friend?

much more to you, both in the flesh [as a servant] and in the Lord [as a fellow believer]. [Col 4:9]

¹⁷So if you consider me a partner, welcome *and* accept him as you would me.

¹⁸But if he has wronged you in any way or owes you anything, charge that to my account;

¹⁹I, Paul, write this with my own hand, I will repay it *in full* (not to mention to you that you owe to me even your own self as well).

²⁰Yes, brother, let me have some benefit *and* joy from you in the Lord; refresh my heart in Christ.

²¹I write to you [perfectly] confident of your obedient compliance, since I know that you will do even more than I ask.

²²At the same time also prepare a guest room for me [in expectation of a visit], for I hope that through your prayers I will be [granted the gracious privilege of] coming to you [at Colossae].

²³Greetings to you from Epaphras, my fellow prisoner here in [the cause of] Christ Jesus,

²⁴and from Mark, Aristarchus, Demas, and Luke, my fellow workers.

²⁵The grace of the Lord Jesus Christ be with your spirit.

speak the Word

Father, I pray that the sharing of my faith may become effective and powerful because of my accurate knowledge of every good thing that is mine in Christ Jesus.
—ADAPTED FROM PHILEMON 6

expect the best

Paul prayed and asked God to allow him to visit Philemon and it is interesting to me that he told Philemon to prepare a guest room in expectation of his visit (see Philemon 22). How does an expectant mother behave? She prepares ahead of time for the child she is expecting but does not have yet. Are you living with expectation? Are you expecting God to do wonderful things in your life? Are you expecting favor everywhere you go? Are you expecting God to enable you to be a blessing to people any time you see a need?

We should all ask ourselves, "What am I expecting?" We might be surprised to find that we are receiving nothing because we expect nothing.

We say we pray in faith, but part of faith is hope and active expectancy. Faith is not asking and then doubting or asking and then being afraid; it is not asking and then worrying. Faith asks and believes God is working, and it expects and looks forward to the answer with joy. The conversation of faith is filled with expectancy, which I like to define as, "a joy-filled looking forward to receiving a desired result." Real faith does not pray for the salvation of a wayward child and then say to a friend over lunch, "I'm so afraid my son is going to get in trouble and ruin his life." Faith says, "I'm expecting my son to change." "I believe God is working in his life and I'm looking forward to the day when he and I can study God's Word together."

The phrase "wait for the Lord," is amplified to include "expect," "look for" and "hope in Him" (Isaiah 40:31). When we read with those additional meanings, we see a better picture of the attitude we need to live with. Waiting on God is not a passive state of doing absolutely nothing. We may do nothing physically, but spiritually we are excited and enthusiastic; we expect and look for God to show up in our circumstances at any moment and we are full of hope, which is joyful and confident expectation.

Let me encourage you to do an attitude check. Are you praying and waiting, but not waiting properly? If so, make a change and start expecting aggressively. Even confess aloud things you expect God to do. Expectancy prepares the way for God's miracle-working power!

Hebrews

Author:
Unknown

Date:
Before AD 70

Everyday Life Principles:
Jesus is superior to everything in heaven and on earth.

In Jesus, we have the best possible covenant and the best possible Mediator of that covenant. When we have Him, we have everything we need.

The blessings of the new covenant are made real in our lives through faith.

Simply put, the book of Hebrews is about "better things." Written to believers under pressure to turn back to their former Jewish faith or to mix Judaism with Christianity, this book emphasizes the new and better covenant we have with God though Jesus Christ and Jesus Himself as the Mediator of that New Covenant. Hebrews exalts Jesus' supremacy over all kinds of former things, such as prophets, angels, and God's spokesmen (Moses, Aaron, and Joshua). It clearly reveals the superiority of the New Covenant over old religious places and things, such as the tabernacle, the sacrificial system, and the Old Covenant.

Hebrews contains a thorough description of Jesus as our Great High Priest and as mankind's once-for-all perfect sacrifice for sin. It also includes and addresses the extreme importance of faith in our lives, for the New Covenant is experienced through faith and includes the "Hall of Faith" in chapter 11 and such well-known verses as: " . . . let us run with endurance and active persistence the race that is set before us" (Hebrews 12:1), and, "Jesus Christ is [eternally changeless, always] the same yesterday and today and forever" (Hebrews 13:8).

As you read the book of Hebrews, I pray that God gives you continual revelation about the New Covenant you have with Him through Jesus Christ and that you are able to receive and enjoy everything that belongs to you through this relationship.

1

GOD, HAVING spoken to the fathers long ago in [the voices and writings of] the prophets in many separate revelations [each of which set forth a portion of the truth], and in many ways, ²has in these last days spoken [with finality] to us in [the person of One who is by His character and nature] His Son [namely Jesus], whom He appointed heir *and* lawful owner of all things, through whom also He created the universe [that is, the universe as a space-time-matter continuum]. ³The Son is the radiance *and* only expression of the glory of [our awesome] God [reflecting God's Shekinah glory, the Light-being, the brilliant light of the divine], and the exact representation *and* perfect imprint of His [Father's] essence, and upholding *and* maintaining *and* propelling all things [the entire physical and spiritual universe] by His powerful word [carrying the universe along to its predetermined goal]. When He [Himself and no other] had [by offering Himself on the cross as a sacrifice for sin] accomplished purification from sins *and* established our freedom from guilt, He sat down [revealing His completed work] at the right hand of the Majesty on high [revealing His Divine authority], ⁴having become as much superior to angels, since He has inherited a more excellent *and* glorious name than they [that is, Son—the name above all names].

⁵For to which of the angels did the Father ever say,

"YOU ARE MY SON,
TODAY I HAVE BEGOTTEN (fathered)
    YOU [established You as a Son,
    with kingly dignity]"?

And again [did He ever say to the angels],

"I SHALL BE A FATHER TO HIM
AND HE SHALL BE A SON TO ME"?
    [2 Sam 7:14; Ps 2:7]

⁶And when He again brings the firstborn [highest-ranking Son] into the world, He says,

"AND ALL THE ANGELS OF GOD ARE
    TO WORSHIP HIM." [Ps 97:7]

⁷And concerning the angels He says,

"WHO MAKES HIS ANGELS WINDS,
AND HIS MINISTERING SERVANTS
    FLAMES OF FIRE [to do His
    bidding]." [Ps 104:4]

⁸But about the Son [the Father says to Him],

"YOUR THRONE, O GOD, IS FOREVER
    AND EVER,
AND THE SCEPTER OF [absolute]
    RIGHTEOUSNESS IS THE SCEPTER
    OF HIS KINGDOM.
⁹"YOU HAVE LOVED RIGHTEOUSNESS
    [integrity, virtue, uprightness
    in purpose] AND HAVE HATED
    LAWLESSNESS [injustice, sin].
THEREFORE GOD, YOUR GOD, HAS
    ANOINTED YOU
WITH THE OIL OF GLADNESS ABOVE
    YOUR COMPANIONS." [Ps 45:6, 7]

¹⁰And,

"YOU, LORD, LAID THE FOUNDATION
    OF THE EARTH IN THE BEGINNING,
AND THE HEAVENS ARE THE WORKS
    OF YOUR HANDS;
¹¹THEY WILL PERISH, BUT YOU
    REMAIN [forever and ever];
AND THEY WILL ALL WEAR OUT LIKE
    A GARMENT,
¹²AND LIKE A ROBE YOU WILL ROLL
    THEM UP;
LIKE A GARMENT THEY WILL BE
    CHANGED.
BUT YOU ARE THE SAME [forever],
AND YOUR YEARS WILL NEVER END."
    [Ps 102:25–27]

¹³But to which of the angels has the Father ever said,

"SIT AT MY RIGHT HAND [together
    with me in royal dignity],
UNTIL I MAKE YOUR ENEMIES

A FOOTSTOOL FOR YOUR FEET [in triumphant conquest]"? [Ps 110:1]

¹⁴Are not all the angels ministering spirits sent out [by God] to serve (accompany, protect) those who will inherit salvation? [Of course they are!]

2 FOR THIS reason [that is, because of God's final revelation in His Son Jesus and because of Jesus' superiority to the angels] we must pay much closer attention than ever to the things that we have heard, so that we do not [in any way] drift away from truth.

²For if the message given through angels [the Law given to Moses] was authentic *and* unalterable, and every violation and disobedient act received an appropriate penalty,

³how will we escape [the penalty] if we ignore such a great salvation [the gospel, the new covenant]? For it was spoken at first by the Lord, and it was confirmed to us *and* proved authentic by those who *personally* heard [Him speak],

⁴[and besides this evidence] God also testifying with them [confirming the message of salvation], both by signs and wonders and by various miracles [carried out by Jesus and the apostles] and by [granting to believers the] gifts of the Holy Spirit according to His own will.

angels are everywhere

What a comfort to know that God provides angels to minister to us and help us (see Hebrews 1:14)! The Bible says that the angels of God are "mighty ones who do His commandments, obeying the voice of His word!" (Psalm 103:20).

Angels are everywhere even though we cannot see them. How can we increase the activity of angels in our lives?

Psalm 91:11 teaches us that God "will command His angels" in regard to us "to protect and defend and guard" us in all our "ways [of obedience and service]." Angels will not help us if we disobey God or live selfish, self-centered lives. But, when we speak God's Word and walk in His will, angels are on the scene, helping us more than we can imagine.

I believe we have angels with us everywhere we go and that they keep us from harm. A friend of mine sat in a folding chair in a fishing boat on the lake. She was reading Psalm 91 and thanking God for her angels when the boat suddenly hit a wave and knocked over her chair. She hit her head on the side of the boat, but she was not really harmed. She was rather distraught by the fact she fell and hit her head, so she asked God, "Where were my angels?" God spoke to her heart and said, "You are not dead are you?" In other words, she may have hit her head, but it could have been much, much worse had her angels not been there.

I wonder how many times our angels save our lives and we do not even know it? How often do we complain about some minor bump in life without realizing that our angels protected us from a major crisis? Let us begin to be more thankful for all the divine, supernatural help that God gives us, including the angels He sends us to assist and protect.

⁵It was not to angels that God subjected the [inhabited] world of the future [when Christ reigns], about which we are speaking.

⁶But one has [solemnly] testified somewhere [in Scripture], saying,

"WHAT IS MAN, THAT YOU ARE
    MINDFUL OF HIM,
OR THE SON OF MAN, THAT YOU
    GRACIOUSLY CARE FOR HIM?
⁷"YOU HAVE MADE HIM FOR A LITTLE
    WHILE LOWER [in status] THAN
    THE ANGELS;
YOU HAVE CROWNED HIM WITH
    GLORY AND HONOR,
AND SET HIM OVER THE WORKS OF
    YOUR HANDS;
⁸YOU HAVE PUT ALL THINGS IN
    SUBJECTION UNDER HIS FEET
    [confirming his supremacy]."

Now in putting all things in subjection to man, He left nothing outside his control. But at present we do not yet see all things subjected to him. [Ps 8:4–6]

⁹But we do see Jesus, who was made lower than the angels for a little while [by taking on the limitations of humanity], crowned with glory and honor because of His suffering of death, so that by the grace of God [extended to sinners] He might experience death for [the sins of] everyone.

¹⁰For it was fitting for God [that is, an act worthy of His divine nature] that He, for whose sake are all things, and through whom are all things, in bringing many sons to glory, should make the author *and* founder of their salvation perfect through suffering [bringing to maturity the human experience necessary for Him to be perfectly equipped for His office as High Priest].

¹¹Both Jesus who sanctifies and those who are sanctified [that is, spiritually transformed, made holy, and set apart for God's purpose] are all from one *Father*; for this reason He is not ashamed to call them brothers and sisters,

¹²saying,

"I WILL DECLARE YOUR (the
    Father's) NAME TO MY BRETHREN
    (believers),
IN THE MIDST OF THE CONGREGATION
    I WILL SING YOUR PRAISE." [Ps
    22:22]

¹³And again [He says],

"MY TRUST *and* CONFIDENT HOPE
    WILL BE PLACED IN HIM."

And again,

"HERE I AM, I AND THE CHILDREN
    WHOM GOD HAS GIVEN ME." [Is
    8:17, 18]

¹⁴Therefore, since [these His] children share in flesh and blood [the physical nature of mankind], He Himself in a similar manner also shared in the same [physical nature, but without sin], so that through [experiencing] death He might make powerless (ineffective, impotent) him who had the power of death—that is, the devil—

¹⁵and [that He] might free all those who through [the haunting] fear of death were held in slavery throughout their lives.

¹⁶For, as we all know, He (Christ) does not take hold of [the fallen] angels [to give them a helping hand], but He does take hold of [the fallen] descendants of Abraham [extending to them His hand of deliverance]. [Is 41:8, 9]

¹⁷Therefore, *it was essential that* He

speak the Word

Thank You, Jesus, that by Your death You have brought the devil to nothing and made him of no effect.
—ADAPTED FROM HEBREWS 2:14

settle down and be faithful

In Hebrews 3:1, 2, we read that during His earthly life, Jesus was faithful to the One Who appointed Him. Yet Jesus went through some silent years. After His miraculous birth and prophetic baptism, we hear nothing about Him again until He reached age twelve, when He was found debating with the teachers in the temple. All we are told about these silent years is that "the Child continued to grow and become strong [in spirit], filled with wisdom; and the grace (favor, spiritual blessing) of God was upon Him" (Luke 2:40). After that, the Bible tells us nothing about what transpired in Jesus' life except that He "kept increasing in wisdom and in stature, and in favor with God and men" (Luke 2:52).

Jesus spent thirty years in preparation for a three-year ministry, a time when He was faithful and obedient to His earthly parents, as well as to His heavenly Father. It was during those silent years that He grew in strength, wisdom, and favor.

The "instant" society that we live in today is ruining people. Because everything is so instant and so easy, we think everything coming from God should be instant and easy. But godly strength, wisdom, knowledge, spiritual maturity, and character are developed in us as we go through tests and continue to do what we know is right, even when it does not feel right or does not feel good to us. If we want to grow up in God and do what He has called us to do, we have to settle down and be faithful.

had to be made like His brothers (mankind) in every respect, so that He might [by experience] become a merciful and faithful High Priest in things related to God, to make atonement (propitiation) for the people's sins [thereby wiping away the sin, satisfying divine justice, and providing a way of reconciliation between God and mankind].

¹⁸Because He Himself [in His humanity] has suffered in being tempted, He is able to help *and* provide immediate assistance to those who are being tempted *and* exposed to suffering.

3 THEREFORE, HOLY brothers and sisters, who share in the heavenly calling, [thoughtfully and attentively] consider the Apostle and High Priest whom we confessed [as ours when we accepted Him as Savior], namely, Jesus;

²He was faithful to Him who appointed Him [Apostle and High Priest], as Moses also was *faithful* in all God's house. [Num 12:7]

³Yet Jesus has been considered worthy of much greater glory *and* honor than Moses, just as the builder of a house has more honor than the house.

⁴For every house is built by someone, but the builder of all things is God.

⁵Now Moses was faithful in [the administration of] all God's house, [but only] as a *ministering* servant, [his ministry serving] as a testimony of the things which were to be spoken

speak the Word

Thank You, Jesus, for helping me and providing immediate assistance when I am being tempted and exposed to suffering.
–ADAPTED FROM HEBREWS 2:18

afterward [the revelation to come in Christ]; [Num 12:7]

6but Christ is faithful as a Son over His [Father's] house. And we are His house if we hold fast our confidence and sense of triumph in our hope [in Christ].

7Therefore, just as the Holy Spirit says,

"TODAY IF YOU HEAR HIS VOICE,
8DO NOT HARDEN YOUR HEARTS
    AS [your fathers did] IN THE
    REBELLION [of Israel at Meribah],
ON THE DAY OF TESTING IN THE
    WILDERNESS,
9WHERE YOUR FATHERS TRIED ME
    BY TESTING [My forbearance and
    tolerance],
AND SAW MY WORKS FOR FORTY
    YEARS
[And found I stood their test].
10"THEREFORE I WAS ANGERED WITH
    THIS GENERATION,
AND I SAID, 'THEY ALWAYS GO
    ASTRAY IN THEIR HEART,
AND THEY DID NOT KNOW MY WAYS
    [nor become progressively better
    and more intimately acquainted
    with them]';
11So I SWORE [an oath] IN MY WRATH,
    'THEY SHALL NOT ENTER MY REST
    [the promised land].'" [Ps 95:7–
    11]

12Take care, brothers and sisters, that there not be in any one of you a wicked, unbelieving heart [which refuses to trust and rely on the Lord, a heart] that turns away from the living God.

the "ifs" and "buts" of biblical faith

I want to call your attention to the word "if" in Hebrews 3:6 because we often do not like to pay attention to the "ifs" and "buts" in the Bible. In scriptures like this one, we see what God will do, *if* we will do what we are supposed to do.

You and I have the awesome privilege of being members of the Father's house, if we remain firm in faith until the end. Going to the altar and praying a sinner's prayer is only the beginning of our walk with Him; we must follow through and continue in faith. We must believe in Him.

Confidence and faith are virtually synonymous; sometimes they can be interchanged without losing the context of what is being said at all. I can give a long fancy definition of faith, but let us boil it down to this: *faith is confidence in God.* In simple terms, faith is the act of knowing that if God says He will do something, He will do it. Even if it does not look like He is doing it right now, it will come to pass in His timing, *if* we remain confident in Him.

The only two things that can interrupt faith are: 1) the manifestation of what is believed; or 2) the manifestation of doubt and unbelief. Once we receive the manifestation of what we have believed for, we no longer need faith, so it ceases. In the same way, the manifestation of doubt and unbelief—that is, receiving the lies of Satan and believing them—interrupts faith, so it ceases to exist.

Our faith must continue even when it seems that everything and everyone is against us. In Christ, we can remain standing firm on the inside because we know that our real life is within us, not in the people or circumstances around us.

life point

When we hear from God, we can choose to respond with humility and trust or we can harden our hearts and ignore Him. Regrettably, when people do not get what they want or when they go through trials and tests, many of them choose to harden their hearts.

This is exactly what happened to the Israelites when they made the trip through the wilderness (see Hebrews 3:7–9). God led them into the wilderness so He could prove to them that He would do good for them and that they could trust Him (see Deuteronomy 8:2, 3). He had great things planned for them, but He tested them first to see if they really would believe Him. That is why He tells us not to harden our hearts as they did. He has great things planned for you too, so keep your heart soft and tender before Him.

¹³But continually encourage one another every day, as long as it is called "Today" [and there is an opportunity], so that none of you will be hardened [into settled rebellion] by the deceitfulness of sin [its cleverness, delusive glamour, and sophistication].

¹⁴For we [believers] have become partakers of Christ [sharing in all that the Messiah has for us], if only we hold firm our newborn confidence [which originally led us to Him] until the end,

¹⁵while it is said,

"TODAY [while there is still opportunity] IF YOU HEAR HIS VOICE,

speak the Word

DO NOT HARDEN YOUR HEART, AS WHEN THEY PROVOKED ME [in the rebellion in the desert at Meribah]." [Ps 95:7, 8]

¹⁶For who were they who heard and yet provoked *Him* [with rebellious acts]? Was it not all those who came out of Egypt led by Moses?

¹⁷And with whom was He angry for forty years? Was it not with those who sinned, whose dead bodies were scattered in the desert?

¹⁸And to whom did He swear [an oath] that they would not enter His rest, but to those who disobeyed [those who would not listen to His word]?

¹⁹So we see that they were not able to enter [into His rest—the promised land] because of unbelief *and* an unwillingness to trust in God. [Num 14:1–35]

4 THEREFORE, WHILE the promise of entering His rest still remains *and* is freely offered today, let us fear, in case any one of you may seem to come short of reaching it *or* think he has come too late.

²For indeed we have had the good news [of salvation] preached to us, just as the Israelites also [when the good news of the promised land came to them]; but the message they heard did not benefit them, because it was not united with faith [in God] by those who heard.

³For we who believe [that is, we who personally trust and confidently rely on God] enter that rest [so we have His inner peace now because we are confident in our salvation, and assured of His power], just as He has said,

Help me, Lord, never to harden my heart to Your voice, but to keep it soft and responsive when You speak.
–ADAPTED FROM HEBREWS 3:15

"As I swore [an oath] in My
    wrath,
They shall not enter My rest,"

[this He said] although His works
were completed from the foundation
of the world [waiting for all who would
believe]. [Ps 95:11]

⁴For somewhere [in Scripture] He
has said this about the seventh day:
"And God rested on the seventh day
from all His works"; [Gen 2:2]

⁵and again in this, "They shall not
enter My rest." [Ps 95:11]

⁶Therefore, since the promise remains for some to enter His rest, and
those who formerly had the good news
preached to them failed to [grasp it
and did not] enter because of [their
unbelief evidenced by] disobedience,

⁷He again sets a definite day, [a new]

putting the Word to work

Hebrews 4:3 teaches that those who
did not listen to God's Word or obey His
instructions would not enter into the
place of rest He offered them. So when
you feel frustrated or upset, or if you
lose your peace and your joy, ask yourself, "Am I believing God's Word?"

The only way we will ever be free
from struggling is to believe the Word
and obey whatever Jesus puts in our
hearts to do. Believing God's Word
delivers us from struggling so we can
rest in God's promises.

Are you in need of God's rest? Adhere to
Him, trust in Him, and rely on Him and experience the rest He has prepared for you.

the rest of God

Hebrews 4:3 teaches that those who believe God enter into His rest. Experiencing
His rest is one way you can tell whether you are really *in* faith, or whether you are
just trying to *have* faith. When you truly enter into the realm of faith, you enter into
the rest of God.

Rest is freedom from excessive reasoning, struggle, fear, inner turmoil, worry, and
frustration, which develop because of our working to do what only God can do.
Being in God's rest is not necessarily resting from physical activity, but resting in
confidence in the midst of everything that goes on in life. It is a rest of the soul in
which the mind, will, and emotions are at peace.

You can rest in God because you know He will take care of you and meet your needs.
You do not know when or how, and you really do not care because you are enjoying
the life you have right now while God works on your problem.

God wants us to live at peace and in His rest. But in order for us to do that, we need
to "believe that God exists and that He rewards those who [earnestly and diligently]
seek Him" (Hebrews 11:6).

If you are worn out, I urge you to enter into God's rest. I encourage you to quit trying to control everyone and everything around you and simply allow God to do for
you what only He can do.

No matter what you face, God wants to help you and give you rest.

Jesus understands

Hebrews 4:15 states that Jesus experienced every emotion and suffered every feeling you and I do, but without committing any sin. Why did He not sin? Because He did not give in to wrong feelings. He knew the Scripture in every area of life because He spent years studying it before He began His ministry.

You and I will never be able to say no to our feelings if we do not have within us a strong knowledge of God's Word. Jesus had the same feelings we do, but He never sinned by giving in to them.

When I am hurt by someone and I feel angry or upset, it is such a comfort to me to lift my face and hands and voice to the Lord and say, "Jesus, I am so glad that You understand what I am feeling right now and that You do not condemn me for feeling this way. I do not want to give vent to my emotions. Help me, Lord, to get over them. Help me to forgive those who have wronged me and not slight them, avoid them, or seek to pay them back for the harm done to me."

Why not bow your head and thank the Lord for understanding you too? Pray with me: "Thank You, God, for understanding me and not condemning me. Thank You for not giving up on me. I ask for Your help, that I may become more understanding, as You are."

"Today," [providing another opportunity to enter that rest by] saying through David after so long a time, just as has been said before [in the words already quoted],

"TODAY IF YOU HEAR HIS VOICE,
DO NOT HARDEN YOUR HEARTS." [Ps 95:7, 8]

8[This mention of a rest was not a reference to their entering into Canaan.] For if Joshua had given them rest, God would not speak about another day [of opportunity] after that.

9So there remains a [full and complete] Sabbath rest for the people of God.

10For the one who has once entered His rest has also rested from [the weariness and pain of] his [human] labors, just as God rested from [those labors uniquely] His own. [Gen 2:2]

11Let us therefore make every effort to enter that rest [of God, to know and experience it for ourselves], so that no one will fall by *following* the same example of disobedience [as those who died in the wilderness].

12For the word of God is living and active *and* full of power [making it operative, energizing, and effective]. It is sharper than any two-edged sword, penetrating as far as the division of the soul and spirit [the completeness of a person], and of both joints and marrow [the deepest parts of our nature],

speak the Word

Thank You, God, that Your Word is living and active and full of power.
It is sharper than any two-edged sword; it divides soul and spirit;
and it judges the thoughts and intentions of the heart.
—ADAPTED FROM HEBREWS 4:12

life point

Jesus understands our human frailty because He was tempted in every way we are, yet without committing any sin (see Hebrews 4:15). How freeing it is to have our High Priest—Who is both sinless and understanding—intercede for us.

exposing *and* judging the very thoughts and intentions of the heart.

¹³And not a creature exists that is concealed from His sight, but all things are open *and* exposed, and revealed to the eyes of Him with whom we have to give account.

¹⁴Inasmuch then as we [believers] have a great High Priest who has [already ascended and] passed through the heavens, Jesus the Son of God, let us hold fast our confession [of faith and cling tenaciously to our absolute trust in Him as Savior].

¹⁵For we do not have a High Priest who is unable to sympathize *and* understand our weaknesses *and* temptations, but One who has been tempted [knowing exactly how it feels to be human] in every respect as *we are, yet* without [committing any] sin.

¹⁶Therefore let us [with privilege] approach the throne of grace [that is, the throne of God's gracious favor] with confidence *and* without fear, so that we may receive mercy [for our failures] and find [His amazing] grace to help in time of need [an appropriate blessing, coming just at the right moment].

5 FOR EVERY high priest chosen from among men is appointed [to act] on behalf of men in things relating to God, so that he may offer both gifts and sacrifices for sins.

²He is able to deal gently with the *spiritually* ignorant and misguided, since he is also subject to *human* weakness;

³and because of this [human weakness] he is required to offer *sacrifices* for sins, for himself as well as for the people.

⁴And besides, one does not appropriate for himself the honor [of being high priest], but he who is called by God, just as Aaron was.

⁵So too Christ did not glorify Himself so as to be made a high priest, but He [was exalted and appointed by the One] who said to Him,

"YOU ARE MY SON,
TODAY I HAVE BEGOTTEN (fathered)
　YOU [declared Your authority
　and rule over the nations]"; [Ps
　2:7]

⁶just as He also says in another place,

"YOU ARE A PRIEST [appointed]
　FOREVER
ACCORDING TO THE ORDER OF
　MELCHIZEDEK." [Ps 110:4]

⁷In the days of His earthly life, Jesus offered up both [specific] petitions and [urgent] supplications [for that which He needed] with fervent crying and tears to the One who was [always] able to save Him from death, and He was heard because of His reverent submission toward God [His sinlessness and

life point

When you and I pray, we need to make sure we approach God as believers, not as beggars. Remember, according to Hebrews 4:16, we are to come to God's throne "with confidence and without fear," not beggarly, but boldly; not cowardly, but confidently.

Be sure to keep the balance. Stay respectful, but be bold. Approach God with confidence and recognize your need for grace. Believe that He delights in your prayers and is ready to answer any request that is in accordance with His will.

His unfailing determination to do the Father's will].

8Although He was a Son [who had never been disobedient to the Father], He learned [active, special] obedience through what He suffered.

9And having been made perfect [uniquely equipped and prepared as Savior and retaining His integrity amid opposition], He became the source of eternal salvation [an eternal inheritance] to all those who obey Him, [Is 45:17]

10being designated by God as High Priest according to the order of Melchizedek. [Ps 110:4]

11Concerning this we have much to say, and it is hard to explain, since you have become dull *and* sluggish in [your spiritual] hearing *and* disinclined to listen.

life point

Hebrews 5:11 warns us that we will miss learning rich life principles if we do not have a listening attitude. We should not limit our hearing only to those times when we desperately need help. (Of course we are always ready to hear from Him if we are in trouble!) God wants to speak to us on a regular basis and we need to hear Him all the time. Do not allow your hearing to become muted; rather keep your spiritual ears open to hear His voice.

12For though by this time you ought to be teachers [because of the time you have had to learn these truths], you actually need someone to teach you again the elementary principles of God's word [from the beginning],

use your pain for gain

Have you ever needed a job, but every employment posting you read asked for someone with experience? You wanted a job but did not have any experience, and it frustrated you. I have been in that situation, and I remember thinking, "How can I get experience if nobody will give me a job?"

God also wants experienced help. When we go to work for God in His kingdom, He will use everything in our past. No matter how painful it was, He considers it experience. Many of us have gone through difficult things, and those things qualify us to help take someone else through them too. Hebrews 5:8, 9 tells us that even Jesus learned and gained experience through the things He suffered.

How could I write to you right now if I had not gone through some difficult things and gained some valuable experience? How could I teach others how to forgive those who have hurt them if I had not first had the experience of forgiving those who hurt me?

I encourage you to look at your pain from a different viewpoint. A right perspective makes all the difference in your life. Take a look at how you can use your pain for someone else's gain. How can your mess become your ministry? Maybe you have gone through so much that you feel you have enough experience to be a specialist in some area. I am a specialist in overcoming shame, guilt, poor self-image, lack of confidence, fear, anger, bitterness, self-pity, et cetera. Let me encourage you to be positive about your past and your pain and realize that it can all be used for good in God's kingdom.

putting the Word to work

Hebrews 5:12–14 teaches us about growing up spiritually. Do adults drink milk from baby bottles or eat only baby food? Of course not! Likewise, let me encourage you as a Christian to be diligent in studying the Bible so you will understand it and be able to apply it to your everyday life. In this way you will grow in faith and move from spiritual "milk" to spiritual "meat." How can you apply a particular truth from God's Word to your life today?

and you have come to be *continually* in need of milk, not solid food.

¹³For everyone who lives on milk is [doctrinally inexperienced and] unskilled in the word of righteousness, since he is a *spiritual* infant.

¹⁴But solid food is for the [spiritually] mature, whose senses are trained by practice to distinguish between what is morally good and *what is* evil.

6 THEREFORE LET us get past the elementary stage in the teachings about the Christ, advancing on to maturity *and* perfection *and* spiritual completeness, [doing this] without laying again a foundation of repentance from dead works and of faith toward God,

²of teaching about washings (ritual purifications), the laying on of hands, the resurrection of the dead, and eternal judgment. [These are all important matters in which you should have been proficient long ago.]

³And we will do this [that is, proceed to maturity], if God permits.

⁴For [it is impossible to restore to repentance] those who have once been enlightened [spiritually] and who have tasted *and* consciously experienced the heavenly gift and have shared in the Holy Spirit,

⁵and have tasted *and* consciously experienced the good word of God and the powers of the age (world) to come,

⁶and then have fallen away—it is impossible to bring them back again to repentance, since they again nail the Son of God on the cross [for as far as they are concerned, they are treating the death of Christ as if they were not saved by it], and are holding Him up again to public disgrace.

⁷For soil that drinks the rain which often falls on it and produces crops useful to those for whose benefit it is cultivated, receives a blessing from God;

⁸but if it persistently produces thorns and thistles, it is worthless and close to being cursed, and it ends up being burned. [Gen 3:17, 18]

⁹But, beloved, even though we speak to you in this way, we are convinced of better things concerning you, and of things that accompany salvation.

¹⁰For God is not unjust so as to forget your work and the love which you have shown for His name in ministering to [the needs of] the saints (God's people), as you do.

¹¹And we desire for each one of you to show the same diligence [all the way through] so as to realize *and* enjoy the full assurance of hope until the end,

life point

I encourage you to take the message of Hebrews 6:11 seriously by following through on the things you start.

It is so easy to begin something, but it takes courage to finish. At the beginning of a new thing, we get excited and often enjoy a lot of support to get it done. But when our emotions wear off and all that is left is hard work and the need for patience, we find out what it takes to truly succeed. Be a person who does succeed and finishes well!

¹²so that you will not be [spiritually] sluggish, but [will instead be] imitators of those who through faith [lean on God with absolute trust and confidence in Him and in His power] and by patient endurance [even when suffering] are [now] inheriting the promises.

¹³For when God made the promise to Abraham, He swore [an oath] by Himself, since He had no one greater by whom to swear,

¹⁴saying, "I WILL SURELY BLESS YOU AND I WILL SURELY MULTIPLY YOU." [Gen 22:16, 17]

¹⁵And so, having patiently waited, he realized the promise [in the miraculous birth of Isaac, as a pledge of what was to come from God].

¹⁶Indeed men swear [an oath] by one greater *than themselves,* and with them [in all disputes] the oath *serves* as confirmation [of what has been said] and is an end of the dispute.

¹⁷In the same way God, in His desire to show to the heirs of the promise the unchangeable nature of His purpose, intervened *and* guaranteed it with an oath,

¹⁸so that by two unchangeable things [His promise and His oath] in which it is impossible for God to lie, we who have fled [to Him] for refuge would have strong encouragement *and* indwelling strength to hold tightly to the hope set before us.

¹⁹This hope [this confident assurance] we have as an anchor of the soul [it cannot slip and it cannot break down under whatever pressure bears upon it]—a safe and steadfast hope that enters within the veil [of the heavenly temple, that most Holy Place in which the very presence of God dwells], [Lev 16:2]

²⁰where Jesus has entered [in advance] as a forerunner for us, having become a High Priest forever according to the order of Melchizedek. [Ps 110:4]

7 FOR THIS Melchizedek, king of Salem, priest of the Most High God, met Abraham as he returned from the slaughter of the kings and blessed him,

²and Abraham gave him a tenth of all [the spoil]. He is, first of all, by the translation *of his name,* king of righteousness, and then he is also king of Salem, which means king of peace.

³Without [any record of] father or mother, nor ancestral line, without [any record of] beginning of days (birth) nor ending of life (death), but having been made like the Son of God, he remains a priest without interruption *and* without successor.

⁴Now pause *and* consider how great this man was to whom Abraham, the patriarch, gave a tenth of the spoils.

⁵It is true that those descendants of Levi who are charged with the priestly office are commanded in the Law to collect tithes from the people—which means, from their kinsmen—though these have descended from Abraham.

⁶But this person [Melchizedek] who is not from their Levitical ancestry received tithes from Abraham and blessed him who possessed the promises [of God].

⁷Yet it is beyond all dispute that the lesser person is *always* blessed by the greater one.

⁸Furthermore, here [in the Levitical priesthood] tithes are received by men who are subject to death; but in that case [concerning Melchizedek], *they are received* by one of whom it is testified that he lives on [perpetually].

⁹A person might even say that Levi [the father of the priestly tribe] himself, who received tithes, paid tithes through Abraham [the father of all Israel and of all who believe],

¹⁰for Levi was still in the loins (unborn) of his forefather [Abraham] when Melchizedek met him (Abraham).

¹¹Now if perfection [a perfect fellowship between God and the worshiper] had been attained through the Levitical priesthood (for under it the people were given the Law) what further need was there for another *and* different kind of priest to arise, one in the manner of Melchizedek, rather than one appointed to the order of Aaron? ¹²For when there is a change in the priesthood, there is of necessity a change of the law [concerning the priesthood] as well. ¹³For the One of whom these things are said belonged [not to the priestly line of Levi but] to another tribe, from which no one has officiated *or* served at the altar. ¹⁴For it is evident that our Lord descended from [the tribe of] Judah, and Moses mentioned nothing about priests in connection with that tribe. ¹⁵And this becomes even more evident if another priest arises in the likeness of Melchizedek, [Ps 110:4] ¹⁶who has become *a priest,* not on the basis of a physical *and* legal requirement in the Law [concerning his ancestry as a descendant of Levi], but on the basis of the power of an indestructible *and* endless life. ¹⁷For it is attested [by God] of Him,

"YOU (Christ) ARE A PRIEST
  FOREVER
ACCORDING TO THE ORDER OF
  MELCHIZEDEK." [Ps 110:4]

¹⁸For, on the one hand, a former commandment is cancelled because of its weakness and uselessness [because of its inability to justify the sinner before God] ¹⁹(for the Law never made anything perfect); while on the other hand a better hope is introduced through which we now *continually* draw near to God. ²⁰And indeed it was not without the taking of an oath [that Christ was made priest] ²¹(for those *Levites* who formerly became priests [received their office] without [its being confirmed by the taking of] an oath, but this One [was designated] with an oath through the One who said to Him,

"THE LORD HAS SWORN
AND WILL NOT CHANGE HIS MIND
  or REGRET IT,
'YOU (Christ) ARE A PRIEST
  FOREVER'"). [Ps 110:4]

²²And so [because of the oath's greater strength and force] Jesus has become the certain guarantee of a better covenant [a more excellent and more advantageous agreement; one that will never be replaced or annulled]. ²³The [former successive line of] priests, on the one hand, existed in greater numbers because they were each prevented by death from continuing [perpetually in office]; ²⁴but, on the other hand, Jesus holds His priesthood permanently *and* without change, because He lives on forever. ²⁵Therefore He is able also to save forever (completely, perfectly, for eternity) those who come to God through Him, since He always lives to intercede *and* intervene on their behalf [with God]. ²⁶It was fitting for us to have such a High Priest [perfectly adapted to our needs], holy, blameless, unstained [by sin], separated from sinners and exalted higher than the heavens;

speak the Word

Thank You, Jesus, that You are able to save forever, completely,
and perfectly those who come to God through You and that You always live
to intercede and intervene with God on my behalf.
—ADAPTED FROM HEBREWS 7:25

[27]who has no day by day need, like those high priests, to offer sacrifices, first of all for his own [personal] sins and then for those of the people, because He [met all the requirements and] did this once for all when He offered up Himself [as a willing sacrifice]. [28]For the Law appoints men as high priests who are weak [frail, sinful, dying men], but the word of the oath [of God], which came after [the institution of] the Law, *permanently appoints* [as priest] a Son who has been made perfect forever. [Ps 110:4]

8 NOW THE main point of what we have to say *is this:* we have such a High Priest, [the Christ] who is seated [in the place of honor] at the right hand of the throne of the Majesty (God) in heaven, [Ps 110:1] [2]a Minister (Officiating Priest) in the holy places and in the true tabernacle, which is erected not by man, but by the Lord. [3]For every high priest is appointed to offer both gifts and sacrifices; so it is essential for this One also to have something to offer. [4]Now if He were [still living] on earth, He would not be a priest at all, for there are priests who offer the gifts [to God] in accordance with the Law. [5]They serve as a pattern and foreshadowing of [what has its true existence and reality in] the heavenly things (sanctuary). For when Moses was about to erect the tabernacle, he was warned *by God,* saying, "SEE THAT YOU MAKE it all [exactly] ACCORDING TO THE PATTERN WHICH WAS SHOWN TO YOU ON THE MOUNTAIN." [Ex 25:40] [6]But as it is, Christ has acquired a [priestly] ministry which is more excellent [than the old Levitical priestly ministry], for He is the Mediator (Arbiter) of a better covenant [uniting God and man], which has been enacted *and* rests on better promises.

[7]For if that first *covenant* had been faultless, there would have been no occasion for a second one *or* an attempt to institute another one [the new covenant].

[8]However, God finds fault with them [showing its inadequacy] when He says,

"BEHOLD, THE DAYS WILL COME,
  SAYS THE LORD,
WHEN I WILL MAKE *and* RATIFY A
  NEW COVENANT
WITH THE HOUSE OF ISRAEL AND
  WITH THE HOUSE OF JUDAH;
[9]NOT LIKE THE COVENANT THAT I
  MADE WITH THEIR FATHERS
ON THE DAY WHEN I TOOK THEM BY
  THE HAND
TO LEAD THEM OUT OF THE LAND OF
  EGYPT;
FOR THEY DID NOT ABIDE IN MY
  COVENANT,
AND SO I WITHDREW MY FAVOR *and*
  DISREGARDED THEM, SAYS THE
  LORD.
[10]"FOR THIS IS THE COVENANT THAT
  I WILL MAKE WITH THE HOUSE OF
  ISRAEL
AFTER THOSE DAYS, SAYS THE LORD:
I WILL IMPRINT MY LAWS UPON
  THEIR MINDS [even upon
  their innermost thoughts and
  understanding],
AND ENGRAVE THEM UPON
  THEIR HEARTS [effecting their
  regeneration].
AND I WILL BE THEIR GOD,
AND THEY SHALL BE MY PEOPLE.
[11]"AND IT WILL NOT BE [necessary]
  FOR EACH ONE TO TEACH HIS
  FELLOW CITIZEN,
OR EACH ONE HIS BROTHER, SAYING,
  'KNOW [by experience, have
  knowledge of] THE LORD,'
FOR ALL WILL KNOW [Me by
  experience and have knowledge
  of] ME,
FROM THE LEAST TO THE GREATEST
  OF THEM.

¹²"FOR I WILL BE MERCIFUL *and*
GRACIOUS TOWARD THEIR
WICKEDNESS,
AND I WILL REMEMBER THEIR SINS
NO MORE." [Jer 31:31–34]

¹³When God speaks of "A new *covenant*," He makes the first one obsolete.
And whatever is becoming obsolete
(out of use, annulled) and growing
old is ready to disappear.

9 NOW EVEN the first *covenant*
had regulations for divine worship and for the earthly sanctuary. [Ex 25:10–40]
²A tabernacle (sacred tent) was put
up, the outer one *or* first section, in
which were the lampstand and the table with [its loaves of] the sacred showbread; this is called the Holy Place.
[Lev 24:5, 6]
³Behind the second veil there was
another tabernacle [the inner one or
second section] known as the Holy of
Holies, [Ex 26:31–33]
⁴having the golden altar of incense
and the ark of the covenant covered
entirely with gold. This contained a
golden jar which held the manna, and
the rod of Aaron that sprouted, and
the [two stone] tablets of the covenant
[inscribed with the Ten Command-
ments]; [Ex 16:32–34; 30:1–6; Num
17:8–10]
⁵and above the ark were the [golden]
cherubim of glory overshadowing the
mercy seat; but we cannot now go into
detail about these things.
⁶Now when these things have been
prepared in this way, the priests continually enter the outer [or first section of the] tabernacle [that is, the Holy

Place] performing [their ritual acts of]
the divine worship,
⁷but into the second [inner tabernacle, the Holy of Holies], only the high
priest *enters* [and then only] once a
year, and never without [bringing a
sacrifice of] blood, which he offers
[as a substitutionary atonement] for
himself and for the sins of the people
committed in ignorance. [Lev 16:15]
⁸By this the Holy Spirit signifies
that the way into the Holy Place [the
true Holy of Holies and the presence
of God] has not yet been disclosed as
long as the first *or* outer tabernacle is
still standing [that is, as long as the
Levitical system of worship remains
a recognized institution],
⁹for this [first or outer tabernacle]
is a symbol [that is, an archetype or
paradigm] for the present time. Accordingly both gifts and sacrifices are
offered which are incapable of perfecting the conscience *and* renewing
the [inner self of the] worshiper.
¹⁰For they [the gifts, sacrifices, and
ceremonies] deal only with [clean and
unclean] food and drink and various ritual washings, [mere] external
regulations for the body imposed [to
help the worshipers] until the time of
reformation [that is, the time of the
new order when Christ will establish
the reality of what these things fore-
shadow—a better covenant].
¹¹But when Christ appeared as a
High Priest of the good things to come
[that is, true spiritual worship], *He
entered* through the greater and more
perfect tabernacle, not made with
hands, that is to say, not a part of this
[material] creation.

speak the Word

Thank You, Lord, for being merciful
and gracious toward my sin when I repent
and for remembering my sin no more.
–ADAPTED FROM HEBREWS 8:12

¹²He went once for all into the Holy Place [the Holy of Holies of heaven, into the presence of God], and not through the blood of goats and calves, but through His own blood, having obtained *and* secured eternal redemption [that is, the salvation of all who personally believe in Him as Savior].

¹³For if the sprinkling of [ceremonially] defiled persons with the blood of goats and bulls and the ashes of a [burnt] heifer is sufficient for the cleansing of the body, [Lev 16:6, 16; Num 19:9, 17, 18]

¹⁴how much more will the blood of Christ, who through the eternal [Holy] Spirit *willingly* offered Himself unblemished [that is, without moral or spiritual imperfection as a sacrifice] to God, cleanse your conscience from dead works *and* lifeless observances to serve the ever living God?

¹⁵For this reason He is the Mediator *and* Negotiator of a new covenant [that is, an entirely new agreement uniting God and man], so that those who have been called [by God] may receive [the fulfillment of] the promised eternal inheritance, since a death has taken place [as the payment] which redeems them from the sins *committed* under the *obsolete* first covenant.

¹⁶For where there is a will *and* testament involved, the death of the one who made it must be established,

life point

Notice that Jesus offered Himself and His blood by the Spirit (see Hebrews 9:14). The Spirit and the blood work together. The promised Holy Spirit could not be poured out on the day of Pentecost until after Jesus' blood was poured out on the cross of Calvary. The blood and the Spirit still work together today. Honor the blood, and you will see the Spirit poured out in your life.

¹⁷for a will *and* testament takes effect [only] at death, since it is never in force as long as the one who made it is alive.

¹⁸So even the first *covenant* was not put in force without [the shedding of] blood.

¹⁹For when every commandment in the Law had been read by Moses to all the people, he took the blood of the calves and goats [which had been sacrificed], together with water and scarlet wool and with a bunch of hyssop, and he sprinkled both the scroll itself and all the people,

²⁰saying, "THIS IS THE BLOOD OF THE COVENANT [that seals and ratifies the agreement] WHICH GOD ORDAINED *and* COMMANDED [me to deliver to] YOU." [Ex 24:6–8]

²¹And in the same way he sprinkled both the tabernacle and all the containers *and* sacred utensils of worship with the blood.

²²In fact under the Law almost everything is cleansed with blood, and without the shedding of blood there is no forgiveness [neither release from sin and its guilt, nor cancellation of the merited punishment].

²³Therefore it was necessary for the [earthly] copies of the heavenly things to be cleansed with these, but the heavenly things themselves required far better sacrifices than these.

²⁴For Christ did not enter into a holy place made with hands, a mere copy of the true one, but [He entered] into heaven itself, now to appear in the very presence of God on our behalf;

²⁵nor did He [enter into the heavenly sanctuary to] offer Himself again and again, as the high priest enters the Holy Place every year with blood that is not his own.

²⁶Otherwise, He would have needed to suffer over and over since the foundation of the world; but now once for all at the consummation of the ages He

has appeared *and* been publicly manifested to put away sin by the sacrifice of Himself.

²⁷And just as it is appointed *and* destined for all men to die once and after this [comes certain] judgment,

²⁸so Christ, having been offered once *and* once for all to bear [as a burden] the sins of many, will appear a second time [when he returns to earth], not to deal with sin, but to bring salvation to those who are eagerly *and* confidently waiting for Him.

10 FOR SINCE the Law has only a shadow [just a pale representation] of the good things to come—not the very image of those things—it can never, by offering the same sacrifices continually year after year, make perfect those who approach [its altars].

²For if it were otherwise, would not these sacrifices have stopped being offered? For the worshipers, having once [for all time] been cleansed, would no longer have a consciousness of sin.

³But [as it is] these [continual] *sacrifices* bring a fresh reminder of sins [to be atoned for] year after year,

⁴for it is impossible for the blood of bulls and goats to take away sins.

⁵Therefore, when Christ enters into the world, He says,

"SACRIFICE AND OFFERING YOU
　HAVE NOT DESIRED,
BUT [instead] YOU HAVE PREPARED
　A BODY FOR ME [to offer];
⁶IN BURNT OFFERINGS AND *sacrifices*
　FOR SIN YOU HAVE TAKEN NO
　DELIGHT.
⁷"THEN I SAID, 'BEHOLD, I HAVE COME
TO DO YOUR WILL, O GOD—
　[TO FULFILL] WHAT IS WRITTEN OF
　ME IN THE SCROLL OF THE BOOK.'"
　[Ps 40:6–8]

⁸After saying [in the citation] above, "YOU HAVE NEITHER DESIRED, NOR HAVE YOU TAKEN DELIGHT IN SACRIFICES AND OFFERINGS AND WHOLE BURNT OFFERINGS AND *sacrifices* FOR SIN" (which are offered according to the Law)

⁹then He said, "BEHOLD, I HAVE COME TO DO YOUR WILL." [And so] He does away with the first [covenant as a means of atoning for sin based on animal sacrifices] so that He may inaugurate *and* establish the second [covenant by means of obedience]. [Ps 40:6–8]

¹⁰And in accordance with this will [of God] we [who believe in the message of salvation] have been sanctified [that is, set apart as holy for God and His purposes] through the offering of the body of Jesus Christ (the Messiah, the Anointed) once for all.

¹¹Every priest stands [at his altar of service] ministering daily, offering the same sacrifices over and over, which are never able to strip away sins [that envelop and cover us];

¹²whereas Christ, having offered the one sacrifice [the all-sufficient sacrifice of Himself] for sins for all time, SAT DOWN [signifying the completion of atonement for sin] AT THE RIGHT HAND OF GOD [the position of honor],

¹³waiting from that time onward UNTIL HIS ENEMIES ARE MADE A FOOTSTOOL FOR HIS FEET. [Ps 110:1]

¹⁴For by the one offering He has perfected forever *and* completely cleansed those who are being sanctified [bringing each believer to spiritual completion and maturity].

¹⁵And the Holy Spirit also adds His testimony to us [in confirmation of this]; for after having said,

¹⁶"THIS IS THE COVENANT THAT I WILL
　MAKE WITH THEM
　AFTER THOSE DAYS, SAYS THE LORD:
　I WILL IMPRINT MY LAWS UPON
　　THEIR HEART,
　AND ON THEIR MIND I WILL INSCRIBE
　　THEM [producing an inward
　　change],"

He then says,

[17]"AND THEIR SINS AND THEIR
    LAWLESS ACTS
  I WILL REMEMBER NO MORE [no
    longer holding their sins against
    them]." [Jer 31:33, 34]

[18]Now where there is [absolute] forgiveness *and* complete cancellation of
the penalty of these things, there is
no longer any offering [to be made to
atone] for sin.

[19]Therefore, believers, since we
have confidence *and* full freedom to
enter the Holy Place [the place where
God dwells] by [means of] the blood
of Jesus,

[20]by this new and living way which
He initiated *and* opened for us through
the veil [as in the Holy of Holies], that
is, through His flesh,

[21]and since we have a great *and* wonderful Priest [Who rules] over the
house of God,

[22]let us approach [God] with a true
and sincere heart in unqualified assurance of faith, having had our
hearts sprinkled *clean* from an evil
conscience and our bodies washed
with pure water.

[23]Let us seize *and* hold tightly the confession of our hope without wavering,

life point

Believing we are made right with God
through our faith in Jesus Christ is a fresh,
new, and living way (see Hebrews 10:20),
one that gives us freedom, boldness,
and confidence. Trying to follow the Law
(trying to do everything right) in order to
earn God's acceptance ministers death
(every kind of misery) to us; but Jesus
offers us His grace, which produces life.

speak the Word

putting the Word to work

Have you ever wondered if you were
truly welcome in God's presence? Take
heart, because through His blood,
Jesus made a "new and living way"
for you to draw near to God with
confidence (Hebrews 10:20). Thank God
for the joy of being in His presence!

for He who promised is reliable *and*
trustworthy *and* faithful [to His word];
[24]and let us consider [thoughtfully]
how we may encourage one another
to love and to do good deeds,

[25]not forsaking our meeting together [as believers for worship and
instruction], as is the habit of some,
but encouraging *one another;* and all
the more [faithfully] as you see the
day [of Christ's return] approaching.

[26]For if we go on willfully *and* deliberately sinning after receiving the
knowledge of the truth, there no longer remains a sacrifice [to atone] for
our sins [that is, no further offering
to anticipate],

putting the Word to work

Sunday morning church services are
great opportunities for Christians to
gather together. However, Hebrews
10:24, 25 encourages us to gather
together often so we can encourage
one another in love and in doing good
deeds. How can you find ways to spend
quality time with other Christians? Be
intentional about including time in your
schedule for gathering together with
other believers. You will be encouraged!

Thank You, Jesus, for shedding Your blood so I could have confidence
and full freedom to enter into God's presence.
—ADAPTED FROM HEBREWS 10:19

²⁷but a kind of awful *and* terrifying expectation of [divine] judgment and THE FURY OF A FIRE *and* BURNING WRATH WHICH WILL CONSUME THE ADVERSARIES [those who put themselves in opposition to God]. [Is 26:11] ²⁸Anyone who has ignored *and* set aside the Law of Moses is put to death without mercy on *the testimony of* two or three witnesses. [Deut 17:2–6] ²⁹How much greater punishment do you think he will deserve who has rejected *and* trampled under foot the Son of God, and has considered unclean *and* common the blood of the covenant that sanctified him, and has insulted the Spirit of grace [who imparts the unmerited favor and blessing of God]? [Ex 24:8] ³⁰For we know Him who said, "VENGEANCE IS MINE [retribution and the deliverance of justice rest with Me], I WILL REPAY [the wrongdoer]." And again, "THE LORD WILL JUDGE HIS PEOPLE." [Deut 32:35, 36] ³¹It is a fearful *and* terrifying thing to fall into the hands of the living God [incurring His judgment and wrath].

³²But remember the earlier days, when, after being [spiritually] enlightened, you [patiently] endured a great conflict of sufferings, ³³sometimes by being made a spectacle, publicly exposed to insults and distress, and sometimes by becoming

life point

Hebrews 10:36 speaks of our need for patience. Who do we need to be patient with? We need to be patient with ourselves because sometimes we are slow in learning; we need to be patient with God because He does not always move in our timing; and we need to be patient with other people for various reasons. Ask God to help you grow in patience. He will.

companions with those who were so treated. ³⁴For you showed sympathy *and* deep concern for those who were imprisoned, and you joyfully accepted the [unjust] seizure of your belongings *and* the confiscation of your property, conscious of the fact that you have a better possession and a lasting one [prepared for you in heaven]. ³⁵Do not, therefore, fling away your [fearless] confidence, for it has a glorious *and* great reward. ³⁶For you have need of patient endurance [to bear up under difficult circumstances without compromising], so that when you have carried out the will of God, you may receive *and* enjoy to the full what is promised.

³⁷FOR YET IN A VERY LITTLE WHILE,
　　HE WHO IS COMING WILL COME, AND
　　WILL NOT DELAY.
³⁸BUT MY RIGHTEOUS ONE [the one
　　justified by faith] SHALL LIVE
　　BY FAITH [respecting man's
　　relationship to God and trusting
　　Him];
　　AND IF HE DRAWS BACK [shrinking
　　in fear], MY SOUL HAS NO DELIGHT
　　IN HIM. [Hab 2:3, 4]

³⁹But our way is not that of those who shrink back to destruction, but [we are] of those who believe [relying on God through faith in Jesus Christ, the Messiah] *and* by this confident faith preserve the soul.

11 NOW FAITH is the assurance (title deed, confirmation) of things hoped for (divinely guaranteed), and the evidence of things not seen [the conviction of their reality—faith comprehends as fact what cannot be experienced by the physical senses]. ²For by this [kind of] faith the men of old gained [divine] approval. ³By faith [that is, with an inherent

trust and enduring confidence in the power, wisdom and goodness of God] we understand that the worlds (universe, ages) were framed *and* created [formed, put in order, and equipped for their intended purpose] by the word of God, so that what is seen was not made out of things which are visible.

⁴By faith Abel offered to God a more acceptable sacrifice than Cain, through which it was testified of him that he was righteous (upright, in right standing with God), and God testified by accepting his gifts. And though he died, yet through [this act of] faith he still speaks. [Gen 4:3–10]

⁵By faith [that pleased God] Enoch was caught up *and* taken to heaven so that he would not have a glimpse of death; AND HE WAS NOT FOUND BECAUSE GOD HAD TAKEN HIM; for even before he was taken [to heaven], he received the testimony [still on record] that he had walked with God *and* pleased Him. [Gen 5:21–24]

⁶But without faith it is impossible to [walk with God and] please Him, for whoever comes [near] to God must [necessarily] believe that God exists and that He rewards those who [earnestly and diligently] seek Him.

⁷By faith [with confidence in God and His word] Noah, being warned *by God* about events not yet seen, in reverence prepared an ark for the salvation of his family. By this [act of

putting the Word to work

Have you ever wondered what faith in action really looks like? Study the lives of the "heroes of faith" in Hebrews 11, and you can see many different ways they lived their faith in their everyday lives. Remember that faith is the assurance of the things we hope for and the evidence of the reality of things we cannot see (see Hebrews 11:1).

life point

Notice in Hebrews 11:6 that without faith it is impossible to please God; therefore, no matter how many good works you offer, God will not be pleased if they were done to try to earn His favor.

Whatever we do for God should be because we love Him, not because we try to get something from Him.

Hebrews 11:6 says that God "rewards those who [earnestly and diligently] seek Him." I rejoiced when I finally realized this! I know I have made many mistakes in the past, but I also know I have diligently sought the Lord with all my heart. That means that I qualify for rewards. I decided a long time ago that even though I did not deserve them, I would receive any blessings that God wanted to give me. I hope you will do the same.

obedience] he condemned the world and became an heir of the righteousness which comes by faith. [Gen 6:13–22]

⁸By faith Abraham, when he was called [by God], obeyed by going to a place which he was to receive as an inheritance; and he went, not knowing where he was going.

⁹By faith he lived as a foreigner in the promised land, as in a strange *land,* living in tents [as nomads] with Isaac and Jacob, who were fellow heirs of the same promise. [Gen 12:1–8]

¹⁰For he was [waiting expectantly and confidently] looking forward to the city which has foundations, [an eternal, heavenly city] whose architect and builder is God.

¹¹By faith even Sarah herself received the ability to conceive [a child], even [when she was long] past the normal age for it, because she considered Him who had given her the promise

to be reliable *and* true [to His word]. [Gen 17:19; 18:11–14; 21:2]

¹²So from one man, though he was [physically] as good as dead, were born *as many descendants* AS THE STARS OF HEAVEN IN NUMBER, AND INNUMERABLE AS THE SAND ON THE SEASHORE. [Gen 15:5, 6; 22:17; 32:12]

¹³All these died in faith [guided and sustained by it], without receiving the [tangible fulfillment of God's] promises, only having seen (anticipated) them and having welcomed them from a distance, and having acknowledged that they were strangers and exiles on the earth. [Gen 23:4; Ps 39:12]

¹⁴Now those who say such things make it clear that they are looking for a country of their own.

¹⁵And if they had been thinking of that *country* from which they departed [as their true home], they would have had [a continuing] opportunity to return.

¹⁶But the truth is that they were longing for a better country, that is, a heavenly one. For that reason God is not ashamed [of them or] to be called their God [even to be surnamed their God—the God of Abraham, Isaac, and Jacob]; for He has prepared a city for them. [Ex 3:6, 15; 4:5]

¹⁷By faith Abraham, when he was tested [that is, as the testing of his faith was still in progress], offered up Isaac, and he who had received the promises [of God] was ready to sacrifice his only son [of promise]; [Gen 22:1–10]

¹⁸to whom it was said, "THROUGH ISAAC YOUR DESCENDANTS SHALL BE CALLED." [Gen 21:12]

¹⁹For he considered [it reasonable to believe] that God was able to raise *Isaac* even from among the dead. [Indeed, in the sense that he was prepared to sacrifice Isaac in obedience to God] Abraham did receive him back [from the dead] figuratively speaking.

²⁰By faith Isaac blessed Jacob and Esau [believing what God revealed to him], even regarding things to come. [Gen 27:27–29, 39, 40]

²¹By faith Jacob, as he was dying, blessed each of the sons of Joseph, and bowed in worship, *leaning* on the top of his staff. [Gen 48]

²²By faith Joseph, when he was dying, referred to [the promise of God for] the exodus of the sons of Israel [from Egypt], and gave instructions concerning [the burial of] his bones [in the land of the promise]. [Gen 50:24, 25; Ex 13:19]

²³By faith Moses, after his birth, was hidden for three months by his parents, because they saw he was a beautiful *and* divinely favored child; and they were not afraid of the king's (Pharaoh's) decree. [Ex 1:22; 2:2; Acts 7:20]

²⁴By faith Moses, when he had grown up, refused to be called the son of Pharaoh's daughter, [Ex 2:10, 15]

²⁵because he preferred to endure the hardship of the people of God rather than to enjoy the passing pleasures of sin.

²⁶He considered the reproach of the Christ [that is, the rebuke he would suffer for his faithful obedience to God] to be greater wealth than all the treasures of Egypt; for he looked ahead to the reward [promised by God].

²⁷By faith he left Egypt, being unafraid of the wrath of the king; for he endured [steadfastly], as seeing Him who is unseen. [Ex 2:15]

²⁸By faith he kept the Passover and the sprinkling of the blood [on the doorposts], so that the destroyer of the firstborn would not touch them (the firstborn of Israel). [Ex 12:21–30]

²⁹By faith the people [of Israel] crossed the Red Sea as though *they were passing* through dry land; but when the Egyptians attempted it they were drowned. [Ex 14:21–31]

³⁰By faith the walls of Jericho fell down after they had been encircled for

seven days [by Joshua and the sons of Israel]. [Josh 6:12–21]

[31]By faith Rahab the prostitute was not destroyed along with those who were disobedient, because she had welcomed the spies [sent by the sons of Israel] in peace. [Josh 2:1–21; 6:22–25]

[32]And what more shall I say? For time will fail me if I tell of Gideon, Barak, Samson, Jephthah, of David and Samuel and the prophets, [Judg 4; 5; 6–8; 11; 12; 13–16; 1 Sam 1–30; 2 Sam 1–24; 1 Kin 1; 2; Acts 3:24]

[33]who by faith [that is, with an enduring trust in God and His promises] subdued kingdoms, administered justice, obtained promised blessings, closed the mouths of lions, [Dan 6]

[34]extinguished the power of [raging] fire, escaped the edge of the sword, out of weakness were made strong, became mighty and unbeatable in battle, putting enemy forces to flight. [Dan 3]

[35]Women received back their dead by resurrection; and others were tortured [to death], refusing to accept release [offered on the condition of denying their faith], so that they would be resurrected to a better life; [1 Kin 17:17–24; 2 Kin 4:25–37]

[36]and others experienced the trial of mocking and scourging [amid torture], and even chains and imprisonment.

[37]They were stoned [to death], they were sawn in two, they were lured with tempting offers [to renounce their faith], they were put to death by the sword; they went about wrapped in the skins of sheep and goats, utterly destitute, oppressed, cruelly treated

[38](people of whom the world was not worthy), wandering in deserts and mountains and [living in] caves and holes in the ground.

[39]And all of these, though they gained [divine] approval through their faith, did not receive [the fulfillment of] what was promised,

[40]because God had us in mind and had something better for us, so that they [these men and women of authentic faith] would not be made perfect [that is, completed in Him] apart from us.

12 THEREFORE, SINCE we are surrounded by so great a cloud of witnesses [who by faith have testified to the truth of God's absolute faithfulness], stripping off every unnecessary weight and the sin which so easily and cleverly entangles us, let us run with endurance and active persistence the race that is set before us,

[2][looking away from all that will distract us and] focusing our eyes on Jesus, who is the Author and Perfecter of faith [the first incentive for our belief and the One who brings our faith to maturity], who for the joy [of accomplishing the goal] set before Him endured the cross, disregarding the shame, and sat down at the right hand of the throne of God [revealing His deity, His authority, and the completion of His work]. [Ps 110:1]

[3]Just consider and meditate on Him who endured from sinners such bitter hostility against Himself [consider it

putting the Word to work

When a runner runs in a race, his focus is not on the people in the stands or on the runners around him, but on the finish line. As a believer, your life is like a race, and as you run, it is important to keep your eyes fixed on Jesus (see Hebrews 12:1, 2). Give Him your undivided attention. Is anything distracting you from God or keeping you from making progress as you grow in faith? What do you need to do in order to focus more fully on Jesus as you run the race of your life?

throw off excess baggage

Hebrews 12:1 tells us that if we are going to run our race, we must lay aside every weight and run the race with "endurance." I have heard this point summarized this way: Running our race with no hindrances means stripping for the contest.

In the days when this verse was written, the writer was drawing a parallel that was much better understood than it is today. In those days, runners conditioned their bodies for a race just as athletes do today. But at the time of the race, they stripped off their clothing, wearing only a loincloth, so that when they ran there was nothing to hinder them. They also oiled their bodies with fine oils.

In the same way, we need to be well oiled or anointed with the Holy Spirit if we want to win our race. We also need to remove from our lives anything that hinders us as we run the race set before us.

There are many different hindrances to running a race to our full potential. Too many commitments is one that keeps us from developing our potential. Letting other people control us keeps us from becoming all we can be. Not knowing how to say no keeps us from developing the potential God has placed in us. Getting overly involved in someone else's goals and vision or becoming entangled in someone else's problems instead of keeping our eyes on our own goals will also keep us from fulfilling our potential.

I find that the devil comes up with a thousand ways every week to entangle me and get me to focus on something that will prevent me from doing what I am supposed to be doing. They all seem like emergencies, and it seems I must be the one to handle them all.

If we want to do what God called us to do we must stay focused, because the world we live in is filled with distractions and entanglements. Let me encourage you to keep your focus on the Lord and be diligent to lay aside everything that might distract you or hold you back.

all in comparison with your trials], so that you will not grow weary and lose heart.

⁴You have not yet struggled to the point of shedding blood in your striving against sin;

⁵and you have forgotten the divine word of encouragement which is addressed to you as sons,

"MY SON, DO NOT MAKE LIGHT OF
  THE DISCIPLINE OF THE LORD,
AND DO NOT LOSE HEART *and* GIVE
  UP WHEN YOU ARE CORRECTED BY
  HIM;

life point

I want to encourage you to keep your eyes off of yourself and the things that distract you. Instead focus firmly on Jesus and His power (see Hebrews 12:2). He already knows your troubles. He is ready, willing, and able to bring about the changes that need to be made in you and in your life. He will bring you to maturity and perfection, if you will simply ask Him and trust Him to do so. You can count on God; He is the Author of your faith and its Perfecter.

life point

Hebrews 12:6 tells us that God disciplines us because He loves us. Jesus Himself verifies this truth about God's correction and discipline of those He loves in Revelation 3:19 when He says, "Those whom I [dearly and tenderly] love, I rebuke and discipline [showing them their faults and instructing them]; so be enthusiastic and repent [change your inner self—your old way of thinking, your sinful behavior—seek God's will]."

Change often requires correction, but people who do not know they are loved have a very difficult time receiving correction. Correction does you no good at all if you cannot receive it. I encourage you to receive the Lord's correction in your life as a sign of His love for you.

⁶FOR THE LORD DISCIPLINES *and* CORRECTS THOSE WHOM HE LOVES, AND HE PUNISHES EVERY SON WHOM HE RECEIVES *and* WELCOMES [TO HIS HEART]." [Prov 3:11, 12]

⁷You must submit to [correction for the purpose of] discipline; God is dealing with you as with sons; for what son is there whom his father does not discipline?

⁸Now if you are exempt from correction *and* without discipline, in which all [of God's children] share, then you are illegitimate children and not sons [at all].

⁹Moreover, we have had earthly fathers who disciplined us, and we submitted *and* respected them [for training us]; shall we not much more willingly submit to the Father of spirits, and live [by learning from His discipline]?

¹⁰For our earthly fathers disciplined us for only a short time as seemed best to them; but He *disciplines us* for our good, so that we may share His holiness.

¹¹For the time being no discipline brings joy, but seems sad *and* painful; yet to those who have been trained by it, afterwards it yields the peaceful fruit of righteousness [right standing with God and a lifestyle and attitude that seeks conformity to God's will and purpose].

¹²So then, strengthen hands that are weak and knees that tremble. [Is 35:3]

¹³Cut through *and* make smooth, straight paths for your feet [that are safe and go in the right direction], so that *the leg* which is lame may not be put out of joint, but rather may be healed.

¹⁴*Continually* pursue peace with everyone, and the sanctification without which no one will [ever] see the Lord.

¹⁵See to it that no one falls short of God's grace; that no root of resentment springs up and causes trouble, and by it many be defiled;

¹⁶and [see to it] that no one is immoral or godless like Esau, who sold his own birthright for a *single* meal. [Gen 25:29–34]

¹⁷For you know that later on, when he wanted [to regain title to] his inheritance of the blessing, he was rejected, for he found no opportunity for repentance [there was no way to repair what he had done, no chance to recall the choice he had made], even

speak the Word

Thank You, Lord, for loving me enough to correct and discipline me. Help me receive Your correction as a reminder of Your love, Your acceptance, and the fact that You deal with me as Your beloved child.
—ADAPTED FROM HEBREWS 12:6, 7

life point

We must refuse to let resentment take root in our hearts (see Hebrews 12:15) or allow ourselves to be offended or remain angry. This means we cannot follow our feelings; we must press past feelings and do what God asks us to do.

If you struggle in this area, I encourage you to pursue God's grace—His unmerited favor and spiritual blessing. Let His grace disintegrate the deep roots of resentment that entangle you.

though he sought for it with [bitter] tears. [Gen 27:30–40] ¹⁸For you have not come [as did the Israelites in the wilderness] to *a mountain* that can be touched and to a blazing fire, and to gloom and darkness and a raging windstorm, ¹⁹and to the blast of a trumpet and a sound of words [such that] those who heard it begged that nothing more be said to them. [Ex 19:12–22; 20:18–21; Deut 4:11, 12; 5:22–27] ²⁰For they could not bear the command, "IF EVEN A WILD ANIMAL TOUCHES THE MOUNTAIN, IT WILL BE STONED [to death]." [Ex 19:12, 13] ²¹In fact, so terrifying was the sight, that Moses said, "I AM FILLED WITH FEAR and trembling." [Deut 9:19] ²²But you have come to Mount Zion and to the city of the living God, the heavenly Jerusalem, and to myriads of angels [in festive gathering], ²³and to the general assembly and assembly of the firstborn who are registered [as citizens] in heaven, and to God, who is Judge of all, and to the spirits of the righteous (the redeemed in heaven) who have been made perfect [bringing them to their final glory], ²⁴and to Jesus, the Mediator of a new covenant [uniting God and man], and to the sprinkled blood, which speaks [of mercy], a better *and* nobler *and* more gracious message than *the blood* of Abel [which cried out for vengeance]. [Gen 4:10] ²⁵See to it that you do not refuse [to listen to] Him who is speaking [to you now]. For if those [sons of Israel] did not escape when they refused [to listen to] him who warned them on earth [revealing God's will], how much less will we *escape* if we turn our backs on Him who warns from heaven? [Heb 2:1–4] ²⁶His voice shook the earth [at Mount Sinai] then, but now He has given a promise, saying, "YET ONCE MORE I WILL SHAKE NOT ONLY THE EARTH, BUT ALSO THE [starry] HEAVEN." [Hag 2:6] ²⁷Now this [expression], "Yet once more," indicates the removal *and* final transformation of all those things which can be shaken—that is, of that which has been created—so that those things which cannot be shaken may remain. [Ps 102:26] ²⁸Therefore, since we receive a kingdom which cannot be shaken, let us show gratitude, and offer to God pleasing service *and* acceptable worship with reverence and awe; ²⁹for our God is [indeed] a consuming fire. [Deut 4:24]

13 LET LOVE of your fellow believers continue. ²Do not neglect to extend hospitality to strangers [especially among the family of believers—being friendly, cordial, and gracious, sharing the comforts of your home and doing

speak the Word

Father, I pray that love for my fellow believers will always continue in my heart.
—ADAPTED FROM HEBREWS 13:1

your part generously], for by this some have entertained angels without knowing it. [Gen 18:1–8; 19:1–3; Judg 6:11–24; 13:6–20]

³Remember those who are in prison, as if you were their fellow prisoner, and those who are mistreated, since you also are in the body [and subject to physical suffering].

⁴Marriage *is to be held* in honor among all [that is, regarded as something of great value], and the *marriage* bed undefiled [by immorality or by any sexual sin]; for God will judge the sexually immoral and adulterous.

⁵Let your character [your moral essence, your inner nature] be free from the love of money [shun greed—be financially ethical], being content with what you have; for He has said, "I WILL NEVER [under any circumstances] DESERT YOU [nor give you up nor leave you without support, nor will I in any degree leave you helpless], NOR WILL I FORSAKE *or* LET YOU DOWN *or* RELAX MY HOLD ON YOU [assuredly not]!" [Josh 1:5]

⁶So we take comfort *and* are encouraged *and* confidently say,

"THE LORD IS MY HELPER [in time
    of need], I WILL NOT BE AFRAID.
WHAT WILL MAN DO TO ME?" [Ps
    27:1; 118:6]

⁷Remember your leaders [for it was they] who brought you the word of God; and consider the result of their conduct [the outcome of their godly lives], and imitate their faith [their conviction that God exists and is the Creator and Ruler of all things, the Provider of eternal salvation through Christ, and imitate their reliance on God with absolute trust and confidence in His power, wisdom, and goodness].

life point

Have you faced times when you wondered if God would really come through and meet your needs? Hebrews 13:5 is an encouraging scripture that will greatly help you in this circumstance. In it, the Lord lets us know that we do not need to have our minds set on money or worry how we will take care of ourselves, because He will take care of these things for us. He promises never to forsake or let us down.

It is important for us to do our part, but we must not try to do God's part. The load is too heavy to bear by ourselves, and if we are not careful, we will break under the weight of it.

Do not worry. Take this verse to heart: "Trust [rely on and have confidence] in the LORD and do good; dwell in the land and feed [securely] on His faithfulness" (Psalm 37:3, 4). There's no need to worry. You can trust God!

⁸Jesus Christ is [eternally changeless, always] the same yesterday and today and forever.

⁹Do not be carried away by diverse and strange teachings; for it is good for the heart to be established *and* strengthened by grace and not by foods [rules of diet and ritualistic meals], which bring no benefit *or* spiritual growth to those who observe them.

¹⁰We have an altar from which those who serve the tabernacle (sacred tent) have no right to eat.

¹¹For the bodies of those animals whose blood is brought into the sanctuary by the high priest *as an offering* for sin, are burned outside the camp. [Lev 16:27]

speak the Word

Thank You, Jesus, for being the same yesterday, today, and forever!
–ADAPTED FROM HEBREWS 13:8

¹²Therefore Jesus also suffered *and* died outside the [city] gate so that He might sanctify *and* set apart for God as holy the people [who believe] through [the shedding of] His own blood.

¹³So, let us go out to Him outside the camp, bearing His contempt [the disgrace and shame that He had to suffer]. [Lev 16:27]

¹⁴For here we have no lasting city, but we are seeking *the city* which is to come.

¹⁵Through Him, therefore, let us at all times offer up to God a sacrifice of praise, which is the fruit of lips that thankfully acknowledge *and* confess *and* glorify His name. [Lev 7:12; Is 57:19; Hos 14:2]

¹⁶Do not neglect to do good, to contribute [to the needy of the church as an expression of fellowship], for such sacrifices are always pleasing to God.

¹⁷Obey your [spiritual] leaders and submit to them [recognizing their authority over you], for they are keeping watch over your souls *and* continually guarding your spiritual welfare as those who will give an account [of their stewardship of you]. Let them do this with joy and not with grief *and* groans, for this would be of no benefit to you.

¹⁸Keep praying for us, for we are convinced that we have a good conscience, seeking to conduct ourselves honorably [that is, with moral courage and personal integrity] in all things.

¹⁹And I urge all of you to pray earnestly, so that I may be restored to you soon.

²⁰Now may the God of peace [the source of serenity and spiritual well-being] who brought up from the dead our Lord Jesus, the great Shepherd of the sheep, through the blood *that sealed and ratified* the eternal covenant, [Is 55:3; 63:11; Ezek 37:26; Zech 9:11]

²¹equip you with every good thing to carry out His will *and* strengthen you [making you complete and perfect as you ought to be], accomplishing in us that which is pleasing in His sight, through Jesus Christ, to whom be the glory forever and ever. Amen.

²²I call on you, brothers and sisters, listen [patiently] to this message of exhortation *and* encouragement, for I have written to you briefly.

²³Notice that our brother Timothy has been released [from prison]. If he comes soon, I will see you [along with him].

²⁴Give our greetings to all of your [spiritual] leaders and to all of the saints (God's people). Those [Christians] from Italy send you their greetings.

²⁵Grace be with you all.

speak the Word

Father, I pray that You, the God of peace, will equip me with everything good to carry out Your will and strengthen me, accomplishing that which is pleasing in Your sight.
—ADAPTED FROM HEBREWS 13:20, 21

James

Author:
James

Date:
Approximately AD 48

Everyday Life Principles:
Genuine faith produces good deeds.
Good works are the fruit of true faith.

Watch your mouth, and remember
that words are powerful.

Heartfelt, persistent prayers are
powerful.

The book of James emphasizes the fact that true faith in God must be accompanied by good works. Let me be quick to point out that good works do not prove a person's belief in God or relationship with Him, but having faith always leads to good works. Faith has to come first because when good works are done in faith, God always gets the glory.

In addition to his focus on unwavering faith and good works, James also provides tremendous practical advice for our everyday lives, including extensive teaching on the joy that is found in suffering and teachings on the mouth and the power of the tongue. He writes about wisdom, about resisting temptation, and about prayer. James penned the familiar words: "Consider it nothing but joy, my brothers and sisters, whenever you fall into various trials" (James 1:2) and, "The heartfelt and persistent prayer of a righteous man (believer) can accomplish much [when put into action and made effective by God—it is dynamic and can have tremendous power]" (James 5:16).

As you read the book of James, I hope it will not only stir your faith, but also inspire you to do good works that glorify God and are motivated by your love for Him. Let it also serve as a reminder of the power of your words and of the necessity of wisdom, and as a call to earnest, heartfelt prayer that makes tremendous power available in your life.

1 JAMES, A bond-servant of God and of the Lord Jesus Christ,
To the twelve [Hebrew] tribes [scattered abroad among the Gentiles] in the dispersion: Greetings (rejoice)!

²Consider it nothing but joy, my brothers and sisters, whenever you fall into various trials.

³Be assured that the testing of your faith [through experience] produces endurance [leading to spiritual maturity, and inner peace].

⁴And let endurance have its perfect result *and* do a thorough work, so that you may be perfect and completely developed [in your faith], lacking in nothing.

⁵If any of you lacks wisdom [to guide

life point

James 1:2, 3 teaches us that we should rejoice in difficult situations, knowing that through them God tests our faith to bring out inner peace. I find that trials do eventually produce inner peace, but first they bring out all kinds of junk to the surface such as pride, anger, rebellion, self-pity, and complaining. We need to face and deal with these ungodly traits before inner peace can come forth.

The Bible talks about purification, sanctification, sacrifice, and suffering. These are not popular words; nevertheless, if we are to be Christlike in character, we must sometimes go through difficult circumstances to learn His ways. I struggled with this process for a long time, but I finally realized that God was not going to do things my way. He placed people and situations in my life that caused me to want to quit this whole process, and He did not want an argument from me. He only wanted to hear, "Yes, Lord. Your will be done."

him through a decision or circumstance], he is to ask of [our benevolent] God, who gives to everyone generously and without rebuke *or* blame, and it will be given to him.

⁶But he must ask [for wisdom] in faith, without doubting [God's willingness to help], for the one who doubts is like a billowing surge of the sea that is blown about and tossed by the wind.

⁷For such a person ought not to think *or* expect that he will receive anything [at all] from the Lord,

⁸*being* a double-minded man, unstable *and* restless in all his ways [in everything he thinks, feels, or decides].

⁹Let the brother in humble circumstances glory in his high position [as a born-again believer, called to the true riches and to be an heir of God];

¹⁰and the rich man *is to glory* in being humbled [by trials revealing human frailty, knowing true riches are found in the grace of God], for like the flower of the grass he will pass away.

¹¹For the sun rises with a scorching wind and withers the grass; its flower falls off and its beauty fades away; so too will the rich man, in the midst of his pursuits, fade away. [Is 40:6, 7]

¹²Blessed [happy, spiritually prosperous, favored by God] is the man who is steadfast under trial *and* perseveres when tempted; for when he has

life point

There are two ways to handle problems—the natural way and the spiritual way. James 1:5, 6 teaches you how to solve your problems the spiritual way. It says if you have trouble, simply ask God what you should do. You may not receive an answer immediately, but you will find that divine wisdom (wisdom beyond your natural understanding) will begin to operate through you, helping you know what to do.

putting the Word to work

James 1:12–15 teaches us about dealing with temptation. When was the last time you were tempted? Are you struggling with temptation right now? It is important to remember that temptation—the desire to have or to do something you know you should avoid—never comes from God. Temptation comes from ungodly desires within us, and such desires, left unchecked, lead to sinful actions. When you are tempted, recognize that God is not testing you; rather He wants to give you strength to overcome the temptation you are facing. Ask Him to do so.

passed the test *and* been approved, he will receive the [victor's] crown of life which *the Lord* has promised to those who love Him.

[13]Let no one say when he is tempted, "I am being tempted by God" [for temptation does not originate from God, but from our own flaws]; for God cannot be tempted by [what is] evil, and He Himself tempts no one.

[14]But each one is tempted when he is dragged away, enticed *and* baited [to commit sin] by his own [worldly] desire (lust, passion).

[15]Then when the illicit desire has conceived, it gives birth to sin; and when sin has run its course, it gives birth to death.

[16]Do not be misled, my beloved brothers and sisters.

[17]Every good thing given and every perfect gift is from above; it comes down from the Father of lights [the Creator and Sustainer of the heavens], in whom there is no variation [no rising or setting] or shadow cast by His turning [for He is perfect and never changes].

[18]It was of His own will that He gave us birth [as His children] by the word of truth, so that we would be a kind of first fruits of His creatures [a prime example of what He created to be set apart to Himself—sanctified, made holy for His divine purposes].

[19]Understand this, my beloved brothers and sisters. Let everyone be quick to hear [be a careful, thoughtful listener], slow to speak [a speaker of carefully chosen words and], slow to anger [patient, reflective, forgiving];

[20]for the [resentful, deep-seated] anger of man does not produce the righteousness of God [that standard of behavior which He requires from us].

[21]So get rid of all uncleanness and all that remains of wickedness, and with a humble spirit receive the word [of God] which is implanted [actually rooted in your heart], which is able to save your souls.

[22]But prove yourselves doers of the word [actively and continually obeying God's precepts], and not merely listeners [who hear the word but fail to internalize its meaning], deluding yourselves [by unsound reasoning contrary to the truth].

[23]For if anyone only listens to the

speak the Word

Father, I thank You that every good thing and every perfect gift in my life comes down from You, and that there is never any variation with You. You are perfect and You never change.
–ADAPTED FROM JAMES 1:17

Help me, Lord, be quick to hear, slow to speak, and slow to anger.
–ADAPTED FROM JAMES 1:19

how to walk in the power of God

We see from James 1:21 that God's Word has the power to save us from a life of sin, but only as we receive and welcome it in our hearts. When we pay wholehearted attention to God's Word, it becomes implanted and rooted in us.

If you and I are to walk in the power of God, we need to heed the advice of James 1:22 to become doers of the Word and not merely listeners. Otherwise we deceive ourselves by reasoning that is contrary to the truth.

It is the truth, and the truth alone, that sets us free and keeps us free. In order for it to work in our lives, and in order for us to receive God's promises from the Word, we must be responsible and obedient to the Word. We cannot try to excuse away our sins and weaknesses. Instead, we must become bond-servants to God and not to our human nature or to other people or things.

The bottom line is this: God is your Helper. He is your Healer. He has a personalized plan for your life. Make sure you know what it is; then begin to walk in obedience to the truth one step at a time. Obeying the Word requires consistency and diligence. It cannot be "hit and miss." You cannot merely try it to see if it works; what's necessary is a dedication and commitment to obey the Word whatever the outcome.

I encourage you today to keep your mind tuned to God's Word more than anything else. Let His Word become planted deep into your heart and listen to what it tells you. Obey Him—then you will be a doer of the Word, not just a hearer of it—and you will walk in the power of God.

word without obeying it, he is like a man who looks very carefully at his natural face in a mirror;

²⁴for *once* he has looked at himself and gone away, he immediately forgets what he looked like.

²⁵But he who looks carefully into the perfect law, the *law* of liberty, and faithfully abides by it, not having become a [careless] listener who forgets but an active doer [who obeys], he will be blessed *and* favored by God in what he does [in his life of obedience].

²⁶If anyone thinks himself to be religious [scrupulously observant of the rituals of his faith], and does not control his tongue but deludes his *own* heart, this person's religion is worthless (futile, barren).

²⁷Pure and unblemished religion [as it is expressed in outward acts] in the sight of our God and Father is this: to visit *and* look after the fatherless and the widows in their distress, and to keep oneself uncontaminated by the [secular] world.

life point

It can be difficult to grasp the idea of the "law of liberty" because law and liberty seem to be opposites: A law says one thing, while liberty says another. I believe the law of liberty mentioned in James 1:25 refers to the freedom of self-control, because God puts a new heart in us, a heart that *wants* to obey His law of love.

With this new heart Jesus gives you, you have the ability to be led by the Spirit, Who gives you the power and freedom to love others. Enjoy your life today by allowing the Lord to love others through you.

life point

Our words are verbal expressions of our souls. Until our mouths are brought under control and submitted to the Lord, He usually does not redeem and restore our souls—our minds, wills, and emotions.

2 MY FELLOW believers, do not practice your faith in our glorious Lord Jesus Christ with *an attitude* of partiality [toward people—show no favoritism, no prejudice, no snobbery].

²For if a man comes into your *meeting place wearing a gold ring and fine clothes, and a poor man in dirty clothes also comes in,

³and you pay special attention to the one who wears the fine clothes, and say to him, "You sit here in this good seat," and you tell the poor man, "You stand over there, or sit down [on the floor] by my footstool,"

⁴have you not discriminated among yourselves, and become judges with wrong motives?

⁵Listen, my beloved brothers and sisters: has not God chosen the poor of this world to be rich in faith and [as believers to be] heirs of the kingdom which He promised to those who love Him?

⁶But you [in contrast] have dishonored the poor man. Is it not the rich who oppress *and* exploit you, and personally drag you into the courts of law?

⁷Do they not blaspheme the precious name [of Christ] by which you are called?

⁸If, however, you are [really] fulfilling the royal law according to the Scripture, "YOU SHALL LOVE YOUR NEIGHBOR AS YOURSELF [that is, if you have an unselfish concern for others and do things for their benefit]" you are doing well. [Lev 19:18]

⁹But if you show partiality [prejudice, favoritism], you are committing sin and are convicted by the Law as offenders.

¹⁰For whoever keeps the whole Law but stumbles in one *point,* he has become guilty of [breaking] all of it.

¹¹For He who said, "DO NOT COMMIT ADULTERY," also said, "DO NOT MURDER." Now if you do not commit adultery, but you murder, you have become guilty of transgressing the [entire] Law. [Ex 20:13, 14; Deut 5:17, 18]

¹²Speak and act [consistently] as people who are going to be judged by the law of liberty [that moral law that frees obedient Christians from the bondage of sin].

¹³For judgment *will be* merciless to one who has shown no mercy; but [to the one who has shown mercy] mercy triumphs [victoriously] over judgment.

¹⁴What is the benefit, my fellow believers, if someone claims to have faith but has no [good] works [as evidence]? Can that [kind of] faith save him? [No, a mere claim of faith is not sufficient—genuine faith produces good works.]

¹⁵If a brother or sister is without [adequate] clothing and lacks [enough] food for each day,

¹⁶and one of you says to them, "Go in peace [with my blessing], [keep] warm and feed yourselves," but he does not give them the necessities for the body, what good does that do?

¹⁷So too, faith, if it does not have works [to back it up], is by itself dead [inoperative and ineffective].

speak the Word

Help me remember, Lord, that faith that does not have works to back it up is dead, inoperative, and ineffective.
—ADAPTED FROM JAMES 2:17

2:2 Lit *synagogue.*

¹⁸But someone may say, "You [claim to] have faith and I have [good] works; show me your [alleged] faith without the works [if you can], and I will show you my faith by my works [that is, by what I do]."

¹⁹You believe that God is one; you do well [to believe that]. The demons also believe [that], and shudder *and* bristle [in awe-filled terror—they have seen His wrath]! [Deut 6:4; 11:13–21; Mark 12:29]

²⁰But are you willing to recognize, you foolish [spiritually shallow] person, that faith without [good] works is useless?

²¹Was our father Abraham not [shown to be] justified by works [of obedience which expressed his faith] when he offered Isaac his son on the altar [as a sacrifice to God]? [Gen 22:1–14]

²²You see that [his] faith was working together with his works, and as a result of the works, his faith was completed [reaching its maturity when he expressed his faith through obedience].

²³And the Scripture was fulfilled which says, "ABRAHAM BELIEVED GOD, AND THIS [faith] WAS CREDITED TO HIM [by God] AS RIGHTEOUSNESS *and* AS

life point

James 3:5–10 teaches us about the power of the tongue. There is power in the tongue indeed, for good or evil. We can bless ourselves or curse ourselves by the way we speak. When we bless, we speak well of something; when we curse, we speak evil of something. By the words of our mouth, you and I can bless our own lives and bring joy to them, or we can curse them and bring misery upon ourselves.

I encourage you to ask God to help you control your tongue. Learn to speak blessing, not cursing. Expect joy to come to your life as a result!

CONFORMITY TO HIS WILL," and he was called the friend of God. [Gen 15:6; 2 Chr 20:7; Is 41:8]

²⁴You see that a man (believer) is justified by works and not by faith alone [that is, by acts of obedience a born-again believer reveals his faith].

²⁵In the same way, was Rahab the prostitute not justified by works too, when she received the [Hebrew] spies as guests *and* protected them, and sent them away [to escape] by a different route? [Josh 2:1–21]

²⁶For just as the [human] body without the spirit is dead, so faith without works [of obedience] is also dead.

3 NOT MANY [of you] should become teachers [serving in an official teaching capacity], my brothers and sisters, for you know that we [who are teachers] will be judged by a higher standard [because we have assumed greater accountability and more condemnation if we teach incorrectly].

²For we all stumble *and* sin in many *ways*. If anyone does not stumble in what he says [never saying the wrong thing], he is a perfect man [fully developed in character, without serious flaws], able to bridle his whole body *and* rein in his entire nature [taming his human faults and weaknesses].

³Now if we put bits into the horses' mouths to make them obey us, we guide their whole body as well.

⁴And look at the ships. Even though they are so large and are driven by strong winds, they are still directed by a very small rudder wherever the impulse of the helmsman determines.

⁵In the same sense, the tongue is a small part of the body, and yet it boasts of great things.

See [by comparison] how great a forest is set on fire by a small spark!

⁶And the tongue is [in a sense] a fire, the *very* world of injustice *and* unrighteousness; the tongue is set among our

members as that which contaminates the entire body, and sets on fire the course of our life [the cycle of man's existence], and is itself set on fire by hell (Gehenna).

⁷For every species of beasts and birds, of reptiles and sea creatures, is tamed and has been tamed by the human race.

⁸But no one can tame the *human* tongue; it is a restless evil [undisciplined, unstable], full of deadly poison.

⁹With it we bless our Lord and Father, and with it we curse men, who have been made in the likeness of God.

¹⁰Out of the same mouth come *both* blessing and cursing. These things, my brothers, should not be this way [for we have a moral obligation to speak in a manner that reflects our fear of God and profound respect for His precepts].

¹¹Does a spring send out from the same opening *both* fresh and bitter *water?*

the power of the tongue

The Bible says a great deal about the tongue and the words of our mouths. The tongue holds the power of death and life (see Proverbs 18:21). The Apostle James said that if any man can control his tongue "he is a perfect man [fully developed in character, without serious flaws] " and can also control his entire being (James 3:2). The tongue is a little member of the body, but it causes tremendous problems. Relationships often end because of things that are said or not said. People lose jobs, cause strife and misunderstanding, and embarrass themselves all with that one tiny organ, the tongue.

No man can tame the tongue, so we need God's help. King David prayed that God would put a guard over his mouth (see Psalm 141:3). He also prayed that the words of his mouth and the meditation of his heart would be acceptable in God's sight (see Psalm 19:14). David knew he could not control his mouth without God's help, and neither can we.

We should avoid "[every form of] wicked (sinful, unjust) speech" (Isaiah 58:9). Jesus said we must take His yoke upon us and learn of Him because He is gentle, meek, and humble, not harsh, hard, sharp, and pressing (see Matthew 11:29, 30, AMPC). According to Proverbs 15:4, "A soothing tongue [speaking words that build up and encourage] is a tree of life, but a perverse tongue [speaking words that overwhelm and depress] crushes the spirit." Even our voice tones are important because they reveal the condition of our hearts.

We can speak words of healing or words that wound; we can edify and build up or discourage and tear down. Words are containers for power and they carry either positive or negative power. The decision is up to us! Words are seeds that we sow and they definitely bring a harvest in our lives. Those who indulge the tongue must eat the fruit of their words, whether they are for death or life (see Proverbs 18:21).

One thing we should strive to do is think before we speak. The Bible says that we are not to be rash with our mouths, but how many times do we say things and then think, "Oh, I wish I had not said that?" But then it is too late because the words are already doing their work. I recommend a thorough study of all these subjects and a sincere prayer asking for God's help to tame the tongue.

¹²Can a fig tree, my brothers, produce olives, or a grapevine produce figs? Nor can salt water produce fresh.

¹³Who among you is wise and intelligent? Let him by his good conduct show his [good] deeds with the gentleness *and* humility of *true* wisdom.

¹⁴But if you have bitter jealousy and selfish ambition in your hearts, do not be arrogant, and [as a result] be in defiance of the truth.

¹⁵This [superficial] wisdom is not that which comes down from above, but is earthly (secular), natural (unspiritual), *even* demonic.

¹⁶For where jealousy and selfish ambition exist, there is disorder [unrest, rebellion] and every evil thing *and* morally degrading practice.

¹⁷But the wisdom from above is first pure [morally and spiritually undefiled], then peace-loving [courteous, considerate], gentle, reasonable [and willing to listen], full of compassion and good fruits. It is unwavering, without [self-righteous] hypocrisy [and self-serving guile].

¹⁸And the seed whose fruit is righteousness (spiritual maturity) is sown in peace by those who make peace [by actively encouraging goodwill between individuals].

4 WHAT LEADS to [the unending] quarrels and conflicts among you? Do they not come from your [hedonistic] desires that wage war in your [bodily] members [fighting for control over you]?

²You are jealous *and* covet [what others have] and your lust goes unfulfilled; so you murder. You are envious and cannot obtain [the object of your

life point

All human beings have evil tendencies, but James 4:6 teaches us that God will give us more and more grace to meet these tendencies.

I spent much of my Christian life trying to overcome my wrong motives and intentions. All my trying brought much frustration. I had to come to a place of humility and learn that God gives grace to the humble, not the proud (see 1 Peter 5:5).

We have our own ideas about what we can accomplish, but often we think more highly of ourselves than we ought. We need humble attitudes, knowing that apart from God, we can do nothing.

If you are planning your own way, trying to make things happen in the strength of your own flesh, then no doubt you are frustrated. You probably have said, "No matter what I do, nothing seems to work!" Nothing will ever work until you learn to trust in God's grace.

Relax. Let God be God. Stop being so hard on yourself. Change is a process; it comes little by little. You are on your way to perfection, so enjoy the trip.

envy]; so you fight and battle. You do not have because you do not ask [it of God]. [1 John 3:15]

³You ask [God for something] and do not receive it, because you ask with wrong motives [out of selfishness or with an unrighteous agenda], so that [when you get what you want] you

speak the Word

Thank You, Lord, that the wisdom You give is first pure and undefiled, then peace-loving, gentle, reasonable, full of compassion and good fruits. It is unwavering and without hypocrisy.
−ADAPTED FROM JAMES 3:17

just ask!

I believe James is saying to us in James 4:1, 2, "You stay upset all the time because you try to get all the things you want through your own efforts. You are never going to get them that way. You are only going to end up being jealous, hating people, and having bad relationships because you want what they have."

Then James summarizes the whole situation in one sentence: "You do not have because you do not ask [it of God]" (James 4:2). Essentially, he points to how we try to get things ourselves instead of asking God for them.

You may think, "But I *have* asked God for things; He just has not given them to me."

If you ask God for something and He does not give it to you, the reason is not that He is holding out on you. It may be that it is not His will or that now is not His time. It may be that there is something better He wants to give you, but you are not yet spiritually mature enough to have it. Whatever the reason, it is never because He does not want you to be blessed.

You are God's child, and He loves you. He is a good God Who does only good things, and He wants to do so much more for you than you could possibly imagine. But He loves you too much to give you things that could hurt you. He loves you too much to give you things that will ultimately make you more carnal or more fleshly or that may even drag you into sin because you are not yet ready to handle them.

Does a loving parent give his children the keys to the car before they are old enough to drive? Of course not, because the parent knows they may get hurt in a wreck through their inexperience. God is the same way with His children. Because He loves us, He will not give us something before we have the spiritual maturity to handle it.

Many people use manipulation and worldly ways to get things they have no business having—and those very things end up ruining them.

I have discovered that the secret of being content is to ask God for what I want and to rest in the knowledge that if it is right, He will bring it to pass at the right time. If it is not right, He will do something much better than what I asked for.

may spend it on your [hedonistic] desires.

⁴You adulteresses [disloyal sinners—flirting with the world and breaking your vow to God]! Do you not know that being the world's friend [that is, loving the things of the world] is being God's enemy? So whoever chooses to be a friend of the world makes himself an enemy of God.

⁵Or do you think that the Scripture says to no purpose that the [human] spirit which He has made to dwell in us lusts with envy? [Gen 6:5]

⁶But He gives us more and more grace [through the power of the Holy Spirit to defy sin and live an obedient life that reflects both our faith and our gratitude for our salvation]. Therefore, it says, "GOD IS OPPOSED TO THE PROUD *and* HAUGHTY, BUT [continually] GIVES [the gift of] GRACE TO THE HUMBLE [who turn away from self-righteousness]." [Prov 3:34]

7So submit to [the authority of] God. Resist the devil [stand firm against him] and he will flee from you.

8Come close to God [with a contrite heart] and He will come close to you. Wash your hands, you sinners; and purify your [unfaithful] hearts, you double-minded [people].

9Be miserable and grieve and weep [over your sin]. Let your [foolish] laughter be turned to mourning and your [reckless] joy to gloom.

life point

We must remember that the devil is not going to sit back and allow us to take new ground without putting up a fight. Any time we make progress in building the kingdom of God, our enemy is going to come against us, but James 4:7 says that he will flee if we resist him.

Many times we make the mistake of trying to use faith to get to the place where we have total freedom from trouble. What we do not realize is that the purpose of faith is not always to keep us from having trouble; it is often to carry us *through* trouble. If we never had trouble, we would never need faith.

Although we are tempted to run away from our problems, the Lord says we are to go through them. The good news is that He promises we will never have to go through them alone. He will always be there to help us in every way. He tells us, "Fear not, for I am with you."

In our daily experience, we must learn to stand our ground and run the devil off our property and drive him out of different areas of our lives. Learning to be stable in hard times is one of the best ways to do this. Remember, the devil will oppose you, but you have the power to resist him—and he will flee!

10Humble yourselves [with an attitude of repentance and insignificance] in the presence of the Lord, and He will exalt you [He will lift you up, He will give you purpose].

11Believers, do not speak against *or* slander one another. He who speaks [self-righteously] against a brother or judges his brother [hypocritically], speaks against the Law and judges the Law. If you judge the Law, you are not a doer of the Law but a judge of it.

12There is *only* one Lawgiver and Judge, the One who is able to save and to destroy [the one God who has the absolute power of life and death]; but who are you to [hypocritically or self-righteously] pass judgment on your neighbor?

13Come now [and pay attention to this], you who say, "Today or tomorrow we will go to such and such a city, and spend a year there and carry on our business and make a profit."

14Yet you do not know [the least thing] about what may happen in your life tomorrow. [What is secure in your life?] You are *merely* a vapor [like a puff of smoke or a wisp of steam from a cooking pot] that is visible for a little while and then vanishes [into thin air].

putting the Word to work

Do you like to plan excessively? Some people seem to have their lives all figured out. They map out a plan for their career, their family, their retirement years, and their financial portfolios. While it is wise to prepare and plan, the Word of God reminds us that we actually do not know what tomorrow will bring (see James 4:13–15). However, we can depend completely on God and trust Him fully with our lives. Ask God to continue to reveal His will for your life to you—and be willing to adjust your plans as He does.

putting the Word to work

Did you know that you can sin by *not* doing something? You can, according to James 4:17. Committing evil deeds is certainly sinful, but so is failing to do what you know God wants you to do. Spend time praying and reading your Bible so you can grow in your understanding of sinful practices to avoid and learn to actively engage in what is pleasing to God.

¹⁵Instead you ought to say, "If the Lord wills, we will live and we will do this or that."

¹⁶But as it is, you boast [vainly] in your pretension *and* arrogance. All such boasting is evil.

¹⁷So any person who knows what is right to do but does not do it, to him it is sin.

5 COME [QUICKLY] now, you rich [who lack true faith and hoard and misuse your resources], weep and howl over the miseries [the woes, the judgments] that are coming upon you.

²Your wealth has rotted *and* is ruined and your [fine] clothes have become moth-eaten.

³Your gold and silver are corroded, and their corrosion will be a witness against you and will consume your flesh like fire. You have stored up your treasure in the last days [when it will do you no good].

⁴Look! The wages that you have [fraudulently] withheld from the laborers who have mowed your fields are crying out [against you for vengeance]; and the cries of the harvesters have come to the ears of the Lord of Sabaoth. [1 Sam 1:3]

⁵On the earth you have lived luxuriously *and* abandoned yourselves to soft living and led a life of wanton pleasure [self-indulgence, self-gratification]; you have fattened your hearts in a day of slaughter.

⁶You have condemned and have put to death the righteous *man;* he offers you no resistance.

⁷So wait patiently, brothers and sisters, until the coming of the Lord. The farmer waits [expectantly] for the precious harvest from the land, being patient about it, until it receives the early and late rains.

⁸You too, be patient; strengthen your hearts [keep them energized and firmly committed to God], because the coming of the Lord is near.

⁹Do not complain against one another, believers, so that you will not be judged [for it]. Look! The Judge is standing right at the door.

¹⁰As an example, brothers and sisters, of suffering and patience, take the prophets who spoke in the name of the Lord [as His messengers and representatives].

¹¹You know we call those blessed [happy, spiritually prosperous, favored by God] who were steadfast *and* endured [difficult circumstances]. You have heard of the *patient* endurance of Job and you have seen the Lord's outcome [how He richly blessed Job]. The Lord is full of compassion and is merciful. [Job 1:21, 22; 42:10; Ps 111:4]

¹²But above all, my fellow believers, do not swear, either by heaven or by

life point

Patience is not just the ability to wait; it is the ability to keep a good attitude while waiting.

James 5:7 does not say to be patient *if* you wait, it says to "wait patiently." Waiting is part of life. Many people do not wait well, yet we actually spend more time in our lives waiting than we do receiving. Ask God to help you wait well!

earth or with any other oath; but let your yes be [a truthful] yes, and your no be [a truthful] no, so that you may not fall under judgment. [Matt 5:34–37]

¹³Is anyone among you suffering? He must pray. Is anyone joyful? He is to sing praises [to God].

¹⁴Is anyone among you sick? He must call for the elders (spiritual leaders) of the church and they are to pray over him, anointing him with oil in the name of the Lord;

¹⁵and the prayer of faith will restore the one who is sick, and the Lord will raise him up; and if he has committed sins, he will be forgiven.

¹⁶Therefore, confess your sins to one another [your false steps, your offenses], and pray for one another, that you may be healed *and* restored. The heartfelt *and* persistent prayer of a righteous man (believer) can accomplish much [when put into action and made effective by God—it is dynamic and can have tremendous power].

¹⁷Elijah was a man with a nature like ours [with the same physical, mental, and spiritual limitations and

worry-free decisions

After making a decision, stand firm. Let your "yes" be a simple yes and your "no" be a simple no.

I believe indecision and double-mindedness not only bring confusion and complication, but, as James 5:12 notes, they also cause feelings of judgment or condemnation. If we believe in our hearts that we should do something and then allow our heads to talk us out of it, we leave an open door for condemnation. We often labor over decisions when actually we just need to pray and then follow our hearts.

Start making decisions without worrying about them. Do not live in fear of being wrong. If your heart is right and you make a decision that is not in accordance with God's will, He will forgive you and get you back on course.

Once you do make a decision, do not let self-doubt torment you. Being double-minded and never deciding anything is complicated. Doubting your decisions after they are made will steal the enjoyment from everything you do.

My husband does not mind shopping with me at all, which is a blessing because most men do not enjoy shopping. He gives me a reasonable amount of time to make my choices, but if I go back and forth too many times, he wants to leave. He says, "Do something. I do not mind being here if we make progress, but just wandering around and never making any choices is a waste of time."

This does not mean it is wrong to take a certain amount of time to look things over and search for a good bargain, but if looking and searching go too far, decision-making becomes complicated. Keep it simple. Buy something and move on to the next thing.

Similarly, make decisions in life as simple as you can, whether your decisions are small ones like I just described, or big decisions that affect your future. Be prayerful and seek to obey God; then make a decision and go on without looking back.

shortcomings], and he prayed intensely for it not to rain, and it did not rain on the earth for three years and six months. [1 Kin 17:1]

¹⁸Then he prayed again, and the sky gave rain and the land produced its crops [as usual]. [1 Kin 18:42–45]

¹⁹My brothers and sisters, if anyone among you strays from the truth *and* falls into error and [another] one turns him back [to God],

²⁰let the [latter] one know that the one who has turned a sinner from the error of his way will save that one's soul from death and cover a multitude of sins [that is, obtain the pardon of the many sins committed by the one who has been restored].

tell the right person

James 5:16 teaches us that confessing our faults to one another aids us in the process of healing and restoration. Many times we receive a release from what is troubling us when we finally tell someone else those things that have been hidden for sometimes years of our lives. Anything we feel we have to hide has power over us, but when things are exposed the truth will make us free. I caution you to use wisdom as you choose a person to confide in. Be Spirit-led. Choose someone you know you can trust, someone who is understanding and will not judge you.

Do not share things with people to help yourself if those things will hurt them. For example, if your grandfather abused you forty years ago, and now your grandmother is eighty-five years old, I advise you not to tell her what happened. That would not be wise. It might help you to release it, but it would burden her. Instead, find a trusted spiritual leader, minister, or counselor.

Using wisdom and balance is so important in these matters. If you are going to share your problems with someone, let God show you who to choose as a confidant. Pick a mature believer, someone who will not be burdened or harmed by what you share or use it to hurt you or make you feel worse about yourself.

We do not always need to confess every fault to someone else but there are times when it is very helpful. I strongly encourage you to follow the biblical instruction to confess your faults to others when you need to in order for you to be healed and restored—just use wisdom as you do.

First Peter

Author:
Peter

Date:
Early AD Sixties

Everyday Life Principles:
Remember that you always have hope in Jesus.

Live a godly life in the midst of an ungodly world.

Be patient and stay faithful in the midst of suffering.

First Peter is such an encouragement to those of us who believe because it reminds us that we always have hope in Jesus. This letter is full of practical advice for everyday living, especially in the midst of hard times, and it urges us to keep the glory of our inheritance in view while we are living here on earth.

First Peter teaches us that there is such a thing as godly suffering. Some suffering is done *in* Christ and some is done *for* Him. When a believer suffers in order to do God's will, that is cause for rejoicing (see 1 Peter 4:13). Saying no to self and suffering in the flesh leads to the death of selfishness, and that kind of hardship yields tremendous freedom and strength.

First Peter also calls us to develop lifestyles that are holy and pleasing to the Lord. It addresses not only our behavior, but also our intentions, and causes us to examine our hearts so we can operate from pure motives. In addition, the words of this book give us nuggets of truth to fight the spiritual war and overcome the enemy. It exhorts us to remember that everything about our lives is a witness that tells others something about God, that we are to live humbly before God, and that above all, we are to love one another fervently (see 1 Peter 4:8).

I hope this book encourages you when you go through trials and difficult times in your life and that it inspires you to develop and maintain godly attitudes and behaviors in every area of your life.

1 PETER, AN apostle (special messenger, personally chosen representative) of Jesus Christ,

To those [elect—both Jewish and Gentile believers] who live as exiles, scattered throughout Pontus, Galatia, Cappadocia, Asia [Minor], and Bithynia, who are chosen [Heb 13:14]

²according to the foreknowledge of God the Father by the sanctifying work of the Spirit to be obedient to Jesus Christ and to be sprinkled with His blood: May grace and peace [that special sense of spiritual well-being] be yours in increasing abundance [as you walk closely with God]. [John 14:27]

³Blessed [gratefully praised and adored] be the God and Father of our Lord Jesus Christ, who according to His abundant *and* boundless mercy has caused us to be born again [that is, to be reborn from above—spiritually transformed, renewed, and set apart for His purpose] to an ever-living hope *and* confident assurance through the resurrection of Jesus Christ from the dead, [Matt 28:1–9; Mark 16:6; Luke 24:6; John 20:1–18]

⁴[born anew] into an inheritance which is imperishable [beyond the reach of change] and undefiled and unfading, reserved in heaven for you,

⁵who are being protected *and* shielded by the power of God through *your* faith for salvation that is ready to be revealed [for you] in the last time.

⁶In this you rejoice greatly, even though now for a little while, if necessary, you have been distressed by various trials,

⁷so that the genuineness of your faith, which is much more precious

life point

When we become born again by accepting Jesus as our Savior, we have an "ever-living hope" in our hearts, according to 1 Peter 1:3.

than gold which is perishable, even though tested *and* purified by fire, may be found to result in [your] praise and glory and honor at the revelation of Jesus Christ.

⁸Though you have not seen Him, you love Him; and though you do not even see Him now, you believe *and* trust in Him and you greatly rejoice *and* delight with inexpressible and glorious joy,

⁹receiving as the result [the outcome, the consummation] of your faith, the salvation of your souls.

¹⁰Regarding this salvation, the prophets who prophesied about the grace [of God] that *was intended for* you, searched carefully and inquired [about this future way of salvation],

¹¹seeking to find out what person or what time the Spirit of Christ within them was indicating as He foretold the sufferings of Christ and the glories [destined] to follow.

¹²It was revealed to them that their services [their prophecies regarding grace] were not [meant] for themselves *and* their time, but for you, in these things [the death, resurrection, and glorification of Jesus Christ] which have now been told to you by those who preached the gospel to you by the [power of the] Holy Spirit [who was] sent from heaven. Into these things even the angels long to look.

¹³So prepare your minds for action, be completely sober [in spirit—steadfast, self-disciplined, spiritually and morally alert], fix your hope completely on the grace [of God] that is coming to you when Jesus Christ is revealed.

¹⁴[Live] as obedient children [of God]; do not be conformed to the evil desires *which governed you* in your ignorance [before you knew the requirements and transforming power of the good news regarding salvation].

¹⁵But like the Holy One who called you, be holy yourselves in all *your* conduct [be set apart from the world by

life point

God never tells us to be holy (see 1 Peter 1:15, 16) without giving us the help we need to become that way. An unholy spirit can never make us holy, so God sends His Holy Spirit into our hearts to do a complete and thorough work in us.

your godly character and moral courage];

¹⁶because it is written, "YOU SHALL BE HOLY (set apart), FOR I AM HOLY." [Lev 11:44, 45; 19:2]

¹⁷If you address as Father, the One who impartially judges according to each one's work, conduct yourselves in [reverent] fear [of Him] *and* with profound respect for Him throughout the time of your stay *on earth*.

¹⁸For you know that you were not redeemed from your useless [spiritually unproductive] way of life inherited [by tradition] from your forefathers with perishable things like silver and gold,

¹⁹but [you were actually purchased] with precious blood, like that of a [sacrificial] lamb unblemished and spotless, *the priceless blood* of Christ. [Lev 22:20]

²⁰For He was foreordained (foreknown) before the foundation of the world, but has appeared [publicly] in these last times for your sake

²¹and through Him you believe [confidently] in God [the heavenly Father], who raised Him from the dead and gave Him glory, so that your faith and hope are [centered and rest] in God.

²²Since by your obedience to the truth you have purified yourselves for a sincere love of the believers, [see that you] love one another from the heart [always unselfishly seeking the best for one another],

²³for you have been born again [that is, reborn from above—spiritually transformed, renewed, and set apart for His purpose] not of seed which is perishable but [from that which is]

imperishable *and* immortal, *that is,* through the living and everlasting word of God.

²⁴For,

"ALL FLESH IS LIKE GRASS,
AND ALL ITS GLORY LIKE THE
    FLOWER OF GRASS.
THE GRASS WITHERS
AND THE FLOWER FALLS OFF,
²⁵BUT THE WORD OF THE LORD
    ENDURES FOREVER."

And this is the word [the good news of salvation] which was preached to you. [Is 40:6–8]

life point

The Holy Spirit, according to 1 Peter 1:22, is the One Who purifies our hearts so we can allow the sincere love of God to flow through us to others. The Holy Spirit's aim is to get us to the place where the sincere love of God flows through us, which helps us to be continually filled with the Holy Spirit.

Walking in the love of God is the ultimate goal of Christianity, and should be the primary pursuit of our lives. We should keep our love for Jesus red-hot. We should also have a fervent, unfailing love for one another (see 1 Peter 4:8). Jesus Himself instructed us to love one another as He loves us (see John 15:12). He said that was the new commandment He came to pronounce and that all other commandments are summed up in the exhortation to love God and to love other people (see John 13:34; Matthew 22:37–40).

When I think of what I can do for myself or how I can get others to bless me, I am filled with me. When I think of other people and how I can bless them, I find myself filled with the Holy Spirit, Who is the Spirit of love.

2 SO PUT aside every trace of malice and all deceit and hypocrisy and envy and all slander *and* hateful speech;

²like newborn babies [you should] long for the pure milk of the word, so that by it you may be nurtured *and* grow in respect to salvation [its ultimate fulfillment],

³if in fact you have [already] tasted the goodness *and* gracious kindness of the Lord. [Ps 34:8]

⁴Come to Him [the risen Lord] as to a living Stone which men rejected *and* threw away, but which is choice and precious in the sight of God. [Ps 118:22; Is 28:16]

⁵You [believers], like living stones, are being built up into a spiritual house for a holy *and* dedicated priesthood, to offer spiritual sacrifices [that are] acceptable *and* pleasing to God through Jesus Christ.

⁶For this is contained in Scripture:

"BEHOLD, I AM LAYING IN ZION
    A CHOSEN STONE, A PRECIOUS
    (honored) CORNERSTONE,
AND HE WHO BELIEVES IN HIM
    [whoever adheres to, trusts
    in, and relies on Him] WILL
    NEVER BE DISAPPOINTED [in his
    expectations]." [Is 28:16]

⁷This precious value, then, is for you who believe [in Him as God's only Son—the Source of salvation]; but for those who disbelieve,

"THE [very] STONE WHICH THE
    BUILDERS REJECTED
HAS BECOME THE CHIEF
    CORNERSTONE," [Ps 118:22]

life point

Like "living stones" (1 Peter 2:5) we are to live dedicated, consecrated lives that include spiritual sacrifices, but only the kind that are acceptable and pleasing to God. The only spiritual sacrifices acceptable and pleasing to God are those done with the right motives, such as a desire to express our love for Him or a desire to honor Him and thank Him for what He has done for us.

⁸and,

"A STONE OF STUMBLING AND A ROCK
    OF OFFENSE";

for they stumble because they disobey the word [of God], and to this they [who reject Him as Savior] were also appointed. [Is 8:14]

⁹But you are A CHOSEN RACE, A royal PRIESTHOOD, A CONSECRATED NATION, A [special] PEOPLE FOR *God's* OWN POSSESSION, so that you may proclaim the excellencies [the wonderful deeds and virtues and perfections] of Him who called you out of darkness into His marvelous light. [Ex 19:5, 6]

¹⁰Once you were NOT A PEOPLE [at all], but now you are GOD'S PEOPLE; once you had NOT RECEIVED MERCY, but now you have RECEIVED MERCY. [Hos 2:23]

¹¹Beloved, I urge you as aliens and strangers [in this world] to abstain from the sensual urges [those dishonorable desires] that wage war against the soul.

¹²Keep your behavior excellent among the [unsaved] Gentiles [conduct

speak the Word

*Lord, I thank You for choosing me and making me
one of Your own special people and for calling me so
I can proclaim the excellencies of You. You are the One
Who called me out of darkness into Your marvelous light.*
—ADAPTED FROM 1 PETER 2:9

yourself honorably, with graciousness and integrity], so that for whatever reason they may slander you as
evildoers, yet by observing your good
deeds they may [instead come to] glorify God in the day of visitation [when
He looks upon them with mercy].

¹³Submit yourselves to [the authority of] every human institution for the
sake of the Lord [to honor His name],
whether it is to a king as one in a position of power,

¹⁴or to governors as sent by him to
bring punishment to those who do
wrong, and to praise *and* encourage
those who do right.

¹⁵For it is the will of God that by
doing right you may silence (muzzle,
gag) the [culpable] ignorance *and* irresponsible criticisms of foolish people.

¹⁶*Live* as free people, but do not use
your freedom as a cover *or* pretext
for evil, but [use it and live] as bond-
servants of God.

it's all in your attitude

Suffering is one of the most difficult things to understand in life and in Christianity.
We know that God is good and we know that He sees everything and is all-powerful,
so why does He allow us to suffer, especially unjustly? This question has been asked
by millions throughout the ages: "Why, God? Why?"

God does not delight in our suffering, but He is honored and pleased when we
endure it with a good attitude (see 1 Peter 2:19, 20). Trust requires unanswered
questions. If we knew all the answers, faith would not be necessary.

Some people become angry with God when tragedy or extreme difficulty comes
their way. This is the worst thing anyone can do because He is the only One Who
can help us. One man I know endured the tragic experience of watching his only
son die of cancer. Afterward, he bitterly asked God, "Where were you when my
son died?" God replied, "The same place I was when Mine died."

God gave His only Son and allowed Him to go through unspeakable suffering He
did not deserve, and He did it for us. There are times when we go through things
God intends to use for our good and for the good of others later in our lives.

During my childhood, I was abused for many years. I prayed and prayed, but no
deliverance came. I did receive strength to endure and a determination to overcome
and to someday do something great with my life. Many character traits developed
in me during those years that have greatly helped me in the ministry I have today.
One of them is that I truly can relate to people who have been hurt by others. I can
teach from experience how important it is to forgive our enemies and help people
know how to do it. Suffering can make us bitter or better; the decision is ours!

The true test of faith is how we behave during trials and tribulations, especially
ones we feel are unfair. Peter said that fiery ordeals will come to test the quality of
our faith and that we are not to think they are strange (see 1 Peter 4:12). Instead
of being concerned about *why* we suffer, let's make the decision to get through
suffering with good attitudes and we will see God work everything together for
good (see Romans 8:28).

¹⁷Show respect for all people [treat them honorably], love the brotherhood [of believers], fear God, honor the king.

¹⁸Servants, be submissive to your masters with all [proper] respect, not only to those who are good and kind, but also to those who are unreasonable.

¹⁹For this *finds* favor, if a person endures the sorrow of suffering unjustly because of an awareness of [the will of] God.

²⁰After all, what kind of credit is there if, when you do wrong and are punished for it, you endure it patiently? But if when you do what is right and patiently bear [undeserved] suffering, this *finds* favor with God.

²¹For [as a believer] you have been called for this purpose, since Christ suffered for you, leaving you an example, so that you may follow in His footsteps.

²²HE COMMITTED NO SIN, NOR WAS DECEIT EVER FOUND IN HIS MOUTH. [Is 53:9]

²³While being reviled *and* insulted, He did not revile *or* insult in return; while suffering, He made no threats [of vengeance], but kept entrusting *Himself* to Him who judges fairly.

²⁴He personally carried our sins in His body on the cross [willingly offering Himself on it, as on an altar of sacrifice], so that we might die to sin [becoming immune from the penalty and power of sin] and live for righteousness; for by His wounds you [who believe] have been healed.

²⁵For you were continually wandering like [so many] sheep, but now you have come back to the Shepherd and Guardian of your souls. [Is 53:5, 6]

3 IN THE same way, you wives, be submissive to your own husbands [subordinate, not as inferior, but out of respect for the responsibilities entrusted to husbands and their accountability to God, and so partnering

with them] so that even if some do not obey the word [of God], they may be won over [to Christ] without discussion by the *godly* lives of their wives, [Eph 5:22]

²when they see your modest and respectful behavior [together with your devotion and appreciation—love your husband, encourage him, and enjoy him as a blessing from God].

³Your adornment must not be *merely* external—with interweaving *and* elaborate knotting of the hair, and wearing gold jewelry, or [being superficially preoccupied with] dressing in *expensive* clothes;

⁴but let it be [the inner beauty of] the hidden person of the heart, with the imperishable quality *and* unfading charm of a gentle and peaceful spirit, [one that is calm and self-controlled, not overanxious, but serene and spiritually mature] which is very precious in the sight of God.

⁵For in this way in former times the holy women, who hoped in God, used to adorn themselves, being submissive to their own husbands *and* adapting themselves to them;

⁶just as Sarah obeyed Abraham [following him and having regard for him as head of their house], calling him lord. And you have become her daughters if you do what is right without being frightened by any fear [that is, being respectful toward your husband but not giving in to intimidation, nor allowing yourself to be led into sin, nor to be harmed].

⁷In the same way, you husbands, live with *your wives* in an understanding way [with great gentleness and tact, and with an intelligent regard for the marriage relationship], as with someone physically weaker, since she is a woman. Show her honor *and* respect as a fellow heir of the grace of life, so that your prayers will not be hindered *or* ineffective.

the hidden person of the heart

First Peter 3:4 talks about "the hidden person of the heart," which means who a person really is underneath his or her appearance. When we interact with others, we should endeavor to know who they really are, in their hearts, and not make hasty judgments against them or judge them according to their appearance. When we do not endeavor to know the "hidden person of the heart," we make a mistake in one of two ways: 1) we approve of someone because they appear to be something they are not; or 2) we disapprove of someone because of some outward appearance or action, when that individual is actually a wonderful person on the inside.

I have found that we all have our little quirks and our odd actions, behaviors, and ways that other people do not easily understand. God Himself does not judge by appearance, and we need to follow His example.

David would have never been chosen by man to be king unless God looked at his heart. Even his own family disregarded him. They did not even include him in the selection process (see 1 Samuel 16:1–13)! But the Lord saw David's heart, the heart of a shepherd. God saw a worshiper, someone with a heart for Him, someone who was pliable and moldable in His hand. These are the qualities He looks for in us.

I often think of the geodes—crude, ugly looking rocks that appear hideous on the outside, but absolutely gorgeous on the inside. Some are actually gemstones inside, but their rough, crusty exteriors are terribly unattractive.

Like the geodes, we are often rough, crusty, and crude on the outside, but God knows He has placed great beauty within us. Just as the gold miner knows he must be patient when digging for nuggets, God knows He must be patient with us as the Holy Spirit continues working with us, digging in our lives, and eventually bringing out the treasures that are within us.

What we sow into the lives of other people, we will surely reap in our own. If we sow harsh, hasty judgment, we will in turn reap harsh, hasty judgment. So, when the temptation to judge or criticize is at the door, resist it. Instead, do your best to look for the best in others and see what God values about each one—the hidden person of the heart.

I also remind you to examine your own heart and be sure you have right motives and heart attitudes. Our secret thoughts and attitudes should be godly. We may hide from other people what is going on inside of us, but we cannot hide anything from God. Our outer man is our reputation with people, but the hidden person of the heart is our reputation with God. We should be much more concerned about our reputations in heaven than we are with our reputations on earth.

⁸Finally, all of you be like-minded [united in spirit], sympathetic, brotherly, kindhearted [courteous and compassionate toward each other as members of one household], and humble in spirit;

⁹and never return evil for evil or insult for insult [avoid scolding, berating,

and any kind of abuse], but on the contrary, give a blessing [pray for one another's well-being, contentment, and protection]; for you have been called for this very purpose, that you might inherit a blessing [from God that brings well-being, happiness, and protection].

¹⁰For,

"THE ONE WHO WANTS TO ENJOY
  LIFE AND SEE GOOD DAYS [good—
  whether apparent or not],
MUST KEEP HIS TONGUE FREE FROM
  EVIL AND HIS LIPS FROM SPEAKING
  GUILE (treachery, deceit).
¹¹"HE MUST TURN AWAY FROM
  WICKEDNESS AND DO WHAT IS
  RIGHT.
HE MUST SEARCH FOR PEACE [with
  God, with self, with others] AND
  PURSUE IT EAGERLY [actively—not
  merely desiring it].
¹²"FOR THE EYES OF THE LORD ARE
  [looking favorably] UPON THE
  RIGHTEOUS (the upright),
AND HIS EARS ARE ATTENTIVE TO
  THEIR PRAYER (eager to answer),
BUT THE FACE OF THE LORD IS
  AGAINST THOSE WHO PRACTICE
  EVIL." [Ps 34:12–16]

¹³Now who is there to hurt you if you become enthusiastic for what is good? ¹⁴But even if you should suffer for the sake of righteousness [though it is not certain that you will], you are still blessed [happy, to be admired and favored by God]. DO NOT BE AFRAID OF THEIR INTIMIDATING THREATS, NOR BE

life point

If we want to enjoy life, which is possible even when there is no apparent reason for us to enjoy it, we must keep our tongues free from evil (see 1 Peter 3:10). If we speak positively and keep the truth of God's Word on our lips, we will have joy even in the midst of difficulties.

TROUBLED or DISTURBED [by their opposition].

¹⁵But in your hearts set Christ apart [as holy—acknowledging Him, giving Him first place in your lives] as Lord. Always be ready to give a [logical] defense to anyone who asks you to account for the hope and confident assurance [elicited by faith] that is within you, yet [do it] with gentleness and respect. [Is 8:12, 13] ¹⁶And see to it that your conscience is entirely clear, so that every time you are slandered or falsely accused, those who attack or disparage your good behavior in Christ will be shamed [by their own words]. ¹⁷For it is better that you suffer [unjustly] for doing what is right, if that should be God's will, than [to suffer justly] for doing wrong. ¹⁸For indeed Christ died for sins once for all, the Just and Righteous for the unjust and unrighteous [the Innocent for the guilty] so that He might bring us to God, having been put to death in the flesh, but made alive in the Spirit; ¹⁹in which He also went and preached to the spirits now in prison, ²⁰who once were disobedient, when the great patience of God was waiting in the days of Noah, during the building of the ark, in which a few, that is, eight persons [Noah's family], were brought safely through the water. [Gen 6–8] ²¹Corresponding to that [rescue through the flood], baptism [which is an expression of a believer's new life in Christ] now saves you, not by removing dirt from the body, but by an appeal to God for a good (clear) conscience, [demonstrating what you believe to be yours] through the resurrection of Jesus Christ, ²²who has gone into heaven and is at the right hand of God [that is, the place of honor and authority], with

[all] angels and authorities and powers made subservient to Him.

4 THEREFORE, SINCE Christ suffered in the flesh [and died for us], arm yourselves [like warriors] with the same purpose [being willing to suffer for doing what is right and pleasing God], because whoever has suffered in the flesh [being like-minded with Christ] is done with [intentional] sin [having stopped pleasing the world],

²so that he can no longer spend the rest of his natural life living for human appetites *and* desires, but [lives] for the will *and* purpose of God.

³For the time already past is [more than] enough for doing what the [unsaved] Gentiles like to do—living [unrestrained as you have done] in

life point

First Peter 4:1, 2 helps us know how to face suffering. *Suffering* and *sacrifice* are not always popular words among Christians, but they are biblical words. Spiritual maturity or Christlikeness cannot be obtained without dying to self, which simply means saying yes to God and no to our flesh when our will and God's will are in opposition.

a course of [shameless] sensuality, lusts, drunkenness, carousing, drinking parties, and wanton idolatries.

⁴In [connection with] all this, they [the unbelievers] are resentful *and* surprised that you do not [think like them, value their values and] run [hand in hand] with *them* into the same excesses

have fervent love

One of the most amazing things I have ever learned, a lesson that still thrills my soul, is that love is actually spiritual warfare. This truth makes spiritual warfare fun, because loving people is very enjoyable.

I have learned that instead of looking like I am oppressed and under something all the time, I can actually look happy. I have found that I can be *on* the attack instead of *under* the attack.

First Peter 4:8 teaches us to have "fervent and unfailing love for one another." The verb form of the Greek word that is translated *fervent* means, "to be hot, to boil." Our love walk needs to be hot, on fire, and boiling over, not tepid, cold, or barely noticeable.

I once heard someone say that even a fly is smart enough to know not to light on a hot stove. If we are hot enough with love, Satan cannot stay around us for long. We might say we will be, "too hot to handle!"

Have you ever let something cook in the microwave for too long and found yourself unable to remove it from the oven because it was too hot to handle? That is the way I want to be. I want the love of God in my heart to be so red-hot that Satan dreads to see me get out of bed in the morning.

Let your love be red-hot. Let it be fervent and unfailing toward God and toward other people, and as you do, you will not only live in obedience to the Word, you will also be too hot and on fire with God's love for the enemy to handle.

of dissipation *and* immoral freedom, and they criticize *and* abuse *and* ridicule you *and* make fun of your values.

⁵But they will [have to] give an account to Him who is ready to judge *and* pass sentence on the living and the dead.

⁶For this is why the good news [of salvation] was preached [in their lifetimes] even to those who are dead, that though they were judged in the flesh as men are, they may live in the spirit according to [the will and purpose of] God.

⁷The end *and* culmination of all things is near. Therefore, be sound-minded and self-controlled for the

purpose of prayer [staying balanced and focused on the things of God so that your communication will be clear, reasonable, specific and pleasing to Him.]

⁸Above all, have fervent *and* unfailing love for one another, because love covers a multitude of sins [it overlooks unkindness and unselfishly seeks the best for others]. [Prov 10:12]

⁹Be hospitable to one another without complaint.

¹⁰Just as each one of you has received a *special* gift [a spiritual talent, an ability graciously given by God], employ it in serving one another as [is appropriate for] good stewards

the Spirit of glory

First Peter 4:14 states that "the Spirit of glory and of God" rests upon us when we are reproached for the name of Christ. Just imagine, we think it is awful when people mistreat us because we are Christians, but God sees that in an entirely different light. God never expects us to suffer for Him without His help. Therefore, we can firmly believe that any time we are reproached or mistreated in any way because of our faith in Christ, God gives us an extra measure of His Spirit to counterbalance the attack.

The Holy Spirit often acts as a shock absorber. Automobiles have shock absorbers to soften the blow of unexpected potholes in the road. The road of life is full of potholes, but God softens the blow and actually comforts us in all our difficult times.

People who are not serving God and trusting Him to meet their needs sometimes look and act as though they are much older than they actually are. Their faces show the strain of the years they have lived without the Holy Spirit's help and protection. Their attitudes are sour due to years of adversity. They often become bitter because they have deemed life unfair. They do not realize that their lives would be different had they served God and leaned on His Spirit to guide and protect them.

Many times in my life I was reproached for the name of Christ, but now I know that the Spirit of glory was always upon me. Right in the middle of attack and adversity, God kept making my life better and better. He loves to take a mess and make something glorious out of it.

If you ask Him, He will take your mess and turn it into your ministry. When the Spirit of glory is upon you and within you, you can help others who face the same kinds of things God has helped you overcome. Your burden can become your blessing, and your weakness can become your weapon.

of God's multi-faceted grace [faithfully using the diverse, varied gifts and abilities granted to Christians by God's unmerited favor].

¹¹Whoever speaks [to the congregation], *is to do so* as one who speaks the oracles (utterances, the very words) of God. Whoever serves [the congregation] *is to do so* as one who serves by the strength which God [abundantly] supplies, so that in all things God may be glorified [honored and magnified] through Jesus Christ, to whom belongs the glory and dominion forever and ever. Amen.

¹²Beloved, do not be surprised at the fiery ordeal which is taking place to test you [that is, to test the quality of your faith], as though something strange *or* unusual were happening to you.

¹³But insofar as you are sharing Christ's sufferings, keep on rejoicing, so that when His glory [filled with His radiance and splendor] is revealed, you may rejoice with great joy.

¹⁴If you are insulted *and* reviled for [bearing] the name of Christ, you are blessed [happy, with life-joy and comfort in God's salvation regardless of your circumstances], because the Spirit of glory and of God is resting on you [and indwelling you—He whom they curse, you glorify]. [Is 11:2]

¹⁵Make sure that none of you suffers as a murderer, or a thief, or any sort of criminal [in response to persecution], or as a troublesome meddler interfering in the affairs of others;

¹⁶but if *anyone suffers* [ill-treatment] as a Christian [because of his belief], he is not to be ashamed, but is to glorify God [because he is considered worthy to suffer] in this name.

¹⁷For it is the time [destined] for judgment to begin with the household of God; and if *it begins* with us, what will the outcome be for those who do not respect *or* believe *or* obey the gospel of God?

¹⁸AND IF IT IS DIFFICULT FOR THE RIGHTEOUS TO BE SAVED, WHAT WILL BECOME OF THE GODLESS AND THE SINNER? [Prov 11:31]

¹⁹Therefore, those who are ill-treated *and* suffer in accordance with the will of God must [continue to] do right and commit their souls [for safekeeping] to the faithful Creator.

5 THEREFORE, I strongly urge the elders among you [pastors, spiritual leaders of the church], as a fellow elder and as an eyewitness [called to testify] of the sufferings of Christ, as well as one who shares in the glory that is to be revealed:

²shepherd *and* guide *and* protect the flock of God among you, exercising oversight not under compulsion, but voluntarily, according to *the will of* God; and not [motivated] for shameful gain, but with wholehearted enthusiasm;

putting the Word to work

To humble yourself "under the mighty hand of God [set aside self-righteous pride], so that He may exalt you" (1 Peter 5:6) means to ask the Lord for what you need and then wait on Him to provide as He sees fit, knowing that His timing is always perfect. Are you humbling yourself under His hand in every situation of your life and trusting that He knows what is best for you? He has great plans for you, so I encourage you to be still, stop striving, and allow Him to show you how to cooperate with His purposes for you.

Also, be sure to cast all your cares upon the Lord (see 1 Peter 5:7). Do not worry about anything because staying peaceful is actually proof that you have humbled yourself and that you trust God to do what needs to be done.

keep your balance

Maintaining balance in all things is so important! If we do not, we open a door to Satan, who prowls around like a hungry lion seeking to devour us (see 1 Peter 5:8). I want to share with you some thoughts that will help you stay balanced in one particular area of your life—your self-image. Of course, there are many other aspects of life that need to be kept in balance, but I want to focus first on self-image because it is such a foundational issue.

In order to develop a balanced, healthy, God-centered self-image, incorporate the thoughts below into the way you think about yourself.

1. I know God created me, and He loves me.

2. I have faults and weaknesses, and I want to change. I believe God is working in my life. He is changing me bit by bit, day by day. While He is working on me, I can still enjoy my life and myself.

3. Everyone has faults, so I am not a complete failure just because I am not perfect.

4. I am going to work with God to overcome my weaknesses, but I realize that I will always have something to deal with; therefore, I will not become discouraged when God convicts me of areas in my life that need improvement.

5. I want to make people happy and have them like me, but my sense of worth is not dependent upon what others think of me. Jesus has already affirmed my value by His willingness to die for me.

6. I will not be controlled by what other people think, say, or do. Even if they totally reject me, I will survive. God has promised never to reject or condemn me as long as I keep believing (see John 6:29).

7. No matter how often I fail, I will not give up, because God is with me to strengthen and sustain me. He has promised never to forsake me (see Hebrews 13:5).

8. I like myself. I do not like everything I do, and I want to change—but I refuse to reject myself.

9. I am right with God through Jesus Christ.

10. God has a good plan for my life. I am going to fulfill my destiny and be all I can be for His glory. I have God-given gifts and talents, and I intend to use them to help others.

11. I am nothing, and yet I am everything! In myself I am nothing, and yet in Jesus I am everything I need to be.

12. I can do everything God calls me to do, through His Son Jesus Christ (see Philippians 4:13).

As I mentioned, there are many other areas where we should strive for balance. We should maintain the balance between work and rest, eat a balanced diet, never spend more than we earn, enjoy people but also have solitude, and although we want to please people and have their approval we must put God and His will first in our lives at all times.

If we do not maintain balance in our lives Satan will take advantage of the door we have opened. Check your life and if you find areas out of balance ask God to help you make the necessary adjustments.

³not lording it over those assigned to your care [do not be arrogant or overbearing], but be examples [of Christian living] to the flock [set a pattern of integrity for your congregation].

⁴And when the Chief Shepherd (Christ) appears, you will receive the [conqueror's] unfading crown of glory.

⁵Likewise, you younger men [of lesser rank and experience], be subject to your elders [seek their counsel]; and all of you, clothe yourselves with humility toward one another [tie on the servant's apron], for GOD IS OPPOSED TO THE PROUD [the disdainful, the presumptuous, and He defeats them], BUT HE GIVES GRACE TO THE HUMBLE. [Prov 3:34]

⁶Therefore humble yourselves under the mighty hand of God [set aside self-righteous pride], so that He may exalt you [to a place of honor in His service] at the appropriate time, [John 3:30]

⁷casting all your cares [all your anxieties, all your worries, and all your concerns, once and for all] on Him, for He cares about you [with deepest affection, and watches over you very carefully]. [Ps 55:22]

⁸Be sober [well balanced and self-disciplined], be alert *and* cautious at all times. That enemy of yours, the devil, prowls around like a roaring lion [fiercely hungry], seeking someone to devour.

⁹But resist him, be firm in *your* faith [against his attack—rooted, established, immovable], knowing that the same experiences of suffering are being experienced by your brothers and sisters throughout the world. [You do not suffer alone.]

¹⁰After you have suffered for a little while, the God of all grace [who imparts His blessing and favor], who called you to His *own* eternal glory in Christ, will Himself complete, confirm, strengthen, and establish you [making you what you ought to be].

¹¹To Him be dominion (power, authority, sovereignty) forever and ever. Amen.

¹²By Silvanus, our faithful brother (as I consider him), I have written to you briefly, to counsel and testify that this is the true grace [the undeserved favor] of God. Stand firm in it!

¹³She [the church] who is in Babylon, chosen together with you, sends you greetings, and *so does* my son [in the faith], Mark.

¹⁴Greet one another with a kiss of love.

To all of you who are in Christ, may there be peace.

Second Peter

Author:
Peter

Date:
AD 65–68

Everyday Life Principles:
Be on guard and do not be deceived.

Study and seek to know the truth.

Be a lifetime learner of the truth of God.

Second Peter was written to people who either did not know the truth of God or were not standing firm in it, so they were in danger of being deceived concerning the second coming of Jesus Christ. The Bible exhorts us in several places in the New Testament not to be deceived. We are living in a day when deception is all around us—and it will only increase as we draw nearer to Jesus' second coming. The only way to avoid being deceived is to know the truth for ourselves. People who think they "know it all" fall into deception.

Let the book of 2 Peter cause you to make a fresh commitment to being a victorious Christian and a "lifetime learner," one who continually seeks and studies the truth of God's Word. Do not simply listen to other people, but be convinced for yourself. Study and read on your own instead of simply believing second-hand information. Stay close to the Word of God. Pray that you will not be deceived, and do whatever it takes to make sure you have accurate knowledge of the Bible. As you pursue deeper and deeper knowledge of the truth, let me encourage you with the words Peter used to close this letter: "But grow [spiritually mature] in the grace and knowledge of our Lord and Savior Jesus Christ. To Him be glory (honor, majesty, splendor) both now and to the day of eternity. Amen" (2 Peter 3:18).

1 SIMON PETER, a bond-servant and apostle (special messenger, personally chosen representative) of Jesus Christ,

To those who have received *and* possess [by God's will] a precious faith of the same kind as ours, by the righteousness of our God and Savior, Jesus Christ:

²Grace and peace [that special sense of spiritual well-being] be multiplied to you in the [true, intimate] knowledge of God and of Jesus our Lord.

³For His divine power has bestowed on us [absolutely] everything necessary for [a dynamic spiritual] life and godliness, through true *and* personal knowledge of Him who called us by His own glory and excellence.

⁴For by these He has bestowed on us His precious and magnificent promises [of inexpressible value], so that by them you may escape from the immoral freedom that is in the world because of disreputable desire, and become sharers of the divine nature.

⁵For this very reason, applying your diligence [to the divine promises, make every effort] in [exercising] your faith to, develop moral excellence, and in moral excellence, knowledge (insight, understanding),

⁶and in *your* knowledge, self-control, and in *your* self-control, steadfastness, and in *your* steadfastness, godliness,

⁷and in *your* godliness, brotherly affection, and in *your* brotherly affection, [develop Christian] love [that

putting the Word to work

If you ever wanted an instruction manual for your life, know that God's power has provided everything you need for a dynamic spiritual life and for godliness (see 2 Peter 1:3). You receive everything you need through knowing Him and reading His Word. Remember that every one of His promises is for you. Which of His promises do you especially need to remember and believe right now?

is, learn to unselfishly seek the best for others and to do things for their benefit].

⁸For as these *qualities* are yours and are increasing [in you as you grow toward spiritual maturity], they will keep you from being useless and unproductive in regard to the true

putting the Word to work

Do you want your Christian life to be effective and bear fruit? Then follow the instructions in 2 Peter 1:5–7: be diligent about God's promises, exercise your faith to develop moral excellence, grow in knowledge, increase in self-control, be steadfast, practice godliness, and show Christian love to others. How can you improve in these areas as you go about your everyday activities and relationships?

speak the Word

Father, I pray that Your grace and peace would be multiplied to me in the true, intimate knowledge of God and of Jesus my Lord.
—ADAPTED FROM 2 PETER 1:2

Thank You, God, that Your divine power has bestowed on me absolutely everything necessary for a dynamic spiritual life and for godliness, through true and personal knowledge of You, who called me by Your own glory and excellence.
—ADAPTED FROM 2 PETER 1:3

everything we need

According to 2 Peter 1:3, God's power provides everything we need to enjoy great and godly lives, but what He provides comes to us through the full, personal knowledge of Him. We cannot know God through someone else. We can know about Him through others, but to know Him for ourselves we must study His Word ourselves and spend time with Him individually.

You can be as close to God as you want to be. He is no respecter of persons and if one person can have a close, intimate relationship with Him, then so can everyone else. Why do some people seem so close to God and yet others do not? I believe it all depends on how much time we are willing to put into developing our personal relationship with Him.

Going to church does not necessarily make us close to God. Going to church is a good and right thing to do, but we need more than an hour on Sunday morning with God if we are going to learn enough to fulfill our destiny and truly enjoy life.

God wants us to have excellent lives, but He also expects us to learn how to behave excellently. Finding the strength to do so only comes as we wait on Him. "Those who wait for the LORD [who expect, look for, and hope in Him] will gain new strength and renew their power" (Isaiah 40:31), and spending time in God's Word teaches us right from wrong. The Bible gives many instructions about how to behave with people and in certain circumstances. It teaches us to be excellent and to go the extra mile and do whatever we do as best we can, unto the Lord.

I once heard, "If you do not read, you will be the same in five years as you are now." That is certainly true where the Bible is concerned. As we study God's Word, we are transformed into His image, from "[one degree of] glory to [even more] glory (2 Corinthians 3:18).

If you will make a commitment of time to God, I believe you will see the life and power that is available to you through His promises. Be a lifetime learner. Refuse to have a second-hand relationship with God; get to know Him for yourself.

knowledge *and* greater understanding of our Lord Jesus Christ.

9For whoever lacks these *qualities* is blind—shortsighted [closing his spiritual eyes to the truth], having become oblivious to the fact that he was cleansed from his old sins.

10Therefore, believers, be all the more diligent to make certain about His calling and choosing you [be sure that your behavior reflects and confirms your relationship with God]; for by doing these things [actively developing these virtues], you will never stumble [in your spiritual growth and will live a life that leads others away from sin];

11for in this way entry into the eternal kingdom of our Lord and Savior Jesus Christ will be abundantly provided to you.

12Therefore, I will always be ready to remind you of these things, even though you *already* know them and are established in the truth which is held firmly in your grasp.

13I think it right, as long as I am in

this *earthly* tent, to inspire you by reminding you,

¹⁴knowing that the laying aside of this *earthly* tent of mine is imminent, as our Lord Jesus Christ has made clear to me.

¹⁵Moreover, I will diligently endeavor [to see to it] that even after my departure you will be able, at all times, to call these things to mind.

¹⁶For we did not follow cleverly devised stories *or* myths when we made known to you the power and coming of our Lord Jesus Christ, but we were eyewitnesses of His majesty [His grandeur, His authority, His sovereignty].

¹⁷For when He was invested with honor and [the radiance of the Shekinah] glory from God the Father, such a voice as this came to Him from the [splendid] Majestic Glory [in the bright cloud that overshadowed Him, saying], "This is My Son, My Beloved Son in whom I am well-pleased *and* delighted"— [Matt 17:5]

¹⁸and we [actually] heard this voice made from heaven when we were together with Him on the holy mountain. [Matt 17:6]

¹⁹So we have the prophetic word made more certain. You do well to pay [close] attention to it as to a lamp shining in a dark place, until the day dawns *and* light breaks through the gloom and the morning star arises in your hearts. [Num 24:17]

²⁰But understand this first of all, that no prophecy of Scripture is *a matter* of *or* comes from one's own [personal or special] interpretation,

²¹for no prophecy was ever made by an act of human will, but men moved by the Holy Spirit spoke from God.

2 BUT [in those days] false prophets arose among the people, just as there will be false teachers among you, who will subtly introduce destructive heresies, even denying the

Master who bought them, bringing swift destruction on themselves.

²Many will follow their shameful ways, and because of them the way of truth will be maligned.

³And in *their* greed they will exploit you with false arguments *and* twisted doctrine. Their sentence [of condemnation which God has decreed] from a time long ago is not idle [but is still in force], and their destruction *and* deepening misery is not asleep [but is on its way].

⁴For if God did not [even] spare angels that sinned, but threw them into hell and sent them to pits of gloom to be kept [there] for judgment;

⁵and if He did not spare the ancient world, but protected Noah, a preacher of righteousness, with seven others, when He brought [the judgment of] a flood upon the world of the ungodly; [Gen 6–8; 1 Pet 3:20]

⁶and if He condemned the cities of Sodom and Gomorrah to destruction by

life point

Second Peter 2:10 comments on people who are presumptuous.

We must always be on guard against presumption—behavior that is arrogant, overconfident, and unreasonably bold. Presumption causes disrespect and rebellious attitudes toward authority.

Presumptuous people talk when they should be quiet. They try to dictate direction to those from whom they should receive counsel. They give orders when they should take orders; and they do things without asking permission.

Presumption is a big problem and comes from a wrong heart. God does not want us to be presumptuous. He wants us to be humble. Eliminate presumption from your life and cultivate humility.

reducing them to ashes, having made them an example to those who would live ungodly *lives* thereafter; [Gen 19:24] ⁷and if He rescued righteous Lot, who was tormented by the immoral conduct of unprincipled *and* ungodly men [Gen 19:16, 29] ⁸(for that just man, while living among them, felt his righteous soul tormented day after day by what he saw and heard of their lawless acts), ⁹then [in light of the fact that all this is true, be sure that] the Lord knows how to rescue the godly from trial, and how to keep the unrighteous under punishment until the day of judgment, ¹⁰and especially those who indulge in the corrupt passions of the sin nature, and despise authority.

Presumptuous *and* reckless, self-willed *and* arrogant [creatures, despising the majesty of the Lord], they do not tremble when they revile angelic majesties, ¹¹whereas *even* angels who are superior in might and power do not bring a reviling (defaming) accusation against them before the Lord. [Jude 8] ¹²But these [false teachers], like unreasoning animals, [mere] creatures of instinct, born to be captured and destroyed, reviling things they do not understand, will also perish in their own corruption [in their destroying they will be destroyed], ¹³suffering wrong [destined for punishment] as the wages of doing wrong. They count it a delight to revel in the daytime [living luxuriously]. They are stains and blemishes [on mankind], reveling in their deceptions even as they feast with you. ¹⁴They have eyes full of adultery, constantly looking for sin, enticing *and* luring away unstable souls. Having hearts trained in greed, [they are] children of a curse. ¹⁵Abandoning the straight road [that is, the right way to live], they have gone

astray; they have followed the way of [the false teacher] Balaam the son of Beor, who loved the reward of wickedness; [Num 22:5, 7] ¹⁶but he was rebuked for his own transgression: a mute donkey spoke with a man's voice and restrained the prophet's madness. [Num 22:21–31] ¹⁷These [false teachers] are springs without water and mists driven by a tempest, for whom is reserved the gloom of black darkness. ¹⁸For uttering arrogant *words* of vanity [pompous words disguised to sound scholarly or profound, but meaning nothing and containing no spiritual truth], they beguile *and* lure *using* lustful desires, by sensuality, those who barely escape from the ones who live in error. ¹⁹They promise them liberty, when they themselves are the slaves of depravity—for by whatever anyone is defeated *and* overcome, to that [person, thing, philosophy, or concept] he is *continually* enslaved. ²⁰For if, after they have escaped the pollutions of the world by [personal] knowledge of our Lord and Savior Jesus Christ, they are again entangled in them and are overcome, their last condition has become worse for them than the first. ²¹For it would have been better for them not to have [personally] known the way of righteousness, than to have known it and then to have turned back from the holy commandment [verbally] handed on to them. ²²The thing spoken of in the true proverb has happened to them, "THE DOG RETURNS TO HIS OWN VOMIT," and, "A sow is washed only to wallow [again] in the mire." [Prov 26:11]

3 BELOVED, I am now writing you this second letter. In this [as in the first one], I am stirring up your untainted mind to remind you,

"when, God, when?"

Second Peter 3:8 reminds us that God has His own sense of timing. God does not move in our timing. He is never late, but He is usually not early either. He is often the God of the midnight hour. He sometimes waits until the last second before He gives us what we need. It is as though we are a drowning person going down for the last time, and God comes through to rescue us at the last moment.

We must learn to trust God's timing. But before we can do that, we must come to the place where we are broken before Him. What I mean is that our self-will and our spirit of independence must be broken before God is free to work His will in our lives and circumstances. Before He intervenes on our behalf, He has to be sure we are not going to take matters into our own hands and do something out of His perfect timing.

Galatians 6:9 says, "Let us not grow weary or become discouraged in doing good, for at the proper time we will reap, if we do not give in." The interesting thing about this scripture is that it always seems to encourage people. Yet really, in this verse, God does not tell us *when* something is going to happen because "the proper time" is not specific. If we start checking references that have to do with timing in the Bible, we will find descriptions like: "at the appointed season, in due time, in due season."

Many times when I am waiting on God in a situation and I grow discouraged about the time it is taking for Him to answer, someone gives me one of those kinds of scriptures and it encourages me. I still do not know any details because "the proper time" is really just the time that God knows as right, but the scripture does remind me to trust God.

David wrote a power passage in Psalm 31:14, 15: "But as for me, I trust [confidently] in You and your greatness, O LORD; I said, 'You are my God.' My times are in Your hands; rescue me from the hand of my enemies and from those who pursue and persecute me." Like David, we must learn to put our confidence in the Lord, trusting Him to deliver us out of our circumstances—and into the next right thing—in His perfect timing.

²that you should remember the words spoken in the past [about the future] by the holy prophets and the commandment of the Lord and Savior *given* by your apostles [His personally chosen representatives].

³First of all, know [without any doubt] that mockers will come in the last days with their mocking, following after their own human desires

⁴and saying, "Where is the promise of His coming [what has become of it]?

For ever since the fathers fell asleep [in death], all things have continued [exactly] as they did from the beginning of creation."

⁵For they willingly forget [the fact] that the heavens existed long ago by the word of God, and the earth was formed out of water and by water,

⁶through which the world at that time was destroyed by being flooded with water. [Gen 1:6–8; 7:11]

⁷But by His word the present heavens

and earth are being reserved for fire, being kept for the day of judgment and destruction of the ungodly people.

⁸Nevertheless, do not let this one *fact* escape your notice, beloved, that with the Lord one day is like a thousand years, and a thousand years is like one day. [Ps 90:4]

⁹The Lord does not delay [as though He were unable to act] *and* is not slow about His promise, as some count slowness, but is [extraordinarily] patient toward you, not wishing for any to perish but for all to come to repentance.

¹⁰But the day of the Lord will come like a thief, and then the heavens will vanish with a [mighty and thunderous] roar, and the [material] elements will be destroyed with intense heat, and the earth and the works that are on it will be burned up.

¹¹Since all these things are to be destroyed in this way, what kind of people ought you to be [in the meantime] in holy behavior [that is, in a pattern of daily life that sets you apart as a believer] and in godliness [displaying profound reverence toward our awesome God],

¹²[while you earnestly] look for and await the coming of the day of God. For on this day the heavens will be destroyed by burning, and the [material] elements will melt with intense heat! [Is 34:4]

¹³But in accordance with His promise we expectantly await new heavens and a new earth, in which righteousness dwells. [Is 65:17; 66:22]

¹⁴So, beloved, since you are looking forward to these things, be diligent *and*

putting the Word to work

Do you ever look at all the evil in the world and wonder why Jesus has not yet returned to earth? The promise of His coming is certain, yet 2 Peter 3:9 tells us that God, in His mercy and patience toward sinners, is waiting. He does not want any person to perish, but wants everyone to come to salvation through repentance and faith in Jesus. Pray for salvation for those in your life who do not yet know Jesus as Lord and Savior.

make every effort to be found by Him [at His return] spotless and blameless, in peace [that is, inwardly calm with a sense of spiritual well-being and confidence, having lived a life of obedience to Him].

¹⁵And consider the patience of our Lord [His delay in judging and avenging wrongs] as salvation [that is, allowing time for more to be saved]; just as our beloved brother Paul also wrote to you according to the wisdom given to him [by God],

¹⁶speaking about these things as he does in all of his letters. In which there are some things that are difficult to understand, which the untaught and unstable [who have fallen into error] twist *and* misinterpret, just as *they do* the rest of the Scriptures, to their own destruction.

¹⁷Therefore, [let me warn you] beloved, knowing these things beforehand, be on your guard so that you are not carried away by the error of unprincipled men [who distort doctrine]

speak the Word

Father, I thank You that You do not delay and You are not slow about what You promise, but you are extraordinarily patient, not wishing for any to perish but for all to come to repentance.
—ADAPTED FROM 2 PETER 3:9

putting the Word to work

What measures do you take to guard your valuables? Perhaps you have an alarm system in your home; you probably lock the doors of your car and keep your money in the bank. Likewise, you should guard the truth of God's Word that you have in your heart so you are not led astray by false teaching (see 2 Peter.3:17). Growing in your relationship with the Lord and in His grace will help you stand firm in the truth.

and fall from your own steadfastness [of mind, knowledge, truth, and faith], [18]but grow [spiritually mature] in the grace and knowledge of our Lord and Savior Jesus Christ. To Him be glory (honor, majesty, splendor), both now and to the day of eternity. Amen.

life point

Once we understand grace, we must grow and learn how to receive it in every situation, as 2 Peter 3:18 encourages us.

We grow in grace by putting our faith in God and receiving His grace in situations that are difficult or impossible for us. Sometimes we put our faith in God, and He gives us grace for deliverance. At other times we put our faith in God, and He gives us grace to "go through." We must leave that choice to Him and know that either way we can have victory, but only by grace through faith.

When you struggle with something in your life, ask yourself honestly if you are putting your faith in God and if you believe His grace will meet the need. Remember, grace is unmerited favor to us sinners. It is God's power coming into our situation to do for us what we cannot do for ourselves.

First John

Author:
John

Date:
Probably between AD 85–95

Everyday Life Principles:
God is light.

God is love.

God loves you.

The letters we call 1, 2, and 3 John were written by the same Apostle John who wrote the Gospel of John and the book of Revelation. This man was a disciple of Jesus Christ; he knew Him personally and was one of three disciples with whom Jesus spent a great deal of time.

Two of 1 John's themes are love and light. In chapter 1, we read that "God is Light" and that there is no darkness in Him (see 1 John 1:5). This is important because it enables believers to have true fellowship with God and with other believers. Just think about that: Living in the light means that we can have deep genuine friendships, honest communication, and good times with each other. When we live in God's light, nothing is hidden; we do not have to try to cover up anything. We can be real before God and before others.

We also read of God's love frequently in 1 John. We see that God loved us long before we ever loved Him and that He loves us as His own sons and daughters (see 1 John 3:1). We read about His love and sacrifice in sending His Son, Jesus, to die for us, and about the total, absolute cleansing power of Jesus' blood.

I pray that 1 John will remind you of how much God loves you and that reading this epistle strengthens your love for others and encourages you to express that love every chance you get.

1 [I AM writing about] what existed from the beginning, what we have heard, what we have seen with our eyes, what we have looked at and touched with our hands, concerning the Word of Life [the One who existed even before the beginning of the world, Christ]—

²and the Life [an aspect of His being] was manifested, and we have seen [it as eyewitnesses] and testify and declare to you [the Life], the eternal Life who was [already existing] with the Father and was [actually] made visible to us [His followers]—

³what we have seen and heard we also proclaim to you, so that you too may have fellowship [as partners] with us. And indeed our fellowship [which is a distinguishing mark of born-again believers] is with the Father, and with His Son Jesus Christ.

⁴We are writing these things to you so that our joy [in seeing you included] may be made complete [by having you share in the joy of salvation].

⁵This is the message [of God's promised revelation] which we have heard from Him and now announce to you, that God is Light [He is holy, His message is truthful, He is perfect in righteousness], and in Him there is no darkness at all [no sin, no wickedness, no imperfection].

⁶If we say that we have fellowship with Him and yet walk in the darkness [of sin], we lie and do not practice the truth;

⁷but if we [really] walk in the Light [that is, live each and every day in conformity with the precepts of God], as He Himself is in the Light, we have [true, unbroken] fellowship with one another [He with us, and we with Him], and the blood of Jesus His Son cleanses us from all sin [by erasing the stain of sin, keeping us cleansed from sin in all its forms and manifestations].

⁸If we say we have no sin [refusing to admit that we are sinners], we delude ourselves and the truth is not in us. [His word does not live in our hearts.]

⁹If we [freely] admit that we have sinned *and* confess our sins, He is faithful and just [true to His own nature and promises], and will forgive our sins and cleanse us *continually* from all unrighteousness [our wrongdoing, everything not in conformity with His will and purpose].

¹⁰If we say that we have not sinned [refusing to admit acts of sin], we make Him [out to be] a liar [by contradicting Him] and His word is not in us.

2 MY LITTLE children (believers, dear ones), I am writing you these things so that you will not sin *and* violate God's law. And if anyone

life point

What happens when we turn on a light in a messy, dirty room? We see bugs scurrying away from the light, and we see clutter and dirt! First John 1:5 says "God is Light." When He gets involved in our lives, He shows us things we may prefer not to look at—things we have hidden, even from ourselves.

We are often deceived, especially about ourselves. We do not want to deal with our faults, nor do we delight in having them exposed. We may feel condemned about them, but at least we feel they are hidden. Anything hidden has power over us because we fear it may be found out. The best and most freeing thing we can do is face up to what God wants to expose and move beyond the fear of it (see 1 John 1:7).

Let the light of God shine on your hidden motives and dark places. He knows about them anyway and in His love He wants to bring you to a place of freedom.

life point

Notice in 1 John 1:9 that we are told if we will confess our sins to God, He will "continually" cleanse us. I believe this is the spiritual correlation to the way our physical blood continuously cleanses our body.

Our blood works for us all the time to keep us cleansed of all poison, and the blood of Jesus works all the time, continuously cleansing us from sin in all its forms and manifestations (see 1 John 1:7). There is power in the shed blood of Jesus Christ! You and I are continually cleansed, not just every once in a while, but frequently and continuously.

The Bible states that there is only one requirement on our part: we must freely admit that we have sinned and confess our sins.

Be quick to repent. Do not try to hide anything from God. He will never reject you. He knows everything anyway, but repentance releases the power of His blood on your behalf and makes it effective in your life. Confess your sins and allow the blood of Jesus to cleanse you on a regular basis.

sins, we have an Advocate [who will intercede for us] with the Father: Jesus Christ the righteous [the upright, the just One, who conforms to the Father's will in every way—purpose, thought, and action].

²And He [that same Jesus] is the propitiation for our sins [the atoning sacrifice that holds back the wrath of God that would otherwise be directed at us because of our sinful nature—our worldliness, our lifestyle]; and not for ours alone, but also for [the sins of all believers throughout] the whole world.

³And this is how we know [daily, by experience] that we have come to know Him [to understand Him and be more deeply acquainted with Him]: if we *habitually* keep [focused on His precepts and obey] His commandments (teachings).

⁴Whoever says, "I have come to know Him," but does not *habitually* keep [focused on His precepts and obey] His commandments (teachings), is a liar, and the truth [of the divine word] is not in him.

⁵But whoever *habitually* keeps His word *and* obeys His precepts [and treasures His message in its entirety], in him the love of God has truly been perfected [it is completed and has reached maturity]. By this we know [for certain] that we are in Him:

⁶whoever says he lives in Christ [that is, whoever says he has accepted Him as God and Savior] ought [as a moral obligation] to walk *and* conduct himself just as He walked *and* conducted Himself.

⁷Beloved, I am not writing a new commandment to you, but an old commandment which you have had from the beginning; the old commandment is the message which you have heard [before from us]. [John 13:34, 35]

⁸On the other hand, I am writing a new commandment to you, which is true *and* realized in Christ and in you, because the darkness [of moral blindness] is clearing away and the true Light [the revelation of God in Christ] is already shining.

⁹The one who says he is in the Light [in consistent fellowship with Christ] and yet *habitually* hates (works against) his brother [in Christ] is in the darkness until now.

¹⁰The one who loves *and* unselfishly seeks the best for his [believing] brother lives in the Light, and in him there is no occasion for stumbling *or* offense [he does not hurt the cause of Christ or lead others to sin].

¹¹But the one who *habitually* hates (works against) his brother [in Christ] is in [spiritual] darkness and is walking in the darkness, and does not know where he is going because the darkness has blinded his eyes.

¹²I am writing to you, little children (believers, dear ones), because your sins have been forgiven for His name's sake [you have been pardoned and released from spiritual debt through His name because you have confessed His name, believing in Him as Savior].

¹³I am writing to you, fathers [those believers who are spiritually mature], because you know Him who has existed from the beginning. I am writing to you, young men [those believers who are growing in spiritual maturity], because you have been victorious *and* have overcome the evil one. I have written to you, children [those who are new believers, those spiritually immature], because you have come to know the Father.

¹⁴I have written to you, fathers,

"in," but not "of"

Jesus said that though we are in the world, we are "not of the world" (John 15:19). We can enjoy the world and the things it offers, but it's important for us to maintain balance and not get too attached to them (see 1 John 2:15). We are to live in the world as strangers and aliens, and remember that we are just passing through; this world is not our home. God is our home and we are on our way to live in His manifest presence for eternity.

One way we can determine if things mean more to us than they should is to watch how we behave when one of our possessions is lost or damaged. It may disappoint us, but it should not devastate us. How would you act if your spouse or child broke your favorite possession? Recently, my daughter and I were thinking about years gone by and she said, "Mom, one of the things you did that really meant a lot to me was what you said when I accidentally broke your new bottle of favorite perfume. You said, 'Do not worry about it. You are more important to me than the perfume.'" Now, I did not always behave so lovingly, but on this occasion I did and she remembered. I urge you not to ever do or say anything that could make people feel they are not as important as things.

I believe God tests us in these areas just to help us maintain right attitudes. The Apostle Paul said that he learned how to be content whether he faced difficult times or abounding in prosperity (see Philippians 4:12). We may experience times of plenty and times of need, but if we remain steady and unchanging no matter what, then we know that things do not have an ungodly hold on us. God wants us to be blessed and to enjoy the best life has to offer, but He wants us to keep Him first in our lives. One man said, "I am very rich, but when I got cancer I called on God, not the First Bank of the U.S."

When everything else is gone, and it will be some day, there will be God. We must keep Him in first place in our lives. We came into the world with nothing and we will leave the same way. We cannot take money and things with us when we go to heaven, so we would be wise not to worship them while we are on earth.

life point

First John 2:15 urges us not to love the things that are in the world. Instead we should love people and use our worldly possessions to bless them. This is hard for us to do if we love things too much! You and I must strive to keep possessions in their proper place in our lives. We must not put earthly goods before people. We must always put people first!

Love is a central theme of 1 John. There are things, as a believer, however, that we are not to love. What does it mean to not love the world or the things in the world (see 1 John 2:15)? It does not mean we should not enjoy the natural beauty of creation, but pursuing what the world offers—things that distract us from God and His purposes for our lives—are pursuits rooted in lust and pride. Ask God to deepen your love for Him and the things of His kingdom.

because you know Him who has existed from the beginning. I have written to you, young men, because you are strong *and* vigorous, and the word of God remains [always] in you, and you have been victorious over the evil one [by accepting Jesus as Savior].

¹⁵Do not love the world [of sin that opposes God and His precepts], nor the things that are in the world. If anyone loves the world, the love of the Father is not in him.

¹⁶For all that is in the world—the lust *and* sensual craving of the flesh and the lust *and* longing of the eyes and the boastful pride of life [pretentious confidence in one's resources or in the stability of earthly things]—these do not come from the Father, but are from the world.

¹⁷The world is passing away, and with it its lusts [the shameful pursuits and ungodly longings]; but the one who does the will of God *and* carries out His purposes lives forever.

¹⁸Children, it is the last hour [the end of this age]; and just as you heard that the antichrist is coming [the one who will oppose Christ and attempt to replace Him], even now many antichrists (false teachers) have appeared, which confirms our belief that it is the last hour.

¹⁹They went out from us [seeming at first to be Christians], but they were not *really* of us [because they were not truly born again and spiritually

transformed]; for if they had been of us, they would have remained with us; but *they went out* [teaching false doctrine], so that it would be clearly shown that none of them are of us.

²⁰But you have an anointing from the Holy One [you have been set apart, specially gifted and prepared by the Holy Spirit], and all of you know [the truth because He teaches us, illuminates our minds, and guards us from error].

²¹I have not written to you because you do not know the truth, but because you do know it, and because no lie [nothing false, no deception] is of the truth.

²²Who is the liar but the one who denies that Jesus is the Christ (the Messiah, the Anointed)? This is the antichrist [the enemy and antagonist of Christ], the one who denies *and* consistently refuses to acknowledge the Father and the Son.

²³Whoever denies *and* repudiates the Son does not have the Father; the one who confesses *and* acknowledges the Son has the Father also.

²⁴As for you, let that remain in you [keeping in your hearts that message of salvation] which you heard from the beginning. If what you heard from the beginning remains in you, you too

will remain in the Son and in the Father [forever].

²⁵This is the promise which He Himself promised us—eternal life.

²⁶These things I have written to you with reference to those who are trying to deceive you [seducing you and leading you away from the truth and sound doctrine].

²⁷As for you, the anointing [the special gift, the preparation] which you received from Him remains [permanently] in you, and you have no need for anyone to teach you. But just as His anointing teaches you [giving you insight through the presence of the Holy Spirit] about all things, and is true and is not a lie, and just as His anointing has taught you, you must remain in Him [being rooted in Him, knit to Him].

²⁸Now, little children (believers, dear ones), remain in Him [with unwavering faith], so that when He appears [at His return], we may have [perfect] confidence and not be ashamed and shrink away from Him at His coming.

²⁹If you know that He is *absolutely* righteous, you know [for certain] that everyone who practices righteousness [doing what is right and conforming to God's will] has been born of Him.

3 SEE WHAT an incredible quality of love the Father has shown to us, that we would [be permitted to] be named *and* called *and* counted the children of God! And so we are! For this reason the world does not know us, because it did not know Him.

²Beloved, we are [even here and] now children of God, and it is not yet made clear what we will be [after His coming]. We know that when He comes *and* is revealed, we will [as His

life point

Sometimes we give more consideration to what people tell us than to what God says to us. If we pray diligently and hear from God, but then start asking everybody else what they think, we are honoring people's opinions above what God says. This attitude prevents us from developing a relationship in which we consistently hear from God.

First John 2:27 confirms that we can trust God to instruct us without needing constant reassurance from others. But is this verse saying we do not need anybody to teach us the Word? No, because God appointed some people to teach in the body of Christ (see Romans 12:6, 7; Ephesians 4:11). But 1 John 2:27 says that if we are in Christ, we have an anointing that abides on the inside of us to teach us and guide us. We might occasionally ask someone for their wisdom, but we do not constantly need to go to other people and ask them about decisions we need to make for our own lives.

children] be like Him, because we will see Him just as He is [in all His glory].

³And everyone who has this hope [confidently placed] in Him purifies himself, just as He is pure (holy, undefiled, guiltless).

⁴Everyone who practices sin also practices lawlessness; and sin is lawlessness [ignoring God's law by action or neglect or by tolerating wrongdoing—being unrestrained by His commands and His will].

⁵You know that He appeared [in visible form as a man] in order to take

speak the Word

Father, I thank You for the incredible quality of love that You have shown me, that I should be named and called and counted as Your child.

—ADAPTED FROM 1 JOHN 3:1

away sins; and in Him there is [absolutely] no sin [for He has neither the sin nature nor has He committed sin or acts worthy of blame].

⁶No one who abides in Him [who remains united in fellowship with Him—deliberately, knowingly, and habitually] practices sin. No one who *habitually* sins has seen Him or known Him.

⁷Little children (believers, dear ones), do not let anyone lead you astray. The one who practices righteousness [the one who strives to live a consistently honorable life—in private as well as in public—and to conform to God's precepts] is righteous, just as He is righteous.

⁸The one who practices sin [separating himself from God, and offending Him by acts of disobedience, indifference, or rebellion] is of the devil [and takes his inner character and moral

life point

I like to teach 1 John 3:9 this way: I used to be a full-time sinner, and once in a while I "accidentally" did something right. But now that I have spent many years developing a deep, personal relationship with God and His Word, I concentrate on being a full-time obedient child of God. I still make mistakes, but not nearly as many as I once did. I am not where I need to be, but thank God, I am not where I used to be.

There are times when I accidentally make mistakes, but it is not the desire of my heart to do wrong. I do not deliberately or knowingly commit sin. I do not habitually sin. So I do not allow those occasions to make me feel insecure. I do not do everything right, but I do know that the attitude of my heart is right. I encourage you to look at the sins and mistakes you make—and at the attitude of your heart— the same way.

putting the Word to work

According to 1 John 3:10, righteousness and loving other believers are two indicators of belonging to God. Is there a fellow Christian in your life with whom you have a hard time getting along? Ask God to show you practical ways to show His love to this person, and as you do these things, ask God to change your heart.

values from him, not God]; for the devil has sinned *and* violated God's law from the beginning. The Son of God appeared for this purpose, to destroy the works of the devil.

⁹No one who is born of God [deliberately, knowingly, and habitually] practices sin, because God's seed [His principle of life, the essence of His righteous character] remains [permanently] in him [who is born again— who is reborn from above—spiritually transformed, renewed, and set apart for His purpose]; and he [who is born again] cannot *habitually* [live a life characterized by] sin, because he is born of God *and* longs to please Him.

¹⁰By this the children of God and the children of the devil are clearly identified: anyone who does not practice righteousness [who does not seek God's will in thought, action, and purpose] is not of God, nor is the one who does not [unselfishly] love his [believing] brother.

¹¹For this is the message which you [believers] have heard from the beginning [of your relationship with Christ], that we should [unselfishly] love *and* seek the best for one another;

¹²and not be like Cain, who was of the evil one and murdered his brother [Abel]. And why did he murder him? Because Cain's deeds were evil, and his brother's were righteous.

¹³Do not be surprised, believers, if the world hates you.

putting the Word to work

First John 3:16–18 teaches us some things about love. How do you define love? Clearly, one aspect of love is helping meet the needs of others. It is important to tell people that God loves them and that you love them; it is also necessary to demonstrate that love through action and good deeds, especially toward fellow believers.

[14]We know that we have passed out of death into Life, because we love the brothers and sisters. He who does not love remains in [spiritual] death.

[15]Everyone who hates (works against) his brother [in Christ] is [at heart] a murderer [by God's standards]; and you know that no murderer has eternal life abiding in him. [Matt 5:21–23]

[16]By this we know [and have come to understand the depth and essence of His precious] love: that He [willingly] laid down His life for us [because He loved us]. And we ought to lay down our lives for the believers.

[17]But whoever has the world's goods (adequate resources), and sees his brother in need, but has no compassion for him, how does the love of God live in him?

[18]Little children (believers, dear ones), let us not love [merely in theory] with word or with tongue [giving lip service to compassion], but in action and in truth [in practice and in sincerity, because practical acts of love are more than words].

[19]By this we will know [without any doubt] that we are of the truth, and will assure our heart *and* quiet our conscience before Him

[20]whenever our heart convicts us [in guilt]; for God is greater than our heart and He knows all things [nothing is hidden from Him because we are in His hands].

[21]Beloved, if our heart does not convict us [of guilt], we have confidence [complete assurance and boldness] before God;

[22]and we receive from Him whatever we ask because we [carefully and consistently] keep His commandments and do the things that are pleasing in His sight [habitually seeking to follow His plan for us].

[23]This is His commandment, that we believe [with personal faith and confident trust] in the name of His Son Jesus Christ, and [that we unselfishly] love *and* seek the best for one another, just as He commanded us.

[24]The one who *habitually* keeps His commandments [obeying His word and following His precepts, abides and] remains in Him, and He in him. By this we know *and* have the proof that He [really] abides in us, by the Spirit whom He has given us [as a gift].

4 BELOVED, DO not believe every spirit [speaking through a self-proclaimed prophet]; instead test the spirits to see whether they are from God, because many false prophets *and* teachers have gone out into the world.

[2]By this you know *and* recognize the Spirit of God: every spirit that acknowledges *and* confesses [the fact] that Jesus Christ has [actually] come in the flesh [as a man] is from God [God is its source];

[3]and every spirit that does not confess Jesus [acknowledging that He has

speak the Word

Father, I pray that I would not love merely in theory or with my words, but in action and in truth.
–ADAPTED FROM 1 JOHN 3:18

come in the flesh, but would deny any of the Son's true nature] is not of God; this is the *spirit* of the antichrist, which you have heard is coming, and is now already in the world.

⁴Little children (believers, dear ones), you are of God *and* you belong to Him and have [already] overcome them [the agents of the antichrist]; because He who is in you is greater than he (Satan) who is in the world [of sinful mankind].

⁵They [who teach twisted doctrine] are of the world *and* belong to it; therefore they speak from the [viewpoint of the] world [with its immoral freedom and baseless theories—demanding compliance with their opinions and ridiculing the values of the upright], and the [gullible one of the] world listens closely *and* pays attention to them.

⁶We [who teach God's word] are from God [energized by the Holy Spirit], and whoever knows God [through personal experience] listens to us [and has a deeper understanding of Him]. Whoever is not of God does not listen to us. By this we know [without any doubt] the spirit of truth [motivated by God] and the spirit of error [motivated by Satan].

⁷Beloved, let us [unselfishly] love *and* seek the best for one another, for love is from God; and everyone who loves [others] is born of God and knows God [through personal experience].

⁸The one who does not love has not become acquainted with God [does not and never did know Him], for God is love. [He is the originator of love, and it is an enduring attribute of His nature.]

⁹By this the love of God was displayed in us, in that God has sent His

speak the Word

life point

The world looks for something real, something tangible. People look for love, and God is love (see 1 John 4:8). Because we know God, we can offer the answer to the searching hearts around us. The love of God mentioned in 1 John 4:8 is that answer.

[One and] only begotten Son [the One who is truly unique, the only One of His kind] into the world so that we might live through Him.

¹⁰In this is love, not that we loved God, but that He loved us and sent His Son to be the propitiation [that is, the atoning sacrifice, and the satisfying offering] for our sins [fulfilling God's requirement for justice against sin and placating His wrath].

¹¹Beloved, if God so loved us [in this incredible way], we also ought to love one another.

¹²No one has seen God at any time. But if we love one another [with un-selfish concern], God abides in us, and His love [the love that is His essence abides in us and] is completed *and* perfected in us.

¹³By this we know [with confident assurance] that we abide in Him and He in us, because He has given to us His [Holy] Spirit.

¹⁴We [who were with Him in person] have seen and testify [as eye-witnesses] that the Father has sent the Son to be the Savior of the world.

¹⁵Whoever confesses *and* acknowledges that Jesus is the Son of God, God abides in him, and he in God.

¹⁶We have come to know [by personal

I pray, Lord, that You would help me unselfishly love and seek the best for other people, for love is from You. Everyone who loves others is born of You and knows You through personal experience.
—ADAPTED FROM 1 JOHN 4:7

enjoying God's love

The Bible says many times that God loves us. But how many of God's children still lack revelation concerning God's love? The truth is, few of God's people really know how much He loves them. If they did, they would act differently.

Many years ago, I began studying how people can learn to receive God's love, and I realized that I was in desperate need of it myself. The Lord led me in my study to 1 John 4:16 and emphasized the importance of being conscious of His love. This means God's love should be something we are actively aware of. But how does one find awareness?

I studied this subject for a long time, and I became conscious of God's love for me through thinking about His love and by confessing it out loud. I learned scriptures about the love of God, and I meditated on them and confessed them with my mouth. I did this over and over for months, and all the time the revelation of His unconditional love for me was becoming more and more of a reality to me.

Now, His love is so real to me that even in hard times, I am comforted by the conscious knowing that He loves me and that I no longer have to live in fear. This can happen to you, too.

I encourage you to know and believe His love for you. Meditate on and speak about God's love, which He expresses to you in His love letters—the Scriptures. Why not start with 1 John 4:16?

observation and experience], and have believed [with deep, consistent faith] the love which God has for us. God is love, and the one who abides in love abides in God, and God abides *continually* in him.

[17]In this [union and fellowship with Him], love is completed *and* perfected with us, so that we may have confidence in the day of judgment [with assurance and boldness to face Him]; because as He is, so are we in this world.

[18]There is no fear in love [dread does not exist]. But perfect (complete, full-grown) love drives out fear, because

fear involves [the expectation of divine] punishment, so the one who is afraid [of God's judgment] is not perfected in love [has not grown into a sufficient understanding of God's love].

[19]We love, because He first loved us.

[20]If anyone says, "I love God," and hates (works against) his [Christian] brother he is a liar; for the one who does not love his brother whom he has seen, cannot love God whom he has not seen.

[21]And this commandment we have from Him, that the one who loves God should also [unselfishly] love his brother *and* seek the best for him.

speak the Word

Thank You, Lord, that there is no fear in love, but that perfect, complete, full-grown love drives out fear.
—ADAPTED FROM 1 JOHN 4:18

5 EVERYONE WHO believes [with a deep, abiding trust in the fact] that Jesus is the Christ (the Messiah, the Anointed) is born of God [that is, reborn from above—spiritually transformed, renewed, and set apart for His purpose], and everyone who loves the Father also loves the *child* born of Him.

²By this we know [without any doubt] that we love the children of God: [expressing that love] when we love God and obey His commandments.

³For the [true] love of God is this: that we *habitually* keep His commandments *and* remain focused on His precepts. And His commandments *and* His precepts are not difficult [to obey].

⁴For *everyone born of God is victorious *and* overcomes the world; and this is the victory that has conquered *and* overcome the world—our [continuing, persistent] faith [in Jesus the Son of God].

⁵Who is the one who is victorious *and* overcomes the world? It is the one who believes *and* recognizes the fact that Jesus is the Son of God.

⁶This is He who came through water and blood [His baptism and death], Jesus Christ—not by the water only, but by the water and the blood. It is the [Holy] Spirit who testifies, because the Spirit is the truth. [He is the essence and origin of truth itself.]

⁷For there are three witnesses:
⁸the Spirit and the water and the blood; and these three are in agreement [their testimony is perfectly consistent].

⁹If we accept [as we do] the testimony of men [that is, if we are willing to take the sworn statements of fallible humans as evidence], the testimony of God is greater [far more authoritative]; for this is the testimony of God, that He has testified regarding His Son.

¹⁰The one who believes in the Son of God [who adheres to, trusts in, and relies confidently on Him as Savior] has the testimony within himself [because he can speak authoritatively about Christ from his own personal experience]. The one who does not believe God [in this way] has made Him [out to be] a liar, because he has not believed in the evidence that God has given regarding His Son.

¹¹And the testimony is this: God has given us eternal life [we already possess it], and this life is in His Son [resulting in our spiritual completeness, and eternal companionship with Him].

¹²He who has the Son [by accepting Him as Lord and Savior] has the life [that is eternal]; he who does not have the Son of God [by personal faith] does not have the life.

¹³These things I have written to you who believe in the name of the Son of God [which represents all that Jesus Christ is and does], so that you will know [with settled and absolute knowledge] that you [already] have eternal life.

¹⁴This is the [remarkable degree of] confidence which we [as believers are entitled to] have before Him: that if we ask anything according to His will, [that is, consistent with His plan and purpose] He hears us.

¹⁵And if we know [for a fact, as indeed we do] that He hears *and* listens to us in

speak the Word

Thank You, God, that I can have confidence that if I ask anything according to Your will—consistent with Your plan and purpose—that You hear me.
—ADAPTED FROM 1 JOHN 5:14

5:4 Lit *everything that is*. John uses the Greek neuter to underscore the fact that everyone who has been born again, regardless of gender or age, is victorious over the world.

life point

When you pray, believe God hears you! This is a promise from 1 John 5:14, 15.

whatever we ask, we [also] know [with settled and absolute knowledge] that we have [granted to us] the requests which we have asked from Him.

¹⁶If anyone sees his brother committing a sin that does not *lead* to death, he will pray *and* ask [on the believer's behalf] and *God* will for him give life to those whose sin is not *leading* to death. There is a sin *that leads* to death; I do not say that one should pray for this [kind of sin].

¹⁷All wrongdoing is sin, and there is sin that does not *lead* to death [one can repent of it and be forgiven].

putting the Word to work

What comes to mind when you think of an idol? Often, people think of statues or figurines representing gods that other cultures worship. However, an idol is anything that you place more importance on or love more than God. It can be your career, money, sports, or a relationship. Do you have any idols in your life? Take time to evaluate your pursuits and priorities; make sure that God is your deepest love and highest priority.

¹⁸We know [with confidence] that anyone born of God does not *habitually* sin; but He (Jesus) who was born of God [carefully] keeps *and* protects him, and the evil one does not touch him.

praying according to God's will

First John 5:14, 15 teach us about prayer and God's will. The Word clearly spells out many things that are part of God's will for our lives. We know we can certainly ask for those things boldly without being concerned about whether or not they are within God's will.

However, we deal daily with many other things that we must pray about, but we do not know God's exact will for those situations. At these times we should pray that His will is done and not ours.

Many times I ask God for something in prayer, but if I do not have a specific Bible verse to back up my request, I tell the Lord, "This is what I think I want—at least, it seems to me that it would be good this way—but if I am wrong in what I am asking, Lord, please do not give it to me. Your will is what I want, not mine."

When learning to pray God's will, it is important for us to consider God's timing. We can pray for something that is the will of God, but until His timing is right in our lives we will not see the physical manifestation of our answer.

Remember: "Now faith is the assurance (title deed, confirmation) of things hoped for (divinely guaranteed), and the evidence of things not seen [the conviction of their reality—faith comprehends as fact what cannot be experienced by the physical senses]" (Hebrews 11:1). If you have the Word of God to back up your requests, stand in faith until you see the results. But remember that real faith causes us to enter the rest of God, so waiting on Him should be a pleasant experience, not one of frustration.

¹⁹We know [for a fact] that we are of God, and the whole world [around us] lies in the power of the evil one [opposing God and His precepts].

²⁰And we [have seen and] know [by personal experience] that the Son of God has [actually] come [to this world], and has given us understanding *and* insight so that we may [progressively and personally] know Him who is true; and we are in Him who is true—in His Son Jesus Christ. This is the true God and eternal life.

²¹Little children (believers, dear ones), guard yourselves from idols— [false teachings, moral compromises, and anything that would take God's place in your heart].

Second John

Author:
John

Date:
Probably between AD 85–95

Everyday Life Principles:
Always remember that Jesus is God's Son in the flesh.

Do not welcome or receive false teachers.

Be a diligent student of God's Word so you will know the truth.

Second John is addressed to "the select (chosen) lady and her children" (2 John 1). Though we do not know if this "lady" was an individual or a group of believers who collectively comprised a church, we do know that John loved this person or these people dearly.

John's reason for writing this letter was that his readers were dealing with false teachers who traveled from place to place, spreading error. They also refused to admit that Jesus Christ ever came to earth in bodily form, in the flesh, and that He was both fully human and fully divine. The recipients of this letter needed strength and encouragement to persevere in their faith and know how to relate to the false teachers. John clearly told them not to receive such ministers (see 2 John 10) and that anyone who did welcome or receive them would participate in the spread of false teaching.

The only way to combat false teaching is to know the truth of God's Word. Concerning that, John wrote that "the truth . . . lives in our hearts and will be with us forever" (2 John 2).

As you read 2 John, I hope you will remember how valuable truth is. Guard the truth you have already, and commit to be a person who is learning to "know and understand the truth" (2 John 1).

¹THE ELDER [of the church addresses this letter] to the elect (chosen) lady and her children, whom I love in truth—and not only I, but also all who know *and* understand the truth—

²because of the truth which lives in our hearts and will be with us forever:

³Grace, mercy, and peace (inner calm, a sense of spiritual well-being) will be with us, from God the Father and from Jesus Christ, the Father's Son, in truth and love.

⁴I was greatly delighted to find *some* of your children walking in truth, just as we have been commanded by the Father.

⁵Now I ask you, lady, not as if *I were* writing to you a new commandment, but [simply reminding you of] the one which we have had from the beginning, that we love *and* unselfishly seek the best for one another.

⁶And this is love: that we walk in accordance with His commandments *and* are guided continually by His precepts. This is the commandment, just as you have heard from the beginning, that you should [always] walk in love.

⁷For many deceivers [heretics, posing as Christians] have gone out into the world, those who do not acknowledge *and* confess the coming of Jesus Christ in the flesh (bodily form). This [person, the kind who does this] is the deceiver and the antichrist [that is, the antagonist of Christ].

⁸Watch yourselves, so that you do not lose what we have accomplished together, but that you may receive

putting the Word to work

Have you ever heard the saying, "If you talk the talk, you have to walk the walk"? As a Christian, it is not enough to know the truth of God's Word; we have to live it. The Word of God is full of ways to practically apply and walk in the truth we know. In what ways can you apply walking in the truth you know to your everyday life right now? Let me encourage you to study the Word diligently and ask God to keep showing you how to walk in the truth more and more.

a full *and* perfect reward [when He grants rewards to faithful believers].

⁹Anyone who runs on ahead and does

putting the Word to work

In this day of e-mail, text messages, and social media, taking time for personal visits is not always a priority. When was the last time you had a face-to-face visit with a Christian friend? While there are many ways to communicate, there is no substitute for taking time to fellowship and to share with one another about what God is teaching you, and to encourage and pray with one another. Whether sharing a meal, going for a walk, or meeting for a cup of coffee, how can you make time to experience the joy of being together with other Christians?

speak the Word

Father, I pray that I will always walk in truth,
just as You have commanded me.
—ADAPTED FROM 2 JOHN 4

God, I pray that I will walk in accordance with and be guided
continually by Your precepts and that I will always walk in love.
—ADAPTED FROM 2 JOHN 6

love leads to obedience

Jesus said that when we love Him, we will obey Him (see John 14:15), and the Apostle John writes that love for God consists of our obedience to Him (see 2 John 6). I like to say that the degree to which we obey Jesus is the degree to which we love Him. I believe our love for Him and obedience to Him can grow—and they do. Everything in our relationship with God after initial salvation is a process. Do not be disappointed with yourself if you are still in the process. Jesus will not be angry when He comes to get you if you have not arrived at the mark of perfection, but He does expect to find all of us pressing on.

The commandment we should strive to obey throughout our lives is to walk in love. Our lives and behavior will change dramatically if all of our thoughts, words, and actions are guided by love. They are to be guided by our love for God, ourselves, and others. God's Word teaches us to love everyone, including ourselves. I like to say, "Do not be *in* love with yourself, but love yourself in a balanced way." If you refuse to love yourself, then you are not receiving the gift God wants to give you. We cannot deserve God's love. It comes to us unconditionally. God loves us first, and He pours His love into us so we can love Him, ourselves, and others. He does not expect us to give away anything we do not have.

Sometimes we make being a Christian very difficult and complicated. We think we must follow hundreds of rules and do multitudes of things, but Jesus said that if we simply walk in love, that is enough (see John 15:12). The reason for this is that if we concentrate on love, all the other things He asks us to do will also get done. Love motivates us to obey, pray, be kind and merciful, give, forgive, repent, and practice other aspects of our Christian faith.

Let me encourage you to study love. Read everything you can about love. Think about it, talk about it, and practice it. God is love and when love is the theme of our lives, He is the theme also.

not remain in the doctrine of Christ [that is, one who is not content with what He taught], does not have God; but the one who *continues* to remain in the teaching [of Christ does have God], he has both the Father and the Son.

¹⁰If anyone comes to you and does not bring this teaching [but diminishes or adds to the doctrine of Christ], do not receive *or* welcome him into your house, and do not give him a greeting *or* any encouragement;

¹¹for the one who gives him a greeting [who encourages him or wishes him success, unwittingly] participates in his evil deeds.

¹²I have many things to write to you, but I prefer not to do so with paper (papyrus) and black (ink); but I hope to come to you and speak with you face to face, so that your joy may be complete. [Num 12:8]

¹³The children of your elect (chosen) sister greet you.

Third John

Author:
John

Date:
Probably between AD 85–95

Everyday Life Principles:
Do what you can to send missionaries and traveling ministers on their way in a manner that is worthy of God's service.

Support the spread of the gospel every way you can.

Imitate good, not evil.

Third John is a brief letter addressed to a man named Gaius, who was most likely a pastor or leader in the early church. Where John has to warn the recipients of his second letter not to associate with false teachers, this letter provides Gaius with instructions on how to treat traveling ministers and missionaries who teach the truth. Specifically, he writes: "You will do well to [assist them and] send them on their way in a manner worthy of God" (3 John 6).

He goes on to say we need to "support such people [welcoming them as guests and providing for them], so that we may be fellow workers for the truth [that is, for the gospel message of salvation]" (3 John 8).

In this letter, John also urges us not to imitate evil, but to imitate good. Those who do good, he writes, are of God, but those who do evil have no experience with Him and do not know Him at all (see 3 John 11).

As you read 3 John, I pray for you as John did for Gaius: "that in every way you may succeed and prosper and be in good health [physically], just as [I know] your soul prospers [spiritually]" (3 John 2). Let these verses inspire you to participate in the work of the ministry and the sharing of the gospel in every way you can. Do your part to support the spread of God's love and truth, just as John urged his readers to do.

¹THE ELDER [of the church addresses this letter] to the beloved *and* esteemed Gaius, whom I love in truth.

²Beloved, I pray that in every way you may succeed *and* prosper and be in good health [physically], just as [I know] your soul prospers [spiritually].

³For I was greatly pleased when [some of the] brothers came [from time to time] and testified to your [faithfulness to the] truth [of the gospel message], *that is,* how you are walking in truth.

⁴I have no greater joy than this, to hear that my [spiritual] children are living [their lives] in the truth.

putting the Word to work

How can you give joy to others as you walk in truth? Walking in truth means living out the truth you read in the Word of God. Others will take note of your faithfulness and it will encourage them.

⁵Beloved, you are acting faithfully in what you are providing for the brothers, and especially *when they are* strangers;

⁶and they have testified before the church of your love *and* friendship. You will do well to [assist them and] send them on their way in a manner worthy of God.

⁷For these [traveling missionaries] went out for the sake of the Name [of Christ], accepting nothing [in the way of assistance] from the Gentiles.

putting the Word to work

There are many people all around the world who work tirelessly for the sake of the gospel. It is important to extend hospitality to such individuals as you have opportunity. Even if you cannot host such a person in your home, what can you do to support these ministries? As you bless them, you share in their work for God's kingdom.

⁸So we ought to support such people [welcoming them as guests and providing for them], so that we may be fellow workers for the truth [that is, for the gospel message of salvation].

⁹I wrote something to the church; but Diotrephes, who loves to put himself first, does not accept what we say *and* refuses to recognize my authority.

¹⁰For this reason, if I come, I will call attention to what he is doing, unjustly accusing us with wicked words *and* unjustified charges. And not satisfied with this, he refuses to receive the

putting the Word to work

To imitate something is to use or follow it as a model. Whose life exhibits goodness you can imitate? Do not imitate those who do evil, who gossip, and who seek to exert control over others. As you do good, you will demonstrate that you belong to God.

speak the Word

Father, I pray that You will cause me to succeed and prosper in every way and be in good health, just as my soul prospers spiritually.
—ADAPTED FROM 3 JOHN 2

Help me, God, to live my life in Your truth.
—ADAPTED FROM 3 JOHN 4

prosper with purpose

One of God's most fervent desires for us is that we prosper in our souls. This means He wants us to mature spiritually, to be full-grown in mind, will, and emotions. He wants us to think with the mind of Christ and according to His Word, to be able to separate our emotions from decisions we need to make, and to use our will to line our lives up with His will for us.

To the degree that we do that, He also wants us to succeed and prosper and be healthy in all areas of life (see 3 John 2). There has been a great deal of discussion over whether God wants His children to prosper. Some believe poverty is a virtue while others believe that all Christians should be rich. I do not believe either one of those extremes. I believe we should concentrate on spiritual maturity and keep God first in our lives and that He will gladly give us everything we need to live happy, generous, blessed, and prosperous lives. God is more concerned with how we behave than with what we own.

Matthew told us to seek first God's "kingdom and His righteousness [His way of doing and being right—the attitude and character of God]" and all these things would be given to us also (Matthew 6:33). God wants us to have things as long as things do not have us. Yes, God wants us to be very blessed and He wants us to be a blessing to other people. We are to have "prosperity with a purpose."

God told Abraham that He would bless him and make him a blessing causing him to be "a source of great good to others" (Genesis 12:2). How can anyone be a blessing if he or she has not first been blessed? We cannot give away something we do not have. The Bible says Abraham was extremely wealthy (see Genesis 13:2), so it is obvious to me that God has no problem with His servants' prospering in every way, including materially, as long as they can handle it properly.

The question often surfaces, "If God wants us to have prosperity, then is a poor person godly?" Of course a poor person can be godly, but we do not have to worship poverty. Sick people can be godly, but that does not keep them from seeking healing. Love God with all of your heart no matter what your station is in life, but seek His best and use it for His purposes.

[missionary] brothers himself, and also forbids those who want to [welcome them] and puts *them* out of the church.

[11]Beloved, do not imitate what is evil, but [imitate] what is good. The one who practices good [exhibiting godly character, moral courage and personal integrity] is of God; the one who practices [or permits or tolerates] evil has not seen God [he has no personal experience with Him and does not know Him at all]. [1 John 3:6]

speak the Word

God, I pray that I will not imitate evil, but that I will imitate good because I am of You.
—ADAPTED FROM 3 JOHN 11

[12]Demetrius has received a *good* testimony *and* commendation from everyone—and from the truth [the standard of God's word] itself; and we add our testimony *and* speak well of him, and you know that our testimony is true.

[13]I had many things [to say when I began] to write to you, but I prefer not to put it down with pen (reed) and black (ink);

[14]but I hope to see you soon, and we will speak face to face. [Num 12:8]

[15]Peace be to you. The friends [here] greet you. Greet the friends [personally] by name.

Jude

Author:
Jude

Date:
AD 65–80

Everyday Life Principles:
Refute error and fight for your faith.

Build yourself up by spending time in God's Word and by praying in the Holy Spirit.

Trust God to keep you from slipping and to hold you firmly in place in your faith as you do your part to walk in truth.

The book of Jude warns believers against false teaching and provides us with a helpful list of characteristics of false teachers and erroneous teaching. False teachers are ungodly; they want to use God's grace as an opportunity for disobedience; and they deny Jesus Christ as Lord and Master (see Jude 4). They reject authority (see Jude 8) and look down on what they do not understand (see Jude 10). They are like "clouds without water" and like "autumn trees without fruit" (Jude 12). Furthermore, they grumble and complain, allow their emotions and passions to control them, brag about themselves, and flatter people in manipulative ways so they can get what they want and cause division.

But Jude knows that false teachers will not succeed and he urges believers to "fight strenuously for [the defense of] the faith" (Jude 3), to fight for what they know is true. To do that, Jude instructs them to "build yourselves up on [the foundation of] your most holy faith [continually progress, rise like an edifice higher and higher], pray in the Holy Spirit" and to "Keep yourselves in the love of God, waiting anxiously and looking forward to the mercy of our Lord Jesus Christ [which will bring you] to eternal life" (Jude 20, 21). We must do our part, and then trust God to keep us from stumbling or slipping as He enables us to continue walking in truth.

¹JUDE, A bond-servant of Jesus Christ, and brother of James, [writes this letter],

To those who are the called (God's chosen ones, the elect), dearly loved by God the Father, and kept [secure and set apart] for Jesus Christ:

²May mercy and peace and love be multiplied to you [filling your heart with the spiritual well-being and serenity experienced by those who walk closely with God].

³Beloved, while I was making every effort to write you about our common salvation, I was compelled to write to you [urgently] appealing that you fight strenuously for [the defense of] the faith which was once for all handed down to the saints [the faith that is the sum of Christian belief that was given verbally to believers].

⁴For certain people have crept in unnoticed [just as if they were sneaking in by a side door]. They are ungodly persons whose condemnation was predicted long ago, for they distort the grace of our God into decadence *and* immoral freedom [viewing it as an opportunity to do whatever they want], and deny *and* disown our only Master and Lord, Jesus Christ.

⁵Now I want to remind you, although you are fully informed once for all, that the Lord, after saving a people out of the land of Egypt, subsequently destroyed those who did not believe [who refused to trust and obey and rely on Him]. [Num 14:27–37]

⁶And angels who did not keep their own designated place of power, but abandoned their proper dwelling place, [these] He has kept in eternal chains under [the thick gloom of

utter] darkness for the judgment of the great day,

⁷just as Sodom and Gomorrah and the adjacent cities, since they in the same way as these *angels* indulged in gross immoral freedom *and* unnatural vice and sensual perversity. They are exhibited [in plain sight] as an example in undergoing the punishment of everlasting fire. [Gen 19:1–29]

⁸Nevertheless in the same way, these dreamers [who are dreaming that God will not punish them] also defile the body, and reject [legitimate] authority, and revile *and* mock angelic majesties.

⁹But even the archangel Michael, when he was disputing with the devil (Satan), and arguing about the body of Moses, did not dare bring an abusive condemnation against him, but [simply] said, "The Lord rebuke you!" [Deut 34:5, 6; Zech 3:2]

¹⁰But these men sneer at anything which they do not understand; and whatever they do know by [mere] instinct, like unreasoning *and* irrational beasts—by these things they are destroyed.

¹¹Woe to them! For they have gone the [defiant] way of Cain, and for profit they have run headlong into the error of Balaam, and perished in the rebellion of [mutinous] Korah. [Gen 4:3–8; Num 16:22–24; 2 Pet 2:15]

¹²These men are hidden reefs [elements of great danger to others] in your love feasts when they feast together with you without fear, looking after [only] themselves; [they are like] clouds without water, swept along by the winds; autumn trees without fruit, doubly dead, uprooted *and* lifeless;

¹³wild waves of the sea, flinging up

speak the Word

God, I pray that I will always fight strenuously for my faith and my Christian beliefs, no matter what.

—ADAPTED FROM JUDE 3

let God decide

What did Cain, Balaam, and Korah (see Jude 11) do that we need to beware of? All of them tried to get something God was not giving them. Cain was jealous of Abel, who had God's approval, so he killed him. He wanted what Abel had, but was not willing to do what Abel did to get it. Abel gave an acceptable offering and Cain did not. When we do not want to give God what He asks for, we cannot resent others who do and are blessed because of it.

Balaam disobeyed God in favor of a promotion promised by an earthly king. He chose a position of earthly honor over doing God's will and became so deceived that God spoke to him through his donkey in order to get his attention.

Korah resented Moses because he wanted his position and power. The world is filled with similar people, who want position and power and compromise their integrity to get it. They do things that war against their conscience and even if they get the things they thought they wanted, they are not happy with them. Korah's rebellion ended up costing him his life.

All of these men sinned against God in order to try to get something that God was not ready to give them. We can ask God for anything, but we must trust Him to give it to us if it is His will and in His timing. God has an individual plan for each of us and it is wrong to look at other people's lives and covet what they have. If we are happy for their blessings and trust God for ourselves, He will take care of us.

We must learn to wait on God and not take matters into our own hands. There is a way that seems right to man but it leads to death (see Proverbs 16:25). Psalm 37:4, 5 says, "Delight yourself in the LORD, and He will give you the desires and petitions of your heart. Commit your way to the LORD; trust in Him also and He will do it."

Enjoy where you are right now on the way to where you are going and do not try to get ahead of God. He has a great plan for you, and even though you may have to wait, you will be blessed in the end.

---

their own shame like foam; wandering stars, for whom the gloom of deep darkness has been reserved forever.

¹⁴It was about these people that Enoch, in the seventh *generation* from Adam, prophesied, when he said, "Look, the Lord came with myriads of His holy ones

¹⁵to execute judgment upon all, and to convict all the ungodly of all the ungodly deeds they have done in an ungodly way, and of all the harsh *and* cruel things ungodly sinners have spoken against Him."

¹⁶These *people* are [habitual] murmurers, griping *and* complaining, following after their own desires [controlled by passion]; they speak arrogantly, [pretending admiration and] flattering people to *gain an* advantage.

¹⁷But as for you, beloved, remember the [prophetic] words spoken by the apostles of our Lord Jesus Christ.

¹⁸They used to say to you, "In the last days there will be scoffers, following after their own ungodly passions." [2 Pet 3:3, 4]

¹⁹These are the ones who are

[agitators] causing divisions—worldly-minded [secular, unspiritual, carnal, merely sensual—unsaved], devoid of the Spirit.

²⁰But you, beloved, build yourselves up on [the foundation of] your most holy faith [continually progress, rise like an edifice higher and higher], pray in the Holy Spirit,

²¹and keep yourselves in the love of God, waiting anxiously *and* looking forward to the mercy of our Lord Jesus Christ [which will bring you] to eternal life.

²²And have mercy on some, who are doubting;

²³save others, snatching them out of the fire; and on some have mercy but with fear, loathing even the clothing spotted *and* polluted by their shameless immoral freedom. [Amos 4:11; Zech 3:2–4]

²⁴Now to Him who is able to keep you from stumbling *or* falling into sin, and to present you unblemished

life point

Jude 20 instructs us to "pray in the Holy Spirit." It is the Holy Spirit of God within us Who motivates us and leads us to pray. We must learn to yield to the leading of the Spirit as soon as we sense it, not later when the moment has passed by. This is part of learning to pray without ceasing, at all times, wherever we may be, and whatever we may be doing (see Ephesians 6:18).

I encourage you to pray in the Holy Spirit, and as you do, you will experience the joy that comes from praying in agreement with God's will.

[blameless and faultless] in the presence of His glory with triumphant joy *and* unspeakable delight,

²⁵to the only God our Savior, through Jesus Christ our Lord, be glory, majesty, dominion, and power, before all time and now and forever. Amen.

speak the Word

Help me, God, to stay built up in my faith, to pray often in the Holy Spirit, and to keep myself in Your love.
—ADAPTED FROM JUDE 20, 21

Thank You, God, that You are able to keep me from stumbling or falling into sin, and to present me blameless and faultless before Your presence with triumphant joy and unspeakable delight.
—ADAPTED FROM JUDE 24

Revelation

Author:
John

Date:
AD 70–95

Everyday Life Principles:
Remember that Jesus loves you and
that you are always victorious in Him.

When reading Revelation, focus on
what you do understand. Pray for
increased understanding, but do not
stumble over problematic passages.

Remember that, in the end, Jesus wins.

There are many different perspectives and interpretations of the book of Revelation, and it can be a difficult book to understand. For our purposes in this Bible, I chose to deal with the practical aspects of this book, and I simply want to point out that Revelation reminds us that we do have an enemy, Satan; that there is a spiritual war being waged between the forces of God and the forces of the enemy; and that, best of all, Jesus wins. As the struggle unfolds, there will be days of deception and an Antichrist will arise. But, through the Holy Spirit, we can live with discernment during these times and look forward to the second coming of Christ. If you are a believer in Jesus Christ, you—along with everyone throughout history who has ever believed in Him as Lord and Savior—are on the winning team and can anticipate an eternity with Him.

We should always remember that the book of Revelation is a revelation—an unveiling, a clearer picture than we previously had—of Jesus Christ. It teaches us about Who He is and what is important to Him. It reveals His mighty power over the enemy and His great love for His bride, the church.

Revelation is the only book of the Bible that specifically promises that those who read it will be blessed (see Revelation 1:3). As you read Revelation, let me encourage you not to get caught up in the parts you do not understand, but focus on its undeniable truths: that Jesus is the Son of God, that He is worthy of all glory and honor and praise, that He loves you, that one day He will return to earth, and that everyone who believes in Him will live forever with Him in a place where there is no more sickness or sadness. Be encouraged to stand strong in your faith, no matter what comes your way, and enjoy God's love for you every day while looking forward to the day when you will live with God in eternity.

1 *THIS IS* the revelation of Jesus Christ [His unveiling of the divine mysteries], which God [the Father] gave to Him to show to His bond-servants (believers) the things which must soon take place [in their entirety]; and He sent and communicated it by His angel (divine messenger) to His bond-servant John,

²who testified *and* gave supporting evidence to the word of God and to the testimony of Jesus Christ, *even* to everything that he saw [in his visions].

³Blessed (happy, prosperous, to be admired) is he who reads and those who hear the words of the prophecy, and who keep the things which are written in it [heeding them and taking them to heart]; for the time [of fulfillment] is near.

⁴John, to the seven churches that are in [the province of] Asia: Grace [be granted] to you and peace [inner calm and spiritual well-being], from Him Who is [existing forever] and Who was [continually existing in the past] and Who is to come, and from the seven Spirits that are before His throne, [Is 11:2]

⁵and from Jesus Christ, the *faithful and* trustworthy Witness, the First-born of the dead, and the Ruler of the kings of the earth. To Him who [always] loves us and who [has once for all] *freed us [or washed us] from our sins by His own blood (His sacrificial death)— [Ps 89:27]

⁶and formed us into a kingdom [as His subjects], priests to His God and Father—to Him be the glory *and* the power *and* the majesty and the dominion

life point

Revelation 1:5 affirms how much Jesus Christ loves us by shedding His own blood that we might be freed from sin and forever be in His presence. The passage communicates this strong message: *You are worth something because Jesus loves you and shed His blood for you.*

Do not allow your sense of worth to be based on the opinions or actions of others. Do not try to find your worth in how you look or what you do. In addition, don't try to find your worth in how other people treat you. Instead, let your sense of worth come through a relationship with Jesus Christ. You are secure in Him. He loves you!

forever and ever. Amen. [Ex 19:6; Is 61:6]

⁷BEHOLD, HE IS COMING WITH THE CLOUDS, and every eye will see Him, even those who pierced Him; and all the tribes (nations) of the earth will mourn over Him [realizing their sin and guilt, and anticipating the coming wrath]. *So it is to be. Amen. [Dan 7:13; Zech 12:10]

⁸"I am the Alpha and the Omega [the Beginning and the End]," says the Lord God, "Who is [existing forever] and Who was [continually existing in the past] and Who is to come, the Almighty [the Omnipotent, the Ruler of all]." [Is 9:6]

⁹I, John, your brother and companion in the tribulation and kingdom and patient endurance *which are* in Jesus, was on the island called Patmos, [exiled

speak the Word

Thank You, Jesus, that You are faithful and trustworthy, that You love me and have once for all freed me from my sins by Your own blood.
– ADAPTED FROM REVELATION 1:5

1:5 Lit *the witness, the faithful.*   **1:5** Some manuscripts use "freed" *(lusanti)* while others use "washed" *(lousanti).* Either reading conveys a similar theological conclusion: Jesus has taken away our sins by His blood. **1:7** Lit *Yes, amen.*

there] because of [my preaching of] the word of God [regarding eternal salvation] and the testimony of Jesus *Christ*.

[10]I was in the *Spirit [in special communication with the Holy Spirit and empowered to receive and record the revelation from Jesus Christ] on the Lord's Day, and I heard behind me a loud voice like the *sound* of a trumpet,

[11]saying, "Write on a scroll what you see [in this revelation], and send it to the seven churches—to Ephesus and to Smyrna and to Pergamum and to Thyatira and to Sardis and to Philadelphia and to Laodicea."

[12]Then I turned to see the voice that was speaking with me. And after turning I saw seven golden lampstands;

[13]and in the midst of the lampstands *I saw* someone like the Son of Man, dressed in a robe reaching to His feet, and with a golden sash wrapped around His chest. [Dan 7:13; 10:5]

[14]His head and His hair were white like white wool, [glistening white] like snow; and His [all-seeing] eyes were [flashing] like a flame of fire [piercing into my being]. [Dan 7:9]

[15]His feet were like burnished [white-hot] bronze, refined in a furnace, and His voice was [powerful] like the sound of many waters. [Dan 10:6]

[16]In His right hand He held seven stars, and from His mouth came a sharp two-edged sword [of judgment]; and His face [reflecting His majesty and the Shekinah glory] was like the sun shining in [all] its power [at midday]. [Ex 34:29]

[17]When I saw Him, I fell at His feet as though dead. And He placed His right hand on me and said, "Do not be afraid; I am the First and the Last [absolute Deity, the Son of God], [Is 44:6]

[18]and the Ever-living One [living in and beyond all time and space]. I died, but see, I am alive forevermore, and I have the keys of [absolute control and victory over] death and of Hades (the realm of the dead).

[19]"So write the things which you have seen [in the vision], and the things which are [now happening], and the things which will take place after these things.

[20]"As for the mystery of the seven stars which you saw in My right hand, and the seven golden lampstands: the seven stars are the angels (divine messengers) of the seven churches, and the seven lampstands are the seven churches.

2 "TO THE angel (divine messenger) of the church in Ephesus write:

"These are the words of the One who holds [firmly] the seven stars [which are the angels or messengers of the seven churches] in His right hand, the One who walks among the seven golden lampstands (the seven churches):

[2]'I know your deeds and your toil, and your patient endurance, and that you cannot tolerate those who are evil, and have tested *and* critically appraised those who call themselves apostles (special messengers, personally chosen representatives, of Christ), and [in fact] are not, and have found them to be liars *and* impostors;

[3]and [I know that] you [who believe] are enduring patiently and are bearing up for My name's sake, and that you have not grown weary [of being faithful to the truth].

[4]'But I have *this* [charge] against you, that you have left your first love [you have lost the depth of love that you first had for Me].

[5]'So remember *the heights* from which you have fallen, and repent [change your inner self—your old way of thinking, your sinful behavior—seek God's

1:10 Or *spirit*. The Greek wording is not decisive, so John could be referring either to being in special communion with the Holy Spirit, or to being in a trance-like state in his own spirit like that experienced by Peter at Joppa (cf Acts 10:10, 11).

putting the Word to work

How did you feel when you first began your relationship with God through Jesus Christ? You probably experienced a variety of feelings such as joy and peace, and you probably felt a new sense of freedom and a desire to love and to follow God with all your heart. God was probably your "first love" (see Revelation 2:4), but it can be easy to let other things in life—relationships, career, studies, even going to church—get in the way of fervently loving God. Let me encourage you to spend some time in prayer inviting God to show you anything or anyone in your life that has become more important to you than He is. Ask His forgiveness and ask Him to help you to make Him your first love once again.

will] and do the works you did at first [when you first knew Me]; otherwise, I will visit you and remove your lampstand (the church, its impact) from its place—unless you repent.

⁶'Yet you have this [to your credit], that you hate the works *and* corrupt teachings of the Nicolaitans [that mislead and delude the people], which I also hate.

⁷'He who has an ear, let him hear *and* heed what the Spirit says to the churches. To him who overcomes [the world through believing that Jesus is the Son of God], I will grant [the privilege] to eat [the fruit] from the tree of life, which is in the Paradise of God.' [Gen 2:9; 3:24; 1 John 5:5]

⁸"And to the angel (divine messenger) of the church in Smyrna write:

"These are the words of the First and the Last [absolute Deity, the Son of God] who died and came to life [again]: [Is 44:6]

⁹'I know your suffering and your poverty (but you are rich), and how you are blasphemed *and* slandered by those who say they are Jews and are not, but are a synagogue of Satan [they are Jews only by blood, and do not believe and truly honor the God whom they claim to worship].

¹⁰'Fear nothing that you are about to suffer. Be aware that the devil is about to throw some of you into prison, that you may be tested [in your faith], and for ten days you will have tribulation. Be faithful to the point of death [if you must die for your faith], and I will give you the crown [consisting] of life. [Rev 3:10, 11]

¹¹'He who has an ear, let him hear *and* heed what the Spirit says to the churches. He who overcomes [the world through believing that Jesus is the Son of God] will not be hurt by the second death (the lake of fire).' [1 John 5:5; Rev 20:14]

¹²"And to the angel (divine messenger) of the church in Pergamum write:

"These are the words of Him who has *and* wields the sharp two-edged sword [in judgment]:

¹³'I know where you dwell, [a place] where Satan sits enthroned. Yet you are holding fast to My name, and you did not deny My faith even in the days of Antipas, My witness, My faithful one, who was killed (martyred) among you, where Satan dwells.

¹⁴'But I have a few things against you, because you have there some [among you] who are holding to the [corrupt] teaching of Balaam, who taught Balak to put a stumbling block

speak the Word

Jesus, I pray that I will never leave You or lose the depth of the love I first had for You.
—ADAPTED FROM REVELATION 2:4

before the sons of Israel, [enticing them] to eat things that had been sacrificed to idols and to commit [acts of sexual] immorality. [Num 25:1, 2; 31:16]

¹⁵'You also have some who in the same way are holding to the teaching of the Nicolaitans.

¹⁶'Therefore repent [change your inner self—your old way of thinking, your sinful behavior—seek God's will]; or else I am coming to you quickly, and I will make war *and* fight against them with the sword of My mouth [in judgment].

¹⁷'He who has an ear, let him hear *and* heed what the Spirit says to the churches. To him who overcomes [the world through believing that Jesus is the Son of God], to him I will give [the privilege of eating] *some* of the hidden manna, and I will give him a white stone with a new name engraved on the stone which no one knows except the one who receives it.' [Ps 78:24; Is 62:2; 1 John 5:5]

¹⁸"And to the angel (divine messenger) of the church in Thyatira write:

"These are the words of the Son of God, who has eyes [that flash] like a flame of fire [in righteous judgment], and whose feet are like burnished [white-hot] bronze: [Dan 10:6]

¹⁹'I know your deeds, your love and faith and service and patient endurance, and that your last deeds are more numerous *and* greater than the first.

²⁰'But I have this [charge] against you, that you tolerate the woman Jezebel, who calls herself a prophetess [claiming to be inspired], and she teaches and misleads My bond-servants so that they commit [acts of sexual] immorality and eat food sacrificed to idols. [1 Kin 16:31; 2 Kin 9:22, 30]

²¹'I gave her time to repent [to change her inner self and her sinful way of thinking], but she has no desire to repent of her immorality *and* refuses to do so.

²²'Listen carefully, I will throw her on a bed *of sickness,* and those who commit adultery with her [I will bring] into great anguish, unless they repent of her deeds.

²³'And I will kill her children (followers) with pestilence [thoroughly annihilating them], and all the churches will know [without any doubt] that I am He who searches the minds and hearts [the innermost thoughts, purposes]; and I will give to each one of you [a reward or punishment] according to your deeds. [Ps 62:12; Jer 17:10]

²⁴'But to the rest of you in Thyatira, who do not hold this teaching, who have not explored *and* known the depths of Satan, as they call them—I place no other burden on you,

²⁵except to hold tightly to what you have until I come.

²⁶'And he who overcomes [the world through believing that Jesus is the Son of God] and he who keeps My deeds [doing things that please Me] until the [very] end, TO HIM I WILL GIVE AUTHORITY *and* POWER OVER THE NATIONS; [1 John 5:5]

²⁷AND HE SHALL SHEPHERD *and* RULE THEM WITH A ROD OF IRON, AS THE EARTHEN POTS ARE BROKEN IN PIECES, as I also have received *authority* [and power to rule them] from My Father; [Ps 2:8, 9]

²⁸and I will give him the Morning Star.

²⁹'He who has an ear, let him hear *and* heed what the Spirit says to the churches.'

3 "TO THE angel (divine messenger) of the church in Sardis write:

"These are the words of Him who has the seven Spirits of God and the seven stars: 'I know your deeds; you have a name (reputation) that you are alive, but [in reality] you are dead.

2114

2'Wake up, and strengthen *and* reaffirm what remains [of your faithful commitment to Me], which is about to die; for I have not found [any of] your deeds completed in the sight of My God *or* meeting His requirements.

3'So remember *and* take to heart the lessons you have received and heard. Keep *and* obey them, and repent [change your sinful way of thinking, and demonstrate your repentance with new behavior that proves a conscious

step out and find out

We all need to hear from God each day about many different issues, but there are critical times in our lives when we especially need to know we are hearing clearly from Him. God wants to speak to us, but we have to be careful that we do not develop a closed mindset about *how* He has to speak to us.

Sometimes God speaks by opening or closing a door to something we want to do, as Revelation 3:7 suggests. My husband Dave and I know from experience that God can open doors of opportunity that no one can close, and He can also close doors that we simply cannot open. I pray that God will open only the doors through which He wants me to pass. I may sincerely think something is right to do, when it may be wrong; therefore, I depend on God to close doors I am trying to walk through if I am in fact making a mistake: "A man's mind plans his way [as he journeys through life], but the LORD directs his steps and establishes them" (Proverbs 16:9).

Sometimes the only way to discover God's will is to practice what I call "stepping out and finding out." If I pray about a situation and do not feel sure about what I should do, I take a step of faith. God has shown me that trusting Him is like standing before the automatic door to a supermarket. We can stand and look at the door all day, but it will not open until we take a step forward and trigger the mechanism that opens the door.

There are times in life when we must take a step forward in order to find out, one way or the other, what we should do. Some doors will never open unless we take a step toward them. At other times we may take a step and find that God will not open the door. If we trust Him for guidance, and the door opens easily, we can trust that He is leading us to enter into the opportunity before us.

In 1 Corinthians 16:9 Paul states that God opened a wide door of opportunity for him. He also mentions that there were many adversaries, so we must not mistake opposition for a closed door.

Paul and his coworkers did not sit and wait for an angel to appear or a vision to be given to them while praying for direction. They took steps in the direction they felt was correct. Many times God did open the door, but there were times when He closed the door. This did not discourage them. They were not afraid of "missing God." They were men of faith and action. They also knew to back off quickly when it became evident that God was not permitting them to follow their own plan. I encourage you to be the same way. Take the steps you believe you need to take in life and see if God opens or shuts the doors.

decision to turn away from sin]. So then, if you do not wake up, I will come like a thief, and you will not know at what hour I will come to you.

⁴'But you [still] have a few people in Sardis who have not soiled their clothes [that is, contaminated their character and personal integrity with sin]; and they will walk with Me [dressed] in white, because they are worthy (righteous).

⁵'He who overcomes [the world through believing that Jesus is the Son of God] will accordingly be dressed in white clothing; and I will never blot out his name from the Book of Life, and I will confess *and* openly acknowledge his name before My Father and before His angels [saying that he is one of Mine]. [Ps 69:28; Dan 12:1; Matt 10:32; 1 John 5:5]

⁶'He who has an ear, let him hear *and* heed what the Spirit says to the churches.'

⁷"And to the angel (divine messenger) of the church in Philadelphia write:

"**T**hese are the words of the Holy One, the True One, He who has the key [to the house] of David, He who opens and no one will [be able to] shut, and He who shuts and no one opens: [Is 22:22]

⁸'I know your deeds. See, I have set before you an open door which no one is able to shut, for you have a little power, and have kept My word, and have not renounced *or* denied My name. [1 Cor 16:9; Col 4:3, 4]

⁹'Take note, I will make *those* of the synagogue of Satan, who say that they are Jews and are not, but lie—I will make them come and bow down at your feet and *make them* know [without any doubt] that I have loved you. [Is 45:14; 49:23; 60:14]

¹⁰'Because you have kept the word of My endurance [My command to persevere], I will keep you [safe] from the hour of trial, that *hour* which is about to come on the whole [inhabited] world, to test those who live on the earth. [Mark 13:9; 2 Thess 2:1–12]

¹¹'I am coming quickly. Hold tight what you have, so that no one will take your crown [by leading you to renounce the faith].

¹²'He who overcomes [the world through believing that Jesus is the Son of God], I will make him a pillar in the temple of My God; he will most certainly never be put out of it, and I will write on him the name of My God, and the name of the city of My God, the new Jerusalem, which descends out of heaven from My God, and My [own] new name. [Is 62:2; Ezek 48:35; 1 John 5:5]

¹³'He who has an ear, let him hear *and* heed what the Spirit says to the churches.'

¹⁴"To the angel (divine messenger) of the church in Laodicea write:

"**T**hese are the words of the Amen, the trusted *and* faithful and true Witness, the Beginning *and* Origin of God's creation:

¹⁵'I know your deeds, that you are neither cold (invigorating, refreshing) nor hot (healing, therapeutic); I wish that you were cold or hot.

¹⁶'So because you are lukewarm (spiritually useless), and neither hot nor cold, I will vomit you out of My mouth [rejecting you with disgust].

¹⁷'Because you say, "I am rich, and have prospered *and* grown wealthy, and have need of nothing," and you do not know that you are wretched and miserable and poor and blind and naked [without hope and in great need], [Hos 12:8]

speak the Word

God, I pray that I will keep Your Word and never renounce or deny Your name.
–ADAPTED FROM REVELATION 3:8

wholehearted service

God wants us to serve Him enthusiastically and wholeheartedly. He does not appreciate halfhearted effort. Revelation 3:15, 16 warn us against being lukewarm and teach us that being neither hot nor cold is not acceptable to God. Actually, He would prefer that we be cold toward Him than lukewarm. His desire is for us to be red-hot, on fire, stirred up, and excited about Him, His Word, His principles, and His will for our lives.

Why would God rather someone be cold than lukewarm? It seems that lukewarm is better than nothing. I believe it is because lukewarm people are easily deceived into thinking they are doing what they should be doing when in fact they are not. They are offering sacrifices, not wholehearted obedience. For example, they might go to church as an obligation but in reality they do not want to be there at all. However, when a person is totally cold toward God at least they know it and can be dealt with more easily than someone who is deceived.

I once taught a message titled, "Get In, Get Out, or Get Run Over." My theory was that God is moving and we can either get on board and move with Him wholeheartedly or remain rebellious and obstinate and get left behind. As far as I am concerned, life is not worth living at all if we are not passionately committed to Jesus Christ. Sadly, many people waste most of their lives before they realize this is true; some never do.

God never does anything halfheartedly and we should not either. Whatever your task may be, work at it wholeheartedly (with all your heart) as something for the Lord (see Colossians 3:23).

The first and principle commandment of God is that we love Him with our whole heart, mind, soul, and strength (see Deuteronomy 6:5). If we do that He will be honored and we will be very fulfilled and blessed. Never lag "behind in diligence," but be "aglow in the Spirit, enthusiastically serving the Lord" (Romans 12:11).

¹⁸I counsel you to buy from Me gold that has been heated red hot *and* refined by fire so that you may become *truly* rich; and white clothes [representing righteousness] to clothe yourself so that the shame of your nakedness will not be seen; and *healing* salve to put on your eyes so that you may see.

¹⁹"Those whom I [dearly and tenderly] love, I rebuke and discipline [showing them their faults and instructing them]; so be enthusiastic and repent [change your inner self—your old way of thinking, your sinful behavior—seek God's will]. [Prov 3:11, 12; Heb 5:8; 12:5–7]

²⁰"Behold, I stand at the door [of the church] and *continually* knock. If anyone hears My voice and opens the door, I will come in and eat with him (restore him), and he with Me.

life point

Revelation 3:20 teaches us that Jesus knocks at the door of many hearts right now, but it's important to remember that the doorknob is on our side. He is a gentleman; He will not force His way into our life. We must welcome Him.

putting the Word to work

Have you ever had your home broken into or known someone who has? There is a terrible sense of intrusion and violation when something like that occurs. Jesus will never enter a place in your life where He is not welcome. God wants to bring healing and wholeness to every area of your life, but He will wait for your invitation (see Revelation 3:20). Ask God to show you where in your life you need Him to do some work, and know that He is eager to bring restoration, healing, and wholeness.

²¹'He who overcomes [the world through believing that Jesus is the Son of God], I will grant to him [the privilege] to sit beside Me on My throne, as I also overcame and sat down beside My Father on His throne. [1 John 5:5] ²²'He who has an ear, let him hear *and* heed what the Spirit says to the churches.'"

4 AFTER THIS I looked, and behold, a door standing open in heaven! And the first voice which I had heard, like *the sound* of a [war] trumpet speaking with me, said, "Come up here, and I will show you what must take place after these things." ²At once I was in [special communication with] the Spirit; and behold, a throne stood in heaven, with One seated on the throne. [Ezek 1:26] ³And He who sat there appeared like [the crystalline sparkle of] a jasper stone and [the fiery redness of] a sardius stone, and encircling the throne *there was* a rainbow that looked like [the color of an] emerald. [Ezek 1:28; Rev 21:11, 19] ⁴Twenty-four [other] thrones surrounded the throne; and seated on these thrones were twenty-four

elders dressed in white clothing, with crowns of gold on their heads. ⁵From the throne came flashes of lightning and [rumbling] sounds and peals of thunder. Seven lamps of fire were burning in front of the throne, which are the seven Spirits of God; [Ex 19:16–20a] ⁶and in front of the throne *there was something* like a sea *or* large expanse of glass, like [the clearest] crystal. In the center and around the throne were four living creatures who were full of eyes in front and behind [seeing everything and knowing everything that is around them]. [Ps 99:1; Is 6:2, 3; Ezek 1:5, 18] ⁷The first living creature was like a lion, the second creature like a calf (ox), the third creature had the face of a man, and the fourth creature was like a flying eagle. [Ezek 1:10] ⁸And the four living creatures, each one of them having six wings, are full of eyes all over and within [underneath their wings]; and day and night they never stop saying,

"HOLY, HOLY, HOLY [is the] LORD GOD, THE ALMIGHTY [the Omnipotent, the Ruler of all], WHO WAS AND WHO IS AND WHO IS TO COME [the unchanging, eternal God]." [Is 6:1–3; Rev 1:4]

life point

Revelation 4:5 speaks of the "seven Spirits of God" that are before God's throne (see also Revelation 1:4; 3:1). We know there is only one Holy Spirit, but the reference to the sevenfold Holy Spirit shows us that He has various ways of manifesting and expressing Himself among us to bring fullness to our lives. Just as the Trinity is one God in three Persons, so the Holy Spirit is one Spirit with different operations or modes of expression.

⁹Whenever the living creatures give glory and honor and thanksgiving to Him who sits on the throne, to Him who lives forever and ever, [Ps 47:8]

¹⁰the twenty-four elders fall down before Him who sits on the throne, and they worship Him who lives forever and ever; and they throw down their crowns before the throne, saying,

¹¹"Worthy are You, our Lord and God, to receive the glory and the honor and the power; for You created all things, and because of Your will they exist, and were created *and* brought into being." [Ps 19:1]

5 I SAW in the right hand of Him who was seated on the throne a scroll written on the inside and on the back, closed *and* sealed with seven seals. [Is 29:11; Ezek 2:9, 10; Dan 12:4]

²And I saw a strong angel announcing with a loud voice, "Who is worthy [having the authority and virtue] to open the scroll and to break its seals?"

³And no one in heaven or on earth or under the earth [in Hades, the realm of the dead] was able to open the scroll or look into it.

⁴And I *began* to weep greatly because no one was found worthy to open the scroll or look into it.

⁵Then one of the [twenty-four] elders said to me, "Stop weeping! Look closely, the Lion of the tribe of Judah, the Root of David, has overcome *and* conquered! He can open the scroll and [break] its seven seals." [Gen 49:9, 10; Is 11:1, 10; Rev 22:16]

⁶And there between the throne (with the four living creatures) and among the elders I saw a Lamb (Christ) standing, [bearing scars and wounds] as though it had been slain, with seven horns (complete power) and with seven eyes (complete knowledge), which are the seven Spirits of God who have been sent [on duty] into all the earth. [Is 53:7; Zech 3:8, 9; 4:10]

⁷And He came and took the scroll from the right hand of Him who sat on the throne.

⁸And when He had taken the scroll, the four living creatures and the twenty-four elders fell down before the Lamb (Christ), each one holding a harp and golden bowls full of fragrant incense, which are the prayers of the saints (God's people).

⁹And they sang a new song [of glorious redemption], saying,

"Worthy *and* deserving are You
  to take the scroll and to break
  its seals; for You were slain
  (sacrificed), and with Your blood
  You purchased *people* for God
  from every tribe and language
  and people and nation. [Ps 33:3]

¹⁰"You have made them to be a
  kingdom [of royal subjects] and
  priests to our God; and they will
  reign on the earth." [Ex 19:6; Is
  61:6; Rev 20:6]

¹¹Then I looked, and I heard the voice of many angels around the throne and [the voice] of the living creatures and the elders; and they numbered myriads of myriads, and thousands of thousands (innumerable), [Dan 7:10]

speak the Word

Lord, I declare that You are worthy to receive glory and honor and power,
for You created all things, and because of Your will they exist,
and were created and brought into being.
–ADAPTED FROM REVELATION 4:11

lion or lamb?

The characteristics of the lion are totally different from those of the lamb, yet the Lord is recognized as having both qualities in Revelation 5:5, 6.

Someone once gave me a picture of a lion and a lamb lying down together, and it reminds me that I am supposed to be a good, godly mixture of both qualities. I never had any trouble with the lion part, but I had a lot of trouble with the lamb part. When we need to communicate with someone, especially concerning confrontational issues, we should first pray for God's grace and mercy to anoint us as lion-hearted lambs. Then we should wait until we have balance in our perspective and approach.

Throughout the Gospels, Jesus seems to act in two contrasting ways. He confronts the moneychangers in the temple with lion-like intensity, overthrowing their tables and firmly demonstrating God's will to all those who watched Him. He said to them, "It is written [in Scripture], 'MY HOUSE SHALL BE CALLED A HOUSE OF PRAYER;' but you are making it a ROBBERS DEN" (Matthew 21:13). Yet in other places, we see Jesus as a lamb, standing falsely accused, without speaking one word in His own defense (Matthew 27:12–14).

What are we to learn from His communication patterns? He was lion-like when He needed to be and yet always a lamb—He never sinned or failed to be excellent in speech. Not defending yourself when someone comes against you is a challenge. It is difficult to ignore insults and shun retaliation.

Isaiah 53:7 says that Jesus "was oppressed and He was afflicted, yet He did not open His mouth [to complain or defend Himself]; like a lamb that is led to the slaughter, and like a sheep that is silent before her shearers, so He did not open His mouth."

Sometimes I find that one of the hardest things God asks us to do is be Christlike in our communication with others. When people are rude and tell you off, mistreat, or insult you, it is hard to look at them with godly love and simply wait on God.

Thank God, He gives us the power to change and to become like Christ, a healthy person who knows when to be a lion and when to be a lamb.

[12]saying in a loud voice,

"Worthy *and* deserving is the Lamb that was sacrificed to receive power and riches and wisdom and might and honor and glory and blessing."

[13]And I heard every created thing that is in heaven or on earth or under the earth [in Hades, the realm of the dead] or on the sea, and everything that is in them, saying [together],

"To Him who sits on the throne, and to the Lamb (Christ), be blessing and honor and glory and dominion forever and ever." [Dan 7:13, 14]

[14]And the four living creatures kept saying, "Amen." And the elders fell

down and worshiped [Him who lives forever and ever].

6 THEN I saw as the Lamb (Christ) broke one of the seven seals [of the scroll initiating the judgments], and I heard one of the four living creatures call out as with a voice of thunder, "Come."

²I looked, and behold, a white horse [of victory] whose rider carried a bow; and a crown [of victory] was given to him, and he rode forth conquering and to conquer. [Ps 45:4, 5; Zech 1:8; 6:1–8]

³When He (the Lamb) broke the second seal, I heard the second living creature call out, "Come."

⁴And another, a fiery red horse [of bloodshed], came out; and its rider was empowered to take peace from the earth, so that men would slaughter one another; and a great sword [of war and violent death] was given to him. [Zech 1:8; 6:1–8]

⁵When He (the Lamb) broke open the third seal, I heard the third living creature call out, "Come." I looked, and behold, a black horse [of famine]; and the rider had in his hand a pair of scales (a balance). [Zech 6:1–8]

⁶And I heard *something* like a voice in the midst of the four living creatures saying, "A quart of wheat for a denarius (a day's wages), and three quarts of barley for a denarius; and do not damage the oil and the wine." [2 Kin 6:25]

⁷When He (the Lamb) broke open the fourth seal, I heard the voice of the fourth living creature call out, "Come."

⁸So I looked, and behold, an ashen (pale greenish gray) horse [like a corpse, representing death and pestilence]; and its rider's name was Death; and Hades (the realm of the dead) was following with him. They were given authority *and* power over a fourth part of the earth, to kill with the sword and with famine and with plague (pesti-

lence, disease) and by the wild beasts of the earth. [Ezek 14:21; Hos 13:14]

⁹When He (the Lamb) broke open the fifth seal, I saw underneath the altar the souls of those who had been slaughtered because of the word of God, and because of the testimony which they had maintained [out of loyalty to Christ].

¹⁰They cried in a loud voice, saying, "O Lord, holy and true, how long now before You will sit in judgment and avenge our blood on those [unregenerate ones] who dwell on the earth?" [Gen 4:10; Ps 79:10; 94:3; Zech 1:12]

¹¹Then they were each given a white robe; and they were told to rest *and* wait quietly for a little while longer, until *the number of* their fellow servants and their brothers and sisters who were to be killed even as they had been, would be completed.

¹²I looked when He (the Lamb) broke open the sixth seal, and there was a great earthquake; and the sun became black as sackcloth [made] of hair, and the whole moon became like blood; [Joel 2:10, 31]

¹³and the stars of the sky fell to the earth, like a fig tree shedding its late [summer] figs when shaken by a strong wind. [Is 34:4]

¹⁴The sky was split [separated from the land] and rolled up like a scroll, and every mountain and island were dislodged *and* moved out of their places.

¹⁵Then the kings of the earth and the great men and the military commanders and the wealthy and the strong and everyone, [whether] slave or free, hid themselves in the caves and among the rocks of the mountains;

¹⁶and they called to the mountains and the rocks, "Fall on us and hide us from the face of Him who sits on the throne, and from the [righteous] wrath *and* indignation of the Lamb; [Is 2:19–21; Hos 10:8]

¹⁷for the great day of their wrath *and*

vengeance *and* retribution has come, and who is able to [face God and] stand [before the wrath of the Lamb]?" [Joel 2:11; Mal 3:2; Jude 14; Rev 19:11–16]

7 AFTER THIS I saw four angels stationed at the four corners of the earth, holding back the four winds of the earth so that no wind would blow on the earth or on the sea or on any tree. [Zech 6:5]

²Then I saw another angel coming up from the rising of the sun, holding the seal of the living God; and with a loud voice he called out to the four angels to whom it was granted [to have authority and power] to harm the earth and the sea,

³saying, "Do not harm the earth nor the sea nor the trees until we seal (mark) the bond-servants of our God on their foreheads." [Ezek 9:4]

⁴And I heard how many were sealed, a hundred and forty-four thousand; [twelve thousand] sealed from every tribe of the sons of Israel:

⁵Twelve thousand were sealed from the tribe of Judah, twelve thousand from the tribe of Reuben, twelve thousand from the tribe of Gad,

⁶twelve thousand from the tribe of Asher, twelve thousand from the tribe of Naphtali, twelve thousand from the tribe of Manasseh,

⁷twelve thousand from the tribe of Simeon, twelve thousand from the tribe of Levi, twelve thousand from the tribe of Issachar,

⁸twelve thousand from the tribe of Zebulun, twelve thousand from the tribe of Joseph, and twelve thousand from the tribe of Benjamin were sealed (marked, redeemed, protected).

⁹After these things I looked, and this is what I saw: a vast multitude which no one could count, [gathered] from every nation and from all the tribes and peoples and languages [of the earth], standing before the throne and before the Lamb (Christ), dressed in white robes, with palm branches in their hands;

¹⁰and in a loud voice they cried out, saying,

"Salvation [belongs] to our God who is seated on the throne, and to the Lamb [our salvation is the Trinity's to give, and to God the Trinity we owe our deliverance]."

¹¹And all the angels were standing around the throne and *around* the [twenty-four] elders and the four living creatures; and they fell to their faces before the throne and worshiped God,

¹²saying,

"Amen! Blessing and glory *and* majesty and wisdom and thanksgiving and honor and power and might belong to our God forever and ever. Amen."

¹³Then one of the elders responded, saying to me, "These who are dressed in the long white robes—who are they, and from where did they come?"

putting the Word to work

Every two years, the eyes of much of the world focus on the Summer or Winter Olympics. Have you ever watched the opening ceremonies and the Parade of Nations? With athletes from more than 175 nations parading under the banner of their nation's flag, it is quite a sight to see! Yet it pales in comparison to the multitude from every nation, tribe, people, and language that will gather together before the throne of God (see Revelation 7:9, 10). Let me encourage you to pray regularly for the nations and people of the world, and for those who take the good news of the gospel to them.

¹⁴I said to him, "My lord, you know [the answer]." And he said to me, "These are the people who come out of the great tribulation (persecution), and they have washed their robes and made them white in the blood of the Lamb [because of His atoning sacrifice]. [Gen 49:11; Dan 12:1]

¹⁵"For this reason, they are [standing] before the throne of God; and they serve Him [in worship] day and night in His temple; and He who sits on the throne will spread His tabernacle over them *and* shelter *and* protect them [with His presence]. [Rev 21:3]

¹⁶"They will hunger no longer, nor thirst anymore; nor will the sun beat down on them, nor any [scorching] heat; [Is 49:10; Ps 121:6]

¹⁷for the Lamb who is in the center of the throne will be their Shepherd, and He will guide them to springs of the waters of life; and God will wipe every tear from their eyes [giving them eternal comfort]." [Ps 23:2; Is 25:8; Ezek 34:23; Rev 21:4]

8 WHEN HE (the Lamb) broke open the seventh seal, there was silence in heaven for about half an hour [in awe of God's impending judgment]. [Zeph 1:7]

²Then I saw the seven angels who stand before God, and seven trumpets were given to them.

³Another angel came and stood at the altar. He had a golden censer, and much incense was given to him, so that he might add it to the prayers of all the saints (God's people) on the golden altar in front of the throne. [Ps 141:2]

⁴And the smoke *and* fragrant aroma of the incense, with the prayers of the saints (God's people), ascended before God from the angel's hand.

⁵So the angel took the censer and filled it with fire from the altar, and hurled it to the earth; and there were peals of thunder *and* loud rumblings and sounds and flashes of lightning and an earthquake. [Lev 16:12; Ezek 10:2]

⁶Then the seven angels who had the seven trumpets prepared themselves to sound them [initiating the judgments].

⁷The first [angel] sounded [his trumpet], and there was [a storm of] hail and fire, mixed with blood, and it was hurled to the earth; and a third of the earth was burned up, and a third of the trees were burned up, and all the green grass was burned up. [Ex 9:13–35]

⁸The second angel sounded [his trumpet], and *something* like a great mountain blazing with fire was hurled into the sea; and a third of the sea was turned to blood; [Jer 51:25]

⁹and a third of the living creatures that were in the sea died, and a third of the ships were destroyed.

¹⁰The third angel sounded [his trumpet], and a great star fell from heaven, burning like a torch [flashing across the sky], and it fell on a third of the rivers and on the springs of [fresh] waters.

¹¹The name of the star is Wormwood; and a third of the waters became wormwood, and many people died from the waters, because they had become bitter (toxic).

¹²Then the fourth angel sounded [his trumpet], and a third of the sun and a third of the moon and a third of the stars were struck, so that a third of them would be darkened and a third of the daylight would not shine, and the night in the same way [would not shine]. [Ex 10:21–23]

¹³Then I looked, and I heard a solitary eagle flying in midheaven [for all to see], saying with a loud voice, "Woe, woe, woe [great wrath is coming] to those who dwell on the earth, because of the remaining blasts of the trumpets which the three angels are about to sound [announcing ever greater judgments]!"

9 THEN THE fifth angel sounded [his trumpet], and I saw a star (angelic being) that had fallen from heaven to the earth; and the key of the bottomless pit (abyss) was given to him (the star-angel). [Rev 20:1]

²He opened the bottomless pit, and smoke like the smoke of a great furnace flowed out of the pit; and the sun and the atmosphere were darkened by the smoke from the pit. [Gen 19:28; Ex 19:18; Joel 2:10]

³Then out of the smoke came locusts upon the earth, and power [to hurt] was given to them, like the power which the earth's scorpions have. [Ex 10:12–15]

⁴They were told not to hurt the grass of the earth, nor any green thing, nor any tree, but [to hurt] only the people who do not have the seal (mark of ownership, protection) of God on their foreheads. [Ezek 9:4]

⁵They were not permitted to kill anyone, but to torment *and* cause them extreme pain for five months; and their torment was like the torment from a scorpion when it stings a man.

⁶And in those days people will seek death and will not find it; and they will long to die [to escape the pain], but [will discover that] death evades them. [Job 3:21]

⁷The locusts resembled horses prepared *and* equipped for battle; and on their heads appeared to be [something like] golden crowns, and their faces resembled human faces. [Joel 2:4]

⁸They had hair like the hair of women, and their teeth were like *the teeth* of lions. [Joel 1:6]

⁹They had breastplates (scales) like breastplates made of iron; and the [whirring] noise of their wings was like the [thunderous] noise of countless horse-drawn chariots charging [at full speed] into battle. [Joel 2:5]

¹⁰They have tails like scorpions, and stingers; and in their tails is their power to hurt people for five months. [Joel 2:6]

¹¹They have as king over them, the angel of the abyss (the bottomless pit); in Hebrew his name is Abaddon (destruction), and in Greek he is called Apollyon (destroyer-king).

¹²The first woe has passed; behold, two woes are still coming after these things.

¹³Then the sixth angel sounded [his trumpet], and I heard a solitary voice from the four horns of the golden altar which stands before God,

¹⁴saying to the sixth angel who had the trumpet, "Release the four angels who are bound at the great river Euphrates."

¹⁵So the four angels, who had been prepared for the [appointed] hour and day and month and year, were released to kill a third of mankind.

¹⁶The number of the troops of cavalry was twice ten thousand times ten thousand (two hundred million); I heard the number of them.

¹⁷And this is how I saw the horses and their riders in my vision: *the riders* had breastplates [the color] of fire and of hyacinth (sapphire blue) and of brimstone (yellow); and the heads of the horses looked like the heads of lions; and from out of their mouths came fire and smoke and brimstone (burning sulfur).

¹⁸A third of mankind was killed by these three plagues—by the fire and the smoke and the brimstone that came from the mouths of the horses.

¹⁹For the power of the horses [to do harm] is in their mouths and in their tails; for their tails are like serpents and have heads, and it is with them that they do harm.

²⁰The rest of mankind, who were not killed by these plagues, did not repent even then of the works of their hands, so as to cease worshiping *and* paying homage to the demons and the idols of gold and of silver and of bronze and of stone and of wood, which can neither

see nor hear nor walk; [Ps 115:4–7; 135:15–17; Is 17:8]

²¹and they did not repent of their murders nor of their sorceries (drugs, intoxications) nor of their [sexual] immorality nor of their thefts.

10

THEN I saw another mighty angel coming down from heaven, clothed in a cloud, with a rainbow (halo) over his head; and his face was like the sun, and his feet (legs) were like columns of fire; [Ex 13:21, 22; Ezek 1:26–28; Dan 7:13; Matt 17:2]

²and he had a little book (scroll) open in his hand. He set his right foot on the sea and his left foot on the land; [Ezek 2:9; Hos 11:10]

³and he shouted with a loud voice, like the roaring of a lion [compelling attention and inspiring awe]; and when he had shouted out, the seven peals of thunder spoke with their own voices [uttering their message in distinct words]. [Ps 29]

⁴And when the seven peals of thunder had spoken, I was about to write; but I heard a voice from heaven saying, "Seal up the things which the seven peals of thunder have spoken and do not write them down." [2 Cor 12:4]

⁵Then the angel whom I had seen standing on the sea and the land raised his right hand [to swear an oath] to heaven, [Deut 32:40; Dan 12:6, 7]

⁶and swore [an oath] by [the name of] Him who lives forever and ever, WHO CREATED HEAVEN AND THE THINGS IN IT, AND THE EARTH AND THE THINGS IN IT, AND THE SEA AND THE THINGS IN IT, that there will be delay no longer, [Neh 9:6]

⁷but when it is time for the trumpet call of the seventh angel, when he is about to sound, then the mystery of God [that is, His hidden purpose and plan] is finished, as He announced the gospel to His servants the prophets. [Dan 12:6; Rom 11:25; 1 Cor 15:55; 2 Thess 2:7]

⁸Then the voice which I heard from heaven, *I heard* again speaking to me, and saying, "Go, take the book (scroll) which is open in the hand of the angel who is standing on the sea and on the land."

⁹So I went up to the angel and told him to give me the little book. And he said to me, "Take it and eat it; it will make your stomach bitter, but in your mouth it will be as sweet as honey." [Ezek 2:8, 9; 3:1–3]

¹⁰So I took the little book from the angel's hand and ate it, and in my mouth it was as sweet as honey; but once I had swallowed it, my stomach was bitter. [Ps 119:103; Jer 15; 16]

¹¹Then they said to me, "You must prophesy again concerning many peoples and nations and languages and kings." [Jer 1:10]

11

THEN THERE was given to me a measuring rod like a staff; and someone said, "Rise and measure the temple of God and the altar [of incense], and [count] those who worship in it. [Ezek 40–42]

²"But leave out the court [of the Gentiles] which is outside the temple and do not measure it, because it has been given to the Gentiles (the nations); and they will trample the holy city for forty-two months (three and one-half years). [Dan 8:9–14; Zech 12:3; Luke 21:24]

³"And I will grant *authority* to My two witnesses, and they will prophesy for twelve hundred and sixty days (forty-two months; three and one-half years), dressed in sackcloth." [Deut 18:18; Mal 4:5; Mark 9:4]

⁴These [witnesses] are the two olive trees and the two lampstands which stand before the Lord of the earth. [Zech 4:3, 11–14]

⁵And if anyone wants to harm them, fire comes out of their mouth and devours their enemies; so if anyone

wants to harm them, he must be killed in this way. [2 Kin 1:10–12; Jer 5:14]

⁶These [two witnesses] have the power [from God] to shut up the sky, so that no rain will fall during the days of their prophesying [regarding judgment and salvation]; and they have power over the waters (seas, rivers) to turn them into blood, and to strike the earth with every [kind of] plague, as often as they wish. [Ex 7:14–19; 1 Kin 17:1]

⁷When they have finished their testimony *and* given their evidence, the beast that comes up out of the abyss (bottomless pit) will wage war with them, and overcome them and kill them. [Dan 7:3, 7, 21]

⁸And their dead bodies *will lie exposed* in the open street of the great city (Jerusalem), which in a spiritual sense is called [by the symbolic and allegorical names of] Sodom and Egypt, where also their Lord was crucified. [Is 1:9]

⁹Those from the peoples and tribes and languages and nations look at their dead bodies for three and a half days, and will not allow their dead bodies to be laid in a tomb.

¹⁰And those [non-believers] who live on the earth will gloat over them and rejoice; and they will send gifts [in celebration] to one another, because these two prophets tormented *and* troubled those who live on the earth.

¹¹But after three and a half days, the breath of life from God came into them, and they stood on their feet; and great fear *and* panic fell on those who were watching them. [Ezek 37:5, 10]

¹²And the two witnesses heard a loud voice from heaven saying to them, "Come up here." Then they ascended into heaven in the cloud, and their enemies watched them. [2 Kin 2:11]

¹³And in that [very] hour there was a great earthquake, and a tenth of the city fell *and* was destroyed; seven thousand people were killed in the earthquake, and the rest [who survived] were overcome with terror, and they glorified the God of heaven [as they recognized His awesome power].

¹⁴The second woe is past; behold, the third woe is coming quickly.

¹⁵Then the seventh angel sounded [his trumpet]; and there were loud voices in heaven, saying,

"The kingdom (dominion, rule) of the world has become *the kingdom* of our Lord and of His Christ; and He will reign forever and ever." [Ps 22:28; Dan 2:31–45; 7:13, 14, 27; Zech 14:9]

¹⁶And the twenty-four elders, who sit on their thrones before God, fell face downward and worshiped God,

¹⁷saying,

"To You we give thanks, O Lord God Almighty [the Omnipotent, the Ruler of all], Who are and Who were, because You have taken Your great power *and* the sovereignty [which is rightly Yours] and have [now] begun to reign.

¹⁸"And the nations (Gentiles) became enraged, and Your wrath *and* indignation came, and the time came for the dead to be judged, and [the time came] to reward Your bond-servants the prophets and the saints (God's people) and those who fear Your name, the small and the great, and [the time came] to destroy the destroyers of the earth." [Ps 2:1; 2 Thess 1:3–12]

¹⁹And the temple of God which is in heaven was opened; and the ark of His covenant appeared in His temple, and there were flashes of lightning, loud rumblings and peals of thunder and an earthquake and a great hailstorm. [1 Kin 8:1–12]

12 AND A great sign [warning of an ominous and frightening future event] appeared in heaven: a woman clothed with the sun, with the moon beneath her feet,

and on her head a crown of twelve stars.

²She was with child (the Messiah) and she cried out, being in labor and in pain to give birth. [Rom 9:4, 5]

³Then another sign [of warning] was seen in heaven: behold, a great fiery red dragon (Satan) with seven heads and ten horns, and on his heads were seven royal crowns (diadems). [Dan 7:7]

⁴And his tail swept [across the sky] *and* dragged away a third of the stars of heaven and flung them to the earth. And the dragon stood in front of the woman who was about to give birth, so that when she gave birth he might devour her child. [Dan 8:10; Rev 12:9]

⁵And she gave birth to a Son, a male *Child,* who is destined to rule (shepherd) all the nations with a rod of iron; and her Child was caught up to God and to His throne. [Ps 2:8, 9; 110:1, 2]

⁶Then the woman fled into the wilderness where she had a place prepared by God, so that she would be nourished there for a thousand two hundred and sixty days (forty-two months; three and one-half years).

⁷And war broke out in heaven, Michael [the archangel] and his angels waging war with the dragon. The dragon and his angels fought,

⁸but they were not strong enough *and* did not prevail, and there was no longer a place found for them in heaven. [2 Pet 2:4; Jude 6]

⁹And the great dragon was thrown down, the age-old serpent who is called the devil and Satan, he who *continually* deceives *and* seduces the entire inhabited world; he was thrown down to the earth, and his angels were thrown down with him. [Gen 3:1, 14, 15; Zech 3:1; John 13:2; 2 Cor 11:3; Rev 20:8]

¹⁰Then I heard a loud voice in heaven, saying,

"Now the salvation, and the power, and the kingdom (dominion, reign)

of our God, and the authority of His Christ have come; for the accuser of our [believing] brothers and sisters has been thrown down [at last], he who accuses them *and* keeps bringing charges [of sinful behavior] against them before our God day and night. [Job 1:6–11]

¹¹"And they overcame *and* conquered him because of the blood of the Lamb and because of the word of their testimony, for they did not love their life *and* renounce their faith even when faced with death. [Zech 3:1–10; Rom 8:33, 34]

¹²"Therefore rejoice, O heavens and you who dwell in them [in the presence of God]. Woe to the earth and the sea, because the devil has come down to you in great wrath, knowing that he has *only* a short time [remaining]!" [Is 44:23; 49:13]

¹³And when the dragon saw that he was thrown down to the earth, he persecuted the woman who had given birth to the male *Child.*

¹⁴But the two wings of the great eagle were given to the woman, so that

life point

In Revelation 12:10, Satan is called "the accuser of our [believing] brothers." He tries to make us feel guilty and condemned. When we feel unhealthy guilt and condemnation, it's important to remember that God does not make us feel that way. God wants us to experience His love and feel the power of His forgiveness.

Guilt depresses us and makes us feel as though we are under a heavy burden. Jesus came to lift us up, to bring good news to us that our sins are forgiven and that the penalty for them has been removed. Stand against guilt and condemnation by embracing the salvation and authority of Christ in your life.

she could fly into the wilderness to her place, where she was nourished for a time and times and half a time (three and one-half years), away from the presence of the serpent (Satan). [Ex 19:4; Deut 32:10, 11; Is 40:31; Dan 7:25; 12:7]

¹⁵And the serpent hurled water like a river out of his mouth after the woman, so that he might cause her to be swept away with the flood.

¹⁶But the earth helped the woman, and the earth opened its mouth and swallowed up the river which the dragon had hurled out of his mouth. [Ex 15:12]

¹⁷So the dragon was enraged with the woman, and he went off to wage war on the rest of her children (seed), those who keep *and* obey the commandments of God and have the testimony of Jesus [holding firmly to it and bearing witness to Him].

13 AND THE dragon (Satan) stood on the sandy shore of the sea. [Dan 7:7]

Then I saw a [vicious] beast coming up out of the sea with ten horns and seven heads, and on his horns were ten royal crowns (diadems), and on his heads were blasphemous names.

²And the beast that I saw resembled a leopard, but his feet were like those of a bear, and his mouth was like that of a lion. And the dragon gave him his power and his throne and great authority.

³*I saw* one of his heads which seemed to have a fatal wound, but his fatal wound was healed; and the entire earth *followed* after the beast in amazement.

⁴They fell down *and* worshiped the dragon because he gave his authority to the beast; they also worshiped the beast, saying, "Who is like (as great as) the beast, and who is able to wage war against him?"

⁵And the beast was given a mouth (the power of speech), uttering great things *and* arrogant and blasphemous words, and he was given freedom *and* authority to act *and* to do as he pleased for forty-two months (three and a half years). [Dan 7:8]

⁶And he opened his mouth to speak blasphemies (abusive speech, slander) against God, to blaspheme His name and His tabernacle, and those who live in heaven.

⁷He was also permitted to wage war against the saints (God's people) and to overcome them, and authority *and* power over every tribe and people and language and nation. [Dan 7:21, 25]

⁸All the inhabitants of the earth will fall down *and* worship him, *everyone* whose name has not been written since the foundation of the world in the Book of Life of the Lamb who has been slain [as a willing sacrifice].

⁹If anyone has an ear, let him hear.

¹⁰If anyone *is destined* for captivity, he will go into captivity; if anyone kills with a sword, he must be killed with a sword. Here is [the call for] the patient endurance and the faithfulness of the saints [which is seen in the response of God's people to difficult times]. [Jer 15:2]

¹¹Then I saw another beast rising up out of the earth; he had two horns like a lamb and he spoke like a dragon. [Matt 7:15, 16]

¹²He exercises all the authority of the first beast in his presence [when the two are together]. And he makes the earth and those who inhabit it worship the first beast, whose deadly wound was healed.

¹³He performs great signs (awe-inspiring acts), even making fire fall from the sky to the earth, right before peoples' eyes.

¹⁴And he deceives those [unconverted ones] who inhabit the earth [into believing him] because of the signs which he is given [by Satan] to perform in

the presence of the [first] beast, telling those who inhabit the earth to make an image to the beast who was wounded [fatally] by the sword and has come back to life. [Deut 13:1–5; Mark 13:22; 2 Thess 2:9, 10]

15And he is given power to give breath to the image of the beast, so that the image of the beast will even [appear to] speak, and cause those who do not bow down *and* worship the image of the beast to be put to death. [Dan 3:5]

16Also he compels all, the small and the great, and the rich and the poor, and the free men and the slaves, to be given a mark on their right hand or on their forehead [signifying allegiance to the beast],

17and that no one will be able to buy or sell, except the one who has the mark, *either* the name of the beast or the number of his name.

18Here is wisdom. Let the person who has enough insight calculate the number of the beast, for it is the [imperfect] number of a man; and his number is six hundred and sixty-six.

14 THEN I looked, and this is what I saw: the Lamb stood [firmly established] on Mount Zion, and with Him a hundred and forty-four thousand who had His name and His Father's name inscribed on their foreheads [signifying God's own possession]. [Joel 2:32]

2And I heard a voice from heaven, like the sound of great waters and like the rumbling of mighty thunder; and the voice that I heard [seemed like music and] was like *the sound* of harpists playing on their harps.

3And they sang a new song before the throne [of God] and before the four living creatures and the elders; and no one could learn the song except the hundred and forty-four thousand who had been purchased (ransomed, redeemed) from the earth. [Rev 7:4–8]

4These are the ones who have not been defiled [by relations] with women, for they are celibate. These are the ones who follow the Lamb wherever He goes. These have been purchased *and* redeemed from among men [of Israel] as the first fruits [sanctified and set apart for special service] for God and the Lamb. [Mark 8:34]

5No lie was found in their mouth, for they are blameless (spotless, untainted, beyond reproach).

6Then I saw another angel flying in midheaven, with an eternal gospel to preach to the inhabitants of the earth, to every nation and tribe and language and people; [Rom 1:1–4; 1 Cor 15:3–5; Gal 1:6, 7]

7and he said with a loud voice, "Fear God [with awe and reverence], and give Him glory [and honor and praise in worship], because the hour of His judgment has come; [with all your heart] worship Him who created the heaven and the earth, the sea and the springs of water."

8Then another angel, a second one, followed, saying, "Fallen, fallen is Babylon the great, she who has made all nations drink the wine of the passion of her immorality [corrupting them with idolatry]." [Is 21:9; Dan 4:30, 31; Rev 17:2]

9Then another angel, a third one, followed them, saying with a loud voice, "Whoever worships the beast and his image and receives the mark [of the beast] on his forehead or on his hand,

10he too will [have to] drink of the wine of the wrath of God, mixed undiluted into the cup of His anger; and he will be tormented with fire and brimstone (flaming sulfur) in the presence of the holy angels and in the presence of the Lamb (Christ). [Gen 19:24; Jer 25:15, 16; Luke 12:9]

11"And the smoke of their torment ascends forever and ever; and they have no rest day and night—those who worship the beast and his image, and whoever receives the mark of his name." [Is 34:10; Mark 9:48]

¹²Here is [encouragement for] the steadfast endurance of the saints (God's people), those who *habitually* keep God's commandments and their faith in Jesus.

¹³Then I heard [the distinct words of] a voice from heaven, saying, "Write, 'Blessed (happy, prosperous, to be admired) are the dead who die in the Lord from now on!'" "Yes, [blessed indeed]," says the Spirit, "so that they may rest *and* have relief from their labors, for their deeds do follow them."

¹⁴Again I looked, and this is what I saw: a white cloud, and sitting on the cloud was One like the Son of Man, with a crown of gold on His head and a sharp sickle [of swift judgment] in His hand. [Dan 7:13, 14; Matt 13:30, 40–42]

¹⁵And another angel came out of the temple, calling with a loud voice to Him who was sitting upon the cloud, "Put in Your sickle and reap [at once], for the hour to reap [in judgment] has arrived, because the earth's harvest is fully ripened." [Joel 3:13]

¹⁶So He who was sitting on the cloud cast His sickle over the earth, and the earth was reaped (judged).

¹⁷Then another angel came out of the temple (sanctuary) in heaven, and he also had a sharp sickle.

¹⁸And another angel came from the altar, the one who has power over fire; and he called with a loud voice to him who had the sharp sickle, saying, "Put in your sharp sickle and reap the clusters of grapes from the vine of the earth, because her grapes are ripe [for judgment]." [Luke 9:54]

¹⁹So the angel swung his sickle to the earth and harvested the grapevine of the earth, and threw the grapes into the great wine press of the wrath *and* indignation of God [as judgment of the rebellious world]. [Is 63:3]

²⁰And *the grapes in* the wine press were trampled *and* crushed outside the city, and blood poured from the wine press, *reaching* up to the horses' bridles, for a distance of sixteen hundred stadia. [Joel 3:13; Heb 13:12]

15 THEN I saw another sign in heaven, great and wonderful [a warning of terrifying and horrible events]: seven angels who had seven plagues (afflictions, calamities), *which are* the last, because with them the wrath of God is finished [that is, it is completely expressed and reaches its zenith]. [Lev 26:21]

²Then I saw something like a sea *or* large expanse of glass mixed with fire, and those who were victorious over the beast and over his image and over the number corresponding to his name were standing on the sea *or* large expanse of glass, holding harps of God [worshiping Him]. [Rev 4:6; 7:9–17]

³And they sang the song of Moses, the bond-servant of God, and the song of the Lamb, saying,

"**G**reat and wonderful *and* awe-inspiring are Your works [in judgment],

O Lord God, the Almighty [the Omnipotent, the Ruler of all];
Righteous and true are Your ways,
O King of the nations! [Ex 15:1–8; Ps 145:17]

speak the Word

Lord, I declare that Your works are great and wonderful and awe-inspiring, and that Your ways are righteous and true.
–ADAPTED FROM REVELATION 15:3

4"Who will not fear [reverently]
   and glorify Your name, O Lord
   [giving You honor and praise in
   worship]?
For You alone are holy;
For ALL THE NATIONS SHALL COME
   AND WORSHIP BEFORE YOU,
FOR YOUR RIGHTEOUS ACTS [Your
   just decrees and judgments]
   HAVE BEEN REVEALED and
   DISPLAYED." [Ps 86:9; Jer 10:7;
   Phil 2:9–11]

5After these things I looked, and the temple (sanctuary) of the tabernacle of the testimony in heaven was opened, 6and the seven angels who had the seven plagues (afflictions, calamities) came out of the temple, arrayed in linen, pure and gleaming, and wrapped around their chests were golden sashes. 7Then one of the four living creatures gave to the seven angels seven golden bowls full of the wrath and indignation of God, who lives forever and ever. [Rev 4:6] 8And the temple was filled with smoke from the glory and radiance and splendor of God and from His power; and no one was able to enter the temple until the seven plagues of the seven angels were finished. [Ex 33:9, 10; 1 Kin 8:10, 11; Is 6:4; Ezek 44:4]

16 THEN I heard a loud voice from the temple, saying to the seven angels, "Go and pour out on the earth the seven bowls of the wrath and indignation of God." [Ps 69:24; Is 66:6] 2So the first angel went and poured out his bowl on the earth; and loathsome and malignant sores came on the people who had the mark of the beast and who worshiped his image. [Ex 9:10, 11; Deut 28:35] 3The second angel poured out his bowl into the sea, and it turned into

blood like that of a corpse [foul and disgusting]; and every living *thing in the sea died. 4Then the third angel poured out his bowl into the rivers and the springs of water; and they turned into blood. [Ex 7:17–21] 5And I heard the angel of the waters saying, "Righteous and just are You, Who are and Who were, O Holy One, because You judged these things; 6for they have poured out the blood of the saints (God's people) and the prophets, and You [in turn] have given them blood to drink. They deserve Your judgment." [Ps 79:3] 7And I heard [another from] the altar saying, "Yes, O Lord God, the Almighty [the Omnipotent, the Ruler of all], Your judgments are true and fair and righteous." [Ps 119:137] 8Then the fourth angel poured out his bowl on the sun, and it was given power to scorch humanity with [raging] fire. 9People were [severely] burned by the great heat; and they reviled the name of God who has power over these plagues, but they did not repent [of their sin] and glorify Him. 10Then the fifth angel poured out his bowl on the throne of the beast, and his kingdom was plunged into darkness; and people gnawed their tongues because of the pain [of their excruciating anguish and severe torment], [Ex 10:21] 11and they blasphemed the God of heaven because of their anguish and their sores (abscesses, boils); and they did not repent of what they had done nor hate their wickedness. 12Then the sixth angel poured out his bowl on the great river, the Euphrates; and its water was dried up, so that the way would be prepared for [the coming of] the kings from the east. [Is 11:15, 16] 13And I saw three loathsome spirits

16:3 Lit soul.

like frogs, *leaping* from the mouth of the dragon (Satan) and from the mouth of the beast (Antichrist, dictator) and from the mouth of the false prophet; [Ex 8:3; 1 Kin 22:21–23]

¹⁴for they are [actually] the spirits of demons, performing [miraculous] signs. And they go out to the kings of the entire inhabited earth, to gather them together for the war of the great day of God, the Almighty.

¹⁵("Behold, I am coming like a thief. Blessed is he who stays awake and who keeps his clothes [that is, stays spiritually ready for the Lord's return], so that he will not be naked—spiritually unprepared—and men will not see his shame.") [Matt 24:42–44; 1 Thess 5:2–4]

¹⁶And they (demons) gathered the kings and armies of the world together at the place which in Hebrew is called Har-Magedon (Armageddon).

¹⁷Then the seventh *angel* poured out his bowl into the air, and a loud voice came out of the temple from the throne [of God], saying, "It is done. [It is all over, it is all accomplished, it has come.]"

¹⁸And there were flashes of lightning and loud rumblings and peals of thunder; and there was a massive earthquake—nothing like it has ever occurred since mankind originated on the earth, so severe and far-reaching was that earthquake. [Ex 19:16–18; Dan 12:1]

¹⁹The great city was split into three parts, and the cities of the nations fell. And God kept in mind Babylon the great, to give her the cup of the wine of His fierce *and* furious wrath.

²⁰Then every island fled away, and no mountains could be found.

²¹And giant hailstones, as heavy as a talent, fell from the sky on the people; and people reviled *and* spoke abusively of God for the plague of the hail, because the plague was so very great. [Ex 9:22–25]

17 THEN ONE of the seven angels who had the seven bowls came and spoke with me, saying, "Come here, I will show you the judgment *and* doom of the great prostitute who is seated on many waters [influencing nations], [Jer 51:13]

²*she* with whom the kings of the earth have committed *acts of* immorality, and the inhabitants of the earth have become intoxicated with the wine of her immorality." [Jer 25:15, 16]

³And the angel carried me away in the Spirit into a wilderness; and I saw a woman sitting on a scarlet beast that was entirely covered with blasphemous names, having seven heads and ten horns. [Acts 10:10, 11]

⁴The woman was dressed in purple and scarlet, and adorned with gold, precious stones and pearls, [and she was] holding in her hand a gold cup full of the abominations and the filth of her [sexual] immorality. [Jer 51:7]

⁵And on her forehead a name was written, a mystery: "BABYLON THE GREAT, THE MOTHER OF PROSTITUTES (false religions, heresies) AND OF THE ABOMINATIONS OF THE EARTH."

⁶I saw that the woman was drunk with the blood of the saints (God's people), and with the blood of the witnesses of Jesus [who were martyred]. When I saw her, I wondered in amazement.

⁷But the angel said to me, "Why do you wonder? I will explain to you the mystery of the woman and of the beast that carries her, which has the seven heads and ten horns.

⁸"The beast that you saw was [once], but [now] is not, and he is about to come up out of the abyss (the bottomless pit, the dwelling place of demons) and go to destruction (perdition). And the inhabitants of the earth, whose names have not been written in the Book of Life from the foundation of the world,

will be astonished when they see the beast, because he was and is not and is yet to come [to earth]. [Dan 7:3]

⁹"Here is the mind which has wisdom [and this is what it knows about the vision]. The seven heads are seven hills on which the woman sits;

¹⁰and they are seven kings: five of whom have fallen, one exists *and* is reigning; the other [the seventh] has not yet come, and when he does come, he must remain a little while.

¹¹"And the beast that [once] was but is not, is himself also an eighth *king* and is one of the seven, and he goes to destruction (perdition).

¹²"The ten horns that you saw are ten kings who have not yet received a kingdom, but [together] they receive authority as kings for a single hour [for a common purpose] along with the beast. [Dan 7:20–24]

¹³"These [kings] have one purpose [one mind, one common goal], and they give their power and authority to the beast.

¹⁴"They will wage war against the Lamb (Christ), and the Lamb will triumph *and* conquer them, because He is Lord of lords and King of kings, and those who are with Him *and* on His side are the called and chosen (elect) and faithful." [Dan 2:47; 1 Tim 6:15; Rev 19:16]

¹⁵Then the angel said to me, "The waters which you saw, where the prostitute is seated, are peoples and multitudes and nations and languages.

¹⁶"And the ten horns which you saw, and the beast, these will hate the prostitute and will make her desolate and naked [stripped of her power and influence], and will eat her flesh and completely consume her with fire.

¹⁷"For God has put it in their hearts to carry out His purpose by agreeing together to surrender their kingdom to the beast, until the [prophetic] words of God will be fulfilled.

¹⁸"The woman whom you saw is the great city, which reigns over *and* dominates *and* controls the kings *and* the political leaders of the earth."

18 AFTER THESE things I saw another angel coming down from heaven, possessing great authority, and the earth was illuminated with his splendor *and* radiance. [Ex 34:29–35; 1 Tim 6:16]

²And he shouted with a mighty voice, saying, "Fallen, fallen [certainly to be destroyed] is Babylon the great! She has become a dwelling place for demons, a dungeon haunted by every unclean spirit, and a prison for every unclean and loathsome bird.

³"For all the nations have drunk from the wine of the passion of her [sexual] immorality, and the kings *and* political leaders of the earth have committed immorality with her, and the merchants of the earth have become rich by the wealth *and* economic power of her sensuous luxury." [Jer 25:15, 27]

⁴And I heard another voice from heaven, saying, "Come out of her, my people, so that you will not be a partner in her sins and receive her plagues; [Is 48:20; Jer 50:8]

⁵for her sins (crimes, transgressions) have piled up as high as heaven, and God has remembered her wickedness *and* crimes [for judgment]. [Jer 51:9]

⁶"Repay to her even as she has repaid *others*, and pay back [to her] double [her torment] in accordance with what she has done; in the cup [of sin and suffering] which she mixed, mix a double portion [of perfect justice] for her. [Ps 137:8]

⁷"To the degree that she glorified herself and reveled *and* gloated in her sensuality [living deliciously and luxuriously], to that same degree impose on her torment *and* anguish, and mourning *and* grief; for in her heart she boasts, 'I SIT AS A QUEEN [on a throne]

AND I AM NOT A WIDOW, and will never, ever see mourning *or* experience grief.' [Is 47:8, 9]

⁸"For this reason in a single day her plagues (afflictions, calamities) will come, pestilence and mourning and famine, and she will be burned up with fire *and* completely consumed; for strong *and* powerful is the Lord God who judges her.

⁹"And the kings *and* political leaders of the earth, who committed immorality and lived luxuriously with her, will weep and beat their chests [in mourning] over her when they see the smoke of her burning, [Ezek 26:16, 17]

¹⁰standing a long way off, in fear of her torment, saying, 'Woe, woe, the great city, the strong city, Babylon! In a single hour your judgment has come.'

¹¹"And merchants of the earth will weep and grieve over her, because no one buys their cargo (goods, merchandise) anymore— [Ezek 27:36]

¹²cargoes of gold and silver and precious stones and pearls and fine linen and purple and silk and scarlet; all *kinds of* citron (scented) wood and every article of ivory and every article of very costly *and* lavish wood and bronze and iron and marble; [Ezek 27:12, 13, 22]

¹³and cinnamon and spices and incense and perfume and frankincense and wine and olive oil and fine flour and wheat; of cattle and sheep, and *cargoes* of horses and chariots *and* carriages; and of slaves and human lives.

¹⁴"The ripe fruits *and* delicacies of your soul's desire have gone from you, and all things that were luxurious and extravagant are lost to you, never again to be found.

¹⁵"The merchants who handled these articles, who grew wealthy from [their business with] her, will stand a long way off in fear of her torment, weeping and mourning aloud,

¹⁶saying, 'Woe, woe, for the great city

that was robed in fine linen, in purple and scarlet, gilded *and* adorned with gold, with precious stones, and with pearls; [Ezek 27:31, 36]

¹⁷because in one hour all the vast wealth has been laid waste.' And every ship captain *or* navigator, and every passenger and sailor, and all who make their living by the sea, stood a long way off, [Is 23:14; Ezek 27:26–30]

¹⁸and exclaimed as they watched the smoke of her burning, saying, 'What could be compared to the great city?'

¹⁹"And they threw dust on their heads and were crying out, weeping and mourning, saying, 'Woe, woe, for the great city, where all who had ships at sea grew rich from her great wealth, because in one hour she has been laid waste!' [Ezek 27:30–34]

²⁰"Rejoice over her, O heaven, and you saints (God's people) and apostles and prophets [who were martyred], because God has executed vengeance for you [through righteous judgment] upon her." [Is 44:23; Jer 51:48, 49]

²¹Then a single powerful angel picked up a boulder like a great millstone and flung it into the sea, saying, "With such violence will Babylon the great city be hurled down [by the sudden, spectacular judgment of God], and will never again be found. [Jer 51:63, 64; Ezek 26:21]

²²"And the sound of harpists and musicians and flutists and trumpeters will never again be heard in you, and no skilled artisan of any craft will ever again be found in you, and the sound of the millstone [grinding grain] will never again be heard in you [for commerce will no longer flourish, and normal life will cease]. [Is 24:8; Ezek 26:13]

²³"And never again will the light of a lamp shine in you, and never again will the voice of the bridegroom and bride be heard in you; for your merchants were the great *and* prominent

men of the earth, because all the nations were deceived *and* misled by your sorcery [your magic spells and poisonous charm].

²⁴"And in Babylon was found the blood of prophets and of saints (God's people) and of all those who have been slaughtered on the earth." [Gen 4:10; Jer 51:49]

19 AFTER THESE things I heard something like the great *and* mighty shout of a vast multitude in heaven, exclaiming,

"Hallelujah! Salvation and glory (splendor, majesty) and power (dominion, might) belong to our God;

²BECAUSE HIS JUDGMENTS ARE TRUE AND RIGHTEOUS. He has judged [convicted and pronounced sentence on] the great prostitute (idolatress) who was corrupting *and* ruining *and* poisoning the earth with her adultery (idolatry), and HE HAS IMPOSED THE PENALTY FOR THE BLOOD OF HIS BONDSERVANTS ON HER." [Deut 32:43; Ps 19:9]

³And a second time they said, "Hallelujah! HER SMOKE SHALL ASCEND FOREVER AND EVER." [Is 34:10]

⁴Then the twenty-four elders and the four living creatures also fell down and worshiped God who sits on the throne, saying, "Amen. Hallelujah (praise the Lord)!" [Ps 106:48]

⁵Then from the throne there came a voice, saying,

"Praise our God, all you bondservants of His, you who fear Him, the small (common) and the great (distinguished)." [Ps 115:13]

⁶Then I heard *something* like the shout of a vast multitude, and like the boom of many pounding waves, and like the roar of mighty peals of thunder, saying,

"Hallelujah! For the Lord our God, the Almighty, [the Omnipotent, the Ruler of all] reigns.

⁷"Let us rejoice and shout for joy! Let us give Him glory *and* honor, for the marriage of the Lamb has come [at last] and His bride (the redeemed) has prepared herself." [Ps 118:24]

⁸She has been permitted to dress in fine linen, dazzling white and clean— for the fine linen signifies the righteous acts of the saints [the ethical conduct, personal integrity, moral courage, and godly character of believers].

⁹Then the angel said to me, "Write, 'Blessed are those who are invited to the marriage supper of the Lamb.' " And he said to me [further], "These are the true *and* exact words of God." [Is 25:6–8; Matt 26:29; Luke 13:29]

¹⁰Then I fell down at his feet to worship him, but he [stopped me and] said to me, "You must not do that; I am a fellow servant with you and your brothers and sisters who have *and* hold the testimony of Jesus. Worship God [alone]. For the testimony of Jesus is the spirit of prophecy [His life and teaching are the heart of prophecy]." [Acts 10:25, 26; 2 Pet 1:21]

¹¹And I saw heaven opened, and behold, a white horse, and He who was riding it is called Faithful and True (trustworthy, loyal, incorruptible, steady), and in righteousness He judges and wages war [on the rebellious nations]. [2 Thess 1:7–10]

speak the Word

God, I worship You.
—ADAPTED FROM REVELATION 19:10

Thank You, Jesus, that You are Faithful and True, trustworthy, loyal, incorruptible, and steady.
—ADAPTED FROM REVELATION 19:11

¹²His eyes are a flame of fire, and on His head are many royal crowns; and He has a name inscribed [on Him] which no one knows *or* understands except Himself.

¹³He is dressed in a robe dipped in blood, and His name is called The Word of God. [John 1:1, 14]

¹⁴And the armies of heaven, dressed in fine linen, [dazzling] white and clean, followed Him on white horses.

¹⁵From His mouth comes a sharp sword (His word) with which He may strike down the nations, and He will rule them with a rod of iron; and He will tread the wine press of the fierce wrath of God, the Almighty [in judgment of the rebellious world]. [Ps 2:9; Is 11:4; Rev 1:16]

¹⁶And on His robe and on His thigh He has a name inscribed, "KING OF KINGS, AND LORD OF LORDS." [Deut 10:17]

¹⁷Then I saw a single angel standing in the sun, and with a loud voice he shouted to all the birds that fly in midheaven, saying, "Come, gather together for the great supper of God, [Ezek 39:4, 17–20]

¹⁸so that you may feast on the flesh of kings, the flesh of commanders, the flesh of powerful *and* mighty men, the flesh of horses and of those who sit on them, and the flesh of all humanity, both free men and slaves, both small and great [in a complete conquest of evil]."

¹⁹Then I saw the beast and the kings *and* political leaders of the earth with their armies gathered to make war against Him who is mounted on the [white] horse and against His army.

²⁰And the beast (Antichrist) was seized *and* overpowered, and with him the false prophet who, in his presence,

life point

Examination of Revelation 19:11–16 readily reveals that Jesus is waging war in the heavenlies (see also Revelation 19:19–21), and that the Word, the name, and the blood are present and being exalted, just as they should be in our daily lives here on earth.

had performed [amazing] signs by which he deceived those who had received the mark of the beast and those who worshiped his image; these two were hurled alive into the lake of fire which blazes with brimstone.

²¹And the rest were killed with the sword which came from the mouth of Him who sat on the horse, and all the birds fed ravenously *and* gorged themselves with their flesh.

20 AND THEN I saw an angel descending from heaven, holding the key of the abyss (the bottomless pit) and a great chain was in his hand.

²And he overpowered *and* laid hold of the dragon, that old serpent [of primeval times], who is the devil and Satan, and bound him [securely] for a thousand years (a millennium); [Rev 12:7–9, 12, 15]

³and the angel hurled him into the abyss, and closed it and sealed it above him [preventing his escape or rescue], so that he would no longer deceive *and* seduce the nations, until the thousand years were at an end. After these things he must be liberated for a short time.

⁴And then I saw thrones, and sitting on them were those to whom judgment [that is, the authority to act as judges]

speak the Word

Jesus, I declare that You are King of kings and Lord of lords.
–ADAPTED FROM REVELATION 19:16

was given. And *I saw* the souls of those who had been beheaded because of their testimony of Jesus and because of the word of God, and those who had refused to worship the beast or his image, and had not accepted his mark on their forehead and on their hand; and they came to life and reigned with Christ for a thousand years. [Dan 7:9, 22, 27]

⁵The rest of the dead [the non-believers] did not come to life again until the thousand years were completed. This is the first resurrection.

⁶Blessed (happy, prosperous, to be admired) and holy is the person who takes part in the first resurrection; over these the second death [which is eternal separation from God, the lake of fire] has no power *or* authority, but they will be priests of God and of Christ and they will reign with Him a thousand years. [Ex 19:6; 1 Pet 2:5, 9; Rev 1:6; 5:10]

⁷And when the thousand years are completed, Satan will be released from his prison (the abyss),

⁸and will come out to deceive *and* mislead the nations which are in the four corners of the earth—[including] Gog and Magog—to gather them together for the war; their number is like the sand of the seashore. [Ezek 38:2; 39:1, 6]

⁹And they swarmed up over the broad plain of the earth and surrounded the camp of the saints (God's people) and the beloved city [Jerusalem]; but fire came down from heaven and consumed them. [2 Kin 1:10–12; Ezek 38:2, 22]

¹⁰And the devil who had deceived them was hurled into the lake of fire and burning brimstone (sulfur), where the beast (Antichrist) and false prophet are also; and they will be tormented day and night, forever and ever.

¹¹And I saw a great white throne and Him who was seated upon it, from whose presence earth and heaven fled

away, and no place was found for them [for this heaven and earth are passing away]. [Is 51:6; Matt 24:35; 2 Pet 3:10–12]

¹²And I saw the dead, the great and the small, standing before the throne, and books were opened. Then another book was opened, which is *the Book* of Life; and the dead were judged according to what they had done as written in the books [that is, everything done while on earth]. [Jer 17:10; Rom 2:6]

¹³And the sea gave up the dead who were in it, and death and Hades (the realm of the dead) surrendered the dead who were in them; and they were judged *and* sentenced, every one according to their deeds.

¹⁴Then death and Hades [the realm of the dead] were thrown into the lake of fire. This is the second death, the lake of fire [the eternal separation from God]. [Matt 25:41; 1 Cor 15:26]

¹⁵And if anyone's name was not found written in the Book of Life, he was hurled into the lake of fire.

21 THEN I saw a new heaven and a new earth; for the first heaven and the first earth had passed away (vanished), and there is no longer any sea. [Is 65:17; 66:22]

²And I saw the holy city, new Jerusalem, coming down out of heaven from God, arrayed like a bride adorned for her husband; [John 14:2, 3; Gal 4:26; Heb 11:10]

³and then I heard a loud voice from the throne, saying, "See! The tabernacle of God is among men, and He will live among them, and they will be His people, and God Himself will be with them [as their God,] [Lev 26:11, 12; Ezek 37:27; John 1:14; 1 Cor 3:16, 17]

⁴and He will wipe away every tear from their eyes; and there will no longer be death; there will no longer be sorrow *and* anguish, or crying, or

putting the Word to work

What do you imagine heaven will be like? One of the wonderful promises about heaven is that we will enjoy unbroken fellowship with God and that there will be no more death, sorrow, anguish, crying, or pain (see Revelation 21:3, 4). God Himself will wipe every tear from your eye. If you are in a difficult season of life, know that God is your very present help in trouble right now (see Psalm 46:1) and the day is coming when you will be troubled no more. Thank God for His promise and receive His strength for today and His hope for tomorrow.

pain; for the former order of things has passed away." [Is 25:8; 35:10]

⁵And He who sits on the throne said, "Behold, I am making all things new." Also He said, "Write, for these words are faithful and true [they are accurate, incorruptible, and trustworthy]." [Is 43:19]

⁶And He said to me, "It is done. I am the Alpha and the Omega, the Beginning and the End. To the one who thirsts I will give [water] from the fountain of the water of life without cost. [Is 55:1]

⁷"He who overcomes [the world by adhering faithfully to Christ Jesus as Lord and Savior] will inherit these things, and I will be his God and he will be My son. [2 Sam 7:14; 1 John 5:5]

⁸"But as for the cowards and unbelieving and abominable [who are devoid of character and personal integrity and practice or tolerate immorality], and murderers, and sorcerers [with intoxicating drugs], and idolaters *and* occultists [who practice and

life point

God is the "Alpha and the Omega, the Beginning and the End" (see Revelation 21:6). Since this is the case, He is also everything in between. He knows our situations and will lead us and guide us if we trust Him to do so. Rely on your heavenly Father to give you what you need, one day at a time.

teach false religions], and all the liars [who knowingly deceive and twist truth], their part will be in the lake that blazes with fire and brimstone, which is the second death."

⁹Then one of the seven angels who had the seven bowls filled with the seven final plagues came and spoke with me, saying, "Come here, I will show you the bride, the wife of the Lamb."

¹⁰And he carried me away in the Spirit to a vast and lofty mountain, and showed me the holy (sanctified) city of Jerusalem coming down out of heaven from God, [Ezek 40:2]

¹¹having God's glory [filled with His radiant light]. The brilliance of it resembled a rare *and* very precious jewel, like jasper, shining *and* clear as crystal.

¹²It had a massive and high wall, with twelve [large] gates, and at the gates [were stationed] twelve angels; and on the gates the names of the twelve tribes of the sons of Israel were written. [Ex 28:21; Ezek 48:30–34]

¹³On the east side [there were] three gates, on the north three gates, on the south three gates, and on the west three gates.

¹⁴And the wall of the city had twelve foundation stones, and on them the twelve names of the twelve apostles of the Lamb (Christ).

speak the Word

Thank You, God, that You are making all things new.
–ADAPTED FROM REVELATION 21:5

15The one who was speaking with me had a gold measuring rod to measure the city, and its gates and its wall.

16The city is laid out as a square, its length being the same as its width; and he measured the city with his rod—twelve thousand stadia (about 1,400 miles); its length and width and height are equal.

17He measured its wall also—a hundred forty-four cubits (about 200 feet), *according to* man's measurements, which are [also] angelic [measurements].

18The wall was built of jasper; and the city was pure gold, transparent like clear crystal. [1 Kin 6:30]

19The foundation stones of the wall of the city were adorned with every kind of precious stone. The first foundation stone was jasper; the second, sapphire; the third, chalcedony; the fourth, emerald; [Ex 28:17–20; Is 54:11, 12]

20the fifth, sardonyx; the sixth, sardius; the seventh, chrysolite (yellow topaz); the eighth, beryl; the ninth, topaz; the tenth, chrysoprase; the eleventh, jacinth; the twelfth, amethyst.

21And the twelve gates were twelve pearls; each separate gate was of one single pearl. And the street (broad way) of the city was pure gold, like transparent crystal.

22I saw no temple in it, for the Lord God Almighty [the Omnipotent, the Ruler of all] and the Lamb are its temple.

23And the city has no need of the sun nor of the moon to give light to it, for the glory (splendor, radiance) of God has illumined it, and the Lamb is its lamp *and* light. [Is 24:23; 60:19, 20]

24The nations [the redeemed people from the earth] will walk by its light, and the kings of the earth will bring into it their glory. [Is 60:1–5]

25By day (for there will be no night there) its gates will never be closed [in fear of evil]; [Is 60:11]

26and they will bring the glory (splendor, majesty) and the honor of the nations into it;

27and nothing that defiles *or* profanes *or* is unwashed will ever enter it, nor anyone who practices abominations [detestable, morally repugnant things] and lying, but only those [will be admitted] whose names have been written in the Lamb's Book of Life. [Dan 12:1]

22 THEN THE angel showed me a river of the water of life, clear as crystal, flowing from the throne of God and of the Lamb (Christ), [Ezek 47:1–12]

2in the middle of its street. On either side of the river was the tree of life, bearing twelve *kinds of* fruit, yielding its fruit every month; and the leaves of the tree were for the healing of the nations. [Gen 2:9; 3:22]

3There will no longer exist anything that is cursed [because sin and illness and death are gone]; and the throne of God and of the Lamb will be in it, and His bond-servants will serve *and* worship Him [with great awe and joy and loving devotion]; [Zech 14:21]

4they will [be privileged to] see His face, and His name will be on their foreheads. [Ps 17:15; Matt 5:48; 1 John 3:2]

5And there will no longer be night; they have no need for lamplight or sunlight, because the Lord God will illumine them; and they will reign [as kings] forever and ever. [Zech 14:7; Rev 1:6]

6Then he said to me, "These words are faithful and true." And the Lord, the God of the spirits of the prophets, has sent His angel [as a representative] to show His bond-servants the things that must soon take place.

7"And behold, I am coming quickly. Blessed (happy, prosperous, to be admired) is the one who heeds *and* takes to heart *and* remembers the words of the prophecy [that is, the predictions, consolations, and warnings] contained in this book (scroll)."

⁸I, John, am the one who heard and saw these things. And when I heard and saw them, I fell down to worship before the feet of the angel who showed me these things.

⁹But he said to me, "Do not do that. I am a fellow servant with you and your brothers the prophets and with those who heed *and* remember [the truths contained in] the words of this book. Worship God."

¹⁰And he said to me, "Do not seal up the words of the prophecy of this book, for the time [of their fulfillment] is near.

¹¹"Let the one who does wrong, still do wrong; and the one who is filthy (vile, impure), still be filthy; and the one who is righteous (just, upright), still be righteous; and the one who is holy, still be holy." [Dan 12:10]

¹²"Behold, I (Jesus) am coming quickly, and My reward is with Me, to give to each one according to the merit of his deeds (earthly works,

payday is coming

Every person, with no exceptions, will one day stand before God and give an account of his or her life (see Romans 14:12). I want to encourage you not to "live like there is no tomorrow," because tomorrow always comes. Jesus will come for us when we least expect it and then it will be too late to do all the things we intended to do but never got around to doing. One of the spiritual laws we see throughout the Word of God is that we reap what we sow. Galatians 6:7, 8 say emphatically that we are not to be deceived and misled for whatever a man sows that and that *only* is what he will reap.

Salvation is a gift of God; it is given by His grace and is to be received by faith. We do not get into heaven because of our good works, but Revelation 22:12 teaches us that our works will be judged and rewarded according to the merit of our deeds.

Our works are not even judged only by what we have done, but by the motives behind them. Works done for impure motives will be burned up. If we give money or things, but do so to be seen or to be admired and well thought of, then we should be sure that satisfies us because it's all the reward we will ever get.

God sees what we do in secret and we will be rewarded openly. Everything that is now done behind closed doors will one day be brought out in the open, so we should be sure that we realize nothing is eternally hidden. The day of reckoning will come.

Some people might think, *Well, as long as I am going to heaven, that is enough.* If this is our only motive in life, then we are living selfishly. We should live for God and His glory. We should realize that we are alive for a purpose and part of that purpose is to be used by God to reconcile others to Him. We are actually created for the good works that God prearranged and prepared for us ahead of time (see Ephesians 2:10). It is God's desire and will that we do good works, but we are to do them because He loves us, not to get Him to love us or to impress people.

Payday is coming! Are you ready?

faithfulness). [Is 40:10; Jer 17:10; Matt 16:27; 2 Cor 5:10]

[13]"I am the Alpha and the Omega, the First and the Last, the Beginning and the End [the Eternal One]." [Is 44:6; 48:12; John 10:30]

[14]Blessed (happy, prosperous, to be admired) are those who wash their robes [in the blood of Christ by believing and trusting in Him—the righteous who do His commandments], so that they may have the right to the tree of life, and may enter by the gates into the city. [Gen 2:9; 3:22, 24]

[15]Outside are the dogs [the godless, the impure, those of low moral character] and the sorcerers [with their intoxicating drugs, and magic arts], and the immoral persons [the perverted, the molesters, and the adulterers], and the murderers, and the idolaters, and everyone who loves and practices lying (deception, cheating).

[16]"I, Jesus, have sent My angel to testify to you and to give you assurance of these things for the churches. I am the Root (the Source, the Life) and the Offspring of David, the radiant and bright Morning Star." [Num 24:17; Is 11:1, 10]

[17]The [Holy] Spirit and the bride (the church, believers) say, "Come." And let the one who hears say, "Come." And let the one who is thirsty come; let the one who wishes take and drink the water of life without cost. [Is 55:1]

[18]I testify and warn everyone who hears the words of the prophecy of this book [its predictions, consolations, and admonitions]: if anyone adds [anything] to them, God will add to him the plagues (afflictions, calamities) which are written in this book; [Deut 4:2]

[19]and if anyone takes away from or distorts the words of the book of this prophecy, God will take away [from that one] his share from the tree of life and from the holy city (new Jerusalem), which are written in this book.

[20]He who testifies and affirms these things says, "Yes, I am coming quickly." Amen. Come, Lord Jesus.

[21]The grace of the Lord Jesus (the Christ, the Messiah) be with all [the saints—all believers, those set apart for God]. Amen.

speak the Word

Come, Lord Jesus!
−ADAPTED FROM REVELATION 22:20

How To Receive Jesus as Your Personal Lord and Savior

God loves you! He created you as a special, unique, one-
of-a-kind individual, and He has a specific purpose and
plan for your life. He wants you to live in
victory. Through a personal relationship with your
Creator—God—you can discover a way of life
that will truly satisfy your soul.

No matter who you are, what you've done, or where you are in your life right now, God's love and grace are greater than your sin (your mistakes). Jesus willingly gave His life so you can receive forgiveness from God and have new life in Him. He's just waiting for you to invite Him to be your Savior and Lord.

If you are ready to commit your life to Jesus and follow Him, all you have to do is ask Him to forgive your sins and give you a fresh start in the life you are meant to live. You can begin right now by praying this prayer:

*Lord Jesus, thank You for giving Your life for me and
forgiving me of my sins so I can have a personal relationship
with You. I am sincerely sorry for the mistakes I've made, and
I know I need You to help me live right.
Your Word says in Romans 10:9, "if you acknowledge and confess with your mouth that Jesus is Lord [recognizing His power,
authority, and majesty as God], and believe in your heart that
God raised Him from the dead, you will be saved."
I believe You are the Son of God, and I confess You as my
Savior and Lord. Take me just as I am, and work in my heart,
making me the person You want me to be. I want to live
for You, Jesus, and I am so grateful to You for giving me
a fresh start in my new life with You today.
I love you, Jesus! Amen.*

It's amazing to know that God loves us so much! He wants to have a deep, intimate relationship with us that grows every day as we spend time with Him in prayer and Bible study.

For more aboutyour new life in Christ, visit www.joycemeyer.org/salva-tion to request at no cost the book A New Way of Living. At joycemeyer.org, you can also find other free resources to help you take your next steps toward everything God has for you.

Congratulations on your fresh start in your life in Christ!

The Word for Your Everyday Life

The Word of God gives us insight, advice, and direction about every area of our lives. In the following pages, you will find a list of topics, needs, or situations you may be facing right now or may face in the future. Let me encourage you to become familiar with the issues in this section so you will know where to look to find biblical answers and encouragement for many circumstances you will likely encounter at some point. Use the verses in this section to strengthen your heart and align your thoughts and words (conversation) with the Word of God so you can have victory in every aspect of your life.

Anger

Psalm 37:8
Psalm 103:8
Proverbs 14:29
Proverbs 15:1
Proverbs 15:18
Proverbs 19:11
Ecclesiastes 7:9
Ephesians 4:26
Ephesians 4:31, 32
Colossians 3:8
James 1:19, 20

Anointing

Psalm 23:5
Psalm 45:7
Psalm 92:10
Isaiah 61:1
Mark 6:13
2 Corinthians 1:21
1 John 2:20
1 John 2:27

Anxiety and Worry

Deuteronomy 31:6
Psalm 86:7
Psalm 139:23, 24
Matthew 6:27
Matthew 6:31–34
Mark 4:19
Philippians 4:6, 7
1 Peter 5:7

Authority of the Believer

Matthew 12:28, 29
Matthew 16:19
Matthew 28:18, 19
Mark 16:17, 18

Luke 10:19
Ephesians 1:17–22
Ephesians 2:6
James 4:7

Civic Responsibility

Deuteronomy 4:7
2 Chronicles 7:14
Proverbs 11:11
Proverbs 24:21
Proverbs 28:7
Jeremiah 29:7
Matthew 22:21
Romans 13:1
Romans 13:7
1 Timothy 2:1–3
Titus 3:1, 2
1 Peter 2:13–17

Compromise

Exodus 34:12
Psalm 1:1
Psalm 119:2, 3
Proverbs 25:26
Acts 23:1
Hebrews 11:25

Confessions for Husbands

Joshua 24:15
Proverbs 3:3
Ecclesiastes 9:9
Mark 10:6–9
Ephesians 4:31, 32
Ephesians 5:25–28
Colossians 3:8–10
Hebrews 13:4
James 5:16
1 Peter 3:7

Confessions for Wives

Proverbs 12:4
Proverbs 19:14
Proverbs 31:10–12
Proverbs 31:26
1 Corinthians 6:20
1 Corinthians 7:3
1 Corinthians 13:1–8
Ephesians 5:33
1 Thessalonians 5:11, 15–18
1 Timothy 3:11
Titus 2:4, 5
1 Peter 3:1–5
1 John 3:18

Confessions for Parents

Deuteronomy 6:2, 5
Deuteronomy 28:13
Deuteronomy 30:19, 20
Proverbs 14:16
Proverbs 17:6
Proverbs 31:28
Jeremiah 18:6
1 Corinthians 15:33
2 Corinthians 6:14
Galatians 5:16
Ephesians 1:17, 18
Ephesians 6:1–4
Philippians 2:14
Colossians 1:3, 5, 9–14
2 Timothy 2:15

Confessions for Singles

Psalm 3:3, 4
Psalm 27:4
Psalm 27:14
Psalm 37:1–5

Psalm 55:22
Psalm 91:14–16
Isaiah 43:1–3
Isaiah 61:1–3
Jeremiah 31:13
Matthew 28:20
Romans 8:25
1 Peter 5:7

Confessions for Families

Deuteronomy 28:8, 11, 12
Joshua 24:15
Proverbs 24:3, 4
Acts 20:32
Ephesians 6:1–3
Colossians 3:13–15
1 John 4:7, 11
3 John 2

What the Bible Says about Confessing the Word

Joshua 1:8
Psalm 119:105
Isaiah 48:6, 7
Isaiah 55:11
Jeremiah 1:12
Mark 11:23
Romans 4:17
Hebrews 4:12
Hebrews 4:14
Hebrews 10:23

Confidence

Joshua 1:9
Psalm 18:29
Psalm 37:3
Psalm 57:7
Psalm 84:12
Psalm 138:3
Proverbs 29:25
Isaiah 30:15
Micah 7:7
Philippians 1:6
Philippians 3:3
Hebrews 4:16
Hebrews 10:35

Contentment

Psalm 16:6
Psalm 17:15
Psalm 84:10
Psalm 92:4, 5
Psalm 107:8, 9
Proverbs 14:30
John 6:35
Philippians 4:10, 11
Philippians 4:19
1 Timothy 6:6–8
Hebrews 13:5, 6

Control

Acts 5:29
Romans 8:9
2 Corinthians 5:14
Galatians 1:10
1 Thessalonians 2:4

Courage

Deuteronomy 31:6
Joshua 1:9
2 Chronicles 32:7, 8
Psalm 27:14
Psalm 31:24
Matthew 14:27
1 Corinthians 16:13
1 John 5:14

Depression

Deuteronomy 31:8
Psalm 3:3
Psalm 34:15, 17
Psalm 40:1–3
Psalm 42:5
Psalm 42:6, 8, 11
Psalm 91:14–16
Isaiah 54:4
Isaiah 60:1
2 Corinthians 7:6
1 Peter 5:6, 7

Determination

Isaiah 40:31
1 Corinthians 2:2
Colossians 3:2
1 Thessalonians 4:11, 12
1 Timothy 6:11–14
1 Peter 5:9

Diligence

Exodus 15:26
Deuteronomy 4:9
Psalm 119:4
Proverbs 4:23
Proverbs 8:17
Proverbs 10:4
Proverbs 12:24
Proverbs 13:4
Proverbs 21:5
Hebrews 11:6

Discouragement and Despair

Psalm 3:3
Psalm 30:11, 12
John 10:10
John 16:33
Romans 8:28
2 Corinthians 1:4
2 Corinthians 4:8–10
2 Corinthians 4:16, 17
2 Corinthians 12:9
Philippians 4:13

Emotions

Psalm 7:9
Psalm 30:5
Psalm 34:18
Psalm 42:5
Psalm 51:8, 12
Psalm 94:13
Psalm 147:3
Romans 8:8
Philippians 4:11
Hebrews 4:15, 16
1 Peter 5:9

Encouragement and Comfort

Psalm 27:5
Psalm 31:7
Psalm 57:1–3
Psalm 62:1, 2
Psalm 119:50
Psalm 138:7, 8
Matthew 5:4
2 Corinthians 1:3, 4
2 Corinthians 4:17, 18
2 Thessalonians 2:16, 17

Faith

Habakkuk 2:4
Matthew 17:20
Mark 11:23
Romans 3:28
Romans 5:2
Romans 10:17
Romans 14:23
Romans 15:13
1 Corinthians 2:5
2 Corinthians 5:7
Galatians 3:24, 25
Ephesians 3:12
Ephesians 6:16
1 Timothy 6:12
Hebrews 10:22, 23
Hebrews 11:1, 3
Hebrews 11:6
James 2:17

Favor

Job 10:12
Psalm 5:12
Psalm 30:7
Psalm 147:11
Proverbs 3:4
Proverbs 11:27
Proverbs 12:2
Proverbs 14:9
Ephesians 2:4–7
Hebrews 4:16

Fear

Psalm 23:4
Psalm 27:1
Psalm 91:4, 5
Psalm 112:7, 8
Proverbs 29:25
Isaiah 41:10
Isaiah 54:14
Luke 12:32
2 Timothy 1:7
Hebrews 13:5, 6
1 Peter 3:14
1 John 4:18

Forgiveness

2 Chronicles 30:9
Matthew 6:14
Mark 11:25, 26
Luke 6:37
Romans 4:7, 8

Ephesians 4:32
Colossians 3:13
James 5:15
1 John 1:9, 10
1 John 2:12

Grace

Psalm 84:11
Acts 13:43
Romans 3:24
Romans 5:15
Romans 5:20, 21
1 Corinthians 3:9–11
Ephesians 2:8
James 4:6

Guilt and Condemnation

Psalm 18:23
Psalm 51:1, 2
Psalm 51:7–9
Isaiah 53:5
Romans 3:11, 12, 21, 22
Romans 8:1, 2
Romans 8:10
Romans 8:33, 34
2 Corinthians 5:21
Hebrews 1:3
Hebrews 10:22, 23
1 John 3:18–20

Health and Healing

Psalm 30:2
Psalm 103:2, 3
Psalm 107:20
Psalm 118:17
Psalm 147:3
Proverbs 4:20–22
Isaiah 58:8
Jeremiah 17:14
Jeremiah 30:17
James 5:14, 15
1 Peter 2:24
3 John 2

Hearing from God

Deuteronomy 28:1
Psalm 40:6
Psalm 95:7, 8

Psalm 119:130
Jeremiah 7:23
Matthew 7:24, 25
Matthew 13:19, 23
John 10:5
John 10:27
Romans 10:17
James 1:22–25

Help

Psalm 28:7
Psalm 34:15, 17
Psalm 50:15
Psalm 55:22
Psalm 94:17–19
Psalm 143:10, 11
Isaiah 41:13
Isaiah 50:7
Nahum 1:7
Hebrews 13:6

Holiness

Leviticus 20:7
Acts 24:16
Romans 6:22
Romans 12:1, 2
1 Corinthians 6:19, 20
Ephesians 1:4
Ephesians 4:23, 24
Colossians 1:22
Hebrews 12:10
Hebrews 12:14
1 Peter 1:14, 15

Hope

Psalm 33:18
Proverbs 13:12
Lamentations 3:24–26
Romans 12:12
Romans 15:4
Romans 15:13
1 Corinthians 13:12, 13
1 Corinthians 15:51, 52, 54
Ephesians 1:18
1 Timothy 4:10
1 Peter 1:13

Humility and Pride

Psalm 25:9

Psalm 69:32
Psalm 147:6
Proverbs 11:2
Proverbs 15:33
Proverbs 16:19
Proverbs 29:23
Micah 6:8
James 4:10
1 Peter 5:6

Insecurity

Psalm 27:1
Psalm 91:1, 4
Proverbs 1:33
Proverbs 14:26
Proverbs 18:10
Isaiah 41:10
Isaiah 54:17
Romans 8:28
Romans 8:37–39
2 Corinthians 12:9
Philippians 4:13
Hebrews 13:6

Integrity

Psalm 15:4
Psalm 25:21
Psalm 26:1–5
Proverbs 11:3
Matthew 5:41
Acts 23:1
Acts 24:16
Romans 9:1
1 Corinthians 12:31
Philippians 1:10, 11
1 Timothy 1:5
1 Timothy 1:19
2 Peter 1:3

Laziness and Passivity

Proverbs 5:23
Proverbs 6:4, 10, 11
Proverbs 20:4
Proverbs 26:15, 16
Ecclesiastes 10:18
Colossians 3:1
Hebrews 6:11, 12
Hebrews 11:6
Revelation 3:15, 16

Loneliness

Genesis 28:15
1 Samuel 12:22
Psalm 25:16
Psalm 27:10
Psalm 46:1
Isaiah 41:10
Matthew 28:20
John 14:18
2 Corinthians 6:18
Hebrews 13:5

Patience

Psalm 37:34
Psalm 40:1
Ecclesiastes 7:8
Romans 5:3, 4
Galatians 6:9
Colossians 1:11, 12
Hebrews 6:11, 12
James 1:2–4
James 5:7, 8

Peace

Job 22:21
Psalm 85:8, 10, 11
Proverbs 16:7
Isaiah 26:3
Isaiah 54:10
Isaiah 58:8
John 14:27
Philippians 4:7
2 Thessalonians 3:16
Hebrews 12:14

Power

Isaiah 40:29
Acts 1:8
1 Corinthians 15:57
2 Corinthians 1:21, 22
2 Corinthians 12:9
Ephesians 1:19
Ephesians 3:16
2 Timothy 1:7

Prayer

Job 22:27
Psalm 34:4
Psalm 38:15
Psalm 145:18, 19

Proverbs 15:29
Isaiah 55:6
Matthew 7:7, 8
Matthew 18:19
Luke 18:1
John 16:24
Romans 8:26
1 Thessalonians 5:17
Hebrews 4:16

Prosperity, Finances, and Giving

Deuteronomy 8:18
Deuteronomy 28:8, 11
Psalm 1:3
Psalm 34:10
Malachi 3:10
Matthew 6:3, 4
Matthew 6:19–21
Luke 6:38
Acts 10:4
Romans 13:8
2 Corinthians 9:6, 7
Philippians 4:19
3 John 2

Protection

Deuteronomy 33:27
Job 11:18, 19
Psalm 9:9
Psalm 32:7
Psalm 52:8, 9
Psalm 91:1, 2
Psalm 91:9–11
Proverbs 14:26

Receiving God's Love

Psalm 86:12, 13, 15
Lamentations 3:22, 23
John 3:16
John 15:9
John 16:27
Romans 5:5
1 Corinthians 8:3
1 Corinthians 16:14
2 Corinthians 5:14, 15
Ephesians 3:17–19
Ephesians 4:15
Ephesians 5:2
1 John 4:16
1 John 4:19

Jude 20, 21

Rejection

Leviticus 26:11
Joshua 1:9
Isaiah 54:17
Matthew 28:20
Luke 10:10, 11
John 15:16
Romans 8:31
Romans 8:37
Ephesians 1:4–6

Seeking God

Deuteronomy 4:29
2 Chronicles 7:14
2 Chronicles 15:2
Psalm 27:4
Lamentations 3:25
Matthew 6:33
Matthew 7:7, 8
Luke 12:29, 31
John 5:30
Colossians 3:1
Hebrews 11:6

Self-Control

Proverbs 15:18
Proverbs 25:28
Proverbs 31:16
Ecclesiastes 5:2
Ecclesiastes 7:9
Lamentations 3:26, 27
Luke 21:19
1 Corinthians 6:12
1 Corinthians 13:4, 5
Galatians 5:22, 23
2 Peter 1:5–7

Selfishness

Genesis 12:2
Proverbs 28:27
Mark 8:34
Romans 12:10
Romans 15:2
1 Corinthians 9:19
1 Corinthians 10:24
1 Corinthians 10:33
2 Corinthians 5:15
Galatians 6:2
Philippians 2:3–7

1 Timothy 5:6
1 John 3:17, 18

Spiritual Warfare

Deuteronomy 28:7
Psalm 35:1–3
Romans 7:23–25
Romans 8:38
2 Corinthians 10:3, 4
Ephesians 6:11
1 Timothy 6:12
1 Peter 5:8

Stress

Psalm 37:5
Psalm 39:6
Psalm 127:2
Isaiah 40:29
Matthew 6:25, 31, 33
Mark 4:19
Luke 12:27
Luke 21:34
1 Corinthians 7:32
Philippians 4:6
Philippians 4:8, 9
1 Peter 5:7

Submission to Authority: God's and Man's

Joshua 24:24
1 Samuel 15:23
Psalm 103:17, 18
Psalm 112:1
Psalm 119:44, 45
Isaiah 1:19, 20
Luke 11:28
Ephesians 6:5
James 4:7, 8
1 Peter 2:18, 19
1 John 3:22

Taking Care of Your Body

Exodus 23:25
Proverbs 3:7, 8
Proverbs 4:10
Proverbs 4:20–22
Proverbs 16:24
Proverbs 17:22
Jeremiah 30:17

1 Corinthians 6:13
1 Corinthians 6:19, 20
1 Thessalonians 5:23
1 Peter 5:8
3 John 2

Temptation

Psalm 138:3
Psalm 143:10
Proverbs 1:10, 15
Proverbs 4:14, 15
Mark 14:38
Luke 22:40
Romans 12:21
James 1:12
James 4:7

The Goodness of God

Psalm 34:8
Psalm 84:11
Psalm 135:3
Psalm 145:9
Jeremiah 29:11
Jeremiah 33:11
Nahum 1:7
Luke 12:32
1 Corinthians 2:9
Philippians 4:19

The Mind

Psalm 139:1–4
Proverbs 3:5, 6
Proverbs 23:7
Romans 12:2
2 Corinthians 10:5
Ephesians 4:22–24
Philippians 4:8
2 Timothy 1:7

The Power of Words

Psalm 19:14
Psalm 34:13
Psalm 141:3
Proverbs 10:11
Proverbs 10:31
Proverbs 13:3
Proverbs 15:1
Proverbs 15:23
Proverbs 16:23
Proverbs 18:21
Proverbs 25:11

Isaiah 50:4
Matthew 12:34–37
Ephesians 4:29
1 Peter 3:10

Trust

2 Samuel 22:31–33
Psalm 18:2, 3
Psalm 20:7
Psalm 31:14, 15
Psalm 56:3, 4
Psalm 62:8
Proverbs 3:5–8
Proverbs 29:25
Isaiah 30:15
Nahum 1:7
Hebrews 2:13

Victory

1 Chronicles 29:11
Proverbs 24:6
Romans 8:37
1 Corinthians 15:54
1 Corinthians 15:57

2 Corinthians 2:14
1 John 5:1–5

Waiting on God and His Timing

Psalm 25:5
Psalm 31:14, 15
Psalm 37:7
Psalm 39:7, 8
Psalm 62:1, 2
Psalm 145:15, 16
Isaiah 30:18
Isaiah 40:31
Habakkuk 2:3

Walking in Love

Deuteronomy 10:12
John 13:34
Ephesians 4:1, 2
Ephesians 5:2
Colossians 3:12–14
1 John 4:7, 8
1 John 4:12
1 John 4:17–19

Wisdom

Psalm 111:10
Proverbs 1:5
Proverbs 2:1–5
Proverbs 3:5–7
Proverbs 3:13–15
Proverbs 3:35
Proverbs 8:11
Proverbs 8:35
Proverbs 19:20
James 1:5

Worship

Psalm 5:7
Psalm 29:2
Psalm 92:1–3
Psalm 95:6
Psalm 96:1–4
Psalm 96:9
Ecclesiastes 3:14
John 4:24
Romans 12:1
Philippians 3:3
Hebrews 12:28
Revelation 5:11–14

Everyday Life Notes

I believe that God will do many things in your life as you read, study, and live according to His Word. For that reason, I wanted to provide the following pages as a place for you to write notes in this Bible. You may want to use them to record your prayer requests and answered prayers, to make a list of your favorite Scripture verses and passages, to jot down understanding or revelation God gives you through His Word, or to keep some sort of diary or journal of your walk with God. Just as this Bible is a compilation of many years of life lessons and ministry experience for me, I hope you will use these pages to write about all the lessons God is teaching you and the experiences you are having with Him during this time of your life.

— Joyce Meyer